THE AUSTRALIAN MODERN OXFORD DICTIONARY

Second Edition

Edited by

FREDERICK LUDOWYK and BRUCE MOORE
at
The Australian National Dictionary Centre

OXFORD
UNIVERSITY PRESS

253 Normanby Road, South Melbourne,
Victoria 3205, Australia

Oxford University Press is a department of the
University of Oxford. It furthers the University's
objective of excellence in research, scholarship,
and education by publishing worldwide in

Oxford New York

Auckland Cape Town Dar es Salaam Delhi
Hong Kong Karachi Kuala Lumpur Madrid
Melbourne Mexico City Nairobi New Delhi
Shanghai Taipei Toronto

With offices in

Argentina Austria Brazil Chile Czech Republic
France Greece Guatemala Hungary Italy Japan
Poland Portugal Singapore South Korea
Switzerland Thailand Turkey Ukraine Vietnam

OXFORD is a trade mark of Oxford University Press
in the UK and in certain other countries

Copyright © Oxford University Press 1998, 2003

First published 1998
Reprinted 2000
Second edition published 2003
Reprinted 2005

Based on *The Australian Oxford Paperback Dictionary*
© 2001 Oxford University Press

Do you have a query about words,
their origin, meaning, use, spelling,
pronunciation, or any other aspect
of international English? Then write
to OWLS at the Australian
National Dictionary Centre,
Australian National University,
Canberra ACT 0200 (email
ANDC@anu.edu.au). All queries
will be answered using the full
resources of *The Australian
National Dictionary* and *The
Oxford English Dictionary*.
The Australian National Dictionary
Centre and Oxford University Press
also produce OZWORDS, a
biannual newsletter which contains
interesting items about Australian
words and language. Subscription
is free – please contact the
OZWORDS subscription manager
at Oxford University Press, GPO
Box 2784Y, Melbourne, VIC
3001, or ozwords.au@oup.com

This book is copyright. Apart from any fair dealing for the purposes of private study,
research, criticism or
review as permitted under the Copyright Act, no part
may be reproduced, stored in a retrieval system, or
transmitted, in any form or by any means, electronic,
mechanical, photocopying, recording or otherwise
without prior written permission. Enquiries to be made
to Oxford University Press.

Copying for educational purposes

Where copies of part or the whole of the book are made under Part VB
of the Copyright Act, the law requires that prescribed procedures be
followed. For information, contact the Copyright Agency Limited.

National Library of Australia

Cataloguing-in-Publication data:

Australian modern Oxford Dictionary.

2nd ed.
ISBN 0 19 551765 2.

1. English language—Dictionaries. I. Ludowyk, Frederick.

423

Typeset by Desktop Concepts P/L, Melbourne
Printed through Golden Cup Printing Co. Ltd, Hong Kong

Contents

Note on Proprietary Terms	iv
Preface	v
How to Use This Dictionary	vi
Pronunciation	viii
Map: Locations of Australian Aboriginal Languages	x
Abbreviations	xii
THE AUSTRALIAN MODERN OXFORD DICTIONARY	1
Appendices	
1. Countries of the World	989
2. Prime Ministers of Australia	995

Note on Proprietary Terms

This dictionary includes some words which are, or are asserted to be, proprietary names or trademarks. Their inclusion does not imply that they have acquired for legal purposes a non-proprietary or general significance, nor is any other judgment implied concerning their legal status. In cases where the editor has some evidence that a word is used as a proprietary name or trademark this is indicated by the designation *trademark*, but no judgment concerning the legal status of such words is made or implied thereby.

Preface

The second edition of the *Australian Modern Oxford Dictionary* draws on two major databases. First, it draws on the comprehensive and continually updated database of Australian English at the Australian National Dictionary Centre at the Australian National University. The Centre was established in 1988 by Oxford University Press Australia and the Australian National University to conduct research into Australian English and to produce the range of Oxford Australian dictionaries. Secondly, it draws on the database of the large *Oxford English Dictionary*, the most comprehensive and authoritative account of international English.

This new edition retains the popular features of the previous edition (including encyclopedic entries), adds many new Australian and international words and meanings, and provides detailed guidance on usage. There is a special emphasis on Australian Aboriginal culture, and for the words that have been borrowed into Australian English from Aboriginal languages, the etymology section specifies the language from which each of the words has been borrowed (and the language can be located on the map provided). A major new feature of the dictionary is the labelling of Australian words and meanings with an *Aust.* marker.

The new words in this edition come from a variety of areas. Sport provides: blood rule, cruciate ligament, erythropoietin (EPO), keirin, madison, onball (player), parapente, tae kwon do, wakeboarding, etc. Health provides: acidophilus, attention deficit disorder, colonoscopy, cryptosporidium, echinacea, economy-class syndrome, giardia, Johne's disease, lyssavirus, reiki, etc. Environmental concerns produce: carbon credit, carbon sink, genetically modified organism, etc. Computing and electronic communication continue to generate many new words and meanings, and often use acronyms and abbreviations. A special attempt has been made to address this semantic area. Additions include: applet, BBS (Bulletin Board System), browser, .com, cybercafé, data casting, domain name, dotcom, cookie, DVD, emoticon, ethernet, extranet, flame, http, JPEG, LOL, mirror site, netsurf, newsgroup, POP, PPP, sig, smiley, URL, virtual memory, webcast, webmaster, etc. The first edition was very strong on Australian lexical items, but this new edition provides proof that Australian English continues to generate new terms. Those added include: bevan, black armband view of history, drop bear, Easter bilby, economic rationalism, long neck, lowset, magic pudding, ningaui, preference against, saltwater people, secret men's business, smoking ceremony, song line, State of Origin, stolen generation(s), trackie daks, wombat crossing, etc.

FREDERICK LUDOWYK
BRUCE MOORE

How to Use This Dictionary

These notes are intended as a brief guide to the conventions adopted in this dictionary. We have adopted the policy of presenting all information in the clearest, most helpful form for the user.

1 Headword

The headword is printed in bold type (**like this**). If the word is not completely naturalised in Australian English, it is printed in bold italic type (***like this***).

Alternative spellings are given before the definition. The form given as the headword is the preferred form. Hence, **colour** *n.* (also **color**); **colourise** *v.* (also **-ize**).

Words that are normally spelled with a capital initial letter are given in this form as the headword. When they are in some senses spelled with a small initial letter and in others with a capital this is indicated by repetition of the full word in the appropriate form within the entry (as at **blue**).

If a sense of a word is always used in the plural form, this is indicated by repetition of the headword in the plural form at the beginning of the appropriate sense (as at **arm²**).

2 Pronunciation

Pronunciation is explained on pp. viii–ix.

3 Part-of-speech Label

A part-of-speech label is given for all main entries and derivatives, but not for encyclopedic entries (which can be assumed to be nouns); it is not given for compounds listed under main entries unless the part of speech is not self-evident.

Different parts of speech of a single word are listed separately, with the second etc. part of speech introduced by a bullet mark (e.g. •*adj.*).

4 Inflections

The plurals of nouns, comparatives ending in *-er* and superlatives ending in *-est* of adjectives and adverbs, and verb forms: these are given only if they are irregular or if there might be doubt about the spelling.

When only two verb forms are given:

    admit *v.* (**admitted, admitting**)

the first form is both the past tense (*he admitted to it*) and the past participle (*it was admitted*), while the second form is the present participle.

When three forms are given:

    come *v.* (**came, come, coming**)

    freeze *v.* (**froze, frozen, freezing**)

the first is the past tense (*he came; his toes froze*), the second is the past participle (*he had come; his toes were frozen*), and the third is the present participle.

5 Subject and usage labels

Subject labels (e.g. *Computing, Music*) are used to help clarify the subject field to which a particular sense applies. They are not used when this is clear from the definition itself.

Words and phrases more common in informal spoken English than in formal written English are labelled *colloq.* ('colloquial'), e.g. **budgie, skite**. Two categories of usage are indicated by special markings: **1** *coarse colloq.* indicates a word that, although widely found, is still unacceptable to many people; **2** *offens.* ('offensive') indicates a use that is offensive because of what it implies about the members of a particular group in society, e.g. **wog**[1]. The inclusion of such terms does not in any way imply that their use is acceptable.

6 Phrases and compounds

Phrases and multi-word compounds are grouped together in alphabetical order at the end of the main word. This section is introduced by the symbol ☐.

If a compound has become so fixed that the preferred form is now as a single word with no space or hyphen (e.g. **bathroom**), it is treated as a main entry with its own headword.

Multi-word compounds (i.e. those consisting of two or more separate or hyphenated words) are usually covered under the headword for the first of the words that make up the compound (e.g. **rat race** will be found at the entry for **rat** and **read between the lines** will be found at the entry for **read**).

7 Derivatives

Words formed by adding an easily understood ending to another word are in many cases listed at the very end of the entry for the main word (e.g. **randomly** is listed under **random**): these derivatives are listed after compounds and phrases (if there are any). In this position they are not defined since they can be understood from the sense of the main word. If definition etc. is needed, such derivatives are treated as main entries in their own right (e.g. **changeable**).

8 Cross-references

A cross-reference to a main entry or to a compound etc. within a main entry is indicated by small capitals, e.g.:

> **mice** *see* MOUSE.
>
> **Rumania, Rumanian** alternative spelling of ROMANIA, ROMANIAN.
>
> **cross off** = CROSS OUT.
>
> **secondary source** a critical book, journal, article, etc., used as supporting evidence in the discussion of a PRIMARY SOURCE.

9 Usage Notes

Usage notes found at the end of some entries give guidance on the current norms of standard Australian English, i.e. the form of written and spoken English most generally accepted as a normal basis of communication in everyday life in Australia. Some of the rules given may legitimately be broken in less formal Australian English, and especially in conversation.

Pronunciation

A guide to pronunciation is given for any word that is difficult to pronounce, or difficult to recognise when read, or spelled the same as another word but pronounced differently. The pronunciation given represents standard Australian speech. Words are broken up into syllables, indicated by hyphens. The syllable that is spoken with most stress in a word of two or more syllables is shown in bold type, like **this**. The pronunciation is shown within slashes, e.g. **galah** /guh-**lah**/.

The sounds represented are as follows:

a	as in **a**nd, b**a**t, c**a**t	oi	as in j**oi**n, v**oi**ce, b**oy**
ah	as in c**a**lm, p**a**th, **ar**m	oo	as in s**oo**n, b**oo**t, **oo**ze
air	as in f**air**, c**are**, th**ere**	oor	as in t**our**
aw	as in l**aw**, f**or**, s**ore**	ow	as in c**ow**, h**ow**, **ou**t
ay	as in pl**ay**, **a**ge, f**a**ce	owuh	as in h**our**, p**ower**
b	as in **b**ed	p	as in **p**eg
ch	as in **ch**in, **ch**ur**ch**, whi**ch**	r	as in **r**ed
d	as in **d**ay	s	as in **s**it, a**ss**
e	as in b**e**d, t**e**n, **e**gg	sh	as in **sh**op, fi**sh**, **ch**arade
ee	as in m**ee**t, m**ea**t, p**i**que	t	as in **t**op
eer	as in b**eer**, h**ere**, f**ear**	th	as in **th**in, me**th**od, bo**th**
er	as in h**er**, b**ir**d	*th*	as in **th**is, ei**th**er, **th**ose
f	as in **f**at	u	as in b**u**n, **u**p
g	as in **g**et, wa**g**on, do**g**	uh	as in **a**bove, c**o**rrect, moth**er**
h	as in **h**at	uu	as in b**oo**k, l**oo**k, p**u**ll
i	as in p**i**n, s**i**t, **i**s	uy	as in cr**y**, l**igh**t
j	as in **j**am, **j**ob, en**j**oy	uyuh	as in f**ire**, w**ire**, sp**ire**
k	as in **k**ing, **c**at, pi**que**	v	as in **v**an, ri**v**er
l	as in **l**eg	w	as in **w**as, **w**ish
m	as in **m**e	y	as in **y**ard, **y**es, **y**ou
n	as in **n**ot	yoo	as in f**ew**, d**ue**, b**eau**ty, t**une**
ng	as in si**ng**, thi**ng**, a**nx**ious	yoor	as in c**ure**, p**ure**, end**ure**
o	as in g**o**t, t**o**p, **o**n	z	as in **z**oo, la**z**y, rai**s**e
oh	as in m**o**st, b**oa**t, g**o**	*zh*	as in divi**s**ion, vi**s**ion, mea**s**ure

Note

1 Alternative pronunciations are separated by a comma within the slashes. Thus:
 belief / bee-**leef**, buh- /
means that this word can be pronounced / bee-**leef** / *or* / buh-**leef** /;
 maladroit / mal-uh-**droit**, **mal**- /
means that this word can be pronounced / mal-uh-**droit** / *or* / **mal**-uh-droit /;

blessed / **bles**-uhd, blest /

means that this word can be pronounced in either of those two ways;

fructose / **fruuk**-tohz, -tohs, **fruk**- /

means that this word can be pronounced / **fruuk**-tohz / *or* / **fruuk**-tohs / *or* / **fruk**-tohz / *or* / **fruk**-tohs /.

2 The indeterminate vowel (or schwa) is often heard in unstressed syllables in Australian speech. It is represented by the symbol 'uh'. It is the sound (marked in *italic*) heard in the following examples: *a*go / uh-**go**/, circ*u*s / **ser**-kuhs /, c*o*rrect / kuh-**rekt** /, d*i*sc*i*pl*e* /duh-**suy**-puhl /, explic*i*t /ek-s**plis**-uht / (*or e*xplic*i*t /uhk-**splis**-uht /), moth*er* /**muth**-uh /, om*i*n*o*us / **om**-uh-nuhs /, omel*e*tte /**om**-luht/, penc*i*l /**pen**-suhl /, prim*i*tive /**prim**-uh-tiv/, princ*i*pal*i*ty /prin-suh-**pal**-uh-tee /, suff*e*red /**suf**-uhd /, tak*e*n /**tay**-kuhn /.

Locations of Australian Aboriginal Languages

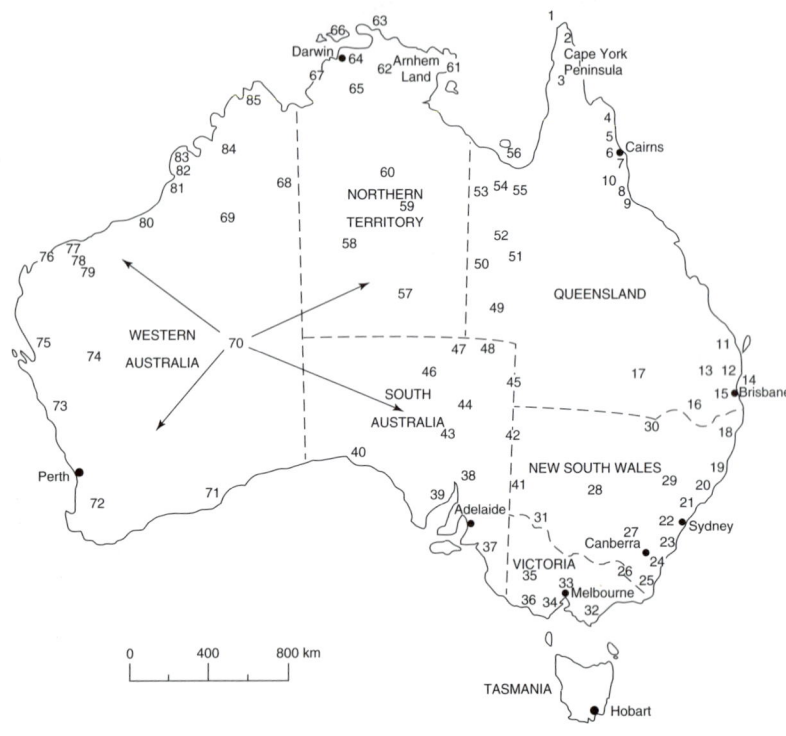

Adnyamathanha	43	Bardi	83
Arabana	46	Bigambil	16
Aranda	57	Dharawal	23
Arrernte	57	Dharuk	22
Awabakal	21	Dhurga	24
Baagandji	41	Diyari	44
Bandjalang	18	Djangati	19
Banggala	39	Djaru	68

Djingulu	60	Pajamal	67
Dyirbal	7	Panyjima	79
Gabi-gabi	12	Pintupi	70
Ganay	32	Pitjantjatjara	70
Gaurna	38	Pitta-pitta	51
Gowar	14	Thawa	25
Gunwinygu	62	Tiwi	66
Gunya	17		
Gureng-gureng	11	Ungarinyin	84
Guugu Yimidhirr	4	Waga-waga	13
Guyani	43	Walmatjari	69
Kalaaku	71	Wangganuru	47
Kala Lagaw Ya	1	Wangka-Yutjuru	50
Kalkatungu	52	Waray	65
Kamilaroi	29	Warlpiri	58
Karadjeri	81	Warrgamay	8
Kattang	20	Warumungu	59
Kuku-Yalanji	5	Warungu	10
Kuurn Kopan Noot	36	Wathawurung	34
Lardil	56	Watjari	74
Luritja	70	Wemba-wemba	35
		Western Desert language	70
Malyangaba	42	Wik-Mungkan	3
Mantjiltjara	70	Wiradhuri	27
Margu	63	Wuna	64
Martuthunira	76	Wunambal	85
Mayi-Kulan	55	Wuywurung	33
Mayi-Kutuna	53		
Mayi-Yapi	54	Yadhaykenu	2
Midhaga	49	Yagara	15
		Yandruwandha	45
Ngaanyatjara	70	Yankunytjatjara	70
Ngamini	48	Yaralde	37
Ngarigo	26	Yawor	82
Ngarluma	77	Yidiny	6
Ngiyambaa	28	Yindjibarndi	78
Nhangka	40	Yingkarta	75
Nhanta	73	Yitha-yitha	31
Nyangumarda	80	Yolngu[2]	61
Nyawaygi	9	Yuwaalaraay	30
Nyungar	72	Yuwaaliyaay	30

Abbreviations

abbr.	abbreviation	*hist.*	historical, history
adj.	adjective	*interj.*	interjection
adv.	adverb	*n.*	noun
Amer.	American	*n.pl.*	plural noun
Archaeol.	Archaeology	*Med.*	Medicine
Archit.	Architecture	*myth.*	Mythology
Aust.	Australian	*offens.*	offensive
Brit.	British	orig.	originally
c.	circa, about	*pl.*	plural
Chem.	Chemistry	*prep.*	preposition
colloq.	colloquial	*pron.*	pronoun
comb.	combination(s)	*Psychol.*	Psychology
comb. form	combining form	*Rom.*	Roman
conj.	conjunction	*Scand.*	Scandinavian
derog.	derogatory	*sing.*	singular
esp.	especially	*US*	United States
foll.	followed	usu.	usually
Geol.	Geology	*v.*	verb
Gk	Greek		

Note

Abbreviations that are in general use (such as etc., km, NW) appear in the dictionary itself. So too do the following abbreviations:

ACT	SA
NSW	Tas.
NT	Vic.
Qld	WA

A *n.* (*pl.* **As** *or* **A's**) **1** the first letter of the alphabet. **2** the first of a series of things; the highest or best grade (of academic marks etc.). **3** *Music* the sixth note of the scale of C major. • *abbr.* **1** ampere(s). **2** answer. □ **A1, A2**, etc. the standard paper size, each half the previous one, e.g. A4 = 297 × 210mm, A5 = 210 × 148mm.

a *adj.* (called the *indefinite article*) **1** one person or thing but not any specific one (*I need a knife*). **2** per (*we pay $40 a year*).

Å *abbr.* ångström(s).

AA *abbr.* = ALCOHOLICS ANONYMOUS.

aardvark / ahd-vahk / *n.* an African animal with a bulky pig-like body and a thick tail, feeding on termites.

Aaron / air-ruhn / (in the Bible) the brother of Moses and traditional founder of the Jewish priesthood.

aback *adv.* □ **taken aback** surprised, shocked.

abacus / ab-uh-kuhs / *n.* (*pl.* **abacuses**) **1** a frame containing parallel rods with beads that slide up and down, used for counting. **2** *Archit.* a flat slab on top of a column or pillar.

abaft / uh-bahft / *adv.* in the stern half of a ship. • *prep.* nearer to the stern than.

abalone / ab-uh-loh-nee / *n.* an edible mollusc with an ear-shaped shell lined with mother-of-pearl.

abandon *v.* **1** go away from (a person or thing or place) without intending to return (*abandon ship*). **2** give up, cease work on (*abandon the attempt*). **3** yield completely to an emotion or impulse (*abandoned himself to despair*). • *n.* careless freedom of manner. □ **abandonment** *n.*

abandoned *adj.* **1** deserted, forsaken. **2** (of behaviour) lacking restraint, depraved.

abase *v.* humiliate, degrade. □ **abasement** *n.*

abashed *adj.* embarrassed, ashamed.

abate *v.* make or become less strong or intense (*the storm abated*).

abattoir / ab-uh-twah / *n.* a slaughterhouse.

abbacy *n.* the office of abbot or abbess.

abbess / ab-es / *n.* a woman who is head of a community of nuns.

abbey *n.* **1** a building occupied by monks or nuns living as a community. **2** the community itself.

abbot *n.* a man who is head of a community of monks.

abbreviate *v.* shorten (especially a word or title).

abbreviation *n.* **1** abbreviating, being abbreviated. **2** a shortened form of a word or title.

ABC *n.* **1** the alphabet. **2** the elementary facts of a subject (*the ABC of carpentry*). **3** an alphabetically arranged guide. • *abbr.* = AUSTRALIAN BROADCASTING CORPORATION.

abdicate *v.* resign from the throne; give up (office, responsibility, etc.). □ **abdication** *n.*

abdomen / ab-duh-muhn / *n.* **1** the part of the body below the chest and diaphragm, containing most of the digestive organs; the belly. **2** the hindmost section of the body of an insect, spider, or crustacean (*head, thorax, and abdomen*). □ **abdominal** / uhb-**dom**-uh-nuhl / *adj.* **abdominally** *adv.*

abduct *v.* carry off (a person) illegally by force or fraud. □ **abduction** *n.* **abductor** *n.*

abeam *adv.* at right angles to a ship's or an aircraft's length.

Abel (in the Bible) the second son of Adam and Eve, murdered by his brother Cain.

aberrant / ab-uh-ruhnt / *adj.* deviating from what is normal or accepted.

aberration / ab-uh-**ray**-shuhn / *n.* **1** a deviation from what is normal. **2** a mental or moral lapse. **3** distortion of an image because of a defect in a lens or mirror. **4** the apparent change in the position of a celestial body caused by the observer's motion and the finite speed of light.

abet *v.* (**abetted, abetting**) (usu. **aid and abet**) encourage or assist (an offender or offence). □ **abetter** (also **abettor**) *n.* **abetment** *n.*

abeyance / uh-**bay**-uhns / *n.* □ **in abeyance** (of a right, rule, or problem etc.) suspended for a time.

abhor / uhb-**haw** / *v.* (**abhorred, abhorring**) detest.

abhorrent / uhb-**ho**-ruhnt / *adj.* detestable. □ **abhorrence** *n.*

abide *v.* (**abided** (in sense 1 **abode**), **abiding**) **1** *archaic* remain; dwell. **2** bear, endure (*I can't abide wasps*). □ **abide by** act in accordance with (a rule, decision, etc.); keep (a promise).

abiding *adj.* long-lasting, permanent.

ability *n.* **1** the capacity or power to do something. **2** cleverness, talent.

ab initio / ab i-**nish**-ee-oh / *adv.* from the beginning. (¶ Latin)

abject / **ab**-jekt / *adj.* **1** wretched, without resources (*abject poverty*). **2** lacking all pride (*an abject coward; an abject apology*). □ **abjectly** *adv.* **abjection** *n.*

abjure / uhb-**joor** / *v.* renounce; repudiate. □ **abjuration** *n.*

ablative / **ab**-luh-tiv / *n.* the grammatical case (especially in Latin) that indicates the agent, instrument, or location of an action.

ablaut

ablaut / **ab**-lowt / *n.* a change of vowel in related words (e.g. *sing, sang, sung*).

ablaze *adj.* blazing.

able *adj.* **1** having the ability to do something. **2** having great ability; competent. ☐ **able-bodied** *adj.* fit, healthy. **able-bodied seaman** an ordinary trained seaman. ☐☐ **ably** *adv.*

abled *adj.* **1** able-bodied. **2** having a particular range of physical abilities (as specified by preceding adverb) (*differently abled*).

ablution / uh-**bloo**-shuhn / *n.* **1** ceremonial washing of hands, vessels, etc. **2** (**ablutions**) *colloq.* **a** ordinary washing of the body (*perform one's ablutions*). **b** a place for doing this.

ABM *abbr.* = ANTI-BALLISTIC MISSILE.

ABN *abbr.* Australian business number, an identifier for companies registered under the Corporations Law and businesses carrying on an enterprise.

abnegate / **ab**-nuh-gayt / *v.* give up or renounce (a pleasure, right, etc.). ☐ **abnegation** *n.*

abnormal *adj.* different from what is normal. ☐ **abnormally** *adv.* **abnormality** / ab-naw-**mal**-uh-tee / *n.*

Abo / **ab**-oh / (also **abo**) *Aust. colloq. offens. n.* (*pl.* **Abos**) an Aborigine. • *adj.* Aboriginal.

aboard *adv.* & *prep.* on or into a ship, aircraft, or train.

abode[1] *n. archaic* a dwelling place.

abode[2] *see* ABIDE.

abolish / uh-**bol**-ish / *v.* put an end to. ☐ **abolition** / ab-uh-**lish**-uhn / *n.*

abolitionist *n.* a person who favours abolishing capital punishment.

A-bomb *n.* an atomic bomb.

abominable *adj.* **1** detestable, loathsome. **2** very bad or unpleasant (*abominable weather*). ☐ **abominably** *adv.*

Abominable Snowman *n.* a large man-like or bear-like animal said to exist in the Himalayas; a yeti.

abominate *v.* detest, loathe.

abomination *n.* **1** loathing. **2** something loathed.

aboriginal *adj.* **1** existing in a land from earliest times or from before the arrival of colonists. **2** (usu. **Aboriginal**) of Australian Aborigines. • *n.* **1** an aboriginal inhabitant. **2** (usu. **Aboriginal**) an Aboriginal inhabitant of Australia. **3** *colloq.* (usu. **Aboriginal**) an Australian Aboriginal language.

Aboriginal and Torres Strait Islander Commission an organisation established in 1990 as the peak representative indigenous agency in Australia, and a Commonwealth statutory authority responsible for the administration of programs for Aboriginal and Torres Strait Islander people.

Aboriginal English *n. Aust.* English, as used by many Aborigines, often in combination with words and constructions from one or more Aboriginal languages.

abracadabra

Aboriginal flag *n.* a flag designed by Harold Thomas. From 1972 it was officially adopted by the Australian Aboriginal people. Its top half is black, representing the people, the bottom half red for the earth, and a central solid yellow circle represents the sun.

Aboriginalisation *n.* (also **-ization**) *Aust.* affirmative action to enable Aborigines to take up positions in organisations etc., esp. organisations dealing with Aboriginal affairs. ☐ **Aboriginalise** *v.*

Aboriginality *n. Aust.* **1** the quality of being Aboriginal. **2** the culture of the Aboriginal people.

aborigine / ab-uh-**rij**-uh-nee / *n.* **1** an aboriginal inhabitant of a country. **2** (usu. **Aborigine**) an Aboriginal inhabitant of Australia.

■ **Usage** There is no consensus on the use of the terms *Aborigine*(*s*) and *Aboriginal*(*s*) to refer to the original people of Australia. Some people prefer *Aboriginal* for a single person and *Aborigines* for more than one. This dictionary uses *Aborigine*(*s*) for the person(s), and *Aboriginal* only as an adjective. *See* KOORI.

abort / uh-**bawt** / *v.* **1** cause an abortion of or to; suffer abortion. **2** end or cause to end prematurely and unsuccessfully.

abortion *n.* **1** the expulsion (either spontaneous or induced) of a foetus from the womb before it is able to survive independently. **2** a misshapen creature or thing.

abortionist *n.* a person who practises abortion, esp. illegally.

abortive *adj.* **1** producing abortion. **2** unsuccessful (*an abortive attempt*).

abound *v.* **1** be plentiful (*fish abound in the river*). **2** (foll. by *in* or *with*) have in great quantities (*the river abounds in fish*).

about *prep.* & *adv.* **1** approximately (*about $10*). **2** in connection with; on the subject of (*what is he talking about?*). **3** all around (*look about you*). **4** somewhere near, not far off (*he's somewhere about*). **5** here and there in (a place) (*papers were lying about the room*). **6** on the move, in circulation (*will soon be about again*). **7** so as to face in the opposite direction (*put the ship about*). **8** in rotation (*on duty week and week about*). ☐ **about-face** (also **about-turn**) a reversal of previous actions or opinions. **be about to** be on the point of doing something.

above *adv.* **1** at or to a higher point; overhead; in heaven. **2** in addition. **3** earlier in a book or article (*mentioned above*). • *prep.* **1** over; higher than; more than. **2** upstream from. **3** beyond the level or reach of (*she is above suspicion*). **4** more important than (*this above all*). ☐ **above board** without deception or concealment, done honourably. **above oneself** conceited, arrogant.

abracadabra / ab-ruh-kuh-**dab**-ruh / *n.* a supposedly magic formula or spell.

abrade / uh-**brayd** / v. scrape or wear away by rubbing.

Abraham the Hebrew patriarch from whom all Jews trace their descent.

abrasion / uh-**bray**-zhuhn / n. abrading; an abraded place.

abrasive / uh-**bray**-siv / adj. **1** causing abrasion. **2** capable of polishing surfaces by rubbing or grinding. **3** harsh, causing angry feelings (*an abrasive personality*). • n. an abrasive substance.

abreast adv. **1** side by side and facing the same way. **2** (foll. by *of*) keeping up with; up to date with (*keep abreast of modern developments*).

abridge v. shorten, esp. by using fewer words. ❏ **abridgment** (also **abridgement**) n.

abroad adv. **1** away from one's own country. **2** far and wide, everywhere (*scattered the seeds abroad*). **3** out and about (*no-one was abroad in the early hours*).

abrogate / **ab**-ruh-gayt / v. cancel, repeal (*abrogate a law*). ❏ **abrogation** n.

abrupt adj. **1** sudden (*came to an abrupt stop*). **2** disconnected, not smooth (*short abrupt sentences*). **3** curt. **4** (of a slope) very steep. ❏ **abruptly** adv. **abruptness** n.

abs / abz / n.pl. colloq. abdominal muscles.

abscess / **ab**-suhs / n. a localised collection of pus within the body.

abscissa / ab-**sis**-uh / n. (pl. **abscissae** or **abscissas**) Maths a coordinate measured parallel to a horizontal axis.

abscond / uhb-**skond** / v. go away secretly, especially after wrongdoing. ❏ **absconder** n.

abseil / **ab**-sayl / v. descend a rock face using a doubled rope fixed at a higher point. • n. this process.

absence n. **1** being away; the period of this. **2** lack, non-existence (*in the absence of proof*). ❏ **absence of mind** inattention.

absent / **ab**-suhnt / adj. **1** not present. **2** non-existent. **3** with one's mind on other things (*stared in an absent way*). ❏ **absent-minded** with one's mind on other things; forgetful. **absent oneself** / uhb-**sent** / stay away. ❏ ❏ **absently** adv. **absent-mindedly** adv.

absentee n. a person who is absent from work etc. ❏ **absentee vote** Aust. a formal vote cast on election day at a polling booth in an electorate other than that in which the elector resides.

absenteeism n. frequent absence from work or school.

absinth / **ab**-sinth / n. **1** wormwood. **2** (usually **absinthe**) a green aniseed-flavoured liqueur based on this.

absolute adj. **1** complete (*absolute silence*). **2** unrestricted (*absolute power*). **3** independent, not relative (*there is no absolute standard for beauty*). **4** colloq. utter, out-and-out (*it's an absolute miracle*). ❏ **absolute majority** a majority over all rivals combined. **absolute pitch** the ability to recognise or sing any given note. **absolute temperature** one measured from absolute zero. **absolute zero** the lowest possible temperature (−273.15°C or zero K).

absolutely adv. **1** completely. **2** without restrictions, unconditionally. **3** colloq. quite so, yes.

absolution / ab-suh-**loo**-shuhn / n. a priest's formal forgiveness of penitents' sins.

absolutism n. **1** the principle of a ruler having complete and unrestricted power. **2** the principle of having a rule etc. that must apply in all cases.

absolve v. **1** clear of blame or guilt. **2** give absolution to (a person). **3** free from an obligation.

absorb v. **1** take in, combine or merge into itself or oneself (*absorb fluid; absorb knowledge; the large firm absorbed the smaller ones*). **2** reduce the effect of (*buffers absorbed most of the shock*). **3** occupy the attention or interest of (*an absorbing book*). ❏ **absorber** n.

absorbent adj. able to absorb moisture etc. ❏ **absorbency** n.

absorption n. **1** absorbing or being absorbed. **2** being engrossed or mentally occupied. ❏ **absorptive** adj.

abstain v. **1** keep oneself from some action or indulgence, especially from drinking alcohol. **2** refrain from using one's vote. ❏ **abstainer** n.

abstemious / uhb-**stee**-mee-uhs / adj. sparing in one's taking of food and drink. ❏ **abstemiously** adv. **abstemiousness** n.

abstention n. abstaining, especially from voting.

abstinence / **ab**-stuh-nuhns / n. abstaining, especially from food or alcohol. ❏ **abstinent** adj.

abstract adj. / ab-**strakt** / **1** having no material existence (*beauty is an abstract quality*). **2** theoretical rather than practical. • n. / **ab**-strakt / **1** an abstract quality or idea. **2** a summary. **3** an example of abstract art. • v. / uhb-**strakt** / **1** take out; separate; remove. **2** make a written summary. ❏ **abstract art** art which does not represent things pictorially but expresses the artist's ideas or sensations. **abstract noun** a noun denoting a quality or state. **in the abstract** regarded theoretically. ❏ ❏ **abstractly** adv. **abstractness** n. **abstractor** n.

abstracted adj. with one's mind on other things, not paying attention. ❏ **abstractedly** adv.

abstraction n. **1** abstracting, removing. **2** an abstract idea. **3** abstractedness.

abstruse / uhb-**stroos** / adj. hard to understand; profound. ❏ **abstrusely** adv. **abstruseness** n.

absurd adj. **1** not in accordance with common sense, very unsuitable. **2** ridiculous, foolish. • n. (**the absurd**) that which is absurd, esp. human existence in a purposeless chaotic universe. ❏ **absurdism** n. **absurdist** n. & adj. **absurdly** adv. **absurdity** n.

Abu Dhabi / ab-oo **dah**-bee / an emirate belonging to the federation of United Arab Emirates; its capital city, also the capital of the UAE.

Abuja / uh-**boo**-juh / the capital of Nigeria.
abundance *n.* a quantity that is more than enough; plenty.
abundant *adj.* **1** more than enough, plentiful. **2** (foll. by *in*) having plenty of something; rich (*a land abundant in minerals*). ☐ **abundantly** *adv.*
abuse *n.* / uh-**byoos** / **1** a misuse. **2** an unjust or corrupt practice. **3** physical, sexual, or emotional maltreatment of another person (*child abuse*). **4** abusive words, insults. • *v.* / uh-**byooz** / **1** make a bad or wrong use of (*abuse one's authority*). **2** illtreat. **3** attack in words, utter insults to or about.
abusive / uh-**byoo**-siv / *adj.* insulting; criticising harshly or angrily. ☐ **abusively** *adv.*
abut / uh-**but** / *v.* (**abutted**, **abutting**) have a common boundary, end or lean against.
abutment *n.* a structure supporting the end of a bridge, arch, etc.
abysmal / uh-**biz**-muhl / *adj.* **1** extreme and deplorable (*abysmal ignorance*). **2** *colloq.* extremely bad (*their taste is abysmal*). ☐ **abysmally** *adv.*
abyss / uh-**bis** / *n.* a hole so deep that it appears bottomless.
abyssal / uh-**bis**-uhl / *adj.* at or of the ocean depths or floor.
Abyssinia the former name of Ethiopia. ☐ **Abyssinian** *adj.* & *n.*
AC *abbr.* **1** (also **a.c.**) alternating current. **2** Companion of the Order of Australia.
Ac *symbol* actinium.
a/c *abbr.* account.
acacia / uh-**kay**-shuh / *n.* **1** the botanical name for all Australian wattles. **2** *Aust.* any of several trees that resemble a wattle.
academe / **ak**-uh-deem / *n. literary* a university environment.
academia *n.* the academic world; scholarly life.
academic / ak-uh-**dem**-ik / *adj.* **1** of a school, college, or university. **2** scholarly as opposed to technical or practical (*academic subjects*). **3** of theoretical interest only, with no practical application. • *n.* an academic person. ☐ **academically** *adv.*
academician / uh-kad-uh-**mish**-uhn / *n.* a member of an Academy.
Academy *n.* a society of distinguished scholars or artists.
academy *n.* a school, especially for specialised training.
Academy Award *n.* a film award given annually by the American Academy of Motion Picture Arts and Sciences. ☐ **Academy Award job** *Aust. colloq.* an exaggerated performance, e.g. a footballer 'playing' for a free kick. **deserve an Academy Award** *colloq. iron.* (of a person's behaviour, performance, etc.) warrant a prize for overacting.
acanthus *n.* a Mediterranean plant with large thistle-like leaves; a representation of the leaf.
a cappella / ah kuh-**pel**-uh / *adj.* & *adv.* (of choral music) unaccompanied.

acca (also **acker**) *Aust. colloq. n.* an academic. • *adj.* academic. • *v.* (**accaed**, **accaing**) study, cram.
ACCC / ay-trip-uhl-**see** / *abbr.* Australian Competition and Consumer Commission.
accede / ak-**seed** / *v.* **1** take office; become monarch. **2** agree to what is proposed.
accelerate / ak-**sel**-uh-rayt / *v.* **1** (of a moving body, esp. a vehicle) move or cause to move more quickly. **2** (of a process) happen or cause to happen more quickly. ☐ **acceleration** *n.*
accelerator *n.* **1** a device for increasing speed. **2** the pedal operating this. **3** *Physics* an apparatus which can make charged particles move at very high speeds.
accelerometer / ak-sel-uh-**rom**-uh-tuh / *n.* an instrument for measuring acceleration or vibrations.
accent *n.* / **ak**-sent / **1** emphasis on a syllable or word. **2** a mark indicating such emphasis or the quality of a vowel sound. **3** a national, local, or individual way of pronouncing words. **4** the emphasis given to something (*the accent is on quality*). • *v.* / ak-**sent** / **1** pronounce with an accent. **2** emphasise. **3** write accents on. ☐ **accentual** / ak-**sen**-choo-uhl / *adj.*
accentuate / uhk-**sen**-choo-ayt / *v.* emphasise. ☐ **accentuation** *n.*
accept *v.* **1** take (a thing offered) willingly; say yes to an offer or invitation. **2** undertake (a responsibility) (*we accept liability for the accident*). **3** treat as welcome (*they were never really accepted by their neighbours*). **4** agree to (*we accept the proposed changes*). **5** take as true (*we do not accept your conclusions*). ☐ **acceptance** *n.* **acceptor** *n.*
acceptable *adj.* **1** worth accepting, welcome. **2** tolerable (*an acceptable risk*). ☐ **acceptably** *adj.* **acceptability** *n.*
access / **ak**-ses / *n.* **1** a way in, a means of approaching or entering. **2** the right or opportunity of reaching or using (*students need access to books*). **3** *Law* enforceable right, usu. of a noncustodial parent, to visit a child. **4** *archaic* an attack of emotion (*a sudden access of rage*). • *adj.* (of broadcasting) allowed to minority or specialinterest groups to undertake (*access radio*). • *v.* retrieve (information stored in a computer). ☐ **access road** a road giving access only to the properties along it. **access time** *Computing* the time taken to retrieve data from storage. **direct access** (also **random access**) the process of storing or retrieving information in a computer without having to read through items stored previously.
accessible / uhk-**ses**-uh-buhl / *adj.* able to be reached or used. ☐ **accessibly** *adv.* **accessibility** *n.*
accession / uhk-**sesh**-uhn / *n.* **1** reaching a rank or position (*accession to high office*). **2** being added; an addition (*recent accessions to the*

accessory 5 **accumulator**

library). • *v.* record the addition of (a new item) to a library or museum.

accessory / uhk-**ses**-uh-ree / *adj.* additional, extra. • *n.* **1** a thing that is extra, useful, or decorative, but not essential; a minor fitting or attachment. **2** a person who helps another in a crime.

accident *n.* **1** an unexpected or undesirable event, especially one causing injury or damage. **2** chance, fortune (*we met by accident*).

accidental *adj.* happening or done by accident. • *n.* a sharp, flat, or natural sign attached to a note in music, showing temporary departure from the key signature. ☐ **accidentally** *adv.*

acclaim / uh-**klaym** / *v.* welcome with shouts of approval; applaud enthusiastically. • *n.* a shout of welcome; applause. ☐ **acclamation** / ak-luh-**may**-shuhn / *n.*

acclimatise *v.* (also **-ize**) make or become used to a new climate or new conditions. ☐ **acclimatisation** *n.*

accolade / **ak**-uh-layd / *n.* **1** praise, approval. **2** a touch on the shoulder with a sword, given when a knighthood is conferred.

accommodate *v.* **1** provide lodging or room for. **2** provide or supply (*the bank will accommodate you with a loan*). **3** adapt; harmonise (*I will accommodate my plans to yours*).

accommodating *adj.* willing to do as one is asked; obliging.

accommodation *n.* **1** lodgings, living premises. **2** the process of accommodating or adapting. **3** provision.

accompaniment *n.* **1** an instrumental part supporting a solo instrument or voice. **2** an accompanying thing.

accompanist *n.* a person who plays a musical accompaniment.

accompany *v.* (**accompanied, accompanying**) **1** go with, travel with as a companion or helper. **2** be present with. **3** provide in addition. **4** play a musical accompaniment to.

accomplice / uh-**kum**-pluhs / *n.* a partner in wrongdoing.

accomplish / uh-**kum**-plish / *v.* succeed in doing, fulfil.

accomplished *adj.* skilled, having many accomplishments.

accomplishment *n.* **1** a skill. **2** accomplishing, completion. **3** a thing accomplished.

accord *n.* consent, agreement. • *v.* **1** be in harmony or consistent. **2** *formal* give or grant (*he was accorded this privilege*). ☐ **of one's own accord** without being asked or compelled. **with one accord** all agreeing; all together.

accordance *n.* agreement, conformity. ☐ **accordant** *adj.*

according *adv.* ☐ **according as** in proportion as; in a manner depending on whether (*he was praised or blamed according as his work was good or bad*). **according to 1** as stated by or in (*according to the Bible*). **2** in a manner consistent with or in proportion to (*grouped according to size*).

accordingly *adv.* **1** according to what is known or stated (*ask what they want and act accordingly*). **2** therefore.

accordion *n.* a portable box-shaped musical instrument with bellows, metal reeds, and keys or buttons. ☐ **accordionist** *n.*

accost / uh-**kost** / *v.* **1** approach and speak to. **2** (of a prostitute) solicit.

account *n.* **1** a statement of money paid or owed. **2** a credit arrangement with a bank or firm. **3** importance (*that is of no account*). **4** a description, a report. • *v.* regard as (*a person is accounted innocent until proved guilty*). ☐ **account for 1** give a reckoning of (money received). **2** explain the cause of; be the explanation of. **3** bring about the death or destruction etc. of. **4** supply or constitute (an amount). **give a good account of oneself** perform well. **keep accounts** keep a systematic record of money spent and received. **on account 1** as an interim payment (*here is $10 on account*). **2** debited to be paid for later (*bought it on account*). **on account of** because of. **on no account** under no circumstances, never. **on one's own account** for one's own purposes and at one's own risk. **take into account** make allowances for. **turn to account** use profitably, make good use of.

accountable *adj.* **1** obliged to give a reckoning or explanation for one's actions etc.; responsible. **2** able to be explained. ☐ **accountability** *n.*

accountant *n.* one whose profession is to keep and examine business accounts. ☐ **accountancy** *n.*

accounting *n.* keeping or examining accounts; accountancy.

accoutrements / uh-**koo**-truh-muhnts / *n.pl.* equipment; a soldier's outfit other than weapons and clothes.

Accra / uh-**krah** / the capital of Ghana.

accredited / uh-**kred**-uh-tuhd / *adj.* **1** officially recognised (*our accredited representative*). **2** generally accepted or believed. **3** certified as being of a prescribed quality.

accretion / uh-**kree**-shuhn / *n.* **1** a growth or increase by means of gradual additions. **2** the growing of separate things into one.

accrual accounting *n.* a system of accounting that requires revenue and costs to be recognised as they are earned or incurred, not as money is received or paid.

accrue / uh-**kroo** / *v.* come as a natural increase or advantage; accumulate (*interest accrues on investments*). ☐ **accrual** *n.*

accumulate *v.* **1** acquire an increasing quantity of. **2** increase in quantity or amount. ☐ **accumulation** *n.* **accumulative** *adj.*

accumulator *n.* **1** a rechargeable battery. **2** a bet placed on a series of events, winnings from each being staked on the next. **3** a storage register in a computer.

accurate *adj.* free from error, conforming exactly to a standard or to truth; careful and exact. ☐ **accurately** *adv.* **accuracy** *n.*

accursed / uh-**ker**-suhd, uh-**kerst** / *adj.* **1** under a curse. **2** *colloq.* detestable, hateful.

accusation *n.* **1** accusing; being accused. **2** a statement accusing a person of a wrongdoing.

accusative / uh-**kyoo**-zuh-tiv / *n. Grammar* the objective form of a word, e.g. *him* in '*we saw him*'.

accuse *v.* state that one lays blame for a fault or wrongdoing on (a named person). ☐ **accuser** *n.* **accusingly** *adv.*

accustom *v.* make used (to something).

accustomed *adj.* **1** (usually foll. by *to*) used to a thing. **2** usual, customary (*in his accustomed seat*).

AC/DC *n.* **1** alternating current/direct current. **2** *colloq.* a bisexual person. • *adj. colloq.* bisexual.

ace *n.* **1** a playing card with one spot. **2** a person who excels at something. **3** (in tennis) a serve that one's opponent does not touch. • *v.* score an ace against (an opponent). • *adj. colloq.* excellent. ☐ **have an ace up one's sleeve** have something effective kept secretly in reserve. **on one's ace** *Aust. colloq.* alone. **within an ace of** on the verge of.

ACE inhibitor *n.* any of a class of drugs used for the treatment of high blood pressure and heart disease. (¶ Angiotensin Converting Enzyme)

acellular / ay-**sel**-yuh-luh / *adj.* having no cells; not consisting of cells.

acerbic / uh-**ser**-bik / *adj.* harsh and sharp, especially in speech or manner. ☐ **acerbity** *n.*

acetaldehyde / as-uh-**tal**-duh-huyd / *n.* a colourless volatile liquid aldehyde.

acetate / **as**-uh-tayt / *n.* **1** a compound derived from acetic acid. **2** a fabric made from cellulose acetate.

acetic / uh-**see**-tik / *adj.* of vinegar. ☐ **acetic acid** the acid that gives vinegar its characteristic taste and smell.

acetone / **as**-uh-tohn / *n.* a colourless liquid used as a solvent.

acetylene / uh-**set**-uh-leen / *n.* a gas that burns with a bright flame, used in cutting and welding metal.

ache / ayk / *v.* **1** suffer a dull continuous physical or mental pain. **2** yearn. • *n.* a dull continuous pain. ☐ **achy** *adj.*

achieve *v.* accomplish, gain or reach by effort. ☐ **achievable** *adj.* **achievement** *n.*

Achilles / uh-**kil**-eez / *Gk myth.* a Greek hero of the Trojan War, whose mother had plunged him in the river Styx during his infancy, making his body invulnerable except for the heel by which she held him. ☐ **Achilles heel** a weak or vulnerable point. **Achilles tendon** the tendon connecting the heel with the calf muscles.

achromatic / ay-kroh-**mat**-ik / *adj.* (in optics) **1** free from colour. **2** transmitting light without decomposing it into constituent colours.

acid *adj.* **1** sharp-tasting, sour. **2** looking or sounding bitter (*acid remarks*). • *n.* **1** any of a class of substances containing hydrogen that can be replaced by a metal to form a salt. **2** a sour substance. **3** *colloq.* the drug LSD. ☐ **acid house** synthesised rock music with a repetitive beat, often associated with the taking of illegal drugs. **acid rain** rain made acidic by contamination from power stations, factories, etc. **acid test** a severe or conclusive test. (¶ Acid is applied to a metal to test whether it is gold or not.) ☐ ☐ **acidly** *adv.*

acidic / uh-**sid**-ik / *adj.* of or like an acid.

acidify / uh-**sid**-uh-fuy / *v.* (**acidified, acidifying**) make or become acid.

acidity / uh-**sid**-uh-tee / *n.* **1** being acid. **2** an over-acid condition of the stomach.

acidophilus / as-uh-**dof**-uh-luhs / *n.* a bacterium used to make yoghurt and to supplement the bacteria naturally inhabiting the intestines.

acidosis / as-uh-**doh**-suhs / *n.* an over-acid condition of the blood or body tissues.

acidulated / uh-**sid**-yoo-lay-tuhd / *adj.* made slightly acid.

acidulous *adj.* somewhat acid.

acknowledge *v.* **1** admit that something is true or valid. **2** confirm the receipt of (a letter etc.). **3** express thanks for (*acknowledged her services to Canberra*). **4** indicate that one has noticed or recognised (*he acknowledged my presence with a sniff*). ☐ **acknowledgment** (also **acknowledgement**) *n.*

acme / **ak**-mee / *n.* the highest point, the peak of perfection.

acne / **ak**-nee / *n.* inflammation of the oil glands of the skin, producing red pimples.

acolyte / **ak**-uh-luyt / *n.* **1** a person who assists a priest in certain church services. **2** an attendant.

aconite / **ak**-uh-nuyt / *n.* **1** a perennial plant of the buttercup family, with a poisonous root. **2** a drug from this.

acorn / **ay**-kawn / *n.* the fruit of the oak tree.

ACOSS / **ay**-kos / *abbr.* = AUSTRALIAN COUNCIL OF SOCIAL SERVICE.

acoustic / uh-**koo**-stik / *adj.* **1** of sound or the sense of hearing; of acoustics. **2** (of a musical instrument etc.) without electrical amplification. • *n.* (**acoustics**) the properties of sound; the qualities of a room that make it good or bad for carrying sound. ☐ **acoustically** *adv.*

acquaint *v.* make aware or familiar (*acquaint him with the facts*). ☐ **be acquainted with** know slightly.

acquaintance *n.* **1** being acquainted. **2** a person one knows slightly.

acquiesce / ak-wee-**es** / *v.* **1** agree without protest; assent. **2** (foll. by *in*) accept as an arrangement.

acquiescent / ak-wee-**es**-uhnt / *adj.* acquiescing. ☐ **acquiescence** *n.*

acquire *v.* gain possession of. ☐ **acquired immune deficiency syndrome** = AIDS. **acquired taste** a liking gained gradually.

acquisition / ak-wuh-**zish**-uhn / *n.* **1** acquiring. **2** something acquired.

acquisitive / uh-**kwiz**-uh-tiv / *adj.* keen to acquire things.

acquit *v.* (**acquitted**, **acquitting**) declare (a person) to be not guilty of the crime with which he or she was charged. ☐ **acquit oneself** conduct oneself; perform (*she acquitted herself well in the test*).

acquittal / uh-**kwit**-uhl / *n.* acquitting; a verdict acquitting a person.

acre / **ay**-kuh / *n.* a measure of land, 4840 sq. yds, 0.405 ha.

acreage / **ay**-kuh-rij / *n.* a number of acres; the extent of a piece of land.

acrid / **ak**-ruhd / *adj.* **1** having a bitter smell or taste. **2** bitter in temper or manner. ☐ **acridity** / uh-**krid**-uh-tee / *n.*

acrimony / **ak**-ruh-muh-nee / *n.* bitterness of manner or words. ☐ **acrimonious** / ak-ruh-**moh**-nee-uhs / *adj.* **acrimoniously** *adv.*

acrobat *n.* a performer of spectacular gymnastic feats. ☐ **acrobatic** *adj.* **acrobatically** *adv.*

acrobatics *n.* (as *pl.*) acrobatic feats; (as *sing.*) the art of performing these.

acronym / **ak**-ruh-nim / *n.* a word formed from the initial letters of other words, e.g. ANZAC.

acrophobia / ak-ruh-**foh**-bee-uh / *n.* an abnormal fear of heights.

acropolis / uh-**krop**-uh-luhs / *n.* **1** the citadel or upper fortified part of an ancient Greek city. **2** (**the Acropolis**) that of Athens.

across *prep.* & *adv.* **1** from one side of a thing to the other. **2** to or on the other side of. **3** so as to be understood or accepted (*got his points across to the audience*). **4** so as to form a cross or intersect (*laid across each other*). ☐ **across the board** applying to all. **be** (*or* **get**) **across** (**something**) be (or become) fully comprehending of the detail or complexity of (an issue etc.) (*the Minister is across her portfolio*).

acrostic / uh-**kros**-tik / *n.* a word puzzle or poem in which the first or last letters of each line form a word or words.

acrylic / uh-**kril**-ik / *adj.* of a synthetic material made from an organic acid (acrylic acid). • *n.* an acrylic fibre, plastic, or resin. ☐ **acrylic acid** a pungent liquid organic acid. **acrylic paint** paint for walls, ceilings, etc. consisting of an emulsion containing acrylic monomer, pigments, etc., which dries to a hard washable finish.

ACT *abbr.* Australian Capital Territory.

act *n.* **1** something done. **2** the process of doing something (*caught in the act*). **3** a decree or law made by a parliament. **4** each of the main divisions of a play. **5** each of a series of short performances in a program (*a circus act*). **6** *colloq.* a pose or pretence (*put on an act*). • *v.* **1** perform actions, behave (*you acted wisely*). **2** function (*the brakes did not act*). **3** have an effect (*acid acts on metal*). **4** portray by actions; perform a part in a play etc. ☐ **act of God** an uncontrollable natural event, e.g. an earthquake. **act up** *colloq.* behave badly; give trouble. **get one's act together** *colloq.* become organised; prepare.

acting *n.* the art or occupation of an actor. • *adj.* serving temporarily, esp. as a substitute (*the acting headmaster*).

actinic / ak-**tin**-ik / *adj.* having photochemical properties, as of short-length radiation.

actinide *n.* any of the series of 15 radioactive elements with atomic numbers between 89 (actinium) and 103 (lawrencium).

actinium / ak-**tin**-ee-uhm / *n.* a radioactive metallic element (symbol Ac) that occurs in pitchblende.

action *n.* **1** the process of doing something, the exertion of energy or influence (*go into action; the action of acid on metal*). **2** a thing done (*generous actions*). **3** a series of events in a story or play (*the action is set in Alice Springs*). **4** a way or manner of moving or functioning; the mechanism of an instrument. **5** a lawsuit. **6** a battle (*he was killed in action*). ☐ **action replay** a playback (at normal or reduced speed) of a televised incident in a sports event. **out of action** not working. **take action** do something.

actionable *adj.* giving cause for a lawsuit.

activate *v.* make active; cause a chemical reaction in; make radioactive. ☐ **activation** *n.* **activator** *n.*

active *adj.* **1** moving about, characterised by energetic action. **2** taking part in activities. **3** functioning, in operation. **4** having an effect (*the active ingredients*). **5** radioactive. • *n.* the form of a verb used when the subject of the sentence is the doer of the action, e.g. *saw* in '*we saw him*'. ☐ **active service** military service in wartime. ☐☐ **actively** *adv.*

activist *n.* one who follows a policy of vigorous action, especially in politics. ☐ **activism** *n.*

activity *n.* **1** being active; busy or energetic action. **2** (often as **activities**) a particular pursuit, action, etc. (*outdoor activities*).

actor *n.* a male or female who performs in a play or a film.

actress *n.* a female actor.

Acts (of the Apostles) the fifth book of the New Testament, relating the early history of the Church in the time of St Peter and St Paul.

ACTU *abbr.* = AUSTRALIAN COUNCIL OF TRADE UNIONS.

actual *adj.* existing in fact, real; current. ☐ **actually** *adv.*

actuality / ak-choo-**al**-uh-tee / *n.* **1** reality. **2** (**actualities**) existing conditions.

actuary / **ak**-choo-uh-ree / *n.* an expert in statistics who calculates insurance risks and premiums. ☐ **actuarial** / ak-choo-**air**-ree-uhl / *adj.*

actuate *v.* **1** activate (a movement or process). **2** be a motive for (a person's actions).

acuity / uh-**kyoo**-uh-tee / *n.* sharpness, acuteness.

acumen / **ak**-yuh-muhn / *n.* sharpness of mind; shrewdness.

acupressure / **ak**-yuh-presh-uh / *n.* applying pressure with the thumbs or fingers to specific points on the body as therapy.

acupuncture / **ak**-yuh-pungk-chuh / *n.* pricking the tissues of the body with fine needles as medical treatment or to relieve pain. ☐ **acupuncturist** *n.*

acute *adj.* **1** very perceptive, having a sharp mind. **2** sharp or severe in its effect (*acute pain; an acute shortage*). **3** (of an illness) coming sharply to a crisis of severity (*acute appendicitis*). ☐ **acute accent** a mark (´) over a vowel, as over *e* in (*café*). **acute angle** an angle of less than 90°. ☐☐ **acutely** *adv.* **acuteness** *n.*

AD *abbr.* (in dates) after the supposed date of Christ's birth. (¶ From the Latin *anno domini* = in the year of the Lord.)

ad *n. colloq.* an advertisement.

adage / **ad**-ij / *n.* a proverb, a saying.

adagio / uh-**dah**-zhee-oh / *adv.* (in music) in slow time. • *n.* (*pl.* **adagios**) a movement to be played in this way.

Adam (in Hebrew tradition) the first man. ☐ **Adam's apple** the lump of cartilage at the front of the neck. **not know a person from Adam** be unable to recognise him or her.

adamant / **ad**-uh-muhnt / *adj.* unyielding to requests; determined.

Adams[1], George (1839–1904), Australian businessman who founded Tattersall's Sweepstakes in 1881.

Adams[2], Gerard ('Gerry') (1948–), Northern Ireland political leader and president of Sinn Féin.

adapt *v.* make or become suitable for a new use or situation. ☐ **adaptation** *n.*

adaptable *adj.* **1** able to be adapted. **2** able to adapt oneself. ☐ **adaptability** *n.*

adaptor *n.* **1** a device that connects pieces of equipment that were not originally designed to be connected. **2** a device for connecting several plugs to one socket.

ADD *abbr.* = ATTENTION DEFICIT DISORDER.

add *v.* **1** join (one thing to another) as an increase or supplement. **2** put numbers or amounts together to get a total. **3** make a further remark. ☐ **add up 1** find the total of. **2** *colloq.* seem consistent or reasonable (*his story doesn't add up*). **add up to 1** yield as a total. **2** *colloq.* result in, be equivalent to.

addendum *n.* (*pl.* **addenda**) something added at the end of a book etc.

adder *n.* **1** a small poisonous snake, a viper. **2** any of various harmless snakes of North America. **3** (also **death adder**) a poisonous snake of the cobra family, found in Australia and nearby islands.

addict / **ad**-ikt / *n.* a person who is addicted to something, especially to drugs.

addicted / uh-**dik**-tuhd / *adj.* **1** doing or using something as a habit or compulsively. **2** devoted to something as a hobby or interest. ☐ **addiction** *n.*

addictive / uh-**dik**-tiv / *adj.* causing addiction.

Addis Ababa / ad-is-**ab**-uh-bah / the capital of Ethiopia.

addition *n.* **1** adding, being added. **2** a thing added to something else. ☐ **in addition** as an extra thing or circumstance.

additional *adj.* added, extra. ☐ **additionally** *adv.*

additive / **ad**-uh-tiv / *n.* a substance added in small amounts, esp. to colour, flavour, or preserve food.

addle *v.* muddle or confuse (*addle one's brains*).

addled *adj.* (of an egg) rotten.

address / uh-**dres** / *n.* **1** the place where a person lives; particulars of where mail should be delivered. **2** a speech delivered to an audience. **3** *Computing* **a** the part of a computer instruction that specifies the location of a piece of stored information. **b** a combination of letters or numbers which identify a person (e.g. an email address: *b.moore@anu.edu.au*), a location on the World Wide Web (e.g. *http://www.anu.edu.au/ANDC*), etc. • *v.* **1** write directions for delivery on (an envelope or parcel). **2** speak or write to (a person, audience, etc.); direct (one's remarks) to a person. **3** apply (oneself) to a task or problem, direct one's attention to (a problem). **4** take aim at (the ball) in golf. **5** store or retrieve (a piece of information) by using an address (see *n.* sense 3).

addressee / ad-res-**ee** / *n.* a person to whom a letter etc. is addressed.

adduce / uh-**dyoos** / *v.* cite as an example or proof. ☐ **adducible** / uh-**dyoos**-uh-buhl / *adj.*

Adelaide the capital of South Australia (former Aboriginal name of the site *Tandarnya* or *Tandarinya*). ☐ **Adelaide Festival** a major cultural event in Australia, held every two years.

Adélie Land / uh-**day**-lee / (also **Adélie Coast**) French territory in the coastal region of Antarctica, south of Australia.

Aden / **ay**-duhn / a seaport and capital of South Yemen (1967–90) prior to unification of North and South Yemen.

adenoids / **ad**-uh-noidz / *n.pl.* enlarged spongy tissue between the back of the nose and the throat, often hindering breathing. ☐ **adenoidal** *adj.*

adept / **ad**-ept, uh-**dept** / *adj.* very skilful; thoroughly proficient. • *n.* one who is very skilful; an expert.

adequate / **ad**-uh-kwuht / *adj.* **1** sufficient, satisfactory. **2** passable, but not outstandingly good. ☐ **adequacy** *n.* **adequately** *adv.*

à deux / uh der / *n.* & *adj.* for two; between two. (¶ French)

ADHD *abbr.* = ATTENTION DEFICIT HYPERACTIVITY DISORDER

adhere / uhd-**heer** / *v.* **1** stick when glued or by suction, or as if by these. **2** remain faithful, continue to give one's support (to a person or cause). **3** (foll. by *to*) keep to and not alter (*we adhered to our plan*).

adherent *adj.* sticking, adhering. • *n.* a supporter of a party or doctrine. ☐ **adherence** *n.*

adhesion / uhd-**hee**-*zh*uhn / *n.* **1** adhering. **2** tissue formed when normally separate tissues of the body grow together as a result of inflammation or injury.

adhesive *adj.* causing things to adhere, sticky (*adhesive tape*). • *n.* an adhesive substance. ☐ **adhesiveness** *n.*

ad hoc *adv.* & *adj.* for a specific purpose (*an ad hoc arrangement*). (¶ Latin, = for this.)

adieu / uh-**dyoo** / *interj.* & *n.* (*pl.* **adieus**) goodbye.

Adi Granth / ah-dee **grunt** / the sacred scripture of Sikhism.

ad infinitum / ad in-fuh-**nuy**-tuhm / *adv.* without limit, for ever. (¶ Latin, = to infinity.)

adipose / **ad**-uh-pohs / *adj.* of animal fat; fatty. ☐ **adiposity** / ad-uh-**pos**-uh-tee / *n.*

adj. *abbr.* adjective.

adjacent *adj.* lying near, adjoining.

adjective / **aj**-ik-tiv / *n.* a word added to a noun to describe a quality or modify a meaning (see panel). ☐ **adjectival** / aj-uhk-**tuy**-vuhl / *adj.* **adjectivally** *adv.*

adjigo / **aj**-i-goh / *n.* a native plant of WA, the edible yams of which supported large populations of Aborigines. (¶ Probably from Nhanta *ajuga* 'vegetable food'.)

adjoin *v.* be next or nearest to.

adjourn / uh-**jern** / *v.* **1** postpone, break off temporarily. **2** break off and go elsewhere (*let's adjourn to the pub*). ☐ **adjournment** *n.*

adjudge *v.* decide or award judicially (*he was adjudged to be guilty*).

adjudicate / uh-**joo**-duh-kayt / *v.* **1** act as judge in a court, tribunal, or competition. **2** judge and pronounce a decision upon. ☐ **adjudication** *n.* **adjudicator** *n.*

adjunct / **aj**-unkt / *n.* something added or attached but subordinate.

adjure / uh-**joor** / *v.* command or urge solemnly (*I adjure you to tell the truth*). ☐ **adjuration** *n.*

adjust *v.* **1** arrange, put into the proper position. **2** alter by a small amount so as to fit or be right for use (*need to adjust the brakes*). **3** adapt or adapt oneself to new circumstances (*he had difficulty in adjusting to civilian life*). **4** assess (loss or damage) in settlement of an insurance claim. ☐ **adjuster** *n.* **adjustment** *n.* **adjustable** *adj.*

adjutant / **aj**-uh-tuhnt / *n.* an army officer assisting a superior officer with administrative work.

ad lib *adv.* as one pleases, without restraint. • *adj.* said or done impromptu; improvised. • *v.* (**ad libbed, ad libbing**) speak impromptu, improvise (remarks or actions). (¶ Latin *ad libitum*, = according to pleasure.)

admin / **ad**-min / *colloq. n.* administration. • *adj.* pertaining to administration (*the admin building*).

administer *v.* **1** manage (business affairs), be an administrator (*administer a person's estate*). **2** give or hand out formally, provide (*administer the sacrament; administer punishment*).

administrate *v.* act as administrator (of).

administration *n.* **1** administering. **2** the management of public or business affairs. **3** the people who administer an organisation etc.; the government.

administrative *adj.* of or involving administration.

administrator *n.* **1** a person responsible for administration; one who has a talent for this. **2** a

Adjective

An adjective is a word that describes a noun or pronoun, e.g.
  red, clever, Tasmanian, depressed, grilled, sticky, shining.
Most can be used either before a noun (in which position they are called *attributive*), e.g.
  the *red house,* a *clever woman,*
or after a verb like *be, seem,* or *call* (in which position they are called *predicative*), e.g.
  The house is *red.*   I wouldn't call him *lazy.*
  She seems very *clever.*
Some can be used only *before* a noun, e.g.
  the *main* reason (one cannot say *the reason is main*).
  Such an adjective is known as an *attributive adjective.*
Some can be used only *after* a verb, e.g.
  The ship is still *afloat* (one cannot say *an afloat ship*).
  Such an adjective is known as a *predicative adjective.*
A few can be used only immediately after a noun, e.g.
  the president *elect* (one cannot say either *an elect president* or *The president is elect*).

person appointed to administer an estate, an insolvent company, etc.

admirable / **ad**-muh-ruh-buhl / *adj.* worthy of admiration, excellent. ☐ **admirably** *adv.*

admiral *n.* **1** a naval officer of high rank, commander of a fleet or squadron. **2** any of various butterflies (*the Australian admiral*).

admire *v.* **1** regard with pleasure or satisfaction; think highly of. **2** express admiration of. ☐ **admiration** *n.* **admirer** *n.*

admissible *adj.* capable of being admitted or allowed.

admission *n.* **1** admitting; being admitted. **2** the charge for this. **3** a statement admitting something, a confession.

admit *v.* (**admitted, admitting**) **1** allow to enter. **2** accept into a school etc. as a pupil or into a hospital as a patient. **3** accept as true or valid. **4** state reluctantly (*we admit that the task is difficult*). ☐ **admit of** leave room for (*the plan does not admit of improvement*).

admittance *n.* being allowed to enter, especially into a private place.

admittedly *adv.* as must be admitted.

admixture *n.* something added as an ingredient.

admonish / uhd-**mon**-ish / *v.* **1** advise or urge seriously. **2** reprove mildly but firmly. ☐ **admonishment** *n.* **admonition** / ad-muh-**nish**-uhn / *n.* **admonitory** / uhd-**mon**-uh-tree / *adj.*

ad nauseam / ad **naw**-see-uhm, -zee- / *adv.* to a sickening extent; excessively. (¶ Latin)

Adnyamathanha / **ad**-nyu-mud-u-nu / *n.* an Aboriginal language of central SA.

ado / uh-**doo** / *n.* fuss, trouble, excitement.

adobe / uh-**doh**-bee / *n.* **1** sun-dried clay brick. **2** clay for making this.

adolescent / ad-uh-**les**-uhnt / *adj.* between childhood and maturity. • *n.* an adolescent person. ☐ **adolescence** *n.*

Adonis / uh-**doh**-nis / *n.* **1** *Gk myth.* a handsome young man, loved by Aphrodite. **2** any beautiful young man.

adopt *v.* **1** take into one's family as a relation, especially as one's child with legal guardianship. **2** choose (a course of action etc.) (*adopted the safer alternative*). **3** take and use as one's own (*adopted this name*). **4** take over (another's idea etc.). **5** approve or accept (a report or financial accounts). ☐ **adoption** *n.*

adoptive *adj.* related by adoption.

adorable *adj.* **1** very lovable. **2** *colloq.* delightful. ☐ **adorably** *adv.*

adore *v.* **1** love deeply. **2** worship as divine. **3** *colloq.* like very much. ☐ **adoration** *n.* **adorer** *n.*

adorn *v.* **1** decorate with ornaments. **2** be an ornament to. ☐ **adornment** *n.*

ADP *abbr.* automatic data processing.

adrenal / uh-**dree**-nuhl / *n.* (in full **adrenal gland**) either of two ductless glands on top of the kidneys, secreting adrenalin.

adrenalin / uh-**dren**-uh-luhn / *n.* (also **adrenaline**) a hormone that stimulates the nervous system, secreted by a part of the adrenal glands or prepared synthetically.

Adriatic / ay-dree-**at**-ik / *adj.* of the Adriatic Sea, between Italy and the former Yugoslavia. • *n.* the Adriatic Sea.

adrift *adv.* & *adj.* **1** drifting. **2** unfastened, loose. **3** wrong; not as planned (*our plans went adrift*).

adroit / uh-**droit** / *adj.* skilful; ingenious. ☐ **adroitly** *adv.* **adroitness** *n.*

adsorb *v.* (of a solid) hold (particles of a gas or liquid) to its surface. ☐ **adsorption** *n.*

adulation / ad-yoo-**lay**-shuhn / *n.* excessive flattery. ☐ **adulatory** / **ad**-yoo-lay-tuh-ree / *adj.*

adult / **ad**-ult / *adj.* grown to full size or strength, mature. • *n.* an adult person. ☐ **adulthood** *n.*

adulterant *n.* a substance added in adulterating something.

adulterate *v.* make impure or poorer in quality by adding another substance. ☐ **adulteration** *n.*

adulterer *n.* a person who commits adultery.

adulteress *n.* a woman who commits adultery.

adultery *n.* the act of being unfaithful to one's wife or husband by voluntarily having sexual intercourse with someone else. ☐ **adulterous** *adj.*

adumbrate *v.* foreshadow. ☐ **adumbration** *n.*

adv. *abbr.* adverb.

advance *v.* **1** move or put forward; make progress. **2** help the progress of (*advance someone's interests*). **3** bring forward or make (*advance a suggestion*). **4** bring (an event) to an earlier date. **5** lend (money), pay before a due date (*advance her a month's salary*). • *n.* **1** a forward movement, progress. **2** an increase in price or amount. **3** a loan, payment beforehand. **4** (**advances**) attempts to establish a sexual relationship or a business agreement. • *adj.* going before others; done or provided in advance (*the advance party; advance bookings*). ☐ **in advance** ahead in place or time. ☐☐ **advancement** *n.*

Advance Australia Fair the national anthem of Australia, composed about 1878, and officially replacing *God Save the Queen* in 1984.

advanced *adj.* **1** far on in progress or in life (*an advanced age*). **2** not elementary (*advanced studies*). **3** (of ideas etc.) new and not yet generally accepted.

advantage *n.* **1** a favourable condition or circumstance. **2** benefit, profit. **3** the next point won after deuce in tennis. **4** *colloq.* a lead (*started the quarter with a 23 point advantage*). ☐ **take advantage of** make use of; exploit.

advantageous / ad-van-**tay**-juhs / *adj.* profitable, beneficial. ☐ **advantageously** *adv.*

Advent *n.* **1** the season (with four Sundays) before Christmas Day. **2** the coming of Christ. **3** (**advent**) the arrival of an important person, event, or development.

Adventist *n.* a member of a sect believing that Christ's second coming is very near.

adventitious / ad-ven-**tish**-uhs / *adj.* **1** accidental, casual. **2** (of roots etc.) occurring in an unusual place.

adventure *n.* **1** an exciting or dangerous experience. **2** willingness to take risks (*the spirit of adventure*). □ **adventurous** *adj.* **adventurously** *adv.*

adventurer *n.* **1** a person who seeks adventures. **2** a person who is ready to make gains by risky or unscrupulous methods.

adverb *n.* a word that qualifies a verb, adjective, or other adverb (see panel). □ **adverbial** *adj.* **adverbially** *adv.*

adversary / **ad**-vuh-suh-ree / *n.* an opponent, an enemy.

adverse / **ad**-vers / *adj.* unfavourable; harmful (*an adverse report; the drug has no adverse effects*). □ **adversely** *adv.*

adversity / uhd-**ver**-suh-tee / *n.* misfortune, trouble.

advert[1] / **ad**-vert / *n. colloq.* an advertisement.

advert[2] / uhd-**vert** / *v.* (foll. by *to*) *literary* refer in speaking or writing.

advertise *v.* **1** make generally known (*advertise a meeting*). **2** promote (goods or services) publicly to encourage people to buy or use them. **3** ask or offer by public notice (*advertise for a secretary*). □ **advertiser** *n.*

advertisement / uhd-**ver**-tuhz-muhnt / *n.* **1** advertising. **2** a public notice advertising something.

advertorial *n.* a commercial advertisement written in the form of a news item, editorial, etc.

advice *n.* **1** an opinion given about what to do or how to behave. **2** a piece of information (*we received advice that the goods had been dispatched*).

advisable *adj.* worth recommending as a course of action. □ **advisability** *n.*

advise *v.* **1** give advice to, recommend. **2** inform, notify.

advisedly / uhd-**vuy**-zuhd-lee / *adv.* after careful thought; deliberately.

adviser *n.* (also **advisor**) a person who advises, esp. officially.

advisory *adj.* giving advice, having the power to advise (*an advisory committee*).

advocaat / ad-vuh-**kaht** / *n.* a liqueur of eggs, sugar, and brandy.

advocacy / **ad**-vuh-kuh-see / *n.* support or argument for a cause, policy, etc.

advocate *v.* / **ad**-vuh-kayt / recommend (*I advocate caution*). • *n.* / **ad**-vuh-kuht / **1** a person who advocates a policy (*an advocate of reform*). **2** a person who pleads on behalf of another; a lawyer presenting a client's case in a lawcourt.

adze / adz / *n.* an axe with a blade at right angles to the handle, used for trimming large pieces of wood.

Aegean / i-**jee**-uhn / *adj.* of the Aegean Sea, between Greece and Turkey. • *n.* the Aegean Sea.

aegis / **ee**-juhs / *n.* protection, sponsorship (*under the aegis of the Republican Movement*).

Aeneas / i-**nee**-uhs / *Gk & Rom. myth.* a Trojan leader, regarded by the Romans as the founder of their State.

Aeneid / i-**nee**-uhd / a Latin epic poem by Virgil, which relates the wanderings of Aeneas after the fall of Troy.

aeolian / ee-**oh**-lee-uhn / *adj.* wind-borne. □ **aeolian harp** a stringed instrument giving musical sounds when exposed to wind. (¶ Named after Aeolus, god of the winds in Greek mythology.)

aeon / **ee**-uhn / *n.* (also **eon**) an immense time.

aerate / **air**-rayt / *v.* **1** expose to the chemical action of air (*aerate the soil by forking it*). **2** add carbon dioxide to (a liquid) under pressure (*aerated water*). □ **aeration** *n.*

aerial / **air**-ree-uhl / *adj.* **1** of or like air. **2** existing in the air; suspended overhead (*an aerial railway*).

Adverb

An adverb is used:
1 with a verb, to indicate:
   a how something happens, e.g. *He walks* quickly.
   b where something happens, e.g. *I live* here.
   c when something happens, e.g. *They visited us* yesterday.
   d how often something happens, e.g. *We usually have coffee.*
2 to strengthen or weaken the meaning of:
   a a verb, e.g. *He really meant it; I almost fell asleep.*
   b an adjective, e.g. *She is very clever; This is a slightly better result.*
   c another adverb, e.g. *It comes off terribly easily; The boys nearly always get home late.*
3 to add to the meaning of a whole sentence, e.g.
    He is probably our best player; Luckily, *no one was hurt.*
In writing or in formal speech, it is **incorrect** to use an adjective instead of an adverb. For example, use
   Do it properly   and not   *Do it* proper.
but note that many words are both an adjective and an adverb, e.g.
   adjective   *adverb*
   a fast *horse*   *He ran* fast.
   a long *time*   *Have you been here* long?

3 by or from aircraft (*aerial bombardment*). • *n.* **1** a wire or rod for transmitting or receiving radio waves. **2** (in *pl.*) a downhill skiing event in which competitors negotiate a ramp and execute somersaults etc. ☐ **aerial ping-pong** *Aust. jocular* Australian Rules football.

aero- *comb. form* air; aircraft (*aero-engine*).

aerobatics *n.pl.* spectacular feats of flying aircraft. ☐ **aerobatic** *adj.*

aerobic / air-**roh**-bik / *adj.* **1** using oxygen from the air. **2** (of exercises) designed to increase the intake of oxygen and strengthen the heart and lungs. • *n.* (**aerobics**) exercises of this kind.

aerodrome *n.* an airfield.

aerodynamics *n.* interaction between airflow and the movement of solid bodies (e.g. aircraft, bullets) through air. ☐ **aerodynamic** *adj.*

aerofoil *n.* an aircraft wing, fin, or tailplane.

aerogramme *n.* (also **aerogram**) an airmail letter in the form of a single sheet folded and sealed.

aeronautics *n.* the scientific study of the flight of aircraft. ☐ **aeronautic** *adj.* **aeronautical** *adj.*

aeroplane *n.* a power-driven aircraft with wings.

aerosol *n.* **1** a substance sealed in a container under pressure, with a device for releasing it as a fine spray. **2** the container itself.

aerospace *n.* **1** the earth's atmosphere and space beyond it. **2** the technology of aviation in this region.

Aeschylus / ee-skuh-luhs / (525–456 BC) Greek dramatist.

Aesop / **ee**-sop / (6th century BC) Greek teller of animal fables with a moral.

aesthete / **ees**-theet, **es**- / *n.* a person who claims to have great understanding and appreciation of what is beautiful.

aesthetic / ees-**thet**-ik, **es**- / *adj.* **1** relating to the appreciation of beauty (*the aesthetic standards of the times*). **2** having or showing such appreciation. **3** artistic, tasteful. • *n.* (**aesthetics**) a branch of philosophy dealing with the principles of beauty and tastefulness. ☐ **aesthetically** *adv.*

aetiology / ee-tee-**ol**-uh-jee / *n.* (also **etiology**) **1** the study of causes or reasons. **2** a scientific account of the causes of a disease. ☐ **aetiological** *adj.* **aetiologically** *adv.*

afar *adv.* far off, far away.

affable *adj.* polite and friendly. ☐ **affably** *adv.* **affability** *n.*

affair *n.* **1** a thing done or to be done; a matter, a concern. **2** *colloq.* an event; a thing (*this camera is a complicated affair*). **3** a temporary sexual relationship between two people who are not married to each other. **4** (**affairs**) public or private business (*current affairs; put your affairs in order*).

affect *v.* **1** have an effect on (*the new tax laws affect us all*). **2** arouse sadness or sympathy in (*the news of his death affected us deeply*). **3** (of a disease) attack or infect (*tuberculosis affected his lungs*). **4** pretend to have or feel (*she affected ignorance*). **5** like and make a display of using or wearing (*he affects velvet jackets*).

■ **Usage** *Affect* should not be confused with *effect* which means 'to bring about, to accomplish', e.g. *The government effected great changes*. Note also that *effect* is commonly used as a noun as well as a verb.

affectation *n.* behaviour that is put on for display and is not natural or genuine.

affected *adj.* **1** full of affectation. **2** pretended.

affection *n.* love; fond feeling.

affectionate *adj.* showing affection, loving. ☐ **affectionately** *adv.*

affiance / uh-**fuy**-uhns / *v. literary* betroth.

affidavit / af-uh-**day**-vit / *n.* a written statement for use as legal evidence, sworn on oath to be true. (¶ Medieval Latin)

affiliate / uh-**fil**-ee-ayt / *v.* connect as a subordinate member or branch (*the club is affiliated to a national society*). • *n.* an affiliated person or organisation. ☐ **affiliation** *n.*

affinity / uh-**fin**-uh-tee / *n.* **1** a strong natural liking or attraction. **2** relationship (especially by marriage) other than blood relationship. **3** similarity; close resemblance or connection (*affinities between different languages*). **4** *Chemistry* the tendency of certain substances to combine with others.

affirm *v.* **1** assert, state as a fact. **2** make an affirmation instead of an oath.

affirmation / af-uh-**may**-shuhn / *n.* **1** affirming. **2** a solemn declaration made instead of an oath by a person who has conscientious objections to swearing an oath or who has no religion.

affirmative / uh-**fer**-muh-tiv / *adj.* affirming, agreeing (*an affirmative reply*). • *n.* an affirmative word or statement (*the answer is in the affirmative*). ☐ **affirmative action** action (esp. in employment, promotion, etc.) favouring those who often suffer from discrimination. ☐ **affirmatively** *adv.*

affirmatory / uh-**fer**-muh-tuh-ree / *adj.* affirming.

affix *v.* / uh-**fiks** / **1** stick on, attach. **2** add in writing (*affix your signature*). • *n.* / **af**-iks / a prefix or suffix.

afflict *v.* distress physically or mentally; be the cause of suffering (*he is afflicted with rheumatism*).

affliction *n.* **1** pain, distress, misery. **2** something that causes this.

affluent / **af**-loo-uhnt / *adj.* rich (*the affluent society*). ☐ **affluently** *adv.* **affluence** *n.*

afford *v.* **1** have enough money, means, or time for a specified purpose (*we can afford to pay $50*). **2** be in a position to do something (*we can't afford to be critical*). **3** *formal* provide (*her diary affords no information*).

afforest *v.* plant with trees to form a forest. ☐ **afforestation** *n.*

affray / uh-**fray** / *n.* a breach of the peace by fighting or rioting in public.

affront / uh-**frunt** / v. **1** insult deliberately; offend or embarrass. **2** face, confront. • n. a deliberate insult or show of disrespect.

Afghan / **af**-gan / n. **1** a native of Afghanistan. **2** the language spoken there, Pashto. **3** (also **Ghan**) *Aust. hist.* an immigrant to Australia from Afghanistan, Pakistan, etc., engaged esp. in camel driving and camel breeding in the outback, and also in storekeeping, selling wares on foot, etc. **4** (**afghan**) a loose sheepskin coat with shaggy fleece lining. ☐ **Afghan hound** a tall breed of dog with long silky hair.

Afghanistan / af-**gan**-uh-stahn / a republic in central Asia.

aficionado / uh-fis-ee-uh-**nah**-doh / n. (pl. **aficionados**) a devotee of a particular sport or pastime. (¶ Spanish)

afield *adv.* far away from home; to or at a distance.

AFL *abbr.* = AUSTRALIAN FOOTBALL LEAGUE.

aflame *adv. & adj.* in flames, burning.

afloat *adv. & adj.* **1** floating. **2** at sea, on board ship (*enjoying life afloat*). **3** out of debt or difficulty. **4** in general circulation; current (*a rumour is afloat that...*). **5** flooded.

afoot *adv. & adj.* progressing, in operation (*there's a scheme afoot to restore Lake Pedder*).

aforementioned *adj.* referred to previously.

aforesaid *adj.* mentioned previously.

aforethought *adj.* premeditated, planned in advance (*with malice aforethought*).

AFP *abbr.* Australian Federal Police.

afraid *adj.* **1** alarmed, frightened, anxious about consequences. **2** politely regretful (*I'm afraid there's none left*).

afresh *adv.* anew, beginning again.

Africa a continent south of the Mediterranean Sea between the Atlantic and Indian Oceans.

African *adj.* of Africa or its people or languages. • n. a native of Africa, especially a black person. ☐ **African violet** an East African plant with purple, pink, or white flowers.

African-American n. a black American. • *adj.* of or relating to black Americans.

African National Congress a South African political party and black nationalist organisation, campaigning for racial equality.

Afrikaans / af-ri-**kahns** / n. a language derived from Dutch, used in South Africa.

Afrikaner / af-ri-**kah**-nuh / n. a white person in South Africa whose native language is Afrikaans.

Afro / **af**-roh / *adj.* (of hair) tightly curled and bushy. • n. (pl. **Afros**) an Afro hairstyle.

Afro- *comb. form* African.

Afro-Asian *adj.* pertaining to the (non-official) affiliation of non-aligned African and Asian countries.

aft *adv.* in or near or towards the stern of a ship or the tail of an aircraft.

after *prep.* **1** behind in place or order. **2** at a later time than. **3** in spite of (*after all I did for him he still ignored me*). **4** as a result of (*after what he did, he doesn't deserve political support*). **5** in pursuit or search of (*run after him*). **6** about, concerning (*he asked after you*). **7** in imitation of (*painted after the manner of Picasso; named after a person*). • *adv.* **1** behind (*Jill came tumbling after*). **2** later (*twenty years after*). • *conj.* at or in a time later than (*they came after I left*). • *adj.* **1** later, following (*in after years*). **2** nearer the stern in a boat (*the after cabins*). • n. (**afters**) *colloq.* dessert. ☐ **after-effect** an effect that arises or persists after its cause has gone.

afterbirth n. the placenta and foetal membrane discharged from the womb after childbirth.

aftercare n. care of a patient after a stay in hospital or of a person on release from prison.

afterlife n. life after death.

aftermath n. events or circumstances that follow and are a consequence of an event (*the aftermath of war*).

afternoon n. the time from noon to evening.

afterpains *n.pl.* pains caused by contraction of the womb after childbirth.

aftershave n. a lotion for use after shaving.

aftershock n. a lesser quake or shock following an earthquake.

aftertaste n. a taste that remains after something has been swallowed.

afterthought n. something thought of or added later.

afterwards *adv.* at a later time.

Ag *symbol* silver.

again *adv.* **1** another time, once more (*try again*). **2** as before, to or in the original place or condition (*you'll soon be well again*). **3** furthermore, besides. **4** on the other hand (*I might, and again I might not*).

against *prep.* **1** in opposition to. **2** in contrast to (*against a dark background*). **3** in preparation for, in anticipation of (*saved against a rainy day*). **4** opposite, so as to cancel or lessen (*allowances to be set against income*). **5** into collision or contact with (*lean against the wall*).

Aga Khan / ah-guh **kahn** / the spiritual leader of Ismaili Muslims.

Agamemnon / ag-uh-**mem**-nuhn / *Gk myth.* king of Mycenae and leader of the Greek expedition against Troy.

agape[1] / uh-**gayp** / *adj.* gaping, open-mouthed.

agape[2] / **ag**-uh-pay / n. **1** an early Christian Eucharistic feast. **2** Christian love. (¶ Greek, = brotherly love.)

agar / **ay**-gar / n. (also **agar-agar**) a substance obtained from seaweed, added to food to thicken it or make it set like jelly; also used as a microbiological medium. Also called *moss-jelly*.

agaric / **ag**-uh-rik / n. a fungus with a cap and stalk, e.g. the common mushroom.

Agassi / **ag**-uh-see /, André (1970–), American tennis player. Tournament wins include Wimbledon

(1992), the US Open (1994, 1999), the French Open (1999), and the Australian Open (1995, 2000–01).

agate / **ag**-uht / *n.* a very hard stone with patches or concentric bands of colour.

age *n.* **1** the length of time a person has lived or a thing has existed. **2** the later part of life, old age. **3** a historical period, a time with special characteristics or events (*the Elizabethan Age; the atomic age*). **4** *colloq.* a very long time (*it took ages; it seemed an age before he came*). • *v.* (**aged, ageing** *or* **aging**) **1** grow old, show signs of age. **2** become mature (*heavy wines age slowly*). **3** cause to become old (*worry aged him rapidly*). **4** allow to mature. ☐ **age of consent** the age at which consent to sexual intercourse is valid in law. **age-old** having existed for a very long time. **of age** having reached the age at which one has an adult's legal rights and obligations. **under age** not yet of age.

aged *adj.* **1** / ayjd / of the age of (*aged 10*). **2** / **ay**-juhd / very old (*an aged man*).

ageism / **ay**-jiz-uhm / *n.* prejudice or discrimination against people solely on the grounds of age. ☐ **ageist** *adj. & n.*

ageless *adj.* not growing or appearing old.

agelong *adj.* existing for a very long time.

agency *n.* **1** the business or place of business of an agent (*a travel agency*). **2** the means through which something is done (*fertilised by the agency of bees*).

agenda / uh-**jen**-duh / *n.* (*pl.* **agendas**) a program of items of business to be dealt with at a meeting.

agent *n.* **1** a person who does something or instigates some activity (*he is a mere instrument, not an agent*). **2** one who acts on behalf of another (*write to our agent in Rome*). **3** something that produces an effect or change (*soda is the active agent*). **4** a spy; a secret agent.

agent orange *n.* a chemical defoliant, esp. as used by US forces during the Vietnam War, so named from the colour coding of its containers. ☐ **agent orange stress syndrome** a complex of physical and psychological illnesses caused by exposure to agent orange.

agent provocateur / ah-zhon pruh-vo-kuh-**ter** / *n.* (*pl.* *agents provocateurs* pronounced the same) a person employed to detect suspected offenders by tempting them to do something illegal.

agglomerate *v.* / uh-**glom**-uh-rayt / collect or become collected into a mass. • *n.* / uh-**glom**-uh-ruht / something composed of clustered fragments. ☐ **agglomeration** *n.*

agglutinate / uh-**gloo**-tuh-nayt / *v.* stick or fuse together. ☐ **agglutination** *n.* **agglutinative** *adj.*

aggrandise / uh-**gran**-duyz, **ag**-ran- / *v.* (also -**ize**) increase the power, wealth, or importance of. ☐ **aggrandisement** *n.*

aggravate *v.* **1** make worse or more serious. **2** *colloq.* annoy. ☐ **aggravation** *n.*

aggregate *adj.* / **ag**-ruh-guht / combined, total (*the aggregate amount*). • *n.* / **ag**-ruh-guht / **1** a total; a mass or amount brought together. **2** hard substances (sand, gravel, broken stone, etc.) mixed with cement to make concrete. • *v.* / **ag**-ruh-gayt / collect or form into an aggregate, unite. ☐ **in the aggregate** as a whole, collectively. ☐☐ **aggregation** *n.*

aggression *n.* **1** unprovoked attacking. **2** a hostile action, hostile behaviour.

aggressive *adj.* **1** apt to make attacks; showing hostility or aggression. **2** self-assertive, forceful (*an aggressive salesman*). ☐ **aggressively** *adv.* **aggressiveness** *n.*

aggressor *n.* a person or country that attacks first or begins hostilities.

aggrieved / uh-**greevd** / *adj.* made resentful by unfair treatment.

aggro *colloq.* *n.* aggressive or hostile behaviour. • *adj.* aggressive, hostile.

aghast / uh-**gahst** / *adj.* filled with consternation.

agile *adj.* nimble, quick-moving. ☐ **agilely** *adv.* **agility** / uh-**jil**-uh-tee / *n.*

agistment / uh-**jist**-muhnt / *n.* **1** the taking in of livestock to feed at a rate of so much a head. **2** the price paid for this. ☐ **agist** *v.*

agitate *v.* **1** shake or move briskly. **2** disturb, cause anxiety to. **3** stir up public interest or concern. ☐ **agitation** *n.* **agitator** *n.*

aglow *adj.* glowing. • *adv.* glowingly.

AGM *abbr.* annual general meeting.

agnail / **ag**-nayl / *n.* a piece of torn skin at the root of a fingernail.

Agni (in Hinduism) the Vedic god of fire, who takes offerings to the gods in the smoke of sacrifice and returns to the earth as lightning.

agnostic / ag-**nos**-tik / *n.* a person who believes that nothing can be known about the existence of God or of anything except material things. ☐ **agnosticism** *n.*

ago *adv.* in the past.

agog / uh-**gog** / *adj.* eager, expectant.

agonise *v.* (also -**ize**) suffer or cause to suffer mental or physical agony (*he agonised over the decision for weeks*). ☐ **agonised** *adj.* expressing agony (*an agonised look*). ☐☐ **agonisingly** *adv.*

agony *n.* extreme mental or physical suffering.

agoraphobia / ag-uh-ruh-**foh**-bee-uh / *n.* abnormal fear of open spaces or public places. ☐ **agoraphobic** *n. & adj.*

Agra / **ah**-gruh / a city on the River Jumna in northern India, site of the Taj Mahal.

agrarian / uh-**grair**-ree-uhn / *adj.* of agricultural land or its cultivation; of landed property.

agree *v.* (**agreed, agreeing**) **1** hold a similar opinion. **2** consent, say that one is willing. **3** get on well together. **4** be consistent, harmonise (*your story agrees with what I've heard already*). **5** suit a person's health or digestion (*curry doesn't agree with me*). **6** correspond in grammatical case, number, gender, or person (*the pronoun 'she'*

agreeable / **aircraft**

agrees with the noun 'woman'; 'he' agrees with 'man').

agreeable *adj.* **1** pleasing, pleasant (*an agreeable voice*). **2** willing to agree (*we'll go if you are agreeable*). ◻ **agreeably** *adv.*

agreement *n.* **1** agreeing. **2** harmony in opinion or feeling. **3** an arrangement agreed between people.

agribusiness / ag-ree-biz-nuhs / *n.* **1** agriculture conducted on strictly commercial principles, esp. using advanced technology. **2** the group of industries dealing with the produce of, and services to, farming.

agriculture *n.* the science or process of cultivating land on a large scale and rearing livestock. ◻ **agricultural** *adj.* **agriculturally** *adv.*

agrifood / ag-ree-food / *n.* **1** any of the products of the agrifood industry. **2** the agrifood industry. ◻ **agrifood industry** an integrated system of food production, including growing, processing, and marketing arrangements.

agronomy / uh-**gron**-uh-mee / *n.* the science of soil management and crop production.

aground *adv.* & *adj.* on or touching the bottom in shallow water (*the ship ran aground*).

ague / **ay**-gyoo / *n.* malarial fever; a fit of shivering.

ah *interj.* an exclamation of surprise, pity, admiration, etc.

aha *interj.* an exclamation of surprise, triumph, or mockery.

ahead *adv.* further forward in space, time, or progress (*try to plan ahead; full speed ahead!*).

ahem *interj.* the noise made when clearing one's throat.

ahimsa / ah-**him**-suh / *n.* (in Hinduism, Buddhism, Jainism) the doctrine of non-violence or non-killing.

-aholic *see* -HOLIC.

ahoy *interj.* a cry used by sailors to call attention.

Ahriman / **ah**-ri-muhn / the evil spirit in Zoroastrianism.

Ahura Mazda / uh-hoor-ruh **maz**-duh / (later called *Ormuzd*) the creator god in Zoroastrianism, the force for good.

aid *v.* help. • *n.* **1** help. **2** something that helps (*a hearing aid*). **3** food, money, etc., sent to a country to help it (*overseas aid*).

aide *n.* **1** an aide-de-camp. **2** an assistant.

aide-de-camp / ayd-duh-**kong** / *n.* (*pl.* **aides-de-camp** / aydz- /) a naval or military officer acting as assistant to a senior officer.

Aids *abbr.* (also **AIDS**) acquired immune deficiency syndrome, an often fatal condition that develops after infection with the Aids virus (*see* HIV), breaking down a person's natural defences against illness. (*See* PWA.)

Aids-related complex *n.* (also **ARC**) second stage of infection by the Aids virus in which fever, weight loss, and malaise become apparent;

sometimes leading to the third stage, always ultimately fatal (FULL-BLOWN AIDS).

Aids virus = HIV.

aikido / uy-**kee**-doh / *n.* a Japanese form of self-defence.

ail *v.* *archaic* make ill or uneasy (*what ails him?*).

aileron / **ay**-luh-ruhn / *n.* a hinged flap on an aeroplane wing, used to control balance.

ailing *adj.* unwell; in poor condition.

ailment *n.* a slight illness.

aim *v.* **1** point or send towards a target; direct (a blow, missile, remark, etc.) towards a specified object or goal. **2** attempt, try (*we aim to please the customers*). • *n.* **1** the act of aiming (*take aim*). **2** purpose, intention (*what is his aim?*).

aimless *adj.* without a purpose. ◻ **aimlessly** *adv.* **aimlessness** *n.*

ain't = am not, is not, are not, has not, have not.

■ **Usage** This word is avoided in standard speech except in humorous use, e.g. *things ain't what they used to be.*

Ainu / **ay**-noo / *n.* (*pl.* **Ainu** or **Ainus**) a member of the non-Mongoloid aboriginal inhabitants of Japan, with very thick wavy hair.

air *n.* **1** the mixture of gases surrounding the earth. **2** the earth's atmosphere; open space in this; this as the place where aircraft operate. **3** an impression given (*an air of mystery*). **4** an impressive manner (*he does things with such an air and flair*). **5** a melody, a tune. • *v.* **1** expose to the air, ventilate (a room etc.) so as to freshen it. **2** put (clothes etc.) into a warm place to finish drying. **3** express publicly (*air one's opinions*). ◻ **air bag** a safety device in a car that fills with air on impact to protect the driver in a collision. **air brake** a brake worked by compressed air. **air conditioned** supplied with air conditioning. **air conditioning** a system controlling the humidity and temperature of the air in a room, building, or vehicle. **air force** a branch of the armed forces that uses aircraft for fighting. **air pocket** a partial vacuum in the air causing aircraft in flight to drop suddenly. **air rifle** an airgun. **air speed** an aircraft's speed relative to the air. **air terminal** a building at an airport with facilities for passengers etc. **air traffic control** airport officials who are responsible for the safe movement of aircraft and who give radio instructions to pilots. **by air** in or by aircraft. **in the air 1** current, exerting an influence (*dissatisfaction is in the air*). **2** (of plans etc.) undecided; uncertain (*these plans are still in the air*). **on the air** broadcast or broadcasting by radio or television. **put on airs** behave in an affected haughty manner.

airbase *n.* a base for military aircraft.

airborne *adj.* **1** transported by the air (*airborne pollen*). **2** in flight after taking off. **3** transported by aircraft (*airborne troops*).

aircraft *n.* (*pl.* **aircraft**) **1** a machine capable of flight. **2** such craft collectively, including aero-

aircraftman planes, gliders, and helicopters. ☐ **aircraft carrier** a ship that carries and acts as a base for aircraft.

aircraftman *n.* (*feminine* **aircraftwoman**) the lowest rank in the RAAF.

airfield *n.* an area of open level ground equipped with hangars and runways for aircraft.

airgun *n.* a gun in which compressed air propels the missile.

airing *n.* **1** exposure to air for drying etc. **2** the public expression of an opinion etc. (*the idea will get an airing at tomorrow's meeting*).

airless *adj.* **1** stuffy. **2** without a breeze, calm and still. ☐ **airlessness** *n.*

airlift *n.* large-scale transport of troops or supplies by aircraft, especially in an emergency. • *v.* transport in this way.

airline *n.* a regular service of air transport for public use; a company providing this.

airliner *n.* a large passenger aircraft.

airlock *n.* **1** a stoppage of the flow in a pump or pipe, caused by an air bubble. **2** a compartment with an airtight door at each end, providing access to a pressurised chamber.

airmail *n.* mail carried by air. • *v.* send by airmail.

airplay *n.* the playing of a record, CD, etc. on radio (*it's had a lot of airplay*).

airport *n.* an airfield with facilities for passengers and goods.

airsick *adj.* made sick or queasy by the motion of an aircraft. ☐ **airsickness** *n.*

airspace *n.* the atmosphere above a country and subject to its control.

airstrip *n.* a strip of ground prepared for aircraft to land and take off.

airtight *adj.* **1** not allowing air to enter or escape. **2** without any flaws (*an airtight alibi*).

airwaves *n.pl. colloq.* radio waves used in broadcasting.

airway *n.* **1** a regular route of aircraft. **2** a ventilating passage in a mine. **3** a passage for air into the lungs; a device to secure this.

airworthy *adj.* (of an aircraft) fit to fly. ☐ **airworthiness** *n.*

airy *adj.* (**airier**, **airiest**) **1** well-ventilated. **2** light as air. **3** careless and light-hearted (*an airy manner*). ☐ **airy-fairy** *adj.* fanciful, impractical. ☐☐ **airily** *adv.* **airiness** *n.*

AIS *abbr.* = AUSTRALIAN INSTITUTE OF SPORT.

aisle / uyl / *n.* **1** a side part of a church. **2 a** a passage between rows of pews or seats. **b** a passage between cabinets and shelves of goods in a supermarket etc.

aitch / aych / *n.* the letter H.

aitchbone *n.* the rump bone of an animal; a cut of beef lying over this.

ajar *adv.* & *adj.* slightly open.

Ajax *Gk myth.* a Greek hero of the Trojan War.

Ajman the smallest emirate of the United Arab Emirates.

aka *abbr.* also known as.

Akihito (1933–), emperor of Japan from 1989.

akimbo / uh-**kim**-boh / *adv.* with hands on hips and elbows pointed outwards.

akin *adj.* (usu. foll. by *to*) related, similar (*a feeling akin to envy*).

akubra / uh-**koo**-bruh / *n. Aust. trademark* a wide-brimmed felt hat.

akudjura / u-**kuj**-uh-ruh / *n.* = BUSH TOMATO. (¶ Taken as a marketing name for products made from bush tomatoes from the Alyawarr language spoken at Hill Station in the Northern Territory.)

Al *symbol* aluminium.

à la *prep.* in the style of. (¶ French)

alabaster / **al**-uh-bah-stuh, -bas-tuh / *n.* a translucent usually white form of gypsum, often carved into ornaments.

à la carte / ah lah **kaht** / *adv.* & *adj.* (of a restaurant meal) ordered as separate items from a menu. (¶ French)

alacrity / uh-**lak**-ruh-tee / *n.* prompt and eager readiness.

Alamein *see* EL ALAMEIN.

à la mode / ah lah **mohd** / *adv.* & *adj.* in fashion, fashionable. (¶ French)

alarm *n.* **1** a warning sound or signal, an apparatus giving this. **2** an alarm clock. **3** fear caused by expectation of danger. • *v.* arouse to a sense of danger; frighten. ☐ **alarm clock** a clock with a device that sounds at a set time.

alarmist *n.* a person who raises unnecessary or excessive alarm.

alas *interj.* an exclamation of sorrow.

alb *n.* a long white vestment worn by some Christian priests.

albacore *n.* an edible sea fish with very long fins, a type of tuna.

Albania a republic between Greece and the former Yugoslavia. ☐ **Albanian** *adj.* & *n.*

albatross *n.* **1** a long-winged sea bird related to the petrel. **2** a constant burden or encumbrance. **3** (in golf) a score of 3 under par at a hole.

albeit / awl-**bee**-it / *conj.* although.

albino / al-**bee**-noh / *n.* (*pl.* **albinos**) a person or animal with no colouring pigment in the skin and hair (which are white) and the eyes (which are pink).

Albion / **al**-bee-uhn / *n. poetic* Britain.

album *n.* **1** a book for autographs, photographs, postage stamps, etc. **2** a long-playing record.

albumen / **al**-byoo-muhn / *n.* white of egg.

albumin *n.* water-soluble protein found in egg white, milk, blood, etc.

Albury-Wodonga a development area on the Murray River, formed in 1974 by amalgamating the cities of Albury (NSW) and Wodonga (Vic.).

alchemy / **al**-kuh-mee / *n.* a medieval form of chemistry, the chief aim of which was to discover how to turn ordinary metals into gold. ☐ **alchemist** *n.*

Alcheringa / al-chuh-**ring**-guh / *see* DREAMTIME. (¶ From Arrernte *altjerre* 'dream', *-nge* 'from, of', the combination meaning 'in the Dreamtime'.)

alcohol *n.* **1** a colourless inflammable liquid, the intoxicant present in wine, beer, whisky, etc. **2** any liquor containing this. **3** a chemical compound of this type.
alcoholic *adj.* **1** of or containing alcohol. **2** caused by drinking alcohol. • *n.* a person suffering from alcoholism.
Alcoholics Anonymous a self-help organisation founded in the US in 1935 for people fighting alcoholism. The organisation, based on a system of local groups, has now spread around the world.
alcoholism *n.* a diseased condition caused by continual heavy drinking of alcohol.
alcove *n.* a recess in a wall.
aldehyde / **al**-duh-huyd / *n.* **1** a fluid with a suffocating smell, obtained from alcohol. **2** a compound with the same structure.
al dente / ul **den**-tay / *adv. & adj.* (of pasta or vegetables) cooked so as to be still firm when bitten. (¶ Italian, = to the tooth.)
alder / **awl**-der / *n.* a tree of the birch family.
alderman / **awl**-duh-muhn / *n.* (*feminine* **alderwoman**) an elected local government councillor, e.g. in some Australian States. □ **aldermanic** *adj.*
ale *n.* beer.
aleatory / **ay**-leer-tree, al-ee-**ay**-tuh-ree / *adj.* depending on random choice.
alembic / uh-**lem**-bik / *n.* an apparatus formerly used in distilling.
alert *adj.* watchful, observant. • *n.* **1** a state of watchfulness or readiness. **2** a warning of danger; notice to stand ready. • *v.* warn of danger, make alert. □ **on the alert** on the lookout, watchful. □□ **alertness** *n.*
Alexander 'the Great' (356–323 BC), king of Macedon from 336 BC.
Alexander technique a method of controlling posture as an aid to well-being. (¶ F.M. Alexander, Australian physiotherapist (1869–1955).)
Alexandria the chief port of Egypt, named after its founder Alexander the Great.
alexandrine / al-uhg-**zan**-druyn, -dreen / *n.* a verse of six iambic feet. • *adj.* of or in this metre.
Alf *n. Aust. derog.* the type of the unthinkingly conservative, anti-intellectual Australian male who holds women in low esteem, despises culture, and is prejudiced against minority groups.
alfalfa / al-**fal**-fuh / *n.* lucerne.
Alfred 'the Great' (849–99), king of Wessex in England from 871.
alfresco / al-**fres**-koh / *adj. & adv.* in the open air (*eating alfresco*). (¶ Italian)
algae / **al**-jee, -gee / *n.pl.* (*sing.* **alga** / **al**-guh /) water plants with no true stems or leaves. □ **algal** *adj.*

■ **Usage** Although *algae* is the plural form of *alga*, it functions as a collective noun, and can take either a singular or plural verb.

algebra / **al**-juh-bruh / *n.* a branch of mathematics in which letters and symbols are used to represent quantities. □ **algebraic** / al-juh-**bray**-ik / *adj.* **algebraically** *adv.*
Algeria a republic in North Africa on the Mediterranean coast. □ **Algerian** *adj. & n.*
Algiers / al-**jeerz** / the capital of Algeria.
Algonquian / al-**gong**-kwee-uhn / *adj.* of or relating to a large scattered group of North American Indian peoples, or their languages. • *n.* **1** a member of any of these peoples. **2** the group of languages spoken by these peoples.
algorithm / **al**-guh-ri*th*-uhm / *n.* a procedure or set of rules for solving a problem, especially by computer. □ **algorithmic** / al-guh-**rith**-mik / *adj.*
alias / **ay**-lee-uhs / *n.* (*pl.* **aliases**) a false name, an assumed name (*Brown had several aliases*). • *adv.* known as; also called (*John Brown, alias Peter Umslopogas*).
Ali Baba / al-ee **bah**-buh / the hero of a story from the *Arabian Nights*, who discovered the magic formula ('Open, Sesame!') which opened the cave in which forty robbers kept their stolen treasure.
alibi / **al**-uh-buy / *n.* (*pl.* **alibis**) **1** evidence that an accused person was elsewhere when a crime was committed. **2** *colloq.* an excuse of any kind.

■ **Usage** The use in sense 2 is considered incorrect by some people.

Alice (usu. **The Alice**) *Aust.* Alice Springs.
Alice Springs a town in Central Australia on the Todd River.
alien / **ay**-lee-uhn / *n.* **1** a person who is not a subject of the country in which he or she is living. **2** a being from another world. • *adj.* **1** foreign, not one's own, unfamiliar (*alien customs*). **2** of a different nature; contrary (*cruelty is alien to her character*).
alienable *adj. Law* able to be transferred to new ownership.
alienate / **ay**-lee-uh-nayt / *v.* cause to become unfriendly or hostile. □ **alienation** *n.*
alight[1] *v.* **1** get down from a horse or a vehicle. **2** descend and settle (*the bird alighted on a branch*).
alight[2] *adj.* on fire, lit up.
align / uh-**luyn** / *v.* **1** place in line, bring into line. **2** join as an ally (*they aligned themselves with Labor*). □ **alignment** *n.*
alike *adj. & adv.* like one another; in the same way.
alimentary / al-uh-**men**-tuh-ree / *adj.* of food or nutrition; nourishing. □ **alimentary canal** the tubular passage through which food passes from mouth to anus in the process of being digested.
alimony / **al**-uh-muh-nee / *n.* an allowance payable to a spouse or former spouse after a legal separation or divorce.

■ **Usage** In Australia this is now called *maintenance*.

aliphatic / al-uh-**fat**-ik / *adj.* (of chemical compounds) related to fats; in which carbon atoms form open chains.

aliquot / **al**-uh-kwot / *Maths adj.* that produces a quotient without a fraction when a given larger number is divided by it. •*n.* **1** an aliquot part. **2** a representative portion of a substance.

alive *adj.* **1** living. **2** (foll. by *to*) alert (*he is alive to the possible dangers*). **3** active, lively. **4** (foll. by *with*) swarming with; full of (*the place was alive with cops*).

alkali / **al**-kuh-luy / *n.* (*pl.* **alkalis**) any of a class of substances (such as caustic soda, potash, and ammonia) that neutralise and are neutralised by acids, have a pH of more than 7, and form caustic or corrosive solutions in water. ☐ **alkaline** / **al**-kuh-luyn / *adj.* **alkalinity** / al-kuh-**lin**-uh-tee / *n.*

alkaloid / **al**-kuh-loid / *n.* any of a large group of nitrogen-containing substances derived from plants, many of which are used in medicine, e.g. morphine, quinine.

alkane *n.* any of a series of saturated aliphatic hydrocarbons, including methane, ethane, and propane.

alkene *n.* any of a series of unsaturated aliphatic hydrocarbons, including ethylene and propene.

alkyl / **al**-kil / *adj.* from or related to a hydrocarbon of the paraffin series.

alkyne *n.* any of a series of unsaturated aliphatic hydrocarbons containing a triple bond, including acetylene.

all *adj.* the whole amount, number, or extent of (*waited all day; beyond all doubt*). •*n.* all persons concerned, everything (*all are agreed; all is lost; the score is four all*). •*adv.* entirely, quite (*dressed all in white; an all-powerful dictator*). ☐ **all but** very little short of; very nearly (*it is all but impossible*). **all-clear** a signal that a danger is over. **all for** *colloq.* much in favour of. **all-in wrestling** freestyle wrestling. **all in all** everything considered. **all one to** a matter of indifference to. **all out** using all possible strength, energy, or speed. **all right 1** as desired, satisfactorily. **2** in good condition; safe and sound. **3** yes, I consent. **all-round** general, not specialised (*a good all-round education; an all-round athlete*). **all there** *colloq.* mentally alert (*not quite all there*). **all the same 1** in spite of this. **2** making no difference. **all-time** unsurpassed (*an all-time record*). **be all eyes** (*or* **ears**) be watching (or listening) intently. **on all fours** crawling on hands and knees.

Allah / **al**-uh, uh-**lah** / the Muslim and Arab name of God.

allay / uh-**lay** / *v.* (**allayed, allaying**) calm, put at rest (*to allay suspicion*).

All Blacks *n.pl.* the New Zealand international Rugby Union team, so called from the colour of their uniforms.

allegation / al-uh-**gay**-shuhn / *n.* a statement or accusation, especially one made without proof.

allege / uh-**lej** / *v.* declare (especially to those doubting one's truthfulness) without proof (*alleging that he was innocent; the alleged culprit*).

allegedly / uh-**lej**-uhd-lee / *adv.* according to allegation.

allegiance / uh-**lee**-juhns / *n.* support of a government, sovereign, cause, etc.

allegorise / **al**-uh-guh-ruyz / *v.* (also -**ize**) treat as an allegory or by means of an allegory.

allegory / **al**-uh-guh-ree, -gree / *n.* a story or description in which the characters and events symbolise some deeper underlying meaning. ☐ **allegorical** / al-uh-**go**-ri-kuhl / *n.* **allegorically** *adv.*

allegretto / al-uh-**gret**-oh / *adv.* (in music) in fairly brisk time. •*n.* (*pl.* **allegrettos**) a movement to be played in this way.

allegro / uh-**lay**-groh, uh-**leg**-roh / *adv.* (in music) fast and lively. •*n.* (*pl.* **allegros**) a movement to be played in this way.

alleluia / al-uh-**loo**-yuh / *interj.* & *n.* (also **hallelujah**) praise to God.

Allen, Peter (original name: Peter Richard Woolnough) (1944–92), AM, Australian songwriter, singer, pianist, and stage entertainer.

allergen / **al**-uh-juhn / *n.* an allergenic substance.

allergenic / al-uh-**jen**-ik / *adj.* causing an allergic reaction.

allergic / uh-**ler**-jik / *adj.* **1** (foll. by *to*) having an allergy to something. **2** caused by an allergy (*allergic reaction*). **3** *colloq.* (foll. by *to*) having a strong dislike of something (*allergic to hard work*).

allergy / **al**-uh-jee / *n.* a damaging immune response by the body to a substance (esp. a particular food, pollen, etc.) to which it has become hypersensitive.

alleviate / uh-**lee**-vee-ayt / *v.* lessen, make less severe (*to alleviate pain*). ☐ **alleviation** *n.*

alley *n.* (*pl.* **alleys**) **1** (also **alleyway**) a narrow passage or street between buildings. **2** a path bordered by hedges or shrubbery. **3** a long channel for balls in games such as tenpin bowling and skittles. **4** (in the game of marbles) a marble of excellent quality.

alliance *n.* a union or association formed for mutual benefit, especially of countries by treaty or families by marriage.

allied *see* ALLY. •*adj.* of the same general kind, similar.

Alligator the name of three rivers in the NT, east of Darwin. The rivers were named by Lieutenant King who mistakenly believed that the saltwater crocodiles found in the estuaries of the rivers were alligators.

alligator *n.* a reptile of the crocodile family, found especially in the rivers of tropical America and China. ☐ **alligator clip** a clip with teeth for gripping.

alliteration / uh-lit-uh-**ray**-shuhn / *n.* the occurrence of the same letter or sound at the beginning of several words in succession, e.g. *sing* *a song of sixpence.* ☐ **alliterative** / uh-**lit**-uh-ruh-tiv / *adj.*

allocate / **al**-uh-kayt / *v.* (usually foll. by *to*) allot or assign to (a person, place, etc.). ☐ **allocation** *n.* **allocator** *n.*

allopathy / uh-**lop**-uh-thee / *n.* the treatment of disease by conventional means, i.e. with drugs having opposite effects to the symptoms (cf. HOMOEOPATHY). ☐ **allopathic** / al-uh-**path**-ik / *adj.*

all ordinaries index *n.* (also **all-ords**) on the Australian Stock Exchange, the weighted average of certain ordinary share prices.

allot / uh-**lot** / *v.* (**allotted**, **allotting**) distribute officially, give as a share of things available or tasks to be done.

allotment *n.* **1** allotting. **2** a share allotted. **3** a small piece of land; a building block.

allotrope / **al**-uh-trohp / *n.* one of the forms of an element that exists in different physical forms (*diamond and graphite are allotropes of carbon*).

allotropy / uh-**lot**-ruh-pee / *n.* the existence of several forms of a chemical element in the same state (gas, liquid, or solid) but with different physical or chemical properties. ☐ **allotropic** / al-uh-**trop**-ik / *adj.*

allow *v.* **1** permit (*dogs are not allowed in the park*). **2** permit to have, give a limited quantity or sum (*allow him $200 a year*). **3** add or deduct in estimating (*allow 10% for inflation; allow for shrinkage*). **4** agree that something is true or acceptable (*I allow that you have been patient*).

allowable *adj.* able to be allowed. ☐ **allowably** *adv.*

allowance *n.* **1** allowing. **2** an amount or sum allowed. ☐ **make allowances for** be lenient towards or because of.

allowedly *adv.* as is generally admitted or agreed.

alloy *n.* / **al**-oy / **1** a metal formed of a mixture of metals or of metal and another substance. **2** an inferior metal mixed with one of greater value. • *v.* / uh-**loy** / (**alloyed**, **alloying**) **1** mix with metal(s) of lower value. **2** weaken or spoil by adding something that reduces value or pleasure.

All Saints' Day 1 November.

All Souls' Day 2 November.

allspice *n.* **1** spice made from the dried and ground berries of the pimento. **2** this berry.

allude / uh-**lood**, -**lyood** / *v.* refer briefly or indirectly in speaking (*he alluded to the troubles in Ireland*).

allure / uh-**loor** / *v.* entice, attract. • *n.* attractiveness. ☐ **allurement** *n.*

alluring *adj.* attractive, charming.

allusion *n.* (often foll. by *to*) a brief or indirect reference to something.

allusive / uh-**loo**-siv / *adj.* containing allusions. ☐ **allusively** *adv.*

alluvial / uh-**loo**-vee-uhl / *adj.* made of soil and sand left by rivers or floods.

alluvium / uh-**loo**-vee-uhm / *n.* an alluvial deposit.

ally *n.* / **al**-uy / **1** a country in alliance with another, esp. (also **Ally**) in war. **2** a person who cooperates with another. • *v.* / uh-**luy** / (**allied**, **allying**) form an alliance. ☐ **the Allies** the nations allied in opposition to Germany and its supporters in each of the two World Wars, or those joined in opposition against Iraq in the Gulf War of 1991.

alma mater / al-muh **mah**-tuh, **may**-tuh / *n.* one's university, college, or school.

almanac / **awl**-muh-nak, **al**- / *n.* (also **almanack**) **1** an annual publication containing a calendar with times of sunrise and sunset, astronomical data, dates of anniversaries, and sometimes other information. **2** usu. annual directory or handbook containing statistical and other information of either general or specialist interest.

almighty *adj.* **1** all-powerful. **2** *colloq.* very great (*an almighty crash*). • *adv. colloq.* very (*almighty glad*). ☐ **the Almighty** God.

almond / **ah**-muhnd / *n.* **1** the kernel of the fruit of a tree related to the peach. **2** this tree.

almoner / **ah**-muh-nuh / *n.* **1** *hist.* an official distributor of alms. **2** a social worker attached to a hospital, seeing to the aftercare of patients.

almost *adv.* all but, nearly.

alms / ahmz / *n. archaic* money and gifts given to the poor.

aloe *n.* **1** a plant with thick sharp-pointed leaves and bitter juice. **2** (**aloes**; in full **bitter aloes**) a strong laxative made from aloe juice. ☐ **aloe vera** a kind of aloe, the leaves of which yield a juice used in skin preparations, shampoos, etc.

aloft *adv.* high up; up in the air.

aloha / uh-**loh**-huh, -hah / *interj.* & *n.* a Hawaiian expression of love or affection, used as a greeting and at parting.

alone *adj.* not with others; without the company or help of others or other things. • *adv.* only, exclusively (*you alone can help*).

along *adv.* **1** onward (*push it along*). **2** through part or the whole of a thing's length (*along by the hedge*). **3** with oneself, or others (*I brought my sister along; I'll be along soon*). • *prep.* **1** close to or parallel with the length of something (*shelves along the wall*). **2** from one end to the other end of (*Australian flags along the route*). **3** on or through any part of the length of (*was walking along the road*). ☐ **along with** together with; in addition to.

alongside *adv.* close to the side of a ship or pier. • *prep.* beside.

aloof *adv.* apart (*he kept aloof*). • *adj.* unconcerned, cool and remote in character, unfriendly. ☐ **aloofly** *adv.* **aloofness** *n.*

alopecia / al-uh-**pee**-shuh / *n. Med.* loss or absence of hair; baldness.

aloud *adv.* in a voice loud enough to be heard, not silently or in a whisper.

ALP *abbr.* = AUSTRALIAN LABOR PARTY.

alp *n.* **1** a high mountain. **2** (**the Alps**) a high range of mountains in south-eastern Australia; a high range of mountains in Switzerland and adjoining countries.

alpaca / al-**pak**-uh / *n.* **1** a llama of South America, with long wool. **2** its wool; fabric made from this.

alpenstock *n.* a long iron-tipped stick used in mountain climbing.

alpha / **al**-fuh / *n.* **1** the first letter of the Greek alphabet (A, α); a first-class mark for a piece of work etc. **2** (in names of stars) the chief star in a constellation. ☐ **alpha and omega** the beginning and the end. **alpha particles** (*or* **rays**) helium nuclei emitted by radioactive substances (originally regarded as rays).

alphabet *n.* **1** the letters used in writing a language. **2** a list of these in a set order.

alphabetical *adj.* in the order of the letters of the alphabet. ☐ **alphabetically** *adv.*

alphabetise *v.* (also **-ize**) put into alphabetical order. ☐ **alphabetisation** *n.*

alphanumeric / al-fuh-**nyoo**-**me**-rik / *adj.* containing both letters and numbers.

alpine *adj.* **1** of high mountains; growing on these. **2** (**Alpine**) of the Alps. • *n.* a plant suited to mountain regions or grown in rock gardens.

already *adv.* **1** before this time (*had already gone*). **2** as early as this (*is he back already?*).

alright *adv.* = ALL RIGHT.

■ **Usage** This spelling is considered incorrect by many people.

Alsatian / al-**say**-shuhn / = GERMAN SHEPHERD.

also *adv.* in addition, besides. ☐ **also-ran** *n.* **1** a horse or dog not among the first three to finish in a race. **2** a person who fails to win distinction.

Altamira / al-tuh-**meer**-ruh / the site of a cave in northern Spain with palaeolithic paintings.

altar *n.* **1** the table on which bread and wine are consecrated in the Mass or in a Communion service. **2** any structure on which sacrifices or offerings are made to a god.

altarpiece *n.* a painting behind an altar.

alter *v.* make or become different, change in character, position, etc. (*alter a garment; alter the clock*). ☐ **alteration** *n.*

altercation / ol-tuh-**kay**-shuhn, awl- / *n.* a noisy dispute or quarrel.

alter ego / awl-tuh **ee**-goh, al- / *n.* **1** one's hidden or second self. **2** an intimate friend.

alternate *adj.* / ol-**ter**-nuht / happening or following in turns, first the one and then the other (*on alternate days*). • *v.* / **ol**-tuh-nayt, **awl**- / **1** arrange, perform, or occur alternately. **2** consist of alternate things. ☐ **alternate angles** two angles, not adjoining one another, formed on opposite sides of a line that intersects two other lines. **alternating current** electric current that reverses its direction at regular intervals. ☐ ☐ **alternately** *adv.* **alternation** *n.*

■ **Usage** *See* the note at ALTERNATIVE.

alternative / ol-**ter**-nuh-tiv, awl- / *adj.* **1** available in place of something else. **2** offering a different approach from the conventional or established one; belonging to the counter-culture (*alternative medicine; alternative lifestyle*). • *n.* one of two or more possibilities. ☐ **alternative energy** energy fuelled in ways that do not use up the earth's natural resources or otherwise harm the environment. ☐ ☐ **alternatively** *adv.*

■ **Usage** Do not confuse *alternative* with *alternate*; *alternative colours* means that one colour can be chosen instead of another or others, *alternate colours* means that there is first one colour then another.

alternator / **ol**-tuh-nay-tuh, **awl**- / *n.* a dynamo giving alternating current.

although *conj.* though.

altimeter / **al**-tuh-mee-tuh / *n.* an instrument used in aircraft showing the height above sea level.

altitude *n.* **1** the height above sea level. **2** the distance of a star etc. above the horizon, measured as an angle.

alto / **al**-toh / *n.* (*pl.* **altos**) **1** the highest adult male singing voice. **2** a contralto. **3** a singer with such a voice; a part written for it. **4** a musical instrument with the second or third highest pitch in its group (*alto saxophone*).

altogether *adv.* **1** entirely, totally. **2** on the whole. ☐ **in the altogether** nude.

■ **Usage** Note that *altogether* means 'in total', whereas *all together* means 'all at once' or 'all in one place'. The phrases *six rooms altogether* (in total) and *six rooms all together* (in one place) illustrate the difference.

altruism / **al**-troo-iz-uhm / *n.* unselfishness. ☐ **altruist** *n.* **altruistic** *adj.* **altruistically** *adv.*

alum / **al**-uhm / *n.* a white mineral salt used in medicine and in dyeing.

alumina / uh-**loo**-muh-nuh / *n.* an oxide of aluminium, e.g. corundum.

aluminium / al-yuh-**min**-ee-uhm / *n.* a chemical element (symbol Al), a lightweight silvery metal.

aluminise / uh-**loo**-muh-nuyz / *v.* (also **-ize**) coat with aluminium.

alumnus / uh-**lum**-nuhs / *n.* (*pl.* **alumni** / -nuy /) a former pupil or student.

alunqua / uh-**lung**-kwuh / *n.* a twining plant of drier Australia producing a fruit (bush cucumber) which was an important food for Aborigines. (¶ Arrernte, the name of the fruit.)

always *adv.* **1** at all times, on all occasions. **2** whatever the circumstances (*you can always sleep on the floor*). **3** repeatedly (*he is always complaining*).

alyssum / **al**-i-suhm, uh-**luy**-suhm / *n.* a plant with small usually yellow or white flowers.

Alzheimer's disease / **alts**-huy-muhz / *n.* a brain disorder causing premature senility. (¶ A. Alzheimer, German neurologist (1864–1915).)

AM *abbr.* **1** Member of the Order of Australia. **2** amplitude modulation.

Am *symbol* americium.

am *see* BE.

a.m. *abbr.* before noon. (¶ From the Latin *ante meridiem.*)

AMA *abbr.* Australian Medical Association.

amalgam *n.* **1** a mixture or blend. **2** an alloy of mercury and another metal or metals, used esp. in dental fillings.

amalgamate *v.* mix; combine. ❏ **amalgamation** *n.*

amanuensis / uh-man-yoo-**en**-sis / *n.* (*pl.* **amanuenses**) a literary assistant, especially one who writes from dictation.

amass / uh-**mas** / *v.* heap up; collect (*amassed a large fortune*).

amateur / **am**-uh-tuh / *n.* a person who does something as a pastime rather than as a profession.

amateurish / **am**-uh-tuh-rish / *adj.* inexpert, lacking professional skill. ❏ **amateurishly** *adv.* **amateurishness** *n.*

amatory / **am**-uh-tuh-ree / *adj.* showing sexual love.

amaze *v.* overwhelm with wonder. ❏ **amazement** *n.*

Amazon 1 *Gk myth.* a woman of a race of female warriors. **2** a great river in South America flowing into the Atlantic Ocean on the north coast of Brazil. (¶ So named because of a legend that a race of female warriors lived somewhere on its banks.) • *n.* (**amazon**) a tall and strong or athletic woman. ❏ **Amazonian** / am-uh-**zoh**-nee-uhn / *adj.*

ambassador *n.* **1** a diplomat sent by one country as a permanent representative or on a special mission to another. **2** an official messenger. ❏ **ambassadorial** / am-bas-uh-**daw**-ree-uhl / *adj.*

amber *n.* **1** a hardened clear yellowish-brown resin used for making ornaments. **2** a yellow traffic light shown as a cautionary signal between red and green. • *adj.* **1** made of amber. **2** coloured like amber. ❏ **amber fluid** *Aust. colloq.* beer.

ambergris / **am**-buh-grees / *n.* a wax-like substance found floating in tropical seas and present in the intestines of sperm whales, used as a fixative in perfumes.

ambidextrous / am-bee-**deks**-truhs / *adj.* able to use either hand equally well.

ambience / **am**-bee-uhns / *n.* surroundings or atmosphere; the character, mood, etc. of a place.

ambient *adj.* surrounding (*ambient temperature*).

ambiguous / am-**big**-yoo-uhs / *adj.* **1** having uncertain (*the outcome is ambiguous*). ❏ **ambiguously** *adv.* **ambiguity** / am-buh-**gyoo**-uh-tee / *n.*

ambit *n.* the bounds, scope, or extent of something. ❏ **ambit claim** a claim, made by employees, which sets the boundaries of an industrial dispute.

ambition *n.* **1** a strong desire to achieve something. **2** the object of this.

ambitious / am-**bish**-uhs / *adj.* full of ambition. ❏ **ambitiously** *adv.*

ambivalent / am-**biv**-uh-luhnt / *adj.* with mixed or opposing feelings towards a certain object or situation. ❏ **ambivalently** *adv.* **ambivalence** *n.*

amble *v.* walk at a slow easy pace. • *n.* a slow easy pace.

ambrosia / am-**broh**-zee-uh / *n.* **1** *Gk* & *Rom. myth.* the food of the gods. **2** something delicious.

ambulance *n.* a vehicle equipped to carry sick or injured people.

ambulant *adj. Med.* (of a patient) able to walk about, not confined to bed.

ambulatory / **am**-byuh-luh-tuh-ree, -tree / *adj.* **1** of or for walking. **2** = AMBULANT. • *n.* a place for walking, as in a cloister.

ambuscade / am-buh-**skayd** / *n.* an ambush. • *v.* ambush.

ambush *n.* **1** the placing of troops etc. in a concealed position to make a surprise attack. **2** such an attack. • *v.* lie in wait for, attack from an ambush.

ameliorate / uh-**mee**-lee-uh-rayt / *v.* make or become better. ❏ **amelioration** *n.*

amen / ah-**men**, ay-**men** / *interj.* (in prayers) so be it.

amenable / uh-**mee**-nuh-buhl, uh-**men**-uh-buhl / *adj.* **1** willing to be guided or controlled by some influence (*he is not amenable to discipline*). **2** subject to a legal authority (*we are all amenable to the law*). ❏ **amenably** *adv.* **amenability** *n.*

amend *v.* correct an error in; make minor alterations in (*they amended the agreement*). ❏ **make amends** compensate or make up for something.

■ **Usage** *Amend* is often confused with *emend*, a more technical word used for the correction of text.

amendment *n.* a minor alteration or addition in a document, statement, etc.

amenity / uh-**mee**-nuh-tee, uh-**men**-uh-tee / *n.* **1** pleasantness of a place or circumstance. **2** a feature of a place etc. that makes life there easy or pleasant. **3** (**amenities**) public toilets.

America 1 (also **the Americas**) a continent of the Western hemisphere consisting of the two great land masses, North America and South America, joined by the narrow isthmus of Central America. **2** the USA. ❏ **America's Cup** an international yachting trophy named after the yacht *America*, which won it in 1851.

American *adj.* **1** of the continent of America. **2** of the USA. • *n.* **1** a native of America. **2** a citizen of the USA. **3** the English language as spoken in the USA. ☐ **American football** a form of football played in the USA between two teams of 11 players with an oval ball and an H-shaped goal, on a field marked out as a gridiron.

American Indian *n.* a member of any of the groups of indigenous peoples of North, Central, and South America, esp. those of North America. • *adj.* of or relating to any of these groups.

■ **Usage** The term *American Indian* has been steadily replaced in the US, esp. in official contexts, by the more recent term *Native American*. However, *American Indian* is still widespread in general use even in the US, perhaps at least partly owing to the fact that it is not normally regarded as offensive by American Indians themselves.

Americanise *v.* (also **-ize**) make American in form or character. ☐ **Americanisation** *n.*

Americanism *n.* a word or phrase of American origin or usage.

americium / am-uh-**ris**-ee-uhm / *n.* an artificially made radioactive metallic element (symbol Am), which emits gamma radiation.

Amerindian *adj.* & *n.* (also **Amerind**) (an) American Indian (*see* AMERICAN INDIAN).

amethyst / **am**-uh-thuhst / *n.* a semiprecious stone, purple or violet quartz.

Amharic / am-**ha**-rik / *n.* the official and trade language of Ethiopia. •*adj.* of this language.

amiable / **ay**-mee-uh-buhl / *adj.* feeling and inspiring friendliness; good-tempered. ☐ **amiably** *adv.* **amiability** *n.*

amicable / **am**-i-kuh-buhl / *adj.* friendly. ☐ **amicably** *adv.* **amicability** *n.*

amid *prep.* (also **amidst**) in the middle of, during (*amid shouts of dismay*).

amide / **am**-uyd / *n.* a compound in which an acid radical or metal atom replaces a hydrogen atom of ammonia.

amidships *adv.* in the middle of a ship.

amine / **ay**-meen / *n.* a compound in which an alkyl or other non-acidic radical replaces a hydrogen atom of ammonia.

amino acid / uh-**mee**-noh / *n.* an organic acid found in proteins.

amir alternative spelling of EMIR.

amiss *adj.* wrong, out of order (*something is amiss*). • *adv.* wrongly; faultily (*don't take this amiss*).

amity *n.* friendly feeling; friendship.

Amman / uh-**mahn** / the capital of Jordan.

ammeter / **am**-ee-tuh / *n.* an instrument that measures electric current, usually in amperes.

ammo *n. colloq.* ammunition.

ammonia *n.* **1** a colourless gas with a strong smell. **2** a solution of this in water.

ammonite / **am**-uh-nuyt / *n.* the fossil of a coil-shaped shell.

ammunition *n.* **1** a supply of bullets, shells, grenades, etc. **2** facts and reasoning used to prove a point.

amnesia / am-**nee**-zee-uh, am-**nee**-zhuh / *n.* loss of memory. ☐ **amnesiac** *adj.* & *n.*

amnesty / **am**-nuh-stee / *n.* a general pardon, especially for offences against the State.

Amnesty International an international organisation whose aim is to publicise violations of human rights and obtain the release of political prisoners.

amniocentesis / am-nee-oh-sen-**tee**-suhs / *n.* a prenatal test for foetal abnormality in which a hollow needle is inserted into the womb to withdraw a sample of the fluid there for analysis.

amnion *n.* (*pl.* **amnia**) the innermost membrane enclosing an embryo.

amniotic fluid *n.* the fluid that surrounds a foetus in the womb.

amoeba / uh-**mee**-buh / *n.* (*pl.* **amoebae** / -bee / *or* **amoebas**) a microscopic organism consisting of a single cell which changes shape constantly.

amok *adv.* (also **amuck**) ☐ **run amok** run wild.

among *prep.* (also **amongst**) **1** surrounded by; in with (*poppies amongst the corn; you are among friends*). **2** in the number of (*this is reckoned among his best works*). **3** within the limits of, between (*we have only $5 amongst us; quarrelled among themselves*).

amoral / ay-**mo**-ruhl / *adj.* not based on moral standards, neither moral nor immoral.

amorous / **am**-uh-ruhs / *adj.* of, showing, or readily feeling sexual love. ☐ **amorously** *adv.*

amorphous / uh-**maw**-fuhs / *adj.* having no definite shape or form.

amortise / uh-**maw**-tuyz / *v.* (also **-ize**) pay off (a debt) gradually by money regularly put aside.

amount *n.* **1** the total of anything. **2** a quantity (*a small amount of salt*). • *v.* (foll. by *to*) **1** add up to. **2** be equivalent to.

amour / uh-**moor** / *n.* a love affair, especially a secret one.

amour propre / a-moor **propr** / *n.* self-respect. (¶ French)

amp *n.* **1** an ampere. **2** *colloq.* an amplifier.

amperage / **am**-puh-rij / *n.* the strength of electric current, measured in amperes.

ampere / **am**-pair / *n.* a unit for measuring electric current (symbol A). (¶ Named after the French physicist A.M. Ampère (1775–1836).)

ampersand *n.* the sign '&' (= and).

amphetamine / am-**fet**-uh-meen, -muhn / *n.* a drug used as a stimulant or to relieve congestion.

amphibian / am-**fib**-ee-uhn / *n.* **1** an animal able to live both on land and in water; one (e.g. a frog) that develops through a stage in which it lives in water, to an adult state in which it breathes air. **2** an aircraft that can take off from and alight

amphibious / am-**fib**-ee-uhs / *adj.* **1** living or operating both on land and in water. **2** involving both sea and land forces (*amphibious operations*).

on both land and water. **3** a vehicle that can move on both land and water.

amphitheatre *n.* an oval or circular unroofed building with tiers of seats surrounding a central arena.

amphometer / am-**fom**-uh-tuh / *n. Aust.* a device for measuring the speed of a vehicle over a fixed distance.

amphora / **am**-fuh-ruh / *n.* (*pl.* **amphorae** / -ree /) an ancient Greek or Roman jar with two handles and a narrow neck.

ample *adj.* **1** plentiful, quite enough (*ample evidence*). **2** large, of generous proportions (*an ample bosom*). ☐ **amply** *adv.*

amplifier *n.* a device that increases the loudness of sounds or the strength of radio signals.

amplify *v.* (**amplified, amplifying**) **1** increase the strength of (*to amplify sound*). **2** make fuller, add details to (*please amplify your story*). ☐ **amplification** *n.*

amplitude *n.* **1** breadth. **2** largeness, abundance. **3** the maximum departure from average of oscillation, alternating current, etc. ☐ **amplitude modulation** the systematic variation of wave amplitude, leaving the frequency unaltered; used especially in broadcasting.

ampoule / **am**-pool / *n.* a small sealed container holding a liquid, esp. for injection.

amputate *v.* cut off by surgical operation. ☐ **amputation** *n.*

amputee *n.* a person who has had a limb amputated.

Amritsar / am-**rit**-suh / a city in Punjab in NW India, the centre of the Sikh faith.

Amsterdam the capital of the Netherlands.

amuck = AMOK.

amulet / **am**-yuh-luht / *n.* a thing worn as a charm against evil.

amulla / uh-**mul**-uh / *n.* a shrub of NSW and Qld with pink or white fruit, an Aboriginal bush food. (¶ Darumbal)

Amundsen / **ah**-muund-suhn / Roald (1872–1928), Norwegian polar explorer, the first to reach the South Pole (December 1911).

amuse *v.* **1** cause to laugh or smile. **2** interest or occupy, keep entertained (*who will amuse the children while I write my novel?*). ☐ **amusing** *adj.*

amusement *n.* **1** something that amuses. **2** being amused. **3** a machine for entertainment at a fairground etc. ☐ **amusement arcade** an indoor area with slot machines, electronic games, etc.

an *adj.* the form of *a* used before vowel sounds other than 'u' / yoo /, *an egg, an hour*, but *a unit*.

anabolic steroid / an-uh-**bol**-ik / *n.* a steroid hormone used to build up bone and muscle tissue.

anabolism / uh-**nab**-uh-liz-uhm / *n.* a biochemical process in which complex molecules are formed from simple ones using energy.

anabranch *n. Aust.* an arm of a river which separates from and later rejoins the main stream.

anachronism / uh-**nak**-ruh-niz-uhm / *n.* **1 a** the placing of an event etc. in the wrong historical period (*Shakespeare wasn't afraid of anachronisms: he made an ancient Roman say 'The clock hath stricken three'*). **b** the thing wrongly placed. **2** a person, custom, or idea regarded as out of date. ☐ **anachronistic** / uh-nak-ruh-**nis**-tik / *adj.*

anaconda / an-uh-**kon**-duh / *n.* a large snake of tropical South America.

anaemia / uh-**nee**-mee-uh / *n.* (also **anemia**) lack of red corpuscles or of their haemoglobin in blood, resulting in paleness and weariness.

anaemic / uh-**nee**-mik / *adj.* (also **anemic**) **1** suffering from anaemia. **2** pale, weak in colour. **3** lacking vigour or positive characteristics. ☐ **anaemically** *adv.*

anaerobic / an-uh-**roh**-bik / *adj.* not requiring air or oxygen.

anaesthesia / an-uhs-**thee**-zee-uh / *n.* (also **anesthesia**) loss of sensation, especially that induced by anaesthetics.

anaesthetic / an-uhs-**thet**-ik / *n.* (also **anesthetic**) a substance that produces loss of sensation and of ability to feel pain. • *adj.* having this effect.

anaesthetise / uh-**nees**-thuh-tuyz / *v.* (also **anaesthetize**; **anesthetise**) administer an anaesthetic to (a person etc.). ☐ **anaesthetisation** *n.*

anaesthetist / uh-**nees**-thuh-tuhst / *n.* (also **anesthetist**) a person trained to administer anaesthetics.

anagram / **an**-uh-gram / *n.* a word or phrase formed from the rearranged letters of another (e.g. *cart-horse* is an anagram of *orchestra*).

anal *adj.* of the anus.

analgesia / an-uhl-**jee**-zee-uh / *n.* loss of ability to feel pain while still conscious.

analgesic / an-uhl-**jee**-zik / *adj.* relieving pain. • *n.* a drug that relieves pain.

analog / **an**-uh-log / *adj.* **1** (of a watch or clock) indicating time by the position of hour and minute hands (cf. DIGITAL). **2** (of a computer etc.) using physical variables which change over a continuum to represent numbers (cf. DIGITAL).

analogous / uh-**nal**-uh-guhs / *adj.* similar in certain respects. ☐ **analogously** *adv.*

analogue / **an**-uh-log / *n.* something that is analogous to something else. • *adj.* = ANALOG.

analogy / uh-**nal**-uh-jee / *n.* partial likeness between two things which are compared (*the analogy between the human heart and a pump*).

analyse *v.* **1** separate (a substance etc.) into its parts to identify it or study its structure. **2** examine and interpret (*tried to analyse the causes of their failure*). **3** psychoanalyse.

analysis n. (pl. **analyses** / uh-**nal**-uh-seez /) **1** analysing. **2** a statement of the result of this. **3** psychoanalysis.

analyst / **an**-uh-luhst / n. **1** a person who is skilled in analysis of chemical substances etc. **2** a psychoanalyst.

analytical / an-uh-**lit**-i-kuhl / adj. (also **analytic**) of or using analysis. ☐ **analytically** adv.

Anangu / ah-**nahn**-goo / n. (pl. the same) an Aborigine. (¶ Western Desert language, = person.)

■ Usage See KOORI.

anapaest / **an**-uh-peest, -pest / n. Poetry a metrical foot with two short or unstressed syllables followed by one long or stressed syllable (as in the word cigarette).

anarchist / **an**-uh-kuhst / n. a person who believes that government is undesirable and should be abolished. ☐ **anarchism** n. **anarchistic** / an-uh-**kis**-tik / adj.

anarchy / **an**-uh-kee / n. **1** absence of government or control, resulting in lawlessness. **2** disorder, confusion. ☐ **anarchic** / uh-**nah**-kik / adj. **anarchical** adj.

anathema / uh-**nath**-uh-muh / n. **1** a detested person or thing (blood sports are anathema to him). **2** a formal curse of the Church, excommunicating someone or condemning something as evil.

anathematise / uh-**nath**-uh-muh-tuyz / v. (also -**ize**) curse.

anatomy n. **1** the scientific study of bodily structures. **2** the bodily structure of an animal or plant. ☐ **anatomical** / an-uh-**tom**-i-kuhl / adj. **anatomically** adv.

anatto alternative spelling of ANNATTO.

ANC abbr. = AFRICAN NATIONAL CONGRESS.

ancestor n. **1** any of the persons from whom a person is descended, especially those more remote than grandparents. **2** an early type of animal, plant, or machine etc., from which later ones have evolved. ☐ **ancestral** adj.

ancestry n. a line of ancestors.

anchor n. **1** a heavy metal structure used to moor a ship to the sea-bottom or a balloon etc. to the ground. **2** anything that gives stability or security. • v. **1** lower an anchor, make secure with an anchor. **2** fix firmly.

anchorage n. **1** a place where ships may anchor safely. **2** the charge for this.

anchorite / **ang**-kuh-ruyt / n. a hermit, a religious recluse.

anchorman n. (feminine **anchorwoman**) **1** a strong member of a sports team who plays a vital part (e.g. at the back of a tug-of-war team or as last runner in a relay race). **2** one who co-ordinates activities. **3** the compère in a broadcast TV or radio program.

anchovy / **an**-chuh-vee, an-**choh**-vee / n. a small strong-flavoured fish of the herring family.

ancient adj. **1** belonging to times long past. **2** having lived or existed for a long time. ☐ **ancient history** history of the period before the end of the Western Roman Empire in AD 476.

ancillary / an-**sil**-uh-ree / adj. helping in a subsidiary way (ancillary services).

AND abbr. = AUSTRALIAN NATIONAL DICTIONARY.

and conj. **1** together with (cakes and pavs). **2** then again repeatedly or increasingly (gets better and better; miles and miles). **3** added to (two and two make four). **4** to (go and buy one). **5** with this consequence (move and I shoot).

Andamooka / an-duh-**moo**-kuh / a town in the heart of SA famous for its opal mining.

andante / an-**dan**-tee / adv. & adj. (of music) in moderately slow time. • n. a movement to be played in this way.

andantino / an-dan-**tee**-noh / adv. & adj. (of music) rather quicker than andante. • n. a movement to be played in this way.

Andersen, Hans Christian (1805–75), Danish writer of fairy tales.

Anderson, John (Duncan) (1956–), Australian politician who in 1999 became leader of the National Party and deputy prime minister.

Andes a range of mountains in western South America. ☐ **Andean** / an-**dee**-uhn / adj.

and/or conj. together with or as an alternative.

Andrew, St (1st century) one of the twelve Apostles.

androgynous / an-**droj**-uh-nuhs / adj. **1** (of a plant, animal, or person) having both male and female reproductive organs. **2** neither distinctively male nor distinctively female in appearance; sexually ambiguous.

android n. (in science fiction) a robot in human form.

Andromeda / an-**drom**-uh-duh / **1** Gk myth. a king's daughter who was fastened to a rock as a sacrifice to a sea monster, and was rescued by Perseus. **2** a constellation conspicuous for its great spiral nebula.

anecdote / **an**-uhk-doht / n. a short amusing or interesting story, especially one that is true.

anemia alternative spelling of ANAEMIA.

anemic alternative spelling of ANAEMIC.

anemometer / an-uh-**mom**-uh-tuh / n. an instrument for measuring the force of wind.

anemone / uh-**nem**-uh-nee / n. a plant related to the buttercup, with white or brightly coloured flowers.

aneroid barometer / **an**-uh-roid / n. a barometer that measures air pressure by the action of air on the lid of a box containing a vacuum, not by the height of a fluid column.

anesthesia etc. alternative spelling of ANAESTHESIA etc.

aneurism / **an**-yuh-riz-uhm / n. (also **aneurysm**) permanent abnormal enlargement of an artery.

anew adv. again; in a new or different way.

angel *n.* **1** an attendant or messenger of God. **2** a very beautiful or kind person. **3** *colloq.* a financial backer of a play etc.

angelfish *n.* a fish with wing-like fins.

angelic *adj.* of or like an angel. ☐ **angelically** *adv.*

angelica / an-**jel**-i-kuh / *n.* **1** a fragrant plant used in cookery and medicine. **2** its candied stalks.

angelus / **an**-juh-luhs / *n.* (in the Catholic Church) **1** a prayer to the Virgin Mary commemorating the Incarnation, said at morning, noon, and sunset. **2** a bell rung as a signal for this.

anger *n.* the strong feeling caused by extreme displeasure. • *v.* make angry.

Angevin / **an**-juh-vuhn / *adj.* **1** of Anjou, a former province of France. **2** of the Plantagenet kings of England from Henry II (son of Geoffrey, Count of Anjou) to Richard II (deposed 1399). • *n.* an Angevin person or ruler.

angina / an-**juy**-nuh / *n.* (in full **angina pectoris** / **pek**-tuh-ruhs /) a sharp pain in the chest caused by over exertion when the heart is diseased.

angiogram / **an**-jee-uh-gram / *n.* a photograph taken by radiography of blood vessels after radio-opaque dyes have been injected.

angiosperm / **an**-jee-uh-sperm / *n.* a member of the group of flowering plants that have seeds enclosed in an ovary.

Angkor / **ang**-kaw / the capital of the ancient kingdom of Khmer, in north-western Cambodia, famous for its temples.

Angle *n.* a member of a North German tribe who settled in England in the 5th century. ☐ **Anglian** *adj.*

angle[1] *n.* **1** the space between two lines or surfaces that meet. **2** a point of view (*written from the woman's angle*). • *v.* **1** move or place in a slanting position. **2** present (news etc.) from a particular point of view.

angle[2] *v.* **1** fish with hook and bait. **2** try to obtain by hinting (*angling for an invitation*). ☐ **angler** *n.*

Anglican *adj.* of the Church of England or any Church in communion with it. • *n.* a member of the Anglican Church. ☐ **Anglicanism** *n.*

anglicise / **ang**-gluh-suyz / *v.* (also **-ize**) make English in form or character.

Anglicism / **ang**-gluh-siz-uhm / *n.* a word or custom peculiar to England.

angling *n.* the sport of fishing.

Anglo *n. Aust.* an Australian whose ancestry is Anglo-Celtic.

Anglo- *comb. form* English, British.

Anglo-Catholic *adj.* of the section of the Anglican Church that stresses its Catholic connection and objects to being called Protestant. • *n.* a member of this section of the Church.

Anglo-Celtic *adj.* of or pertaining to a person whose origins were in Britain and/or Ireland (and not in Europe, Asia, etc.). ☐ **Anglo-Celt** *n.*

Anglo-French *adj.* English (or British) and French. • *n.* the French language as developed in England after the Norman Conquest.

Anglo-Norman *adj.* English and Norman. • *n.* the Norman dialect used in England after the Norman conquest.

Anglo-Saxon *n.* **1** an English person of the period before the Norman Conquest. **2** the English language of this period, also called *Old English*. • *adj.* of the Anglo-Saxons or their language.

Angola / an-**goh**-luh / a republic on the west coast of Africa. ☐ **Angolan** *adj.* & *n.*

angophora / ang-**gof**-uh-ruh / *n.* an Australian tree, closely related to eucalypts, which bears a profusion of white flowers.

angora *n.* **1** yarn or fabric made from the hair of angora goats or rabbits. **2** a long-haired variety of cat, goat, or rabbit.

angostura / ang-guh-**styoor**-ruh / *n.* the bitter bark of a South American tree, used as a flavouring.

angry *adj.* (**angrier**, **angriest**) **1** feeling or showing anger. **2** inflamed (*an angry sore*). ☐ **angrily** *adv.*

angst *n.* anxiety; a feeling of guilt or remorse.

angstrom / **ang**-struhm / *n.* a unit of length used in measuring wavelengths. (¶ Named after A.J. Ångström (1814–74), Swedish physicist.)

anguish *n.* severe physical or mental pain.

anguished *adj.* feeling anguish.

angular *adj.* **1** having angles or sharp corners. **2** lacking plumpness or smoothness. **3** measured by angle (*the angular distance*). ☐ **angularity** / ang-gyuh-**la**-ruh-tee / *n.*

anhydrous *adj. Chem.* without water.

anigozanthos / an-uh-goh-**zan**-thuhs / *n.* any plant of the WA genus *Anigozanthos*, commonly called a *kangaroo paw*.

aniline / **an**-uh-leen / *n.* an oily liquid obtained from nitrobenzene, used in the manufacture of dyes and plastics.

anilingus *n.* oral stimulation of the anus.

anima *n.* the feminine part of a man's personality (cf. ANIMUS).

animadvert / an-uh-mad-**vert** / *v. literary* make hostile criticisms. ☐ **animadversion** *n.*

animal *n.* **1** a living thing that can feel and move voluntarily. **2** such a being other than a human being. **3** a four-footed animal distinguished from a bird, fish, reptile, or insect. **4** a brutish or uncivilised person. • *adj.* of, from, or relating to animal life. ☐ **animal husbandry** the science of breeding and caring for farm animals. **animal liberation** the movement aimed at securing animal rights, esp. to ensure their well-being on farms etc. and to prevent them being used experimentally in scientific etc. research. **animal magnetism** sex appeal; sexual attractiveness. **animal rights** the natural right of animals to live free from human exploitation.

animalism *n.* **1** the nature and activity of animals; concern with physical matters; sensuality. **2** the belief that humans are not superior to other animals.

animate *adj.* / **an**-uh-muht / living. • *v.* / **an**-uh-mayt / **1** give life or movement to; make lively (*an animated discussion*). **2** motivate (*he was animated by loyalty*). **3** produce as an animated cartoon. ☐ **animated cartoon** a film made by photographing a series of drawings, giving an illusion of movement. ☐☐ **animator** *n.*

animation *n.* **1** animating. **2** liveliness.

animism *n.* the belief that all beings and natural things such as rocks, streams, and winds have a living soul. ☐ **animistic** *adj.*

animosity / an-uh-**mos**-uh-tee / *n.* a spirit of hostility.

animus / **an**-uh-muhs / *n.* **1** animosity shown in speech or action. **2** the masculine part of a woman's personality (cf. ANIMA).

anion / **an**-uy-uhn / *n.* an ion with a negative charge. ☐ **anionic** / an-uy-**on**-ik / *adj.*

anise / **an**-is / *n.* a plant with aromatic seeds.

aniseed *n.* the sweet-smelling seed of the plant anise, used for flavouring.

Ankara / **ang**-kuh-ruh / the capital of Turkey.

ankle *n.* **1** the joint connecting the foot with the leg. **2** the slender part between this and the calf. ☐ **ankle-biter** *n. US & Aust. colloq.* a very small child.

anklet *n.* an ornamental chain or band worn around the ankle.

ankylosaur / **ang**-kuh-luh-saw / *n.* a plant-eating dinosaur armoured with heavy plates.

ankylosis / ang-kuh-**loh**-suhs / *n.* stiffening of a joint by fusion of the bones.

annals / **an**-uhlz / *n.pl.* a history of events year by year; historical records. ☐ **annalist** *n.*

Annan / **an**-uhn, uh-**nahn** /, Kofi (1938–), Ghanaian international civil servant who in 1997 became secretary-general of the United Nations.

annatto *n.* (also **anatto**) an orange-red dye from the pulp of a tropical fruit, used for colouring foods.

Anne, St (in Christian tradition) the mother of the Virgin Mary.

anneal *v.* heat (metal or glass) and cool it slowly, especially to toughen it.

annex / uh-**neks** / *v.* **1** add or join to a larger thing. **2** take possession of (*to annex territory*). ☐ **annexation** *n.*

annexe / **an**-eks / *n.* a building attached to a larger one or forming a subordinate part of a main building.

Annie *n.* ☐ **upstairs in Annie's room** *Aust. colloq.* the supposed location of something that cannot be found.

annihilate / uh-**nuy**-uh-layt / *v.* destroy completely. ☐ **annihilation** *n.* **annihilator** *n.*

anniversary *n.* the yearly return of the date of an event; a celebration of this.

Anno Domini / an-oh **dom**-uh-nuy, -nee / *adv.* in the year of the Lord; indicating a date after Christ's birth (usually shortened to AD).

annotate / **an**-oh-tayt, **an**-uh-tayt / *v.* add notes of explanation to (*an annotated edition*). ☐ **annotation** *n.*

announce *v.* **1** make known publicly or to an audience. **2** make known the presence or arrival of. ☐ **announcement** *n.*

announcer *n.* a person who announces items in a broadcast.

annoy *v.* **1** cause slight anger to. **2** be troublesome to, harass. ☐ **annoyance** *n.*

annoyed *adj.* slightly angry.

annual *adj.* **1** coming or happening once every year (*annual general meeting*). **2** of one year, reckoned by the year (*annual subscription*). **3** lasting only one year or season (*annual plants*). • *n.* **1** a plant that lives for one year or one season. **2** a book or periodical published in yearly issues. ☐ **annually** *adv.*

annualised *adj.* (also **-ized**) (of rates of interest, inflation, etc.) calculated on an annual basis from information about figures given for a shorter period.

annuity / uh-**nyoo**-uh-tee / *n.* a fixed annual allowance, especially one provided by a form of investment.

annul / uh-**nul** / *v.* (**annulled, annulling**) make null and void, destroy the validity of (*the marriage was annulled*). ☐ **annulment** *n.*

annular / **an**-yuh-luh / *adj.* ring-like. ☐ **annular eclipse** a solar eclipse in which a ring of light remains visible.

annulate *adj.* marked with or formed of rings.

Annunciation *n.* **1** the announcement by the angel Gabriel to the Virgin Mary that she was to be the mother of Christ. **2** the festival commemorating this (25 March).

anode / **an**-ohd / *n.* the electrode by which current enters a device.

anodise / **an**-uh-duyz / *v.* (also **-ize**) coat (metal) with a protective layer by electrolysis.

anodyne / **an**-uh-duyn / *n.* **1** a drug that relieves pain. **2** anything that relieves pain or distress. • *adj.* relieving pain or distress.

anoint *v.* **1** apply holy oil or chrism to, especially ritually (e.g. in sacraments such as baptism and the Anointing of the Sick or extreme unction). **2** smear or rub with grease.

anomaly / uh-**nom**-uh-lee / *n.* something that deviates from the general rule or the usual type, an irregularity or inconsistency (*the many anomalies in our tax system*). ☐ **anomalous** *adj.*

anon / uh-**non** / *adv. archaic* soon, presently (*I will say more of this anon*).

anon. *abbr.* anonymous (author).

anonymity / an-uh-**nim**-uh-tee / *n.* being anonymous.

anonymous / uh-**non**-uh-muhs / *adj.* **1** with a name that is not known or not made public (*an*

anopheles / uh-**nof**-uh-leez / *n.* a species of mosquito which can carry the malaria parasite and infect humans.

anorak / **an**-uh-rak / *n.* a waterproof jacket, usually with a hood attached.

anorexia / an-uh-**rek**-see-uh / *n.* lack of appetite, esp. (in full **anorexia nervosa**) a medical condition characterised by an obsessive desire to lose weight and refusal to eat normally. ☐ **anorexic** *adj. & n.*

another *adj.* **1** additional, one more. **2** different (*fit another pipe, this one leaks*). **3** some or any other (*will not do another man's work*). **4** person like (*another Hitler*). • *pron.* another person or thing.

Ansett, Sir Reginald Myles (1909–81), Australian aviator and company director, founder of Ansett Airlines in 1936.

answer *n.* something said, needed, or done to deal with a question, accusation, or problem. • *v.* **1** make an answer to; say, write, or do something in return. **2** suffice or be suitable for (*a piece of old pantihose answers very well for tying plants to stakes*). **3** (foll. by *to, for*) take responsibility; vouch (*they must answer for their crimes; I will answer for his honesty*). **4** (foll. by *to*) correspond (*this bag answers to the description of the stolen one*). ☐ **answer back** answer a rebuke cheekily. **answering machine** a machine that answers telephone calls and records messages.

answerable *adj.* **1** able to be answered. **2** responsible (*you will be answerable to me for any breakages*).

ant *n.* a very small insect of which there are many species, all of which form and live in highly organised groups.

antacid / ant-**as**-uhd / *n.* a substance that prevents or corrects acidity.

antagonise *v.* (also **-ize**) arouse antagonism in.

antagonism / an-**tag**-uh-niz-uhm / *n.* active opposition, hostility.

antagonist / an-**tag**-uh-nist / *n.* an opponent; one who is hostile to something. ☐ **antagonistic** / an-tag-uh-**nis**-tik / *adj.* **antagonistically** *adv.*

Antananarivo / an-tuh-nuh-nuh-**ree**-voh / the capital of Madagascar.

Antarctic *adj.* of the regions round the South Pole. • *n.* **1** these regions. **2** the Antarctic Ocean, the sea surrounding Antarctica. ☐ **Antarctic Circle** an imaginary line round the Antarctic region, the line of latitude 60° 33′ S.

Antarctica the continent mainly within the Antarctic Circle.

antbed *n. Aust.* **1** the large earth mound built by termites to house their nest. **2** earth from termite mounds, esp. as used for floors.

ant cap *n. Aust.* a shield placed on top of the supports of a building (piers, stumps, etc.) to discourage termites from entering the building from below. • *v.* put ant caps on the supports of a building. ☐ **ant capping** *n.*

ante / **an**-tee / *n.* **1** a stake put up by a poker player before drawing new cards. **2** an amount payable in advance. • *v.* put up an ante; pay up. ☐ **up** (*or* **raise**) **the ante** increase the amount; increase the requirements.

ante- / **an**-tee / *comb. form* before.

anteater *n.* an animal that feeds on ants and termites, esp. the echidna and the numbat.

antecedent / **an**-tuh-see-duhnt / *n.* **1** a preceding thing or circumstance (*the war and its antecedents; I know nothing of his antecedents*). **2** a noun, clause, or sentence to which a following pronoun refers (in *the book which I have*, 'book' is the antecedent of 'which'). • *adj.* previous.

antechamber *n.* a small room leading to a main one.

antechinus / an-tee-**kuy**-nuhs / *n.* (*pl.* **antechinuses**) an Australian marsupial mouse.

antedate *v.* **1** precede in time. **2** put an earlier date on (a document) than that on which it was issued.

antediluvian / an-tee-duh-**loo**-vee-uhn / *adj.* **1** of the time before Noah's Flood. **2** *colloq.* completely out of date.

antelope *n.* a swift-running animal (e.g. chamois, gazelle) resembling a deer, found especially in Africa.

antenatal *adj.* **1** before birth. **2** during pregnancy (*antenatal care*).

antenna *n.* **1** (*pl.* **antennae** / an-**ten**-ee /) each of a pair of flexible sensitive projections on the heads of insects, crustaceans, etc.; a feeler. **2** (*pl.* **antennas**) an aerial.

antepenultimate / an-tee-puh-**nul**-tuh-muht / *adj.* last but two.

anterior *adj.* coming before in position or time.

ante-room *n.* a small room leading to a main one.

anthem *n.* **1** an elaborate choral composition usually based on sacred scripture. **2** a solemn hymn of praise etc., esp. = NATIONAL ANTHEM.

anther *n.* the part of a flower's stamen that contains pollen.

anthill *n.* **1** a moundlike nest built by ants or termites. **2** a community teeming with people. ☐ **anthill parrot** any of three Australian parrots which make their nests in termites' mounds.

anthologist *n.* a person who compiles an anthology.

anthology / an-**thol**-uh-jee / *n.* a collection of passages from literature, especially poems.

Anthony, St (of Padua, 1195–1231), Franciscan friar, invoked as the finder of lost objects.

anthouse plant *n.* any of several Queensland epiphytic plants with tall, fleshy stems. The stems spring from bloated bases, honeycombed with passages which ants use as nests.

anthracite *n.* a hard form of coal that burns with little flame or smoke.

anthrax *n.* a disease of sheep and cattle that can be transmitted to people.

anthropocentric *adj.* regarding human beings as the centre of existence.

anthropoid / **an**-thruh-poid / *adj.* human in form. • *n.* an anthropoid ape such as a gorilla or chimpanzee.

anthropologist *n.* an expert in anthropology.

anthropology / an-thruh-**pol**-uh-jee / *n.* the scientific study of mankind, especially of human origins, development, customs, and beliefs. ☐ **anthropological** / an-thruh-puh-**loj**-i-kuhl / *adj.* **anthropologically** *adv.*

anthropomorphism / an-thruh-puh-**maw**-fiz-uhm / *adj.* the attributing of human form or personality to a god, animal, or object. ☐ **anthropomorphic** *adj.*

anthropomorphous / an-thruh-puh-**maw**-fuhs / *adj.* in human form.

anti *n.* (*pl.* **antis**) a person who opposes a particular policy, cause, group, etc. • *prep.* opposed to.

anti- *comb. form* **1** opposed to (*anti-nuclear*). **2** preventing, counteracting (*antiperspirant*). **3** opposite of (*anticlimax*). **4** rival (*antipope*). **5** unlike the conventional form (*anti-hero; anti-novel*).

anti-abortion *adj.* opposing abortion. ☐ **anti-abortionist** *n.*

anti-aircraft *adj.* used against enemy aircraft.

anti-ballistic missile *n.* a missile that can destroy ballistic missiles in the air.

antibiotic / an-tee-buy-**ot**-ik / *n.* a substance capable of destroying or preventing the growth of bacteria. • *adj.* functioning in this way.

antibody / **an**-tee-bod-ee / *n.* a protein formed in the blood in reaction to certain substances which it then attacks and destroys. ☐ **antibody negative** not showing antibodies to a virus, and therefore not indicating the presence of the virus in the body. **antibody positive** showing antibodies to a virus, and therefore indicating infection by the virus.

antic *n.* (usu. as **antics**) absurd or foolish behaviour, esp. movements intended to cause amusement.

Antichrist *n.* the ultimate antagonist of Christ in the world; any enemy of Christ.

anticipate *v.* **1** deal with or use before the proper time (*anticipate one's income*). **2** take action before someone else has had time to do so (*others may have anticipated Columbus in the discovery of America*). **3** notice what needs doing and take action in advance (*anticipate someone's needs; the boxer anticipated the blow*). **4** expect (*we anticipate that Australia will soon become a republic*). ☐ **anticipation** *n.* **anticipatory** / an-tis-uh-**pay**-tuh-ree / *adj.*

■ **Usage** Many people regard the use in sense 4 as unacceptable, but it is very common in informal use.

anticlimax *n.* a disappointing ending or outcome of events where a climax was expected. ☐ **anticlimactic** *adj.*

anticlockwise *adv.* & *adj.* moving in a curve from right to left, in the opposite direction to the hands of a clock.

anticoagulant *n.* a substance that prevents or slows down the clotting of blood.

anticyclone *n.* an area in which atmospheric pressure is high, producing fine settled weather, with an outward flow of air.

antidepressant *n.* a drug that counteracts mental depression.

antidote / **an**-tee-doht / *n.* **1** a substance that counteracts the effects of a poison or a disease. **2** anything that counteracts unpleasant effects.

antifreeze *n.* a substance added to water to lower its freezing point, used especially in a vehicle's radiator to prevent freezing.

antigen / **an**-tuh-juhn / *n.* a substance (e.g. a toxin) that causes the body to produce antibodies.

Antigua and Barbuda / an-**tee**-guh, bah-**boo**-duh / a country consisting of three islands in the Caribbean Sea. ☐ **Antiguan** *adj.* & *n.* **Barbudan** *adj.* & *n.*

anti-hero *n.* a central character in a story or drama who lacks conventional heroic attitudes.

antihistamine / an-tee-**his**-tuh-meen / *n.* a substance that counteracts the effects of histamine, used in treating allergies.

antiknock *n.* a substance added to motor fuel to prevent or reduce knocking.

Antill, John Henry (1904–86), Australian composer, best known for his music to the ballet *Corroboree*.

anti-lock *adj.* (of brakes) designed to prevent locking and skidding when applied suddenly.

antilog *n. colloq.* an antilogarithm.

antilogarithm *n.* the number to which a given logarithm belongs.

antimacassar / an-tee-muh-**kas**-uh / *n.* a small protective cover for the backs or arms of chairs etc. (¶ Originally a protection against the Macassar oil that was used on hair.)

antimatter *n.* matter composed solely of antiparticles.

antimony / **an**-tuh-muh-nee / *n.* a chemical element (symbol Sb), a brittle silvery metal used in alloys.

antinomy / an-**tin**-uh-mee / *n.* contradiction between two reasonable beliefs or conclusions.

antinovel *n.* a work of fiction that deliberately avoids the normal patterns and conventions of most novels.

anti-nuclear *adj.* opposed to the development and use of nuclear weapons or power.

antioxidant / an-tee-**ok**-suh-duhnt / *n.* **1** an agent that inhibits oxidation, esp. used to counteract deterioration of stored food products. **2** a substance (e.g. vitamin C or E) that removes potentially damaging oxidising agents in a living organism.

antiparticle *n.* an elementary particle with the same mass as another particle but opposite electrical charge and magnetic properties.

antipasto *n.* (*pl.* **antipastos** *or* **antipasti**) a starter or appetiser, esp. as part of an Italian meal.

antipathy / an-**tip**-uh-thee / *n.* **1** a strong and settled dislike. **2** the object of this.

antiperspirant / an-tee-**pers**-puh-ruhnt / *n.* a substance that prevents or reduces sweating.

antiphon / **an**-tuh-fuhn, -fon / *n.* a verse of a psalm etc. sung by part of a choir in response to one sung by the other part. ☐ **antiphonal** / an-**tif**-uh-nuhl / *adj.*

antipodean / an-tip-uh-**dee**-uhn / *adj.* Australian. •*n.* an Australian.

antipodes / an-**tip**-uh-deez / *n.pl.* **1** places on opposite sides of the earth. **2** (**the Antipodes**) the Australasian regions, almost diametrically opposite Europe.

antipope *n.* a person set up as pope in opposition to the one chosen by canon law.

antipyretic *adj.* (of a drug) preventing or reducing fever.

antiquary / **an**-tuh-kwuh-ree / *n.* one who studies or collects antiques or antiquities. ☐ **antiquarian** / an-tuh-**kwair**-ree-uhn / *adj.* & *n.*

antiquated / **an**-tuh-kway-tuhd / *adj.* old-fashioned, out of date.

antique / an-**teek** / *adj.* belonging to the distant past, in the style of past times. •*n.* an antique object, especially furniture or a decorative object of a kind sought by collectors.

antiquity / an-**tik**-wuh-tee / *n.* **1** ancient times, especially before the Middle Ages. **2** (**antiquities**) objects dating from ancient times. **3** great age.

antiscorbutic / an-tee-skaw-**byoo**-tik / *adj.* preventing or curing scurvy.

anti-Semitic / an-tee-suh-**mit**-ik / *adj.* hostile to or prejudiced against Jews. ☐ **anti-Semitism** / an-tee-**sem**-uh-tiz-uhm / *n.*

antiseptic *adj.* **1** preventing the growth of bacteria etc. that cause things to become septic. **2** thoroughly clean and free from germs. •*n.* a substance with an antiseptic effect.

antiserum *n.* serum containing a large number of antibodies.

antisocial *adj.* **1** opposed to the social institutions and laws of an organised community. **2** interfering with amenities enjoyed by others (*it's antisocial to leave litter*). **3** unsociable, withdrawing oneself from others. ☐ **antisocially** *adv.*

antistatic *adj.* counteracting the effects of static electricity.

antitetanus *adj.* effective against tetanus.

antithesis / an-**tith**-uh-suhs / *n.* (*pl.* **antitheses**) **1** the direct opposite of something; an opposition or contrast (*slavery is the antithesis of freedom*). **2** contrast of ideas emphasised by choice of words or by their arrangement. ☐ **antithetical** *adj.* **antithetically** *adv.*

antitoxin *n.* a substance that neutralises a toxin and prevents it from having a harmful effect. ☐ **antitoxic** *adj.*

antitrades *n.pl.* winds blowing in the opposite direction to trade winds.

antivenene *n.* (also **antivenin**) = ANTIVENOM.

antivenom *n.* an antiserum containing antibodies against specific poisons in the venom of snakes, spiders, etc.

antler *n.* a branched horn; one of a pair of these on a stag or other deer. ☐ **antlered** *adj.*

antonym / **an**-tuh-nim / *n.* a word that is opposite in meaning to another.

ANU *abbr.* = AUSTRALIAN NATIONAL UNIVERSITY.

Anuradhapura / u-nuu-**rah**-juh-puu-ruh / the ancient capital of Sri Lanka (4th century BC–AD 760), site of numerous Buddhist foundations.

anus / **ay**-nuhs / *n.* the opening at the end of the alimentary canal, through which solid waste matter passes out of the body.

anvil *n.* a block of iron on which a smith hammers metal into shape.

anxiety *n.* **1** the state of being anxious. **2** something causing this.

anxious *adj.* **1** troubled and uneasy in mind. **2** causing worry, filled with such feeling (*an anxious moment*). **3** eager (*anxious to please*). ☐ **anxiously** *adv.*

any *adj.* **1** one or some (but no matter which) from several. **2** every, whichever you choose (*any fool knows that*). **3** in a significant amount (*did not stay any length of time*). •*pron.* any person, thing, or amount (*I can't find any of them; we haven't any*). •*adv.* at all, in some degree (*he isn't any better*). ☐ **any more** to any further extent.

anybody *n.* & *pron.* **1** any person. **2** a person of importance (*is he anybody?*).

anyhow *adv.* **1** anyway. **2** not in an orderly manner (*work was done all anyhow*).

anyone *n.* & *pron.* anybody.

anything *n.* & *pron.* any thing (*anything will do*). ☐ **anything but** not at all; far from being (*it's anything but cheap*). **like anything** with great intensity.

anyway *adv.* **1** in any manner. **2** at any rate. **3** to resume (*anyway, as I was saying*).

anywhere *adv.* in or to any place. •*pron.* any place.

Anzac *n.* **1** a soldier of the Australian and New Zealand Army Corps who served in the Gallipoli Campaign during the First World War (1914–18). **2** an Australian (or New Zealand) soldier or ex-soldier. (¶ Named from the initial letters of the Corps.) ☐ **Anzac biscuit** a biscuit made of rolled oats, flour, golden syrup, desiccated coconut, butter, and sugar. **Anzac Day** 25 April, the anniversary of the landing at Anzac Cove in the Gallipoli peninsula of Australian and New Zealand troops: a national public holiday commemorating all Australia's war dead.

AO *abbr.* Officer of the Order of Australia.

aorta / ay-**aw**-tuh / *n.* the major artery through which blood is carried from the left side of the heart. ☐ **aortic** *adj.*

Aotearoa / ow-tay-uh-**roh**-uh / the Maori name for NEW ZEALAND. It means 'land of the long white cloud'.

apace *adv. literary* swiftly (*work proceeded apace*).

Apache / uh-**pach**-ee / *n.* a member of a tribe of North American Indians inhabiting the south-western part of the USA.

apart *adv.* **1** aside, separately, to or at a distance. **2** into pieces (*it came apart*). ☐ **apart from** independently of, other than (*has no books apart from these*). **joking apart** speaking seriously, without joking.

apartheid / uh-**pah**-tayt / *n.* a policy (especially formerly in South Africa) of racial segregation, separating Europeans and non-Europeans.

apartment *n.* **1** a room or a set of rooms. **2** a flat.

apathy / **ap**-uh-thee / *n.* lack of interest or concern. ☐ **apathetic** / ap-uh-**thet**-ik / *adj.* **apathetically** *adv.*

ape *n.* any of the four primates (gorilla, chimpanzee, orang-utan, gibbon) most closely related to man. •*v.* to imitate, to mimic.

APEC / **ay**-pek / *abbr.* Asia Pacific Economic Cooperation.

apeman *n.* an extinct primate thought to have been the forerunner of humans.

aperient / uh-**peer**-ree-uhnt / *adj.* laxative. •*n.* a laxative medicine.

aperitif / uh-pe-ruh-**teef** / *n.* an alcoholic drink taken before a meal.

aperture / **ap**-uh-chuh / *n.* an opening, especially one that admits light.

apex[1] *n.* a system of reduced fares for scheduled flights when paid for in advance. (¶ From *a*dvance *p*urchase *ex*cursion.)

apex[2] / **ay**-peks / *n.* (*pl.* **apexes** or **apices** / **ay**-puh-seez /) the tip or highest point, the pointed end (*the apex of a triangle*).

aphasia / uh-**fay**-zee-uh, -*zh*uh / *n.* loss of the ability to speak or understand language as a result of brain damage.

aphelion / ap-**hee**-lee-uhn, uh-**fee**-lee-uhn / *n.* (*pl.* **aphelia**) the point in a planet's or comet's orbit when it is furthest from the sun.

aphid / **ay**-fuhd / *n.* any of several small insects gathering in large numbers to suck sap from the leaves, stems, etc. of plants.

aphis / **ay**-fuhs / *n.* (*pl.* **aphides** / **ay**-fuh-deez /) an aphid.

aphorism / **af**-uh-riz-uhm / *n.* a short wise saying, a maxim.

aphrodisiac / af-ruh-**diz**-ee-ak / *adj.* arousing sexual desire. •*n.* an aphrodisiac substance.

Aphrodite / af-ruh-**duy**-tee / *Gk myth.* the goddess of beauty, fertility, and sexual love, identified by the Romans with Venus.

Apia / ah-**pee**-uh / the capital of Samoa.

apiary / **ay**-pee-uh-ree / *n.* a place with a number of hives where bees are kept.

apiculture *n.* bee-keeping.

apiece *adv.* to each, for or by each one of a group (*cost $5 apiece*).

aplomb / uh-**plom** / *n.* dignity and confidence.

apnoea / **ap**-nee-uh, ap-**nee**-uh / *n.* (also **apnea**) a temporary cessation of breathing.

apocalypse / uh-**pok**-uh-lips / *n.* **1** (**the Apocalypse**) Revelation, the last book in the New Testament, containing a prophetic description of the end of the world. **2** a violent and destructive event.

apocalyptic / uh-pok-uh-**lip**-tik / *adj.* of or like an apocalypse; prophesying events of this kind.

Apocrypha / uh-**pok**-ruh-fuh / *n.pl.* the Biblical books received by the early Church as part of the Greek version of the Old Testament and included in the Latin version, but not included in the Hebrew Scriptures or in later Protestant versions.

apocryphal / uh-**pok**-ruh-fuhl / *adj.* unlikely to be true (*an apocryphal account of his travels*).

apogee / **ap**-uh-jee / *n.* **1** the point in the orbit of the moon or any planet when it is at its furthest point from earth. **2** the highest or most distant point; a climax.

apolitical / ay-puh-**lit**-i-kuhl / *adj.* not political, not concerned with politics.

Apollo 1 *Gk myth.* a god associated with the sun, music, and prophecy, represented in art as the ideal type of male beauty. **2** the American space program for landing people on the moon, which achieved its object on 20 July 1969.

Apollyon / uh-**pol**-yuhn / the Devil.

apologetic *adj.* making an apology. • *n.* (**apologetics**) a reasoned defence, especially of Christianity. ☐ **apologetically** *adv.*

apologia / ap-uh-**loh**-jee-uh / *n.* a formal defence of belief or conduct.

apologise *v.* (also **-ize**) make an apology.

apologist *n.* a person who explains or defends something by reasoned argument.

apology *n.* **1** a statement of regret for having done wrong. **2** an explanation or defence of one's beliefs. **3** a poor or scanty specimen (*this feeble apology for a meal*).

apophthegm / **ap**-uh-them / *n.* a terse or pithy saying.

apoplectic / ap-uh-**plek**-tik / *adj.* **1** of apoplexy. **2** suffering from apoplexy. **3** *colloq.* furious, enraged.

apoplexy / **ap**-uh-plek-see / *n.* **1** sudden inability to feel and move, caused by blockage or rupture of an artery in the brain; a stroke. **2** *colloq.* a rush of extreme emotion, esp. anger.

apostasy / uh-**pos**-tuh-see / *n.* renunciation of one's beliefs, principles, or party.

apostate / uh-**pos**-tayt / *n.* a person who renounces a former belief, principle, etc.

a posteriori / ay pos-teer-ree-**aw**-ruy / *adj.* (of reasoning in logic) proceeding from effect to cause; inductive. (¶ Latin, = from what comes after.)

Apostle *n.* **1** any of the twelve men sent out by Christ to preach the Gospel. **2** (**apostle**) a leader or teacher of a new faith or movement.

apostolic / ap-uh-**stol**-ik / *adj.* **1** of or relating to the Apostles or their teaching. **2** of or relating to the pope. ☐ **apostolic succession** the uninterrupted transmission of spiritual authority from the Apostles through successive popes and bishops.

apostrophe / uh-**pos**-truh-fee / *n.* **1** a punctuation mark (') used to show that letters or numbers have been omitted, or showing the possessive case, or the plurals of letters (see panel). **2** a passage in a speech or poem etc. addressing an absent person or an abstract idea.

apostrophise / uh-**pos**-truh-fuyz / *v.* (also **-ize**) to address in an apostrophe.

apothecary / uh-**poth**-uh-kuh-ree / *n. archaic* a pharmaceutical chemist.

apotheosis / uh-poth-ee-**oh**-suhs / *n.* (*pl.* **apotheoses** / -seez /) **1** elevation to the status of a god, deification. **2** a thing's highest development; an ideal, a perfect example.

appal / uh-**pawl** / *v.* (**appalled**, **appalling**) fill with horror or dismay, shock deeply.

appalling *adj. colloq.* shocking, unpleasant.

apparatus / ap-uh-**rah**-tuhs, -**ray**- / *n.* **1** the equipment used for doing something; the instruments etc. used in scientific experiments. **2** a complex organisation or system (*the Labor apparatus*).

apparel *n.* clothing.

apparent / uh-**pa**-ruhnt / *adj.* **1** clearly seen or understood; obvious (*it became apparent*). **2** seeming but not real (*his reluctance was only apparent*). ☐ **heir apparent** *see* HEIR. ☐☐ **apparently** *adv.*

apparition / ap-uh-**rish**-uhn / *n.* **1** something that appears, especially something remarkable or unexpected. **2** a ghost.

appeal *v.* (**appealed**, **appealing**) **1** make an earnest or formal request (*appealed for contributions*). **2** ask a person or go to a recognised authority for an opinion (*appealed to the chairman*). **3** take a case to a higher court for judicial review of a lower court's decision. **4** be of interest, attract (*the idea of an Australian Republic appeals to us greatly*). • *n.* **1** the act of appealing. **2** a judicial review of a case by a higher court; a request for this. **3** attraction, interest, pleasantness. **4** a request for public donations to a cause.

appealing *adj.* attractive, likeable.

appear *v.* **1** become or be visible. **2** present oneself, especially formally or publicly (*the Aboriginal group 'Yothu Yindi' is appearing at the Opera House tonight*). **3** act as counsel in a lawcourt (*I appear for the defendant*). **4** be published (*the story appeared in the newspapers*). **5** give a certain impression (*you appear to have forgotten*).

Apostrophe '

An apostrophe is used:
1 to indicate possession:
   with a singular noun:
   the boy's book; a week's work; the boss's salary;
   with a plural already ending with s:
   a girls' school; two weeks' newspapers; the bosses' salaries;
   with a plural not already ending with s:
   the children's shoes; women's liberation;
   with a singular name:
   Gavin's hat; Louise's coat; Thomas's (or *Thomas'*) *book; Keats' poems;*
   with a name ending in -es that is pronounced /-uhz/:
   Bridges' poems; Moses' mother;
   and before the word *sake*:
   for God's sake; for goodness' sake; for Nicholas' sake;
   but it is often omitted in a business or place name:
   Smiths Bookshop; Crows Nest.
2 to mark an omission of one or more letters or numbers:
   he's (*he is* or *he has*)   *haven't* (*have not*)
   can't (*cannot*)   *we'll* (*we shall*)
   won't (*will not*)   *o'clock* (*of the clock*)
   the summer of '96 (*1996*)
3 when letters or numbers are referred to in plural form:
   mind your p's and q's; find all the number 7's.
   but it is unnecessary in, e.g.,
   MPs; the 1940s.

appearance *n.* **1** appearing. **2** an outward sign, form, or impression (*has an appearance of prosperity*). ☐ **keep up appearances** keep an outward show of prosperity or good behaviour. **put in an appearance** be present, especially for only a short time. **to all appearances** so far as can be seen (*he was to all appearances dead*).

appease *v.* make calm or quiet by making concessions or by satisfying demands. ☐ **appeasement** *n.*

appellant / uh-**pel**-uhnt / *n.* a person making an appeal to a higher court.

appellate / uh-**pel**-uht / *adj.* (especially of a court) concerned with appeals.

appellation / ap-uh-**lay**-shuhn / *n. formal* **1** naming. **2** a name or title.

append *v.* **1** attach. **2** add at the end (*append one's signature*).

appendage / uh-**pen**-dij / *n.* a thing added to or forming a natural part of something larger or more important.

appendectomy *n.* (also **appendicectomy**) the surgical removal of the appendix.

appendicitis *n.* inflammation of the appendix of the intestine.

appendix *n.* **1** (*pl.* **appendices** / uh-**pen**-duh-seez /) a section with supplementary information at the end of a book or document. **2** (*pl.* **appendixes**) a small tube of tissue closed at one end, forming an outgrowth of the intestine.

appertain / ap-uh-**tayn** / *v.* (foll. by *to*) relate, belong, or be appropriate to.

appetiser *n.* (also **-izer**) something eaten or drunk to stimulate the appetite.

appetising *adj.* (also **-izing**) stimulating the appetite (*an appetising smell*). ☐ **appetisingly** *adv.*

appetite *n.* **1** physical desire, especially for food. **2** a craving (*an appetite for sex*).

applaud *v.* **1** show approval of (a thing) by clapping one's hands. **2** praise (*we applaud your decision*).

applause *n.* **1** hand clapping by people applauding. **2** warm approval.

apple *n.* **1** a round firm fruit with crisp juicy flesh. **2** the tree that bears this. **3** any of several Australian trees or shrubs thought by early settlers to resemble an apple tree, esp. trees of the genus *Angophora*. ☐ **apple of one's eye** a cherished person or thing. **apple-pie order** extreme neatness. **upset the apple cart** spoil carefully laid plans.

Apple Isle *n.* Tasmania, so called because of its identification as an apple-growing region. ☐ **Apple Islander** *n.*

applet / **ap**-luht / *n.* a small computer program, particularly one executing a single task within a larger suite of applications.

appliance *n.* a device, an instrument; a machine or piece of equipment.

applicable / **ap**-lik-uh-buhl, uh-**plik**-uh-buhl / *adj.* able to be applied; appropriate. ☐ **applicability** / uh-plik-uh-**bil**-uh-tee / *n.*

applicant / **ap**-luh-kuhnt / *n.* a person who applies for something, especially a job.

application *n.* **1** applying something, putting one thing on another (*ointment for external application only*). **2** the thing applied. **3** making a formal request; the request itself (*his application was refused*). **4** bringing a rule into use; putting something to practical use; relevance. **5** the ability to apply oneself.

applicator *n.* a device for applying something.

applied *see* APPLY. • *adj.* put to practical use; not merely theoretical (*applied science; applied mathematics*).

appliqué / **ap**-luh-kay / *n.* **1** a piece of cut-out material sewn or fixed ornamentally to another. **2** needlework of this kind. • *v.* (**appliquéd**, **appliquéing**) decorate with appliqué.

apply *v.* (**applied**, **applying**) **1** put (a thing) into contact with another; spread on a surface. **2** bring into use or action; put into effect (*apply economic sanctions*). **3** be relevant (*what I said does not apply to you*). **4** make a formal request (*to apply for a job*). ☐ **apply oneself** give one's attention and energy to a task.

appoint *v.* **1** choose (a person) for a job; set up by choosing members (*appoint a committee*). **2** fix or decide by authority (*they appointed a time for the next meeting*). ☐ **well-appointed** *adj.* well equipped or furnished.

appointee *n.* the person appointed.

appointment *n.* **1** an arrangement to meet or visit at a particular time. **2** appointing a person to a job. **3** the job or position itself. **4** (**appointments**) equipment, furniture.

apportion / uh-**paw**-shuhn / *v.* divide into shares, allot. ☐ **apportionment** *n.*

apposite / **ap**-uh-zuht / *adj.* (of a remark) appropriate for a purpose or occasion. ☐ **appositely** *adv.* **appositeness** *n.*

apposition / ap-uh-**zish**-uhn / *n.* **1** placing side by side. **2** a grammatical relationship in which a word or phrase is placed with another which it describes, e.g. in 'William the Conqueror', *the Conqueror* is in apposition to *William*.

appraise *v.* estimate or assess the value or quality of. ☐ **appraisal** *n.*

appreciable / uh-**pree**-shuh-buhl / *adj.* able to be seen or felt; considerable (*an appreciable change in temperature*). ☐ **appreciably** *adv.*

appreciate *v.* **1** value greatly, be grateful for. **2** enjoy intelligently (*to appreciate Aboriginal art*). **3** understand (*we appreciate their reluctance to give details*). **4** rise or raise in value (*the investments have appreciated greatly*). ☐ **appreciation** *n.*

appreciative / uh-**pree**-shuh-tiv / *adj.* feeling or showing grateful recognition or enjoyment. ☐ **appreciatively** *adv.*

appreciatory / uh-**pree**-shuh-tree / *adj.* showing appreciation.

apprehend / ap-ruh-**hend** / *v.* **1** seize, arrest. **2** grasp the meaning of, understand.

apprehended violence order *n. Aust.* an order made by a court that protects a person who has a reasonable fear of violence, harassment, etc., from a specified person.

apprehension / ap-ruh-**hen**-shuhn / *n.* **1** a feeling of fear about a possible danger or difficulty. **2** understanding. **3** arrest.

apprehensive / ap-ruh-**hen**-siv / *adj.* feeling apprehension, anxious. □**apprehensively** *adv.* **apprehensiveness** *n.*

apprentice *n.* **1** a person learning a trade etc. by working in it for an agreed period. **2** a novice. • *v.* (usually as **apprenticed to**) working as an apprentice for an employer (*he was apprenticed to a builder*). □**apprenticeship** *n.*

apprise / uh-**pruyz** / *v. formal* inform.

appro / **ap**-roh / *n. colloq.* □ **on appro** on approval.

approach *v.* **1** come near or nearer in space or time. **2** set about doing or tackling (*approach the problem in a practical way*). **3** go to with a request or offer (*approach your bank for a loan*). **4** be similar to (*a dislike that approaches hatred*). • *n.* **1** approaching (*watched their approach*). **2** a way of reaching a place. **3** the final part of an aircraft's flight before landing. **4** a method of doing or tackling something. **5** an effort to establish an agreement or friendly relations. **6** an approximation (*his closest approach to an apology*).

approachable *adj.* able to be approached; friendly and easy to talk to. □**approachability** *n.*

approbation / ap-ruh-**bay**-shuhn / *n.* approval.

appropriate[1] / uh-**proh**-pree-uht / *adj.* suitable, proper. □**appropriately** *adv.* **appropriateness** *n.*

appropriate[2] / uh-**proh**-pree-ayt / *v.* **1** take and use as one's own. **2** set aside for a special purpose (*$500 was appropriated to Aids research*). □**appropriation** *n.* **appropriator** *n.*

approval *n.* feeling, showing, or saying that one considers something to be good or acceptable. □**on approval** (of goods) taken by a customer for examination without obligation to buy unless satisfied.

approve *v.* **1** say or feel that something is good or suitable. **2** sanction, agree to (*the committee approved the expenditure*).

approx. *abbr.* approximate; approximately.

approximate *adj.* / uh-**prok**-suh-muht / almost exact or correct but not completely so. • *v.* / uh-**prok**-suh-mayt / **1** be almost the same (*a story that approximated to the truth*). **2** make approximately the same. □**approximately** *adv.* **approximation** *n.*

appurtenance / uh-**per**-tuh-nuhns / *n.* (usually as **appurtenances**) a minor piece of property, or a right or privilege, that goes with a more important one.

après-ski / ap-ray-**skee** / *n.* social activities following a day's skiing. (¶ French)

apricot *n.* **1** a juicy stone fruit related to the plum and peach, orange-pink when ripe. **2** this colour.

April *n.* the fourth month of the year. □**April fool** a person who is hoaxed on April Fool's Day (1 April).

a priori / ay pruy-**aw**-ruy, ay pree-**aw**-ree / *adj.* **1** (of reasoning in logic) from cause to effect; deductive. **2** (of concepts) not derived from experience. **3** assumed without investigation. • *adv.* **1** deductively; logically. **2** as far as one knows. (¶ Latin, = from what is before.)

apron *n.* **1** a garment worn over the front part of the body to protect the wearer's clothes. **2** an extension of a theatre stage in front of the curtain. **3** a hard-surfaced area on an airfield, where aircraft are manoeuvred or loaded and unloaded.

apropos / **ap**-ruh-poh, -**poh** / *adv.* appropriately, to the point. • *adj.* suitable or relevant to what is being said or done. □**apropos of** concerning, with reference to (*apropos of elections, who is to be our new candidate?*).

apse *n.* a recess with an arched or domed roof, especially in a church.

apsis *n.* (*pl.* **apsides** / **ap**-suh-deez /) each of the points on the orbit of a planet or satellite etc. that are nearest to or furthest from the body round which it moves.

apt *adj.* **1** suitable, appropriate (*an apt quotation*). **2** having a certain tendency; likely (*he is apt to be careless*). **3** quick at learning. □**aptly** *adv.* **aptness** *n.*

aptitude *n.* a natural ability or skill.

aqua *n.* the colour aquamarine.

aquaculture / **ak**-wuh-kul-chuh / *n.* the cultivation or rearing of aquatic plants or animals.

aqualung *n.* a diver's portable breathing apparatus consisting of cylinders of compressed air connected to a face mask.

aquamarine / ak-wuh-muh-**reen** / *n.* **1** a bluish-green gemstone. **2** its colour.

aquaplane *n.* a board on which a person stands to be towed by a speedboat. • *v.* **1** ride on such a board. **2** glide uncontrollably on a wet road surface.

aqua regia / **ree**-jee-uh / *n.* a highly corrosive mixture of acids.

aquarium / uh-**kwair**-ree-uhm / *n.* (*pl.* **aquariums**) a tank in which fish are kept for display; a building containing a lot of these.

Aquarius / uh-**kwair**-ree-uhs / *n.* the eleventh sign of the zodiac, the Water-carrier. □**Aquarian** *adj.* & *n.*

aquatic / uh-**kwot**-ik / *adj.* **1** growing or living in or near water (*aquatic plants*). **2** taking place in or on water (*aquatic sports*).

aqua vitae / **vee**-tay / *n.* strong alcoholic spirit, especially brandy. (¶ Latin, = water of life.)

aqueduct / **ak**-wuh-dukt / *n.* an artificial channel carrying water across country, especially one like a bridge over a valley or road.

aqueous / **ay**-kwee-uhs, **ak**-wee-uhs / *adj.* **1** of or like water. **2** produced by water. ☐ **aqueous humour** clear fluid in the eye between the lens and the cornea.

aquiline / **ak**-wuh-luyn / *adj.* hooked like an eagle's beak (*an aquiline nose*).

Aquinas / uh-**kwuy**-nuhs /, St Thomas (1225–74), Italian theologian, Doctor of the Church, a Dominican friar.

Ar *symbol* argon.

Arab *n.* **1** a member of a Semitic people originating in Saudi Arabia and neighbouring countries, now widespread throughout the Middle East and North Africa. **2** a horse of a breed native to Arabia. • *adj.* of Arabs.

Arabana / u-ru-**bun**-u / *n.* an Aboriginal language of a vast area west of Lake Eyre in the north-eastern region of SA.

arabesque / a-ruh-**besk** / *n.* **1** an elaborate design with intertwined leaves, branches, and scrolls. **2** a ballet dancer's posture poised on one leg with the other stretched backwards horizontally. **3** a short elaborate piece of music.

Arabia a peninsula in the Middle East between the Red Sea and the Persian Gulf.

Arabian *adj.* of Arabia. ☐ **Arabian Nights** the popular title of a collection of Oriental folk tales mostly dating from the 9th century.

Arabic *adj.* of the Arabs or their language. • *n.* the language of the Arabs. ☐ **Arabic numerals** the symbols 1, 2, 3, 4, 5, etc.

arable / **a**-ruh-buhl / *adj.* (of land) suitable for growing crops. • *n.* arable land.

arachnid / uh-**rak**-nid / *n.* a member of the class of animals including spiders, scorpions, and mites.

arachnophobia *n.* an abnormal fear of spiders.

Arafat / **a**-ruh-fat /, Yasser (1929–), leader of the Palestine Liberation Organisation from 1968.

Arafura Sea / ay-ruh-**fyoor**-ruh / a sea, of strategic importance to Australia, lying between the western half of New Guinea, the northern coast of Australia, and the easternmost islands of Indonesia.

arak alternative spelling of ARRACK.

Araldite *n.* *trademark* an epoxy resin used as a strong heatproof cement to mend china, plastic, etc.

Aramaic / a-ruh-**may**-ik / *n.* a Semitic language spoken in Syria and Palestine in New Testament times.

Aranda / u-**run**-tu, a-ruhn-du / *n.* alternative spelling of ARRERNTE.

Ararat / **a**-ruh-rat / either of two mountain peaks in eastern Turkey, where Noah's ark is said to have rested after the Flood.

arbiter / **ah**-buh-tuh / *n.* **1** a person who has the power to decide what shall be done or accepted, one with entire control (*designers who are the arbiters of fashion*). **2** an arbitrator.

arbitrary / **ah**-buh-truh-ree, -tree / *adj.* **1** based on random choice or impulse, not on reason (*an arbitrary selection*). **2** despotic, unrestrained (*arbitrary powers*). ☐ **arbitrarily** *adv.* **arbitrariness** *n.*

arbitrate *v.* act as an arbitrator.

arbitration *n.* settlement of a dispute by a person or persons acting as arbitrators. ☐ **arbitration award** *Aust.* a determination made by a court of industrial arbitration. **arbitration court** *Aust.* a tribunal for the resolution of industrial disputes etc. **arbitration system** *Aust.* the organisation and method of resolving industrial disputes, determining industrial awards, etc.

arbitrator *n.* an impartial person chosen to settle a dispute between two parties.

arbor *n.* an axle or spindle on which a wheel etc. revolves in mechanism.

arboreal / ah-**baw**-ree-uhl / *adj.* **1** of trees. **2** living in trees.

arboretum / ah-baw-**ree**-tuhm / *n.* (*pl.* **arboreta**) a place where rare trees are grown for study and display.

arboriculture *n.* cultivation of trees and shrubs.

arborio rice / ah-**baw**-ree-oh / *n.* a kind of plump round-grained rice originally grown in Italy, esp. for use in risotto.

arbour / **ah**-buh / *n.* (also **arbor**) a shady place among trees, especially in a garden with climbing plants growing over a framework.

ARC *abbr.* = AIDS-RELATED COMPLEX.

arc *n.* **1** part of the circumference of a circle or other curve. **2** anything shaped like this. **3** a luminous electric current passing across a gap between two terminals. • *v.* (**arced**, **arcing**) **1** form an arc; move in a curve. **2** form an electric arc. ☐ **arc lamp** (*or* **light**) lighting using an electric arc. **arc welding** welding by means of an electric arc.

arcade *n.* **1** a covered passage or area, usually with shops on both sides. **2** a series of arches supporting or along a wall.

Arcadia / ah-**kay**-dee-uh / a mountainous area in the central Peloponnese in Greece, in poetic fantasy the idyllic home of song-loving shepherds.

Arcadian *n.* a country dweller with a peaceful life. • *adj.* poetically rural.

arcane / ah-**kayn** / *adj.* mysterious, secret.

arch[1] *n.* **1** a curved structure supporting the weight of what is above it or used ornamentally. **2** something shaped like this. **3** the curved underpart of the foot. • *v.* form into an arch.

arch[2] *adj.* consciously or affectedly playful (*an arch smile*). ☐ **archly** *adv.*

arch- *comb. form* **1** chief. **2** extreme.

Archaean / ah-**kee**-uhn / *adj.* of the earliest geological era.

archaeologist *n.* an expert in archaeology.

archaeology / ar-kee-**ol**-uh-jee / n. the scientific study of civilisations through their material remains. ☐ **archaeological** adj.
archaeopteryx / ah-kee-**op**-tuh-riks / n. a fossil bird with teeth, feathers, and a long bony tail.
archaic / ah-**kay**-ik / adj. belonging to former or ancient times.
archaism / **ah**-kay-iz-uhm / n. an archaic word or expression.
archangel n. an angelic being ranking higher than an angel.
archbishop n. a bishop ranking above other bishops in a province of the Church.
archbishopric n. the office or diocese of an archbishop.
archdeacon n. an Anglican cleric ranking next below a bishop. ☐ **archdeaconry** n.
archdiocese / ahch-**duy**-uh-suhs / n. the diocese of an archbishop.
archduke n. hist. chief duke, especially as the title of a son of an Austrian Emperor.
Archer, Robyn (1948–), AO, Australian actor, singer, writer, musician, and director.
archer n. **1** a person who shoots with bow and arrows. **2** (**the Archer**) a sign of the zodiac, Sagittarius.
archery n. the sport of shooting with bows and arrows.
archetype / **ah**-kuh-tuyp / n. an original model from which others are copied. ☐ **archetypal** adj.
Archibald Prize a prize established in 1921 for a portrait in oil or watercolour by an Australian artist, preferably of some man or woman distinguished in Australian art, letters, or politics. (¶ Jules François Archibald (1856–1919), Australian journalist, co-founder of the *Bulletin*.)
archidiaconal / ah-kee-duy-**ak**-uh-nuhl / adj. of an archdeacon.
archiepiscopal / ah-kee-uh-**pis**-kuh-puhl / adj. of an archbishop or archbishopric.
archimandrite / ah-kee-**man**-druyt / n. the head of a large monastery in the Orthodox Church.
Archimedes / ah-kuh-**mee**-deez / (3rd century BC) Greek mathematician and inventor.
archipelago / ah-kuh-**pel**-uh-goh / n. (pl. **archipelagos**) **1** a group of many islands. **2** a sea containing such a group.
architect n. **1** a designer of buildings. **2** (foll. by *of*) a person who brings about a specified thing (*architect of peace*).
architecture n. **1** the art or science of designing buildings. **2** the design or style of a building or buildings. ☐ **architectural** adj. **architecturally** adv.
architrave / **ah**-kuh-trayv / n. **1** the horizontal piece resting on the columns of a building. **2** the surround of a doorway or window.
archive / **ah**-kuyv / n. (often **archives**) the records or historical documents of an institution or community.
archivist / **ah**-kuh-vuhst / n. a person trained to deal with archives.
archway n. a passageway under an arch.
Arctic adj. **1** of the regions round the North Pole. **2** (**arctic**) very cold (*the weather was arctic*). • n. **1** the Arctic regions. **2** the Arctic Ocean, the ocean surrounding the North Pole, lying within the Arctic Circle. ☐ **Arctic Circle** an imaginary line round the Arctic region, the line of latitude 66° 33′ N.
ardent / **ah**-duhnt / adj. full of ardour; enthusiastic. ☐ **ardently** adv.
ardour / **ah**-duh / n. great warmth of feeling.
arduous / **ah**-dyoo-uhs / adj. needing much effort; laborious. ☐ **arduously** adv.
are[1] see BE.
are[2] / ah / n. an area of 100 square metres.
area n. **1** the extent or measurement of a surface. **2** a region; a space for a specific purpose (*picnic area*). **3** the scope or range of an activity or study (*working in the area of Aboriginal linguistics*).
arena / uh-**ree**-nuh / n. the level area in the centre of a sports stadium or an amphitheatre.
aren't = ARE NOT.

■ **Usage** The phrase *aren't I?* is a recognised colloquialism for *am I not?*

areola / uh-**reer**-luh / n. (pl. **areolae**) a circular coloured area, especially around a nipple.
Areopagus / ah-ree-**op**-uh-guhs / **1** a hill at Athens. **2** a council or judicial court of ancient Athens meeting on this hill.
Ares / **air**-reez / Gk myth. the god of war, identified by the Romans with Mars.
arête / uh-**rayt**, -**ret** / n. a sharp ridge on a mountain.
Argentina / ah-juhn-**tee**-nuh / a republic in the southern part of South America. ☐ **Argentine** / **ah**-juhn-tuyn / adj. & n. **Argentinian** / ah-juhn-**tin**-ee-uhn / adj. & n.
Argentine ant n. a destructive South American ant now a pest in Australia.
argon n. a chemical element (symbol Ar), an inert gas used e.g. in electric-light bulbs and in arc welding.
Argonauts / **ah**-guh-nawts / n.pl. Gk myth. the heroes who accompanied Jason on the ship *Argo* in quest of the Golden Fleece.
argosy / **ah**-guh-see / n. poetic a large merchant ship.
argot / **ah**-goh / n. the special jargon of a group.
arguable adj. **1** able to be asserted. **2** open to doubt or dispute, not certain. ☐ **arguably** adv.
argue v. **1** express disagreement, exchange angry words. **2** give reasons for or against something, debate. **3** (foll. by *into*, *out of*) persuade by talking (*argued him into going*). **4** indicate (*their lifestyle argues that they are well off*).
argument n. **1** a discussion involving disagreement; a quarrel. **2** a reason put forward. **3** a theme or chain of reasoning.

argumentation *n.* arguing.

argumentative / ah-gyuh-**men**-tuh-tiv / *adj.* fond of arguing. ☐ **argumentatively** *adv.*

Argus *Gk myth.* a monster with many eyes, slain by Hermes.

aria / **ah**-ree-uh / *n.* an operatic song for one voice.

Arianism / **air**-ree-uh-niz-uhm / *n.* the principal heresy denying the divinity of Christ, named after its author Arius (*c.*250–*c.*336), priest of Alexandria. ☐ **Arian** *adj.* & *n.*

arid / a-ruhd / *adj.* **1** dry, parched (*arid regions*). **2** uninteresting (*an arid discussion*). ☐ **aridly** *adv.* **aridness** *n.* **aridity** / uh-**rid**-uh-tee / *n.*

Aries / **air**-reez / *n.* the first sign of the zodiac, the Ram. ☐ **Arian** / **air**-ree-uhn / *adj.* & *n.*

aright *adv.* rightly.

arise *v.* (**arose**, **arisen**) **1** come into existence, come to people's notice (*problems arose*). **2** *archaic* get up, stand up; rise from the dead.

aristocracy / a-ruh-**stok**-ruh-see / *n.* **1** hereditary upper classes in some countries; the nobility. **2** a country ruled by these. **3** the best of a category.

aristocrat / a-ruh-stuh-krat / *n.* a member of the aristocracy, a noble.

aristocratic / a-ruh-stuh-**krat**-ik / *adj.* **1** of the aristocracy. **2** noble in style. ☐ **aristocratically** *adv.*

Aristophanes / a-ruh-**stof**-uh-neez / (*c.*450–*c.*385 BC), Greek comic playwright.

Aristotle (384–322 BC), Greek philosopher. ☐ **Aristotelian** *adj.* & *n.*

arithmetic *n.* / uh-**rith**-muh-tik / the science of numbers; calculating by means of numbers. •*adj.* / a-rith-**met**-ik / (also **arithmetical**) of arithmetic. ☐ **arithmetic mean** = AVERAGE (sense 1). **arithmetic progression** a sequence of numbers with constant intervals (e.g. 9, 7, 5, 3, etc.). ☐ **arithmetically** *adv.*

ark *n.* Noah's boat or a model of this.

Ark of the Covenant a wooden chest in which the writings of Jewish Law were kept.

ARL *abbr.* Australian Rugby League.

arm[1] *n.* **1** either of the two upper limbs of the human body. **2** a sleeve of a garment. **3** something shaped like an arm or projecting from a main part (*an arm of a sea; the arms of a chair*). ☐ **at arm's length** at a distance. **with open arms** cordially.

arm[2] *v.* **1** supply or fit with weapons. **2** make (a bomb etc.) ready to explode (*the device was not yet armed*). •*n.* **1** a branch of military forces. **2** (**arms**) weapons. **3** (**arms**) = COAT OF ARMS. ☐ **arms race** competition among nations in accumulating weapons. **under arms** equipped for war. **up in arms** protesting vigorously.

armada / ah-**mah**-duh / *n.* a fleet of warships. ☐ **the (Spanish) Armada** a naval invasion force sent by Spain against England in 1588.

armadillo / ah-muh-**dil**-oh / *n.* (*pl.* **armadillos**) a small burrowing animal of South America with a body covered with a shell of bony plates.

Armageddon *n.* **1** (in the Bible) the scene of the final conflict between the forces of good and evil at the end of the world. **2** a bloody battle on a huge scale.

armament *n.* **1** the weapons with which an army or a ship, aircraft, or fighting vehicle is equipped. **2** the process of equipping for war.

armature / **ah**-muh-chuh / *n.* **1** the wire-wound core of a dynamo or electric motor. **2** a bar placed in contact with the poles of a magnet to preserve its power or transmit force to support a load. **3** a framework round which a clay or plaster sculpture is modelled.

armband *n.* a band worn round the arm or sleeve.

armchair *n.* **1** a chair with arms or raised sides. **2** (used as *adj.*) theoretical rather than active; reading about something rather than doing it (*armchair gardeners; an armchair traveller*).

Armenia a republic to the east of the Black Sea, bordering on Turkey. ☐ **Armenian** *adj.* & *n.*

armful *n.* (*pl.* **armfuls**) as much as the arms can hold.

armhole *n.* an opening in a garment through which the arm is inserted.

armistice *n.* an agreement during a war or battle to stop fighting for a time.

armlet *n.* an armband.

armor etc. variant spelling of ARMOUR etc.

armorial *adj.* of heraldry or coats of arms.

armour *n.* **1** a protective covering for the body, formerly worn in fighting. **2** metal plates covering a warship, car, or tank to protect it from missiles. **3** armoured fighting vehicles collectively.

armoured *adj.* **1** covered or protected with armour (*an armoured car*). **2** equipped with armoured vehicles (*armoured divisions*).

armoury / **ah**-muh-ree / *n.* a place where weapons and ammunition are stored.

armpit *n.* the hollow under the arm below the shoulder.

army *n.* **1** an organised force equipped for fighting on land. **2** a vast group (*an army of locusts*). **3** a body of people organised for a particular purpose (*an army of helpers*).

Arnhem Land / **ah**-nuhm / a name generally applied to the eastern half of the large peninsula on the north coast of the NT; specifically to the Aboriginal Reserve, one of the largest in Australia, which covers most of the upland in the region. Arnhem Land consists of heath, scrub, and rainforests and has sustained Aboriginal life for at least 25,000 years. (¶ Named by Matthew Flinders in 1803 in allusion to the early 17th century Dutch discoverers of the region.)

arnica *n.* **1** a plant with yellow flowers. **2** a substance prepared from this, used to treat bruises.

aroma / uh-**roh**-muh / *n*. a smell, esp. a pleasant one.

aromatherapy *n*. the use of essential plant oils in massage.

aromatic *adj*. **1** fragrant, spicy. **2** (of organic compounds) having an unsaturated ring of atoms, esp. containing a benzene ring. • *n*. an aromatic substance or plant.

arose *see* ARISE.

around *adv*. & *prep*. **1** all round, on every side, in every direction. **2** about, here and there (*he's somewhere around*). **3** about, approximately at (*be here around five o'clock*).

arouse *v*. rouse; sexually stimulate. ◻ **arousal** *n*.

arpeggio / ah-**pej**-ee-oh / *n*. (*pl*. **arpeggios**) the notes of a musical chord played in succession instead of simultaneously.

arrack *n*. (also **arak**) an alcoholic spirit, esp. one made from the nectar tapped from coconut flowers or from rice.

arraign *v*. accuse; find fault with. ◻ **arraignment** *n*.

arrange *v*. **1** put into a certain order, adjust; place attractively. **2** form plans; settle the details of; prepare (*arrange to be there; arrange a meeting*). **3** adapt (a musical composition) for voices or instruments other than those for which it was written. ◻ **arrangement** *n*. **arranger** *n*.

arrant / **a**-ruhnt / *adj*. downright, out-and-out (*this is arrant nonsense!*).

arras / **a**-ruhs / *n*. a richly decorated tapestry or wall hanging.

array *v*. **1** arrange in order (*arrayed his forces along the river*). **2** dress (*arrayed in all her finery*). • *n*. **1** an imposing series; a display (*a fine array of tools*). **2** an ordered arrangement. **3** an arrangement of data in a computer, so constructed that a program can extract the items by means of a key.

arrears *n.pl*. **1** money that is owing and ought to have been paid earlier (*arrears of rent*). **2** work that should have been finished but is still waiting to be dealt with (*arrears of correspondence*). ◻ **in arrears** behind with payment or work.

Arrernte / u-**run**-tu, **a**-ruhn-du / *n*. **1** a member of an Aboriginal people of central Australia. **2** their language.

arrest *v*. **1** stop or check (a process or movement). **2** attract (a person's attention). **3** seize by authority of the law. • *n*. **1** stoppage (*cardiac arrest*). **2** seizure, legal arresting of an offender (*he is under arrest*).

arrester *n*. (also **arrestor**) a device for slowing an aircraft after landing.

arris / **a**-ruhs / *n*. the sharp edge formed where two surfaces meet to form an angle, especially in architecture.

arrival *n*. **1** arriving. **2** a person or thing that has arrived.

arrive *v*. **1** reach one's destination or a point on a journey. **2** come at last, make an appearance (*the great day arrived; the baby arrived on Tuesday*). **3** (foll. by *at*) reach (a conclusion, decision, etc.). **4** be recognised as having achieved success in the world.

arrogant / a-ruh-guhnt / *adj*. proud and overbearing through an exaggerated feeling of one's superiority. ◻ **arrogantly** *adv*. **arrogance** *n*.

arrogate / a-ruh-gayt / *v*. claim or seize without having the right to do so. **2** attribute or assign to another person unjustly. ◻ **arrogation** *n*.

arrow *n*. **1** a straight thin pointed shaft to be shot from a bow. **2** a line with an outward-pointing V at the end, used to show direction or position.

arrowhead *n*. the head of an arrow.

arrowroot *n*. an edible starch prepared from the root of a plant.

arse *coarse colloq*. *n*. the buttocks or rump. •*v*. **1** (usu. **arse about** *or* **arse around**) play the fool. **2** *Aust*. dismiss without ceremony.

arsehole *coarse colloq*. *n*. **1** the anus. **2** *offens*. a contemptible person. • *v*. *Aust*. dismiss (a person) from employment etc.

arsenal *n*. a place where weapons and ammunition are stored or manufactured.

arsenic / **ah**-suh-nik / *n*. **1** a chemical element (symbol As), a brittle steel-grey substance. **2** a highly poisonous white compound of this. ◻ **arsenical** / ah-**sen**-i-kuhl / *adj*.

arsey (also **arsie**, **arsy**) *adj*. *Aust*. *colloq*. extremely lucky.

arson *n*. the act of setting fire to a house or other property intentionally and unlawfully. ◻ **arsonist** *n*.

art[1] *n*. **1** human creative skill or its application. **2** works such as paintings or sculptures showing such skill. **3** (**the arts**) creative activities such as painting, music, theatre, writing. **4** (**arts**) subjects (e.g. languages, literature, history) associated with creative skill as opposed to sciences where exact measurements and calculations are used. **5** any practical skill; a knack (*the art of sailing*). **6** cunning, artfulness. ◻ **art deco** a style of decorative art and architecture popular in the 1920s and 1930s, characterised by geometric patterns, sharp edges, and bright colours. **art gallery** a gallery where paintings or pieces of sculpture are displayed. **art nouveau** / aht noo-**voh** / an art style of the late 19th century characterised by flowing lines and natural forms.

art[2] *archaic* the present tense of **be**, used with *thou*.

artefact / **ah**-tuh-fakt / *n*. (also **artifact**) **1** a product of human art and workmanship. **2** a simple prehistoric tool or weapon.

arterial / ah-**teer**-ree-uhl / *adj*. of an artery. ◻ **arterial road** an important main road.

arteriosclerosis / ah-teer-ree-oh-skluh-**roh**-suhs / *n*. a condition in which the walls of arteries become thicker and less elastic so that blood circulation is hindered.

artery *n.* **1** any of the tubes carrying blood away from the heart to all parts of the body. **2** an important transport route.

artesian basin *n. Aust.* a geological structure in which water is confined under pressure.

artesian bore / ah-**tee**-zhuhn / *n.* (also **artesian well**) *Aust.* a well bored vertically into a place where a constant supply of water will rise to the earth's surface with little or no pumping.

artful *adj.* crafty; cunningly clever at getting what one wants. ☐ **artfully** *adv.* **artfulness** *n.*

arthritis / ah-**thruy**-tuhs / *n.* a condition in which there is pain and stiffness in the joints. ☐ **arthritic** / ah-**thrit**-ik / *adj. & n.*

arthropod / **ahth**-ruh-pod / *n.* an animal of the group that includes insects, spiders, crustaceans, and centipedes.

arthroscope / **ahth**-ruh-skohp / *n. Med.* an instrument for insertion into the cavity of a joint to inspect its contents before a surgical operation or biopsy.

Arthur[1] reputed king of the Britons (perhaps 5th or 6th century), legendary leader of the Knights of the Round Table at his court at Camelot. ☐ **Arthurian** / ah-**thyoor**-ree-uhn / *adj. & n.*

Arthur[2] *n.* ☐ **not to know whether one is Arthur or Martha** *Aust. colloq.* to be in a state of confusion.

Arthur[3], Sir George (1784–1854), Lieutenant-Governor of Van Diemen's Land (1824–36): he founded new penal settlements at Maria Island and at Port Arthur, and organised the white settlers in a massive drive against the Aborigines which came to be known as the 'Black War'.

artichoke *n.* a plant related to the thistle, with a flower consisting of thick leaf-like scales used as a vegetable (also called *globe artichoke*). Cf. JERUSALEM ARTICHOKE.

article *n.* **1** a particular or separate thing (*articles of clothing; toilet articles*). **2** a piece of writing, complete in itself, in a newspaper or periodical (*an article on immigration*). **3** a separate clause or item in an agreement. **4** *Grammar* a word used before a noun to identify what it refers to (e.g. *a*, *the*). • *v.* employ under contract as a trainee. ☐ **definite article** the word 'the'. **indefinite article** the words 'a' or 'an'.

articled clerk *n.* a trainee solicitor.

articular / ah-**tik**-yuh-luh / *adj.* of a joint or joints of the body.

articulate *adj.* / ah-**tik**-yuh-luht / **1** spoken clearly, in words. **2** able to express ideas clearly. • *v.* / ah-**tik**-yuh-layt / **1** say or speak distinctly (*articulating each word with care*). **2** form a joint, connect by joints (*this bone is articulated with another*). ☐ **articulated vehicle** one that has sections connected by a flexible joint or joints. ☐ ☐ **articulately** *adv.* **articulation** *n.*

artifact alternative spelling of ARTEFACT.

artifice / **ah**-tuh-fuhs / *n.* trickery; a clever trick intended to mislead someone.

artificer / ah-**tif**-uh-suh / *n.* a skilled craftsman or mechanic.

artificial *adj.* not originating naturally; made by human skill in imitation of something natural. ☐ **artificial insemination** injection of semen into the womb artificially so that conception may take place without sexual intercourse. **artificial intelligence** the development of computers to do things that normally need human intelligence, such as using language. **artificial respiration** the process of forcing air into and out of the lungs to start natural breathing or stimulate it when it has failed. ☐ ☐ **artificially** *adv.* **artificiality** / ah-tuh-fish-ee-**al**-uh-tee / *n.*

artillery *n.* **1** large guns used in fighting on land. **2** a branch of an army that uses these. ☐ **artilleryman** *n.*

artisan / ah-tuh-**zan**, **ah**-tuh-zuhn / *n.* a skilled manual worker, craftsman, or craftswoman.

artist *n.* **1** a person who produces works of art, especially paintings. **2** a person who does something with exceptional skill. **3** a professional entertainer. **4** *colloq.* (as the final element in compounds) a habitual practiser of a specified (usu. reprehensible) activity (*booze artist; bull artist; con artist*).

artiste / ah-**teest** / *n.* a professional entertainer.

artistic *adj.* **1** showing or done with skill and good taste. **2** of art or artists. ☐ **artistically** *adv.*

artistry *n.* artistic skill.

artless *adj.* free from artfulness; simple and natural. ☐ **artlessly** *adv.* **artlessness** *n.*

artwork *n.* **1** pictures and diagrams in books, advertisements etc. **2** paintings, sculptures, etc. (*an exhibition of children's artwork*).

arty *adj. colloq.* with an exaggerated and often affected display of artistic style or interests. ☐ **artiness** *n.*

arty-crafty *adj. colloq.* arty; artistic but having no functional value.

arum / **air**-ruhm / *n.* a plant with a flower consisting of a single petal-like part surrounding a central spike.

arvo *n. Aust. colloq.* afternoon (*see you this arvo!*).

Aryan / **air**-ree-uhn / *adj.* **1** of the original Indo-European language; of its speakers or their descendants. **2** (in Nazi ideology) of non-Jewish white Nordic extraction. • *n.* an Aryan person. (¶ Sanskrit *aryas* noble.)

As *symbol* arsenic.

as *adv.* **1** in the same degree, equally. **2** similarly, like. **3** in the character of (*Olivier as Hamlet*). • *conj.* **1** at the same time that (*they came as I left*). **2** because, for the reason that (*as he refuses, we can do nothing*). **3** in the way in which (*do as I do*). • *relative pron.* that, who, which (*I had the same trouble as you; he was a foreigner, as I knew from his accent*). ☐ **as for** with regard to (*as for you, you're hopeless!*). **as from** from the date stated (*your salary will be increased as from 1 April*). **as if** as it would be if (*he said it as if he meant it*). **as it was**

in the actual circumstances. **as it were** as if it was actually so (*he became, as it were, a man without a country*). **as of** at the date mentioned (*that was the position as of last Monday*). **as though** as if. **as to** with regard to (*said nothing as to holidays*). **as well 1** in addition, too. **2** desirable (*it might be as well to go*). **as well as** in addition to. **as yet** up to this time.

asafoetida / as-uh-fuh-**tee**-duh / *n*. a strong-smelling plant gum, used as a cooking spice and formerly in medicine.

asap / **ay**-sap / *abbr*. (also **a.s.a.p.**) as soon as possible.

asbestos *n*. **1** a soft fibrous mineral substance. **2** this as formerly used as a heat-resistant or insulating material.

asbestosis / as-bes-**toh**-suhs / *n*. a lung disease caused by inhaling asbestos particles.

ascend *v*. go or come up. ❏ **ascend the throne** become king or queen.

ascendancy / uh-**sen**-duhn-see / *n*. the state of being dominant.

ascendant *adj*. **1** ascending, rising. **2** *Astronomy* rising towards a point above the observer. **3** *Astrology* just above the eastern horizon. ❏ **in the ascendant** rising in power or influence.

ascension / uh-**sen**-shuhn / *n*. **1** ascent. **2** (**the Ascension**) the taking up of Christ into heaven, witnessed by the Apostles.

Ascension Day the Thursday on which the Ascension of Christ is commemorated, the 40th day after Easter.

ascent *n*. **1** ascending. **2** a way up, an upward slope or path.

ascertain / as-uh-**tayn** / *v*. find out by making enquiries. ❏ **ascertainment** *n*.

ascetic / uh-**set**-ik / *adj*. self-denying, not allowing oneself pleasures and luxuries. • *n*. a person who leads a severely simple life without ordinary pleasures, often for religious reasons. ❏ **asceticism** / uh-**set**-uh-siz-uhm / *n*.

ASCII / **as**-kee / *abbr*. (also **ASCII code**) *Computing* American Standard Code for Information Interchange: a code assigning a different number to each letter and character for computing purposes.

ascorbic acid / uh-**skaw**-bik / vitamin C, found especially in citrus fruits and in vegetables.

ascribe / uh-**skruyb** / *v*. attribute. ❏ **ascription** / uh-**skrip**-shuhn / *n*.

ASEAN / **az**-ee-an / *abbr*. = ASSOCIATION OF SOUTH-EAST ASIAN NATIONS.

asepsis / ay-**sep**-suhs, uh-**sep**-suhs / *n*. aseptic methods or conditions.

aseptic / ay-**sep**-tik / *adj*. free from bacteria that cause something to become septic; surgically clean. ❏ **aseptically** *adv*.

asexual / ay-**sek**-shoo-uhl / *adj*. without sex, sex organs, or sexuality. ❏ **asexually** *adv*.

Asgard / **az**-gahd / *Scand. myth*. a region in the centre of the universe, inhabited by the gods.

ash *n*. **1** a tree of the Northern hemisphere with silver-grey bark and close-grained wood. **2** any of many Australian trees (usu. eucalypts) having a similar wood (*alpine ash*). **3** the powder that remains after something has burnt. **4** (usu. in *pl*.) human remains after cremation. **5** (**the Ashes**) a trophy for the winner of a series of test matches in cricket between Australia and England. The ashes, kept in a small urn in England (and never allowed to be taken to Australia when Australia wins), are those of a bail (or ball) cremated in Melbourne to memorialise the demise of English cricket.

ashamed *adj*. feeling shame.

Ashburton a river in the north-west of WA. It was named by F.T. Gregory in 1861 after Lord Ashburton, the then president of the Royal Geographical Society.

ashen *adj*. pale as ashes.

Ashkenazi / ash-kuh-**nah**-zee / *n*. (*pl*. **Ashkenazim**) a Jew of northern or eastern Europe, as distinct from a Sephardi. ❏ **Ashkenazic** *adj*.

ashlar *n*. square-cut stones; masonry made of these.

Ashmore and Cartier Islands an external territory of Australia in the Indian Ocean, comprising the uninhabited Ashmore Reef and Cartier Islands. The area is designated a nature reserve.

ashore *adv*. to or on shore.

ashram *n*. a place of religious learning or retreat for Hindus.

Ash Wednesday *n*. the first day of Lent (from the ritual of the priest marking the foreheads of churchgoers with blest ashes on that day).

ashy *adj*. **1** ashen. **2** covered with ash.

Asia / **ay**-zhuh / the largest of the continents, extending from Europe to the Pacific Ocean. ❏ **Asian** *adj*. & *n*.

Asia Minor a peninsula of western Asia between the Mediterranean and the Black Sea, including most of Turkey.

Asianise *v*. (also **-ize**) **1** (of a culture, population, etc.) introduce Asian elements to. **2** make Asian in character etc. ❏ **Asianisation** *n*.

Asiatic / ay-zhee-**at**-ik / *adj*. of Asia. • *n*. an Asian.

■ Usage *Asian* is the preferred word when used of people.

aside *adv*. **1** to or on one side, away from the main part or group (*pull it aside; step aside*). **2** away from one's thoughts or from consideration. **3** in reserve (*put money aside for a holiday*). • *n*. words spoken so that only certain people will hear.

Asimov / **as**-uh-mov /, Isaac (1920–95), Russian-born American writer of science fiction.

asinine / **as**-uh-nuyn / *adj*. silly, stupid.

ASIO / **ay**-zee-oh / *abbr*. = AUSTRALIAN SECURITY INTELLIGENCE ORGANISATION.

ASIS / **ay**-suhs / *abbr*. = AUSTRALIAN SECRET INTELLIGENCE SERVICE.

ask *v*. **1** call for an answer to or about, address a question to (a person). **2** seek to obtain from another person (*ask a favour of him; asked $5 for the book*). **3** invite (*ask him to dinner*). • *n. colloq.* a task; a requirement (*an impossible ask, mate*). ☐ **a big ask** *Aust. colloq.* a difficult task. **ask after** inquire about (a person). **ask for it** *colloq.* behave in such a way that trouble is likely. **asking price** the price at which something is offered for sale.

askance / uh-**skans** / *adv.* sideways. ☐ **look askance at** regard with distrust or disapproval.

askew *adv.* & *adj.* not straight or level.

aslant *adv.* on a slant, obliquely. • *prep.* obliquely across.

asleep *adv.* & *adj.* **1** in or into a state of sleep. **2** numbed (*my foot is asleep*).

Asmara / as-**mah**-ruh / the capital of Eritrea.

asocial / ay-**soh**-shuhl / *adj.* **1** not social, not sociable. **2** *colloq.* inconsiderate.

asp *n.* a small poisonous snake.

asparagus / uh-**spa**-ruh-guhs / *n.* a plant whose young shoots are cooked and eaten as a vegetable.

aspect *n.* **1** a viewpoint; a feature to be considered (*this aspect of the problem*). **2** the look or appearance of a person or thing (*the forest had a sinister aspect*). **3** the direction a thing faces, a side facing this way (*the house has a southern aspect*). **4** (in astrology) the relative position of a star or group of stars, regarded as having influence on events.

aspen *n.* a poplar with leaves that move in the slightest wind.

asperity / uh-**spe**-ruh-tee / *n.* harshness or severity, especially of manner.

aspersions / uh-**sper**-shuhnz, -zhuhnz / *n.pl.* ☐ **cast aspersions on** attack the reputation of.

asphalt / **ash**-felt, **as**-felt / *n.* **1** a black sticky substance like coal tar. **2** a mixture of this with gravel etc. used for paving. • *v.* surface with asphalt.

asphodel / **as**-fuh-del / *n.* a plant of the lily family.

asphyxia / as-**fik**-see-uh / *n.* a condition caused by lack of air in the lungs; suffocation.

asphyxiate / as-**fik**-see-ayt / *v.* suffocate. ☐ **asphyxiation** *n.*

aspic *n.* a savoury jelly used for coating meats, eggs, etc.

aspidistra *n.* a house plant with broad tapering leaves.

aspirant / **as**-puh-ruhnt, uh-**spuy**-uh-ruhnt / *n.* a person who aspires to something.

aspirate *n.* / **as**-puh-ruht / the sound of *h.* • *v.* / **as**-puh-rayt / **1** pronounce with an *h.* **2** draw out with an aspirator.

aspiration / as-puh-**ray**-shuhn / *n.* **1** ambition, strong desire. **2** aspirating. **3** the drawing of breath.

aspirator *n.* a device used to suck fluid from a cavity.

aspire *v.* have a high ambition (*he aspires to become president; aspires to the presidency*).

aspirin *n.* a medicinal drug used to relieve pain and reduce fever; a tablet of this.

Aspro *n. trademark* a form of aspirin developed in Australia by Melbourne pharmacist George Nicholas (1884–1960) when supplies from the German company Bayer were disrupted during the First World War.

ass *n.* **1** a donkey. **2** *colloq.* a stupid person.

assagai alternative spelling of ASSEGAI.

assail / uh-**sayl** / *v.* **1** attack violently and persistently. **2** begin (a task) resolutely.

assailant *n.* an attacker.

assassin *n.* a killer, especially of a political or religious leader.

assassinate *v.* kill (an important person) by violent means, usually from political or religious motives. ☐ **assassination** *n.*

assault *n.* **1** a violent attack. **2** an unlawful personal attack on another person, even if only with menacing words. • *v.* make an assault on. ☐ **assault and battery** *Law* a threatening act resulting in physical harm to someone. **assault course** an obstacle course used e.g. for training soldiers.

assay / uh-**say**, **as**-ay / *n.* a test of metal or ore for quality. • *v.* make an assay of.

assegai / **as**-uh-guy / *n.* (also **assagai**) a light iron-tipped spear of South African peoples.

assemblage *n.* **1** assembling. **2** an assembled group.

assemble *v.* **1** bring or come together. **2** fit or put together.

assembler *n.* **1** a worker who assembles a machine, garment, etc. **2** a computer program that translates instructions from a low-level language into a form that can be understood and executed by the computer. **3** the low-level language itself; assembly language.

assembly *n.* **1** assembling. **2** an assembled group, esp. of people meeting for a specific purpose. ☐ **assembly language** *Computing* a low-level symbolic code converted by an assembler. **assembly line** a sequence of machines and workers through which parts of a product move to be assembled in successive stages.

assent *v.* consent, express agreement. • *n.* (official) consent or approval.

assert *v.* **1** declare as true, state (*asserted his innocence*). **2** enforce a claim to (rights etc.) (*asserted his authority*). ☐ **assert oneself** take effective action; use one's authority; insist on one's rights.

assertion *n.* **1** asserting. **2** a statement that something is a fact.

assertive *adj.* asserting oneself, self-assertive; positive, confident. ☐ **assertively** *adv.* **assertiveness** *n.*

assess *v.* **1** decide or fix the amount or value of. **2** estimate the worth, quality, or likelihood of. ☐ **assessment** *n.*

assessor *n.* **1** a person who assesses, especially for tax and insurance. **2** one who advises a judge in court on technical matters.

asset / **as**-et / *n.* **1** any property that has money value. **2** a useful or valuable quality or skill; a person or thing regarded as useful. ☐ **asset-stripping** the practice of taking over a company and selling off its assets to make a profit.

asseverate / uh-**sev**-uh-rayt / *v. formal* assert solemnly. ☐ **asseveration** *n.*

assiduous / uh-**sid**-yoo-uhs / *adj.* diligent and persevering. ☐ **assiduously** *adv.* **assiduity** / as-i-**dyoo**-uh-tee / *n.*

assign *v.* **1** allot (*rooms were assigned to us*). **2** appoint or designate to perform a task etc. (*assign your best investigator to the job*). **3** ascribe, regard as belonging to (*we cannot assign an exact date to the first arrival of the Aborigines in Australia*).

assignation / as-ig-**nay**-shuhn / *n.* **1** assigning; being assigned. **2** an arrangement to meet, esp. by lovers in secret; an appointment.

assignment *n.* **1** a task or mission. **2** a written task etc. required from a student. **3** assigning; being assigned. **4** *Aust. hist.* the making over to a private individual of the services of a convict.

assimilate *v.* **1** absorb and digest (food etc.) into the body. **2** absorb (information etc.) into the mind. **3** absorb (people) into a larger group. ☐ **assimilable** *adj.*

assimilation *n.* **1** the act or process of assimilating. **2** the acceptance by immigrant minorities of prevailing cultural values; the integration of such minorities into a society. **3** *Aust. hist.* the integration of Aborigines into white Australian society.

assist *v.* help. ☐ **assistance** *n.*

assistant *n.* **1** a person who assists, a helper. **2** a person who serves customers in a shop. • *adj.* assisting, helping, and ranking next below a senior person (*the assistant manager*).

assizes *n.pl. Brit.* until 1972, a court sitting periodically in each county in England and Wales to deal with civil and criminal cases.

associate *v.* / uh-**soh**-shee-ayt, -see-ayt / **1** join or cause to join as a companion, colleague, or supporter. **2** (usually foll. by *with*) have frequent dealings; spend a lot of time with (*he associates with dishonest dealers*). **3** connect in one's mind (*we associate the smell of gum leaves with Australia*). • *n.* / uh-**soh**-shee-uht, -see-uht / **1** a partner, colleague, or companion. **2** one who has been admitted to a lower level of membership of an association without the status of a full member. • *adj.* / uh-**soh**-shee-uht, -see-uht / **1** associated. **2** of lower status (*associate professor*). ☐ **associative** *adj.*

association *n.* **1** associating; being associated; companionship. **2** a group of people organised for some common purpose. **3** a mental connection between ideas.

Association of South-East Asian Nations a regional organisation formed by Indonesia, Malaysia, the Philippines, Singapore, and Thailand through the Bangkok Declaration of 1967, designed to promote economic cooperation. Brunei joined the organisation in 1984.

assonance / **as**-uh-nuhns / *n.* resemblance of sound between two syllables; a rhyme depending on similarity of vowel sounds in syllables that do not form a complete rhyme (as in *vermin/furnish*) or in consonants only (as in *killed/cold*).

assort *v.* **1** arrange in sorts, classify. **2** suit or harmonise (with another person or thing).

assorted *adj.* of different sorts put together (*assorted chocolates*).

assortment *n.* **1** a collection composed of several sorts. **2** classification.

assuage / uh-**swayj** / *v.* soothe, make less severe (*to assuage one's thirst*). ☐ **assuagement** *n.*

assume *v.* **1** take as true or sure to happen before there is proof (*we assume that we shall win*). **2** take on, undertake (*he assumed the extra responsibility*). **3** put on (*assumed a serious expression*).

assuming *adj.* presumptuous. • *conj.* (often foll. by *that*) if we assume that something is the case or will happen (*assuming that we finish it today, we can deliver it tomorrow*).

assumption *n.* **1** assuming. **2** something taken for granted, something assumed but not proved. **3** (**the Assumption**) the reception of the Virgin Mary bodily into heaven after she died; the festival commemorating this (15 August).

assurance *n.* **1** a formal declaration or promise given to inspire confidence. **2** life insurance. **3** self-confidence.

assure / uh-**shaw** / *v.* **1** declare confidently, promise (*I assure you there is no danger*). **2** cause to know for certain (*tried the door to assure himself that it was locked*). **3** make certain, ensure (*this will assure your success*). **4** insure by means of an assurance policy.

assured / uh-**shawd** / *adj.* **1** sure. **2** confident (*has an assured manner*). **3** payable under an assurance policy (*the sum assured*).

assuredly / uh-**shaw**-ruhd-lee / *adv.* certainly.

Assyria an ancient country in what is now northern Iraq. ☐ **Assyrian** *adj.* & *n.*

astatine / **as**-tuh-teen / *n.* a radioactive element (symbol At).

aster *n.* a garden plant with daisy-like flowers of various colours.

asterisk *n.* a star-shaped symbol (*) used to draw attention to something or as a reference mark. • *v.* mark with an asterisk.

astern *adv.* **1** in, at, or towards the stern of a ship or the tail of an aircraft; behind. **2** backwards (*full speed astern!*).

asteroid / **as**-tuh-roid / *n.* any of the small planets revolving round the sun, especially between the orbits of Mars and Jupiter.

asthma / as-muh / *n.* a chronic condition causing difficulty in breathing.

asthmatic / as-**mat**-ik / *adj.* **1** of asthma. **2** suffering from asthma. • *n.* an asthmatic person.

astigmatism / uh-**stig**-muh-tiz-uhm / *n.* a defect in an eye or lens, preventing proper focusing. □ **astigmatic** / as-tig-**mat**-ik / *adj.*

astir *adv.* & *adj.* in motion, moving.

Astley, William, *see* WARUNG.

astonish *v.* surprise very greatly. □ **astonishment** *n.*

astound *v.* shock with surprise.

astraddle *adv.* astride.

astrakhan / as-truh-**kan** / *n.* the dark tightly-curled fleece of lambs from Astrakhan in Russia; fabric imitating this.

astral / **as**-truhl / *adj.* of or from the stars.

astray *adv.* & *adj.* away from the right path. □ **go astray** (of things) be mislaid. **lead astray** lead into error or wrongdoing.

astride *adv.* **1** with legs wide apart. **2** with one leg on either side of something. • *prep.* astride of; extending across.

astringent / uh-**strin**-juhnt / *adj.* **1** causing skin or body tissue to contract, stopping bleeding. **2** harsh, severe. • *n.* an astringent substance, used medically or in cosmetics. □ **astringency** *n.*

astro- *comb. form* of the stars; relating to outer space.

astrolabe / **as**-truh-layb / *n.* an instrument formerly used for measuring the altitudes of stars.

astrology / uh-**strol**-uh-jee / *n.* study of the supposed influence of stars on human affairs. □ **astrologer** *n.* **astrologist** *n.* **astrological** *adj.*

astronaut *n.* a crew member of a spacecraft.

astronautics *n.* the scientific study of space travel and its technology.

astronomical *adj.* **1** of astronomy. **2** enormous in amount (*an astronomical sum of money*). □ **astronomically** *adv.*

astronomy / uh-**stron**-uh-mee / *n.* the scientific study of the stars and planets and their movements. □ **astronomer** *n.*

astrophysics / as-troh-**fiz**-iks / *n.* the branch of astronomy concerned with the physics and chemistry of the heavenly bodies. □ **astrophysical** *adj.* **astrophysicist** *n.*

Astroturf *n. trademark* an artificial grass surface for sports fields.

astute / uh-**styoot** / *adj.* shrewd, quick at seeing how to gain an advantage. □ **astutely** *adv.* **astuteness** *n.*

Asunción / uh-suun-see-**ohn** / the capital of Paraguay.

asunder / uh-**sun**-duh / *adv. literary* apart, into pieces (*torn asunder*).

asylum *n.* **1** refuge and safety; a place of refuge. **2** *archaic* a mental home or institution. □ **political asylum** protection given by a nation to a person who has fled from political persecution in another country.

asymmetry / ay-**sim**-uh-tree / *n.* lack of symmetry. □ **asymmetric** *adj.* **asymmetrical** *adj.*

At *symbol* astatine.

at *prep.* expressing position or state: **1** of place, order, or time of day (*at the top; came at midnight*). **2** of condition or occupation (*at ease; they are at dinner*). **3** of price, amount, or age, etc. (*sold at $1 each; left school at 15*). **4** of cause (*was annoyed at his failure*). **5** of direction towards (*aimed at the target*). □ **at all** in any way, to any extent, of any kind. **at it 1** engaged in an activity; working hard. **2** *colloq.* repeating a habitual (usu. disapproved of) activity (*found them at it again*). **at that 1** at that point. **2** moreover. **where it's at** *colloq.* a fashionable scene or with-it activity.

atavism / **at**-uh-viz-uhm / *n.* likeness to remote ancestors rather than to parents; reversion to an earlier type.

atavistic / at-uh-**vis**-tik / *adj.* like a remote ancestor.

ataxia *n. Med.* difficulty in controlling bodily movements.

ate *see* EAT.

atheist / **ay**-thee-uhst / *n.* a person who believes that there is no God. □ **atheism** *n.* **atheistic** / ay-thee-**is**-tik / *adj.*

Athene / uh-**thee**-nee / *Gk myth.* the goddess of wisdom, identified by the Romans with Minerva.

Athens the capital of Greece.

atherosclerosis / ah-tuh-roh-skluh-**roh**-suhs / *n.* damage to the arteries caused by a build-up of fatty deposits.

Atherton Tableland a high plateau of weathered basalt in north-eastern Qld, west of Cairns, supporting various crops and dairying.

athlete *n.* a person who is good at athletics. □ **athlete's foot** an infectious fungal condition affecting the feet.

athletic *adj.* **1** of athletes. **2** physically strong and active, muscular in build. • *n.* (**athletics**) (treated as *pl.* or *sing.*) physical exercises and sports, esp. competitions in running, jumping, etc. □ **athletically** *adv.* **athleticism** *n.*

-athon *suffix* (also **-thon** after a vowel which is sounded) indicating an extended activity, usu. involving much endurance, as specified in the first part (such activity being used for fund-raising, breaking records, etc.) (*walkathon; sleepathon; telethon*). (¶ Falsely derived from the *-athon* in *marathon*.)

Athos / **a**-thos, **ay**-thos / a mountainous peninsula on the coast of Macedonia, an autonomous district of Greece inhabited by monks of the Orthodox Church. □ **Athonite** *adj.* & *n.*

Atlantic *adj.* of the Atlantic Ocean. • *n.* (in full **Atlantic Ocean**) the ocean lying between the Americas and Europe/Africa.

Atlantis *Gk myth.* a beautiful and prosperous island in the Atlantic Ocean, overwhelmed by the sea.

Atlas *Gk myth.* one of the Titans, who was punished for his part in their revolt against Zeus by being made to support the heavens.

atlas *n.* a book of maps.

ATM *abbr.* = AUTOMATED TELLER MACHINE.

atmosphere *n.* **1** the mixture of gases surrounding the earth or any star or planet. **2** the air in any place. **3** a psychological environment; a feeling or tone conveyed by something (*an atmosphere of peace and calm*). **4** a unit of pressure, equal to the pressure of the atmosphere at sea level. ☐ **atmospheric** *adj.*

atmospherics *n.pl.* **1** electrical disturbances in the atmosphere; crackling sounds or other interference in telecommunications caused by these. **2 a** actions intended to create a particular atmosphere or mood. **b** deliberately created atmosphere or mood.

atoll / **at**-ol / *n.* a ring-shaped coral reef enclosing a lagoon.

atom *n.* **1** the smallest particle of a chemical element. **2** this as a source of atomic energy. **3** a very small quantity or thing (*there's not an atom of truth in it*). ☐ **atom bomb** = ATOMIC BOMB.

atomic *adj.* of an atom or atoms. ☐ **atomic bomb** a bomb that derives its destructive power from atomic energy. **atomic energy** energy obtained as the result of nuclear fission. **atomic mass** the mass of an atom measured in atomic mass units. **atomic mass unit** a unit of mass used to express atomic and molecular weights, equal to one-twelfth of the mass of an atom of carbon-12. **atomic number** the number of protons in the nucleus of an atom. **atomic theory** the theory that all matter consists of atoms. **atomic weight** = RELATIVE ATOMIC MASS.

atomise *v.* (also **-ize**) reduce to atoms or fine particles.

atomiser *n.* (also **-izer**) a device for reducing liquids to a fine spray.

atonal / ay-**toh**-nuhl, uh-**toh**-nuhl / *adj.* (of music) not written in any particular key or scale-system. ☐ **atonality** / ay-toh-**nal**-uh-tee / *n.*

atone *v.* make amends; make up for some error or deficiency.

atonement *n.* **1** atoning. **2** (**the Atonement**) the expiation of mankind's sin by Christ. ☐ **Day of Atonement** see YOM KIPPUR.

atrium / **ay**-tree-uhm, **a**-tree-uhm / *n.* (*pl.* **atria** *or* **atriums**) **1** the central court of an ancient Roman house. **2** either of the two upper cavities in the heart.

atrocious / uh-**troh**-shuhs / *adj.* **1** extremely wicked; brutal, savage. **2** *colloq.* very bad or unpleasant. ☐ **atrociously** *adv.*

atrocity / uh-**tros**-uh-tee / *n.* wickedness; a wicked or cruel act.

atrophy / **at**-ruh-fee / *n.* wasting away through undernourishment or lack of use. • *v.* (**atrophied**, **atrophying**) **1** cause atrophy in. **2** suffer atrophy.

atropine / **at**-ruh-peen, -puhn / *n.* a poisonous alkaloid in deadly nightshade.

ATSIC *abbr.* = ABORIGINAL AND TORRES STRAIT ISLANDER COMMISSION.

attach *v.* (often foll. by *to*) **1** fix to something else. **2** join as a companion or member; assign (a person) to a particular group. **3** attribute (*we attach no importance to the matter*). **4** be ascribed, be attributable (*no blame attaches to the company*). **5** make a legal attachment of (money or goods).

attaché / uh-**tash**-ay / *n.* a person who is attached to the staff of an ambassador in some specific field of activity (*the military attaché*). ☐ **attaché case** a small rectangular case for carrying documents etc.

attached *adj.* **1** fastened on. **2** bound by affection or loyalty (*she is very attached to her cousin*).

attachment *n.* **1** attaching; being attached. **2** something attached; an extra part that fixes on. **3** affection, devotion. **4** legal seizure of property.

attack *v.* **1** act violently against; start a fight. **2** criticise strongly. **3** act harmfully on (*rust attacks metals*). **4** begin vigorous work on. • *n.* **1** a violent attempt to hurt, overcome, or defeat. **2** strong criticism. **3** a sudden onset of illness (*an attack of flu*). ☐ **attacker** *n.*

attain *v.* succeed in doing or getting. ☐ **attainable** *adj.*

attainment *n.* **1** attaining. **2** something attained; a personal achievement.

attar / **at**-ah / *n.* fragrant oil obtained from flowers (*attar of roses*).

attempt *v.* **1** make an effort to accomplish (*that's attempting the impossible*). **2** try to climb or master (a mountain etc.) (*will attempt Everest again next year*). • *n.* **1** an effort to accomplish, overcome, or surpass something. **2** an attack (*made an attempt on my life*).

attend *v.* **1** be present at; go regularly to (*attend school*). **2** (usu. foll. by *to*) apply one's mind to, give care and thought to; deal with (*attend to what I say; attend to the matter*). **3** (usu. foll. by *on*) look after (*which doctor is attending on you?*). **4** (usu. in *passive*) follow as a result of (*the error was attended by serious consequences*). **5** accompany as an attendant.

attendance *n.* **1** attending. **2** the number of people present.

attendant *n.* a person who is present as a companion or whose function is to provide service. • *adj.* accompanying; being in attendance (on a person).

attention *n.* **1** applying one's mind to something, mental concentration. **2** awareness (*it attracts attention*). **3** consideration, care (*she shall have every attention*). **4** action to repair or improve something (*this chair needs some attention*). **5** a soldier's erect attitude of readiness with feet together and arms stretched downwards (*stand at attention*). **6** (**attentions**) small acts of kindness or courtesy. • *interj.* an exclamation used to call people to take notice or to assume an attitude of attention. ☐ **attention deficit disorder** (also **attention deficit hyperactivity disorder**) any of a range of behavioural disorders occurring primarily in children, including such symptoms as poor concentration, hyperactivity, and learning difficulties.

attentive *adj.* **1** paying attention, watchful. **2** devotedly showing consideration or courtesy to another person. ☐ **attentively** *adv.* **attentiveness** *n.*

attenuate / uh-**ten**-yoo-ayt / *v.* **1** make slender or thin. **2** make weaker, reduce the force or value of. ☐ **attenuation** *n.*

attest / uh-**test** / *v.* **1** provide clear proof of. **2** declare to be true or genuine. ☐ **attestation** / at-es-**tay**-shuhn / *n.*

Attic *adj.* of ancient Athens or Attica, or the form of Greek used there.

attic *n.* a room in the top storey of a house, immediately below the roof.

Attica the easternmost part of central Greece, in ancient times the territory of Athens (its chief city).

Attila / **at**-il-uh, uh-**til**-uh / king of the Huns 434–53, who inflicted great devastation on much of the Roman Empire.

attire *n. formal* clothes. • *v. formal* clothe.

attitude *n.* **1** a way of thinking or behaving. **2** a position of the body or its parts. **3** *colloq.* **a** aggressive or uncooperative behaviour; resentful or antagonistic manner. **b** any highly independent or individual outlook, approach, appearance, etc.; self-possession; style, swagger. **4** the position of an aircraft etc. in relation to given points. ☐ **attitude problem** an unhelpful attitude or approach.

attitudinise *v.* (also -**ize**) behave in an artificial, affected way; pose.

attorney / uh-**ter**-nee / *n.* (*pl.* **attorneys**) a person who is appointed to act on behalf of another in business or legal matters. ☐ **attorney-general** *n.* (*pl.* **attorneys-general**) **1** (chief) law minister in an Australian government. **2** chief legal officer in some countries.

attract *v.* **1** draw towards itself by unseen force (*a magnet attracts iron*). **2** get the attention of. **3** arouse the interest or pleasure of.

attraction *n.* **1** attracting. **2** the ability to attract. **3** something that attracts by arousing interest or pleasure.

attractive *adj.* **1** able to attract, pleasing in appearance or effect. **2** having the ability to draw towards itself by unseen force (*the attractive force of a magnet*). ☐ **attractively** *adv.* **attractiveness** *n.*

attribute *v.* / uh-**trib**-yoot / regard as belonging to, originated by, or written or said by (*this play is attributed to Shakespeare*). • *n.* / **at**-ruh-byoot / **1** a quality that is characteristic of a person or thing (*kindness is one of his attributes*). **2** an object regularly associated with a person or thing (*a pair of scales is an attribute of Justice*). ☐ **attributable** / uh-**trib**-yuh-tuh-buhl / *adj.* **attribution** / at-ruh-**byoo**-shuhn / *n.*

attributive / uh-**trib**-yuh-tiv / *adj. Grammar* expressing an attribute and placed before the word it describes, e.g. 'old' in *the old dog* but not in *the dog is old.* ☐ **attributively** *adv.*

attrition / uh-**trish**-uhn / *n.* **1** wearing something away by rubbing. **2** a gradual wearing down of strength and morale by continuous harassment (*a war of attrition*).

attune *v.* harmonise or adapt (one's mind etc.) to a matter, situation, or idea (*I am not attuned to the latest trends*).

atypical / ay-**tip**-i-kuhl / *adj.* not typical; not conforming to a type. ☐ **atypically** *adv.*

Au *symbol* gold.

aubergine / **oh**-buh-zheen / *n.* a plant with deep purple or white egg-shaped fruit used as a vegetable. Also called EGGPLANT.

auburn / **aw**-buhn / *adj.* (of hair) reddish-brown.

Auckland the largest city and chief seaport of New Zealand.

auction / **ok**-shuhn / *n.* a public sale in which articles are sold to the highest bidder. • *v.* sell by auction.

auctioneer *n.* a person who conducts an auction.

audacious / aw-**day**-shuhs / *adj.* bold, daring. ☐ **audaciously** *adv.* **audacity** / aw-**das**-uh-tee / *n.*

audible *adj.* loud enough to be heard. ☐ **audibly** *adv.* **audibility** *n.*

audience *n.* **1** people who have gathered to hear or watch something. **2** people within hearing. **3** a formal interview with the pope or with a ruler or other important person.

audio *n.* (*pl.* **audios**) sound or its reproduction. ☐ **audio frequency** a frequency comparable to that of ordinary sound.

audio- *comb. form* hearing or sound.

audiotape *n.* (also **audio tape**) magnetic tape for recording sound; a recording on this.

audio-visual *adj.* (of teaching aids etc.) using both sight and sound.

audit *n.* **1** an official examination of accounts to see that they are in order. **2** a systematic review (*a safety audit*). • *v.* (**audited**, **auditing**) make an audit of.

audition *n.* a trial to test the ability of a prospective performer. • *v.* **1** hold an audition. **2** be tested in an audition.

auditor *n.* a person who makes an audit.

auditorium / aw-duh-**taw**-ree-uhm / *n*. (*pl.* **auditoriums** *or* **auditoria**) the part of a theatre etc. in which an audience sits.

auditory / **aw**-duh-tuh-ree, -tree / *adj*. of or concerned with hearing.

au fait / oh **fay** / *adj*. (usu. foll. by *with*) well acquainted with (a subject) (*I'm not au fait with the rules*). (¶ French)

Augean / aw-**jee**-uhn / *adj*. **1** of the legendary king Augeus or his filthy stables, which Hercules cleaned in a day by diverting a river through them. **2** filthy.

auger / **aw**-guh / *n*. a tool with a spiral point for boring holes in wood.

aught / awt / *n. archaic* anything (*for aught I know*).

augment / awg-**ment** / *v*. add to; increase. ▫ **augmentation** *n*.

au gratin / oh **grat**-uhn / *adj*. cooked with a crust of breadcrumbs or melted cheese. (¶ French)

augur / **aw**-guh / *v*. foretell, be a sign of (*this augurs well for your future*).

augury *n*. **1** an omen. **2** interpretation of omens.

August *n*. the eighth month of the year.

august / aw-**gust** / *adj*. majestic, imposing.

Augustan / aw-**gus**-tuhn / *adj*. **1** of the reign of Augustus. **2** (of any national literature) classical, stylish; (in English literature) of the 17th–18th centuries. • *n*. a writer of an Augustan period.

Augustine[1] / aw-**gus**-tuhn /, St (of Canterbury, d. *c*.604): sent by Pope St. Gregory the Great to convert England, he became the first Archbishop of Canterbury.

Augustine[2] / aw-**gus**-tuhn /, St (of Hippo in North Africa, 354–430), bishop and theologian, who profoundly influenced all later Western theology.

Augustinian / aw-guhs-**tin**-nee-uhn / *adj*. of St Augustine of Hippo. • *n*. a member of any of the religious orders of the Catholic Church which observe a rule based on his writings.

Augustus / aw-**gus**-tuhs / (63 BC–AD 14), the first Roman emperor.

auk *n*. a Northern hemisphere sea bird with small narrow wings.

auld lang syne *n. Scottish* days of long ago.

au naturel / oh nach-uh-**rel** / *adj*. **1** uncooked (*ate a dozen oysters au naturel*). **2** cooked in the most natural or simple way. **3** naked. (¶ French, = in the natural state.)

Aung San Suu Kyi / owng sahn soo **chee** / (1945–), Burmese political leader. Her party, the National League for Democracy, won 80 per cent of the seats in the democratic elections of 1990, but the ruling military government refused to recognise the victory. She was awarded the Nobel Peace Prize in 1991.

aunt *n*. **1** a sister or sister-in-law of one's father or mother. **2** *children's colloq*. an unrelated woman friend of the family.

auntie *n*. (also **aunty**) **1** *colloq*. an aunt. **2** (in Aboriginal English) a respectful mode of address to an older woman. **3** *colloq*. (**Auntie**) any institution considered to be conservative or cautious, esp. the ABC.

Aunt Sally **1** a figure used as a target in a throwing game. **2** a target of general abuse or criticism.

au pair / oh **pair** / *n*. a young person, esp. from overseas, helping with housework and receiving board and lodging in return. (¶ French, = on equal terms.)

aura / **aw**-ruh / *n*. a distinctive atmosphere surrounding a person or thing (*an aura of happiness*).

aural / **aw**-ruhl / *adj*. of the ear or hearing. ▫ **aurally** *adv*.

aureate / aw-ree-**uht** / *adj. poetic* **1** golden; brilliant. **2** (of language) flowery, elaborate.

aureole / **aw**-ree-ohl / *n*. (also **aureola** / aw-ree-uh-luh /) **1** a celestial crown or halo, especially on a painting etc. of a divine figure. **2** a corona round the sun or moon.

au revoir / oh ruh-**vwah** / *interj*. & *n*. goodbye (until we meet again). (¶ French)

auricle / **aw**-ri-kuhl / *n*. **1** the external part of the ear. **2** an atrium of the heart.

auricular / aw-**rik**-yuh-luh / *adj*. **1** of or relating to the ear or hearing. **2** spoken aloud to the hearing (*auricular confession to a priest*). **3** of or relating to the auricle of the heart. **4** shaped like an auricle.

auriferous / aw-**rif**-uh-ruhs / *adj*. yielding gold.

aurochs / **aw**-ruhks / *n*. an extinct European wild ox.

Aurora / aw-**raw**-ruh / *Rom. myth*. the goddess of the dawn, corresponding to the Greek Eos.

aurora / aw-**raw** ruh / *n*. bands of coloured light appearing in the sky at night and probably caused by electrical radiation from the north and south magnetic poles. ▫ **aurora australis** (also called the **southern lights**) these lights in the Southern hemisphere (irregularly visible esp. in the southern parts of Australia). **aurora borealis** / baw-ree-**ah**-luhs / (also called the **northern lights**) these lights in the Northern hemisphere.

Auschwitz / **owsh**-vitz / a town in Poland, site of a Nazi concentration camp in the Second World War.

auscultation / aw-skuhl-**tay**-shuhn / *n*. listening to the sounds of the heart, lungs, etc., for medical diagnosis.

Auslan / **oz**-lan / Australian Sign Language, the preferred language of the Australian deaf community.

auspice / **aw**-spis / *n*. **1** an omen. **2** (**auspices**) (usu. **under the auspices of**) patronage (*under the auspices of the Red Cross*).

auspicious / aw-**spish**-uhs / *adj*. showing signs that promise success. ▫ **auspiciously** *adv*.

AUSSAT / **oz**-sat / *abbr*. Australia's domestic satellite system. (¶ *Aus*tralia, *sat*ellite.)

Aussie / oz-ee / *Aust. colloq. n.* **1** an Australian. **2** Australia. **3** Australian English. • *adj.* Australian. ☐ **Aussie battler** (also **little Aussie battler**) *colloq.* typical, esp. working class, Australian who survives against any odds. **Aussie Rules** = AUSTRALIAN RULES.

Austen, Jane (1775–1817), English novelist.

austere / os-**teer** / *adj.* severely simple and plain without ornament or comfort. ☐ **austerely** *adv.*

austerity / o-**ste**-ruh-tee / *n.* being austere, an austere condition (*the austerities of life in wartime*).

Austin Friar *n.* an Augustinian Friar.

Austral, Florence (1894–1968), stage name of Florence Mary Wilson, Australian dramatic soprano who was internationally acclaimed for her performances in opera and on the concert platform.

austral / **o**-struhl / *adj.* **1** southern. **2** (**Austral**) Australian; Australasian. **3** (**Austral**) the first element in the names of various Australian plants (*Austral bluebell; Austral pincushion*).

Australasia / o-struh-**lay**-zhuh / *n.* Australia, New Zealand, and neighbouring islands in the South Pacific. ☐ **Australasian** *adj.* & *n.*

Australia / o-**stray**-lyuh, uh- / *n.* the continent in the Southern hemisphere bounded by the Indian, Southern, and Pacific Oceans (in early use often restricted to the mainland or to NSW as the only known part of the mainland); the sovereign nation comprising the mainland and the island of Tasmania; the federated States and Territories which together make up the Commonwealth of Australia. (¶ Latin (*Terra*) *Australis* the Southern Land.)

Australia Council the statutory authority established by the Federal Government to encourage the development of the arts in Australia, provide grants to individuals and to organisations, etc.

Australia Day 26 January, the day on which the landing of Governor Phillip at Sydney Cove in 1788 is commemorated.

Australia Felix / **fee**-liks / *n. hist.* the name given by the explorer Thomas Mitchell in 1836 to the region south of the Murray River which, in 1851, was separated from NSW and named Victoria. (¶ Latin *felix* 'happy, productive, fertile'.)

Australian / o-**stray**-lee-uhn, o-**stray**-lyuhn, uh- / *n.* **1** *hist.* an Aborigine. **2** a native or national of Australia. **3** a person of Australian descent. **4** = AUSTRALIAN ENGLISH. • *adj.* **1** characteristic of or belonging to Australia. **2** used as the first element in the names of some fauna and flora.

Australiana / o-stray-lee-**ah**-nuh, uh- / *n.* books, documents, artefacts, etc., relating to or characteristic of Australia and its history.

Australian adjective *see* GREAT AUSTRALIAN ADJECTIVE.

Australian Alps the section of the Great Dividing Range from the Brindabella Range in south-eastern New South Wales to the Victorian Alps, which contains Australia's highest alpine peaks, including Mount Kosciuszko (2228 metres) and Mount Townsend (2209 metres).

Australian Antarctic Territory an area of Antarctica administered by Australia as an external territory. Bases for scientific and other research are established at Mawson, Davis, and Casey.

Australian arbo-encephalitis / ah-boh-en-**kef**-uh-luy-tuhs / *n.* a viral disease of the brain transmitted by mosquitoes.

Australian Ballet Australia's national ballet company, founded in 1962.

Australian Broadcasting Corporation Australia's national and international broadcaster, a statutory authority responsible for a national television network, radio services both domestic and overseas, etc.

Australian Capital Territory federal territory in south-eastern Australia comprising 2402.5 square kilometres: the Territory includes Jervis Bay on the east coast and Canberra, the Capital of Australia.

Australian cattle dog *see* BLUE HEELER.

Australian Conservation Foundation a non-government organisation founded in 1965 to heighten awareness of the need for conservation and to deal with all matters relating to conservation.

Australian Council of Social Service the national body representing welfare organisations all around Australia.

Australian Council of Trade Unions the national organisation governing Australian trade unions.

Australian crawl *n.* a fast swimming stroke in which the body is prone, the arms reach forward alternately in an overarm action and pull back through the water, and the legs maintain a flutter kick.

Australian Democrats a centrist political party espousing liberal principles, founded in 1977.

Australian English *n.* the dialect of English spoken by Australians, with distinctive features differentiating it from British, American, and other Englishes.

Australian Football League 1 the regulating body for Australian National Football: *see* AUSTRALIAN RULES. **2** the national competition run by this organisation.

Australian Heritage Commission a commission set up in 1976 with the responsibility of advising the Federal Government on all matters related to conserving the national estate.

Australian Inland Mission an organisation founded by John Flynn to provide a safety network of medical and other support to people in remote outback areas.

Australian Institute of Sport a government-funded program providing facilities and assistance for elite athletes in many sports with its headquarters in Canberra.

Australianise v. (also **-ize**) make (a person, an institution, etc.) Australian in character.

Australianism n. **1** a distinctively Australian word or phrase. **2** pride in Australian nationalism. **3** character distinctively Australian.

Australian Labor Party a democratic socialist political party commonly known as the ALP, the first political party to be established in Australia. One of the major political parties today, the ALP represents the interests esp. of the working people.

Australian language n. **1** an Aboriginal language. **2** = AUSTRALIAN ENGLISH.

Australian National Dictionary a dictionary of Australianisms published in 1988. It contains some 10,000 Australian words and meanings, illustrated by more than 60,000 dated and referenced quotations from more than 9,000 sources.

Australian National Flag a blue flag with the Union Jack of the United Kingdom occupying the upper quarter next to the flagstaff, differenced by a large seven-pointed white star, the Federation Star (representing the six States of Australia and the Territories), and five smaller white stars (four with seven points and one with five points), representing the Southern Cross constellation. The flag was officially adopted in 1953.

Australian National University established in Canberra as a national university for postgraduate research in 1946, the ANU (as it is commonly called) has, since 1960, offered undergraduate degrees as well.

Australian Rules a form of football originating in the mid-19th century in Vic., played with an oval ball by teams of eighteen.

Australian salute see GREAT AUSTRALIAN SALUTE.

Australian Secret Intelligence Service (abbr. **ASIS**) an organisation established in 1952, responsible for external security functions. It reports to the Minister for Foreign Affairs.

Australian Security Intelligence Organisation (abbr. **ASIO**) an organisation established in 1949 and given a statutory basis in 1956, responsible for internal security functions. It reports to the Attorney-General.

Australian Sign Language see AUSLAN.

Australian silky terrier n. (also **Sydney silky**) a small terrier with long silky bluish hair.

Australian terrier n. a small, sturdy dog with a coat of coarse bluish hair.

Australian War Memorial an institution, located in Canberra, established to commemorate the service of Australians who died in the First World War, and later expanded to include the service of Australians in every war in which Australia has participated.

Australite n. any of several small pieces of dark meteoric glass found in Australia.

Australoid adj. of, allied to, or resembling the ethnological type of the Aborigines of Australia.
• n. a person possessing the physical characteristics of this ethnic group.

Australorp n. an Australian breed of Orpington fowl.

Austria / **os**-tree-uh / a republic in central Europe. □ **Austrian** adj. & n.

Austronesian n. (also **Malayo-Polynesian**) a family of at least 500 languages with around 200 million speakers, covering a vast geographical area from Madagascar to Easter Island, Taiwan to Hawaii and New Zealand. It is usually divided into two main groups, Western (Western Malayo-Polynesian) and Eastern (Oceanic).

autarchy / **aw**-tah-kee / n. a system of government with unrestricted powers; autocracy.

autarky / **aw**-tah-kee / n. self-sufficiency, especially in economic affairs.

authentic adj. genuine, known to be true. □ **authentically** adv. **authenticity** n.

authenticate v. prove the truth or authenticity of. □ **authentication** n.

author n. **1** the writer of a book or books etc. **2** the originator of a plan or policy. **3** the originator or creator of anything (he is the author of all my woes). • v. be the author of (a book or piece of writing). □ **authorial** adj. **authoring** n. **authorship** n.

authorise v. (also **-ize**) **1** give authority to. **2** give authority for, sanction (I authorised this payment). □ **authorisation** n.

Authorised Version the English translation of the Bible (1611) made by order of King James I.

authoritarian / aw-tho-ruh-**tair**-ree-uhn, uh- / adj. favouring or enforcing complete obedience to authority. • n. a supporter of such principles.

authoritative / aw-**tho**-ruh-tuh-tiv, uh- / adj. having or using authority. □ **authoritatively** adv.

authority n. **1** the power or right to give orders and make others obey, or to take specific action. **2** a person or group with such power. **3** a person with specialised knowledge; a book etc. that can supply reliable information (he is an authority on spiders).

autistic / aw-**tis**-tik / adj. having a form of mental illness that causes a person to withdraw into a private world and be unable to communicate with others or respond to the real environment (autistic children). □ **autism** / aw-tiz-uhm / n.

auto[1] n. automatic control.

auto[2] adj. automobile (auto parts; auto repairs).

auto[3] n. (pl. **autos**) colloq. a motor car.

auto- comb. form **1** self; own (autobiography). **2** of or by oneself or itself, automatic (auto-suggestion; automobile).

autobiography *n.* the story of a person's life written by himself or herself. ☐ **autobiographical** *adj.*

autoclave / **aw**-tuh-klayv / *n.* a steriliser using high-pressure steam.

autocracy / aw-**tok**-ruh-see / *n.* rule by an autocrat; dictatorship.

autocrat / **aw**-tuh-krat / *n.* a person with unlimited power; a dictatorial person. ☐ **autocratic** / aw-tuh-**krat**-ik / *adj.* **autocratically** *adv.*

autocross *n.* motor racing across country.

autocue *n. trademark* a device showing a television speaker the script as an aid to memory.

auto-da-fé / aw-toh-dah-**fay** / *n.* (*pl.* *autos-da-fé*) **1** *hist.* the ceremonial judgment of heretics by the Spanish Inquisition. **2** the execution of heretics by public burning. (¶ Portuguese, = act of the faith.)

auto-electrician *n. Aust.* a person who specialises in the maintenance of the electrical systems of motor vehicles.

autograph *n.* a person's signature, esp. that of a celebrity. •*v.* sign one's name on or in (*the author will autograph copies of his book tomorrow*).

autoimmune *adj.* (of a disease) caused by the action of antibodies produced against substances naturally present in the body. ☐ **autoimmunity** *n.*

automate *v.* control or operate by automation (*the process is fully automated*). ☐ **automated teller machine** an automatic machine from which customers of a bank etc. may withdraw cash, esp. by using a keycard.

automatic *adj.* **1** working of itself without direct human control, self-regulating. **2** firing repeatedly until pressure on the trigger is released (*an automatic pistol*). **3** done without thought, done from habit or routine (*made an automatic gesture of apology*). •*n.* **1** an automatic machine, tool, or firearm. **2** a vehicle with a system for automatic gear-change. ☐ **automatic control** operation of a machine, device, etc. with little or no direct human intervention. **automatic pilot** a device in an aircraft or ship to keep it on a set course. **automatic transmission** a system in a vehicle for changing gear automatically. ☐☐ **automatically** *adv.*

automation *n.* the use of automatic methods or equipment to save labour.

automatism / aw-**tom**-uh-tiz-uhm / *n.* **1** involuntary action. **2** unthinking routine.

automaton / aw-**tom**-uh-tuhn / *n.* (*pl.* **automata** *or* **automatons**) a robot; a person who seems to act like one, mechanically and without thinking.

automobile / aw-tuh-muh-beel / *n.* a motor car.

automotive / aw-tuh-**moh**-tiv / *adj.* concerned with motor vehicles.

autonomous / aw-**ton**-uh-muhs / *adj.* self-governing.

autonomy *n.* **1** self-government. **2** personal freedom.

autopilot = AUTOMATIC PILOT.

autopsy / **aw**-top-see / *n.* a post-mortem.

auto-suggestion *n.* a self-induced or subconscious suggestion affecting reaction, behaviour, etc.

autumn *n.* the season between summer and winter. ☐ **autumn** (*or* **autumnal**) **equinox** the equinox in autumn, about 20 March in the southern hemisphere. ☐☐ **autumnal** / aw-**tum**-nuhl / *adj.*

auxiliary / og-**zil**-yuh-ree, awg- / *adj.* giving help or support (*auxiliary services*). •*n.* **1** a helper. **2** (**auxiliaries**) foreign or allied troops employed by a country at war. ☐ **auxiliary verb** one used in forming parts of other verbs (see panel).

avail *v.* be of help or advantage (*nothing availed against the storm*). •*n.* effectiveness, advantage (*it was of no avail*). ☐ **avail oneself of** make use of.

available *adj.* ready or able to be used; obtainable. ☐ **availability** *n.*

avalanche / **av**-uh-lahnsh, -lansh / *n.* **1** a mass of snow or rock pouring down a mountainside. **2** a great onrush (*an avalanche of letters*).

Avalon / **av**-uh-lon / **1** (in Arthurian legend) the place to which King Arthur was conveyed after death. **2** *Welsh myth.* an island paradise of the blessed dead.

avant-garde / av-ong-**gahd** / *adj.* using or favouring an ultra-modern style, especially in art or literature; new, innovative. •*n.* an avant-garde group.

avarice / **av**-uh-ruhs / *n.* greed for gain. ☐ **avaricious** / av-uh-**rish**-uhs / *adj.*

avatar / **av**-uh-tah / *n.* (in Hinduism) the descent to earth of a deity in human, animal, or superhuman form.

Auxiliary verb

An auxiliary verb is used in front of another verb to alter its meaning. Mainly, it expresses:
1. when something happens, by forming a tense of the main verb, e.g. *I shall go. He was going.*
2. permission, obligation, or ability to do something, e.g. *They may go. You must go. I can't go.*
3. The likelihood of something happening, e.g. *I might go. She would go if she could.*

The principal auxiliary verbs are:

be	*have*	*must*	*will*
can	*let*	*ought*	*would*
could	*may*	*shall*	
do	*might*	*should*	

Ave / **ah**-vay / *n.* (in full **Ave Maria** / muh-**ree**-uh /) Hail Mary, a prayer to the Virgin Mary. (¶ Latin)

avenge *v.* take vengeance for (a wrongdoing). □ **avenger** *n.*

avenue *n.* **1** a wide street or road, esp. one lined with trees. **2** any road or street. **3** a way of approaching or making progress (*other avenues to fame*).

aver / uh-**ver** / *v.* (**averred**, **averring**) assert, state as true. □ **averment** *n.*

average *n.* **1** the value arrived at by adding several quantities together and dividing the total by the number of quantities. **2** the standard or level regarded as usual. **3** *Law* damage to or loss of a ship or cargo. • *adj.* **1** found by making an average (*the average age of the pupils is fifteen*). **2** of the ordinary or usual standard (*people of average intelligence*). • *v.* **1** amount to or produce as an average (*the car averaged 100 kilometres an hour*). **2** calculate the average of. □ **on average** (or **on an average**) as an estimated average rate; normally.

averse / uh-**vers** / *adj.* (usu. foll. by *to*) unwilling, disinclined (*he is averse to hard work*).

aversion / uh-**ver**-*zh*uhn, -shuhn / *n.* **1** (usu. foll. by *to* or *for*) a strong dislike. **2** something disliked.

avert / uh-**vert** / *v.* **1** turn away (*people averted their eyes*). **2** prevent, ward off (*managed to avert disaster*).

Avesta / uh-**ves**-tuh / *n.* the sacred writings of Zoroastrianism.

Avestan / uh-**ves**-tuhn / *n.* the ancient east-Iranian language in which the Avesta is written. • *adj.* of Avestan or the Avesta.

aviary / **ay**-vuh-ree, -vyuh- / *n.* a large cage or building for keeping birds.

aviation / ay-vee-**ay**-shuhn / *n.* the practice or science of flying aircraft.

aviator / **ay**-vee-ay-tuh / *n.* a pilot or member of an aircraft crew in the early days of aviation.

avid / **av**-uhd / *adj.* eager, greedy; keen (*an avid photographer; avid for more news*). □ **avidly** *adv.* **avidity** / uh-**vid**-uh-tee / *n.*

avionics / ay-vee-**on**-iks / *n.* the application of electronics in aviation.

avocado / av-uh-**kah**-doh / *n.* (*pl.* **avocados**) a usually dark green pear-shaped fruit with creamy edible flesh.

avocation / av-uh-**kay**-shuhn / *n.* **1** a secondary activity done in addition to one's main work. **2** *colloq.* one's occupation.

avocet / **av**-uh-set / *n.* a wading bird with long legs and an upturned bill (*the Australian red-necked avocet*).

avoid *v.* **1** keep oneself away from (something dangerous or undesirable). **2** refrain from (*avoid making rash promises*). □ **avoidable** *adj.*

avoidance *n.* an act of shunning or averting. □ **avoidance relationship** an association that is forbidden in traditional Aboriginal society, e.g. that between mother-in-law and son-in-law. **avoidance rules** the complex of laws governing an avoidance relationship.

avoirdupois / av-uh-duh-**poiz** / *n.* (in full **avoirdupois weight**) a system of weights based on a pound of 16 ounces or 7000 grains.

avow *v. formal* admit, declare openly. □ **avowal** *n.* **avowedly** / uh-**vow**-uhd-lee / *adv.*

AVS *abbr.* (on the Internet) age verification service.

avuncular / uh-**vung**-kyuh-luh / *adj.* of or like a kindly uncle; friendly, caring.

Awabakal / u-**wub**-u-kul / *n.* an Aboriginal language of a large area of eastern NSW north of Sydney.

await *v.* **1** wait for (*I await your reply*). **2** be waiting for (*a surprise awaits you*).

awake *v.* (**awoke**, **awoken**) **1** wake, cease to sleep. **2** become active. **3** rouse from sleep. • *adj.* **1** not yet asleep, no longer asleep. **2** alert, aware (*he is awake to the possible danger*).

awaken *v.* awake. □ **awakening** *n.*

award *v.* give by official decision as a payment or prize. • *n.* **1** a decision of this kind. **2** a thing awarded. **3** *Aust.* the determination made by an industrial court, commission, or tribunal. **4** *Aust.* a judicial decision. □ **award wage** *Aust.* the amount fixed by an industrial tribunal etc. as remuneration to be paid to specified workers (in an occupation, industry, etc.)

aware *adj.* **1** having knowledge or realisation (*I am aware of this possibility*). **2** well-informed. **3** (of a person, social group, etc.) fully informed about current issues of concern in a particular field (*an environmentally aware industry*). **4** (of a product) designed, manufactured, or marketed in such a way as to take account of current concerns and attitudes (*an ecologically aware detergent*). □ **awareness** *n.*

awash *adj.* **1** covered by water; flooded. **2** (foll. by *with*) overflowing, full (*the place was awash with journalists*).

away *adv.* **1** to or at a distance. **2** out of existence (*the water has boiled away*). **3** constantly, persistently (*we worked away at it*). • *adj.* played or playing on an opponent's ground (*an away match*).

awe *n.* respect combined with fear or wonder. • *v.* fill with awe. □ **awe-inspiring** *adj.* magnificent; causing awe.

aweigh / uh-**way** / *adv.* (of an anchor) hanging just clear of the sea-bottom.

awesome *adj.* **1** inspiring awe; dreaded. **2** *colloq.* excellent.

awestricken *adj.* (also **awestruck**) suddenly filled with awe.

awful *adj.* **1** extremely bad or unpleasant (*an awful accident*). **2** *colloq.* extreme, very great (*that's an awful lot of money*).

awfully *adv.* **1** badly; unpleasantly. **2** *colloq.* very; very much.

awhile *adv.* for a short time.
awkward *adj.* **1** difficult to use or deal with. **2** clumsy, having little skill. **3** inconvenient (*came at an awkward time*). **4** embarrassed (*I feel awkward about it*). ❑ **awkwardly** *adv.* **awkwardness** *n.*
awl *n.* a small pointed tool for making holes, especially in leather or wood.
awn *n.* the bristly head of the sheath of barley and other grasses.
awning *n.* a roof of canvas etc. stretched on a frame as a shelter against sun or rain.
awoke, awoken *see* AWAKE.
AWOL / **ay**-wol / *abbr.* absent without leave (*gone AWOL*).
awry / uh-**ruy** / *adv.* **1** twisted towards one side. **2** amiss (*plans went awry*). • *adj.* crooked; wrong.
AWU *abbr.* the Australian Workers' Union. Formed in 1891 by rural workers, esp. shearers, the AWU is now one of Australia's largest unions.
axe *n.* **1** a chopping tool with a heavy blade. **2** (**the axe**) dismissal (of employees); abandonment of a project etc. • *v.* cut (costs or staff) drastically; dismiss; abandon (*the project was axed*). ❑ **have an axe to grind** have some personal interest involved and be anxious to take care of it.
axes *see* AXIS.
axial *adj.* **1** of or forming an axis. **2** round an axis. ❑ **axially** *adv.*
axil *n.* the angle where a leaf joins a stem.
axiom / **ak**-see-uhm / *n.* an accepted general truth or principle.
axiomatic / ak-see-uh-**mat**-ik / *adj.* **1** of or like an axiom. **2** self-evident.
axis *n.* (*pl.* **axes** / **ak**-seez /) **1** an imaginary line through the centre of an object, round which it rotates when spinning. **2** a line about which a regular figure is symmetrically arranged. **3** a reference line for the measurement of coordinates etc. **4** the relation between countries, regarded as a common pivot on which they move; (**the Axis**) the alliance between Germany and Italy (and later Japan) in the Second World War.
axle *n.* the bar or rod on which a wheel or group of wheels is fixed.
axolotl / ak-suh-**lot**-uhl / *n.* a newt-like amphibian found in Mexican lakes.
ayah *n.* a native nurse or maidservant, esp. formerly in Sri Lanka and India.
ayatollah / uy-uh-**tol**-uh / *n.* a Shi'ite Muslim religious leader in Iran.
aye[1] / uy / (also **ay**) *adv. archaic* yes. • *n.* a vote in favour of a proposal (*the ayes have it*).
aye[2] / ay / *adv. archaic* always.
Ayers Rock / airz / the former name for ULURU.
azalea / uh-**zay**-lee-uh, uh-**zay**-lyuh / *n.* a shrub-like flowering plant of the rhododendron family.
Azerbaijan / az-uh-buy-**jahn** / a republic of Eastern Europe between the Black Sea and the Caspian Sea.
azimuth / **az**-uh-muhth / *n.* **1** an arc of the sky from the zenith to the horizon. **2** the angle between this arc and the meridian. **3** a directional bearing. ❑ **azimuthal** *adj.*
Azrael / **az**-rayl / *Jewish* & *Muslim myth.* the angel who severs the soul from the body at death.
AZT *abbr.* a drug developed for use in the treatment of Aids.
Aztec *n.* **1** a member of an Indian people of Mexico before the Spanish conquest (1521). **2** the language of this people. • *adj.* of the Aztecs or their language.
azure / **ay**-zhuh, uh-**zyoor** / *adj.* & *n.* sky-blue.

B

B *n.* (*pl.* **Bs** *or* **B's**) **1** the second letter of the alphabet. **2** *Music* the seventh note of the scale of C major. **3** the second point, example, etc.; the second highest category (of academic marks etc.). **4** (**B**, **2B**, **3B**, etc.) (of a pencil lead) soft; softer than H and HB (the higher the number, the softer and blacker the lead). •*symbol* boron.

b. *abbr.* born.

BA *abbr.* Bachelor of Arts

Ba *symbol* barium.

baa *n.* the cry of a sheep or lamb.

Baagandji / **bah**-gun-jee / *n.* an Aboriginal language of a vast area on both sides of the Darling River in NSW from Bourke to Menindee, and extending into SA.

babble *v.* **1** chatter in a thoughtless or confused way. **2** make a continuous murmuring sound (*a babbling brook*). •*n.* babbling talk or sound.

babe *n.* **1** *literary* a baby. **2** *colloq.* a girlfriend, a young woman. **3** *teenage colloq.* a sexually attractive young male or female.

babel / **bay**-buhl / *n.* a confused noise or scene. □ **Tower of Babel** (in the Old Testament) a high tower built in an attempt to reach heaven, which God frustrated by confusing the languages of its builders so that they could not understand one another.

baboon *n.* a large long-nosed African or Arabian monkey.

baby *n.* **1** a very young child or animal. **2** a babyish or timid person. **3** something small of its kind. **4** something that is one's personal concern or creation. • *v.* (**babied**, **babying**) treat like a baby, pamper. □ **baby boom** a temporary marked increase in the birth rate. **baby boomer** a person born during a baby boom, esp. that which occurred after the Second World War. **baby grand** the smallest kind of grand piano. **be left holding the baby** *colloq.* be left with an unwelcome responsibility. □□ **babyhood** *n.*

babyish *adj.* like a baby.

Babylon the capital of Babylonia.

Babylonia the ancient name for southern Mesopotamia, a powerful kingdom until 538 BC. □ **Babylonian** *adj.* & *n.*

babysit *v.* look after a child in its home while its parents are out. □ **babysitter** *n.*

baccarat / **bak**-uh-rah / *n.* a gambling card game.

Bacchanalia *n.pl.* **1** the Roman festival of Bacchus, the god of wine. **2** (**bacchanalia**) drunken revelry.

Bacchus / **bak**-uhs / *Gk myth.* another name for Dionysus.

Bach / bahk /, Johann Sebastian (1685–1750), and his sons Carl Philipp Emanuel (1714–88), and Johann Christian (1735–82), German composers.

bach see BATCH².

bachelor *n.* **1** an unmarried man. **2** a person who holds a university first degree (*Bachelor of Arts*). □ **bachelorhood** *n.*

bacillus / buh-**sil**-uhs / *n.* (*pl.* **bacilli** / buh-**sil**-uy /) a rod-like bacterium.

back *n.* **1** the rear surface of the human body from neck to hip; the corresponding part of an animal's body. **2** that part of a chair etc. against which a seated person's back rests. **3** the part or surface of an object that is less used or less important; the part furthest from the front. **4** *Aust.* a part of the interior which is remote from settlements or from water. **5** the part of a garment covering the back. **6** a defensive player near the goal in football etc.; this position. •*adj.* **1** situated behind; remote (*the back teeth; backstreets; back country*). **2** of or for a past time (*back pay*). •*adv.* **1** at or towards the rear, away from the front or centre (*go back a bit*). **2** in check (*hold it back*). **3** in or into a previous time or position or condition (*I'll be back at six*). **4** in return (*pay it back*). •*v.* **1** go or cause to go backwards. **2** (of wind) change gradually in an anticlockwise direction. **3** give one's support to, assist. **4** give financial support to (*he is backing the play*). **5** lay a bet on. **6** cover the back of (*the rug is backed with canvas*). □ **at the back of** being the underlying cause or motive of (a thing). **back-door** secret, underhand (*did a back-door deal*). **back down** give up a claim; withdraw one's argument. **back number 1** an old issue of a periodical. **2** an out-of-date person or idea. **back of** (**a place**) *Aust.* behind, beyond (*back of Woolloomooloo*). **back of beyond** esp. *Aust.* a very remote place; the outback. **back of Bourke** any remote part of Australia. **back out** withdraw from an agreement. **back paddock** *Aust.* a paddock distant from the station homestead. **back-pedal** *v.* change one's mind; try to reverse one's previous decision or commitment. **back road** (also **back track**) a little used, often indirect, road or track. **back seat 1** a seat at the back. **2** a less prominent position. **back-seat driver** a person who has no responsibility but is eager to give orders to one who has. **back to front** with the back placed where the front should be. **back up 1** give one's support to; confirm (a statement). **2** *Computing* make a backup copy of (a file, disk, etc.). **have one's back to the wall** be fighting for survival in a desperate situation. **on the back-burner** left aside for consideration at a later date; postponed. **put** (*or* **get**) **a person's back up** offend or antagonise him or her.

backbencher *n.* an ordinary MP who does not hold a senior office (cf. FRONTBENCHER).

backbiting *n.* spiteful talk, especially about a person who is not present.

backblocks *n.pl. Aust.* **1** land in the remote and sparsely inhabited interior. **2** the outer suburbs of a city. **3** (as *adj.*) located in a sparsely populated inland district; characteristic of those who live in such a place (*a backblocks pub; backblocks customs*).

backbone *n.* **1** the column of small bones down the centre of the back, the spine. **2** strength of character.

backburn *v. Aust.* burn undergrowth etc. in the path of a bushfire to check its advance.

backchat *n. colloq.* cheeky words in response to a rebuke.

backcloth = BACKDROP.

backdate *v.* declare that (a thing) is to be regarded as valid from some date in the past.

backdrop *n.* **1** a flat painted curtain at the back of a stage set. **2** the background to a scene or situation.

backer *n.* a person who supports another, especially financially.

backfire *v.* **1** ignite or explode prematurely, especially in an internal combustion engine. **2** produce an undesired effect, especially upon the originators (*their plan backfired*). • *n.* an instance of backfiring.

backflip *n.* **1** a backward somersault done in the air with the arms and legs stretched out straight. **2** a complete reversal.

backgammon *n.* a game played on a double board with draughts and dice.

background *n.* **1** the back part of a scene or picture; the setting for the chief objects or people. **2** an inconspicuous position (*he was kept in the background; background music*). **3** the conditions and events surrounding and influencing something; a person's family life, education, experience, etc.

backhand *adj.* (of a stroke or blow) made with the back of the hand turned outwards. • *n.* a backhand stroke or blow.

backhanded *adj.* **1** backhand. **2** indirect; ambiguous (*a backhanded compliment*).

backhander *n.* **1** a backhanded stroke, blow, or remark. **2** *colloq.* a bribe, a reward for services rendered.

backing *n.* **1** help, support. **2** material used to support or line a thing's back. **3** a musical accompaniment to a pop singer.

backlash *n.* **1** a violent and usu. hostile reaction to some event or development. **2** a recoil in machinery; excessive play between parts.

backlist *n.* a publisher's list of books still available.

backlog *n.* arrears of work.

backpack *n.* **1** a rucksack. **2** a package of equipment carried similarly. ▫ **backpacker** *n.*

backside *n. colloq.* the buttocks.

backslide *v.* slip back from good behaviour into bad.

backspace *v.* cause a typewriter carriage, computer cursor, etc. to move one space back.

backspin *n.* a backward spinning movement of a ball, reducing its speed as it bounces.

backstage *adj. & adv.* behind the stage of a theatre, in the wings or dressing rooms.

backstitch *v.* sew by inserting the needle each time behind the place where it has just been brought out. • *n.* a stitch made in this way.

backstreet *n.* a side street, an alley.

backstroke *n.* a swimming stroke done lying on the back.

backtrack *v.* **1** go back the same way that one came. **2** back down from an argument or policy, reverse one's previous action.

backup *n.* (often used as *adj.*) **1** support; reserve (*a backup team*). **2** *Computing* the copying of data, files, disks, etc. for safety; the copy itself.

backward *adj.* **1** directed towards the back or the starting point. **2** having made less than normal progress. **3** diffident, not putting oneself forward. • *adv.* backwards. ▫ **backwardness** *n.*

backwards *adv.* **1** away from one's front, towards the back. **2** with the back foremost; in a reverse direction or order. ▫ **bend** (*or* **fall** *or* **lean**) **over backwards** *colloq.* do one's utmost.

backwash *n.* **1** a backward flow of water. **2** the after-effects of an action or event.

backwater *n.* **1** a stretch of stagnant water joining a stream. **2** a place unaffected by progress or new ideas.

backwoods *n.* **1** remote uncleared forest land. **2** a remote or backward area. ▫ **backwoodsman** *n.*

backyard *n.* an enclosure, usu. including a garden, at the back of a house. • *adj.* illegal, illicit (*backyard abortions*).

bacon *n.* salted or smoked meat from the back or sides of a pig. ▫ **bacon-and-eggs** any of several Australian shrubs, widespread in the bush, bearing yellow and reddy-brown pea-flowers suggesting the foods in question. **bring home the bacon** *colloq.* **1** achieve success in an undertaking. **2** provide financial support for one's family.

bacteriology *n.* the scientific study of bacteria. ▫ **bacteriological** *adj.* **bacteriologist** *n.*

bacterium / bak-**teer**-ree-uhm / *n.* (*pl.* **bacteria**) a microscopic organism. ▫ **bacterial** *adj.*

■ **Usage** A common mistake is the use of the plural form *bacteria* as the singular. This should be avoided.

Bactrian camel *n.* a two-humped camel of central Asia.

bad *adj.* (**worse**, **worst**) **1** wicked, evil. **2** unpleasant; unwelcome (*bad weather; bad news*). **3** serious, severe (*a bad mistake; a bad headache*). **4** inadequate, defective (*a bad light*). **5** harmful (*smoking is bad for the lungs*). **6** unskilled; lacking competence (*bad at cricket; bad at maths*). **7** (of food) decayed. **8** *colloq.* ill, injured (*feeling bad today; a bad back*). **9** morally unacceptable (*bad desires; bad language*). **10** naughty (*you bad boy!*). **11** not valid (*passing bad cheques*). **11** (**badder**, **baddest**) esp. *US colloq.* good, excellent. • *adv. colloq.* badly (*is he hurt bad?*). • *n.* that which is bad or unfortunate. ☐ **bad blood** ill feeling, enmity. **bad debt** one that will not be repaid. **bad-mouth** *v.* insult, put down. **bad news** *colloq.* an unpleasant or troublesome person or thing (*that boyfriend of hers is bad news*). **be in a bad way** be ill or in trouble. **not bad** *colloq.* quite good. **too bad** *colloq.* regrettable. ☐☐ **badness** *n.*
baddy *n. colloq.* a villain.
bade *see* BID².
Baden-Powell, Robert (Stephenson Smyth), 1st Baron (1857–1941), English soldier, founder of the Boy Scouts (1908) and Girl Guides (1910).
badge *n.* **1** a thing worn to show one's rank, membership of an organisation, support for a cause, etc. **2** a thing that reveals a condition or quality (*bleached hair is the badge of a surfie*).
badger *n.* a nocturnal animal of Europe etc. that has a black and white striped head and lives in a burrow (or set). • *v.* pester, harass.
badinage / **bad**-uh-nah*zh* / *n.* banter. (¶ French)
badly *adv.* (**worse**, **worst**) **1** in an inferior, unsuitable, or defective way. **2** so as to inflict much injury; severely. **3** *colloq.* very much.
badminton *n.* a game played with racquets and shuttlecocks across a high net.
baffle *v.* **1** puzzle, perplex. **2** frustrate (*baffled their attempts*). • *n.* a screen placed so as to hinder or control the passage of sound, light, or fluid. ☐ **bafflement** *n.*
bag *n.* **1** a container made of flexible material, used for holding or carrying things. **2** something resembling a bag (*bags under the eyes*). **3** *colloq. offens.* a woman. **4** the amount of game shot by one person. **5** (**bags**) *colloq.* plenty (*bags of room*). • *v.* (**bagged**, **bagging**) **1** put into a bag or bags. **2** kill or capture (*bagged a feral cat*). **3** *colloq.* take possession of, stake a claim to. **4** hang loosely. **5** *Aust. colloq.* criticise; disparage. ☐ **bag lady** a homeless woman who carries her possessions in shopping bags. **in the bag** *colloq.* achieved, secured as now wished.
bagatelle / bag-uh-**tel** / *n.* **1** a board game in which small balls are struck into holes. **2** something small and unimportant. **3** a short piece of music.
bagel / **bay**-guhl / *n.* a hard bread roll in the shape of a ring.

bagful *n.* (*pl.* **bagfuls**) as much as a bag will hold.
baggage *n.* **1** luggage. **2** portable equipment. **3** mental encumbrances.
baggy *adj.* (**baggier**, **baggiest**) hanging in loose folds. ☐ **baggily** *adv.* **bagginess** *n.*
Baghdad / bag-**dad** / the capital of Iraq.
bagman *n.* **1** *Aust.* a swagman. **2** *Aust.* a bookmaker's clerk. **3** chiefly *US* & *Aust. colloq.* an agent who collects or distributes money for illicit purposes.
bagpipe *n.* (also **bagpipes**) a musical instrument with air stored in a bag and pressed out through pipes.
baguette / ba-**get** / *n.* a long thin French loaf.
bah *interj.* an exclamation of contempt or disgust.
Baha'i / buh-**hah**-ee / *n.* **1** a religion founded in Persia in the 19th century by Baha'ullah (1817–92) and his son, whose quest is for world peace and unity. **2** a follower of this religion.
Bahamas / buh-**hah**-muhz / a nation consisting of a group of islands in the West Indies. ☐ **Bahamian** *adj.* & *n.*
Bahasa Indonesia / bah-**hah**-suh / *n.* the official language of Indonesia.
Bahrain / bah-**rayn** / a sheikhdom consisting of a group of islands in the Persian Gulf. ☐ **Bahraini** *adj.* & *n.*
baht *n.* (*pl.* same) the basic monetary unit of Thailand.
bail¹ *n.* **1** money or property pledged as security that a person accused of a crime will return to stand trial. **2** permission for a person's release on such security. • *v.* **1** obtain or allow (a person's) release on bail. **2** (foll. by *out*) relieve by financial help in an emergency (*bail the firm out*). ☐ **jump bail** *colloq.* fail to appear for trial after being released on bail. **on bail** released after payment of bail. **stand** (*or* **go**) **bail for** pledge money as bail for (a person).
bail² *n.* **1** either of the two cross-pieces resting on the three stumps in cricket. **2** a bar separating horses in an open stable. **3** a bar holding paper against the platen of a typewriter. **4** *Aust.* a framework for securing the head of a cow during milking. ☐ **bail up!** **1** the call with which a cow is encouraged into the bail to be milked. **2** *hist.* a bushranger's challenge, requiring those addressed to submit to being 'milked'. **bail up** *v. Aust.* **1** secure (a cow) in the bail during milking. **2** *hist.* (of a bushranger) make a person hold up his or her arms to be robbed. **3** buttonhole (a person) (*nuns collecting for charity bailed me up in the street*). **4** bring (an animal) to bay (*the dogs bailed up a wallaroo*).
bail³ *v.* (also **bale**) scoop out (water that has entered a boat); clear (a boat) in this way.
bailey *n.* the outer wall of a castle; a courtyard enclosed by this.
Bailey bridge *n.* a bridge made in prefabricated sections designed for rapid assembly. (¶ Named after its designer Sir Donald Bailey (1901–85).)

bailiff *n.* a law officer who helps a sheriff, serving writs and performing arrests.

bailiwick *n.* **1** the authority or territory of a bailiff. **2** a person's particular interest.

bailout *n.* financial assistance given to a failing business or economy by a government, bank, etc. so as to save it from collapse.

bain-marie / ban-muh-**ree** / *n.* (*pl.* **bains-marie** pronounced the same) a vessel of hot water in which a dish of food is placed for slow cooking. (¶ French)

Baird, John Logie (1888–1946), Scottish pioneer of television.

bairn *n.* (esp. *Scottish*) a child.

bait *n.* **1** food placed to attract prey. **2** food treated with poison to eradicate pests etc. **3** an enticement. • *v.* **1** place bait on or in (*bait the trap*). **2** torment by jeering.

baize *n.* thick woollen green cloth, used for covering tables.

bake *v.* **1** cook or be cooked by dry heat, especially in an oven. **2** expose to great heat; harden or be hardened by heat.

Bakelite / **bay**-kuh-luyt / *n. trademark* a hard plastic. (¶ Named after its Belgian-American inventor L.H. Baekeland (1863–1944).)

baker *n.* one who bakes and sells bread. □ **baker's dozen** thirteen. (¶ From the former custom of allowing the retailer to receive thirteen loaves for each twelve paid for.)

bakery *n.* a place where bread and cakes are baked or sold.

Bakery Hill a hill in the Ballarat goldfields: here, in 1854, angry miners held mass meetings which were a preamble to the EUREKA STOCKADE. Here too, in 1858, the famous Welcome Nugget was found. It weighed 68,956 grams.

baking *adj. colloq.* (of weather etc.) very hot.

baking powder *n.* a mixture of powders used as a raising agent for cakes etc.

baking soda *n.* sodium bicarbonate, used in baking.

baklava / **buk**-luh-vuh / *n.* a rich cake of flaky pastry, honey, and nuts. (¶ Turkish)

Baku / ba-**koo** / the capital of Azerbaijan on the shore of the Caspian Sea.

Balaclava / bal-uh-**klah**-vuh / a Crimean village, scene of a battle (1854) in the Crimean War. • *n.* (**balaclava**) a woollen cap covering the head and neck, with an opening for the face.

balalaika / bal-uh-**luy**-kuh / *n.* a guitar-like instrument with a triangular body. (¶ Russian)

balance *n.* **1** a weighing-apparatus with two pans hanging from a cross bar. **2** a balance wheel. **3** an even distribution of weight or amount, a steady position. **4** the difference between credits and debits. **5** money remaining after payment of a debt. • *v.* **1** consider by comparing (*balance one argument against another*). **2** be or put or keep (a thing) in a state of balance. **3** compare the debits and credits of an account and make the entry needed to equalise these; have these equal. □ **balance of payments** the difference between the amount paid to foreign countries for imports and services and the amount received from them for exports etc. in a given period. **balance of power 1** a situation in which the chief nations have roughly equal power. **2** the power to decide events, held by a small group when the larger groups are of equal strength to each other. **balance of trade** the difference in value between imports and exports. **balance sheet** a written statement of assets and liabilities. **balance wheel** a wheel regulating the speed of a clock or watch. **in the balance** with the outcome still uncertain. **off balance** in danger of falling. **on balance** taking everything into consideration.

balander / buh-**lan**-duh / *n. Aust.* (in Aboriginal English) a white man. (¶ A corruption of *Hollander.*)

balcony / **bal**-kuh-nee / *n.* **1** a platform with a rail or parapet, projecting outside an upper storey of a building. **2** an upper floor of seats in a cinema or above the dress circle in a theatre. □ **balconied** *adj.*

bald *adj.* **1** with the scalp wholly or partly hairless. **2** (of animals) lacking the usual hair or feathers. **3** (of tyres) with the tread worn away. **4** bare, without details (*bald facts*). **5** (of an animal) marked with white, esp. on the face. □ **bald eagle** an eagle with white feathers on its head and neck, the emblem of the USA. □ □ **baldly** *adv.* **baldness** *n.*

Balder / **bol**-duh, **bahl**-duh / *Scand. myth.* the beautiful young God of the Summer Sun, a son of Odin.

balderdash *n.* nonsense.

balding *adj.* becoming bald.

baldy *n.* **1** *Aust.* a Hereford. **2** any white-faced beast. • *adj.* **1** *Aust.* Hereford (*a mob of baldy bullocks*). **2** (of cattle) with white markings on the face.

bale[1] *n.* **1** a large bundle of straw etc. bound with cord or wire. **2** a large package of goods. • *v.* make into a bale. □ **bale out** make a parachute descent from an aircraft in an emergency.

bale[2] alternative spelling of BAIL[3].

baleen / buh-**leen** / *n.* whalebone.

baleful *adj.* menacing; destructive (*a baleful look*). □ **balefully** *adv.*

Bali / **bah**-lee / an island of Indonesia. □ **Bali belly** *colloq.* a diarrhoea caught by a tourist in Bali or elsewhere in Asia. Also known as a *Delhi belly.* □ □ **Balinese** *adj.* & *n.*

balk alternative spelling of BAULK.

Balkan / **bawl**-kuhn / *adj.* of the peninsula in SE Europe bounded by the Adriatic, Aegean, and Black Seas, or of its people or countries. • *n.* (**the Balkans**) the Balkan countries.

ball[1] *n.* **1** a solid or hollow sphere. **2** a single delivery of the ball by the bowler in cricket or by the pitcher in baseball. **3** a rounded part (*the ball*

ball of the foot). **4** (**balls**) *coarse colloq.* the testicles. **5** (**balls**) *coarse colloq.* courage, 'guts'. **6** (**balls**) (usu. as *interj.*) *coarse colloq.* nonsense. • *v.* form into a ball. ◻ **ball-and-socket joint** a joint in which a rounded end lies in a concave socket, allowing wide movement. **ball bearing** *n.* a bearing using small steel balls; one of these balls. **ball game 1** a game played with a ball. **2** *colloq.* a situation; a matter (*a whole new ball game*). **ball up** *Aust. Rules* the bouncing of the ball by the field umpire to start or restart play. **balls up** *v. colloq.* bungle, make a mess of. **balls-up** *n. colloq.* something done badly; a mess. **on the ball** *colloq.* alert, competent. **start the ball rolling** start a discussion or activity.

ball[2] *n.* a formal social gathering for dancing. ◻ **have a ball** *colloq.* enjoy oneself.

ballad *n.* **1** a simple song or poem; one telling a story. **2** a slow sentimental song.

ballade / ba-**lahd** / *n.* a poem with sets of three verses each ending with the same refrain line.

ballast / **bal**-uhst / *n.* **1** heavy material placed in a ship's hold to improve its stability. **2** coarse stones etc. forming the bed of a railway or road. **3** a device to stabilise current in an electric circuit.

ballcock *n.* a device with a floating ball controlling the water level in a toilet cistern.

ballerina / bal-uh-**ree**-nuh / *n.* a female ballet dancer.

ballet / **bal**-ay / *n.* a form of dancing and mime to music; a performance of this. ◻ **balletic** / buh-**let**-ik / *adj.*

ballistic / buh-**lis**-tik / *adj.* of projectiles such as bullets and missiles. • *n.* (**ballistics**) (usu. treated as *sing.*) the scientific study of projectiles and firearms. ◻ **ballistic missile** a missile that is powered and directed at its launch stage and falls by gravity onto its target. **go ballistic** *colloq.* become furious.

balloon *n.* **1** a small inflatable rubber bag, used as a child's toy or a decoration. **2** a large inflatable sphere often carrying a basket in which passengers may ride. **3** a balloon-shaped line enclosing the words or thoughts of a character in a comic strip or cartoon. • *v.* swell like a balloon.

balloonist *n.* a person who travels by balloon.

ballot *n.* **1** the process of (usually secret) voting by means of papers or tokens. **2** a paper or token used in this. **3** the number of such votes recorded. • *v.* (**balloted**, **balloting**) **1** vote by ballot. **2** take a ballot of (*balloting their members*). ◻ **ballot box** a container for ballot papers. **ballot paper** a paper used in voting by ballot.

ballpoint *n.* (in full **ballpoint pen**) a pen with a tiny ball as its writing point.

ballroom *n.* a large room where dances are held. ◻ **ballroom dancing** formal social dancing for couples; e.g. the waltz, foxtrot, etc.

ballyhoo *n.* **1** loud noise; fuss. **2** extravagant publicity.

balm / bahm / *n.* **1** = BALSAM (sense 1). **2** a fragrant ointment. **3** a healing or soothing influence. **4** (also **lemon balm**) a herb with lemon-scented leaves.

Balmain bug / **bal**-mayn / *n.* an edible marine crustacean (of southern Australian waters) having an oddly flattened body.

balmy / **bah**-mee / *adj.* (**balmier**, **balmiest**) **1** like balm, fragrant. **2** soft and warm (*balmy air*).

baloney / buh-**loh**-nee / *n.* (also **boloney**) *colloq.* nonsense.

balsa / **bawl**-suh, **bol**-suh / *n.* (also **balsa wood**) very lightweight wood from a tropical American tree.

balsam / **bawl**-suhm, **bol**-suhm / *n.* **1** a fragrant medicinal gum exuded by certain trees. **2** a tree producing this. **3** a kind of flowering plant. ◻ **balsamic** / -**sam**-ik / *adj.*

balsamic vinegar *n.* an Italian vinegar made from wines and musts and aged in wooden casks.

Baltic / **bawl**-tik, **bol**-tik / *adj.* of the **Baltic Sea**, an almost land-locked sea of NE Europe. • *n.* the Baltic Sea.

baluster / **bal**-uh-stuh / *n.* a short post or pillar supporting a rail.

balustrade / bal-uh-**strayd** / *n.* a row of short posts or pillars supporting a rail or stone coping round a balcony or terrace.

Balzac / **bal**-zak /, Honoré de (1799–1850), French novelist.

Bama / **bam**-uh / *n.* (also **Pama**) an Aborigine. (¶ Many north Qld languages *bama* 'person, man.')

■ **Usage** *See* KOORI.

Bamako / **bam**-uh-koh / the capital of Mali.

bamboo / bam-**boo** / *n.* a giant tropical woody grass with hollow stems. ◻ **bamboo shoot** the young shoot of a bamboo, eaten as a vegetable.

bamboozle *v. colloq.* **1** hoax, cheat. **2** mystify. ◻ **bamboozlement** *n.*

ban *v.* (**banned**, **banning**) forbid officially. • *n.* an order that bans something.

banal / buh-**nahl** / *adj.* commonplace, uninteresting. ◻ **banality** *n.*

banana *n.* the finger-shaped fruit of a tropical tree. ◻ **banana bender** *Aust. colloq.* a Queenslander (one who puts the bend in the bananas). **banana kick** *Aust. Rules* a shot at goal from a difficult angle in which the ball describes an arc. **banana prawn** a large Australian prawn with banana-like coloration. **banana republic** *derog.* a small country dependent on foreign capital and regarded as economically unstable. **go bananas** *colloq.* go crazy.

Bananaland *n. Aust. colloq.* Queensland. ◻ **Bananalander** *n.*

band *n.* **1** a narrow strip, hoop, or loop. **2** a range of values, wavelengths, etc. within a series. **3** an organised group of people with a common purpose. **4** a set of people playing music together.

bandage

• *v.* **1** put a band of metal, paper, etc. on or round. **2** unite in an organised group (*they banded together*).

bandage *n.* a strip of material for binding up a wound. •*v.* bind up with this.

bandaid *adj.* temporary; makeshift; of the nature of a patch-up (*bandaid solutions to the unemployment problem*). (¶ Band-Aid *trademark* a small adhesive patch for a superficial wound.)

bandanna / ban-**dan**-uh / *n.* a large coloured handkerchief or scarf.

Bandaranaike / bun-dah-ruh-**nah**-yuh-kuh /, Sirimavo Ratwatte Dias (1916–2000), Sinhalese stateswoman, prime minister of Sri Lanka 1960–65 and 1970–77, the world's first woman prime minister.

Bandar Seri Begawan / ban-dah se-ree buh-**gah**-wuhn / the capital of Brunei.

b & b *abbr.* bed and breakfast.

bandeau / ban-**doh** / *n.* (*pl.* **bandeaux** / ban-**dohz** /) a strip of material worn round the head.

bandicoot *n.* **1** any of various cat-sized Australian marsupials with a long, pointed head, nocturnal in habit. **2** a very large cat-sized rat of Sri Lanka and India. •*v. Aust.* fossick, esp. in a previously worked mining area. ☐ **as bald as a bandicoot** *Aust. colloq.* totally bald. **as lousy as a bandicoot** *Aust. colloq.* stingy, utterly mean. **as miserable as a bandicoot** *Aust. colloq.* thoroughly wretched; destitute.

bandit *n.* a member of a band of robbers. ☐ **banditry** *n.*

Bandjalang / **ban**-ju-lang / *n.* an Aboriginal language of a large area covering north-eastern NSW and south-eastern Qld.

Bandler, Faith (1918–), AM, Australian writer and Aboriginal activist, daughter of an Aboriginal mother and New Hebridean islander father (brought to the Queensland canefields by blackbirders in 1883).

bandmaster *n.* the conductor of a musical band.

bandolier / ban-duh-**leer** / *n.* (also **bandoleer**) a shoulder belt with loops for ammunition.

bandsaw *n.* a power saw consisting of a toothed steel belt running over wheels.

bandsman *n.* a member of a jazz band, brass band, etc.

bandstand *n.* a covered outdoor platform for a musical band.

bandwagon *n.* ☐ **climb** (*or* **jump**) **on the bandwagon** join a party, cause, or group that seems likely to succeed; get in on the winning side.

bandwidth *n.* a range of frequencies in telecommunications etc.

bandy *v.* (**bandied, bandying**) **1** pass to and fro (*the story was bandied about*). **2** exchange (words) in quarrelling. • *adj.* (**bandier, bandiest**) (of legs) curving apart at the knees. ☐ **bandy-legged** *adj.* having bandy legs. ☐☐ **bandiness** *n.*

banker

bandy-bandy *n.* either of two small venomous Australian snakes patterned with black and white bands around the body. (¶ Probably Kattang)

bane *n.* a cause of trouble, misery, or anxiety. ☐ **baneful** *adj.*

bang *v.* **1** make a sudden loud noise like an explosion. **2** strike or shut noisily. **3** (foll. by *into, against*, etc.) collide with, bump into. **4** *coarse colloq.* have sexual intercourse (with). •*n.* **1** a sudden loud noise of or like an explosion. **2** a sharp blow. •*adv.* **1** with a bang, abruptly (*bang go my chances*). **2** *colloq.* exactly (*bang in the middle*). ☐ **bang on** *colloq.* exactly right. **go with a bang** be very successful or impressive.

bangalay / **bang**-guh-lay / *n.* a shady gum tree of NSW and Vic. (¶ Probably from Dharawal.)

bangalow / **bang**-guh-loh / *n.* a tall palm of NSW and Qld, having arching feather-like fronds, lilac flowers, and bright red fruits. (¶ Dharawal)

banger *n.* **1** *colloq.* a sausage. **2** alternative spelling of BUNGER.

Banggala / **bung**-gu-lu / *n.* an Aboriginal language of southern SA.

Bangkok / bang-**kok** / the capital of Thailand.

Bangladesh / bung-gluh-**desh** / a republic in SE Asia bordering on northern India. ☐ **Bangladeshi** *adj.* & *n.*

bangle *n.* a rigid bracelet or anklet.

Bangui / **bang**-gee / the capital of the Central African Republic.

banian alternative spelling of BANYAN.

banish *v.* **1** condemn to exile. **2** dismiss from one's presence or one's mind (*banish care*). ☐ **banishment** *n.*

banister *n.* (also **bannister**) **1** each of the uprights supporting the handrail of a stair. **2** (**banisters**) these uprights and the rail together.

banjo / **ban**-joh / *n.* (*pl.* **banjos**) a stringed instrument like a guitar with a circular body.

Banjul / ban-**jool** / the capital of Gambia.

bank[1] *n.* **1** a slope, especially at the side of a river. **2** a raised mass of sand etc. in a river bed. **3** a long mass of cloud, snow, or other soft substance. **4** a row or series of lights, switches, etc. •*v.* **1** (often foll. by *up*) build or form a bank (*bank up the fire*). **2** (of a motorcycle, aircraft, etc.) tilt or be tilted sideways in rounding a curve. ☐ **bank up** pile up, accumulate (*the traffic had banked up bumper to bumper because of the accident*). **bank-up** an accumulation; a backlog.

bank[2] *n.* **1** an establishment for depositing, withdrawing, and borrowing money. **2** the money held by the banker in some gambling games. **3** a place for storing a reserve supply (*a blood bank*). •*v.* **1** place or keep money in a bank. **2** (foll. by *on*) base one's hopes on (*we are banking on your success*).

bankcard *n.* a credit card issued by a bank.

banker[1] *n.* **1** a person who runs a bank. **2** the keeper of a bank in some gambling games. ☐ **banker's order** an instruction to a bank to make regular fixed payments from an account usu. to another party.

banker[2] *n. Aust.* a river flooded to the top of its banks. ☐ **run a banker** *v.* (of a river) swell to the top of, or over, its banks.

banking *n.* the business of running a bank.

banknote *n.* a piece of paper money.

bankrupt *n.* **1** a person who is unable to pay his or her debts in full and whose assets are administered and distributed for the benefit of creditors. **2** a person exhausted of or deficient in a certain attribute (*a moral bankrupt*). •*adj.* **1** declared by a lawcourt to be a bankrupt. **2** (often foll. by *of*) exhausted or drained (of some quality etc.); deficient, lacking (*bankrupt of ideas; morally bankrupt*). •*v.* make bankrupt. ☐ **bankruptcy** *n.*

Banks, Sir Joseph (1743–1820), English naturalist who joined Cook's *Endeavour* voyage in 1768 and made botanical records, observations, and collections in eastern Australia. The genus *Banksia* was named after him.

banksia *n.* any tree or shrub of the Australian genus *Banksia* (over 60 species), having usu. leathery leaves and large dense flower-spikes (varying in colour from greenish to yellow to scarlet) which form thick woody cones. ☐ **banksia man** *Aust.* the popular name for the large woody cone of several species of *Banksia*. (¶ May Gibbs, in her books for children, personified the banksia cones as wicked *banksia men*.)

banner *n.* **1** a flag. **2** a strip of cloth bearing an emblem or slogan, hung up or carried in a procession etc. ☐ **banner headline** a large front-page newspaper headline.

bannister alternative spelling of BANISTER.

banns *n.pl.* a public announcement in church of a forthcoming marriage between two named people.

banquet *n.* **1** a sumptuous, esp. formal, feast or dinner. **2** a set-priced meal for a group in a Chinese etc. restaurant, allowing diners to sample a wide range of dishes. •*v.* (**banqueted, banqueting**) take part in a banquet.

banshee / **ban**-shee / *n.* a wailing female spirit (of Irish and Scottish folk tradition) warning of death in a house.

bantam *n.* a small domestic fowl.

bantamweight *n.* a weight in certain sports between featherweight and flyweight, in boxing 51–4 kg.

banter *n.* good-humoured teasing. •*v.* joke in a good-humoured way.

Bantu / ban-**too** / *n.* (*pl.* **Bantu** *or* **Bantus**) (often *offens.*) one of a group of African black peoples or their languages.

banyan *n.* (also **banian**) an Indian fig tree whose branches send roots down to the ground, these roots eventually acquiring the thickness of trunks.

baobab / **bay**-oh-bab / *n.* **1** a tree of north WA with a massive trunk swollen at the base and tangy, yellowish to blue, edible fruits. **2** a related African tree.

baptise *v.* (also **-ize**) **1** administer baptism to. **2** give a name or nickname to.

baptism *n.* the sacrament of symbolic admission to the Christian Church, with the ceremonial use of water and usu. name giving. ☐ **baptism of fire** **1** a soldier's experience of fighting for the first time. **2** a painful first experience. ☐☐ **baptismal** *adj.*

Baptist *n.* **1** a member of a Protestant religious denomination believing that baptism should be by total immersion of the adult being baptised. **2** (**the Baptist**) St John, who baptised Christ.

baptistery / **bap**-tis-tuh-ree / *n.* a building or part of a church used for baptism.

bar *n.* **1** a long piece of solid material. **2** a narrow strip (*bars of colour*). **3** *Aust.* a sandbank. **4** each of the vertical lines dividing a piece of music into equal units; a unit contained by these. **5** a partition (real or imaginary) across a court of justice separating the judge, jury, and certain lawyers from the public. **6** (**the Bar**) barristers. **7** a barrier. **8** a restriction (*colour bar; bar to promotion*). **9** a counter or room where alcohol is served. **10** a place where refreshments are served across a counter (*a snack bar*). **11** a shop counter selling a single type of commodity or service (*bra bar*). **12** a unit of pressure used in meteorology. •*v.* (**barred, barring**) **1** fasten with a bar or bars. **2** keep in or out by this. **3** obstruct (*barred the way*). **4** prevent or prohibit. •*prep.* except (*it's all over bar the shouting*). ☐ **be called to the Bar** become a barrister. **not have a bar of** *Aust. colloq.* be unable to tolerate (a person etc.); dislike intensely; reject utterly (a course of action).

Barak / **ba**-rak /, William (1824–1903), Australian Aboriginal painter and spokesman for the tribes of central and south-western Vic. whose culture he explicated.

Barassi / buh-**ras**-ee /, Ron(ald Dale) (1936–), AM, Australian Rules footballer and coach.

barb *n.* **1** the backward-pointing part of an arrowhead, fish-hook, etc. that makes it difficult to withdraw. **2** a wounding remark. **3** a small pointed projecting part or filament.

Barbados / bah-**bay**-dos / an island nation in the West Indies. ☐ **Barbadian** *adj.* & *n.*

barbarian *n.* an uncivilised person. • *adj.* of barbarians.

barbaric / bah-**ba**-rik / *adj.* suitable for barbarians, rough and wild. ☐ **barbarically** *adv.*

barbarism / **bah**-buh-riz-uhm / *n.* **1** an uncivilised condition or practice. **2** an unacceptable use of words.

barbarity / bah-**ba**-ruh-tee / *n.* savage cruelty; a savagely cruel act.

barbarous / **bah**-buh-ruhs / *adj.* uncivilised, cruel. ☐ **barbarously** *adv.*

Barbary an old name for the western part of North Africa. ☐ **Barbary ape** a macaque of North Africa and Gibraltar.

barbecue / bah-buh-kyoo / (also **barbeque**) *n.* **1** a device for cooking food outdoors consisting of a grid suspended over an open fire or other source of heat. **2** an open-air party at which food is cooked on this. **3** the food itself. • *v.* cook on a barbecue.

barbed *adj.* having a barb or barbs. ☐ **barbed wire** wire with short sharp points at intervals.

barbel *n.* a beard-like filament at the mouth of certain fishes.

barbell *n.* a metal rod used in weightlifting, with adjustable weighted discs at each end.

barber *n.* a men's hairdresser. ☐ **barber-shop** (**quartet**) *n.* close harmony singing for four male voices.

barbican *n.* an outer defence of a castle or city, especially a double tower over a gate or bridge.

barbie *n. Aust. colloq.* a barbecue.

barbiturate / bah-**bich**-uh-ruht / *n.* a sedative drug.

barbituric acid / bah-buh-**choor**-rik / *n.* an acid from which barbiturates are obtained.

Barbuda see ANTIGUA AND BARBUDA.

barcarole / bah-kuh-**rohl** / *n.* (also **barcarolle**) **1** a gondolier's song. **2** a piece of music with a steady lilting rhythm.

barcode *n.* a pattern of stripes (on packaging etc.) containing information for processing by a computer. ☐ **barcoded** *adj.*

Barcoo / bah-**koo** / *adj. Aust.* relating to or characteristic of the remote inland of Australia, its people and its living conditions. ☐ **Barcoo rot** a form of scurvy characterised by chronic sores. **Barcoo sore** an illness characteristic of Barcoo rot. (¶ Barcoo River in western Qld.)

bard *n.* **1** *hist.* a Celtic minstrel. **2** *formal* a poet. **3** a prizewinner at an Eisteddfod. ☐ **bardic** *adj.*

Bardi / bahr-dee / *n.* an Aboriginal language of northern WA.

bardi / bah-dee / *n. Aust.* the edible larva or pupa of a species of beetle or of various species of moth (*see* WITCHETTY). (¶ Nyungar and many other languages in WA and SA.)

Bard of Avon Shakespeare.

Bardot / bah-**doh** /, Brigitte (original name: Camille Javal) (1934–), French film actor.

bare *adj.* **1** without clothing or covering (*the trees were bare; with one's bare hands*). **2** plain, without detail; undisguised (*the bare facts*). **3** empty (*the cupboard was bare*). **4** only just sufficient (*the bare necessities of life*). • *v.* uncover; reveal (*bared his teeth; bared his soul*). ☐ **bareness** *n.*

bareback *adj. & adv.* on a horse without a saddle.

barebelly *n. Aust.* a sheep with bare belly and legs, the result of a defect in the fibre-structure of the wool. ☐ **barebellied** *adj.*

barefaced *adj.* shameless; undisguised.

barefoot *adj. & adv.* wearing nothing on the feet.

bareheaded *adj.* not wearing a hat.

barely *adv.* **1** scarcely, only just. **2** scantily (*barely furnished*).

barf *colloq. v.* vomit. • *n.* an attack of vomiting.

bargain *n.* **1** an agreement. **2** something obtained as a result of this. **3** a thing got cheaply. • *v.* discuss the terms of an agreement. ☐ **bargain for** (*or* **on**) be prepared for, expect (*didn't bargain on his arriving so early; got more than he bargained for*). **into the bargain** in addition to other things.

barge *n.* a large flat-bottomed boat for use on canals or rivers, especially for carrying goods. • *v.* move clumsily or heavily. ☐ **barge in** intrude.

bargepole *n.* a long pole for pushing from a barge. ☐ **would not touch with a bargepole** *colloq.* refuse to have anything to do with.

barista / buh-**ris**-tuh / *n.* (*pl.* **baristas** *or* **baristi**) a person who makes coffee (esp. espresso) professionally. (¶ Italian, = bartender.)

baritone *n.* **1** a male voice between tenor and bass. **2** a singer with such a voice; a part written for this.

barium / **bair**-ree-uhm / *n.* a chemical element (symbol Ba), a soft silvery-white metal. ☐ **barium meal** a mixture of barium sulphate and water swallowed to reveal the stomach and intestines in X-rays.

bark¹ *n.* the outer layer of tree trunks and branches. • *v.* **1** peel bark from. **2** scrape the skin off accidentally (*barked my knuckles*). ☐ **bark painting** *Aust.* a picture painted on bark as part of the ceremonial art of Arnhem Land Aborigines; now a widely practised Aboriginal art form.

bark² *n.* **1** the sharp explosive cry of a dog etc. **2** a sound like this (*a short bark of laughter*). • *v.* **1** make this sound. **2** speak in a sharp commanding voice (*barked out orders*). ☐ **barking lizard** *Aust.* any of several lizards which make barking noises. **barking spider** *Aust.* a spider which utters a loud whistling sound and which is also reputed to bark. **bark up the wrong tree** direct one's effort or complaint in the wrong direction.

barker *n.* a tout outside a nightclub, at a side-show, etc.

barley *n.* a cereal plant; its grain. ☐ **barley sugar** a sweet made of boiled sugar.

barleycorn *n.* a grain of barley.

barm *n.* froth on fermenting malt liquor.

bar mitzvah / **mits**-vuh / *n.* **1** a Jewish boy aged 13, when he takes on the responsibilities of an adult under Jewish law. **2** the solemnisation of this event by calling upon the boy to read from the Scriptures in a synagogue service. (¶ Hebrew, = son of commandment.)

barmy *adv. colloq.* crazy; stupid.

barn *n.* a simple roofed building for storing grain etc. on a farm. ☐ **barn dance** a kind of country dance; a social gathering for dancing, originally held in a barn.

barnacle *n.* a shellfish that attaches itself to objects under water.

Barnard, Christiaan (Neethling) (1922–), South African surgeon, pioneer of human heart transplantation (1967).

Barnardo, Thomas John (1845–1905), British philanthropist, founder of a chain of homes for destitute children.

barney *n. colloq.* a noisy quarrel. • *v.* argue, quarrel.

barnstorm *v.* tour rural districts as an actor or political campaigner. ☐ **barnstormer** *n.*

barnyard *n.* a yard beside a barn.

barograph / **ba**-ruh-grahf, -graf / *n.* a barometer that produces a graph showing the atmospheric pressure.

barometer / buh-**rom**-uh-tuh / *n.* an instrument measuring atmospheric pressure, used for forecasting the weather. ☐ **barometric** / ba-ruh-**met**-rik / *adj.*

baron *n.* **1** a member of the lowest rank of the nobility. **2** a powerful businessman, entrepreneur, etc. (*beer baron; a newspaper baron*). ☐ **baronial** / buh-**roh**-nee-uhl / *adj.*

baroness *n.* **1** a woman holding the rank of baron. **2** a baron's wife or widow.

baronet *n.* a holder of a British hereditary title ranking below a baron but above a knight, having the title 'Sir'. ☐ **baronetcy** *n.*

baroque / buh-**rok**, buh-**rohk** / *adj.* of the ornate architectural style of the 17th and 18th centuries, or of comparable musical developments from about 1600 to 1750 (the death of J.S. Bach). • *n.* this style of ornamentation.

Barossa Valley a valley in the Mount Lofty Ranges in SA in which are a number of Australia's finest vineyards.

barouche / buh-**roosh** / *n.* a four-wheeled horse-drawn carriage with seats for two couples facing each other.

barque / bark / *n.* a sailing ship with the rear mast fore-and-aft rigged and other masts square-rigged. **2** *poet.* a boat.

barrack[1] *n.* (usu. in *pl.*, often treated as *sing.*) **1** a large building or group of buildings for soldiers to live in. **2** a large, plain, and ugly building. • *v.* lodge (soldiers etc.) in barracks.

barrack[2] *v.* **1** shout or jeer at (players, a speaker, etc.). **2** (foll. by *for*) *Aust.* cheer for, encourage (a team etc.).

barracouta / ba-ruh-**koo**-tuh / *n.* (*pl.* **barracouta** *or* **barracoutas**) a long slender fish of southern oceans, including those of southern Australia.

barracuda / ba-ruh-**koo**-duh / *n.* (*pl.* **barracuda** *or* **barracudas**) a large tropical marine fish.

barrage / **ba**-rah*zh* / *n.* **1** an artificial barrier, especially one damming a river. **2** a heavy continuous bombardment by artillery. **3** a rapid fire of questions or comments.

barramundi / ba-ruh-**mun**-dee / *n.* (*pl.* **barramundi** *or* **barramundis**) any of various Australian fishes of tropical rivers and estuaries, all highly valued for eating. (¶ Probably from an Aboriginal language of central Qld.)

barratry / **ba**-ruh-tree / *n.* fraud or gross negligence by a ship's master or crew at the expense of the owner or user.

barre *n.* a horizontal bar used by ballet dancers while exercising.

barrel *n.* **1** a large round container with flat ends. **2** the amount this contains; (as a measure of mineral oil) about 159 litres (35 gallons). **3** a tube-like part, especially of a gun. • *v.* (**barrelled**, **barrelling**) **1** put into a barrel or barrels. **2** *colloq.* (often foll. by *along*) drive fast. **3** *colloq.* fell or flatten (a person). **4** *colloq.* (often foll. by *away*) press, demand, etc., persistently. ☐ **barrel organ** a mechanical musical instrument, played by turning a handle to rotate a pin-studded cylinder which acts on keys, pipes, or strings to sound notes. **over a barrel** *colloq.* in a helpless position.

barren *adj.* **1** not fertile enough to produce crops (*barren land*). **2** not producing fruit or seeds (*a barren tree*). **3** unable to have young. **4** unproductive; unstimulating. ☐ **barrenness** *n.*

barricade *n.* a barrier, especially one hastily erected as a defence. • *v.* block or defend with a barricade.

barrier *n.* **1** a fence etc. that bars advance or access. **2** an obstacle or circumstance that keeps people or things apart, or prevents communication (*class barriers; language barrier*). ☐ **barrier reef** a coral reef with a channel between it and the land.

Barrier Reef see GREAT BARRIER REEF.

barring *prep.* except, not including.

barrister / **ba**-ruh-stuh / *n.* a lawyer entitled to practise as an advocate in any court.

barrow *n.* **1** a wheelbarrow. **2** a small cart with two wheels, pulled or pushed by hand. **3** a prehistoric burial mound.

bartender *n.* a person who serves drinks behind a bar.

barter *v.* trade by exchanging goods etc. for other goods, not for money. • *n.* trading by exchange.

Bartholomew[1], St (1st century), one of the twelve Apostles.

Bartholomew[2], Wayne ('Rabbit') (1955–), Australian surfer, world champion in 1978.

Bartók / **bah**-tok /, Béla (1881–1945), Hungarian composer.

Barton, Sir Edmund (1849–1920), Australian statesman and judge. He was Australia's first prime minister (1901–03).

baryon / **ba**-ree-on / *n.* a heavy elementary particle of mass equal to or greater than a proton.

baryta / buh-**ruy**-tuh / *n.* barium oxide or hydroxide.

barytes / buh-**ruy**-teez / *n.* barium sulphate, used in some white paints.

BAS *abbr.* business activity statement, a compliance statement by means of which a business reports its obligations to the Australian Taxation Office.

basal / **bay**-suhl / *adj.* of, at, or forming the base of something.

basalt / **ba**-sawlt / *n.* a dark rock of volcanic origin. □ **basaltic** / buh-**sawl**-tik / *adj.*

base *n.* **1** the lowest part of anything; the part on which it rests or is supported. **2** a starting point. **3** the headquarters of an expedition or other enterprise. **4** a substance into which other things are mixed (*some paints have an oil base*). **5** a cream or liquid applied to the skin as a foundation for make-up. **6** a substance (e.g. an alkali) capable of combining with an acid to form a salt. **7** each of the four stations to be reached by a runner in baseball. **8** the number on which a system of counting is based (e.g. 10 in decimal counting). • *v.* use as a base or foundation or as evidence for a forecast. • *adj.* **1** dishonourable (*base motives*). **2** of inferior value (*base metals*). **3** debased, not of acceptable quality (*base coins*). □ **baseness** *n.*

baseball *n.* a team game in which runs are scored by hitting a ball and running round a series of four bases.

baseless *adj.* without foundation (*baseless rumours*).

baseline *n.* **1** a line used as a base or starting point. **2** the line at each end of a tennis court.

basement *n.* the lowest storey of a building, below ground level.

bases *see* BASIS.

bash *v.* **1** strike violently. **2** attack with blows, words, or hostile actions. • *n.* a violent blow or knock. □ **have** (*or* **give it**) **a bash** *colloq.* have (or give it) a try.

bashful *adj.* shy and self-conscious. □ **bashfully** *adv.* **bashfulness** *n.*

BASIC *n.* a computer programming language using familiar English words. (¶ From the initials of Beginners' All-purpose Symbolic Instruction Code.)

basic *adj.* forming a base or starting point, fundamental (*basic principles; basic rates of pay*). • *n.pl.* (**basics**) basic facts or principles etc. □ **basic wage** *Aust.* the minimum living wage for an adult unskilled worker as determined by an industrial tribunal. □ □ **basically** *adv.*

Basil, St, 'the Great' (*c.*330–79), Greek bishop, whose monastic rule is the basis of that followed in the Orthodox Church.

basil *n.* a sweet-smelling herb.

basilica / buh-**zil**-i-kuh, -**sil**- / *n.* **1** an ancient Roman hall with an apse and colonnades, used as a lawcourt etc. **2** a (usu. large) Christian church having special privileges from the Pope. **3** a church (usu. ancient) which has the nave on a higher elevation than the aisles.

basilisk / **baz**-uh-lisk, **bas**- / *n.* a mythical reptile with keen eyesight and advanced halitosis: its glance causes instant death and its breath causes death by slow degrees.

basin *n.* **1** a round open dish. **2** the amount a basin contains. **3** a washbasin. **4** a sunken place where water collects; the area drained by a river. **5** an almost landlocked harbour (*a yacht basin*). □ **basinful** *n.* (*pl.* **basinfuls**).

basis *n.* (*pl.* **bases** / **bay**-seez /) a foundation or support; a main principle.

bask *v.* **1** expose oneself comfortably to a pleasant warmth. **2** (foll. by *in*) enjoy (approval, success, etc.) (*basking in glory*).

basket *n.* **1** a container made of interwoven cane, wire, etc. **2** this with its contents. **3** the hoop through which players try to throw the ball in basketball; a point scored in this way. **4** an assorted set (*a basket of currencies*). □ **basket case** *colloq.* a mentally disturbed or eccentric person. **basket weave** a weave resembling basketwork.

basketball *n.* a team game in which points are scored by putting the ball through a high hoop.

basketful *n.* (*pl.* **basketfuls**) the amount a basket will hold.

basketry *n.* basketwork.

basketwork *n.* the craft of weaving baskets; the work produced.

basmati / bas-**mah**-tee, baz- / *n.* (in full **basmati rice**) a superior kind of Indian rice. (¶ Hindi, = fragrant.)

Basque / bahsk / *n.* **1** a member of a people living in the western Pyrenees area of Spain and France. **2** their language.

bas-relief / **bas**-ruh-leef / *n.* a sculpture or carving with figures projecting slightly from the background.

Bass / bas /, George (1771–*c.*1803), English naval surgeon and explorer who explored much of the south-eastern coast of Australia. *Bass Strait* was named in his honour.

bass[1] / bas / *n.* (*pl.* **bass**) **1** a marine fish of eastern Australian waters. **2** a freshwater fish of eastern Australia. **3** a Northern hemisphere fish of the perch family.

bass[2] / bays / *adj.* deep-sounding; of the lowest pitch in music. • *n.* **1** the lowest male voice; a singer with such a voice; a part written for this. **2** the lowest-pitched member of a group of similar musical instruments. **3** *colloq.* a double bass; a bass guitar. □ **bass clef** *Music* a clef placing F below middle C on the second highest line of the stave.

basset / **bas**-uht / *n.* (also **basset hound**) a long-bodied short-legged hound.

bassinet *n.* a baby's (usu. wicker) cradle or carrying basket.

basso *n.* (*pl.* **bassos** *or* **bassi**) a singer with a bass voice.

bassoon / buh-**soon** / *n.* a deep-toned woodwind instrument. □ **bassoonist** *n.*

Bass Strait / bas / a strait between the Australian mainland and Tasmania.

bast *n.* fibrous material obtained from the inner bark of the lime-tree or other sources, used for matting etc.

bastard *n.* (often *offens.*) **1** person born of an unmarried mother. **2** *colloq.* used variously of a person in Australia: sometimes *derog.* (but without any suggestion of illegitimacy), frequently good-humoured if sometimes edged, often even affectionate: **a** an unpleasant or despicable person. **b** a person of a specified kind (*poor bastard; lucky bastard*). **c** any person. **d** a mate (*c'mon, you bastard, let's get going!*). **3** *colloq.* a difficult or awkward or unpleasant thing. •*adj.* **1** of illegitimate birth. **2** hybrid. **3** (of a plant or animal in Australia) resembling the foreign species whose name is taken (*bastard mahogany; bastard dory*). ☐ **bastardy** *n.* (in sense 1 of noun).

bastardisation *n.* (also **-ization**) *Aust.* (in certain educational institutions, the armed services, etc.) the ritual physical and psychological harassment of those newly enrolled.

bastardise *v.* (also **-ize**) **1** corrupt; debase. **2** *Aust.* initiate into a school, regiment, etc., by practising bastardisation.

bastardry / **bah**-stuhd-ree / *n. Aust.* cruel, despicable, or malicious behaviour.

baste / bayst / *v.* **1** sew together temporarily with long loose stitches; tack. **2** moisten (meat) with fat etc. during cooking.

Bastille / bas-**teel** / *hist.* a prison in Paris: its storming on 14 July 1789 marked the start of the French Revolution. ☐ **Bastille Day** the anniversary of this event, kept as a national holiday in France.

bastinado / bas-tuh-**nay**-doh / *n.* a form of torture, the victim being caned on the soles of the feet. •*v.* torture a person in this way.

bastion / **bas**-tee-uhn / *n.* **1** a projecting part of a fortification. **2** a fortified place near hostile territory. **3** something serving as a stronghold (*a bastion of democracy*).

bat[1] *n.* **1** a shaped wooden implement for striking the ball in games. **2** a turn at using this. **3** a batsman. •*v.* (**batted**, **batting**) **1** use a bat. **2** strike with a bat; hit. ☐ **off one's own bat** without prompting or help from another person.

bat[2] *n.* a small flying mammal with a mouselike body.

bat[3] *v.* flutter (*it batted its wings*). ☐ **not bat an eyelid** show no reaction or emotion.

batch[1] *n.* **1** a number of things produced at the same time. **2** a number of people or things dealt with as a group. •*v.* group (items) for batch processing. ☐ **batch processing** the processing by a computer etc. of similar transactions in batches in order to make economical use of time.

batch[2] *v.* (also **bach**; **batch it**) *colloq.* live on one's own; provide for oneself (in a rough and ready way, without the usual domestic conveniences). (¶ From *bachelor*.)

bated / **bay**-tuhd / *adj.* ☐ **with bated breath** very anxiously.

Bates, Daisy May (1863–1951), Irish-born journalist and social worker among Australian Aborigines from about 1899 onwards. From 1912 to 1945 she mostly lived among the Aborigines.

bath *n.* **1** a (usu. plumbed-in) container for sitting in and washing the body all over; its contents; the act of washing the body in this. **2** a liquid in which something is immersed; its container. **3** (**baths**) a public building with baths or a swimming pool. •*v.* wash (especially a baby) in a bath.

bathe *v.* **1** immerse oneself in water, esp. to swim or wash oneself. **2** immerse in, wash, or treat with liquid (*he bathed his sore eyes*). **3** make wet or bright all over (*fields were bathed in sunlight*).

bathers *n.pl. Aust.* a swimming costume.

bathos / **bay**-thos / *n.* a lapse in mood from the sublime to the absurd or trivial; an anticlimax. ☐ **bathetic** *adj.*

bathrobe *n.* a dressing gown, especially one made of towelling.

bathroom *n.* **1** a room containing a bath, wash basin, etc. **2** a room with a toilet.

Bathsheba / bath-**shee**-buh / the wife of Uriah the Hittite (2 Sam. 11). King David desired her and so caused Uriah to be killed in battle. David then took her to wife. She became the mother of King Solomon.

Bathurst Island a mangrove-bordered island of about 2600 square kilometres some 80 kilometres north of Darwin. The entire island is an Aboriginal reserve and is the home of the Tiwi people.

bathyscaphe / **bath**-ee-skayf / *n.* a manned vessel for deep-sea diving, with special buoyancy gear.

bathysphere / **bath**-ee-sfeer / *n.* a spherical diving vessel for deep-sea observation.

batik / ba-**teek**, **bah**-tik / *n.* **1** a method (originating in Java) of printing coloured designs on textiles by waxing the parts not to be dyed. **2** fabric treated in this way.

batiste / ba-**teest** / *n.* a very soft fine woven fabric.

Batman, John (1801–39), Australian farmer and pioneer, a founder of Melbourne. He explored the Port Phillip district and was the first to recognise the potential of the site now occupied by Melbourne.

batman *n.* (*pl.* **batmen**) a soldier acting as an army officer's personal servant.

bat mitzvah / baht **mits**-vuh / *n.* a religious initiation ceremony for a Jewish girl aged twelve years and one day, regarded as the age of religious maturity.

baton / **bat**-uhn, buh-**ton** / *n.* **1** a short thick stick, especially one serving as a symbol of

batrachian | 62 | **Bayreuth**

authority; a truncheon. **2** a thin stick used by the conductor of an orchestra for beating time. **3** a short stick or tube carried in relay races.

batrachian / buh-**tray**-kee-uhn / *n.* an amphibian (such as a frog or toad) that discards its gills and tail when adult.

bats *adj. colloq.* crazy.

batsman *n.* (*pl.* **batsmen**) a player who is batting in cricket or baseball; one who specialises in batting.

batt *n.* insulation material (e.g. fibreglass) packed into a usu. rectangular shape ready for installation in ceilings etc.

battalion *n.* an army unit made up of several companies and forming part of a regiment.

batten *n.* a strip of wood or metal fastening or holding something in place. • *v.* **1** fasten with battens; close securely (*batten down the hatches*). **2** feed greedily; thrive or prosper at the expense of others or so as to injure them (*galahs battening on the crops*).

batter[1] *v.* hit hard and often; subject to repeated violence (*battered babies; battered wives*). • *n.* a beaten mixture of flour, eggs, and milk, for cooking. ☐ **batterer** *n.*

batter[2] *n. Sport* a player batting.

battering ram *n.* an iron-headed beam, originally with the striking end in the form of a ram's head, formerly used in war to breach walls or gates by battering them.

battery *n.* **1** a group of big guns on land or on a warship. **2** an artillery unit of guns, men, and vehicles. **3** a set of similar or connected units of equipment, or of cages for the intensive breeding of poultry etc. **4** an electric cell or group of cells supplying current. **5** *Law* unlawful physical violence against a person.

battle *n.* **1** a fight between large organised forces. **2** any struggle or contest (*a battle of wits*). • *v.* **1** engage in battle with. **2** struggle persistently against (*battling Aids; battling for women's rights*). ☐ **battle royal 1** a fight involving a lot of people. **2** a heated and prolonged argument.

battleaxe *n.* **1** a heavy axe used as a weapon in ancient times. **2** *colloq. derog.* a formidable aggressive woman.

battlecry *n.* a war cry; a slogan.

battledore *n.* a small racquet used with a shuttlecock in the ancient volleying game **battledore and shuttlecock.**

battledress *n.* the everyday uniform of a soldier.

battlefield *n.* a place where a battle is fought.

battleground *n.* a battlefield.

battlements *n.pl.* a parapet with gaps at intervals, originally for firing from.

battler *n. Aust.* a person who strives long and hard and doggedly against the odds (*little Aussie battler*).

battleship *n.* the most heavily armed kind of warship.

batty *adj. colloq.* crazy.

batwing *adj.* (of a sleeve) triangular in shape, narrow at the wrist and wide at the top.

bauble *n.* a showy but valueless ornament or fancy article.

Baudelaire / boh-duh-**lair** /, Charles (1821–67), French poet and critic.

bauera / **bow**uh-ruh / *n.* any shrub of the Australian genus *Bauera*, having a spreading habit and often extremely showy flowers.

Bauhaus / **bow**-hows / a German school of architecture and design established in 1919.

bauhinia / boh-**hin**-ee-uh / *n.* a deciduous shrub or small tree of mainly Qld which, when leafless, has masses of white flowers yielding a sweet nectar used as a drink by the Aborigines.

baulk / bawk / (also **balk**) *v.* **1** shirk, jib at (*baulked the problem; the horse baulked at the fence*). **2** frustrate, thwart; disappoint (*baulked in his ambition; her hopes were baulked*). • *n.* **1** a stumbling block, a hindrance. **2** a roughly squared timber beam. **3** the area of a billiard table within which the cue balls are placed at the start of a game.

bauxite / **bawk**-suyt / *n.* the clay-like substance from which aluminium is obtained.

bawdy *adj.* (**bawdier**, **bawdiest**) humorous in a coarse or indecent way. ☐ **bawdily** *adv.* **bawdiness** *n.*

bawl *v.* **1** shout or cry loudly. **2** weep noisily, howl. ☐ **bawl out** *colloq.* scold severely.

bay[1] *n.* a laurel with dark green leaves which are used for flavouring food.

bay[2] *n.* part of the sea or of a large lake within a wide curve of the shore.

bay[3] *n.* **1** each of a series of compartments in a building, structure, or area. **2** a recess in a room or building. **3** an area off a road for parking or unloading. ☐ **bay window** a window projecting from the outside wall of a house.

bay[4] *n.* the deep drawn-out cry of a large dog or of hounds in pursuit of a hunted animal. • *v.* make this sound. ☐ **at bay** forced to face attackers in a desperate situation. **keep at bay** hold off (a pursuer).

bay[5] *adj.* reddish-brown. • *n.* a bay horse.

Baynton, Barbara (Jane) (1857–1929), Australian author, esp. known for the collection of stories *Bush Life*, in which the horrors of bush life, especially for women, are depicted with grim realism.

bayonet / **bay**-uh-net, **bay**-nuht, / *n.* a dagger-like blade that can be fixed to the muzzle of a rifle and used in hand-to-hand fighting. • *v.* (**bayoneted**, **bayoneting**) stab with a bayonet. ☐ **bayonet fitting** an electrical fitting pushed into a socket and twisted.

Bayreuth / **buy**-roit / a town in Bavaria closely associated with Wagner. Festivals of his operas are held regularly in a theatre specially built to house the *Ring* Cycle.

bazaar

bazaar *n.* **1** a group of shops or stalls in an Oriental country. **2** a sale of goods to raise funds.

bazooka / buh-**zoo**-kuh / *n.* a portable weapon for firing anti-tank rockets.

BBQ *abbr.* barbecue.

BBS *abbr.* = BULLETIN BOARD SYSTEM.

BC *abbr.* (in dates) before Christ.

BCG *abbr.* Bacillus Calmette-Guérin, an anti-tuberculosis vaccine.

bdellium / **del**-ee-uhm / *n.* **1** a resin used as a perfume. **2** the tree producing this.

Be *symbol* beryllium.

be *v.* (**am**, **are**, **is**; **was**, **were**; **been**, **being**) **1** exist, occur, live; occupy a position. **2** have a certain identity, quality, or condition. **3** become. • *auxiliary v.* used to form parts of other verbs (*it is rising; he was killed*). ▫ **be-all and end-all** the supreme purpose or essence.

beach *n.* the usu. sandy shore of (esp.) the sea; the seashore as a place for sunbathing and other recreation. • *v.* **1** bring on shore from out of the water. **2** (as **beached** *adj.*) (of a whale etc.) stranded out of the water. ▫ **beach bum** *colloq.* a habitual frequenter of beaches, and therefore regarded as lazy etc.

beachcomber / **beech**-koh-muh / *n.* **1** a person who searches beaches for useful or valuable things. **2** a long wave rolling in from the sea.

beachhead *n.* a fortified position set up on a beach by landing forces.

beacon *n.* **1** a fire or light on a hill or tower, used as a signal or warning. **2** a signal station such as a lighthouse.

bead *n.* **1** a small shaped piece of hard material pierced for threading with others on a string, or for sewing on to fabric. **2** a drop of liquid on a surface. **3** a small knob forming the sight of a gun. **4** a strip on the inner edge of a pneumatic tyre, for gripping the wheel. **5** a small round moulding, often applied in moulds like a series of beads. **6** (**beads**) a necklace of beads; a rosary. ▫ **draw a bead on** take aim at.

beaded *adj.* **1** decorated with beads. **2** forming or covered with beads of moisture.

beading *n.* **1** a decoration of beads. **2** a moulding or carving like a series of beads. **3** a strip of wood or plastic with one side rounded, used as a trimming. **4** the bead of a tyre.

beadle *n. hist.* a minor disciplinary officer in a parish.

beady *adj.* like beads; (of eyes) small and bright. ▫ **beadily** *adv.*

beagle *n.* a small short-haired hound used for hunting.

beak *n.* **1** a bird's horny projecting jaws. **2** a similar projection such as the jaw of a turtle or platypus, or the pouring lip of a jug. **3** *colloq.* a person's nose. **4** *colloq.* a magistrate, a judge, or a schoolmaster.

beard

beaker *n.* **1** a small open glass vessel with straight sides and a lip for pouring liquids, used in laboratories. **2** a tall cup or tumbler.

beakie *n.* Aust. *colloq.* a garfish.

beam *n.* **1** a long piece of squared timber or other solid material, supported at both ends and carrying the weight of part of a building or other structure. **2** a narrow, raised horizontal piece of squared timber on which a gymnast balances while performing exercises. **3** a ship's breadth at its widest part. **4** the crosspiece of a balance, from which the scales hang. **5** a ray or stream of light or other radiation; a radio signal used to direct the course of an aircraft. **6** a radiant smile. • *v.* **1** send out (light or other radiation). **2** smile radiantly.

bean *n.* **1** a plant bearing kidney-shaped seeds in long pods. **2** its seed used as a vegetable. **3** a similar seed of coffee and other plants. ▫ **bean curd** a jelly or paste made from soya beans, used esp. in Asian cookery. **bean shoot** (also **bean-sprout**) the sprout of a bean seed, esp. of the mung bean, used in salads and as a vegetable. **full of beans** *colloq.* in high spirits.

beanbag *n.* **1** a small bag filled with dried beans and used for throwing or carrying in games. **2** a large bag filled usu. with polystyrene pieces and used as a seat.

beanfeast *n. colloq.* a celebration.

beanie *n.* a small close-fitting knitted cap.

bear[1] *n.* **1** a large heavy animal with thick fur. **2** a child's cuddly toy like this animal. **3 a** a rough ill-mannered person. **b** *colloq.* a man with a lot of body hair. **4** *Stock Exchange* a person who sells shares, hoping to buy them back more cheaply (cf. BULL sense 4). ▫ **bear hug** a big hug; a tight embrace. **bear market** a situation where share prices are falling rapidly. **Great Bear**, **Little Bear** constellations near the North Pole.

bear[2] *v.* (**bore**, **borne**, **bearing**; *see* the note under BORNE) **1** carry, support. **2** have or show a certain mark or characteristic (*he still bears the scar*). **3** have in one's heart or mind (*bear a grudge; I will bear it in mind*). **4** bring, provide. **5** endure, tolerate (*grin and bear it*). **6** be fit for (*his language won't bear repeating*). **7** produce, give birth to (*land bears crops; she had borne him two sons*). **8** turn, diverge (*bear right when the road forks*). ▫ **bear down** press downwards. **bear down on** move rapidly or purposefully towards. **bear on** be relevant to (*matters bearing on public health*). **bear out** confirm. **bear up** be strong enough not to give way or despair. **bear with** tolerate patiently. **bear witness to** provide evidence of the truth of.

bearable *adj.* able to be borne, endurable. ▫ **bearably** *adv.*

beard *n.* **1** hair on and round a man's chin. **2** a similar hairy or bristly growth of hair on an animal or plant. • *v.* confront boldly (*bearded him in his study*). ▫ **bearded** *adj.*

bearded dragon *n.* a lizard of eastern Australia having large spiny scales on the throat pouch and other parts of the body.

beardie *n. Aust.* = LING (so called because of its beard-like barbels).

bearer *n.* **1** one who carries or bears something (*cheque is payable to bearer*). **2** one who helps to carry something (e.g. a coffin to the grave, a stretcher).

bearing *n.* **1** deportment, behaviour (*soldierly bearing*). **2** relationship, relevance (*it has no bearing on this problem*). **3** a compass direction. **4** a device reducing friction in a part of a machine where another part turns. **5** a heraldic emblem. □ **get one's bearings** find out where one is by recognising landmarks etc.

Béarnaise sauce / *bair*-nayz / *n.* a rich sauce thickened with egg yolks.

bearpit *n.* (also **bear house**) a place (esp. the floor of parliament) where intense debate etc. occurs.

beast *n.* **1** a large four-footed animal. **2** a cruel or disgusting person. **3** *colloq.* a disliked person or thing; something difficult. **4** (**the beast**) the animal nature in humans (*it brought out the beast in him*).

beastly *adj.* (**beastlier, beastliest**) **1** like a beast or its ways. **2** *colloq.* abominable, very unpleasant. • *adv. colloq.* very, unpleasantly (*it was beastly cold*).

beat *v.* (**beat, beaten, beating**) **1** hit repeatedly, especially with a stick. **2** shape or flatten by blows (*beat a path*). **3** mix vigorously to a frothy or smooth consistency (*beat the eggs*). **4** (of the heart) expand and contract rhythmically. **5** overcome, do better than. **6** be too hard for; perplex (*beats me how you can take it lying down*). **7** sail towards the direction from which the wind is blowing, by tacking in alternate directions. • *n.* **1** a regular repeated stroke; a sound of this; recurring emphasis marking rhythm in music or poetry. **2 a** a police officer's route or area; a person's habitual round. **b** *Aust.* a habitual area for making sexual liaisons. • *adj. colloq.* exhausted, tired out. □ **beat about the bush** discuss a subject without coming to the point. **beat a retreat** go away defeated. **beat down 1** cause (a seller) to lower the price by bargaining. **2** (of the sun, rain, etc.) shine or fall fiercely, heavily, etc. **beaten track** a well-worn path (*off the beaten track*). **beat it** *colloq.* go away. **beat off** drive off by fighting. **beat up** assault violently. **beat-up** a highly exaggerated press report.

beater *n.* an implement for beating (eggs, batter, etc.).

beatific / bee-uh-*tif*-ik / *adj.* showing great happiness (*a beatific smile*).

beatification *n.* the Pope's official statement that a dead person is among the Blessed, the final step before canonisation.

beatify / bee-*at*-uh-fy / *v.* (**beatified, beatifying**) honour by beatification.

beatitude / bee-*at*-uh-tyood / *n.* **1** blessedness. **2** (**the Beatitudes**) the declarations made by Christ in the Sermon on the Mount, beginning 'Blessed are...'.

Beatles an English rock group consisting of George Harrison (1943–), John Lennon (1940–80), Paul McCartney (1942–), and Ringo Starr (Richard Starkey, 1940–), whose music and ideas became popular with their generation throughout the world in the 1960s.

beatnik *n.* a member of a movement of socially unconventional young people in the 1950s.

Beatrix / bee-uh-triks / (1938–), (Beatrix Wilhelmina Armgard), Queen of the Netherlands since 1980.

beau / boh / *n.* (*pl.* **beaux** / bohz /) **1** a boyfriend. **2** a fop, a dandy.

Beaufort scale / **boh**-fuht / *n.* a scale and description of wind velocity ranging from 0 (calm) to 12 (hurricane). (¶ Sir Francis Beaufort, English admiral (1774–1857) who devised it)

beaujolais / boh-*zhuh*-lay / *n.* a red or white burgundy wine from Beaujolais, France.

beaut / byoot / *Aust. colloq. n.* an excellent or admirable person or thing. • *adj.* excellent; exciting admiration. □ **you beaut!** an exclamation indicating enthusiastic approval etc.

beauteous *adj. poetic* beautiful.

beautician / byoo-*tish*-uhn / *n.* a person who gives beauty treatment.

beautiful *adj.* **1** having beauty, giving pleasure to the senses or the mind. **2** very satisfactory. □ **beautifully** *adv.*

beautify *v.* (**beautified, beautifying**) make beautiful. □ **beautification** *n.*

beauty *n.* **1** a combination of qualities that give pleasure to the sight or other senses or to the mind. **2** a person or thing having this; a beautiful woman. **3** a fine specimen (*here's a beauty*). **4** a beautiful feature (*that's the beauty of it*). **5** *colloq.* (esp. as *Aust.* **bewdy** / byoo-dee /) (esp. as an exclamation of approval) an excellent specimen (*you bewdy!; gave him a bewdy right in the eye*). • *adj.* (also *Aust.* **bewdy**) *colloq.* excellent; highly pleasing (*bewdy bottler!*). □ **beauty parlour** a beauty salon. **beauty salon** an establishment for giving cosmetic treatments to the face, body, etc. **beauty spot 1** a place with beautiful scenery. **2** a birthmark or artificial patch on the face, said to heighten beauty.

Beauvoir / boh-*vwah* /, Simone de (1908–86), French existentialist novelist and feminist.

beaux *see* BEAU.

beaver *n.* **1** an animal of Europe etc. with soft fur and strong teeth that lives both on land and in water and cuts down trees with its teeth to dam rivers. **2** its brown fur. • *v.* (usu. foll. by *away*) work hard.

Beazley / **bee**-zlee /, Kim (Christian) (1948–), Federal Australian Labor politician who became leader of the opposition in 1996.

bebop *n.* a type of 1940s jazz music.

becalmed / buh-**kahmd** / *adj.* (of a sailing boat) unable to move because there is no wind.

became *see* BECOME.

because *conj.* for the reason that (*did it because I was asked*). ☐ **because of** by reason of, on account of (*because of his age*).

béchamel sauce / **besh**-uh-muhl / *n.* a thick white sauce.

beck *n. archaic* a gesture. ☐ **at someone's beck and call** always ready and waiting to obey his or her orders.

Beckett, Samuel (Barclay) (1906–89), Irish dramatist, novelist, and poet, author of the play *Waiting for Godot*.

beckon *v.* (**beckoned**, **beckoning**) signal or summon by a gesture.

become *v.* (**became**, **become**, **becoming**) **1** come or grow to be; begin to be. **2** look well on, suit (*blue becomes him*). **3** befit (*it ill becomes you to complain*).

becoming *adj.* giving a pleasing appearance or effect, suitable. ☐ **becomingly** *adv.*

becquerel / b e k - u h - r u h l / *n.* a unit of radioactivity. (¶ Named after A.H. Becquerel (1852–1908), French physicist.)

bed *n.* **1** a thing to sleep or rest on, a piece of furniture with a mattress and coverings. **2** the use of a bed; being in bed (*it's time for bed!*). **3** a flat base on which something rests, a foundation. **4** the bottom of the sea or a river etc. **5** a layer (*a bed of clay*). **6** a garden plot for plants. •*v.* (**bedded**, **bedding**) **1** provide with a place to sleep; put or go to bed. **2** place or fix in a foundation (*the bricks are bedded in concrete*). **3** plant in a garden bed (*he was bedding out seedlings*). ☐ **bed and breakfast** a room and breakfast in a guest house, hotel etc.; an establishment providing this. **go to bed with** have sexual intercourse with.

BEd *abbr.* Bachelor of Education.

bedaub *v.* smear all over.

bedbug *n.* a bug infesting beds.

bedclothes *n.pl.* sheets and quilts etc.

bedding *n.* mattresses and bedclothes. ☐ **bedding plant** a plant suitable for planting when it is in flower as part of a display, discarded at the end of the season.

bedevil *v.* (**bedevilled**, **bedevilling**) **1** cause trouble or difficulties for (*the show has been bedevilled with problems*). **2** confound, confuse. ☐ **bedevilment** *n.*

bedfellow *n.* **1** a person who shares one's bed. **2** an associate.

bedlam / **bed**-luhm / *n.* uproar.

Bedouin / **bed**-uh-wuhn / *n.* (also **Beduin**) (*pl.* **Bedouin**) a member of an Arab people living in tents in the desert.

Bedourie / buh-**doo**-ree / *n. Aust.* **1** a dust storm. **2** a type of portable camp oven with a lid (which can be used as a frying pan). (¶ Bedourie, a town in south-western Qld.)

bedpan *n.* a pan for use as a portable toilet by a person confined to bed.

bedpost *n.* one of the upright supports of a bedstead.

bedraggled / buh-**drag**-uhld / *adj.* hanging in a limp untidy way, esp. when wet; dishevelled, untidy.

bedridden *adj.* confined to bed through illness or weakness.

bedrock *n.* **1** solid rock beneath loose soil. **2** basic facts or principles.

bedroom *n.* a room for sleeping in.

bedside *n.* a position by a bed.

bedsitter *n.* a one-roomed unit of accommodation used for both living and sleeping in, and having cooking facilities.

bedsore *n.* a sore caused by pressure, developed by lying in bed for a long time.

bedspread *n.* a covering spread over a bed.

bedstead *n.* a framework supporting the springs and mattress of a bed.

Beduin alternative spelling of BEDOUIN.

bedwetting *n.* involuntary urination when asleep in bed.

bee *n.* **1** a four-winged stinging insect that produces wax and honey after gathering nectar and pollen from flowers. **2** esp. *US & Aust.* a meeting for communal work etc. (*a working bee*). ☐ **bee-eater** any of many bright-plumaged insect-eating birds, including the Australian rainbow bird. **bee-keeper** a person who keeps bees in hives. **have a bee in one's bonnet** have a particular idea that occupies one's thoughts continually. **the bee's knees** *colloq.* something excellent, outstanding (*he thinks he's the bee's knees*).

beech *n.* **1** a European tree with smooth bark and glossy leaves. **2** any of several Australian trees (*Antarctic beech; white beech*).

beef *n.* **1** the flesh of a bull or cow used as meat. **2** (in Aboriginal English) meat of any kind. **3** (*pl.* **beeves**) a bull or a cow bred for meat. **4** *colloq.* well-developed male muscle; brawn. **5** *colloq.* a grumble or complaint. •*v. colloq.* grumble or complain. ☐ **beef up** *colloq.* strengthen, reinforce (*need to beef up the system*).

beefcake *n. colloq.* attractive men with well-developed muscles.

beefeater *n.* a warder in the Tower of London wearing Tudor dress as uniform.

beefwood *n.* any of several Australian trees which yield a dark red, beef-like, close-grained timber.

beefy *adj.* (**beefier**, **beefiest**) **1** like beef. **2** having a solid muscular body. ☐ **beefiness** *n.*

Bee Gees a pop group formed in the 1950s by the Australian (British-born) Gibb brothers,

Barry (1947–) and the twins Robin and Maurice (1949–).

beehive *n.* **1** an artificial shelter for a colony of bees. **2** a busy place.

beeline *n.* ☐ **make a beeline for** go straight or rapidly towards.

Beelzebub / bee-**el**-zuh-bub / (in the New Testament) the Devil; (in the Old Testament) a Philistine god. (¶ Hebrew, = Lord of the Flies.)

been see BE.

Been There, Done That see BT, DT.

beep *n.* a short light sound (*a beep on the horn*). • *v.* emit a beep.

beer *n.* **1** an alcoholic drink made from malt and flavoured with hops. **2** a glass etc. of this. ☐ **beer gut** *colloq.* a (beer drinker's) distended belly; a pot.

beery *adj.* (**beerier**, **beeriest**) **1** affected by beer drinking. **2** like beer.

beeswax *n.* a yellowish substance secreted by bees, used for polishing wood.

beet *n.* a plant with a fleshy root used as a vegetable or for making sugar.

Beethoven / **bayt**-hoh-vuhn /, Ludwig van (1770–1827), German composer.

beetle *n.* **1** an insect with hard wing-covers. **2** any similar, usu. black, insect.

beetle-browed *adj.* with shaggy, projecting, or scowling eyebrows.

beetling *adj.* overhanging, projecting (*beetling cliffs; beetling brows*).

beetroot *n.* the fleshy dark red root of a beet, used as a vegetable.

befall / bee-**fawl**, buh- / *v.* (**befell**, **befallen**, **befalling**) *formal* happen, happen to.

befit / bee-**fit**, buh- / *v.* (**befitted**, **befitting**) be right and suitable for.

before *adv., prep.,* & *conj.* **1** at an earlier time; earlier than. **2** ahead; ahead of; in front of (*they sailed before the wind*). **3** rather than, in preference to (*death before dishonour!*).

Before Christ *adv.* (of dates) reckoned backwards from the year of the birth of Christ.

beforehand *adv.* in advance, in readiness.

befriend *v.* act as a friend to; help.

befuddle *v.* stupefy, make confused.

beg *v.* (**begged**, **begging**) **1** ask for as charity or as a gift; obtain a living in this way. **2** request earnestly, humbly, or formally (*I beg your pardon; beg to differ*). **3** (of a dog) sit up expectantly with forepaws off the ground. ☐ **beg off** ask to be excused from doing something. **beg the question** use circular reasoning; assume the truth of something needing proof, without arguing it or proving it. **go begging** (of things) be available but unwanted.

■ **Usage** Many people use the phrase *beg the question* in the disputed sense 'pose the question'. It originally meant, and still means, 'to assume the truth of the thing that is to be proved', e.g. *By devoting such a large part of the budget for the fight against drug addiction to education, we are begging the question of its significance in the battle against drugs* (i.e. we are assuming that through education we can radically reduce drug-taking). Over the years *beg the question* has been misunderstood and another meaning has arisen, 'to raise the question', or 'invite the obvious question', and this is now the more common use of the phrase, e.g. *Most people continue to live in cities, which begs the question as to whether city life or country life is more desirable.*

began see BEGIN.

beget / bee-**get**, buh- / *v.* (**begot**, **begotten**, **begetting**) *literary* **1** be the father of. **2** give rise to (*war begets misery and ruin*).

beggar *n.* **1** a person who lives by begging. **2** *colloq.* a person (*you lucky beggar!*). • *v.* **1** reduce to poverty. **2** make poor or inadequate (*the scenery beggars description*).

beggarly *adj.* mean and insufficient.

begin *v.* (**began**, **begun**, **beginning**) **1** perform the earliest or first part of (some activity); start speaking; be the first to do something. **2** come into existence. **3** have as its first element or starting point. ☐ **not begin to** not in any way; be totally unable to (*I can't begin to thank you enough; this doesn't begin to explain why*). **to begin with** as the first thing.

beginner *n.* a person who is just beginning to learn a skill.

beginning *n.* **1** the first part. **2** the starting point, the source or origin.

begone / bee-**gon**, buh- / *interj. poetic* go away immediately (*begone, dull care!*).

begonia / buh-**goh**-nyuh / *n.* a garden plant with colourful flowers and often ornamental leaves.

begot, begotten see BEGET.

begrudge *v.* grudge.

beguile / bee-**guyl**, buh- / *v.* **1** win the attention or interest of, charm. **2** delude; cheat. ☐ **beguiling** *adj.*

beguine / bee-**geen**, buh- / *n.* a West Indian dance.

begum / **bay**-guhm / *n.* (in Pakistan and India) **1** the title of a Muslim married woman. **2** a Muslim woman of high rank.

begun see BEGIN.

behalf *n.* ☐ **on behalf of** (*or* **on a person's behalf**) in aid of; as the representative of (*speaking on behalf of his client*).

behave *v.* **1** act or react in some specified way; function. **2** show good manners (*the child must learn to behave*).

behaviour *n.* (also **behavior**) a way of behaving; treatment of others; manners. ☐ **behavioural** *adj.*

behavioural science *n.* the study of human behaviour.

behaviourism *n.* the psychological theory that human behaviour is determined by conditioning rather than by thoughts or feelings, and that

behead *v.* cut the head from; execute (a person) in this way.

beheld *see* BEHOLD.

behest *n. formal* a command; a request (*at the behest of the Governor-General*).

behind *adv.* **1** in or to the rear. **2** remaining after others have gone. **3** in arrears; late in finishing a task etc.; backward. •*prep.* **1** in the rear of, on the further side of. **2** causing. **3** supporting. **4** having made less progress than (*some countries are behind others in development*). **5** later than (*we are behind schedule*). •*n.* **1** *colloq.* the buttocks. **2** *Aust. Rules* a scoring kick which scores one point. ☐ **behind post** *Aust. Rules* each of a pair of posts flanking the goal posts. **behind the scenes** backstage; hidden from public view or knowledge. **behind time** late. **behind the times** old-fashioned, out of date.

behold *v.* (**beheld**, **beholding**) *archaic* see, observe. ☐ **beholder** *n.*

beholden *adj.* under obligation (*we don't want to be beholden to anybody*).

behove *v. formal* be incumbent on; befit (*it ill behoves him to protest*).

beige / bayzh / *n.* a light sandy fawn colour. •*adj.* of this colour.

Beijing / bay-**jing** / (the official Chinese form of **Peking**) capital of the People's Republic of China. ☐ **Beijing Massacre** the massacre by the Chinese military on 3 June 1989 of several of the hundreds of students involved in a peaceful political demonstration in Tiananmen Square.

being *n.* **1** existence. **2** essence or nature. **3** something that exists and has life, esp. a person.

Beirut / bay-**root** / the capital of Lebanon.

bejewelled *adj.* adorned with jewels.

bel *n.* a unit (= 10 decibels) used in comparing power levels in electrical communication.

belabour *v.* (also **belabor**) **1** attack with blows or words. **2** argue or elaborate (a subject) in excessive detail (*you don't need to belabour the point*).

belah / buh-**lah** / *n.* any of several casuarinas of drier Australia with slender jointed branches and woody cones. (¶ Wiradhuri)

Belarus / bel-uh-**roos** / (also **Belorussia**) a republic in Eastern Europe. ☐ **Belarussian** *adj.*

belated / bee-**lay**-tuhd, buh- / *adj.* coming very late or too late. ☐ **belatedly** *adv.*

belay *v.* secure (a rope) by winding it round a peg or spike. •*n.* the securing of a rope in this way.

bel canto *n.* a rich-toned and lyrical style of operatic singing concentrating on beauty of sound and vocal technique.

belch *v.* **1** send out wind from the stomach noisily through the mouth. **2** send out from an opening or funnel; gush (*a chimney belching smoke*). •*n.* an act or sound of belching.

beleaguer / bee-**lee**-guh, buh- / *v.* **1** besiege. **2** harass, oppress.

Belfast the capital of Northern Ireland.

belfry *n.* a bell tower, a space for bells in a tower.

Belgium a kingdom in western Europe. ☐ **Belgian** *adj.* & *n.*

Belgrade the chief city of Serbia and capital of the former Yugoslavia.

belie *v.* (**belied**, **belying**) **1** fail to confirm, show to be untrue. **2** give a false idea of.

belief *n.* **1** the feeling that something is real and true; trust, confidence. **2** something accepted as true; what one believes. **3** acceptance of the teachings of a religion etc.; these teachings.

believe *v.* **1** accept as true or as speaking or conveying truth. **2** think, suppose (*I believe it's raining*). **3** have religious faith. ☐ **believe in** have faith in the existence of; feel sure of the value or worth of. ☐ ☐ **believable** *adj.* **believer** *n.*

belittle *v.* imply that (a thing) is unimportant or of little value. ☐ **belittlement** *n.*

Belize / buh-**leez** / a country in Central America, on the Caribbean coast. ☐ **Belizean** / buh-**lee**-zh uhn / *adj.* & *n.*

Bell[1], Alexander Graham (1847–1922), Scottish-American inventor of the telephone.

Bell[2], John (Anthony) (1940–), AM, Australian actor and director.

bell *n.* **1** a cup-shaped metal instrument that makes a ringing sound when struck; a device making a ringing or buzzing sound to attract attention in a house etc. **2** the sound of this, esp. as a signal. **3** a bell-shaped thing. **4** *colloq.* a telephone call. ☐ **bell-bottomed** *adj.* (of trousers) widening from knee to ankle. **bell jar** a bell-shaped glass cover or container. **bells and whistles** attractive additional features or trimmings; gimmicks.

belladonna *n.* **1** deadly nightshade. **2** a medicinal drug prepared from this.

bellbird *n.* either of two Australian birds with a pure penetrating bell-like call.

belle / bel / *n.* a beautiful woman.

belles-lettres / bel-**letr** / *n.pl.* literary writings or studies.

bellicose / **bel**-uh-kohz, -kohs / *adj.* eager to fight; warlike.

belligerent / buh-**lij**-uh-ruhnt / *adj.* **1** waging a war (*the belligerent nations*). **2** aggressive, showing eagerness to fight (*a belligerent reply*). ☐ **belligerently** *adv.* **belligerence** *n.*

bellow *n.* **1** the loud deep sound made by a bull. **2** a deep shout. •*v.* utter a bellow.

bellows *n.pl.* **1** an apparatus for driving air into or through something. **2** a device or part that can be expanded or flattened in a series of folds.

belly *n.* **1** the abdomen. **2** the stomach. **3** bulging or rounded part of something. •*v.* (**bellied**, **bellying**) swell, bulge (*the sails bellied out*). ☐ **belly button** *colloq.* the navel. **belly dance** an oriental dance by a woman, with erotic movement of the belly. **belly laugh** a deep loud laugh.

bellyache *colloq. n.* **1** a pain in the belly; colic. **2** a grumble, a whinge. • *v.* grumble or whinge.

bellyflop *n.* an awkward dive in which the body hits the water almost horizontally.

bellyful *n.* **1** as much as one wants or can eat. **2** *colloq.* more than one can tolerate.

Belmopan / **bel**-moh-puhn / the capital of Belize.

Belo, Carlos (Felipe Ximenes) (1948–), East-Timorese Catholic bishop. He was a strong critic of Indonesia's role in East Timor, and shared the 1996 Nobel Peace Prize with José Ramos Horta.

belong *v.* **1** (foll. by *to*) be rightly assigned as property or as a part or inhabitant etc. (*the house belongs to me; that lid belongs to this jar*). **2** be a member (*we belong to the club*). **3** have a rightful or usual place (*the pans belong in the kitchen*).

belongings *n.pl.* personal possessions.

Belorussia *see* BELARUS.

beloved *adj.* / bee-**luv**-uhd, -**luvd**, buh- / dearly loved (*she was beloved by all*). • *n.* darling (*he's my beloved*).

below *adv.* **1** at or to a lower position; downstream. **2** at the foot of a page; further on in a book or article (*see chapter 6 below*). • *prep.* **1** lower in position, amount, or rank etc. than. **2** downstream from (*the bridge is below the billabong*).

Belsen a village in Germany, site of a Nazi concentration camp in the Second World War.

belt *n.* **1** a strip of leather or other material worn round the waist. **2** a continuous moving strap passing over pulleys and so driving machinery (*a fan belt*). **3** a long narrow region or strip (*a belt of rain will move eastwards*). **4** *colloq.* a heavy blow. • *v.* **1** put a belt round. **2** attach with a belt. **3** thrash with a belt; *colloq.* hit. **4** *colloq.* hurry, rush. □ **below the belt** unfair, unfairly. **belt out** *colloq.* sing or play loudly (*belting out pop songs*). **belt up 1** wear a seatbelt. **2** *colloq.* be quiet. **tighten one's belt** live more frugally. **under one's belt** *colloq.* obtained or achieved.

beltman *n. Aust.* the member of a surf lifesaving team who has a lifeline attached to his belt when he swims out to rescue a swimmer in difficulties.

beluga / buh-**loo**-guh / *n.* **1** a large sturgeon. **2** caviare from this. **3** a white whale.

belvedere / **bel**-vuh-deer / *n.* a raised turret or summerhouse from which to view scenery.

bemoan *v.* lament, complain of.

bemused / bee-**myoozd**, buh- / *adj.* **1** bewildered. **2** lost in thought.

Benaud, Richie (full name: Richard Benaud) (1930–), Australian test cricketer and test captain, writer, and television commentator.

bench *n.* **1** a long seat of wood or stone. **2** a work table of various kinds (in the kitchen, in a laboratory, etc.). **3** a lawcourt. **4** the judges or magistrates hearing a case.

benchmark *n.* **1** a surveyor's mark used as a reference point in measuring altitudes. **2** a standard or point of reference (*the Mabo decision by the High Court was a benchmark*).

bend[1] *v.* (**bent**, **bending**) **1** force out of straightness, make curved or angular. **2** become curved or angular. **3** turn downwards, stoop. **4** turn in a new direction (*they bent their steps homeward*). • *n.* **1** a curve or turn. **2** (**the bends**) sickness due to too rapid decompression, e.g. after diving. □ **bend the elbow** *colloq.* drink (esp. beer). **bend the rules** interpret them loosely to suit oneself. **round the bend** *colloq.* crazy. □□ **bendy** *adj.*

bend[2] *n.* **1** any of various knots. **2** (in heraldry) a stripe from the dexter chief to the sinister base. • *v.* (**bent**, **bending**) attach (a rope or sail etc.) with a knot.

bender *n. colloq.* a wild drinking spree.

beneath *adv. & prep.* **1** below, under, underneath. **2** not worthy of, not befitting.

Benedict, St (*c.*480–*c.*550), an Italian hermit who founded a monastic order.

Benedictine *n.* **1** / ben-uh-**dik**-tuhn / a monk or nun following the monastic rule of St Benedict. **2** / ben-uh-**dik**-teen / *trademark* a liqueur originally made by monks of this order. • *adj.* of St Benedict or the Benedictines.

benediction / ben-uh-**dik**-shuhn / *n.* **1** a spoken blessing at the end of Mass or other religious service. **2** (**Benediction**) a special Catholic service in which the priest blesses the people with the Blessed Sacrament in a monstrance. □ **benedictory** *adj.*

benefaction *n.* **1** a donation; a gift. **2** giving; doing good.

benefactor *n.* a person who gives financial or other help.

benefactress *n.* a female benefactor.

benefice / **ben**-uh-fuhs / *n.* a position that provides a clergyman with a livelihood.

beneficent / buh-**nef**-uh-suhnt / *adj.* conferring blessings or favours. □ **beneficence** *n.*

beneficial *adj.* **1** having a helpful or useful effect. **2** improving the health. □ **beneficially** *adv.*

beneficiary / ben-uh-**fish**-uh-ree / *n.* a person who receives a benefit; one who is left a legacy under someone's will.

benefit *n.* **1** something helpful, favourable, or profitable. **2** an allowance of money etc. to which a person is entitled from an insurance policy or government funds. **3** a performance or game held to raise money for a charitable cause. • *v.* (**benefited**, **benefiting**) **1** do good to. **2** receive benefit. □ **benefit of the doubt** the assumption that a person is innocent (or right) rather than guilty (or wrong) when nothing can be fully proved either way.

Benelux / **ben**-uh-luks / a collective name for Belgium, the Netherlands, and Luxembourg.

benevolent *adj.* **1** wishing to do good to others; kindly and helpful. **2** charitable (*a benevolent fund*). ☐ **benevolently** *adv.* **benevolence** *n.*

benighted *adj.* **1** overtaken by night. **2** intellectually or morally ignorant.

benign / buh-**nuyn** / *adj.* **1** kindly. **2 a** mild and gentle in its effect. **b** (of a tumour) not malignant. ☐ **benignly** *adv.*

benignant / buh-**nig**-nuhnt / *adj.* kindly.

benignity / buh-**nig**-nuh-tee / *n.* kindliness.

Benin / buh-**neen** / a republic in West Africa. ☐ **Beninese** *adj.* & *n.*

Bennelong (?–1813), an Australian Aborigine captured on Governor Phillip's orders in 1789 as part of an attempt to learn more of the customs and language of the indigenous people. A small hut was built for him at Bennelong Point (the site on which the Sydney Opera House is now built). He was taken to England by Phillip in 1792 and was even introduced to George III. Returned to Sydney in 1795, he could not re-integrate with his people or be accepted by the whites.

bent *see* BEND[1]. • *n.* a natural skill or liking (*she has a bent for music*). • *adj. colloq.* dishonest. ☐ **bent on** determined or seeking to do something (*bent on mischief*).

benumb *v.* make numb.

benzene / **ben**-zeen / *n.* a colourless liquid obtained from petroleum and coal tar, used as a solvent, as fuel, and in the manufacture of plastics.

benzine / **ben**-zeen / *n.* a colourless liquid mixture of hydrocarbons obtained from petroleum and used as a solvent in dry-cleaning.

benzoin *n.* a strong-smelling resin from a tropical tree. ☐ **benzoic** / ben-**zoh**-ik / *adj.*

benzol *n.* benzene, esp. in the unrefined state.

bequeath / bee-**kwee***th*, buh- / *v.* leave as a legacy.

bequest / bee-**kwest**, buh- / *n.* a legacy.

berate / bee-**rayt**, buh- / *v.* scold.

Berber *n.* **1** a member of a group of North African peoples. **2** their language.

berceuse / buh-**serz** / *n.* a piece of music in the style of a lullaby.

bereave *v.* deprive, esp. of a relative, by death (*the bereaved husband*). ☐ **bereavement** *n.*

bereft *adj.* (foll. by *of*) deprived (*bereft of reason*).

Beresford, Bruce (1940–), Australian film director.

beret / **be**-ray / *n.* a soft round flat cap with no peak.

bergamot / **ber**-guh-mot / *n.* **1** a perfume from the rind of a citrus fruit. **2** the tree bearing this. **3** a fragrant herb.

Bergman, Ingrid (1915–82), Swedish film and stage actor.

beriberi *n.* a disease affecting the nervous system, caused by lack of vitamin B_1.

berk *n. colloq.* a stupid person.

berkelium / ber-**kee**-lee-uhm / *n.* an artificially made radioactive metallic element (symbol Bk).

berley *n. Aust.* chopped or ground fish bait. • *v.* (also **berley-up**) scatter berley on the water to attract fish to the area.

Berlin the capital of Germany.

Berlioz / **bair**-lee-ohz /, Hector (1803–69), French composer.

Bermuda a group of islands in the West Atlantic. ☐ **Bermuda shorts** (also **Bermudas**) knee-length shorts. **Bermuda Triangle** an area of the western Atlantic between Bermuda and Florida, credited since the mid-19th century with a number of unexplained (supposedly supernatural) disappearances of ships and aircraft. ☐☐ **Bermudian** *adj.*

Bern alternative spelling of BERNE.

Bernard, St (*c.*996–*c.*1081), a French monk who founded two hospices in the Alps to aid travellers. St Bernard dogs are named after him.

Berne / bern / (also **Bern**) the capital of Switzerland.

Bernhardt / **bairn**-haht /, Sarah (original name: Rosine Bernard) (1844–1923), French actor, known as 'the divine Sarah'.

Bernstein / **bern**-stuyn, -steen /, Leonard (1918–90), American conductor and composer.

berry *n.* **1** any small roundish juicy stoneless fruit. **2** *Bot.* any fruit with its seeds enclosed in pulp (e.g. a banana or a tomato).

berserk / buh-**serk**, -zerk / *adj.* frenzied. ☐ **go berserk** go into an uncontrollable and destructive rage.

berth *n.* **1** a bunk or sleeping-place in a ship or train. **2** a place for a boat to moor. **3** adequate room for a ship. • *v.* moor at a berth. ☐ **give a wide berth to** keep at a safe distance from.

Bertrand, John (Edwin) (1946–), AM, captain of the yacht *Australia II* in the successful challenge for the America's Cup in 1983.

beryl *n.* a transparent usu. green precious stone.

beryllium / buh-**ril**-ee-uhm / *n.* a very light hard greyish-white metallic element (symbol Be), used in alloys where lightness and a high melting point are important.

beseech *v.* (**besought**, **beseeching**) implore; beg earnestly.

beset *v.* (**beset**, **besetting**) hem in, surround; afflict (a person) persistently (*the temptations that beset people*).

beside *prep.* **1** at the side of, close to. **2** compared with (*beside him I am an angel*). ☐ **beside oneself** frantic with worry; overwhelmed. **beside the point** having nothing to do with the point, irrelevant.

besides *prep.* in addition to; other than (*he has no income besides his pension*). • *adv.* also.

besiege *v.* **1** lay siege to. **2** crowd round with requests or questions.

besmirch *v.* **1** dirty, discolour. **2** dishonour; damage (a person's reputation).

besom / **bee**-zuhm / *n.* a broom made by tying a bundle of twigs to a long handle.

besotted / bee-**sot**-uhd, buh- / *adj.* infatuated.
besought *see* BESEECH.
bespeak *v.* (**bespoke, bespoken, bespeaking**) **1** engage beforehand. **2** order (goods). **3** be evidence of (*his gift bespeaks a kind heart*).
bespectacled *adj.* wearing spectacles.
bespoke *see* BESPEAK. •*adj.* (of clothes) made to order; (of a tailor etc.) making such clothes.
best *adj.* of the most excellent kind; most satisfactory. •*adv.* in the best manner, to the greatest degree. •*n.* **1** that which is best; the chief merit or advantage. **2** (foll. by *of*) the winning majority of (games played etc.) (*the best of three games*). **3** one's best clothes. •*v. colloq.* defeat, outdo, outwit. □ **at best** taking the most hopeful view. **best boy** the assistant to the chief electrician of a film crew. **best man** the bridegroom's chief attendant at a wedding. **best-seller** a book that sells in very large numbers. **he had best. . ., it is best. . ., etc.** the most sensible thing to do is … (*we had best go; it is best ignored*).
bestial / **bes**-tee-uhl / *adj.* **1** brutish, cruel. **2** of or like a beast.
bestiality *n.* **1** bestial behaviour. **2** sexual intercourse between a person and an animal.
bestiary / **bes**-tee-uh-ree / *n.* a medieval collection of moralising descriptions of real and imaginary beasts.
bestir *v.* (**bestirred, bestirring**) □ **bestir oneself** rouse or exert oneself.
bestow *v.* present as a gift. □ **bestowal** *n.*
bestrew *v.* **1** strew. **2** lie scattered over. □ **bestrewn** *adj.*
bestride *v.* (**bestrode, bestridden, bestriding**) sit or stand astride over.
bet *n.* **1** an agreement pledging something that will be forfeited if one's forecast of some event proves wrong. **2** the money etc. pledged. **3** *colloq.* a choice, possibility, or course of action (*your best bet is to come in person*). **4** *colloq.* a prediction, an opinion (*my bet is that he won't come*). •*v.* (**bet** or **betted, betting**) **1** make a bet; pledge in a bet. **2** *colloq.* predict, think most likely. □ **you bet** *colloq.* you may be sure.
beta / **bee**-tuh / *n.* **1** the second letter of the Greek alphabet (Β, β). **2** (*attrib.*) denoting the second of a series of items, categories, forms of a chemical compound, etc. **3** a second-class mark in an examination. **4** (in names of stars) the second-brightest in a constellation. □ **beta blocker** a drug used to prevent increased cardiac activity. **beta particles** fast-moving electrons emitted by radioactive substances.
betake *v.* (**betook, betaken, betaking**) □ **betake oneself** go.
betatron *n.* an apparatus for accelerating electrons in a circular path.
betel / **bee**-tuhl / *n.* an aromatic leaf chewed in tropical Asia together with shavings from the **betel nut** (the areca nut).

Betelgeuse / **bee**-tuhl-jerz / a large variable star in the constellation Orion.
bête noire / bayt **nwah** / *n.* (*pl.* **bêtes noires** pronounced the same) a thing or person that one dislikes or fears very much. (¶ French, = black beast.)
bethink *v.* (**bethought, bethinking**) □ **bethink oneself** *literary* remind oneself, remember.
Bethlehem a small town near Jerusalem, the reputed birthplace of Jesus Christ.
betide *v.* happen to; *see* WOE BETIDE.
betimes *adv. formal* in good time, early.
betoken *v.* be a sign of.
betook *see* BETAKE.
betray *v.* **1** give up or reveal (a person, secrets, etc.) treacherously to an enemy. **2** be disloyal to. **3** show unintentionally (*betray one's feelings*). □ **betrayal** *n.* **betrayer** *n.*
betroth / bee-**troh**th, buh- / *v. formal* engage with a promise to marry. □ **betrothal** *n.*
better[1] *adj.* **1** of a more excellent kind; more satisfactory. **2** partly or fully recovered from an illness. •*adv.* in a better manner, to a better degree; more usefully. •*n.* **1** that which is better. **2** (**betters**) people who are of higher status than oneself. •*v.* improve, do better than. □ **go one better** do better than someone else's effort. **had better** would find it wiser or more sensible to.
better[2] *n.* a person who bets.
betterment *n.* making or becoming better, improvement.
bettong *n.* a rat-kangaroo. (¶ Dharuk)
between *prep.* & *adv.* **1** in the space bounded by two or more points, lines, or objects. **2** intermediate to, esp. in time, quantity, or quality. **3** separating (*the difference between right and wrong*). **4** to and from (*the ferry travels between the Opera House and Manly*). **5** connecting (*the great love between them*). **6** shared by (*$50 between you and me*). **7** taking one and rejecting the other (*choose between them*). □ **between ourselves, between you and me** in confidence; to be kept secret.

■ **Usage** Use in sense 6 with reference to more than two people or things is established and acceptable (e.g. *relations between Australia, New Zealand, and Papua New Guinea*).

betwixt *prep.* & *adv. archaic* between.
beurre manié / ber mun-**yay** / *n.* a mixture of butter and flour, kneaded together and used to thicken sauces etc. (¶ French *beurre* 'butter', *manié* 'handled'.)
bevan *n. Aust. colloq.* a person who is regarded as uncultured, lacking in style, etc.
bevel / **bev**-uhl / *n.* **1** a sloping edge or surface. **2** a tool for making such slopes. •*v.* (**bevelled, bevelling**) give a sloping edge to.
beverage / **bev**-uh-rij / *n.* any drink.
bevy / **bev**-ee / *n.* a company, a large group.
bewail *v.* wail over; mourn for.

beware *v.* be on one's guard.

bewdy / **byoo**-dee / *Aust. colloq.* variant of BEAUTY.

bewilder *v.* puzzle, confuse. ☐ **bewilderment** *n.*

bewitch *v.* **1** put under a magic spell. **2** delight very much.

beyond *adv.* & *prep.* **1** at or to the further side of; further on. **2** outside; outside the scope or understanding of (*this is beyond repair; it is beyond me; he lives beyond his income*). **3** besides, except. ☐ **beyond doubt** quite certain; unquestionably.

bezel / **bez**-uhl / *n.* **1** the sloping edge of a chisel; an oblique face of a cut gem. **2** a rim holding a gem in position.

bezique / buh-**zeek** / *n.* a card game for two players.

Bh *symbol* bohrium.

Bhagavadgita / bah-guh-vahd-**gee**-tuh / *n.* the 'Song of the Lord' (i.e. Krishna), the most famous religious text of Hinduism.

bhakti / **bahk**-tee / *n.* (in Hinduism) worship directed to one supreme deity, usu. Vishnu or Siva.

bhang / bang / *n.* the dried leaves and flower-tops of Indian hemp smoked or chewed as a narcotic and intoxicant.

Bhopal / boh-**pahl** / a city in central India where in 1984 leakage of poisonous gas from an American-owned pesticide factory caused thousands of deaths and injuries.

BHP *abbr.* the Broken Hill Proprietary Company Limited, an Australian mining company, which became BHP Billiton in 2001.

b.h.p. *abbr.* brake horse power.

Bhumibol Adulyadej / boo-mee-pawl uh-doo-lyuh-**day** / (1927–), King of Thailand since 1946.

Bhutan / boo-**tahn** / a kingdom between India and Tibet. ☐ **Bhutanese** *adj.* & *n.* (*pl.* **Bhutanese**).

Bhutto / **boo**-toh /, Benazir (1953–), Pakistani stateswoman, prime minister 1988–90 and 1993–96.

Bi *symbol* bismuth.

bi *colloq. adj.* bisexual. •*n.* a bisexual person.

bi- *comb. form* two; twice.

biannual *adj.* appearing or happening twice a year. ☐ **biannually** *adv.*

bias *n.* **1** (often foll. by *towards*, *against*) an opinion or influence that strongly favours one side in an argument or one item in a group or series. **2** the slanting direction across threads of woven material. **3** the tendency of a ball in the game of bowls to swerve because of the way it is weighted. •*v.* (**biased**, **biasing**) **1** (esp. as **biased** *adj.*) influence (usu. unfairly); prejudice. **2** give a bias to. ☐ **cut on the bias** (of fabric) cut with the threads running slantwise across the up-and-down line of a garment. **bias binding** a strip of fabric cut on the bias and used to bind edges.

biathlon *n.* a contest in cycling and running or skiing and shooting.

bib *n.* **1** a cloth or plastic covering put under a young child's chin to protect the front of its clothes while it is eating; any similar covering. **2** the front part of an apron, dungarees, etc., above the waist.

Bible *n.* **1** (**the Bible**) the Christian scriptures; the Jewish scriptures. **2** (**bible**) a copy of either of these. **3** a book regarded as authoritative (*this will be the footy fan's bible*). ☐ **Bible-bashing** (also **Bible-thumping**) *colloq.* aggressive fundamentalist preaching or moralising, or the attempt to force one's own moral views on everyone.

biblical *adj.* of or in the Bible.

bibliography / bib-lee-**og**-ruh-fee / *n.* **1** a list of books or articles about a particular subject or by a particular author. **2** the study of the history of books and their production. ☐ **bibliographer** *n.* **bibliographical** / bib-lee-uh-**graf**-i-kuhl / *adj.*

bibliomania / bib-lee-oh-**may**-nee-uh / *n.* an extreme enthusiasm for collecting and possessing books.

bibliophile / **bib**-lee-uh-fuyl / *n.* a lover of books.

bibulous / **bib**-yuh-luhs / *adj.* addicted to alcoholic drink.

bicameral / buy-**kam**-uh-ruhl / *adj.* (of a parliament etc.) having two chambers.

bicarb *colloq.* = BICARBONATE OF SODA.

bicarbonate *n.* any acid salt of carbonic acid. ☐ **bicarbonate of soda** sodium bicarbonate, used in baking powder or to correct acidity.

bicentenary / buy-sen-**tee**-nuh-ree / *n.* a 200th anniversary.

bicentennial / buy-sen-**ten**-ee-uhl / *adj.* of a bicentenary. •*n.* a bicentenary.

biceps / **buy**-seps / *n.* the large muscle at the front of the upper arm, which bends the elbow.

bicker *v.* quarrel constantly about unimportant things.

bickie *n.* (also **bikkie**) *colloq.* a biscuit. ☐ **big bickies** *Aust.* a large sum of money.

bicuspid / buy-**kus**-puhd / *adj.* having two cusps. •*n.* a bicuspid tooth; a premolar.

bicycle *n.* a two-wheeled vehicle driven by pedals. •*v.* ride on a bicycle. ☐ **bicycle lizard** name for an Australian dragon lizard (esp. the frill-necked lizard), so called from its habit of using only its hind legs for movement.

bicyclist *n.* a person who rides a bicycle.

bid[1] *n.* **1** an offer of a price to buy something, esp. at an auction. **2** a statement of the number of tricks a player proposes to win in a card game. **3** an effort to obtain something (*made a bid for popular support*). •*v.* (**bid**, **bidding**) make a bid. ☐ **bidder** *n.*

bid[2] *v.* (**bid**, *literary* **bade** / bad /; **bid** *or* **bidden**, **bidding**) **1** command (*go, bid the soldiers shoot; they bade her begin*). **2** say as a greeting or farewell (*bidding them good night*).

biddable *adj.* willing to obey.

bidding *n.* **1** a command or request. **2** bids in an auction or card game.

biddy *n.* ◻ **old biddy** *colloq.* an elderly woman.

bide *v.* ◻ **bide one's time** wait for a good opportunity.

bidet / **bee**-day / *n.* a low narrow basin that one can sit on to wash the genital area.

biennale / bee-uh-**nah**-lee / *n.* an exhibition of art etc. held every two years.

biennial / buy-**en**-ee-uhl / *adj.* **1** lasting or living for two years. **2** happening every second year. •*n.* a plant that lives for two years, flowering and dying in the second. ◻ **biennially** *adv.*

bier / beer / *n.* a movable stand on which a coffin or a dead body is placed before burial.

biff *colloq. v.* hit. •*n.* a blow.

bifid / **buy**-fuhd / *adj.* divided by a deep cleft into two parts.

bifocal / buy-**foh**-kuhl / *adj.* having two focuses. •*n.* (**bifocals**) spectacles with each lens made in two sections, the upper part for looking at distant objects and the lower part for reading and other close work.

bifurcate / **buy**-fuh-kayt / *v.* divide into two branches. ◻ **bifurcation** *n.*

big *adj.* (**bigger**, **biggest**) **1** large in size, amount, or intensity. **2** more grown up, elder (*my big sister*). **3** important (*the big match*). **4** boastful, pretentious (*big talk*). **5** *colloq.* generous (*that's big of you*). •*adv. colloq.* on a large scale (*think big*). ◻ **big bang theory** the theory that the universe began with a massive explosion of dense matter. **big bin** a large plastic bin for garbage or for recyclable waste. **big deal!** *colloq.* I am not impressed. **big dipper** a roller coaster. **big dry** the dry season in any part of Australia. **big end** the end of a connecting rod that encircles the crank shaft in an engine. **big mob** (originally Australian pidgin) a large number or quantity (*a big mob of galahs*). **big-note** *v. Aust. colloq.* display one's wealth ostentatiously; promote or talk big about oneself, esp. offensively or tediously. **big-noter** *Aust. colloq.* a person who big-notes. **big picture** the overall or long-term view. **big smoke** (originally Australian pidgin) any large Australian city. **big top** the main tent at a circus. **big wet** the wet season in any part of Australia. ◻ ◻ **biggish** *adj.*

Bigambil / **bi**-gahm-bil / *n.* an Aboriginal language of the Darling Downs region of Qld and north-eastern NSW.

bigamist *n.* a person guilty of bigamy.

bigamy *n.* the crime of marrying while still married to another person. ◻ **bigamous** *adj.* **bigamously** *adv.*

Big Brother *n.* a dictator who exercises close control of everything while pretending to be kindly.

bight / buyt / *n.* **1** a long inward curve in a coast (*the Great Australian Bight*). **2** a loop of rope.

bigot / **big**-uht / *n.* a person who holds an opinion obstinately and is intolerant towards those who think differently. ◻ **bigoted** *adj.* **bigotry** *n.*

Big Sunday *n. Aust.* (in Aboriginal English) any major religious ceremony.

bigwig *n. colloq.* an important person.

bike *colloq. n.* a bicycle or motorcycle. •*v.* travel on a bike.

bikie / **buy**-kee / *n. Aust.* a member of a gang of motorcyclists.

bikini *n.* a woman's two-piece swimming costume consisting of a bra and briefs.

bilateral / buy-**lat**-uh-ruhl / *adj.* of or on two sides; having two sides (*a bilateral agreement*). ◻ **bilaterally** *adv.*

bilby *n.* a small burrowing marsupial bandicoot of drier mainland Australia. (¶ Yuwaalaraay)

bile *n.* a bitter yellowish liquid produced by the liver and stored in the gall bladder, aiding digestion of fats.

bilge / bilj / *n.* **1** a ship's bottom, inside and outside. **2** the water that collects there. **3** *colloq.* worthless ideas or talk.

bilharzia / bil-**hah**-zee-uh / *n.* a tropical disease caused by a parasitic flatworm.

bilingual / buy-**ling**-gwuhl / *adj.* **1** written in two languages. **2** able to speak two languages.

bilious / **bil**-yuhs / *adj.* **1** affected by nausea etc. assumed to be caused by too much bile. **2** of a sickly yellowish colour or shade (*a bilious green*). ◻ **biliousness** *n.*

bilk *v. colloq.* escape paying one's debts to; defraud.

Bill *n.* (usu. **the Bill** *or* **the Old Bill**) *Brit. colloq.* the police. (¶ Origin uncertain: the term is possibly a transfer from *Old Bill* in the sense 'a grumbling veteran soldier, usu. having a large moustache', which derives from a cartoon character created during the First World War by B. Bairnsfather, British cartoonist (1888–1959).)

bill[1] *n.* **1** a written statement of charges for goods supplied or services rendered. **2** a poster or placard. **3** a program of entertainment. **4** the draft of a proposed law, to be discussed by a parliament (and called an Act when passed). **5** a banknote (*a ten-dollar bill*). •*v.* **1** announce in a bill or poster (*Olivier was billed to appear as Hamlet*). **2** send a note of charges to. ◻ **bill of exchange** a written order to pay a specified sum of money on a particular date to a named person or to the bearer. **bill of fare** a menu. **bill of lading** a list giving details of a ship's cargo. **fill the bill** be or do what is required.

bill[2] *n.* **1** a bird's beak. **2** the muzzle of a platypus. •*v.* (of doves) stroke each other with their bills.

billabong *n. Aust.* **1** an arm of a river, made by water flowing from the main stream, usu. only in time of flood, to form a backwater, blind creek, anabranch, or, when the water level falls, a pool or lagoon. **2** the dry bed of such a formation. (¶ Wiradhuri)

billboard *n.* a hoarding for advertisements.

billet *n.* **1** a lodging for troops or evacuees, esp. in a private house. **2** a lodging in a private house for a member of a sporting team etc. **3** the person so billeted. **4** *colloq.* a position, a job. **5** a thick piece of firewood. • *v.* (**billeted**, **billeting**) lodge (a soldier etc.) in a billet.

billet-doux / bil-ay-**doo** / *n.* (*pl.* **billets-doux** pronounced the same) a love letter.

billfish *n.* any of several large fish with a streamlined body and a long pointed spear-like snout. It is a popular sporting fish.

billhook *n.* a long-handled tool with a curved blade for lopping trees.

billiards *n.* a game played with cues and three balls on a cloth-covered table.

billion *n.* **1** a million million. **2** a thousand million. ☐ **billionth** *adj.* & *n.*

billionaire *n.* a person who has over a billion dollars etc.

bill of rights *n.* a statement of the rights of the people of a nation.

billow *n.* a great wave. • *v.* rise or roll like waves (*smoke billowed forth*). ☐ **billowy** *adj.*

billposter *n.* a person who sticks advertisements or notices onto walls, shop windows, or hoardings.

billy *n.* (also **billycan**) *Aust.* a tin can or enamelled container with a lid and wire handle, used as an outdoor cooking pot, esp. for boiling water and making tea. ☐ **billy tea** tea brewed in a billy.

billy buttons *n.* an Australian plant with button-like yellow flowers.

billycart *n. Aust.* **1** a small handcart. **2** a roughly built child's four-wheeled play vehicle, usu. without brakes and steered by a rope attached to the front axle.

billy goat *n.* a male goat.

bimble *n.* (in full **bimble box**) a poplar-like eucalypt of NSW and Qld. (¶ Wiradhuri)

bimbo *n.* (*pl.* **bimbos** or **bimboes**) *colloq.* an attractive but unintelligent young woman.

bimetallic *adj.* using or made of two metals.

bimonthly *adj.* **1** happening every second month. **2** happening twice a month.

bin *n.* **1** a large rigid container or enclosed space, usu. with a lid, used for storing coal, grain, flour, etc. **2** a receptacle for rubbish or litter.

binary / **buy**-nuh-ree / *adj.* **1** of a pair or pairs. **2** of the binary system. • *n.* something having two parts. ☐ **binary digit** (or **number**) either of the two digits, 0 and 1, used in the binary system. **binary star** two stars that revolve round each other. **binary system** a system using the numbers 0 and 1 to code information, esp. in computing.

bind *v.* (**bound**, **binding**) **1** tie or fasten; tie up. **2** hold together; unite (*bound by ties of friendship*). **3** encircle with a strip or band of material (*bind up the wound*). **4** cover the edge of (a thing) in order to strengthen it or as a decoration. **5** fasten the pages of (a book) into a cover. **6** stick together in a solid mass (*bind the mixture with egg yolk*). **7** place under an obligation or a legal agreement. • *n. colloq.* a bore, a nuisance. ☐ **bind over** *Law* order to keep the peace. **in a bind** in trouble; in a dilemma or fix.

binder *n.* **1** a person or thing that binds. **2** a loose cover for papers. **3** a bookbinder. **4** *hist.* a machine for binding harvested grain into sheaves.

bindery *n.* a workshop where books are bound.

bindi-eye *n.* **1** any of several Australian plants bearing barbed fruits. **2** the fruit of these plants. (¶ Kamilaroi and Yuwaalaraay *bindayaa*.)

binding *n.* **1** fabric used for binding edges. **2** the strong covering holding the leaves of a book together. • *adj.* making a legal obligation (*the agreement is binding on both parties*).

bindweed *n.* a wild convolvulus.

binge / binj / *colloq. n.* a bout of excessive eating, drinking, etc. • *v.* indulge in a binge.

bingle *n. Aust. colloq.* **1** a collision. **2** a fight or skirmish

bingo *n.* a gambling game in which each player has a card with numbers to be marked off as they are called. • *interj.* **1** an exclamation made by a person winning a game of bingo. **2** an exclamation of triumph, success, etc. in other contexts.

bingy / **bin**-jee / *n. Aust. colloq.* the stomach; belly. (¶ Dharuk)

binnacle / **bin**-uh-kuhl / *n.* a non-magnetic stand for a ship's compass.

binocular / buh-**nok**-yuh-luh / *adj.* for or using both eyes. • *n.* (**binoculars**) an instrument with lenses for both eyes, making distant objects seem nearer.

binomial / buy-**noh**-mee-uhl / *n.* an algebraic expression consisting of two terms linked by a plus or minus sign. • *adj.* consisting of two terms or names. ☐ **binomial theorem** a formula for finding any power of a binomial.

bio- *comb. form* **1** life. **2** of living things.

biochemistry *n.* chemistry of living organisms. ☐ **biochemical** *adj.* **biochemist** *n.*

biodegradable / buy-oh-duh-**gray**-duh-buhl / *adj.* able to be broken down by bacteria in the environment.

biodiversity / buy-oh-duh-**ver**-suh-tee / *n.* diversity of plant and animal life.

bioengineering *n.* the application of engineering techniques to biological processes.

bioethics *n.pl.* (treated as *sing.*) the ethics of medical and biological research.

biogenesis *n.* **1** the hypothesis that a living thing originates only from a similar living thing. **2** the production of substances by living things.

biogeography *n.* the scientific study of the geographical distribution of plants and animals.

biographer *n.* a person who writes a biography.

biography *n.* the story of a person's life written by another. ☐ **biographical** *adj.*

biological *adj.* of biology or living organisms. ☐ **biological clock** an internal mechanism

biology 74 **bishop**

controlling the rhythmic pattern of activities of a living thing. **biological control** control of plant pests by introducing natural predators. **biological warfare** the use of organisms against an enemy to spread disease. ☐ ☐ **biologically** *adv.*

biology *n.* the scientific study of the life and structure of living things. ☐ **biologist** *n.*

biomass *n.* the total quantity or weight of organisms in a given area or volume.

biome / **buy**-ohm / *n.* **1** a large, naturally occurring community of fauna and flora adapted to the particular conditions in which they occur, e.g. an Australian rainforest. **2** the geographical region containing such a community.

bionic / buy-**on**-ik / *adj.* **1** of bionics. **2** (of a person or faculties) operated by electronic means, not naturally. • *n.* (**bionics**) the study of mechanical systems that function like parts of living beings.

biophysics *n.* the scientific study of the properties of physics in living organisms, and investigation of biological matters by means of modern physics. ☐ **biophysical** *adj.* **biophysicist** *n.*

biopic / **buy**-oh-pik / *n.* a film biography for television or cinema.

biopsy / **buy**-op-see / *n.* examination of tissue cut from a living body.

biorhythm / **buy**-oh-ri*th*-uhm / *n.* any of the recurring cycles of physical, emotional, and intellectual activity said to occur in people's lives.

biosphere / **buy**-oh-sfeer / *n.* the regions of the earth's crust and atmosphere occupied by living things.

biosynthesis *n.* the production of organic molecules by living things. ☐ **biosynthetic** *adj.*

biotechnology *n.* the use of living microorganisms and biological processes in industrial and commercial production.

biotin *n.* a vitamin of the B complex, found in egg yolk, liver, and yeast.

bipartisan / buy-**pah**-tuh-zuhn / *adj.* of or involving two political or other parties.

bipartite / buy-**pah**-tuyt / *adj.* having two parts, shared by or involving two groups.

biped / **buy**-ped / *n.* a two-footed animal.

biplane / **buy**-playn / *n.* an aeroplane with two sets of wings, one above the other.

birch *n.* **1** a deciduous European tree with smooth bark and slender branches. **2** a bundle of birch twigs used for flogging. • *v.* flog with a birch.

bird *n.* **1** a feathered animal with two wings and two legs. **2** *colloq.* a person (*he's a cunning old bird*). **3** *colloq.* a young woman; girlfriend. ☐ **bird-eating spider** a large venomous Australian spider (the female having a body often larger than a mouse) which captures large prey such as birds, frogs, etc. **bird of paradise** a bird of Australia and New Guinea, the male of which has brilliantly coloured plumage. **bird of prey** a bird which hunts animals for food. **bird's-eye view** a general view from above. **bird's nest fern** an Australian rainforest fern having long fronds radiating out from a central base and forming a bowl-shaped whole.

birdbrain *n. colloq.* a stupid or flighty person. ☐ **birdbrained** *adj.*

birdcage *n.* **1** a cage for birds. **2** the enclosure at a racecourse in which jockeys mount and dismount.

birdie *n.* a score of one stroke under par for a hole at golf.

birdlime *n.* a sticky substance spread to trap birds.

birdo *n.* (*pl.* **birdos**) *Aust. colloq.* a birdwatcher; a bird fancier.

Birdsville Track a 500 km stockroute from Birdsville in south-western Qld to Marree in SA.

birdwatcher *n.* one who studies the habits of birds in their natural surroundings.

birdwing *n.* a large colourful butterfly of north-eastern coastal Australia.

biretta / buh-**ret**-uh / *n.* a square cap worn by Catholic priests.

biriani / bi-ree-**yah**-nee / *n.* (also **buriani**) a dish (originally Indian) consisting of highly seasoned rice and meat (usu. lamb) etc.

biro *n. trademark* a ballpoint pen.

birth *n.* **1** the emergence of young from the mother's body. **2** origin, parentage (*he is of convict birth*). ☐ **birth certificate** an official document giving the date and place of a person's birth. **birth control** prevention of unwanted pregnancy; contraception. **birth rate** the number of births in one year for every 1000 persons. **give birth to 1** produce (young). **2** be the cause of, originate.

birthday *n.* an anniversary of the day of one's birth. ☐ **in one's birthday suit** naked.

birthmark *n.* an unusual coloured mark on a person's skin at birth.

birthplace *n.* the house or district where one was born.

birthright *n.* a privilege or property to which a person has a right through being born into a particular family or country.

birthstain *n. Aust. hist.* the stigma once attached to convict ancestry in Australia.

birthstone *n.* a gem popularly associated with a particular month or with a sign of the zodiac.

biscuit / **bis**-kuht / *n.* **1** a small flat thin piece of a pastry or cake-like substance, savoury or sweet, baked crisp. **2** fired unglazed pottery. **3** light-brown colour.

bisect / buy-**sekt** / *v.* divide into two equal parts. ☐ **bisection** *n.* **bisector** *n.*

bisexual / buy-**sek**-shoo-uhl / *adj.* **1** sexually attracted to people of both sexes. **2** *Biol.* having both male and female sexual organs in one individual; hermaphrodite. • *n.* a bisexual person. ☐ **bisexuality** *n.*

bishop *n.* **1** a senior Christian clergyman, usu. with authority over the work of the Church in a city or district (his diocese) and empowered to confer holy orders. **2** a chess piece shaped like a mitre.

bishopric *n.* the office or diocese of a bishop.

bismuth / **biz**-muhth / *n.* **1** a chemical element (symbol Bi), a greyish-white metal used in alloys. **2** a compound of this used in medicines.

bison / **buy**-suhn / *n.* (*pl.* **bison**) a wild hump-backed ox of Europe or North America.

bisque / bisk / *n.* **1** an extra turn, stroke, etc., allowed to an inferior player in some games. **2** unglazed white porcelain. **3** a rich soup made from shellfish.

bistre / **bis**-tuh / *n.* **1** a brown pigment prepared from soot. **2** its colour.

bistro / **bis**-troh / *n.* (*pl.* **bistros**) **1** a small informal restaurant. **2** a wine bar.

bit[1] *n.* **1** a small piece or amount. **2** a short time or distance (*wait a bit*). ☐ **a bit on the side** *colloq.* a sexual relationship involving infidelity. **bit part** a small part in a play or film. **a bit rough** *colloq.* **1** (of language, a joke, etc.) indecent; not seemly in the circumstances. **2** unjust; unfair.

bit[2] *n.* **1** a metal bar forming the mouthpiece of a bridle. **2** the part of a tool that cuts or grips when twisted; the boring piece of a drill. ☐ **take the bit between one's teeth** take decisive action.

bit[3] *n. Computing* a unit of information expressed as a choice between two possibilities. (¶ From *bi*nary digi*t*.)

bit[4] *see* BITE.

bitch *n.* **1** a female dog; a female fox, wolf, otter, etc. **2** *derog.* a spiteful person. **3** *colloq.* an unpleasant or difficult thing or situation. • *v. colloq.* speak spitefully; complain; whinge. ☐ **bitchy** *adj.* **bitchiness** *n.*

bite *v.* (**bit**, **bitten**, **biting**) **1** cut into or nip with the teeth. **2** (of an insect) sting; (of a snake) pierce with its fangs. **3** accept bait (*the fish are biting*). **4** grip or act effectively (*wheels can't bite on a slippery surface*). **5** *colloq.* swindle (*was bitten by a con man*). **6** *colloq.* be infected by (enthusiasm, love, etc.). **7** *Aust. colloq.* cadge, borrow money from. • *n.* **1** an act of biting. **2** a wound made by this. **3** a mouthful cut off by biting. **4** food to eat, a small meal. **5** the taking of bait by a fish. **6** a firm grip or hold (*this drill has no bite*). **7** the way the teeth close in biting (*he has a faulty bite*). **8** sharpness, effectiveness.

biting *adj.* **1** causing a smarting pain (*a biting wind*). **2** (of remarks) sharp and critical.

bitmap *Computing n.* a representation in which each item is shown by one or more bits of information, esp. a display of the contents of a memory store.

bitser *n. Aust. colloq.* a mongrel dog.

bitten *see* BITE.

bitter *adj.* **1** tasting sharp; not sweet. **2** showing, feeling, causing, or caused by mental pain or resentment (*bitter remarks*). **3** piercingly cold (*a bitter wind*). • *n.* **1** beer flavoured with hops and tasting slightly bitter. **2** (**bitters**) liquor flavoured with bitter herbs to give a stimulating taste. ☐ **bitter-sweet** *adj.* sweet but with a bitter taste at the end; pleasant but with a mixture of something unpleasant. ☐☐ **bitterly** *adv.* **bitterness** *n.*

bittern *n.* any of many wading birds related to the heron, including many Australian species.

bitty *adv.* made up of unrelated bits.

bitumen / **bich**-uh-muhn / *n.* a black sticky substance obtained from petroleum, used for covering roads etc. ☐ **bituminous** *adj.*

bivalve / **buy**-valv / *n.* a shellfish with a hinged double shell.

bivouac / **biv**-oo-ak / *n.* a temporary camp without tents or other cover. • *v.* (**bivouacked**, **bivouacking**) camp in a bivouac.

biweekly *adj.* **1** happening every second week. **2** happening twice a week.

biz *n. colloq.* business.

bizarre / buh-**zah** / *adj.* strikingly odd.

Bk *symbol* berkelium.

blab *v.* (**blabbed**, **blabbing**) talk indiscreetly, let out a secret.

blabber *n.* (also **blabbermouth**) a person who blabs. • *v.* (often foll. by *on*) talk at length about trivial things.

blachan / **bluch**-ahn / *n.* (also **blacan**) *see* TRASI.

black *adj.* **1** of the very darkest colour, like coal or soot. **2** having a black skin. **3** (also **Black**) of the human group with dark-coloured skin, esp. of Aboriginal or African descent. **4** soiled with dirt. **5** dismal; hostile; not hopeful; disastrous. **6** evil, wicked. **7** not to be handled by trade unionists while others are on strike (*declared the cargo black*). • *n.* **1** black colour. **2** a black substance or material; black clothes. **3** the black ball in snooker etc. **4** the black pieces in chess etc.; the player using these. **5** the credit side of an account. **6** (also **Black**) a member of a dark-skinned race, esp. an Aborigine or an African. • *v.* **1** make black. **2** polish with blacking. ☐ **black armband** a black band worn around the upper arm to indicate mourning. **black armband view of history** *Aust.* over-emphasis on the negative aspects of Australian history, esp. on the dispossession and ill-treatment of the indigenous people. **black bean** a fermented soya bean, used as flavouring in Asian cooking. **black belt** the highest grade of proficiency in judo, karate, etc.; the holder of this. **black box** an electronic device in an aircraft recording information about its flight. **black comedy** comedy presenting a tragic theme or situation in comic terms. **black crow** *Aust. hist.* an Aborigine (esp. in the phrase *black crow shooting*, the practice by whites of shooting Aborigines for sport). **black economy** goods and services paid for by cash, which cash is not declared as part of taxable income. **black eye** an eye with the skin round it darkened by a bruise. **black game** *Aust. hist.* an Aborigine regarded by whites as an animal to be shot as a trophy or for sport (*as late as 1895, A.C. Bicknell wrote: 'I might get a brace or two of black game before the morning'*). **black hole** a region in outer space with a gravitational field so intense that no matter or radiation can escape from it. **black ice** hard thin transparent ice on roads. **black magic** magic involving the invocation of evil spirits. **black mark** a mark of disapproval. **black market** the illegal buying and selling of goods or currencies. **black marketeer** one who trades in the black market. **black out 1** cover windows etc. so that no light can penetrate. **2** suffer temporary loss of consciousness or sight or memory. **black pepper** pepper from the whole of the pepper berry including the outer husk. **black prince** *Aust.* a large black cicada. **black pudding** a large dark sausage containing blood, suet, etc. **black sheep** a member of a family or other group regarded as a disgrace or failure. **black snake** a highly venomous Australian snake. **black spot 1** a place where conditions are dangerous or difficult. **2** a fungal plant disease producing black spots. **black swan** a large Australian swan with black plumage and a red bill. **black tea** tea that is fully fermented before drying (cf. GREEN TEA). **black tie** a man's black bow tie worn with a dinner jacket. **black widow** a poisonous spider found in tropical and subtropical regions. (¶ The female of a North American species devours its mate.). **in the black** having a credit balance. □□ **blackly** *adv.* **blackness** *n.*

■ **Usage** When referring to dark-skinned people, *black* (rather than *negro* or *coloured*) is now the preferred term. In Britain and the US it is generally used to designate people of African descent while in Australia it is used of Aborigines. The term *African-American* is also common in the US for people of African descent. In order to avoid offence the terms *negro* and *coloured* should not be used.

blackball *v.* prevent (a person) from being elected as a member of a club by voting against him or her at a secret ballot.

black ban *n. Aust.* **1** a refusal (by suppliers, trade unions, etc.) to supply or provide goods or services, usu. as part of an industrial dispute or protest. **2** a prohibition (esp. as imposed by a trade union) which prevents work (on a site etc.) from proceeding.

blackberry *n.* **1** the bramble. **2** its small dark sweet berry.

blackbird[1] *n.* the common European thrush, introduced into Australia.

blackbird[2] *n. Aust. hist.* **1** an Aborigine (esp. in the phrase *blackbird shooting*, the practice whereby parties of whites would go out to hunt and murder Aborigines). **2** a Pacific Islander as victim of kidnapping and enslavement by white Australians.

blackbirding *n. Aust. hist.* the act or practice of kidnapping Pacific Islanders and selling them as slave labour, mainly for the Qld cotton and sugar plantations. □ **blackbirder** *n.*

blackboard *n.* a board with a smooth dark surface for writing on with chalk.

blackboy *n. Aust.* = XANTHORRHOEA.

Black Death *n.* an epidemic of plague in Europe during the 14th century.

blacken *v.* **1** make or become black. **2** say unpleasant things about (*blackened his character*).

blackfellow *n. Aust.* (also **blackfella, blackfeller**) (in white use often *offens.*) an Aborigine.

Black Friar a Dominican Friar, so called from his black cloak.

blackguard / *blag*-ahd, -uhd / *n.* a scoundrel. • *v.* scold or abuse vehemently. □ **blackguardly** *adv.*

blackhead *n.* a small black-topped lump blocking a pore in the skin.

blackjack = PONTOON.

blacklead *n.* graphite.

blackleg *n.* a person who works while fellow workers are on strike. • *v.* (**blacklegged, blacklegging**) act as a blackleg.

Black Line *Aust. hist.* a dragnet operation in 1830 in which the military and police, aided by settlers and their convict servants, moved systematically across eastern Tasmania in an attempt to round up the Aboriginal population. (*See* BLACK WAR.)

blacklist *n.* a list of people who are disapproved of. • *v.* put on a blacklist.

blackmail *v.* demand payment or action from (a person) by threats esp. of revealing a discreditable secret. • *n.* the crime of demanding payment in this way; the money itself. □ **blackmailer** *n.*

Blackman, Charles Raymond (1928–), Australian artist.

Black Mass *n.* a blasphemous misrepresentation of the Mass, in worship of Satan.

blackout *n.* **1** a temporary loss of consciousness or memory. **2** a loss of electric power, radio reception, etc. **3** a temporary suppression of news. **4** compulsory darkness at night during wartime.

Black Power *n.* a militant movement supporting civil rights, political power, etc., for blacks.

Black Rod *n.* the usher of the Australian Senate, so called from the ebony rod of office.

blackshirt *n. hist.* a member of a Fascist organisation.

blacksmith *n.* a smith who works in iron.

black stump *n. Aust.* an imaginary marker at the limits of settled (and, by implication, civilised) country in Australia. □ **beyond the black stump** in the remote outback. **this side of the black stump** in the world known to the speaker.

Black War *Aust. hist.* the final years of the clashes between Europeans and Aborigines in Van Diemen's Land (1828–32), at the end of which full-blooded Aborigines had been all but wiped out.

blackwattle *n. Aust.* a small native tree, unrelated to the true wattle, used by early settlers for their wattle-and-daub huts.

blackwood *n. Aust.* a tall wattle with reddish-brown wood.

bladder *n.* **1** a sac in which urine collects in human and animal bodies. **2** an inflatable bag, e.g. in a football.

blade *n.* **1** the flattened cutting part of a knife, sword, chisel, etc. **2** the flat wide part of an oar, spade, propeller, etc. **3** a flat narrow leaf, esp. of grass and cereals. **4** a broad flattish bone (*shoulder blade*).

Blair[1], Harold (1924–76), AO, Aboriginal tenor and music teacher.

Blair[2], Tony (full name: Anthony Charles Lynton Blair) (1953–), British Labour statesman who became prime minister in 1997.

Blake, William (1757–1827), English artist and poet.

Blake Prize a prize awarded annually for a religious painting, drawing, or sculpture by an Australian. (¶ Named after William Blake.)

blame *v.* hold responsible and criticise for a fault. • *n.* responsibility for a fault; criticism for doing wrong.

blameless *adj.* deserving no blame, innocent.

Blamey, Sir Thomas (Albert) (1884–1951), Australian soldier who served in the First and Second World Wars, in 1942 becoming Commander-in-Chief of the Australian Military Forces and Commander of Allied Forces in the South-West Pacific under General MacArthur.

blanch *v.* **1** make or become white or pale. **2** whiten (a plant) by depriving it of light. **3** immerse (vegetables) briefly in boiling water. **4** peel (almonds etc.) by scalding.

Blanchett / blan-**shet** /, Cate (1969–), Australian actor.

blancmange / bluh-**mon**z*h*, -**monj** / *n.* a flavoured jelly-like pudding made with milk.

bland *adj.* **1** mild in flavour; tasteless and dull (*bland foods*). **2** gentle and casual in manner, not irritating or stimulating. ◻ **blandly** *adv.* **blandness** *n.*

blandish *v.* flatter, coax. ◻ **blandishment** *n.*

blank *adj.* **1** not written or printed on; unmarked; (of a wall) without ornament or opening. **2** without interest or expression; without result. • *n.* **1** a blank space or paper; an empty surface (*his mind was a blank*). **2** a blank cartridge. ◻ **blank cartridge** one that contains no bullet. **blank cheque 1** a cheque with the amount left blank, to be filled in by the payee. **2** *colloq.* unlimited freedom of action. **blank off** seal (an opening). **blank out** cross out; obscure. **blank verse** verse written in lines of usu. ten syllables, without rhyme. ◻ ◻ **blankly** *adv.* **blankness** *n.*

blanket *n.* **1** a thick covering made of woollen or other fabric. **2** a thick covering mass (*a blanket of fog*). • *adj.* covering everything; inclusive (*a blanket agreement*). • *v.* (**blanketed, blanketing**) **1** cover with a blanket. **2** stifle, suppress (*blanketed all discussion.*) ◻ **blanket stitch** an embroidery stitch suitable for finishing a raw edge.

blare *n.* a harsh loud sound like that of a trumpet. • *v.* make such a sound.

blarney *n.* smooth talk that flatters and deceives people. • *v.* flatter, cajole.

blasé / **blah**-zay / *adj.* bored or unimpressed by things because one has experienced or seen them so often.

blaspheme *v.* utter a blasphemy. ◻ **blasphemer** *n.*

blasphemy / **blas**-fuh-mee / *n.* contemptuous or irreverent talk about God or sacred things. ◻ **blasphemous** *adj.* **blasphemously** *adv.*

blast *n.* **1** a sudden strong rush of wind or air, a wave of air from an explosion. **2** a single emission of sound by a wind instrument, whistle, car horn, etc. **3** *colloq.* a severe reprimand. • *v.* **1** blow up with explosives. **2** cause to wither, blight, destroy. • *interj.* damn. ◻ **at full blast** at maximum power or speed. **blast furnace** a furnace for smelting ore, with compressed hot air driven in. **blast off** (of a spacecraft) take off from a launching site. **blast-off** the launching of a spacecraft.

blasted *adj. colloq.* damned; annoying.

blatant / **blay**-tuhnt / *adj.* **1** attracting attention in a loud, obtrusive way. **2** obvious and unashamed (*a blatant lie*). ◻ **blatantly** *adv.*

blather *colloq. v.* chatter foolishly. • *n.* foolish chatter.

Blaxland, Gregory (1778–1853), English-born free settler who joined Lawson and Wentworth in their successful expedition across the Blue Mountains.

blaze[1] *n.* **1** a bright flame or fire. **2** a bright light, a brightly coloured display. **3** an outburst (*a blaze of anger*). **4** (**blazes**) *colloq.* hell (*what the blazes is that?*). • *v.* **1** burn or shine brightly. **2** have an outburst of intense feeling or anger. ◻ **blaze away** fire a gun continuously.

blaze[2] *n.* **1** a white mark on an animal's face. **2** a mark chipped in the bark of a tree to mark a route. • *v.* mark (a tree or route) with blazes. ◻ **blaze a trail** make such marks; pioneer and show the way for others to follow.

blazer *n.* a jacket without matching trousers, often in the colours of a school, club, or team.

blazon / **blay**-zuhn / *n.* a heraldic shield, a coat of arms. • *v.* **1** proclaim. **2** describe or paint (a coat of arms); inscribe with arms, names, etc., in colours.

bleach *v.* whiten by sunlight or chemicals. • *n.* a bleaching substance.

bleak *adj.* cold and cheerless (*the future looks bleak*). ◻ **bleakly** *adv.* **bleakness** *n.*

bleary *adj.* watery and seeing indistinctly (*bleary eyes*). ☐ **blearily** *adv.* **bleariness** *n.*

bleat *n.* the cry of a sheep, goat, or calf. • *v.* **1** make this cry. **2** speak or say plaintively.

Bledisloe Cup / bled-uhs-loh / the prize for a Rugby Union competition between Australia and New Zealand. It was first awarded by Lord Bledisloe, governor-general of New Zealand, in 1931.

bleed *v.* (**bled**, **bleeding**) **1** leak blood or other fluid. **2** draw blood or fluid from. **3** (of dye) come out in water; run. **4** extort money from.

bleeding *adj.* & *adv. colloq.* bloody, damned.

bleep *n.* a short high-pitched sound used as a signal. • *v.* make this sound.

bleeper *n.* a small electronic device that bleeps to contact the person carrying it.

blemish *n.* a flaw that spoils a thing's perfection. • *v.* spoil with a blemish.

blench *v.* flinch.

blend *v.* **1** mix in order to get a certain quality. **2** mingle, become a mixture. **3** have no sharp or unpleasant contrast (*the colours blend well*). • *n.* a mixture of different sorts (*a blend of tea*).

blender *n.* **1** something that blends things. **2** a kitchen appliance for liquidising or puréeing food.

blenny *n.* any of many small spiny-finned scaleless marine fish of Australian coastal waters and elsewhere.

bless *v.* (past & past participle **blessed** or **blest** pronounced the same) **1** make sacred or holy with the sign of the Cross. **2** call holy; thank (*they blessed God; blest the day he met her*). **3** call God's favour upon (*bless this house*). ☐ **be blessed with** be fortunate in having (*he was blest with good health*).

blessed / bles-uhd / *adj.* **1** holy, sacred (*the Blessed Virgin*). **2** *Catholic Church* beatified (*Blessed Mary McKillop*). **3** revered (*of blessed memory*). **4** fortunate (*blessed are the meek*). **5** *colloq.* damned (*the blessed thing slipped*). ☐ **blessedness** *n.*

blessing *n.* **1** God's favour; a prayer for this. **2** something one is glad of (*a blessing in disguise*).

blew see BLOW¹.

Bligh, William (1754–1817), British naval officer, commander of HMS *Bounty* whose crew mutinied in 1789. He became the Governor of NSW in 1806.

blight *n.* **1** a disease that withers plants. **2** a fungus or insect causing this disease. **3** = SANDY BLIGHT. **4** a malignant influence. **5** an unsightly area. • *v.* **1** affect with blight. **2** harm, destroy; spoil (*he blighted my hopes*).

blighter *n. colloq.* a person, esp. an annoying one.

blimp *n.* **1** a small non-rigid airship. **2** a soundproof cover for a cine-camera.

blind *adj.* **1** without sight. **2** without foresight or understanding; without adequate information (*blind obedience*). **3** concealed (*blind hemming*). **4** (in cookery) without filling (*bake it blind*). **5** (of a tube, road, etc.) closed at one end. • *adv.* blindly. • *v.* **1** make blind; dazzle with bright light. **2** take away the power of judgment; overawe (*blinded by success*). • *n.* **1** a screen, esp. on a roller, for a window. **2** a thing used to conceal the truth (*he's a spy: his job is just a blind*). ☐ **blind alley 1** an alley that is closed at one end. **2** a situation with no prospects of improvement or success. **blind bend** a road bend where it is impossible to see what is coming. **blind date** a date between people who have not met before. **blind drunk** *colloq.* very drunk indeed. **blind man's buff** a game in which a blindfolded player tries to catch others. **blind spot 1** a point on the eye that is insensitive to light. **2** an area where understanding is lacking. **3** an area cut off from a motorist's vision. **turn a blind eye** pretend not to notice. ☐☐ **blindly** *adv.* **blindness** *n.*

blinder *n. colloq.* **1 a** an excellent piece of play in a game. **b** an excellent game. **2** a bout of drinking to excess.

blindfold *adj.* & *adv.* with the eyes covered with a cloth to block one's sight. • *n.* a cloth used for this. • *v.* cover the eyes with a cloth.

Blind Freddy *n. Aust. colloq.* a most unperceptive person.

blink *v.* **1** open and shut the eyes rapidly. **2** shine unsteadily; flicker. • *n.* **1** an act of blinking. **2** a quick gleam. ☐ **on the blink** *colloq.* not working properly; out of order.

blinker *v.* obstruct the sight or understanding of. • *n.* a device that blinks, esp. a car's indicators. *n.pl.* (**blinkers**) leather pieces fixed on a bridle to prevent a horse from seeing sideways.

blinking *adj.* & *adv. colloq.* damned.

blip *n.* **1** a spot of light on a radar screen. **2** a quick electronic popping sound. **3** a minor problem, mistake, or change. • *v.* (**blipped**, **blipping**) make a blip.

bliss *n.* perfect happiness. ☐ **blissful** *adj.* **blissfully** *adv.*

blister *n.* **1** a bubble-like swelling on the skin, filled with watery liquid. **2** a raised swelling, e.g. on a painted surface. • *v.* **1** cause a blister on; be affected with blisters. **2** criticise severely.

blithe / bluy*th* / *adj.* casual and carefree. ☐ **blithely** *adv.*

blithering *adj. colloq.* hopeless, contemptible (*blithering idiot*).

BLitt *abbr.* Bachelor of Letters.

blitz *n.* **1** a violent attack, esp. from aircraft. **2** any intensive attack (*the police blitz on drink-driving*). **3** an intensive period of work (*have a blitz on this room*). **4** (**the Blitz**) German air raids on London in 1940. • *v.* **1** attack or damage in a blitz. **2** defeat convincingly.

blitzkrieg / blits-kreeg / *n.* an intense military campaign intended to bring about a swift victory.

blizzard *n.* a severe snowstorm.

bloat *v.* cause to swell out with fat, gas, or liquid. • *n.* a disease of livestock characterised by an

bloated

accumulation of gases in the stomach, usu. caused by eating too much green fodder.

bloated *adj.* **1** swollen with fat, gas, or liquid. **2** puffed up with pride or self-indulgence.

blob *n.* a drop of liquid; a round mass or spot.

bloc *n.* a group of parties or countries who unite to support a particular interest.

block *n.* **1** a solid piece of wood, stone, or other hard substance. **2** a large piece of wood for chopping or hammering on; that on which condemned people were beheaded. **3** *Aust.* a large tract of land in a rural area or a building allotment in a suburb etc. **4** a compact mass of buildings bounded by streets (*drive round the block*). **5** a large building divided into separate flats or offices. **6** a large section of shares, seats, etc. as a unit. **7** a pad of paper for drawing or writing on. **8** an obstruction. **9** *colloq.* the head. • *v.* **1** obstruct, prevent the movement or use of. **2** stop (a bowled ball) with the bat. □ **block and tackle** a system of pulleys and ropes used for lifting things. **block capitals** = BLOCK LETTERS. **block diagram** a diagram showing the general arrangement of parts in an apparatus. **block in** sketch in roughly. **block letters** plain capital letters. **do one's block** *Aust. colloq.* lose one's temper.

blockade *n.* the blocking of access to a place in order to prevent the entry of goods etc. • *v.* set up a blockade of.

blockage *n.* **1** something that blocks. **2** the state of being blocked.

blockbuster *n.* **1** something very powerful or successful. **2** a huge bomb.

blockhead *n.* a stupid person.

blockhole *n. Cricket* the spot on which a batsman blocks the ball before the wicket, and rests the bat before playing.

bloke *n. colloq.* a person.

blokey *adj.* (**blokier**, **blokiest**) *Aust. colloq.* **1** male-centred; exclusively male. **2** = OCKER.

blond (of a woman or her hair **blonde**) *adj.* fair-haired; (of hair) fair. • *n.* a fair-haired person.

blood *n.* **1** the red oxygen-bearing liquid circulating in the bodies of animals. **2** bloodshed; the guilt for this. **3** temper; courage (*his blood is up*). **4** race, descent, parentage (*they are my own blood*). • *v.* initiate (a person) by experience. □ **blood bank** a store of blood for transfusion. **blood bath** a massacre. **blood bin** *Sport* any place off the field of play to which a player is sent to comply with the blood rule. **blood brother 1** a brother by birth. **2** an intimate friend to whom one has sworn loyalty by the ceremonial mingling of blood. **blood count** the number of corpuscles in a specific amount of blood. **blood-curdling** horrifying. **blood donor** a person who gives blood for transfusion. **blood group** any of the classes or types of human blood. **blood heat** normal human temperature, about 37°C or 98.4°F. **blood-letting 1** removal of some of a patient's blood. **2** bloodshed; killing. **blood poisoning** the condition that results when the bloodstream is infected with harmful micro-organisms. **blood pressure** the pressure of blood within the arteries and veins; abnormally high pressure of this kind. **blood rule** *Sport* the rule by which a competitor who is bleeding, or whose clothing is marked with fresh blood, is sent from the field of play to prevent the spread of blood-borne disease. **blood sports** sports involving killing or wounding animals. **blood sugar** the amount of glucose in the blood. **blood vessel** a vein, artery, or capillary tube carrying blood.

blooded *adj.* **1** initiated. **2** (in *combinations*) having blood or a disposition of a specified kind (*cold-blooded; red-blooded*).

bloodhound *n.* a large keen-scented dog formerly used in tracking.

bloodless *adj.* **1** having no blood; looking pale, drained of blood. **2** without bloodshed. **3** without vitality.

bloodshed *n.* the killing or wounding of people.

bloodshot *adj.* (of eyes) red from dilated veins.

bloodstain *n.* a stain made by blood.

bloodstained *adj.* **1** stained with blood. **2** disgraced by bloodshed.

bloodstock *n.* thoroughbred horses.

bloodstream *n.* the blood circulating in the body.

bloodsucker *n.* **1** a creature that sucks blood. **2** a person who extorts money.

Bloodsworth, James (?–1804), a master bricklayer and builder who arrived as a convict on the First Fleet and was soon responsible for the design and construction of many of the Colony's earliest buildings, including Government House. He was pardoned in 1790.

bloodthirsty *adj.* eager for bloodshed.

bloodwood *n. Aust.* any of many eucalypts, typically having a rough tessellated bark and bleeding a viscous red fluid when damaged.

bloody *adj.* **1** of, like, running with, or smeared with blood. **2** with much bloodshed (*a bloody battle*). **3** bloodthirsty, cruel. **4** *colloq.* expressing annoyance or antipathy, or as an intensifier expressing approval or disapproval (*bloody idiot; a bloody marvel; a bloody sight better*). • *adv. colloq.* (as an intensifier) (*bloody awful; you'd bloody well better!*). • *v.* (**bloodied, bloodying**) stain with blood. □ **bloody-minded** deliberately unco-operative. □□ **bloodily** *adv.* **bloodiness** *n.*

bloom *n.* **1** a flower. **2** beauty, perfection (*he's in the full bloom of youth*). **3** a healthy glow of the complexion. **4** a fine powder on fresh ripe grapes etc. • *v.* **1** bear flowers, be in bloom. **2** be in full beauty. □ **in bloom** in flower, flowering.

bloomer *n.* **1** *colloq.* a blunder. **2** a plant that blooms in a specified way (*an autumn bloomer*). **3** (**bloomers**) *colloq.* knickers with legs.

blooming *adj.* & *adv. colloq.* damned; really.

blossom *n.* **1** a flower, esp. of a fruit tree. **2** a mass of such flowers. • *v.* **1** open into flowers. **2** develop and flourish.

blot *n.* **1** a spot of ink etc. **2** something ugly (*a blot on the landscape*). **3** a fault, a disgraceful act or quality. • *v.* (**blotted**, **blotting**) **1** make a blot or blots on. **2** dry with blotting paper, soak up. ☐ **blot out 1** destroy, obliterate (*blot out the memory*). **2** obscure (*mist blotted out the view*).

blotting paper absorbent paper for drying ink writing.

blotch *n.* a large irregular mark. ☐ **blotched** *adj.* **blotchy** *adj.*

blotto *adj. colloq.* very drunk.

blouse *n.* **1** a shirt-like garment worn by women. **2** a waist-length coat forming part of a military uniform. • *v.* **1** make (a thing) full like a blouse. **2** (foll. by *out*) fill with air and billow.

blouson / **bloo**-zon / *n.* a short full jacket gathered in at the waist.

blow[1] *v.* (**blew**, **blown**, **blowing**) **1** send out a current of air or breath; move or be moved by this. **2** move or flow as a current of air does. **3** sound or be sounded by blowing (*blow the trumpet; the whistle blew*). **4** shape (molten glass) by blowing into it. **5** puff and pant. **6** swell. **7** melt with too strong an electric current (*blow the fuse; a fuse has blown*). **8** break with explosives. **9** *colloq.* reveal (*the spy's cover was blown*). **10** *colloq.* spend recklessly (*blew $100*). **11** *colloq.* bungle (an opportunity etc.); fail (*blew his chances; blew the exam*). **12** register (a reading of one's blood-alcohol level) by blowing into a breathalyser (*he blew .06*). **13** *coarse colloq.* fellate. **14** *coarse colloq.* (of a male) ejaculate; (cause to) achieve orgasm. • *n.* **1** an act of blowing. **2** exposure to fresh air. ☐ **blow-dry** use a hand-held drier to style (washed hair) while drying it. **blow job** *coarse colloq.* fellatio. **blow-out 1** a burst tyre. **2** a melted fuse. **3** a rapid uncontrolled upward rush of oil or gas from a well. **4** *Econ.* (of expenditure estimates, a budget deficit, etc.) an increase in size. **blow over** die down without serious consequences. **blow the mind** produce hallucinations; astound. **blow through** *Aust. colloq.* depart suddenly. **blow up 1** inflate. **2** exaggerate (*you've blown this problem up out of all proportion*). **3** make an enlargement of (a photograph). **4** explode; shatter by an explosion. **5** lose one's temper; reprimand severely. **6** become a crisis (*this problem has blown up recently*). **blow-up** *colloq.* an enlargement of a photograph. **2** an explosion.

blow[2] *n.* **1** a stroke with a hand or weapon. **2** a shock, a disaster. ☐ **blow-by-blow** *adj.* telling all the details of an event in their order of occurrence.

blower *n.* **1** a person or thing that blows. **2** *colloq.* a telephone.

blowfly *n.* a large fly that lays its eggs on meat, wounds, the flesh of animals, etc.

blowhole *n.* **1** the nostril of a whale. **2** (in coastal rock) a hole through which air or water rushes in response to the action of waves. **3** (in inland Australia) a vent through which air passes out forcefully from an underground reservoir of air. **4** a hole (esp. in ice) for breathing or fishing through.

blowie *n. Aust. colloq.* = BLOWFLY.

blowlamp *n.* a portable burner producing a very hot flame that can be directed on a selected spot.

blown see BLOW[1].

blowpipe *n.* **1** a tube through which air is blown. **2** a tube for sending out darts or pellets by blowing.

blowtorch = BLOWLAMP.

blowy *adj.* windy.

blowzy / **blow**-zee / *adj.* **1** red-faced and coarse-looking. **2** slovenly.

blubber *n.* whale fat. • *v.* weep noisily. • *adj.* (of lips) thick, swollen.

bludge *Aust. colloq. v.* **1** evade one's responsibilities. **2** (foll. by *on*) live off the efforts of others; impose on others. **3** avoid work, be idle, usu. (by implication) at someone else's expense. **4** cadge or scrounge (money, food, etc.). • *n.* **1** an undemanding job. **2** (usu. foll. by *on*) the act or an instance of imposing on (a person). ☐ **bludging** *adj.* & *n.*

bludgeon / **bluj**-uhn / *n.* a short stick with a thickened end, used as a weapon. • *v.* **1** strike with a bludgeon. **2** compel forcefully; bully.

bludger *n. Aust. colloq.* **1** *hist.* a man who lives on the earnings of a prostitute. **2** a person who lives off the efforts of others. **3** an idler, a loafer. **4** a person who cadges (money etc.) or who does not contribute his or her fair share (of a cost, of work, etc.). **5** a generalised term of abuse.

blue *adj.* **1** of the colour of the sky on a cloudless day. **2** unhappy, depressed. **3** indecent, obscene (*blue jokes*). • *n.* **1** blue colour. **2** a blue substance or material; blue clothes. **3** *Aust. colloq.* an argument, a row, a fight. **4** *Aust. colloq.* a mistake, a blunder. **5** the award for achievement in a university sport. **6** (**Blue**) *Aust.* (as a nickname) a red-headed person. **7** (**the blues**) a state of depression. **8** (**blues**) (treated as *sing.* or *pl.*) melancholy music of African-American origin. • *v.* (**blued**, **blueing**) **1** make blue. **2** *colloq.* squander (*blued his wages at the pub*). ☐ **blue baby** one with blueness of the skin from a heart defect. **blue blood** aristocratic descent. **blue cheese** cheese with veins of blue mould. **blue-chip** *adj.* (of shares) fairly reliable as an investment though less secure than gilt-edged. (¶ So called from the high-valued blue chips in the game of poker.) **blue-collar worker** a manual or industrial worker. **blue duck** *Aust.* a lost cause, a failure. **blue-eyed boy** *colloq.* a favourite. **blue flyer** *Aust.* an adult female red kangaroo. **blue gum** *Aust.* any of several eucalypts having a smooth bluish-grey bark or bluish-grey juvenile foliage. **blue heeler** a breed of highly intelligent cattle (or sheep) dog having a blue or red-flecked coat, developed in Australia in the 19th century by crossing native dingo with merle collie from Scotland and subsequently with dalmatian and black-and-tan kelpie. **blue pointer** a large bluish shark of southern Australian waters. **blue ribbon** *n.* a high honour; a prize. **blue-ribbon** *adj.* *Politics* relating to an electorate which is held very comfortably by a particular political party (*a blue-ribbon Labor seat*). **2** prize-winning. **blue whale** *n.* a rorqual, the largest known living animal. **out of the blue** unexpectedly. **stack on** (or **bung on**) **a blue** *Aust. colloq.* create a disturbance; have a row or a fight. **true blue** faithful, loyal. □□ **blueness** *n.*

bluebell *n.* **1** any of various plants with bell-shaped blue flowers. **2** = WAHLENBERGIA.

blueberry *n.* **1** a shrub with edible blue berries. **2** its fruit.

bluebottle *n.* **1** *see* PORTUGUESE MAN-OF-WAR. **2** a large fly with a bluish body.

bluegrass *n.* instrumental music influenced by American folk and country music.

blue-green algae *n.* a poisonous bacterium (not an alga) which infests rivers etc. with a mantle of blue-green scum.

Blue Mountains a plateau on the eastern side of the Great Dividing Range, west of Sydney, so called because of the mountains' striking blue haze.

blueprint *n.* **1** a blue photographic print of building plans. **2** a detailed plan or scheme.

blue-ringed octopus *n.* a very small highly venomous octopus of Australian coasts, having bands of bluish-purple on the tentacles.

bluestocking *n.* a learned woman. (¶ Named after the 'Blue Stocking Club', an 18th-century London literary group, many of whose male members wore grey or 'blue' worsted stockings instead of the black silk of formal dress.)

bluetongue *n.* any of several large Australian lizards with a broad blue tongue prominently displayed when the animal is threatened.

bluey *adj.* rather blue (*bluey-green*). •*n. Aust.* **1** a swag (so called because the outer covering was traditionally a blue blanket). **2** luggage. **3** a swagman's (traditionally blue) blanket. **4** a heavy grey-blue woollen outer garment or coat. **5** a nickname for a red-haired person.

bluff[1] *adj.* **1** with a broad steep front (*a bluff headland*). **2** abrupt, frank, and hearty in manner. •*n.* a bluff headland or cliff. □ **bluffness** *n.*

bluff[2] *v.* deceive someone by making a pretence, esp. of strength. •*n.* bluffing, a threat intended to get results without being carried out.

bluish *adj.* rather blue.

Blundell, Graeme (1945–), Australian actor, director (stage and screen), and writer.

blunder *v.* **1** move clumsily and uncertainly. **2** make a blunder. •*n.* a mistake made esp. through ignorance or carelessness. □ **blunderer** *n.*

blunderbuss *n.* an old type of gun firing many balls at one shot.

blunnies *n.pl. Aust. colloq.* a pair of stout leather working boots. (¶ From Blundstone, name of manufacturer.)

blunt *adj.* **1** not sharp or pointed. **2** speaking or expressed in plain terms (*a blunt refusal*). •*v.* **1** make or become blunt. **2** weaken the force or effect of (*his tears blunted her anger*). □ **bluntly** *adv.* **bluntness** *n.*

blur *n.* **1** a confused or indistinct appearance. **2** a smear. •*v.* (**blurred, blurring**) **1** make or become indistinct. **2** smear.

blurb *n.* a description of something, praising it, e.g. on the jacket of a book.

blurt *v.* (usu. foll. by *out*) utter abruptly or tactlessly (*blurted it out*).

blush *v.* become red in the face from shame or embarrassment. •*n.* such reddening of the face.

bluster *v.* **1** be windy, blow in gusts. **2** talk aggressively, esp. with empty threats. •*n.* such talk. □ **blustery** *adj.*

B-lymphocyte / bee-**lim**-fuh-suyt / *n.* a lymphocyte not processed by the thymus gland, and responsible for producing antibodies (cf. T-LYMPHOCYTE). (¶ *B* for *bursa*, referring to an organ in birds where it was first identified.)

BMX *n.* **1** organised bicycle racing on a dirt track. **2** a kind of bicycle for use in this.

BO *abbr. colloq.* body odour.

boa / **boh**-uh / *n.* a large non-poisonous South American snake that squeezes its prey to suffocate it. □ **boa constrictor** a Brazilian species of boa.

boar *n.* **1** a wild pig. **2** an uncastrated domestic male pig.

board *n.* **1** a thin flat piece of sawn timber. **2** a flat piece of wood or stiff material for a special purpose, e.g. a noticeboard, a surfboard, an ironing board, a chessboard. **3** thick stiff paper used for book covers. **4** daily meals obtained in return for payment or services (*board and lodging*). **5** a committee, e.g. the directors of a company or a group of examiners. **6** *Aust.* the part of the floor of a shearing shed upon which sheep are shorn. •*v.* **1** cover with boards. **2** go on board (a ship, aircraft, etc.). **3** receive or provide with meals and accommodation for payment. □ **board game** a game played on a specially marked board. **board up** block with fixed boards. **go by the board** be ignored or rejected. **on board** on or in a ship, aircraft, etc. **take on board** accept (a new idea etc.) and consider or act upon it.

boarder *n.* **1** a person who boards, esp. a resident pupil at a boarding school. **2** a person who boards a ship, esp. an enemy. **3** a person who rides a surfboard or snowboard.

boardie *n. colloq.* a surfboard rider.

boardies *n.pl. Aust. colloq.* boardshorts.

boarding *n.* **1** boards. **2** a structure or covering made of these.

boarding house *n.* a house at which board and lodging may be obtained for payment.

boarding school *n.* a school in which pupils receive board and lodging.

boardroom *n.* a room where the meetings of the board of a company etc. are held.

boardshorts *n.pl.* long shorts, originally as used by surfboard riders.

boast *v.* **1** speak with great pride and try to impress people, esp. about oneself. **2** possess as something to be proud of (*the town boasts a fine park*). • *n.* **1** a boastful statement. **2** something one is proud of. ☐ **boaster** *n.*

boastful *adj.* boasting frequently, full of boasting. ☐ **boastfully** *adv.* **boastfulness** *n.*

boat *n.* **1** a small vessel for travelling on water; *loosely* a ship. **2** a boat-shaped serving dish for sauce or gravy. ☐ **boat people** refugees leaving a country by sea. **boat race** *Aust.* a team competition which involves a race to drink quantities of beer etc. **in the same boat** suffering the same troubles.

boatie *n.* esp. *Aust. colloq.* **1** a person who sails a boat for pleasure. **2** a yachting enthusiast.

boatswain / boh-**suhn** / *n.* (also **bosun, bo'sun**) a ship's officer in charge of rigging, boats, anchors, etc.

bob *v.* (**bobbed, bobbing**) **1** make a jerky movement, move quickly up and down. **2** cut (hair) in a bob. • *n.* **1** a bobbing movement. **2** a straight hairstyle with the hair cut at the same length just above the shoulders. **3** (*pl.* **bob**) *colloq. hist.* a shilling.

bobbin *n.* a small spool holding thread or wire in a machine.

bobble *n.* a small ornamental woolly ball.

bobby pin *n.* a flat hairpin; a hairgrip.

bobcat *n.* a small four-wheeled earth-moving machine.

bobsleigh / bob-slay / *n.* (also **bobsled**) a sledge with two sets of runners, esp. with mechanical steering, used for tobogganing. ☐ **bobsleighing** *n.*

bobtail *n.* **1** a docked tail. **2** a slow-moving lizard of southern mainland Australia, having large ridged scales on the back and a very short knob of a tail.

Boccaccio / buh-**kah**-chee-oh /, Luigi (1313–75), Italian novelist, poet, and humanist.

bocce / **boch**-ay / *n.* an Italian game similar to bowls. (¶ Italian *pl.* of *boccia* 'ball'.)

Boche / bosh / *n. colloq. offens.* a German, esp. a soldier.

bod *n. colloq.* a person.

bodacious / boh-**day**-shuhs / *adj. colloq.* remarkable, excellent.

bode *v. literary* be a sign of, promise (*it boded well for their future*).

bodgie *n. Aust.* **1** something flawed or worthless. **2** a larrikin young Australian male of the 1950s. • *adj.* **1** worthless; flawed; inferior; false (*a bodgie second-hand car with bodgie number plates*). **2** (of names) assumed.

Bodhisattva / bod-uh-**saht**-vuh / *n.* (in Buddhism) one who is destined to become enlightened.

bodice / **bod**-uhs / *n.* **1** the upper part of a woman's dress, down to the waist. **2** a woman's vest-like undergarment.

bodily *adj.* of the human body or physical nature. • *adv.* **1** in person, physically. **2** as a whole (*the bridge was moved bodily 50 metres downstream*).

bodkin *n.* a blunt thick needle with a large eye, for drawing tape etc. through a hem.

body *n.* **1** the structure of bones, flesh, etc., of a human being or animal, living or dead. **2** the physical aspects of a human being (as distinct from the soul). **3** the trunk, the main part of a body apart from the head and limbs. **4** the main part of anything (*the body of a concert hall*). **5** *colloq.* a person (*she's a cheerful old body*). **6** a group or quantity of people, things, or matter, regarded as a unit. **7** a distinct piece of matter; an object in space. **8** full or substantial quality of flavour, tone, etc. (*this wine lacks body*). ☐ **body blow** a severe setback. **body corporate 1** *Law* a corporation. **2** *Aust.* an association of individual owners responsible for the maintenance and administration of property held in common, e.g. a block of home units held on strata title, a group of townhouses, etc. **body double** a stand-in for a film actor in physical or nude scenes. **body language** involuntary movements or attitudes by which a person communicates his or her feelings or moods etc. **body odour** the smell of the human body, esp. when unpleasant. **body politic** the nation regarded as a political unit.

bodyboard *n.* a short flexible surfboard, usu. ridden lying down. ☐ **bodyboarder** *n.* **bodyboarding** *n.*

bodybuilder *n.* a person who develops the muscles of the body by systematic exercise. ☐ **bodybuilding** *n.*

bodyguard *n.* an escort or personal guard to protect a person's life.

bodysuit *n.* a close-fitting one-piece stretch garment used mainly for sport.

bodysurf *v.* ride a wave towards the beach, streamlining the body and holding it rigid like a board. ☐ **bodysurfer** *n.*

bodywork *n.* the shell of a motor vehicle.

Boer / baw, boor / *n.* **1** an Afrikaner. **2** *archaic* an early Dutch inhabitant of the Cape. • *adj.* of Boers. ☐ **Boer War** either of two wars fought by Britain in South Africa, 1880–81 and 1899–1902.

boffin *n. colloq.* a person expert in some field, esp. a research scientist.

bog *n.* **1** an area of ground that is permanently wet and spongy. **2** *colloq.* a toilet. ☐ **bog down** (**bogged, bogging**) cause to be stuck and unable to make progress. **bog in** (or **into**) *Aust. colloq.*

Bogan engage in (a task or activity) with vigour and enthusiasm (esp. begin eating). □□ **boggy** adj.

Bogan / **boh**-guhn / the name of a river in New South Wales. It rises near Parkes and flows 595 km north-west, joining the Barwon near Bourke. □ **Bogan gate** a makeshift gate of barbed wire and sticks. **Bogan shower** a dust storm.

bogan n. Aust. colloq. a person who is not 'with it' in terms of behaviour and appearance, and hence perceived as not being 'one of us'; a contemptible person.

bogey[1] n. (pl. **bogeys**) **1** (in golf) a score of one stroke over par at a hole. **2** (also **bogy**) an evil or mischievous spirit; something that causes fear or trouble.

bogey[2] n. Aust. **1** a swim or a bathe. **2** (in full **bogey hole**) a swimming hole. • v. swim, bathe. (¶ Dharuk bugi 'swim' or 'dive'.)

bogeyman n. (also **bogyman**) an imaginary person feared by children.

boggi / **bog**-uy / n. Aust. a name for the Australian sleepy lizard. (¶ Wiradhuri)

boggle v. be surprised or baffled (the mind boggles at the idea).

bogie / **boh**-gee / n. **1** an undercarriage fitted below a railway vehicle, pivoted at the end for going round curves. **2** a small truck used for carrying coal, rubble, etc.

Bogle / **boh**-guhl / Eric (1944–), AM, Australian songwriter and musician. His best-known song is 'And the Band Played Waltzing Maltilda', a powerful anti-war song.

bogong / **boh**-gong / n. a large brown moth which breeds on plains in southern Australia; the adults, which mass-migrate to the hills where they gather in rock crevices, were eaten by Aborigines. (¶ Ngarigo).

Bogotá / bog-uh-**tah** / n. the capital of Colombia.

bogus / **boh**-gus / adj. sham, counterfeit.

Bohemia an area of the Czech Republic.

Bohemian adj. **1** of Bohemia. **2** (also **bohemian**) unconventional in one's way of living. • n. **1** a native or inhabitant of Bohemia. **2** (also **bohemian**) a socially unconventional person, esp. an artist or a writer.

bohrium / **baw**-ree-uhm / n. an unstable element (symbol Bh) made by high-energy atomic collisions. (¶ Named after N. Bohr, Danish physicist (1885–1962).)

boil v. **1** bubble up and change into vapour through being heated. **2** heat (a liquid or its container) so that the liquid boils; cook, wash, or process in this way; be heated or cooked etc. in this way. **3** seethe like boiling liquid; be hot with anger. • n. **1** boiling point (on the boil; off the boil). **2** an inflamed swelling under the skin, producing pus. □ **boil down 1** reduce or be reduced in quantity by boiling. **2** express or be expressed in fewer words. **boiled sweet** a sweet made of boiled sugar. **boiling point 1** the temperature at which a liquid boils. **2** a state of great anger or excitement.

boiler n. **1** a container in which water is heated. **2** a water-tank in which a hot-water supply is stored. **3** a closed metal tub for boiling laundry. **4** a fowl too tough to roast but suitable for boiling. □ **boiler suit** a one-piece garment combining overalls and shirt, worn for rough work.

boilermaker n. a person who makes boilers; a metalworker in heavy industry.

boilover n. Aust. (orig. Horse racing) a surprise result; the unexpected defeat of a favourite.

boisterous adj. **1** noisy and cheerful (boisterous children). **2** stormy; windy. □ **boisterously** adv.

bok choy / **bok** choi / n. a plant of the mustard family, having a loose cluster of dark green leaves on white stalks. (¶ Chinese)

bold adj. **1** confident and courageous. **2** without feelings of shame, impudent. **3** (of colours) strong and vivid. • n. boldface type. □ **boldly** adv. **boldness** n.

boldface n. a thick black typeface as in the headword 'boldface'.

Boldrewood, Rolf, pseudonym of Thomas Alexander Browne (1826–1915), Australian novelist best known for Robbery Under Arms.

bole n. the trunk of a tree.

bolero n. (pl. **boleros**) **1** / buh-**lair**-roh / a Spanish dance; the music for this. **2** / bol-uh-roh / a woman's short jacket with no front fastening.

Bolivia / buh-**liv**-ee-uh / a landlocked republic in South America. □ **Bolivian** adj. & n.

boll n. the round seed vessel of the cotton or flax plant etc.

bollard / **bol**-ahd / n. **1** a short thick post to which a ship's mooring rope may be tied. **2** a short post for keeping traffic off a path, traffic island, etc.

bollocks n.pl. colloq. **1** (usu. as interj.) rubbish, nonsense. **2** testicles.

boloney / buh-**loh**-nee / n. (also **baloney**) colloq. nonsense.

Bolshevik n. **1** a member of the extremist faction of the Russian socialist party which was renamed the (Russian) Communist Party in 1918. **2** any socialist extremist. □ **Bolshevism** n. **Bolshevist** n.

bolshie adj. colloq. Bolshevik, left-wing. □ **bolshiness** n.

Bolshoi Ballet / **bol**-shoi / a Moscow ballet company dating from 1776. (¶ Russian, = great.)

bolster n. a long under-pillow for the head of a bed. • v. support, prop (bolster up confidence).

bolt n. **1** a sliding bar for fastening a door. **2** the sliding part of a rifle-breech. **3** a strong metal pin for fastening things together. **4** a shaft of lightning. **5** a roll of fabric. **6** an arrow shot from a crossbow. **7** the act of bolting. • v. **1** fasten with a bolt or bolts. **2** run away; (of a horse) run off out of control. **3** (of plants) run to seed. **4** gulp down (food) hastily. □ **a bolt from the blue** a complete (usu. unwelcome) surprise. **bolt upright** quite upright.

bolter *n. Aust.* **1** *hist.* a runaway convict. **2** *colloq.* a horse with only a remote chance of winning a race. **3** *colloq.* the unexpected winner of a horse race.

bolwarra / bol-**wo**-ruh / *n.* a small Australian tree which bears aromatic edible fruit. Also called *native guava*. (¶ Probably from an Aboriginal language.)

bomb *n.* **1** a container filled with explosive or incendiary material to be set off by impact or by a timing device. **2** (**the bomb**) an atomic or hydrogen bomb. **3** *Aust. colloq.* an old or unreliable motor vehicle. • *v.* **1** attack with bombs. **2** *colloq.* fail badly (*the show bombed*). ▢ **bomb out** *colloq.* fail badly (*bombed out in Maths*).

bombard *v.* **1** attack with many missiles, esp. from big guns. **2** send a stream of high-speed particles against. **3** attack with questions or complaints. ▢ **bombardment** *n.*

bombardier / bom-buh-**deer** / *n.* a non-commissioned officer in the artillery.

bombasine / **bom**-buh-zeen / *n.* (also **bombazine**) a twilled worsted dress-material, esp. the black kind formerly much used for mourning.

bombast / **bom**-bast / *n.* pompous words or speech. ▢ **bombastic** / bom-**bas**-tik / *adj.*

Bombay the capital of the state of Maharashtra in India. In 1995 the city's official name was changed to the Hindi form 'Mumbai'.

Bombay duck *n.* a kind of dried fish eaten as a pungent relish, esp. with rice and curry. (¶ Alteration of *bummalo*, the name of the fish.)

bomber *n.* **1** an aircraft that carries and drops bombs. **2** a person who throws or plants bombs.

bombora / bom-**baw**-ruh / *n. Aust.* **1** a dangerous stretch of broken water forming over a submerged offshore reef or rock. **2** the reef or rock itself. (¶ Perhaps Dharuk)

bombshell *n.* something that comes as a great surprise and shock.

bona fide / boh-nuh **fuy**-dee / *adj.* genuine, without fraud (*bona fide customers*). • *n.* (**bona fides**) (treated as *pl.*) *colloq.* guarantees of good faith; credentials (*his bona fides are good*).

bonanza / buh-**nan**-zuh / *n.* a source of sudden great wealth or luck; a windfall.

Bonaparte / **boh**-nuh-paht / the name of a Corsican family including the three French rulers named Napoleon.

bonbon *n.* **1** a paper cylinder pulled apart, esp. at Christmas, with a sharp noise and releasing a hat, joke, etc. **2** a lolly, a sweet.

bond *n.* **1** something that binds, attaches, or restrains, e.g. a rope. **2** something that unites people. **3** a binding agreement; a document containing this. **4** money deposited as a guarantee. **5** a document issued by a government or public company acknowledging that money has been lent to it and will be repaid usu. with interest. **6** writing paper of high quality. • *v.* **1** connect or unite with a bond, link with an emotional bond. **2** put into a customs warehouse. **3** insure a contract etc. by means of a financial bond. ▢ **in bond** stored in a customs warehouse until duties are paid.

bondage *n.* **1** slavery, captivity. **2** sado-masochistic practices involving constraint.

Bondi / **bon**-duy / a suburb of Sydney famous for its beach. ▢ **shoot through like a Bondi tram** *Aust.* depart hurriedly.

bondi / **bon**-duy / *n. Aust.* a heavy Aboriginal club with a knob on the end. ▢ **give** (**a person**) **bondi** attack him or her savagely. (¶ Wiradhuri)

bonding *n.* **1** the process by which a mother becomes emotionally attached to her child. **2** the process by which any couple or the members of a group become emotionally attached one to the other(s) (*male bonding*).

bone *n.* **1** any of the hard parts (other than teeth, nails, horns, and cartilage) of an animal's body, making up the skeleton in vertebrates. **2** the substance from which such parts are made; a similar hard substance. **3** *Aust.* (in Aboriginal ritual practice) a bone pointed at a person whose death is wished. • *v.* **1** remove the bones from. **2** *colloq.* steal. **3** (also **point the bone**) *Aust.* (in Aboriginal ritual practice) influence (a person at whom a bone is pointed) with the intention of causing (that person's) death. ▢ **the bare bones** the essentials. **bone china** fine china made of clay mixed with bone ash. **bone-dry** quite dry. **bone-idle** very lazy. **bone of contention** the subject of a dispute. **bone marrow** = MARROW (sense 1). **bone up** (often foll. by *on*) *colloq.* study (a subject) intensively. **have a bone to pick** (usu. foll. by *with*) have something to argue or complain about. **make no bones about 1** raise no objection to. **2** speak frankly about. **to the bone** thoroughly, completely; to the bare minimum. ▢▢ **boneless** *adj.*

boner *n. colloq.* a stupid mistake.

boneseed *n.* a South African shrub introduced to Vic. in 1858, now naturalised and declared a noxious weed in southern Australia including Tas.

boneshaker *n.* a decrepit or uncomfortable old vehicle.

bonfire *n.* a large fire built in the open air.

bong *n.* a water pipe used for smoking marijuana or other drugs. (¶ Thai *baung* 'cylindrical wooden tube'.)

bongo *n.* (*pl.* **bongos** or **bongoes**) each of a pair of small drums played with the fingers.

bonhomie / **bon**-uh-mee / *n.* a genial manner. (¶ French)

bonito / buh-**nee**-toh / *n.* any of several tuna-like fish.

bonk *colloq. v.* **1** make an abrupt thudding sound; bump. **2** have sexual intercourse with; copulate. • *n.* **1** a bump. **2** sexual intercourse.

bonkers *adj. colloq.* crazy.

Bonn a city in Germany, the former capital of West Germany.

Bonner, Neville (Thomas) (1922–99), AO, Australian Aboriginal senator and writer, the first Aborigine to hold a seat in federal parliament.

bonnet *n.* **1** a hat with strings that tie under the chin. **2** a hinged cover over the engine etc. of a motor vehicle

Bonney, Maude Rose Lores (1897–1994), AM, Australian pioneer aviator who set several records including first round-Australia flight by a woman (1932), first Australia-England flight by a woman (1933), and she was the first person to fly solo from Australia to South Africa (1937).

bonny *adj.* (**bonnier**, **bonniest**) **1** healthy-looking. **2** *Scottish* & *N. England* good-looking.

bonsai / **bon**-suy / *n.* **1** a pair or tree grown in miniature form in a pot by artificially restricting its growth. **2** the method of cultivating this. (¶ Japanese)

bonus *n.* (*pl.* **bonuses**) a payment or benefit in addition to what is usual or expected.

■ Usage The phrase *added bonus*, although common, is regarded as tautologous by some people and is to be avoided in formal usage.

bon voyage / bon vwah-**yah**zh, bon voi-**yah**zh / *interj.* & *n.* an expression of good wishes to someone starting a journey. (¶ French)

bony *adj.* (**bonier**, **boniest**) **1** like bones. **2** having large or prominent bones, having bones with little flesh. **3** full of bones. ▫ **boniness** *n.*

Bonynge / **bon**-ning /, Richard (Alan) (1930–), AO, Australian pianist and conductor. He helped form the operatic career of Joan Sutherland whom he married in 1954.

bonze *n.* a Buddhist priest in Japan or China.

bonzer *Aust. colloq. n.* something or someone exciting admiration. • *adj.* excellent, first-rate.

boo *interj.* **1** a sound made to show disapproval or contempt. **2** an exclamation used to startle someone. • *v.* show disapproval by shouting 'boo'.

boob *colloq. n.* **1** a foolish person. **2** (also **booboo**) a stupid mistake. **3** a woman's breast. • *v.* (also **booboo**) make a stupid mistake.

boobialla / boo-bee-**al**-uh / *n.* any of several Australian plants (genus *Myoporum*) varying in form from ground-covers to tall shrubs or small trees, having usu. highly glossy leaves. (¶ From the Aboriginal language of south-eastern Tas.)

boobook / boo-buuk / *n.* the smallest and most widespread of the Australian owls, having a characteristic two-note call suggested by its name. (¶ Dharuk)

booby *n.* **1** a foolish or childish person. **2** a large seabird. ▫ **booby prize** a prize given as a joke to the competitor with the lowest score. **booby trap** **1** a hidden trap rigged up for a practical joke. **2** a hidden bomb placed so that it will explode when some apparently harmless object is touched or moved.

boodie *n.* a burrowing rat-kangaroo, formerly widespread on mainland Australia, now rare or extinct except on islands off the WA coast. (¶ Nyungar)

boofhead / buuf-hed / *n. Aust. colloq.* **1** a fool, a simpleton. **2** a person or animal having a large head.

boogie *v. colloq.* dance to pop music. ▫ **boogie board** a short light type of surfboard ridden in a prone position. **boogie-woogie** *n.* a style of playing blues or jazz on the piano, marked by a persistent bass rhythm.

book *n.* **1** a series of written or printed or plain sheets of paper fastened together at one edge and enclosed in a cover. **2** a literary work that would fill such a book or books if printed (*he is working on his book*). **3** a number of cheques, stamps, tickets, matches, etc. fastened together in the shape of a book. **4** each of the main divisions of a written work. **5** a libretto; the script of a play. **6** a record of bets made. • *v.* **1** reserve (a seat or accommodation etc.); buy (tickets) in advance; make a reservation. **2** engage a performer. **3** take the personal details of (an offender or rule breaker). **4** enter in a book or list. ▫ **book in** register at a hotel etc. **bring to book** make (a person) answer for his or her conduct. **by the book** in strict accordance with the correct procedure. **in a person's good** (*or* **bad**) **books** in (or out of) favour with him or her. **in my book** in my opinion. **take a leaf out of a person's book** imitate him or her. **throw the book at a person** charge a person or punish him or her to the utmost.

bookbinding *n.* binding books professionally. ▫ **bookbinder** *n.*

bookcase *n.* a piece of furniture with shelves for books.

Booker Prize a literary prize awarded annually for a novel published by a British or Commonwealth citizen during the previous year. It was founded in 1969 and financed by the multi-national company Booker McConnell.

bookie *n. colloq.* a bookmaker.

booking *n.* a reservation; an engagement to perform somewhere.

bookish *adj.* **1** studious; fond of reading. **2** having knowledge mainly from books.

bookkeeping *n.* the systematic recording of business transactions. ▫ **bookkeeper** *n.*

booklet *n.* a small thin usu. paper-covered book.

bookmaker *n.* a person whose business is taking bets. ▫ **bookmaking** *n.*

bookmark *n.* a strip of paper or other material placed between the pages of a book to mark a place.

bookplate *n.* a decorative label in a book bearing the owner's name.

bookworm *n.* **1** a grub that eats holes in books. **2** a person who is very fond of reading.

Boolean / **boo**-lee-uhn / *adj.* denoting a system of algebraic notation to represent logical propositions. ❑ **Boolean logic** the use of 'and', 'or', and 'not' in retrieving information from a database. (¶ George Boole, English mathematician (1815–64).)

Booligal a town in south-western NSW. The name is used to refer to any place which is hellishly hot and desolate (from Banjo Paterson's poem 'Hay and Hell in Booligal').

boom[1] *v.* **1** make a hollow deep resonant sound. **2** have a period of prosperity or rapid economic growth. • *n.* **1** a booming sound. **2** a period of increased growth, prosperity, or value.

boom[2] *n.* **1** a long pole used to keep the bottom of a sail stretched. **2** a floating barrier or a heavy chain across a river or a harbour entrance. **3** a long pole carrying a microphone.

boomer *n. Aust.* **1** a large adult male kangaroo. **2** anything exceptionally large or outstanding of its kind (*a boomer of a day; that wave was a boomer*).

boomerang *n. esp. Aust.* **1** a curved flat hardwood missile used by Aborigines in hunting prey, in warfare, and in recreation, and often of a kind able to return in flight to the thrower. **2** a plan or scheme that causes unexpected harm to its originator. **3** a thing (esp. a book) lent or borrowed which the lender insists has to be returned. **4** a dud cheque (which is returned to the sender). • *v.* act as a boomerang (*the cheque boomeranged*). (¶ Dharuk)

boon *n.* a benefit. ❑ **boon companion** an intimate friend or favourite social companion.

boondoggle *US colloq. n.* an unnecessary or wasteful project. • *v.* waste money or time on such projects.

boong / buung / *n. Aust. offens.* **1** an Aborigine. **2** any dark-skinned person.

boongarry / **buung**-guh-ree / *n. Aust.* a tree kangaroo. (¶ Warrgamay)

boor *n.* an ill-mannered person. ❑ **boorish** *adj.* **boorishly** *adv.* **boorishness** *n.*

boost *v.* **1** push upwards. **2** increase the strength, value, or good reputation of; promote. • *n.* **1** an upward thrust. **2** an increase.

booster *n.* **1** a device for increasing power or voltage. **2** an auxiliary engine or rocket for extra initial speed. **3** a second injection renewing the effect of the first one.

boot[1] *n.* **1** a shoe or outer covering for the foot and ankle or leg. **2** a compartment for luggage in a car. **3** (**the boot**) *colloq.* dismissal. • *v.* **1** kick. **2** (often foll. by *out*) eject forcefully. **3** (usu. foll. by *up*) make (a computer) ready. ❑ **boots and all** *Aust.* without reservation; with no holds barred. **put** (or **sink**) **the boot in** orig. *Aust.* **1** kick brutally. **2** attack savagely (verbally or physically), esp. when the opponent is at a disadvantage.

boot[2] *n.* ❑ **to boot** as well, in addition.

bootee *n.* a baby's knitted or crocheted boot.

Booth, William (1829–1912), founder of the Salvation Army.

booth *n.* **1** a small temporary shelter at a market or fair. **2** an enclosure for a public telephone. **3** a compartment in a large room, e.g. for voting at elections.

bootleg *v.* (**bootlegged**, **bootlegging**) **1** smuggle (alcohol). **2** make and sell (alcohol etc.) illicitly. • *adj.* smuggled or sold illicitly. ❑ **bootlegger** *n.*

bootscooting = LINE DANCING. ❑ **bootscooter** *n.*

booty *n.* loot.

booyong / **boo**-yong / *n.* any of several Australian ornamental and timber trees of the same genus, esp. the tulip oak. (¶ Bandjalang)

booze *colloq. v.* drink alcohol, esp. in large quantities. • *n.* alcoholic drink. ❑ **booze bus** *Aust.* a police vehicle carrying equipment for the random breath testing of motorists. **booze-up** a drinking session. ❑❑ **boozy** *adj.*

boozer *n. colloq.* **1** a person who boozes. **2** a hotel.

bop *n.* **1** *colloq.* a dance. **2** = BEBOP. • *v. colloq.* dance, esp. to pop music.

bora / **baw**-ruh / *n. Aust.* **1** the initiation ceremony by which an Aboriginal boy is admitted to the privileges as well as the responsibilities of manhood. **2** the sacred site at which the bora is performed. (¶ Kamilaroi)

boracic *adj.* = BORIC.

borage / **bo**-rij / *n.* a plant with blue flowers and hairy leaves, used in salads etc.

borak / **baw**-rak / *n. adv. Aust. archaic* no; not. • *n.* nonsense; rubbish; derision (*not going to take any more borak from you lot*). ❑ **poke borak at** make fun of; mock. (¶ Wathawurung *burag* 'no' or 'not'.)

borax *n.* a soluble white powder that is a compound of boron, used in making glass, enamels, and detergents.

bordeaux / baw-**doh** / *n.* a red or white wine from Bordeaux in SW France.

Border, Allan (Robert) (1955–), AO, Australian cricketer. A batsman, he made 156 test match appearances (93 as captain) and scored 11,174 runs (all three figures being world records at the time of his retirement in 1994). He was test captain 1984–94.

border *n.* **1** an edge or boundary, the part near this. **2** the line dividing two countries; the boundary between two States in Australia; the area near this. **3** a strip (esp. ornamental) round an edge. **4** a strip of ground round a garden or a part of it. • *v.* put or be a border to. ❑ **border on 1** be next to. **2** come close to (*it borders on the absurd*).

borderland *n.* the district near a boundary.

borderline *n.* **1** the line dividing two (often extreme) conditions, e.g. decency and indecency, pass and fail. **2** the line that marks a boundary. • *adj.* on the boundary between two opposed conditions; barely acceptable (*that joke was very borderline; a borderline pass in the exam*).

bore[1] *v.* **1** make (a hole or well etc.) with a revolving tool or by digging out soil. **2** pierce or penetrate in this way. • *n.* **1** the hollow inside of a gun barrel or engine cylinder; its diameter. **2** a hole made by boring. **3** *Aust.* a deep hole made esp. to find water; an artesian bore.

bore[2] *v.* make (a person) feel tired or uninterested by being dull or tedious. • *n.* a boring person or thing. ☐ **boredom** *n.* **boring** *adj.*

bore[3] *n.* a tidal wave with a steep front that moves up some estuaries.

bore[4] *see* BEAR[2].

boree / baw-ree, baw-**ree** / *n.* any of several Australian wattles, esp. a myall. (¶ Wiradhuri and Kamilaroi.)

borer *n.* **1** any of several insects, insect larvae, etc., which bore into wood, other plant material, etc. **2** a tool for boring.

boric / baw-rik / *adj.* of boron. ☐ **boric acid** a substance derived from boron, used as a mild antiseptic.

born (*See* the note at BORNE.) • *adj.* **1** destined by birth (*born to suffer; born to be king*). **2** having a certain order, status, or place of birth (*first-born; well-born; Australian-born*). **3** having a natural quality or ability (*a born leader*). ☐ **be born** be brought forth by birth. **born-again** *adj.* having experienced a revival of faith etc. **born of** originating from (*their courage was born of despair*). **not born yesterday** experienced in people's ways and not easy to deceive.

borne *see* BEAR[2]. • *adj.* (in *combinations*) carried by (*airborne; mosquito-borne*).

■ **Usage** The word *borne* is used as part of the verb *to bear* when it comes before *by* or after *have*, *has*, or *had*, e.g. *children (who were) borne by Eve; she had borne him a son*. The word *born* is used in *a son was born*.

Borneo a large island of the Malay Archipelago.
boron / baw-ron / *n.* a chemical element (symbol B) that is very resistant to high temperatures.
boronia *n.* any of several related shrubs endemic to Australia, several bearing masses of colourful flowers, and one, the brown boronia, having brown flowers with, reputedly, the strongest and headiest perfume in the world.
borough / bu-ruh / *n.* (in Australia) an urban local government area in Vic. corresponding to a municipality in the other Australian States.
borrow *v.* **1** get the temporary use of, on the understanding that the thing received is to be returned. **2** use without being the inventor; copy (*borrow their methods*). **3** (of a language) adopt words from another language (*Australian English has borrowed many words from Aboriginal languages*). ☐ **borrower** *n.*

borsch alternative spelling of BORSCHT.
borscht / bawch / *n.* (also **borsch**) a highly seasoned Russian or Polish soup of beetroot, cabbage, and other ingredients.
Bosch / bosh /, Hieronymus (*c.*1450–1516), Dutch painter whose works are typically crowded with fantastic creatures, half-human, half-animal, as well as with human figures, prefiguring the style of the surrealists.
bosh *n.* & *interj. colloq.* nonsense.
Bosnia-Herzegovina / boz-nee-uh, herts-uh-**gov**-uh-nuh / a republic of Eastern Europe, formerly part of Yugoslavia. ☐ **Bosnian** *adj.* & *n.*
bosom *n.* **1** a person's breast. **2** the part of a garment covering this. **3** the centre or inmost part (*returned to the bosom of his family*). ☐ **bosom friend** one who is intimate.
boss[1] *n.* a person who controls or gives orders to workers. • *v.* be the boss of; give orders to (*boss someone about*).
boss[2] *n.* a round projecting knob or stud.
bossa nova *n.* a dance similar to the samba; the music for this.
bossy *adj.* (**bossier**, **bossiest**) *colloq.* fond of ordering people about; doing this continually. ☐ **bossily** *adv.* **bossiness** *n.*
bosun, bo'sun alternative spellings of BOATSWAIN.
bot *n.* **1** any of various parasitic larvae infesting horses, sheep, etc. **2** *Aust. colloq.* a person who persistently borrows or cadges from others. • *v. Aust. colloq.* **1** cadge. **2** 'borrow' (*can I bot a drink?—I'm parched*).
botanical / buh-**tan**-i-kuhl / *adj.* of botany. ☐ **botanical gardens** gardens where plants and trees are grown for scientific study.
botanist *n.* an expert in botany.
botany *n.* the scientific study of plants.
Botany Bay 1 a bay, near Sydney, which was the site of James Cook's landing in 1770 (so called because of the many botanical specimens collected there by Joseph Banks). **2** *hist.* a name used variously to refer to Sydney, to NSW, and to other Australian colonies. **3** *hist.* penal servitude; any Australian penal colony.
botch *v.* (also **bodge**) spoil by poor or clumsy work. • *n.* a clumsy piece of work.
both *adj.*, *pron.*, & *adv.* the two, not only the one.
bother *v.* **1** cause trouble, worry, or annoyance to; pester. **2** take trouble, feel concern. • *interj.* an exclamation of annoyance. • *n.* **1** worry; minor trouble. **2** a person or thing causing this.
botheration *interj.* & *n.* bother.
bothersome *adj.* causing bother.
bo tree *n.* a species of fig tree sacred to Buddhists. (¶ Representing Sinhalese *bo gaha* 'tree of knowledge', the Buddha's enlightenment having occurred beneath such a tree.)

Botswana / bot-**swah**-nuh / an inland republic of southern Africa.

Botticelli / bot-uh-**chel**-ee /, Sandro (Alessandro) (1445–1510), Florentine painter.

bottle *n.* **1** a narrow-necked container for storing liquid. **2** the amount contained in this. **3** a baby's feeding bottle; milk from this. **4** a hot-water bottle. **5** (**the bottle**) drinking alcoholic drinks (*too fond of the bottle*). • *v.* **1** store in bottles. **2** preserve in glass jars (*bottled fruit*). ◻ **bottle-fed** *adj.* fed with milk from a feeding-bottle. **bottle green** dark green. **bottle shop** *Aust.* a shop (or section of a hotel) which sells beer, wine, etc. to be taken away. **bottle tree 1** a Qld tree which develops a large swollen trunk (widest at the base) resembling a bottle. **2** = BAOBAB. **bottle up** *v.* conceal or restrain (esp. a feeling).

bottlebrush *n.* **1** any shrub or small tree of the Australian genus *Callistemon*, the flower-spikes of which are shaped like a cylindrical brush. **2** any of several other Australian plants with similar flowers, esp. of the genera *Melaleuca* and *Banksia*.

■ **Usage** The application of the term 'bottlebrush' to plants other than the callistemons is considered incorrect.

bottleneck *n.* **1** a narrow stretch of road where traffic cannot flow freely. **2** anything similarly obstructing progress.

bottler *n. Aust. colloq.* an excellent person or thing.

bottom *n.* **1** the lowest part of anything, the part on which it rests; the lowest place; the end furthest away (*the bottom of the garden*). **2** the buttocks, the part of the body on which one sits. **3** the ground under a stretch of water. **4** bottom gear. **5** a ship's keel or hull. • *adj.* lowest in position, rank, or degree. • *v.* **1** provide with a bottom. **2** reach or touch bottom. ◻ **at bottom** basically, really. **be at the bottom of** be the underlying cause or originator of. **bottom line 1** the amount of total assets after profit and loss etc. have been calculated. **2** the basic essential requirement. **get to the bottom of** find out the cause or origin of. **bottom out** reach the lowest level (*the recession has bottomed out*).

bottomless *adj.* **1** extremely deep. **2** inexhaustible (*a bottomless purse*).

bottommost *adj.* lowest.

botulism / **boch**-uh-liz-uhm / *n.* a kind of food poisoning.

bouclé / **boo**-klay / *n.* **1** yarn with one of its strands looped at intervals. **2** fabric made from this.

boudoir / **boo**-dwah / *n.* a woman's private room.

bouffant / **boo**-fon / *adj.* (of hair) puffed out, backcombed.

Bougainville / **boh**-guhn-vil / the largest of the Solomon Islands. It constitutes the North Solomons province of Papua New Guinea.

bougainvillea / boh-guhn-**vil**-ee-uh / *n.* (also **bougainvillaea**) a tropical shrub with red, purple, etc. bracts.

bough *n.* a large branch coming from the trunk of a tree.

bought *see* BUY.

bouillon / **boo**-yon / *n.* thin clear soup, broth.

boulder / **bohl**-duh / *n.* a large smooth rounded rock.

boule / bool / *n.* (also **boules** pronounced the same) a French game similar to bowls played on rough ground with heavy metal balls.

boulevard / **boo**-luh-vahd / *n.* a wide street, often with trees on each side.

bounce *v.* **1** spring back when sent against something hard; cause to do this. **2** (of a cheque) be sent back by the bank because there is not enough money in the account to pay it. **3** jump suddenly; move in a lively manner. • *n.* **1** bouncing; the power of bouncing. **2** a strongly self-confident manner. **3** *Aust. Rules* = BALL UP. ◻ **bouncy** *adj.*

bouncer *n.* **1** a bowled ball that bounces forcefully. **2** a person employed to expel troublesome people from a club etc.

bouncing *adj.* big and healthy, boisterous.

bound[1] *v.* limit, be the boundary of. • *n.pl.* (**bounds**) limits. ◻ **out of bounds** outside the area one is allowed to enter.

bound[2] *v.* jump or spring; run with jumping movements. • *n.* a bounding movement.

bound[3] *adj.* going or heading towards (*bound for Ballarat; northbound traffic*).

bound[4] *see* BIND. • *adj.* obstructed or hindered by (*fog-bound*). ◻ **bound to** certain to. **bound up with** closely associated with. **I'll be bound** I feel certain.

boundary *n.* **1** a line that marks a limit. **2** a hit to or over the boundary of the field in cricket. ◻ **boundary rider** *Aust.* **1** a person employed to ride round the extensive fences etc. of a cattle or sheep station and keep them in good order. **2** a roving reporter at a football game, esp. one based on the playing field boundary and having specialist knowledge of the game.

bounden *adj.* obligatory. ◻ **one's bounden duty** a duty dictated by one's conscience.

boundless *adj.* without limits.

bountiful *adj.* **1** giving generously. **2** abundant.

bounty *n.* **1** generosity in giving. **2** a generous gift. **3** a reward or payment given as an inducement.

bouquet / boo-**kay**, boh- / *n.* **1** a bunch of flowers, esp. professionally arranged. **2** a compliment, praise. **3** the scent of wine. ◻ **bouquet garni** / gah-**nee** / (*pl.* **bouquets garnis** pronounced the same) a bunch of herbs used for flavouring.

bourbon / **ber**-buhn / *n.* a whisky made from maize and rye.

bourgeois /boor-*zh*wah / *adj.* **1** conventionally middle-class; selfishly materialistic. **2** capitalist. • *n.* a bourgeois person.

bourgeoisie /boor-*zh*wah-zee / *n. derog.* **1** the capitalist class. **2** the middle class.

Bourke[1], Sir Richard (1777–1855), Irish military officer, Governor of NSW. An able administrator and a notable reformer, he was also responsible for the foundation of a town on the banks of the Yarra. He directed that this town be called 'Melbourne'.

Bourke[2] □ **back of Bourke** the remote and sparsely populated inland of Australia. (¶ A town in north-western NSW.)

bourn / bawn / *n.* (also **bourne**) *archaic* or *poetic* **1** a goal, a destination. **2** a realm or territory. **3** a limit.

bourse / boors / *n.* a money market.

bout *n.* **1** a period of activity, work, or illness. **2** a boxing contest.

boutique / boo-teek / *n.* a small shop selling clothes etc. of the latest fashion. • *adj.* (of a business) producing individual or high-class products (*a boutique brewery; a boutique winery*).

bouzouki / buh-**zoo**-kee / *n.* (*pl.* **bouzoukis**) a Greek stringed instrument of the lute family.

bovine / **boh**-vuyn / *adj.* **1** of or like cattle. **2** dull and stupid.

bow[1] / boh / *n.* **1** a piece of wood, plastic, etc., curved by a tight string joining its ends, used for shooting arrows. **2** a rod with horsehair stretched between its ends, used for playing the violin etc. **3** a knot made with a loop or loops; ribbon etc. tied in this way. • *v.* use a bow on (a violin etc.). □ **bow-legged** having bandy legs. **bow tie** a man's necktie tied into a bow. **bow window** a curved bay window.

bow[2] / bow / *n.* bending of the head or body in greeting, respect, agreement, etc. • *v.* **1** make a bow; bend in greeting etc. **2** bend downwards under a weight. **3** submit or give in (*must bow to the inevitable*). □ **bow and scrape** be obsequiously polite; grovel.

bow[3] / bow / *n.* **1** the front or forward end of a boat or ship. **2** the oarsman nearest the bow.

bowdlerise / **bowd**-luh-ruyz / *v.* (also **-ize**) remove words or scenes considered improper from (a book etc.); censor. (¶ Named after T. Bowdler who in 1818 produced a censored version of Shakespeare's plays.)

bowel *n.* **1** the intestine. **2** (**bowels**) the innermost parts (*in the bowels of the earth*).

bower / bowuh / *n.* a leafy shelter.

bowerbird *n.* **1** any of various birds of Australia and New Guinea, the males of which construct elaborate 'bowers' decorated with feathers, grasses, shells, etc. during courtship. **2** *Aust.* **a** a person who collects useless objects etc. **b** a thief.

bowie knife / **boh**-ee / *n.* a long hunting knife with a double-edged point.

bowl[1] *n.* **1** a basin for holding food or liquid. **2** this with its contents; the amount it contains. **3** any deep-sided container shaped like a bowl (*toilet bowl*). **4** the hollow rounded part of a spoon, tobacco pipe, etc. **5** a bowl-shaped region or building, esp. an amphitheatre (*Myer Music Bowl*).

bowl[2] *n.* **1** a heavy ball that is slightly asymmetrical, so that it rolls in a curve, used in the game of bowls. **2** a large, heavy ball with indents for gripping, used in tenpin bowling. **3** a spell or turn of bowling in cricket. • *v.* **1** send rolling along the ground. **2** be carried fast and smoothly by car etc. (*bowling along the Hume Highway*). **3** send a ball to be played by a batsman; dismiss by knocking down a wicket with this. **4** (**bowls**) a game played by rolling asymmetrical bowls towards a jack. □ **bowl over 1** knock down. **2** overwhelm with surprise or emotion.

bowler *n.* **1** a person who bowls in cricket. **2** a person who plays bowls. **3** (in full **bowler hat**) *Brit.* a stiff felt hat with a rounded top.

bowline / **boh**-luhn / *n.* a simple knot for forming a non-slipping loop at the end of a rope.

bowling *n.* playing bowls, tenpin bowling, or a similar game. □ **bowling alley** a long narrow enclosure for tenpin bowling. **bowling green** a lawn for playing bowls.

bowser / **bow**-zuh / *n. Aust.* **1** a petrol pump. **2** a tanker used for fuelling aircraft etc.

bowsprit / **boh**-sprit / *n.* a long pole projecting from the stem of a ship, to which ropes from the front mast and sails are fastened.

bow-wow *interj.* an imitation of a dog's bark. • *n.* a child's word for a dog.

box[1] *n.* **1** a container with a flat base and usu. a lid. **2** the amount it contains. **3** a receptacle or enclosure for a special purpose (*money box; post-office box; telephone box*). **4** a compartment, e.g. with seats for several persons in a theatre, for a horse in a stable or vehicle, for the jury or witnesses in a lawcourt. **5** a small hut or shelter (*sentry box*). **6** a receptacle at a newspaper office for replies to an advertisement. **7** *Aust. hist.* a movable box-like prison (a little more than 2m wide) in which up to 28 convicts were confined at night. **8** (**the box**) *colloq.* television. **9** a light shield for the genitals in cricket etc. • *v.* put into a box. □ **box girder** a girder made of metal plates fastened in a box shape. **box in** (*or* **up**) shut into a small space, preventing free movement. **box jellyfish** a jelly-like sea animal with a box-shaped body and stinging tentacles. **box number** a number used to identify a box in a newspaper office or post office to which letters may be sent. **box office** an office for booking seats at a theatre etc. **box pleat** an arrangement of parallel pleats folding in alternate directions, forming a raised strip. **box spring** each of a set of vertical springs in a mattress.

**box² **v. fight with the fists; engage in boxing. •*n.* a slap with the open hand.

box³ **n. **1 a small evergreen European shrub. **2** its wood. **3** any of several Australian trees, esp. some eucalypts, having a close-grained timber resembling that of the European box.

boxer **n. **1 a person who boxes, esp. as a sport. **2** a dog of a breed resembling the bulldog. ☐ **boxer shorts** men's loose underpants like shorts. ☐☐ **boxing **n.

Boxing Day the day after Christmas Day, when Christmas boxes used to be presented to servants etc.

boy **n. **1 a male child. **2** a young man. **3** a young male employee (*a delivery boy*). **4** (in some countries) a male servant. **5** (in *pl.*) a man's male friends (*out with the boys again!*). •*interj.* an exclamation of surprise or joy. ☐ **boy scout** = SCOUT¹ (sense 4). ☐☐ **boyhood **n.

boycott / **boi**-kot / v. refuse to have social or commercial relations with (a person, group, country, etc.) usu. as punishment or coercion. •*n.* boycotting, treatment of this kind.

Boyd the name of an Australian family notable as artists and writers. It includes Martin (à Beckett) Boyd (1893–1972), novelist, author of *A Difficult Young Man*, etc.; and Arthur (Merric Bloomfield) Boyd (1920–99), AC, painter, sculptor, and potter. In 1990 the Federal Government accepted Arthur Boyd's gift to the nation of his extensive properties, the Riversdale estate and the adjoining Bundanon, to be used as a work centre for creative artists and as a bushland reserve.

**boyfriend **n. a person's regular male companion or lover.

**boyish **adj. like a boy. ☐ **boyishly **adv. **boyishness **n.

Boyle, Raelene (Ann) (1951–), Australian sprinter who won seven gold medals in four Commonwealth Games, and three silver medals in three Olympic Games.

Boyle, Robert (1627–91), English scientist. ☐ **Boyle's law** the volume of a fixed quantity of gas at constant temperature is inversely proportional to its pressure.

BP *abbr.* (in geological dating) before the present.
Bq *abbr.* becquerel.
Br *symbol* bromine.

**bra **n. a woman's undergarment worn to cover and support the breasts.

Brabham, Sir Jack (full name: John Arthur Brabham) (1926–), Australian motor-racing driver, three times world champion.

brace **n. **1 a device that clamps things together or holds and supports them in position. **2** (*pl.* **brace**) a pair (*five brace of partridge*). **3** a connecting mark used in printing or }. **4** (**braces**) straps used to keep trousers up, fastened to the waistband and passing over the shoulders. **5** (**braces**) a wire device fitted over teeth to straighten them. •*v.* support, give firmness to. ☐ **brace and bit** a revolving tool for boring holes, with a D-shaped central handle. **brace oneself** (also **brace up**) steady oneself in order to meet a blow or shock.

bracelet **n. an ornamental band or chain worn on the wrist or arm. ☐ **bracelet honey myrtle an extremely common melaleuca of Qld, NSW, and Vic., often used as a windbreak.

brachiosaurus / bray-kee-uh-**saw**-ruhs / n. (*pl.* **brachiosauruses**) a huge dinosaur with forelegs longer than its hind legs.

brachycome / brak-ee-**koh**-mee / n. any of several small, hardy, extremely showy Australian plants bearing masses of usu. blue daisy flowers.

**bracing **adv. invigorating, stimulating.

**bracken **n. a large coarse perennial fern widespread in Australia; a mass of such ferns.

bracket **n. **1 a support projecting from an upright surface. **2** any of the marks used in pairs for enclosing words or figures, ( ), [ ], { } (see panel). **3** a group bracketed together as similar or falling between certain limits (*an income bracket*). •*v.* (**bracketed**, **bracketing**) **1** enclose or join by brackets. **2** put together to imply connection or equality. ☐ **bracket creep** esp. *Aust.* the situation

---

Brackets ( ) [ ]

Round brackets, also called parentheses, are used mainly to enclose:
1   explanations and extra information or comment, e.g.
        Myanmar (formerly Burma)
        He is (as he always was) a rebel.
        This is done using integrated circuits (see page 38).
2   optional words or parts of words, e.g.
        crossword (puzzle)   *king-size(d)*.
In this dictionary round brackets are used to indicate typical objects of transitive verbs, e.g.
    cream *v.* beat (ingredients) to a creamy consistency.
and to indicate the type of word which can be used with the word being defined, e.g.
    crown *v.* (of a bushfire) move rapidly through the tops of trees (*the fire's beginning to crown*).
Square brackets are used mainly to enclose:
1   words added by someone other than the original writer, e.g.
        Then the man said, 'He [the police officer] can't prove I did it'.
2   various special types of information, such as stage directions, e.g.
        HEDLEY: Goodbye! [Exit].

brackish

in which a wage increase pushes a wage earner into a higher marginal tax bracket which, with the effects of inflation, reduces or cancels the increase.

brackish *adj.* slightly salty (*brackish water*).

bract *n.* a leaf-like part of a plant, often highly coloured and often mistaken for a flower, which usu. encloses the (tiny) true flower, e.g. in bougainvillea and poinsettia.

bradawl *n.* a small tool for boring holes by hand.

Bradman, Sir Don(ald George) (1908–2001), AC, Australian cricketer. A batsman, his test match average of 99.94 is well above that of any other cricketer of any era. He was test captain 1936–48.

Bradshaw *n.* each of an ancient series of human figures painted on sandstone with mulberry tree juice in the remote Kimberley area of Western Australia. Also known by local Aboriginal people as Gwion Gwion. (¶ Named after Joseph Bradshaw, Australian explorer, who first described them in 1892.)

brae / bray / *n. Scottish* a hillside.

brag *v.* (**bragged**, **bragging**) boast. • *n.* a boast.

braggart *n.* a person who brags.

Brahma *n.* **1** the Hindu creator. **2** = BRAHMAN (sense 2).

Brahman / brah-muhn / *n.* **1** (also **brahman**, **Brahmin**) a member of the highest or priestly Hindu caste. **2** the supreme divine Hindu reality. □ **Brahmanic** *adj.* **Brahmanism** *n.*

Brahms, Johannes (1833–97), German composer and pianist.

braid *n.* **1** a woven ornamental trimming. **2** a plait of hair. • *v.* **1** plait. **2** trim with braid.

Braille / brayl / *n.* a system of representing letters etc. by raised dots which blind people can read by touch. (¶ Named after its inventor, Louis Braille, who perfected it in 1834.)

brain *n.* **1** the organ that is the centre of the nervous system in animals, a mass of soft grey matter in the skull. **2** (often **brains**) the mind or intellect, intelligence. **3** an intelligent person; (also **brains**) one who originates a complex plan or idea. • *v.* kill by a heavy blow on the head. □ **brain death** incurable brain damage resulting in the person being unable to breathe independently. **brain drain** the loss of clever and skilled people by emigration. **brain-teaser** a puzzle or problem. **on the brain** obsessively in one's thoughts (*he has sex on the brain*).

brainchild *n.* a person's clever idea or invention.

brainless *adj.* stupid.

brainpower *n.* mental ability, intelligence.

brainstorm *n.* **1** a sudden violent mental disturbance. **2** a sudden bright idea. **3** a mental lapse; sudden inability to remember. **4** (also **brainstorming**) a spontaneous discussion in search of new ideas. • *v.* engage in a brainstorming session.

brass

brainwash *v.* force (a person) to reject old beliefs and accept new ones by subjecting him or her to intense psychological pressure.

brainwave *n.* **1** an electrical impulse in the brain. **2** a sudden bright idea.

brainy *adj.* (**brainier**, **brainiest**) clever, intelligent.

braise *v.* cook slowly with very little liquid in a closed container.

brake *n.* **1** a device for reducing the speed of something or stopping its motion. **2** the pedal etc. operating this. **3** a thicket. • *v.* slow down by means of a brake. □ **brake drum** a cylinder attached to a wheel, on which the brake shoe presses. **brake horsepower** the power of an engine measured by the force needed to brake it. **brake lining** a strip of fabric attached to a brake shoe to increase the friction.

bramble *n.* any wild thorny shrub, esp. the blackberry.

bran *n.* coarse meal consisting of the ground inner husks of grain, sifted out from flour.

branch *n.* **1** an arm-like part of a tree. **2** a similar part of anything; a lateral extension of a river, road, railway, etc. **3** a subdivision of a family, group of languages, or subject. **4** a local shop or office etc. belonging to a larger organisation. • *v.* send out branches; divide into branches. □ **branch off** leave a main route and take a minor one. **branch out** begin a new line of activity.

branchlet *n.* a small branch of a tree etc.

brand *n.* **1** a trademark; a particular make of goods. **2** a mark of identification made with a hot iron; the iron used for this. **3** a piece of burning or charred wood. • *v.* **1** mark with a hot iron; label with a trademark. **2** give a bad name to (*he was branded a troublemaker*). **3** impress on the memory. □ **brand-new** *adj.* completely new.

brandish *v.* wave (a thing) in display or threateningly.

Brando, Marlon (1924–), American film actor.

brandy *n.* a strong alcoholic spirit distilled from wine or fermented fruit juice.

Braque / brahk /, Georges (1882–1963), French painter who, with Picasso, inaugurated cubism.

brash *adj.* vulgarly self-assertive; impudent. □ **brashly** *adv.* **brashness** *n.*

Brasilia the capital of Brazil.

brass *n.* **1** a yellow alloy of copper and zinc. **2** a thing or things made of this. **3** the brass wind instruments of an orchestra. **4** a brass memorial tablet in a church. **5** *colloq.* money. **6** *colloq.* impudence. **7** *colloq.* high-ranking officers or officials (*the top brass*). • *adj.* made of brass. □ **brass band** a band playing brass and percussion instruments only. **brass razoo** see RAZOO. **brass rubbing** an impression of a brass memorial tablet taken by rubbing heelball over paper. **get down to brass tacks** *colloq.* consider the basic facts or practical details.

brasserie / bras-uh-ree / *n.* a bar where food can be obtained as well as drinks; an informal licensed restaurant.

brassica *n.* a plant of the family that includes cabbage and turnip.

brassière / braz-ee-uh / *n.* a bra.

brassy *adj.* (**brassier**, **brassiest**) **1** like brass in appearance or sound. **2** bold and vulgar. ☐ **brassiness** *n.*

brat *n. derog.* a child, esp. a badly-behaved one.

Bratislava the capital of the Slovak Republic.

bravado / bruh-**vah**-doh / *n.* a show of boldness.

brave *adj.* **1** able to face and endure danger or pain. **2** spectacular (*a brave show of wattle bloom*). • *n.* a North American Indian warrior. • *v.* face and endure with bravery. ☐ **bravely** *adv.* **bravery** *n.*

bravo *interj.* & *n.* (*pl.* **bravos**) a cry of 'well done!'

bravura / bruh-**vyoo**-ruh / *n.* **1** a brilliant or ambitious performance. **2** a style of music requiring brilliant technique, esp. in singing. **3** bravado.

brawl *n.* a noisy quarrel or fight. • *v.* take part in a brawl.

brawn *n.* **1** muscular strength. **2** jellied chopped meat from a pig's head pressed in a mould.

brawny *adj.* (**brawnier**, **brawniest**) strong and muscular.

bray *n.* the cry of a donkey; a sound like this. • *v.* make this cry or sound.

braze *v.* solder with an alloy of brass and zinc.

brazen / **bray**-zuhn / *adj.* **1** made of brass, like brass. **2** shameless, impudent. ☐ **brazen it out** behave, after doing wrong, as if one has nothing to be ashamed of.

brazier / **bray**-zee-uh / *n.* a basket-like stand for holding burning coals.

Brazil a republic in NE South America. • *n.* a Brazil nut. ☐ **Brazil nut** a large three-sided nut. ☐☐ **Brazilian** *adj.* & *n.*

Brazzaville the capital of the Congo.

breach *n.* **1** the breaking or neglect of a rule or agreement etc. **2** an estrangement. **3** a broken place, a gap. • *v.* break through, make a gap in. ☐ **breach of the peace** the crime of causing a public disturbance. **step into the breach** give help in a crisis.

bread *n.* **1** a food made of flour and liquid, usu. leavened by yeast, and baked. **2** *colloq.* money. ☐ **bread and butter** one's livelihood; a basic income.

breadcrumbs *n.pl.* bread (fresh or dried) crumbled or ground for use in cooking.

breaded *adj.* coated with breadcrumbs.

breadfruit *n.* the fruit of a tropical tree, with white pulp which becomes soft like new bread when roasted.

breadline *n.* ☐ **on the breadline** living in extreme poverty.

breadth *n.* width, broadness.

breadwinner *n.* the member of a family who earns the money to support the others.

break *v.* (**broke**, **broken**, **breaking**) **1** fall into pieces; cause to do this. **2** damage, make or become unusable. **3** fail to keep (a promise). **4** stop for a time, make or become discontinuous (*broke the silence; we broke for coffee; broke the strike*). **5** make a way suddenly or violently. **6** emerge or appear suddenly. **7** reveal (news etc.); become known (*the story broke*). **8** surpass (*broke the world record*). **9** make or become weak; overwhelm with grief etc.; destroy (*the scandal broke him*). **10** (of a voice) change its even tone, either with emotion or (of a boy's voice) by becoming suddenly deeper at puberty. **11** (of a ball) change direction after touching the ground. **12** (of waves) fall in foam. **13** (of boxers) come out of a clinch. • *n.* **1** act or process of breaking. **2** an escape; a sudden dash. **3** a gap, a broken place. **4** an interval, e.g. between periods of work or exercise. **5** points scored continuously in billiards, snooker, etc. **6** *colloq.* a piece of luck. **7** a fair chance (*give him a break*). ☐ **break-dancing** an acrobatic style of dancing to rock music. **break down 1** demolish. **2** cease to function; (of a person's health) collapse. **3** give way to emotion. **4** act upon chemically and reduce to constituent parts. **5** analyse (*break down the expenditure*). **break even** make gains and losses that balance exactly. **break in 1** force one's way into a building. **2** interrupt. **3** accustom to a new routine. **4** accustom (a horse) to saddle and bridle etc. **break-in** *n.* a forcible entry, esp. by a thief. **breaking point** the point at which a person or thing gives way under stress. **break into 1** enter forcibly. **2** burst into (song, laughter, etc.). **3** change pace for (a faster one) (*broke into a run*). **break out 1** begin suddenly. **2** exclaim. **3** force one's way out. **4** develop (a rash etc.). **break service** win a game at tennis when one's opponent is serving. **break the ice** overcome formality. **break wind** expel wind from the anus. ☐☐ **breakable** *adj.*

breakage *n.* **1** breaking. **2** something broken.

breakaway *n.* **1** becoming separate or free. **2** *Aust.* a stampede of cattle, esp. at the sight of water. • *adj.* that breaks or has broken away (*a breakaway group*).

breakdown *n.* **1** mechanical failure. **2** a weakening. **3** a collapse of health or mental stability. **4** an analysis of statistics.

breaker *n.* a heavy ocean wave that breaks on the coast or over a reef.

breakfast *n.* the first meal of the day. • *v.* eat breakfast.

breakneck *adj.* (of speed) dangerously fast.

breakthrough *n.* **1** the act of breaking through an obstacle etc. **2** a major advance in knowledge.

breakup *n.* breaking up; collapse; dispersal.

breakwater *n.* a wall built out into the sea to protect a harbour or coast against heavy waves.

breakwind *n. Aust.* an Aboriginal shelter.
bream / brim / *n.* **1** any of several Australian marine fish, valued for sport and eating. **2** any of several Australian freshwater perch. **3** / breem / a similar marine and freshwater fish of Europe etc.
breast *n.* **1** either of the two milk-producing organs on the upper front of a woman's body; the corresponding part of a man's body. **2** the upper front part of the human body or of a garment covering this. **3** the corresponding part in animals. **4** the breast as a source of nourishment or emotion. • *v.* face and advance against (*breasted the waves*). ☐ **breast-feed** feed (a baby) by allowing it to suckle at the mother's breast.
breastbone *n.* the flat vertical bone in the chest or breast, joined to the ribs.
breastplate *n.* a piece of armour covering the breast.
breaststroke *n.* a swimming stroke performed face downwards, with horizontal sweeping movements of the arms.
breastwork *n.* a low temporary defensive wall or parapet.
breath / breth / *n.* **1** air drawn into and sent out of the lungs. **2** breathing in (*take six deep breaths*). **3** breath as perceived by the senses (*her breath steaming in the cold air; bad breath*). **4** a gentle blowing (*a breath of wind*). **5** a hint or slight rumour (*not a breath of scandal*). ☐ **breath test** a test for alcohol on the breath, using a breathalyser. **catch one's breath 1** cease breathing momentarily in surprise etc. **2** rest to restore normal breathing. **out of breath** panting after exercise. **save one's breath** refrain from useless discussion. **take one's breath away** surprise or delight. **under one's breath** in a whisper.
breathalyse *v.* test with a breathalyser.
breathalyser *n. trademark* a device that measures the amount of alcohol in a person's breath as he or she breathes out.
breathe / breeth / *v.* **1** draw air into the lungs and send it out again; (of plants) respire. **2** take into or send out of the lungs (*breathing other people's cigarette smoke*). **3** utter (*don't breathe a word of it*). ☐ **breathe again** feel relieved of fear or anxiety. **breathing space** room to breathe; a pause to recover from fear.
breather / bree-*th*uh / *n.* **1** a pause for rest. **2** a short period in the fresh air.
breathless *adj.* **1** out of breath, panting. **2** holding one's breath with excitement. ☐ **breathlessly** *adv.* **breathlessness** *n.*
breathtaking *adj.* very exciting, spectacular.
breathy / breth-ee / *adj.* with a noticeable sound of breathing.
Brecht / brekt /, Bertolt (1898–1956), German dramatist, producer, and poet.
bred see BREED.
breech *n.* **1** the back part of a gun barrel. **2** *archaic* the buttocks. ☐ **breech birth** (also **breech delivery**) a birth in which the baby's buttocks or feet appear first.
breeches / brich-uhz / *n.pl.* trousers reaching to just below the knee.
breed *v.* (**bred**, **breeding**) **1** produce offspring. **2** keep (animals) for the purpose of producing young. **3** train, bring up. **4** give rise to. **5** create (fissile material) by nuclear reaction. • *n.* a variety of animals or plants within a species, having similar appearance.
breeder *n.* a person who breeds animals. ☐ **breeder reactor** a nuclear reactor that produces more fissile material than it uses in operating.
breeding *n.* **1** the production of young from animals, propagation. **2** good manners resulting from training or background.
breeze *n.* **1** a light wind. **2** *colloq.* an easy task. • *v. colloq.* move in a lively or casual manner (*they breezed in*).
breezy *adj.* (**breezier**, **breeziest**) **1** exposed to wind. **2** pleasantly windy. **3** lively, jovial. ☐ **breezily** *adv.* **breeziness** *n.*
Bren gun *n.* a lightweight machine-gun.
Brennan, Christopher John (1870–1932), Australian poet and philosopher.
Brereton, John Le Gay (1871–1933), Australian poet and scholar.
brethren *n.pl. archaic* brothers.
Breton / bret-uhn / *adj.* of Brittany or its people or language. • *n.* **1** a native of Brittany. **2** the Celtic language of Brittany.
breve / breev / *n.* **1** a mark placed over a short or unstressed vowel (e.g. ŏ). **2** a note in music, equal to two semibreves.
breviary / bree-vyuh-ree, brev-yuh- / *n.* a book of prayers to be read or recited daily by Catholic priests.
brevity / brev-uh-tee / *n.* shortness, briefness.
brew *v.* **1** make (beer) by boiling and fermentation; make (tea) by infusion. **2** undergo this process (*the tea is brewing*). **3** bring about; develop (*trouble is brewing*). • *n.* **1** liquid made by brewing. **2** an amount brewed.
brewer *n.* a person whose trade is brewing beer.
brewery *n.* a building in which beer is brewed.
briar *n.* (also **brier**) **1** a thorny bush, the wild rose. **2** a shrub with a hard woody root used for making tobacco pipes; a pipe made of this.
bribe *n.* something offered in order to influence a person to act in favour of the giver. • *v.* persuade by a bribe. ☐ **bribery** *n.*
bric-à-brac / brik-uh-brak / *n.* odd items of furniture, ornaments, etc., of no great value.
brick *n.* **1** a block of baked or dried clay or other substance used to build walls; building work consisting of such blocks. **2** a child's toy building block. **3** a rectangular block of something. **4** *colloq.* a kind-hearted, helpful person. • *adj.* **1** built of brick. **2** brick-red. • *v.* block with brickwork. ☐ **a brick short of a load** mentally

brickbat

deficient. **brick-red** of the red colour of bricks. **brick veneer** (a house with) a timber frame and a brick exterior that is not part of the structure. **drop a brick** *colloq.* say something tactless or indiscreet.

brickbat *n.* **1** a piece of brick, esp. one used as a missile. **2** an uncomplimentary remark; a criticism.

brickfielder *n. Aust.* **1** a hot, dry, north wind. **2** *hist.* (in Sydney) a sudden squally wind from the south bringing storms of dust. (¶ Brickfield Hill in Sydney, site of a brickworks.)

brickie *n. colloq.* a bricklayer.

bricklayer *n.* a worker who builds with bricks.

brickwork *n.* **1** a structure made of bricks. **2** (**brickworks**) a place where bricks are made.

bridal *adj.* of a bride or wedding.

bride *n.* a woman on her wedding day; a newly married woman.

bridegroom *n.* a man on his wedding day; a newly married man.

bridesmaid *n.* an unmarried woman or girl attending the bride at a wedding.

bridge *n.* **1** a structure providing a way across a river, railway, etc. **2** the raised platform on a ship from which the captain and officers direct its course. **3** the bony upper part of the nose. **4** the piece of wood on a violin etc. over which the strings are stretched. **5** something that joins, connects, or supports other parts. **6** a card game developed from whist. • *v.* make or form a bridge over. ☐ **bridging loan** a loan given for the period between two transactions, e.g. between buying a new house and selling one's own.

bridgehead *n.* a fortified area established in enemy territory, esp. on the far side of a river.

bridgework *n.* a dental structure made to cover a gap, joined to the teeth on either side.

bridle *n.* the part of a horse's harness that goes on its head. • *v.* **1** put a bridle on. **2** restrain, keep under control. **3** draw one's head up in anger, pride, or scorn.

brie / bree / *n.* a soft white cheese.

brief *adj.* **1** lasting only for a short time. **2** concise. **3** short in length. **4** abrupt, brusque (*was rather brief with me*). • *n.* **1** a summary of the facts of a case, drawn up for a barrister. **2** a case given to a barrister. **3** instructions and information given in advance. **4** (**briefs**) women's brief underpants or knickers; men's close-fitting underpants covering only the genitals and buttocks. **5** a papal letter regarding some issue of discipline. • *v.* **1** give a legal brief to. **2** instruct or inform concisely in advance. ☐ **hold no brief for** not be obliged to support. **in brief** in a few words. ☐☐ **briefly** *adv.* **briefness** *n.*

briefcase *n.* a flat case for carrying documents.

brier alternative spelling of BRIAR.

brig *n.* a square-rigged sailing-vessel with two masts.

bring

brigade / bruh-**gayd** / *n.* **1** an army unit forming part of a division. **2** a group of people organised for a particular purpose (*fire brigade*).

brigadier / brig-uh-**deer** / *n.* an officer commanding an army brigade; a staff officer of similar status.

brigalow / **brig**-uh-loh / *n.* **1** any of several Australian wattles having a dark furrowed bark and silver foliage. **2** (**the brigalow** *or* **brigalow country**) large areas of country dominated by brigalow. (¶ Perhaps from Kamilaroi *buriigal.*)

brigand / **brig**-uhnd / *n.* a member of a band of robbers. ☐ **brigandage** *n.*

brigantine *n.* a two-masted ship with a square-rigged foremast and a fore-and-aft rigged mainmast.

bright *adj.* **1** giving out or reflecting much light; shining. **2** intense, vivid. **3** cheerful. **4** quick-witted, clever. • *adv.* brightly. ☐ **brightly** *adv.* **brightness** *n.*

brighten *v.* make or become brighter.

Bright's disease *n.* a kidney disease. (¶ Richard Bright (1789–1858), English surgeon.)

brilliant *adj.* **1** very bright or sparkling. **2** outstandingly talented or intelligent. **3** *colloq.* excellent, superb. • *n.* a cut diamond with many facets. ☐ **brilliantly** *adv.* **brilliance** *n.* **brilliancy** *n.*

brilliantine *n.* a substance used to make the hair glossy.

brim *n.* **1** the top edge of a cup, hollow, or channel. **2** the projecting edge of a hat. • *v.* (**brimmed**, **brimming**) fill or be full to the brim. ☐ **brim over** overflow.

brimful *adj.* filled to the brim.

brimstone *n. archaic* sulphur.

brindled / **brin**-duhld / *adj.* brown with streaks of other colour (*the brindled cow*).

brine *n.* salt water.

bring *v.* (**brought**, **bringing**) **1** cause to come, esp. with oneself, by carrying, leading, or attracting. **2** produce as profit or income. **3** result in, cause (*war brought famine*). **4** put forward (charges etc.) in a lawcourt (*they brought an action for libel*). **5** cause to arrive at a particular state (*bring it to the boil*). **6** adduce (evidence, an argument, etc.). ☐ **bring about** cause to happen. **bring back** restore; make one remember. **bring down 1** cause to fall. **2** introduce legislation in parliament. **bring forth** give birth to; cause; *archaic* produce. **bring forward 1** arrange for (a thing) to happen earlier than was intended. **2** call attention to (a matter). **3** transfer from a previous page or account. **bring in 1** initiate, introduce. **2** produce as profit or income. **3** pronounce as a verdict in court. **bring off** do successfully. **bring out 1** cause to appear, show clearly. **2** publish. **bring the house down** get loud applause in a theatre etc. **bring to bear** concentrate as an influence (*pressure was brought to bear on the dissenters*). **bring up 1** look after and train (grow-

brinjal / brin-jawl / n. an eggplant.
brink n. 1 the edge of a steep place or of a stretch of water. 2 the verge, the edge of something unknown, dangerous, or exciting.
brinkmanship n. the art of pursuing a dangerous policy to the brink of disaster.
briny adj. salty.
brio / bree-oh / n. dash, verve, vivacity. (¶ Italian)
brioche / bree-osh / n. a small round sweet bread roll.
briquette / bri-ket / n. a block of compressed coal dust as fuel.
Brisbane the seaport and capital city of the State of Queensland. □ **Brisbane Line** an imaginary diagonal line connecting a point north of Brisbane to a point north of Adelaide. During the Second World War the military planned to defend only that part of the country which lies south of the line in the event of an enemy invasion.
brisk adj. active, lively, moving quickly. □ **briskly** adv. **briskness** n.
brisket / bris-kuht / n. a joint of beef cut from the breast.
bristle n. 1 a short stiff hair. 2 any of the stiff pieces of hair or wire etc. in a brush. •v. 1 (of an animal) raise the bristles in anger or fear. 2 show indignation. 3 be thickly set with bristles. □ **bristle with** be full of (*the place was bristling with security guards*). □□ **bristly** adj.
bristlebird n. any of three species of brownish birds of mainland Australia having prominent bristles on the face.
Brit n. colloq. a British person.
Britain (in full **Great Britain**) England, Wales, and Scotland.
Britannia the personification of Britain, shown as a woman with a shield, helmet, and trident.
Briticism / brit-uh-siz-uhm / n. an English word or idiom used only in Britain.
British adj. of Britain or its inhabitants. •n. (**the British**) British people. □ **British disease** colloq. derog. militant union activity.
Briton n. 1 a native or inhabitant of southern Britain before the Roman conquest. 2 a British person.
Brittany a district of NW France.
Britten, (Edward) Benjamin, Lord Britten of Aldeburgh (1913–76), English composer, conductor, and pianist.
brittle adj. hard but easily broken. •n. a brittle sweet made of nuts and melted sugar. □ **brittle-bone disease** = OSTEOPOROSIS. □□ **brittleness** n.
broach v. 1 make a hole in and draw out liquid. 2 begin a discussion of (*broached the topic*). 3 veer or cause (a ship) to veer and present its side to the wind and waves. •n. 1 a bit used for boring. 2 a roasting spit.

broad adj. 1 large across, wide. 2 measuring from side to side (*2 metres broad*). 3 full and complete; strong (*broad daylight; a broad hint; a broad Aussie accent*). 4 in general terms, not detailed (*in broad outline*). 5 rather coarse (*broad humour*). 6 tolerant, liberal (*a broad view*). •n. the broad part (*broad of the back*). □ **broad Australian** that pronunciation of Australian English which most obviously exhibits distinctive Australian features.
broad bean an edible bean with large flat seeds.
broad-minded adj. having tolerant views. □□ **broadness** n.
broadacre farming n. esp. *Aust.* the practice of farming vast extents of land in the one operation in order to achieve economies of scale.
broadband adj. relating to or using signals over a broad range of frequencies, esp. in high-capacity telecommunications.
broadcast v. (**broadcast**, **broadcasting**) 1 send out by radio or television. 2 speak or appear in a radio or television program. 3 make generally known. 4 sow (seed) by scattering, not in drills. 5 transmit (a message) to all nodes in a computer network. •n. a broadcast program. •adv. scattered freely. □ **broadcaster** n.
broaden v. make or become broad.
broadloom adj. (esp. of carpets) woven in broad widths.
broadly adv. 1 in a broad way. 2 in a general way (*broadly speaking*).
broadsheet n. 1 a large-sized newspaper. 2 a large sheet of paper printed on one side only, esp. with information.
broadside n. 1 the firing of all guns on one side of a ship. 2 a strong attack in words. 3 the side of a ship above the water. □ **broadside on** sideways on.
broadsword n. a sword with a broad blade, used for cutting rather than thrusting.
Broadway a long street in New York City, famous for its theatres.
brocade / bruh-kayd / n. a rich fabric woven with raised patterns. □ **brocaded** adj.
broccoli / brok-uh-lee / n. a vegetable with tightly packed green or purple flower heads.
brochette / broh-shet, bruh- / n. a skewer on which chunks of meat or vegetable are grilled or barbecued.
brochure / broh-shuh, bruh-shoor / n. a booklet or pamphlet containing information.
Brock, Peter (Geoffrey) (1945–), AM, Australian professional racing driver.
broderie anglaise / broh-duh-ree on-glayz / n. open embroidery on white linen or other fabric.
brogue / brohg / n. 1 a strong shoe with patterns of little holes. 2 a dialectal accent, esp. Irish.
broil v. 1 (esp. *US*) grill (meat). 2 make or be very hot, esp. from the sun.
broiler n. a young chicken suitable for broiling or roasting.

broke see BREAK. •*adj. colloq.* having no money. ❑ **go for broke** *colloq.* risk everything.

broken see BREAK. •*adj.* **1** having been broken. **2** reduced to despair; beaten. **3** (of language) badly spoken by a foreigner (*broken English*). **4** interrupted (*broken sleep*). ❑ **broken-down** *adj.* worn out; not functioning. **broken home** a family lacking one parent through divorce or separation. ❑❑ **brokenly** *adv.*

Broken Hill a major mining district in the arid far west of NSW served by the city of the same name (nicknamed the Silver City). The area contains probably the world's richest deposits of silver-lead-zinc ore.

broker *n.* **1** an agent who buys and sells things on behalf of others; a middleman. **2** a member of the Stock Exchange dealing in stocks and shares.

brokerage *n.* a broker's fee or commission.

brolga *n.* a large crane living near water in eastern and northern Australia, having grey plumage and red skin on its head. (¶ Kamilaroi (and other languages across to Lake Eyre) *burralga*.)

brolly *n. colloq.* an umbrella.

bromide / broh-**muyd** / *n.* **1** a compound of bromine, used in medicine to calm the nerves. **2** a boring or obvious remark. **3** a reproduction on paper coated with silver bromide emulsion.

bromine / broh-**meen** / *n.* a dark-red liquid chemical element (symbol Br), compounds of which are used in medicine and photography.

bronchial / **brong**-kee-uhl / *adj.* of the branched tubes into which the windpipe divides, leading into the lungs.

bronchitis / brong-**kuy**-tuhs / *n.* inflammation of the mucous membrane inside the bronchial tubes.

bronchus *n.* (*pl.* **bronchi**) either of the two major branches of the windpipe.

bronco / **brong**-koh / *n.* (*pl.* **broncos**) a wild or half-tamed horse, originally of western North America.

Bronhill, June (1929–), Australian soprano with an illustrious career in opera etc. She changed her name (Gough) to a contraction of Broken Hill, her native city, when its citizens raised money for her further study in England in 1952.

Brontë / **bron**-tee /, Charlotte (1816–55), Emily (1818–48), and Anne (1820–49), English novelists.

brontosaurus / bron-tuh-**saw**-ruhs / *n.* (*pl.* **brontosauruses**) a large plant-eating dinosaur with a long whiplike tail.

bronze *n.* **1** an alloy of copper and tin. **2** its brownish colour. **3** a thing made of bronze; a bronze sculpture; a bronze medal (awarded as third prize). •*adj.* made of bronze; bronze-coloured. •*v.* make or become tanned by sun. ❑ **bronzed Aussie** *Aust.* (stereotype of) the sun-loving, healthy, Australian male.

Bronze Age the period when weapons and tools were made of bronze.

brooch / brohch / *n.* an ornamental hinged pin fastened with a clasp.

brood *n.* **1** the young birds or other animals produced at one hatching or birth. **2** a family of children. •*v.* **1** sit on eggs to hatch them. **2** think long and deeply or resentfully. ❑ **brood mare** a mare kept for breeding.

broody *adj.* **1** (of a hen) wanting to brood. **2** sullenly thoughtful or depressed. **3** *colloq.* wanting to have a baby.

brook *n.* a small stream. •*v.* tolerate (*he would brook no interference*).

■ **Usage** In Australia (with the exception of WA) the noun *brook* has been replaced by *creek*.

broom *n.* **1** any of several shrubs, often with yellow flowers. **2** a long-handled brush for sweeping floors. ❑ **new broom** a newly appointed official who gets rid of old methods etc.

broomstick *n.* a broom-handle.

Bros *abbr.* Brothers.

broth *n.* the water in which meat or fish has been boiled; soup made with this.

brothel / **broth**-uhl / *n.* **1** a house where prostitutes work. **2** an untidy or messy room etc.

brother *n.* **1** a son of the same parents as another person. **2** a man who is a fellow member of a trade union or other association. **3** a monk who is not a priest; (**Brother**) his title. ❑ **brother-in-law** *n.* (*pl.* **brothers-in-law**) the brother of one's husband or wife; the husband of one's sister. ❑❑ **brotherly** *adj.*

brotherhood *n.* **1** the relationship of brothers. **2** brotherliness, comradeship. **3** an association of men; its members.

Brotherhood of St Lawrence an Australian social welfare organisation connected with the Anglican Church.

brought see BRING.

brougham / **broo**-uhm / *n.* a horse-drawn closed carriage with a driver perched outside in front.

brouhaha / **broo**-hah-hah / *n.* a commotion; a sensation.

brow *n.* **1** an eyebrow. **2** the forehead. **3** a projecting or overhanging part; the summit of a hill.

browbeat *v.* (**browbeat**, **browbeaten**, **browbeating**) intimidate.

Brown[1], Bryan (1948–), Australian actor of stage and esp. screen.

Brown[2], Noeline (1938–), Australian comedy actor.

brown *adj.* **1** of a colour between orange and black. **2** having skin of this colour; sun-tanned. **3** (of bread) made with wholemeal or wheatmeal flour. •*n.* **1** brown colour or pigment. **2** a brown substance, material, or thing; brown clothes. **3** the brown ball in snooker etc. •*v.* make or become brown. ❑ **browned off** *colloq.* bored, fed up.

brown paper strong coarse paper for wrapping

parcels etc. **brown rice** unprocessed rice with only the outer husk of the grain removed. **brown snake** any of several Australian snakes, more or less brown and highly venomous. **brown sugar** sugar that is only partly refined. ☐☐ **brownish** *adj.*

brownie *n.* **1** a benevolent elf. **2** a small square chocolate cake. **3** (**Brownie**, in full **Brownie Guide**) a member of a junior branch of the Guides. ☐ **earn Brownie points** *colloq.* do good deeds in order to earn recognition.

Brownlow Medal *n.* a medal awarded annually to the best and fairest player of the season in the Australian Football League. (¶ Named after Charles Brownlow (1861–1924), captain and coach of the Geelong team.)

browse / browz / *v.* **1** feed as animals do, on leaves or grass etc. **2** look through a book, or examine items for sale, in a casual leisurely way. **3** *Computing* read or survey (data files), typically via a network.

browser *n.* **1** a person or animal that browses. **2** *Computing* a program, usu. with a graphical user interface for displaying HTML files, used to search for and access documents on the World Wide Web.

Bruce[1], Mary Grant (1878–1958), Australian writer, best known for her Billabong series of children's books.

Bruce[2], Stanley Melbourne, Viscount Bruce of Melbourne (1883–1967), Australian statesman, prime minister 1923–29.

brucellosis / broo-suh-**loh**-suhs / *n.* a bacterial disease causing abortion in cattle and fever in humans.

bruise / brooz / *n.* **1** an injury caused by a knock or by pressure that discolours the skin without breaking it. **2** similar damage on a fruit etc. • *v.* **1** cause a bruise or bruises on. **2** show the effects of a knock etc.; be susceptible to bruises. **3** hurt mentally (*the rejection bruised his ego*).

bruiser *n. colloq.* **1** a large tough-looking person. **2** a boxer.

bruit / broot / *v. archaic* spread (a report or rumour).

brumby *n. Aust.* a wild unbroken horse. (¶ Possibly from an Aboriginal language of southern Qld or northern NSW.)

brummy *adj. Aust. colloq.* counterfeit; cheaply or shoddily made.

brunch *n.* a meal combining breakfast and lunch.

Brunei / **broo**-nuy / an independent country on the island of Borneo. ☐ **Bruneian** *adj.*

brunet / broo-**net** / *n.* a male with dark-brown hair.

brunette / broo-**net** / *n.* a female with dark-brown hair.

brunt *n.* the chief stress or strain (*bore the brunt of the attack*).

brush[1] *n.* **1** an implement with bristles of hair, wire, or nylon, etc., set in a solid base, used for cleaning or painting, grooming the hair, etc. **2** an act of brushing. **3** a brush-like piece of carbon or metal for making a good electrical connection. **4** a fox's bushy tail. **5** each of a pair of thin sticks with long wire bristles for striking a drum, cymbal, etc. **6** a short esp. unpleasant encounter (*a brush with the law*). • *v.* **1** use a brush on, remove with a brush or by passing something lightly over the surface of. **2** touch lightly in passing. ☐ **brush aside** reject casually or curtly. **brush off** reject curtly, snub. **brush-off** *n.* a curt rejection, a snub. **brush up 1** smarten. **2** study and revive one's former knowledge of.

brush[2] *n.* **1** a tract of dense natural vegetation (originally applied chiefly to the understorey, later to forest, esp. rainforest). **2** generally low and apparently stunted forms of vegetation, often thick; land covered with this. **3** = BRUSHWOOD 2. ☐ **brush fence** a fence made of sections of brushwood wired together. **brush turkey** a large mound-building bird of eastern Australia, having a bare red head and neck, yellow or bluish white wattles, and black plumage.

brushed *adj.* with raised nap (*brushed nylon*).

brushtail *n.* (also **brush-tailed possum**) a common possum, a widespread arboreal marsupial found in all Australian States, cat-sized with a long prehensile tail.

brushwood *n.* **1** undergrowth, a thicket. **2** (also **brush**) dead or felled vegetation used for building purposes, esp. the construction of fences.

brushwork *n.* the style of the strokes made with a painter's brush.

brusque / bruusk, brusk / *adj.* curt and offhand in manner. ☐ **brusquely** *adv.* **brusqueness** *n.*

Brussels the capital of Belgium; headquarters of the European Commission. ☐ **Brussels sprout** a plant of the cabbage family having small cabbage-like buds growing close to the stem; such a bud used as a vegetable.

brutal *adj.* savagely cruel, merciless. ☐ **brutally** *adv.* **brutality** *n.*

brutalise *v.* (also **-ize**) **1** make or become brutal. **2** treat brutally. ☐ **brutalisation** *n.*

brute *n.* **1** an animal other than a human. **2** a brutal person. **3** *colloq.* an unpleasant or difficult person or thing. ☐ **brute force** cruel and unthinking force. ☐☐ **brutish** *adj.*

Brutus / **broo**-tuhs /, Marcus Junius (85–42 BC), Roman senator, who with Cassius led the conspirators who assassinated Julius Caesar in 44 BC.

Brythonic / bruy-**thon**-ik / *adj.* of the Celts of southern Britain or their languages. • *n.* the southern group of the Celtic languages, including Welsh, Cornish, and Breton.

BS *abbr.* Bachelor of Surgery.

BSc *abbr.* Bachelor of Science.

BSE *abbr.* bovine spongiform encephalopathy, a usu. fatal disease of cattle, affecting the nervous system (also known as 'mad cow disease').

BT, DT *abbr.* Been There, Done That, an expression (usu. in response to a suggestion that something be done etc.) indicating bored rejection = I've experienced it already.

BTW *abbr.* (esp. in electronic communications) by the way.

bubble *n.* **1** a thin ball of liquid enclosing air or gas. **2** a small ball of air in a liquid or in a solidified liquid, such as glass. **3** a transparent domed cover. • *v.* **1** send up bubbles; rise in bubbles; make the sound of these. **2** show great liveliness. ☐ **bubble gum** chewing gum that can be blown into large bubbles. **bubble wrap** sheets of transparent, flexible plastic containing bubbles of air, used for packaging, insulation, etc.

bubbler *n. Aust.* a drinking fountain.

bubbly *adj.* full of bubbles. • *n. colloq.* champagne.

bubo / byoo-boh / *n.* (*pl.* **buboes**) an inflamed swelling in the groin or armpit.

bubonic plague / byoo-**bon**-ik / *n.* a contagious disease with buboes, spread by rats etc.

buccaneer *n.* a pirate, an unscrupulous adventurer. ☐ **buccaneering** *adj. & n.*

Bucharest / buuk-uh-**rest** / the capital of Romania.

Buchenwald / **buuk**-uhn-vahlt / a village in eastern Germany, site of a Nazi concentration camp in the Second World War.

buck[1] *n.* **1** the male of a deer, hare, or rabbit. **2** a young man. **3** an act or instance of bucking; a buckjump. • *v.* **1** (of a horse) jump with the back arched. **2** (usu. foll. by *off*) throw (a rider) in this way. **3** *colloq.* resist or oppose (*bucking the system*). **4** (usu. foll. by *up*) *colloq.* cheer (a person) up (*bucked him up no end*). **5** (usu. foll. by *up*) *colloq.* hurry up; make an effort (*buck up!—we haven't got all day*). ☐ **buck's party** *Aust.* a party for males only given for a bridegroom, usu. on the eve of his wedding, by his male friends. **buck-teeth** *n.* front upper teeth that stick out.

buck[2] *n. colloq.* (in poker) an article placed as a reminder before the next dealer. ☐ **the buck stops here** this is where the ultimate responsibility lies. **pass the buck** shift responsibility (and possible blame) to someone else.

buck[3] *n. US & Aust. colloq.* a dollar. ☐ **a fast buck** *colloq.* easy money.

bucket *n.* **1** a round open container with a handle. **2** this with its contents; the amount it contains. **3** (**buckets**) *colloq.* large quantities, esp. of rain or tears (*wept buckets*). • *v. colloq.* **1** pour heavily (*rain was bucketing down*). **2** *Aust.* denigrate (a person etc.) (*the national pastime of bucketing Canberra*). ☐ **bucket seat** a seat with a rounded back, for one person. **drop** (*or* **tip**) **the bucket on** *Aust. colloq.* make damaging revelations about (e.g. a political opponent). ☐☐ **bucketful** *n.* (*pl.* **bucketfuls**).

Buckingham Palace the London residence of the British sovereign since 1837.

buckjump *v.* (of a horse) leap with head down, legs drawn together, and back arched in an attempt to throw the rider. • *n.* **1** an act or an instance of buckjumping. **2** a buckjumping event.

buckjumper *n.* a horse which buckjumps habitually.

buckle *n.* a device usu. with a hinged pin, through which a belt or strap is threaded to secure it. • *v.* **1** fasten with a buckle. **2** crumple under pressure; cause to do this. ☐ **buckle down to** set about doing; get on with. **buckle up** fasten one's seat belt.

buckler *n.* a small round shield with a handle.

Buckley, William (?1780–1856), English convict who escaped from Port Phillip in 1803, was rescued by Aborigines, and lived with them in the Geelong area for nearly 32 years (1803–35).

Buckley's *n.* (in full **Buckley's chance** *or* **hope** etc.) *Aust.* a forlorn hope; no chance whatever (*you've got Buckley's of getting the job, mate!*). (¶ Perhaps from William BUCKLEY, with a punning reference to the Melbourne firm 'Buckley & Nunn' (*none*).)

buckram / **buk**-ruhm / *n.* stiffened cloth, esp. that used for binding books.

buckshot *n.* coarse lead shot.

buckskin *n.* **1** leather from a buck's skin (now also from a sheepskin). **2** a thick smooth cotton or woollen fabric.

buckwheat *n.* the dark seed of a particular cereal plant used to make flour or cooked as a grain.

bucolic / byoo-**kol**-ik / *adj.* characteristic of country life.

bud *n.* **1** a small knob that will develop into a branch, leaf-cluster, or flower. **2** a flower or leaf not fully open. • *v.* (**budded, budding**) **1** form buds. **2** graft a bud of (a plant) on to another.

Budapest / buud-uh-**pest** / the capital of Hungary.

Buddha / **buud**-uh, **buuth**- / *n.* **1** the title meaning 'enlightened one' (often treated as a name) of the Indian philosopher Gautama (5th century BC), and of a series of teachers of Buddhism. **2** a statue or carving representing Gautama the Buddha.

buddha / **bud**-uh / (also **budda**) *n.* a small tree of inland Australia, the leaves and timber of which smell strongly of sandalwood; the wood of this plant. (¶ Wiradhuri and Yuwaalaraay.)

Buddhism / **buud**-iz-uhm / *n.* an Asian religion based on the teachings of the Buddha. ☐ **Buddhist** *adj. & n.*

budding *adj.* beginning to develop (*a budding poet*).

buddleia / **bud**-lee-uh / *n.* a shrub (commonly called 'butterfly bush' because it attracts butterflies) with fragrant lilac, red, or yellow flowers.

buddy *n. colloq.* a friend, a mate.

budge *v.* **1** move slightly. **2** cause to alter a position or opinion.

budgeree / **buj**-uh-ree, **buuj**-uh-ree / *adj.* (also **boodgery, boojeree, budgeri**) *Aust.* (originally in Australian pidgin) good. (¶ Dharuk)

budgerigar / **buj**-uh-ree-gah / *n.* a small green and yellow Australian parrot (now bred with other colours as well), occurring usu. in large flocks in drier mainland areas, and popular as a cage bird. (¶ Perhaps an alteration of Kamilaroi *gijirrigaa.*)

budget *n.* **1** an estimate or plan of income and expenditure. **2** (**the Budget**) that made annually by the Federal government and by State governments. **3** the amount allotted for a particular purpose. • *v.* (**budgeted, budgeting**) plan or allot in a budget. ◻ **budgetary** *adj.*

budgie *n. colloq.* a budgerigar.

Buenos Aires / bwah-nuhs **air**-reez / the capital of Argentina.

buff *n.* **1** strong velvety dull-yellow leather. **2** a yellowish beige colour. **3** the bare skin (*stripped to the buff*). **4** *colloq.* an enthusiast (*film buffs*). (¶ Originally, an enthusiast for going to fires, from the buff-coloured uniforms once worn by New York volunteer firemen.) • *adj.* **1** yellowish beige. **2** (also **buffed**) (of a person or their body) in good physical shape with well-developed muscles. • *v.* polish with soft material.

buffalo *n.* (*pl.* **buffaloes** *or* **buffalo**) **1** a wild ox found in Asia and Africa. **2** a North American bison.

buffer *n.* **1** something that lessens the effect of an impact; a device for this purpose on a railway engine or at the end of a track. **2** a person or thing that protects against or reduces the effect of (damage, hostile forces, etc.) (*a buffer against inflation*). **3** *Computing* a temporary memory area or queue for data. • *v.* act as a buffer to. ◻ **buffer State** a small country between two powerful ones, thought to reduce the chance of war between them.

buffet[1] / **buuf**-ay, **buf**-ay / *n.* **1** a counter where food and drink may be bought and consumed. **2** provision of food where guests serve themselves (*buffet lunch*). **3** a sideboard or a cupboard in a recess, for dishes etc. ◻ **buffet car** a railway coach serving refreshments.

buffet[2] / **buf**-uht / *n.* a blow, esp. with the hand. • *v.* (**buffeted, buffeting**) strike or jolt repeatedly.

buffoon / buh-**foon** / *n.* a person who plays the fool. ◻ **buffoonery** *n.*

bug *n.* **1** an insect with mouthparts adapted for piercing and sucking; any small insect. **2** *colloq.* a micro-organism, esp. one causing disease. **3** *colloq.* a great enthusiasm. **4** a small hidden microphone installed secretly. **5** *colloq.* an error in a computer program or system etc. • *v.* (**bugged, bugging**) **1** fit with a hidden microphone secretly so that conversations etc. can be overheard. **2** annoy.

bugbear *n.* something feared or disliked.

bugeen / **bug**-een / *n.* a devil or evil spirit. (¶ Probably from Wiradhuri *baginny* 'evil spirit'; but cf. British dialect *bugan* 'evil spirit'.)

bugger *n.* (*colloq.* except in sense 3 of *n.* and *v.*) **1** an unpleasant or difficult person or thing (*a bugger of a job!*). **2** a person of a specified kind (*clever bugger!*). **3** a person who practises buggery. • *v.* **1** (often foll. by *up*) spoil, ruin. **2** exhaust (*I'm buggered!*). **3** penetrate anally. • *interj.* damn. ◻ **bugger-all** *n.* nothing. **bugger about** (*or* **around**) (often foll. by *with*) mess about. **bugger off** go away. **play silly buggers** fool about.

buggerise *v.* (also **-ize**) (often foll. by *around*) *coarse colloq.* mess about; fool aimlessly (with).

buggery *n.* **1** anal intercourse, sodomy. **2** sexual intercourse between a person and an animal. **3** *colloq.* hell (*go to buggery!*; *hurt like buggery*).

buggy *n.* **1** *archaic* a light horse-drawn carriage. **2** a small sturdy vehicle (*beach buggy*).

bugle *n.* a brass instrument like a small trumpet, used for sounding military signals. ◻ **bugler** *n.*

build *v.* (**built, building**) construct by putting parts or material together. • *n.* bodily shape (*of slender build*). ◻ **build in** incorporate. **build on 1** rely on. **2** add (an extension etc.). **build up 1** accumulate; establish gradually. **2** fill in with buildings. **3** boost with praise or flattering publicity. **build-up** *n.* **1** advance publicity. **2** a gradual approach to a climax. **3** an increase. **4** (in northern Australia) a period of increasing humidity which precedes the wet season.

builder *n.* a person who builds; one whose trade is building houses etc.

building *n.* **1** the constructing of houses etc. **2** a permanent built structure that can be entered. ◻ **building society** an organisation that accepts deposits and lends out money, esp. to people wishing to buy a house.

built *see* BUILD. • *adj.* having a specified build (*sturdily built*). ◻ **built-in** incorporated as part of a structure. **built-up** filled in with buildings; densely developed (*a built-up area*).

Bujumbura / boo-juhm-**boor**-ruh / the capital of Burundi.

bulb *n.* **1** a thick rounded mass of scale-like leaves from which a stem grows up and roots grow down. **2** a plant grown from this. **3** a bulb-shaped object. **4** a glass globe containing an inert gas and a metal filament, providing light when an electric current is passed through it.

bulbous / **bul**-buhs / *adj.* shaped like a bulb; fat and bulging.

Bulgar / **bul**-gah / *adj. & n.* = BULGARIAN.

bulgar alternative spelling of BULGUR.

Bulgaria a republic in SE Europe, on the Black Sea. ◻ **Bulgarian** *adj. & n.*

bulge *n.* a rounded swelling, an outward curve. • *v.* form a bulge, cause to swell out.

bulgur *n.* (also **bulghur**) wheat grains that have been partly boiled and dried, so that they only need to be soaked before being eaten.

bulimia / byoo-**lim**-ee-uh, buh- / *n.* (in full **bulimia nervosa**) a psychological condition causing bouts of compulsive overeating followed by self-induced vomiting, purging, or fasting. □ **bulimic** *adj.* & *n.*

bulk *n.* **1** size or magnitude, esp. when great. **2** the greater part, the majority. **3** a large shape or body or person. • *v.* **1** seem (in size or importance) (*bulks large*). **2** increase the size or thickness of (*bulk it out*). • *adj. Aust. colloq.* many; a lot of (*bulk people at the party*). □ **bulk bill** *v. Aust.* (of a medical practitioner) bill (the health insurance agency) for the scheduled fee for treating a number of patients (who pay nothing). **bulk billing** *Aust.* this practice. **in bulk** in large amounts; in a mass, not packaged.

bulkhead *n.* an upright partition in a ship, aircraft, or vehicle.

bulky *adj.* (**bulkier**, **bulkiest**) taking up much space. □ **bulkiness** *n.*

bull *n.* 1 an uncastrated male of any animal of the ox family. 2 the male of the whale, elephant, and other large animals. 3 (the Bull) a sign of the zodiac, Taurus. 4 *Stock Exchange* a person who buys shares hoping to sell them at a higher price (compare BEAR[1] sense 4). 5 the bull's-eye of a target. 6 an official edict issued by the pope. 7 *colloq.* an obviously absurd statement; lies, nonsense. □ **bull ant** (also **bulldog ant**) a large, aggressive, primitive Australian ant capable of inflicting an extremely painful sting. **bull artist** *Aust. colloq.* a person noted for boasting, exaggeration, etc. **bull bird** a swamp bird, a bittern, with a loud booming call, occurring in southern Australia. **bull market** a situation where share prices are rising rapidly. **bull terrier** a dog of a breed originally produced by crossing a bulldog and a terrier. □□ **bullish** *adj.*

Bullamakanka / buul-uh-muh-**kang**-kuh / *n. Aust.* an imaginary town, remote and backward, typifying real towns of this kind.

bullan-bullan[1] / **buul**-uhn-buul-uhn / *n.* (also **buln-buln**) *Aust.* any of several predominantly green Australian parrots having a narrow yellow collar on the neck. (¶ Yuwaalaraay)

bullan-bullan[2] / **buul**-uhn-buul-uhn / *n.* (also **buln-buln**) *Aust.* the superb lyrebird. (¶ Wuywurung)

bullbar *n.* orig. *Aust.* a strong metal bar or frame in front of a vehicle to reduce damage in the event of a collision with an animal etc.

bulldog *n.* a dog of a powerful breed with a short muzzle and a short thick neck. □ **bulldog clip** a spring clip that closes very strongly.

bulldoze *v.* **1** clear with a bulldozer. **2** *colloq.* force or intimidate (*he bulldozed them into accepting it*). **3** make (one's way) forcibly; force, push (*bulldozed his way through the crowd*; *bulldozed the bill through parliament*).

bulldozer *n.* a powerful tractor with a broad steel sheet mounted in front, used for shifting earth or clearing ground.

bulldust *n. Aust.* **1** a kind of fine powdery dust found in inland Australia. **2** *euphemism* = BULLSHIT.

bullet *n.* a small round or conical missile used in a rifle or revolver.

Bulletin an Australian magazine issued weekly. Founded in 1880 as a literary journal, it promoted Australian art and writing, playing an important role in the development of a distinctively Australian style, and was radical and nationalistic in its stance. It is now a news and financial magazine.

bulletin *n.* **1** a short official statement of news. **2** a society's regular list of information and news. □ **bulletin board system** an information storage system for any authorised computer user to access and add to from a remote terminal.

bulletproof *adj.* designed to protect people from bullets.

bullfight *n.* the sport of baiting and killing bulls for public entertainment, as in Spain. □ **bullfighter** *n.* **bullfighting** *n.*

bullfrog *n.* any of several large frogs with a bellowing or booming cry.

bullion *n.* gold or silver in bulk or bars, before coining or manufacture.

bullock *n.* a bull after castration. • *v. Aust.* work tirelessly (*we bullocked away for hours*). □ **bullocking** *n.*

bullocky *n. Aust.* the driver of a team of bullocks. • *adj.* of or pertaining to bullock driving or rural life in general (*the bullocky life*; *bullocky yarns*).

bullring *n.* an arena for bullfights.

bullroarer *n.* a sacred object of Aboriginal ritual, a carved, flat, oval piece of wood tied to a string at one end and whirled round and round to produce a loud roaring noise. (¶ From the name of a child's toy to which this ritual object has a fancied resemblance.)

bull's-eye *n.* **1** the centre of a target. **2** a large hard round peppermint sweet. **3** a hemisphere or thick disc of glass as a window.

bullsh *n. colloq.* = BULLSHIT.

bullshit *coarse colloq. n.* (often as *interj.*) rubbish, nonsense. • *v.* (**bullshitted**, **bullshitting**) talk rubbish; try to convince (a person) of something when one knows nothing about it. □ **bullshitter** *n.*

bullswool *n. Aust.* **1** fibrous bark, esp. that of some stringybarks. **2** *euphemism* = BULLSHIT.

Bullwinkel, Vivian (1915–2000), Australian nurse and prisoner-of-war. She survived a massacre by Japanese soldiers, and subsequent imprisonment, and has come to symbolise Australian determination in the face of Japanese wartime brutality.

bully *n.* a person who uses strength or power to hurt or frighten others. • *v.* (**bullied**, **bullying**) behave as a bully towards, intimidate. ☐ **bully for you!** *colloq.* bravo! **bully off** *v.* start play in hockey, where two opposing players tap the ground and each other's stick alternately three times before hitting the ball. **bully-off** *n.* this procedure.

buln-buln = BULLAN-BULLAN.

bulrush *n.* a tall rush with a thick velvety head.

bulwaddy / buul-**wod**-ee / *n.* a tree of northern Australia that forms dense thickets. (¶ Probably from a NT Aboriginal language.)

bulwark / buul-**wuhk** / *n.* **1** a wall of earth built as a defence. **2** something that acts as a protection or defence. **3** (**bulwarks**) a ship's side above the level of the deck.

bum *colloq. n.* 1 the buttocks. 2 a beggar, a loafer. • *v.* 1 (often foll. by *around*) loaf or wander around. 2 cadge; live off (someone). *adj.* bad; of poor quality. ☐ **bum chum** *Aust. colloq.* the close male friend of a male.

bumbag *n. colloq.* a small pouch strapped around the waist or hips.

bumble *v.* **1** move or act in a blundering or inept way. **2** ramble in speaking. ☐ **bumbling** *adj.*

bumblebee *n.* a large bee with a loud hum.

bumble tree *n.* any of several Australian trees and shrubs bearing sweet-smelling flowers and rounded edible fruit. Also called *native orange*. (¶ Kamilaroi and nearby languages.)

bumf *n.* (also **bumph**) *colloq.*, usu. *derog.* documents, papers; paperwork. (¶ Abbreviation of *bum-fodder*, = toilet paper.)

bummer *n. colloq.* an unpleasant experience; a disappointment (*the party was a bummer; a bummer of a day*).

bump *v.* **1** knock with a dull-sounding blow; hurt by this. **2** travel with a jolting movement. • *n.* **1** a bumping sound, knock, or movement. **2** a raised mark left by a blow. **3** a swelling or lump on a surface. ☐ **bump into** *colloq.* meet by chance. **bump off** *colloq.* kill. **bump up** *colloq.* raise (*bumped up the price*).

bumper *n.* **1** (usu. used as *adj.*) unusually large or plentiful (*a bumper crop*). **2** a horizontal bar attached to the front or back of a motor vehicle to lessen the effect of a collision. **3** a ball in cricket that rises high after pitching.

bumph alternative spelling of BUMF.

bumpkin *n.* a country person with awkward manners.

bumptious / **bump**-shuhs / *adj.* offensively self-assertive or conceited.

bumpy *adj.* (**bumpier, bumpiest**) full of bumps; causing jolts.

bun *n.* **1** a small round sweet bread roll or cake. **2** hair twisted into a bun shape at the back of the head. **3** (**buns**) *colloq.* buttocks.

bunch *n.* **1** a cluster (*a bunch of grapes*). **2** a number of small similar things held or fastened together (*a bunch of keys*). **3** *colloq.* a mob, a gang. • *v.* come or bring together into a bunch or in folds.

bunchy *adj.* gathered in clumsy folds.

bundle *n.* **1** a collection of things loosely fastened or wrapped together. **2** *colloq.* a large amount of money. **3** *Computing* a set of software and hardware sold together. • *v.* **1** make into a bundle. **2** put away hastily and untidily, push hurriedly (*bundled him into a taxi*). **3** (usu. as **bundled** *adj.*) (foll. by *with*) *Computing* sell (items of hardware and software) as a package with. ☐ **drop one's bundle** *Aust. colloq.* give up hope; go to pieces mentally.

bundy[1] *n.* any of several eucalypts of south-eastern Australia.

bundy[2] *n.* (also **Bundy**) *Aust. trademark* a time clock which employees activate to record the time they start and finish work.

bung[1] *n.* a stopper for closing a hole in a barrel or cask. • *v.* **1** close with a bung. **2** *colloq.* throw or toss (*bung some more sausages on the barbie*). ☐ **bunged up** blocked. **bung it on** *Aust.* assume a style of speech or behaviour that is pretentious or ostentatious (*bunging it on like a pom—who does he think he is?*).

bung[2] *adj.* broken down; useless (*the telly's bung*). ☐ **go bung** *v.* **1** break down (*telly's gone bung again*). **2** fail; go bankrupt. (¶ Originally Australian pidgin, = dead; probably Yagara.)

bungalow *n.* a cottage, shack, or sleepout.

bungarra / **bung**-a-ruh / *n.* a widespread Australian monitor lizard, usu. having a dark horizontal stripe through the eye, bordered by pale lines. (¶ Nhanta)

bungee / **bun**-jee / *n.* an elasticated rope used for securing baggage or in bungee jumping. ☐ **bungee jumping** the sport of jumping from a height attached to a bungee.

bunger *n.* a firework designed to go bang.

bungle *v.* spoil by lack of skill; tackle clumsily and without success. • *n.* a bungled attempt. ☐ **bungler** *n.*

bungwall *n.* an Australian fern of swampy land, the root of which is an important traditional Aboriginal food. (¶ Yagara)

bunion *n.* a swelling at the base of the big toe, with thickened skin.

bunji-man *n. Aust.* a white man with a predilection for Aboriginal women. (¶ Perhaps from a WA Aboriginal language; perhaps from English *fancy-man*.)

bunk *n.* **1** a built-in shelf-like bed, e.g. on a ship. **2** *colloq.* nonsense, rubbish. ☐ **do a bunk** *colloq.* run away.

bunker *n.* **1** a container for fuel. **2** a sandy hollow forming a hazard on a golf course. **3** a reinforced underground shelter.

bunkum *n.* nonsense, rubbish.

Bunn, Anna Maria (1808–89), Irish-born author of *The Guardian*, the first novel to be published (1838) in mainland Australia.

Bunny, Rupert (Charles Wulsten) (1864–1947), Australian artist.

bunny *n.* **1** a child's word for a rabbit. **2** *Aust.* a victim or dupe; a scapegoat.

Bunsen, Robert Wilhelm Eberhard (1811–99), German chemist, a pioneer of spectral analysis. ❏ **Bunsen burner** a laboratory instrument devised by Bunsen, with a vertical tube burning a mixture of air and gas.

bunting *n.* **1** flags and streamers for decorating streets and buildings. **2** a loosely-woven fabric used for making these.

bunya *n.* (also **bunya-bunya**) **1** an Australian conifer, the cones of which contain seeds which are eaten raw, roasted, or pounded to a flour. **2** (also **bunya nut**) the seed of this tree. (¶ Yagara *bunya-bunya*; Gabi-gabi and Waga-waga *bunyi*.)

Bunyan, John (1628–88), English writer, author of *The Pilgrim's Progress*.

bunyip *n. Aust.* a monster of Aboriginal legend, said to inhabit some swamps and lagoons. ❏ **bunyip aristocracy** a derisive term for Australians who consider themselves aristocrats. (¶ Wemba-wemba.)

buoy / boi / *n.* an anchored floating object marking a navigable channel, showing the position of submerged rocks etc. • *v.* **1** mark with a buoy or buoys. **2** (usu. foll. by *up*) keep (a thing) afloat. **3** encourage, uplift (*buoyed up with new hope*).

buoyant / **boi**-uhnt / *adj.* **1** able to float. **2** light-hearted, cheerful. ❏ **buoyantly** *adv.* **buoyancy** *n.*

burble *v.* **1** make a gentle murmuring sound. **2** speak in a rambling way. • *n.* **1** a burbling noise. **2** long-winded or rambling speech.

Burchett, Wilfred Graham (1911–83), Australian journalist, war correspondent, and author. He was the first to give an eye-witness account of the effects of the atom bomb on Hiroshima.

Burdekin / **ber**-duh-kuhn / a major river system in north-eastern Qld, rising near Ingham some 60 km from the coast, and flowing some 700 km before reaching the sea near Ayr.

burden *n.* **1** something carried, a heavy load. **2** something difficult to bear (*the heavy burden of taxation*). **3** the chief theme of a speech etc. • *v.* **1** load, put a burden on. **2** oppress. ❏ **beast of burden** an animal that carries packs on its back. **the burden of proof** the obligation to prove what one says.

burdensome *adj.* troublesome, tiring.

bureau / **byoo**-roh / *n.* (*pl.* **bureaux** *or* **bureaus**) **1** a piece of furniture with drawers and a hinged flap for use as a desk. **2** an office or department (*a travel bureau*).

bureaucracy / byoo-**rok**-ruh-see / *n.* **1** government by State officials not by elected representatives. **2** these officials. **3** excessive official routine, esp. because there are too many offices or departments.

bureaucrat / **byoo**-ruh-krat / *n.* **1** an official who works in a government office. **2** one who applies the rules of a department without exercising much judgment.

bureaucratic / byoo-ruh-**krat**-ik / *adj.* **1** of bureaucracy. **2** of or like bureaucrats.

burette / byoo-**ret** / *n.* a graduated glass tube with a tap, used for measuring small quantities of liquid.

burgeon / **ber**-juhn / *v.* begin to grow rapidly; flourish.

burger *n. colloq.* a hamburger.

burgher *n.* **1** a citizen, esp. of a town in continental Europe. **2** a descendant of a Dutch colonist in Sri Lanka, esp. as settled in Australia. • *adj.* of or pertaining to a burgher.

burghul / **ber**-guul / = BULGUR.

burglar *n.* a person who enters a building illegally, esp. in order to steal. ❏ **burglary** *n.*

burgle *v.* rob as a burglar.

burgomaster / **ber**-guh-mah-stuh / *n.* the mayor of a Dutch or Flemish town.

burgundy *n.* **1** (also **Burgundy**) a red or white wine from Burgundy in France; a similar wine from elsewhere. **2** a dark purplish red colour.

burial *n.* **1** burying; being buried; a funeral. **2** a grave or its remains.

buriani = BIRIANI.

burin / **byoo**-ruhn / *n.* an engraving tool.

Burke, Robert O' Hara (1821–61), Australian explorer (born in Ireland). In 1860–1 he successfully crossed Australia from south to north in the company of W.J. Wills and others. All members of the exploring party (except John King, who survived by living with Aborigines) died on the return journey.

Burkina Faso / ber-kee-nuh **fa**-soh / an inland republic of western Africa. ❏ **Burkinese** *adj.* & *n.*

burl *n. Aust. colloq.* a try, an attempt. ❏ **give it a burl** venture an attempt, have a go.

burlesque / ber-**lesk** / *n.* a mocking imitation, a parody. • *v.* (**burlesques**, **burlesqued**, **burlesquing**) parody.

Burley Griffin, Lake an artificial lake in Canberra, ACT. Although it was part of Griffin's original plan for the city, it was not formed until 1964, with the damming of the Molonglo River.

burly *adj.* (**burlier**, **burliest**) with a strong heavy body, sturdy.

Burma (from 1989 officially called **Myanmar**) a republic of SE Asia, on the Bay of Bengal.

Burmese *n.* (*pl.* **Burmese**) **1** a person from Burma. **2** the language of Burma. • *adj.* of Burma or its people or language.

burn *v.* (**burned** *or* **burnt** (see note at end of entry), **burning**) **1** blaze or glow with fire. **2** produce heat or light; be alight. **3** damage, hurt, or destroy by fire, heat, or the action of chemicals; be injured or damaged in this way. **4** use as fuel. **5** be able to be set on fire. **6** feel or cause to feel hot. **7** make or become brown from heat or light. **8** (often foll. by *with*) feel or cause to feel great emotion or passion (*burn with shame*). **9** record data on a CD or DVD. • *n.* **1** a mark or sore made by burning. **2** *colloq.* a fast drive (*went for a burn in* *his car*). ◻ **burn off** *US. & Aust.* clear land of vegetation by burning. **burn-off** *n. Aust.* an area of forest etc. cleared by burning. **burn-out** *n.* physical or emotional exhaustion. **burn the midnight oil** study far into the night.

■ Usage The form *burnt* (not *burned*) is always used for adjectival uses of the past participle, e.g. in *a burnt offering*. For the verb, either *burned* or *burnt* may be used.

burner *n.* the part of a lamp or cooker that emits and shapes the flame.

Burnet, Sir (Frank) Macfarlane (1899–1985), AK, Australian medical scientist and writer, joint winner of the Nobel Prize for medicine in 1960 for his work on immunology.

burning *see* BURN. •*adj.* **1** intense (*a burning desire*). **2** hotly discussed, vital (*a burning question*).

burnish *v.* polish by rubbing.

burnous / ber-**noos** / *n.* an Arab or Moorish hooded cloak.

Burns, Robert (1759–96), Scottish poet and songwriter.

burnt *see* BURN. •*adj.* of a deep shade (*burnt sienna, burnt umber*).

Burnum Burnum (1936–97), Australian Aboriginal activist. He was one of the founders of the Aboriginal Tent Embassy in Canberra in 1972.

burp *n. colloq.* a belch, a belching sound. •*v.* **1** *colloq.* belch. **2** cause (a baby) to bring up wind from the stomach.

burr[1] *n.* **1** a whirring sound. **2** the strong pronunciation of 'r'. **3** a small drill. •*v.* make a whirring sound.

burr[2] *n.* **1** a prickly, clinging seed case or flower head; any plant having this. **2** a clinging person.

burramys / bu-ruh-muhs / *n.* the rare mountain pygmy possum, a small terrestrial marsupial which had been known only from fossils until a small colony was discovered in Mount Hotham, Vic., in the 1960s.

burrawang / bu-ruh-wang / *n.* any of several Australian plants with palm-like fronds and pineapple-like cones producing poisonous nuts eaten by Aborigines after the nuts had been subjected to special treatment. (¶ Dharuk).

burrow *n.* a hole or tunnel dug by a rabbit etc. as a dwelling. •*v.* **1** dig a burrow, tunnel. **2** form by tunnelling. **3** search deeply, delve.

Burrows, Don(ald Vernon) (1928–), AO, Australian jazz musician, founder of the Burrows Quartet, pre-eminent in Australian jazz.

bursar / ber-suh / *n.* **1** a person who manages the finances and other business of a school or college. **2** a student who holds a bursary.

bursary / ber-suh-ree / *n.* a grant given to a student.

burst *v.* (**burst**, **bursting**) **1** force or be forced open; fly violently apart because of pressure inside (*buds are bursting*). **2** appear or come suddenly and forcefully (*burst into flame*). **3** let out a violent expression of feeling (*burst into tears; burst out laughing*). •*n.* **1** a bursting, a split. **2** an explosion or outbreak; a series of shots (*a burst of gunfire*). **3** a brief violent effort; a spurt.

bursting *adj.* full to breaking point (*sacks bursting with grain; bursting with energy*).

Burundi / buh-**ruun**-dee / a republic in East Africa. ◻ **Burundian** *adj. & n.*

bury *v.* (**buried**, **burying**) **1** place (a dead body) in the earth, a tomb, or the sea. **2** put underground, hide in earth etc. **3** cover up; put in an obscure place to be forgotten (*buried himself in the outback*). **4** put (a feeling, idea, etc.) out of one's mind. **5** involve oneself deeply (*buried in a book; buried herself in her work*). ◻ **bury the hatchet** forget grievances and make peace.

bus *n.* (*pl.* **buses**) **1** a long-bodied passenger vehicle. **2** *Computing* a defined set of conductors carrying data and control signals within a computer. •*v.* (**bused**, **busing** *or* **bussed**, **bussing**) **1** travel by bus. **2** transport by bus.

Bush, George W(alker) (1946–), American Republican statesman, 43rd president of the USA from 2001.

bush[1] *n.* **1** a shrub. **2** a thick growth or clump (*a bush of hair*). **3** esp. *Aust.* wild uncultivated land with natural vegetation. **4** esp. *Aust.* rural as opposed to urban life. •*adj. Aust.* **1** of or pertaining to natural vegetation. **2** made with branches, saplings, etc. (*a bush gate*). **3** (of Aborigines) living outside white society. **4** (of animals and plants) native to Australia (*bush animal; bush tucker*). **5** (of domestic animals) having become wild (*bush cattle*). **6** rural as opposed to urban (*bush race meeting*). **7** (in Aboriginal English) traditional or Aboriginal as opposed to European. ◻ **bush band** a band which specialises in Australian folk music, and which uses distinctively Australian instruments, e.g. the lagerphone. **bush bash** *Aust.* **1** ride at speed through the bush, esp. in pursuit of wild or straying cattle. **2** make a track through the bush; travel cross-country. **bush capital** Canberra. **bush carpenter** *Aust.* an amateur, rough-and-ready carpenter. **bush fly** *Aust.* a small fly which settles persistently on the eyes, mouth, etc. of humans and animals. **bush food** *Aust.* traditional Aboriginal food, esp. if hunted or gathered in traditional fashion. **bush lawyer** *Aust.* **1** a person claiming legal knowledge but with no legal qualifications. **2** an argumentative person who produces specious arguments in support of a case; a pompous know-all. **bush medicine** *Aust.* traditional Aboriginal medicine. **bush tucker** *Aust.* traditional Aboriginal food. **bush turkey** = BRUSH TURKEY. **go bush** *Aust.* **1** escape or disappear from one's usual haunts. **2** (of Aborigines) return to traditional life. **3** leave urban life for that of the country; visit the country. **4** (of fauna and flora) become wild (*brumbies are* *horses that had gone bush*). **take to the bush** *Aust.* **1** (originally of convicts) escape from custody; run away. **2** (of animals) run wild.

bush² *n.* **1** a metal lining for a round hole in which something fits or revolves. **2** an electrically insulating sleeve. • *v.* fit with a bush.

bushcraft *n. Aust.* knowledge of how to live or survive in the bush.

bushed *adj. Aust. colloq.* **1** lost in the bush. **2** tired out, exhausted. **3** bewildered (*the problem has me bushed*).

bushel *n.* a measure for grain and fruit in the imperial system (8 gallons or 36.4 litres). ☐ **hide one's light under a bushel** conceal one's abilities.

bushfire *n.* a fire which burns through (often extensive) areas of natural vegetation, often causing loss of life and property. ☐ **bushfire brigade** *Aust.* a volunteer fire-fighting organisation operating outside city areas.

bushido / boo-**shee**-doh / *n.* the strict ethical code of the Japanese samurai, involving military skill, fearlessness, and obedience to authority.

bushie *adj. Aust.* countrified; lacking the (supposed) refinements of urban life. • *n.* a person who lives in the country as opposed to the city; a person whose manner or appearance indicates this.

bushman *n.* (*pl.* **bushmen**) **1** *Aust.* a person skilled and experienced in travelling through bush country. **2** *Aust.* a person who lives in the bush. **3** (**Bushman**) a member of or the language of an aboriginal people in South Africa. ☐ **bushmanship** *n.*

bushranger *n. Aust.* **1** *hist.* a person who engages in armed robbery, escaping into, or living in, the bush in the manner of an outlaw. **2** a person or business seen as making extortionate demands or charging exorbitant prices. ☐ **bushrange** *v.* **bushranging** *n.*

bush telegraph *n. Aust.* **1** *hist.* a person who alerts a bushranger to police movements or to a potential victim. **2** an informal network by which information is conveyed in remote areas; the information so conveyed; rumour. **3** a means of very effective long-distance communication used by Aborigines, usu. employing smoke signals; the message so conveyed. • *v.* communicate (information) by means of bush telegraphy. ☐ **bush telegraphy** *n.*

bushwalk *n. Aust.* **1** (of an Aborigine) a walkabout. **2** a hike in the bush, esp. including camping out etc. • *v.* **1** (of an Aborigine) go walkabout. **2** take a (usu. extended) hike in the bush. ☐ **bushwalker** *n.* **bushwalking** *n.*

bush week *n. Aust.* **1** a (fictitious) time when people from the bush come to town and are easy targets for con men etc. **2** (at some universities) a period of student festivity, pranks, etc. ☐ **what do you think this—bush week?** a response to a request etc., implying that one is being unfairly imposed upon or taken for a (rustic) fool.

bushwhack *v.* **1** clear land in bush country. **2** live or travel in bush country. **3** (as **bushwhacked** *adj.*) utterly exhausted. ☐ **bushwhacking** *n.*

bushwhacker *n.* **1** a person who clears land in bush country by felling etc. **2** a person who lives or travels in bush country, a bushie.

bushy *adj.* (**bushier**, **bushiest**) **1** growing thickly. **2** covered with bushes.

business *n.* **1** a trade, a profession; a person's usual occupation. **2** one's own concern (*that's my business*). **3** buying and selling, trade. **4** a commercial firm; a shop (*they own a grocery business*). **5** a thing needing to be dealt with; the agenda. **6** *Aust.* (in Aboriginal English) traditional lore and ritual (*see also* SUNDAY BUSINESS). **7** a (difficult or unpleasant) matter or affair (*sick of the whole business*). **8** *Theatre* action on stage. ☐ **business ground** *Aust.* (in Aboriginal English) a ceremonial site for traditional ritual etc. **have no business to** have no right to (do something). **mean business** *colloq.* be in earnest.

businesslike *adj.* practical, systematic, rational.

businessman *n.* a man engaged in trade or commerce, esp. at a senior level.

businesswoman *n.* a woman engaged in trade or commerce, esp. at a senior level.

busk *v.* perform in the street to entertain passers-by and collect money. ☐ **busker** *n.*

bust *n.* **1** a sculpture of the head, shoulders, and chest. **2** the bosom. **3** the measurement round a woman's body at the bosom. **4** *colloq.* a raid or an arrest made by the police. • *v.* (**busted** *or* **bust**, **busting**) *colloq.* **1** break; burst. **2** raid, search. **3** arrest. **4** break, tame (a brumby etc.). • *adj. colloq.* (also **busted**) **1** burst, broken. **2** bankrupt. ☐ **be busting** *colloq.* **1** be hard pressed to urinate. **2** be very keen (to do something). **bust up** *colloq.* **1** bring or come to collapse; explode. **2** (esp. of a couple in a relationship) quarrel and separate. **3** wreck. **4** disrupt (a meeting, a gathering etc.).

bust-up *n. colloq.* **1** a violent quarrel. **2** (esp. of a couple in a relationship) an acrimonious separation. **3** (of a business etc.) a collapse. **4** a wild party.

bustard *n.* **1** a large, swift-running bird of Europe and Asia. **2** an Australian bird of the same family, the plain turkey.

buster *n.* **1** *colloq.* (often *derog.*) mate; fellow. **2** *Aust.* a strong squally wind, esp. from the south. **3** a heavy fall.

-buster *comb. form* indicating that which: **1** eradicates (*dirt-buster*). **2** destroys (*the pre-Christmas sale was a door-buster*). **3** stretches to the full (*brain-buster*).

bustier *n.* a strapless close-fitting bodice.

bustle *v.* **1** make a show of hurrying. **2** cause to hurry. • *n.* **1** excited activity. **2** padding formerly

busty   105   **buzzard**

used to puff out the top of a woman's skirt at the back.

busty *adj.* (**bustier**, **bustiest**) having a large bust.

busy *adj.* (**busier**, **busiest**) **1** working, occupied; having much to do. **2** full of activity (*a busy day*). **3** (of a telephone line) engaged. **4** (of a picture or design) too full of detail. •*v.* (**busied**, **busying**) keep busy (*busy oneself*). ◻ **busily** *adv.*

busybody *n.* a meddlesome person.

but *conj.* however; on the other hand. •*prep.* except (*there's no one here but me*). •*adv.* **1** without the result that (*it never rains but it pours*). **2** only, no more than (*we can but try*). •*n.* an objection (*ifs and buts*). ◻ **but for** were it not for (*I'd have drowned but for you*). **but one** (or **two** etc.) excluding one (or two etc.) from the number (*next door but one; last but one*).

butane / **byoo**-tayn / *n.* an inflammable gas produced from petroleum, used in liquid form as a fuel.

butch *adj. colloq.* tough-looking; masculine, mannish.

butcher *n.* **1** a person whose trade is to slaughter animals for food; one who cuts up and sells animal flesh. **2** a brutal murderer. •*v.* **1** slaughter or cut up (an animal) for meat. **2** kill wantonly or brutally. **3** *colloq.* ruin, make a mess of.

butcherbird *n.* any of several Australian birds having black and white plumage and hook-tipped bills, noted for their predatory habits (including impaling lizards etc. on twigs in order to tear them apart).

butchery *n.* **1** a butcher's trade. **2** needless or brutal killing.

butler *n.* the chief manservant of a household.

butt[1] *n.* **1** the thicker end of a tool or weapon. **2** a short remnant, a stub. **3** a large cask or barrel. **4** the mound of earth behind the targets on a shooting-range. **5** a person or thing that is a target for ridicule or teasing. **6** (**butts**) a shooting range. **7** *colloq.* the buttocks.

butt[2] *v.* **1** push with the head or horns like a ram or goat. **2** meet or place edge to edge (*the strips should be butted against each other, not overlapping*). •*n.* **1** an act of butting. **2** a butted join. ◻ **butt in** interrupt; meddle. **butt out** *colloq.* cease to interfere or meddle.

butter *n.* **1** solidified churned cream, used as a spread and in cooking. **2** a similar substance made from other materials (*peanut butter*). •*v.* spread, cook, or serve with butter. ◻ **butter bean** a large pale flat bean. **butter muslin** a thin looselywoven fabric. **butter up** *colloq.* flatter.

buttercup *n.* a plant with yellow cup-shaped flowers.

butterfingers *n.pl.* used as *sing. colloq.* a person likely to drop things.

butterfly *n.* **1** an insect with four often brightly coloured wings and knobbed feelers. **2** (in full **butterfly stroke**) a swimming stroke in which both arms are lifted at the same time. ◻ **butterfly bush** = BUDDLEIA. **butterfly nut** a kind of wing nut. **have butterflies in the stomach** feel nervous tremors.

Butterley, Nigel (Henry) (1935–), AM, Australian composer, pianist, and teacher.

buttermilk *n.* the liquid left after butter has been churned from milk.

butterscotch *n.* a hard toffee made from butter, brown sugar, etc.

buttery *adj.* like or containing butter.

buttock *n.* either of the two fleshy rounded parts at the lower or rear end of the back of the human or an animal body.

button *n.* **1** a knob or disc sewn on a garment as a fastener or ornament. **2** a small rounded object; a knob pressed to operate an electric bell etc. •*v.* (**buttoned**, **buttoning**) fasten with a button or buttons. ◻ **button mushroom** a small unopened mushroom. **button up 1** fasten with buttons. **2** *colloq.* complete satisfactorily. **3** *colloq.* be silent.

buttonhole *n.* **1** a slit through which a button is passed to fasten clothing. **2** a flower worn in the buttonhole of a lapel. •*v.* accost and detain (a reluctant listener) with conversation.

buttress *n.* **1** a support built against a wall. **2** a thing that supports or reinforces something. •*v.* prop up.

Buttrose, Ita (Clare) (1942–), AO, Australian journalist, editor, writer, and broadcaster.

butyl / **byoo**-tuhl / *n.* the univalent alkyl radical C_4H_9. ◻ **butyl rubber** synthetic rubber used to make tyre inner tubes.

buxom *adj.* plump and healthy-looking; busty.

buy *v.* (**bought**, **buying**) **1** obtain in exchange for money or by some sacrifice. **2** win over by bribery. **3** *colloq.* believe, accept the truth of (*no one would buy that excuse*). **4** *colloq.* receive as a punishment. •*n.* a purchase (*a good buy*). ◻ **buy in** buy a stock of. **buy into 1** pay for a share in (an enterprise). **2** (also **buy in**) *colloq.* involve oneself in (an activity). **buy off** get rid of by payment. **buy out** obtain full ownership by paying (another person) to give up his or her share. **buy up** buy all or as much as possible of.

buyer *n.* **1** a person who buys something. **2** an agent choosing and buying stock for a large shop. ◻ **buyers' market** a state of affairs when goods are plentiful and prices are low.

buyout *n.* the purchase of a controlling share in a company; the buying of a company by people who work there (*a management buyout*).

Buzo, Alex(ander John) (1944–), Australian playwright.

buzz *n.* **1** a vibrating humming sound. **2** *colloq.* a rumour. **3** a stir of excitement etc. **4** *colloq.* a telephone call (*give me a buzz*). **5** *colloq.* a thrill. •*v.* **1** make a buzz. **2** be filled with a buzzing noise. **3** go about quickly and busily. **4** threaten (an aircraft) by flying close to it. ◻ **buzz off** *colloq.* go away. **buzz saw** a circular saw.

buzzard *n.* a large bird of the hawk family.

buzzer *n.* a device that produces a buzzing note as a signal.

buzzword *n. colloq.* a piece of fashionable jargon.

by *prep.* **1** near, beside. **2** via; past. **3** during (*came by night*). **4** through the agency or means of; (of an animal) having as its sire. **5** (of numbers or measurements) taking it together with (*multiply six by four*); expressing dimensions (*it measures ten centimetres by eight*). **6** not later than. **7** according to (*judging by appearances; sold by the dozen*). **8** after, succeeding (*bit by bit*). **9** to the extent of (*missed it by inches*). **10** in respect of (*a tailor, Jones by name; pull it up by the roots*). **11** in the belief of (*swear by God*). **12** between the compass points indicated (*north by north-west*). • *adv.* **1** near (*sat by*). **2** aside; in reserve (*put $50 by*). **3** past (*walked by*). ▫ **by and by** before long. **by and large** on the whole, considering everything. **by the bye** (*or* **by**) incidentally.

bye *n.* **1** a run scored in cricket from a ball that passes the batsman without being hit. **2** a hole or holes remaining unplayed when a golf match is ended. **3** the status of having no opponent for one round in a tournament and so advancing to the next as if having won. **4** (in a competition with an uneven number of teams) the status of a team not having a match in a particular round. • *interj.* (also **bye-bye**) *colloq.* goodbye.

bycatch *n.* an unwanted species of sea creatures caught incidental to commercial fishing operations.

by-election *n.* an election to fill a vacancy caused by the death or resignation of an MP.

Byelorussia alternative name for BELARUS. ▫ **Byelorussian** *adj.* & *n.*

bygone *adj.* belonging to the past. • *n.pl.* (**bygones**) things belonging to the past (*let bygones be bygones*).

by-law *n.* a regulation made by a local government authority or corporation. (¶ Obsolete *by* 'town'.)

byline *n.* **1** a line in a newspaper etc. naming the writer of an article. **2** a secondary line of work. **3** the goal line or touch line of a soccer etc. pitch.

BYO *n.* & *adj. abbr.* bring your own: **1** an intimation to patrons of an unlicensed restaurant that they may bring their own liquor. **2** such a restaurant. **3** pertaining to a barbecue, party, etc. to which people bring their own liquor (*a BYO barbie at Bob's*).

bypass *n.* **1** a main road passing round a town or its centre. **2** a secondary channel allowing something to flow when the main route is blocked. **3** a surgical operation to redirect the flow of blood away from a damaged part of the heart. • *v.* **1** avoid by means of a bypass. **2** omit or ignore (procedures, regulations, etc.) in order to act quickly.

byplay *n.* action, usu. without speech, of minor characters in a play etc.

by-product *n.* **1** a substance produced during the making of something else. **2** a secondary result.

byroad *n.* a minor road.

Byron, George Gordon, 6th Baron (1788–1824), English Romantic and satirical poet.

byssinosis / bi-suh-**noh**-suhs / *n.* a lung disease caused by much breathing in of textile fibre dust.

bystander *n.* a person standing near but taking no part when something happens; an onlooker.

byte / buyt / *n.* a fixed number of bits (= binary digits) in a computer, often representing a single character.

byway *n.* a little used or secluded road or path.

byword *n.* **1** a person or thing spoken of as a notable example (*the firm became a byword for mismanagement*). **2** a familiar saying.

Byzantine / **biz**-uhn-teen, -tuyn, bi-**zan**-tuyn, buy- / *adj.* **1** of Byzantium or the Eastern Roman Empire. **2** (of a situation, attitude, etc.) complicated, inflexible, underhand.

Byzantium / bi-**zan**-tee-uhm, buy-**zan**- / an ancient Greek city on the Bosporus, refounded by Constantine the Great as Constantinople (modern Istanbul).

C

C *n.* (*pl.* **Cs** or **C's**) **1** *Music* the first note of the scale of C major. **2** the third highest category, academic mark, etc.; the third example, item in a list, etc. **3** (as a Roman numeral) 100. • *abbr.* **1** Celsius, centigrade. **2** coulomb(s). **3** capacitance. • *symbol* carbon.

© *symbol* copyright.

c. *abbr.* **1** century. **2** cent(s).

c. *abbr. circa*, about.

Ca *symbol* calcium.

cab *n.* **1** a taxi. **2** a compartment for the driver of a train, lorry, or crane.

cabal / kuh-**bahl**, -**bal** / *n.* a secret (esp. political) plot; the people engaged in it.

cabana / kuh-**bah**-nuh / *n.* a spicy sausage, eaten cold.

cabanossi / kab-uh-**nos**-ee / *n.* a spicy sausage, eaten cold.

cabaret / **kab**-uh-ray / *n.* an entertainment provided in a restaurant or nightclub.

cabbage *n.* **1** a vegetable with green or purple leaves usu. forming a round head. **2** *colloq.* a person who is inactive, or who lives without interests or ambition. □ **cabbage garden** (or **patch**) *Aust.* a nickname for the State of Victoria. **cabbage tree** a palm of northern and eastern Australia etc., the young growing shoots or central mass of which can be eaten. **cabbage-tree hat** *Aust. hist.* a wide-brimmed hat woven from cabbage-tree leaves and worn by (esp. young) Australians as a mark of distinctive Australianness.

cabbala / kuh-**bah**-luh, **kab**-uh-luh / *n.* (also **kabbala**) **1** a Jewish mystical tradition. **2** any esoteric doctrine or occult lore. □ **cabbalism** *n.* **cabbalist** *n.*

cabbalistic / ka-buh-**lis**-tik / *adj.* having a mystical sense; occult.

cabby *n.* (also **cabbie**) *colloq.* a taxi driver.

caber / **kay**-buh / *n.* a roughly-trimmed tree trunk used in the Scottish sport of tossing the caber.

cabernet sauvignon / kab-uh-nay **soh**-vin-yon / *n.* a black grape used in winemaking; a red wine made from these grapes.

cabin *n.* **1** a small dwelling or shelter, esp. of wood. **2** a compartment in a ship or aircraft or spacecraft. **3** a driver's cab. □ **cabin cruiser** a large motor boat with a cabin or cabins.

cabinet *n.* **1** a cupboard or container for storing or displaying things. **2** (**Cabinet**) the group of ministers chosen by the prime minister to be responsible for government policy.

cabinetmaker *n.* a skilled joiner; a maker of high-quality furniture.

cable *n.* **1** a thick rope of fibre or wire. **2** an anchor chain. **3** a set of insulated wires for carrying electricity or electronic signals. **4** a telegram sent abroad. **5** (in full **cable stitch**) a knitted pattern looking like twisted rope. • *v.* send a telegram to (a person) abroad; transmit (money or information) in this way. □ **cable car** any of the cars in a **cable railway**, a railway with cars drawn by an endless cable by means of a stationary engine. **cable television** the transmission of television programs by cable to subscribers.

caboodle / kuh-**boo**-duhl / *n.* □ **the whole** (**kit and**) **caboodle** *colloq.* the whole lot.

caboose / kuh-**boos** / *n.* a kitchen on a ship's deck.

cabriole / **kab**-ree-ohl / *n.* a curved leg on furniture.

cabriolet / **kab**-ree-oh-lay / *n.* **1** a car with a folding top. **2** a light two-wheeled one-horse carriage with a hood.

cacao / kuh-**kay**-oh / *n.* (*pl.* **cacaos**) **1** a tropical tree producing a seed from which cocoa and chocolate are made. **2** its seed.

cacciatore / kach-uh-**taw**-ray, -ree / *adj.* (of poultry or game) cooked in a tomato and wine based sauce (*chicken cacciatore*). (¶ Italian, = hunter.)

cachalot / **kash**-uh-lot, -loht / *n.* a sperm whale.

cache / kash / *n.* **1** a hiding place for treasure or stores; the hidden items. **2** / kaysh / *Computing* an area of memory which improves the speed of a computer system by anticipating what the computer will be requested to do. • *v.* place in a cache.

cachet / **kash**-ay / *n.* **1** a distinguishing mark or seal. **2** prestige. **3** a flat capsule enclosing an unpleasant medicine.

cack-handed *adj. colloq.* **1** left-handed. **2** clumsy.

cackle *n.* **1** the loud clucking noise a hen makes after laying. **2** a loud silly laugh. **3** noisy chatter. • *v.* **1** give a cackle. **2** chatter noisily.

cacophony / kuh-**kof**-uh-nee / *n.* a harsh discordant sound. □ **cacophonous** *adj.*

cactoblastis / kak-toh-**blah**-stuhs / *n.* South American moth whose larvae are used in Australia as a biological control for prickly pear.

cactus *n.* (*pl.* **cactuses** or **cacti** / **kak**-tuy /) a plant from a hot dry climate, with a fleshy stem and usu. prickles but no leaves. ☐ **in the cactus** *Aust. colloq.* in difficulty; in trouble.

cad *n. archaic* a man who behaves dishonourably. ☐ **caddish** *adj.*

cadaver / kuh-**dah**-vuh, -**dav**-uh / *n.* a corpse.

cadaverous / kuh-**dav**-uh-ruhs / *adj.* gaunt and pale, like a corpse.

caddie (also **caddy**) *n.* a person who carries a golfer's clubs during a game. • *v.* (**caddied**, **caddying**) act as caddie.

caddis-fly *n.* a four-winged insect living near water.

caddy[1] *n.* a small container for tea.

caddy[2] *see* CADDIE.

cadence / **kay**-duhns / *n.* **1** rhythm in sound. **2** the rise and fall of the voice in speaking. **3** the end of a musical phrase.

cadenza / kuh-**den**-zuh / *n.* an elaborate passage for a solo instrument or voice, showing off the performer's skill.

cadet / kuh-**det** / *n.* **1** a young trainee for the armed services, police force, etc. **2** a member of a military training corps in a secondary school. **3** *Aust.* **a** a trainee journalist or newspaper photographer. **b** a young person employed by a large enterprise as a trainee, usually in a discipline requiring university study (*engineering cadet*). **c** a novice surfer. ☐ **cadetship** *n.*

cadge *v.* ask for as a gift; get or seek by begging or 'borrowing'.

cadi / **cah**-dee, **cay**- / *n.* a judge in a Muslim country.

Cadman's Cottage a building dating from Macquarie's time, the oldest extant house in Sydney. It was built about 1815 for John Cadman and is now cared for by the National Trust of Australia.

cadmium / **kad**-mee-uhm / *n.* a chemical element (symbol Cd) that looks like tin.

cadre / **kah**-duh / *n.* **1** a basic unit, esp. of servicemen. **2** a group of political activists.

caecum / **see**-kuhm / *n.* (*pl.* **caeca**) a tubular pouch forming the first part of the large intestine.

Caenozoic = CENOZOIC.

Caesar / **see**-zuh / *see* JULIUS CAESAR. • *n.* a title of the Roman emperors.

Caesarean / suh-**zair**-ree-uhn / *n.* (also **Caesarian**) (in full **Caesarean section**) a surgical operation by which a child is taken from the womb by cutting through the wall of the abdomen and into the womb. (¶ So called from the story that Julius Caesar was born in this way.)

caesium / **see**-zee-uhm / *n.* a soft silver-white metallic element (symbol Cs).

caesura / suh-**zhoo**-ruh / *n.* a short pause in a line of verse.

café / **ka**-fay / *n.* a small coffee house or restaurant.

cafeteria / kaf-uh-**teer**-ree-uh / *n.* a café where customers serve themselves from a counter.

caffeine / **kaf**-een / *n.* a stimulant found in tea and coffee.

caffe latte / ka-fay **lah**-tay / *n.* (also **caffé latte**) coffee with milk, white coffee.

caftan / **kaf**-tan / *n.* (also **kaftan**) **1** a long coat-like garment worn by men in SW Asia. **2** a long loose dress or shirt.

cage *n.* **1** a framework with wires or bars in which birds or animals are kept. **2** any similar structure; the enclosed platform in which people travel in a lift or the shaft of a mine. • *v.* put or keep in a cage.

cagey *adj.* (**cagier**, **cagiest**) (also **cagy**) *colloq.* cautious about giving information, secretive. ☐ **cagily** *adv.* **caginess** *n.*

cahoots / kuh-**hoots** / *n.pl. colloq.* ☐ **in cahoots with** in league with.

Cain the eldest son of Adam, and murderer of his brother Abel.

Cainozoic = CENOZOIC.

cairn *n.* a pyramid of rough stones set up as a landmark or a monument.

Cairo the capital of Egypt.

caisson / **kay**-suhn / *n.* a watertight chamber inside which work can be carried out on underwater structures.

cajole / kuh-**johl** / *v.* coax. ☐ **cajolery** *n.*

Cajun / **kay**-juhn / *adj.* (of music, food, culture, etc.) in the style of French Louisiana in the US.

cake *n.* **1** a baked sweet bread-like food made from a mixture of flour, fats, sugar, eggs, etc. **2** a mixture cooked in a round flat shape (*fish cakes*). **3** a shaped or hardened mass (*a cake of soap*). • *v.* **1** harden into a compact mass. **2** encrust with a hardened mass. ☐ **a piece of cake** *colloq.* something easily achieved. **sell** (*or* **go**) **like hot cakes** *colloq.* sell very quickly.

cakewalk *n.* **1** an obsolete African-American dance. **2** *colloq.* an easy task.

Cal *abbr.* large calorie(s).

cal *abbr.* small calorie(s).

calabash / **kal**-uh-bash / *n.* **1** a tropical American tree with fruit in the form of large gourds. **2** this or a similar gourd whose shell serves for holding liquid etc. **3** a bowl or pipe made from a gourd.

caladenia / kal-uh-**dee**-nee-uh / *n.* any of nearly 70 species of Australian orchid having extremely showy flowers (some species being known also as spider orchids).

calamari / kal-uh-**mah**-ree / *n.* (*pl.* the same) a squid used as food.

calamine *n.* a pink powder, chiefly zinc carbonate or oxide, used in skin lotions.

calamity *n.* a disaster. ☐ **calamitous** *adj.*

calcareous / kal-**kair**-ree-uhs / *adj.* of or containing calcium carbonate.

calces *see* CALX.

calciferol *n.* vitamin D_2, essential for the depositing of calcium in the bones.

calciferous *adj.* yielding calcium salts, esp. calcium carbonate.

calcify / kal-suh-fuy / *v.* (**calcified**, **calcifying**) harden by a deposit of calcium salts. ☐ **calcification** *n.*

calcine / **kal**-suhn, -suyn / *v.* reduce (a substance) or be reduced to quicklime or powder by heating to a high temperature without melting it. ☐ **calcination** *n.*

calcite *n.* natural crystalline calcium carbonate.

calcium *n.* a greyish-white chemical element (symbol Ca), present in bones and teeth and forming the basis of lime. ☐ **calcium carbonate** a white insoluble solid occurring as chalk, marble, etc.

calculable *adj.* able to be calculated.

calculate *v.* **1** find out by using mathematics, count. **2** plan deliberately; intend. **3** (foll. by *on*) rely on (*calculated on a quick response*). ☐ **calculation** *n.*

calculated *adj.* **1** (of an action) done deliberately or with foreknowledge. **2** intended or designed to have a particular effect (*a speech calculated to cause trouble for the government*).

calculating *adj.* (of people) shrewd, scheming.

calculator *n.* **1** a device, esp. a small electronic one, used in making calculations. **2** one who calculates.

calculus / **kal**-kyuh-luhs / *n.* (*pl.* **calculi** *or* **calculuses**) **1** a branch of mathematics that deals with problems involving rates of variation. **2** a stone formed in the body.

caldron alternative spelling of CAULDRON.

Caledonian / kal-uh-**doh**-nee-uhn / *adj.* of Scotland. •*n. literary* a person from Scotland.

calendar *n.* **1** a chart showing the days, weeks, and months of a particular year. **2** a device displaying the date. **3** a list of dates or events of a particular kind (*the Racing Calendar*). **4** the system by which time is divided into fixed periods (*the Gregorian calendar*). ☐ **calendar year** the period from 1 January to 31 December inclusive.

calender *n.* a machine in which cloth or paper is pressed by rollers to glaze or smooth it. •*v.* press in a calender.

calends *n.pl.* (also **kalends**) the first day of the month in the ancient Roman calendar.

calendula *n.* a plant with orange or yellow flowers; the marigold.

calf *n.* (*pl.* **calves**) **1** the young of cattle, also of the elephant, whale, and certain other animals. **2** calfskin. **3** the fleshy back part of the leg below the knee. ☐ **calf-love** childish romantic love.

calfskin *n.* leather made from the skin of a calf.

calibrate / kal-uh-brayt / *v.* **1** mark or correct units of measurement on a gauge. **2** measure the calibre of. ☐ **calibration** *n.* **calibrator** *n.*

calibre / **kal**-uh-buh / *n.* **1** the diameter of the inside of a tube or gun barrel. **2** the diameter of a bullet or shell. **3** ability, importance (*we need a woman of your calibre*).

calices *see* CALIX.

calicivirus / kuh-**lee**-see / *n.* any of a number of viruses characterised by having cup-like indentations. ☐ **feline calicivirus** such a virus which causes an influenza-like disease in cats. **rabbit calicivirus** such a virus, first detected in Europe and Asia, which kills rabbits. It was being tested for use in Australia, when it was accidentally released in 1995. (¶ Latin *calix*, = cup, chalice.)

calico *n.* (*pl.* **calicoes**) cotton cloth, esp. plain white or unbleached. •*adj.* made of calico.

Californian poppy *n.* a small cultivated yellow or orange poppy.

californium *n.* an artificially made radioactive metallic element (symbol Cf), used in industry and medicine as a source of neutrons.

Caligula / kuh-**lig**-yoo-luh / the nickname of Gaius, Roman emperor 37–41, whose reign has become a byword for tyrannical excess.

caliper alternative spelling of CALLIPER.

caliph / **kay**-luhf, **ka**- / *n.* the former title of certain Muslim leaders.

calisthenics alternative spelling of CALLISTHENICS.

calix / kay-liks / *n.* (*pl.* **calices** / kay-luh-seez /) a cup-like cavity or organ.

calk alternative spelling of CAULK.

call *n.* **1** a shout or cry. **2** the characteristic cry of a bird. **3** a signal on a bugle etc. **4** *Aust.* the broad-cast description of a race in progress. **5** a short visit. **6** a summons; an invitation. **7** a demand, a claim (*I have many calls on my time*). **8** a need, occasion; reason (*there's no call for you to worry*). **9** a declaration of trumps etc. in card games; a player's right or turn to make this. **10** an act of telephoning, a conversation on the telephone. •*v.* **1** shout or speak loudly. **2** utter a call. **3** *Aust.* broadcast a description of a race as it is being run. **4** pay a short visit. **5** name; describe or address as (*I call that cheating*). **6** declare (a trump suit etc.) in card games. **7** rouse deliberately; summon to get up. **8** summon (*call the fire brigade*). **9** command or invite, urge as if by commanding (*call a strike; duty calls*). **10** communicate with by telephone or radio. ☐ **call a person's bluff** challenge him or her to carry out a threat. **call for 1** demand, require. **2** come and collect. **call girl** a prostitute who accepts appointments by telephone. **call in 1** pay a casual visit. **2** seek the advice or services of (*call in a plumber*). **3** order the return of, take out of circulation. **call it a day** stop working. **call off 1** call away. **2** cancel (*the strike was called off*). **call of nature** a need to go to the toilet. **call on 1** make a short visit to (a person). **2** appeal to; request. **call out** summon to action; order to come out on strike. **call the tune** (*or* **the shots**) control the proceedings. **call to mind** remember; cause to remember. **call up** *v.* **1** telephone. **2** bring back to one's mind. **3** summon for military service. **call-up** *n.* a summons for military service. **on call** available to be called out

Callas

on duty. **within call** near enough to be summoned by calling. □□ **caller** n.

Callas, Maria (original name: Maria Cecilia Anna Kallageropoulos) (1923–77), operatic coloratura soprano, born in America of Greek parents.

calligraphy / kuh-**lig**-ruh-fee / n. **1** beautiful handwriting; the art of producing this. **2** handwriting. □ **calligrapher** n.

calling n. an occupation, a profession or trade; a vocation.

Calliope / kuh-**luy**-uh-pee / Gk myth. the Muse of Epic Poetry. Her name means 'beautiful-voiced'.

calliper / kal-uh-puh / n. (also **caliper**) **1** a metal support for a weak or injured leg. **2** (**callipers**) compasses for measuring the diameter of tubes or of round objects.

callistemon / kuh-**lis**-tuh-muhn / n. an Australian shrub or small tree, popularly called a 'bottlebrush'.

callisthenics n.pl. (also **calisthenics**) exercises to develop elegance and grace of movement.

callitris / kuh-**luy**-truhs / n. a mainly Australian genus of coniferous trees, each commonly called a 'cypress pine'.

callosity / kuh-**los**-uh-tee / n. a callus.

callous / **kal**-uhs / adj. **1** unsympathetic. **2** (also **calloused**) hardened, having calluses. □ **callously** adv. **callousness** n.

callow / kal-oh / adj. immature and inexperienced. □ **callowness** n.

callus / **kal**-uhs / n. (pl. **calluses**) an area of thick hardened skin or tissue.

calm adj. **1** quiet and still, not windy. **2** not excited or agitated. **3** casual and confident. •n. a calm condition or period, lack of strong winds. • v. make or become calm. □ **calmly** adv. **calmness** n.

calomel / kal-uh-mel, -muhl / n. a compound of mercury, used as a laxative.

calorie n. a unit of quantity of heat, the amount needed to raise the temperature of one gram (*small calorie*) or one kilogram (*large calorie*) of water by 1°C, often used to measure the energy value of foods. □ **caloric** adj.

calorific adj. producing heat.

calorimeter / kal-uh-**rim**-uh-tuh / n. an instrument for measuring the quantity of heat.

calothamnus / kal-oh-**tham**-nuhs / n. any of several small related shrubs endemic to WA, having red or yellow bottlebrush-like flowers on one side only of the stem (popular name: *one-sided bottlebrush*).

calumniate / kuh-**lum**-nee-ayt / v. slander. □ **calumniation** n.

calumny / kal-uhm-nee / n. **1** slander. **2** a slanderous statement.

Calvary the place (just outside ancient Jerusalem) where Christ was crucified.

calve v. give birth to a calf.

Calvin, John (1509–64), French Protestant religious reformer, living in Switzerland.

Calvinism n. the theology of John Calvin or his followers, stressing predestination. □ **Calvinist** n. **Calvinistic** adj.

calx / kalks / n. (pl. **calces** / kal-seez /) the powdery or crumbling substance left after the burning of a metal or mineral.

calypso n. (pl. **calypsos**) a West Indian song with a variable rhythm and topical usu. improvised lyrics.

calyx / **kay**-liks, **kal**-iks / n. (pl. **calyxes** or **calyces** / **kay**-luh-seez /) **1** a ring of leaves (sepals) enclosing an unopened flower bud. **2** *Biology* = CALIX.

cam n. a projecting part on a wheel or shaft, shaped or mounted so that its circular motion, as it turns, transmits an up-and-down or back-and-forth motion to another part.

camaraderie / kam-uh-**rah**-duh-ree / n. comradeship, friendship.

camber n. a slight arch or upward curve given to a surface, esp. of a road. □ **cambered** adj.

Cambodia / kam-**boh**-dee-uh / a republic in SE Asia between Thailand and the south of Vietnam; formerly called Kampuchea. □ **Cambodian** adj. & n.

Cambrian adj. **1** Welsh. **2** *Geol.* of the first period of the Palaeozoic era. •n. this period.

cambric n. thin linen or cotton cloth.

Cambridge, Ada (1844–1926), English-born Australian writer whose writings include the novels *A Marked Man* and *The Three Miss Kings*, as well as the volume of poems *Unspoken Thoughts*, published anonymously in 1887 and soon after suppressed because of its frank concerns with sexuality, marriage, and other social issues.

camcorder n. a combined video camera and sound recorder.

came see COME.

camel n. **1** a long-necked animal with either one or two humps on its back, used in desert countries for riding and for carrying goods. **2** a fawn colour. □ **camel hair** n. fine soft hair used in artists' brushes; fabric made of this.

camellia / kuh-**meel**-yuh, kuh-**mee**-lee-uh / n. any of several evergreen shrubs native to E. Asia, with shiny leaves and showy flowers, the tea bush being one of the species.

Camelot / **kam**-uh-lot / (in legend) the place where King Arthur held his court.

camembert / **kam**-uhm-bair / n. a soft rich pungent cheese.

cameo / **kam**-ee-oh / n. (pl. **cameos**) **1** a small piece of hard stone carved with a raised design. **2** something small but well executed, e.g. a short description or a part in a play.

camera n. an apparatus for taking photographs, moving pictures, or television pictures. □ **in**

camera (of the hearing of evidence or lawsuits) in the judge's private room; in private, in secret.

cameraman *n.* a person whose job is to operate a film camera or television camera.

Cameroon / kam-uh-**roon** / a republic on the west coast of Africa. ☐ **Cameroonian** *adj.* & *n.*

camisole / **kam**-uh-sohl / *n.* a woman's bodice-like garment or undergarment with shoulder straps.

camomile / **kam**-uh-muyl, -meel / *n.* (also **chamomile**) a sweet-smelling plant with daisy-like flowers which are dried for use in medicine as a tonic.

camouflage / **kam**-uh-flah*zh* / *n.* **1** a method of disguising or concealing objects by colouring or covering them so that they look like part of their surroundings. **2** pretence (*his friendliness is all camouflage*). • *v.* conceal in this way.

camp¹ *n.* **1** a place where holidaymakers, detainees, etc. live temporarily in tents, huts, or similar shelters; a place where troops are lodged or trained. **2** the occupants of such a place. **3** *Aust.* an Aboriginal living place, temporary or permanent. **4** *Aust.* an assembly place of sheep or cattle. **5** supporters of a particular party or cause etc., regarded collectively (*the Labor camp*). • *v.* **1** sleep in a tent; live in a camp. **2** live temporarily as if in a camp. **3** *Aust.* (of sheep or cattle) flock together, esp. for rest. ☐ **camp bed** a folding portable bed. **camp draft** (also **camp drafting**) *Aust.* a competitive equestrian event in which a steer is driven round a set course. **camp follower 1** a hanger-on providing services to a military camp etc. **2** a person who is sympathetic to a group without officially being a member. **camp oven** *Aust.* a heavy, iron, three-legged cooking vessel which stands in an open fire and has a flat, usu. recessed, lid on top of which hot coals can be placed.

camp² *adj.* **1** effeminate; exaggerated in style, esp. for humorous effect. **2** homosexual. • *n.* such a style or manner. *v.* behave or do in a camp way. ☐ **camp it up** deliberately overact; behave affectedly. ☐ ☐ **campy** *adj.*

campaign *n.* **1** a series of military operations with a set purpose, usu. in one area. **2** a similar series of planned activities (*an advertising campaign*). • *v.* take part in a campaign. ☐ **campaigner** *n.*

campanile / kam-puh-**nee**-lee / *n.* a bell tower, esp. a free-standing one in Italy.

campanology / kam-puh-**nol**-uh-jee / *n.* **1** the study of bells (their ringing, founding, etc.). **2** bell-ringing. ☐ **campanologist** *n.*

campanula / kam-**pan**-yuh-luh / *n.* a plant with bell-shaped usu. blue or white flowers.

camper *n.* **1** a person who is camping. **2** (in full **campervan**) a large motor vehicle with beds, cooking stove, etc.

camphor *n.* a strong-smelling white substance used in medicine and mothballs and in making plastics.

campsite *n.* a place for camping, esp. one equipped for holidaymakers.

campus *n.* (*pl.* **campuses**) the grounds of a university or college.

camshaft *n.* a shaft carrying cams.

Camus / kuh-**moo** /, Albert (1913–60), French writer of novels, plays, and essays.

can¹ *n.* **1** a metal or plastic container for liquids. **2** a sealed tin in which food or drink is preserved. **3** either of these with its contents; the amount it contains. **4** (**cans**) *colloq.* headphones. **5** (**the can**) *colloq.* prison. • *v.* (**canned, canning**) **1** preserve in a sealed can. **2** *colloq.* disparage (*the critics canned his latest film*). **3** *colloq.* cancel; shelve (*they've canned tonight's meeting*). ☐ **carry the can** *colloq.* bear the responsibility or blame. **in the can** *colloq.* finished, ready.

can² *auxiliary v.* (*past* **could**) expressing ability or knowledge of how to do something (*he can play the violin*), or permission (*you can go*), or desire or liberty to act (*we cannot allow this*).

■ **Usage** When expressing permission, *may* is a more formal alternative to *can*.

Canaan / **kay**-nuhn / *n.* a promised land (originally that west of the River Jordan, the Promised Land of the Israelites).

Canada a country in North America. ☐ **Canadian** *adj.* & *n.*

canal *n.* **1** a channel cut through land for navigation or irrigation. **2** a tubular passage through which food or air passes in a plant or animal body (*the alimentary canal*).

canapé / **kan**-uh-pay / *n.* a small piece of bread or pastry with a savoury topping.

canard *n.* a false rumour or story.

canary *n.* **1** a small yellow songbird. **2** *Aust. hist.* a convict (from the yellow clothing worn).

canasta / kuh-**nas**-tuh / *n.* a card game played with two packs of cards including the jokers.

Canberra / **kan**-buh-ruh, -bruh / the name of the capital city of Australia and of the Australian Capital Territory. (¶ From an Aboriginal language. Popularly said to be = 'woman's breasts' with reference to the peaks of Mount Ainslie and Black Hill; or *Nganbirra* a meeting place; or *Kembery* or *Gnabra*, supposed Aboriginal names for the area.)

cancan *n.* a lively stage dance involving high kicking.

cancel *v.* (**cancelled, cancelling**) **1** say that (something already decided on or arranged) will not be done or take place. **2** order (a thing) to be discontinued. **3** cross out. **4** mark (a stamp or ticket) in order to prevent further use. ☐ **cancel out** counter balance, neutralise (each other). ☐ ☐ **cancellation** *n.*

cancer n. **1** a malignant tumour of body cells. **2** a disease in which malignant growths form. **3** something evil that spreads destructively (*the cancer of racial hatred*). **4** (**Cancer**) the fourth sign of the zodiac, the Crab. □ **tropic of Cancer** see TROPIC. □□ **cancerous** adj.

candela / kan-**dee**-luh, -**day**-luh / n. a unit for measuring the brightness of a source of light.

candelabrum / kan-duh-**lah**-bruhm / n. (also **candelabra**) (pl. **candelabra**) a large branched candlestick or holder for lights.

■ **Usage** The form *candelabra* is, strictly speaking, the plural. However, *candelabra* (singular) and *candelabras* (plural) are often found in informal use.

candid adj. **1** frank, not hiding one's thoughts. **2** (of a photograph) taken informally, usu. without the subject's knowledge. □ **candidly** adv. **candidness** n.

candida n. a fungus causing thrush.

candidate n. **1** a person who seeks or is nominated for appointment to an office or position. **2** a person taking an examination. **3** colloq. a likely prospect (*smoking as much as he does, he's a candidate for lung cancer*). □ **candidacy** n. **candidature** n.

candied / **kan**-deed / adj. encrusted with sugar, preserved in sugar. □ **candied peel** peel of citrus fruits candied for use in cooking.

candle n. a stick of wax with a wick through it, giving light when burning.

candlelight n. light from candles. □ **candlelit** adj.

Candlemas n. the feast of the Purification of the Virgin Mary, when candles are blessed (2 February).

candlenut n. a tree of Qld and the Pacific Islands yielding a hard, oily, edible nut used, when grated, to thicken some Asian curries (and formerly to provide a candle-like light when a wick is inserted in the nut and set alight).

candlepower n. a unit of measurement of light, expressed in candelas.

candlestick n. a holder for one or more candles.

candlewick n. **1** a fabric with a raised tufted pattern worked in soft cotton yarn. **2** this yarn.

candour / **kan**-duh / n. (also **candor**) frankness; openness.

candy n. **1** (also **sugar candy**) sugar crystallised by repeated boiling and slow evaporation. **2** esp. US sweets, confectionery. • v. preserve (fruit etc.) in candy.

candyfloss n. Brit. = FAIRY FLOSS.

candystripe n. alternate stripes of white and a colour. □ **candystriped** adj.

cane n. **1** the hollow jointed stem of tall reeds and grasses (e.g. bamboo, rattan); the solid stem of slender palms. **2** = SUGAR CANE. **3** cane (such as rattan) used for making furniture etc. **4** a stem or a length of it; a slender rod; a walking stick. **5** the stem of a raspberry or blackberry etc. plant. • v. **1** punish by beating with a cane. **2** weave cane into (a chair etc.). □ **cane beetle** a beetle, the larvae of which attack the roots of sugar cane. **cane sugar** sugar obtained from the juice of sugar cane. **cane toad** a very large toad, native to S. America, introduced from north-eastern Australia to combat the cane beetle, and now a serious pest.

canecutter n. an itinerant worker employed in the harvesting of sugar cane.

canegrower n. the proprietor of a sugar cane farm.

canine / **kay**-nuyn, **kan**-uyn / adj. of a dog or dogs; of or belonging to the animal family which includes dingoes, dogs, wolves, foxes, etc. • n. **1** a dog. **2** (in full **canine tooth**) a strong pointed tooth next to the incisors.

caning n. **1** a beating with a cane. **2** a verbal attack or rebuff. **3** an overwhelming defeat (*Australia gave the poms a caning in the last cricket Test*).

canister n. **1** a small container for tea etc. **2** a cylinder, filled with shot or tear gas, that bursts and releases its contents when fired from a gun or thrown.

canker n. **1** a disease that destroys the wood of plants and trees. **2** a disease that causes ulcerous sores in animals. **3** a corrupting influence.

cannabis / **kan**-uh-buhs / n. **1** a hemp plant. **2** a preparation of this for smoking or chewing as an intoxicant drug; marijuana.

canned see CAN[1]. • adj. **1** recorded for reproduction (*canned music*). **2** sold in a can (*canned beer*). **3** colloq. drunk. **4** colloq. cancelled.

cannelloni / kan-uh-**loh**-nee / n.pl. rolls of pasta with a savoury filling.

cannery n. a canning factory.

cannibal n. a person who eats human flesh; an animal that eats its own kind. □ **cannibalism** n. **cannibalistic** adj.

cannibalise v. (also **-ize**) dismantle (a machine etc.) in order to provide spare parts for others. □ **cannibalisation** n.

cannon n. **1** (pl. **cannon**) an old type of large heavy gun firing solid metal balls. **2** an automatic shell-firing gun used in aircraft. **3** a shot in billiards in which the player's ball hits the two other balls in succession. • v. (**cannoned**, **cannoning**) **1** collide heavily. **2** make a cannon at billiards. □ **cannon fodder** soldiers regarded merely as material to be expended in war.

cannonade n. continuous heavy gunfire. • v. bombard with a cannonade.

cannonball n. a large ball fired from a cannon.

cannot = can not.

canny adj. (**cannier**, **canniest**) shrewd, worldly-wise; thrifty. □ **cannily** adv. **canniness** n.

canoe n. a light narrow boat propelled by paddles. • v. (**canoed**, **canoeing**) paddle or travel in a canoe. □ **canoeist** n.

canon n. **1** a general principle. **2** a law or decree of the Church. **3** a body of sacred writings accepted as genuine (*Biblical canon*). **4** the recognised genuine works of a particular author. **5** a member of certain Catholic religious orders. **6** a member of a cathedral chapter. **7** the central unchanging part of the Catholic mass. **8** the list of canonised saints. **9** a passage or piece of music in which a theme is taken up by several parts in succession. □ **canon law** Church law as laid down by decrees of the popes, councils of the Church, etc.

canonical / kuh-**non**-i-kuhl / *adj.* **1** ordered by canon law. **2** included in the canon of Scripture. **3** authoritative, standard, accepted. □ **canonically** *adv.*

canonise *v.* (also **-ize**) (of the pope) declare (a person who has died) officially to be a saint. □ **canonisation** n.

canoodle *v. colloq.* kiss and cuddle.

canopied *adj.* having a canopy.

canopy n. **1** a hanging cover forming a shelter above a throne, bed, or person etc. **2** any similar covering. **3** the part of a parachute that spreads in the air. **4** the uppermost layers of foliage etc. in a forest.

cant *v.* slope, tilt. •n. **1** a tilted or sloping position. **2** insincere pious or moral talk. **3** jargon.

can't = can not.

cantabile / kan-**tah**-buh-lee, -lay / *adv.* & *adj. Music* in smooth flowing style.

cantaloupe / **kan**-tuh-lohp, -loop / n. (also **cantaloup**) a small round melon with orange-coloured flesh, a rock melon.

cantankerous / kan-**tang**-kuh-ruhs / *adj.* bad-tempered, quarrelsome. □ **cantankerously** *adv.* **cantankerousness** n.

cantata / kan-**tah**-tuh / n. a musical composition for singers, like an oratorio but shorter.

canteen n. **1** a restaurant for the employees of a factory, office, etc.; a shop for provisions in a barracks or camp. **2** a school shop selling lunches. **3** a case or box containing a set of cutlery. **4** a soldier's or camper's water flask.

canter n. a slow easy gallop. •v. ride at a canter, gallop gently.

canticle / **kan**-tik-uhl / n. a song or chant with words taken from the Bible.

cantilever / **kan**-tuh-lee-vuh / n. a projecting beam or girder fixed at one end only, supporting a balcony or similar structure. □ **cantilever bridge** a bridge made of cantilevers projecting from piers and connected by girders.

canto n. (*pl.* **cantos**) each of the sections into which a long poem is divided.

canton n. a division of a country, esp. of Switzerland.

Cantonese n. **1** (*pl.* **Cantonese**) a native or inhabitant of the city of Canton in China. **2** a Chinese language spoken in southern China and in Hong Kong. •*adj.* of Canton or its people or language or distinctive cuisine.

cantor n. **1** the leader of the prayers of a congregation in a synagogue; one who chants the liturgy. **2** a church choir leader.

canvas n. **1** strong coarse cloth used for making tents and sails etc. and by artists for painting on. **2** a piece of canvas for painting on; an oil painting. □ **under canvas 1** in tents. **2** with sails spread.

canvass *v.* **1** visit in order to ask for votes, orders for goods, or opinions. **2** propose (a plan). •n. canvassing. □ **canvasser** n.

canyon / **kan**-yuhn / n. (also **cañon**) a deep gorge, usu. with a river flowing through it.

canyoning n. the sport of jumping into a fast-flowing mountain stream and allowing oneself to be carried downstream at high speed.

cap n. **1** a soft covering for the head, without a brim but often with a peak. **2** an academic headdress, a mortar board. **3** a cap as the sign of membership of a sports team. **4** a cap-like cover; a top for a bottle, pen, etc. **5** = PERCUSSION CAP. **6** a dental crown. •*v.* (**capped**, **capping**) **1** put a cap on; cover the top or end of. **2** excel, outdo.

capability n. **1** ability, power. **2** an undeveloped or unused faculty or ability.

capable *adj.* **1** competent. **2** (foll. by *of*) having a certain ability or capacity (*quite capable of lying*). □ **capably** *adv.*

capacious / kuh-**pay**-shuhs / *adj.* roomy, able to hold much. □ **capaciously** *adv.* **capaciousness** n.

capacitance n. **1** ability to store an electric charge. **2** the measure of this; the ratio of the change in the electric charge of a body to a corresponding change in its potential (symbol C).

capacitor / kuh-**pas**-uh-tuh / n. a device storing a charge of electricity.

capacity n. **1** the ability to contain or accommodate, the amount that can be contained. **2** ability, capability (*working at full capacity*). **3** a position or function (*signed it in his capacity as chairman*). □ **to capacity** fully (*the hall was filled to capacity*).

caparison / kuh-**pa**-ruh-suhn / *literary v.* deck out. •n. **1** a horse's trappings. **2** equipment, finery.

cape[1] n. **1** a cloak. **2** a very short part of a coat etc., covering the shoulders.

cape[2] n. a headland, a promontory. □ **the Cape** = CAPE OF GOOD HOPE

Cape Barren Island an island in Bass Strait. □ **Cape Barren goose** a grey waterbird that breeds on the islands off the south coast of the Australian mainland.

Cape Horn the southernmost point of South America, on an island south of Tierra del Fuego, belonging to Chile.

Cape of Good Hope a mountainous promontory near the southern extremity of South Africa, south of Cape Town.

caper[1] *v.* jump or run about playfully. • *n.* **1** capering. **2** *colloq.* an activity, an occupation, an escapade.

caper[2] *n.* **1** a bramble-like shrub. **2** one of its buds pickled for use as a flavouring.

Cape Town one of the two capital cities of South Africa; the legislative capital.

Cape Verde Islands / kayp **verd** / a republic consisting of a group of islands off the west coast of Africa. □ **Cape Verdean** *adj.* & *n.*

Cape York Peninsula a peninsula in Qld, about 650 kilometres long, which forms the northernmost point of mainland Australia.

capillarity *n.* the rise or depression of a liquid in a narrow tube.

capillary / kuh-**pil**-uh-ree / *n.* any of the very fine branching blood vessels that connect veins and arteries. • *adj.* of or like a capillary. □ **capillary action** = CAPILLARITY.

capital *adj.* **1** principal, most important. **2** *colloq.* excellent. **3** involving the death penalty (*a capital offence; capital punishment*). **4** very serious; fatal (*a capital error*). **5** (of letters) of the form and size used to begin a name or a sentence. • *n.* **1** the chief town or city of a country, State, or region, usu. its seat of government and administrative centre. **2** a capital letter. **3** the head or top part of a pillar. **4** wealth or property that is used or invested to produce more wealth; the money with which a business etc. is started. □ **capital gain** profit from the sale of investments or property. **capital goods** goods such as ships, railways, machinery, etc., used in producing consumer goods.

capitalise / **kap**-uh-tuh-luyz / *v.* (also **-ize**) **1** write or print as a capital letter. **2** convert into capital; provide with capital. □ **capitalise on** profit by, use (a thing) to one's advantage. □ **capitalisation** *n.*

capitalism / **kap**-uh-tuh-liz-uhm / *n.* an economic system in which trade and industry are controlled by private owners for profit.

capitalist / **kap**-uh-tuhl-uhst / *n.* **1 a** one who has much capital invested. **b** *derog.* a rich person. **2** a person who favours capitalism. • *adj.* of or favouring capitalism. □ **capitalistic** *adj.*

Capitol 1 the building in Washington DC in which the Congress of the USA meets. **2** the temple of Jupiter in ancient Rome.

capitulate *v.* surrender. □ **capitulation** *n.*

capo / **ka**-poh, **kay**- / *n.* (*pl.* **capos**) a device fitted across the strings of a guitar, banjo, etc. to raise their pitch equally.

capon / **kay**-pon / *n.* a domestic cock castrated and fattened for eating.

cappuccino / kap-uh-**chee**-noh / *n.* (*pl.* **cappuccinos**) coffee with milk made frothy with pressurised steam. (¶ Italian)

caprice / kuh-**prees** / *n.* **1** a whim. **2** a piece of music in a lively fanciful style.

capricious / kuh-**prish**-uhs / *adj.* **1** guided by caprice, impulsive. **2** changeable (*a capricious breeze*). □ **capriciously** *adv.* **capriciousness** *n.*

Capricorn *n.* the tenth sign of the zodiac, the Goat. □ **tropic of Capricorn** *see* TROPIC. □ □ **Capricornian** *adj.* & *n.*

capsicum / **kap**-suh-kuhm / *n.* **1** a plant with hollow edible fruits, esp. varieties of sweet pepper. **2** the fruits themselves, usu. red, green, or yellow, used as a vegetable. □ **capsicum spray** an oil extracted from cayenne pepper, causing temporary intense pain and burning sensations, used esp. by police to ward off attackers, disarm violent offenders, etc.

capsize *v.* overturn (*a wave capsized the boat; the boat capsized*).

capstan / **kap**-stuhn / *n.* **1** a thick revolving post used to pull in a rope or cable that winds round it as it turns, e.g. for raising a ship's anchor. **2** a revolving spindle on a tape recorder. □ **capstan lathe** a lathe with a revolving tool-holder.

capsule *n.* **1** a small soluble case in which a dose of medicine is enclosed for swallowing. **2** a plant's seed case that splits open when ripe. **3** a detachable compartment of a spacecraft, containing instruments or crew.

capsulise *v.* (also **-ize**) put (information etc.) into a compact form.

Capt. *abbr.* Captain.

captain *n.* **1** a person given authority over a group or team. **2** an army officer ranking below a major and above a lieutenant. **3** a naval officer ranking below a rear admiral and above a commander. **4** the person commanding a ship. **5** the pilot of a civil aircraft. • *v.* act as captain of; lead. □ **captaincy** *n.*

Captain Cook *n. Aust. rhyming slang* a look (*took a Captain Cook at the files*).

caption / **kap**-shuhn / *n.* **1** a short title or heading. **2** a description or explanation printed with an illustration etc. **3** words shown on a cinema or television screen. • *v.* provide with a caption.

captious / **kap**-shuhs / *adj.* fond of finding fault or raising objections about trivial matters. □ **captiously** *adv.* **captiousness** *n.*

captivate *v.* fascinate, charm. □ **captivation** *n.*

captive *adj.* **1** taken prisoner. **2** kept as a prisoner, unable to escape. • *n.* a captive person or animal. □ **captive audience** people who cannot get away easily and therefore cannot avoid being addressed.

captivity *n.* the state of being held captive.

captor *n.* one who captures a person or animal.

capture *v.* **1** make a prisoner of. **2** take or obtain by force, trickery, attraction, or skill. **3** portray; record on film etc. **4** put (data) into a form accessible by computer. • *n.* **1** capturing. **2** a person or thing captured.

Capuchin / kap-yuh-chuhn / *n.* **1** a Franciscan friar of the new Rule of 1529. **2** (**capuchin**) a monkey or pigeon with a hood-like crown.

car *n.* **1** a motor car. **2** a carriage of a specified type (*dining car*). **3** the passenger compartment of an airship, balloon, cable railway, or lift. □ **car park** an area for parking cars. **car phone** a cellular phone for use in a car. **car seat** a special protective seat secured to a main car seat and intended to protect a very small child.

Caracas / kuh-**rak**-uhs / the capital of Venezuela.

carafe / kuh-**rahf**, -**raf** / *n.* a glass bottle in which wine or water is served at the table.

carambola / ka-ruhm-**boh**-luh / *n.* **1** a small tree native to SE Asia, bearing golden-yellow ribbed fruit. **2** this fruit. Also called *star fruit*.

caramel *n.* **1** burnt sugar used for colouring and flavouring food. **2** a kind of toffee tasting like this.

caramelise *v.* (also **-ize**) turn or be turned into caramel. □ **caramelisation** *n.*

carapace / **ka**-ruh-pays / *n.* the shell on the back of a tortoise or crustacean.

carat / **ka**-ruht / *n.* **1** a unit of weight for precious stones, 200 milligrams. **2** a measure of the purity of gold, pure gold being 24 carat.

Caravaggio / ka-ruh-**vah**-jee-oh /, Michelangelo Merisi da (1571–1610), Italian painter, noted for his realistic depiction of traditional religious subjects.

caravan *n.* **1** a vehicle equipped for living in and usu. towed by a car. **2** a company of people (e.g. merchants) travelling together across desert country. □ **caravanning** *n.*

caravanserai / ka-ruh-**van**-suh-ruy / *n.* (in Asia, N. Africa, etc.) an inn with a large central courtyard for accommodation of travelling caravans.

caraway *n.* a plant with spicy seeds that are used for flavouring cakes etc.

carbeen *n.* a large eucalypt with a pattern like tiles on its bark, occurring in north-eastern Australia. (¶ Kamilaroi and Yuwaalaraay.)

carbide / **kah**-buyd / *n.* a compound of carbon, the compound used in making acetylene gas.

carbine / **kah**-buyn / *n.* a short light automatic rifle.

carbohydrate *n.* **1** an organic compound, such as the sugars and starches, composed of carbon, oxygen, and hydrogen. **2** (**carbohydrates**) starchy foods.

carbolic *n.* (in full **carbolic acid**) phenol, esp. when used as a disinfectant.

carbon *n.* **1** a chemical element (symbol C) that is present in all living matter and occurs in its pure form as diamond and graphite. **2** a rod of carbon in an arc lamp. **3** carbon paper; a copy made with this. □ **carbon copy 1** a copy made with carbon paper. **2** an exact copy. **carbon credit** a credit for something (such as the planting of a forest) that reduces or absorbs carbon monoxide, such a credit being set off against a country's requirements to reduce greenhouse gas emissions. **carbon dating** a method of deciding the age of prehistoric objects by measuring the decay of radiocarbon in them. **carbon dioxide** a colourless odourless gas formed by the burning of carbon or breathed out by animals in respiration. **carbon fibre** a thin strong filament of carbon, used as a strengthening material and in protective clothing. **carbon-14** a radioisotope used in carbon dating. **carbon monoxide** a very poisonous gas formed when carbon burns incompletely, occurring e.g. in the exhaust of motor engines. **carbon paper** thin paper coated with pigment, placed between sheets of writing paper for making copies of what is written or typed on the top sheet. **carbon sink** an area (such as a forest) that stores carbon dioxide, and therefore prevents it from collecting in the atmosphere. **carbon tetrachloride** a colourless liquid used as a solvent in dry cleaning etc. **carbon-12** a stable isotope of carbon, used as a standard in calculating atomic mass.

carbonaceous / kah-buh-**nay**-shuhs / *adj.* **1** consisting of or containing carbon. **2** of or like coal or charcoal.

carbonate *n.* a compound that releases carbon dioxide when mixed with acid.

carbonated *adj.* charged with carbon dioxide; (of drinks) made fizzy with this.

carbonic *adj.* of carbon. □ **carbonic acid** a weak acid formed from carbon dioxide and water.

carboniferous / kah-buh-**nif**-uh-ruhs / *adj.* **1** producing coal. **2** (**Carboniferous**) of the geological period in the Palaeozoic era when many coal deposits were created. • *n.* (**Carboniferous**) this period.

carbonise *v.* (also **-ize**) **1** convert (a substance that contains carbon) into carbon alone, e.g. by heating or burning it. **2** coat with carbon. □ **carbonisation** *n.*

carborundum / kah-buh-**run**-duhm / *n.* a hard compound of carbon and silicon used for polishing and grinding things.

carboy / **kah**-boi / *n.* a large round bottle surrounded by a protecting framework, used for transporting liquids safely.

carbuncle *n.* **1** a severe abscess in the skin. **2** a bright red gem cut in a knob-like shape.

carburettor *n.* an apparatus for mixing fuel and air in an internal-combustion engine.

carcass *n.* (also **carcase**) **1** the dead body of an animal, esp. one prepared for cutting up as meat. **2** the bony part of the body of a bird before or after cooking. **3** the framework or skeleton of a building, ship, etc. **4** *colloq.* a person's body; a corpse. **5** the worthless remains of something.

carcinogen / kah-**sin**-uh-juhn / *n.* a cancer-producing substance.

carcinogenic / kah-sin-uh-**jen**-ik / *adj.* producing cancer.

carcinoma / kah-suh-**noh**-muh / *n.* (*pl.* **carcinomata** *or* **carcinomas**) a cancerous growth.

card[1] *n.* **1** thick stiff paper or thin cardboard; a small piece of this used e.g. to send messages or greetings, or to record information such as a person's name or the title of a book and used for identification or in a card index. **2** a small flat sq. rectangular piece of plastic issued by a bank etc. with personal (often machine-readable) data on it, chiefly to obtain cash or credit. **3** a program of events at a race meeting. **4** a playing card. **5** *colloq.* an odd or amusing person. **6** (**cards**) card playing, card games. ☐ **be on the cards** be likely or probable. **card-carrying member** a registered member of a political party, trade union, etc. **card index** an index in which each item is entered on a separate card. **card sharp** (*or* **sharper**) a person who makes a living by cheating at card games. **card swipe** an electronic reader through which a credit card, security pass, etc. is passed to record its number etc. **have a card up one's sleeve** have something held in reserve secretly. **put one's cards on the table** be frank about one's resources and intentions.

card[2] *n.* a wire brush or toothed instrument for cleaning or combing wool. • *v.* clean or comb with this.

cardamom / **kah**-duh-muhm / *n.* spice from the seed-capsules of a plant of the ginger family from Sri Lanka etc.

cardboard *n.* pasteboard or stiff paper, esp. for making into boxes.

Carden, Joan (1930–), AO, Australian soprano in opera.

cardiac / **kah**-dee-ak / *adj.* of the heart.

cardigan *n.* a knitted jacket. (¶ Named after the 7th Earl of Cardigan (1797–1868) who led the disastrous Charge of the Light Brigade in the Crimean War.)

cardinal *adj.* **1** chief, most important (*the cardinal virtues*). **2** deep scarlet. • *n.* a member of the Sacred College of the Catholic Church, which elects the pope. ☐ **cardinal numbers** the whole numbers, 1, 2, 3, etc. (as distinct from the ordinal numbers, 1st, 2nd, 3rd, etc.). **cardinal points** the four main points of the compass, North, South, East, and West.

cardiogram *n.* an electrocardiogram.

cardiograph *n.* a device recording heart movements; an electrocardiograph.

cardiology / kah-dee-**ol**-uh-jee / *n.* the branch of medicine dealing with diseases and abnormalities of the heart. ☐ **cardiological** *adj.* **cardiologist** *n.*

cardiovascular *adj.* of the heart and blood vessels.

cardphone *n.* a public telephone operated by a machine-readable card instead of money.

care *n.* **1** serious attention and thought (*planned with care*). **2** caution to avoid damage or loss (*handle with care*). **3** protection, charge, supervision (*left the child in her sister's care*). **4** worry, anxiety (*freedom from care*). • *v.* **1** feel concern or interest. **2** feel affection or liking. **3** feel willing; like (*would you care to try one?*). ☐ **care for** have in one's care; take care of. **care of** (*abbr.* **c/o**) to the address of (someone who will deliver or forward things) (*write to him care of his bank*). **take care of 1** take charge of; see to the safety or well-being of. **2** deal with.

careen / kuh-**reen** / *v.* **1** tilt or keel over to one side. **2** swerve about.

career *n.* **1** progress through life, esp. in a profession. **2** an occupation, a way of making a living, esp. one with opportunities for advancement or promotion. **3** (used as *adj.*) following a career; working permanently in a profession (*a career woman*). **4** quick or violent forward movement. • *v.* move swiftly or wildly.

careerist *n.* a person who is keen to advance in a career.

carefree *adj.* light-hearted through being free from anxiety or responsibility.

careful *adj.* **1** giving serious attention and thought, painstaking (*a careful worker*). **2** done with care (*careful work*). **3** cautious, avoiding damage or loss. ☐ **carefully** *adv.*

careless *adj.* **1** not careful. **2** unthinking, insensitive. **3** casual and light-hearted. ☐ **carelessly** *adv.* **carelessness** *n.*

carer *n.* a person who looks after a sick or disabled person at home.

caress / kuh-**res** / *n.* a loving touch. • *v.* touch lovingly.

caret / **ka**-ruht / *n.* a mark (∧, ⋏) indicating a proposed insertion in printing or writing.

caretaker *n.* **1** a person employed to look after a house or building. **2** (usu. used as *adj.*) having temporary authority or power (*a caretaker government*).

careworn *adj.* showing signs of prolonged worry.

Carey[1], George Leonard (1935–), Archbishop of Canterbury from 1991.

Carey[2], Peter (1944–), Australian writer of short stories and novels, winner of the Booker Prize for *Oscar and Lucinda* in 1988. His other novels include *Illywhacker* (1985), *Jack Maggs* (1997), and *True History of the Kelly Gang* (2000).

cargo *n.* (*pl.* **cargoes** *or* **cargos**) goods carried on a ship or aircraft.

Carib / **ka**-rib / *n.* **1** a member of a group of American Indian inhabitants of the Lesser Antilles and parts of the neighbouring South American coast, or their descendants. **2** their language.

Caribbean / ka-ruh-**bee**-uhn, kuh-**rib**-ee-uhn / *adj.* of the Caribbean Sea, a part of the Atlantic off Central America. • *n.* the Caribbean Sea.

caribou / **ka**-ruh-boo / *n.* (*pl.* **caribou**) a North American reindeer.

caricature / **ka**-ruh-kuh-tyor, -choor / *n.* **1** a picture, description, or imitation of a person or thing that exaggerates certain characteristics, esp.

caricaturist *n.* a person who makes caricatures.
caries / **kair**-reez / *n.* (*pl.* **caries**) decay in bones or teeth (*dental caries*).
carillon / kuh-**ril**-yuhn / *n.* a set of bells sounded either from a keyboard or mechanically.
caring *adj.* **1** kind, humane; committed, compassionate (*a caring society*). **2** concerned with looking after people (*the caring professions*).
carioca / ka-ree-**oh**-kuh / *n.* a Brazilian dance resembling the samba.
carjack *v.* steal (an occupied car) by threatening the driver with violence. □ **carjacking** *n.*
cark *v.* **1** (of a crow etc.) caw. **2** (of a person) speak raucously. **3** *Aust.* alternative spelling of KARK.
Carmelite / **kah**-muhl-luyt / *n.* **1** a friar of the order of Our Lady of Mount Carmel, following a rule of extreme asceticism (also called a *White Friar*, from the colour of his cloak). **2** a nun of the corresponding order of nuns. • *adj.* of this order.
carminative / **kah**-muh-nuh-tiv / *adj.* curing flatulence. • *n.* a carminative drug.
carmine / **kah**-muyn / *adj.* deep red. • *n.* **1** this colour. **2** carmine pigment made from cochineal.
carn *v. Aust. colloq.* (in barracking at sporting fixtures) 'come on!'.
carnage / **kah**-nij / *n.* the killing of many people.
Carnac / **kah**-nak / the site in NW France, in Brittany near the Atlantic coast, of a group of stone monuments dating from the neolithic period.
carnal / **kah**-nuhl / *adj.* of the body or flesh, not spiritual (*carnal desires*). □ **carnal knowledge** *Law* sexual intercourse. □□ **carnally** *adv.*
Carnarvon Range 1 a range in south-eastern Qld of approximately 150 km, forming part of the Great Dividing Range **2** a range in central WA.
carnation *n.* a cultivated clove-scented pink.
carnelian *n.* = CORNELIAN.
carnet / **kah**-nay / *n.* a permit to drive across a frontier
carnival *n.* **1** festivities and public merrymaking, usu. with a procession. **2** a series of sporting events (*swimming carnival; surf carnival*).
carnivore / **kah**-nuh-vaw / *n.* a carnivorous animal or plant.
carnivorous / kah-**niv**-uh-ruhs / *adj.* feeding on flesh or other animal matter.
carob / **ka**-ruhb / *n.* the horn-shaped edible pod of a Mediterranean evergreen tree, similar in taste to chocolate.
carol *n.* a joyful song, esp. a Christmas hymn. • *v.* (**carolled, carolling**) **1** sing carols. **2** sing joyfully.
Carolingian *adj.* of the Frankish dynasty founded by Charlemagne. • *n.* a member of this dynasty.
carotene *n.* an orange-coloured pigment found in carrots, tomatoes, etc., a source of vitamin A.

carotid / kuh-**rot**-uhd / *n.* either of the two great arteries (one on either side of the neck) carrying blood to the head. • *adj.* of these arteries.
carouse / kuh-**rowz** / *v.* drink and be merry. □ **carousal** *n.* **carouser** *n.*
carousel / ka-ruh-**sel** / *n.* **1** a merry-go-round. **2** a rotating conveyor or delivery system for luggage at an airport etc.
carp *n.* (*pl.* **carp**) an edible coarse-fleshed freshwater fish of Europe etc.; introduced to Australia and now numerous in rivers etc. • *v.* keep finding fault, raise petty objections.
carpal / **kah**-puhl / *adj.* of the wrist joint. • *n.* a wrist bone.
carpe diem / kah-pay **dee**-uhm / *interj.* used to urge someone to make the most of the present time and give little thought to the future. (¶ Latin, = seize the day!, a quotation from Horace (*Odes* I.xi).)
carpel / **kah**-puhl / *n.* the female reproductive organ (pistil) of a flower, the part in which the seeds develop.
Carpentaria *see* GULF OF CARPENTARIA.
carpenter *n.* a person who makes or repairs wooden objects and structures. • *v.* do or make by carpenter's work. □ **carpentry** *n.*
carpet *n.* **1** a thick textile covering for floors. **2** a thick layer underfoot (*a carpet of leaves*). • *v.* (**carpeted, carpeting**) **1** cover with a carpet. **2** *colloq.* reprimand. □ **carpet shark** a slow-moving, bottom-dwelling, eastern Australian shark with a variegated patterning on its skin. Also called *wobbegong*. **carpet snake** a python with variegated skin patterning, widespread in Australia. **sweep under the carpet** conceal (a problem or difficulty).
carpetbagger *n. colloq.* **1** esp. *US* a political candidate etc. without local connections (orig. a northerner in southern US after the Civil War). **2** an unscrupulous opportunist.
carpeting *n.* material for carpets.
carport *n.* an open-sided shelter for a car.
carpus *n.* (*pl.* **carpi**) the set of small bones forming the wrist.
carrel *n.* a small reading cubicle in a library.
Carreras / kuh-**rair**-ruhs /, José (1946–), Spanish operatic tenor.
carriage *n.* **1** a wheeled vehicle, usu. horse-drawn, for carrying passengers. **2** a railway vehicle for passengers. **3** the carrying of goods from place to place; the cost of this. **4** a gun carriage. **5** a moving part carrying or holding something in a machine; the roller of a typewriter. **6** the posture of the body when walking.
carriageway *n.* the part of the road on which vehicles travel.
carrier *n.* **1** a person or thing that carries something. **2** a person or company that transports goods or people. **3** a support for luggage or a seat for a passenger on a bicycle etc. **4** a person or animal that transmits a disease to others without

being affected by it. **5** an aircraft carrier. ☐ **carrier bag** a paper or plastic bag with handles, for holding shopping etc. **carrier pigeon** a pigeon trained to carry messages. **carrier wave** *Radio* a high-frequency wave that is modulated either in amplitude or frequency to convey a signal.

carrion / ka-ree-uhn / *n.* dead and decaying flesh. • *adj.* rotten; loathsome.

Carroll[1], Lewis (pseudonym of Charles Lutwidge Dodgson) (1832–98), English writer, author of *Alice's Adventures in Wonderland* and *Through the Looking-Glass*.

Carroll[2], Tom (1961–), Australian surfer who won the world championship in 1983 and 1984.

carrot *n.* **1** a plant with a tapering orange-coloured root. **2** this root, used as a vegetable. **3** a means of enticing someone to do something.

carroty *adj.* orange-red.

Carruthers, Jimmy (full name: James William Carruthers) (1929–90), Australian world champion bantamweight boxer.

carry *v.* (**carried, carrying**) **1** take from one place to another. **2** have on one's person (*he is carrying a gun*). **3** conduct; take (*wires carry electric current*). **4** support the weight of, bear. **5** involve, entail (*the crime carries a life sentence*). **6** extend (*don't carry modesty too far*). **7** reckon in the next column when adding figures. **8** win, capture; approve (a motion) (*the motion was carried*). **9** (of a newspaper or broadcast) contain (*all the tabloids carried the story*). **10** hold and move (the body) in a certain way. **11** be transmitted clearly (*sound carries across water*). **12** be the driving force behind or mainstay of (*she carries the department*). • *n.* **1** carrying. **2** (in golf) the flight of a ball before it pitches. ☐ **carry forward** transfer to a new page of accounts in bookkeeping. **carry off 1** cause the death of (*plague carried off most of the village.*) **2** win (a prize). **3** deal with (a situation) successfully. **carry on 1** continue; take part in (a conversation); manage or conduct (a business etc.). **2** *colloq.* behave excitedly; complain lengthily. **carry-on** *n.* (also **carryings-on**) *colloq.* **1** fuss; excitement. **2** questionable behaviour. **3** flirtation or love-affair. **carry on with** *colloq.* have an affair with; flirt with. **carry out** put into practice, accomplish. **carry over 1** carry forward in bookkeeping. **2** postpone. **get carried away** get very excited.

carsick *adj.* made sick or queasy by the motion of a car. ☐ **carsickness** *n.*

cart *n.* **1** a two-wheeled vehicle used for carrying loads, pulled by a horse etc. **2** a light vehicle with a shaft, pushed or drawn by hand. • *v.* **1** carry in a cart, transport. **2** *colloq.* carry laboriously, lug (*carted the corpse up the cliff*). ☐ **put the cart before the horse** put a thing first when it should logically come second.

carte blanche / kaht **blonsh** / *n.* full power to act as one thinks best. (¶ French, = blank paper.)

cartel / kah-**tel** / *n.* a combination of business firms to control production, marketing, etc., and avoid competing with one another.

Cartesian / kah-**tee**-zhuhn / *adj.* of the philosopher Descartes (17th century) or his theories. • *n.* a follower of Descartes. ☐ **Cartesian coordinates** a system for locating a point by reference to its distance from axes intersecting at right angles.

carthorse *n.* a strong horse fit for heavy work.

Carthusian / kah-**thyoo**-zee-uhn / *n.* a member of a contemplative order of monks founded at La Grande Chartreuse near Grenoble, France, in 1084 by St Bruno. • *adj.* of this order.

cartilage / **kah**-tuh-lij / *n.* tough white flexible tissue attached to the bones of animals. ☐ **cartilaginous** *adj.*

cartography / kah-**tog**-ruh-fee / *n.* map drawing. ☐ **cartographer** *n.* **cartographic** / kah-tuh-**graf**-ik / *adj.*

carton *n.* a cardboard or plastic container.

cartoon *n.* **1** an amusing drawing in a newspaper etc., esp. as a comment on public matters. **2** a sequence of these telling a comic or serial story. **3** an animated cartoon. **4** a drawing made by an artist as a preliminary sketch for a painting etc. • *v.* draw cartoons; represent in a cartoon.

cartoonist *n.* a person who draws cartoons.

cartouche / kah-**toosh** / *n.* **1** a scroll-like ornamentation in architecture etc. **2** an oval emblem of an ancient Egyptian king.

cartridge *n.* **1** a tube or case containing explosive for firearms or blasting, with bullet or shot if for a rifle etc. **2** a sealed case holding film, recording tape, etc., put into an apparatus and removed from it as a unit. **3** the detachable head of a pick-up on a record player, holding the stylus. **4** an ink container for insertion in a pen. ☐ **cartridge paper** thick strong paper for drawing.

cartwheel *n.* **1** the wheel of a cart. **2** a circular sideways handspring with arms and legs extended.

Caruso / kuh-**roo**-soh /, Enrico (1873–1921), Italian operatic tenor.

carve *v.* **1** form or inscribe by cutting solid material. **2** cut (cooked meat) into slices for eating. ☐ **carve out** make by great effort (*carve out a career for himself*). **carve up 1** divide into parts or shares; subdivide (territory etc.). **2** *colloq.* defeat soundly (*the prime minister carved up the Opposition at question time*).

carvel-built *adj.* (of a boat) made with planks joined smoothly and not overlapping.

carver *n.* **1** a person who carves. **2** a knife for carving meat.

carvery *n.* a buffet or restaurant where meat is carved from a joint as required.

carving *n.* a carved object or design.

caryatid / ka-ree-**at**-uhd / *n.* (*pl.* **caryatides** / ka-ree-**at**-uh-deez / *or* **caryatids**) a sculptured female figure used as a supporting pillar.

CASA / kah-zuh / *abbr. Aust.* Civil Aviation Safety Authority.

Casals / kuh-**salz**, -**sahlz** /, Pablo (1876–1973), Spanish cellist, conductor, and composer.

Casanova / kas-uh-**noh**-vuh / *n.* a man with a reputation for having many love affairs; a womaniser. (¶ Named after an 18th-century Italian adventurer.)

casbah alternative spelling of KASBAH.

cascade / kas-**kayd** / *n.* **1** a waterfall. **2** something falling or hanging like this. • *v.* fall as or like a cascade.

Cascade Brewery Australia's oldest manufacturing concern, built in Hobart in 1824.

case[1] **1** an instance or example of the occurrence of something; an actual state of affairs. **2** a condition of disease or injury; a person suffering from this (*two cases of measles*). **3** something being investigated by police etc. (*a murder case*). **4** a lawsuit. **5** a set of facts or arguments supporting something. **6** *Grammar* the form of a noun or pronoun that shows its relationship to another word, e.g. in *Mary's hat*, *'s* shows the possessive case. ▫ **case history** a record of the past history of a patient etc. **case law** as established by cases decided. **in any case** whatever the facts are; whatever may happen. **in case** lest something should happen.

case[2] *n.* **1** a container or protective covering. **2** this with its contents, the amount it contains. **3** a suitcase. • *v.* **1** enclose in a case. **2** *colloq.* reconnoitre (a house etc.) before burgling (it).

casein / **kay**-see-uhn, **kay**-seen / *n.* a protein found in milk, the basis of cheese.

casement *n.* a window that opens on hinges at the side, like a door.

casemix *n.* a health care management tool which makes comparisons (of kinds of patients, cost of treatment, quality of care, etc.) between hospitals etc.

casework *n.* social work that involves studying a person's family and background. ▫ **caseworker** *n.*

Casey Station the Australian station for scientific and meteorological research in the Antarctic, established in 1969, and now replaced by a new complex a kilometre to the south.

Cash, Pat(rick Hart) (1965–), Australian tennis player, winner of the men's singles title at Wimbledon in 1987.

cash *n.* **1** money in coin or notes. **2** immediate payment for goods, as opposed to hire purchase etc. **3** *colloq.* money, wealth (*they're short of cash*). • *v.* give or get cash for (*cashed a cheque*). ▫ **cash cow** *colloq.* a business, or part of one, that provides a steady cash flow. **cash crop** a crop grown for selling. **cash economy** = BLACK ECONOMY. **cashed up** *Aust. colloq.* well supplied with money. **cash flow** the movement of money out of and into a business as goods are bought and sold. **cash in on** make a large profit from; turn to one's advantage. **cash on delivery** payment to be made when goods are delivered, not at the time of purchase. **cash register** a machine in a shop etc. for recording the amount of each sale.

cashable *adj.* able to be cashed.

cashew / **kash**-oo / *n.* the small edible kidney-shaped nut of a tropical tree.

cashier *n.* a person employed to receive and pay out money in a bank, shop, etc. • *v.* dismiss from service, esp. with disgrace.

cashmere *n.* **1** a very fine soft wool, esp. that from the Kashmir goat. **2** fabric made from this.

casing *n.* **1** a protective covering or wrapping. **2** the material from which this is made.

casino *n.* (*pl.* **casinos**) a public building for gambling.

cask *n.* **1** *Aust.* **a** (in full **wine cask**) a plastic or foil-lined container for table wine, enclosed within a cardboard pack, and having a spigot so that wine not drawn off remains under a vacuum. **b** such a container for fruit juice etc. **2 a** a barrel, esp. for alcohol. **b** its contents. ▫ **cask wine** *Aust.* wine from a cask.

casket *n.* **1** a small usu. ornamental box for holding valuables etc. **2** a coffin.

Cassandra / kuh-**san**-druh / *n.* a person who prophesies disaster. (¶ Named after a prophetess in Greek mythology who foretold evil events but was doomed never to be believed.)

cassata / kuh-**sah**-tuh / *n.* ice cream containing candied or dried fruit and nuts.

cassava / kuh-**sah**-vuh / *n.* a tropical plant with starchy roots from which tapioca is obtained.

casserole *n.* **1** a covered dish for cooking food in the oven. **2** food cooked in this. • *v.* cook (food) in a casserole.

cassette / kuh-**set**, ka- / *n.* a small sealed case containing a reel of film or magnetic tape.

cassia *n.* **1** any of several related Australian shrubs and trees having pinnate leaves and golden flowers. **2** a related tree native to Sudan yielding senna (used as a laxative). **3** the cinnamon-like bark of an unrelated tree, used as a spice.

Cassiopeia / kas-ee-uh-**pay**-uh / a W-shaped northern constellation, named after the mother of Andromeda in Greek mythology.

cassis / ka-**sees** / *n.* blackcurrant-flavoured syrup, often alcoholic, as a drink. (¶ French)

cassock *n.* a long garment worn by priests, altar servers, etc.

cassoulet / **kas**-uh-lay / *n.* a stew of meat and beans.

cassowary / **kas**-uh-wuh-ree / *n.* a large flightless Australasian bird; the Australian cassowary (black with a bare blue neck and red wattles) inhabits rainforest in northern Qld.

cast *v.* (**cast**, **casting**) **1** throw, emit (*cast a net*; *cast a shadow*). **2** shed. **3** turn or send in a particular direction (*cast your eye over this*). **4** record or register (one's vote). **5** make (an object) by pouring metal etc. into a mould and letting it harden. **6** calculate (*cast a horoscope*). **7** select actors for a play etc.; assign a role to. **8** *Aust.* (in mustering) direct (a sheepdog) to make a wide sweep. •*n.* **1** an act of casting; the throwing of a missile, dice, fishing line or net, etc. **2** something made by putting soft material into a mould to harden; a plaster cast (*see* PLASTER). **3** a set of actors cast for parts in a play. **4** the form, type, or quality (of features, the mind, etc.). **5** a tinge of colour (*it has a reddish cast*). **6** a slight squint. **7** the mass of earth etc. excreted by a worm. □ **cast about** (*or* **around**) **for** search or look for. **cast down** depress, cause dejection in. **cast iron** a hard alloy of iron made by casting in a mould. **cast-iron** *adj.* **1** made of cast iron. **2** very strong. **cast off 1** abandon; discard. **2** release a ship from its moorings. **3** (in knitting) loop stitches off a needle to finish off a piece of knitting. **cast on** (in knitting) create stitches, looping them on to a needle.

castanets / kas-tuh-**nets** / *n.pl.* a pair of shell-shaped pieces of wood etc., struck together with the fingers, esp. as an accompaniment to a Spanish dance.

castaway *n.* a shipwrecked person.

caste / kahst / *n.* **1** each of the hereditary Hindu social divisions or classes. **2** any exclusive social class.

castellated / **kas**-tuh-lay-tuhd / *adj.* having turrets or battlements like a castle. □ **castellation** *n.*

caster *n.* (also **castor**) **1** a small container for sugar or salt, with a perforated top for sprinkling from. **2** a small swivelled wheel fixed to each leg of a piece of furniture so that it can be moved easily. □ **caster sugar** finely granulated white sugar.

castigate / **kas**-tuh-gayt / *v.* punish or criticise severely. □ **castigation** *n.* **castigator** *n.*

Castile / kas-**teel** / the central plateau of the Iberian peninsula, a former Spanish kingdom.

Castilian / kas-**til**-ee-uhn / *n.* **1** a native or inhabitant of Castile. **2** the language of Castile; standard literary Spanish. •*adj.* of Castile or its people or language.

casting *n.* **1** a cast, esp. of molten metal; the object so cast. **2** the process of choosing actors for a film etc.

casting vote *n.* a vote that decides the issue when votes on each side are equal.

castle *n.* **1** a large fortified building or group of buildings. **2** a chess piece also called a rook. •*v.* (in chess) move the king two squares towards a rook and the rook to the square the king has crossed. □ **castles in the air** daydreams.

Castlereagh / **kah**-suhl-ray, **kas**-uhl- / a river of 550 km in north-central NSW.

Castor 1 *Gk myth.* the twin brother of POLLUX. **2** a bright star in the constellation Gemini.

castor alternative spelling of CASTER.

castor oil *n.* oil from the seeds of a tropical plant, used as a purgative and as a lubricant.

castrate / kas-**trayt**, **kah**-strayt / *v.* **1** remove the testicles of; geld. **2** deprive of vigour (*the editor castrated my article by cutting out so much*). □ **castration** *n.*

castrato *n.* (*pl.* **castrati**) *hist.* a male singer who had been castrated before puberty so that he would retain a pure soprano or alto voice.

Castries / kas-**trees** / the capital of St Lucia.

Castro, Fidel (1927–), Cuban statesman, leader of the Communist regime in Cuba since 1959.

casual *adj.* **1** happening by chance (*a casual encounter*). **2** made or done without forethought; not serious; not methodical (*a casual remark; a casual inspection*). **3** informal, for informal occasions (*casual clothes*). **4** irregular, not permanent (*found some casual work; casual labourers*). •*n.* (**casuals**) casual clothes; casual shoes. □ **casual sex** sexual activity between persons who are not regular or established sexual partners. □□ **casually** *adv.* **casualness** *n.*

casualty *n.* **1** a person who is killed or injured in a war or accident. **2** a thing lost or destroyed. **3** an accident or mishap. **4** (in full **casualty department**) the part of a hospital where victims of accidents are treated.

casuarina / **kazh**-yuh-ree-nuh / *n.* any of about 30 related Australian shrubs and trees, having distinctive foliage on slender jointed branchlets resembling horsetails. Also called *she-oak*.

casuist / **kaz**-yoo-uhst / *n.* a person who uses clever but false reasoning, esp. on moral issues. □ **casuistic** *adj.* **casuistry** *n.*

CAT *abbr.* (in full **computerised axial tomography**) a medical technology which provides a series of cross-sectional pictures of internal organs and builds these up into a detailed picture using an X-ray machine controlled by a computer. □ **CAT scan** *v.* use this process on a patient. **CAT scanner** the machine which uses this process.

cat *n.* **1** a small furry domesticated animal often kept as a pet. **2** a wild animal related to this, e.g. lion, tiger. **3** *colloq.* a spiteful or malicious woman. **4** the cat-o'-nine-tails. **5** *colloq.* a jazz enthusiast. □ **cat burglar** a burglar who enters by climbing to an upper floor. **cat-o'-nine-tails** a whip with nine knotted lashes, formerly used for flogging people. **cat's eye 1** a precious stone. **2** each of a line of reflector studs marking the centre or edge of a road. **cat's paw** a person who is used by another to do something risky. (¶ From the fable of the monkey who used the paw of his friend the cat to rake hot chestnuts out of the fire.) **the cat's whiskers** *colloq.* an excellent person or thing.

catabolism / kuh-**tab**-uh-liz-uhm / *n.* destructive metabolism, the breaking down of complex substances in the body. □ **catabolic** / kat-uh-**bol**-ik / *adj.*

catachresis / kat-uh-**kree**-suhs / *n.* incorrect use of words. □ **catachrestic** *adj.*

cataclysm / **kat**-uh-kliz-uhm / *n.* a violent upheaval or disaster. ☐ **cataclysmic** / kat-uh-**kliz**-mik / *adj.*

catacombs / **kat**-uh-kohmz, -koomz / *n.pl.* a series of underground galleries (esp. Roman) with side recesses for tombs.

catafalque / **kat**-uh-falk / *n.* a decorated platform on which the coffin of a distinguished person stands during the funeral or lying in state, or on which it is drawn in procession.

catalepsy / **kat**-uh-lep-see / *n.* a condition in which a person becomes rigid and unconscious. ☐ **cataleptic** / kat-uh-**lep**-tik / *adj.*

catalogue *n.* a list of items, usu. in systematic order and with a description of each. • *v.* (**catalogued**, **cataloguing**) list in a catalogue. ☐ **cataloguer** *n.*

catalyse / **kat**-uh-luyz / *v.* (also **-lyze**) accelerate or produce by catalysis.

catalysis / kuh-**tal**-uh-suhs / *n.* (*pl.* **catalyses**) the action of a catalyst.

catalyst / **kat**-uh-luhst / *n.* **1** a substance that aids or speeds up a chemical reaction while remaining unchanged itself. **2** a person or thing that precipitates a change.

catalytic *adj.* of or involving catalysis. ☐ **catalytic converter** part of an exhaust system that converts pollutant gases into harmless products.

catamaran / **kat**-uh-muh-ran / *n.* **1** a boat with parallel twin hulls. **2** a raft of yoked logs or boats.

catamite *n.* a passive partner (esp. a boy or youth) in homosexual intercourse. (¶ From the Latin name for GANYMEDE.)

catapult *n.* **1** a device with elastic for shooting small stones. **2** a device for launching a glider, or an aircraft from the deck of a carrier. • *v.* **1** hurl from a catapult; fling forcibly. **2** rush violently.

cataract *n.* **1** a large waterfall; a rush of water. **2** a condition in which the lens of the eye becomes cloudy and obscures sight; this opaque area.

catarrh / kuh-**tah** / *n.* inflammation of the mucous membrane, esp. of the nose and throat, accompanied by a watery discharge. ☐ **catarrhal** *adj.*

catastrophe / kuh-**tas**-truh-fee / *n.* a sudden great disaster. ☐ **catastrophic** / ka-tuh-**strof**-ik / *adj.* **catastrophically** *adv.*

catatonia *n.* **1** schizophrenia with intervals of catalepsy and sometimes violence. **2** catalepsy. ☐ **catatonic** *adj.*

catbird *n.* a bird of Australian rainforests with a miaow-like call.

catcall *n.* a shrill whistle of disapproval.

catch *v.* (**caught**, **catching**) **1** capture in a net or snare or after a chase. **2** overtake. **3** grasp and hold (something moving). **4** come unexpectedly upon; take by surprise; detect; trap into a mistake or contradiction etc. **5** be in time for and get on (a train etc.). **6** *colloq.* hear (a broadcast); watch (a film). **7** get briefly (*caught a glimpse of it*). **8** become or cause to become fixed or prevented from moving. **9** hit (*the blow caught him on the nose*). **10** begin to burn. **11** become infected with (*caught a cold*). • *n.* **1** the act of catching. **2** something caught or worth catching (*he's a good catch*). **3** a concealed difficulty or disadvantage. **4** a device for fastening something. **5** a round for singing by three or more voices. ☐ **catch-all** *n.* something designed to catch or include many items. *adj.* meant to be all-inclusive (*catch-all remedies rarely catch anything*). **catch it** *colloq.* be scolded or punished. **catch on** *colloq.* **1** become popular. **2** understand what is meant. **catch out** detect in a mistake. **catch up 1** reach (someone ahead). **2** do or complete arrears of work.

catcher *n.* **1** one who catches. **2** a baseball fielder positioned behind the batter.

catching *adj.* **1** infectious. **2** likely to be imitated. **3** attractive; captivating.

catchment area *n.* **1** an area from which rainfall drains into a river or reservoir. **2** an area from which a hospital draws its patients or a school its pupils.

catchphrase *n.* a phrase in frequent current use, a catchword or slogan.

catch-22 *n.* a dilemma where the victim is bound to suffer, no matter which course of action is chosen. (¶ From the title of a comic novel by J. Heller (1961), set in the Second World War, in which the hero wishes to avoid flying any more missions and decides to go crazy, only to be told that anyone who wants to get out of combat duty is not really crazy.)

catchword *n.* a memorable word or phrase that is often used, a slogan.

catchy *adj. colloq.* (**catchier**, **catchiest**) pleasant and easy to remember (*a catchy tune*).

catechise / **kat**-uh-kuyz / *v.* (also **-ize**) **1** put a series of questions to (a person). **2** instruct by using a catechism. ☐ **catechist** *n.*

catechism / **kat**-uh-kiz-uhm / *n.* **1** a summary of the principles of a religion in the form of questions and answers; a book containing this. **2** a series of questions.

catechumen / kat-uh-**kyoo**-muhn / *n.* a convert to Christianity who is being instructed before baptism.

categorical / kat-uh-**go**-ri-kuhl / *adj.* absolute, unconditional (*a categorical refusal*). ☐ **categorically** *adv.*

categorise / **kat**-uh-guh-ruyz / *v.* (also **-ize**) place in a particular category. ☐ **categorisation** *n.*

category / **kat**-uh-guh-ree, -gree / *n.* a class of things.

cater / **kay**-tuh / *v.* provide what is needed or wanted, esp. food or entertainment (*cater for 50 people*). ☐ **cater to** pander to (people's bad inclinations).

caterer *n.* one whose trade is to supply food for social events.

caterpillar *n.* **1** the larva of a butterfly or moth. **2** (**Caterpillar**, in full **Caterpillar track** *or* **tread**) *trademark* a steel band passing round two wheels of a tractor or tank, enabling it to travel over very rough ground.

caterwaul *v.* make a cat's howling cry. • *n.* this noise.

catfish *n.* any of various marine and freshwater fish having whisker-like barbels round the mouth and harmful spines.

catgut *n.* a fine strong cord made from the dried intestines of the sheep, horse, etc. (but not cat), used for the strings of musical instruments and for sewing up surgical incisions.

catharsis / kuh-**thah**-suhs / *n.* **1** relief of strong feelings or tension, e.g. by giving vent to them in drama or art etc. **2** *Psychol.* the freeing and elimination of repressed emotion.

cathartic *adj.* **1** producing or causing catharsis. **2** laxative. • *n.* a laxative.

Cathay / kath-ay / *poetic* the name by which China was known in medieval Europe.

cathedral *n.* the principal church of a diocese.

catherine wheel *n.* a rotating firework. (¶ Named after St Catherine (d. *c.*307) who was tortured on a spiked rotating wheel.)

catheter / kath-uh-tuh / *n.* a tube inserted into a body cavity to introduce or to drain fluid, esp. into the bladder to extract urine.

cathode / kath-ohd / *n.* the electrode by which current leaves a device. ☐ **cathode-ray tube** a vacuum tube in which beams of electrons are directed against a fluorescent screen where they produce a luminous image, e.g. the picture tube of a television set.

catholic *adj.* **1** all-embracing; of wide sympathies or interests (*his tastes are catholic*). **2** universal, of interest or use to all. **3** (**Catholic**) of the largest section of the Christian Church acknowledging the pope as its head (often particularised by those not of this Church as *Roman Catholic*). **4** (**Catholic**) of the ancient Church before divisions occurred; of all present Churches claiming apostolic succession. • *n.* (**Catholic**) a Roman Catholic. ☐ **Catholicism** / kuh-**thol**-uh-siz-uhm / *n.* **catholicity** / kath-uh-**lis**-uh-tee / *n.*

cation / **kat**-uy-uhn / *n.* an ion with a positive charge. ☐ **cationic** / kat-uy-**on**-ik / *adj.*

catkin *n.* a spike of small soft flowers hanging from trees such as willow and hazel.

catnap *n.* a short nap. • *v.* (**catnapped**, **catnapping**) have a catnap.

catnip *n.* a plant with a strong smell that is attractive to cats.

catspaw *n.* a WA plant related to the kangaroo paw but having smaller, furry, clawlike flowers.

cattery *n.* a place where cats are bred or boarded.

cattle *n.pl.* large ruminant animals with horns and cloven hoofs, bred for their milk or meat. ☐ **cattle grid** *n.* a grid covering a ditch so that people and vehicles can pass but not cattle or sheep etc. **cattle station** *Aust.* a large cattle-raising establishment.

catty *adj.* (**cattier**, **cattiest**) spiteful, speaking spitefully. ☐ **cattily** *adv.* **cattiness** *n.*

Catullus / kuh-**tul**-uhs /, Gaius Valerius (*c.*84–*c.*54 BC), Roman poet.

catwalk *n.* a raised narrow pathway.

Caucasian / kaw-**kay**-zhuhn / *adj.* **1** of the Caucasus. **2** of the so-called white or light-skinned race. • *n.* a Caucasian person.

Caucasoid / **kaw**-kuh-zoid / *adj.* of Caucasians.

Caucasus / **kaw**-kuh-suhs / a mountain range following the boundary between Georgia and Russia, between the Black Sea and the Caspian Sea.

caucus / **kaw**-kuhs / esp. *US* & *Aust.* *n.* **1** a meeting of the members of a political party. **2** collectively, those eligible to attend such a meeting. • *v.* (of a group of delegates to a meeting) meet beforehand to discuss tactics etc.

caudal / **kaw**-duhl / *adj.* of or at the tail.

caudate *adj.* having a tail.

caught *see* CATCH.

caul / kawl / *n.* **1** a membrane enclosing a foetus in the womb. **2** part of this occasionally found on a child's head at birth.

cauldron *n.* (also **caldron**) a large deep pot for boiling things in.

cauli *n. colloq.* a cauliflower.

cauliflower *n.* a cabbage with a large white flower head. ☐ **cauliflower ear** an ear thickened by repeated blows, e.g. in boxing.

caulk / kawk / *v.* (also **calk**) make (a boat) watertight by filling seams or joints with waterproof material, or by driving edges of plating together.

causal *adj.* **1** of or forming a cause. **2** relating to cause and effect. ☐ **causally** *adv.*

causality / kaw-**zal**-uh-tee / *n.* the relationship between cause and effect.

causation *n.* **1** the act of causing. **2** causality.

causative / **kaw**-zuh-tiv / *adj.* acting as or expressing a cause.

cause *n.* **1** a person or thing that makes something happen or produces an effect. **2** a reason (*he has no cause for complaint*). **3** a purpose or aim for which efforts are made; a movement or charity (*a good cause*). **4** a lawsuit; a case. • *v.* be the cause of, produce, make happen.

cause célèbre / kawz suh-**leb**-ruh / *n.* (*pl.* *causes célèbres* pronounced the same) a lawsuit or other issue that rouses great interest. (¶ French)

causeway *n.* a raised road across low or wet ground.

caustic *adj.* **1** able to burn or corrode things by chemical action. **2** sarcastic, biting. • *n.* a caustic substance. ☐ **caustic soda** sodium hydroxide. ☐☐ **caustically** *adv.* **causticity** / kaws-**tis**-uh-tee / *n.*

cauterise

cauterise *v.* (also **-ize**) burn the surface of (living tissue) with a caustic substance or a heated instrument in order to destroy infection or stop bleeding. ☐ **cauterisation** *n.*

caution *n.* **1** avoidance of rashness, attention to safety. **2** a warning against danger etc. **3** a warning and reprimand (*let him off with a caution*). • *v.* **1** warn. **2** warn and reprimand.

cautionary *adj.* conveying a warning; *a cautionary tale.*

cautious *adj.* having or showing caution. ☐ **cautiously** *adv.* **cautiousness** *n.*

cavalcade / kav-uhl-**kayd** / *n.* a procession, esp. of people on horseback or in cars.

cavalier *n.* **1** (**Cavalier**) a supporter of Charles I in the English Civil War. **2** a courtly gentleman. **3** *archaic* a horseman. • *adj.* arrogant, offhand (*a cavalier attitude*).

cavalry *n.* troops who fight on horseback or in armoured vehicles.

cave *n.* a natural hollow in the side of a hill or cliff, or underground. • *v.* (**caving**) explore caves. ☐ **cave in 1** fall inwards, collapse. **2** cause to do this. **3** withdraw one's opposition; give up.

caveat / **kav**-ee-uht, **kay**-vee-uht / *n.* a warning. (¶ Latin, = let him beware.)

caveat emptor *n.* the principle that the buyer alone is responsible if dissatisfied. (¶ Latin, = let the buyer beware.)

caveman *n.* **1** a person of prehistoric times living in caves. **2** a crude or old fashioned person.

cavern *n.* a large cave.

cavernous *adj.* like a cavern; large and dark or hollow.

caviare / **kav**-ee-ah / *n.* (also **caviar**) the pickled roe of sturgeon or other large fish.

cavil *v.* (**cavilled, cavilling**) raise petty objections. • *n.* a petty objection.

caving *n.* the sport of exploring caves.

cavity *n.* **1** a hollow within a solid body. **2** a decayed part of a tooth. ☐ **cavity wall** a double wall with a space between.

cavort / kuh-**vawt** / *v.* caper about excitedly.

caw *n.* the harsh cry of a crow etc. • *v.* make this sound.

Cawley, Evonne (original name: Evonne Fay Goolagong) (1951–), AO, Aboriginal Australian tennis player. She won the Wimbledon singles title in 1971 and 1980.

Caxton, William (*c.*1422–91), the first English printer.

Cayenne the capital of French Guiana.

cayenne / kay-**en** / *n.* (in full **cayenne pepper**) a hot red powdered pepper.

Cayley, Neville William (1886–1950), Australian artist and ornithologist, leading painter of Australian birds.

cayman *n.* (*pl.* **caymans**) (also **caiman**) a reptile similar to an alligator, found in South America.

Cazaly / cuh-**zay**-lee /, Roy (1893–1963), Australian Rules footballer with a reputation for taking extremely high marks. ☐ **up there Cazaly!** *Aust.* a cry of encouragement (originally to players from spectators) (originally in Australian Rules, but now also in other sports and in other contexts).

CB *abbr.* citizens' band.

cc *abbr.* (also **c.c.**) **1** copy or copies.(to). **2** cubic centimetre(s).

CD *abbr.* compact disc. ☐ **CD-ROM** a compact disc storing data for use as a read-only memory (for display on a computer screen). **CD-video 1** a system of simultaneously reproducing high-quality sound and video pictures from a compact disc. **2** such a compact disc.

Cd *symbol* cadmium.

cd *abbr.* candela.

Ce *symbol* cerium.

cease *v.* come or bring to an end, stop. • *n.* ceasing.

ceasefire *n.* a temporary suspension of fighting, typically one during which peace talks take place; a truce.

ceaseless *adj.* not ceasing, going on continually. ☐ **ceaselessly** *adv.*

Cecilia / suh-**see**-lyuh /, St (2nd or 3rd century), a martyr in the early Roman Church, patron saint of church music.

cedar / **see**-duh / *n.* **1** an evergreen conifer of Europe etc. with hard sweet-smelling wood. **2** its wood. **3** any of several Australian trees resembling cedar in the colour, grain, or fragrance of the wood, esp. the rainforest tree *red cedar*, now extremely rare because of indiscriminate logging.

cede / seed / *v.* give up one's rights to or possession of (*they were compelled to cede certain territories*).

cedilla / suh-**dil**-uh / *n.* a mark written under *c* in certain languages to show that it is pronounced as *s* (as in *façade*).

ceiling *n.* **1** the under-surface of the top of a room. **2** the maximum altitude at which a particular aircraft can fly. **3** an upper limit or level (*wage ceilings*).

celebrant *n.* a person who performs a rite, esp. the officiating priest at Mass etc., or a secular person authorised to conduct civil marriages or funerals.

celebrate *v.* **1** mark (a special day or event) in some way, esp. with festivities; make merry on such an occasion. **2** officiate at (a religious ceremony). **3** praise publicly. ☐ **celebration** *n.* **celebratory** / sel-uh-**bray**-tuh-ree / *adj.*

celebrated *adj.* famous.

celebrity / suh-**leb**-ruh-tee / *n.* **1** a well-known person. **2** fame, being famous.

celeriac / suh-**le**-ree-ak / *n.* a kind of celery with an edible turnip-like root.

celerity / suh-**le**-ruh-tee / *n. literary* swiftness.

celery *n.* a garden plant with crisp juicy stems used in salads or as a vegetable.

celesta / suh-**les**-tuh / *n.* a small keyboard instrument with hammers striking metal plates to produce a bell-like sound.

celestial *adj.* **1** of the sky. **2** of heaven, divine. □ **celestial equator** the circle of the sky in the plane perpendicular to the earth's axis.

celibate / **sel**-uh-buht / *adj.* remaining unmarried or abstaining from sexual relations, esp. for religious reasons (*celibate priesthood*). • *n.* a celibate person. □ **celibacy** / **sel**-uh-buh-see / *n.*

cell *n.* **1** a very small room, e.g. for a monk in a monastery or for confining a prisoner. **2** a compartment in a honeycomb. **3** a device for producing electric current by chemical action. **4** a microscopic unit of living matter. **5** a small group of people forming a centre or nucleus of political activities.

cellar *n.* **1** an underground room used for storing things. **2** such a room in which wine is stored; the stock of wine it contains.

cellist / **chel**-uhst / *n.* a person who plays the cello.

cello / **chel**-oh / *n.* (*pl.* **cellos**) an instrument like a large violin, played held upright between the knees of the seated player.

cellophane / **sel**-uh-fayn / *n. trademark* thin moisture-proof transparent material used for wrapping things.

cellphone *n.* a small portable telephone having access to a cellular radio system.

cellular / **sel**-yuh-luh / *adj.* **1** of cells, composed of cells. **2** woven with an open mesh (*cellular blankets*). □ **cellular radio** (*or* **telephone**) a system of mobile telephone transmission with an area divided into cells, each served by a small transmitter.

cellule *n.* a small cell or cavity.

cellulite / **sel**-yuh-luyt / *n.* a lumpy form of fat, esp. on the hips and thighs of women, producing puckering of the skin.

celluloid / **sel**-yuh-loid / *n.* **1** a plastic made from cellulose nitrate and camphor. **2** cinema film.

cellulose / **sel**-yuh-lohz, -lohs / *n.* **1** an organic substance found in all plant tissues and in textile fibres derived from these; this used in making plastics. **2** paint or lacquer made from this.

Celsius / **sel**-see-uhs / *adj.* of a scale of temperature on which water freezes at 0° and boils at 100°. (¶ Named after A. Celsius, Swedish astronomer (1701–44), who devised the scale.)

■ **Usage** See note at CENTIGRADE.

Celt / kelt / *n.* a member of an ethnic group, including the inhabitants of Ireland, Wales, Cornwall, Scotland, and Brittany.

Celtic / **kel**-tik, **sel**- / *adj.* of the Celts. • *n.* a group of languages spoken by these, now with two main divisions, (i) Irish, Scots Gaelic, and Manx, (ii) Welsh, Cornish, and Breton.

cement *n.* **1** a grey powder, made by burning lime and clay, that sets to a stone-like mass when mixed with water and is used for building. **2** any similar soft substance that sets firm. • *v.* **1** put cement on or in, join with cement. **2** establish or strengthen (a friendship etc.); unite firmly.

cemetery *n.* a public burial ground.

cenobite variant spelling of COENOBITE.

cenotaph / **sen**-uh-tahf, -taf / *n.* a tomb-like monument to a person buried elsewhere.

Cenozoic / see-nuh-**zoh**-ik / *adj.* (also **Caenozoic**, **Cainozoic**) of the third and most recent geological era, lasting from about 65 million years ago to the present day. • *n.* this era.

censer / **sen**-suh / *n.* a container in which incense is burnt, swung on chains at High Mass or other religious ceremony to disperse its fragrance.

censor / **sen**-suh / *n.* a person authorised to examine letters, books, films, etc. and remove or ban anything regarded as harmful. • *v.* subject to such examination or removal. □ **censorship** *n.*

■ **Usage** Do not confuse with *censure*.

censorious / sen-**saw**-ree-uhs / *adj.* severely critical. □ **censoriously** *adv.*

censure / **sen**-shuh / *n.* strong criticism or condemnation. • *v.* blame or rebuke.

■ **Usage** Do not confuse with *censor*.

census / **sen**-suhs / *n.* an official count of the population or of things (e.g. traffic).

cent *n.* **1** one 100th of a dollar or of certain other metric units of currency; a coin of this value. **2** *colloq.* a very small amount of money (*I haven't a cent*).

centaur / **sen**-taw / *n.* **1** a creature in Greek mythology with the upper half of a man and the lower half of a horse. **2** (**the Centaur**) the southern constellation Centaurus.

centenarian / sen-tuh-**nair**-ree-uhn / *n.* a person who is 100 years old or more.

centenary / sen-**tee**-nuh-ree, -**ten**-uh-ree / *n.* a 100th anniversary; a celebration of this. • *adj.* **1** of a centenary. **2** occurring every hundred years.

centennial / sen-**ten**-ee-uhl / *adj.* **1** lasting for a hundred years. **2** occurring every hundred years. **3** completing or marking a hundred years.

centesimal / sen-**tes**-uh-muhl / *adj.* reckoning or reckoned by hundreds.

centi- / **sen**-tee / *comb. form* one 100th; a hundred.

centigrade / **sen**-tuh-grayd / *adj.* **1** = CELSIUS. **2** of or using a scale divided into 100 degrees.

■ **Usage** In sense 1, *Celsius* is preferred in technical contexts.

centigram *n.* (also **centigramme**) one 100th of a gram.

centilitre *n.* one 100th of a litre.

centimetre *n.* one 100th of a metre, about 0.4 inch.

centipede *n.* a small crawling creature with a long thin segmented body and many legs, one pair on each segment.

central *adj.* **1** of or at or forming the centre. **2** chief, most important (*the central character in this novel*). □ **central bank** a national (not commercial) bank, issuing currency. **central heating** a system of heating a building with pipes, radiators, etc., fed from a single central source. **central nervous system** the brain and spinal cord. **central processor** (also **central processing unit**) the part of a computer that controls and coordinates the activities of other units and performs the actions specified in the program. □□ **centrally** *adv.* **centrality** / sen-**tral**-uh-tee / *n.*

Central African Republic a republic in central equatorial Africa.

Central America the narrow southern part of North America, south of Mexico.

Centralia *Aust.* a name originally proposed for SA but now applied to the area around Alice Springs. □ **Centralian** *adj. & n.*

centralise *v.* (also **-ize**) **1** concentrate (esp. administration) at a single centre. **2** subject (a nation) to this system. □ **centralisation** *n.*

centralism *n.* a centralising policy, esp. in administration. □ **centralist** *n.*

Central Land Council a statutory body established in 1977 to represent the interests of some sixty Aboriginal communities from the southern half of the Northern Territory.

Central Standard Time the time zone lying on the 147th meridian which covers the Northern Territory and South Australia. It is nine and a half hours ahead of Greenwich Mean Time, a half hour behind Eastern Standard Time, and one and a half hours ahead of Western Standard Time, the Western Australian time zone.

centre *n.* **1** the middle point or part. **2** a point towards which interest is directed or from which administration etc. is organised. **3** a place where certain activities or facilities are concentrated (*a shopping centre*). **4** (with a preceding word) equipment for a number of connected functions (*a music centre*). **5** (**The Centre**) (also **The Red Centre**) *Aust.* the arid central region of Australia. **6** a political party or group holding moderate opinions between two extremes. **7** *Sport* the middle player in a line in some field games; a kick or a hit from the side to the centre of a pitch; *Australian Rules* a player occupying the position in the centre of the field. • *adj.* of or at the centre. • *v.* (**centred**, **centring**) **1** place in or at the centre. **2** concentrate or be concentrated at one point (*the debate centred on the new proposals*). □ **centre of gravity** (also **centre of mass**) the central point in an object about which its mass is evenly balanced. **centre spread** two facing middle pages of a magazine, newspaper, etc.

centreboard *n.* a retractable keel in a sailing boat or sailboard.

centrefold *n.* a centre spread of a magazine, newspaper, etc., esp. with nude photographs.

centric *adj.* (also **centrical**) **1** at or near the centre. **2** from a centre.

centricity / sen-**tris**-uh-tee / *n.* being central or a centre.

centrifugal / sen-truh-**fyoo**-guhl, sen-**trif**-uh-guhl / *adj.* moving away from the centre or axis. □ **centrifugal force** a force that appears to cause a body that is travelling round a centre to fly outwards and off its circular path. □□ **centrifugally** *adv.*

centrifuge / **sen**-truh-fyooj, -fyoozh / *n.* a machine using centrifugal force to separate substances, e.g. milk and cream.

centripetal / sen-**trip**-uh-tuhl / *adj.* moving towards the centre or axis. □ **centripetal force** a force acting on a body causing it to move towards a centre.

centrist *n.* a person who adopts a central position in politics etc. □ **centrism** *n.*

centuple / **sen**-chuh-puhl / *n.* a hundredfold amount. • *adj.* increased a hundredfold. • *v.* multiply by a hundred; increase a hundredfold.

centurion / sen-**tyoo**-ree-uhn / *n.* an officer in the ancient Roman army, originally one commanding 100 infantrymen.

century *n.* **1** a period of 100 years; one of these periods reckoned from the birth of Christ (*twentieth century* = 1901–2000; *fifth century* BC = 500–401 BC). **2** 100 runs made by a batsman in one innings at cricket.

■ **Usage** Strictly speaking, since the first century ran from the year 0–100, the first year of a given century should be that ending in 01. However, in popular use this has been moved back a year, and so the twenty-first century will commonly be regarded as running from 2000–2099.

CEO *abbr.* chief executive officer.

cephalic / suh-**fal**-ik, ke- / *adj.* of or in the head.

cephalopod / **sef**-uh-luh-pod / *n.* a mollusc (such as the octopus) which has a distinct head with a ring of tentacles round the mouth.

ceramic / suh-**ram**-ik, kuh- / *adj.* of pottery or similar substances. • *n.* **1** a ceramic substance. **2** (**ceramics**) the art of making pottery.

Cerberus / **ser**-buh-ruhs / *Gk myth.* the monstrous three-headed watchdog guarding the entrance to Hades.

cereal *n.* **1** a grass, such as wheat, rye, oats, or rice, producing an edible grain. **2** its seed. **3** a breakfast food made from such grain. • *adj.* of edible grain.

cerebellum / se-ruh-**bel**-uhm / *n.* (*pl.* **cerebellums** *or* **cerebella**) a small part of the brain, located in the back of the skull, which coordinates and regulates muscular activity.

cerebral / se-ruh-bruhl / adj. **1** of the brain. **2** intellectual rather than emotional. □ **cerebral palsy** paralysis resulting from brain damage before or at birth, involving muscle spasms and involuntary movements.

cerebration / se-ruh-**bray**-shuhn / n. activity of the brain, thought.

cerebrospinal / se-ruh-broh-**spuy**-nuhl / adj. of the brain and spinal cord.

cerebrum / se-**ruh**-bruhm / n. (pl. **cerebra**) the principal part of the brain, located in the front of the skull, which integrates complex sensory and neural functions.

ceremonial adj. of a ceremony; used in ceremonies; formal. •n. **1** ceremony. **2** a system of rules for ceremonies. □ **ceremonially** adv.

ceremonious adj. **1** characterised by ceremony; formal. **2** excessively polite. □ **ceremoniously** adv.

ceremony / se-ruh-muh-nee / n. **1** a set of formal acts, esp. those used on religious or public occasions. **2** excessively polite behaviour (*bowed low with great ceremony*).

Ceres / **seer**-reez / **1** *Rom. myth.* a cereal goddess. **2** the largest of the asteroids.

cerise / suh-**rees**, -**reez** / adj. & n. light clear red.

cerium / **seer**-ree-uhm / n. a chemical element (symbol Ce), a soft grey metal used in cigarette lighter flints and as a polishing agent.

cert n. *colloq.* a certainty, something sure to happen or to be successful (*a dead cert*).

certain adj. **1** feeling sure, convinced. **2** known without doubt. **3** able to be relied on to come or happen or be effective. **4** specific but not named or stated for various reasons. **5** small in amount but definitely there (*I feel a certain reluctance*). **6** existing but not well known (*a certain John Smith*). □ **for certain** without doubt, as a certainty.

certainly adv. **1** without doubt. **2** yes.

certainty n. **1** being certain. **2** something that is certain. **3** absolute conviction (*I can say that with certainty*).

certifiable adj. able to be certified; deserving to be certified as insane. □ **certifiably** adv.

certificate n. an official written or printed statement giving certain facts (*birth certificate*). □ **certificated** adj.

certify v. (**certified**, **certifying**) **1** declare formally. **2** declare by certificate (that a person is qualified or competent). **3** officially declare insane. □ **certified mail** a Post Office service in which the despatch and receipt of a letter or parcel are officially recorded. □ **certification** n.

certitude / **ser**-tuh-tyood / n. a feeling of absolute certainty or conviction.

cerulean / suh-**roo**-lee-uhn / adj. *literary* sky-blue.

cerumen / suh-**roo**-muhn / n. a yellow-brown waxy substance in the outer ear; earwax.

Cervantes / suh-**van**-teez /, Miguel de (1547–1616), Spanish novelist and dramatist, author of *Don Quixote*.

cervical / ser-**vuy**-kuhl, **ser**-vi-kuhl / adj. **1** of the neck (*cervical vertebrae*). **2** of a cervix, of the cervix of the womb. □ **cervical smear** (also **pap smear**, **smear test**) a smear taken from the neck of the womb as a routine examination for cervical cancer.

cervix / **ser**-viks / n. (pl. **cervices** / **ser**-vuh-seez /) **1** the neck. **2** a neck-like structure; the neck of the womb.

cessation / se-**say**-shuhn / n. ceasing.

cession / **sesh**-uhn / n. ceding, giving up.

cesspit n. (also **cesspool**) a covered pit where liquid waste or sewage is stored temporarily.

cetacean / suh-**tay**-shuhn / n. a member of the order of animals that contains whales, dolphins, and porpoises. •adj. of this order.

cetane n. a liquid hydrocarbon used in standardising ratings of diesel fuel.

Ceylon the former name of Sri Lanka. □ **Ceylon moss** a red seaweed which yields a gelatinous substance used in desserts etc. □□ **Ceylonese** adj. & n.

Cézanne / say-**zan** /, Paul (1839–1906), French painter, a forerunner of cubism.

Cf *symbol* californium.

cf. abbr. compare (¶ Short for the Latin *confer*.)

CFC abbr. chlorofluorocarbon, a usu. gaseous compound of carbon, hydrogen, and fluorine, used in refrigerants, aerosols, etc., and opposed as harmful to the ozone layer in the earth's atmosphere.

CFS abbr. = CHRONIC FATIGUE SYNDROME.

cg abbr. centigram(s).

chablis / **shah**-blee, **shab**-lee / n. a very dry white wine.

cha-cha n. (also **cha-cha-cha**) a Latin American dance.

chaconne n. a set of musical variations over a ground bass.

Chad a republic in North Africa. □ **Chadian** adj. & n.

chafe / chayf / v. **1** warm by rubbing. **2** make or become sore from rubbing. **3** become irritated or impatient.

chafer / **chay**-fuh / n. a large slow-moving beetle.

chaff / chahf / n. **1** husks separated from the seed of cereals by threshing or winnowing. **2** hay or straw cut up as food for cattle. **3** good-humoured teasing or joking. **4** worthless things; rubbish. •v. tease or joke in a good-humoured way.

chafing dish / **chay**-fing-dish / n. a pan with a heater under it for cooking food or keeping it warm at the table.

chagrin / shag-**ruhn**, shuh-**green** / n. a feeling of annoyance and embarrassment or disappointment. •v. affect with chagrin.

chain n. **1** a connected flexible series of esp. metal links. **2** a thing resembling this (*formed a human*

chain). **3** a connected series or sequence (*a chain of mountains; a chain of events*). **4** a number of shops or hotels etc. owned by the same company. **5** (in the imperial system) a unit of length for measuring land, 66 ft., 20.1168 m. • *v.* **1** make fast with a chain or chains. **2** confine or restrict (a person) (*is chained to the office*). ☐ **chain gang** *Aust. hist.* a team of convicts chained together to work out of doors. **chain letter** a letter of which the recipient is asked to make copies and send these to other people, who will do the same. **chain mail** armour made of interlaced rings. **chain reaction** a chemical or other change forming products that themselves cause more changes; a series of events each of which causes or influences the next. **chain-smoke** *v.* smoke many cigarettes in a continuous succession. **chain-smoker** a person who chain-smokes. **chain stitch** a looped stitch that looks like a chain, in crochet or embroidery. **chain store** one of a series of similar shops owned by one firm.

chainsaw *n.* a saw with teeth set on an endless chain.

chair *n.* **1** a movable seat, with a back, for one person. **2** (non-sexist way of saying) chairman or chairwoman; a chairperson (*resigned as chair of the society*). **3** the seat or office of a chairperson. **4** a professorship. **5** *US* the electric chair. • *v.* **1** seat in a chair of honour. **2** carry in triumph on the shoulders of a group. **3** act as chairperson of.

chairlift *n.* a series of chairs suspended from an endless cable, for carrying people up a mountain.

chairman *n.* **1** a person who presides over a meeting or a committee. **2** the president of a board of directors. ☐ **chairmanship** *n.*

chairperson *n.* a chairman or chairwoman.

chairwoman *n.* **1** a woman who presides over a meeting. **2** a woman who is president of a board of directors.

chaise longue / shayz **long** / *n.* (*pl.* **chaise longues** or **chaises longues**, pronounced the same) a chair with a very long seat on which one can lie back and stretch out one's legs.

chakra / **chuk**-ruh / *n.* each of the centres of spiritual power in the human body, recognised in yoga. (¶ Sanskrit)

chalcedony / kal-**sed**-uh-nee / *n.* a type of quartz including many varieties regarded as precious stones, e.g. onyx and jasper.

chalet / **shal**-ay / *n.* **1** a Swiss mountain hut or cottage with overhanging eaves. **2** a house in a similar style. **3** a dwelling in a holiday camp etc., esp. at a ski resort.

chalice / **chal**-uhs / *n.* **1** a cup for the wine at Mass or (in non-Catholic Churches) for communion. **2** *literary* a goblet.

chalk *n.* **1** a soft white limestone. **2** a piece of this or of similar substance, white or coloured, used in crayons for drawing. • *v.* write, draw, or mark with chalk, rub with chalk. ☐ **by a long chalk** by far. **chalk up 1** make a note of something. **2** achieve (*chalked up another victory*). ☐ ☐ **chalky** *adj.*

challenge *n.* **1** a call to demonstrate one's ability or strength. **2** a call or demand to respond; a sentry's call for a person to identify himself or herself. **3** a formal objection, e.g. to a prospective jury member. **4** a difficult or demanding task. • *v.* **1** issue a challenge to. **2** raise a formal objection to. **3** question the truth or rightness of. ☐ **challenger** *n.*

challenging *adj.* offering problems that test one's ability; stimulating.

chamber *n.* **1** an assembly hall; the hall used for meetings of a parliament etc.; the members of the group using it. **2** a cavity or compartment in the body of an animal or plant, or in machinery. **3** *archaic* a room, a bedroom. **4** (**chambers**) a set of rooms; a judge's room for hearing cases that do not need to be taken in court. ☐ **chamber music** music written for a small group of players. **chamber pot** a receptacle for urine etc., used in the bedroom.

Chamberlain, Lindy (full name: Alice Lynne Chamberlain) (1948–), Australian woman who was convicted in 1982 for the murder of her baby, Azaria, who she maintained had been carried away by a dingo from their tent at Ayers Rock in 1980. She was sentenced to life imprisonment with hard labour. The sentence was quashed in 1988.

chamberlain / **chaym**-buh-luhn / *n.* an official who manages a royal or noble household.

chambermaid *n.* a woman employed to clean bedrooms in a hotel.

Chamber of Commerce *n.* an association to promote local commercial interests.

chameleon / kuh-**mee**-lee-uhn / *n.* **1** a small lizard that can change colour according to its surroundings. **2** a variable or inconstant person.

chamfer / **cham**-fuh / *v.* bevel the edge or corner of. • *n.* a bevelled surface at an edge.

chamois *n.* (*pl.* **chamois**) **1** / **sham**-wah / a small wild antelope found in the mountains of Europe and Asia. **2** / **sham**-ee / (in full **chamois leather**) a piece of soft yellowish leather made from the skin of sheep, goats, and deer and used for washing and polishing things.

chamomile alternative spelling of CAMOMILE.

champ *v.* munch noisily, make a chewing action or noise. • *n. colloq.* a champion. ☐ **champ at the bit** be restlessly impatient.

champagne *n.* **1** a sparkling white wine from Champagne in France or elsewhere. **2** its pale straw colour.

■ **Usage** Since the EU-Australia Wine Treaty was signed in January 1994, the use by Australian winemakers of European geographical indicators, such as champagne, burgundy, marsala, etc., as generic wine names has been phased out. They have been replaced by varietal names, e.g. cabernet sauvignon, pinot noir, chardonnay, etc., or by local names, e.g. Clover Hill Sparkling Wine, Coonawarra Red.

champignon / **sham**-pin-yong / alternative name for a BUTTON MUSHROOM.

champion *n.* **1** a person or thing that has defeated all others in a competition. **2** a person who fights, argues, or speaks in support of another or of a cause. •*adj.* & *adv. colloq.* splendid, splendidly. •*v.* support as a champion.

championship *n.* **1** (often as **championships**) a contest to decide the champion in a sport etc. **2** the position of champion.

chana / **chun**-uh / *n.* (also **channa**) chickpeas, esp. when roasted and prepared as a snack. (¶ Hindi)

chance *n.* **1** the way things happen through no known cause or agency; luck, fate. **2** a possibility, likelihood. **3** an opportunity, an occasion when success seems very probable. •*v.* **1** happen without plan or intention. **2** *colloq.* risk (*let's chance it*). •*adj.* coming or happening by chance (*a chance meeting*). □ **by chance** as it happens or happened, without being planned. **chance on** come upon or find by chance. **chance one's arm** *colloq.* take a chance although failure is probable.

chancel / **chahn**-suhl, **chan**-suhl / *n.* the part of a church near the altar.

chancellery / **chahn**-suhl-ree, **chan**- / *n.* (also **chancelry**) a chancellor's position, department, or official residence.

chancellor *n.* **1** (chiefly *Brit.*) a government or law official of various kinds. **2** the head of government in some European countries. **3** the non-resident honorary head of a university. □ **chancellorship** *n.*

chancre / **chang**-kuh / *n.* a painless ulcer developing in a person who has syphilis.

chancy *adj.* (**chancier**, **chanciest**) risky, uncertain.

chandelier / shan-duh-**leer** / *n.* an ornamental hanging fixture with supports for several lights.

chandler *n.* a dealer in ropes, canvas, and other supplies for ships.

Chang, Victor Peter (1936–91), AC, Australian heart and lung surgeon who performed more than 260 heart transplants, and was Australian of the year in 1986. He was fatally shot in a failed extortion attempt.

change *v.* **1** make or become different. **2** pass from one form or phase into another. **3** take or use another instead of. **4** put fresh clothes or coverings etc. on. **5** go from one to another (*change trains*). **6** exchange; give small money in change for notes or larger coins. •*n.* **1** changing, alteration. **2** a substitution of one thing for another; variety. **3** a fresh occupation or surroundings. **4** money in small units. **5** money returned as the balance when the price is less than the amount offered in payment. **6** (**changes**) the different orders in which a peal of bells can be rung. □ **change hands** pass into another person's possession. **change over** change from one system or position to another. **get no change out of** *colloq.* **1** fail to get the better of. **2** fail to get information from. **the change (of life)** the menopause.

changeable *adj.* **1** able to be changed. **2** altering frequently (*changeable weather*).

changeling / **chaynj**-ling / *n.* a child or thing believed to have been substituted secretly for another.

changeover *n.* a change from one system or situation to another.

Changi / **chang**-ee / an area in eastern Singapore used by the Japanese during the Second World War as a prisoner-of-war camp.

channel *n.* **1** the sunken bed of a stream of water. **2** the navigable part of a waterway, deeper than the parts on either side. **3** a stretch of water, wider than a strait, connecting two seas. **4** a passage along which a liquid may flow, a sunken course or line along which something may move. **5** any course by which news or information etc. may travel. **6** a band of frequencies used in radio and television transmission, esp. by a particular station. **7** a circuit for transmitting electrical signals. **8** a lengthwise section of recording tape. **9** *Computing* an information route in input/output operations or data transmission. •*v.* (**channelled**, **channelling**) **1** form a channel or channels in. **2** direct through a channel or desired route.

chant *n.* **1** a tune to which the words of psalms or other works with irregular rhythm are fitted by singing several syllables or words to the same note. **2** a monotonous song. **3** a rhythmic call or shout. •*v.* **1** sing, esp. a chant. **2** call or shout rhythmically.

chanter *n.* **1** a person who chants. **2** the melody-pipe of bagpipes.

chantry *n.* a chapel founded for priests to say or sing masses for the founder's soul.

chaos / **kay**-os / *n.* great disorder and confusion.

chaotic / kay-**ot**-ik / *adj.* confused; disordered. □ **chaotically** *adv.*

chap *v.* (**chapped**, **chapping**) (of skin) split or crack, become cracked. •*n.* **1** a crack in the skin. **2** *colloq.* a man or boy, fellow. **3** (**chaps**) long leather leggings worn by cowboys.

chaparral / chap-uh-**ral**, shap- / *n. US* dense tangled brushwood, esp. in south-western USA and Mexico.

chapati / chuh-**pah**-tee / *n.* (also **chapatti**) a thin flat circle of unleavened bread, usu. eaten with an Indian meal.

chapel *n.* **1** a place for private Christian worship in a cathedral or large church, with its own altar. **2** this attached to a school, hospital, etc. **3** the members or branch of a printers' trade union at a place of work.

chaperone / **shap**-uh-rohn / (also **chaperon**) *n.* an older woman ensuring propriety by accompanying a girl or young unmarried woman on social occasions. • *v.* act as chaperone to. □ **chaperonage** *n.*

chaplain / **chap**-luhn / *n.* a member of the clergy attached to a private chapel, institution, ship, regiment, etc. □ **chaplaincy** *n.*

chaplet / **chap**-luht / *n.* **1** a wreath for the head. **2** a short rosary (five of the fifteen decades).

Chaplin, Charlie (full name: Sir Charles Spencer Chaplin) (1889–1977), English comic film actor and director.

Chappell[1], Greg(ory Stephen) (1948–), Australian cricketer. A batsman, he was the first Australian to score more than 7,000 test runs. He was test captain 1975–77 and 1979–83.

Chappell[2], Ian (Michael) (1943–), Australian cricketer. A batsman, he was test captain 1971–75.

chapter *n.* **1** a division of a book, usu. numbered. **2** the canons of a cathedral or the members of a monastic order; a meeting of these. □ **chapter and verse** an exact reference to a passage or authority.

char *n.* **1** *Brit.* a charwoman. • *v.* (**charred**, **charring**) make or become black by burning; scorch.

charabanc / **sha**-ruh-bangk / *n.* an early form of bus with bench seats, used for outings.

character *n.* **1** all those qualities that make a person, group, or thing what he, she, or it is and different from others. **2** a person's moral nature. **3** moral strength. **4** a person, esp. a noticeable or eccentric one. **5** a person in a novel or play etc. **6** a description of a person's qualities, a testimonial. **7** a letter, sign, or mark used in a system of writing or printing etc. **8** a physical characteristic of a plant or animal. □ **in character** appropriate to a person's general character. **out of character** not consistent with a person's character.

characterise *v.* (also **-ize**) **1** describe the character of. **2** be a characteristic of. □ **characterisation** *n.*

characteristic *adj.* forming part of the character of a person or thing, showing a distinctive feature. • *n.* **1** a characteristic feature or quality. **2** *Maths* a whole number or integral part of a logarithm. □ **characteristically** *adv.*

characterless *adj.* lacking any positive character.

charade / shuh-**rahd**, -**rayd** / *n.* **1** (usu. as **charades**, treated as *sing.*) a game which involves guessing a word from acted clues. **2** an absurd pretence.

charcoal *n.* a black substance made by burning wood slowly in an oven with little air, used as a filtering material, as fuel, or for drawing. □ **charcoal grey** very dark grey.

chard *n.* a kind of beet with edible leaves and stalks.

chardonnay / **shah**-duh-nay / *n.* a variety of white grape; the wine made from this.

charge *n.* **1** the price asked for goods or services. **2** the quantity of material that an apparatus holds at one time; the amount of explosive needed for one explosion. **3** the electricity contained in a substance; energy stored chemically for conversion into electricity. **4** a task or duty; custody (*he is in my charge*). **5** a person or thing entrusted. **6** formal instructions about one's duty or responsibility. **7** an accusation, esp. of having committed a crime. **8** a rushing attack, esp. in battle; the signal for this. **9** *colloq.* a glass of alcoholic drink, esp. spirits. **10** *colloq.* a thrill, a 'kick' (*he gets a charge out of surfing*). • *v.* **1** ask as a price. **2** record as a debt (*charge it to my account*). **3** load or fill; put a charge into. **4** give an electric charge to; store energy in. **5** give as a task or duty; entrust. **6** accuse formally. **7** move wildly and rapidly; rush (*children charging around all over the place*). **8** rush forward in attack. □ **in charge** in command. **take charge** take control.

chargeable *adj.* able to be charged.

chargé d'affaires / shah-zhay duh-**fair** / *n.* (*pl.* **chargés d'affaires** pronounced the same) **1** an ambassador's deputy. **2** an envoy to a minor country.

charger *n.* **1** a cavalry horse. **2** an apparatus for charging a battery.

chariot *n.* a two-wheeled horse-drawn carriage used in ancient times in battle and in racing.

charioteer *n.* the driver of a chariot.

charisma / kuh-**riz**-muh / *n.* the power to inspire devotion and enthusiasm; great charm.

charismatic / ka-ruhz-**mat**-ik / *adj.* **1** having charisma. **2** (of Christian worship) characterised by spontaneity and utterances made while in religious ecstasy.

charitable *adj.* **1** generous in giving to the needy. **2** of or belonging to charities (*charitable institutions*). **3** unwilling to think badly of people or acts. □ **charitably** *adv.*

charity *n.* **1** leniency or tolerance in judging others; unwillingness to think badly of people or acts. **2** generosity in giving to the needy. **3** an institution or fund for helping the needy. **4** loving kindness towards others.

charlatan / **shah**-luh-tuhn / *n.* a person who falsely claims to be an expert.

Charlemagne / **shah**-luh-mayn / (742–814), ruler of the Franks in northern Europe from 768, and emperor from 800.

Charles, Prince, (other names, Philip Arthur George), Prince of Wales (1948–), eldest son of Elizabeth II and Prince Philip.

charleston *n.* (also **Charleston**) a lively dance of the 1920s, with side kicks from the knee.

charlie *n. colloq.* **1** a fool. **2** *Aust.* a girl, a woman.

Charlton, Eddie (full name: Edward Francis Charlton) (1929–), AM, Australian snooker champion.

charm n. **1** attractiveness; the power of arousing admiration. **2** an act or object or words believed to have magic power. **3** a small ornament worn on a chain or bracelet. • v. **1** give pleasure to. **2** influence by personal charm. **3** influence as if by magic. ☐ **charmer** n.

charming adj. delightful.

charnel house / char-nuhl / n. a place in which the bodies or bones of the dead are kept.

Charon / kair-ron / Gk myth. the aged ferryman who conveys the souls of the dead across the river Styx to Hades.

chart n. **1** a map designed for navigators on water or in the air. **2** an outline map showing special information (*a weather chart*). **3** a diagram, graph, or table giving information in an orderly form (*a temperature chart*). **4** (**the charts**) a listing of the recordings that are currently most popular. • v. make a chart of, map.

charter n. **1** a document from a ruler or government granting certain rights or defining the form of an institution. **2** the chartering of a ship, aircraft, or vehicle. • v. **1** grant a charter to, found by charter. **2** let or hire a ship, aircraft, or vehicle. ☐ **charter flight** a flight by chartered aircraft as opposed to a regular scheduled flight.

chartered adj. (of an accountant, engineer, librarian, etc.) qualified according to the rules of a professional association which has a royal charter.

chartreuse / shah-**trerz** / n. a fragrant green or yellow liqueur made by Carthusian monks at La Grande Chartreuse, their monastery in France.

charwoman n. Brit. a woman employed as a cleaner in a house or offices.

chary / **chair**-ree / adj. **1** cautious, wary. **2** sparing (*chary of giving praise*).

Charybdis / kuh-**rib**-duhs / Gk myth. a dangerous whirlpool in a narrow channel, opposite the cave of SCYLLA.

chase v. **1** go quickly after in order to capture, overtake, or drive away. **2** hurry (*chasing round the shops*). **3** colloq. **a** try to attain (*chasing gold at the Olympics*). **b** court persistently (*has been chasing her for months*). **4** engrave or emboss (metal). • n. chasing, pursuit. ☐ **chase up** colloq. **1** pursue (a thing overdue); try to hasten (suppliers or supplies). **2** try to locate; look for (*he's chasing up some references in the library*). **give chase** begin to pursue.

chaser n. colloq. a drink taken after a drink of another kind, e.g. beer after spirits.

chasm / kaz-uhm / n. **1** a deep opening or gap, esp. in earth or rock. **2** a wide difference of feeling, interests, etc.; a gulf. ☐ **chasmic** adj.

chassis / shaz-ee, shas-ee / n. (pl. **chassis** / -eez /) **1** a base frame, esp. of a vehicle, on which other parts are mounted. **2** a frame to carry radio etc. components.

chaste / chayst / adj. **1** virgin, celibate. **2** not having sexual intercourse except with the person to whom one is married. **3** simple in style, not ornate. ☐ **chastely** adv. **chasteness** n.

chasten / **chay**-suhn / v. **1** discipline, punish by inflicting suffering. **2** subdue the pride of (*a chastening experience*).

chastise / chas-**tuyz** / v. **1** scold severely. **2** punish, esp. by beating. ☐ **chastisement** n.

chastity n. **1** being chaste; virginity, celibacy. **2** simplicity of style.

chasuble / **chaz**-yuh-buhl / n. a loose sleeveless usu. ornate garment worn over all other vestments by a priest celebrating Mass or a minister (e.g. in some Anglican churches) celebrating the Eucharist.

chat[1] n. a pleasant informal conversation. • v. (**chatted, chatting**) have a chat; converse informally. ☐ **chat show** a broadcast program in which celebrities are interviewed informally. **chat up** colloq. chat to (a person) flirtatiously or with an ulterior motive.

chat[2] n. **1** any of various small and colourful Australian birds with a metallic ringing or chattering call (*crimson chat, gibber chat, yellow chat*, etc.). **2** any of various small birds of Europe etc. with harsh calls.

chat[3] Aust. colloq. n. **1** a louse. **2** a debased person; a drunk. • v. (**chatted, chatting**) remove lice from one's person.

chat[4] n. Aust. a small potato.

chateau / sha-**toh** / n. (also **château**) (pl. **chateaux** / sha-**tohz** /) a castle or large country house in France.

chatelaine / **shat**-uh-layn / n. the mistress of a large house.

Chater, Gordon (Maitland) (1922–99), AM, Australian stage and television actor.

chattel n. (usu. as **chattels**) a movable possession (as opposed to a house or land).

chatter v. **1** talk quickly and continuously about unimportant matters. **2** (of a bird, monkey, etc.) emit short quick sounds. **3** (of teeth) click repeatedly together. • n. **1** chattering talk. **2** a chattering sound. ☐ **chatterer** n.

chatterbox n. a talkative person.

chatty adj. (**chattier, chattiest**) **1** fond of chatting. **2** resembling chat; informal (*a chatty letter*). **3** Aust. colloq. afflicted with lice (see CHAT[3]). ☐ **chattily** adv. **chattiness** n.

Chaucer, Geoffrey (*c.*1342–1400), English poet, author of *The Canterbury Tales*.

chauffeur / shoh-fuh, shoh-**fer** / n. a person employed to drive a car. • v. drive as chauffeur.

Chauvel, Charles (Edward) (1897–1959), Australian film and television director and producer.

chauvinism / **shoh**-vuh-niz-uhm / n. **1** exaggerated or aggressive patriotism. **2** a pompous, self-satisfied belief that one's own sex or group is superior (*male chauvinism*).

chauvinist n. **1** a person exhibiting chauvinism. **2** (in full **male chauvinist**) a man showing

cheap   131   **cheesecake**

excessive loyalty to men and prejudice against women. ☐ **chauvinistic** *adj.*

cheap *adj.* **1** low in price, worth more than its cost. **2** charging low prices, offering good value (*a cheap restaurant*). **3** poor in quality, of low value (*cheap housing*). **4 a** costing little effort, or acquired by discreditable means, and hence of little worth (*cheap popularity; a cheap joke*). **b** contemptible, despicable (*a cheap act of revenge*). • *adv.* cheaply (*we got it cheap*). ☐ **on the cheap** cheaply. ☐☐ **cheaply** *adv.* **cheapness** *n.*

cheapen *v.* **1** make or become cheap. **2** depreciate; degrade (*your behaviour cheapens you*).

cheapie *n. colloq.* any cheap article, esp. a car.

cheapish *adj.* rather cheap.

cheapo *see* EL CHEAPO.

cheapskate *n. colloq.* a mean stingy person.

cheat *v.* **1** act dishonestly or unfairly in order to win some profit or advantage. **2** trick, deceive; deprive by deceit (*cheated him of his rights*). **3** avoid (something undesirable) by luck or skill (*cheated death*). • *n.* **1** a person who cheats, an unfair player. **2** a deception. ☐ **cheat on** *colloq.* be sexually unfaithful to.

check[1] *v.* **1** stop or slow the motion of suddenly; restrain. **2** make a sudden stop. **3** threaten (an opponent's king) at chess. **4** test or examine to make sure that something is correct or in good condition. **5** make sure, verify (*check that the doors are locked*). **6** correspond when compared (*your version doesn't check with mine*). **7** *Aust. Rules* keep a close watch etc. on an opposing player to stop him gaining the ball etc. **8** (usu. in *imperative*) *colloq.* look at, notice (*check the socks that guy's wearing!*). • *n.* **1** a stopping or slowing of motion, a pause. **2** a rebuff. **3** a person or thing that restrains. **4** a control to secure accuracy; a test or examination to see whether something is correct or in good working order. **5** (in chess) exposure of a king to possible capture. ☐ **check digit** (also **check character**) *Computing* an extra digit which when added to a sequence enables the accuracy of the sequence to be validated. **check in** *v.* register on arrival, e.g. as a passenger at an airport or as a guest at a hotel. **check-in** *n.* the act of checking in; the place where this is done. **check off** mark (items) on a list as correct, dealt with, etc. **check on** (or **up** or **up on**) examine or investigate the correctness of; keep watch on. **check out 1** register on departure (from a hotel etc.) or at the dispatch (of goods etc.). **2** check on. **check up** *v.* make sure, verify. **check-up** *n.* a thorough examination, esp. a medical one. **keep in check** keep under control.

check[2] *n.* a pattern of squares like a chessboard, or of crossing lines.

checked *adj.* having a check pattern.

checker *n.* a person who examines and checks work in a factory etc.

checklist *n.* a complete list of items, used for reference.

checkmate *n.* **1** (in chess) = MATE[2]. **2** a complete defeat. • *v.* **1** put into checkmate in chess. **2** defeat finally, foil.

checkout *n.* **1** the act of checking out. **2** a place where goods are paid for by customers in a supermarket.

checkpoint *n.* **1** a place or barrier where documents, vehicles, etc. are checked or inspected. **2** a point in a computer process where interim results are stored, and at which reprocessing may be started.

cheddar *n.* a kind of firm smooth cheese. ☐ **stiff cheddar!** (also **stiff cheese!**) too bad!, bad luck! (used either to express sympathy, concern, etc., or to express a decided lack of sympathy, to snub, rebuff).

cheek *n.* **1 a** either side of the face below the eye. **b** the side wall of the mouth (*I bit my cheek*). **2** *colloq.* a buttock. **3 a** impertinence; cool confidence. **b** impudent speech. • *v.* be impertinent to. ☐ **cheek by jowl** close together, intimate; in close association.

cheekbone *n.* the bone below the eye.

cheeky *adj.* (**cheekier**, **cheekiest**) **1** showing bold or cheerful lack of respect; impertinent. **2** *Aust.* (in Aboriginal English) threatening, dangerous. ☐ **cheekily** *adv.* **cheekiness** *n.*

cheep *n.* a weak shrill cry like that made by a young bird. • *v.* make such a cry.

cheer *n.* **1** a shout of encouragement or applause. **2** mood, disposition (*in good cheer*). **3** cheerfulness. **4** (**cheers!**) *colloq.* **a** expressing good wishes before parting or before drinking. **b** expressing gratitude. • *v.* **1 a** applaud with shouts. **b** (usu. foll. by *on*) urge with shouts. **2** shout for joy. **3** comfort, gladden (*this cheers my heart*). ☐ **cheer up** make or become more cheerful.

cheerful *adj.* **1** visibly happy, contented, in good spirits. **2** pleasantly bright (*a cheerful room*). ☐ **cheerfully** *adv.* **cheerfulness** *n.*

cheerio[1] *interj. colloq.* goodbye.

cheerio[2] *n.* esp. *Qld colloq.* a small sausage of the frankfurter type.

cheerleader *n.* a person who encourages an audience to cheer and applaud.

cheerless *adj.* gloomy, dreary.

cheery *adj.* in good spirits; cheerful. ☐ **cheerily** *adv.* **cheeriness** *n.*

cheese *n.* **1** a food made from milk curds. **2** a shaped mass of this with rind. **3** thick stiff jam (*damson cheese*). ☐ **cheese-paring** *adj.* stingy. **cheese tree** a tree of Qld and NSW bearing fruits that resemble small cheeses. **say cheese!** smile (for the camera). **stiff** (or **hard**) **cheese** *see* CHEDDAR.

cheeseburger *n.* a hamburger with cheese in or on it.

cheesecake *n.* **1** a tart with a filling of cream cheese or curd cheese, often flavoured with fruit. **2**

cheesecloth

colloq. the portrayal of women in a sexually stimulating manner (cf. BEEFCAKE).

cheesecloth *n.* a thin loosely-woven cotton fabric.

cheesed *adj. colloq.* (often foll. by *off*) bored, exasperated (*cheesed off with work*).

cheesy *adj.* **1** like cheese in taste, smell, or appearance. **2** *colloq.* smelly. ☐ **cheesy smile** (or **grin**) a forced or artificial smile (or grin).

cheetah / **chee**-tuh / *n.* a swift-running, spotted, leopard-like feline of Africa and western Asia.

chef / shef / *n.* a professional cook; the chief cook in a restaurant etc. ☐ **chef's hat correa** a NSW correa having light green flowers with an unusual calyx that gives each flower the appearance of a chef's traditional hat.

chef-d'œuvre / shef-**der**-vruh / *n.* (*pl.* ***chefs-d'œuvre*** pronounced the same) a masterpiece. (¶ French)

Chekhov / **chek**-of /, Anton (Pavlovich) (1860–1904), Russian dramatist and short-story writer, whose plays include *Uncle Vanya* and *The Cherry Orchard*.

chemical *adj.* of, using, or produced by chemistry. • *n.* a substance obtained by or used in a chemical process. ☐ **chemical engineering** the design, manufacture, and operation of industrial chemical plants. **chemical warfare** warfare using poison gas and other chemicals. ☐☐ **chemically** *adv.*

chemise / shuh-**meez** / *n.* a loose-fitting undergarment or dress formerly worn by women, hanging straight from the shoulders.

chemist *n.* **1 a** an authorised dispenser of medicinal drugs. **b** the shop at which a chemist operates and which also has cosmetics etc. for sale. **2** a scientist skilled in chemistry.

chemistry *n.* **1** the scientific study of substances and their elements and of how they react when combined or in contact with one another. **2** chemical structure, properties, and reactions. **3** *colloq.* the relationship between people; sexual attraction.

chemotherapy / kee-moh-**the**-ruh-pee, kem-oh- / *n.* the treatment of disease, esp. cancer, by use of chemical substances.

chenille / shuh-**neel** / *n.* a fabric with a long velvety pile, used for furnishings.

cheongsam / chong-**sam** / *n.* a Chinese woman's garment with a high neck and slit skirt.

Cheops / **kee**-ops / = KHUFU.

cheque *n.* **1** a written order to a bank to pay out money from an account. **2** the printed form on which this is written. **3** *Aust.* the total sum received by a rural worker at the end of a seasonal contract (*he drank his entire cheque*). ☐ **cheque book** a book of printed cheques. **cheque-book journalism** the payment of large sums for exclusive rights to material for (esp. personal) newspaper stories.

chequer / **chek**-uh / *n.* a pattern of squares, esp. of alternate squares of colour.

chequered *adj.* **1** marked with a pattern of squares. **2** with varied fortunes (*a chequered career*).

cherish *v.* **1** look after lovingly. **2** be fond of. **3** keep in one's heart (*we cherish hopes of his return*).

Chernobyl / **cher**-nuh-bil / a city near Kiev in Ukraine, where in 1986 explosions at a nuclear power station resulted in a serious escape of radioactivity which spread to a number of countries in Europe.

Cherokee *n.* a member of an American Indian tribe of the southern USA.

cheroot / shuh-**root** / *n.* a cigar with both ends open.

cherry *n.* **1** a small soft round fruit with a stone. **2** any of several trees of the genus *Prunus* producing this or grown for its ornamental flowers. **3** the wood of this tree. **4** deep red. • *adj.* deep red. ☐ **cherry ballart** = NATIVE CHERRY. **cherry nose** a dark-coloured Australian cicada with a bright red nose. Also called *whisky drinker*. **cherry picker** a crane for raising and lowering people. **cherry tomato** a miniature tomato with a strong flavour.

cherub *n.* **1** (*pl.* **cherubim**) an angelic being of the second order of the heavenly hierarchy, usu. grouped with the seraphim. **2** (*pl.* **cherubs**) **a** a representation (in art) of a chubby infant with wings. **b** a beautiful or innocent child.

cherubic / chuh-**roo**-bik / *adj.* like a cherub, with a plump innocent face.

chervil *n.* a herb used for flavouring.

cheshire / **chesh**-uh / *n.* a kind of firm crumbly cheese. ☐ **like a cheshire cat** with a broad fixed grin.

chess *n.* a game of skill for two players with 16 pieces each, played on a chessboard.

chessboard *n.* a chequered board of 64 squares on which chess is played.

chessman *n.* any of the pieces with which chess is played.

chest *n.* **1** a large strong box for storing or shipping things in. **2** the upper front surface of the body; the part containing the heart and lungs. **3** a small cabinet for medicines etc. ☐ **chest of drawers** a piece of furniture with drawers for storing clothes etc. **play it close to one's chest** be secretive.

chesterfield *n.* a sofa with arms and back of the same height.

chestnut *n.* **1** a tree with hard brown edible nuts. **2** the wood of this tree. **3** its nut. **4** deep reddish brown. **5** a horse of a reddish-brown colour. **6** an old joke or story. • *adj.* deep reddish-brown.

chesty *adj. colloq.* inclined to suffer from bronchial diseases; showing symptoms of these. ☐ **chestiness** *n.*

cheval glass / shuh-**val** glahs / *n.* a tall mirror mounted in a frame so that it can be tilted.

chevalier / shev-uh-**leer**, shuh-**val**-yay / *n*. **1** a member of certain orders of knighthood (e.g. conferred by the pope), or of the French Legion of Honour etc. **2** *hist*. a knight.

chèvre / **shair**-vruh / *n*. cheese made from goat's milk.

chevron / **shev**-ruhn / *n*. a V shaped stripe or bar, esp. as a badge on a uniform indicating rank etc.

chew *v*. work or grind between the teeth; make this movement. •*n*. **1** the act of chewing. **2** something for chewing. ◻ **chewing gum** a sticky substance flavoured for prolonged chewing. **chew on 1** work continuously between the teeth. **2** think about (*I'll chew on that for a while*). **chew over 1** discuss, talk over (*we need to chew this over*). **2** think about. **chew the fat** *colloq*. chat.

chewie alternative spelling of CHEWY *n*.

chewy *adj*. **1** suitable for chewing. **2** needing much chewing, tough. •*n*. (also **chewie**) *colloq*. (a piece of) chewing gum. ◻ **chewie on your boot** *Aust*. a barracker's call intended to discourage or deride a player. ◻◻ **chewiness** *n*.

chez / shay / *prep*. at the home of. (¶ French)

chi / kuy / *n*. the twenty-second letter of the Greek alphabet (Χ, χ).

Chiang Kai-shek (1887–1975), Chinese leader who opposed the Communists.

chiack / **chuy**-ak / (also **chyack**) *Aust*. *v*. taunt, barrack, or tease (a person). •*n*. a barracking. ◻ **chiacking** *n*.

chianti / kee-**an**-tee / *n*. a dry red Italian wine.

chiaroscuro / kee-ah-ruh-**skyoo**-roh / *n*. **1** the treatment of light and shade in a drawing or painting. **2** light and shade effects in nature. **3** use of contrast in literature etc.

chic / sheek / *adj*. stylish and elegant. •*n*. stylishness and elegance.

chicane / shuh-**kayn** / *n*. **1** chicanery. **2** an artificial barrier or obstacle on a motor-racing course. **3** *Bridge* a hand without trumps, or without cards of one suit. •*v*. use chicanery, cheat.

chicanery / shuh-**kay**-nuh-ree / *n*. **1** trickery used to gain an advantage. **2** clever but misleading talk.

chick *n*. **1** a young bird before or after hatching. **2** *colloq*. a young woman.

chicken *n*. **1** a young bird, esp. of the domestic fowl. **2** the flesh of domestic fowl as food. **3** a young person. **4** *colloq*. a coward. •*adj*. *colloq*. afraid to do something, cowardly. ◻ **be no chicken** *colloq*. be no longer young. **chicken feed** (also **chickenfeed**) **1** food for poultry. **2** *colloq*. something that is small in amount. **chicken-hearted** cowardly. **chicken out** *colloq*. withdraw through cowardice. **chicken wire** lightweight wire netting.

chickenpox *n*. an infectious disease, esp. of children, with a rash of small blisters.

chickpea *n*. a dwarf pea with yellow seeds used as a vegetable.

chicle / **chik**-uhl / *n*. the milky juice of a tropical American tree, used chiefly in chewing gum.

chicory *n*. a blue-flowered plant, cultivated for its salad leaves and for its root, which is roasted, ground, and used with or instead of coffee.

chide *v*. (**chided** *or* **chid**, **chided** *or* **chidden**, **chiding**) *archaic* scold, rebuke.

chief *n*. **1** a leader or ruler. **2** a person with the highest authority. •*adj*. **1** highest in rank or authority. **2** most important.

chiefly *adv*. above all; mainly but not exclusively.

chieftain / **cheef**-tuhn / *n*. the chief of a tribe, clan, or other group. ◻ **chieftaincy** *n*.

chiffon / **shif**-on, shuh-**fon** / *n*. a thin almost transparent fabric of silk or nylon etc.

chiffonier / shif-uh-**neer** / *n*. a movable low cupboard with a top used as a sideboard.

Chifley, Ben (full name: Joseph Benedict Chifley) (1885–1951), Australian Labor statesman, prime minister 1945–49.

chignon / **shee**-nyon / *n*. a knot or roll of long hair, worn at the back of the head by women.

chigoe *n*. a tropical flea that burrows into the skin.

chihuahua / chuh-**wah**-wuh / *n*. a very small smooth-haired dog of a breed that originated in Mexico.

chilblain *n*. a painful itching swelling on the hand, foot, or ear, caused by exposure to cold and by poor circulation.

child *n*. (*pl*. **children**) **1** a young human being below the age of puberty; a boy or girl. **2** a son or daughter. **3** a person regarded as a product of something (*he's a child of the times*). ◻ **child abuse** maltreatment of a child, esp. by emotional or physical violence or sexual interference. **child care** the care of children, esp. in a crèche or day care centre.

childbearing *n*. pregnancy and childbirth.

childbirth *n*. the process of giving birth to a child.

childhood *n*. the condition or period of being a child. ◻ **second childhood** a person's dotage.

childish *adj*. like a child; unsuitable for a grown person. ◻ **childishly** *adv*. **childishness** *n*.

childless *adj*. having no children.

childlike *adj*. having the good qualities of a child, simple and innocent.

children *see* CHILD.

Children's Court *n*. a court for the trial of children (in Australia, under 17).

children's python *n*. a small nocturnal python of northern Australia. (¶ J.G. Children, English naturalist (1777–1852).)

Chile / **chil**-ee / a republic in South America, on the Pacific coast. ◻ **Chilean** *adj*. & *n*.

chill *n*. **1** unpleasant coldness. **2** an illness with feverish shivering. **3** a depressing influence (*cast a chill over the merrymaking*). •*adj*. chilly. •*v*. preserve at a low temperature without freezing (*chilled beef*). ◻ **chill out** *colloq*. calm down, relax.

chilli *n.* (*pl.* **chillies**) (also **chili**) a small hot-tasting green or red pod of a variety of capsicum, used fresh (*green chilli; red chilli*) or dried (usu. in powdered form) in curries etc. • *adj.* (also **chillied**) having chilli as a main ingredient (*chilli beef; chillied prawns*). ☐ **chilli con carne** / kah-nee / a dish of minced or cubed beef and beans spiced with chillies.

chilly *adj.* (**chillier**, **chilliest**) **1** rather cold, unpleasantly cold. **2** cold and unfriendly in manner. ☐ **chilliness** *n.*

chime *n.* **1** a tuned set of bells; a series of notes sounded by these. **2** (usu. **chimes**) a set of attuned bells as a doorbell. • *v.* **1** (of bells) ring. **2** (of a clock) show the hour by chiming. ☐ **chime in** insert an unexpected remark when others are talking. **chime with** (*or* **in with**) agree or correspond with.

chimera / kuh-**meer**-ruh / *n.* **1** *Gk myth.* a monster with a lion's head, goat's body, and serpent's tail. **2** a wild or fantastic creation of the mind.

chimney *n.* (*pl.* **chimneys**) **1** a structure carrying off smoke or gases from a fire; the part of this above a roof. **2** a narrow vertical crack in a rock face, used by mountaineers to ascend. ☐ **chimney sweep** a person whose trade is to remove soot from inside chimneys.

chimp *n. colloq.* a chimpanzee.

chimpanzee *n.* an African ape, smaller than a gorilla.

chin *n.* the front of the lower jaw. ☐ **keep one's chin up** *colloq.* remain cheerful. **take (something) on the chin** endure (something) courageously.

China (official name **People's Republic of China**) a country in eastern Asia, the third largest and most populous in the world.

china *n.* **1** fine earthenware porcelain. **2** articles made of this. **3** (in full **china plate**) *rhyming slang* a mate. • *adj.* made of china. ☐ **china clay** kaolin.

Chinaman *n.* (*archaic*, now usu. *offens.*) a Chinese man.

China, Republic of the official name for TAIWAN.

China Sea a part of the Pacific Ocean off the coast of China, divided by the island of Taiwan into the **East China Sea** in the north and the **South China Sea** in the south.

Chinatown a section of a town in which the Chinese live as a group.

chinchilla / chin-**chil**-uh / *n.* **1** a small squirrel-like South American rodent. **2** its soft grey fur. **3** a breed of cat or rabbit.

chine *n.* **1** an animal's backbone; a joint of meat containing part of this. **2** a mountain ridge. • *v.* cut along and separate the backbone in (a joint of meat).

Chinese *adj.* of China or its people or language. • *n.* **1** (*pl.* **Chinese**) a native of China, a person of Chinese descent. **2** the language of China. ☐ **Chinese cabbage** a vegetable with long pale cabbage-like leaves that can be cooked or eaten raw in salads. **Chinese lantern** a collapsible paper lantern; a plant with an orange-coloured calyx resembling this.

chink *n.* **1** a narrow opening or slit. **2** a sound like glasses or coins being struck together. • *v.* make or cause to make this sound.

chinless *adj. colloq.* weak or feeble in character.

chinoiserie / shee-**nwah**-zuh-ree / *n.* imitation Chinese motifs in furniture or decoration.

Chinook / chuh-**nuuk** / *n.* (*pl.* **Chinook**) a member of a North American Indian people of the Pacific coast.

chintz *n.* a cotton cloth with a printed pattern, usu. glazed, used for furnishings.

chintzy *adj.* **1** like chintz; characteristic of a decorating style associated with chintz. **2** cheap, gaudy.

chinwag *colloq. n.* a chat. • *v.* chat. ☐ **chinwagger** *n.* **chinwagging** *n.*

chip *n.* **1** a thin piece cut or broken off something hard. **2** a place from which a chip has been broken. **3** a fried oblong strip of potato; a potato crisp. **4** a counter used to represent money, esp. in gambling. **5** a microchip. **6** *Soccer etc.* & *Golf* a short kick, pass, or shot, with the ball describing an arc. • *v.* (**chipped**, **chipping**) **1** cut or break at the surface or edge; shape or carve by doing this. **2** be apt to break at the edge (*careful!—it will chip easily*). **3** make (potatoes) into chips. **4** *Soccer etc.* & *Golf* kick or strike (the ball) with a chip. ☐ **chip heater** *Aust.* a domestic water heater which uses small pieces of wood as fuel. **chip in** *colloq.* **1** interrupt with a remark when someone is speaking. **2** contribute money. **have a chip on one's shoulder** *colloq.* be touchy or embittered. **have had one's chips** *colloq.* be defeated; die. **when the chips are down** *colloq.* when it comes to the point.

chipboard *n.* thin material made of compressed wood chips and resin.

chipmunk *n.* a small striped squirrel-like animal of North America.

chipolata / chip-uh-**lah**-tuh / *n.* a small sausage.

Chipp, Don(ald Leslie) (1925–), AO, one of the founders of the Australian Democrats party.

Chippendale *n.* an 18th-century style of English furniture, named after its designer Thomas Chippendale (1718–79).

Chirac / shuh-**rahk** /, Jacques (René) (1932–), French statesman, prime minister 1974–76 and 1986–88, and president since 1995.

chiromancy / **kuy**-roh-man-see / *n.* palmistry. ☐ **chiromancer** *n.*

chiropody / kuh-**rop**-uh-dee / *n.* the treatment of ailments of the feet. ☐ **chiropodist** *n.*

chiropractic / **kuy**-roh-prak-tik / *n.* the treatment of certain disorders by manipulation of the joints, esp. those of the spine, not by medicinal drugs or surgery. ◻ **chiropractor** *n.*

chirp *n.* the short sharp note made by a small bird or a grasshopper. •*v.* **1** (of birds etc.) make this sound. **2** speak or utter merrily.

chirpy *adj.* lively and cheerful. ◻ **chirpily** *adv.* **chirpiness** *n.*

chirrup *n.* a series of chirps. •*v.* make this sound.

chisel *n.* a tool with a bevelled edge for shaping wood, stone, or metal. •*v.* (**chiselled**, **chiselling**) **1** cut or shape with a chisel. **2** *colloq.* treat unfairly, swindle. **3** (as **chiselled** *adj.*) (of facial features) clean-cut, fine.

Chisholm / **chiz**-uhm /, Caroline (1808–77), English philanthropist who came to Australia in 1838, where the plight of many stranded immigrants led her to found a Female Immigrants' Home in Sydney in 1841; her charitable work continued through the depression of the 1840s, and she was especially concerned with the plight of women.

chit *n.* **1** (often *derog.*) a young child, a small young woman (*only a chit of a girl*). **2** a short written order or memorandum. **3** a note containing an order or statement of money owed.

chit-chat *n.* chat, gossip. •*v.* engage in this.

chitin / **kuy**-tuhn / *n.* a substance forming the horny constituent in the hard outer covering of certain insects, spiders, and crustaceans.

chitterlings *n.pl.* the small intestines of a pig, cooked as food.

chivalry / **shiv**-uhl-ree / *n.* courtesy and considerate behaviour, esp. towards weaker people. ◻ **chivalrous** *adj.*

chive / chuyv / *n.* a herb with long tubular onion- or garlic-flavoured leaves.

chivvy *v.* (**chivvied**, **chivvying**) keep urging (a person) to hurry; harass, nag.

chlamydia / kluh-**mid**-ee-uh / *n.* (*pl.* **chlamydiae**) a parasitic bacterium which causes diseases such as trachoma, psittacosis, and (the usu. sexually transmitted) non-specific urethritis in men, and infection of the cervix and PID (*see* PELVIC INFLAMMATORY DISEASE) and infertility in women.

Chloe / **kloh**-ee / *n.* ◻ **as drunk as Chloe** *colloq.* very drunk. (¶ The idiom appears in the early 19th c., but its popularity in Australia derives from the nude painting *Chloe* which was brought to Melbourne for the Great Exhibition of 1880. The painting caused a furore when it was exhibited at the Melbourne Art Gallery. Subsequently it was displayed for many years in the saloon bar of Young and Jackson's Hotel at the corner of Flinders and Swanston Streets.)

chloral / **klaw**-ruhl / *n.* **1** a colourless liquid used in making DDT. **2** (also **chloral hydrate**) a white crystalline compound made from this liquid and used as a sedative or an anaesthetic.

chloride / **klaw**-ruyd / *n.* a compound of chlorine and one other element.

chlorinate / **klaw**-ruh-nayt, **klo**- / *v.* treat or sterilise with chlorine. ◻ **chlorination** *n.*

chlorine / **klaw**-reen / *n.* a chemical element (symbol Cl), a poisonous gas used in sterilising water and in industry.

chlorofluorocarbon *see* CFC.

chloroform / **klo**-ruh-fawm / *n.* a liquid that gives off vapour which causes unconsciousness when breathed in. •*v.* make unconscious by this.

chlorophyll / **klo**-ruh-fil / *n.* the green pigment found in most plants, responsible for the absorption of light to provide energy for photosynthesis.

chlorosis / kluh-**roh**-suhs / *n.* the reduction or loss of the normal green coloration of plants, caused by an iron deficiency in the soil.

chock *n.* a block or wedge used to prevent something from moving. •*v.* wedge with a chock or chocks. ◻ **chock-a-block** *adv.* & *adj.* crammed or crowded together. **chock-full** *adj.* crammed full.

chocolate *n.* **1** a powdered or solid food made from roasted ground cacao seeds. **2** a drink made with this. **3** a sweet made of or covered with this. **4** dark brown colour. •*adj.* **1** flavoured or coated with chocolate. **2** dark brown. ◻ **chocolate lily** an Australian perennial of the lily family, having purple flowers giving off a strong sweet chocolate scent; its tubers are an Aboriginal bush food.

CHOGM / **chog**-uhm / *abbr.* Commonwealth Heads of Government Meeting (held every two years).

choice *n.* **1** choosing; the right of choosing. **2** a variety from which to choose (*a wide choice of holidays*). **3** a person or thing chosen (*this is my choice*). •*adj.* of the best quality (*the choicest cuts of meat*).

choir *n.* **1** a regular group of singers, esp. in a church. **2** that part of a cathedral or large church between the altar and the nave.

choirboy *n.* (*feminine* **choirgirl**) a boy soprano or alto in a church choir, a chorister.

choke *v.* **1** cause to stop breathing by squeezing or blocking the windpipe or (of smoke etc.) by being unfit to breathe. **2** be unable to breathe from such causes. **3** make or become speechless from emotion. **4** clog, smother (*the garden is choked with weeds*). •*n.* **1** a valve controlling the flow of air into a petrol engine. **2** *Electronics* a device for smoothing the variations of an alternating current. ◻ **choke back** suppress (feelings) with difficulty.

choker *n.* **1** a high stiff collar. **2** a close-fitting necklace.

choko *n. Aust.* a succulent green pear-shaped vegetable like a cucumber in flavour.

choler / **kol**-uh / *n. archaic* **1** one of the four humours, bile. **2** anger, bad temper.

cholera / **kol**-uh-ruh / *n.* an infectious and often fatal disease causing severe vomiting and diarrhoea.

choleric / **kol**-uh-rik / *adj.* easily angered, often angry.

cholesterol / kuh-**les**-tuh-rol / *n.* a fatty substance found in animal tissues, thought to cause hardening of the arteries in high concentration.

chomp *v.* munch noisily.

choof / chuuf / *v. Aust. colloq.* go or move. ☐ **choof off** leave, depart.

chook / chuuk / *n. Aust. colloq.* a chicken or fowl.

choom / chuum / *n. Aust. colloq.* a pom. (¶ Mockingly reproducing a British dialectal pronunciation of *chum*.)

choose *v.* (**chose**, **chosen**, **choosing**) **1** select out of a greater number of things. **2** decide; prefer; desire.

choosy *adj. colloq.* careful and cautious in choosing; hard to please, fussy.

chop *v.* (**chopped**, **chopping**) **1** cut by a blow with an axe or knife. **2** hit with a short downward stroke or blow. • *n.* **1** a cutting stroke, esp. with an axe. **2** a chopping blow. **3** a thick slice of meat, (esp. pork or lamb) usu. including a rib. **4** *Aust.* an event or a series of events in which axemen compete in a contest of speed. **5** *colloq.* a share (usu. of winnings) (*he'll be in for his chop*). **6** (**chops**) the jaws of an animal. ☐ **get the chop** *colloq.* **1** be axed; be dismissed. **2** be murdered. **not much chop** *Aust. colloq.* no good; not up to much.

Chopin / shoh-**pan** /, Frédéric (1810–49), Polish composer, whose works are chiefly for the piano.

chopper *n.* **1** a chopping tool such as a butcher's cleaver; a short axe with a large blade. **2** *colloq.* a helicopter. **3** *colloq.* a type of bicycle or motorcycle with high handlebars. **4** (**choppers**) *colloq.* teeth. **5** *Aust. colloq.* = ROCK CHOPPER.

choppy *adj.* **1** full of short broken waves. **2** jerky, not smooth. ☐ **choppiness** *n.*

chopstick *n.* each of a pair of sticks used by the Chinese and Japanese to lift food to the mouth.

chopsuey / chop-**soo**-ee / *n.* a Chinese-style dish made with small pieces of meat fried with rice and vegetables.

choral / **kaw**-ruhl, **ko**-ruhl / *adj.* written for a choir or chorus; sung or spoken by these. ☐ **chorally** *adv.*

chorale / kuh-**rahl** / *n.* a choral composition, using the words of a hymn.

chord / kawd / *n.* **1** a combination of notes sounded together in harmony. **2** a straight line joining two points on a curve. ☐ **strike a chord** elicit a sympathetic response.

chore / chaw / *n.* a routine or tedious task, esp. domestic.

choreograph / **ko**-ree-uh-grahf, -graf / *v.* provide choreography for.

choreography / ko-ree-**og**-ruh-fee / *n.* the design of ballets or stage dances; the sequence of steps involved in this. ☐ **choreographer** *n.* **choreographic** *adj.*

chorister / **ko**-ruh-stuh / *n.* a member of a choir, esp. a choirboy.

chorizema / **ko**-ruh-zee-muh / *n.* any of several small, related, Australian shrubs with vivid bi-coloured pea-flowers, flame-red and bright orange. Also called *flame pea*.

chorizo / chuh-**ree**-zoh / *n.* (*pl.* **chorizos**) a hot, spicy, pork sausage, originally as used in Spanish cookery. (¶ Spanish)

chortle *n.* a loud gleeful chuckle. • *v.* utter a chortle.

chorus *n.* **1** a group of singers. **2** a piece of music for these. **3** something spoken or sung by many people together (*a chorus of approval*). **4** the refrain or main part of a song. **5** a group of singing dancers in a musical comedy. • *v.* (**chorused**, **chorusing**) sing, speak, or say in chorus. ☐ **in chorus** speaking or singing all together.

chose, chosen *see* CHOOSE.

Chou En-lai / choh en-**luy** / former spelling of ZHOU ENLAI.

chough / chuf / *n.* **1** a bird of eastern Australia with black plumage and white wing-markings. **2** a bird of Europe etc.

choux pastry / shoo / very light pastry enriched with eggs.

chow *n.* **1** a long-haired dog of a Chinese breed. **2** *colloq.* food.

chowchilla / chow-**chil**-uh / *n.* a dark-coloured perching bird whose distinctive call is heard at dusk and dawn in the rainforests of north-eastern Qld. Also called *logrunner*. (¶ Dyirbal and Yidiny.)

chow chow *n.* a Chinese preserve of ginger, carrot, melon, etc. in a sugar syrup, used as an ingredient in Christmas cake etc.

chowder *n.* a thick soup or stew usu. of fish, clams, corn, with bacon, onions, etc.

chow mein / ming, min / *n.* a Chinese-style dish of fried noodles with shredded meat or prawns etc. and vegetables.

chrism *n.* consecrated oil used esp. for anointing in Catholic and Orthodox rites and sacraments.

Chrissie / **kris**-ee / *n. & adj. Aust. colloq.* Christmas.

Christ *n.* **1** the title of Jesus (= 'the anointed one'), now treated as a name. **2** the Messiah as prophesied in the Old Testament. • *interj. colloq.* expressing surprise or anger.

christen *v.* **1** admit to the Christian Church by baptism. **2** give a name or nickname to. **3** *colloq.* use for the first time (*let's christen our new spa*). ☐ **christening** *n.*

Christendom / **kris**-uhn-duhm / *n.* all Christians, all Christian countries.

Christian *adj.* **1** of Christ's teaching; believing in or based on this. **2** showing the qualities associated with Christ's teaching. **3** *colloq.* kind, fair, decent. • *n.* **1** a person who believes in Christianity. **2** a kindly or humane person.

Christian name a name given at a christening; a person's given name.
Christian Brothers *n.pl.* an Order of lay religious in the Catholic Church dedicated to the education of boys.
Christianity *n.* **1** the religion based on the belief that Christ was the incarnate Son of God, and on his teachings. **2** being a Christian.
Christian Science *n.* a religious sect claiming that health and healing can be achieved through the mental effect of faith, without medical treatment, and that matter is an illusion.
Christmas *n.* (*pl.* **Christmases**) the Christian festival (celebrated on 25 December) commemorating Christ's birth; the period about this time. ☐ **Christmas beetle** any of several Australian scarab beetles, so called because the adults emerge in summer. **Christmas box** a small present or gratuity given at Christmas, esp. to employees. **Christmas tree 1** an evergreen (or artificial) tree decorated at Christmas. **2** *see* NUYTSIA.
Christmas Day 25 December.
Christmas Eve 24 December.
Christmas Island an Australian territory of about 135 sq. km in the Indian Ocean, about 360 km south of Java and 1400 km from NW Australia.
Christopher, St, a legendary martyr, adopted as the patron saint of travellers. His feast day (25 July) was dropped from the Roman calendar in 1969.
chromatic / kruh-**mat**-ik / *adj.* of colour, in colours. ☐ **chromatic scale** (in music) a scale that ascends or descends by semitones.
chromatin *n.* chromosome material in a cell nucleus that takes up stain easily, making it visible under a microscope.
chromatography / kroh-muh-**tog**-ruh-fee / *n.* separation of a mixture into its component substances by passing it over material which absorbs these at different rates so that they appear as layers, often of different colours.
chrome / krohm / *n.* **1** chromium. **2** (in full **chrome yellow**) yellow colouring-matter obtained from a compound of chromium.
chromite *n.* a mineral of chromium and iron oxides.
chromium / **kroh**-mee-uhm / *n.* a chemical element (symbol Cr), a hard metal used in making stainless steel and for coating other metals (*chromium-plated*).
chromosome / **kroh**-muh-sohm / *n.* one of the tiny thread-like structures in animal and plant cells, carrying genes.
chronic *adj.* **1** (of a disease etc.) affecting a person for a long time, constantly recurring. **2** having had an illness or a habit for a long time (*a chronic invalid*). **3** *colloq.* very unpleasant (*chronic weather*). **4** *colloq.* habitual (*a chronic liar*). ☐ **chronically** *adv.*

chronic fatigue syndrome *n.* (also **CFS** and **ME**) a benign but severely debilitating and often long-lasting condition which usually occurs after a viral infection and causes headaches, fever, muscular pain, incapacitating fatigue, and depression.
chronicle / **kron**-i-kuhl / *n.* **1** a record of events in the order of their happening. **2** (**Chronicles**) either of two books of the Old Testament recording the history of Israel and Judah. • *v.* record in a chronicle. ☐ **chronicler** *n.*
chronological / kron-uh-**loj**-i-kuhl / *adj.* arranged in the order in which things occurred. ☐ **chronologically** *adv.*
chronology / kruh-**nol**-uh-jee / *n.* **1** the study of historical records to establish the dates of past events. **2** the arrangement of events in the order in which they occurred.
chronometer / kruh-**nom**-uh-tuh / *n.* a time-measuring instrument, esp. one used in navigation.
chrysalis / **kris**-uh-luhs / *n.* (*pl.* **chrysalises**) the stage in an insect's life when it forms a sheath inside which it changes from a grub to an adult insect, esp. a butterfly or moth.
chrysanthemum *n.* a garden plant of the daisy family with brightly coloured flowers.
chrysoberyl / kris-uh-**be**-ruhl / *n.* a yellowish-green gem.
chrysolite / **kris**-uh-luyt / *n.* a precious stone, a variety of olivine.
chrysoprase / **kris**-uh-prayz / *n.* an apple-green variety of chalcedony.
chubby *adj.* (**chubbier**, **chubbiest**) round and plump. ☐ **chubbiness** *n.*
chuck *v.* **1** *colloq.* throw carelessly or casually. **2** *colloq.* give up, resign. **3** touch playfully under the chin. **4** *Aust. colloq.* vomit. **5** (foll. by *in*) *colloq.* contribute (*each of them chucked in ten dollars*). **6** *colloq.* perform with vigour, speed, etc. (*chuck a uey*). • *n.* **1** a playful touch under the chin. **2** the part of a lathe that grips the drill; the part of a drill that holds the bit. **3** a cut of beef from the neck to the ribs (*chuck steak*). **4** (**the chuck**) *colloq.* dismissal; rejection. **5** *Aust. colloq.* a bout of vomiting. ☐ **chuck it in** *colloq.* give up; stop; cease work.
chuckle *n.* a quiet or half-suppressed laugh. • *v.* give a chuckle.
chuditch / **choo**-dich / *n.* the western quoll, a cat-sized marsupial once widely distributed across the continent but now found only in the south-western corner of Australia. (¶ Nyungar)
chuff *v.* (of an engine) work with a regular sharp puffing sound.
chuffed *adj. colloq.* delighted.
chug *v.* (**chugged**, **chugging**) make a dull short repeated sound, like an engine running slowly. • *n.* this sound.
chukker *n.* (also **chukka**) a period of play in polo.

chum *n. colloq.* a close friend, a mate.
chummy *adj.* very friendly.
chump *n.* **1** *colloq.* a foolish person. **2** the thick end of a loin of lamb or mutton (*chump chop*). **3** a short thick block of wood.
chunder *v. & n. Aust. colloq.* vomit. (¶ Rhyming slang *Chunder Loo of Akim Foo* for 'spew', after a cartoon figure drawn by the Australian artist Norman Lindsay.)
chunk *n.* **1** a thick piece of something. **2** a substantial amount.
chunky *adj.* **1** short and sturdy. **2** in chunks; containing chunks.
church *n.* **1** a building for public Christian worship. **2** a religious service in this (*see you after church*). **3** (**the Church**) the whole body of Christian believers; a particular group of these; the clergy.
Churchill[1], Clive (Bernard), (1927–85), AO, Australian Rugby League player.
Churchill[2], Sir Winston (Leonard Spencer) (1874–1965), British Conservative statesman, prime minister 1940–45, 1951–55. ☐ **Churchill Fellowship** a program of overseas scholarships designed to provide training in a wide range of fields, awarded in Australia since 1963 by the Winston Churchill Memorial Trust.
Church of England the established English Protestant Church, recognised by the State and having the Sovereign as its head.
Church of Rome (also **Catholic Church**) a Christian Church maintaining apostolic succession and having the pope as its head.
churchyard *n.* the enclosed land round a church, often used for burials.
churinga / chuh-**ring**-guh / *n.* (also **tjuringa**, **churinga stone**) a sacred object, normally carved or painted, of Aboriginal ceremonial. (¶ Arrernte *jwerrenge* 'object from the Dreaming'.)
churl *n.* **1** an ill-bred person. **2** *archaic* a peasant.
churlish *adj.* ill-mannered, surly. ☐ **churlishly** *adv.* **churlishness** *n.*
churn *n.* **1** a large milk can. **2** a machine for making butter, ice cream, etc. • *v.* **1** agitate (milk or cream) in a churn; produce (butter) in a churn. **2** stir or swirl violently. **3** cause distress to; upset; agitate (*my stomach churns at the sight of blood; he's all churned up about the loss*). ☐ **churn out** produce in large quantities.
chute / shoot / *n.* **1** a sloping or vertical channel down which things can slide or be dropped. **2** a slide into a swimming pool. **3** *colloq.* a parachute.
chutney *n.* a pungent orig. Indian condiment of fruit, vinegar, chillies, sugar, spices, etc.
chutzpah / **chuts**-pah / *n. colloq.* shameless cheek; impudence.
Ci *abbr.* curie.
CIA *abbr.* (in the USA) Central Intelligence Agency.
ciabatta / chuh-**bah**-tuh / *n.* (*pl.* **ciabattas**) **1** a type of moist aerated Italian bread made with olive oil. **2** a loaf of this. (¶ Italian, literally 'slipper'.)
ciao / chow / *interj. colloq.* **1** goodbye. **2** hello.
ciborium *n.* (*pl.* **ciboria**) a vessel with an arched cover used to hold the Eucharist.
cicada / suh-**kah**-duh, -**kay**-duh / *n.* a grasshopper-like insect that makes a shrill chirping sound.
cicatrice / **sik**-uh-truhs / *n.* the scar left by a healed wound.
cicerone / chich-uh-**roh**-nee, sis-**uh**- / *n.* (*pl.* **ciceroni**) a guide who shows antiquities to visitors.
Cid / sid /, **el** or **the** the title in Spanish literature of Ruy Diaz, 11th-century champion of Christianity against the Moors.
cider *n.* an alcoholic drink made from fermented apples. ☐ **cider gum** any of several eucalypts yielding a sweet sap which is drinkable, and which can be fermented.
c.i.f. *abbr.* cost, insurance, freight.
cigar *n.* a roll of tobacco leaves for smoking.
cigarette *n.* a roll of shredded tobacco enclosed in thin paper for smoking.
ciliate / **sil**-ee-uht / *adj.* having cilia.
cilium / **sil**-ee-uhm / *n.* (*pl.* **cilia**) **1** each of the minute hairs fringing a leaf, an insect's wing, etc. **2** a hairlike vibrating organ on animal or vegetable tissue. **3** an eyelash. ☐ **ciliary** *adj.*
cinch / sinch / *n. colloq.* **1** a certainty. **2** an easy task.
cinchona / sing-**koh**-nuh / *n.* **1** a South American evergreen tree or shrub whose bark is the source of quinine. **2** this bark.
cincture / **singk**-chuh / *n.* **1** *literary* a girdle, belt, or border. **2** the white rope worn round the waist by a priest at Mass.
cinder *n.* **1** a small piece of partly burnt coal or wood. **2** (**cinders**) ashes.
Cinderella *n.* a person or thing that is persistently neglected in favour of others. (¶ Named after a girl in a fairy tale.)
cine- / **sin**-ee / *comb. form* cinematographic (*cine-camera; cine-film; cine-projector*).
cinema *n.* **1** a theatre where motion pictures are shown. **2** films as an art form or an industry. ☐ **cinematic** *adj.*
cinematographic / sin-uh-mat-uh-**graf**-ik / *adj.* for taking or projecting motion pictures.
cinematography / sin-uh-muh-**tog**-ruh-fee / *n.* the art of making motion-picture films. ☐ **cinematographer** *n.*
cineol / **sin**-ee-ol / *n.* a colourless terpene ether found in oil extracted from eucalypts, used in medicine etc.
cineraria / sin-uh-**rair**-ree-uh / *n.* a plant of the Canary Islands with brightly coloured daisy-like flowers.
cinerary urn / **sin**-uh-ruh-ree / *n.* an urn for holding a person's ashes after cremation.

cinnabar / sin-uh-bah / *n.* **1** red mercuric sulphide; the pigment obtained from this. **2** vermilion.

cinnamon / sin-uh-muhn / *n.* **1** an aromatic spice consisting of the peeled, rolled, and dried inner bark of a tree native to Sri Lanka. **2** its colour, yellowish-brown.

cinque / singk / *n.* the five on dice.

cinquefoil / singk-foil / *n.* **1** a plant with a compound leaf of five leaflets. **2** an ornament with five cusps in a circle or arch.

cipher / suy-fuh / *n.* (also **cypher**) **1** a symbol (0), representing nought or zero. **2** any Arabic numeral. **3** a person or thing of no importance. **4** a set of letters or symbols representing others, used to conceal the meaning of a message etc. • *v.* write in cipher.

circa / ser-kuh / *prep.* (preceding a date) about (*was born circa 1300*).

circadian / ser-kay-dee-uhn / *adj.* (of biological processes) occurring about once a day.

Circe / ser-see / *Gk myth.* an enchantress who detained Odysseus on her island and changed his companions into swine.

circle *n.* **1** a perfectly round plane figure. **2** the line enclosing it, every point on which is the same distance from the centre. **3** a circular or roundish enclosure, structure, or road. **4** curved rows of seats rising in tiers at a theatre etc. above the lowest level. **5** a number of people bound together by similar interests (*in business circles*). **6** a set or restricted group (*not done in the best circles*). • *v.* move in a circle, form a circle round. ☐ **come full circle** pass through a series of events etc. and return to the starting point.

circlet / ser-kluht / *n.* a circular band worn as an ornament, esp. round the head.

circuit / ser-kuht / *n.* **1** a line, route, or distance round a place; a motor-racing track. **2** a closed path for an electric current; an apparatus with conductors, valves, etc., through which electric current passes. **3** the journey of a judge round a non-metropolitan area to hold courts; the area itself. **4** a street which is circular. **5** a sequence of sporting events (*tennis circuit*). **6** a roundabout journey. ☐ **circuit-breaker** a device for interrupting an electric current.

circuitous / ser-kyoo-uh-tuhs / *adj.* roundabout, indirect. ☐ **circuitously** *adv.*

circuitry / ser-kuh-tree / *n.* electric circuits; the equipment forming these.

circular *adj.* **1** shaped like a circle. **2** moving round a circle; following a route that brings travellers back to the starting point. **3** (of reasoning) using as evidence for its conclusion the very thing that it is trying to prove, hence invalid. **4** addressed to a number of people (*a circular letter*). • *n.* a circular letter or advertising leaflet. ☐ **circular saw** a power saw with a rotating toothed disc. ☐ ☐ **circularity** / ser-kyuh-la-ruh-tee / *n.*

circularise *v.* (also **-ize**) send a circular to.

circulate *v.* **1** be in circulation; spread (*a rumour is circulating*). **2** pass from place to place; move about among guests etc. **3** cause to move round; send round (*we will circulate this letter*). **4** circularise (*we will circulate these people*).

circulation *n.* **1** circulating, being circulated. **2** the movement of blood round the body, pumped by the heart. **3** the number of copies sold or distributed, esp. of a newspaper. ☐ **in** (*or* **out of**) **circulation** active (or not active) socially.

circulatory *adj.* of the circulation of blood.

circum- *comb. form* around, about.

circumcise *v.* **1** cut off the foreskin of (a male person) as a surgical operation or as an Aboriginal or Jewish or Muslim rite. **2** cut off the clitoris of (a female) as a religious rite. ☐ **circumcision** *n.*

circumference / suh-**kum**-fuh-ruhns / *n.* the boundary of a circle, the distance round this. ☐ **circumferential** / suh-kum-fuh-**ren**-shuhl / *adj.*

circumflex / ser-kuhm-fleks / *n.* (in full **circumflex accent**) a mark (ˆ) over a vowel, as over *e* in *fête*.

circumlocution / ser-kuhm-luh-**kyoo**-shuhn / *n.* **1** the use of many words where a few would do. **2** evasive talk. ☐ **circumlocutory** / ser-kuhm-lok-yuh-tuh-ree, -tree / *adj.*

circumnavigate *v.* sail completely round. ☐ **circumnavigation** *n.*

circumscribe *v.* **1** draw a line round. **2** mark the limits of; restrict (*our sightseeing was circumscribed by lack of time*).

circumscription *n.* circumscribing.

circumspect / ser-kuhm-spekt / *adj.* cautious and watchful, wary. ☐ **circumspection** *n.*

circumstance *n.* **1** any of the conditions or facts connected with an event, person, or action (*he was a victim of circumstances*). **2** (**circumstances**) one's financial situation (*what are his circumstances?*). **3** ceremony; fuss (*pomp and circumstance*). ☐ **circumstanced** *adj.*

circumstantial / ser-kuhm-**stan**-shuhl / *adj.* **1** giving full details. **2** consisting of facts that strongly suggest something but do not provide direct proof (*circumstantial evidence*). ☐ **circumstantially** *adv.* **circumstantiality** *n.*

circumvent / ser-kuhm-**vent** / *v.* evade, find a way round (*managed to circumvent the rules*). ☐ **circumvention** *n.*

circus *n.* **1** a travelling show with performing acrobats, clowns, and often animals. **2** *colloq.* a scene of lively or disorderly action. **3** (in ancient Rome) an arena for sports and games.

cirque / serk / *n.* a bowl-shaped hollow on a mountain.

cirrhosis / si-**roh**-suhs, suh- / *n.* a chronic disease, as a result of alcoholism, hepatitis, etc., in which the liver hardens into many small projections. ☐ **cirrhotic** / si-**rot**-ik / *adj.*

cirrus / **si**-ruhs / *n.* (*pl.* **cirri**) light wispy clouds.

CIS *abbr.* Commonwealth of Independent States, a loose confederation of former constituent republics of the USSR.

Cistercian / si-**ster**-shuhn / *n.* a monk or nun of the order founded in 1098 at Citeaux in France as a stricter branch of the Benedictines. •*adj.* of this order.

cistern / **sis**-tuhn / *n.* **1** a tank or other vessel for storing water; the tank above a toilet bowl. **2** an underground reservoir.

citadel / **sit**-uh-del / *n.* a fortress overlooking a city.

citation *n.* **1** citing; a passage cited. **2** *Military* an official mention or award for bravery etc. **3** description of the reasons for an award.

cite *v.* **1** quote or mention as an example or to support an argument. **2** mention in an official dispatch. **3** summon to appear in court.

citizen *n.* **1** a person who has full rights in a nation by birth or by naturalisation. **2** an inhabitant of a city. ☐ **citizens' band** radio frequencies to be used by private individuals for local communication. ☐☐ **citizenship** *n.*

citizenry *n.* citizens collectively.

citrate *n.* a salt of citric acid.

citric acid / **sit**-rik / *n.* the acid in the juice of lemons, limes, etc.

citronella *n.* a lemon-scented grass from S. Asia which yields an oil used as an insect repellent and a fragrance.

citrus / **sit**-ruhs / *n.* any of a group of related trees including lemon, orange, and grapefruit. ☐ **citrus fruit** fruit from such a tree.

city *n.* **1** a large town. **2** *Aust.* a town qualified for city status (on the basis of population etc. requirements varying from State to State in Australia). **3** *Aust.* a similar area within a large city, e.g. the City of Dandenong within the Melbourne metropolitan area. **4** the business centre of a city. **5** the inhabitants of a city (*almost the entire city turned up to watch*). ☐ **city slicker** (usu. *derog.*) a smart and sophisticated city dweller. **city state** (usu. *hist.*) a city that with its surrounding territory forms an independent State (*Vatican City is a city state*).

civet / **siv**-uht / *n.* **1** (also **civet cat**) a cat-like animal of Central Africa. **2** a musky-smelling substance obtained from its glands, used in making perfumes.

civic / **siv**-ik / *adj.* of or proper to a city or town; of citizens or citizenship. •*n.* (**civics**) the study of municipal government and the rights and duties of citizens. ☐ **civic centre** an area containing municipal offices and other public buildings. ☐☐ **civically** *adv.*

civil *adj.* **1** belonging to citizens. **2** of the general public, not the armed forces or the Church (*civil aviation; civil marriage*). **3** involving civil law not criminal law (*a civil dispute*). **4** polite and obliging, not rude. ☐ **civil defence** the organising of civilians for protection during wartime attacks or in a natural disaster. **civil disobedience** a form of peaceful protest involving refusal to comply with certain laws. **civil engineering** the designing and construction of roads, bridges, canals, etc. **civil law** law dealing with the private rights of citizens, not with crime. **civil liberties** freedom of action and speech; basic rights of the individual. **civil rights** the rights of citizens to political and social freedom and equality. **civil war** war between groups of citizens of the same country. ☐☐ **civilly** *adv.*

civilian *n.* a person not serving in the armed forces or police force. •*adj.* of or for civilians.

civilisation *n.* (also **-ization**) **1** making or becoming civilised. **2** a stage in the evolution of organised society; a particular type of this (*ancient civilisations*). **3** civilised conditions or society (*far from civilisation*).

civilise *v.* (also **-ize**) **1** cause to improve from a savage or primitive stage of human society to a more developed one. **2** impose upon (esp. an indigenous people) a way of life alien to them. **3** enlighten; refine and educate.

civility *n.* politeness; an act of politeness.

civvies / **siv**-eez / *n.pl. colloq.* civilian clothes.

civvy street *n. colloq.* civilian life.

Cl *symbol* chlorine.

cl *abbr.* centilitre(s).

clack *n.* **1** a short sharp sound like that made by boards struck together. **2** the noise of chatter. •*v.* make such a sound or noise.

clad *adj.* **1** clothed (*warmly clad*). **2** covered with cladding (*iron-clad*).

cladding *n.* material applied to the surface of another as a protective covering.

cladistics / kluh-**dis**-tiks / *n.* a method of studying the relationship of groups of living things by tracing the course of their development from a common ancestor, by analysis of shared features.

cladode *n.* a flattened plant-stem which looks like a leaf.

claim *v.* **1** request as one's right or due. **2** declare that something is true or has been achieved; state without being able to prove. **3** have as an achievement or consequence (*the floods claimed many lives*). •*n.* **1** a request for something as one's right (*lay claim to*). **2** an application for compensation under the terms of an insurance policy. **3** the right to something (*a widow has a claim on her deceased husband's estate*). **4** a statement claiming that something is true, an assertion. **5** a thing claimed. **6** a piece of land formally claimed and taken up for mining purposes. ☐ **claim jumper** a person who occupies or takes summary possession of another's mining claim.

claimant *n.* a person who makes a claim, esp. in law.

clairvoyance / klair-**voi**-uhns / *n.* the supposed power of seeing in the mind either future events or things that are happening or existing out of sight. ❑ **clairvoyant** *n.* & *adj.*

clam *n.* **1** a large shellfish with a hinged shell. **2** *colloq.* a shy or withdrawn or secretive person. ❑ **clam up** (**clammed**, **clamming**) *colloq.* refuse to talk.

clamber *v.* climb with some difficulty using the hands and feet. •*n.* a difficult climb.

clammy *adj.* unpleasantly moist and sticky. ❑ **clammily** *adv.* **clamminess** *n.*

clamour *n.* (also **clamor**) **1** a loud confused noise, esp. of shouting. **2** a loud protest or demand. •*v.* make a loud protest or demand. ❑ **clamorous** *adj.*

clamp *n.* **1** a device for holding things tightly, often with a screw. **2** (in full **wheel clamp**) a device for immobilising an illegally parked vehicle. •*v.* **1** grip with a clamp; fix firmly. **2** immobilise (a vehicle) by attaching a wheel clamp to it. ❑ **clamp down on** become stricter about; put a stop to.

clampdown *n.* a sudden policy (or act) of suppression.

clan *n.* **1** a group of people with a common ancestor, esp. among Aboriginal groups and in the Scottish Highlands. **2** a large family as a social group.

Clancy, Edward Bede (1923–), AC, Australian archbishop and cardinal.

clandestine / klan-**des**-tuhn / *adj.* kept secret, done secretly. ❑ **clandestinely** *adv.*

clang *n.* a loud ringing sound. •*v.* make a clang.

clanger *n. colloq.* a blunder. ❑ **drop a clanger** commit a conspicuous indiscretion.

clangour / **klang**-guh, -uh / *n.* (also **clangor**) a prolonged or repeated clanging noise. ❑ **clangorous** *adj.*

clank *n.* a metallic sound like that of metal striking metal. •*v.* (cause to) make a clank.

clannish *adj.* showing clan feeling, clinging together and excluding others.

clap[1] *n.* **1** the sharp noise of thunder. **2** the sound of the palms of the hands being struck together, esp. in applause. **3** a friendly slap (*gave him a clap on the shoulder*). •*v.* (**clapped**, **clapping**) **1** strike the palms loudly together, esp. in applause. **2** give a friendly slap. **3** put or place quickly or with determination (*clapped him in prison; clapped a tax on books*). ❑ **clap eyes on** *colloq.* catch sight of. **clap on the speed** increase (*clapped on the speed*). **clapped out** *colloq.* worn out; exhausted. **clap stick** (also **music stick**) *Aust.* an Aboriginal percussion instrument consisting of two sticks of resonant wood clapped rhythmically together.

clap[2] *n. colloq.* venereal disease, esp. gonorrhoea.

clapper *n.* the tongue or striker of a bell.

clapperboard *n.* a device in film-making of hinged boards struck together to synchronise the starting of the picture and sound.

claptrap *n.* pretentious talk or ideas; nonsense.

claque / klak / *n.* a group of people hired to applaud something.

Clare, St (1194–1253), foundress of the 'Poor Clares', an order of Franciscan nuns. In 1958 Pope Pius XII proclaimed her patron saint of television.

claret / **kla**-ruht / *n.* **1** a dry red wine, from Bordeaux in France; a similar wine from elsewhere. **2** a purplish-red. ❑ **claret ash** an ornamental ash tree with purple-red autumn leaves, orig. cultivated in SA.

clarify *v.* (**clarified**, **clarifying**) **1** make or become clear or easier to understand. **2** remove impurities from (stock, fats, etc.), e.g. by heating; make transparent. ❑ **clarification** *n.*

clarinet / kla-ruh-**net** / *n.* a woodwind instrument with a single reed.

clarinettist *n.* a person who plays the clarinet.

clarion / **kla**-ree-uhn / *n.* **1** a loud clear rousing sound. **2** *archaic* a shrill war trumpet. •*adj.* clear and loud.

clarity *n.* clearness.

Clark[1], (Charles) Manning (Hope) (1915–91), AC, Australian historian, author of the six-volume *A History of Australia* (1962–87).

Clark[2], Helen (1950–), New Zealand Labour stateswoman who became prime minister in 1999.

Clarke, Marcus (Andrew Hislop) (1846–81), Australian writer (born in England), author of *For the Term of His Natural Life*.

clash *v.* **1** strike making a loud harsh sound like that of cymbals. **2** conflict; disagree. **3** take place inconveniently at the same time as something else. **4** (of colours) produce an unpleasant visual effect by not being harmonious. •*n.* **1** a sound of clashing. **2** a conflict; a disagreement. **3** a clashing of colours.

clasp *n.* **1** a device for fastening things, with interlocking parts. **2** a grasp, a handshake; an embrace. •*v.* **1** fasten; join with a clasp. **2** grasp; hold or embrace closely. ❑ **clasp knife** *n.* a folding knife with a catch to hold the blade open.

class *n.* **1** people, animals, or things with some characteristics in common. **2** people of the same social or economic level (*the working class; the middle class*). **3** a set of students taught together; a session when these are taught. **4** a division according to quality (*first class; tourist class*). **5** distinction, high quality (*a tennis player with class*). •*v.* **1** place in a class, classify. **2** *Aust.* grade (fleeces). ❑ **class action** legal action brought against a company etc. by a group of people, each with the same complaint.

classic *adj.* **1** having a high quality that is recognised and unquestioned (*Hardy's classic novel*). **2** very typical (*a classic case of malnutrition*). **3** (of style in art, music, etc.) simple, harmonious, well-proportioned. **4** (of clothes) made in a simple elegant style not much affected by changes in fashion. •*n.* **1** a classic writer, artist,

classical work, or example. **2** (**classics**) the study of ancient Greek and Latin literature, culture, etc.

classical adj. **1** of ancient Greek and Roman art, literature, and culture (*a classical scholar*). **2** restrained, traditional, or standard in style. **3** (of music) serious or conventional, or of the period c.1750–1800. **4** (of a language) having the form used by ancient standard authors. □ **classically** adv.

classicism n. **1** following of the classic style. **2** classical scholarship. **3** ancient Greek or Latin idiom.

classicist n. a classical scholar.

classificatory adj. of or involving classification.

classified adj. **1** arranged in classes or categories. **2** (of newspaper advertisements) arranged according to subject matter. **3** (of information etc.) designated as officially secret. • n. (**classifieds**) small advertisements placed in a newspaper and organised in categories.

classify v. (**classified, classifying**) **1** arrange systematically in classes or groups, put into a particular class. **2** designate as officially secret or not for general disclosure. □ **classification** n. **classifiable** adj.

classless adj. without distinctions of social class.

classroom n. a room where a class of students is taught.

classy adj. colloq. stylish, superior. □ **classily** adv. **classiness** n.

clatter n. **1** a sound like that of plates rattled together. **2** noisy talk. • v. make or cause to make a clatter.

clause n. **1** a single part in a treaty, law, or contract. **2** *Grammar* a part of a sentence, with its own finite verb (see panel). □ **clausal** adj.

claustrophobia / klos-truh-**foh**-bee-uh, klaw-struh- / n. abnormal fear of being in an enclosed space. □ **claustrophobic** adj.

clavichord / **klav**-uh-kawd / n. an early small stringed keyboard instrument with a very soft tone.

clavicle / **klav**-i-kuhl / n. the collar bone.

claw n. **1** the pointed nail on an animal's or bird's foot; a foot with such nails. **2** the pincers of a shellfish (*a crab's claw*). **3** a device like a claw, used for grappling and holding things. • v. grasp, scratch, or pull with a claw or the hands. □ **claw back 1** regain laboriously or gradually. **2** recoup (money etc.) that has just been given away (e.g. in taxation). **claw hammer** a hammer with a head divided at one end for pulling out nails.

clawback n. **1** an act of clawing back. **2** money recovered in this way.

clay n. **1** stiff sticky earth that becomes hard when baked, used for making bricks and pottery. **2** *literary* the substance of the human body. □ **clay pigeon** a breakable disc thrown up as a target for shooting. □□ **clayey** adj.

claypan n. Aust. a natural hollow in clay soil, retaining water after rain.

Clayton's n. Aust. trademark something which is largely illusory or exists in name only; imitation (*Australian English is not a Clayton's English—it's dinkum*). (¶ From the advertising slogan used by the manufacturer of a non-alcoholic drink: 'It's the drink you have when you're not having a drink.')

clean adj. **1** free from dirt or impurities, not soiled. **2** not yet used (*a clean page*). **3** free from indecency (*clean jokes*). **4** attentive to personal hygiene and cleanliness, with clean habits. **5** entire, complete, clear-cut (*a clean sweep; a clean break*). **6** showing no record of crime, disease, drug use etc.; (of a licence) with no endorsements. **7** keeping to the rules; not unfair (*a clean fighter*). **8** (of a car etc.) streamlined; (of a person) well-formed, slender and shapely (*the car has clean lines; clean-limbed Aussie surfies*). **9** (of timber) free from knots. **10** adroit, skilful (*a clean bit of fielding*). **11** (of a nuclear bomb) producing relatively little fallout. • adv. completely, entirely (*I clean forgot*). • v. make or become clean. • n. an act of cleaning. □ **clean-bowl** v. *Cricket* bowl out (a batsman) with a ball that hits the wicket without having touched the bat or body of the batsman. **clean-cut** sharply outlined or defined (*clean-cut features*). **clean out 1** clean the inside of. **2** *colloq.* use up all the supplies or money of. **clean-shaven** without beard, moustache, or whiskers. **clean up 1** make clean and tidy. **2** rid of crime and corruption. **3** *colloq.* make a gain or profit. **4** *colloq.* defeat thoroughly (*cleaned them up in the final quarter*). **come clean** *colloq.* confess. **make a clean breast of** confess fully about. □□ **cleanness** n.

cleaner n. **1** a device or substance used for cleaning things. **2** a person employed to clean rooms. **3** (**cleaners**) a dry-cleaning establishment etc. □ **take to the cleaners** *colloq.* **1** rob or defraud. **2** criticise strongly.

cleanly[1] / **kleen**-lee / adv. **1** in a clean way (*make the break cleanly*). **2** efficiently; without difficulty.

Clause
A clause is a group of words that includes a main verb. If it makes complete sense by itself, it is known as a main clause, e.g.
> *The sun came out.*

Otherwise, although it makes some sense, it must be attached to a main clause: this is known as a subordinate clause, e.g.
> *when the sun came out*
> (as in *When the sun came out, we went outside*).

cleanly² / klen-lee / *adj.* attentive to cleanness, with clean habits. ☐ **cleanliness** *n.*

cleanse / klenz / *v.* make thoroughly clean. ☐ **cleanser** *n.*

cleanskin *n. Aust.* **1** an unbranded animal. **2** a person who has no criminal record. **3** a person new to (a situation or activity) and lacking experience. **4** *colloq.* an unlabelled bottle of wine.

clear *adj.* **1** transparent; not cloudy (*clear glass; clear water; clear soup*). **2** free from blemishes (*a clear complexion*). **3** free from guilt (*a clear conscience*). **4** easily seen, heard, or understood; distinct. **5** evident (*a clear case of cheating*). **6** free from doubt, not confused. **7** free from obstruction or from something undesirable. **8** net, without deductions (*a clear $1000*). **9** complete (*give 3 clear days' notice*). •*adv.* **1** clearly. **2** completely. **3** apart, not in contact (*stand clear!*). •*v.* **1** make or become clear. **2** make or become free from obstruction etc. **3** free (land) for cultivation or building by cutting down trees etc. **4** cause people to leave (a room etc.) (*police moved in to clear the street*). **5** (often foll. by *of*) show (a person) to be innocent. **6** approve (a person etc.) for a special duty, access to information, etc. **7** free (one's throat) of phlegm or huskiness by a slight cough. **8** pass over or by, safely or without touching, esp. by jumping. **9** pass through (customs etc.). **10** pass (a cheque) through a clearing house. **11** make as net gain or profit. ☐ **clear-cut** very distinct; not open to doubt. **clear off** *colloq.* go away. **clear the air** remove suspicion, tension, etc. **clear up 1** tidy up. **2** become better or brighter. **3** solve (a mystery, problem, etc.). **in the clear** free of suspicion or difficulty. ☐☐ **clearly** *adv.* **clearness** *n.*

clearance *n.* **1** clearing. **2** authorisation, permission. **3** the space left clear when one object moves within or past another.

clearing *n.* an open space from which trees have been cleared in a forest.

clearway *n.* a road on which vehicles, at stated times, may not stop.

cleat *n.* **1** a short piece of wood or metal with projecting ends round which a rope may be fastened. **2** a strip or other projecting piece fixed to a gangway etc. or to footwear, to prevent slipping. **3** a wedge. •*v.* fasten to a cleat.

cleavage *n.* **1** a split, a division made by cleaving. **2** the hollow between a woman's breasts.

cleave¹ *v.* **1** divide by chopping; split or become split. **2** make a way through.

■ **Usage** The past tense may be *cleaved* or *clove* or *cleft, has cloven* or *has cleft* (*he cleaved it in two, he clove it in two, he cleft it in two*). *Clove* and *cleft* are rather old-fashioned. In the past perfect, both are used. The adjectives *cloven* and *cleft* are used of different objects (*see* CLEFT *and* CLOVEN).

cleave² *v. literary* adhere, cling (*she cleaves to her principles; I will cleave to him through thick and thin*).

cleaver *n.* a butcher's chopper.

clef *n.* a symbol on a stave in a musical score, showing the pitch of the notes (e.g. treble, bass).

cleft *see* CLEAVE¹. •*adj.* split, partly divided; with a V shaped hollow (*a cleft stick*). •*n.* a split, a cleavage. ☐ **cleft palate** a defect in the roof of the mouth where two sides of the palate failed to join before birth. **in a cleft stick** in a difficult dilemma.

clematis / kluh-**may**-tuhs / *n.* a flowering climbing plant.

clemency / **klem**-uhn-see / *n.* **1** mildness, esp. of weather. **2** mercy.

Clement, St (1st century AD), bishop of Rome, the third pope after St Peter.

clement *adj.* **1** (of weather) mild, pleasant. **2** merciful.

clench *v.* **1** close (the teeth or fingers) tightly. **2** grasp tightly. **3** fasten (a nail or rivet) by hammering the point sideways after it is driven through. •*n.* a clenching action; a clenched state.

Cleopatra (69–30 BC), ruler of Egypt from 51 BC.

clerestory / **kleer**-stuh-ree, -staw-ree / *n.* an upper row of windows in a large church, above the level of the roofs of the aisles.

clergy *n.* people who have been ordained for religious duties.

clergyman *n.* (*feminine* **clergywoman**) a member of the clergy.

cleric / **kle**-rik / *n.* a member of the clergy.

clerical *adj.* **1** of clerks. **2** of the clergy.

clerk / klahk / *n.* **1** a person employed to keep records or accounts etc. in an office. **2** an official who keeps the records of a court or council etc.

clever *adj.* **1** quick at learning and understanding things, talented. **2** showing skill (*a clever plan*). **3** *Aust.* (in Aboriginal English) wise, learned in traditional lore, and spiritually powerful. **4** oversmart; cocky (*don't you get clever with me, mate!*). ☐ **clever man** *Aust.* (in Aboriginal English) an Aborigine with recognised skills in traditional medicine and (frequently) a role in ceremonial life. ☐☐ **cleverly** *adv.* **cleverness** *n.*

cliché / klee-shay / *n.* a hackneyed phrase or idea. ☐ **clichéd** *adj.* (also **cliché'd**).

click¹ *n.* a short sharp sound like that of billiard balls colliding. •*v.* **1** make or cause to make a click; fasten with a click. **2** *colloq.* be a success. **3** *colloq.* become understood (*it all suddenly clicked*). **4** *colloq.* get on well (*he and I clicked from the moment we met*). **5** *Computing* **a** press a button on a mouse. **b** select (an item represented on screen, a particular function, etc.) by so doing.

click² *n.* (also **klick**) *colloq.* a kilometre.

client *n.* **1** a person using the services of a lawyer, architect, or other professional person. **2** a customer.

clientele / kluy-uhn-**tel**, klee- / *n.* clients, customers.

cliff *n.* a steep rock face, esp. on a coast.

cliffhanger *n.* **1** a story etc. with a strong element of suspense. **2** a sporting contest, election, etc. in which the result is very close.

climacteric / kluy-**mak**-tuh-rik, kluy-muhk-**te**-rik / *n.* the period of life when fertility and sexual activity begin to decline.

climactic / kluy-**mak**-tik / *adj.* of a climax.

climate *n.* **1** the regular weather conditions of an area. **2** an area with certain weather conditions (*living in a hot climate*). **3** a general attitude or feeling; an atmosphere (*a climate of hostility*). □ **climatic** / kluy-**mat**-ik / *adj.* **climatically** *adv.*

climax *n.* **1** the event or point of greatest interest or intensity; a culmination. **2** an orgasm. **3** *Ecology* a state of equilibrium reached by a plant or animal community. • *v.* reach or bring to a climax.

climb *v.* **1** go up or over; move upwards. **2** grow up a support (*a climbing rose*). **3** slope upwards (*the road climbs sharply here*). • *n.* an ascent made by climbing. □ **climb down** *v.* **1** go downwards by effort. **2** retreat from a position taken up in argument.

climbdown *n.* a retreat from a position taken up in an argument or negotiation.

climber *n.* **1** one who climbs, a mountaineer. **2** a climbing plant.

clime *n. literary* **1** a region. **2** a climate.

clinch *v.* **1** fasten securely; clench (a nail or rivet). **2** (in boxing) be too close together for a full-arm blow. **3** settle (an argument, bargain, etc.) conclusively (*clinched the deal*). • *n.* **1** a clinching position in boxing. **2** *colloq.* an embrace.

clincher *n.* a decisive point that settles an argument, proposition, etc.

cling *v.* (**clung**, **clinging**) **1** hold on tightly. **2** become attached, stick. **3** remain close or in contact; be emotionally attached or dependent. **4** refuse to abandon (*clinging to hopes of rescue*). □ **cling wrap** thin clinging polythene used as a wrapping for food.

clinic *n.* **1** a private or specialised hospital. **2** a place or session at which specialised treatment or advice is given to visiting persons (*antenatal clinic; tennis clinic*).

clinical *adj.* **1** of a clinic. **2** of or used in the treatment of patients. **3** of or based on observed signs and symptoms (*clinical medicine; clinical death*). **4** (of a room, building etc.) looking bare and hygienic. **5** unemotional, cool and detached. □ **clinically** *adv.*

clink[1] *n.* a thin sharp sound like glasses striking together. • *v.* make or cause to make this sound.

clink[2] *n. colloq.* prison (*in the clink*).

clinker *n.* a mass of slag or lava; rough stony material left after coal has burnt.

clinker-built *adj.* (of a boat) made with the outside planks overlapping downwards.

Clinton, Bill (full name: William Jefferson Clinton) (1946–), American Democratic statesman, 42nd president of the USA from 1993 to 2001.

Clio *Gk & Rom. myth.* the Muse of history.

clip[1] *n.* **1** a device for holding things tightly or together; a paper clip. **2** a magazine for a firearm. **3** an ornament fastened by a clip. • *v.* (**clipped**, **clipping**) fix or fasten with a clip. □ **clip-on** *adj.* attached by a clip.

clip[2] *v.* (**clipped**, **clipping**) **1** cut or trim with shears or scissors. **2** punch a small piece from (a ticket) to show that it has been used. **3** cut from a newspaper etc. **4** *colloq.* hit smartly (*clipped him on the ear*). • *n.* **1** the act or process of clipping; a piece clipped off or out. **2** the wool cut from a sheep or flock at one shearing. **3** an extract from a film. **4** = VIDEO CLIP. **5** *colloq.* a sharp blow. **6** a rapid pace (*going at quite a clip*). □ **clip joint** *colloq.* a club etc. charging exorbitant prices.

clipboard *n.* a portable board with a spring clip at the top for holding papers.

clipper *n.* **1** a fast sailing ship. **2** (**clippers**) an instrument for clipping hair etc.

clipping *n.* a piece clipped off or out, esp. from a newspaper.

clique / kleek, klik / *n.* a small exclusive group. □ **cliquey** *adj.* **cliquish** *adj.*

clitoris / **klit**-uh-ruhs / *n.* a small sensitive erectile part of the female genitals, at the upper end of the vulva. □ **clitoral** *adj.*

cloaca / kloh-**ay**-kuh / *n.* the excretory opening at the end of the intestinal canal in birds, reptiles, etc.

cloak *n.* **1** a loose sleeveless outdoor garment. **2** something that conceals (*under the cloak of darkness*). • *v.* cover or conceal. □ **cloak-and-dagger** *adj.* involving intrigue and espionage.

cloakroom *n.* **1** a room where outdoor clothes and luggage etc. may be left temporarily. **2** a toilet.

clobber *colloq. n.* clothing and equipment. • *v.* **1** hit repeatedly. **2** defeat. **3** criticise severely.

clock *n.* **1** an instrument (other than a watch) for measuring and showing the time. **2** a measuring device resembling this, e.g. a speedometer, stopwatch, etc. **3** time considered as something to be beaten (*run against the clock*). • *v.* **1** time (a race or competitor). **2** *colloq.* (often foll. by *up*) achieve as a speed (*he clocked up 10 seconds for the 100 metres*). **3** *colloq.* hit (*clocked him one*). □ **clock in** (or **on**) register one's arrival at work. **clock off** (or **out**) register one's departure from work. **round the clock** all day and night.

clockwise *adv. & adj.* moving in a curve from left to right, in the same direction as the hands of a clock.

clockwork *n.* a mechanism with wheels and springs (*clockwork toys*). □ **like clockwork** with perfect regularity and precision; smoothly.

clod *n.* **1** a lump of earth or clay. **2** *colloq.* a foolish person.

cloddish *adj.* loutish, foolish, clumsy.

clodhopper *n. colloq.* **1** a large heavy shoe. **2** a foolish or clumsy person.

clog *n.* **1** a wooden-soled shoe. **2** a block of wood to impede an animal's movement. •*v.* (**clogged**, **clogging**) **1** cause an obstruction in. **2** become blocked.

cloister *n.* **1** a covered walk round a quadrangle, esp. in a convent, monastery, college, etc. **2** a monastery or convent; secluded life in this. •*v.* seclude in, or as if in, a monastery or convent (*he cloisters himself in his home*). ☐ **cloistral** *adj.*

cloistered *adj.* sheltered, secluded.

clomp *v.* walk with a heavy tread; clump.

clone *n.* **1** a group of plants or organisms produced asexually from one ancestor; a member of this group. **2** *colloq.* one of several people who look identical because of the way they dress etc.; one of several seemingly identical things. •*v.* propagate or become propagated as a clone. ☐ **clonal** *adj.*

clonk *n.* an abrupt heavy sound of impact. •*v.* **1** make this sound. **2** *colloq.* hit.

close[1] / **klohs** / *adj.* **1** near in space or time. **2** near in relationship (*a close relative*). **3** near or intimate in association (*a close friend; we are very close*). **4** nearly alike (*a close resemblance*). **5** in which the competitors are nearly equal (*a close contest*). **6** dense, compact, with no or only slight intervals (*close formation*). **7** leaving no gaps or weaknesses, rigorous (*close reasoning*). **8** concentrated, searching (*close examination*). **9** secretive. **10** stingy, mean. **11** humid; without fresh air. **12** (of a danger etc.) directly threatening, narrowly avoided (*that was close; a close call*). •*adv.* closely, in a near position (*they live close by*). •*n.* **1** a cul-de-sac. **2** the grounds round a cathedral or abbey etc., usu. with its buildings (houses etc.). ☐ **at close quarters** very close together. **close-knit** tightly interlocked; closely united in friendship. **close shave** *colloq.* a narrow escape. **close-up** a photograph giving a detailed view of something. ☐☐ **closely** *adv.* **closeness** *n.*

close[2] / **klohz** / *v.* **1** shut, block up. **2** be or declare to be not open to the public. **3** bring or come to an end. **4** bring or come closer or into contact (*close the ranks*). **5** make (an electric circuit) continuous. •*n.* a conclusion, an end. ☐ **closed book** a subject one does not understand. **closed-circuit television** that transmitted by wires, not waves, to a restricted number of screens. **close down** shut completely; cease working. **closed shop** the system whereby membership of a trade union is a condition of employment. **close in (on)** approach from all sides. **close with** accept (an offer); accept the offer made by (a person).

closet *n.* **1** a cupboard. **2** a small room. **3** = WATER CLOSET. **4** (used as *adj.*) secret (*a closet homosexual*). •*v.* (**closeted**, **closeting**) shut away in private conference or study.

closure / **kloh**-*zh*uh / *n.* **1** closing; a closed condition. **2** a decision in parliament to take a vote without further debate.

clot *n.* **1** a small thickened mass of blood or other liquid. **2** *colloq.* a stupid person. •*v.* (**clotted**, **clotting**) form clots.

cloth *n.* **1** woven or felted material. **2** a piece of this for a special purpose; a dishcloth, tablecloth, etc. **3** the clergy (*respect for the cloth*).

clothe *v.* (**clothed** or **clad**, **clothing**) **1** put clothes upon; provide with clothes. **2** cover as with clothes.

clothes *n.pl.* **1** things worn to cover the body and limbs. **2** bedclothes. ☐ **clothes hoist** (also **rotary hoist**) a rotating clothes drier consisting of a square frame between the arms of which run lengths of clothes line, turning about a central pole and adjustable in height. **clothes horse** a frame for airing washed clothes. **clothes line** a rope or wire on which washed clothes are hung to dry. **clothes peg** a clip for securing clothes to a clothes line.

clothier / **kloh**-*th*ee-uh / *n.* a seller of men's clothes.

clothing *n.* clothes, garments.

cloud *n.* **1** a visible mass of condensed watery vapour, floating in the sky. **2** a mass of smoke, mist, dust, etc. **3** a mass of things moving in the air (*a cloud of insects*). **4** a state of gloom, trouble, or suspicion (*casting a cloud over the festivities*). •*v.* **1** cover or darken with clouds or gloom or trouble. **2** (often foll. by *over*) become overcast, indistinct, or gloomy. ☐ **cloud chamber** a device containing vapour for tracking the paths of charged particles, X-rays, and gamma rays. **cloud cuckoo land** a fanciful or ideal place. **on cloud nine** *colloq.* extremely happy. **under a cloud** out of favour; under suspicion.

cloudburst *n.* a sudden violent rainstorm.

cloudless *adj.* free from clouds.

cloudy *adj.* (**cloudier**, **cloudiest**) **1** covered with clouds. **2** not transparent (*a cloudy liquid*). ☐ **cloudily** *adv.* **cloudiness** *n.*

clout *n.* **1** a heavy blow. **2** power of effective action (*trade unions with clout*). •*v.* hit hard.

clove see CLEAVE[1]. •*n.* **1** one of the small bulbs making up a compound bulb (*a clove of garlic*). **2** the dried unopened flower bud of tropical myrtle, used as a spice. ☐ **clove hitch** a knot used to secure a rope round a spar or pole.

cloven see CLEAVE[1]. ☐ **cloven hoof** one that is divided, like those of oxen, sheep, goats, or the Devil.

clover *n.* a plant with three-lobed leaves, used for fodder. ☐ **in clover** in ease and luxury.

clown *n.* **1** a performer who does comical tricks and actions. **2** a person who is always behaving comically. •*v.* (often foll. by *about*, *around*) behave as a clown; act foolishly or playfully. ☐ **clownery** *n.* **clownish** *adj.*

cloy v. sicken by glutting with sweetness, richness, pleasure, sentimentality, etc. (*cloy the appetite*). ☐ **cloying** adj. **cloyingly** adv.

club n. **1** a heavy stick with one end thicker than the other, used as a weapon. **2** a stick with a shaped head used to hit the ball in golf. **3** a playing card of the suit (**clubs**) marked with black clover leaves. **4** an organisation offering members sporting facilities, entertainment, etc.; their premises. •v. (**clubbed, clubbing**) **1** strike with a club. **2** join in subscribing (*we clubbed together to buy a boat*). **3** *colloq.* go out to nightclubs. ☐ **club foot** a deformed foot. **club moss** a moss-like plant of tropical Australia etc., having upright stems a metre or more high, and nearly identical with fossils 400 million years old. **club sandwich** a three-decker sandwich.

clubber n. *colloq.* **1** a member of a club (e.g. a surf lifesaving club). **2** a frequenter of social clubs.

clubhouse n. the premises of a (usu. sporting) club.

cluck n. the throaty cry of a hen. •v. utter a cluck.

clucky adj. **1** (of a hen) sitting on eggs. **2** *Aust.* (of a woman) wanting to have a baby; broody.

clue n. **1** a fact or idea that gives a guide to the solution of a problem. **2** a piece of evidence etc. in the detection of a crime. **3** a word or words indicating what is to be inserted in a crossword puzzle. •v. provide with a clue. ☐ **clue up** (*or* **in**) *colloq.* inform.

clueless adj. **1** without a clue. **2** *colloq.* stupid or incompetent.

cluey adj. *Aust. colloq.* knowledgable; alert (to the possibilities of a situation).

clump n. **1** a cluster or mass (esp. of trees or shrubs). **2** a clumping sound. •v. **1** form a clump; arrange in a clump. **2** walk with a heavy tread; clomp.

clumsy adj. (**clumsier, clumsiest**) **1** awkward in movement or shape; ungainly; lacking in skill. **2** large and difficult to handle or use. **3** done without tact or skill (*a clumsy apology*). ☐ **clumsily** adv. **clumsiness** n.

clung see CLING.

clunk n. a dull sound like thick metal objects striking together. •v. make this sound.

cluster n. a close group or bunch of similar people or things. •v. bring or come together in a cluster. ☐ **cluster headache** an intense recurring headache behind one eye or temple, occurring in a cluster of several days or weeks, followed by several weeks of remission. **cluster house** any of several houses in a cluster housing complex. **cluster housing complex** a group of several detached houses on a single large site with shared private roads and open space, the entire site having been developed as a single entity.

clutch[1] v. grasp tightly; seize eagerly. •n. **1** a tight grasp; a clutching movement. **2** (in *plural*) cruel or relentless grasp or control (*I've been in his clutches for a long while*). **3** a device for connecting and disconnecting certain working parts in machinery, esp. the engine and the transmission in a vehicle; the pedal or other device operating this.

clutch[2] n. **1** a set of eggs for hatching. **2** the chickens hatched from these.

clutter n. **1** things lying about untidily. **2** a crowded untidy state. •v. fill with clutter, crowd untidily.

Cm *symbol* curium.

cm *abbr.* centimetre(s).

CO *abbr.* Commanding Officer.

Co *symbol* cobalt.

Co. *abbr.* Company (*Cobb & Co*).

c/o *abbr.* (also **c/–**) *Aust.* care of (*see* CARE).

co- *comb. form* together with, jointly (*co-author; coexistence*).

coach n. **1** a bus, usu. comfortably equipped, for long journeys. **2** a large four-wheeled horse-drawn carriage. **3** a railway carriage. **4** an instructor or trainer in a sport. **5** a teacher giving private specialised tuition. **6** *Aust.* = COACHER. •v. **1** train or teach as a coach. **2** give hints to (*don't coach the contestant*). **3** use tame cattle etc. as a lure for wild cattle etc.

coacher n. *Aust.* a tame beast used as a lure in the attempt to catch wild ones, esp. wild cattle and brumbies.

coagulant / koh-**ag**-yoo-luhnt / n. a substance that causes coagulation.

coagulate / koh-**ag**-yoo-layt / v. change from a liquid to a semisolid; clot, curdle. ☐ **coagulation** n.

coal n. **1** a hard black mineral used for burning to supply heat. **2** a piece of this. ☐ **carry coals to Newcastle** take a thing to a place where it is already plentiful (since Newcastle in England used to be a coal-mining area). **coal scuttle** a container for coal to supply a domestic fire. **coal tar** tar produced when gas is made from coal. **haul over the coals** reprimand severely.

coalesce / koh-uh-**les** / v. combine and form one whole. ☐ **coalescence** n. **coalescent** adj.

coalface n. **1** the exposed working surface of coal in a mine. **2** *colloq.* any place where 'real' work is performed (as distinct from theorising etc.), the workplace as opposed to administration etc.

coalfield n. an area where coal occurs naturally.

coalition / koh-uh-**lish**-uhn / n. **1** union. **2** a temporary alliance, esp. of political parties.

coalmine n. a mine where coal is dug. ☐ **coalminer** n.

coarse adj. **1** composed of large particles, rough or loose in texture. **2** (of a person's features) rough or large. **3** rough or crude in manner or behaviour, not refined; crude, obscene (*coarse humour*). ☐ **coarsely** adv. **coarseness** n.

coarsen v. make or become coarse.

coast n. the seashore and the land near it; its outline. •v. **1** ride down a hill without using

coastal adj. of or near the coast.

coaster n. **1** a ship that travels along the coast from port to port. **2** a tray for a decanter; a small mat for a glass.

coastguard n. **1** an organisation that polices the coast to report passing ships, save lives at sea, prevent smuggling, etc. **2** any of its members.

coastline n. the shape or outline of a coast (*a rugged coastline*).

coat n. **1** an outdoor garment with sleeves. **2** an animal's hair or fur. **3** a covering layer (*a coat of paint*). • v. cover with a layer; form a covering to. ❑ **coat of arms** a design on a shield, used as an emblem by a family, city, or institution. **coat of mail** a jacket made of chain mail.

coathanger n. **1** *see* HANGER (sense 3). **2** (**the Coathanger**) Sydney Harbour Bridge (from its resemblance to the shape of a coathanger).

coating n. a covering layer (of paint etc.).

coax v. **1** persuade gently or gradually. **2** obtain in this way (*coaxed a smile out of her*).

coaxial / koh-**ak**-see-uhl / adj. having an axis in common. ❑ **coaxial cable** an electric cable in which there are two conductors, one inside the other with a layer of insulating material between.

cob n. **1** a roundish lump of coal etc. **2** = CORN COB. **3** a sturdy short-legged horse for riding. **4** a male swan.

cobalt / **koh**-bawlt, -bolt / n. **1** a chemical element (symbol Co), a hard white metal used in many alloys and with radioactive forms used in medicine and industry. **2** colouring matter made from this; its deep-blue colour.

Cobb & Co. an Australian coaching company founded in Melbourne in 1853 by four Americans. It serviced the goldfields and eventually the three eastern colonies, with 6,000 horses harnessed each day. The last service ran in 1924.

cobber *Aust.* n. (often used as a mode of address) friend, mate. • v. (often foll. by *up*) make friends (with).

cobble n. (in full **cobblestone**) a rounded stone used for paving. • v. **1** pave with cobblestones. **2** put together or mend roughly.

cobbler n. **1** a shoe repairer. **2** stewed fruit topped with a crust. **3** an iced drink of wine, sugar, etc. **4** *Aust.* a sheep that is difficult to shear and therefore the last to be shorn. **5** a WA freshwater catfish and a SA marine fish, both with harmful spiny fins. **6** (**cobblers**) *colloq.* nonsense (*what a load of cobblers!*). (¶ Sense 4 is a shortened form of *cobbler's last* as a pun on *last*.)

COBOL / **koh**-bol / n. a high-level computer language designed for use in business. (¶ *Common Business Oriented Language*.)

cobra[1] / **koh**-bruh, **kob**-ruh / n. a highly venomous snake of India and Sri Lanka as well as Africa which rears up and spreads its neck like a hood when excited.

cobra[2] / **kob**-ruh / n. *Aust.* a shipworm, a mollusc native to mangroves, boring into wood in brackish or sea water and traditionally eaten by Aborigines. (¶ Probably from Djangati.)

cobweb n. the fine network spun by a spider; a strand of this. ❑ **cobwebby** adj.

coca / **koh**-kuh / n. a South American shrub with leaves that are chewed as a stimulant.

cocaine / koh-**kayn** / n. a drug made from coca or prepared synthetically, used as a local anaesthetic or as a stimulant.

coccyx / **kok**-siks / n. (*pl.* **coccyges** / kok-**suy**-jeez /) a small triangular bone at the base of the spine.

cochineal / koch-uh-neel, koch-uh-**neel** / n. bright red colouring-matter made from the dried bodies of certain insects.

cochlea / **kok**-lee-uh / n. (*pl.* **cochleae**) the spiral cavity of the inner ear.

cock n. **1** a male bird, esp. of the domestic fowl. **2** a tap or valve for controlling the flow of a liquid. **3** *coarse colloq.* the penis. **4** a lever in a gun, raised ready to be released by the trigger. **5** *colloq.* (as a form of address) friend; fellow. **6** *colloq.* nonsense. • v. **1** raise or make upright or erect. **2** turn or move (the eye or ear) attentively or knowingly (*the dog cocked his ears*). **3** raise the cock of (a gun) ready for firing; set (the shutter of a camera) ready for release. ❑ **at half cock** only half ready. **cock-a-hoop** adj. pleased and triumphant. **cock-and-bull story** a foolish story that one should not believe. **cock a snook** *see* SNOOK. **cock-eyed** *colloq.* **1** crooked, askew. **2** absurd, not practical. **cock up** *colloq.* make a mess of, bungle. **cock-up** n. *colloq.* a muddle or a bungle.

cockade / ko-**kayd** / n. a rosette of ribbon worn on a hat as a badge.

cockatiel n. (also **cockateel**) a small Australian parrot with a long tapering crest.

cockatoo n. (*pl.* **cockatoos**) **1** any of several large parrots of Australia etc. having powerful beaks and erectile crests. **2** *Aust.* a lookout posted by those engaged in an illegal activity. **3** *Aust.* a farmer with a small holding. **4** *Aust. hist.* a convict serving a sentence on Cockatoo Island. • v. *Aust.* act as a lookout for others.

Cockatoo Island an island of about 16 hectares in the mouth of the Parramatta River, near Sydney Harbour. It was used in the early days of settlement as a prison for intractable convicts.

cockatrice / **kok**-uh-truhs, -truys / n. **1** = BASILISK. **2** a fabulous animal hatched by a snake from an egg laid by a cock, and having the body of a snake with the head, wings, and legs of a cock, and a glance that instantly kills.

cockerel n. a young male bird.

cocker spaniel n. a small spaniel with a silky coat.

cockie n. *Aust. colloq.* a cockroach.

cockle *n.* **1** an edible bivalve shellfish of Europe; its shell. **2** (in full **cockleshell**) a small shallow boat. **3** a pucker or wrinkle in paper, glass, etc. □ **warm the cockles of one's heart** make one contented.

cockney *n.* (*pl.* **cockneys**) **1** a native of London, esp. of the East End or speaking its dialect. **2** the dialect or accent used by cockneys. **3** *Aust.* a young schnapper. • *adj.* of cockneys or cockney. (¶ From *cokeney* 'cock's egg'.)

cockpit *n.* **1** the compartment for the pilot and crew of an aircraft or spacecraft. **2** the well where the wheel is situated in certain small yachts etc. **3** the driver's seat in a racing car. **4** a place made for cock fighting.

cockroach *n.* a flat brown beetle-like insect that infests kitchens etc.

cockscomb *n.* the fleshy crest of a cock.

cocksure *adj.* over-confident; arrogant.

cocktail *n.* **1** a mixed alcoholic drink. **2** an appetiser containing shellfish or fruit (*prawn cocktail*). **3** any mixture of diverse elements.

cocky[1] *adj.* (**cockier**, **cockiest**) conceited and arrogant. □ **cockily** *adv.* **cockiness** *n.*

cocky[2] *n. Aust. colloq.* a cockatoo. □ **cocky apple** a tree of northern Australia having an edible egg-shaped fruit (often eaten by cockatoos).

cocky[3] *n. Aust.* **1** a farmer with a small holding (*cow cocky; fruit cocky*). **2** (now often applied to) a substantial farmer or the rural interests generally (*cockies protesting outside Parliament*). **3** (as *adj.*) pertaining to farmers (*the cocky vote*). • *v.* farm, esp. in a small way. □ **cocky country** a district chiefly devoted to small farming. **cocky gate** (also **cocky's gate**) an improvised gate. **cocky's joy** (also **cocky's delight**) treacle or golden syrup.

coco *n.* (*pl.* **cocos**) a coconut palm.

cocoa *n.* **1** powder made from crushed cacao seeds. **2** a drink made from this. □ **cocoa bean** a cacao seed.

coconut *n.* **1** the hard-shelled nut of the coco palm, containing a sweetish pale grey water. **2** its edible white lining. **3** *Aust.* (in Aboriginal English) an Aborigine living in a manner perceived as repudiating Aboriginal identity (*a coconut is brown on the outside and white underneath*). □ **coconut matting** matting made from the tough fibre of the coconut's outer husk. **coconut milk 1** the thick milky juice squeezed from the grated flesh of the coconut and used in cooking, esp. in curries. **2** coconut water. **coconut water** the drinkable sweetish watery liquid exuded when the coconut is cracked.

cocoon / kuh-**koon** / *n.* **1** the silky sheath round a chrysalis. **2** a protective wrapping. • *v.* protect by wrapping or enclosing (*he lives a sheltered life, cocooned from the world*).

Cocos Islands / **koh**-kuhs / (also **Keeling Islands**) a group of about twenty small islands in the Indian Ocean, administered by Australia 1955–84, and becoming part of Australia in 1984.

cocotte / koh-**kot** / *n.* a small fireproof dish for cooking and serving food.

COD *abbr.* cash on delivery.

cod[1] *n.* (*pl.* **cod**) **1** any of a number of large sea fish such as the Atlantic cod, used as food, including the bearded rock cod and the beardie (or ling) of southern Australian waters. **2** any of several unrelated Australian fish such as the Murray cod. □ **cod-liver oil** oil obtained from cod livers, rich in vitamins A and D.

cod[2] *n.* (usu. in *plural*) the scrotum; testicle(s).

coda / **koh**-duh / *n.* the concluding passage of a piece of music.

coddle *v.* **1** cherish and protect carefully; pamper. **2** cook (eggs) in water just below boiling point.

code *n.* **1** a prearranged word or phrase representing a message, for secrecy. **2** a system of words, letters, or symbols used to represent others, esp. in order to send messages by machine (e.g. the *Morse code*). **3** a set of laws or rules (*a code of practice for advertisers*). **4** a set of program instructions for use in a computer. • *v.* put into code.

codeine / **koh**-deen / *n.* a white substance made from opium, used to relieve pain or induce sleep.

codex / **koh**-deks / *n.* (*pl.* **codices** / **koh**-duh-seez /) **1** an ancient manuscript text in book form, not in a continuous roll. **2** a collection of pharmaceutical descriptions of drugs etc.

codger *n. colloq.* a person, esp. a strange one.

codicil / **koh**-duh-sil, **kod**-uh- / *n.* an addition to a will.

codify / **koh**-duh-fuy / *v.* (**codified**, **codifying**) arrange (laws or rules) systematically into a code. □ **codification** *n.* **codifier** *n.*

codlin *n.* **1** (also **codling**) a kind of cooking apple. **2** a moth whose larva feeds on apples. **3** a small codfish.

codpiece *n. hist.* a bag or flap at the front of a man's breeches to enclose the genitals.

codswallop *n. colloq.* nonsense, rubbish.

coed *adj. colloq.* coeducational. • *n.* a school for both sexes.

coeducation *n.* education of boys and girls in the same classes. □ **coeducational** *adj.*

coefficient / koh-uh-**fish**-uhnt / *n.* **1** *Maths* a quantity placed before and multiplying an algebraic expression. **2** *Physics* a multiplier or factor by which a property is measured (*coefficient of expansion*).

coelacanth / **see**-luh-kanth / *n.* a large sea fish formerly thought to be extinct.

coelenterate / suh-**len** tuh-rayt, -ruht / *n.* a sea animal with a simple tube-shaped or cup-shaped body (including sea anemones, jellyfish, and corals).

coeliac disease / **see**-lee-ak / *n.* a disease causing inability to digest gluten.

coenobite / **see**-nuh-buyt / *n.* (also **cenobite**) a monk who lives as a member of a monastic community.

coequal *adj.* equal to one another.

coerce / koh-**ers** / *v.* compel by threats or force. □ **coercion** / koh-**er**-shuhn / *n.*

coercive / koh-**er**-siv / *adj.* using coercion.

coeval / koh-**ee**-vuhl / *adj.* having the same age; existing at the same epoch. •*n.* a coeval person, a contemporary. □ **coevally** *adv.*

coexist *v.* exist together, esp. in peace despite different views. □ **coexistence** *n.* **coexistent** *adj.*

coextensive *adj.* extending over the same space or time.

coffee *n.* **1** the bean-like seeds of a tropical shrub, roasted and ground for making a drink. **2** this drink. **3** light brown colour.

coffer *n.* **1** a large strong box for valuables. **2** (**coffers**) funds, financial resources.

Coffey, Essie (original name: Essiena Goodgabah) (1942–98), AO, Aboriginal Australian activist who made the internationally acclaimed film *My Survival as an Aboriginal*.

coffin *n.* a box in which a dead body is placed for burial or cremation.

cog *n.* each of a series of teeth on the edge of a wheel, fitting into and pushing those on another wheel.

cogent / **koh**-juhnt / *adj.* convincing, compelling belief (*a cogent argument*). □ **cogently** *adv.* **cogency** *n.*

cogitate / **koj**-uh-tayt / *v.* think deeply. □ **cogitation** *n.*

cognac / **kon**-yak / *n.* high-quality brandy, esp. that made in Cognac, France.

cognate / **kog**-nayt / *adj.* **1** related; descended from a common ancestor. **2** (of words) having the same linguistic family or derivation (e.g. English *father*, German *Vater*, Latin *pater*, Sanskrit *pitr̥*, Sinhalese *pitha*, etc.). •*n.* **1** a relative. **2** a cognate word.

cognisant / **kog**-nuh-zuhnt / *adj.* aware, having knowledge. □ **cognisance** *n.*

cognition / kog-**nish**-uhn / *n.* the faculty of knowing or perceiving things.

cognitive / **kog**-nuh-tiv / *adj.* of cognition.

cognomen / kog-**noh**-muhn / *n.* **1** a nickname. **2** an ancient Roman's personal name or epithet.

cognoscente / kon-yuh-**shen**-tee / *n.* (*pl.* *cognoscenti*) a connoisseur. (¶ Italian)

cohabit *v.* live together as husband and wife (esp. of a couple who are not married to each other). □ **cohabitation** *n.* **cohabitee** *n.*

cohere / koh-**heer** / *v.* **1** stick together, remain united in a mass (*the particles cohere*). **2** be logical or consistent.

coherent / koh-**heer**-ruhnt / *adj.* **1** cohering. **2** connected logically, not rambling in speech or in reasoning. □ **coherently** *adv.* **coherence** *n.*

cohesion / koh-**hee**-zhuhn / *n.* cohering, a tendency to stick together. □ **cohesive** *adj.*

cohort *n.* **1** a division of the ancient Roman army, one-tenth of a legion. **2** persons grouped together; a group having a common statistical characteristic.

coif *n. archaic* a close-fitting cap.

coiffed / kwahft / *adj.* (of the hair) arranged, done.

coiffeur / kwah-**fer** / *n.* a hairdresser. (¶ French)

coiffeuse / kwah-**ferz** / *n.* a female hairdresser.

coiffure / kwah-**fyoor** / *n.* a hairstyle.

coign / coin / *n.* □ **coign of vantage** a favourable position for observation or action.

coil *v.* wind into rings or a spiral. •*n.* **1** something coiled. **2** one ring or turn in this. **3** a length of wire wound in a spiral to conduct electric current. **4** a contraceptive device for insertion into the womb.

coin *n.* a small stamped piece of metal as official money; coins collectively. •*v.* **1** make (coins) by stamping metal. **2** *colloq.* make (money) in large quantities. **3** invent (a word or phrase).

coinage *n.* **1** coining. **2** coins; the system of coins in use. **3** a coined word or phrase.

coincide / koh-uhn-**suyd** / *v.* **1** occur at the same time (*his holidays don't coincide with mine*). **2** occupy the same portion of space. **3** agree (*our tastes coincide*).

coincidence / koh-**in**-suh-duhns / *n.* **1** coinciding. **2** occurrence of similar events at the same time by chance.

coincident / koh-**in**-suh-duhnt / *adj.* coinciding.

coincidental / koh-in-suh-**den**-tuhl / *adj.* happening by coincidence. □ **coincidentally** *adv.*

coir / **koi**-uh / *n.* fibre from the outer husk of the coconut, used for ropes, matting, etc.

coition / koh-**ish**-uhn / *n.* sexual intercourse.

coitus / **koh**-uh-tuhs / *n.* coition. □ **coitus interruptus** sexual intercourse with withdrawal of the penis before ejaculation. □ □ **coital** *adj.*

coke *n.* **1** the solid substance left after coal gas and coal tar have been extracted from coal, used as fuel. **2** *colloq.* cocaine.

Col. *abbr.* Colonel.

col *n.* a depression in a range of mountains.

cola / **koh**-luh / *n.* (also **kola**) **1** a West African tree bearing seeds containing caffeine. **2** a carbonated drink usu. flavoured with these.

colander / **kul**-uhn-duh, **kol**- / *n.* a container with holes for straining water from foods.

colane / kuh-**layn**, **kol**-ayn / *n. Aust.* = EMU APPLE (sense 1). (¶ Wiradhuri)

cold *adj.* **1** at or having a low temperature. **2** not heated, having cooled after being heated or cooked (*my tea's cold*). **3** *colloq.* unconscious (*knocked him cold*). **4** without friendliness, affection, or enthusiasm (*got a cold reception*). **5** (of colours) suggesting coldness. **6** (of the scent in hunting) faint because no longer fresh. **7** (in children's games) far from finding or guessing what is sought. •*adv.* unrehearsed (*I can't do it cold*). •*n.* **1** lack of heat or warmth; low temperature. **2** an infectious illness causing catarrh and sneezing. ☐ **cold-blooded 1** having a body temperature that varies with the temperature of surroundings. **2** unfeeling, deliberately ruthless (*a cold-blooded killer*). **cold chisel** a chisel for cutting metal, stone, or brick. **cold front** the forward edge of an advancing mass of cold air. **cold fusion** nuclear fusion at room temperature, esp. as a possible energy source. **cold shoulder** deliberate unfriendliness. **cold-shoulder** *v.* treat with deliberate unfriendliness. **cold sore** inflammation and blistering around the mouth, caused by the *herpes simplex* virus. **cold storage 1** storage in a refrigerated place. **2** postponement (of plans etc.). **cold sweat** sweating induced by fear or illness. **cold turkey** *colloq.* the sudden withdrawal of narcotic drugs from an addict. **cold war** intense hostility between nations without actual fighting. **get cold feet** feel afraid or reluctant. ☐ ☐ **coldly** *adv.* **coldness** *n.*

coldie *n. Aust. colloq.* a glass, bottle, or can of well-chilled beer.

Cole, Edward William (1832–1918), Australian founder of a chain of bookshops and author of the popular *Cole's Funny Picture Book*.

Colebee one of two Aborigines captured in 1789 by Governor Arthur Phillip as part of an attempt to learn about Aboriginal life and language (*see* BENNELONG).

Coleridge, Samuel Taylor (1772–1834), English poet.

Coles the surname of five Australian brothers who from a small beginning in 1914 developed what is now one of Australia's largest retail chains, Coles Ltd.

coleslaw *n.* finely shredded raw cabbage with carrots etc. coated in dressing, as a salad.

Colette / ko-**let** / (born Sidonie Gabrielle Claudine) (1873–1954), French novelist.

coleus / **koh**-lee-uhs / *n.* a plant with coloured leaves.

colic *n.* severe spasmodic abdominal pain. ☐ **colicky** *adj.*

colitis / kuh-**luy**-tuhs / *n.* inflammation of the lining of the colon.

collaborate *v.* **1** work in partnership. **2** cooperate with an enemy. ☐ **collaboration** *n.* **collaborator** *n.*

collage / ko-**lah**zh, kuh-**lah**zh / *n.* an artistic composition made by fixing bits of paper, cloth, string, etc. to a surface.

collagen / **kol**-uh-juhn / *n.* a protein substance found in bone and tissue, yielding gelatin on boiling.

collapse *v.* **1** fall down or in suddenly. **2** lose strength, force, or value suddenly (*enemy resistance collapsed*). **3** fold or be foldable. **4** cause to collapse. •*n.* collapsing; a breakdown.

collapsible *adj.* made so as to fold together compactly (*a collapsible canoe*).

collar *n.* **1** a band round the neck of a garment. **2** a band of leather etc. put round the neck of an animal. **3** a band, ring, or pipe holding part of a machine. **4** a coloured marking resembling a collar round the neck of a bird or animal. •*v.* **1** gain control over (*he's collared the market in cherry-pits*). **2** *colloq.* take for oneself; seize.

collarbone *n.* the bone joining the breastbone and shoulder blade; the clavicle.

collate / kuh-**layt**, ko- / *v.* **1** compare in detail. **2** collect and arrange systematically (*collate information*). ☐ **collator** *n.*

collateral / kuh-**lat**-uh-ruhl / *adj.* **1** side by side, parallel. **2** additional but subordinate (*collateral evidence*). **3** descended from the same ancestor but by a different line (*a collateral branch of the family*). •*n.* a collateral person or security. ☐ **collateral damage** destruction or injury beyond that intended or expected, esp. around a military target. **collateral security** an additional security pledged; security lodged by a third party, or consisting of stocks, shares, property, etc. as opposed to a personal guarantee. ☐ ☐ **collaterally** *adv.*

collation *n.* **1** collating; something collated. **2** a light meal.

colleague *n.* a fellow official or worker, esp. in a business or profession.

collect[1] / **kol**-ekt / *n.* a short prayer or set of prayers said at Mass etc. in the Catholic and Anglican Churches.

collect[2] / kuh-**lekt** / *v.* **1** bring or come together. **2** get from a number of people; ask for (payment or contributions) from people. **3** seek and obtain specimens of, esp. as a hobby or for study. **4** fetch (*collect the children from school*). **5** gather (one's thoughts) into systematic order or control. **6** *colloq.* win (*with this lucky lottery ticket, I'm bound to collect*). **7** *Aust. colloq.* (esp. of a motor vehicle) collide with (*lost control of the ute and collected two cats and a cow*). •*adj.* & *adv.* (of a parcel, telephone call, etc.) to be paid for by the recipient.

collectable *adj.* (also **collectible**) suitable for being collected as a hobby etc. •*n.* an item sought by collectors.

collected *adj.* **1** grouped or gathered together. **2** calm and self-controlled. ☐ **collectedly** *adv.*

collection *n.* **1** collecting. **2** money collected at a church service, or for a charity, etc. **3** objects collected systematically or placed together; an accumulation (*a stamp collection; a collection of dust*).

collective *adj.* of a group taken as a whole (*our collective impression of the new plan*). •*n.* a cooperative enterprise; its members (*women's collective*). ☐ **collective bargaining** bargaining by an organised group of employees. **collective**

collectivise

farm a farm or group of smallholdings organised and run by its workers, usu. under State control.

collective noun a noun that is singular in form but denotes many individuals, e.g. *army, cattle, committee, herd*. **collective ownership** ownership of land etc. by all and for the benefit of all. □ **collectively** *adv.*

collectivise *v.* (also **-ize**) bring from private into collective ownership. □ **collectivisation** *n.*

collectivism *n.* the theory or practice of collective ownership of land and the means of production. □ **collectivist** *n.*

collector *n.* **1** a person who collects things of interest. **2** a person who collects money etc. due (*rent collector; ticket collector*).

colleen / ko-**leen** / *n. Irish* a girl.

college *n.* **1** an educational establishment for higher or professional education. **2** a residential part of a university. **3** (in names) a senior secondary school (*Xavier College*). **4** the buildings of any of these. **5** an organised body of professional people with common purposes and privileges (*College of Physicians*).

College of Cardinals (in full **Sacred College of Cardinals**) **1** all the cardinals of the Catholic Church as constituting the pope's council. **2** those cardinals (under a certain age) eligible to elect a new pope from among their number.

collegiate / kuh-**lee**-juht / *adj.* of or constituted as a college; corporate.

collide *v.* **1** (of a moving object) strike violently against something; meet and strike. **2** (of interests or opinions) conflict; (of persons etc.) have such a conflict.

collie *n.* a sheepdog with a long pointed muzzle and shaggy hair.

collier *n.* **1** a coalminer. **2** a ship that carries coal as its cargo; a member of its crew.

colliery *n.* a coalmine and its buildings.

Collins, David (1756–1810), English naval officer, Deputy Judge-Advocate of Botany Bay, and Lieutenant-Governor of Van Diemen's Land (1803–10), author of *An Account of the English Colony of NSW* (1798, 1802).

Collins Street cocky *n.* (usu. *derog.*) a person whose interests are in the city but who buys rural property, farms, etc., usu. as a tax write-off. (¶ *Collins Street* a principal business street in Melbourne.)

colonial

collision *n.* **1** the violent impact of a moving body with another or with a fixed object. **2** a clash of interests etc.

collocate *v.* **1** place together or side by side. **2** bring together for purposes of comparison. **3** juxtapose (a word etc.) with another so as to form a collocation. □ **collocator** *n.*

collocation *n.* **1** collocating. **2** *Linguistics* **a** the customary association of a particular word with other particular words, e.g. *as bold as brass*. **b** any short group of words (*the collocation 'a round square' seems to make no sense*).

colloid *n.* **1** a substance consisting of ultra-microscopic particles. **2** a mixture of such particles dispersed in another substance. **3** a gluey substance. □ **colloidal** *adj.*

colloquial / kuh-**loh**-kwee-uhl / *adj.* suitable for ordinary conversation but not for formal speech or writing. □ **colloquially** *adv.*

colloquialism *n.* a colloquial word or phrase.

colloquy / **kol**-uh-kwee / *n. formal* a conversation.

collude *v.* conspire together.

collusion / kuh-**loo**-*zh*uhn / *n.* an agreement between two or more people for a deceitful or fraudulent purpose. □ **collusive** *adj.*

collywobbles *n.pl. colloq.* **1** a rumbling or pain in the stomach. **2** nervousness.

cologne / kuh-**lohn** / *n.* eau-de-cologne or other lightly scented liquid, used to cool and scent the skin.

Colombia a republic in South America. □ **Colombian** *adj.* & *n.*

Colombo / kuh-**lum**-boh / the capital of Sri Lanka.

colon / **koh**-luhn / *n.* **1** the lower and greater part of the large intestine. **2** a punctuation mark (:) (see panel).

colonel / **ker**-nuhl / *n.* an army officer commanding a regiment, ranking next below a brigadier. □ **colonelcy** *n.*

colonial *adj.* **1** of a colony or colonies; of colonialism. **2** *Aust. hist.* of an Australian Colony or Colonies before Federation. **3** *Aust. hist.* Australian, usu. as distinct from British. **4** (of architecture, furniture, etc.) of, belonging to, or characteristic of pre-Federation Australia. • *n.* **1** an inhabitant of a colony. **2** *Aust.* (chiefly *hist.*) a person born in Australia of immigrant descent (as

Colon :

A colon is used:
1   between two main clauses of which the second explains, enlarges on, or follows from the first, e.g.
        It was not easy: to begin with I had to find the right house.
2   to introduce a list of items (a dash should not be added), and after expressions such as *namely, for example, to resume, to sum up, and the following*, e.g.
        You will need: a tent, a sleeping bag, cooking equipment, and insect repellent.
3   before a quotation, e.g.
        The anthem begins: 'Australians all, let us rejoice'.
4   between numbers that are in proportion,
        e.g. 1:2 = 2:4.

opposed to an immigrant from Britain). ❑ **colonial experience** *Aust. hist.* **1** first-hand knowledge of life in outback Australia. **2** (also **colonial experiencer**) a British youth trying to acquire this. **colonial goose** a boned and stuffed roast leg of mutton. **colonial youth** *Aust. hist.* a young person born in Australia (as opposed to an immigrant); such persons collectively (also known as 'currency').

colonialism *n.* the policy of acquiring or maintaining colonies.

colonic / koh-**lon**-ik / *adj.* of the intestinal colon.

colonise *v.* (also **-ize**) **1** establish a colony in; join a colony. **2** (of plants and animals) become established in an area. ❑ **colonisation** *n.*

colonist *n.* a pioneer settler in a colony.

colonnade *n.* a row of columns.

colonoscopy / kol-uh-**nos**-kuh-pee / *n.* an examination of the colon and rectum, using a video-camera instrument etc. introduced through the anus.

colony *n.* **1** an area of land settled or conquered by a distant nation and controlled by it. **2** its inhabitants. **3** (prior to Federation) one of the British Colonies in Australia or these collectively; (after Federation) used loosely of Australia as a former British Colony. **4** people of one nationality or occupation etc. living in a particular area; the area itself (*the artists' colony*). **5** a separate or segregated group (*a nudist colony*). **6** a group of animals or organisms living close together.

colophon / **kol**-uh-fon, -fuhn / *n.* **1** a decoration at the end of a chapter or book etc., giving the writer's or printer's name. **2** a publisher's or printer's imprint, esp. on a title page.

coloration *n.* (also **colouration**) colouring.

coloratura / kol-uh-ruh-**too**-ruh, -**tyoo**-ruh / *n.* **1** elaborate ornamentation of a vocal melody. **2** a soprano skilled in singing this.

colossal *adj.* **1** immense. **2** *colloq.* remarkable, splendid. ❑ **colossally** *adv.*

Colosseum / kol-uh-**see**-uhm / a vast amphitheatre in Rome, begun *c*.AD 75.

colossus / kuh-**los**-uhs / *n.* (*pl.* **colossi** / kuh-**los**-uy / *or* **colossuses**) **1** an immense statue. **2** a person of immense importance and influence.

colostomy / kuh-**los**-tuh-mee / *n.* an operation to make an opening in the abdominal wall through which the bowel can empty.

colour (also **color**) *n.* **1** the sensation produced by rays of light of different wavelengths; a particular variety of this. **2** the use of all colours, not only black and white (*a colour film*). **3** the pigmentation of the skin, esp. if dark; this as ground for prejudice or discrimination. **4** ruddiness of complexion. **5** pigment, paint, or dye. **6** the flag of a ship or regiment. **7** (**colours**) a coloured ribbon or uniform etc. worn to signify membership of a school, club, team, etc. • *v.* **1** put colour on; paint, stain, or dye. **2** change colour; blush. **3** give a special character or bias to (*his political opinions colour his writings*). ❑ **colour bar** racial discrimination against non-White people. **colour-blind** unable to see the difference between certain colours. **colour sergeant** a senior sergeant of an infantry company. **give** (*or* **lend**) **colour to** give an appearance of truth to.

colourant *n.* (also **colorant**) colouring matter.

colouration alternative spelling of COLORATION.

coloured (also **colored**) *adj.* **1** having colour. **2** wholly or partly of non-white descent. **3** (also **Coloured**) (in South Africa) of mixed white and non-white descent. • *n.* **1** a coloured person. **2** (**Coloured**) (in South Africa) a person of mixed white and non-white descent.

colourful *adj.* (also **colorful**) **1** full of colour. **2** with vivid details (*a colourful account of his journey*). ❑ **colourfully** *adv.*

colouring *n.* (also **coloring**) **1** the way in which something is coloured. **2** a substance used to colour things.

colourise *v.* (also **-ize**) add colour to a black and white film by means of a computer process.

colourless *adj.* (also **colorless**) **1** without colour. **2** lacking character or interest (*a colourless personality*).

colposcopy *n.* medical examination of the vagina and neck of the womb. ❑ **colposcope** *n.*

colt *n.* **1** a young male horse. **2** *Sport* an inexperienced player. ❑ **coltish** *adj.*

columbine *n.* a garden plant bearing purple-blue etc. flowers with pointed spurs at the back of each one. Also called *granny bonnet.*

Columbus, Christopher (1451–1506), Italian explorer in the service of Spain, who in 1492 discovered the New World.

column *n.* **1** a round pillar. **2** something shaped like this (*a column of smoke*). **3** a vertical section of a printed page (*there are two columns on this page*). **4** a regular feature in a newspaper. **5** a long narrow formation of troops or vehicles etc. ❑ **columnar** / kuh-**lum**-nuh / *adj.* **columned** *adj.*

columnist / **kol**-uhm-nuhst / *n.* a journalist who regularly writes a column.

.com *abbr.* denoting an email address or a site on the Internet that is commercial in nature.

coma / **koh**-muh / *n.* a state of deep unconsciousness.

Comanche / kuh-**man**-chee / *n.* **1** a North American Indian people. **2** their language.

comatose / **koh**-muh-tohz, -tohs / *adj.* **1** in a coma. **2** drowsy.

comb *n.* **1** a strip of plastic etc. with teeth, used for tidying the hair or holding it in place. **2** something shaped or used like this, e.g. for separating strands of wool or cotton. **3** *Aust.* the lower, fixed, and toothed part of the cutting-piece of a shearing machine, either of the standard breadth of 63.5 mm (*narrow comb*) or of greater breadth (*wide comb*). **4** the fleshy crest of a fowl. **5** a honeycomb. • *v.* **1** tidy or untangle with a comb. **2** search thoroughly (*combed the bush for the missing boy*).

☐ **comb out 1** arrange hair loosely by combing. **2** remove with a comb. **3** search out and get rid of.

combat *n.* a fight or contest. •*v.* (**combated, combating**) **1** engage in combat with. **2** oppose; strive against (*combat the spread of racism*).

combatant / **kom**-buh-tuhnt / *adj.* fighting. •*n.* one who is engaged in fighting.

combative / **kom**-buh-tiv / *adj.* eager to fight, aggressive.

comber *n.* **1** a person or thing that combs. **2** a long curling wave; a breaker.

combi *n. colloq.* (in full **combivan**) a small light van. (¶ From *Kombivan* trademark.)

combination *n.* **1** combining, being combined. **2** a number of people or things that are combined. **3** a sequence of numbers or letters used in opening a combination lock. ☐ **combination lock** a lock that can be opened only by turning one or more dials into a particular series of positions.

combine *v.* / kuhm-**buyn** / join or be joined into a group, set, or mixture. •*n.* / **kom**-buyn / **1** a combination of people or firms acting together in business. **2** (in full **combine harvester**) a combined reaping and threshing machine.

combings *n.pl.* loose hair removed by a comb or brush.

combining form *n.* a word or partial word used in combination with another to form a different word (e.g. *Anglo-* = English, *bio-* = life, *-graphy* = writing).

combo *n.* (*pl.* **combos**) *colloq.* **1** a small jazz or dance band. **2** *Aust.* **a** a white man who lives with an Aboriginal woman. **b** a white man who sexually exploits Aboriginal women. **3** a combination; a combined unit.

combustible / kuhm-**bus**-tuh-buhl / *adj.* capable of catching fire and burning; used for burning. •*n.* a combustible substance. ☐ **combustibility** *n.*

combustion / kuhm-**bus**-chuhn / *n.* **1** the process of burning. **2** a chemical process (accompanied by heat) in which substances combine with oxygen in air.

come *v.* (**came, come, coming**) **1** move or be brought towards the speaker or a place or point. **2** (of an illness) begin to develop. **3** arrive, reach a point, condition, or result; happen (*when winter comes; we came to a decision*). **4** be available (*the dress comes in 3 sizes*). **5** occur as a result (*that's what comes of being too confident*). **6** (foll. by *of*) be descended (*she comes of an old convict family*). **7** (foll. by *from*) be or have been a native or resident of (*I come from Sri Lanka*). **8** *colloq.* play the part of; behave like (*don't come the raw prawn with me!*). **9** *coarse colloq.* have an orgasm; ejaculate semen. •*interj.* think again, don't be hasty (*oh come, it's not that bad!*). •*n.* (also **cum**) *coarse colloq.* semen ejaculated. ☐ **come across 1** find or meet unexpectedly. **2** *colloq.* be effective or understood; give a specified impression (*she came across very well; he comes across as a bit of a dill*). **3** *colloq.* hand over, contribute (money, information, etc.) (*will he come across, do you think?*). **come again?** *colloq.* what did you say? **come by** obtain (a thing). **come clean** *colloq.* confess fully. **come down 1** collapse; fall, become lower. **2** decide (*came down in favour of spending it all*). **3** (of a river) be in flood. **come-hither** *adj.* enticing, flirtatious. **come in 1** take a specified position in a race or competition (*he came in third*). **2** be received as income. **3** have a part to play, serve a purpose (*it will come in useful; where do I come in?*). **come in for** receive a share of. **come in spinner!** *Aust.* the invitation to toss the coins in two-up. **come into** inherit. **come of age** reach adult status. **come off it!** *colloq.* stop talking or behaving like that. **come-on** *n. colloq.* an enticement. **come out 1** emerge with a specified result. **2** (of the sun, moon, etc.) emerge from behind clouds. **3** become known; be published; be solved. **4** erupt; become covered (in a rash). **5** declare one's opinions or feelings publicly (*came out in favour of the plan*). **6** openly declare that one is a homosexual (*I've come out to my family and friends*). **7** go on strike. **come out of the closet** stop concealing the fact that one is homosexual. **come round 1** make a casual or informal visit. **2** recover from faintness or bad temper. **3** be converted to another person's opinion. **4** recur. **come to 1** amount to, be equivalent to. **2** regain consciousness. **come up** arise for discussion etc., occur (*a problem has come up*). **how come?** *colloq.* why? how is it that?

comeback *n.* **1** a return to one's former successful position. **2** *colloq.* a reply or retort. **3** *Aust.* a sheep bred from crossbred and purebred parents for both wool and meat.

comedian *n.* **1** an actor who plays comic parts. **2** a humorous entertainer. **3** a person who behaves humorously.

comedienne / kuh-mee-dee-**en** / *n.* a female comedian.

comedown *n.* **1** a loss of status. **2** a disappointment.

comedy *n.* **1** a light amusing play or film. **2** the branch of drama that consists of such plays. **3** humour.

comely / **kum**-lee / *adj. archaic* handsome, good-looking. ☐ **comeliness** *n.*

comer / **kum**-uh / *n.* one who comes, esp. an applicant (*the first comers; all comers*).

comestibles / kuh-**mes**-tuh-buhlz / *n.pl. formal* things to eat.

comet / **kom**-uht / *n.* an object in space that orbits the sun, usu. with a bright, burning centre and a long, hazy tail pointing away from the sun.

comeuppance *n. colloq.* deserved punishment.

comfort *n.* **1** a state of ease and contentment. **2** relief of suffering or grief. **3** a person or thing that gives this. •*v.* give comfort to.

comfortable *adj.* **1** giving ease and contentment. **2** not close or restricted (*won by a comfortable margin*). **3** feeling at ease, in a state of comfort. **4** having or providing freedom from financial worry (*a comfortable income*). □ **comfortably** *adv.*

comforter *n.* **1** a person who comforts. **2** *archaic* a woollen scarf.

comfrey / **kum**-free / *n.* a tall plant with bell-shaped purple or white flowers.

comfy *adj. colloq.* comfortable.

comic *adj.* **1** causing amusement or laughter. **2** of comedy. •*n.* **1** a comedian. **2** a paper (usu. for children) with series of strip cartoons. □ **comic strip** a sequence of drawings telling a story. □□ **comical** *adj.* **comically** *adv.*

coming *see* COME. •*adj.* **1** approaching, next (*the coming week*). **2** likely to be important in the near future (*a coming man*). •*n.* arriving (*comings and goings*).

comity / **kom**-uh-tee / *n. formal* **1** courtesy, friendship. **2** an association of nations etc. for their mutual benefit. □ **comity of nations** nations' friendly recognition of each other's laws and customs.

comma *n.* a punctuation mark (,) indicating a slight pause or break between parts of a sentence, or separating words or figures in a list (see panel).

command *n.* **1** an order, an instruction. **2** an instruction to a computer. **3** the right to control others, authority (*she is in command*). **4** ability to use something, mastery (*he has a good command of languages*). **5** a body of troops or staff. •*v.* **1** give a command or order to. **2** have authority over. **3** have at one's disposal (*the firm commands great resources*). **4** deserve and get (*they command our respect*). **5** look down over or dominate from a strategic position (*the tower commands the harbour*). □ **command module** the control compartment in a spacecraft.

commandant / **kom**-uhn-dant, -dahnt / *n.* the officer in command, esp. of a military academy.

commandeer *v.* **1** seize for military purposes. **2** seize for one's own purposes.

Comma ,

The comma marks a slight break between words, phrases, etc. In particular, it is used:
1. to separate items in a list, e.g.
    red, white, and blue
    We bought some shoes, socks, gloves, and handkerchiefs.
    Will you have potatoes, peas, or carrots?
2. to separate adjectives that describe something in the same way, e.g.
    It is a hot, dry, dusty place.
    but not if they describe it in different ways, e.g.
    a distinguished foreign author
    or if one adjective adds to or alters the meaning of another, e.g.
    a bright red tie
3. to separate main clauses, e.g.
    Cars will park here, and buses will turn left.
4. to separate a name or word used to address someone, e.g.
    David, I'm here.
    Well, Mr Jones, we meet again.
    Have you seen this, my friends?
5. to separate a phrase, e.g.
    Having had lunch, we went back to work.
    especially in order to clarify meaning, e.g.
    In the valley below, the town looked very small.
6. after words that introduce direct speech, or after direct speech where there is no question mark or exclamation mark, e.g.
    They answered, 'Here we are'.
    'Here we are', they answered.
7. after *Dear Sir, Dear Sarah*, etc., and *Yours faithfully, Yours sincerely*, etc. in letters.
8. to separate a word, phrase, or clause that is secondary or adds information or a comment, e.g.
    I am sure, however, that it will not happen.
    Fred, who happens to be skinny, complained of the cold.
    but not with a relative clause (one usually beginning with who, which, or that) that restricts the meaning of the noun it follows, e.g.
    Men who are skinny feel the cold more than men who are fat.

No comma is needed between a month and a year in dates, e.g.
in December 1993
or between a number and a road in addresses, e.g.
17 Warragamba Drive.

commander *n.* **1** a person who commands. **2** a naval officer ranking next below a captain. ☐ **commander-in-chief** *n.* the supreme commander, esp. of a nation's forces.

commanding *adj.* **1** impressive (*she has a commanding presence*). **2** (of a location) giving a wide view. **3** substantial (*Labor has a commanding lead*).

commandment *n.* a divine command.

commando *n.* (*pl.* **commandos**) **1** a military unit specially trained for making raids and assaults. **2** a member of such a unit.

commemorate *v.* **1** keep in the memory by means of a celebration or ceremony. **2** be a memorial to (*a plaque commemorates the victory*). ☐ **commemoration** *n.* **commemorative** *adj.*

commence *v.* begin. ☐ **commencement** *n.*

commend *v.* **1** praise. **2** recommend. **3** entrust, commit (*commending his soul to God*). ☐ **commendation** *n.*

commendable *adj.* worthy of praise. ☐ **commendably** *adv.*

commensurable / kuh-**men**-shuh-ruh-buhl / *adj.* able to be measured by the same standard.

commensurate / kuh-**men**-shuh-ruht / *adj.* **1** of the same size or extent. **2** proportionate (*the salary is commensurate with the responsibilities*).

comment *n.* an opinion given briefly about an event or in explanation or criticism. • *v.* utter or write comments.

commentary *n.* **1** a descriptive spoken account of an event or performance as it happens. **2** a collection of explanatory comments on a text etc.

commentate *v.* act as commentator.

commentator *n.* **1** a person who broadcasts a commentary. **2** a person who comments on current events.

commerce / **kom**-ers / *n.* all forms of trade and the services that assist trading, e.g. banking and insurance.

commercial *adj.* **1** of or engaged in commerce. **2** (of broadcasting) financed by firms etc. whose advertisements are included (*commercial radio*). **3** having financial profit as its primary aim rather than artistic etc. value; viewed as a matter of business. • *n.* a broadcast advertisement. ☐ **commercial traveller** a firm's representative who visits shops etc. to show samples and get orders. ☐☐ **commercially** *adv.*

commercialise *v.* (also **-ize**) make commercial; exploit or spoil for profit (*Christmas has been completely commercialised*). ☐☐ **commercialisation** *n.*

commercialism *n.* commercial practices and attitudes.

commie *n.* & *adj. colloq.* communist.

commination *n. literary* threatening of divine vengeance. ☐ **comminatory** / kom-uh-nuh-tuh-ree, -tree / *adj.*

commingle *v. literary* mingle.

comminute *v.* reduce to small portions or fragments. ☐ **comminution** *n.*

commiserate / kuh-**miz**-uh-rayt / *v.* express pity for, sympathise. ☐ **commiseration** *n.*

commissar / **kom**-uh-sar / *n. hist.* head of a Soviet government department.

commissariat / kom-uh-**sair**-ree-uht, -at / *n.* **1** a stock of food. **2** a military department supplying this. **3** *hist.* a government department of the USSR.

commissary / **kom**-uh-suh-ree / *n.* **1** a deputy; a delegate. **2** *Military* an officer responsible for the supply of food etc. to soldiers.

commission *n.* **1** the authority to perform a certain task or duty. **2** the task etc. given (*a commission to paint a portrait*). **3** the body of people to whom such authority is given. **4** a warrant conferring authority esp. on officers above a certain rank in the armed forces. **5** performance, committing (*the commission of a crime*). **6** payment to an agent for selling goods or services etc., often calculated in proportion to the amount sold. • *v.* **1** give a commission to. **2** place an order for (*commissioned a portrait*). ☐ **commission house** *Aust.* (in some States) a government owned house for people on low incomes. **in commission** ready for service. **out of commission** not in commission; not in working order.

commissionaire / kuh-mish-uh-**nair** / *n.* a uniformed attendant at the entrance to a theatre, hotel, etc.

commissioner *n.* **1** a person appointed by commission (e.g. the head of a police force etc.). **2** a member of a government commission. **3** a government official in charge of a district abroad.

commit *v.* (**committed**, **committing**) **1** do, perform (*commit a crime*). **2** entrust for safe keeping or treatment. **3** send (an accused person) to trial; send to prison. **4** pledge, bind with an obligation; (**commit oneself**) give a definite statement or opinion.

commitment *n.* **1** committing. **2** the state of being involved in an obligation. **3** an obligation or pledge.

committal *n.* **1** committing, esp. to prison or a psychiatric institution. **2** the burial of a dead person. ☐ **committal hearing** proceedings before a magistrate to determine whether a case should go for trial.

committed *adj.* **1** dedicated or pledged, esp. to support a doctrine or cause. **2** under obligation (*felt committed to stay*).

committee *n.* **1** a group of people appointed for a special function by (and usu. out of) a larger body. **2** (**Committee**) the whole House of Representatives when sitting as a committee during the committee stage of a bill. ☐ **committee stage** a stage of a bill's progress through parliament, following its second reading, when it may be considered in detail and amendments may be made.

commo *n. Aust. colloq.* a communist.

commode / kuh-**mohd** / *n.* a chamber pot mounted in a chair with a cover.

commodious / kuh-**moh**-dee-uhs / *adj.* roomy and comfortable.

commodity *n.* an article of trade, a product.

commodore / **kom**-uh-daw / *n.* **1** a naval officer ranking above a captain and below a rear admiral. **2** the commander of a squadron or other division of a fleet. **3** the president of a yacht club.

common *adj.* **1** of or affecting the whole community. **2** belonging to or shared by two or more people or things (*common knowledge*). **3** occurring frequently; familiar (*a common weed; the common cold*). **4** without special distinction, ordinary (*the common house spider*). **5** ill-bred, not refined in behaviour or style. ☐ **common denominator 1** *Maths* a common multiple of the numbers below the line of several fractions. **2** a common feature of several situations, members of a group, etc. **common heath** *Aust.* a small epacris with white, pink, or deep-red tube-like flowers, the floral emblem of Victoria. **common law** unwritten law based on custom and former court decisions. **common noun** *Grammar* a name denoting a class of objects or a concept, not a particular individual. **common or garden** *colloq.* ordinary. **common room** a room for the social use of students or teachers at a college etc. **common time** (in music) four crotchet beats in a bar. **in common** in joint use; shared as a possession, characteristic, or interest. ☐☐ **commonly** *adv.* **commonness** *n.*

commonality *n.* **1** the sharing of a characteristic. **2** a common occurrence. **3** = COMMONALTY.

commonalty / **kom**-uh-nuhl-tee / *n.* **1** the common people. **2** the general body (esp. of mankind).

commoner *n.* one of the common people.

Common Market the European Community.

commonplace *adj.* ordinary, usual; lacking originality. • *n.* something commonplace.

commonsense *n.* (also **common sense**) normal good sense in practical matters, gained by experience. • *adj.* (also **common-sense**) having or marked by commonsense.

commonsensical *adj.* having or marked by commonsense.

commonwealth *n.* **1** an independent nation or community, esp. a democratic republic. **2** (**the Commonwealth**) the title of the federated States and Territories of Australia. **3** (**Commonwealth**) the government of this Australian federation (also used as *adj.*). **4** (**the Commonwealth**) (in full **Commonwealth of Nations**) a loose international association, the members of which are nations that were previously part of the British Empire, as well as the United Kingdom, and dependencies. **5** *hist.* the republican government of Britain between the execution of Charles I in 1649 and the restoration of the monarchy in 1660.

Commonwealth Constitution the constitution of the Commonwealth of Australia, drawn up at two constitutional conventions, one in 1891, and the other in 1897–98, which, with only minor amendments, was enacted by the British parliament on 9 July 1900 and came into operation on 1 January 1901.

Commonwealth Games a competition for the best athletes of the Commonwealth of Nations, modelled on the Olympic Games and held every four years.

Commonwealth Scientific and Industrial Research Organisation (*abbr.* **CSIRO**) an Australian statutory body established in 1949 to carry out, for the Commonwealth, a wide range of scientific research activities.

commotion *n.* an uproar; fuss and disturbance.

communal / **kom**-yuh-nuhl, kuh-**myoo**-nuhl / *adj.* shared between members of a group or community (*a communal playground*). ☐ **communally** *adv.*

commune *n.* / **kom**-yoon / **1** a group of people sharing accommodation, goods etc., esp. as a political act. **2** a communal settlement, esp. for the pursuit of shared interests. • *v.* / kuh-**myoon** / communicate mentally or spiritually (*communing with the spirit of Uluru at dawn*).

communicable *adj.* able to be communicated or passed on.

communicant *n.* **1** a person who receives Holy Communion. **2** a person who communicates information.

communicate *v.* **1** make known. **2** transfer, transmit (*communicated the disease to others*). **3** (often foll. by *with*) pass news and information to and fro; have social dealings; have a meaningful relationship (*young people cannot always communicate with older ones*). **4** be connected (*the passage communicates with the hall and stairs*).

communication *n.* **1** communicating. **2** something that communicates information, a letter or message. **3** a means of communicating, e.g. a road, railway, telegraph line, radio, or other link between places. ☐ **communication cord** a cord or chain inside a train, to be pulled to stop the train in an emergency. **communication(s) satellite** a satellite used to relay telephone circuits or broadcast programs.

communicative / kuh-**myoo**-nuh-kuh-tiv / *adj.* ready and willing to talk and give information.

communion *n.* **1** fellowship, having ideas or beliefs in common (*Churches in communion with one another*). **2** social dealings between people. **3** a Christian denomination (*the Methodist communion*). **4** (**Communion** *or* **Holy Communion**) the Eucharist.

communiqué / kuh-**myoo**-nuh-kay / *n.* an official communication giving a report.

communism *n.* **1** a social system in which property is owned by the community and each member works for the common benefit. **2** (**Communism**) the form of socialist society established in Cuba, China, etc., and previously in the former Soviet Union.

communist *n.* **1** a supporter of communism. **2** (**Communist**) a member of the **Communist Party**, a political party supporting Communism. ☐ **communistic** *adj.*

community *n.* **1** a body of people living in one place or country and considered as a whole. **2** a group with common interests or origins (*Melbourne's large Greek community*). **3** fellowship, being alike in some way (*community of interests*). **4** a monastic etc. body practising common ownership; (*a community of nuns*). **5** a group of animals or plants living or growing together in the same area. ☐ **community centre** a place providing social, recreational, and educational facilities for a neighbourhood. **community language** any language (other than English or an Aboriginal language) spoken by Australians, e.g. Greek, Italian, Vietnamese, Yiddish. **community service** performance of specified unpaid services to the community, esp. as an alternative to serving a prison sentence.

commutable *adj.* **1** exchangeable, able to be exchanged for money. **2** (of a punishment) able to be commuted.

commute *v.* **1** travel some distance to and from one's daily work. **2** exchange for something else (*commuted part of his pension for a lump sum*). **3** change (a punishment) into something less severe. ☐ **commutation** *n.*

commuter *n.* a person who commutes to and from work.

Comoros / kom-uh-rohz / a republic consisting of a group of islands in the Indian Ocean north of Madagascar; capital, Moroni. ☐ **Comoran** *adj.* & *n.*

compact *n.* / kom-pakt / **1** an agreement, a contract. **2** a small flat container for face powder. • *adj.* / kuhm-**pakt** / **1** closely or neatly packed together. **2** concise. **3** (of a person) small but well-proportioned. • *v.* / kuhm-**pakt** / make compact; join or press firmly together or into a small space. ☐ **compact disc** a disc without grooves, on which sound or information is recorded digitally for reproduction by means of a laser beam directed on to it. ☐ ☐ **compacted** *adj.* **compaction** *n.* **compactly** *adv.* **compactness** *n.*

companion *n.* **1** a person who accompanies another or who shares in his or her work, pleasures, or misfortunes etc. **2** a person employed to live with and assist another. **3** a handbook or reference book. **4** each of two things that match or go together (*the companion volume will be published later*). **5** *euphemistic* a person's lover. **6** (**Companion**) a member of the highest General or Military Division of the Order of Australia. ☐ **companion plants** plants of different species which are supposed to benefit one another when planted side by side. **companion planting** the practice of planting companion plants side by side.

companionable *adj.* friendly, sociable. ☐ **companionably** *adv.*

companionship *n.* the state of being companions, the friendly feeling of being with another or others.

companionway *n.* a staircase from a ship's deck to the saloon or cabins.

company *n.* **1** companionship (*travel with us for company*). **2** a number of people assembled; guests. **3** the people with whom one spends one's time (*got into bad company*). **4** people working together or united for business purposes, a firm (*the ship's company*). **5** a subdivision of an infantry battalion.

comparable / kom-puh-ruh-buhl, -pruh-buhl / *adj.* (often foll. by *to*, *with*) able or suitable to be compared, similar. ☐ **comparably** *adv.* **comparability** *n.*

comparative *adj.* **1** involving comparison (*a comparative study of the output of two firms*). **2** estimated by comparison; relative (*their comparative merits; living in comparative comfort*). **3** of a grammatical form used in comparing, expressing 'more', e.g. *bigger, greater, worse*. • *n.* a comparative form of a word. ☐ **comparatively** *adv.*

compare *v.* judge the similarity between (one thing and another). ☐ **beyond compare** without equal. **compare notes** exchange ideas or conclusions. **compare to** liken, declare to be similar (*he compared the human body to a machine*). **compare with 1** consider (things or people) together so as to judge their similarities and differences. **2** be worthy of comparison (*he cannot compare with Patrick White as a novelist*).

comparison *n.* comparing. ☐ **beyond comparison** not comparable because one is so much better than the other(s).

compartment *n.* **1** one of the spaces into which a structure or other object is divided, separated by partitions. **2** such a division of a railway carriage. **3** an administrative unit of a forest.

compartmental / kom-paht-**men**-tuhl / *adj.* of or divided into compartments or categories.

compartmentalise *v.* (also -**ize**) divide into compartments or categories.

compass *n.* **1** a device for determining direction, with a needle that points to the magnetic north. **2** circumference, boundary; range, scope (*that's beyond my compass*). **3** (**compasses**) an instrument used for drawing circles, usu. with two legs joined at one end. • *v.* encompass.

compassion *n.* a feeling of pity that makes one want to help or show mercy. ☐ **compassionate** *adj.* **compassionately** *adv.*

compassionate leave *n.* leave granted on the grounds of bereavement etc.

compatible / kuhm-**pat**-uh-buhl / *adj.* **1** capable of living together harmoniously. **2** able to exist or be used together (*at a speed compatible with safety*). ☐ **compatibly** *adv.* **compatibility** *n.*

compatriot / kuhm-**pat**-ree-uht, -**pay**-tree-uht / *n.* a person from the same country as another.

compel *v.* (**compelled**, **compelling**) **1** use force or influence to cause (a person) to do something; allow no choice of action. **2** arouse irresistibly (*his courage compels admiration*).

compendious / kuhm-**pen**-dee-uhs / *adj.* giving much information concisely.

compendium / kuhm-**pen**-dee-uhm / *n.* (*pl.* **compendiums** *or* **compendia**) **1** a concise and comprehensive summary. **2** a collection of table games.

compensate *v.* **1** make a suitable payment in return for (loss or damage). **2** serve as a counterbalance (*our present success compensates for earlier failures*).

compensation *n.* **1** compensating or being compensated. **2** money etc. given to compensate for loss or damage.

compensatory / kom-**puhn**-say-tuh-ree / *adj.* compensating.

compère / **kom**-pair / *n.* a person who introduces the performers in a variety show etc. • *v.* act as compère (to).

compete *v.* take part in a competition or other contest; strive for superiority or supremacy.

competence / **kom**-puh-tuhns / *n.* (also **competency**) **1 a** the quality of being competent; ability. **b** an area in which a person is competent; a skill. **2** the legal capacity (of a court etc.) to deal with a matter. **3** a comfortably adequate income.

competent / **kom**-puh-tuhnt / *adj.* **1** having the ability or authority to do what is required. **2** adequate, satisfactory (*a competent knowledge of Japanese*). **3** (of a judge or court) authorised to deal with a matter; (of a person) having legal capacity and qualification. ☐ **competently** *adv.*

competition *n.* **1** a contest in which people try to do better than their rivals. **2** competing (*competition for export markets*). **3** those competing with oneself (*we have strong foreign competition*).

competitive *adj.* **1** of or involving competition (*competitive sports; the competitive spirit*). **2** (of a price) one which compares favourably with those of rivals. **3** having a strong urge to win. ☐ **competitively** *adv.* **competitiveness** *n.*

competitor *n.* one who competes; a rival, esp. in business.

compile *v.* **1** collect and arrange (information) into a list or book. **2** make up (a book etc.) in this way. **3** accumulate (*compiled a score of 160 runs*). **4** *Computing* translate (a programming language) into machine code. ☐ **compilation** / kom-puh-**lay**-shuhn / *n.*

compiler *n.* **1** a person who compiles information into a list or book. **2** *Computing* a program that translates instructions from a high-level language into a form which can be understood by the computer.

complacent / kuhm-**play**-suhnt / *adj.* smugly self-satisfied or calmly content. ☐ **complacently** *adv.* **complacency** *n.*

■ **Usage** Do not confuse with *complaisant*.

complain *v.* **1** say that one is dissatisfied, protest that something is wrong. **2** (foll. by *of*) state that one is suffering from (a pain etc.); state a grievance concerning (*complained of the delay*).

complainant *n.* the plaintiff (in certain lawsuits).

complaint *n.* **1** a statement saying that one is dissatisfied, a protest. **2** a cause of dissatisfaction (*a list of complaints*). **3** an illness.

complaisant / kuhm-**play**-zuhnt, -suhnt / *adj.* willing to do what pleases others. ☐ **complaisance** *n.*

■ **Usage** Do not confuse with *complacent*.

complement / **kom**-pluh-muhnt / *n.* **1** that which makes a thing complete. **2** the number or quantity needed to fill something (*the bus had its full complement of passengers*). **3** *Grammar* the word(s) added to a verb to complete the predicate. **4** the number of degrees needed to make up an angle to 90°. • *v.* make complete; form a complement to (*the hat complements the outfit*).

■ **Usage** Do not confuse with *compliment*.

complementary *adj.* completing, forming a complement. ☐ **complementary colours** two colours of light which when mixed have the appearance of white light (e.g. blue and yellow).

■ **Usage** Do not confuse with *complimentary*.

complete *adj.* **1** having all its parts, not lacking anything. **2** finished (*the work is now complete*). **3** thorough; in every way (*a complete stranger*). • *v.* **1** add what is lacking to (a thing) and make it complete. **2** finish (a piece of work etc.). **3** add what is required to (a thing) (*complete the questionnaire*). ☐ **completely** *adv.* **completeness** *n.*

completion / kuhm-**plee**-shuhn / *n.* completing, being completed.

complex / **kom**-pleks / *adj.* **1** made up of parts. **2** complicated. • *n.* **1** a complex whole. **2** *Psychology* a connected group of feelings or ideas that influence a person's behaviour or mental attitude (*a persecution complex; Oedipus complex*). **3** (in general use) a preoccupation; a feeling of inadequacy (*he has a complex about his legs being*

complexion   159   **comprehensive**

skinny). **4** a set of buildings (*a shopping complex*). ☐ **complexity** / kuhm-**plek**-suh-tee / *n.*

complexion *n.* **1** the colour, texture, and appearance of the skin of the face. **2** the general character or nature of things (*that puts a different complexion on the matter*).

compliance *n.* **1** obedience to a request or command. **2** a tendency or willingness to yield. ☐ **compliance plate** a metal plate near the engine of a car etc., indicating date of manufacture, design compliance, etc.

compliant / kuhm-**pluy**-uhnt / *adj.* complying, obedient.

complicate *v.* make complex or complicated.

complicated *adj.* made up of many parts; difficult to understand or use because of this.

complication *n.* **1** complicating; being made complicated. **2** a complex combination of things. **3** something that complicates or adds difficulties. **4** an illness or condition that arises during the course of another and makes it worse.

complicity / kuhm-**plis**-uh-tee / *n.* partnership or involvement in wrongdoing.

compliment *n.* **1** an expression of praise or admiration. **2** (**compliments**) formal greetings. • *v.* pay a compliment to, congratulate.

■ Usage Do not confuse with *complement*.

complimentary *adj.* **1** expressing a compliment. **2** given free of charge.

■ Usage Do not confuse with *complementary*.

compline / **kom**-pluhn, -pluyn / *n.* the last service of the day in the Catholic Church, said or chanted after vespers; a similar service in the High Anglican Church.

comply / kuhm-**pluy** / *v.* (**complied**, **complying**) (often foll. by *with*) do as one is asked or ordered (*comply with the rules*).

compo *n. Aust. colloq.* a payment or a series of payments made under a workers' compensation scheme. ☐ **on compo** in receipt of workers' compensation.

component / kuhm-**poh**-nuhnt / *n.* each of the parts of which a thing is composed. • *adj.* being a component.

comport *v.* ☐ **comport oneself** *literary* behave; conduct oneself (*I would comport myself hysterically were I an early Christian contemplating his first lion*). **comport with** suit, befit (*such behaviour does not comport with your principles*). ☐☐ **comportment** *n.*

compose *v.* **1** form, make up (*a footy team is composed of 18 players*). **2** create in music or literature. **3** arrange into good order. **4** make calm (*to compose oneself*). **5** *Printing* set up (type).

■ Usage See note at *comprise*.

composed *adj.* calm, with one's feelings under control. ☐ **composedly** / kuhm-**pohz**-uhd-lee / *adv.*

composer *n.* a person who composes music etc.

composite / **kom**-puh-zuht / *adj.* **1** made up of a number of parts or styles. **2** (of a plant) having a head of many flowers forming one bloom (e.g. the daisy). • *n.* **1** something made up of a number of parts. **2** a composite plant.

composition *n.* **1** putting together into a whole, composing. **2** something composed; a piece of music or writing; a short essay written as a school exercise. **3** the parts of which something is made up (*the composition of the soil*). **4** artistic arrangement (of the parts of a picture, subjects for a photograph, etc.). **5** mental constitution; character (*jealousy is not in his composition*). **6** a compound artificial substance. ☐ **compositional** *adj.*

compositor *n.* a person who sets up type for printing.

compos mentis *adj.* in one's right mind, sane. (¶ Latin)

compost *n.* **1** a mixture of decayed organic matter added to soil to improve it. **2** a mixture usu. of soil and other ingredients for growing seedlings, cuttings, etc. • *v.* treat with compost; make into compost.

composure *n.* calmness of mind or manner.

compote / **kom**-pot, -poht / *n.* fruit preserved or cooked in syrup.

compound[1] / **kom**-pownd / *adj.* made up of several parts or ingredients. • *n.* a compound thing or substance. ☐ **compound fracture** one where the fractured bone has pierced the skin. **compound interest** interest paid on the original capital and on the interest that has been added to it. **compound time** (in music) that with a subdivision of the unit into three, six, or nine.

compound[2] / kuhm-**pownd** / *v.* **1** put together to form a whole, combine (*grief compounded with fear*). **2** add to or increase (*your anxiety is only compounding the problem*). **3** come to an agreement, settle (*he compounded with his creditors*). **4** agree to refrain from revealing (a crime) (*compounding a felony*).

compound[3] / **kom**-pownd / *n.* **1** a fenced-in enclosure. **2** (in India, China, etc.) an enclosure in which a house or factory stands.

comprehend *v.* **1** grasp mentally, understand. **2** include (*this new TV documentary will comprehend many aspects of multicultural Australia*).

comprehensible *adj.* able to be understood. ☐ **comprehensibly** *adv.* **comprehensibility** *n.*

comprehension *n.* **1** understanding. **2** a text set as a test of understanding. **3** inclusion.

comprehensive *adj.* **1** inclusive; including much or all. **2** (of motor insurance) providing protection against most risks. ☐ **comprehensively** *adv.* **comprehensiveness** *n.*

compress *v.* / kuhm-**pres** / squeeze together to force into less space or shorter time. • *n.* / **kom**-pres / a pad or cloth pressed on the body to stop bleeding or to cool inflammation etc.

compressible *adj.* able to be compressed.

compression *n.* **1** compressing. **2** reduction in volume of the fuel mixture in an internal-combustion engine before ignition.

compressor *n.* a machine for compressing air or other gases.

comprise / kuhm-**pruyz** / *v.* **1** include. **2** consist of. **3** make up, compose.

■ **Usage** Note that it is incorrect to use *comprise* with *of*: *compose* should be used instead. Thus, while *a footy team comprises 18 players* (sense 2) is acceptable, *a footy team is comprised of 18 players* (sense 3) is not. Say *a footy team is composed of 18 players*.

compromise / **kom**-pruh-muyz / *n.* **1** making a settlement by each side giving up part of its demands. **2** a settlement made in this way. **3** something that is half-way between opposite opinions or courses of action etc. • *v.* **1** settle a dispute by a compromise. **2** expose to danger, suspicion, or scandal by unwise action.

comptroller / kuhn-**troh**-luh / *n.* (in titles of some financial officers) controller.

compulsion *n.* **1** compelling, being compelled. **2** an irresistible urge.

compulsive *adj.* **1** compelling; irresistible (*this novel makes for compulsive reading*). **2** acting as if from compulsion (*a compulsive gambler*). ☐ **compulsively** *adv.*

compulsory *adj.* that must be done, required by the rules etc. ☐ **compulsorily** *adv.*

compunction *n.* the pricking of conscience; a slight regret or scruple.

computable *adj.* able to be computed.

compute *v.* **1** reckon mathematically, calculate. **2** use a computer. ☐ **computation** *n.* **computational** *adj.*

computer *n.* an electronic machine for making calculations, storing and analysing information fed into it, or controlling machinery automatically. ☐ **computer language** any of numerous systems of rules, words, and symbols for writing computer programs or representing instructions etc. **computer-literate** (also **computerate**) knowledgable about and able to use computers efficiently (as opposed to **computer-illiterate**). **computer programmer** a person who writes computer programs. **computer science** the study of the principles and use of computers. **computer virus** *see* VIRUS (sense 3).

computerate / kuhm-**pyoo**-tuh-ruht / *adj.* = COMPUTER-LITERATE.

computerise *v.* (also **-ize**) equip with, perform, or produce by computer. ☐ **computerisation** *n.*

comrade *n.* **1** a companion in some activity; a friend. **2** a fellow socialist or Communist; a fellow member of the Australian Labor Party (often as a form of address). ☐ **comradely** *adv.* **comradeship** *n.*

con[1] *colloq. v.* (**conned**, **conning**) persuade or swindle after winning a person's confidence. • *n.* **1** a confidence trick. **2** a convict. ☐ **con artist** a con man. **con man** a confidence trickster.

con[2] *n.* (usu. as **cons**) reasons against (*consider the pros and cons*).

Conakry / **ko**-nuh-kree / the capital of Guinea.

concatenate / kuhn-**kat**-uh-nayt / *v.* link together (a chain of events, things, computer data, etc.), form a sequence or combination of. • *adj.* joined, linked. ☐ **concatenation** *n.*

concave *adj.* curving like the surface of a ball as seen from the inside. ☐ **concavity** / kon-**kav**-uh-tee / *n.*

conceal *v.* keep secret or hidden. ☐ **concealment** *n.*

concede / kuhn-**seed** / *v.* **1** admit to be true. **2** grant, allow; yield (*they conceded us the right to cross their land*). **3** admit defeat in, esp. before the official end of a contest.

conceit *n.* **1** too much pride in oneself. **2** *literary* a far-fetched comparison; a complex or surprising metaphor ('*the Antipodes in shoes/Have shod their heads in their canoes*' *is a conceit that doesn't work*).

conceited *adj.* being too proud of oneself. ☐ **conceitedly** *adv.*

conceivable *adj.* able to be imagined or believed. ☐ **conceivably** *adv.*

conceive *v.* **1** become pregnant. **2** form (an idea or plan etc.) in the mind; think, imagine.

concelebrate *v.* (of two or more priests) celebrate the Mass together.

concentrate *v.* **1** employ all one's thought, attention, or effort on something. **2** bring or come together to one place. **3** make less dilute. • *n.* a concentrated substance or solution.

concentrated *adj.* **1** (of a solution etc.) having a large proportion of effective elements, not dilute. **2** intense (*concentrated hatred*).

concentration *n.* **1** concentrating or being concentrated. **2** mental attention. **3** a concentrate. **4** the amount of a substance contained in another substance. ☐ **concentration camp** a place where civilian political prisoners, racial groups, etc. are brought together and confined, esp. in Nazi Germany for the mass extermination of Jews etc.

concentric / kuhn-**sen**-trik / *adj.* having the same centre (*concentric circles*). ☐ **concentrically** *adv.* **concentricity** / kon-sen-**tris**-uh-tee / *n.*

concept / **kon**-sept / *n.* an idea, a general notion (*the concept of freedom*).

conception *n.* **1** conceiving; being conceived. **2** an idea, plan.

conceptual *adj.* of mental concepts. ☐ **conceptually** *adv.*

conceptualise v. (also -**ize**) form a mental concept of. ▫ **conceptualisation** n.

concern v. **1** be about, have as its subject (*the story concerns a group of rabbits*). **2** be of importance to, affect. **3** take up the time or attention of. • n. **1** something of interest or importance, a responsibility (*it's no concern of mine*). **2** a connection, a share (*he has a concern in industry*). **3** worry, anxiety. **4** a business, a firm (*a going concern*).

concerned adj. **1** worried, anxious. **2** involved, interested. ▫ **concernedly** adv. **concernedness** n.

concerning prep. about, in regard to.

concert n. a musical performance of usu. several separate compositions. ▫ **concert pitch 1** *Music* the pitch internationally agreed whereby A above middle C = 440 Hz. **2** a state of keyed-up readiness, efficiency, keenness (for action etc.). **in concert** in combination, together.

concerted / kuhn-**ser**-tuhd / adj. **1** jointly arranged; done in cooperation. **2** (of music) arranged in parts for voices or instruments.

concertina n. **1** a portable musical instrument with hexagonal ends and bellows, played by squeezing while pressing studs at each end. **2** *colloq.* a side of lamb. • v. (**concertinaed**, **concertinaing**) fold or collapse like the bellows of a concertina.

concertise v. (also -**ize**) give a concert performance of music.

concerto / kuhn-**sher**-toh, -**cher**-toh / n. (pl. **concertos** or **concerti**) a musical composition for one or more solo instruments and an orchestra.

concession n. **1** conceding. **2** something conceded. **3** a right given by the owners of land to extract minerals etc. from it or to sell goods there (*an oil concession*). **4** a reduction in price for certain categories of person. ▫ **concessionary** adj.

concessionaire n. the holder of a concession.

conch n. the spiral shell of a kind of shellfish, sometimes used as a horn.

conchie *Aust. colloq. derog.* n. a conscientious objector. • adj. conscientious.

conchology / kong-**kol**-uh-jee / n. the study of shells and shellfish. ▫ **conchologist** n.

concierge / kon-see-**airzh** / n. **1** (in France and French-speaking countries) a doorkeeper or porter, esp. in a block of flats. **2** a person in a hotel employed to assist guests by booking tours, making reservations, etc.

conciliate v. **1** overcome the anger or hostility of, win the goodwill of. **2** reconcile (people who disagree). **3** (esp. in a dispute between employers and employees) attempt to bring the disputing parties to an agreement. ▫ **conciliation** n. **conciliator** n. **conciliatory** / kuhn-**sil**-yuh-tuh-ree, -tree / adj.

concise / kuhn-**suys** / adj. brief, giving much information in few words. ▫ **concisely** adv. **conciseness** n.

conclave / **kon**-klayv / n. **1** a private meeting. **2** *Catholic Church* an assembly of cardinals for the election of a pope; the meeting place for this (a building etc. into which the cardinals are locked until the new pope is elected).

conclude v. **1** bring or come to an end. **2** arrange, settle finally (*they concluded a treaty*). **3** arrive at a belief or opinion by reasoning.

conclusion n. **1** ending, an end (*at the conclusion of his speech*). **2** arrangement, settling (*conclusion of the treaty*). **3** a belief or opinion based on reasoning. ▫ **in conclusion** lastly, to conclude.

conclusive adj. ending doubt, completely convincing (*conclusive evidence of his guilt*). ▫ **conclusively** adv.

concoct / kuhn-**kokt** / v. **1** prepare by putting ingredients together. **2** invent (*concocted an excuse*). ▫ **concoction** n.

concomitant / kuhn-**kom**-uh-tuhnt / adj. accompanying; occurring together (*malnutrition is concomitant with poverty*). • n. an accompanying thing (*luxury is a concomitant of wealth*). ▫ **concomitance** n.

concord n. agreement or harmony between people or things. ▫ **concordant** / kuhn-**kaw**-duhnt / adj.

concordance / kuhn-**kaw**-duhns, kuhng- / n. **1** agreement. **2** an alphabetical index of all the words used in a book or by an author in all his writings (*a concordance to Shakespeare*).

concordat / kon-**kaw**-dat, kong- / n. an agreement made, esp. between the Vatican and a nation.

concourse / **kon**-kaws, **kong**- / n. **1** a crowd, a gathering. **2** an open area through which people pass, e.g. at a railway terminus.

concrete / **kon**-kreet, **kong**- / n. a mixture of cement with sand and gravel, used for building and paving. • adj. **1** existing in material form, able to be touched and felt. **2** definite, positive (*concrete evidence*). • v. cover with or embed in concrete.

concretion / kuhn-**kree**-shuhn / n. a hard solid mass.

concubine / **kong**-kyoo-buyn / n. **1** a secondary wife in countries where polygamy is customary. **2** a woman who lives with a man as his wife. ▫ **concubinage** / kuhn-**kyoo**-buh-nij, kon- / n.

concupiscence / kon-**kyoo**-puh-suhns / n. *formal* lust; sexual desire. ▫ **concupiscent** adj.

concur / kuhn-**ker** / v. (**concurred**, **concurring**) **1** agree in opinion. **2** happen together, coincide.

concurrence / kuhn-**ku**-ruhns / n. **1** agreement (*concurrence of opinion*). **2** simultaneous occurrence of events.

concurrent / kuhn-**ku**-ruhnt / adj. existing or occurring at the same time. ▫ **concurrently** adv.

concuss / kuhn-**kus** / v. affect with concussion.

concussion / kuhn-**kush**-uhn / n. **1** injury to the brain caused by a hard blow. **2** violent shaking.

Condamine a river of 690 km in south-western Qld.

condemn v. **1** express strong disapproval of. **2** pronounce guilty, convict. **3** sentence (*was condemned to death*). **4** destine to an unhappy fate. **5** declare unfit for use or uninhabitable (*condemned buildings*). ☐ **condemned cell** a cell for a prisoner condemned to death. ☐☐ **condemnation** / kon-dem-**nay**-shuhn / n.

condemnatory / kuhn-**dem**-nuh-tuh-ree, kon-dem-**nay**-tuh-ree, -tree / adj. expressing condemnation.

condensation n. **1** condensing or being condensed. **2** condensed liquid (esp. tiny droplets of water on a cold surface).

condense v. **1** make denser or more concentrated. **2** change or be changed from gas or vapour into liquid. **3** express in fewer words (*a condensed report on the meeting*). ☐ **condensed milk** milk made thick by evaporation and sweetened.

condenser n. **1** an apparatus for condensing vapour. **2** *Electricity* = CAPACITOR. **3** a lens for concentrating light.

Conder, Charles (1868–1909), Australian painter who was influenced by the impressionistic style of artists of the Heidelberg School in Melbourne, of which he became a member.

condescend v. behave in a way that shows one's feeling of dignity or superiority. ☐ **condescension** n.

condign / kuhn-**duyn** / adj. (of a punishment etc.) severe and well-deserved.

condiment / **kon**-duh-muhnt / n. a seasoning (such as salt or pepper) or a relish (such as chutney) for food.

condition n. **1** the state in which a person or thing is with regard to characteristics and circumstances. **2** a state of physical fitness or (of things) fitness for use (*get into condition; out of condition*). **3** an illness or abnormality (*she has a heart condition*). **4** something required as part of an agreement. **5** (**conditions**) the facts, situations, or surroundings that affect something (*working conditions are good*). • v. **1** bring into a desired condition; make physically fit; put into a proper state for work or use. **2** have a strong effect on. **3** train, accustom. ☐ **conditioned reflex** (*or* **response**) a reaction produced by training, not a natural one. **on condition that** provided that (a thing will be done).

conditional adj. containing a condition or stipulation (*a conditional offer*). ☐ **conditional emancipation** (also **conditional pardon**) *Aust. hist.* remission of a convict's sentence subject to certain conditions, but always precluding return to the British Isles until the expiration of the original sentence. ☐ **conditionally** adv.

conditioner n. a substance that conditions hair, fabric, etc.

condole / kuhn-**dohl** / v. (foll. by *with*) express sympathy. ☐ **condolatory** / kuhn-**doh**-luh-tree / adj. **condolingly** adv.

■ Usage *Condole* is often confused with *console¹*.

condolence n. (often as **condolences**) expression of sympathy.

condom / **kon**-dom / n. a rubber etc. sheath worn on the penis during sexual intercourse either as a contraceptive or as a safe sex measure to prevent infection by Aids etc.

condominium / kon-duh-**min**-ee-uhm / n. **1** joint control of a nation's affairs by two or more other nations. **2** a building containing individually owned flats.

condone / kuhn-**dohn** / v. **1** forgive or overlook (an offence or wrongdoing). **2** approve or sanction, usu. reluctantly (*condoned the use of force against the demonstrators*).

condor n. **1** a large vulture of South America. **2** a smaller vulture of North America.

conducive / kuhn-**dyoo**-siv / adj. (often foll. by *to*) helping to cause or produce (*smoking is not conducive to good health*).

conduct v. / kuhn-**dukt** / **1** lead or guide. **2** be the conductor of (a choir, orchestra, etc.). **3** manage or direct (business, negotiations, or an experiment). **4** have the property of allowing heat, light, sound, or electricity to pass along or through. • n. / **kon**-dukt / **1** a person's behaviour. **2** managing or directing affairs (*the conduct of the war*). ☐ **conduct oneself** behave.

conductance n. the power of a specified material to conduct electricity.

conduction n. the transmission or conducting of heat or electricity etc.

conductive adj. able to conduct heat or electricity. ☐ **conductivity** n.

conductor n. **1** a person who directs the performance of an orchestra or choir etc. by gestures. **2** one who collects the fares in a bus etc. **3** a substance that conducts heat or electricity etc.

conduit / **kon**-dit, **kon**-joo-uht / n. **1** a pipe or channel for conveying liquids. **2** a tube or trough protecting insulated electric wires.

cone n. **1** a solid body that narrows to a point from a round flat base. **2** something shaped like this. **3** the dry fruit of certain evergreen trees, consisting of woody scales arranged in a shape suggesting a cone.

conesticks n. any of about 40 species of plants native to WA having showy flowers followed by striking woody cones.

confab / **kon**-fab / *colloq.* n. a chat. • v. chat.

confabulate v. converse, chat. ☐ **confabulation** n.

confection n. a sweet dish or delicacy.

confectioner *n.* a maker or retailer of confectionery.

confectionery *n.* sweets, cakes, and pastries.

confederacy *n.* **1** a league or alliance, esp. of confederate States, a confederation. **2** a coming together for an unlawful or evil purpose.

confederate *adj.* allied, joined by agreement or treaty. •*n.* **1** a member of a confederacy. **2** an ally (esp. in a bad sense), an accomplice.

confederated *adj.* united by agreement or treaty.

Confederate States the 11 southern States which seceded from the United States in 1860–61 and formed a confederacy of their own (thus precipitating the American Civil War); it was overthrown in 1865.

confederation *n.* **1** joining in an alliance. **2** a confederated group of people, organisations, or States.

confer *v.* (**conferred**, **conferring**) **1** grant, bestow. **2** hold a conference or discussion. ☐ **conferrable** / kuhn-**fer**-ruh-buhl / *adj.*

conference *n.* a meeting for discussion. •*v.* take part in a conference.

conferment / kuhn-**fer**-muhnt / *n.* granting, bestowing.

confess *v.* **1** (often foll. by *to*) state formally that one has done wrong or has a weakness (*confessed to the crime*). **2** state one's attitude or reaction reluctantly (*I must confess that I am puzzled*). **3** declare one's sins formally to a priest in the sacrament of penance. **4** (of a priest) hear the confession of (*Father Brown confessed me this morning*).

confessedly / kuhn-**fes**-uhd-lee / *adv.* admittedly; by one's own confession.

confession *n.* **1** confessing. **2** a thing confessed, a statement of one's wrongdoing. **3** a declaration of one's beliefs (*a confession of faith*).

confessional *n.* an enclosed stall in a church, where a priest sits to hear confessions.

confessor *n.* **1** a priest who hears confessions and is empowered to give absolution. **2** a person who keeps to the Christian faith despite persecution, but not suffering martyrdom.

confetti *n.* bits of coloured paper thrown by wedding guests at the bride and groom.

confidant / **kon**-fuh-dant, -**dant** / *n.* a person in whom one confides.

confidante *n.* a woman in whom one confides.

confide *v.* **1** (foll. by *in*) talk confidentially to (*confided in his friend*). **2** (usu. foll. by *to*) tell (a secret) in confidence. **3** (foll. by *to*) entrust (an object, task, etc.) to.

confidence *n.* **1** firm trust. **2** a feeling of certainty, self-reliance, boldness (*he lacks confidence*). **3** something told confidentially (*has listened to many confidences*). ☐ **confidence man** a man who robs by means of a confidence trick. **confidence trick** a swindle in which the victim is persuaded to trust the swindler. **confidence trickster** a person who defrauds or tricks people, a swindler. **in a person's confidence** trusted with his or her secrets. **in confidence** as a secret.

confident *adj.* feeling confidence, bold. ☐ **confidently** *adv.*

confidential *adj.* **1** spoken or written in confidence, to be kept secret. **2** entrusted with secrets (*a confidential secretary*). **3** confiding (*spoke in a confidential tone*). ☐ **confidentially** *adv.* **confidentiality** *n.*

configuration *n.* **1** a method of arrangement (e.g. of apparatus or parts of a computer system). **2** a shape or outline.

configure *v.* set up (a computer system, apparatus, etc.) for a particular purpose.

confine *v.* / kuhn-**fuyn** / **1** keep or restrict within certain limits. **2** keep shut up. •*n.* (**confines**) / **kon**-fuynz / the limits or boundaries of an area.

confined *adj.* narrow, restricted (*a confined space*).

confinement *n.* **1** confining; being confined. **2** the time during which a woman is giving birth to a baby.

confirm *v.* **1** provide supporting evidence for the truth or correctness of; prove. **2** establish more firmly (*it confirmed him in his dislike of cats*). **3** make definite or valid formally (*bookings made by telephone must be confirmed in writing*). **4** administer the sacrament or religious rite of confirmation to.

confirmation *n.* **1** confirming. **2** something that confirms. **3** a sacrament or rite confirming a baptised person as a member of a particular Christian Church. **4** a ceremony confirming a person in the Jewish faith.

confirmed *adj.* firmly settled in some habit or condition (*a confirmed bachelor*).

confiscate / **kon**-fuhs-kayt / *v.* take or seize by authority. ☐ **confiscation** *n.*

conflagration / kon-fluh-**gray**-shuhn / *n.* a great and destructive fire.

conflate *v.* combine or blend together (esp. two variant texts into one). ☐ **conflation** *n.*

conflict *n.* / **kon**-flikt / **1** a fight, a struggle. **2** disagreement between people with different ideas or beliefs. •*v.* / kuhn-**flikt** / **1** fight, struggle. **2** be in opposition or disagreement.

confluence / **kon**-floo-uhns / *n.* a place where two rivers join.

confluent / **kon**-floo-uhnt / *adj.* flowing together, uniting.

conform *v.* **1** keep to rules or general custom (*he refuses to conform*). **2** (foll. by *to*, *with*) comply with; be in accordance with (*it doesn't conform to my idea of art*).

conformable *adj.* **1** similar. **2** consistent; adaptable.

conformation *n.* the way a thing is formed, its structure.

conformist / kuhn-**faw**-muhst / *n.* a person who readily conforms to established rules or standards etc.; a conventional person. ☐ **conformism** *n.*

conformity *n.* conforming to established rules or standards etc.

confound *v.* **1** astonish and perplex. **2** confuse. **3** *archaic* defeat, overthrow. •*interj.* an exclamation of annoyance (*confound it!*).

confounded *adj. colloq.* damned (*a confounded nuisance*).

confront / kuhn-**frunt** / *v.* **1** be or come face to face with (*the problems confronting us*). **2** face boldly as an enemy or in defiance. **3** bring face to face (*we confronted him with his accusers*). ☐ **confrontation** / kon-fruhn-**tay**-shuhn / *n.* **confrontational** *adj.*

Confucianism / kuhn-**fyoo**-shuh-niz-uhm / *n.* the moral and religious system founded by Confucius. ☐ **Confucian** *adj.* & *n.*

Confucius / kuhn-**fyoo**-shuhs / (551–479 BC), the most influential Chinese philosopher.

confuse *v.* **1** throw into disorder, mix up. **2** throw the mind or feelings of (a person) into disorder; destroy the composure of. **3** fail to distinguish between. **4** make unclear (*confuse the issue*). ☐ **confusable** *adj.*

confused *adj.* (of a person) not mentally sound or alert.

confusedly / kuhn-**fyoo**-zuhd-lee / *adv.* in a confused way.

confusion *n.* **1** confusing. **2** a confused state.

confute / kuhn-**fyoot** / *v.* prove (a person or argument) to be wrong. ☐ **confutation** / kon-fyoo-**tay**-shuhn / *n.*

conga *n.* **1** a Latin-American dance in which people form a long winding line. **2** a tall narrow drum beaten with the hands.

congeal / kuhn-**jeel** / *v.* make or become semi-solid instead of liquid. ☐ **congealment** *n.* **congelation** / kon-juh-**lay**-shuhn / *n.*

congenial / kuhn-**jee**-nee-uhl / *adj.* **1** pleasant because similar to oneself (*a congenial companion*). **2** suited or agreeable to oneself (*a congenial climate*). ☐ **congenially** *adv.* **congeniality** *n.*

congenital / kuhn-**jen**-uh-tuhl / *adj.* **1** existing since a person's birth (*a congenital deformity*). **2** as (or as if) such from birth (*a congenital liar*). ☐ **congenitally** *adv.*

conger / **kong**-guh / *n.* (in full **conger eel**) a large sea eel.

congested *adj.* **1** too full, overcrowded. **2** (of an organ or tissue of the body) abnormally full of blood or mucus.

congestion / kuhn-**jes**-chuhn / *n.* a congested condition.

conglomerate *adj.* / kuhn-**glom**-uh-ruht / gathered into a mass. •*n.* **1** a conglomerate mass. **2** a group formed by merging several different firms. •*v.* / kuhn-**glom**-uh-rayt / gather into a mass.

conglomeration *n.* a mass of different things put together.

Congo a republic in central Africa. ☐ **Congolese** *adj.* & *n.*

Congo, Democratic Republic of a republic in central Africa. From 1971 to 1997 it was known as Zaire.

congolli / kuhng-**goh**-lee / *n. Aust.* = TUPONG. (¶ Probably from an Aboriginal language.)

congratulate *v.* express pleasure to (a person) about his or her achievement or good fortune.

congratulation *n.* **1** congratulating. **2** (usu. in *plural*) an expression of this.

congratulatory *adj.* expressing congratulations.

congregate *v.* flock together; collect into a crowd.

congregation *n.* **1** a gathering of people, esp. for religious worship. **2** a committee of the College of Cardinals. ☐ **congregational** *adj.*

Congregationalism *n.* a form of Protestant church organisation in which each local church is independent. ☐ **Congregationalist** *n.*

congress *n.* **1** a formal meeting of delegates (from societies, nations, etc.) for discussion. **2** (**Congress**) the law-making body of a country, esp. of the USA. **3** *Literary* sexual intercourse.

congressional / kuhn-**gresh**-uh-nuhl / *adj.* of a congress.

congruent / **kong**-groo-uhnt / *adj.* **1** suitable, consistent. **2** (of geometrical figures) having exactly the same shape and size. ☐ **congruence** *n.* **congruency** *n.* **congruity** *n.*

conic / **kon**-ik / *adj.* of a cone.

conical *adj.* cone-shaped. ☐ **conically** *adv.*

conifer / **kon**-uh-fuh / *n.* a coniferous tree, including pines, firs, cedars, etc.

coniferous / kuh-**nif**-uh-ruhs / *adj.* bearing cones.

conjectural *adj.* based on conjecture.

conjecture *v.* guess. •*n.* a guess.

conjoin *v. formal* join together.

conjugal / **kon**-juh-guhl / *adj.* of marriage; of the relationship between husband and wife. ☐ **conjugally** *adv.*

conjugate *v.* / **kon**-juh-gayt / **1** give the different forms of (a verb). **2** unite, become fused; unite sexually. •*adj.* / **kon**-juh-guht / joined together, fused. ☐ **conjugation** *n.*

conjunct *adj.* joined together; combined; associated.

conjunction *n.* **1** a word that joins words, phrases, or sentences (see panel). **2** combination, union (*the four countries acted in conjunction*). **3** the occurrence of events etc. at the same time. **4** the apparent nearness of two or more heavenly bodies to each other.

conjunctiva / kon-jungk-**tuy**-vuh / *n.* the mucous membrane covering the eyeball and inner eyelid.

conjunctive *adj.* joining.

conjunctivitis *n.* inflammation of the surface of the conjunctiva.

conjure[1] / **kun**-juh / *v.* **1** perform tricks which appear to be magical (*conjuring tricks*). **2** summon (a spirit) to appear. ☐ **conjure up 1** produce as if from nothing (*they managed to conjure up a meal*). **2** produce in the mind (*mention of the Antarctic conjures up visions of snow and ice*).

conjure[2] / kuhn-**joor** / *v. formal* appeal solemnly to (*conjured them to keep the peace*).

conjuror *n.* (also **conjurer**) a person who performs conjuring tricks.

conk *colloq. n.* **1** the nose; the head. **2** a punch on the nose or head. •*v.* hit on the nose or head (*I'll conk you one*). ☐ **conk out** *colloq.* **1** (of a machine) break down, fail. **2** (of a person) become exhausted and give up; fall asleep; faint; die.

conkerberry *n.* either of two small trees of northern Australia, having perfumed flowers and sweet, black, edible berries. (¶ Mayi-Yapi and Mayi-Kulan *ganggabarri*.)

connect *v.* **1** join or be joined. **2** (of a train etc.) be timed to arrive so that passengers from one train etc. can catch another to continue their journey. **3** put into communication by telephone. **4** think of (things or persons) as being associated with each other. **5** *colloq.* hit or strike effectively.

connection *n.* **1** connecting, being connected. **2** a place where things connect; a connecting part. **3** a train etc. timed to connect with another. **4** a link, esp. by telephone. **5** (often as **connections**) a relative or associate, esp. with influence. **6** a link or relationship between ideas. **7** (often as **connections**) the owners etc. of a racehorse etc. ☐ **in connection with** with reference to, concerning.

connective *adj.* connecting (*connective tissue*).

connector *n.* a thing that connects others.

conning tower *n.* **1** a raised structure on a submarine, containing the periscope. **2** an armoured pilot house on a warship.

connive / kuh-**nuyv** / *v.* **1** (foll. by *at*) take no notice of (wrongdoing), thus seeming to consent to it. **2** (foll. by *with*) conspire (*connived with them to rob the bank*). ☐ **connivance** *n.*

connoisseur / kon-uh-**ser** / *n.* a person with great experience and appreciation of artistic and similar subjects.

connote / kuh-**noht** / *v.* imply in addition to the literal meaning. ☐ **connotation** *n.* **connotative** / **kon**-uh-tay-tiv, kuh-**noh**-tuh-tiv / *adj.*

connubial / kuh-**nyoo**-bee-uhl / *adj.* of marriage; of the relationship between husband and wife.

conquer *v.* **1** overcome in war, win. **2** overcome by effort (*conquer one's fear*). ☐ **conqueror** *n.*

conquest *n.* **1** conquering. **2** (**the Conquest** or **Norman Conquest**) the conquest of England by the Normans in 1066. **3** something got by conquering.

conquistador / kon-**kwis**-tuh-daw / *n.* (*pl.* **conquistadores** / kon-kwis-tuh-**daw**-reez / or **conquistadors**) a conqueror, esp. a member of the Spanish soldiers and adventurers who conquered South America in the 16th c.

Conrad, Joseph (1857–1924), Polish-born British novelist.

consanguineous / kon-sang-**gwin**-ee-uhs / *adj.* descended from the same ancestor. ☐ **consanguinity** *n.*

conscience *n.* **1** a person's sense of what is right and wrong, esp. in his or her own behaviour. **2** a feeling of remorse. ☐ **conscience money** money paid by a person who feels guilty, esp. about having evaded payment previously. **on one's conscience** causing one to feel guilty or remorseful. **prisoner of conscience** a person imprisoned for his or her political or religious views.

conscientious / kon-shee-**en**-shuhs / *adj.* showing (or done with) careful attention. ☐ **conscientious objector** one who refuses to do something (esp. to serve in the armed forces in a war) because he or she believes it is morally wrong. ☐☐ **conscientiously** *adv.* **conscientiousness** *n.*

conscious *adj.* **1** with one's mental faculties awake, aware of one's surroundings and identity. **2** aware of (*he was conscious of his failings; fashion-conscious*). **3** realised by oneself, intentional (*a conscious insult*). ☐ **consciousness-raising** the

Conjunction

A conjunction is used to join parts of sentences which usually, but not always, contain their own verbs, e.g.

He found it difficult **but** *I helped him.*
They made lunch **for** *Alice* **and** *Mary.*
I waited **until** *you came.*

The most common conjunctions are:

after	for	since	unless
although	if	so	until
and	in order that	so that	when
as	like	than	where
because	now	that	whether
before	once	though	while
but	or	till	

activity of raising people's social or political sensitivity or awareness. ☐ ☐ **consciously** *adv.* **consciousness** *n.*

conscript *v.* / kuhn-**skript** / summon for compulsory military service. • *n.* / **kon**-skript / a conscripted recruit. ☐ **conscription** *n.*

consecrate *v.* **1** make or declare sacred; dedicate formally to a religious or divine purpose. **2** (in Christian belief) transform (the substance of bread and wine) into the substance of the body and blood of Christ. **3** (foll. by *to*) devote to (a purpose) (*consecrated her life to serving the dying*). **4** ordain (a priest) as bishop. ☐ **consecration** *n.*

consecutive / kuhn-**sek**-yuh-tiv / *adj.* following continuously, in unbroken order. ☐ **consecutively** *adv.*

consensus / kuhn-**sen**-suhs / *n.* general agreement in opinion.

consent *v.* say that one is willing to do or allow what someone wishes. • *n.* agreement, permission. ☐ **age of consent** the age at which consent to sexual intercourse becomes valid in law.

consequence *n.* **1** a result produced by some action or condition. **2** importance (*a person of consequence; the matter is of no consequence*). ☐ **in consequence** as a result.

consequent *adj.* following as a result.

consequential / kon-suh-**kwen**-shuhl / *adj.* **1** following as a result. **2** important. ☐ **consequentially** *adv.*

consequently *adv.* as a result, therefore.

conservation *n.* **1** conserving, being conserved. **2** the preservation of the natural environment. **3** the preservation of works of art, documents, etc.

conservationist *n.* a person who supports environmental conservation.

conservatism *n.* a conservative attitude; conservative principles (general or political).

conservative *adj.* **1** disliking or opposed to change, esp. if rapid; tending to want to maintain existing institutions etc. **2** moderate, avoiding extremes (*conservative in his dress*). **3** (of an estimate etc.) purposely low. • *n.* **1** a conservative person. **2** a person having conservative political views. ☐ **conservatively** *adv.*

conservatorium / kuhn-**ser**-vuh-taw-ree-uhm / *n. Aust.* a school of music.

conservator / **kon**-ser-vay-tuh, kuhn-**serv**-uh-tuh / *n.* a person who conserves or keeps something safe; one who preserves and restores articles in a museum etc.

conservatory *n.* a greenhouse for tender plants.

conserve *v.* / kuhn-**serv** / keep from harm, decay, or loss, for future use. • *n.* / **kon**-serv / jam made from fresh fruit and sugar.

consider *v.* **1** think about, esp. in order to make a decision; weigh the merits of. **2** make allowances for (*consider people's feelings*). **3** think to be, suppose (*consider yourself lucky*). **4** (foll. by *that*) have the opinion (*he considers that the world is flat*).

considered *adj.* formed after careful thought (*a considered opinion*).

considerable *adj.* fairly great in amount or extent (*in considerable pain; of considerable importance*). ☐ **considerably** *adv.*

considerate *adj.* taking care not to inconvenience or hurt others. ☐ **considerately** *adv.*

consideration *n.* **1** careful thought. **2** being considerate, kindness. **3** a fact that must be kept in mind (*time is now an important consideration*). **4** payment given as a reward (*he will do it for a consideration*). ☐ **in consideration of** in return for; on account of. **take into consideration** allow for. **under consideration** being considered.

considering *prep.* taking into consideration (*she is very active, considering her age*). • *adv. colloq.* taking everything into account (*you've done very well, considering*).

consign *v.* **1** hand over or deliver formally. **2** give into someone's care. **3** assign; commit (*consign it to the rubbish bin*).

consignee / kon-suy-**nee** / *n.* the person to whom goods etc. are consigned.

consignment *n.* **1** consigning. **2** a batch of goods etc. consigned.

consignor *n.* one who consigns goods etc. to another.

consist *v.* **1** (foll. by *of*) be made up of (*the flat consists of 3 rooms*). **2** (foll. by *in*) have as its basis or essential feature (*its beauty consists in its use of colour*).

consistency *n.* **1** the degree of thickness, firmness, or solidity (*mix it to the consistency of thick cream*). **2** being consistent.

consistent *adj.* **1** conforming to a regular pattern or style, unchanging (*they have no consistent policy*). **2** not contradictory (*their reforms are consistent with their general policies*). ☐ **consistently** *adv.*

consistory *n.* a council of cardinals, or of the pope and cardinals.

consolable *adj.* able to be consoled.

consolation *n.* consoling; being consoled. ☐ **consolation prize** a prize given to a competitor who has just missed winning one of the main prizes.

console[1] / kuhn-**sohl** / *v.* comfort in time of sorrow or disappointment.

■ **Usage** *Console* is often confused with *condole*, which is different in that it is always followed by *with*.

console[2] / **kon**-sohl / *n.* **1** a bracket to support a shelf. **2** a frame containing the keyboards and stops etc. of an organ. **3** a panel holding the controls of electrical or other equipment; a workstation from which the operation of a computer

consolidate can be monitored and controlled. **4** a cabinet for a television etc.

consolidate v. **1** make or become secure and strong (*consolidating his position as leader*). **2** combine (territories, companies, debts, etc.) into one whole. ☐ **consolidated revenue** the main fund operated by a government into which tax revenue is paid. ☐☐ **consolidation** n.

consommé / **kon**-suh-may, kunh-**soh**-may / n. clear meat soup.

consonance / **kon**-suh-nuhns / n. agreement, harmony, esp. of a combination of notes in music.

consonant n. **1** a letter of the alphabet other than a vowel. **2** the speech sound it represents. • adj. consistent, harmonious (*actions that are consonant with his beliefs*). ☐ **consonantal** adj.

consort n. / **kon**-sawt / **1** a husband or wife, esp. of a monarch. **2** a small group of players, singers, or instruments. • v. / kuhn-**sawt** / associate, keep company (*consorting with criminals*).

consortium / kuhn-**saw**-tee-uhm, -shee-uhm / n. (pl. **consortia** or **consortiums**) a combination of countries, companies, or other groups acting together.

conspicuous adj. **1** easily seen, attracting attention. **2** worthy of notice. ☐ **conspicuously** adv. **conspicuousness** n.

conspiracy n. **1** conspiring. **2** a plan made by conspiring.

conspirator n. a person who conspires. ☐ **conspiratorial** adj. **conspiratorially** adv.

conspire v. **1** plan secretly with others, esp. for some unlawful purpose. **2** (of events) seem to combine (*events conspired to bring about his downfall*).

constable n. a police officer of the lowest rank.

constabulary / kuhn-**stab**-yuh-luh-ree / n. a police force.

constancy n. **1** the quality of being constant and unchanging. **2** faithfulness.

constant adj. **1** happening or continuing all the time; happening repeatedly. **2** unchanging, faithful (*remained constant to his principles*). • n. something that is constant and does not vary. ☐ **constantly** adv.

Constantine (d. 337), Roman emperor from 306, who encouraged toleration of the Christian faith.

Constantinople the former name of Istanbul.

constellation n. **1** a group of fixed stars whose outline is regarded as forming a particular figure, e.g. the Southern Cross. **2** a group of associated persons noteworthy in some way (*a constellation of young Australian musicians*).

consternation n. anxiety or dismay causing mental confusion.

constipate v. (usu. as **constipated** adj.) affect with constipation.

constipation n. a condition with hardened faeces and difficulty in emptying the bowels.

constituency n. **1** = ELECTORA... customers, supporters, etc.

constituent adj. **1** forming part of a v... *constituent parts*). **2** able to make or ch... constitution (*constituent assembly*). **3** appoin... or electing. • n. **1** a constituent part. **2** a membe... of a constituency.

constitute v. **1** make up, form (*12 months constitute a year*). **2** appoint (*they constituted him chief adviser*). **3** establish or be (*this does not constitute a precedent*).

constitution n. **1** constituting. **2** composition. **3** the body of fundamental principles according to which a country is organised. **4** general condition and character, esp. of a person's body (*she has a strong constitution*).

constitutional adj. **1** of a country's constitution; established, permitted, or limited by this (*a constitutional crisis; constitutional government*). **2** of or produced by a person's physical or mental constitution (*a constitutional weakness*). • n. a regular walk taken for the sake of one's health. ☐ **constitutionally** adv. **constitutionality** n.

constitutive adj. **1** able to form or appoint; constituent. **2** essential.

constrain v. **1** compel; oblige (*I am constrained to agree*). **2** confine; restrict (*the injury constrains her freedom of movement*).

constrained adj. (of the voice, manner, etc.) strained; forced, embarrassed; showing constraint.

constraint n. **1** constraining, being constrained; compulsion. **2** a strained manner caused by holding back one's natural feelings.

constrict v. tighten by making narrower, squeeze. ☐ **constriction** n. **constrictive** adj.

constrictor n. **1** a snake (esp. a boa) that kills by squeezing its prey to prevent it breathing. **2** a muscle that contracts an organ or part of the body.

construct v. / kuhn-**strukt** / make by placing parts together. • n. / **kon**-strukt / something constructed, esp. by the mind. ☐ **constructor** n.

construction n. **1** constructing; being constructed. **2** something constructed. **3** two or more words put together to form a phrase, clause, or sentence. **4** an interpretation (*put a bad construction on their refusal*). ☐ **constructional** adj.

constructive adj. offering helpful suggestions (*they made constructive criticisms*). ☐ **constructively** adv.

construe / kuhn-**stroo** / v. **1** interpret, explain (*her words were construed as a refusal*). **2** combine (words with others) grammatically. **3** analyse the syntax of. **4** translate word for word.

consul n. **1** either of the two chief magistrates in ancient Rome. **2** an official appointed to live in a foreign city to assist and protect his or her countrymen who live or visit there and to help

consultant.

consultant *n.* **1** a person qualified to give expert professional advice. **2** a senior medical specialist in a hospital.

consultative / kuhn-**sul**-tuh-tiv / *adj.* for consultation (*a consultative committee*).

consulting *adj.* giving professional advice (*a consulting physician*). □ **consulting room** a room in which a doctor interviews patients.

consume *v.* **1** use up (*much time was consumed in waiting*). **2** eat or drink up. **3** destroy completely; overwhelm (*fire consumed the buildings*). □ **consumable** *adj.* & *n.*

consumer *n.* a person who buys or uses goods or services. □ **consumer goods** those bought and used by individual consumers rather than used for producing other goods. **consumer price index** *Aust.* a measure of the cost of living based on a standard set of prices.

consumerism *n.* **1** the protection of consumers' interests. **2** high consumption of goods etc.

consuming *adj.* overwhelming, dominating (*a consuming ambition*).

consummate *v.* / **kon**-suh-mayt / **1** accomplish, make complete. **2** complete (a marriage) by sexual intercourse between the partners. • *adj.* / kuhn-**sum**-uht / supremely skilled (*a consummate artist*). □ **consummation** *n.*

consumption *n.* **1** consuming, using up, destruction. **2** the amount consumed. **3** use by a particular group (*a film unfit for children's consumption*). **4** *archaic* tuberculosis of the lungs.

consumptive *adj.* *archaic* suffering from tuberculosis of the lungs. • *n.* a person with tuberculosis.

cont. *abbr.* **1** continued. **2** contents.

contact / **kon**-takt / *n.* **1** touching, coming together. **2** being in touch, communication. **3** a connection for the passage of electric current. **4** a person who has recently been near someone with a contagious disease and may carry infection. **5** an acquaintance who may be contacted when one needs information or help. • *v.* get in touch with (a person). □ **contact lens** a small lens worn directly on the eyeball to correct vision. **contact period** *Aust.* the period when Aborigines and Europeans first interacted in a particular place.

contagion / kuhn-**tay**-juhn / *n.* **1** the spreading of disease by bodily contact or close association. **2** a disease spread in this way. **3** a corrupting influence.

contagious / kuhn-**tay**-juhs / *adj.* **1** able to be spread by contact or close association (*a contagious disease*). **2** capable of spreading disease in this way (*all these children are now contagious*). **3** (of emotions etc.) likely to be spread (*their enthusiasm was contagious*).

contain *v.* **1** have within itself (*the atlas contains 40 maps*). **2** consist of, be equal to (*a tablespoon contains 20 ml*). **3** restrain (*contained his anger with difficulty*). **4** keep within limits (*enemy troops were contained in the valley*).

container *n.* **1** a box or bottle etc. designed to contain a substance or goods. **2** a large metal box for transporting goods.

containerise *v.* (also **-ize**) transport by container; convert to this method of transporting goods. □ **containerisation** *n.*

containment *n.* the policy of preventing the expansion of a hostile country or influence.

contaminant *n.* a substance that contaminates or pollutes.

contaminate *v.* pollute (esp. with radioactivity). □ **contamination** *n.* **contaminator** *n.*

contemplate / **kon**-tuhm-playt / *v.* **1** gaze at thoughtfully. **2** consider. **3** intend (*he doesn't contemplate retiring*). **4** meditate. □ **contemplation** *n.*

contemplative / kuhn-**tem**-pluh-tiv / *adj.* thoughtful; devoted to religious contemplation. • *n.* a person devoted to religious contemplation, esp. a monk or nun of one of the contemplative orders of the Catholic Church. □ **contemplative order** an order of monks or nuns (e.g. the Trappist Order, the Carmelite Order) in which religious contemplation is central to the way of life.

contemporaneous *adj.* existing or occurring at the same time. □ **contemporaneously** *adv.* **contemporaneity** *n.*

contemporary / kuhn-**tem**-puh-ruh-ree, -puh-ree, -pree / *adj.* **1** living or occurring at the same time; of roughly the same age. **2** modern in style or design. • *n.* a person contemporary with another (*Ned Kelly and his contemporaries*).

contempt *n.* **1** the process or feeling of despising a person or thing. **2** the condition of being despised (*fell into contempt*). **3** disrespect. □ **contempt of court** disobedience or disrespect towards a court of law or its processes.

contemptible *adj.* deserving contempt. □ **contemptibly** *adv.* **contemptibility** *n.*

contemptuous *adj.* feeling or showing contempt. □ **contemptuously** *adv.*

contend *v.* **1** strive or fight in competition or against difficulties. **2** assert, argue (*the defendant contends that he is innocent*). □ **contender** *n.*

content[1] / kuhn-**tent** / *adj.* contented, satisfied with what one has. • *n.* being contented, satisfaction. • *v.* make content, satisfy.

content[2] / **kon**-tent / *n.* what is contained in something (*the contents of the barrel; butter has a high fat content*).

contented *adj.* happy with what one has; satisfied. ◻**contentedly** *adv.*
contention *n.* **1** contending; quarrelling, arguing. **2** an assertion made in arguing.
contentious / kuhn-**ten**-shuhs / *adj.* **1** quarrelsome. **2** likely to cause contention. ◻**contentiously** *adv.*
contentment *n.* a contented state; tranquil happiness.
conterminous *adj.* (often foll. by *with*) having a common boundary; coextensive.
contest *n.* / **kon**-test / **1** a struggle for superiority or victory. **2** a competition, a test of skill or ability etc. between rivals. •*v.* / kuhn-**test** / **1** compete for or in (*contest a seat at an election; contest an election*). **2** dispute, challenge (*contest a statement; contest a will*).
contestant *n.* one who takes part in a contest, a competitor.
context *n.* **1** the words that come before and after a particular word or phrase and help to fix its meaning. **2** the circumstances in which an event occurs (*shortages were tolerated in the context of war*). ◻**out of context** without the surrounding words and therefore giving a false impression of the meaning.
contiguous / kuhn-**tig**-yoo-uhs / *adj.* (usu. foll. by *to, with*) adjoining, in contact (*New South Wales and Victoria are contiguous States; Tasmania is not contiguous with mainland Australia*). ◻**contiguously** *adv.* **contiguity** / kon-tuh-**gyoo**-uh-tee / *n.*
continent[1] *n.* any of the world's seven main continuous expanses of land (Africa, Antarctica, Asia, Australia, Europe, N. and S. America).
continent[2] *adj.* **1** able to control the excretion of one's urine and faeces. **2** exercising self-restraint, esp. sexually. ◻**continence** *n.*
continental[1] *adj.* of a continent. ◻**continental breakfast** a light breakfast of coffee and rolls etc. **continental drift** the hypothesis that the continents are moving slowly over the surface of the earth. **continental quilt** a doona. **continental shelf** the shallow seabed bordering a continent.
continental[2] *n. US hist.* a currency note issued during the American War of Independence (and which depreciated sharply afterwards). ◻**not give** (or **care**) **a continental** *colloq.* not care at all; not give a damn.
contingency / kuhn-**tin**-juhn-see / *n.* **1** something unforeseen. **2** a possibility, something that may occur at a future date.
contingent / kuhn-**tin**-juhnt / *adj.* **1** happening by chance. **2** possible, liable to occur but not certain. **3** (usu. foll. by *on, upon*) depending on something that may or may not happen. •*n.* **1** a body of troops or ships etc. contributed to form part of a force. **2** a group of people forming part of a gathering (*the Australian contingent among the spectators at the Olympics*).

continual *adj.* constantly or frequently recurring; always happening. ◻**continually** *adv.*

■ **Usage** *Continual* is often confused with *continuous*. *Continual* is used of something that happens very frequently (e.g. *there were continual interruptions to the telecast*), while *continuous* is used of something that happens without a pause (e.g. *continuous rain all day*).

continuance *n.* **1** continuing. **2** duration.
continuation *n.* **1** continuing, starting again after ceasing. **2** a thing that continues something else (*the proposed continuation of the railway line*).
continue *v.* **1** keep up (an action etc.); do something without ceasing (*continued to read; continue the struggle*). **2** remain in a certain place or condition (*he will continue as manager*). **3** go further (*the road continues beyond the bridge*). **4** begin again after stopping (*the discussion will continue next week*).
continuity / kon-tuh-**nyoo**-uh-tee / *n.* **1** being continuous. **2** the uninterrupted succession of things. **3** the detailed scenario of a film or broadcast. **4** linkage between broadcast items.
continuo *n.* (*pl.* **continuos**) *Music* an accompaniment providing a bass line in Baroque music, usu. played on a keyboard instrument, e.g. a harpsichord.
continuous *adj.* continuing, without a break; uninterrupted, unbroken. ◻**continuously** *adv.*

■ **Usage** See note at *continual*.

continuum / kuhn-**tin**-yoo-uhm / *n.* (*pl.* **continua**) something that extends continuously.
contort / kuhn-**tawt** / *v.* force or twist out of the usual shape. ◻**contortion** / kuhn-**taw**-shuhn / *n.*
contortionist / kon-**taw**-shuhn-uhst / *n.* an entertainer who twists his or her body into unusual postures.
contour / **kon**-toor / *n.* **1** a line (on a map) joining the points that are the same height above sea-level. **2** an outline.
contra- *comb. form* against; opposite.
contraband *n.* **1** smuggled goods. **2** smuggling. •*adj.* forbidden to be imported or exported.
contraception / kon-truh-**sep**-shuhn / *n.* the prevention of pregnancy; the use of contraceptives.
contraceptive / kon-truh-**sep**-tiv / *adj.* preventing pregnancy. •*n.* a contraceptive drug or device.
contract *n.* / **kon**-trakt / **1** a formal agreement between people or groups or countries, esp. one enforceable by law. **2** a document setting out the terms of such an agreement. •*v.* / kuhn-**trakt** / **1** make or become smaller or shorter. **2** arrange or undertake by contract (*they contracted to supply oil to the factory*). **3** catch (an illness); form or acquire (a habit, a debt, etc.). ◻**contract in** (or **out**) choose to enter (or not enter) a scheme or commitment.

contractable *adj.* (of a disease) able to be contracted.

contractible *adj.* able to be shrunk or drawn together.

contractile *adj.* able to contract or to produce contraction. ☐ **contractility** *n.*

contraction *n.* 1 contracting. 2 a shortened form of a word or words (e.g. *he's*). 3 shortening of the uterine muscles during childbirth.

contractor *n.* one who makes a contract, esp. for constructing a building.

contractual / kuhn-**trak**-choo-uhl / *adj.* of a contract. ☐ **contractually** *adv.*

contradict *v.* 1 state that (what is said) is untrue or that (a person) is wrong. 2 state the opposite of, be contrary to (*these rumours contradict previous ones*). ☐ **contradiction** *n.* **contradictory** *adj.*

contradistinction *n.* a distinction made by contrasting.

contralto / kuhn-**trahl**-toh / *n.* (*pl.* **contraltos**) 1 the lowest female singing voice. 2 a singer with such a voice; a part written for it.

contraption *n. colloq.* an odd-looking gadget or machine.

contrapuntal *adj.* of or in counterpoint. ☐ **contrapuntally** *adv.*

contrariwise *adv.* / **kon**-truh-ree-wuyz / 1 on the other hand. 2 in the opposite way. 3 / kuhn-**trair**-ree-wuyz / perversely.

contrary / **kon**-truh-ree / *adj.* 1 opposite in nature; opposed (*the result was contrary to expectation*). 2 opposite in direction (*delayed by contrary winds*). 3 / kuhn-**trair**-ree / doing the opposite of what is expected or advised, wilful. • *n.* the opposite. • *adv.* in opposition, against (*acting contrary to instructions*). ☐ **on the contrary** in denial of what has just been said or implied and stating that the opposite is true. **to the contrary** proving or indicating the opposite (*there is no evidence to the contrary*). ☐ ☐ **contrarily** / **kon**-truh-ruh-lee / *adv.* / kuhn-**trair**-ruh-lee / *adj.* **contrariness** *n.*

contrast *n.* / **kon**-trahst / 1 the act of contrasting. 2 a difference clearly seen when things are put together. 3 something showing such a difference. 4 the degree of difference between tones or colours (e.g. in a television picture or photograph). • *v.* / kuhn-**trahst** / 1 compare or oppose two things so as to show their differences. 2 show a striking difference when compared.

contravene / kon-truh-**veen** / *v.* act in opposition to, conflict with (*contravening the law*). ☐ **contravention** / kon-truh-**ven**-shuhn / *n.*

contretemps / **kon**-truh-tong / *n.* 1 an unfortunate happening; a mishap. 2 a dispute or disagreement.

contribute / kuhn-**trib**-yoot / *v.* 1 give jointly with others, esp. to a common fund. 2 supply for publication in a newspaper or magazine book. 3 help to bring about (*drink contributed to his ruin*). ☐ **contribution** / kon-truh-**byoo**-shuhn / *n.* **contributor** / kuhn-**trib**-yoo-tuh / *n.*

contributory / kuhn-**trib**-yoo-tuh-ree, -tree / *adj.* 1 contributing to a result. 2 involving contributions to a fund (*a contributory pension scheme*).

contrite / **kon**-truyt, kuhn-**truyt** / *adj.* penitent, feeling great guilt. ☐ **contritely** *adv.* **contrition** / kuhn-**trish**-uhn / *n.*

contrivance / kuhn-**truy**-vuhns / *n.* 1 contriving. 2 something contrived, a plan. 3 a mechanical device.

contrive *v.* 1 plan cleverly; achieve in a clever or resourceful way. 2 manage (*contrived to make matters worse*). ☐ **contriver** *n.*

contrived *adj.* planned so carefully as to seem artificial, forced (*the plot of your novel sounds contrived*).

control *n.* 1 the power to give orders or to restrain something. 2 a means of restraining or regulating; a device by which a machine is operated. 3 restraint, self-restraint. 4 a standard of comparison for checking the results of an experiment. 5 a place where cars taking part in a race must stop for inspection etc. • *v.* (**controlled, controlling**) 1 have control of, regulate. 2 restrain. 3 check, verify (*the results of an experiment*). ☐ **controlling interest** ownership of so many shares etc. in a business that the holder can control its policies. **control tower** a tall building from which air traffic is controlled at an airport.

controllable *adj.* able to be controlled.

controller *n.* 1 a person or thing that controls. 2 a person in charge of expenditure.

controversial / kon-truh-**ver**-shuhl / *adj.* causing controversy.

controversy / **kon**-truh-ver-see, kuhn-**trov**-uh-see / *n.* a prolonged argument or dispute.

■ **Usage** The second pronunciation, stressed on the second syllable, is considered incorrect by some people.

controvert / **kon**-truh-vert, -**vert** / *v.* deny the truth of; contradict. ☐ **controvertible** *adj.*

contumacy / **kon**-choo-muh-see, -tyoo- / *n.* stubborn refusal to obey or comply. ☐ **contumacious** / kon-choo-**may**-shuhs, -tyoo- / *adj.*

contumely / **kon**-tyoo-muh-lee, -choo- / *n.* 1 an insult. 2 a disgrace.

contuse / kuhn-**tyooz** / *v.* injure without breaking the skin, bruise.

contusion / kuhn-**tyoo**-zhuhn / *n.* a bruise.

conundrum / kuh-**nun**-druhm / *n.* a hard or puzzling question; a riddle.

conurbation / kon-er-**bay**-shuhn / *n.* a large urban area, esp. consisting of several towns and merging suburbs.

convalesce *v.* regain health after illness. ☐ **convalescence** *n.* **convalescent** *adj.* & *n.*

convection *n.* the transmission of heat within a liquid or gas by movement of the heated parts. ☐ **convective** *adj.*

convector *n.* a heating appliance that circulates warmed air by convection.

convene *v.* assemble, cause to assemble.

convener alternative spelling of CONVENOR.

convenience *n.* **1** the quality of being convenient. **2** something that is convenient. **3** a toilet, esp. a public one. ☐ **at your convenience** whenever or however you find convenient.

convenient *adj.* **1** easy to use or deal with, not troublesome. **2** available or occurring at a suitable time or place; with easy access (*convenient for station and shops*). ☐ **conveniently** *adv.*

convenor *n.* (also **convener**) a person who convenes a meeting etc.

convent *n.* **1** a religious community esp. of nuns (but also of friars). **2** the building in which they live. **3** (in full **convent school**) a school run by the nuns of a convent.

convention *n.* **1** a formal assembly. **2** a formal agreement, esp. between countries (*the Geneva Convention*). **3** an accepted custom.

conventional *adj.* **1** done or doing things according to conventions; traditional; bound by social conventions. **2** not spontaneous or sincere or original (*a very conventional production of the play*). ☐ **conventional weapons** non-nuclear weapons. ☐☐ **conventionally** *adv.* **conventionalism** *n.* **conventionality** *n.*

converge *v.* come to or towards the same point. ☐ **convergence** *n.*

convergent *adj.* **1** converging. **2** *Biology* (of unrelated organisms) having the tendency to become similar while adapting to the same environment.

conversant / kuhn-**ver**-suhnt, **kon**-vuh-suhnt / *adj.* (foll. by *with*) having a knowledge of (*I'm not conversant with the local customs*).

conversation *n.* informal talk between people. ☐ **conversational** *adj.* **conversationally** *adv.*

conversationalist *n.* a person who is good at conversation.

converse[1] / kuhn-**vers** / *v.* hold a conversation.

converse[2] / **kon**-vers / *adj.* opposite, contrary. • *n.* an idea or statement that is the opposite of another. ☐ **conversely** *adv.*

conversion *n.* **1** converting or being converted, esp. in belief or religion. **2** the transformation of fertile into fissile material in a nuclear reactor. **3** *Rugby* the scoring of points by a successful kick at goal after scoring a try.

convert *v.* / kuhn-**vert** / **1** change from one form, use, or character to another. **2** be able to be changed (*the sofa converts into a bed*). **3** cause (a person) to change his or her attitude or beliefs (*several Anglicans were converted to Catholicism*). **4** score a goal from (a try in Rugby football). • *n.* / **kon**-vert / a person who is converted, esp. to a religious faith.

converter *n.* (also **convertor**) **1** a person or thing that converts. **2** an electrical apparatus that converts alternating current to direct current and vice versa. ☐ **converter reactor** a nuclear reactor that converts fertile material into fissile material.

convertible *adj.* able to be converted. • *n.* a car with a roof that can be folded down or removed. ☐ **convertible note** an unsecured note paying fixed interest and convertible on maturity to cash or ordinary shares. ☐☐ **convertibility** *n.*

convex / **kon**-veks / *adj.* curving like the surface of a ball as seen from the outside. ☐ **convexity** / kuhn-**vek**-suh-tee / *n.*

convey *v.* **1** carry, transport, or transmit. **2** communicate as an idea or meaning. ☐ **conveyable** *adj.*

conveyance *n.* **1** conveying. **2** a means of transport; a vehicle. **3** transfer of the legal ownership of land etc.; a document effecting this.

conveyancing *n.* the business of transferring the legal ownership of property. ☐ **conveyancer** *n.*

conveyor *n.* (also **conveyer**) a person or thing that conveys. ☐ **conveyor belt** a continuous moving belt for conveying objects in a factory etc.

convict *v.* / kuhn-**vikt** / prove or declare (a person) to be guilty of a crime. • *n.* / **kon**-vikt / **1** a person serving a prison sentence. **2** *Aust. hist.* a person sentenced in the British Isles to a term of penal servitude in an Australian Colony. • *adj. Aust. hist.* of or relating to a convict or convicts (sense 2) (*convict station*). ☐ **convict boy** *Aust. hist.* a boy sentenced in the British Isles to penal servitude in Australia. **convict colony** *Aust. hist.* an Australian Colony regarded primarily as a place of punishment for British convicts. **convict settler** *Aust. hist.* a person transported as a convict who has subsequently taken up land in Australia.

conviction *n.* **1** convicting; being convicted. **2** being convinced. **3** a firm opinion or belief. ☐ **carry conviction** be convincing.

convince *v.* **1** make (a person) feel certain that something is true (*I am convinced of his honesty*). **2** (as **convinced** *adj.*) firmly persuaded (*a convinced Australian republican*). ☐ **convincible** *adj.* **convincing** *adj.* **convincingly** *adv.*

convivial / kuhn-**viv**-ee-uhl / *adj.* sociable and lively; festive. ☐ **convivially** *adv.* **conviviality** / kuhn-viv-ee-**al**-uh-tee / *n.*

convocation *n.* **1** convoking. **2** an assembly convoked.

convoke *v. formal* summon (people) to assemble.

convoluted / kon-vuh-**loo**-tuhd / *adj.* **1** coiled, twisted. **2** complicated, involved (*a convoluted style of writing*).

convolution / kon-vuh-**loo**-shuhn / *n.* **1** a coil, a twist. **2** complexity.

convolvulus *n.* a twining plant with trumpet-shaped flowers. Also called *bindweed*, *morning glory*.

convoy / **kon**-voi / *v.* escort and protect, esp. with an armed force or warships. •*n.* a group of ships or vehicles travelling under escort or together.

convulse *v.* **1** cause violent movement in. **2** cause to double up with laughter.

convulsion *n.* **1** a violent movement of the body, esp. caused by muscles contracting involuntarily. **2** a violent upheaval or disturbance. **3** (**convulsions**) a violent fit of laughter.

convulsive *adj.* like a convulsion; producing upheaval. ☐ **convulsively** *adv.*

cony *n.* (also **coney**) rabbit fur used in making clothes.

coo *n.* a soft murmuring sound as of a dove. •*v.* emit a coo; talk or say in a soft, amorous voice.

cooba *n.* any of several Australian wattles having a willow-like weeping foliage. (¶ Wiradhuri)

Coober Pedy / koo-buh **pee**-dee / an opal-mining area in northern South Australia. Many of the miners live in underground dwellings.

cooee *Aust. n.* / **koo**-ee / a long loud call ending on a shrill, rising jerk on the 'ee', used to attract attention, esp. in the bush and at a distance (originally a call used by an Aborigine to communicate with a distant person, later adopted by settlers and now widely used). •*interj.* / koo-**ee** / the uttering of such a call. •*v.* / **koo**-ee / utter such a call. ☐ **not** (**come**) **within** (**a**) **cooee** (**of**) not (come) near achieving something desired. **within cooee** (*or* **a cooee of**) very near to. (¶ Dharuk *guuu-wi* 'come here!')

Cook¹, James (1728–79), English naval explorer who aboard the *Endeavour* discovered, mapped, and explored the east coast of Australia.

Cook², Sir Joseph (1860–1947), Australian Labor politician, later a Liberal, prime minister 1913–14.

cook *v.* **1** prepare (food) for eating, by using heat. **2** undergo this preparation (*lunch is cooking*). **3** *colloq.* alter or falsify in order to produce a desired result (*cook the books*). •*n.* a person who cooks, esp. as a job. ☐ **cook up** *colloq.* concoct; invent (*cook up an excuse*). **what's cooking?** *colloq.* what is happening or being planned?

cookbook *n.* a book containing recipes and other information about cooking.

cooker *n.* an appliance or vessel for cooking food.

cookery *n.* the art and practice of cooking.

cookie *n.* **1** (esp. *US*) a sweet biscuit. **2** *colloq.* a person (*he's a tough cookie*). **3** *Computing* a packet of data sent by an Internet server to a browser, which is returned by the browser each time it subsequently accesses the same server, used to identify the user or track their access to the server. ☐ **the way** (*or* **how**) **the cookie crumbles** *colloq.* how things turn out; the unalterable state of affairs.

Cooktown orchid *n.* an Australian dendrobium having brilliant purple flowers, the floral emblem of Qld.

cool *adj.* **1** moderately cold, not hot or warm. **2** (of colours) suggesting coolness. **3** calm and unexcited. **4** not enthusiastic (*got a cool reception*). **5** casual and confident; calmly audacious (*a cool request for a loan*). **6** *colloq.* excellent (*the party was cool*). •*n.* **1** coolness; cool air, a cool place (*the cool of the evening*). **2** *colloq.* calmness, composure (*keep your cool*). •*v.* make or become cool. ☐ **cool change** a cool wind which lowers the temperture markedly on a very hot day. **cooling-off period** an interval to allow for a change of mind before action. **cooling tower** a tower for cooling hot water in an industrial process so that it can be reused. **cool it** *colloq.* calm down. **that's cool with me** *colloq.* that's fine as far as I'm concerned. ☐☐ **coolly** *adv.* **coolness** *n.*

coolabah alternative spelling of COOLIBAH.

coolamon / koo-luh-muhn / *n.* a basin-like vessel of wood or bark used by Aborigines to hold water etc., and for carrying a baby etc. Also called *pitchi*. (¶ Kamilaroi and nearby languages.)

coolant *n.* a fluid used for cooling machinery etc.

cooler *n.* **1** a piece of equipment in which things are cooled. **2** *colloq.* a prison cell.

Coolgardie *n.* (in full **Coolgardie safe**) *Aust.* a safe consisting of a frame covered with hessian etc. kept constantly wet with a water-drip system, used for keeping foodstuffs cool esp. in the outback. (¶ Coolgardie, a town in WA.)

coolibah / **koo**-luh-bah / *n.* any of several esp. blue-leaved eucalypts found across central and northern Australia. (¶ Yuwaaliyaay and nearby languages.)

coolie *n.* an unskilled native labourer in some Asian countries.

Cooloolah monster *n. Aust.* a large, cricket-like insect, discovered in the late 1970s in Cooloolah National Park, south-eastern Qld.

coomb *n.* (chiefly *Brit.*) a valley on the side of a hill.

Coombs, Herbert Cole ('Nugget') (1906–97), AC, Australian economist and writer, former chairman of the Reserve Bank, active in the arts and Aboriginal affairs, and supporter of environmental concerns.

coop *n.* a cage for poultry. •*v.* (usu. foll. by *up*) confine or shut in (*he is cooped up in his room*).

co-op *n. colloq.* a cooperative society or shop.

Cooper, William (?1861–1941), Aboriginal activist who campaigned vigorously for the enfranchisement of Aborigines, for land rights, and for Aboriginal representation in parliament.

cooper *n.* a person whose job is making and repairing casks, barrels, etc.

cooperate *v.* (also **co-operate**) work with another or others. ☐ **cooperation** *n.* **cooperator** *n.*

cooperative (also **co-operative**) *adj.* **1** of or providing cooperation. **2** willing to cooperate. **3** (of a business etc.) owned and run jointly by its members with profits shared. •*n.* a society, business, etc. organised on a cooperative basis. ☐ **cooperatively** *adv.*

Cooper Creek a river flowing from south-western Qld to the north-east of SA and, in very wet seasons, reaching across the Channel Country to Lake Eyre. The Creek has many literary associations; the best known is with Banjo Paterson's drover 'down the Cooper', Clancy of the Overflow.

co-opt *v.* appoint to become a member of a group by the invitation of its existing members. ❏ **co-option** *n.* **co-optive** *adj.*

coordinate (also **co-ordinate**) *adj.* / koh-**aw**-duh-nuht / equal in importance. • *n.* / koh-**aw**-duh-nuht / **1** a coordinate thing. **2** any of the magnitudes used to give the position of a point etc., e.g. latitude and longitude. **3** (**coordinates**) matching items of clothing designed to be worn together. • *v.* / koh-**aw**-duh-nayt / bring (parts etc.) into a proper relationship; work or cause to work together efficiently. ❏ **coordination** *n.* **coordinator** *n.*

coot *n.* **1** a black aquatic bird with a horny white plate on the forehead. **2** *colloq.* a stupid person.

coota *n.* (also **couta**) *Aust. colloq.* = BARRA-COUTA.

Cootamundra wattle *n. Aust.* the wattle *Acacia baileyana*, having bluish-grey true leaves and a spectacular display of fluffy golden ball-flowers.

cop *colloq. n.* **1** a police officer. **2** capture or arrest (*it's a fair cop*). • *v.* (**copped**, **copping**) **1** catch or arrest (an offender). **2** receive, suffer (*copped a lot of criticism; copped a punch in the jaw*). **3** take, seize (*copped the best bits for himself*). **4** put up with (*I'm not going to cop any more of your cheek!*). **5** (*imperative*) take note of (*cop the guy with the purple hair!*). ❏ **cop it** get into trouble, be punished. **cop it sweet** *Aust.* **1** be lucky. **2** accept without complaint. **cop out** back out; fail to do what one promised. **cop-out** an evasion or failure of this kind. **not much cop** of little value or use.

copal / **koh**-puhl, -pal / *n.* the resin of various tropical trees, used for varnish.

copartner *n.* a partner; an associate. ❏ **copartnership** *n.*

cope¹ *v.* (often foll. by *with*) deal effectively with; manage successfully.

cope² *n.* a long loose ceremonial cloak worn by Christian clergy.

copeck / **koh**-pek / *n.* (also **kopek**, **kopeck**) a Russian coin, one hundredth of a rouble.

Copenhagen / koh-puhn-**hay**-guhn / the capital of Denmark.

Copernicus / kuh-**per**-ni-kuhs /, Nicolaus (1473–1543), Polish astronomer, who rejected the orthodox view that the Earth was the centre of the universe and suggested that planets orbit the sun.

copier *n.* a copying machine, a photocopier.

copilot *n.* a second pilot in an aircraft.

coping / **koh**-ping / *n.* the top row of masonry (usu. sloping) in a wall. ❏ **coping saw** a D-shaped saw for cutting curves in wood. **coping stone** one of the stones forming the top of a wall.

copious *adj.* **1** existing in large amounts; plentiful. **2** producing much (*this cow's a copious milker; a copious writer*). ❏ **copiously** *adv.*

copper¹ *n.* **1** a chemical element (symbol Cu), a reddish-brown metal. **2** a coin made of copper or a copper alloy. **3** a reddish-brown colour. **4** a large metal vessel for boiling things, esp. laundry. • *adj.* **1** made of copper. **2** reddish-brown. ❏ **copper sulphate** a blue crystalline solid used in electroplating, dyeing, and plant sprays.

copper² *n. colloq.* a police officer.

copperhead *n.* **1** a venomous snake of south-eastern Australia. **2** a venomous viper of N. America.

copperplate *n.* a type of elaborate, clear handwriting.

coppice *n.* an area of undergrowth and small trees. • *v.* **1** cut back (eucalypts etc.) to stimulate growth. **2** (of a tree which has been cut back or cut down to stump level) put forth new growth.

copra *n.* the dried kernels of coconuts.

copse *n.* a coppice.

Copt *n.* **1** an Egyptian of the period from the mid 4th century BC onwards. **2** a member of the Coptic Church.

Coptic *adj.* **1** of the Copts. **2** of Coptic. • *n.* the language of the Copts, now used only as the liturgical language of the Coptic Church.

copula *n. Grammar* a connecting word, esp. a part of the verb *to be* connecting the predicate with the subject.

copulate / **kop**-yuh-layt / *v.* have sexual intercourse; (of animals) mate. ❏ **copulation** *n.*

copy *n.* **1** a thing made to look like another. **2** one specimen of a book or document or newspaper. **3** material for printing; material for newspaper reporting. **4** the text of an advertisement. • *v.* (**copied**, **copying**) **1** make a copy of. **2** try to do the same as, imitate.

copybook *n.* a book containing models of hand-writing for learners to imitate. • *adj.* very good, model (*scored a copybook century*).

copycat *n. colloq.* a person who copies another.

copyist *n.* a person who makes copies of documents etc.

copyright *n.* the sole legal right to print, publish, perform, film, or record a literary or artistic or musical work, including sound recordings, films, television and radio broadcasts, and computer software. • *adj.* (of material) protected by copyright. • *v.* secure copyright for (material).

copywriter *n.* a person who writes or prepares advertising copy for publication.

coq au vin / kok oh **van** / *n.* a casserole of chicken pieces in wine. (¶ French)

coquette / ko-**ket**, koh-**ket** / *n.* a woman who flirts. ❏ **coquetry** *n.* **coquettish** *adj.*

coracle / **ko**-ruh-kuhl / *n.* a small, round wickerwork boat covered with watertight material.

coral *n.* **1** a hard red, pink, or white substance formed by the skeletons of tiny sea creatures. **2** yellowish- or reddish-pink colour. •*adj.* **1** red or pink, like coral. **2** used as a descriptive epithet for fauna and flora with reference either to habitat or to a fancied resemblance (*coral fern; coral gum; coral pea; coral snake; coral tree; coral trout*).

coralline *adj.* of or like coral. •*n.* a seaweed with a hard jointed stem.

coral reef *n.* a reef formed by the growth of coral.

Coral Sea a part of the Pacific lying between Australia, New Guinea, and Vanuatu that includes the waters of Torres Strait and the Great Barrier Reef. In 1969 Australia proclaimed a Coral Sea Islands Territory which includes 15 reefs and island groups, and in 1982 it proclaimed two national nature reserves, the Coringa-Herald, and the Lihou Reef. □ **Battle of the Coral Sea** a crucial battle in May 1942 between Australian-American forces and Japanese forces in which both sides suffered damage. The battle however prevented the Japanese from establishing a major base less than 400 km from the Qld coast.

cor anglais / kawr **ahng**-glay / *n.* (*pl.* **cors anglais** pronounced the same) an alto woodwind instrument of the oboe family.

corbel / **kaw**-buhl / *n.* a stone or timber projection from a wall, to support something. □ **corbelled** *adj.*

cord *n.* **1** long thin flexible material made from twisted strands; a piece of this; electric flex. **2** a similar structure in the body. **3** corduroy material. **4** (**cords**) *colloq.* corduroy trousers. •*v.* fasten or bind with cord.

corded *adj.* (of fabric) with raised ridges.

cordial *n.* **1** a concentrated sweet syrup flavoured with fruit etc. and diluted to make a drink. **2** (in Tas.) a soft drink. •*adj.* warm and friendly. □ **cordially** *adv.* **cordiality** / kaw-dee-**al**-uh-tee / *n.*

cordite / **kaw**-duyt / *n.* a smokeless explosive used in bullets and shells.

cordless *adj.* powered by a charging unit rather than an electric cable (*cordless phone*).

cordon *n.* **1** a ring of people or military posts etc. enclosing or guarding something. **2** an ornamental cord or braid worn as a badge of honour. **3** a fruit tree with its branches pruned so that it grows as a single stem. •*v.* enclose with a cordon.

cordon bleu / kaw-don **bler** / *adj.* of the highest degree of excellence in cookery. (¶ French, = blue ribbon.)

corduroy *n.* **1** cotton cloth with velvety ridges. **2** (**corduroys**) trousers made of corduroy fabric.

core *n.* **1** the horny central part of certain fruits, containing the seeds. **2** the central or most important part of something. **3** a unit in the structure of a computer memory storing one bit of data. **4** the part of a nuclear reactor that contains the fissile material. •*v.* remove the core from. □ **to the core** thoroughly, entirely. □□ **corer** *n.*

corella / kuh-**rel**-uh / *n.* either of two large white Australian crested parrots, the little corella and the long-billed corella. (¶ Wiradhuri)

co-respondent / koh-ruh-**spon**-duhnt / *n.* the person with whom the person proceeded against in a divorce suit (the *respondent*) is said to have committed adultery.

corgi *n.* (*pl.* **corgis**) a dog of a small Welsh breed with a foxlike head.

coriander / ko-ree-**an**-duh / *n.* **1** an aromatic plant with leaves used for flavouring in eastern dishes, and small round fruit. **2** its powdered seeds used for flavouring in curries and as the major ingredient in Sri Lankan etc. curry powder.

Corinthian / kuh-**rin**-thee-uhn / *adj.* **1** of Corinth, a city of Ancient Greece. **2** of the most ornate of the five classical orders of architecture.

cork¹ *n.* **1** a light tough substance, the thick outer bark of a South European oak. **2** a piece of this used as a float. **3** a bottle stopper made of this or similar material. •*v.* stop up with a cork.

cork² *v. Aust.* bruise badly (*corked his thigh playing footy*).

corkage *n.* a charge made by a restaurant for serving wine brought by the customers.

corked *adj.* **1** (of wine) contaminated by a decayed cork. **2** *colloq.* drunk. **3** *Aust.* bruised.

corker *n. colloq.* an excellent person or thing.

corkie *n. Aust. colloq.* a bad bruise.

corkscrew *n.* **1** a tool for extracting corks from bottles. **2** a spiral thing.

corkwood *n.* an Australian shrub or small tree (genus *Duboisia*, from the leaves of which the important alkaloid *duboisine* is extracted), having a rough corky bark.

corm *n.* a rounded underground base of a stem, from the top of which buds sprout.

cormorant *n.* any of various diving waterbirds having black or pied plumage, including the Australian little black cormorant and pied cormoran.

corn *n.* **1** maize or Indian corn. **2** (chiefly *Brit.*) wheat or oats. **3** cereal plants before or after harvesting. **4** a single grain of a cereal plant or a seed of pepper etc. **5** *colloq.* something corny or trite. **6** a small tender area of horny hardened skin on the foot. □ **corn cob** the cylindrical centre of a maize ear on which the grains grow. **corn on the cob** maize cooked and eaten from the cob.

corncrake *n.* a bird (a rail) of Australia and elsewhere, inhabiting marshes and nesting on the ground.

cornea / **kaw**-nee-uh / *n.* the tough transparent outer covering of the eyeball. □ **corneal** *adj.*

corned *adj.* preserved in salt (*corned beef*).

cornelian *n.* (also **carnelian**) a reddish or white semi-precious stone.

corner *n.* **1** the angle or area where two lines or sides or streets etc. meet. **2** a difficult position, one with no escape. **3** a hidden or remote place. **4** a free hit or kick from the corner of the field in hockey or soccer. **5** the corner of the ring where a contestant rests between rounds in boxing and wrestling. **6** (**the Corner**) = CORNER COUNTRY. **7** a virtual monopoly of a certain type of goods or services, enabling the holder to control the price. • *v.* **1** drive into a corner; force into a position from which there is no escape. **2** obtain (all or most of something) for oneself; establish a monopoly of. **3** move round a corner (*the car had cornered too fast*). ☐ **round the corner** nearby; about to occur. **turn the corner** begin to improve; start recovering from an illness.

Corner Country (also **the Corner**) the area in which the borders of NSW, Qld, and SA meet.

cornerstone *n.* **1** a stone in the projecting angle of a wall; a foundation stone. **2** an indispensable part or basis.

cornet *n.* **1** a brass musical instrument like a small trumpet. **2** a cone-shaped wafer holding ice cream.

cornflakes *n.pl.* a breakfast cereal of toasted maize flakes.

cornflour *n.* flour made from maize or rice, used to thicken sauces.

Cornforth, Sir John Warcup (1917–), AC, Australian organic chemist who worked on penicillin etc. during the Second World War and shared the Nobel Prize for chemistry in 1975.

cornice / **kaw**-nuhs / *n.* a band of ornamental moulding round the wall of a room just below the ceiling or crowning a building.

Cornish *adj.* of Cornwall (a county of SW England) or its people or language. • *n.* the ancient Celtic language of Cornwall. ☐ **Cornish pastie** a mixture of meat and vegetables wrapped in pastry.

cornstalk *n. Aust.* **1** *hist.* nickname for a non-Aboriginal native-born Australian (as opposed to a recent British immigrant), the Australians purportedly being remarkable for their tallness and leanness. **2** nickname for a person native to or resident in NSW.

cornucopia / kaw-nyuh-**koh**-pee-uh / *n.* **1** a horn of plenty, a horn-shaped container overflowing with fruit and flowers. **2** an abundant supply.

corny *adj.* (**cornier, corniest**) *colloq.* repeated so often that people are tired of it; over-sentimental. ☐ **cornily** *adv.* **corniness** *n.*

corolla / kuh-**rol**-uh / *n.* the petals of a flower.

corollary / kuh-**rol**-uh-ree / *n.* a natural consequence or result; something that follows logically after something else is proved.

corona / kuh-**roh**-nuh / *n.* a small circle or glow of light round something.

coronary / **ko**-ruh-nuh-ree, -ruhn-ree / *adj.* of the arteries supplying blood to the heart. • *n.* **1** a coronary artery. **2** (in full **coronary thrombosis**) blockage of a coronary artery by a clot of blood.

coronation *n.* the ceremony of crowning a king, queen, or consort.

coroner / **ko**-ruh-nuh / *n.* an official who holds an inquest into the cause of a death which is not clearly the result of natural causes.

coronet *n.* **1** a small crown. **2** a band of gold or jewels etc. for the head.

coronial *adj.* of or relating to a coroner.

corpora *see* CORPUS.

corporal[1] *adj.* of the human body. ☐ **corporal punishment** punishment by whipping or beating. ☐ ☐ **corporality** *n.*

corporal[2] *n.* a non-commissioned officer ranking just below sergeant in the army or air force.

corporate / **kaw**-puh-ruht / *adj.* **1** shared by members of a group (*corporate responsibility*). **2** united in one group (*a corporate body*). **3** of or relating to a large company or group. ☐ **corporate raider** a person who makes an unwelcome takeover bid by buying up a company's shares on the stock market.

corporation *n.* a group of people authorised to act as an individual, esp. in business.

corporative *adj.* of a corporation.

corporeal / kaw-**paw**-ree-uhl / *adj.* bodily, physical; material. ☐ **corporeally** *adv.* **corporeality** *n.*

corps / kaw / *n.* (*pl.* **corps** / kawz /) **1** the main subdivision of an army in the field. **2** a body of troops with special duties (*intelligence corps*). **3** a body of people engaged in a special activity (*the diplomatic corps*).

corps de ballet / kaw duh **bal**-ay / *n.* a group of ensemble dancers in a ballet.

corpse *n.* a dead body.

corpulent / **kawp**-yuh-luhnt / *adj.* having a bulky body; fat. ☐ **corpulence** *n.*

corpus *n.* (*pl.* **corpora**) a large collection of writings etc.

Corpus Christi a Catholic festival in honour of the Eucharist, celebrated on the Thursday after Trinity Sunday.

corpuscle / **kaw**-puh-suhl / *n.* any of the red or white cells in the blood. ☐ **corpuscular** / kaw-**pus**-kyuh-luh / *adj.*

corpus delicti / kaw-puhs duh-**lik**-tuy / *n. Law* the facts and circumstances constituting a breach of a law. (¶ Latin, = body of offence.)

corral / ko-**rahl** / *n.* an enclosure for horses, cattle, etc. • *v.* (**corralled, corralling**) put into a corral.

correa / **ko**-ree-uh / *n.* a decorative shrub mainly of south-eastern Australia bearing usu. tubular flowers of yellow, red, green, or a mixture of these.

correct *adj.* **1** true, accurate. **2** proper, in accordance with an approved way of behaving or working. •*v.* **1** make correct, set right. **2** mark the errors in. **3** point out faults in (a person); punish (a person or a fault). ☐ **correctly** *adv.* **correctness** *n.* **corrector** *n.*

correction *n.* **1** correcting; being corrected. **2** an alteration made to something that was incorrect.

correctitude *n.* being correct; consciously correct behaviour.

corrective *adj.* correcting what is bad or harmful. •*n.* something that corrects.

correlate / **ko**-ruh-layt / *v.* (usu. foll. by *with*) **1** compare or connect systematically. **2** have a systematic connection. •*n.* each of two related or complementary things (*liver damage is a correlate of alcohol abuse*). ☐ **correlation** *n.* **correlative** / ko-**rel**-uh-tiv, kuh- / *adj.*

correspond *v.* **1** (usu. foll. by *with, to*) be in harmony or agreement (*this corresponds with what I've heard*). **2** (usu. foll. by *to*) be similar or equivalent (*the Australian Senate does not correspond to the British House of Lords*). **3** write letters to each other. ☐ **correspondingly** *adv.*

correspondence *n.* **1** agreement; similarity. **2** communicating by writing letters; the letters themselves. ☐ **correspondence course** instruction by means of materials sent by post.

correspondent *n.* **1** a person who writes letters. **2** a person employed to contribute news reports to a newspaper or radio station etc.

corridor *n.* **1** a long narrow passage, esp. one from which doors open into rooms or compartments. **2** a route which an aircraft must follow, esp. over a foreign country. ☐ **corridors of power** institutions and people said to have hidden influence on government.

corrigendum / ko-ruh-**gen**-duhm / *n.* (*pl.* **corrigenda**) an error, esp. in a printed book, for which a correction is printed.

corrigible / **ko**-ruh-juh-buhl / *adj.* **1** able to be corrected. **2** docile, open to correction. ☐ **corrigibly** *adv.* **corrigibility** *n.*

Corris, Peter (1942–), Australian writer of detective fiction.

corroborate / kuh-**rob**-uh-rayt / *v.* get or give supporting evidence. ☐ **corroboration** *n.* **corroborative** / kuh-**rob**-uh-ruh-tiv / *adj.* **corroborator** *n.* **corroboratory** *adj.*

corroboree / kuh-**rob**-uh-ree / *n. Aust.* **1** an Aboriginal dance ceremony, of which song and rhythmical musical accompaniment are an integral part, and which may be sacred and ritualised or non-sacred, occasional, and informal. **2** in transferred senses (*a dozen magpies holding a corroboree of warbling; the weird, wonderful corroboree each year at Flemington to celebrate the Melbourne Cup*). **3** *colloq.* any noisy celebration or gathering. •*v.* (**corroboreed, corroboreeing**) **1** (of Aborigines) perform a corroboree. **2** in transferred senses (*surfies corroboreeing on the beach around a bonfire; mozzies corroboreed around my ears all night*). ☐ **corroboree frog** a small Australian frog with black and yellow markings thought to resemble Aboriginal body painting. (¶ Dharuk *garabari* 'a style of dancing'.)

corrode *v.* destroy gradually by chemical action (*rust corrodes metal*).

corrosion *n.* **1** corroding or being corroded. **2** a corroded area. ☐ **corrosive** *adj.*

corrugated *adj.* shaped into alternate ridges and grooves (*corrugated iron*). ☐ **corrugation** *n.*

corrupt *adj.* **1** dishonest, accepting bribes. **2** immoral, wicked. **3** (of a text or computer data) made unreliable by errors, alterations, electrical faults, etc. **4** rotten. •*v.* **1** cause to become dishonest or immoral, persuade to accept bribes. **2** spoil, taint. ☐ **corruptness** *n.* **corruptibility** *n.* **corruptive** *adj.* **corruptible** *adj.* **corruptly** *adv.*

corruption *n.* **1** moral deterioration, esp. widespread. **2** the use of corrupt practices, esp. bribery or fraud (*alleged corruption in the police force*). **3** irregular alteration (of a text, computer data, etc.) from its original state. **4** decomposition, esp. of a corpse or other organic matter.

corsage *n.* / kaw-**sah**zh / a small bouquet of flowers worn by women on formal occasions.

corsair / **kaw**-sair / *n. archaic* **1** a pirate ship. **2** a pirate.

corset *n.* a close-fitting undergarment worn to shape or support the body. ☐ **corsetry** *n.*

cortège / kaw-**tay**zh / *n.* a funeral procession.

cortex *n.* (*pl.* **cortices** / **kaw**-tuh-seez /) **1** an outer layer of tissue (e.g. of a kidney or a plant stem); the bark of a tree. **2** the outer grey matter of the brain.

cortical *adj.* of the cortex.

cortisone / **kaw**-tuh-zohn / *n.* a hormone from the adrenal cortex or made synthetically, used against inflammation and allergy.

corundum / kuh-**run**-duhm / *n.* extremely hard alumina, used esp. as an abrasive.

coruscate / **ko**-ruh-skayt / *v.* give off flashing light; sparkle. ☐ **coruscation** *n.*

corvette / kaw-**vet** / *n.* a small warship designed for convoy escort duty.

corymb / **ko**-rimb, **ko**-rim / *n.* a flat-topped cluster of flowers with the flower stalks proportionally longer lower down the stem.

corymbia / ko-**rimb**-bee-uh / *n.* any of many bloodwoods and ghost gums of the genus *Corymbia* of Australia and New Guinea, recognised by their compound flowers and formerly classified as *Eucalyptus*. The classification of this group of trees was revised in January 1996.

cos[1] / kos / *n.* a lettuce with long crisp leaves.

cos[2] / koz, kos / *n. abbr.* cosine.

cos[3] / koz / *adv.* & *conj. colloq.* because.

cosh *n.* a weighted weapon for hitting people. •*v.* hit with a cosh.

co-signatory *n.* a person or State signing a treaty etc. jointly with others.

cosine / koh-suyn / *n.* (in a right-angled triangle) the ratio of the length of a side adjacent to one of the acute angles to the length of the hypotenuse.

cosmetic *n.* a substance for beautifying the body, esp. the face. •*adj.* **1** for beautifying or improving the appearance (*cosmetic surgery*). **2** intended to improve only appearances; superficially improving (*these are only cosmetic changes to this law*). □ **cosmetically** *adv.*

cosmic *adj.* of the universe. □ **cosmic rays** (*or* **radiation**) high-energy radiation that reaches the earth from outer space.

cosmogony / koz-**mog**-uh-nee / *n.* the origin of the universe; a theory about this.

cosmology / koz-**mol**-uh-jee / *n.* the scientific study of the creation and development of the universe. □ **cosmological** *adj.* **cosmologist** *n.*

cosmonaut *n.* a Russian astronaut.

cosmopolitan *adj.* **1** of or from many parts of the world, containing people from many countries (*Sydney is a very cosmopolitan city*). **2** free from national prejudices and at home in all parts of the world (*a cosmopolitan outlook*). •*n.* a cosmopolitan person. □ **cosmopolitanism** *n.*

cosmos / **koz**-mos / *n.* the universe.

Cossack / **kos**-ak / *n.* a member of a people of south Russia, famous as horsemen.

cosset / **kos**-uht / *v.* (**cosseted, cosseting**) pamper.

cossie / **koz**-ee / *n. Aust. colloq.* a swimming costume.

cost *n.* **1** an amount given or required as payment. **2** an expenditure of time or labour; a loss suffered in achieving something. **3** (**costs**) the expenses involved in having something settled in a lawcourt. •*v.* (**cost** (in sense 3 **costed**), **costing**) **1** be obtainable at a certain price. **2** require a certain effort or loss etc. (*cost them much effort; cost him his life*). **3** estimate the cost involved (*costed the repairs at $500*). **4** *colloq.* be costly (to) (*it'll cost you*). □ **at all costs** (also **at any cost**) no matter what the risk or loss involved may be. **at cost** at cost price. **cost-effective** (*or* **cost-efficient**) *adj.* producing useful results in relation to its cost. **to one's cost** involving bitter experience.

costal *adj.* of the ribs.

Costa Rica / kos-tuh **ree**-kuh / a republic in Central America. □ **Costa Rican** *adj. & n.*

costermonger / **kos**-tuh-mung-guh / *n. Brit.* a person who sells fruit etc. from a barrow.

costing *n.* estimation of costs.

costive *adj.* constipated.

costly *adj.* (**costlier, costliest**) costing much, expensive. □ **costliness** *n.*

costume *n.* **1** a style of clothes belonging to a particular place, period, or group, or suitable for a particular activity. **2** special garments worn by an actor. •*v.* provide with a costume. □ **costume jewellery** artificial jewellery.

costumier / kos-**tyoo**-mee-uh / *n.* a person who makes or deals in costumes.

cosy *adj.* (**cosier, cosiest**) warm and comfortable; snug. •*n.* a cover for a teapot or boiled egg to keep it hot. □ **cosily** *adv.* **cosiness** *n.*

cot[1] *n.* **1** a child's bed with high sides. **2** a small light bed. □ **cot-case** *n.* **1** a person too ill to leave his or her bed. **2** *colloq.* a person incapacitated by drink. **3** *colloq.* an eccentric or mad person. **cot death** (also **SIDS, sudden infant death syndrome**) the sudden, unexplained death of a sleeping baby.

cot[2] *abbr.* cotangent.

cotangent / koh-**tan**-juhnt / *n.* the ratio of the side adjacent to an acute angle (in a right-angled triangle) to the opposite side.

cote *n.* a small shelter built for birds or animals.

coterie / **koh**-tuh-ree / *n.* an exclusive group of people sharing interests.

cotoneaster / kuh-toh-nee-**as**-tuh / *n.* a shrub (of Europe etc.) with red or orange berries.

cottage *n.* **1** a small simple house, esp. in the country. **2** *Aust.* a detached, single-storeyed suburban house. □ **cottage cheese** soft white cheese made from curds without pressing. **cottage industry** one that can be carried on at home.

cottager *n.* a person who lives in a cottage.

Cottee, Kay (1954–), AO, Australian sailor. She was the first woman to complete a solo, non-stop, unassisted circumnavigation of the globe, completing the voyage at Sydney on 5 June 1988 after 189 days at sea.

cotter *n.* **1** a bolt or wedge for securing parts of machinery etc. **2** (in full **cotter pin**) a split pin that can be opened after passing through a hole.

Cotton, Olive (1911–), Australian photographer.

cotton *n.* **1** a soft white substance round the seeds of a tropical plant. **2** the plant itself. **3** thread made from this. **4** fabric made from this thread. □ **cotton bud** *trademark* a small stick with cotton wool at each end, suitable for applying medication to the mouth, nostril, etc. **cotton on** (**to**) *colloq.* **1** begin to understand. **2** form a liking for. **cotton wool** fluffy wadding of a kind originally made from raw cotton. □□ **cottony** *adj.*

cottony cushion scale *n.* an Australian scale insect which infests fruit trees, wattles, etc., covering its eggs with a white wax-like substance.

cotyledon / kot-uh-**lee**-duhn / *n.* the first leaf growing from a seed.

coucal / **koo**-kal / *n.* = PHEASANT COUCAL.

couch[1] *n.* **1** an upholstered piece of furniture for several people; a sofa. **2** a long padded seat or bed-like structure with a headrest at one end (*a psychiatrist's couch*). •*v.* **1** express in words of a certain kind (*the request was couched in polite terms*). **2** lower (a lance etc.) to the position for attack. **3** *Med.* treat (a cataract) by displacing the lens of the eye. □ **couch potato** *colloq.* a person who spends leisure time passively (e.g. by sitting watching television), eats junk food, and takes no physical exercise.

couch[2] / kooch / n. (in full **couch grass**) a grass with long creeping roots.

cougar / **koo**-guh / n. US a puma.

cough v. **1** send out air or other matter from the lungs with a sudden sharp sound. **2** (of an engine etc.) make a similar sound. •n. **1** an act or sound of coughing. **2** an illness causing frequent coughing. □ **cough up 1** eject with coughs. **2** colloq. give (money or information) with some reluctance.

could auxiliary v. **1** used as the past tense of CAN[2]. **2** feel inclined to (*I could murder him*). **3** might (*he could have been delayed*).

couldn't = could not.

coulomb / **koo**-lom / n. a unit of electric charge (abbr. **C**). (¶ Named after C.A. de Coulomb, French engineer (1736–1806).)

coulter / **kohl**-tuh / n. a vertical blade in front of a ploughshare.

council n. **1** an assembly of people to advise on, discuss, or organise something. **2** the local administrative body of a town etc.

■ Usage Do not confuse with *counsel*.

Council for Aboriginal Reconciliation a council established by an act of the Australian Commonwealth Parliament in 1991 to facilitate the reconciliation of indigenous and non-indigenous Australians.

councillor n. a member of a (esp. local) council.

■ Usage Do not confuse with *counsellor*.

counsel n. **1** advice, suggestions (*give counsel*). **2** (pl. **counsel**) a barrister or group of barristers giving advice in a legal case. •v. (**counselled**, **counselling**) **1** advise, recommend. **2** give professional guidance to (a person in need of psychological help). □ **keep one's own counsel** not confide in others.

■ Usage Do not confuse with *council*.

counsellor n. an adviser; a person giving professional guidance on personal problems (*marriage guidance counsellor*).

■ Usage Do not confuse with *councillor*.

count[1] v. **1** find the total of. **2** say the numbers in order. **3** include or be included in a reckoning (*six of us, counting the dog*). **4** be important; be worth reckoning (*fine words count for nothing*). **5** regard or consider (*I should count it an honour*). •n. **1** counting; a calculation. **2** a number reached by counting, a total. **3** any of the points being considered; each of the charges against an accused person (*he was found guilty on all counts*). □ **count noun** Grammar a countable noun; see COUNTABLE (sense 2). **count on** rely on; expect confidently. **count out 1** count one by one from a stock. **2** exclude from a reckoning (*you can count me out*). **3** (of a referee) count up to ten seconds over (a boxer or wrestler who has been knocked or fallen to the floor). **4** count (sheep or cattle) as they leave a pen or paddock. **out for the count 1** defeated, demoralised. **2** unconscious; asleep.

count[2] n. (in some European countries) a nobleman.

countable adj. **1** able to be counted. **2** Grammar (of a noun such as *book*, *kindness*, etc.) that can form a plural or be used with the indefinite article.

countdown n. **1** counting numerals backwards to zero, as in the procedure for launching a spacecraft etc. **2** the period immediately before an event (*countdown to the Grand Final*).

countenance n. **1** the expression of the face. **2** composure (*he kept his countenance while being heckled*). **3** approval, moral support (*I shall lend no countenance to such a scheme*). •v. give approval to (*I cannot countenance this breach of the rules*).

counter n. **1** a flat-topped fitment over which goods are sold or business is transacted. **2** a small disc used in table games. **3** a token representing a coin. **4** an apparatus for counting things. •adv. in the opposite direction. •adj. opposed. •v. **1** oppose, contradict. **2** hinder or defeat by an opposing action. □ **counter lunch** (or **tea**) Aust. a usu. cheap but substantial midday (or evening) meal in a local hotel or pub (originally at the bar or counter). **under the counter** transacted in an underhand way, esp. illegally.

counter- comb. form denoting **1** opposition; rivalry (*a counter-threat*). **2** opposite direction (*counter-clockwise*). **3** correspondence; similarity (*counterpart; countersign*).

counteract v. reduce or prevent the effects of. □ **counteraction** n. **counteractive** adj.

counter-attack n. an attack directed against an enemy who has already attacked or invaded. •v. make a counter-attack (on).

counterbalance n. a weight or influence that balances another. •v. act as a counterbalance to.

counter-claim n. a claim made in opposition to another claim.

counter-clockwise adj. & adv. anticlockwise.

counter-culture n. a radical, alternative culture, esp. among young people, that seeks out new values to replace the established and conventional values of society. □ **counter-culturalist** n.

counter-espionage n. action taken to uncover and counteract enemy espionage.

counterfeit / **kown**-tuh-fuht, -feet / adj. fake. •n. a fake. •v. fake.

counterfoil n. a detachable section of a cheque or receipt etc. kept by the payer as a record.

counter-intelligence = COUNTER-ESPIONAGE.

countermand v. cancel (a command or order). •n. a command or order cancelling a previous one.

countermeasure *n.* action taken to counteract a threat or danger etc.

countermove *n.* a move or action taken in opposition to another.

counter-offensive *n.* a large-scale counter-attack.

counterpane *n.* a bedspread.

counterpart *n.* **1** a person or thing corresponding to another in position or use. **2** a duplicate.

counterpoint *n.* **1** a melody added as an accompaniment to another. **2** a method of combining melodies according to fixed rules. • *v.* set in contrast.

counterpoise *n.* a counterbalance. • *v.* counterbalance.

counter-productive *adj.* having the opposite of the desired effect.

Counter-Reformation *n.* the reformation within the Catholic Church following on the Protestant Reformation.

counter-revolution *n.* a revolution opposing a former one or reversing its results.

countersign *n.* a password; a mark of identification. • *v.* add another signature to (a document) to give it authority.

countersink *v.* (**countersunk, countersinking**) enlarge the top of (a hole) so that the head of a screw or bolt will lie level with or below the surface; sink (a screw etc.) in such a hole.

counter-tenor *n.* a male singing voice higher than tenor; a singer with this.

countervail *v.* **1** counterbalance. **2** oppose forcefully and usu. successfully.

counterweight *n.* a counterbalancing weight or influence. • *v.* **1** counterbalance. **2** fit with a counterweight.

countess *n.* **1** the wife or widow of a count or earl. **2** a woman holding the rank of count or earl.

countless *adj.* too many to be counted.

countrified *adj.* (also **countryfied**) (often *derog.*) rural or rustic, esp. in manners, appearance, etc.

country *n.* **1** a nation or state with its own government; the land it occupies. **2** rural districts as opposed to towns or the capital. **3** the land of a person's birth or citizenship. **4** an area of land with certain features (*central Australia, typical Namatjira country*). **5** the national population, esp. as voters (*the country won't stand for it*). **6** *Aust.* the traditional territory of an Aboriginal people. **7** country-and-western. □ **country and western** *n.* a type of rural folk music originated by whites in the southern US. **country town** a small rural town. **go** (or **appeal**) **to the country** test public opinion by dissolving parliament and holding a general election.

countryman *n.* (*feminine* **countrywoman**) **1** a person living in a rural area. **2** (also **fellow-countryman, fellow-countrywoman**) a person of one's own country. **3** *Aust.* a person from an Aborigine's own country (*see* COUNTRY 6). **4** *Aust.* a person with whom an Aborigine has extremely close ritual etc. bonding, involving responsibility of one for the other.

Country Party the former name of the National Party of Australia.

countryside *n.* rural areas.

countrywide *adj.* & *adv.* (extending) throughout a nation.

Country Women's Association a non-sectarian, non-political organisation, founded in NSW in 1922 and now operating in all States, which aims to improve the welfare of country women and children.

county *n.* a territorial division in some countries, usu. forming the chief unit of local administration.

County Court (in Vic.) = DISTRICT COURT.

coup / koo / *n.* (*pl.* **coups** / kooz /) **1** a successful stroke or action. **2** a coup d'état.

coup de grâce / koo duh **grahs** / *n.* **1** the finishing stroke to kill a wounded animal or person. **2** an action etc. that settles or puts an end to something. (¶ French)

coup d'état / koo day-**tah** / *n.* (*pl.* **coups d'état** pronounced the same) the sudden overthrowing of a government by force or by illegal means. (¶ French)

coupe / koop / *n.* an area of forest set aside for felling.

coupé / **koo**-pay / *n.* a closed two-door car with a sloping back.

couple *n.* **1** two people or things considered together. **2** two people who are married to, or in a sexual relationship with, each other. **3** a pair of partners in a dance etc. • *v.* **1** fasten or link together; join by a coupling. **2** copulate.

couplet / **kup**-luht / *n.* two successive lines of verse, esp. when these rhyme and have the same metre.

coupling *n.* **1** a device for connecting two railway carriages or parts of machinery. **2** copulation.

coupon *n.* **1** a voucher, ticket, etc. that entitles the holder to receive something or that can be used as an application form. **2** an entry form for a competition etc.

courage *n.* the ability to control fear when facing danger or pain; bravery.

courageous / kuh-**ray**-juhs / *adj.* having or showing courage. □ **courageously** *adv.*

courgette / kaw-**zhet** / = ZUCCHINI.

courier / **kuu**-ree-uh, **koo**- / *n.* **1** a messenger carrying news or important papers. **2** a person employed to guide and assist a group of tourists. **3** a person who works for a courier service. □ **courier service** a branch of the post office or a private firm which picks up and delivers parcels etc., esp. with speedy service.

course *n.* **1** an onward movement in space or time (*in the ordinary course of events*). **2** the direction taken or intended (*the course of the river;*

the ship was off course). **3** a series of things one can do to achieve something (*your best course is to start again*). **4** a series of talks, lessons, or treatment etc. **5** a golf course; a stretch of land or water over which a race takes place. **6** a continuous layer of brick or stone in a wall. **7** each of the successive parts of a meal. • *v.* **1** follow a course. **2** move or flow freely (*blood coursed through his veins*). ☐ **in course of** in the process of (*the bridge is in course of construction*). **in the course of** during. **of course** without a doubt, as was to be expected; admittedly.

courser *n.* poetic a fast horse.

courseware *see* -WARE.

coursework *n.* work done during a course of study, esp. when counting towards a student's final assessment.

Court, Margaret (original name: Margaret Smith) (1942–), Australian tennis champion, the first Australian woman to win the Wimbledon championship, the first woman ever to win the Grand Slam (1970), thrice a winner at Wimbledon.

court *n.* **1** a courtyard. **2** a short street. **3** an enclosed area for certain games, e.g. squash, tennis. **4** a sovereign's establishment with attendants, councillors, etc. **5** a lawcourt; the judges in this. **6** the attention paid to a person whose favour etc. is sought (*paid court to her*). • *v.* **1** try to win the favour or support of. **2** *archaic* try to win the affection of, esp. in order to marry. **3** (of animals) try to attract sexually. **4** behave as though trying to provoke something harmful (*courting danger*). ☐ **court card** the king, queen, or jack in playing cards. **court martial** (*pl.* **courts martial**) **1** a court for trying offences against military law. **2** trial by such a court. **court-martial** *v.* (**court-martialled, court-martialling**) try by a court martial. **court of summary jurisdiction** a court having the authority to use summary proceedings and arrive at a judgment or conviction. **court order** a direction issued by a court or a judge. **court shoe** a woman's low-cut shoe with no straps, fastenings, etc. **hold court** preside over one's admirers. **out of court 1** without reaching trial (*was settled out of court*). **2** not worthy of consideration (*that suggestion is quite out of court*).

courteous / **ker**-tee-uhs / *adj.* polite. ☐ **courteously** *adv.*

courtesan / kaw-tuh-**zan** / *n. archaic* a prostitute with wealthy or upper-class clients.

courtesy / **ker**-tuh-see / *n.* courteous behaviour; a courteous act. ☐ **by courtesy of** by the permission or favour of.

courthouse *n.* a building in which a judicial court is held.

courtier / **kaw**-tee-uh / *n.* one of a sovereign's companions at court.

courtly / **kawt**-lee / *adj.* refined and polite. ☐ **courtliness** *n.*

Court of Appeal *n.* a court hearing appeals against judgments made in lower courts of the Australian States.

Court of Disputed Returns *n.* a court for determining disputes about elections.

Court of Petty Sessions *n.* an Australian State court of summary jurisdiction, usu. presided over by a magistrate.

courtroom *n.* a room in which a court of law meets.

courtship *n.* **1** courting, wooing; the period during which this takes place. **2** the courting behaviour of animals, birds, etc.

courtyard *n.* a space enclosed by walls or buildings.

couscous / **kuus**-kuus / *n.* **1** dry, pre-cooked, durum-wheat semolina, available in fine or coarse grains. **2** a North African dish of couscous steamed over a spicy meat etc. broth, and served with the meat and broth.

cousin *n.* **1** (also **first cousin**) a child of one's uncle or aunt. **2** *Aust.* (in Aboriginal English) any of several more distant relatives. **3** a person of a related race or nation.

couture / koo-**tyoor** / *n.* the design and making of high-class fashionable clothes.

couturier / koo-**tyoo**-ree-ay, koo-**toor**-ree-uh / *n.* a designer of high-class fashionable clothes.

Couvreur, Jessie (Catherine) (1848–97), Australian writer. Her novels included *Uncle Piper of Piper's Hill* (1889), a portrayal of middle class society in colonial Melbourne.

covalency *n.* **1** the linking of atoms by a bond in which pairs of electrons are shared by two atoms in a molecule. **2** the number of pairs of electrons an atom can share with another. ☐ **covalent** *adj.*

cove *n.* **1** a small bay or inlet on a coast. **2** a curved moulding at a junction of a ceiling and a wall. **3** *colloq.* a man, bloke, chap. • *v.* **1** provide (a room etc.) with a cove. **2** slope (the sides of a fireplace) inwards.

coven / **kuv**-uhn / *n.* an assembly of witches.

covenant / **kuv**-uh-nuhnt / *n.* a formal agreement, a contract. • *v.* undertake by covenant. ☐ **covenanter** *n.*

Coventry / **kuv**-uhn-tree / a city in England. ☐ **send a person to Coventry** refuse to speak to or associate with him or her.

cover *v.* **1** protect or conceal with a cloth, lid, etc. **2** strew thickly (*covered the floor with straw*). **3** lie or extend over; occupy the surface of (*the factory covers a large area; he's covered in dirt*). **4** travel over (a distance) (*we covered sixty kilometres*). **5** guard; protect by dominating the approach to; have within range of one's gun(s); keep a gun aimed at. **6** protect by providing insurance or a guarantee (*covering you against fire or theft*). **7** be enough money to pay for (*$20 should cover it*). **8** include, deal with (*this book covers all the main topics*). **9** envelop (*covered in confusion; this will cover us in glory*). **10** investigate or report for a

coverage

newspaper etc. (*who is covering the conference?*). **11** (of a stallion etc.) copulate with. •*n.* **1** a thing that covers. **2** the binding of a book etc.; either half of this. **3** a wrapper or envelope. **4** shelter, protection (*there was no cover*). **5** a supporting force etc. protecting another from attack (*fighter cover*). **6** a screen or pretence (*under cover of friendship*). **7** insurance against loss or damage etc. ☐ **cover charge** a service charge per person in a restaurant etc. **cover for** deputise temporarily for. **covering letter** (also **covering note**) an explanatory letter sent with a document or goods. **cover much ground 1** travel far. **2** deal with a variety of topics. **cover note** a temporary certificate of insurance. **cover oneself** take measures to protect oneself (*I had covered myself by saying I might be late*). **cover point** (in cricket) a fieldsman covering point; this position. **cover story 1** a magazine article advertised on the front cover. **2** the main story in a television current affairs program. **cover up** conceal (a thing or fact). **cover-up** *n.* concealment, esp. of facts. **cover version** a recording of a previously re-corded song etc. made by a different artist. **take cover** find shelter. **under separate cover** in a separate envelope or package.

coverage *n.* **1** the act or fact of covering. **2** the area or amount covered. **3** the reporting of events in a newspaper or broadcast.

coveralls *n.* a full-length protective garment.

coverlet *n.* a bedspread.

covert / koh-vert, kuv-uht / *n.* **1** an area of thick undergrowth in which animals hide. **2** a bird's feather covering the base of another. •*adj.* concealed, done secretly (*gave him covert glances; covert operations*). ☐ **covertly** *adv.*

covet / kuv-uht / *v.* (**coveted, coveting**) desire eagerly, esp. something belonging to another person.

covetous / kuv-uh-tuhs / *adj.* **1** coveting. **2** grasping; avaricious. ☐ **covetously** *adv.* **covetousness** *n.*

covey / kuv-ee / *n.* (*pl.* **coveys**) **1** a brood or small flock of partridges. **2** a small group of people or things.

cow *n.* **1** the fully-grown female of cattle or of certain other large animals (e.g. elephant, whale, seal). **2** *colloq. offens.* a woman one dislikes. **3** *Aust. colloq.* a term of abuse applied to any person, animal, situation, or thing to which the speaker takes violent exception (*it's a cow of a job*). •*v.* subdue by frightening with threats or force. ☐ **cow cocky** *Aust.* a dairy farmer.

cowabunga / kow-uh-**bung**-guh / *interj. colloq.* an exclamation of exhilaration or satisfaction. (¶ Originally *Kawabonga* etc., an exclamation of anger in a 1950s US cartoon; it has been suggested that the word came from a NSW Aboriginal language (*kauwul* 'big', *bong* 'death', *gubba* 'good') and migrated to the US through surfing contacts.)

Cr

cowal / kow-uhl / *n. Aust.* a tree-covered swampy depression in country with reddish soil. (¶ Kamilaroi)

Cowan, Dame Edith (Dircksey) (1861–1932), Australian social worker and the first woman member of an Australian parliament.

coward *n.* **1** a person who lacks courage. **2** one who attacks only those who cannot retaliate.

cowardice *n.* cowardly feelings or actions.

cowardly *adj.* of or like a coward. ☐ **cowardliness** *n.*

cowboy *n.* **1** a man who herds and tends cattle, esp. in the western US. **2** *colloq.* a person who uses reckless or unscrupulous methods in business etc. **3** *Aust.* a worker on a station who performs such tasks as milking cows etc.

Cowen, Sir Zelman (1919–), AK, Australian jurist, writer, and academic, Governor-General of Australia 1977–82.

cower *v.* crouch or shrink back in fear.

cowgirl *n.* a female who herds and tends cattle.

cowhide *n.* **1** a cow's hide. **2** leather or a whip made from this.

cowl *n.* **1** a monk's hood or hooded robe. **2** a hood-shaped covering, e.g. on a chimney.

cowlick *n.* a lock of hair that stands out over the forehead.

cowling *n.* a removable metal cover over an engine.

cowpat *n.* a flat round piece of cow dung.

cowrie *n.* **1** a mollusc found in tropical seas, with a glossy often brightly-coloured shell. **2** its shell, esp. when used as money in parts of Africa and S. Asia.

cowslip *n.* a wild plant with clusters of small yellow flowers. ☐ **cowslip orchid** an Australian orchid bearing large, bright yellow flowers.

cox *n.* a coxswain. •*v.* act as cox of a racing boat.

coxcomb *n.* a conceited young man; a show-off.

coxswain / kok-suhn, -swayn / *n.* **1** a person who steers a rowing boat. **2** a sailor in charge of a ship's boat. **3** a senior petty officer on certain naval vessels.

coy *n.* pretending to be shy or embarrassed, bashful. ☐ **coyly** *adv.* **coyness** *n.*

coyote / kuy-**oh**-tee, **koi**-oht / *n.* a North American wolf-like wild dog.

coypu / **koi**-poo / *n.* a beaver-like water animal, originally from South America.

coz / kuz / *n.* (*archaic* except in Aboriginal English) cousin.

cozen / **kuz**-uhn / *v. literary* cheat; act deceitfully. ☐ **cozenage** *n.* **cozener** *n.*

cozzie alternative spelling of COSSIE.

CPI *abbr.* = CONSUMER PRICE INDEX.

Cpl *abbr.* Corporal.

cps *abbr.* **1** *Computing* characters per second. **2** *Science* cycles per second.

CPU *abbr. Computing* central processing unit.

Cr *symbol* chromium.

crab n. **1** a ten-footed shellfish with the first pair of legs as pincers. **2** its flesh as food. **3** (**the Crab**) a sign of the zodiac, Cancer. **4** (also **crab louse**) (usu. as **crabs**) a parasitic louse sexually transmitted esp. to the pubic hair. **5** = CRAB APPLE. **6** a sour person. •v. (**crabbed, crabbing**) colloq. **1** find fault with, grumble. **2** spoil (*the mistake crabbed his chances*). ◻ **catch a crab** get an oar jammed or miss the water by a faulty stroke in rowing. **crab apple** a small sour apple.

crabbed / krabd / adj. **1** bad-tempered. **2** (of writing) difficult to read or decipher.

crabby adj. bad-tempered. ◻ **crabbily** adv. **crabbiness** n.

crabhole n. Aust. **1** a hole in the ground made by a land crab; any similar hole. **2** = GILGAI.

crabwise adj. & adv. sideways or backwards.

crack n. **1** a sudden sharp explosive noise. **2** a sharp blow. **3** a sudden change in vocal pitch (*had a crack in his voice*). **4** colloq. a wisecrack, a joke. **5** a chink. **6** a line of division where something is broken but has not come completely apart. **7** colloq. a first-rate player, horse, etc. **8** a very strong form of cocaine used as a stimulant. •adj. colloq. first-rate. •v. **1** make or cause to make a sudden sharp explosive sound; hit sharply (*cracked his head against the wall*). **2** tell (a joke). **3** break with a sharp sound. **4** break into (a safe etc.). **5** open and consume (a bottle of wine, a can of beer, etc.) (*cracked a few tinnies*). **6** find the solution to (a code or problem). **7** colloq. obtain (*did you crack an invite to the party?*). **8** break without coming completely apart. **9** (of a voice) become suddenly harsh, esp. with emotion; (of an adolescent boy's voice) change pitch suddenly. **10** collapse under strain, cease to resist (*cracked under torture*). **11** Surfing catch and ride (a wave). ◻ **crack a fat** Aust. colloq. have an erection of the penis. **crack down on** colloq. take severe measures against. **crack hardy** colloq. put on a brave front. **crack it** Aust. colloq. succeed (in an enterprise etc.). **crack on to** Aust. colloq. make amorous advances to. **crack up** colloq. **1** Aust. praise highly (*not what it's cracked up to be*). **2** have a physical or mental breakdown. **3** laugh uncontrollably. **have a crack at** colloq. attempt.

crackdown n. colloq. severe measures, esp. against lawbreakers.

cracked adj. colloq. crazy.

cracker n. **1** a firework that explodes with a sharp crack. **2** a small paper tube that explodes harmlessly when the ends are pulled, releasing a hat, joke, etc., a bonbon. **3** a thin dry biscuit. **4** (usu. in *pl.*) an instrument for cracking. **5** colloq. a person or thing that is exceptionally attractive, fine, etc. **6** a cracking or rattling pace (*the pace is a cracker*). **7** Aust. the smallest imaginable amount of money (*stranded in the back of Bourke without a cracker*). •adj. (**crackers**) Aust. colloq. crazy. ◻ **not worth a cracker** completely worthless.

crackerjack colloq. n. **1** something that is exceptionally fine or splendid. **2** a person who is exceptionally skilful or expert. •adj. exceptional (*she's a crackerjack cricketer*).

cracking adj. colloq. **1** excellent. **2** fast and exciting (*set a cracking pace*). •adv. outstandingly (*is cracking good at it*).

crackle v. make or cause to make a series of slight cracking sounds (*the radio crackled; the fire is crackling*). •n. these sounds.

crackling n. crisp skin on roast pork.

Cracknell, Ruth (Winifred) (1925–), AM, Australian actor in serious as well as comic roles in theatre, television, and films, for which she has won many awards. Most widely known for her lead role in the television series *Mother and Son*.

crackpot adj. colloq. crazy, unpractical. •n. a person with crazy or unpractical ideas.

cradle n. **1** a small bed for a baby, usu. on rockers. **2** a place where something originates (*the cradle of civilisation*). **3** a supporting framework or structure. **4** Aust. a box-like apparatus for separating gold from sand, gravel, etc. •v. **1** place in a cradle; hold or support as if in a cradle. **2** Aust. wash (gold-containing gravel etc.) in a miner's cradle. ◻ **cradle-snatcher** n. colloq. the admirer or lover of a much younger person.

craft n. **1** an occupation in which skill is needed. **2** such a skill. **3** cunning, deceit. **4** (*pl.* **craft**) a boat or raft; an aircraft or spacecraft. •v. make skilfully (*crafted a poem*).

craftsman n. a person who is skilled in a craft. ◻ **craftsmanship** n.

crafty adj. (**craftier, craftiest**) cunning, using underhand methods; ingenious. ◻ **craftily** adv. **craftiness** n.

crag n. a steep or rugged rock.

craggy adj. (of facial features or landscape) rugged; rough-textured. ◻ **cragginess** n.

crake n. any of various birds of the rail family inhabiting esp. reedbeds and swamps.

cram v. (**crammed, cramming**) **1** force into too small a space so that the container is overfull. **2** overfill in this way. **3** study intensively for an examination.

cramp n. **1** sudden painful involuntary tightening of a muscle. **2** a metal bar with bent ends for holding masonry etc. together. •v. **1** affect with cramp. **2** keep within too narrow limits. **3** fasten with a cramp. ◻ **cramp a person's style** prevent him or her from acting freely or naturally.

cramped adj. **1** without room to move. **2** (of a space) too narrow. **3** (of writing) small and with letters close together.

crampon / kram-puhn / n. an iron plate with spikes, worn on boots for walking or climbing on ice.

cranberry n. **1** the small acid red berry of a shrub, used for making jelly and sauce. **2** = NATIVE CRANBERRY.

crane n. **1** an apparatus for moving heavy objects, usu. by suspending them from a jib by ropes or chains. **2** a large wading bird with long legs, neck, and bill. •v. stretch (one's neck) to see something.

cranesbill n. a wild geranium.

cranium / **kray**-nee-uhm / n. (pl. **craniums** or **crania**) the bones enclosing the brain; the skull. □ **cranial** adj.

crank n. **1** an L-shaped part for converting to-and-fro motion into circular motion. **2** a person with very strange ideas. •v. cause to move by means of a crank.

crankshaft n. a shaft driven by a crank.

cranky adj. **1** eccentric; strange. **2** working badly; shaky. **3** grumpy, irritable. **4** Aust. (in Aboriginal English) mad, crazy. □ **cranky fan** a mostly grey fantail, widespread throughout Australia, so called because of its rapid changes of direction as it flies after insects. □□ **crankiness** n.

cranny n. a crevice. □ **crannied** adj.

crap coarse colloq. n. **1** faeces. **2** nonsense, rubbish. **3** odds and ends; things (*don't leave your crap lying around the house*). •v. (**crapped**, **crapping**) defecate. □ **crap on** talk nonsense. □□ **crappy** adj.

crape n. black crêpe formerly used for mourning.

crapulent / **krap**-yuh-luhnt / adj. drunken; caused by drunkenness. □ **crapulence** n. **crapulous** adj.

crash n. **1** a sudden violent noise like that of something breaking by impact. **2** a violent collision or fall. **3** a sudden drop or failure; a financial collapse. **4** *Computing* the unexpected failure of a machine or system. •v. **1** make a crash; move or go with a crash. **2** cause (a vehicle or aircraft) to have a collision; be involved in a crash. **3** colloq. enter without permission, gatecrash. **4** drop or fail suddenly; collapse financially. **5** colloq. (often foll. by *out*) sleep, esp. on a floor etc. **6** *Computing* (of a machine or system) (cause to) fail unexpectedly. •adj. involving intense effort to achieve something rapidly (*a crash program*). □ **crash barrier** a protective fence erected where there is danger of vehicles leaving a road. **crash-dive** n. a sudden dive by an aircraft or submarine. v. dive in this way. **crash helmet** a padded helmet worn esp. by cyclists and motorcyclists to protect the head in case of a crash. **crash hot** colloq. excellent. **crash-land** v. land (an aircraft) in an emergency, esp. with damage to it; be landed in this way.

crashing adj. colloq. overwhelming (*a crashing bore*).

crass adj. **1** gross (*crass stupidity*). **2** very stupid. □ **crassly** adv. **crassness** n.

crate n. **1** a packing case made of wooden slats. **2** colloq. an old aircraft or car. **3** a divided container for bottles.

crater n. a bowl-shaped cavity or hollow.

cravat / kruh-**vat** / n. a man's scarf worn inside an open-necked shirt.

crave v. **1** long for, have a strong desire. **2** *archaic* ask earnestly for (*crave mercy*).

craven adj. cowardly. •n. a cowardly person.

craving n. a strong desire, a longing.

craw n. the crop of a bird or insect. □ **stick in one's craw** be unacceptable.

Crawford, Hector (William) (1913–91), AO, Australian radio and television producer, winner of many awards for his productions.

crawl v. **1** move as snakes or ants do, with the body close to the ground. **2** move on hands and knees. **3** move slowly or with difficulty. **4** colloq. seek favour by behaving in a servile way (*he crawls to the boss*). **5** be covered with crawling things (*the shed is crawling with triantelopes*). **6** (esp. of the skin) feel a creepy sensation (*he makes my skin crawl*). •n. **1** a crawling movement. **2** a very slow pace (*at a crawl*). **3** = AUSTRALIAN CRAWL. □ **crawler** n.

cray n. Aust. = CRAYFISH.

crayfish n. (pl. **crayfish**) **1** an Australian freshwater crustacean like a small lobster, esteemed as food (e.g. YABBY, MARRON). **2** any of several Australian marine crustaceans, some very large, esteemed as food (e.g. rock lobster).

crayon n. a stick of coloured wax etc. for drawing. •v. draw or colour with crayons.

craze n. **1** a great but short-lived enthusiasm for something. **2** the object of this.

crazed adj. driven insane (*crazed with grief*).

crazy adj. (**crazier**, **craziest**) **1** insane. **2** foolish, not sensible (*this crazy plan*). **3** extremely enthusiastic; extravagantly in love with (*crazy about hang-gliding; crazy about him*). □ **crazy paving** paving made up of oddly-shaped pieces fitted together. □□ **crazily** adv. **craziness** n.

Creaghe / krayk /, Emily Caroline (1860–1944), Australian explorer and diarist: she was a member of the expedition which in 1882 explored the unknown territory at the base of the Gulf of Carpentaria.

creak n. a harsh squeak like that of an unoiled hinge. •v. **1** make such a sound. **2** be badly constructed (*the plot of this play creaks*). □ **creaky** adj. **creakily** adv.

cream n. **1** the fatty part of milk. **2** its colour, yellowish white. **3** a food containing or like cream. **4** a soft cream-like substance, esp. as a cosmetic. **5** the best part of something (*the cream of the nation's youth*). •adj. cream-coloured. •v. **1** remove the cream from. **2** make creamy; beat (ingredients) to a creamy consistency. **3** apply a cream to. **4** form cream, froth, or scum. **5** colloq. defeat thoroughly (*we creamed the opposition*). □ **cream cheese** soft rich cheese made from curds of cream and unskimmed milk. **cream off** remove (the best or a required part). **cream of tartar** a compound of potassium used in medicine and in baking powder.

creamery *n.* **1** a factory producing butter and cheese. **2** a dairy.

creamy *adj.* (**creamier, creamiest**) **1** rich in cream. **2** like cream. ☐ **creaminess** *n.*

crease *n.* **1** a line caused by crushing, folding, or ironing. **2** a line marking the limit of the bowler's and batsman's positions in cricket. • *v.* **1** make a crease or creases in. **2** develop creases.

create *v.* **1** bring into existence; originate. **2** give rise to; produce by what one does (*create a good impression*). **3** give a new rank or position to (*created the garbo a duke*). **4** *colloq.* make a fuss, grumble.

creation *n.* **1** creating or being created. **2** (**the Creation**) God's creating of the universe. **3** (**Creation**) the universe; all things. **4** a product of the imagination, art, fashion, etc.; something created.

creationism *n.* the theory attributing all matter, biological species, etc., to separate acts of creation by God, rather than to evolution. ☐ **creationist** *n.*

creative *adj.* **1** having the power or ability to create things. **2** showing imagination and originality (*creative work*). ☐ **creative accounting** modification of accounts so as to present figures in a misleadingly favourable light. ☐☐ **creatively** *adv.*

creator *n.* **1** one who creates something. **2** (**the Creator**) God.

creature *n.* **1** a living being, esp. an animal. **2** a person (*a poor creature*). ☐ **creature comforts** things that make one's life comfortable.

crèche / kraysh, kresh / *n.* a day nursery.

cred *n. colloq.* credibility.

credence / kree-duhns / *n.* **1** belief. **2** (in full **credence table**) a small side table, shelf, or niche which holds the elements of the Eucharist before they are consecrated.

credentials / kruh-**den**-shuhlz / *n.pl.* **1** letters or papers showing that a person is who or what he or she claims to be. **2** evidence of achievements or trustworthiness.

credibility *n.* the quality of being credible.

credible *adj.* that can be believed; convincing. ☐ **credibly** *adv.*

credit *n.* **1** honour or acknowledgment given for some achievement or good quality. **2** a source of honour (*a credit to the school*). **3** credibility, confidence in a person or his or her actions etc. **4** a system of doing business by trusting that a person will pay at a later date for goods or services supplied (*buy on credit*). **5** the power to buy in this way. **6** the amount of money in a person's bank account or entered in an account book as paid to the holder. **7** an educational course counting towards a degree or other qualification. **8** (**credits**) a list of acknowledgments shown at the end of a film or television program. • *v.* (**credited, crediting**) **1** believe. **2** attribute (*scholars credit Strauss with this waltz*). **3** enter as credit in an account book. ☐ **credit card** a card authorising a person to buy on credit. **credit note** a document crediting a sum of money to a customer, e.g. for goods returned. **credit rating** an estimate of a person's suitability for credit or a loan. **credit union** a non-profit-making organisation which handles some of the functions of a bank, usu. for a group of employees.

creditable *adj.* deserving praise. ☐ **creditably** *adv.*

creditor *n.* a person to whom money is owed.

creditworthy *adj.* considered suitable to receive credit or a loan.

credo / **kray**-doh, **kree**- / *n.* (*pl.* **credos**) a creed.

credulous / **kred**-yuh-luhs / *adj.* too ready to believe things. ☐ **credulously** *adv.* **credulity** / kruh-**dyoo**-luh-tee / *n.*

creed *n.* **1** a formal summary of Christian beliefs. **2** a set of beliefs or principles.

creek *n.* **1** *US* & *Aust.* a watercourse, esp. a stream, or tributary of a river. **2** *Brit.* a small bay; a narrow inlet on a sea coast. ☐ **up the creek** *colloq.* **1** in difficulties. **2** crazy.

creel *n.* a fisherman's wicker basket for carrying fish.

creep *v.* (**crept, creeping**) **1** move with the body close to the ground. **2** move timidly, slowly, or stealthily; come on gradually. **3** *colloq.* seek to gain advancement by acting in a servile way. **4** (of plants) grow along the ground. **5** feel as if covered with crawling things (*it will make your flesh creep*). • *n.* **1** creeping. **2** *colloq.* a person one dislikes; one who seeks favour by behaving in a servile way. **3** a gradual change in the shape of metal under stress. **4** (**the creeps**) *colloq.* a nervous feeling produced by fear or dislike.

creeper *n.* **1** a creeping or climbing plant. **2** a bird that climbs, esp. a treecreeper.

creepy *adj.* (**creepier, creepiest**) making one's flesh creep; feeling this sensation. ☐ **creepy-crawly** *colloq.* **1** a crawling insect etc. **2** (**creepy-crawlies**) a feeling of fear or loathing (*that guy gives me the creepy-crawlies*). ☐☐ **creepily** *adv.* **creepiness** *n.*

cremate *v.* burn (a corpse) to ashes. ☐ **cremation** *n.*

crematorium / krem-uh-**taw**-ree-uhm / *n.* (*pl.* **crematoria** *or* **crematoriums**) a place where corpses are cremated.

crème / krem / *n.* **1** a food containing or like cream. **2** used in the names of various liqueurs. ☐ **crème brûlée** / **broo**-lay / baked cream or custard pudding coated with caramel. **crème caramel** custard coated with caramel. **crème de la crème** the very best; the best part. **crème de menthe** / month, mont / peppermint liqueur.

crenellated / **kren**-uh-lay-tuhd / *adj.* (of a tower etc.) having battlements. ☐ **crenellation** / kren-uh-**lay**-shuhn / *n.*

Creole / **kree**-ohl / *n.* (also **creole**) **1** a descendant of European settlers in the West Indies or Central or South America; a white descendant of French settlers in the southern USA. **2** a person of mixed European and Black descent. **3** a language formed from a European language and another language, as Torres Strait Creole (*see* KRIOL). •*adj.* **1** of Creole or Creoles. **2** (**creole**) of Creole origin etc. (*creole cooking*).

creosote / **kree**-uh-soht / *n.* **1** a thick brown oily liquid obtained from coal tar, used as a preservative for wood. **2** a colourless liquid obtained from wood tar, used as an antiseptic. •*v.* treat with creosote.

crêpe / krayp / *n.* **1** fabric with a wrinkled surface. **2** rubber with a wrinkled texture, used for shoe soles. **3** a thin pancake with a sweet or savoury filling. ☐ **crêpe de Chine** / duh **sheen** / fine silk crêpe. **crêpe paper** thin crinkled paper. **crêpe Suzette** a small sweet pancake flamed in alcohol. ☐☐ **crêpey** *adj.* (also **crêpy**).

crepitate *v.* make a crackling sound. ☐ **crepitation** *n.*

crepitus *n. Med.* **1** a grating noise from the ends of a fractured bone rubbing together. **2** a similar sound heard from the chest in pneumonia etc.

crept *see* CREEP.

crepuscular / kruh-**pus**-kyuh-luh / *adj.* of twilight; appearing or active at dusk.

Cres. *abbr.* Crescent.

crescendo / kruh-**shen**-doh / *adj. & adv.* gradually becoming louder. •*n.* (*pl.* **crescendos**) **1** a gradual increase in loudness. **2** progress towards a climax (*a crescendo of passion*).

■ *Usage Crescendo* is sometimes wrongly used to mean the climax itself (e.g. *reached a crescendo and then died away*) rather than progress towards it.

crescent *n.* **1** the waxing or waning moon, seen as a narrow curved shape tapering to a point at each end. **2** something shaped like this. **3** a curved street.

cress *n.* a plant with small leaves used in salads.

crest *n.* **1** a tuft or fleshy outgrowth on a bird's or animal's head. **2** a plume on a helmet. **3** the top of a slope or hill; the white top of a large wave. **4** a design above the shield on a coat of arms, or used separately to on a seal or notepaper etc.; such a device as used by schools, colleges, etc. (*the school crest*). •*v.* **1** reach the crest of (a hill, wave, etc.). **2** provide with a crest or serve as a crest to. **3** (of a wave) form a crest. ☐ **on the crest of a wave** at the most favourable time in one's progress.

crested *adj.* **1** having a crest. **2** as a distinguishing epithet in the names of some birds (*crested bellbird*).

crestfallen *adj.* downcast, disappointed at failure.

cretaceous / kruh-**tay**-shuhs / *adj.* **1** of or like chalk. **2** (**Cretaceous**) of the geological period in the Mesozoic era when chalk was deposited. •*n.* (**Cretaceous**) this period.

cretin / **kret**-uhn / *n.* **1** a person who is deformed and mentally undeveloped through lack of thyroid hormone. **2** *colloq.* a very stupid person. ☐ **cretinism** *n.* **cretinous** *adj.*

cretonne / kre-**ton**, **kret**-on / *n.* heavy cotton cloth with a printed pattern, used in furnishings.

Creutzfeldt-Jakob Disease *n.* a degenerative disease affecting nerve cells in the brain. (¶ H.G. Creutzfeldt (1885–1964) and A. Jakob (1884–1931), German physicians.)

crevasse / kruh-**vas** / *n.* a deep open crack, esp. in the ice of a glacier.

crevice / **krev**-uhs / *n.* a narrow opening or crack, esp. in a rock or wall.

crew[1] *see* CROW[2].

crew[2] *n.* **1** the people working a ship or aircraft. **2** all these except the officers. **3** a group of people working together (*the camera crew*). **4** a company of people, a gang (*had the crew from the shop over for a barbie*). •*v.* **1** act as crew (for). **2** supply a crew for. ☐ **crew cut** a closely cropped style of haircut. **crew neck** a closely fitting round neckline of a knitted garment.

crewel / **kroo**-uhl / *n.* fine worsted yarn used for tapestry and embroidery.

crib *n.* **1** a wooden framework from which animals can pull out fodder. **2** a baby's cot. **3** a model of the manger scene at Bethlehem. **4** the cards given by other players to the dealer at cribbage. **5** *colloq.* cribbage. **6** something copied from another person's work. **7** a literal translation (for use by students) of something written in a foreign language. **8** *Aust.* **a** a light meal or refreshment, packed to be eaten during a break from work. **b** the break itself. •*v.* (**cribbed**, **cribbing**) **1** copy unfairly or without acknowledgment; pilfer. **2** confine in a small space.

cribbage *n.* a card game in which the dealer scores also from cards in the crib (*see* CRIB sense 4).

crick *n.* a sudden painful stiffness in the neck or back. •*v.* cause a crick in.

cricket[1] *n.* an outdoor game played with a ball, bats, and wickets, between two sides of 11 players. ☐ **not cricket** *colloq.* not fair play. ☐☐ **cricketer** *n.*

cricket[2] *n.* a brown grasshopper-like insect that makes a shrill chirping sound.

cri de cœur / kree duh **ker** / *n.* (*pl. cris de cœur* pronounced the same) a passionate appeal, complaint, or protest. (¶ French, = cry from the heart.)

crier *n.* (also **cryer**) one who cries, esp. *hist.* an official making public announcements in the streets etc. (*town crier*).

crikey *interj. colloq.* an exclamation of astonishment. (¶ Euphemism for *Christ*.)

crim *n. & adj. Aust. colloq.* = CRIMINAL.

crime *n.* **1** a serious offence, one for which there is punishment by law. **2** such offences, serious law-breaking (*the detection of crime*). **3** *colloq.* a shame, a senseless act (*it would be a crime to miss such a chance*).

Crimea / kruy-**mee**-uh / *a peninsula in southern Ukraine.* □ **Crimean** *adj.*

Crimean shirt *n. Aust. hist.* a coloured flannel shirt formerly popular among workers in the bush.

Crimean War a war fought mainly in the Crimea in 1853–56, between Russia and an alliance of Great Britain, France, Sardinia, and Turkey.

criminal *n.* a person who is guilty of crime. •*adj.* **1** of or involving crime (*a criminal offence*). **2** concerned with crime and its punishment (*criminal law*). **3** *colloq.* scandalous, deplorable.

criminology *n.* the scientific study of crime. □ **criminologist** *n.*

crimp *v.* press into small folds or ridges.

crimson *adj.* **1** of a rich deep red. **2** used as a distinguishing epithet in the names of fauna and flora (*crimson chat; crimson sun-orchid*). •*n.* this colour. □ **crimson bottlebrush** the commonest callistemon in cultivation, a shrub, native to eastern Australia, bearing crimson bottlebrush flowers. **crimson rosella** a crimson and vivid blue parrot of eastern Australia

cringe *v.* **1** shrink back in fear, cower. **2** shrink in sheer embarrassment and distaste. **3** behave in a servile fawning way (*he's cringing to the boss again*). •*n.* an act or instance of cringing.

crinkle *v.* make or become wrinkled. •*n.* a wrinkle, a crease. □ **crinkle-cut** *adj.* with wavy edges. □□ **crinkly** *adj.*

crinoline / **krin**-uh-luhn / *n.* a light framework formerly worn to make a long skirt stand out; a skirt shaped by this.

cripes *interj. colloq.* an exclamation of astonishment. (¶ An alteration of *Christ.*)

cripple *n.* a person who is permanently lame. •*v.* **1** make a cripple of. **2** disable; weaken or damage seriously (*the business was crippled by lack of money*).

crisis *n.* (*pl.* **crises** / **kruy**-seez /) **1** a decisive time. **2** a time of acute difficulty or danger.

crisp *adj.* **1** brittle, breaking with a snap (*crisp pastry*). **2** stiff and crackling (*a crisp $100 note*). **3** cold and bracing (*a crisp winter morning*). **4** brisk and decisive (*a crisp manner*). •*n.* a thin fried slice of potato (usu. sold in packets). •*v.* make or become crisp. □ **crisply** *adv.* **crispness** *n.*

crispbread *n.* a thin crisp biscuit of crushed rye etc.

crispy *adj.* (**crispier**, **crispiest**) crisp.

criss-cross *n.* a pattern of crossing lines. •*adj.* with crossing lines. •*v.* mark or form or move in this pattern. (¶ An alteration of *Christ's cross.*)

criterion / kruy-**teer**-ree-uhn / *n.* (*pl.* **criteria**) a principle or standard by which a thing is judged (*the sole criterion is 'will it work?'*).

■ **Usage** Note that *criteria* is a plural; it is incorrect to speak of *a criteria* or *this criteria*, or of *criterias*.

criterium / kruy-**teer**-ree-uhm / *n.* a cycling race of multiple laps of a circuit, often as a stage in a touring race.

critic *n.* **1** a person who forms and expresses judgments about books, art, musical works, etc., esp. regularly or professionally. **2** a person who finds fault with something.

critical *adj.* **1** looking for faults. **2** expressing criticism (*a critical evaluation of the short stories of Henry Lawson*). **3** providing textual criticism (*a critical edition of Henry Lawson*). **4** of or at a crisis; at an important point when there will be a decisive change; risky; dangerous (*the patient's condition is critical*). **5** (of a nuclear reactor) having reached the stage of maintaining a self-sustaining chain reaction. □ **critical path** a sequence of stages determining the minimum time needed for an operation. □□ **critically** *adv.*

criticise *v.* (also **-ize**) **1** find fault (with). **2** examine critically; express judgments about.

criticism *n.* **1** finding fault; a remark pointing out a fault. **2** the work of a critic; judgments about books, art, music, etc.

critique / kri-**teek**, kruh-**teek** / *n.* a critical essay or review.

croak *n.* a deep hoarse cry or sound, like that of a frog. •*v.* **1** utter or speak with a croak. **2** *colloq.* die. □ **croaky** *adj.* **croakiness** *n.*

Croat / **kroh**-at / *n.* **1** a native or inhabitant of Croatia. **2** the Slavonic language of the Croats.

Croatia / kroh-**ay**-shuh / *a republic in south-eastern Europe, formerly part of Yugoslavia.* □ **Croatian** *adj.* & *n.*

croc *colloq.* a crocodile.

crochet / **kroh**-shay, **kroh**-shuh / *n.* a kind of needlework in which thread is looped into a lacy pattern of connected stitches by means of a hooked needle. •*v.* (**crocheted**, **crocheting**) do this needlework; make (an article) by this.

crock *n.* **1** an earthenware pot or jar. **2** a broken piece of this. **3** *colloq.* an old, worn-out person, horse, vehicle, etc.

crockery *n.* household china.

crocodile *n.* **1** a large tropical amphibian reptile with a thick skin, long tail, and huge jaws. **2** its skin, used to make bags, shoes, etc. **3** a long line of schoolchildren walking in pairs. □ **crocodile tears** insincere sorrow. (¶ So called from the belief that the crocodile wept while devouring its victim or to allure it.)

crocus *n.* (*pl.* **crocuses**) a small plant growing from a corm, with yellow, purple, or white flowers, the stigmas of *Crocus sativus* yielding the spice saffron.

Croesus / **kree**-suhs / *n.* an extremely wealthy person. (¶ The name of a king of ancient Lydia.)

croissant / krwah-song / *n.* a light crescent-shaped bread roll made of rich yeast dough.

Croker Island / kroh-kuh / an Australian island 250 km north-east of Darwin. In 1998 the Federal Court ruled that native title could exist over the surrounding areas of the sea and the seabed, although native title rights did not override the interests of other parties.

Cro-Magnon / kroh-**man**-yon, -**mag**-nuhn / *adj. Anthropology* of a tall broad-faced European race of late palaeolithic times. (¶ The name of a hill in France where remains were found in 1868.)

cromlech / krom-lek / *n.* **1** = DOLMEN. **2** a circle of upright prehistoric stones.

crone *n.* a withered old woman.

crony *n.* a close friend or companion.

crook *n.* **1** a hooked stick or staff, used by a shepherd or bishop. **2** something bent or curved (*carried it in the crook of her arm*). **3** *colloq.* a dishonest person; a criminal. •*adj. Aust. colloq.* **1** unwell; injured. **2** bad; unpleasant (*things are really crook on the land*). **3** out of order; broken. **4** bad-tempered; angry. **5** dishonest. •*v.* bend into the shape of a crook (*crooked his finger to summon me*). ☐ **crook on** (also **crooked on**) *Aust. colloq.* infuriated with; hostile to. **go crook** *Aust. colloq.* **1** lose one's temper; become angry with (*went crook at me*). **2** go out of order, cease functioning.

crooked *adj.* **1** not straight or level; having curves, bends, or twists. **2** dishonest, not straightforward. ☐ **crookedly** *adv.* **crookedness** *n.*

croon *v.* sing, hum, or say in a low sentimental voice. •*n.* singing etc. of this kind. ☐ **crooner** *n.*

crop *n.* **1** a batch of plants grown for their produce. **2** the harvest from this. **3** a group or quantity appearing or produced at one time (*this year's crop of students*). **4** the bag-like part of a bird's throat where food is broken up for digestion before passing into the stomach. **5** the handle of a whip; a whip with a loop instead of a lash. **6** a very short haircut. •*v.* (**cropped**, **cropping**) **1** cut or bite off (*sheep crop the grass closely*). **2** cut (hair) very short. **3** (of land) bear a crop. ☐ **crop dusting** the spraying of insecticide on crops, esp. from the air. **crop-eared** with the ears (of animals) cut short; with hair cut short enough to reveal the ears. **crop up** occur unexpectedly or by chance.

cropper *n.* a plant producing a crop of a specified quality. ☐ **come a cropper** *colloq.* fall heavily; fail badly.

croquet / kroh-kay / *n.* a game played on a lawn with wooden balls that are driven through hoops with mallets.

croquette / kroh-ket / *n.* a fried ball or roll of potato, meat, or fish.

Crosby, Bing (original name: Harry Lillis Crosby) (1904–77), American crooner and film actor.

crosier / kroh-zee-uh / *n.* (also **crozier**) a hooked staff carried by a bishop or a mitred abbot as a symbol of office.

cross *n.* **1** a mark made by drawing one line across another, (×) or (+). **2** an upright post with another piece of wood across it, used in ancient times for crucifixion; (**the Cross**) that on which Christ died. **3** a model of this as a Christian emblem. **4** an annoying thing one has to bear. **5** a cross-shaped military etc. decoration. **6** an animal or plant produced by cross-breeding. **7** a mixture of two different things (*he's a cross between a larrikin and a dandy*). **8** (**the Cross**)*Aust.* = SOUTHERN CROSS. **9** (**the Cross**) Kings Cross, a district of Sydney noted for its cosmopolitan character. •*v.* **1** go or extend across. **2** place crosswise (*crossed his legs*). **3** draw a line across (*cross the t's*). **4** mark (a cheque) with two parallel lines so that it must be paid into a bank or building society account. **5** make the sign of the Cross on or over (*cross oneself*). **6** oppose the wishes or plans of. **7** cross-breed (animals); cross-fertilise (plants). •*adj.* **1** passing from side to side. **2** annoyed, showing bad temper. **3** contrary, opposed; reciprocal (*crosswind*; *crossfire*). ☐ **at cross purposes** misunderstanding or conflicting with each other. **cross off** = CROSS OUT. **cross one's mind** come briefly into one's mind. **cross out** draw a line through (an item on a list) to show that it is no longer valid. **crossed line** a faulty telephone link in which another person's conversation can be heard. **on the cross** crosswise, on the bias. ☐☐ **crossly** *adv.* **crossness** *n.*

crossbar *n.* a horizontal bar, e.g. over a pair of goalposts or on a bicycle.

cross-bench *n.* a bench in parliament for members not belonging to the government or main opposition. ☐ **cross-bencher** *n.*

crossbow *n.* a powerful bow with mechanism for drawing and releasing the string.

cross-breed *v.* (**cross-bred**, **cross-breeding**) produce by mating an animal with one of a different kind. •*n.* an animal produced in this way.

cross-check *v.* check by a different method. •*n.* a check of this kind.

cross-country *adj. & adv.* across paddocks or countryside, not keeping to main roads or to a direct road.

cross-dressing *n.* the practice of dressing in the clothes of the opposite sex.

crosse *n.* a lacrosse stick.

cross-examine *v.* cross-question, esp. in a lawcourt. ☐ **cross-examination** *n.*

cross-eyed *adj.* having one or both eyes turned towards the nose.

cross-fertilise *v.* (also **-ize**) fertilise (an animal or plant) from one of a different kind. ☐ **cross-fertilisation** *n.*

crossfire *n.* the firing of guns from two or more points so that the lines of fire cross.

cross-grained *adj.* **1** (of wood) with the grain in crossing directions. **2** bad-tempered.

cross-hatch *v.* shade (e.g. a drawing) with crossing parallel lines.

crossing *n.* **1** a journey across water (*we had a smooth crossing*). **2** a place where things cross. **3** a place at which one may cross; a place for pedestrians to cross a road.

cross-legged *adj. & adv.* (sitting) with legs folded one across the other.

crosspatch *n. colloq.* a bad-tempered person.

crosspiece *n.* a transverse beam, bar, section, etc.

cross-ply *adj.* (of tyres) having fabric layers with cords lying crosswise (cf. RADIAL-PLY).

cross-question *v.* question closely in order to test answers given to previous questions.

cross-refer *v.* (**cross-referred, cross-referring**) refer from one part of a book, document, etc. to another.

cross-reference *n.* a note directing people to another part of a book, index, etc. for further information.

crossroads *n.* a place where two or more roads intersect.

cross-section *n.* **1** a diagram showing the internal structure of something as though it has been cut through. **2** a representative sample.

cross stitch *n.* a stitch formed by two crossing stitches.

crossways *adv.* = CROSSWISE.

crosswind *n.* a wind blowing across the direction of travel.

crosswise *adj. & adv.* **1** in the form of a cross; intersecting. **2** diagonal or diagonally.

crossword *n.* a puzzle in which intersecting words, indicated by clues, have to be inserted into blank squares in a grid.

crotch *n.* **1** a place where things fork. **2** the part of the body or of a garment where the legs fork.

crotchet / kroch-uht / *n.* a note in music, equal to half a minim.

crotchety *adj.* peevish, irritable.

crouch *v.* lower the body with the limbs bent and close to it; be in this position. •*n.* an act of crouching; a crouching position.

croup / kroop / *n.* **1** a children's disease in which inflammation of the windpipe causes a hard cough and difficulty in breathing. **2** the rump, esp. of a horse.

croupier / **kroo**-pee-uh, -ay / *n.* a person who rakes in the money at a gambling table and pays out winnings.

crouton / **kroo**-ton / *n.* a small piece of fried or toasted bread served with soup etc.

crow[1] *n.* a large black bird of a family that includes the raven etc., including two Australian species. ☐ **as the crow flies** in a straight line. **crow's ash** a tall Australian rainforest tree with a durable timber resembling teak. **crow's feet** wrinkles in the skin at the side of the eyes. **crow shrike** the pied currawong. **crow's nest** a protected lookout platform high on the mast of a ship.

crow[2] *v.* (**crowed** or **crew, crowing**) **1** (of a rooster) make a loud shrill cry. **2** (of a baby) make sounds of pleasure. **3** express gleeful triumph. •*n.* a crowing cry or sound.

crowbar *n.* a bar of iron with a flattened or beak-like end, used as a lever.

crowd *n.* **1** a large number of people in one place. **2** *colloq.* a particular set of people (*met the crowd from the sales department*). •*v.* **1** come together in a crowd. **2** fill or occupy fully; cram with people or things. **3** inconvenience by crowding or coming aggressively close (*stop crowding me, mate!*). ☐ **crowd surf** (esp. at a rock concert) ride the body of a crowd as if it were a wave, by being passed over the heads of individual crowd members. ☐ ☐ **crowded** *adj.*

Crowe, Russell (Ira) (1964–), New Zealand-born Australian actor. His films include *Gladiator* (2000), for which he won a best-actor Oscar.

crowea / kroh-ee-uh / *n.* an Australian shrub with showy starflowers, white to deep rose.

croweater *n. Aust. colloq.* a South Australian.

crown *n.* **1** an ornamental headdress worn by a monarch. **2** (**the Crown**) a monarch as head of State, e.g. in Britain, or in an independent nation such as Australia which is still under a monarchy. **3** a wreath worn on the head, esp. as a symbol of victory. **4** a crown-shaped object or ornament. **5** the top part of something (e.g. of the head or a hat); the highest part of something arched. **6** the part of a tooth visible above the gum; an artificial replacement for this. **7** a former Australian coin worth 5 shillings. •*v.* **1** put a crown on (a person or head) as a symbol of royal power or victory in sport etc. **2** form, cover, or ornament the top part of. **3** make a successful conclusion to (*our efforts were crowned with success*). **4** put an artificial top on (a tooth). **5** *Aust.* (of a bushfire) move (rapidly) through the tops of trees (*the fire's beginning to crown*). **6** *colloq.* hit on the head. ☐ **crown fire** a bushfire which moves through the tops of trees. **crown land** (in Australia) land which has never been bought or sold and is owned by a State government. **crown of thorns starfish** *Aust.* a spiny coral-eating starfish of tropical regions including the Great Barrier Reef, so called because of a fancied resemblance to Christ's crown of thorns.

crozier alternative spelling of CROSIER.

CRT *abbr.* cathode ray tube.

cruces *see* CRUX.

crucial / kroo-shuhl / *adj.* **1** decisive, critical. **2** *colloq.* very important. ☐ **crucially** *adv.*

cruciate ligament *n.* either of a pair of ligaments in the knee which cross each other and connect the femur and the tibia.

crucible / **kroo**-suh-buhl / *n.* a pot in which metals are melted.

cruciferous / kroo-**sif**-uh-ruhs / *adj.* of the family of plants bearing flowers with four equal petals arranged crosswise.

crucifix *n.* a model of the Cross or of Christ on the Cross.

crucifixion *n.* **1** crucifying, being crucified. **2** (**the Crucifixion**) that of Christ.

cruciform / kroo-suh-fawm / *adj.* cross-shaped.

crucify *v.* (**crucified, crucifying**) **1** put to death by nailing or binding to a cross. **2** persecute, torment. **3** *colloq.* defeat thoroughly in an argument, match, etc.; humiliate.

crud *n. colloq.* **1** a deposit of grease, dirt, etc. **2** an unpleasant person. **3** nonsense.

cruddy *adj. colloq.* **1** filthy. **2** of inferior quality; shoddy (*bought this cruddy watch*).

crude *adj.* **1** in a natural state, not refined (*crude oil*). **2** not well finished or worked out, rough (*a crude carving*). **3** without good manners, vulgar. • *n.* crude oil. ☐ **crudely** *adv.* **crudity** *n.*

crudités / **kroo**-di-tay / *n.pl.* a starter of mixed raw vegetables cut into small pieces, often with a special sauce to dip them in.

cruel *adj.* (**crueller, cruellest**) **1** feeling pleasure in another's suffering. **2** causing pain or suffering (*this cruel war*). • *v. colloq.* spoil (an opportunity etc.); ruin (*he has just cruelled his chances of promotion*). ☐ **cruelly** *adv.* **cruelty** *n.*

cruet *n.* **1 a** a set of small salt, pepper, etc. containers for use at the table. **b** such a container. **2** *Aust. colloq.* the head.

Cruise, Tom (original name: Thomas Cruise Mapother IV) (1962–), American actor. His films include *Top Gun* (1986) and *Magnolia* (1999).

cruise *v.* **1** sail about for pleasure or on patrol. **2** (of a vehicle or aircraft) travel at a moderate speed that is economical of fuel. **3** drive at moderate speed, or at random when looking for passengers etc. **4** *colloq.* search for a sexual (esp. homosexual) partner in bars etc. **5** achieve an objective, esp. win a race etc. with ease. • *n.* a cruising voyage. ☐ **be cruising** *colloq.* be doing or performing effortlessly. **cruise missile** a missile that is able to fly at low altitude and guide itself by reference to the features of the region traversed.

cruiser *n.* a high-speed warship.

crumb *n.* **1** a small fragment, esp. of bread or other food. **2** the soft inner part of bread. **3** *colloq.* an objectionable person. • *v.* **1** cover with breadcrumbs. **2** crumble (bread). ☐ **pick up** (*or* **gather**) **the crumbs** *Aust. Rules* pick up a loose ball.

crumble *v.* break or fall into small fragments. • *n.* fruit cooked with a crumbly topping (*apple crumble*).

crumbly *adj.* easily crumbled.

crumhorn alternative spelling of KRUMMHORN.

crummy *adj.* (**crummier, crummiest**) *colloq.* **1** dirty, squalid. **2** inferior, worthless. ☐ **crumminess** *n.*

crumpet *n.* **1** a soft cake of yeast mixture, eaten toasted and buttered. **2** *colloq. offens.* a sexually attractive woman; women regarded merely as the object of male sexual desire.

crumple *v.* **1** crush or become crushed into creases. **2** collapse loosely.

crunch *v.* **1** crush noisily with the teeth. **2** walk or move with a sound of crushing; make such a sound. • *n.* **1** crunching; a crunching sound. **2** *colloq.* a decisive event, a showdown. ☐ **crunchy** *adj.*

crupper *n.* a strap for holding a harness back, passing under a horse's tail.

crusade / kroo-**sayd** / *n.* **1** any of the military expeditions made by Europeans in the Middle Ages to recover the Holy Land from the Muslims. **2** a vigorous campaign for a cause. • *v.* take part in a crusade. ☐ **crusader** *n.*

crush *v.* **1** press so as to break, injure, or wrinkle; squeeze tightly. **2** pound into small fragments. **3** become crushed. **4** defeat or subdue completely. • *n.* **1** a crowd of people pressed together. **2** *Aust.* a narrow passage in a stockyard through which animals can pass only in single file. **3** a drink made from crushed fruit. **4** *colloq.* an infatuation. ☐ **crushable** *adj.*

crust *n.* **1** the hard outer layer of something, esp. bread, a pie, etc. **2** the rocky outer portion of the earth. **3** a deposit, esp. from wine on a bottle. **4** *colloq.* impudence. **5** esp. *Aust. colloq.* livelihood (*what do you do for a crust?*).

crustacean / krus-**tay**-shuhn / *n.* an animal that has a hard shell (e.g. crab, crayfish, prawn, yabby).

crusty *adj.* (**crustier, crustiest**) **1** having a crisp crust. **2** having a harsh manner. ☐ **crustily** *adv.* **crustiness** *n.*

crutch *n.* **1** a support for a lame person, usu. fitting under the armpit. **2** the crotch of the body or of a garment. **3** esp. *Aust.* the hindquarters of a sheep. • *v.* esp. *Aust.* remove wool from about the tail of a sheep to prevent fouling and esp. to prevent blowfly strike.

crutchings *n.pl. Aust.* the wool clipped from the hindquarters of a sheep.

crux *n.* (*pl.* **cruxes** *or* **cruces** / kroo-seez /) the vital part of a problem; a decisive point.

cry *n.* **1** a loud wordless sound expressing pain, grief, joy, etc. **2** a shout. **3** the call of a bird or animal. **4** an appeal, a demand. **5** a battle-cry. **6** a spell of weeping (*have a good cry*). • *v.* (**cried, crying**) **1** shed tears. **2** call out loudly in words. **3** appeal, demand. **4** (of an animal) utter its cry. ☐ **a crying shame** a terrible injustice; one demanding attention. **a far cry 1** a long way (*it's quite a far cry away*). **2** a very different thing (*liberty is a far cry from licence*). **cry down** decry. **cry off** withdraw from a promise or arrangement.

cryer alternative spelling of CRIER.

cryogenics / kruy-oh-**jen**-iks / *n.* the scientific study of very low temperatures and their effects. ☐ **cryogenic** *adj.*

cryonics / kruy-**on**-iks / *n.* the use of extreme cold to preserve living tissue.

crypt / kript / *n.* a room below the floor of a church; a vault used as a burial place.

cryptic / **krip**-tik / *adj.* concealing its meaning in a puzzling way; secret, mysterious. ☐ **cryptically** *adv.*

cryptogam / **krip**-tuh-gam / *n.* a flowerless plant such as a fern, moss, or fungus. ☐ **cryptogamous** / krip-**tog**-uh-muhs / *adj.*

cryptogram / **krip**-tuh-gram / *n.* something written in code or cipher.

cryptography / krip-**tog**-ruh-fee / *n.* the art of writing in codes or ciphers or of deciphering these. ☐ **cryptographer** *n.* **cryptographic** *adj.*

cryptosporidium / krip-toh-spuh-**rid**-ee-uhm / *n.* a parasite infecting the small intestine of mammals, including humans, and causing diarrhoea, abdominal cramps, etc.

crystal *n.* **1** a clear transparent colourless mineral. **2** very clear glass of high quality. **3** each of the pieces into which certain substances solidify (*crystals of ice*). • *adj.* made of crystal; like or clear as crystal. ☐ **crystal ball** a globe of glass used in crystal-gazing. **crystal-gazing** *n.* looking into a crystal ball in an attempt to see future events pictured there.

crystalline / **kris**-tuh-luyn / *adj.* **1** like or containing crystals. **2** transparent, very clear.

crystallise *v.* (also **-ize**) **1** form crystals. **2** (of ideas or plans) become clear and definite in form. ☐ **crystallised fruit** fruit preserved in and coated with sugar. ☐ ☐ **crystallisation** *n.*

crystallography *n.* the science of crystal formation and structure. ☐ **crystallographer** *n.*

crystalloid *n.* a substance that in solution is able to pass through a semi-permeable membrane.

Cs *symbol* caesium.

c/s *abbr.* cycles per second.

CSIRO *abbr.* = COMMONWEALTH SCIENTIFIC AND INDUSTRIAL RESEARCH ORGANISATION.

Cu *symbol* copper.

cu. *abbr.* cubic.

cub *n.* **1** the young of certain animals, e.g. fox, bear, lion. **2** (**Cub**) (in full **Cub Scout**) a member of the junior branch of the Scout Association. **3** *colloq.* a young newspaper reporter. • *v.* (**cubbed**, **cubbing**) give birth to (cubs).

Cuba a Caribbean republic, the largest and furthest west of the islands of the West Indies. ☐ **Cuban** *adj.* & *n.*

cubby-hole *n.* a small room or compartment.

cubby-house *n.* a child's playhouse.

cube *n.* **1** a solid body with six equal square faces. **2** a block shaped like this. **3** the product of a number multiplied by itself twice (*the cube of 3 is 27*). • *v.* **1** cut (food) into small cubes. **2** find the cube of (a number). ☐ **cube root** a number which produces a given number when cubed (*the cube root of 27 is 3*).

cubic *adj.* of three dimensions. ☐ **cubic metre** etc., the volume of a cube with sides one metre etc. long.

cubical *adj.* cube-shaped.

cubicle *n.* a small division of a large room; an enclosed space screened for privacy.

cubism *n.* a style in art in which objects are represented as geometrical shapes. ☐ **cubist** *n.* & *adj.*

cubit / **kyoo**-buht / *n.* an ancient measure of length, approximately equal to the length of the arm from elbow to fingertips.

cuboid / **kyoo**-boid / *adj.* cube-shaped, like a cube. • *n.* a solid body with six rectangular sides.

cuckold / **kuk**-uhld / *n.* a man whose wife has committed adultery during their marriage. • *v.* make a cuckold of (a married man).

cuckoo *n.* a bird (including a number of Australian species) having a call sounding similar to its name, and often laying its eggs in the nests of other birds. ☐ **cuckoo-shrike** a bird of Australia and elsewhere having a mostly grey plumage with black markings. **cuckoo spit** a froth exuded by the larvae of certain insects on leaves, stems, etc.

cucumber *n.* **1** a long green-skinned fleshy fruit eaten as salad or pickled. **2** the plant producing this.

cucurbit / kyoo-**ker**-buht / *n.* any of various plants of the gourd family, including melons, pumpkins, ornamental gourds, etc.

cud *n.* the food that cattle etc. bring back from the stomach into the mouth and chew again.

cuddle *v.* hold closely and lovingly in one's arms. • *n.* a prolonged and loving hug.

cuddlesome *adj.* (also **cuddly**) pleasant to cuddle.

cudgel / **kuj**-uhl / *n.* a short thick stick used as a weapon. • *v.* (**cudgelled**, **cudgelling**) beat with a cudgel. ☐ **cudgel one's brains** think hard about a problem. **take up the cudgels** (often foll. by *for*) make a vigorous defence (of someone or something).

cudgerie *n.* any of several Australian rainforest trees, esp. bumpy ash. (¶ Probably from Bandjalang.)

cue[1] *n.* something said or done which serves as a signal for something else to be done, e.g. for an actor to speak in a play. • *v.* (**cued**, **cueing**) give a cue to. ☐ **on cue** at the correct moment.

cue[2] *n.* a long rod for striking the ball in billiards and similar games. ☐ **cue ball** the ball to be struck with a cue.

cue[3] *Aust. n.* a shoe for a bullock. • *v.* shoe (a bullock) with a cue.

cuff[1] *n.* **1** the end part of a sleeve. **2** a trouser turn-up. **3** (**cuffs**) handcuffs. ☐ **cuff link** *n.* each of a pair of fasteners for shirt-cuffs, used instead of buttons. **off the cuff** *colloq.* without rehearsal or preparation.

cuff[2] *v.* strike with the open hand. • *n.* a cuffing blow.

Cufic alternative spelling of KUFIC.

cuirass / kwuh-**ras** / *n.* a piece of armour consisting of a breastplate and a similar plate protecting the back.

cuisine / kwuh-**zeen** / *n.* a style of cooking.

cul-de-sac / **kul**-duh-sak / *n.* (*pl.* **culs-de-sac** pronounced the same, *or* **cul-de-sacs**) a street with an opening at one end only.

culinary / **kul**-uhn-ree / *adj.* of a kitchen or cooking; used in cooking (*culinary herbs*).

cull *v.* **1** pick (flowers). **2** select. **3** pick out and kill (surplus animals) from a herd or flock. • *n.* culling; things culled.

culminate *v.* reach its highest point or degree (*the argument culminated in a fight*). ◻ **culmination** *n.*

Culotta, Nino, the pen-name of John Patrick O'Grady (1907-81), Australian comic writer, best known for his novel *They're a Weird Mob* (1957) which demonstrated O'Grady's keen ear for Australian idiom.

culottes / kuh-**lots** / *n.pl.* women's trousers or shorts styled to look like a skirt.

culpable / **kul**-puh-buhl / *adj.* deserving blame. ◻ **culpably** *adv.* **culpability** *n.*

culprit *n.* a person who has done something wrong.

cult *n.* **1** a religious system, sect, etc. **2** devotion to or admiration of a person or thing. **3** (often used as *adj.*) popular with a particular group or clique (*a cult film*).

cultivar *n.* a variety of plant produced by cultivation.

cultivate *v.* **1** prepare and use (land) for crops. **2** produce (crops) by tending them. **3** spend time and care in developing and encouraging (a friendship, person, etc.). ◻ **cultivation** *n.*

Cultivated Australian English *n.* the prestige pronunciation of Australian English.

cultivator *n.* **1** a device for breaking up ground for cultivation. **2** a person who cultivates.

cultural *adj.* of culture. ◻ **cultural cringe** *Aust.* an attitude characterised by deference to the cultural achievements of other countries and disparagement of Australian culture. ◻ ◻ **culturally** *adv.*

Cultural Revolution a political upheaval in China (1966–68) in support of the theories of Mao Zedong.

culture *n.* **1** the appreciation and understanding of literature, arts, music, etc. **2** the customs and civilisation of a particular people or group (*Chinese culture*). **3** improvement by care and training. **4** the cultivating of plants, the rearing of bees, silkworms, etc. **5** a quantity of bacteria grown for study. • *v.* grow (bacteria) for study. ◻ **culture shock** confusion and discomfort felt by a person subjected to an unfamiliar way of life.

cultured *adj.* educated to appreciate literature, arts, music, etc. ◻ **cultured pearls** pearls formed by an oyster when a foreign body is inserted artificially into its shell.

culvert / **kul**-vuht / *n.* a drain that crosses under a road or railway etc.

cum[1] *prep.* with; combined with; also used as (*a bedroom-cum-study*).

cum[2] *coarse colloq. n.* emitted semen. • *v.* emit semen.

cumbersome / **kum**-buh-suhm / *adj.* (also **cumbrous**) clumsy to carry, wear, or manage.

cumbungi / kum-**bun**-gee / *n.* a tall reed-like plant with spear-like flower spikes, found in or near water in all Australian States. (¶ Wembawemba)

cummerbund *n.* a sash worn round the waist.

cummin *n.* (also **cumin**) a plant with aromatic seeds used as flavouring, esp. ground as an ingredient of curry powder.

Cummings, Bart (full name: James Bartholomew Cummings) (1927–), AM, Australian racehorse trainer.

cumquat / **kum**-kwot / *n.* (also **kumquat**) a small orange-like fruit used in preserves etc.; the shrub or small tree yielding this.

cumulative / **kyoo**-myuh-luh-tiv / *adj.* increasing in amount by one addition after another. ◻ **cumulatively** *adv.*

cumulus *n.* (*pl.* **cumuli**) a form of cloud consisting of rounded masses heaped on a horizontal base.

cuneiform / **kyoo**-nuh-fawm / *adj.* of or written in the wedge-shaped strokes used in the inscriptions of ancient Assyria, Persia, etc. • *n.* cuneiform writing.

cunjevoi[1] / **kun**-juh-voy / *n.* an Australian sea squirt found on intertidal rocks and used as bait. (¶ Probably from a NSW Aboriginal language.)

cunjevoi[2] *n.* a rainforest plant of NSW and Qld, having extremely large leaves and arum-lily-like flowers, the stem tissue providing a staple food for Aborigines after it had been carefully treated to rid it of its very high toxicity. (¶ Probably from Bandjalang.)

cunmerrie / **kun**-muh-ree / *n. Aust.* (in Aboriginal lore) a huge winged spirit which carries off people and animals. (¶ Pitta-pitta (and other languages).)

cunnilingus *n.* oral stimulation of the female genitals.

cunning *adj.* **1** skilled at deceiving people, crafty. **2** ingenious (*a cunning device*). • *n.* craftiness. ◻ **cunningly** *adv.*

cunt *n. coarse colloq.* **1** the female genitals. **2** *offens.* an unpleasant person or thing.

cup *n.* **1** a small open container for drinking from. **2** its contents; the amount it contains (used as a measure in cookery: *see* CUPFUL). **3** something shaped like a cup. **4** (**the Cup**) the Melbourne Cup. **5** an ornamental goblet-shaped vessel

cupboard awarded as a prize. **6** flavoured wine or cider etc. (*claret cup*). •*v.* (**cupped, cupping**) **1** form into a cup-like shape (*cupped his hands*). **2** hold as if in a cup (*with her chin cupped in her hands*). □ **not my cup of tea** *colloq.* not what I like; not what interests me.

cupboard *n.* a recess or piece of furniture with a door, in which things may be stored.

Cup Day the day on which the Melbourne Cup is run, celebrated Australia-wide.

cupful *n.* (*pl.* **cupfuls**) **1** an amount held by a cup; esp. as a measure (250 ml) in cookery. **2** a full cup.

Cupid the Roman god of love. •*n.* a picture or statue of a beautiful boy with wings and a bow and arrows. □ **play Cupid** indulge in matchmaking.

cupidity / kyoo-**pid**-uh-tee / *n.* greed for gain.

cupola / **kyoo**-puh-luh / *n.* **1** a small dome on a roof. **2** a revolving dome protecting mounted guns.

cuppa *n. colloq.* a cup of tea.

cupreous / **kyoo**-pree-uhs / *adj.* of or like copper.

cupric / **kyoo**-prik / *adj.* of copper.

cupro-nickel *n.* an alloy of copper and nickel.

cur *n.* **1** a bad-tempered or worthless dog. **2** a contemptible person.

curable *adj.* able to be cured.

curaçao / kyoo-ruh-**soh** / *n.* an orange-flavoured liqueur.

curacy *n.* the position of a curate.

curare / kyoo-**rah**-ree / *n.* a bitter substance obtained from certain South American plants, used by S. American Indians to poison arrows.

curate *n.* a member of the clergy who assists a parish priest. □ **curate's egg** something of very mixed character, partly good and partly bad.

curative / **kyoo**-ruh-tiv / *adj.* helping to cure illness.

curator / kyoo-**ray**-tuh / *n.* a person in charge of a museum or other collection. □ **curatorship** *n.*

curb *n.* **1** something that restrains (*put a curb on spending*). **2** a chain or strap passing under a horse's lower jaw, used to restrain it. •*v.* restrain.

curd *n.* **1** (often **curds**) the thick soft substance formed when milk turns sour. **2** any similar substance (*bean curd; lemon curd*). **3** the edible head of a cauliflower.

curdle *v.* form or cause to form curds. □ **make one's blood curdle** fill one with horror.

cure *v.* **1** restore to health. **2** rid (of a disease or troublesome condition). **3** preserve (meat, fruit, tobacco, or skins) by salting, drying, etc. **4** vulcanise (rubber). •*n.* **1** curing, being cured. **2** a substance or treatment that cures a disease; a remedy.

curettage / kyoo-**ret**-ij, -ruh-**tahj** / *n.* scraping surgically to remove tissue or growths.

curette / kyoo-**ret** / *n.* a surgeon's small scraping instrument. •*v.* scrape with this.

curfew *n.* **1** a signal or time after which people must remain indoors until the next day. **2** *hist.* a signal at a fixed time for all fires to be extinguished.

Curia *n.* (also **curia**) the papal court, the government department of the Vatican.

Curie, Marie (1867–1934) and Pierre (1859–1906), French pioneers of the study of radioactivity.

curie *n.* **1** a unit of radioactivity (symbol Ci). **2** a quantity of radioactive substance having this. (¶ Named after Marie and Pierre Curie.)

curio *n.* (*pl.* **curios**) an object that is interesting because it is rare or unusual.

curiosity *n.* **1** a desire to find out and know things. **2** something that is of interest because it is rare or unusual.

curious *adj.* **1** eager to learn or know something. **2** strange, unusual. □ **curiously** *adv.*

curium *n.* an artificially made radioactive metallic element (symbol Cm).

curl *v.* **1** bend, coil into a spiral. **2** move in a spiral form (*smoke curled upwards*). •*n.* **1** something curved inwards or coiled. **2** a coiled lock of hair. **3** a curling movement. □ **curl up 1** lie or sit with the knees drawn up comfortably. **2** writhe with horror or embarrassment.

curler *n.* a pin or roller for curling the hair.

curlew / **ker**-lyoo / *n.* a wading bird with a long slender curved bill.

curlicue / **ker**-lee-kyoo / *n.* a curly ornamental line.

curling *n.* a game played with large flat round stones which are sent along ice towards a mark.

curly *adj.* (**curlier, curliest**) curling, full of curls. □ **curliness** *n.*

curmudgeon / kuh-**muj**-uhn / *n.* a bad-tempered person. □ **curmudgeonly** *adj.*

currant *n.* **1** the dried fruit of a small seedless grape. **2** a small round red, white, or black berry; the shrub that produces it.

currawong / **ku**-ruh-wong / *n.* any of three species of Australian birds, having predominantly black or grey plumage, yellow eyes, and a loud, melodious, ringing call. Also called *bell magpie*. (¶ Probably from Yagara (and neighbouring languages), or perhaps from Dharuk.)

currency *n.* **1** money in actual use in a country; some other commodity used as money. **2** *Aust. hist.* money other than sterling circulating in the Australian Colonies and discounted against sterling. **3** *Aust. hist.* a native-born Australian as opposed to a British immigrant (dubbed *sterling*). **4** the state of being in common use or generally accepted (*the rumour gained currency*). □ **currency lad** (or **boy**) (*feminine* **currency lass**) *Aust. hist.* a native-born Australian as opposed to a British-born immigrant.

current *adj.* **1** belonging to the present time, happening now (*current events*). **2** in general use (*words that are no longer current*). •*n.* **1** water or air etc. moving in a certain direction; a running stream. **2** the flow of electricity through something or along a wire or cable. **3** a general tendency or course (*the current of opinion runs in favour of an Australian Republic*). ❑ **current account 1** transactions in goods etc. that make up a part of a country's balance of payments. **2** a bank account offering instant access to one's money and the use of a cheque book.

currently *adv.* at the present time.

curriculum / kuh-**rik**-yuh-luhm / *n.* (*pl.* **curricula**) subjects included in a course of study. ❑ **curriculum vitae** / **vee**-tuy / (*pl.* **curricula vitae** *or* **curriculum vitaes**) a brief account of one's education and previous career. (¶ Latin, = course of life.)

curry[1] *n.* an Asian dish of meat, vegetables, etc., cooked in a spicy-hot sauce, and usu. served as the main accompaniment to rice. • *v.* (**curried, currying**) cook (meat etc.) in a curry sauce. ❑ **curry powder** a mixture of ground coriander, chilli, cummin, fennel, and other spices, used for making curry. **give a person curry** *colloq.* make life difficult or 'hot' for a person, esp. by attacking physically or verbally.

curry[2] *v.* (**curried, currying**) **1** groom (a horse) with a curry-comb. **2** treat (tanned leather) to improve its properties. ❑ **curry-comb** a pad with rubber or plastic projections. **curry favour** win favour by flattery.

curse *n.* **1** a call for evil to come upon a person or thing. **2** the evil produced by this. **3** a violent exclamation of anger. **4** something that causes evil or harm. • *v.* **1** utter a curse against. **2** exclaim violently in anger. ❑ **the curse** *colloq.* menstruation. **be cursed with** be afflicted or burdened with.

cursed / ker-suhd, kerst / *adj.* damnable.

cursive *adj.* (of writing) done with joined letters. • *n.* cursive writing.

cursor *n.* **1** an indicator on a VDU screen showing a specific position, usu. the point at which the next keystroke will be entered. **2** the transparent slide, bearing the reference line, on a slide rule.

cursory / **ker**-suh-ree / *adj.* hasty and not thorough (*a cursory inspection*). ❑ **cursorily** *adv.*

curt *adj.* noticeably or rudely brief. ❑ **curtly** *adv.* **curtness** *n.*

curtail *v.* cut short, reduce. ❑ **curtailment** *n.*

curtain *n.* **1** a piece of cloth or other material hung as a screen, esp. at a window or between the stage and auditorium of a theatre. **2** the fall of a stage curtain at the end of an act or scene. **3** a curtain call. **4** (**curtains**) *colloq.* the end. • *v.* provide or shut off with a curtain or curtains. ❑ **curtain call** *n.* applause calling for an actor etc. to take a bow after the curtain has been lowered.

curtain-raiser a short piece before the main performance; a preliminary event.

Curtin, John (Joseph) (1885–1945), Australian Labor statesman, prime minister 1941–45.

curtsy *n.* (also **curtsey**) a movement of respect made by women and girls, bending the knees and lowering the body with one foot forward. • *v.* (**curtsied, curtsying**) make a curtsy.

curvaceous / ker-**vay**-shuhs / *adj. colloq.* (of a woman) having a shapely figure.

curvature / **ker**-vuh-chuh / *n.* curving; a curved form (*the curvature of the earth*).

curve *n.* **1** a line of which no part is straight. **2** a smooth continuous surface of which no part is flat. **3** a curved form or thing. • *v.* bend or shape so as to form a curve. ❑ **curvy** *adj.*

curvet / ker-**vet** / *n.* a horse's short frisky leap. • *v.* (**curvetted, curvetting** *or* **curveted, curveting**) **1** make a curvet. **2** leap or frisk (about) (*the young man curveted past me into the room*).

curvilinear *adj.* contained by or consisting of curved lines.

Cusack / **kyoo**-zak /, (Ellen) Dymphna (1902–81), AM, Australian novelist and playwright esp. concerned with social issues.

cuscus / **kus**-kuhs / *n.* any of several nocturnal marsupial mammals of northern Australia and New Guinea.

cushion *n.* **1** a bag filled with soft material, used to make a seat more comfortable. **2** a soft pad or other means of support or of protection against jarring or shock. **3** the padded border round a billiard table, from which the balls rebound. **4** the body of air supporting a hovercraft etc. • *v.* **1** provide or protect with a cushion or cushions. **2** lessen the impact of (a blow, shock, or something harmful).

cushy *adj.* (**cushier, cushiest**) *colloq.* pleasant and easy (*a cushy job*).

cusp *n.* a pointed end where two curves meet, e.g. the horn of a crescent moon.

cuss *colloq. v.* curse. • *n.* **1** a curse. **2** a difficult person (*an awkward cuss*).

cussed / **kus**-uhd / *adj. colloq.* awkward and stubborn. ❑ **cussedness** *n.*

custard *n.* **1** a dish or sauce made with beaten eggs and milk. **2** a sweet sauce made with milk and flavoured cornflour.

custodian / kus-**toh**-dee-uhn / *n.* a guardian or keeper, esp. of a public building.

custody *n.* **1** the right or duty of taking care of something; guardianship. **2** imprisonment. ❑ **take into custody** arrest. ❑❑ **custodial** *adj.*

custom *n.* **1** a usual way of behaving or of doing something. **2** the regular support given to a business by customers. ❑ **custom-built** (also **custom-made**) made according to a customer's order.

customary *adj.* in accordance with custom, usual. ❑ **customary law** *Aust.* Aboriginal traditional practices. ❑❑ **customarily** *adv.*

customer *n.* **1** a person who buys goods or services from a shop or business. **2** *colloq.* a person

customise of a specified kind (*awkward customer; cool customer*).

customise *v.* (also **-ize**) make or modify to personal requirements.

customs *n.* (treated as *pl.* or *sing.*) **1** duty charged on goods imported from other countries. **2** the government department dealing with this. **3** the area at a port or airport where officials examine goods and baggage.

cut *v.* (**cut**, **cutting**) **1** divide, wound, or detach with an edged instrument. **2** shape, make, or shorten in this way. **3** be able to be cut. **4** have (a tooth) appear through the gum. **5** cross, intersect; go (through or across), esp. as a shorter way. **6** reduce by removing part (*cut taxes; two scenes were cut by the censor*). **7** go directly to another shot in a film. **8** switch off (electric power, an engine, etc.). **9** lift and turn up part of a pack of cards, e.g. in deciding who is to deal. **10** hit a ball with a chopping movement in cricket etc. **11** stay away deliberately from (*cut the lecture*). **12** ignore (a person) deliberately. **13** record (a song or album). **14** *Aust.* (in Aboriginal English) ritually circumcise (a boy) to initiate into manhood. **15** castrate, neuter (an animal). • *n.* **1** the act of cutting; a division or wound made by this. **2** a stroke with a sword, whip, or cane. **3** a stroke made by cutting a ball in cricket etc. **4** a piece of meat cut from the carcass of an animal. **5** the way a thing is cut; the style in which clothes are made by cutting. **6** a cutting remark. **7** a reduction; a temporary stoppage. **8** the cutting out of part of a play or film etc. **9** *colloq.* a share of profits. **10** *Aust.* a harvest, esp. of sugar cane etc. • *adj.* **1** gashed or wounded (*a cut finger*). **2** divided into pieces (*cut firewood*). **3** castrated, neutered. **4** *colloq.* circumcised (*are you cut or uncut?*). □ **a cut above** noticeably superior to. **cut and dried** planned or prepared in advance. **cut back** reduce; prune. **cut-back** *n.* a reduction. **cut both ways** have two appropriate and opposite ways of being applied. **cut a corner** pass round it as closely as possible. **cut corners** fail to do something properly, esp. to save time. **cut down 1** bring or throw down by cutting; kill by sword etc. or by disease. **2** reduce (wages etc.). **3** reduce the length of (*cut down trousers to make shorts*). **4** reduce consumption (*I must cut down on beer*). **cut glass** glass with patterns cut in it. **cut in 1** interrupt. **2** return too soon to one's own side of the road, obstructing the path of an overtaken vehicle. **cut it fine** allow very little margin of time etc. **cut no ice** *colloq.* have no influence or effect. **cut off 1** prevent from continuing. **2** keep from union or contact. **3** leave (a person) a very small amount in a will instead of a large inheritance. **cut one's losses** abandon an unprofitable scheme before one loses too much. **cut out 1** shape by cutting. **2** outdo (a rival). **3** cease or cause to cease functioning (*the engine cut out*). **4** stop doing or using (something) (*cut out chocolate; cut out the rough stuff*). **5** *Aust.* separate (animals) from a mob. **6** come to an end (*the road cuts out in 2 kilometres*). **7.** *colloq.* be finished or used up (*the party ended when the grog cut out*). **cut-out** *n.* **1** a shape cut out of paper etc. **2** a device that disconnects an appliance automatically. **cut out for** having the qualities and abilities needed for. **cut-price** *adj.* (also **cut-rate**) for sale at a reduced price. **cut up 1** cut into pieces. **2** (usu. as **be cut up**) *colloq.* be greatly distressed. **cut up rough** *colloq.* show anger or resentment.

cutaneous / kyoo-**tay**-nee-uhs / *adj.* of the skin.

cutaway *adj.* (of a diagram, model, etc.) with parts of the outside missing to reveal the interior.

cute *adj. colloq.* **1** attractive. **2** sexy (*he's really cute*). **3** (often sarcastic) ingenious, clever (*who's the cute bastard who put itching-powder in my jocks?*). □ **cutely** *adv.* **cuteness** *n.*

Cuthbert, Betty (1938–), AM, Australian sprinter, winner of four Olympic gold medals.

cuticle / **kyoo**-ti-kuhl / *n.* hardened skin at the base of a fingernail or toenail.

cutie *n. colloq.* a male or female who is CUTE (sense 2).

cutis / **kyoo**-tuhs / *n.* the true skin beneath the epidermis.

cutlass *n.* a short sword with a slightly curved blade.

cutler *n.* a maker or seller of cutlery.

cutlery *n.* knives, forks, and spoons used in eating and serving food.

cutlet *n.* **1** a neck chop of mutton or lamb. **2** a piece of veal etc. for frying. **3** a fish steak.

cutoffs *n.pl.* jeans which have been roughly cut above the knee and left to fray.

cutter *n.* **1** a person or tool that cuts (e.g. a shearer, canecutter, timber-getter, etc.). **2** a small fast sailing ship. **3** a small boat carried by a large ship.

cutthroat *n.* a person who cuts throats, a murderer. • *adj.* **1** intense and merciless (*cutthroat competition*). **2** (of card games) three-handed. **3** (of a razor) having a long blade set in a handle.

cutting see CUT. • *adj.* (of words) hurtful (*cutting remarks*). • *n.* **1** a piece cut from something; a section cut from a newspaper etc. and kept for reference. **2** an excavation through high ground for a road or railway. **3** a piece cut from a plant for replanting to form a new plant.

cuttlebone *n.* the internal shell of the cuttlefish, used (crushed) for polishing or to supplement the diet of caged birds.

cuttlefish *n.* (*pl.* **cuttlefish** or **cuttlefishes**) a mollusc similar to a squid which squirts out a black liquid when threatened.

cutworm *n.* any of several caterpillars that eat through the stems of young plants level with the ground.

cuvée / kyoo-**vay** / *n.* a blend or batch of wine.

c.v. *abbr.* (also **CV**) curriculum vitae.

CWA *abbr. Aust.* Country Women's Association.

cwt *abbr.* hundredweight (approx. 51 kg).

cyan / **suy**-uhn / *adj.* & *n.* (in photography) greenish-blue.

cyanic / suy-**an**-ik / *adj.* of or containing cyanogen. ☐ **cyanic acid** an unstable colourless strong-smelling acid gas.

cyanide / **suy**-uh-nuyd / *n.* a very poisonous chemical substance used in the extraction of gold and silver.

cyanogen / suy-**an**-uh-juhn / *n.* an inflammable poisonous gas.

cyanosis / suy-uh-**noh**-suhs / *n.* a condition in which the skin appears blue, caused by lack of oxygen in the blood.

cyathea / suy-uh-**thee**-uh / *n.* any of several Australian tree ferns, having tall, slender trunks and long fronds radiating from the summit.

cybercafé *n.* a café where customers can sit at computer terminals and log on to the Internet while eating and drinking.

cybernetics / suy-buh-**net**-iks / *n.* the science of communication and control in animals (e.g. by the nervous system) and in machines (e.g. computers). ☐ **cybernetic** *adj.*

cyberpunk *n.* a style of science fiction writing combining high-tech plots (in which the world is controlled by artificial intelligence) with unconventional or nihilistic social values.

cybersex *n.* sexual arousal by means of computer technology, esp. by using virtual reality equipment or by real-time interaction on the Internet.

cyberspace *n.* **1** the notional space within which electronic communication occurs, esp. when represented as the inside of a computer system. **2** space perceived as such by an observer but generated by a computer system and having no real existence; the space of virtual reality.

cyborg *n.* a person whose physical abilities are extended beyond normal human limits by a machine; an integrated man-machine.

cycad *n.* a palmlike plant often growing to a great height.

cyclamate *n.* a former artificial sweetener.

cyclamen / **suy**-kluh-muhn, **sik**-luh- / *n.* a plant with pink, red, or white flowers with petals that turn back.

cycle *n.* **1** a series of events or operations that are regularly repeated in the same order (*the cycle of the seasons*). **2** the time needed for one such series. **3** one complete occurrence of a continually recurring process such as electrical oscillation or alternation of electric current. **4** a complete set or series, e.g. of songs or poems. **5** a bicycle or motorcycle. •*v.* **1** ride a bicycle etc. **2** move in cycles. ☐ **cycle track** (also **cycleway**, **cycle path**) a path for bicycles, often marked as such on a main road.

cyclic / **suy**-klik, **sik**-lik / *adj.* (also **cyclical**) **1** recurring in cycles or series. **2** forming a cycle. ☐ **cyclically** *adv.*

cyclist *n.* a person who rides a bicycle.

cyclone / **suy**-klohn / *n.* **1** a system of winds rotating round a calm central area. **2** a violent destructive form of this. ☐ **cyclone fence** *Aust. trademark* a fence made with interlocking wire in metal frames. ☐☐ **cyclonic** / suy-**klon**-ik / *adj.*

Cyclops / **suy**-klops / (*pl.* **Cyclops** or **Cyclopes**) *Gk myth.* a member of a race of one-eyed giants.

cyclotron / **suy**-kluh-tron / *n.* an apparatus for accelerating charged particles by making them move spirally in a magnetic field.

cygnet / **sig**-nuht / *n.* a young swan.

cylinder *n.* **1** a solid or hollow object with straight sides and circular ends. **2** a machine part shaped like this; the chamber in which a piston moves in an engine. ☐ **cylindrical** *adj.*

cymbal *n.* a percussion instrument consisting of a brass plate struck with another or with a stick. ☐ **cymbalist** *n.*

cymbidium *n.* a tropical orchid having large, showy flowers, three species being endemic to Australia.

cyme / suym / *n.* a flower cluster with one flower on the end of each stem. ☐ **cymose** *adj.*

Cymric / **kim**-rik / *adj.* Welsh.

cynic / **sin**-ik / *n.* **1** a person with a pessimistic view of human nature and little faith in human sincerity or goodness. **2** (**Cynic**) a member of a sect of ancient Greek philosophers who despised ease and wealth. ☐ **cynical** *adj.* **cynically** *adv.*

cynicism / **sin**-uh-siz-uhm / *n.* the attitude of a cynic.

cynosure / **sin**-uh-shoor, -zhoor / *n.* a centre of attraction or admiration.

cypher alternative spelling of CIPHER.

cypress *n.* a coniferous evergreen tree with dark feathery leaves. ☐ **cypress pine** any of several Australian trees of the genus *Callitris*, the wood of which is often termite-resistant.

Cypriot / **sip**-ree-uht / (also **Cypriote** / **sip**-ree-oht /) *n.* a native or national of Cyprus. •*adj.* of Cyprus.

Cyprus an island republic in the East Mediterranean.

Cyrillic / suh-**ril**-ik / *adj.* of the alphabet used by Slavonic peoples of the Eastern Church, named after St Cyril (9th c.), Greek missionary, who is said to have introduced it; now used chiefly for Russian and Bulgarian. •*n.* this alphabet.

cyst / sist / *n.* an abnormal sac formed in or on the body, containing fluid or semi-solid matter.

cystic / **sis**-tik / *adj.* **1** of the bladder. **2** like a cyst. ☐ **cystic fibrosis** a hereditary disease, usu. causing breathing disorders.

cystitis / sis-**tuy**-tuhs / *n.* inflammation of the bladder.

cytology / suy-**tol**-uh-jee / *n.* the scientific study of biological cells. ☐ **cytological** *adj.*

cytoplasm / **suy**-toh-plaz-uhm / *n.* the content of a biological cell other than the nucleus. ☐ **cytoplasmic** *adj.*

czar alternative spelling of TSAR.

Czech / chek / *n.* **1** a native or the language of the Czech Republic. **2** (formerly) a citizen of Czechoslovakia.

Czechoslovakia a former country in central Europe which divided into the independent Czech and Slovak Republics in 1993. ☐ **Czechoslovak** / chek-uh-**sloh**-vak / *adj.* & *n.* **Czechoslovakian** *adj.* & *n.*

Czech Republic the western of the two republics into which the former Czechoslovakia is divided.

D

D *n.* (*pl.* **Ds** or **D's**) **1** *Music* the second note of the scale of C major. **2** (as a Roman numeral) 500. **3** the fourth highest class or category (of academic marks etc.); the fourth example, item in a list, etc. • *symbol* deuterium.

d. *abbr. hist.* (pre-decimal) penny, pence. (¶ Short for Latin *denarius*.)

'd *colloq.* = had; would (*I'd; she'd*).

dab *n.* **1** a light or feeble blow, a tap. **2** quick gentle pressure on a surface with something soft (*a dab with a sponge*). **3** a small amount of a soft substance applied to a surface. • *v.* (**dabbed, dabbing**) **1** strike lightly or feebly. **2** press briefly and lightly with a cloth etc. **3** apply by dabbing (*dab some lotion on the rash*). ☐ **dab hand** *colloq.* an expert (*she's a dab hand at fixing computers*).

dabble *v.* **1** wet by splashing or by putting in and out of water. **2** move the feet, hands, etc. lightly in water. ☐ **dabble in** study or work at casually, not seriously. ☐☐ **dabbler** *n.*

dabchick *n.* a small waterbird of the grebe family.

da capo / dah **kah**-poh / *adv. Music* repeat from the beginning.

Dachau / **dak**-ow / a Nazi concentration camp in southern Bavaria, Germany, from 1933 to 1945.

dachshund / **daks**-huund, **dash**-huhnd / *n.* a small dog with a long body and very short legs.

dacoit / duh-**koyt** / *n.* (in India or Burma) a member of a band of armed robbers. (¶ Hindi)

dactyl / **dak**-til / *n.* a metrical foot with one long or stressed syllable followed by two short or unstressed syllables. ☐ **dactylic** / dak-**til**-ik / *adj.*

dad *n. colloq.* father.

Dada / **dah**-dah / *n.* an international movement in art and literature of about 1915–20, mocking conventions. ☐ **Dadaism** *n.* **Dadaist** *n.* & *adj.*

Dad and Dave *adj. Aust.* pertaining to bush matters (esp. comic ones). (¶ Characters in the stories of Steele Rudd (1868–1935).)

daddy *n. colloq.* father.

daddy-long-legs *n.* a small house-spider with very long thin legs.

dado / **day**-doh / *n.* (*pl.* **dados**) **1** the lower part of the wall of a room or corridor when it is coloured or faced differently from the upper part. **2** the plinth of a column. **3** the cube of a pedestal.

daff *n. colloq.* = DAFFODIL.

daffodil *n.* a usu. yellow flower with a trumpet-shaped central part, growing from a bulb.

daft *adj. colloq.* silly, foolish, crazy.

dag[1] *Aust. n.* a lump of matted wool and dung hanging from the hinder parts of a sheep; such a lump cut from a sheep. • *v.* **1** remove dags from (a sheep). **2** castrate baby lambs with a knife. ☐ **dag-picker** a person employed in a shearing shed to pick over dags in order to separate wool from the dung.

dag[2] *n. Aust. colloq.* **1** an entertainingly interesting person; a character. **2** an unfashionable and behind-the-times person. **3** an untidy or dirty-looking person. **4** a socially awkward adolescent.

da Gama *see* GAMA.

dagger *n.* a short pointed two-edged weapon used for stabbing.

daggy *adj. Aust.* **1** (of a sheep) fouled with dags. **2** *colloq.* (of a person) slovenly; unfashionable; stupid.

dago / **day**-goh / *n.* (*pl.* **dagos**) *colloq. offens.* a foreigner, esp. one from southern Europe.

daguerreotype / duh-**gair**-ruh-tuyp / *n.* an early kind of photograph taken on a silver-coated copper plate, giving an image of white on silver. (¶ Named after its French inventor, Louis Daguerre (1789–1851).)

dahlia / **day**-lee-uh / *n.* a garden plant with large brightly-coloured flowers and tuberous roots.

Dáil / doil / *n.* (in full **Dáil Éireann** / **air**-uhn /) the lower house of parliament in the Republic of Ireland.

daily *adj.* happening or appearing on every day (or every weekday). • *adv.* **1** once a day. **2** progressively. • *n.* **1** a daily newspaper.

Daintree an ecologically significant area within the wet tropics of north-eastern Qld, where coastal rainforest is fringed by a coral reef. Logging operations etc. are endangering the environmental balance of the region, which is habitat for numerous plant and animal species found only in the Daintree, e.g. the tube-nosed bat, the world's rarest living mammal.

dainty *adj.* (**daintier, daintiest**) **1** small and pretty, delicate. **2** fastidious, esp. about food. **3** (**dainties**) choice foods, delicacies. ☐ **daintily** *adv.* **daintiness** *n.*

daiquiri / **dak**-uh-ree / *n.* (*pl.* **daiquiris**) a cocktail of rum, lime juice, etc.

dairy *n.* a room or building where milk and milk products are processed, distributed, or sold. • *adj.* of milk or milk products (*dairy cow*). ☐ **dairying** *n.*

dais / **day**-uhs / *n.* a low platform, esp. at one end of a hall.

daisy *n.* a 'flower' with many petal-like rays surrounding a central disk containing a mass of tightly-packed true flowers.

Dakar / **dak**-ah / the capital of Senegal.

daks / daks / *n.pl. Aust. trademark colloq.* trousers.

Dalai Lama / dal-uy **lah**-muh / the chief lama of Tibet.

dale *n.* (chiefly *Brit.*) a valley.

dalgite / **dal**-guyt / *n.* (also **dalgyte**) WA name for the bilby. (¶ Nyungar)

Dali / **dah**-lee /, Salvador (1904–89), Spanish painter whose surrealist pictures are said to derive from the subconscious.

dally *v.* (**dallied, dallying**) **1** idle, dawdle. **2** amuse oneself; flirt. ☐ **dalliance** *n.*

Dalmatian / dal-**may**-shuhn / *adj.* of Dalmatia, a coastal region of southern Croatia. •*n.* a large white dog with dark spots.

dal segno / dal **say**-nyoh / *adv. Music* repeat from the point marked by a sign.

Daly / **day**-lee / a major river (320 km) in the NT that flows from south-west of Katherine north-west to Anson Bay.

dam[1] *n.* **1** *Aust.* an artificial pond or reservoir for the storage of usu. run-off rainwater, esp. to provide water for stock. **2** a barrier built across a river etc. to hold back water and control its flow or form a reservoir. •*v.* (**dammed, damming**) **1** hold back with a dam. **2** block up; obstruct.

dam[2] *n.* the mother of a four-footed animal.

damage *n.* **1** harm or injury. **2** *colloq.* the cost or charge (*what's the damage?*). **3** (**damages**) money claimed or paid as compensation for an injury. •*v.* cause damage to.

damascene / **dam**-uh-seen / *v.* decorate (metal) with inlaid or wavy patterns.

Damascus the capital of Syria.

damask / **dam**-uhsk / *n.* silk or linen material woven with a pattern that is visible on either side. •*adj.* **1** made of damask. **2** coloured like a damask rose, velvety pink. ☐ **damask rose** an old sweet-scented variety of rose.

dame *n.* **1** (**Dame**) the title of a woman who has been awarded a knighthood in the Order of Australia (no longer bestowed) or in a comparable British order. **2** *colloq.* a woman. **3** a comic female character in pantomime, usu. played by a man.

damn *v.* **1** condemn to eternal punishment in hell. **2** condemn as a failure. **3** swear at, curse. •*interj.* an exclamation of anger or annoyance. •*n.* 'damn' said as a curse. •*adj.* & *adv.* damned. ☐ **damn with faint praise** praise feebly and so imply disapproval.

damnable *adj.* hateful, annoying. ☐ **damnably** *adv.*

damnation *n.* being damned or condemned to hell. •*interj.* an exclamation of anger or annoyance.

damned *adj. colloq.* damnable. •*adv.* damnably, extremely (*it's damned hot*). ☐ **do one's damnedest** do one's very best.

Damocles / **dam**-uh-kleez / ☐ **sword of Damocles** imminent danger. (¶ From the story of Damocles, a Greek of the 4th century BC, above whose head a sword was once hung by a hair while he ate.)

damp *n.* **1** slight moisture, esp. when unwelcome. **2** foul or explosive gas in a mine. •*adj.* slightly or moderately wet. •*v.* **1** make damp. **2** make sad or dull; discourage (*damped their enthusiasm*). **3** reduce the vibration of (a string in music). ☐ **damp course** (also **damp-proof course**) a layer of damp-proof material built into a wall near the ground to prevent damp from rising. **damp off** (of a seedling) die suddenly from a fungus disease, esp. in damp conditions. **damping-off** this disease. **damp squib** an unsuccessful attempt to impress etc. ☐ ☐ **damply** *adv.* **dampness** *n.*

dampen *v.* damp.

damper[1] *n. Aust.* a simple kind of bush bread, traditionally unleavened, baked in the ashes of an outdoor fire.

damper[2] *n.* **1** a movable metal plate that regulates the flow of air into the fire in a stove or furnace. **2** an influence that discourages enthusiasm (*cast a damper over the proceedings*). **3** a small pad that presses against a piano string to stop it vibrating.

Dampier, William (1652–1715), English pirate and adventurer who was commissioned by the British government in 1699 to explore the unknown Australian coast. He made no important discoveries in Australia. His importance rests on his writings, of which *A Voyage to New Holland* (i.e. Australia) *in the Year 1699* may be said to have increased that interest in New Holland which led to its colonisation by Britain.

dampiera *n.* any of several small Australian shrubs or ground covers, bearing blue to purple flowers.

damsel / **dam**-zuhl / *n. archaic* a young woman.

dan *n.* **1** a grade of proficiency in judo. **2** one who reaches this.

dance *v.* **1** move with rhythmical steps or movements, usu. to music; perform in this way. **2** move in a quick or lively way; bob up and down. •*n.* **1** a piece of dancing. **2** a piece of music for dancing to. **3** a social gathering for the purpose of dancing. ☐ **dancer** *n.*

d and c *abbr.* dilatation (of the cervix) and curettage (of the womb); a minor operation to remove matter from the womb.

dandelion *n.* a weed with edible leaves and bright yellow flowers.

Dandenong Ranges a low range of hills near Melbourne in Victoria.

dander *n. colloq.* fighting spirit. ☐ **get one's dander up** become angry.

dandified *adj.* like a dandy.

dandle *v.* dance (a child) in one's arms or on one's knee.

dandruff *n.* flakes of dead skin on the scalp and amongst the hair.

dandy *n.* a man who pays excessive attention to the smartness of his appearance and clothes. • *adj. colloq.* very good; splendid.

Dane *n.* **1** a native of Denmark. **2** a Viking invader of England in the 9th–11th centuries.

danger *n.* **1** liability or exposure to harm or death. **2** a person or thing that causes this.

dangerous *adj.* involving or causing danger. □ **dangerously** *adv.*

dangle *v.* **1** hang loosely. **2** hold or carry (a thing) so that it swings loosely. **3** hold out (hopes) to a person temptingly.

Danish *adj.* of Denmark or its people or language. • *n.* the language of Denmark. □ **Danish blue** soft white cheese with veins of blue mould. **Danish pastry** a yeast cake topped with icing, nuts, etc.

dank *adj.* unpleasantly damp and cold. □ **dankness** *n.*

Dante / **dan**-tee / (full name: Dante Alighieri) (1265–1321), Italian poet and philosopher.

Danube a river in central and SE Europe.

daphne / **daf**-nee / *n.* a shrub with highly scented flowers.

dapper *adj.* precise, esp. in appearance; sprightly.

dapple *v.* mark with spots or patches of shade or a different colour. □ **dapple-grey** *adj.* grey with darker markings.

dare *v.* **1** have the courage or impudence to do something. **2** take the risk of, face as a danger. **3** challenge (a person) to do something risky. • *n.* a challenge to do something risky.

daredevil *n.* a recklessly daring person.

dargawarra / dah-guh-**wo**-ruh / *n. Aust.* a small hopping mouse of arid central and western Australia. (¶ Western Desert language)

Dargie, Sir William Alexander (1912–), Australian painter specialising in portraits and a many-times winner of the Archibald Prize.

daring *n.* boldness. • *adj.* **1** bold, taking risks boldly. **2** boldly dramatic or unconventional. □ **daringly** *adv.*

dariole / **da**-ree-ohl / *n.* a dish cooked in a small mould.

Dark, Eleanor (1901–86), AO, Australian writer, best known for her trilogy of novels tracing the development of white settlement from 1788–1814 from both the Aboriginal and the European points of view.

dark *adj.* **1** with little or no light. **2** (of colour) of a deep shade. **3** (of a person) with brown or black hair or complexion. **4** gloomy, cheerless, dismal (*dark thoughts*). **5** evil, sinister (*dark deeds*). **6** secret (*keep it dark*). **7** mysterious; remote and unexplored (*in darkest Africa*). • *n.* **1** absence of light. **2** a time of darkness, night or nightfall (*out after dark*). **3** a dark colour. □ **dark horse** a successful competitor of whose abilities little was known before the contest. **dark on** *colloq.* furious with (*dark on her for standing him up*). **in the dark** having no information about something. □ **darkly** *adv.* **darkness** *n.*

Dark Ages the early part of the Middle Ages in Europe (about 500–1100), when government and culture were supposedly in decline.

darken *v.* make or become dark or darker.

darkroom *n.* a room where light is excluded so that photographs can be processed.

Darling a river in central eastern Australia. With its catchment area in Qld, and flowing 2,757 km through western NSW in a generally southerly direction to join the Murray River at Wentworth, the Darling is Australia's longest river.

darling *n.* a dearly loved or lovable person or thing; a favourite. • *adj.* dearly loved; *colloq.* charming.

darn[1] *v.* mend (cloth etc.) by filling a hole with stitching. • *n.* a place mended by darning.

darn[2] *interj.* & *adj.* = DAMN, DAMNED.

darned *adj.* = DAMNED.

Dart *n.* (in full **Old Dart**) *Aust.* Britain, esp. England. (¶ A British dialect pronunciation of *dirt*.)

dart *n.* **1** a small pointed missile. **2** a small metal-tipped object used in the game of darts. **3** (**darts**) an indoor game in which darts are thrown at a target. **4** a darting movement. **5** a tapering stitched tuck in a garment. **6** any of several fish of warmer Australian waters. • *v.* **1** move suddenly and rapidly. **2** send out rapidly (*darted an angry look at him*).

dartboard *n.* a circular board used as a target in the game of darts.

darter *n.* any of various large waterbirds having a narrow head and long thin neck.

Darwin[1] the capital city of the Northern Territory. □ **Darwin rig** semi-formal male attire (in Darwin): long-sleeved white shirt with or without tie, long trousers (or shorts with long white socks), no coat. **Darwin stubby** *Aust. trademark* a very large bottle of beer (usu. 2 litres) (cf. STUBBY *n.*, sense 1).

Darwin[2], Charles Robert (1809–82), English naturalist who put forward the theory of the evolution of species by the action of natural selection (cf. CREATIONISM). □ **Darwinian** *adj.* & *n.* **Darwinism** *n.* **Darwinist** *n.*

dash *v.* **1** run rapidly, rush. **2** strike or fling forcefully, esp. so as to shatter. **3** destroy; ruin (*our hopes were dashed*). • *interj. colloq.* damn. • *n.* **1** a short rapid run; a rush. **2** a small amount of liquid or flavouring added. **3** a dashboard. **4** lively spirit or appearance. **5** a punctuation mark (–) used to show a break in sense (see panel on next page). **6** the longer of the two signals used in the Morse code. **7** a sprinting race. □ **dash off** write or draw hurriedly. **do one's dash** *Aust.* exhaust one's energies or opportunities.

dashboard *n.* a panel below the windscreen of a motor vehicle, carrying various instruments and controls.

dashi *n.* a basic stock of dried kelp and flakes of dried bonito, used in Japanese cooking.

dashing *adj.* spirited, showy.

dastardly *adj.* contemptible and cowardly.

dasyure / **das**-ee-yoor, **daz**- / *n.* (also **dasyurid**) any of various small carnivorous marsupials, including the Australian native cats.

data / **day**-tuh, **dah**-tuh / *n.pl.* facts or information to be used as a basis for discussing or deciding something, or prepared for being processed by a computer etc. ☐ **data bank** a store or source of computerised data. **data bus** a signal route used to transmit data in parallel from one part of a computer to another. **data capture** the entering of data into a computer. **data casting** a service (other than traditional broadcasting services) that delivers information in the form of data, speech, images etc. via the established television broadcasting bands. **data processing** the performance of operations on data, esp. using a computer, to obtain information, solutions to problems, etc.

■ **Usage** This word is now often used with a singular verb (as is 'information'), esp. in the context of computers, e.g. *the data is entered here*, but it is by origin a Latin plural (the singular is *datum*) and in other contexts should be used (as 'facts' is used) with a plural verb, *these data are from official sources*.

database *n.* an organised store of computerised data.

datable *adj.* able to be dated.

date[1] *n.* **1** the day on which something happened or was written or is to happen etc.; a statement of this in terms of day, month, and year (or any of these). **2** the period to which something belongs (*objects of prehistoric date*). **3** an appointment to meet socially. **4** a person (usu. of the opposite sex) with whom one has a social engagement. •*v.* **1** mark with a date. **2** assign a date to. **3** originate from a particular date (*the custom dates from medieval times*). **4** show signs of becoming out of date (*some fashions date quickly*). **5** make a social engagement (with); go out together as sexual partners. ☐ **date rape** rape committed on a person who has accepted a social invitation for a date. **out of date** *see* OUT. **to date** until now (*here are our sales figures to date*).

date[2] *n.* a small brown sweet edible fruit. ☐ **date palm** a palm tree of North Africa and SW Asia bearing this fruit.

dateless *adj.* **1** having no date. **2** not becoming out of date.

Date Line *n.* (also **International Date Line**) a line from north to south roughly along the meridian 180° from Greenwich, east and west of which the date differs (east being one day earlier).

dative *n.* the grammatical case of a word expressing the indirect object or a recipient, e.g. *me* in 'give me the book'.

datum / **day**-tuhm, **dah**-tuhm / *n.* (*pl.* **data**; see the entry for DATA) an item of information; a unit of data.

daub *v.* cover or smear roughly with a soft substance; paint clumsily. •*n.* **1** a clumsily-painted picture. **2** a covering or smear of something soft.

daughter *n.* **1** a girl or woman in relation to her parents. **2** a female descendant or inheritor of a quality etc. (*a true daughter of the revolution*). ☐ **daughter-in-law** *n.* (*pl.* **daughters-in-law**) a son's wife. ☐☐ **daughterly** *adj.*

daunt *v.* make afraid or discouraged. ☐ **daunting** *adj.*

dauntless *adj.* brave, not to be daunted.

dauphin / **daw**-fin, doh-**fan** / *n.* the title of the eldest son of the king of France in the days when France was ruled by a king.

David king of the Hebrews after Saul.

Davis[1] an Australian Antarctic Research Base established in 1957.

Davis[2], Jack (Leonard) (1918–2000), AM, Aboriginal poet and playwright whose work is concerned with the resolution of racial problems, esp. those of the urban Aborigine.

Davis[3], Judy (1956–), Australian stage, television, and film actor, winner of many awards. Her films include *My Brilliant Career* and *A Passage to India*.

Davis Cup an annual award for a men's international lawn tennis team competition, donated by a leading American player, Dwight F. Davis, in 1900.

davit / **dav**-uht / *n.* a small crane on board ship.

Davy, Sir Humphry (1778–1829), English chemist. ☐ **Davy lamp** an early type of safety lamp for miners, invented by Davy in 1816.

Davy Jones *colloq.* the evil spirit of the sea. ☐ **Davy Jones's locker** the bottom of the sea as

---

Dash —

A dash is used:
1. to mark the beginning and end of an interruption in the structure of a sentence:
   My son—where has he gone?—would like to meet you.
2. to show faltering speech in conversation:
   Yes—well—I would—only you see—it's not easy.
3. to show other kinds of break in a sentence, where a comma, semicolon, or colon would traditionally be used, e.g.
   Come tomorrow—if you can.
   The most important thing is this—don't rush the work.

dawdle v. walk slowly and idly; take one's time. ◻ **dawdler** n.

Dawe, (Donald) Bruce (1930–), AO, Australian poet whose poems reflect his antipathy to regimes and institutions that oppress, as well as his concern for the individual.

dawn n. **1** the first light of day. **2** the beginning (*the dawn of civilisation*). •v. **1** begin to grow light. **2** (often foll. by *on*) begin to appear or become evident (to) (*it finally dawned on her that…*). ◻ **dawn parade** (also **dawn service**) *Aust.* a memorial service at dawn on Anzac Day.

Dawson[1], Andrew (1863–1910), Australian mining unionist and Labor politician. Dawson was premier of Qld for six days in 1899, making him the first person to form a Labor government in Australia.

Dawson[2], Peter (1882–1961), Australian baritone, singer of opera and ballads, and composer of ballads and songs.

Dawson[3], Smoky (original name: Herbert Henry Dawson) (1913–), AM, Australian country music singer and songwriter.

day n. **1** the time during which the sun is above the horizon. **2** the time for one rotation of the earth; a period of 24 hours. **3** the hours given to work (*an eight-hour day*). **4** a specified or appointed day (*graduation day*). **5** a period or era (*in Gough Whitlam's day; in my young days*). **6** a period of success (*racism has had its day*). **7** victory in a contest (*win the day*). ◻ **all in a day's work** part of the normal routine. **at the end of the day** when all is said and done. **call it a day** end a period of activity. **day care** care of young children, the elderly, the handicapped, etc. during the working day. **that will be the day** *colloq.* that will never happen.

daybreak n. the first light of day, dawn.

daydream n. idle and pleasant thoughts. •v. have day-dreams.

daylight n. **1** the light of day. **2** dawn. **3** understanding or knowledge that has dawned. **4** (**daylights**) *colloq.* life, consciousness (*scared the daylights out of me*). ◻ **daylight robbery** unashamed swindling. **daylight saving** longer summer evening daylight achieved by putting clocks forward.

Day of Atonement see YOM KIPPUR.

Day of Judgment see JUDGMENT DAY.

Day of Mourning (in Aboriginal culture) Australia Day. The first formal Day of Mourning was held on 26 January 1938, the sesquicentenary of the arrival of the First Fleet.

daytime n. the time of daylight.

day trip n. an excursion etc. completed in one day ◻ **day tripper** n.

daze v. make (a person) feel stunned or bewildered. •n. a dazed state.

dazzle v. **1** make (a person) unable to see clearly because of too much bright light. **2** amaze and impress or confuse (a person) by a splendid display. •n. bright confusing light. ◻ **dazzling** *adj.* **dazzlingly** *adv.*

dazzler n. *colloq.* anything exceptionally good, brilliant, etc.

Db *symbol* dubnium.

dB *abbr.* decibel(s).

DC *abbr.* **1** (also **dc**) direct current. **2** *Music* da capo.

D-Day n. **1** the day (6 June 1944) on which Allied forces invaded northern France in the Second World War. **2** the date on which an important operation is planned to begin.

DDT n. a white chlorinated hydrocarbon used as an insecticide.

deacon n. **1** a member of the clergy ranking below a priest. **2** a layman attending to church business in Nonconformist churches.

deaconess n. a woman with duties similar to those of a deacon.

deactivate v. make inactive or less reactive.

dead *adj.* **1** no longer alive. **2** numb, without feeling. **3** no longer used (*a dead language*). **4** lifeless and without lustre, resonance, or warmth. **5** no longer active or functioning (*the microphone went dead*). **6** dull; without interest, movement, or activity. **7** (of a ball in games) out of play. **8** complete, abrupt, exact (*dead silence; a dead stop; dead centre*). •*adv.* **1** completely, exactly (*dead drunk; dead level*). **2** *colloq.* very, extremely (*it's dead easy*). •n. an inactive or silent time (*the dead of night*). ◻ **dead beat** *colloq.* tired out. **deadbeat** n. *colloq.* a down-and-out. **dead end** the closed end of a road or passage; a blind alley. **dead-end job** a job with no prospects of advancement. **dead finish** *Aust.* **1** a small wattle of drier Australia which can form tangled prickly thickets. **2** the limit; the end. **dead heat** the result of a race in which two or more competitors finish exactly even. **dead letter 1** a rule or law that is no longer observed. **2** a letter which lies unclaimed at a post office or which cannot be delivered because of a faulty address etc. **dead loss** *colloq.* a useless person or thing. **dead man's handle** (or **pedal**) a controlling device (on a train etc.) that disconnects the driving power if it is released. **dead march** a funeral march. **dead men** *colloq.* bottles after the contents (the 'spirits') have been drunk. **dead nark** *Aust. colloq.* a spoilsport. **dead on** exactly right. **dead reckoning** calculating a ship's position by log and compass etc. when observations are impossible. **dead ringer** see RINGER. **dead set** a determined attack. **dead-set** *Aust. adj.* genuine; absolute (*he's the dead-set image of his father*). *adv.* truly (*I'm dead-set worried*). **dead weight** a heavy inert weight.

Dead Centre n. (also **Dead Heart**) *Aust.* the arid interior of Australia.

deaden *v.* deprive of or lose vitality, loudness, feeling, etc.

deadhead *v.* remove dead flower heads from (rose bushes etc.).

deadline *n.* a time limit. (¶ Originally this meant the line round a military prison beyond which a prisoner was liable to be shot.)

deadlock *n.* a complete standstill or lack of progress. •*v.* reach a deadlock; cause to do this.

deadly *adj.* (**deadlier, deadliest**) **1** causing or capable of causing fatal injury, death, or serious damage. **2** death-like (*a deadly silence*). **3** *colloq.* very dreary. **4** *Aust.* fantastic, terrific (*a deadly shirt*). •*adv.* **1** as if dead (*deadly pale*). **2** extremely (*deadly serious*). ☐ **deadly nightshade** a plant with poisonous black berries. **the seven deadly sins** those that result in damnation for a person's soul (traditionally pride, covetousness, lust, envy, gluttony, anger, sloth). ☐☐ **deadliness** *n.*

deadpan *adj.* & *adv. colloq.* with an expressionless face.

Dead Sea an inland salt lake in the Jordan valley on the Israel-Jordan border. ☐ **Dead Sea scrolls** a collection of Hebrew and Aramaic manuscripts discovered (chiefly in fragments) in caves near the Dead Sea.

deaf *adj.* **1** wholly or partly without the sense of hearing; unable to hear. **2** refusing to listen (*deaf to all advice; turned a deaf ear to our requests*). ☐ **deaf mute** a person who is both deaf and dumb. ☐☐ **deafness** *n.*

deafen *v.* make deaf or unable to hear by a very loud noise. ☐ **deafening** *adj.* **deafeningly** *adv.*

Deakin, Alfred (1856–1919), Australian statesman, prime minister 1903–04, 1905–08, 1909–10. Deakin is claimed by many to be the founder of the Liberal Party.

deal[1] *v.* (**dealt, dealing**) **1** distribute among several people; hand out (cards) to players in a card game. **2** give, inflict (*dealt him a severe blow*). **3** do business; trade (*they deal in colonial furniture*). •*n.* **1** dealing; a player's turn to deal; a round of play after dealing. **2** a business transaction. **3** treatment (*didn't get a fair deal*). **4** (also **a good deal, a great deal**) a large amount. ☐ **deal with 1** do business with. **2** take action about or be what is needed by (a problem etc.); discuss (a subject) in a book or speech etc.

deal[2] *n.* **1** sawn fir or pine timber. **2** a deal board of standard size.

dealer *n.* **1** a person who deals. **2** one who deals at cards. **3** a trader in (esp. retail) goods. **4** a trafficker in drugs.

dealings *n.pl.* a person's transactions with another.

dealt *see* DEAL.

dean *n.* **1** a college or university official with disciplinary and advisory functions. **2** the head of a university faculty or department or of a medical school. **3** the head of a cathedral chapter etc.

dear *adj.* **1** much loved, cherished. **2** esteemed; as a polite expression beginning a letter (*Dear Sir*). **3** costing more than it is worth, not cheap. •*n.* a dear person. •*adv.* dearly, at a high price. •*interj.* an exclamation of surprise or distress. ☐ **dearly** *adv.* **dearness** *n.*

Dear John *n.* (in full **Dear John letter**) *colloq.* a letter from a woman to a man terminating a personal relationship.

dearth / derth / *n.* a scarcity.

death *n.* **1** the process of dying, the end of life; final cessation of vital functions. **2** the state of being dead. **3** a cause of death (*smoking was the death of him*). **4** the ending or destruction of something (*the death of our hopes*). ☐ **death adder** any of three species of venomous snake of Australia and Papua New Guinea. **death certificate** an official statement of the date, place, and cause of a person's death. **death duty** tax levied on property after the owner's death. **death mask** a cast taken of a dead person's face. **death penalty** punishment for a crime by being put to death. **death rate** the number of deaths in one year for every 1000 persons. **death rattle** a gurgling in the throat sometimes heard at death. **death row** (esp. *US*) a prison area housing prisoners sentenced to death. **death trap** a dangerous place, vehicle, etc. **death warrant 1** an order for the execution of a condemned person. **2** something that causes the end of an established practice etc. **death-watch beetle** a beetle whose larva bores holes in old wood and makes a ticking sound formerly supposed to be a sign of an imminent death. **death wish** a desire (usu. unconscious) for the death of oneself or another person. **to death** extremely, to the utmost limit (*bored to death*).

deathbed *n.* the bed on which a person dies.

deathblow *n.* **1** a blow etc. causing death. **2** an event or action that destroys or ends something.

deathly *adj.* & *adv.* like death (*a deathly hush; deathly pale*).

deb *abbr. colloq.* a debutante.

debacle / day-**bah**-kuhl, duh- / *n.* (also **débâcle**) a sudden disastrous collapse, defeat, or failure.

debag *v.* (**debagged, debagging**) *colloq.* remove the trousers of (a person) as a joke.

debar *v.* (**debarred, debarring**) exclude, prohibit. ☐ **debarment** *n.*

debark *v.* disembark. ☐ **debarkation** *n.*

debase *v.* lower in quality or value; reduce the value of (coins) by using an alloy or inferior metal. ☐ **debasement** *n.*

debatable *adj.* questionable, open to dispute.

debate *n.* **1** a formal discussion on a particular matter (esp. in a legislative assembly etc.). **2** discussion (*that's open to debate*). •*v.* **1** hold a debate about. **2** discuss, consider.

debauch / duh-**bawch** / *v.* make dissolute, lead into debauchery. •*n.* a bout of sensual (esp. sexual) indulgence.

debauchery / duh-**baw**-chuh-ree / *n*. over-indulgence in sensual (esp. sexual) pleasures.

debenture / duh-**ben**-chuh / *n*. a certificate or bond acknowledging a debt on which fixed interest is being paid.

debilitate *v*. cause debility in.

debility *n*. feebleness, weakness.

debit *n*. **1** an entry in an account-book of a sum owed by the holder. **2** the sum itself; the total of such sums. • *v*. (**debited**, **debiting**) enter as a debit in an account.

debonair / deb-uh-**nair** / *adj*. having a carefree self-confident manner.

debouch / duh-**bowch**, -**boosh** / *v*. **1** (of troops or a stream) come out into open ground. **2** (often foll. by *into*) (of a river, road, etc.) merge into a larger body or area. ☐ **debouchment** *n*.

debrief *v. colloq.* question (a person) in order to obtain information about a mission just completed.

debris / **deb**-ree, **day**-bree / *n*. scattered broken pieces.

debt *n*. something owed by one person to another. ☐ **in debt** owing something.

debtor *n*. a person who owes money to another.

debug *v*. (**debugged**, **debugging**) **1** remove concealed listening devices from (a room etc.). **2** remove defects from (a computer program). **3** = DELOUSE.

debunk *v. colloq.* show up (a claim or theory, or a good reputation) as exaggerated or false.

Debussy / duh-**boo**-see /, (Achille) Claude (1862–1918), French composer and critic.

debut / **day**-byoo, duh-**byoo**, duh-**boo** / *n*. (also **début**) a first public appearance.

debutante / **deb**-yoo-tont, **day**-byoo- / *n*. (also **débutante**) a young woman making her first appearance in society.

deca- *comb. form* ten.

decade / **dek**-ayd, duh-**kayd** / *n*. **1** a period of ten years. **2** a set, series, or group of ten (*a decade of the rosary*). ☐ **decadal** *adj*.

■ **Usage** The second pronunciation given, with the stress on the second syllable, is considered incorrect by some people.

decadent / **dek**-uh-duhnt / *adj*. **1** becoming less worthy; deteriorating in standard. **2** self-indulgent; immoral. ☐ **decadence** *n*.

decaffeinated / dee-**kaf**-uh-nay-tuhd, duh- / *adj*. with the caffeine removed or reduced.

decagon *n*. a geometric figure with ten sides. ☐ **decagonal** / duh-**kag**-uh-nuhl / *adj*.

decahedron / dek-uh-**hee**-druhn / *n*. a solid geometric figure with ten faces. ☐ **decahedral** *adj*.

decalitre *n*. a unit of 10 litres.

Decalogue / **dek**-uh-log / *n*. the Ten Commandments.

decametre / **dek**-uh-mee-tuh / *n*. a unit of length equal to 10 metres.

decamp *v*. **1** break up camp; leave camp. **2** go away suddenly or secretly.

decant / duh-**kant** / *v*. pour (liquid) gently from one container into another without disturbing the sediment.

decanter / duh-**kan**-tuh / *n*. a stoppered glass bottle into which wine etc. may be decanted.

decapitate / dee-**kap**-uh-tayt, duh- / *v*. behead. ☐ **decapitation** *n*.

decapod / **dek**-uh-pod / *n*. **1** a crustacean with ten feet, e.g. a crab, prawn, crayfish. **2** a mollusc with ten tentacles, e.g. a squid.

decarbonise *v*. (also -**ize**) remove the carbon deposit from (an engine etc.). ☐ **decarbonisation** *n*.

decathlete *n*. a competitor in a decathlon.

decathlon / dek-**kath**-lon / *n*. an athletic contest in which each competitor takes part in the ten events it includes.

decay *v*. **1** become rotten; cause to rot. **2** lose quality or strength. **3** (of a substance) undergo change by radioactivity. • *n*. **1** decaying, rot. **2** decline in health or quality. **3** radioactive change.

decease / duh-**sees** / *n. formal* death. • *v*. die.

deceased *adj*. dead. • *n*. (**the deceased**) the person(s) who died recently.

deceit *n*. deceiving; a deception.

deceitful *adj*. deceiving people. ☐ **deceitfully** *adv*. **deceitfulness** *n*.

deceive *v*. **1** cause (a person) to believe something that is not true. **2** be sexually unfaithful to. ☐ **deceive oneself** persist in a mistaken belief. ☐☐ **deceiver** *n*.

decelerate / dee-**sel**-uh-rayt / *v*. cause to slow down; decrease one's speed. ☐ **deceleration** *n*.

December *n*. the twelfth month of the year.

decency *n*. **1** being decent. **2** (**decencies**) the requirements of respectable behaviour in society.

decennial / duh-**sen**-ee-uhl / *adj*. **1** lasting for ten years. **2** happening every tenth year.

decent *adj*. **1** conforming to the accepted standards of what is proper; not immodest or obscene. **2** respectable (*he comes from a decent background*). **3** quite good (*earns a decent salary*). **4** kind, generous, obliging (*was decent enough to apologise*). ☐ **decently** *adv*.

decentralise *v*. (also -**ize**) divide and distribute (powers etc.) from a central authority to places or branches away from the centre. ☐ **decentralisation** *n*.

deception *n*. **1** deceiving; being deceived. **2** something that deceives people.

deceptive *adj*. deceiving; easily mistaken for something else. ☐ **deceptively** *adv*.

decibel / **des**-uh-bel / *n*. a unit for measuring the relative loudness of sound or power levels of electrical signals.

decide *v*. **1** think about and make a choice or judgment; come to a decision. **2** settle by giving victory to one side (*this goal decided the match*). **3** cause to reach a decision (*that decided me*).

decided *adj.* **1** having clear opinions; determined. **2** clear, definite (*a decided difference*). □ **decidedly** *adv.*

decider *n.* a game or race to decide which of the competitors who finished equal in a previous contest should be the final winner.

deciduous / duh-**sid**-yoo-uhs / *adj.* **1** (of a tree) shedding its leaves annually. **2** falling off or shed after a time (*a deer has deciduous antlers*).

decigram *n.* (also **decigramme**) one-tenth of a gram.

decilitre *n.* one-tenth of a litre.

decimal / **des**-uh-muhl / *adj.* reckoned in tens or tenths. • *n.* a decimal fraction. □ **decimal currency** currency in which each unit is ten or one hundred times the value of the one next below it. **decimal fraction** a fraction whose denominator is a power of 10, expressed in figures after a dot (the **decimal point**), e.g. $0.5 = {}^{5}/_{10}$, $0.52 = {}^{52}/_{100}$. **decimal system** a system of weights and measures with each unit ten times that immediately below it.

decimalise *v.* (also **-ize**) **1** express as a decimal. **2** convert to a decimal system. □ **decimalisation** *n.*

decimate / **des**-uh-mayt / *v.* **1** destroy one-tenth of. **2** destroy a large proportion of. □ **decimation** *n.* (¶ From the practice of putting to death one in every ten of a body of soldiers guilty of mutiny or other crime—a practice in the ancient Roman army, sometimes followed in later times.)

■ **Usage** The looser and more general use in terms of 'a large proportion' is now widespread, but strictly speaking is incorrect. This word should not be used to mean 'destroy totally'.

decimetre *n.* one-tenth of a metre.

decipher / duh-**suy**-fuh / *v.* make out the meaning of (a coded message, bad handwriting, or something difficult to interpret). □ **decipherable** *adj.*

decision *n.* **1** deciding, making a reasoned judgment about something. **2** the judgment itself. **3** the ability to form clear opinions and act on them (*he acted with decision*).

decisive / duh-**suy**-siv / *adj.* **1** settling something conclusively (*a decisive battle*). **2** showing decision and firmness. □ **decisively** *adv.* **decisiveness** *n.*

deck *n.* **1** any of the horizontal floors in a ship. **2** a similar floor or platform, esp. one of two or more (*the top deck of a bus*). **3** a piece of equipment for playing discs or tapes as part of a sound system. **4** a pack of cards. **5** *colloq.* the ground (*hit the deck*). • *v.* **1** decorate; dress up (*decked with flags; decked out in her finest clothes*). **2** *US* & *Aust. colloq.* floor (a person) by hitting (*I decked him*). □ **on deck** *colloq.* ready for action, work, etc. (*I'm back on deck*).

deckchair *n.* a portable folding chair of canvas on a wood or metal frame.

deckhand *n.* a cleaner on a ship's deck.

decking *n.* **1** planking etc. forming the deck of a ship. **2** anything compared to this, e.g. the floor of a pergola.

deckle edge *n.* a ragged edge like that on handmade paper. □ **deckle-edged** *adj.*

declaim / duh-**klaym** / *v.* speak or say impressively or dramatically. □ **declamation** / dek-luh-**may**-shuhn / *n.* **declamatory** *adj.*

declaration *n.* **1** declaring. **2** a formal or emphatic statement. **3** (in full **declaration of the poll**) the public official announcement of the votes cast for candidates in an election. **4** the act of declaring an innings closed in cricket.

declare *v.* **1** make known; announce openly, formally, or explicitly. **2** state firmly (*he declares that he is innocent*). **3** inform customs officials that one has (goods) on which duty may be payable. **4** choose to close one's side's innings at cricket before ten wickets have fallen. **5** name the trump suit in a card game. □ **declarative** *adj.* **declaratory** *adj.*

declassify *v.* declare (information, documents, etc.) to be no longer secret. □ **declassification** *n.*

declension *n.* **1** variation of the form of a noun etc. to give its grammatical case; the class by which a noun etc. is declined. **2** decrease, deterioration (*the gradual declension of his mental faculties*).

declination / dek-luh-**nay**-shuhn / *n.* **1** a downward turn or bend. **2** the angle between the true north and the magnetic north. **3** the angle between the direction of a star etc. and the celestial equator.

decline *v.* **1** refuse (*decline the invitation*). **2** slope downwards. **3** decrease, lose strength or vigour (*one's declining years*). **4** give the forms of (a noun or adjective) corresponding to the grammatical cases. • *n.* a gradual decrease or loss of strength. □ **in decline** decreasing.

declivity / duh-**kliv**-uh-tee / *n.* a downward slope.

declutch *v.* disengage the clutch of a motor vehicle.

decoction *n.* boiling down to extract an essence; the extract itself.

decode *v.* put (a coded message) into plain language; translate (coded characters in a computer).

decoder *n.* **1** a person or machine that decodes messages etc. **2** a device for analysing stereophonic signals and passing them to separate amplifier channels.

decoke *v. colloq.* decarbonise.

décolletage / day-**kol**-tah*zh* / *n.* a low neckline. (¶ French)

décolleté / day-**kol**-tay / *adj.* having a low neckline. (¶ French)

decompose *v.* **1** decay; cause to decay. **2** separate (a substance) into its elements. □ **decomposition** *n.*

decompress *v.* subject to decompression.

decompression *n.* **1** release from compression. **2** the gradual and safe reduction of air pressure on

decongestant

a person who has been in compressed air (e.g. deep under water). ☐ **decompression chamber** an enclosed space where this can be done. **decompression sickness** a painful condition caused by the sudden lowering of air pressure and the formation of bubbles in the blood.

decongestant / dee-kuhn-**jes**-tuhnt / *n.* a medicinal substance that relieves congestion.

deconstruction *n.* **1** the action of undoing the construction of a thing. **2** *Philosophy & Literary Theory* the strategy of critical analysis directed towards exposing unquestioned metaphysical assumptions and internal contradictions in philosophical and literary language. ☐ **deconstruct** *v.* **deconstructionism** *n.* **deconstructionist** *adj.* & *n.*

decontaminate *v.* remove radioactive or other contamination from (an area, person, clothes, etc.). ☐ **decontamination** *n.*

decor / **day**-kaw / *n.* (also **décor**) the style of furnishings and decoration used in a room, a stage set, etc.

decorate *v.* **1** make (a thing) look attractive or festive by adding objects or details. **2** put fresh paint or paper on the walls etc. of (a room). **3** confer a medal or other award upon.

decoration *n.* **1** decorating. **2** something that decorates. **3** a medal etc. awarded and worn as an honour. **4** (**decorations**) flags and other decorative objects put up on festive occasions.

decorative / **dek**-uh-ruh-tiv / *adj.* ornamental, pleasing to look at. ☐ **decoratively** *adv.*

decorator *n.* **1** a person who decorates, esp. one whose job is to paint and paper houses. **2** a person who offers professional advice on the decor for rooms etc.

decorous / **dek**-uh-ruhs / *adj.* polite and well-behaved; decent. ☐ **decorously** *adv.*

decorum / duh-**kaw**-ruhm / *n.* correctness and dignity of behaviour or procedure etc.

decoupage / day-koo-**pahzh** / *n.* (also **découpage**) the decoration of surfaces with paper etc. cut-outs; an object so decorated. • *v.* decorate (an object) in this way.

decoy *n.* / **dee**-koi / something used to lure an animal or person into a trap. • *v.* / duh-**koi** / lure by means of a decoy.

decrease *v.* make or become shorter, smaller, or fewer. • *n.* **1** decreasing. **2** the amount by which something decreases. ☐ **decreasingly** *adv.*

decree *n.* **1** an order given by a government or other authority and having the force of a law. **2** a judgment or decision of certain lawcourts. • *v.* (**decreed**, **decreeing**) order by decree.

decrepit / duh-**krep**-uht / *adj.* made weak by old age or hard use; dilapidated. ☐ **decrepitude** *n.*

decrescendo = DIMINUENDO.

decretal / duh-**kree**-tuhl / *n.* **1** a papal decree. **2** (**decretals**) a collection of these, forming part of canon law.

deep

decriminalise *v.* (also **-ize**) pass a law causing (an action etc.) to cease to be treated as a crime. ☐ **decriminalisation** *n.*

decry / duh-**kruy** / *v.* (**decried**, **decrying**) disparage, belittle.

dedicate *v.* **1** devote (a building etc.) to a saint or to a sacred use (*they dedicated the church to St Peter*). **2** devote (one's time and energy) to a special purpose. **3** (of an author etc.) address (a book or piece of music etc.) to a person as a compliment, putting his or her name at the beginning. ☐ **dedicator** *n.*

dedicated *adj.* **1** devoted to a vocation, cause, etc. (*a dedicated scientist*). **2** having single-minded loyalty.

dedication *n.* **1** dedicating. **2** the words with which a book etc. is dedicated.

dedicatory / **ded**-uh-kay-tuh-ree, -tree / *adj.* making a dedication (*a dedicatory inscription*).

deduce / duh-**dyoos** / *v.* arrive at (knowledge or a conclusion) by reasoning from observed facts. ☐ **deducible** *adj.*

deduct *v.* take away (an amount or quantity); subtract.

deductible *adj.* able to be deducted, esp. from tax or taxable income.

deduction *n.* **1** deducting; something that is deducted. **2** deducing; a conclusion reached by reasoning. **3** logical reasoning that something must be true because it is a particular case of a general law that is known to be true.

deductive *adj.* based on reasoning.

deed *n.* **1** something done, an act. **2** a legal agreement, esp. one giving ownership or rights, bearing the giver's signature and seal. ☐ **deed of covenant** an undertaking to make an annual subscription for a period of years to a charity etc. which is allowed to reclaim, in addition, the tax paid on this amount by the contributor. **deed poll** a deed made by one party only, making a formal declaration, esp. to change a name.

deem *v. formal* believe, consider, or judge (*I deem it my duty*).

deeming *n. Aust.* the calculation of income to determine eligibility for social security benefits etc. by assuming a prescribed rate of return on assets. ☐ **deeming rate** the assumed rate of return on personal investments, set by government for the purposes of calculating social security benefits.

deep *adj.* **1** going or situated far down or back or in (*a deep cut; deep shelves; a deep sigh*). **2** (in cricket) distant from the batsman. **3** intense, extreme (*deep sleep; deep interest*). **4** low-pitched and resonant, not shrill (*a deep voice*). **5** fully absorbed or overwhelmed (*deep in thought*). **6** heartfelt (*deep sympathy*). **7** difficult to understand, obscure (*that's too deep for me*). **8** *colloq.* cunning or secretive (*he's a deep one*). • *adv.* deeply far down or in (*dig deep*). • *n.* **1** a deep place or state. **2** (**the deep**) *poetic* the sea.

☐ **deep-freeze** n. a freezer. v. freeze or store in a deep-freeze. **deep-fry** v. fry (food) in oil that covers it. **deep-rooted** (also **deep-seated**) adj. (of opinions, beliefs, etc.) firmly established; not superficial (*a deep-seated distrust*). **deep vein thrombosis** (*abbr.* **DVT**) the formation of a blood clot within a vein, esp. in the thigh or calf. **go off the deep end** *colloq.* become very angry or emotional. **in deep water** in trouble or difficulty. ☐☐ **deeply** adv. **deepness** n.

deepen v. make or become deep or deeper.

deer n. (pl. **deer**) a grazing animal, the male of which usu. has antlers.

deerstalker n. a soft cloth peaked cap with ear-flaps.

de-escalate v. (of a dispute, crisis, etc.) make or become less intense or dangerous. ☐ **de-escalation** n.

deface v. spoil or damage the surface of. ☐ **defacement** n.

de facto / dee **fak**-toh / adv. in fact (whether by right or not). •adj. that exists or is such in fact (*a de facto wife*). •n. Aust. a person living with another as if married (*he's my de facto*). (¶ Latin)

defalcate / **dee**-fal-kayt / v. *formal* misappropriate funds. ☐ **defalcator** n.

defalcation / dee-fal-**kay**-shuhn / n. *formal* misappropriation of funds; a breach of trust concerning money.

defamatory / duh-**fam**-uh-tuh-ree, -tree / adj. defaming.

defame / dee-**faym** / v. attack the good reputation of, speak ill of. ☐ **defamation** / def-uh-**may**-shuhn / n.

default n. **1** failure to appear (e.g. in court on the day assigned), pay (a debt), or act as one should. **2** a preselected choice or action taken by a computer program when no alternative is specified. •v. **1** fail to fulfil an obligation. **2** fail to take part in scheduled in a sporting match etc.; lose a match in this way. ☐ **by default** because there is no alternative or opposition. **in default of** because of the absence of. ☐☐ **defaulter** n.

defeat v. **1** win a victory over. **2** cause to fail, frustrate (*this defeats our hopes for reform*). **3** baffle (*the problem defeats me*). •n. **1** defeating others. **2** being defeated; a lost battle or contest.

defeatist n. a person who expects to be defeated or accepts defeat too easily. ☐ **defeatism** n.

defecate / **def**-uh-kayt / v. discharge waste matter from the bowels. ☐ **defecation** n.

defect n. / **dee**-fekt, duh-**fekt** / a deficiency; an imperfection. •v. / duh-**fekt** / desert one's country; abandon one's allegiance to a cause. ☐ **defection** n. **defector** n.

defective adj. **1** having defects; imperfect; incomplete. **2** mentally subnormal. ☐ **defectively** adv. **defectiveness** n.

defence n. **1** defending from or resisting attack. **2** something that defends or protects against attack. **3** the military reserves of a country. **4** a justification put forward in response to an accusation. **5** the defendant's case in a lawsuit; the lawyer(s) representing an accused person. **6** the players in a defending position in a game. ☐ **defence mechanism 1** the body's resistance to disease. **2** a usu. unconscious mental process to avoid conscious conflict or anxiety. ☐☐ **defenceless** adj. **defencelessness** n.

defend v. **1** protect by warding off an attack. **2** to preserve (*the champion is defending his title*). **3** uphold by argument, put forward a justification of. **4** represent the defendant in a lawsuit.

defendant n. a person accused or sued in a lawsuit (opposed to the *plaintiff*).

defender n. a person who defends something.

Defender of the Faith a title (translation of Latin *Fidei defensor*) conferred by the pope on Henry VIII in 1521 and assumed by all subsequent British sovereigns.

defensible adj. able to be defended. ☐ **defensibly** adv. **defensibility** n.

defensive adj. **1** used or done for defence, protective. **2** anxious to challenge or avoid criticism. ☐ **on the defensive** in an attitude of defence; expecting criticism. ☐☐ **defensively** adv. **defensiveness** n.

defer[1] v. (**deferred, deferring**) put off to a later time, postpone. ☐ **deferment** n. **deferral** n.

defer[2] v. (**deferred, deferring**) (foll. by *to*) give way to a person's wishes or authority; yield.

deference / **def**-uh-ruhns / n. polite respect; compliance with another person's wishes. ☐ **in deference to** out of respect for.

deferential / def-uh-**ren**-shuhl / adj. showing deference. ☐ **deferentially** adv.

defiance n. defying, open disobedience, bold resistance.

defiant adj. showing defiance. ☐ **defiantly** adv.

deficiency / duh-**fish**-uhn-see / n. **1** being deficient. **2** a lack or shortage; a thing lacking; the amount by which something falls short of what is required. ☐ **deficiency disease** a disease caused by lack of vitamins or other essential elements in food.

deficient / duh-**fish**-uhnt / adj. **1** not having enough (*deficient in vitamins*). **2** insufficient or not present at all.

deficit / **def**-uh-suht / n. **1** the amount by which a total falls short of what is required. **2** the excess of expenditure over income, or of liabilities over assets.

defile[1] / duh-**fuyl** / v. **1** make dirty, pollute. **2** desecrate, profane. ☐ **defilement** n.

defile[2] / duh-**fuyl** / n. a narrow gorge or pass. •v. march in file.

define v. **1** give the exact meaning of (a word etc.). **2** state or explain the scope of (*customers' rights are defined by the law*). **3** outline clearly, mark out the boundary of. ☐ **definable** adj.

definite adj. **1** having exact limits. **2** clear and unmistakable, not vague (*I want a definite*

definition

answer). **3** certain, settled (*is it definite that we are to move?*). ☐ **definite article** *Grammar* the word 'the'. ☐☐ **definitely** *adv*.

■ **Usage** See the note at *definitive*.

definition *n*. **1** a statement of the exact meaning of a word or phrase, or of the nature of a thing. **2** making or being distinct; clearness of outline.

definitive / duh-**fin**-uh-tiv / *adj*. finally fixing or settling something; conclusive.

■ **Usage** This word is sometimes confused with *definite*. A *definite* offer is one that is clearly stated. A *definitive* offer is one that must be accepted or refused without trying to alter its terms. A *definitive edition* is one with authoritative status.

deflate *v*. **1** let out air or gas from (an inflated tyre etc.). **2** cause (a person) to lose confidence or self-esteem. **3** counteract inflation in (a country's economy), e.g. by reducing the amount of money in circulation. **4** become deflated. ☐ **deflation** *n*. **deflationary** *adj*.

deflect *v*. turn or cause to turn aside. ☐ **deflection** (also **deflexion**) *n*. **deflector** *n*.

deflower *v*. *literary* **1** deprive (a person) of virginity. **2** spoil the perfection of, ravage.

Defoe / duh-**foh** /, Daniel (1660–1731), English novelist, author of *Robinson Crusoe*.

defoliant / duh-**foh**-lee-uhnt / *n*. a chemical substance that destroys foliage.

defoliate / dee-**foh**-lee-ayt / *v*. strip of leaves; destroy the foliage of by chemical means. ☐ **defoliation** *n*.

deforest *v*. clear of forests or trees. ☐ **deforestation** *n*.

deform *v*. spoil the form or appearance of; put out of shape. ☐ **deformation** / dee-faw-**may**-shuhn / *n*.

deformed *adj*. badly or abnormally shaped.

deformity *n*. **1** being deformed. **2** a deformed part of the body.

defraud *v*. deprive by fraud.

defray *v*. provide money to pay (costs or expenses). ☐ **defrayal** *n*. **defrayment** *n*.

defrock *v*. dismiss (a priest) from office.

defrost *v*. **1** remove frost or ice from. **2** unfreeze (*defrost the chicken; let the chicken defrost*).

deft *adj*. skilful; handling things neatly. ☐ **deftly** *adv*. **deftness** *n*.

defunct / dee-**fungkt** / *adj*. **1** dead. **2** no longer existing, used, or functioning.

defuse *v*. **1** remove the fuse of; make (an explosive) unable to explode. **2** reduce the dangerous tension in (a situation).

defy *v*. (**defied**, **defying**) **1** refuse to obey. **2** challenge (a person) to try and do something that one believes he or she cannot or will not do (*I defy you to prove this*). **3** offer difficulties that cannot be overcome by (*the door defied all attempts to open it*).

dejected

degauss / dec-**gows** / *v*. remove unwanted magnetism from (esp. a television set) by encircling with a conductor carrying electric current.

degenerate *v*. / dee-**jen**-uh-rayt, duh- / become worse or lower in standard; lose good qualities. • *adj*. / duh-**jen**-uh-ruht / having degenerated; immoral, degraded. • *n*. / duh-**jen**-uh-ruht / a degenerate person or animal. ☐ **degeneration** *n*. **degeneracy** *n*.

degradable *adj*. (of waste products etc.) able to be broken down by chemical or biological processes.

degrade *v*. **1** reduce to a lower rank or status. **2** bring disgrace or contempt on. **3** (of soils) reduce to a lower quality (due to erosion, overuse, etc.). **4** reduce to a simpler molecular structure. ☐ **degradation** / deg-ruh-**day**-shuhn / *n*.

degrading *adj*. shaming, humiliating.

degree *n*. **1** a step or stage in an ascending or descending series. **2** a stage in intensity or amount (*a high degree of skill*). **3** an academic rank awarded to a person who has successfully completed a course of study or as an honour. **4** a unit of measurement for angles or arcs, indicated by the symbol °, e.g. 45°. **5** a unit of measurement in a scale e.g. of temperatures. ☐ **to a degree** *colloq*. considerably; to a certain extent (*I'm with you to a degree*).

dehisce / dee-**his**, duh- / *v*. (esp. of seed-vessels) gape, burst open. ☐ **dehiscence** *n*. **dehiscent** *adj*.

dehumanise *v*. (also **-ize**) take away human qualities from; make impersonal or machine-like. ☐ **dehumanisation** *n*.

dehydrate *v*. **1** remove the moisture content from (esp. foods). **2** lose moisture. ☐ **dehydration** *n*.

de-ice *v*. remove or prevent the formation of ice on (a windscreen or other surface). ☐ **de-icer** *n*.

deify / **dee**-uh-fuy, **day**- / *v*. (**deified**, **deifying**) make a god of; treat as a god. ☐ **deification** *n*.

deign / dayn / *v*. condescend; be kind or gracious enough to do something (*she did not deign to reply*).

deinstitutionalise *v*. (also **-ize**) remove (a person) from an institution or help (him or her) recover from the effects of being in an institution (such as an orphanage, a prison, etc.). ☐ **deinstitutionalisation** *n*.

deism / **dee**-iz-uhm, **day**- / *n*. belief in the existence of a god (creator of the world) without accepting divine revelation (*see* THEISM). ☐ **deist** *n*. **deistic** *adj*.

deity / **dee**-uh-tee, **day**- / *n*. **1** a god or goddess (*Roman deities*). **2** divinity. **3** (**the Deity**) God.

déjà vu / day-zhah **voo** / *n*. a feeling of having experienced the present situation before. • *adj*. boringly familiar. (¶ French, = already seen.)

dejected *adj*. in low spirits; depressed. ☐ **dejectedly** *adv*. **dejection** *n*.

de jure / dee **joor**-ree, day-**yoor**-ray / *adj.* rightful (*the de jure pope*). • *adv.* rightfully, by right. (¶ Latin)

dekko *n. colloq.* a look.

de Klerk, F(rederik) W(illem) (1936–), South African statesman, president 1989–94. In 1993 he shared the Nobel Peace Prize with Nelson Mandela.

delay *v.* **1** make or be late; hinder. **2** put off until later, postpone. **3** wait, linger. • *n.* **1** delaying, being delayed. **2** the amount of time for which something is delayed (*a two-hour delay*). ☐ **delayed-action** *adj.* operating after a set interval of time.

delectable *adj.* delightful, enjoyable. ☐ **delectably** *adv.*

delectation / dee-lek-**tay**-shuhn / *n.* enjoyment, delight (*for your delectation*).

delegate *n.* / **del**-uh-guht / a person who represents others and acts according to their instructions. • *v.* / **del**-uh-gayt / **1** entrust (a task, power, or responsibility) to an agent. **2** appoint or send as a representative.

delegation / del-uh-**gay**-shuhn / *n.* **1** delegating. **2** a group representing others.

delete / duh-**leet** / *v.* **1** cross out (something written or printed). **2** *Computing* remove or overwrite a record or item of data. ☐ **deletion** *n.*

deleterious / del-uh-**teer**-ree-uhs / *adj.* harmful to the body or mind.

delft *n.* (also **delftware**) glazed earthenware, usu. decorated in blue, made at Delft in Holland.

Delhi / **del**-ee / (in full **New Delhi**) the capital of India.

deli *n.* (*pl.* **delis**) *colloq.* a delicatessen.

deliberate *adj.* / duh-**lib**-uh-ruht / **1** done or said on purpose, intentional (*a deliberate insult*). **2** slow and careful, unhurried (*entered with deliberate steps*). • *v.* / duh-**lib**-uh-rayt / think over or discuss carefully before reaching a decision. ☐ **deliberately** *adv.*

deliberation *n.* **1** careful consideration or discussion. **2** careful slowness.

deliberative / duh-**lib**-uh-ruh-tiv / *adj.* for the purpose of deliberating or discussing things (*a deliberative assembly*).

delicacy *n.* **1** being delicate (in all senses). **2** avoidance of what is immodest or offensive or hurtful to others. **3** a choice or expensive food.

delicate *adj.* **1** fine in texture; soft; slender. **2** of fine quality or workmanship. **3** (of colour or flavour) pleasant and not strong or intense. **4** easily injured; liable to illness; (of plants) unable to withstand cold. **5** requiring careful handling (*a delicate operation; the situation is delicate*). **6** skilful and sensitive (*has a delicate touch*). **7** taking great care to avoid what is immodest, offensive, or hurtful to others. ☐ **delicately** *adv.* **delicateness** *n.*

delicatessen / del-uh-kuh-**tes**-uhn / *n.* a shop or part of a supermarket selling speciality cheeses, cooked meats, etc.

delicious *adj.* delightful, esp. to the senses of taste or smell. ☐ **deliciously** *adv.*

delight *v.* **1** please greatly. **2** (foll. by *in*) take great pleasure in (*she delights in giving surprises*). • *n.* **1** great pleasure. **2** something that causes this.

delightful *adj.* giving delight. ☐ **delightfully** *adv.*

Delilah / duh-**luy**-luh / *n.* a seductive and treacherous woman. (¶ Named after a woman in the Bible, who betrayed Samson to the Philistines.)

delimit / dee-**lim**-uht / *v.* fix the limits or boundaries of. ☐ **delimitation** *n.*

delineate / duh-**lin**-ee-ayt / *v.* show by drawing or by describing. ☐ **delineation** *n.*

delinquent / duh-**ling**-kwuhnt / *adj.* committing an offence; failing to perform a duty. • *n.* a delinquent person, esp. a young offender against the law. ☐ **delinquency** *n.*

deliquesce / del-i-**kwes** / *v.* **1** become liquid, melt. **2** dissolve in moisture absorbed from the air. ☐ **deliquescence** *n.* **deliquescent** *adj.*

delirious / duh-**li**-ree-uhs, duh-**leer**- / *adj.* **1** affected with delirium, raving. **2** wildly excited. ☐ **deliriously** *adv.*

delirium / duh-**leer**-ree-uhm / *n.* **1** a disordered state of mind, esp. during feverish illness. **2** wild excitement or emotion. ☐ **delirium tremens** / **trem**-enz, -uhnz /, a form of delirium with tremors and terrifying delusions, caused by heavy drinking.

deliver *v.* **1** take (letters, goods, etc.) to the addressee or purchaser. **2** hand over; present. **3** utter (a speech). **4** aim or launch (a blow, an attack); bowl (a ball) in cricket etc. **5** rescue, save, or set free. **6** assist at the birth of or in giving birth. **7** give birth to. ☐ **deliverer** *n.*

deliverance *n.* rescue, setting free; being rescued.

delivery *n.* **1** delivering; being delivered. **2** a periodical distribution of letters or goods etc. **3** the manner of delivering a speech. **4** the manner of bowling a ball in cricket etc.

dell *n.* a small wooded hollow or valley.

delouse *v.* remove lice from (a person or animal).

Delphi / **del**-fee / an ancient Greek city on the southern slopes of Mount Parnassus, site of the most famous oracle of Apollo.

Delphic *adj.* (also **Delphian**) of or like the ancient Greek oracle at Parnassus, which often gave obscure and enigmatic prophecies.

delphinium *n.* a garden plant with tall spikes of flowers, usu. blue.

delta *n.* **1** the fourth letter of the Greek alphabet (Δ, δ). **2** a triangular patch of land accumulated at the mouth of a river between two or more of its branches (*the Nile Delta*).

delude / duh-**lood** / v. deceive, mislead.
deluge / **del**-yooj / n. **1** a great flood; a heavy fall of rain. **2** (**the Deluge**) the flood in Noah's time. **3** anything coming in a heavy rush (*a deluge of questions*). • v. flood, come down on like a deluge.
delusion n. **1** a false belief or opinion. **2** a hallucination. □ **delusory** adj.
delusive adj. deceptive, raising vain hopes.
de luxe adj. of very high quality, luxurious.
delve v. **1** *archaic* dig. **2** search deeply for information.
demagogue / **dem**-uh-gog / n. a leader or agitator who wins support by appealing to people's feelings and prejudices rather than by reasoning. □ **demagogic** adj. **demagogy** n.
demand n. **1** a request made imperiously or as if one had a right. **2** a desire for goods or services by people who wish to buy or use these (*an increased demand for new houses*). **3** an urgent claim (*there are many demands on my time*). • v. **1** make a demand for. **2** need (*the work demands great skill*). □ **in demand** sought after. **on demand** as soon as the demand is made (*payable on demand*).
demanding adj. **1** making many demands. **2** requiring a great deal of skill or effort (*a demanding job*).
demarcation / dee-mah-**kay**-shuhn / n. **1** marking of the boundary or limits of something. **2** trade-union practice of restricting a specific job to one union. □ **demarcate** v.
dematerialise v. (also -**ize**) make or become non-material; vanish.
demean v. lower the dignity of (*I wouldn't demean myself to ask for it*).
demeanour n. a person's behaviour or bearing.
demented adj. driven mad, crazy. □ **dementedly** adv.
dementia / di-**men**-shuh / n. chronic disorder of the mental processes marked by memory loss, personality changes, etc. (*senile dementia*). □ **dementia praecox** / **pree**-koks / *formal* schizophrenia.
demerara / dem-uh-**rair**-ruh / n. brown raw cane sugar.
demerit n. **1** a fault, a defect. **2** a mark awarded against an offender.
demesne / duh-**meen**, -**mayn** / n. **1** a territory; a domain. **2** landed property.
Demeter / di-**mee**-tuh / *Gk myth.* the cereal goddess, mother of Persephone, identified by the Romans with Ceres.
demi- *comb. form* half; partly.
Demidenko, Helen, the Ukrainian name assumed by the Australian writer Helen Darville (1971–) for her novel *The Hand That Signed the Paper*, the winner of a number of major literary awards. A literary controversy erupted in 1995 when her true identity was revealed.
demigod n. **1** a partly divine being. **2** a person regarded as godlike.
demijohn n. a large bottle, often in a wicker case.

demilitarise v. (also -**ize**) remove military installations or forces from (an area). □ **demilitarisation** n.
demi-monde / **dem**-ee-mond / n. **1** women of doubtful repute in society. **2** a group behaving with doubtful legality or respectability. (¶ French, = half-world.)
demise / duh-**muyz** / n. *formal* **1** death. **2** termination; failure.
demisemiquaver n. a note in music, equal to half a semiquaver.
demist v. clear mist from (a windscreen etc.). □ **demister** n.
demo n. (*pl.* **demos**) *colloq.* a demonstration.
demob v. (**demobbed**, **demobbing**) *colloq.* demobilise.
demobilise v. (also -**ize**) release from military service. □ **demobilisation** n.
democracy n. **1** government by the whole people of a country, esp. through representatives whom they elect. **2** a country governed in this way. **3** a form of society etc. characterised by social equality and tolerance.
democrat n. **1** a person who favours democracy. **2** (**Democrat**) **a** *Aust.* a member of the Australian Democrats. **b** *US* a member of the Democratic Party.
democratic adj. **1** of, like, or supporting democracy. **2** in accordance with the principle of equal rights for all (*a democratic decision*). □ **democratically** adv.
Democratic Party the more liberal of the two main political parties in the USA.
democratise / duh-**mok**-ruh-tuyz / v. (also -**ize**) make democratic. □ **democratisation** n.
demodulation n. the process of extracting a modulating radio signal from a modulated wave etc.
demography / duh-**mog**-ruh-fee / n. the study of statistics of births, deaths, diseases, etc., as illustrating the conditions of life in communities. □ **demographic** adj. **demographically** adv. **demographics** n.pl.
demolish v. **1** pull or knock down (a building). **2** destroy (a person's argument or theory etc.); put an end to (an institution). **3** *colloq.* eat up. □ **demolition** / dem-uh-**lish**-uhn / n.
demon n. **1** a devil or evil spirit. **2** a cruel person. **3** (usu. used as adj.) very skilful or forceful (*a demon bowler*). □ **demonic** / duh-**mon**-ik / adj.
demonetise / dee-**mun**-uh-tuyz / v. (also -**ize**) withdraw (a coin etc.) from use as money. □ **demonetisation** n.
demoniac / duh-**moh**-nee-ak / adj. (also **demoniacal** / dee-muh-**nuy**-uh-kuhl /) **1** of or like a demon. **2** possessed by an evil spirit. **3** fiercely energetic, frenzied. □ **demoniacally** adv.
demonise / dee-muh-**nuyz** / v. (also -**ize**) **1** make into or like a demon. **2** represent as a demon.

demonolatry / dee-muh-**nol**-uh-tree / n. worship of demons.

demonology n. the study of beliefs about demons.

demonstrable / duh-**mon**-struh-buhl, **dem**-uhn- / adj. able to be shown or proved. ☐ **demonstrably** adv.

demonstrate v. 1 show evidence of, prove. 2 describe and explain by doing an experiment, by showing (a machine) in practical use, etc. 3 take part in a public demonstration.

demonstration n. 1 demonstrating. 2 a show of feeling. 3 an organised gathering or procession to express the opinion of a group publicly. 4 a display of military force.

demonstrative / duh-**mon**-struh-tiv / adj. 1 showing or proving. 2 expressing one's feelings openly (*he's very demonstrative for a man*). 3 *Grammar* (of an adjective or pronoun) indicating the person or thing referred to (e.g. *this*, *those*). ☐ **demonstratively** adv. **demonstrativeness** n.

demonstrator n. 1 a person who demonstrates politically etc. 2 a person who demonstrates machines etc. to potential customers. 3 a person who teaches by esp. scientific demonstration.

demoralise v. (also **-ize**) weaken the morale of, dishearten. ☐ **demoralisation** n.

demote / dee-**moht**, duh- / v. reduce to a lower rank or category. ☐ **demotion** n.

demotic / duh-**mot**-ik / adj. (of language or writing) of the popular form. • n. 1 a cursive script of ancient Egypt. 2 the popular form of modern Greek.

demotivate v. cause to lose motivation or incentive. ☐ **demotivation** n.

demountable n. a transportable building, used as temporary office or school etc. accommodation.

demur / duh-**mer** / v. (**demurred**, **demurring**) (often foll. by *to*, *at*) raise objections (*they demurred at working on Sundays*). • n. an objection raised (*they went without demur*).

demure / duh-**myoor** / adj. quiet and serious or pretending to be so. ☐ **demurely** adv. **demureness** n.

demurrer / duh-**mu**-ruh / n. a legal objection to the relevance of an opponent's point.

demutualise / dee-**myoo**-choo-uh-luyz, -tyoo- / v. (also **-ize**) change (a mutual organisation, such as a building society) to one of a different kind. ☐ **demutualisation** / -zay-shuhn / n.

demystify v. remove the mystery from; make simple (*judicial proceedings need to be demystified*).

den n. 1 a wild animal's lair. 2 a place where people gather for some illegal activity (*an opium den; a den of vice*). 3 a small private room where a person goes to work or relax.

denarius / duh-**nair**-ree-uhs, duh-**nah**- / n. (pl. **denarii**) an ancient Roman silver coin.

denary / **dee**-nuh-ree / adj. of ten; decimal.

denationalise v. (also **-ize**) transfer (an industry) from national to private ownership. ☐ **denationalisation** n.

denature v. 1 change the natural qualities of. 2 make (alcohol) unfit for drinking.

dendrobium n. any of a large genus of orchids in SE Asia, India, and Australia (which has about 50 species).

dendrochronology n. a method of dating timber by study of its annual growth rings.

dendrocnide / den-droh-**knuy**-dee / n. a tree having large leaves covered in stinging hairs (which cause severe pain and glandular swelling when touched), and showy, edible, and very tasty fruit: four species are recorded for Australia, the best known being the gympie.

dendrology n. the study of trees.

dengue / **deng**-gee / n. an infectious tropical fever causing acute pain in the joints.

Deng Xiaoping / dung show-**ping** / (1904–97), Chinese Communist leader, who remained influential following his official retirement in 1987. In 1989 his orders led to the massacre of some 2,000 pro-democracy demonstrators in Beijing's Tiananmen Square.

deniable adj. able to be denied.

denial n. 1 denying. 2 a statement that a thing is not true. 3 refusal of a request or wish. 4 = SELF-DENIAL. 5 disavowal of a leader etc. (*Peter's denial of Christ*).

denier / **den**-ee-uh / n. a unit of weight by which the fineness of silk, rayon, or nylon yarn is measured.

Deniehy, Daniel (Henry) (1828–65), Australian orator and writer. He undermined W.C. Wentworth's plan to institute an Australian aristocracy modelled on the English and coined the phrase *bunyip aristocracy* for the proposed Australian nobles.

denigrate / **den**-uh-grayt / v. blacken the reputation of; sneer at. ☐ **denigration** n.

denim n. 1 a strong twilled cotton fabric used for making clothes. 2 (**denims**) trousers made of denim.

denizen / **den**-uh-zuhn / n. 1 an inhabitant or occupant (*denizens of the outback*). 2 a foreigner having certain rights in an adopted country. 3 a naturalised foreign word, animal, or plant.

Denmark a monarchy in northern Europe.

Dennis, C.J. (full name: Clarence Michael James Dennis) (1876–1938), Australian poet and journalist. His stories in verse, *The Songs of A Sentimental Bloke* (with the character Ginger Mick) and *The Moods of Ginger Mick*, established his reputation.

denominate v. give a name to; call or describe as.

denomination n. 1 a name or title. 2 a distinctively named Church or religious sect (*Baptists and other Protestant denominations*). 3 a unit of measurement or money (*coins of small denomination*).

denominational adj. of a particular religious denomination.

denominator n. the number written below the line in a fraction, e.g. 4 in ¼, showing how many parts the whole is divided into.

denote / duh-**noht** / v. be the sign, symbol, or name of; indicate (*in road signs, P denotes a parking area*). ☐ **denotation** / dee-noh-**tay**-shuhn / n.

denouement / day-**noo**-mon, duh- / n. (also **dénouement**) the clearing up, at the end of a play or story, of the complications of the plot.

denounce v. **1** speak publicly against. **2** give information against (*denounced him as a spy*). **3** announce that one is ending (a treaty or agreement).

dense adj. **1** thick, not easy to see through (*dense fog*). **2** massed closely together (*dense crowds*). **3** stupid. ☐ **densely** adv. **denseness** n.

density n. **1** a dense or concentrated condition (*the density of the fog*). **2** stupidity. **3** *Physics* the relation of mass to volume.

dent n. **1** a depression left by a blow or by pressure (*a dent in the car*). **2** a (detrimental) reduction (*a dent in our funds*). •v. **1** make a dent in. **2** become dented. **3** have an adverse effect on, damage (*that's dented his pride*).

dental adj. **1** of or for the teeth. **2** of dentistry (*a dental practice*). ☐ **dental floss** strong thread used for cleaning between the teeth.

dentate adj. *Zoology* & *Botany* having teeth or toothlike notches.

dentine / **den**-teen / n. the hard dense tissue forming the main part of teeth.

dentist n. a person who is qualified to treat the teeth, fit artificial ones, etc.

dentistry n. the work or profession of a dentist.

dentition n. **1** the type and arrangement of teeth in a species etc. of animals. **2** teething.

D'Entrecasteaux / don-truh-kas-**toh** /, Joseph-Antoine Raymond de Bruni (1739–93), French navigator who in 1791–93 led an expedition in search of La Perouse, in the course of which he charted Australian waters, esp. around Tas.

denture n. a set of artificial teeth.

denuclearise v. (also **-ize**) remove nuclear weapons from (a country etc.). ☐ **denuclearisation** n.

denude v. **1** make naked or bare, strip the cover from (*the trees were denuded of their leaves*). **2** take all of something away from (a person) (*creditors denuded him of every cent*). ☐ **denudation** / den-yoo-**day**-shuhn / n.

denunciation / dee-nun-see-**ay**-shuhn, duh- / n. denouncing.

deny v. (**denied, denying**) **1** say that (a thing) is not true or does not exist. **2** disown, refuse to acknowledge (*Peter denied Christ*). **3** refuse to give what is asked for or needed, prevent from having (*no one can deny you your rights*). ☐ **deny oneself** restrict one's food, drink, or pleasure.

deodorant / dee-**oh**-duh-ruhnt / n. a substance that removes or conceals unwanted smells. •adj. deodorising.

deodorise v. (also **-ize**) destroy the odour of. ☐ **deodorisation** n.

deoxyribonucleic acid / dee-ok-see-ruy-boh-**nyoo**-klee-ik / *see* DNA.

depart v. **1** go away, leave. **2** (of trains or buses) start, begin a journey. **3** cease following a particular course (*departed from our normal procedure*).

departed adj. **1** bygone (*departed glories*). **2** (**the departed**) the dead.

department n. **1** any of the units, each with a specialised function, into which an organisation, university, business, shop, etc. is divided (*Department of Defence; English Department; hardware department*). **2** an area of activity, expertise, etc. (*that's hardly my department*). ☐ **department store** a large shop with many departments dealing in different goods.

departmental / dee-paht-**men**-tuhl / adj. of a department. ☐ **departmentally** adv.

departure n. **1** departing, going away. **2** setting out on a new course of action or thought.

depend v. (often foll. by *on* or *upon*) **1** be controlled or determined by (*whether we can have a barbecue depends on the fire restrictions*). **2** be unable to do without (*she depends on my help*). **3** trust confidently, feel certain about (*you can depend on John to be there when he's needed*).

dependable adj. able to be relied on. ☐ **dependably** adv. **dependability** n.

dependant n. one who depends on another for financial support (*he has four dependants*).

dependence n. depending, being dependent.

dependency n. **1** a country that is controlled by another. **2** = DEPENDENCE.

dependent adj. **1** (usu. foll. by *on, upon*) depending, conditional (*promotion is dependent on ability*). **2** (usu. foll. by *on, upon*) needing the help of; unable to do without (*he is dependent on heroin*). **3** maintained at another's cost; controlled by another, not independent (*dependent territories*). **4** (of a clause, phrase, or word) in a subordinate relation to a sentence or word.

depict v. **1** show in the form of a picture. **2** describe in words. ☐ **depicter** or **depictor** n. **depiction** n.

depilate / **dep**-uh-layt / v. remove hair from. ☐ **depilation** n.

depilatory / duh-**pil**-uh-tuh-ree, -tree / n. a substance that removes hair. •adj. removing hair.

deplete / duh-**pleet** / v. use up large quantities of; reduce in number or quantity. ☐ **depletion** n.

deplorable adj. **1** regrettable. **2** exceedingly bad, shocking. ☐ **deplorably** adv.

deplore v. **1** regret deeply. **2** be scandalised by (*we deplore the sale of cigarettes to minors*).

deploy v. spread out; bring or come into action systematically (*deploying troops; deploying* *resources in the most effective way*). ☐ **deployment** *n.*

depoliticise *v.* (also **-ize**) make (an issue etc.) non-political. ☐ **depoliticisation** *n.*

deponent / duh-**poh**-nuhnt / *n.* a person making a deposition under oath.

depopulate *v.* reduce the population of. ☐ **depopulation** *n.*

deport *v.* remove (an unwanted person) from a country. ☐ **deport oneself** behave in a specified manner. ☐☐ **deportation** *n.*

deportee *n.* a deported person.

deportment *n.* behaviour; a person's way of holding himself or herself in standing and walking.

depose *v.* **1** remove from power (*the king was deposed*). **2** testify or bear witness, esp. on oath in court.

deposit *n.* **1** a thing deposited for safe keeping. **2** a sum of money paid into an account. **3** a sum paid as a guarantee or a first instalment. **4** a layer of matter deposited or accumulated naturally (*new deposits of copper were found*). •*v.* (**deposited, depositing**) **1** lay or put down (*she deposited the books on the desk*). **2** store or entrust for safe keeping; pay (money) into an account. **3** pay as a guarantee or first instalment. **4** leave as a layer or covering of matter (*floods deposited mud on the land*).

depositary *n.* a person to whom a thing is entrusted.

deposition *n.* **1** deposing or being deposed from power. **2** a statement made on oath. **3** depositing. **4** (**the Deposition**) the taking down of Christ from the Cross.

depositor *n.* a person who deposits money or property.

depository *n.* **1** a storehouse. **2** = DEPOSITARY.

depot / **dep**-oh / *n.* **1** a storehouse, esp. for military supplies. **2** the headquarters of a regiment. **3** a place where buses or trams are kept.

deprave / duh-**prayv** / *v.* make morally bad, corrupt. ☐ **depravation** / dep-ruh-**vay**-shuhn / *n.*

depraved *adj.* immoral, wicked.

depravity / duh-**prav**-uh-tee / *n.* moral corruption, wickedness.

deprecate / **dep**-ruh-kayt / *v.* **1** feel and express disapproval of. **2** try to turn aside (praise or blame etc.) politely. ☐ **deprecation** *n.* **deprecatory** *adj.*

■ Usage Do not confuse with *depreciate*.

depreciate / duh-**pree**-shee-ayt, -see-ayt / *v.* **1** make or become lower in value. **2** belittle, disparage. ☐ **depreciatory** *adj.*

■ Usage Do not confuse with *deprecate*.

depreciation *n.* **1** a decline in value, esp. that due to wear and tear. **2** the allowance made for this.

depredation / dep-ruh-**day**-shuhn / *n.* plundering; damage.

depress *v.* **1** make sad, lower the spirits of. **2** reduce the activity of (trade, businesses, etc.). **3** press down; lower (*he depressed the lever*).

depressant *n.* a substance that reduces the activity of the nervous system, a sedative.

depressed *adj.* undergoing depression.

depression *n.* **1** *Psychol.* a state of extreme sadness or hopelessness, often with physical symptoms. **2** a long period of inactivity in business and trade, with widespread unemployment. **3** (**the Depression**) the severe worldwide economic depression of 1929–34. **4** a lowering of atmospheric pressure; an area of low pressure which may bring rain. **5** a sunken place or hollow on a surface. **6** pressing down.

depressive *adj.* **1** depressing. **2** involving mental depression. •*n.* a person suffering from mental depression.

deprival / duh-**pruy**-vuhl / *n.* depriving; being deprived.

deprivation / dep-ruh-**vay**-shuhn / *n.* **1** deprival. **2** a keenly felt loss.

deprive *v.* **1** take a thing away from; prevent from using or enjoying something (*the prisoner had been deprived of food*). **2** (as **deprived** *adj.*) lacking what is needed; underprivileged (*a deprived child; deprived areas*).

Dept *abbr.* Department.

depth *n.* **1** being deep. **2** the distance from the top down, or from the surface inwards, or from front to back. **3** deep learning, thought, or feeling. **4** intensity of colour or darkness. **5** lowness of pitch in a voice or sound. **6** the deepest or most central part (*living in the depths of the country*). ☐ **depth charge** a bomb that will explode under water. **in depth** with thorough and intensive investigations (*studied it in depth*). **in-depth** *adj.* thorough and intensive. **out of one's depth 1** in water that is too deep to stand in. **2** attempting something that is beyond one's ability.

deputation *n.* a body of people appointed to go on a mission on behalf of others.

depute / duh-**pyoot** / *v.* **1** delegate (a task) to a person. **2** appoint (a person) to act as one's representative.

deputise *v.* (also **-ize**) act as deputy.

deputy *n.* **1** a person appointed to act as substitute for another. **2** a member of a parliament in certain countries.

derail *v.* (**derailed, derailing**) cause (a train) to leave the rails. ☐ **derailment** *n.*

derange *v.* **1** throw into confusion, disrupt. **2** make insane. ☐ **derangement** *n.*

derby / **dah**-bee / *n.* **1** a major horse race for three-year-olds. **2** an important sporting contest.

deregulate *v.* remove (esp. government) regulations from (an industry etc.). ☐ **deregulation** *n.*

derelict *adj.* deserted and left to fall into ruin. • *n.* **1** an abandoned property, esp. a ship. **2** a vagrant; a tramp.

dereliction / de-ruh-**lik**-shuhn / *n.* **1** neglect of duty. **2** abandoning; being abandoned.

derestrict *v.* remove restrictions (esp. speed limits) from (a road, an area, etc.). ☐ **derestriction** *n.*

deride / duh-**ruyd** / *v.* laugh at scornfully, treat with scorn.

de rigueur / duh ri-**ger** / *adj.* required by custom or etiquette (*evening dress is de rigueur*). (¶ French, = of strictness.)

derision / duh-**rizh**-uhn / *n.* scorn, ridicule.

derisive / duh-**ruy**-siv / *adj.* scornful, showing derision (*derisive cheers*). ☐ **derisively** *adv.*

derisory / duh-**ruy**-zuh-ree / *adj.* **1** showing derision. **2** deserving derision; too insignificant for serious consideration (*a derisory offer*).

derivation / de-ruh-**vay**-shuhn / *n.* **1** deriving. **2** origin (*what is the derivation of the word 'pommy'?*).

derivative / de-**riv**-uh-tiv / *adj.* derived from another source; not original (*his music is derivative*). • *n.* **1** a thing that is derived from another. **2** *Maths* a quantity measuring the rate of change of another.

derive *v.* (usu. foll. by *from*) **1** get or trace from a source (*she derived great pleasure from music*). **2** arise from, originate in (*happiness derives from many things*). **3** show or state the origin of (a word, phrase, etc.) (*the English word 'anaconda' derives from the Sinhalese word 'henakandaya'*).

dermatitis / der-muh-**tuy**-tuhs / *n.* inflammation of the skin.

dermatology / der-muh-**tol**-uh-jee / *n.* the study of the skin and its diseases. ☐ **dermatologist** *n.*

dermis *n.* the layer of skin below the epidermis.

dero *n.* (also **derro**) *Aust. colloq.* a vagrant, esp. one dependent upon alcohol.

derogate / **de**-ruh-gayt / *v.* detract (from a merit or right etc.) (*this new law is not intended to derogate from the right to free speech*). ☐ **derogation** *n.*

derogatory / duh-**rog**-uh-tuh-ree, -tree / *adj.* critical, scornful, insulting.

derrick *n.* **1** a crane with an arm pivoted to the base of a central post or to a floor. **2** a framework over an oil well or bore hole, holding the drilling machinery.

derrière / de-ree-**air** / *n. colloq.* buttocks.

derris *n.* **1** a tropical climbing plant. **2** an insecticide made from its powdered root.

dervish *n.* a member of a Muslim religious order vowed to poverty, and which uses wild dancing etc. as part of its ceremonies.

Derwent a river in south-eastern Tas., rising in Lake St Clair in the centre of the island and flowing 190 km south-east to enter the sea at Storm Bay. In its final stages it bisects the city of Hobart.

desalinate *v.* remove the salt from (sea water etc.). ☐ **desalination** *n.*

descant / **des**-kant / *n.* **1** a harmonising higher-pitched melody sung or played in accompaniment to the main melody. **2** a melody; a song. • *v.* / des-**kant** / talk lengthily, esp. in praise of (*descanting on the charms of the Apple Isle*).

Descartes / day-**kaht** /, René (1596–1650), French philosopher, mathematician, and scientist.

descend *v.* **1** come or go down. **2** slope downwards. **3** (usu. foll. by *on*) make a sudden attack or an unexpected and usu. unwelcome visit (*hope they don't descend on us at the weekend*). **4** sink or stoop to unworthy behaviour (*they would never descend to cheating*). **5** be passed down by inheritance (*the title descended to his son*). ☐ **be descended from** come by descent from (a specified person, people, or people).

descendant *n.* a person who is descended from another.

descendent *adj.* descending.

descent *n.* **1** descending. **2** a way by which one may descend. **3** a downward slope. **4** a sudden attack or invasion. **5** ancestry, family origin (*of convict descent*).

describe *v.* **1** set forth in words; say what something is like. **2** mark out or draw the outline of; move in a certain pattern (*described a complete circle*).

description *n.* **1** describing. **2** an account or picture in words. **3** a kind or class of thing (*there's no food of any description*).

descriptive *adj.* giving a description.

descry / duh-**skruy** / *v.* catch sight of, discern.

desecrate / **des**-uh-krayt / *v.* treat (a sacred place or thing) with irreverence or disrespect; violate (*the council desecrated an Aboriginal sacred site by building a road through it*). ☐ **desecration** *n.* **desecrator** *n.*

desegregate *v.* end segregation of (people, classes, races, etc.). ☐ **desegregation** *n.*

desensitise *v.* (also **-ize**) reduce or destroy sensitivity towards (an allergen, a phobia, violence, etc.) (*it is argued that watching violence on TV desensitises us to violence*).

desert[1] / **dez**-uht / *n.* **1** a dry barren often sand-covered area of land. **2** an uninteresting or barren subject, period, etc. (*a cultural desert*). • *adj.* **1** barren and uncultivated; uninhabited. **2** used as a descriptive epithet in the names of plants and animals inhabiting arid areas (*desert gum; desert chat*). ☐ **desert boots** suede ankle-high boots.

desert lime an Australian shrub of the citrus family, bearing edible lime-like fruit. **desert rat** *colloq.* any Allied soldier who fought in the African desert campaign of 1941–42.

desert[2] / duh-**zert** / *v.* **1** abandon; leave without intending to return; forsake. **2** leave service in the armed forces without permission. ☐ **deserter** *n.* **desertion** *n.*

desertification *n.* the changing of fertile land into desert or barren waste through overstocking, clearing, felling, etc.

deserts / duh-**zerts** / *n.pl.* what one deserves.

deserve *v.* be worthy of or entitled to (a thing) because of actions or qualities.

deservedly / duh-**zer**-vuhd-lee / *adv.* according to what is deserved, justly.

deserving *adj.* worthy, worth rewarding or supporting (*a deserving charity; those who are deserving of our sympathy*).

desex *v.* castrate or spay (an animal).

déshabillé / day-zah-**bee**-ay / *n.* (also **déshabille** / day-zah-**beel** /, **dishabille** / dis-uh-**beel** /) the state of being only partly dressed. (¶ French)

desiccate *v.* / **des**-uh-kayt / dry out the moisture from; dry (solid food) in order to preserve it (*desiccated coconut*). ☐ **desiccation** *n.*

desideratum / duh-zid-uh-**rah**-tuhm, -**ray**-tuhm / *n.* (*pl.* **desiderata**) something that is lacking but needed or desired.

design *n.* **1** a drawing or plan that shows how something is to be made. **2** the art of making such drawings (*she studied design*). **3** the general form or arrangement of something (*the design of the building is good*). **4** a combination of lines or shapes to form a decoration. **5** a mental plan, a purpose. • *v.* **1** prepare a drawing or design for (a thing). **2** plan, intend for a specific purpose (*the book is designed for students*). ☐ **have designs on** plan to get possession of (a thing), seduce (a person), etc.

designate *v.* / **dez**-ig-nayt / **1** mark or point out clearly, specify (*the river was designated as the western boundary*). **2** describe as; give a name or title to. **3** appoint to a position (*designated Smith as his successor*). • *adj.* / **dez**-ig-nuht / appointed but not yet installed in office (*the bishop designate*).

designation / dez-ig-**nay**-shuhn / *n.* **1** designating. **2** a name or title.

designedly / duh-**zuy**-nuhd-lee / *adv.* intentionally.

designer *n.* **1** a person who designs things. **2** (used as *adj.*) designed by a famous, fashionable designer (*designer T-shirts*). ☐ **designer drug** a drug that has the narcotic effects of an illegal drug, but is sufficiently different to be outside legal control.

designing *adj.* crafty, scheming.

desirable *adj.* **1** arousing desire; attractive (*a desirable riverside house*). **2** sexually attractive. **3** advisable, worth doing (*it is desirable that you should be present*). ☐ **desirably** *adv.* **desirability** *n.*

desire *n.* **1** a feeling that one would get pleasure or satisfaction by obtaining or possessing something. **2** an expressed wish, a request (*at the desire of the Governor-General*). **3** an object of desire (*all your heart's desires*). **4** sexual urge. • *v.* **1** have a desire for. **2** ask for.

desirous *adj.* having a desire, desiring.

desist / duh-**zist** / *v.* (often foll. by *from*) cease (from an action etc.).

desk *n.* **1** a piece of furniture with a flat top and often drawers, used when reading or writing etc. **2** a counter behind which a cashier or receptionist etc. sits (*ask at the information desk*). **3** the section of a newspaper office dealing with specified topics. **4** a unit of two orchestral players sharing a stand.

desktop *n.* **1 a** the working surface of a desk. **b** *Computing* the working area of a computer screen viewed as a representation of the top of a desk, used with icons resembling familiar office equipment. **2** (often used as *adj.*) (esp. of a computer) small enough for use on a desk. ☐ **desktop publishing** designing and printing documents, booklets, etc. with a desktop computer and a high-quality printer.

desolate / **des**-uh-luht / *adj.* **1** solitary, lonely. **2** deserted, uninhabited, barren, dismal (*a desolate landscape*). **3** forlorn and unhappy.

desolated / **des**-uh-layt-uhd / *adj.* feeling lonely and wretched.

desolation *n.* **1** a desolate or barren condition. **2** loneliness. **3** grief, wretchedness.

despair *n.* **1** complete loss or lack of hope. **2** a thing that causes this. • *v.* lose all hope.

despatch alternative spelling of DISPATCH.

desperado / des-puh-**rah**-doh / *n.* (*pl.* **desperadoes**) a reckless criminal.

desperate *adj.* **1** leaving little or no hope, extremely serious (*the situation is desperate*). **2** made reckless by despair or urgency (*a desperate criminal; they are desperate for food*). **3** done or used in a nearly hopeless situation (*a desperate remedy*). ☐ **desperately** *adv.*

desperation *n.* **1** hopelessness. **2** being desperate; recklessness caused by despair.

despicable / **des**-pik-uh-buhl, duh-**spik**- / *adj.* deserving to be despised, contemptible. ☐ **despicably** *adv.*

despise *v.* regard as inferior or worthless, feel disrespect for.

despite *prep.* in spite of.

despoil *v. literary* plunder, rob. ☐ **despoliation** *n.*

despondent *adj.* in low spirits, dejected. ☐ **despondently** *adv.* **despondency** *n.*

despot / **des**-pot / *n.* a tyrant, a ruler who has unrestricted power.

despotic / des-**pot**-ik / *adj.* having unrestricted power. ☐ **despotically** *adv.*

despotism / **des**-puh-tiz-uhm / *n.* **1** tyranny, government by a despot. **2** a country ruled by a despot.

dessert / duh-**zert** / *n.* the sweet or fruit course of a meal.

dessertspoon *n.* a medium-sized spoon used in eating dessert etc. and as a measurement in cooking etc. (10 ml or 2 teaspoons). ☐ **dessertspoonful** *n.* (*pl.* **dessertspoonfuls**).

destabilise *v.* (also **-ize**) **1** make unstable. **2** overthrow or weaken (a government).

destination *n.* the place to which a person or thing is going.

destine *v.* settle or determine the future of, set apart for a purpose (*he was destined to be a star*).

destiny *n.* **1** fate considered as a power. **2** that which happens to a person or thing, thought of as determined in advance by fate.

destitute *adj.* **1** poverty-stricken, without the necessaries of life. **2** lacking in something (*a landscape destitute of trees*).

destitution *n.* being destitute; extreme poverty.

destroy *v.* **1** pull or break down; reduce to a useless form; spoil completely. **2** kill (a sick or unwanted animal) deliberately (*the cat had to be destroyed*). **3** put out of existence (*it destroyed our chances*).

destroyer *n.* **1** a person or thing that destroys. **2** a fast warship designed to protect other ships.

destruct *v.* esp. *Astronautics* destroy (one's own rocket, equipment, etc.) or be destroyed deliberately, esp. for safety. • *n.* an act of destrucing.

destructible *adj.* able to be destroyed.

destruction *n.* **1** destroying, being destroyed. **2** a cause of destruction or ruin (*gambling was his destruction*).

destructive *adj.* **1** destroying; causing destruction. **2** (of criticism etc.) disproving or discrediting something without offering amendments or alternatives.

desuetude / duh-**syoo**-uh-tyood / *n.* formal a state of disuse (*the custom fell into desuetude*).

desultory / **dez**-uhl-tuh-ree, **des**-, -tree / *adj.* going constantly from one subject to another, not systematic. ☐ **desultorily** *adv.*

detach *v.* release or remove from something else or from a group. ☐ **detachable** *adj.*

detached *adj.* **1** (of a house) not joined to another. **2** (of the mind or opinions) free from bias or emotion.

detachment *n.* **1** detaching; being detached. **2** freedom from bias or emotion; aloofness, lack of concern. **3** a group of people or ships etc. detached from a larger group for a special duty.

detail *n.* **1** an individual item; a small or subordinate particular. **2** a number of such particulars (*the description is full of detail*). **3** the minor decoration in a building or picture etc. (*look at the detail in the carvings*). **4** a small military detachment assigned to special duty. • *v.* **1** give particulars of, describe fully. **2** assign to special duty. ☐ **go into details** explain things in detail. **in detail** describing the individual parts or events etc. fully.

detailed *adj.* giving or showing many details.

detailing *n.* a process by which a new car is given extras to enhance its appearance or durability (e.g. rust-proofing, fabric protection) or an old car is refurbished.

detain *v.* **1** keep in confinement or under restraint. **2** keep waiting; cause delay to; keep from proceeding.

detainee / dee-tay-**nee**, duh-**tay**-nee / *n.* a person detained in custody, esp. for political reasons.

detect *v.* **1** discover the existence or presence of. **2** find (a person) doing something bad or secret. ☐ **detectable** *adj.*

detection *n.* **1** detecting, being detected. **2** the work of a detective.

detective *n.* a person, esp. a police officer, whose job is to investigate crimes.

detector *n.* a device for detecting the presence of something (*a smoke detector*).

détente / day-**tont** / *n.* the easing of strained relations between countries.

detention *n.* **1** detaining; being detained. **2** being kept in custody. **3** being kept in school after hours as a punishment.

deter *v.* (**deterred**, **deterring**) discourage or prevent from doing something through fear of the consequences. ☐ **determent** *n.*

detergent *n.* a cleansing substance, esp. a synthetic substance other than soap. • *adj.* having a cleansing effect.

deteriorate *v.* become worse. ☐ **deterioration** *n.*

determinable *adj.* able to be settled or calculated (*its age is not determinable*).

determinant *adj.* determining, decisive. • *n.* **1** a decisive factor. **2** *Maths* the quantity obtained by adding the products of the elements of a square matrix according to a certain rule.

determinate / duh-**ter**-muh-nuht / *adj.* limited, of fixed and definite scope or nature. ☐ **determinacy** *n.*

determination *n.* **1** firmness of purpose. **2** the process of deciding or calculating. **3** the conclusion of a dispute by the decision of an arbitrator; the decision so reached. **4** a judicial decision or sentence.

determine *v.* **1** find out or calculate precisely (*we must determine the height of the mountain*). **2** settle, decide (*determine what is to be done*). **3** settle or resolve (a dispute etc.), esp. by means of an arbitrator. **4** be the decisive factor or influence on (*income determines one's standard of living*). **5** decide firmly (*he determined to become a doctor*).

determined *adj.* showing determination; firm and resolute. ☐ **determinedly** *adv.*

determinism *n.* the theory that human action is not free but is determined by external forces acting on the will. ☐ **determinist** *n.* **deterministic** *adj.*

deterrent / duh-**te**-ruhnt / *adj.* deterring. • *n.* a thing that deters; a weapon that deters countries

detest

from attacking the one who has it. ☐ **deterrence** *n.*

detest *v.* dislike intensely, hate. ☐ **detestation** *n.*

detestable *adj.* intensely disliked, hateful.

dethatch *v.* esp. *Aust.* remove a matted layer of plant debris (from a lawn) in order to improve aeration and water penetration.

dethatcher *n.* esp. *Aust.* a machine with hooked blades which rotate vertically, removing matted plant debris from a lawn.

dethrone *v.* remove from a throne; depose. ☐ **dethronement** *n.*

detonate / **det**-uh-nayt / *v.* explode or cause to explode. ☐ **detonation** *n.*

detonator *n.* a device for detonating an explosive.

detour / **dee**-toor / *n.* a deviation from one's direct or intended course.

detoxify *v.* remove poison or harmful substances from. ☐ **detoxification** *n.*

detract *v.* (foll. by *from*) take away a part or amount from, lessen (a quantity, value, etc.) (*it will not detract from our pleasure*). ☐ **detraction** *n.*

detractor *n.* a person who criticises something, esp. unfairly (*the plan has its detractors*).

detriment / **det**-ruh-muhnt / *n.* **1** harm, damage. **2** something causing this.

detrimental / det-ruh-**men**-tuhl / *adj.* causing harm (*smoking is detrimental to health*). ☐ **detrimentally** *adv.*

detritus / duh-**truy**-tuhs / *n.* debris; loose matter (e.g. gravel) produced by erosion.

de trop / duh **troh** / *adj.* not wanted; in the way (*racial remarks are decidedly de trop*). (¶ French, = excessive.)

deuce[1] *n.* **1** (in tennis) the score of 40 all. **2** the two on dice.

deuce[2] *n. colloq.* (in exclamations of surprise or annoyance) the Devil (*where the deuce is it?*).

deus ex machina / day-uus eks **mak**-i-nuh / *n.* a power, event, or person arriving in the nick of time to save a seemingly impossible situation; a providential (often rather contrived) interposition, esp. in a novel or play. (¶ Latin, = god from the machinery, with reference to the machinery by which, in ancient Greek theatre, gods were shown descending in the air to impose a divine solution on an insoluble human dilemma.)

deuterium / dyoo-**teer**-ree-uhm / *n.* a heavy form of hydrogen (symbol D or ^{2}H), used as a moderator in nuclear reactors and a fuel in thermonuclear bombs.

Deutschmark / **doich**-mahk / *n.* (also **Deutsche Mark**) the unit of money in Germany.

de Valera / duh vuh-**lair**-ruh /, Eamon (1882–1975), Irish statesman, a leader of the Easter 1916 uprising against the British, who formed the Fianna Fáil party and served several times as president and as prime minister of his country.

devil

devalue *v.* **1** reduce the value of. **2** reduce the value of (a currency) in relation to other currencies or to gold. ☐ **devaluation** *n.*

Devanagari / day-vuh-**nah**-guh-ree / *n.* the alphabet in which Sanskrit, Hindi, and several North Indian languages are usu. written.

devastate *v.* **1** lay waste; cause great destruction to. **2** overwhelm with shock or grief. ☐ **devastation** *n.*

devastating *adj.* **1** causing destruction. **2** overwhelming (*a devastating loss*).

devein *v.* remove the dorsal vein from (a prawn).

develop *v.* (**developed**, **developing**) **1** make or become larger, fuller, or more mature or organised. **2** bring or come gradually into existence (*a storm developed*). **3** begin to exhibit or suffer from, acquire gradually (*develop measles; develop bad habits*). **4** convert (land) to a new purpose so as to use its resources; use (an area) for the building of houses, shops, factories, etc. **5** treat (a photographic film or plate etc.) so as to make the picture visible. ☐ **developing country** a poor country that is developing better economic and social conditions.

developer *n.* **1** one who develops. **2** a person or firm that develops land. **3** a substance used for developing photographic film etc.

development *n.* **1** developing; being developed. **2** something that has developed or been developed (*the latest developments in foreign affairs*). ☐ **developmental** *adj.*

Devi / **day**-vee / the supreme Hindu goddess, often identified with Parvati and Sakti.

deviant / **dee**-vee-uhnt / *adj.* deviating from what is regarded by most as normal or usual, esp. sexually. •*n.* a deviant person or thing.

deviate / **dee**-vee-ayt / *v.* turn aside or diverge from a course of action, a rule, truth, etc. ☐ **deviation** *n.* **deviator** *n.*

device *n.* **1** a thing that is made or used for a particular purpose (*labour-saving devices*). **2** a plan or scheme for achieving something. **3** a design used as a decoration or emblem. ☐ **left to one's own devices** left to do as one wishes without interference or help.

devil *n.* **1** (**the Devil**) (in Jewish and Christian teaching) the supreme spirit of evil and enemy of God. **2** an evil spirit. **3** a wicked or annoying person. **4** a mischievously clever person. **5** *colloq.* something difficult or hard to manage (*this door's a devil to open*). **6** *colloq.* a person (*you little devil; lucky devil*). **7** *colloq.* used in exclamations of surprise or annoyance (*where the devil is it?*). **8** a person who devils for an author etc.; a junior legal counsel. •*v.* (**devilled**, **devilling**) **1** cook (food) with chilli or other hot seasoning (*devilled prawns*). **2** do research or other work for an author or barrister. ☐ **devil-may-care** *adj.* cheerful and reckless. **play the devil with** cause severe damage to. **the devil to pay** trouble to be expected.

devil-devil *n.* (also **debil-debil**) *Aust.* **1** (in Aboriginal English) an evil spirit; a manifestation of evil. **2** (in full **devil-devil country**) = GILGAI.

devilish *adj.* **1** of or like a devil. **2** mischievous. • *adv. colloq.* very. ◻ **devilishly** *adv.*

devilment *n.* mischief, wild spirits.

devilry *n.* **1** wickedness. **2** devilment.

devil's advocate *n.* **1** *Catholic Church* a person who presents and argues the case against a dead person's canonisation or beatification. **2** one who tests a theory by putting forward possible objections to it.

Devine, Tilly (full name: Matilda Mary Devine) (1900–70) notorious Sydney prostitute and madam who by the start of the Second World War had achieved great wealth and cult status. Her brothels serviced wartime Sydney's needs and she donated money generously to the war effort.

devious / **dee**-vee-uhs / *adj.* **1** winding, round about. **2** not straightforward, underhand. ◻ **deviously** *adv.* **deviousness** *n.*

devise / duh-**vyz** / *v.* **1** think out, plan, invent. **2** *Law* leave (real estate) by will.

devoid / duh-**void** / *adj.* (foll. by *of*) lacking or free from something (*devoid of merit*).

devolution / dee-vuh-**loo**-shuhn / *n.* **1** the delegation or transference of work or power from a central administration to a local or regional one. **2** the descent by natural or due succession from one to another of property or qualities. **3** *Biology* degeneration (the opposite of EVOLUTION). ◻ **devolutionist** *adj.* & *n.*

devolve *v.* pass or be passed on to a deputy or successor (*this work will devolve on the new manager*).

devon *n.* a large bland sausage eaten cold.

Devonian / duh-**voh**-nee-uhn / *Geol. adj.* of the fourth period of the Palaeozoic era. • *n.* this period.

Devonshire tea *n.* esp. *Aust.* scones with jam and cream, served with tea or coffee.

devote *v.* give or use for a particular activity or purpose (*devoted himself to sport*).

devoted *adj.* showing devotion, very loyal or loving. ◻ **devotedly** *adv.*

devotee / dev-uh-**tee** / *n.* a person who is devoted to something, an enthusiast.

devotion *n.* **1** great love or loyalty; enthusiastic zeal. **2** a form of prayer (*the devotion known as the Way of the Cross*). **3** (**devotions**) prayers. ◻ **devotional** *adj.*

devour *v.* **1** eat hungrily or greedily. **2** destroy completely, consume (*fire devoured the forest*). **3** take in greedily with the eyes or ears (*they devoured the story*). **4** absorb the attention of (*she was devoured by curiosity*).

devout *adj.* **1** earnestly religious (*a devout Buddhist*). **2** earnest, sincere (*a devout supporter*). ◻ **devoutly** *adv.* **devoutness** *n.*

dew *n.* **1** small drops of moisture that condense on cool surfaces during the night from water vapour in the air. **2** moisture in small drops on a surface.

dewclaw *n.* a small claw on the inner side of a dog's leg, not reaching the ground in walking.

dewdrop *n.* a drop of dew.

Dewey system *n.* a decimal system for classifying books in libraries. (¶ Named after Melville Dewey (1851–1931), the American librarian who devised it.)

dewlap *n.* a fold of loose skin that hangs from the throat of cattle and other animals.

dewy *adj.* wet with dew. ◻ **dewy-eyed** *adj.* innocently trusting or sentimental.

dexter *adj.* (in heraldry) of or on the right-hand side (the observer's left) of a shield etc.

dexterity / dek-**ste**-ruh-tee / *n.* skill in using one's hands; mental adroitness.

dexterous / **deks**-truhs / *adj.* (also **dextrous**) showing dexterity. ◻ **dexterously** *adv.*

dextrin *n.* a sticky substance used as a thickening agent, adhesive, etc.

dextrose *n.* a form of glucose.

Dhaka / **dak**-uh / (also **Dacca**) the capital of Bangladesh.

dhal / dahl / *n.* **1** a kind of small, red split pulse, common in India, Sri Lanka, etc. Also called *red lentils*. **2** a dish made with this.

Dharawal / **du**-ru-wol / *n.* an Aboriginal language of the Illawarra region of NSW, from the southern shore of Botany Bay to Jervis Bay, including the modern towns of Wollongong and Nowra.

dharma / **dahr**-muh / *n.* **1** social custom; correct behaviour. **2** the Buddhist truth. **3** the Hindu moral law.

Dharuk / du-**ruuk** / *n.* an Aboriginal language of the Sydney region, from Port Jackson to the north side of Botany Bay, and inland at least as far as Camden and Penrith.

d'Hondt / dont / *n.* a voting system based on proportional representation. (¶ Victor d'Hondt, a Belgian mathematician (1841–1901).)

dhoti / **doh**-tee / *n.* (*pl.* **dhotis**) a loincloth worn by male Hindus.

dhow / dow / *n.* a lateen-rigged ship used on the Arabian sea.

dhufish *n. Aust.* = JEWFISH.

Dhurga / **duur**-gu / *n.* an Aboriginal language of a wide area of NSW from Jervis Bay to Lake Wallaga.

di- *comb. form* two; double.

diabetes / duy-uh-**bee**-teez / *n.* a disease in which sugar and starch are not properly absorbed by the body.

diabetic / duy-uh-**bet**-ik / *adj.* of diabetes. • *n.* a person suffering from diabetes.

diabolical / duy-uh-**bol**-i-kuhl / *adj.* (also **diabolic**) **1** like a devil, very cruel or wicked. **2** fiendishly clever, cunning, or annoying. ◻ **diabolically** *adv.*

diabolism / duy-**ab**-uh-liz-uhm / *n.* **1** worship of the Devil. **2** sorcery.

diachronic / duy-uh-**kron**-ik / *adj.* of or studying the historical development of a subject (esp. a language).

diaconal / duy-**ak**-uh-nuhl / *adj.* of a deacon.

diaconate / duy-**ak**-uh-nayt, -nuht / *n.* **1** the office of a deacon. **2** the body of deacons.

diacritic / duy-uh-**krit**-ik / *n.* a sign (e.g. an accent or cedilla) indicating different sounds or values of a letter.

diacritical *adj.* distinguishing, distinctive. ☐ **diacritical mark** *or* **sign** = DIACRITIC.

diadem / **duy**-uh-dem / *n.* a crown or headband, usu. as a sign of sovereignty.

diaeresis / duy-**eer**-ruh-suhs, -**e**-ruh-suhs / *n.* (*pl.* **diaereses**) (also **dieresis**) a mark placed over a vowel to show that it is sounded separately, as in *naïve*.

Diaghilev / dee-**ag**-uh-lef /, Serge Pavlovich (1872–1929), Russian ballet impresario, who introduced Russian ballet to western Europe.

diagnose / **duy**-uhg-nohz / *v.* make a diagnosis of (*the doctor diagnosed measles; diagnosed an iron deficiency in the soil*).

diagnosis / duy-uhg-**noh**-suhs / *n.* (*pl.* **diagnoses** / -seez /) a statement of the nature of a disease or other condition made after observing its signs and symptoms.

diagnostic / duy-uhg-**nos**-tik / *adj.* of or used in diagnosis (*diagnostic procedures*). ☐ **diagnostically** *adv.*

diagnostics *n.* **1** (treated as *pl.*) *Computing* programs etc. used to identify faults in hardware or software. **2** (treated as *sing.*) the science of diagnosing disease.

diagonal / duy-**ag**-uh-nuhl / *adj.* slanting, crossing from corner to corner. •*n.* a straight line joining two opposite corners. ☐ **diagonally** *adv.*

diagram *n.* an outline drawing or plan that shows the parts of something or how it works.

diagrammatic / duy-uh-gruh-**mat**-ik / *adj.* in the form of a diagram. ☐ **diagrammatically** *adv.*

dial *n.* **1** the face of a clock or watch. **2** a marked scale indicating measurements, selections, etc. by means of a pointer. **3** a selection disc, control knob, etc. on a piece of equipment. **4** a movable numbered disc on a telephone used for selecting the correct number. **5** *colloq.* a person's face. •*v.* (**dialled, dialling**) **1** select or regulate by means of a dial. **2** make a telephone connection by using a dial or numbered buttons. ☐ **dialling tone** a sound heard on a telephone indicating that a caller may dial.

dialect / **duy**-uh-lekt / *n.* a form of speech peculiar to a particular region or social group; a variety of a language showing sufficient differences from the standard language in vocabulary, pronunciation, or idiom for it to be considered as distinct. ☐ **dialectal** *adj.*

dialectic / duy-uh-**lek**-tik / *n.* investigation of truths in philosophy etc. by systematic reasoning.

dialectical / duy-uh-**lek**-ti-kuhl / *adj.* of dialectic. ☐ **dialectical materialism** the theory, put forward by Marx and Engels, that political and social conditions result from a conflict of social forces (the 'class struggle') produced by economic factors. ☐☐ **dialectically** *adv.*

dialogue / **duy**-uh-log / *n.* **1** a conversation; a discussion (e.g. between the representatives of two nations or groups with differing opinions). **2** the words spoken by characters in a play or story.

dialysis / duy-**al**-uh-suhs / *n.* **1** the separation of particles in a liquid by differences in their ability to pass through a membrane into another liquid. **2** (in cases of kidney failure) the removal of waste matter from the blood by this technique, esp. outside the body in an artificial kidney. **3** an occasion of undergoing this process.

diamanté / duy-uh-**mon**-tee, dee-uh- / *adj.* decorated with fragments of crystal or other sparkling substance. (¶ French)

Diamantina / duy-uh-man-**tee**-nuh / a river in western Qld (about 900 km after rain). It rises near Longreach and flows south-west into SA.

diameter / duy-**am**-uh-tuh / *n.* **1** a straight line passing from side to side through the centre of a circle or sphere. **2** the length of this.

diametrical / duy-uh-**met**-ri-kuhl / *adj.* (also **diametric**) **1** of or along a diameter. **2** (of opposites) complete; absolutely opposed. ☐ **diametrically** *adv.*

diamond *n.* **1** a very hard brilliant precious stone of pure crystallised carbon. **2** a figure with four equal sides and with angles that are not right angles. **3** something shaped like this. **4** a playing card of the suit (**diamonds**) marked with red figures of this shape. •*adj.* made of or set with diamonds. ☐ **diamond wedding** the 60th (or 75th) anniversary of a wedding.

Diana *Rom. myth.* an early Italian goddess identified with Artemis and associated with hunting, virginity, and the moon.

Diana, Princess of Wales (original name: Lady Diana Frances Spencer) (1961–97), former wife of Prince Charles. She died in a car crash in Paris.

dianthus *n.* a flowering plant of a kind that includes the carnation.

diapason / duy-uh-**pay**-zuhn, -suhn / *n.* **1** the entire range of a musical instrument or a voice. **2** a fixed standard of musical pitch. **3** either of the two main organ stops extending through the whole range.

diaper / **duy**-uh-puh / *n. US* a baby's nappy.

diaphanous / duy-**af**-uh-nuhs / *adj.* (of fabric) light, delicate, and almost transparent.

diaphragm / **duy**-uh-fram / *n.* **1** the midriff, the internal muscular partition that separates the chest from the abdomen and is used in breathing. **2** a vibrating disc in a microphone or telephone

diapositive   219   **didn't**

receiver etc. **3** a device for varying the aperture of a camera lens. **4** a thin contraceptive cap fitting over the neck of the womb.

diapositive *n.* a positive photographic slide or transparency.

diarist / duy-uh-ruhst / *n.* a person who keeps a diary.

diarrhoea / duy-uh-**ree**-uh / *n.* a condition in which bowel movements are excessively frequent and fluid.

diary *n.* **1** a daily record of events or thoughts. **2** a book for this or for noting engagements.

Diaspora / duy-**as**-puh-ruh / *n.* **1 a** the Dispersion of the Jews after their exile in 538 BC. **b** the Jews dispersed in this. **2** the dispersion of any people from their original homeland.

diastase / duy-uh-stayz / *n.* the enzyme (important in digestion) that converts starch into sugar.

diastole / duy-**as**-tuh-lee / *n.* the period between two contractions of the heart when the heart muscle relaxes and allows the chambers to fill with blood: diastole alternates with systole to form the pulse. ❏ **diastolic** / duy-uh-**stol**-ik / *adj.*

diatom / **duy**-uh-tuhm / *n.* a microscopic alga found as plankton and forming fossil deposits.

diatomic / duy-uh-**tom**-ik / *adj.* consisting of two atoms.

diatonic / duy-uh-**ton**-ik / *adj.* (in music) using the notes of the major or minor scale only, not of the chromatic scale.

diatribe / **duy**-uh-truyb / *n.* a violent attack in words; abusive criticism.

dibble *n.* (also **dibber**) a hand tool used to make holes in the ground for seeds or young plants. • *v.* plant with a dibble.

dibbler *n.* a small, spotted, Australian marsupial mouse, once numerous in the extreme south west but now almost extinct. (¶ From a dialect of Nyungar.)

DiCaprio, Leonardo (Wilhelm) (1974–), American actor. His films include *Romeo and Juliet* (1996) and *Titanic* (1997).

dice *n.* **1** (properly the plural of DIE², but often used as a singular, *pl.* **dice**) a small cube marked on each side with a number of spots (usu. 1–6), used in games of chance. **2** a game played with these. • *v.* **1** take great risks (*dicing with death*). **2** cut into small cubes (*dice the carrots*). **3** *Aust. colloq.* reject, abandon (*she's diced me*). ❏ **no dice** *colloq.* not a chance.

dicey *adj.* (**dicier**, **diciest**) *colloq.* risky, unreliable.

dichotomy / duy-**kot**-uh-mee / *n.* division into two (esp. sharply defined) parts or kinds.

dichromatic / duy-kroh-**mat**-ik / *adj.* **1** two-coloured. **2** having vision that is sensitive to only two of the three primary colours.

dick *n. colloq.* **1** (in certain set phrases) person (*clever dick*). **2** *coarse colloq.* the penis. **3** *coarse colloq.* a dickhead. **4** a detective.

Dickens, Charles (Huffham) (1812–70), English novelist.

dickens *n. colloq.* (in exclamations of surprise or annoyance) deuce, the Devil (*where the dickens is it?*).

Dickensian / duh-**ken**-zee-uhn / *adj.* of Charles Dickens, his works, or the conditions portrayed in them, esp. poverty and social injustice.

dickhead *n. coarse colloq.* a fool, an idiot.

Dickless Tracy *n. Aust. colloq.* a female police officer. (¶ Punning on the cartoon-strip private eye *Dick Tracy* and *dick* 'penis'.)

dickstickers *n.pl. Aust. colloq.* a skimpy male swimming costume.

dicky *adj. colloq.* **1** unsound, unhealthy (*I have a dicky heart*). **2** difficult; awkward; tricky (*this leaves us in a dicky situation*).

dicotyledon / duy-kot-uh-**lee**-duhn / *n.* a flowering plant that has two cotyledons. ❏ **dicotyledonous** *adj.*

dicta *see* DICTUM.

dictaphone *n. trademark* a machine that records and plays back dictation.

dictate *v.* **1** say or read aloud (words) to be written down by a person or recorded by a machine. **2** state or order with the force of authority (*dictate terms to a defeated enemy*). **3** give orders officiously (*I will not be dictated to*). • *n.pl.* (**dictates**) authoritative commands (*the dictates of conscience*). ❏ **dictation** *n.*

dictator *n.* **1** a ruler who has unrestricted authority, esp. one who has taken control by force. **2** a person with supreme authority in any sphere. **3** a domineering person. ❏ **dictatorship** *n.*

dictatorial / dik-tuh-**taw**-ree-uhl / *adj.* **1** of or like a dictator. **2** domineering. ❏ **dictatorially** *adv.*

diction / **dik**-shuhn / *n.* a person's manner of uttering or pronouncing words in speaking or singing; a person's choice of words.

dictionary *n.* a book that lists and explains the words of a language or a particular subject, or that gives their equivalents in another language, usu. in alphabetical order.

dictum *n.* (*pl.* **dicta** *or* **dictums**) **1** a formal expression of opinion. **2** a saying.

did *see* DO.

didactic / duy-**dak**-tik, duh- / *adj.* **1** giving instruction. **2** having the manner of one who is lecturing pupils; tediously pedantic. ❏ **didactically** *adv.* **didacticism** *n.*

diddle *v. colloq.* cheat, swindle.

didgeridoo *n.* a long tubular Australian Aboriginal wind instrument made of wood: it produces a low-pitched resonant sound and is capable of complex rhythmic patterns. (¶ The name is not Aboriginal: it probably evolved from white people's imitation of the sound of the instrument.)

didn't = did not.

die[1] *v.* (**died, dying**) **1** cease to be alive; have one's vital functions cease finally. **2** cease to exist. **3** cease to function; stop (*the engine sputtered and died*). **4** (of a fire or flame) go out. **5** become exhausted (*I'm dying of boredom; we were dying with laughter*). **6** feel an intense longing (*we are dying to go; dying for a drink*). **7** feel an extreme of embarrassment etc. □ **die away** become fainter or weaker and then cease (*the noise died away*). **die back** (of plants) decay from the tip towards the root. **die-back** *n.* the disease which causes plants to die back. **die down** become less loud or less violent (*the excitement died down*). **die hard** die reluctantly (*old habits die hard*). **die out** pass out of existence (*the custom has died out; the family has died out*). **to-die-for** *see* TO.

die[2] *n.* **1** a dice (*see* DICE). **2** an engraved device that stamps a design on coins or medals etc.; a device that stamps or cuts or moulds material into a particular shape. □ **die-cast** *adj.* made by casting metal in a mould. **die-casting** this process. **the die is cast** a step has been taken and its consequences must follow.

diehard *n.* a person who obstinately refuses to abandon old theories or policies, one who resists change.

dielectric *adj.* that does not conduct electricity. • *n.* a dielectric substance usable for insulating things.

dieresis alternative spelling of DIAERESIS.

diesel / dee-zuhl / *n.* **1** a diesel engine; a vehicle driven by this. **2** fuel for a diesel engine. □ **diesel engine** an oil-burning engine in which ignition is produced by the heat of highly compressed air. (¶ Named after the German engineer Rudolf Diesel (1858–1913).)

Dies irae / dee-ez ee-ray / *n.* a Latin sequence sung in a solemn Mass for the dead, the melody of which had often been used by composers to evoke desolation etc. in their works. (¶ Latin (the hymn's first words), = day of wrath (i.e. Judgment Day).)

diet[1] *n.* **1** the foods usu. eaten by a person, animal, or community. **2** a selection of food to which a person is restricted. **3** something regularly offered (*a diet of half-truths*). • *v.* (**dieted, dieting**) **1** restrict oneself to a special diet, esp. in order to control one's weight. **2** restrict (a person) to a special diet. □ **dieter** *n.*

diet[2] *n.* a congress; a parliamentary assembly in certain countries, e.g. Japan.

dietary / duy-uh-tree / *adj.* of or involving diet (*special dietary requirements*). □ **dietary fibre** (also **fibre**) food material such as bran that is not broken down by the process of digestion; roughage.

dietetic / duy-uh-**tet**-ik / *adj.* of diet and nutrition. • *n.pl.* (**dietetics**) the study of diet and nutrition.

dietitian / duy-uh-**tish**-uhn / *n.* an expert in dietetics.

Dietrich / dee-trik /, Marlene (original name: Maria Magdalene von Losch) (1901–90), German-born American film actor.

diff *n. colloq.* **1** difference (*it makes no diff*). **2** differential gear.

differ *v.* **1** be unlike, be distinguishable from something else. **2** disagree in opinion.

difference *n.* **1** the state of being different or unlike. **2** the point in which things differ; the amount or degree of unlikeness. **3** the quantity by which amounts differ; the remainder left after subtraction (*the difference between 8 and 5 is 3*). **4** a disagreement in opinion, a quarrel.

different *adj.* **1** unlike, of other nature or form or quality (*your version is quite different from mine*). **2** separate, distinct (*several different people*). **3** unusual (*I must say this music's certainly different*). □ **differently** *adv.*

■ **Usage** In sense 1, *different from* is generally regarded as the most acceptable collocation; *different to* is common in less formal Australian use; *different than* is established in US use and also found in Australian use, esp. when followed by a clause, e.g. *I am a different person than I was a year ago.*

differential / dif-uh-**ren**-shuhl / *adj.* **1** of, showing, or depending on a difference. **2** *Maths* relating to infinitesimal differences. • *n.* **1** an agreed difference in wages between industries or between different classes of workers in the same industry (*wage differential*). **2** a differential gear. □ **differential calculus** a method of calculating rates of change, maximum or minimum values, etc. **differential gear** an arrangement of gears that allows a motor vehicle's driven wheels to revolve at different speeds in rounding corners.

differentiate / dif-uh-**ren**-shee-ayt / *v.* **1** be a difference between, make different (*the features that differentiate one breed from another*). **2** recognise as different, distinguish; discriminate (*the pension scheme does not differentiate between male and female employees*). **3** develop differences, become different. **4** *Maths* calculate the derivative of. □ **differentiation** *n.*

difficult *adj.* **1** needing much effort or skill, not easy. **2** troublesome, perplexing (*these are difficult times*). **3** not easy to please or satisfy (*a difficult employer*).

difficulty *n.* **1** being difficult. **2** a difficult problem or thing. **3** a difficult state of affairs, trouble (*in financial difficulties*).

diffident / **dif**-uh-duhnt / *adj.* lacking self-confidence, hesitating to put oneself or one's ideas forward. □ **diffidently** *adv.* **diffidence** *n.*

diffract *v.* **1** break up (a beam of light) into a series of dark and light bands or the coloured bands of the spectrum. **2** break up (a beam of radiation or particles) into a series of high and low intensities. □ **diffraction** *n.* **diffractive** *adj.*

diffuse *adj.* / duh-**fyoos** / **1** spread out, diffused, not concentrated (*diffuse light*). **2** wordy, not concise (*a diffuse style*). •*v.* / duh-**fyooz** / **1** spread (light, heat, knowledge, etc.) widely or thinly throughout something. **2** mix (liquids or gases) slowly, become intermingled. □ **diffusely** *adv.* **diffusible** *adj.* **diffusive** *adj.*

diffusion *n.* **1** diffusing or being diffused. **2** *Physics* the natural random movement and mingling of atoms and particles through a substance.

dig *v.* (**dug**, **digging**) **1** break up and move (ground) with a tool, claws, etc.; make (a way or a hole) by doing this. **2** remove by digging (*dig potatoes*). **3** excavate archaeologically. **4** (often foll. by *up* or *out*) seek or discover by investigation (*dug up some useful information*). **5** thrust, plunge; prod (*dig a knife into it; dug him in the ribs*). **6** *colloq.* appreciate, enjoy (*she really digs sci-fi*). **7** *colloq.* understand (*I don't dig a word you say*). **8** *colloq.* look at; take notice of (*dig that guy with the tattoos on his nose!*). •*n.* **1** a piece of digging. **2** an archaeological excavation. **3** a thrust, a poke (*a dig in the ribs*). **4** a cutting remark (*that was a dig at me*). **5** (**digs**) *colloq.* lodgings. **6** *Aust.* = DIGGER (sense 4). □ **dig in** *colloq.* begin eating or working energetically. **dig one's heels in** become obstinate, refuse to give way.

digest *v.* / duy-**jest** / **1** dissolve (food) in the stomach etc. so that it can be absorbed by the body. **2** think over, absorb into the mind (*digesting the information*). **3** summarise methodically. •*n.* / **duy**-jest / **1** a methodical summary. **2** a periodical publication giving excerpts and summaries of news, writings, etc.

digestible *adj.* able to be digested. □ **digestibility** *n.*

digestion *n.* **1** the process of digesting. **2** the power of digesting food (*has a good digestion*).

digestive *adj.* **1** of or aiding digestion. **2** having the function of digesting food (*the digestive system*). •*n.* a substance that aids digestion.

digger *n.* **1** a person or machine that digs, esp. a mechanical excavator. **2** a miner, esp. a gold-digger on the Australian goldfields. **3** *Aust.* a soldier (esp. a private) from Australia or New Zealand (increasingly, an Australian soldier exclusively). **4** (also **dig**) *Aust.* (as a form of address in Australia, originally to a fellow soldier, later also more generally) mate. □ **digger's hat** *Aust.* the felt slouch hat worn as part of the Australian soldier's uniform.

diggings *n.pl. Aust.* **1** (also **diggins**) an Australian goldfield. **2** a mine. **3** the material dug out of a mine etc.

digging stick *n.* (also **yam stick**) *Aust.* (among Aborigines in the outback) a tool made from a rod of wood pointed at each end and used to excavate yams etc.

diggins alternative spelling of DIGGINGS (sense 1).

digit / **dij**-uht / *n.* **1** any numeral from 0 to 9. **2** a finger or toe.

digital / **dij**-uh-tuhl / *adj.* **1** of digits. **2** (of a clock, watch, etc.) showing the time by displaying a row of figures. **3** (of a computer) operating on data represented as a series of usu. binary digits. **4** (of a recording) converting sound into electrical pulses (representing binary digits) for more reliable transmission. □ **digitally** *adv.*

digitalis / dij-uh-**tay**-luhs, -**tah**-luhs / *n.* a drug prepared from dried foxglove leaves, used as a heart stimulant.

digitise *v.* (also **-ize**) convert data into digital form, esp. for a computer. □ **digitisation** *n.*

dignified *adj.* having or showing dignity.

dignify *v.* (**dignified**, **dignifying**) **1** give dignity to. **2** make (a thing) sound more important than it is (*they dignified the school with the name of 'college'*).

dignitary / **dig**-nuh-tuh-ree, -tree / *n.* a person holding a high rank or position.

dignity *n.* **1** a calm and serious manner or style. **2** worthiness (*the dignity of labour*). **3** a high rank or position.

digraph / **duy**-grahf, -graf / *n.* two letters representing one sound (as *ph* in *phone, ea* in *bean*).

digress / duy-**gres** / *v.* depart from the main subject temporarily in speaking or writing. □ **digression** *n.*

dike alternative spelling of DYKE.

diktat *n.* a firm statement or decree.

dilapidated *adj.* falling to pieces, in a state of disrepair.

dilapidation *n.* a state of disrepair; bringing or being brought into this state.

dilatation / duy-luh-**tay**-shuhn / *n.* **1** dilation. **2** widening of the neck of the womb, e.g. for surgical curettage.

dilate / duy-**layt** / *v.* **1** make or become wider or larger. **2** speak or write at length (*dilating upon this subject*). □ **dilation** *n.*

dilatory / **dil**-uh-tuh-ree, -tree / *adj.* **1** slow in doing something. **2** designed to cause delay. □ **dilatorily** *adv.* **dilatoriness** *n.*

dildo / **dil**-doh / *n.* (*pl.* **dildos**) an artificial erect penis used for sexual stimulation.

dilemma / dil-**em**-uh, duy- / *n.* **1** a perplexing situation, in which a choice has to be made between alternatives that are equally undesirable. **2** a problem or difficult choice (*what to do with one's spare time is a modern dilemma*).

■ **Usage** Many people regard the use in sense 2 as unacceptable.

dilettante / dil-uh-**tan**-tee / *n.* (*pl.* **dilettantes** or **dilettanti**) a person who dabbles in a subject for enjoyment and without serious study. □ **dilettantism** *n.*

Dili capital of East Timor. □ **Dili Massacre** the massacre by members of the Indonesian army of

diligent / dil-uh-juhnt / *adj.* **1** hard-working, putting care and effort into what one does. **2** done with care and effort (*a diligent search*). ☐ **diligently** *adv.* **diligence** *n.*

dill[1] *n.* a herb with feathery leaves and spicy seeds used for flavouring. ☐ **dill weed** the leaves of dill used fresh or dried in cooking.

dill[2] *n. Aust. colloq.* a fool.

dillon bush *n. Aust.* a rigid, spreading shrub of all mainland States (but not the NT), bearing edible fruits. (¶ Wemba-wemba)

dillybag *n. Aust.* **1** an Aboriginal bag or basket made from woven vine, grass, or fibre. **2** (in general use) a bag of any sort, usu. small and usu. for carrying provisions etc. (¶ Yagara *dili* 'coarse grass or reeds; a bag woven of this'.)

dilly-dally *v. colloq.* **1** dawdle. **2** waste time by not making up one's mind.

dilute / duy-**lyoot**, -**loot** / *v.* **1** thin down, make (a liquid) less concentrated by adding water or other liquid. **2** weaken or reduce the forcefulness of. • *adj.* diluted (*a dilute acid*). ☐ **dilution** *n.*

diluvial / duy-**loo**-vee-uhl, duh- / *adj.* of a flood, esp. the Flood in Genesis.

dim *adj.* (**dimmer**, **dimmest**) **1** faintly lit, luminous but not bright. **2** indistinct, not clearly seen, heard, or remembered. **3** not seeing clearly (*eyes dim with tears*). **4** *colloq.* stupid. • *v.* (**dimmed**, **dimming**) make or become dim. ☐ **take a dim view of** *colloq.* disapprove of. ☐ ☐ **dimly** *adv.* **dimness** *n.*

dime *n.* a ten-cent coin of the USA.

dimension / duy-**men**-shuhn, duh- / *n.* **1** a measurable extent such as length, breadth, thickness, area, or volume. **2** size. **3** extent; scope; aspect (*gave the problem a new dimension*). ☐ **dimensional** *adj.*

diminish *v.* make or become smaller or less.

diminuendo / duh-min-yoo-**en**-doh / *adj. & adv.* (in music) gradually becoming quieter. • *n.* (*pl.* **diminuendos**) a gradual decrease in loudness.

diminution / dim-uh-**nyoo**-shuhn / *n.* **1** diminishing; being diminished. **2** a decrease.

diminutive / duh-**min**-yuh-tiv / *adj.* remarkably small. • *n.* a word for a small specimen of something (e.g. *booklet, duckling*), or an affectionate or familiar form of a name etc. (e.g. *Johnnie, Bluey* (for a redhead), *matey, footy, tinnie*, etc.).

dimity *n.* a cotton fabric woven with checks or stripes of heavier thread.

dimmer *n.* a device for varying the brightness of electric lights.

dimple *n.* a small hollow or dent, esp. a natural one in the skin of the cheek or chin. • *v.* **1** produce dimples in. **2** show dimples.

dim sum / dim sum / *n.* (also **dim sim**) **1** a meal or course of savoury Cantonese-style snacks. **2** (now usu. **dim sim** in Australia) a small roll of seasoned meat etc. wrapped in thin dough and steamed or fried.

dimwit *n. colloq.* a stupid person. ☐ **dim-witted** *adj.*

DIN *n.* any of a series of German technical standards for electrical connections, film speeds, and paper sizes.

din *n.* a loud, resonant, and annoying noise. • *v.* (**dinned**, **dinning**) **1** make a din. **2** force (information) into a person by continually repeating it (*din it into him*).

dinar / **dee**-nah / *n.* a unit of currency in the former Yugoslavia and in various countries of the Middle East and North Africa.

dine *v.* **1** eat dinner. **2** eat for dinner (*dined on barramundi and emu steak*). **3** entertain to dinner (*we were wined and dined*). ☐ **dining car** a railway carriage in which meals are served.

diner *n.* **1** a person who dines. **2** a dining car on a train. **3** a small restaurant.

ding[1] *v.* make a ringing sound. • *n.* a ringing sound.

ding[2] *Aust. colloq. n.* **1** a minor collision of motor vehicles etc. **2** a dent (in a surfboard, motor vehicle, etc.). • *v.* dent or damage; smash (*dinged the car*).

dingbat *n. US & Aust. colloq.* a stupid or eccentric person. ☐ **be** (or **have the**) **dingbats** *Aust.* be mad, stupid, eccentric, etc. **give a person the dingbats** *Aust.* infuriate or irritate him or her.

ding-dong *n.* **1** the sound of two chimes, esp. of a doorbell. **2** *colloq.* a heated argument or fight. • *adj. & adv.* with vigorous and alternating action (*a ding-dong contest*).

dinghy / **ding**-gee / *n.* (*pl.* **dinghies**) **1** a small open boat driven by oars or sails. **2** a small inflatable rubber boat.

dingle *n.* a deep wooded valley or hollow.

Dingo, Ernie (full name: Ernest Ashly Dingo) (1956–), AM, Aboriginal Australian film, television, and stage actor and comedian.

dingo *n.* (*pl.* **dingoes**) **1** a wolf-like native dog (*Canis familiaris dingo*) of mainland Australia, introduced by the Aborigines. Also called *warrigal*. **2** *Aust.* a cowardly or treacherous person. • *v. Aust.* behave in a cowardly manner. ☐ **dingo it** *Aust.* act the coward; back away (*he didn't dingo it, but stood and fought*). **dingo on** (**a person**) *Aust.* betray (a person), let (a person) down. (¶ Dharuk *din-gu* or *dayn-gu* 'a domesticated dingo'.)

dingy / **din**-jee / *adj.* (**dingier**, **dingiest**) dirty-looking, not fresh or cheerful. ☐ **dingily** *adv.* **dinginess** *n.*

dink[1] (also **double-dink**) *Aust. colloq. n.* a lift on a bicycle etc. ridden by another. • *v.* carry (a passenger) on a bicycle etc. (*he dinked me to school*).

dink[2] *abbr.* (also **dinks**) *Aust.* = DINKUM.

dink[3] *n. colloq.* either partner of a career couple with no children, both of whom work and who are therefore viewed as affluent consumers. (¶ double (or dual) income, no kids.)

dinkum *Aust. colloq. adj.* reliable, genuine, honest, true (*if you're dinkum, I'll help you; the roo's a dinkum Aussie*). • *adv.* really, truly; really?, truly? (*it's dinkum good stuff, goanna oil is; 'It was like that, dinkum?' —'Dinkum, I kid you not!'*). ☐ **dinkum oil** the truth. **fair dinkum** (also **fair dinks**) (frequently as interjection) **1** fair play (*let's have some fair dinkum, you guys*). **2** genuine(ly), honest(ly), true, truly (*he's a fair dinkum bushie; 'It's God's own truth.' —'Fair dinkum?' —'Fair dinkum!'*). (¶ Probably from British dialect *dinkum* 'work, a due share of work'; the popular etymology, that it is from Cantonese *ding kam* 'top gold', is without foundation.)

dinky *adj. colloq.* neat and attractive; small, dainty.

dinky-di *adj., adv. & interj. Aust.* = DINKUM in all senses.

dinner *n.* **1** the chief meal of the day, either at midday or esp. in the evening. **2** a meal eaten at midday, but not the principal meal of the day; lunch. **3** (in full **dinner party**) a formal evening meal, esp. with guests.

dinnyhayser / din-ee-**hay**-zuh / *n. Aust.* **1** a knockout blow. **2** anything that is significant, powerful, etc. (*a dinnyhayser of a storm; the party was a dinnyhayser*). (¶ Origin uncertain: perhaps from a 19th-c. boxer Dinny Hays.)

dinosaur / **duy**-nuh-saw / *n.* an extinct reptile of the Mesozoic era, often of enormous size.

dint *n.* a dent. • *v.* mark with dints. ☐ **by dint of** by means of.

diocese / **duy**-uh-suhs / *n.* a district under the pastoral care of a bishop. ☐ **diocesan** / duy-**os**-uh-suhn / *adj.*

diode / **duy**-ohd / *n.* **1** a simple thermionic valve with only two electrodes. **2** a rectifier made of semiconducting materials and having two terminals.

Dionysian / duy-uh-**nis**-ee-uhn, -**niz**- / *adj.* **1** wildly sensual; unrestrained. **2** of or relating to the god Dionysus.

Dionysus / duy-uh-**nuy**-suhs / *Gk myth.* the young and beautiful god of wine and fertility; worshipped by the Romans as Bacchus.

dioptre / duy-**op**-tuh / *n.* a unit of refractive power of a lens.

diorama / duy-uh-**rah**-muh / *n.* **1** a small model of a scene etc. with three-dimensional figures, viewed through a window. **2** any small-scale model (e.g. of a building project); a miniature film set. **3** a scenic painting in which changing lighting simulates sunrise etc.

dioxide / duy-**ok**-suyd / *n.* an oxide with two atoms of oxygen to one of a metal or other element.

dioxin / duy-**ok**-suhn / *n.* any of several chemical compounds, derivatives of which are used in herbicides.

Dip. *abbr.* diploma.

dip *v.* (**dipped**, **dipping**) **1** put or lower into liquid. **2** go under water and emerge quickly. **3** go down (*the sun dipped below the horizon*). **4** put a hand or ladle etc. into something in order to take something out. **5** lower (*dip the flag; dip headlights*). **6** slope or extend downwards (*the path dips down to the river*). **7** (foll. by *into*) read short passages here and there in a book (*I've dipped into 'War and Peace'*). **8** (foll. by *into*) use part of (one's savings, resources, etc.). **9** wash (sheep) in a vermin-killing liquid. • *n.* **1** dipping; being dipped. **2** a quick plunge; a short bathe. **3** a downward slope. **4 a** a plunge bath for sheep, containing vermin-killing liquid. **b** the contents of such a bath. **5** a creamy mixture into which food is dipped.

diphtheria / dif-**theer**-ree-uh, dip- / *n.* an acute infectious disease causing severe inflammation of a mucous membrane, esp. in the throat.

diphthong / **dif**-thong / *n.* a compound vowel sound produced by combining two simple ones, e.g. *oi* in *point*, *ou* in *loud*.

diplodocus / dip-**lod**-uh-kuhs, dip-loh-**doh**-kuhs / *n.* a giant plant-eating dinosaur with a long neck and tail.

diploma *n.* a certificate awarded by a college etc. to a person who has successfully completed a course of study.

diplomacy / duh-**ploh**-muh-see / *n.* **1** the handling of international relations; skill in this. **2** deftness in personal relations; tact.

diplomat / **dip**-luh-mat / *n.* **1** a member of the diplomatic service. **2** a tactful person.

diplomatic / dip-luh-**mat**-ik / *adj.* **1** of or engaged in diplomacy. **2** tactful (*a diplomatic reply*). ☐ **diplomatic corps** a body of diplomats representing other countries at a seat of government. **diplomatic immunity** the exemption of diplomatic staff abroad from arrest, taxation, etc. **diplomatic service** officials who represent their country abroad. ☐☐ **diplomatically** *adv.*

diplomatist / duh-**ploh**-muh-tuhst / *n.* a diplomat.

dipole *n.* **1** two equal and oppositely charged or magnetised poles separated by a distance. **2** a molecule in which a concentration of positive charges is separated from a concentration of negative charges. **3** an aerial consisting of a horizontal rod with a connecting wire at its core.

dipper *n.* a ladle.

diprotodon / duy-**proh**-tuh-don / *n.* an extinct, gigantic, herbivorous, Australian quadruped marsupial having two prominent incisors in the lower jaw.

dipso *n. colloq.* an alcoholic.

dipsomania / dip-suh-**may**-nee-uh / *n*. an uncontrollable craving for alcohol. □ **dipsomaniac** *n*.

dipstick *n*. **1** a rod for measuring the depth of oil in a vehicle's engine. **2** *colloq*. a fool; a crazy or unliked person.

dipterous / dip-tuh-ruhs / *adj*. **1** (of insects) having two wings. **2** (of seeds) having two wing-like parts.

diptych / **dip**-tik / *n*. a painting, esp. an altarpiece, on two surfaces that fold like a book.

dire *adj*. **1** dreadful, terrible (*in dire peril*). **2** ominous, predicting trouble (*dire warnings*). **3** extreme and urgent (*in dire need*). **4** *colloq*. very bad (*this party is dire*).

direct *adj*. **1** going in a straight line; not curved or roundabout (*the direct route*). **2** with nothing or no one in between; in an unbroken line (*in direct contact*). **3** straightforward, frank, going straight to the point (*a direct way of speaking*). **4** exact, complete (*the direct opposite*). • *adv*. by a direct route (*travelled to Rome direct*). • *v*. **1** tell or show how to do something or get somewhere (*can you direct me to the station?*). **2** address (a letter or parcel etc.). **3** cause to have a specified direction or target. **4** control, manage (*there was no one to direct the workmen*). **5** command, order (*directed his men to advance*). **6** supervise the acting, filming, etc. of (a film, play, etc.). □ **direct access** the direct and immediate retrieval of data from any part of a computer file. **direct bill** *v*. *Aust*. (of a doctor) use direct billing. **direct billing** *Aust*. the system (put in place under Medicare) by which doctors choosing to do so bill Medicare for the services they have given to patients instead of charging the patients themselves. **direct current** electric current flowing in one direction only. **direct object** *Grammar* the primary object of the action of a transitive verb; the person or thing that is directly affected. **direct speech** words actually spoken, not as they are reported. **direct tax** tax paid directly to the government (e.g. on income) as opposed to tax on goods and services. □□ **directness** *n*.

direction *n*. **1** directing, aiming, guiding, managing. **2** the line along which something moves or faces (*in the direction of Sydney Harbour Bridge*). **3** (**directions**) instructions.

directional *adj*. **1** of or indicating direction. **2** operating or sending radio signals in one direction only.

directive *n*. a general instruction issued by an authority.

directly *adv*. **1** in a direct line, in a direct manner. **2** without delay. **3** very soon. • *conj*. *colloq*. as soon as (*I went directly I knew*).

director *n*. **1** a person who supervises or manages things, esp. a member of the board managing a business company on behalf of shareholders. **2** a person who directs a film or play. □ **directorial** *adj*. **directorship** *n*.

directorate *n*. **1** the position of director. **2** a board of directors.

Director of Public Prosecutions (*abbr*. **DPP**) (in the Federal jurisdiction and in some States in Australia) the law officer who heads a government authority responsible for instituting and conducting criminal proceedings in the public interest.

directory *n*. a book containing a list of telephone subscribers, inhabitants of a district, members of a profession, business firms, etc.

dirge / derj / *n*. a slow mournful song; a lament for the dead.

dirham / **der**-ham / *n*. the main unit of money in Morocco and the United Arab Emirates.

dirigible / **di**-rij-uh-buhl, duh-**rij**- / *adj*. capable of being guided. • *n*. a dirigible balloon or airship.

dirk *n*. a short dagger.

Dirk Hartog Island a long narrow island, 77 km long and from 5 to 11 km wide, in the Indian Ocean off the coast of WA at the entrance to Shark Bay. It was named after the Dutch sea captain, Dirck Hartog, who landed there in 1616, the first European known to have set foot on the west coast of Australia. West Point on the island is the westernmost point of Australia.

dirt *n*. **1** unclean matter that soils something. **2** earth, soil. **3** a person or thing considered worthless. **4** foul words or talk; scandal. **5** excrement.

dirty *adj*. (**dirtier**, **dirtiest**) **1** soiled, unclean; (of a job etc.) causing the doer to become dirty. **2** not having clean habits. **3** dishonourable, mean, unfair (*a dirty trick; a dirty fighter*). **4** (of weather) rough and stormy. **5** lewd, obscene (*dirty jokes*). **6** (of a nuclear weapon) producing considerable radioactive fallout. **7** *colloq*. resentful; very angry. • *adv*. *colloq*. **1** extremely (*a dirty great diamond*). **2** in an obscene or mean manner (*talk dirty; acted dirty towards his mates*). • *v*. (**dirtied**, **dirtying**) make or become dirty. □ **dirty linen** (also **dirty washing**) intimate secrets, esp. of a scandalous nature. **dirty on** *Aust*. *colloq*. angry with (*he's dirty on you for what you said*). **dirty weekend** *colloq*. a weekend spent secretly with a lover. **do the dirty on** play a mean trick on. □□ **dirtily** *adv*. **dirtiness** *n*.

dis *v*. (also **diss**) (**dissed**, **dissing**) esp. *US colloq*. act or speak in a disrespectful way towards. (¶ Abbreviation of DISRESPECT.)

disability *n*. something that disables or disqualifies a person, a physical incapacity caused by injury or disease etc.

disable *v*. deprive of some ability, make unfit or useless. □ **disablement** *n*.

disabled *adj*. having a physical disability.

disablist *adj*. showing discrimination or prejudice against disabled people. • *n*. a person who shows such prejudice etc.

disabuse / dis-uh-**byooz** / *v*. (usu. foll. by *of*) disillusion, free from a false idea (*disabused him of his belief that he is God's gift to women*).

disadvantage *n.* **1** an unfavourable condition or circumstance (*at a disadvantage*). **2** damage to one's interest or reputation (*to our disadvantage*). • *v.* put at a disadvantage.

disadvantaged *adj.* lacking normal opportunities through poverty, disability, etc.

disadvantageous / dis-ad-vuhn-**tay**-juhs / *adj.* causing disadvantage.

disaffected *adj.* discontented (esp. politically); having lost one's feelings of loyalty. □ **disaffection** *n.*

disaffiliate / dis-uh-**fil**-ee-ayt / *v.* **1 a** end the affiliation of (*the Perth branch was disaffiliated from the Society*). **b** end one's affiliation (*the Perth branch decided to disaffiliate*). **2** detach. □ **disaffiliation** / -**ay**-shuhn / *n.*

disagree *v.* (**disagreed**, **disagreeing**) **1** have a different opinion. **2** be unlike, fail to correspond. **3** quarrel. □ **disagree with 1** differ in opinion from. **2** (of food or climate) have bad effects on.

disagreeable *adj.* **1** unpleasant. **2** badtempered. □ **disagreeably** *adv.*

disagreement *n.* **1** disagreeing. **2** a quarrel; a dispute.

disallow *v.* refuse to allow or accept as valid (*the judge disallowed the claim*).

disappear *v.* cease to be visible, pass from sight or from existence. □ **disappearance** *n.*

disappoint *v.* fail to do or be equal to what was hoped, desired, or expected. □ **disappointed** *adj.* **disappointing** *adj.*

disappointment *n.* **1** a person or thing that disappoints. **2** being disappointed.

disapprobation / dis-ap-ruh-**bay**-shuhn / *n.* formal disapproval.

disapprove *v.* have or express an unfavourable opinion. □ **disapproval** *n.*

disarm *v.* **1** deprive of weapons or of the means of defence. **2** disband or reduce armed forces. **3** defuse (a bomb). **4** make less angry, hostile, etc.; charm, win over (*disarmed me with his smile*).

disarmament *n.* reduction of a country's armed forces or weapons of war.

disarrange *v.* put into disorder, disorganise. □ **disarrangement** *n.*

disarray *n.* disorder. • *v.* disarrange.

disassociate = DISSOCIATE.

disaster *n.* **1** a sudden great misfortune. **2** a complete failure (*the performance was a disaster*). □ **disaster area** an area in which a major disaster (e.g. an earthquake) has recently occurred. □ □ **disastrous** / di-**zah**-struhs / *adj.* **disastrously** *adv.*

disavow *v.* disclaim. □ **disavowal** *n.*

disband *v.* break up, separate (*disbanded the choir; the troops disbanded*). □ **disbandment** *n.*

disbar *v.* (**disbarred**, **disbarring**) deprive (a barrister) of the right to practise law; *colloq.* expel (a person) from; prevent entry to (*he ought to be disbarred from the bushwalking society*). □ **disbarment** *n.*

disbelieve *v.* refuse or be unable to believe. □ **disbelief** *n.*

disburse *v.* pay out (money). □ **disbursal** *n.* **disbursement** *n.*

disc *n.* **1** a thin circular plate of any material. **2** something shaped or looking like this (*the sun's disc*). **3** a layer of cartilage between vertebrae. **4** a gramophone record. **5** (in full **optical disc**) a disc for data recorded and read by laser. **6** a compact disc. **7** *Computing* = DISK. **8** *Computing* = FLOPPY *n.* □ **disc brake** one in which a flat plate presses against a plate at the centre of a wheel. **disc jockey** a person who plays and introduces pop records on radio, at a disco, etc.

discalced / dis-**kalst** / *adj.* (of a Catholic friar or nun) barefoot or wearing only sandals (*the Order of discalced Carmelites*).

discard / dis-**kahd** / *v.* throw away, put aside as useless or unwanted. • *n.* / **dis**-kahd / a discarded item or person.

discern / duh-**sern** / *v.* perceive clearly with the mind or senses. □ **discernible** *adj.* **discernment** *n.*

discerning / duh-**ser**-ning / *adj.* perceptive, showing good judgment.

discharge *v.* / dis-**chahj** / **1** give or send out (*the pipes discharge their contents into the river; the river discharges into the sea; the wound is discharging pus*). **2** give out an electric charge; cause to do this. **3** fire (a missile or gun). **4** dismiss from employment. **5** allow to leave (*the patient was discharged from hospital*). **6** pay (a debt); perform or fulfil (a duty or contract). • *n.* / **dis**-chahj / **1** discharging; being discharged. **2** something that is discharged (*the discharge from the wound*). **3** the release of an electric charge, esp. with a spark. **4** a written certificate of release or dismissal.

disciple / duh-**suy**-puhl / *n.* **1** any of the original followers of Christ. **2** a person who follows the teachings of a leader.

disciplinarian / dis-uh-pluh-**nair**-ree-uhn / *n.* one who enforces or believes in strict discipline.

disciplinary / **dis**-uh-pluh-nuh-ree, -pluhn-ree / *adj.* of or for discipline.

discipline / **dis**-uh-pluhn / *n.* **1** training that produces obedience, self-control, or a particular skill. **2** controlled behaviour produced by such training. **3** punishment given to correct a person or enforce obedience. **4** a branch of instruction or learning (*Philosophy is a hard discipline*). • *v.* **1** train to be obedient and orderly. **2** punish.

disclaim *v.* disown; deny (*they disclaim responsibility for the accident*).

disclaimer *n.* a statement disclaiming something.

disclose *v.* expose to view, reveal, make known. □ **disclosure** *n.*

disco *n.* (*pl.* **discos**) a discothèque. • *v.* (**discoes**, **discoing**) dance to disco music. □ **disco music** a popular dance music with a heavy bass rhythm.

discolour v. (also **discolor**) **1** spoil the colour of, stain. **2** become changed in colour or stained. □ **discolouration** n.

discomfit / dis-**kum**-fit, -fuht / v. (**discomfited**, **discomfiting**) disconcert; frustrate; baffle (*he was discomfited by the question put to him at the interview*). □ **discomfiture** / dis-**kum**-fuh-chuh, -tyoor / n.

discomfort n. **1** being uncomfortable in body or mind. **2** something that causes this. • v. make uncomfortable ('*These wads of wool in your mouth*', *said the dentist*, '*may discomfort you a bit*.').

■ **Usage** As a verb, *discomfort* is sometimes confused with *discomfit*.

discommode / dis-kuh-**mohd** / v. inconvenience (a person etc.). □ **discommodious** adj.

discompose v. disturb the composure of, agitate. □ **discomposure** n.

disconcert / dis-kuhn-**sert** / v. upset the composure of; fluster.

disconnect v. break the connection of; put (an electrical appliance) out of action by disconnecting certain parts, esp. by pulling out the plug. □ **disconnection** n.

disconnected adj. lacking orderly connection between its parts (*a disconnected speech*).

disconsolate / dis-**kon**-suh-luht / adj. unhappy at the loss of something, disappointed. □ **disconsolately** adv.

discontent n. dissatisfaction, lack of contentment. □ **discontented** adj. **discontentment** n.

discontinue v. put an end to, come to an end. □ **discontinuance** n.

discontinuous adj. not continuous. □ **discontinuity** / dis-kon-tuh-**nyoo**-uh-tee / n.

discord / **dis**-kawd / n. **1** disagreement, quarrelling. **2** a combination of musical notes producing a harsh or unpleasant sound. □ **discordance** n. **discordant** / dis-**kaw**-duhnt / adj. **discordantly** adv.

discothèque / **dis**-kuh-tek / n. **1** a club or party etc. where amplified recorded music is played for dancing. **2** the equipment used for this.

discount n. / **dis**-kownt / an amount of money taken off the full price or total. • v. / dis-**kownt** / **1** disregard partly or wholly (*we cannot discount this possibility*). **2** deduct an amount from (a price, goods, etc.); reduce in price. □ **at a discount 1** below the nominal or usual price. **2** not valued as it used to be (*is honesty at a discount nowadays?*).

discountenance v. **1** fluster, confuse, worry (*I was discountenanced by his stare*). **2** refuse to approve of.

discourage v. **1** dishearten. **2** dissuade. **3** deter. □ **discouragement** n.

discourse n. / **dis**-kaws / **1** *formal* a conversation. **2** a speech or lecture. **3** a written treatise on a subject. **4** a connected series of utterances; a text. • v. / dis-**kaws** / utter or write a discourse.

discourteous / dis-**ker**-tee-uhs / adj. lacking courtesy; rude. □ **discourteously** adv. **discourtesy** n.

discover v. **1** obtain sight or knowledge of, esp. by searching or other effort. **2** be the first to do this (*who discovered America?*). **3** (in show business etc.) find and promote as a new performer. □ **discoverer** n.

discovery n. **1** discovering; being discovered. **2** a person or thing that is discovered.

discredit v. (**discredited**, **discrediting**) **1** damage the good reputation of. **2** refuse to believe (*I discredit it utterly*). **3** cause to be disbelieved (*this new information discredits her story*). • n. **1** damage to reputation (*brought discredit on the firm*). **2** a person or thing that causes this (*he is a discredit to the family*). **3** doubt, lack of credibility (*threw discredit on her story*).

discreditable adj. bringing discredit, shameful. □ **discreditably** adv.

discreet adj. **1** showing caution and good judgment in what one does; not giving away secrets. **2** not showy or obtrusive. □ **discreetly** adv.

■ **Usage** Do not confuse with *discrete*.

discrepancy / duh-**skrep**-uhn-see / n. difference, inconsistency, failure to tally (*there were several discrepancies between the two accounts*). □ **discrepant** adj.

discrete / dis-**kreet** / adj. discontinuous, individually distinct. □ **discretely** adv.

■ **Usage** Do not confuse with *discreet*.

discretion / duh-**skresh**-uhn / n. **1** being discreet in one's speech, keeping secrets. **2** good judgment (*he acted with discretion*). **3** freedom or authority to act according to one's judgment (*the treasurer has full discretion*). □ **at a person's discretion** in accordance with his or her decision.

discretionary / duh-**skresh**-uhn-uh-ree, -uhn-ree / adj. done or used at a person's discretion (*discretionary powers*).

discriminate v. **1** (often foll. by *between*) make or see a distinction. **2** (usu. foll. by *against* or *in favour of*) treat unfavourably or favourably, esp. on the basis of race, gender, sexual preference, etc. (*employers who discriminate against women; we need to discriminate in favour of minorities*). □ **discriminatory** adj.

discriminating adj. showing good judgment or taste.

discrimination n. **1** unfair treatment based on racial, sexual, etc. prejudice. **2** good taste or judgment.

discursive adj. rambling from one subject to another.

discus n. a heavy thick-centred disc, thrown in athletic contests.

discuss v. examine by means of argument; talk or write about. □ **discussion** n.

disdain *n.* scorn, contempt. • *v.* **1** regard with disdain, treat as unworthy of notice. **2** refrain out of disdain (*she disdained his offer*). ☐ **disdainful** *adj.* **disdainfully** *adv.*

disease *n.* an unhealthy condition caused by infection or diet or by faulty functioning of a bodily process.

diseased *adj.* affected with disease.

disembark *v.* put or go ashore; get off an aircraft, bus, etc. ☐ **disembarkation** *n.*

disembodied *adj.* (of the soul or spirit) freed from the body. ☐ **disembodiment** *n.*

disembowel *v.* (**disembowelled, disembowelling**) take out the bowels or entrails of.

disempower / dis-em-**powuh** / *v.* remove the power to act from (a person, group, etc). ☐ **disempowerment** *n.*

disenchant *v.* free from enchantment; disillusion (*they are disenchanted with the government*). ☐ **disenchantment** *n.*

disenfranchise *v.* (also **disfranchise**) deprive (a person) of the right to vote, the right to be represented, or other rights of a citizen. ☐ **disenfranchisement** *n.*

disengage *v.* free from engagement; detach (*disengaged the clutch*). ☐ **disengagement** *n.*

disengaged *adj.* not engaged in attending to another person or to business; free.

disentangle *v.* free from tangles or confusion, extricate. ☐ **disentanglement** *n.*

disestablish *v.* end the established state of; deprive (a Church) of its official connection with the State. ☐ **disestablishment** *n.*

disfavour (also **disfavor**) *n.* dislike, disapproval. • *v.* regard or treat with disfavour.

disfigure *v.* spoil the appearance of. ☐ **disfigurement** *n.*

disfranchise = DISENFRANCHISE.

disgorge *v.* **1** throw out from the throat (*the whale swallowed Jonah and then disgorged him*). **2** pour forth (*tourist buses disgorging tourists*). **3** *colloq.* hand over (*made him disgorge the stolen property*).

disgrace *n.* **1** loss of favour or respect. **2** something that causes this. • *v.* bring disgrace upon, humiliate.

disgraceful *adj.* causing disgrace. ☐ **disgracefully** *adv.*

disgruntled *adj.* discontented, resentful. ☐ **disgruntlement** *n.*

disguise *v.* **1** conceal the identity of (*disguised himself as a policewoman; disguised the taste by adding sugar*). **2** conceal (*there's no disguising the fact*). • *n.* **1** something worn or used for disguising. **2** disguising; a disguised condition.

disgust *n.* a strong feeling of dislike; finding a thing very unpleasant or against one's principles. • *v.* cause disgust in.

disgusted *adj.* feeling disgust.

disgusting *adj.* revolting, repugnant; terrible, awful. ☐ **disgustingly** *adv.*

dish *n.* **1** a shallow flat- holding or serving food; utensils in general (*it's yo... dishes*). **2** the amount a dish co. itself; a particular kind of food *n. dish tasted wonderful*). **4** a shallow c... ...ject. **5** = SATELLITE DISH. **6** a vessel in wh... alluvial soil, gravel, etc. is washed to separate out gold. **7** *colloq.* a sexually attractive person (*he's a dish*). • *v.* = DISH UP (sense 1) (*I'm ready to dish the food*). ☐ **dish it out (to)** *colloq.* **1** deal out punishment, reprimands, etc. (*really dished it out to them*). **2** fight hard (*he can dish it out with the best of them*). **dish out** *colloq.* distribute. **dish up 1** serve (food). **2** *colloq.* serve up as facts etc. (*they dished up the usual excuses*).

dishabille = DÉSHABILLÉ.

disharmony *n.* lack of harmony. ☐ **disharmonious** *adj.*

dishcloth *n.* a usu. open-weave cloth for washing dishes.

dishearten *v.* cause to lose hope or confidence. ☐ **disheartened** *adj.* **disheartening** *adj.* **disheartenment** *n.*

dishevelled / di-**shev**-uhld / *adj.* ruffled and untidy. ☐ **dishevelment** *n.*

dishonest *adj.* not honest. ☐ **dishonestly** *adv.* **dishonesty** *n.*

dishonour (also **dishonor**) *n.* **1** loss of honour or respect, disgrace. **2** something that causes this. • *v.* **1** bring dishonour on, disgrace. **2** refuse to accept or pay (a cheque etc.).

dishonourable *adj.* (also **dishonorable**) not honourable, shameful. ☐ **dishonourably** *adv.*

dishwasher *n.* a machine (or person) that washes dishes etc.

dishy *adj.* (**dishier, dishiest**) *colloq.* sexually attractive.

disillusion *v.* set free from mistaken beliefs or illusion. • *n.* the state of being disillusioned. ☐ **disillusionment** *n.*

disincentive *n.* something that discourages an action or effort.

disincline *v.* make (a person) feel reluctant or unwilling to do something. ☐ **disinclination** *n.*

disinfect *v.* clean (something) with disinfectant. ☐ **disinfection** *n.*

disinfectant *n.* a substance that destroys germs etc.

disinformation *n.* deliberately false information.

disingenuous / dis-in-**jen**-yoo-uhs / *adj.* insincere, not frank. ☐ **disingenuously** *adv.*

disinherit *v.* deprive (a person) of an inheritance. ☐ **disinheritance** *n.*

disintegrate *v.* break or cause to break into small parts or pieces. ☐ **disintegration** *n.*

disinter / dis-in-**ter** / *v.* (**disinterred, disinterring**) dig up (something buried, esp. a corpse).

disinterest *n.* **1** impartiality. **2** lack of interest.

·age See the note at *disinterested*.

disinterested *adj.* **1** impartial, unbiased, not influenced by self-interest. **2** uninterested, uncaring. ◻ **disinterestedly** *adv.*

■ **Usage** The use in sense 2 is widely regarded as unacceptable because it obscures a useful distinction between *disinterested* and *uninterested*. The use of the noun *disinterest* to mean 'lack of interest' is also objected to, but it is seldom used in any other sense and the alternative *uninterest* is rare.

disjoint *v.* **1** take apart at the joints (*disjointed the chook*). **2** disturb the working of; disrupt.

disjointed *adj.* (of talk) disconnected.

disjunction *n.* disjoining, separation.

disjunctive *adj.* **1** involving separation. **2** (of a conjunction) expressing an alternative, e.g. *or* in *is it wet or dry?*

disk *n.* (in full **magnetic disk**) a flat circular device coated with magnetic material on which computer data can be stored. ◻ **disk drive** *Computing* a mechanism for spinning a disk and reading data from or writing data to it.

diskette *n. Computing* a floppy disk.

dislike *n.* **1** a feeling of not liking some person or thing. **2** the object of this. •*v.* feel dislike for.

dislocate *v.* **1** put (a thing) out of place in relation to connecting parts; displace (a bone) from its proper position in a joint. **2** put out of order, disrupt (*fog dislocated traffic*). ◻ **dislocation** *n.*

dislodge *v.* move or force (a person or thing) from an established position. ◻ **dislodgment** (also **dislodgement**) *n.*

disloyal *adj.* not loyal. ◻ **disloyally** *adv.* **disloyalty** *n.*

dismal *adj.* **1** causing or showing gloom; dreary. **2** *colloq.* feeble (*a dismal attempt at humour*). ◻ **dismally** *adv.*

dismantle *v.* **1** take to pieces; pull down. **2** deprive of defences or equipment.

dismay *n.* a feeling of surprise and discouragement. •*v.* fill with dismay.

dismember *v.* **1** remove the limbs of. **2** divide into parts; partition (a country etc.). ◻ **dismemberment** *n.*

dismiss *v.* **1** send away from one's presence or employment. **2** put out of one's thoughts; mention or discuss only briefly. **3** reject without further hearing (*the case was dismissed for lack of evidence*). **4** put (a batsman or side) out in cricket. ◻ **dismissal** *n.*

Dismissal, the the sacking in 1975 of the Labor government (led by E.G. Whitlam) by the governor-general, Sir John Kerr. Kerr acted after the opposition had taken the unprecedented action of blocking supply in the Senate.

dismissive *adj.* dismissing rudely or casually; disdainful. ◻ **dismissively** *adv.* **dismissiveness** *n.*

dismount *v.* **1** get off or down from something on which one is riding. **2** cause to fall off, unseat. **3** remove (a gun etc.) from its mounting.

Disney, Walt (full name: Walter Elias Disney) (1901–66), American animator and film producer, famous for the creation of cartoon characters such as Mickey Mouse and Donald Duck and pioneer of feature-length cartoon films.

disobedient *adj.* not obedient. ◻ **disobediently** *adv.* **disobedience** *n.*

disobey *v.* (**disobeyed**, **disobeying**) disregard orders, fail to obey.

disoblige *v.* refuse to help or cooperate with (a person).

disorder *n.* **1** lack of order, untidiness. **2** a disturbance of public order, a riot. **3** disturbance of the normal working of body or mind (*a nervous disorder*). •*v.* throw into disorder, upset. ◻ **disorderly** *adj.*

disorganise *v.* (also **-ize**) throw into confusion, upset the orderly system or arrangement of. ◻ **disorganisation** *n.*

disorganised *adj.* (also **-ized**) lacking organisation or an orderly system.

disorient = DISORIENTATE.

disorientate / dis-o-ree-uhn-tayt / *v.* (also **disorient**) confuse and make (a person) lose his or her bearings. ◻ **disorientation** *n.*

disown *v.* refuse to acknowledge as one's own, reject all connection with.

disparage / dis-**pa**-rij / *v.* speak of in a slighting way, belittle. ◻ **disparagingly** *adv.* **disparagement** *n.*

disparate / **dis**-puh-ruht / *adj.* different in kind.

disparity / dis-**pa**-ruh-tee / *n.* inequality, difference.

dispassionate *adj.* free from emotion, calm, impartial. ◻ **dispassionately** *adv.*

dispatch (also **despatch**) *v.* **1** send off to a destination or for a purpose. **2** kill (*dispatched him with a boomerang*). **3** complete or dispose of quickly (*dispatched the day's work by noon*). •*n.* **1** dispatching; being dispatched. **2** promptness, speed (*he acted with dispatch*). **3** an official message or report sent with speed. **4** a news report sent to a newspaper or news agency etc.

dispel *v.* (**dispelled**, **dispelling**) drive away, scatter (*wind dispelled the fog; how can we dispel their fears?*).

dispensable *adj.* not essential.

dispensary *n.* a place where medicines are dispensed (*the hospital dispensary*).

dispensation *n.* **1** dispensing, distributing. **2** exemption from a penalty, rule, or duty; an instance of this. **3** (in the Catholic Church) exemption from a religious observance on a particular occasion; an instance of this. **4** a reli-

dispense

gious or political system (*the old dispensation before Christianity was founded*).

dispense *v.* **1** distribute, deal out (*dispense justice*). **2** prepare and give out (medicine etc.) according to a doctor's prescription. ☐ **dispense with** do without; make unnecessary (*let's dispense with formalities*).

dispersal *n.* **1** dispersing. **2** *Aust. hist.* the euphemistic name given by whites to: the forced expulsion of Aborigines from their traditional territories, and the hunting down and mass slaughter of Aborigines.

disperse *v.* scatter, go, drive, or send in different directions. ☐ **dispersal** *n.*

dispersion *n.* **1** dispersing; being dispersed. **2** (**the Dispersion**) = DIASPORA.

dispirit *v.* (esp. as **dispiriting**, **dispirited** *adjectives*) depress, dishearten.

displace *v.* **1** shift from its place. **2** take the place of, oust. ☐ **displaced person** a refugee in war or from persecution.

displacement *n.* **1** displacing or being displaced. **2** the amount of fluid displaced by an object placed in it.

display *v.* **1** show; arrange (a thing) so that it can be seen. **2** reveal (*displayed his ignorance*). **3** (of birds and animals) make a display (*see sense 3 below*). •*n.* **1** displaying; being displayed. **2** something displayed conspicuously. **3** a special pattern of behaviour used by birds and animals as a means of visual communication, esp. in a mating ritual.

displease *v.* offend, arouse the disapproval or anger of.

displeasure *n.* a displeased feeling, dissatisfaction.

disport *v. formal* (usu. **disport oneself**) play; amuse oneself (*disporting themselves on the beach*).

disposable *adj.* **1** able to be disposed of. **2** at one's disposal. **3** designed to be thrown away after being used once. ☐ **disposable income** income remaining after tax and other fixed payments.

disposal *n.* disposing of something. ☐ **at one's disposal** available for one's use.

dispose *v.* **1** place suitably or in order (*disposed the troops in two lines*). **2** determine the course of events (*man proposes, God disposes*). **3** make willing or ready to do something, incline (*their friendliness disposed us to accept the invitation; we felt disposed to accept*). ☐ **be well disposed towards** be friendly towards, favour. **dispose of 1** deal with; get rid of; finish; kill. **2** sell. **3** prove (an argument etc.) incorrect.

disposition *n.* **1** setting in order, arrangement (*the disposition of troops*). **2** a person's natural qualities of mind and character (*he has a cheerful disposition*). **3** a natural tendency or inclination (*a disposition to overeat*).

dispossess *v.* deprive (a person) of the possession of something. ☐ **dispossession** *n.*

disproof *n.* disproving; a refutation.

229

disseminate

disproportion *n.* lack of proper proportion; being out of proportion.

disproportionate *adj.* out of proportion, relatively too large or too small. ☐ **disproportionately** *adv.*

disprove *v.* show to be false or wrong; refute.

disputable / dis-**pyoo**-tuh-buhl, **dis**-pyuh- / *adj.* able to be disputed, questionable. ☐ **disputably** *adv.*

disputant / dis-**pyoo**-tuhnt / *n.* a person engaged in a dispute.

disputation *n.* argument, debate.

disputatious *adj.* argumentative.

dispute / duhs-**pyoot**, dis- / *v.* **1** argue, debate. **2** quarrel. **3** question the truth or validity of (*dispute a claim; the disputed territory*). •*n.* **1** an argument or debate. **2** a quarrel. **3** a disagreement leading to industrial action. ☐ **in dispute 1** being argued about. **2** involved in a dispute.

disqualify *v.* (**disqualified**, **disqualifying**) **1** debar from a competition because of an infringement of the rules. **2** make unsuitable or ineligible (*weak eyesight disqualifies him for military service*). ☐ **disqualification** *n.*

disquiet *n.* uneasiness, anxiety. •*v.* make uneasy or anxious.

disquietude *n.* disquiet.

disquisition / dis-kwuh-**zish**-uhn / *n.* a long elaborate spoken or written account of something.

disregard *v.* pay no attention to, treat as of no importance. •*n.* lack of attention; treating something as of no importance (*complete disregard for his own safety*).

disrepair *n.* a bad condition caused by lack of repairs (*in a state of disrepair*).

disreputable / dis-**rep**-yuh-tuh-buhl / *adj.* having a bad reputation, not respectable. ☐ **disreputably** *adv.*

disrepute / dis-ruh-**pyoot** / *n.* lack of good reputation, discredit (*fell into disrepute*).

disrespect *n.* lack of respect, rudeness. ☐ **disrespectful** *adj.* **disrespectfully** *adv.*

disrobe *v.* take off official or ceremonial robes; undress.

disrupt *v.* cause to break up, throw into disorder, interrupt the flow or continuity of (*disputes about Mabo disrupted the coalition; floods disrupted traffic*). ☐ **disruption** *n.*

disruptive *adj.* causing disruption.

dissatisfaction *n.* lack of satisfaction.

dissatisfied *adj.* not satisfied, feeling dissatisfaction.

dissect / duy-**sekt**, duh- / *v.* **1** cut apart, esp. in order to examine internal structure. **2** examine (a theory etc.) critically and in detail. ☐ **dissection** *n.* **dissector** *n.*

dissemble *v.* conceal (one's feelings); be insincere.

disseminate / duh-**sem**-uh-nayt / *v.* spread (ideas etc.) widely. ☐ **dissemination** *n.*

dissension *n.* disagreement that gives rise to strife.

dissent *v.* have or express a different opinion. • *n.* **1** a difference in opinion; the expression of this. **2** refusal to accept the doctrines of an established church; nonconformity. ☐ **dissenter** *n.*

dissentient / duh-**sen**-shuhnt / *adj.* dissenting from the majority. • *n.* one who dissents.

dissertation *n.* **1** a lengthy essay or a thesis, esp. one submitted towards an academic degree. **2** a speech.

disservice *n.* an ill turn; an injury, esp. done when trying to help.

dissident / **dis**-uh-duhnt / *adj.* disagreeing, esp. with an established government, system, etc. • *n.* one who disagrees; one who opposes the authorities. ☐ **dissidence** *n.*

dissimilar *adj.* unlike. ☐ **dissimilarity** *n.*

dissimulate *v.* dissemble. ☐ **dissimulation** *n.*

dissipate / **dis**-uh-payt / *v.* **1** dispel, disperse. **2** squander or fritter away (money, energy, etc.).

dissipated *adj.* indulging one's vices, living a dissolute life.

dissipation *n.* **1** dissipating; being dissipated. **2** dissolute or debauched living.

dissociate / di-**soh**-shee-ayt, -see-ayt / *v.* **1** separate in one's thoughts (*it is difficult to dissociate the man from his work*). **2** become disconnected. ☐ **dissociate oneself from** declare that one has no connection with (a person, organisation, activity, etc.). ☐ ☐ **dissociation** *n.* **dissociative** *adj.*

dissoluble *adj.* able to be dissolved, disintegrated, loosened, or disconnected; soluble.

dissolute / **dis**-uh-loot, -lyoot / *adj.* lacking moral restraint or self-discipline; licentious.

dissolution *n.* **1** the dissolving of a bond, esp. a marriage, partnership, or alliance. **2** the dismissal or dispersal of an assembly, esp. of a parliament at the end of its term. **3** death; destruction. **4** bringing or coming to an end; fading away.

dissolve *v.* **1** make or become liquid; disperse or cause to be dispersed in a liquid. **2** (cause to) disappear; disappear gradually. **3** dismiss or disperse (an assembly, e.g. parliament); annul or put an end to (a partnership, e.g. a marriage). **4** give way to emotion (*she dissolved into tears*).

dissonant / **dis**-uh-nuhnt / *adj.* harsh-toned; unharmonious. ☐ **dissonance** *n.*

dissuade *v.* discourage or persuade against a course of action (*dissuaded him from going*). ☐ **dissuasion** *n.*

dissuasive *adj.* dissuading.

distaff / **dis**-tahf / *n.* a cleft stick holding wool etc. for spinning. ☐ **the distaff side** the mother's side of a family.

distance *n.* **1** the length of space between one point and another. **2** a distant part (*in the distance*). **3** gap or gulf (*there's quite a distance between living frugally and being destitute*). **4** being distant, remoteness; aloofness of manner. • *v.* **1** outdistance in a race. **2** be aloof (*he distanced himself from them*). ☐ **keep one's distance 1** remain at a safe distance. **2** behave aloofly, be unfriendly.

distant *adj.* **1** at a specified or considerable distance away (*three kilometres distant*). **2** remote, much apart in space, time, or relationship etc. (*the distant past; a distant cousin*). **3** not friendly, aloof. **4** abstracted (*a distant look on her face*). ☐ **distantly** *adv.*

distaste *n.* dislike.

distasteful *adj.* unpleasant, arousing distaste. ☐ **distastefully** *adv.*

distemper *n.* **1** a viral disease of dogs and certain other animals, with coughing and weakness. **2** a paint made from powdered colouring matter mixed with glue or size. • *v.* paint with this.

distend *v.* swell or become swollen by pressure from within (*distended stomach*). ☐ **distension** *n.*

distich / **dis**-tik / *n.* a verse couplet.

distil *v.* (**distilled**, **distilling**) **1** treat by distillation; make, produce, or purify in this way. **2** undergo distillation.

distillate *n.* a substance produced by distillation.

distillation *n.* **1** the process of turning a substance to vapour by heat, then cooling the vapour so that it condenses and collecting the resulting liquid, in order to purify it, separate its constituents, or extract an essence. **2** something distilled.

distiller *n.* a person who distils; one who makes alcoholic liquor by distillation.

distillery *n.* a place where alcoholic liquor is distilled.

distinct *adj.* **1** able to be perceived clearly by the senses or the mind, definite and unmistakable (*a distinct improvement*). **2** different in kind, separate (*the two wattles are quite distinct from each other*). ☐ **distinctly** *adv.* **distinctness** *n.*

distinction *n.* **1** an act or instance of discriminating or distinguishing. **2** the difference between two things (*there is a clear distinction between the true leaves and the phyllodes of a wattle*). **3** a thing that differentiates or distinguishes, esp. a mark, name, or title. **4** special consideration or honour (*treat him with distinction*). **5** excellence (*a person of distinction*). **6** a grade in an examination denoting great excellence.

distinctive *adj.* characteristic, serving to distinguish a thing by making it different from others.

■ **Usage** Do not confuse with *distinct*. A *distinct* sign is one that can be seen clearly; a *distinctive* sign is one not commonly found elsewhere.

distingué / dis-**tang**-gay / *adj.* distinguished or dignified in appearance, manner, etc. (¶ French)

distinguish *v.* **1** see or point out a difference between; draw distinctions (*we must distinguish facts from rumours*). **2** make different, be a charac-

distinguished

teristic mark or property of (*speech distinguishes humans from animals*). **3** make out by listening or looking (*unable to distinguish distant objects*). **4** make notable, bring honour to (*he distinguished himself by his bravery*). ❑ **distinguishable** *adj.*

distinguished *adj.* **1** showing excellence. **2** famous for great achievements. **3** having an air of distinction and dignity.

Distinguished Service Cross an Australian Commonwealth Government award for distinguished command and leadership in action.

Distinguished Service Medal an Australian Commonwealth Government award for distinguished leadership in action.

distort *v.* **1** pull or twist out of its usual shape. **2** misrepresent, alter (facts). **3** transmit (sound or pictures) inaccurately. ❑ **distortion** *n.*

distract *v.* **1** draw away the attention of. **2** confuse, bewilder. **3** amuse, esp. to divert from pain etc. (*these colouring books may distract the child*).

distracted *adj.* distraught; confused.

distraction *n.* **1** something that distracts the attention and prevents concentration. **2** an amusement or entertainment. **3** mental upset or distress. ❑ **to distraction** almost to a state of frenzy (*your whistling is driving me to distraction*).

distrain *v.* levy a distraint (upon a person or goods).

distraint *n.* seizure of a person's possessions as payment for what he or she owes, or in order to sell them to meet his or her debts.

distraught /duhs-**trawt**, dis-/ *adj.* greatly upset, nearly crazy with grief or worry.

distress *n.* **1** suffering caused by pain, worry, illness, or exhaustion. **2** poverty. **3** *Law* = DISTRAINT. • *v.* make worried, upset, or unhappy.

distressed *adj.* **1** upset, unhappy, worried. **2** impoverished.

distributary *n.* a branch of a river or glacier that does not return to it after leaving the main stream (e.g. in a delta).

distribute *v.* **1** divide and give a share to each of a number, deal out. **2** spread or scatter; place at different points. ❑ **distribution** *n.*

distributive *adj.* of or concerned with distribution.

distributor *n.* **1** a person or thing that distributes, esp. goods. **2** a device for passing current to each of the spark plugs in an engine. **3** a main road carrying traffic from a busy centre and leading to several minor roads.

district *n.* **1** an area marked off as an administrative unit (*a postal district*). **2** an area or region which has a particular feature (*winegrowing district*). ❑ **district attorney** (in the US) prosecuting officer of a district.

District Court *n.* (in NSW, Qld, and WA) an intermediate State court between Courts of Petty Sessions and Supreme Courts, presided over by a judge.

dive

distrust *n.* lack of trust, suspicion. • *v.* feel distrust in. ❑ **distrustful** *adj.*

disturb *v.* **1** break the rest, quiet, or calm of. **2** cause to move from a settled position.

disturbance *n.* **1** disturbing; being disturbed. **2** a commotion; an outbreak of social or political disorder.

disturbed *adj.* emotionally or mentally unstable or abnormal.

disunion *n.* **1** separation, lack of union. **2** discord.

disunite *v.* **1** remove unity from. **2** cause to separate. **3** experience separation.

disunity *n.* lack of unity.

disuse *n.* the state of not being used (*rusty from disuse*). ❑ **disused** *adj.*

ditch *n.* **1** a trench for drainage or irrigation. **2** a watercourse, stream, etc. • *v.* **1** make or repair ditches. **2** *colloq.* abandon; discard (*ditched her boyfriend; the plans have been ditched*). **3** bring (an aircraft) down on the sea in an emergency; (of an aircraft) make a forced landing on the sea.

dither *v.* hesitate indecisively. • *n.* a state of dithering; nervous excitement or fear (*all of a dither*). ❑ **ditherer** *n.* **dithery** *adj.*

ditto *n.* **1** (used in lists to avoid repeating something) the same again. **2** *colloq.* (used to avoid repetition) the same (*came late today and ditto yesterday*). ❑ **ditto marks** two small marks (") placed under the item to be repeated.

ditty *n.* a short simple song.

diuretic / duy-yoo-**ret**-ik / *n.* a substance that causes more urine to be secreted.

diurnal / duy-**er**-nuhl / *adj.* **1** of the day, not nocturnal. **2** daily. **3** occupying one day. **4** (of animals) active in the daytime.

diva / **dee**-vuh / *n.* a great or famous woman opera singer, a prima donna.

divalent / duy-**vay**-luhnt / *adj. Chem.* having a valency of two.

divan / duh-**van** / *n.* a low couch without a raised back or ends; a bed resembling this.

dive *v.* (**dived, diving**) **1** plunge head first into water. **2** (of an aircraft) plunge steeply downwards. **3** (of a submarine or diver) go under water. **4** put one's hand quickly into (a pocket, handbag, etc.). **5** move suddenly (*dived into a shop*). • *n.* **1** an act of diving. **2** a sharp downward movement or fall (*share prices took a dive*). **3** *colloq.* a disreputable nightclub, bar, etc. ❑ **dive-bomb** *v.* bomb (a target) from a diving aircraft.

dive-bomber an aircraft designed to dive-bomb.

diving bell an open-bottomed structure supplied with air, in which a diver can be lowered into deep water. **diving suit** a watertight suit, usu. with a helmet and air supply, for work under water.

■ **Usage** In Canada and parts of the United States *dove* is acceptable as the past tense of *dive*. While it is often heard in Australia, it is non-standard.

diver *n.* **1** one who dives. **2** a person who works underwater in a diving suit. **3** a diving bird.

diverge / duy-**verj** / *v.* **1** go in different directions from a common point or from each other; become further apart. **2** go aside from a path (*diverge from the truth*). ☐ **divergent** *adj.* **divergence** *n.*

divers / **duy**-verz / *adj. archaic* several, various.

diverse / duy-**vers**, **duy**-, duh- / *adj.* of different kinds.

diversify *v.* (**diversified, diversifying**) introduce variety into, vary. ☐ **diversification** *n.*

diversion *n.* **1** diverting something from its course. **2** diverting of attention (*create a diversion*). **3** a recreation, an entertainment. **4** an alternative route when a road is temporarily closed; a detour. ☐ **diversionary** *adj.*

diversity / duy-**ver**-suh-tee, duh- / *n.* variety.

divert *v.* **1** turn (a thing) from its course (*divert the stream; divert attention; divert traffic*). **2** entertain or amuse with recreations.

diverticulitis / duy-ver-tik-yoo-**luy**-tis / *n.* inflammation of a side branch (*diverticulum*) of a cavity or passage in the body, esp. in the alimentary tract.

divertimento *n.* (*pl.* **divertimentos** *or* **divertimenti**) a light entertaining piece of music, often for a chamber orchestra.

diverting *adj.* entertaining, amusing.

divest / duy-**vest** / *v.* **1** strip of clothes (*divested himself of his robes*). **2** take away, deprive (*divested him of his power*).

divide *v.* **1** separate into parts, split or break up (*divide the money between you; the river divides into two channels*). **2** separate (one thing) from another (*divide the sheep from the goats*). **3** arrange in separate groups, classify. **4** cause to disagree (*this controversy divided the party*). **5** (in Parliament) part in order to vote (*the House divided*). **6** find how many times one number contains another (*divide 12 by 3*). **7** be able to be divided. • *n.* **1** a dividing or boundary line (*the divide between rich and poor*). **2** a watershed.

dividend *n.* **1** a number that is to be divided. **2** a share of profits paid to shareholders or to winners in a totalisator pool etc. **3** a benefit from an action (*his long training paid dividends*).

divider *n.* **1** something that divides; a screen or piece of furniture to divide a room into two parts. **2** (**dividers**) a measuring compass.

dividing range *n. Aust.* a stretch of high country forming a division between adjacent river systems.

divination / div-uh-**nay**-shuhn / *n.* divining, foretelling future events or discovering hidden knowledge.

divine *adj.* **1** of, from, or like God or a god. **2** sacred (*the divine office*). **3** supremely gifted or beautiful (*he has a divine talent*). **4** *colloq.* excellent, delightful (*that outfit is simply divine*). • *v.* discover or learn about future events by what are alleged to be magical means, or by inspiration or guessing. ☐ **divine office** *Catholic Church* the daily recital by priests etc. of the prayers, psalms, readings from scripture, etc. in the breviary. **divine right of kings** the doctrine that a monarch in the hereditary line of succession derives his or her sovereignty and authority directly from God, independently of his or her subjects' will. **divining rod** a forked stick or rod used in dowsing. ☐☐ **divinely** *adv.*

diviner *n.* a person who practises divination.

divinity *n.* **1** being divine. **2** a god.

divisible / duh-**viz**-uh-buhl / *adj.* able to be divided. ☐ **divisibility** *n.*

division *n.* **1** dividing; being divided. **2** (in Parliament) separation of members into two sections for counting votes. **3** a dividing line, a partition. **4** one of the parts into which a thing is divided. **5** a major unit of administration, esp.: **a** a group of army brigades or regiments. **b** *Sport* a grouping of teams within a competition, usu. by ability. **c** a section within an industry, business, etc. (*the marketing division*). ☐ **division sign** a sign (÷) (as in 12 ÷ 4) indicating that one quantity is to be divided by another. ☐☐ **divisional** *adj.*

divisional van *n.* (in Vic.) a police van.

divisive / duh-**vuy**-siv / *adj.* tending to cause disagreement among members of a group. ☐ **divisiveness** *n.*

divisor / duh-**vuy**-zuh / *n.* a number by which another is divided.

divorce *n.* **1** the legal termination of a marriage. **2** separation (*the divorce between thought and feeling*). • *v.* **1** end a marriage with (one's husband or wife) by divorce. **2** separate (*he is divorced from reality*).

divorcee / duh-vaw-**see** / *n.* a divorced person.

divot / **div**-uht / *n.* a piece of turf cut out by a golf club in making a stroke.

divulge / duy-**vulj**, duh- / *v.* reveal (information). ☐ **divulgence** *n.*

divvy *colloq. n.* a dividend. • *v.* (**divvied, divvying**) **1** (often foll. by *up*) share out (*divvied up the spoils*). **2** (often foll. by *with*) share (*I'll divvy with you*).

Diwali / dee-**wah**-lee / *n.* a Hindu religious festival at which lamps are lit, held in October or November.

Dixie *n.* the southern States of the USA.

dixie *n.* **1** a large iron cooking pot used by campers etc. **2** a utensil used by a soldier in the field to eat from, cook in, etc.

Dixieland *n.* **1** Dixie. **2** a kind of traditional jazz with a strong two-beat rhythm.

DIY *abbr.* do-it-yourself.

Diyari / **deer**-ree / *n.* an Aboriginal language of a large region of east-central SA.

dizzy *adj.* (**dizzier, dizziest**) **1** giddy, feeling confused. **2** causing giddiness (*dizzy heights*). **3** *colloq.* stupid. ☐ **dizzily** *adv.* **dizziness** *n.*

DJ *abbr.* disc jockey.

Djakarta alternative spelling of JAKARTA.

Djangati /jun-gu-tee/ *n.* an Aboriginal language of north-eastern NSW.

Djaru /jah-roo/ *n.* an Aboriginal language of a large area of north-eastern WA.

djellaba /jel-u-buh/ *n.* (also **jellaba**) a loose hooded cloak as worn by Arab men.

Djibouti /juh-**boo**-tee/ **1** a republic on the NE coast of Africa. **2** its capital city.

Djingulu /jing-uu-loo/ *n.* an Aboriginal language of a vast area of the central region of the NT.

djinn = JINNEE.

DLitt *abbr.* Doctor of Letters.

DM *abbr.* Deutschmark.

DMus *abbr.* Doctor of Music.

DNA *abbr.* deoxyribonucleic acid, a substance in chromosomes that stores genetic information.

D-notice *n.* an official government notice to news editors not to publish items on specified subjects, for reasons of security.

do *v.* (**did**, **done**, **doing**) **1** perform, carry out, fulfil or complete (a work, duty, etc.). **2** produce, make (*do five copies; we do lunches*). **3** deal with, set in order, solve (*do a crossword; do the dishes*). **4** cover (a distance) in travelling (*did 50 kilometres today*). **5** travel at a specified speed (*was doing eighty*). **6** *colloq.* visit, see the sights of (*we did Rome last year*). **7** *colloq.* undergo (*did time for robbery*). **8** *colloq.* provide food etc. for (*they do you well here*). **9** act or proceed (*do as you like*). **10** fare, get on, achieve something (*they did well out of it*). **11** be suitable or acceptable. **12** be in progress; be happening (*what's doing?*). **13** act or behave like; play the part of (*he's done a Melba; I'm doing Lady Macbeth*). **14** produce a play, opera, etc. (*we're doing 'Dimboola' at Dimboola*). **15** *colloq.* rob, swindle (*you were done!*). **16** *colloq.* prosecute, convict (*done for shoplifting*). **17** *colloq.* take (drugs). • *auxiliary v.* **1** used to indicate present or past tense (*what does he think?; what did he think?*). **2** used for emphasis (*I do like nuts*). **3** used to avoid repetition of a verb just used (*we work as hard as they do*). • *n.* (pl. **dos** or **do's**) **1** *colloq.* an entertainment, a party. **2** alternative spelling of DOH. ▫ **do-gooder** a person who is well-meaning but unrealistic or officious in trying to promote social work or reform. **do-it-yourself** *n.* work (on a house etc.) done by an amateur handyman. ▫▫ **doable** *adj.*

do. *abbr.* ditto.

dob *v.* (**dobbed**, **dobbing**) *Aust. Rules* kick accurately (*dobbed the ball through the centre*). ▫ **dob in** *Aust. colloq.* **1** incriminate (a person) by informing on him or her. **2** impose (a responsibility) upon (*dobbed him in to do the cleaning*). **3** contribute (money) towards a common cause (*everyone dobbed in to help him out*). **dob on** *Aust. colloq.* inform on; betray (*I'll dob on you if you don't stop doing that*). ▫▫ **dobber** *n.*

Dobell, Sir William (1899–1970), Australian painter, esp. of portraits.

Dobermann pinscher *n.* a large dog of a German breed with a smooth coat.

Dobson, Rosemary (1920–), AO, Australian poet.

doc *n. colloq.* **1** doctor. **2** documentary.

docile / **doh**-suyl/ *adj.* willing to obey. ▫ **docilely** *adv.* **docility** / duh-**sil**-uh-tee / *n.*

dock[1] *n.* a weed with broad leaves.

dock[2] *v.* **1** cut short (an animal's tail). **2** reduce or take away part of (wages, supplies, etc.).

dock[3] *n.* **1** an artificially enclosed body of water where ships are admitted for loading, unloading, or repair. **2** (**docks**) a dockyard. • *v.* **1** bring or come into dock. **2** join (two or more spacecraft) together in space; become joined thus.

dock[4] *n.* an enclosure in a criminal court for a prisoner on trial.

docker *n.* a waterside worker.

docket *n.* a document or label listing goods delivered, jobs done, the contents of a package, or recording payment of customs dues etc. • *v.* (**docketed**, **docketing**) enter on a docket; label with a docket.

dockland *n.* the district near docks or former docks.

dockyard *n.* an area with docks and equipment for building and repairing ships.

doco *n. colloq.* documentary.

docs *n.pl.* (in full **Doc Martens**) *trade name* a type of heavy (esp. laced) boot or shoe with a cushioned sole. (¶ Dr Klaus Maertens, German inventor of the sole.)

doctor *n.* **1** a person who is qualified to be a practitioner of medicine, a physician. **2** a person who holds a doctorate (*Doctor of Philosophy*). **3** *Aust.* a cool, refreshing sea breeze (*Albany doctor; Fremantle doctor*). **4** *Aust.* (in Aboriginal English) = CLEVER MAN. • *v.* **1** treat medically. **2** castrate or spay. **3** patch up (machinery etc.). **4** tamper with or falsify (*doctored the evidence*). **5** adulterate (*he doctored my drink*).

doctoral *adj.* of or for the degree of doctor.

doctorate / **dok**-tuh-ruht / *n.* the highest degree at a university, entitling the holder to the title of 'doctor'.

doctrinaire / dok-truh-**nair** / *adj.* applying theories or principles without regard for practical considerations.

doctrine / **dok**-truhn / *n.* a principle or set of principles and beliefs held by a religious, political, or other group. ▫ **doctrinal** / dok-**truy**-nuhl, **dok**-truh-nuhl / *adj.*

docudrama *n.* a television drama based on real events.

document *n.* a paper giving information or evidence about something. • *v.* prove by or support with documents (*a heavily documented report*).

documentary / dok-yoo-**men**-tuh-ree, -tree / *adj.* **1** consisting of documents (*documentary*

documentation   234   **Doherty**

evidence). **2** giving a factual filmed report of a subject or activity. • *n.* a documentary film.

documentation *n.* **1** the collection and classification of information. **2** the documents collected in this way. **3** the material used to prove or support an argument etc. (*this essay has inadequate documentation*). **4** booklets or other material explaining how to use a computer, a piece of software, etc.

dodder[1] *v.* tremble or totter because of age or frailty. ☐ **dodderer** *n.* **doddery** *adj.*

dodder[2] *n.* (in full **dodder-laurel**) a parasitic perennial climber of all Australian States. Also called *devil's twine*.

dodecagon / doh-**dek**-uh-guhn / *n.* a geometric figure with twelve sides.

dodecahedron / doh-dek-uh-**hee**-druhn / *n.* a solid body with twelve faces.

dodge *v.* **1** move quickly to one side; change position or direction in order to avoid something. **2** evade by cunning or trickery (*dodged paying the fare*). • *n.* **1** a quick movement to avoid something. **2** *colloq.* a clever trick. ☐ **dodger** *n.*

dodgem / **doj**-uhm / *n.* a small electrically driven car in an enclosure at a funfair, in which the driver tries to bump other cars.

dodgy *adj.* (**dodgier**, **dodgiest**) *colloq.* **1** awkward; unreliable, risky. **2** cunning, artful.

dodo / **doh**-doh / *n.* (*pl.* **dodos**) a large non-flying bird that formerly lived in Mauritius but has been extinct since the 18th century.

Dodoma / duh-**doh**-muh / the capital of Tanzania.

Dodson[1], Mick (full name: Michael James Dodson) (1950–), Australian Aboriginal barrister and activist. He is the brother of Pat Dodson.

Dodson[2], Pat (full name: Patrick Lionel Minnira Dodson) (1947–), Australian Aboriginal lawyer and activist. He is the brother of Mick Dodson.

doe *n.* (*pl.* **doe** or **does**) a female fallow deer, kangaroo, reindeer, hare, or rabbit.

doer *n.* a person who does something; one who takes action rather than just thinking or talking about what might be done.

doesn't = does not.

doff *v.* remove (a hat or clothes). (¶ From *do off*.)

dog *n.* **1** a four-legged carnivorous animal akin to the fox and wolf, and of many breeds. **2** the male of this or of the wolf or fox. **3** *colloq.* **a** a despicable person. **b** *US* & *Aust.* an informer; a traitor. **c** a person of a specified kind (*lucky dog*). **4** a mechanical device for gripping things. **5** (**the dogs**) *colloq.* greyhound racing. • *v.* (**dogged**, **dogging**) **1** follow closely or persistently (*this weirdo dogged my heels all the way home*). **2** annoy; trouble; plague (*this project has been dogged by misfortune from the start*). **3** *Aust.* hunt dingoes. ☐ **dog collar** *colloq.* a priest's back-to-front collar. **dog-eared** (of a book) having the corners of the pages turned down through use. **dog-eat-dog** *adj.* ruthlessly competitive. **dog-leg** a sharp bend.

dog licence (*or* **certificate** *or* **ticket**) *Aust. hist.* a certificate exempting a few Aborigines from legislation pertaining specifically to Aborigines only (e.g. prohibiting the sale of alcohol to Aborigines). **dog-paddle** a simple swimming stroke like that of a dog. **dog rose 1** (also **river rose**) a shrub of NSW, Tas., and Vic., having a profusion of rose-like pink flowers almost all the year round. **2** a wild rose with single flowers. **dog's breakfast** (*or* **dinner**) *colloq.* a mess. **dog's life** a life of misery or harassment. **dog star** the star Sirius. **dog-tired** tired out. **go to the dogs** *colloq.* become worthless; be ruined. **not a dog's chance** no chance at all. **turn dog on** *Aust. colloq.* inform on; betray.

doge / dohj / *n. hist.* the former ruler of Venice or of Genoa.

dogfight *n.* **1** a rough fight. **2** close combat between fighter aircraft.

dogfish *n.* (*pl.* **dogfish** or **dogfishes**) a kind of small shark.

dogged / **dog**-uhd / *adj.* determined, not giving up easily. ☐ **doggedly** *adv.* **doggedness** *n.*

dogger *n. Aust.* a person who hunts dingoes.

doggerel / **dog**-uh-ruhl / *n.* bad verse.

doggo *adv.* ☐ **lie doggo** *colloq.* lie motionless or hidden.

doggy *adj.* **1** of dogs. **2** *colloq.* devoted to dogs (*a doggy person*). • *n.* (also **doggie**) *colloq.* a child's name for a dog. ☐ **doggy bag** a bag provided at a restaurant so that customers may take home leftovers.

doghouse *n.* a dog's kennel. ☐ **in the doghouse** *colloq.* in disgrace.

dogma *n.* a doctrine or doctrines put forward by some authority, esp. the Church or a political party, to be accepted as true without question.

dogman *n. Aust.* a worker who rides on the hook of a crane (or on a girder etc. being lifted by a crane) and gives signals to the crane operator.

dogmatic / dog-**mat**-ik / *adj.* putting forward opinions in an authoritative, intolerant, or arrogant way. ☐ **dogmatically** *adv.*

dogmatise / **dog**-muh-tuyz / *v.* (also **-ize**) make dogmatic statements.

dogmatism / **dog**-muh-tiz-uhm / *n.* being dogmatic.

dogsbody *n. colloq.* a person who runs errands and does boring jobs for others.

dogwatch *n.* either of two short watches on a ship (4–6 p.m. or 6–8 p.m.).

doh *n.* (also **do**) *Music* the first note of a major scale in music, or the note C.

d'oh / doh / *interj. colloq.* used to comment on an action perceived as foolish or stupid. (¶ From the US television series *The Simpsons*.)

Doha / **doh**-huh / the capital of Qatar.

Doherty / doh-uh-tee /, Peter (Charles) (1940–), AC, Australian immunologist. He shared the 1996 Nobel Prize for physiology or medicine with R.M. Zinkernagel (1944–) for their discoveries concerning the way the immune system recognises virus-infected cells.

doily *n.* (also **doyley**) a small ornamental paper or lace mat placed under cakes etc. on a dish.

doings *n.* (treated as *pl.*) *colloq.* necessary things, ingredients (*have we got all the doings?*).

Dolby *n. trademark* a system used in tape-recording to reduce unwanted sounds at high frequency. (¶ Name of its inventor R.M. Dolby (1933–).)

doldrums *n.pl.* (usu. as **the doldrums**) **1** the ocean regions near the equator where there is little or no wind. **2** a period of inactivity. ☐ **in the doldrums** in low spirits.

dole *v.* (usu. foll. by *out*) distribute sparingly. •*n.* an unemployment benefit. ☐ **dole bludger** *Aust. colloq.* **1** a person who exploits the system of unemployment benefits by avoiding gainful employment. **2** a person who allegedly prefers the dole to work. **on the dole** receiving unemployment benefits.

doleful *adj.* mournful, sad. ☐ **dolefully** *adv.*

doley *n. Aust. colloq.* a person receiving the dole.

doll *n.* **1** a small model of a human figure, esp. as a child's toy. **2** a ventriloquist's dummy. **3** *colloq.* an attractive person of either sex (formerly only of a woman) (*he's a real doll*). •*v.* (foll. by *up*) *colloq.* dress smartly (*all dolled up and nowhere to go*).

dollar *n.* **1** the chief monetary unit in Australia since 1966. **2** the chief monetary unit in the US, Canada, various countries in SE Asia, etc.

dollop *n. colloq.* a shapeless lump of something soft.

dolly *n.* **1** a child's name for a doll. **2** a movable platform for a cine-camera. **3** *Aust.* an apparatus for crushing auriferous quartz in order to extract the gold. **4** *Cricket* an easy catch.

dolma *n.* (*pl.* **dolmas** or **dolmades** / dol-**mah**-deez /) an E. European delicacy of spiced rice and minced lamb etc. wrapped in vine or cabbage leaves and cooked in stock.

dolman sleeve *n.* a loose sleeve cut in one piece with the body of a garment.

dolmen / **dol**-muhn / *n.* a prehistoric tomb with a large flat stone laid on upright ones.

dolomite / **dol**-uh-muyt / *n.* a mineral or rock of calcium magnesium carbonate.

dolour / **do**-luh / *n.* (also **dolor**) *literary* sorrow, distress. ☐ **dolorous** *adj.*

dolphin *n.* a sea mammal like a porpoise but larger and with a beak-like snout.

dolt / dohlt / *n.* a stupid person. ☐ **doltish** *adj.*

Dom *n.* a title put before the names of some Catholic dignitaries and of Benedictine and Carthusian monks.

domain / duh-**mayn** / *n.* **1** a district or area under someone's control; a range of influence. **2** a field of thought or activity (*the domain of science*). **3** (**the Domain**) the land (now a public park) which surrounds Government House in Sydney; a traditional forum for speakers of all kinds.

☐ **domain name** a sequence of words etc. forming an address on the Internet.

dome *n.* **1** a rounded roof with a circular base. **2** something shaped like this. •*v.* cover with or shape into a dome. ☐ **domed** *adj.*

Dome of the Rock an Islamic shrine in Jerusalem.

domestic *adj.* **1** of the home or household or family affairs. **2** of one's own country, not foreign or international. **3** (of animals) kept by humans, not wild. **4** fond of home life. •*n.* **1** a domestic disturbance, esp. an argument or fight between a husband and wife etc. **2** a servant in a household. ☐ **domestic science** home economics; the study of household management. ☐ ☐ **domestically** *adv.*

domesticated *adj.* **1** (of animals) trained to live with and be kept by humans. **2** (of people) enjoying household work and home life.

domesticity / do-mes-**tis**-uh-tee, doh- / *n.* being domestic; domestic or home life.

domicile / **dom**-uh-suyl / *n.* a person's place of residence. •*v.* (usu. as **domiciled** *adj.*) living (in a place).

domiciliary / dom-uh-**sil**-yuh-ree / *adj.* **1** of a dwelling place. **2** visiting a patient etc. at home (*domiciliary physiotherapist*).

dominant *adj.* dominating. •*n.* (in music) the fifth note of the diatonic scale of any key. ☐ **dominance** *n.* **dominantly** *adv.*

dominate *v.* **1** have a commanding influence over. **2** be the most influential or conspicuous person or thing. **3** (of a high place) tower over (*the mountain dominates the whole valley*). ☐ **domination** *n.*

domineer *v.* behave in a forceful way, making others obey.

Domingo, Placido (1941–), Spanish operatic tenor.

Dominica / dom-i-**nee**-kuh / a mountainous island in the West Indies, an independent Republic within the Commonwealth. ☐ **Dominican** / dom-i-**nee**-kuhn / *adj.* & *n.*

Dominican / duh-**min**-i-kuhn / *n.* a member of an order of friars (also called **Black Friars**) founded by a Spanish priest, St Dominic (*c.*1170–1221), or of a corresponding order of nuns.

Dominican Republic / duh-**min**-i-kuhn / a country in the West Indies. ☐ **Dominican** *adj.* & *n.*

dominion *n.* **1** authority to rule; control. **2** territory controlled by a ruler or government; a domain. **3** *hist.* the title of Australia and other self-governing territories of the British Empire.

domino *n.* (*pl.* **dominoes**) **1** each of the small oblong pieces marked with up to 6 pips on each half, used in the game of **dominoes**. **2** a loose cloak with a mask for the upper part of the face, formerly worn at masquerades. ☐ **domino effect** an effect whereby (or theory that) one event triggers off a cascading series of related events, like a row of falling dominoes, esp. the notion that a political event etc. in one country will cause similar events in neighbouring countries.

Don *n.* a Spanish title put before a man's Christian name.

don[1] *v.* (**donned**, **donning**) put on (clothing).

don[2] *n.* a university teacher.

Donald Duck a cartoon character created by Walt Disney. His lines were quacked by Clarence Nash (1904–85).

donate *v.* give as a donation.

Donatello / don-uh-**tel**-oh /, Donato di Niccolo (1386–1466), Florentine sculptor.

donation *n.* **1** an act of donating. **2** a gift of money etc. to a fund or institution.

Done, / dohn / Ken(neth Stephen) (1940–), AM, Australian designer and artist.

done *see* DO. • *adj.* **1** completed. **2** cooked sufficiently. **3** *colloq.* tired out. **4** *colloq.* socially acceptable (*the done thing; it isn't done*). • *interj.* (in reply to an offer) I accept.

doner kebab / **do**-nuh, **doh**-nuh / *n.* spiced lamb cooked on a spit and served in slices, often with pitta bread.

dong[1] *n.* **1** the deep sound of a large bell. **2** *Aust. colloq.* a heavy blow. **3** (also **donger**) *coarse colloq.* a penis. • *v.* **1** make the deep sound of a large bell. **2** *Aust. colloq.* hit, punch (*donged him one*).

dong[2] *n.* the chief monetary unit of Vietnam.

donga *n.* **1** a dry watercourse. **2** *Aust.* **a** a broad, shallow, often circular depression most often found in dry country. **b** the bush. **3** *Aust.* a makeshift or temporary dwelling.

donjon *n.* the great tower or keep of a castle.

Don Juan / joo-uhn, wahn / *n.* **1** legendary Spanish nobleman of dissolute life. **2** a seducer of women.

donk *n. colloq.* **1** a donkey. **2 a** a small, usu. subsidiary engine (abbr. of DONKEY ENGINE). **b** any engine.

donkey *n.* (*pl.* **donkeys**) **1** an animal of the horse family, with long ears. **2** *colloq.* a stupid or utterly stubborn person. **3** (in SA) *colloq.* a lift on a bicycle etc. ridden by another. • *v.* (in SA) *colloq.* carry (a passenger) on a bicycle etc. ❑ **donkey engine** a small auxiliary engine. **donkey's years** *colloq.* a very long time. **donkey vote** *Aust.* **1** a vote recorded by merely allocating preferences according to the order in which candidates are listed on the ballot paper. **2** such votes viewed collectively.

donks *n.* ❑ **in** (or **for**) **donks** *colloq.* in (or for) a very long time (*haven't seen him in donks*). (¶ Abbreviation of *donkey's years.*)

Donna *n.* the title of an Italian, Spanish, or Portuguese lady.

donnish *adj.* like a university don; pedantic.

Donohoe, / **don**-uh-hyoo / Jack (?1806–30), a young Australian bushranger (born in Dublin) who became a folklore hero (*Bold Jack Donohoe*) in Australia. His exploits are commemorated in numerous songs and ballads, among them *The Wild Colonial Boy*. He was shot dead by a trooper in the bush near Campbelltown on 1 September 1830.

donor *n.* **1** one who gives or donates something. **2** one who provides blood for transfusion, semen for insemination, or tissue for transplantation. ❑ **donor card** an official card authorising the use of the card carrier's organs for transplants in the event of his or her death.

Don Quixote *see* QUIXOTIC.

don't = do not. • *n.* a prohibition (*do's and don'ts*).

doodle *v.* scribble aimlessly or absent-mindedly. • *n.* a drawing or marks made by doodling.

doofus / **doo**-fuhs / *n. colloq.* a fool, a stupid person.

Doohan, Michael (Sydney) (1965–), AM, Australian world champion 500cc motorcycle racer.

doom *n.* a grim fate; death or ruin. • *v.* destine to a grim fate.

doomsday *n.* the day of the Last Judgment, the end of the world.

doona *n. Aust. trademark* a thick soft quilt with a detachable cover, used instead of an upper sheet and blankets.

door *n.* **1** a hinged, sliding, or revolving barrier for closing and opening the entrance to a building, room, cupboard, etc. **2** this as representing a house etc. (*lives two doors away*). **3** a doorway. **4** a means of obtaining or approaching something (*closed the door to any agreement*). ❑ **door-to-door** *adj.* (of selling etc.) done at each house in turn.

doorknock *n. Aust.* **1** an appeal in which agents for a (charitable) cause go from house to house soliciting contributions. **2** a campaign in support of a political party. • *adj.* of or concerning such an appeal. • *v.* conduct a doorknock.

doormat *n.* **1** a mat placed at a door, for wiping dirt from shoes. **2** *colloq.* a very submissive person.

doorstop *n.* a device for keeping a door open or preventing it from striking a wall when it opens. • *v.* wait at the entrance of a building for (a person) in order to interview (him or her).

doover *n. Aust. colloq.* any object when one does not know or cannot remember what it is called; a thingummyjig.

doorway *n.* an opening filled by a door.

dopamine / **doh**-puh-meen / *n.* a compound found in nervous tissue, acting as a neurotransmitter and a precursor of other substances including adrenalin.

dope *n.* **1** *colloq.* a medicine or drug; a narcotic; marijuana; a drug given to an athlete, horse, etc. to affect performance. **2** *colloq.* information. **3** *colloq.* a stupid person. **4** a thick liquid used as a lubricant etc. • *v.* **1** treat with dope. **2** give a narcotic or stimulant to.

dopey *adj.* (also **dopy**) *colloq.* **1** half asleep, stupefied by a drug. **2** stupid. ❑ **dopiness** *n.*

doppelgänger / **dop**-uhl-geng-uh, -gang- / *n.* an apparition or double of a living person. (¶ German, = double-goer.)

Doppler effect *n.* the apparent increase (or decrease) in the frequency of light or other radiation, e.g. the pitch of sound, when the source and the observer are becoming closer (or more distant). (¶ Named after the Austrian physicist C.J. Doppler (1803–53).)

Doric *adj.* of the oldest and simplest of the five classical orders of architecture.

dork *n. colloq.* a stupid or ineffectual person.

dormant *adj.* **1** sleeping; lying inactive as if in sleep. **2** (of plants) alive but not actively growing. **3** temporarily inactive (*a dormant volcano*).

dormer *n.* (in full **dormer window**) an upright window under a gable built out from a sloping roof.

dormitory *n.* a sleeping room with a number of beds, esp. in a school or institution.

dormouse *n.* (*pl.* **dormice**) a mouselike animal that hibernates in winter.

Dorothy Dix *n.* (also **Dorothy Dixer**) *Aust.* a prearranged parliamentary question asked so as to allow a minister to deliver a prepared speech. (¶ Dorothy Dix (1870–1951), US writer of a question-and-answer column.)

dorsal *adj.* of or on the back of an animal or plant (*a dorsal fin; a dorsal petal*).

dory *n.* any of various edible sea fish, esp. the John Dory.

DOS *n. Computing* one of the operating systems available for manipulating information on a disk. (¶ Abbreviation of *disk operating system.*)

dosa / **doh**-suh / *n.* (*pl.* **dosas** or **dosai**) (in southern Indian cookery) a rice flour pancake served usu. with a spiced vegetable filling.

dosage *n.* **1** the giving of medicine in doses. **2** the size of a dose.

dose *n.* **1** an amount of medicine to be taken at one time. **2** an amount of radiation received. **3** a quantity (or the experience) of something regarded as being as unpleasant as a dose of medicine (*a dose of flu*). **4** (**a dose**) *colloq.* a venereal infection. • *v.* treat with medicine, give a dose of medicine to.

doss *colloq. v.* sleep in cheap lodgings. ◻ **doss down** sleep on a makeshift bed (*some of you guys will have to doss down on the floor*).

dossier / **dos**-ee-uh, **dos**-ee-ay / *n.* a set of documents containing information about a person or event.

Dostoevsky / dos-toi-**ef**-skee /, Fedor Mikhailovich (1821–81), Russian novelist.

dot *n.* **1** a small round mark, a point; this as part of *i* or *j*, as a decimal point, full stop, etc. **2** the shorter of the two signals used in the Morse code. **3** *Music* a dot used to indicate the lengthening of a note or rest, or to indicate staccato. • *v.* (**dotted, dotting**) **1** mark with a dot or dots, place a dot over a letter. **2** scatter here and there (*dot them about; the sea was dotted with ships*). **3** *colloq.* hit (*dotted him one*). ◻ **dot ball** *Cricket* a ball from which no run is scored, indicated by a dot on the scoresheet. **dot painting** a style of Aboriginal painting with dots of colour, from central Australia. **dotted line** a line of dots showing where a signature etc. is to be entered on a document. **on the dot** exactly on time. **the year dot** *colloq.* a very long time ago.

dotage / **doh**-tij / *n.* a state of weakness of mind caused by old age (*in his dotage*).

dotard / **doh**-tuhd / *n.* a person who is in his or her dotage.

dotcom *adj.* of or pertaining to a commercial enterprise operating via the Internet. • *n.* such an enterprise. (¶ .COM)

dote *v.* (often foll. by *on*) be excessively fond of.

doth *v. archaic* does.

dotterel *n.* any of various small wading birds (often also called plovers), some of which are resident in Australia and some migrants.

dottle *n.* unburnt tobacco left in a pipe.

dotty *adj.* (**dottier, dottiest**) *colloq.* **1** crazy; eccentric. **2** (foll. by *about*) infatuated with. ◻ **dottiness** *n.*

double *adj.* **1** consisting of two things or parts that form a pair. **2** twice as much or as many; twice the standard portion. **3** designed for two people or things (*a double bed*). **4** combining two things or qualities (*it has a double meaning*). **5** (of flowers) having more than one circle of petals. **6** (of musical instruments) lower in pitch by an octave (*double bassoon*). • *adv.* **1** twice the amount or quantity (*it costs double what it cost last year*). **2** in twos (*see double*). • *n.* **1** a double quantity or thing. **2** a person or thing that looks very like another. **3** a hit between the two outer circles of the board in darts, scoring double. **4** a bet where the winnings and stake from one race are re-staked on another. **5** (at a motel etc.) a room for two. **6** (**doubles**) a game between two pairs of players. • *v.* **1** make or become twice as much or as many. **2** bend or fold in two. **3** (often foll. by *back*) turn sharply back from a course (*the dingo doubled back on its tracks*). **4** act two parts in the same play etc. **5** (often foll. by *for*) be an understudy etc. **6** (often foll. by *as*) play a twofold role (*the chairman doubled as secretary at the meeting*). **7** increase a bid (in cards) or bet etc. twofold. ◻ **at** (or **on**) **the double** running, hurrying. **double agent** one who spies for two rival countries. **double bank** *Aust.* = DINK[1]. **double-barrelled** *adj.* **1** (of a gun) having two barrels. **2** (of a surname) having two parts. **3** having a twofold purpose, meaning, etc. (*a double-barrelled question*). **double bass** the largest lowest-pitched instrument of the violin family. **double blind** a test or experiment in which neither the tester nor the subject has knowledge of identities etc. which might lead to bias. **double bluff** a genuine action or statement disguised as bluff. **double-breasted** (of a coat) having fronts that overlap to fasten across the breast. **double-cross** v. deceive or cheat a person with whom one pretends to be collaborating; n. the act of doing this. **double-dealing** deceit, esp. in business. **double-dipping** US & Aust. the practice by which a retired person draws income from two publicly funded sources. **double dissolution** Aust. the simultaneous dissolution of the upper and lower houses of a parliament preparatory to an election. **double drummer** a large black and yellow cicada of southern and eastern Australia, so called from the two large organs which produce its characteristic sound. **double-faced 1** insincere. **2** (of a fabric or material) finished on both sides so that either may be used as the right side. **double glazing** two layers of glass in a window, with an air space between. **double header 1** Sport two matches in succession between the same opponents or between different opponents. **2** a coin with a head on both sides. **double helix** a pair of parallel helices with a common axis, esp. in the structure of a DNA molecule. **double-jointed** having very flexible joints that allow the fingers, arms, or legs to bend in unusual ways. **double negative** Grammar a negative statement containing two negative elements, considered incorrect in standard English (e.g. *he didn't say nothing*). **double-park** park a car alongside one already parked at the side of a street. **double pneumonia** pneumonia affecting both lungs. **double standard** a rule or principle applied more strictly to some people than to others (or to oneself). **double take** a delayed reaction to a situation etc., coming immediately after one's first reaction. **double time** payment of an employee at twice the normal rate. **double up 1** (cause to) bend or curl up with pain or laughter. **2** share (or assign to) a shared room, quarters, etc.; sleep two in the same single bed. □□ **doubly** adv.

double entendre / doo-buhl ahn-**tahn**-druh, dub-uhl on-**ton**-druh / n. a phrase with two meanings, one of which is usu. indecent. (¶ French)

doublet / **dub**-luht / n. **1** a man's close-fitting jacket, with or without sleeves, worn in the 15th–17th centuries. **2** either of a pair of similar things.

doubloon / dub-**loon** / n. a former Spanish gold coin.

doubt n. **1** a feeling of uncertainty about something, an undecided state of mind. **2** a feeling of disbelief. **3** an uncertain state (*all is in doubt*). **4** lack of full proof or clear indication (*benefit of the doubt*). • v. **1** feel uncertain or undecided about. **2** hesitate to believe. □ **doubter** n.

doubtful adj. **1** feeling doubt. **2** causing doubt; unreliable (*a doubtful ally*). □ **doubtfully** adv.

doubtless adv. no doubt.

douche / doosh / n. **1** a jet of liquid applied to a part of the body to cleanse it or for medical purposes. **2** a device for applying this. • v. treat with a douche; use a douche.

dough / doh / n. **1** a thick mixture of flour etc. and liquid, to be baked as bread, pastry, etc. **2** *colloq.* money. □ **doughy** adv.

doughnut n. (also **donut**) **1** a small sweetened fried cake of dough, usu. in the shape of a ring or ball. **2** *colloq.* a tight 360° turn in a vehicle, usu. executed with much wheelspin.

doughty / **dow**-tee / adj. archaic valiant, stouthearted.

dour / door / adj. stern, severe, gloomy-looking. □ **dourness** n.

douse / dows / v. (also **dowse**) **1** put into water; throw water over. **2** extinguish (a light).

dove n. **1** a bird with short legs, a small head, and a thick body, that makes a cooing sound, including the Australian *diamond dove*, *emerald dove*, and *peaceful dove*. **2** a person who favours a policy of peace and negotiation rather than violence (*the doves versus the hawks*).

dovecote n. (also **dovecot**) a shelter for domesticated pigeons.

dovetail n. a wedge-shaped joint interlocking two pieces of wood. • v. **1** join by such a joint. **2** fit closely together, combine neatly (*my plans dovetailed with hers*).

dowager / **dow**-uh-juh / n. **1** a woman who holds a title or property from her dead husband (*the dowager duchess*). **2** *colloq.* a dignified elderly woman.

dowak / **dow**-uhk / n. Aust. a weapon used by Aborigines, a wooden club abruptly pointed at each end. (¶ Nyungar)

dowdy adj. (**dowdier**, **dowdiest**) **1** (of clothes) unattractively dull, not stylish. **2** dressed in dowdy clothes. □ **dowdily** adv. **dowdiness** n.

dowel / dowl, **dow**-uhl / n. a headless wooden or metal pin for holding two pieces of wood or stone together by fitting into a corresponding hole in each. • v. (**dowelled**, **dowelling**) fasten with a dowel.

dowelling n. round rods for cutting into dowels.

dower n. a widow's share for life of her husband's estate.

Dow-Jones index (also **Dow-Jones average**) a figure indicating the relative price of shares on the New York Stock Exchange. (¶ Named after C.H. Dow (1851–1902) and E.D. Jones (1856–1920), American economists.)

down[1] adv. **1** from an upright position to a horizontal one (*fell down*). **2** to, in, or at a lower level, value, or condition; to a smaller size (*they are two goals down; we are $5 down on the transaction; I'm down to my last penny; grind it down*). **3** to or in a place regarded as lower, esp.: **a** southwards. **b** away from a major city (*travelling down from Melbourne*). **4** so as to be more settled (*quieten down; calm down*). **5** so as to be quieter or more mild (*turn down the volume; tone down your criticism*). **6** incapacitated by illness (*is down with* *flu*). **7** in a weaker condition (*hit a man when he's down*). **8** (of a computer) out of action. **9** from an earlier to a later time (*Aboriginal customs handed down; down to the present day*). **10** in writing; listed (*copy it down; down to speak next*). **11** to the source or the place where something is (*track it down*). **12** as a deposit or part (*$5 down, $20 to pay; three down, six to go*). •*prep.* **1** downwards along or through or into, along, from top to bottom of. **2** at a lower part of (*Echuca is further down the river*). •*adj.* **1** directed downwards (*a down draught*). **2** travelling away from a capital or centre (*a down train*). **3** *colloq.* depressed; miserable (*I'm really down*). •*v. colloq.* **1** knock or bring down. **2** swallow; drink (*down it in one gulp; down a few tinnies*). •*n.* **1** misfortune (*ups and downs*). **2** *colloq.* a period of depression (*he's in one of his downs*). **3** a throw in wrestling. **4** *colloq.* a feeling of dislike or hostility; a grudge. ☐ **be down on** (*or* **have a down on**) *Aust. colloq.* show animosity towards (*he is down on Asians; he has a down on Aborigines*). **come down** *Aust.* (of a watercourse) flood, be in spate. **down and out** completely destitute. **down-and-out** *n.* a destitute person. **down at** (*or* **down to**) **1** at (*or* to) (*works down at the pub; gone down to the coast*). **2** (with omission of the preposition *at* or *to*) (*works down the pub weekends; going down the pub for a beer?*). **down-country** *adj. Aust.* of or from the more closely settled areas of Australia. **down-market** *adj. & adv.* of or towards the cheaper end of the market. **down payment** a partial initial payment. **down the track** *colloq.* in the future, later on. **down time** the time during which a machine, esp. a computer, is out of action or unavailable for use. **down tools** *colloq.* cease work, go on strike. **down to the wire** *see* WIRE.

down[2] *n.* **1** the first covering of young birds. **2** a bird's soft under-plumage. **3** fine soft hair as the first growth of hair on a boy's face and body after puberty. **4** a fine soft fuzz on some plants and fruits, etc.

down[3] *n.* (often in the *plural* and usu. preceded by *the*) open rolling land (*the Darling Downs*).

downbeat *adj.* **1** pessimistic, gloomy. **2** relaxed, casual. •*n. Music* an accented beat, usu. the first of the bar.

downcast *adj.* **1** looking downwards (*downcast eyes*). **2** (of a person) dejected.

downer *n. colloq.* **1** a depressant or tranquillising drug. **2** a depressing person or experience; a failure. **3** = DOWNTURN. ☐ **on a downer** depressed.

downfall *n.* **1** a fall from prosperity or power; something that causes this. **2** a sudden heavy fall of rain etc.

downgrade *v.* **1** reduce to a lower grade or status. **2** speak disparagingly of. •*n.* a downward slope. ☐ **on the downgrade** in decline.

downhearted *adj.* dejected, disappointed. ☐ **downheartedly** *adv.* **downheartedness** *n.*

downhill *adv.* in a downward direction; further down a slope. •*adj.* going or sloping downwards. •*n.* **1** a downhill race in skiing. **2** a downward slope.

download *v. Computing* transfer (software or data) from a central storage device or controlling system to a smaller machine. •*n.* the action or process of downloading software or data. ☐ **downloadable** *adj.*

downpipe *n.* a pipe for carrying rainwater from a roof to a drain.

downpour *n.* a heavy fall of rain.

downright *adj.* **1** frank, straightforward. **2** thorough, complete (*a downright lie*). •*adv.* thoroughly (*felt downright scared*).

downside *n.* a negative or adverse aspect of a situation etc.

downsize *v.* reduce in size.

Down syndrome *n.* (also **Down's syndrome**) a congenital disorder causing intellectual impairment and physical abnormalities. (¶ Named after J.L.H. Down, English physician (1828–96).)

downstage *adj. & adv.* nearer the front of a theatre stage.

downstairs *adv.* down the stairs; to or on a lower floor. •*adj.* (also **downstair**) situated downstairs.

downstream *adj. & adv.* in the direction in which a stream or river flows.

downtown *adj.* of a lower or more central part of a town or city. •*adv.* in or into this part. •*n.* a downtown area.

downtrodden *adj.* trampled underfoot; oppressed.

downturn *n.* a decline in activity or prosperity.

down under (also **Down Under**) *Aust. adv.* in or to the antipodes (as seen from the Northern hemisphere), esp. Australia. •*n.* Australia (and sometimes New Zealand). •*adj.* (**down-under**) Australian etc.

downward *adj.* moving, leading, or pointing towards what is lower, less important, or later. •*adv.* (also **downwards**) towards what is lower, less important, or later.

downwind *adj. & adv.* in the direction towards which the wind is blowing.

downy *adj.* (**downier**, **downiest**) like or covered with soft down.

dowry / **dow**-ree, **dowuh**-ree / *n.* property or money brought by a bride to her husband.

dowse / dowz / *v.* **1** search for underground water or minerals by using a Y-shaped stick or rod which is supposed to dip abruptly when it is over the right spot. **2** alternative spelling of DOUSE. ☐ **dowser** *n.*

doxology *n.* a formula of praise to God used in prayer.

doyen / **doi**-uhn / *n.* a man who is the senior member of his staff, profession, etc.

doyenne *n.* a woman who is the senior member of her profession, staff, etc.

Doyle, Sir Arthur Conan (1859–1930), Scottish-born novelist, creator of the fictional private detective Sherlock Holmes and his friend Dr Watson.

doyley alternative spelling of DOILY.

doze v. sleep lightly. •n. a short light sleep.

dozen n. **1** a set of twelve (*pack them in dozens*). **2** (**dozens**) very many (*dozens of things*). ☐ **talk nineteen to the dozen** talk incessantly.

■ Usage Correct use is *ten dozen* (not *ten dozens*).

dozy adj. **1** drowsy. **2** *colloq.* stupid; lazy.

DPhil abbr. Doctor of Philosophy.

DPP abbr. Director of Public Prosecutions.

Dr abbr. **1** Doctor. **2** Drive.

drab adj. **1** dull, uninteresting. **2** of a dull greyish-brown colour. •n. drab colour. ☐ **drably** adv. **drabness** n.

drachm / dram / n. one-eighth of an ounce or of a fluid ounce.

drachma / **drak**-muh / n. the unit of money in Greece.

drack *Aust. colloq.* adj. **1** (of a person) unattractive; dressed in a slovenly way. **2** dreary, dull. •n. an unattractive or slovenly person.

draconian / druh-**koh**-nee-uhn / adj. very harsh (*draconian laws*). (¶ Named after *Draco*, who is said to have established severe laws in ancient Athens in the 6th century BC.)

Dracula, **Count** the chief of the vampires in Bram Stoker's novel *Dracula* (1897).

draft n. **1** a rough preliminary written version (*a draft of a speech*). **2** a written order for the payment of money by a bank; the drawing of money by this. **3** a group detached from a larger group for special duty; the selection of these. **4** *Aust.* an animal or a number of animals separated from the main flock or herd for a specific purpose. **5** conscription. •v. **1** prepare a written draft of. **2** select for a special duty (*he was drafted to the Paris branch*). **3** conscript.

draftsman n. **1** a person who drafts documents. **2** = DRAUGHTSMAN (sense 1).

drag v. (**dragged**, **dragging**) **1** pull along with effort or difficulty. **2** trail or allow to trail along the ground; move slowly and with effort. **3** search the bottom of water with grapnels, dragnets, etc. (*drag the river*). **4** continue slowly in a dull manner (*the speeches dragged on*). **5** draw on a cigarette etc. **6** *colloq.* take part in a drag race. •n. **1** something that is made for pulling along the ground, e.g. a heavy harrow, a dragnet. **2** *Aeronautics* the longitudinal retarding force created by air. **3** something that slows progress (*he was a real drag on her career*). **4** *colloq.* a boring person, duty, etc. **5** *colloq.* inhalation of a cigarette etc. **6** *colloq.* women's clothes worn by men; a party etc. at which these are worn. **7** *colloq.* a street or road (*the main drag*). **8** a drag race. ☐ **drag in** introduce (a subject) unnecessarily or in an artificial way. **drag queen** *colloq.* a male homosexual who dresses in women's clothes.

drag race a race between cars, usu. over a set distance, to see which can accelerate fastest from a standstill.

draggle v. make wet or dirty by trailing on the ground.

dragnet n. **1** a net drawn through a river or across ground to trap fish or game, or to find a drowned person, etc. **2** a systematic hunt for criminals etc.

dragon n. **1** a mythical monster resembling a reptile, usu. with wings and able to breathe out fire. **2** any of various lizards of Australia and elsewhere, often having crests, spines, and neck frills (*bearded dragon; mallee dragon*). **3** a fierce woman.

dragonet n. any of various spiny sea fish, the males often being brightly coloured, including Australian species.

dragonfly n. a large insect with a long body and two pairs of transparent wings.

dragoon n. **1** a cavalryman. **2** a fierce person. •v. bully or force into doing something (*dragooned him into going to the opera*).

dragster n. a car built or modified to take part in drag races.

drain v. **1** draw off (liquid) by means of channels or pipes etc. **2** flow or trickle away. **3** dry or become dried when liquid flows away. **4** deprive gradually of (strength or resources). **5** drink; empty (a glass etc.) by drinking its contents. •n. **1** a channel or pipe through which liquid or sewage is carried away. **2** something that drains one's strength or resources.

drainage n. **1** draining. **2** a system of drains. **3** what is drained off.

drainpipe n. **1** a pipe used in a system of drains. **2** (**drainpipes**) very narrow trousers.

drake n. a male duck.

dram n. **1** a drachm. **2** a small drink of spirits.

drama / **drah**-muh / n. **1** a play for acting on the stage or for broadcasting. **2** plays as a branch of literature; their composition and performance. **3** a dramatic series of events. **4** dramatic quality (*the drama of the situation*).

dramatic adj. **1** of drama. **2** exciting; impressive (*a dramatic change*). •n. (**dramatics**) (often treated as *sing.*) **1** the performance of plays. **2** exaggerated behaviour. ☐ **dramatically** adv.

dramatise v. (also **-ize**) **1** make (a story etc.) into a play. **2** make (a thing) seem dramatic. ☐ **dramatisation** n.

dramatis personae / dram-uh-tuhs per-**soh**-nuy, -nee / n.pl. the characters in a play. (¶ Latin)

dramatist n. a writer of plays.

drank see DRINK.

drape v. **1** cover loosely or decorate with cloth etc. **2** arrange loosely or in graceful folds. **3** position (one's limbs etc.) loosely or casually (*draped himself all over the sofa*). •n. **1** the way a fabric hangs in folds. **2** (**drapes**) curtains.

draper *n.* a retailer of fabrics.

drapery *n.* **1** a draper's trade or fabrics. **2** fabric arranged in loose folds.

drastic *adj.* having a strong or violent effect. ☐ **drastically** *adv.*

drat *interj. colloq.* an expression of annoyance or frustration. (¶ An alteration of *(Go)d rot.*)

dratted *adj. colloq.* cursed; damn (*the dratted thing won't work!*).

draught / drahft / *n.* **1** a current of air in an enclosed place. **2** pulling. **3** the pulling in of a net of fish; the fish caught in this. **4** the depth of water needed to float a ship. **5** the drawing of liquor from a cask etc. **6** one continuous process of swallowing liquid; the amount swallowed. **7** (**draughts**) a game for two players using 24 round pieces, played on a draughtboard. **8** = DRAFT (esp. *n.* sense 1). •*v.* = DRAFT (esp. *v.* sense 1). ☐ **draught beer 1** beer drawn from a cask, not bottled or canned. **2** beer with the properties etc. of draught beer sold in bottles or cans. **draught horse** a horse used for pulling heavy loads.

draughtboard *n.* a chequered games board of 64 squares.

draughtsman *n.* (*pl.* **draughtsmen**) **1** one who makes drawings, plans, or sketches. **2** a piece used in the game of draughts. ☐ **draughtsmanship** *n.*

draughty *adj.* (**draughtier**, **draughtiest**) letting in sharp currents of air. ☐ **draughtiness** *n.*

Dravidian / druh-**vid**-ee-uhn / *n.* **1** a member of an indigenous people of southern India and Sri Lanka. **2** the group of languages spoken by them (including Tamil, Telugu, and Kanarese). •*adj.* of the Dravidians or their languages.

draw *v.* (**drew**, **drawn**, **drawing**) **1** pull (*draw a bow; draw the curtains*). **2** attract (*draw attention; felt drawn to him*). **3** take in (*draw breath*). **4** take out (*drew the cork; draw water; draw $10 from the account*). **5** draw lots; select (a raffle ticket). **6** get information from (*tried to draw him about his plans*). **7** finish a contest with neither side winning. **8** require (a certain depth of water) in which to float (*the ship draws 10 feet*). **9** produce a picture or diagram by making marks on a surface. **10** formulate (*draw a conclusion*). **11** write out (a cheque etc.) **12** make one's way (*draw near; the train drew in*). **13** (of tea) infuse. •*n.* **1** the act of drawing. **2** a person or thing that draws custom, an attraction (*she will be a big draw at our concert*). **3 a** a drawing of lots, a raffle. **b** *Sport* a schedule of competition matches (*when will the footy draw be released?*). **4** a drawn game. ☐ **draw in** (of the time of daylight) become shorter. **draw out 1** prolong (a discussion etc.); encourage (a person) to talk. **2** (of the time of daylight) become longer. **draw the line at** refuse to do or tolerate. **draw up 1** come to a halt. **2** compose (a contract etc.). **3** make (oneself) stiffly erect.

drawback *n.* a disadvantage.

drawbridge *n.* a bridge over a moat, hinged at one end so that it can be drawn up.

drawcard *n.* a person, event, etc. that attracts a large audience.

drawer / **draw**-uh / *n.* **1** a person who draws something; one who writes out a cheque. **2** (also / draw /) a boxlike compartment without a lid, that can be slid horizontally in and out of a piece of furniture. **3** (**drawers**) *archaic* knickers; underpants.

drawing *n.* a picture etc. drawn but not coloured. ☐ **drawing board** a flat board on which paper is stretched while a drawing is made. **drawing pin** a flat-headed pin for fastening paper etc. to a surface. **drawing room** a room in a private house for sitting or entertaining in.

drawl *v.* speak lazily or with drawn-out vowel sounds. •*n.* a drawling manner of speaking.

drawn *see* DRAW. •*adj.* (of a person's features) looking strained from tiredness or worry.

drawstring *n.* a cord threaded through a waistband, bag opening, etc. and pulled to tighten it.

dray *n.* a strong low flat cart for heavy loads.

dread *n.* great fear. •*v.* fear greatly. •*adj. archaic* dreaded, dreadful.

dreaded *adj.* **1** regarded with fear, apprehension, or awe. **2** *colloq.* regarded with mock fear.

dreadful *adj.* **1** causing dread. **2** *colloq.* very annoying, very bad (*dreadful weather*). ☐ **dreadfully** *adv.*

dreadlocks *n.pl.* a Rastafarian hairstyle with hair hanging in tight braids.

dream *n.* **1** a series of pictures or events in a sleeping person's mind. **2** the state of mind of one dreaming or daydreaming (*he goes round in a dream*). **3** an ambition, an ideal. **4** a beautiful person or thing. •*v.* (**dreamt** / dremt / *or* **dreamed**, **dreaming**) **1** have a dream or dreams while sleeping. **2** have an ambition (*dream of being champion*). **3** think of as a possibility (*never dreamt it would happen*). ☐ **dream up** imagine, invent. ☐☐ **dreamer** *n.*

dreamboat *n. colloq.* a sexually attractive person.

Dreaming *n. Aust.* = DREAMTIME, esp. as manifested in the natural world and celebrated in Aboriginal ritual; the spiritual identification an Aborigine makes with a place, a species of plant or animal etc.; a place, a species, or a being so regarded; the spiritual significance of a place (often as *adj.*), e.g. *Dreaming place*; *Dreaming site*; *Dreaming track*.

Dreamtime *n. Aust.* (in Aboriginal belief) a collection of events beyond living memory which shaped the physical, spiritual, and moral world; the era in which these events occurred; an Aborigine's consciousness of the enduring nature of that era even in the present day. (¶ A translation of ALCHERINGA.)

dreamy *adj.* **1** daydreaming. **2** dreamlike, vague. **3** *colloq.* wonderful (*he's dreamy*). □ **dreamily** *adv.* **dreaminess** *n.*

dreary *adj.* (**drearier, dreariest**) dull, boring; (of places etc.) gloomy. □ **drearily** *adv.* **dreariness** *n.*

dreck *n.* (also **drek**) *colloq.* rubbish, trash. □ **dreckish** *adj.* **drecky** *adj.* (¶ Yiddish)

dredge *n.* an apparatus for scooping things from the bottom of a river or the sea. •*v.* **1** bring up or clean out (mud etc.) with a dredge. **2** (often foll. by *up*) bring up (something forgotten) (*why dredge up the past?*). **3** find or locate with difficulty (*where did you dredge up that excuse?*). **4** sprinkle with flour, sugar, etc.

dredger *n.* **1** a boat with a dredge; the dredge itself. **2** a container with a perforated lid for sprinkling flour, sugar, etc.

dregs *n.pl.* **1** bits of worthless matter that sink to the bottom of a liquid. **2** the worst and most useless part (*the dregs of society*).

drench *v.* **1** make wet through and through. **2** force (an animal) to take medicine. •*n.* **1** a thorough soaking. **2** a dose of medicine for an animal.

Dresden china *n.* fine china made at Meissen, near Dresden in Germany.

dress *n.* **1** clothing, esp. the visible part of it (*fussy about his dress*). **2** a woman's or girl's garment with a bodice and skirt. **3** external covering; outward form (*birds in their winter dress*). •*v.* **1** put clothes upon; put on one's clothes; provide clothes for. **2** put on evening dress (*they dress for dinner*). **3** decorate (*dress a shop window*). **4** put a dressing on (a wound etc.). **5** groom and arrange (hair). **6** finish or treat the surface of (*to dress leather*). **7** prepare (poultry, crab, etc.) for cooking or eating; coat (salad) with dressing. **8** apply manure etc. to a paddock, garden, etc. **9** arrange (soldiers) into a straight line. □ **dress circle** the first gallery in theatres, where evening dress was formerly required. **dress down** *colloq.* **1** reprimand or scold severely. **2** dress informally. **dress rehearsal** a rehearsal in full costume. **dress up 1** put on special clothes. **2** make (a thing) look more interesting.

dressage / **dres**-ah*zh* / *n.* the management of a horse to show its obedience and deportment.

dresser *n.* **1** one who dresses a person or thing. **2** a person who dresses in a specified way (*a snappy dresser*). **3** a sideboard with shelves above for dishes etc.

dressing *n.* **1** a sauce or stuffing for food. **2** (also **top dressing**) compost, loam, etc. spread over land. **3** a bandage, ointment, etc. for a wound. **4** a substance used to stiffen fabrics during manufacture. □ **dressing down** a scolding, a thrashing. **dressing gown** a loose gown worn when one is not fully dressed. **dressing room** a room for dressing or changing one's clothes, esp. in a theatre or sports ground, or attached to a bedroom. **dressing shed** *Aust.* a changing room at a swimming pool etc. **dressing table** a piece of bedroom furniture with a mirror and drawers.

dressmaker *n.* a person who makes women's clothes. □ **dressmaking** *n.*

dressy *adj.* (**dressier, dressiest**) **1** wearing stylish clothes. **2** (of clothes) elegant, elaborate.

drew *see* DRAW.

drey / dray / *n.* (*pl.* **dreys**) a squirrel's nest.

Dreyfus, George (1928–), AM, Australian composer.

dribble *v.* **1** allow saliva to flow from the mouth. **2** flow or allow to flow in drops. **3** move the ball forward in football or hockey with slight touches of the feet or stick. •*n.* **1** an act of dribbling. **2** a dribbling flow.

driblet *n.* a small amount.

dribs and drabs *n.pl. colloq.* small amounts.

dried *see* DRY. •*adj.* (of foods) preserved by drying (*dried apricots*).

drier *n.* (also **dryer**) a device for drying hair, laundry, etc. •*adj. see* DRY.

drift *v.* **1** be carried by or as if by a current of water or air. **2** proceed casually or aimlessly (*drifted into teaching*). **3** be piled into drifts by wind etc. (*the snow had drifted*). **4** cause to drift. •*n.* **1** a drifting movement (*the drift of people from the country to the cities; the drift of public opinion*). **2** a mass of snow or sand piled up by wind. **3** deviation from a set course. **4** the general tendency or meaning of what is said (*I didn't catch his drift*). □ **drift net** *n.* a large net for sea fishing, allowed to drift with the tide.

drifter *n.* **1** a boat used for fishing with a drift net. **2** an aimless person.

driftwood *n.* wood floating on the sea or washed ashore by it.

drill[1] *n.* **1 a** a pointed tool or a machine used for boring holes or sinking wells. **b** a dentist's rotary tool for cutting away part of a tooth etc. **2** training in military exercises. **3** thorough training by practical exercises, usu. with much repetition. **4 a** a routine procedure in an emergency (*fire drill*). **b** *colloq.* a routine procedure to be followed (*what's the drill?*). •*v.* **1** use a drill; make (a hole) with a drill. **2** train or be trained by means of drill.

drill[2] *n.* **1** a furrow. **2** a machine for making or sowing seed in furrows. **3** a row of seeds sown in this way. •*v.* plant in drills.

drill[3] *n.* strong twilled linen or cotton cloth.

drill[4] *n.* a baboon found in West Africa, related to the mandrill.

drily *adv.* (also **dryly**) (said) in a dry way.

drink *v.* (**drank, drunk, drinking**) **1** swallow (liquid). **2** (of plants, the soil, etc.) take in or absorb liquid. **3** take alcohol, esp. in excess (*drank himself to death*). **4** pledge good wishes to by drinking (*drank his health*). •*n.* **1** liquid for drinking. **2** alcoholic liquor; excessive use of this. **3** *colloq.* the sea. □ **drink in** watch or listen to with delight or eagerness. □□ **drinker** *n.*

drink-drive v. drive (a vehicle) having drunk more than the legal limit of alcohol. □ **drink-driver** a person who drives in this state. □□ **drink-driving** n.

drip v. (**dripped**, **dripping**) fall or let fall in drops. • n. **1** liquid falling in drops; each of these drops. **2** the sound of this. **3** a drip-feed. **4** *colloq.* a weak or dull person. □ **drip irrigation** the drip-by-drip form of the localised watering of plants.

drip-dry v. (**drip-dried**, **drip-drying**) (of fabric etc.) dry crease-free when hung up to drip. • *adj.* made of fabric that will drip-dry.

drip-feed n. **1** feeding by liquid a drop at a time, esp. intravenously. **2** apparatus for this. • v. feed in this way.

dripping n. fat melted from roasted meat.

drippy *adj. colloq.* (of a person) ineffectual; sloppily sentimental.

drive v. (**drove**, **driven**, **driving**) **1** urge or send in some direction, esp. in a forceful way. **2** strike and propel (a ball etc.) forcibly. **3** force to penetrate (*drove a stake into his heart*). **4** operate (a vehicle or locomotive) and direct its course; travel or convey in a vehicle (*he drove me to the station*). **5** (of electricity or other power) keep (machinery) going. **6** cause, compel (*was driven by hunger to steal*; *drove him mad*). **7** rush, move or be moved rapidly (*driving rain*). **8** effect or conclude forcibly (*drove his point home*). • n. **1** a journey in a vehicle. **2** a stroke made by driving in cricket or golf etc. **3** the transmission of power to machinery (*front-wheel drive; left-hand drive*). **4** energy, persistence; a psychological urge (*the sex drive*). **5** an organised effort (for fund-raising etc.) (*a lamington drive*). **6** a social gathering to play card games etc., changing partners and tables. **7** a (esp. scenic) street or road; a private road through a garden to a house etc. □ **drive at** intend to convey as a meaning (*what was he driving at?*). **drive-in** *adj.* (of a cinema, bottle shop, etc.) able to be used without getting out of one's car. *n.* a cinema, bottle shop, etc., of this kind. **driver's licence** a licence permitting one to drive a vehicle.

drivel n. silly talk, nonsense. • v. (**drivelled**, **drivelling**) talk or write drivel.

driven see DRIVE.

driver n. **1** a person who drives, esp. one who drives a motor vehicle. **2** a golf club for driving from a tee.

drivetime *adj.* (of a radio program) intended for people driving home from work in the evening.

driveway n. **1** a private road through a garden to a house etc. **2** the area in front of a service station where a customer can get driveway service.

drizzle n. very fine rain. • v. (of rain) fall in very fine drops. □ **drizzly** *adj.*

droll / drohl / *adj.* amusing in an odd way. □ **drolly** *adv.*

drollery / **drohl**-uh-ree / n. droll humour.

dromedary / **drom**-uh-duh-ree, drum- / n. a one-humped camel bred for riding.

drone n. **1** a male honey bee. **2** an idler. **3** a deep humming sound. **4** a monotonous speaking tone. **5** the bass pipe of a bagpipe; its continuous note. • v. **1** make a deep humming sound. **2** speak or utter monotonously.

drongo n. (*pl.* **drongos** or **drongoes**) **1** any of various black birds of Australia and elsewhere having elongated tail feathers like a fish's tail (*the spangled drongo*). **2** *Aust. colloq.* a fool, a simpleton.

droob n. *Aust. colloq.* a hopeless-looking ineffectual person. □ **drooby** *adj.*

drool v. **1** water at the mouth, dribble. **2** (often foll. by *over*) admire extravagantly.

droop v. bend or hang downwards through tiredness or weakness. • n. a drooping attitude. □ **droopy** *adj.*

drop n. **1** a small rounded or pear-shaped portion of liquid. **2** something shaped like this, e.g. a sweet or a hanging ornament. **3** a very small quantity (*I'll have just a drop; not a drop of pity*). **4** (**drops**) liquid medicine to be measured and given in drops. **5** the act of dropping; a fall (*a drop in prices*). **6** a steep or vertical descent; the distance of this (*a drop of 10 metres from the window*). **7** a curtain or scenery let down on to a stage. **8** the number of lambs or calves born on a station in a season. **9** the act of delivering goods (*this is our last drop for the day*). • v. (**dropped**, **dropping**) **1** fall by force of gravity through not being held; allow to fall (*his tears dropped; he dropped lightly from the branch; he dropped his trousers*). **2** sink from exhaustion (*feel ready to drop*). **3** fall naturally (*he dropped into the habit*). **4** (cause to) cease or lapse; abandon (*the project has been dropped; drop everything and come at once!*). **5** form a steep or vertical descent (*the cliff drops sharply to the sea*). **6** lower, become lower or weaker (*drop the hem; prices dropped*). **7** allow oneself to move to a position further back (*dropped behind the others*). **8** utter or send casually (*drop a hint; drop me a line*). **9** fail to pronounce or insert (*drop one's h's*). **10** set down (a passenger or parcel etc.). **11** give up; reject; cease to associate with (*dropped the habit; has dropped his friends*). **12** dismiss or omit (*dropped from the team*). **13** (of animals) give birth to (offspring). **14** lose (a game or point). **15** *Aust. colloq.* do, perform (*drop a uey; drop a wheelie*). □ **drop bear** *Aust. jocular* an animal similar in appearance to a koala, but about 1.5 metres in height, with very sharp claws and teeth, and purported to devour tourists. **drop-dead** *attrib.adj. colloq.* stunningly beautiful; brilliant, excellent (also used as *adv.*: *drop-dead gorgeous*). **drop in** *colloq.* **1** (also **drop by**) pay a casual visit. **2** *Surfing* **a** (also **drop in on**) obstruct another surfer by beginning one's surf ride in his or her path. **b** slide down the face of a wave immediately after take-off. **drop kick** n. **1** *Aust. Rules* & *Rugby* a

droplet 244 **dry**

kick made by dropping a football and kicking it as it comes up from the ground. **2** *colloq.* a contemptible person. **drop off 1** fall asleep. **2** set down (a passenger) (*drop me off at the intersection*). **3** decline (*sales have dropped off*). **drop out** cease to participate; opt out from society. **drop-out** *n.* one who drops out from a course of study or from conventional society. **drop punt 1** *Aust. Rules* a kick made with the ball held vertically before dropping it onto the foot. **2** *colloq.* a contemptible person. **drop scone** a pikelet. **drop shot** *n.* (in tennis) a shot which drops abruptly just over the net. **get** (or **have**) **the drop on** *colloq.* get (or have) a person at a disadvantage (esp. because of what one knows about him or her).

droplet *n.* a small drop of liquid.

dropper *n.* **1** a device for releasing liquid in drops. **2** *Aust. & S.Afr.* a vertical batten placed at regular intervals between the posts of a wire fence to keep the wires braced.

droppings *n.pl.* dung of animals or birds.

dropsy *n.* a disease in which watery fluid collects in the body. □ **dropsical** *adj.*

dross *n.* **1** scum on molten metal. **2** impurities; rubbish.

drought *n.* **1** continuous dry weather. **2** the prolonged lack of something. □ **drought-declared** *Aust.* (of a district) officially recognised as being affected by drought for the purposes of relief payments, taxation concessions, etc.

Droughtmaster *n. Aust.* a breed of cattle developed in Australia to withstand dry conditions. It is a cross between the tropical Brahman and British breeds.

drove see DRIVE. • *n.* **1** a moving herd, flock, or crowd. **2** (**droves**) very many; a great number (*they came in droves*). • *v.* (**droved, droving**) *Aust.* drive (a herd or flock), esp. over a great distance (*she droved the cattle overland for 3,000 kilometres*).

drover *n. Aust.* a person who drives a herd or flock, esp. over a great distance. □ **drover's dog** *n.* a drudge; a person who earns no respect (*even a drover's dog could have won the election, but he lost it*).

droving *n. Aust.* **1** the act of driving a herd or flock over a great distance. **2** the occupation of a drover.

drown *v.* **1** kill or be killed by suffocating in water or other liquid. **2** flood, drench (*drowned the yard in half a metre of water*). **3** deaden (grief etc.) with drink (*drown one's sorrows*). **4** overpower (a sound) with greater loudness.

drowse / drowz / *v.* be half asleep.

drowsy *adj.* (**drowsier, drowsiest**) sleepy, half asleep. □ **drowsily** *adv.* **drowsiness** *n.*

drub *v.* (**drubbed, drubbing**) **1** thrash. **2** defeat thoroughly.

drubbing *n.* a beating; a severe defeat.

drudge *n.* a person who does dull, laborious, or menial work. • *v.* do such work. □ **drudgery** *n.*

drug *n.* **1** a substance used in medicine. **2** a substance that acts on the nervous system, e.g. a narcotic or stimulant, esp. one causing addiction. • *v.* (**drugged, drugging**) **1** add a drug to (food or drink). **2** give drugs to; stupefy.

druggie *n. colloq.* a drug addict.

druggist *n.* a pharmaceutical chemist.

Druid / droo-uhd / *n.* **1** a priest of an ancient Celtic religion. **2** a member of a modern Druidic order. □ **Druidism** *n.* **Druidic** *adj.* **Druidical** *adj.*

drum *n.* **1** a percussion instrument consisting of a skin stretched tightly across a round frame. **2** the sound of this being struck; a similar sound. **3** a cylindrical structure or object or container. **4** *Aust.* a swagman's bundle of possessions; swag. **5** the eardrum. **6** (also **the drum**) *Aust. colloq.* a piece of reliable information, esp. a racing tip. • *v.* (**drummed, drumming**) **1** play a drum or drums. **2** make a drumming sound; tap or thump continuously or rhythmically. **3** drive (facts etc.) into a person's mind by constant repetition. □ **drum brake** one in which curved pads on a vehicle press against the inner cylindrical part of a wheel. **drum out** dismiss in disgrace. **drum up** obtain through vigorous effort (*drum up support*).

drummer *n.* **1** a person who plays drums. **2** any of several sea fish able to make a drumming noise (*Queensland drummer; silver drummer*).

drumstick *n.* **1** a stick for beating a drum. **2** the lower part of a cooked fowl's leg. □ **drumsticks** see ISOPOGON.

drunk see DRINK. • *adj.* **1** excited or stupefied with alcoholic drink. **2** (often foll. by *with*) overcome with joy, power, etc. (*drunk with success*). • *n.* a drunken person.

■ Usage See the note under *drunken*.

drunkard *n.* a person who is often drunk.

drunken *adj.* **1** intoxicated; frequently in this condition. **2** happening during or because of drunkenness (*a drunken brawl*). □ **drunkenly** *adv.* **drunkenness** *n.*

■ Usage This word is used before a noun (e.g. *a drunken man*), whereas *drunk* is usu. used after a verb (e.g. *he is drunk*).

drupe / droop / *n.* a fruit with juicy flesh round a stone with a kernel, e.g. a peach.

Druse *n.* a member of a political and religious sect of Muslim origin, concentrated in Lebanon, with smaller groups in Syria and Israel, considered heretics by the general Muslim community.

druthers / dru*th*-uhz / *n.pl. colloq.* a choice, a preference (*if I had my druthers I'd leave immediately*). (¶ Alteration of *I* (etc.) *would rather*.)

dry *adj.* (**drier, driest**) **1** without water or moisture. **2** (of cows) not producing milk. **3** eaten without butter etc. (*dry toast*). **4** thirsty or thirst-making (*I feel dry; this is really dry work*). **5** (of wine) not sweet. **6** uninteresting (*a dry book*). **7**

dryad 245 **duct**

expressed with pretended seriousness (*dry humour*). **8** not allowing the sale of alcohol; without alcohol (*a dry area; a dry wedding breakfast*). **9** of, or being, a political 'dry' (*the party's dry economic policies*). •*v.* (**dried, drying**) **1** make or become dry. **2** preserve (food) by removing its moisture. •*n.* (*pl.* **dries**) **1** the process or an instance of drying. **2** a politician who advocates individual responsibility, free trade, economic stringency, etc., and opposes high government spending on social welfare etc. (as opposed to *wet*) (*see* WET *n.*, sense 4). **3** (**the dry**) *Aust.* (in northern and central Australia) the dry season. **4** (**the dry**) a desert area; waterless country. **5** a dry spot (*come here into the dry*). ☐ **dried out** *Aust.* **1** (of land) parched by drought. **2** (of people) driven off drought-stricken land. **dry battery** (also **dry cell**) an electric battery or cell in which the electrolyte is absorbed in a solid. **dry-clean** *v.* clean (clothes etc.) by a solvent which evaporates very quickly, not by water. **dry diggings** *Aust.* a place removed from running water where gold is found on or near the surface. **dry dock** a dock which can be emptied of water, used for repairing ships. **dry farmer** *US* & *Aust.* a person who farms in dry country. **dry heart** *Aust.* central Australia. **dry ice** solid carbon dioxide used as a refrigerant. **dry rot** decay of wood that is not well ventilated; the fungi that cause this. **dry run** *colloq.* a dummy run; a rehearsal. **dry-shod** without wetting one's shoes. **dry up 1** dry washed dishes. **2** *colloq.* cease talking; (of an actor) forget one's lines. **3** become unproductive. **4** (of supplies) run out. ☐☐ **dryness** *n.*
dryad *n.* a wood nymph.
dryandra *n.* any of several WA shrubs (related to the banksias) with large and spectacular flowers.
dryblow / **druy**-bloh / *v. Aust.* separate (particles of a mineral, esp. gold) from the surrounding material, using a current of air. ☐ **dryblower** *n.* **dryblowing** *n.*
dryer alternative spelling of DRIER.
dryly alternative spelling of DRILY.
Drysdale, Sir (George) Russell (1912–81), AC, Australian artist, noted for his dramatic paintings of the harsh Australian outback and its stoic inhabitants.
drystone *adj.* (of a stone or rubble wall) built without mortar.
DSC *abbr.* Distinguished Service Cross.
DSc *abbr.* Doctor of Science.
DSM *abbr.* Distinguished Service Medal.
DT *abbr.* (also **DTs**) delirium tremens.
dual *adj.* composed of two parts, double. ☐ **dual carriageway** a road with a dividing strip between traffic flowing in opposite directions. **dual control** two linked sets of controls, enabling either of two persons to operate a car or aircraft. ☐☐ **duality** / dyoo-**al**-uh-tee / *n.*
dualism *n.* **1** being twofold; duality. **2** *Philosophy* the theory that in any domain of reality there are two independent underlying principles, e.g. mind and matter, form and content. **3** *Theology* the theory that the forces of good and evil are equally balanced in the universe.
dub[1] *v.* (**dubbed, dubbing**) **1** make (a person) a knight by touching the shoulders with a sword. **2** give a nickname to. **3** smear (leather) with grease.
dub[2] *v.* (**dubbed, dubbing**) **1** replace the soundtrack of (a film), esp. in a different language. **2** add (sound effects or music) to a film or broadcast. **3** copy (a recording).
Dubai / dyoo-**buy** / an emirate belonging to the federation of United Arab Emirates.
dubbo *Aust. colloq. n.* **1** a person who appears to be a bit of a country bumpkin. **2** an idiot; an imbecile. •*adj.* loutish; imbecilic. (¶ *Dubbo* a country town in NSW.)
dubiety / dyoo-**buy**-uh-tee / *n. literary* doubt.
dubious / **dyoo**-bee-uhs / *adj.* doubtful. ☐ **dubiously** *adv.* **dubiousness** *n.*
dubnium / **dub**-nee-uhm / *n.* an unstable chemical element (symbol Db) made by high-energy atomic collisions.
Dublin the capital of the Republic of Ireland.
ducal *adj.* of or like a duke.
ducat / **duk**-uht / *n.* a gold coin formerly current in most European countries.
duchess *n.* **1** a duke's wife or widow; a woman whose rank is equal to that of a duke. **2** a stately or imposing woman. **3** (esp. in Qld) a dressing table with a pivoting mirror. •*v. Aust.* **1** entertain (esp. a visiting dignitary) lavishly and with ceremony. **2** *colloq.* fawn on (a person), treat (him or her) obsequiously in order to curry favour etc.
duchy *n.* the territory of a duke or duchess.
duck[1] *n.* **1** a swimming bird of various kinds. **2** the female of this. **3** its flesh as food. **4** a batsman's score of 0 (orig. short for *duck's egg*, used for the figure 0 because of its similar shape). •*v.* **1** dip the head briefly under water; push (a person) under water. **2** bob down, esp. to avoid being seen or hit. **3** dodge, avoid (a task etc.). ☐ **duck into** (or **out**) *colloq.* go in(to) (or out) for a brief time (*I'll just duck into this shop; I'm ducking out for a few minutes*). **duck-shove** *Aust. colloq.* evade (responsibilities), esp. by shifting them to someone else; avoid (an issue that has to be dealt with). **duck-shover** *Aust. colloq.* a person who duck-shoves.
duck[2] *n.* a strong linen or cotton fabric.
duckbill *n.* (also **duck-billed platypus**) = PLATYPUS.
duckling *n.* a young duck.
duckweed *n.* a plant that grows on the surface of ponds etc.
duco / **dyoo**-koh / *n. Aust. trademark* a kind of paint, used esp. on the body of a car etc. •*v.* (**ducoed, ducoing**) paint (a car etc.) with duco.
duct *n.* **1** a tube or channel for conveying liquid, gas, cable, etc. **2** a tube in the body through which

ductile

fluid passes (*tear ducts*). • *v.* convey through a duct.

ductile *adj.* **1** (of metal) able to be drawn out into fine strands. **2** (of a substance) easily moulded. **3** (of a person) easily led; gullible. □ **ductility** *n.*

ductless *adj.* without a duct. □ **ductless glands** glands that pour their secretions directly into the blood, not through a duct.

dud *colloq. n.* **1** something that is useless or counterfeit or that fails to work. **2** (**duds**) clothes. • *adj.* useless, defective. • *v. Aust.* trick, defraud, deceive.

dude / dyood, dood / *n.* **1** a person, guy, fellow (*I don't like those dudes*). **2** (as a form of address) friend, mate (*let's go, dudes*). □ **cool dude** a fashionable or otherwise attractive or desirable person (esp. a male). (¶ Originally US, from German dialect *dude* 'a fool'.)

dudgeon / **duj**-uhn / *n.* resentment, indignation. □ **in high dudgeon** very angry.

due *adj.* **1** owed as a debt or obligation. **2** payable immediately (*it has become due*). **3** that ought to be given to a person; rightful, adequate (*with due respect; after due consideration*). **4** scheduled to do something or to arrive (*he is due to speak tonight; the train is due at 7.30*). • *adv.* exactly (*sailed due east*). • *n.* **1** a person's right; what is owed to a person (*give him his due*). **2** (**dues**) a fee; what one owes (*pay one's dues*). □ **in due course** in the proper order; at the appropriate time. **due to** caused by (*his lateness was due to a car accident*).

■ **Usage** The phrase *due to* is often used to mean *because of*, e.g. *play was stopped due to rain*. Some people regard this usage as unacceptable and maintain that *due to* should be used only after a noun (often with a linking verb), e.g. *the stoppage was due to rain*. Alternatively, *owing to* could be used, e.g. *play was stopped owing to rain*.

duel *n.* **1** a fight with weapons between two people, usu. to the death. **2** a contest between two people or sides. • *v.* (**duelled**, **duelling**) fight a duel. □ **duellist** *n.*

duet *n.* a musical composition for two performers.

duff *v. Aust.* **1** steal and alter brands on (cattle etc.). **2** pasture (stock) illegally on another's land. **3** alter the appearance etc. of stolen goods. □ **duffing** *n.*

duffer[1] *n. colloq.* an inefficient or stupid person; a dunce.

duffer[2] *n. Aust.* **1** a person who steals stock and alters brand marks. **2** an unproductive mine or claim. • *v.* (of a mine etc.) prove unproductive; peter out.

duffle *n.* (also **duffel**) heavy woollen cloth. □ **duffle coat** *n.* a hooded overcoat made of duffle, fastened with toggles.

dug[1] *see* DIG.

dug[2] *n.* an udder, a teat.

dun

dugite / **doo**-guyt / *n.* a highly venomous, predominantly grey, olive, or brown snake of south-western Australia. (¶ Nyungar)

dugong / **doo**-gong / *n.* (*pl.* **dugong** or **dugongs**) an Asian sea mammal; a sea cow.

dugout *n.* **1** an underground shelter. **2** a canoe made by hollowing a tree trunk.

duke *n.* **1** a nobleman of the highest hereditary rank. **2** a sovereign prince ruling a duchy or small nation.

dukedom *n.* the position or lands of a duke.

dulcet / **dul**-suht / *adj.* sweet-sounding.

dulcimer / **dul**-suh-muh / *n.* a musical instrument with strings struck by two hand-held hammers.

dull *adj.* **1** not bright or clear. **2** slow in understanding, stupid. **3** not sharp; (of sound) not resonant. **4** not interesting or exciting, boring. • *v.* make or become dull. □ **dully** *adv.* **dullness** *n.*

dullard *n.* a mentally dull person.

duly / **dyoo**-lee / *adv.* in a correct or suitable way.

dumb *adj.* **1** unable to speak. **2** temporarily silent (*struck dumb by the news*). **3** *colloq.* stupid. **4** giving no sound (*some keys on this piano are dumb*). □ **dumb-bell** a short bar with a weight at each end, lifted to exercise the muscles. **dumb down** *colloq.* simplify or reduce the intellectual content (of something) so as to make it accessible to a larger audience. **dumb show** gestures without words. **dumb waiter** a small lift for conveying food from kitchen to dining room. □□ **dumbly** *adv.* **dumbness** *n.*

dumbfound *v.* astonish, strike dumb with surprise.

dumbo *n.* (*pl.* **dumbos**) *colloq.* a stupid person.

dumbstruck *adj.* speechless with surprise.

dumdum *n.* (in full **dumdum bullet**) a soft-nosed bullet that expands on impact.

dummy *n.* **1** a sham article. **2** a model of the human figure, used to display clothes. **3** a rubber teat for a baby to suck. **4** a stupid person. **5** a person taking no real part, a figurehead. **6** (in card games) a player whose cards are placed upwards on the table and played by a partner. **7** (also **dummy pass**) *Rugby* a pretended pass or move. • *adj.* sham; imitation. • *v.* (**dummies**, **dummied**) make a pretended pass or swerve in rugby etc. □ **dummy run** a trial run, a practice.

dump *v.* **1** deposit as rubbish. **2** put down carelessly. **3** get rid of (something unwanted). **4** market goods abroad at a lower price than is charged in the home market. • *n.* **1** a rubbish heap; a place where rubbish may be deposited. **2** a temporary store (*ammunition dump*). **3** *colloq.* a dull or unattractive place. □ **down in the dumps** *colloq.* miserable, gloomy.

dumpling *n.* **1** a ball of dough cooked in stew etc. or baked with fruit inside it. **2** a small fat person.

dumpy *adj.* short and fat. □ **dumpiness** *n.*

dun[1] *adj.* & *n.* greyish-brown.

dun[2] *v.* (**dunned**, **dunning**) ask persistently for payment of a debt.

dunce *n.* a person who is slow at learning.

dunderhead *n.* a stupid person.

dune / dyoon / *n.* a mound or ridge of sand formed by the wind.

dung *n.* animal excrement. ☐ **dung beetle** *n.* a beetle whose larvae develop in dung.

dungarees / dung-guh-**reez** / *n.pl.* overalls or trousers of coarse cotton cloth.

dungeon / **dun**-juhn / *n.* a strong underground cell for prisoners.

dunghill *n.* a heap of dung.

dunk *v.* dip (a biscuit etc.) into liquid.

Dunkirk (French **Dunquerque**) a seaport in northern France from which British troops were evacuated in 1940.

Dunlop, Sir Ernest Edward ('Weary') (1907–93), AC, Australian surgeon. He was captured by the Japanese in 1943 and sent to work on the notorious Burma Railway, where he provided medical treatment for prisoners under appalling conditions. His courage and loyalty earned him great respect.

dunnart *n.* any of the narrow-footed marsupial mice of all Australian States. (¶ Nyungar)

dunny *n. Aust.* **1** (orig.) an unsewered outdoor toilet. **2** any toilet. ☐ **dunny can** a removable receptacle in an outdoor toilet. **dunny cart** (esp. in unsewered areas and formerly) a vehicle for the collection and disposal of human excrement. **dunny man** a man who mans a dunny cart and collects dunny cans.

duo / **dyoo**-oh / *n.* (*pl.* **duos**) **1** a pair of performers. **2** a duet.

duodecimal / dyoo-oh-**des**-uh-muhl / *adj.* based on 12; reckoning by twelves.

duodenum / dyoo-uh-**dee**-nuhm / *n.* the first part of the small intestine, immediately below the stomach. ☐ **duodenal** *adj.*

duologue / **dyoo**-uh-log / *n.* a dialogue between two people.

dupe *n.* a person who is deceived or tricked. • *v.* deceive, trick.

duple / **dyoo**-puhl / *adj.* of or having two parts. ☐ **duple time** (in music) rhythm with two beats to the bar.

duplex / **dyoo**-pleks / *adj.* **1** having two parts. **2** *Computing* (of a circuit) allowing simultaneous two-way transmission of signals. • *n.* **1** (in some parts of Australia) either of two semi-detached houses. **2** a flat on two floors.

duplicate *n.* / **dyoo**-pluh-kuht / **1** one of two or more things that are exactly alike. **2** an exact copy. • *adj.* **dyoo**-pluh-kuht / exactly like another thing; being a duplicate. • *v.* / **dyoo**-pluh-kayt / **1** make or be an exact copy of. **2** repeat or do twice. ☐ **in duplicate** as two identical copies. ☐ **duplication** *n.*

duplicity / dyoo-**plis**-uh-tee / *n.* double-dealing, deceitfulness.

durable *adj.* likely to last, not wearing out or decaying quickly. • *n.pl.* (**durables**) durable goods. ☐ **durably** *adv.* **durability** *n.*

dura mater / dyoo-ruh **mah**-tuh / *n.* the tough outermost membrane covering the brain and the spinal cord.

duration *n.* the time during which a thing continues.

duress / dyoo-**res**, **dyoo**- / *n.* **1** the use of violence or threats to procure something. **2** imprisonment.

Durga a fierce Hindu goddess (often identified with Kali), wife of Siva.

durian / **doo**-ree-uhn / *n.* a large tree, native to SE Asia, bearing oval spiny fruits containing a creamy pulp with a fetid smell and an agreeable taste.

during *prep.* throughout or at a point in the continuance of.

durry *n. Aust. colloq.* a cigarette.

dusk *n.* the darker stage of twilight.

dusky *adj.* (**duskier**, **duskiest**) **1** shadowy, dim. **2** dark-coloured. ☐ **duskiness** *n.*

dust *n.* **1** fine particles of earth or other matter. **2** a dead person's remains. **3** confusion, turmoil (*the news raised quite a dust*). **4** *Aust. colloq.* silicosis. **5** *Aust.* gold dust. • *v.* **1** sprinkle with sugar, powder, etc. **2** clear (furniture etc.) of dust by wiping. **3** *colloq.* defeat thoroughly, thrash (*our team got dusted*). ☐ **dust bowl** a desert made by drought or erosion. **dust cover** (or **jacket**) a paper cover on a hardback book. **dust-up** *n. colloq.* a noisy argument; a fight.

dusted *adj. Aust. colloq.* suffering from silicosis.

duster *n.* **1** a cloth for dusting furniture etc. **2** a wooden block with a thick pad of felt, used in schools for wiping a blackboard clean.

dustpan *n.* a pan into which dust is brushed from a floor.

Dusty, Slim (original name: David Gordon Kirkpatrick) (1927–), AO, Australian country music singer and songwriter.

dusty *adj.* (**dustier**, **dustiest**) **1** full of dust; covered with dust. **2** (of a colour) greyish (*dusty pink*). ☐ **dusty miller** an Australian shrub with white flowers and very large leaf-like bracts which look as if they have been dusted with flour. ☐ ☐ **dustiness** *n.*

Dutch *adj.* of the Netherlands or its people or language. • *n.* **1** the Dutch language. **2** (**the Dutch**) Dutch people. ☐ **Dutch auction** one in which the price asked is gradually reduced until a buyer is found. **Dutch cap** a flexible dome-shaped contraceptive device inserted to fit over a woman's cervix. **Dutch courage** that obtained by drinking alcohol. **Dutch elm disease** a disease of elm trees, caused by a fungus. **Dutch oven 1** a covered dish for cooking meat etc. slowly. **2** a metal box with the open side facing a fire. **Dutch treat** a party, outing, etc. where people pay for themselves. **go Dutch** share expenses on an outing etc. ☐ ☐ **Dutchman** *n.* **Dutchwoman** *n.*

duteous / **dyoo**-tee-uhs / *adj. literary* dutiful.

dutiable / **dyoo**-tee-uh-buhl / *adj.* on which customs or other duties must be paid.

dutiful *adj.* doing one's duty, showing due obedience. ☐ **dutifully** *adv.*

Dutton, Geoffrey (Piers Henry) (1922–98), AO, Australian novelist, poet, and academic.

duty *n.* **1** a moral or legal obligation. **2** a task that must be done, action required from a particular person (*teachers on yard duty during school recesses*). **3** a tax charged on certain goods or on imports. ☐ **do duty for** serve as (something else).

duty-free *adj.* (of goods) on which duty is not charged. **duty-free shop** a shop at an airport etc. selling duty-free goods.

duvet / **doo**-vay / *n.* = DOONA.

dux *n.* the top pupil in a class or in a school.

DVD *abbr.* digital versatile disc (formerly, digital video disc).

Dvořák / **dvawr**-zhak /, Antonin (1841–1904), Czech composer.

dwarf *n.* (*pl.* **dwarfs** or **dwarves**) **1** a person, animal, or plant much below the usual size. **2** (in fairy tales and fantasy novels) a short manlike non-human being, often with magic powers. **3** a small usu. dense star. •*adj.* of a kind that is very small in size. •*v.* **1** stunt in growth. **2** make seem small by contrast or distance.

dweeb *n.* a contemptible or boring person, esp. one who is studious, puny, or unfashionable.

dwell *v.* (**dwelt** or **dwelled**, **dwelling**) live as an inhabitant. ☐ **dwell on** (or **upon**) think, speak, or write lengthily about; brood or harp on (*always dwelling on his grievances*). ☐☐ **dweller** *n.*

dwelling *n. formal* a house etc. to live in.

dwindle *v.* become gradually less or smaller; lose importance; decline.

Dy *symbol* dysprosium.

dybbuk / **dib**-uhk / *n.* (in Jewish folklore) the malevolent spirit of a dead person that enters and controls the body of a living person until exorcised.

dye *v.* (**dyed**, **dyeing**) **1** colour, esp. by dipping in a liquid. **2** absorb dye (*this fabric dyes well*). •*n.* **1** a substance used for dyeing. **2** a colour given by dyeing. ☐ **dyed-in-the-wool** *adj.* unchangeable, confirmed in one's beliefs (*a dyed-in-the-wool socialist*). ☐☐ **dyer** *n.*

dying *see* DIE[1].

Dyirbal / **jeer**-bahl / *n.* an Aboriginal language (with regional dialects) of a vast area of northern Qld, from Cardwell to beyond Innisfail along the coast, and inland to Malanda and Herberton.

dyke (also **dike**) *n.* **1** an embankment built to prevent flooding. **2** a ditch. **3** a low wall of turf or stone. **4** *colloq.* a lesbian. **5** *Aust. colloq.* a toilet. •*v.* (**dyking**) provide or protect with a dyke or dykes.

Dylan / **dil**-uhn /, Bob (original name: Robert Allen Zimmerman) (1941–), American folk and rock singer and songwriter.

dynamic *adj.* **1** (of force) producing motion (as opposed to *static*). **2** (of a person) energetic, having force of character. **3** *Computing* capable of change while the system or program continues to run. •*n.* (**dynamics**) **1** (usu. treated as *sing.*) a branch of physics that deals with matter in motion. **2** *Music* (treated as *pl.*) varying degrees of loudness in musical performance. ☐ **dynamically** *adv.*

dynamism / **duy**-nuh-miz-uhm / *n.* energising or dynamic action or power.

dynamite *n.* **1** a powerful explosive made of nitroglycerine. **2** something likely to cause violent or dangerous reactions (*the frontier question is dynamite*). **3** a person or thing with great vitality or effectiveness. •*v.* fit with a charge of dynamite, blow up with dynamite.

dynamo *n.* (*pl.* **dynamos**) **1** a generator producing electric current. **2** *colloq.* an energetic dynamic person.

dynamometer / duy-nuh-**mom**-uh-tuh / *n.* an instrument measuring energy expended.

dynast / **din**-uhst, **duy**-nuhst / *n.* a hereditary ruler, a member of a dynasty.

dynasty / **din**-uh-stee / *n.* **1** a line of hereditary rulers. **2** a succession of leaders in any field. ☐ **dynastic** *adj.*

dyne *n. Physics* the force required to give a mass of one gram an acceleration of one centimetre per second per second.

dysentery / **dis**-uhn-tree / *n.* a disease with inflammation of the intestines, causing severe diarrhoea with blood and mucus.

dysfunction / dis-**fungk**-shuhn / *n.* failure to function normally.

dyslexia / dis-**lek**-see-uh / *n.* abnormal difficulty in reading and spelling, caused by a condition of the brain. ☐ **dyslexic** *adj.* & *n.*

dysmenorrhoea / dis-men-uh-**ree**-uh / *n.* painful or difficult menstruation.

dyspepsia / dis-**pep**-see-uh / *n.* indigestion. ☐ **dyspeptic** *adj.* & *n.*

dysphasia / dis-**fay**-zee-uh / *n.* difficulty in coordinating speech as a result of brain damage.

dysprosium / dis-**proh**-zee-uhm / *n.* a chemical element (symbol Dy), a soft metal used in certain magnetic alloys.

dystopia / dis-**toh**-pee-uh / *n.* a nightmare vision of society (opp. UTOPIA), often as one dominated by a totalitarian or technological state. ☐ **dystopian** *adj.* & *n.* (¶ DYS- + UTOPIA)

dystrophy / **dis**-truh-fee / *n.* defective nutrition. *See also* MUSCULAR DYSTROPHY.

Dzongkha / **zonk**-uh / *n.* a Tibetan dialect that is the official language of Bhutan.

E

E *n.* (*pl.* **Es** *or* **E's**) *Music* the third note of the scale of C major. • *abbr.* (also **E.**) East; Eastern.

e- *prefix* denoting the use of electronic data transfer in cyberspace for information exchange and financial transactions, esp. through the Internet (*e-commerce; e-retailing*).

each *adj.* every one of two or more people or things (*each child*). • *pron.* each person or thing (*each of them; give them two each*). ☐ **each other** one another. **each way** (of a bet) backing a horse etc. to win and to be placed.

eager *adj.* full of strong desire, enthusiastic. ☐ **eagerly** *adv.* **eagerness** *n.*

eagle *n.* **1** a large bird of prey. **2** = WEDGE-TAILED EAGLE. **3** a score of two strokes under par for a hole at golf. ☐ **eagle hawk** *Aust.* = WEDGE-TAILED EAGLE.

eaglet *n.* a young eagle.

Eales, John (Anthony) (1970–), AM, Australian rugby union player who became captain of the Australian team in 1996.

ear[1] *n.* **1** the organ of hearing in humans and certain animals; the external part of this. **2** the ability to distinguish sounds accurately or with great sensitivity (*she has an ear for music*). **3** sympathetic attention (*give ear to; have a person's ear*). ☐ **by ear** (the performance of music) without reference to the written score etc. **have** (*or* **keep**) **one's ear to the ground** be alert to rumours or trends of opinion.

ear[2] *n.* the seed-bearing part of a cereal plant.

earache *n.* pain in the eardrum.

earbash *v.* (also **ear-bash**) *Aust.* subject (a person) to a torrent of words; talk at great length to; harangue. ☐ **earbasher** *n.* **earbashing** *n.*

eardrum *n.* a membrane inside the middle ear that vibrates when sound waves strike it.

earful *n. colloq.* **1** a large amount of talk. **2** a strong reprimand.

earl *n.* (in the UK) a male ranking between marquis and viscount.

earldom *n.* the position or lands of an earl.

early *adj.* & *adv.* (**earlier**, **earliest**) **1** before the usual or expected time. **2** not far on in a period of time or development or a series (*early evening; at the earliest opportunity; early man; his early years; the early chapters*). **3** used with reference to the earliest period of white settlement in Australia (*early settlers*). • *n.* (usu. in the *plural*) an early fruit or vegetable. ☐ **early days** too soon to expect results etc. **early mark** approval to leave work early as a reward. ☐☐ **earliness** *n.*

earmark *n.* a distinguishing mark. • *v.* **1** put a distinguishing mark on. **2** set aside for a particular purpose (*funds earmarked for Aids research*).

earn *v.* (**earned**, **earning**) **1** get or deserve as a reward for one's work or merit. **2** (of money lent or invested) gain as interest. ☐ **earned income** income derived from paid employment. ☐☐ **earner** *n.*

earnest[1] *adj.* showing serious feeling or intentions. ☐ **in earnest** seriously, not jokingly; with determination, intensively. ☐☐ **earnestly** *adv.* **earnestness** *n.*

earnest[2] *n.* **1** money paid as an instalment, esp. to confirm a contract etc. **2** a token or foretaste of what is to come (*I give you this as an earnest of my determination to help*).

earnings *n.pl.* money earned.

earphone *n.* (usu. as **earphones**) a device applied to the ear to receive radio or telephone communications.

earpiece *n.* the part of a telephone etc. which is applied to the ear.

earplug *n.* a piece of wax or other material placed in the ear to keep out noise or water.

earring *n.* a piece of jewellery worn on the lobe or edge of the ear.

earshot *n.* range of hearing (*within earshot*).

earth *n.* **1** (also **Earth**) the planet on which we live; the world in which we live. **2** its surface, dry land, the ground. **3** soil. **4** the hole of a fox etc. **5** an oxide with little taste or smell. **6** connection to the ground as completion of an electrical circuit. • *v.* connect (an electrical circuit) to earth. ☐ **earth science** a science such as geology or geography concerned with the structure and age of the earth. **go to earth** go into hiding. **on earth** (used for emphasis in questions) ever (*what on earth is that?*).

earthbound *adj.* **1** attached to the earth or earthly things. **2** moving towards the earth.

earthen *adj.* **1** made of earth. **2** made of baked clay.

earthenware *n.* pottery made of coarse baked clay.

earthling *n.* an inhabitant of the earth, esp. in science fiction.

earthly *adj.* of this earth; of human life on it. ☐ **not an earthly** *colloq.* no chance at all. ☐☐ **earthliness** *n.*

earthquake *n.* a violent natural movement of a part of the earth's crust.

earthwork *n.* an artificial bank of earth.

earthworm *n.* a common worm that lives in the soil.

earthy *adj.* **1** like earth or soil. **2** gross, coarse (*earthy humour*). □ **earthiness** *n.*

earwig *n.* **1** a small insect with pincers at the end of its body. **2** *colloq.* an eavesdropper.

ease *n.* **1** freedom from pain, trouble, or anxiety. **2** relief from pain. **3** absence of painful effort (*did it with ease*). **4** freedom or relief from constraint or formality (*his ease of manner put us at our ease*). • *v.* **1** relieve from pain or anxiety. **2** make less tight, forceful, or burdensome. **3** move gently or gradually (*ease it in*). **4** slacken, reduce in severity or pressure etc. (*it will ease off*). □ **at ease 1** free from anxiety, in comfort. **2** (of a soldier) standing with feet apart rather than to attention. **ease up** slow down, moderate one's behaviour etc. (*ease up, mate, or you'll have a heart attack*).

easel *n.* a wooden frame to support a painting or a blackboard etc.

easement *n.* a legal right of way or similar right over another person's ground or property.

easily *adv.* **1** in an easy way, with ease. **2** by far (*easily the best*). **3** very probably (*it could easily snow*).

east *n.* **1** the point on the horizon where the sun rises; the direction in which this point lies. **2** the eastern part of something. **3** (**the East**) Asia, China, etc. **4** the eastern part of a country, city, etc. • *adj.* **1** towards or in the east. **2** (of a wind) blowing from the east. • *adv.* towards or in the east.

eastbound *adj.* travelling or leading eastwards.

Easter *n.* the Christian festival (celebrated on a Sunday in March or April) commemorating Christ's resurrection; the period about this time. □ **Easter bilby** the Australian equivalent of the Easter bunny; a chocolate representation of this. **Easter bunny** (a representation of) a rabbit popularly said to bring gifts at Easter. (¶ Apparently from *Eostre*, goddess of dawn, whose festival was kept at the vernal equinox.)

Easter Island an island in the SE Pacific west of Chile, famous for its many monolithic statues of human heads (up to 10 metres high).

easterly *adj.* **1** in or towards the east. **2** (of a wind) blowing from the east. • *n.* an easterly wind.

eastern *adj.* of or in the east. □ **eastern grey** (also **great grey**) an extremely large kangaroo (the male may stand nearly 2 metres tall) of eastern Australia, with silvery grey fur.

Eastern Church the Orthodox Church.

easterner *n.* a native or inhabitant of the east.

easternmost *adj.* furthest east.

Eastern Standard Time the standard time used in eastern Australia.

Eastern Stater *n.* (in WA) a person from the Eastern States, i.e. Australia excluding WA (and sometimes SA and NT).

East Indies the many islands off the SE coast of Asia, now often called the Malay Archipelago.

East Timor a former Portuguese colony (capital Dili) comprising the eastern section of the island of Timor. The region declared itself independent in 1975. It was invaded by Indonesia, who annexed and claimed it in 1976. This was followed by bitter pro-independence resistance and fighting. After a referendum in 1999 which voted overwhelmingly for independence, East Timor was granted independence. (*See* DILI MASSACRE.) □ **East Timorese** *n.* & *adj.*

eastward *adj.* & *adv.* (also **eastwards**) towards the east.

easy *adj.* (**easier**, **easiest**) **1** not difficult, done or obtained without great effort. **2** free from pain, trouble, or anxiety (*with an easy mind; in easy circumstances*). **3** compliant, obliging; easily persuaded (*Mum's an easy touch; he's easy game*). **4** *colloq.* of loose morals; promiscuous. • *adv.* in an easy way, with ease. □ **I'm easy** *colloq.* I'm ready to go along (with whatever is proposed); I have no preference. □□ **easiness** *n.*

easygoing *adj.* placid and tolerant, not strict.

Easy Street *n. colloq.* affluence.

eat *v.* (**ate**, **eaten**, **eating**) **1** take food into the mouth and swallow it; chew and swallow. **2** have a meal (*when do we eat?*). **3** destroy gradually, consume (*acids eat into metals*). **4** *colloq.* trouble, vex (*what's eating you?*). • *n.pl.* (**eats**) *colloq.* food. □ **eat crow** submit to humiliation, eat humble pie. **eat one's words** be obliged to withdraw what one has said. **eat up 1** eat completely. **2** use or deal with rapidly or wastefully (*this car eats up petrol*).

eatable *adj.* fit to be eaten (because of its condition). • *n.pl.* (**eatables**) food.

eater *n.* one who eats (*a big eater*).

eating disorder *n.* any of a range of psychological disorders characterised by abnormal or disturbed eating habits.

eau-de-Cologne / oh-duh-kuh-**lohn** / *n.* an alcohol-based perfume originally made at Cologne.

eau-de-vie / oh-duh-**vee** / *n.* spirits, esp. brandy.

eaves *n.pl.* the underside of a projecting roof.

eavesdrop *v.* (**eavesdropped**, **eavesdropping**) listen secretly to a private conversation. □ **eavesdropper** *n.*

ebb *n.* **1** the outward movement of the tide, away from the land. **2** a condition of lowness or decline. • *v.* **1** (of tides) flow away from the land. **2** become lower, weaken (*his strength ebbed*).

Ebola virus / uh-**boh**-luh / *n.* a virus which first appeared in Zaire and Sudan in 1976. It causes uncontrollable internal and external bleeding in humans and usu. death. (¶ Named after a river in the Democratic Republic of Congo.)

Ebonics / ee-**bon**-iks / *n.* African-American vernacular English.

ebonite *n.* vulcanite.

ebony *n.* the hard black wood of a tropical tree. • *adj.* made of ebony; as black as ebony.

ebullient / uh-**buul**-ee-uhnt, uh-**bul**- / *adj.* exuberant, bubbling over with high spirits. ◻ **ebullience** *n.* **ebulliency** *n.* **ebulliently** *adv.*

ecad / **ee**-kad / *n. Ecology* an organism modified by its environment.

eccentric *adj.* **1** unconventional in appearance or behaviour. **2** (of circles) not concentric; (of orbits) not circular; (of a pivot) not placed centrally. • *n.* **1** an eccentric person. **2** a disc fixed off centre on a revolving shaft, for changing rotary motion to to-and-fro motion. ◻ **eccentrically** *adv.* **eccentricity** *n.*

Eccles, Sir John Carew (1903–97), AC, Australian neurophysiologist, co-winner of the Nobel Prize for medicine in 1963.

ecclesiastic / uh-klee-zee-**as**-tik / *n.* a priest or clergyman.

ecclesiastical / uh-klee-zee-**as**-ti-kuhl / *adj.* of the Church or the clergy.

ECG *abbr.* = ELECTROCARDIOGRAM or ELECTROCARDIOGRAPH.

echelon / **esh**-uh-lon / *n.* **1** a wedge-shaped formation of troops, aircraft, etc. **2** a level of rank or authority (*the upper echelons of the Public Service*).

echidna / uh-**kid**-nuh / *n.* any of several egg-laying pouch-bearing Australian mammals with a covering of spines and a long snout and long claws. Also called *spiny anteater*.

echinacea / ek-uh-**nay**-shuh / *n.* a plant of the daisy family, used in herbal medicine, largely for its antibiotic and wound-healing properties.

echinoderm / uh-**kuy**-nuh-derm, **ek**-uh- / *n.* an animal of the group that includes starfish and sea urchins.

echo *n.* (*pl.* **echoes**) **1** repetition of sound by the reflection of sound waves; a secondary sound produced in this way. **2** a reflected radio or radar beam. **3** a close imitation or imitator. • *v.* (**echoed**, **echoing**) **1** repeat (sound) by echo, resound. **2** repeat or imitate. ◻ **echo sounder** *n.* a sounding apparatus for finding the depth of the sea beneath a ship by measuring the time taken for an echo to be received.

echoic / e-**koh**-ik / *adj.* (of a word) imitating the sound it represents, onomatopoeic (e.g. *boom*).

éclair / ay-**klair**, uh- / *n.* a finger-shaped iced cake of choux pastry with cream filling.

eclampsia / uh-**klamp**-see-uh / *n.* a kind of epileptic convulsion affecting women in pregnancy or childbirth.

éclat / ay-**klah** / *n.* **1** brilliant display (*she played the concerto with éclat*). **2** social distinction, conspicuous success; universal acclaim (*was received with great éclat*). (¶ French)

eclectic / e-**klek**-tik / *adj.* choosing or accepting ideas, beliefs, etc. from various sources. • *n.* an eclectic person or philosopher. ◻ **eclectically** *adv.* **eclecticism** *n.*

eclipse *n.* **1** the blocking of light from one heavenly body by another. **2** a loss of brilliance, power, or reputation. • *v.* **1** cause an eclipse of. **2** outshine, throw into obscurity.

ecliptic / uh-**klip**-tik, ee- / *n.* the sun's apparent path among stars during the year.

eclogue / **ek**-log / *n.* a short usu. pastoral poem.

eco- *comb. form* relating to ecology and environmental issues.

E. coli / ee **koh**-luy / *n.* a bacterium commonly found in the intestines of humans and other animals, where it usually causes no harm. Some strains can cause severe food poisoning.

ecology / ee-**kol**-uh-jee / *n.* **1** the scientific study of living things in relation to each other and to their environment. **2** this relationship. ◻ **ecological** / ee-kuh-**loj**-i-kuhl / *adj.* **ecologically** *adv.* **ecologist** *n.*

econocrat *n.* a person who believes that a nation's economy must take first place in government planning and override even the immediate welfare of its citizens.

economic / ee-kuh-**nom**-ik, ek-uh- / *adj.* **1** of economics (*the government's economic policies*). **2** sufficient to give a good return for the money or effort laid out (*an economic rent*). • *n.* (**economics**) **1** (treated as *sing.*) the science concerned with the production and consumption or use of goods and services. **2** (treated as *pl.*) the financial aspects of something (*the economics of farming*).

economical / ee-kuh-**nom**-i-kuhl, ek-uh- / *adj.* thrifty, avoiding waste. ◻ **economically** *adv.*

economic rationalism *n. Aust.* a government's free-market approach to economic management typically reflected in the adoption of privatisation, deregulation, user pays, and low government spending as indicators of economic success. ◻ **economic rationalist** *n.*

economise *v.* (also **-ize**) be economical, use or spend less than before.

economist / uh-**kon**-uh-muhst / *n.* an expert in economics.

economy *n.* **1** being economical (*practise economy*). **2** an instance of this, a saving (*make economies*). **3** a community's system of wealth creation (*a capitalist economy*). **4** (**the economy**) the state of a country's prosperity (*this could have a disastrous effect on the economy*). ◻ **economy class** the cheapest class of air travel. **economy class syndrome** = DEEP VEIN THROMBOSIS.

ecorat / **ek**-oh-rat / *n. Aust.* an economic rationalist.

ecosphere *n.* a region of space including planets where conditions are such that living things can exist.

ecosystem *n.* a biological community of interacting organisms and their environment.

ecotourism *n.* a form of tourism which uses but does not exploit ecologically sensitive areas.

ecru / **ay**-kroo, e-**kroo** / *n.* a very light fawn colour.

ecstasy *n.* **1** a feeling of intense delight. **2** *colloq.* a drug used as a stimulant and hallucinogen. ☐ **ecstatic** *adj.* **ecstatically** *adv.*

ECT *abbr.* = ELECTROCONVULSIVE THERAPY.

ectopic / ek-**top**-ik / *adj.* in an abnormal place. ☐ **ectopic pregnancy** a pregnancy in which the fertilised egg develops outside the womb.

ectoplasm / **ek**-toh-plaz-uhm, **ek**-tuh- / *n.* **1** the outer portion of the matter of an animal or vegetable cell. **2** a substance supposed to be exuded from a spiritualist medium during a trance.

Ecuador / **ek**-wuh-daw / a republic in South America, on the Pacific coast. ☐ **Ecuadorean** *adj.* & *n.*

ecumenical / ee-kyoo-**men**-uh-kuhl, ek-yoo / *adj.* **1** of or representing the whole Christian world. **2** seeking worldwide Christian unity (*the ecumenical movement*). ☐ **ecumenism** / ee-**kyoo**-muh-niz-uhm / *n.*

Ecumenical Council *n.* an assembly of the bishops of the world convened by the pope to consider questions of doctrine and practice, the conclusions of such a Council being binding upon the whole Church.

eczema / **ek**-suh-muh / *n.* a skin disease causing scaly itching patches.

edam / **ee**-dam, -duhm / *n.* a round originally Dutch cheese with a red rind.

Edda / **ed**-uh / a body of ancient Icelandic literature compiled in the 13th century, chief source of our knowledge of Scandinavian mythology.

eddy *n.* a swirling patch of water, air, fog, etc. •*v.* (**eddied**, **eddying**) swirl in eddies.

edelweiss / **ay**-duhl-vuys / *n.* a plant with white flowers, growing in the European Alps.

Eden *n.* (also **the Garden of Eden**) **1** in the biblical account of the creation, the place where Adam and Eve lived. **2** a place or state of great happiness and innocence.

edge *n.* **1** the sharpened side of a blade. **2** its sharpness (*the knife has lost its edge*). **3** the line where two surfaces meet at an angle. **4** a rim, the narrow surface of a thin or flat object (*the pages have gilt edges*). **5** the outer limit or boundary of an area. **6** the brink of a precipice. **7** effectiveness, incisiveness; excitement (*the argument had real edge to it*). **8** *Cricket* **a** a ball struck off the edge of the bat. **b** such a stroke. •*v.* **1** supply with a border; form the border of. **2** move gradually (*edging towards the door*). ☐ **be on edge** be tense and irritable. **have the edge on** *colloq.* have an advantage over. **set a person's teeth on edge** upset his or her nerves by causing an unpleasant sensation. **take the edge off** dull or soften (a feeling) (*seeing you devein those prawns has taken the edge off my appetite*).

edgeways *adv.* (also **edgewise**) with the edge forwards or outwards. ☐ **get a word in edgeways** contribute to a conversation during a pause by the dominant speaker.

edging *n.* something placed round an edge to define or strengthen or decorate it.

edgy *adj.* with nerves on edge, irritable. ☐ **edginess** *n.*

edible *adj.* fit to be eaten. ☐ **edibility** *n.*

edict / **ee**-dikt / *n.* an order proclaimed by an authority.

edifice / **ed**-uh-fuhs / *n.* a large or imposing building.

edify / **ed**-uh-fuy / *v.* (**edified**, **edifying**) be an uplifting moral or intellectual influence on (*an edifying discussion*). ☐ **edification** *n.*

Edison, Thomas (Alva) (1847–1931), American inventor, among whose most important inventions were the carbon microphone for telephones, the phonograph (precursor of the gramophone), and the carbon filament lamp.

edit *v.* (**edited**, **editing**) **1** act as editor of (a newspaper etc.). **2** prepare (written material) for publication. **3** prepare an edition of (an author's work). **4** reword in order to correct or to change the emphasis. **5** prepare (data) for processing by computer. **6** alter or add to (a text entered in a word processor). **7** prepare (a film or recording) by selecting individual sections and arranging them in sequence.

edition *n.* **1** the form in which something is published (*a pocket edition*). **2** the copies of a book or newspaper printed from one set of type. **3** the total number of a product (e.g. a commemorative medal) issued at one time (*a limited edition*). **4** an instance of a regular broadcast (*the Sunday edition*). **5** a person or thing similar to another (*she's a miniature edition of her mother*).

editor *n.* **1** a person who edits material for publication. **2** a person who is responsible for the content and writing of a newspaper or a broadcast news program or a particular section of one. **3** one who edits written material for publication. **4** one who edits cinema film or recording tape. **5** a computer program for entering and modifying textual data. ☐ **editorship** *n.*

editorial *adj.* of editing or an editor (*editorial work*). •*n.* a newspaper article giving the editor's comments on a current topic. ☐ **editorially** *adv.*

EDP *abbr.* electronic data processing.

.edu *abbr.* denoting an email address or a site on the Internet that is educational in nature (e.g. a university).

educable *adj.* able to be educated.

educate *v.* **1** train the mind and abilities of, provide education for. **2** train (a person, a physical faculty or organ, etc.), so as to develop some special aptitude, taste, etc. (*his ear needs educating; I'm educating myself to like cheese that smells of dirty socks*). ☐ **educator** *n.*

educated *adj.* **1** having had an (esp. good) education. **2** resulting from this (*an educated feel for Australian history*). **3** based on experience or study (*an educated guess*). **4** trained (to appreciate art, good food, etc.) (*an educated eye and ear; an educated palate*).

education *n.* systematic training and instruction designed to impart knowledge and develop skill. ☐ **educational** *adj.* **educationally** *adv.*

educationist *n.* (also **educationalist**) an expert in educational methods.

educative / **ed**-yuh-kuh-tiv / *adj.* informative or instructive.

Edward VIII (1894–1972), British king who reigned for eleven months in 1936 before being forced to abdicate because he intended to marry a divorced woman, the American commoner Mrs Wallis Simpson.

Edwardian / ed-**waw**-dee-uhn / *adj.* of the time of the British King Edward VII (1901–10). • *n.* a person living at this time.

EEC *abbr.* European Economic Community.

EEG *abbr.* ELECTROENCEPHALOGRAM or ELECTROENCEPHALOGRAPH.

eel *n.* a snake-like fish.

Eelam / **ee**-luhm / *n.* the proposed homeland of the Tamil people of Sri Lanka in the north and east of the country where there is a Tamil majority.

EEO *abbr.* Equal Employment Opportunity: Australian government policy that people should be employed, promoted, etc., on merit alone and without regard to factors such as sex, race, physical disability, etc. ☐ **EEO officer** a person employed or appointed to ensure the implementation etc. of EEO policy.

eerie *adj.* (**eerier**, **eeriest**) causing a feeling of mystery and fear (*eerie silence*). ☐ **eerily** *adv.* **eeriness** *n.*

efface *v.* rub out, obliterate. ☐ **effacement** *n.*

effect *n.* **1** a change produced by an action or cause, a result. **2** an impression produced on a spectator or hearer etc. (*special lighting gave the effect of moonlight*). **3** a state of being operative (*the law came into effect last week*). **4** a physical phenomenon (*Doppler effect; greenhouse effect*). **5** (**effects**) property (*personal effects*). **6** (**effects**) sounds and lighting etc. provided to accompany a play, a broadcast, or a film. • *v.* bring about, accomplish (*effect one's purpose; effect a cure*). ☐ **for effect** in order to impress people (*he only does it for effect*). **in effect** in fact, really (*it is, in effect, a refusal*). **take effect** produce its effect(s); become operative. **to that effect** with that implication (*words to that effect*). **with effect from** coming into operation at (a stated time).

■ **Usage** *Effect* should not be confused with *affect* which, as a verb, has more meanings and is more common, but which does not exist as a noun. *Effected the cure* means 'brought about the cure; cured', but *affected the cure* means 'had an effect on a cure' (which was already in place).

effective *adj.* **1 a** producing an effect, powerful in its effect. **b** efficient. **2** making a striking impression. **3** actual, existing (*the effective membership is higher than one would expect*). **4** operative (*the law is effective from 1 April*). ☐ **effectively** *adv.* **effectiveness** *n.*

effectual *adj.* answering its purpose, sufficient to produce the required effect. ☐ **effectually** *adv.*

effeminate / ee-**fem**-uh-nuht / *adj.* (of a man) unmasculine, having qualities associated with women. ☐ **effeminately** *adv.* **effeminacy** *n.*

effervesce / ef-uh-**ves** / *v.* **1** give off small bubbles of gas. **2** (of a person) be lively or energetic. ☐ **effervescent** *adj.* **effervescence** *n.*

effete / uh-**feet** / *adj.* feeble; having lost vitality. ☐ **effeteness** *n.*

efficacious / ef-uh-**kay**-shuhs / *adj.* producing the desired result. ☐ **efficacy** / **ef**-uh-kuh-see / *n.*

efficient / uh-**fish**-uhnt / *adj.* acting effectively, producing results with little waste of effort. ☐ **efficiently** *adv.* **efficiency** *n.*

effigy / **ef**-uh-jee / *n.* a sculpture or model of a person.

effloresce / ef-law-**res** / *v.* **1** burst into flower. **2** turn to fine powder when exposed to air; (of salts) come to the surface and crystallise. **3** (of a surface) become covered with such salt particles. ☐ **efflorescence** *n.* **efflorescent** *adj.*

effluence *n.* **1** a flowing out of light or electricity etc. **2** that which flows out.

effluent / **ef**-loo-uhnt / *adj.* flowing out. • *n.* **1** sewage or industrial waste discharged into a river etc. **2** a stream or lake flowing from a larger body of water.

effluvium / uh-**floo**-vee-uhm / *n.* (*pl.* **effluvia**) an unpleasant or harmful odour or outflow of a substance.

effort *n.* **1** the use of physical or mental energy to achieve something. **2** the energy exerted (*it was quite an effort to give up smoking*). **3** something produced by this (*this painting isn't bad for a first effort*).

effortless *adj.* done without effort. ☐ **effortlessly** *adv.* **effortlessness** *n.*

effrontery / uh-**frun**-tuh-ree / *n.* shameless insolence.

effulgent / uh-**ful**-juhnt, ee- / *adj. literary* radiant, bright. ☐ **effulgence** *n.*

effuse / uh-**fyooz**, ee- / *v.* pour forth; flow out.

effusion / ee-**fyoo**-zhuhn, uh- / *n.* **1** a pouring forth. **2** an unrestrained outpouring of thought or feeling.

effusive / uh-**fyoo**-siv, -ziv, ee- / *adj.* gushing; expressing emotions in an unrestrained way. ☐ **effusively** *adv.* **effusiveness** *n.*

EFL *abbr.* English as a foreign language.

EFT *abbr.* electronic funds transfer.

EFTPOS *abbr.* electronic funds transfer at point of sale.

e.g. *abbr.* for example. (¶ From the Latin *exempli gratia*.)

egalitarian / uh-gal-uh-**tair**-ree-uhn, ee- / *adj.* holding the principle of equal rights for all persons. • *n.* one who holds this principle. ☐ **egalitarianism** *n.*

egg *n.* **1** a reproductive cell produced by the female of mammals, birds, fish, reptiles, etc. **2** the hard-shelled egg of a domestic hen, used as food. ☐ **egg on** *v.* encourage to do something daring or foolish. ☐☐ **eggy** *adj.*

eggcup *n.* a cup for holding a boiled egg.

egghead *n. colloq.* an intellectual person; an expert.

eggplant *n.* (a plant bearing) a deep purple or white egg-shaped fruit used as a vegetable. Also called *aubergine*.

eggshell *n.* the shell of an egg. • *adj.* **1** (of china) very fragile. **2** (of paint) with a slightly glossy finish.

ego / **ee**-goh / *n.* (*pl.* **egos**) **1** the self; the part of the mind that reacts to reality and has a sense of individuality. **2** (in general use) self-esteem, conceit (*he has a swollen ego*). ☐ **ego trip** *n. colloq.* an activity devoted to boosting one's self-esteem or indulging one's feelings.

egocentric / ee-goh-**sen**-trik / *adj.* self-centred. ☐ **egocentricity** *n.*

egoism / **ee**-goh-iz-uhm / *n.* **1** self-interest as the moral basis of behaviour. **2** = EGOTISM. ☐ **egoist** *n.* **egoistic** *adj.* **egoistically** *adv.*

■ Usage The meanings of *egoism* and *egotism* overlap, but *egoism* alone is used as a term in philosophy and psychology to mean self-interest (often contrasted with *altruism*).

egotism / **ee**-guh-tiz-uhm / *n.* the practice of talking too much about oneself; conceit. ☐ **egotist** *n.* **egotistic** *adj.* **egotistical** *adj.* **egotistically** *adv.*

■ Usage See note at *egoism*.

egregious / uh-**gree**-juhs / *adj.* outstandingly bad (*egregious stupidity*).

egress / **ee**-gres / *n.* an exit.

egret / **ee**-gruht / *n.* a kind of heron with long white feathers, including several Australian species (*cattle egret; plumed egret*).

Egypt a republic in NE Africa. ☐ **Egyptian** *adj.* & *n.*

Egyptology *n.* the study of Egyptian antiquities. ☐ **Egyptologist** *n.*

eh / ay / *interj. colloq.* an exclamation of enquiry or surprise.

eider / **uy**-duh / *n.* a large duck of the Northern hemisphere.

eiderdown *n.* a quilt stuffed with down (originally from the eider) or some other soft material.

Eiffel Tower / **uy**-fuhl / a wrought-iron structure 300 metres tall that is a landmark in Paris, designed and built by the French engineer A.G. Eiffel for the exhibition of 1889.

eight *adj.* & *n.* **1** one more than seven (8, VIII). **2** an eight-oared rowing boat or its crew.

eight ball *n.* a black ball, numbered eight, in the US variety of pool. ☐ **behind the eight ball** at a disadvantage; 'snookered'.

eighteen *adj.* & *n.* **1** one more than seventeen (18, XVIII). **2** *Aust. Rules* a team (*the Geelong eighteen*). ☐ **eighteenth** *adj.* & *n.*

eightfold *adj.* & *adv.* **1** eight times as much or as many. **2** consisting of eight parts.

eighth *adj.* & *n.* **1** next after seventh. **2** one of eight equal parts of a thing. ☐ **eighthly** *adv.*

eighty *adj.* & *n.* **1** eight times ten (80, LXXX). **2** (**eighties**) the numbers from 80 to 89, esp. the years of a century or of a person's life. ☐ **eightieth** *adj.* & *n.*

Einstein / **uyn**-styn /, Albert (1879–1955), German-born theoretical physicist, founder of the theory of relativity.

einsteinium / uyn-**stuy**-nee-uhm / *n.* an artificially made radioactive metallic element (symbol Es).

Eire / **air**-ruh / a former name of the Republic of Ireland, still often used to distinguish the country from Northern Ireland.

EIS *abbr. see* ENVIRONMENTAL.

Eisenstein / **uy**-zuhn-styn /, Sergei Mikhailovich (1898–1948), Russian film director.

eisteddfod / uy-**sted**-fuhd / *n.* (*pl.* **eisteddfods** *or* **eisteddfodau** / uy-sted-**vod**-uy /) **1** a congress of Welsh poets and musicians. **2** any festival for musical competitions etc.

either / **uy**-ther, **ee**-ther / *adj.* & *pron.* **1** one or the other of two (*either of you can go*). **2** each of two (*there are houses on either side of the road*). • *adv.* & *conj.* **1** as one alternative (*he is either mad or drunk*). **2** likewise, any more than the other (*the new lid doesn't fit, either*). **3** moreover (*there is no time to lose, either*).

ejaculate / ee-**jak**-yuh-layt / *v.* **1** say suddenly and briefly. **2** eject semen during orgasm. ☐ **ejaculation** *n.* **ejaculatory** *adj.*

eject *v.* **1** thrust or send out forcefully (*the gun ejects the spent cartridges*). **2** expel, compel to leave. **3** exit from an aircraft using an ejector seat. **4** cause to be removed, drop out, or pop up automatically from a gun, cassette player, etc. ☐ **ejection** *n.*

ejector *n.* a device for ejecting. ☐ **ejector seat** a seat that can eject the occupant out of an aircraft in an emergency to descend by parachute.

eke / eek / *v.* (foll. by *out*) **1** supplement (*eke out the meat with lots of vegetables*). **2** make (a living) laboriously (*eke out a livelihood from the stony soil*).

elaborate *adj.* / uh-**lab**-uh-ruht / with many parts or details, complicated (*an elaborate* *pattern*). • *v.* / uh-**lab**-uh-rayt, ee- / work out or describe in detail. ☐ **elaborately** *adv.* **elaborateness** *n.* **elaboration** *n.*

El Alamein / **al**-uh-mayn / the site of the Allied victory of the North African campaign of 1940–43, 90 km west of Alexandria.

élan / ay-**lahn** / *n.* (also **elan**) vivacity. (¶ French)

eland / **ee**-luhnd / *n.* (*pl.* **eland** *or* **elands**) a large African antelope with spirally twisted horns.

elapse *v.* (of time) pass by.

elastic *adj.* **1** going back to its original length or shape after being stretched or squeezed. **2** adaptable, not rigid (*the rules are somewhat elastic*). • *n.* cord or material made elastic by interweaving strands of rubber etc. ☐ **elastically** *adv.* **elasticity** *n.*

elasticated *adj.* made elastic by being interwoven with elastic thread.

elate *v.* make intensely delighted or proud. ☐ **elated** *adj.* **elation** *n.*

Elba a small island off the west coast of Italy, famous as the place of Napoleon's first exile 1814–15.

elbow *n.* **1** the joint between the forearm and upper arm; its outer part. **2** a sharp bend in a pipe etc. • *v.* jostle or thrust with one's elbow. ☐ **elbow grease** *n.* vigorous polishing; hard work. **elbow room** *n.* enough room to work or move.

el cheapo *colloq. adj.* cheap, inferior (*buy an el cheapo watch and you get an el cheapo watch*). • *n.* a thing (a restaurant etc.) that is el cheapo (*a bit broke, so we ate out at an el cheapo*).

elder[1] *adj.* older (*elder sister*). • *n.* **1** an older person (*respect your elders*). **2** an official in certain Churches. **3** *Aust.* a person of recognised authority in an Aboriginal community.

elder[2] *n.* a tree of the Northern hemisphere with edible white flowers and dark edible berries.

elderberry *n.* the berry of the elder tree, used for making wine etc.

elderly *adj.* rather old; past middle age.

eldest *adj.* oldest, first-born (*eldest son*).

eldorado / el-duh-**rah**-doh / *n.* (*pl.* **eldorados**) a place of great wealth, abundance, or opportunity. (¶ From the name of a fictitious country or city rich in gold, once believed to exist on the River Amazon.)

eldritch *adj.* **1** weird. **2** hideous (*an eldritch shriek in the night*).

elect *v.* **1** choose by voting (*elect a treasurer*). **2** choose as a course, decide (*he elected to become a lawyer*). • *adj.* **1** chosen (*the elect few*). **2** (after the noun) chosen but not yet in office (*the president elect*).

election *n.* **1** choosing or being chosen by voting. **2** the process of electing representatives, esp. Members of Parliament.

electioneer *v.* take part in an election campaign. ☐ **electioneering** *n.*

elective *adj.* **1** chosen by or derived from election. **2** (of a body) having the power to elect. **3** (of a course of study) chosen by the student; optional. **4** (of a surgical operation etc.) optional; not urgently necessary (*the waiting list for elective surgery*). • *n.* an elective course of study at a school or university.

elector *n.* a person who has the right to vote in an election.

electoral *adj.* of electors.

electorate *n.* **1** the entire body of electors. **2** *Aust.* the area represented by one Member of Parliament.

Electra *Gk myth.* the daughter of Agamemnon and Clytemnestra. Agamemnon was murdered by Clytemnestra and her lover Aegisthus. Distraught at the death of her father and hating her mother, Electra succeeded in persuading her brother Orestes to murder Clytemnestra and Aegisthus. ☐ **Electra complex** *Psychol.* a daughter's subconscious sexual attraction to her father and hostility towards her mother, corresponding to the Oedipus complex in a son.

electric *adj.* **1** of or producing electricity. **2** worked by electricity. **3** causing sudden excitement (*the news had an electric effect*). ☐ **electric chair** a chair in which criminals are executed by electrocution. **electric eel 1** an eel-like fish able to give an electric shock. **2** a device for clearing drainage pipes of blockages. **electric eye** a photoelectric cell operating a relay when a beam of light is broken. **electric guitar** a solid-bodied guitar that is amplified electrically rather than acoustically. **electric shock** the effect of a sudden discharge of electricity through the body. **electric storm** a violent disturbance of the electrical condition of the atmosphere.

electrical *adj.* of or concerned with electricity (*electrical engineering*). ☐ **electrically** *adv.*

electrician / ee-lek-**trish**-uhn, el-, uh- / *n.* a person whose job is installing and maintaining electricity supplies and electrical equipment.

electricity *n.* **1** a form of energy produced by the flow of electrons in matter and causing it to accumulate a charge. **2** a supply of electric current for lighting, heating, etc. **3** excitement.

electrify *v.* (**electrified**, **electrifying**) **1** charge with electricity. **2** convert (a place) to the use of electric power. **3** startle or excite. ☐ **electrification** *n.*

electrocardiogram *n.* the pattern traced by an electrocardiograph.

electrocardiograph *n.* an instrument for detecting and recording the electric currents generated by heartbeats.

electroconvulsive therapy *n.* the treatment of mental illness by means of electric shocks that produce convulsions.

electrocute *v.* kill by electricity. ☐ **electrocution** *n.*

electrode / uh-**lek**-trohd, ee- / *n.* **1** a solid conductor through which electricity enters or leaves a vacuum tube etc. **2** a small electrical

electrodynamics conductor attached to a person's skin enabling pulse rate, heartbeat, etc. to be monitored on a machine.

electrodynamics *n*. the study of the interactions between electrical and mechanical forces.

electroencephalogram *n*. the pattern traced by an electroencephalograph.

electroencephalograph *n*. an instrument for detecting and recording the electric currents generated by activity of the brain.

electrolyse / uh-**lek**-truh-luyz / *v*. subject to or treat by electrolysis.

electrolysis / ee-lek-**trol**-uh-sis / *n*. **1** chemical decomposition by electric current. **2** the breaking up of tumours, hair roots, etc. by electric current. □ **electrolytic** / ee-lek-truh-**lit**-ik, uh- / *adj*.

electrolyte / uh-**lek**-truh-luyt, ee- / *n*. a solution that conducts electric current, esp. in an electric cell or battery.

electromagnet *n*. a soft metal core made into a magnet by passing an electric current through a coil wound round it.

electromagnetic *adj*. having both electrical and magnetic properties. □ **electromagnetically** *adv*.

electromagnetism *n*. **1** magnetic forces produced by electricity. **2** the study of these.

electrometer / ee-lek-**trom**-uh-tuh, el- / *n*. an instrument for measuring electrical potential without drawing any current from the circuit.

electromotive *adj*. producing electric current. □ **electromotive force** a force set up in an electric circuit by a difference in potential.

electron / ee-**lek**-tron, uh- / *n*. a negatively charged particle that occurs in all atoms and is the primary carrier of electricity. □ **electron microscope** a high-powered microscope that uses a beam of electrons instead of light.

electronic / ee-lek-**tron**-ik, el- / *adj*. **1** produced or worked by a flow of electrons. **2** of or concerned with electronics (*electronic engineering*). •*n*. (**electronics**) **1** (treated as *sing*.) the development and application of electronic devices, e.g. in transistors, computers, etc. **2** (treated as *pl*.) electronic circuits. □ **electronic funds transfer** a computerised bank system for the transfer of funds. **electronic mail** = EMAIL. **electronic publishing** publication of books in machine-readable form rather than on paper. **electronic tagging** the attaching of electronic markers to people or goods, enabling them to be tracked down. □□ **electronically** *adv*.

electronvolt *n*. a unit of energy, the amount of energy gained by an electron when accelerated through a potential difference of one volt.

electroplate *v*. coat with a thin layer of silver etc. by electrolysis. •*n*. objects plated in this way.

electro-shock *adj*. (of medical treatment) by means of electric shocks (*electro-shock therapy*).

electrostatics *n*. the study of static electricity.

electrotechnology *n*. the science of the application of electricity in technology.

electrotherapy *n*. the treatment of diseases by the use of electricity.

elegant *adj*. tasteful, refined, and dignified in appearance or style. □ **elegantly** *adv*. **elegance** *n*.

elegiac / el-uh-**juy**-ik / *adj*. used for elegies; mournful. □ **elegiacally** *adv*.

elegy / **el**-uh-jee / *n*. a sorrowful poem or song, esp. for the dead.

element *n*. **1** any of the parts that make up a whole. **2** any of the 100 or so substances that cannot be chemically separated into simpler substances. **3** any of the four basic substances (earth, water, air, and fire) in ancient and medieval philosophy. **4** the natural environment or habitat for a particular creature (*air is the element of the birds*). **5** a trace (*there's an element of truth in the story*). **6** the wire that gives out heat in an electric heater, cooker, etc. **7** (**the elements**) atmospheric forces, e.g. wind, rain (*exposed to the elements*). **8** (**elements**) the basic or elementary principles of a subject. **9** (**elements**) the bread and wine used in the Eucharist, each element being changed at the Consecration into the substance of the body and blood of Christ (or, in Protestant belief, a representation of that body and blood). □ **in one's element** absorbed in doing what one enjoys most.

elemental *adj*. **1** of or like the elements or the forces of nature; powerful. **2** basic, essential. •*n*. an entity or force which manifests itself in physical form (through magic etc.).

elementary *adj*. **1** dealing with the simplest facts of a subject; introductory (*elementary maths*). **2** simple (*it's elementary, my dear Watson!*). □ **elementary particle** any of the subatomic particles that are not known to be composed of simpler particles.

elephant *n*. the largest living land animal, with grey skin, a trunk, and ivory tusks.

elephantiasis / el-uh-fuhn-**tuy**-uh-suhs / *n*. a tropical disease in which parts of the body, esp. the limbs, become grossly enlarged.

elephantine / el-uh-**fan**-tuyn / *adj*. **1** of or like elephants. **2** very large or clumsy (*elephantine movements; elephantine humour*).

elevate *v*. **1** raise to a higher place or position, lift up. **2** raise to a higher moral or intellectual level.

elevation *n*. **1** elevating; being elevated. **2** the altitude of a place. **3** a piece of rising ground, a hill. **4** the angle that the direction of something (e.g. a gun) makes with the horizontal. **5** a drawing or diagram showing a structure or object as viewed from the side (cf. PLAN). **6** (**Elevation**) the raising up for adoration by the people of the Host and then the chalice immediately after Consecration in the Mass. **7** *Ballet* the capacity of a dancer to attain height in springing movements;

elevator | 257 | **El Salvador**

the action of tightening the muscles and uplifting the body.

elevator *n.* **1** something that hoists or raises things. **2** the movable part of a tailplane, used for changing an aircraft's altitude. **3** a lift.

eleven *adj. & n.* **1** one more than ten (11, XI). **2** a team of eleven players at cricket, soccer, etc.

eleventh *adj. & n.* **1** next after tenth. **2** one of eleven equal parts of a thing. ☐ **the eleventh hour** the latest possible moment.

elf *n.* (*pl.* **elves**) **1** a mythological magical being that is minuscule and mischievous. **2** (in recent fantasy literature) a human-sized being of great beauty, wisdom, etc., belonging to a magical non-human race. ☐ **elfish** *adj.* (also **elvish**). *See also* ELVEN.

elfin *adj.* like an elf (sense 1); small and delicate.

El Greco / **grek**-oh / (1541–1614), (= 'the Greek') Spanish painter of Greek origin (original name: Domenikos Theotokopoulos), noted for his use of elongated human forms and bright discordant colour.

elicit / uh-**lis**-uht / *v.* draw out (information, a response, etc.).

elide *v.* (**eliding**) omit (a vowel or syllable) in pronunciation.

eligible / el-uh-juh-buhl / *adj.* **1** qualified to be chosen for a position or allowed a privilege etc. (*he is eligible for a pension*). **2** regarded as suitable or desirable, esp. for marriage. ☐ **eligibility** *n.*

eliminate / uh-**lim**-uh-nayt, ee- / *v.* **1** get rid of; remove (*eliminate errors; he must be eliminated*). **2** exclude from a further stage of a competition etc. through defeat (*was eliminated in the fourth round*). **3** discharge (waste matter from the body); excrete. ☐ **elimination** *n.* **eliminator** *n.*

Eliot[1], George (pseudonym of Mary Ann Evans) (1819–80), English novelist.

Eliot[2], T(homas) S(tearns) (1888–1965), Anglo-American poet, critic, and dramatist.

elision / uh-**lizh**-uhn / *n.* omission of part of a word in pronouncing it (e.g. *I'm* = I am).

elite / ay-**leet**, uh-, ee- / (also **élite**) *n.* the best of a group; a select group or class. •*adj.* **1** of or belonging to the elite (*an elite athlete*). **2** exclusive (*an elite club*).

elitist *n.* one who advocates selecting and treating certain people as an elite. •*adj.* advocating the selection and treatment of certain people as an elite. ☐ **elitism** *n.*

elixir / uh-**lik**-suh / *n.* **1** a fragrant liquid used as a medicine. **2** an alchemist's preparation believed to cure all ills or (**elixir of life**) to prolong life indefinitely.

Elizabeth I (1533–1603), queen of England and Ireland 1558–1603.

Elizabeth II (1926–), queen of the UK from 1952; head of state of Australia.

Elizabethan *adj.* of the time of Elizabeth I's reign (1558–1603). •*n.* a person living at this time.

Elizabeth Farm the oldest surviving European building in Australia, built in 1793 by John Macarthur at Parramatta, NSW, and named after his wife.

elk *n.* a large deer of northern Europe and Asia.

elkhorn *n.* a large epiphytic fern of Qld and NSW, forming often enormous clumps on trees and rocks, and having large lobed fronds resembling the horns of an elk.

Elkins, Margreta (Anne Enid) (1930–), AM, Australian operatic mezzo-soprano.

ell *n. archaic* a measure of length, = 114 cm (45 inches).

Ella Brothers three Aboriginal brothers who have represented Australia in Rugby Union: Mark Gordon (1959–), AM, captain of the Australian team 1982–84; Glen Joseph (1959–); Gary Albert (1960–).

Ellington, Duke (full name: Edward Kennedy Ellington) (1899–1974), American composer, pianist, and jazz band-leader

Elliott, Herb(ert James) (1938–), Australian athlete, called the greatest mile runner in history. He won the gold medal in the 1500 metres at the 1960 Olympics.

ellipse / uh-**lips**, ee- / *n.* a regular oval that can be divided into four identical quarters.

ellipsis / uh-**lip**-suhs, ee- / *n.* (*pl.* **ellipses** / uh-**lip**-seez /) **1** the omission of words needed to complete a meaning or a grammatical construction. **2** a set of three dots etc. indicating omission.

elliptical / uh-**lip**-ti-kuhl, ee- / *adj.* **1** of or shaped like an ellipse. **2** containing an ellipsis, having omissions. **3** (of speech, style, etc.) condensed (to the point of producing ambiguity or obscuring meaning). ☐ **elliptically** *adv.*

elm *n.* a deciduous tree (of Europe etc.) with rough serrated leaves.

Elms, Lauris (Margaret) (1931–), AM, Australian mezzo-soprano in opera and on the concert stage.

El Niño / el **nin**-yoh / *n.* an irregular warming of the southern Pacific Ocean surface that causes unusually dry to severe drought conditions in Australia. (¶ A shortening of Spanish *El Niño de Navidad* 'the Christmas Child'.)

elocution / el-uh-**kyoo**-shuhn / *n.* a person's style of speaking; the art of speaking expressively. ☐ **elocutionary** *adj.* **elocutionist** *n.*

elongate / **ee**-long-gayt / *v.* lengthen, prolong. ☐ **elongation** *n.*

elope / ee-**lohp**, uh- / *v.* run away secretly with a lover, esp. in order to get married. ☐ **elopement** *n.*

eloquence / **el**-uh-kwuhns / *n.* the fluent and effective use of language.

eloquent / **el**-uh-kwuhnt / *adj.* **1** using language fluently and effectively. **2** expressive. ☐ **eloquently** *adv.*

El Salvador / el **sal**-vuh-daw / a republic in Central America, on the Pacific coast.

else *adv.* **1** besides, other (*someone else*). **2** otherwise, if not (*run or else you'll be late*).
elsewhere *adv.* somewhere else.
elucidate / uh-**loo**-suh-dayt, ee- / *v.* throw light on (a problem); make clear. ☐ **elucidation** *n.* **elucidatory** *adj.*
elude / uh-**lood**, ee- / *v.* **1** escape skilfully from, avoid (*eluded his pursuers*). **2** baffle (a person or memory etc.) (*the answer eludes me*). ☐ **elusion** *n.*
elusive / uh-**loo**-siv, ee- / *adj.* **1** difficult to find or catch. **2** difficult to remember. ☐ **elusiveness** *n.*
elven *adj.* of an elf, concerning an elf (sense 2). (*See* ELF.)
elver *n.* a young eel.
elves *see* ELF.
Elysium / uh-**liz**-ee-uhm, ee- / **1** *Gk myth.* the place where certain favoured heroes, exempted from death, were taken by the gods; the abode of the blessed after death. **2** a place of ideal happiness. ☐ **Elysian** *adj.*
em *n.* (in printing) a unit of measurement equal to the width of an M.
'em *pron. colloq.* = THEM.
emaciated / ee-**may**-see-ay-tuhd, uh- / *adj.* very thin from illness or starvation. ☐ **emaciation** *n.*
email *n.* (also **e-mail**) messages transmitted within and between networks of computer users and displayed on-screen.
emanate / **em**-uh-nayt / *v.* **1** issue or originate from a source (*pleasant smells emanated from the kitchen*). **2** cause to do this. ☐ **emanation** *n.*
emancipate / uh-**man**-suh-payt, ee- / *v.* **1** liberate, set free from slavery or some form of social or political restraint. **2** (usu. as **emancipated** *adj.*) free from the inhibitions of moral or social conventions. **3** *Aust. hist.* discharge as free (a convict who has received a pardon). ☐ **emancipator** *n.* **emancipatory** *adj.* **emancipist** *n.*
emancipation *n.* **1** emancipating. **2** *Aust. hist.* the act of setting free a convict who has received a pardon.
emasculate / ee-**mas**-kyuh-layt, uh- / *v.* **1** castrate. **2** deprive of force (*an emasculated law*). • *adj.* / ee-**mas**-kyuh-luht, uh- / **1** castrated; deprived of force. **2** effeminate. ☐ **emasculation** *n.*
embalm / em-**bahm** / *v.* preserve (a corpse) from decay. ☐ **embalmment** *n.*
embankment *n.* a long mound of earth or a stone structure to keep a river from spreading or to carry a road or railway.
embargo / em-**bah**-goh / *n.* (*pl.* **embargoes**) **1** an order forbidding ships to enter or leave a country's ports. **2** an official suspension of commerce or other activity. • *v.* (**embargoed**, **embargoing**) place under embargo.
embark *v.* **1** put or go on board a ship or aircraft at the start of a journey. **2** (usu. foll. by *on*) begin an undertaking (*they embarked on a program of expansion*). ☐ **embarkation** *n.*
embarrass *v.* make (a person) feel awkward or ashamed. ☐ **embarrassment** *n.*
embassy *n.* **1** an ambassador and his or her staff. **2** the official headquarters of an ambassador. **3** a deputation sent to a foreign government.
embattled *adj.* **1** prepared for battle (*embattled troops*). **2** fortified against attack. **3** under pressure or in trying circumstances.
embed *v.* (also **imbed**) (**embedded**, **embedding**) fix firmly in a surrounding mass.
embellish / em-**bel**-ish / *v.* **1** ornament. **2** improve (a story etc.) by adding details that are entertaining but invented. ☐ **embellishment** *n.*
ember *n.* (usu. in *pl.*) a small piece of live coal or wood in a dying fire.
Ember days *n.pl.* any of the days traditionally reserved for fasting and prayer in the Christian Church.
embezzle *v.* take fraudulently for one's own use (money or property placed in one's care). ☐ **embezzlement** *n.* **embezzler** *n.*
embitter *v.* arouse bitter feelings in. ☐ **embitterment** *n.*
emblazon / em-**blay**-zuhn / *v.* ornament with heraldic or other devices.
emblem *n.* a symbol; a device that represents something.
emblematic / em-bluh-**mat**-ik / *adj.* serving as an emblem, symbolic.
embody *v.* (**embodied**, **embodying**) **1** express (principles or ideas) in a visible form (*the house embodied her idea of a home*). **2** incorporate, include (*parts of the old treaty are embodied in the new one*). ☐ **embodiment** *n.*
embolden *v.* make bold, encourage.
embolism / em-buh-liz-uhm / *n.* obstruction of an artery or vein by a clot of blood, air bubble, etc.
embolus / **em**-buh-luhs / *n.* (*pl.* **emboli**) a thing causing an embolism.
emboss *v.* decorate with a raised design. ☐ **embossment** *n.*
embrace *v.* **1** hold closely and affectionately in one's arms; (of two people) do this to each other. **2** accept eagerly (*embraced the opportunity*). **3** adopt (a religion etc.) (*embraced Buddhism*). **4** include (*this new plan embraces several features of the previous one*). • *n.* the act of embracing, a hug.
embrasure / em-**bray**-zhuh / *n.* **1** an opening in a wall for a door or window, with splayed sides. **2** a similar opening for a gun, widening towards the outside.
embrocation *n.* a liquid for rubbing on the body to relieve aches or bruises.
embroider *v.* **1** ornament with needlework. **2** embellish (a story) with fictitious additions.
embroidery *n.* **1** embroidering. **2** embroidered material.
embroil *v.* involve in an argument or quarrel etc. ☐ **embroilment** *n.*

embryo / **em**-bree-oh / n. (pl. **embryos**) **1** an animal in the early stage of its development, before birth or emergence from an egg (used of a child in the first eight weeks of its development in the womb). **2** a rudimentary plant contained in a seed. **3** something in its very early stages. ☐ **in embryo** existing but undeveloped.

embryology / em-bree-**ol**-uh-jee / n. the study of embryos.

embryonic / em-bree-**on**-ik / adj. existing in embryo.

emend / ee-**mend**, uh- / v. alter (something written) in order to remove errors. ☐ **emendation** / ee-men-**day**-shuhn / n.

■ **Usage** See note at *amend*.

emerald n. **1** a bright green precious stone. **2** its colour. ☐ **the Emerald Isle** *poetic* Ireland.

emerge / ee-**merj**, uh- / v. **1** come up or out into view. **2** (of facts or ideas) be revealed by investigation, become obvious. ☐ **emergence** n. **emergent** adj.

emergency n. **1** a serious happening or situation needing prompt action. **2** a condition needing immediate treatment; a patient with this. **3** *Aust.* **a** *Sport* a reserve player. **b** *Horse racing* a reserve runner.

emeritus / ee-**me**-ruh-tuhs, uh- / adj. retired but retaining one's title as an honour (*emeritus professor*).

Emerson, Roy (Stanley) (1936–), Australian tennis player and Wimbledon champion (1964–65).

emery / **em**-uh-ree / n. a coarse abrasive used for polishing metal or wood etc. ☐ **emery board** a small stiff strip of wood or cardboard coated with emery, used for filing the nails.

emetic / uh-**met**-ik / n. medicine used to cause vomiting. • adj. that causes vomiting.

emf abbr. (also **EMF**) electromotive force.

emigrant n. a person who emigrates.

emigrate v. leave one country and go to settle in another. ☐ **emigration** n.

émigré / **em**-uh-gray / n. an emigrant, esp. a political exile.

Emily's List 1 *US* an organisation (established in 1985) which identifies talented Democratic women and supports their election with funding, campaign advice, etc. **2** *Aust.* a similar organisation for Australian Labor women, established in 1996. (¶ Acronym from 'Early money is like yeast' i.e. it makes the 'dough' rise.)

eminence / **em**-uh-nuhns / n. **1** the state of being famous or distinguished (*a surgeon of great eminence*). **2** a piece of rising ground. **3** (**Eminence**) the title used in addressing or referring to a cardinal (*Your Eminence; His Eminence Edward Cardinal Clancy*).

éminence grise / ay-muh-nons **greez** / n. (pl. **éminences grises** pronounced the same) a person who exercises power or influence without holding office. (¶ French, = grey cardinal (originally used of Cardinal Richelieu's secretary in the 17th century).)

eminent / **em**-uh-nuhnt / adj. **1** famous, distinguished. **2** conspicuous, outstanding (*a man of eminent goodness*). ☐ **eminently** adv.

emir / e-**meer**, uh- / n. (also **amir**) the title of various Muslim rulers.

emirate / **em**-uh-ruht / n. the territory of an emir.

emissary / **em**-uh-suh-ree / n. a person sent on a special (usu. diplomatic) mission.

emission n. **1** emitting. **2** a thing emitted. **3** a discharge of fluid from the body, esp. semen (*nocturnal emissions*). ☐ **emission control** the control (by government regulation) of the release of air-borne pollutants from cars, factories, incinerators, etc.

emit / ee-**mit**, uh- / v. (**emitted**, **emitting**) **1** send out (light, heat, fumes, a smell, lava, etc.); discharge. **2** utter (*she emitted a shriek*). ☐ **emissive** adj. **emitter** n.

emmental / **em**-uhn-tahl / n. (also **emmenthal**) a hard Swiss cheese with holes in it.

emollient / ee-**mol**-ee-uhnt, uh-, ee-**moh**-lee-uhnt / adj. softening or soothing the skin, feelings, etc. • n. an emollient substance for the skin.

emolument / ee-**mol**-yuh-muhnt, uh- / n. a fee received, a salary.

emote / ee-**moht**, uh- / v. act or say with a show of emotion.

emoticon / uh-**moh**-tuh-kon / n. a representation of a facial expression (such as a smile or a frown), made with standard keyboard characters, and used to convey the writer's feelings in electronic messages etc.

emotion n. **1** a strong instinctive feeling, e.g. love or fear. **2** emotional intensity (*spoke with emotion*).

emotional adj. **1** of the emotions. **2** especially liable to emotion (*he's a very emotional man*). **3** expressing or based on emotion (*he became very emotional; an emotional appeal*). **4** arousing emotion (*a highly emotional issue*). ☐ **emotionally** adv. **emotionalism** n.

■ **Usage** See note at *emotive*.

emotive / ee-**moh**-tiv, uh- / adj. **1** arousing emotion. **2** of or characterised by emotion. **3** (of language etc.) arousing feeling; not purely descriptive or neutral.

■ **Usage** Although the meanings of *emotive* and *emotional* overlap, *emotive* is more common in the sense 'arousing emotion', as in *an emotive issue*, and is not used at all in sense 2 of *emotional*.

empanel / em-**pan**-uhl / v. (also **impanel**) (**empanelled**, **empanelling**) list or select for service on a jury.

empathise / **em**-puh-thuyz / v. (also **-ize**) feel empathy (*I can empathise with you*).

empathy / **em**-puh-thee / n. the ability to identify oneself mentally with a person or thing and so understand his or her feelings or its meaning. ☐ **empathetic** adj. **empathic** / em-**path**-ik / adj.

emperor n. **1** the male ruler of an empire. **2** any of several tropical Australian fish. ☐ **emperor gum moth** a large moth of eastern Australia, having a conspicuous spot on each wing, the large larvae of the moth feeding mainly on eucalypts. **emperor penguin** an Antarctic penguin of the largest known species.

emphasis / **em**-fuh-suhs / n. (pl. **emphases** / **em**-fuh-seez /) **1** special importance given to something; prominence (*the emphasis is on quality*). **2** vigour of expression, feeling, or action (*nodded his head with emphasis*). **3** the extra force used in speaking a particular syllable or word to make the meaning clear or to show importance; the extra force placed on a sound in music.

emphasise / **em**-fuh-suyz / v. (also **-ize**) lay emphasis on; stress.

emphatic / em-**fat**-ik / adj. using or showing emphasis, expressing oneself with emphasis. ☐ **emphatically** adv.

emphysema / em-fuh-**see**-muh / n. **1** a condition (brought on by smoking etc.) in which the air sacs in the lungs become enlarged, causing breathlessness. **2** a swelling caused by the presence of air in the connective tissues of the body.

empire n. **1** a group of countries ruled by a single supreme authority. **2** supreme power. **3** a large commercial organisation controlled by one person or group. ☐ **empire building** n. the process of deliberately acquiring extra territory or authority etc.

empirical / em-**pi**-ri-kuhl / adj. (also **empiric**) (of knowledge) based on observation, experience, or experiment, not on theory. ☐ **empirically** adv.

empiricism / em-**pi**-ruh-siz-uhm / n. **1** the use of empirical methods. **2** the theory that sensory experience is the only source of knowledge. ☐ **empiricist** n.

emplacement n. a place or platform for a gun or battery of guns.

employ v. **1** give work to, use the services of (a person) in return for payment. **2** make use of (*how do you employ your spare time?*). **3** keep (a person) occupied. ☐ **in the employ of** employed by.

employable adj. able to be employed or worth employing.

employee / em-ploi-**ee**, em-**ploi**-ee / n. a person who works for another in return for wages.

employer n. a person or firm that employs people.

employment n. **1** employing. **2** the state of being employed. **3** work done as an occupation or to earn a livelihood (*what's your employment?*).

emporium / em-**paw**-ree-uhm / n. (pl. **emporia** or **emporiums**) **1** a centre of commerce. **2** a large retail store selling a wide variety of goods.

empower v. give power or authority to (*police are empowered to arrest people*).

empress n. **1** the female ruler of an empire. **2** the wife or widow of an emperor.

empty adj. **1** containing nothing. **2** (of a house etc.) without occupants or furnishings. **3** unoccupied (*rows of empty seats; empty streets*). **4** ineffective or insincere (*empty threats; empty promises*). **5** without purpose or value (*an empty existence*). **6** lacking good sense or intelligence (*an empty head*). **7** colloq. hungry (*I feel rather empty*). • v. (**emptied, emptying**) **1** make or become empty. **2** transfer (the contents of one thing) into another. **3** (of a river) discharge itself (into the sea etc.). • n.pl. (**empties**) emptied boxes, bottles, etc. ☐ **empty-handed** adj. bringing or taking away nothing. ☐☐ **emptily** adv. **emptiness** n.

empyrean / em-puy-**ree**-uhn / n. **1** the highest heaven, as the sphere of fire in ancient cosmology or the abode of God in early Christianity. **2** the visible heavens. • adj. of the empyrean. ☐ **empyreal** adj.

emu / **ee**-myoo / n. **1** a large Australian flightless bird up to 2 metres tall, having exposed blue skin on the neck and long grey-brown feathers on the back, and capable of running at high speed. **2** *Aust. colloq.* a person who collects discarded betting tickets at racecourses etc. in the hope of finding a winning ticket. ☐ **emu apple 1 a** a small tree of central Australia. Also called *colane, sour plum*. **b** its edible apple-like fruit with bitter red flesh, so called because it is eaten by emus. **2** any of several other similar Australian plants. **emu-bob** v. *Aust.* **1** pick up pieces of timber, roots, etc., after clearing or burning. **2** collect litter. **emu-bobber** *Aust.* a person who emu-bobs. **emu bush** *Aust.* **1** any of many shrubs of the mainland Australian genus *Eremophila*, some species of which bear fruits eaten by the emu. **2** = PITURI. **emu parade** *Aust.* an assembly (esp. of soldiers) for the purpose of picking up litter etc. **emu wren** any of several long-tailed birds of southern Australia (*mallee emu wren; southern emu wren*) or of central Australia (*rufous-crowned emu wren*), so called because its long tail feathers resemble the feathers of an emu.

emulate / **em**-yoo-layt, em-**yuh**-layt / v. try to do as well as or better than; imitate. ☐ **emulation** n. **emulative** adj. **emulator** n.

emulous / **em**-yuh-luhs / adj. **1** imitating in an eager or jealous way. **2** motivated by rivalry.

emulsifier n. **1** any substance that stabilises an emulsion, esp. a food additive used to stabilise processed foods. **2** an apparatus for producing an emulsion.

emulsify v. (**emulsified, emulsifying**) convert or be converted into an emulsion.

emulsion / ee-**mul**-shuhn / *n.* **1** a creamy liquid in which particles of oil or fat are evenly distributed. **2** a medicine or paint in this form. **3** the light-sensitive coating on photographic film.

en *n. Printing* a unit of measurement equal to half an em.

enable *v.* **1** give (a person) the means or authority to do something. **2** make possible. **3** (esp. *Computing*) make (a device) operational; switch on.

enact *v.* **1** decree, make into a law. **2** perform, act (a play etc.). ☐ **enactive** *adj.*

enactment *n.* a law enacted.

enamel *n.* **1** a glass-like substance used for coating metal or pottery. **2** paint that dries hard and glossy. **3** the hard outer covering of teeth. **4** a painting done in enamel. • *v.* (**enamelled, enamelling**) coat or decorate with enamel. ☐ **enamel orchid** either of two WA terrestrial orchids having highly shining or glazed enamel-like flowers, purple or rose-pink.

enamoured / e-**nam**-uhd / *adj.* (also **enamored**) (usu. foll. by *of*) feeling great fondness or love (*he was enamoured of the sound of his own voice*).

en bloc / on **blok** / *adv.* in a block, all at the same time. (¶ French)

encamp *v.* settle in a (esp. military) camp.

encampment *n.* a camp.

encapsulate *v.* **1** enclose in or as if in a capsule. **2** summarise. ☐ **encapsulation** *n.*

encase *v.* enclose in or as if in a case. ☐ **encasement** *n.*

encephalitis / en-sef-uh-**luy**-tuhs, en-kef- / *n.* inflammation of the brain.

encephalogram / en-**sef**-uh-luh-gram, en-**kef**- / *n.* an electroencephalogram.

encephalograph / en-**sef**-uh-luh-grahf, en-**kef**-, -graf / *n.* an electroencephalograph.

enchant *v.* **1** put under a magic spell. **2** fill with intense delight. ☐ **enchantment** *n.*

enchanter *n.* a man who enchants; a wizard.

enchantress *n.* a woman who enchants, esp. sexually; a sorceress.

enchilada / en-chi-**lah**-duh / *n.* a tortilla with chilli sauce and usu. containing a filling, esp. meat.

encircle *v.* surround. ☐ **encirclement** *n.*

enclave / **en**-klayv, **on**- / *n.* **1** a small territory belonging to one nation but lying wholly within the boundaries of another. **2** a group of people who are culturally, intellectually, or socially distinct from those surrounding them.

enclitic / en-**klit**-ik / *adj.* (of a word) pronounced with so little emphasis that it forms part of the preceding word. • *n.* such a word, e.g. *not* in *cannot*.

enclose *v.* **1** put a wall or fence etc. round; shut in on all sides. **2** shut up in a receptacle; put into an envelope along with a letter or into a parcel along with the contents.

enclosed *adj.* (of a religious community) living in isolation from the outside world (*an enclosed Order of nuns*).

enclosure *n.* **1** enclosing. **2** an enclosed area, esp. for a special class of persons at a sporting event. **3** something enclosed with a letter etc.

encode *v.* put into code; put (data) into a coded form for processing by computer. ☐ **encoder** *n.*

encomium / en-**koh**-mee-uhm / *n.* (*pl.* **encomiums**) high praise given in a speech or writing.

encompass *v.* **1** surround, encircle (*I am encompassed by idiots*). **2** contain, include (*this book encompasses all aspects of the subject*).

encore / **ong**-kaw / *interj.* an audience's call for repetition of a performance or for a further item. • *n.* **1** this call. **2** the item performed in response to it. • *v.* call for such a repetition of (an item); call back (a performer) for this.

encounter *v.* **1** meet, esp. by chance or unexpectedly. **2** find oneself faced with (*encounter difficulties*). **3** meet in battle. • *n.* **1** a sudden or unexpected meeting. **2** a battle.

encourage *v.* **1** give hope or confidence to. **2** urge (*encouraged him to try*). **3** stimulate, help to develop (*competitiveness will help to encourage exports*). ☐ **encouragement** *n.*

encroach *v.* **1** intrude on someone's territory, rights, or time. **2** advance beyond the original or proper limits (*the sea encroached gradually upon the land*). ☐ **encroachment** *n.*

encrust *v.* **1** cover with a crust of hard material. **2** ornament with a layer of jewels etc. (*encrusted with pearls*). ☐ **encrustation** *n.*

encumber *v.* be a burden to, hamper.

encumbrance *n.* a burden or hindrance.

encyclical / en-**sik**-li-kuhl / *adj.* for wide circulation. • *n.* a formal epistle from the pope to all the bishops of the Catholic Church.

encyclopedia *n.* (also **-paedia**) a book or set of books giving information on all branches of knowledge or on many aspects of one subject, usu. arranged alphabetically.

encyclopedic *adj.* (also **-paedic**) (of knowledge or information) comprehensive.

end *n.* **1** the extreme limit of something (*end of the road; to the ends of the earth*). **2** the part or surface forming an extremity (*a plank with a nail at one end*). **3** (**the end**) *colloq.* the limit of what one can endure. **4** either half of a sports pitch or court, defended or occupied by one side or player. **5** the finish or conclusion of something; the latter or final part (*no end to his misery; towards the end of his reign*). **6** destruction, downfall, death. **7** a purpose or aim (*to gain his own ends*). **8** result, outcome (*what was the end of your discussions?*). **9** the part with which a person is concerned (*no problem at my end*). • *v.* **1** bring to an end, put an end to. **2** come to an end. ☐ **end on** with the end facing one or adjoining the end of the next object.

end product the final product of a manufacturing process. **end up** reach a specified place or state eventually. **keep one's end up** do one's part in spite of difficulties. **make ends meet** keep one's expenditure within one's income. **on end 1** upright (*his hair stood on end*). **2** continuously (*for three weeks on end*).

endanger *v.* cause danger to. □ **endangered species** a species in danger of extinction.

endear *v.* cause to be loved (*endeared himself to everyone he met*).

endearing *adj.* inspiring affection.

endearment *n.* **1** a word or words expressing love. **2** liking, affection.

Endeavour[1] the name of the ship captained by James Cook when he discovered the eastern coast of Australia in April 1770.

Endeavour[2] a river in north-east Qld rising about 35 km west of Cooktown and flowing into the Pacific. It was named after James Cook's ship *Endeavour*.

endeavour / en-**dev**-uh / (also **endeavor**) *v.* attempt, try earnestly. • *n.* an earnest attempt.

endemic / en-**dem**-ik / *adj.* commonly found in a particular country, district, or group of people (*the disease is endemic in Africa*). • *n.* an endemic disease or plant. □ **endemically** *adv.*

Enderby Land a part of Antarctica, claimed by Australia.

ending *n.* the final part.

endive / en-duyv / *n.* a curly-leaved plant used in salads.

endless *adj.* **1** infinite, without end. **2** continual (*endless complaints*). **3** interminable (*an endless sermon*). **4** *colloq.* numerous (*endless demands on my time*).

endmost *adj.* nearest the end.

endocrine / **en**-doh-kruyn / *adj.* (of a gland) secreting straight into the blood, not through a duct.

endogamy / en-**dog**-uh-mee / *n.* **1** *Anthropology* marrying within the same tribe. **2** *Botany* pollination from the same plant.

endogenous / en-**doj**-uh-nuhs / *adj.* originating from within.

endometrium / en-doh-**mee**-tree-uhm / *n.* membrane lining the womb.

endorphin / en-**daw**-fuhn / *n.* any of a group of peptide neurotransmitters occurring naturally in the brain and having pain-relieving properties.

endorse *v.* **1** sign or add a comment on (a document); sign the back of (a cheque) in order to obtain the money indicated. **2** make an official entry on (a driver's licence) about a motoring offence by the holder. **3** confirm (a statement); declare one's approval of. **4** *Aust.* select as a candidate for an election (*the endorsed candidate for Wills*). □ **endorsement** *n.*

endoscope / **en**-doh-skohp / *n.* an instrument for viewing the internal parts of the body when inserted, e.g. through the anus into the rectum and beyond.

endow *v.* **1** provide with a permanent income (*endow a school*). **2** provide with a power, ability, or quality (*was endowed with great talents*).

endowment *n.* **1** endowing. **2** an endowed income. **3** a natural ability.

endpaper *n.* a strong leaf of paper fixed across the beginning or end of a book and the inside of the cover.

endue *v. formal* (also **indue**) provide with a talent or quality etc. (*endued with herculean strength*).

endurable *adj.* able to be endured.

endurance *n.* ability to withstand pain or hardship or prolonged use or strain.

endure *v.* **1** experience (pain or hardship), bear patiently. **2** tolerate (*I can't endure him*). **3** remain in existence, last (*your luck will not endure for ever*).

endways *adv.* (also **endwise**) **1** with its end foremost. **2** end to end.

enema / **en**-uh-muh / *n.* **1** the insertion of liquid into the rectum through the anus by means of a syringe, esp. to flush out its contents. **2** this liquid or syringe.

enemy *n.* **1** a person who is actively hostile towards another. **2** a member of a hostile army or nation etc. **3** (**the enemy**) an opposing military force, ship, aircraft, etc., or a group or organisation considered to be hostile. **4** an opponent of something (*enemy of progress*). • *adj.* of or belonging to the enemy.

energetic *adj.* full of energy, done with energy. □ **energetically** *adv.*

energise / en-uh-juyz / *v.* (also **-ize**) **1** give energy to. **2** cause electricity to flow to.

energy *n.* **1** the capacity for vigorous activity. **2** force or vigour of expression (*I admire the energy of his style*). **3** the ability of matter or radiation to do work because of its motion, its mass, or its electric charge. **4** fuel and other resources used for the operation of machinery etc. (*the country's energy requirements*).

enervate / **en**-uh-vayt / *v.* deprive of vigour or vitality (*an enervating climate; an enervated style of writing*). □ **enervation** *n.*

enfant terrible / on-fon tuh-**ree**-bluh / *n.* (*pl.* **enfants terribles** pronounced the same) a person whose behaviour is embarrassing, indiscreet, or irresponsible. (¶ French, = terrible child.)

enfeeble *v.* make feeble. □ **enfeeblement** *n.*

enfilade / en-fuh-**layd** / *n.* gunfire directed along a line from end to end. • *v.* rake with gunfire.

enfold *v.* **1** wrap up. **2** clasp (*enfolded him in his arms*).

enforce *v.* compel obedience to; impose by force or compulsion (*the law was firmly enforced*). □ **enforcement** *n.* **enforcer** *n.*

enforceable *adj.* able to be enforced.

enforcer *n.* **1** a person, organisation, etc., that enforces something. **2** *colloq.* a person who imposes his will on others by violence and intimi-

enfranchise

dation, esp. as a member of a criminal gang. **3** *Sport* a person with a reputation for aggressive physical play, strong-arm tactics, etc.

enfranchise *v.* **1** give (a person) the right to vote in elections. **2** free (a slave etc.). ☐ **enfranchisement** *n.*

engage *v.* **1** take (a person) into one's employment. **2** arrange beforehand to occupy (a seat etc.). **3** promise, pledge (*he engaged to get the matter attended to*). **4** occupy the attention of (*engaged her in conversation*). **5** occupy oneself (*he engages in politics*). **6** begin a battle against (*engaged the enemy troops*). **7** interlock (parts of a gear) so that it transmits power; become interlocked in this way.

engaged *adj.* **1** having promised to marry (*an engaged couple*). **2 a** occupied or reserved by a person. **b** occupied with business etc. (*I'm afraid the manager is engaged*). **3** (of a telephone line) already in use.

engagement *n.* **1** engaging something; being engaged. **2** an appointment made with another person. **3** a promise to marry a specified person. **4** a battle.

engaging *adj.* attractive, charming.

Engels / **en**-guhlz /, Friedrich (1820–95), German socialist, founder with Karl Marx of modern Communism.

engender / en-**jen**-duh / *v.* give rise to (*he engendered much hostility in his audience*).

engine *n.* **1** a mechanical device consisting of several parts working together, esp. as a source of power. **2** the engine of a railway train.

engineer *n.* **1** a person who is skilled in a branch of engineering. **2** one who is in charge of machines and engines, e.g. on a ship. **3** a person who designs and constructs military works, esp. a soldier so trained. **4** one who contrives or brings about something (*he's the engineer of all our woes*). • *v.* **1** construct or control as an engineer. **2** contrive or bring about (*he engineered a meeting between them*).

engineering *n.* the application of scientific knowledge to the design, building, and use of machines (**mechanical engineering**), roads and bridges (**civil engineering**), or electrical equipment (**electrical engineering**).

England the country forming the southern part of Great Britain.

English *adj.* of England or its people or language. • *n.* **1 a** the language of England, now used in many varieties in the British Isles. **b** (*pl.* **Englishes**) a variety of this, as used in the United States, most Commonwealth or ex-Commonwealth countries, and often internationally (*Australian English; world Englishes*). **2** (**the English**) English people.

engorged *adj.* **1** crammed full. **2** congested with blood (*the penis when engorged becomes erect*).

engraft *v.* **1** insert (a shoot) as a graft. **2** implant. **3** incorporate.

263

enormity

engrave *v.* **1** cut or carve (a design) into a hard surface; ornament with a design in this way. **2** fix deeply in the mind or memory. ☐ **engraver** *n.*

engraving *n.* a print made from an engraved plate.

engross / en-**grohs** / *v.* **1** occupy fully by absorbing the attention (*the problem engrossed him for hours*). **2** write out (a document etc.) in larger letters or in legal form. ☐ **engrossment** *n.*

engulf *v.* **1** surround or cause to disappear by flowing round or over, swamp. **2** overwhelm.

enhance *v.* increase the attractiveness or other qualities of; improve. ☐ **enhancement** *n.*

enigma / uh-**nig**-muh / *n.* a puzzling thing or person; a riddle or paradox.

enigmatic / en-ig-**mat**-ik / *adj.* mysterious or puzzling. ☐ **enigmatically** *adv.*

enjoin *v.* **1** order, command (*I enjoin you to keep the peace*). **2** (often foll. by *on*) impose (an action or conduct) (*enjoined on them the need for secrecy*). **3** prohibit (from doing something) by an official injunction.

enjoy *v.* **1** get pleasure from. **2** have as an advantage or benefit (*to enjoy good health*). ☐ **enjoyment** *n.*

enjoyable *adj.* giving enjoyment, pleasant. ☐ **enjoyably** *adv.*

enkephalin / en-**kef**-uh-luhn / *n.* either of two morphine-like substances found in the brain and thought to be concerned with the control of pain.

enkindle *v.* cause to flare up, arouse.

enlarge *v.* **1** make or become larger. **2** reproduce (a photograph) on a larger scale. **3** say more about something (*enlarge upon this matter*). ☐ **enlargement** *n.*

enlighten *v.* give knowledge to, inform. ☐ **enlightenment** *n.*

enlightened *adj.* freed from ignorance or prejudice, progressive (*in these enlightened days*).

Enlightenment, the an 18th-century philosophy of reason and individualism.

enlist *v.* **1** take into or join the armed forces (*enlist as a soldier*). **2** secure as a means of help or support (*enlisted their sympathy*). ☐ **enlistment** *n.*

enliven *v.* make more lively. ☐ **enlivenment** *n.*

en masse / on **mas** / *adv.* all together. (¶ French)

enmesh *v.* entangle in or as if in a net.

enmity *n.* hostility between opposing people, groups, nations, etc.

ennoble *v.* **1** make (a person or thing) noble or more dignified (*her courage has ennobled her*). **2** make (a person) a noble. ☐ **ennoblement** *n.*

ennui / **on**-wee, on-**wee** / *n.* boredom. (¶ French)

enormity / ee-**naw**-muh-tee, uh- / *n.* **1** great wickedness (*the enormity of this crime*). **2** a serious crime or error. **3** enormous size, magnitude (*the enormity of their task*).

■ **Usage** Many people regard the use in sense 3 as unacceptable.

enormous *adj.* very large, huge. ☐ **enormously** *adv.* **enormousness** *n.*

enough *adj.* & *n.* as much or as many as necessary. •*adv.* **1** to the required degree (*are you warm enough?*). **2** fairly (*she sings well enough*). **3** quite (*you know well enough what I mean*).

en passant / on pa-**son** / *adv.* in passing; by the way (e.g. to mention something *en passant*). (¶ French)

enquire *v.* ask. ☐ **enquiry** *n.*

■ Usage Although these words are often used in exactly the same way as *inquire* and *inquiry*, there is a tendency to use *enquire* as a formal word for 'ask' and *inquire* to refer to an investigation, esp. an official one.

enrage *v.* make furious.

enrapture *v.* fill with intense delight.

enrich *v.* **1** make richer. **2** improve the quality of by adding things (*this food is enriched with vitamins; Australian English has been enriched with borrowings from Aboriginal languages*). **3** increase the content of an isotope in (material), esp. enrich uranium with isotope U-235. ☐ **enrichment** *n.*

enrobe *v.* put a robe on.

enrol *v.* (**enrolled**, **enrolling**) **1** enlist; write the name of (a person) on a list. **2** become a member of a society, institution, etc.; admit as a member. **3** register oneself, esp. for a course of study. ☐ **enrolment** *n.*

en route / on **root** / *adv.* on the way (*met him en route from Rome to Rio*). (¶ French)

ensconce / en-**skons** / *v.* establish or settle comfortably (*ensconced himself in his favourite armchair*).

ensemble / on-**som**-buhl / *n.* **1** a thing viewed as a whole. **2** a group of musicians who perform together; a passage of music for such a group. **3** a group of actors, dancers, etc. working together. **4** a set of clothes worn together.

enshrine *v.* **1** enclose in a shrine. **2** serve as a shrine for. **3** preserve and cherish, as at a shrine (*the memory of Elvis, enshrined at Graceland*).

enshroud *v. literary* **1** cover with or as with a shroud. **2** cover completely, hide from view (*fog has enshrouded the valley*).

ensign / **en**-suyn, -suhn / *n.* **1** a military or naval flag; a special form of the national flag flown by ships. **2** *hist.* a standard-bearer.

ensilage / **en**-suh-lij / *n.* silage.

enslave *v.* make a slave of. ☐ **enslavement** *n.*

ensnare *v.* catch in or as if in a snare.

ensorcell / en-**saw**-suhl / *v.* (also **-el**) use sorcery or magic on. ☐ **ensorcellment** *n.*

ensue / en-**syoo** / *v.* **1** happen afterwards (*what ensued?*). **2** happen as a result (*a brawl ensued from his drunken taunts*).

en suite / **on** sweet / *n.* esp. *Aust.* a bathroom and toilet attached to a bedroom. (¶ French)

ensure *v.* **1** make certain, secure (*I have taken steps to ensure his silence*). **2** make safe (against harm, risks, etc.).

ENT *abbr.* ear, nose, and throat.

entablature / en-**tab**-luh-chuh / *n. Archit.* the section including the architrave, frieze, and cornice of a building or structure, above the supporting columns.

entail / en-**tayl** / *v.* **1** make necessary, involve (*these plans entail great expense*). **2** *Law* leave (land) to a line of heirs so that none of them can give it away or sell it. •*n.* the entailing of landed property; the property itself.

entangle *v.* **1** tangle. **2** entwine in something that it is difficult to escape from. **3** involve in something complicated. ☐ **entanglement** *n.*

Entebbe / en-**teb**-bee / the former capital of Uganda: the airport was the scene of a raid by Israeli commandos in 1976 to rescue the passengers on a hijacked plane.

entente / on-**tont** / *n.* (also **entente cordiale** / kaw-**dyahl** /) a friendly understanding between countries.

enter *v.* **1** go or come in or into. **2** come on stage (also as a direction: *enter Macbeth*). **3** penetrate (*the bullet entered his lung*). **4** become a member of (a society or profession) (*he entered a Dominican monastery*). **5** put (a name, details, etc.) on a list or in a book. **6** register as a competitor (*entered for the long jump*). **7** record formally, present for consideration (*entered a plea of not guilty; entered a protest*). ☐ **enter into 1** take part in (a conversation, an agreement, etc.). **2** form part of (calculations, plans, etc.). **enter on 1** begin (a process, a stage of work, etc.). **2** take possession of (an inheritance, an appointment, etc.).

enteric / en-**te**-rik / *adj.* of the intestines.

enteritis / en-tuh-**ruy**-tuhs / *n.* inflammation of the intestines.

enterprise *n.* **1** an undertaking, esp. a bold or difficult one. **2** initiative. **3** a business firm; business activity (*private enterprise*). ☐ **enterprise bargaining** *Aust.* negotiations on wages and conditions conducted between the employer and the employees of a particular enterprise, any agreement reached being confined to that enterprise, with no flow-on to other enterprises.

enterprising *adj.* full of initiative.

entertain *v.* **1** amuse, occupy agreeably. **2** receive (a person) with hospitality (*they entertained me to lunch; they entertain a great deal*). **3** have in the mind (*entertain doubts*). **4** consider favourably (*refused to entertain the idea*).

entertainer *n.* one who performs in entertainments, esp. as an occupation.

entertainment *n.* **1** entertaining; being entertained. **2** amusement. **3** something performed before an audience to amuse or interest them.

enthral / en-**thrawl** / v. (**enthralled, enthralling**) captivate, please greatly. ◻ **enthralment** n.

enthrone v. place (a king, bishop, etc.) on a throne, esp. ceremonially. ◻ **enthronement** n.

enthuse / en-**thooz**, -**thyooz** / v. **1** show enthusiasm. **2** fill with enthusiasm.

enthusiasm n. **1** a feeling of eager liking for or interest in something. **2** the object of this (*one of my enthusiasms*).

enthusiast n. a person who is full of enthusiasm for something (*a sports enthusiast*).

enthusiastic adj. full of enthusiasm. ◻ **enthusiastically** adv.

entice v. attract, lure, or persuade by offering something pleasant. ◻ **enticement** n.

entire adj. whole, complete. ◻ **entirely** adv.

entirety / en-**tuyuh**-ruh-tee / n. completeness, the total. ◻ **in its entirety** in its complete form.

entitle v. **1** give a title to (a book etc.) (*the book is entitled 'Understanding Shakespeare' by E.F.C. Ludowyk*). **2** give a right (*the ticket entitles you to a seat*). ◻ **entitlement** n.

entity / **en**-tuh-tee / n. a thing with distinct existence (as opposed to a quality etc.); a thing's existence in itself.

entomb / en-**toom** / v. place in (or as if in) a tomb. ◻ **entombment** n.

entomology / en-tuh-**mol**-uh-jee / n. the study of insects. ◻ **entomological** / en-tuh-muh-**loj**-i-kuhl / adj. **entomologist** n.

entourage / on-toor-**rahzh** / n. the people accompanying an important person.

entr'acte / on-trakt / n. **1** an interval between the acts of a play. **2** a dance or music etc. performed then.

entrails / **en**-traylz / n.pl. **1** bowels, intestines. **2** the innermost parts of a thing (*went down into the entrails of the earth*).

entrance[1] / **en**-truhns / n. **1** entering. **2** a door or passage by which one enters. **3** the coming of an actor on stage. **4** the right of admission; the fee charged for this.

entrance[2] / en-**trahns**, -**trans** / v. **1** fill with intense delight. **2** put into a trance. ◻ **entrancement** n.

entrant n. a person who enters (an examination, a profession, a competition, etc.).

entrap v. (**entrapped, entrapping**) **1** catch in or as if in a trap. **2** trick, beguile. ◻ **entrapment** n.

entreat v. request earnestly or emotionally. ◻ **entreaty** n.

entrecôte / **on**-truh-koht / n. boned steak cut off the sirloin.

entrée / **on**-tray / n. **1** the right or privilege of admission. **2** a dish served before the main course of a meal.

entrench / en-**trench** / v. **1** establish firmly in a well-defended position or in a job, office, etc. **2** surround with a trench for defence.

entrenched adj. (of attitudes, ideas, etc.) firmly established and not easily modified.

entrenchment n. **1** entrenching; being entrenched. **2** a trench made for defence.

entrepreneur / on-truh-pruh-**ner** / n. **1** a person who organises and manages a commercial undertaking, esp. one involving commercial risk. **2** a contractor acting as intermediary. **3** a person who organises entertainments, esp. musical shows. ◻ **entrepreneurial** adj.

entropy / **en**-truh-pee / n. *Physics* a measure of disorder indicating the amount of energy that, rather than being concentrated, has become more evenly distributed and so cannot be used to do work (within a particular system, or in the universe as a whole).

entrust v. give as a responsibility; place (a person or thing) in a person's care.

entry n. **1** entering. **2** a place of entrance; a door, gate, etc. **3** the coming of an actor on stage. **4** a ceremonial entrance (*made a grand entry*). **5** liberty to go or come in (*he has entry to my home any time he pleases*). **6** an item entered in a list, diary, etc. **7** a person or thing entered in a race or competition. **8** the number of entrants in a competition.

entwine v. twine round, interweave.

enumerate / uh-**nyoo**-muh-rayt, ee- / v. count, mention (items) one by one. ◻ **enumeration** n. **enumerator** n. **enumerative** adj.

enunciate / uh-**nun**-see-ayt, ee- / v. **1** pronounce (words) clearly. **2** express (a proposition or theory) in definite terms. **3** proclaim. ◻ **enunciation** n.

enuresis / en-yoo-**ree**-suhs / n. involuntary passing of urine; bedwetting.

envelop / en-**vel**-uhp / v. (**enveloped, enveloping**) wrap up; cover on all sides (*the hill was enveloped in mist*). ◻ **envelopment** n.

envelope / **en**-vuh-lohp, **on**- / n. **1** a wrapper or covering, esp. a folded paper container for a letter. **2** the gas container of a balloon or airship. ◻ **push the envelope** (*or* **the edge of the envelope**) *colloq.* approach or extend the limits of what is possible.

envenom v. **1** put poison on or into; make poisonous (*the arrows were envenomed*). **2** infuse venom or bitterness into (feelings, words, or actions) (*an envenomed reply*).

enviable / **en**-vee-uh-buhl / adj. desirable enough to arouse envy. ◻ **enviably** adv.

envious adj. full of envy. ◻ **enviously** adv.

environment n. **1** physical surroundings and conditions, esp. those affecting people's lives (*an urban environment; the home environment*). **2** (**the environment**) the external conditions affecting the growth, development, and well-being of plants, animals, and humans (*a threat to the environment*). **3** *Computing* the overall structure within which a user, computer, or program operates. ◻ **environment-unfriendly** *see* UNFRIENDLY.

environmental *adj.* **1** of an environment or environments. **2** concerned with the conservation of the natural environment; not harmful to the environment, environmentally friendly. ❑ **environmental impact study** research undertaken to assess whether any proposed new development etc. will damage the ecological balance of a particular environment. The results of this research are published in an **environmental impact statement** *or* **EIS**.

environmentalism *n.* concern with, or support for, the conservation of the natural environment; green politics.

environmentalist *n.* a person who is committed to the study and conservation of the natural environment.

environmentally *adv.* as regards the conservation of the natural environment. ❑ **environmentally aware** (of a person or group) informed about contemporary concerns for the environment; sensitive to the effect upon the environment of a product, activity, etc. **environmentally friendly** (also **environmentally sound**) (of a product etc.) causing little harm to the natural environment, ecologically sound. **environmentally sensitive** (of a geographical area) recognised as containing a habitat for rare species, or some other natural feature, which needs to be protected from damage or destruction.

environs / en-**vuy**-ruhnz / *n.pl.* the surrounding districts, esp. round a town.

envisage / en-**viz**-ij / *v.* **1** visualise, imagine (a thing not yet existing). **2** foresee (*changes are envisaged*).

envoy / **en**-voi / *n.* **1** a messenger or representative. **2** (in full **envoy extraordinary**) a diplomatic agent ranking below an ambassador.

envy *n.* **1** a feeling of discontent aroused by someone else's possession of things one would like to have oneself. **2** the object of this (*his car is the envy of the neighbourhood*). • *v.* (**envied**, **envying**) feel envy of (a person, their circumstances) (*I envy you your good luck*).

Enzed *n. Aust. colloq.* **1** New Zealand. **2** a New Zealander. ❑ **Enzedder** a New Zealander.

enzyme / **en**-zuym / *n.* **1** a protein formed in living cells and assisting chemical processes (e.g. in digestion). **2** a similar substance produced synthetically for use in chemical processes, household detergents, etc.

Eocene / **ee**-oh-seen / *adj.* of the second epoch of the Tertiary period of geological time, about 55 million years ago, with evidence of an abundance of mammals including horses, bats, and whales. • *n.* this epoch.

eolithic / ee-uh-**lith**-ik / *adj.* of the period preceding the palaeolithic age, thought to include the earliest use by man of flint tools.

eon alternative spelling of AEON.

Eora / ay-**or**-ruh / *n.* (also **Iora**) **1** a member of an Aboriginal people of what is now the Sydney region of NSW; this people. **2** the language of the Eora.

EPA *abbr.* Environment Protection Agency.

epacris / uh-**pak**-ruhs / *n.* any shrub of the south-eastern Australian genus *Epacris*, including the common heath, the floral emblem of Victoria.

epaulette / **ep**-uh-luht, ep-uh-**let** / *n.* an ornamental shoulder piece on a jacket, shirt, etc., esp. on a uniform.

épée / **ay**-pay, **ep**-ay / *n.* a sharp-pointed sword used (with the end blunted) in fencing.

ephedrine / **ef**-uh-dreen, -druyn / *n.* an alkaloid drug used to relieve asthma, hay fever, etc.

ephemera / ee-**fem**-uh-ruh / *n.pl.* things of only short-lived usefulness.

ephemeral / ee-**fem**-uh-ruhl / *adj.* lasting only a very short time.

ephod / **ee**-fod / *n.* a Jewish priestly vestment.

epic *n.* **1** a long poem or other literary work telling of great events or heroic deeds. **2** a book or film resembling this. **3** a subject fit to be told in an epic. • *adj.* of or like an epic, on a grand scale.

epicene / **ep**-ee-seen / *adj.* **1** of or for both sexes. **2** having the characteristics of both sexes or of neither sex. **3** effete, effeminate. • *n.* an epicene person.

epicentre *n.* **1** the point at which an earthquake reaches the earth's surface. **2** the central point of a difficulty.

epicure / **ep**-ee-kyoor, **ep**-uh- / *n.* a person with refined tastes, esp. in food and drink. ❑ **epicurism** *n.*

Epicurean / ep-ee-kyoo-**ree**-uhn, ep-uh- / *adj.* **1** of the Greek philosopher Epicurus (*c.*300 BC), who sought freedom from anxiety and disturbance. **2** (**epicurean**) devoted to sensuous pleasure and luxury. • *n.* **1** a follower or student of Epicurus. **2** (**epicurean**) an epicurean person.

Epidaurus / ep-ee-**daw**-ruhs / an ancient Greek city and port on the NE coast of the Peloponnese, site of a temple dedicated to Asclepius and a well-preserved Greek theatre dating from the 4th century BC.

epidemic *n.* **1** an outbreak of a disease etc. spreading rapidly through a community. **2** a spate of something usu. regarded as undesirable (*an epidemic of burglaries in Tuggeranong*).

epidemiology / ep-uh-dee-mee-**ol**-uh-jee / *n.* the branch of medicine concerned with the control of epidemics.

epidermis / ep-ee-**der**-muhs, ep-uh- / *n.* the outer layer of the skin. ❑ **epidermal** *adj.*

epidiascope / ep-ee-**duy**-uh-skohp / *n.* a projector giving images of both opaque and transparent objects.

epidural / ep-ee-**dyoo**-ruhl / *adj.* (of an anaesthetic) injected round the nerves of the spinal cord and having the effect of anaesthetising

epiglottis the lower part of the body. • *n.* an epidural injection, used esp. in childbirth.

epiglottis / ep-ee-**glot**-uhs / *n.* the cartilage at the root of the tongue, that descends to cover the windpipe in swallowing.

epigram *n.* a short witty saying. □ **epigrammatic** *adj.*

epigraph *n.* an inscription on a statue, a quotation at the beginning of a book or chapter, etc.

epilepsy *n.* a disorder of the nervous system causing convulsions, sometimes with loss of consciousness.

epileptic *n.* a person with epilepsy. • *adj.* of epilepsy.

epilogue / **ep**-ee-log, **ep**-uh- / *n.* a short concluding section in a literary work.

epiphany / uh-**pif**-uh-nee / *n.* **1** any manifestation of a god or demigod. **2** (**Epiphany**) the Christian festival commemorating the showing of Christ to the Magi, celebrated on 6 January.

epiphyte / **ep**-ee-fuyt, **ep**-uh- / *n.* a plant growing on (but not parasitic on) another, e.g. a moss, various Australian orchids growing on trees. □ **epiphytic** / ep-ee-**fit**-ik / *adj.*

episcopacy / uh-**pis**-kuh-puh-see / *n.* **1** government of a Church by bishops. **2** (**the episcopacy**) bishops.

episcopal / uh-**pis**-kuh-puhl / *adj.* of a bishop or bishops; governed by bishops.

episcopalian / uh-pis-kuh-**pay**-lee-uhn / *adj.* of or advocating the government of a Church by bishops.

episcopate / uh-**pis**-kuh-puht / *n.* **1** the office or tenure of a bishop. **2** (**the episcopate**) bishops collectively.

episiotomy / e-pee-zee-**ot**-uh-mee, uh- / *n.* a cut made at the opening of the vagina during childbirth, to aid delivery of the baby.

episode *n.* **1** an incident or event forming one part of a sequence. **2** an incident in a story; one part of a serial.

episodic / ep-uh-**sod**-ik / *adj.* **1** occurring irregularly. **2** consisting of episodes. □ **episodically** *adv.*

epistemology / uh-pis-tuh-**mol**-uh-jee / *n.* the philosophy of knowledge, esp. with regard to its methods and validation. □ **epistemological** / uh-pis-tuh-muh-**loj**-i-kuhl / *adj.*

epistle / uh-**pis**-uhl / *n.* **1** *humorous* a letter. **2** (**Epistle**) any of the books in the New Testament written as Letters by the Apostles. **3** a poem etc. in the form of a letter.

epistolary / uh-**pis**-tuh-luh-ree / *adj.* of letters; in the form of a letter.

epitaph / **ep**-uh-tahf, -taf / *n.* words inscribed on a tomb or describing a dead person.

epithalamium / ep-uh-thuh-**lay**-mee-uhm / *n.* (*pl.* **epithalamiums** *or* **epithalamia** / -mee-uh /) a song or poem celebrating a marriage. (¶ Greek, = at the bridal chamber.)

epithelium / ep-ee-**thee**-lee-uhm / *n.* (*pl.* **epithelia** *or* **epitheliums**) the tissue forming the outer layer of the body or of an open cavity. □ **epithelial** *adj.*

epithet / **ep**-uh-thet / *n.* **1** a descriptive word or phrase added to a name, e.g. 'the Great' in *Alfred the Great*. **2** a descriptive word, esp. abusive (*she hurled some choice epithets at him*).

epitome / uh-**pit**-uh-mee / *n.* **1** a person or thing embodying perfectly a stated quality or idea (*she is the epitome of common sense*). **2** a thing that shows well on a small scale the qualities of something much larger (*the Elves in his fantasy novel are an epitome of the human race*).

epitomise / uh-**pit**-uh-muyz / *v.* (also **-ize**) be an epitome of; typify.

EPNS *abbr.* electroplated nickel silver.

EPO *abbr.* erythropoietin, esp. when isolated as a drug for medical use or as an illegal performance enhancer for athletes.

epoch / **ee**-pok / *n.* **1** a particular period of history. **2** a division of a geological period. □ **epoch-making** *adj.* very important or remarkable. □ □ **epochal** / **ep**-uh-kuhl / *adj.*

eponym / **ep**-uh-nim / *n.* **1** a word, place name, etc. derived from a person's name (e.g. *Tasmania* from Abel *Tasman*). **2** a person's name that is used in this way. □ **eponymous** / uh-**pon**-uh-muhs / *adj.*

epoxy / ee-**pok**-see / *adj.* related to or derived from a compound with one oxygen atom and two carbon atoms bonded in a triangle. □ **epoxy resin** a synthetic thermosetting resin.

epsilon / **ep**-si-lon / *n.* the fifth letter of the Greek alphabet (Ε, ε).

Epsom salts *n.pl.* magnesium sulphate, used as a purgative and to green the leaves of plants.

equable / **ek**-wuh-buhl / *adj.* **1** moderate or unvarying (*an equable climate*). **2** (of a person) not easily disturbed or angered. □ **equably** *adv.*

equal *adj.* **1** the same in size, amount, value, etc. **2** evenly balanced (*an equal contest*). **3** having the same rights or status. • *n.* a person or thing that is equal to another. • *v.* (**equalled**, **equalling**) **1** be equal to. **2** produce or achieve something to match (*no one has equalled this score*). □ **be equal to** have enough strength, courage, or ability etc. for (*she was equal to the task*). □ □ **equally** *adv.*

Equal Employment Opportunity *see* EEO.

equalise *v.* (also **-ize**) **1** make or become equal. **2** (in games) equal an opponent's score. □ **equalisation** *n.*

equaliser *n.* (also **-izer**) an equalising goal etc.

equality *n.* being equal.

equanimity / ek-wuh-**nim**-uh-tee, ee-kwuh- / *n.* calmness of mind or temper.

equate / ee-**kwayt**, uh- / *v.* consider to be equal or equivalent. □ **equatable** *adj.*

equation / ee-**kway**-zhuhn, uh- / *n*. **1** a mathematical statement that two expressions (connected by the sign =) are equal. **2** a formula indicating a chemical reaction by the use of symbols. **3** making equal.

equator / ee-**kway**-tuh / *n*. an imaginary line round the earth at an equal distance from the North and South Poles.

equatorial / ek-wuh-**taw**-ree-uhl / *adj*. of or near the equator.

Equatorial Guinea a republic on the west coast of Africa.

equestrian / uh-**kwes**-tree-uhn / *adj*. of or relating to horses and horse riding.

equiangular *adj*. having equal angles.

equidistant / ee-kwee-**dis**-tuhnt, ek-wee- / *adj*. at an equal distance.

equilateral / ee-kwuh-**lat**-uh-ruhl / *adj*. having all sides equal.

equilibrium / ee-kwuh-**lib**-ree-uhm, ek- / *n*. (*pl*. **equilibria** *or* **equilibriums**) **1** a state of physical balance. **2** a state of mental or emotional stability.

equine / **ee**-kwuyn, **ek**-wuyn / *adj*. of or like a horse.

equinoctial / ee-kwuh-**nok**-shuhl, ek-wuh- / *adj*. occurring at an equinox. • *n*. (in full **equinoctial line**) = CELESTIAL EQUATOR.

equinox / **ee**-kwuh-noks, **ek**-wuh- / *n*. the time (twice each year) when day and night are of equal length (about 20 March and 22 September).

equip *v*. (**equipped**, **equipping**) supply with what is needed.

equipment *n*. **1** the outfit, tools, and other things needed for a particular job or expedition etc. **2** equipping.

equipoise / **ek**-wuh-poiz, **ee**-kwuh- / *n*. **1** equilibrium. **2** a counterbalance.

equitable / **ek**-wi-tuh-buhl / *adj*. **1** fair and just. **2** *Law* valid in equity as distinct from law. □ **equitably** *adv*.

equity / **ek**-wi-tee / *n*. **1** fairness, impartiality. **2** principles of justice used to correct or supplement the law. **3** *Law* a body of principles and rules developed in England since medieval times and followed in Australia in contrast to the principles and rules of the common law. **4** (**Equity**) the actors' trade union. **5** the value of the shares issued by a company. **6** (**equities**) stocks and shares not bearing fixed interest.

equivalent *adj*. equal in value, importance, meaning, etc. • *n*. an equivalent thing, amount, or word. □ **equivalence** *n*.

equivocal / ee-**kwiv**-uh-kuhl, uh- / *adj*. **1** able to be interpreted in two ways, ambiguous. **2** questionable, suspicious (*an equivocal character*). □ **equivocally** *adv*.

equivocate / ee-**kwiv**-uh-kayt, uh- / *v*. use ambiguous words in order to conceal the truth; avoid committing oneself. □ **equivocation** *n*.

ER *abbr*. Queen Elizabeth. (¶ Latin *Elizabetha Regina*.)

Er *symbol* erbium.

er *interj*. an expression of hesitation.

era / **eer**-ruh / *n*. **1** a distinct period of history (*the pre-Roman era*). **2** a division of geological time (*the mesozoic era*).

eradicable *adj*. able to be eradicated.

eradicate / ee-**rad**-uh-kayt, uh- / *v*. get rid of, remove all traces of. □ **eradication** *n*. **eradicator** *n*.

erase / ee-**rayz**, uh- / *v*. **1** rub or scrape out (marks, writing, etc.). **2** wipe out a recorded signal from (a magnetic tape or disk). **3** remove all traces of (*erased it from my memory*).

eraser *n*. a thing that erases, esp. a piece of rubber for rubbing out marks or writing.

erasure / ee-**ray**-zhuh, uh- / *n*. **1** erasing. **2** a word etc. that has been erased.

erbium / **er**-bee-uhm / *n*. a soft metallic element (symbol Er).

ere / air / *prep*. & *conj*. *poetic* before.

Erebus (in full **Mount Erebus**) a volcano on Ross Island in Antarctica.

erect *adj*. **1** standing on end, upright, vertical. **2** (of the penis, nipples, or clitoris) enlarged and rigid from sexual excitement. • *v*. set up, build. □ **erectly** *adv*. **erectness** *n*.

erectile / ee-**rek**-tuyl, uh- / *adj*. (of parts of the body) able to become enlarged and rigid from sexual excitement.

erection *n*. **1** erecting; being erected. **2** something erected, such as a building. **3** swelling and hardening (esp. of the penis) in sexual excitement.

erector *n*. **1** a person or thing that erects something. **2** a muscle causing erection.

eremophila / e-ruh-**mof**-uh-luh / *n*. a shrub or small tree of the large Australian genus *Eremophila*, bearing showy usu. tubular bell-flowers in cream, pink, purple, or red.

erg *n*. a unit of work or energy.

ergo *adv*. therefore. (¶ Latin)

ergonomics / er-guh-**nom**-iks / *n*. the study of work and its environment and conditions in order to achieve maximum efficiency. □ **ergonomic** *adj*. **ergonomically** *adv*.

ergot / **er**-guht / *n*. a fungus affecting rye and other cereals; a drug (such as ergotamine) prepared from this fungus.

Erin / **e**-rin, **eer**-rin / an ancient or poetic name for Ireland.

Eritrea / e-ruh-**tray**-uh / an independent state in NE Africa, on the Red Sea.

erl-king *n*. *Germanic myth*. a bearded, golden-crowned blond figure who entices children to play with him and then leads them to the land of death.

ermine *n*. **1** an animal of the weasel family, with brown fur that turns white in winter. **2** this white fur.

Ern Malley a non-existent Australian poet, invented in 1944 by the poets James McAuley and Harold Stewart who published a series of 'nonsense' modern poems supposed to be by Malley in order to see whether the experts would see through the hoax. These concocted pieces were taken seriously by many of the avant garde writers of the time, and aroused heated debate between modernists and conservatives.

erode / uh-**rohd**, ee- / *v.* wear away or destroy gradually (*wind and water have eroded the slope; his confidence was eroded by her laughter*). ☐ **erosion** / ee-**roh**-zhuhn, uh- / *n.* **erosive** *adj.*

erogenous / uh-**roj**-uh-nuhs, ee- / *adj.* **1** (of a part of the body) particularly sensitive to sexual stimulation. **2** giving rise to sexual desire or excitement. ☐ **erogenous zones** those parts of the body which provide sexual pleasure when stimulated by touch etc.

Eros / **eer**-ros / **1** *Gk myth.* the young god of sexual love. **2** (**eros**) (in Freudian psychology) the urge towards self-preservation and sexual pleasure.

erotic / uh-**rot**-ik, e-, ee- / *adj.* of sexual love; arousing sexual desire. ☐ **erotically** *adv.*

erotica / uh-**rot**-i-kuh, e-, ee- / *n.pl.* erotic literature or art.

eroticism / uh-**rot**-uh-siz-uhm, e-, ee- / *n.* erotic nature or character; the use of (or response to) erotic images or erotic stimulation.

erotogenic / uh-rot-oh-**jen**-ik, e- / *adj.* = EROGENOUS.

err / er / *v.* (**erred**, **erring**) **1** make a mistake, be incorrect. **2** sin.

errand *n.* **1** a short journey on which a person goes or is sent to carry a message or deliver goods etc. **2** the object of such a journey.

errant / **e**-ruhnt / *adj.* **1** erring, misbehaving. **2** *literary* travelling in search of adventure (*a knight errant*). ☐ **errantry** *n.* (in sense 2).

erratic / uh-**rat**-ik, ee- / *adj.* irregular or uneven in movement, quality, habit, etc. ☐ **erratically** *adv.*

erratum / uh-**rah**-tuhm, e- / *n.* (*pl.* **errata**) an error in printing or writing.

erroneous / uh-**roh**-nee-uhs, e- / *adj.* mistaken, incorrect. ☐ **erroneously** *adv.*

error *n.* **1** a mistake. **2** the condition of being wrong in opinion or conduct. **3** the amount of inaccuracy in a calculation or a measuring-device (*an error of 2 per cent*). ☐ **error message** *Computing* a message that reports a software, hardware, or operator error.

ersatz / **er**-zats, -sats / *adj.* made in imitation (*ersatz coffee*). •*n.* an ersatz thing or substance. (¶ German)

Erse *n.* & *adj.* Gaelic.

erstwhile *adj.* former (*his erstwhile lover*).

eructation / ee-ruk-**tay**-shuhn / *n. formal* belching.

erudite / **e**-ruh-duyt / *adj.* having or showing great learning. ☐ **erudition** / e-roo-**dish**-uhn / *n.*

erupt *v.* **1** break out suddenly and violently. **2** (of a volcano) shoot forth lava etc.; (of a geyser) spurt water or steam. **3** (of a rash or blemish) appear on the skin. ☐ **eruption** *n.* **eruptive** *adj.*

erysipelas / e-ruh-**sip**-uh-luhs / *n.* a disease causing fever and inflammation of the skin.

erythrocyte / uh-**rith**-roh-suyt / *n.* a red blood cell.

erythromycin / uh-rith-roh-**muy**-suhn / *n.* a broad spectrum antibiotic similar in its effects to penicillin.

erythropoietin / uh-rith-roh-poi-**et**-uhn / *n.* a hormone secreted by the kidneys that increases the rate of production of red blood cells in response to falling levels of oxygen in the tissues. *See also* EPO.

Es *symbol* einsteinium.

escalate / **es**-kuh-layt / *v.* increase or cause to increase in intensity or extent. ☐ **escalation** *n.*

escalator *n.* a moving staircase consisting of a circulating belt forming steps.

escalope / **es**-kuh-lop / *n.* a thin slice of boneless meat, esp. veal.

escapade / es-kuh-**payd**, **es**- / *n.* a piece of reckless or mischievous conduct.

escape *v.* **1** get oneself free from confinement or control. **2** (of gas etc.) leak. **3** succeed in avoiding (danger, punishment, etc.) (*escaped by the skin of my teeth*). **4** avoid a commitment etc. (*escaped doing the dishes*). **5** be forgotten or unnoticed by (*his name escapes me*). **6** (of words, a sigh, etc.) be uttered unintentionally. •*n.* **1** the act of escaping, the fact of having escaped. **2** a means of escaping. **3** a leakage of liquid or gas. **4** a temporary distraction or relief from reality or worry (*he surfs the Internet as an escape*). ☐ **escape clause** a clause releasing a person from a contract under certain conditions. **escape velocity** the minimum velocity needed to escape from the gravitational field of a planet or other body.

escapee / es-kuh-**pee**, e-skay-pee / *n.* a person who has escaped.

escapement *n.* a mechanism regulating the movement of a watch or clock.

escapist *n.* one who likes to escape from the realities of life by absorbing the mind in entertainment or fantasy. ☐ **escapism** *n.*

escapology / es-kuh-**pol**-uh-jee / *n.* the methods and technique of escaping from captivity or confinement, esp. as entertainment. ☐ **escapologist** *n.*

escarpment *n.* a steep slope at the edge of a plateau.

eschatology / es-kuh-**tol**-uh-jee / *n.* theology concerning death and final destiny. ☐ **eschatological** *adj.*

eschew / es-**choo**, uhs- / *v. formal* avoid or abstain from (certain kinds of action or food etc.) (*eschewed sex for Lent*). ☐ **eschewal** *n.*

escort *n.* / **es**-kawt / **1** one or more persons or ships etc. accompanying a person or thing to give protection or as an honour. **2** a person accompanying a member of the opposite sex socially. **3** a person hired to accompany a person socially. **4** a male or female prostitute. •*v.* / uh-**skawt** / act as an escort to. ☐ **escort agency** an establishment which hires or rents out males or females for purely social (or, more commonly, sexual) purposes.

escritoire / es-kri-**twah** / *n.* a writing desk with drawers.

escudo / es-**kyoo**-doh / *n.* (*pl.* **escudos**) the chief unit of money in Portugal.

escutcheon / uh-**skuch**-uhn / *n.* a shield or emblem bearing a coat of arms.

ESD *abbr.* ecologically sustainable development.

Eskimo *n.* (*pl.* **Eskimos** *or* **Eskimo**) **1** a member of a people living near the Arctic coast of America and eastern Siberia. **2** their language. (¶ Algonquian, = people speaking a different language.)

■ **Usage** In Canada and, increasingly, elsewhere the term *Inuit* is used to refer to Canadian Eskimos and also to Eskimos generally. The term *Eskimo* may offend some people.

esky *n. Aust. trademark* a portable insulated container for keeping food or drink cool. ☐ **esky lid** a bodyboard. **esky lidder** a bodyboarder.

esophagus alternative spelling of OESOPHAGUS.

esoteric / ee-soh-**te**-rik, es-uh- / *adj.* **1** intelligible only to people with special knowledge (*esoteric jargon*). **2** (of a belief etc.) intended only for the initiated. ☐ **esoterically** *adv.*

ESP *abbr.* extrasensory perception.

espadrille / es-puh-**dril** / *n.* a canvas shoe with a sole of plaited fibre.

espalier / es-**pal**-yuh / *n.* **1** latticework etc. along which the branches of a fruit tree etc. are trained to grow flat against a wall etc. **2** a fruit tree or shrub so trained. •*v.* train a fruit tree etc. to grow in this way (*espaliered two apple trees and a peach*).

especial *adj.* **1** special, outstanding (*of especial interest*). **2** belonging chiefly to one person or thing (*for your especial benefit*).

especially *adv.* chiefly, more than in other cases.

Esperanto / es-puh-**ran**-toh / *n.* an artificial language designed for international use.

espionage / **es**-pee-uh-nah*zh* / *n.* spying or using spies to obtain secret information.

esplanade / es-pluh-**nahd**, -**nayd** / *n.* a long open level area for walking, esp. beside the sea.

espouse / uh-**spowz**, es- / *v.* **1** adopt or support (a cause). **2** marry. ☐ **espousal** *n.*

espresso *n.* (also **expresso**) (*pl.* **espressos**) **1** strong coffee made by forcing steam through ground coffee. **2** a machine for making this.

esprit / es-**pree**, uh- / *n.* liveliness, wit. ☐ **esprit de corps** / duh **kaw** / loyalty and devotion uniting the members of a group. (¶ French)

espy *v.* (**espied**, **espying**) catch sight of.

Esq. *abbr.* Esquire; a courtesy title (in formal use) placed after a man's surname where no title is used before his name.

-ess *suffix* forming nouns denoting females (*hostess*; *lioness*).

■ **Usage** In many contexts, sex-based suffixes of this kind are no longer acceptable, e.g. *authoress*, *poetess*.

essay *n.* / **es**-ay / **1** a short piece of writing on a given subject. **2** *formal* an attempt. •*v.* / uh-**say** / *formal* attempt (*essayed the north face of the mountain*).

essayist *n.* a writer of essays.

essence *n.* **1** all that makes a thing what it is, its nature. **2** an indispensable quality or element. **3** a concentrated extract of something, often obtained by distillation. **4** a liquid perfume.

essential *adj.* **1** indispensable. **2** of or constituting a thing's essence (*its essential qualities*). •*n.pl.* (**essentials**) indispensable elements or things. ☐ **essential oil** a volatile oil that is extracted from a plant, with its characteristic smell. ☐☐ **essentially** *adv.*

essentialism *n.* **1** *Philosophy* the belief that things have a set of characteristics which make them what they are, and that the task of science and philosophy are their discovery and expression. **2** the view that categories of people (e.g. women and men, heterosexuals and homosexuals) have intrinsically different and characteristic natures or dispositions. ☐ **essentialist** *n.* & *adj.*

establish *v.* **1** set up (a business, a system, etc.) on a permanent basis. **2** settle (a person or oneself) in a place or position. **3** cause people to accept (a custom or belief etc.). **4** show to be true, prove (*established his innocence*).

establishment *n.* **1** establishing; being established. **2** an organised body of people maintained for a purpose, a household or staff etc. **3** a business firm or public institution, its members or employees or premises. **4** a Church system established by law. **5** (**the Establishment**) people in positions of power and authority, exercising influence and generally resisting changes (e.g. those controlling the public service, the armed services, the mainstream Churches, as well as the judiciary, etc.).

estate *n.* **1** landed property. **2** a residential or industrial district planned as a unit. **3** *Law* interest in land measured by duration, such as fee simple or leasehold; all that a person owns, esp. at his or her death. **4** a property where rubber, tea, grapes, etc. are cultivated. **5** *archaic* condition (*the holy estate of matrimony*). ☐ **estate agent** one whose business is the selling or letting of buildings and land.

esteem *v.* **1** think highly of. **2** *formal* consider or regard (*I should esteem it an honour*). •*n.* favourable opinion, respect.

ester / **es**-tuh / *n.* a chemical compound formed when an acid and an alcohol interact in a certain way.

estimable / es-tuh-muh-buhl / *adj.* worthy of esteem.

estimate *n.* / **es**-tuh-muht / **1** a judgment of a thing's approximate value or amount etc. **2** a contractor's statement of the approximate charge for work to be undertaken. **3** a judgment of character or qualities. •*v.* / es-tuh-mayt / form an estimate of. ▫ **estimator** *n.*

estimation *n.* **1** estimating. **2** judgment of a person's or thing's worth.

Estonia / es-**toh**-nee-uh / a republic in eastern Europe on the Gulf of Finland, formerly a republic of the USSR.

Estonian *adj.* of Estonia or its people or language. •*n.* **1** a person from Estonia. **2** the language of Estonia.

estrange *v.* cause (people formerly friendly or loving) to become unfriendly or indifferent. ▫ **estrangement** *n.*

estrogen variant spelling of OESTROGEN.

estuary / **es**-choo-ree / *n.* the tidal mouth of a large river.

ET *abbr.* extraterrestrial.

ETA *abbr.* **1** estimated time of arrival. **2** / **ee**-tuh / a Basque separatist movement.

eta / **ee**-tuh / *n.* the seventh letter of the Greek alphabet (Η, η).

et al. *abbr.* = and others. (¶ Latin *et alii*.)

etc. *abbr.* = ET CETERA.

et cetera / et-**se**-tuh-ruh, -**set**-ruh / *adv.* and other similar things; and so on. •*n.pl.* (**etceteras**) the usual extras. (¶ Latin, = and the rest.)

etch *v.* **1** make (a pattern or picture) by engraving a metal plate with acid, esp. so that copies can be printed from this. **2** impress deeply (*the scene is etched on my mind*). ▫ **etcher** *n.*

etching *n.* a print made from an etched plate.

eternal *adj.* **1** existing always without beginning or end. **2** unchanging, too frequent. **3** *colloq.* ceaseless, too frequent (*these eternal arguments*). ▫ **eternal triangle** a complex emotional or sexual relationship involving two men and a woman or two women and a man. ▫▫ **eternally** *adv.*

Eternal City, the Rome.

eternity *n.* **1** infinite (esp. future) time. **2** the endless period of life after death. **3** *colloq.* a very long time (*you're taking an eternity to finish that job*).

ethane *n.* a gaseous hydrocarbon of the alkane series, occurring in natural gas.

ethanoic acid / eth-uh-**noh**-ik / *n.* acetic acid.

ethanol / **eth**-uh-nol / *n.* alcohol.

ether / **ee**-thuh / *n.* **1** the clear sky, the upper regions beyond the clouds. **2** a substance formerly thought to fill all space and act as a medium for transmission of radio waves etc. **3** a colourless volatile liquid used as an anaesthetic and as a solvent.

ethereal / ee-**theer**-ree-uhl / *adj.* **1** light and delicate, esp. in appearance. **2** of heaven, heavenly. ▫ **ethereally** *adv.*

ethernet / **ee**-thuh-net / *n. Computing* a system of communication for local area networks by coaxial cable that prevents simultaneous transmission by more than one station.

ethic / **eth**-ik / *adj.* of or involving morals. •*n.* a moral principle or set of principles.

ethical / **eth**-i-kuhl / *adj.* **1** of ethics. **2** morally correct, honourable. ▫ **ethically** *adv.*

ethics *n.* **1** (treated as *sing.*) moral philosophy. **2** (treated as *pl.*) moral principles (*medical ethics*).

Ethiopia a country of NE Africa. ▫ **Ethiopian** *adj.* & *n.*

Ethiopic / ee-thee-**op**-ik / *n.* the liturgical language of the Coptic Church of Ethiopia.

ethnic *adj.* **1** (of a social group) having common national, racial, cultural, religious, or linguistic characteristics; esp. (in Australia) designating a social group of migrants (or their descendants) whose original language is not English. **2** (of music, clothes, etc.) inspired by or resembling those of an exotic people (*ethnic dancing*). **3** of ethnic groups (*ethnic radio*). **4** denoting origin by birth or descent rather than nationality (*ethnic Turks; ethnic origins*). •*n.* a member of an ethnic group. ▫ **ethnic cleansing** euphemism for the practice of mass expulsion or massacre of people from opposing ethnic or religious groups within a certain area. ▫▫ **ethnically** *adv.*

ethnocentric *adj.* regarding one's own race or ethnic group as of supreme importance and superior to all others; evaluating other races and cultures by criteria specific to one's own. ▫ **ethnocentricity** / eth-no-sen-**tris**-uh-tee / *n.* **ethnocentrism** *n.*

ethnologist *n.* an expert in ethnology.

ethnology / eth-**nol**-uh-jee / *n.* the study of human races and their characteristics. ▫ **ethnological** / eth-nuh-**loj**-i-kuhl / *adj.*

ethos / **ee**-thos / *n.* the characteristic spirit and beliefs of a community etc.

ethyl / **eth**-uhl / *n.* a radical present in alcohol and ether. ▫ **ethyl alcohol** alcohol.

ethylene / **eth**-uh-leen / *n.* a hydrocarbon of the alkene series, occurring in natural gas and used in the manufacture of polythene.

etiolate / ee-tee-oh-layt / *v.* make (a plant) pale through lack of light; give a sickly colour to (a person). ▫ **etiolation** *n.*

etiology variant spelling of AETIOLOGY.

etiquette / **et**-uh-kuht, et-**ee**- / *n.* the rules of correct behaviour in society or among the members of a profession.

Etna, Mount a volcano in eastern Sicily, rising to 3,323 metres. It is the highest and most active volcano in Europe.

Etruscan / uh-**trus**-kuhn / *n.* **1** a native of ancient Etruria (modern Tuscany). **2** the language of the Etruscans.

et seq. *abbr.* and the following (pages etc.). (¶ Latin *et sequentia*.)

étude / **ay**-tyood, ay-**tyood** / *n.* a short musical composition.

etymology / et-uh-**mol**-uh-jee / *n.* **1** an account of the origin and development of a word (cf. FOLK ETYMOLOGY). **2** the study of words and their origins. ☐ **etymological** / et-uh-muh-**loj**-i-kuhl / *adj.* **etymologically** *adv.* **etymologist** *n.*

Eu *symbol* europium.

euc / yook / *colloq.* = EUCALYPT.

eucalypt / **yoo**-kuh-lipt / *n.* an Australian tree of the genus *Eucalyptus* (also used as *adj.*: *eucalypt forests*).

eucalyptol *n.* the common (and formerly scientific) name for the volatile oil cineol, a principal component of pharmaceutical-grade eucalyptus oil.

eucalyptus / yoo-kuh-**lip**-tuhs / *n.* (*pl.* **eucalyptuses** or **eucalypti**) (also **eucalypt**) **1** an essentially Australian genus (*Eucalyptus*) of trees (and some shrubs), consisting of some 600 classified species. **2** any tree (or shrub) of this genus, evergreen, cultivated for its timber and for the oil from its leaves (*see also* GUM TREE). ☐ **eucalyptus oil** any of several volatile oils extracted from the leaves of certain eucalypts and valued for their medicinal and germicidal properties etc.

Eucharist / **yoo**-kuh-ruhst / *n.* **1** the Christian sacrament in which consecrated bread (or bread and wine in some Churches) is consumed. **2** the consecrated elements, esp. the bread. ☐ **Eucharistic** *adj.*

euchre / **yoo**-kuh / *n.* a card game. • *v.* **1** (in the card game) gain the advantage over (another player) when that player fails to take three tricks. **2** *colloq.* outwit, deceive (a person). ☐ **euchred** *adj. Aust. colloq.* exhausted; done for.

Euclid / **yoo**-klid / (*c*.300 BC), Greek mathematician, whose *Elements* was the standard work on geometry until recent times. ☐ **Euclidean** / yoo-**klid**-ee-uhn / *adj.*

Eucumbene, Lake created mainly by the damming of the Eucumbene River, Lake Eucumbene near Cooma is the main water-storage for the Snowy Mountains Hydro-Electric Scheme and has several tourist resorts on its shores.

eugenics / yoo-**jen**-iks, yoo-**jee**-niks / *n.* (treated as *sing.* or *pl.*) the science of developing a human or animal population using controlled breeding. ☐ **eugenic** *adj.* **eugenically** *adv.*

eulogise / **yoo**-luh-juyz / *v.* (also **-ize**) write or utter a eulogy of. ☐ **eulogistic** *adj.*

eulogy / **yoo**-luh-jee / *n.* a speech or piece of writing in praise of a person or thing.

eunuch / **yoo**-nuhk / *n.* **1** a castrated man. **2** a person lacking effectiveness (*he's a political eunuch*).

euphemism / **yoo**-fuh-miz-uhm / *n.* a mild or roundabout expression substituted for one considered improper or too direct (*'pass away' is a euphemism for 'die'*). ☐ **euphemistic** / yoo-fuh-**mis**-tik / *adj.* **euphemistically** *adv.*

euphonium / yoo-**foh**-nee-uhm / *n.* a large brass wind instrument of the tuba family.

euphony / **yoo**-fuh-nee / *n.* pleasantness of sounds, esp. in words. ☐ **euphonious** / yoo-**foh**-nee-uhs / *adj.*

euphoria / yoo-**faw**-ree-uh / *n.* an intense feeling of well-being and excitement. ☐ **euphoric** / yoo-**fo**-rik / *adj.*

eurabbie / yoo-**rab**-ee / *n.* a tall eucalypt of south-eastern Australia. (¶ Possibly from an Aboriginal language.)

Eurasian / yoo-**ray**-zhuhn / *adj.* **1** of Europe and Asia. **2** of mixed European and Asian parentage. • *n.* a Eurasian person.

eureka / yoo-**ree**-kuh / *interj.* **1** I have found it (an exclamation of triumph at a discovery). **2** (**Eureka**) *Aust.* the clash between gold miners and the police and military at Ballarat in 1854, now a symbol of republicanism in Australia. (¶ *Eureka* is said to have been uttered in his bath by the Greek mathematician Archimedes (3rd century BC) on realising that the volume of an object can be calculated by the amount of water it displaces.)

Eureka Flag a blue flag bearing a white cross with a star at the end of each arm, first raised at the Eureka Stockade; now associated with the Australian republican cause.

Eureka Stockade the name and place of the insurrection at the Ballarat goldfields in Vic. on 3 December 1854. It was caused mainly by the diggers' resentment of the monthly licence fee introduced by Lieutenant-Governor La Trobe in 1851 and of the harsh methods used to collect it. When James Scobie, a digger, was murdered and charges against his police-officer murderers were dismissed, the diggers formed the Ballarat Reform League, which was led by Peter Lalor. Lalor and a group of diggers built a stockade and proclaimed a Republic of Victoria. In the early hours of morning the stockade was attacked by infantry, cavalry, and police, and the brief rebellion was soon crushed.

eurhythmics / yoo-**rith**-miks / *n.* (treated as *sing.* or *pl.*) harmony of bodily movement, developed with music and dance into a system of education.

Euripides / yoo-**rip**-uh-deez / (5th century BC), Greek dramatist.

euro[1] / **yoo**-roh / *n.* the single European currency introduced in the European Union in 1999.

euro[2] / **yoo**-roh / *n.* a reddish, short-haired macropod of drier Australia west of the Great Dividing Range, a sub-species of wallaroo. (¶ Adnyamathanha)

Euro- *comb. form* Europe; European.

Europa / yoo-**roh**-puh / *Gk myth.* a woman who was wooed by Zeus in the form of a bull and carried off by him to Crete.

Europe a continent extending from Asia to the Atlantic Ocean. ☐ **European wasp** a very dangerous bee-sized wasp with yellow and black bands, able to sting repeatedly; originally of Europe etc., but now well-established in Australia. Also called *killer wasp*. ☐☐ **European** *adj.* & *n.*

European Union *n.* an economic and political association of certain European countries as a unit with internal free trade and common external tariffs.

europium / yoo-**roh**-pee-uhm / *n.* a soft metallic element (symbol Eu).

Eurydice / yoo-**rid**-uh-see / *Gk myth.* the wife of Orpheus.

Eustachian tube / yoo-**stay**-shuhn / *n.* the narrow passage from the pharynx to the cavity of the middle ear.

euthanase *v.* (also **-ise**, **-ize**) perform euthanasia upon.

euthanasia / yoo-thuh-**nay**-zhee-uh, -zhuh / *n.* the bringing about of a gentle death for a person suffering from a painful incurable disease.

eV *abbr.* electronvolt.

evacuate *v.* **1** send (people) away from a place considered dangerous; remove the occupants of (a place). **2** empty (a vessel) of air etc. **3** empty (the bowels etc.). ☐ **evacuation** *n.*

evacuee *n.* an evacuated person.

evade / ee-**vayd**, uh- / *v.* avoid by cleverness or trickery (*evade the police; evade arrest*).

evaluate *v.* find out or state the value of, assess. ☐ **evaluation** *n.*

evanesce / ev-uh-**nes** / *v. literary* fade from sight, disappear. ☐ **evanescent** *adj.* **evanescence** *n.*

evangelical / ee-van-**jel**-i-kuhl / *adj.* **1** of or according to the teaching of the gospel. **2** of the Protestant movement that lays stress on personal conversion and salvation by faith. • *n.* a member of this movement. ☐ **evangelicalism** *n.* **evangelically** *adv.*

evangelise *v.* (also **-ize**) preach or spread the gospel to, win over to Christianity. ☐ **evangelisation** *n.*

evangelism / ee-**van**-juh-liz-uhm, uh- / *n.* preaching or spreading of the gospel.

evangelist / ee-**van**-juh-list / *n.* **1** any of the authors of the four Gospels (Matthew, Mark, Luke, John). **2** a preacher of the gospel. ☐ **evangelistic** *adj.*

Evans, Ada Emily (1872–1947), Australian lawyer, the first woman to qualify (1902) as a lawyer in Australia (although by the law of that time she was not allowed to practise).

evaporate *v.* **1** turn or be turned into vapour. **2** lose or cause to lose moisture in this way. **3** cease to exist (*their enthusiasm evaporated*). ☐ **evaporated milk** unsweetened milk thickened by partial evaporation and tinned. ☐☐ **evaporation** *n.*

evasion / ee-**vay**-zhuhn, uh- / *n.* **1** evading (*tax evasion*). **2** an evasive answer or excuse.

evasive / ee-**vay**-siv, uh- / *adj.* evading, not frank or straightforward. ☐ **evasively** *adv.* **evasiveness** *n.*

Evatt[1], Elizabeth (Andreas) (1933–), AO, niece of Herbert Vere Evatt, became Chief Judge of the Family Court of Australia in 1976, the first woman in Australia to do so.

Evatt[2], Herbert Vere ('Doc') (1894–1965), Australian judge, writer, and politician, the youngest ever Justice of the High Court of Australia, Federal Labor politician and Leader of the Australian Labor Party after the death of Chifley in 1951.

Eve (in Biblical tradition) the first woman, formed of Adam's rib.

eve *n.* **1** the evening or day before a festival (*Christmas Eve*). **2** the time just before an event (*on the eve of an election*). **3** *archaic* evening.

even[1] *adj.* **1** level, free from irregularities, smooth. **2** uniform in quality. **3** (of temper) calm, not easily upset. **4** equally balanced or matched. **5** equal in number or amount. **6** (of a number) exactly divisible by two; bearing such a number (*no parking on even dates*). **7** (of money or time or quantity) exact, not involving fractions (*an even dozen*). • *adv.* **1** (used to emphasise a comparison) to a greater degree (*ran even faster*). **2** (used to introduce a particularly extreme case or example) (*does he even suspect the danger?; even a child could understand that*). • *v.* (often foll. by *out* or *up*) make or become even. • *n.pl.* (**evens**) = EVEN MONEY. ☐ **be** (or **get**) **even with** have one's revenge on. **even as** at the very moment that (*even as he was bucketing the bishop, he kicked the bucket*). **even-handed** impartial. **even money 1** betting odds offering the chance to win the amount one has staked. **2** equally likely to happen or not (*it's even money he won't turn up*). **even-stevens** *adj.* & *adv.* an intensive form of 'even' in various senses; fifty-fifty (*my chances of getting the job are even-stevens; let's split the money even-stevens*). ☐☐ **evenly** *adv.* **evenness** *n.*

even[2] *n. poetic* evening.

evening *n.* **1** the end part of the day between late afternoon and bedtime. **2** a time compared with this, esp. the last part of a person's life. ☐ **evening dress** clothing usu. worn for formal occasions in the evening; a woman's long formal dress. **evening primrose** a plant with pale yellow flowers that open in the evening. **evening primrose oil** an extract of evening primrose, supposedly good for certain ailments. **evening star** a planet (esp. Venus) when conspicuous in the west after sunset.

evensong *n.* the service of evening prayer in the Anglican Church.

event *n.* **1** something that happens, esp. something important. **2** the fact of a thing happening. **3** an item in a sports program. ☐ **at all events** (also **in any event**) in any case. **in the event of** if (a specified thing) happens (*in the event of a bushfire, don't run blindly*).

eventful *adj.* full of incidents.

eventide *n.* poetic evening.

eventing *n.* participation in equestrian competitions, esp. dressage and showjumping.

eventual *adj.* coming at last, ultimate (*his eventual success*). ☐ **eventually** *adv.*

eventuality / ee-ven-choo-**al**-uh-tee, uh- / *n.* a possible event (*prepared for every eventuality*).

eventuate *v.* result, be the outcome (*what will eventuate if I press this button?*).

ever *adv.* **1** at all times, always (*ever hopeful*). **2** at any time (*have you ever been to Baddaginnie?*). **3** (used for emphasis) in any way, at all (*how ever did you do it?*). **4** (in *combinations*) constantly (*ever-present*). **5** (foll. by the comparative) constantly, increasingly (*grew ever larger*).

■ **Usage** When *ever* is used with a question word for emphasis it is written separately (see sense 3). When used with a relative pronoun or adverb to give it indefinite or general force, *ever* is written as one word with the relative pronoun or adverb, e.g. *however it's done, it's difficult*.

Everage, Dame Edna (1955–), an Australian housewife who has become a cult-figure. Known as 'La Stupenda of Suburbia' and 'The Megastar of Moonee Ponds' (a Melbourne suburb), she became an international jet-setter after she was created a Dame of the British Empire by the Queen in 1974. (*See also* Barry HUMPHRIES.)

Everest, Mount the world's highest mountain (8,848 m), in the Himalayas on the border of Nepal and Tibet.

evergreen *adj.* **1** (of a tree or shrub) having green leaves throughout the year. **2** always fresh; popular for a long time (*an evergreen song*). • *n.* **1** an evergreen tree or shrub. **2** a thing which remains popular for a long time ('*Waltzing Matilda' is an evergreen*).

everlasting *adj.* **1** lasting for ever. **2** lasting a very long time. **3** lasting too long, repeated too often (*his everlasting complaints*). **4** (of flowers) keeping shape and colour when dried. • *n.* **1** eternity. **2** = PAPER DAISY. ☐ **everlastingly** *adv.*

evermore *adv.* for ever, always.

every *adj.* **1** each single one without exception (*enjoyed every minute*). **2** each in a series (*he comes every fourth day*). **3** all possible (*she shall be given every care*). ☐ **every bit as** *colloq.* (in comparisons) quite as (*every bit as handsome as his brother*). **every one** each one. **every other day** (*or* **week** etc.) on alternate days (or weeks etc.).

everybody *pron.* every person.

everyday *adj.* **1** worn or used on ordinary days. **2** usual, commonplace (*an everyday activity*).

Everyman *n.* the ordinary or typical person. (¶ The name of the main character in a 15th-century morality play.)

everyone *pron.* everybody.

■ **Usage** Do not confuse with *every one* = each one (*see* EVERY).

everything *pron.* **1** all things. **2** the most important thing (*speed is everything*).

everywhere *adv.* in or to every place; in or to several places (*I've been everywhere except to Toogoolawah*).

evict / ee-**vikt**, uh- / *v.* expel (a tenant) by legal process. ☐ **eviction** *n.*

evidence *n.* **1** anything that establishes a fact or gives reason for believing something. **2** statements made or objects produced in a lawcourt as proof or to support a case. • *v.* indicate, be evidence of. ☐ **be in evidence** be conspicuous.

evident *adj.* plain or obvious. ☐ **evidently** *adv.*

evidential / ev-uh-**den**-shuhl / *adj.* of, based on, or providing evidence.

evil *adj.* **1** morally bad, wicked. **2** harmful or tending to harm, esp. characteristically (*smoking is evil*). **3** very unpleasant or troublesome (*an evil temper*). **4** unlucky (*an evil omen*). • *n.* an evil thing; sin; harm. ☐ **the evil eye** a gaze or stare superstitiously believed to cause harm. ☐ ☐ **evilly** *adv.*

evildoer *n.* one who does evil things. ☐ **evildoing** *n.*

evince / ee-**vins**, uh- / *v.* indicate or display (a quality, feeling, etc.) (*evinced a desire to eat a live witchetty grub*).

eviscerate / ee-**vis**-uh-rayt, uh- / *v.* disembowel. ☐ **evisceration** *n.*

evocative / ee-**vok**-uh-tiv, uh- / *adj.* tending to evoke (esp. feelings or memories) (*clothes evocative of the sixties*).

evoke / ee-**vohk**, uh- / *v.* call up or inspire (memories, feelings, a response, etc.) (*evoked the past; his tears evoked no response from her*). ☐ **evocation** / ev-uh-**kay**-shuhn / *n.*

evolution / ee-vuh-**loo**-shuhn, ev-uh- / *n.* **1** a gradual development, esp. from a simple to a more complex form (*the evolution of the computer*). **2** the origination of plant and animal species by development from earlier forms, rather than by a special act of creation by God. ☐ **evolutionary** *adv.*

evolutionist *n.* a person who regards evolution as explaining the origin of plant and animal species.

evolve / ee-**volv**, uh- / *v.* **1** develop or work out gradually (*evolved a scheme to extract sunbeams from cucumbers*). **2** (of plants and animals) develop from lower to higher forms. **3** give off (heat, gas, etc.).

ewe *n.* a female sheep.

ewer / **yoo**-uh / *n.* a wide-mouthed water jug.

ex prep. **1** (of goods) sold from (*ex warehouse*). **2** without, excluding. • *n. colloq.* a former husband or wife, boyfriend or girlfriend. ☐ **ex dividend** (of stocks or shares) not including a dividend that is about to be paid.

ex- *comb. form* former (*ex-convict; ex-president*).

exacerbate / ek-**sas**-uh-bayt / *v.* **1** make (pain, disease, etc.) worse. **2** irritate (a person). ☐ **exacerbation** *n.*

exact *adj.* **1** correct in every detail, free from error. **2** giving all details (*gave me exact instructions*). **3** capable of being precise (*the exact sciences*). • *v.* insist on and obtain (*exacted payment*). ☐ **exactness** *n.*

exacting *adj.* making great demands or requiring great effort (*an exacting task*).

exaction *n.* **1** the exacting of money etc. **2** the thing exacted. **3** an illegal or outrageous demand, extortion.

exactitude *n.* exactness.

exactly *adv.* **1** in an exact manner. **2** (said in agreement) quite so, as you say. **3** just (*that's exactly what I like*).

exaggerate *v.* **1** make (a thing) seem greater or more extreme than it really is. **2** (usu. as **exaggerated** *adj.*) beyond what is normal or appropriate (*exaggerated politeness*). ☐ **exaggeration** *n.* **exaggerative** *adj.*

exalt / eg-**zawlt**, uhg- / *v.* **1** raise (a person) in rank, power, or dignity. **2** praise highly. **3** (usu. as **exalted** *adj.*) lofty or noble (*exalted aims; an exalted style*).

■ **Usage** *Exalt* is often confused with *exult*.

exaltation *n.* **1** exalting; being exalted. **2** elation, spiritual delight.

exam *n.* an examination (sense 2).

examination *n.* **1** examining; being examined or looked at (e.g. medically). **2** the testing of knowledge or ability by oral or written questions or by exercises. **3** a formal questioning of a witness or an accused person in a lawcourt.

examine *v.* **1** look at closely; inspect, investigate. **2** test formally (a person's knowledge or ability). **3** question formally in order to get information. ☐ **examiner** *n.*

examinee *n.* a person being tested in an examination.

example *n.* **1** a fact that illustrates a general rule; a thing that shows the quality or characteristics of others in the same group or of the same kind. **2** something (esp. conduct) that is worthy of imitation (*his courage is an example to us all*). ☐ **for example** by way of illustrating a general rule. **make an example of** punish as a warning to others.

exasperate *v.* annoy greatly. ☐ **exasperation** *n.*

Excalibur (in legend) the name of King Arthur's magic sword.

ex cathedra / eks kuh-**thee**-druh / *adj. & adv.* (of a pronouncement by the pope) with full authority (involving infallibility as doctrinally defined). (¶ Latin, = from the chair (of St. Peter).)

excavate *v.* **1** make (a hole or channel) by digging; dig out (soil). **2** reveal or extract by digging. ☐ **excavation** *n.* **excavator** *n.*

exceed *v.* **1** be greater or more numerous than. **2** go beyond the limit of, do more than is warranted by (*exceeded his authority*).

exceedingly *adv.* very, extremely.

excel *v.* (**excelled**, **excelling**) **1** be better than. **2** be very good at something. ☐ **excel oneself** do better than one has ever done before.

excellence *n.* very great merit or quality.

Excellency *n.* (usu. preceded by *Your*, *His*, or *Her*) the title of high officials such as ambassadors and governors.

excellent *adj.* extremely good. ☐ **excellently** *adv.*

except *prep.* not including (*they all left except me*). • *v.* exclude from a statement, condition, etc. (*excepted him from the amnesty; present company excepted*).

excepting *prep.* except.

■ **Usage** *Excepting* should be used only after *not* and *always*; otherwise, *except* should be used (*all are to blame, not excepting you; no-one is to blame except you*).

exception *n.* **1** excepting; being excepted. **2** a thing that does not follow the general rule. ☐ **take exception to** object to. **with the exception of** except.

exceptionable *adj.* open to objection (*your morals are highly exceptionable—they are like those of an alley-cat!*).

■ **Usage** *Exceptionable* is sometimes confused with *exceptional*.

exceptional *adj.* **1** forming an exception, very unusual (*exceptional circumstances*). **2** outstandingly good (*an exceptional athlete*). ☐ **exceptionally** *adv.*

■ **Usage** See note at *exceptionable*.

excerpt *n.* / **ek**-serpt / a short extract from a book, film, piece of music, etc. • *v.* / ek-**serpt** / select excerpts from. ☐ **excerption** *n.*

excess *n.* **1** the exceeding of due limits. **2** the amount by which one number or quantity etc. exceeds another. **3** an agreed amount subtracted by an insurer from the total payment to be made to an insured person who makes a claim. **4** (**excesses**) immoderation in eating or drinking. **5** (**excesses**) outrageous behaviour. ☐ **in excess of** more than.

excessive *adj.* greater than what is normal or necessary, too much. ☐ **excessively** *adv.*

exchange *v.* **1** give or receive (one thing) in place of another. **2** give to and receive from another person (*they exchanged greetings*). • *n.* **1**

exchequer

exchanging (goods, prisoners, words, blows, etc.). **2** the exchanging of money for its equivalent in another currency; the relation in value between the money of two or more countries. **3** a place where merchants or bankers etc. assemble to do business (*stock exchange*). **4** the central telephone office of a district. ☐ **exchange rate** the value of one currency in terms of another. ☐ **exchangeable** *adj.*

exchequer *n.* **1** the treasury of a nation. **2** a person's supply of money.

excise *n.* / **ek**-suyz, **ek**-suys / duty or tax levied on certain goods and licences etc. • *v.* / ek-**suyz** / remove by cutting out or away (*excise tissue from the body; excise a passage from a book*). ☐ **excision** / ek-**sizh**-uhn / *n.*

excitable *adj.* (of a person) easily excited. ☐ **excitability** *n.*

excite *v.* **1** rouse the feelings of; cause (a person) to feel strongly; arouse sexually; make eager. **2** cause (a feeling or reaction) (*it excited curiosity*). **3** produce activity in (a nerve or organ of the body etc.). ☐ **excitation** *n.* **excitative** *adj.* **excitatory** / ek-**suy**-tuh-tuh-ree, ek-suy-**tay**-tuh-ree, -tree / *adj.*

excited *adj.* feeling or showing excitement. ☐ **excitedly** *adv.*

excitement *n.* **1** a state of great emotion, esp. that caused by something pleasant. **2** something causing this.

exciting *adj.* causing great interest or eagerness. ☐ **excitingly** *adv.*

exclaim *v.* cry out or utter suddenly from pain, pleasure, surprise, etc.

exclamation *n.* **1** exclaiming. **2** a word or words exclaimed. **3** a strong sudden cry. ☐ **exclamation mark** the punctuation mark (!) placed after an exclamation (see panel).

exclamatory / eks-**klam**-uh-tuh-ree, uhks-, -tree / *adj.* of, containing, or serving as an exclamation.

exclude *v.* **1** keep out (a person or thing) from a place, group, or privilege etc. **2** omit, ignore as irrelevant (*do not exclude this possibility*). **3** make impossible, prevent (*his explanation excluded all doubt*). ☐ **exclusion** *n.*

exclusive *adj.* **1** not admitting something else; excluding other things. **2** (of groups or societies) admitting only certain carefully selected people to membership. **3** (of shops or their goods) high-class, catering only for the wealthy, expensive. **4** (of an article in a newspaper or goods in a shop) not published or obtainable elsewhere. **5** done or held etc. so as to exclude everything else, not shared (*we have the exclusive rights*). **6** (foll. by *of*) not including (*20 men exclusive of our own*). • *n.* an article or story released by only one newspaper, TV channel, etc. ☐ **exclusively** *adv.* **exclusiveness** *n.* **exclusivity** *n.*

excommunicate *v.* officially exclude (a person) from participation in a Church, esp. in its sacraments. ☐ **excommunication** *n.*

excoriate / eks-**kaw**-ree-ayt / *v.* **1** remove skin from (a person etc.), e.g. by grazing; strip of (skin). **2** criticise severely. ☐ **excoriation** *n.*

excrement / **eks**-kruh-muhnt / *n.* faeces. ☐ **excremental** *adj.*

excrescence / ek-**skres**-uhns / *n.* **1** an abnormal outgrowth on the body or a plant. **2** an ugly addition (*this new house is an excrescence in our old street*). ☐ **excrescent** *adj.*

excreta / ek-**skree**-tuh / *n.pl.* faeces and urine.

excrete / ek-**kreet** / *v.* (of an animal or plant) expel (waste matter). ☐ **excretion** *n.* **excretory** *adj.*

excruciating / ek-**skroo**-shee-ay-ting, uhk- / *adj.* **1** intensely painful. **2** *colloq.* extremely bad.

exculpate / **eks**-kul-payt / *v.* free (a person) from blame, clear of a charge of wrongdoing. ☐ **exculpation** *n.*

excursion *n.* **1** a short journey to a place and back; a pleasure trip, an outing. **2** a digression (*the physicist made a brief excursion into fantasy at the end of his lecture*).

excursive *adj. literary* digressive.

excusable *adj.* able to be excused. ☐ **excusably** *adv.*

excuse *v.* / ek-**skyooz**, uhk- / **1** forgive or overlook (an offence or the person committing it). **2** (of a thing or circumstance) justify a fault or error (*nothing can excuse such rudeness*). **3** release from an obligation or duty; grant exemption to. • *n.* / ek-**skyoos**, uhk- / a reason put forward to justify a fault or error. ☐ **be excused** be allowed to leave. **excuse me** a polite apology for interrupting or disagreeing etc.

ex-directory *adj.* not listed in a telephone directory, at one's own request.

execrable / ek-suh-kruh-buhl / *adj.* abominable (*execrable behaviour*). ☐ **execrably** *adv.*

execrate / **ek**-suh-krayt / *v.* detest greatly; utter curses upon. ☐ **execration** *n.* **execrative** *adj.*

execute *v.* **1** carry out (an order); put (a plan etc.) into effect. **2** perform (an action or manoeuvre). **3** produce (a work of art). **4** make legally valid e.g. by signing (*execute a will*). **5** carry out a death sentence on.

Exclamation mark !

An exclamation mark is used instead of a full stop at the end of a sentence to show that the speaker or writer is very angry, enthusiastic, insistent, disappointed, hurt, surprised, etc., e.g.

I am not pleased at all!   *I wish I could have gone!*
I just love lollies!   *Ouch!*
Go away!   *He didn't even say goodbye!*

execution *n.* **1** the carrying out or performance of something. **2** skill in playing music (*her execution was flawless*). **3** executing a condemned person.

executioner *n.* an official who executes a condemned person.

executive / eg-**zek**-yuh-tiv, uhg- / *n.* **1** a person or group that has administrative or managerial powers in a business or commercial organisation. **2** the branch of a government or other organisation concerned with putting laws, agreements, etc. into effect. • *adj.* having the powers to execute plans or to put laws or agreements etc. into effect.

Executive Council *n.* the constitutional body in the Commonwealth of Australia (presided over by the governor-general and consisting of government ministers) responsible for the implementation of the laws.

executor / eg-**zek**-yuh-tuh, uhg- / *n.* a person appointed by a testator to carry out the terms of his or her will.

exegesis / ek-suh-**jee**-suhs / *n.* (*pl.* **exegeses** / -seez /) a critical explanation of a text, esp. of Scripture. ☐ **exegetic** / ek-suh-**jet**-ik / *adj.* **exegetical** *adj.*

exemplar / eg-**zem**-pluh, uhg- / *n.* **1** a model, a type. **2** a typical or parallel instance.

exemplary / eg-**zem**-pluh-ree, uhg- / *adj.* **1** outstandingly good (*exemplary conduct*). **2** serving as a warning to others (*exemplary punishment*). **3** illustrative.

exemplify / eg-**zem**-pluh-fuy, uhg- / *v.* (**exemplified, exemplifying**) **1** serve as an example of (*this exemplifies the need for greater security*). **2** illustrate by example (*you need to exemplify this point by quoting from the novel*). ☐ **exemplification** *n.*

exemplum / eg-**zem**-pluhm, uhg- / *n.* (*pl.* **exempla**) an example or model, esp. a moral or illustrative story.

exempt *adj.* (often foll. by *from*) free from an obligation or payment etc. that is required of others. • *v.* make exempt. ☐ **exemption** *n.*

exequies / **ek**-suh-kweez / *n.pl. formal* funeral rites.

exercise *n.* **1** activity requiring physical exertion, done for the sake of health. **2** concentrated mental or spiritual activity (*the spiritual exercises of St. Ignatius*). **3** a task or set of tasks devised to train technique etc. (*Czerny's piano exercises*). **4** a short essay or translation written by school students etc. **5** the practice of an ability, quality, etc. (*the exercise of tolerance*). **6** (often as **exercises**) a military training manoeuvre. • *v.* **1** use or employ (a faculty, rights, influence, etc.) (*exercised his intuition; exercised their right to keep silent; exercised her authority*). **2** take or cause to take exercise; train by means of exercises. **3** perplex, worry (*he was much exercised by fear for her safety*).

exert *v.* bring (a quality or influence etc.) into use (*exert all one's strength*). ☐ **exert oneself** make an effort.

exertion *n.* **1** exerting; being exerted. **2** a great effort.

exeunt / **ek**-see-uunt / *v.* (as a stage direction) they leave the stage. (¶ Latin, = they go out.)

exfoliate *v.* **1** (of bone, the skin, a mineral, etc.) come off in scales or layers. **2** (of a tree) throw off layers of bark. ☐ **exfoliation** *n.*

ex gratia / eks **gray**-shuh / *adv.* & *adj.* done or given as a favour; not from legal or other obligation (*an ex gratia payment*). (¶ Latin, = from favour.)

exhale *v.* breathe out. ☐ **exhalation** *n.*

exhaust *v.* **1** use up completely. **2** empty, draw out the contents of (*exhaust a well*). **3** tire out (*he has exhausted my patience; this work is exhausting*). **4** find out or say all there is to say about (a subject) (*exhaust the possibilities*). • *n.* **1** waste gases or steam expelled from an engine etc. **2** the system through which they are sent out. ☐ **exhaustible** *adj.*

exhaustion / eg-**zaws**-chuhn, uhg- / *n.* **1** exhausting something; being exhausted. **2** total loss of strength.

exhaustive *adj.* thorough, trying all possibilities (*we made an exhaustive search*). ☐ **exhaustively** *adv.*

exhibit / eg-**zib**-uht, uhg- / *v.* display, present for the public to see. • *n.* a thing or collection of things exhibited. ☐ **exhibitor** *n.*

exhibition *n.* **1** exhibiting, being exhibited. **2** a display or show (*an exhibition of temper*). **3** a public display of works of art or industrial products etc. or of a skilled performance. **4** a scholarship. ☐ **make an exhibition of oneself** behave so that one appears ridiculous.

exhibitionism *n.* **1** a tendency towards attention-seeking behaviour. **2** *Psychol.* a compulsion to display one's genitals in public. ☐ **exhibitionist** *n.*

exhilarate / eg-**zil**-uh-rayt, uhg- / *v.* make very happy or lively. ☐ **exhilaration** *n.*

exhort / eg-**zawt**, uhg- / *v.* urge or advise earnestly. ☐ **exhortation** / eg-zaw-**tay**-shuhn / *n.* **exhortative** *adj.* **exhortatory** *adj.*

exhume / eks-**hyoom** / *v.* dig up (esp. a dead body). ☐ **exhumation** *n.*

exigency / **ek**-suh-juhn-see, uhg-**zij**-uhn-see / *n.* (also **exigence**) **1** an urgent need (*the exigencies of the long-term unemployed*). **2** an emergency (*we need quick help in this exigency*).

exigent / **ek**-suh-juhnt / *adj.* **1** urgent. **2** exacting, requiring much.

exiguous / eg-**zig**-yoo-uhs, uhg- / *adj.* very small, scanty (*trying to make do on an exiguous income*). ☐ **exiguity** *n.*

exile *n.* **1** being sent away from one's country as a punishment. **2** long absence from one's country

exist

or home. **3** an exiled person. •*v.* send (a person) into exile.

exist *v.* **1** have a place as part of what is real (*do ghosts exist?*). **2** occur or be found (*air cannot exist in a vacuum; as long as these conditions exist*). **3** continue living (*we cannot exist without food*). **4** live with no pleasure, barely maintain life (*he felt he was merely existing, not living*).

existence *n.* **1** the state of existing, occurrence, presence (*no longer in existence*). **2** continuance in life or being (*the struggle for existence*). **3** the manner of one's existence or living, esp. under adverse conditions (*a wretched existence*). **4** all that exists.

existent *adj.* existing, actual, current.

existential / eg-zis-**ten**-shuhl / *adj.* **1** of existence. **2** of human experience as viewed by existentialism. □ **existentially** *adv.*

existentialism / eg-zis-**ten**-shuh-liz-uhm / *n.* a philosophical theory emphasising that people are responsible for their own actions and free to choose their development and destiny. □ **existentialist** *n.* & *adj.*

exit *n.* **1** the act of going away or out, departure from a place or position. **2** a passage or door to go out by. **3** a place where vehicles can leave a major road etc. **4** an actor's or performer's departure from the stage. •*v.* (**exited, exiting**) make one's exit, leave (also as a stage-direction: *exit Macbeth*). □ **exit poll** a poll of people leaving a polling station, asking how they voted.

ex libris *n.* (*pl.* same) a usu. decorated label bearing the owner's name, pasted into the front of a book. (¶ Latin, = among the books of.)

Exocet *n.* **1** *trademark* a kind of rocket-propelled short-range guided anti-ship missile which travels at almost the speed of sound. **2** (**exocet**) something devastating and unexpected, a 'bombshell' (*she then launched her exocet: the news that she was leaving me*). •*v.* (**exocet**) (**exoceted, exoceting**) **1** deliver an attack on (something) as if with an Exocet. **2** move seemingly as fast as an Exocet.

exocrine / **ek**-soh-kruyn / *adj.* (of a gland) secreting through a duct.

exodus *n.* **1** a mass departure of people. **2** (**Exodus**) the Biblical departure of the Israelites from Egypt.

ex officio / eks uh-**fish**-ee-oh / *adv.* & *adj.* because of one's official position (*the director is a member of this committee ex officio; an ex-officio member*). (¶ Latin)

exogamy / ek-**sog**-uh-mee / *n.* **1** the custom by which a marriage partner is chosen from outside one's own tribe or group (as opposed to ENDOGAMY). **2** *Biology* the fusion of reproductive cells from distantly related or unrelated individuals.

exonerate / eg-**zon**-uh-rayt, uhg- / *v.* free from blame, declare (a person) to be blameless. □ **exoneration** *n.*

278

expectant

exorbitant / eg-**zaw**-buh-tuhnt, uhg / *adj.* (of a price or demand) much too great.

exorcise / **ek**-saw-suyz / *v.* (also -**ize**) **1** drive out (a supposed evil spirit) by religious rituals etc. **2** free (a person or place) of evil spirits. □ **exorcism** *n.* **exorcist** *n.*

exordium / ek-**saw**-dee-uhm / *n.* (*pl.* **exordiums** or **exordia**) an introductory part, esp. of a discourse or treatise.

exoskeleton *n.* an external bony or leathery covering on an animal, e.g. the shell of a lobster.

exosphere *n.* the layer of atmosphere furthest from the earth.

exotic / eg-**zot**-ik, ugh- / *adj.* **1** (of plants, words, etc.) introduced from abroad, not native. **2** attractively or remarkably strange or unusual. •*n.* an exotic plant, person, or thing. □ **exotically** *adv.*

exotica *n.pl.* strange or rare objects, esp. as a collection.

expand *v.* **1** make or become larger, increase in bulk or importance. **2** unfold or spread out. **3** give a fuller account of, write out in full (*what is condensed or abbreviated*). **4** become genial, throw off one's reserve (*after a drink or two, he began to expand*). □ **expandable** *adj.*

expanse *n.* a wide area or extent of open land or space.

expansible *adj.* able to be expanded.

expansion *n.* **1** expanding, increase, extension. **2** enlargement or development of a business.

expansionism *n.* the practice of expanding (esp. a nation's) territory or area of influence. □ **expansionist** *n.* & *adj.*

expansive *adj.* **1** able or tending to expand. **2** (of a person or manner) genial, communicating thoughts and feelings readily. □ **expansively** *adv.* **expansiveness** *n.*

expatiate / ek-**spay**-shee-ayt, uhk- / *v.* speak or write about (a subject) at length (*expatiated on the un-Australianness of racism*). □ **expatiation** *n.* **expatiatory** *adj.*

expatriate *v.* / eks-**pat**-ree-ayt / banish (a person); withdraw (oneself) from one's native country and live abroad. •*adj.* / eks-**pat**-ree-uht / expatriated, living abroad; exiled. •*n.* / eks-**pat**-ree-uht, -**pay**-tree-uht / an expatriate person. □ **expatriation** *n.*

expect *v.* **1** regard as likely. **2** regard as appropriate or due to one (*he expects obedience*). **3** think, suppose. □ **be expecting** *colloq.* be pregnant.

expectancy *n.* **1** a state of expectation. **2** a prospect (*a life expectancy of 70 years*). **3** (foll. by *of*) an expected chance (*the expectancy of a better life after death*).

expectant *adj.* **1** filled with expectation. **2** having a baby (said of the mother or father). □ **expectantly** *adv.*

expectation *n.* **1** expecting, looking forward with hope or pleasure. **2** a thing that is expected to happen. **3** the probability that a thing will happen.

expectorant *n.* a medicine that causes a person to expectorate. • *adj.* causing expectoration.

expectorate *v.* cough and spit out phlegm from the throat or lungs; spit. ☐ **expectoration** *n.*

expedient / ek-**spee**-dee-uhnt / *adj.* **1** suitable for a particular purpose. **2** advantageous rather than right or just (*it may be expedient to deny that you were there*). • *n.* a means of achieving something (*when every expedient had been exhausted, he tried blackmail*). ☐ **expediently** *adv.* **expedience** *n.* **expediency** *n.*

expedite / **eks**-puh-duyt / *v.* help or hurry the progress of (business etc.), perform (business) quickly.

expedition *n.* **1** a journey or voyage for a particular purpose. **2** the people or ships etc. making this. **3** promptness, speed (*solved it with expedition*).

expeditionary *adj.* of or used in an expedition (*an expeditionary force*).

expeditious / ek-spuh-**dish**-uhs / *adj.* acting or done speedily or efficiently. ☐ **expeditiously** *adv.*

expel *v.* (**expelled**, **expelling**) **1** force or drive out. **2** compel (a person) to leave a school or country etc.

expend *v.* spend (money, time, etc.), use up.

expendable *adj.* **1** able to be expended. **2** not worth preserving, suitable for sacrificing in order to gain an objective (*he considered their lives expendable*).

expenditure *n.* **1** the process or an instance of spending or using up. **2** the thing (esp. money) expended.

expense *n.* **1** the cost or price of an activity. **2** a cause of spending money (*the car was a great expense*). **3** (**expenses**) the amount spent in doing a job etc. **4** (**expenses**) the amount paid to reimburse what has been spent (*$100 per day in expenses*). **5** expenditure (of other than money) (*at great expense of time and energy*). ☐ **at the expense of** so as to cause loss, damage, or discredit to (*succeeded but at the expense of his health; had a good laugh at my expense*).

expensive *adj.* costing or charging a great deal. ☐ **expensively** *adv.* **expensiveness** *n.*

experience *n.* **1** actual observation of facts or events; activity or practice in doing something (*has little experience of life; school has a work experience program*). **2** skill or knowledge gained in this way (*most job ads call for people with experience*). **3** an event or activity that gives one experience. • *v.* **1** observe or share in (an event etc.) personally (*he thinks he's experiencing a mid-life crisis*). **2** be affected by (a feeling) (*experienced sheer terror*).

experienced *adj.* having knowledge or skill gained from much experience.

experiential / ek-speer-ree-**en**-shuhl / *adj.* involving or based on experience.

experiment *n.* **1** a test or trial carried out to see how something works, to find out what happens, or to demonstrate a known fact. **2** the act or an instance of trying out something new. • *v.* conduct an experiment. ☐ **experimentation** *n.*

experimental *adj.* **1** of, used in, or based on experiments. **2** still being tested. ☐ **experimentally** *adv.* **experimentalism** *n.*

expert *n.* **1** a person with great knowledge or skill in a particular thing. **2** *Aust.* a person responsible for maintaining machinery, esp. in a shearing shed. • *adj.* **1** having great knowledge or skill. **2** involving or resulting from this (*expert advice*). • *v. Aust.* maintain the machinery in a shearing shed. ☐ **expert system** *Computing* a system, used to simulate highly specialised tasks, which infers new facts from a given information base and which has the ability to explain its reasoning processes. ☐☐ **expertly** *adv.*

expertise / ek-sper-**teez** / *n.* expert knowledge, skill, or judgment.

expiable / **eks**-pee-uh-buhl / *adj.* able to be expiated.

expiate / **eks**-pee-ayt / *v.* make amends for (wrongdoing). ☐ **expiation** *n.*

expire *v.* **1** breathe out (air). **2** breathe one's last, die. **3** come to the end of its period of validity (*this licence has expired*). ☐ **expiration** / ek-spuh-**ray**-shuhn / *n.*

expiry *n.* the end of a period of validity, e.g. of a licence or contract.

explain *v.* **1** make plain or clear, show the meaning of. **2** account for (*that explains his absence*). ☐ **explain away** minimise the significance of by offering reasons or excuses.

explanation *n.* **1** explaining. **2** a statement or fact that explains something.

explanatory / ek-**splan**-uh-tuh-ree, uhk-, -tree / *adj.* serving or intended to explain something.

expletive / ek-**splee**-tiv / *n.* a swear word or exclamation.

explicable / eks-**plik**-uh-buhl / *adj.* able to be explained.

explicate / **eks**-pluh-kayt / *v.* bring out the implicit meaning of (an idea or statement) more fully or clearly. ☐ **explication** *n.*

explicit / ek-**splis**-uht, uhk- / *adj.* **1** stated or shown directly rather than being implied. **2** detailed and definite. **3** (of a person, a book, etc.) expressing views unreservedly; outspoken. **4** graphic, leaving nothing to the imagination (*explicit sex-scenes*). ☐ **explicitly** *adv.* **explicitness** *n.*

explode *v.* **1** expand or burst violently and with a loud noise; cause to do this. **2** (of feelings) burst out; (of a person) show sudden violent emotion (*exploded with laughter*). **3** (of a population, supply of goods, etc.) increase suddenly or rapidly. **4** destroy (a theory) by showing it to be false

exploit

(*exploded his contention that the holocaust never took place*). ☐ **exploded diagram** one showing the parts of a structure in their relative positions but slightly separated from each other.

exploit *n.* / **ek**-sploit / a bold or notable deed. • *v.* / ek-**sploit** / **1** work or develop (mines and other natural resources). **2** take full advantage of, use (employees etc.) for one's own advantage and their disadvantage. ☐ **exploitation** *n.*

exploratory / ek-**splo**-ruh-tuh-ree, uhk-, -tree / *adj.* for the purpose of exploring.

explore *v.* **1** travel into or through (a country etc.) in order to learn about it. **2** examine by touch. **3** examine or investigate (a problem, possibilities, etc.). ☐ **exploration** *n.* **explorer** *n.*

explosion *n.* **1** exploding; being exploded; a loud noise caused by this. **2** a sudden outburst of anger, laughter, etc. **3** a sudden great increase (*the population explosion*).

explosive *adj.* **1** able to explode, tending to explode. **2** likely to cause violent and dangerous reactions, dangerously tense (*an explosive situation*). • *n.* an explosive substance. ☐ **explosively** *adv.*

Expo *n.* (also **expo**) (*pl.* **Expos**) a large international exhibition.

exponent / ek-**spoh**-nuhnt, uhk- / *n.* **1** a person who sets out the facts or interprets something. **2** one who favours a particular theory or policy (*he's an exponent of harsh censorship laws*). **3** *Maths* a raised figure or other symbol beside a number etc. indicating how many times the number is to be multiplied by itself.

exponential *adj.* **1** of or indicated by a mathematical exponent. **2** (of an increase) more and more rapid.

export *v.* / ek-**spawt**, uhk-, **ek**-spawt / send (goods etc.) to another country for sale. • *n.* / **ek**-spawt / **1** exporting. **2** a thing exported. ☐ **exporter** *n.* **exportation** *n.* **exportable** *adj.*

expose *v.* **1** leave (a person or thing) uncovered or unprotected, esp. from the weather. **2** (often foll. by *to*) subject to a risk, an influence, etc. (*exposed to great danger; Mozart was exposed to music from infancy*). **3** allow light to reach (photographic film or plate). **4** make visible, reveal. **5** make known or reveal (a crime, impostor, etc.); reveal the wrongdoings of (a person). ☐ **expose oneself** display one's body, esp. one's genitals, indecently in public.

exposé / ek-spoh-**zay** / *n.* **1** an orderly statement of facts. **2** revelation of a discreditable thing.

exposed *adj.* **1** (of a place) not sheltered. **2** vulnerable to danger or criticism.

exposition *n.* **1** expounding; an explanatory account of a plan or theory etc. **2** a large public exhibition. **3** (in music) the part of a movement in which themes are presented. ☐ **expositional** *adj.*

expulsion

expostulate / ek-**spos**-tyoo-layt, uhk- / *v.* make a protest, reason or argue with a person. ☐ **expostulation** *n.* **expostulatory** *adj.*

exposure *n.* **1** exposing or being exposed. **2** a physical condition resulting from being exposed to the elements (*died of exposure*). **3** the exposing of photographic film or plate to the light; the length of time for which this is done. **4** a section of film exposed as a unit. **5** publicity, good or bad. **6** aspect or outlook (*has a fine southern exposure*). ☐ **exposure meter** a device measuring light and indicating the length of time needed for a photographic exposure.

expound *v.* set forth or explain in detail.

express *adj.* **1** definitely stated, not merely implied (*those are his express instructions*). **2** done, made, or sent for a special purpose (*did it with the express intention of humiliating his wife*). **3** going or sent quickly; designed for high speed; (of a train etc.) travelling rapidly to its destination with few or no intermediate stops. **4** (of a letter or parcel) delivered quickly by a special messenger or service. • *adv.* at high speed; by express service. • *n.* an express train etc. • *v.* **1** make known (feelings or qualities) (*expressed dissatisfaction; his body language expresses unease*). **2** put (a thought etc.) into words (*she expresses her ideas well*). **3** represent by means of symbols, e.g. in mathematics. **4** press or squeeze out. **5** send by express service. ☐ **express oneself** communicate one's thoughts or feelings (*expressed himself of the view that Australia should be a Republic*). ☐ **expressible** *adj.*

expression *n.* **1** expressing, being expressed. **2** a word or phrase. **3** a look that expresses one's feelings. **4** the conveying of feeling in music, speaking, dance, etc.; the depiction of feeling etc. in art. **5** a collection of mathematical symbols expressing a quantity.

expressionism *n.* a style of painting, drama, or music seeking to express the artist's or writer's emotional experience rather than to represent the physical world realistically. ☐ **expressionist** *n.* & *adj.* **expressionistic** *adj.*

expressionless *adj.* without positive expression, not revealing one's thoughts or feelings (*an expressionless face*).

expressive *adj.* **1** serving to express (*a tone expressive of contempt*). **2** full of expression (*an expressive voice*). ☐ **expressively** *adv.* **expressiveness** *n.*

expressly *adv.* **1** explicitly. **2** for a particular purpose.

expresso = ESPRESSO.

expressway *n.* *US & Aust.* a road designed for fast traffic.

expropriate / eks-**proh**-pree-ayt / *v.* **1** take away (property) from its owner. **2** dispossess (a person). ☐ **expropriation** *n.*

expulsion *n.* expelling; being expelled. ☐ **expulsive** *adj.*

expunge / ek-**spunj** / v. wipe or rub out, delete.

expurgate / **eks**-puh-gayt / v. remove what one considers to be objectionable matter from (a book etc.); remove (such matter). ☐ **expurgation** n. **expurgator** n.

exquisite / **eks**-kwuh-zuht, ek-**skwiz**-uht / adj. **1** having special beauty. **2** having excellent discrimination (*exquisite taste in dress*). **3** acute, keenly felt (*exquisite pain*). ☐ **exquisitely** adv.

ex-serviceman n. a man formerly a member of the armed forces.

ex-servicewoman n. a woman formerly a member of the armed forces.

extant / ek-**stant**, **ek**-stuhnt / adj. still existing (*the only extant manuscript*).

extemporaneous / ek-stem-puh-**ray**-nee-uhs, uhk- / adj. spoken or done without preparation. ☐ **extemporaneously** adv.

extemporary / ek-**stem**-puh-ruh-ree, uhk-, -pruh-ree / adj. extemporaneous.

extempore / ek-**stem**-puh-ree, uhk- / adv. & adj. (spoken or done) without preparation, impromptu.

extemporise / ek-**stem**-puh-ruyz, uhk- / v. (also **-ize**) speak or produce extempore. ☐ **extemporisation** n.

extend v. **1** make longer in space or time. **2** stretch out (a hand, foot, etc.). **3** reach, be continuous over an area or from one point to another (*our land extends to the river; his power extends from Moscow to London*). **4** enlarge, increase the scope of. **5** offer or grant (*extend a welcome*). **6** (of a task) stretch the ability of (a person) fully. ☐ **extended family** a family including relatives in addition to parents and children. ☐☐ **extendible** adj. **extensible** adj.

extension n. **1** extending; being extended. **2** extent, range. **3** an addition or section extended from the main part of a building etc. **4** an additional period of time allowed (*got an extension on my essay*). **5** a subsidiary telephone on the same line as the main one; its number. **6** extramural instruction by a university or college (*extension lectures*).

extensive adj. **1** large in area (*extensive gardens*). **2** wide-ranging, large in scope (*extensive knowledge*). ☐ **extensively** adv. **extensiveness** n.

extent n. **1** the space over which a thing extends. **2** the range or scope of something (*the full extent of his power*). **3** a large area (*an extent of marsh*).

extenuate / ek-**sten**-yoo-ayt, uhk- / v. make (a person's guilt or offence) seem less serious by providing an explanation or excuse (*there were extenuating circumstances*). ☐ **extenuation** n.

exterior adj. on or coming from the outside. ● n. an external surface, part, or appearance.

exterminate v. destroy utterly (esp. a living thing). ☐ **extermination** n. **exterminator** n.

external adj. **1** of or on the outside or visible part of something. **2** of or on the outside of the body (*for external use only*). **3** coming or obtained from an independent source (*external influences*). **4** relating to a country's foreign affairs. **5** belonging to the world outside a person or people, not in the mind. **6** for or concerning students taking the examinations of a university without attending it. ● n.pl. (**externals**) outward appearances; external circumstances. ☐ **externally** adv.

externalise v. (also **-ize**) give or attribute external existence to. ☐ **externalisation** n.

extinct adj. **1** having died out (*extinct animals*). **2** (of a volcano) no longer active. **3** no longer burning.

extinction n. **1** extinguishing, being extinguished. **2** making or becoming extinct.

extinguish v. **1** put out (a light, fire, or flame). **2** end the existence of (hope, passion, etc.).

extinguisher = FIRE EXTINGUISHER.

extirpate / **ek**-stuh-payt / v. root out and destroy completely. ☐ **extirpation** n.

extol / ek-**stohl**, uhk- / v. (**extolled**, **extolling**) praise enthusiastically.

extort v. obtain (esp. money) by force, threats, or intimidation. ☐ **extortion** n. **extortioner** n.

extortionate / ek-**staw**-shuh-nuht, uhk- / adj. excessively high in price; (of demands) excessive. ☐ **extortionately** adv.

extra adj. additional, more than is usual or expected. ● adv. **1** more than usually (*extra strong*). **2** in addition (*postage extra*). ● n. **1** an extra thing, something additional. **2** a thing for which an additional charge is made (*salad's an extra*). **3** a run in cricket scored otherwise than from a hit by the bat. **4** a special issue of a newspaper etc. **5** a person engaged temporarily for a minor part or to form one of a crowd in a cinema film. **6** a lesson taken by a teacher for an absent colleague. ☐ **extra time** *Sport* **1** added playing time to make up for time lost through interruptions to play. **2** an additional period of play so that a result may be achieved.

extra- *comb. form* **1** outside or beyond (a boundary) (*extraterrestrial*). **2** beyond the scope of (*extracurricular*).

extract v. / ek-**strakt**, uhk- / **1** take out by force or effort (something firmly fixed). **2** obtain (money, information, etc.) from someone unwilling to give it. **3** obtain (juice) by suction or pressure; obtain (a substance) as an extract. **4** obtain (information from a book etc.); take or copy passages from (a book). **5** derive (pleasure etc.). ● n. / **ek**-strakt / **1** a substance separated from another by dissolving it or by other treatment. **2** a concentrated substance prepared from another. **3** a passage from a book, play, film, or piece of music.

extraction n. **1** extracting. **2** descent, lineage (*he is of Sri Lankan extraction*). **3** a removal of a tooth.

extractive adj. of or involving extraction; extracting minerals from the ground.

extractor *n.* **1** a person or machine that extracts. **2** (usu. used as *adj.*) (of a device) extracting stale or polluted air (*extractor fan*).

extracurricular / eks-truh-kuh-**rik**-yuh-luh / *adj.* not part of the normal curriculum.

extraditable / eks-truh-**duy**-tuh-buhl / *adj.* liable to extradition; (of a crime) warranting extradition.

extradite / **eks**-truh-duyt / *v.* **1** hand over (a person accused or convicted of a crime) to the foreign country, State, etc. where the crime was committed (*Tasmania extradited him to Victoria*). **2** obtain (such a person) for trial or punishment. □ **extradition** / eks-truh-**dish**-uhn / *n.*

extramarital / eks-truh-**ma**-ruh-tuhl / *adj.* (esp. of sexual relationships) occurring outside marriage.

extramural / eks-truh-**myoo**-ruhl / *adj.* (of university teaching or studies) for students who are non-resident or who are not members of the university.

extraneous / ek-**stray**-nee-uhs / *adj.* **1** of external origin. **2** not belonging to the matter or subject in hand. □ **extraneously** *adv.*

extranet *n.* *Computing* a secure network that supplements a closed intranet by allowing access to suppliers, customers, etc., outside the company or organisation.

extraordinaire / ek-straw-duh-**nair** / *adj.* (always following the *noun*) of exceptional skill or talent (*a chef extraordinaire*).

extraordinary *adj.* **1** very unusual or remarkable. **2** beyond what is usual or ordinary (*an extraordinary general meeting*). □ **extraordinarily** *adv.*

extrapolate / ek-**strap**-uh-layt / *v.* make an estimate of (something unknown and outside the range of one's data) on the basis of available data. □ **extrapolation** *n.*

extrasensory *adj.* achieved by some means other than the known senses. □ **extrasensory perception** the supposed faculties of telepathy, clairvoyance, etc.

extraterrestrial *adj.* **1** of or from outside the earth or its atmosphere. **2** *Science Fiction* of or from outer space. • *n.* *Science Fiction* a being from outer space.

extravagant *adj.* **1** spending much more than is necessary. **2** (of prices) excessively high. **3** (of ideas, praise, behaviour, etc.) going beyond what is reasonable, not properly controlled. **4** flamboyant, showy (*an extravagant display*). □ **extravagantly** *adv.* **extravagance** *n.*

extravaganza / ek-strav-uh-**gan**-zuh, uhk- / *n.* **1** a lavish spectacular film or theatrical production. **2** a fanciful composition in music.

extreme *adj.* **1** very great or intense (*extreme cold*). **2** at the end(s), furthest, outermost (*the extreme edge*). **3** going to great lengths in actions or views, not moderate (*extreme measures*). **4** on the far left or right of a political party (*the extreme right of the Liberal Party*). • *n.* **1** either end of anything. **2** an extreme degree, act, or condition. □ **extreme sport** a sport performed in a hazardous environment. **extreme unction** the last rites for the dying in the Catholic and Orthodox Churches. □ **extremely** *adv.*

extremist *n.* a person with extreme or fanatical political or religious views, esp. one who resorts to or advocates extreme action. □ **extremism** *n.*

extremity / ek-**strem**-uh-tee, uhk- / *n.* **1** an extreme point, the end of something. **2** an extreme degree of feeling, need, danger, etc. **3** (**extremities**) the hands and feet.

extricate / **eks**-truh-kayt / *v.* disentangle or release from an entanglement or difficulty etc. □ **extrication** *n.* **extricable** *adj.*

extrinsic / ek-**strin**-zik / *adj.* **1** not inherent or intrinsic; not essential. **2** (often foll. by *to*) extraneous; not belonging.

extrovert / **eks**-truh-vert / *n.* **1** a person more interested in the people and things around him or her than in his or her own thoughts and feelings. **2** a lively sociable person. • *adj.* (also **extroverted**) having these characteristics. □ **extroversion** *n.*

extrude *v.* **1** thrust or squeeze out. **2** shape (metal or plastic etc.) by forcing through a die. **3** jut out, protrude. □ **extrusion** *n.*

exuberant / eg-**zyoo**-buh-ruhnt / *adj.* **1** full of high spirits, very lively. **2** growing profusely (*plants with exuberant foliage*). □ **exuberantly** *adv.* **exuberance** *n.*

exude / eg-**zyood** / *v.* **1** (of a liquid etc.) ooze out (*the pus exuding from the wound*). **2** send out (a liquid etc.) (*exuding sweat from every pore*). **3** emit (a smell). **4** show (an emotion etc.) freely (*exuding confidence*). □ **exudation** / eks-yoo-**day**-shuhn / *n.*

exult / eg-**zult** / *v.* **1** rejoice greatly (*exulting in their freedom*). **2** have a feeling of triumph (over a person) (*exulted over their downfall*). □ **exultation** *n.*

■ **Usage** *Exult* is often confused with *exalt*.

exultant *adj.* exulting.

eye *n.* **1** the organ of sight in humans and animals. **2** the eye characterised by the colour of the iris (*I have blue eyes*). **3** the region round the eye (*gave him a black eye*). **4** (also as **eyes**) the power of seeing, observation (*sharp eyes; a good eye*). **5** a thing like an eye; a spot on a peacock's tail; a leaf bud on a potato. **6** the calm region at the centre of a storm or hurricane. **7** the hole in a needle, through which thread is passed. • *v.* (**eyed**, **eyeing** or **eying**) look at, watch (*eyed him with suspicion*). □ **all eyes** watching intently. **eye-catching** *colloq.* striking. **eye off** *colloq.* **1** watch (a thing) closely (esp. with the intention of stealing it). **2** look at (a person) with interest, esp. sexual interest. **eye-opener** *colloq.* a fact or circumstance that brings enlightenment or great surprise. **eye shadow** a cosmetic applied to the eyelids and skin round the eyes. **get** (*or* **keep**) **one's eye in** accustom oneself (*or* keep oneself accustomed) to conditions requiring expertise (in sport etc.). **have an eye for** be capable of recognising or appreciating (*he has an eye for beauty; has a good eye for a bargain*). **have an eye to** be alert to (*he has an eye to the main chance*). **have eyes for** be interested in (*he has eyes for no-one but me*). **have one's eye on** wish or plan to buy (*she has her eye on a diamond ring*). **in the eyes of** in the opinion or judgment of. **pick the eyes out of** select the best parts of. **see eye to eye** be in full agreement with a person. **up to the eyes** (*or* **one's eyes**) **in** deeply involved or occupied in (something). **with an eye to** with the aim or intention of. **with one's eyes shut** (*or* **closed**) with the greatest ease (*I can do it with my eyes shut*).

eyeball *n.* the ball of the eye, within the lids. • *v.* stare at.

eyebrow *n.* the line of hair growing on the ridge above the eye-socket. ☐ **raise one's eyebrows** show surprise or disapproval.

eyeful *n.* (*pl.* **eyefuls**) **1** something thrown or blown into one's eye (*got an eyeful of sand*). **2** *colloq.* a thorough look (*having an eyeful*). **3** *colloq.* a visually attractive person or thing (*he's quite an eyeful*).

eyeglass *n.* a lens to aid defective sight.

eyelash *n.* one of the fringe of hairs on the edge of each eyelid.

eyelet *n.* **1** a small hole through which a rope or cord is passed. **2** a metal ring strengthening this.

eyelid *n.* the upper or lower fold of skin closing to cover the eyeball.

eyeliner *n.* a cosmetic applied as a line round the eye.

eyepiece *n.* the lens or lenses to which the eye is applied at the end of a telescope or other optical instrument.

eyeshade *n.* a visor worn on the forehead to protect the eyes from strong light.

eyesight *n.* **1** the ability to see. **2** range of vision (*within eyesight*).

eyesore *n.* a thing that is ugly to look at, esp. a building.

eyetooth *n.* a canine tooth in the upper jaw, under the eye.

eyewash *n.* **1** a lotion for the eyes. **2** *colloq.* nonsense; insincere talk.

eyewitness *n.* a person who saw an event and can describe it.

Eyre[1], Edward John (1815–1901), Australian explorer and writer (born in England). He made the first Sydney-Adelaide overland crossing and later made the epic journey into central Australia and overland around the Great Australian Bight to King George Sound in WA.

Eyre[2], John (?1771–?), Australian artist (transported from England as a convict in 1801) who is famed for his watercolours and drawings of Sydney and its surrounds.

Eyre, Lake a salt lake in SA in two parts connected by the Goyder Channel; usually dry; the largest lake in Australia (5,800 square km). Lake Eyre was first sighted by Edward John Eyre in 1840.

eyrie / **eer**-ree, **air**-ree / *n.* **1** the high nest of an eagle or other bird of prey. **2** a house etc. perched high up.

e-zine / ee-zeen / *n.* an electronic magazine, distributed by means of a computer network.

F

F *n.* (*pl.* **Fs** *or* **F's**) *Music* the fourth note of the scale of C major. • *abbr.* Fahrenheit. • *symbol* fluorine.

f *abbr.* (also **f.**) **1** female; feminine. **2** *Music* forte. **3** focal length. **4** following page etc.

fa alternative spelling of FAH.

fab *adj. colloq.* fabulous, marvellous.

fable *n.* **1** a short (usu. supernatural) story not based on fact, often with animals as characters and conveying a moral. **2** these stories or legends collectively. **3** untrue statements (*sort out fact from fable*).

fabled *adj.* told of in fables, legendary.

fabric *n.* **1** cloth; woven or knitted or felted material. **2** the walls, floors, and roof of a building. **3** the essential structure or essence of a thing (*the fabric of society*).

fabricate *v.* **1** construct, manufacture. **2** invent (a story); forge (a document). ☐ **fabrication** *n.* **fabricator** *n.*

fabulous *adj.* **1** told of in fables; legendary (*the fabulous bunyip*). **2** incredibly great (*fabulous wealth*). **3** *colloq.* wonderful, marvellous. ☐ **fabulously** *adv.*

façade / fuh-**sahd** / *n.* (also **facade**) **1** the face or front of a building. **2** an outward appearance, esp. a deceptive one.

face *n.* **1** the front part of the head from forehead to chin. **2** the expression shown by its features (*a cheerful face; made a face*). **3** coolness, effrontery. **4** the outward show or aspect of something (*the unacceptable face of capitalism*). **5** the front, façade, or right side of something; the dial of a clock; the distinctive side of a playing card. **6** a coalface. **7** *Aust.* the front of a bushfire. **8** the striking surface of a bat etc.; the working surface of a tool. **9** *Aust.* the side of a mob of cattle etc. that is being worked. • *v.* **1** have or turn the face towards (a certain direction). **2** be opposite to (*facing page 20*). **3** meet confidently or defiantly; accept and be prepared to deal with (unpleasant facts or problems). **4** meet (an opponent) in a contest. **5** present itself to (*the problem that faces us*). **6** cover (a surface) with a layer of different material; put a facing on (a garment etc.). ☐ **face the music** face unpleasant consequences bravely. **face value 1** the value printed or stamped on money. **2** the superficial appearance or outward impression of a thing. **lose face** be humiliated. **save face** avoid humiliation.

facecloth *n.* (also **face flannel**, **face washer**) a cloth for washing one's face.

faceless *adj.* **1** without identity or character. **2** deliberately not identifiable.

facelift *n.* **1** cosmetic surgery to remove wrinkles etc. **2** an alteration etc. that improves the appearance, e.g. of a building.

facer *n. colloq.* a sudden great difficulty.

facet / **fas**-uht / *n.* **1** each of the many sides of a cut stone or jewel. **2** each aspect of a situation or problem.

facetious / fuh-**see**-shuhs / *adj.* intended or intending to be amusing, esp. inappropriately. ☐ **facetiously** *adv.* **facetiousness** *n.*

facia alternative spelling of FASCIA.

facial / **fay**-shuhl / *adj.* of or for the face. • *n.* a beauty treatment for the face. ☐ **facially** *adv.*

facile / **fas**-uyl / *adj.* **1** easily achieved but of little value (*a facile solution*). **2** glib, fluent.

facilitate / fuh-**sil**-uh-tayt / *v.* make easier. ☐ **facilitation** *n.*

facilitator *n.* a person or thing that facilitates something, esp. a person who helps others to develop business plans etc.

facility / fuh-**sil**-uh-tee / *n.* **1** the quality of being easy; absence of difficulty. **2** ease in doing something, aptitude (*facility of expression*). **3** (often as **facilities**) an opportunity, the equipment, or the resources for doing something (*sports facilities*).

facing *n.* **1** an outer layer covering a surface. **2** a layer of material covering part of a garment etc. for contrast or strengthening.

facsimile / fak-**sim**-uh-lee / *n.* an exact copy of a document, book, painting, etc. (*see also* FAX).

fact *n.* **1** something known to have happened, to be true, or to exist. **2** a thing asserted to be true as a basis for reasoning (*his facts are disputed*). ☐ **before** (*or* **after**) **the fact** before (or after) the committing of a crime. **fact of life** something that must be accepted. **facts of life** information about sexual functions and practices.

faction / **fak**-shuhn / *n.* **1** a small united group within a larger one, esp. in politics. **2** dissent within a group. ☐ **factional** *adj.* **factionally** *adv.*

factious / **fak**-shuhs / *adj.* characterised by or inclined to faction.

factitious / fak-**tish**-uhs / *adj.* **1** made for a special purpose; contrived. **2** artificial (*factitious grief*). ☐ **factitiously** *adv.*

factor *n.* **1** a circumstance or influence that contributes towards a result (*safety factor*). **2** any of the numbers or mathematical expressions by which a larger number etc. can be divided exactly (*2, 3, 4, and 6 are factors of 12*). **3** a business agent.

factorise v. (also **-ize**) convert into factors. ☐ **factorisation** n.

factory n. a building or buildings in which goods are manufactured. ☐ **factory floor** the workers in a factory or industry as distinct from the management.

factotum / fak-**toh**-tuhm / n. an employee who does all kinds of work.

factual adj. based on or concerning facts. ☐ **factually** adv.

faculty / **fak**-uhl-tee / n. **1** a power of the body or mind (*the faculty of sight*). **2** a particular aptitude or ability (*a faculty for learning languages*). **3** a department teaching a particular subject or group of related subjects in a university or college (*the law faculty*). **4** the academic staff of these departments.

fad n. **1** a particular like or dislike, a craze. **2** a peculiar notion. ☐ **faddish** adj.

Fadden, Sir Arthur (William) (1895–1973), Australian Country Party statesman, prime minister for five weeks in 1941.

faddy adj. having petty likes and dislikes, e.g. about food. ☐ **faddiness** n.

fade v. **1** lose or cause to lose colour, freshness, or vigour. **2** (often foll. by *away*) disappear gradually; become indistinct; languish or grow thin; die gradually. **3** (foll. by *out, in*) cause (the sound or picture in broadcasting or cinema) to decrease or increase gradually. **4** angle a surfboard towards the breaking part of a wave. • n. an act or sound of fading.

faeces / **fee**-seez / n.pl. waste matter discharged from the bowels. ☐ **faecal** / **fee**-kuhl / adj.

faerie n. **1** (**Faerie**) the enchanted realm peopled by elves etc. **2** (also **faery**) poetic a fairy. • adj. poetic (also **faery**) fairy.

fag v. (**fagged, fagging**) make tired. • n. **1** colloq. tiring work, drudgery (*what a fag!*). **2** exhaustion (*brain-fag*). **3** colloq. a cigarette. **4** colloq. offens. a male homosexual. ☐ **fag end 1** the last bit; a useless remnant. **2** a cigarette butt. **fagged** or **fagged out** tired out.

faggot n. **1** a bundle of sticks or twigs bound together. **2** a ball of chopped seasoned liver, served baked. **3** a bundle of herbs for seasoning, a bouquet garni. **4** colloq. offens. a male homosexual.

fah n. (also **fa**) *Music* the fourth note of a major scale.

Fahd ibn Abdul Aziz, (?1922–), the king and prime minister of Saudi Arabia.

Fahrenheit / fa-ruhn-huyt / adj. of a temperature scale with the freezing point of water at 32° and the boiling point at 212°. (¶ Named after the German physicist G. Fahrenheit (1686–1736).)

faience / **fuy**-ahns / n. pottery decorated with an opaque glaze.

fail v. **1** be unsuccessful in what is attempted. **2** be or become insufficient; (of crops) produce a very poor harvest. **3** become weak or ineffective, cease functioning (*the engine failed*). **4** neglect, forget, or be unable to do something (*he failed to appear*). **5** disappoint the hopes of. **6** become bankrupt. **7** judge (a candidate) not to have passed an examination. • n. failure in an examination. ☐ **fail-safe** adj. (of equipment) reverting to a danger-free condition in the event of a breakdown or other failure.

failed adj. unsuccessful (*a failed author*).

failing n. a weakness or fault. • prep. if (a thing) does not happen; if (a person) is not available.

failure n. **1** failing, non-performance of something, lack of success. **2** breakdown of a mechanism; the ceasing of a part of the body etc. to function (*heart failure*). **3** bankruptcy, collapse. **4** an unsuccessful person, thing, or attempt.

fain adj. & adv. archaic willing or willingly under the circumstances.

faint adj. **1** not clearly perceived by the senses, indistinct; not intense in colour, sound, or smell. **2** weak, vague (*a faint hope*). **3** timid, feeble. **4** about to lose consciousness. • v. lose consciousness temporarily through failure in the supply of blood to the brain. • n. an act or state of fainting. ☐ **faintly** adv. **faintness** n.

fair n. **1** a periodical gathering for the sale of goods, often with entertainments. **2** an exhibition of commercial or industrial goods. **3** a funfair. • adj. **1** (of the hair or skin) light in colour; (of a person) having fair hair. **2** archaic beautiful. **3** (of weather) fine, (of winds) favourable. **4** just, unbiased, in accordance with the rules. **5** of moderate quality or amount. • adv. in a fair manner. ☐ **a fair cop** colloq. the discovery of someone in the act of doing something wrong. **a fair cow** Aust. colloq. anything unpleasant or difficult (*a fair cow of a job!*). **a fair treat** colloq. excessively; lavishly (*she bucketed him a fair treat*). **fair dinkum** Aust. adj. true, genuine, reliable, DINKUM. interj. (also **fair dink**) an assertion of utter reliability (*I wouldn't lie to you, mate, fair dink!*). **fair game** a person or thing crying out for criticism or attack (*after his obnoxiously racist remarks, he's fair game*). **fair go** Aust. colloq. n. a fair chance; fair treatment. exclamation (a plea for fair treatment) steady on!; be reasonable! **fair suck** (in full **fair suck of the sauce bottle**) Aust. colloq. = FAIR GO exclamation. **in a fair way to** likely to. **fair-weather** adj. reliable only when things go well, unreliable in times of trouble (*a fair-weather friend*). ☐☐ **fairness** n.

Fairfax the name of an Australian family notable as newspaper proprietors and philanthropists.

fairing n. a structure added to the exterior of a ship or aircraft etc. to streamline it.

fair isle n. (also **Fair Isle**) a knitting design in coloured wools (orig. from the Shetland Island of the same name).

fairly adv. **1** in a fair manner. **2** moderately (*fairly difficult*). **3** actually (*fairly jumped for joy*).

fairway *n.* **1** a navigable channel. **2** part of a golf course between tee and green, kept free of rough grass.

fairy *n.* **1** a tiny imaginary being with wings. **2** *colloq. offens.* **a** an effeminate man. **b** an effeminate male homosexual. • *adj.* **1** of fairies, fairy-like, delicate, small. **2** (in the names of flora and fauna) small, finely formed (*fairy grass; fairy possum; fairy prion; fairy tern*). ☐ **fairy bread** *Aust.* bread buttered and sprinkled with hundreds and thousands. **fairy floss** *Aust. n.* **1** airy spun sugar on a stick. **2** an inconsequential person or thing. *adj.* lacking in substance, strength (of character) etc.; trivial; of no consequence. **fairy godmother** a benefactress who provides a sudden unexpected gift. **fairy penguin** a small penguin with steel-blue back and white front found on the southern coasts of Australia. **fairy possum** a small possum inhabiting tree hollows in south-eastern Australia. **fairy story** (*or* **tale**) **1** a tale about fairies or magic. **2** an incredible story; a falsehood. **fairy toast** = MELBA TOAST. **fairy wren** any of several Australian wrens, the breeding male having bright variously coloured plumage.

fairyland *n.* **1** the world of fairies. **2** a very beautiful place.

fait accompli / fayt ah-kom-**plee** / *n.* a thing that is already done and not reversible. (¶ French)

faith *n.* **1** reliance or trust. **2** firm (esp. religious) belief not based on proof. **3** a system of religious belief (*the Christian faith*). **4** a promise; loyalty, sincerity. **5** (used as *adj.*) concerned with curing by faith and prayer rather than medical treatment (*faith healing*). ☐ **in bad faith** with intent to deceive. **in good faith** with honest intention.

faithful *adj.* **1** loyal, trustworthy, conscientious. **2** true to the facts, accurate (*a faithful account*). **3** maintaining sexual fidelity, having sex with no-one but one's lover or spouse. **4** (**the faithful**) **a** the believers in a religion. **b** loyal supporters. ☐ **faithfulness** *n.*

faithfully *adv.* in a faithful manner. ☐ **Yours faithfully** the formula for ending a formal letter when it begins 'Dear Sir' or 'Dear Madam'.

faithless *adj.* **1** false to promises, disloyal. **2** lacking religious faith.

fake *n.* a person or thing that is not genuine. • *adj.* faked, not genuine. • *v.* **1** make (a thing) that looks genuine, in order to deceive people. **2** pretend (*he faked illness*). ☐ **faker** *n.*

fakir / **fay**-keer / *n.* a Muslim or (rarely) Hindu religious beggar or ascetic regarded as a holy man.

falcon / **fal**-kuhn / *n.* a small long-winged hawk.

falconry *n.* the breeding and training of hawks.

Falk, Leib Aisack (1889–1957), Australian rabbi at the Great Synagogue in Sydney and chaplain to the Australian Military Forces in the Second World War. ☐ **the Rabbi Falk Memorial Library** the library, housed in the Great Synagogue, which contains Rabbi Falk's collection of books on Judaism etc., the largest such collection in the Southern hemisphere.

fall *v.* (**fell, fallen, falling**) **1** come or go down freely, e.g. by force of weight, loss of balance, or becoming detached. **2** come as if by falling (*silence fell*). **3** lose one's position or office (*fell from power*). **4** (of hair, clothing, etc.) hang down. **5** decrease in amount, number, or intensity (*prices fell; her spirits fell; the barometer is falling*). **6** slope downwards. **7** (of the face) show dismay. **8** cease to stand (*six wickets fell*). **9** die in battle. **10** (of a fortress or city) be captured. **11** take a specified direction or place (*his glance fell on me; the stress falls on the second syllable*). **12** come by chance or be assigned as what one must have or do (*the honour falls to you*). **13** happen to come (*fell into bad company*). **14** pass into a specified state, become (*fall in love; fell asleep; she fell pregnant*). **15** occur, have as a date (*Easter fell early*). • *n.* **1** the act of falling. **2** giving way to temptation. **3** the amount by which something falls. **4** *US* autumn. **5** a wrestling bout; a throw that causes the opponent to remain on the ground for a specified time. **6** (**falls**) a waterfall. ☐ **fall about** *colloq.* be helpless with laughter. **fall back on** retreat to; turn to for help when something else has failed. **fall for 1** fall in love with. **2** be taken in by (a deception). **fall foul of** come into conflict with. **fall guy** *colloq.* an easy victim; a scapegoat. **fall in** take one's place in a military formation. **falling star** a meteor. **fall in with 1** meet by chance. **2** agree to. **fall off** decrease in size, number, or quality. **fall off the back of a truck** *Aust. colloq.* be stolen or otherwise dishonestly obtained (*that trannie you bought at the pub fell off the back of a truck*). **fall out 1** quarrel. **2** happen. **3** leave one's place in a military formation. **fall pregnant** *Aust.* become pregnant. **fall short** be insufficient or inadequate. **fall short of** fail to obtain or reach. **fall through** (of a plan) fail, come to nothing. **fall to** begin working, fighting, or eating.

Fall, the (also **the Fall of Man**) in Christian and Jewish theology, the lapse into a sinful state which resulted from the first act of disobedience by Adam and Eve, the eating of the fruit of the tree of knowledge (Genesis 2 ff.).

fallacious / fuh-**lay**-shuhs / *adj.* containing a fallacy. ☐ **fallaciously** *adv.* **fallaciousness** *n.*

fallacy / **fal**-uh-see / *n.* **1** a false or mistaken belief. **2** faulty reasoning.

fallible / **fal**-uh-buhl / *adj.* capable of making mistakes. ☐ **fallibly** *adv.* **fallibility** / fal-uh-**bil**-uh-tee / *n.*

Fallopian tube / fuh-**loh**-pee-uhn / *n.* either of the two tubes in female mammals carrying ova from the ovaries to the womb.

fallout *n.* **1** radioactive debris from a nuclear explosion. **2** the adverse side-effects of a situation etc.

fallow / **fal**-oh / *adj.* (of land) ploughed but left unplanted in order to restore its fertility. ❑ **fallow deer** a small deer, white-spotted in summer.

Falun Gong a Chinese religious movement founded in 1992, and drawing on Taoist and Buddhist traditions.

false *adj.* **1** wrong, incorrect. **2** deceitful, lying, unfaithful. **3** not genuine, illusory; sham, artificial (*false teeth; false economy*). **4** improperly so called (*the false acacia*). ❑ **false pretences** acts intended to deceive. **false sarsaparilla** an Australian hardenbergia with purple flowers. ❑ **falsely** *adv.* **falseness** *n.*

falsehood *n.* **1** an untrue statement, a lie. **2** telling lies.

falsetto / fol-**set**-oh / *n.* (*pl.* **falsettos**) a high-pitched voice above one's natural range, esp. when used by male singers. • *adv.* in a falsetto voice.

falsify *v.* (**falsified, falsifying**) **1** alter (a document) fraudulently. **2** misrepresent (facts). ❑ **falsification** *n.*

falsity *n.* **1** falseness. **2** a falsehood, an error.

falter *v.* **1** go or function unsteadily. **2** become weaker, begin to give way (*his courage faltered*). **3** speak or utter hesitatingly, stammer.

fame *n.* **1** the condition of being known to many people. **2** reputation (*a house of ill fame*).

Famechon, Johnny (full name: Jean Pierre Famechon) (1945–), Australian featherweight boxer. He won the World Championship title in 1969, and successfully defended it twice.

famed *adj.* famous.

familial / fuh-**mil**-yuhl / *adj.* of a family or its members.

familiar *adj.* **1** well known, often seen or experienced (*a familiar sight*). **2** (foll. by *with*) knowing well, well acquainted with (*am familiar with all the problems*). **3** lacking formality, friendly and informal (*addressed him in familiar terms*). **4** too informal, assuming a greater degree of informality or friendship than is proper. • *n.* (in full **familiar spirit**) a demon serving a witch etc. ❑ **familiarly** *adv.* **familiarity** *n.*

familiarise *v.* (also **-ize**) make well acquainted (with a person or thing). ❑ **familiarisation** *n.*

family *n.* **1** parents and their children. **2** a person's children (*they have a large family*). **3** a set of relatives. **4** all the descendants of a common ancestor; their line of descent. **5** a group of things that are alike in some way. **6** a group of related plants or animals (*lions belong to the cat family*). ❑ **family allowance** any of various government schemes in Australia offering financial assistance with the rearing of children. **family law** that section of federal law in Australia which deals with the rights of parents and children, esp. in cases of dispute etc. **family planning** birth control. **family reunion 1** a get-together for the extended members of a family. **2** *Aust.* an immigration policy which favours immigrants who have members of their family already settled in Australia. **family tree** a diagram showing how people in a family are related.

Family Court of Australia *n.* the court which administers family law.

famine *n.* extreme scarcity (esp. of food) in a region.

famished *adj. colloq.* (also **famishing**) extremely hungry.

famous *adj.* **1** known to very many people. **2** *colloq.* excellent. ❑ **famously** *adv.*

fan[1] *n.* **1** a device waved in the hand or operated mechanically to create a current of air. **2** anything spread out like a semicircular fan. • *v.* (**fanned, fanning**) **1** drive a current of air upon, with, or as if with, a fan. **2** stimulate (flames etc.) in this way. **3** (usu. foll. by *out*) spread from a central point (*troops fanned out*). ❑ **fan belt** a belt driving the fan that cools the radiator of a motor vehicle. **fan flower** a small Australian shrub with profuse fan-shaped usu. bluish flowers. **fan-forced** (of a convection oven) fitted with a fan that distributes the heat evenly throughout. **fan palm** a Qld palm with large circular leaves.

fan[2] *n.* an enthusiastic admirer or supporter (*footy fan*). (¶ Originally short for *fanatic*.)

fanatic / fuh-**nat**-ik / *n.* a person obsessively and unreasonably devoted to a religious etc. belief, an activity, etc. ❑ **fanatical** *adj.* **fanatically** *adv.*

fanaticism / fuh-**nat**-uh-siz-uhm / *n.* obsessive and unreasoning zeal.

fancier *n.* a person with special knowledge of and love for something, a connoisseur (*a dog fancier*).

fanciful *adj.* **1** (of people) using the imagination freely, imagining things. **2** imaginary. **3** designed in a quaint or imaginative style. ❑ **fancifully** *adv.*

fancy *n.* **1** the power of imagining things, esp. of an unreal or fantastic sort. **2** something imagined, an unfounded idea or belief. **3** an unreasoning desire for something. **4** a liking. • *adj.* **1** ornamental, not plain; elaborate. **2** based on imagination, not fact. • *v.* (**fancied, fancying**) **1** imagine. **2** be inclined to believe or suppose. **3** *colloq.* take a fancy to, like, desire; find (a person) sexually attractive. ❑ **fancy dress** a costume worn for a party etc. where the guests dress to represent characters of history or fiction etc. **fancy-free** *adj.* not in love. **fancy oneself** *colloq.* be rather conceited, admire oneself. **take a person's fancy** attract or please him or her.

fandango *n.* (*pl.* **fandangoes** or **fandangos**) a lively Spanish dance for two people.

fanfare *n.* a short showy or ceremonious sounding of trumpets.

fang[1] *n.* **1** a long sharp tooth, esp. of dogs and wolves. **2** a snake's tooth with which it injects venom. **3** the root of a tooth; either of its prongs. • *v. Aust. colloq.* **1** borrow in a pressurising way (*he fanged me for forty bucks*). **2** grab, take control of (*the Kiwis have fanged a large slice of the Aussie banana-skin market*). ❑ **put the fangs in** *Aust. colloq.* attempt to cadge or borrow; importune.

fang² *Aust. colloq. n.* a high-speed drive in a car (*took the Jag for a fang*). • *v.* **1** (often foll. by *around*) drive at high speed in a car. **2** drive (a car) at high speed (*fanged the Ford all the way*). (¶ J.M. Fangio, Argentinian motor-racing driver (1911–95).)

fanlight *n.* a small, originally semicircular window above a door or another window.

fanny *n. coarse colloq.* the female genitals.

fantail *n.* **1** a pigeon with a semi-circular tail. **2** an Australian flycatcher with a fan-shaped tail, e.g. *grey fantail*, *rufous fantail*.

fantasia / fan-**tay**-zee-uh, fan-**tay**-*zh*uh / *n.* an imaginative musical or other composition.

fantasise / **fan**-tuh-suyz / *v.* (also **-ize**) imagine in fantasy; create a fantasy about; daydream.

fantastic *adj.* (also **fantastical**) **1** absurdly fanciful. **2** designed in a very imaginative style. **3** *colloq.* remarkable, excellent. ☐ **fantastically** *adv.*

fantasy *n.* **1** imagination, esp. when unrelated to reality. **2** a wild or fantastic product of the imagination, a daydream. **3** a fanciful design; a fantasia. **4** a special category of fiction concerned with imaginative, often magical worlds. • *adj.* dealing with imaginative, magical worlds (*a fantasy novel; fantasy literature*). ☐ **fantasy sport** a competition in which participants select imaginary teams from among the real players in an actual league and score points according to the actual performance of their players, e.g. fantasy football.

fanzine / **fan**-zeen / *n.* a magazine, usually produced by amateurs, for fans of a particular performer, group, or form of entertainment, or fans of science fiction and fantasy.

FAQ *abbr. Computing* frequently asked questions; a text file containing a list of questions and answers about a particular subject, esp. one giving basic information for users of an Internet newsgroup.

far *adv.* (**farther** *or* **further**, **farthest** *or* **furthest**; *see also* the note at **farther**) **1** at, to, or by a great distance (*far away*; *far off*; *far out*; *are you travelling far?*). **2** by much (*far better*; *far too early*). • *adj.* **1** distant, remote (*far country*). **2** more distant (*the far end of the hall*). **3** extreme (*the far Left of the Labor Party*). ☐ **a far cry from** greatly different from. **far-fetched** (of an explanation etc.) unconvincing, incredible. **far-flung 1** widely scattered. **2** remote. **far from** very different from; almost the opposite of (*far from being fat*). **far gone** *colloq.* very ill or drunk. **far out** *adj.* **1** distant. **2** *colloq.* unconventional, avant-garde. **3** *colloq.* excellent. **far-reaching** having a wide range, influence, or effect. **far-sighted** having foresight, prudent. **in so far as** *see* IN.

farad / **fa**-ruhd / *n.* a unit of electric capacitance. (¶ Named after FARADAY.)

Faraday, Michael (1791–1867), English physicist and chemist, discoverer of electromagnetic induction (the condition under which a permanent magnet can generate electricity), the key to the development of the electric dynamo and motor.

farce *n.* **1** a light comedy. **2** this kind of drama. **3** absurd and useless proceedings; a pretence. ☐ **farcical** / **fah**-suh-kuhl / *adj.* **farcically** *adv.*

fare *n.* **1** the price charged for a passenger to travel. **2** a passenger who pays a fare, esp. for a hired vehicle. **3** a range of food. • *v.* **1** progress, get on (*how did they fare?*). **2** happen (*what fared at the meeting?*).

farewell *interj.* goodbye. • *n.* **1** leave-taking. **2** a function organised to mark a person's departure. • *adj.* valedictory (*a farewell address*). • *v.* say goodbye to.

farina / fuh-**ree**-nuh / *n.* flour or meal of cereal, nuts, or starchy roots.

farinaceous / fa-ruh-**nay**-shuhs / *adj.* of or like farina, starchy.

farm *n.* **1** an area of land and its buildings used under one management for raising crops or livestock. **2** such land etc. for a specified purpose (*a trout farm*). • *v.* **1** grow crops or raise livestock. **2** use (land) for this purpose. **3** breed (fish etc.) commercially. **4** (often foll. by *out*) delegate or subcontract (work) to others. ☐ **buy back the farm** *Aust.* retrieve Australian land, companies, etc. from foreign ownership. **sell off the farm** *Aust.* sell the capital assets of Australia to foreign interests. ☐☐ **farmable** *adj.* **farming** *n.* & *adj.*

Farmer, Graham ('Polly') (1935–), Australian Aboriginal football player in the Australian Rules code, an outstanding ruckman.

farmer *n.* a person who owns or manages a farm, esp. one whose principal occupation is the cultivation of crops.

farmhand *n.* a worker on a farm.

farmhouse *n.* a dwelling place attached to a farm.

farmstead / **fahm**-sted / *n.* a farm and its buildings.

farmyard *n.* the yard of a farmhouse.

farnarkel / fah-**nah**-kuhl / *v.* (**farnarkeled**, **farnarkeling**) *Aust. colloq.* (often foll. by *around*) create the public impression of working industriously and to great effect while getting little or nothing done in fact.

Farnham, John (Peter) (1949–), AO, Australian rock and pop singer.

farrago / fuh-**rah**-goh / *n.* (*pl.* **farragos**) a hotchpotch.

Farrelly, Bernard ('Midget') (1944–), Australian surfer, world champion in 1964.

farrier / **fa**-ree-uh / *n.* a smith who shoes horses.

farrow / **fa**-roh / *v.* (of a sow) give birth to young pigs. • *n.* **1** farrowing. **2** a litter of young pigs.

Farsi *n.* the Persian language.

fart *coarse colloq. v.* **1** send out wind through the anus. **2** (foll. by *about* or *around*) behave foolishly. • *n.* **1** an emission of wind from the anus. **2** an unpleasant or foolish person.

farther *adv.* & *adj.* at or to a greater distance, more remote. ☐ **farthest** *adv.* & *adj.*

■ Usage *Further* and *furthest* are used more commonly than these words except where the sense of physical distance is involved.

farthing *n.* **1** *hist.* a coin worth one-quarter of a penny. **2** a trifling amount (*not worth a farthing*).

farthingale *n.* a hooped petticoat formerly worn under a skirt to make it stand out.

fasces / **fa**-seez / *n.pl.* (in ancient Rome) a bundle of rods with a projecting axe-blade, as a symbol of a magistrate's power.

fascia / **fay**-shuh / *n.* (also **facia**) **1** a stripe or band. **2** a long flat surface in classical architecture. **3** a flat surface, usu. of wood, covering the ends of rafters.

fascicle / **fas**-uh-kuhl / *n.* each section of a book that is published in instalments.

fascinate *v.* **1** attract and hold the interest of; charm greatly. **2** deprive (a victim) of the power of escape by a fixed look, as a snake does. ☐ **fascination** *n.* **fascinator** *n.*

fascinating *adj.* having great attraction or charm.

Fascism / **fash**-iz-uhm / *n.* (also **fascism**) a system of extreme right-wing dictatorial government. ☐ **Fascist** *n.* **Fascistic** *adj.*

fashion *n.* **1** a manner or way of doing something (*continue working in this fashion*). **2** the popular style of dress, customs, etc. at a given time. • *v.* make into a particular form or shape. ☐ **after** (*or* **in**) **a fashion** to some extent but not very satisfactorily.

fashionable *adj.* **1** in or adopting a style that is currently popular. **2** frequented or used by stylish people (*a fashionable hotel*). ☐ **fashionably** *adv.*

fast[1] *adj.* **1** moving or done quickly. **2** producing or allowing quick movement (*a fast car; the fast lane*). **3** (of a clock etc.) showing a time ahead of the correct one. **4** (of a person) spending too much time and energy on pleasure; immoral. **5** (of photographic film) very sensitive to light; (of a lens) having a large aperture, allowing a short exposure to be used. **6** (of a cricket pitch etc.) causing the ball to bounce quickly; (of a racecourse) firm and dry, enabling fast times. **7** firmly fixed or attached (*is the knot fast?; fast friendship*). **8** (of colours or dyes) unlikely to fade or run. • *adv.* **1** quickly. **2** firmly, tightly, securely (*stuck fast; fast asleep*). **3** close, immediately (*fast on their heels*). ☐ **fast breeder reactor** one using fast neutrons to produce the same fissile material it uses. **fast buck** *colloq.* money made quickly and usu. dishonestly. **fast food** quickly-prepared food, esp. that served or cooked in a restaurant. **fast-forward** *adj.* producing onward accelerated motion of a tape etc., esp. in order to reach a particular place in a recording; *n.* (**fast forward**) the switching device (on a video etc.) which produces this onward motion; *v.* run (a videotape etc.) swiftly forward. **fast neutron** one with high kinetic energy. **pull a fast one** (*or* **a fastie** *or* **a swiftie**) *Aust. colloq.* try to deceive or gain an unfair advantage.

fast[2] *v.* go without food or without certain kinds of food, esp. as a religious duty. • *n.* **1** fasting. **2** a day or season appointed for this.

fasten *v.* **1** fix firmly, tie or join together. **2** (foll. by *in*, *up*) lock securely; shut in. **3** fix (one's glance or attention) intently. **4** become fastened (*the door fastens with a latch*). ☐ **fasten off** tie or secure the end of a thread etc. **fasten on** **1** lay hold of. **2** single out for attack. **3** seize as a pretext.

fastener *n.* (also **fastening**) a device for fastening something.

fastidious / fas-**tid**-ee-uhs / *adj.* **1** selecting carefully, choosing only what is good. **2** easily disgusted. ☐ **fastidiously** *adv.* **fastidiousness** *n.*

fastie *n. Aust. colloq.* a deceitful act.

fast lane *n.* **1** a lane on a highway for overtaking or for travelling fast. **2** the quickest route to social and financial success. ☐ **life in the fast lane** life lived at a hectic pace.

fastness *n.* **1** the state of being fast or secure (*colour fastness*). **2** a stronghold, a fortress.

fastskin *n. trademark* **1** a fabric designed to imitate a shark's skin. **2** a swimmer's close-fitting bodysuit made from this.

fast-talk *v.* deceive by confusing the listener with a rapid flow of talk. ☐ **fast-talk**(**ing**) *n.*

fast track *n.* = FAST LANE. • *v.* (**fast-track**) bring about the completion of something very speedily (*they want the government to fast-track the building of the bypass*). • *adj.* (**fast-track**) pertaining to FAST TRACK *n.* (*fast-track yuppies on the go*).

fat *n.* **1** a natural oily substance, insoluble in water, found in animal bodies and certain seeds. **2** that part of meat etc. containing this. **3** this substance prepared for use in cooking. **4** an excessive presence of fat in a person or animal; corpulence (*work off the fat*). **5** *coarse colloq.* an erection of the penis. **6** (in *pl.*) *Aust.* fat cattle or sheep. • *adj.* (**fatter**, **fattest**) **1** containing much fat, covered with fat. **2** excessively plump. **3** (of an animal) made plump for slaughter; fatted. **4** thick (*a fat book*). **5** substantial (*a fat cheque*). **6** (of land or resources) fertile, rich. **7** richly rewarded (*a nice fat job*). **8** *colloq.* ironic very little; not much (*a fat chance; a fat lot you care!*). ☐ **crack a fat** *coarse colloq.* have an erection of the penis. **fat cat** *derog.* **1** a person who is accustomed to special privileges because of status or influence. **2** a member of the higher echelons of the public service in Australia. **live off** (*or* **on**) **the fat of the land** have the best of everything. **the fat is in the fire** trouble is imminent. ☐☐ **fatless** *adj.* **fatness** *n.*

fatal *adj.* **1** causing or ending in death. **2** causing disaster (*a fatal mistake*). **3** fateful (*the fatal day*). ☐ **fatally** *adv.*

fatalist *n.* a person who accepts and submits to what happens, regarding it as inevitable. □ **fatalism** *n.* **fatalistic** *adj.*

fatality / fuh-**tal**-uh-tee / *n.* **1** death caused by accident or in war etc. **2** a person killed in this way. **3** a fatal influence; a liability to disaster.

fate *n.* **1** a power thought to control all events and impossible to resist. **2** a person's destiny. **3** (**the Fates**) *Gk myth.* the three goddesses who presided over people's lives and deaths.

fated *adj.* destined by fate, doomed.

fateful *adj.* bringing or producing great and usu. unpleasant events. □ **fatefully** *adv.*

father *n.* **1** a male parent. **2** a male ancestor (*land of our fathers*). **3** the founder or originator of something. **4** (**the Father**) God, the first person of the Trinity. **5** (also **Father**) the title of Catholic etc. priests. • *v.* **1** beget, be the father of. **2** found or originate (an idea or plan etc.). □ **father-figure** an older man who is respected and trusted like a father. **father-in-law** (*pl.* **fathers-in-law**) the father of one's wife or husband. □□ **fatherly** *adj.* **fatherhood** *n.* **fatherless** *adj.*

fatherland *n.* one's native country.

Father's Day a day (usu. the first Sunday in September) on which special tribute is paid to fathers.

fathom *n.* a measure of 6 feet (1.8288 m), used in stating the depth of water. • *v.* **1** measure the depth of. **2** get to the bottom of, understand.

fathomless *adj.* too deep to fathom.

fatigue *n.* **1** tiredness resulting from hard work or exercise. **2** weakness in metals etc. caused by repeated stress. **3 a** any of the non-military duties of soldiers, e.g. cooking, cleaning. **b** (**fatigues**) clothing worn for these duties or when on active service. • *v.* cause fatigue to.

fatted *adj.* (of animals) fattened as food.

fatten *v.* make or become fat.

fattish *adj.* rather fat.

fatty *adj.* like fat, containing fat. • *n. colloq.* a fat person. □ **fatty acid** an organic compound consisting of a hydrocarbon chain and a terminal carboxyl group.

fatuous / **fat**-yoo-uhs / *adj.* foolish, silly. □ **fatuously** *adv.* **fatuousness** *n.* **fatuity** / fuh-**tyoo**-uh-tee / *n.*

fatwa *n.* a legal decision or ruling by an Islamic religious leader.

faucet / **faw**-suht / *n.* (esp. *US*) a tap of any kind.

fault *n.* **1** a defect or imperfection. **2** an offence, something wrongly done. **3** the responsibility for something wrong. **4** a break in the continuity of layers of rock, caused by movement of the earth's crust. **5** an incorrect serve in tennis etc. • *v.* **1** find fault with, criticise. **2** *Geol.* break the continuity of (strata). □ **to a fault** excessively (*generous to a fault*). □□ **faultless** *adj.* **faultlessly** *adv.*

faulty *adj.* (**faultier**, **faultiest**) having a fault or faults, imperfect. □ **faultily** *adv.* **faultiness** *n.*

faun / fawn / *n. Rom. myth.* any of a class of gods of the woods and fields, with a goat's horns, legs, and tail. (¶ From the name of the Latin god Faunus, identified with the Greek Pan.)

fauna *n.* (*pl.* **faunae** or **faunas**) the animals of an area or period of time.

faunal emblem *n.* an animal officially adopted by a country (and in Australia also by a State or Territory) as a symbol, hence: **1** (of Australia) the kangaroo and the emu. **2** (of the ACT) the gang-gang cockatoo. **3** (of NSW) the platypus and the kookaburra. **4** (of the NT) the red kangaroo and the wedge-tailed eagle. **5** (of Qld) the koala and the brolga. **6** (of SA) the hairy-nosed wombat and piping shrike. **7** (of Tasmania) (unofficial) the Tasmanian tiger or Tasmanian devil. **8** (of Vic.) Leadbeater's possum and the helmeted honeyeater. **9** (of WA) the numbat and the black swan. (*See also* FLORAL EMBLEM.)

Fauré / **faw**-ray /, Gabriel (1845–1924), French composer, noted for his songs and Requiem Mass.

Faust / fowst / a wandering astronomer and magician who lived in Germany *c.*1488–1541, and was reputed to have sold his soul to the Devil. He was the hero of dramas by Marlowe and Goethe and of an opera by Gounod.

faux pas / foh **pah** / *n.* (*pl.* **faux pas** / foh **pahz** /) an embarrassing blunder. (¶ French, = false step.)

fave *n.* & *adj. colloq.* favourite.

Favenc, Ernest (1845–1908), Australian explorer (in Qld, WA, the NT), bushman, journalist, author, and poet.

favour *n.* (also **favor**) **1** liking, goodwill, approval. **2** an act of kindness. **3** support or preference given to one person or group at the expense of another. **4** an ornament or badge etc. worn to show that one supports a certain political or other party. • *v.* **1** regard or treat with favour. **2** be in favour of. **3** (foll. by *with*) oblige (*favour us with a song*). **4** (of events or circumstances) make possible or easy, be advantageous to. **5** resemble (one parent etc.) (*the boy favours his father*).

favourable *adj.* (also **favorable**) **1** giving or showing approval. **2** pleasing, satisfactory (*made a favourable impression*). **3** helpful, advantageous (*favourable winds*). □ **favourably** *adv.*

favourite *adj.* (also **favorite**) liked or preferred above others. • *n.* **1** a favoured person or thing. **2** a competitor generally expected to win.

favouritism *n.* (also **favoritism**) unfair favouring of one person or group at the expense of another.

Fawkner, John Pascoe (1792–1869), Australian pioneer, newspaper proprietor, and a founder of Melbourne, who arrived in Australia with his convict father in 1801.

fawn *n.* **1** a fallow deer in its first year. **2** light yellowish brown. • *adj.* fawn-coloured. • *v.* **1** (of a dog etc.) show extreme affection. **2** try to win favour by obsequious behaviour.

fax *n.* **1** transmission of exact copies of documents electronically. **2** a copy produced by this. **3** (also **fax machine**) a machine for sending and receiving faxes. •*v.* transmit (a document) by this process.

fay *n. poetic* a fairy.

faze *v.* fluster; daunt.

Fe *symbol* iron.

fealty / **fee**-uhl-tee / *n.* loyalty, allegiance (originally the duty of a feudal tenant or vassal to his lord).

fear *n.* **1** an unpleasant emotion caused by the nearness of danger or the expectation of pain etc. **2** reverence or awe. **3** a danger, a likelihood. •*v.* **1** feel fear of, be afraid. **2** show reverence towards (God). **3** have an uneasy feeling; be politely regretful (*I fear there's none left*). ▫ **for fear of** because of the risk of.

fearful *adj.* **1** causing horror. **2** feeling fear. **3** *colloq.* very great, extremely bad. ▫ **fearfully** *adv.*

fearless *adj.* feeling no fear. ▫ **fearlessly** *adv.* **fearlessness** *n.*

fearsome *adj.* frightening or alarming in appearance, very great (*a fearsome task*).

feasible / **fee**-zuh-buhl / *adj.* **1** able to be done, possible. **2** likely, plausible (*a feasible explanation*). ▫ **feasibly** *adv.* **feasibility** / fee-zuh-**bil**-uh-tee / *n.*

feast *n.* **1** a large elaborate meal. **2** (also **Feast**) an annual religious celebration (*the Christian Feast of the Nativity; the Jewish Feast of Tabernacles; the Hindu Feast of Lanterns*). •*v.* **1** eat heartily. **2** give a feast to.

feat *n.* a remarkable action or achievement.

feather *n.* **1** any of the structures that grow from a bird's skin and cover its body, consisting of a central shaft with a fringe of fine strands on each side. **2** plumage. •*v.* **1** cover or fit with feathers. **2** turn (an oar) so that the blade passes through the air edgeways. **3** make (propeller blades) rotate in such a way as to lessen the resistance of the air or water. ▫ **feather bed** a mattress stuffed with feathers. **feather-bed** *v.* (**feather-bedded, feather-bedding**) make things financially easy for, pamper. ▫▫ **feathery** *adj.*

feathering *n.* **1** plumage. **2** the feathers of an arrow. **3** a feather-like structure or marking.

featherweight *n.* **1** a weight in certain sports between bantamweight and lightweight, in amateur boxing 54–57 kg. **2** a very lightweight thing or person. **3** (usu. used as *adj.*) of little or no influence.

feature *n.* **1** any of the parts of the face (e.g. mouth, nose, eyes) which together make up its appearance. **2** a distinctive or noticeable quality of a thing. **3** a prominent article in a newspaper etc. **4** (in full **feature film**) the main film in a cinema program. **5** a broadcast based on one specific theme. •*v.* **1** give special prominence to. **2** be a feature. ▫ **featureless** *adj.*

febrile / **fee**-bruyl / *adj.* of or involving fever, feverish.

February *n.* the second month of the year.

feckless *adj.* feeble and incompetent; irresponsible. ▫ **fecklessly** *adv.* **fecklessness** *n.*

fecund / **fek**-uhnd / *adj.* **1** producing many offspring. **2** producing many ideas etc. ▫ **fecundity** / fuh-**kun**-duh-tee / *n.*

fecundate / **fek**-uhn-dayt / *v.* make fecund, fertilise. ▫ **fecundation** *n.*

fed[1] *see* FEED. ▫ **fed up** (**to the back teeth**) *colloq.* bored or discontented.

fed[2] *n. colloq.* **1** *Aust.* an officer of the Australian Federal Police. **2** *Aust.* a member of the Federal parliament (as distinct from a State parliament). **3** *US* a federal official, esp. a member of the FBI.

federal *adj.* **1** of a system of government in which several States unite under a central authority but remain independent in internal affairs. **2** belonging to this group as a whole (not to its separate parts) (*federal laws*). **3** of or pertaining to the Commonwealth of Australia, as distinct from the States (*federal election; federal parliament; Canberra, the federal capital*). **4** of an association of units that are largely independent. ▫ **federally** *adv.*

Federal Court of Australia *n.* a court of limited jurisdiction established by the Commonwealth Parliament in 1976 to exercise the judicial power of the Commonwealth. It deals mainly with matters of industrial relations, bankruptcy, and trade practices.

federalism *n.* **1** being federal. **2** favouring a federal system. ▫ **federalist** *n.*

federalise *v.* (also **-ize**) make federal, organise in a federal system. ▫ **federalisation** *n.*

federate *v.* / **fed**-uh-rayt / organise or be organised on a federal basis. •*adj.* / **fed**-uh-ruht / federally organised.

federation *n.* **1** federating. **2** a federated society or group of States. **3** (**Federation**) the association of the six Australian colonies in a federal union. **4** (**Federation**) the formation of the Commonwealth of Australia on 1 January 1901. ▫ **federation style 1** the style of Australian domestic architecture flourishing between 1895 and 1915. **2** an imitation of this. ▫▫ **federationist** *n.*

federative *adj.* federated, federal.

fee *n.* **1** a sum payable to an official or a professional person for advice or services. **2** a sum payable for membership of a society, entrance for an examination, etc. **3** (**fees**) regular payments (esp. to a school).

feeble *adj.* weak, without strength, force, or effectiveness. ▫ **feeble-minded** *adj.* mentally deficient. ▫▫ **feebly** *adv.* **feebleness** *n.*

feed *v.* (**fed, feeding**) **1** give food to; put food into the mouth of. **2** give as food to animals (*feed oats to horses*). **3** (often foll. by *on*) (esp. of animals, or *colloquial* of people) take food (*they*

feedback

feed on nuts and seeds). **4** serve as food for, nourish. **5** supply, pass a supply of material to (*feed the fire; feed more coins into the parking meter*). **6** (of a river etc.) flow into a lake etc. **7** supply (an actor etc.) with cues. **8** send passes to (a player) in football etc. **9** gratify (vanity etc.). **10** provide (advice, information, etc.) to. •*n.* **1** an amount of food (chiefly for animals or babies). **2** an act or instance of feeding; the giving of food. **3** *colloq.* a meal. **4** a pipe or channel etc. by which material is carried to a machine; the material itself. □ **feed up** fatten.

feedback *n.* **1** *Electronics* return of part of the output of a system to its source, esp. so as to modify the output. **2** the return of information about a product etc.; response. •*v.* (**feed back**) produce feedback.

feeder *n.* **1** (of plants and animals) one that takes in food in a certain way (*some plants are gross feeders*). **2** a baby's bib. **3** a hopper or feeding apparatus in a machine. **4** a branch road, railway line, etc., linking outlying areas with a central line or service.

feedlot *n.* an area in which cattle etc. are massed in order to fatten them by hand-feeding, esp. for the grain-fed beef market. •*v.* hand-feed (cattle etc.) in a feedlot, esp. with grain. □ **feedlotter** *n.* **feedlotting** *n.*

feel *v.* (**felt, feeling**) **1** explore or perceive by touch. **2** be conscious of, be aware of being (*feel a pain; feel happy*). **3** be affected by (*feels the cold badly*). **4** give a certain sensation or impression (*the water feels warm*). **5** have a vague conviction or impression of something. **6** have as an opinion, consider (*we felt it was necessary to do this*). **7** (foll. by *for*) sympathise with. •*n.* **1** the sense of touch. **2** the act of feeling. **3** the sensation produced by something touched (*silk has a soft feel*). □ **feel free** *colloq.* an expression of permission. **feel like** *colloq.* be in the mood for. **feel one's way** proceed cautiously. **feel out** explore tentatively in order to judge possible reactions. **get the feel of** become accustomed to using.

feeler *n.* **1** a long slender part or organ in certain animals, used for testing things by touch. **2** a cautious proposal or suggestion put forward to test people's reactions.

feeling *n.* **1** the power and capacity to feel (*lost all feeling in his legs*). **2** mental or physical awareness, emotion. **3** an idea or belief not wholly based on reason (*I had a feeling she would*). **4** sensitivity, sympathy (*showed no feeling for the sufferings of others*). **5** opinion, attitude (*the feeling of the meeting was against it*). **6** (**feelings**) the emotional side of a person's nature (contrasted with the intellect) (*hurt my feelings; had strong feelings about it*). •*adj.* sensitive, sympathetic; heartfelt.

feet *see* FOOT.

feign / faynt / *v.* pretend.

feijoa / fuy-**joh**-uh, fee- / *n.* **1** any evergreen shrub or tree of the genus *Feijoa*, bearing edible guava-like fruit. **2** this fruit.

feint / faynt / *n.* a slight attack or movement made to divert attention from the main attack coming elsewhere. •*v.* make a feint. •*adj.* (of ruled lines) faint.

feisty / **fuy**-stee / *adj.* (**feistier, feistiest**) aggressive, excitable.

felafel / fuh-**lah**-fuhl / *n.* (also **falafel**) a hot and spicy dish of fried rissoles made from mashed chick peas, chillies, etc.

feldspar *n.* (also **felspar**) any of a group of usu. white or red rock-forming minerals that are aluminium silicates combined with various other metallic ions.

felicitate / fuh-**lis**-uh-tayt / *v.* congratulate. □ **felicitation** *n.*

felicitous / fuh-**lis**-uh-tuhs / *adj.* (of words or remarks) well chosen, apt. □ **felicitously** *adv.*

felicity *n.* **1** being happy, great happiness. **2** a pleasing manner or style (*expressed himself with great felicity*).

feline / **fee**-luyn / *adj.* of cats, catlike. •*n.* an animal of the cat family. □ **felinity** / fuh-**lin**-uh-tee / *n.*

fell[1] *v.* **1** strike down by a blow. **2** cut (a tree) down. •*adj. poetical* ruthless, cruel, destructive. □ **at** (or **in**) **one fell swoop** in a single (orig. deadly) action.

fell[2] *see* FALL.

fella = FELLOW (senses 1 & 4).

fellate *v.* perform fellatio (on).

fellatio / fuh-**lay**-shee-oh / *n.* a sexual practice in which a person stimulates the penis of another with lips, mouth, and tongue.

feller = FELLOW (senses 1 & 4).

fellow *n.* **1** (also **fella, feller**) *colloq.* a man or a boy or an animal (*poor fellow!*). **2** *colloq.* a boyfriend (*he's my fellow*). **3** (usu. in *plural*) a person in a group etc.; a comrade (*separated from their fellows*). **4** *Aust.* (in Aboriginal English) (usu. as **fella** or **feller**) a person. **5** a thing of the same class or kind, the other of a pair. **6** an equal; one's peer. **7** a graduate paid to do research at a university etc. **8** (usu. **Fellow**) a member of a learned society (*Fellow of the Royal Australasian College of Physicians*). •*adj.* of the same group etc. (*my fellow Australians*). □ **fellow-feeling** sympathy. **fellow-traveller** a sympathiser with the Communist Party.

fellowship *n.* **1** friendly association with others, companionship. **2** a number of people associated together, a society; membership of this. **3** the position of a university fellow.

felon / **fel**-uhn / *n.* a person who has committed a felony.

felonry *n.* **1** the class of felons. **2** *Aust. hist.* the convict population in Australia.

felony / **fel**-uh-nee / *n.* a serious, usu. violent, crime. □ **felonious** / fuh-**loh**-nee-uhs / *adj.*

felspar = FELDSPAR.

felt[1] *n.* a kind of cloth made by matting and pressing fibres. •*v.* **1** make or become matted together like felt. **2** cover with felt. ☐ **felt-tipped** (or **felt-tip**) **pen** one with a writing point made of fibre.

felt[2] *see* FEEL.

felucca / fuh-**luk**-uh / *n.* a small Mediterranean ship with lateen sails and/or oars.

female *adj.* **1** of the sex that can bear offspring or produce eggs. **2** (of plants) fruit-bearing, having a pistil and no stamens. **3** of a woman or women. **4** (of parts of machinery etc.) made hollow to receive a corresponding inserted (male) part. •*n.* a female person, animal, or plant.

feminine *adj.* **1** of, like, or suitable for women; having the qualities or appearance considered characteristic of a woman. **2** having the grammatical form suitable for the names of females or for words corresponding to these (*'lioness' is the feminine noun corresponding to 'lion'*). •*n.* a feminine word or gender. ☐ **femininity** *n.*

feminist *n.* a supporter of women's demand to be given rights equal to those of men. ☐ **feminism** *n.*

femme fatale / fam fuh-**tahl** / *n.* (*pl.* ***femmes fatales*** pronounced the same) a dangerously seductive woman. (¶ French)

femocrat / **fem**-uh-crat / *n.* a woman who espouses feminist principles in the bureaucratic workplace.

femur / **fee**-muh / *n.* (*pl.* **femurs** *or* **femora** / **fem**-uh-ruh /) the thigh bone. ☐ **femoral** *adj.*

fen *n. Brit.* a low-lying, flooded, or marshy tract of land.

fence *n.* **1** a barrier, railing, or other upright structure put round a field or garden to mark a boundary or keep animals from straying. **2** a raised structure for a horse to jump. **3** a person who knowingly buys and re-sells stolen goods. •*v.* **1** surround with or as with a fence. **2** act as a fence for (stolen goods). **3** engage in fencing. **4** evade answering (a person or question). ☐ **over the fence** *colloq.* unacceptable (*that remark was a bit over the fence!*). **sit on the fence** *see* SIT. ☐☐ **fencer** *n.*

fencing *n.* **1** fences; a length of fence. **2** the sport of fighting with foils or other kinds of sword.

fend *v.* ☐ **fend for** provide a livelihood for; look after. **fend off** ward off (an attack etc.).

fender *n.* **1** a low frame bordering a fireplace to keep in falling coals etc. **2** the bumper bar of a car.

Fenech, Jeff(rey) (1964–), Australian boxer, world champion in three weight divisions, nicknamed 'the Marrickville Mauler'.

feng shui / feng **shoo**-ee, **shway** / *n.* (in Chinese thought) a system of laws considered to govern spatial arrangements and orientation in relation to the flow of energy, and whose effects are taken into account when siting and designing buildings and their interiors. (¶ Chinese)

fennel *n.* a fragrant aniseed-flavoured herb; its bulbous stem, used as a vegetable; its seeds ground and used as an ingredient in curry powder.

fenugreek / **fen**-yoo-greek / *n.* a plant with white flowers and fragrant seeds used for flavouring, esp. in curries.

feral / **fe**-ruhl / *adj.* **1** (of an animal or plant) wild, untamed, uncultivated. **2 a** (of an animal) in a wild state after escape from captivity. **b** born in the wild of such an animal. **3** *Aust. colloq.* **a** (of a young person) living outside the home environment, often as a streetkid. **b** (of a person) wild in behaviour. **c** (of a person) living an alternative, esp. hippy-like, lifestyle. **d** hungry (*feeling a bit feral*). **e** out of hand; unruly (*the party became a bit feral*). **f** excellent. **4** brutal. •*n. colloq.* a feral animal or person.

ferial / **feer**-ree-uhl / *adj.* (of a day) not a festival or a fast.

ferment *v.* / fer-**ment** / **1** undergo fermentation; cause fermentation in. **2** seethe with excitement or agitation. •*n.* / **fer**-ment / **1** fermentation. **2** something that causes this. **3** excitement or agitation.

fermentation *n.* a chemical change caused by the action of an organic substance such as yeast, involving effervescence and the production of heat, e.g. when sugar is converted into alcohol. ☐ **fermentative** / fer-**men**-tuh-tiv / *adj.*

fermium *n.* an artificially made radioactive metallic element (symbol Fm).

fern *n.* a flowerless plant usu. having feathery fronds. ☐ **fern gully** *Aust.* a small valley in a damp forest where tree ferns flourish. ☐☐ **ferny** *adj.*

fernery *n.* (*pl.* **ferneries**) a sheltered place in the garden where ferns are grown; a shadehouse etc. for growing ferns.

ferocious *adj.* fierce, savage. ☐ **ferociously** *adv.* **ferocity** / fuh-**ros**-uh-tee / *n.*

ferret *n.* **1** a small polecat used in catching rabbits, rats, etc. **2** a person who searches assiduously. •*v.* (**ferreted**, **ferreting**) **1** hunt with ferrets. **2** rummage; search out (secrets, criminals, etc.). ☐ **ferret out** discover by searching or rummaging.

ferric *adj.* of or containing iron.

ferroconcrete *n.* reinforced concrete.

ferrous / **fe**-ruhs / *adj.* containing iron (*ferrous metals*).

ferrule / **fe**-rool / *n.* a metal ring or cap strengthening the lower end of a stick, umbrella, etc.

ferry *v.* (**ferried**, **ferrying**) **1** convey (people or things) in a boat etc. across a stretch of water. **2** transport from one place to another, esp. as a regular service. •*n.* **1** a boat etc. used for ferrying. **2** the place where it operates. **3** the service it provides. ☐ **ferryman** *n.*

fertile *adj.* **1** (of soil) rich in the materials needed to support vegetation. **2** (of plants) able to produce fruit; (of animals) able or likely to conceive young. **3** (of seeds or eggs) capable of developing into a new plant or animal, fertilised. **4** (of the mind) able to produce ideas, inventive. **5** (of nuclear material) able to become fissile by the capture of neutrons. ☐ **fertility** *n.*

fertilise *v.* (also **-ize**) **1** make (soil etc.) fertile or productive. **2** introduce pollen or sperm into (a plant, egg, or female animal) so that it develops seed or young. ☐ **fertilisation** *n.*

fertiliser *n.* (also **-izer**) material (natural or artificial) added to soil to make it more fertile.

fervent / **fer**-vuhnt / *adj.* showing warmth of feeling; intense. ☐ **fervently** *adv.* **fervency** *n.*

fervid *adj.* **1** burning; intensely passionate (*fervid lovemaking*). **2** *poetic* hot, glowing. ☐ **fervidly** *adv.*

fervour *n.* (also **fervor**) warmth and intensity of feeling, zeal.

fescue / **fes**-kyoo / *n.* a pasture and lawn grass.

fess / fes / *v. colloq.* confess, own up.

festal *adj.* **1** joyous, merry. **2** of a feast or festival. ☐ **festally** *adv.*

fester *v.* **1** make or become septic and filled with pus. **2** cause continuing resentment. **3** rot, stagnate.

festival *n.* **1** a day or time of celebration. **2** a series of performances of music, drama, etc., given periodically (*the Adelaide Festival*).

festive *adj.* **1** of or suitable for a festival. **2** joyous. ☐ **festively** *adv.* **festiveness** *n.*

festivity *n.* a festive occasion or celebration.

festoon *n.* a chain of flowers, ribbons, etc., hung in a curve or loop as a decoration. • *v.* decorate with hanging ornaments.

Festschrift / **fest**-shrift / *n.* (*pl.* **Festschriften** or **Festschrifts**) a collection of writings published in honour of a scholar. (¶ German, = festival writing.)

feta / **fet**-uh / *n.* a soft white esp. ewe's-milk salty cheese made esp. in Greece.

fetch *v.* **1** go for and bring back (*fetch a doctor*). **2** cause to come out (*fetched a sigh; fetch tears to the eyes*). **3** (of goods) sell for (a price) (*your books won't fetch much*). **4** *colloq.* give (a blow) to (*fetched him a slap*). • *n.* **1** a dodge, a trick. **2** the ghostly apparition of a (usu. living) person; a spectre. ☐ **fetch and carry** do menial tasks. **fetch up** *colloq.* **1** arrive or end up at a place or in a certain position. **2** vomit.

fetching *adj.* attractive. ☐ **fetchingly** *adv.*

fete / fayt / (also **fête**) *n.* **1** an outdoor entertainment or sale, usu. to raise funds for a cause or charity. **2** a festival. • *v.* (**feted, feting**) honour or entertain (a person) lavishly.

fetid / **fet**-uhd, **fee**-tuhd / *adj.* (also **foetid**) stinking.

fetish / **fet**-ish / *n.* **1** an object worshipped by primitive peoples for its supposed magical powers or as being inhabited by a spirit. **2** a non-sexual object (e.g. underwear) or a non-sexual part of the body (e.g. feet) which arouses sexual desire. **3** sexual desire for such an object etc. (*he has a strong fetish for feet*). **4** anything to which abnormally excessive attention is given (*he makes a fetish of punctuality*). ☐ **fetishism** *n.* **fetishist** *n.* **fetishistic** *adj.*

fetlock *n.* the part of a horse's leg above and behind the hoof.

fetter *n.* a chain or shackle for a prisoner's ankles. • *v.* **1** put into fetters. **2** impede or restrict (*fettered by all these petty rules*).

fettle *n.* condition, trim (*in fine fettle*).

fettucine / fe-tuh-**chee**-nee / *n.* ribbons of pasta; an Italian dish consisting of this with a sauce.

fetus alternative spelling of FOETUS.

feud / fyood / *n.* **1** lasting hostility, esp. between families, tribes, etc. **2** a prolonged or bitter quarrel or dispute (*his feud with the tax department*). • *v.* carry on a feud.

feudal / **fyoo**-duhl / *adj.* **1** of or according to the **feudal system**, a method of holding land (during the Middle Ages in Europe) by giving one's services to the owner. **2** reactionary (*his attitude to law reform is positively feudal*). ☐ **feudalism** *n.* **feudalistic** *adj.*

fever *n.* **1** an abnormally high body temperature. **2** a disease characterised by this (*scarlet fever*). **3** a state of nervous excitement or agitation. ☐ **fever bark** (also **fever tree**) a tree of north Qld, the bitter bark of which was used by Aborigines to make a medicine. **fever pitch** a high level of excitement.

fevered *adj.* affected with fever; excited.

feverish *adj.* **1** having a fever; caused or accompanied by a fever. **2** restless with excitement or agitation. ☐ **feverishly** *adv.* **feverishness** *n.*

few *adj.* & *n.* not many.

■ **Usage** *See* the note under *less*.

fey / fay / *adj.* **1** clairvoyant. **2** having a strange other-worldly charm; whimsical. **3** doomed to die soon (as manifested by strange, exultant behaviour which is supposed to portend death).

fez / fez / *n.* (*pl.* **fezzes**) a high flat-topped red cap with a tassel, worn by men in certain Muslim countries.

ff *abbr.* Music fortissimo.

ff. *abbr.* and the following (pages etc.).

fiancé, fiancée / fee-**on**-say / *n.* a man (*fiancé*) or a woman (*fiancée*) to whom one is engaged to be married.

Fianna Fáil / fee-uh-nuh **foil** / an Irish political party formed by de Valera in 1926 from moderate members of Sinn Fein. (¶ Irish, interpreted by its founders to mean 'soldiers of destiny'.)

fiasco / fee-**as**-koh / *n.* (*pl.* **fiascos**) a ludicrous or humiliating failure.

fiat / **fee**-at, -uht / *n.* an order or decree. (¶ Latin, = let it be done.)

fib *n.* an unimportant lie. • *v.* (**fibbed, fibbing**) tell a fib. ☐ **fibber** *n.*

fibre *n.* **1** one of the thin strands of which animal and vegetable tissue or textile substance is made; a

fibreboard · 295 · **fiend**

threadlike piece of glass. **2** a substance consisting of fibres; fibrous food material in plants, roughage. **3** strength of character (*moral fibre*). ☐ **fibre optics** the use of thin flexible fibres of glass or other transparent solids to transmit light signals.

fibreboard *n*. board made of compressed fibres.

fibreglass *n*. **1** textile fabric made from woven glass fibres. **2** plastic containing glass fibres.

fibril / **fuy**-bruhl / *n*. a small fibre.

fibro *n*. *Aust*. **1** = FIBRO-CEMENT. **2** a house made of sheets of fibro. •*adj*. made of fibro (*a fibro house*). ☐ **fibro-cement** a building material manufactured in sheet form from a mixture of sand, cement, and cellulose fibre.

fibroid / **fuy**-broid / *adj*. consisting of fibrous tissue. •*n*. a benign fibroid tumour in the womb.

fibrosis / fuy-**broh**-suhs / *n*. a thickening and scarring of connective tissue, usu. as a result of injury.

fibrositis / fuy-bruh-**suy**-tuhs / *n*. rheumatic pain in any tissue other than bones and joints.

fibrous / **fuy**-bruhs / *adj*. like fibres; made of fibres.

fibula / **fib**-yoo-luh / *n*. (*pl*. **fibulae** or **fibulas**) the bone on the outer side of the lower part of the leg.

fiche / feesh / *n*. (*pl*. **fiche** or **fiches**) a microfiche.

fickle *adj*. often changing, not constant or loyal. ☐ **fickleness** *n*.

fiction *n*. **1** a product of the imagination. **2** an invented story. **3** a class of literature consisting of books containing such stories, esp. novels. ☐ **fictional** *adj*. **fictionally** *adv*.

fictionalise *v*. (also **-ize**) make into a fictional narrative. ☐ **fictionalisation** *n*.

fictitious / fik-**tish**-uhs / *adj*. imagined, not real, not genuine (*gave a fictitious account of his movements*). ☐ **fictitiously** *adv*.

ficus / **fuy**-kuhs / *n*. (also **fig**) any tree, shrub, or vine of the genus *Ficus*, having a milky sap, and tiny flowers and seeds inside a fruit-like receptacle called a fig, e.g. the banyan tree, the sacred bo tree, the rubber plant, and several Australian trees, e.g. the Moreton Bay fig, the Port Jackson fig, the sandpaper fig.

FID *abbr*. = FINANCIAL INSTITUTIONS DUTY.

fiddle *n*. **1** a violin or other stringed instrument, esp. when played as a folk instrument. **2** a piece of cheating, a swindle. •*v*. **1** play the fiddle. **2** (often foll. by *with*) fidget with something; handle a thing aimlessly; adjust, tinker, tamper with a thing. **3** (often foll. by *about*) move aimlessly; waste time. **4** *colloq*. cheat or swindle; falsify (accounts etc.); get by cheating.

fiddler *n*. **1** a fiddle player. **2** *colloq*. a swindler, a cheat. **3** any of several fish (rays) of Australian waters with a flattened, fiddle-shaped body.

fiddlesticks *interj*. nonsense.

fiddling *adj*. **1** petty, trivial. **2** *colloq*. = FIDDLY.

fiddly *adj*. *colloq*. small and awkward to use or do.

fidelity / fuh-**del**-uh-tee / *n*. **1** faithfulness, loyalty. **2** accuracy, truthfulness. **3** the quality or precision of the reproduction of sound (*high fidelity*).

fidget *v*. (**fidgeted**, **fidgeting**) **1** make small restless movements. **2** be uneasy, make (a person) uneasy, worry. •*n*. **1** a person who fidgets. **2** (**fidgets**) fidgeting movements; a restless mood. ☐ **fidgety** *adj*.

fiduciary / fuh-**dyoo**-shuh-ree / *adj*. of, held, or given in trust. •*n*. a trustee.

fief / feef / *n*. **1** land held under a feudal system or in absolute ownership. **2** one's sphere of operation or control.

field *n*. **1** a piece of open ground, esp. one used for pasture or cultivation. **2** an area rich in some natural product; a coalfield, goldfield, oilfield, etc. **3** a battlefield. **4** a sports ground; the playing area marked out on this (*footy field*). **5** the space within which an electric, magnetic, or gravitational influence can be felt; the force of that influence. **6** the area that can be seen or observed (*one's field of vision*). **7** the range of a subject or activity or interest (*an expert in the field of music*). **8** (in computers) one section of a record, representing a unit of information. **9** the scene or area of fieldwork (*field archaeology; a field trip*). **10** all the competitors in a contest, race, or sport, or all except the one(s) specified (*Tonetto and Nguyen are far ahead of the field*). **11** the fielding side in cricket. •*v*. **1** act as a fielder in cricket etc. **2** stop and return (the ball) in cricket etc. **3** select (a player or team) to play in a game. **4** deal successfully with (a series of questions). ☐ **field day 1** an exciting or successful time. **2** *Aust*. a day set aside for the display of agricultural machinery. **3** a military exercise or review. **field events** athletic sports other than races, e.g. jumping, shot-putting, etc. **field goal** a goal in rugby scored with a drop kick. **field marshal** an army officer of the highest rank. **field mouse** a mouse which inhabits paddocks etc. (as distinct from the house mouse). **field umpire** *Aust. Rules* the umpire (or one of three umpires in major games) in control of the match. **play the field** *colloq*. date many partners.

fielder *n*. a member of the side not batting in cricket etc.

fieldsman *n*. a fielder.

fieldwork *n*. **1** practical work done outside libraries and laboratories, e.g. by surveyors, scientists, and social workers who visit people in their homes. **2** a temporary fortification. ☐ **fieldworker** *n*.

fiend / feend / *n*. **1** an evil spirit, a demon. **2** (**the Fiend**) the Devil. **3** a very wicked or cruel person. **4** a mischievous or annoying person. **5** *colloq*. a devotee or addict (*a fitness fiend*). **6** a difficult or unpleasant thing. ☐ **fiendish** *adj*. **fiendishly** *adv*.

fierce *adj.* **1** violent in temper, manner, or action; not gentle. **2** eager, intense (*fierce competition*). **3** unpleasantly strong or extreme (*fierce heat*). □ **fiercely** *adv.* **fierceness** *n.*

fiery *adj.* **1** consisting of fire, flaming. **2** looking like fire, bright red. **3** intensely hot, producing a burning sensation. **4** intense, passionate (*a fiery speech*). **5** easily roused to anger. □ **fierily** *adv.* **fieriness** *n.*

fiesta / fee-es-tuh / *n.* a holiday, a festivity, or a religious festival.

FIFA *abbr.* International Football Federation. (¶ French, = *Fédération Internationale de Football Association*.)

fife *n.* a small shrill flute used with a drum in military music.

fifteen *adj.* & *n.* **1** one more than fourteen (15, XV). **2** a Rugby Union football team of fifteen players. □ **fifteenth** *adj.* & *n.*

fifth *adj.* & *n.* **1** next after fourth. **2** one of five equal parts of a thing. □ **fifth column** an organised body working for the enemy within a country at war. (¶ General Mola, leading four columns of troops towards Madrid in the Spanish Civil War, declared that he had a fifth column inside the city.) **fifth columnist** a member of such a group. □□ **fifthly** *adv.*

fifty *adj.* & *n.* **1** five times ten (50, L). **2** (**fifties**) the numbers from 50 to 59, esp. the years of a century or of a person's life. □ **fifty-fifty** *adj.* & *adv. colloq.* shared or sharing equally between two; with equal chances. □□ **fiftieth** *adj.* & *n.*

fig *n.* **1** a soft pulpy fruit with many seeds. **2** (in full **fig tree**) a tree of the genus *Ficus* bearing figs. □ **fig leaf** a representation of a leaf of a fig tree used in art to cover the genitals of nude figures. **not care** (*or* **give**) **a fig** not care at all.

fig. *abbr.* **1** figure. **2** figurative. **3** figuratively.

figbird *n.* a greenish-coloured fruit-eating bird, usu. with red eyepatch, of eastern and northern Australia.

fight *v.* (**fought, fighting**) **1** struggle against (a person or country) in physical combat or in war. **2** carry on (a battle). **3** struggle or contend in any way; strive to obtain or accomplish something. **4** strive to overcome or destroy (*they fought the fire*). **5** make one's way by fighting or effort. • *n.* **1** fighting, a battle. **2** a struggle, contest, or conflict of any kind. **3** a boxing match. **4** the power or the inclination to fight (*he has no fight left in him*). □ **fight back 1** counter-attack. **2** suppress (feelings etc.) (*fought back his tears*). **fighting chance** a chance of succeeding by great effort. **fighting fit** very fit. **fight off** drive away with effort. **fight shy of** avoid (a task etc.).

fighter *n.* **1** a person who fights. **2** a fast military aircraft designed for attacking other aircraft.

figment *n.* a thing that only exists in the imagination.

figurative / **fig**-yoor-ruh-tiv / *adj.* **1** using or containing a figure of speech; metaphorical, not literal. **2** of pictorial or sculptural representation. □ **figurative style** *Aust.* a style of (esp. ancient) Aboriginal art in which human, animal, or mythological figures predominate, as distinct from Aboriginal art consisting of circles, lines, and other such non-figurative elements. □□ **figuratively** *adv.*

figure *n.* **1** the written symbol of a number. **2** a diagram. **3** a decorative pattern; a pattern traced in dancing or skating. **4** a representation of a person or animal in drawing, sculpture, etc. **5** a person seen in outline but not identified (*saw a figure leaning against the door*). **6** a person of a specified kind or appearance (*the most terrible figure in our history*). **7** external form or shape, bodily shape (*has a good figure*). **8** a geometrical shape enclosed by lines or surfaces. **9** (**figures**) arithmetic (*no good at figures*). **10** amount, estimated value (*cannot put a figure on it*). **11** *Music* a short succession of notes producing a single impression; a brief melodic formula out of which longer passages are developed. • *v.* **1** represent in a diagram or picture. **2** picture mentally, imagine. **3** form part of a plan etc.; appear or be mentioned (*he figures in all books on the subject*). **4** understand; consider. **5** *colloq.* make sense; be likely (*that figures*). □ **figure of speech** a word or phrase used for vivid or dramatic effect and not literally; a metaphor. **figure on** count on, expect. **figure out** work out by arithmetic or logic. **2** interpret, understand. **figure skater** a person who practises figure skating. **figure skating** skating in prescribed patterns.

figured *adj.* ornamented, decorated (*figured silk*). □ **figured bass** *Music* = CONTINUO.

figurehead *n.* **1** a carved image at the prow of a ship. **2** a person at the head of an organisation etc. but without real power.

figurine / fig-uh-**reen** / *n.* a statuette.

Fiji / fee-jee / a republic consisting of about 100 inhabited islands in the South Pacific. □ **Fijian** / fee-jee-uhn / *adj.* & *n.*

filament *n.* **1** a threadlike strand. **2** a fine wire in an electric lamp, giving off light when heated by the current.

filch *v.* pilfer, steal (something of small value).

file[1] *n.* a tool with a roughened surface for shaping or smoothing wood, fingernails, etc. • *v.* shape or smooth with a file.

file[2] *n.* **1** a holder, cover, or box for keeping papers arranged for reference purposes. **2** its contents. **3** a collection of related data stored under one reference in a computer. **4** a line of people or things one behind the other (*in single file*). • *v.* **1** place in a file. **2** place on record (*file an application*). **3** (of a reporter) send in (a story etc.). **4** march in file (*they filed out*). □ **on file** placed in order for easy reference.

filial / fil-ee-uhl / *adj.* of (or due from) a son or daughter (*filial duty*). □ **filially** *adv.*

filibuster *n.* **1** a person who obstructs the passage of a parliamentary bill by making long speeches. **2** this action. •*v.* obstruct things in this way. ☐ **filibusterer** *n.*

filigree / fil-uh-**gree** / *n.* **1** ornamental lace-like work in gold or other metal wire. **2** delicate work of a similar kind. ☐ **filigreed** *adj.*

filing cabinet *n.* a metal or wooden container with drawers for filing documents.

filings *n.pl.* particles rubbed off by a file.

Filipino / fil-uh-**pee**-noh / *n.* (also *feminine* **Filipina**) (*pl.* **Filipinos**, **Filipinas**) a native of the Philippine Islands. •*adj.* of the Philippine Islands or their inhabitants.

fill *v.* **1** make or become full; occupy the whole of. **2** block up (a hole or cavity). **3** spread over or through (*smoke began to fill the room*). **4** hold (a position); appoint a person to (a vacant post). **5** occupy (vacant time). •*n.* **1** enough to fill something. **2** enough to satisfy a person's appetite or desire (*eat your fill*). ☐ **fill in 1** complete by writing or drawing inside an outline; complete (an unfinished document, a form, etc.). **2** *colloq.* inform (a person) more fully. **3** (often foll. by *for*) act as a substitute.

filler *n.* **1** an object or material used to fill a cavity or to increase the bulk of something. **2** paste or a similar substance used to fill in holes or cracks prior to painting a surface. **3** a small item filling space in a newspaper etc.

fillet *n.* **1** a piece of boneless meat from near the loins or ribs; a thick boneless piece of fish. **2** a strip of ribbon etc. worn round the head. **3** (in architecture) a narrow flat band between mouldings. •*v.* (**filleted**, **filleting**) **1** remove the bones from (fish etc.). **2** bind or provide with fillet(s).

filling *n.* **1** material used to fill a tooth cavity; the process of inserting this. **2** material used to fill a sandwich, a pie, etc. ☐ **filling station** a place where petrol is supplied to motorists from pumps.

fillip *n.* **1** a quick smart blow or stroke given with a finger. **2** a stimulus or incentive (to trade etc.). •*v.* (**filliped**, **filliping**) propel with a fillip; stimulate (*let me fillip your memory*).

filly *n.* a young female horse.

film *n.* **1** a thin coating or covering layer. **2** a rolled strip or sheet coated with light-sensitive material used for taking photographs or making a motion picture; a single roll of this. **3** a motion picture. **4** (**films**) the cinema industry. **5** a fine haze or blur. •*v.* **1** cover or become covered with a thin coating or covering layer. **2** make a film of (a story etc.).

filmstrip *n.* a series of transparencies for projection.

filmy *adj.* (**filmier**, **filmiest**) thin and almost transparent. ☐ **filminess** *n.*

filo pastry / **fee**-loh, **fuy**-loh / *n.* a tissue-thin pastry used in Greek etc. cooking.

filter *n.* **1** a device or substance for holding back the impurities in a liquid or gas passed through it. **2** a screen for preventing light of certain wavelengths from passing through. **3** a device for suppressing electrical or sound waves of frequencies other than the ones required. •*v.* **1** pass or cause to pass through a filter; remove (impurities) in this way. **2** make a way in or out gradually (*news filtered out; people filtered into the hall*). ☐ **filter paper** *n.* porous paper for filtering.

filth *n.* **1** disgusting dirt. **2** obscenity.

filthy *adj.* (**filthier**, **filthiest**) **1** disgustingly dirty. **2** obscene. **3** *colloq.* very unpleasant; vile (*filthy weather; a filthy mood*). **4** *colloq.* excellent (*the surf is filthy today*). •*adv.* **1** filthily (*filthy dirty*). **2** extremely (*he's filthy rich*). ☐ **filthily** *adv.* **filthiness** *n.*

filtrate *n.* filtered liquid. •*v.* filter. ☐ **filtration** *n.*

fin *n.* **1** a thin flat projection from the body of a fish etc., used by the animal for propelling and steering itself in the water. **2** an underwater swimmer's rubber flipper. **3** a small projection shaped like a fish's fin, e.g. to improve the stability of an aircraft, a surfboard, etc. ☐ **finned** *adj.*

FINA / **fee**-nuh / *abbr.* the international controlling body of amateur competitive aquatic sports, including swimming, diving, and water polo. (¶ French, = *Fédération Internationale de Natation Amateur.*)

finagle / fuh-**nay**-guhl / *v. colloq.* behave or obtain dishonestly. ☐ **finagler** *n.*

final *adj.* **1** at the end, coming last. **2** putting an end to doubt or argument. •*n.* **1** the last of a series of contests in sports or a competition. **2** the edition of a newspaper published latest in the day. **3** (**finals**) the last set of examinations in a series. ☐ **final solution** the euphemistic term used by the Nazis for their policy (1941-45) of exterminating European Jews. ☐☐ **finally** *adv.*

finale / fuh-**nah**-lee / *n.* the final section of a musical composition or a drama.

finalise *v.* (also -**ize**) **1** bring to an end. **2** put into its final form. ☐ **finalisation** *n.*

finalist *n.* one who competes in a final.

finality / fuy-**nal**-uh-tee / *n.* the quality or fact of being final.

finance / **fuy**-nans / *n.* **1** the management of money. **2** money as support for an undertaking. **3** (**finances**) the money resources of a country, company, or person. •*v.* provide the money for. ☐ **finance company** a company concerned mainly with lending money esp. for hire-purchase transactions.

financial / fuy-**nan**-shuhl / *adj.* **1** of finance. **2** *Aust. colloq.* having ready money. **3** (of a club member etc.) with fees or dues fully paid to date. ☐ **financial institutions duty** (*abbr.* **FID**) *Aust. hist.* a state government tax levied on transactions with financial institutions, e.g. bank deposits, credit card payments, etc. **financial year** the twelve-monthly period for which accounts are made up, taxes, paid, etc. (in Australia 1 July to 30 June). ☐ **financially** *adv.*

Financial Times index (*abbr.* **FT–SE**) (also called **FT Index, Footsie**) in Britain, the Financial Times–Stock Exchange 100 share index, an index based on the share values of Britain's one hundred largest public companies.

financier / fuy-**nan**-see-uh / *n.* a person engaged in financing business etc. on a large scale.

Finch, Peter (Ingle) (1916–77), Australian actor in theatre and in film. He won a posthumous Oscar for his role in the film *Network*.

finch *n.* any of many small seed-eating birds, often with brightly coloured plumage, including Australian species, e.g. *the blue-faced finch, the crimson finch, the Gouldian finch, the zebra finch*.

find *v.* (**found, finding**) **1** discover by search or effort or by chance. **2** become aware of, discover (a fact). **3** arrive at naturally (*water finds its own level*). **4** succeed in obtaining (*can't find time to do it*). **5** supply, provide (*who will find the money for the expedition?*). **6** (of a jury etc.) decide and declare (*found him innocent; found for the plaintiff*). **7** experience (*find difficulty in breathing*). •*n.* a discovery; a thing found; a valued thing or person newly discovered. ☐ **find out 1** get information about. **2** detect (a person) who has done wrong. **3** discover (a deception or fraud).

finder *n.* **1** one who finds something. **2** the viewfinder of a camera. **3** a small telescope attached to a larger one to locate an object for observation.

findings *n.pl.* the conclusions reached by means of an inquiry.

fine[1] *n.* a sum of money fixed as a penalty for an offence. •*v.* punish by a fine.

fine[2] *adj.* **1** of high quality. **2** excellent, of great merit. **3** (of weather) bright and clear, free from rain and fog etc. **4** of slender thread or thickness; small-sized; consisting of small particles. **5** requiring very skilful workmanship. **6** difficult to perceive (*making fine distinctions*). **7** complimentary, esp. in an insincere way (*said fine things about them*). **8** in good health, comfortable (*I'm fine, thank you*). •*adv.* **1** finely. **2** *colloq.* very well (*that will suit me fine*). •*v.* make or become finer, thinner, or less coarse. ☐ **fine arts** those appealing to the sense of beauty, esp. painting, sculpture, and architecture. **fine-drawn 1** subtle (*a fine-drawn distinction*). **2** (of a wire etc.) extremely thin. **fine print** detailed information printed small, esp. in legal documents etc. **fine-tooth comb** a comb with narrow close-set teeth. **fine-tune** make delicate adjustments to (a mechanism, plan, etc.) in order to improve it. **fine up** *Aust.* become fine (esp. of weather). **fine-woolled** esp. *Aust.* (of a sheep etc.) having wool with fibres less than 18.05 microns thick. **go over with a fine-tooth comb** examine closely and thoroughly. **not to put too fine a point on it** to express it bluntly. ☐☐ **finely** *adv.* **fineness** *n.*

finery *n.* fine clothes or decorations.

fines herbes / feen **zairb** / *n.pl.* mixed herbs used in cooking. (¶ French)

finesse / fuh-**nes** / *n.* **1** refinement. **2** subtle manipulation. **3** tact and cleverness in dealing with a situation. **4** (in card games) an attempt to win a trick by playing a card that is not the highest held. •*v.* **1** achieve by finesse. **2** (in card games) make a finesse; play (a card) as a finesse.

finger *n.* **1** any of the five parts extending from each hand; any of these other than the thumb. **2** the part of a glove that fits over a finger. **3** a finger-like object (*fish finger*). **4** *colloq.* the breadth of a finger as a measure of alcohol in a glass. •*v.* touch or feel with the fingers. ☐ **finger cherry** the elongated cherry-like fruit of a Qld tree. **finger flower** a small Australian shrub having deep violet flowers with long gold anthers resembling fingers. **finger food** food served in such a form and style that it can conveniently be eaten with the fingers; savouries. **finger lime** a small Australian rainforest tree of the citrus family which bears long, finger-like, edible limes. **get** (*or* **pull**) **one's finger out** *colloq.* start to act. **put one's finger on** locate or identify exactly. **put the finger on** *colloq.* name or inform on someone to the police.

fingerboard *n.* the part of the neck of a stringed instrument on which the strings are pressed by the fingers.

fingering *n.* **1** a method of using the fingers in playing a musical instrument or in typing. **2** indication of this in a musical score, usu. by numbers.

fingerling *n.* a very young, finger-sized fish.

fingernail *n.* the nail on a finger.

fingerprint *n.* an impression of the ridges of the skin on the pad of a finger, esp. as a means of identification. •*v.* record the fingerprints of.

fingerstall *n.* a sheath to cover an injured finger.

fingertalk *n.* *Aust.* an Aboriginal sign language.

fingertip *n.* the tip of a finger. ☐ **have at one's fingertips** be thoroughly familiar with (facts etc.).

finial *n.* an ornamental top to a gable, canopy, etc.

finical *adj.* finicky.

finicking *adj.* & *n.* being finicky.

finicky *adj.* **1** excessively detailed, fiddly. **2** over-particular, fastidious.

finis / **fin**-is / *n.* the end, esp. of a book.

finish *v.* **1** bring or come to an end, complete. **2** reach the end of a task or race etc. **3** consume or get through all of (*finish the pie*). **4** put the final touches to; complete the manufacture of (woodwork, cloth, etc.) by surface treatment. •*n.* **1** the last stage of something. **2** the point at which a race etc. ends. **3** the state of being finished or perfect. **4** the method, texture, or material used for finishing woodwork etc. ☐ **finish off 1** end. **2** *colloq.* kill. **finish with** complete one's use of; end one's association with.

finite / **fuy**-nuyt / *adj.* **1** limited, not infinite. **2** *Grammar* (of a part of a verb) having a specific number and person.

fink *n. colloq.* **1** a despicable person, esp. one who goes back on his or her word. **2** a strikebreaker, a blackleg.

Finland a republic of NE Europe.

Finn *n.* a native of Finland.

Finnish *adj.* of the Finns or their language. • *n.* the language of the Finns.

fiord / **fee**-awd / *n.* (also **fjord**) a long narrow inlet of the sea between high cliffs as in Norway.

fipple *n.* the mouthpiece of a wind instrument. ☐ **fipple flute** a flute played by blowing the end, e.g. a recorder.

fir *n.* **1** an evergreen cone-bearing tree with needle-like leaves on its shoots. **2** its wood.

fire *n.* **1** combustion producing light and heat. **2** destructive burning (*bushfire*). **3** burning fuel in a grate or furnace etc.; an electric or gas fire. **4** anger or excited feeling, enthusiasm. **5** the firing of guns (*hold your fire*). • *v.* **1** send a bullet or shell from a gun etc.; send out (a missile); detonate. **2** deliver or utter in rapid succession (*fired insults*). **3** dismiss (an employee) from a job. **4** set fire to with the intention of destroying. **5** *Aust.* (esp. of Aborigines) set fire to the bush in a controlled way in order to trap animals or to maintain grassland and promote regrowth (*see* FIRESTICK FARMING). **6** catch fire; (of an internal-combustion engine) undergo ignition. **7** supply (a furnace etc.) with fuel. **8** bake (pottery or bricks); cure (tea or tobacco) by artificial heat. **9** excite, stimulate (*fired them with enthusiasm*). **10** cause to glow, redden. ☐ **fire away** *colloq.* begin, go ahead. **fire ban** the official prohibition of the lighting of fires in the open on days of high fire risk. **fire brigade** an organised body of people trained and employed to extinguish fires. **fire door** a fire-resistant door preventing the spread of fire. **fire drill** rehearsal of the procedure to be used in case of fire. **fire engine** a vehicle fitted with equipment used for fighting large fires. **fire escape** a staircase or apparatus for escape from a building etc. in case of fire. **fire extinguisher** an apparatus for spraying foam etc. to put out a fire. **fire risk 1** the likelihood of bushfires. **2** the risk of the loss of property by fire. **3** a building etc. which because of its condition is in danger of catching fire. **fire station** the headquarters of a fire brigade. **fire trail** a permanent track through the bush providing access for firefighters. **fire trap** a building without sufficient exits in case of fire. **fire watcher** a person keeping watch for fires, esp. bushfires. **under fire 1** being fired on. **2** being rigorously criticised or questioned.

firearm *n.* a gun, esp. a rifle or pistol.

fireball *n.* **1** a large meteor. **2** a ball of flame (esp. from a nuclear explosion or in a bushfire). **3** a ball of lightning.

firebrand *n.* **1** a piece of burning wood. **2** a person who stirs up trouble.

firebreak *n.* an obstacle (esp. a strip that has been cleared) to the spread of fire in a forest etc.

firebug *n. colloq.* a person who deliberately sets fire to the bush on days of high fire danger or sets buildings etc. alight.

firecracker *n.* an explosive firework.

firedamp *n.* the miners' name for methane, which is explosive when mixed in certain proportions with air.

firedog *n.* an iron support (usu. one of a pair) for holding logs in a fireplace.

firedrake *n.* a fire-breathing dragon.

firefighter *n.* a member of a team employed to put out fires, esp. bushfires.

firelighter *n.* a piece of flammable material to help start a fire in a fireplace or barbecue.

firefly *n.* a beetle that gives off a phosphorescent light.

fireman *n.* **1** a firefighter. **2** a person who tends a steam engine or the furnace of a steamship.

Firenze *see* FLORENCE.

fireplace *n.* **1** an open recess for a domestic fire, at the base of a chimney. **2** the surrounding structure. **3** a structure provided at a picnic place, rest area, etc., in which a cooking fire may be lit.

fireplough *n.* an implement that cuts a furrow wide enough to form a firebreak.

firepower *n.* the destructive capacity of guns etc.

fireproof *adj.* able to resist fire or great heat (*fireproof dishes*). • *v.* make fireproof.

firescreen *n.* an ornamental and/or protective screen for a domestic fireplace.

firestick *n. Aust.* a smouldering stick used to light a fire, esp. as carried by an Aborigine. ☐ **firestick farming** a method of vegetation control and bushland regeneration, esp. as practised for centuries by Aborigines.

firetail *n.* any of several often colourful Australian finches having red rumps.

firewall *n.* **1** a fireproof wall to inhibit or prevent the spread of fire. **2** *Computing* software which protects a computer network against unauthorised access.

fireweed *n.* any of several plants, esp. of the genus *Senecio*, which reappear rapidly after a bushfire.

firewheel tree *n.* a tree of eastern Australia remarkable for its whorls of fire-red flowers.

firewood *n.* wood for use as fuel.

firework *n.* **1** a device containing chemicals that burn or explode with spectacular effect, used at celebrations. **2** (**fireworks**) an outburst of anger.

firing line *n.* **1** the front line of a battle, from which troops fire at the enemy. **2** the forefront of an activity.

firing squad *n.* a group ordered to fire a salute during a military funeral, or to shoot a condemned person.

firm *n.* a partnership for carrying on a business; a commercial establishment. • *adj.* **1** not yielding when pressed, hard, solid. **2** steady, not shaking. **3** securely fixed. **4** established, not easily changed or influenced (*a firm belief; a firm offer*). **5** steadfast (*a firm friend*). • *adv.* firmly (*stand firm*). • *v.* make or become firm or compact; fix firmly.

firmament *n. poetic* the sky with its clouds and stars.

firmware *n. Computing* system software programmed into a read-only memory.

first *adj.* coming before all others in time, order, or importance. • *n.* **1** something that is first; the first day of a month; the first occurrence or achievement of something. **2** first-class honours in a university degree. **3** first gear. • *adv.* **1** before all others. **2** before another event or time (*finish this work first*). **3** for the first time (*when did you first see him?*). **4** in preference (*will see him damned first*). **5** first class (*I usually travel first*). ☐ **at first hand** directly from the original source. **first aid** treatment given to an injured person before a doctor comes. **first class 1** a set of persons or things grouped together as better than others. **2** the best accommodation in a train, aircraft, etc. **3** the highest division in examination results. **4** (used as *adv.*) in or by first class. **first-class** *adj.* **1** of the best quality; very good. **2** of or using first-class accommodation etc. **first cousin** *see* COUSIN. **first-degree burn** a non-serious surface burn. **first floor** the floor above the ground floor. **first fruits 1** the first of a season's agricultural products. **2** the first results of work etc. **first-generation** *see* GENERATION. **first name** a personal or Christian name. **first night** the first public performance of a play etc. **first offender** a criminal with no previous convictions. **first past the post** (of an electoral system) selecting a candidate or a party by a simple majority. **first person** *see* PERSON. **first-rate** *adj.* of the best class; excellent. *adv. colloq.* very well (*feeling first-rate*).

First Australian *n.* an Aborigine.

firstborn *adj. & n.* eldest; the eldest child.

First Fleet *n.* the first British ships to bring convicts, civilians, marines, to Australia (1788). ☐ **First Fleeter 1** a person who came to Australia with the First Fleet. **2** a descendant of such a person.

firsthand *adj. & adv.* directly from the original source.

firstly *adv.* first, as a first consideration.

firth *n.* an estuary or a narrow inlet of the sea.

fiscal *adj.* **1** of public revenue. **2** financial (*the fiscal year*).

fish[1] *n.* (*pl.* **fish** *or* **fishes**) **1** a cold-blooded animal living wholly in water. **2** its flesh as food. **3** *colloq.* a person (*an odd fish*). **4** (**the Fish** *or* **Fishes**) a sign of the zodiac, Pisces. • *v.* **1** try to catch fish. **2** search for something under water or by reaching into something; bring out or up in this way (*fished out his keys*). **3** (usu. foll. by *for*) try to obtain by hinting or indirect questioning (*fishing for information*). ☐ **fish-eye lens** a very wide-angled lens producing a distorting effect. **fish finger** a small oblong piece of fish in batter or breadcrumbs. **fish-hook** a barbed hook for catching fish. **fish out of water** a person out of his or her element. **fish spear** an implement, sometimes barbed, used by Aboriginal men and women for spearing fish, dugong, turtles, etc. **have other fish to fry** have more important business to attend to. ☐☐ **fisher** *n.*

fish[2] *n.* a piece of wood or iron etc. to strengthen a mast or beam.

Fisher, Andrew (1862–1928), Australian Labor statesman and prime minister 1908–09, 1910–13, 1914–15. His social reforms included the provision of maternity allowances, the extension of old age and invalid pensions, and the establishment of the Commonwealth Bank.

fisherman *n.* a person who catches fish for a living or as a sport.

fishery *n.* **1** a place where fish are caught or reared. **2** the industry of fishing or breeding fish.

fishing *n.* trying to catch fish. ☐ **fishing line** a thread with a baited hook for catching fish. **fishing rod** a long rod to which a line is attached, used for fishing. **fishing weir** *Aust.* a barrier built by Aborigines across a watercourse to catch fish. **go on a fishing expedition** question or investigate merely in the hope of uncovering something detrimental.

fishmonger *n.* a dealer in fish.

fishnet *adj.* (of fabric) made in a kind of open mesh (*fishnet stockings*).

fishplate *n.* a flat plate of iron etc. connecting the rails of a railway.

fishtail palm *n.* a tall palm of Qld rainforests having leaves like fishtails and spikes of yellow and purple flowers.

fishwife *n.* a coarse-mannered or noisy woman.

fishy *adj.* (**fishier**, **fishiest**) **1** like fish, smelling or tasting of fish. **2** *colloq.* causing disbelief or suspicion (*a fishy story*). ☐ **fishily** *adv.* **fishiness** *n.*

fissile / **fis**-uyl / *adj.* **1** tending to split. **2** capable of undergoing nuclear fission.

fission *n.* **1** splitting of the nucleus of certain atoms, with release of energy. **2** splitting or division of biological cells as a method of reproduction. ☐ **fission bomb** the atom bomb.

fissionable *adj.* capable of undergoing nuclear fission.

fissure / **fish**-uh / *n.* a cleft made by splitting or separation of parts.

fist *n.* the hand when tightly closed, with the fingers bent into the palm. ☐ **make a good** (*or* **poor**) **fist of something** do something well (or badly).

fisticuffs *n.pl.* fighting with the fists.

fistula / fis-tyoo-luh / *n.* (*pl.* **fistulas** *or* **fistulae**) **1** a long pipe-like ulcer. **2** an abnormal or surgically made passage in the body. **3** a natural pipe or spout in whales, insects, etc. ☐ **fistular** *adj.*

fit[1] *n.* **1** a brief spell of an illness or its symptoms (*a fit of coughing*). **2** a sudden violent seizure of epilepsy, apoplexy, etc., with convulsions or loss of consciousness. **3** an attack of strong feeling (*a fit of rage*). **4** a short period of a certain feeling or activity, an impulse (*a fit of energy*). ☐ **by** (*or* **in**) **fits and starts** in short bursts of activity, not steadily or regularly. **have a fit** *colloq.* be outraged. **in fits** laughing uncontrollably.

fit[2] *adj.* (**fitter**, **fittest**) **1** suitable or well adapted for something, good enough. **2** right and proper, fitting. **3** feeling in a suitable condition to do something (*worked till they were fit to drop*). **4** in good athletic condition or health. • *v.* (**fitted**, **fitting**) **1** be the right shape and size for something. **2** put clothing on (a person) and adjust to the right shape and size. **3** put into place (*fit a lock on the door*). **4** (usu. foll. by *for*) make or be suitable or competent (*his training fitted him for the position*). • *n.* the way a thing fits (*the coat is a good fit*). ☐ **fit as a fiddle** *colloq.* extremely healthy. **fit as a mallee bull** *Aust. colloq.* extremely fit. **fit in 1** make room or time etc. for. **2** be or cause to be harmonious or in a suitable relationship. **fit out** *or* **up** supply or equip. **fit to be tied** *colloq.* extremely angry; ropeable. **see** (*or* **think**) **fit** decide or choose to do something. ☐☐ **fitly** *adv.* **fitness** *n.*

fitful *adj.* occurring in short periods, not regularly or steadily. ☐ **fitfully** *adv.*

fitment *n.* a piece of fixed furniture.

fitted *adj.* **1** made to fit closely or exactly (*fitted carpet*). **2** provided with built-in fittings etc. (*a fitted kitchen*). **3** built-in (*fitted cupboards*). ☐ **fitted sheet** a bed sheet with elastic at the corners to keep attachment to the mattress secure.

fitter *n.* **1** a mechanic who fits together and adjusts machinery. **2** a supervisor of the cutting and fitting of garments.

fitting *adj.* proper, suitable. • *n.* **1** the process of having a garment etc. fitted. **2** (**fittings**) the fixtures and fitments of a building or room.

Fitton, Dame Doris (Alice) (1897–1985), Australian actor and stage director.

Fitzgerald[1], Ella (1918–96), American jazz singer.

Fitzgerald[2], R(obert) D(avid) (1902–87), AM, Australian poet.

Fitzroy 1 a river in northern Western Australia, rising in the Kimberleys and flowing about 640 km west to King Sound. **2** a river in north-eastern Queensland, rising on the confluence of the Dawson and Mackenzie rivers and flowing about 480 km north then south-east to Keppel Bay.

five *adj.* & *n.* one more than four (5, V). ☐ **five-eighth** esp. *Aust. Rugby* either of two players between the scrum-half and the centre three-quarter. **take five** *colloq.* take a short break.

fivefold *adj.* & *adv.* **1** five times as much or as many. **2** consisting of five parts.

fix *v.* **1** fasten firmly. **2** implant (facts or ideas) firmly in the mind or memory. **3** direct (the eyes or attention) steadily. **4** establish, specify (*fixed a time for the meeting; how are you fixed for cash?*). **5** treat (a photographic image or a colour etc.) with a substance that prevents it from fading or changing colour. **6** repair. **7** *colloq.* deal with, get even with. **8** *colloq.* use bribery or deception or improper influence on, arrange (the result of a race etc.) fraudulently. **9** *colloq.* inject a narcotic. **10** *colloq.* prepare (food or drink). • *n.* **1** *colloq.* an awkward situation (*be in a fix*). **2** the finding of the position of a ship or aircraft etc. by taking bearings; the position found. **3** *colloq.* an addict's dose of a narcotic drug. **4** a dishonest act; a bribe. ☐ **be fixed** *colloq.* be situated (regarding) (*how is he fixed for money?*). **fixed interest** an interest rate which does not vary over the term of a loan. **fixed star** an ordinary star, one that (unlike the sun and planets) is so far from the earth that it seems to have no motion of its own. **fix on** (*or* **upon**) choose, decide on. **fix up 1** arrange; organise. **2** accommodate; provide for (*fixed him up for the night; fixed me up with a job*).

fixated *adj.* having a fixation.

fixation *n.* **1** fixing, being fixed. **2** an abnormal emotional attachment to a person or thing. **3** concentration on one idea, an obsession.

fixative *adj.* tending to fix or secure. • *n.* **1** a substance for keeping things in position. **2** a substance for fixing colours etc., or for preventing perfumes from evaporating too quickly.

fixedly / fik-suhd-lee / *adv.* in a fixed way; intently.

fixer *n.* **1** a person or thing that fixes something. **2** a substance for fixing photographic images. **3** *colloq.* a person who makes arrangements, esp. of an illicit kind.

fixity *n.* a fixed state, stability, permanence.

fixture *n.* **1** a thing that is fixed in position. **2** a person or thing that is firmly established and unlikely to leave. **3** a date appointed for a match or race etc.; the match or race itself. **4** (**fixtures**) articles attached to a house or land and regarded as legally part of it.

fizgig *n. Aust.* an informer to the police.

fizz *v.* make a hissing or splluttering sound as when gas escapes in bubbles from a liquid. • *n.* **1** this sound. **2** a fizzy drink, esp. champagne. ☐ **fizzy** *adj.* **fizziness** *n.*

fizzer[1] *n. colloq.* **1** a firecracker that does not explode. **2** *Aust.* a failure, a fiasco (*the party was a fizzer*).

fizzer[2] *n. Aust. colloq.* an informer to the police. (¶ From FIZGIG.)

fizzle *v.* make a feeble fizzing sound. ☐ **fizzle out** end feebly or unsuccessfully.

fjord alternative spelling of FIORD.

fl. *abbr.* **1** floruit. **2** fluid.

flab *n. colloq.* fat; flabbiness.

flabbergast *v. colloq.* astonish, astound.

flabby *adj.* (**flabbier, flabbiest**) **1** (of flesh etc.) fat and limp, not firm. **2** (of language or character etc.) feeble. ☐ **flabbily** *adv.* **flabbiness** *n.*

flaccid / **flak**-suhd, **flas**-uhd / *adj.* hanging loose or wrinkled, not rigid or erect (*a flaccid penis*). ☐ **flaccidly** *adv.* **flaccidity** *n.*

flag *n.* **1** a usu. oblong or square piece of cloth with particular colours and often symbols, used as the emblem or standard of a country etc. **2** a similar device for signalling or indicating (*goal umpire's flags*). **3** an adjustable oblong strip of metal etc. used as a signal that a taxi is for hire. **4** (**the flag**) *Aust. Rules* the pennant awarded for winning the premiership; the premiership itself. **5** a plant with blade-like leaves, esp. an iris. **6** a flagstone. • *v.* (**flagged, flagging**) **1** mark out with or as if with a flag or flags. **2** signal with or as if with a flag. **3** hang down limply, droop. **4** lose vigour, become weak (*interest flagged*). **5** pave with flagstones. ☐ **flag down** signal to stop. **flag of convenience** a foreign flag of the nationality under which a ship is registered to evade taxation or certain regulations. **flag-waving** *n.* populist agitation; chauvinism. *adj.* aggressively patriotic, chauvinistic. **flying the Australian flag** *Aust. colloq.* with shirt tail untucked and hanging out. **show the flag** *colloq.* rally round; make an appearance.

flagellant / **flaj**-uh-luhnt, fluh-**jel**-uhnt / *n.* a person who scourges himself, herself, or others as a religious discipline or as a sexual stimulus. • *adj.* of flagellation.

flagellate / **flaj**-uh-layt / *v.* scourge, whip. ☐ **flagellation** *n.*

flageolet / flaj-uh-**let** / *n.* a small flute like a recorder.

flagfall *n. Aust.* the initial (pre-trip) charge for the hire of a taxi.

flagon *n.* **1** a large rounded bottle in which wine etc. is sold. **2** a vessel with a handle, lip, and lid for serving wine.

flagpole *n.* a pole on which a flag is hoisted.

flagrant / **flay**-gruhnt / *adj.* (of an offence or an offender) very bad and obvious. ☐ **flagrantly** *adv.* **flagrancy** *n.*

flagship *n.* **1** a ship that carries an admiral. **2** the principal vessel of a shipping line. **3** a firm's best or most important product.

flagstaff *n.* a flagpole.

flagstone *n.* a flat slab of rock used for paving.

flail *n.* an old-fashioned tool for threshing grain, consisting of a strong stick hinged on a long handle. • *v.* **1** beat with or as if with a flail. **2** wave or swing about wildly (*with arms flailing*).

flair *n.* **1** a natural ability to do something well or to select what is good or useful etc. **2** style, finesse.

flak *n.* **1** shells fired by anti-aircraft guns. **2** adverse criticism; abuse. ☐ **cop the** (or **some**) **flak** come in for heavy criticism or abuse.

flake *n.* **1** a small thin light piece of snow etc. **2** a thin broad piece peeled or split off. **3** flesh of the school shark and other Australian sharks etc., sold as food. • *v.* **1** take off or come away in flakes. **2** sprinkle with or fall in flakes. ☐ **flake out** *colloq.* fall asleep or drop from exhaustion; faint. ☐☐ **flaky** *adj.*

flambé / **flom**-bay / *adj.* (of food) covered with alcohol and served alight (*pancakes flambé*). • *v.* set (food) alight (*flambé the pancakes with brandy*). (¶ French, = singed.)

flamboyant *adj.* **1** coloured or decorated in a very showy way. **2** (of people) having a very showy appearance or manner. ☐ **flamboyantly** *adv.* **flamboyance** *n.*

flame *n.* **1** a bright tongue-shaped portion of ignited gases burning visibly. **2** (often in *plural*) visible combustion (*burst into flames*). **3** a brilliant orange-red colour. **4** *Aust.* the brilliant flashes of red found in some Australian opals; such an opal. **5** a strong passion, esp. love (*fan the flame*). **6** *colloq.* a sweetheart. • *v.* **1** burn with flames, send out flames. **2** become bright or glowing (*his face flamed with anger*). **3** shine or glow like flame (*the sky flamed at sunset*). **4** *Computing* send abusive messages to a newsgroup etc. on the Internet. ☐ **flame pea** a mainly WA genus of shrubs or twining plants bearing spectacular orange and red pea-flowers. **flame-thrower** a weapon throwing a jet of flame. **flame tree** (in full **Illawarra flame tree**) a deciduous eastern Australian tree with spectacular flame-coloured flowers.

flamenco / fluh-**men**-koh / *n.* (*pl.* **flamencos**) a Spanish gypsy style of song or dance.

flaming *adj.* **1** emitting flames. **2** very hot or bright. **3** *colloq.* passionate (*a flaming row*). **4** *colloq.* a euphemism for *bloody, fucking,* etc. (*flaming idiot!*; *stone the flaming crows!*).

flamingo / fluh-**ming**-goh / *n.* (*pl.* **flamingoes**) a long-legged wading bird with a long neck and pinkish feathers.

flammable *adj.* able to be set on fire, inflammable. ☐ **flammability** *n.*

■ **Usage** *Flammable* and *inflammable* mean the same. However, *flammable* is often preferred because *inflammable* can be mistaken for the negative. The true negative of *flammable* is *non-flammable*.

flan *n.* **1** an open pastry case with a sweet or savoury filling. **2** a sponge base with a sweet topping.

Flanders an area in the SW of the Low Countries, now divided between Belgium, France, and Holland, the scene of much fighting in the First World War. ☐ **Flanders poppy 1** a blood-red poppy with a black centre; used as an emblem of Allied forces who died in the First World War. **2**

an artificial red poppy for wearing on Remembrance Day, sold by the RSL in aid of needy ex-service people.

flange / flanj / n. a projecting rim or edge.

flank n. **1** the fleshy part of the side of the body between the last rib and the hip. **2** the side of a building or mountain. **3** the right or left side of a body of troops etc. **4** *Aust. Rules* an outside position, e.g. half-forward flank. • *v.* place or be situated at the side of.

flannel n. **1** a kind of loosely woven woollen fabric. **2** a cloth used for washing the face etc. ☐ **flannel flower** an Australian plant with divided silvery leaves and large white star-flowers with attractive flannel-like bracts.

flannelette n. cotton fabric made to look and feel like flannel.

flap v. (**flapped**, **flapping**) **1** move or be moved up and down like wings; beat. **2** give a light blow with a flexible flat object (*flapped him with the towel*). **3** *colloq.* be agitated or in a panic. **4** sway; flutter (*flags flapping in the wind*). • *n.* **1** the action or sound of flapping. **2** a light blow with something flat. **3** a broad piece hinged or attached at one side (e.g. a pocket-cover, the folded part of an envelope); a hinged or sliding section on an aircraft wing etc. used to control lift, an aileron. **4** *colloq.* a state of agitation or fuss (*he is in a flap*). ☐ **with ears flapping** *colloq.* listening eagerly. ☐☐ **flappy** *adj.*

flapjack n. a small thick pancake.

flapper n. *hist.* (in the 1920s) a young unconventional woman.

flare v. **1** blaze with a sudden irregular flame. **2** burst into sudden activity or anger (*tempers flared*). **3** widen gradually outwards (*flared trousers*). • *n.* **1** a sudden outburst of flame. **2** a device producing a flaring light as a signal or for illumination. **3** a flared shape, a gradual widening. **4** (**flares**) wide-bottomed trousers. ☐ **flare path** the line of lights on a runway to guide aircraft. **flare up 1** burst into flame. **2** become suddenly angry. **flare-up** n. **1** a violent row or argument. **2** a sudden outburst of flame, temper, activity, etc.

flash v. **1** (cause to) give out a brief or intermittent bright light. **2** send or reflect like a sudden flame (*her eyes flashed fire*). **3** come suddenly into view or into the mind (*the idea flashed upon me*). **4** move rapidly (*the train flashed past*). **5** (of water) rush along, rise and flow. **6** signal with a light or lights. **7** send (news etc.) by radio or telegraph. **8** *colloq.* show ostentatiously (*flashed her ring*). **9** *colloq.* (of a man) expose his penis briefly in an indecent way. • *n.* **1** a sudden burst of flame or light, e.g. of lightning. **2** a display of wit, a sudden brief feeling, etc. (*a flash of hope*). **3** a very brief time (*in a flash*). **4** a rush of water. **5** a brief news item sent out by radio etc. **6** a device producing a brief bright light in photography. **7** a coloured patch of cloth as an emblem on a military uniform etc. • *adj. colloq.* **1** gaudy and vulgar, flashy (*a flash car*). **2** smart, with-it (*flash jacket you're wearing*). ☐ **flash flood** a sudden destructive flood. **flash in the pan** something that makes a promising start and then fails. (¶ Originally an explosion of gunpowder in the 'pan' of an old gun without actually firing the charge.)

flashback n. the changing of the scene in a story or film to a scene at an earlier time.

flashbulb n. a bulb giving a bright light for flashlight photography.

flasher n. **1** an automatic device for flashing a light on and off. **2** *colloq.* a man who briefly exposes his penis in public.

flashgun n. a device operating a camera flashlight.

flashing n. a strip of metal to prevent water entering at a joint in roofing etc.

flashlight n. **1** an intensely bright flash of light used for photography. **2** a torch.

flashpoint n. **1** the temperature at which vapour from oil etc. will ignite. **2** the point at which anger is ready to break out.

flashy *adj.* showy, gaudy, cheaply attractive. ☐ **flashily** *adv.* **flashiness** n.

flask n. **1** a narrow-necked bulbous bottle for wine etc. or used in chemistry. **2** a hip flask.

flat[1] *adj.* (**flatter**, **flattest**) **1** horizontal, level. **2** spread out; lying at full length. **3** smooth and even; with a broad level surface; without projection etc. (*a flat stomach; a flat cap*). **4** (of a tyre) deflated because of a puncture etc. **5** absolute, unqualified (*a flat refusal*). **6** dull, monotonous (*spoke in a flat tone of voice*). **7** dejected (*feeling flat*). **8** (of a fizzy drink) having lost its effervescence. **9** (of paint) not glossy, having a matt finish. **10** (of a battery etc.) unable to generate any more electric current. **11** (in music) **a** below the correct pitch (*the violins are flat*). **b** (as D flat etc.) a semitone lower than the note or key stated. • *adv.* **1** in a flat manner. **2** *colloq.* completely (*I am flat broke*). **3** *colloq.* exactly (*in ten seconds flat*). **4** below the correct pitch in music (*he was singing flat*). • *n.* **1** a flat thing or part (*flat of the hand*). **2** level ground, esp. a plain or swamp. **3** (in music) a note that is a semitone lower than the corresponding one of natural pitch; the sign (♭) indicating this. **4** (in theatre) flat scenery on a frame. **5** *colloq.* a flat tyre. ☐ **flat feet** feet with less than the normal arch beneath. **flat-footed 1** having flat feet. **2** *colloq.* uninspired; clumsy. **3** *colloq.* unprepared (*their sudden arrival caught us flat-footed*). **flat racing** horse racing over level ground, without jumps. **flat rate** a rate that is the same in all cases, not proportional. **flat spin 1** a nearly horizontal spinning descent of an aircraft, usu. uncontrollable. **2** a state of agitation or panic. **flat strap** (also **flat chat**) *Aust. colloq.* at full speed (*he drove flat strap to get her to the hospital in time*). **that's**

flat *colloq.* that is definite. ☐ ☐ **flatly** *adv.* **flatness** *n.*

flat² *n.* a set of rooms, usu. on one floor, as a residence. • *v. Aust.* live in a flat; share accommodation (with) (*I'm flatting by myself; she flats with her sister*).

flatette *n. Aust.* a tiny residential flat.

flatfish *n.* sole, plaice, etc. with both eyes on one side of a thin, flattened body.

flathead *n.* a marine food fish with a flattened head.

flatlet *n.* = FLATETTE.

flatmate *n.* a person sharing a flat, house, etc.

flatten *v.* 1 make or become flat. 2 *colloq.* humiliate. 3 *colloq.* knock down.

flatter *v.* 1 compliment (a person) excessively or insincerely, esp. in order to win favour. 2 gratify by honouring (*we were flattered to receive an invitation*). 3 enhance the appearance of (*that blouse flatters you*). 4 represent (a person or thing) favourably in a portrait etc. so that good looks are exaggerated. ☐ **flatter oneself** please or delude oneself with a belief (*he flatters himself that he can sing*). ☐ ☐ **flatterer** *n.*

flattery *n.* 1 flattering. 2 excessive or insincere compliments.

flattie *n. colloq.* 1 *Aust.* = FLATHEAD. 2 *Aust.* a flat tyre. 3 (**flatties**) low-heeled or heel-less shoes.

flattish *adj.* rather flat.

flatulent / **flatch**-uh-luhnt, **flat**-yoo- / *adj.* 1 causing or suffering from the formation of gas in the digestive tract. 2 (of speech etc.) pretentious. ☐ **flatulence** *n.*

flatworm *n.* a worm with a flattened body.

flaunt *v.* display proudly; show off; parade (*flaunting himself in his bathers*).

■ **Usage** This word is sometimes used incorrectly in place of *flout*.

flautist / **flaw**-tuhst / *n.* a flute player.

flavour *n.* (also **flavor**) 1 a distinctive taste. 2 a special quality or characteristic (*the story has a romantic flavour*). • *v.* give flavour to, season. ☐ **flavour of the month** (also **flavour of the week**) a temporary trend or fashion; a currently popular person.

flavouring *n.* (also **flavoring**) a substance used to give flavour to food.

flavoursome *adj.* (also **flavorsome**) full of flavour; extremely tasty.

flaw *n.* 1 an imperfection; a blemish; a crack. 2 an invalidating defect in a legal document etc. • *v.* crack; damage; spoil.

flawless *adj.* without a flaw; perfect. ☐ **flawlessly** *adv.*

flax *n.* 1 a blue-flowered plant cultivated for the textile fibre obtained from its stem and for its seeds (linseed). 2 its fibre.

flaxen *adj.* 1 made of flax. 2 pale yellow in colour like dressed flax (*flaxen hair*).

flay *v.* 1 strip off the skin or hide of. 2 criticise severely.

flea *n.* a small wingless jumping insect that feeds on human and animal blood. ☐ **a flea in one's ear** *colloq.* a stinging rebuke. **flea market** a street market selling second-hand goods.

fleabag *n. colloq.* 1 a sleeping bag. 2 a flea-ridden animal. 3 a shabby or unattractive person or thing.

fleck *n.* 1 a very small patch of colour or light. 2 a small particle, a speck. • *v.* mark with flecks.

fled *see* FLEE.

fledge *v.* 1 bring up (a young bird) until it can fly. 2 provide or deck (an arrow etc.) with feathers.

fledged *adj.* (of young birds) with fully grown wing-feathers, able to fly. ☐ **fully-fledged** mature; trained and experienced (*a fully-fledged engineer*).

fledgling *n.* (also **fledgeling**) 1 a young bird that is just fledged. 2 an inexperienced person.

flee *v.* (**fled**, **fleeing**) 1 run or hurry away. 2 run away from (*fled the country*). 3 pass away swiftly, vanish (*all hope had fled*).

fleece *n.* 1 the woolly hair of a sheep or similar animal. 2 the wool sheared from a sheep at one time. 3 a soft fabric used for linings etc. • *v.* 1 strip (a person) of money, valuables, etc.; swindle. 2 remove the fleece from (a sheep). 3 cover as if with a fleece (*a sky fleeced with clouds*). ☐ **fleecy** *adj.*

fleet *n.* 1 the naval force of a country; a number of warships under one commander. 2 a number of ships or aircraft or buses or taxis etc. moving or working under one command or ownership. • *adj. literary* moving swiftly, nimble.

fleeting *adj.* passing quickly, brief (*a fleeting glimpse*). ☐ **fleetingly** *adv.*

Fleming¹ *n.* a native of Flanders or of Flemish-speaking Belgium.

Fleming², Alexander (1881–1955), Scottish doctor and scientist, co-discoverer of penicillin with the Australian pathologist Howard Walter Florey.

Flemish *adj.* of Flanders or its people or language. • *n.* the Flemish language, one of the two official languages of Belgium.

flesh *n.* 1 the soft substance of an animal or human body, consisting of muscle and fat. 2 plumpness, fat (*he's put on flesh*). 3 the body as opposed to mind or soul, esp. considered as sinful. 4 the pulpy part of fruits and vegetables. 5 the visible surface of the human body. 6 animal or human life. ☐ **flesh and blood** *n.* 1 humankind. 2 human nature, people with all their motions and weaknesses (*more than flesh and blood can stand*). 3 near relatives; descendants (*one's own flesh and blood*). *adj.* real, not imaginary. **flesh out** 1 make or become substantial. 2 expand, amplify (*flesh out your story with more detail*).

flesh wound *n.* a wound that does not reach a bone or vital organ.

fleshly

fleshly *adj.* **1** bodily; sensual (*fleshly lusts*). **2** worldly rather than spiritual.

fleshpots *n.pl.* places of sensual indulgence.

fleshy *adj.* **1** of or like flesh. **2** having much flesh, plump; (of plants or fruits etc.) pulpy. □ **fleshiness** *n.*

fleur-de-lis / fler-duh-**lee** / *n.* (also **fleur-de-lys**) (*pl.* **fleurs-de-lis** pronounced the same) a design of a lily with three petals used in heraldry.

flew see FLY².

flews *n.pl.* the hanging lips of a bloodhound or other dog.

flex¹ *v.* bend (a joint or limb); move (a muscle) so that it bends a joint. • *n.* flexible insulated wire used for carrying electric current to a lamp or other appliance.

flex² *n.* = FLEXI. • *v.* (foll. by *off*) take time off from work under the flexitime system (*he's flexing off today*).

flexi *n. colloq.* a flexiday (*I'm having a flexi tomorrow*).

flexible *adj.* **1** able to bend easily without breaking. **2** adaptable, able to be changed to suit circumstances. □ **flexibly** *adv.* **flexibility** *n.*

flexiday *n.* a day taken off from work under the flexitime system.

flexion *n.* bending, a bent state, esp. of a joint or limb.

flexitime *n.* a system of flexible working hours.

flibbertigibbet *n.* a gossiping or frivolous person.

flick *n.* **1** a quick light blow or stroke, e.g. with a whip. **2** *colloq.* a cinema film. **3** (**the flicks**) *colloq.* the cinema. • *v.* **1** strike or remove with a quick light blow. **2** make a flicking movement. □ **flick knife** a weapon with a blade that springs out when a button is pressed. **flick pass** *Aust. Rules* a handpass in which the ball is struck with the open hand (instead of with a closed fist). **flick through 1** turn over (pages etc.) quickly. **2** glance through (a book etc.).

flicker *v.* **1** burn or shine unsteadily. **2** (of hope etc.) occur briefly. **3** quiver, move quickly to and fro. • *n.* a flickering movement or light; a brief occurrence of hope etc. □ **flicker out** die away.

flier alternative spelling of FLYER.

flight *n.* **1** the process of flying; the movement or path of a thing through the air. **2** a journey made by air; transport in an aircraft making a particular journey. **3** a flock of birds or insects. **4** a series of stairs in a straight line or between two landings; a series of hurdles etc. in a race. **5** swift passage (of time). **6** a mental soaring (*a flight of the imagination*). **7** the feathers etc. on a dart or arrow. **8** a volley (*a flight of arrows*). **9** fleeing, running or going away. • *v.* **1** fix feathers onto a dart or arrow. **2** give (a ball etc.) a certain path through the air. □ **flight attendant** a steward or stewardess on a passenger aircraft. **flight deck 1** the deck of an aircraft carrier. **2** the cockpit of a large aircraft. **flight lieutenant** a rank of officer in

flip

the RAAF immediately below squadron leader. **flight path** the planned course of an aircraft. **flight recorder** an electronic device in an aircraft, recording technical details about its flight.

flightless *adj.* (of birds, e.g. penguins) unable to fly.

flighty *adj.* (**flightier, flightiest**) frivolous, fickle, changeable. □ **flightiness** *n.*

flimsy *adj.* (**flimsier, flimsiest**) **1** insubstantial, rickety (*a flimsy structure*). **2** unconvincing (*a flimsy excuse*). **3** (of clothing) thin. □ **flimsily** *adv.* **flimsiness** *n.*

flinch *v.* **1** draw back in fear, wince. **2** shrink from one's duty etc.

Flinders¹ the longest river in Qld (840 km), named after Matthew Flinders. It flows from the Great Dividing Range to the sea on the Gulf of Carpentaria.

Flinders², Matthew (1774–1814), English naval officer, navigator and explorer who with George Bass was the first to circumnavigate Van Diemen's Land in 1798. In 1802 Flinders mapped the coast of the southern continent, eventually circumnavigating it for the first time. He wrote *A Voyage to Terra Australis* (1814) in which he advocated the term 'Australia', afterwards generally adopted.

Flinders Island an island in Bass Strait, 64 km long and 29 km wide, north-east of Tas. In 1830 what were considered to be the last of Tasmania's Aborigines were exiled to this island.

Flinders Ranges the most extensive mountain chain in SA, extending over 500 km from Crystal Brook to the Lake Eyre basin.

fling *v.* (**flung, flinging**) **1** throw violently, angrily, or hurriedly. **2** put or send suddenly or forcefully (*was flung into gaol*). **3** rush, go angrily or violently (*she flung out of the room*). **4** utter (words) forcefully (*he flung out the accusation*). **5** (foll. by *on*, *off*) put on or take off (clothes) carelessly or rapidly. • *n.* **1** the act or movement of flinging. **2** a spell of indulgence in pleasure (*have a fling*). **3** an attempt at something, esp. when uncertain of success (*oh well, I'll give it a fling*). **4** a vigorous Scottish dance.

flint *n.* **1** a very hard kind of stone that can produce sparks when struck against steel. **2** a piece of this, esp. as a primitive tool or weapon. **3** a piece of hard alloy used to produce a spark. **4** anything hard and unyielding. □ **flinty** *adj.*

flintlock *n.* an old type of gun fired by a spark from a flint.

flip¹ *v.* (**flipped, flipping**) **1** flick. **2** toss (a thing) with a sharp movement so that it turns over in the air. **3** = FLIP ONE'S LID. • *n.* **1** the action of flipping something. **2** a somersault. • *adj. colloq.* glib, flippant. □ **flip a person for** *colloq.* toss a coin with a person for something or to determine an issue (*flip you to see who does the dishes*). **flip one's lid** *colloq.* show great anger; go mad. **flip over a person** (*or* **thing**) *colloq.* be passionately fond of.

flip side 1 the reverse side of a gramophone

flip record. **2** the reverse or less important side of something. **flip through** = FLICK THROUGH.

flip² n. a drink of raw egg beaten in milk.

flippant adj. not showing proper seriousness; disrespectful. ☐ **flippantly** adv. **flippancy** n.

flipper n. **1** a limb of certain sea animals (e.g. seals, turtles, penguins), used in swimming. **2** one of a pair of large flat rubber attachments worn on the feet for underwater swimming. **3** *Cricket* a topspinner given an extra flip of the fingers.

flipping adj. & adv. colloq. expressing annoyance or used as an intensifier (*flipping idiot!; I flipping well will!*).

flirt v. **1** (often foll. by *with*) behave in a frivolously amorous or sexually enticing manner. **2** (usu. foll. by *with*) superficially interest oneself (*flirted with politics*); trifle (with danger etc.) (*flirting with death*). • n. a person who flirts. ☐ **flirtation** n.

flirtatious adj. flirting, fond of flirting. ☐ **flirtatiously** adv. **flirtatiousness** n.

flit v. (**flitted**, **flitting**) **1** fly or move lightly and quickly. **2** disappear in a stealthy way (to escape creditors etc.). • n. a stealthy move of this kind. ☐ **do a flit** colloq. depart surreptitiously.

flitch n. a side of bacon.

flitter v. flit about; flutter.

float v. **1** rest or drift on the surface of a liquid without sinking; be held up freely in air or gas. **2** cause to do this. **3** move lightly or casually. **4** have or allow (currency) to have a variable rate of exchange. **5** launch (a business company or a scheme), esp. by getting financial support from the sale of shares. **6** circulate (a rumour or idea) or cause (such) to circulate. • n. **1** a thing designed to float on liquid; a cork, plastic ball or quill used on a fishing line to show when the bait has been taken; any of the corks supporting the edge of a fishing net. **2** a floating device to control the flow of water, petrol, etc. **3** a structure to enable an aircraft to float on water. **4** a decorated platform or tableau on a truck in a procession etc. **5** (in full **horse float**) a closed vehicle for transporting a horse or horses. **6** a supply of loose change in a shop, at a fête, etc.; petty cash.

floatation alternative spelling of FLOTATION.

floater n. **1** a person or thing that floats. **2** a cheque that bounces. **3** a person who frequently changes jobs. **4** *Aust.* (in two-up) a coin that fails to spin when tossed. **5** *Aust.* a piece of ore that has come to the surface. **6** (in SA) a meat pie served floating in gravy and peas.

floaties n.pl. inflatable floats fixed on the arms of a child learning to swim.

floating adj. not settled; variable (*floating population*). ☐ **floating dock** a floating structure usable as a dry dock. **floating kidney** an abnormally movable kidney. **floating rib** a lower rib not joined to the breastbone.

flocculent adj. like tufts of wool, downy; in tufts or showing tufts. ☐ **flocculence** n.

flock n. **1** a number of animals of one kind, esp. birds, feeding or travelling together. **2** a number of domestic animals, esp. sheep, goats, or geese, kept together. **3** a large number of people together. **4** a number of people in the care of a priest or teacher etc. • v. gather or go in a flock. ☐ **flock pigeon 1** mainly brown nomadic pigeon of inland north Australia. **2** a mainly grey pigeon of eastern Australian rainforests.

floe n. a sheet of floating ice.

flog v. (**flogged**, **flogging**) **1** beat severely with a whip, stick, etc. **2** make (something) work through violent effort; overuse (*flogging the engine*). **3** (often foll. by *off*) colloq. sell. **4** colloq. steal. ☐ **flog a dead horse 1** try to do something quite useless. **2** try to raise or revive interest in a dead issue etc. ☐ ☐ **flogging** n.

flogger n. (esp. in *Aust. Rules*) streamers (in the colours of a team) attached to a rod and waved by cheerleaders and supporters.

flood n. **1** the coming of a great quantity of water over a place that is usu. dry; the water itself. **2** (**the Flood**) that of the time of Noah, described in Genesis. **3** a great outpouring or outburst (*a flood of abuse*). **4** the inflow of the tide. **5** a floodlight. • v. **1** cover or fill with a flood, overflow. **2** (of a river etc.) become flooded. **3** come in great quantities (*letters flooded in*). **4** have a haemorrhage of the womb. **5** overfill (a carburettor) with petrol.

floodgate n. **1** a gate that can be opened or closed to control the flow of water, esp. the lower gate of a lock. **2** (usu. as **floodgates**) a last restraint holding back tears, rain, anger, etc.

floodlight n. a lamp used for producing a broad bright beam of light to light up a stage or building etc. • v. (**floodlit**, **floodlighting**) illuminate with this.

floor n. **1** the lower surface of a room, the part on which one stands. **2** the bottom of the sea or of a cave etc; the ground. **3** (in a legislative chamber) the place where members sit and speak. **4** a minimum level for wages or prices. **5** a storey of a building. • v. **1** put a floor into (a building); pave. **2** knock down in a fight. **3** colloq. baffle, overwhelm (a person) with a problem or argument. ☐ **floor manager** the stage manager of a television production. **floor show** an entertainment in a nightclub. **from the floor** (of a speech etc.) given by a member of the audience. **take the floor 1** begin to dance. **2** speak in a debate.

floorboard n. one of the wooden boards forming the floor of a room.

flooring n. boards etc. used as a floor.

flop v. (**flopped**, **flopping**) **1** hang or sway heavily and loosely (*his hair flopped over his face*). **2** fall or move or sit down clumsily. **3** colloq. be a failure. • n. **1** a flopping movement or sound. **2** colloq. a failure. • adv. with a flop.

floppy *adj.* (**floppier, floppiest**) hanging heavily and loosely, not firm or rigid. •*n.* (in full **floppy disk**) *Computing* a flexible magnetic disk for the storage of data. □ **floppiness** *n.*

Flora *Rom. myth.* the goddess of flowering plants.

flora *n.* the plants of an area or period of time.

floral *adj.* decorated with or depicting flowers.

floral emblem *n.* a plant officially adopted by a country (and in Australia also by a State or Territory) as a symbol, hence: **1** (of Australia) the golden wattle *Acacia pycnantha*. **2** (of the ACT) the royal bluebell *Wahlenbergia gloriosa*. **3** (of the NT) Sturt's desert rose *Gossypium sturtianum*. **4** (of NSW) the waratah *Telopea speciosissima*. **5** (of Qld) the Cooktown orchid *Dendrobium bigibbum*. **6** (of SA) Sturt's desert pea *Clianthus formosus*. **7** (of Tas.) the Tasmanian blue gum *Eucalyptus globulus*. **8** (of Vic.) the common heath *Epacris impressa*. **9** (of WA) the red-and-green kangaroo paw *Anigozanthos manglesii*. (*See also* FAUNAL EMBLEM.)

Florence (Italian **Firenze**) a city of north Italy, a leading centre of the Italian Renaissance from the 14th to the 16th century.

Florentine / **flo**-ruhn-tuyn / *adj.* of Florence. •*n.* a native of Florence.

floret *n.* **1** each of the small flowers making up a composite flower head. **2** each stem of a head of cauliflower, broccoli, etc. **3** a small flower.

Florey, Howard (Walter), Baron Florey of Adelaide and Marston (1898–1968), Australian pathologist, co-discoverer of penicillin with Alexander Fleming. Awarded the Nobel Prize in 1945.

floribunda / flo-ruh-**bun**-duh / *n.* a rose or other plant bearing dense clusters of flowers.

florid *adj.* **1** elaborate and ornate. **2** (of the complexion) ruddy.

florin *n. hist.* a silver two-shilling coin.

florist *n.* a person whose business is the selling or growing of flowers.

floruit / **flo**-roo-uht, **flaw**- / *v.* (*abbr.* **fl.**) flourished; lived and worked (of a painter, writer, etc. whose exact dates are unknown). (¶ Latin)

floss *n.* **1** a mass of silky fibres. **2** silk thread with little or no twist, used in embroidery. **3** = DENTAL FLOSS. •*v.* clean (teeth) with dental floss. □ **flossy** *adj.*

flotation *n.* (also **floatation**) the launching or financing of a commercial venture.

flotilla / fluh-**til**-uh / *n.* **1** a small fleet. **2** a fleet of boats or small ships.

flotsam *n.* wreckage found floating. □ **flotsam and jetsam** *n.* **1** wreckage found floating as well as cast ashore. **2** odds and ends.

flounce *v.* go in an impatient annoyed manner (*flounced out of the room*). •*n.* **1** a flouncing movement. **2** a deep frill of material sewn by its upper edge to a skirt etc.

flounced *adj.* trimmed with a flounce.

flounder *n.* a small edible flatfish, including species found in coastal Australian waters. •*v.* **1** move clumsily and with difficulty as if wading in mud. **2** make mistakes or become confused when trying to do something.

flour *n.* fine meal or powder made from ground wheat or other grain. •*v.* cover or sprinkle with flour. □ **floury baker** a common cicada of coastal eastern Australia, so called because of its floury scales. □□ **floury** *adj.* **flouriness** *n.*

flourish *v.* **1** thrive in growth or development. **2** prosper, be successful. **3** (of famous people) be alive and working at a certain time (*Beethoven flourished in the early 19th century*). **4** wave (a thing) dramatically. •*n.* **1** a dramatic sweeping gesture. **2** a flowing ornamental curve in writing etc. **3** a fanfare.

flout *v.* disobey openly and scornfully.

■ **Usage** See the note under *flaunt*.

flow *v.* **1** glide along as a stream, move freely like a liquid or gas; circulate. **2** proceed steadily and continuously (*keep the traffic flowing*). **3** (of talk or literary style) proceed smoothly and evenly. **4** hang loosely; (of a line or curve) be smoothly continuous. **5** gush forth; (of the tide) come in, rise. **6** come (from a source), be the result (*his failure flows from his shyness*). •*n.* **1** a flowing movement or mass. **2** the amount that flows. **3** an outpouring, a copious supply. **4** the inward movement of the tide towards the land (*ebb and flow*). □ **flow chart** (or **diagram** or **sheet**) a diagram showing the movement of things through a series of processes, e.g. in manufacturing. **flow-on** *Aust.* a wage increase granted to other sections of the workforce because the increase had previously been granted to one section of the workforce.

flower *n.* **1** the part of a plant from which seed or fruit develops. **2** a blossom and its stem for use as a decoration etc., usu. in groups. **3** a plant that is cultivated or noted for its fine flowers. **4** the best part of something. •*v.* **1** (of a plant) produce flowers. **2** reach a peak. □ **flowering gum** *Aust.* any of several eucalypts noted for their beauty while flowering, esp. the red-flowering gum *Eucalyptus ficifolia*. **flower people** hippies with flowers as symbols of peace and love. **flower power** peace and love, esp. as a political idea. **in flower** with the flowers out. □□ **flowered** *adj.*

flowery *adj.* **1** (of language) full of ornamental phrases. **2** full of flowers.

flowing *adj.* **1** (of style etc.) fluent; easy. **2** (of a line, curve, etc.) smoothly continuous. **3** (of hair etc.) unconfined. □ **flowingly** *adv.*

flown *see* FLY².

flu *n.* influenza.

fluctuate *v.* (of levels, prices, etc.) vary irregularly, rise and fall. □ **fluctuation** *n.*

flue *n.* **1** a smoke duct in a chimney. **2** a channel for conveying heat.

fluent / floo-uhnt / *adj.* **1** (of a person) able to speak smoothly and readily, esp. in a foreign language (*fluent in German*). **2** (of speech) coming smoothly and readily. □ **fluently** *adv.* **fluency** *n.*

fluff *n.* **1** a light soft downy substance. **2** *colloq.* a bungled attempt; a mistake in speaking. • *v.* **1** shake into a soft mass. **2** *colloq.* bungle.

fluffy *adj.* (**fluffier, fluffiest**) having or covered with a soft mass of fur or fibres. □ **fluffiness** *n.*

fluid *n.* a substance that is able to flow freely as liquids and gases do. • *adj.* **1** able to flow freely, not solid or rigid. **2** (of a situation) not stable. □ **fluid ounce** *Brit.* one-twentieth of a pint or *US* one-sixteenth of a pint (approximately 0.028 litre). □ □ **fluidity** / floo-**id**-uh-tee / *n.*

fluke *n.* **1** an accidental stroke of good luck. **2** the broad triangular flat end of each arm of an anchor. **3** the barbed head of a harpoon etc. **4** one of the lobes of a whale's tail. **5** a flatfish, esp. the flounder. **6** a flatworm found as a parasite in sheep's liver. • *v.* achieve (something) by an accidental stroke of good luck.

flummery *n.* **1** a sweet made with milk, beaten eggs, etc. **2** flattery; nonsense, empty talk.

flummox *v. colloq.* baffle.

flung see FLING.

flunk *v. colloq.* fail, esp. in an examination. □ **flunk out** give up, get out of (*he flunked out of the swimming trials*).

flunkey *n.* (also **flunky**) (*pl.* **flunkeys** or **flunkies**) *colloq. derog.* **1** a liveried servant. **2** a servile toady, a crawler.

fluoresce / floor-**res**, fluh- / *v.* become fluorescent.

fluorescent / floor-**res**-uhnt / *adj.* (of substances) taking in radiations and sending them out in the form of light; (of lamps) containing such a substance; (of a screen) coated with this. □ **fluorescence** *n.*

fluoridate / **floor**-ruh-dayt, **floo**- / *v.* add traces of fluoride to (drinking water, toothpaste, etc.) to prevent tooth decay. □ **fluoridation** *n.*

fluoride *n.* a compound of fluorine and one other element. • *adj.* containing fluoride.

fluorine / **floor**-reen, **floo**- / *n.* a chemical element (symbol F), a pale yellow corrosive gas.

fluorocarbon *n.* a compound of a hydrocarbon with fluorine atoms. Fluorocarbons are known to cause environmental damage.

flurry *n.* **1** a short sudden rush of wind, rain, or snow. **2** a commotion. **3** a state of nervous agitation. • *v.* (**flurried, flurrying**) fluster, agitate.

flush *v.* **1** become red in the face because of a rush of blood to the skin. **2** cause (the face) to redden in this way. **3** fill with pride (*flushed with success*). **4** cleanse (a drain or toilet etc.) with a flow of water; dispose of in this way. **5** (of water) rush out in a flood. **6** cause (a bird) to fly up and away. • *n.* **1** flushing of the face, a blush. **2** excitement caused by emotion (*the first flush of victory*). **3** freshness, vigour (*in the first flush of manhood*). **4** (also **hot flush**) a sudden feeling of heat which may occur during menopause. **5** a feverish redness. **6** a rush of water. **7** fresh growth of vegetation. **8** (in poker) a hand of cards all of one suit. • *adj.* **1** level, in the same plane, without projections (*doors that are flush with the walls*). **2** *colloq.* well supplied with money. • *adv.* squarely, exactly (*I hit him flush on the nose*). □ **flush out** reveal, bring into the open. **2** drive out. **royal flush** (in poker) a straight flush headed by an ace. **straight flush** (in poker) a flush that is a straight sequence.

fluster *v.* make or become nervous and confused (*stop flustering me; he flusters easily*). • *n.* a flustered state.

flute *n.* **1** a wind instrument consisting of a long pipe held sideways with holes stopped by fingers or keys and a mouth-hole at the side. **2** an ornamental groove in a column. • *v.* **1** play, or play (a tune etc. on), the flute. **2** speak or utter in high flute-like tones. **3** make ornamental grooves in.

fluting *n.* ornamental grooves.

flutist = FLAUTIST.

flutter *v.* **1** move the wings hurriedly in flying or trying to fly. **2** fall quiveringly (*leaves fluttering to the ground*). **3** wave or flap quickly and irregularly; (of the heart) beat feebly and irregularly. • *n.* **1** a fluttering movement; a fluttering heartbeat. **2** a state of nervous excitement. **3** a stir, a sensation. **4** *colloq.* a small bet (*have a flutter*). **5** rapid variation in the pitch or loudness of reproduced sound.

fluty *adj.* flute-like in sound.

fluvial / **floo**-vee-uhl / *adj.* of or found in rivers.

flux *n.* **1** a continuous succession of changes (*in a state of flux*). **2** the process of flowing or flowing out. **3** an abnormal discharge of blood, excrement, etc. from the body.

fly[1] *n.* **1** a two-winged insect; the housefly. **2** some other winged insect, e.g. a firefly. **3** a natural or artificial fly used as bait in fishing. • *adj. colloq.* astute, knowing. □ **fly-blown** (*or* **flyblown** *or* **flystruck**) *adj.* (of meat etc.) tainted by flies' eggs. **fly-fishing** fishing with flies as bait. **fly in the ointment** one small thing that spoils enjoyment. **fly on the wall** an unnoticed observer. **like flies** in large numbers (*dying like flies*). **there are no flies on him** *colloq.* he is very astute.

fly[2] *v.* (**flew, flown, flying**) **1** move through the air by means of wings as a bird does. **2** travel through the air or through space. **3** travel in an aircraft. **4** direct or control the flight of (an aircraft etc.); transport in an aircraft. **5** raise (a flag) so that it waves; (of a flag) wave in the air. **6** make (a kite) rise and stay aloft. **7** go or move quickly, rush along; (of time) pass quickly. **8** be scattered violently (*sparks flew in all directions*). **9** become angry etc. quickly (*flew into a rage*). **10** flee from (*must fly the country*). **11** *colloq.* depart (*I really must fly*). • *n.* **1** flying. **2** (often as **flies**) a concealing flap, esp. over the opening in a pair of trousers; this opening (*your fly's undone*). **3** a flap at the entrance of a tent. **4** a speed-regulating device in clockwork or machinery. **5** (**flies**) the space above a stage where scenery and lighting are suspended. **6** an act of flying in a plane (*going for a fly this arvo*). ☐ **fly a kite** *colloq.* do something to test public opinion. **fly at** (*or* **into**) attack violently, either physically or with words. **fly-away** (of hair) fine and difficult to control. **fly-half** *n.* a stand-off half in Rugby football. **fly in the face of** disregard or disobey openly. **fly off the handle** *colloq.* lose one's temper. **fly-past** *n.* a ceremonial flight of aircraft.

flycatcher *n.* a type of bird that catches insects in the air, including several Australian species, e.g. the *restless flycatcher*.

flyer *n.* (also **flier**) **1** a bird etc. that flies. **2** an animal (esp. a kangaroo) or a vehicle that moves very fast. **3** an aviator. **4** an ambitious or outstanding person (*a high-flyer*). **5** a small promotional handbill.

flying *adj.* able to fly. ☐ **flying boat** a boatlike seaplane. **flying buttress** a buttress that springs from a separate structure, usu. forming an arch with the wall it supports. **flying colours** great credit gained in a test etc. **flying doctor** *Aust.* a doctor who visits patients (e.g. in the Australian outback) by air. **flying duck orchid** an Australian terrestrial orchid having reddish brown flowers remarkably like a duck in flight, the glossy 'beak' being a sensitive pollinating mechanism that snaps downwards when touched. **flying fish** a tropical fish with wing-like fins, able to rise into the air. **flying fox 1** any of various fruit-eating bats of Australia and elsewhere with a foxlike head. **2** *Aust.* an overhead cable and apparatus for the transport of materials etc. over difficult terrain. **flying mouse** Australia's smallest gliding marsupial. Also called *feathertail glider, pygmy glider.* **flying officer** RAAF rank next below flight lieutenant. **flying possum** (also **flying phalanger**) any of various tree-climbing Australian marsupials, esp. one that glides through the air using flaps of skin between the fore and hind limbs as parachutes. **flying saucer** an unidentified saucer-shaped object reported as seen in the sky and imagined to come from outer space. **flying squad** a detachment of police etc. organised for rapid movement. **flying start 1** a start (of a race) in which the competitors cross the starting line at full speed but are disqualified if they cross that line before the starting signal sounds. **2** a distinct initial advantage (*his knowledge of Bahasa Indonesia gave him a flying start over the other candidates*). **flying visit** a brief or hasty visit.

flyleaf *n.* a blank leaf at the beginning or end of a book.

Flynn[1], Errol (1909–59), Australian-born American film actor whose usual role was the swashbuckling hero of romantic costume dramas. ☐ **in like Flynn** *Aust. colloq.* **1** (of a male) achieving the object of one's sexual desire. **2** achieving success in any activity.

Flynn[2], John (1880–1951), Australian clergyman who founded the Royal Flying Doctor Service.

flyover *n.* a bridge that carries one road or railway over another.

flypaper *n.* sticky paper for trapping or poisoning flies.

flyscreen *n.* a fine mesh-frame over a window or door to permit ventilation but exclude flies and other insects.

flystrike *n.* an infestation of the skin and flesh of sheep with the maggots of blowflies.

flytrap *n.* a plant that catches and digests flies etc. (*Venus flytrap*).

flyweight *n.* a boxing weight (48–51 kg) below bantamweight.

flywheel *n.* a heavy wheel revolving on a shaft to regulate machinery.

flywire *n.* screening of very fine wire mesh designed to keep out insects, esp. flies.

FM *abbr.* frequency modulation.

Fm *symbol* fermium.

FNQ *abbr.* Far North Queensland.

f-number *n.* a ratio used in photography to calculate the amount of light passing through the lens.

foal *n.* the young of a horse or of a related animal. • *v.* give birth to a foal. ☐ **in foal** (of a mare) pregnant.

foam *n.* **1** a collection of small bubbles formed in or on a liquid. **2** the froth of saliva or perspiration. **3** rubber or plastic in a light spongy form. • *v.* form or send out foam. ☐ **foam bark** a rainforest tree of Qld and NSW, the bark of which contains a substance that foams in the water and was used by the Aborigines to stun fish. ☐☐ **foamy** *adj.*

fob *n.* **1** an ornament worn hanging from a watch chain etc. **2** a tab on a key ring. ☐ **fob off** (**fobbed, fobbing**) **1** (often foll. by *with*) put off or deter (a person) (*don't fob me off with fast-talk*). **2** (often foll. by *with* a thing) deceive (a person) into accepting something inferior (*fobbed me off with a wonder-camera that doesn't work*). **3** (often foll. by *on* or *on to* a person) offload (an unwanted thing).

focaccia / fuh-**kah**-chuh / *n.* a type of flat savoury Italian bread made with yeast and oil and usu. seasoned with herbs etc.

focal *adj.* of or at a focus. ☐ **focal distance** (*or* **length**) the distance between the centre of a mirror or lens and its focus. **focal point 1** = FOCUS *n.* (sense 1). **2** the centre of interest or activity.

fo'c's'le alternative spelling of FORECASTLE.

focus / foh-kuhs / *n.* (*pl.* **focuses** *or* **foci** / foh-suy /) **1** the point at which rays meet or from which they appear to proceed. **2** the point or distance at which an object is most clearly seen by the eye or through a lens (*bring into focus*). **3** an adjustment on a lens to produce a clear image at varying distances. **4** the principal site of an infection or disease. **5** the centre of interest of activity, focal point. **6** the place of origin of an earthquake. • *v.* (**focused, focusing** or **focussed, focussing**) **1** adjust the focus of (a lens or the eye). **2** bring into focus. **3** concentrate or be concentrated or directed (on a centre etc.).

fodder *n.* dried food, hay, etc. for horses and farm animals.

foe *n.* an enemy.

foetid alternative spelling of FETID.

foetus / **fee**-tuhs / *n.* (also **fetus**) (*pl.* **foetuses**) a developed embryo in the womb or egg; a human embryo more than 8 weeks after conception. ☐ **foetal** *adj.*

fog *n.* **1** thick mist that is difficult to see through. **2** cloudiness on a photographic negative etc., obscuring the image. **3** an uncertain or confused position or state. • *v.* (**fogged, fogging**) **1** cover or become covered with fog or condensed vapour. **2** cause cloudiness on (a negative etc.). **3** bewilder or confuse (as if with a fog). ☐ **fogged up** (of a windscreen, mirror, etc.) clouded with condensed vapour.

fogbound *adj.* unable to travel because of fog.

fogey alternative spelling of FOGY.

foggy *adj.* (**foggier, foggiest**) **1** full of fog. **2** made opaque by condensed vapour etc.; clouded. **3** obscure, vague (*only a foggy idea*). ☐ **not have the foggiest** *colloq.* have no idea at all. ☐☐ **fogginess** *n.*

foghorn *n.* a sounding instrument for warning ships in fog.

fogy *n.* (also **fogey**) (*pl.* **fogies**) a person with old-fashioned ideas (esp. *old fogy*).

FOI *abbr.* = FREEDOM OF INFORMATION.

foible / **foi**-buhl / *n.* a harmless peculiarity or minor weakness in a person's character.

foil *n.* **1** metal hammered or rolled into a thin sheet (*tin foil*). **2** (in full **aluminium foil**) a very thin sheet of aluminium which comes in a roll and is used esp. in the kitchen for wrapping food etc. and for baking in etc. **3** a person or thing that contrasts strongly with another and therefore makes the other's qualities more obvious. **4** a long thin sword with a button on the point, used in fencing. • *v.* thwart, frustrate (*foiled their plans*).

foist *v.* force (a thing or oneself on to an unwilling person) (*the job was foisted on me*; *foisted himself on us for a week*).

fold *v.* **1** bend or turn (a flexible thing) so that one part lies on another; close or flatten by pressing parts together. **2** become folded; be able to be folded. **3** clasp (the arms etc.) about; hold close to one's chest. **4** envelop. **5** blend (an ingredient) in cooking by turning it over carefully with a spoon. **6** collapse, cease to function (*the business had folded*). • *n.* **1** a folded part. **2** a line made by folding. **3** a hollow among hills. **4** an enclosure for sheep. **5** an established body of believers or members of a Church.

-fold *comb. form* forming adjectives and adverbs from numbers: **1** in an amount multiplied by (*repaid tenfold*). **2** with so many parts (*threefold blessing*).

folder *n.* **1** a folding cover for loose papers. **2** a folded leaflet.

Foley, Gary (Edward) (1950–), Australian Aboriginal activist and actor.

foliaceous / foh-lee-**ay**-shuhs / *adj.* of or like leaves.

foliage / **foh**-lee-ij / *n.* the leaves of a tree or plant.

foliar / **foh**-lee-uh / *adj.* of leaves.

foliate *adj.* / **foh**-lee-uht / leaflike, having leaves. • *v.* / **foh**-lee-ayt / split or beat into thin layers. ☐ **foliation** *n.*

folic acid / **foh**-lik / *n.* a vitamin of the B-group, deficiency of which causes anaemia.

folio / **foh**-lee-oh / *n.* (*pl.* **folios**) **1** a large sheet of paper folded once, making two leaves of a book. **2** a book made of such sheets, the largest-sized volume. **3** the page number of a printed book.

folk / fohk / *n.* **1** people in general. **2** the people of a certain group or nation etc. (*country folk*). **3** (**folk** or **folks**) one's relatives. **4** folk music (*he sings folk*). ☐ **folk dance** a dance of popular origin or in the traditional style of a country. **folk etymology 1** a popular modifying of the form of a word or phrase to make it seem to be derived from a more familiar word, e.g. FORLORN HOPE. **2** a spurious explanation of the origin of a word. **folk music** music of traditional origin, transmitted orally from generation to generation. **folk singer** a singer of folk songs. **folk song** a song of popular or traditional origin or style. **folk tale** a traditional story.

folkie *n. colloq.* a player or follower of folk music.

folklore *n.* the traditional beliefs and tales of a people; the study of these. ☐ **folklorist** *n.*

folksy *adj.* **1** of or like folk art or culture. **2** friendly, unpretentious.

folkweave *n.* loosely woven fabric used chiefly for furnishings.

follicle / **fol**-i-kuhl / *n.* a very small sac or cavity in the body, esp. one containing a hair root. ☐ **follicular** / fo-**lik**-yuh-luh / *adj.*

follow *v.* **1** go or come after. **2** go along (a path or road etc.). **3** come after in order or time (*dessert followed; proceed as follows*). **4** provide with a sequel or successor. **5** take as a guide or leader or example; conform to (*follow the fashion*). **6** grasp the meaning of, understand. **7** take an interest in the progress of (events, a team, etc.). **8** happen as a result, result from. **9** be necessarily true in consequence of something else. ☐ **follow on** (of a side in cricket) have to bat again immediately after the first innings. **follow-on** *n.* an example of this. **follow out** carry out (instructions etc.). **follow suit 1** play a card of the suit led. **2** follow a person's example. **follow through 1** continue to a

follower

conclusion. **2** continue the movement of a stroke after hitting the ball. **follow-through** *n.* the continuing movement of a stroke after hitting the ball. **follow up 1** add a further action etc. to a previous one. **2** perform further work or investigation upon. **follow-up** *n.* subsequent or continued action.

follower *n.* **1** one who follows. **2** a person who believes in or supports a religion, teacher, team, or cause. **3** *Aust. Rules* either of the two players who, with the rover, does not have a fixed position and so follows the play.

following *n.* a body of believers or supporters. • *adj.* now to be mentioned (*answer the following questions*). • *prep.* as a sequel to, after (*following the fall of the dollar, prices rose sharply*).

folly *n.* **1** foolishness; a foolish act. **2** an ornamental building serving no practical purpose.

foment / fuh-**ment** / *v.* **1** stir up or stimulate (trouble, discontent, etc.). **2** bathe (a limb etc.) with warm or medicated liquid to relieve pain or inflammation; supply warmth (to a limb etc.) for the same reason. ☐ **fomentation** *n.*

fond *adj.* **1** affectionate, loving, doting. **2** (of hopes) cherished but unlikely to be fulfilled; naive. ☐ **fondly** *adv.* **fondness** *n.*

fondant *n.* a soft sweet made of flavoured sugar.

fondle *v.* touch or stroke lovingly.

fondue / **fon**-doo / *n.* **1** a dish of flavoured melted cheese into which pieces of bread are dipped. **2** any other dish in which small pieces of food are dipped in hot oil or sauce.

font *n.* **1** a basin or vessel in a church, to hold water for baptism. **2** a set of printing type of the same face and size.

fontanelle / fon-tuh-**nel** / *n.* a space under the skin on the top of an infant's head where the bones of the skull have not yet grown together.

fontware *see* WARE.

food *n.* any substance that can be taken into an animal or plant to maintain its life and growth. **2** a solid substance of this kind (*food and drink*). ☐ **food additive** a substance, esp. a chemical, added to food by manufacturers to colour or flavour or preserve it etc. **food chain** a series of organisms each dependent on the next for food. **food poisoning** illness caused by bacteria or toxins in food. **food processor** an electric machine with blades for mixing and chopping food.

foodie *n. colloq.* a gourmet; one who is specially interested in food.

foodstuff *n.* a substance used as food.

fool *n.* **1** a person who acts unwisely; one who lacks good sense or judgment. **2** a jester or clown in a household during the Middle Ages. • *v.* **1** behave in a joking or teasing way. **2** (foll. by *about*, *around*) play about idly. **3** trick or deceive (a person). **4** (foll. by *around with*) dally sexually

311

foothold

with. ☐ **fool's paradise** happiness that is based on an illusion.

foolery *n.* foolish behaviour.

foolhardy *adj.* bold but rash, delighting in taking unnecessary risks. ☐ **foolhardiness** *n.*

foolish *adj.* **1** lacking good sense or judgment. **2** (of actions) unwise. **3** ridiculous (*felt foolish*). ☐ **foolishly** *adv.* **foolishness** *n.*

foolproof *adj.* **1** (of rules or instructions) plain and simple and unable to be misinterpreted. **2** (of machinery) very simple to operate.

foolscap *n.* a large size of paper. (¶ So called from the use of a *fool's cap* (a jester's cap with bells) as a watermark.)

foot *n.* (*pl.* **feet**) **1** the end part of the leg below the ankle. **2** a similar part in animals, used in moving or to attach itself to things. **3** the lower end of a table or bed etc., the end opposite the head. **4** the part of a sock etc. covering the foot. **5** a person's step or tread or pace of movement (*fleet of foot*). **6** a lower usu. projecting part of something (e.g. of a table leg); the part of a sewing machine that is lowered on to the material to hold it steady. **7** the lowest part of something that has height or length; the bottom of a hill, ladder, page, list, etc. **8** a measure of length in the imperial system, = 12 inches (30.48 cm). **9** a unit of rhythm in a line of poetry, usu. containing a stressed syllable, e.g. each of the four divisions in *Jack/and Jill/went up/the hill*. • *v.* go on foot; walk (*shall have to foot it*). ☐ **feet of clay** a great weakness in a person or thing that is honoured. **foot-and-mouth disease 1** a contagious disease of cattle etc. **2** (also **foot-in-mouth disease**) *Aust. colloq.* a proneness to put one's foot in one's mouth. **foot fault** *n. Tennis* putting the foot illegally over the baseline while serving. **foot-fault** *v.* make a foot fault. **foot the bill** pay the bill. **have both feet on the ground** be practical. **put one's foot down** *colloq.* **1** insist. **2** accelerate a vehicle. **put one's foot in one's mouth** (*or* **in it**) *colloq.* make a tactless blunder.

footage *n.* a length measured in feet, esp. of cinema or television film.

football *n.* **1** a large inflated leather or plastic ball. **2** a game played with this on a field, between two teams of players. ☐ **footballer** *n.*

footbrake *n.* a brake operated by the foot in a motor vehicle.

footbridge *n.* a bridge for pedestrians.

footer *n.* **1** (in *combinations*) a person or thing of so many feet in length or height (*six-footer*). **2** (in word processing) words etc. programmed to appear at the foot of every page (as opposed to HEADER).

footfall *n.* the sound of a footstep.

foothill *n.* one of the low hills near the bottom of a mountain or range.

foothold *n.* **1** a place wide enough for a foot to be placed on when climbing etc. **2** a secure position gained in a business etc.

footie alternative spelling of FOOTY.

footing n. **1** a placing of the feet, a foothold (*lost his footing*). **2** status; conditions (*they were on a friendly footing; put the army on a war footing*).

footlights n.pl. a row of lights along the front of a stage floor.

footling / foot-ling / adj. colloq. trivial, petty.

footloose adj. independent, without responsibilities.

footman n. a manservant (usu. in livery) who admits visitors, waits at table, etc.

footmark n. a footprint.

footnote n. a note printed at the bottom of a page.

footpath n. a path for pedestrians, a pavement.

footplate n. a platform for the driver etc. operating a locomotive.

footprint n. an impression left by a foot or shoe.

footrace n. a running or walking race.

footsie n. colloq. a foot. ☐ **play footsie(s) with 1** touch someone secretly with one's feet as part of amorous play. **2** flirt, have an affair.

footsore adj. having feet that are sore from walking.

footstep n. a step taken in walking; the sound of this.

footstool n. a stool for resting the feet on when sitting.

footwalk v. Aust. (in Aboriginal English) travel on foot.

footwear n. shoes, socks, stockings, etc.

footwork n. the manner of moving the feet in dancing, boxing, football, etc.

footy (also **footie**) n. Aust. colloq. **1** the game of football, esp. Australian Rules. **2** a football, esp. the oval ball used in Australian Rules.

foo yong n. a Chinese dish or sauce made with eggs and other ingredients.

fop n. a man obsessed with fashion, clothes, appearance, etc., a dandy. ☐ **foppery** n. **foppish** adj.

for prep. **1** representing or in place of (*the MP for Corio; I'm here for my uncle*). **2** as a consequence of (*was fined for speeding; decorated for bravery; here's $5 for your trouble*). **3** in defence, support, or favour of (*fight for one's rights*). **4** with a view to, in order to obtain (*went for a walk; looking for a job*). **5** with regard to, in respect of (*ready for dinner*). **6** in the direction of (*set out for home*). **7** intended to be received by or belong to (*bought shoes for the children*). **8** so as to happen at (*an appointment for two o'clock*). **9** on account of (*famous for its Aboriginal rock paintings; could not speak for laughing*). **10** to the extent or duration of (*walked for two kilometres; it will last for years*). **11** suitable or appropriate to (*a dance for beginners; it's not for me to say*). **12** in exchange with, at the price of, corresponding to (*swapped it for a didgeridoo; give me $50 for it; word for word*). **13** as being (*for the last time; I for one refuse*). **14** in spite of; notwithstanding (*for all your fine words*). **15** considering or making due allowances in respect of (*excellent work for a beginner*). •conj. because (*they hesitated, for they were afraid*). ☐ **be for it** colloq. be about to meet with punishment or trouble. **for ever** for all time; continually, repeatedly.

forage / fo-rij / n. **1** food for horses and cattle. **2** a search for food. •v. go searching, rummage (esp. for food); get by foraging. ☐ **forager** n.

foray / fo-ray / n. a sudden attack or raid. •v. make a foray.

forbade see FORBID.

forbear v. (**forbore, forborne, forbearing**) archaic refrain (*could not forbear (from) criticising; forbore to mention it*).

forbearance n. patience, tolerance.

forbearing adj. patient or tolerant.

forbid v. (**forbade** / faw-**bad** /, **forbidden, forbidding**) **1** order (a person) not to do something or not to enter (*forbid him to go; forbid him this house*). **2** refuse to allow (*forbid the marriage; he is forbidden wine*). ☐ **forbidden fruit** something highly desired, esp. because not allowed.

forbidding adj. uninviting, stern.

forbore, forborne see FORBEAR.

force n. **1** strength, power, intense effort. **2** in scientific use) a measurable influence tending to cause movement of a body; its intensity. **3** a body of troops or police. **4** a body of people organised or available for a purpose (*a labour force*). **5** compulsion. **6** effectiveness, legal validity (*the new rules come into force next week*). •v. **1** use force in order to get or do something, compel, oblige. **2** exert force on, break open by force (*forced the lock*). **3** strain to the utmost, overstrain. **4** impose, inflict. **5** cause or produce by effort (*forced a smile*). **6** cause (plants etc.) to reach maturity earlier than is normal. ☐ **forced landing** an emergency landing of an aircraft. **force-feed** (**force-fed, force-feeding**) feed (a prisoner etc.) against his or her will. **force the issue** make an immediate decision necessary. **in force 1** valid, current (*the laws now in force*). **2** in great strength or numbers (*attacked in force*).

forceful adj. powerful and vigorous, effective. ☐ **forcefully** adv. **forcefulness** n.

force majeure / mah-**zher** / n. **1** irresistible compulsion or coercion. **2** an unforeseeable course of events that excuses a person from the fulfilment of a contract. (¶ French, = superior strength.)

forcemeat n. finely chopped meat seasoned and used as stuffing.

forceps / **faw**-seps / n. (pl. **forceps**) surgical pincers or tongs used for gripping things.

forcible adj. done by force, forceful. ☐ **forcibly** adv.

Ford, Henry (1863–1947), American pioneer of mass production for motor vehicles.

ford *n.* a shallow place where a river may be crossed by wading or riding or driving through. • *v.* cross in this way. □ **fordable** *adj.*

Forde, Francis Michael (1890–1983), Australian Labor statesman, prime minister from 6–12 July 1945, Australia's shortest-serving prime minister.

fore *adj.* situated in front. • *adv.* in, at, or towards the front. • *n.* the fore part. • *interj.* a cry to warn a person who may be hit by a golf ball that is about to be played. □ **fore-and-aft** *adj.* (of sails) set lengthwise on a ship or boat (as opposed to *square-rigged*). **to the fore** in front; conspicuous.

forearm *n.* / **faw**-rahm / the arm from elbow to wrist or fingertips. • *v.* / fawr-**ahm** / arm or prepare in advance against possible danger etc.

forebears *n.pl.* ancestors.

forebode *v.* be an advance sign or token of (trouble).

foreboding *n.* a feeling that trouble is coming.

forecast *v.* (**forecast**, **forecasting**) tell in advance (what is likely to happen). • *n.* a statement that forecasts something, esp. the weather.

forecastle / **fohk**-suhl / *n.* (also **fo'c's'le**) the forward part of certain ships, where formerly the crew had their accommodation.

foreclose *v.* **1** (of a firm etc. that has lent money on mortgage) take possession of property when the loan is not duly repaid (*the Bank decided to foreclose the mortgage*). **2** bar from a privilege. □ **foreclosure** *n.*

forecourt *n.* an enclosed space in front of a large building; an outer court.

forefathers *n.pl.* ancestors.

forefinger *n.* the finger next to the thumb.

forefoot *n.* (*pl.* **forefeet**) an animal's front foot.

forefront *n.* the very front.

forego alternative spelling of FORGO.

foregoing *adj.* preceding, previously mentioned.

foregone conclusion *n.* a result that can be foreseen easily and with certainty.

foreground *n.* **1** the part of a scene or picture that is nearest to an observer. **2** the most conspicuous position. • *v.* place in the foreground; make prominent.

forehand *adj.* **1** (of a stroke in tennis etc.) played with the palm of the hand facing the opponent. **2** on the side on which this is made. • *n.* a forehand stroke. □ **forehanded** *adj.*

forehead / **fo**-ruhd, **faw**-hed / *n.* the part of the face above the eyebrows.

foreign *adj.* **1** of, in, or from another country; not of one's own country. **2** dealing with or involving other countries (*foreign affairs*). **3** not belonging naturally (*jealousy is foreign to her nature*). **4** coming from outside (*a foreign body in the eye*). □ **foreign exchange** the currencies of other countries; dealings in these. □□ **foreignness** *n.*

foreigner *n.* a person who was born in or comes from another country.

foreknowledge *n.* knowledge of something before it occurs.

foreland *n.* a cape or promontory.

foreleg *n.* an animal's front leg.

forelock *n.* a lock of hair just above the forehead.

foreman *n.* **1** a worker who supervises other workers. **2** the member of a jury who presides over its deliberations and speaks on its behalf.

foremast *n.* the mast nearest to the bow in a sailing-ship.

foremost *adj.* **1** most advanced in position or rank. **2** most important. • *adv.* in the foremost position etc.

forename *n.* a person's personal name as distinct from the surname or family name; (among Christians) a Christian name.

forenoon *n. literary* the morning.

forensic / fuh-**ren**-sik, -zik / *adj.* **1** of or used in lawcourts. **2** of or involving **forensic medicine**, the medical knowledge needed in legal matters or police investigations (e.g. in a poisoning case). □ **forensically** *adv.*

foreordain *v.* destine beforehand (*it was foreordained by God*).

forepaw *n.* an animal's front paw.

foreplay *n.* sexual stimulation before intercourse.

forerunner *n.* a person or thing that comes in advance of another; a predecessor.

foresail *n.* the principal sail on a foremast.

foresee *v.* (**foresaw**, **foreseen**, **foreseeing**) be aware of or realise beforehand. □ **foreseeable** *adj.*

foreshadow *v.* be a sign of (something that is to come).

foreshore *n.* the shore between high-water mark and low-water mark.

foreshorten *v.* represent (an object, when drawing it) by shortening of certain lines to give an effect of distance.

foresight *n.* **1** the ability to foresee and prepare for future needs. **2** the front sight of a gun.

foreskin *n.* the loose retractable fold of skin covering the end of the penis; prepuce.

forest *n.* **1** a large area of trees and undergrowth; the trees in this. **2** a tract of open well-grassed land with occasional stands of trees. **3** a large number or dense mass. • *v.* plant with trees; convert into a forest. □ **forest oak** a casuarina of eastern Australia having drooping reddening branchlets and red timber.

forestall *v.* prevent or foil (a person or his or her plans) by taking action first.

forestay *n.* a stay from the head of the mast or foremast to a ship's deck.

forested *adj.* covered in forest.

forester *n.* **1** a person managing a forest or skilled in forestry. **2** *Aust.* the eastern grey kangaroo.

forestry *n.* the science or practice of planting and caring for forests.

foretaste *n.* a small preliminary experience of what is to come (*a foretaste of the pleasure ahead; a foretaste of hell*).

foretell *v.* (**foretold, foretelling**) predict, forecast; prophesy.

forethought *n.* careful thought and planning for the future.

forever *adv.* continually; without end.

forewarn *v.* warn beforehand.

forewoman *n.* **1** a woman who supervises other workers. **2** a woman acting as president and spokeswoman of a jury.

foreword *n.* introductory remarks at the beginning of a book, usu. written by someone other than the author.

forfeit / faw-fuht / *n.* something that has to be paid or given up as a penalty. •*adj.* paid or given up in this way. •*v.* pay or give up as a forfeit. ☐ **forfeiture** *n.*

forgather *v.* assemble.

forgave *see* FORGIVE.

forge *n.* **1** a workshop with a fire and an anvil where metals are heated and shaped, esp. one used by a smith for shoeing horses and working iron. **2** a furnace or hearth for melting or refining metal; the workshop containing it. •*v.* **1** shape by heating in fire and hammering. **2** make an imitation or copy of (a thing) in order to pass it off fraudulently as real. **3** make one's way forward gradually or steadily (*forged ahead*). ☐ **forger** *n.*

forgery *n.* **1** forging, imitating fraudulently. **2** a fraudulent copy.

forget *v.* (**forgot, forgotten, forgetting**) **1** lose remembrance of (a thing or duty etc.). **2** put out of one's mind, stop thinking about (*decided to forget our quarrels*).

forgetful *adj.* **1** apt to forget, absent-minded. **2** (often foll. by *of*) neglectful (*forgetful of his duties*). ☐ **forgetfully** *adv.* **forgetfulness** *n.*

forget-me-not *n.* a plant with small blue flowers, so called because those wearing the flower were supposed never to be forgotten by their lovers.

forgive *v.* (**forgave, forgiven, forgiving**) cease to feel angry or bitter towards (a person) or about (an offence); pardon. ☐ **forgiveness** *n.*

forgiving *adj.* willing to forgive.

forgo *v.* (also **forego**) (**forwent, forgone, forgoing**) give up; go without.

forgot, forgotten *see* FORGET.

fork *n.* **1** a pronged instrument used in eating or cooking. **2** a pronged agricultural implement used for digging or lifting things. **3** a thing shaped like this (*tuning fork*). **4** a place where something (a tree branch, a road, etc.) separates into two parts; either of these parts (*take the left fork*). •*v.* **1** lift or dig with a fork. **2** (of an object or road etc.) form a fork by separating into two parts. **3** follow one of these branches (*fork left*). ☐ **fork out** (*or* **over** *or* **up**) *colloq.* hand over; pay out money reluctantly.

forked lightning *n.* a lightning flash in the form of a zigzag or branching line.

forklift *n.* (in full **forklift truck**) a truck with a fork-like mechanical device for lifting and moving heavy objects.

forlorn *adj.* **1** sad and abandoned. **2** in a pitiful state. **3** desperate, hopeless (*a forlorn attempt*). ☐ **forlornly** *adv.* (¶ From *lorn* the past participle of the obsolete *leese* 'lose'.)

forlorn hope *n.* a faint remaining hope or chance. (¶ Not from *forlorn* but from the Dutch *verloren hoop* 'lost troop'.)

form *n.* **1** the shape of something; its outward or visible appearance. **2** its structure, arrangement, or style. **3** a person or animal as it can be seen or touched. **4** the way in which a thing exists (*ice is a form of water*). **5** a class in a school. **6** a fixed or usual method of doing something, a formality; a set order of words in a ritual etc. **7** a document with blank spaces that are to be filled in with information. **8** (of a horse or athlete) condition of health and training (*is in good form*). **9** details of previous performances (*study form before betting*). **10** general state or disposition (*he was in great form at the party*). **11** a person's reputation or record (including criminal). **12** a long low bench. **13** a hare's lair. •*v.* **1** shape, mould; produce, construct. **2** bring into existence, constitute (*form a committee*). **3** be the material of. **4** come into existence; take shape, become solid (*icicles formed*). **5** develop in the mind (*formed a plan*). **6** arrange in a certain formation.

formal *adj.* **1** conforming to accepted rules or customs; showing or requiring formality (*a formal greeting; a formal occasion*). **2** prim or stiff in manner. **3** outward (*only a formal resemblance*). **4** regular or geometrical in design (*formal gardens*). **5** valid (*a formal vote*). **6** explicit and definite (*a formal agreement*). **7** (of education) obtained in a recognised establishment. •*n.* (esp. at secondary schools etc.) an official dance or social get-together at which usu. formal dress is to be worn. ☐ **formally** *adv.*

formaldehyde / faw-**mal**-duh-huyd / *n.* a colourless gas used in solution as a preservative and disinfectant.

formalin *n.* a solution of formaldehyde in water.

formalise *v.* (also -**ize**) make formal or official. ☐ **formalisation** *n.*

formalism *n.* strict or excessive adherence to the outward form (as opposed to the content) of something (esp. in art). ☐ **formalist** *n.*

formality / faw-**mal**-uh-tee / *n.* **1** strict observance of rules and conventions. **2** a formal act, something required by law or custom (often with an implied lack of real significance) (*legal formalities; it's just a formality*). **3** ceremony; elaborate procedure.

format / **faw**-mat / *n.* **1** the shape and size of a book etc. **2** a style of arrangement or procedure. **3** an arrangement of data etc. for processing or

formation / 315 / **forty**

storage by computer. • *v.* (**formatted, formatting**) **1** arrange or put into a format. **2** *Computing* prepare (a storage medium) to receive data.

formation *n.* **1** forming; being formed. **2** a thing formed. **3** a particular arrangement or order (e.g. of troops). **4** rocks or strata with a common characteristic.

formative / faw-muh-tiv / *adj.* serving to form or fashion; of formation (*a child's formative years*).

former *adj.* **1** of an earlier period (*in former times*). **2** having been previously (*her former husband*). ☐ **the former** the first or first mentioned of two.

formerly *adv.* in former times.

formica / faw-**muy**-kuh / *n.* trademark a hard heat-resistant plastic used on surfaces.

formic acid *n.* a colourless irritant acid contained in fluid emitted by ants.

formidable / faw-muh-duh-buhl, faw-**mid**-uh-buhl / *adj.* **1** inspiring fear or awe. **2** difficult to do or overcome (*a formidable task*). ☐ **formidably** *adv.*

■ **Usage** The second pronunciation given is considered incorrect by some people.

formless *adj.* without distinct or regular form.

formula *n.* (*pl.* **formulas** *or* in scientific usage **formulae** / **for**-myoo-lee /) **1** a set of chemical symbols showing the constituents of a substance. **2** a mathematical rule or statement expressed in algebraic symbols. **3** a fixed series of words, esp. one used on social or ceremonial occasions. **4** a form or set of words that embody an agreement or enable it to be made. **5** an established and successful mode (*the film followed the usual formula: sex and violence*). **6** a list of ingredients. **7** the classification of a racing car, esp. by its engine capacity. **8** an infant's food made according to a prescribed recipe. ☐ **formulaic** / faw-myuh-**lay**-ik / *adj.*

formulary / **faw**-myuh-luh-ree / *n.* **1** a collection of esp. religious formulas or set forms. **2** *Pharmacology* a compendium of drug formulae.

formulate *v.* express in a formula; express clearly and exactly. ☐ **formulation** *n.*

fornicate / **faw**-nuh-kayt / *v. archaic* (of people not married to each other) have sexual intercourse. ☐ **fornication** *n.* **fornicator** *n.*

forsake *v.* (**forsook, forsaken, forsaking**) **1** give up, renounce (*forsaking their former way of life*). **2** withdraw one's help, friendship, or companionship from (*he forsook his wife and children*).

forsooth / faw-**sooth** / *adv. archaic* indeed, no doubt.

Forster, E(dward) M(organ) (1879–1970), English novelist.

forswear *v.* (**forswore, forsworn, forswearing**) **1** abjure; renounce an oath. **2** (as **forsworn** *adj.*) perjured. ☐ **forswear oneself** perjure oneself.

fort *n.* a fortified building or position. ☐ **hold the fort** keep things going as normal (esp. in the absence of a person in charge).

Fort Denison a small island in Sydney Harbour, used from 1788 as a prison for troublesome convicts who, while there, were kept on short rations, hence its early name, 'Pinchgut'.

forte / **faw**-tay / *n.* a person's strong point. • *adv.* (in music) loudly.

fortescue / **faw**-tuh-skyoo / *n.* a fish of eastern Australian coastal waters, having venomous spines.

forth *adv.* **1** forward; into view (*bring forth; come forth*). **2** onwards in time (*from this day forth*). **3** out from a starting point (*set forth*). ☐ **and so forth** and so on.

forthcoming *adj.* **1** about to come or appear (*forthcoming events*). **2** made available when needed (*money was not forthcoming*). **3** *colloq.* willing to give information; responsive (*the girl was not very forthcoming*).

forthright *adj.* **1** outspoken; straightforward. **2** decisive, unhesitating.

forthwith *adv.* immediately.

fortieth *see* FORTY.

fortification *n.* **1** fortifying. **2** a wall or building constructed to defend a place.

fortify *v.* (**fortified, fortifying**) **1** strengthen (a place) against attack, esp. by constructing fortifications. **2** strengthen (a person) mentally or morally; increase the vigour of. **3** increase the food value of (bread etc.) by adding vitamins; strengthen (wine) with alcohol.

fortissimo *adv.* (in music) very loudly.

fortitude *n.* courage in bearing pain or trouble.

fortnight *n.* a period of two weeks.

fortnightly *adv.* & *adj.* happening or appearing once a fortnight.

Fortran *n.* a high-level computer language used esp. in scientific work. (¶ From the first letters of *Formula Translation*.)

fortress *n.* a fortified building or town.

fortuitous / faw-**tyoo**-uh-tuhs / *adj.* happening by chance. ☐ **fortuitously** *adv.* **fortuitousness** *n.* **fortuity** *n.*

fortunate *adj.* having, bringing, or brought by good fortune.

fortunately *adv.* **1** luckily; successfully. **2** (qualifying a whole sentence) it is fortunate that (*fortunately, he didn't realise that I was there*).

fortune *n.* **1** the events that chance brings to a person or undertaking. **2** chance as a power in the affairs of mankind. **3** a person's destiny. **4** prosperity, success (*seek one's fortune*). **5** a great amount of wealth (*left him a fortune*). ☐ **a small fortune** *colloq.* a vast amount of wealth. **fortune-teller** a person who claims to foretell future events in people's lives.

forty *adj.* & *n.* **1** four times ten (40, XL). **2** (**forties**) the numbers from 40 to 49, esp. the years of a century or of a person's life. ☐☐ **forty winks** a short sleep or nap. ☐ **fortieth** *adj.* & *n.*

forum *n.* **1** the public square or marketplace in an ancient Roman city. **2** a place or meeting where a public discussion is held.

forward *adj.* **1** continuing in one's line of motion; directed or moving towards the front; situated in the front. **2** of or relating to the future (*forward buying*). **3** having made more than the normal progress. **4** too bold in one's manner, presumptuous. • *n.* **1** an attacking player near the front in football or hockey (= striker); this position. **2** *Aust. Rules* any of the six players (e.g. full forward) in a position to attack the goal. **3** any of the players who make up the scrum in rugby. • *adv.* forwards; in advance, ahead; towards the future (*move forward; sent them forward; from this time forward*). • *v.* **1** send on (a letter etc.) to a new address. **2** send or dispatch (goods) to a customer. **3** help to advance (a person's interests). ☐ **forwardness** *n.*

forwards *adv.* **1** towards the front, onward so as to make progress. **2** with the front foremost.

forwent *see* FORGO.

fosse / fos / *n.* a long ditch or trench, esp. in fortification.

fossick *v. Aust.* **1** search for gold etc., esp. in claims abandoned by others. **2** (often foll. by *about*) search likewise for anything (*fossicking in the box for a needle; fossicking about for his specs*). ☐ **fossicker** *n.* **fossicking** *n.*

fossil *n.* **1** the remains or impression of a prehistoric animal or plant once buried in earth and now hardened in rock. **2** *colloq.* a person who is out of date and unable to accept new ideas. ☐ **fossil fuel** natural fuel, such as coal, oil, or gas, formed in the past from the remains of living organisms.

fossilise *v.* (also **-ize**) turn or be turned into a fossil. ☐ **fossilisation** *n.*

Foster, David (1944–), Australian writer whose novel *The Glade Within the Grove* won the 1997 Miles Franklin Award.

foster *v.* **1** promote the growth or development of. **2** encourage or harbour (a feeling) (*fostering racial hate*). **3** take care of and bring up (a child that is not one's own). **4** (often foll. by *out*) (of a government agency etc.) assign (a child) to be fostered. • *adj.* having a family connection by fostering and not by birth (*foster brother; foster child; foster parent*). ☐ **foster home** a family home in which a foster child is brought up.

fought *see* FIGHT.

foul *adj.* **1** causing disgust, having an offensive smell or taste. **2** soiled, filthy. **3** morally offensive, evil. **4** (of language) disgusting, obscene. **5** (of weather) rough, stormy. **6** clogged, choked; overgrown with barnacles etc. **7** in collision; entangled. **8** unfair, against the rules of a game (*a foul stroke*). • *n.* **1** a foul stroke or blow etc., breaking the rules of a game. **2** a collision or entanglement, esp. in riding, rowing, or running. • *v.* **1** make or become foul. **2** (of an animal) deposit excrement on (*fouled the carpet*). **3** entangle or collide with, obstruct. **4** commit a foul against (a player) in a game. ☐ **foul-mouthed** *adj.* using foul language. **foul play 1** a foul in sport. **2** a violent crime, esp. murder. **foul up 1** become or cause to become entangled or blocked. **2** spoil, bungle. **foul-up** an entanglement or blockage; a muddle or bungle. ☐☐ **foully** *adv.* **foulness** *n.*

found[1] *v.* **1** establish, originate; provide money for starting (an institution etc.). **2** base or construct (*a novel that is founded on fact*). **3** melt and mould (metal); fuse (materials for glass). **4** make (an object) in this way. ☐ **founder** *n.*

found[2] *see* FIND.

foundation *n.* **1** the founding of an institution etc. **2** the institution itself; a fund of money established for a charitable purpose. **3** the solid ground or base from which a building is built up; (also **foundations**) the lowest part of a building, usu. below ground level. **4** a cosmetic applied to the skin as the first layer of make-up. **5** the underlying principle or idea etc. on which something is based. **6** the material or part on which others are overlaid. **7** a foundation garment. ☐ **foundation garment** a woman's supporting undergarment, e.g. a corset. **foundation stone** a stone laid ceremonially to celebrate the founding of a building.

founder[1] *v.* **1** stumble or fall. **2** (of a ship) fill with water and sink. **3** fail completely (*the plan foundered*).

founder[2] *n.* a person who has founded an institution, etc.

foundling *n.* a deserted child of unknown parents.

foundry *n.* a factory or workshop where metal or glass is founded.

fount *n.* **1** (also **font**) a set of printing type of one style and size. **2** a source. **3** *poetic* a spring; a fountain.

fountain *n.* **1** a spring of water, esp. a jet of water made to spout artificially as an ornament. **2** a structure providing a supply of drinking water in a public place. **3** the source (*the fountain of wisdom*). ☐ **fountain pen** a pen that can be filled with a supply of ink.

fountainhead *n.* the source.

four *adj.* & *n.* **1** one more than three (4, IV). **2** a four-oared boat or its crew. ☐ **four-letter word 1** a short word referring to sexual or excretory functions and regarded as obscene (esp. the word *fuck*). **2** anything unpleasant (*the boys in this class consider 'study' a four-letter word*). **four-poster** a bed with four posts to support a canopy. **four-square** *adj.* solidly based, steady; *adv.* squarely. **four-stroke** *adj.* (of an engine) having a cycle of four strokes of the piston with the cylinder firing once. *n.* a four-stroke engine or vehicle. **four-**

fourfold 317 **Francis**

wheel drive *n.* **1** drive acting on all four wheels of a vehicle. **2** (also **4WD**) a vehicle having this.
fourfold *adj.* & *adv.* **1** four times as much or as many. **2** consisting of four parts.
foursome *n.* **1** four people who get together for some purpose. **2** a golf match between two pairs, with partners playing the same ball.
fourteen *adj.* & *n.* one more than thirteen (14, XIV). ☐ **fourteenth** *adj.* & *n.*
fourth *adj.* next after third. • *n.* **1** something that is fourth. **2** one of four equal parts of a thing. ☐ **fourth dimension 1** a postulated dimension additional to those determining area and volume. **2** time regarded as equivalent to linear dimensions. **fourth generation language** (usu. as **4GL**) *Computing* a type of high-level programming language designed for non-programmers and used mainly for database and report generation applications. ☐☐ **fourthly** *adv.*
fowl *n.* (*pl.* **fowls** *or* **fowl**) **1** a chicken kept to supply eggs and flesh for food. **2** poultry as food. **3** *archaic* (except in combinations) a bird (*guinea fowl; wildfowl*). • *v.* catch or hunt wildfowl.
fowling *n.* catching, shooting, or snaring wildfowl. ☐ **fowler** *n.*
Fox, George (1624–91), founder of the Society of Friends (also called **Quakers**).
fox *n.* **1** a wild animal of the dog family (introduced into Australia) with a pointed snout, reddish fur, and a bushy tail. **2** its fur. **3** a crafty person. • *v.* deceive or puzzle by acting craftily.
foxed *adj.* (of things, e.g. the pages of a book) discoloured by brown spots caused by damp.
foxglove *n.* a tall plant (of the genus *Digitalis*) with purple or white flowers like glove-fingers.
foxhole *n.* an excavated hole in the ground used as a shelter etc. in battle.
fox terrier *n.* a short-haired terrier.
foxtrot *n.* a ballroom dance with slow and quick steps; the music for this. • *v.* (**foxtrotted**, **foxtrotting**) dance a foxtrot.
foxy *adj.* (**foxier**, **foxiest**) **1** looking like a fox. **2** sly or cunning. **3** reddish-brown. **4** *colloq.* (of a woman) sexually attractive. ☐ **foxily** *adv.* **foxiness** *n.*
foyer / **foi**-uh / *n.* the entrance hall of a theatre or cinema or of a hotel.
Fr *symbol* francium.
Fr. *abbr.* **1** Father. **2** French.
fracas / **frak**-ah / *n.* (*pl.* **fracas** / **frak**-ahz /) a noisy quarrel or disturbance.
fractal / **frak**-tuhl / *n.* *Maths* a curve or geometrical figure, each part of which has the same statistical character as the whole.
fraction *n.* **1** a number that is not a whole number, e.g. ¼, 0.5. **2** a very small part, piece, or amount. **3** the act or an instance of breaking.
fractional *adj.* **1** of a fraction. **2** very small (*a fractional difference*). ☐ **fractional distillation** separation of a mixture into its constituent parts by making use of their different physical properties. ☐☐ **fractionally** *adv.*
fractious / **frak**-shuhs / *adj.* irritable, peevish. ☐ **fractiously** *adv.* **fractiousness** *n.*
fracture *n.* breakage, esp. of a bone. • *v.* cause a fracture in; suffer a fracture.
fragile *adj.* **1** easily damaged or broken. **2** of delicate constitution, not strong. ☐ **fragilely** *adv.* **fragility** / fruh-**jil**-uh-tee / *n.*
fragment *n.* / **frag**-muhnt / **1** a piece broken off something. **2** an isolated part (*a fragment of the conversation*). • *v.* / frag-**ment** / break or be broken into fragments.
fragmentary / **frag**-muhn-tuh-ree / *adj.* consisting of fragments.
fragmentation *n.* **1** the process or an instance of breaking into fragments. **2** *Computing* the creation of many small often unusable areas of memory; an instance of this.
fragrance *n.* **1** sweetness of smell. **2** something fragrant; perfume.
fragrant *adj.* having a pleasant smell. ☐ **fragrantly** *adv.*
frail *adj.* not strong, physically weak.
frailty *n.* **1** being frail, weakness. **2** moral weakness, liability to yield to temptation.
frame *n.* **1** a rigid structure forming a support for other parts e.g. of a building, vehicle, or piece of furniture. **2** an open case or a border in which a picture, door, pane of glass, etc. may be set. **3** (**frames**) the structure holding the lenses in a pair of spectacles. **4** the human or an animal body with reference to its size (*he has a small frame*). **5** a single exposure on a strip of cinema film. **6** a boxlike structure used for protecting plants from the cold. **7** a triangular structure for setting up balls in snooker etc.; a round of play using this. **8** a frame-up. • *v.* **1** put or form a frame round. **2** construct. **3** compose, express in words (*frame a treaty*). **4** arrange false evidence against. ☐ **frame of mind** a temporary state of mind. **frame of reference** a set of principles or standards by which ideas and behaviour etc. are evaluated.
frame-up *n.* the arrangement of false evidence against an innocent person.
framework *n.* **1** the supporting frame of a building or other construction. **2** the structural basis of an organisation, the structure of a plan etc.
franc *n.* the unit of money in France, Belgium, Switzerland, and certain other countries.
France a republic in western Europe.
franchise / **fran**-chuyz / *n.* **1** the right to vote at public elections. **2** authorisation to sell a company's goods or services in a particular area. • *v.* grant a franchise to.
Francis[1], St, of Assisi (1181–1226), the Catholic friar who founded the Franciscan order of friars and nuns, noted for his simple faith and love of nature.
Francis[2], St, of Sales / sahl / (1567–1622), French bishop of Geneva and one of the leaders of the

Counter-Reformation. He co-founded the Order of the Visitation for nuns. The Salesian order is named after him.

Franciscan / fran-**sis**-kuhn / *n.* a member of the order of friars (also called *Grey Friars*) founded by St Francis of Assisi, or of a corresponding order of nuns.

Francis Xavier, St, *see* XAVIER.

francium / **fran**-see-uhm / *n.* a radioactive metallic element (symbol Fr).

Franco, Francisco (1892–1975), Spanish dictator 1939–75.

Franco- *comb. form* **1** French (*a Franco-German treaty*). **2** regarding France or the French (*Francophile*).

franger *n. Aust. colloq.* a condom.

frangipani / fran-juh-**pa**-nee / *n.* a tropical American tree with fragrant cream, pink, or yellow flowers; a perfume made from these flowers.

Frank *n.* a member of a Germanic people that conquered Gaul in the 6th century. ▫ **Frankish** *adj.*

frank[1] *adj.* showing one's thoughts and feelings openly. •*v.* mark (a letter) to record the payment of postage. •*n.* a franking signature or mark. ▫ **frankly** *adv.* **frankness** *n.*

frank[2] *colloq.* = FRANKFURT.

Frankenstein / **frank**-uhn-stuyn / *n.* (in full **Frankenstein's monster**) a thing that becomes terrifying to its creator. (¶ The name of a person in Mary Shelley's novel *Frankenstein* (1818), who constructed a human monster and endowed it with life. It became filled with hatred for its creator and eventually killed him.)

frankfurt *n.* (also **frankfurter**, **frank**) a seasoned smoked sausage. (¶ Originally made at Frankfurt in Germany.)

frankincense *n.* a sweet-smelling gum resin burnt as incense.

Franklin[1], Benjamin (1706–90), American statesman, inventor, and scientist, one of the signatories to the peace between the USA and Britain after the War of American Independence.

Franklin[2], (Stella Maria Sarah) Miles (1879–1954), Australian novelist, feminist, and cultural nationalist, her best known work probably being *My Brilliant Career* (1901) which was made into a film in 1979. Many of her novels were written under the pseudonym 'Brent of Bin Bin'. Under the terms of her will the Miles Franklin Award is presented each year to the novel which best presents 'Australian life, in any of its phases'.

Franklin a river rising in the mountains of south-western Tas. and flowing south through limestone gorges in densely forested and mountainous country to join the Gordon river. The Tasmanian government's proposal to dam the Gordon below the Franklin (which would have flooded the valleys of the Franklin and the Gordon) created widespread controversy in the 1970s and early 80s. The Federal Liberal Government opposed the proposal. It was with the election of a Federal Labor Government in 1983, however, that the project was cancelled and the region given a World Heritage listing.

frantic *adj.* **1** wildly excited or agitated by anxiety etc.; frenzied. **2** *colloq.* extreme. ▫ **frantically** *adv.*

Fraser[1], Dawn (1937–), AO, Australian swimmer, who at three consecutive Olympic games (1956, 1960, and 1964) won gold medals for the 110 yards/100 metres freestyle event. In 1962 she was the first woman to break the one-minute barrier for 110 yards (and 100 metres).

Fraser[2], (John) Malcolm (1930–), AC, Australian Liberal statesman, prime minister 1975–83, following the dismissal of the Whitlam Government. In 1985 he represented Australia in a Commonwealth group formed to negotiate the peaceful dismantling of South Africa's apartheid policy, and has since served as president of CARE International and chaired CARE Australia.

Fraser[3], Neale (Andrew) (1933–), AO, Australian tennis player, Wimbledon and Davis Cup champion.

Fraser Island a 166,000 hectare island off the south-east coast of Qld. It is the largest sand island in the world.

fraternal / fruh-**ter**-nuhl / *adj.* of a brother or brothers; comradely. ▫ **fraternal twins** twins developed from separate ova and not necessarily similar. ▫▫ **fraternally** *adv.*

fraternise / **frat**-uh-nuyz / *v.* (also **-ize**) (often foll. by *with*) **1** associate with others in a friendly way. **2** enter into friendly relations with enemies etc. ▫ **fraternisation** *n.*

fraternity / fruh-**ter**-nuh-tee / *n.* **1** being fraternal, brotherly feeling. **2** a religious brotherhood. **3** a group or company of people with common interests, or of the same professional class (*the medical fraternity*).

fratricide / **frat**-ruh-suyd / *n.* **1** the act of killing one's own brother. **2** a person who is guilty of this. ▫ **fratricidal** *adj.*

Frau / frow / *n.* (*pl.* **Frauen**) (the title of) a married or widowed German woman; Mrs.

fraud *n.* **1** criminal deception; a dishonest trick. **2** a person or thing that is not what it seems or pretends to be; an impostor.

fraudster *n.* a person who commits fraud, esp. in business dealings.

fraudulent / **fraw**-dyuh-luhnt / *adj.* acting with fraud; involving fraud; obtained by fraud. ▫ **fraudulently** *adv.* **fraudulence** *n.*

fraught / frawt / *adj.* **1** (foll. by *with*) filled, involving (*fraught with danger*). **2** *colloq.* anxious; distressing.

Fräulein / **froi**-luyn / *n.* (the title of) a German unmarried woman; Miss.

fray *n.* a fight, a conflict (*ready for the fray*). •*v.* (**frayed**, **fraying**) **1** make worn so that there are

frazzle loose threads, esp. at the edge. **2** strain or upset (nerves or temper). **3** become frayed.

frazzle *colloq. n.* a completely exhausted state; a shrivelled state (*worn to a frazzle; burnt to a frazzle*). • *v.* (usu. as **frazzled** *adj.*) completely wear out, exhaust.

freak *n.* **1** a person or thing that is abnormal in form. **2** (usu. used as *adj.*) very unusual or irregular (*a freak storm*). **3** a person who dresses absurdly. **4** one who freaks out; a drug addict. **5** a person who is obsessed with something specified (*a health freak*). • *v.* **1** (usu. foll. by *out*) experience (or cause another to experience) strong emotions, whether good or bad (*he'll freak (out) when we tell him he won the car; his failure freaked him out*). **2** (usu. foll. by *out*) get into a panic or rage. **3** (always foll. by *out*) (cause to) undergo hallucinations etc. from narcotic drugs (*dope has freaked him out; he's freaked out on marijuana*). **4** (always foll. by *out*) adopt an unconventional lifestyle. □**freakish** *adj.***freaky** *adj.*

freckle *n.* **1** a small light brown spot on the skin. **2** *Aust. coarse colloq.* the anal pucker, the anus. • *v.* become or cause to become spotted with freckles (sense 1).

free *adj.* (**freer**,**freest**) **1** (of a person) not a slave, not in the power of another or others; having social and political liberty. **2** (of a country or its citizens or institutions) not controlled by a foreign or despotic government; having representative government; having private rights which are respected. **3** *Aust. hist.* (of a convict in Australia) released from penal servitude; (of a settler in Australia) not transported hither as a convict. **4** not fixed or held down, able to move without hindrance. **5** unrestricted, not controlled by rules. **6** (foll. by *from* or *of*) without, not subject to or affected by (*free from blame; this food is free of preservatives*). **7** without payment, costing nothing. **8** (of place or time) not occupied, not being used; (of a person) without engagements or things to do. **9** coming, given, or giving readily (*he is very free with his advice*). **10** unmetrical (*free verse*). **11** (of translation) not literal. **12** familiar, impudent (*that child's far too free with the adults*). • *n.* = FREE KICK. • *v.* (**freed**, **freeing**) **1** make free, liberate. **2** (foll. by *from* or *of*) relieve, rid or ease (*freed him from suspicion*). **3** clear, disengage or disentangle. □**free enterprise** freedom of private business to operate without government control.**free fall 1** the unrestricted fall of a body towards earth under the force of gravity; the period of descent by parachute before the parachute opens. **2** a dramatic and uncontrollable fall in money and commodity values, stock market prices, etc.**free-for-all 1** a fight or brawl involving many or most of those present. **2** a discussion, argument, etc. involving many and hence chaotic.**free hand** the right of taking what action one chooses.**free-handed** generous.**free kick 1** a kick in football taken without interference from opponents, as a minor penalty. **2** esp. *Polit.* tactical or other advantage unwittingly conceded by one party to another. **free love** sexual relations according to choice and without restraints such as marriage etc.; sexual freedom. **free market** a market governed by unrestricted competition.**free port** one open to all traders alike, or free from duty on goods in transit.**free radical** an atom or group of atoms in which there is one or more unpaired electrons; an unstable element in the human body which, it is thought, can be overproduced as a result of chemical pollution and may then cause cell damage.**free-range** *adj.* (of hens) allowed to range freely in search of food, not kept in a battery; (of eggs) from such hens.**free-select** *Aust. hist.* acquire land under a free-selection scheme. **free-selection** *Aust. hist.* the scheme under which Australian land suitable for farming could be acquired on favourable terms (in contrast to land acquired by squatting or by grant from the Crown).**free-selector** *Aust. hist.* a small farmer who acquired a tract of land under a free-selection scheme. **free speech** the right to express opinions freely. **free spirit** an independent or uninhibited person. **free-spoken** forthright. **free-standing** not supported by another structure.**free trade 1** international trade with no restrictions on imports or exports, and without subsidies by producing nations. **2** unrestricted trade between Australian States.**free vote** a parliamentary vote in which members are not subject to party discipline. **free will 1** the doctrine that human beings have the power to act freely and at will, without being constrained by necessity or fate or God's predetermination. **2** the ability to act without coercion (*did it of my own free will*). □□**freely** *adv.*

-free (as the second part of a hyphenated adjective) not containing or involving the undesirable ingredient or factor named in the word before the hyphen (*cholesterol-free; gluten-free; sugar-free; nuclear-free*).

freebie *n. colloq.* something that is given free of charge.

freebooter *n.* a pirate.

freeborn *adj.* **1** not born a slave. **2** *Aust. hist.* (of a person born in an Australian colony) free of any association with the convict system.

freedom *n.* **1** the condition of being free; independence. **2** frankness, outspokenness. **3** exemption from a defect or duty etc. **4** (foll. by *of*) unrestricted use (*has the freedom of the library*). □**freedom fighter** one who takes part in violent resistance to an established political regime. **freedom of information** the public's legal right of access to information about decisions taken, or certain material held, by government organisations.

freehand *adj.* (of a drawing) done without ruler or compasses etc. • *adv.* in a freehand manner.

freehold *n.* **1** the holding of land or property in absolute ownership for an unlimited period. **2** such land or property. • *adj.* owned thus. ☐ **freeholder** *n.*

freelance *n.* (also **freelancer**) a self-employed person who works for several employers on particular assignments. • *adj.* working in this way (*a freelance journalist*). • *v.* work as a freelance.

freeloader *n. colloq.* a sponger.

Freeman, Cathy (full name: Catherine Astrid Salome Freeman) (1973–), OAM, Australian Aboriginal athlete. She won a silver medal in the 400 metres at the 1996 Olympics, and a gold medal in the same event at the 2000 Olympics.

Freemason *n.* a member of an international fraternity for mutual help and fellowship, with elaborate secret rituals. ☐ **Freemasonry** *n.*

freepost *n.* a system of business post where postage is paid by the firm or business receiving the thing posted.

freesia *n.* a fragrant flowering plant growing from a bulb.

freestyle *n.* **1** a swimming race in which any stroke may be used. **2** wrestling allowing almost any hold. **3** a skateboarding competition in which each competitor is required to perform a solo routine consisting of movements and tricks. **4** a skiing competition in which competitors are required to perform in one or all of three categories: acrobatic skiing, ballet skiing, and moguls.

freethinker *n.* a person who refuses to allow his or her reasoning process to be controlled by religious or other authorities; a rationalist.

Freetown the capital of Sierra Leone.

freeware *see* -WARE.

freeway *n.* a main road, with separate carriageways and limited access, designed for fast traffic.

freewheel *n.* the driving wheel of a bicycle, able to revolve with the pedals at rest. • *v.* **1** ride a bicycle with the pedals at rest. **2** act without constraint. ☐ **freewheeler** *n.* **freewheeling** *adj.*

freeze *v.* (**froze**, **frozen**, **freezing**) **1** be so cold that water turns to ice. **2** change or be changed from a liquid to a solid by extreme cold; become full of ice or covered in ice. **3** become very cold, or rigid from cold or fear etc.; chill by cold or fear etc. **4** preserve (food) by refrigeration to below freezing point. **5** make (credits or assets) unable to be realised. **6** hold (prices, wages, etc.) at a fixed level. **7** stop (the movement in a videotape etc.). • *n.* **1** a period of freezing weather. **2** the freezing of prices, wages, etc. **3** = FREEZE-FRAME. ☐ **freeze-dry** *v.* freeze and dry by evaporation of ice in a vacuum. **freeze-frame** *n.* a still picture forming part of a motion sequence; a facility on video recorders allowing one to stop the action and view the picture currently on the screen as a still; *v.* use the freeze-frame facility; pause (action or a picture) in this way. **freeze out** exclude from business, society, etc., by severe competition, chilling behaviour, etc. **freezing point** the temperature at which a liquid, esp. water, freezes. **freezing works** *Aust.* a building where animals are slaughtered and carcases frozen, esp. for export.

freezer *n.* a refrigerated container for preserving and storing perishable goods by keeping them at a very low temperature.

freight / frayt / *n.* **1** the transport of goods in containers or by water, land, or air. **2** the goods transported, cargo. **3** the charge for this. • *v.* transport as freight or load with freight.

freighter / **fray**-tuh / *n.* a ship or aircraft carrying mainly freight.

Fremantle the chief port of the State of Western Australia, situated on the mouth of the Swan River, 17 km from the capital, Perth. ☐ **Fremantle doctor** (in Perth) a cool, refreshing sea breeze which brings relief from summer heat.

French[1], Leonard (William) (1928–), Australian artist and designer.

French[2] *adj.* **1** of France or its people or language. **2** having French characteristics. • *n.* **1** the French language. **2** (**the French**) (as *pl.*) French people. ☐ **French bean** a kidney bean or haricot bean, used as a vegetable both as unripe pods and as ripe seeds. **French bread** = FRENCH STICK. **French Canadian** a native of the French-speaking area of Canada. **french chalk** finely powdered talc used as a lubricant etc. **French dressing** salad dressing of seasoned oil and vinegar. **French fries** thin strips of fried potato. **French horn** a coiled brass wind instrument with a wide bell. **French kiss** a kiss in which one partner's tongue is inserted in the other's mouth or where both tongues intertwine. **French leave** absence without permission. **French letter** *colloq.* a condom. **French polish** *n.* a shellac polish for wood. *v.* polish (wood) with French polish. **French stick** a long roll of white bread with a crisp crust. **French window** one of a pair of long windows used as doors. ☐ ☐ **Frenchman** *n.* **Frenchwoman** *n.*

frenetic / fruh-**net**-ik / *adj.* frantic, frenzied. ☐ **frenetically** *adv.*

frenzied *adj.* in a state of frenzy, wildly excited or agitated. ☐ **frenziedly** *adv.*

frenzy *n.* violent excitement or agitation.

frequency *n.* **1** the state of being frequent, frequent occurrence. **2** the rate of the occurrence or repetition of something. **3** the number of cycles per second of a carrier wave; a band or group of similar frequencies. ☐ **frequency modulation** *Electronics* a modulation in which the frequency of the carrier wave is varied; used esp. in broadcasting.

frequent *v.* / fruh-**kwent** / go frequently to, be often in (a place). • *adj.* / **free**-kwuhnt / happening or appearing often. ☐ **frequently** *adv.*

frequentative / fruh-**kwen**-tuh-tiv / *adj. Grammar* (of a verb) expressing frequent

fresco repetition or intensity of an action. • *n.* a frequentative verb.

fresco / fres-koh / *n.* (*pl.* **frescos**) a picture painted on a wall or ceiling before the plaster is dry.

fresh *adj.* **1** newly made, produced, or gathered; not stale. **2** newly arrived. **3** new or different, not previously known or used. **4** (of food) not preserved by salting, pickling, tinning, or freezing etc. **5** not salty, not bitter. **6** (of air or weather) cool, refreshing; (of wind) moderately strong. **7** bright and pure in colour, not dull or faded. **8** not weary; feeling vigorous. **9** *colloq.* cheeky; amorously impudent. ☐ **freshly** *adv.* **freshness** *n.*

freshen *v.* make or become fresh.

fresher *n.* a first-year student at a university.

freshet *n.* **1** a stream of fresh water flowing into the sea. **2** a flood of a river.

freshie *n.* (also **freshy**) *Aust. colloq.* a freshwater crocodile.

freshwater *adj.* of fresh water, not of the sea (*freshwater fish*). ☐ **freshwater people** *Aust.* an Aboriginal people who live along inland watercourses (opp. SALTWATER PEOPLE).

fret[1] *v.* (**fretted**, **fretting**) **1** make or become unhappy, worry, vex. **2** wear away by gnawing or rubbing. • *n.* a state of unhappiness or worry.

fret[2] *n.* **1** a bar or ridge on the fingerboard of a guitar, banjo, etc., as a guide for the fingers to press the strings at the correct place. **2** an ornamental pattern of straight lines joined usu. at right angles. • *v.* (**fretted**, **fretting**) ornament with this or with carved or embossed work. ☐ **fretted** *adj.*

fretful *adj.* anxious or distressed. ☐ **fretfully** *adv.* **fretfulness** *n.*

Fretilin / fret-uh-luhn / a movement for independence in East Timor. Fretilin's ascendancy in the country led to the invasion and annexation of East Timor by Indonesia in 1975. See EAST TIMOR.

fretsaw *n.* a narrow saw fixed in a frame, used for cutting thin wood in patterns.

fretwork *n.* carved work in decorative patterns, esp. in wood cut with a fretsaw.

Freud / froid /, Sigmund (1856–1939), Austrian psychiatrist, the founder of psychoanalysis.

Freudian / froi-dee-uhn / *adj.* of Sigmund Freud or his theories. • *n.* a follower of Freud. ☐ **Freudian slip** an absent-minded remark that seems to reveal subconscious feelings.

Frey *Scand. myth.* the god of fertility and dispenser of rain and sunshine.

Freya *Scand. myth.* the goddess of love and of the night, sister of Frey. She is often identified with Frigga.

friable / fruy-uh-buhl / *adj.* easily crumbled. ☐ **friability** *n.*

friar *n.* a member of certain Catholic male religious orders (esp. the Augustinians, Carmelites, Dominicans, and Franciscans), working among people in the outside world and not as enclosed orders. ☐ **friar bird** any of four large Australian honeyeaters having bare skin on the head (suggesting a tonsured friar), a knob on the bill, and a raucous call. **friar's balsam** a tincture of benzoin etc. used esp. as an inhalant.

friary *n.* a monastery of friars.

fricassee / frik-uh-see / *n.* a dish of pieces of meat served in a thick sauce. • *v.* (**fricasseed**, **fricasseeing**) make a fricassee of.

fricative *n. Phonetics* a consonant sounded by the friction of breath in a narrow opening, e.g. *f*, *th*.

friction *n.* **1** the rubbing of one thing against another. **2** the resistance of one surface to another that moves over it. **3** conflict between people with different ideas or personalities. ☐ **frictional** *adj.*

Friday *n.* the day of the week following Thursday. • *adv. colloq.* **1** on Friday. **2** (**Fridays**) on Fridays; each Friday. ☐ **girl** (*or* **man**) **Friday** an assistant doing general duties in an office etc. (¶ Named after Man Friday in Defoe's *Robinson Crusoe*.)

fridge *n. colloq.* a refrigerator.

fried see FRY.

Friend, Donald (Stuart Leslie) (1915–89), Australian artist and writer. His paintings often depict his favourite subjects, the native peoples (especially youths) of Bali, Sri Lanka, and the Torres Strait Islands.

friend *n.* **1** a person with whom one is on terms of mutual affection independently of sexual or family love. **2** a helpful thing or quality (*darkness was our friend*). **3** a helper, sympathiser, or patron (*Friends of the Australian Opera*). **4** (**Friend**) a member of the Society of Friends, a Quaker. ☐ **friendship** *n.* **friendless** *adj.*

friendly *adj.* (**friendlier**, **friendliest**) **1** like a friend, kindly. **2** (of things) favourable, helpful. ☐ **friendly fire** gunfire from one's own side in a conflict. ☐ ☐ **friendliness** *n.*

-friendly *comb. form* (as the second word in a hyphenated adjective) **1** adapted, designed, or made easy for what is named in the first word (*user-friendly*). **2** safe for, not harmful to what is named in the first word (*environment-friendly*; *ozone-friendly*).

Friendly Islands Tonga.

Friendly Society *n.* a society for the mutual benefit of its members, e.g. during illness or old age.

frier alternative spelling of FRYER.

Friesian / free-zhuhn / *n.* an animal of a breed of large black-and-white dairy cattle originally from Friesland, a province of the Netherlands.

frieze *n.* a band of sculpture or decoration round the top of a wall or building.

frig[1] *coarse colloq. v.* **1** masturbate. **2** have sexual intercourse (with). **3** (usu. foll. by *around*) mess about; fool around. **4** (often foll. by *up*) confuse; mess up. **5** (sometimes foll. by *up*) break, damage (*you've frigged the fridge with your tampering*). **6** (foll. by *off*) go away, get lost. **7** (as **frigging** *adj.*)

frig (*euphemism* for) fucking. • *n.* an act or an instance of frigging.

frig² / frij / = REFRIGERATOR.

frigate / **frig**-uht / *n.* a small fast naval escort vessel or a small destroyer.

Frigga *Scand. myth.* the wife of Odin and goddess of married love and the hearth.

fright *n.* **1** sudden great fear. **2** a grotesque or ridiculous-looking person or thing.

frighten *v.* **1** cause fright to. **2** feel fright (*he doesn't frighten easily*). **3** drive or compel by fright (*frightened them into concealing it*). □ **frightened of** afraid of. □ □ **frightening** *adj.* **frighteningly** *adv.*

frightful *adj.* **1** causing horror; revolting. **2** *colloq.* extremely bad (*a frightful idea*). **3** *colloq.* very great (*I'm in a frightful rush*). □ **frightfully** *adv.*

frigid / **frij**-uhd / *adj.* **1** intensely cold. **2** very cold and formal in manner. **3** (of a woman) unresponsive sexually. □ **frigid zones** those parts of the earth south of the Antarctic Circle and north of the Arctic Circle. □ □ **frigidly** *adv.* **frigidity** / fruh-**jid**-uh-tee / *n.*

frijoles / free-**hoh**-les / *n.pl.* (esp. in Mexican cookery) (a dish of) beans.

frill *n.* **1** a gathered or pleated strip of trimming attached at one edge. **2** (**frills**) unnecessary extras (*simple accommodation with no frills*). • *v.* decorate with a frill. □ **frill-necked lizard** (also **frillie**) a large northern Australian lizard with an erectile membrane around the neck. □ □ **frilled** *adj.* **frilly** *adj.*

fringe *n.* **1** an ornamental edging of hanging threads or cords etc. **2** something resembling this. **3** front hair cut short to hang over the forehead. **4** the edge of an area, group, sphere of activity, etc.; (as *adj.*) existing on such an edge (*fringe dweller; fringe theatre*). **5** an area of sparse settlement bordering the arid Australian inland. **6** an unimportant area or part. • *v.* **1** decorate with a fringe. **2** form a fringe to. □ **fringe benefits** benefits that are provided for an employee in addition to wages or salary. **fringe dweller** *Aust.* **1** a person who lives in wretched conditions on the outskirts of a city or town. **2** a person who by choice lives on the outskirts of a city or town. **fringe lily** any of several small Australian plants of the genus *Thysanotus* bearing blue or purple flowers, the three broad petals of which are finely fringed. **fringe medicine** systems of treating disease, injury, etc. that are not regarded as orthodox by the medical profession. **fringe myrtle** any of several shrubs of the Australian genus *Calytrix* with pink, red, yellow, or violet starry fringed flowers.

frippery *n.* **1** showy unnecessary finery or ornament, esp. in dress. **2** unnecessary display in speech, literary style, etc. **3** (**fripperies**) knick-knacks, trifles.

frisbee *n. trademark* a concave plastic disc for skimming through the air as an outdoor game.

Frisian / **friz**-ee-uhn / *adj.* of Friesland, a province of the Netherlands, or its people or language. • *n.* **1** a native of Friesland. **2** the Germanic language spoken there.

frisk *v.* **1** leap or skip playfully. **2** *colloq.* pass one's hands over (a person) in order to search for concealed weapons etc.

frisky *adj.* (**friskier**, **friskiest**) **1** lively, playful. **2** *colloq.* sexually aroused. □ **friskily** *adv.* **friskiness** *n.*

frisson / **free**-son, **fri**-son / *n.* an emotional thrill. (¶ French, = shiver.)

frittata / fri-**tah**-tuh / *n.* a thick unfolded omelette topped with herbs, seasonings, and potatoes or other vegetables.

fritter *n.* a small flat fried cake of batter containing sliced fruit or meat etc. • *v.* (usu. foll. by *away*) waste little by little, esp. on trivial things (*fritter away one's money*).

fritz *n.* a bland sausage usu. sliced and eaten cold.

frivolous *adj.* **1** not serious, silly, shallow (*a frivolous character*). **2** paltry, trifling (*arrested on a frivolous charge*). □ **frivolously** *adv.* **frivolity** *n.*

frizz *v.* curl (hair) into a wiry mass. • *n.* a frizzed condition; frizzed hair. □ **frizzy** *adj.* **frizziness** *n.*

frizzle *v.* **1** fry or cook with a sizzling noise. **2** burn or shrivel by burning. **3** frizz. • *n.* frizzed hair. □ **frizzly** *adj.*

fro *adv.* □ **to and fro** see TO.

frock *n.* **1** a woman's or girl's dress. **2** a monk's or priest's gown. **3** a smock. • *v.* invest with priestly office (cf. DEFROCK).

frog *n.* **1** a small smooth tailless cold-blooded jumping animal living both in water and on land. **2** a horny substance in the sole of a horse's foot. **3** a coat fastener consisting of a button and an ornamentally looped cord. **4** (**Frog**) *colloq. offens.* a French person. □ **have a frog in one's throat** *colloq.* be unable to speak except hoarsely.

frogman *n.* a swimmer equipped with a rubber suit, flippers, and an oxygen supply for swimming and working under water.

frogmarch *v.* hustle (a person) forward forcibly with his or her arms held fast behind the back. • *n.* this process.

frogmouth *n.* any of various nocturnal Australian and Asian birds having large wide beaks resembling the mouth of a frog and brown or grey marbled plumage.

frolic *v.* (**frolicked**, **frolicking**) play about in a lively cheerful way. • *n.* **1** lively cheerful playing or entertainment. **2** a prank. □ **frolicker** *n.*

frolicsome *adj.* merry, playful.

from *prep.* expressing separation or origin: **1** indicating the place, time, or limit that is the starting point (*travelled from Hobart; from ten o'clock*). **2** indicating a specified distance etc. (*5 miles from Gundagai; far from sure*). **3** indicating source or origin (*took water from the well; a gift from Dad*). **4** indicating separation, prevention, escape, etc. (*was released from prison; cannot*

fromage frais   323   **fruitful**

refrain from laughing). **5** indicating difference or discrimination (*can't tell red from green*). **6** indicating a lower limit (*from 10 to 20 boats*). **7** indicating a state changed from another (*from being poor he became rich*). **8** indicating cause, agent, or means (*died from starvation*). **9** indicating the position of a person who observes or considers (*saw it from the roof; from her point of view*). **10** indicating material used in a process (*wine is made from grapes*). **11** adverb or preposition of time or place (*from long ago; from abroad; from under the bed*).

fromage frais / fro-mah*zh* fray / *n.* smooth soft fresh cheese with the consistency of thick yoghurt.

frond *n.* a leaflike part of a fern or other flowerless plant, or of a palm tree.

front *n.* **1** the foremost or most important side or surface. **2** the part normally nearer or towards the spectator or line of motion (*the front of a bus*). **3** the area where fighting is taking place in a war; the foremost line of an army etc. **4** an organised sector of activity (compared to a military front) (*on the domestic front*). **5** an outward appearance or show; something serving as a cover for secret or illegal activities (*putting on a bold front; his massage parlour was a front for a brothel*). **6** the forward edge of an advancing mass of cold or warm air. **7** the forward edge of a bushfire. **8** land facing a road, a river, the sea, etc. **9** the part of a garment covering the front of the body (*spilt soup all down his front*). **10** the part of a theatre where the audience sits, in front of the stage. **11** (in names) an organised political group (*the Patriotic Front*). **12** *Aust. colloq.* impudence. •*adj.* of the front; situated in front. •*v.* **1** face, have the front towards (*a hotel fronting the sea*). **2** *colloq.* be a front or cover for secret activities. **3** (often foll. by *up*) *Aust. colloq.* turn up, make an appearance (*he had to front up before the principal*). **4** lead (a band, an organisation, etc.). ◻ **front line** the foremost part of an army. **front-line** *adj.* prominent; in the forefront. **front runner** the contestant who seems most likely to succeed. **in front** at the front of something. **in front of 1** ahead of, in advance of. **2** in the presence of. **up front** in advance (*payment up front*).

frontage *n.* **1** the front of a building. **2** the land bordering its front. **3** land next to a street or water etc. **4** the way a thing faces; outlook.

frontal *adj.* **1** of or on the front (*frontal view; fully frontal nudity; a frontal attack*). **2** of the forehead (*frontal bone*).

frontbench *n.* those seats in parliament which are reserved for government ministers and members of the shadow cabinet (cf. BACK-BENCH). •*adj.* pertaining to the frontbench or frontbenchers.

frontbencher *n.* a government minister or opposition shadow minister occupying the frontbench (cf. BACKBENCHER).

frontier *n.* **1** the land border between two countries. **2** the district on each side of this. **3** the limit of attainment or knowledge in a subject. ◻ **frontiersman** *n.*

frontispiece / **frun**-tuhs-pees / *n.* an illustration placed opposite the title page of a book.

frost *n.* **1** a weather condition with temperature below the freezing point of water. **2** a white powder-like coating of frozen vapour produced by this. **3** a chilling influence; great coolness of manner, unfriendliness. •*v.* **1** injure (a plant etc.) with frost. **2** cover with frost or frosting. **3** make (glass) opaque by roughening the surface.

frostbite *n.* injury to tissue of the body from freezing. ◻ **frostbitten** *adj.*

frostie *n. Aust. colloq.* an ice-cold can or bottle of beer.

frosting *n.* sugar icing.

frosty *adj.* (**frostier**, **frostiest**) **1** cold with frost. **2** covered by frost. **3** unfriendly or cold in manner. ◻ **frostily** *adv.* **frostiness** *n.*

froth *n.* **1** foam. **2** idle talk or ideas. **3** anything unsubstantial or of little worth. •*v.* **1** (of beer etc.) emit or gather froth; foam. **2** cause (beer etc.) to foam. ◻ **frothy** *adj.*

frown *v.* wrinkle one's brow in thought or disapproval. •*n.* a frowning movement or look. ◻ **frown at** (*or* **on**) disapprove of.

frowsty *adj.* fusty, stuffy.

frowzy *adj.* (also **frowsy**) **1** fusty. **2** slatternly, dingy.

frozen *see* FREEZE.

fructify / **fruk**-tuh-fuy / *v.* (**fructifies**, **fructified**) **1** bear fruit. **2** make fruitful.

fructose / **fruuk**-tohz, -tohs, **fruk**- / *n.* a simple sugar found in honey and fruits.

frugal / **froo**-guhl / *adj.* **1** careful and economical. **2** scanty, costing little (*a frugal meal*). ◻ **frugally** *adv.* **frugality** / froo-**gal**-uh-tee / *n.*

fruit *n.* **1** the seed-containing part of a plant or tree; this as food. **2** these collectively. **3** any plant product used as food (*the fruits of the earth*). **4** the product or rewarding outcome of labour. **5** currants etc. used in food. **6** *colloq. offens.* a homosexual male. •*v.* **1** (of a plant) produce fruit. **2** cause (a plant) to produce fruit. ◻ **fruit cocky** *Aust.* a fruit farmer. **fruit dove** any of several Australian fruit-eating pigeons, often found in rainforest areas, e.g. the *rose-crowned fruit dove*. **fruit fly** any of various flies which lay their eggs in fruit, esp. the Qld fruit fly which is a serious pest. **fruit salad** various fruits cut up and mixed.

fruitbat *n.* any of various large fruit-eating bats (of Australia and elsewhere), including the flying fox.

fruitcake *n.* **1** a cake containing dried fruit. **2** *colloq.* an eccentric or mad person.

fruiterer *n.* a shopkeeper who deals in fruit.

fruitful *adj.* **1** producing much fruit. **2** producing good results. ◻ **fruitfully** *adv.*

fruition / froo-**ish**-uhn / n. **1** the fulfilment of hopes; results attained by work. **2** the bearing of fruit.

fruitless adj. **1** producing little or no result. **2** not bearing fruit. ☐ **fruitlessly** adv.

fruity adj. (**fruitier, fruitiest**) **1** like fruit in smell or taste. **2** of full rich quality (*a fruity voice*). **3** colloq. slightly indecent or sexually suggestive (*fruity jokes*).

frump n. a dowdily-dressed unattractive woman. ☐ **frumpish** adj. **frumpy** adj.

frustrate v. prevent (a person) from achieving a purpose; make (efforts) useless.

frustrated adj. **1** discontented because of being unable to achieve something. **2** sexually unfulfilled. ☐ **frustration** n.

frustum n. (pl. **frusta** or **frustums**) the lower part of a cone or pyramid whose top is cut off parallel to the base.

fry v. (**fried, frying**) cook or be cooked in boiling oil or fat. • n. **1** offal, usu. eaten fried (*lamb's fry*). **2** fried food, esp. meat. **3** (as pl.) young or newly hatched fishes; the young of other creatures produced in large numbers, e.g. bees or frogs. ☐ **small fry 1** people of little importance. **2** children.

fryer n. (also **frier**) **1** a person who fries things. **2** a vessel for frying fish etc.

frying pan n. a shallow pan used in frying.

frypan n. **1** an electric frying pan. **2** = FRYING PAN.

ft abbr. foot or feet (as a measure).

FTP abbr. *Computing* file-transfer protocol, a standard for the exchange of program and data files across a computer network.

FT-SE abbr. see FINANCIAL TIMES INDEX.

fuchsia / **fyoo**-shuh / n. an ornamental shrub with red, purple, or white drooping flowers.

fuck coarse colloq. v. **1** have sexual intercourse with. **2** (expressing annoyance) damn, curse. **3** (foll. by *about, around*) mess about; fool around. **4** (as **fucking** adj. & adv.) used as an intensifier expressing approval (*it's a fucking miracle*) as well as disapproval (*he's a fucking liar*). • n. **1** an act of sexual intercourse. **2** a partner in this. **3** the slightest amount (*he doesn't give a fuck*). ☐ **fuck-all** nothing. **fuck off** go away. **fuck-up** a complete bungle, a muddle. ☐☐ **fucker** n.

■ **Usage** Although widely used, *fuck* is still considered by many to be one of the most offensive of words. In discussions about bad language it is frequently referred to as *the 'f' word*.

fuckwit n. coarse colloq. a nitwit, a stupid idiot.

fuddle v. stupefy, esp. with alcoholic drink. • n. **1** confusion. **2** intoxication.

fuddy-duddy colloq. adj. old-fashioned; quaintly fussy. • n. a person of this kind.

fudge n. **1** a soft sweet made of milk, sugar, and butter, etc. **2** a piece of dishonesty or faking. • v. put together in a makeshift or dishonest way; fake (*he fudged the results*).

fuehrer alternative spelling of FÜHRER.

fuel n. **1** material for burning or lighting as a source of warmth, light, or energy, or used as a source of nuclear energy. **2** something that increases anger or other strong feelings. • v. (**fuelled, fuelling**) **1** supply with, take in, or get, fuel (*fuelled the car; will have to fuel up soon*). **2** inflame (feelings etc.). ☐ **fuel cell** a cell producing electricity directly from a chemical reaction.

fug n. colloq. close stuffy air in a room. ☐ **fuggy** adj.

fugitive / **fyoo**-juh-tiv / n. a person fleeing or escaping from something. • adj. **1** fleeing, escaping. **2** transient.

fugue / fyoog / n. a musical composition in which one or more themes are introduced and then repeated in a complex pattern. ☐ **fugal** adj.

führer / **fyoo**-ruh / n. (also **fuehrer**) a tyrannical leader. (¶ German, = leader: the title taken by Hitler.)

Fujairah / foo-**juy**-ruh / n. an emirate belonging to the federation of United Arab Emirates.

Fujiyama / foo-jee-**yah**-muh / the highest mountain in Japan, a cone-shaped dormant or extinct volcano.

Fulbright n. (in full **Fulbright Scholarship**) a scholarship awarded to US citizens for study or research in other countries; a similar scholarship awarded to the citizens of other countries for study or research in the US. (¶ James William Fulbright (1905–95), US politician.)

fulcrum / **fuul**-kruhm / n. (pl. **fulcra** or **fulcrums**) the point on which a lever turns.

fulfil v. (**fulfilled, fulfilling**) **1** accomplish, carry out (a task, a promise, etc.). **2** do what is required by (a treaty etc.); satisfy the requirements of. **3** make (a prophecy) come true. ☐ **fulfilled** adj. completely happy or contented. ☐☐ **fulfilment** n.

full[1] adj. **1** holding or having as much as the limits will allow. **2** (often foll. by *of*) having much or many, crowded (*full of vitality*). **3** (foll. by *of*) completely occupied with, engrossed in (*full of himself; full of the news*). **4** fed to satisfaction (*ate till he was full*). **5** copious (*give full details*). **6** complete, reaching the usual or specified extent or limit (*in full bloom; waited a full hour*). **7** plump, rounded (*a full figure*). **8** (of clothes) fitting loosely, made with much material hanging in folds. **9** (of tone) deep and mellow. **10** (of motion etc.) vigorous (*at full gallop*). **11** colloq. drunk. • adv. **1** very (*knows full well*). **2** quite, fully (*full six kilometres*). **3** completely (*full-grown*). **4** exactly (*hit him full on the nose*). ☐ **full back** one of the defensive players near the goal in football, hockey, etc. **full blood 1** a person of unmixed race. **2** a pure-bred animal. **full-blown** fully developed (*a full-blown rose; full-blown Aids*). **full board** provision of bed and all meals at a hotel etc. **full-bodied** adj. rich in quality, tone, or flavour.

full forward *Aust. Rules* a position in front of the goal on the forward line of the attacking team; a player in this position. **full-frontal** *adj.* 1 (of a naked figure) turned front-on so that the genitals are fully exposed. 2 explicit, unrestrained. **full house** 1 maximum attendance at a theatre etc. 2 (in poker) a hand with three of a kind and a pair. **full moon** the moon with its whole disc illuminated; the time when this occurs. **full-scale** *adj.* not reduced in size; complete. **full stop** 1 the punctuation mark (.) used at the end of a sentence or abbreviation (see panel). 2 a complete cessation. **full term** the completion of a normal pregnancy. **full time** *n.* the end of a football etc. match. **full-time** *adj.* 1 for or during the whole of a working day or week (*a full-time job*). 2 of or pertaining to the time a football etc. match is scheduled to end (*the full-time siren*). *adv.* on a full-time basis (*he works full-time*). **full-timer** a person employed to work a full working week. **full toss** *Cricket* a ball pitched right up to the batsman without touching the ground. **to the full** thoroughly, completely.

full[2] *v.* clean and thicken freshly-woven cloth.

full-blown Aids *n.* a stage of Aids (reached by some persons who have been infected with the Aids virus) that is ultimately fatal and is characterised by the breaking down of the body's natural defences against infection and sometimes by the development of tumours etc. (*See also* AIDS[1], AIDS-RELATED COMPLEX.)

fuller *n.* a person who fulls cloth. □ **fuller's earth** a type of clay used for this process.

fullness *n.* being full.

fully *adv.* 1 completely, entirely. 2 no less than (*fully sixty years of age*).

fulminant / ful-muh-nuhnt, fuul- / *adj.* 1 fulminating. 2 (of a disease) developing suddenly.

fulminate / ful-muh-nayt, fuul- / *v.* 1 (often foll. by *against*) attack or condemn loudly and forcefully (*fulminating from the pulpit against the Sydney Gay and Lesbian Mardi Gras*). 2 explode violently; flash. □ **fulmination** *n.*

fulsome / fuul-suhm / *adj.* sickeningly excessive, cloying, insincere (*fulsome praise*).

■ **Usage** The phrase *fulsome praise* is often wrongly used to mean 'generous praise' rather than 'excessive praise'.

Fulton, Bobby (full name: Robert Sebastian Fulton) (1948–), AM, Australian Rugby League player and a test captain (1978) and test coach (1989–98).

fumble *v.* 1 touch or handle awkwardly (*fumbled the ball*). 2 grope about. •*n.* an act of fumbling.

fume *n.* (usu. as **fumes**) strong-smelling smoke, gas, or vapour. •*v.* 1 treat with chemical fumes, esp. to darken wood (*fumed oak*). 2 emit fumes. 3 seethe with anger.

fumigate / **fyoo**-muh-gayt / *v.* disinfect by means of fumes. □ **fumigation** *n.* **fumigator** *n.*

fun *n.* 1 light-hearted amusement. 2 a source of this. 3 mockery, ridicule (*turned him into a figure of fun*). •*adj. colloq.* amusing, enjoyable (*a fun thing to do*). □ **for fun** (*or* **for the fun of it**) as a source of amusement, not seriously. **fun run** an organised long-distance footrace, including both serious competitors and those in it just for enjoyment, and often run to raise money for charity. **in fun** as a joke, not seriously.

■ **Usage** The use of *fun* as an attributive adjective (e.g. *a fun party*) is common in informal use, but is considered incorrect by some people.

Funafuti / foo-nuh-**foo**-tee / the capital of Tuvalu, situated on an island of the same name.

Full stop .
A full stop is used:
1 at the end of a sentence, e.g.
   I am going to the movies tonight.
   The film begins at seven.
   The full stop is replaced by a question mark at the end of a question, and by an exclamation mark at the end of an exclamation.
2 after an abbreviation, e.g.
   E.G. Whitlam   *p. 19 (= page 19)*   *Sun. (= Sunday)*
   Ex. 6 (= Exercise 6).
Full stops are **not** used with:
   a numerical abbreviations, e.g. *1st, 2nd, 15th, 23rd*
   b acronyms, e.g. *ASEAN, UNESCO*
   c abbreviations that are used as ordinary words, e.g. con, demo, recap
   d chemical symbols, e.g. *Fe, K, H$_2$O*
Full stops are not essential for:
   a abbreviations consisting entirely of capitals, e.g. *SBS, AD, BC, CES*
   b *C (= Celsius), F (= Fahrenheit)*
   c measures of length, weight, time, etc., except for *in. (= inch), st. (= stone)*
   d an abbreviation which concludes with the last letter of the full word: *Dr, Revd* (but note *Rev.*), *Mr, Mrs, Ms, Mme, Mlle, St (= Saint)*

function *n.* **1** the special activity or purpose of a person or thing. **2** an important social or official gathering. **3** *Computing* a program unit that computes a single value. **4** *Maths* a quantity whose value depends on the varying values of others. • *v.* **1** perform a function, operate; be in working order. **2** (foll. by *as*) do the work or perform the role (of someone or something else).

functional *adj.* **1** of a function or functions. **2** designed to perform a particular function without being decorative or luxurious; practical. **3** in working order. **4** (esp. of a disease) affecting the function of a bodily organ but not its structure. □ **functionally** *adv.*

functionalism *n.* belief in or stress on the practical application of a thing, esp. in architecture and furniture design. □ **functionalist** *n.* & *adj.*

functionary *n.* an official.

fund *n.* **1** a stock of money, esp. that available for a particular purpose. **2** an available stock or supply (*a fund of jokes*). **3** (**funds**) money resources. • *v.* provide with money.

fundament *n.* the anus.

fundamental *adj.* **1** of the basis or foundation of a subject etc., serving as a starting point. **2** very important, essential. • *n.pl.* (**fundamentals**) fundamental facts or principles. □ **fundamental note** *Music* the lowest note of a chord. **fundamental particle** an elementary particle. □□ **fundamentally** *adv.*

fundamentalism *n.* **1** strict maintenance of the belief that every detail of the Bible is literally true and should be accepted as the basis of Protestant Christianity. **2** (in Islam) a movement which demands rigorous adherence to Islamic laws. □ **fundamentalist** *n.* & *adj.*

funeral *n.* **1** the ceremony of burying or cremating the dead. **2** a procession to this. **3** *colloq.* a person's unpleasant responsibility or concern (*that's your funeral*). □ **funeral director** an undertaker. **funeral parlour 1** an undertaker's establishment where corpses are prepared for funerals. **2** a place where non-church funeral services are conducted.

funerary / **fyoo**-nuh-ruh-ree / *adj.* of or used for burial or a funeral.

funereal / fyoo-**neer**-ree-uhl / *adj.* suitable for a funeral; dismal, dark. □ **funereally** *adv.*

fungal *adj.* **1** of, relating to, or caused by a fungus (*a fungal infection*). **2** like a fungus.

fungicide / **fung**-guh-suyd / *n.* a fungus-destroying substance. □ **fungicidal** *adj.*

fungoid / **fung**-goid / *adj.* like a fungus. • *n.* a fungoid plant.

fungous / **fung**-guhs / *adj.* **1** = FUNGAL. **2** springing up like a mushroom; transitory.

fungus *n.* (*pl.* **fungi** / **fung**-gee, -guy / *or* **funguses**) a plant without leaves, flowers, or green colouring matter, growing on other plants or on decaying matter and including mushrooms, toadstools, and moulds.

funicular / fuh-**nik**-yuh-luh / *n.* a cable railway with ascending and descending cars counter-balancing each other.

funk *n. colloq.* **1** fear. **2** a coward. **3** funky music. • *v. colloq.* show fear; fear and shirk.

funky *adj. colloq.* **1** (of jazz or rock) earthy, soulful, emotional, with a heavy rhythm. **2** exciting, excellent.

funnel *n.* **1** a tube or pipe, wide at the top and narrow at the bottom, for pouring liquids, powders, etc. into small openings. **2** a metal chimney on a steam engine or steamship. • *v.* (**funnelled**, **funnelling**) move through a funnel or a narrowing space.

funnel-web *n.* (in full **funnel-web spider**) a large, black, aggressive, highly venomous spider of eastern Australia with a potentially fatal bite: it builds a funnel-shaped web.

funny *adj.* (**funnier**, **funniest**) **1** causing amusement. **2** puzzling, hard to account for. **3** *colloq.* slightly unwell or insane. **4** *colloq.* impertinent (*don't be funny!*). • *n. colloq.* a joke (*he's cracked a funny*). □ **funny business** trickery; dubious doings. □□ **funnily** *adv.* **funniness** *n.*

funnybone *n.* part of the elbow over which a very sensitive nerve passes.

fur *n.* **1** the short fine soft hair covering the bodies of certain animals. **2** animal skin with the fur on it, esp. when used for making or trimming clothes. **3** fabric imitating this. **4** a coat or other garment of real or imitation fur. **5** a coating formed on a sick or unhealthy person's tongue. **6** the coating formed by hard water on the inside of a kettle or pipes. • *v.* (**furred**, **furring**) cover or become covered with fur.

furbelows *n.pl.* showy trimmings (*frills and furbelows*).

furbish *v.* polish, clean or renovate.

furcate / **fer**-kayt / *adj.* forked, branched. • *v.* fork, divide. □ **furcation** *n.*

Furies, the / **fyoo**-reez / *Gk myth.* the spirits of punishment, often represented as three goddesses (Alecto, Megaera, and Tisiphone) with hair composed of snakes.

furious *adj.* **1** full of anger. **2** violent, intense (*a furious pace*). □ **furiously** *adv.*

furl *v.* (**furled**, **furling**) roll up and fasten (a sail, flag, or umbrella).

furlong *n.* (in the imperial system) one-eighth of a mile, 220 yards (201.168 m).

furlough / **fer**-loh / *n.* leave of absence, esp. military.

furnace *n.* **1** an enclosed structure for intense heating by fire, esp. of metals or water. **2** a very hot place (*this room's a furnace*).

Furneaux Group / **fer**-noh / a group of islands extending over 100 km north–south in eastern Bass Strait, including Flinders and Cape Barren Islands.

furnish

furnish v. **1** equip (a room or house etc.) with furniture. **2** (often foll. by *with*) provide or supply.
furnished adj. (also **fully furnished**) (of a house etc.) let with furniture.
furnishings n.pl. furniture and fitments, curtains, etc. in a room or house.
furniture n. **1** the movable articles (such as tables, chairs, beds) needed in a room or house etc. **2** a ship's equipment. **3** accessories, e.g. the handles and lock on a door.
furore / fyoo-raw, fyoo-**raw**-ree / n. **1** uproar; fury. **2** a wave of enthusiastic admiration; a craze.
furph n. Aust. colloq. = FURPHY.
Furphy, Joseph (1843–1912), Australian writer, farmer, bullock driver, and iron foundry worker. He wrote under the pseudonym *Tom Collins* which was at the time a synonym for an absurd rumour or a rumour-monger. (Coincidentally, his own name came to mean the same thing because of his brother John's water carts: *see* FURPHY.)
furphy n. (pl. **furphies**) *Aust.* **1** a false report or rumour. **2** an absurd story. • adj. (**furphier**, **furphiest**) absurdly false, unbelievable (*that's the furphiest bit of news I ever heard*). (¶ From the water and sanitary *Furphy* carts (centres of gossip for troops during the First World War) manufactured by the Australian firm J(ohn) Furphy & Sons.)
furrier / **fu**-ree-uh / n. a person who deals in furs or fur clothes or who dresses furs.
furrow n. **1** a long cut in the ground made by a plough or other implement. **2** a groove resembling this; a deep wrinkle in the skin. • v. plough; make furrows in.
furry / **fer**-ree / adj. (**furrier**, **furriest**) **1** like fur. **2** covered with fur.
further adv. (also **farther**) **1** more far in space or time (*unsafe to proceed any further*). **2** at a greater distance (*nothing was further from my mind*). **3** to a greater extent, more (*shall enquire further*). **4** in addition (*I may add further that...*). • adj. (also **farther**) **1** more distant or advanced (*on the further shore*). **2** more, additional (*further details*). • v. help the progress of (*further someone's interests*). ❏ **further education** education beyond secondary school.

■ **Usage** The form *farther* is used esp. with reference to physical distance, although *further* is preferred by many people even in this sense.

furtherance n. the furthering of someone's interests etc.
furthermore adv. in addition, moreover.
furthermost adj. most distant.
furthest (also **farthest**) adj. most distant. • adv. to or at the greatest distance.

■ **Usage** The form *farthest* is used esp. with reference to physical distance, although *furthest* is preferred by many people even in this sense.

future

furtive adj. sly, stealthy. ❏ **furtively** adv. **furtiveness** n.
fury n. **1** wild anger; a fit of rage. **2** violence of the weather, a disease, etc. (*the storm's fury*). **3** a violently angry person, esp. a woman.
fuse¹ n. (in an electric circuit) (also **safety fuse**) a short piece of wire designed to melt and break the circuit if the current exceeds a safe level. • v. **1** blend or amalgamate (metals, living bones, institutions, etc.) into a whole. **2** fit (a circuit or appliance) with a fuse. **3** cease or cause to cease functioning through the melting of a fuse. ❏ **fuse box** a box containing the fuses of an electrical system.
fuse² n. (also **fuze**) a length of easily burnt material for igniting a bomb or an explosive charge. • v. fit a fuse to.
fuselage / **fyoo**-zuh-lah*zh* / n. the body of an aeroplane.
fusible adj. able to be fused. ❏ **fusibility** n.
fusil / **fyoo**-zuhl / n. *hist.* a light musket.
fusiliers / fyoo-zuh-**leerz** / n.pl. any of several Brit. infantry regiments formerly armed with fusils.
fusillade / fyoo-zuh-**layd** / n. **1** a continuous firing of guns. **2** a great outburst of questions, criticism, etc.
fusion / **fyoo**-*zh*uhn / n. **1** fusing, the blending or uniting of different things into a whole. **2** the union of atomic nuclei to form a heavier nucleus, usu. with release of energy.
fuss n. **1** unnecessary excitement or activity. **2** a display of worry about something unimportant. **3** a vigorous protest or dispute. • v. make a fuss; bother (a person) with unimportant matters or by fussing. ❏ **fusser** n.
fussed adj. worried, concerned, bothered (*I can't be fussed*).
fusspot n. colloq. a person who fusses habitually.
fussy adj. (**fussier**, **fussiest**) **1** often fussing. **2** fastidious. **3** full of unnecessary detail or decoration. ❏ **fussily** adv. **fussiness** n.
fustian n. **1** a thick twilled cotton (usu. dark) cloth. **2** pompous language.
fusty adj. (**fustier**, **fustiest**) **1** musty, stuffy. **2** old-fashioned in ideas etc. ❏ **fustiness** n.
futile / **fyoo**-tuyl / adj. producing no result, useless. ❏ **futility** / fyoo-**til**-uh-tee / n.
futon / **foo**-ton / n. a Japanese quilted mattress used as a bed; this with a frame of wooden slats.
futsal / **fuut**-suhl / n. indoor soccer. (¶ Blend of Spanish *fútbol* 'football' (i.e. soccer) and *sala* 'salon, indoor room'.)
future adj. belonging or referring to the time coming after the present; *Grammar* (of a tense) describing an event yet to happen. • n. **1** the time to come. **2** future events. **3** the future condition of a person, country, etc. **4** prospect of success etc. (*there's no future in it*). **5** *Grammar* future tense. **6** (**futures**) *Stock Exchange* goods, stocks, etc. sold for future delivery; the contracts for these.

☐ **future perfect** *Grammar* a tense giving the sense 'will have done'. **future shock** a state of distress or disorientation arising from a person's inability to cope with rapid technological or social change.

futurism *n.* an artistic movement launched in Italy in 1909 that departed from traditional forms so as to express movement, growth, and celebration of new technology. ☐ **futurist** *n.*

futuristic / fyoo-chuh-**ris**-tik / *adj.* **1** looking suitable for the future, not traditional; ultramodern. **2** of futurism.

futurity / fyoo-**choo**-ruh-tee / *n. literary* **1** future time. **2** (in *singular* or *plural*) future events.

futurology *n.* the forecasting of the future, esp. from present trends in society.

fuze alternative spelling of FUSE[2].

fuzz *n.* **1** fluff. **2** something fluffy or frizzed, e.g. hair. **3** (**the fuzz**) *colloq.* the police. **4** *colloq.* a police officer. **5** *colloq.* a haze, a blur.

fuzzy *adj.* (**fuzzier**, **fuzziest**) **1** like fuzz; covered with fuzz. **2** frizzy. **3** blurred, indistinct. ☐ **fuzzily** *adv.* **fuzziness** *n.*

fuzzy wuzzy *n. Aust. colloq.* a New Guinean. ☐ **fuzzy-wuzzy angel** *hist.* any New Guinean who helped Australian service personnel (esp. the wounded) during the Second World War.

Fysh, Sir (Wilmot) Hudson (1895–1974), Australian pioneer airman, co-founder of Qantas in 1920, writer and historian.

G

G¹ *n.* (*pl.* **Gs** or **G's**) *Music* the fifth note of the scale of C major.

G² *abbr.* (also **G.**) **1** gauss. **2** giga-. **3** gravitational constant.

g *abbr.* (also **g.**) **1** gram(s). **2** gravity; the acceleration due to this.

G7 *see* GROUP OF SEVEN.

Ga *symbol* gallium.

gab *colloq. n.* **1** talk, idle chitchat. **2** fast-talking, smooth (perhaps suspicious) eloquence (*he has the gift of the gab*). • *v.* talk idly, chitchat.

gabardine alternative spelling of GABERDINE.

Gabba (preceded by **the**) *abbr. colloq.* the Queensland Cricket Association ground at Woolloongabba, Brisbane.

gabble *v.* talk quickly and indistinctly. • *n.* fast unintelligible talk. ☐ **gabbler** *n.*

gaberdine / **gab**-uh-deen / *n.* (also **gabardine**) **1** a strong fabric woven in a twill pattern. **2** a raincoat etc. made of this.

gabfest *n.* a lengthy discussion, conference, etc., at which much is said but little is achieved.

Gabi-gabi / **gu**-bee-gu-bee / *n.* an Aboriginal language of south-eastern Qld, north of Brisbane.

gable *n.* the triangular upper part of an outside wall at the end of a ridged roof. ☐ **gabled** *adj.*

Gabon / guh-**bon** / a republic on the west coast of Africa. ☐ **Gabonese** / gab-uh-**neez** / *adj.* & *n.* (*pl.* **Gabonese**).

Gaborone / gab-uh-**roh**-nee / the capital of Botswana.

Gabriel / **gay**-bree-uhl / (in the Bible) the archangel who foretold the birth of Jesus to the Virgin Mary (Luke 1:26–38).

gad *v.* (**gadded**, **gadding**) (usu. foll. by *about*) go about aimlessly or in search of pleasure.

gadabout *n.* a person who gads about.

Gadaffi / guh-**dah**-fee /, Muammar al- (1942–), head of the republic of Libya since 1970.

gadfly *n.* **1** a fly that bites horses and cattle. **2** a stingingly critical and/or irritating person.

gadget *n.* a small mechanical device or tool. ☐ **gadgetry** *n.*

gadolinium / gad-uh-**lin**-ee-uhm / *n.* a metallic element (symbol Gd) resembling steel in appearance.

Gael / gayl / *n.* **1** a Scots Celt. **2** a Gaelic-speaking Celt.

Gaelic / **gay**-lik / *n.* **1** (also / **gal**-ik /) the Celtic language of the Scots. **2** the Celtic language of the Irish. • *adj.* of or in Gaelic.

gaff *n.* **1** a stick with an iron hook for landing large fish caught with rod and line. **2** a barbed fishing spear. **3** the spar to which the head of a fore-and-aft sail is bent. • *v.* seize with a gaff (*gaffing a barramundi*). ☐ **blow the gaff** *colloq.* reveal a plot or secret.

gaffe *n.* a blunder; an indiscreet act or remark.

gaffer *n.* the chief electrician in a film or television production unit.

gag *n.* **1** something put into a person's mouth or tied across it to prevent speaking or crying out. **2** anything that prevents freedom of speech or of writing. **3** government closure of debate in parliament when opposition members wish the debate to be prolonged. **4** a joke or funny story, esp. as part of a comedian's act. • *v.* (**gagged**, **gagging**) **1** put a gag into or over the mouth of. **2** prevent from having freedom of speech or of writing (*we cannot gag the press*). **3** apply the gag in parliament. **4** retch or choke.

gaga / **gah**-gah / *adj. colloq.* **1** senile. **2** slightly crazed. **3** crazy (about), infatuated (*he's gone gaga over her*).

Gagarin / guh-**gah**-ruhn /, Yuri Alekseevich (1934–68), Russian cosmonaut, who in 1961 made the first manned space flight.

gage *n.* **1** a pledge, a thing given as security. **2** the symbol of a challenge to fight, esp. a glove thrown down.

gaggle *n.* **1** a flock of geese. **2** *colloq.* a disorderly group of people.

Gaia / **guy**-uh, **gay**-uh / *n.* the earth viewed as a vast self-regulating organism in which the whole range of living matter defines the conditions for its own survival, modifying the physical environment to suit its needs. ☐ **Gaia theory** the theory that this is how the global ecosystem functions. ☐ ☐ **Gaian** *adj.* & *n.* **Gaiaist** *adj.* (¶ *Gaia* the earth goddess, earth mother, in Greek mythology (the daughter of Chaos).)

gaiety *n.* **1** cheerfulness, a happy and light hearted manner. **2** merrymaking.

gai lum / **guy** lum / *n.* Chinese broccoli.

gaily *adv.* **1** in a cheerful light-hearted manner. **2** in bright colours (*gaily decorated*).

gain *v.* **1** obtain, esp. something desirable (*gain recognition; gained the advantage*). **2** make a profit (*gained $50 on the deal*). **3** achieve (*you will gain nothing by sulking*). **4** acquire gradually, become more of (*gained strength after illness*). **5** (of a clock etc.) become ahead of the correct time. **6** (often foll. by *on*) get nearer in racing or pursuit (*our horse was gaining on the favourite*). **7** reach (a desired place) (*gained the shore*). • *n.* **1** an increase in wealth or possessions. **2** an improvement, an increase in

gainful adj. profitable. ☐ **gainfully** adv.

gainsay v. (**gainsaid**, **gainsaying**) formal deny or contradict (there is no gainsaying it).

gait n. a manner of walking or running.

gala / **gah**-luh / n. a festive occasion (the Geelong gala). • adj. festive, celebratory (a gala occasion).

galactic / guh-**lak**-tik / adj. of a galaxy or galaxies.

galah / guh-**lah** / n. **1** a grey-backed, pink-breasted cockatoo occurring in most parts of Australia. **2** Aust. colloq. a fool, an idiot. ☐ **mad as a gum tree full of galahs** Aust. colloq. completely crazy. **make a proper galah of oneself** Aust. colloq. make a complete fool of oneself. (¶ Yuwaalaraay)

Galahad (in legends of King Arthur) a knight of immaculate purity, destined to retrieve the Holy Grail.

galangal / guh-**lang**-guhl / n. the aromatic rhizome of certain plants of the ginger family, used in Asian cooking.

galantine / **gal**-uhn-teen / n. white meat or fish boned and spiced and cooked in the form of a roll, served cold.

Galapagos Islands / guh-**lap**-uh-guhs / a group of islands in the Pacific on the Equator, west of Ecuador (to which they belong). The abundant and unique wildlife on the islands includes giant tortoises, flightless cormorants, etc. The observations made here by Charles Darwin in 1835 helped him to form his theory of natural selection.

galaxias / guh-**lak**-see-uhs / n. (pl. same) a small freshwater Australian fish.

galaxy / **gal**-uhk-see / n. **1** any of the large independent systems of stars existing in space. **2** a brilliant company (a galaxy of talent). **3** (**the Galaxy**) the galaxy containing the Earth. **4** (**the Galaxy**) the Milky Way.

gale n. **1** a very strong wind (gale-force winds). **2** a noisy outburst (gales of laughter).

Galilean adj. of Galileo. ☐ **Galilean satellites** the four largest moons of Jupiter, discovered by Galileo in 1610.

Galilee the northern part of ancient Palestine west of the Jordan, now in Israel. ☐ **Sea of Galilee** (also called **Lake Tiberias**) an inland lake in northern Israel. ☐☐ **Galilean** adj. & n.

Galileo Galilei / gal-uh-**lay**-oh gal-uh-**lay**-ee / (1564–1642), Italian astronomer and physicist, one of the founders of modern science.

gall¹ / gawl / n. **1** bile. **2** bitterness of feeling. **3** impudence. **4** rancour. ☐ **gall bladder** an organ attached to the liver, storing and releasing bile.

gall² / gawl / n. **1** a sore made by chafing, esp. on the skin of an animal. **2** a place rubbed bare. • v. **1** rub and make sore. **2** vex or humiliate.

gall³ / gawl / n. an abnormal growth produced by insects, bacteria, etc. on plants and trees, esp. on eucalypts and wattles.

gallant / **gal**-uhnt / adj. **1** brave. **2** fine, stately (our gallant ship). **3** / guh-**lant** / chivalrous, very attentive to women. • n. / guh-**lant** / a ladies' man. ☐ **gallantly** adv.

gallantry n. (pl. **gallantries**) **1** bravery. **2** devotion to women. **3** a chivalrous or polite action or speech.

galleon / **gal**-ee-uhn / n. a large Spanish sailing ship used in the 15th–17th centuries.

galleria / gal-uh-**ree**-uh / n. a collection of small shops under one roof.

gallery n. **1** a room or building for showing works of art. **2** a balcony, esp. in a church or hall (minstrels' gallery). **3** the highest balcony in a theatre containing the cheapest seats; the audience seated there. **4** a covered walk partly open at the side; a colonnade. **5** a long room or passage, esp. one used for a special purpose (a shooting gallery). **6** the spectators at a golf match. **7** an underground passage in a mine. ☐ **play to the gallery** try to win favour by appealing to the taste of the general public.

Gallery Hill a granite hill in the Pilbara area of WA on which are engraved thousands of figures, many of them ancient, many of them linking to form a series, a highly significant gallery of Aboriginal art. The figures include mythological beings such as the rainbow snake, animals, and above all humans, mostly depicted in the Gurangara style.

galley n. (pl. **galleys**) **1** a long low medieval ship, usu. rowed by slaves or criminals. **2** an ancient Greek or Roman warship propelled by oars. **3** the kitchen in a ship or aircraft. **4** an oblong tray for holding type for printing. ☐ **galley proof** a printed proof made from type set in a galley. **galley slave 1** hist. a slave chained and forced to row in a galley. **2** a drudge, one who is overworked.

Gallic / **gal**-ik / adj. **1** of ancient Gaul. **2** of France; typically French (Gallic wit).

gallinaceous / gal-uh-**nay**-shuhs / adj. of the group of birds that includes domestic poultry, pheasants, etc.

galling / **gaw**-ling / adj. vexing, humiliating.

Gallipoli / guh-**lip**-uh-lee / a peninsula on the European side of the Dardanelles, the scene of heavy fighting in 1915–16 during the First World War.

gallium n. a soft bluish-white metallic element (symbol Ga).

gallivant v. gad about, esp. with amorous pleasure in mind.

Gallo- / **ga**-loh / comb. form **1** French; French and. **2** Gaul (Gallo-Roman). (¶ Latin Gallus 'a Gaul'.)

gallon n. **1** a measure for liquids in the imperial system, = 8 pints (4.546 litres in Australia, or 3.785

gallop

litres in the USA). **2** (**gallons**) *colloq.* a large amount.

gallop *n.* **1** a horse's fastest pace, with all four feet off the ground simultaneously in each stride. **2** a ride at this pace. •*v.* (**galloped, galloping**) **1** go at a gallop, cause a horse to do this. **2** read, talk, etc. very fast. **3** progress rapidly (*galloping inflation*).

gallows *n.* **1** a framework with a suspended noose for the hanging of criminals. **2** (**the gallows**) execution by hanging. **3** *Aust.* the structure from which the carcase of a slaughtered beast is hung.

gallstone *n.* a small hard mass that sometimes forms in the gall bladder.

Gallup poll an opinion poll, used esp. to forecast how people will vote in an election. (¶ Named after G.H. Gallup (1901–84), American statistician who devised it.)

galore *adv.* in plenty (*whisky galore*).

■ Usage *Galore* always follows the noun, e.g. *parties galore, sales galore.*

galoshes *n.pl.* (also **goloshes**) overshoes, usu. made of rubber.

Galvani / gal-**vah**-nee /, Luigi (1737–98), Italian anatomist, pioneer of research into the electrical properties of living things. (¶ The words *galvanic, galvanise,* and *galvanometer* embody his name.)

galvanic / gal-**van**-ik / *adj.* **1** producing an electric current by chemical action (*a galvanic cell*); (of electricity) produced by chemical action. **2** sudden and remarkable (*had a galvanic effect*). **3** stimulating; full of energy. ☐ **galvanically** *adv.*

galvanise *v.* (also **-ize**) **1** rouse forcefully, esp. by shock or excitement (*was galvanised into action*). **2** stimulate by or as by electricity. **3** coat (iron) with zinc in order to protect it from rust. ☐ **galvanised iron** zinc-coated sheets of corrugated iron used as a roofing, fencing, etc. material. ☐☐ **galvanisation** *n.*

galvanometer / gal-vuh-**nom**-uh-tuh / *n.* an instrument for detecting and measuring small electric currents.

galvo *n. Aust. colloq.* = GALVANISED IRON.

Gama / **gah**-muh /, Vasco da (*c.*1469–1524), Portuguese explorer, the first European to sail round the Cape of Good Hope.

Gambia (also **the Gambia**) a republic in West Africa. ☐ **Gambian** *adj.* & *n.*

Gambier, Mount an extinct volcano in southeastern SA. Its crater contains four lakes, one of which, Blue Lake, is a popular tourist attraction.

gambit *n.* **1** an opening sequence of moves in chess in which a player deliberately sacrifices a pawn or piece in order to gain an advantage. **2** an opening move in a discussion etc. **3** an action or statement intended to secure some advantage.

gamble *v.* **1** play games of chance for money. **2** stake or risk money etc. in the hope of great gain.

gammon

3 (foll. by *on*) stake one's hopes (*gambled on its being a fine day*). •*n.* **1** a spell of gambling. **2** a risky attempt or undertaking. ☐ **gambler** *n.*

gamboge / gam-**bohj** / *n.* a gum resin used as a yellow pigment and as a purgative.

gambol *v.* (**gambolled, gambolling**) jump or skip about in play. •*n.* a gambolling movement; a frolic, a caper.

game[1] *n.* **1** a form of play or sport, esp. one with rules. **2** a single section forming a scoring unit in some games (e.g. in tennis or bridge). **3** a scheme or plan, a trick (*so that's his little game!*). **4** a piece of fun, a jest (*didn't mean to upset you—it was only a game*). **5** a type of activity or business (*she has been in the antiques game a long time*). **6** (**games**) a series of athletics or sports contests (*the Olympic Games*). **7** wild animals or birds hunted for sport or food. **8** their flesh as food. •*v.* gamble for money stakes. •*adj.* **1** brave. **2** having spirit or energy (*are you game for a lark?*). ☐ **easy game** easily hoodwinked or seduced. **game point** the stage in a game when one side will win if it gains the next point. **game theory** the branch of mathematics that deals with the selection of best strategies for participants in competitive situations where the outcome of a person's choice of action depends critically on the actions of other players. **give the game away** reveal a secret or scheme. **lift one's game** perform better; try harder. **the game's up** the secret or deception is revealed. **the name of the game** the main point; the salient aim (*winning votes is the name of the game in politics*). ☐☐ **gamely** *adv.*

game[2] *adj.* lame (*a game leg*).

gamelan / **gam**-uh-lan / *n.* **1** the standard instrumental group of Indonesia, consisting of sets of tuned gongs and other percussion instruments as well as string and woodwind instruments. **2** a type of xylophone used in this group.

gamesmanship *n.* the art of winning contests by upsetting the confidence of one's opponent.

gamete / **gam**-eet / *n.* a sexual cell capable of fusing with another in reproduction. ☐ **gametic** / guh-**met**-ik / *adj.*

gamin / **gam**-uhn / *n.* **1** a street urchin. **2** a mischievous but likeable boy.

gamine / gam-**een** / *n.* **1** a female street urchin. **2** a mischievous but likeable girl who looks like a boy, a tomboy.

gaming *n.* **1** gambling. **2** taking part in a ROLE-PLAYING GAME.

gamma *n.* **1** the third letter of the Greek alphabet (Γ, γ). **2** a third-class mark in an examination etc. ☐ **gamma radiation** (*or* **rays**) X-rays of very short wavelength emitted by radioactive substances.

gammon[1] *n.* **1** the bottom piece of a flitch of bacon, including a hind leg. **2** cured or smoked ham.

gammon² / **gam**-uhn / *colloq. n.* humbug, deception. •*v.* **1 a** talk speciously. **b** pretend. **2** hoax, deceive.

■ **Usage** This word is archaic in standard Australian English, but was used in 19th-c. Australian pidgin English, and is used in Aboriginal English.

gammy *adj. colloq.* = GAME².

gamut / **gam**-uht / *n.* the whole series, range, or scope of anything (*the whole gamut of emotion*). ☐ **run the gamut of** experience or perform the complete range of.

Ganapati / gun-uh-**put**-ee / = GANESHA.

Ganay / **gu**-nuy / *n.* an Aboriginal language of a very large area of south-eastern Vic.

gander *n.* a male goose.

Gandhi¹ / **gahn**-dee /, Indira (1917–84), Indian stateswoman, prime minister 1966–77 and 1980–84. She was assassinated by her own Sikh bodyguards. Her son Rajiv (1944–91) was prime minister 1984–89. He was assassinated during the 1991 election campaign.

Gandhi² / **gahn**-dee /, Mahatma (original name: Mohandas Karamchand Gandhi) (1869–1948), Indian statesman who became the leader and symbol of the nationalist movement in opposition to British rule. He was assassinated by a Hindu following his agreement to the creation of the state of Pakistan for the Muslim minority.

Ganesha / guh-**nay**-shuh / (also **Ganapati**) an elephant-headed Hindu god, son of Siva and Parvati, worshipped as the remover of obstacles and as patron of learning.

gang *n.* **1** a band of people going about or working together, esp. for some antisocial or criminal purpose. **2** a group of friends who go about together. **3** a group of slaves or prisoners; a group of workers (*a road gang*). ☐ **gang-bang** *colloq.* (of several males) have sexual intercourse in turn with (one other person). **gang rape** the rape of one person by several people in succession. **gang up** *colloq.* **1** (often foll. by *with*) act together. **2** (foll. by *on*) combine in a group (against a person) (*they ganged up on him*). ☐☐ **ganger** *n.*

Ganges / **gan**-jeez / a river in the north of India, held sacred by Hindus, flowing from the Himalayas through Bangladesh to the Bay of Bengal.

gang-gang *n.* a grey cockatoo of south-eastern Australia, the male having an orange-red crest and head. (¶ Wiradhuri)

gangling *adj.* (of a person) tall, thin, and awkward-looking.

ganglion *n.* (*pl.* **ganglia** *or* **ganglions**) **1** a group of nerve cells from which nerve fibres radiate. **2** a cyst on a tendon sheath. ☐ **ganglionic** / gang-glee-**on**-ik / *adj.*

gangly *adj.* = GANGLING.

gangplank *n.* a movable plank used as a bridge for walking onto or off a boat, etc.

gangrene *n.* death and decay of body tissue, usu. caused by blockage of the blood supply. ☐ **gangrenous** / **gang**-gruh-nuhs / *adj.*

gangster *n.* a member of a gang of violent criminals.

gangway *n.* **1** a passage, esp. between rows of seats. **2** a movable bridge from a ship to the land; the opening in a ship's side into which this fits. •*interj.* make way!

ganja / **gun**-juh / *n.* marijuana.

gannet / **gan**-uht / *n.* any of various large diving sea birds, including the *Australian gannet*.

gantry *n.* a light bridge-like overhead framework for supporting a travelling crane, railway signals over several tracks, road signals, rocket-launching equipment, etc.

Ganymede / **gan**-ee-meed / *n.* **1** *Gk myth.* a Trojan youth who was so beautiful that Zeus (Jupiter) carried him off to be his cupbearer and lover. **2** the largest satellite of the planet Jupiter. **3** *colloq.* a good-looking young male homosexual.

gaol alternative spelling of JAIL.

gap *n.* **1** a break or opening in something continuous such as a hedge or fence. **2** a gorge or pass; a ravine. **3** an unfilled space or interval (*a gap between programs*). **4** something lacking (*a gap in one's education*). **5** a wide difference in ideas (*generation gap*). ☐ **gap insurance** *Aust.* private medical insurance taken to bridge the gap between the Medicare pay-out and the scheduled fee for hospital service by a doctor. ☐☐ **gappy** *adj.*

gape *v.* **1** open the mouth wide. **2** stare in surprise or wonder. **3** open or be open wide (*a gaping chasm*). •*n.* **1** an open-mouthed stare. **2** a rent or opening.

garage / **ga**-rah*zh*, guh-**rah***zh* / *n.* **1** a building in which to keep a motor vehicle or vehicles. **2** a commercial establishment where motor vehicles are repaired and serviced. **3** a roadside establishment selling petrol and oil etc. •*v.* put or keep in a garage. ☐ **garage sale** *US & Aust.* a sale of household goods, often held in the garage of a private house.

garam masala / ga-ruhm muh-**sah**-luh / *n.* a fragrant mixture of ground spices used in Indian cooking.

garb *n.* **1** clothing, esp. of a distinctive kind (*a man in clerical garb*). **2** external semblance; form. •*v.* clothe.

garbage *n.* **1** refuse, esp. kitchen waste. **2** *colloq.* nonsense. **3** *colloq.* trash, worthless stuff. ☐ **garbage man** *Aust.* a person employed to clear household refuse left outside for disposal.

garbanzo / gah-**ban**-zoh / *n.* chickpea.

garble *v.* **1** give a confused account of something, so that a message or story is distorted or misunderstood. **2** make a (usu. unfair) selection from (facts, statements, etc.). ☐☐ **garbler** *n.*

Garbo, Greta (original name: Greta Gustafsson) (1905–90), Swedish film actor.

garbo *n. Aust. colloq.* a garbage man.
garden *n.* **1** a piece of cultivated ground, esp. attached to a house. **2** (**gardens**) ornamental public grounds. • *v.* tend a garden. ☐ **lead up the garden path** entice, mislead deliberately.
gardener *n.* a person who tends a garden, either as a job or as a hobby.
gardenia / gar-**dee**-nyuh / *n.* a tree or shrub with large fragrant white flowers.
Garden State, the Victoria.
Gardiner, Frank (full name: Francis Christie Gardiner) (1830–?1903), Australian bushranger. He features in Australian ballads and was a model for a character in Boldrewood's novel *Robbery Under Arms* (1888).
Gardner, Wayne (Michael) (1959–), AM, Australian 500cc motorcyclist, world champion in 1987.
garfish *n.* (*pl.* **garfish** or **garfishes**) any of various fishes found in Australian waters and elsewhere, having a long spearlike snout.
gargantuan / gah-**gan**-choo-uhn / *adj.* gigantic.
gargle *v.* wash or rinse the inside of the throat with liquid held there by air breathed out from the lungs. • *n.* a liquid used for this.
gargoyle *n.* a grotesque carved face or figure, esp. as a gutter-spout carrying water clear of a wall.
garish / **gair**-rish, **gah**- / *adj.* excessively bright, gaudy, over-decorated. ☐ **garishly** *adv.*
Garland, Judy (original name: Frances Gumm) (1922–69), American film actor and singer.
garland *n.* a wreath of flowers etc. worn or hung as a decoration. • *v.* adorn with a garland or garlands.
garlic *n.* **1** an onion-like plant. **2** its bulbous root that has a strong taste and smell, used for flavouring. • *adj.* containing garlic (*garlic bread*). ☐ **garlicky** *adj.*
garment *n.* an article of clothing.
Garner, Helen (1942–), Australian writer and telescript writer. Her novel *Monkey Grip* (1977) was made into a film, and her book *The First Stone* (1995) aroused great controversy.
garner *v.* **1** collect. **2** store up. • *n. literary* a storehouse or granary.
garnet *n.* a semiprecious stone of deep transparent red.
garnish *v.* decorate (esp. food for the table). • *n.* something used for garnishing.
garotte alternative spelling of GARROTTE.
garret *n.* an attic.
Garrett, Peter (Robert) (1953–), lead-singer of the Australian pop and rock group Midnight Oil, political activist, anti-nuclear campaigner, a president of the Australian Conservation Foundation.
garrison *n.* **1** troops stationed in a town or fort to defend it (*a garrison town*). **2** the building or fort they occupy. • *v.* **1** place a garrison in. **2** occupy and defend (*troops garrisoned the town*).

garrotte / guh-**rot** / (also **garotte**) *v.* execute or kill by strangulation, esp. with a wire around the neck. • *n.* a device used for this.
garrulous / ga-ruh-luhs / *adj.* talkative. ☐ **garrulously** *adv.* **garrulousness** *n.* **garrulity** / guh-**roo**-luh-tee / *n.*
garter *n.* a band esp. of elastic worn round the leg to keep a stocking up. ☐ **garter stitch** rows of plain stitch in knitting.
garuda / guh-**roo**-duh / *n.* **1** a fabulous, partly human bird of Indian myth. **2** this as the national emblem of Indonesia (hence *Garuda Airline*).
gas *n.* (*pl.* **gases**) **1** an airlike substance with particles that can move freely, i.e. not a liquid or solid. **2** any of the gases or mixtures of gases used for lighting, heating, or cooking (*gas cooker; gas fire*). **3** poisonous gas used to disable an enemy in war. **4** nitrous oxide or other gas used as an anaesthetic. **5** *colloq.* idle talk. **6** *colloq.* something wonderful, successful (*the barbie was a gas*). • *adj. colloq.* excellent (*that's a gas notion*). • *v.* (**gassed**, **gassing**) **1** expose to gas, poison or overcome by gas. **2** *colloq.* talk idly for a long time. **3** boast. ☐ **gas chamber** a room that can be filled with poisonous gas to kill animals or prisoners. **gas-fired** heated by burning gas. **gas mask** a device worn over the face to protect the wearer against poisonous gas. **gas permeable** (esp. of contact lenses) capable of penetration by gases.
gasbag *n. colloq.* **1** a person who talks too much. **2** an empty boaster.
gaseous / **gas**-ee-uhs / *adj.* of or like a gas.
gash *n.* a long deep slash, cut, or wound. • *v.* make a gash in; cut.
gasket *n.* a flat sheet or ring of rubber or other soft material used for sealing a joint between metal surfaces to prevent gas, steam, or liquid from entering or escaping. ☐ **blow a gasket** *colloq.* explode with anger.
Gasnier, Reg(inald William) (1939–), AM, Australian Rugby League player, the youngest ever to captain an Australian test team (1962, aged 23).
gasoline *n.* (also **gasolene**) *US* petrol.
gasometer / ga-**som**-uh-tuh / *n.* a large tank in which gas is stored and from which it is distributed through pipes.
gasp *v.* **1** struggle for breath with the mouth open. **2** draw in the breath sharply in astonishment etc. **3** speak in a breathless way. **4** be filled with desire for, crave (*gasping for a drink*). • *n.* a breath drawn in sharply.
gassy *adj.* **1** of or like a gas. **2** full of gas.
gastric *adj.* of the stomach. ☐ **gastric brooding frog** (also **platypus frog**) a rare Qld frog which swallows its fertilised eggs, turns its stomach into a uterus, and spits the fully formed young out of its mouth. **gastric flu** sickness and diarrhoea of unknown cause. **gastric juice** digestive fluid secreted by the stomach.
gastritis / gas-**truy**-tuhs / *n.* inflammation of the stomach.

gastro / **gas**-troh / *n. Aust. colloq.* gastroenteritis.
gastroenteritis / gas-troh-en-tuh-**ruy**-tuhs / *n.* inflammation of the stomach and intestines.
gastronome / **gas**-truh-nohm / *n.* a gourmet.
gastronomy / gas-**tron**-uh-mee / *n.* the science or art of good eating and drinking. ☐ **gastronomic** / gas-truh-**nom**-ik / *adj.*
gastropod / **gas**-truh-pod / *n.* a mollusc (such as a snail or limpet) that moves by means of a muscular organ on its ventral surface.
gastroscope / **gas**-truh-skohp / *n.* an instrument that can be passed down the throat for looking inside the stomach.
gasworks *n.* a place where gas for lighting and heating is manufactured.
gate *n.* **1** a movable barrier, usu. on hinges, serving as a door in a wall or fence, or regulating the passage of water etc. **2** a means of entrance or exit. **3** a numbered place of access to aircraft at an airport. **4** an arrangement of slots controlling the movement of a gear lever in a motor vehicle. **5** an electrical device that controls the passage of electrical signals; (in computers) a circuit with one output that is activated only by a combination of input signals. **6 a** the number of spectators entering by payment at the gates of a sports ground etc. **b** (in full **gate money**) the amount of money taken thus. • *v.* confine to college or school as a punishment.
-gate *comb. form* describing scandals comparable in some way to the Watergate scandal of 1972 (*Dianagate*; *Irangate*).
gateau / **gat**-oh / *n.* (*pl.* **gateaus** or **gateaux** / gat-ohz /) a large rich cake filled with cream etc.
gatecrash *v.* go to a private party etc. without being invited. ☐ **gatecrasher** *n.*
Gates, Bill (full name: William Henry Gates) (1955–), American computer entrepreneur, co-founder of the software company Microsoft.
gateway *n.* **1** an opening or structure framing a gate. **2** any means of access (*Wodonga, the gateway to Victoria*; *the gateway to success*). **3** *Computing* a device that interconnects two networks and whose presence is visible to users.
gather *v.* **1** bring or come together; accumulate (*gathering swallows twitter in the skies*). **2** pick or collect, esp. as harvest (*gather the crop*). **3** increase gradually (*gather speed*). **4** understand or conclude (*I gather that the Premier is set to resign*). **5** collect (*gather dust*). **6** draw (parts) together (*his brow was gathered in thought*). **7** come to a head (*there's a storm gathering*). **8** pull fabric into gathers (*a gathered skirt*). **9** (of a sore) swell up and form pus. • *n.* a fold or pleat. ☐ **gather dust** be neglected or unused. **gather up** bring together; pick up from the ground; draw into a small compass.
gathering *n.* **1** an assembly of people. **2** an inflamed swelling with pus in it.
GATT *abbr.* General Agreement on Tariffs and Trade; a treaty to which more than 100 countries were parties, to promote trade and economic development. GATT was superseded in 1994 by WTO.
gauche / gohsh / *adj.* **1** socially awkward. **2** tactless.
gaucherie / **goh**-shuh-ree / *n.* gauche manners; a gauche action.
gaucho / **gow**-choh / *n.* (*pl.* **gauchos**) a cowboy from the South American pampas.
Gaudron, Mary Genevieve (1943–), the first woman to become a justice of the High Court of Australia.
gaudy *adj.* (**gaudier**, **gaudiest**) showy or bright in a tasteless way. ☐ **gaudily** *adv.* **gaudiness** *n.*
gauge / gayj / *n.* **1** a standard measure of contents, fineness of textiles, thickness of sheet metal, or diameter of bullets. **2** the distance between pairs of rails or between opposite wheels. **3** an instrument used for measuring, marked with regular divisions or units of measurement. **4** capacity, extent. **5** a means of estimating something; a criterion. • *v.* **1** measure exactly. **2** estimate, form a judgment of (*gauge the mood of the electorate*).
Gauguin / goh-**gan** /, Paul (1848–1903), French painter.
Gaul an ancient region of Europe corresponding roughly to modern France and Belgium. • *n.* a native or inhabitant of Gaul.
Gaulle / gawl /, Charles Joseph de (1890–1970), French general and statesman, president of the French Republic 1959–69.
gaunt *adj.* **1** lean and haggard. **2** grim or desolate-looking. ☐ **gauntness** *n.*
gauntlet *n.* **1** a glove with a wide cuff covering the wrist. **2** a glove with metal plates worn by soldiers in the Middle Ages. ☐ **run the gauntlet** be exposed to continuous severe criticism or risk. (¶ The phrase is derived from a former military and naval punishment in which the victim was made to pass between two rows of men who struck him as he passed.) **throw down** (*or* **take up**) **the gauntlet** issue (or accept) a challenge.
Gaurna / **gowrh**-nu / *n.* an Aboriginal language of a vast area of south-eastern SA, including what is now Adelaide (and hence referred to as 'the Adelaide language').
gauss / gows / *n.* (*pl.* **gauss**) a unit of magnetic flux density. (¶ Named after K.F. Gauss (1777–1855), German mathematician, astronomer, and physicist.)
Gautama / **gow**-tuh-muh / the family name of the Buddha.
gauze / gawz / *n.* **1** thin transparent woven material of silk or cotton etc. **2** fine wire mesh. ☐ **gauzy** *adj.*
gave *see* GIVE.
gavel / **gav**-uhl / *n.* a hammer used by an auctioneer, chairman, or judge to call for attention or order.
gavotte / guh-**vot** / *n.* an old French dance.

gawk *v. colloq.* stare stupidly or obtrusively. •*n.* an awkward or bashful person.

gawky *adj.* awkward and ungainly. ☐ **gawkiness** *n.*

Gawler Ranges a range of sparsely covered hills, rising about 150 metres and extending for about 180 km across the north of Eyre Peninsula, SA.

gawp *v. colloq.* gawk.

gay *adj.* **1** homosexual (*he is gay*). **2** intended for or used by homosexuals (*a gay bar*). **3** light-hearted, cheerful. **4** brightly coloured. **5** careless, thoughtless (*gay abandon*). •*n.* a homosexual (esp. male) (*many gays take pride in their gayness*). ☐ **gay lib** (in full **gay liberation**) a social and political movement for the liberation of homo-sexuals from social stigma and discrimination. ☐☐ **gayness** *n.*

■ Usage Senses 3, 4, and 5 of the adjective have now been superseded almost entirely by senses 1 and 2. In many instances it is restricted in application to male homosexuals and contrasted with *lesbian* when discussing homosexuals as a group, e.g. *The message from gays and lesbians living in rural Australia was one of a sense of isolation.*

Gay and Lesbian Mardi Gras an annual celebration of gayness held in Sydney. It features exhibitions of art etc. and culminates in a televised parade in which Australian and overseas organisations etc. participate, the largest event of its kind in the world.

Gaza Strip / **gah**-zuh / a strip of coastal territory on the SE Mediterranean, including the town of Gaza.

Gaze, Andrew (Barry Casson) (1965–), Australian basketballer.

gaze *v.* look long and steadily. •*n.* a long steady look.

gazebo / guh-**zee**-boh / *n.* (*pl.* **gazebos**) a free-standing garden structure, e.g. a summer-house, affording an enjoyable view.

gazelle *n.* a small graceful Asian or African antelope.

gazette *n.* the title of certain newspapers, or of official journals that contain public notices and lists of government appointments. •*v.* (**gazetted**, **gazetting**) announce or name in an official gazette.

gazetteer / gaz-uh-**teer** / *n.* an index of geographical names and statistics.

gazpacho / guhz-**pah**-choh / *n.* a cold Spanish soup with uncooked tomato, onion, cucumber, garlic, etc., as well as oil and vinegar.

gazump *v. colloq.* **1** raise the price of a property after accepting an offer from (a buyer). **2** swindle.

gazunder *v. colloq.* (of a buyer) lower the amount of an offer made to (the seller) for a property, esp. just before exchange of contracts.

Gd *symbol* gadolinium.

g'day / guh-**day** / *interj. Aust.* = GOOD DAY.

GDP *abbr.* gross domestic product.

Ge *symbol* germanium.

gear *n.* **1** (often as **gears**) a set of toothed wheels working together in a machine to transmit rotary motion, esp. those connecting the engine of a motor vehicle to the road wheels. **2** a particular setting of these (*first gear*). **3** apparatus or equipment (*aircraft landing gear*). **4** personal belongings, esp. movable items. **5** *colloq.* clothes. •*v.* **1** provide with or connect by gears. **2** put in gear. **3** (foll. by *to*) adjust or adapt (*a factory geared to the export trade*). **4** (foll. by *up*) get ready (*the resort is gearing up for the tourist season*).

gearbox *n.* a case enclosing a gear mechanism.

gearing *n.* a set or arrangement of gears.

gearstick *n.* (also **gearshift**, **gear lever**) a lever used to engage or change gear.

gecko / **gek**-oh / *n.* (*pl.* **geckos**) a small lizard frequenting houses in warm climates, able to climb walls by the adhesive pads on its toes.

geebung / **jee**-bung / *n.* **1** the edible fruit of any of several Australian shrubs or small trees of the genus *Persoonia*. **2** this shrub or tree. (¶ Dharuk)

geek / geek / *n. colloq.* **1** *Aust.* a look (*take a geek at that!*). **2** a dull or socially inept person. **3** a computer fanatic.

Geelong / juh-**long** / the largest provincial city in Vic., situated on Corio Bay 75 km south-west of Melbourne.

geese *see* GOOSE.

geez / jeez / *interj.* an expression of surprise etc. (¶ Probably an abbreviation of *Jesus*.)

geezer / **gee**-zuh / *n. colloq.* **1** a person, a bloke. **2** a peculiar person. **3** an old man.

Gehenna / guh-**hen**-uh / (in Judaism and the New Testament) a name for hell as a place of fiery torment for the wicked.

Geiger counter / **guy**-guh / *n.* a device for detecting and measuring radioactivity. (¶ Named after H.J.W. Geiger (1882–1945), German nuclear physicist, who developed the first device of this kind.)

geisha / **gay**-shuh, gee- / *n.* a Japanese hostess trained to entertain men by dancing and singing.

gel / jel / *n.* **1** a semi-solid jelly-like colloid. **2** a jelly-like substance used for setting the hair. **3** a semi-liquid soap for use in the shower. •*v.* (**gelled**, **gelling**) **1** form a gel. **2** use gel (in hair) to create a hairdo. **3** = JELL 2.

gelatine *n.* (also **gelatin**) a clear tasteless substance made by boiling the bones, skins, and connective tissue of animals, used in foods, medicine, and photographic film.

gelatinise / juh-**lat**-uh-nuyz / *v.* (also -**ize**) make or become gelatinous. ☐ **gelatinisation** *n.*

gelatinous / juh-**lat**-uh-nuhs / *adj.* of or like gelatine, jelly-like.

gelato / juh-**lah**-toh / n. (pl. **gelati** or **gelatos**) a kind of Italian ice cream made with water (sometimes with milk).

■ **Usage** The Italian plural *gelati* is often treated as a singular in Australian usage and given a new plural *gelatis*.

geld / geld / v. castrate (an animal).

gelding n. a gelded animal, esp. a horse.

gelignite / **jel**-ig-nuyt / n. an explosive containing nitroglycerine.

gelled adj. (of hair) set with GEL (*boys with hair gelled in spikes*).

gem n. **1** a precious stone, esp. when cut and polished. **2** something valued because of its excellence or beauty (*the gem of the collection*).

gemfish n. a popular food fish, found off the coast of NSW and Vic. Also called *hake*.

geminate / **jem**-uh-nayt / v. **1** double, repeat. **2** arrange in pairs. • adj. / **jem**-uh-nuht / combined in pairs. ☐ **gemination** n.

Gemini / **jem**-uh-nuy / the third sign of the zodiac, the Twins. ☐ **Geminian** adj. & n.

gemma / **jem**-uh / (pl. **gemmae** / **jem**-ee /) a small cellular body, in plants such as mosses, that separates from the mother-plant and starts a new one.

gemmation / juh-**may**-shuhn / n. reproduction by gemmae.

gemstone n. a precious stone used as a gem.

gen / jen / n. colloq. information. • v. (**gen up**) (**genned**, **genning**) colloq. gain information; give information to.

gendarme / **zhon**-dahm / n. a French police officer.

gender n. **1** the class in which a noun is placed in grammatical grouping in certain languages, in particular masculine, feminine, or neuter. **2** a person's sex. ☐ **gender gap** the purported divergence between males and females in customs, attitudes, patterns of behaviour, etc.

gene / jeen / n. each of the factors controlling heredity, carried by a chromosome. ☐ **gene therapy** the introduction of normal genes into cells in place of defective or missing ones in order to correct genetic disorders.

genealogy / jee-nee-**al**-uh-jee / n. **1** an account of descent from an ancestor given by listing the intermediate persons; pedigree. **2** the science or study of family pedigrees. **3** an organism's line of development from earlier forms. ☐ **genealogical** / jee-nee-uh-**loj**-i-kuhl / adj. **genealogist** n.

genera see GENUS.

general adj. **1** of or affecting all or nearly all; not partial, local, or particular. **2** involving various kinds, not specialised (*a general education*). **3** involving only main features, not detailed or specific (*spoke only in general terms*). **4** chief, head (*the general manager*). • n. **1** an army officer ranking below a field marshal. **2** a lieutenant general or major-general. **3** the chief of the Jesuits or other religious order. ☐ **general anaesthetic** one affecting the whole body, usu. with loss of consciousness. **general election** an election for representatives in Parliament from the whole country. **general knowledge** knowledge of a wide variety of subjects. **general meeting** one open to all members. **general practitioner** a community doctor who treats cases of all kinds in the first instance (as opposed to a specialist). **general store** *Aust.* a shop which stocks a wide range of miscellaneous goods, esp. in a country town. **general strike** a simultaneous strike by workers in all or most trades and industries. **in general 1** as a normal rule; usually. **2** for the most part.

General Australian the pronunciation of Australian English used by the majority of Australians.

generalise v. (also **-ize**) **1** draw a general conclusion from particular instances. **2** speak in general terms, use generalities. **3** bring into general use. ☐ **generalisation** n.

generality / je-nuh-**ral**-uh-tee / n. **1** being general. **2** a general statement or rule. **3** general applicability. **4** lack of detail. **5** (foll. by *of*) the main body or a majority (*the generality of Australians favour a republic.*)

generally adv. **1** usually; as a general rule. **2** widely, for the most part (*the plan was generally welcomed*). **3** in a general sense, without regard to details (*speaking generally*).

generate v. bring into existence; produce.

generation n. **1** generating; being generated. **2** a single stage in descent or pedigree, for example, children, parents, or grandparents. **3** a stage in an immigrant family's lineage (*first generation Australian*). **4** all people born about the same time and therefore of the same age. **5** the average period (regarded as about 30 years) in which children grow up and take the former place of their parents. **6** (of machinery etc.) a set of models at one stage of development (*fourth-generation computers*). **7** the production, esp. of electricity. **8** procreation. ☐ **generation gap** lack of understanding between people of different generations.

Generation X n. the group of young adults who were born in the mid 1960s to the mid 1970s (after the baby boomers), typically perceived to be disaffected and directionless.

generative adj. **1** of procreation. **2** productive.

generator n. **1** an apparatus for producing gases, steam, etc. **2** a machine for converting mechanical energy into electricity.

generic / juh-**ne**-rik / adj. **1** characteristic of or relating to a class; general, not specific or special. **2** characteristic of or belonging to a genus. **3** (of e.g. supermarket goods) having no brand name. • n. such a product (in e.g. a supermarket) sold under the name of the product itself (e.g. coffee) and not under a brand name. ☐ **generically** adv.

generous *adj.* **1** giving or ready to give freely, free from meanness or prejudice. **2** given freely; plentiful (*a generous gift; a generous portion*). □ **generously** *adv.* **generosity** *n.*

genesis / **je**-nuh-suhs / *n.* **1** a beginning or origin. **2** (**Genesis**) the first book of the Old Testament, telling of the creation of the world.

Genet / *zh*uh-**nay** /, Jean (1910–86), French novelist, poet, and dramatist.

genetic / juh-**net**-ik / *adj.* **1** of genes. **2** of genetics. **3** of or in origin. • *n.pl.* (treated as *sing.*) (**genetics**) the study of heredity and the variation of inherited characteristics. □ **genetically modified** (of an organism) with an alteration of the genetic structure to improve yield, taste, resistance to disease, etc. **genetic code** the system of storage of genetic information in chromosomes. **genetic engineering** deliberate modification of hereditary features by treatment to transfer certain genes. **genetic fingerprinting** (or **profiling**) an analysis of body tissue or fluid to discover its cell-structure, used for identifying criminals or for proving a family relationship. □ □ **genetically** *adv.*

geneticist / juh-**net**-uh-suhst / *n.* an expert in genetics.

Geneva / juh-**nee**-vuh / a city in SW Switzerland, on the Lake of Geneva.

Geneva Conventions a series of international agreements made at Geneva between 1846 and 1949 governing the status and treatment of hospitals, ambulances, wounded persons, etc. during times of war.

Genghis Khan / geng-guhs **kahn** / (1162–1227), founder of the Mongol empire, which by the time of his death stretched from the Pacific to the Black Sea.

genial / **jee**-nee-uhl / *adj.* **1** kindly, pleasant, and cheerful. **2** mild, pleasantly warm (*a genial climate*). □ **genially** *adv.* **geniality** / jee-nee-**al**-uh-tee / *n.*

genie / **jee**-nee / *n.* (in Arabian tales) a spirit or goblin with magical powers.

genital / **jen**-uh-tuhl / *adj.* of animal reproduction or the reproductive organs. • *n.pl.* (**genitals**) (also **genitalia** / jen-uh-**tay**-lee-uh /) *n.* the external sex organs of people and animals. □ **genital herpes** a sexually transmitted disease caused by the herpes simplex virus and characterised by genital blisters.

genitive / **jen**-uh-tiv / *n.* the grammatical case showing source or possession in certain languages, corresponding to the use of *of* or *from* in English.

genius[1] *n.* (*pl.* **geniuses**) **1** exceptionally great intellectual or creative ability; any great natural ability. **2** a person possessing this. **3** a person powerfully influencing another for good or evil (*he was my evil genius*). **4** a natural aptitude, talent, or inclination (*he had a genius for dropping in just when dinner was about to be served*).

genius[2] *n.* (*pl.* **genii** / **jee**-nee-uy /) **1** the tutelary spirit of a person, place, etc. **2** a spirit powerfully influencing a person for good or evil.

genocide / **jen**-uh-suyd / *n.* the deliberate extermination of a race of people. □ **genocidal** *adj.*

genome / **jee**-nohm / *n.* **1** the haploid set of chromosomes of an organism. **2** the genetic material of an organism.

genre / *zh*on-ruh / *n.* **1** a particular kind or style of art or literature. **2** (also **genre painting**) a style of painting depicting scenes of ordinary life.

gent *n. colloq.* **1** a man, a gentleman. **2** (**the gents**) a men's public toilet.

genteel / jen-**teel** / *adj.* **1** cultured, well-bred, well-mannered. **2** *ironic* of or appropriate to the upper classes. **3** affected, excessively refined or stylish. □ **genteelly** *adv.*

gentian / **jen**-shuhn / *n.* a mountain plant usu. with blue bell-like flowers. □ **gentian violet** a dye used as an antiseptic.

gentile / **jen**-tuyl / *n.* a person who is not Jewish. • *adj.* of gentiles.

gentility / jen-**til**-uh-tee / *n.* **1** social superiority. **2** genteel manners or behaviour.

gentle *adj.* **1** mild, moderate, not rough or severe (*a gentle nature*). **2** moderate (*a gentle breeze*). **3** *archaic* of good family (*of gentle birth*). **4** quiet; requiring patience (*the gentle art of persuasion*). □ **gently** *adv.* **gentleness** *n.*

gentleman *n.* **1** a man of honourable and kindly behaviour. **2** a man of good social position. **3** (in polite use) a man. **4** (in *plural*) as a form of address) the male members of an audience etc. □ **gentleman convict** *Aust. hist.* a convict in Australia fitted by prior training for employment in a clerical or professional capacity. **gentleman's agreement** one that is regarded as binding in honour but not enforceable at law. □ □ **gentlemanly** *adj.*

gentrification *n.* the upgrading of a working-class urban area by the arrival of more affluent residents. □ **gentrify** *v.*

gentry *n.pl.* **1** people on the upper levels of society. **2** *Brit.* people next below the nobility.

genuflect / **jen**-yoo-flekt / *v.* bend the knee and lower the body, esp. in worship. □ **genuflection** (also **genuflexion**) *n.*

genuine *adj.* really what it is said to be (*genuine pearls; with genuine pleasure*). □ **genuinely** *adv.* **genuineness** *n.*

genus / **jee**-nuhs / *n.* (*pl.* **genera** / **jen**-uh-ruh /) **1** a group of animals or plants with common characteristics, usu. containing several species. **2** *colloq.* a kind or sort. **3** (in logic) a class of things including subordinate kinds or species.

geocentric / jee-oh-**sen**-trik / *adj.* **1** considered as viewed from the earth's centre. **2** having the earth as its centre. □ **geocentrically** *adv.*

geode / **jee**-ohd / *n.* **1** a small cavity lined with crystals. **2** a rock containing this.

geodesic / jee-oh-**dee**-zik / *adj.* (also **geodetic** / jee-oh-**det**-ik /) of geodesy. ☐ **geodesic dome** a dome built of short struts holding flat or triangular polygonal pieces, fitted together to form a rough hemisphere. **geodesic line** the shortest possible line between two points on a curved surface.

geodesy / jee-**od**-uh-see / *n.* the scientific study of the earth's shape and size.

Geoghegan / **gay**-guhn /, Edward (?1813–?), Australian convict, playwright, and adapter of plays. A medical student in Dublin, he was convicted of obtaining goods under false pretences and transported. He produced ten plays, written or adapted by him, and was certainly the author of the best known *The Currency Lass*, a musical comedy.

geographical *adj.* (also **geographic**) of geography. ☐ **geographically** *adv.*

geography *n.* **1** the scientific study of the earth's surface and its physical features, climate, products, and population. **2** the physical features and arrangement of a place. ☐ **geographer** *n.*

geologist *n.* an expert in geology.

geology / jee-**ol**-uh-jee / *n.* **1** the scientific study of the earth's crust, strata, origins of its rocks, etc. **2** the geological features of an area. ☐ **geological** *adj.* **geologically** *adv.*

geometric *adj.* (also **geometrical**) **1** of geometry. **2** (of a design etc.) having regular lines and shapes. ☐ **geometric progression** a progression with a constant ratio between successive quantities (as 1, 3, 9, 27). ☐☐ **geometrically** *adv.*

geometry / jee-**om**-uh-tree / *n.* the branch of mathematics dealing with the properties and relations of lines, angles, surfaces, and solids.

George, Lake a lake 30 km north-east of the ACT, at an altitude of 650 metres. It is about 25 km long and 10 km wide when full.

Georgetown the capital of Guyana.

georgette / jaw-**jet** / *n.* a thin dress-material similar to crêpe.

Georgia a republic between the Black Sea and the Caspian Sea. ☐ **Georgian** *adj.*

geothermal / jee-oh-**ther**-muhl / *adj.* of or using the heat produced in the earth's interior.

Geraldton wax *n.* a spreading WA shrub having large waxy flowers ranging in colour from white to pink to deep purple.

geranium *n.* **1** a herb or shrub bearing fruit shaped like a crane's bill. **2** (in general use) a cultivated garden plant with showy red, pink, or white flowers, properly known as PELARGONIUM.

gerbera / **jer**-buh-ruh, **ger**- / *n.* a plant with daisy-like flowers usu. in garish colours.

gerbil / **jer**-buhl / *n.* (also **jerbil**) a mouse-like desert rodent with long hind legs.

geriatric *adj.* / je-ree-**at**-rik / **1** of or pertaining to GERIATRICS. **2** *colloq. offens.* of old people. **3** *colloq.* old, outdated. •*n.* **1** an old person under geriatric care. **2** *colloq. offens.* any elderly person.

■ **Usage** The use of the adjective and noun *geriatric* in any sense other than the technical (*see* GERIATRICS) is considered offensive by most people.

geriatrics *n.pl.* (usu. treated as *sing.*) the branch of medicine or social science dealing with the health and care of old people.

geriatrician / je-ree-uh-**trish**-uhn / *n.* a specialist in geriatrics.

germ *n.* **1** a micro-organism, esp. one causing disease. **2** a portion of a living organism capable of becoming a new organism; the embryo of a seed (*wheat germ*). **3** a beginning or basis from which something may develop (*the germ of an idea*). ☐ **germ warfare** the use of germs to spread disease in war.

German *adj.* of Germany or its people or language. •*n.* **1** a native of Germany. **2** the language of Germany. ☐ **German measles** a contagious disease like mild measles; rubella. **German sausage** a large bland sausage eaten cold. **German shepherd** a large wolf-like dog, much used as a police dog, a guard dog, etc.

german *adj.* ☐ **brother** (*or* **sister**) **german** one having the same parents, not a half-brother (or half-sister). **cousin german** a first cousin.

germane / jer-**mayn** / *adj.* relevant.

Germanic / jer-**man**-ik / *adj.* **1** having German characteristics. **2** of the Scandinavians, Anglo-Saxons, or Germans. •*n.* the branch of Indo-European languages which includes English, German, Dutch, and the Scandinavian languages.

germanium / jer-**may**-nee-uhm / *n.* a brittle greyish-white semi-metallic element (symbol Ge).

Germany a republic in Europe. The Federal Republic of Germany (= West Germany) and the German Democratic Republic (= East Germany) were reunited in October 1990.

germicide / **jer**-muh-suyd / *n.* a substance that kills germs or micro-organisms. ☐ **germicidal** *adj.*

germinal *adj.* **1** of germs. **2** in the earliest stage of development. **3** productive of new ideas.

germinate *v.* **1** begin to develop and grow, put forth shoots. **2** cause to do this. ☐ **germination** *n.* **germinator** *n.* **germinative** *adj.*

gerontology / je-ron-**tol**-uh-jee / *n.* the study of old age and the process of ageing.

gerrymander / je-ree-**man**-duh / *v.* manipulate the boundaries of (an electorate etc.) so as to give undue influence to some party in elections. •*n.* / je-ree-man-duh / this practice. (¶ Named after Governor Gerry of Massachusetts, who rearranged boundaries for this purpose in 1812.)

Gershwin, George (1898–1937), American composer and pianist, of Russian-Jewish family (Gershovitz).

gerund / **je**-ruhnd / *n.* a verbal noun, in English ending in *-ing*, as in *I'll do the cooking*.

gesso / jes-oh / *n.* gypsum as used in painting or sculpture.

gestalt / guh-**shtult** / *n. Psychol.* an organised whole that is perceived as more than the sum of its parts. ❑ **gestalt psychology** a system maintaining that perceptions, reactions, etc., are gestalts.

Gestapo / guh-**stah**-poh / *n.* the German secret police of the Nazi regime.

gestation / jes-**tay**-shuhn / *n.* **1** the process or period of carrying or being carried in the womb. **2** development of a plan etc. ❑ **gestate** *v.*

gesticulate / jes-**tik**-yuh-layt / *v.* make expressive movements of the hands and arms instead of speech or to reinforce speech. ❑ **gesticulation** *n.*

gesture / **jes**-chuh / *n.* **1** an expressive movement of any part of the body. **2** something done to convey one's intentions or attitude (*a gesture of friendship*). **3** a token or not very committed response (*he made a gesture towards reconciliation*). • *v.* make a gesture.

get *v.* (**got**, **getting**) **1** come into possession of; obtain or receive; earn (*get a job; got $400 a week*). **2** fetch or procure (*get your coat; got a new car*). **3** suffer (a punishment etc.) (*she got ten years in prison*). **4** contract (an illness). **5** go to reach or catch (a bus, train, etc.). **6** catch, punish, or have revenge on (*I'll get him for that*). **7** hit (*the bullet got him in the leg*). **8** *colloq.* understand (*I don't get your meaning; do you get me?*). **9** prepare (a meal). **10** bring or come into a certain condition; cause to happen (*got rich; got married; got wet; got his legs waxed; get the fire going*). **11** move in a particular direction; (cause to) succeed in coming or going (*get off the grass; we'll get you there somehow; got absolutely nowhere; got home at last*). **12** succeed in bringing or persuading (*got a message to her; got her to agree*). **13** (preceded by *have*) possess (*haven't got a cent*). **14** (preceded by *have*) be bound or obliged (*I have got to see you*). **15** obtain as a result of calculation (*if you take 3 from 10, what do you get?*). **16** establish contact by telephone etc. with; receive (a broadcast signal) (*get him on the phone; getting ABC FM loud and clear*). **17** *colloq.* annoy (*it gets me the way you pick your nose in public*). **18** *colloq.* affect emotionally (*Bach really gets me*). **19** *colloq.* attract (*she gets me, fair dinkum, so how do I get to meet her?*). **20** develop an inclination (*I'm getting to like it*). **21** establish (an idea etc.) in one's mind (*he's got it in his head that he's Queen Elizabeth*). **22** catch in an argument; corner; puzzle (*that riddle's got me!*). **23** begin (*get going*). **24** *colloq.* be off; go away (*go on, get!*). ❑ **get about** (or **around**) **1** travel extensively or fast; go from place to place. **2** (of news, rumours, etc.) spread. **3** begin walking etc. (esp. after illness). **get across** communicate, convey (an idea, etc.). **get ahead** make progress (esp. in a career etc.). **get along** get on. **get at 1** reach; get hold of. **2** *colloq.* mean, imply (*what are you getting at?*). **3** *colloq.* nag; criticise (*he keeps getting at the trade unions*). **4** *colloq.* corrupt, as by bribery etc. (*they say the jury was got at*). **get away with** escape blame or punishment for. **get back 1** return; get in touch with again. **2** receive as profit etc. **get back at** *colloq.* retaliate against. **get by** *colloq.* pass, be accepted; manage to survive. **get down 1** swallow (a thing). **2** record in writing. **3** *colloq.* cause depression in (a person). **get down to** begin working on. **get in** arrive; obtain a place in a university etc. **get in on the act** (or **action**) *colloq.* involve oneself in. **get into** *colloq.* become deeply interested in (*I just can't get into classical music and all that jazz*). **get it (all) together** *colloq.* succeed in acquiring equilibrium of body, mind, will, etc.; become efficient. **get off 1** begin a journey. **2** escape with little or no punishment; obtain an acquittal for (*a clever lawyer got him off*). **get off with** *colloq.* form a romantic or sexual relationship with (a person), esp. quickly. **get on 1** manage; make progress. **2** be on friendly or harmonious terms. **3** advance in age (*he is getting on in years*). **get on to** *colloq.* **1** make contact with. **2** understand; become aware of. **3** (as *interjection*) just look at! (*get on to that guy with the green hair!*). **get out of** avoid or get round (a duty etc.). **get over** overcome (a difficulty); recover from (an illness or shock etc.). **get round 1** influence in one's favour, coax. **2** evade (a law or rule) without actually breaking it. **get round to** find time to deal with. **get somewhere** make progress; be initially successful. **get through 1** finish or use up. **2** pass an examination. **3** make contact by telephone. **get through to** make (a person) understand. **get to** *colloq.* affect (a person) emotionally (*the baby's crying was really getting to him*). **get together** gather, assemble. **get-together** *n. colloq.* a social gathering. **get up 1** stand after sitting or kneeling etc., get out of bed or from one's chair. **2** (of wind etc.) begin to be strong. **3** prepare or organise. **4** produce or stimulate (*get up steam*). **5** (often *reflexive*) dress or arrange elaborately; arrange the appearance of. **6** (foll. by *to*) indulge or become involved in (*always getting up to mischief*). **7** *Aust.* win a race etc. (*did your horse get up in the Melbourne Cup?*). **get-up** *n. colloq.* **1** style or arrangement of dress etc. **2** clothing, outfit (*his get-up was weird*). **3** style or layout (*the get-up of his kitchen was quite stunning*).

get-at-able *adj. colloq.* accessible, able to be reached.

getaway *n.* **1** escape, esp. after committing a crime. **2** a holiday involving travel. • *adj.* pertaining to a getaway (*getaway car; a getaway holiday on the Gold Coast; getaway tours*).

Gethsemane, Garden of / geth-**sem**-uh-nee / a garden lying in the valley between Jerusalem and the Mount of Olives, where Jesus went with his disciples after the Last Supper and which was the scene of his agony and betrayal (Matthew 26:36–46).

get-up-and-go *n. colloq.* energy, enthusiasm.

geyser *n.* / **gee**-zuh, **guy**- / a natural spring sending up a column of hot water or steam at intervals.

Ghan *n.* **1** = AFGHAN. **2** (**the Ghan**) *Aust.* the train running on the Central Australian Railway.

Ghana / **gah**-nuh / a republic in West Africa. ▫ **Ghanaian** / gah-**nay**-uhn / *adj.* & *n.*

ghastly *adj.* **1** causing horror or fear (*a ghastly accident*). **2** *colloq.* very unpleasant, very bad (*a ghastly mistake*). **3** pale and ill-looking. ▫ **ghastliness** *n.*

ghat / gaht / *n.* (in India) **1** a flight of steps down to a river, a landing-place. **2** a mountain pass. ▫ **burning ghat** a level area at the top of a river ghat where Hindus burn their dead.

ghee / gee / *n.* Indian clarified butter, esp. from the milk of a buffalo or cow, used extensively in cooking.

gherkin / **ger**-kuhn / *n.* a small pickled cucumber.

ghetto / **get**-oh / *n.* (*pl.* **ghettos**) **1** part of a city occupied by a minority group. **2** *hist.* a Jewish quarter in a city. **3** a segregated group or area. ▫ **ghetto blaster** *n.* a large portable stereo radio etc., esp. for playing loud pop music.

ghost *n.* **1** a dead person's spirit or apparition. **2** a shadow or semblance (*he hasn't the ghost of a chance*). **3** a duplicated image in a defective telescope or television picture. • *v.* write as a ghost writer. ▫ **ghost gum** a northern Australian eucalypt with a smooth, shimmering white bark. **ghost town** a town abandoned by all or most of its former inhabitants. **ghost writer** a person who writes a book, article, or speech for another to pass off as his or her own. **give up the ghost 1** die. **2** (of equipment etc.) cease functioning. ▫ ▫ **ghostly** *adj.* **ghostliness** *n.*

ghosting *n.* the appearance of a 'ghost' image in a television picture.

ghoul / gool / *n.* **1** a person who enjoys gruesome things. **2** an evil spirit or phantom. **3** (in Muslim folklore) a spirit that robs graves and devours the corpses in them. ▫ **ghoulish** *adj.* **ghoulishly** *adv.*

GI *n.* a soldier in the US Army. (¶ Short for *government* (or *general*) *issue*.)

giant *n.* **1** (in fairy tales) a man of very great height and size. **2** a person, animal, or plant that is much larger than the usual size. **3** a person of outstanding ability or influence. **4** (**Giants**) *Gk myth.* a race of monstrous appearance and great strength who tried unsuccessfully to overthrow the Olympian gods. • *adj.* gigantic; of a very large kind.

giantess *n.* a female giant.

giardia / jee-**ah**-dee-uh / *n.* a protozoan of the genus *Giardia* which can infect the intestine and cause diarrhoea and other symptoms. (¶ From A. Giard (1846–1908), French biologist.)

gibber[1] / **jib**-uh / *v.* make unintelligible or meaningless sounds, esp. when shocked or terrified.

gibber[2] / **gib**-uh / *n.* a large stone, rock, or boulder. ▫ **gibber bird** (also **gibber chat**, **desert chat**) a small yellow and brown bird inhabiting the gibber country in central Australia. **gibber country** = GIBBER PLAIN. **gibber gunyah** a shallow cave used for shelter. **gibber plain** an arid, stony area of low relief in central Australia etc. in which stones form a surface layer. (¶ Dharuk)

gibberish / **jib**-uh-rish / *n.* unintelligible talk or sounds, nonsense.

gibbet / **jib**-uht / *n.* **1** a gallows. **2** an upright post with an arm from which executed criminals were formerly hanged. **3** (**the gibbet**) death by hanging. • *v.* (**gibbeted**, **gibbeting**) **1** put to death by hanging. **2** expose or hang up on a gibbet.

gibbon *n.* a long-armed anthropoid ape of SE Asia.

gibbous / **gib**-uhs / *adj.* **1** convex, protuberant, humped. **2** (of a moon or planet) having more than half (but less than the whole) of its disc illuminated.

Gibbs, May (1876–1969), Australian author and artist. Her illustrated story *Gumnut Babies* (1916) was followed by others including *Snugglepot and Cuddlepie* (1918). Her bush creatures, such as the evil 'banksia men' and the blossom babies, delighted many generations of Australian children.

gibe / juyb / (also **jibe**) *v.* jeer. • *n.* a jeering remark.

giblets / **jib**-luhts / *n.pl.* the edible organs (heart, gizzard, liver) of a bird, taken out and usu. cooked separately.

Gibraltar a fortified town and rocky headland at the southern tip of Spain on the Strait of Gibraltar that forms the outlet of the Mediterranean Sea to the Atlantic. ▫ **Gibraltarian** / jib-rol-**tair**-ree-uhn / *adj.* & *n.*

Gibson, Mel (original name: Columcille Gerard Gibson) (1956–), AO, Australian film actor.

Gibson Desert a desert in central eastern Western Australia, lying between the Great Victoria Desert in the south and the Great Sandy Desert in the north.

gidday / guh-**day** / *Aust.* = GOOD DAY.

giddy *adj.* (**giddier**, **giddiest**) **1** having the feeling that everything is spinning round. **2** causing this feeling (*giddy heights*). **3** mentally intoxicated (*giddy with success*). **4** frivolous, flighty. ▫ **giddily** *adv.* **giddiness** *n.*

Gide / zheed / , André (1869–1951), French novelist and critic.

gidgee *n. Aust.* **1** a wattle which at times emits a disagreeable smell, the stink wattle. **2** an Aboriginal spear. (¶ Yuwaalaraay)

Gielgud / geel-guud /, Sir (Arthur) John (1904–2000), English actor, famous for his Shakespearean roles.

GIF / gif / *n.* *Computing* a format for viewing graphics files. (¶ Acronym from *Graphics Interchange Format*.)

gift *n.* **1** a thing given or received without payment. **2** a natural ability (*has a gift for languages*). **3** *colloq.* an easy task. **4** esp. *Aust.* a handicapped footrace for professional athletes. • *v.* give as a gift. ▫ **look a gift-horse in the mouth** accept a gift, good fortune, etc. ungratefully, examining it for faults.

gifted *adj.* having great natural ability.

gift-wrap *v.* (**gift-wrapped**, **gift-wrapping**) **1** wrap (a gift) in attractive paper etc. **2** present something inferior in an attractive way (*his argument was gift-wrapped in fine-sounding words*). • *n.* (also **gift-wrapping**) attractive covering for a gift etc.

gig[1] *n.* **1** a light two-wheeled horse-drawn carriage. **2** a light ship's boat for rowing or sailing. **3** a rowing boat chiefly used for racing.

gig[2] *n.* an engagement to perform music etc., esp. for a single performance. • *v.* (**gigged**, **gigging**) perform a gig.

gig[3] *Aust. colloq. n.* **1** a fool; a figure of fun. **2** an inquisitive look (*having a gig at the neighbours*). • *v.* **1** mock or make fun of. **2** peek at inquisitively.

gig[4] *abbr.* gigabyte.

giga- *comb. form* one thousand million (10^9).

gigabyte *n. Computing* one thousand megabytes.

gigaflop *n. Computing* a unit of computing speed equal to one thousand million floating-point operations per second.

gigantic *adj.* very large, giantlike. ▫ **gigantically** *adv.*

giggle *v.* laugh in a silly or nervous way. • *n.* **1** this kind of laugh. **2** *colloq.* an amusing person or thing; a joke (*did it for a giggle*).

gigolo / jig-uh-loh, zhig-uh-loh / *n.* (*pl.* **gigolos**) **1** a (usu. young) man who is paid by an older woman to be her escort or lover. **2** *colloq.* a womaniser.

Gilbert[1], Kevin (1933–93), Australian Aboriginal writer, playwright, poet, painter, and political activist for the recognition of the rights of Aborigines.

Gilbert[2], Sir W(illiam) S(chwenck) (1836–1911), English comic dramatist and writer of humorous verse, who collaborated with the composer Sir Arthur Sullivan, writing the libretti for 14 comic operas (e.g. *The Mikado*).

gild *v.* **1** cover with a thin layer of gold or gold paint; tinge with a golden colour. **2** give a false brilliance to. ▫ **gild the lily** spoil something already beautiful by trying to improve it.

gilgai / gil-guy / *n. Aust.* **1** low-relief terrain in inland Australia characterised by hollows and mounds formed by expansion and contraction of the surface. **2** a hollow in such a terrain in which water collects; a waterhole. (¶ Wiradhuri and Kamilaroi.)

Gilgamesh / gil-guh-mesh / *n.* a legendary king of Sumeria in the third millennium BC, hero of the Gilgamesh Epic, one of the best-known works of ancient literature. This Epic recounts Gilgamesh's adventures in his finally futile quest for immortality. It also contains an account of a flood which has remarkable parallels with the Bible story of Noah.

gilgie / jil-gee / *n.* (also **jilgie**) the WA name for a yabby. (¶ Nyungar)

Gill, Samuel Thomas (1818–80), Australian artist, famous for his often humorous sketches, watercolours, and lithographs of the Vic. goldfields and of town and bush life.

gill[1] / gil / *n.* (usu. **gills**) **1** the organ with which a fish breathes in water. **2** (one of) the vertical radial plates on the underside of a mushroom etc. **3** the flesh below a person's jaws and ears. ▫ **fed up to the gills** *colloq.* utterly discontented or frustrated. **green at** (or **about** or **around**) **the gills** *colloq.* **1** thoroughly nauseous and showing it. **2** inexperienced. **white at** (or **about** or **around**) **the gills** *colloq.* white-faced because of fear or exhaustion.

gill[2] / jil / *n.* (in the imperial system) one quarter of a pint (142 ml).

Gillies, Max (1941–), AM, Australian actor of stage, television, and film, noted for his comedy roles and esp. for his satire (as in the television series *The Gillies Report*).

Gilmore, Dame Mary (Jean) (1865–1962), Australian writer, poet, journalist, socialist reformer and crusader for such causes as women's suffrage, the improved treatment of Aborigines, and invalid pensions.

Gilroy, His Eminence Sir Norman Thomas (1896–1977), Cardinal Archbishop of Sydney, Australia's first Australian-born Cardinal.

gilt *adj.* gilded, gold-coloured. • *n.* **1** gold or goldlike material used for gilding. **2** a young sow. ▫ **gilt-edged** *adj.* (of investments) considered to be very safe.

gimbals / jim-buhlz / *n.pl.* a contrivance of rings and pivots for keeping instruments horizontal in a moving ship, etc.

gimcrack / jim-krak / *adj.* showy, worthless, and flimsy (*gimcrack ornaments*).

gimlet / gim-luht / *n.* **1** a small tool with a screw-like tip for boring holes. **2** a slender WA eucalypt, the trunk of which is bronze-coloured and shiny and characteristically very twisted. ▫ **gimlet-eyed** having a piercing or penetrating glance.

gimmick / gim-ik / *n.* a trick or device, used esp. for attracting notice or publicity. ▫ **gimmickry** *n.* **gimmicky** *adj.*

gin[1] / jin / *n.* **1** a trap or snare for catching animals. **2** a machine for separating raw cotton from its seeds. **3** a kind of crane and windlass. • *v.*

(**ginned**, **ginning**) **1** treat (cotton) in a gin. **2** snare.

gin² / jin / n. a colourless alcoholic spirit flavoured with juniper berries. □ **gin rummy** a form of rummy for two players.

gin³ / jin / n. (now *offens.*) an Aboriginal woman. (¶ Dharuk *diyin* 'woman, wife'.)

ging / ging / n. *Aust.* a child's catapult, a shanghai.

gingelly / **jin**-juh-lee / n. (also **gingili**) **1** sesame. **2** sesame oil. (¶ Hindi)

ginger n. **1** the hot-tasting spicy root of a tropical plant, used fresh or powdered in cooking (esp. in curries), or preserved in syrup. **2** liveliness. **3** light reddish yellow. •v. **1** flavour with ginger. **2** (foll. by *up*) make more lively (*ginger things up*). •adj. ginger-coloured. □ **ginger group** a group within a larger group, urging a more active or livelier policy (*the Labor ginger group in caucus*). □□ **gingery** adj.

gingerbread n. ginger-flavoured treacle cake. •adj. gaudy, tawdry.

gingerly adv. cautiously. •adj. cautious.

Ginger Meggs a very popular Australian comic-strip character created by the artist J.C. Bancks (1889–1952). Ginger Meggs represents the idealised Australian boy, honest, good-hearted, but mischievous.

gingham / **ging**-uhm / n. a cotton fabric often with a striped or checked pattern.

gingivitis / jin-juh-**vuy**-tuhs / n. inflammation of the gums.

ginkgo / **ging**-koh / n. (pl. **ginkgos** or **ginkgoes**) a tree with fan-shaped leaves and yellow flowers, originally from China and Japan. Also called *maidenhair tree*.

ginormous / juy-**naw**-muhs / adj. *colloq.* enormous.

ginseng / **jin**-seng / n. the root of a plant found in eastern Asia and North America, used in medicine.

Gippsland a fertile agricultural and pastoral district in the east of Victoria, comprising the country between the Dividing Range and the coast, extending from the New South Wales border almost to Westernport.

gipsy alternative spelling of GYPSY.

giraffe n. a large four-legged African animal with a spotted skin, a long neck and long forelegs.

gird v. **1** encircle or attach with a belt or band (*he girded on his sword*). **2** enclose or encircle. **3** (foll. by *round*) place (a cord etc.) round. **4** (often foll. by *up*) prepare for action. □ **gird** (or **gird up**) **one's loins** prepare for action.

girder n. a metal beam supporting part of a building or a bridge.

girdle n. **1** a belt or cord worn round the waist. **2** an elastic corset. **3** a connected ring of bones in the body (*the pelvic girdle*). •v. surround.

girl n. **1** a female child, a daughter. **2** a young woman. **3** *colloq.* a girlfriend. □ **the girls** a woman's close circle of female friends. □□ **girlhood** n. **girly** adj.

girlfriend n. a female friend, esp. a man's usual companion or lover.

girlie n. *colloq.* a girl. □ **girlie magazine** a magazine containing erotic pictures of young women.

girlish adj. like a girl. □ **girlishly** adv. **girlishness** n.

giro / **juy**-roh / n. (pl. **giros**) **1** a system of credit transfer between banks, post offices, etc. **2** a cheque or payment by giro. •v. (**giroes**, **giroed**) pay by giro. (¶ German from Italian.)

girt adj. *poetic* girded.

girth n. **1** the distance round a thing. **2** a band passing under a horse's belly, holding the saddle in place.

gismo n. (also **gizmo**) (pl. **gismos**) *colloq.* a gadget.

gist / jist / n. the essential points or general sense of anything.

git n. *colloq.* a silly or contemptible person.

give v. (**gave**, **given**, **giving**) **1** transfer the possession of freely; hand over as a present; donate. **2** transfer temporarily; provide with (*gave him the dog to hold; gave her a new hip*). **3** administer medicine. **4** deliver (a message) (*give her my best wishes*). **5** *colloq.* tell what one knows (*you've got ten seconds: give!*). **6** utter; declare (*gave a shriek; gave the batsman out*). **7** pledge (*give one's word*). **8** make over in exchange or payment (*gave him $30 for the bicycle*). **9** confer, grant (a benefit, an honour, etc.). **10** accord, bestow (love, time, etc.). **11** award, administer (praise, blame, etc.) (*gave him my blessing; gave them the sack; I'll give him a scolding*). **12** perform (an action etc.) (*gave a jump; gave a performance; gave the door a kick*). **13** consign, put (*gave him into custody*). **14** sanction the marriage of (a daughter etc.). **15** devote, dedicate (*gave her life to the cause*). **16** present; offer; show; hold out (*gives no sign of life; gave her his arm; give me an example*). **17** provide (a meal or party) as host. **18** yield as a product or result (*this paddock gives feed for 20 cows; the lamp gives a poor light; gives an average of 7*). **19** impart; be the source of; cause (*gave him my sore throat; gave me trouble; gives much pain*). **20** permit a view of or access to (*the window gives on to the street*). **21** concede (*I give you the benefit of the doubt*). **22** declare (judgment) authoritatively (*gave his verdict*). **23** be flexible, yield when pressed or pulled; collapse (*woollen fabric gives; the tent's beginning to give*). **24** *colloq.* be happening (*so what gives in your neck of the woods?*). **25** *colloq.* tell; mention as excuse or explanation (*don't give me that!*). •n. capacity to yield or comply; elasticity (*there's no give in his attitudes; this rubber band's lost its give*). □ **give and take 1** an exchange of words, ideas, blows, etc. **2** willingness on both sides to make concessions. **give away 1** give as a present. **2** hand over (the bride) to the

given 343 **glaucoma**

groom at a wedding. **3** reveal (a secret etc.) unintentionally. **4** betray (*don't give me away*). **5** *Aust.* abandon (*he's had to give surfing away*). **give-away** *n. colloq.* **1** a thing given without charge or at a low price. **2** something that reveals a secret. **give in** acknowledge that one is defeated. **give it to a person** *colloq.* scold or punish him or her. **give it to a person straight** *colloq.* tell the full, blunt truth to him or her with no evasion. **give me** I prefer (*give me Greece any day*). **give off** produce and emit (*petrol gives off fumes*). **give oneself away** disclose something about oneself unintentionally; make a FREUDIAN SLIP. **give or take** *colloq.* add or subtract (an amount) in estimating (*took him ten years to build, give or take a few months*). **give over 1** devote (*afternoons are given over to sport*). **2** *colloq.* cease doing something. **give up 1** cease (doing something). **2** part with; surrender. **3** abandon hope. **4** declare a person to be incurable or a problem to be too difficult for oneself to solve. □□ **giver** *n.*

given see GIVE. • *adj.* **1** specified or stated; assumed or granted (*all the people in a given area; given the circumstances*). **2** (foll. by *to*) having a certain tendency (*he is given to swearing*). □ **given name** a first name (given in addition to the family name or surname).

Giza /gee-zuh/, **El** a city south-west of Cairo in northern Egypt, site of three great pyramids and of the Sphinx.

gizmo alternative spelling of GISMO.

gizzard *n.* a bird's second stomach, in which food is ground.

glacé /glas-ay, glah-say/ *adj.* iced with sugar, preserved in sugar (*glacé cherries*).

glacial /glay-shuhl, -see-uhl/ *adj.* **1** icy. **2** of or from glaciers or other ice (*glacial deposits*). □ **glacial epoch** (*or* **glacial period**) the period when a large part of the earth's surface was covered by ice; the ice age. □□ **glacially** *adv.*

glaciated /glay-see-ay-tuhd, glay-shee-, glas-ee-/ *adj.* covered with glaciers; affected by their action. □ **glaciation** *n.*

glacier /glay-see-uh, glas-ee-uh/ *n.* a river of ice moving very slowly, formed by an accumulation of snow on high ground.

glad[1] *adj.* (**gladder, gladdest**) **1** pleased, expressing joy. **2** giving joy (*the glad news*). □ **be glad of** be grateful for. **glad eye** *colloq.* an inviting or seductive look. **glad rags** *colloq.* dressy clothes. □□ **gladly** *adv.* **gladness** *n.*

glad[2] *n. Aust. colloq.* a gladiolus.

gladden *v.* make or become glad.

gladdie *n. Aust. colloq.* a gladiolus.

glade *n.* an open space in a forest.

gladiator /glad-ee-ay-tuh/ *n.* a trained fighter in ancient Roman shows. □ **gladiatorial** /glad-ee-uh-taw-ree-uhl/ *adj.*

gladiolus *n.* (*pl.* **gladioli** *or* **gladioluses**) a garden plant with spikes of brightly coloured flowers.

gladsome *adj. poetic* cheerful, joyous.

gladwrap *n. Aust. trademark* a thin, self-clinging, transparent plastic sheeting used for wrapping food, newspapers for delivery, etc.

glair *n.* white of egg; a thick substance made of or resembling this.

glamorise *v.* (also **-ize**) make glamorous or attractive.

glamour *n.* (also **glamor**) **1** alluring beauty. **2** attractive and exciting qualities that arouse envy. □ **glamorous** *adj.* **glamorously** *adv.*

glance *v.* **1** look briefly. **2** strike at an angle and glide off an object (*a glancing blow; the ball glanced off his bat*). **3** (of light etc.) flash or dart. • *n.* **1** a brief look. **2** a stroke in cricket with the bat's face turned slantwise to the ball. **3** a flash or gleam.

gland *n.* **1** an organ that separates from the blood substances that are to be used by the body or expelled from it. **2** a similar organ in a plant.

glanders *n.* a contagious disease of horses and related animals.

glandular /**glan**-dyoo-luh, -juh-/ *adj.* of or like a gland. □ **glandular fever** a feverish illness in which the lymph glands are swollen.

glans *n.* (*pl.* **glandes** /**glan**-deez/) the rounded part forming the end of the penis or of the clitoris.

Glanville-Hicks, Peggy (1912–90), Australian composer. Her compositions include five ballets, four operas, film scores, and chamber and orchestral works.

glare *v.* **1** shine with an unpleasant dazzling light. **2** stare angrily or fiercely. • *n.* **1** a strong unpleasant light. **2** oppressive attention (*the glare of publicity*). **3** an angry or fierce stare.

glaring *adj.* **1** bright and dazzling. **2** very obvious (*a glaring error*). □ **glaringly** *adv.*

glasnost /**glaz**-nost/ *n.* (in the former Soviet Union) a policy of more open government and greater openness in the reporting of news etc. (¶ Russian, = openness.)

Glass, Philip (1937–), American composer.

glass *n.* **1** a hard brittle substance (as used in windows), usu. transparent. **2** an object made of this, e.g. a mirror. **3** a glass container for drinking from. **4** a barometer. **5** (**glasses**) spectacles; binoculars. • *v.* fit or enclose with glass. □ **glassblowing** shaping semi-molten glass by blowing air into it through a tube. **glass ceiling** an invisible barrier which prevents progress upwards (esp. of women in a career). **glass fibre** fabric woven from glass filaments; plastic reinforced with glass filaments.

glasshouse *n.* a greenhouse.

glasspaper *n.* paper coated with glass particles, used for smoothing things.

glassware *n.* articles made of glass.

glassy *adj.* **1** like glass in appearance. **2** with a dull expressionless stare (*glassy-eyed*). □ **glassily** *adv.* **glassiness** *n.*

glaucoma /glaw-**koh**-muh/ *n.* a condition caused by increased pressure of the fluid within

glaze the eyeball, causing weakening or loss of sight. □ **glaucomatous** adj.

glaze v. **1** fit (a window etc.) with glass or (a building) with windows. **2** cover (pottery etc.) with a glaze (sense 1). **3** cover (pastry, meat, etc.) with a glaze (sense 2). **4** cover a painted surface etc. with a glaze (sense 3). **5** (often foll. by *over*) (of the eyes) become glassy. **6** give a glassy surface to. • n. **1** a vitreous substance for glazing pottery. **2** a smooth shiny coating of milk, sugar, egg white, etc. on food. **3** a thin coat of transparent paint to modify an underlying tone. **4** a shiny surface formed by glazing.

glazier / **glay**-zee-uh / n. a person whose trade is to fit glass in windows etc.

gleam n. **1** a beam or ray of soft light, esp. one that comes and goes. **2** a brief show of some quality (*a gleam of hope*). • v. **1** send out gleams, shine. **2** (of a quality) be indicated (*fear gleamed in his eyes*).

glean v. **1** pick up (grain left by harvesters). **2** gather (information) in small amounts. □ **gleaner** n.

gleanings n.pl. things gleaned, esp. facts.

glee n. **1** lively or triumphant joy. **2** a part-song for three or more (esp. male) voices. □ **glee club** a type of choral society.

gleeful adj. full of glee. □ **gleefully** adv.

glen n. a narrow valley.

Glenrowan a town 290 km north-east of Melbourne. On 29 June 1880, Ned Kelly was captured here, and the rest of his gang killed, when police laid siege to the Glenrowan hotel.

glib adj. ready with words but insincere or superficial (*a glib tongue; a glib excuse*). □ **glibly** adv. **glibness** n.

glide v. **1** move along smoothly. **2** fly in a glider or in an aeroplane without engine power. **3** pass gradually or imperceptibly. **4** go stealthily. **5** cause to glide. • n. a gliding movement. □ **glide path** an aircraft's line of descent to land.

glider n. **1** a person who or a thing which glides. **2** a light aircraft without an engine. **3** any of various tree-dwelling Australian marsupials (e.g. the flying possum, the sugar glider, etc.) that glide through the air using flaps of skin between the fore and hind limbs as 'parachutes'.

glimmer n. **1** a faint gleam. **2** (also **glimmering**) (usu. foll. by *of*) a small sign (of hope etc.). • v. gleam faintly.

glimpse n. **1** a brief view or look. **2** a faint transient appearance (*glimpses of the truth*). • v. have a brief view of (*glimpsed his face in the crowd*).

glint n. a very brief flash of light; a sparkle. • v. send out a glint.

glissade / gli-**sahd**, -**sayd** / v. **1** glide or slide skilfully down a steep slope, esp. in mountaineering. **2** make a gliding step in ballet. • n. a glissading movement or step.

glisten v. shine like something wet or polished.

glitch n. colloq. a malfunction, a hitch.

glitter v. **1** shine with a bright reflected light; sparkle. **2** (usu. foll. by *with*) be showy or splendid. • n. **1** a sparkle. **2** showiness. **3** tiny pieces of sparkling material as decoration etc. □ **glitteringly** adv. **glittery** adj.

glitterati / glit-uh-**rah**-tee / n.pl. colloq. rich and fashionable people; celebrities.

glitz n. colloq. showy glamour; over-ostentatious display of wealth and luxury. □ **glitzy** adj.

gloaming n. poetic the evening twilight.

gloat v. be full of greedy or malicious delight. • n. an act of gloating.

glob n. colloq. a small mass or lump of semi-liquid substance, e.g. mud; a dollop.

global adj. **1** of the whole world, world wide (*a global conflict*). **2** relating to or affecting the Earth as an ecological unit (*global consciousness*). **3** all-embracing. **4** *Computing* relating to an entire program, the whole of a set of data, etc.; total (*a global change*). □ **global consciousness** receptiveness to (and understanding of) cultures other than one's own (since all cultures are part of the global village). **global English** English as the world's pre-eminent language. **global village** the entire inhabited world seen as a single community. **global warming** the increase in the temperature of the earth's atmosphere caused by the greenhouse effect. □□ **globally** adv.

globalise v. (also **-ize**) make global, internationalise. □ **globalisation** n.

globe n. **1** an object shaped like a ball, esp. one with a map of the earth on it. **2** the world (*travelled all over the globe*). **3** a hollow round glass object, e.g. a fishbowl. **4** a light bulb. □ **globe artichoke** the edible flower of an artichoke.

Globe Theatre a theatre in London, erected in 1599, in which Shakespeare had a share and where he acted.

globetrotter n. colloq. a person who travels widely. □ **globetrot** v. **globetrotting** n. & adj.

globular / **glob**-yuh-luh / adj. **1** shaped like a globe. **2** composed of globules.

globule / **glob**-yool / n. a small globe or rounded drop.

globulin / **glob**-yuh-luhn / n. a molecule-transporting protein found in plant and animal tissue.

glockenspiel / **glok**-uhn-speel, -shpeel / n. a musical instrument consisting of bells or metal bars struck by hammers.

gloom n. **1** semi-darkness. **2** a feeling of sadness and depression. • v. **1** become dark or threatening; lour. **2** become depressed and sad; frown.

gloomy adj. (**gloomier**, **gloomiest**) **1** almost dark, unlighted. **2** depressed, sullen. **3** dismal, depressing. □ **gloomily** adv. **gloominess** n.

glorify v. (**glorified**, **glorifying**) **1** praise highly. **2** worship. **3** make something seem more splendid than it is (*their patio is only a glorified backyard*). □ **glorification** n.

glorious *adj.* **1** possessing or bringing glory. **2** splendid, great (*a glorious view; a glorious muddle*). □ **gloriously** *adv.*

glory *n.* **1** fame and honour won by great deeds. **2** adoration and praise. **3** beauty, magnificence (*the glory of a sunset*). **4** a thing deserving praise and honour. • *v.* (**gloried**, **glorying**) (foll. by *in*) rejoice or pride oneself (*glorying in their success*). □ **glory box** *Aust.* a box in which young women put away linen, clothes, and other necessaries in anticipation of marriage. **glory hole** *colloq.* a room, cupboard, etc., in which things can be bundled away out of sight; a messy room or cupboard.

gloss[1] *n.* **1** the shine on a smooth surface. **2** a deceptively attractive appearance. **3** (in full **gloss paint**) a paint which gives a glossy finish. • *v.* make glossy. □ **gloss over** seek to cover up (a mistake or fault), esp. by mentioning only briefly.

gloss[2] *n.* **1** an explanatory comment added to a text, e.g. in the margin. **2** an interpretation or paraphrase. • *v.* add a gloss to (a text, a word, etc.).

glossary / **glos**-uh-ree / *n.* **1** a list of technical or special words with their definitions. **2** a collection of glosses.

glossolalia / glos-uh-**lay**-lee-uh / *n.* babbling, meaningless 'speech' associated with some schizophrenic disorders and certain religious states (e.g. in the modern phenomenon known as 'speaking with tongues').

glossy *adj.* (**glossier**, **glossiest**) smooth and shiny (*glossy paper*). • *n.* (*pl.* **glossies**) a glossy magazine or photograph. □ **glossy magazine** one printed on glossy paper, with many illustrations. □□ **glossily** *adv.* **glossiness** *n.*

glottal *adj.* of the glottis. □ **glottal stop** a sound in speech made by suddenly opening or shutting the glottis.

glottis *n.* the opening of the upper end of the windpipe between the vocal cords.

glove *n.* **1** a covering for the hand, usu. with separate divisions for each finger and the thumb. **2** a boxing glove. • *v.* (**gloved**, **gloving**) cover or provide with gloves. □ **glove box** a recess for small articles in the dashboard of a car.

Glover, John (1767–1849), a pioneer of Australian landscape painting, esp. in Tas.

glover *n.* a maker of gloves.

glow *v.* **1** send out light and heat without flame. **2** have a warm or flushed look or colour. **3** show or feel strong emotion (*glowed with pride*). **4** (as **glowing** *adj.*) very enthusiastic or favourable (*a glowing report*). • *n.* **1** a glowing state. **2** bright warm colour. **3** a feeling of satisfaction or well-being. □ **glow-worm** *n.* a kind of beetle whose female can give out a greenish light at its tail.

glower / glowuh / *v.* **1** scowl, stare angrily. **2** look dark or threatening. • *n.* a glowering look.

Gluck / gluuk /, Christoph Willibald von (1714–87), German composer of operas.

glucose / **gloo**-kohz, -kohs / *n.* a form of sugar found in the blood or in fruit juice etc.

glue *n.* a sticky substance used for joining things. • *v.* (**glued**, **gluing** *or* **glueing**) **1** fasten with glue. **2** attach or hold closely (*his ear was glued to the keyhole*). **3** stick fast (to something) through intense interest, habit, etc. (*glued to the telly; glued to his book*). □ **glue ear** a blocking of the Eustachian tube, esp. in children. **glue-sniffer** a person who practises glue-sniffing. **glue-sniffing** inhaling the fumes of plastic glue for their narcotic effects.

gluey *adj.* (**gluier**, **gluiest**) resembling glue; viscous, sticky. □ **glueyness** *n.*

gluggy *adj. colloq.* gluey, sticky (*gluggy rice*).

glum *adj.* (**glummer**, **glummest**) sad and gloomy. □ **glumly** *adv.* **glumness** *n.*

glut *v.* (**glutted**, **glutting**) **1** supply with much more than is needed (*glut the market*). **2** satisfy fully with food (*glut oneself; glut one's appetite*). **3** indulge (a desire etc.) to the full. • *n.* **1** an excessive supply (*a glut of apples*). **2** indulgence to the full; surfeit.

glutamate / **gloo**-tuh-mayt / *n.* a substance used to bring out the flavour in food.

gluten / **gloo**-tuhn / *n.* a sticky protein substance present in cereal grains, which remains when starch is washed out of flour.

glutinous / **gloo**-tuh-nuhs / *adj.* glue-like, sticky (*glutinous rice is a must in some Asian cuisines*).

glutton *n.* **1** a person who eats far too much. **2** a person with a great desire or capacity for something (*a glutton for punishment; a glutton for work*). □ **gluttonise** (also **-ize**) *v.* **gluttonous** *adj.* **gluttony** *n.*

glycerine / **glis**-uh-reen, **glis**-uh-ruhn / *n.* (also **glycerol**) a thick sweet colourless liquid used in ointments, medicines, and explosives.

Glyndebourne / **gluynd**-bawn / an estate in Sussex, England, where an annual festival of opera is held.

GM *abbr.* genetically modified.

gm *abbr.* gram(s).

GMO *abbr.* genetically modified organism.

GMT *abbr.* = GREENWICH MEAN TIME.

gnamma / **nam**-uh / *n.* (also **namma**) (in full **gnamma hole**) *Aust.* a hole (commonly in granite) in which rainwater collects. (¶ Nyungar)

gnarled / nahld / *adj.* (of a tree or hands) covered with knobbly lumps; twisted and misshapen.

gnash *v.* **1** grind (one's teeth). **2** (of teeth) strike together.

gnat *n.* a small two-winged biting fly.

gnaw *v.* (**gnawed**, **gnawed** *or* **gnawn**, **gnawing**) **1** bite persistently at something hard. **2** corrode; wear away. **3** (of pain, fear, etc.) torment (*was gnawed by doubt*). **4** (as **gnawing** *adj.*) persistent, continuously worrying (*a gnawing pain*).

gneiss / nuys / *n.* a kind of coarse-grained rock of feldspar, quartz, and mica.

gnocchi / **nok**-ee, **nyok**-ee / *n.pl.* (in Italian cuisine) tiny dumplings made with mashed potato and flour, or with semolina, etc., and eaten in a soup or with a sauce.

gnome *n.* **1** a kind of dwarf in fairy tales, living underground. **2** a model of such a dwarf as a garden ornament. **3** *colloq.* a person with secret influence, esp. in finance (*the gnomes of Zurich*).

gnomic / **noh**-mik, **nom**-ik / *adj.* consisting of or using aphorisms or maxims; sententious.

gnomon / **noh**-mon / *n.* the rod of a sundial, showing the time by its shadow.

gnosis / **noh**-suhs / *n.* knowledge of spiritual mysteries.

gnostic / **nos**-tik / *adj.* **1** of knowledge. **2** having special mystical knowledge. •*n.* (**Gnostic**) an early Christian heretic claiming mystical knowledge. □ **Gnosticism** *n.*

GNP *abbr.* = GROSS NATIONAL PRODUCT.

gnu / noo / *n.* an ox-like antelope.

go *v.* (**goes, went, gone, going**) **1** begin to move; be moving; pass from one point to another; make a trip for a specific purpose (*we must go at one o'clock; go skiing*). **2** extend or lead from one place to another (*the road goes to Gundagai*). **3** leave, depart (*they had to go*). **4** be in a specified state (*they went hungry; went in fear of his life*). **5** be functioning (*that clock doesn't go*). **6** make a movement or sound, often of a specified kind (*go like this with your foot; the gun went bang; the doorbell's gone*). **7** (of an animal) make its characteristic cry (*a cow goes 'moo'*). **8** *colloq.* say (*so he goes to me 'Why don't you like it?'*). **9** (foll. by *and* + verb) *colloq.* expressing annoyance (*you went and told him!*). **10** (of time) pass; (of a distance) be traversed or accomplished (*ten days to go; that last kilometre went quickly*). **11** be allowable or acceptable (*anything goes; what she says, goes; that goes without saying*). **12** belong in some place or position (*plates go on the shelf*). **13** (of a story or tune etc.) have a certain wording or content (*I forget how the chorus goes*). **14** be current or accepted (*so the story goes*). **15** be suitable; fit; match (*the shoes don't go with the hat; those pinks don't go*). **16** pass into a certain condition (*the fruit went bad; he's gone to sleep*). **17** proceed or escape in a specified condition (*the poet went unrecognised*). **18** turn out, proceed; take a course or view (*all went well; NSW went Labor*). **19** be successful (*made the party go*). **20** be sold (*it's going cheap; went for $1*). **21** (of money or supplies) be spent or used up (*$200 went on a new jacket; the sugar's all gone*). **22** be given up, dismissed, abolished, or lost (*some luxuries must go; half the employees will have to go*). **23** fail, decline; give way, collapse (*his sight is going; the light globe has gone*). **24** carry an action to a certain point (*that's going too far; I'll go to $50 for it*). **25** be able to be put (*your clothes won't go into that suitcase; 6 into 5 won't go*). **26** be given or allotted (*first prize went to the girl; his property will go to his nephew*). **27** serve; contribute to (*it all goes to prove what I said; this will go towards your holiday*). **28** be guided by; judge or act on or in harmony with (*I have nothing to go on; a good rule to go by*). **29** attend regularly (*goes to school*). **30** (foll. by the *present participle*) *colloq.* proceed (often foolishly) to do (*went running to the police; don't go making him angry*). **31** (in the *imperative*) begin motion (a starter's order in a race) (*ready, steady, go!*). **32** be known or called (*he goes by the name of Ocker*). **33** *colloq.* proceed to (*go jump in the lake!*). **34** (foll. by *for*) apply to (*that goes for me too*). •*n.* (pl. **goes**) **1** energy (*full of go*). **2** a turn or try (*he's had two goes already*). **3** *colloq.* a success (*make a go of it*). **4** vigorous activity (*it's all go from now on*). **5** a bout (of illness) (*a bad go of flu*). **6** *colloq.* a fixture, a firm arrangement (*next week's match against the Cats is now a go*). •*adj. colloq.* functioning properly (*all systems are go*). □ **all the go** *colloq.* in the height of current fashion, all the rage. **as a person** (or **thing**) **goes** as the average is (*he's a bit skinny as rugby players go*). **as far** (or **so far**) **as it goes** an expression of caution against taking a statement too positively (*the work is good as far as it goes*). **give it a go** *colloq.* **1** attempt, have a go at. **2** (a plea for fair treatment) steady on, be reasonable (*give it a go, mate, he's too small for you to pick on!*). **go-ahead** *n.* a signal to proceed immediately. *adj.* energetic, willing to try new methods. **go all the way** **1** (foll. by *with*) agree or support unreservedly (*I go all the way with you on this*). **2** *colloq.* have sexual intercourse. **go along with** agree with. **go around** (also **go round**) suffice for everyone (*is there enough beer to go around?*). **go around with** **1** be regularly in the company of (*he goes around with Johnno*). **2** have a (usu. sexual) relationship with (*he goes around with Kylie*). **go at** take in hand energetically (*went at it with a will*). **go back on** fail to keep (a promise, etc.). **go-between** *n.* one who acts as a messenger or negotiator. **go down 1** descend. **2** (of a ship) sink, (of the sun) appear to descend towards the horizon, set, (of a flood) subside, (of an amount) become less through use (*the coffee bottle's gone down a lot*), (of a theatre curtain) fall. **3** decrease in price. **4** deteriorate; (of a computer system etc.) cease to function. **5** be written down. **6** *colloq.* be remembered (*he'll go down as the biggest ratbag in Oz*). **7** be swallowed. **8** be received or accepted (*the suggestion went down very well*). **9** *colloq.* go to prison. **go down to** be defeated by (*the Sydney Swans went down to Geelong's Cats*). **go down with** become ill with (a disease). **go for 1** like, prefer, choose (*that's the one I go for*). **2** attack (*the dog went for him*). **3** go to fetch. **4** pass for or be accounted as (*your opinion goes for nothing*). **5** *colloq.* strive to attain (*go for it!*). **go off 1** explode, discharge. **2** (esp. of foodstuffs) lose quality, become stale or spoiled. **3** lose popular appeal (*that café's gone off the last few weeks—it's no longer in*). **4** (of an actor) go off-stage. **5** fall asleep. **6** proceed (*the party went off well*). **7** dislike what one liked formerly (*I've gone off tea lately; I've gone off him*). **go off at** *Aust. colloq.* reprimand, scold. **go on 1** continue, persevere (*decided to go on with it; went on trying*). **2** happen (*what went on at the meeting?*). **3** (of an actor) enter onstage. **4** talk lengthily. **5** proceed (*went on to become a star*). **6** conduct oneself (*shameful the way they went on*). **7** (also **go upon**) use as evidence (*the police have nothing to go on*). **8** *colloq.* approach (*he's twelve going on thirteen; it must be going on noon*). **go on at** *colloq.* nag. **go out 1** leave (a house, room, etc.). **2** be broadcast (*the program goes out live*). **3** be extinguished (*the fire's gone out*). **4** cease to be fashionable (*moustaches are going out*). **5** *colloq.* lose consciousness (*he went out like a light*). **6** (foll. by *to*) (of the heart etc.) expand with sympathy etc. towards (*my heart went out to them in their plight*). **7** (of a tide) ebb to low tide. **8** go on strike (*going out over unsafe working conditions*). **go out with** have (a person) as a regular (usu. sexual) partner. **go over 1** inspect the details of; rehearse; retouch. **2** be received (as specified) (*the play went over very well in Cootamundra.*) **3** change sides, loyalties, religion, etc. (*some Labor supporters are going over to the Greens*). **go round 1** spin, revolve. **2** be enough for everyone (*I don't think the savs will go round*). **3** (usu. foll. by *to*) visit informally (*let's go round to Bill's*). **go slow** work at a deliberately slow pace as a form of industrial protest. **go-slow** *n.* a deliberately slow pace of this kind. **go through 1** be dealt with or completed. **2** discuss or scrutinise in detail. **3** perform. **4** undergo; endure (*after what I've gone through, I've a right to be bitter*). **5** *colloq.* use up; spend (money etc.). **6** (of a book) be successfully published (in so many editions). **go with 1** match, harmonise with (*blue doesn't go with green*). **2** be courting, dating, etc.; be in a sexual relationship with (*John's going with Sally; he's been going with Peter for years*). **have a go** *Aust.* **1** (foll. by *at*) attack; criticise. **2** (often foll. by *at*) attempt; try harder. **let go 1** release. **2** *colloq.* be uninhibited; loosen up (*let go, matey, and have some fun*). **let oneself go 1** neglect one's appearance etc.; become slovenly. **2** behave freely or spontaneously. **make a go of** *colloq.* make a success of. **no go** *colloq.* impossible; not feasible; not on.

goad *n.* **1** a pointed stick for prodding cattle to move onwards. **2** something stimulating a person to activity. • *v.* **1** urge on with a goad. **2** act as a stimulus to (*goaded her into answering back*).

goal *n.* **1** a structure or area into which players try to send a ball in certain games. **2** point(s) scored in this way. **3** an object of ambition or effort; a destination. • *v.* score a goal (*he goaled in the first three minutes*). ☐ **goal sneak** *Aust. Rules* a player who adroitly sneaks in a goal, catching the opposing players by surprise. **goal umpire** *Aust.*
Rules one of two umpires (one at each goal) who judges when a goal or a behind is scored. ☐☐ **goalless** *adj.*

goalie *n. colloq.* a goalkeeper.

goalkeeper *n.* a player whose task is to keep the ball out of the goal.

goalpost *n.* either of the pair of upright posts of a goal.

goanna / goh-**an**-uh / *n.* any of various Australian monitor lizards, typically large and fast-moving. ☐ **goanna oil** oil supposedly from goanna fat, a bush panacea.

goat *n.* **1** a domesticated cud-chewing mammal with horns and (in the male) a beard, kept for its milk and its meat. **2** a lecherous man. **3** *colloq.* a foolish person. **4** (**the Goat**) a sign of the zodiac, Capricorn. ☐ **get** (**on**) **a person's goat** *colloq.* irritate him or her intensely.

goatee / goh-**tee** / *n.* a short pointed beard.

goatherd *n.* a person who looks after a herd of goats.

goatish *adj.* **1** goat-like. **2** lustful. ☐ **goatishly** *adv.* **goatishness** *n.*

gob *colloq. n.* **1** a clot of a slimy substance. **2** the mouth. • *v.* (**gobbed, gobbing**) spit.

gobbet *n.* **1** a lump or piece of flesh, food, etc. **2** an extract from a text.

gobble *v.* **1** eat quickly and greedily. **2** (of a turkeycock) make a characteristic throaty sound. ☐ **gobble up 1** take over, seize control of (*retail giants gobbling up the small shopkeepers*). **2** read eagerly, devour (a book etc.).

gobbledegook *n.* (also **gobbledygook**) *colloq.* pompous or unintelligible language used by officials.

goblet *n.* a drinking glass with a stem and a foot.

goblin *n.* a mischievous ugly dwarflike creature in fairy tales etc.

gobsmacked *adj. colloq.* astounded, flabbergasted; speechless with amazement.

gobstopper *n.* a large sweet for sucking.

goby / **goh**-bee / *n.* a small fish with the ventral fins joined to form a disc or sucker.

go-cart alternative spelling of GO-KART.

god *n.* **1** a superhuman being regarded and worshipped as having power over nature and human affairs (*Mars was the Roman god of war*). **2** (**God**) the creator and ruler of the universe in Christian, Jewish, and Muslim teaching. **3** an image of a god, an idol. **4** a person or thing that is greatly admired or adored (*money is his god*). **5** (**the gods**) the gallery of a theatre. **6** (**God!**) an exclamation of surprise, anger, etc. ☐ **God-forsaken** *adj.* wretched, dismal; inaccessible. **God's gift** *colloq.* (usu. *ironical*) a godsend (*he thinks he's God's gift to women!*).

godchild *n.* (*pl.* **godchildren**) a child in relation to its godparent(s).

god-daughter *n.* a female godchild.

goddess *n.* a female god.

godfather *n.* **1** a male godparent. **2** the mastermind behind an illegal organisation, esp. the Mafia.

godhead *n.* **1** divine nature. **2** (**the Godhead**) God.

Godiva / guh-**duy**-vuh /, Lady (d.1080), English noblewoman. According to a 13th-century legend, she agreed to her husband's proposition that he would reduce some particularly unpopular taxes only if she rode naked on horseback through the marketplace of Coventry. Peeping Tom, the only person to take a look at her, was struck blind.

godless *adj.* **1** not having belief in God. **2** wicked. □ **godlessly** *adv.* **godlessness** *n.*

godlike *adj.* like God or a god.

godly *adj.* (**godlier**, **godliest**) sincerely religious. □ **godliness** *n.*

godmother *n.* a female godparent.

godparent *n.* a person who undertakes, when a child is baptised, to see that it is brought up as a Christian.

godsend *n.* a piece of unexpected good fortune.

godson *n.* a male godchild.

godspeed *n.* an expression of good wishes to a person starting a journey.

Godwin-Austen, Mount *see* K2.

godwit *n.* any of various wading birds with long legs, some of which are summer visitors to Australia from Asia etc.

Godzone *n. Aust. jocular* God's Own Country (used esp. of Australia or New Zealand) (*can't wait to get back to Godzone!*).

Goebbels, (Paul) Joseph (1897–1945), German Nazi leader and politician, who became Hitler's propaganda minister in 1933.

goer *n.* **1** a person or thing that goes (*a slow goer; churchgoers*). **2** *colloq.* a lively or persevering person. **3** *Aust. colloq.* a project likely to be accepted or to succeed. **4** a person or thing that goes very fast (*that horse in race three's a real goer*).

Goering, Hermann Wilhelm (1893–1946), German Nazi leader, who became the commander of the German air force in 1934 and founded the Gestapo.

Goethe / **ger**-tuh /, Johann Wolfgang von (1749–1832), German writer, scholar, and statesman.

gofer *n.* (also **gopher**) *colloq.* **1** a person who does menial jobs for others, runs errands, etc. **2** a toady, a crawler. (¶ Alteration of *go for*, glancing at GOPHER, sense 1.)

goggle *v.* stare with wide-open eyes. □ **goggle-eyed** *adj.* with wide-open eyes.

goggles *n.pl.* spectacles for protecting the eyes from wind, dust, water, etc.

go-go *adj. colloq.* (of dancers, music, etc.) in a modern style; lively, erotic, and rhythmic.

Gogh *see* VAN GOGH.

going *see* GO. • *n.* **1** moving away, departing (*comings and goings*). **2** the state of the ground for walking or riding on (*rough going*). **3** rate of progress (*it was good going to get there by lunchtime*). • *adj.* **1** in or into action (*set the clock going*). **2** existing, available (*there's cold beef going*). **3** current (*the going rate*). **4** active and prosperous (*a going concern*). □ **be going to** be about to, be likely to. **going-over** *colloq.* **1** an inspection or overhaul. **2** a thrashing. **goings-on** **1** surprising or mysterious or morally suspect behaviour. **2** current news, happenings, etc. (*the goings-on in Bosnia*).

goitre / **goi**-tuh / *n.* an enlarged thyroid gland, often showing as a swelling in the neck.

go-kart *n.* (also **go-cart**) a miniature racing car with a skeleton body.

Golan Heights a range of hills on the border between Syria and Israel, north-east of the Sea of Galilee. Formerly under Syrian control, the area was occupied by Israel in 1967 and annexed in 1981.

gold *n.* **1** a chemical element (symbol Au), a yellow metal of very high value. **2** coins or other articles made of gold. **3** its colour. **4** a gold medal (awarded as first prize) (*going for gold at the Olympics*). **5** something very good or precious. • *adj.* made of gold; coloured like gold. □ **gold-digger** **1** a person who digs for gold in a goldfield. **2** *colloq.* a woman who uses her attractions to obtain money from men. **gold dust** gold found naturally in fine particles. **gold foil** (also **gold leaf**) gold beaten into a very thin sheet. **gold medal** a medal of gold, usu. awarded as first prize. **gold plate** **1** vessels made of gold. **2** material coated with gold. **gold-plate** *v.* coat with gold. **gold reserve** gold held by a central bank to guarantee the value of a country's currency. **gold standard** a system by which the value of money is based on that of gold.

Gold Coast **1** a coastal strip, some 42 kilometres long, which forms the City of the Gold Coast in Qld and is one of Australia's main tourist areas. The strip stretches from Paradise Point in the north to Coolangatta in the south, with Surfers Paradise (near the centre) being the area of greatest tourist concentration. **2** *hist.* the name given by European traders to a coastal area of West Africa (now Ghana) that was an important source of gold.

golden *adj.* **1** made of gold. **2** yielding gold. **3** coloured like gold. **4** precious, excellent (*a golden opportunity*). □ **golden age** **1** a supposed past age when people were happy and innocent. **2** the period of a nation's greatest prosperity, cultural merit, etc. **golden boy** (or **girl**) a popular or successful person. **golden goal** a method of deciding a drawn match in soccer etc. where the first goal scored in extra time decides the winner. **golden handshake** *colloq.* money given by a firm to an employee as compensation for being dismissed or forced to retire. **golden jubilee** a 50th anniversary. **golden mean** **1** neither too much nor too little. **2** = GOLDEN SECTION. **golden**

moths (also **snake orchid**) an Australian terrestrial orchid bearing golden moth-like flowers on long, slender, snake-like stems. **golden oldie** *colloq.* an old hit record, film, etc. that is still well-known and popular. **golden rule** a basic principle of action, esp. 'do as you would be done by'. **golden section** the division of a line so that the whole is to the greater part as that part is to the smaller part. **golden staph** a virulent species of (the staphylococcus) bacterium which has developed a resistance to many antibiotics. **golden syrup** a kind of thick golden treacle. **golden wattle** a heavily flowering small tree (*Acacia pycnantha*), the golden flower of which is popularly regarded as the floral emblem of Australia. **golden wedding** the 50th anniversary of a wedding.

Golden Calf **1** (in the Bible) an image of gold in the shape of a calf, made by Aaron in response to the Israelites' pleas for a god as they awaited Moses' return from Mount Sinai, where he was receiving the Ten Commandments (Exodus 32). **2** (**golden calf**) wealth as an object of worship.

Golden Fleece *Gk myth.* the fleece of a winged golden ram, sought by Jason and the Argonauts.

Golden Mile an area (3 km by 1 km) south of Kalgoorlie in WA, supposed to be the richest gold-bearing terrain in the world.

Golden Temple a sacred Sikh shrine in Amritsar, India.

Golden Triangle the area at the meeting point of Burma (Myanmar), Laos, and Thailand, where much opium is grown.

goldfield *n.* a district in which gold occurs naturally.

goldfinch *n.* a European songbird with a band of yellow across each wing, introduced to Australia and now common.

goldfish *n.* (*pl.* **goldfish** or **goldfishes**) a small reddish-golden Chinese carp kept in a bowl or pond. ☐ **goldfish bowl** **1** a globular glass container for goldfish. **2** a situation in which privacy is completely lacking.

goldmine *n.* **1** a place where gold is mined. **2** a source of wealth, income, profit, or of anything that is sought after. ☐ **goldminer** *n.*

goldrush *n.* a rush to a newly-discovered gold-field.

goldsmith *n.* a person whose trade is making articles in gold.

Goldstein, Vida (Jane Mary) (1869–1949), Australian feminist, suffragist, and pacifist, leader of the radical women's movement in Australia.

golem / **goh**-luhm / *n.* **1** a manikin made of clay etc. and (according to Jewish legend) magically brought to life by human intervention. **2** a robot; an automaton.

golf *n.* a game in which a small hard ball is struck with clubs towards and into a series of (18 or 9) holes with the fewest possible strokes. • *v.* play golf. ☐ **golfer** *n.*

Golgotha / gol-**goth**-uh, gol-guh-thuh / the Aramaic name of Calvary.

Goliath / guh-**luy**-uhth / a Philistine giant, traditionally slain by the boy David with a stone from a sling.

golliwog *n.* a black-faced soft doll with fuzzy hair.

gonad / **goh**-nad / *n.* an animal sex gland (such as a testis or ovary) producing gametes.

gondola / **gon**-duh-luh / *n.* **1** a boat with high pointed ends, used on the canals in Venice. **2** a basket-like structure suspended beneath a balloon or airship, or attached to a ski lift, for carrying passengers etc.

gondolier / gon-duh-**leer** / *n.* a person who propels a gondola by means of a pole.

Gondwana (also **Gondwanaland**) a super-continent existing at the time present-day Australia, Antarctica, South America, India, and Arabia were joined. (Australia became a separate continent about 50 million years ago, gradually moving north.) (¶ From *Gondwana* land of the Gonds, a Dravidian people of central India.)

gone *see* GO. • *adj.* **1** departed; past (*it's gone six o'clock*). **2** lost, hopeless; dead. **3** *colloq.* pregnant for a specified time (*she is six months gone*). **4** consumed, used up (*the butter's just about gone*). **5** *colloq.* completely enthralled or entranced, esp. by rhythmic music, drugs, etc. ☐ **a bit gone** *colloq.* somewhat mad; eccentric (*he's been a bit gone ever since the clock fell on his head*). **be gone** be away (temporarily) (*I'll be gone for about 10 minutes, in case anyone rings*) (cf. BEGONE). **far gone** *colloq.* **1** thoroughly mad or insane. **2** totally drunk. **3** utterly weary. **4** near death. **5** in a state of terminal disrepair (*your fridge is far gone, mate—not worth fixing*). **6** far advanced. **gone missing** *colloq.* lost, not to be found. **gone on** *colloq.* infatuated with (*he's gone on heavy metal; gone on the guy next door*).

goner *n. colloq.* a person or thing that is dead, ruined, or doomed.

gong *n.* **1** a round metal plate that resounds when struck. **2** *colloq.* a medal.

gonorrhoea / gon-uh-**ree**-uh / *n.* (also **gonor-rhea**) a venereal disease causing a thick discharge from the sexual organs. ☐ **gonorrhoeal** *adj.*

goo *n. colloq.* **1** a sticky or slimy substance. **2** sickly sentiment.

good *adj.* (**better, best**) **1** having the right or desirable qualities (*a good wine*). **2** adequate (*his results were just good*). **3** efficient, competent (*good at French; a good driver*). **4** effective, reliable (*good brakes*). **5** (of health etc.) strong (*he has a good constitution*). **6** kind, benevolent (*good of you to come*). **7** morally correct, virtuous (*a good deed*). **8** (of a child) well-behaved. **9** loyal, reliable (*a good friend*). **10** *colloq.* in good health ('*How's your wife?*' —'*She's good, thanks.*'). **11** gratifying, enjoyable, beneficial (*have a good time; good morning*). **12** thorough (*a good beating; a good wash*). **13** not less than, full (*walked a good ten* miles). **14** considerable in number (*a good many people*). **15** beneficial (*milk is good for you*). **16** valid, sound (*a good reason*). **17** financially sound (*his credit is good*). **18** used in exclamations (*good God!*). **19** right, expedient (*thought it good to have a try*). **20** fresh, untainted (*is the meat still good?*). **21** commendable, worthy (*a good reputation; my regards to your good lady*). **22** attractive (*good looks*). **23** suited to the purpose (*now's a good time to water the garden*). •*adv. colloq.* well (*doing pretty good, thanks*). •*n.* (*See also* GOODS.) **1** that which is morally right. **2** profit, benefit (*it will do him good; life is a doubtful good to many*). **3** (**the good**) virtuous people. ☐ **all to the good** *colloq.* in (a person's) best interests (often used to justify an unpleasant occurrence) (*well, you didn't get that cushy job, but it might be all to the good*). **as good as** practically, almost (*the war was as good as over*). **come good** *colloq.* fulfil an expectation (*he'll come good in the end*); improve after a poor start (*the business finally came good*). **good day** (usu. elliptical in Australia as **g'day** or **gidday**) a familiar greeting. **good for 1** beneficial to; having a good effect on. **2** able to pay or undertake (*he is good for $100; they are good for a 10-kilometre hike*). **3** *colloq.* able to be counted on (*Mum's always good for a few bucks*). **4** valid (*your pass is good for another two trips*). **good-for-nothing** *adj.* worthless. *n.* a worthless person. **good-hearted** kindly, well-meaning. **good humour** a genial mood. **good-humoured** cheerful, amiable. **good-looker** (also **looker**) *colloq.* a good-looking person. **good-looking** handsome; physically attractive. **good nature** a friendly disposition. **good-natured** kind, patient; easygoing. **good oil** *Aust. colloq.* reliable information (*the good oil for the Melbourne Cup is 'Tantanoola Tiger'*). **good one!** *Aust. colloq.* **1** an exclamation of admiration, agreement, praise, etc. **2** an ironical exclamation indicating that the person on the receiving end has just made a tactless remark, done something tactless, etc. (*good one, Bill!—didn't you know her husband's left her?*). **good on you!** (or **him!** or **her!** etc.) *Aust. colloq.* an exclamation of approval and encouragement. **good question** *colloq.* an extraordinarily difficult question to answer (*good question, mate!—no idea where the beer's all gone*). **in good with a person** *colloq.* in his or her favour.

goodbye *interj.* & *n.* farewell, an expression used when parting or at the end of a telephone call.

Good Friday the Friday before Easter, commemorating the Crucifixion.

goodie *colloq. n.* (also **goody**) **1** a good or favoured person, esp. a hero in a film etc. (*the goodies and the baddies*). **2** (usu. **goodies**) something good or attractive, esp. to eat. **3** = GOODY-GOODY. •*interj.* expressing childish or affected delight.

goodish *adj.* **1** fairly good. **2** somewhat considerable (*a goodish distance away*).

goodness *n.* **1** virtue; excellence. **2** kindness (*he had the goodness to wait*). **3** the good part of something (*the goodness is in the gravy*). **4** used instead of 'God' in exclamations (*goodness knows*).

good-o (also **good-oh**) *Aust. colloq. adj.* pleasing; fine; satisfactory (*things are pretty good-o at present*). •*adv.* well; satisfactorily (*the barbie was going good-o until it began to rain*). •*interj.* okay!; fine!

goods *n.pl.* **1** movable property. **2** articles of trade (*leather goods*). **3** things to be carried by road and rail (*goods train*). **4** (**the goods**) *colloq.* the genuine article, the real thing (*he's the goods*). ☐ **deliver the goods** *colloq.* produce what one has promised. **have the goods on** (**a person**) *colloq.* **1** have incriminating evidence against (him or her) (*the police have the goods on him at last*). **2** have information which gives one a hold over (him or her).

goodwill *n.* **1** a friendly feeling. **2** the established custom or popularity of a business, considered as an asset. **3** cheerful consent; readiness (*he minded my kids all day with great goodwill*). •*adj.* showing or intending to foster goodwill (*a goodwill gesture*).

goody-goody *colloq. adj.* smugly virtuous. •*n.* a goody-goody person.

gooey *adj. colloq.* **1** viscous, sticky. **2** sickly sentimental.

goof / goof, guuf / *colloq. n.* **1** a stupid person. **2** a mistake. •*v.* bungle; blunder. ☐ **goof around** fool around, act the clown. **goof up** bungle or mess (something) up (*goofed up the entire works with his carelessness*).

goofy *adj. colloq.* stupid; bungling (*a goofy thing to do*). ☐ **goofiness** *n.*

goofy-foot *n.* a person who rides a surfboard, skateboard, etc. with the right (instead of the left) foot forward. ☐ **goofy-footer** *n.*

goog / guug / *n. Aust. colloq.* **1** an egg. **2** an idiot. ☐ **full as a goog 1** extremely full (*the car was packed full as a goog*). **2** totally drunk. **3** (of a person) filled with food.

googie / guu-gee / *n. Aust. colloq.* an egg.

googly / goo-glee / *n.* (*pl.* **googlies**) *Cricket* an off-break ball bowled with apparent leg-break action.

googol *n.* ten raised to the hundredth power (10^{100}).

Goolagong, Evonne *see* CAWLEY.

goolie *n. colloq.* **1** *Aust.* a pebble, a stone. **2** a testicle.

goon *n. colloq.* **1** a stupid person. **2** a hired ruffian.

goose *n.* (*pl.* **geese**) **1** a large waterbird with webbed feet and a broad bill. **2** its flesh as food. **3** a female goose (cf. GANDER). **4** *colloq.* a stupid person. ☐ **cook a person's goose** *colloq.* bring his or her plans, hopes, etc. to naught. **one's goose is cooked** one is ruined, finished, done for.

gooseberry *n.* **1** a thorny shrub. **2** its edible yellowish-green berry with juicy flesh.

gooseflesh *n.* (also **goosebumps, goose pimples**) a bristling state of the skin produced by cold, fright, etc.

gooya / **goo**-yuh / *n. Aust.* = EMU APPLE. (¶ Yuwaalaraay)

gopher / **goh**-fuh / *n.* **1** an American burrowing rodent, burrowing ground squirrel, burrowing tortoise, or burrowing snake. **2** = GOFER.

Gorbachev / **gaw**-buh-chof /, Mikhail (Sergeevich) (1931–), Soviet statesman, general secretary of the Communist Party of the USSR 1985–91, president 1988–91. He was awarded the Nobel Peace Prize in 1990.

Gordian *adj.* ◻ **cut the Gordian knot** solve a seemingly insoluble problem forcefully or by evading the conditions. (¶ An intricate knot which no-one could unravel was tied by Gordius, king of ancient Phrygia. Challenged to undo the knot, Alexander the Great cut through it with his sword.)

Gordon, Adam Lindsay (1833–70), Australian poet, steeplechaser, and horsebreaker. His poetry, including *Bush Ballads and Galloping Rhymes* (1870), evokes the Australian outback.

Gordon River *see* FRANKLIN.

gore *n.* **1** thickened blood from a cut or wound. **2** a triangular or tapering section of a skirt, sail, or umbrella. • *v.* pierce with a horn or tusk.

gorge *n.* **1** a narrow steep-sided valley. **2** the act of gorging; a feast. **3** the contents of the stomach. **4** the food passage extending from the back of the throat to the stomach. • *v.* **1** eat greedily (*don't gorge*). **2** (often *reflexive*) glut, satiate (*gorged himself on meat pies at the footy*). **3** devour (something) greedily (*he gorged the entire duck*). **4** (as **gorged**) filled, choked, blocked up. ◻ **make a person's gorge rise** sicken or disgust him or her.

gorgeous *adj.* **1** richly coloured, magnificent. **2** *colloq.* very pleasant (*gorgeous weather*). **3** strikingly beautiful. ◻ **gorgeously** *adv.*

gorgon *n.* **1** *Gk myth.* any of three snake-haired sisters (esp. Medusa) whose looks turned to stone anyone who saw them. **2** a terrifying woman.

gorgonzola / gaw-guhn-**zoh**-luh / *n.* a rich strong blue-veined cheese, originally from Gorgonzola in north Italy.

gorilla *n.* the largest of the anthropoid apes, native to Africa.

gormandise / **gaw**-muhn-duyz / *v.* (also **-ize**) eat greedily. ◻ **gormandiser** *n.*

gormless *adj. colloq.* stupid.

gorse *n.* a wild evergreen shrub with yellow flowers and sharp thorns. ◻ **gorsy** *adj.*

Gorton, Sir John (Grey) (1911–), AC, Australian Liberal statesman, prime minister 1968–71.

gory *adj.* **1** covered with blood. **2** involving bloodshed (*a gory battle*). **3** *colloq.* nasty; unpleasant. ◻ **gorily** *adv.* **goriness** *n.*

gosh *interj.* an exclamation of surprise.

goshawk / **gos**-hawk / *n.* any of various large hawks with long tails and short wings, including some Australian species (e.g. *the brown goshawk, the red goshawk*).

gosling / **goz**-ling / *n.* a young goose.

gospel *n.* **1** the teachings of Christ recorded in the first four books of the New Testament. **2** (**Gospel**) any of these books. **3** (also **gospel truth**) a thing one may safely believe (*you can take it as gospel*). **4** (in full **gospel music**) African-American religious singing.

goss *n. Aust. colloq.* **1** gossip. **2** a gossiper.

gossamer *n.* **1** a fine filmy piece of cobweb made by small spiders. **2** any flimsy delicate material. • *adj.* light and flimsy as gossamer.

gossip *n.* **1** casual talk, esp. about other people's affairs or social incidents. **2** a person who is fond of gossiping. **3** groundless rumour. • *v.* engage in or spread gossip. ◻ **gossiper** *n.* **gossipy** *adj.*

got *see* GET. ◻ **have got into a person** *colloq.* causing a person to be grumpy, irritable, etc. (*what's got into you this past hour?*). **have got it in a person to** possess the ability, skill, potential, etc. to (*he's got it in him to go to uni but he won't do the work*). **have got it in for a person** *colloq.* be filled with spite, animosity, etc. against a person (*the teachers have got it in for me—why else would I have failed in every subject?*). **have got to** must.

Goth *n.* **1** a member of a Germanic tribe which invaded the Roman Empire from the east in the 3rd–5th centuries. **2** an uncivilised or ignorant person.

goth *n.* **1** a style of rock music with an intense or droning sound and mystical lyrics. **2** a performer or follower of this music, often favouring black clothing and a white-painted face with black make-up.

Gothic / **goth**-ik / *adj.* **1** of the Goths. **2** of the style of architecture common in western Europe in the 12th–16th centuries, with pointed arches and rich stone carving. • *n.* **1** this style. **2** the language of the Goths. ◻ **Gothic novel** a kind of novel with sensational or horrifying events, popular in the 18th–19th centuries.

gotten *US* = GOT.

■ **Usage** Non-standard in Australian English, except in *ill-gotten*.

Götterdämmerung / ger-tuh-**dem**-uh-ruung / *n.* the twilight of the gods (*see* TWILIGHT); the complete downfall of a regime etc. (¶ German)

gouache / goo-**ahsh** / *n.* **1** painting with opaque pigments ground in water and thickened with gum and honey. **2** these pigments.

gouda / **gow**-duh, **goo**- / *n.* a flat round Dutch cheese.

gouge / gowj / *n.* **1** a chisel with a concave blade, used for cutting grooves. **2** a groove etc. made with such a tool. • *v.* **1** cut out with a gouge. **2** (foll. by *out*) scoop or force out (e.g. an eye with the thumb). **3** *Aust.* dig for opal.

gouging *n.* (in football, esp. in rugby) the infringement of poking a finger into an opponent's eye.

goujons / goo-*zh*awn / *n.pl.* narrow deep-fried strips of fish or meat.

goulash / goo-lash / *n.* a stew (orig. Hungarian) of meat and vegetables, seasoned with paprika.

Goulburn / gohl-buhn / **1** a city in south-eastern NSW. **2** a river in north central Victoria. **3** a river in central east NSW.

Gould[1], Elizabeth (1804–41), English natural history artist, and John (1804–81), English zoologist, wife and husband. The Goulds were in Australia from 1838 to 1840 and produced their major work, the 7-volume *Birds of Australia* (1840–8), which Elizabeth Gould illustrated until her death. John Gould later published *The Mammals of Australia* (1865). Elizabeth is remembered in the beautiful *Gouldian finch* and John is remembered in the nationwide Australian society, the Gould League (of Bird Lovers).

Gould[2], Shane (Elizabeth) (1956–), Australian swimmer who broke every world freestyle record from 100 to 1500 metres and won 3 gold medals in record-breaking times at the 1972 Olympics.

Gould[3], William Buelow (1801–53), Australian convict artist, noted esp. for his paintings of flowers.

Gouldian finch *n.* a strikingly beautiful multi-coloured finch of northern Australia.

Gounod / goo-noh /, Charles François (1818–93), French composer.

gourd / goord, gawd / *n.* **1** the hard-skinned fleshy fruit of a climbing plant. **2** a bowl or container made from the dried hollowed-out rind of this fruit.

gourmand / gaw-**mond**, gaw-muhnd / *n.* **1** a glutton. **2** a gourmet.

■ **Usage** The use of *gourmand* in sense 2 is considered incorrect by some people. *Gourmand* is often applied to a person contemptuously, whereas *gourmet* is not.

gourmandise / gaw-muhn-deez, goor- / *n.* love of food, gluttony.

gourmet / gaw-may, goor- / *n.* a connoisseur of good food and drink.

■ **Usage** See the note under *gourmand*.

gout *n.* a disease causing inflammation of the joints, esp. the toes. ☐ **gouty** *adj.*

.gov *abbr.* denoting an email address or a site on the Internet that is governmental.

Gove Peninsula a peninsula on the north-east point of Arnhem Land, NT, which is an Aboriginal Reserve.

govern *v.* **1** rule with authority; conduct the affairs of a country or an organisation. **2** keep under control (*to govern one's temper*). **3** influence or direct (*be governed by the experts' advice*).

governance *n.* governing, control.

government / **guv**-uhn-muhnt, **guv**-muhnt, guv-uh-muhnt / *n.* **1** governing, the system or method of governing. **2** the group or organisation governing a country. **3** (usu. **Government**) a particular ministry in office. **4** the State as an agent (*a government grant*). •*adj.* of or pertaining to the government (*government department*). ☐ **governmental** *adj.*

■ **Usage** The second and third pronunciations given are extremely common in Australia, but are non-standard.

Governor, Jimmy (1875–1901), Australian Aboriginal bushranger, hanged in Darlinghurst jail on January 18, 1901: his life was the subject of the novel by Thomas Keneally *The Chant of Jimmie Blacksmith* (1972).

governor *n.* **1** a person who governs. **2** the representative of the British monarch: **a** in each Australian State; **b** in a colony or former colony. **3** the head or a member of the governing body of an institution (*the Governor of the Reserve Bank*). **4** the official in charge of a prison. **5** *colloq.* one's employer. **6** *colloq.* one's father. **7** a mechanism that automatically controls speed or the intake of gas or water etc. in a machine. ☐ **governor-general** (*pl.* **governors-general** *or* **governor-generals**) the representative of the British monarch: **a** in the Commonwealth of Australia; **b** in any other country of the Commonwealth that regards the British monarch as Head of State. ☐☐ **governorship** *n.*

govie / **guv**-ee / *Aust. colloq. adj.* (also **guvvie**) government (*a govie car*). •*n.* (also **govie flat** *or* **house**) a flat or house originally built or bought by the government for low-cost or subsidised rental.

Gowar / **guu**-wahr / *n.* an Aboriginal language of Moreton Island in Moreton Bay, Qld.

gown *n.* **1** a loose flowing garment, esp. a woman's long dress. **2** a loose outer garment that is the official robe of members of a university, judges, etc. **3** a surgeon's overall.

gowned *adj.* wearing a gown.

goy *n.* (*pl.* **goyim** *or* **goys**) a Jewish name for a person who is not a Jew.

Goya (in full Francisco José de Goya y Lucientes) (1746–1828), Spanish painter and etcher.

GP *abbr.* general practitioner.

GPO *abbr.* General Post Office.

gr *abbr.* (also **gr.**) **1** gram(s). **2** grains. **3** gross.

grab *v.* (**grabbed**, **grabbing**) **1** grasp suddenly. **2** take something greedily or unfairly. **3** operate harshly or jerkily (*the brakes are grabbing*). **4** *colloq.* make an impression on (*how does that music grab you?*). **5** (foll. by *at*) snatch at. •*n.* **1** a sudden clutch or an attempt to seize. **2** a mechanical device for gripping or lifting things. **3 a** a brief attention-grabbing or headline-grabbing statement, esp. one made by a politician at a doorstop interview etc. **b** such a statement or interview in a television news or other broadcast. ▫ **grab bag** *n.* a miscellaneous collection (*made a grab bag of promises*). **up for grabs** *colloq.* available for anyone to take. ▫▫ **grabber** *n.*

Grace, Dr W(illiam) G(ilbert) (1848–1915), English cricketer.

grace *n.* **1** the quality of being attractive, esp. in movement, manner, or design. **2** elegance of manner, politeness (*he had the grace to apologise*). **3** favour, goodwill. **4** a delay granted as a favour (*give him a week's grace*). **5** (in Christianity) the unmerited favour of God. **6** a short prayer of thanks before or after a meal. • *v.* add grace to; confer honour or dignity on (*graced us with his presence*). ▫ **grace note** a music note that is added as an embellishment. **His Grace**, **Your Grace**, etc. the title used in speaking of or to a duke, duchess, or archbishop. **in a person's good** (*or* **bad**) **graces** regarded by that person with favour (or disfavour). **put on airs and graces** show snobbish pride; display affected mannerisms. **with** (**a**) **good** (*or* **bad**) **grace** as if willingly (or reluctantly).

graceful *adj.* having or showing grace or elegance. ▫ **gracefully** *adv.* **gracefulness** *n.*

graceless *adj.* **1** lacking grace, elegance, or charm. **2** ungracious; boorish.

Graces *n.pl. Gk myth.* three beautiful sister goddesses, givers of beauty, charm, and skill.

gracious *adj.* **1** kind. **2** indulgent to inferiors (*the Queen being gracious to commoners*). **3** showing divine grace, merciful. **4** showing qualities associated with good taste and elegant comfort (*gracious living*). ▫ **graciously** *adv.* **graciousness** *n.*

gradate / gruh-**dayt** / *v.* **1** pass or cause to pass by gradations into the next colour or stage etc. **2** arrange in gradations.

gradation / gruh-**day**-shuhn / *n.* **1** a series following successive stages in rank, merit, intensity, etc. **2** arrangement in this way. **3** a process of gradual change; a stage in such a process (*the gradations of colour between green and blue*). ▫ **gradational** *adj.*

grade *n.* **1** a step, stage, or degree in some rank, quality, or value (*Grade A eggs*). **2** a class of people or things of the same rank or quality etc. **3** a mark indicating the quality of a student's work. **4** a gradient, a slope. **5** a class in school. • *v.* **1** arrange in grades. **2** give a grade to a student. **3** adjust the gradient of (a road). **4** pass gradually into a grade or between grades. • *adj. Aust.* (of sports) organised in grades according to level of ability (*grade cricket*). ▫ **make the grade** reach the desired standard.

grader *n.* **1** a person or thing that grades. **2** a wheeled, motor-driven machine for levelling the ground, esp. in roadmaking.

gradient / **gray**-dee-uhnt / *n.* **1** the amount of slope in a road, railway, or line or curve on a graph (*the road has a gradient of 1 in 10*). **2** a sloping road or railway.

gradual *adj.* taking place by degrees, not rapid, sudden, or steep. • *n.* a response sung or recited between the Epistle and the Gospel in the Mass. ▫ **gradually** *adv.*

graduate *n.* / **graj**-oo-uht / a person who holds an academic degree. • *v.* / **graj**-oo-ayt / **1** obtain an academic degree. **2** (foll. by *to*) move up to (a higher grade of activity etc.). **3** mark out in degrees or parts. **4** arrange in gradations; apportion (e.g. tax) according to a scale. ▫ **graduation** *n.*

Graeco-Roman / gree-koh-**roh**-muhn / *adj.* of the ancient Greeks and Romans.

Graf, Steffi (full name: Stephanie Maria Graf) (1969–), German tennis player.

graffiti / gruh-**fee**-tee / *n.pl.* (*sing.* **graffito**) words or drawings scratched, scribbled, or sprayed on a surface.

■ **Usage** *Graffiti* is, in formal terms, a plural noun and as such should be used with a plural verb. However, the most common use of *graffiti* is as a collective or mass noun, referring to inscriptions in general or as a group. As such, this word is usually found with a singular verb, e.g. *Graffiti is an increasing problem*. Most people find this use natural and acceptable, as they do the collective use of the word *data*.

graft *n.* **1** a shoot from one tree fixed into a cut in another to form a new growth. **2** a piece of living tissue transplanted surgically to replace diseased or damaged tissue. **3** *Aust. colloq.* hard work. **4** advantage in business or politics obtained by bribery, unfair influence, or other shady means. • *v.* **1** put a graft in or on. **2** join (a thing) inseparably to another. **3** *Aust. colloq.* work hard (*grafting for opals at Coober Pedy*). **4** seek or gain advantage through bribery etc.

Grail *n.* (in full **Holy Grail**) **1** the cup or platter used (according to legend) by Christ at the Last Supper and in which Joseph of Arimathea received drops of Christ's blood at the Crucifixion, sought in prolonged quests by knights in medieval legends. **2** the object of a quest.

grain *n.* **1** a small hard seed of a food plant such as wheat or rice. **2** such plants themselves. **3** a small hard particle of salt, sand, gold, etc. **4** a unit of weight, about 65 milligrams. **5** the smallest possible amount (*he hasn't a grain of sense*). **6** the texture produced by the particles in flesh, stone, etc. or in photographic prints. **7** the pattern of lines made by fibres in wood or by layers in rock or coal etc.; the direction of threads in woven fabric. ▫ **against the grain** contrary to one's natural inclinations. ▫▫ **grainy** *adj.*

Grainger, Percy (Aldridge) (1882–1961), Australian pianist and composer.

gram[1] *n.* a unit of mass in the metric system, one-thousandth of a kilogram.

gram² n. any of various pulses (such as chickpeas, split peas, etc.) used as food (*green gram; black gram*).

-gram¹ *comb. form* **1** forming nouns denoting a thing written or recorded (often in a certain way) (*anagram; epigram; telegram*). **2** meaning *telegram* and denoting one intended to amuse or embarrass the receiver since it is delivered in public (e.g. at a birthday party) by a specified messenger, e.g. a clown, a singer, one who delivers with a kiss, a derelict, etc.; hence *clownogram, sing-a-gram, kissogram, dero-gram*, etc.

-gram² *comb. form* denoting grams (*kilogram*).

graminaceous / gram-uh-**nay**-shuhs / *adj.* of or like grass.

graminivorous / gram-uh-**niv**-uh-ruhs / *adj.* (of an animal) feeding on grass.

gramma n. *Aust.* a variety of pumpkin with sweet orange flesh.

grammar n. **1** the study of words and of the rules for their formation and their relationships to each other in sentences. **2** the rules themselves. **3** a book about these. **4** speech or writing judged as good or bad according to these rules (*his grammar is appalling*). ◻ **grammar school** a secondary school in Australia, usu. a private Church school (*Geelong Grammar*).

grammarian n. an expert in grammar or linguistics.

grammatical *adj.* in accordance with the rules of grammar. ◻ **grammatically** *adv.*

gramme alternative spelling of GRAM¹.

gramophone n. a record player, esp. the kind that is not operated electrically.

Grampians a range of westward-tilting, sandstone mountains in western Vic., important as a scenic resource and including Vic.'s largest national park.

grampus n. (*pl.* **grampuses**) a large dolphin-like sea animal with a blunt snout.

granary n. a storehouse for threshed grain.

grand *adj.* **1** splendid, magnificent; dignified, imposing. **2** main; of chief importance (*footy grand final*). **3** of the highest rank (*grand duke; grand master in chess*). **4** *colloq.* very enjoyable or satisfactory (*we had a grand time*). **5** (in *combinations*) (in names of family relationships) denoting the second degree of ascent or descent (*grandfather; granddaughter*). **6** including everything, final (*the grand total*). •n. **1** a grand piano. **2** *colloq.* a thousand dollars (*five grand*). ◻ **grand final** *Aust.* the concluding match of a competition. **grand opera** opera in which everything is sung and there are no spoken parts. **grand piano** a large full-toned piano standing on three legs, with the strings arranged horizontally. **grand slam** *see* SLAM. ◻◻ **grandly** *adv.* **grandness** n.

grandchild n. (*pl.* **grandchildren**) the child of a person's son or daughter.

granddaughter n. the daughter of a person's son or daughter.

grandee / gran-**dee** / n. **1** a Spanish or Portuguese noble. **2** a person of high rank.

grandeur / **gran**-juh / n. splendour, magnificence, grandness.

grandfather n. the father of a person's father or mother. ◻ **grandfather clock** a clock in a tall wooden case, worked by weights.

grandiloquent / gran-**dil**-uh-kwuhnt / *adj.* using pompous, flowery language. ◻ **grandiloquently** *adv.* **grandiloquence** n.

grandiose / **gran**-dee-ohs / *adj.* **1** imposing, planned on a large scale. **2** trying to be grand, pompous. ◻ **grandiosity** / gran-dee-**os**-uh-tee / n.

grand mal / gron **mal** / n. epilepsy with loss of consciousness. (¶ French, = great sickness.)

grandmother n. the mother of a person's father or mother.

grandparent n. a grandfather or grandmother.

grand prix / gron **pree** / n. (*pl.* **grands prix** pronounced the same) **1** the highest award in a show, a competition, etc. **2** (usu. **Grand Prix**) any of various important international motor or motorcycle racing events. (¶ French, = great or chief prize.)

grandson n. the son of a person's son or daughter.

grandstand n. the principal roofed building with rows of seats for spectators at a racetrack or sports ground. •v. act in an ostentatious, self-important manner in order to impress (*as soon as he saw the TV cameras, he began to grandstand outrageously*). •*adj.* advantageous for observing (*from his second-floor window he had a grandstand view of the accident*). ◻ **grandstand finish** a close and exciting finish to a race, an election, etc.

graniferous / gruh-**nif**-uh-ruhs / *adj.* producing grain or grainlike seed.

granite n. a hard grey stone for building.

granivorous / gruh-**niv**-uh-ruhs / *adj.* feeding on grains.

granny n. (also **grannie**) *colloq.* **1** grandmother. **2** *Aust.* (in Aboriginal English) an elderly relative or a community elder. ◻ **granny bonnet** (also **granny's bonnet**) **1** = COLUMBINE. **2** (also **pimelea**) an eastern Australian shrub with showy heads of white flowers. **granny flat** a self-contained flat in (or an addition to) someone's house where an elderly relative can live independently but close to the family. **granny knot** a reef knot with the strings crossed the wrong way and therefore likely to slip.

Granny Smith n. a large Australian green-skinned apple excellent for eating raw or for cooking. (¶ Maria Ann ('Granny') Smith (1801–70) who first produced them in Sydney.)

grant v. **1** give or allow as a privilege (*grant a request*). **2** give formally, transfer legally. **3** admit or agree that something is true (*I grant that your* offer is generous). •*n.* something granted, esp. a sum of money given by the government. ❑ **take for granted** assume that (a thing) is true or sure to happen; be so used to having (a thing) that one no longer appreciates it.

Granth n. = ADI GRANTH.

grantor *n.* a person by whom something is legally transferred.

granular / gran-yuh-luh / *adj.* **1** of or like grains or granules. **2** having a granulated surface or structure. ❑ **granularity** *n.*

granulate / gran-yuh-layt / *v.* **1** form into grains or granules (*granulated sugar*). **2** make rough and grainy on the surface. ❑ **granulation** *n.*

granule / gran-yool / *n.* a small grain.

grape *n.* a green or purple berry growing in clusters on vines, used for eating and for making wine. ❑ **grape hyacinth** a small hyacinth-like plant with clusters of rounded usu. blue flowers.

grapefruit *n.* (*pl.* **grapefruit**) a large round yellow citrus fruit with an acid juicy pulp.

grapevine *n.* **1** a vine on which grapes grow. **2** a way by which news is passed on unofficially (*heard it on the grapevine*).

graph *n.* a diagram consisting of a line or lines showing the relationship between corresponding values of two quantities. •*v.* draw a graph of. ❑ **graph paper** paper ruled into small squares, used for plotting graphs.

graphic / graf-ik / *adj.* **1** of drawing, painting, lettering, or engraving (*the graphic arts; a graphic artist*). **2** giving a vivid description (*a graphic account of the fight*). •*n.* (**graphics**) **1** (as *sing.*) the use of diagrams in calculation or in design. **2** (as *pl.*) lettering and drawings (*the graphics are by John James*). ❑ **computer graphics** a mode of processing and output in which a significant part of the information is in pictorial form. **graphic equaliser** a device for varying the quality of an audio signal by controlling the strength of individual radio frequency bands. **graphic novel** a novel in comic-strip format.

graphical / graf-i-kuhl / *adj.* **1** using diagrams or graphs. **2** = GRAPHIC (sense 1). ❑ **graphically** *adv.*

graphite *n.* a soft black form of carbon used in lubrication, as a moderator in nuclear reactors, and in lead pencils.

graphology / gruh-fol-uh-jee / *n.* the study of handwriting, esp. as a supposed guide to the writer's character. ❑ **graphological** *adj.* **graphologist** *n.*

grapnel *n.* **1** a hooked grappling instrument used in dragging the bed of a lake or river. **2** a small anchor with three or more flukes.

grapple *v.* **1** seize or hold firmly. **2** (often foll. by *with*) struggle at close quarters. **3** (foll. by *with*) try to manage or deal with (*grapple with a problem*). ❑ **grappling iron** a grapnel.

grasp *v.* **1** seize and hold firmly, esp. with one's hands or arms. **2** understand (*he couldn't grasp what we meant*). •*n.* **1** a firm hold or grip (*within her grasp*). **2** a mental hold, understanding (*a thorough grasp of the subject*). ❑ **grasp at** snatch at. **grasp the nettle** tackle a difficulty boldly.

grasping *adj.* greedy for money or possessions.

grass *n.* **1** any of a group of common wild low-growing plants with green blades and stalks that are eaten by animals. **2** a plant of the family which includes cereal plants, reeds, and bamboos. **3** ground covered with grass, lawn, or pasture. **4** grazing (*out to grass*). **5** *colloq.* marijuana. **6** *colloq.* a person who grasses; an act of betraying. •*v.* **1** cover with grass; provide with pasture. **2** *colloq.* betray a conspiracy, turn informer. ❑ **grass-fed** *Aust.* (of a horse) inexperienced, not trained as a racehorse. **grass fighter** *Aust. colloq.* a person who fights with no holds barred. **grass parrot** (also **grass parakeet**) any of various Australian parrots frequenting grassy country and feeding mainly on grass seeds (e.g. the budgerigar). **grass tree** any of many small woody-trunked Australian trees bearing a very tall flowering spike arising from a crown of grass-like leaves, and yielding a yellowish resin. Also called *blackboy, xanthorrhoea, yakka*. **grass widow** (or **widower**) a wife (or husband) whose spouse is absent for some time. **grass wren** any of several large ground-dwelling Australian wrens inhabiting mainly spinifex country. **put out to grass 1** (of a racehorse) retire it from racing when it is past its prime. **2** *colloq.* retire a person.

grasshopper *n.* a jumping insect that makes a shrill chirping noise.

grassland *n.* a wide area covered in grass and with few trees, esp. used for grazing.

grassroots *n.pl.* **1** the fundamental level or source. **2** ordinary people; the rank and file of an organisation, esp. a political party. •*adj.* pertaining to or deriving from ordinary people (*grassroots opposition to the new tax*).

grassy *adj.* like grass; covered with grass.

grate *n.* **1** a metal framework that keeps fuel in a fireplace. **2** a fireplace or furnace. •*v.* **1** shred into small pieces by rubbing against a jagged surface. **2** make a harsh noise by rubbing; sound harshly (*a grating laugh*). **3** have an unpleasant irritating effect.

grateful *adj.* **1** feeling or showing that one values a kindness or benefit received. **2** pleasant; acceptable (*a grateful breeze*). ❑ **gratefully** *adv.*

grater *n.* a device with a jagged surface for grating food.

gratify *v.* (**gratified, gratifying**) give pleasure to, satisfy (wishes etc.). ❑ **gratification** *n.*

grating *n.* a screen of spaced metal or wooden bars placed across an opening.

gratis / grah-tuhs / *adv.* & *adj.* free of charge (*you can have the leaflet gratis*).

gratitude *n.* being grateful.

gratuitous / gruh-tyoo-uh-tuhs / *adj.* **1** given or done without payment. **2** given or done without

gratuity 356 **Great Barrier Reef**

good reason (*a gratuitous insult*). ☐ **gratuitously** *adv.* **gratuitousness** *n.*

gratuity / gruh-**tyoo**-uh-tee / *n.* money given in recognition of services rendered, a tip.

gravamen / gruh-**vay**-men / *n.* (*pl.* **gravamens** or **gravamina**) **1** the essence or most serious part of an argument. **2** a grievance.

grave *n.* **1** a hole dug in the ground to bury a corpse; a mound or memorial stone placed over this. **2** (**the grave**) death, being dead. •*adj.* **1** serious, causing great anxiety (*grave news*). **2** solemn, not smiling. ☐ **grave accent** / grahv / a mark (`) over a vowel, as over *a* in *à la carte*. ☐☐ **gravely** *adv.*

gravel *n.* **1** coarse sand with small stones, as used for roads and paths. **2** *Med.* hard crystals forming in the urinary tract. •*v.* (**gravelled, gravelling**) cover with gravel.

gravelly *adv.* **1** like gravel. **2** rough-sounding (*a gravelly voice*).

graven *adj.* **1** carved (*a graven image*). **2** firmly fixed (*graven on my memory*).

gravestone *n.* a stone monument over a grave.

graveyard *n.* a burial ground. ☐ **graveyard shift** a work shift scheduled to begin very late at night or at dawn.

gravid / **grav**-uhd / *adj. Med.* pregnant.

gravitate *v.* **1** move or be attracted towards (*gravitated towards the pub*). **2** move or tend by force of gravity towards; sink by or as if by gravity.

gravitation *n.* **1** the force of attraction between any particle of matter in the universe and any other. **2** the effect of this, esp. the falling of bodies to the earth. ☐ **gravitational** *adj.*

gravity *n.* **1** the force that attracts bodies towards the centre of the earth; the intensity of this. **2** seriousness (*the gravity of Aids is not realised by many*). **3** solemnity. ☐ **centre of gravity** *see* CENTRE.

gravy *n.* **1** juice that comes out of meat while it is cooking. **2** sauce made from this. **3** *colloq.* money or profit easily or unexpectedly acquired. ☐ **gravy beef** *Aust.* a lesser quality but flavoursome meat from shank or shin used for making stock, broth, etc. **gravy train** *colloq.* a source of easy money.

grayling *n.* a silver-grey freshwater fish of SE Australia.

graze[1] *v.* **1** eat growing grass (*cattle grazing in the fields*). **2** put (animals) into a field to eat the grass. ☐ **grazing country** *Aust.* land suitable to or used for the raising of sheep or cattle. **grazing district** *Aust.* an area in which the principal industry is sheep raising or cattle raising.

graze[2] *v.* **1** touch or scrape lightly in passing. **2** scrape the skin from. •*n.* a raw place where the skin has been scraped.

grazier / **gray**-zee-uh / *n. Aust.* the owner of a large-scale property on which sheep or cattle are raised. ☐ **grazier's alert** a warning of cold weather ahead issued by the weather bureau to graziers, esp. when it is lambing season.

grease / grees / *n.* **1** oily or fatty matter, esp. as a lubricant. **2** the melted fat of a dead animal. •*v.* (also / greez /) put grease on or in. ☐ **grease the palm of** *colloq.* bribe.

greasepaint *n.* make-up used by actors and other performers.

greaseproof *adj.* impervious to grease (*grease-proof paper*).

greaser / **gree**-zuh / *n. colloq.* an obsequious person, a crawler.

greasies / **gree**-zeez / *n.pl. Aust. colloq.* **1** fish and chips. **2** any take-away food, esp. if oily.

greasy / **gree**-zee, -see / *adj.* (**greasier, greasiest**) **1** covered with or containing much grease. **2** slippery. **3** oily in manner; unctuous. •*n. Aust. colloq.* **1** a person who cooks for a number of people, as an army cook. **2** a shearer. ☐ **greasily** *adv.* **greasiness** *n.*

great *adj.* **1** much above average in size, amount, extent, or intensity. **2** (also **greater**) larger than others of similar kind (*the great grey kangaroo; the greater glider*). **3** of remarkable ability or character, etc. (*one of the great painters; Pope St Gregory the Great*). **4** distinguished (*a great statesman*). **5** with implied admiration, contempt, etc., esp. in exclamations (*you great idiot!; great stuff!*). **6** reinforcing words that denote size, quantity, etc. (*a great big hole; a great many*). **7** important, main (*the great thing is not to get caught*). **8** grand, imposing (*this great occasion*). **9** (foll. by *at*, *on*) competent, well-informed (*great at chess; great on Aboriginal languages*). **10** elaborate, intense (*told in great detail*). **11** doing something frequently or intensively or very well (*a great reader; a great believer in tolerance*). **12** *colloq.* very enjoyable or satisfactory (*we had a great time*). **13** of a family relationship that is one generation removed in ancestry or descent (*great-aunt; great-niece; great-great-grandfather*). •*n.* an outstanding person or thing (*he is one of the greats*). •*adv. colloq.* well, successfully (*she's going great in the exams*). ☐ **great circle** a circle on the surface of a sphere whose plane passes through the sphere's centre. **great one for** *colloq.* very keen on; very skilled at (*he's a great one for computer games*). **the greatest thing since sliced bread** *colloq.* (of a person or thing) wonderful, pre-eminent, first rate. ☐☐ **greatness** *n.*

Great Artesian Basin the world's largest water-bearing basin covering an area of nearly 1.7 million square kilometres and ranging from Qld through NSW and SA to the NT.

great Australian adjective *n.* the epithet 'bloody'.

Great Australian Bight a wide bay (1,200 km east to west) on the south coast of Australia, bounded by Cape Pasley, WA, and West Point, SA.

great Australian salute *n.* a frequently seen wave of the hand brushing flies off the face.

Great Barrier Reef the largest coral reef in the world, stretching for about 2,000 km roughly

Great Britain

parallel to the NE coast of Australia. Since 1981 it has been on the World Heritage List.
Great Britain England, Wales, and Scotland considered as a unit.
greatcoat *n.* a heavy overcoat.
Great Dane *n.* a very large powerful smooth-haired breed of dog.
Great Dividing Range the crest of the eastern highlands of Australia, roughly parallel to the coast for most of its north–south length from Cape York to western Vic.
greater glider *n.* a large gliding possum of mainland Australia.
great grey kangaroo *n.* (also **great kangaroo**, **eastern grey kangaroo**) an extremely large kangaroo (the male may stand nearly 2 metres tall) of eastern Australia, with silvery grey fur.
Great Lake Australia's largest freshwater lake, situated on the central plateau of Tas. It is 24 km long and up to 8 km wide.
greatly *adv.* much; by a considerable amount.
Great Sandy Desert a large arid desert in the north-east of WA.
great sun orchid *n.* an Australian terrestrial orchid, *Thelymitra grandiflora*, bearing numerous large flowers of a magnificent blue, a colour rare in the orchid family.
Great Victoria Desert a large desert area north of the Nullarbor Plain, extending from north-west SA well into WA.
Great Wall of China a long defensive wall in northern China extending for some 2,400 kilometres. It has the distinction of being the only man-made structure on earth visible from the moon.
Great War the First World War.
greave *n.* a piece of armour worn on the leg to protect the shin.
grebe / greeb / *n.* any of various diving birds (of Australia, Europe, etc.) with a long neck, lobed toes, and almost no tail (e.g., in Australia, *the great crested grebe*, *the hoary-headed grebe*).
Grecian / gree-shuhn / *adj.* pertaining to ancient Greece (esp. its art, architecture, etc.) (*Grecian urn*). □ **Grecian nose** a straight nose (as portrayed in ancient Greek statues) that continues the line of the forehead without a dip.
Greece a republic in SE Europe comprising a peninsula bounded by the Ionian, Mediterranean, and Aegean Seas, and numerous outlying islands.
greed *n.* an excessive desire, esp. for food or wealth.
greedy *adj.* (**greedier**, **greediest**) **1** having or showing greed. **2** very eager or keen for something. □ **greedily** *adv.* **greediness** *n.*
Greek *adj.* of Greece or its people or language; Hellenic. •*n.* **1** a member of the people living in ancient or modern Greece. **2** their language. □ **Greek cross** a cross with four equal arms. **it's Greek to me** *colloq.* I cannot understand its meaning.

Greek Orthodox Church that branch of the Orthodox Church which is the established Church of Greece.
green *adj.* **1** of the colour between blue and yellow in the spectrum, the colour of growing grass. **2** covered with grass or with growing leaves. **3** (of fruit or wood) unripe or unseasoned. **4** not dried, smoked, cured, or tanned. **5** raw, uncooked (*green prawns*). **6** immature, inexperienced, easily deceived. **7** (of the complexion) pale and sickly-looking. **8** jealous, envious. **9** young, flourishing. **10** not withered or worn out (*in his green old age*). **11** (also **Green**) concerned with protection of the environment; (of a product, a process, etc.) not harmful to the environment; environment-friendly. •*n.* **1** green colour or pigment. **2** a green substance or material; green clothes. **3** a green light. **4** *Brit.* a piece of grassy public land (*the village green*). **5** a grassy area used for a special purpose (*a putting green*). **6** (also **Green**) a supporter of an environmentalist group or party. **7** (**Greens**) the Green Party (*see below*). **8** (**greens**) green vegetables. •*v.* **1** make or become green. **2** make (an urban area) fresh and green by planting trees etc. **3** make (people, a society, etc.) aware of ecological issues or able to act on ecological principles; change the policies of (a party, a government, etc.) so as to minimise harm to the environment. □ **green and golden bell frog** *Aust.* a rare frog of eastern NSW and eastern Vic. **green ban** *Aust.* action (esp. by trade unions) which prevents construction work from proceeding in a green belt or which prevents the demolition or marring of a building of historical or cultural etc. significance. **green belt** an area of open land round a city, designated for preservation. **green drought** *Aust.* new but insubstantial growth (of forage) following rain. **green fingers** skill in making plants grow. **green gram** mung beans. **green leek** any of several predominantly green or green-faced Australian parakeets. **green light 1** a signal to proceed on a road or railway. **2** *colloq.* permission to go ahead with a project. **green mallee** a small eucalypt of inland eastern Australia with vividly green leaves, one of the species from which eucalyptus oil is obtained. **green monday** *Aust.* = GREENGROCER (sense 2). **green pick** *Aust.* new growth (of forage) promoted by rain. **green room** a room in a theatre, for the use of actors when they are not on the stage. **green shoot** new growth of vegetation immediately after a bushfire. **green tea** tea made from leaves that are steam-dried, not fermented (cf. BLACK TEA). **green tree ant** (also **green ant**) a green ant of northern Australia which makes large intricate nests of leaves in trees. □□ **greenish** *adj.* **greenly** *adv.* **greenness** *n.*
Greene, (Henry) Graham (1904–91), English novelist.
greenery *n.* green foliage or growing plants.

greenfinch *n.* a finch with green and yellow feathers, introduced to Australia.

greenfly *n.* (*pl.* **greenfly**) a small green aphid that sucks juices from plants.

greengage *n.* a round plum with a greenish skin.

greengrocer *n.* **1** a shopkeeper selling fruit and vegetables. **2** a species of large Australian cicada when in its green stage. Also called *green monday.* (cf. YELLOW MONDAY). ☐ **greengrocery** *n.*

greenhood *n.* any of many species of terrestrial Australian orchid of the genus *Pterostylis*, having a hooded greenish (often translucent) flower.

greenhorn *n.* an inexperienced person.

greenhouse *n.* a building with glass sides and roof in order to trap heat from the sun, used for rearing plants. ☐ **greenhouse effect** the trapping of the sun's warmth in the lower atmosphere of the earth, caused by an increase in pollutants such as carbon dioxide, methane, etc., with the result that global warming occurs. **greenhouse gas** any of the gases, esp. carbon dioxide and methane, that contribute to the greenhouse effect.

greenie *n. colloq.* a member or supporter of an environmentalist group or party; a conservationist.

Greenland an island lying north-east of North America and mostly within the Arctic Circle, a part of Denmark but with internal autonomy. ☐ **Greenlander** *n.*

Green Party (also **the Greens**) a political party of environmentalists and ecologists.

Greenpeace an international organisation concerned with the general conservation and safety of the environment.

greenstick fracture a kind of fracture, usu. in children, in which the bone is partly broken and partly only bent.

Greenway, Francis (1777–1837), Australian architect. He was transported to Australia from England as a convict in 1814. He soon received his ticket-of-leave and under Governor Macquarie's patronage became government civil architect. He designed 40 buildings (e.g. St Matthew's church, Windsor, NSW), the first buildings in Australia to have a truly Australian character.

Greenwich / gren-ich / a suburb of London, the former site of the Royal Observatory. ☐ **Greenwich Mean Time** time on the line of longitude which passes through Greenwich, used as a basis for calculating time throughout the world.

greeny *adj.* greenish. • *n.* = GREENIE.

Greer, Germaine (1939–), Australian writer, lecturer, and feminist. Her book, *The Female Eunuch* (1971), a feminist analysis of sexual stereotyping, is a landmark of the women's liberation movement.

greet *v.* **1** address (a person) politely or with welcome on meeting or arrival. **2** receive with a certain reaction (*the news was greeted with dismay*). **3** present itself to one's sight or hearing (*the sight that greeted our eyes*).

greeting *n.* **1** words or gestures used to greet a person. **2** (often in *pl.*) an expression of goodwill (*birthday greetings*).

gregarious / gruh-**gair**-ree-uhs / *adj.* **1** living in flocks or communities. **2** fond of company. ☐ **gregariously** *adv.* **gregariousness** *n.*

Gregorian calendar / gruh-**gaw**-ree-uhn / *n.* the calendar introduced by Pope Gregory XIII in 1582, replacing the Julian calendar and still in general use.

Gregorian chant *n.* plainsong church music, named after Pope St Gregory I, 'the Great' (*see* PLAINCHANT).

Gregory I, St, 'the Great' (*c.*540–604), pope from 590 and a Doctor of the Church, who sent St Augustine as head of a mission to convert England to the Christian faith, and is credited with the invention of plainsong.

gremlin *n.* a mischievous sprite said to cause mishaps to machinery etc.

gremmie *n.* (also **gremmy**) *colloq.* a young surfer, esp. an inexperienced one.

Grenada / gruh-**nay**-duh / an independent State in the West Indies. ☐ **Grenadian** *adj.* & *n.*

grenade / gruh-**nayd** / *n.* a small bomb thrown by hand or fired from a rifle.

grevillea / gruh-**vil**-ee-uh / *n.* any ground cover, shrub, or tree of the large chiefly Australian genus of the same name, many of which have extremely showy flowers and are widely cultivated as ornamentals.

grew *see* GROW.

grey *adj.* **1** of the colour between black and white, coloured like ashes or lead. **2** having hair which is turning white with age. **3** dull, dismal (*grey skies*). **4** indeterminate, unidentifiable (*grey area*). • *n.* **1** grey colour or pigment. **2** a grey substance or material; grey clothes. **3** a grey horse. • *v.* make or become grey. ☐ **grey area** a situation or topic not clearly defined; a vague area between two extremes. **grey butcherbird** a woodland butcherbird, widespread in Australia, having black, grey and white plumage, and noted for its beautiful song. **grey matter 1** the material of the brain and spinal cord. **2** *colloq.* intelligence. **grey nurse** a common shark of SE Australian waters. **grey power** the influence (esp. political) exerted by senior citizens, esp. through the organisations representing them. **grey thrush** a predominantly grey woodland bird of Australia (not a member of the thrush family) zoologically named *harmonica* after the beauty of its song. ☐ ☐ **greyish** *adj.* **greyness** *n.*

Grey Friar *n.* a Franciscan friar, so called from his grey cloak.

greyhound *n.* a slender smooth-haired dog noted for its swiftness, used in racing.

grid *n.* **1** a grating. **2** *Aust.* (in an opening in a fence) a set of metal rails fixed on the ground over a shallow trench, and so spaced as to prevent the passage of stock. **3** a network of squares on maps, numbered for reference. **4** any network of lines; an arrangement of electric-powered cables or gas-supply lines for distributing current or supplies over a large area. **5** a pattern of lines marking the starting places on a motor racing track. **6** a perforated electrode controlling the flow of electrons in a thermionic valve etc. **7** the arrangement of town streets in a rectangular pattern.

gridded *adj.* marked with a grid.

griddle *n.* a circular iron plate placed over a source of heat for cooking etc.

gridiron / **grid**-uyuhn / *n.* **1** a framework of metal bars for grilling food on. **2** American football.

gridlock *n.* an urban traffic jam caused by continuous intersecting lines of traffic. ☐ **gridlocked** *adj.*

grief *n.* **1 a** deep sorrow. **b** something causing this. **2** *colloq.* trouble; annoyance. ☐ **come to grief** meet with disaster.

Grieg / greeg /, Edvard (1843–1907), Norwegian composer.

grievance *n.* a real or imagined cause of complaint. ☐ **grievance debate** *Aust.* a period set aside during a parliamentary session when members can speak on topics of their own choosing.

grieve *v.* **1** cause grief to. **2** feel grief. ☐ **griever** *n.*

grievous / gree-vuhs / *adj.* **1** (of pain, injury, etc.) severe. **2** causing grief (*wept at the grievous news*). **3** (of a fault, crime, etc.) flagrant, heinous. ☐ **grievous bodily harm** *Law* serious injury afflicted intentionally. ☐☐ **grievously** *adv.*

Griffin, Walter Burley (1876–1937), Australian architect and landscape architect (born in America) who in 1912 won the international competition for the design of the Australian Capital, Canberra.

griffin *n.* (also **gryphon**) a mythical creature with an eagle's head and wings on a lion's body.

griffon = GRIFFIN.

grill *n.* **1** a device in a cooker for radiating heat downwards. **2** meat, fish, or vegetables cooked under this or on a gridiron. **3** a gridiron for cooking on. **4** (in full **grill room**) a restaurant specialising in grilled food. • *v.* **1** cook under a grill or on a gridiron. **2** be exposed to great heat. **3** question closely and severely (*grilled the suspect*). ☐ **griller** *n.* **grilling** *n.*

grille *n.* (also **grill**) **1** a grating, esp. in a door or window. **2** a metal grid protecting the radiator of a vehicle.

grilse *n.* (*pl.* **grilse** or **grilses**) a young salmon returning from the sea to fresh water to spawn for the first time.

grim *adj.* (**grimmer**, **grimmest**) **1** stern or severe in appearance. **2** severe, unrelenting, merciless (*held on like grim death*). **3** without cheerfulness, unattractive (*a grim prospect*). ☐ **grimly** *adv.* **grimness** *n.*

grimace / **grim**-uhs, gruh-**mays** / *n.* a contortion of the face expressing pain or disgust, or intended to cause amusement. • *v.* make a grimace.

grime *n.* dirt or soot ingrained in a surface or in the skin. • *v.* blacken with grime. ☐ **grimy** *adj.* **griminess** *n.*

Grimm, Jacob (Ludwig Carl) (1785–1863) and brother Wilhelm (Carl) (1786–1859), German linguistics scholars who inaugurated a dictionary of German on historical principles and are remembered also for the anthology of folk fairy tales which they compiled.

grin *v.* (**grinned**, **grinning**) **1** smile broadly, showing the teeth. **2** express by a grin (*he grinned his approval*). • *n.* a broad smile. ☐ **grinner** *n.*

grind *v.* (**ground**, **grinding**) **1** crush or be crushed into grains or powder. **2** produce in this way. **3** oppress or crush by cruelty. **4** sharpen or smooth by friction (*grind the axe*). **5** rub gratingly together (*ground his teeth in rage*). **6** (often foll. by *down*) oppress, harass with exorbitant demands (*ground down by debt; grinding poverty*). **7** (often foll. by *away*) study hard (*grinding away at his algebra*). • *n.* **1** the act of grinding. **2** the size of ground particles (*a coarse grind*). **3** *colloq.* hard monotonous work (*the daily grind*). ☐ **grind out** produce with effort (*grinding out excuses*).

grinder *n.* **1** a person or thing that grinds. **2** a molar tooth.

grindstone *n.* a thick revolving disc used for sharpening or grinding things. ☐ **keep one's nose to the grindstone** work hard without rest.

grip *v.* (**gripped**, **gripping**) **1** take a firm hold of. **2** hold a person's attention (*his story gripped us*). **3** (of a feeling or emotion) deeply affect (a person); (*was gripped by fear*). • *n.* **1** a firm grasp or hold. **2** the power of gripping; a way of grasping or holding. **3** intellectual mastery, understanding (*has a good grip of her subject*). **4** effective control of one's behaviour etc. (*lose one's grip*). **5** the part of a tool or machine etc. that grips things. **6** the part (of a weapon or device) designed to be held. **7** a travelling bag. ☐ **come** (or **get**) **to grips with** begin to cope with, deal with (a problem) firmly.

gripe *v.* **1** *colloq.* grumble, complain. **2** affect with gastric pain. • *n.* **1** (usu. **gripes**) gastric pain, colic. **2** *colloq.* a complaint.

grisly *adj.* causing fear, horror, or disgust (*all the grisly details*). ☐ **grisliness** *n.*

grist *n.* grain to be ground or already ground. ☐ **grist to one's mill** a source of profit or advantage.

gristle *n.* tough flexible tissue of animal bodies, esp. in meat. ☐ **gristly** *adj.*

grit *n.* **1** particles of stone or sand. **2** courage and endurance. • *v.* (**gritted**, **gritting**) **1** clench (*grit one's teeth*). **2** make a grating sound. ☐ **gritty** *adj.* **grittiness** *n.*

grizzle v. colloq. **1** (esp. of a child) whimper or cry fretfully. **2** complain whiningly, whinge. □ **grizzle-guts** n. colloq. a constant whinger or complainer. □□ **grizzly** adj.

grizzled adj. grey-haired or partly so.

grizzly adj. **1** grey, grey-haired. **2** in a whining or complaining mood. • n. (in full **grizzly bear**) a large variety of brown bear of North America and North Russia.

groan v. **1** make a long deep sound expressing pain, grief, or disapproval. **2** utter with groans. **3** (usu. foll. by *under*, *beneath*, *with*) be loaded or oppressed. • n. **1** the sound made in groaning. **2** colloq. a boring person or thing (*he's such a groan; the party was a real groan*).

grocer n. a shopkeeper who sells foods and household provisions.

grocery n. **1** a grocer's trade or shop. **2** (**groceries**) goods sold by a grocer.

grog colloq. n. **1** Aust. beer. **2** Aust. any other alcoholic drink. **3** hist. a drink of rum (or other spirit) mixed with water. • v. Aust. drink beer (or some other alcoholic beverage). □ **grog artist** Aust. a heavy drinker (*see* ARTIST sense 4). **grog on** v. Aust. engage in a prolonged drinking session. **grog-on** n. (also **grog-up**) Aust. a prolonged drinking session. **grog shanty** Aust. hist. a roughly run (unlicensed) hotel, esp. on a goldfield. **grog shop** Aust. a shop selling alcohol, a bottle shop. **on the grog** Aust. **1** taken to drinking (*he's on the grog in spite of his doctor's warning*). **2** engaged in a bout of heavy drinking.

groggy adj. **1** incapable or unsteady from being dazed etc. (*the boxer was groggy after the uppercut*). **2** colloq. drunk. □ **groggily** adv. **grogginess** n.

groin n. **1** the part of the body where each thigh joins the trunk. **2** Archit. the curved edge where two vaults meet in a roof; an arch supporting a vault.

groined adj. built with groins.

grommet n. **1** (also **grummet**) a metal, plastic, or rubber eyelet placed in a hole to protect or insulate a rope or cable passed through it. **2** (also **grummet**) a tube passed through the eardrum in surgery to drain and ventilate the middle ear. **3** esp. Aust. colloq. a young, inexperienced surfer or skateboarder.

groom n. **1** a person employed to look after horses. **2** a bridegroom. • v. **1** clean and brush (an animal). **2** give a neat appearance to (a person etc.). **3** prepare or train (a person) for a career or for a particular purpose. **4** (of an ape etc.) clean the fur of (its fellow) with its fingers.

Groote Eylandt an island (about 70 km long and 50 km wide) off the east coast of Arnhem Land, NT, in the Gulf of Carpentaria, home of the Enindhilyagwa Aboriginal people. The entire island is Aboriginal land.

groove n. **1** a long narrow channel in the surface of hard material. **2** a spiral cut on a gramophone record for the needle or stylus. **3** a way of living that has become a habit, a rut (*he's got into a groove*). • v. **1** make a groove or grooves in. **2** colloq. enjoy oneself.

groovy adj. colloq. **1** excellent; exciting. **2** trendy.

grope v. **1** feel about as one does in the dark; (foll. by *for*) seek by feeling. **2** (foll. by *for*, *after*) search mentally with some uncertainty (*groping for an answer*). **3** colloq. feel or fondle (a person) clumsily with sexual intent. • n. an act of groping. □ **groper** n. **gropingly** adv.

groper[1] n. any of several large Australian etc. sea fish with heavy body, big head, and enormously wide mouth.

groper[2] n. colloq. = SANDGROPER.

grosgrain / **groh**-grayn / n. corded fabric of silky thread, used for ribbons, etc.

gros point / groh / n. an embroidery stitch worked over two or more horizontal and vertical threads of the canvas.

gross / grohs / adj. **1** thick, large-bodied. **2** overfed, bloated. **3** coarse, unrefined, or indecent (*gross manners; his behaviour was gross*). **4** glaringly obvious, outrageous (*gross negligence*). **5** total, whole, without deductions (*gross income*). **6** (of the senses etc.) dull. **7** colloq. repulsive; off-putting (*wearing ties is really gross*). • n. (pl. **gross**) twelve dozen (144) items. • v. produce or earn as total profit. • interj. colloq. an exclamation indicating revulsion etc. □ **gross domestic product** (abbr. **GDP**) the total value of goods produced and services provided in a country in one year. **gross national product** (abbr. **GNP**) the gross domestic product plus the total of net income from abroad. **gross out** v. colloq. feel or cause intense disgust (*he grossed out at the sight of all the blood; that really grosses me out*). □□ **grossly** adv. **grossness** n.

grot n. **1** colloq. filth; a filthy person. **2** poetic a grotto.

grotesque / groh-**tesk** / adj. **1** comically or repulsively distorted. **2** incongruous, absurd. • n. **1** a comically distorted figure. **2** a design using fantastic human, animal, and plant forms. □ **grotesquely** adv. **grotesqueness** n.

grotto / **grot**-oh / n. (pl. **grottoes** or **grottos**) **1** a picturesque cave. **2** an artificial ornamental cave.

grotty adj. colloq. unpleasant, dirty, shabby, unattractive.

grouch colloq. v. grumble; complain. • n. **1** a discontented person. **2** a fit of grumbling or the sulks. **3** a complaint (*what's your grouch?*). □ **grouchy** adj.

ground[1] n. **1** the solid surface of the earth, esp. contrasted with the air surrounding it. **2** an area, position, or distance on the earth's surface (*the explorers covered a lot of ground in inland Australia*). **3** the extent of a subject dealt with (*this book covers a lot of ground*). **4** a foundation or reason for a theory or action (*there are no grounds for suspicion*). **5** an area or basis for agreement etc. (*managed to find some common ground*). **6** soil,

ground   361   **grow**

earth (*marshy ground*). **7** an area used for a particular purpose (*a football ground; fishing grounds*). **8** the underlying part; a surface worked upon in embroidery or painting. **9** (**grounds**) an area of enclosed land belonging to a large house or an institution. **10** (**grounds**) solid particles that sink to the bottom of a liquid (*coffee grounds*). **11** connection to the earth as the completion of an electrical circuit. **12** (in combinations) **a** (of animals) living on or in the ground; typically seen on the ground (*ground parrot*). **b** (of plants) dwarfish or trailing (*ground cover*). •*v*. **1** run (a ship) aground, strand; (of a ship) run aground. **2** prevent (a pilot or an aircraft) from flying (*all aircraft were grounded because of the fog*). **3** (foll. by *in*) teach thoroughly (in a subject) (*grounding him in mathematics*). **4** base (*it is grounded on fact*). **5** withdraw privileges etc. as a punishment (*grounded both boys for a week*). **6** connect (an electrical circuit) to the earth. ❑ **down to the ground** completely (*the job suits me down to the ground*). **go to ground** retire from the public eye for a prolonged period. **ground bass** *Music* a short bass line constantly repeated. **ground control** the personnel directing the landing etc. of an aircraft or spacecraft from the ground. **ground cover** a low, rapidly spreading plant grown to suppress weeds. **ground floor** the floor at ground level in a building. **ground glass** **1** glass made non-transparent by grinding etc. **2** glass ground to a powder. **ground plan** **1** a plan of a building at ground level. **2** an outline or general design of a scheme. **ground rule** a basic rule, code of conduct, etc. (*these are the ground rules for this excursion*). **ground speed** an aircraft's speed relative to the ground. **ground state** *Physics* the lowest energy state of an atom etc. **ground zero** the point on the ground under an exploding (usu. nuclear) bomb. **hold** (or **stand**) **one's ground** not retreat or give way. **old stamping ground** *colloq.* a place one used to frequent, esp. in one's youth. **on the grounds of** because of (*retired on the grounds of ill-health*).

ground[2] *see* GRIND.

grounding *n*. thorough teaching, basic training (*a good grounding in arithmetic*).

groundless *adj*. without basis, without good reason (*your fears are groundless*). ❑ **groundlessly** *adv*.

groundnut *n*. a peanut.

groundsheet *n*. a waterproof sheet for spreading on the ground.

groundsman *n*. a man employed to look after a sports ground.

groundswell *n*. **1** heavy slow-moving waves caused by a distant or recent storm or an earthquake. **2** an increasingly forceful presence (esp. of public opinion) (*the groundswell of support for an Australian Republic*).

groundwork *n*. preliminary or basic work.

group *n*. **1** a number of people or things gathered, placed, or classed together, or working together for some purpose. **2** a number of commercial companies under one owner. **3** a number of musicians and singer(s) performing esp. pop, rock, or jazz. **4** = BLOOD GROUP. •*v*. **1** form or gather into a group or groups. **2** place in a group; organise into groups. ❑ **group captain** an officer in the RAAF next below commodore. **group certificate** an annual record of salary etc. and of tax deducted, given to an employee for submission with a tax return. **group practice** a medical practice in which several doctors are associated. **group therapy** therapy in which patients with a similar condition are brought together to assist one another psychologically.

grouper = GROPER[1].

groupie *n. colloq*. **1** an ardent follower of touring pop groups, esp. a (female) fan following a group and providing sexual favours. **2** a fan, a follower of sports stars and other celebrities.

Group of Seven (*abbr*. **G7**) the seven leading industrial nations outside the former Communist bloc, i.e. the US, Japan, (West) Germany, France, the UK, Italy, and Canada.

groupware *see* -WARE.

grouse[1] / grows / *n*. (*pl*. **grouse**) **1** a game bird with a plump body and feathered feet. **2** its flesh as food.

grouse[2] / grows, growz / *colloq. v*. grumble or complain. •*n*. a complaint. ❑ **grouser** *n*.

grouse[3] / grows / *adj. Aust. colloq*. very good of its kind (*that film was grouse*). ❑ **extra grouse** excellent, terrific.

Grout, Wally (full name: Arthur Theodore Wallace Grout) (1927–67), Australian test cricketer. ❑ **your Wally Grout** *Aust. rhyming slang* your shout (i.e. your turn to pay for the next round of drinks).

grout *n*. thin fluid mortar used to fill narrow cavities such as joints between stones or wall tiles. •*v*. fill with grout.

grouter *n. Aust. colloq*. an unfair advantage. ❑ **come in on the grouter** start with or take an unfair advantage.

grove *n*. a group of trees, a small wood.

grovel *v*. (**grovelled**, **grovelling**) **1** humble oneself; behave obsequiously. **2** lie or crawl with the face downwards in a show of humility or fear.

grow *v*. (**grew**, **grown**, **growing**) **1** increase in size or quantity; become greater. **2** develop (*the seeds are growing*). **3** be capable of developing as a plant, flourish (*rice grows in warm climates*). **4** become gradually (*she grew rich*). **5** cause or allow to grow, produce by cultivation (*grow a beard; grow roses*). ❑ **growing pains 1** neuralgic pain in children's legs, usu. caused by tiredness. **2** problems arising because a project or development is in its early stages. **grow on** (of an idea etc.) become more acceptable to (*gardening has grown on me*). **grow out of 1** (of a growing child) become too large to wear (certain clothes). **2** become too mature for (*grew out of childish habits*). **3** have as a source, arise or develop from. **grow up 1** develop, become adult or mature. **2** (of a custom) arise. **3** *Aust.* (in Aboriginal English) rear (*his father grew me up*).

grower *n.* **1** a person who grows plants, fruit, or vegetables commercially. **2** a plant that grows in a certain way (*a rapid grower*).

growl *v.* **1** make a low threatening sound. **2** speak or say in a growling manner, grumble. **3** rumble (*my stomach's growling*). **4** *Aust.* (in Aboriginal English) criticise or threaten. • *n.* **1** a growling sound. **2** an angry murmur; a grumble. **3** a rumble.

grown *see* GROW. • *adj.* **1** fully developed, adult (*a grown man*). **2** (foll. by *over*) covered with a growth (*a wall grown over with ivy*). ▫ **grown-up** *adj.* adult. *n.* an adult person.

growth *n.* **1** the process of growing, development. **2** cultivation of produce. **3** something that grows or has grown (*a thick growth of weeds*). **4** an abnormal formation of tissue in the body, a tumour. ▫ **growth hormone** a substance which stimulates the growth of a plant or animal. **growth industry** one developing rapidly.

groyne *n.* a structure of wood, stone, or concrete built at right angles to the coast and towards the sea to check beach erosion.

grub *n.* **1** the thick-bodied worm-like larva of certain insects. **2** = WITCHETTY. **3** *colloq.* food. **4** *colloq.* a dirty or untidy child. • *v.* (**grubbed**, **grubbing**) **1** dig superficially, clear away roots, etc. (*grub that paddock*). **2** (foll. by *up*, *out*) extract by digging, uproot (*grub up that gum-tree stump*). **3** search laboriously; rummage (*grubbing for scraps*). **4** (foll. by *on*, *along*, *away*) toil, plod.

grubber *n.* **1** a person or thing that grubs. **2** = MULLYGRUBBER. **3** *Rugby* a deliberate kick, usu. to touch, intended to send the ball slowly endforward along the ground.

grubby *adj.* (**grubbier**, **grubbiest**) dirty, unwashed. ▫ **grubbily** *adv.* **grubbiness** *n.*

grudge *v.* resent having to give or allow something (*I don't grudge him his success*). • *n.* a feeling of resentment or ill will. ▫ **grudging** *adj.* **grudgingly** *adv.*

gruel / **groo**-uhl / *n.* a thin porridge made by boiling oatmeal in milk or water.

gruelling / **groo**-uh-ling / *adj.* very tiring, exhausting.

gruesome / **groo**-suhm / *adj.* horrifying, disgusting, revolting (*the gruesome details of the murder*).

gruff *adj.* **1** (of the voice) low and harsh, hoarse. **2** having a gruff voice. **3** surly in manner. ▫ **gruffly** *adv.* **gruffness** *n.*

gruie / **groo**-ee / *n. Aust.* an emu apple. (¶ Kamilaroi)

grumble *v.* **1** complain in a bad-tempered way. **2** rumble (*thunder was grumbling in the distance*).

• *n.* **1** a complaint, esp. a bad-tempered one. **2** a rumble. ▫ **grumbling appendix** *colloq.* one that causes pain from time to time without developing into appendicitis. ▫▫ **grumbler** *n.*

grummet = GROMMET.

grump *colloq. n.* **1** an irritable, grumpy person; a grouch. **2** (**grumps**) a fit of the sulks. • *v.* grumble, whinge, complain.

grumpy *adj.* bad-tempered and gloomy. ▫ **grumpily** *adv.* **grumpiness** *n.*

Grundy, Reginald (1924–), Australian television producer.

grunge *n. colloq.* **1** grime, dirt. **2** a raucous style of rock music; a ragged style of clothing associated with this music. ▫ **grunge novel** a usu. sexually explicit novel dealing with the sleazier side of life.

grunt *v.* **1** make the gruff snorting sound characteristic of a pig. **2** speak or utter with such a sound (*he grunted a reply*). • *n.* **1** a grunting sound. **3** esp. *US* an infantry soldier.

grunter *n.* **1** a pig. **2** a person or animal that grunts. **3** any of many Australian freshwater fish that grunt when caught (e.g. *the silver perch, the spangled grunter*).

gruyère / **groo**-yuh, groo-**yair** / *n.* a firm pale cheese with holes.

gryphon = GRIFFIN.

GST *abbr.* goods and services tax.

G-string *n.* **1** a string on a musical instrument, tuned to the note G. **2** a narrow strip of cloth covering only the genitals, attached to a string round the waist.

G-suit *n.* a close-fitting inflatable suit worn by pilots and astronauts flying at high speed to prevent blood from draining away from the head and causing blackouts (G = gravity).

GT *abbr.* gran turismo; a high-performance saloon car. (¶ Italian, = grand touring.)

guacamole / gwah-kuh-**moh**-lee / *n.* a dish of mashed avocado mixed with chopped onion, tomatoes, chilli peppers, and seasoning.

guano / **gwah**-noh / *n.* **1** the excrement of sea birds, used as manure. **2** an artificial manure, esp. made from fish.

guarantee *n.* **1** a formal promise to do what has been agreed, or that a thing is of specified quality and durability, with penalties for failure. **2** = GUARANTY. **3** = GUARANTOR. **4** that which acts as does a guaranty (*hard work is a guarantee of success*). • *v.* (**guaranteed**, **guaranteeing**) **1** give or be a guarantee for. **2** promise, state with certainty.

guarantor *n.* a person who gives a guarantee.

guaranty *n.* **1** a formal promise given by one person to another that he or she will be responsible for something that is to be done or for a debt that is to be paid by a third person. **2** something offered or accepted as security.

guard *v.* **1** watch over and protect, keep safe. **2** watch over and supervise or prevent from escaping. **3** keep in check, restrain (*guard your*

guarded / **guinea fowl**

tongue). **4** take precautions (*guard against errors*). • *n.* **1** a state of watchfulness or alertness for possible danger. **2** a defensive attitude in boxing, fencing, cricket, etc. **3** a protector, a sentry. **4** a railway official in charge of a train. **5** a body of soldiers or others guarding a place or a person, or serving as escort, or forming a separate part of an army. **6** a protecting part or device (*fire guard*).

guarded *adj.* cautious, discreet (*a guarded statement*).

guardian *n.* **1** one who guards or protects. **2** a person who undertakes legal responsibility for someone who is not able to manage his or her own affairs, such as an orphaned child. □ **guardian-ship** *n.*

Guatemala / gwah-tuh-**mah**-luh / **1** a republic in the north of Central America. **2** its capital city. □ **Guatemalan** *adj.* & *n.*

guava / **gwah**-vuh / *n.* the edible pale orange fruit of a tropical American tree.

gubba *n.* (also **gub**, **gubbar**, **gubber**) *Aust.* the name (often derogatory) given by Aborigines to a white person. (¶ Probably an abbreviation of GOVERNMENT.)

guck *n. colloq.* dirt; slime.

gudgeon[1] / **guj**-uhn / *n.* **1** a small easily caught freshwater fish of Europe. **2** any of several similar Australian fish. **3** a credulous or easily fooled person.

gudgeon[2] / **guj**-uhn / *n.* **1** a kind of pivot. **2** a socket for a rudder. **3** the tubular part of a hinge. **4** a pin holding two blocks of stone etc. together.

Guernsey / **gern**-zee / *n.* **1** one of a breed of dairy cattle originally from Guernsey in the Channel Islands. **2** (**guernsey**) *Aust.* a thick knitted woollen sweater. **3** (**guernsey**) *Aust.* a football jersey, esp. the (often sleeveless) jumper in team colours worn by a player of Australian Rules football. □ **get a** (or **the**) **guernsey** *Aust.* **1** be selected for a football team. **2** win approval, recognition, etc. (*in this list of the best places to live in Australia, why didn't Canberra get a guernsey?*).

guerrilla / guh-**ril**-uh / *n.* (also **guerilla**) a member of a small independently acting (usu. political) group taking part in irregular fighting (usu. against a stronger more organised force). □ **guerrilla war** (or **warfare**) fighting by or with guerrillas.

guess *v.* **1** form an opinion, make a statement, or give an answer without calculating or measuring and without definite knowledge. **2** think likely. • *n.* an opinion formed by guessing. □ **I guess** *colloq.* I think it likely; I suppose. □□ **guesser** *n.*

guesstimate alternative spelling of GUESTIMATE.

guesswork *n.* the process of guessing; an example of this.

guest *n.* **1** a person staying at another's house or visiting by invitation or being entertained to a meal. **2** a person lodging at a hotel. **3** a visiting performer taking part in an entertainment (*a guest artist*). □ **be my guest!** *colloq.* you are welcome (to take the action indicated)!

guestimate / ges-tuh-muht / *n.* (also **guesstimate**) *colloq.* an estimate based on a mixture of guesswork and calculation.

guff *n. colloq.* empty talk, nonsense.

guffaw *n.* a coarse noisy laugh. • *v.* give a guffaw.

guidance *n.* **1** guiding, being guided. **2** advising or advice on problems.

guide *n.* **1** a person who shows others the way. **2** one employed to point out interesting sights on a journey or visit. **3** an adviser. **4** a person or thing that directs or influences one's behaviour (*one's feelings are a bad guide*). **5** a book of information about a place or a subject (*A Guide to Italy*). **6** a thing that marks a position, guides the eye, or steers moving parts. **7** (**Guide**) a member of a girls' organisation corresponding to the Scout Association. • *v.* **1** act as guide to. **2** be the principle or motive of (*anger guided his actions*). □ **guided missile** a missile that is under remote control or directed by equipment within itself. **guide dog** a dog trained to guide a blind person.

guidebook *n.* a book of information about a place, for travellers or visitors.

guideline *n.* a statement of principle giving general guidance.

guild *n.* (also **gild**) **1** a society of people with similar interests and aims. **2** any of the associations of craftsmen or merchants in the Middle Ages.

guilder / **gil**-duh / *n.* a unit of money in the Netherlands, a florin.

guile / guyl / *n.* treacherous cunning, craftiness. □ **guileful** *adj.* **guileless** *adj.*

guillotine / **gil**-uh-teen / *n.* **1** a machine with a heavy blade sliding down in grooves, used for beheading people. **2** a machine with a long blade for cutting paper or metal. **3** a method of preventing delay in the discussion of a bill in parliament by fixing times at which various parts of it must be voted on. • *v.* use a guillotine on.

guilt *n.* **1** the fact of having committed some offence. **2** a feeling that one is to blame for something.

guiltless *adj.* innocent.

guilty *adj.* (**guiltier**, **guiltiest**) **1** having done wrong. **2** feeling or showing guilt. □ **guiltily** *adv.* **guiltiness** *n.*

Guinea a republic on the west coast of Africa.

guinea / **gin**-ee / *n.* **1** *hist.* the sum of twenty-one shillings. **2** a former British gold coin first coined for the African trade. □ **guinea flower** any Australian plant of the genus *Hibbertia*, esp. *H. scandens* bearing large gold flowers.

Guinea-Bissau / **bis**-ow / a republic on the west coast of Africa between Guinea and Senegal.

guinea fowl *n.* a domestic fowl of the pheasant family, with grey feathers spotted with white.

guinea pig 1 a short-eared animal like a large rat, kept as a pet or for biological experiments. **2** a person or thing used as a subject for experiment.

Guinevere / gwin-uh-veer / (in legends of King Arthur) the wife of King Arthur and mistress of Lancelot.

guipure / gi-**pyoor**, guh- / *n*. a heavy lace of linen pieces joined by embroidery.

guise / guyz / *n*. an outward manner or appearance put on in order to conceal the truth, a pretence (*they exploited him under the guise of friendship*).

guitar / guh-**tah**, gi- / *n*. a stringed musical instrument, played by plucking with the fingers or a plectrum. ☐ **electric guitar** one with a built-in microphone. ☐☐ **guitarist** *n*.

Gulag *n*. the system of detention camps which operated in the former Soviet Union 1930–55.

gulf *n*. **1** an area of sea (larger than a bay) that is partly surrounded by land. **2** (**the Gulf**) the Gulf of Carpentaria. **3** a deep hollow or chasm. **4** a wide difference in opinions or outlook; a wide separation (*the gulf between the haves and the have-nots*).

Gulf of Carpentaria a large indentation 480 km wide and extending over 600 km southwards, between Arnhem Land in the west and Queensland's Cape York in the east. ☐ **Gulf Country** the Gulf's low-lying, mangrove-fringed southern shores and adjacent plains. **Gulf fever** malaria.

Gulf War 1 the war between Iraq and Iran, in the general area of the Persian Gulf, 1980–8. **2** the war of Jan.–Feb. 1991, between Iraq and an international coalition of forces based in Saudi Arabia, after Iraq's invasion of Kuwait in Aug. 1990.

gull *n*. **1** a large seabird with long wings and webbed feet. **2** a dupe, a fool. •*v*. to dupe, fool.

gullet *n*. **1** the food passage extending from the mouth to the stomach; the oesophagus. **2** the throat.

gullible / gul-uh-buhl / *adj*. easily deceived. ☐ **gullibility** / gul-uh-**bil**-uh-tee / *n*.

gully *n*. **1** a water-worn ravine. **2** *Aust*. an eroded watercourse; an elongated water-worn depression; a (small) river valley. **3** a gutter or drain. **4** *Cricket* a fieldsman between point and slips; this position. ☐ **gully-rake** *Aust*. **1** muster unbranded cattle from country not readily accessible. **2** steal such cattle. **gully-raker** *Aust*. a cattle thief. **gully trap** (also **gulley trap**) *Aust*. a water-sealed trap (against the return of gases) through which household drainage flows to outside drains.

gulp *v*. **1** swallow (food or drink) hastily, greedily, or with effort. **2** (foll. by *back*, *down*) suppress (*he gulped back his tears*). **3** make a gulping movement, choke or gasp (*gulping for breath*). •*n*. **1** the act of gulping. **2** a large mouthful of liquid.

Gulpilil / gul-puh-lil /, David (1953–), AO, Australian Aboriginal actor and dancer.

gum[1] *n*. the firm flesh in which the teeth are rooted.

gum[2] *n*. **1** *Aust*. a gum tree, often with a distinguishing *adj*., as apple gum, blue gum, fluted gum, red gum, etc. **2** a sticky substance exuded by some trees and shrubs; an adhesive made from this. **3** chewing gum. **4** = GUM ARABIC. **5** glue. •*v*. (**gummed**, **gumming**) smear or cover with gum; stick together with gum. ☐ **gum arabic** gum exuded by some kinds of acacia and used as a glue and in incense. **gum up** *colloq*. cause confusion or delay in, spoil. **gum up the works** interfere with the smooth running of something.

gumboil *n*. a small abscess on the gum.

gumboot *n*. a rubber boot, a wellington.

gumleaf *n*. *Aust*. a leaf of a gum tree, esp. as used to make musical sounds as of a single reed or double reed musical instrument when the leaf is placed between the lips and blown against. ☐ **gumleaf band** a band of musicians playing gumleaves.

gummy *adj*. **1** sticky with gum or exuding gum. **2** showing the gums, toothless. •*n*. **1** (in full **gummy shark**) a small shark with rounded teeth. **2** a toothless sheep.

gumnut *n*. *Aust*. the woody seed case of the gum tree.

gumption / **gump**-shuhn / *n*. *colloq*. **1** common sense. **2** initiative.

gumsucker *n*. *Aust*. (mainly *hist*.) **1** a nickname for a native-born, non-Aboriginal Australian (as opposed to esp. an immigrant from Britain). **2** a Victorian.

gum tree *n*. (also **gum**) **1** any tree of the large, chiefly Australian genus *Eucalyptus*, the dominant tree genus of Australian forests and woodlands, esp. those eucalypts which have a smooth trunk (as opposed to rough-barked eucalypts such as the stringybark, box, etc.). **2** any other tree which exudes gum. ☐ **up a gum tree** *Aust*. *colloq*. **1** in great difficulties. **2** thoroughly baffled.

gun *n*. **1** a firearm that sends shells or bullets from a metal tube. **2** a starting pistol. **3** a device that forces out insecticide, grease, electrons, etc. in the required direction. **4** a person using a sporting gun as a member of a shooting party. **5** (in full **gun shearer**) *Aust*. a shearer with a high daily tally of sheep shorn. •*v*. (**gunned**, **gunning**) **1** (foll. by *down*) shoot with a gun (*gunned him down*). **2** *colloq*. accelerate or rev (an engine or vehicle). **3** (foll. by *for*) search for determinedly in order to attack or rebuke (a person) (*she was really gunning for him after his gambling spree*). •*adj*. *Aust*. pre-eminent (in an occupation or activity); exceptionally talented or skilled (*gun fencer; gun surfer; gun entertainer*). ☐ **go great guns** *colloq*. succeed, do well. **gun cotton** an explosive made by steeping cotton in nitric and sulphuric acids. **in the gun** *Aust*. *colloq*. in bad favour; likely to attract criticism or punishment (*don't get caught or we'll all be in the gun*). **stick to one's guns** *colloq.* maintain one's position under attack.

gunboat *n.* a small armed vessel with heavy guns. ☐ **gunboat diplomacy** diplomacy backed by the threat of force.

gundy[1] *n.* (also **goondie**) *Aust.* a gunyah. (¶ Yuwaaliyaay and Kamilaroi *gundhi* 'house, hut'; also Wiradhuri *gunday* 'stringybark', and a shelter made from this.)

gundy[2] *n. Aust.* ☐ **no good to gundy** no good at all. (¶ Origin unknown.)

gunfire *n.* the firing of guns.

gung-ho *adj.* arrogantly eager; over-zealous.

gungurru / gung-guh-**roo** / *n.* (also **gungunnu** / gung-guh-**noo** /) a small WA eucalypt with large spectacular gold-tipped pink flowers. (¶ Probably Kalaaku.)

gunk *n. colloq.* **1** junk food, esp. foods filled with sugar. **2** nonsense (*don't give me all that gunk!*). **3** sticky or viscous matter (ointment, face creams, etc.) (*smeared her face with gunk*).

gunman *n.* (*pl.* **gunmen**) a man armed with a gun.

gunmetal *n.* **1** a dull bluish-grey colour. **2** an alloy formerly used for guns.

Gunn, Mrs Aeneas (Jeannie) (1870–1961), Australian novelist, noted for *We of the Never Never* (1908) a fictionalised account of her experiences on a remote station in the NT.

gunnel alternative spelling of GUNWALE.

gunner *n.* **1** a soldier in an artillery unit, the official term for a private. **2** a warrant officer in the navy, in charge of a battery of guns. **3** a member of an aircraft crew who operates a gun (*rear gunner*).

gunnery *n.* the construction and firing of large guns.

gunny *n.* **1** a coarse material, usu. jute fibre, used for making sacks. **2** (also **gunny bag**, **gunny sack**) a sack made from this.

gunpoint *n.* ☐ **at gunpoint** under threat of being shot by a gun held ready.

gunpowder *n.* an explosive of saltpetre, sulphur, and charcoal.

gunrunner *n.* a person engaged in smuggling guns and ammunition into a country. ☐ **gunrunning** *n.*

gunshot *n.* **1** a shot fired from a gun. **2** the range of a gun (*within gunshot*).

gunsmith *n.* a maker and repairer of small firearms.

gunwale / gun-uhl / *n.* (also **gunnel**) the upper edge of a small ship's or boat's side.

Gunwinygu / guun-win-goo / *n.* an Aboriginal language of Arnhem Land in the north of the NT.

Gunya / gun-yu / *n.* an Aboriginal language of a vast region of southern Qld.

gunyah / gun-yuh / *n. Aust.* a temporary shelter of the Aborigines, usu. a simple frame of branches covered with bark, leaves, or grass. (¶ Dharuk)

gunyang / gun-yang / *n.* any of several Australian plants bearing a green to ivory-coloured globular berry which is edible. Also called *kangaroo apple*. (¶ Ganay)

guppy *n.* a small freshwater West Indian fish which gives birth to live young, often kept in aquariums.

Gurangara art a style of ancient Aboriginal art from the Pilbara region of WA, consisting mostly of detailed and lively rock-engravings depicting esp. animals and humans, the latter often with sexual organs carefully depicted and sometimes seemingly in the act of sexual intercourse.

gurdwara / gerd-**wah**-ruh / *n.* a Sikh temple.

Gureng-gureng / guu-reng guu-reng / *n.* an Aboriginal language of a large area of southeastern Qld, including present-day Bundaberg.

gurgle *n.* a low bubbling sound as of water from a bottle. • *v.* make this sound.

gurgler *n. Aust. colloq.* the plughole in a sink; a drain. ☐ **down the gurgler** down the drain; irretrievably lost.

Gurindji / guu-rin-jee / *n.* an Aboriginal people of the Victoria River area, NT. From the mid-nineteenth century their land was occupied by the British pastoral company Vestey Ltd. Many of the Gurindji worked for Vestey's and lived at Wave Hill pastoral station. In 1965 they walked off the station, protesting against working conditions and claiming ownership of their land. Their claim was unsuccessful, but in 1975 the Whitlam government granted the Gurindji leasehold rights to 3,300 sq. km of their land, and this was converted to inalienable freehold title in 1986.

Gurkha / ger-kuh / *n.* **1** a member of a Hindu people in Nepal who speak a Sanskritic language. **2** a Nepalese soldier serving in the Indian etc. army.

guru / guu-roo, goo- / *n.* (*pl.* **gurus**) **1** a Hindu spiritual teacher or head of a religious sect. **2** an influential or revered teacher (*Mrs Smith was my guru at uni*).

gush *v.* **1** flow or pour out suddenly or in great quantities. **2** talk with extravagant enthusiasm or emotion, esp. in an affected manner. • *n.* **1** a sudden or great outflow. **2** an outpouring of feeling, effusiveness.

gusher *n.* **1** an effusive person. **2** an oil well from which oil flows strongly without needing to be pumped.

gushy *adj.* excessively emotional, effusive; highly sentimental. ☐ **gushily** *adv.* **gushiness** *n.*

Gusmão / guuz-mow /, Xanana (1946–), a leader of the East-Timorese resistance against Indonesian rule.

gusset *n.* **1** a piece of cloth inserted in a garment to strengthen or enlarge it. **2** a bracket strengthening an angle of a structure.

gust *n.* **1** a sudden rush of wind. **2** a burst of rain, smoke, emotion, etc. • *v.* blow in gusts. ☐ **gusty** *adj.* **gustily** *adv.*

gusto *n.* zest, great enjoyment in doing something.

gut *n.* **1** the lower part of the alimentary canal from the stomach to the anus, the intestine. **2** (**guts**) the bowel or entrails. **3** *colloq.* the stomach, the belly. **4** a thread made from the intestines of animals, used surgically and for violin and racquet strings. **5** material for fishing lines made from the silk glands of silkworms. **6** (**guts**) the contents of a thing; the essence (of e.g. an issue or problem) (*tinkering with the guts of the clock; getting down to the guts of the matter*). **7** (**guts**) *colloq.* courage and determination. **8** (**guts**) *colloq.* **a** a glutton. **b** a greedy person (one who takes the lion's share of anything). •*adj.* **1** fundamental, basic (*a gut issue*). **2** instinctive (*a gut reaction*). **3** (**guts**) *colloq.* full of determination, vigour, etc. (*made a guts effort to win the cup*). •*v.* (**gutted**, **gutting**) **1** remove the guts from (a fish). **2** remove or destroy the internal fittings or parts of (a building) (*the shop was gutted by fire*). □ **good guts** *Aust. colloq.* information, the facts (of a matter) (*gave us the good guts about the fracas*). **have a gutful** *colloq.* have as much as one can take (*I've had a gutful of your whingeing*). **rough as guts** *Aust. colloq.* lacking in refinement. **spill one's guts** *colloq.* confess; admit everything. **work one's guts out** *colloq.* work extremely hard.

Gutenberg / goo-tuhn-berg /, Johann (*c.*1400–68), German printer, inventor of movable type.

gutless *adj. colloq.* lacking courage and determination; lacking energy (*our representative was gutless; this car's really gutless going up a hill*).

gutser *n.* alternative spelling of GUTZER.

gutsy *adj. colloq.* **1** courageous (*a gutsy effort*). **2** strong, full of character (*a gutsy soup, wine, etc.*) **3** greedy.

gutta-percha *n.* a tough rubber-like substance made from the juice of various Malayan trees.

gutter *n.* **1** a shallow trough under the eaves of a building, or a channel at the side of a street, for carrying off rainwater. **2** (**the gutter**) a poor or degraded background or environment. **3** an open conduit. **4** a groove. **5** *Aust.* the lowest part of a former watercourse, where gold is most likely to be concentrated. •*v.* **1** to furrow or channel (as water does). **2** (of a candle) burn unsteadily so that melted wax flows freely down the sides. □ **gutter press** newspapers seeking sensationalism, e.g. concerning people's private lives.

guttering *n.* the gutters of a building; material for gutters.

guttersnipe *n.* **1** a street urchin. **2** one who speaks or acts as a street urchin is supposed to do.

guttural / gut-uh-ruhl / *adj.* **1** throaty, harsh-sounding (*a guttural voice*). **2** *Phonetics* (of a consonant) pronounced in the back of the throat. •*n.* a guttural consonant (e.g. *g*, *k*). □ **gutturally** *adv.*

gutzer *n.* (also **gutser**) *Aust. colloq.* **1** a heavy fall. **2** a failure. □ **come a gutzer** fail as a result of miscalculation, 'come a cropper'.

Guugu Yimidhirr / goo-goo **yim**-i-dee-r / *n.* an Aboriginal language of the Cooktown region of far northern Qld, this language contributing the first Aboriginal loan into English in 1770, *kangaroo*.

guv *n. colloq.* governor (in the sense one's employer or one's father).

guvvie alternative spelling of GOVIE.

guy[1] *n.* a rope or chain used to keep something steady or secured. •*v.* secure with a guy or guys.

guy[2] *n.* **1** *colloq.* a man; a fellow. **2** *colloq.* any person, female as well as male. **3** *Brit.* an effigy of Guy Fawkes burnt on 5 November. •*v.* ridicule, esp. by comic imitation.

Guyana / guy-**ah**-nuh, guy-**an**-uh / *n.* a republic on the NE coast of South America. □ **Guyanese** / guy-uh-**neez** / *adj.* & *n.* (*pl.* **Guyanese**)

Guyani / **guu**-yun-ee / *n.* an Aboriginal language, a dialect of Adnyamathanha, of central SA between Lake Torrens and Lake Eyre.

guzzle *v.* eat or drink greedily. □ **guzzler** *n.*

gybe / juyb / *v.* (also **jibe**) **1** (of a sail or boom) swing across. **2** make (a sail) do this. **3** change course; change the course of (a ship) so that this happens.

gym / jim / *colloq. n.* **1** a gymnasium. **2** gymnastics. •*adj.* pertaining to gymnastics (*gym boots; gym gear*).

gymea lily / **guy**-mee-uh / *n.* a spectacular eastern Australian plant with sword-like leaves 1 metre in length surrounding a 4 metre high flower spike bearing a cluster of scarlet flowers each 10 cm in width. Also called *giant lily*, *gigantic lily*.

gymkhana / jim-**kah**-nuh / *n.* **1** horse-riding events with races and various games, competitions, etc. **2** a gymnastic and athletics meet.

gymnasium *n.* (*pl.* **gymnasiums** or **gymnasia**) a room or building equipped for gymnastics.

gymnast / **jim**-nast, -nuhst / *n.* an expert performer of gymnastics.

gymnastic *adj.* of gymnastics. □ **gymnastically** *adv.*

gymnastics *n.pl.* (also treated as *sing.*) exercises performed to develop the muscles or demonstrate agility. □ **mental gymnastics** mental agility, elaborate reasoning.

gymnosperm / **jim**-noh-sperm / *n.* a member of the group of plants (mainly trees such as conifers, cycads, and ginkgos) that have seeds not enclosed in an ovary.

gympie / **gim**-pee / *n.* a shrub of northern NSW and Qld, the hairs of which inflict an extremely painful recurring sting. (¶ Gabi-gabi.)

gynaecology / guy-nuh-**kol**-uh-jee / *n.* (also **gynecology**) the science of the female reproductive system and functions and diseases specific to women. □ **gynaecological** *adj.* **gynaecologist** *n.*

gyp / jip / *colloq. n.* **1** a swindle. **2** a swindler. **3** pain or severe discomfort. **4** a scolding (*she gave him gyp*). •*v.* defraud or cheat.

gyprock / **jip**-rok / *n.* esp. *Aust.* plaster sheeting made from gypsum.

gypsum / **jip**-suhm / *n.* a chalk-like mineral from which plaster of Paris is made.

gypsy / **jip**-see / *n.* (also **gipsy**) (*pl.* **gypsies**) **1** (usu. **Gypsy**) a member of a nomadic people of Europe and North America, of Hindu origin, with dark skin and hair. **2** one whose looks, lifestyle, etc. suggest a Gypsy. •*adj.* of or pertaining to the Gypsies.

gyrate / juy-**rayt** / *v.* move round in circles or spirals, revolve, whirl. ☐ **gyration** / juy-**ray**-shuhn / *n.*

gyratory / **juy**-ruh-tuh-ree, juy-**ray**- / *adj.* gyrating, following a circular or spiral path.

gyro / **juy**-roh / *n.* (*pl.* **gyros**) *colloq.* a gyroscope.

gyrocompass / **juy**-ruh-kum-puhs / *n.* a navigation compass using a gyroscope and so independent of the earth's rotation.

gyroscope / **juy**-ruh-skohp / *n.* a device consisting of a heavy wheel which, when spinning fast, keeps the direction of its axis unchanged, used in navigation instruments in ships and in spacecraft etc.

H

H. *abbr.* **1** (of a pencil lead) hard. **2** *colloq.* heroin. • *symbol* hydrogen.

h. *abbr.* (also **h**) **1** height. **2** hour.

Ha *symbol* hahnium.

ha *interj.* (also **hah**) an exclamation of triumph, derision, or surprise. • *abbr.* hectare(s).

habanera / hub-uh-**nair**-ruh / *n.* **1** a Cuban dance in slow duple time. **2** the music for this. (¶ Spanish, = of HAVANA.)

habeas corpus / hay-bee-uhs **kaw**-puhs / *n.* an order requiring a person to be brought before a judge or into court, esp. in order to investigate the right of the authorities to keep him or her imprisoned. (¶ Latin, = you must have the body.)

haberdasher *n.* a shopkeeper dealing in dress accessories and in sewing goods. ☐ **haberdashery** *n.*

habiliments / huh-**bil**-uh-muhnts / *n.pl. archaic* clothing, garments.

habit *n.* **1** a settled way of behaving. **2** something done frequently and almost without thinking. **3** something that is hard to give up. **4** the long dress worn by a monk or nun. ☐ **habit-forming** *adj.* causing addiction.

habitable *adj.* suitable for living in.

habitat / **hab**-uh-tat / *n.* the natural environment of an animal or plant.

habitation *n.* **1** a place to live in. **2** inhabiting, being inhabited.

habitual *adj.* **1** done constantly; like or resulting from a habit. **2** regular, usual (*in his habitual place*). **3** doing something as a habit (*a habitual smoker*). ☐ **habitually** *adv.*

habituate *v.* accustom. ☐ **habituation** *n.*

habitué / huh-**bit**-yoo-ay / *n.* one who visits a place frequently or lives there. (¶ French)

háček / **hach**-ek / *n.* a mark (ˇ) placed over a letter to modify its sound in some languages (e.g. the name *Dvořak*).

hachures / ha-**shoor** / *n.pl.* parallel lines used on maps to indicate the degree of slope in hills.

hacienda / ha-see-**en**-duh / *n.* (in Spanish-speaking countries) a large estate with a dwelling house.

hack[1] *v.* **1** cut or chop roughly. **2** deal a rough blow or kick (*hacked at his shins*). **3** savagely cut, shorten (a piece of writing etc.) (*hacked my report to pieces*). **4** *colloq.* (often foll. by *into*) gain unauthorised access to (computer files). **5** *colloq.* manage, cope with; tolerate (*they couldn't hack the pace*). • *n.* **1** a kick given with the toe of a boot. **2** a gash or wound. **3** = HACKER 2b. **4** a mattock. **5** a miner's pick.

hack[2] *n.* **1** a horse for ordinary riding; a horse that may be hired; an old or decrepit horse, a jade. **2** a person paid to do hard and uninteresting work, esp. as a writer. • *v.* ride on horseback at an ordinary pace, esp. along roads.

hacker *n.* **1** a person or thing that hacks or cuts roughly. **2** *colloq.* **a** a person whose hobby is computing or computer programming; **b** a person who gains unauthorised access to a computer network and uses or alters data etc.

Hackett, Grant (1980–), OAM, Australian swimmer. He won a gold medal in the 1500 metres freestyle at the 2000 Sydney Olympic Games.

hacking *adj.* (of a cough) short, dry, and frequent.

hackles *n.pl.* **1** erectile hairs on the back of an animal's neck which rise when it is angry or alarmed. **2** the long feathers on the neck of a domestic cock and other birds. ☐ **have one's hackles up** be extremely angry, fighting mad. **make one's hackles rise** cause one to be angry or indignant.

hackney *n.* a horse for ordinary riding.

hackneyed / **hak**-need / *adj.* (of a saying etc.) having lost its original impact through long overuse.

hacksaw *n.* a saw for cutting metal, with a short blade in a frame.

hackwork *n.* work (esp. artistic or literary) which is routine, uninspired (*his latest novel is just hackwork*).

had *see* HAVE.

haddock *n.* (*pl.* **haddock**) a North Atlantic sea fish like cod but smaller, used for food.

Hades / **hay**-deez / *n. Gk myth.* **1** the underworld, the place where the spirits of the dead go. **2** (also **Pluto**) the god who rules the underworld.

hadn't = had not.

haemal / **hee**-muhl / *adj.* (also **hemal**) of the blood.

haematic / hee-**mat**-ik / *adj.* (also **hematic**) of or containing blood.

haematite / **hee**-muh-tuyt / *n.* (also **hematite**) ferric oxide as ore; iron ore.

haematology / hee-muh-**tol**-uh-jee / *n.* (also **hematology**) the study of blood and its diseases. ☐ **haematologist** *n.*

haemoglobin / hee-muh-**gloh**-buhn / *n.* (also **hemoglobin**) the red oxygen-carrying substance in the blood.

haemophilia / hee-muh-**fil**-ee-uh / *n.* (also **hemophilia**) a tendency (usu. inherited) to bleed

haemophiliac

severely from even slight injury, through failure of the blood to clot quickly.

haemophiliac / hee-muh-**fil**-ee-ak / *n.* (also **hemophiliac**) a person suffering from haemophilia.

haemorrhage / **hem**-uh-rij / *n.* (also **hemorrhage**) bleeding, esp. when this is heavy. • *v.* bleed heavily.

haemorrhoids / **hem**-uh-roidz / *n.pl.* (also **hemorrhoids**) swollen veins in the wall of the anus; piles.

hafnium / **haf**-nee-uhm / *n.* a metallic element (symbol Hf), used in control rods of nuclear reactors.

haft *n.* the handle of a knife, dagger, or cutting tool.

hag *n.* **1** an ugly old woman. **2** a witch.

haggard *adj.* looking exhausted and distraught.

haggis *n.* a Scottish dish made from offal boiled in a sheep's stomach with suet, oatmeal, etc.

haggle *v.* argue about price or terms when settling a bargain.

hagiography / hag-ee-**og**-ruh-fee / *n.* writing about saints' lives. ☐ **hagiographer** *n.*

hagiology *n.* literature about the lives and legends of saints.

hagridden *adj.* afflicted by nightmares or fear.

Hague, The / hayg / the seat of government of the Netherlands.

hah alternative spelling of HA.

ha ha *interj.* representing an outburst of laughter (*ironic* when spoken) (*ha ha! that's not funny!*).

ha-ha *n.* a ditch with a wall in it, forming a boundary or fence without interrupting the view.

hahnium / **hah**-nee-uhm / *n.* an artificially produced radioactive element (symbol Ha).

haiku / **huy**-koo / *n.* a Japanese three-line poem of 17 syllables.

hail[1] *v.* **1** signal to (a taxi etc.) to stop. **2** greet enthusiastically. **3** originate, have come (*where does he hail from?*). **4** acclaim (*hailed him King of Moomba*). • *interj. archaic* or *jocular* an exclamation of greeting.

hail[2] *n.* **1** pellets of frozen rain falling in a shower. **2** something coming in great numbers (*a hail of bullets*). • *v.* **1** send down hail (*it is hailing*). **2** come or send down like hail (*stones hailed down on us; hailed blows on his body*).

Hail Mary *n.* a prayer to the Virgin Mary beginning with these words.

hailstone *n.* a pellet of hail.

hailstorm *n.* a storm of hail.

hair *n.* **1** each of the fine threadlike strands that grow from the skin of people and animals or on certain plants. **2** a mass of these, esp. on the human head. **3** a very small quantity or extent (*won by a hair*). ☐ **hair of the dog** a further alcoholic drink taken to cure a hangover. **hair-raising** terrifying. **hair's breadth** a tiny amount (*escaped death by a hair's breadth*). **hair shirt** a shirt of haircloth, worn formerly by penitents and ascetics. **hair-splitting** *n.* & *adj.* splitting hairs (*see below*). **hair-trigger** *n.* a trigger that causes a gun to fire at the very slightest pressure. *adj.* very quick (*he has hair-trigger reactions*). **let one's hair down** *colloq.* enjoy oneself without restraint. **not turn a hair** remain unmoved or unaffected. **split hairs** make distinctions of meaning that are too small to be of any real importance.

haircloth *n.* stiff cloth woven from hair.

haircut *n.* **1** shortening the hair by cutting it. **2** the style in which it is cut.

hairdo *n.* (*pl.* **hairdos**) a hairstyle; the process of styling hair.

hairdresser *n.* a person who cuts and styles hair. ☐ **hairdressing** *n.*

hairless *adj.* without hair, bald.

hairline *n.* **1** the edge of a person's hair around the face. **2** a very narrow line, esp. a crack. ☐ **hairline fracture** a fracture in bone, metal, etc. which shows itself as a hairline on the surface.

hairpiece *n.* a wig worn to conceal baldness.

hairpin *n.* a U-shaped pin for keeping the hair in place. ☐ **hairpin bend** a sharp U-shaped bend in a road.

hairspring *n.* a fine spring regulating the balance wheel in a watch.

hairstyle *n.* a style in which hair is arranged. ☐ **hairstylist** *n.*

hairy *adj.* (**hairier**, **hairiest**) **1** having much hair. **2** *colloq.* frightening, dangerous (*a hairy ride in a car with no brakes*). **3** *colloq.* very difficult (*quite a hairy problem*). ☐ **hairy-nosed wombat** either of two wombats of southern and eastern Australia with fine hairs on the snout. ☐ ☐ **hairiness** *n.*

Haiti / **hay**-tee / a republic in the West Indies. ☐ **Haitian** / **hay**-shuhn / *adj.* & *n.*

hajj *n.* (also **hadj**) an Islamic pilgrimage to Mecca.

hajji / **haj**-ee / *n.* (also **hadji**) a Muslim who has made the pilgrimage to Mecca.

haka / **hah**-kuh / *n. NZ* a Maori ceremonial war dance with chanting; an imitation of this by a sports team before a match.

hake *n.* (*pl.* **hake**) **1** a marine fish of the cod family, used as food. **2** a gemfish.

hakea / **hay**-kee-uh / *n.* any Australian shrub of the large genus *Hakea*, having spiny and usu. very showy flowers followed by woody fruits. (¶ Baron von Hake, patron of botany (1745–1818).)

halal / hah-**lahl** / *v.* (**halalled**, **halalling**) (also **hallal**) kill (an animal for meat) according to Muslim law. • *n.* meat from an animal so killed.

halberd *n.* an ancient weapon that is a combined spear and battleaxe.

halcyon / **hal**-see-uhn / *adj.* (of a period) happy and peaceful (*halcyon days*). (¶ Named after a bird formerly believed to have the power of calming wind and waves while it nested on the sea.)

hale *adj.* strong and healthy (*hale and hearty*). • *v.* draw or drag forcibly (*haled him into the room by the scruff of his neck*).

half *n.* (*pl.* **halves**) **1** each of two equal or corresponding parts into which a thing is divided. **2** *colloq.* a half-back. **3** *Sport* either of two equal periods of play. •*adj.* amounting to a half (*half the men; a half share*). •*adv.* **1** to the extent of a half, partly (*half-cooked; I'm half inclined to agree*). **2** (in reckoning time) by the amount of half (an hour) (*half past two*). **3** *colloq.* half past (*half seven*). □ **by half** excessively (*too clever by half*). **by halves** imperfectly or incompletely (*they never do things by halves*). **go halves** share a thing equally. **half-back** **1** *Sport* a position between the forwards and the full backs. **2** *Aust. Rules* a position between the back and centre lines. **half-baked** *colloq.* not competently planned; foolish. **half-breed** *offens.* = HALF-CASTE. **half-brother** a brother with whom one has only one parent in common. **half-caste** *offens.* a person of mixed race. **half-forward** *Aust. Rules* a position between the forward and centre lines. **half-hearted** lacking in enthusiasm. **half hitch** a knot for tying a rope round a post etc., formed by passing the short end round the main length of rope and then through the loop. **half-life** the time it takes the radioactivity of a substance to fall to half its original value. **half mast** a position of a flag halfway down a mast, as a mark of respect for a dead person. **half measures** a policy lacking thoroughness. **half-moon** the moon when half its surface is illuminated. **half nelson** *see* NELSON. **half-sister** a sister with whom one has only one parent in common. **half-time** the interval between the two halves of a game. **half-truth** a statement that (esp. deliberately) conveys only part of the truth. **half-volley** (in ball games) a return of the ball as soon as it has reached the ground.

halfpenny / **hayp**-nee / *n.* (*pl.* **halfpennies** for separate coins, **halfpence** for a sum of money) a former coin worth half a penny.

halftone *n.* a black-and-white illustration in which light and dark shades are reproduced by means of small and large dots.

halfway *adv.* **1** at a point between and equally distant from two others (*halfway there*). **2** to some extent, more or less (*halfway acceptable*). •*adj.* situated halfway (*reached the halfway mark*). □ **halfway house 1** a compromise. **2** the halfway point in a progression. **3** a home in which ex-prisoners, mental patients, drug addicts, etc. can live until they are equipped to re-enter the outside world.

halfwit *n.* a foolish or stupid person. □ **half-witted** *adj.*

halibut *n.* (*pl.* **halibut**) **1** a large marine flatfish used for food. **2** (also **Queensland halibut**) a fine food fish found in tropical Australian waters.

halitosis / hal-uh-**toh**-suhs / *n.* breath that smells unpleasant.

Hall[1], Ben(jamin) (1837–65), Australian bushranger whose reckless courage and courtesy to women have inspired several ballads, novels (including Boldrewood's *Robbery Under Arms*), a play, films, and a television series.

Hall[2], Ken(neth George) (1901–94), AO, Australian Oscar-winning film director and producer.

Hall[3], Rodney (1935–), AM, Australian writer. His novel *Just Relations* (1982) won the Miles Franklin Award.

hall *n.* **1** an area into which the front entrance of a house etc. opens; a corridor or passage in a house or other building. **2** a large room or building for meetings, concerts, etc. **3** *Brit.* a large country house. □ **hall of residence** a building for university students to live in.

hallal alternative spelling of HALAL.

hallelujah = ALLELUIA.

Halley / **hal**-ee /, Edmond (1656–1742), English astronomer. □ **Halley's comet** a bright comet that orbits the sun in about 76 years, whose reappearance in 1758 was predicted by Halley.

halliard alternative spelling of HALYARD.

hallmark *n.* **1** a mark indicating the standard of gold, silver, and platinum. **2** a distinguishing characteristic (*generosity was the hallmark of his life*).

hallmarked *adj.* marked with a hallmark.

hallo alternative spelling of HELLO.

hallow *v.* **1** make holy. **2** honour as holy.

Halloween *n.* (also **Hallowe'en**) 31 October, the eve of All Saints' Day.

hallucinate / huh-**loo**-suh-nayt / *v.* experience hallucinations. □ **hallucinant** *adj. & n.*

hallucination / huh-loo-suh-**nay**-shuhn / *n.* the illusion of seeing or hearing something when no such thing is present. □ **hallucinatory** / huh-loo-suh-nuh-tree, huh-loo-suh-**nay**-tuh-ree / *adj.*

hallucinogen / huh-**loo**-suh-nuh-juhn / *n.* a drug causing hallucinations. □ **hallucinogenic** / huh-loo-suh-nuh-**jen**-ik / *adj.*

hallway *n.* an entrance area or corridor.

halm alternative spelling of HAULM.

halo *n.* (*pl.* **haloes**) **1** a disc or ring of light shown round the head of a sacred figure in paintings etc. **2** glory associated with an idealised person etc. **3** a disc of diffused light round a luminous body such as the sun or moon. □ **haloed** *adj.*

halogen / **hal**-uh-juhn / *n.* any of the five chemically related elements, fluorine, chlorine, bromine, iodine, and astatine, which form salts when combined with a metal. •*adj.* (of lamps and radiant heat sources) using a filament surrounded by a halogen, usu. iodine vapour.

halon / **hay**-lon / *n.* any of various gaseous compounds of carbon, bromine, and other halogens, used to extinguish fires.

halt *n.* **1** a temporary stop, an interruption of progress (*work came to a halt*). **2** a minor stopping place on a local railway line. •*v.* come or bring to a halt.

halter *n.* **1** a length of rope or a leather strap for leading or tying up a horse. **2** a rope with a noose

halting

for hanging a person; execution by this means. **3** (also **halter-neck**) a strap passing round the back of the neck holding a dress or top up and leaving the back and shoulders bare. • *v.* put a halter on (a horse).

halting *adj.* hesitant (*a halting explanation*). □ **haltingly** *adv.*

halva *n.* (also **halwa**) a sweet (orig. from the Middle East) made of ground sesame seeds and honey.

halve *v.* **1** divide or share equally between two. **2** reduce by half. **3** *Golf* use the same number of strokes as an opponent in (a hole or match).

halves *see* HALF.

halyard / **hal**-yuhd / *n.* (also **halliard**) a rope or tackle for raising or lowering a sail, yard, or flag.

ham *n.* **1** the upper part of a pig's leg, dried and salted or smoked for food. **2** the back of the thigh and buttock. **3** *colloq.* a poor actor or performer. **4** *colloq.* the operator of an amateur radio station (*a radio ham*). • *v.* (**hammed**, **hamming**) *colloq.* overact, exaggerate one's actions deliberately (*hamming it up*). □ **ham-fisted** (also **ham-handed**) *adj. colloq.* clumsy.

hamadryad / ham-uh-**druy**-uhd / *n.* a king cobra.

hamartia / huh-**mah**-tee-uh / *n.* (in Greek tragedy) the fatal flaw leading to the destruction of the tragic hero or heroine.

hamburger *n.* a flat round cake of seasoned minced beef, usu. fried or grilled and eaten in a soft bread roll.

Hamersley Range / **ham**-uhz-lee / a range in the north-west of WA, rich in iron ore deposits.

Hamite / **ham**-uyt / *n.* a member of a group of North African peoples including the ancient Egyptians and the present-day Berbers. □ **Hamitic** / huh-**mit**-ik / *adj.*

hamlet *n.* a small village.

hammer[1] *n.* **1** a tool with a heavy metal head used for breaking things, driving nails in, etc. **2** something shaped or used like this, e.g. an auctioneer's mallet, part of the firing device in a gun, a lever striking the string in a piano. **3** a metal ball attached to a wire for throwing as an athletic contest. • *v.* **1** hit or beat with or as with a hammer, strike loudly. **2** impress (an idea etc.) strongly upon a person (*hammered the idea into her*). **3** *colloq.* defeat utterly; beat up. **4** (foll. by *at*, *away at*) work hard or persistently at. □ **come** (or **go**) **under the hammer** be sold by auction. **hammer and sickle** the symbols of manual worker and peasant used as the emblem of the former USSR and international communism. **hammer and tongs** with great energy and noise. **hammer out 1** work out the details of (a plan etc.) with great effort. **2** play (a tune, esp. on the piano) loudly or clumsily. **hammer toe** a toe that is permanently bent downwards.

hammer[2] *n. colloq.* a person's back. □ **on a person's hammer** in hot pursuit of him or her; hounding or pestering him or her.

hammerhead *n.* a shark with a flattened head and with eyes in lateral extensions of the head (thereby resembling a double-headed hammer).

hammering *n. colloq.* a thorough defeat; a thrashing.

hammerlock *n.* a hold in which a wrestler's arm is bent behind the back.

hammock *n.* a hanging bed of canvas or rope network.

Hammond, Dame Joan (1912–96), Australian soprano (born in NZ) who achieved international fame in opera and on the concert stage.

hammy *adj. colloq.* over-theatrical.

hamper *n.* a large basket, usu. with a hinged lid, for containing food. • *v.* prevent the free movement or activity of, hinder.

hamster *n.* a small mouselike rodent with cheek pouches for storing food.

hamstring *n.* **1** any of the five tendons at the back of the human knee. **2** the great tendon at the back of an animal's hock. • *v.* (**hamstrung**, **hamstringing**) **1** cripple by cutting the hamstring(s). **2** impair the activity or efficiency of (*we were hamstrung by the lack of proper equipment*).

hand *n.* **1** the end part of the arm beyond the wrist. **2** part of an animal's foreleg. **3** possession, control, care (*the child is in good hands*). **4** influence, activity (*many people had a hand in it*). **5** active help (*give him a hand*). **6** a pledge of marriage (*asked for her hand*). **7** a manual worker in a factory or farm etc.; a member of a ship's crew. **8** skill or style of workmanship; a person with reference to skill (*has a light hand with pastry; an old hand at this*). **9** style of handwriting. **10** a pointer on a clock etc. **11** side or direction; each of two contrasted sides in an argument etc. (*on the left hand side; on the other hand*). **12** a unit of 10.16 cm (4 inches) used in measuring a horse's height. **13** the cards dealt to a player in a card game. **14** *colloq.* applause (*got a big hand*). **15** done, operated, or carried etc. by hand (*hand-knitted; hand luggage*). **16** a cluster or bunch (*a hand of bananas*). **17** a forehock of pork. • *v.* give or pass with one's hand(s) or otherwise (*hand me the scissors; handed them the advantage*). □ **at hand 1** close by. **2** about to happen. **dead hand at** *colloq.* expert at. **hand and foot** completely (*waited on them hand and foot*). **hand in glove with** working in close association with. **hand it to** *colloq.* award praise to, admire. **hand-me-down** an article of clothing etc. passed on from another person. **hand over fist** *colloq.* with rapid progress (*making money hand over fist*). **hand-picked** carefully chosen. **hands down** (of a victory won) easily, completely. **hands off!** do not touch or interfere. **hands-off** *adj. Computing etc.* not requiring the manual use of controls. **hands-on** *adj.* **1** (of experience etc.) practical, working or operating a thing (esp. a keyboard) directly. **2** *Computing etc.* of or requiring personal operation at a keyboard. **hands up!** an order to raise one's hand (e.g. in agreement) or both hands in surrender. **hand-to-hand** (of fighting) at close quarters. **in hand 1** in one's possession. **2** in control. **3** (of business) being dealt with. **on hand** available. **on one's hands** resting on one as a responsibility. **out of hand 1** out of control. **2** without delay or preparation (*rejected it out of hand*). **show one's hand** reveal one's plans. **to hand** within reach; available.

handbag *n.* a small bag for holding a purse and personal articles.

handball *n.* **1** a game with a ball thrown by hand among players or against a wall. **2** *Aust. Rules* a handpass. **3** *Soccer* intentional touching of the ball, constituting a foul. • *v. Aust. Rules* to handpass.

handbook *n.* a small book giving useful facts.

handbrake *n.* a brake operated by hand.

handclap *n.* a clapping of the hands, applause. □ **slow handclap** *n.* a round of very slow rhythmic clapping expressing disapproval. *v.* express disapproval (of) by clapping in this way.

handcraft *v.* make by handicraft.

handcuff *n.* each of a pair of linked metal rings for securing a prisoner's wrists. • *v.* put handcuffs on (a prisoner).

Handel, George Frederick (1685–1759), German-born composer who settled in England.

handfeed *v.* **1** rear (a young animal etc.) by giving food by hand; poddy (a young animal etc.). **2** assist (students etc.) to an excessive degree, thus sapping initiative.

handful *n.* (*pl.* **handfuls**) **1** a quantity that fills the hand. **2** a small number of people or things. **3** *colloq.* a person who is difficult to control; a troublesome task.

handicap *n.* **1** a physical or mental disability. **2** a disadvantage imposed on a superior competitor in order to equalise chances; a race or contest in which this is imposed. **3** the number of strokes by which a golfer normally exceeds par for the course. **4** anything that lessens one's chance of success or makes progress difficult. • *v.* (**handicapped, handicapping**) impose or be a handicap on.

handicapped *adj.* suffering from a physical or mental disability.

handicraft *n.* work that needs both skill with the hands and artistic design, e.g. woodwork, needlework, pottery.

handiwork *n.* something done or made by the hands, or by a named person.

handkerchief *n.* (*pl.* **handkerchiefs** *or* **handkerchieves**) a small square of cloth for wiping the nose etc.

handle *n.* **1** the part of a thing by which it is to be held, carried, or controlled. **2** a fact that may be taken advantage of (*gave a handle to his critics*). **3** *colloq.* a personal title or name. • *v.* **1** touch, feel, or move with the hands. **2** be able to be operated (*the car handles well*). **3** manage, deal with (*knows how to handle people*). **4** deal in (goods). **5** discuss or write about (a subject). □ **fly off the handle** see FLY². **get a handle on** *colloq.* understand the basis of or the reason for a situation etc.

handlebar *n.* the steering bar of a bicycle etc.

handler *n.* **1** a person who handles or deals in something. **2** a person who trains and looks after an animal (esp. a police dog).

handmaid *n.* (also **handmaiden**) *archaic* a female servant.

handout *n.* **1** something distributed free of charge to a needy person. **2** notes given out in a class etc. **3** a statement issued to the press etc.

handover *n.* handing over.

handpass *n. Aust. Rules* a pass (to a team mate) in which the ball is held in one hand and struck with the other. • *v.* deliver a handpass.

handrail *n.* a narrow rail for people to hold as a support.

handset *n.* a telephone mouthpiece and earpiece as one unit.

handshake *n.* grasping and shaking a person's hand with one's own as a greeting.

handsome *adj.* **1** (usu. of a man) good-looking. **2** generous (*a handsome present*). **3** (of a price or fortune etc.) very large. □ **handsomely** *adv.*

handspring *n.* a gymnastic feat consisting of a handstand, somersaulting, and landing in a standing position.

handstand *n.* balancing on one's hands with the feet in the air.

handwriting *n.* **1** writing done by hand with a pen or pencil. **2** a person's style of this.

handwritten *adj.* written by hand.

handy *adj.* (**handier, handiest**) **1** convenient to handle or use. **2** conveniently placed for being reached or used. **3** clever with one's hands. □ **handily** *adv.* **handiness** *n.*

handyman *n.* a person who is clever at doing household repairs etc. or who is employed to do odd jobs.

hang *v.* (**hung** (in senses 5 and 6 **hanged**), **hanging**) **1** support or be supported from above so that the lower end is free. **2** cause (a door or gate) to rest on hinges so that it swings freely to and fro; be placed in this way. **3** stick (wallpaper) to a wall. **4** decorate with drapery or hanging ornaments. **5** kill by suspending from a rope that tightens round the neck; be executed in this way. **6** *colloq.* damn (*I'm hanged if I know*). **7** let droop; lean over (*hang one's head; people hung over the gate*). **8** be present, esp. oppressively or threateningly (*smoke hung over the area; the threat is hanging over him*). **9** *colloq.* blame (a thing) on (a person) (*you can't hang that on me*). • *n.* the way something hangs or falls (*the hang of the drapes*). □ **get the hang of** *colloq.* get the knack of; get the meaning or sense of. **hang about** (*or* **around**) loiter; linger near (a person or place). **2** (usu. foll. by *with*) *colloq.* associate closely with (*he hangs around with Jeff*). **hang back** show reluctance to take action or to advance. **hang five** *colloq.* ride standing on the nose of a surfboard with the toes of one foot dangling over the edge. **hang-glider** the frame used in hang-gliding. **hang-gliding** the sport of being suspended in an airborne frame controlled by one's own movements. **hang in** *colloq.* **1** persist, persevere. **2** ride a surfboard close to the breaking part of a wave. **hang loose** *colloq.* be relaxed or uninhibited. **hang on 1** continue to hold or grasp. **2** (foll. by *to*) retain; fail to give back. **3** listen closely to (*he hangs on my every word*). **4** depend on (*everything hangs on his reply*). **5** *colloq.* continue; persevere. **6** *colloq.* wait for a short time (*hang on a sec*). **7** *colloq.* (in telephoning) not ring off during a pause in the conversation. **hang out 1** suspend from a window, clothes line, etc. **2 a** protrude downwards (*shirt hanging out*). **b** (foll. by *of*) lean out of (a window etc.). **3** *colloq.* frequent a place (*he hangs out at the games arcade*). **b** live in a place (*he hangs out somewhere near Wagga Wagga*). **hang-out** *colloq.* a place in which a person is usu. found. **hang ten** *colloq.* ride standing on the nose of a surfboard with the toes of both feet dangling over the edge. **hang together** (of people) help or support one another; (of statements) fit well together, be consistent. **hang** (or **do**) **a uey** *Aust. colloq.* make a U-turn in a vehicle. **hang up 1** end a telephone conversation by replacing the receiver (*he hung up on me*). **2** (as **hung up**) (foll. by *on*) *colloq.* have a psychological problem or an obsession for (*she is hung up on her father*). **3** *Aust.* tether a horse. **hang-up** *n. colloq.* an emotional problem or inhibition. **let it all hang out** *colloq.* be uninhibited or relaxed.

hangar *n.* a building for housing aircraft.

hangdog *adj.* shamefaced.

hanger *n.* **1** a person who hangs things. **2** a loop or hook by which something is hung. **3** (in full **coathanger**) a shaped piece of wood, wire, etc. for hanging a garment on. ☐ **hanger-on** (*pl.* **hangers-on**) an unwanted follower or dependant.

hangi / hahng-ee, hang-ee / *n.* chiefly *NZ* **1** an earth-covered pit in which food is cooked on heated stones. **2** the food cooked in such an oven. **3** a banquet consisting of such food. (¶ Maori)

hanging *n.* **1** execution by suspending a person by the neck. **2** a drapery hung on a wall.

Hanging Gardens of Babylon the terraced gardens at Babylon, watered by pumps from the Euphrates, whose construction was ascribed to Nebuchadnezzar (*c.*600 BC). They were one of the Seven Wonders of the World.

hangman *n.* a man whose job is to hang persons condemned to death.

hangnail *n.* a piece of torn skin at the base of a fingernail.

hangover *n.* **1** a severe headache or other unpleasant after-effects from drinking too much alcohol. **2** something left from an earlier time.

Hang Seng index an index based on the average price of selected securities on the Hong Kong stock exchange.

hank *n.* a coil or length of wool or thread etc.

hanker *v.* (usu. foll. by *for* or *after*) crave, feel a longing.

Hanks, Tom (full name: Thomas J. Hanks) (1956–), American film actor. He won best actor Oscars for *Philadelphia* (1993) and *Forrest Gump* (1994).

hanky *n.* (also **hankie**) *colloq.* a handkerchief.

hanky-panky *n. colloq.* **1** trickery, dishonest dealing. **2** naughtiness, esp. sexual.

Hannan, Paddy (full name: Patrick Hannan) (1842–1925), Australian prospector (born in Ireland) who discovered gold in WA and precipitated the goldrush which established Kalgoorlie as Australia's richest goldfield.

Hanoi the capital of Vietnam.

Hansard *n.* the official reports of the proceedings of parliament. (¶ Named after the English printer whose firm originally compiled it.)

Hansen's disease *n.* leprosy. (¶ Named after the Norwegian physician G.H.A. Hansen (1841–1912), who discovered the leprosy bacillus.)

hansom *n.* (in full **hansom cab**) *archaic* a two-wheeled horse-drawn cab.

Hanson, Pauline (Lee) (1954–), Australian politician and founder of the One Nation party. She won the seat of Oxley in the Commonwealth parliament in 1996, but was defeated when she stood for the seat of Blair in 1998.

Hanukkah / **hah**-nuh-kuh / *n.* an eight-day Jewish festival of lights, beginning in December, commemorating the rededication of the Temple at Jerusalem in 165 BC after its desecration by the Syrian king.

hanuman / hah-noo-**mahn** / *n.* **1** an Indian monkey venerated by Hindus. **2** (**Hanuman**) (in Hinduism) a semi-divine monkey-like being to whom extraordinary powers are attributed.

haphazard / hap-**haz**-uhd / *adj.* done or chosen at random, without planning. ☐ **haphazardly** *adv.*

hapless *adj.* unlucky.

happen *v.* **1** occur (by chance or otherwise). **2** have the (good or bad) fortune to do something (*we happened to see him*). **3** be the fate or experience of (*what happened to you?*). **4** (foll. by *on*) find by chance.

happening *n.* **1** an event. **2** an improvised or spontaneous theatrical etc. performance.

happy *adj.* (**happier**, **happiest**) **1** feeling or showing pleasure or contentment. **2** fortunate. **3** (of words or behaviour) very suitable, pleasing. ☐ **happy-go-lucky** *adj.* cheerfully casual. **happy hour** a time in the day when drinks are served at reduced prices. **happy medium** something that

hara-kiri achieves satisfactory avoidance of extremes; a compromise. **happy wanderer** *Aust.* a common term for the hardenbergia. ☐☐ **happily** *adv.* **happiness** *n.*

hara-kiri / hah-ruh-**ki**-ree, ha- / *n.* suicide involving disembowelment, formerly practised by Japanese samurai when in disgrace or under sentence of death.

harangue / huh-**rang** / *n.* a lengthy ranting speech. •*v.* make a harangue to; lecture, scold, verbally abuse.

Harare / huh-**rah**-ree / the capital of Zimbabwe.

harass / **ha**-ruhs, huh-**ras** / *v.* **1** trouble and annoy continually. **2** make repeated attacks on (an enemy). ☐ **harassed** *adj.* **harassment** *n.*

■ **Usage** The second pronunciation given, with the stress on the second syllable, is considered incorrect by some people but is now acceptable in Australian English.

harbinger / **hah**-bin-juh / *n.* a person or thing whose presence announces the approach of another; a forerunner; an omen.

harbour (also **harbor**) *n.* a place of shelter for ships. •*v.* **1** give shelter to, conceal (a criminal etc.). **2** keep in one's mind (*harbour a grudge*).

hard *adj.* **1** firm, not yielding to pressure; not easily cut. **2** difficult to do or understand or answer. **3** causing unhappiness, difficult to bear. **4** severe, harsh, unsympathetic. **5** energetic (*a hard worker*). **6** (of currency) not likely to drop suddenly in value. **7** (of drinks) strongly alcoholic. **8** (of drugs) strong and likely to cause addiction. **9** (of water) containing mineral salts that prevent soap from lathering freely and cause a hard coating to form inside kettles, water tanks, etc. **10** (of colours or sounds) harsh to the eye or ear. **11** (of consonants) sounding sharp not soft (*the letter 'g' is hard in 'gun' and soft in 'gin'*). **12** (of pornography) highly obscene. **13** (in politics) extreme; most radical (*the hard right*). •*adv.* **1** with great effort, intensively (*worked hard; it's raining hard*). **2** with difficulty (*hard-earned money*). **3** so as to be hard (*hard-baked*). ☐ **hard and fast rules** rules that cannot be altered to fit special cases. **hard-boiled 1** (of eggs) boiled until white and yolk have become solid. **2** (of people) callous. **hard by** close by. **hard cash** coins and banknotes, not a cheque or a promise to pay later. **hard copy** material printed, esp. by a computer, on paper. **hard core** *n.* the stubborn unyielding nucleus of a group (*the hard core of the ALP Left*). *adj.* (also **hardcore**) **1** blatant, uncompromising; stubborn, highly committed. **2** (of pornography) explicit, obscene. **hard disk** (in computers) a rigid disk, installed permanently, capable of holding more data than a floppy disk. **hard-headed** practical, not sentimental. **hard-hit** *adj.* badly affected (*hard-hit by the drought*). **hard labour** heavy manual work as a punishment, esp. in a prison. **hard line** unyielding adherence to a firm policy. **hard of hearing** slightly deaf. **hard-on** *coarse colloq.* an erection of the penis. **hard palate** the bony front part of the palate. **hard-pressed 1** in difficulty; burdened. **2** closely pursued. **hard rock** *colloq.* rock music with a heavy beat. **hard sell** aggressive salesmanship. **hard up** *colloq.* short of money. **hard yards** (originally in Rugby) preliminary or ground-breaking work or effort (*let them do the hard yards to secure a wage increase and we'll enjoy the benefits*). ☐☐ **hardness** *n.*

hardback *adj.* bound in stiff covers. •*n.* a book bound in this way.

hardbitten *adj.* tough and realistic.

hardboard *n.* stiff board made of compressed wood pulp.

harden *v.* **1** make or become hard or harder. **2** make or become unyielding (*attitudes have hardened in the dispute*). **3** (of prices etc.) cease to fall or fluctuate. ☐ **hardening of the arteries** = ARTERIOSCLEROSIS. **harden off** accustom (a plant) to the cold by gradually increasing its exposure.

hardenbergia / hah-duhn-**ber**-jee-uh, -ber-gee-uh / *n.* an Australian climbing or trailing plant with masses of usu. purple pea-flowers. Also called *purple coral pea, false sarsaparilla*.

hardihood *n.* boldness, daring.

hardliner *n.* a person (esp. a politician) who takes a hard line on an issue.

hardly *adv.* **1** only with difficulty (*can hardly see*). **2** scarcely (*hardly recognised me*). **3** surely not (*can hardly have realised*).

hardship *n.* **1** severe discomfort or lack of the necessities of life. **2** a circumstance causing this.

hardware *n.* **1** tools and household implements etc. sold by a shop. **2** weapons, machinery. **3** the mechanical and electronic parts of a computer.

hardwood *n.* the hard heavy wood obtained from a eucalypt or from deciduous trees, e.g. teak.

Hardy[1], Frank (full name: Francis Joseph Hardy) (1917–94), Australian writer who frequently addressed the theme of corruption in financial, political, and legal circles. His works include the novel *Power Without Glory*.

Hardy[2], Thomas (1840–1928), English novelist and poet.

hardy *adj.* (**hardier, hardiest**) **1** capable of enduring cold or difficult conditions. **2** (of plants) able to grow in the open air all the year round. ☐ **hardiness** *n.*

hare *n.* a field animal like a rabbit but larger. •*v.* run rapidly. ☐ **hare-brained** *adj.* wild and foolish, rash. **hare wallaby** any of several small hare-like wallabies of mainland Australia.

Hare-Clark system an electoral system first used in the 1909 elections for the Tasmanian House of Assembly. A form of proportional representation based on the 'single transferable vote', the system increases the likelihood of parliamentary representation for minority groups. (¶ From Thomas Hare (1806–91) and Andrew

Inglis Clark (1848–1907), political reformers and advocates of proportional representation.)

Hare Krishna / hah-ree-**krish**-nuh / the title of a love chant or mantra based on the name of the Hindu god Vishnu, used as an incantation by members of a religious sect founded in the USA in 1966.

harelip n. (often *offens.*) a deformed lip (usu. the upper lip) with a vertical slit in it.

harem / **hair**-ruhm, hah-**reem** / n. **1** the women of a Muslim household, living in a separate part of the house. **2** their quarters.

haricot / **ha**-ruh-koh / n. (in full **haricot bean**) the edible white dried seed of a kind of bean.

Harijan / **hu**-ree-juhn / n. a member of the class of untouchables in the Indian subcontinent.

harissa / huh-**ris**-uh / n. a hot spicy paste of red chillis and olive oil, used in North African cookery.

hark v. *archaic* listen. ☐ **hark back** return to an earlier subject.

harlequin n. **1** (**Harlequin**) a mute pantomime character, usu. masked and dressed in a diamond-patterned costume. **2** *Aust.* a highly-prized form of Australian opal. • *adj.* in varied colours.

harlot n. *archaic* a prostitute. ☐ **harlotry** n.

harm n. damage, injury. • v. cause harm to.

harmful *adj.* causing harm. ☐ **harmfully** *adv.*

harmless *adj.* **1** unlikely to cause harm. **2** inoffensive. ☐ **harmlessly** *adv.* **harmlessness** n.

harmonic *adj.* **1** of harmony in music. **2** harmonious. • n. a tone produced by vibration of a string etc. in any of certain fractions (half, third, quarter, fifth, etc.) of its length.

harmonica n. a small rectangular musical instrument played by blowing and sucking air through it.

harmonious *adj.* **1** forming a pleasing or consistent whole. **2** free from disagreement or ill feeling. **3** sweet-sounding, tuneful. ☐ **harmoniously** *adv.*

harmonise v. (also -**ize**) **1** make or be harmonious. **2** produce an agreeable artistic effect. **3** add notes to (a melody) to form chords. ☐ **harmonisation** n.

harmonium n. a musical instrument with a keyboard, in which notes are produced by air pumped through reeds.

harmony n. **1** the state of being harmonious. **2** the combination of musical notes to produce chords. **3** a sweet or melodious sound.

harness n. **1** the straps and fittings by which a horse is controlled and fastened to the cart etc. that it pulls. **2** fastenings resembling this for attaching a thing to a person's body. • v. **1** put harness on (a horse); attach by a harness. **2** control and use (a river or other natural force), esp. to produce power. ☐ **harness racing** see TROTTING.

harp n. a large upright musical instrument consisting of strings stretched on a roughly triangular frame, played by plucking with the fingers. ☐ **harp on** talk repeatedly and tiresomely (about a subject). ☐☐ **harpist** n.

harpoon n. a spear-like missile with a rope attached, for catching whales etc. • v. spear with a harpoon.

harpsichord / **hahp**-suh-kawd / n. a keyboard instrument with horizontal strings plucked mechanically. ☐ **harpsichordist** n.

harpy n. a grasping unscrupulous person. (¶ Named after the Harpies, creatures in Greek mythology with a woman's filthy head and body and a bird's wings and claws.)

harridan / **ha**-ruh-duhn / n. a bad-tempered old woman.

harrier n. **1** a hound used for hunting hares. **2** a hawk-like bird of prey, including some Australian species. **3** any of a group of cross-country runners.

Harris, Rolf (1930–), AM, Australian entertainer and musician whose recording of *Tie me Kangaroo Down, Sport* (1960) had worldwide success.

harrow n. a heavy frame with metal spikes or discs for breaking up clods of soil. • v. **1** draw a harrow over (land). **2** distress greatly.

Harrowing of Hell (in medieval Christian theology) the defeat of the powers of evil and the release of its victims, by the descent of Christ into hell after his death.

harry v. (**harried**, **harrying**) **1** ravage or despoil. **2** harass.

harsh *adj.* **1** rough and disagreeable, esp. to the senses (*a harsh texture; a harsh voice*). **2** severe, cruel (*harsh treatment*). ☐ **harshly** *adv.* **harshness** n.

Hart, Pro (original name: Kevin Charles Hart) (1928–), Australian artist whose paintings often depict bush scenes in vivid colours.

hart n. (*pl.* **hart** or **harts**) an adult male deer.

hartebeest / **hah**-tuh-beest / n. a large African antelope with curving horns.

harum-scarum *colloq. adj.* wild and reckless. • n. a wild and reckless person.

harvest n. **1** the gathering of a crop or crops; the season when this is done. **2** the season's yield of any natural product. **3** the product of any action. • v. gather a crop, reap.

harvester n. **1** a reaper. **2** a reaping-machine.

Harvey, William (1578–1657), English physician who discovered that blood circulates in the veins and is not (as contemporary theory held) absorbed as food.

has see HAVE. ☐ **has-been** n. (*pl.* **has-beens**) *colloq.* a person or thing that is no longer as famous or successful as formerly.

hash[1] n. **1** a dish of cooked or preserved meat cut into small pieces and recooked. **2** a jumble, a mixture. **3** recycled material. **4** *colloq.* hashish. ☐ **make a hash of** *colloq.* make a mess of, bungle.

hash[2] n. (also **hash sign**) the symbol #.

hashish *n.* the resinous product of the top leaves and tender parts of hemp, smoked or chewed as a narcotic.

hasn't = has not.

hasp *n.* a hinged metal strip with a slit in it that fits over a U-shaped staple through which a pin or padlock is then passed.

hassium / **has**-ee-uhm / *n.* an unstable chemical element (symbol Hs) made by high-energy atomic collisions. (¶ Modern Latin *Hassia* 'Hesse', the German State in which it was discovered.)

hassle *colloq. n.* a quarrel or struggle. •*v.* **1** quarrel. **2** annoy; harass.

hassock *n.* a thick firm cushion for kneeling on in church.

hast *archaic* the present tense of HAVE, used with *thou*.

haste *n.* urgency of movement or action, hurry. •*v. archaic* = HASTEN (sense 1).

hasten *v.* **1** hurry. **2** cause (a thing) to be done earlier or to happen earlier.

hasty *adj.* (**hastier, hastiest**) **1** hurried, acting quickly. **2** done too quickly. ☐ **hastily** *adv.* **hastiness** *n.*

hat *n.* **1** a covering for the head, usu. worn out of doors. **2** this thought of as symbolising a person's official position (*wearing her managerial hat*). ☐ **hat trick** the taking of 3 wickets in cricket by 3 successive balls from the same bowler; the scoring of 3 goals or winning of 3 victories by one person. **take one's hat off to** *colloq.* admire, congratulate.

hatch[1] *n.* **1** an opening in a wall between kitchen and dining room for serving food. **2** an opening or trapdoor in a floor, roof, etc.; the cover for this. **3** an opening or door in an aircraft etc. **4** a hatchway; a movable cover for this (often in plural: *batten the hatches*). ☐ **down the hatch!** *colloq.* (as a toast) drink up, cheers!

hatch[2] *v.* **1** (of a young bird or fish etc.) emerge from an egg; (of an egg) produce a young animal. **2** cause (eggs) to produce young by incubating them. **3** devise (a plot). •*n.* hatching; a brood hatched.

hatch[3] *v.* mark with close parallel lines. ☐ **hatching** *n.*

hatchback *n.* a car with a sloping back hinged at the top to form a door.

hatchery *n.* a place for hatching eggs, esp. of fish (*a trout hatchery*).

hatchet *n.* a light short-handled axe. ☐ **hatchet job** a fierce verbal attack on a person, esp. in print. **hatchet man** *colloq.* a person hired by an employer to do unpleasant tasks on his or her behalf, such as firing employees, cutting costs, etc.

hatchway *n.* an opening in a ship's deck through which cargo is lowered or raised.

hate *n.* **1** hatred. **2** *colloq.* a hated person or thing. •*v.* **1** feel hatred towards. **2** dislike greatly. **3** be reluctant (*I hate to interrupt you, but it's time to go*).

hateful *adj.* arousing hatred.

hath *archaic* has.

hatred *n.* extreme dislike or enmity.

hatter *n.* a person whose trade is making or selling hats.

haughty / **haw**-tee / *adj.* (**haughtier, haughtiest**) proud of oneself and looking down on other people. ☐ **haughtily** *adv.* **haughtiness** *n.*

haul *v.* **1** pull or drag forcibly. **2** transport by a truck etc. **3** turn a ship's course. •*n.* **1** hauling. **2** the amount gained as a result of effort; booty (*made a good haul*). **3** a distance to be travelled (*it's only a short haul from here*).

haulage *n.* transport of goods; the charge for this.

haulier / **haw**-lee-uh / *n.* a person or firm whose trade is transporting goods by road.

haulm / hawm, hahm / *n.* (also **halm**) **1** a stalk or stem. **2** the stems of plants such as potatoes, beans, and peas.

haunch *n.* **1** the fleshy part of the buttock and thigh. **2** the leg and loin of deer etc. as food.

haunt *v.* **1** (of ghosts) be frequently in (a place) with manifestations of their presence and influence. **2** be persistently in (a place) (*he haunts the disco*). **3** linger in the mind of (*the memory haunts me*). **4** distress; torment (*haunted by guilt*). •*n.* a place often visited by the person(s) or animal(s) named (*that bistro is a favourite haunt of journos*).

haunted *adj.* frequented by a ghost or ghosts.

haunting *adj.* (of a memory, melody, etc.) lingering in the mind; evocative.

haute couture / oht koo-**tyoor** / *n.* high-class fashion; products of the leading fashion houses. (¶ French)

haute cuisine / oht kwuh-**zeen** / *n.* high-class cookery. (¶ French)

hauteur / oh-**ter** / *n.* haughtiness.

Havana / huh-**van**-uh / the capital of Cuba.

have *v.* (**has, had, having**) **1** be in possession of (a thing or quality); possess in a certain relationship (*he has many enemies*). **2** contain (*the house has six rooms*). **3** experience, undergo (*had a shock*). **4** give birth to. **5** put into a certain condition (*you had me worried*). **6** defeat; have at a disadvantage (*you have me there*). **7** *colloq.* cheat or deceive (*we've been had*). **8** have sexual intercourse with. **9** engage in, carry on (*had a talk with him*). **10** eat (*had breakfast*). **11** allow, tolerate (*won't have him bullied*). **12** show (a quality) (*have pity on him*). **13** receive, accept (*we had news of her; will you have another drink?*). **14** cause a thing to be done (*have one's hair cut; have three copies made*). •*auxiliary v.*, used to form past tenses of verbs (*he has gone; we had expected it*). ☐ **had better** would find it wiser to. **have had (a person or thing)** *colloq.* be thoroughly fed up with. **have had it** *colloq.* **1** have missed one's chance. **2** be near death; have been killed, defeated, etc.; be broken or no longer usable, etc. **3** be utterly exhausted. **have it 1** (foll. by *that*)

Havel 377 **head**

maintain that (*he has it that the drought has been caused by pollution in the atmosphere*). **2** have a sudden inspiration about a problem etc. (*I have it!*). **3** win a decision in a vote (*the ayes have it*). **have it in for** *colloq.* show ill will towards (a person). **have it out** (**with a person**) settle a problem by frank discussion. **have on** *colloq.* hoax (*you're having me on*). **have oneself on** *colloq.* be so conceited as to delude oneself. **haves and have-nots** people with and without wealth or privilege. **have to** be obliged to, must. **have up** bring (a person) before a court of justice or an interviewer.

Havel / **hah**-vuhl /, Václav (1936–), Czech dramatist and statesman, who was president of Czechoslovakia 1989–92, and who became president of the Czech Republic in 1993.

haven *n.* a refuge.

haven't = have not.

haversack *n.* a strong bag carried on the back or over the shoulder.

havoc / **hav**-uhk / *n.* widespread destruction; great disorder.

haw *v. see* HUM.

Hawaii / huh-**wuy**-ee / a State of the USA consisting of a group of islands in the Pacific. □ **Hawaiian** / huh-**wuy**-uhn / *adj.* & *n.*

hawk[1] *n.* **1** a bird of prey with rounded wings shorter than a falcon's. **2** *Politics* a person who advocates aggressive (esp. military) policies (as opposed to a DOVE). □ **hawk-eyed** *adj.* keen-sighted. □ □ **hawkish** *adj.*

hawk[2] *v.* **1** clear the throat noisily, esp. to bring up phlegm. **2** carry (goods) about for sale. **3** (often foll. by *about*) spread (news, gossip, etc.) freely.

Hawke, Robert James Lee ('Bob') (1929–), AC, Australian Labor statesman, prime minister 1983–91.

hawker *n.* a person who hawks goods for a living.

Hawkesbury a river in central eastern NSW, flowing into Broken Bay north of Sydney.

hawser / **haw**-zuh / *n.* a heavy rope or cable for mooring or towing a ship.

hawthorn *n.* a thorny tree or shrub with small red berries.

Hawthorne, Nathaniel (1804–64), American novelist.

hay *n.* grass cut and dried for fodder. □ **hay fever** an allergy with asthmatic symptoms caused by pollen or dust. **make hay while the sun shines** seize opportunities for profit.

Hayden, William George ('Bill') (1933–), Australian Labor politician and leader of the opposition in Federal parliament (1977–83), governor-general of Australia 1989–96.

Haydn / **huy**-duhn /, Franz Joseph (1732–1809), Austrian-born composer.

Hayman Island an island and popular tourist resort off the east coast of north Qld.

hayrick *n.* a haystack.

haystack *n.* a regularly shaped pile of hay firmly packed for storing, with a pointed or ridged top.

haywire *adj. colloq.* badly disorganised; out of order; out of control, berserk.

hazard / **haz**-uhd / *n.* **1** risk, danger; a source of this. **2** an obstacle (e.g. a pond or bunker) on a golf course. • *v.* risk, venture (*hazard a guess*).

hazardous *adj.* risky.

hazchem / **haz**-kem / *n.* a notice or label warning that hazardous chemicals are used or stored where the notice or label is displayed.

haze *n.* **1** thin mist. **2** mental confusion or obscurity. • *v.* subject (newcomers to a group, first-year students at a university, etc.) to a period of organised bullying, ridicule, abuse, etc. as part of initiation.

hazel *n.* **1** a bush with small edible nuts. **2** greenish-brown.

hazelnut *n.* the nut of the hazel.

Hazlehurst, Noni (1954–), AM, Australian stage, television, and film actor and film director.

hazy *adj.* (**hazier**, **haziest**) **1** misty. **2** vague, indistinct. **3** feeling confused or uncertain. □ **hazily** *adv.* **haziness** *n.*

HB *abbr.* (of a pencil lead) hard black.

H-bomb *n.* a hydrogen bomb.

HCF *abbr.* highest common factor.

He *symbol* helium.

he *pron.* **1** the male person or animal mentioned. **2** a person (male or female) (*he who hesitates is lost*). • *adj.* male (*a he-goat*). □ **he-man** a masterful or muscular or virile man.

head *n.* **1** the part of the human body containing the eyes, nose, mouth, and brain; the corresponding part of an animal's body. **2** this as a measure of length (*the horse won by a head*). **3** the intellect, the imagination, the mind (*use your head*). **4** a mental ability or faculty (*has a good head for figures; no head for heights*). **5** the side of a coin bearing the image of a head; (**heads**) this side turned upwards after being tossed. **6** *colloq.* a headache. **7** a person, an individual person or animal (*it costs $1 per head*). **8** (*pl.* **head**) a number of animals (*20 head of cattle*). **9** a thing like a head in form or position, e.g. the rounded end of a pin, the glans of the penis, the cutting or striking part of a tool etc., a rounded mass of leaves or petals etc. at the top of a stem, the flat surface of a drum or cask. **10** foam on top of beer etc. **11** the top of something long (e.g. a stair or mast) or of a list. **12** the top part of a boil where it tends to break. **13** the upper end or part of a table (where the host sits) or of a lake (where a river enters) or of a bed etc. (where a person's head rests); or the front part of a queue. **14** a confined body of steam for exerting pressure in an engine. **15** the leading part in a procession or army. **16** (in place names) a promontory (*Barwon Heads*). **17** the chief person of a group or organisation etc.; a headmaster or headmistress. **18 a** the part of a video recorder that touches the moving tape and converts signals. **b** the part of a record player that holds the playing cartridge and stylus. **c** *Computing* (also **printhead**) the part of a disk drive, tape drive, or printer that reads or writes. • *v.* **1** be at the head or top of. **2** strike (a ball) with one's head in football. **3** move in a certain direction (*we headed south; heading for disaster*). **4** (often foll. by *off*) force to turn back or aside by getting in front of (*head him off*). □ **come to a head** (of matters) reach a crisis. **give a person his or her head** let him or her act freely. **go to a person's head 1** (of alcohol) make him or her dizzy or slightly drunk. **2** (of success) make him or her conceited. **head-on** *adj.* & *adv.* with the head pointed directly towards something; colliding head to head. **head on down** *v.* go (*let's head on down to the beach*). **head over turkey** (*or* **head over heels**) **1** turning one's body upside down in a circular movement (*tumbled head over turkey down the stairs*). **2** completely, utterly (*he is head over heels in love*). **head start** an early advantage. **head them** *Aust.* make both coins in the game of two-up land with head upwards; play the game of two-up. **head wind** a wind blowing from directly in front. **keep** (*or* **lose**) **one's head** remain (*or* fail to remain) calm in a crisis. **make head or tail of** (usu. with *negative* or as a question) be able to understand at all. **need one's head read** *colloq.* be crazy. **off the top of one's head** *colloq.* impromptu; unrehearsed. **over one's head 1** beyond one's understanding. **2** without one's rightful knowledge or involvement, esp. of action taken by a subordinate consulting one's own superior (*he went over my head to the managing director*). **put heads together** pool ideas. **turn a person's head** make him or her vain.

-head *suffix colloq.* indicating a person who has a certain character etc. (*thickhead* a fool), or who has a particular partiality to something (*waxhead* a surfing fanatic).

headache *n.* **1** continuous pain in the head. **2** *colloq.* a worrying problem, person, or thing. □ **headachy** *adj.*

headbanger *n. colloq.* **1** a person who shakes his or her head violently to loud rock music. **2** a crazy or eccentric person.

headbutt *n.* a thrust with the head into the chin or body of another person. • *v.* attack with a headbutt.

headcount *n.* **1** a counting of individual people. **2** a tally of the total number of a group.

headdress *n.* an ornamental covering for the head.

header *n.* **1** heading of the ball in soccer. **2** a dive or plunge with head first. **3** a brick laid at right angles to the face of a wall. **4** (in word processing) a heading programmed to appear at the top of every page (as opposed to FOOTER).

headgear *n.* a hat or headdress.

headhigh tackle *n.* Rugby an illegal tackle taken about an opponent's head or neck.

headhunting *n.* **1** cutting off and preserving the heads of enemies as trophies. **2** seeking to recruit experienced staff by approaching people employed elsewhere. **3** getting rid of (esp. political) opponents. **4** seeking a scapegoat. □ **headhunt** *v.* **headhunter** *n.*

heading *n.* **1** a word or words put at the top of a section of printed or written matters as a title etc. **2** a horizontal passage in a mine.

headlamp = HEADLIGHT.

headland *n.* a promontory.

headlight *n.* a powerful light mounted on the front of a vehicle; the beam from this.

headline *n.* **1** a heading in a newspaper, esp. the largest one at the top of the front page. **2** (**headlines**) a brief broadcast summary of news.

headlong *adv.* & *adj.* **1** falling or plunging with the head first. **2** in a hasty and rash way.

headmaster *n.* a male in charge of a school.

headmistress *n.* a female in charge of a school.

headphones *n.pl.* a set of earphones fitting over the head, for listening to audio equipment etc.

headquarters *n.* (as *sing.* or *pl.*) the place from which an organisation is controlled.

headroom *n.* clearance above the head of a person or the top of a vehicle etc.

headset *n.* headphones, often with a microphone attached.

headshrinker *n. colloq.* a psychiatrist.

headstall *n.* the part of a bridle or halter fitting round a horse's head.

headstone *n.* a stone set up at the head of a grave.

headstrong *adj.* self-willed and obstinate.

headwaters *n.pl.* the streams forming the sources of a river.

headway *n.* **1** progress. **2** headroom.

headword *n.* a word forming a heading esp. to an entry in a dictionary.

heady *adj.* (**headier**, **headiest**) **1** (of drinks) likely to intoxicate people. **2** (of success etc.) exciting. **3** rash, impulsive. □ **headily** *adv.* **headiness** *n.*

heal *v.* **1** (of sore or wounded parts) form healthy flesh again. **2** cause to do this. **3** cure (*heal the sick*). **4** put right (differences etc.). □ **healer** *n.*

health *n.* **1** the state of being well and free from illness (*was restored to health*). **2** the condition of the body (*ill health*). □ **health centre** the headquarters of a group of local medical services. **health food** food thought to have health-giving qualities; natural unprocessed foods. **health kick** *colloq.* an obsession with one's health (*he's on a health kick and eats only green vegies*).

healthful *adj.* producing good health, beneficial.

healthy *adj.* (**healthier**, **healthiest**) **1** having, showing, or producing good health. **2** beneficial. **3** (of things) functioning well. **4** substantial (*a healthy amount*). □ **healthily** *adv.* **healthiness** *n.*

heap *n.* **1** a number of things lying on one another; a mass of material so shaped. **2** (**heaps**) *colloq.* a great amount; plenty (*there's heaps of time*). **3** *colloq.* a dilapidated vehicle. •*v.* **1** pile or become piled in a heap. **2** load with large quantities, give large quantities of (*heaped the plate with food; they heaped insults on him*).

hear *v.* (**heard**, **hearing**) **1** perceive (sounds) with the ear. **2** listen or pay attention to. **3** listen to and try (a case) in a lawcourt. **4** receive information or a message or letter etc. ☐ **have heard of** have knowledge or information about (*we have never heard of this firm*). **hear! hear!** I agree. **not hear of** refuse to allow (*won't hear of my paying for it*). ☐☐ **hearer** *n.*

Heard and McDonald Islands an Australian Antarctic territory, situated 2,500 nautical miles south-west of Fremantle. Heard Island is formed about Big Ben (2,700 metres), the only active volcano on Australian territory.

hearing *n.* **1** the ability to hear. **2** the range within which sounds may be heard (*within hearing*). **3** an opportunity to state one's case (*got a fair hearing*). **4** the trial of a case in a lawcourt. ☐ **hearing aid** a small device worn by a partially deaf person to amplify sound.

hearken / hah-kuhn / *v. archaic* listen.

hearsay *n.* rumour or gossip.

hearse / hers / *n.* a vehicle for carrying the coffin at a funeral.

heart *n.* **1** the hollow muscular organ that keeps blood circulating in the body by contracting rhythmically. **2** the part of the body where this is, the breast. **3** the centre of a person's emotions or affections or inmost thoughts (*knew it in her heart*). **4** the ability to feel emotion (*a tender heart*). **5** courage (*take heart*). **6** enthusiasm (*his heart isn't in it*). **7** a mood or feeling (*a change of heart*). **8** the central or innermost part of a thing (*the heart of the city*). **9** the essence (*the heart of the matter*). **10** the compact tender inner part of a lettuce etc. **11** a symmetrical figure conventionally representing a heart. **12** a red figure shaped like this on playing cards; a playing card of the suit (**hearts**) marked with these. ☐ **at heart 1** in one's inmost feelings. **2** basically. **by heart** memorised thoroughly. **have a change of heart** reverse one's previous decision or attitude. **heart attack** (*or* **failure**) sudden failure of the heart to function normally. **heart-rending** very distressing. **heart-searching** examination by oneself of one's own feelings and motives. **heart-to-heart** *adj.* frank and personal (*a heart-to-heart talk*). *n.* such a talk. (**not**) **have the heart to** (not) be insensitive or hard-hearted enough to (do something).

heartache *n.* mental pain, deep sorrow.

heartbeat *n.* the pulsation of the heart.

heartbreak *n.* overwhelming unhappiness. ☐ **heartbreaking** *adj.* **heartbroken** *adj.*

heartburn *n.* a burning sensation in the lower part of the chest from indigestion.

hearten *v.* make (a person) feel encouraged.

heartfelt *adj.* felt deeply or earnestly.

hearth / hahth / *n.* **1** the floor of a fireplace. **2** the home.

heartily *adv.* **1** in a hearty way. **2** very (*heartily sick of it*).

heartland *n.* the central or most important part of an area etc.

heartless *adj.* not feeling pity or sympathy. ☐ **heartlessly** *adv.* **heartlessness** *n.*

heartsick *adj.* despondent.

heartstrings *n.pl.* one's deepest feelings of love or pity.

heartthrob *n. colloq.* a person for whom one has (esp. immature) romantic feelings.

heartwood *n.* the dense inner part of a tree trunk, yielding the hardest timber.

hearty *adj.* (**heartier**, **heartiest**) **1** showing warmth of feeling, enthusiastic. **2** vigorous, strong (*hale and hearty*). **3** (of meals or appetites) large. ☐ **heartiness** *n.*

heat *n.* **1** a form of energy produced by the movement of molecules. **2** the sensation produced by this, hotness. **3** hot weather. **4** an intense feeling (esp. of anger), tension. **5** the most intense part or period of activity (*the heat of battle*). **6** a preliminary race etc. whose winners take part in further contests or the final. •*v.* make or become hot or warm. ☐ **on heat** (of mammals, esp. females) sexually receptive; ready to mate.

heated *adj.* (of a person or discussion) angry. ☐ **heatedly** *adv.*

heater *n.* a stove or other heating device.

heath *n.* **1** an area of flat uncultivated land with low shrubs. **2** a small shrubby plant of the heather kind. **3** any of several plants occurring in the Australian bush, esp. the epacris, a low shrub bearing tube-shaped white, pink, or scarlet flowers, including *Epacris impressa*, the floral emblem of Victoria.

heathen / hee-*th*uhn / *n.* **1** a person who does not belong to a widely-held religion (esp. a religion which proclaims that there is only one God) as regarded by those who do belong to such a religion; a pagan. **2** a person regarded as lacking culture or moral principles. •*adj.* **1** of heathens. **2** having no 'proper' religion; unenlightened.

heather *n.* any of various European shrubs growing esp. on moors and heaths, e.g. Scotch heather.

heating *n.* **1** the imparting or generation of heat. **2** the equipment used to heat a building etc.

heatproof *adj.* able to resist great heat. •*v.* make heatproof.

heatstroke *n.* a feverish condition caused by excessive exposure to heat.

heatwave *n.* a period of very hot weather.

heave *v.* (**heaved** (in sense 6 **hove**), **heaving**) **1** lift or haul (something heavy) with great effort. **2**

heaven 380 **heel**

utter with effort (*heaved a sigh*). **3** *colloq.* throw (*heave a brick at him*). **4** rise and fall regularly like waves at sea. **5** pant; retch. **6** (in nautical use) come (*hove in sight*). • *n.* the act of heaving.

heaven *n.* **1** the place regarded in some religions as the abode of God and the angels, and of the blessed after death, often characterised as above the sky. **2** (**Heaven**) God, Providence. **3** a place or state of supreme bliss. **4** *colloq.* something delightful (*this reclining chair is simply heaven*). **5** (**the heavens**) the sky as seen from the earth, in which the sun, moon, and stars appear. ☐ **to high heaven** to an extreme extent (*those prawns are off—they stink to high heaven*).

heavenly *adj.* **1** of heaven, divine. **2** of the heavens or sky. **3** *colloq.* very pleasing. ☐ **heavenly bodies** the sun and stars etc.

heavy *adj.* (**heavier, heaviest**) **1** having great weight, difficult to lift, carry, or move. **2** of more than average amount or force (*heavy artillery; heavy rain*). **3** (of work) needing much physical effort. **4** severe, intense (*a heavy sleeper*). **5** grave, serious (*a heavy responsibility*). **6** doing a thing to excess (*a heavy drinker*). **7** dense (*a heavy mist*). **8** (of ground) clinging, difficult to travel over. **9** (of food) stodgy and difficult to digest. **10** (of a book etc.) hard to read or understand. **11** dull and tedious; serious in tone. **12** clumsy or ungraceful in appearance, effect, or movement. **13** oppressive (*heavy demands*). **14** weighted down with care or grief (*my heart is heavy*). **15** pronounced, marked (*a heavy accent*). • *n.* **1** *colloq.* a large violent person; a hired thug. **2** a villainous role in a film or play; an actor who plays such a role. **3** a strong-arm man such as a bodyguard or a bouncer. **4** *colloq.* a person at the top of a profession etc.; a bigwig (*all the military heavies were there*). • *v. Aust.* put pressure on or harass (*heavied him into doing things their way*). ☐ **heavy-duty** *adj.* intended to withstand hard use. **heavy going** progress made only with difficulty. **heavy-handed 1** clumsy. **2** overbearing, oppressive. **heavy hydrogen** = DEUTERIUM. **heavy industry** industry producing metal, machines, etc. **heavy metal 1** metal of a high density. **2** a type of loud rock music with a heavy beat. **heavy on** using a lot of (*heavy on petrol*). **heavy water** deuterium oxide, a substance with the same chemical properties as water but greater density. **make heavy weather of** exaggerate (a difficulty or problem). ☐☐ **heavily** *adv.* **heaviness** *n.*

heavyweight *n.* **1** a person of more than average weight. **2** a weight in certain sports, in amateur boxing over 81 kg. **3** *colloq.* a person of great influence.

hebdomadal / heb-**dom**-uh-duhl / *adj. formal* weekly.

Hebe / **hee**-bee / *Gk myth.* the gods' cupbearer, daughter of Zeus and Hera.

hebe / **hee**-bee / *n.* a small shrub with blue, violet, or white flowers in spikes.

Hebraic / hee-**bray**-ik / *adj.* of Hebrew or the Hebrews.

Hebraist / **hee**-bray-ist / *n.* an expert in Hebrew.

Hebrew *n.* **1** a member of a Semitic people in ancient Palestine; an Israelite. **2** their language; a modern form of this used in Israel. • *adj.* **1** of the Hebrews or the Jews. **2** of or in Hebrew.

Hecate / **hek**-uh-tee / *Gk myth.* a goddess associated with uncanny things, the ghost world, and witchcraft.

heck *interj. colloq.* a mild exclamation of surprise or dismay.

heckle *v.* interrupt and harass (a public speaker) with aggressive questions and abuse. ☐ **heckler** *n.*

HECS *abbr. Aust.* Higher Education Contribution Scheme.

hectare / **hek**-tair / *n.* a unit of area, 10,000 sq. metres (2.471 acres).

hectic *adj.* involving feverish activity (*a hectic day*). ☐ **hectically** *adv.*

hectogram *n.* one hundred grams.

Hector *Gk myth.* a Trojan prince, killed by Achilles at the siege of Troy.

hector *v.* intimidate by bullying.

Hecuba / **hek**-yoo-buh / *Gk myth.* wife of Priam, king of Troy.

he'd = **1** he had. **2** he would.

hedge *n.* **1** a fence of closely planted bushes or shrubs. **2** a means of protecting oneself against possible loss (*bought diamonds as a hedge against inflation*). • *v.* **1** surround or bound with a hedge. **2** reduce the possible loss on (a bet etc.) by another speculation. **3** avoid giving a direct answer or commitment. ☐ **hedge-hop** *v.* fly at a very low altitude. ☐☐ **hedger** *n.*

hedgehog *n.* a small insect-eating animal with a piglike snout and a back covered in stiff spines, able to roll itself up into a ball when attacked.

hedgerow *n.* a row of bushes etc. forming a hedge.

hedonist / **hee**-duh-nist, **hed**-uh-nist / *n.* one who believes that pleasure is the chief good in life. ☐ **hedonism** *n.* **hedonistic** *adj.*

heebie-jeebies *n.pl.* (preceded by *the*) *colloq.* **1** nervous anxiety; fear, revulsion. **2** delirium tremens.

heed *v.* pay attention to. • *n.* careful attention (*take heed*). ☐ **heedful** *adj.* **heedless** *adj.* **heedlessly** *adv.*

hee-haw *n.* a donkey's bray; a rude donkey-like laugh. • *v.* bray like a donkey; bray with laughter.

heel[1] *n.* **1** the rounded back part of the human foot. **2** the corresponding part in vertebrate animals. **3** the part of a sock etc. covering the heel. **4** a built-up part of a boot or shoe that supports a person's heel. **5** something like a heel in shape or position (*the heel of the hand*). **6** *colloq.* a person regarded with contempt. **7** a small fragment of the parent branch left at the end of a shoot taken as a cutting. • *v.* **1** repair the heels of (shoes etc.). **2** (foll. by *out*) (in Rugby football) pass the ball with the heel. **3** (usu. foll. by *in*) = HELE. **4** (**heel!**) the command to a dog to walk close to its owner's heel. ☐ **at** (*or* **to**) **heel** (of a dog) close behind; under control. **down at heel 1** (of a shoe) with the heel worn down. **2** (of a person) shabby in dress etc.; impoverished. **heel cutting 1** a type of cutting (for plant propagation) in which a shoot is so removed that a fragment (the heel) of the parent branch is left at the base of the shoot. **2** a shoot or cutting removed in this way. **well-heeled** rich.

heel[2] *v.* tilt (a ship) or become tilted to one side (*heeled over*). • *n.* the act or amount of this.

heel[3] = HELE.

hefty *adj.* (**heftier, heftiest**) **1** (of a person) big and strong. **2** (of a thing) large, heavy; powerful. ☐ **heftily** *adv.* **heftiness** *n.*

Hegel / **hay**-guhl /, Georg Wilhelm Friedrich (1770–1831), German idealist philosopher. ☐ **Hegelian** / huh-**gay**-lee-uhn / *adj.*

hegemony / **hej**-uh-muh-nee, **heg**-, huh-**gem**-uh-nee / *n.* leadership, domination, esp. by one State of a confederacy over the others.

Hegira / **hej**-uh-ruh / *n.* (also **Hejira**) the flight of Mohammed from Mecca (AD 622), from which the Muslim era is reckoned.

Heidelberg School the name of a group of Australian impressionists in the late 1880s (including Arthur Streeton, Charles Conder, Louis Abrahams, Tom Roberts, and Frederick McCubbin) that was the first to paint the Australian bush in terms other than those based on European ideas of the picturesque.

heifer / **hef**-uh / *n.* a cow under three years of age that has not produced a calf.

height *n.* **1** measurement from base to top or head to foot. **2** the distance (of an object or position) above ground level or sea level. **3** a high place or area (*afraid of heights*). **4** the highest degree of something (*the height of fashion*). **5** the most intense part or period (*the height of the tourist season*).

heighten *v.* make or become higher or more intense.

heinous / **hay**-nuhs, **hee**- / *adj.* very wicked.

heir / air / *n.* a person who inherits property or rank etc. from its former owner. ☐ **heir apparent** the legal heir whose claim cannot be set aside by the birth of another heir. **heir presumptive** one whose claim may be set aside in this way.

heiress / **air**-res / *n.* a female heir.

heirloom / **air**-loom / *n.* a possession that has been handed down in a family for several generations.

heist / huyst / (also **hoist**) *colloq. v.* steal; shoplift. • *n.* a robbery.

Hejira alternative spelling of HEGIRA.

held *see* HOLD[1].

hele / heel / *v.* (**heled, heling**) (also commonly **heel**) (usu. foll. by *in*) preserve a plant or cutting by burying its rooting end in loose soil until one is ready to plant it in its permanent position.

■ **Usage** The spelling 'heel' for this verb is etymologically incorrect, although its use is widespread.

Helen *Gk myth.* the wife of Menelaus king of Sparta, whose abduction by Paris led to the Trojan War.

Helena, St (AD *c.*255–*c.*330), Roman empress and mother of Constantine the Great. She was a convert to Christianity and later tradition ascribes to her the finding of the cross on which Christ was crucified

helical / **hel**-i-kuhl / *adj.* like a helix.

helichrysum / hel-ee-**kruy**-suhm / *n.* any of many related Australian plants with usu. large white, gold, or pink papery flowers and silvery foliage.

helicopter / **hel**-ee-kop-tuh, **hel**-uh- / *n.* a wingless aircraft obtaining lift and propulsion from horizontal revolving overhead blades.

heliocentric / hee-lee-oh-**sen**-trik / *adj.* **1** considered as viewed from the sun's centre. **2** regarding the sun as the centre.

heliograph / **hee**-lee-uh-grahf, -graf / *n.* **1** a signalling device reflecting the sun's rays in flashes. **2** a message sent by this.

Helios / **hee**-lee-os / *Gk myth.* the sun personified as a god, father of Phaethon. He is generally represented as a charioteer driving daily from east to west across the sky.

heliotrope / **hee**-lee-uh-trohp, **hel**-ee- / *n.* a European plant with small sweet-smelling purple flowers.

heliport / **hel**-ee-pawt / *n.* (also **helipad**) a place where helicopters take off and land.

helipterum / he-**lip**-tuh-ruhm / *n.* any of several Australian everlastings or 'paper flowers' with white, yellow, pink, or red blooms.

helium / **hee**-lee-uhm / *n.* a chemical element (symbol He), a light colourless gas that does not burn, used in airships and as a coolant.

helix / **hee**-liks / *n.* (*pl.* **helices** / **hee**-luh-seez /) a spiral, esp. a three-dimensional one, either like a corkscrew or flat like a watch spring.

hell *n.* **1** a place (of fire and other torments) regarded in some religions as the abode of the dead, or of devils and condemned sinners. **2** a place or state of supreme misery; something extremely unpleasant (*it's hell gardening in winter*). **3** *colloq.* used to express anger or intensify a meaning or indicate something extreme (*what the hell does he want?; ran like hell*). • *interj.* an exclamation of anger or surprise. ☐ **a** (*or* **one**) **hell of a** *colloq.* an outstanding example of (*a hell of a mess; one hell of a party*). **for the hell of it** just for fun. **hell-bent** recklessly determined. **hell for leather** at full speed. **hell's angel** a member of a gang of motorcycle enthusiasts notorious for disorderly or violent behaviour. **hell to pay** *colloq.* serious consequences to face.

he'll = he will.

Hellas / **hel**-as / *n.* the ancient and modern Greek name for Greece.

Hellene / **hel**-een / *n.* a Greek. ☐ **Hellenic** / huh-**len**-ik / *adj.*

Hellenistic *adj.* of the Greek language and culture of the 4th–1st centuries BC.

Heller, Joseph (1923–99), American novelist, whose most famous novel was *Catch-22* (1961).

Hellespont / **hel**-uhs-pont / *n.* the ancient name for a narrow strait between Europe and Asiatic Turkey; now called the Dardanelles.

hellish *adj. colloq.* very difficult or unpleasant. ☐ **hellishly** *adv.*

hello *interj.* & *n.* (also **hallo, hullo**) (*pl.* **hellos**) an expression used in greeting or to call attention or express surprise.

helm *n.* the tiller or wheel by which a ship's rudder is controlled. ☐ **at the helm** at the head of an organisation etc., in control.

helmet *n.* a protective head covering worn by soldiers, cyclists, motorcyclists, construction workers, etc.

helmeted honeyeater *n.* an extremely rare nectar-eating bird occurring only in a small area east of Melbourne, and a faunal emblem of Vic.: it has olive-black colouring on its upper surface, and the yellow feathers on its head form what looks like a helmet.

helmsman *n.* a person who steers a ship.

helot / **hel**-uht / *n.* a serf in ancient Sparta.

help *v.* **1** make it easier for (a person) to do something or for (a thing) to happen. **2** do something for the benefit of (someone in need). **3** prevent, refrain from, remedy (*it can't be helped; I couldn't help myself*). **4** (often foll. by *to*) serve (a person with food) (*may I help you to more greens?*). • *n.* **1** the action of helping or being helped. **2** a person or thing that helps. **3** a person employed to help with housework. **4** remedy or escape (*there is no help for it*). ☐ **help oneself to 1** serve oneself with (food) at a meal. **2** take without seeking assistance or permission. **help out** give help (esp. in a crisis). ☐☐ **helper** *n.*

helpful *adj.* giving help, useful. ☐ **helpfully** *adv.* **helpfulness** *n.*

helping *n.* a portion of food given to one person at a meal. • *adj.* providing support, aid, etc. (*a helping hand*).

helpless *adj.* **1** unable to manage without help, dependent on others. **2** incapable of action; indicating this (*helpless with laughter; gave him a helpless glance*). ☐ **helplessly** *adv.* **helplessness** *n.*

Helpmann, Sir Robert (Murray) (1909–86), Australian ballet dancer, choreographer, director, and stage and film actor.

helpmate *n.* a helper, a companion or partner who helps.

Helsinki / hel-**sing**-kee / the capital of Finland.

helter-skelter *adv.* in disorderly haste.

hem[1] *n.* the border of cloth where the edge is turned under and sewn or fixed down. • *v.* (**hemmed, hemming**) turn and sew a hem on. ☐ **hem in** surround and restrict the movement of (*enemy forces hemmed them in*).

hem[2] *interj.* = AHEM.

hemal etc. alternative spelling of HAEMAL etc.

hemi- *comb. form* half.

Hemingway, Ernest (Miller) (1899–1961), American novelist and writer.

hemiplegia *n.* paralysis of one side of the body.

hemipterous / huh-**mip**-tuh-ruhs / *adj.* of those insects (such as aphids, bugs, and cicadas) with piercing or sucking mouthparts.

hemisphere *n.* **1** half a sphere. **2** either of the halves into which the earth is divided either by the equator (the *Northern* and *Southern hemisphere*) or by a line passing through the poles (the *Eastern* and *Western hemisphere*).

hemispherical / hem-uhs-**fe**-ruh-kuhl / *adj.* shaped like a hemisphere.

hemline *n.* the lower edge of a skirt or dress.

hemlock *n.* a poisonous plant with small white flowers.

hemp *n.* **1** a plant from which coarse fibres are obtained for the manufacture of rope and cloth. **2** any of several narcotic drugs made from this plant (e.g. hashish, marijuana). ☐ **hempen** *adj.*

hen *n.* a female bird, esp. of a domestic fowl. ☐ **hens' party** *n. colloq.* (also **hen party**) a social gathering of women only.

hen-and-chickens fern *n.* an eastern Australian fern very popular for cultivation: the parent plant (the hen) grows an abundance of plantlets (the chickens) at the ends of its leaves, and these can be removed and grown separately.

hence *adv.* **1** from this time (*five years hence*). **2** for this reason. **3** *archaic* from here.

henceforth *adv.* (also **henceforward**) from this time on, in future.

henchman *n.* (*pl.* **henchmen**) a faithful supporter.

Henderson, Moya Patricia (1941–), AM, Australian composer.

Hendrix, Jimi (original name: James Marshall Hendrix) (1942–70), American rock guitarist and singer.

Henley-on-Todd a mock rowing regatta held each year on the dry bed of the Todd River in Alice Springs. (¶ A send-up of the royal regatta held each year at Henley-on-Thames in England.)

henna *n.* a reddish-brown dye used esp. on the hair, obtained from a tropical shrub. ☐ **hennaed** / **hen**-uhd / *adj.*

henpeck *v.* (of a wife) constantly nag at and dominate her husband. ☐ **henpecked** *adj.*

Henry VIII (1491–1547), king of England who had six wives, two of whom he had executed. Reigned 1509–47.

henry *n.* (*pl.* **henries**) a unit of electric inductance. (¶ Named after the American physicist J. Henry (1797–1878).)

hep = HIP⁴.

hepatic / huh-**pat**-ik / *adj.* of the liver.

hepatitis / hep-uh-**tuy**-tuhs / *n.* a serious disease, marked by inflammation of the liver, caused by viruses etc. ☐ **hepatitis A** caused by the hepatitis A virus transmitted by contaminated food or drink. **hepatitis B** caused by the hepatitis B virus transmitted by infected blood or other body fluids, e.g. in intravenous drug use or through sexual contact. **hepatitis C** caused by the hepatitis C virus and transmitted in the same way as hepatitis B.

Hephaestus / huh-**fuys**-tuhs, -**fees**- / *Gk myth.* the god of fire, called Vulcan by the Romans.

hepta- *comb. form* seven.

heptagon / **hep**-tuh-guhn / *n.* a geometric figure with seven sides. ☐ **heptagonal** / hep-**tag**-uh-nuhl / *adj.*

heptathlon *n.* an athletic contest in which each competitor takes part in the seven events it includes. ☐ **heptathlete** *n.*

her *pron.* **1** the objective case of SHE (*we saw her*). **2** *colloq.* = SHE (*it's her all right*). •*adj.* of or belonging to her.

Hera / **heer**-ruh / *Gk myth.* a goddess, sister and wife of Zeus and queen of the Olympian gods, identified by the Romans with Juno.

Heracles / **he**-ruh-kleez / the Greek form of the name Hercules.

herald *n.* **1** an official in former times who made announcements and carried messages from a ruler. **2** a person or thing indicating the approach of something (*heralds of spring*). **3** an official who records people's pedigrees and grants coats of arms. •*v.* proclaim the approach of, usher in.

heraldic / huh-**ral**-dik / *adj.* of heralds or heraldry.

heraldry *n.* the study of coats of arms and the right to bear them.

herb¹ *n.* **1** a soft-stemmed plant that dies down to the ground after flowering. **2** a plant with leaves or seeds etc. that are used as food or in medicine or for flavouring. ☐ **herby** *adj.*

herb² *Aust. colloq. v.* **1** drive (or travel in) a car fast (*herbing along the Hume Highway*). **2** (foll. by *over*) hand (something) over (usu. at great speed or urgently) (*herb me over a towel or something, the pan's on fire*). •*n.* (**herbs**) the horsepower of a car engine (*my new car has heaps of herbs*).

herbaceous / her-**bay**-shuhs / *adj.* of or like herbs (the plants). ☐ **herbaceous border** a garden border containing perennial flowering plants.

herbage *n.* grass and other field plants.

herbal *adj.* of herbs used in medicine or for flavouring. •*n.* a book with descriptions of these.

herbalist *n.* a dealer in medicinal herbs.

herbarium / her-**bair**-ree-uhm / *n.* (*pl.* **herbaria**) **1** a systematic collection of dried plants. **2** a book, case, or room for these.

Herbert¹ a river about 240 km long in north Qld, flowing into the Coral Sea.

Herbert², (Alfred Francis) Xavier (1901–84), Australian novelist, noted esp. for the novels *Capricornia* and *Poor Fellow My Country*.

herbicide *n.* a substance that is poisonous to plants, used to destroy unwanted vegetation.

herbivore / **her**-buh-vaw / *n.* an animal that feeds on plants.

herbivorous / her-**biv**-uh-ruhs / *adj.* feeding on plants.

herculean / her-kyuh-**lee**-uhn / *adj.* having or needing great strength or effort (*a herculean task*).

Hercules / **her**-kyuh-leez / *Gk myth.* a hero, noted for his great strength and courage, who performed twelve immense tasks ('labours') imposed upon him.

herd *n.* **1** a number of cattle or other animals feeding, travelling, or staying together. **2** (**the herd**) *derog.* a large mob of people; the rabble. •*v.* **1** gather, stay, or drive as a group. **2** tend (a herd of animals). ☐ **herd instinct** the instinct to think and behave like the majority of people.

herdsman *n.* a person who tends a herd of animals.

here *adv.* **1** in, at, or to this place. **2** at this point in a process or a series of events. •*interj.* an exclamation calling attention to something or making a protest, or used as a reply (= I am here) in answer to a roll-call. •*n.* this place (*lives near here*). ☐ **here's to** I drink to the health of. **neither here nor there** of no importance.

hereabouts *adv.* (also **hereabout**) somewhere near here.

hereafter *adv.* in future, from now on. •*n.* (**the hereafter**) the future; life after death.

hereby *adv.* by this means, as a result of this.

hereditary / huh-**red**-uh-tuh-ree, -tree / *adj.* **1** inherited, able to be passed or received from one generation to another (*hereditary characteristics*). **2** holding a position by inheritance (*hereditary owner*).

heredity / huh-**red**-uh-tee / *n.* inheritance of physical or mental characteristics from parents or ancestors.

Hereford *n.* an animal of a breed of red and white beef cattle.

herein *adv. formal* in this place, document, etc.

hereinafter *adv. formal* from this point on; in a later part of this document etc.

hereof *adv. formal* of this.

heresy / **he**-ruh-see / *n.* **1** an opinion that is contrary to the accepted beliefs of a religion, esp. of the Catholic Church. **2** opinion contrary to what is normally accepted.

heretic / **he**-ruh-tik / *n.* a person believing in or practising heresy. ◻ **heretical** / huh-**ret**-i-kuhl / *adj.*
hereto *adv. formal* to this.
heretofore *adv. formal* formerly.
hereupon *adv. formal* after or in consequence of this.
herewith *adv. formal* with this (*enclosed herewith*).
heritable *adj.* able to be inherited or to inherit.
heritage *n.* **1** that which has been or may be inherited. **2** inherited circumstances or benefits. **3** a nation's historic buildings, monuments, countryside, etc., esp. when regarded as worthy of preservation.
hermaphrodite / her-**maf**-ruh-duyt / *n.* an animal or plant that has both male and female sexual organs in one individual. ◻ **hermaphroditic** / her-maf-ruh-**dit**-ik / *adj.*
hermeneutics / her-muh-**nyoo**-tiks / *n.pl.* (also treated as *sing.*) the branch of knowledge that deals with (theories of) interpretation, esp. of Scripture or literary texts.
Hermes / **her**-meez / *Gk myth.* the messenger of the gods, identified by the Romans with Mercury.
hermetic *adj.* **1** with an airtight closure (*hermetic seal*). **2** relating to alchemy, magic, etc. (*the hermetic arts*). ◻ **hermetically** *adv.*
hermit *n.* a person who has withdrawn from human society and lives in solitude (esp. for religious reasons). ◻ **hermit crab** *n.* a crab that lives in a cast-off shell to protect its soft hinder parts.
hermitage *n.* a hermit's dwelling.
hernia *n.* a protrusion of a part or organ of the body through a wall of the cavity (esp. the abdomen) that normally contains it; a rupture.
hero *n.* (*pl.* **heroes**) **1** a person admired for nobility, courage, outstanding achievements, etc. **2** the chief male character in a story, play, or poem. ◻ **hero worship** *n.* excessive devotion to an admired person. **hero-worship** *v.* idolise.
Herod the name of four rulers in ancient Palestine, including Herod the Great, in whose reign Christ was born.
heroic *adj.* having the characteristics of a hero, very brave. • *n.pl.* (**heroics**) over dramatic talk or behaviour. ◻ **heroically** *adv.*
heroin *n.* a highly addictive analgesic drug prepared from morphine.
heroine *n.* a female hero.
heroism *n.* heroic conduct or qualities.
heron *n.* a long-legged long-necked wading bird.
herpes / **her**-peez / *n.* a virus disease causing blisters on the skin. ◻ **herpes simplex 1** a cold sore. **2** a form of herpes occurring on the genitals. **herpes zoster** shingles.
herpetology / her-puh-**tol**-uh-jee / *n.* the study of reptiles. ◻ **herpetologist** *n.*
Herr / hair / *n.* (*pl.* **Herren**) the title of a German man; Mr.

herring *n.* (*pl.* **herring** or **herrings**) **1** a North Atlantic fish. **2** a similar Australian fish used for food. ◻ **herring-bone** *n.* a zigzag pattern or arrangement.
hers *possessive pron.* the one or ones of or belonging to her (*it is hers; hers are best*). ◻ **of hers** belonging to her.
herself *pron.* **1** the emphatic and reflexive form of *she* and *her* (*she herself went; she hurt herself*). **2** in her normal state (*not herself today*). ◻ **by herself** *see* ONESELF.
herstory / **her**-stuh-ree / *n.* (*pl.* **-ies**) history viewed from a female or specifically feminist perspective.
hertz *n.* (*pl.* **hertz**) a unit of frequency of electromagnetic waves, = one cycle per second. (¶ Named after H.R. Hertz, German physicist (1857–94).)
he's = **1** he is. **2** he has.
Hesiod / **hee**-see-uhd / (*c.*700 BC) one of the oldest known Greek poets.
hesitant *adj.* hesitating. ◻ **hesitantly** *adv.* **hesitancy** *n.*
hesitate *v.* **1** show or feel indecision or uncertainty, pause in doubt. **2** be reluctant, scruple (*wouldn't hesitate to break the rules if it suited him*). ◻ **hesitation** *n.*
hessian *n.* strong coarse cloth made of hemp or jute; sackcloth.
hetero / **het**-uh-roh / *adj.* & *n. colloq.* heterosexual; a heterosexual person.
heterodox / **het**-uh-ruh-doks / *adj.* not orthodox. ◻ **heterodoxy** *n.*
heterodyne / **het**-uh-roh-duyn / *adj.* of or involved in the production of a lower radio frequency from a combination of two high frequencies.
heterogeneous / het-uh-roh-**jee**-nee-uhs / *adj.* made up of people or things that are unlike each other. ◻ **heterogeneity** / het-uh-roh-juh-**nee**-uh-tee / *n.*

■ **Usage** The less common form *heterogenous* is considered incorrect by some people and is best avoided.

heteromorphic / het-uh-roh-**maw**-fik / *adj.* (also **heteromorphous**) *Biology* **1** of dissimilar forms. **2** (of insects) existing in different forms at different stages in their life cycle. ◻ **heteromorphism** *n.*
heterosexual *adj.* feeling or involving sexual attraction to persons of the opposite sex. • *n.* a heterosexual person. ◻ **heterosexuality** *n.*
het up *adj. colloq.* excited, overwrought.
heuristic / hyoo-**ris**-tik, hyor- / *adj.* **1** serving or helping to find out or discover something. **2** proceeding by trial and error.
hew *v.* (**hewed**, **hewn** or **hewed**, **hewing**) **1** chop or cut with an axe or sword etc. **2** cut into shape.

Hewett, Dorothy (1923–), AO, Australian poet and playwright.

hex *n.* a magic spell, a curse. • *v.* **1** bewitch. **2** practise witchcraft.

hexa- *comb. form* six.

hexadecimal / hek-suh-**des**-uh-muhl / *adj. Computing* of a number system that has 16 (the figures 0 to 9 and the letters A to F) rather than 10 as a base.

hexagon / **hek**-suh-guhn / *n.* a geometric figure with six sides. ☐ **hexagonal** / hek-**sag**-uh-nuhl / *adj.*

hexagram *n.* a six-pointed star formed by two intersecting equilateral triangles.

hexameter / hek-**sam**-uh-tuh / *n.* a line of verse with six metrical feet.

Hexham grey *n.* a large grey mosquito, the largest biting mosquito in Australia.

hey *interj.* an exclamation calling attention to or expressing surprise or enquiry.

heyday *n.* the time of greatest success or prosperity (*it was in its heyday*).

Heysen, Sir Hans (1877–1968), Australian artist whose watercolour landscapes are distinguished by a sensitivity to the effects of light, esp. on gum trees.

Hezbollah / hez-buh-**lah** / *n.* (also **Hizbollah**) an extreme Shi'ite Muslim group, active esp. in Lebanon. (¶ From Arabic, = party of God.)

HF *abbr.* high frequency.

Hf *symbol* hafnium.

Hg *symbol* mercury.

hg *abbr.* hectogram(s).

HH *abbr.* (of a pencil lead) double hard.

hi *interj.* an exclamation calling attention or expressing greeting.

hiatus / huy-**ay**-tuhs / *n.* (*pl.* **hiatuses**) a break or gap in a sequence or series.

hibachi / hi-**bah**-chee / *n.* a Japanese cooking pot in which charcoal is burned and food cooked on a grill on top of the pot.

Hibberd, Jack (full name: John Charles Hibberd) (1940–), Australian playwright and director, best known for his play *Dimboola*.

hibbertia / hi-**ber**-shuh / *n.* any of several temperate Australian shrubs with gold or orange flowers (*see* GUINEA FLOWER).

hibernate / **huy**-buh-nayt / *v.* (of certain animals) spend the winter in a state like deep sleep. ☐ **hibernation** *n.*

Hibernian / huy-**ber**-nee-uhn / *adj. poetic* of Ireland. • *n.* an Irish person.

hibiscus / huy-**bis**-kuhs / *n.* (*pl.* **hibiscuses**) a cultivated shrub with large brightly coloured flowers, some native to Australia.

hiccup (also **hiccough**) *n.* **1** a sudden spasm of the diaphragm causing a characteristic sound 'hic'. **2** (**hiccups**) an attack of hiccuping. **3** a brief hitch. • *v.* (**hiccuped**, **hiccuping**) make a hiccup.

hick *n. colloq.* a country bumpkin, a provincial.

hickey / **hik**-ee / *n. colloq.* a skin blemish, esp. a mark caused by a love bite.

hickory *n.* **1** a North American tree related to the walnut. **2** its hard wood.

hid *see* HIDE[2].

hide[1] *n.* **1** an animal's skin, esp. when tanned or dressed. **2** *colloq.* the human skin, esp. of the backside (*I'll tan your hide!*). **3** *Aust. colloq.* impertinence, effrontery (*he's got a hide coming here after what he's done*).

hide[2] *v.* (**hid**, **hidden**, **hiding**) **1** put or keep out of sight, prevent from being seen. **2** keep secret. **3** conceal oneself. • *n.* a place of concealment used when observing wildlife. ☐ **hidden agenda** a secret motivation behind a policy, statement, etc.; an ulterior motive. **hide-out** *n. colloq.* a hiding place.

hideaway *n.* a hiding place or a place of retreat.

hidebound *adj.* narrow-minded, refusing to abandon old customs and prejudices.

hideous *adj.* **1** very ugly; revolting. **2** *colloq.* unpleasant. ☐ **hideously** *adv.*

hiding[1] *n. colloq.* a thrashing; a sound defeat.

hiding[2] *n.* the state of being or remaining hidden (*went into hiding*).

hierarchy / **huyuh**-rah-kee / *n.* a system with grades of status or authority ranking one above another in a series. ☐ **hierarchical** / huyuh-**rah**-ki-kuhl / *adj.*

hieratic / huyuh-**rat**-ik / *adj.* of priests. • *n.* a form of hieroglyphs used in ancient Egypt, originally for religious texts.

hieroglyph / **huyuh**-ruh-glif / *n.* **1** one of the pictures or symbols used in ancient Egypt and elsewhere to represent sounds, words, or ideas. **2** a written symbol with a secret or cryptic meaning.

hieroglyphic / huyuh-ruh-**glif**-ik / *adj.* of or written in hieroglyphs. • *n.pl.* (**hieroglyphics**) hieroglyphs.

hi-fi *colloq. adj.* high fidelity. • *n.* a set of hi-fi equipment.

higgledy-piggledy *adj.* & *adv.* mixed up, in disorder.

high *adj.* **1** extending far upwards, extending above the normal or average level. **2** situated far above the ground or above sea level. **3** measuring a specified distance from base to top (*one inch high; waist high*). **4** ranking above others in importance or quality (*high officials; high society*). **5** lavish; superior (*high living; high fashion*). **6** extreme, intense, greater than what is normal or average (*high temperatures; high prices; formed a high opinion of her*). **7** extreme or very traditional in religious opinion (*high Anglican*). **8** (of a time or period) fully reached, at its peak (*high noon; it's high time we left; High Renaissance*). **9** noble, virtuous (*high ideals*). **10** (of a sound or voice) of high frequency; shrill. **11** (of meat) beginning to go bad; *Brit.* (of game) hung until slightly decomposed and ready to cook. **12** *colloq.* intoxicated; under the influence of drugs. • *n.* **1** a high level or figure (*exports reached a new high*). **2** an area of high barometric pressure. **3** *colloq.* a state of great excitement or happiness, esp. drug-induced (*I'm on a high*). **4** the top gear of a motor vehicle (*shift into high*). **5** a high school (*Caroline Chisholm High*). •*adv.* **1** in, at, or to a high level or position. **2** in or to a high degree. **3** at a high price. **4** (of a sound) at or to a high pitch. □ **high altar** the chief altar of a church. **high and dry** aground; stranded, isolated. **high and low** everywhere (*searched high and low*). **high-blocked** (of a house) built on very high foundations, as in northern Australia. **high-class** of high quality or social class. **high colour** a flushed complexion. **high country** *Aust.* hilly country in a mountainous region, esp. as used for sheep and cattle raising. **high explosive** explosive with a violently shattering effect. **high-fibre** of or pertaining to foods that contain a high proportion of plant fibre for roughage. **high fidelity** reproduction of sound with little or no distortion. **high-five** *n.* a gesture of celebration or greeting in which two people slap each other's palms with their arms extended over their heads. *v.* greet with a high-five. **high-flown** (of language etc.) extravagant, pretentious. **high-flyer** (also **high-flier**) **1** an ambitious person. **2** a person or thing with capacity for great achievements. **high frequency** (in radio) 3 to 30 megahertz. **high gear** a gear such that the driven end of a transmission revolves faster than the driving end. **high-grade 1** of high quality. **2** (of ore) yielding a relatively high amount of metal. **high ground** (usu. preceded by an explanatory adjective such as *moral, intellectual*, etc.) a position of superiority or advantage in a debate, election campaign, etc. **high-handed** disregarding others' feelings. **high jinks** boisterous fun. **high jump 1** an athletic competition of jumping over a high horizontal bar. **2** *colloq.* drastic punishment (*you're for the high jump*). **high-level 1** (of negotiations) conducted by people of high rank. **2** (of a computer language) not machine-dependent and usu. close to natural language. **high-minded** having high moral principles. **high-octane** *adj.* (of fuel used in internal-combustion engines) not detonating readily during the power stroke. **high-pitched** (of a voice or sound) high. **high-powered 1** using great power or energy. **2** important or influential. **high pressure 1** a high degree of activity or exertion. **2** an atmospheric condition with the pressure above average. **high priest** a chief priest. **high-profile** *adj.* (of a public figure) having much exposure to public attention, publicity, etc. **high-rise** (of a building) with many storeys. **high road** a main road. **high school** a secondary school. **high sea** (or **seas**) the open seas not under any country's jurisdiction. **high season** the busiest period at a resort etc. **high-spirited** lively, cheerful. **high street** the principal shopping street of a town. **high table** a table at a public dinner or in a college etc. for the most important guests or members. **high-tech** using or involving advanced technological development, esp. in electronics. **high tension** = HIGH VOLTAGE. **high tide** the tide at its highest level. **high time** time that is overdue (*it is high time they arrived*). **high treason** treason against one's country. **high voltage** electrical potential large enough to injure or damage. **high water** high tide. **high-water mark 1** the level reached at high water. **2** a maximum recorded value or the highest point of excellence. **high wire** a high tightrope.

highbrow *adj.* intellectual, highly cultured. •*n.* a highbrow person.

High Church *n.* (also called **Anglo-Catholic Church**) that section of the Anglican Church that gives an important place to ritual, sacraments, and to the authority of bishops and priests.

High Court *n.* (in full **High Court of Australia**) the supreme Federal Court established by the Constitution as the final arbiter of constitutional questions and the final court of appeal from the Supreme Courts of the States and from Federal Courts.

High Mass *n.* (esp. in the Catholic Church) a mass celebrated by a priest, usu. attended by deacon and subdeacon, with ritual chanting, the burning of incense, etc.

higher *adj.* & *adv.* more high. •*adv.* in or to a higher position etc. □ **higher animals** (*or* **plants**) those which are highly developed and of complex structure. **higher education** education above the level given in schools, e.g. at university.

highfalutin *adj.* (also **highfaluting**) pompous, pretentious.

highland *adj.* of or in a mountainous region. • *n.pl.* (**highlands**) mountainous country. □ **highlander** *n.*

highlight *n.* **1** a light or bright area in a painting etc. **2** the brightest or most outstanding feature of something (*the highlight of the tour*). **3** (usu. as **highlights**) a light streak in the hair produced by bleaching. •*v.* **1** draw special attention to. **2** mark with a bright colour or with a highlighter.

highlighter *n.* a marker pen for emphasising a printed word etc. by overlaying it with (usu. fluorescent) colour.

highly *adv.* **1** in a high degree, extremely (*highly amusing; highly commended*). **2** very favourably (*thinks highly of her*). □ **highly-strung** *adj.* (also **high-strung**) (of a person) very sensitive or nervous.

Highness *n.* the title used in speaking of or to a prince or princess (*Her Highness; Your Royal Highness*).

highset esp. *Qld adj.* (of a house) high-blocked. • *n.* such a house.

hightail *v.* (usu. foll. by *it*) depart speedily.

highway *n.* **1** a public road. **2** a main route. **3** a direct course of action (*on the highway to success*).

highwayman *n.* a man (usu. on horseback) who robbed passing travellers in former times.

hijack *v.* **1** seize control of (a vehicle) in order to steal its goods, take its passengers hostage, or force it to a new destination. **2** take control of (talks etc.) by force or subterfuge. • *n.* a hijacking. ☐ **hijacker** *n.*

hike *n.* **1** a long walk, esp. a cross-country walk taken for pleasure. **2** an increase (*a price hike*). • *v.* **1** go for a hike. **2** walk laboriously. **3** (usu. foll. by *up*) raise; increase. ☐ **hiker** *n.*

hilarious *adj.* **1** noisily merry. **2** extremely funny. ☐ **hilariously** *adv.* **hilarity** / huh-**la**-ruh-tee / *n.*

Hill[1], Alfred Francis (1870–1960), Australian composer, conductor, and violinist.

Hill[2], Lance (Leonard) (1902–86), Australian inventor, the first to manufacture the rotary clothes hoist.

hill *n.* **1** a natural elevation of the earth's surface not as high as a mountain. **2** a slope in a road etc. **3** a heap or mound. **4** (**the hill**) *Aust.* an uncovered area of rising ground for spectators at a sports ground. ☐ **over the hill 1** past the prime of life; declining. **2** past a crisis.

Hillary, Sir Edmund (1919–), New Zealand mountaineer, who (with Tenzing Norgay) was the first to reach the summit of Mount Everest (1953).

hillbilly *n.* **1** folk music like that of the southern USA. **2** *US colloq.* a person from a remote mountain area in a southern State.

hillite *n. Aust. colloq.* a sports spectator who views from the hill (*see* HILL, sense 4).

hillock *n.* a small hill, a mound.

hills hoist *Aust. n.* = CLOTHES HOIST. Also called *hoist, rotary hoist.* • *adj.* (**hills-hoist**) characterised socially by the use of such a hoist (*a traditional hills-hoist backyard; hills-hoist suburbia*). (¶ HILL[2])

hillside *n.* the sloping side of a hill.

hilly *adj.* full of hills. ☐ **hilliness** *n.*

hilt *n.* the handle of a sword or dagger etc. ☐ **to the hilt** completely (*his guilt was proved to the hilt*).

him *pron.* **1** the objective case of HE (*we saw him*). **2** *colloq.* = HE (*it's him all right*).

Himalayas / him-uh-**lay**-uhz / *n.pl.* a system of high mountains in Nepal and adjacent countries. ☐ **Himalayan** *adj.*

himbo *n. colloq.* a young man whose main asset is good looks, but who lacks intelligence; the male equivalent of a bimbo.

himself *pron.* **1** the emphatic and reflexive form of *he* and *him* (*he told me himself; he cut himself*). **2** in his normal state (*he is not himself today*). ☐ **by himself** *see* ONESELF.

hind *n.* a female deer. • *adj.* situated at the back (*hind legs*).

hinder[1] / **hin**-duh / *v.* keep (a person or thing) back by delaying progress.

hinder[2] / **huyn**-duh / *adj.* hind (*the hinder part*).

Hindi / **hin**-dee / *n.* **1** one of the official languages of India, a literary form of Hindustani. **2** a group of spoken languages of northern India.

Hindmarsh Island a large island (about 14 km in length and 6 km in width) which lies within the mouth of the Murray River in SA. In the early 1990s it became the focus of national attention when a group of Ngarrindjeri women invoked its spiritual significance in their attempts to block construction of a bridge connecting the island to the mainland.

hindmost *adj.* furthest behind.

hindquarters *n.pl.* the hind legs and parts adjoining these of a four-legged animal.

hindrance *n.* **1** something that hinders. **2** hindering, being hindered (*went forward without hindrance*).

hindsight *n.* wisdom about an event after it has occurred.

Hindu *n.* a person whose religion is Hinduism. • *adj.* of the Hindus.

Hinduism / **hin**-doo-iz-uhm / *n.* a religion and philosophy of India, with a caste system and belief in reincarnation.

Hindustani / hin-doo-**stah**-nee / *n.* the language of much of northern India and (as colloquial Urdu) Pakistan.

hinge *n.* **1** a joint on which a lid, door, etc. turns or swings. **2** a principle on which all depends. • *v.* **1** attach or be attached by a hinge or hinges. **2** (foll. by *on*) depend (*everything hinges on this meeting*).

hinny *n.* the offspring of a female donkey and a male horse.

hint *n.* **1** a slight indication, a suggestion made indirectly. **2** a small piece of practical information (*household hints*). • *v.* make a hint. ☐ **hint at** refer indirectly to.

hinterland *n.* **1** a district lying behind a coast etc. **2** an area served by a port or other centre. **3** a remote or fringe area.

hip[1] *n.* **1** the projection formed by the pelvis and upper part of the thigh-bone on each side of the body. **2** (**hips**) the circumference of the body at the buttocks (*has slim hips*). ☐ **hip bone** the bone forming the hip. **hip flask** a small flask for spirits etc. **hip pocket** *n.* **1** trouser pocket just behind the hip and where one's wallet usu. resides. **2** one's finances, bank balance (*hit in the hip pocket by the latest budget*). **hip-pocket** *adj.* pertaining to one's income (*voters are concerned about hip-pocket issues*). **hip-pocket nerve** an imaginary nerve which twinges sharply whenever demands are made on one's money.

hip[2] *n.* the fruit (red when ripe) of a rose, esp. a wild rose.

hip[3] *interj.* used in cheering (*hip, hip, hooray*).

hip[4] *adj. colloq.* **1** trendy, stylish. **2** (often foll. by *to*) knowledgable about; alert to (*hip to the latest trends in jazz*). ☐ **hip hop** a style of popular music of US black and Hispanic origin, featuring rap with an electronic backing.

hippie n. (also **hippy**) colloq. (esp. in the 1960s) a person rejecting conventional ideas and clothes, typically with long hair, beads, etc., and using hallucinogenic drugs.

hippo n. (pl. **hippos**) colloq. a hippopotamus.

Hippocratic / hip-uh-**krat**-ik / adj. of Hippocrates, a Greek physician of the 5th century BC. □ **Hippocratic oath** an oath (formerly taken by those beginning medical practice) to observe the code of professional behaviour.

hippodrome n. **1** (in names) a music hall or dance hall. **2** (in classical antiquity) a course for chariot races etc.

hippopotamus n. (pl. **hippopotamuses** or **hippopotami**) a large African river animal with a wide muzzle, short legs, and thick dark skin.

hippy alternative spelling of HIPPIE.

hipsters n.pl. trousers or underpants hanging from the hips rather than from the waist.

hire v. **1** purchase the temporary use of (a thing) (hired a van). **2** employ (a person). •n. hiring; payment for this. □ **for hire** (or **on hire**) available to be hired. **hire out** grant the temporary use of (a thing) for payment. **hire purchase** a system by which a person may purchase a thing by paying in instalments while having the use of it. □□ **hirer** n.

hireling n. derog. a person who does anything (only) for money.

Hirohito / hi-roh-**hee**-toh / (1901–1989), emperor of Japan 1926–89.

Hiroshima / hi-**rosh**-uh-muh, hi-roh-**shee**-muh / a Japanese city, target of the first atomic bomb (6 August 1945).

hirsute / **her**-syoot / adj. hairy; shaggy.

his adj. & possessive pron. of or belonging to him; the thing(s) belonging to him.

Hispanic / his-**pan**-ik / adj. of Spain and other Spanish-speaking countries. •n. a Hispanic person.

Hispaniola / his-pan-ee-**oh**-luh / an island in the West Indies, divided into the States of Haiti and the Dominican Republic.

hiss n. a sound like that of s. •v. **1** make this sound. **2** express disapproval in this way.

hissy fit n. colloq. a tantrum.

histamine / **his**-tuh-meen / n. a chemical compound present in body tissues, associated with some allergic reactions.

histogram / **his**-tuh-gram / n. a diagram used in statistics, showing the value of a number of variables by means of columns.

histology / his-**tol**-uh-jee / n. the study of organic tissues. □ **histological** adj.

historian n. an expert in history; a writer of history.

historic adj. famous or important in history or potentially so (this is a historic moment).

historical adj. **1** belonging to or dealing with history or past events (as opposed to legend or prehistory) (historical novels). **2** concerned with history (a historical society). □ **historically** adv.

historicism / his-**to**-ruh-siz-uhm / n. **1** the belief that historical events occur in accordance with certain laws of development. **2** a tendency to stress the importance of historical development and the influence of the past.

historicity / his-tuh-**ris**-uh-tee / n. the historical genuineness of an alleged event, etc.

historiography / his-to-ree-**og**-ruh-fee / n. the writing of history; the study of this. □ **historiographer** n.

history n. **1** a continuous methodical record of important or public events. **2** the study of past events, esp. of human affairs. **3** past events; those connected with a person or thing. **4** an interesting or eventful past (this house has a history). **5** (foll. by of) a past record (has a history of illness). □ **be history** colloq. be broken or damaged beyond repair (my new car was history after the accident; their marriage is history). **make history** do something memorable.

histrionic / his-tree-**on**-ik / adj. dramatic or theatrical in manner. •n.pl. (**histrionics**) insincere and dramatic behaviour intended to impress people.

hit v. (**hit**, **hitting**) **1** strike with a blow or missile; aim a blow etc.; come against (a thing) with force. **2** propel (a ball etc.) with a bat or club; score runs or points in this way. **3** have an effect on (a person); cause to suffer (the loss hit him hard). **4** get at, come to (a thing aimed at), find or reach (what is sought) (can't hit the high notes). **5 a** encounter, come upon (hit a snag; hit the right road at last). **b** arrive at (hit town). **6** colloq. demand or wrest money from (the tax department has hit me for $2000). **7** occur forcefully to (the true meaning only hit him later). •n. **1** a blow, a stroke. **2** a shot etc. that hits its target. **3** a success. **4** colloq. a shot or dose of some drug. □ **hit-and-run** adj. causing harm or damage and making off immediately. **hit back** retaliate. **hit home** make a strong impression on (a person). **hit it off** get on well (with a person). **hit list** colloq. **1** a list of people to be killed or eliminated. **2** a list of things against which action is planned. **hit man** colloq. a hired assassin. **hit on** discover suddenly or by chance. **hit-or-miss** erratic; random.

hitch v. **1** fasten or be fastened with a loop or hook etc. **2** move (a thing) with a slight jerk. **3** = HITCHHIKE. •n. **1** a noose or knot of various kinds. **2** a temporary stoppage, a snag. **3** a slight jerk. **4** colloq. a free ride in a vehicle. □ **get hitched** colloq. get married.

Hitchcock, Sir Alfred (Joseph) (1899–1980), British film director, specialising in suspense thrillers.

hitchhike v. travel by seeking free rides in passing vehicles. □ **hitchhiker** n.

hi-tech = HIGH-TECH.
hither *adv. formal* to or towards this place.
hitherto *adv.* until this time.
Hitler, Adolf (1889–1945), Austrian-born German dictator, leader of the National Socialist (Nazi) party, whose expansionist foreign policy led to the Second World War.
HIV *abbr.* human immunodeficiency virus, either of two retroviruses which cause a breakdown of the body's immune system, leading in some cases to the development of Aids.
hive *n.* **1** a beehive. **2** the bees living in this. **3** a busy swarming place (*a hive of industry*). **4** (**hives**) a skin eruption, esp. nettle rash. •*v.* gather or live in a hive. ☐ **hive off** separate from a larger group. **hive up** hoard for future use.
Hizbollah alternative spelling of HEZBOLLAH.
HMAS *abbr.* Her (or His) Majesty's Australian Ship.
Ho *symbol* holmium.
ho *interj.* an exclamation of triumph or scorn, or calling attention.
hoard *n.* a carefully saved and guarded store of money, food, or treasured objects. •*v.* save and store away. ☐ **hoarder** *n.*
hoarding *n.* **1** a large, usu. wooden, structure used to carry advertisements etc. **2** a temporary fence around a building site etc.
hoar frost *n.* frozen water vapour on vegetation etc.
hoarse *adj.* **1** (of the voice) sounding rough, as if from a dry throat. **2** (of a person) having a hoarse voice. ☐ **hoarsely** *adv.* **hoarseness** *n.*
hoary *adj.* (**hoarier**, **hoariest**) **1** white or grey (*hoary hair*). **2** with hoary hair, aged. **3** (of a joke etc.) old and trite.
hoax *v.* deceive jokingly. •*n.* a joking or malicious deception. ☐ **hoaxer** *n.*
hob *n.* **1** a flat heating surface on a cooker. **2** a flat metal shelf at the side of a fireplace, where a pan etc. can be heated.
Hobart the capital city of the State of Tasmania.
hobbit *n.* a member of an imaginary race of half-sized people in the fantasy novels of J.R.R. Tolkien.
hobble *v.* **1** walk lamely; proceed haltingly in speech or action. **2** fasten the legs of (a horse etc.) so as to limit movement and prevent it from straying. •*n.* **1** a hobbling walk. **2** a rope etc. for hobbling a horse.
hobby *n.* an activity pursued for pleasure in one's spare time. ☐ **hobby farm** *Aust.* a farm maintained as a hobby, not as the main source of income.
hobby horse *n.* **1** a stick with a horse's head, used as a toy. **2** a topic that a person is esp. fond of discussing.
hobgoblin *n.* a mischievous imp.
hobnail *n.* a heavy-headed nail for boot soles.
hobnob *v.* (**hobnobbed**, **hobnobbing**) mix socially or informally (*people hobnobbing with the prime minister on the street*).

hobo *n.* (*pl.* **hoboes** or **hobos**) a wandering worker; a tramp.
Hobson's choice *n.* a situation in which there is no alternative to the thing offered. (¶ Thomas Hobson (17th century) hired out horses and made people take the one nearest the stable door or go without.)
Ho Chi Minh (original name: Nguyen That Thanh) (1890–1969), Vietnamese Communist statesman, who led his country in its struggle for independence.
Ho Chi Minh City a city (formerly called Saigon) in southern Vietnam.
hock[1] *n.* the middle joint of an animal's hind leg.
hock[2] *n.* a dry white wine.
hock[3] *v. colloq.* **1** pawn. **2** sell, esp. illegally. ☐ **in hock 1** in pawn. **2** in debt.
hockey *n.* a game played on a field between two teams of players with curved sticks and a small hard ball.
hockeyroos *n.pl.* **1** the Australian women's international hockey team. **2** (in *sing.*) a member of this team.
hocus-pocus *n.* trickery.
hod *n.* **1** a trough on a pole used by bricklayers for carrying mortar or bricks. **2** a cylindrical container for shovelling and holding coal.
hoddie *n. Aust.* a bricklayer's labourer; a hodman.
hodgepodge = HOTCHPOTCH.
Hodgkin's disease *n.* a malignant disease of the lymphatic tissues, usu. characterised by enlargement of the lymph nodes. (¶ T. Hodgkin (1798–1866), English physician.)
hodman = HODDIE.
hoe *n.* a tool with a blade on a long handle, used for loosening soil or scraping up weeds. •*v.* (**hoed**, **hoeing**) **1** dig or scrape with a hoe. **2** (**hoe in**) *Aust. colloq.* begin to eat eagerly; begin working with vigour. **3** (**hoe into**) *Aust. colloq.* attack (one's food) with gusto; attack (a task etc.) with vigour; attack (a person) verbally.
Hoffman, Dustin (Lee) (1937–), American stage and film actor.
hog *n.* **1** a castrated male pig reared for meat. **2** *colloq.* a greedy or selfish person. •*v.* (**hogged**, **hogging**) *colloq.* take more than one's fair share of; hoard selfishly; monopolise (*conversation* etc.). ☐ **go the whole hog** *colloq.* do something thoroughly. ☐☐ **hoggish** *adj.*
Hogan, Paul (1940–), AM, Australian television and film actor, esp. in comedy roles.
hogget *n.* **1** a yearling sheep. **2** its meat.
hogmanay / **hog**-muh-nay, hog-muh-**nay** / *n.* Scottish New Year's Eve.
hogshead *n.* **1** a large cask. **2** a liquid or dry measure (about 236 litres, 50 gallons).
hogtie *v.* **1** secure by fastening the hands and feet or all four feet together. **2** restrain, impede (*all these rules have me hogtied*).
hogwash *n. colloq.* nonsense, rubbish.

ho-hum *adj. colloq.* boring (*the lecture was utterly ho-hum*).

hoick *v. colloq.* lift or bring out, esp. with a jerk (*hoicked him out of bed*).

hoi polloi / hoi puh-**loi** / *n.* the common people, the masses. (¶ Greek, = the many.)

■ **Usage** This phrase is usually preceded by *the*, which is, strictly speaking, unnecessary, since *hoi* means 'the'.

hoisin / **hoi**-sin / *n.* (in full **hoisin sauce**) a thick red sauce of soybeans, vinegar, sugar, garlic, etc., much used in southern Chinese cookery.

hoist *v.* **1** raise or haul up; lift with ropes and pulleys etc. **2** *colloq.* steal; shoplift. **3** *colloq.* throw (*hoisted it out of the window*). • *n.* **1** an apparatus for hoisting things. **2** a pull or haul up (*give it a hoist*). **3** *Aust.* a rotary clothes hoist. **4** *colloq.* a theft. □ **hoist with one's own petard** caught by one's own trick etc.

hokum / **hoh**-kuhm / *n. colloq.* **1** sentimental, sensational, or unreal material in a play, film, etc. **2** nonsense.

hold[1] *v.* (**held**, **holding**) **1** take and keep in one's arms, hand(s), etc. **2** keep in a particular position; grasp or keep so as to control; detain in custody. **3** dominate (*held the stage*). **4** keep (a person) in a certain condition (*he held us all in suspense*). **5** be able to contain (*this jug holds two pints*). **6** have in one's possession or as something one has gained (*he holds the record for the high jump*). **7** keep or reserve (*please hold our seats*). **8** support, bear the weight of. **9** remain unbroken under strain (*the rope failed to hold*). **10** be able to drink (alcohol) without effect (*can't hold his grog*). **11** continue, remain valid (*will the fine weather hold?; the law still holds*). **12** keep possession of (a place or position etc.) against attack. **13** keep (a person's attention) by being interesting. **14** have the position of, occupy (a job etc.) (*held the directorship*). **15** cause to take place, conduct (*hold a meeting*). **16** restrain, cause to cease action or movement etc. **17** believe, consider; assert. **18** (in telephoning) = HOLD THE LINE (*see also* ON HOLD). • *n.* **1** the act or manner of holding something. **2** an opportunity or means of holding. **3** (foll. by *on*, *over*) a means of exerting influence on a person. □ **get hold of 1** acquire. **2** make contact with (a person). **hold back 1** prevent (a person) from doing something. **2** hesitate; refrain. **3** keep for oneself. **hold down** be competent enough to keep (one's job). **hold forth** speak lengthily. **hold good** remain valid. **hold it!** cease action etc. **hold off** wait, not begin (*the rain held off*). **hold on 1** keep one's grasp of something. **2** refrain from ringing off (on the telephone). **3** *colloq.* wait! **hold one's tongue** keep silent. **hold out 1** offer (an inducement or hope). **2** last (*if supplies hold out*). **hold out for** refuse to accept anything other than. **hold out on** *colloq.* conceal something from; refuse the requests etc. of. **hold over** postpone. **hold the fort** act as a temporary substitute; cope in an emergency. **hold the line** refrain from ringing off (on the telephone). **hold up 1** support or sustain. **2** hinder. **3** stop by the use of threats or force for the purpose of robbery. **hold-up 1** a stoppage or delay. **2** robbery by armed robbers. **hold water** (of reasoning) be sound. **hold with** *colloq.* approve of (*we don't hold with bribery*). **no holds barred** all methods are permitted. **on hold 1** postponed; awaiting action. **2** (of a telephone connection) held open automatically until the person called is free to deal with the call. **take hold** grasp; become established. □ □ **holder** *n.*

hold[2] *n.* a cavity in the lower part of a ship or aircraft, where cargo is stored.

holdall *n.* a large soft travelling bag.

holding *n.* something held or owned; land held by an owner or tenant. □ **holding company** one formed to hold the shares of other companies which it then controls. **holding paddock** (or **holding pen** or **holding yard**) *Aust.* an enclosure in which livestock is kept for a special purpose.

hole *n.* **1** an empty place in a solid body or mass; a sunken place on a surface. **2** an animal's burrow. **3** a small, dark, or wretched place. **4** *colloq.* an awkward situation. **5** *colloq.* a flaw; a fallacy (*your argument is full of holes*). **6** a hollow or cavity into which a ball etc. must be sent in various games. **7** a section of a golf course between the tee and the hole in the putting green; a point scored by a player who reaches the hole with the fewest strokes. **8** an opening in or through something. • *v.* **1** make a hole or holes in (*the ship was holed*). **2** put into a hole. □ **hole-and-corner** *adj.* underhand. **hole in the heart** *colloq.* a congenital defect in the heart membrane. **hole up** *colloq.* hide oneself.

holey *adj.* full of holes. □ **holey dollar** (also **holy dollar**) *Aust. hist.* a coin made from a Spanish silver dollar by punching out its centre (or DUMP), used in Australia between 1814 and 1828.

Holi / **hoh**-lee / *n.* a Hindu spring festival celebrated in February or March.

-holic (or **-aholic**) *suffix colloq.* addicted to (*bingoholic; workaholic*). (¶ Erroneously formed on *alcoholic*.)

holiday *n.* **1** (also **holidays**) an extended period of recreation, esp. spent away from home or travelling; a break from work. **2** a day of festivity or recreation, when no work is done. • *v.* (**holidayed**, **holidaying**) spend a holiday.

holidaymaker *n.* a person on holiday.

holiness *n.* being holy or sacred. □ **His Holiness** (or **Your Holiness**) the title used when referring to (or addressing) the pope.

holism / **hoh**-liz-uhm / *n.* (also **wholism**) **1** the theory that certain wholes are greater than the sum of their parts. **2** *Med.* treating of the whole person rather than the symptoms of a disease. □ **holistic** / hoh-**lis**-tik / *adj.*

Holland the Netherlands.
hollandaise / hol-uhn-dayz / *n.* a creamy sauce containing butter, egg yolks, and vinegar.
holler *colloq. v.* shout. •*n.* a shout.
Hollingworth, Peter (John) (1935–), AO, Australian Anglican archbishop. He became governor-general of Australia in 2001.
hollow *adj.* **1** having a hole inside, not solid. **2** sunken (*hollow cheeks*). **3** (of sound) echoing, as if from something hollow. **4** empty, worthless (*a hollow triumph*). **5** insincere (*a hollow laugh*). •*n.* a hollow or sunken place, a hole, a valley. •*adv.* completely (*beat them hollow*). •*v.* (often foll. by *out*) make or become hollow. ☐ **hollowly** *adv.* **hollowness** *n.*
Hollows, Fred(erick Cossom) (1930–93), AC, Australian ophthalmologist (born in New Zealand) who worked and campaigned vigorously to eliminate blindness amongst the Aborigines in outback Australia and later extended the campaign to Eritrea.
holly *n.* an evergreen shrub with prickly leaves and red berries.
hollyhock *n.* a plant with large showy flowers on a tall stem.
Hollywood a district of Los Angeles, centre of the American film-making industry.
Holmes, Sherlock, a fictional private detective, the central figure in a number of stories by Conan Doyle.
holmium / hol-mee-uhm / *n.* a silvery soft metallic element (symbol Ho).
holocaust / hol-uh-kawst, -kost / *n.* **1** large-scale destruction, esp. by fire or nuclear war. **2** (**the Holocaust**) the mass murder of Jews (and other persecuted groups such as gypsies and homosexuals) by the Nazis in 1939–45.
Holocene / hol-uh-seen / *adj. Geol.* of the second of the two epochs of the Quaternary period, lasting from about 10,000 years ago to the present day. •*n.* this epoch.
hologram / hol-uh-gram / *n.* an image produced (without using lenses) on photographic film in such a way that under suitable illumination a three-dimensional representation of an object is seen. ☐ **holographic** *adj.* **holography** *n.*
holograph / hol-uh-grahf, -graf / *n.* a document that is handwritten by its author.
holster / hohl-stuh / *n.* a leather case for a pistol or revolver, worn fixed to a belt.
Holt, Harold (Edward) (1908–67), Australian Liberal statesman, prime minister 1966–67.
holy *adj.* (**holier**, **holiest**) **1** morally and spiritually excellent or perfect, and to be revered. **2** consecrated, sacred (*holy water*). **3** devoted to God (*a holy man*). ☐ **holier-than-thou** self-righteous. **holy cross toad** a yellowish frog of inland south-eastern Australia with a warty cross on its back. Also known as the *Catholic frog*. **holy of holies 1** a place or thing regarded as most sacred. **2** the sacred inner chamber of the Jewish temple. **holy orders** the sacrament of ordination, esp. to the priesthood; the status of a bishop, priest, or deacon.
Holy Communion *see* COMMUNION.
Holy Father *n.* the pope.
Holy Ghost *n.* = HOLY SPIRIT.
Holy Grail *see* GRAIL.
Holy Land the part of Palestine west of the Jordan, revered by Christians.
Holy Roman Empire the empire set up in western Europe following the coronation of Charlemagne (800 AD) and ruled by Frankish or German rulers bearing the title of Emperor until abolished by Napoleon in 1806.
Holy See 1 the See of Rome; the jurisdiction and office of the pope. **2** the papal court; those people associated with the pope in the government of the Catholic Church at its headquarters in Rome.
Holy Spirit *n.* the Third Person of the Trinity, God acting spiritually.
Holy Week *n.* the week before Easter Sunday.
Holy Writ *n.* the Bible.
Holy Year *n.* a period of remission from the penal consequences of sin, granted by the pope, under certain conditions, for a year usu. at intervals of 25 years.
homage *n.* things said as a mark of respect (*paid homage to his achievements*).
homburg *n.* a man's felt hat with a narrow curled brim and a lengthwise dent in the crown.
home *n.* **1** the place where one lives, esp. with one's family. **2** one's native land; the district where one was born or where one has lived for a long time or to which one feels attached. **3** a dwelling-house. **4** an institution where those needing care may live (*an old people's home*). **5** the natural environment of an animal or plant. **6** the place to be reached by a runner in a race or in certain games. •*adj.* **1** of or connected with one's own home or country; done or produced there (*home industries; home produce*). **2** played on one's own ground (*a home match*). •*adv.* **1** to or at one's home or country (*go home*). **2** to the point aimed at, right in (*the thrust went home; drive a nail home*). •*v.* **1** (of a trained pigeon) fly home. **2** (often foll. by *in on*) be guided to a target; make for a particular destination. ☐ **at home 1** in one's own home or country. **2** at ease; comfortable or familiar. **3** available to visitors. **bring home to** cause to realise fully. **home and hosed** (*or* **home and dry**) having achieved one's aim. **home brew** a drink (esp. beer) brewed at home. **home economics** the study of household management. **home help** a person who helps with housework etc., esp. one provided by a welfare agency. **home invasion** a gang robbery of a suburban house, usu. including violence and threats to the householders. **home paddock** *Aust.* a paddock adjacent to a homestead. **home page** the main page of a document on the World Wide Web; such a page representing an individual or organisation.

home rule government of a country by its own citizens. **home run** a hit in baseball that allows the batter to make a complete circuit of the bases. **home station** *Aust.* the principal residence on a large stock-raising property. **home straight** (*or* **stretch**) the stretch of a racecourse between the last turn and the finishing line. **home truth** an unpleasant truth that a person is made to realise about himself or herself. **home unit** *Aust.* a self-contained apartment (one of several in the same building) with separate title and usu. occupied by the owner.

homeboy *n.* = HOMIE.

homecoming *n.* arrival at home.

homeland *n.* one's native land. ☐ **homeland centre** *Aust.* the traditional lands of an Aboriginal community to which members of that community have returned to live. **homeland movement** *Aust.* the forming of homeland centres.

homeless *adj.* lacking a home. ☐ **homelessness** *n.*

homely *adj.* **1** simple and informal, not pretentious. **2** (of a person's appearance) plain, not beautiful. **3** comfortable, cosy. ☐ **homeliness** *n.*

homeopathy alternative spelling of HOMOEOPATHY.

Homer (?c.700 BC) Greek epic poet, traditionally the author of the *Iliad* and the *Odyssey*.

Homeric / hoh-**me**-rik / *adj.* of the writings or heroes of Homer.

homesick *adj.* feeling depressed through longing for one's home when one is away from it. ☐ **homesickness** *n.*

homespun *adj.* **1** made of yarn spun at home. **2** plain, simple. • *n.* homespun fabric.

homestead / **hohm**-sted / *n.* **1** a house, esp. a farmhouse, and its outbuildings. **2** = HOME STATION.

homeward *adj.* going towards home. • *adv.* (also **homewards**) towards home.

homework *n.* **1** work that a pupil is required to do away from school. **2** preparatory work to be done before a discussion etc. takes place.

homey *adj.* (also **homy**) like home, homely.

homicide / **hom**-uh-suyd / *n.* **1** the killing of one person by another. **2** a person who kills another. ☐ **homicidal** *adj.*

homie / **hoh**-mee / *n.* (also **homeboy**) *colloq.* **1** (in young people's slang) a member of one's own gang. **2** (in the usage of outsiders) a member of a teenage gang, esp. one associated with violence.

homily *n.* a sermon, a moralising lecture. ☐ **homiletic** / hom-uh-**let**-ik / *adj.*

homing *adj.* **1** (of a pigeon) trained to fly home. **2** (of a device) for guiding to a target etc.

hominid / **hom**-uh-nid / *n.* a member of the zoological family that includes humans and their extinct ancestors. • *adj.* of this family.

hominoid / **hom**-uh-noid / *n.* an animal resembling a human. • *adj.* like a human.

homo / **hoh**-moh / *n.* (*pl.* **homos**) *colloq. offens.* a homosexual.

homoeopathy / hoh-mee-**op**-uh-thee, hom-ee- / *n.* (also **homeopathy**) treatment of disease with very small doses of drugs etc. that in a healthy person would produce symptoms like those of the disease itself. ☐ **homoeopath** / **hoh**-mee-oh-path, **hom**-ee- / *n.* **homoeopathic** *adj.* **homoeopathist** *n.*

homogeneous / hoh-muh-**jee**-nee-uhs, hom-uh- / *adj.* of the same kind as the others; formed of parts that are all of the same kind. ☐ **homogeneity** / hoh-muh-juh-**nee**-uh-tee, hom-uh- / *n.*

homogenise / huh-**moj**-uh-nuyz / *v.* (also **-ize**) treat (milk) so that the particles of fat are broken down and the cream does not separate. ☐ **homogenisation** *n.*

homograph / **hom**-uh-grahf, -graf / *n.* a word that is spelt like another but has a different meaning or origin, e.g. *bat* (a flying animal) and *bat* (for striking a ball).

homologous / huh-**mol**-uh-guhs / *adj.* **1** having the same relation or relative position, corresponding. **2** *Biology* (of organs etc.) similar in position or structure but not in function.

homology / huh-**mol**-uh-jee / *n.* a homologous state or relation.

homonym / **hom**-uh-nim / *n.* a word of the same spelling or sound as another but with a different meaning, e.g. *grate* (= fireplace), *grate* (= to rub), *great* (= large).

homophobia / hoh-muh-**foh**-bee-uh, hom-uh- / *n.* hatred or fear of homosexuals. ☐ **homophobe** *n.* **homophobic** *adj.*

homophone / **hom**-uh-fohn / *n.* a word with the same sound as another, e.g. *son, sun.*

Homo sapiens / hoh-moh **sap**-ee-enz / *n.* modern humans regarded as a species. (¶ Latin, = wise man.)

homosexual / hoh-muh-**sek**-shoo-uhl, hom-uh- / *adj.* feeling sexually attracted only to people of the same sex as oneself. • *n.* a homosexual person. ☐ **homosexuality** *n.*

homy alternative spelling of HOMEY.

Hon. *abbr.* **1** Honorary. **2** Honourable.

Honduras / hon-**dyoor**-ruhs / *n.* a republic in Central America. ☐ **Honduran** *adj.* & *n.*

hone *n.* a fine-grained stone used for sharpening razors and tools. • *v.* **1** sharpen on this. **2** polish or refine (reasoning etc.).

honest *adj.* **1** fair and just; not cheating or stealing. **2** free of deceit and lies; sincere. **3** (of gain etc.) got by fair means (*earn an honest living*). • *adv. colloq.* genuinely, really ('*Won a million dollars.*' —'*Honest?*'). ☐ **honest-to-goodness** *adj. colloq.* genuine, straightforward.

honestly *adv.* **1** in an honest way. **2** really (*that's all I know, honestly*).

honesty *n.* **1** being honest. **2** a plant with seeds that form in flat round translucent pods.

honey *n.* (*pl.* **honeys**) **1** a sweet sticky yellowish substance made by bees from nectar. **2** its colour. **3** sweetness, pleasantness; a sweet thing. **4** darling. **5** a person or thing exciting admiration (*he's a honey*). ◻ **honey ant** (also **honey-bag ant**) any of several Australian ants able to store a honey-like liquid in its crop: a delicacy for Aborigines who hold the living ant by its head and bite off the abdomen. **honey bag** (also **sugar bag**) the honeycomb of the wild Australian stingless bee, much valued by Aborigines. **honey bee** *n.* the common bee that lives in a hive.

honeycomb *n.* **1** a bees' wax structure of six-sided cells for holding their honey and eggs. **2** a pattern or arrangement of six-sided sections. **3** tripe from the second stomach of a ruminant. • *v.* **1** fill with holes or tunnels (*the rock was honeycombed with passages*). **2** mark or sew in a honeycomb pattern.

honeydew *n.* **1** a sweet sticky substance found on leaves and stems, secreted by aphids. **2** a variety of melon with pale skin and sweet green flesh.

honeyeater *n.* any of numerous Australian birds having a long brush-tipped tongue for feeding on flower nectar and other foods.

honeyed *adj.* flattering, pleasant (*honeyed words*).

honeymoon *n.* **1** a holiday spent together by a newly-married couple. **2** an initial period of enthusiasm or goodwill. • *v.* spend a honeymoon. ◻ **honeymooner** *n.*

honeysuckle *n.* a climbing shrub with fragrant yellow or pink flowers.

Hong Kong a former British dependency on the SE coast of China. China resumed sovereignty in 1997, and it became an administrative district of China.

Honiara / hon-ee-**ah**-ruh / the capital of the Solomon Islands.

honk *n.* a loud harsh sound; the cry of the wild goose; the sound made by a car horn. • *v.* make a honk, sound (a horn).

honky-tonk *n.* ragtime piano music.

Honolulu the capital of Hawaii.

honor alternative spelling of HONOUR.

honorable alternative spelling of HONOURABLE.

honorarium / on-uh-**rair**-ree-uhm / *n.* (*pl.* **honorariums** *or* **honoraria**) a voluntary payment made for services where no fee is legally required.

honorary / **on**-uh-ruh-ree / *adj.* **1** given as an honour (*an honorary degree*). **2** (of an office or its holder) unpaid (*the honorary treasurer*).

honorific / on-uh-**rif**-ik / *adj.* **1** conferring honour. **2** (esp. of Oriental forms of speech) implying respect. **3** a title of formal respect, as *Doctor, Professor,* etc.

honour *n.* (also **honor**) **1** great respect, high public regard. **2** a mark of this; a privilege given or received (*had the honour of being invited*). **3** a source of this; a person or thing that brings honour (*an honour to her profession*). **4** a thing conferred as a distinction, esp. an official award for bravery or achievement. **5** good personal character; a reputation for honesty and loyalty etc. **6** a title of respect given to certain judges or people of importance (*your Honour*). **7** the right of driving off first in golf, held by the player who won the previous hole. **8** (in certain card games) any of the four or five cards of the highest value. **9** (**honours**) a specialised degree course or special distinction in an examination. • *v.* **1** respect highly. **2** confer honour on. **3** acknowledge and pay (a cheque etc. when it is due). **4** observe the terms of (an agreement). ◻ **do the honours** perform the usual civilities to guests or visitors etc. **honours degree** a university degree requiring a higher level of attainment than a pass degree. **honours list** a list of people awarded honours in recognition of their achievements. **in honour bound** (*or* **on one's honour**) under a moral obligation to do something.

honourable *adj.* (also **honorable**) **1** deserving honour. **2** possessing or showing honour. • *adj.* (**Honourable**) the courtesy title of certain high officials and members of parliament, and used during debates by MPs to one another. ◻ **honourably** *adv.*

hood / huud / *n.* **1** a covering for the head and neck, esp. as part of a garment. **2** a separate hoodlike garment worn over an academic gown to indicate the wearer's degree and university. **3** something resembling a hood in shape or use, e.g. a folding roof over a car, the expanded neck of a cobra, etc. **4** *colloq.* = HOODLUM. • *v.* cover with or as with a hood.

hooded *adj.* **1** having a hood. **2** (of animals) having a hoodlike part.

hoodlum / **hood**-luhm / *n.* **1** a hooligan, a young thug. **2** a gangster.

hoodoo / **hoo**-doo / *n.* **1** a thing or person thought to cause bad luck. **2** = VOODOO. • *v.* (**hoodooed**, **hoodooing**) make unlucky; bewitch.

hoodwink / huud-wingk / *v.* deceive.

hooey *n. colloq.* nonsense.

hoof / huuf / *n.* (*pl.* **hoofs** *or* **hooves** / hoovz /) the horny part of the foot of a horse and other animals. ◻ **hoof it** *colloq.* go on foot. **on the hoof** (of livestock) not yet slaughtered.

hoo-ha *n. colloq.* a commotion.

hook *n.* **1** a bent or curved piece of metal etc. for catching hold of or for hanging things on. **2** something shaped like this, e.g. a fish-hook. **3** a bend in a river or road, a curved strip of land. **4** a curved cutting tool (*reaping hook*). **5** (in cricket or golf) a hooked stroke. **6** (in boxing) a short swinging blow with the elbow bent. • *v.* **1** grasp or catch with a hook; fasten with a hook or hooks. **2** connect (apparatus etc.) to a power source. **3** be or become attached as with a hook (*he's hooked on*

hookah 394 **hopeless**

comics). **4** catch with or as with a hook (*hooked a fish; hooked a husband*). **5** *colloq.* obtain; steal. **6** propel (a ball) in a curving path. **7** (in Rugby) pass (the ball) backward with the foot. □ **by hook or by crook** by some means no matter what happens. **hook and eye** a small metal hook and loop for fastening a garment. **hook, line, and sinker** entirely. **hook-up** *n. colloq.* interconnection of broadcasting equipment. **off the hook 1** *colloq.* freed from a difficulty. **2** (of a telephone receiver) not on its rest. **3** (of clothes) ready-made. **put the hooks into** *Aust. colloq.* borrow or cadge from.

hookah / **huuk**-uh / *n.* an oriental tobacco pipe with a long tube passing through a glass container of water that cools the smoke as it is drawn through.

hooked *adj.* **1** hook-shaped (*a hooked nose*). **2** (often foll. by *on*) *colloq.* addicted or captivated.

hooker *n.* **1** *Rugby* a player in the front row of the scrum, who tries to get the ball by hooking it. **2** *colloq.* a prostitute.

hookworm *n.* a worm with hooklike mouth parts, which can infest the intestines of humans and animals.

hooky *n.* (also **hookey**) □ **play hooky** *colloq.* play truant.

hooligan *n.* a young ruffian. □ **hooliganism** *n.*

hoon *Aust. colloq. n.* **1** a hooligan. **2** a show-off, an exhibitionist. **3** a bludger. • *v.* (also **hoon around**) drive dangerously or at reckless speed in order to show off.

hoop *n.* **1** a band of metal or wood etc. forming part of a framework. **2** this used as a child's toy for bowling along the ground, or for circus performers to jump through. **3** *Basketball* the metal ring from which the net is suspended; the goal ring. **3 a** a band in contrasting colour on a jockey's blouse, etc. **b** *Aust. colloq.* a jockey. • *v.* bind or encircle with hoops. □ **be put** (or **go**) **through the hoops** undergo a test or ordeal.

hoop-la *n.* a game in which rings are thrown to encircle a prize.

hoopoe / **hoo**-poo / *n.* a bird with a fan-like crest and striped wings and tail.

hooray¹ = HURRAH.
hooray² = HOOROO.

hooroo / **hoo**-roo / *interj.* & *n. Aust. colloq.* a conventional form of farewell, goodbye ('*Hooroo!*' *he said as he left; give my hooroos to all*).

hoot *n.* **1** the cry of an owl. **2** the sound made by a vehicle's horn or a steam whistle. **3** a cry expressing scorn or disapproval. **4** *colloq.* laughter; a cause of this. • *v.* **1** make a hoot or hoots. **2** receive or drive away with scornful hoots. **3** laugh raucously (*hooted with laughter*). **4** sound (a horn). □ **not care** (or **give**) **a hoot** (or **two hoots**) *colloq.* not care at all.

hooter *n.* **1** a thing that hoots, e.g. a car horn. **2** *colloq.* a nose.

hoover *n. trademark* a vacuum cleaner. • *v.* (**hoover**) clean (a carpet etc.) with a vacuum cleaner.

hooves *see* HOOF.

hop¹ *v.* (**hopped**, **hopping**) **1** (of an animal) spring from all feet at once. **2** (of a person) jump on one foot. **3** cross a ditch, fence, etc. by hopping. **4** move or go quickly (*hop over to the milk bar and get me some sugar*). **5** take a quick flight or trip (*hopped over to Tassie for the day*). **6** *colloq.* obtain a lift (*can I hop a ride with you?*). • *n.* **1** a hopping movement. **2** an informal dance. **3** a short journey, esp. a flight. □ **hop in** (or **out**) *colloq.* get into or out of a car, train, etc. **hop into** *Aust. colloq.* **1** begin (a meal, an activity, etc.) with enthusiasm. **2** get into (clothes) rapidly (*hang on till I hop into my bathers!*). **hop it** *colloq.* go away.

hopping mouse any of several native Australian mice having long hind legs and a rapid kangaroo-like hopping gait. **hop, step, and jump 1** = TRIPLE JUMP. **2** a short distance. **on the hop** *colloq.* unprepared (*we were caught on the hop*).

hop² *n.* **1** a climbing plant cultivated for its cones which are used for giving a bitter flavour to beer. **2** (**hops**) the ripe cones of this plant. □ **hop bush** any shrub of the Australian genus *Dodonaea* with bitter three-angled fruits used by the early settlers for making beer. **on the hops** *colloq.* engaged in a drinking session.

Hope¹, A(lec) D(erwent) (1907–2000), AC, Australian poet and literary critic.

Hope², Bob (original name: Leslie Townes Hope) (1903–), American film actor and comedian.

hope *n.* **1** a feeling of expectation and desire combined; a desire for certain events to happen. **2** a person, thing, or circumstance that gives cause for this. **3** what is hoped for. • *v.* feel hope; expect and desire; feel fairly confident.

hopeful *adj.* **1** feeling hope. **2** causing hope, seeming likely to be favourable or successful. • *n.* a person who hopes or seems likely to succeed (*young hopefuls*).

hopefully *adv.* **1** in a hopeful way. **2** it is to be hoped (*hopefully, we shall be there by one o'clock*).

■ **Usage** The use of *hopefully* in sense 2 is extremely common, but it is still considered incorrect by some people. The main reason is that other such adverbs, e.g. *regrettably*, *fortunately*, etc., can be converted to the form *it is regrettable*, *it is fortunate*, etc., but *hopefully* converts to *it is to be hoped*. This use of *hopefully* probably arose as a translation of German *hoffentlich*, used in the same way, and first became popular in America in the late 1960s. Its use is best restricted to informal contexts.

hopeless *adj.* **1** feeling no hope. **2** admitting no hope (*a hopeless case*). **3** inadequate, incompetent (*is hopeless at tennis*). **4** not possible to solve or resolve (*a hopeless mess*). □ **hopelessly** *adv.* **hopelessness** *n.*

Hopman, Harry (full name: Henry Christian Hopman) (1906–85), Australian tennis player. He was captain of the Davis Cup team 1938–39, and non-playing captain 1950–69.

hopper *n*. **1** a hopping insect. **2** a V-shaped container with an opening at the base through which its contents can be discharged into a machine etc.

hopscotch *n*. a children's game of hopping and jumping over marked squares to retrieve a stone tossed into these.

horde *n*. a large group or crowd.

horizon *n*. **1** the line at which earth and sky appear to meet. **2** the limit of a person's experience, knowledge, or interests. ☐ **on the horizon** (of an event) about to happen, just becoming apparent.

horizontal *adj*. parallel to the horizon; at right angles to the vertical. ☐ **horizontally** *adv*.

hormone / **haw**-mohn / *n*. a regulatory substance produced within the body of an animal or plant (or made synthetically) and carried by the blood or sap to stimulate cells or tissues into action. ☐ **hormone replacement therapy** treatment to relieve menopausal symptoms by boosting a woman's oestrogen levels. ☐ ☐ **hormonal** / haw-**moh**-nuhl / *adj*.

horn *n*. **1** a hard pointed outgrowth on the heads of certain animals. **2** the hard smooth substance of which this consists. **3** a projection resembling a horn. **4** any of various wind instruments (originally made of horn, now usu. of brass) with a trumpet-shaped end; the French horn (*see* FRENCH). **5** a device for sounding a warning signal. ☐ **horn in** *colloq*. intrude, butt in. **horn of plenty** a cornucopia; an abundant supply. **horn-rimmed** *adj*. (of spectacles) with frames made of a material like horn or tortoiseshell. ☐ ☐ **horned** *adj*.

hornblende *n*. a black, green, or dark brown mineral.

Horne, Donald (Richmond) (1921–), AO, Australian academic and writer, author of *The Lucky Country*.

hornet *n*. a large kind of wasp inflicting a serious sting. ☐ **stir up a hornets' nest** cause an outbreak of angry feeling.

hornpipe *n*. a lively dance usu. for one person, traditionally associated with sailors.

horny *adj*. (**hornier**, **horniest**) **1** of or like horn. **2** hardened and calloused (*horny hands*). **3** *colloq*. sexually excited. • *n*. (*pl*. **hornies**) *Aust*. a bullock.

horology / huh-**rol**-uh-jee / *n*. the art of measuring time or of making clocks and watches. ☐ **horological** *adj*.

horoscope *n*. a forecast of a person's future, based on an astrologer's diagram showing the relative positions of the planets and stars at a particular time.

horrendous *adj*. horrifying. ☐ **horrendously** *adv*.

horrible *adj*. **1** causing horror. **2** *colloq*. unpleasant. ☐ **horribly** *adv*.

horrid *adj*. horrible. ☐ **horridly** *adv*.

horrific *adj*. horrifying. ☐ **horrifically** *adv*.

horrify *v*. (**horrified**, **horrifying**) arouse horror in; shock. ☐ **horrifying** *adj*.

horror *n*. **1** a feeling of loathing and fear. **2** intense dislike or dismay. **3** a person or thing causing horror. **4** (**the horrors**) a fit of horror or depression. ☐ **horror film** one full of violent or supernatural scenes presented sensationally for entertainment.

hors d'oeuvre / aw-**derv** / *n*. food served as an appetiser at the start of a meal. (¶ French)

horse *n*. **1** a four-legged animal with a flowing mane and tail, used for riding on or to carry or pull loads. **2** an adult male horse. **3** a frame on which something is supported (*clothes horse*). **4** a vaulting block. ☐ **get on** (*or* **off**) **one's high horse** be (or cease to be) arrogant, pompous. **horse around** *colloq*. fool about. **horse duffer** *hist*. a horse thief. **horse float** a closed trailer or van for transporting a horse or horses. **horse laugh** *n*. a loud, raucous (esp. jeering) laugh. **horse mackerel** any of several sea fish, esp. the jack mackerel and the bonito, abundant along the east coast of Australia. **horse plant** *Aust*. a team of working horses. **horse race** a race between horses with riders. **horse racing** the sport of conducting horse races. **horse sense** *colloq*. plain common sense. **straight from the horse's mouth** (of information) from a first-hand source.

horseflesh *n*. **1** the flesh of horses, as food. **2** horses (*a good judge of horseflesh*).

horsehair *n*. hair from a horse's mane or tail, used for padding furniture etc.

horseman *n*. (*feminine* **horsewoman**) a rider on horseback, esp. a skilled one. ☐ **horsemanship** *n*.

horseplay *n*. boisterous play.

horsepower *n*. (*pl*. **horsepower**) a unit for measuring the power of an engine (550 foot-pounds per second, about 750 watts).

horseradish *n*. a plant with a strong-tasting root used to make a sauce.

horseshoe *n*. **1** a U-shaped strip of metal nailed to a horse's hoof. **2** anything shaped like this.

horsetailer *n*. *Aust*. a person responsible for the care of working horses. ☐ **horsetailing** *n*.

horsewhip *n*. a whip for horses. • *v*. (**horsewhipped**, **horsewhipping**) beat with a horsewhip.

horsy *adj*. **1** of or like a horse. **2** interested in horses. **3** (of a person) resembling a horse (with large face and teeth etc.).

hortative / **haw**-tuh-tiv / *adj*. = HORTATORY.

hortatory / **haw**-tuh-tuh-ree / *adj*. exhorting, encouraging.

horticulture *n*. the art of garden cultivation. ☐ **horticultural** *adj*. **horticulturist** *n*.

hosanna *interj*. & *n*. a cry of adoration.

hose *n.* **1** (also **hosepipe**) a flexible tube for conveying water etc. **2** stockings and socks. **3** *archaic* breeches (*doublet and hose*). • *v.* (often foll. by *down*) **1** water or spray with a hose (*hose the car down*). **2** reduce the fervour of; defuse (*tried to hose down their anger*).

hosier *n.* a dealer in hosiery.

hosiery *n.* stockings and socks.

hospice / **hos**-pis / *n.* **1** a home for destitute or sick people, esp. the terminally ill. **2** a lodging house for travellers, esp. one kept by a religious order.

hospitable / hos-**pit**-uh-buhl / *adj.* giving hospitality, welcoming. ☐ **hospitably** *adv.*

hospital *n.* **1** an institution providing medical and surgical treatment for people who are ill or injured. **2** *archaic* a hospice.

hospitalise / **hos**-pi-tuh-luyz / *v.* (also **-ize**) send or admit (a patient) to a hospital. ☐ **hospitalisation** *n.*

hospitality *n.* friendly and generous reception and entertainment of guests.

host[1] *n.* a large number of people or things.

host[2] *n.* **1** a person who receives and entertains another as a guest. **2** a compère. **3** an organism on which another organism lives as a parasite. **4** the recipient of a transplanted organ etc. • *v.* act as host to (a person) or at (an event).

host[3] *n.* (often **the Host**) the bread consecrated in the sacrifice of the Mass or in the Eucharist.

hostage *n.* a person held as security that the holder's demands will be satisfied.

hostel *n.* a lodging house for young travellers, students, or other special groups.

hostelling *n.* the practice of staying in youth hostels. ☐ **hosteller** *n.*

hostelry *n. archaic* an inn.

hostess *n.* **1** a woman who receives and entertains a person as her guest. **2** a woman employed to welcome and entertain people at a nightclub etc.

hostile *adj.* **1** of an enemy (*hostile aircraft*). **2** unfriendly, opposed (*a hostile glance; they are hostile towards reform*). ☐ **hostilely** *adv.*

hostility *n.* **1** being hostile, enmity. **2** (**hostilities**) acts of warfare.

hot *adj.* (**hotter**, **hottest**) **1** having great heat or high temperature; giving off heat; feeling heat. **2** producing a burning sensation to the taste (*red hot Sri Lankan curries*). **3** angry; excited, excitable (*a hot temper*). **4** (often foll. by *on*) eager, keen (*in hot pursuit; he's hot on punctuality*). **5** *colloq.* exciting, trendy (*hot new clothes*). **6** (of the scent in hunting) fresh and strong; (of news) fresh, recent; (of information) unusually reliable (*a hot tip*). **7** (of a player) very skilful; (of a competitor) strongly favoured to win. **8** (foll. by *on*) knowledgable about. **9** (of jazz etc.) strongly rhythmical and emotional. **10** radioactive. **11** *colloq.* (of goods etc.) recently stolen, difficult to dispose of because identifiable; (of persons) wanted by the police. ☐ **have the hots for** *colloq.* be sexually attracted to. **hot air** *colloq.* empty or boastful talk. **hot cross bun** a bun marked with a cross, traditionally eaten hot on Good Friday. **hot dog** a frankfurt in a soft roll. **hot potato** *colloq.* a situation etc. likely to cause trouble to the person handling it. **hot rod** a motor vehicle modified to have extra power and speed. **hot seat** *colloq.* **1** the position of someone who has difficult responsibilities. **2** the electric chair. **hot up** *v.* **1** make or become hot. **2** make or become more active, exciting, or dangerous. **3** escalate or be escalated (*the war's hotting up*). **4** modify (a car etc.) to achieve high speed. **in hot water** *colloq.* in trouble or disgrace. ☐ ☐ **hotly** *adv.* **hotness** *n.*

hotbed *n.* **1** a bed of earth heated by fermenting manure. **2** a place favourable to the growth of vice, intrigue, etc.

hotchpotch *n.* (also **hodgepodge**) a jumble.

hotel *n.* **1** *Aust.* a public house, a pub. **2** a building where meals and rooms are provided for payment.

hotelier / hoh-**tel**-ee-uh / *n.* a hotel-keeper.

hotfoot *adv.* in eager haste. ☐ **hotfoot it** *v.* hurry eagerly.

hothead *n.* an impetuous person. ☐ **hotheaded** *adj.*

hothouse *n.* a heated building made of glass, for growing plants in a warm temperature.

hotline *n.* a direct exclusive telephone line, esp. for emergencies.

hotplate *n.* a heated surface for cooking food or keeping it hot.

hotpot *n.* a stew containing meat with potatoes and other vegetables.

Hottentot *n.* **1** a member of a people of SW Africa. **2** their language.

Houdini / hoo-**dee**-nee /, Harry (original name: Eric Weiss) (1874–1926), American escapologist.

houmous alternative spelling of HUMMUS.

hound *n.* a dog used in hunting. • *v.* harass or pursue.

hour *n.* **1** a twenty-fourth part of a day and night, 60 minutes. **2** a time of day, a point of time (*always comes at the same hour*). **3** a short period of time; the time for action (*the hour has come*). **4** (in the Catholic Church) prayers to be said at one of the seven times of day appointed for prayer (*a book of hours*). **5** a period for a specified activity (*the lunch hour*). **6** an hour's travelling time (*we are an hour from Brisbane*). **7** (**hours**, preceded by numerals in the form 18.00, 20.30, etc.) this number of hours and minutes past midnight on the 24-hour clock (*assemble at 20.00 hours*). **8** (**hours**) a fixed period for daily work (*office hours are 9 to 5; after hours*). ☐ **on the hour** when the clock indicates a whole number of hours after midnight (*buses leave on the hour*).

hourglass *n.* a wasp-waisted glass container holding a quantity of fine sand that takes one hour to trickle from the upper to the lower section.

houri / **hoor**-ree, **hoo**-ree / *n.* a young and beautiful woman of the Muslim Paradise.

hourly *adj.* **1** done or occurring once an hour (*an hourly bus service*). **2** continual, frequent (*lives in hourly dread of discovery*). **3** per hour (*hourly wage*). • *adv.* every hour.

house *n.* / hows / **1** a building made for people to live in, a home. **2** the people living in this, a household. **3** a building for a particular purpose or for animals (*opera house; hen house*). **4** a religious community; its buildings. **5** (**the house**) *Aust.* the principal residence on a rural property (as distinct from accommodation provided for employees). **6** a boarding-school residence; the pupils in this; each of the divisions of a day school for sports competitions etc. **7** a building used by a legislative assembly; the assembly itself (*the House of Representatives*). **8** a business firm (*a banking house*). **9** the audience of a theatre or cinema (*a full house*). **10** a family or dynasty (*the House of Orange*). **11** each of the twelve parts into which the heavens are divided in astrology. • *adj.* of or relating to a house (*house mouse; house guest*). • *v.* / howz / **1** provide accommodation for. **2** store (goods etc.). **3** encase (a part or fixture). ☐ **house arrest** detention in one's own house, not in prison. **house guest** a visitor staying for some days in one's home. **house husband** a man who does a wife's traditional household duties. **house lights** lights in a theatre auditorium. **house mouse** the common domestic mouse. **house music** a style of pop music, typically using drum machines and synthesised bass lines with sparse repetitive vocals and a fast beat. **house of cards** an insecure scheme. **house paddock** a paddock adjacent to the house, usu. for horses. **house-proud** attentive to (or excessively preoccupied with) the care and appearance of the home. **house-sit** live in and look after a house while its owner is away. **house sitter** a person who house-sits. **house-trained** (of animals) trained to be clean in the house. **house-warming** a party to celebrate a move to a new home. **house wine** bulk wine selected by the management of a restaurant, hotel, etc. to be offered at a special price. **on the house** (of drinks) free. **put** (*or* **set**) **one's house in order** make the necessary reforms. **run of the house** complete freedom of the house given to a guest.

houseboat *n.* a boat fitted up for living in.

housebound *adj.* confined to one's house through illness etc.

housebreaking *n.* the act of breaking into a building to commit a crime. ☐ **housebreaker** *n.*

housebroken *adj.* (of animals) trained to be clean in the house.

housefly *n.* a common fly often found in houses.

household *n.* **1** all the occupants of a house living as a family. **2** a house and its affairs. ☐ **household word** (*or* **name**) a well-known saying or name or person or thing.

householder *n.* a person owning or renting a house; the head of a household.

housekeeper *n.* a person, esp. a woman, employed to look after a household.

housekeeping *n.* **1** management of household affairs. **2** money to be used for this. **3** operations of maintenance, record-keeping, etc., in an organisation. **4** *Computing* the actions performed within a program or system to maintain internal orderliness.

housemaid *n.* a female servant in a house, esp. one who cleans rooms. ☐ **housemaid's knee** inflammation of the kneecap, often caused by excessive kneeling.

House of Assembly the lower legislative house in SA and Tas.

House of Representatives the lower legislative house of the federal parliament of Australia.

housetop the roof of a house. ☐ **shout** etc. **from the housetops** announce publicly.

housewife *n.* (*pl.* **housewives**) **1** a woman who manages a household and usu. does not have a full-time paid job. **2** / **huz**-if / a case for needles, threads, etc. ☐ **housewifely** *adv.*

housework *n.* the regular cleaning and cooking etc. done in housekeeping.

housey-housey (also **housie-housie**, **housie**) = BINGO.

housing *n.* **1** dwelling houses collectively; the provision of these. **2** shelter, lodging. **3** a rigid casing enclosing machinery. **4** a shallow trench or groove cut in a piece of wood to receive an insertion. ☐ **housing development** (*or* **estate**) a number of houses in an area planned as a unit.

hove see HEAVE.

hovea / **hoh**-vee-uh / *n.* an Australian shrub bearing purple or blue pea-flowers in spring.

hovel / **hov**-uhl / *n.* a small miserable dwelling.

Hovell, William Hilton (1786–1875), Australian explorer (born in England) who in 1824 joined Hamilton Hume on an overland exploration of the territory between Goulburn in NSW and Port Phillip (Vic.).

hover *v.* **1** (of a bird etc.) remain in one place in the air. **2** wait about, linger, wait close at hand. **3** waver (*hovering between life and death*).

hovercraft *n.* a vehicle that travels over land or water supported on an air cushion provided by a downward blast from its engines.

how *adv.* **1** by what means, in what way. **2** to what extent or amount etc. **3** in what condition (*how are you?*). • *conj. colloq.* that (*he told us how he'd been in India*). ☐ **how are you going?** (*or* **how goes it?**) an informal version of HOW DO YOU DO? **how come** *colloq.* why, how did it happen? **how do you do?** a formal greeting. **how's that 1** what is your opinion or explanation? **2** *Cricket* (also **howzat**) (an appeal to the umpire) is the batsman out? **how's things** (*or* **tricks**)? an

Howard   398   **human**

informal version of HOW DO YOU DO? **how-to-vote card** *Aust.* (in preferential voting) a card issued to voters by a political party or independent candidate indicating how that party or candidate would wish voters to mark their preferences on the ballot paper.

Howard, John (Winston) (1939–), Australian Liberal statesman who became prime minister in 1996.

howdah / **how**-duh / *n.* a seat, usu. with a canopy, for riding on an elephant or camel.

however *adv.* **1** in whatever way, to whatever extent (*he'll not succeed, however hard he tries*). **2** all the same, nevertheless (*later, however, she decided to go*).

howitzer *n.* a short gun firing shells, with a steep angle of fire.

howl *n.* **1** the long loud wailing cry of a dog etc. **2** a loud cry of amusement, pain, or scorn. **3** a similar noise made by a strong wind or in an electrical amplifier. • *v.* **1** make a howl. **2** weep loudly. **3** utter with a howl. **4** drive away with howls (*howled him off the stage*).

howler *n. colloq.* a glaring mistake.

hoy[1] *interj.* an exclamation used to call attention.

hoy[2] *n. Aust.* a game of chance resembling bingo, using playing cards.

hoya *n.* a climbing plant, native to tropical Asia and Australia, with fleshy leaves and clusters of thick waxy pink, yellow, or maroon flowers, sometimes scented.

hoyden *n.* a girl who behaves boisterously.

Hoyts *n.* □ **the man outside Hoyts** *Aust. jocular* **1** a mythical person who is the authority for reports, rumours, etc. (*must be true, but—heard it from the man outside Hoyts*). **2** an important person. (¶ Originally the commissionaire outside Hoyts Theatre in Melbourne.)

h.p. *abbr.* (also **hp**) **1** hire purchase. **2** horsepower.

HQ *abbr.* headquarters.

hr. *abbr.* hour.

HRT *abbr.* hormone replacement therapy.

Hs *symbol* hassium.

HT *abbr.* high tension.

HTML *abbr.* = HYPERTEXT MARKUP LANGUAGE.

http *abbr.* = HYPERTEXT TRANSFER PROTOCOL.

hub *n.* **1** the central part of a wheel, from which spokes radiate. **2** a central point of activity (*the hub of the universe*).

Hubble, Edwin Powell (1889–1953), American astronomer, whose researches established that the universe is continually expanding so that the galaxies are carried further apart.

hubbub *n.* a loud confused noise of voices.

hubcap *n.* a round metal cover over the hub of a car wheel.

hubris / **hyoo**-bruhs / *n.* arrogant pride or presumption. □ **hubristic** *adj.*

huckleberry *n.* a low shrub of North America with blue or black fruit.

huckster *n.* an aggressive salesman; a hawker. • *verb* **1** haggle. **2** hawk (goods).

huddle *v.* **1** crowd together; nestle closely (*huddled up to him*). **2** (often foll. by *up*) curl one's body into a small space. **3** heap together in a muddle. • *n.* a confused mass. □ **go into a huddle** hold a close or secret conference.

hue / hyoo / *n.* a colour, a tint. □ **hue and cry** a general outcry of alarm, demand, or protest.

huff *n.* a fit of annoyance. • *v.* **1** blow. **2** (esp. as **huff and puff**) bluster self-importantly but ineffectually. □ **in a huff** annoyed and offended.

huffy *adj.* (also **huffish**) **1** apt to take offence. **2** offended. □ **huffily** *adv.*

hug *v.* (**hugged**, **hugging**) **1** squeeze tightly in one's arms. **2** keep close to (*the ship hugged the shore*). • *n.* a strong clasp with the arms.

huge *adj.* extremely large, enormous. □ **hugely** *adv.*

hugger-mugger *adj.* & *adv.* **1** in secret. **2** in disorder. • *n.* **1** confusion. **2** secrecy.

Hughes, William Morris ('Billy', 'The Little Digger') (1862–1952), Australian statesman, Labor and then Nationalist prime minister 1915–23.

Hughie *n.* (also **Huey**) *Aust. jocular* the water god up above who controls rain for farmers and good waves for surfers (*surfing will be great—I've spoken to Hughie about it*). □ **send her down, Hughie!** let there be rain! **send 'em up** (or **whip 'em up**), **Hughie!** *Surfing* let the waves be huge!

Hugo, Victor-Marie (1802–85), French poet, novelist, and dramatist, whose novels include *Notre Dame de Paris* and *Les Misérables*.

Huguenot / **hyoo**-guh-noh / *n.* a member of the Calvinist French Protestants *c.*1560 who were involved in almost continuous civil war with the Catholic majority.

huh *interj.* an expression of disgust or surprise.

hula *n.* a Polynesian dance performed by women.

hulk *n.* **1** the body of an old ship. **2** *hist.* this as a prison for convicts. **3** a large clumsy-looking person or thing.

hulking *adj. colloq.* bulky, clumsy.

hull *n.* **1** the framework of a ship or airship. **2** the green calyx of a ripe strawberry etc. **3** the pod of peas and beans. • *v.* remove the hulls of (strawberries etc.).

hullabaloo *n.* an uproar.

hullo alternative spelling of HELLO.

hum *v.* (**hummed**, **humming**) **1** make a low steady continuous sound like that of a bee. **2** utter a slight sound in hesitating. **3** sing with closed lips. **4** *colloq.* be in a state of activity (*things started humming; make things hum*). **5** *colloq.* give off a bad smell. • *interj.* an exclamation of hesitation. • *n.* **1** a humming sound. **2** an exclamation of hesitation. **3** *colloq.* a bad smell. □ **hum and haw** (or **ha**) hesitate.

human *adj.* **1** of or consisting of human beings (*the human race*). **2** having the qualities that distinguish humankind; not divine, animal, or mechanical. **3** of or characteristic of humans, esp. as being weak, fallible, etc. (*he's only human*). **4** kind, sympathetic, etc. (*is very human*). • *n.* a human being. ❑ **human being** a man, woman, or child. **human nature** the general characteristics and feelings of humankind. **human rights** the rights held to be claimable by any living person, irrespective of race, status, etc. **human shield** a person (or people) placed in a line of fire in order to discourage attack.

humane / hyoo-**mayn** / *adj.* **1** kind-hearted, compassionate, merciful. **2** inflicting the minimum of pain. **3** (of learning etc.) tending to civilise or confer refinement (*literature is one of the humane studies*). ❑ **humanely** *adv.*

humanise *v.* (also -**ize**) make human or humane. ❑ **humanisation** *n.*

humanism / **hyoo**-muh-niz-uhm / *n.* **1** a non-religious philosophy based on liberal human values. **2** (often **Humanism**) literary culture, esp. that of the Renaissance. ❑ **humanist** *n.* **humanistic** *adj.*

humanitarian / hyoo-man-uh-**tair**-ree-uhn / *adj.* concerned with human welfare and the reduction of suffering. • *n.* a humanitarian person. ❑ **humanitarianism** *n.*

humanity *n.* **1** the human race, people (*crimes against humanity*). **2** being human, human nature. **3** being humane, kindheartedness. **4** (**humanities**) subjects concerned with human culture, e.g. language, literature, and history, as opposed to the sciences.

humankind *n.* human beings collectively.

humanly *adv.* **1** in a human way. **2** by human means, with human limitations (*as accurate as is humanly possible*).

humanoid *adj.* having a human form or human characteristics. • *n.* a humanoid thing.

humble *adj.* **1** having or showing a modest estimate of one's own importance, not proud. **2** having or showing low self-esteem. **3** offered with or affected by such low self-esteem (or the pretence of it) (*in my humble opinion*). **4** of low social or political rank (*of humble origins*). **5** (of a thing) not large or showy or elaborate (*a humble cottage*). • *v.* **1** bring low; abase. **2** lower the rank or self-importance of. **3** make humble (*was humbled by the knowledge that he had erred*). ❑ **eat humble pie** make a humble apology; accept humiliation. (¶ From *umble pie*, that made with 'umbles', the offal of deer.) ❑❑ **humbly** *adv.* **humbleness** *n.*

humbug *n.* **1** lying or deception; hypocrisy; nonsense. **2** (in Aboriginal English) trouble, difficulty. **3** an impostor, a hypocrite. **4** a hard, boiled, striped sweet, usu. flavoured with peppermint. • *v.* **1** be or behave like an impostor. **2** *Aust.* be sexually predatory (esp. of a white man with an Aboriginal woman). **3** deceive, hoax. ❑ **humbugger** *n.* **humbuggery** *n.*

humdinger *n. colloq.* a remarkable person or thing.

humdrum *adj.* dull, commonplace, monotonous.

Hume, Hamilton (1797–1873), Australian explorer who in 1824 joined William Hilton Hovell on the important overland exploration of the territory between Goulburn in NSW and Port Phillip (Vic.).

humerus / **hyoo**-muh-ruhs / *n.* (*pl.* **humeri** / **hyoo**-muh-ruy /) the bone in the upper arm, from shoulder to elbow. ❑ **humeral** *adj.*

humid / **hyoo**-muhd / *adj.* (of the air or climate) damp.

humidicrib / hyoo-**mid**-ee-krib / *n.* a small, completely enclosed cot, with devices to monitor and control warmth and humidity, in which premature infants are kept until they are able to survive outside it.

humidifier / hyoo-**mid**-uh-fuy-uh / *n.* a device for keeping the air moist in a room or enclosed space.

humidify / hyoo-**mid**-uh-fuy / *v.* (**humidified**, **humidifying**) make humid.

humidity / hyoo-**mid**-uh-tee / *n.* dampness of the air.

humiliate *v.* cause (a person) to feel disgraced. ❑ **humiliation** *n.*

humility *n.* a humble condition or attitude of mind.

hummingbird *n.* a small tropical bird that vibrates its wings rapidly, producing a humming sound.

hummock *n.* a hump in the ground.

hummus / **huum**-uhs / *n.* (also **houmous**) a dip or appetiser made from ground chickpeas and sesame oil flavoured with lemon and garlic.

humongous / hyoo-**mung**-guhs / *adj.* (also **humungous**) *colloq.* huge, enormous.

humor alternative spelling of HUMOUR.

humoresque / hyoo-muh-**resk** / *n.* a light and lively musical composition.

humorist *n.* a writer or speaker noted for his or her humour.

humorous *adj.* full of humour. ❑ **humorously** *adv.*

humour *n.* (also **humor**) **1** the quality of being amusing. **2** (in full **sense of humour**) the ability to perceive and enjoy amusement and to take a joke. **3** a state of mind (*in a good humour*). **4** (in full **cardinal humour**) *archaic* each of the four bodily fluids (blood, phlegm, choler, and melancholy) formerly believed to determine a person's physical and mental qualities. • *v.* keep (a person) contented by giving way to his or her wishes. ❑ **aqueous humour** the clear fluid between the lens of the eye and the cornea. **vitreous humour** the transparent jelly-like tissue filling the eyeball.

hump *n.* **1** a rounded projecting part as on a camel's back. **2** a deformity on a person's back, where there is abnormal curvature of the spine. **3** a raised bump across the width of a road to slow traffic down at that point. • *v.* **1** form into a hump. **2** hoist or carry (one's pack etc.). □ **hump it** (or **hump one's swag** or **bluey** or **Matilda**) *Aust. colloq.* travel on foot, carrying one's possessions.

humpback *n.* **1** a hunchback. **2** a whale with a hump on its back. □ **humpback bridge** a small steeply-arched bridge. □□ **humpbacked** *adj.*

humph *interj.* & *n.* a sound expressing doubt or dissatisfaction.

Humphries, (John) Barry (1934–), AO, Australian actor and writer, best known for his satirical creation Dame Edna Everage.

humpy *n.* (*pl.* **humpies**) *Aust.* a temporary bush shelter of the Aborigines made from saplings, boughs, etc., a gunyah; an oversmall or substandard house. (¶ Yagara)

humus / hyoo-muhs / *n.* a rich dark organic material, formed by the decay of dead leaves and plants etc. and essential to the fertility of soil.

Hun *n.* **1** *offens.* a German. **2** a member of an Asiatic people who ravaged Europe in the 4th–5th centuries.

hunch *v.* bend into a hump (*hunched his back*). • *n.* **1** a hump. **2** a feeling based on intuition.

hunchback *n.* **1** a person with a hump on his or her back. **2** this hump.

hundred *adj.* & *n.* (*pl.* **hundreds** or **hundred**) ten times ten (100, C) (*a few hundred*). □ **hundred per cent** entirely, completely. **hundreds and thousands** tiny coloured sugar strands used for decorating cakes etc. □□ **hundredth** *adj.* & *n.*

hundredfold *adj.* & *adv.* one hundred times as much or as many.

hundredweight *n.* (*pl.* **hundredweight** or **hundredweights**) **1** a measure of weight in the imperial system, 112 lb (50.802 kg). **2** (in full **metric hundredweight**) a unit of weight equal to 50 kg.

hung see HANG. • *adj.* (in full **well-hung**) *colloq.* (of a male) having a large penis (*he's hung*). □ **hung-over** *colloq.* having a hangover. **hung parliament** one that cannot reach decisions because there is no clear majority in voting. **hung-up** *colloq.* beset by worries; having acute inhibitions, anxieties, etc.

Hungarian / hung-**gair**-ree-uhn / *adj.* of Hungary or its people or language. • *n.* **1** a person from Hungary. **2** the language of Hungary.

Hungary a republic in central Europe.

hunger *n.* **1** need for food, the uncomfortable sensation felt when one has not eaten for some time. **2** a strong desire for something. • *v.* feel hunger; (foll. by *for, after*) crave or desire. □ **hunger strike** refusal of food as a form of protest.

hungry *adj.* (**hungrier**, **hungriest**) feeling hunger. □ **hungrily** *adv.*

hunk *n.* **1** a large roughly cut piece. **2** *colloq.* a sexually attractive (usu. young) man. □ **hunky** *adj.*

hunky-dory *adj. colloq.* excellent.

Hun Sen / huun **sen** / (1951–), Cambodian statesman who, after being co-equal prime minister (1985–93), and second prime minister (1993–98), became prime minister after a coup in 1998.

hunt *v.* **1** pursue (wild animals) for food or sport; (of a wild animal) chase (its prey). **2** make a search (for) (*hunted for it everywhere; hunt it out*). **3** (foll. by *away, from,* etc.) drive off by pursuit (*the Aborigines were hunted from their traditional lands*). • *n.* **1** hunting. □ **hunt down** pursue and capture. **hunt up** search for; look (something) up (in a book etc.).

hunted *adj.* (of a look etc.) terrified as if being hunted.

hunter *n.* **1** one who hunts. **2** a person who seeks something (*fortune hunter*).

huntsman *n.* (*pl.* **huntsmen**) **1** a hunter (sense 1). **2** (in full **huntsman spider**) *Aust.* a large, hairy spider which typically stalks and pounces upon its prey.

huon pine *n.* a tall Tas. conifer exploited for its valuable pale yellow timber. (¶ Huon River in Tas.)

hurdle *n.* **1** one of a series of light upright frames to be jumped over by athletes in a race. **2** a portable rectangular frame with bars, used for a temporary fence. **3** an obstacle or difficulty. **4** (**hurdles**) a hurdle race. • *v.* jump over a hurdle or anything else.

hurdler *n.* a person who runs in hurdle races.

hurdy-gurdy *n.* **1** a musical instrument with a droning sound, played by turning a handle. **2** *colloq.* a barrel organ.

hurl *v.* **1** throw violently. **2** utter vehemently (*hurl insults*). • *n.* a forceful throw.

hurly-burly *n.* a rough bustle of activity.

hurrah *interj.* & *n.* (also **hooray**, **hurray**) an exclamation of joy or approval. • *v.* shout 'hurrah', cheer.

hurricane / **hu**-ruh-kuhn / *n.* **1** a storm with a violent wind, esp. a cyclone. **2** a wind of 65 knots (117 km/h) or more, force 12 on the Beaufort scale. □ **hurricane lamp** a paraffin lamp with the flame protected from high wind.

hurried *adj.* done with great haste. □ **hurriedly** *adv.*

hurry *n.* great haste; the need for this. • *v.* (**hurried**, **hurrying**) **1** move or do something with eager haste or too quickly. **2** cause to move etc. in this way. □ **hurry up** (or **along**) *v.* (cause to) make haste. **hurry-up** *n.* a spur to action. *adj.* providing a spur to action. **in a hurry** **1** hurrying. **2** easily or willingly (*you won't beat that in a hurry; shan't ask again in a hurry*). □□ **hurriedly** *adv.*

hurt v. (**hurt, hurting**) **1** cause pain, damage, or injury to. **2** cause mental pain to, distress. **3** suffer pain (*my leg hurts*). •*n.* **1** injury. **2** harm, wrong.

hurtful *adj.* causing hurt, esp. mental. ☐ **hurtfully** *adv.*

hurtle *v.* move rapidly or noisily; come with a crash (*rain hurtling down; hurtled into the fence*).

husband *n.* a married man in relation to his wife. • *v.* use economically, try to save (*husband one's resources*).

husbandry *n.* **1** farming. **2** careful management of resources.

hush *v.* **1** make or become silent or quiet. **2** (foll. by *up*) prevent (a thing) from becoming generally known. • *interj.* a call for silence. • *n.* silence. ☐ **hush-hush** *adj. colloq.* kept very secret. **hush money** money paid to prevent something from being revealed.

husk *n.* the dry outer covering of certain seeds and fruits. • *v.* remove the husk(s) from.

husky[1] *adj.* (**huskier, huskiest**) **1** (of a person or voice) dry in the throat, hoarse. **2** big and strong, burly. ☐ **huskily** *adv.* **huskiness** *n.*

husky[2] *n.* a dog of a powerful breed used in the Arctic for pulling sledges.

hussar / huu-**zah**, huh- / *n.* a member of a light cavalry regiment.

Hussein[1], ibn Talal (1935–99), King of Jordan from 1953 to 1999.

Hussein[2], Saddam (full name: Saddam bin Hussein at-Takriti) (1937–), Iraqi leader, president from 1979.

hussy *n. derog.* an impudent or promiscuous girl or woman.

hustings *n.* parliamentary election campaign or proceedings. (¶ Originally a temporary platform from which candidates for parliament could address the electors.)

hustle *v.* **1** jostle, push roughly. **2** hurry. **3** make (a person) act quickly and without time to consider things (*hustled him into a decision*). **4** *colloq.* solicit business aggressively. •*n.* hustling; bustle. ☐ **hustler** *n.*

hut *n.* **1** a small roughly-made house or shelter. **2** a large house for lodging skiers.

hutch *n.* a box or cage for rabbits or other small animals.

Hutu / **hoo**-too / *n.* (*pl.* the same or **Hutus**) a member of a Bantu-speaking people who form the majority of the population in Rwanda and Burundi, but who were formerly dominated by the Tutsi minority.

hyacinth *n.* **1** a plant with fragrant bell-shaped flowers, growing from a bulb. **2** purplish blue. ☐ **hyacinth orchid** a leafless Australian orchid consisting of a tall stalk on which are 60 or more large deep pink flowers with darker pink spots. (¶ From HYACINTHUS.)

Hyacinthus *Gk myth.* a beautiful boy loved by the god Apollo and accidentally killed by Apollo with a discus: from his blood the grieving god caused the hyacinth flower to spring.

hyaena alternative spelling of HYENA.

hybrid *n.* **1** an animal or plant that is the offspring of two different species or varieties. **2** something made by combining two different elements. •*adj.* produced in this way, cross-bred. ☐ **hybridism** *n.*

hybridise *v.* (also **-ize**) **1** subject (a species etc.) to cross-breeding. **2** produce hybrids. **3** (of animals or plants) interbreed. ☐ **hybridisation** *n.*

Hyde, Edward, *see* JEKYLL.

Hyde, Miriam (1913–), AO, Australian composer.

hydra *n.* **1** a freshwater polyp with a tubular body and tentacles round the mouth. **2** a thing that is hard to get rid of. (¶ Named after the Hydra in Greek mythology, a water snake with many heads that grew again if cut off.)

hydrangea / huy-**drayn**-juh / *n.* a shrub with white, pink, or blue flowers growing in clusters.

hydrant *n.* a pipe from a water main (esp. in a street) with a nozzle to which a hose can be attached for firefighting etc.

hydrate *n.* / **huy**-drayt / a chemical compound of water with another compound or element. •*v.* / huy-**drayt** / combine chemically with water; cause to absorb water. ☐ **hydration** *n.*

hydraulic / huy-**dro**-lik / *adj.* **1** of water conveyed through pipes or channels. **2** operated by the movement of water or other fluid (*a hydraulic lift*). **3** concerned with the use of water etc. in this way (*hydraulic engineer*). **4** hardening under water (*hydraulic cement*). **5** (**hydraulics**) the science of the conveyance of liquids through pipes etc., esp. as motive power. ☐ **hydraulically** *adv.*

hydride *n.* a compound of hydrogen with an element.

hydro *n.* (*pl.* **hydros**) *colloq.* **1** a hydroelectric power plant. **2** (in Tas.) hydroelectricity.

hydrocarbon *n.* any of a class of compounds of hydrogen and carbon which are found in petrol, coal, and natural gas.

hydrocephalus / huy-druh-**kef**-uh-luhs, -**sef**-uh-luhs / *n.* a condition (esp. of children) in which fluid accumulates on the brain. ☐ **hydrocephalic** *adj.*

hydrochloric acid / huy-druh-**klaw**-rik, -**klo**-rik / a colourless corrosive acid, a solution of hydrogen chloride gas in water.

hydrodynamics *n.* the science of forces exerted by a moving liquid, esp. water. ☐ **hydro-dynamic** *adj.*

hydroelectric *adj.* using water power to produce electricity. ☐ **hydroelectricity** *n.*

hydrofoil *n.* a boat equipped with a structure designed to raise the hull out of the water when the boat is in motion, enabling it to travel fast and economically.

hydrogen *n.* a chemical element (symbol H), a colourless odourless tasteless gas, the lightest

hydrogenate / huy-**droj**-uh-nayt, **huy**-druh-juh-nayt / *v.* charge with or cause to combine with hydrogen. ❑ **hydrogenation** *n.*

substance known, combining with oxygen to form water. ❑ **hydrogen bomb** an immensely powerful bomb releasing energy by fusion of hydrogen nuclei. **hydrogen peroxide** a viscous unstable liquid with strong oxidising properties, used as a bleach. **hydrogen sulphide** a poisonous unpleasant-smelling gas formed by rotting animal matter.

hydrogenous / huy-**droj**-uh-nuhs / *adj.* of or containing hydrogen.

hydrography / huy-**drog**-ruh-fee / *n.* the scientific study of seas, lakes, rivers, etc. ❑ **hydrographer** *n.* **hydrographic** *adj.*

hydrology / huy-**drol**-uh-jee / *n.* the study of the properties of water, esp. of its movement in relation to the land. ❑ **hydrological** *adj.* **hydrologist** *n.*

hydrolyse / **huy**-druh-luyz / *v.* (also -**yze**) decompose by hydrolysis.

hydrolysis / huy-**drol**-uh-suhs / *n.* a chemical reaction of a substance with water, usu. resulting in decomposition.

hydrometer / huy-**drom**-uh-tuh / *n.* an instrument that measures the density of liquids.

hydropathy / huy-**drop**-uh-thee / *n.* the use of water (internally and externally) in the treatment of disease and abnormal physical conditions. ❑ **hydropathic** / huy-druh-**path**-ik / *adj.*

hydrophilic / huy-druh-**fil**-ik / *adj.* having a tendency to combine with water; able to be wetted by water.

hydrophobia / huy-druh-**foh**-bee-uh / *n.* **1** abnormal fear of water, esp. as a symptom of rabies in humans. **2** rabies. ❑ **hydrophobic** *adj.*

hydroplane *n.* **1** a light fast motor boat designed to skim over the surface of water. **2** a finlike attachment enabling a submarine to rise and descend.

hydroponics / huy-druh-**pon**-iks / *n.* the art of growing plants without soil in sand, gravel, or liquid to which nutrients have been added.

hydrosphere *n.* the waters of the earth's surface.

hydrostatic *adj.* of the pressure and other characteristics of water or other liquid at rest. • *n.* (**hydrostatics**) the study of these characteristics.

hydrotherapy *n.* the use of water, esp. swimming, in the treatment of arthritis, paralysis, etc.

hydrous / **huy**-druhs / *adj.* (of substances) containing water.

hydroxide *n.* a compound containing oxygen and hydrogen either as a hydroxide ion or a hydroxyl group.

hydroxyl / huy-**drok**-suhl / *n.* a univalent group containing hydrogen and oxygen.

hyena *n.* (also **hyaena**) a flesh-eating animal like a dog or wolf, with a howl that sounds like wild laughter.

hygiene / **huy**-jeen / *n.* the practice or conditions of cleanliness which help to maintain health and prevent disease. ❑ **hygienic** *adj.* **hygienically** *adv.*

hygienist / **huy**-jee-nuhst / *n.* an expert in hygiene.

hygrometer / huy-**grom**-uh-tuh / *n.* an instrument that measures humidity.

hygroscope / **huy**-gruh-skohp / *n.* an instrument indicating but not measuring the humidity of the air.

hygroscopic / huy-gruh-**skop**-ik / *adj.* **1** of the hygroscope. **2** (of a substance) having a tendency to absorb moisture from the air.

Hymen *Gk myth.* the god of marriage, represented as a strikingly handsome young man.

hymen *n.* a membrane partly closing the external opening of the vagina, usu. broken at the first occurrence of sexual intercourse.

hymenopterous / huy-muh-**nop**-tuh-ruhs / *adj.* of the kind of insects that includes ants, bees, and wasps, having four transparent wings.

hymenosporum / huy-muh-**nos**-puh-ruhm / *n.* the Australian native frangipani.

hymn *n.* a song of (esp. Christian) praise. • *v.* praise or celebrate in hymns.

hymnal *n.* a book of hymns.

hyoscine / **huy**-uh-seen / *n.* a poisonous substance from which a sedative is made, found in plants of the nightshade family.

hype *colloq. n.* **1** extravagant or intensive promotion of a product etc. **2** cheating; a swindle. • *v.* publicise or promote with hype.

hyped up *adj. colloq.* **1** nervously excited or stimulated. **2** (of a car etc. engine) modified and tuned to increase speed, power, etc.

hyper *adj. colloq.* hyperactive, highly-strung.

hyper- *comb. form* above, over; excessively.

hyperactive *adj.* (of a person) abnormally and excessively active. ❑ **hyperactivity** *n.*

hyperbola / huy-**per**-buh-luh / *n.* (*pl.* **hyperbolas** or **hyperbolae**) the curve produced when a cone is cut by a plane that makes a larger angle with the base than the side of the cone does. ❑ **hyperbolic** / huy-puh-**bol**-ik / *adj.*

hyperbole / huy-**per**-buh-lee / *n.* an exaggerated statement that is not meant to be taken literally, e.g. *a stack of work a mile high.* ❑ **hyperbolical** / huy-puh-**bol**-i-kuhl / *adj.*

hypercritical *adj.* excessively critical. ❑ **hypercritically** *adv.*

hyperglycaemia / huy-puh-gluy-**see**-mee-uh / *n.* (also **hyperglycemia**) excess glucose in the bloodstream.

hypermedia *n.* the provision of several media (e.g. audio, video, and graphics) on one computer system.

hypersensitive *adj.* excessively sensitive. ❑ **hypersensitivity** *n.*

hypersonic *adj.* **1** of speeds more than five times that of sound. **2** of sound frequencies above 1,000 megahertz.

hypertension *n.* **1** abnormally high blood pressure. **2** great emotional tension.

hypertext *n.* the provision of several texts on one computer system. □ **hypertext markup language** (**HTML** *or* **html**) a computer programming markup language used esp. for World Wide Web applications, involving the linking of text, graphical display, video clips, etc., and cross-referencing between pages or sections of a website, home page, etc. **hypertext transfer protocol 1** a method of transferring documents on the World Wide Web. **2** (in its abbreviated form **http**) the beginning of an address on the World Wide Web.

hyperthermia *n.* abnormally high body temperature.

hyperventilation *n.* abnormally rapid breathing. □ **hyperventilate** *v.*

hyphen *n.* a sign (-) used to join two words together or to indicate the division of a word (see panel).

hyphenate *v.* separate (a word) or join (words) with a hyphen. □ **hyphenation** *n.*

Hypnos *Gk myth.* the god of sleep, son of Nyx (Night). (¶ Greek *hupnos* 'sleep'.)

hypnosis / hip-**noh**-suhs / *n.* a sleep-like state produced in a person who is then very susceptible to suggestion and acts only if told to do so.

hypnotherapy *n.* the treatment of disease etc. by hypnosis. □ **hypnotherapist** *n.*

hypnotic / hip-**not**-ik / *adj.* **1** of or producing hypnosis or a similar condition. **2** (of a drug) producing sleep. • *n.* a hypnotic drug. □ **hypnotically** *adv.*

hypnotise / **hip**-nuh-tuyz / *v.* (also **-ize**) **1** produce hypnosis in (a person). **2** fascinate, dominate the mind or will of.

hypnotism / **hip**-nuh-tiz-uhm / *n.* the production of hypnosis. □ **hypnotist** / **hip**-nuh-tuhst / *n.*

hypo *n.* **1** sodium thiosulphate (incorrectly called hyposulphite) used as a photographic fixer. **2** *colloq.* (*pl.* **hypos**) a hypodermic syringe or injection.

hypo- *comb. form* under; below normal.

hypocaust / **huy**-puh-kawst / *n.* a system of underfloor heating by hot air, used in ancient Roman houses.

hypochondria / huy-puh-**kon**-dree-uh / *n.* abnormal and ill-founded anxiety about one's health.

hypochondriac *n.* one who suffers from hypochondria. • *adj.* of or affected by hypochondria.

hypocrisy / hi-**pok**-ruh-see / *n.* falsely pretending to be virtuous, insincerity.

hypocrite / **hip**-uh-krit / *n.* a person who is given to hypocrisy. □ **hypocritical** / hip-uh-**krit**-i-kuhl / *adj.* **hypocritically** *adv.*

hypodermic *adj.* injected beneath the skin; used for such injections. • *n.* **1** (in full **hypodermic syringe**) a syringe fitted with a hollow needle through which a liquid can be injected beneath the skin. **2** an injection with this. □ **hypodermically** *adv.*

hypotension *n.* abnormally low blood pressure.

hypotenuse / huy-**pot**-uh-nyooz / *n.* the side opposite the right angle in a right-angled triangle.

Hyphen -

A hyphen is used:

1. to join two or more words so as to form a compound or single expression, e.g.
   mother-in-law, non-stick, dressing-table
   This use is growing less common; often you can do without such hyphens:
   nonstick, treelike, dressing table
2. to join words in an attributive compound (i.e. one put before a noun, like an adjective), e.g.
   a well-known man (but *the man is well known*)
   an out-of-date list (but *the list is out of date*)
3. to join a prefix etc. to a proper name, e.g.
   anti-Darwinian; non-Aboriginal; neo-Nazi; ex-Premier
4. to make a meaning clear by linking words, e.g.
   twenty-odd people (as opposed to *twenty odd people*)
   or by separating a prefix, e.g.
   re-cover (as opposed to *recover*); *re-present* (as opposed to *represent*); *re-sign* (as opposed to *resign*)
5. to separate two identical letters in adjacent parts of a word, e.g.
   pre-exist, co-opt
6. to represent a common second element in the items of a list, e.g.
   two-, three-, or *fourfold*
7. to divide a word if there is no room to complete it at the end of the line, e.g.
   . . . diction-
   ary . . .

The hyphen comes at the end of the line, not at the beginning of the next line. In general, words should be divided at the end of a syllable: dicti-onary would be quite wrong. In handwriting, typing and word-processing, it is safest (and often neatest) not to divide words at all.

hypothalamus *n.* (*pl.* **hypothalami**) the part of the brain controlling body temperature, thirst, hunger, etc.

hypothermia *n.* the condition of having an abnormally low body temperature.

hypothesis / huy-**poth**-uh-suhs / *n.* (*pl.* **hypotheses** / -seez /) a supposition or guess put forward to account for certain facts and used as a basis for further investigation by which it may be proved or disproved.

hypothesise / huy-**poth**-uh-suyz / *v.* (also -**ize**) form or assume a hypothesis.

hypothetical / huy-puh-**thet**-i-kuhl / *adj.* **1** of or based on a hypothesis. **2** supposed but not necessarily true. □ **hypothetically** *adv.*

hypoventilation / huy-poh-ven-tuh-**lay**-shuhn / *n.* abnormally slow breathing.

hyssop / **his**-uhp / *n.* **1** a small fragrant bushy herb formerly used in medicine. **2** a plant used for sprinkling in ancient Jewish rites.

hysterectomy / his-tuh-**rek**-tuh-mee / *n.* surgical removal of the womb.

hysteria / his-**teer**-ree-uh / *n.* **1** wild uncontrollable emotion or excitement. **2** a functional disturbance of the nervous system marked by emotional outbursts.

hysteric / his-**te**-rik / *n.* **1** a hysterical person. **2** (**hysterics**) **a** a hysterical outburst. **b** *colloq.* uncontrollable laughter.

hysterical / his-**te**-ri-kuhl / *adj.* **1** caused by hysteria; suffering from this. **2** (of laughter) uncontrollable. **3** *colloq.* extremely funny. □ **hysterically** *adv.*

Hz *abbr.* hertz.

I *pron.* the person who is speaking or writing and referring to himself or herself. • *n.* (as a Roman numeral) 1. • *symbol* iodine.

-i *suffix* forming the plural of nouns from Latin in *-us* or from Italian in *-e* or *-o* (*foci*; *dilettanti*; *timpani*).

■ **Usage** Plurals in *-s* or *-es* are often also possible especially when the word is well established in English, e.g. *cactus*, plural *cacti* or *cactuses*.

iamb / **uy**-amb / *n.* an iambus.

iambic / uy-**am**-bik / *adj.* of or using iambuses. • *n.pl.* (**iambics**) lines of verse in iambic metre.

iambus / uy-**am**-buhs / *n.* (*pl.* **iambuses** or **iambi**) a metrical foot with one short or unstressed syllable followed by one long or stressed syllable.

iatrogenic / uy-**at**-ruh-jen-ik / *adj.* (of a disease etc.) caused by medical examination or treatment. (¶ Greek *iatros* 'physician'.)

Iberia / uy-**beer**-ree-uh / the ancient name for the peninsula in SW Europe comprising Spain and Portugal. ❑ **Iberian** *adj.* & *n.*

ibex / **uy**-beks / *n.* (*pl.* **ibexes**) a mountain goat with long curving horns.

ibid. *abbr.* ibidem; in the same book or passage etc. (¶ Latin)

ibis / **uy**-buhs / *n.* (*pl.* **ibises**) a wading bird with a long curved bill and long legs.

Ibo / **ee**-boh / *n.* (also **Igbo**) (*pl.* **Ibo** or **Ibos**) **1** a member of a black people of SE Nigeria. **2** their language.

Ibsen / **ib**-suhn /, Henrik (1828–1906), Norwegian dramatist.

ICAC *abbr.* Independent Commission Against Corruption.

Icarus / **ik**-uh-ruhs / *Gk myth.* the son of Daedalus, who escaped from Crete on wings made by his father but was killed when he flew too near the sun and the wax attaching his wings melted.

ice *n.* **1** frozen water, a brittle transparent solid. **2** esp. *Brit.* a portion of ice cream or water ice. • *v.* **1** (foll. by *over* or *up*) become covered with ice (*the pond iced over*). **2** cover or mix with ice; make very cold (*iced drinks*). **3** decorate with icing. ❑ **ice age** a period when much of the Northern hemisphere was covered with glaciers. **ice blue** *adj.* & *n.* very pale blue. **ice-breaker 1** a ship designed to break through ice. **2** a joke, incident, etc. that breaks reserve or tension. **ice-cold** as cold as ice. **ice cream** a sweet creamy frozen food. **ice field** a large expanse of floating ice. **ice hockey** a form of hockey played on ice. **ice pack 1** = PACK ICE. **2** ice applied to the body for medical purposes. **ice skate** *n.* a boot with a blade underneath, for skating on ice. *v.* skate on ice. **on ice** *colloq.* in reserve; temporarily shelved (*our holiday plans had to be put on ice*). **on thin ice** in a risky situation.

iceberg *n.* a huge mass of ice floating in the sea with the greater part under water. ❑ **iceberg lettuce** a crisp round type of lettuce. **the tip of the iceberg** a small evident part of something much larger or more complex.

iceblock *n. Aust.* a confection of flavoured and frozen water.

icecap *n.* the permanent covering of ice in polar regions.

Icehouse Australian rock and pop group with Iva Davies as lead vocalist and songwriter.

Iceland an island republic in the North Atlantic. ❑ **Icelander** *n.*

Icelandic *adj.* of Iceland or its people or language. • *n.* the language of Iceland.

ichthyology / ik-thee-**ol**-uh-jee / *n.* the study of fishes. ❑ **ichthyological** *adj.* **ichthyologist** *n.*

ichthyosaurus / ik-thee-uh-**saw**-ruhs / *n.* (also **ichthyosaur**) (*pl.* **ichthyosauruses**) an extinct sea reptile with a long head, four flippers, and a large tail.

icicle *n.* a pointed piece of ice hanging down, formed when dripping water freezes.

icing *n.* a coating of sugar etc. on cakes or biscuits. ❑ **icing on the cake** an attractive addition or bonus. **icing sugar** powdered sugar used for making icing.

icon / **uy**-kon / *n.* (also **ikon**) **1** an image or statue. **2** (in the Orthodox Church) a painting or mosaic of a holy figure. **3** *Computing* a symbol on a screen of a program, option, or window for selection. **4** an object of particular admiration, esp. as a representative symbol of something (*a literary icon of the 1970s*; *the shed has become an icon in Australia*). ❑ **iconic** *adj.*

iconoclast / uy-**kon**-uh-klast / *n.* **1** a person who attacks cherished beliefs. **2** a destroyer of religious images. ❑ **iconoclasm** *n.* **iconoclastic** *adj.*

iconography / uy-kuh-**nog**-ruh-fee / *n.* **1** the illustration of a subject by drawings. **2** the study of portraits, or of artistic images or symbols.

iconostasis / uy-kuh-**nos**-tuh-suhs / *n.* (*pl.* **iconostases** / -stuh-seez /) (in the Orthodox Church) a screen bearing icons and separating the sanctuary from the nave.

icosahedron / uy-koh-suh-**hee**-druhn / n. a solid figure with twenty faces.

icy adj. (**icier, iciest**) **1** very cold (*icy winds*). **2** covered with ice (*icy roads*). **3** very cold and unfriendly in manner (*an icy voice*). □ **icy pole** *Aust. trademark* = ICEBLOCK. □□ **icily** adv. **iciness** n.

ID abbr. identification, identity.

I'd = **1** I had. **2** I should; I would.

id n. a person's inherited psychological impulses considered as part of the unconscious. (¶ Latin, = that.)

id. abbr. idem.

idea n. **1** a plan etc. formed in the mind by thinking. **2** a mental impression (*give him an idea of what is needed*). **3** intention or purpose (*the idea is to make money*). **4** an opinion (*tries to force his ideas on us*). **5** a vague belief or fancy, a feeling that something is likely (*I have an idea that we shall be late*).

ideal adj. **1** satisfying one's idea of what is perfect (*ideal weather for sailing*). **2** existing only in an idea, visionary (*in an ideal world there would be no disease*). • n. a person, thing, or idea that is regarded as perfect or as a standard for attainment or imitation. □ **ideally** adv.

idealise v. (also **-ize**) regard or represent as perfect. □ **idealisation** n.

idealist / uy-**deer**-luhst / n. a person who has high ideals and tries in an unrealistic way to achieve these. □ **idealism** n. **idealistic** adj.

idée fixe / ee-day **feeks** / n. (pl. **idées fixes** pronounced the same) an idea that is dominant or keeps recurring obsessively. (¶ French, = fixed idea.)

idem / **id**-em, **uy**-dem / adv. in the same author as previously mentioned. • n. the same word or author as previously mentioned. (¶ Latin)

identical adj. **1** the same (*this is the identical place we stayed in last year*). **2** similar in every detail, exactly alike (*no two people have identical fingerprints*). □ **identical twins** twins developed from a single fertilised ovum and therefore of the same sex and very similar in appearance. □□ **identically** adv.

identify v. (**identified, identifying**) **1** establish the identity of, recognise as being a specified person or thing. **2** consider to be identical, equate (*one cannot identify riches and happiness*). **3** (foll. by *with*) **a** associate very closely in feeling or interest (*he has identified himself with the progress of the firm*). **b** (esp. of an indigenous person, and, in Australia, esp. of an Aborigine) associate (oneself or one's people) inseparably with (traditional land and its spiritual associations etc.). **4** (foll. by *with*) regard oneself as sharing the characteristics or fortunes of another person (or another people) (*people like to identify with the characters in a film*). □ **identifier** n. **1** a person or thing that identifies. **2** *Computing* a sequence of characters used to identify or refer to an element of a program. □□ **identification** n. **identifiable** adj.

identikit n. *trademark* a set of pictures of features that can be put together to form a likeness (esp. of a person who is sought by the police) constructed from descriptions.

identity n. **1** the state of being identical. **2** the condition or fact of being a particular person or thing (*many Aborigines have not lost their identity in spite of persecution*). **3** identification or the result of it (*mistaken identity; identity card*). **4** individuality, personality. **5** *colloq.* a well-known person.

ideogram / **id**-ee-oh-gram / n. a symbol indicating the idea (not the sounds forming the name) of a thing, e.g. numerals, Chinese characters, and symbols used in road signs.

ideograph / **id**-ee-oh-grahf, -graf / n. an ideogram. □ **ideographic** adj. **ideography** n.

ideologue / **uy**-dee-uh-log / n. (often *derog.*) a person who fervently supports an ideology.

ideology / uy-dee-**ol**-uh-jee, id-ee- / n. the ideas that form the basis of an economic or political theory etc. (*in Marxist ideology*). □ **ideological** adj. **ideologist** n.

ides / uydz / n.pl. the 15th day of March, May, July, and October, the 13th of other months, in the ancient Roman calendar.

idiocy n. **1** the state of being an idiot. **2** stupid behaviour; a stupid action.

idiom / **id**-ee-uhm / n. **1** a phrase that must be taken as a whole, usu. having a meaning that is not clear from the meanings of the individual words, e.g. *foot the bill* and *a change of heart*. **2** the language used by a people or group (*in the scientific idiom*). **3** a characteristic style of expression in art or music etc.

idiomatic / id-ee-uh-**mat**-ik / adj. **1** relating to or conforming to idiom. **2** characteristic of a particular language. □ **idiomatically** adv.

idiosyncrasy / id-ee-oh-**sing**-kruh-see / n. a person's attitude or behaviour that is unlike that of others; an eccentricity. □ **idiosyncratic** / id-ee-oh-sing-**krat**-ik / adj.

idiot n. **1** a mentally deficient person incapable of rational conduct. **2** a stupid person. □ **idiot board** *colloq.* a board privately displaying to a television newsreader etc. the words to be said during the broadcast. **idiot box** *colloq.* a television set. □□ **idiotic** adj. **idiotically** adv.

idle adj. **1** doing no work, not employed; not active or in use. **2** (of time) not spent in doing something. **3** avoiding work, lazy. **4** worthless, having no special purpose (*idle gossip; idle curiosity*). • v. **1** pass (time) without working, be idle. **2** (of an engine) run slowly in a neutral gear. □ **idly** adv. **idleness** n. **idler** n.

idol n. **1** an image of a god, used as an object of worship. **2** a person or thing that is the object of intense admiration or devotion.

idolater / uy-**dol**-uh-tuh / *n.* a person who worships an idol or idols. □ **idolatry** *n.* **idolatrous** *adj.*

idolise *v.* (also **-ize**) feel excessive admiration or devotion to (a person or thing). □ **idolisation** *n.*

idyll / **id**-uhl, **uy**-duhl / *n.* **1** a short description (usu. in verse) of a peaceful or romantic scene or incident, esp. in country life. **2** a scene or incident of this kind.

idyllic / i-**dil**-ik, uy-**dil**-ik / *adj.* like an idyll, peaceful and happy. □ **idyllically** *adv.*

-ie *see* **-y**.

i.e. *abbr.* = that is. (¶ From the Latin *id est*.)

if *conj.* **1** on condition that (*he'll do it only if you pay him*). **2** in the event that (*if you are tired we will rest*). **3** supposing or granting that (*even if she said it she didn't mean it*). **4** even though (*I'll finish it, if it takes me all day*). **5** whether (*see if you can turn the handle*). **6** in exclamations of wish or surprise (*well, if it isn't Simon!*). • *n.* a condition or supposition (*too many ifs about it*). □ **iffy** *adj. colloq.* uncertain; dubious. **if only 1** expressing regret; I wish that. **2** even if for no other reason than (*I'll come if only to see her*).

Igbo alternative spelling of IBO.

igloo *n.* a dome-shaped Inuit house built of blocks of hard snow.

Ignatius Loyola / ig-nay-shuhs loi-**oh**-luh /, St (1491–1556), Spanish theologian, founder of the Jesuits and their first superior general.

igneous / **ig**-nee-uhs / *adj.* **1** of fire; fiery. **2** (of rocks) formed when molten matter has solidified; volcanic.

ignite / ig-**nuyt** / *v.* **1** set fire to. **2** catch fire.

ignition / ig-**nish**-uhn / *n.* **1** igniting; being ignited. **2** the mechanism providing the spark that ignites the fuel in an internal-combustion engine.

ignoble *adj.* dishonourable in character, aims, purpose, or reputation. □ **ignobly** *adv.*

ignominious / ig-nuh-**min**-ee-uhs / *adj.* bringing contempt or disgrace, humiliating. □ **ignominiously** *adv.*

ignominy / **ig**-nuh-muh-nee / *n.* disgrace, dishonour.

ignoramus / ig-nuh-**ray**-muhs / *n.* (*pl.* **ignoramuses**) an ignorant person.

ignorant *adj.* **1** lacking knowledge. **2** behaving rudely through lack of knowledge of good manners. □ **ignorantly** *adv.* **ignorance** *n.*

ignore *v.* take no notice of, disregard deliberately.

iguana / ig-**wah**-nuh / *n.* a large tree-climbing lizard of the West Indies and tropical America.

iguanodon / ig-**wah**-nuh-don / *n.* a large dinosaur that fed on plants.

ijjecka alternative spelling of ADJIGO.

ikebana / ik-uh-**bah**-nuh / *n.* the art of Japanese flower arrangement.

ikon alternative spelling of ICON.

ileum / **il**-ee-uhm / *n.* (*pl.* **ilea**) the lowest part of the small intestine.

iliac / **il**-ee-ak / *adj.* of the lower body or flanks.

Iliad / **il**-ee-ad / a Greek epic poem, traditionally ascribed to Homer, telling of the climax of the war at Troy (Ilium) between Greeks and Trojans.

ilk *n.* (usu. *derog.*) sort, family, class, etc. (*you and all your ilk ought to be prosecuted*).

I'll = I shall, I will.

ill *adj.* **1** physically or mentally unwell. **2** harmful (*no ill effects*). **3** not favourable (*ill luck*). **4** hostile, unkind (*no ill feelings*). • *adv.* **1** badly, wrongly. **2** unfavourably. **3** imperfectly, scarcely (*ill provided for; can ill afford to do this*). • *n.* evil, harm, injury. □ **ill-advised** unwise. **ill at ease** uncomfortable, embarrassed. **ill-bred** having bad manners. **ill-equipped** not adequately equipped or qualified. **ill-favoured** unattractive. **ill-gotten** gained by evil or unlawful means. **ill health** poor physical or mental condition. **ill-natured** unkind. **ill-treat** (*or* **ill-use**) treat badly or cruelly. **ill will** hostility, unkind feeling. **ill wind** an unfavourable or untoward circumstance.

Illawarra / il-uh-**wo**-ruh / *n.* (in full **Illawarra shorthorn**) a breed of dairy cattle with a red coat developed in the Illawarra district south of Sydney.

illegal *adj.* against the law. □ **illegally** *adv.* **illegality** / il-ee-**gal**-uh-tee / *n.*

illegible / i-**lej**-uh-buhl / *adj.* not legible. □ **illegibly** *adv.* **illegibility** *n.*

illegitimate / il-uh-**jit**-uh-muht / *adj.* **1** born of parents not married to each other. **2** contrary to law or to rules. **3** (of a conclusion in an argument etc.) not logical, wrongly inferred. □ **illegitimately** *adv.* **illegitimacy** *n.*

illiberal / i-**lib**-uh-ruhl / *adj.* **1** intolerant, narrow-minded. **2** without liberal culture; vulgar. **3** stingy. □ **illiberally** *adv.* **illiberality** *n.*

illicit / i-**lis**-uht / *adj.* **1** unlawful, not allowed. **2** unlicensed. □ **illicitly** *adv.*

illiterate / i-**lit**-uh-ruht / *adj.* unable to read and write; showing lack of education. • *n.* an illiterate person. □ **illiterately** *adv.* **illiteracy** *n.*

illness *n.* **1** the state of being ill in body or mind. **2** a particular form of ill health.

illogical *adj.* not logical, contrary to logic. □ **illogically** *adv.* **illogicality** / i-loj-i-**kal**-uh-tee / *n.*

illuminate *v.* **1** light up, make bright. **2** throw light on (a subject), make understandable. **3** decorate (a street or building etc.) with lights. **4** decorate (a manuscript) with gold, coloured designs, etc. □ **illumination** *n.* **illuminative** *adj.*

illumine *v. literary* **1** light up. **2** enlighten spiritually.

illusion / i-**loo**-zhuhn / *n.* **1** something that a person wrongly supposes to exist. **2** a false belief about the nature of something.

illusionist *n.* a person who produces illusions, a conjuror.

illusive / i-**loo**-siv / *adj.* illusory.

illusory / i-**loo**-zuh-ree / *adj.* based on illusion, not real.

illustrate *v.* **1** supply (a book or newspaper etc.) with drawings or pictures. **2** make clear or explain by examples or pictures. **3** serve as an example of. ☐ **illustrator** *n.*

illustration *n.* **1** illustrating. **2** a drawing or picture in a book etc. **3** an example used to explain something.

illustrative / il-uh-struh-tiv / *adj.* serving as an illustration or example. ☐ **illustratively** *adv.*

illustrious / i-**lus**-tree-uhs / *adj.* famous and distinguished. ☐ **illustriousness** *n.*

illywhacker / **il**-ee-wak-uh / *n. Aust.* a small-time confidence trickster.

I'm = I am.

image *n.* **1** a representation of the outward form of a person or thing, e.g. a statue. **2** the optical appearance of something, produced in a mirror or through a lens etc. **3** a mental picture. **4** the general impression of a person, firm, etc. as perceived by the public; a reputation. **5** a simile or metaphor. **6** a semblance, a likeness. • *v.* portray; reflect. ☐ **be the image of** look exactly like. **spitting image** an exact copy or lookalike.

imagery *n.* **1** the use of metaphorical language to produce pictures in the minds of readers or hearers. **2** images; statuary, carving.

imaginary *adj.* existing only in the imagination, not real.

imagination *n.* imagining, the ability to imagine creatively or to use this ability in a practical way.

imaginative *adj.* having or showing imagination. ☐ **imaginatively** *adv.*

imagine *v.* **1** form a mental image of, picture in one's mind. **2** think or believe; suppose (*don't imagine you'll get away with it*). **3** guess (*can't imagine where it has gone*). ☐ **imaginable** *adj.*

imago / i-**may**-goh / *n.* (*pl.* **imagos** or **imagines** / i-**may**-juh-neez /) **1** the fully developed stage of an insect's life, e.g. a butterfly. **2** *Psychol.* **a** an idealised mental picture of oneself or others, esp. a parent. **b** an unconscious image of an archetype.

imam / i-**mahm** / *n.* **1** the leader of prayers in a mosque. **2** the title of various Muslim religious leaders.

Imax / **uy**-maks / *n.* (also **IMAX**) *trademark* a technique of wide-screen cinematography which produces an image approximately ten times larger than that from standard 35-mm film.

imbalance *n.* lack of balance, disproportion.

imbecile / **im**-buh-seel, -suyl / *n.* **1** a mentally deficient person; an adult whose intelligence is equal to that of an average five-year-old child. **2** a stupid person. • *adj.* idiotic. ☐ **imbecility** / im-buh-**sil**-uh-tee / *n.*

imbed alternative spelling of EMBED.

imbibe / im-**buyb** / *v.* **1** drink. **2** absorb (ideas etc.) into the mind. **3** inhale (air).

imbroglio / im-**broh**-lee-oh / *n.* (*pl.* **imbroglios**) **1** a confused situation, usu. involving a disagreement. **2** a confused heap.

imbue / im-**byoo** / *v.* **1** fill (a person) with certain feelings, qualities, or opinions. **2** saturate or dye (with a colour etc.).

IMF *abbr.* International Monetary Fund.

IMHO *abbr.* (esp. in electronic communications) in my humble opinion.

imitable *adj.* able to be imitated.

imitate *v.* **1** copy the behaviour of, take as an example that should be followed. **2** mimic playfully or for entertainment. **3** make a copy of; be like (something else). ☐ **imitator** *n.*

imitation *n.* **1** imitating. **2** something produced by this, a copy. **3** (usu. used as *adj.*) fake, counterfeit (*imitation leather*). **4** the act of mimicking a person or thing for entertainment (*he does imitations*).

imitative / **im**-uh-tuh-tiv / *adj.* imitating.

immaculate *adj.* **1** spotlessly clean. **2** free from moral blemish. **3** free from fault, right in every detail. ☐ **immaculately** *adv.*

Immaculate Conception the Catholic doctrine that the Virgin Mary, from the moment of her conception by her mother, was and remains free from original sin.

immanent / **im**-uh-nuhnt / *adj.* **1** (of qualities) inherent. **2** (of God) permanently pervading the universe. ☐ **immanence** *n.*

■ **Usage** Do not confuse with *imminent*.

Immanuel / i-**man**-yoo-uhl / the name given to Christ as the deliverer of Judah prophesied by Isaiah (Isaiah 7:14, 8:8; Matthew 1:23).

immaterial *adj.* **1** having no physical substance (*as immaterial as a ghost*). **2** of no importance or relevance (*it is now immaterial whether he goes or stays*). ☐ **immateriality** *n.*

immature *adj.* not mature; undeveloped. ☐ **immaturity** *n.*

immeasurable *adj.* not measurable; immense. ☐ **immeasurably** *adv.*

immediate *adj.* **1** occurring or done at once, without delay. **2** nearest, next; direct (*the immediate neighbourhood; my immediate family*). **3** most pressing or urgent (*our immediate concern*). ☐ **immediacy** *n.*

immediately *adv.* **1** without delay. **2** without an intermediary. • *conj.* as soon as.

immemorial *adj.* existing from before what can be remembered or found recorded (*from time immemorial*).

immense *adj.* exceedingly great. ☐ **immensely** *adv.* **immensity** *n.*

immerse *v.* (often foll. by *in*) **1** put completely into water or other liquid. **2** absorb or involve deeply in thought or business etc. **3** embed.

immersion *n.* **1** immersing; being immersed. **2** baptism by putting the whole body into water.

immigrant *n.* a person who immigrates. • *adj.* of immigrants.

immigrate *v.* come into a foreign country as a permanent resident. ☐ **immigration** *n.*

imminent *adj.* (of events) about to occur, likely to occur at any moment. ☐ **imminence** *n.*

■ **Usage** Do not confuse with *immanent*.

immiscible / i-**mis**-uh-buhl / *adj.* (often foll. by *with*) not able to be mixed with another substance.

immobile *adj.* **1** unable to move or be moved. **2** not moving. ☐ **immobility** *n.*

immobilise *v.* (also -**ize**) make or keep immobile. ☐ **immobilisation** *n.*

immoderate *adj.* excessive, lacking moderation. ☐ **immoderately** *adv.*

immodest *adj.* **1** lacking in modesty, indecent. **2** conceited. ☐ **immodestly** *adv.* **immodesty** *n.*

immolate / **im**-uh-layt / *v.* kill or offer as a sacrifice. ☐ **immolation** *n.*

immoral *adj.* not conforming to the accepted rules of morality, morally wrong (esp. in sexual matters). ☐ **immorally** *adv.* **immorality** / i-muh-**ral**-uh-tee / *n.*

immortal *adj.* **1** living for ever, not mortal. **2** famous for all time. • *n.* an immortal being or person. ☐ **immortality** *n.*

immortalise *v.* (also -**ize**) make immortal.

immovable *adj.* (also **immoveable**) **1** unable to be moved. **2** unyielding, not changing in one's purpose; not moved emotionally. **3** (of property) consisting of land, houses, etc. ☐ **immovably** *adv.* **immovability** *n.*

immune *adj.* **1** protected against infection through inoculation etc. **2** relating to immunity (*the immune system*). **3** (foll. by *from*, *to*) exempt from or proof against (a charge, duty, criticism, etc.). ☐ **immune system** those functions in the body responsible for maintaining immunity.

immunise *v.* (also -**ize**) make immune against infection, esp. by inoculation. ☐ **immunisation** *n.*

immunity *n.* **1** the ability of an animal or plant to resist infection by means of antibodies and white blood cells. **2** special exemption from a tax, duty, or penalty.

immunodeficiency *n.* reduction in the body's normal immune defences.

immunology / im-yoo-**nol**-uh-jee / *n.* the scientific study of resistance to infection. ☐ **immunological** *adj.* **immunologist** *n.*

immunotherapy *n.* the prevention or treatment of disease with substances that stimulate the immune response.

immure / i-**myoor** / *v.* imprison, shut in.

immutable / i-**myoo**-tuh-buhl / *adj.* unchangeable. ☐ **immutably** *adv.* **immutability** *n.*

imp *n.* **1** a small devil. **2** a mischievous child.

impact *n.* / **im**-pakt / **1** a collision. **2** the force exerted when one body collides with another. **3** the force exerted by the influence of new ideas. • *v.* / im-**pakt** / pack, drive, or wedge firmly into something or together. ☐ **impact on** *v.* have a strong effect on. ☐☐ **impaction** *n.*

impacted *adj.* (of a tooth) wedged between another tooth and the jaw.

impair *v.* damage, cause weakening of (*impair one's health*). ☐ **impairment** *n.*

impaired *adj.* (in *comb.*) having a disability of a specified kind.

impala / im-**pah**-luh / *n.* (*pl.* **impala** or **impalas**) a small African antelope.

impale *v.* fix or pierce through with a sharp-pointed object. ☐ **impalement** *n.*

impalpable / im-**pal**-puh-buhl / *adj.* **1** unable to be felt by touch. **2** not easily grasped by the mind. **3** (of a powder) so fine that grains cannot be felt. ☐ **impalpably** *adv.* **impalpability** *n.*

impanel alternative spelling of EMPANEL.

impart *v.* **1** give. **2** reveal or make (information etc.) known.

impartial / im-**pah**-shuhl / *adj.* not favouring one more than another. ☐ **impartially** *adv.* **impartiality** / im-pah-shee-**al**-uh-tee / *n.*

impassable *adj.* (of roads or barriers) impossible to travel on or over. ☐ **impassably** *adv.* **impassability** *n.*

impasse / **im**-pahs / *n.* a deadlock.

impassible / im-**pas**-uh-buhl / *adj.* incapable of feeling, emotion, or injury; impassive. ☐ **impassibly** *adv.* **impassibility** *n.*

impassioned / im-**pash**-uhnd / *adj.* full of deep feeling (*an impassioned appeal*).

impassive *adj.* not feeling or showing emotion. ☐ **impassively** *adv.* **impassiveness** *n.* **impassivity** *n.*

impasto *n.* a technique in art of laying on paint thickly.

impatiens *n.* any of several flowering plants including balsam and busy Lizzie.

impatient *adj.* **1** unable to wait patiently; restlessly eager. **2** showing lack of patience, irritated (*got an impatient reply*). **3** (foll. by *of*) intolerant (*impatient of delay*). ☐ **impatiently** *adv.* **impatience** *n.*

impeach *v.* **1** accuse of treason or other serious crime against the nation, and bring for trial. **2** call in question, disparage (a person's integrity, etc.). ☐ **impeachment** *n.*

impeccable *adj.* faultless. ☐ **impeccably** *adv.* **impeccability** *n.*

impecunious / im-puh-**kyoo**-nee-uhs / *adj.* having little or no money. ☐ **impecuniosity** *n.*

impedance / im-**pee**-duhns / *n.* the total resistance of an electric circuit to the flow of alternating current.

■ **Usage** Do not confuse with *impediment*.

impede *v.* hinder.

impediment *n.* **1** a hindrance, an obstruction. **2** a defect in speech, e.g. a lisp or stammer.

■ **Usage** Do not confuse with *impedance*.

impedimenta / im-ped-i-**men**-tuh / *n.pl.* encumbrances; travelling equipment, esp. of an army.

impel *v.* (**impelled, impelling**) **1** urge or drive to do something (*curiosity impelled her to investigate*). **2** send or drive forward, propel.

impending *adj.* (of an event or danger) imminent, about to happen.

impenetrable *adj.* **1** unable to be penetrated. **2** incomprehensible. **3** inaccessible to ideas etc. □ **impenetrably** *adv.* **impenetrability** *n.*

impenitent *adj.* not sorry, not repentant. □ **impenitence** *n.*

imperative / im-**pe**-ruh-tiv / *adj.* **1** expressing a command. **2** essential, obligatory (*further economies are imperative*). •*n.* **1** a command. **2** *Grammar* a form of a verb used in making commands (e.g. *come* in *come here!*). **3** something essential or obligatory (*survival is the first imperative*).

imperceptible *adj.* not perceptible; very slight or gradual and therefore difficult to see. □ **imperceptibly** *adv.* **imperceptibility** *n.*

impercipient *adj.* lacking in perception. □ **impercipience** *n.*

imperfect *adj.* **1** not perfect; incomplete. **2** *Grammar* of the tense of a verb used to denote action going on but not completed, esp. in the past, e.g. *she was singing*. •*n. Grammar* the imperfect tense.

imperfection *n.* **1** being imperfect. **2** a mark or fault.

imperial *adj.* **1** of an empire or an emperor or empress. **2** majestic. **3** (of weights and measures) used by statute in the UK, formerly for all goods and still for certain goods (*an imperial gallon*). □ **imperially** *adv.*

imperialism *n.* **1** belief in the desirability of acquiring colonies and dependencies. **2** imperial rule or authority. □ **imperialist** *n.* **imperialistic** *adj.*

imperil *v.* (**imperilled, imperilling**) endanger.

imperious / im-**peer**-ree-uhs / *adj.* commanding, bossy. □ **imperiously** *adv.* **imperiousness** *n.*

imperishable *adj.* not able to perish, indestructible.

impermanent *adj.* not permanent. □ **impermanence** *n.* **impermanency** *n.*

impermeable / im-**per**-mee-uh-buhl / *adj.* not able to be penetrated, esp. by liquid. □ **impermeability** *n.*

impersonal *adj.* **1** not influenced by personal feeling, showing no emotion. **2** not referring to any particular person. **3** having no existence as a person (*nature's impersonal forces*). **4** *Grammar* (of verbs) used with 'it' to make general statements such as 'it is raining'. □ **impersonally** *adv.* **impersonality** *n.*

impersonate *v.* **1** play the part of. **2** pretend to be (another person) for entertainment or in fraud. □ **impersonation** *n.* **impersonator** *n.*

impertinent *adj.* insolent, not showing proper respect. □ **impertinently** *adv.* **impertinence** *n.*

imperturbable / im-puh-**ter**-buh-buhl / *adj.* not excitable, calm. □ **imperturbably** *adv.* **imperturbability** *n.*

impervious / im-**per**-vee-uhs / *adj.* (usu. foll. by *to*) **1** not able to be penetrated (*impervious to water*). **2** not influenced, not responsive (*impervious to argument*).

impetigo / im-puh-**tuy**-goh / *n.* a contagious skin disease causing spots that form yellowish crusts.

impetuous / im-**pe**-choo-uhs, -**pet**-yoo-uhs / *adj.* **1** moving quickly or violently (*an impetuous dash*). **2** acting or done on impulse. □ **impetuously** *adv.* **impetuosity** *n.*

impetus / **im**-puh-tuhs / *n.* (*pl.* **impetuses**) **1** the force or energy with which a body moves. **2** a driving force (*the treaty gave an impetus to trade*).

impiety / im-**puy**-uh-tee / *n.* lack of reverence.

impinge *v.* (usu. foll. by *on* or *upon*) **1** make an impact. **2** encroach (*your statement impinges on the absurd*).

impious / **im**-pee-uhs / *adj.* not reverent; wicked. □ **impiously** *adv.*

impish *adj.* of or like an imp; mischievous. □ **impishly** *adv.* **impishness** *n.*

implacable / im-**plak**-uh-buhl / *adj.* not able to be placated, relentless. □ **implacably** *adv.* **implacability** *adv.*

implant *v.* / im-**plahnt**, -**plant** / **1** plant, insert. **2** insert or fix (ideas etc.) in the mind. **3** insert (tissue or other substance) in a living thing. •*n.* / **im**-plahnt, -plant / a thing implanted, implanted tissue etc. □ **implantation** *n.*

implausible *adj.* not plausible. □ **implausibly** *adv.* **implausibility** *n.*

implement *n.* / **im**-pluh-muhnt / a tool or instrument for working with. •*v.* / **im**-pluh-ment / put into effect (*we implemented the scheme*). □ **implementation** *n.*

implicate *v.* **1** involve or show (a person) to be involved in a crime etc. **2** lead to as a consequence or inference; imply.

implication *n.* **1** implicating; being implicated. **2** implying; being implied. **3** something that is implied.

implicit / im-**plis**-uht / *adj.* **1** implied though not made explicit. **2** absolute, unquestioning (*expect implicit obedience*). □ **implicitly** *adv.*

implode *v.* burst or cause to burst inwards. □ **implosion** *n.*

implore *v.* request earnestly, entreat. □ **imploringly** *adv.*

imply *v.* (**implied, implying**) **1** suggest without stating directly, hint. **2** mean (*silence implies guilt*). **3** involve the truth or existence of (*the beauty of the carving implies that they had skilled craftsmen*).

impolite *adj.* ill-mannered, rude. ◻ **impolitely** *adv.*

impolitic / im-**pol**-uh-tik / *adj.* unwise, inexpedient.

imponderable / im-**pon**-druh-buhl, -duh-ruh-buhl / *adj.* **1** not able to be estimated. **2** weightless, very light. • *n.* (usu. as **imponderables**) something difficult or impossible to assess.

import *v.* / im-**pawt**, **im**- / **1** bring in from abroad or from an outside source. **2** imply, indicate. • *n.* / **im**-pawt / **1** the importing of goods etc., something imported. **2** what is implied; meaning (*what is the import of his remark?*). **3** importance. ◻ **importation** *n.* **importer** *n.*

important *adj.* **1** having or able to have a great effect; momentous. **2** (of a person) having great authority or influence. **3** pompous (*he has an important manner*). ◻ **importantly** *adv.* **importance** *n.*

importunate / im-**paw**-chuh-nuht, -tyoo-nuht / *adj.* making persistent or pressing requests. ◻ **importunity** *n.*

importune / im-**paw**-tyoon, im-puh-**tyoon** / *v.* **1** pester (a person) with requests, demands, etc. **2** solicit as a prostitute.

impose *v.* **1** (often foll. by *on*) put (a tax or obligation etc.) (*imposed heavy duties on tobacco*). **2** (often foll. by *on*) inflict (*imposed a great strain on our resources*). **3** force to be accepted (*imposed his ideas on the group*). **4** (foll. by *on*) take unfair advantage of (*we don't want to impose on your hospitality*).

imposing *adj.* impressive, formidable, esp. in appearance.

imposition *n.* **1** the act of imposing something. **2** something imposed, e.g. a tax or duty. **3** a burden imposed unfairly.

impossible *adj.* **1** not possible, unable to be done or to exist. **2** *colloq.* outrageous, unendurable (*an impossible person*). ◻ **impossibly** *adv.* **impossibility** *n.*

impost / **im**-post, -pohst / *n.* **1** a tax or duty levied. **2** the upper course of a pillar, carrying an arch.

impostor *n.* (also **imposter**) a person who fraudulently pretends to be someone else.

imposture *n.* a fraudulent deception.

impotent / **im**-puh-tuhnt / *adj.* **1** powerless, unable to take action. **2** (of a man) unable to achieve an erection or orgasm. ◻ **impotence** *n.*

impound *v.* **1** take (another person's property) into legal custody, confiscate. **2** shut up (animals etc.) in a pound.

impoverish *v.* **1** cause to become poor. **2** exhaust the natural strength or fertility of (*impoverished soil*). ◻ **impoverishment** *n.*

impracticable *adj.* incapable of being put into practice. ◻ **impracticably** *adv.* **impracticability** *n.*

impractical *adj.* not practical, unwise. ◻ **impracticality** *n.*

imprecation / im-pruh-**kay**-shuhn / *n.* a spoken curse.

imprecise *adj.* not precise. ◻ **imprecisely** *adv.* **imprecision** *n.*

impregnable / im-**preg**-nuh-buhl / *adj.* safe against attack (*an impregnable fortress; an impregnable argument*). ◻ **impregnably** *adv.* **impregnability** *n.*

impregnate / im-**preg**-nayt / *v.* **1** introduce sperm or pollen into and fertilise (a female animal or plant); make pregnant. **2** penetrate all parts of (a substance), fill or saturate (*the water was impregnated with salts*). ◻ **impregnation** *n.*

impresario / im-pruh-**sah**-ree-oh / *n.* (*pl.* **impresarios**) an organiser of public entertainment; the manager of a theatre or music company.

impress *v.* / im-**pres** / **1** make (a person) form a strong (usu. favourable) opinion of something. **2** (often foll. by *on*) fix firmly in the mind (*impressed on them the need for haste*). **3** press a mark into, stamp with a mark. • *n.* / **im**-pres / **1** an impressed mark. **2** a characteristic mark or quality.

impression *n.* **1** an effect produced on the mind. **2** an uncertain idea, belief, or memory. **3** an imitation of a person or sound, done for entertainment. **4** the impressing of a mark; an impressed mark. **5** a reprint of a book etc. made with few or no alterations to its contents. ◻ **be under the impression** think (that something is a fact).

impressionable *adj.* easily influenced. ◻ **impressionably** *adv.* **impressionability** *n.*

Impressionism *n.* **1** a style of painting in the late 19th century giving the general impression of a subject, esp. by using the effects of light, without elaborate detail. **2** a similar style in music or literature. ◻ **Impressionist** *n.*

impressionistic *adj.* **1** (**Impressionistic**) in the style of Impressionism. **2** subjective, unsystematic. ◻ **impressionistically** *adv.*

impressive *adj.* making a strong impression; arousing admiration and approval. ◻ **impressively** *adv.*

imprimatur / im-pruh-**mah**-tuh, -**may**-tuh / *n.* **1** *Catholic Church* an official licence to print (a religious book etc.). **2** official approval (*the headmaster gave our project his imprimatur*).

imprint *n.* / **im**-print / **1** a mark made by pressing or stamping a surface (*the imprint of a foot*). **2** a publisher's name etc. printed in a book. • *v.* / im-**print** / **1** impress or stamp a mark etc. on. **2** establish firmly in the mind.

imprison *v.* **1** put into prison. **2** confine (*imprisoned all day in the house*). ◻ **imprisonment** *n.*

improbable *adj.* not likely to be true or to happen. ◻ **improbably** *adv.* **improbability** *n.*

improbity / im-**proh**-buh-tee / *n.* dishonesty, wickedness.

impromptu / im-**promp**-tyoo / *adv.* & *adj.* without preparation or rehearsal. •*n.* **1** a short instrumental composition, often improvisatory in style. **2** an impromptu performance or speech.

improper *adj.* **1** wrong, incorrect (*improper use of the word 'infer'*). **2** not conforming to the rules of social or lawful conduct. **3** indecent. ☐ **improper fraction** one with the numerator greater than the denominator, e.g. 5/3. ☐ **improperly** *adv.*

impropriety / im-pruh-**pruy**-uh-tee / *n.* being improper; an improper act or remark.

improve *v.* **1** make or become better. **2** make good use of (opportunities etc.) (*we must improve the occasion*). **3** (as **improving** *adj.*) giving moral benefit (*improving literature*). ☐ **improved value** (of land) the value with the addition of betterments (e.g. a house). **on the improve** *Aust.* showing signs of betterment. ☐ ☐ **improvable** *adj.* **improver** *n.*

improvement *n.* **1** improving, being improved. **2** an addition or alteration that improves something or adds to its value.

improvident / im-**prov**-uh-duhnt / *adj.* not providing for future needs; wasteful. ☐ **improvidently** *adv.* **improvidence** *n.*

improvise / **im**-pruh-vuyz / *v.* **1** compose or perform (music, verse, etc.) extempore. **2** provide or construct using whatever materials are at hand (*improvised a bed from cushions and rugs*). ☐ **improvisation** *n.* **improviser** *n.* **improvisatory** *adj.*

imprudent / im-**proo**-duhnt / *adj.* unwise, rash. ☐ **imprudently** *adv.* **imprudence** *n.*

impudent / **im**-pyoo-duhnt / *adj.* impertinent, cheeky. ☐ **impudently** *adv.* **impudence** *n.*

impugn / im-**pyoon** / *v.* express doubts about the truth or honesty of; try to discredit (*we do not impugn their motives*). ☐ **impugnment** *n.*

impulse *n.* **1** a sudden inclination to act, without thought for the consequences (*did it on impulse*). **2** a push or thrust; impetus. **3** a stimulating force in a nerve, causing a muscle to react. ☐ **impulse buying** buying of goods on impulse and not because of previous planning.

impulsion *n.* **1** impelling, a push; impetus. **2** a mental impulse.

impulsive *adj.* **1** (of a person) habitually acting on impulse. **2** (of an action) done on impulse. ☐ **impulsively** *adv.* **impulsiveness** *n.*

impunity / im-**pyoo**-nuh-tee / *n.* freedom from punishment or injury.

impure *adj.* **1** adulterated; mixed with foreign matter. **2** unchaste; obscene (*impure thoughts*).

impurity *n.* **1** being impure. **2** an impure substance or element.

imputation *n.* **1** an instance of imputing. **2** (in full **dividend imputation**) *Aust.* the crediting to shareholders of tax a company has paid on profits it distributes as dividends to those shareholders, thereby eliminating or reducing the tax liability of those shareholders.

impute / im-**pyoot** / *v.* attribute (a fault etc.) to (*imputed his bankruptcy to mere bad luck*).

In *symbol* indium.

in *prep.* expressing position or state: **1** of inclusion within the limits of space, time, circumstance, or surroundings. **2** of quantity or proportion (*they are packed in tens*). **3** of form or arrangement (*hanging in folds*). **4** of activity, occupation, or membership (*he is in the army*). **5** wearing as dress or colour etc. (*in gumboots*). **6** of method or means of expression (*spoke in French*). **7** with the instrument or means of (*written in ink*). **8** with the identity of (*found a friend in Mary*). **9** under the influence of (*spoke in anger*). **10** having the condition of; affected by (*in bad health; in danger*). **11** (of an animal) pregnant with (*in calf*). **12** with respect to (*lacking in courage*). **13** as the content of (*there's not much in it*). **14** after the time of (*back in ten minutes*). **15** into. •*adv.* **1** expressing position bounded by certain limits, or motion to a point enclosed by these (*come in*). **2** at home (*will you be in?*). **3** on or towards the inside (*with the fur side in*). **4** in fashion, season, or office; elected; in effective or favourable action (*long hair is in; Labor is in; my luck was in*). **5** (of the tide) at the highest point. **6** (in cricket and baseball) batting (*which side is in?*). **7** having arrived or been gathered or received (*the train is in; harvest is in*). •*adj.* **1** internal; living etc. inside. **2** fashionable (*it's the in thing to do*). ☐ **be in for** be about to experience (*she is in for a surprise*). **be in on** *colloq.* be aware of or sharing in (a secret or activity). **in all** in total number. **ins and outs** the details of an activity or procedure. **in so far as** to the extent that (*he carried out orders only in so far as he did not openly disobey them*). **in with** on good terms with.

in. *abbr.* inch(es).

inability *n.* being unable.

in absentia / ab-**sen**-tee-uh / *adv.* in his, her, or their absence. (¶ Latin)

inaccessible *adj.* not accessible; unapproachable. ☐ **inaccessibly** *adv.* **inaccessibility** *n.*

inaccurate *adj.* not accurate. ☐ **inaccurately** *adv.* **inaccuracy** *n.*

inaction *n.* lack of action, doing nothing.

inactive *adj.* **1** not active. **2** not operating. **3** indolent. ☐ **inactively** *adv.* **inactivity** *n.*

inadequate *adj.* **1** not adequate, insufficient. **2** not sufficiently able or competent (*felt inadequate*). ☐ **inadequately** *adv.* **inadequacy** *n.*

inadmissible *adj.* not allowable. ☐ **inadmissibly** *adv.* **inadmissibility** *n.*

inadvertent / in-uhd-**ver**-tuhnt / *adj.* **1** unintentional. **2** negligent, inattentive. ☐ **inadvertently** *adv.* **inadvertence** *n.*

inadvisable *adj.* not advisable. ☐ **inadvisability** *n.*

inalienable / in-**ay**-lyuh-nuh-buhl / *adj.* not able to be given away or taken away (*an inalienable right*).

inamorata / in-am-uh-**rah**-tah / *n.* (*pl.* **inamoratas**) *literary* a female lover.

inamorato *n. literary* a male lover.

inane *adj.* **1** silly, lacking sense. **2** empty, void. ☐ **inanely** *adv.* **inanity** / in-**an**-uh-tee / *n.*

inanimate / in-**an**-uh-muht / *adj.* **1** (of rocks and other objects) lifeless; (of plants) lacking animal life. **2** showing no sign of life.

inapplicable / in-uh-**plik**-uh-buhl, in-**ap**-li-kuh-buhl / *adj.* not applicable.

inapposite / in-**ap**-uh-zuht / *adj.* not apposite, unsuitable. ☐ **inappositely** *adv.*

inappreciable / in-uh-**pree**-shuh-buhl / *adj.* **1** imperceptible; not worth reckoning (*the difference was so slight as to be inappreciable*). **2** that cannot be appreciated. ☐ **inappreciably** *adv.*

inappropriate / in-uh-**proh**-pree-uht / *adj.* unsuitable. ☐ **inappropriately** *adv.* **inappropriateness** *n.*

inapt / in-**apt** / *adj.* **1** not apt or suitable. **2** unskilful. ☐ **inaptitude** *n.* **inaptly** *adv.* **inaptness** *n.*

■ **Usage** See usage note at INEPT.

inarticulate / in-ah-**tik**-yoo-luht / *adj.* **1** not expressed in words (*an inarticulate cry*). **2** unable to speak distinctly (*was inarticulate with rage*). **3** unable to express one's ideas clearly. ☐ **inarticulately** *adv.*

inasmuch as 1 since, because. **2** in so far as.

inattention *n.* lack of attention, neglect.

inattentive *adj.* not attentive, not paying attention. ☐ **inattentively** *adv.* **inattentiveness** *n.*

inaudible / in-**aw**-duh-buhl / *adj.* not audible, unable to be heard. ☐ **inaudibly** *adv.*

inaugural / in-**aw**-gyuh-ruhl / *adj.* of or for an inauguration (*the inaugural ceremony*).

inaugurate / in-**aw**-gyuh-rayt / *v.* **1** admit (a person) to office with a ceremony. **2** enter ceremonially upon (an undertaking); open (a building or exhibition etc.) formally. **3** be the beginning of, introduce. ☐ **inauguration** *n.* **inaugurator** *n.*

inauspicious / in-aw-**spish**-uhs / *adj.* not auspicious; unlucky. ☐ **inauspiciously** *adv.* **inauspiciousness** *n.*

inborn *adj.* existing in a person or animal from birth; natural (*an inborn ability*).

inbred *adj.* **1** produced by inbreeding. **2** inborn.

inbreeding *n.* breeding from closely related animals or persons.

inbuilt *adj.* built-in.

Inc. *abbr.* US & *Aust.* Incorporated.

Inca *n.* a member of an American Indian people in Peru before the Spanish conquest.

incalculable *adj.* unable to be calculated. ☐ **incalculably** *adv.* **incalculability** *n.*

incandesce / in-kan-**des** / *v.* glow with heat; cause to do this.

incandescent / in-kan-**des**-uhnt / *adj.* glowing with heat, shining. ☐ **incandescence** *n.*

incantation / in-kan-**tay**-shuhn / *n.* words or sounds to be uttered as a magic spell.

incapable *adj.* **1** not capable. **2** helpless, powerless. ☐ **incapably** *adv.* **incapability** *n.*

incapacitate / in-kuh-**pas**-uh-tayt / *v.* **1** disable. **2** make ineligible.

incapacity *n.* inability, lack of sufficient strength or power.

incarcerate / in-**kah**-suh-rayt / *v.* imprison. ☐ **incarceration** *n.*

incarnate *adj.* / in-**kah**-nuht / embodied in flesh, esp. in human form (*a devil incarnate*). • *v.* / in-**kah**-nayt, in-**kah**- / **1** embody in flesh. **2** put (an idea etc.) into concrete form. **3** be a living embodiment of (a quality etc.).

incarnation / in-kah-**nay**-shuhn / *n.* **1** embodiment, esp. in human form. **2** (**the Incarnation**) the embodiment of God in human form as the Christ.

incautious / in-**kaw**-shuhs / *adj.* not cautious, rash. ☐ **incautiously** *adv.* **incautiousness** *n.*

incendiary / in-**sen**-dyuh-ree / *adj.* **1** (of a bomb etc.) designed to cause a fire; containing chemicals that ignite. **2** of arson; guilty of arson. **3** tending to stir up strife, inflammatory. • *n.* **1** an incendiary bomb. **2** an arsonist; an agitator or troublemaker.

incense[1] / **in**-sens / *n.* **1** a substance that produces a sweet smell when burning. **2** its smoke, used esp. in religious ceremonies.

incense[2] / in-**sens** / *v.* make angry.

incentive / in-**sen**-tiv / *n.* something that rouses or encourages a person to some action or effort. • *adj.* acting as an incentive, inciting.

inception / in-**sep**-shuhn / *n.* the beginning of the existence of something.

inceptive / in-**sep**-tiv / *adj.* beginning, initial.

incessant / in-**ses**-uhnt / *adj.* unceasing, continually repeated. ☐ **incessantly** *adv.*

incest / **in**-sest / *n.* sexual intercourse between people regarded as too closely related to marry each other.

incestuous / in-**ses**-choo-uhs, -tyoo- / *adj.* **1** involving incest. **2** guilty of incest.

inch *n.* **1** a measure of length, one twelfth of a foot (= 2.54 cm). **2** an amount of rainfall that would cover a surface to a depth of 1 inch. **3** a very small amount (*would not yield an inch*). • *v.* move slowly and gradually (*they inched forward*). ☐ **every inch** entirely (*looked every inch a soldier*). **within an inch of** almost to the point of.

inchoate / **in**-koh-ayt, in-**koh**- / *adj.* **1** just begun. **2** not yet fully developed. ☐ **inchoation** *n.*

incidence / **in**-suh-duhns / *n.* **1** the rate at which something occurs or affects people or things (*studied the incidence of the disease*). **2** the falling of something (e.g. a ray of light) on a surface.

incident *n.* **1** an event, esp. a minor one. **2** a piece of hostile activity (*frontier incidents*). **3** a public disturbance or accident (*the protest march took place without incident*). **4** an event that attracts general attention. • *adj.* **1** (often foll. by *to*) liable

incidental to happen; accompanying something (*the risks incident to a pilot's career*). **2** (of rays of light etc.) falling on a surface.

incidental *adj.* **1** occurring as a minor accompaniment (*incidental expenses*). **2** liable to occur in consequence of or in connection with something (*the incidental hazards of exploration*). **3** casual, occurring by chance. ☐ **incidental music** music played as a background to the action of a film or play.

incidentally *adv.* **1** in an incidental way. **2** as an unconnected comment; by the way.

incinerate / in-**sin**-uh-rayt / *v.* burn to ashes. ☐ **incineration** *n.*

incinerator / in-**sin**-uh-ray-tuh / *n.* a furnace or enclosed device for burning rubbish.

incipient / in-**sip**-ee-uhnt / *adj.* in its early stages, beginning (*incipient decay*).

incise / in-**suyz** / *v.* **1** make a cut in (a surface). **2** engrave by cutting.

incision / in-**siz***h*-uhn / *n.* **1** incising. **2** a cut, esp. one made surgically into the body.

incisive / in-**suy**-siv / *adj.* clear and decisive (*made incisive comments*). ☐ **incisively** *adv.* **incisiveness** *n.*

incisor / in-**suy**-zuh / *n.* a sharp-edged cutting tooth at the front of the mouth.

incite / in-**suyt** / *v.* urge on to action, stir up. ☐ **incitement** *n.*

incivility *n.* **1** lack of civility. **2** an impolite act or remark.

inclement / in-**klem**-uhnt / *adj.* (of weather) cold, wet, or stormy. ☐ **inclemency** *n.*

inclination *n.* **1** a slope or slant; a leaning or bending movement. **2** a tendency. **3** a liking or preference.

incline *v.* / in-**kluyn** / **1** lean, slope. **2** bend (the head or body) forward. **3** have or cause a certain tendency, influence (*his manner inclines me to believe him*). • *n.* / **in**-kluyn / a slope. ☐ **be inclined** have a certain tendency or willingness (*the door is inclined to bang; I'm inclined to agree*).

include *v.* **1** have or regard or treat as part of a whole. **2** put into a certain category or list etc.

inclusion *n.* **1** the action of including. **2** the fact or condition of being included. **3** that which is included. **4** (in *pl.*) *Aust.* soft furnishings as included in the purchase price of a house.

inclusive *adj.* **1** including the limits mentioned and the part between (*pages 7 to 26 inclusive*). **2** (often foll. by *of*) including. **3** (of language) nonsexist; deliberately worded so as to include both women and men explicitly rather than using masculine forms to cover both. ☐ **inclusively** *adv.*

incognisant / in-**kog**-ni-zuhnt / *adj.* (also **incognizant**) unaware. ☐ **incognisance** *n.*

incognito / in-kog-**nee**-toh / *adj.* & *adv.* with one's identity kept secret (*she was travelling incognito*). • *n.* (*pl.* **incognitos**) the identity assumed by one who is incognito.

incoherent / in-koh-**heer**-ruhnt / *adj.* rambling in speech or in reasoning. ☐ **incoherently** *adv.* **incoherence** *n.*

incombustible *adj.* not able to be burnt.

income *n.* money received during a certain period (esp. a year) as wages or salary, interest on investments, etc. ☐ **income tax** tax that must be paid on annual income.

-incomer *combining form* earning a specified level of income (*middle-incomer; low-incomers*).

incoming *adj.* **1** coming in (*the incoming tide*). **2** succeeding another person (*the incoming president*). • *n.* (**incomings**) revenue, income.

incommensurable *adj.* not commensurable. ☐ **incommensurability** *n.*

incommensurate *adj.* **1** not commensurate; disproportionate, inadequate. **2** incommensurable.

incommode / in-kuh-**mohd** / *v.* inconvenience, disturb.

incommodious / in-kuh-**moh**-dee-uhs / *adj. formal* too small for comfort; inconvenient.

incommunicable *adj.* unable to be communicated.

incommunicado / in-kuh-myoo-nuh-**kah**-doh / *adj.* not allowed to (or not in a position to) communicate with others (*the prisoner was held incommunicado*).

incomparable / in-**kom**-puh-ruh-buhl, -pruh-buhl / *adj.* without an equal, beyond comparison. ☐ **incomparably** *adv.* **incomparability** *n.*

incompatible / in-kuhm-**pat**-uh-buhl / *adj.* **1** not compatible; conflicting or inconsistent (*the two statements are incompatible*). **2** (of persons) unable to live, work, etc. together in harmony. **3** (of an organ, tissue, blood, etc.) not suitable for transplant, grafting, transfusion, etc. because donor and recipient are not well matched. ☐ **incompatibly** *adv.* **incompatibility** *n.*

incompetent / in-**kom**-puh-tuhnt / *adj.* not competent, lacking the necessary skill. • *n.* an incompetent person. ☐ **incompetently** *adv.* **incompetence** *n.*

incomplete *adj.* not complete. ☐ **incompletely** *adv.* **incompleteness** *n.*

incomprehensible / in-kom-pruh-**hen**-suh-buhl / *adj.* not able to be understood. ☐ **incomprehensibly** *adv.*

incomprehension / in-kom-pruh-**hen**-shuhn / *n.* failure to understand.

inconceivable *adj.* **1** unable to be imagined. **2** *colloq.* impossible to believe, most unlikely. ☐ **inconceivably** *adv.*

inconclusive *adj.* (of evidence or an argument etc.) not fully convincing, not decisive. ☐ **inconclusively** *adv.*

incongruous / in-**kong**-groo-uhs / *adj.* unsuitable; out of place. ☐ **incongruously** *adv.* **incongruity** / in-kong-**groo**-uh-tee / *n.*

inconsequent / in-**kon**-suh-kwuhnt / *adj.* not following logically; irrelevant. ☐ **inconsequently** *adv.* **inconsequence** *n.*

inconsequential / in-kon-suh-**kwen**-shuhl / *adj.* **1** not following logically; irrelevant. **2** unimportant. ☐ **inconsequentially** *adv.*

inconsiderable *adj.* not worth considering; of small size, amount, or value. ☐ **inconsiderably** *adv.*

inconsiderate *adj.* not considerate towards other people; thoughtless. ☐ **inconsiderately** *adv.* **inconsiderateness** *n.*

inconsistent *adj.* not consistent. ☐ **inconsistently** *adv.* **inconsistency** *n.*

inconsolable / in-kuhn-**soh**-luh-buhl / *adj.* not able to be consoled. ☐ **inconsolably** *adv.*

inconspicuous *adj.* not conspicuous, not easily noticed. ☐ **inconspicuously** *adv.* **inconspicuousness** *n.*

inconstant *adj.* **1** fickle, changeable. **2** variable, not fixed. ☐ **inconstancy** *n.*

incontestable / in-kuhn-**tes**-tuh-buhl / *adj.* indisputable. ☐ **incontestably** *adv.*

incontinent *adj.* **1** unable to control the bladder or bowels. **2** lacking self-restraint (esp. in regard to one's sexual appetite). ☐ **incontinence** *n.*

incontrovertible / in-kon-truh-**ver**-tuh-buhl / *adj.* indisputable, undeniable. ☐ **incontrovertibly** *adv.*

inconvenience *n.* **1** being inconvenient. **2** a circumstance that is inconvenient. • *v.* cause inconvenience or slight difficulty to.

inconvenient *adj.* not convenient, not suiting one's needs or requirements; slightly troublesome. ☐ **inconveniently** *adv.*

incorporate *v.* / in-**kaw**-puh-rayt / **1** include as a part (*your suggestions will be incorporated in the plan*). **2** form into a legal corporation. • *adj.* / in-**kaw**-puh-ruht / incorporated. ☐ **incorporation** *n.*

incorrect *adj.* **1** wrong; not true. **2** improper, unsuitable. ☐ **incorrectly** *adv.* **incorrectness** *n.*

incorrigible / in-**ko**-ruh-juh-buhl / *adj.* (of a person or habit) not able to be reformed or improved (*an incorrigible liar*). ☐ **incorrigibly** *adv.* **incorrigibility** *n.*

incorruptible / in-kuh-**rup**-tuh-buhl / *adj.* **1** not able to be corrupted morally, e.g. by bribes. **2** not liable to decay. ☐ **incorruptibility** *n.*

increase *v.* / in-**krees** / make or become greater in size, amount, or intensity. • *n.* / **in**-krees / **1** the process of increasing. **2** the amount by which something increases.

increasingly *adv.* more and more.

incredible *adj.* **1** unbelievable. **2** *colloq.* amazing; extremely good. ☐ **incredibly** *adv.*

incredulous / in-**krej**-yuh-luhs, -**kred**-yuh- / *adj.* unbelieving, showing disbelief. ☐ **incredulously** *adv.* **incredulity** / in-kruh-**joo**-luh-tee, -**dyoo**- / *n.*

increment / **in**-kruh-muhnt / *n.* an increase, an added amount (*a salary with annual increments of $400*). ☐ **incremental** / in-kruh-**men**-tuhl / *adj.*

incriminate *v.* **1** indicate as involved in wrongdoing (*his statement incriminated the guard*). **2** charge with a crime. ☐ **incrimination** *n.* **incriminatory** *adj.*

incrustation *n.* **1** encrusting, being encrusted. **2** a crust or deposit formed on a surface.

incubate *v.* **1** hatch (eggs) by warmth of a bird's body as it sits on them or by artificial heat. **2** cause (bacteria) to develop in suitable conditions. **3** develop slowly.

incubation *n.* incubating. ☐ **incubation period** the time it takes for symptoms of a disease to become apparent in an infected person.

incubator *n.* **1** an apparatus for hatching eggs or developing bacteria by artificial warmth. **2** an apparatus in which babies born prematurely can be kept in a constant controlled heat and supplied with oxygen etc.

incubus / **ing**-kyoo-buhs, **in**- / *n.* (*pl.* **incubuses** or **incubi**) **1** a burdensome person or thing. **2** a demon formerly believed to have sexual intercourse with sleeping women (cf. SUCCUBUS).

inculcate / **in**-kul-kayt / *v.* implant (ideas or habits) by persistent urging (*desiring to inculcate obedience in the young*). ☐ **inculcation** *n.*

incumbency / in-**kum**-buhn-see / *n.* the position of an incumbent.

incumbent / in-**kum**-buhnt / *adj.* (often foll. by *on*) forming an obligation or duty (*it is incumbent on you to warn people of the danger*). • *n.* the holder of an office or post.

incunabulum / in-kyoo-**nab**-yoo-luhm / *n.* (*pl.* **incunabula**) an early printed book, esp. from before 1501.

incur *v.* (**incurred**, **incurring**) bring (something unpleasant) on oneself (*incurred great expense*).

incurable *adj.* unable to be cured. • *n.* a person with an incurable disease. ☐ **incurably** *adv.* **incurability** *n.*

incurious *adj.* feeling or showing no curiosity. ☐ **incuriously** *adv.*

incursion *n.* a raid or brief invasion. ☐ **incursive** *adj.*

indebted *adj.* owing money or gratitude. ☐ **indebtedness** *n.*

indecent *adj.* **1** offending against recognised standards of decency. **2** unseemly (*with indecent haste*). ☐ **indecent assault** sexual assault on a person not involving rape. **indecent exposure** exposing one's genitals in public. ☐ ☐ **indecently** *adv.* **indecency** *n.*

indecipherable *adj.* unable to be deciphered.

indecision *n.* inability to make up one's mind; hesitation.

indecisive *adj.* **1** (of a person) not decisive; hesitating. **2** not conclusive (*an indecisive battle*). ☐ **indecisively** *adv.* **indecisiveness** *n.*

indecorous / in-**dek**-uh-ruhs / *adj.* improper; not in good taste. ☐ **indecorously** *adv.*

indeed *adv.* **1** truly, really (*it was indeed remarkable*). **2** used to intensify a meaning (*very nice indeed*). **3** admittedly (*it is, indeed, his first attempt*). **4** used to express surprise or contempt (*does she indeed!*).

indefatigable / in-duh-**fat**-i-guh-buhl / *adj.* untiring, unflagging. ☐ **indefatigably** *adv.*

indefeasible / in-duh-**fee**-zuh-buhl / *adj. literary* (of a right or possession) unable to be annulled or forfeited. ☐ **indefeasibly** *adv.*

indefensible *adj.* unable to be defended or justified. ☐ **indefensibly** *adv.* **indefensibility** *n.*

indefinable / in-duh-**fuy**-nuh-buhl / *adj.* unable to be defined or described clearly. ☐ **indefinably** *adv.*

indefinite *adj.* not clearly defined, stated, or decided; vague. ☐ **indefinite article** *Grammar* the word 'a' or 'an'.

indefinitely *adv.* **1** in an indefinite way. **2** for an unlimited period.

indelible *adj.* **1** (of a mark, stain, or feeling) unable to be removed or washed away. **2** (of ink etc.) making an indelible mark. ☐ **indelibly** *adv.*

indelicate *adj.* **1** slightly indecent; coarse, unrefined. **2** tactless. ☐ **indelicately** *adv.* **indelicacy** *n.*

indemnify / in-**dem**-nuh-fuy / *v.* (**indemnified**, **indemnifying**) **1** protect or insure (a person) against penalties incurred by his or her actions etc. **2** compensate (a person) for injury suffered, expenses incurred, etc. ☐ **indemnification** *n.*

indemnity *n.* **1** protection or insurance against penalties incurred by one's actions. **2** compensation for damage done.

indent *v.* / in-**dent** / **1** make recesses or tooth-like notches in (*an indented coastline*). **2** start (a line of print or writing) further from the margin than the others (*indent the first line of each paragraph*). **3** place an indent for goods or stores. • *n.* / **in**-dent / **1** an official order for goods or stores. **2** an indentation. **3** an indenture. ☐ **indentation** *n.*

indenture / in-**den**-chuh / *n.* **1** a written contract or agreement. **2** (**indentures**) an agreement binding an apprentice to work for someone. • *v.* bind by indentures.

independent *adj.* **1** (often foll. by *of*) not dependent on or controlled by another person or thing (*he is now independent of his parents*). **2** not depending on something else for its validity or operation (*independent proof*). **3** self-governing. **4** having or providing a sufficient income to make it unnecessary for the possessor to earn a living (*he has independent means*). **5** not influenced by others in one's ideas or conduct. **6** unwilling to be under an obligation to others. **7** (of a school) non-government. • *n.* a politician who is not committed to any political party. ☐ **independence** *n.* **independently** *adv.*

Independent Commission Against Corruption an independent body, esp. one having judicial powers similar to those of a Royal Commission, established by a government to investigate allegations of improper or corrupt behaviour by public officials.

in-depth *adj.* thorough, very detailed (*an in-depth survey*).

indescribable *adj.* unable to be described, too great or bad etc. to be described. ☐ **indescribably** *adv.*

indestructible *adj.* unable to be destroyed. ☐ **indestructibly** *adv.* **indestructibility** *n.*

indeterminable *adj.* **1** that cannot be ascertained. **2** (of a dispute etc.) that cannot be settled. ☐ **indeterminably** *adv.*

indeterminate *adj.* not fixed in extent or character etc.; vague, left doubtful. ☐ **indeterminately** *adv.* **indeterminacy** *n.*

index *n.* (*pl.* **indexes** *or* (in sense 2, and always in sense 3) **indices** / **in**-duh-seez /) **1** a list of names, titles, subjects, etc., esp. an alphabetical list indicating where in a book etc. each can be found. **2** a figure indicating the relative level of prices or wages compared with that at a previous date. **3** *Maths* the exponent of a number. **4** a sign or indication of something (*this is the real index of his worth*). • *v.* **1** make an index to (a book or collection of books etc.). **2** enter in an index. **3** relate (wages, pensions, etc.) to a price index. ☐ **index finger** the forefinger. ☐ ☐ **indexer** *n.*

indexation *n.* the practice of making wages, pensions, etc. index-linked.

India 1 a large peninsula of Asia south of the Himalayas, forming a subcontinent. **2** a federal republic consisting of the greater part of this.

Indian *adj.* of India or Indians. • *n.* **1** a native of India. **2** (in full **American Indian**) any of the original inhabitants of the continent of America (other than Eskimos) or their descendants. ☐ **Indian clubs** a pair of heavy bottle-shaped clubs for swinging to exercise the arms. **Indian corn** maize. **Indian file** single file. **Indian ink** ink made with a black pigment (made originally in China and Japan). **Indian Ocean** the ocean to the south of India, extending from the east coast of Africa to the East Indies and Australia. **Indian summer 1** a period of dry sunny weather in late autumn. **2** a period of tranquil enjoyment late in life.

indiarubber *n.* a rubber for rubbing out pencil or ink marks.

Indic *adj.* of the branch of Indo-European languages consisting of Sanskrit and the modern languages of India, Pakistan, and Sri Lanka which are its descendants. • *n.* this group of languages.

indicate *v.* **1** point out, make known. **2** be a sign of, show the presence of. **3** show the need of, require (*stronger measures are indicated*). **4** state briefly. **5** use a vehicle's indicator (*booked for failing to indicate*). ☐ **indication** *n.*

indicative / in-**dik**-uh-tiv / *adj.* **1** (foll. by *of*) giving an indication (*fine 'sawdust' at the base of a tree is often indicative of borers*). **2** *Grammar* (of a form of a verb) used in making a statement, not in a command or wish etc., e.g. *he said* or *he is coming*. • *n.* this form of a verb.

indicator *n.* **1** a flashing light on a vehicle showing the direction in which it is about to turn. **2** a thing that indicates or points to something. **3** a meter or other device giving information about the functioning of a machine etc.

indices *see* INDEX.

indict / in-**duyt** / *v.* make an indictment against (a person).

indictable / in-**duy**-tuh-buhl / *adj.* (of an action) making the doer liable to be charged with a crime; (of a person) liable to this.

indictment / in-**duyt**-muhnt / *n.* **1** a written statement of charges against an accused person. **2** an accusation, esp. of serious wrongdoing. **3** a thing that serves to condemn or censure (*the appalling living conditions of so many Aborigines is an indictment of our society*).

indie / **in**-dee / *colloq. adj.* (of a pop group or record label) independent, not belonging to one of the major companies. • *n.* such a group or label. (¶ Abbreviation of INDEPENDENT.)

Indies, the *archaic* India and adjacent regions. ❏ **East Indies, West Indies** *see* separate entries.

indifferent *adj.* **1** feeling or showing no interest or sympathy; unconcerned. **2** neither good nor bad. **3** not of good quality or ability (*he is an indifferent footballer*). ❏ **indifferently** *adv.* **indifference** *n.*

indigenous / in-**dij**-uh nuhs / *adj.* (of plants, animals, or inhabitants) native or belonging naturally to a place (as opposed to those coming later) (*Aborigines are indigenous to Australia; Australia's indigenous fauna and flora*).

indigent / **in**-di-juhnt / *adj.* needy, poverty-stricken. ❏ **indigence** *n.*

indigestible / in-duh-**jes**-tuh-buhl / *adj.* difficult or impossible to digest. ❏ **indigestibility** *n.*

indigestion / in-duh-**jes**-chuhn / *n.* pain caused by difficulty in digesting food.

indignant *adj.* feeling or showing indignation. ❏ **indignantly** *adv.*

indignation *n.* anger aroused by something thought to be unjust or wrong.

indignity *n.* **1** treatment that makes a person feel undignified or humiliated; an insult. **2** the quality of being humiliating

indigo *n.* a deep blue dye or colour.

indirect *adj.* not direct. ❏ **indirect object** *Grammar* a person or thing indirectly affected by the action of a verb, e.g. *him* in (*give him the book*). **indirect speech** = REPORTED SPEECH. **indirect taxes** those paid in the form of increased prices for goods and services, not on income or capital. ❏ ❏ **indirectly** *adv.*

indiscernible / in-duh-**ser**-nuh-buhl / *adj.* not discernible.

indiscipline *n.* lack of discipline.

indiscreet *adj.* **1** not discreet, revealing secrets. **2** not cautious, unwise. ❏ **indiscreetly** *adv.*

indiscretion / in-duh-**skresh**-uhn / *n.* **1** lack of discretion. **2** an indiscreet action or statement.

indiscriminate *adj.* making no distinctions; done or acting at random (*indiscriminate shooting*). ❏ **indiscriminately** *adv.* **indiscrimination** *n.*

indispensable *adj.* not able to be dispensed with; essential. ❏ **indispensably** *adv.* **indispensability** *n.*

indisposed *adj.* **1** slightly ill. **2** unwilling (*they seem indisposed to help us*). ❏ **indisposition** *n.*

indisputable / in-duh-**spyoo**-tuh-buhl / *adj.* not able to be disputed, undeniable. ❏ **indisputably** *adv.* **indisputability** *n.*

indissoluble / in-duh-**sol**-yuh-buhl / *adj.* firm and lasting; not able to be dissolved or destroyed (*indissoluble bonds of friendship*). ❏ **indissolubly** *adv.*

indistinct *adj.* not distinct; unclear, obscure. ❏ **indistinctly** *adv.* **indistinctness** *n.*

indistinguishable *adj.* not distinguishable. ❏ **indistinguishably** *adv.*

indite / in-**duyt** / *v. archaic* put into words, compose and write (a letter etc.).

indium / **in**-dee-uhm / *n.* a soft silvery metallic element (symbol In), used in alloys and semi-conductor devices.

individual *adj.* **1** single, separate (*each individual strand*). **2** of or for one person (*baked in individual portions*). **3** characteristic of one particular person or thing (*has a very individual style*). • *n.* **1** one person, plant, or animal considered separately. **2** *colloq.* a person (*a most unpleasant individual*).

individualise *v.* (also **-ize**) **1** give an individual character to. **2** (esp. as **individualised** *adj.*) personalise (*individualised notepaper*).

individualism *n.* **1** a social theory favouring free action by individuals. **2** being independent or different. **3** self-centred feeling or conduct; egoism.

individualist *n.* a person who is very independent in thought or action. ❏ **individualistic** *adj.*

individuality / in-duh-vid-yoo-**al**-uh-tee / *n.* **1** individual personality or character, esp. when strongly marked. **2** the fact or condition of existing as an individual; separate existence.

individually *adv.* **1** singly, one by one (*individually we are weak, but as a group we can be strong*). **2** personally (*to me, individually, it makes no difference*). **3** in an individual or distinctive manner.

indivisible / in-duh-**viz**-uh-buhl / *adj.* not divisible. ❏ **indivisibly** *adv.* **indivisibility** *n.*

Indo- *comb. form* Indian (and).

Indo-China 1 the peninsula of SE Asia between India and China, containing Burma (Myanmar), Thailand, Malaya, Laos, Cambodia, and Vietnam. **2** a former French dependency, the region that now consists of Laos, Cambodia, and Vietnam. □ **Indo-Chinese** adj. & n.

indoctrinate / in-**dok**-truh-nayt / v. teach (a person) to accept a particular belief uncritically. □ **indoctrination** n.

Indo-European adj. **1** of the family of languages which includes most European and many Asian ones. **2** of the hypothetical parent language of this family. • n. **1** this family of languages. **2** the hypothetical parent language of these.

indolent / **in**-duh-luhnt / adj. lazy. □ **indolently** adv. **indolence** n.

indomitable / in-**dom**-uh-tuh-buhl / adj. having an unyielding spirit, stubbornly persistent when faced with difficulty or opposition. □ **indomitably** adv.

Indonesia / in-duh-**nee**-zhuh / a republic consisting of a large group of islands in SE Asia.

Indonesian / in-duh-**nee**-zhuhn / n. **1 a** a native or national of Indonesia in SE Asia. **b** a person of Indonesian descent. **2** = BAHASA INDONESIA. • adj. of or relating to Indonesia or its people or language(s).

indoor adj. situated, used, or done inside a building (*indoor games; an indoor aerial*).

indoors adv. inside a building.

indrawn adj. (of breath etc.) drawn in.

indubitable / in-**dyoo**-buh-tuh-buhl / adj. that cannot reasonably be doubted. □ **indubitably** adv.

induce / in-**dyoos** / v. **1** persuade. **2** produce or cause. **3** bring on (labour in childbirth) by artificial means. □ **inducible** adj.

inducement n. **1** inducing; being induced. **2** an attraction or incentive.

induct v. introduce (a person) formally into office; install.

inductance n. the property of producing an electric current by induction.

induction n. **1** inducting. **2** inducing. **3** logical reasoning that a general law exists because particular cases that seem to be examples of it exist. **4** production of an electric or magnetic state in an object by bringing an electrified or magnetic object close to but not touching it. **5** the drawing of a fuel mixture into the cylinders of an internal-combustion engine. **6** production of an electric current in a circuit by varying the magnetic field. **7** formal introduction to a new job or position.

inductive adj. **1** of or using induction (*inductive reasoning*). **2** of electric or magnetic induction.

inductor n. a component in an electric circuit having inductance.

indulge v. **1** allow (a person) to have what he or she wishes. **2** gratify (a wish). **3** *colloq*. take alcoholic drink. □ **indulge in** allow oneself the pleasure of (*he indulges in a cigar after lunch*).

indulgence n. **1** indulging. **2** being indulgent. **3** something allowed as a pleasure or privilege. **4** (in the Catholic Church) remission of the punishment in purgatory still due for sins even after absolution has been given.

indulgent adj. indulging a person's wishes too freely; kind and lenient. □ **indulgently** adv.

industrial adj. **1** of or engaged in industries (*industrial workers*). **2** for use in industries. **3** having many highly developed industries (*an industrial country*). □ **industrial action** a strike or work to rule etc. undertaken by workers for better pay, conditions, safety in the workplace, etc. **industrial estate** an area of land zoned for industrial and business enterprises. **industrial relations** relations between management and workers. □□ **industrially** adv.

industrialised adj. (also **-ized**) (of a country or area) made industrial. □ **industrialisation** n.

industrialism n. a system in which manufacturing industries are predominant.

industrialist n. a person who owns or manages an industrial business.

industrious adj. hard-working. □ **industriously** adv. **industriousness** n.

industry n. **1** the manufacture or production of goods. **2** a particular branch of this; any business activity (*the tourist industry*). **3** the quality of being industrious; diligence.

Indy / **in**-dee / n. chiefly American form of motor racing, usu. at very high speeds on oval circuits (often attrib.: *Indy racing*). (¶ Indianapolis in the US, where the principal Indy race is held.)

inebriate / in-**ee**-bree-uht / adj. drunken. • n. a drunken person; a drunkard.

inebriated / in-**ee**-bree-ay-tuhd / adj. drunken. □ **inebriation** n.

inedible adj. not edible, not suitable for eating.

ineducable / in-**ed**-yuh-kuh-buhl / adj. incapable of being educated, esp. through mental inadequacy.

ineffable / in-**ef**-uh-buhl / adj. too great to be described; unutterable (*ineffable joy*). □ **ineffably** adv.

ineffective adj. **1** not effective. **2** (of a person) inefficient. □ **ineffectively** adv.

ineffectual adj. having no effect. □ **ineffectually** adv.

inefficacious / in-ef-uh-**kay**-shuhs / adj. (of a remedy etc.) not producing the desired effect. □ **inefficacy** n.

inefficient adj. not efficient; wasteful. □ **inefficiently** adv. **inefficiency** n.

inelegant adj. not elegant; unrefined. □ **inelegantly** adv. **inelegance** n.

ineligible adj. not eligible or qualified. □ **ineligibility** n.

ineluctable / in-uh-**luk**-tuh-buhl / adj. inescapable, unavoidable.

inept adj. **1** clumsy, unskilful. **2** unsuitable, absurd. □ **ineptly** adv. **ineptitude** n.

■ **Usage** *Inept* and *inapt* are easily confused because they have virtually the same meanings. However, *inept* is a far commoner word than *inapt* and is usually used in sense 1 'clumsy, unskilful'. *Inapt* is more often used to mean 'unsuitable, inappropriate'. This difference is illustrated by the example *His after-dinner speech was both inept and inapt*, i.e. it was both clumsy and inappropriate.

inequable / in-**ek**-wuh-buhl / *adj.* **1** unfair. **2** not uniform.

inequality *n.* **1** lack of equality in size, standard, etc. **2** unevenness.

inequitable / in-**ek**-wuh-tuh-buhl / *adj.* unfair, unjust. ◻ **inequitably** *adv.*

inequity / in-**ek**-wuh-tee / *n.* unfairness.

ineradicable / in-uh-**rad**-uh-kuh-buhl / *adj.* unable to be removed or rooted out. ◻ **ineradicably** *adv.*

inert *adj.* **1** (of matter) without power to move or act. **2** without active chemical or other properties, incapable of reacting (*an inert gas*). **3** not moving; slow to move or take action. ◻ **inertly** *adv.* **inertness** *n.*

inertia / in-**er**-shuh / *n.* **1** inertness, slowness to take action. **2** *Physics* the property of matter by which it remains in its existing state of rest or motion unless acted upon by an external force. ◻ **inertia reel** a reel round which one end of a safety belt is wound so that the belt will tighten automatically over the wearer if it is pulled suddenly. **inertia selling** the sending of goods to a person who has not ordered them, in the hope that he or she will not take action to refuse them and must later make payment. ◻◻ **inertial** *adj.*

inescapable *adj.* unavoidable. ◻ **inescapably** *adv.*

inessential *adj.* not essential. • *n.* an inessential thing.

inestimable / in-**es**-tuh-muh-buhl / *adj.* too great, precious, etc. to be estimated. ◻ **inestimably** *adv.*

inevitable / in-**ev**-uh-tuh-buhl / *adj.* **1** not able to be prevented, sure to happen or appear. **2** *colloq.* tiresomely familiar (*the tourist with his inevitable camera*). • *n.* (**the inevitable**) something that is unavoidable. ◻ **inevitably** *adv.* **inevitability** *n.*

inexact *adj.* not exact. ◻ **inexactly** *adv.* **inexactitude** *n.*

inexcusable *adj.* unable to be excused or justified. ◻ **inexcusably** *adv.*

inexhaustible *adj.* not able to be totally used up; available in unlimited quantity.

inexorable / in-**ek**-suh-ruh-buhl / *adj.* relentless; unable to be persuaded by request or entreaty. ◻ **inexorably** *adv.*

inexpedient *adj.* not expedient.

inexpensive *adj.* not expensive, offering good value for the price.

inexperience *n.* lack of experience. ◻ **inexperienced** *adj.*

inexpert *adj.* not expert, unskilful. ◻ **inexpertly** *adv.*

inexpiable / in-**ek**-spee-uh-buhl / *adj.* unable to be expiated or appeased.

inexplicable / in-ek-**splik**-uh-buhl / *adj.* unable to be explained or accounted for. ◻ **inexplicably** *adv.*

inexpressible *adj.* unable to be expressed in words.

in extremis / in ek-**stree**-mis / *adj.* **1** at the point of death. **2** in very great difficulties. (¶ Latin)

inextricable / in-ek-**strik**-uh-buhl, in-**ek**-stri-kuh-buhl / *adj.* **1** inescapable. **2** unable to be disentangled or sorted out. ◻ **inextricably** *adv.*

infallible / in-**fal**-uh-buhl / *adj.* **1** incapable of making a mistake or being wrong. **2** never failing (*an infallible remedy*). **3** (of the pope) not able to err when proclaiming, *ex cathedra*, a doctrine of faith or morals. ◻ **infallibly** *adv.* **infallibility** / in-fal-uh-**bil**-uh-tee / *n.*

infamous / **in**-fuh-muhs / *adj.* having or deserving a very bad reputation; notorious. ◻ **infamy** / **in**-fuh-mee / *n.*

infancy *n.* **1** early childhood, babyhood. **2** an early stage of development.

infant *n.* **1** a child during the earliest period of its life. **2** (also **minor**) *Law* a person under 18.

infanta / in-**fan**-tuh / *n. hist.* a daughter of the Spanish or Portuguese king.

infanticide / in-**fan**-tuh-suyd / *n.* **1** the act of killing an infant soon after its birth. **2** a person who is guilty of this.

infantile / **in**-fuhn-tuyl / *adj.* **1** of infants or infancy. **2** childish. ◻ **infantile paralysis** polio.

infantilism *n.* **1** childish behaviour. **2** *Psychol.* the persistence of infantile characteristics or behaviour in adult life.

infantry *n.* troops who fight on foot.

infantryman *n.* a member of an infantry regiment.

infarct / in-**fahkt** / *n.* (also **infarction**) a region of dead tissue caused by the blocking of an artery or other vessel.

infatuated *adj.* temporarily filled with an intense unreasoning love for a person or thing. ◻ **infatuation** *n.*

infect *v.* **1** affect or contaminate with a germ, virus, or disease. **2** affect (others) with one's own feeling(s) (*she infected us with her enthusiasm*).

infection *n.* **1** infecting, being infected. **2** the spreading of disease, esp. by air or water etc. **3** a disease that is spread in this way; a diseased condition.

infectious *adj.* **1** (of a disease) able to spread by air or water etc. **2** infecting with disease. **3** quickly spreading to others (*his fear was infectious*).

infelicity / in-fuh-**lis**-uh-tee / *n.* **1** an inappropriate remark or expression. **2** unhappiness; misfortune. ◻ **infelicitous** *adj.*

infer v. (**inferred**, **inferring**) **1** reach (an opinion) from facts or reasoning; deduce. **2** imply, suggest. □ **inferable** adj.

■ **Usage** The use of *infer* in sense 2 is considered incorrect by many people since it is the reverse of the primary sense of the verb. It should be avoided by using *imply* or *suggest*.

inference / in-fuh-ruhns / n. **1** inferring. **2** a thing inferred. **3** colloq. something implied. □ **inferential** / in-fuh-**ren**-shuhl / adj.

inferior adj. low or lower in rank, importance, quality, or ability. • n. a person who is inferior to another, esp. in rank.

inferiority n. being inferior. □ **inferiority complex** a feeling of general inferiority, sometimes with aggressive behaviour in compensation.

infernal adj. **1** of hell (*the infernal regions*). **2** colloq. detestable, tiresome (*an infernal nuisance*). □ **infernally** adv.

inferno / in-**fer**-noh / n. (pl. **infernos**) **1** a raging fire. **2** somewhere intensely hot. **3** a place resembling hell.

infertile adj. **1** not fertile. **2** unable to have offspring. □ **infertility** n.

infest v. (of pests or vermin etc.) be numerous and troublesome in (a place); overrun. □ **infestation** n.

infidel / **in**-fuh-del / n. a person who does not believe in esp. the supposed true religion. • adj. **1** of infidels. **2** unbelieving.

infidelity n. unfaithfulness, esp. adultery.

infield n. (in cricket) the part of the ground near the wicket.

infighting n. **1** hidden conflict within an organisation. **2** boxing with an opponent nearer than arm's length.

infill n. material used to fill a hole, gap, etc. • v. fill in (a cavity etc.).

infiltrate / **in**-fuhl-trayt / v. **1** enter (a territory, a political party, etc.) gradually and without being noticed, esp. to spy or to subvert. **2** cause to do this. **3** pass (fluid) by filtration. □ **infiltration** n. **infiltrator** n.

infinite / **in**-fuh-nuht / adj. **1** having no limit, endless. **2** very great or many. □ **infinitely** adv.

infinitesimal / in-fin-uh-**tez**-uh-muhl, -**tes**- / adj. extremely small. □ **infinitesimally** adv.

infinitive / in-**fin**-uh-tiv / n. a form of a verb that does not indicate a particular tense or number or person, in English used with or without *to*, e.g. *go* in *let him go* or *allow him to go*.

infinitude n. literary being infinite; infinity.

infinity / in-**fin**-uh-tee / n. **1** an infinite number, extent, or time. **2** being infinite; boundlessness. **3** a very great distance.

infirm adj. **1** physically weak, esp. from old age. **2** weak of will, faltering, irresolute.

infirmary n. **1** a hospital. **2** a room or rooms for sick people in a monastery, school etc.

infirmity n. **1** being infirm. **2** a particular physical weakness.

infix v. fasten or fix in.

in flagrante delicto / in fluh-gran-tee duh-**lik**-toh / adv. in the very act of committing an offence. (¶ Latin, = in blazing crime.)

inflame v. **1** provoke to strong feeling or emotion; arouse anger in. **2** cause inflammation in. **3** aggravate, intensify. **4** catch or set on fire.

inflammable adj. **1** easily set on fire; flammable. **2** easily excited.

■ **Usage** This word means the same as *flammable*. Its opposite is *non-inflammable*.

inflammation n. **1** redness, heat, and pain produced in the body, esp. as a reaction to injury or infection. **2** inflaming.

inflammatory / in-**flam**-uh-tuh-ree, -tree / adj. **1** likely to arouse strong feeling or anger (*inflammatory speeches*). **2** causing or involving inflammation.

inflatable / in-**flay**-tuh-buhl / adj. able to be inflated. • n. an inflatable object.

inflate v. **1** fill or become filled with air or gas and swell up. **2** exaggerate the importance of; puff up (with pride etc.). **3** increase (a price etc.) artificially. **4** resort to inflation (of currency).

inflation n. **1** inflating; being inflated. **2** a general increase of prices and fall in the purchasing value of money. □ **inflationary** adj.

inflect v. **1** change the pitch of (the voice) in speaking. **2** change the ending or form of (a word) to show its grammatical relation or number etc., e.g. *sing* to *sang* or *sung*; *child* to *children*. □ **inflection** (or **inflexion**) n.

inflective adj. of or involving grammatical inflection.

inflexible adj. **1** not flexible, unable to be bent. **2** not able to be altered (*an inflexible rule*). **3** refusing to alter one's demands etc., unyielding. □ **inflexibly** adv. **inflexibility** n.

inflict v. **1** deal out (a blow or wound). **2** (usu. foll. by *on*) impose (something unpleasant) (*shall not inflict myself on you any longer*). □ **infliction** n. **inflictor** n.

inflight adj. occurring or provided during a flight.

inflorescence / in-fluh-**res**-uhns / n. **1** a flowering. **2** the flowers of a plant; their arrangement on a stem etc.

inflow n. an inward flow; the amount that flows in (*a large inflow of cash*).

influence n. **1** the power to produce an effect (*the influence of the moon on the tides*). **2** the ability to affect someone's character or beliefs or actions. **3** a person or thing with this ability. • v. exert influence on. □ **under the influence** colloq. drunk.

influential / in-floo-**en**-shuhl / adj. having great influence. □ **influentially** adv.

influenza n. a virus disease causing fever, muscular pain, and catarrh.

influx *n.* an inflow, esp. of people or things into a place.

info *n. colloq.* information.

infomercial / in-fuh-**mer**-shuhl / *n.* (also **informercial**) an advertising film, esp. on television, which promotes a product in an informative and purportedly objective style.

inform *v.* **1** give information to. **2** (usu. foll. by *against* or *on*) give incriminating information about a person to the authorities.

informal *adj.* **1** without formality or ceremony. **2** (of clothing etc.) everyday; not formal. **3** (of a vote) not valid. □ **vote informal** mark a ballot paper incorrectly (or leave it blank) with the result that the vote is invalid. □ □ **informally** *adv.* **informality** / in-faw-**mal**-uh-tee / *n.*

informant *n.* a person who gives information.

information *n.* **1** facts told or discovered. **2** facts fed into a computer etc.; data. **3** a charge or complaint lodged with a court etc. □ **information science** the study of the processes for storing and retrieving information. **information superhighway** a means of rapid transfer of information in different digital forms (e.g. video, sound, and graphics) via an extensive electronic network, esp. the Internet. **information technology** the study or use of systems (esp. computers, telecommunications, etc.) for storing, retrieving, and sending information.

informative *adj.* giving information; instructive.

informed *adj.* having good or sufficient knowledge of something (*informed opinion*).

informer *n.* a person who informs against someone.

infotainment *n.* broadcast material intended both to entertain and to inform.

infotech *n. & adj.* = INFORMATION TECHNOLOGY.

infra *adv.* below or further on in a book etc. (¶ Latin, = below.)

infraction / in-**frak**-shuhn / *n.* an infringement.

infra dig *adj. colloq.* beneath one's dignity. (¶ From the Latin *infra dignitatem*.)

infrangible / in-**fran**-juh-buhl / *adj.* **1** unbreakable. **2** inviolable.

infrared *adj.* of or using rays with a wavelength slightly longer than the red end of the visible spectrum.

infrastructure *n.* **1** the basic structural foundations of a society or enterprise. **2** the facilities (such as roads, bridges, sewers, etc.) regarded as a country's economic foundation.

infrequent *adj.* not frequent. □ **infrequently** *adv.* **infrequency** *n.*

infringe *v.* **1** break or act against (a rule or agreement etc.); violate. **2** (foll. by *on* or *upon*) encroach, trespass (*TV cameras often infringe on people's privacy*). □ **infringement** *n.*

infuriate *v.* enrage. □ **infuriating** *adj.* **infuriatingly** *adv.*

infuse *v.* **1** imbue, instil (*infused them with courage; infused life into them*). **2** steep (tea or herbs etc.) in a liquid in order to make flavour or soluble constituents pass into the liquid; (of tea etc.) undergo this process.

infusible *adj.* not able to be melted. □ **infusibility** *n.*

infusion *n.* **1** infusing, being infused. **2** a liquid made by infusing. **3** something added or introduced into a stock (*an infusion of new blood to improve the breed*).

ingenious *adj.* **1** clever at inventing new things or methods. **2** cleverly contrived (*an ingenious machine*). □ **ingeniously** *adv.*

■ **Usage** *Ingenious* is sometimes confused with *ingenuous*.

ingénue / **an**-zhay-nyoo / *n.* an unsophisticated or innocent young woman, esp. as a role in a play. (¶ French)

ingenuity / in-juh-**nyoo**-uh-tee / *n.* skill in devising or contriving; ingeniousness.

ingenuous / in-**jen**-yoo-uhs / *adj.* **1** unsophisticated, innocent (*an ingenuous manner*). **2** frank. □ **ingenuously** *adv.*

■ **Usage** Do not confuse with *ingenious*.

ingest / in-**jest** / *v.* take in as food. □ **ingestion** *n.*

inglorious *adj.* **1** ignominious. **2** not famous; obscure.

in-goal *n.* (in full **in-goal area**) *Rugby* the area between the goal line and the dead ball line.

ingoing *adj.* going in.

ingot / **ing**-guht, -got / *n.* a brick-shaped lump of cast metal, esp. gold.

ingrained *adj.* **1** (of habits, feelings, or tendencies) firmly fixed. **2** (of dirt) marking a surface deeply.

ingrate / **in**-grayt / *n.* an ungrateful person.

ingratiate / in-**gray**-shee-ayt / *v.* (**ingratiate oneself**) (usu. foll. by *with*) bring oneself into a person's favour, esp. in order to gain an advantage. □ **ingratiating** *adj.* **ingratiatingly** *adv.*

ingratitude *n.* lack of due gratitude.

ingredient *n.* any of the parts or elements in a mixture.

ingress *n.* **1** going in. **2** the right to go in. **3** the place through which one goes in.

in-ground *adj.* (esp. of an open-air domestic swimming pool) constructed in an excavated pit with the top of the pool level with the ground surface.

in-group *n.* a small exclusive group or clique of people with a common interest.

ingrowing *adj.* growing abnormally into the flesh (*an ingrowing toenail*). □ **ingrown** *adj.*

inguinal / **ing**-gwuh-nuhl / *adj.* of the groin.

inhabit *v.* (of a person or animal) dwell in; occupy (a region, house, etc.). □ **inhabitable** *adj.*

inhabitant *n.* a person etc. who inhabits a place.

inhalant / in-**hay**-luhnt / *n.* **1** a medicinal substance to be inhaled. **2** = INHALER.

inhale v. breathe in, draw into the lungs by breathing. ☐ **inhalation** / in-huh-**lay**-shuhn / n.

inhaler n. a device that sends out a medicinal vapour to be inhaled, esp. to relieve asthma.

inharmonious adj. not harmonious; discordant.

inhere / in-**heer** / v. be inherent.

inherent / in-**heer**-ruhnt, in-**he**-ruhnt / adj. existing in something as a natural or permanent characteristic or quality. ☐ **inherently** adv. **inherence** n.

inherit v. **1** receive (property or a title etc.) by legal right of succession or by a will when its previous owner or holder has died. **2** receive from a predecessor (*this government inherited many problems from the last one*). **3** receive (a characteristic) from one's parents or ancestors. ☐ **inheritable** adj. **inheritor** n.

inheritance n. **1** inheriting. **2** a thing that is inherited.

inhibit v. **1** restrain, prevent (*this substance inhibits the growth of moss*). **2** hinder the impulses of (a person); cause inhibitions in.

inhibited adj. suffering from inhibition.

inhibition / in-hi-**bish**-uhn, in-uh-**bish**-uhn / n. **1** inhibiting; being inhibited. **2** *Psychol.* repression of or resistance to an instinct, impulse, or feeling. **3** emotional resistance to a thought, action, etc. (*has inhibitions about singing in front of others*).

inhospitable / in-hos-**pit**-uh-buhl / adj. **1** not hospitable. **2** (of a place or climate) giving no shelter or no favourable conditions.

in-house adv. & adj. within an institution or company (*saw an in-house video at the motel*).

inhuman adj. brutal; lacking normal human qualities of kindness, pity, etc. ☐ **inhumanity** n.

inhumane / in-hyoo-**mayn** / adj. not humane; cruel.

inhumation / in-hyoo-**may**-shuhn / n. **1 a** the action or practice of burying the dead (opp. CREMATION). **b** the fact of being buried; interment. **2** the burying of something in or under the ground.

inimical / i-**nim**-uh-kuhl / adj. **1** hostile. **2** harmful (*smoking is inimical to health*). ☐ **inimically** adv.

inimitable / i-**nim**-uh-tuh-buhl / adj. impossible to imitate. ☐ **inimitably** adv.

iniquitous / i-**nik**-wuh-tuhs / adj. very unjust.

iniquity / i-**nik**-wuh-tee / n. **1** great injustice. **2** wickedness.

initial / i-**nish**-uhl / adj. of or at the beginning (*the initial stages of the work*). •n. the first letter of a word, esp. of a person's name. •v. (**initialled**, **initialling**) sign or mark with initials. ☐ **initially** adv.

initialise v. (also -**ize**) *Computing* set the value of (a variable or a storage location) at the start of an operation.

initialism n. a group of initial letters used as an abbreviation for a name or expression, each letter being pronounced separately (e.g. *ABC* for 'Australian Broadcasting Corporation') (cf. ACRONYM).

initiate v. / i-**nish**-ee-ayt / **1** cause to begin, start (a scheme) working (*he initiated certain reforms*). **2** admit (a person) into membership of a society etc., often with special ceremonies. **3** give (a person) basic instruction or information about something. •n. / i-**nish**-ee-uht / an initiated person; a person undergoing initiation. ☐ **initiation** n. **initiator** n. **initiatory** adj.

initiative / i-**nish**-uh-tiv, i-**nish**-ee-uh-tiv / n. **1** the first step in a process. **2** the power or right to begin something. **3** the ability to initiate things; enterprise (*he lacks initiative*). ☐ **have the initiative** be in a position to control the course of events, e.g. in a war. **on one's own initiative** without being prompted by others.

inject v. **1** force or drive (a liquid etc.) into something, esp. by means of a syringe; administer medicine etc. to (a person) in this way. **2** (foll. by *into*) introduce (a new element or quality) (*may I inject a note of realism into this discussion?*). ☐ **injector** n.

injection n. injecting; an instance of this. ☐ **fuel injection** the spraying of liquid fuel into the cylinders of an internal-combustion engine.

in-joke n. a joke or allusion understood only by an in-group and baffling to outsiders.

injudicious / in-joo-**dish**-uhs / adj. showing lack of good judgment, unwise. ☐ **injudiciously** adv.

injunction n. an order or command, esp. an order from a lawcourt restraining a person or group from some act or compelling redress to an injured party.

injure v. **1** hurt. **2** do wrong to.

injurious / in-**joo**-ree-uhs / adj. **1** hurtful. **2** insulting.

injury n. **1** damage, harm. **2** a particular form of this (*a leg injury*). **3** a wrong or unjust act.

injustice n. **1** lack of justice. **2** an unjust action or treatment. ☐ **do a person an injustice** make an unfair judgment about him or her.

ink n. **1** a coloured liquid or paste used in writing, printing, etc. **2** a black liquid squirted by a cuttlefish or octopus for concealment. •v. mark or cover with ink.

Inkatha / in-**kah**-tuh / a Zulu political organisation in South Africa.

inkling n. a hint, a slight knowledge or suspicion.

inky adj. **1** covered or stained with ink. **2** very black. ☐ **inkiness** n.

INLA abbr. Irish National Liberation Army, an organisation seeking to achieve union between Northern Ireland and the Irish Republic.

inlaid see INLAY.

inland adj. & adv. in or towards the interior of a country. •n. **1** (**the Inland**) **a** the Australian outback. **b** the inhabitants of this region collectively (*all the Inland listened to the broadcast*). **2** the parts of a country remote from the sea or frontiers.

inlander *n.* a person who lives in the sparsely populated interior of Australia, the Inland.

in-laws *n.pl.* a person's relatives by marriage.

inlay *v.* / in-**lay** / (**inlaid**, **inlaying**) **1** set (pieces of wood or metal etc.) into a surface so that they lie flush with it and form a design. **2** decorate (a thing with inlaid work). **3** (as **inlaid** *adj.*) ornamented by inlaying (*an inlaid table*). • *n.* inlay / **1** inlaid material. **2** a design formed by this. **3** a dental filling shaped to fit a tooth cavity.

inlet *n.* **1** a strip of water extending into the land from a sea or lake, or between islands. **2** a way in, e.g. for water into a tank (*the inlet pipe*).

in loco parentis / in loh-koh puh-**ren**-tis / *adv.* acting in place of a parent. (¶ Latin)

inmate *n.* one of a number of inhabitants of a hospital, prison, or other institution.

in medias res / in mee-dee-as **rayz** / *adv.* **1** into the midst of things. **2** into the middle of a story, without preamble. (¶ Latin)

in memoriam / muh-**maw**-ree-uhm / *prep.* in memory of (a dead person). • *n.* a written article etc. in memory of a dead person; an obituary notice. (¶ Latin)

inmost *adj.* furthest inward.

inn *n.* a small hotel providing liquor, food, and accommodation for travellers (*an outback inn*).

innards *n.pl. colloq.* **1** entrails. **2** the inner parts of a thing.

innate / in-**ayt** / *adj.* inborn, natural (*an innate talent*). ☐ **innately** *adv.*

inner *adj.* **1** nearer to the centre or inside, interior, internal. **2** (of thoughts etc.) deeper (*inner motives*). • *n.* (in archery) the division of a target next to the bull's-eye; a shot that strikes this. ☐ **inner city** the central area of a city, often associated with overcrowding, poverty, etc. **inner tube** a separate inflatable tube inside a pneumatic tyre.

innermost *adj.* furthest inward.

innings *n.* (*pl.* **innings**) **1** a batsman's or side's turn at batting in cricket. **2** a period of power or of opportunity to show one's ability (*he had a long innings in politics*).

innkeeper *n.* a person who keeps an inn.

innocent *adj.* **1** not guilty of a particular crime etc. **2** free of all evil or wrongdoing (*as innocent as a new-born babe*). **3** harmless (*innocent amusements*). **4** not deliberate or maliciously intended (*an innocent mistake*). **5** foolishly trustful. • *n.* a person (esp. a child) who is free of all evil or who is foolishly trustful. ☐ **innocently** *adv.* **innocence** *n.*

innocuous / i-**nok**-yoo-uhs / *adj.* harmless. ☐ **innocuously** *adv.*

innovate *v.* introduce a new process or way of doing things. ☐ **innovation** *n.* **innovator** *n.* **innovatory** *adj.*

innuendo / in-yoo-**en**-doh / *n.* (*pl.* **innuendoes** *or* **innuendos**) an unpleasant insinuation.

Innuit alternative spelling of INUIT.

innumerable *adj.* too many to be counted. ☐ **innumerably** *adv.*

innumerate *adj.* having no knowledge of basic mathematics. ☐ **innumeracy** *n.*

inoculate *v.* treat (a person or animal) with vaccine or serum to promote immunity against a disease. ☐ **inoculation** *n.*

inoffensive *adj.* not offensive, harmless.

inoperable / in-**op**-uh-ruh-buhl / *adj.* **1** unable to be cured by surgical operation (*inoperable cancer*). **2** that cannot be worked or operated (*the machine was inoperable*).

inoperative *adj.* not functioning.

inopportune / in-**op**-uh-tyoon / *adj.* coming or happening at an unsuitable time. ☐ **inopportunely** *adv.*

inordinate / in-**aw**-duh-nuht / *adj.* excessive. ☐ **inordinately** *adv.*

inorganic / in-aw-**gan**-ik / *adj.* **1** of mineral origin, not organic. **2** without organised physical structure. ☐ **inorganic chemistry** a branch of chemistry dealing with inorganic compounds.

in-patient *n.* a patient who remains resident in a hospital while undergoing treatment.

input *n.* **1** what is put in. **2** the place where energy or information etc. enters a system. **3** the data, programs, etc. supplied to a computer. • *v.* (**input** *or* **inputted**, **inputting**) put in; supply (data, programs, etc.) to a computer.

inquest *n.* **1** an inquiry by a coroner's court into a death, esp. a death which may not be the result of natural causes. **2** a judicial inquiry to discover the facts relating to an incident etc. **3** *colloq.* a detailed discussion of something that is over, e.g. a game, an election result, etc. (*footy inquest*).

inquietude / in-**kwuy**-uh-tyood / *n.* uneasiness of mind.

inquire *v.* make an inquiry, seek information. ☐ **inquirer** *n.*

■ **Usage** *See* the note under *enquire*.

inquiry *n.* an investigation, esp. an official one.

inquisition / in-kwuh-**zish**-uhn / *n.* **1** a detailed questioning or investigation. **2** (**the Inquisition**) *hist.* a tribunal of the Catholic Church in the Middle Ages, esp. the very severe one in Spain, to discover and punish heretics. ☐ **inquisitional** *adj.*

inquisitive *adj.* **1** eagerly seeking knowledge. **2** prying. ☐ **inquisitively** *adv.*

inquisitor / in-**kwiz**-uh-tuh / *n.* **1** a person who questions another searchingly. **2** *hist.* an officer of the Inquisition.

inquisitorial / in-kwiz-uh-**taw**-ree-uhl / *adj.* of or like an inquisitor, prying. ☐ **inquisitorially** *adv.*

inquorate / in-**kwor**-rayt / *adj.* not constituting a quorum.

INRI *abbr.* Jesus of Nazareth, King of the Jews. (¶ Latin *Iesus Nazarenus Rex Iudaeorum*.)

inroad *n.* a sudden attack made into a country. ☐ **make inroads on** (*or* **into**) use up large quantities (of resources etc.).

inrush *n.* a rush in, a violent influx.

insalubrious / in-suh-**loo**-bree-uhs / *adj.* (of a place or climate) unhealthy.

insane *adj.* **1** not sane, mad. **2** extremely foolish. **3** *colloq.* wonderful. ☐ **insanely** *adv.* **insanity** *n.*

insanitary *adj.* unclean and likely to be harmful to health.

insatiable / in-**say**-shuh-buhl / *adj.* unable to be satisfied (*an insatiable appetite*). ☐ **insatiably** *adv.* **insatiability** *n.*

insatiate / in-**say**-shee-uht / *adj.* never satisfied (*an insatiate greed for wealth*).

inscribe *v.* **1** write or cut (words etc.) on (a surface) (*inscribed their names on the stone; inscribed it with their names*). **2** draw (one geometrical figure) within another so that certain points of their boundaries coincide. **3** enter (a name) on a list or in a book.

inscription *n.* **1** words inscribed on a monument, coin, etc. **2** inscribing.

inscrutable / in-**skroo**-tuh-buhl / *adj.* impossible to understand or interpret; mysterious. ☐ **inscrutably** *adv.* **inscrutability** *n.*

insect *n.* a small animal with six legs, no backbone, and a body divided into three parts (head, thorax, abdomen).

insecticide *n.* a substance for killing insects.

insectivore / in-**sek**-tuh-vaw / *n.* an animal or plant that feeds on insects. ☐ **insectivorous** / in-sek-**tiv**-uh-ruhs / *adj.*

insecure *adj.* **1** not secure or safe. **2** uncertain; lacking confidence. ☐ **insecurely** *adv.* **insecurity** *n.*

inseminate / in-**sem**-uh-nayt / *v.* insert semen into. ☐ **insemination** *n.*

insensate / in-**sen**-sayt / *adj.* **1** without sensibility, unfeeling. **2** stupid. **3** without physical sensation.

insensible *adj.* **1** unconscious. **2** without feeling, unaware (*seemed insensible of his danger*). **3** callous. **4** (of changes) imperceptible. ☐ **insensibly** *adv.* **insensibility** *n.*

insensitive *adj.* not sensitive; unfeeling. ☐ **insensitively** *adv.* **insensitivity** *n.*

inseparable *adj.* **1** unable to be separated. **2** liking to be constantly together (*inseparable companions*). ☐ **inseparably** *adv.* **inseparability** *n.*

insert *v.* / in-**sert** / put (a thing) into or in or between or among other things (*inserted the key into the keyhole; inserted an ad in the newspaper*). • *n.* / **in**-sert / a thing inserted (e.g. a loose page in a magazine, a piece of cloth in a garment, etc.). ☐ **insertion** *n.*

in-service *adj.* (of training) for people actively working in the profession or activity concerned.

inset *v.* / **in**-set / (**inset** *or* **insetted, insetting**) set or place in; decorate with an inset (*the crown was inset with jewels*). • *n.* / **in**-set / something set into a larger thing, e.g. a small map within the border of a larger one.

inshore *adv.* & *adj.* at sea but near to the shore.

inside *n.* **1** the inner side, surface, or part. **2** the side away from the road and nearest the kerb (*don't overtake a car on the inside*). **3** (usu. as **insides**) *colloq.* the organs in the abdomen; the stomach and bowels. **4** *colloq.* a position affording inside information (*knows someone on the inside*). • *adj.* on or coming from the inside. • *adv.* **1** on, in, or to the inside. **2** *Aust.* within a more settled part of Australia (as opposed to the outback) (*came inside after two years in the Northern Territory*). **3** *colloq.* in prison. • *prep.* on the inner side of, within (*inside an hour*). ☐ **inside country** *Aust.* comparatively closely settled parts of Australia as opposed to the outback. **inside information** information that is not available to outsiders. **inside job** *colloq.* a crime committed by someone living or working on the premises where it occurred. **inside out 1** with the inner surface turned to face the outside. **2** thoroughly (*know a subject inside out*). **3** in utter confusion; topsy-turvy. **inside track 1** the lane (on a racecourse etc.) which is shorter because of the curve. **2** a position of advantage.

insider *n.* an accepted member of a certain group or profession etc. ☐ **insider trading** the illegal practice of trading on the stock exchange to one's own advantage through having access to confidential information.

insidious / in-**sid**-ee-uhs / *adj.* **1** proceeding inconspicuously but with harmful effect (*an insidious disease*). **2** treacherous; crafty. ☐ **insidiously** *adv.* **insidiousness** *n.*

insight *n.* **1** the ability to perceive and understand the true nature of something. **2** knowledge obtained by this.

insignia / in-**sig**-nee-uh / *n.* (treated as *sing.* or *pl.*) a badge or distinguishing mark of rank, office, etc.

insignificant *adj.* having little or no importance, value, or influence. ☐ **insignificantly** *adv.* **insignificance** *n.*

insincere *adj.* not sincere; hypocritical. ☐ **insincerely** *adv.* **insincerity** *n.*

insinuate / in-**sin**-yoo-ayt / *v.* **1** hint artfully or unpleasantly. **2** introduce gradually or craftily (*insinuate oneself into a person's good graces*). ☐ **insinuation** *n.*

insipid / in-**sip**-uhd / *adj.* **1** lacking in flavour. **2** lacking in interest or liveliness. ☐ **insipidity** / in-si-**pid**-uh-tee / *n.*

insist *v.* declare or demand emphatically (*insist on your being there*).

insistent *adj.* **1** insisting, declaring or demanding something emphatically. **2** forcing itself on one's attention (*the insistent throb of the engines*). ☐ **insistently** *adv.* **insistence** *n.*

in situ / **sit**-yoo / *adv.* in its original place. (¶ Latin)

insobriety / in-suh-**bruy**-uh-tee / *n.* lack of sobriety, drunkenness.

insofar as = in so far as (*see* IN).

insole *n.* **1** the inner sole of a boot or shoe. **2** a loose piece of material laid in the bottom of a shoe for warmth or comfort.

insolent *adj.* behaving insultingly; arrogant, contemptuous. ☐ **insolently** *adv.* **insolence** *n.*

insoluble *adj.* **1** unable to be dissolved. **2** unable to be solved (*an insoluble problem*). ☐ **insolubly** *adv.* **insolubility** *n.*

insolvent *adj.* unable to pay one's debts; bankrupt. ☐ **insolvency** *n.*

insomnia *n.* habitual inability to sleep.

insomniac *n.* a person who suffers from insomnia.

insomuch *adv.* **1** (foll. by *that*) to such an extent. **2** (foll. by *as*) inasmuch as.

insouciant / in-**soo**-see-uhnt / *adj.* carefree, unconcerned. ☐ **insouciance** *n.*

inspect *v.* **1** look at closely, esp. looking for flaws. **2** examine officially; visit in order to make sure that rules and standards are being observed. ☐ **inspection** *n.*

inspector *n.* **1** a person whose job is to inspect things or supervise services etc. **2** a police officer next above sergeant in rank. ☐ **inspectorate** *n.*

inspiration *n.* **1** inspiring. **2** an inspiring influence. **3** a sudden brilliant idea.

inspire *v.* **1** stimulate (a person) to creative or other activity or to express certain ideas. **2** fill or arouse with (a certain feeling or reaction) (*he inspires confidence in us; inspired me with determination*).

inspiriting *adj.* encouraging.

inst. *abbr.* instant, = of the current month (*on the 6th inst.*).

instability *n.* lack of stability.

install *v.* (also **instal**) **1** place (a person) in office, esp. with ceremonies. **2** set (apparatus) in position and ready for use. **3** settle in a place (*he was comfortably installed in an armchair*). ☐ **installation** / in-stuh-**lay**-shuhn / *n.*

instalment *n.* **1** any of a number of payments made to clear a debt over a period of time. **2** any of several parts, esp. of a broadcast or published story.

instance *n.* **1** an example or illustration of something. **2** a particular case (*that's not true in this instance*). • *v.* mention as an instance (*he instanced his previous record*). ☐ **for instance** as an example. **in the first instance** firstly.

instant *adj.* **1** occurring immediately (*there was instant relief*). **2** (of food) designed to be prepared quickly and easily. **3** (in commerce) of the current month (*the 6th instant*). • *n.* **1** an exact moment (*come here this instant!*). **2** a very short space of time, a moment (*not an instant too soon*). ☐ **instant replay** the immediate repetition on television of part of a filmed sports event, often in slow motion.

instantaneous / in-stuhn-**tay**-nee-uhs / *adj.* occurring or done instantly (*death was instantaneous*). ☐ **instantaneously** *adv.*

instantly *adv.* immediately.

instate *v.* (often foll. by *in*) install; establish.

instead *adv.* as an alternative or substitute. ☐ **instead of** in place of.

instep *n.* **1** the upper surface of the foot between toes and ankle. **2** the part of a shoe etc. over or under this.

instigate *v.* urge or incite; bring about by persuasion (*instigated them to strike; instigated an inquiry*). ☐ **instigation** *n.* **instigator** *n.*

instil *v.* (**instilled, instilling**) introduce (ideas etc.) into a person's mind gradually (*instilled fear into them all*). ☐ **instillation** *n.* **instilment** *n.*

instinct *n.* **1** an inborn impulse or tendency to perform certain acts or behave in certain ways. **2** a natural ability (*has an instinct for finding a good place*). **3** intuition. ☐ **instinct with** imbued with, filled with (*his poetry is instinct with passion*). ☐☐ **instinctive** *adj.* **instinctively** *adv.*

instinctual *adj.* instinctive. ☐ **instinctually** *adv.*

institute *n.* **1** a society or organisation for promotion of a scientific, educational, or social etc. activity. **2** the building used by this. • *v.* **1** establish, found. **2** cause (an inquiry or a custom) to be started.

institution *n.* **1** instituting; being instituted. **2** an institute, esp. for a charitable or social activity. **3** an established law, custom, or practice. **4** *colloq.* a person who has become a familiar figure in some activity.

institutional *adj.* **1** of or like an institution. **2** typical of institutions (*institutional food*). ☐ **institutionally** *adv.*

institutionalise *v.* (also **-ize**) **1** make (a thing) institutional. **2** place or keep (a person) in an institution that will provide the care needed. ☐ **institutionalisation** *n.*

institutionalised *adj.* so used to living in an institution that one cannot live independently.

instruct *v.* **1** give (a person) instruction in a subject or skill. **2** inform (*we are instructed by our agents that you owe us $50*). **3** give instructions to. **4** authorise (a solicitor or counsel) to act on one's behalf. ☐ **instructor** *n.*

instruction *n.* **1** teaching; education. **2** (often as **instructions**) a direction; an order. **3** expression in a computer program defining and effecting an operation. ☐ **instructional** *adj.*

instructive *adj.* giving or containing instruction; enlightening. ☐ **instructively** *adv.*

instrument *n.* **1** a tool or implement, esp. for delicate or scientific work. **2** a measuring device giving information about the operation of an engine etc. or used in navigation. **3** (in full **musical instrument**) a device designed for producing musical sounds. **4** a person or thing used or controlled to perform an action (*he is merely an instrument of the tobacco industry*). **5** a formal or legal document.

instrumental *adj.* **1** serving as an instrument or means of doing something (*was instrumental in finding her a job*). **2** performed on musical instruments (*instrumental music*). **3** of or arising from an instrument (*the plane crash was caused by instrumental error*).

instrumentalist *n.* a person who plays a musical instrument.

instrumentality *n.* agency or means.

instrumentation *n.* **1** the arrangement or composition of music for instruments. **2** the provision or use of mechanical or scientific instruments.

insubordinate *adj.* disobedient, rebellious. ☐ **insubordination** *n.*

insubstantial *adj.* **1** not existing in reality, imaginary. **2** not made of a strong or solid substance; flimsy (*insubstantial evidence*).

insufferable *adj.* **1** unbearable. **2** unbearably conceited or arrogant. ☐ **insufferably** *adv.*

insufficient *adj.* not sufficient; inadequate. ☐ **insufficiently** *adv.* **insufficiency** *n.*

insular / **in**-syoo-luh, -shoo-luh / *adj.* **1** of or on an island. **2** narrow-minded (*insular prejudices*). ☐ **insularity** / in-syoo-**la**-ruh-tee / *n.*

insulate / **in**-syoo-layt, **in**-shoo- / *v.* **1** cover or protect (a thing) with a substance or device that prevents the passage of electricity or sound or the loss of heat (*insulating tape*). **2** isolate (a person or place) from influences. ☐ **insulation** *n.* **insulator** *n.*

insulin / **in**-syuh-luhn, **in**-suh-, **in**-shuh- / *n.* a hormone produced in the pancreas, controlling the absorption of sugar by the body.

insult *v.* / in-**sult** / speak or act in a way that hurts the feelings or pride of (a person). •*n.* / **in**-sult / an insulting remark or action. ☐ **insulting** *adj.* **insultingly** *adv.*

insuperable / in-**soo**-puh-ruh-buhl, -**syoo**-, -pruh-buhl / *adj.* unable to be overcome (*an insuperable difficulty*). ☐ **insuperably** *adv.* **insuperability** *n.*

insupportable *adj.* **1** unable to be endured. **2** unjustifiable.

insurance *n.* **1** a contract undertaking to provide compensation for loss, damage, or injury etc., in return for payment made in advance. **2** the business of providing such contracts. **3** the amount payable to the company etc. providing the contract; a premium. **4** the amount payable by the company etc. in compensation. **5** a measure taken to provide for a possible contingency (*take an umbrella as insurance*).

■ **Usage** *See* the note under *assurance.*

insure *v.* **1** protect by a contract of insurance. **2** provide for (a possible contingency). ☐ **insurer** *n.* **insurable** *adj.*

insurgent / in-**ser**-juhnt / *adj.* rebellious, rising in revolt. •*n.* a rebel. ☐ **insurgence** *n.*

insurmountable / in-suh-**mown**-tuh-buhl / *adj.* unable to be surmounted, insuperable.

insurrection / in-suh-**rek**-shuhn / *n.* rising against established authority, rebellion. ☐ **insurrectionist** *n.*

inswinger *n.* **1** *Cricket* **a** a ball bowled with a curve or swing from off to leg. **b** a bowler who bowls such balls. **2** *Soccer* a pass or kick that sends the ball curving towards the goal.

intact *adj.* undamaged; complete.

intaglio / in-**tah**-lee-oh / *n.* (*pl.* **intaglios**) **1** a carving in which the design is sunk below the surface. **2** a gem carved in this way.

intake *n.* **1** the process of taking something in. **2** the place where liquid or air etc. is channelled into something. **3** the number of people or things accepted or received (*a school's annual intake of pupils*).

intangible / in-**tan**-juh-buhl / *adj.* **1** unable to be felt by touching. **2** unable to be grasped mentally. •*n.* a thing that cannot be precisely assessed or defined. ☐ **intangibly** *adv.*

integer / **in**-tuh-juh / *n.* a whole number, not a fraction.

integral / **in**-tuh-gruhl, in-**teg**-ruhl / *adj.* **1** (of a part) constituent, necessary to the completeness of a whole (*Tasmania is an integral part of Australia*). **2** complete, forming a whole (*an integral design*). **3** of or denoted by an integer. •*n.* *Maths* a quantity of which a given function is the derivative. ☐ **integrally** *adv.*

■ **Usage** The alternative pronunciation given for the adjective, stressed on the second syllable, is considered incorrect by some people.

integrate / **in**-tuh-grayt / *v.* **1** combine or form (a part or parts) into a whole. **2** bring or come into equal membership of a community. **3** desegregate, esp. racially (e.g. a school). **4** *Maths* calculate the integral of. ☐ **integrated circuit** a small chip of material replacing a conventional electronic circuit of many components. **integrated services digital network** a telecommunications network through which sound, images, and data can be transmitted as digitised signals. ☐ ☐ **integration** *n.*

integrity / in-**teg**-ruh-tee / *n.* **1** honesty, incorruptibility. **2** wholeness, soundness.

integument / in-**teg**-yoo-muhnt / *n.* skin or other natural outer covering.

intellect / **in**-tuh-lekt / *n.* **1** the mind's power of reasoning and acquiring knowledge. **2** a clever or knowledgable person.

intellectual / in-tuh-**lek**-choo-uhl / *adj.* **1** of the intellect. **2** needing use of the intellect (*an intellectual occupation*). **3** having a well-developed intellect and a taste for advanced knowledge. •*n.* an intellectual person. ☐ **intellectual property** *Law* non-tangible property that is the result of creativity, such as patents, copyrights, etc. □ □ **intellectually** *adv.* **intellectuality** *n.*

intelligence *n.* **1** mental ability; the power of learning and understanding. **2** information, esp. that of military value. **3** the people engaged in collecting this. □ **intelligence quotient** (*abbr.* **IQ**) a number that shows how a person's intelligence compares with the average.

intelligent *adj.* **1** having great mental ability. **2** (of a device in a computer system) containing in itself a capacity to process information. □ **intelligently** *adv.*

intelligentsia / in-tel-uh-**jent**-see-uh / *n.* intellectual people regarded as a class.

intelligible / in-**tel**-uh-juh-buhl / *adj.* able to be understood. □ **intelligibly** *adv.* **intelligibility** *n.*

intemperate *adj.* **1** drinking alcohol excessively. **2** immoderate. □ **intemperance** *n.*

intend *v.* **1** have in mind as what one wishes to do or achieve. **2** plan that (a thing) shall be used or interpreted in a particular way (*we intended this room for you; the remark was intended as an insult*).

intended *adj.* done on purpose. •*n. colloq.* one's fiancé or fiancée.

intense *adj.* **1** strong in quality or degree (*intense heat*). **2** (of a person) emotional. □ **intensely** *adv.* **intenseness** *n.*

intensifier *n. Grammar* a word used to give force or emphasis, e.g. *really* in *I'm really hot.*

intensify *v.* (**intensified, intensifying**) make or become more intense. □ **intensification** *n.*

intensity *n.* **1** intenseness. **2** the amount of some quality such as force or brightness.

intensive *adj.* **1** employing much effort; concentrated. **2** serving to increase production (*intensive farming*). **3** *Grammar* (of a word) used to give force or emphasis, e.g. *really* in *I'm really hot.* □ **intensive care 1** medical treatment with constant supervision of a seriously ill patient. **2** the part of a hospital devoted to this. □ □ **intensively** *adv.* **intensiveness** *n.*

intensivist *n.* a doctor specially trained to treat patients in an intensive care unit.

intent *n.* intention (*with intent to kill*). •*adj.* **1** (foll. by *on* or *upon*) intending, having one's mind fixed on some purpose (*intent on killing*). **2** with one's attention concentrated (*an intent gaze*). □ **to all intents and purposes** practically, virtually. □ □ **intently** *adv.* **intentness** *n.*

intention *n.* what one intends to do or achieve; one's purpose.

intentional *adj.* done on purpose; not accidental. □ **intentionally** *adv.*

inter / in-**ter** / *v.* (**interred, interring**) bury (a dead body) in the earth or in a tomb.

inter- *comb. form* between, among.

interact *v.* have an effect upon each other. □ **interaction** *n.*

interactive *adj.* **1** interacting. **2** (in computers) allowing information to be transferred immediately both to and from a computer system and its user.

inter alia / **ay**-lee-uh / *adv.* among other things. (¶ Latin)

interbreed *v.* (**interbred, interbreeding**) **1** (cause to) breed with members of a different plant or animal species etc. to produce a hybrid; crossbreed. **2** breed within one family etc.

intercede / in-tuh-**seed** / *v.* intervene on behalf of another person or as a peacemaker.

intercept / in-tuh-**sept** / *v.* stop or catch (a person or thing) on the way from one place to another. □ **interception** *n.* **interceptor** *n.*

intercession / in-tuh-**sesh**-uhn / *n.* interceding. □ **intercessor** *n.*

interchange *v.* / in-tuh-**chaynj** / **1** put (each of two things) into the other's place. **2** make an exchange of, give and receive (one thing for another). **3** alternate. •*n.* / **in**-tuh-chaynj / **1** interchanging. **2** alternation. **3** *Aust. Rules* (in full **interchange player**) a player not on the field who may be substituted for an active player in his team at any point in the game. **4** *Aust. Rules* (in full **interchange bench**) **a** the bench on which an interchange player waits to enter play. **b** (collectively) a team's interchange players. **5** a major road junction □ **interchangeable** *adj.* **interchangeability** *n.*

inter-city *adj.* existing or travelling between cities.

intercom / **in**-tuh-kom / *n.* a system of communication by radio or telephone between or within offices, ships, etc.; the instrument used for this.

intercommunicate *v.* **1** communicate with each other. **2** (of rooms etc.) have access into each other. □ **intercommunication** *n.*

interconnect *v.* connect with each other. □ **interconnection** *n.*

intercontinental *adj.* connecting or travelling between continents.

intercourse *n.* **1** dealings or communication between people or countries. **2** sexual intercourse (*see* SEXUAL), copulation.

interdenominational *adj.* of or involving more than one religious denomination.

interdepartmental *adj.* of or involving more than one department.

interdependent *adj.* dependent on each other. □ **interdependence** *n.*

interdict *v.* / in-tuh-**dikt** / prohibit or forbid authoritatively. •*n.* / **in**-tuh-dikt / **1** an authoritative prohibition. **2** (in the Catholic Church) a sentence excluding a person or place from certain ecclesiastical functions and privileges. □ **interdiction** *n.*

interdisciplinary *adj.* of or involving different branches of learning.

interdominion *adj.* (of sports matches, diplomatic relations, etc.) occurring or carried on

interest *n.* **1** curiosity or concern about something. **2** the quality of arousing such a feeling (*the subject has no interest for me*). **3** a subject or hobby in which one is concerned (*his interests are knitting and playing Rugby*). **4** advantage, benefit (*she looks after her own interests*). **5** a legal right to a share in something; a financial stake in a business etc. **6** money paid for the use of money lent. •*v.* **1** arouse the interest of. **2** cause to take an interest in (*interested herself in welfare work*).

interested *adj.* **1** feeling or showing interest or curiosity. **2** having a private interest in something (*interested parties in this dispute*).

interesting *adj.* arousing interest. ☐ **interestingly** *adv.*

interface *n.* **1** a surface forming a boundary between two regions. **2** a place or piece of equipment where interaction occurs between two processes etc. **3** *Computing* a program or apparatus for connecting two pieces of equipment so that they can be operated jointly or for enabling a user to access a program. •*v.* connect by means of an interface.

interfere *v.* **1** (usu. foll. by *with*) meddle; obstruct a process etc. **2** intervene, esp. without invitation. **3** (foll. by *with*) molest sexually. **4** *Physics* cause interference.

interference *n.* **1** interfering. **2** the fading of received radio signals because of atmospherics or unwanted signals. **3** *Physics* the meeting of wave motions to form a wave in which the displacement is reinforced or cancelled.

interferon / in-tuh-**feer**-ron / *n.* a protein substance that prevents the development of a virus in living cells.

interfuse *v.* **1** intersperse. **2** blend or fuse together. ☐ **interfusion** *n.*

intergalactic *adj.* between galaxies.

interim / **in**-tuh-ruhm / *n.* an intervening period of time (*in the interim*). •*adj.* temporary, provisional (*an interim report*).

interior *adj.* **1** nearer to the centre, inner. **2** internal; domestic. •*n.* **1** an interior part or region; the central or inland part of a country. **2** the inside of a building or room. ☐ **interior decoration** (*or* **design**) decoration or design of the interior of a building.

interject *v.* put in (a remark) when someone is speaking.

interjection *n.* **1** interjecting. **2** an interjected remark. **3** an exclamation such as *oh!* or *good heavens!*

interlace *v.* weave or lace together.

interlard *v.* insert contrasting remarks throughout (a speech etc.) (*interlarded his speech with quotations*).

interleave *v.* insert leaves (usu. blank) between the pages of (a book).

interline *v.* put an extra layer of material between the fabric of (a garment) and its lining. ☐ **interlining** *n.*

interlink *v.* connect together.

interlock *v.* fit into each other, esp. so that parts engage. •*n.* **1** machine-knitted fabric with fine stitches. **2** a mechanism for preventing a set of operations from being performed in the wrong sequence.

interlocutor / in-tuh-**lok**-yuh-tuh / *n.* a person who takes part in a conversation.

interloper *n.* **1** an intruder. **2** one who interferes in the affairs of others.

interlude *n.* **1** an interval between parts of a play etc. **2** something (such as a piece of music) performed during this. **3** an intervening time or event etc. of a different kind from the main one.

intermarry *v.* (**intermarried**, **intermarrying**) **1** (of races, castes, families, etc.) become connected by marriage. **2** marry within one's own family. ☐ **intermarriage** *n.*

intermediary / in-tuh-**mee**-dyuh-ree / *n.* a mediator, a go-between. •*adj.* **1** acting as an intermediary. **2** intermediate.

intermediate *adj.* coming between two things in time, place, or order. •*n.* an intermediate thing.

interment / in-**ter**-muhnt / *n.* burial.

■ **Usage** Do not confuse with *internment*.

intermezzo / in-tuh-**met**-soh / *n.* (*pl.* **intermezzi** *or* **intermezzos**) a short musical composition to be played between acts of a play etc. or between sections of a larger work, or independently.

interminable / in-**ter**-muh-nuh-buhl / *adj.* endless; long and boring. ☐ **interminably** *adv.*

intermingle *v.* mix together.

intermission *n.* an interval; a pause in work or action.

intermittent *adj.* occurring at intervals, not continuous (*intermittent rain*). ☐ **intermittently** *adv.*

intern *v.* / in-**tern** / compel (an enemy alien or prisoner of war etc.) to live in a special area or camp. •*n.* / **in**-tern / (also **interne**) **1** a resident junior doctor at a hospital. **2** esp. *US* a student or trainee who works, sometimes without pay, at a trade or occupation in order to gain work experience or satisfy requirements for a qualification.

internal *adj.* **1** of or in the inside of a thing. **2** of or in the interior of the body (*internal organs*). **3** of the domestic affairs of a country. **4** used or applying within an organisation. **5** of the mind or soul. ☐ **internal-combustion engine** an engine that produces power by the explosion of gases or vapour with air in a cylinder. **internal evidence** evidence contained in the thing being discussed. ☐ ☐ **internally** *adv.*

internalise *v.* (also **-ize**) **1** learn, absorb into the mind as a fact, attitude, etc. **2** suppress (an emotion etc.) (*internalised his grief*). ☐ **internalisation** *n.*

international *adj.* of or existing or agreed between two or more countries. • *n.* **1** a sports contest between players representing different countries. **2** any of these players. **3** (**International**) any of several international socialist organisations, of which the first was formed by Karl Marx in London in 1864. ☐ **internationally** *adv.*

International Court of Justice a judicial court of the United Nations which meets at The Hague.

internationalism *n.* **1** being international. **2** support and cooperation between nations.

internationalise *v.* (also **-ize**) make international.

International Monetary Fund an international organisation, with headquarters in Washington, DC, for promoting international trade and monetary cooperation and the stabilisation of exchange rates.

International Phonetic Alphabet a set of phonetic symbols for international use.

International System (**of units**) *see* SI.

interne alternative spelling of INTERN *n.*

internecine / in-ter-**nee**-suyn / *adj.* destructive to each of the parties involved (*internecine war*).

internee / in-ter-**nee** / *n.* a person who is interned.

Internet *n.* (also **internet**) *trademark* an international computer network linking computers from educational institutions, government agencies, industry, etc., accessible to the general public via modem links. ☐ **Internet relay chat** a tool on the Internet which enables people to take part in a discussion on a particular topic etc. in real time. **Internet service provider** a company which provides access to the Internet for users.

internment *n.* interning; being interned.

■ **Usage** Do not confuse with *interment*.

interpenetrate *v.* **1** penetrate each other. **2** pervade. ☐ **interpenetration** *n.*

interpersonal *adj.* between persons; social.

interplanetary *adj.* between planets.

interplay *n.* interaction; reciprocal action.

Interpol International Criminal Police Commission, an organisation that co-ordinates investigations (made by the police forces of member countries) into crimes with an international basis.

interpolate / in-**ter**-puh-layt / *v.* **1** interject. **2** insert (new material) into a book etc. **3** estimate (values) between known ones in the same range. ☐ **interpolation** *n.* **interpolator** *n.*

interpose *v.* **1** insert between; interject. **2** intervene. ☐ **interposition** *n.*

interpret *v.* **1** explain the meaning of. **2** understand in a specified way (*interpreted his gesture as mocking*). **3** act as interpreter. ☐ **interpretation** *n.*

interpretative / in-**ter**-pruh-tuh-tiv / *adj.* interpreting.

interpreter *n.* **1** a person whose job is to translate a speech etc. into another language orally. **2** *Computing* a language processor that analyses and executes a program on a line by line basis.

interpretive *adj.* interpretative.

interracial *adj.* between or affecting different races.

interregnum / in-tuh-**reg**-nuhm / *n.* **1** an interval when the normal government or leadership is suspended, esp. between successive reigns or regimes. **2** an interval, a pause.

interrelated *adj.* related to each other. ☐ **interrelation** *n.*

interrogate / in-**te**-ruh-gayt / *v.* question closely or formally. ☐ **interrogation** *n.* **interrogator** *n.*

interrogative / in-tuh-**rog**-uh-tiv / *adj.* questioning; having the form of a question (*an interrogative tone*). • *n.* an interrogative word (e.g. *what?*).

interrogatory / in-tuh-**rog**-uh-tuh-ree, -tree / *adj.* questioning. • *n.* a formal set of questions.

interrupt *v.* **1** break the continuity of. **2** break the flow of a speech etc. by inserting a remark. **3** obstruct (a view etc.). • *n. Computing* the action of interrupting the execution of a program. ☐ **interruption** *n.*

interrupter *n.* (also **interruptor**) **1** a person or thing that interrupts. **2** a device for opening and closing an electric circuit.

intersect *v.* **1** divide (a thing) by passing or lying across it. **2** (of lines or roads etc.) cross each other.

intersection *n.* **1** intersecting. **2** a place where lines or roads etc. intersect.

intersperse *v.* insert contrasting material here and there in (a thing); scatter.

interstate *adj.* existing or carried on between States, e.g. those of Australia. • *adv.* in, into, or from a State other than that in which one usually lives (*he's moved interstate*).

interstellar *adj.* between stars.

interstice / in-**ter**-stuhs / *n.* a small intervening space; a crevice.

interstitial / in-tuh-**stish**-uhl / *adj.* of, forming, or occupying interstices.

intertwine *v.* twine together, entwine.

interval *n.* **1** a time between two events or parts of an action. **2** a pause between two parts of a performance. **3** a space between two objects or points. **4** the difference in musical pitch between two notes. ☐ **at intervals** with some time or distance between; now and then. ☐ ☐ **intervallic** / in-tuh-**val**-ik / *adj.*

intervene / in-tuh-**veen** / *v.* **1** occur in the time between events (*in the intervening years*). **2** cause hindrance by occurring (*we should have finished harvesting but a storm intervened*). **3** enter a

intervention discussion or dispute etc. in order to change its course or resolve it.

intervention / in-tuh-**ven**-shuhn / *n.* intervening, esp. by one country in the internal affairs of another.

interventionist *n.* a person who favours intervention.

interview *n.* a formal meeting or conversation with a person, held in order to assess his or her merits as a candidate etc. or to obtain comments and information. • *v.* hold an interview with. ☐ **interviewer** *n.*

interviewee *n.* a person who is interviewed.

interwar *adj.* in the period between two wars.

interweave *v.* (**interwove**, **interwoven**, **interweaving**) **1** weave together. **2** blend intimately (*fact interwoven with fiction*).

intestate / in-**tes**-tayt, in-**tes**-tuht / *adj.* not having made a valid will before death (*he died intestate*). ☐ **intestacy** / in-**tes**-tuh-see / *n.*

intestine / in-**tes**-tuhn, -tuyn / *n.* the long tubular section of the alimentary canal, extending from the outlet of the stomach to the anus. ☐ **large intestine** the broader and shorter part of this, including the colon and rectum. **small intestine** the narrower and longer part. ☐☐ **intestinal** *adj.*

intestinal flora *n.* the bacteria naturally inhabiting the gut.

in-thing *colloq.* (usu. preceded by *the*) a currently fashionable or trendy thing (*rap dancing is the in-thing these days*).

intifada / in-ti-**fah**-duh / *n.* an uprising by Arabs.

intimate[1] / **in**-tuh-muht / *adj.* **1** having a close acquaintance or friendship with a person. **2** having a sexual relationship with a person, esp. outside marriage. **3** private and personal. **4** (of knowledge) detailed and obtained by much study or experience. **5** (of a place etc.) friendly (*an intimate restaurant*). • *n.* an intimate friend. ☐ **intimately** *adv.* **intimacy** *n.*

intimate[2] / **in**-tuh-mayt / *v.* make known, esp. by hinting. ☐ **intimation** *n.*

intimidate / in-**tim**-uh-dayt / *v.* subdue or influence by frightening with threats or force. ☐ **intimidation** *n.*

into *prep.* **1** to the inside of, to a point within (*went into the house; fell into the river; far into the night*). **2** to a particular state, condition, or occupation (*got into trouble; grew into an adult; went into banking*). **3** *colloq.* actively interested and participating in (*he is into rock music*). **4** *Maths* indicating division (*4 into 20 is 5*).

intolerable *adj.* unbearable. ☐ **intolerably** *adv.*

intolerant *adj.* not tolerant, esp. of ideas or beliefs etc. that differ from one's own (*intolerant of opposition*). ☐ **intolerantly** *adv.* **intolerance** *n.*

intonation / in-tuh-**nay**-shuhn / *n.* **1** intoning. **2** the tone or pitch of the voice in speaking. **3** a slight accent (*a Welsh intonation*).

intone *v.* recite (prayers etc.) in a chanting voice, esp. on one note.

in toto *adv.* completely. (¶ Latin)

intoxicant *adj.* causing intoxication. • *n.* an intoxicating substance.

intoxicated *adj.* **1** (of a person) drunk. **2** made greatly excited or reckless (*intoxicated by success*). ☐ **intoxication** *n.*

intra- *comb. form* within.

intractable / in-**trak**-tuh-buhl / *adj.* unmanageable, hard to deal with or control (*an intractable difficulty; intractable children*). ☐ **intractability** *n.*

intramural / in-truh-**myoo**-ruhl / *adj.* **1** situated or done within the walls of an institution etc. **2** forming part of ordinary university work.

intramuscular / in-truh-**mus**-kyuh-luh / *adj.* in or into muscle tissue (*an intramuscular injection*).

intranet *n.* *Computing* a local or restricted communications network, esp. a private network created using World Wide Web software.

intransigent / in-**tran**-suh-juhnt, -zuh- / *adj.* unwilling to compromise, stubborn. ☐ **intransigence** *n.*

intransitive / in-**tran**-suh-tiv, -zuh-tiv / *adj.* (of a verb) used without being followed by a direct object, e.g. *hear* in *we can hear* (but not in *we can hear you*). ☐ **intransitively** *adv.*

intrauterine / in-truh-**yoo**-tuh-ruyn / *adj.* within the uterus. ☐ **intrauterine device** a contraceptive device fitted inside the uterus and physically preventing the implantation of fertilised ova.

intravenous / in-truh-**vee**-nuhs / *adj.* within or into a vein (*an intravenous injection*). ☐ **intravenously** *adv.*

in-tray *n.* a tray to hold incoming documents awaiting attention.

intrepid / in-**trep**-uhd / *adj.* fearless, brave. ☐ **intrepidly** *adv.* **intrepidity** / in-truh-**pid**-uh-tee / *n.*

intricate *adj.* very complicated. ☐ **intricately** *adv.* **intricacy** / **in**-truh-kuh-see / *n.*

intrigue *v.* / in-**treeg** / **1** plot with someone in an underhand way; use secret influence. **2** rouse the interest or curiosity of (*the subject intrigues me*). • *n.* / **in**-treeg / **1** underhand plotting; an underhand plot. **2** *archaic* a secret love affair. ☐ **intriguing** *adj.* **intriguingly** *adv.*

intrinsic / in-**trin**-zik / *adj.* belonging to the basic nature of a person or thing. ☐ **intrinsically** *adv.*

intro *n.* *colloq.* an introduction.

introduce *v.* **1** make (a person) known by name to others. **2** announce (a speaker or broadcast program etc.) to an audience. **3** bring (a bill) before Parliament. **4** cause (a person) to become acquainted with a subject. **5** bring (a custom or idea etc.) into use or into a system. **6** bring or put in (*introduce the needle into a vein*).

introduction *n.* **1** introducing; being introduced. **2** the formal presentation of one person

introductory

another. **3** an introductory or explanatory section at the beginning of a book, speech, etc. **4** an introductory treatise (*An Introduction to Aboriginal Culture*).

introductory *adj.* introducing a person or subject; preliminary.

introit / **in**-troit / *n.* a psalm or antiphon sung or said while the priest approaches the altar for the Mass; any introductory psalm, anthem, etc.

introspection *n.* examination of one's own thoughts and feelings. ☐ **introspective** *adj.*

introvert / **in**-truh-vert / *n.* **1** a person concerned more with his or her own thoughts and feelings than with the people and things round him or her. **2** a shy person. •*adj.* (also **introverted**) having these characteristics. ☐ **introversion** *n.*

intrude *v.* come or join in without being invited or wanted.

intruder *n.* **1** a person who intrudes. **2** a burglar.

intrusion *n.* **1** intruding. **2** an influx of molten rock between existing strata. ☐ **intrusive** *adj.*

intuition / in-tyoo-**ish**-uhn / *n.* the power of knowing or understanding something immediately without reasoning or being taught. ☐ **intuitional** *adj.*

intuitive / in-**tyoo**-uh-tiv / *adj.* of, possessing, or based on intuition. ☐ **intuitively** *adv.*

Inuit / **in**-yoo-uht / *n.* (also **Innuit**) (*pl.* **Inuit** or **Inuits**) **1** an Eskimo, esp. in Canada. **2** the languages of the Eskimos, esp. the language of the Canadian Eskimos.

inundate / **in**-uhn-dayt / *v.* **1** flood, cover with water. **2** overwhelm (*inundated with enquiries*). ☐ **inundation** *n.*

inure / i-**nyoor** / *v.* **1** accustom, esp. to something unpleasant. **2** (in law) take effect. ☐ **inurement** *n.*

invade *v.* **1** enter (territory) with armed forces in order to attack or occupy it. **2** crowd into (*tourists invaded the city*). **3** penetrate harmfully (*the disease had invaded all parts of the body*). ☐ **invader** *n.*

invalid[1] / **in**-vuh-lid, -leed / *n.* a person who is weakened by illness or injury. •*v.* **1** remove from active service because of ill health or injury (*he was invalided out of the army*). **2** disable by illness.

invalid[2] / in-**val**-uhd / *adj.* not valid.

invalidate / in-**val**-uh-dayt / *v.* make (a claim, argument, law, etc.) ineffective or not valid. ☐ **invalidation** *n.*

invalidity / in-vuh-**lid**-uh-tee / *n.* **1** lack of validity. **2** being an invalid.

invaluable *adj.* having a value that is too great to be measured; priceless. ☐ **invaluably** *adv.*

invariable / in-**vair**-ree-uh-buhl / *adj.* not variable; always the same. ☐ **invariably** *adv.*

invasion *n.* invading, being invaded.

invasive / in-**vay**-siv, -ziv / *adj.* **1** (of weeds, cancer cells, etc.) tending to spread. **2** (of surgery) involving large incisions, the introduction of instruments into the body, etc. **3** tending to encroach.

invective / in-**vek**-tiv / *n.* a violent attack in words; abusive language.

inveigh / in-**vay** / *v.* (foll. by *against*) attack violently or bitterly in words.

inveigle / in-**vay**-guhl, -**vee**-guhl / *v.* entice; persuade by guile (*inveigled me into going with him*). ☐ **inveiglement** *n.*

invent *v.* **1** create by thought; make or design (something original). **2** construct (a false or fictional story) (*invented an excuse*). ☐ **inventor** *n.*

invention *n.* **1** inventing; being invented. **2** something invented. **3** a false story. **4** inventiveness in literature etc.

Invention of the Cross the Christian festival, held on 3 May, commemorating the finding by St Helena of Christ's Cross.

inventive *adj.* able to invent things; imaginative. ☐ **inventiveness** *n.*

inventory / **in**-vuhn-tree / *n.* a detailed list of goods or furniture etc. •*v.* (**inventoried**, **inventorying**) make an inventory of; enter in an inventory.

inverse *adj.* reversed in position, order, or relation. •*n.* **1** an inverse state. **2** a thing that is the exact opposite of another. ☐ **in inverse proportion** with one quantity increasing in proportion as the other decreases. ☐☐ **inversely** *adv.*

inversion *n.* **1** inverting; being inverted. **2** something that is inverted.

invert *v.* turn (a thing) upside down; reverse the position, order, or relationship of. ☐ **inverted commas** quotation marks (' ' or " "). **inverted snob** a person who likes, or takes pride in, what a snob might be expected to disapprove of.

invertebrate / in-**ver**-tuh-bruht, -brayt / *adj.* not having a backbone. •*n.* an invertebrate animal.

invest *v.* **1** use (money) to buy stocks, shares, or property in order to earn interest or bring profit for the buyer. **2** (often foll. by *in*) spend money, time, or effort on something that will be useful (*invest in a freezer*). **3** confer a rank, office, or power upon (a person). **4** (foll. by *with*) provide or credit (a person) with a quality (*invested him with more intelligence than he had*). **5** cover as with a garment (*mist investing the garden with mystery*). ☐ **investor** *n.*

investigate *v.* **1** make a careful study of (a thing) in order to discover the facts about it. **2** make a search or systematic inquiry. ☐ **investigation** *n.* **investigator** *n.* **investigative** / in-**ves**-tuh-guh-tiv / *adj.* **investigatory** *adj.*

investiture / in-**ves**-tuh-chuh / *n.* the process of investing a person with honours or rank.

investment *n.* **1** investing. **2** a sum of money invested. **3** something in which money, time, or effort is invested.

inveterate / in-**vet**-uh-ruht / *adj.* **1** habitual (*an inveterate gambler*). **2** firmly established (*inveterate prejudices*). □ **inveteracy** *n.*

invidious / in-**vid**-ee-uhs / *adj.* likely to cause resentment or anger (*in an invidious position; an invidious task*).

invigilate / in-**vij**-uh-layt / *v.* supervise people taking an examination. □ **invigilation** *n.* **invigilator** *n.*

invigorate / in-**vig**-uh-rayt / *v.* give vigour or strength to. □ **invigorating** *adj.*

invincible / in-**vin**-suh-buhl / *adj.* unconquerable (*an invincible army; invincible stupidity*). □ **invincibly** *adv.* **invincibility** *n.*

inviolable / in-**vuy**-uh-luh-buhl / *adj.* not to be violated or dishonoured. □ **inviolably** *adv.* **inviolability** *n.*

inviolate / in-**vuy**-uh-luht / *adj.* not violated; safe. □ **inviolacy** *n.*

invisible *adj.* not visible, unable to be seen. □ **invisible exports** (*or* **imports**) payment for services (such as insurance or shipping) made to (or by) another country. □ □ **invisibly** *adv.* **invisibility** *n.*

invite *v.* / in-**vuyt** / **1** ask (a person) in a friendly way to come to one's house or to a gathering etc. **2** ask (a person) formally to do something. **3** ask for (comments, suggestions, etc.). **4** act so as to be likely to cause (a thing) unintentionally (*you are inviting disaster*). **5** attract, tempt. • *n.* / **in**-vuyt / *colloq.* an invitation. □ **invitation** *n.* **invitational** *adj.* & *n.*

inviting *adj.* attracting one to do something, pleasant and tempting. □ **invitingly** *adv.*

in vitro / vee-troh / *adv.* (of biological processes) taking place in a test tube or other laboratory environment. □ **in vitro fertilisation** the fertilisation of a human egg by a sperm in a test tube so that the embryo which results might be implanted in a uterus. (¶ Latin, = in glass.)

invocation / in-vuh-**kay**-shuhn / *n.* invoking; calling upon God or the saints in prayer. □ **invocatory** *adj.*

invoice *n.* a list of goods sent or services performed, with prices and charges. • *v.* **1** make an invoice of (goods). **2** send an invoice to (a person).

invoke / in-**vohk** / *v.* **1** call upon (a deity etc.) in prayer. **2** call for the help or protection of (*invoked the law*). **3** summon up (a spirit) with words. **4** ask earnestly for (vengeance etc.).

involuntary *adj.* done without intention or without conscious effort of the will (*an involuntary twitch*). □ **involuntarily** *adv.*

involute / in-vuh-loot / *adj.* **1** complex, intricate. **2** curled spirally.

involution *n.* **1** the process of involving. **2** entanglement; intricacy. **3** a curling inwards; a part that curls inwards. **4** a reduction in size or activity of esp. the sexual organs in old age.

involve *v.* **1** contain within itself, make necessary as a condition or result (*the plan involves much expense*). **2** cause to share in an experience or effect; include or affect in its operation (*the safety of the nation is involved*). **3** bring into difficulties (*it will involve us in much expense*). **4** show (a person) to be concerned in a crime etc. □ **involvement** *n.*

involved *adj.* **1** complicated. **2** concerned in something. **3** intimately (esp. sexually) associated (*how long have you been involved with Jim?*).

invulnerable / in-**vul**-nuh-ruh-buhl / *adj.* unable to be wounded or damaged. □ **invulnerability** *n.*

inward *adj.* **1** situated on the inside. **2** going towards the inside. **3** in the mind or spirit (*inward happiness*). • *adv.* (also **inwards**) **1** towards the inside. **2** in the mind or spirit.

inwardly *adv.* **1** on the inside. **2** in the mind or spirit.

inwrought / in-**rawt** / *adj.* **1** (of fabric etc.) with a pattern worked into it. **2** (of a pattern) worked into something.

INXS / in-ek-**ses** / an Australian rock band formed in Sydney in 1977. The lead singer was Michael Hutchence (1960–97).

iodine / **uy**-uh-deen, -duyn / *n.* a bluish-black chemical element (symbol I), found in sea water and seaweed and used in solution as an antiseptic.

iodise / **uy**-uh-duyz / *v.* (also -**ize**) treat or impregnate with iodine.

ion / **uy**-uhn / *n.* an electrically charged atom or group of atoms that has lost or gained one or more electrons.

Ionesco / ee-uh-**nes**-koh /, Eugène (1912–94), French dramatist, a leading exponent of the Theatre of the Absurd.

Ionia / uy-**oh**-nee-uh / the ancient Greek name for the central part of the west coast of Asia Minor. □ **Ionian** *adj.* & *n.*

Ionic / uy-**on**-ik / *adj.* of the **Ionic order**, one of the five classical orders of architecture, characterised by columns with a scroll-like ornamentation at the top.

ionic / uy-**on**-ik / *adj.* of or using ions.

ionise / **uy**-uh-nuyz / *v.* (also -**ize**) convert or be converted into ions. □ **ionisation** *n.* **ioniser** *n.*

ionosphere / uy-**on**-uh-sfeer / *n.* an ionised region of the upper atmosphere, able to reflect radio waves for transmission to another part of the earth. □ **ionospheric** *adj.*

iota / uy-**oh**-tuh / *n.* **1** the ninth letter of the Greek alphabet (Ι, ι). **2** the smallest possible amount; a jot (*it doesn't make an iota of difference*).

IOU *n.* a signed paper acknowledging that one owes a sum of money to the holder (= *I owe you*).

IPA *abbr.* International Phonetic Alphabet.

ipecacuanha / i-puh-kak-yoo-**ah**-nuh / *n.* the dried root of a South American plant, used as an emetic or purgative.

ipso facto / ip-soh **fak**-toh / *adv.* by that very fact. (¶ Latin)

IQ *abbr.* intelligence quotient.

Ir *symbol* iridium.

IRA *abbr.* Irish Republican Army, an organisation seeking to achieve a united Ireland independent of Britain.

Iran / i-**rahn** / a republic in SW Asia, formerly called Persia. ☐ **Iranian** / i-**ray**-nee-uhn / *adj.* & *n.*

Irangate a US political scandal of 1987 involving the sale of arms to Iran (and subsequent release of American hostages) and use of the proceeds to supply arms to the anti-Communist Contras in Nicaragua.

Iraq / i-**rahk** / a republic lying between Iran and Saudi Arabia. ☐ **Iraqi** / i-**rah**-kee / *adj.* & *n.* (*pl.* **Iraqis**).

irascible / i-**ras**-uh-buhl / *adj.* irritable, hot-tempered. ☐ **irascibly** *adv.* **irascibility** *n.*

irate / uy-**rayt** / *adj.* angry, enraged. ☐ **irately** *adv.*

IRC *abbr.* = INTERNET RELAY CHAT.

ire *n. literary* anger.

Ireland[1] an island west of Great Britain, divided into Northern Ireland (which forms part of the UK) and the Republic of Ireland which occupies four-fifths of the island.

Ireland[2], David (1927–), AO, Australian novelist.

Irian Jaya / i-ree-an **juy**-uh / a province of Indonesia, making up the western half of the island of New Guinea. Also called *West Papua*.

iridaceous / i-ruh-**day**-shuhs / *adj.* of the iris family.

iridescent / i-ruh-**des**-uhnt / *adj.* **1** showing rainbow-like colours. **2** showing a change of colour when its position is altered. ☐ **iridescence** *n.*

iridium / i-**rid**-ee-uhm / *n.* a hard white metallic element (symbol Ir).

iridology / uy-ruh-**dol**-uh-jee / *n.* (in alternative medicine) diagnosis by examination of the iris of the eye.

Iris *Gk myth.* the goddess of the rainbow.

iris *n.* **1** the circular coloured membrane in the eye, with a circular opening (the pupil) in the centre. **2** a plant with sword-shaped leaves and showy flowers.

Irish *adj.* of Ireland or its people or language. •*n.* **1** the Celtic language of Ireland, a distinct variety of Gaelic. **2** (**the Irish**) Irish people. ☐ **get one's Irish up** *colloq.* become very angry. **Irish coffee** coffee with cream and Irish whisky. **Irish stew** stew of mutton, potatoes, and onions. **luck of the Irish** *colloq.* extreme good fortune occurring against all the odds. ☐ **Irishman** *n.* **Irishwoman** *n.*

irk *v.* annoy, be tiresome to.

irksome *adj.* annoying, tiresome.

iron *n.* **1** a metallic element (symbol Fe), a very common hard grey metal capable of being magnetised. **2** a tool made of this (*branding iron*). **3** a golf club with an iron or steel head. **4** an implement with a flat base that is heated for smoothing clothes etc. **5** a metal splint or support worn on the leg. **6** (**irons**) fetters. **7** great strength (*a will of iron*). •*adj.* **1** made of iron. **2** strong or unyielding (*an iron constitution; an iron will*). **3** *Aust.* made wholly or partly of sheets of corrugated iron (*a fibro and iron house*). •*v.* **1** smooth (clothes etc.) with an iron. **2** *Aust. colloq.* knock down; defeat (*ironed the opposition*). ☐ **iron-fisted 1** miserly, stingy. **2** harshly severe; ruthless. **iron lace** *Aust.* delicate-looking cast-iron decorative work orig. used in 19th-century terrace houses. **iron lung** a rigid case fitting over a patient's body, used for administering artificial respiration for a prolonged period by means of mechanical pumps. **iron man** (*or* **iron woman**) the winner of an Iron Man (*or* Iron Woman) competition (an endurance event involving swimming, board-riding, beach running, etc.). **iron out** deal with and remove (difficulties etc.). **iron rations** a small emergency supply of food. **many irons in the fire** many undertakings or opportunities.

Iron Age the prehistoric period when weapons and tools were made of iron.

ironbark *n.* an eastern Australian eucalypt with a thick, hard, usu. black bark and hard, dense timber.

ironclad *adj.* **1** covered or protected with iron. **2** impregnable; rigorous (*an ironclad alibi*).

Iron Curtain *hist.* a former barrier of secrecy and restriction preventing the free passage of people and information between the USSR (and countries under its influence) and the Western world.

ironed gang *n.* (also **iron gang**) *Aust. hist.* a detachment of convicts assigned to hard labour in fetters.

ironic / uy-**ron**-ik / *adj.* (also **ironical**) using or expressing irony. ☐ **ironically** *adv.*

ironing *n.* clothes etc. for ironing or just ironed. ☐ **ironing board** a narrow flat stand on which clothes etc. are ironed.

ironmonger / **uy**-uhn-mung-guh / *n.* a person who sells tools and household implements etc. ☐ **ironmongery** *n.*

ironstone *n.* **1** rock containing iron ore. **2** (esp. in Australia) a hard sandstone, siltstone, or shale rich in iron oxides and reddish to purplish in colour. **3** a kind of hard white pottery.

ironware *n.* things made of iron.

ironwood *n.* any of several Australian trees yielding a very hard, heavy timber, esp. two species of wattle in northern Australia; the wood of these trees.

ironwork *n.* articles made of iron, such as gratings or railings.

ironworks *n.* a place where iron is smelted or iron goods are made.

irony / **uy**-ruh-nee / *n.* **1** a form of speech in which the real and intended meaning (which may be humorous, sardonic, cutting, etc.) is belied by the words used (which may at first seem innocent

irradiate

or guileless). **2** sarcasm. **3** the quality of an occurrence being so unexpected or ill-timed that it appears to be deliberately perverse.

irradiate / i-**ray**-dee-ayt / v. **1** subject to (any form of) radiation. **2** treat food with radiation. **3** shine upon; light up, illuminate. **4** throw light on (a subject).

irradiation n. **1** the process of irradiating. **2** the treatment of food with a small dose of radiation (in the form of gamma rays) to arrest the development of bacteria and so extend the food's shelf life.

irrational / i-**rash**-uh-nuhl / adj. **1** not rational, not guided by reasoning, illogical (*irrational fears or behaviour*). **2** not capable of reasoning. ☐ **irrationally** adv. **irrationality** n.

irreconcilable adj. unable to be reconciled; opposed or incompatible. ☐ **irreconcilably** adv. **irreconcilability** n.

irrecoverable adj. unable to be recovered or remedied. ☐ **irrecoverably** adv.

irredeemable adj. **1** unable to be redeemed. **2** hopeless. ☐ **irredeemably** adv.

irreducible / i-ruh-**dyoo**-suh-buhl / adj. unable to be reduced or simplified (*an irreducible minimum*).

irrefutable / i-**ref**-yuh-tuh-buhl, i-ruh-**fyoo**- / adj. unable to be refuted. ☐ **irrefutably** adv.

irregular adj. **1** not regular; uneven; varying. **2** contrary to rules or to established custom. **3** (of troops) not belonging to the regular armed forces. **4** (of a word) not inflected according to the usual rules. **5** disorderly. ☐ **irregularly** adv. **irregularity** n.

irrelevant / i-**rel**-uh-vuhnt / adj. not relevant. ☐ **irrelevance** n. **irrelevancy** n.

irreligious / i-ruh-**lij**-uhs / adj. **1** not religious. **2** indifferent or hostile to religion; irreverent.

irremediable / i-ruh-**mee**-dee-uh-buhl / adj. not able to be remedied. ☐ **irremediably** adv.

irremovable / i-ruh-**moo**-vuh-buhl / adj. unable to be removed. ☐ **irremovably** adv.

irreparable / i-**rep**-uh-ruh-buhl, i-**rep**-ruh-buhl / adj. unable to be repaired or made good (*irreparable damage*). ☐ **irreparably** adv.

irreplaceable adj. unable to be replaced.

irrepressible / i-ruh-**pres**-uh-buhl / adj. unable to be repressed or restrained. ☐ **irrepressibly** adv.

irreproachable adj. blameless, faultless. ☐ **irreproachably** adv.

irresistible adj. too strong, convincing, or delightful to be resisted. ☐ **irresistibly** adv.

irresolute / i-**rez**-uh-loot / adj. showing uncertainty; hesitating. ☐ **irresolutely** adv. **irresoluteness** n. **irresolution** n.

irrespective adj. (foll. by *of*) not taking into account (*prizes are awarded to winners irrespective of nationality*).

irresponsible adj. not showing a proper sense of responsibility. ☐ **irresponsibly** adv. **irresponsibility** n.

Islam

irretrievable adj. unable to be retrieved or restored. ☐ **irretrievably** adv.

irreverent adj. not reverent, not respectful. ☐ **irreverently** adv. **irreverence** n.

irreversible adj. not reversible, unable to be altered or revoked. ☐ **irreversibly** adv.

irrevocable / i-**rev**-uh-kuh-buhl / adj. **1** unable to be revoked; final and unalterable. **2** gone beyond recall (*the past is irrevocable*). ☐ **irrevocably** adv.

irrigate v. **1** supply (land or crops) with water by means of streams, channels, etc. **2** wash (a wound) with a constant flow of liquid. ☐ **irrigation** n. **irrigator** n.

irritable adj. **1** easily annoyed, bad-tempered. **2** (of an organ etc.) sensitive. • **irritable bowel syndrome** recurrent abdominal pain and constipation or diarrhoea, often associated with stress. ☐ ☐ **irritably** adv. **irritability** n.

irritant adj. causing irritation. • n. something that causes irritation.

irritate v. **1** annoy, rouse impatience or slight anger in (a person). **2** cause itching or other discomfort in (a part of the body). **3** *Biology* stimulate (an organ) to action. ☐ **irritation** n.

irrits n.pl. Aust. colloq. (**the irrits**) feelings of annoyance or extreme irritation (*he has the irrits*).

irrupt v. enter forcibly or violently. ☐ **irruption** n.

is see BE.

Isaiah / uy-**zuy**-uh / **1** a Hebrew major prophet of the 8th century BC. **2** a book of the Old Testament that bears his name.

ISBN abbr. international standard book number.

ISDN abbr. = INTEGRATED SERVICES DIGITAL NETWORK.

-ise suffix (also **-ize**) forming verbs meaning: **1** make or become such (*Americanise*; *realise*). **2** treat in such a way (*monopolise*). **3** follow a special practice (*economise*). **4** have a specified feeling (*sympathise*). **5** affect with, provide with, or subject to (*oxidise*; *hospitalise*). ☐ **-isation** suffix

■ **Usage** Both *-ise* and *-ize* have long histories of use in English. The *-ise* spelling is preferred in Australia, and is compulsory in certain cases: **a** where it forms part of a larger word-element, such as *-mise* (= sending) in e.g. *compromise*, and *-prise* (= taking) in e.g. *surprise*; **b** in verbs corresponding to nouns with *-s-* in the stem, such as *advertise* and *televise*. The *-ize* spelling is preferred in American English and by some British publishing houses but is compulsory only in a very small number of cases, e.g. *capsize*, *prize* (in the sense 'value highly'). This dictionary gives both when both are valid but prefers *-ise*; it does not matter which you prefer as long as you are consistent in your usage.

isinglass / **uy**-zing-glahs / n. **1** a kind of gelatine obtained from fish. **2** mica.

Islam / **iz**-lahm, -lam / n. **1** the Muslim religion, based on the teaching of Mohammed. **2** the Muslim world. ☐ **Islamic** / iz-**lam**-ik / adj.

Islamabad / iz-**lahm**-uh-bahd / the capital of Pakistan.

island / **uy**-luhnd / n. **1** a piece of land surrounded by water. **2** something detached or isolated. ☐ **traffic island** a paved or raised area in the middle of a road, for pedestrians to use in crossing.

islander / **uy**-luhn-duh / n. **1** an inhabitant of an island. **2** (**Islander**) **a** an indigenous inhabitant of the Torres Strait Islands. **b** a person indigenous to a Pacific island.

isle / uyl / n. (*poetic* except in place-names) an island (*the Apple Isle*).

islet / **uy**-luht / n. a small island. ☐ **islets of Langerhans** groups of pancreatic cells secreting insulin.

ism n. *colloq.* (usu. *derog.*) a doctrine or practice, esp. one with a name ending in -*ism*.

Ismaili / iz-**muy**-lee / n. a member of any of various Shi'ite Muslim sects, of which the best known is that headed by the Aga Khan.

isn't = is not.

isobar / **uy**-suh-bah / n. a line on a map connecting places that have the same atmospheric pressure. ☐ **isobaric** adj.

isochronous / uy-**sok**-ruh-nuhs / adj. **1** occupying an equal time. **2** occurring at the same time.

isolate v. **1** place apart or alone. **2** separate (an infectious person) from others. **3** separate (a substance) from a mixture. ☐ **isolation** n.

isolationism n. the policy of holding aloof from other countries or groups. ☐ **isolationist** n.

isomer / **uy**-suh-muh / n. one of two or more substances whose molecules have the same atoms in different arrangements. ☐ **isomeric** / uy-suh-**me**-rik / adj. **isomerism** / uy-**som**-uh-riz-uhm / n.

isometric / uy-suh-**met**-rik / adj. **1** (of muscle action) developing tension while the muscle is prevented from contracting. **2** (of a drawing or projection) drawing a three-dimensional object, without perspective, so that equal lengths along the three axes are drawn equal. **3** of equal measure.

isometrics n.pl. a system of physical exercises in which muscles are caused to act against each other or against a fixed object.

isomorph / **uy**-suh-mawf / n. a substance having the same form or composition as another. ☐ **isomorphic** adj. **isomorphism** n.

isopogon / uy-suh-**poh**-guhn / n. any of about 35 species of Australian shrubs with yellow to deep pink flowers followed by the large globe-shaped fruit cones which give most of the species the popular name 'drumsticks'.

isosceles / uy-**sos**-uh-leez / adj. (of a triangle) having two sides of equal length.

isotherm / **uy**-suh-therm / n. a line on a map connecting places that have the same temperature. ☐ **isothermal** adj.

isotope / **uy**-suh-tohp / n. one of two or more forms of a chemical element with different atomic weight and different nuclear properties but the same chemical properties. ☐ **isotopic** / uy-suh-**top**-ik / adj.

isotropic / uy-suh-**trop**-ik / adj. having the same physical properties in all directions. ☐ **isotropy** / uy-**sot**-ruh-pee / n.

ISP abbr. = INTERNET SERVICE PROVIDER.

Israel[1] the Hebrew nation or people (also called **children of Israel**) traditionally descended from Jacob. ☐ **Israelite** adj. & n.

Israel[2] a republic in SW Asia, at the eastern end of the Mediterranean Sea. ☐ **Israeli** / iz-**ray**-lee / adj. & n. (pl. **Israelis**).

issue n. **1** an outgoing or outflow. **2** the giving out of things for use or for sale. **3** one set of publications in a regular series (*the May issue*). **4** a result, an outcome. **5** the point in question; an important topic for discussion (*what are the real issues?*). **6** offspring (*died without male issue*). •v. **1** come or flow out. **2** supply or distribute for use (*campers were issued with blankets*). **3** put out for sale; publish. **4** send out (*issue orders*). **5** result, originate (*this disaster issued from your incompetence; the confrontation issued in violence*). ☐ **at issue** being discussed or disputed. **join** (or **take**) **issue** argue or disagree. **make an issue of** make a fuss about.

Istanbul a port and the former capital of Turkey.

isthmus / **is**-muhs / n. (pl. **isthmuses**) a narrow strip of land connecting two masses of land.

IT abbr. = INFORMATION TECHNOLOGY.

it pron. **1** the thing or animal mentioned or being discussed. **2** the person in question (*who is it?; it's me*). **3** used as the subject of a verb making a general statement about the weather (e.g. *it is raining*) or about circumstances etc. (e.g. *it is 6 kilometres to Bendigo*), or as an indefinite object (*run for it!*). **4** used as the subject or object of a verb, with reference to a following clause or phrase, e.g. *it is seldom that he fails; I take it that you agree*. **5** exactly what is needed (*that's absolutely it*). **6 a** (in children's games) the player who has to perform a required feat. **b** a person selected for a (usu. unwelcome) task (*someone has to tell the boss and you're it!*). **7** *colloq.* (usu. *sarcastic*) someone perfect (*thinks he's it and a bit*). **8** *colloq.* sexual intercourse. **9** *colloq.* sex appeal.

■ **Usage** See the note under *its*.

Italian adj. of Italy or its people or language. •n. **1** a native of Italy. **2** the Romance language of Italy.

Italianate / i-**tal**-yuh-nayt / adj. Italian in style or appearance.

italic / i-**tal**-ik / adj. **1** (of printed letters) sloping (*like this*). **2** (of handwriting) compact and pointed like an early form of Italian handwriting. **3** (**Italic**) of ancient Italy. •n.pl. (**italics**) sloping printed letters (*like these*).

italicise / i-**tal**-uh-suyz / *v.* (also **-ize**) **1** put into italics. **2** emphasise (*the silence of the people in the room was italicised by the sound of a dripping tap.*)

Italy a republic in southern Europe consisting of a peninsula that juts south into the Mediterranean Sea and offshore islands of which the largest are Sicily and Sardinia.

itch *n.* **1** an irritation or tickling feeling in the skin. **2** a restless desire or longing. • *v.* **1** have or feel a tickling sensation in the skin, causing a desire to scratch the affected part. **2** feel a restless desire or longing.

itchy *adj.* having or causing an itch. ☐ **have itchy feet** *colloq.* be restless; have a desire to travel. **itchy grub** *Aust.* any of many caterpillars in Australia capable of causing skin irritation. ☐☐ **itchiness** *n.*

it'd = **1** it had. **2** it would.

item *n.* **1** a single thing in a list or number of things. **2** a single piece of news.

itemise *v.* (also **-ize**) list, state item by item. ☐ **itemisation** *n.*

iterate / **it**-uh-rayt / *v.* repeat, state repeatedly. ☐ **iteration** *n.* **iterative** *adj.*

Ithaca / **ith**-uh-kuh / an island off the western coast of Greece, legendary home of Odysseus.

ithyphallic / ith-uh-**fa**-lik / *adj. Gk Hist.* **1 a** of the phallus carried in Bacchic festivals. **b** (of a statue etc.) having an erect penis. **2** lewd, licentious.

itinerant / uy-**tin**-uh-ruhnt / *adj.* travelling from place to place. • *n.* an itinerant person.

itinerary / uy-**tin**-uh-ruh-ree / *n.* **1** a route, a list of places to be visited on a journey. **2** a record of travel. **3** a guidebook.

its *possessive pron.* of or belonging to it.

■ **Usage** Do not confuse with *it's*, which has a different meaning (*see* the next entry). The word *its* is the possessive form of *it*, and (like *hers, ours, theirs, yours*) has no apostrophe; correct usage is *the dog wagged its tail* (not *it's*), *the dog is hers* (not *her's*), *these are ours* (not *our's*).

it's = **1** it is (*it's very hot*). **2** it has (*it's broken all records*).

■ **Usage** Do not confuse with *its*.

itself *pron.* the emphatic and reflexive form of *it* (*the meal itself was good; the money doubled itself*). ☐ **in itself** viewed in its essential qualities (*not in itself a bad thing*).

IUD *abbr.* = INTRAUTERINE DEVICE.

I've = I have.

IVF *abbr.* = IN VITRO FERTILISATION.

ivory *n.* **1** the hard creamy-white substance forming the tusks of elephants etc. **2** a creamy-white colour. • *adj.* creamy-white. ☐ **ivory tower** a place or situation where people live secluded from the harsh realities of everyday life.

Ivory Coast (official name **Côte d'Ivoire**) a republic in West Africa.

ivy *n.* a climbing evergreen shrub with shiny five-pointed leaves. ☐ **ivied** *adj.*

J

J *abbr.* joule(s).

jab *v.* (**jabbed**, **jabbing**) poke roughly, thrust. • *n.* **1** a rough blow or thrust, esp. with something pointed. **2** *colloq.* a hypodermic injection.

jabber *v.* **1** speak or say rapidly and unintelligibly. **2** chatter continuously. • *n.* jabbering talk or sound.

jabberwocky *n.* **1** a piece of nonsensical writing or speech. **2** *colloq.* nonsense, drivel (*what you've said is a load of jabberwocky*). (¶ The title of a poem in Lewis Carroll's *Through the Looking Glass*.)

Jabiluka / jab-uh-**loo**-kuh / a uranium mining deposit in the Alligator Rivers region of the NT.

jabiru / **jab**-uh-roo / *n.* a large Australian stork, with glossy greenish-black and white plumage and red legs, occurring along the north and east coast. Also called *policeman bird*.

jabot / **zhab**-oh / *n.* an ornamental frill down the front of a shirt, blouse, or dress.

jacana / juh-**kah**-nuh / *n.* the lotus bird.

jacaranda / jak-uh-**ran**-duh / *n.* a tropical American tree with hard scented wood and blue flowers.

jacinth / **jas**-inth, **jay**-sinth / *n.* a reddish-orange gem, a variety of zircon.

jack *n.* **1** a portable device for raising heavy weights off the ground, esp. one for raising the axle of a motor vehicle so that a wheel may be changed. **2** a ship's flag (smaller than an ensign) flown at the bow of a ship to show its nationality. **3** a playing card with a picture of a soldier, page, etc., ranking below a queen in card games. **4** a small white ball aimed at in the game of bowls. **5** a device using a single-pronged plug to connect an electrical circuit. **6** (**Jack**) a familiar form of *John*, esp. typifying the common man, a male animal, etc. (*I'm all right, Jack*). **7** (also **jacky** and **jacko**) *Aust.* nickname for a kookaburra. • *v.* (usu. foll. by *up*) **1** raise with a jack. **2** *colloq.* raise (prices etc.). **3** *Aust. colloq.* refuse to cooperate (*jacked up when I asked him to take out the garbage*). ❑ **every man Jack** every individual person. **jacked up** *colloq.* fed up (*I'm jacked up with this job*). **jack in** *colloq.* abandon (an attempt etc.). **jack-in-the-box** a toy figure that jumps out of a box when the lid is lifted. **jack of** *Aust. colloq.* fed up with, sick and tired of (*I'm jack of all this housework*). **jack of all trades** one who can do many different kinds of work.

jackal / **jak**-uhl, -awl / *n.* a wild flesh-eating animal of Africa and Asia, related to the dog, scavenging in packs for food.

jackanapes *n. archaic* a rascal.

jackaroo = JACKEROO.

jackass *n.* **1** a male donkey. **2** a stupid or foolish person. **3** (in full **laughing jackass**) *Aust.* a kookaburra. ❑ **jackass fish** a marine food fish, widely distributed in Australian waters, having an elongated ray of the pectoral fin. Also called *morwong*.

jackboot *n.* **1** a military boot reaching above the knee. **2** military oppression, bullying behaviour.

jackdaw *n.* a black, grey-headed European bird of the crow family.

jackeroo / jak-uh-**roo** / *Aust. n.* **1** (also **jackaroo**) *hist.* a young man (usu. English and of independent means) gaining experience by working as a trainee on an Australian sheep or cattle station. **2** a trainee in station management. • *v.* (**jackerooed**, **jackerooing**) work as a jackeroo.

jacket *n.* **1** a short coat, usu. reaching to the hips. **2** a protective or supporting garment (*life jacket*). **3** an outer covering round a boiler etc. to lessen loss of heat. **4** = DUST JACKET. **5** the skin of a potato.

jackfruit *n.* (also **jakfruit**, **jack**, **jak**) an East Indian tree bearing fruit resembling breadfruit; this fruit.

jackhammer *n.* a pneumatic hammer or drill.

jackjumper *n. Aust.* = JUMPER[1] sense 1.

jackknife *n.* **1** a large clasp-knife. **2** a dive in which the body is first bent double and then straightened. • *v.* (of an articulated vehicle) fold against itself in an accident.

jackpot *n.* a large prize, esp. the accumulated stakes in a lottery, various games, etc., increasing in value until won. • *v.* (of prize money in a lottery etc.) accumulate (if not won) (*first prize jackpotted to $1,000,000*).

jackshea / **jak**-shay / *n.* (also **jackshay**) *Aust.* a tin vessel holding a quart and incorporating a smaller drinking vessel, used by those in the bush for brewing tea etc.

Jackson[1], Marjorie (1931–), Australian sprinter who won three gold medals at the 1952 Olympics; nicknamed 'the Lithgow Flash' and 'the Lithgow Flyer'.

Jackson[2], Michael (1958–), American singer and songwriter.

Jack the Ripper a notorious murderer, never identified, who carried out a series of grisly murders of women in the East End of London in 1888–89.

jacky *n.* used in the names of small animals. ▫ **jacky lizard** a small, grey, mainly tree-dwelling dragon lizard of eastern Australia. **jacky winter** a small grey-brown and white flycatcher of mainland Australia.

Jacky Howe *n. Aust.* a navy or black sleeveless singlet worn esp. by shearers, rural workers, etc. (¶ John Howe, champion Qld shearer (1853–1920).)

Jacky Jacky *n. Aust. colloq. offens.* **1** a nickname for a male Aboriginal person. **2** = COCONUT (sense 3).

Jacob a Hebrew patriarch also called Israel (see ISRAEL¹).

Jacobean / jak-uh-**bee**-uhn / *adj.* **1** of the reign of James I of England (1603–25). **2** (of furniture) heavy and dark in style.

jacquard / **jak**-ahd / *n.* a fabric woven with an intricate figured pattern.

jacuzzi / juh-**koo**-zee / *n. trademark* a large bath with underwater jets of water which massage the body.

jade¹ *n.* **1** a hard green, blue, or white stone from which ornaments are carved. **2** its green colour.

jade² *n.* **1** a poor worn-out horse. **2** a disreputable or bad-tempered woman.

jaded *adj.* tired and bored; lacking zest.

jaffa *n.* **1** a large oval thick-skinned variety of orange, originally grown near the port of Jaffa in Israel. **2** *Aust. trademark* a hard round orange-flavoured sweet with a chocolate centre. **3** *Aust. Cricket* a perfect delivery of the ball.

jaffle *n.* a sandwich with a savoury or sweet filling sealed and toasted over a fire in a jaffle iron (or in an electric jaffle-maker). ▫ **jaffle iron** *trademark* a long-handled device for toasting jaffles, consisting of two saucer-shaped moulds, hinged, and locking together.

Jaffna a city and port on the Jaffna peninsula at the northern tip of Sri Lanka. It has a predominantly Tamil population and until the 17th century was the capital of a Tamil monarchy.

jag¹ *n.* a sharp projection of rock etc. • *v.* **1** cut or tear unevenly. **2** make indentations in.

jag² *n. colloq.* **1** a drinking bout. **2** a period of indulgence in a particular activity, emotion, etc.

jagged / **jag**-uhd / *adj.* having an uneven edge or outline with sharp projections.

jaggery / **jag**-uh-ree, -gree / *n.* a strong-flavoured dark brown sugar made from the nectar of the palmyrah palm or the coconut palm.

jaguar *n.* a large flesh-eating animal of the cat family, found in tropical America.

jail / jayl / (also **gaol**) *n.* **1** prison. **2** imprisonment. • *v.* put in jail.

jailbait *n.* (*collect.*) *colloq.* girl(s) or boy(s) under the legal age of consent.

jailbird *n.* (also **gaolbird**) a prisoner or habitual criminal.

jailbreak *n.* (also **gaolbreak**) a prison breakout, an escape from jail.

jailer *n.* (also **gaoler**) = WARDER.

Jain / juyn, jayn / *n.* a member of an Indian religion with doctrines like those of Buddhism. • *adj.* of this religion. ▫ **Jainism** *n.* **Jainist** *n. & adj.*

Jakarta (also **Djakarta**) the capital of Indonesia.

jake *adj.* esp. *Aust. colloq.* all right; fine. ▫ **she'll be jake** all will be well.

jalapeno / hal-uh-**pay**-noh / *n.* (*pl.* **jalapenos**) a very hot green chilli, used esp. in Mexican cooking.

jalebi / juh-**lay**-bee / *n.* an Indian sweet consisting of a porous saffron coil of fried batter, sugar-crisp on the outside and filled inside with flavoured syrup. (¶ Hindustani).

jalopy / juh-**lop**-ee / *n.* a battered old car.

jam¹ *v.* (**jammed, jamming**) **1** squeeze or wedge into a space; become wedged. **2** make (part of a machine) immovable so that the machine will not work; become unworkable in this way. **3** crowd or block (a passage, road, etc.) with people or things. **4** (usu. foll. by *on*) thrust or apply forcibly (*jammed on the brakes*). **5** cause interference to (a radio transmission), making it unintelligible. **6** *colloq.* (in jazz and popular music) improvise with other musicians. • *n.* **1** a squeeze, crush, or stoppage caused by jamming. **2** a crowded mass making movement difficult (*traffic jams*). **3** *colloq.* a difficult situation (*I'm in a jam*). ▫ **jam-packed** *adj. colloq.* packed full and tightly. **jam session** *colloq.* improvised playing by a group of jazz musicians.

jam² *n.* **1** a sweet substance made by boiling fruit with sugar to a thick consistency. **2** *colloq.* something easy or pleasant (*money for jam*). **3** *Aust.* = RASPBERRY JAM. ▫ **jam tree** *Aust.* = RASPBERRY JAM. **jamwood** *Aust.* = RASPBERRY JAM. ▫▫ **jammy** *adj.*

jam³ *n.* affectation; pretentious display. ▫ **put on jam** adopt an affected way of speaking or an affected manner. ▫▫ **jammy** *adj.*

Jamaica an island country in the Caribbean Sea. ▫ **Jamaican** *adj. & n.*

jamb / jam / *n.* the vertical side post of a doorway or window frame.

jambalaya / jum-buh-**luy**-uh / *n.* a dish of rice with shrimps, chicken, etc.

jamboree / jam-buh-**ree** / *n.* **1** a celebration; a spree. **2** a large rally of Scouts.

James¹, Clive (Vivian Leopold) (1939–), AM, Australian writer, literary critic, and television broadcaster.

James², St **1** 'the Great', an Apostle, martyred in AD 44. **2** 'the Less', an Apostle. **3** a person described as 'the Lord's brother', put to death in AD 62, to whom is ascribed the **Epistle of St James**, a book of the New Testament.

Janáček / **yan**-uh-chek /, Leoš (1854–1928), Czech composer and conductor.

jangle *n.* a harsh metallic sound. • *v.* **1** make or cause to make this sound. **2** cause irritation to (nerves etc.) by discord.

janitor / jan-uh-tuh / *n.* **1** the caretaker of a building. **2** a doorkeeper.

January *n.* the first month of the year.

Janus / jay-nuhs / *Rom. myth.* a god who was the guardian of doorways, gates, and beginnings, usu. shown with two faces that look in opposite directions. January is named after him.

Jap *n.* & *adj. colloq. offens.* = JAPANESE.

Japan a monarchy in eastern Asia.

japan *n.* a hard usu. black varnish, originally from Japan. • *v.* (**japanned**, **japanning**) coat with japan.

Japanese *n.* (*pl.* **Japanese**) **1** a native or national of Japan. **2** the language of Japan. • *adj.* of Japan, its people, or its language.

jape *n.* a practical joke. • *v.* play a joke.

japonaiserie / jap-uh-**nay**-zuh-ree / *n.* (also **Japanesery**) **1** Japanese characteristics or fashion (in decor, film, etc.). **2** (in *pl.*) Japanese ornaments, knick-knacks, etc.

japonica / juh-**pon**-i-kuh / *n.* an ornamental variety of quince, with red or pink flowers.

jar[1] *n.* a cylindrical container made of glass or earthenware; the contents of this.

jar[2] *v.* (**jarred**, **jarring**) **1** (often foll. by *on*) make a sound that has a discordant or painful effect. **2** (often foll. by *with*) (of an action etc.) be out of harmony, have a harsh or disagreeable effect. **3** (often foll. by *against* or *on*) cause an unpleasant jolt or a sudden shock. • *n.* a jarring movement or effect.

jardinière / zhah-duh-**nyair** / *n.* **1** a large ornamental pot for holding indoor plants. **2** a dish of mixed vegetables.

jargon *n.* **1** words or expressions developed for use within a particular group, hard for outsiders to understand (*scientists' jargon*). **2** ugly or pretentious language; nonsense; gibberish.

jarrah / ja-ruh / *n. Aust.* a tall WA eucalypt with hard, dark-red wood; the wood of this tree, native mahogany. (¶ Nyungar)

jasmine *n.* a shrub or climber with yellow or white flowers, usu. highly fragrant.

Jason *Gk myth.* the leader of the Argonauts in quest of the Golden Fleece.

jasper *n.* an opaque variety of quartz, usu. red, yellow, or brown.

Jataka / **jah**-tuh-kuh / *n.* any of the various stories of the Buddha found in Buddhist literature.

jaundice / jawn-duhs / *n.* a condition in which the skin becomes abnormally yellow as a result of excessive bile in the bloodstream.

jaundiced *adj.* **1** discoloured by jaundice. **2** filled with resentment or jealousy.

jaunt *n.* a short pleasure-trip. • *v.* take a jaunt.

jaunty *adj.* (**jauntier**, **jauntiest**) **1** cheerful and self-confident in manner; sprightly. **2** (of clothes) stylish and cheerful. ☐ **jauntily** *adv.* **jauntiness** *n.*

Java[1] / **jah**-vuh / *an island of Indonesia.* ☐ **Javanese** *adj.* & *n.* (*pl.* **Javanese**). **Javan** *adj.*

Java[2] *n. trademark Computing* a general-purpose computer programming language designed to produce programs that will run on any computer system.

javelin / **jav**-uh-luhn, **jav**-luhn / *n.* a light spear thrown in sport or, formerly, as a weapon. ☐ **javelin fish** a marine food fish of northern Australia having an enlarged anal fin resembling a javelin.

jaw *n.* **1** either of the two bones that form the framework of the mouth and in which the teeth are set. **2** the lower of these; the part of the face covering it. **3** (**jaws**) the narrow mouth of a valley, channel, etc. **4** (**jaws**) the gripping parts of a tool etc. **5** (**jaws**) a grip (*in the jaws of death*). **6** *colloq.* tedious talk (*hold your jaw*). • *v. colloq.* talk long and boringly; gossip. ☐ **jaws-of-life** a powerful jaw-like tool used after car crashes etc. to cut away metal in order to rescue trapped persons.

jawbone *n.* the lower jaw in most mammals.

jawbreaker *n. colloq.* **1** a word that is very long or hard to pronounce. **2** a large, hard, or sticky sweet.

Jawoyn / **ju**-woyn, **yu**- / *n.* **1** a member of an Aboriginal people of the north of the NT; this people. **2** the language of the Jawoyn. • *adj.* of or relating to the people or their language.

jay *n.* **1** any of several Australian birds with a loud call, such as the grey currawong and the white-winged chough. **2** a noisy European bird.

jaywalk *v.* walk carelessly in a road, without regard for traffic or signals. ☐ **jaywalker** *n.*

jazz *n.* **1** a type of music of African-American origin with strong rhythm and syncopation, often improvised. **2** *colloq.* a matter, esp. something regarded as pretentious or as nonsense (*talked of the honour of the firm and all that jazz*). • *v.* play or dance to jazz. ☐ **jazz up** brighten, enliven.

jazzy *adj.* **1** of or like jazz. **2** flashy, showy (*a jazzy sports car*).

jealous / **jel**-uhs / *adj.* **1** feeling or showing resentment towards a person whom one thinks of as a rival (esp. in love) or as having advantages. **2** possessive and taking watchful care (*is very jealous of his own rights*). ☐ **jealously** *adv.* **jealousy** *n.*

jeans *n.pl.* casual trousers, esp. made of denim.

jeep *n.* **1** *trademark* a small sturdy motor vehicle, esp. in military use, with four-wheel drive. **2** = SHOPPING JEEP.

jeer *v.* laugh or shout at rudely and scornfully. • *n.* a jeering remark or shout.

jeez! *interj.* an expression of surprise etc. (¶ Probably an abbreviation of *Jesus*.)

Jefferson, Thomas (1743–1826), 3rd president of the USA 1801–09, who drafted the Declaration of Independence (1775–76).

jehad alternative spelling of JIHAD.

Jehovah / juh-**hoh**-vuh / *the name of God in the Old Testament* (cf. YAHWEH). ☐ **Jehovah's**

jejune / juh-**joon** / *adj.* **1** scanty, poor; (of land) barren. **2** unsatisfying to the mind.

Jekyll and Hyde a person in whom two personalities (one good, one evil) alternate. (¶ Named after the hero of a story (by R.L. Stevenson) who could transform himself from the respectable Dr Jekyll into the evil Mr Hyde by means of a potion which he drank.)

jell *v. colloq.* **1** set as jelly. **2** take definite form (*our ideas began to jell*).

jellaba alternative spelling of DJELLABA.

jellify *v.* turn into jelly; make or become like jelly.

jelly *n.* **1** a soft solid food made of liquid set with gelatine, esp. one prepared in a mould as a sweet dish. **2** a kind of jam made of strained fruit juice and sugar. **3** a substance of similar consistency (*petroleum jelly*). **4** *colloq.* gelignite. •*v.* (cause to) set as or in a jelly, congeal. □ **jelly blubber** *Aust.* a jellyfish.

jellyfish *n.* (*pl.* **jellyfish** or **jellyfishes**) **1** a sea animal with a jelly-like body and stinging tentacles. **2** *colloq.* a cowardly, spineless person.

jemmy *n.* a short crowbar used by burglars to force doors, windows, and drawers. •*v.* force open with a jemmy.

je ne sais quoi / *zh*uh nuh say **kwah** / *n.* an indefinable something. (¶ French, = I do not know what.)

jenny *n.* a female donkey.

Jenolan Caves / juh-**noh**-luhn / a series of spectacular limestone caves in the Great Dividing Range west of Sydney.

jeopardise / **jep**-uh-duyz / *v.* (also -**ize**) endanger.

jeopardy / **jep**-uh-dee / *n.* danger.

jerbil alternative spelling of GERBIL.

jerboa / jer-**boh**-uh / *n.* a small desert rodent with long hind legs used for leaping.

jeremiad / je-ruh-**muy**-uhd / *n.* a long mournful lament about one's troubles. (¶ Named after JEREMIAH.)

Jeremiah / je-ruh-**muy**-uh / **1** a Hebrew major prophet (*c.*650–*c.*585 BC). **2** the book of the Old Testament containing his account of the troubles of the Jews at that time. **3** a dismal, pessimistic person.

Jerez / he-reth / a town in Andalusia, Spain, centre of the sherry-making industry.

Jericho an ancient city north of the Dead Sea, on the West Bank.

jerk *n.* **1** a sudden sharp movement; an abrupt pull, push, or throw. **2 a** (**jerks**) exercises (*physical jerks*). **b** (in full **clean and jerk**) (in weightlifting) raising of a weight to above the head following an initial lift to shoulder level. **3** *colloq.* a stupid or obnoxious person. •*v.* **1** pull, throw, or stop with a jerk; move with a jerk or in short uneven movements. **2** cure (beef etc.) by cutting it into long slices and drying it in the sun. □ **jerk off** *colloq.* masturbate; **jerk** (**a person**) **off** masturbate (oneself or another). **jerk-off** *colloq.* an act of masturbation.

jerkin *n.* a sleeveless jacket.

jerky[1] *adj.* making abrupt starts and stops, not moving or acting smoothly. □ **jerkily** *adv.* **jerkiness** *n.*

jerky[2] *n.* meat that has been cured by being cut into long, thin strips and dried.

jeroboam / je-ruh-**boh**-uhm / *n.* a wine bottle of 4–12 times the ordinary size. (¶ Named after a king of Israel (10th century BC) whose name means 'mighty man of valour'.)

Jerome / juh-**rohm** /, St (*c.*342–420), a scholar and monk, Doctor of the Church, who translated the Bible from the original Hebrew and Greek into the language (Latin) of the people of his own time (*see* VULGATE).

jerry[1] *n. colloq.* a chamber pot; a toilet.

jerry[2] *v. Aust. colloq.* (**jerried**, **jerrying**) (often foll. by *to*) realise; understand.

jerry-built *adj.* built badly and with poor materials. □ **jerry-build** *v.* **jerry-builder** *n.* **jerry-building** *n.*

jerrycan *n.* (also **jerrican**) a rectangular can for carrying petrol or water.

jersey *n.* **1** plain machine-knitted fabric used for making clothes. **2** (*pl.* **jerseys**) a close-fitting woollen pullover with sleeves. **3** (**Jersey**) a light brown dairy cow, originally from Jersey, one of the Channel Islands.

Jerusalem a city in the Judaean hills considered holy by Jews, Christians, and Muslims, the capital of the State of Israel.

Jerusalem artichoke *n.* a kind of sunflower with edible underground tubers; this tuber as a vegetable. (¶ Corruption of Italian *girasole* 'sunflower'.)

Jervis Bay / **jer**-vuhs, **jah**- / a large inlet and popular holiday destination on the south coast of NSW, part of the ACT.

jess *n.* a short strap put round the leg of a hawk used in falconry.

Jesse / **jes**-ee / (in the Bible) the father of David (1 Samuel 16), hence represented as the first in the genealogy of Jesus Christ.

jest *n.* **1** a joke; fun. **2** an object of derision. •*v.* make jokes. □ **in jest** in fun, not seriously.

jester *n.* **1** *hist.* a professional clown at a medieval court etc. **2** a person who jests, or speaks or acts in jest; a person given to uttering jests or witticisms, a joker.

Jesu *archaic* = Jesus.

Jesuit / **jez**-yoo-uht / *n.* a member of the Society of Jesus, a Catholic male religious order founded by St IGNATIUS LOYOLA.

Jesuitical / jez-yoo-**it**-uh-kuhl / *adj.* **1** of or like Jesuits. **2** often *offens.* using clever but false

reasoning (such as the Jesuits were once accused of by their enemies).

Jesus (also **Jesus Christ**) the central figure of the Christian religion believed by Christians to be the Son of God, a Jew living in Palestine at the beginning of the 1st century AD. • *interj. colloq.* an exclamation of surprise, dismay, etc.

jet[1] *n.* a hard black mineral that can be polished, used as a gem. □ **jet black** *adj.* & *n.* deep glossy black.

jet[2] *n.* **1** a stream of water, gas, flame, etc., shot out from a small opening. **2** a spout or opening from which this comes, e.g. a burner on a gas cooker. **3** a jet engine or jet plane. • *v.* (**jetted**, **jetting**) **1** spurt in jets. **2** *colloq.* travel or convey by jet-propelled aircraft. □ **jet-about** *adj.* of, using, or including travel by air (*won a jet-about holiday; jet-about members of parliament*). **jet engine** an engine using jet propulsion to give forward thrust. **jet lag** delayed physical effects of tiredness etc. felt after a long flight by aircraft across time zones. **jet-propelled** propelled by jet engines; very fast. **jet propulsion** propulsion by engines that give forward thrust by sending out a high-speed jet of gases at the back. **jet set** wealthy people who travel widely, esp. for pleasure. **jet-setter** a member of the jet set. **jet ski** *n.* a jet-propelled vehicle like a motorbike, for riding across water. **jet-ski** *v.* ride on a jet ski. **jet stream 1** a jet from a jet engine. **2** a strong wind blowing in a narrow range of altitudes in the upper atmosphere.

jeté / zhuh-**tay** / *n. Ballet* a spring or leap with one leg forward and the other stretched backwards.

jetsam *n.* goods thrown overboard from a ship in distress to lighten it, esp. those that are washed ashore.

jettison *v.* **1** throw (goods) overboard or (goods or fuel) from an aircraft, esp. to lighten a ship or aircraft in distress. **2** discard (what is unwanted).

jetty *n.* **1** a breakwater built to protect a harbour, coast, etc. **2** a landing pier.

Jew *n.* a person of Hebrew descent, or one whose religion is Judaism.

jewel *n.* **1** a precious stone. **2** an ornament for wearing, containing one or more precious stones. **3** a person or thing that is highly valued. □ **jewel beetle** any of many brilliantly coloured and jewel-like Australian beetles.

jewelled *adj.* ornamented or set with jewels.

jeweller *n.* a person who makes or deals in jewels or jewellery. □ **jeweller's shop** a rich deposit of gold or opal.

jewellery / **joo**-uhl-ree / *n.* jewels or similar ornaments to be worn.

jewfish *n.* (also **dhufish**) **1** any of several large, edible sea fish found only off the WA coast. **2** a mulloway.

Jewish *adj.* of Jews or Judaism.

Jewry *n.* Jews collectively.

jew's harp *n.* a musical instrument held in the teeth while a projecting metal strip is twanged with a finger. (¶ The name of the instrument is an ancient one, but no connection with Jews has been established with certainty.)

jewy (also **jewie**) = JEWFISH.

jezebel / **jez**-uh-bel / *n.* a shameless or immoral woman. (¶ From Jezebel in the Old Testament, wife of Ahab, king of Israel.)

jib[1] *n.* **1** a triangular sail stretching forward from the mast. **2** the projecting arm of a crane.

jib[2] *v.* (**jibbed**, **jibbing**) **1** (esp. of a horse) stop and refuse to go on; (of a person) refuse to continue. **2** (foll. by *at*) show reluctance and dislike for (a course of action).

jibe 1 alternative spelling of GIBE. **2** alternative spelling of GYBE.

jiffy *n.* (also **jiff**) *colloq.* a moment (*in a jiffy*). □ **jiffy bag** *trademark* a padded envelope. **jiffy pot** *trademark* a compressed round pellet of peat etc. which when wetted expands into a plant pot.

jig[1] *n.* **1** a lively jumping dance; the music for this. **2** a device that holds a piece of work and guides the tools working on it. • *v.* (**jigged**, **jigging**) **1** dance a jig. **2** move up and down rapidly and jerkily; fidget. **3** work on or equip with a jig or jigs. □ **the jig is up** *colloq.* the game's up; one has been caught red-handed.

jig[2] *v. Aust. colloq.* play truant (from school). □ **jigger** *n.*

jigger *n.* **1** *colloq.* the name for a tool, device, etc. (when one cannot remember its proper name) (*I'll use this jigger here to do the job*). **2** a measure of spirits etc.; a glass holding this amount. **3** a cue rest used in billiards. **4** *Aust. colloq.* (in prisons) an improvised radio receiver. **5** *Aust. colloq.* a device for administering an illegal electric shock to a horse during a race. • *v. colloq.* break, ruin (*you'll jigger it if you keep on fiddling*).

jiggered *adj. colloq.* broken, ruined. □ **I'll be jiggered** *colloq.* an exclamation of astonishment.

jiggery-pokery *n. colloq.* trickery, underhand dealing.

jiggle *v.* rock or jerk lightly.

jiggler *n. colloq.* a tea bag for a tea cup.

jigsaw *n.* **1** a mechanical fretsaw with a fine blade. **2** (in full **jigsaw puzzle**) a picture pasted on board and cut with a jigsaw into irregular pieces which are then shuffled and reassembled as a pastime.

jihad / juh-**hahd** / *n.* (also **jehad**) (in Islam) a holy war against unbelievers.

jilleroo *n.* (also **jillaroo**) *Aust.* a female jackeroo. • *v.* (**jillerooed**, **jillerooing**) work as a jilleroo.

jilt *v.* abruptly reject or abandon (esp. a lover).

jimmies *n.pl. Aust. colloq.* = JIMMY BRITS.

Jimmy Brits *n.pl. Aust. colloq.* **1** the shits. **2** a state of extreme anxiety (*the exams are giving him the Jimmy Brits*). (¶ Rhyming slang.)

jimmygrant *n.* (also **jimmigrant**, **Jimmy Grant**) *Aust. hist.* an immigrant to Australia, esp. from Britain. (¶ Rhyming slang.)

Jimmy Woodser *n. Aust. colloq.* **1** a person who drinks alone. **2** a drink taken on one's own. (¶ *Jimmy Wood*, the name of a character in the poem of that name by the Australian poet Barcroft Boake (1866–92).)

Jindyworobak / jin-dee-**wo**-ruh-bak / *n. Aust.* a member of a literary group formed by the poet Rex Ingamells to promote Australianism in art and literature. (¶ Wuywurung)

jingera / **jin**-juh-ruh / *n. Aust.* remote and mountainous bush-covered country. •*adj.* of such terrain. (¶ Possibly from an Aboriginal language.)

jingle *v.* make or cause to make a metallic ringing or clinking sound. •*n.* **1** a jingling sound. **2** a verse or words with simple catchy rhymes or repetitive sounds.

jingoism / **jing**-goh-iz-uhm / *n.* blustering aggressive patriotism. ☐ **jingoist** *n.* **jingoistic** *adj.*

jink *v.* dodge by turning suddenly and sharply. •*n.* an act of jinking. ☐ **high jinks** noisy merrymaking, boisterous fun.

jinker *n. Aust.* a wheeled conveyance for moving heavy logs.

Jinnah / **jin**-uh /, Muhammad Ali (Lord Jinnah) (1876–1948), founder and first governor-general of Pakistan.

jinnee *n.* (also **jinn**, **djinn**) (*pl.* **jinn** or **djinn**) *Islamic myth.* any of the supernatural beings able to appear in human and animal form and to help or hinder human beings.

jinx *colloq. n.* a person or thing that is thought to bring bad luck. •*v.* (usu. used as **jinxed** *adj.*) subjected to bad luck.

jism / **jiz**-uhm / *n. colloq.* **1** emitted semen; sperm. **2** energy, strength.

jitta *n.* (also **ghittoe**) **1** an Australian rainforest tree yielding a tough flexible flammable timber easily burnt when green. **2** its wood, used by Aborigines for a musical instrument (accompanying a special style of love song) and for spears etc. (¶ Dyirbal and Warrgamay.)

jitter *colloq. v.* feel nervous, behave nervously. •*n.pl.* (**the jitters**) nervousness. ☐ **jittery** *adj.* **jitteriness** *n.*

jitterbug *n.* **1** a nervous person. **2** a fast dance popular in the early 1940s. •*v.* (**jitterbugged**, **jitterbugging**) dance the jitterbug.

jiu-jitsu alternative spelling of JU-JITSU.

jive *n.* fast lively jazz music; dancing to this. •*v.* dance to such music. ☐ **jiver** *n.*

Jnr. *abbr.* Junior.

Joachim / **joh**-uh-kim /, St, the husband of St Anne and father of the Virgin Mary.

Joan of Arc, St (1412–31), French national heroine, who led French forces against the English in the Hundred Years War, and relieved Orleans. After being captured she was tried and burnt at the stake as a heretic.

Job / johb / **1** a prosperous Hebrew leader who, despite enduring many undeserved misfortunes, ultimately remained convinced of the goodness of God. **2** a book of the Old Testament giving an account of this. ☐ **Job's comforter** a person who aggravates the distress of the person he or she is supposed to be comforting, like those who counselled Job.

job *n.* **1** a piece of work to be done. **2** a paid position of employment (*got a job at the factory*). **3** something one has to do, a responsibility (*it's your job to lock the gates*). **4** something completed, a product of work (*a neat little job*). **5** *colloq.* a crime, esp. a robbery. **6** *colloq.* a difficult task (*you'll have a job to move it*). **7** a state of affairs (*gave it up as a bad job*). •*v.* (**jobbed**, **jobbing**) **1** do jobs, do piecework. **2** buy or sell (stock or goods) as a middleman. ☐ **job lot** a collection of miscellaneous articles bought together. **jobs for the boys** *colloq.* the assurance of gain or profitable positions for one's friends. **job-sharing** the sharing of a full-time job by two or more people.

jobber *n.* **1** a person who jobs. **2** a wholesale merchant. **3** a pieceworker.

jobbery *n.* corrupt dealing.

jobbing *adj.* doing single specific pieces of work for payment (*a jobbing gardener*).

job-control language *n. Computing* a language enabling the user to determine the tasks to be undertaken by the operating system.

jobless *adj.* unemployed, out of work.

jock *n.* **1** (**jocks**) a jockstrap. **2** a male athlete. **3** a disc jockey.

jockettes / jo-**kets** / *n.pl. Aust. colloq.* men's brief underpants.

jockey *n.* (*pl.* **jockeys**) **1** a person who rides horses in horse races, esp. a professional rider. **2** (**jockeys**) close-fitting briefs worn by men. **3** *Aust.* an assistant to a carrier, a taxi driver, etc. •*v.* (**jockeyed**, **jockeying**) **1** manoeuvre in order to gain an advantage (*jockeying for position; jockeyed him into doing it*). **2** trick, cheat, or outwit. ☐ **jockey shorts** a man's brief underpants or shorts.

jocks *n.pl. colloq.* **1** = JOCKEY SHORTS. **2** = JOCKSTRAP.

jockstrap *n.* a support for the male genitals, covering these but not the buttocks, and worn esp. for sport.

jocose / juh-**kohs** / *adj.* joking, playful. ☐ **jocosely** *adv.* **jocosity** *n.*

jocular / **jok**-yuh-luh / *adj.* joking, avoiding seriousness. ☐ **jocularly** *adv.* **jocularity** / jok-yuh-**la**-ruh-tee / *n.*

jocund / **jok**-uhnd / *adj. literary* merry, cheerful. ☐ **jocundity** / juh-**kun**-duh-tee / *n.*

jodhpurs / **jod**-puhz / *n.pl.* long breeches for riding, fitting closely below the knee and loosely above it.

joe[1] *n. Aust.* a ewe (*the bare-bellied joe*).

joe² ** *n. Aust. hist.* **1 a policeman, trooper, etc., esp. one charged with implementing licensing regulations on the Vic. goldfields. **2** a cry warning of the approach of a joe. **3** a term of derision or abuse. • *v.* jeer at, abuse. (¶ Probably from Charles Joseph La Trobe, governor of Victoria (1851–54).)

Joe Blake *n. Aust. colloq.* **1** (also **Joe**) a snake. **2** (in *pl.*) the shakes. (¶ Rhyming slang.)

Joe Blow *n. colloq.* a hypothetical average citizen, an average member of the public.

joes *n.pl. Aust. colloq.* **1** the shakes; delirium tremens. **2** a fit of depression; low spirits. (¶ Abbreviation of JOE BLAKE(S).)

joey *n.* (*pl.* **joeys**) *Aust.* **1** a young kangaroo, wallaby, or possum. **2** any young animal. **3** a baby or young child.

jog *v.* (**jogged, jogging**) **1** give a slight knock or push to; shake with a push or jerk. **2** rouse or stimulate (*jogged his memory*). **3** (of a horse) trot. **4** run at a leisurely pace with short strides, as a form of exercise. • *n.* **1** a slight shake or push, a nudge. **2** a slow run or trot; a spell of jogging.

jogger *n.* **1** a person who jogs, esp. one who runs for physical exercise. **2** (in *pl.*) shoes specially designed for jogging.

joggle *v.* shake slightly; move by slight jerks. • *n.* a joggling movement, a slight shake.

jogtrot *n.* a slow regular trot.

John, St **1** an Apostle, credited with the authorship of the fourth Gospel, the Apocalypse, and three epistles of the New Testament. **2** the fourth Gospel. **3** any of the three epistles attributed to St John.

john¹ *n.* a policeman. (¶ Abbreviation of *johndarme*, Australian pronunciation of the French *gendarme*.)

john² *n. colloq.* **1** a toilet. **2** the male client of a male or female prostitute.

John Dory *n.* (*pl.* the same *or* **Dories**) **1** a much valued marine food fish of Australian waters. **2** a similar fish found elsewhere.

Johne's disease / *yoh*-nuhz / *n.* a form of chronic diarrhoea in sheep and cattle caused by a bacterium. (¶ H.A. Johne, German veterinary surgeon (1839–1910).)

johnny *n. colloq.* a fellow, a bloke. ☐ **johnny cake** a small, usu. thin damper. **johnny-come-lately** *n.* a newcomer, an upstart.

John Paul II (original name: Karol Józef Wojtylá) (1920–), Polish cardinal who was elected pope in 1978 and took this name.

Johnson¹, Amy (1903–41), English aviator, who established several records with her solo flights to Australia (1930), Tokyo (1932), and the Cape of Good Hope (1936).

Johnson², Michael (1967–), American sprinter. He won the 200 and 400 metres at the 1996 Olympics, and the 400 metres at the 2000 Olympics.

Johnson³, Samuel (1709–84), English poet, critic, and lexicographer, whose celebrated *Dictionary* was published in 1755.

John the Baptist, St, a preacher (cousin of Jesus Christ, whom he baptised); beheaded by Herod Antipas.

joie de vivre / *zh*wah duh **vee**-vruh / *n.* a feeling of great enjoyment of life. (¶ French, = joy of living.)

join *v.* **1** put together; fasten, unite, or connect. **2** (often foll. by *with*) come together; be united. **3** (of a river, road, etc.) become continuous or connected with (another). **4** take part with others in doing something (*joined in the chorus*). **5** come into the company of (*join us for lunch*). **6** become a member of (*joined the Navy*). **7** take or resume one's place in (*joined his ship*). • *n.* a point, line, or surface where things join. ☐ **join battle** begin fighting. **join up 1** enlist in the armed forces. **2** connect, unite.

joiner *n.* a person who makes furniture, house fittings, and other finished woodwork.

joinery *n.* the work of a joiner.

joint *adj.* **1** shared, held, or done by two or more people together (*a joint account*). **2** sharing in an activity etc. (*joint authors*). • *n.* **1** a place or device at which two parts of a structure are joined. **2** a structure in an animal body by which bones are fitted together. **3** any of the parts into which a butcher divides a carcass as meat. **4** *colloq.* a place where people meet for gambling or drinking etc. **5** *colloq.* a marijuana cigarette. • *v.* **1** connect by a joint or joints. **2** divide (meat) into joints. ☐ **out of joint 1** (of a bone) dislocated. **2** in disorder.

jointly *adv.* so as to be shared or done by two or more people together.

joist *n.* any of the parallel beams, extending from wall to wall, on which floorboards or ceiling laths are fixed.

jojoba / hoh-**hoh**-buh / *n.* a plant with seeds yielding an oily extract used in cosmetics etc.

joke *n.* **1** something said or done to cause laughter. **2** a ridiculous person, thing, or circumstance. • *v.* make jokes. ☐ **jokingly** *adv.*

joker *n.* **1** a person who jokes. **2** *Aust. colloq.* a fellow. **3** an extra playing card used in certain games as the highest trump.

joky *adj.* (also **jokey**) joking, not serious.

Jolley, Elizabeth (1923–), AO, Australian novelist and short-story writer.

jollify *v.* (**jollified, jollifying**) be or cause to be jolly. ☐ **jollification** *n.*

jollity *n.* being jolly, merriment, merrymaking.

jolly *adv.* (**jollier, jolliest**) **1** cheerful, merry. **2** festive, jovial. **3** very pleasant, delightful. • *adv. colloq.* very. ☐ **jolly (along)** (**jollied, jollying**) *colloq.* keep (a person) in a good humour, esp. in order to win cooperation (*jollied him into coming with us*).

Jolson / jol-suhn /, Al (original name: Asa Yoelson) (1886–1950), Russian-born American singer and film actor.

jolt v. **1** shake or dislodge with a jerk. **2** move along jerkily, as on a rough road. **3** give a mental shock to. •n. **1** a jolting movement or effect. **2** a surprise or shock.

Jonah / joh-nuh / **1** a Hebrew minor prophet. **2** a book of the Old Testament telling of his attempted escape from God's call, in which he was thrown overboard, swallowed by a great fish, and vomited out on to dry land. •n. (**jonah**) a person who is believed to bring bad luck.

Jonathan (in the Bible) the son of Saul and bosom friend of David, killed at the battle of Mount Gilboa (1 Samuel 13 ff.).

Jones, Marion (1975–), American athlete. She won the 100 and 200 metres at the 2000 Olympics.

Joneses n.pl. a person's neighbours or social equals. ☐ **keep up with the Joneses** try to emulate or try not to be outdone by one's neighbours or social peers.

jonquil / jong-kwil / n. a narcissus with fragrant yellow or white flowers.

joonda n. the wild almond tree of Australia, the poisonous plum-like fruit of which can be made edible by leaching. (¶ Kuku-Yalanji)

Jordan[1], Michael (Jeffery) (1963–), US basketball player.

Jordan[2] **1** a river rising in Syria and Lebanon and flowing south through the Sea of Galilee to the Dead Sea. **2** (in full **Hashemite Kingdom of Jordan**) a kingdom in the Middle East, bordering on the east of Israel. ☐ **Jordanian** / jaw-**day**-nee-uhn / adj. & n.

Joseph, St, a carpenter of Nazareth, husband of the Virgin Mary to whom he was betrothed at the time of the Annunciation.

josh colloq. v. hoax; tease in a good-natured way. •n. good-natured teasing.

joss n. a Chinese idol. ☐ **joss house** a Chinese temple. **joss stick** a thin stick that burns to give off a smell of incense.

jostle v. **1** push roughly, esp. when in a crowd. **2** (foll. by *with*) struggle roughly. •n. the act of jostling.

jot n. a very small amount (*not one jot*). •v. (**jotted**, **jotting**) write briefly or hastily (*jot it down*).

jotter n. a small pad or notebook.

jottings n.pl. jotted notes.

joule / jool / n. a unit of work or energy (symbol J). (¶ J.P. Joule, English physicist (1818–89).)

journal / jer-nuhl / n. **1** a daily record of news, events, or business transactions. **2** a newspaper or periodical.

journalese / jer-nuh-**leez** / n. hackneyed writing characteristic of some newspapers.

journalist / **jer**-nuh-list / n. a person employed in writing for a newspaper or magazine. ☐ **journalism** n. **journalistic** adj.

journey n. (pl. **journeys**) **1** an act of going from one place to another, esp. at a long distance. **2** the distance travelled or the time required for this (*a day's or 4 days' journey*). •v. (**journeyed**, **journeying**) make a journey.

journeyman n. **1** a qualified mechanic or artisan who works for another. **2** a reliable but not outstanding worker.

journo n. Aust. colloq. a journalist.

joust / jowst / v. hist. fight on horseback with lances.

Jove Jupiter, the king of the gods in Roman mythology.

jovial / **joh**-vee-uhl / adj. full of cheerful good humour. ☐ **jovially** adv. **joviality** / joh-vee-**al**-uh-tee / n.

jowl n. **1** the jaw or jawbone. **2** the cheek. **3** an animal's dewlap; similar loose skin on a person's throat. ☐ **jowly** adj.

joy n. **1** pleasure, extreme gladness. **2** a thing that causes this. ☐ **no joy** colloq. no satisfaction or success. ☐☐ **joyful** adj. **joyfully** adv. **joyfulness** n. **joyless** adj.

Joyce[1], Eileen (1912–91), Australian concert pianist with an international reputation who also made many acclaimed recordings.

Joyce[2], James (Augustine Aloysius) (1882–1941), Irish novelist, whose most important novels, *Ulysses* and *Finnegans Wake*, revolutionised the form and structure of the modern novel. ☐ **Joycean** adj.

joyous adj. joyful. ☐ **joyously** adv.

joyride n. a ride taken for pleasure in a (usu. stolen) car. ☐ **joyrider** n. **joyriding** n.

joystick n. **1** the control lever of an aircraft. **2** a device for moving a cursor on a VDU screen.

JP abbr. Justice of the Peace.

JPEG / **jay**-peg / n. Computing a format for compressing images. (¶ Acronym from Joint Photographic Experts Group.)

Jr abbr. Junior.

jube / joob / n. Aust. = JUJUBE.

jubilant adj. showing joy, rejoicing.

jubilation n. rejoicing.

jubilee n. **1** a special anniversary, esp. the 25th (*silver*), 50th (*golden*), or 60th (*diamond jubilee*). **2** a time of rejoicing. **3** *Jewish Hist.* a year of emancipation and rejoicing, kept every 50 years. **4** (in the Catholic Church) a period of remission from the penal consequences of sin, granted under certain conditions for a year, usu. every 25 years.

Judaea / joo-**dee**-uh / hist. the name for the southern district of ancient Palestine, west of the Jordan. ☐ **Judaean** adj.

Judaic / joo-**day**-ik / adj. of or characteristic of the Jews or Judaism.

Judaism / joo-day-iz-uhm / n. the religion of the Jewish people, with belief in one God and based on the teachings of Moses and the Talmud.

judas n. **1** a traitor; a person who betrays a friend. **2** *Aust.* a docile domestic animal used to lead animals into an abattoir, stockyard, etc. (¶ JUDAS ISCARIOT.)

Judas Iscariot an Apostle, who betrayed Jesus to the Jewish authorities in return for thirty pieces of silver.

judder v. shake noisily or violently. • n. a juddering movement or effect.

judge n. **1** a public officer appointed to hear and try legal cases. **2** a person appointed to decide who has won a contest. **3** a person who is able to give an authoritative opinion on the merits of something (*a good judge of art*). • v. **1** try (a case) in a lawcourt. **2** act as judge of (a contest). **3** form and give an opinion about. **4** estimate (*judged the distance accurately*).

judgment n. (also **judgement**) **1** judging, being judged. **2** the decision of a judge etc. in a lawcourt (*the judgment was in his favour*). **3** ability to judge wisely, good sense (*he lacks judgment*). **4** misfortune considered or jokingly said to be a punishment sent by God (*it's a judgment on you!*). **5** an opinion (*in the judgment of most people*). □ **against one's better judgment** contrary to what one really thinks to be advisable.

judgmental / juj-**men**-tuhl / adj. (also **judgemental**) **1** involving judgment. **2** condemning, critical.

Judgment Day (also **Day of Judgment**) (in Judaism, Christianity, and Islam) the day of the Last Judgment, when God will judge all mankind.

judicature / **joo**-duh-kuh-chuh, joo-**dik**-uh-chuh / n. **1** the administration of justice. **2** a judge's position. **3** a body of judges.

judicial / joo-**dish**-uhl / adj. **1** of lawcourts or the administration of justice. **2** of a judge or judgment. **3** able to judge things wisely (*a judicial mind*). □ **judicially** adv.

judiciary / joo-**dish**-uh-ree / n. the whole body of judges in a country.

judicious / joo-**dish**-uhs / adj. judging wisely, showing good sense. □ **judiciously** adv.

judo n. a Japanese sport of unarmed combat, developed from ju-jitsu.

jug n. **1** a vessel for holding and pouring liquids, with a handle and a shaped lip. **2** *colloq.* prison. • v. (**jugged**, **jugging**) **1** cook (hare or rabbit) by stewing it (formerly in a jug or jar). **2** *colloq.* imprison. □ **jugful** n. (pl. **jugfuls**).

juggernaut n. **1** a very large heavy semitrailer etc. **2** an overwhelming force or object. **3** an institution or notion to which people blindly sacrifice themselves or others. (¶ Hindi *Jagannath*, = Lord of the World: the name of a statue of the God Krishna carried in procession on a massive cart under the wheels of which devotees are said to have formerly thrown themselves to be crushed.)

juggle v. **1** toss and catch a number of objects skilfully, keeping one or more in the air at one time. **2** deal with (several activities) at once. **3** rearrange (facts or figures) to suit a purpose or to deceive people (*juggled the accounts*).

juggler n. **1** a person who juggles. **2** an impostor, a fraud. □ **jugglery** n.

jugular / **jug**-yuh-luh / adj. of the neck or throat. • n. (in full **jugular vein**) a large vein in the neck carrying blood from the head.

juice n. **1** the liquid content of fruits, vegetables, or meat. **2** liquid secreted by an organ of the body (*digestive juices*). **3** *colloq.* petrol; electricity. • v. extract juice from (*juiced the oranges*).

juicer / **joo**-suh / n. an (electrical) appliance used to extract juice from fruit and vegetables.

juicy adj. (**juicier**, **juiciest**) **1** full of juice. **2** *colloq.* interesting, esp. because of its scandalous nature (*juicy gossip*). **3** *colloq.* profitable. □ **juicily** adv. **juiciness** n.

ju-jitsu / joo-**jit**-soo / n. (also **jiu-jitsu**, **ju-jutsu**) a Japanese method of unarmed self-defence using throws, punches, etc.

ju-ju / **joo**-joo / n. **1** an object venerated in parts of West Africa as a charm or fetish. **2** the magic attributed to this.

jujube n. a jelly-like sweet.

jukebox n. a machine that automatically plays a selected musical recording when a coin is inserted.

julep / **joo**-lep / n. **1** a medicated drink. **2** *US* a drink of iced and flavoured spirits and water (*mint julep*).

Julian calendar n. the calendar introduced by Julius Caesar, replaced by the Gregorian calendar.

julienne / joo-lee-**en** / n. vegetables or other food cut into thin strips. • adj. cut into thin strips.

Julius Caesar, Gaius (100–44 BC), Roman general and statesman, who completed the conquest of Gaul and established himself in supreme authority in Rome. July, the month in which he was born, is named after him.

July n. the seventh month of the year.

jumble v. mix in a confused way. • n. a confused state or heap; a muddle. □ **jumble sale** a sale of miscellaneous second-hand goods to raise money, esp. for a charity.

jumbo n. (pl. **jumbos**) **1** something very large of its kind (*a jumbo packet*). **2** (in full **jumbo jet**) a very large jet aircraft able to carry several hundred passengers (usu. specifically a Boeing 747).

jumbuck n. *Aust.* a sheep. (¶ Originally in Australian pidgin, perhaps from *jump up*.)

jump v. **1** move up off the ground etc. by bending and then extending the legs or (of fish) by a movement of the tail. **2** move suddenly with a jump or bound; get quickly into a car etc. **3** pass over by jumping; use (a horse) for jumping. **4** pass over (a thing) to a point beyond; skip (part of a book etc.) in reading or studying. **5** give a sudden movement from shock or excitement. **6** rise suddenly in amount or in price or value. **7**

jumper | 446 | **jurisprudence**

leave (rails or a track) accidentally. **8** pounce on, attack suddenly. **9** pass (a red traffic light etc.). **10** get on or off (a train etc.) quickly, esp. illegally or dangerously. **11** seize (a goldmining claim etc.) in the absence of the former occupant or by resort to legal technicalities. •*n.* **1** a jumping movement. **2** a sudden movement caused by shock etc. **3** a sudden rise in amount or price or value. **4** a sudden change to a different condition or set of circumstances; a gap in a series etc. **5** an obstacle to be jumped over. □ **jump at** accept eagerly. **jump bail** fail to come for trial when summoned after being released on bail. **jumped-up** *adj.* having risen suddenly from a low position or status and appearing arrogant. **jump-jet** a jet aircraft that can take off directly upwards. **jump lead** = JUMPER LEAD. **jump ship** (of a seaman) desert one's ship. **jump-start** start (a vehicle) by pushing it or with jumper leads. **jump suit** a one-piece garment for the whole body. **jump the gun** start or act prematurely. **jump the queue** obtain something without waiting for one's proper turn. **jump to conclusions** reach them too hastily. **jump-up** *n. Aust.* a sudden steep rise; an escarpment.

jumper[1] *n.* **1** (also **jackjumper**) any of several smaller species of Australian ant capable of jumping and inflicting a painful sting. **2** a person or animal that jumps. **3** a person who jumps a goldmining claim. **4** a short wire used to make or break an electrical circuit. □ **jumper lead** either of a pair of cables for conveying current from one battery to another.

jumper[2] *n.* **1** a knitted pullover. **2** a loose outer jacket worn by sailors. **3** *Aust. hist.* a smock-like outer garment, distinctive as part of the conventional attire of a goldminer.

jump up *v. Aust.* (in Aboriginal English) come back to life. □ **jump up whitefellow** be reincarnated as a white person.

jumpy *adj.* **1** nervous. **2** making sudden movements.

junction *n.* **1** a place where things join. **2** a place where roads or railways lines etc. meet and unite. □ **junction box** a box containing a junction of electric cables etc.

juncture / jungk-chuh / *n.* **1** a point of time; a critical convergence of events. **2** joining; a joining point.

June *n.* the sixth month of the year.

Jung / yuung /, Carl (Gustav) (1875–1961), Swiss psychologist, who originated the concepts of two types of personality (introvert and extrovert) and of the existence of a 'collective unconscious' derived from ancestral experiences. □ **Jungian** *adj.* & *n.*

junga / juung-uh, jung-uh / *n. Aust.* a parakeeliya. (¶ Panyjima)

jungle *n.* **1** land overgrown with tangled vegetation, esp. in the tropics. **2** a wild tangled mass. **3** a scene of bewildering complexity or confusion, or of ruthless struggle (*the concrete jungle*). □ **jungle fowl** (*or* **hen**) **1** *Aust.* = SCRUB FOWL. **2** an Indian etc. wild bird from which the domestic fowl is said to have been derived. □ **jungled** *adj.* **jungly** *adj.*

junior *adj.* **1** younger in age. **2** added to a son's name to distinguish him from his father when the names are the same. **3** lower in rank or authority (*junior partner*). **4** for younger children (*junior school*). •*n.* **1** a person younger than oneself (*he is two years my junior*). **2** a person employed to work in a junior capacity (*the office junior*).

juniper / joo-nuh-puh / *n.* an evergreen coniferous shrub with prickly leaves and dark-purple berry-like cones used in cooking and to flavour gin.

junk[1] *n.* **1** discarded material, rubbish. **2** *colloq.* anything regarded as useless or of little value. **3** *colloq.* a narcotic drug, esp. heroin. •*v.* discard as junk. □ **junk bond** a bond bearing high interest but considered to be a very risky investment. **junk food** food with low nutritional value. **junk mail** unrequested advertising matter sent by post or email, or hand-delivered to letter boxes. **junk shop** a shop selling miscellaneous second-hand goods or cheap antiques.

junk[2] *n.* a flat-bottomed ship with sails, used in the China seas.

junket *n.* **1** a sweet custard-like food made of milk curdled with rennet and flavoured. **2** a feast, merrymaking. **3** a pleasure outing. **4** an official's tour at public expense. •*v.* (**junketed, junketing**) **1** feast, make merry. **2** hold a picnic or outing.

junkie *n.* (also **junky**) *colloq.* **1** a drug addict, esp. a heroin addict. **2** (with modifier) a person with a compulsive habit or obsessive dependency on something (*food junkie; gym junkie*).

Juno / joo-noh / *Rom. myth.* a great goddess of the Roman State, identified with Hera.

junta / jun-tuh, huun-tuh / *n.* a group of people who combine to rule a country, esp. having seized power after a revolution.

Jupiter / joo-puh-tuh / **1** (also **Jove**) *Rom. myth.* the chief of the gods, identified with Zeus. **2** the largest planet of the solar system, orbiting between Mars and Saturn.

jural / joor-ruhl, joo- / *adj.* **1** of the law. **2** of (moral) rights and obligations.

Jurassic / joor-**ras**-ik, joo- / *adj. Geol.* of the second period of the Mesozoic era. •*n.* this period.

juridical / joo-**rid**-i-kuhl / *adj.* (also **juridic**) of the law or judicial proceedings.

jurisdiction / joor-ruhs-**dik**-shuhn, joo-ruhs- / *n.* **1** the administration of justice. **2** official power exercised within a particular sphere of activity. **3** the extent or territory over which legal or other power extends.

jurisprudence / joor-ruhs-**proo**-duhns, joo-ruhs- / *n.* the science or philosophy of law.

jurist

☐ **jurisprudential** / joor-ruhs-proo-**den**-shuhl / adj.

jurist / **joor**-ruhst, **joo**- / n. a person who is skilled in the law. ☐ **juristic** adj.

juror / **joor**-ruh, **joo**- / n. **1** a member of a jury. **2** a person taking an oath.

jury n. **1** a body of people sworn to give a verdict on a case presented to them in a court of law. **2** a body of people appointed to judge a competition. ☐ **jury box** n. an enclosure for the jury in a lawcourt.

jus / zhoos / n. a sauce consisting of the natural juices exuded by meat etc. during cooking.

just adj. **1** giving proper consideration to the claims of everyone concerned. **2** deserved, right in amount etc. (*a just reward*). **3** well grounded in fact; justified (*his just anger*). • adv. **1** exactly (*just what I need*). **2** barely, no more than, by only a short distance (*I just managed it; just below the knee*). **3** at this moment or only a little time ago (*he has just gone*). **4** colloq. simply, merely (*we are just good friends*). **5** quite (*not just yet*). **6** colloq. really, positively (*it's just splendid*). ☐ **just about** colloq. almost exactly or completely. **just now 1** at this moment. **2** a little time ago. **just so 1** exactly arranged (*she likes everything just so*). **2** it is exactly as you say. ☐ ☐ **justly** adv. **justness** n.

justice n. **1** just treatment, fairness. **2** legal proceedings (*a court of justice*). **3** a judge or magistrate; the title of a judge (*Mr Justice Smith*). ☐ **do justice to 1** show (a thing) to advantage. **2** show appreciation of.

Justice of the Peace n. a person authorised to witness oaths, statutory declarations, etc.

justifiable adj. able to be justified. ☐ **justifiably** adv.

justify v. (**justified, justifying**) **1** show (a person, statement, or act etc.) to be right or just or reasonable. **2** be a good or sufficient reason for (*increased production justifies an increase in wages*). **3** adjust (a line of type in printing) so that it fills a space evenly, gives even margins, etc. ☐ **justification** n. **justificatory** adj.

jut v. (**jutted, jutting**) (often foll. by *out*) protrude, project. • n. a projection, a thing that protrudes.

jute n. **1** fibre from the bark of certain tropical plants, used for making sacks etc. **2** sacking etc. made from this; gunny.

Juvenal / **joo**-vuh-nuhl / (*c*.60–*c*.130), Roman satirist, who attacked the vice and folly of Roman society.

juvenile / **joo**-vuh-nuyl / adj. **1** youthful, childish; immature. **2** for young people. • n. **1** a young person. **2** an actor playing the parts of young people. ☐ **juvenile delinquent** a young offender against the law, below the age when he or she may be held legally responsible for his or her actions. **juvenile delinquency** offences of this kind.

juvenilia / joo-vuh-**nil**-ee-uh / n. pl. the youthful works of an author or an artist.

juxtapose / juk-stuh-**pohz** / v. put (things) side by side. ☐ **juxtaposition** n.

K

K *abbr.* **1** kelvin(s). **2** King. **3** one thousand (dollars etc.) (*32 K*). **4** *Computing* a unit of 1,024 (i.e. 2^{10}) bytes or bits, or loosely 1,000. **5** Köchel (catalogue of Mozart's works). **6** kindergarten. • *symbol* potassium.

k¹ *abbr.* **1** kilo-. **2** knot(s).

k² *n.* (*pl.* **k** *or* **ks** / kayz /) kilometre (cf. KM).

Kaaba / kah-uh-buh / *n.* a shrine at Mecca containing a sacred black stone.

kabana alternative spelling of CABANA.

kabbala alternative spelling of CABBALA.

kabuki / kuh-**boo**-kee / *n.* a form of classical Japanese theatre.

Kabul / **kah**-buul / the capital of Afghanistan.

kadaitcha / kuh-**duy**-chuh / *n.* (also **kurdaitcha**) *Aust.* **1** a malignant spirit of Aboriginal lore. **2** an Aboriginal mission of execution or punishment (against an Aborigine who has been judged guilty of a serious offence against customary Law). **3** the ritual accompanying this. ☐ **kadaitcha man** an Aborigine empowered by the elders to carry out the sentence of execution etc. against the man found guilty. **kadaitcha shoes** shoes made of emu feathers stuck with blood and worn by the kadaitcha man so that he will leave no tracks when he carries out the sentence on the guilty person. (¶ Perhaps from Arrernte.)

Kaddish / **ka**-dish / *n.* **1** a Jewish mourner's prayer. **2** a doxology recited in the synagogue service.

Kaffir *n. hist.* **1** a member or language of a Bantu people of South Africa. **2** *South African, offens.* a black African.

Kafka, Franz (1883–1924), German-speaking Jewish novelist born in Prague, whose works often portray an enigmatic reality where the individual is seen as lonely, perplexed, and threatened. ☐ **Kafkaesque** *adj.*

kaftan alternative spelling of CAFTAN.

kahili ginger / kuh-**hee**-lee / *n.* a herb native to India, a member of the ginger family, bearing highly scented yellow-and-red flowers.

kaiser / **kuy**-zuh / *n. hist.* an emperor, esp. of Germany, Austria, or the Holy Roman Empire.

Kakadu / kak-uh-**doo** / a national park (12,000 sq. km) in Arnhem Land, traditionally owned by the Gagudju people and leased by them to the Australian National Parks and Wildlife Service. The park is world-famous for its rock paintings (many dating back some 18,000 years), esp. those in the famed X-ray style.

kakka *n.* (also **cacker**) (in WA) an undersized crayfish or other crustacean.

Kalaaku / ku-**lah**-koo / *n.* an Aboriginal language of southern WA at Israelite Bay and inland around the Fraser Range and Norseman.

Kala Lagaw Ya / **kah**-lah lah-gow yah / *n.* an Aboriginal language of the Torres Strait islands off the far north of Qld.

kale *n.* a kind of cabbage with curly leaves that do not form a compact head.

kaleidoscope / kuh-**luy**-duh-skohp / *n.* a toy consisting of a tube containing small brightly coloured fragments of glass etc. and mirrors which reflect these to form changing patterns. ☐ **kaleidoscopic** / kuh-luy-duh-**skop**-ik / *adj.*

kalends alternative spelling of CALENDS.

Kalgoorlie / kal-**goor**-lee / a goldmining town in WA, some 600 km east of Perth.

Kali / **kah**-lee / (in Hinduism) the most terrifying goddess, wife of Siva, often identified with Durga and usu. portrayed as black, naked, old, and hideous, with a necklace of skulls, a belt of severed hands, and a protruding bloodstained tongue.

Kalkatungu / kal-kah-tuung-oo / *n.* an Aboriginal language of a wide area of west-central Qld.

kalsomine / **kal**-suh-muyn / (also **calcimine**) *n.* a kind of white or coloured wash for walls. • *v.* coat or wash with kalsomine

Kama / **kah**-muh / (in Hinduism) the god of sexual love, usu. portrayed as a beautiful youth with a bow of sugar cane, a bowstring of bees, and arrows of flowers.

Kamahl / kuh-**mahl** / (1937–), AM, Australian popular singer (born in Malaysia).

Kama Sutra / kah-muh **soo**-truh / an ancient Sanskrit treatise on the art of love and sexual technique, a sex manual.

kamikaze / kam-uh-**kah**-zee / *n.* (in the Second World War) **1** a Japanese aircraft laden with explosives and suicidally crashed on a target by its pilot. **2** the pilot of this. • *adj.* reckless, esp. suicidal.

Kamilaroi / **kam**-i-lu-roi / *n.* an Aboriginal language of a vast area of east-central NSW and extending into southern Qld.

Kampala / kam-**pah**-luh / the capital of Uganda.

kampong / **kam**-pong / *n.* a Malayan enclosure or village.

Kampuchea / kam-poo-**chee**-uh / the former name for Cambodia. ☐ **Kampuchean** *adj.* & *n.*

Kanaka / kuh-**nak**-uh / *n.* a Pacific Islander, esp. (formerly) one kidnapped and forced to serve as an indentured labourer in the sugar and cotton industries of Qld.

Kanchenjunga / kan-chuhn-**juung**-guh / the third-highest peak in the world, situated east of Mount Everest in the Himalayas.

Kandy a city in the highlands of central Sri Lanka. It contains one of the most sacred Buddhist shrines, the Dalada Maligava (Temple of the Tooth).

kanga / kang-guh / *n. Aust. colloq.* **1** a kangaroo. **2** kanga cricket. **3** (rhyming slang on *screw*) a prison warder. **4** cash. **5** a jackhammer. ▫ **kanga cricket** a game of cricket with rules and equipment specially modified for young players.

kangaroo *n.* **1** any of the larger plant-eating marsupials of Australia, having short forelimbs, a large thick tail for support and balance, long feet, and powerful limbs enabling a swift bounding motion; (loosely) any member of the family, including wallaroos and wallabies. **2** (with distinguishing name) any of the main types of kangaroo: *brush* (kangaroo); *bush*; *eastern grey*; *great grey*; *hill*; *Kangaroo Island*; *red*; *western grey*. **3** an Australian, esp. one who represents Australia in sport. **4** (**Kangaroos**) the Australian international Rugby League team. •*v.* (**kangarooed**, **kangarooing**) *Aust.* **1** hunt kangaroos. **2** leap like a kangaroo. **3** (of a car etc.) move forward in jerks. ▫ **have kangaroos in the** (*or* **your** etc.) **top paddock** *Aust. colloq.* be crazy or eccentric. **kangaroo apple** any of several Australian shrubs (esp. those known as *gunyang*) bearing egg-shaped fruit edible when fully ripe. **kangaroo bar** (also **roo bar**) *Aust.* a strong metal bar or frame mounted at the front of a vehicle to protect it in the event of a collision with a kangaroo etc., esp. at night. **kangaroo bush** *Aust.* = PUNTY. **kangaroo court** a court formed illegally by a group of people (e.g. prisoners or strikers) to settle disputes among themselves. **kangaroo drive** *Aust.* an operation (usu. illegal) in which kangaroos are herded, trapped, and slaughtered. **kangaroo fence** *Aust.* a fence (2.1–3 metres high) made to exclude kangaroos etc. from pastoral properties. **kangaroo grass** a tall tussocky perennial Australian grass eaten by kangaroos and useful for stock. **kangaroo-hop** *Aust.* **1** proceed in short hops or stages (*kangaroo-hopped his way across Australia in a jeep*). **2** (of a car etc.) move forward in jerks. **kangaroo mouse** = HOPPING MOUSE. **kangaroo paw** any plant of the genera *Anigozanthos* and *Macropidia* of WA with woolly flowers shaped like the paw of a kangaroo, esp *A. manglesii* with red stems and vivid green flowers, the floral emblem of WA. **kangaroo thorn** a wattle with stiff spines on the stems and golden ball-flowers, often planted as a hedge. **rat-kangaroo** any of several small rabbit-sized kangaroos, including the *bettong* and the *potoroo*. (¶ Guugu Yimidhirr)

kangarooer / kang-guh-**roo**-uh / *n.* a person who takes part in a kangaroo drive; a person who shoots kangaroos.

Kangaroo Island an island about 80 km south-west of Adelaide. ▫ **Kangaroo Island kangaroo** a very large sooty-brown kangaroo restricted to Kangaroo Island.

kaolin / **kay**-uh-lin / *n.* a fine white clay used in making porcelain and in medicine.

kapok / **kay**-pok / *n.* a cottonwool-like substance from a tropical tree, used for padding.

kappa / **kap**-uh / *n.* the tenth letter of the Greek alphabet (Κ, κ).

kaput / kuh-**puut** / *adj. colloq.* ruined, broken; out of order.

Karadjeri / kah-ru-je-ree / *n.* an Aboriginal language of northern WA.

karakul / **ka**-ruh-kuul, -kuhl / *n.* **1** an Asian sheep whose lambs have a dark curled fleece. **2** a fur made from or resembling this.

karaoke / ka-ree-**oh**-kay, -oh-kee / *n.* a form of entertainment in pubs, clubs, etc., in which a customer has the chance to sing along to a backing track.

karara / kuh-**rah**-ruh / *n.* a small wattle of drier Australia which forms tangled thickets. Also called *dead finish*. (¶ Panyjima)

karate / kuh-**rah**-tee / *n.* a Japanese system of unarmed combat in which the hands and feet are used as weapons.

kark *v.* (also **cark**) *Aust. colloq.* (often followed by *it*) **1** die. **2** break down (*the car's finally carked it*).

karkalla / kah-**kal**-uh / *n.* any of several species of Australian pigface bearing edible fruit. (¶ Gaurna)

karma *n.* (in Buddhism and Hinduism) the sum of a person's actions in a previous existence, thought to decide his or her fate in future existences.

karpe / **kah**-pee / *n.* a parasitic Australian fig tree with glossy leaves and edible fruit: the bark was used by Aborigines to make blankets. (¶ Dyirbal)

karri / **ka**-ree / *n.* a tall WA eucalypt with a straight, silky-smooth grey trunk; the hard, heavy, red wood of this tree. (¶ Probably from Nyungar.)

karst *n.* a limestone region with underground streams and many cavities.

kart *n.* a small four-wheeled motor-racing vehicle usually consisting of a tubular frame with a rear-mounted engine, used in the sport of karting.

karting *n.* a motor-racing sport using karts, begun in the US in 1956.

kasbah / **kaz**-bah / *n.* (also **casbah**) the citadel of an Arab city in North Africa, or the old crowded part near this.

Kashmir a former State on the northern border of India, since 1947 disputed between India and Pakistan.

Kasparov, Gary (original name: Gary Weinstein) (1963–), Russian chess player, world champion from 1985.

Kata Tjuta / kah-tuh **joo**-tu / a group of giant monoliths of brilliant red conglomerate rock in the south-western NT. Also called *the Olgas*.

Katherine Gorge a deep sandstone gorge 30 km from the town of Katherine (which is 350 km south-east of Darwin in the NT).

Kathmandu / kat-man-**doo** / the capital of Nepal.

Kattang / **kut**-ung / *n.* an Aboriginal language of coastal eastern NSW from Port Stephens to Port Macquarie.

katsuo / **kut**-swoh / *n.* a bonito, important as a food fish in Japan, esp. dried. (¶ Japanese)

katsuobushi / kut-swoh-**buush**-ee / *n.* dried flakes of katsuo, an essential ingredient in Japanese cooking, esp. in dashi (stock). (¶ Japanese)

kauri / **kow**-ree / *n.* a coniferous tree of New Zealand, yielding a resin. □ **kauri pine** any of three tall coniferous trees of the Australian rainforest yielding a pale, light, easily worked wood.

Kaurna alternative spelling of GAURNA.

kava / **kah**-vuh / *n.* **1** a Polynesian shrub. **2** an intoxicating drink made from the crushed roots of this.

kayak / **kuy**-ak / *n.* a canoe of a type used originally by the Inuit, made of a light frame with a watertight covering having a small opening in the top to sit in. • *v.* (**kayaked**, **kayaking**) travel by kayak; paddle a kayak.

Kazakhstan / kaz-ahk-**stahn** / an independent republic in central Asia (formerly part of the USSR), lying east of the Caspian Sea.

kc/s *abbr.* kilocycles per second.

Keating, Paul (John), (1944–), Australian Labor statesman, prime minister 1991–96.

Keats, John (1795–1821), English poet, a principal figure of the Romantic movement.

kebab / kuh-**bab** / *n.* small pieces of meat, vegetables, etc. cooked on a skewer.

kedge *v.* move (a boat) or be moved by means of a hawser attached to a small anchor. • *n.* this anchor.

kedgeree / kej-uh-ree / *n.* **1** an Indian dish of rice, split peas, onions, eggs, etc. **2** a westernised dish resembling this, usu. with fish.

keel *n.* the timber or steel structure along the base of a ship, on which the ship's framework is built up. • *v.* **1** (often foll. by *over*) become tilted; overturn, collapse. **2** turn keel upwards. □ **on an even keel** steady, balanced.

keelhaul *v.* **1** haul (a person) under the keel of a ship as a punishment. **2** rebuke severely.

Keeling Islands = COCOS ISLANDS.

keelson *n.* (also **kelson**) the line of timber fixing a ship's floor-timbers to the keel.

keen[1] *adj.* **1** sharp, having a sharp edge or point. **2** (of sound or light) acute, penetrating. **3** piercingly cold (*keen wind*). **4** (of prices) low because of competition. **5** intense (*keen interest*). **6** showing or feeling intense interest or desire (*a keen swimmer; is keen to go*). **7** perceiving things very distinctly (*keen sight*). □ **keenly** *adv.* **keenness** *n.*

keen[2] *n.* an Irish funeral song accompanied by wailing. • *v.* wail mournfully.

keep *v.* (**kept**, **keeping**) **1** remain or cause to remain in a specified state, position, or condition. **2** prevent or hold back from doing something, detain (*what kept you?*). **3** put aside for a future time. **4** respect, honour, abide by (*keep the law; keep a promise*). **5** celebrate (a feast or ceremony). **6** guard or protect (a person or place), keep safe. **7** continue to have; have and not give away (*keep the change*). **8** provide with the necessities of life; maintain (a person) as one's lover etc. (*a kept woman*). **9** own and look after (animals) for one's use or enjoyment (*keep hens*). **10** manage (*keep a shop*). **11** have (a commodity) regularly in stock or for sale. **12** make entries in (a diary or accounts etc.). **13** continue doing something, do frequently or repeatedly (*the strap keeps breaking*). **14** continue in a specified direction (*keep straight on*). **15** (of food) remain in good condition. **16** be able to be put aside for later (*the news will keep*). • *n.* **1** provision of the necessities of life, the food required for this (*he earns his keep*). **2** the central tower or other strongly fortified structure in a castle. □ **for keeps** *colloq.* permanently. **keep at** persist or cause to persist with. **keep down 1** keep low in amount or number (*it keeps the weeds down*). **2** continue in (*keep down a job*). **3** eat and not vomit (food). **keep in with** remain on good terms with. **keep the peace** obey the laws and refrain from causing trouble. **keep to oneself 1** keep (a thing) secret. **2** avoid meeting people (*keeps himself to himself*). **keep up 1** progress at the same pace as others. **2** continue to observe, carry on (*keep up old customs*). **3** continue (*our troops kept up the attack all day*). **4** maintain in proper condition (*the cost of keeping up a large house*). **5** prevent from going to bed.

keeper *n.* **1** a person who looks after or is in charge of animals, people, or a thing. **2** the custodian of a museum, forest, etc. **3 a** a wicketkeeper. **b** a goalkeeper. **4** a sleeper in a pierced ear.

keeping *n.* **1** custody, charge (*in safe keeping*). **2** harmony, conformity (*a style that is in keeping with his dignity*). □ **keeping place** an Aboriginal cultural centre, so called because its function is to keep alive the culture of a particular group.

keepsake *n.* a thing that is kept in memory of the giver.

keg *n.* **1** a small barrel. **2** a barrel of beer.

keirin / **keer**-ruhn / *n.* (in full **keirin racing**) *Cycling* a track race of usu. 2 km in which 8–10 cyclists jostle for position as a motorcyclist sets the pace in the first laps, and then sprint for the finish after the motorcyclist leaves them. (¶ Japanese)

Kelly, Ned (Edward) (1855–80), a young Australian bushranger, leader of the Kelly Gang (who equipped themselves with armour made from plough mould-boards). Wounded in a prolonged shoot-out, captured, and hanged, Ned Kelly has become an Australian folk hero and symbol of the reckless defiance of the underdog towards the authorities (whom he wrote of as 'big ugly fat-necked wombat headed big bellied magpie legged narrow hipped splay-footed sons of Irish baillifs of English landlords'). □ **Kelly country** the district in north-eastern Vic. in which Ned Kelly and his gang were active as bushrangers. **Kelly Gang** Ned's brother Dan Kelly (1861–80), Joseph Byrne (1857–80), and Stephen Hart (1859–80).

kelp *n.* a large brown seaweed suitable for manure.

kelpie *n.* an Australian breed of short-haired, prick-eared dog, noted for its ability to work sheep.

Kelt alternative spelling of CELT.

kelvin *n.* the SI unit of thermodynamic temperature, equal in magnitude to the degree celsius. □ **Kelvin scale** a scale of temperature with absolute zero as zero and the triple point of water exactly 273.16. (¶ Lord Kelvin, British physicist (1824–1907).)

kemiri / **kem**-uh-ree / *n.* = CANDLENUT.

ken *n.* the range of sight or knowledge (*beyond my ken*).

Kendall, Henry (1839–82), Australian poet who celebrated the Australian countryside and anticipated Henry Lawson and Banjo Paterson in drawing lightly satiric portraits of outback types.

kendo *n.* the Japanese art of fencing with two-handed bamboo swords.

Keneally, Tom (full name: Thomas Michael Keneally) (1935–), AO, Australian novelist. His novels include *The Chant of Jimmie Blacksmith* and *Schindler's Ark*.

kennedia / kuh-**nee**-dee-uh / *n. Aust.* any plant of the genus of climbing or trailing perennials *Kennedia*, some species being cultivated for their colourful pea-flowers. (¶ J. Kennedy, London nurseryman (1759–1842).)

Kennedy[1], Graham (Cyril) (1934–), Australian television compere and film actor.

Kennedy[2], John Fitzgerald (1917–63), 35th president of the USA 1961–63, assassinated at Dallas, Texas.

kennel *n.* **1** a shelter for a dog. **2** (**kennels**) a breeding or boarding place for dogs. • *v.* (**kennelled**, **kennelling**) put into a kennel.

keno / **kee**-noh / *n.* game of chance resembling bingo or lotto. (¶ French *quine* 'set of five winning numbers in a lottery'.)

Kenya / **ken**-yuh, **kee**-nyuh / a republic in East Africa. □ **Kenyan** *adj.* & *n.*

kept see KEEP.

ker- *prefix colloq.* forming nouns and interjections imitative of the sound or the effect of the fall of some heavy body, as *kerplunk*, *kerslam*, *kersplash*, *kerthump*, etc.

keratin / **ke**-ruh-tuhn / *n.* a strong protein substance forming the basis of horns, claws, nails, feathers, hair, etc.

keratosis / ke-ruh-**toh**-suhs / *n.* (*pl.* **keratoses** / -**toh**-seez /) **1** a horny growth, esp. on the skin (e.g. a wart). **2** a condition marked by such growths.

kerb *n.* a stone edging to a pavement or raised path.

kerbcrawl *v.* (of usu. a male) drive slowly near the edge of the road in an attempt to engage a prostitute or harass esp. female passers-by. □ **kerbcrawler** *n.* **kerbcrawling** *n.*

kerchief *n.* **1** a headscarf or neckerchief. **2** *poetic* a handkerchief.

kerfuffle *n. colloq.* fuss, commotion.

Kern, Jerome (1885–1945), American composer of popular melodies and songs, including 'Ol' Man River'.

kernel *n.* **1** the softer (usu. edible) part inside the shell of a nut or fruit stone. **2** the part of a grain or seed within the husk. **3** the central or important part of a subject, plan, problem, etc.

kero *abbr. Aust.* kerosene.

kerosene / **ke**-ruh-seen / *n.* (also **kerosine**) a fuel oil distilled from petroleum etc. □ **kerosene wood** (also **kerosene tree**) *Aust.* = JITTA.

kestrel *n.* a small hovering falcon.

ketch *n.* a small sailing boat with two masts.

ketchup *n.* a thick sauce made from tomatoes and vinegar etc., used as a seasoning.

ketone / **kee**-tohn / *n.* any of a class of organic compounds including acetone.

kettle *n.* a container with a spout and handle, for boiling water in. □ **a fine** (*or* **pretty**) **kettle of fish** an awkward state of affairs.

kettledrum *n.* a large bowl-shaped drum.

key[1] *n.* **1** a small piece of metal shaped so that it will move the bolt of a lock and so lock or unlock something. **2** a similar instrument for grasping and turning something, e.g. for winding a clock or tightening a spring. **3** something that provides access or control or insight (*the key to success*). **4** a set of answers to problems; a word or set of symbols for interpreting a map, code, etc., or for extracting items of data from a computer. **5** a system of related notes in music, based on a particular note (*the key of C major*). **6** the general tone or degree of intensity of something (*low-key discussions*). **7** roughness of surface helping plaster or paint to adhere to it. **8** a piece of wood or metal inserted between others to hold them secure. **9** each of a set of levers to be pressed by the fingers in playing a musical instrument or operating a typewriter etc. **10** a device for making or breaking an electric circuit, e.g. in telegraphy, or to operate the ignition in a motor vehicle. • *adj.* essential (*a key element in the plan*). • *v.* (**keyed**, **keying**) **1** fasten with a pin, bolt, etc. **2** (often foll. by *in*) enter (data) by means of a computer keyboard. **3** roughen (a surface) so that plaster or paint will adhere well. **4** (foll. by *to*) link closely with something else (*the factory is keyed to the export trade*). □ **keyed up** stimulated, nervously tense. **key grip** a person in charge of moving equipment to the correct positions in a film or television studio. **key signature** *Music* any of several combinations of sharps or flats indicating the key of a composition.

key² *n.* a reef, a low island.

keyboard *n.* **1** the set of keys on a piano, typewriter, computer, etc. **2** an electronic musical instrument with keys arranged as on a piano. •*v.* enter (data) by means of a computer keyboard.

keyboarder *n.* a person who operates a (computer) keyboard, a person who enters data on a keyboard.

keyboardist *n.* a musician who performs on an electronic keyboard.

keyhole *n.* the hole by which a key is put into a lock. □ **keyhole surgery** surgery carried out through a very small incision.

Keynes / kaynz /, John Maynard (1883–1946), English economist, advocate of the planned economy with positive intervention by the State. □ **Keynesian** *adj.*

keynote *n.* **1** the note on which a key in music is based. **2** the prevailing tone or idea of a speech, conference, etc. (*gave the keynote address*).

keypad *n.* a small keyboard of numbered buttons on a telephone, remote control device, etc.

keystone *n.* **1** the central wedge-shaped stone at the summit of an arch, locking the others in position. **2** the central principle of a system, policy, etc.

keystroke *n.* a single depression of a key on a (computer etc.) keyboard, esp. as a measure of work.

keyword *n.* **1** the key to a cipher etc. **2** a significant word, esp. when used in indexing, information retrieval, etc.

kg *abbr.* kilogram(s).

KGB *abbr.* the secret police of the former USSR.

khaki / **kah**-kee, kah-**kee** / *adj.* & *n.* dull brownish-yellow, the colour used for some military uniforms.

khan / kahn / *n.* the title of rulers and officials in Central Asia.

Khartoum / kah-**toom** / the capital of Sudan.

Khmer / kuh-**mair** / *n.* **1** a native or inhabitant of the ancient kingdom of Khmer in SE Asia or of the Khmer Republic (the official name in 1970–5 of what is now Cambodia). **2** their language, the official language of Cambodia. □ **Khmer Rouge** / roozh / the Communist guerrilla organisation in the wars there in the 1960s and 1970s, holding power 1975–9.

Khomeini / hom-**ay**-nee /, Ruhollah (1900–89), known as Ayatollah Khomeini, Iranian Shiite Muslim leader who in 1979 established a fundamentalist Islamic regime after the overthrow of the Shah.

Khufu / **koo**-foo / (*c.*2551–2528 BC), a pharaoh in ancient Egypt, who commissioned the building of the great pyramid at Giza. Also known as *Cheops*.

kHz *abbr.* kilohertz.

kia ora / keer **aw**-ruh / *interj.* NZ (a greeting) expressing good will, or wishing good health. (¶ Maori)

kibble *v.* grind coarsely (*kibbled wheat*).

kibbutz / kuh-**buuts** / *n.* (*pl.* **kibbutzim** / kuh-buut-**seem** /) a communal (esp. farming) settlement in Israel.

kibbutznik *n.* a member of a kibbutz.

kibosh / **kuy**-bosh / *n.* (also **kybosh**) □ **put the kibosh on** *colloq.* put an end to.

kick *v.* **1** strike, thrust, or propel with the foot or hoof. **2** move the legs about vigorously. **3** *Football* score (a goal) by a kick. **4** (of a gun) recoil when fired. **5** *colloq.* protest at; rebel against. **6** *colloq.* give up (a habit). •*n.* **1** an act of kicking; a blow from being kicked. **2** *colloq.* a thrill, a pleasurable effect. **3** *colloq.* an interest or activity (*the health food kick*). **4** the recoil of a gun when it is fired. **5** *colloq.* a sharp stimulant effect, esp. of alcohol. □ **get a kick out of** *colloq.* receive much satisfaction from. **kick about** (or **around**) *colloq.* **1** treat roughly or inconsiderately. **2** discuss unsystematically. **3** go idly from place to place. **4** be unused or unwanted. **kick in** contribute (esp. money); pay one's share. **kick off 1** start a football game by kicking the ball. **2** *colloq.* begin proceedings. **kick-off** kicking off in football. **kick on** *Aust.* maintain (or gain) momentum (*the party's kicking on nicely*). **kick one's heels** be kept waiting. **kick the bucket** *colloq.* die. **kick upstairs** promote (a person) to a higher position in order to get rid of him or her.

kickback *n.* **1** a recoil. **2** *colloq.* (usu. illegal) payment for help or favours, esp. in business.

kickboxing *n.* a form of boxing characterised by the use of blows with the feet as well as with gloved fists. □ **kickboxer** *n.*

kickout *n.* (also **kick-out**) **1** *Aust. Rules* a kick to put the ball back into play, taken by the defending full back or another back after a behind has been scored. **2** *Surfing* a manoeuvre executed by thrusting down on the rear of one's surfboard and pivoting on its tail so as to ride up and over the top of a wave.

kick-start *v.* **1** start (the engine of a motorcycle etc.) by pushing down a lever with one's foot. **2** start or restart (a process etc.) by providing some initial impetus. •*n.* (also **kick-starter**) a device for starting an engine in this way.

kid *n.* **1** a young goat. **2** leather made from its skin. **3** *colloq.* a child. •*v.* (**kidded**, **kidding**) deceive (esp. for fun), tease. □ **handle with kid gloves** treat tactfully.

Kidman, Nicole (Mary) (1967–), Australian actor. Her films include *To Die For* (1995) and *Eyes Wide Shut* (1999).

kidnap *v.* (**kidnapped**, **kidnapping**) carry off (a person) by force or fraud in order to obtain a ransom. □ **kidnapper** *n.*

kidney *n.* (*pl.* **kidneys**) **1** either of a pair of glandular organs that remove waste products from the blood and secrete urine. **2** an animal's kidney as food. □ **kidney bean** a red-skinned dried bean. **kidney machine** an apparatus able to take over the functions of a damaged kidney.

kidstakes *n.pl. Aust. colloq.* nonsense; pretence.

kidult *n.* an adult who has the tastes, interests, etc. of a child. •*adj.* **1** consisting of kidults (*television seems to cater for a kidult society*). **2** geared to kidults (*kidult programs on telly*). **3** designed to appeal to all age groups.

Kiev / kee-ef / the capital of Ukraine.

Kigali / ki-**gah**-lee / the capital of Rwanda.

kill *v.* **1** cause the death of (a person or animal); destroy the vitality of (a plant etc.). **2** put an end to (a feeling etc.). **3** make (a colour, noise, etc.) ineffective. **4** spend (time) while waiting for something (*an hour to kill*). **5** *colloq.* cause severe pain to (*my feet are killing me*). **6** *colloq.* overwhelm with amusement etc. **7** switch off (a light, engine, etc.). **8** *Computing colloq.* delete. •*n.* **1** the act of killing. **2** the animal(s) killed by a hunter. □ **dressed to kill** dressed showily or alluringly. **in at the kill** present at the time of victory.

killer *n.* **1** a person, animal, or thing that kills. **2** *Aust.* an animal, esp. a bullock or sheep, selected and killed for immediate consumption. **3** *colloq.* an impressive, formidable, or excellent thing. **4** an extremely difficult or tortuous etc. thing (*the exam paper was a real killer*). □ **killer instinct 1** an inborn tendency to kill. **2** a ruthless streak. **killer whale** a black and white whale with a prominent dorsal fin.

killing *adj. colloq.* **1** very amusing. **2** exhausting. •*n.* an act of causing death. □ **make a killing** have a great financial success.

killjoy *n.* a person who spoils or questions the enjoyment of others, a wowser.

kiln *n.* an oven for hardening or drying things such as pottery, bricks, or hops, or for burning lime.

kilo / kee-loh / *n.* (*pl.* **kilos**) a kilogram.

kilo- / kil-uh / *comb. form* one thousand.

kilobyte *n. Computing* 1,024 bytes as a measure of memory size etc.

kilocalorie *n.* the amount of heat needed to raise the temperature of 1kg of water by 1°C.

kilogram *n.* the basic unit of mass in the International System of Units (approx. 2.205 lb).

kilohertz *n.* a unit of frequency of electromagnetic waves, = 1,000 cycles per second.

kilojoule *n.* 1,000 joules, esp. as a measure of the energy value of foods.

kilolitre *n.* 1,000 litres (220 imperial gallons).

kilometre / **kil**-uh-mee-tuh, kuh-**lom**-uh-tuh / *n.* a distance of 1,000 metres (approx. 0.62 miles). □ **kilometric** *adj.*

■ **Usage** Some people object to the second pronunciation on the grounds that units of measurement (cf. *kilogram*) should be stressed on the first syllable, while measuring instruments (cf. *speedometer*) should be stressed on the second or a later syllable. In the case of *kilometre*, the two pronunciations given are firmly established in Australian English.

kiloton / **kil**-uh-ton / *n.* (also **kilotonne**) a unit of explosive force equal to 1,000 tons of TNT.

kilovolt *n.* 1,000 volts.

kilowatt *n.* 1,000 watts. □ **kilowatt-hour** *n.* an amount of energy equal to a power consumption of 1,000 watts for one hour.

kilt *n.* a knee-length pleated skirt of tartan wool, worn as part of a Scottish Highland man's dress or by women and children. •*v.* **1** tuck up (skirts) round the body. **2** arrange in vertical pleats.

kilter *n.* (also **kelter**) good working order (*out of kilter*).

Kimberley an extensive and sparsely settled region, often referred to as 'the Kimberleys', in tropical north-west WA, bounded by the Ord River valley on the east, the Fitzroy River valley to the south, and the Timor Sea to the north and north-east. The great sandstone plateau of the area is interspersed with old volcanic rocks, the dominating feature being the King Leopold Ranges.

kimchi / **kim**-chee / *n.* a raw, strongly flavoured cabbage-pickle, the Korean national dish.

Kim Dae Jung / kim day **yuung** / (1924–), South Korean statesman. He became president of South Korea in 1998.

Kim Jong Il / kim jong **il** / (1942–), North Korean politician. He became president in 1994, on the death of his father Kim Il Sung (1912–94).

kimono / kuh-**moh**-noh, **kim**-uh-noh / *n.* (*pl.* **kimonos**) **1** a long loose Japanese robe with wide sleeves, worn with a sash. **2** a dressing gown resembling this.

kin *n.* a person's relatives.

kina / **kee**-nuh / *n.* the chief monetary unit of Papua New Guinea.

kind *n.* a class of similar things or animals, a type. •*adj.* friendly, generous, or considerate. □ **a kind of** something that belongs (approximately) to the class named (*he's a kind of doctor*). **in kind 1** in the same form (*repaid his insolence in kind*). **2** (of payment) in goods or labour, not money. **kind of** *colloq.* slightly (*I felt kind of sorry for him*). **of a kind** similar. □ □ **kindness** *n.*

kinder / **kin**-duh / *n. Aust.* kindergarten.

kindergarten *n.* a school for very young children.

kindie alternative spelling of KINDY.

kindle v. **1** set on fire; cause (a fire) to begin burning. **2** arouse or stimulate (*kindled our hopes*). **3** become kindled.

kindling n. small pieces of wood for lighting fires.

kindly adj. (**kindlier**, **kindliest**) kind in character, manner, or appearance. • adv. **1** in a kind way. **2** please (*kindly shut the door*). □ **not take kindly to** be displeased by. □□ **kindliness** n.

kindred / **kin**-druhd / n. **1** a person's relatives. **2** blood relationship. **3** resemblance in character. • adj. **1** related. **2** of a similar kind (*chemistry and kindred subjects*). □ **kindred spirit** a person whose tastes are similar to one's own.

kindy n. Aust. colloq. (also **kindie**) kindergarten.

kine n.pl. archaic cows, cattle.

kinematic / kin-uh-**mat**-ik / adj. of motion considered abstractly without reference to force or mass. • n. (**kinematics**) the science of pure motion.

kinetic / kuh-**net**-ik, kuy- / adj. of or produced by movement; characterised by movement. • n. (**kinetics**) **1** the science of the relations between the motions of objects and the forces acting upon them. **2** the study of the mechanisms and rates of chemical reactions or other processes. □ **kinetic art** art that depends for its effect on the movement of some of its parts. **kinetic energy** energy of motion.

King, Martin Luther (1929–68), African-American Baptist minister and civil rights leader. He was awarded the Nobel Peace Prize in 1964. He was assassinated in 1968.

king n. **1** a male sovereign, esp. a hereditary ruler. **2** a person or thing regarded as supreme in some way. **3** Aust. hist. the title given by colonists to the male leader of an Aboriginal community. **4** a large species of plant or animal (*king penguin*). **5** Aust. colloq. = KINGFISH. **6** the piece in chess that has to be protected from checkmate. **7** a piece in draughts that has been crowned on reaching the opponent's end of the board. **8** a playing card bearing a picture of a king and ranking next above queen. • v. = KING-HIT (v. sense 1). □ **king brown** a large brown extremely venomous snake occurring throughout northern and drier southern mainland Australia. Also called *mulga snake*. **king fern** either of two very large Australian ferns. **king parrot** a large scarlet-and-green parrot of eastern Australia. **king prawn** a very large Australian prawn highly valued for eating. **king-size** (or **king-sized**) extra large. **king tide** Aust. a spring tide; an unusually high tide. □□ **kingly** adj. **kingship** n.

King Billy n. Aust. hist. a generic term for an Aboriginal leader. (¶ Probably in jocular allusion to the British king William IV.)

kingdom n. **1** a country ruled by a king or queen. **2** the spiritual reign of God (*thy Kingdom come*). **3** a division of the natural world (*the animal kingdom*). **4** a specified mental or emotional province (*kingdom of the heart*).

kingfish n. any of several very large food fish of Australian waters, esp. the yellowtail and the mulloway.

kingfisher n. a small bird with brightly coloured plumage, which dives to catch fish.

King George Sound a large inlet 400 km south-east of Perth. In 1827 it was the site of the first settlement in the west of Australia when a penal colony was established there.

king-hit Aust. colloq. n. **1** a knock-out punch. **2** any sudden catastrophe etc. • v. **1** (also **king**) punch (a person) suddenly and hard. **2** (metaphorically) deliver a telling blow (*was king-hit by the recession*).

kingie n. Aust. colloq. **1** = KINGFISH. **2** = KING PRAWN.

King Island an island in Bass Strait to the north-west of Tas.

kingpin n. **1** a vertical bolt used as a pivot. **2** an indispensable person or thing.

Kings Cross a small district in the Sydney suburb of Darlinghurst which has attained a worldwide reputation for its cosmopolitan character, bohemianism, night life, and, more recently, drugs trade.

Kingsford Smith, Sir Charles Edward ('Smithy') (1897–1935), Australian pioneer aviator.

Kingston the capital of Jamaica.

kink n. **1** a short twist in a wire, rope, hair etc. **2** a mental or moral peculiarity. **3** a flaw, a weak spot (*a few kinks in the plan need to be ironed out*). • v. form or cause to form kinks.

kinky adj. (**kinkier**, **kinkiest**) **1** full of kinks. **2** colloq. bizarre, eccentric, esp. in sexual behaviour.

kinsfolk n.pl. a person's relatives. □ **kinsman** n. **kinswoman** n.

Kinshasa / kin-**shah**-suh / the capital of the Democratic Republic of Congo.

kinship n. **1** blood relationship. **2** likeness; sympathy.

kiosk / **kee**-osk / n. a small light open structure where newspapers, refreshments, tickets, etc. are sold.

kip[1] colloq. n. **1** a sleep; a nap. **2** a bed or cheap lodgings. • v. (**kipped**) (often foll. by *down*) sleep.

kip[2] n. a small piece of wood from which coins are spun in the game of two-up.

Kipling, Rudyard (1865–1936), English writer and poet (born in India), the first English writer to be awarded the Nobel Prize for literature (1907).

kipper[1] Aust. hist. n. **1** an Aboriginal boy who has been initiated into manhood. **2** the ceremony in which such initiation takes place. • v. initiate (an Aboriginal boy) into manhood. □ **kipper ground** (or **kipper ring**) the place reserved for such an initiation ceremony. (¶ Dharuk *gibarra* 'an initiated boy'.)

kipper² *n.* a fish, esp. a herring, cured by splitting, cleaning, and drying it in the open air or in smoke. • *v.* cure (a fish) in this way.

Kirghizia / ker-**gee**-zee-uh / an independent republic (formerly part of the USSR) in Asia, on the Chinese frontier.

Kiribati / **ki**-ruh-bas / a republic consisting of a group of islands in the Pacific NE of Australia. • *adj.* of Kiribati or its inhabitants.

kirk *n. Scottish* a church.

kirsch / keersh, kersh / *n.* a colourless brandy made from the juice of cherries.

kismet / **kiz**-met / *n.* destiny, fate.

kiss *n.* **1** a touch or caress given with the lips. **2** a light touch. • *v.* **1** touch with the lips in affection or as a greeting or in reverence. **2** greet each other in this way. **3** touch gently. ☐ **kiss and tell** recount one's sexual exploits. **kiss-curl** *n.* a small curl of hair on the forehead, cheek, or nape. **kiss of death** an apparently friendly act causing ruin. **kiss of life** mouth-to-mouth resuscitation.

kissogram *see* -GRAM¹ (sense 2).

kit *n.* **1** specialised clothing or uniform, esp. military. **2** the equipment needed for a particular activity or situation (*a first-aid kit*). **3** a set of parts sold together to be assembled (*in kit form*). • *v.* (**kitted, kitting**) (often foll. by *out* or *up*) equip with kit. ☐ **the whole kit and caboodle** *see* CABOODLE.

kitbag *n.* a large usu. cylindrical bag for holding a soldier's or traveller's kit.

kitchen *n.* a room in which food is prepared and cooked. ☐ **kitchen sink** *n.* a sink in the kitchen. *adj.* (**kitchen-sink**) (in art forms) depicting extreme realism, esp. drabness or sordidness (*kitchen-sink school of painting; kitchen-sink drama*). **kitchen tea** a party, given for a bride-to-be, to which the (usu. female) guests bring gifts of kitchen equipment.

kitchenware *n.* cooking utensils.

kite *n.* **1** a large bird of prey of the hawk family. **2** a toy consisting of a light framework to be flown in a wind on the end of a long string.

kitehawk *n.* a predominantly brown, carrion-eating bird common in Australia.

kith *n.* ☐ **kith and kin** kinsfolk; friends and relations.

kitsch / kich / *n.* (often as *adj.*) vulgar, pretentious art, literature, décor, etc., lacking in good taste. ☐ **kitschy** *adj.*

kitten *n.* the young of a cat, ferret, etc. • *v.* (of a cat etc.) give birth (to). ☐ **have kittens** *colloq.* be very agitated or nervous.

kittenish *adj.* playful, lively, or flirtatious.

kitty *n.* **1** the pool of stakes to be played for in some card games. **2** a fund of money for communal use.

kitul / **kith**-uul / *n.* **1** the jaggery palm. **2** (*attrib.*) of or pertaining to the nectar tapped from the flowers of this palm (*kitul jaggery; kitul syrup*). (¶ Sinhalese)

kiwi / **kee**-wee / *n.* **1** a New Zealand bird that does not fly, with a long bill and no tail. **2** (**Kiwi**) *colloq.* a New Zealander. ☐ **kiwi fruit** the fruit of a kind of vine, with thin hairy skin and green flesh. Also called *Chinese gooseberry*.

kJ *abbr.* kilojoule(s).

kl *abbr.* kilolitre(s).

klaxon *n. trademark* a horn or warning hooter.

kleptomania / klep-tuh-**may**-nee-uh / *n.* an uncontrollable tendency to steal things, with no desire to use or profit by them. ☐ **kleptomaniac** *n.*

klick alternative spelling of CLICK².

km *abbr.* kilometre(s) (cf. K²). ☐ **km/h** kilometres per hour. **km/s** kilometres per second.

knack *n.* **1** the ability to do something skilfully. **2** a habit (*a knack of offending people*).

knacker *n.* **1** a buyer of useless horses etc. for slaughter, or of old houses, ships, etc. for the materials. **2** (**knackers**) *colloq.* testicles. • *v. colloq.* (esp. as **knackered** *adj.*) **1** exhaust, wear out (*homework knackers me; I'm knackered*). **2** broken, not working (*the telly's knackered*). **3** castrated (*has your cat been knackered yet?*).

knapsack *n.* a hiker's or soldier's usu. canvas bag worn strapped on the back.

knave *n.* **1** *archaic* a rogue. **2** the jack in playing cards. ☐ **knavish** *adj.* **knavery** *n.*

knead *v.* **1** work (moist flour or clay) into dough or paste by pressing and stretching it with the hands. **2** make (bread etc.) in this way. **3** massage (the body, muscles, etc.) with kneading movements.

knee *n.* **1** the joint between the thigh and the lower part of the human leg; the corresponding joint in animals. **2** the part of a garment covering this. **3** the upper surface of the thigh of a sitting person (*sit on my knee*). • *v.* touch or strike with the knee. ☐ **bring a person to his** *or* **her knees** reduce him or her to submission or a state of weakness. **knee-deep 1** of or in sufficient depth to cover a person up to the knees. **2** deeply involved (*knee-deep in work*). **knee-jerk** an involuntary jerk of the leg when a tendon below the knee is struck. **knee-jerk reaction** one that is automatic, predictable, or stereotyped.

kneeboard *n.* a short surfboard ridden in a kneeling position. • *v.* ride a kneeboard. ☐ **kneeboarder** *n.* **kneeboarding** *n.*

kneecap *n.* **1** the small bone covering the front of the knee-joint. **2** a protective covering for the knee. • *v.* (**kneecapped, kneecapping**) *colloq.* shoot (a person) in the knee or leg as a punishment.

kneel *v.* (**knelt** *or* **kneeled, kneeling**) fall or rest on the knees or a knee.

kneepad *n.* a protective pad worn on the knees, e.g. by skateboarders etc.

knell *n.* **1** the sound of a bell tolled solemnly after a death or at a funeral. **2** an announcement, event, etc., regarded as an ill omen. •v. **1** ring a knell. **2** announce by a knell.

knelt see KNEEL.

Knesset / **knes**-uht / n. the parliament of the State of Israel.

knew see KNOW.

Kngwarreye / nuh-**wah**-ray /, Emily Kame (c.1910–96), Australian Aboriginal painter with an international reputation.

knickerbockers n.pl. loose-fitting breeches gathered in at the knee or calf.

knickers n.pl. = PANTIES.

knick-knack n. (also **nick-nack**) a small ornamental article.

knife n. (pl. **knives**) **1** a cutting instrument or weapon consisting of a sharp blade with a handle. **2** the cutting blade of a machine. **3** (as **the knife**) a surgical operation. •v. **1** cut or stab with a knife. **2** betray, double-cross (esp. a friend or ally). ☐ **knife pleats** narrow flat pleats. **on a knife-edge** in a situation involving extreme tension or anxiety about the outcome.

knight n. **1** a man awarded a non-hereditary title (*Sir*) by a sovereign. **2** *hist.* a man raised to an honourable military rank by a sovereign. **3** a chess piece, usu. shaped like a horse's head. •v. confer a knighthood on. ☐ **knight errant** a medieval knight or chivalrous man in search of adventures. **knight of the road** *Aust.* **1** *hist.* a bushranger. **2** a swagman. ☐☐ **knighthood** n. **knightly** adj. poetic

Knights Templars (also **Knights Templar**) a military order founded in 1118 to protect pilgrims from bandits in the Holy Land.

knit v. (**knitted** or **knit**, **knitting**) **1** make (a garment or fabric etc.) from yarn formed into interlocking loops either by long hand-held needles or on a machine. **2** form (yarn) into fabric etc. in this way. **3** make a plain (not purl) stitch in knitting. **4** unite or grow together (*the broken bones had knit well*). ☐ **knit one's brow** frown. ☐☐ **knitter** n.

knitting n. work in the process of being knitted. ☐ **knitting needle** n. each of the long needles used for knitting by hand.

knitwear n. knitted garments.

knives see KNIFE.

knob n. **1** a rounded projecting part, esp. one forming the handle of a door or drawer or for turning to adjust a dial-setting etc. **2** a small lump of butter etc. ☐ **with knobs on** *colloq.* that and more. ☐☐ **knobby** adj.

knobbly adj. hard and lumpy.

knock v. **1** strike with an audible sharp blow. **2** make a noise by striking something, e.g. at a door to gain admittance. **3** (of an engine) make a thumping or rattling noise while running, ping. **4** drive by striking (*knocked the ball into the hole; knocked those ideas out of him; knocked her hand away*). **5** *colloq.* criticise (*don't knock it till you've tried it*). •n. **1** an act or sound of knocking. **2** a sharp blow. **3** (in an engine) knocking, pinging. ☐ **knock about** (or **around**) *colloq.* **1** treat roughly. **2** wander aimlessly or adventurously. **3** be present, esp. by chance (*the keys?—they're knocking about somewhere*). **knock back 1** *colloq.* swallow (food or drink), esp. quickly. **2** *colloq.* refuse, rebuff. **3** thwart or impede. **knock-back** n. a refusal, a rebuff. **knock down 1** dispose of (an article) at auction. **2** lower the price of (an article). **knock-down** adj. **1** (of a blow, misfortune, argument, etc.) overwhelming. **2** (of a price) very low; (of a price at auction) reserve. **3** (of furniture) easy to dismantle and reassemble. **knock knees** an abnormal inward curving of the legs at the knees. **knock off 1** *colloq.* finish work. **2** *colloq.* produce (a work of art etc.) or do (a task) rapidly. **3** deduct (an amount) from a price. **4** *colloq.* steal. **5** *colloq.* kill. **knock-off** n. time set for the day's work to finish. **knock-on effect** an alteration that causes similar alterations elsewhere. **knock out 1** make unconscious by hitting on the head. **2** defeat (a boxer) by knocking him down for a count of 10. **3** defeat in a knockout competition; exhaust or disable. **4** *colloq.* astonish. **knock up 1** rouse by knocking at the door. **2** make or arrange hastily. **3** practise tennis etc. before formal play begins. **knock-up** n. a practice or casual game at tennis etc.

knockabout adj. **1** *Aust.* pertaining to an unskilled labourer on a rural property (*worked as a knockabout man*). **2** (of comedy) boisterous; slapstick. **3** (of clothes) hard-wearing. •n. **1** *Aust.* an unskilled rural labourer. **2** a loafer; a tramp.

knocker n. **1** a hinged metal instrument on a door for knocking with. **2** a carping critic (*I'm sick of all these knockers!*). ☐ **on the knocker** *Aust. colloq.* **1** (payment made) immediately, on demand. **2** punctually (*be there at 6 on the knocker*).

knockout adj. **1** that knocks a boxer etc. out (*a knockout blow*). **2** (of a competition) in which the loser of each successive round is eliminated. •n. **1** a blow that knocks a boxer out. **2** a knock-out competition. **3** *colloq.* an outstanding or irresistible person or thing.

knoll / nohl, nol / n. a hillock, a mound.

Knossos / **knos**-uhs / the principal city of Crete in Minoan times, containing the remains of the Palace of Minos.

knot n. **1** an intertwining of one or more pieces of thread or rope etc. to fasten them together; knotted ribbon etc. as an ornament. **2** a tangle. **3** a hard mass in something, esp. on a tree trunk where a branch joins it. **4** a round cross-grained spot in timber where a branch joined. **5** a cluster of people or things. **6** a unit of speed used by ships at sea and by aircraft, = one nautical mile per hour. **7** the central point in a problem etc. •v. (**knotted**, **knotting**) **1** tie or fasten with a knot. **2** entangle. ☐ **at a rate of knots** *colloq.* very rapidly. **tie in knots** *colloq.* baffle or confuse.

knothole *n.* a hole in timber where a knot has fallen out.

knotty *adj.* (**knottier**, **knottiest**) **1** full of knots. **2** puzzling, full of problems or difficulties.

know *v.* (**knew**, **known**, **knowing**) **1** have in one's mind or memory as a result of experience, learning, or information. **2** feel certain (*I know I left it here!*). **3** recognise (a person); have had social contact with; be familiar with (a place). **4** recognise with certainty (*knows a bargain when she sees one*). **5** understand and be able to use (a subject, language, or skill). **6** experience; be subject to (*her joy knew no bounds*). ▫ **in the know** *colloq.* having inside information. **know-all** *colloq.* a person who behaves as if he or she knows everything. **know-how** practical knowledge or skill. •*v.* **you never know** it is always possible. ▫▫ **knowable** *adj.*

knowing *adj.* showing knowledge; shrewd; showing that one has inside information (*a knowing look*). ▫ **knowingly** *adv.*

knowledgable *adj.* (also **knowledgeable**) well-informed.

knowledge *n.* **1** knowing. **2** all that a person knows. **3** all that is known, an organised body of information. ▫ **to my knowledge** as far as I know.

known *see* KNOW.

knuckle *n.* **1** a finger joint. **2** the knee joint of an animal, or the part joining the leg to the foot, esp. as a joint of meat. •*v.* strike, press, or rub with the knuckles. ▫ **knuckle down** begin to work earnestly. **knuckle under** yield, submit.

knuckleduster *n.* a metal device worn over the knuckles to protect them and increase the injury done by a blow.

knurl / nerl / *n.* a small projecting ridge or knob.

KO *abbr.* knockout. ▫ **KO'd** knocked out.

koala / koh-**ah**-luh / *n.* (also often but incorrectly **koala bear**) a small, slow, tree-dwelling marsupial native to eastern Australia, having a stout body, thick grey-brown fur, large rounded furry ears, a leathery nose, strong claws, and a vestigial tail. It is the faunal emblem of Qld. (¶ Dharuk)

kobold / **koh**-bold / *n.* (in German mythology) **1** a goblin or brownie. **2** an underground spirit inhabiting mines etc.

Koch / kosh /, Christopher (John) (1932–), AO, Australian novelist whose works include *The Year of Living Dangerously* (1978), and *Highway to a War* (1996).

Köchel number / **ker**-chuhl / *n.* a number given to each of Mozart's compositions in the complete catalogue of his works compiled by L. von Köchel (1800–77) and his successors.

koel / **koh**-uhl / *n.* a large black Indian cuckoo migrating to northern and eastern Australia each summer and having a call said to be similar to the human call 'cooee'. Also called *cooee bird*.

Koestler / **kerst**-luh /, Arthur (1905–83), Hungarian-born essayist and novelist, whose best-known novel *Darkness at Noon* exposed the Stalinist purges of the 1930s.

kofta / **kof**-tuh / *n.* a kind of spiced meat or fish rissole.

Kohl, Helmut (1930–), German statesman, Chancellor of the Federal Republic of Germany 1982–90, and of the united Germany from 1990–98.

kohl *n.* a black powder used as eye make-up, esp. in Eastern countries.

kohlrabi / kohl-**rah**-bee / *n.* (*pl.* **kohlrabies**) a cabbage with an edible turnip-shaped stem.

koi / koi / *n.* any of various colourful carp bred in Japan for their ornamental value.

koine / **koi**-nee / *n.* **1** the common language of the Greeks from the close of the classical period to the Byzantine era. **2** a common language shared by various peoples; a lingua franca.

Kokoda Track (also popularly known as the *Kokoda Trail*) a 240 km foot-track linking Port Moresby with Kokoda village: in 1942 Australian and Papuan soldiers successfully resisted the southward advance of the Japanese army along this track.

kola alternative spelling of COLA.

komodo dragon / kuh-**moh**-doh / *n.* a large monitor lizard, native to the East Indies.

koodoo alternative spelling of KUDU.

kook *n.* esp. *US colloq.* a crazy or eccentric person. ▫ **kooky** *adj.* (**kookier**, **kookiest**).

kookaburra *n.* either of two Australian kingfishers: the large brown and white *laughing jackass* of southern and eastern Australia having a loud call resembling raucous and somewhat manic human laughter, and the *blue-winged kookaburra* of woodlands in northern Australia. (¶ Wiradhuri)

Koori / **kuu**-ree, **koor**-ree / *n.* (*pl.* **Kooris**) *Aust.* an Aborigine. (¶ Awabakal *gurri* 'an Aboriginal person'.)

■ **Usage** Many Aborigines understandably dislike the use of 'Aborigine' or 'Aboriginal' since these terms have been foisted on them and can carry pejorative overtones: they prefer to use the word for 'person' from a local language. Because of the wide variety of Aboriginal languages, however, *Koori* has not gained Australia-wide acceptance, being confined to most of NSW and to Vic. Other terms are preferred in other regions: *Murri* over most of south and central Qld, *Bama* in north Qld, *Nunga* in southern SA, *Yura* in SA, *Nyoongah* around Perth, *Mulba* in the Pilbara region, *Wongi* in the Kalgoorlie region, *Yammagi* in the Murchison River region, *Yolngu* in Arnhem Land, *Anangu* in central Australia, and *Yuin* on the south coast of NSW.

koori *n. Aust.* a young Aboriginal woman. (¶ Probably from Panyjima *kurri* 'a marriageable teenage girl' or *kurri* 'spouse, sexual partner'.)

kopeck, kopek alternative spellings of COPECK.
kopi / koh-puy, -pee / *n. Aust.* **1** a fine powdery gypsum used in ritual Aboriginal mourning. **2** a more cohesive gypsum-rich mass found where opal is mined. (¶ Marawara dialect of Baagandji.)
koradji / kuh-**raj**-ee / *n. Aust.* an Aborigine having recognised skills in traditional medicine and a role in ceremonial life. (¶ Dharuk)
Koran / kaw-**rahn**, kuh- / *n.* the sacred book of Islam containing the revelations of Mohammed, written in Arabic.
Korea / kuh-**ree**-uh / a country in Asia, divided between the Republic of Korea (= South Korea) and the Democratic People's Republic of Korea (= North Korea).
Korean *adj.* of Korea or its people or language. • *n.* **1** a person from North or South Korea. **2** the language of Korea.
korma / **kaw**-muh / *n.* a richly spiced Indian dish of braised mutton, chicken, etc., cooked in yoghurt or curds.
Kosciuszko / koz-ee-**os**-koh, ko-**shuush**-koh / Australia's highest mountain (2228 m), situated in the Snowy Mountains, NSW. It was formerly spelt *Kosciusko.*
kosher / **koh**-shuh, **kosh**-uh / *adj.* **1** (of food or a food shop) conforming to the requirements of Jewish dietary laws. **2** *colloq.* genuine, correct, legitimate. • *n.* kosher food or shop.
Kosovo / **kos**-uh-voh / a province of Serbia. ▫ **Kosovar** *n. & adj.*
Kostunica / kos-tuh-**nits**-uh /, Vojislav (1944–), Yugoslavian statesman who became president in 2000.
kowari / kuh-**wah**-ree / *n.* a small yellow-brown carnivorous marsupial with a striking black brush on its tail and occurring in the gibber deserts of central Australia. (¶ Diyari and Ngamini)
kowhai / **koh**-uy / *n.* a New Zealand tree or shrub with golden flowers.
kowtow *v.* behave with exaggerated respect towards a person. (¶ The *kowtow* was a former Chinese custom of touching the ground with the forehead as a sign of worship or submission.)
Kr *symbol* krypton.
kraal / krahl / *n.* (in South Africa) **1** a village of huts enclosed by a fence. **2** an enclosure for cattle or sheep.
krait / krayt / *n.* a venomous snake of Eastern Asia.
kransky / **kran**-skee / *n. Aust.* a smoked pork and veal sausage, usu. eaten fried or grilled.
kremlin *n.* **1** a citadel within a Russian town. **2** (**the Kremlin**) that of Moscow; the Russian government.
krill *n.* the mass of tiny planktonic crustaceans that forms the principal food of certain whales.
Kriol *n. Aust.* a creolised language (*see* CREOLE) spoken by more than 15,000 Aborigines across northern Australia.
kris *n.* a Malay or Indonesian dagger with a wavy blade.

Krishna (in Hinduism) one of the most popular gods, the eighth and most important avatar of Vishnu.
krona / **kroh**-nuh / *n.* the unit of money in Sweden (*pl.* **kronor**) and Iceland (*pl.* **kronur**).
krone / **kroh**-nuh / *n.* (*pl.* **kroner**) the unit of money in Denmark and Norway.
krummhorn *n.* (also **crumhorn**) a medieval wind instrument with a double reed.
krypton / **krip**-ton / *n.* a chemical element (symbol Kr), a colourless odourless gas used in various types of lamps and bulbs.
K/T boundary *n. Geol.* the boundary between the Cretaceous and Tertiary periods, marked by the extinction of many groups of organisms, including dinosaurs. (¶ From symbols for Cretaceous and Tertiary.)
K2 the second-highest peak in the world, in the western Himalayas.
Kuala Lumpur / kwah-luh **luum**-puh / the capital of Malaysia.
Kublai Khan / koo-bluh **kahn** / (1216–94), Mongol emperor of China from 1259, grandson of Genghis Khan.
kudos / **kyoo**-dos / *n. colloq.* honour and glory.
kudu / **koo**-doo / *n.* (also **koodoo**) a large African antelope with white stripes and spiral horns.
Kufic / **kyoo**-fik / *n.* (also **Cufic**) an early form of the Arabic alphabet, found esp. in inscriptions.
Ku Klux Klan an American secret society of Protestant ultra-racist Whites using terrorism and violence against esp. Blacks, originally formed in the southern States after the Civil War.
Kuku-Yalanji / goo-goo-**yal**-uhn-jee / *n.* an Aboriginal language of the Bloomfield River region of northern Qld.
kultarr / **kuul**-tah / *n.* an Australian marsupial mouse which bounds rapidly from short forelegs to long hindlegs. (¶ Probably Yitha-yitha)
Kumaratunga / kuu-mah-ruh-**tuung**-guh /, Chandrika (Bandaranaike) (1945–), Sri Lankan stateswoman. She was prime minister in 1994 and became president later that year.
kumarl / **kuum**-al / *n.* (also **goomal**) the common Australian brushtail possum. (¶ Nyungar)
kümmel / **kuum**-uhl / *n.* a sweet liqueur flavoured with caraway and cummin seeds.
kumquat = CUMQUAT.
kung fu / kuung **foo**, kung- / *n.* a Chinese form of unarmed combat, similar to karate.
kunzea / **kun**-zee-uh / *n.* a temperate Australian shrub having white, yellow, or red bottlebrush or ball flowers with striking (usu. gold-tipped) anthers.
Kuomintang / kwoh-min-**tang** / *n.* a nationalist party founded in China in 1912, eventually defeated by the Communist Party in 1949 and subsequently forming the central administration of Taiwan.

Kurd *n.* a member of a pastoral people of Kurdistan.

kurdaitcha = KADAITCHA.

Kurdish *adj.* of the Kurds or their language. •*n.* the language of the Kurds.

Kurdistan a mountainous region inhabited by the Kurds, covering parts of Turkey, Iraq, Iran, Syria, and the former USSR.

Kurnai alternative spelling of GANAY.

kurrajong / **ku**-ruh-jong / *n.* **1** an Australian evergreen tree with glossy leaves and cream bell-flowers red on the inside. **2** any Australian plant (of this genus and others) producing (like this) a useful fibre. (¶ Dharuk *garrajung* referring to 'fishing line', since Aborigines used kurrajong fibre for such lines, as well as for nets and bags.)

Kuurn Kopan Noot / **kuurn** kuup-ahn nuut / *n.* an Aboriginal language of a wide area in the Portland/Warrnambool region of Vic.

Kuwait / koo-**wayt** / **1** a monarchy bordering on the Persian Gulf. **2** its capital city. ☐ **Kuwaiti** *adj.* & *n.*

kV *abbr.* kilovolt(s).

kvass / kvahs / *n.* (esp. in Russia) a fermented beverage, low in alcohol, made from rye flour or bread with malt.

kwashiorkor / kwash-ee-**aw**-kuh / *n.* a form of malnutrition caused by lack of protein in the diet, esp. in young children in the tropics.

kW *abbr.* kilowatt(s).

kwongan / **kwong**-gan / *n.* esp. *WA* an area of dry scrubland with woody evergreen vegetation, having leaves that are hard and tough, and usually small and thick, thus reducing the rate of loss of water. (¶ Nyungar)

kWh *abbr.* kilowatt-hour(s).

kylie / **kuy**-lee / *n. Aust.* a boomerang (the girl's name *Kylie* is thought to be based on this word). (¶ Nyungar)

Kyrie / **keer**-ree-ay / *n.* (in full **Kyrie eleison**) a short repeated invocation used in the Catholic and Greek Orthodox Churches, esp. at the beginning of Mass. (¶ Greek, = Lord, have mercy.)

L

L *abbr.* learner driver. •*n.* (as a Roman numeral) 50.

l *abbr.* (also **l.**) litre(s).

£ *abbr.* pound(s) (of money). (¶ Latin *libra*.)

La *symbol* lanthanum.

la alternative spelling of LAH.

lab *n. colloq.* a laboratory.

label *n.* **1** a slip of paper or other material fixed on or beside an object and showing its nature, owner, name, destination, or other information about it. **2** a descriptive word or phrase classifying people etc. •*v.* (**labelled, labelling**) **1** attach a label to. **2** describe or classify (*he was labelled (as) a troublemaker*).

labellum / luh-**bel**-uhm / *n.* (*pl.* **labella**) a large central petal at the base of an orchid flower, usu. large and unlike the others.

labia / **lay**-bee-uh / *n.pl.* the lips of the female genitals.

labial / **lay**-bee-uhl / *adj.* of the lips. •*n.* a speech sound involving closure of the lips (e.g. *p*, *m*).

laboratory / luh-**bo**-ruh-tuh-ree, -tree / *n.* a room or building equipped for scientific experiments or research etc.

laborious *adj.* **1** needing much effort or perseverance. **2** showing signs of great effort, not spontaneous, forced. ☐ **laboriously** *adv.*

Labor Party *n.* (*abbr.* **ALP**; in full **Australian Labor Party**) a major Australian political party, the oldest in Australia, representing the interests esp. of working people and, in its ideals, located to the left of the political spectrum.

labour *n.* (also **labor**) **1** physical or mental work, exertion. **2** a task. **3** the pains or contractions of the womb at childbirth. **4** workers, working people distinguished from management or considered as a political force. •*v.* **1** exert oneself, work hard. **2** have to make a great effort, operate or progress only with difficulty (*the engine was labouring*). **3** treat at great length or in excessive detail (*I will not labour the point*). ☐ **labour-intensive** *adj.* **1** (of an industry) needing to employ many people. **2** (of a job or type of manual work) time-consuming. **labour of love** a demanding task done for satisfaction rather than payment.

■ **Usage** Except in the name of the political party, the *-our* spelling is generally preferred in Australia.

Labour Day 1 a day celebrated in honour of workers, often 1 May. **2** in the Australian States a public holiday on various dates; a commemoration of the campaign conducted by trade unions in the 19th century to achieve an eight-hour working day.

laboured *adj.* showing signs of great effort, not spontaneous.

labourer *n.* a person employed to do unskilled manual work or to assist a skilled worker.

labrador / **lab**-ruh-daw / *n.* a retriever dog of a breed with a smooth black or golden coat.

labyrinth / **lab**-uh-rinth / *n.* **1** a complicated network of paths through which it is difficult to find one's way. **2** the complex cavity of the inner ear. ☐ **labyrinthine** / lab-uh-**rin**-thuyn / *adj.*

lac *n.* a resinous substance secreted by an insect of SE Asia as a protective covering and used to make shellac.

lace *n.* **1** fabric or trimming made in an ornamental openwork design. **2** a cord or narrow leather strip threaded through holes or hooks for pulling opposite edges together and securing them. •*v.* **1** fasten with a lace or laces. **2** pass (a cord) through; intertwine. **3** add spirits to (a drink or food). ☐ **lace monitor** a large, tree-climbing goanna of mainland Australia, dark green in colour with a lacy pattern of yellow spots.

lacerate / **las**-uh-rayt / *v.* **1** injure (flesh) by tearing. **2** wound (feelings). ☐ **laceration** *n.*

lacewing *n.* an insect with lacy wings whose larvae feed on aphids etc.

Lachesis / **lak**-uh-sis / *Gk myth.* one of the three Fates.

Lachlan / **lok**-luhn / the chief tributary river of the Murrumbidgee River, NSW, having a length of nearly 1,500 km.

lachrymal / **lak**-ruh-muhl / *adj.* (also **lacrimal**) of tears, secreting tears (*lachrymal ducts*).

lachrymose / **lak**-ruh-mohs / *adj. formal* tearful.

lack *n.* the state or fact of not having something. •*v.* be without or not have (a thing) when it is needed. ☐ **be lacking 1** be undesirably absent (*money was lacking*). **2** be deficient (*he is lacking in courage*).

lackadaisical / lak-uh-**day**-zi-kuhl / *adj.* lacking vigour or determination, unenthusiastic. ☐ **lackadaisically** *adv.*

lackerband / lak-uh-**band** / *n. Aust. colloq.* = RUBBER BAND.

lackey *n.* (*pl.* **lackeys**) **1** a footman, a servant. **2** a person's servile follower.

lacklustre *adj.* lacking in force or vitality; dull (*a lacklustre performance*).

laconic / luh-**kon**-ik / *adj.* using few words, terse. ☐ **laconically** *adv.*

lacquer / lak-uh / *n.* **1** a hard glossy varnish. **2** a substance sprayed on the hair to keep it in place. • *v.* coat with lacquer.

lacrimal alternative spelling of LACHRYMAL.

lacrosse / luh-**kros** / *n.* a game resembling hockey but with players using a netted crook (a crosse) to catch, carry, or throw the ball.

lactate *v.* / lak-**tayt** / secrete milk. • *n.* / **lak**-tayt / a salt or ester of lactic acid.

lactation / lak-**tay**-shuhn / *n.* the secreting of milk in breasts or udder; the period during which this occurs.

lacteal *adj.* of milk. • *n.pl.* (**lacteals**) vessels in the intestine which absorb fats.

lactic *adj.* of milk. ☐ **lactic acid** the acid found in sour milk and produced in the muscles during strenuous exercise.

lactose *n.* a sugar present in milk.

lacuna / luh-**kyoo**-nuh / *n.* (*pl.* **lacunas** or **lacunae** / luh-**kyoo**-nee /) a gap, a section missing from a book or argument etc.

lacy *adj.* like lace.

lad *n.* **1** a boy or youth. **2** *colloq.* a man (*one of the lads*).

ladder *n.* **1** a set of horizontal bars fixed between two uprights, used for climbing up or down. **2** a vertical strip of unravelled stitching in a stocking etc. **3** a means or series of stages by which a person may advance in his or her career etc. (*the political ladder*). • *v.* cause a ladder in (a stocking etc.); develop a ladder.

lade *v.* (**laded**, **laden**, **lading**) load (a ship); (of a ship) take on cargo.

laden *adj.* (of a vehicle, person, tree, table, etc.) heavily loaded; (of the conscience, spirit, etc.) painfully burdened.

lading / **lay**-ding / *n.* cargo.

ladle *n.* a deep long-handled spoon used for serving liquids. • *v.* (often foll. by *out*) transfer with a ladle.

lady *n.* **1** a woman considered to be of good social position or to have refined manners. **2** (often used as *adj.*) a woman (*a lady doctor; a cleaning lady; ask that lady*). **3** (**Lady**) (in the Brit. system) a title used by peeresses, female relatives of peers, wives and widows of knights, etc. ☐ **the Ladies** (or **Ladies'**) a women's public lavatory. **Lady chapel** a chapel within a large church, dedicated to the Virgin Mary. **lady's finger** (also **lady finger**) **1** a variety of banana of commercial importance in Australia. **2** a variety of large, elongated dessert grape. **3** okra. **Our Lady** the Virgin Mary.

ladybird *n.* a small flying beetle, usu. red with black spots.

Lady Day the Feast of the Annunciation, 25 March.

ladylike *adj.* polite and suitable for a lady (*ladylike manners*).

ladyship *n.* a title used in speaking to or about a woman of the rank of Lady (*your ladyship*).

La Fontaine / lah fon-**tayn** /, Jean de (1621–95), French poet, author of *Fables*.

lag[1] *v.* (**lagged**, **lagging**) **1** go too slow, fail to keep up with others. **2** (of a chat service etc. on the Internet) go into a state of (temporary) stasis. • *n.* lagging; a delay.

lag[2] *v.* (**lagged**, **lagging**) encase (pipes or a boiler etc.) in a layer of insulating material to prevent loss of heat.

lag[3] *colloq. n. Aust. hist.* a convict (*old lags*). • *v.* (**lagged**, **lagging**) **1** *Aust. hist.* transport (a convict) to a penal settlement in Australia. **2** send to prison. **3** arrest. **4** *Aust.* inform against.

lager / **lah**-guh / *n.* a kind of beer, effervescent and light in colour and body.

lagerphone *n. Aust.* an improvised musical instrument made by loosely fixing beer bottle-tops to a pole which is then banged to create a jingling percussive effect.

laggard *n.* a person who lags behind.

lagger *n. Aust. colloq.* a police informer, esp. a prisoner who informs against a fellow prisoner.

lagging *n.* material used to lag pipes etc.

lagoon *n.* **1** *US* & *Aust.* an expanse of fresh water, usu. shallow. **2** a saltwater lake separated from the sea by a sandbank or coral reef etc.

lah *n.* (also **la**) *Music* the sixth note of a major scale.

laid *see* LAY[3]. ☐ **laid-back** *adj. colloq.* easygoing, relaxed. **laid up** *adj.* confined to bed or the house.

lain *see* LIE[2].

lair[1] *n.* **1** a sheltered place where a wild animal regularly sleeps or rests. **2** a person's hiding place.

lair[2] *Aust. colloq. n.* a youth or man who dresses flashily and shows off; a larrikin. • *adj.* vulgarly flamboyant (*a lair paint-job*). • *v.* (often with *up*) (also **lairise**) **1** behave as a lair (*lairing (lairising) with his mates*). **2** decorate, paint, etc. in bad taste (*laired up his car in purple and green*). ☐ **mug lair** a person who is both stupid and vulgar; a general term of abuse.

lairy *adj. Aust.* flashy; vulgar; socially unacceptable.

laissez-faire / la-say-**fair** / *n.* (also **laisser-faire**) the policy of non-interference, esp. in politics or economics. (¶ French, = allow to do.)

laity / **lay**-uh-tee / *n.* lay people as distinct from the clergy.

lake[1] *n.* a large body of water entirely surrounded by land.

lake[2] *n.* a kind of pigment, esp. a reddish pigment originally made from lac.

lakh / lak / *n.* (in India and Sri Lanka) a hundred thousand (*a lakh of rupees*).

Lakshmi / **luk**-shmee / (in Hinduism) the goddess of prosperity, consort of Vishnu.

Lalor / **law**-luh /, Peter (1827–89), Australian politician, leader of the Eureka rebellion at the Eureka Stockade on 3 December 1854 at which he lost an arm.

lam v. (**lammed**, **lamming**) *colloq.* hit hard, thrash.

lama / **lah**-muh / n. a priest or monk of the form of Buddhism found in Tibet and Mongolia.

Lamarck / la-**mahk** /, Jean Baptiste de (1744–1829), French botanist and zoologist who (among others) anticipated Darwin's theory of organic evolution.

lamasery / **lah**-muh-suh-ree / n. a monastery of lamas.

lamb n. **1** a young sheep. **2** its flesh as food. **3** a gentle or endearing person. • v. give birth to a lamb. ☐ **lamb down 1** tend ewes at lambing time. **2** *Aust. colloq.* squander one's earnings on liquor. **lamb marker** *Aust.* a person who performs lamb marking. **lamb marking** *Aust.* **1** marking the ear of a lamb with the owner's brand. **2** completing other processes (castrating, docking, etc.) at the same time. **lamb's fry** lamb's liver as food. **lambs' tails** (also **lambswool**) a WA shrub with felt-like leaves and tall spikes of white, woolly flowers.

lambada / lam-**bah**-duh / n. a fast erotic Brazilian dance in which couples dance with their stomachs touching each other.

lambaste / lam-**bayst** / (also **lambast**) v. *colloq.* beat or reprimand severely.

lambda / **lam**-duh / n. the eleventh letter of the Greek alphabet (Λ, λ).

lambent *adj.* **1** (of a flame or light) playing about a surface. **2** (of the eyes, wit, etc.) gently brilliant. ☐ **lambency** n.

lambertia / lam-**ber**-shuh / n. any of ten species of WA shrubs of the genus *Lambertia*, with attractive flowers and often bizarre woody fruits. Also called *honey flower*.

lambing n. (of ewes) giving birth to lambs.

Lambing Flat riots a series of anti-Chinese riots in 1860 and 1861, on the Burrangong goldfields, NSW, the site of the present town of Young.

lame *adj.* **1** unable to walk normally because of an injury or defect, esp. in a foot or leg. **2** (of an excuse or argument) weak, unconvincing. • v. make lame. ☐ **lame duck** a person or firm etc. that is in difficulties and unable to manage without help. ☐☐ **lamely** *adv.* **lameness** n.

lamé / **lah**-may / n. a fabric in which gold or silver thread etc. is interwoven.

lament n. **1** a passionate expression of grief. **2** a song or poem expressing grief. • v. feel or express grief or regret.

lamentable / **lam**-uhn-tuh-buhl / *adj.* regrettable, deplorable. ☐ **lamentably** *adv.*

lamentation / lam-uhn-**tay**-shuhn / n. **1** lamenting. **2** a lament, an expression of grief.

lamented *adj.* (esp. of a dead person) mourned for.

lamina / **lam**-uh-nuh / n. (pl. **laminae**) a thin plate, scale, or layer. ☐ **laminar** *adj.*

laminate v. / **lam**-uh-nayt / **1** flatten or split (a material) into thin sheets or layers. **2** form (a sheet of material) by pressing together several layers. **3** overlay (a surface or material) with a thin sheet or layer of another material. • n. / **lam**-uh-nuht / a material formed from several layers pressed together. ☐ **lamination** n.

laminex n. *Aust. trademark* a hard, durable, plastic laminate used as a surfacing material for tables etc.

lamington n. *Aust.* a cube of sponge cake covered all over in chocolate icing and coated with desiccated coconut. ☐ **lamington drive** an organised effort (by a community group) to raise money by the sale of lamingtons. (¶ Possibly from Baron Lamington, Governor of Qld 1895–1901.)

lamp n. **1** a device for giving light, either by the use of electricity or gas or by burning oil or spirit. **2** a glass container enclosing a filament that is made to glow by electricity. **3** an electrical device producing radiation (*an infrared lamp*).

lamplighter n. an Australian cicada with three ruby-coloured spots on the head.

lampoon / lam-**poon** / n. a piece of writing that attacks a person by ridiculing him or her. • v. ridicule in a lampoon.

lamprey n. (pl. **lampreys**) a small eel-like water animal with a round mouth used as a sucker for attaching itself to things.

LAN *abbr. Computing* local area network.

lance n. a long spear used esp. by horsemen. • v. **1** pierce with a lance. **2** prick or cut open with a surgical lancet. ☐ **lance corporal** lowest rank of NCO in the army.

Lancelot / **lan**-suh-lot, **lahn**- / (in legends of King Arthur) the most famous of Arthur's knights, lover of Queen Guinevere.

lancet n. a pointed two-edged knife used by surgeons. ☐ **lancet arch** (*or* **window**) a tall narrow pointed arch (or window).

lancewood n. any of several Australian trees yielding a tough, durable timber.

land n. **1** the solid part of the earth's surface, the part not covered by water. **2** the ground or soil as used for farming etc. **3** an expanse of country (*forest land*). **4** a country, State, or nation. **5** property consisting of land. • v. **1** arrive or put on land from a ship. **2** bring (an aircraft or its passengers etc.) down to the ground or other surface; come down in this way. **3** alight after a jump or fall. **4** bring (a fish) to land; win (a prize) or obtain (an appointment etc.) (*landed an excellent job*). **5** (often foll. by *up*) arrive or cause to arrive at a certain place, stage, or position (*landed up in gaol; landed us all in a mess; landed up in Wagga Wagga*). **6** *colloq.* strike with a blow (*landed him one in the eye*). **7** present with a problem etc. (*landed us with the job of sorting it out*). ☐ **land claim** *Aust.* a claim by Aborigines to ownership of land based on LAND RIGHTS. **land council** *Aust.* a body appointed to represent the interests of Aborigines in Aboriginal land. **land crab** (*or* **crayfish**) any of several small freshwater crayfish of eastern Australia. **land mass** a large continuous area of land. **land mullet** a large mullet-like skink of eastern Australia. **land rights** *Aust.* the entitlement of Aborigines to possess their traditional territory; the acknowledgment of this. **land train** *Aust.* = ROAD TRAIN.

Landcare *n.* (also **landcare**) *Aust.* a joint Federal–State project promoting community, industry, and government involvement in the sustainable management of land, water, and living natural resources.

landed *adj.* **1** owning land (*landed gentry*). **2** consisting of land.

landfall *n.* approach to land after a journey by sea or air.

landfill *n.* **1** waste material etc. used to landscape or reclaim land. **2** this process of waste disposal.

landing *n.* **1** the process of coming or bringing something to land. **2** a place where people and goods may be landed from a boat etc. **3** a level area at the top of a flight of stairs or between flights. ▫ **landing craft** a vehicle designed for putting ashore troops and equipment. **landing gear** the undercarriage of an aircraft.

landlady *n.* **1** a woman who owns and lets land or premises. **2** a woman who keeps a boarding house etc.

landlocked *adj.* almost or entirely surrounded by land.

landlord *n.* **1** a man who owns and lets land or premises. **2** a man who keeps a boarding house etc.

landlubber *n.* a person who is unfamiliar with the sea or sailing.

landmark *n.* **1** a conspicuous and easily recognised feature of a landscape. **2** an event that marks a stage or change in the history of something.

landmine *n.* an explosive mine laid in or on the ground.

landowner *n.* an owner of (esp. much) land. ▫ **landowning** *adj.* & *n.*

landscape *n.* **1** the scenery of a land area. **2** a picture of this; this type of painting. • *v.* lay out (an area) attractively, with natural features. ▫ **landscape gardening** the laying out of grounds to resemble natural scenery.

landslide *n.* **1** a landslip. **2** an overwhelming majority of votes for one side in an election.

landslip *n.* the sliding down of a mass of land from a slope or mountain.

landward *adj.* & *adv.* towards the land. ▫ **landwards** *adv.*

Landy, John (Michael) (1930–), AC, Australian middle-distance runner and the second person in the world to break the four-minute mile.

lane *n.* **1** a narrow road. **2** a strip of road for a single line of traffic (*a four-lane highway*). **3** a strip of track or water for a runner, rower, or swimmer in a race. **4** a route prescribed for or regularly followed by ships or aircraft (*shipping lanes*). **5** a passage made or left between rows of people. **6** *Aust.* an enclosure in a stockyard from which animals may be fed into the appropriate pen.

laneway *n.* **1** = LANE (sense 1). **2** *Aust.* strip of land running between paddocks and providing access to them.

language *n.* **1** the use of words in an agreed way as a method of human communication. **2** a system of words of a particular community or country etc. **3** *Aust.* (in Aboriginal English) an Aboriginal language (*she speaks language*). **4** a system of signs or symbols used for conveying information. **5** a system of words, phrases, and symbols by means of which a computer can be programmed. **6** a particular style of wording. **7** the vocabulary of a particular group of people (*medical language*).

languid / **lang**-gwuhd / *adj.* lacking vigour or vitality. ▫ **languidly** *adv.*

languish / **lang**-gwish / *v.* **1** lose or lack vitality. **2** live under miserable conditions, be neglected. **3** pine.

languor / **lang**-guh / *n.* **1** tiredness, listlessness, lack of vitality. **2** a languishing expression. **3** oppressive stillness of the air. ▫ **languorous** *adj.*

laniferous / luh-**nif**-uh-ruhs / *adj.* wool-bearing.

langur / **lung**-goor / *n.* any of various Asian long-tailed monkeys.

La Niña / lah **nee**-nyah / *n.* a climatic phenomenon associated with extensive cooling of the central and eastern Pacific Ocean, stronger than normal trade winds, high positive values on the Southern Oscillation Index, and increased likelihood of wet conditions in Australia. Cf. EL NIÑO. (¶ Spanish, = the (girl) child.)

lank *adj.* **1** tall and lean. **2** (of hair or grass) long and limp.

lanky *adj.* (**lankier**, **lankiest**) ungracefully lean and long or tall. ▫ **lankiness** *n.*

Lanney, William (1834–69), Tasmanian Aborigine, regarded by the white community as the last full-blooded male Tasmanian Aborigine. His body was stolen for 'scientific' research.

lanolin / **lan**-uh-luhn / *n.* fat extracted from sheep's wool and used as a basis for cosmetics etc.

lantern *n.* **1** a transparent case for holding a light and shielding it against wind etc. outdoors. **2** the light-chamber of a lighthouse. **3** a projection with windows on each side, on top of a dome or room.

lanthanide / **lan**-thuh-nuyd / *n.* any of a series of chemically related elements from lanthanum to lutetium (atomic numbers 57–71).

lanthanum / **lan**-thuh-nuhm / *n.* a silvery-white metallic element (symbol La).

lanyard *n.* **1** a short rope or line used on a ship to fasten something or secure it. **2** a cord worn round the neck or on the shoulder, to which a knife or whistle etc. may be attached. **3** a woven cord worn round the shoulder in some military uniforms.

Laos / lows / a small landlocked republic in SE Asia. ☐ **Laotian** / lah-**oh**-shuhn / *adj.* & *n.*

Lao-tzu / low-**tsoo** / **1** the legendary founder of Taoism and traditional author of its most sacred scripture. **2** this scripture.

lap[1] *n.* **1** the flat area formed by the upper part of the thighs of a seated person. **2** the part of a dress etc. covering this. ☐ **in a person's lap** as his or her responsibility. **in the lap of luxury** in great luxury.

lap[2] *n.* **1** an overlapping part; the amount of overlap. **2** a single circuit e.g. of a racecourse. **3** one section of a journey (*the last lap*). • *v.* (**lapped**, **lapping**) **1** fold or wrap round. **2** overlap. **3** be one or more laps ahead of (another competitor) in a race. ☐ **lap of honour** a ceremonial circuit of a racetrack etc. by the winner.

lap[3] *v.* (**lapped**, **lapping**) **1** take up (liquid) by movements of the tongue, as a cat does. **2** flow with ripples making a gentle splashing sound (*waves lapped the shore*). ☐ **lap up** drink (liquid) greedily. **2** consume (gossip, praise, etc.) eagerly.

laparoscope / lap-uh-ruh-skohp / *n.* a fibre optic instrument inserted through the abdomen to view the internal organs. ☐ **laparoscopy** / lap-uh-**ros**-kuh-pee / *n.*

laparotomy / lap-uh-**rot**-uh-mee / *n.* surgical cutting through the abdominal wall for access to the internal organs.

La Paz the capital of Bolivia.

lapdog *n.* a small pet dog.

lapel / luh-**pel** / *n.* a flap at the edge of each front of a coat etc., folded back to lie against its outer surface. ☐ **lapelled** *adj.*

La Perouse, Jean François de Galaup, Comte de (1741–88), French explorer in Australia who reached Botany Bay in 1788 and set up camp in the area now known as La Perouse.

lapidary / **lap**-uh-duh-ree / *adj.* of stones, engraved on stone. • *n.* a cutter, polisher, or engraver of gems.

lapin / **lap**-uhn / *n.* rabbit fur used for jackets, coats, etc. (¶ French, = rabbit)

lapis lazuli / lap-uhs **laz**-yoo-lee, -luy / *n.* a bright blue semi-precious stone.

Lapland the region inhabited by the Lapps at the north of Scandinavia. ☐ **Laplander** *n.*

lap-lap *n.* a cloth worn around the waist or loins in Papua New Guinea etc.

Lapp *n.* **1** a Laplander. **2** the language of Lapland. ☐ **Lappish** *adj.*

■ **Usage** The Lapps' own name for themselves, *Sami*, is now often preferred with reference to the people.

lappet *n.* a flap or fold of a garment etc. or of flesh.

lapse *n.* **1** a slight error, esp. one caused by forgetfulness, weakness, or inattention. **2** backsliding, a decline into an inferior state. **3** the passage of a period of time (*after a lapse of six months*). **4** the termination of a privilege or legal right through disuse. • *v.* **1** fail to maintain one's position or standard. **2** (foll. by *into*) fall back into an inferior or previous state (*he lapsed into bad habits*). **3** (of rights and privileges) be lost or no longer valid because not used, claimed, or renewed.

laptop *n.* (often used as *adj.*) a portable microcomputer, suitable for use while travelling etc.

lapunyah / luh-**pun**-yuh / *n.* (also **yapunyah**) any of various eucalypts occurring along watercourses in Qld and the NT. (¶ Gunya)

lapwing *n.* a peewit, including two Australian species.

larboard *n. archaic* = PORT[3].

larceny / **lah**-suh-nee / *n.* theft of personal goods. ☐ **larcenous** *adj.*

■ **Usage** Except in NSW and SA, 'larceny' has been replaced as a statutory crime by *theft*.

larch *n.* a deciduous coniferous tree of the genus *Larix*, with bright foliage and producing tough timber.

lard *n.* a white greasy substance prepared from pig fat and used in cooking. • *v.* **1** place strips of fat or bacon in or on (meat) before cooking, in order to prevent it from becoming dry while roasting. **2** garnish (talk or writing) with strange terms.

larder *n.* a room or cupboard for storing food.

Lardil / **lahr**-dil, **ler**- / *n.* the Aboriginal language of the Lardil people on Mornington Island in the Gulf of Carpentaria.

lardon *n.* (also **lardoon**) a strip of fat bacon used to lard meat.

largamente / lah-guh-**men**-tay / *adv.* & *adj. Music* in a slow dignified style. (¶ Italian, = broadly.)

large *adj.* **1** of considerable size or extent. **2** of the larger kind (*the large intestine*). **3** acting on a large scale (*large manufacturer*). • *adv.* in a large way, on a large scale (*loom large*). ☐ **at large 1** free to roam about, not in confinement. **2** in a general way, at random. **3** as a whole, in general (*is popular with the country at large*). **large as life** in person, esp. when prominent. **larger than life** seeming extreme or exaggerated. **large-scale** *adj.* **1** drawn to a large scale so that many details can be shown (*a large-scale map*). **2** extensive, involving large quantities etc. (*large-scale operations*). ☐☐ **largeness** *n.* **largish** *adj.*

largely *adv.* to a great extent (*his success was largely due to luck*).

largesse / lah-**zhes**, -**jes** / *n.* money or gifts generously given.

largish *adj.* fairly large.

largo *adj.* & *adv. Music* in a slow tempo and dignified style. • *n.* (*pl.* **largos**) a largo passage or movement.

lariat / **la**-ree-uht / *n.* **1** a lasso. **2** a rope used to tether a horse etc.

lark[1] *n.* **1** any of several small sandy-brown songbirds, esp. the skylark.

lark 465 **latch**

lark[2] *colloq. n.* **1** a playful adventurous action. **2** a type of activity etc. (*I'm fed up with this digging lark*). •*v.* play tricks (*larking about*).

Larrakia / la-**ruh**-kee-uh / *n.* **1** a member of an Aboriginal people of the far north of the Northern Territory; this people. **2** the language of the Larrakia.

larrikin *n. Aust.* **1** *hist.* a young urban rough, a hooligan. **2** a mischief-making youth; a troublemaker. **3** a person who acts with apparent disregard for social or political conventions. □ **larrikinism** *n.*

■ **Usage** In the second half of the nineteenth century the name 'larrikin' was used to describe young men of rowdy, delinquent behaviour who roamed the streets of Sydney and Melbourne in 'pushes' or gangs. More an urban than a Australian phenomenon, for they had much in common with young male gangs in the northern hemisphere at the time, nevertheless the larrikins have a place in the Australian quest for identity, the 'larrikin spirit' often being presented as nationalistic and anti-authoritarian. Nowadays the 'hooligan' connotations have disappeared, and the term is applied to extroverted and irreverent people (usu. males) of all ages.

Larry *n.* □ **as happy as Larry** *Aust.* extremely happy.
larry-doo *n. Aust.* = LARRY DOOLEY.
Larry Dooley *n. Aust. colloq.* **1** a beating. **2** a disturbance or fracas. □ **give** (**a person** *or* **a thing**) **Larry Dooley** beat; treat roughly.
larva *n.* (*pl.* **larvae** / **lah**-vee /) an insect in the first stage of its life after coming out of the egg. □ **larval** *adj.*
laryngeal / la-**rin**-jee-uhl, la-ruhn-**jee**-uhl / *adj.* of the larynx.
laryngitis / la-ruhn-**juy**-tuhs / *n.* inflammation of the larynx.
larynx / **la**-ringks / *n.* the part of the throat containing the vocal cords.
lasagne / luh-**sahn**-yuh / *n.* **1** pasta formed into sheets. **2** a dish of this pasta layered with minced meat and cheese sauce.
La Scala / lah **skah**-luh / an opera house in Milan, Italy, one of the most famous in the world.
Lascaux / lah-**skoh** / the site of a cave in SW France with palaeolithic paintings.
lascivious / luh-**siv**-ee-uhs / *adj.* lustful; arousing lust. □ **lasciviously** *adv.* **lasciviousness** *n.*
laser / **lay**-zuh / *n.* a device that generates an intense and highly concentrated beam of light or other electromagnetic radiation. □ **laser printer** a computer printer that uses a laser beam to print quietly and accurately.
lash *v.* **1** move in a whip-like movement (*lashed its tail*). **2** strike with a whip; beat or strike violently (*rain lashed against the windows*). **3** attack violently in words. **4** fasten or secure with cord etc. (*lashed them together*). •*n.* **1** a stroke with a whip etc. **2** the flexible part of a whip. **3** an eyelash. □ **lash out 1** attack with blows or words. **2** spend lavishly.
lashings *n.pl. colloq.* a lot (*lashings of cream*).
lass *n.* a girl.
Lassa fever *n.* an acute and often fatal disease of tropical Africa, caused by a virus. (¶ Named after Lassa in Nigeria.)
Lasseter's Reef an extremely rich reef of gold claimed to have been discovered by goldseeker Harry Lasseter (1880–1931) in central Australia. Numerous expeditions to rediscover this reef have failed.
lassitude *n.* tiredness, listlessness.
lasso / la-**soo** / *n.* (*pl.* **lassos** *or* **lassoes**) a rope with a running noose, used for catching cattle, brumbies, etc. •*v.* (**lassoed**, **lassoing**) catch with a lasso.
last[1] *adj.* & *adv.* **1** after all others in position or time, coming at the end. **2** latest, most recent, most recently (*last night*). **3** remaining as the only one(s) left (*our last hope*). **4** least likely or suitable (*she is the last person I'd have chosen*). •*n.* **1** a person or thing that is last. **2** the last performance of certain actions (*breathe one's last*). **3** the last mention or sight of something (*shall never hear the last of it*). □ **at last** (*or* **at long last**) in the end, after much delay. **last-ditch** *adj.* (of an attempt etc.) final, desperate. **last-minute** *adj.* at the latest possible time. **last post** a military bugle call sounded at sunset and at military funerals. **last rites** (*or* **sacraments**) the sacraments of penance, viaticum, and extreme unction administered to a person about to die. **last straw** a slight addition to one's difficulties that makes them finally unbearable. **last word 1** the final statement in a dispute. **2** a definitive statement. **3** the latest fashion.
last[2] *v.* **1** continue for a period of time, endure (*the rain lasted all day*). **2** be sufficient for one's needs (*enough food to last us for three days*). □ **last out** be strong enough or sufficient to last.
last[3] *n.* a block of wood or metal shaped like a foot, used in making and repairing shoes.
'lastic-sides *n.pl.* (in full **elastic sides**) *Aust.* a pair of boots without laces and having a piece of elastic inset into each side: part of the traditional Australian bush costume.
lasting *adj.* able to last for a long time.
Last Judgment *see* JUDGMENT DAY.
lastly *adv.* in the last place, finally.
Last Supper the final meal of Jesus with his Apostles on the night before the Crucifixion.
lat *n.* (usu. in *pl.*) *colloq.* (in bodybuilding) a latissimus muscle.
lat. *abbr.* latitude.
latch *n.* **1** a small bar fastening a door or gate, lifted from its catch by a lever. **2** a spring lock that catches when a door is closed. •*v.* fasten or be

latchet | 466 | **laughter**

fastened with a latch. ❑ **latch on to** *colloq.* **1** cling to. **2** take in as an idea.

latchet *n.* an edible marine fish of southern Australian coastal waters, having large pectoral fins and a reddish skin.

latchkey *n.* the key of an outer door. ❑ **latchkey child** (*or* **kid**) a child who is alone at home after school until a parent returns from work.

late *adj. & adv.* **1** after the proper or usual time. **2** flowering or ripening late in the season. **3** far on in the day or night or a period of time or a series etc. (*in the late 1920s*). **4** of recent date or time (*the latest news*). **5** no longer alive; no longer holding a certain position (*my late husband; I just met the late prime minister*). **6** formerly but not now (*late of the Alice*). ❑ **late in the day** at a late stage in the proceedings. **of late** lately. ❑❑ **lateness** *n.*

latecomer *n.* a person who arrives late.

lateen / luh-**teen** / *adj.* (of a sail) triangular and hung on a long spar at an angle of 45° to the mast.

lately *adv.* in recent times, not long ago.

latent / **lay**-tuhnt / *adj.* existing but not active, developed, or visible. ❑ **latent heat** *Physics* heat required to turn a solid into a liquid or vapour, or a liquid into a vapour, without change of temperature. ❑❑ **latency** *n.*

lateral / **lat**-uh-ruhl / *adj.* of, at, or towards the side(s). ❑ **lateral thinking** a method of solving problems without using conventional logic. ❑❑ **laterally** *adv.*

Lateran / **lat**-uh-ruhn / the site in Rome containing the basilica dedicated to St John the Baptist and St John the Evangelist, which is the cathedral church of Rome.

latex / **lay**-teks / *n.* **1** a milky fluid exuded from the cut surfaces of certain plants, e.g. the rubber tree. **2** a synthetic product resembling this, used in paints and adhesives.

lath / lahth / *n.* a narrow thin strip of wood, used in trellises or as a support for plaster etc.

lathe / layth / *n.* a machine for holding and turning pieces of wood or metal etc. against a tool that shapes them.

lather / **lath**-uh, **lah**-*th*uh / *n.* **1** a froth produced by soap or detergent mixed with water. **2** frothy sweat. **3** a state of agitation. • *v.* **1** cover with lather. **2** form a lather.

Latin *n.* the language of the ancient Romans. • *adj.* **1** of or in Latin. **2** of the countries or peoples (e.g. France, Spain, Portugal, Italy) using languages developed from Latin. **3** of the Catholic Church (*Latin rite*). ❑ **Latin cross** a plain cross with the lowest member longer than the other three.

Latin America the parts of Central and South America where Spanish or Portuguese is the main language. ❑ **Latin American** *adj. & n.*

latish *adj. & adv.* rather late.

latissimus / lah-**tis**-uh-muhs / *n.* (*pl.* **latissimi**) (in full **latissimus dorsi** / **daw**-suy, -see /) either of a pair of large, roughly triangular, muscles covering the lower part of the back.

latitude *n.* **1** the distance of a place from the equator, measured in degrees. **2** (usu. as **latitudes**) a region or climate. **3** freedom from restrictions on actions or opinions.

latitudinarian / lat-uh-tyoo-duh-**nair**-ree-uhn / *adj.* allowing great freedom of belief or opinion, esp. in religion. • *n.* a person of this kind.

latrine / luh-**treen** / *n.* a communal toilet in a camp or barracks etc.

La Trobe, Charles Joseph (1801–75), lieutenant-governor of Victoria 1851–54. With the discovery of gold in Vic. in 1851, La Trobe adopted the NSW licence system, thereby sowing the seeds of the Eureka rebellion.

latter *adj.* **1** the second of two (people, things etc.) mentioned. **2** nearer to the end (*the latter half of the twentieth century*). ❑ **latter-day** *adj.* modern, recent.

■ **Usage** When referring to the last of three or more, *the last*, not *the latter*, should be used.

latterly *adv.* of late, nowadays.

lattice / **lat**-uhs / *n.* **1** a framework of crossed laths or bars with spaces between, used as a screen or fence etc. **2** a structure resembling this.

Latvia a republic in eastern Europe on the shore of the Baltic Sea, formerly a republic of the USSR.

Latvian *adj.* of Latvia or its people or language. • *n.* **1** a person from Latvia. **2** the language of Latvia.

laud *v. formal* praise. • *n.* **1** praise; a hymn of praise. **2** (**lauds**) the first service of the day in the Catholic Church.

laudable / **law**-duh-buhl / *adj.* praiseworthy, commendable. ❑ **laudably** *adv.*

laudanum / **lawd**-nuhm / *n.* a solution containing opium, prepared for use as a sedative.

laudatory / **law**-duh-tuh-ree, -tree / *adj.* expressing praise.

■ **Usage** Do not confuse with *laudable*.

laugh *v.* **1** make the sounds and movements that express lively amusement or amused scorn. **2** express (a feeling) by laughing. **3** (foll. by *at*) ridicule, make fun of. • *n.* **1** an act, sound, or manner of laughing. **2** *colloq.* an amusing incident. ❑ **be laughing** *colloq.* be in a fortunate or successful position. **laughing gas** nitrous oxide used as an anaesthetic, which can cause involuntary laughter when inhaled. **laughing jackass** *Aust.* the kookaburra. **laughing owl** any of several Australian nightjars with loud laughing calls. **laughing stock** a person or thing that is ridiculed. **laugh off** get rid of (embarrassment) by joking.

laughable *adj.* so ridiculous as to be amusing.

laughter *n.* the act, sound, or manner of laughing.

Launceston / **lon**-ses-tuhn, **lawn**- / a city in northern Tasmania.

launch v. **1** send on its course by hurling or thrusting (*launch a rocket*). **2** set (a vessel) afloat. **3** put into action (*launch an attack*). **4** publicly introduce (a new product, a new book, etc.) or begin (a new enterprise). **5** enter boldly or freely into a course of action. • n. **1** the process of launching a ship or spacecraft. **2** a large motor boat. **3** a warship's largest boat. **4** the occasion of launching a new product, book, business, etc. ☐ **launching pad** (*or* **launch pad**) a concrete platform from which spacecraft are launched. **launch out** spend money freely; start on an ambitious enterprise.

launder v. **1** wash and iron (clothes etc.). **2** transfer (funds etc.) to conceal their dubious or illegal origin.

laundromat / **lawn**-druh-mat / n. an establishment with coin-operated washing machines and driers for public use.

laundry n. **1** a place where clothes etc. are laundered; a business establishment that launders things for customers. **2** clothes etc. for laundering; clothes etc. newly laundered.

laureate / **lo**-ree-uht / *adj. poetic* wreathed with laurel as an honour. • n. = POET LAUREATE. ☐ **laureateship** n.

laurel / **lo**-ruhl / n. **1** an evergreen shrub with smooth glossy leaves, = BAY[1]. **2** (also **laurels**) a wreath of laurel leaves as an emblem of victory or poetic merit. ☐ **look to one's laurels** beware of losing one's position of superiority. **rest on one's laurels** be satisfied with what one has done and not seek further success. (¶ From the ancient use of a branch or wreath of laurel as a token of victory.)

lav n. *colloq.* a lavatory.

lava / **lah**-vuh / n. flowing molten rock discharged from a volcano; the solid substance formed when this cools.

lavatorial *adj.* (esp. of humour) relating to or preoccupied with excretion.

lavatory n. = TOILET.

lave / layv / v. *literary* **1** wash, bathe. **2** flow against.

lavender n. **1** a shrub with fragrant purple flowers that are dried and used to scent linen etc. **2** light purple. ☐ **lavender bug** an Australian beetle which when distressed squirts out a corrosive fluid that supposedly smells like lavender. **lavender water** a light perfume made from lavender.

Laver, Rod(ney George) (1938–), Australian tennis player. He won the international grand slam twice (1962, 1969).

lavish / **lav**-ish / *adj.* **1** giving or producing something in large quantities. **2** plentiful (*a lavish display*). • v. bestow lavishly. ☐ **lavishly** *adv.* **lavishness** n.

law n. **1** a rule established among a community by authority or custom. **2** a body of such rules. **3** their controlling influence, their operation as providing a remedy against wrongs (*law and order*). **4** the subject or study of such rules. **5** (**the law**) *colloq.* the police. **6** something that must be obeyed (*her word was law*). **7** a general statement about consistently-occurring natural events (*the laws of nature; the law of gravity*). ☐ **law-abiding** obeying the law. **a law unto oneself** (*or* **itself**) a person (or thing) that does not behave in the accepted fashion.

lawbreaker n. a person who breaks the law. ☐ **lawbreaking** n. & *adj.*

lawcourt n. a court of law.

lawful *adj.* permitted or recognised by law (*lawful business; his lawful wife*). ☐ **lawfully** *adv.*

Lawler, Ray(mond Evenor) (1921–), Australian playwright, best known for *The Summer of the Seventeenth Doll*.

lawless *adj.* **1** (of a country) where laws do not exist or are not applied. **2** disregarding the law, uncontrolled (*lawless hooligans*). ☐ **lawlessly** *adv.* **lawlessness** n.

lawman n. *Aust.* (in Aboriginal English) a spiritual leader.

lawn n. **1** an area of closely-cut grass in a garden or park. **2** fine woven cotton or synthetic material. ☐ **lawn sale** *Aust.* a sale (of miscellaneous household goods) held on the lawn of a private house.

lawnmower n. a machine for cutting lawns.

Lawrence[1], D(avid) H(erbert) (1885–1930), English novelist, poet, critic, and painter.

Lawrence[2], Marjorie Florence (1908–79), Australian dramatic soprano in opera who contracted polio at the height of her international fame and was paralysed: she continued to sing on stage from a wheelchair, however, and her autobiography *Interrupted Melody* was made into a film.

lawrencium / luh-**ren**-see-uhm / n. a radioactive metallic element (symbol Lw).

Lawson[1], Henry (1867–1922), Australian writer of poetry and prose, noted esp. for his short-story collections (e.g. *While the Billy Boils*) which evoke life in the harsh Australian bush.

Lawson[2], Louisa (1848–1920), Australian feminist, writer, and publisher. She published *Republican*, a radical monthly, and *Dawn*, Australia's first feminist journal. She was the mother of Henry Lawson.

Lawson[3], William (1774–1850), Australian explorer who in 1813 joined Blaxland and Wentworth in a successful attempt to cross the Blue Mountains.

lawsuit n. the process of bringing a dispute or claim before a court of law for settlement.

lawyer n. a legal practitioner, as a solicitor or a barrister. ☐ **lawyer palm** any of several Australian climbing palms and vines with barbs which hook

lax *adj.* slack, not strict or severe (*discipline was lax*). ☐ **laxly** *adv.* **laxity** *n.*

laxative / **lak**-suh-tiv / *n.* a medicine that stimulates the bowels to empty. •*adj.* having this effect.

lay[1] *n. archaic* a poem meant to be sung, a ballad.

lay[2] *adj.* **1** not ordained into the clergy. **2** not professionally qualified, esp. in law or medicine (*lay opinion*).

lay[3] *v.* (**laid, laying**) **1** place on a surface, esp. horizontally or in a particular place. **2** put down into the required place (*lay a carpet*). **3** make by putting down (*lay foundations*). **4** (of a hen bird) produce (an egg). **5** cause to subside or lie flat. **6** (usu. foll. by *on*) attribute or place (*laid the blame on me*). **7** prepare (a plan or trap). **8** prepare (a table) for a meal. **9** arrange the materials for (a fire). **10** put down as a bet; stake. **11** (foll. by *with*) coat or scatter over (a surface). **12** deal with to remove (a ghost, fears, etc.). **13** *coarse colloq.* have sexual relations with (a person). •*n.* **1** the way in which something lies. **2** *coarse colloq.* sexual intercourse; a partner in this. ☐ **lay bare** expose, reveal. **lay claim to** claim as one's right. **lay down 1** put on a flat surface. **2** give up (office). **3** establish as a rule or instruction. **4** store (wine) in a cellar for future use. **5** sacrifice (one's life). **lay in** provide oneself with a stock of. **lay into** *colloq.* thrash; reprimand harshly. **lay it on the line** *colloq.* offer without reserve; speak frankly. **lay it on thick** (or **with a trowel**) *colloq.* exaggerate greatly; flatter a person excessively. **lay low 1** overthrow; humble. **2** incapacitate by illness. **lay off 1** discharge (workers) temporarily owing to shortage of work. **2** *colloq.* cease, esp. from causing trouble or annoyance. **lay-off** *n.* a temporary discharge of workers; a redundancy. **lay out 1** arrange according to a plan. **2** prepare (a body) for burial. **3** spend (money) for a purpose. **4** knock unconscious. **lay to rest** bury. **lay up 1** store or save. **2** cause to be confined to bed or unfit for work. **lay waste** destroy or ruin (a place or area).

■ **Usage** Do not confuse *lay* (= put down; past tense is *laid*) with *lie* (= recline; past tense is *lay*). Correct uses are as follows: *go and lie down*; *she went and lay down*; *please lay it on the floor*; *they laid it on the floor*. Incorrect use is *go and lay down*; *she was laying on the floor*.

lay[4] see LIE[2].

layabout *n.* a habitually idle person.

lay-by *n.* (*pl.* **lay-bys**) **1** *Aust.* **a** the system of paying a deposit on an article which is then reserved by the retailer until the full price is paid, usu. in instalments. **b** an article bought in this way. **2** *Brit.* & *WA* = REST AREA. •*v. Aust.* buy (an article) using lay-by. ☐ **on lay-by** *Aust.* (of an article) in the process of being so purchased.

layer *n.* **1** a thickness of material (often one of several) covering a surface. **2** a person etc. that lays something (*a bricklayer*). **3** a hen that lays eggs. **4** a shoot of a plant fastened down for propagation by layering. •*v.* **1** arrange in layers. **2** cut (hair) in layers. **3** propagate (a plant) by fastening down a shoot to take root while still attached to the parent plant.

layette *n.* the clothes and bedding etc. prepared for a newborn baby.

lay figure *n.* a jointed wooden figure of the human body, used by artists for arranging drapery on etc. (¶ From an old Dutch word *led* = joint.)

layman *n.* (*feminine* **laywoman**) a lay person (*see* LAY[2]).

layout *n.* the way in which a thing or place is arranged or set out.

laze *v.* **1** spend time idly. **2** (foll. by *away*) pass (time) idly. •*n.* an act or period of lazing.

lazy *adj.* (**lazier, laziest**) **1** unwilling to work; doing little work. **2** showing or characterised by lack of energy (*a lazy yawn*). ☐ **lazily** *adv.* **laziness** *n.*

lazybones *n.* (*pl.* **lazybones**) *colloq.* a lazy person.

lb *abbr.* = pound(s) weight. (¶ From the Latin *libra*.)

lbw *abbr.* leg before wicket.

l.c. *abbr.* lower case.

LCD *abbr.* **1** liquid crystal display. **2** lowest common denominator.

LCM *abbr.* lowest (or least) common multiple.

lea / lee / *n. poetic* a meadow, a field.

leach *v.* make (liquid) percolate through soil or ore etc.; remove (soluble matter) in this way.

lead[1] / leed / *v.* (**led, leading**) **1** cause to go with oneself; guide, esp. by going in front. **2** influence the actions or opinions of (*what led you to believe this?*). **3** be a route or means of access (*the door leads into a passage*). **4** have as its result (*this led to confusion*). **5** live or pass (one's life) (*he was leading a double life*). **6** be in first place or position in, be ahead (*they lead the world in electronics*). **7** be the leader or head of, control. **8** (foll. by *with* or *on*) (of a newspaper or news program) have as its main story or feature (*led with the unemployment figures*). **9** (in card games) play as one's first card; be the first player. •*n.* **1** guidance given by going in front, an example. **2** *Aust.* the front of a travelling mob of sheep. **3** a clue (*it gave us a lead*). **4** a leading place, leadership (*take the lead*). **5** the amount by which one competitor is in front (*a lead of 5 points*). **6** an electrical cable or wire carrying current to an appliance. **7** a strap or cord etc. for leading and restraining a dog or other animal. **8** the act or right of playing one's card first in a card game; the card played. **9** the chief part in a play or other performance, one who takes this part (*play the lead*; *the lead singer*). ☐ **lead by the nose** control the actions of (a person) completely. **lead-in** *n.* an introduction or opening. **lead off**

begin. **lead on** entice. **lead up the garden path** mislead. **lead up to** 1 serve as an introduction to or preparation for. 2 direct the conversation towards.

lead² / led / *n.* 1 a chemical element (symbol Pb), a heavy soft greyish metal. 2 a thin stick of graphite in a pencil. 3 a lump of lead used in taking soundings in water. 4 (**leads**) strips of lead used to cover a roof. 5 (**leads**) a piece of lead-covered roof. 6 (**leads**) a framework of lead strips holding pieces of stained glass etc. in a window. ☐ **lead-free** (of petrol) without added lead compounds. **lead pencil** a pencil of graphite in wood. **lead-poisoning** poisoning by absorption of lead into the body. **swing (the) lead** malinger, avoid one's share of work.

Leadbeater's possum / **led**-be-tuhz / *n.* a rare possum restricted to mountain ash forests in Vic.; faunal emblem of Vic. (¶ John Leadbeater, naturalist (*c.*1832–88).)

leaded / **led**-uhd / *adj.* 1 covered or framed with lead. 2 (esp. of petrol) containing lead.

leaden / **led**-uhn / *adj.* 1 made of lead. 2 heavy, slow as if weighted with lead. 3 lead-coloured, dark grey (*leaden skies*).

leader *n.* 1 a person or thing that leads. 2 one who has the principal part in something; the head of a group etc.; (in an orchestra) the principal first-violin player. 3 one whose example is followed (*a leader of fashion*). 4 a leading article in a newspaper; an editorial. 5 a shoot of a plant growing from the stem or main branch. 6 a bullock placed at the front in a team or pair.

leadership *n.* 1 being a leader. 2 ability to be a leader. 3 the leaders of a group.

leading¹ / **lee**-ding / *see* LEAD¹. ☐ **leading aircraftman** the rank above aircraftman in the RAAF. **leading article** a long article in a newspaper, giving editorial opinions. **leading lady** (*or* **man**) one taking the chief part in a play etc. **leading light** a prominent member of a group. **leading question** a question that prompts a person to give the answer the questioner wants.

■ Usage *Leading question* does not mean a 'principal' or 'loaded' or 'searching' question.

leading² / **led**-ing / *n.* a covering or framework of lead (metal).

leaf *n.* (*pl.* **leaves**) 1 a flat organ (usu. green) growing from the stem or branch of a plant or directly from the root. 2 the state of having leaves out (*the trees are in leaf*). 3 a single thickness of the paper forming the pages of a book. 4 a very thin sheet of metal (*gold leaf*). 5 a hinged flap of a table; an extra section inserted to extend a table. • *v.* put forth leaves. ☐ **leaf-cutting bee** any of several Australian bees which cut and use pieces of leaf to construct cells for their eggs. **leaf mould** soil or compost consisting chiefly of decayed leaves. **leaf through** turn over the leaves of a book. **take a leaf out of someone's book**

follow his or her example. ☐☐ **leafage** *n.* **leafy** *adj.* **leafless** *adj.*

leaflet *n.* 1 a sheet of paper or pamphlet giving information. 2 a young leaf. 3 a division of a compound leaf. • *v.* (**leafleted, leafleting**) distribute leaflets to.

league¹ *n.* 1 a group of people or countries who combine formally for a particular purpose. 2 a group of sports clubs which compete against each other for a championship. 3 a class of contestants (*he is out of his league*). • *v.* form a league. ☐ **in league with** allied with; conspiring with. **league football** 1 Australian Rules football. 2 Rugby League.

league² *n. archaic* a varying measure of distance, usu. about 5 kilometres.

leak *n.* 1 a hole or crack etc. through which liquid or gas may accidentally pass in or out. 2 the liquid or gas passing through this. 3 such an escape of liquid or gas. 4 a similar escape of an electric charge; the charge itself. 5 an intentional disclosure of secret information to the press etc. 6 *colloq.* an act of passing urine. • *v.* 1 (of liquid or gas etc.) escape through an opening. 2 (of a container) allow such an escape, let out (liquid or gas). 3 intentionally disclose (secret information) (*he leaked the news to a reporter*). 4 *colloq.* urinate. ☐ **leak out** (of a secret) become known despite efforts to keep it secret.

leakage *n.* 1 leaking. 2 a thing or amount that has leaked out.

leaky *adj.* liable to leak.

lean¹ *adj.* 1 (of a person or animal) without much flesh. 2 (of meat) containing little or no fat. 3 scanty (*a lean harvest*). • *n.* the lean part of meat. ☐ **leanness** *n.*

lean² *v.* (**leaned** *or* **leant, leaning**) 1 put or be in a sloping position. 2 rest against or on something for support. 3 rely or depend for help. 4 be inclined or partial to (*she leans towards Catholicism*). ☐ **lean on** *colloq.* seek to influence by intimidation. **lean-to** a building with its roof resting against the side of a larger building.

leangle / lee-**ang**-guhl / *n. Aust.* an Aboriginal fighting club with a hooked striking head. (¶ Wemba-wemba and Wuywurung *lienggel*, related to *lia* 'tooth', describing the head of the club.)

leaning *n.* a tendency or preference (*she has leanings towards socialism*).

leap *v.* (**leaped** *or* **leapt, leaping**) jump vigorously (*leapt forward; leaped the fence*). • *n.* a vigorous jump. ☐ **leap in the dark** an uninformed act of daring. **by leaps and bounds** with very rapid progress. **leap year** a year with an extra day (29 February), occurring every four years.

leap-frog *n.* a game in which each player in turn vaults with parted legs over another who is bending down. • *v.* (**leap-frogged, leap-**

frogging) **1** perform this vault. **2** overtake alternately.

learn v. (**learned** / lernd / or **learnt** / lernt / **learning**) **1** gain knowledge of or skill in (a subject etc.) by study or experience or by being taught. **2** become aware by information or from observation.

learned / **ler**-nuhd / adj. **1** having much knowledge acquired by study (*learned men*). **2** of or for learned people (*a learned society*). ☐ **learnedly** adv.

learner n. a person who is learning a subject or skill. ☐ **learner driver** one who is learning to drive a motor vehicle but has not yet passed the driving test.

learning n. knowledge obtained by study.

lease n. **1** a contract by which the owner of land or a building etc. allows another person to use it for a specified time, usu. in return for payment. **2** *US & Aust.* an area leased for farming, mining, etc. • v. **1** grant the use of (a property) by lease. **2** obtain or hold (a property) by lease. ☐ **a new lease of life** a longer and better prospect of life, or of use after repair.

leasehold n. **1** the holding of land or a house or flat etc. by means of a lease. **2** the property held by lease. ☐ **leaseholder** n.

leash n. a strap for holding a dog etc.; a lead. • v. hold on a leash.

least adj. **1** smallest in amount or degree. **2** lowest in rank or importance. • n. the least amount or degree. • adv. in the least degree. ☐ **at least 1** not less than what is stated. **2** anyway. **in the least** at all, in the smallest degree (*not in the least offended*). **to say the least** putting the case moderately.

leather n. **1** material made from animal skins by tanning or a similar process. **2** (often as **leathers**) leather clothing, esp. for motorcyclists. • v. cover with leather.

leatherhead n. any of several Australian friar birds having a featherless head covered with a leatherlike skin, esp. the noisy friar bird.

leatherjacket n. **1** any of many sea fish with a tough skin. **2** *Aust. hist.* a thin flour-and-water cake cooked with fat in a pan over the fire, esp. in the bush. **3** any of several Australian trees with a very tough bark.

leatherwood n. a Tasmanian rainforest tree bearing highly scented white flowers from which bees make a distinctive honey.

leathery adj. as tough as leather.

leave[1] v. (**left**, **leaving**) **1** go away from; go away finally or permanently. **2** cease to belong to (a group) or live at (a place); cease working for an employer. **3** cause or allow to remain (*left the door open; left my gloves in the bus*). **4** give as a legacy. **5** have remaining after one's death (*he leaves a wife and two children*). **6** allow to stay or proceed without interference (*left him to get on with it; leave the dog alone*). **7** refrain from consuming or dealing with (*left all the fat; let's leave the washing-up*). **8** entrust or commit to another person (*leave it to me*). **9** deposit for collection, repair, or transmission (*leave a message*). **10** abandon, desert (*was left to clear up the mess*). ☐ **leave off** make an end; discontinue. **leave out** omit, not include.

leave[2] n. **1** permission. **2** official permission to be absent from duty; the period for which this lasts. ☐ **leave loading** *Aust.* a payment added to a person's wage when annual leave is taken. **leave-taking** taking one's leave, departure. **on leave** absent with official permission. **take leave of one's senses** go mad. **take one's leave** say farewell and go away.

leaved adj. **1** having leaves. **2** (in *comb.*) having a leaf or leaves of a specified kind or number (*four-leaved clover*).

leaven / **lev**-uhn / n. **1** a substance (e.g. yeast) that produces fermentation in dough. **2** a quality or influence that lightens or enlivens something. • v. **1** add leaven to. **2** modify by an addition; enliven.

leavings n.pl. what is left.

Lebanon / **leb**-uh-non / a republic at the eastern end of the Mediterranean Sea. ☐ **Lebanese** adj. & n. (pl. **Lebanese**).

lechenaultia / lesh-uh-**nol**-tee-uh / n. (also **leschenaultia**) a group of mainly WA plants with vivid blue (or red, orange, etc.) flowers which are extremely showy.

lecher n. a lecherous person.

lecherous adj. of or characterised by lechery.

lechery n. unrestrained sexual desire.

lecithin / **les**-uh-thuhn / n. a compound found in plant and animal tissue and used as an emulsifier and stabiliser in food products.

lectern n. a stand with a sloping top to hold a book in a church or a lecturer's notes etc.

lecture n. **1** a speech giving information about a subject to an audience or class. **2** a long serious speech, esp. one giving reproof or warning. • v. **1** give a lecture or series of lectures. **2** talk to (a person) seriously or reprovingly. ☐ **lecturer** n.

LED abbr. light-emitting diode.

led see LEAD[1].

Leda / **lee**-duh / *Gk myth.* queen of Sparta, loved by Zeus who had sex with her while he was in the form of a swan.

lederhosen / **lay**-duh-hoh-zuhn / n.pl. leather shorts traditionally worn by men in Bavaria etc. (¶ German).

ledge n. a narrow horizontal projection, a narrow shelf.

ledger n. a tall narrow book used as an account book or to record transactions.

lee n. shelter, the sheltered side or part of something (*under the lee of the hedge*).

leech n. **1** a small blood-sucking worm usu. living in water. **2** a person who drains the resources of another.

leek

leek *n.* a plant related to the onion but with broader leaves and a cylindrical white bulb.

leer *v.* look slyly, maliciously, or lustfully. •*n.* a leering look.

leery *adj. colloq.* wary, suspicious.

lees / leez / *n.pl.* sediment that settles at the bottom of wine etc.

leeward / lee-wuhd / (in nautical use / **loo**-uhd /) *adj.* situated on the side turned away from the wind. •*n.* the leeward side or region.

leeway *n.* **1** a ship's sideways drift from its course. **2** a degree of freedom of action (*these instructions give us plenty of leeway*).

left[1] *see* LEAVE[1]. ❑ **left luggage** luggage deposited temporarily at a railway station etc.

left[2] *adj.* & *adv.* on or towards the left-hand side. •*n.* **1** the left-hand side or region. **2** the left hand; a blow with this. **3** (in marching) the left foot. **4** (often **Left**) the left wing of a political party or other group. ❑ **have two left feet** be extremely clumsy. **left hand** the hand that in most people is less used, on the west side of the body when facing north. **left-hand** *adj.* of or towards this side of a person or the corresponding side of a thing. **left-handed** *adj.* **1** naturally using the left hand for writing etc. **2** (of a blow or tool) made with or operated by the left hand. **3** (of a screw) to be tightened by turning towards the left. **4** (of a compliment) ambiguous in meaning, backhanded. **left-hander** a left-handed person or blow. **left wing 1** the more socialist section of a political party or system. **2** the left side of a football etc. team on the field. **left-wing** *Politics* socialist, radical, politically progressive. **left-winger** a left-wing person.

leftist *n.* a supporter of socialism; one who belongs to the left of a socialist group. •*adj.* of the left wing in politics etc. ❑ **leftism** *n.*

leftover *n.* (usu. in *pl.*) an item (esp. of food) remaining after the rest has been used. •*adj.* remaining over, surplus.

leftward *adv.* & *adj.* towards or facing the left. ❑ **leftwards** *adv.*

lefty *n.* (also **leftie**) *colloq.* **1** a left-handed person. **2** a left-winger.

leg *n.* **1** each of the limbs on which a human or animal stands or walks. **2** the leg of a bird or animal as food. **3** the part of a garment covering a leg. **4** a projecting support beneath a chair, table, etc. **5** a section of a journey. **6** a stage of a competition. **7** (in cricket) the half of the field, when divided lengthways, in which the batsman's feet are placed. ❑ **get one's** (*or* **a**) **leg in the door** make a start towards succeeding in something. **give a leg up** help to mount a horse etc., or to get over an obstacle or difficulty. **leg before wicket** (of a batsman in cricket) out because of illegally obstructing the ball. **leg bye** *Cricket* a run scored from a ball that touches the batsman. **leg it** *colloq.* **1** walk or run rapidly. **2** go on foot. **leg-pull** *colloq.* a hoax. **leg-room** space for the legs of a seated person. **leg-rope** *n.* **1** a noosed rope used to secure an animal by one hind leg. **2** a rope used by a surfer to secure one leg to the surfboard. *v.* secure with a leg-rope. **leg spin** *Cricket* a type of spin which causes the ball to deviate from the leg side after bouncing. **leg spinner** *Cricket* a bowler who uses leg spin.

Legacy an Australian organisation formed initially to care for the dependants of servicemen killed in the First World War, but, by the 1970s, extended to cover the families of service personnel who had served in any war area.

legacy / **leg**-uh-see / *n.* **1** money or an article left to someone in a will. **2** something received from a predecessor or because of earlier events etc. (*a legacy of distrust*).

legal *adj.* **1** of or based on law. **2** in accordance with the law; authorised or required by law. ❑ **legal aid** payment from public funds towards the cost of legal advice or proceedings. **legal limit 1** the blood-alcohol level which one must not exceed if in control of a motor vehicle, boat, etc. **2** the maximum speed allowed for a motor vehicle in a particular area. **legal tender** officially recognised currency that cannot be refused in payment of a debt. ❑❑ **legally** *adv.* **legality** / luh-**gal**-uh-tee, lee- / *n.*

legalese *n.* the technical style of language used in legal documents.

legalise *v.* (also -**ize**) make legal. ❑ **legalisation** *n.*

legalistic *adj.* adhering too closely to laws or rules. ❑ **legalism** *n.*

legate / **leg**-uht / *n.* an ambassador representing the pope.

legatee / leg-uh-**tee** / *n.* a person who receives a legacy.

legation / luh-**gay**-shuhn / *n.* **1** a diplomatic minister and staff. **2** his or her official residence.

legato / luh-**gah**-toh / *adv. Music* in a smooth even manner.

legend / **lej**-uhnd / *n.* **1** a traditional story or myth. **2** a famous or remarkable person or event (*became a rock legend*). **3** an inscription on a coin or medal. **4** an explanation on a map etc. of the symbols used.

legendary / **lej**-uhn-duh-ree, -dree / *adj.* **1** of or based on legends; described in a legend. **2** famous, often talked about.

legerdemain / lej-uh-duh-**mayn** / *n.* sleight of hand, conjuring tricks.

leger line / **lej**-uh / *n.* a short line added in a musical score for notes above or below the range of the stave.

leggy *adj.* **1** having noticeably long legs. **2** (of a plant) long-stemmed and weak.

legible / **lej**-uh-buhl / *adj.* (of print or handwriting) clear enough to read, readable. ❑ **legibly** *adv.* **legibility** *n.*

legion / **lee**-juhn / *n.* **1** a division (3,000–6,000 men) of the ancient Roman army. **2** a large

legionary | 472 | **Leningrad**

organised body. • *adj.* great in number (*such stories are legion*).

legionary / **lee**-juh-nuh-ree, juhn-ree / *adj.* of legions or a legion. • *n.* a member of a legion.

legionella / lee-juh-**nel**-uh / *n.* the bacterium which causes legionnaires' disease.

legionnaire / lee-juh-**nair** / *n.* a member of a legion. ☐ **legionnaires' disease** a form of bacterial pneumonia first identified in an outbreak at a meeting of the American Legion in 1976.

legislate / **lej**-uhs-layt / *v.* make laws.

legislation / lej-uhs-**lay**-shuhn / *n.* **1** legislating. **2** the laws themselves.

legislative / **lej**-uhs-luh-tiv / *adj.* making laws (*a legislative body*).

Legislative Assembly the lower house of the parliaments of NSW, Vic., and WA, and the sole house of the parliaments of Qld, the NT, and the ACT.

Legislative Council the upper house of the parliaments of all Australian States except Qld.

legislator / **lej**-uhs-lay-tuh / *n.* one who makes laws.

legislature / **lej**-uhs-lay-chuh, -luh-chuh / *n.* the legislative body of a State, nation, etc.

legit / luh-**jit** / *adj. colloq.* legitimate (in sense 1).

legitimate / luh-**jit**-uh-muht / *adj.* **1** in accordance with the law or rules. **2** logical, justifiable (*a legitimate reason for absence*). **3** (of a child) born of parents who are married to each other. • *n. Aust. hist.* a person who came to Australia as a convict, i.e. one who had a *legal* reason for coming (as opposed to an *illegitimate*, a person who freely migrated to Australia). ☐ **legitimately** *adv.* **legitimacy** *n.*

legitimatise / luh-**jit**-uh-muh-tuyz / *v.* (also -**ize**) legitimise.

legitimise / luh-**jit**-uh-muyz / *v.* (also -**ize**) **1** make legitimate. **2** serve as a justification for.

legume / **leg**-yoom, **lay**-gyoom / *n.* **1** a leguminous plant. **2** a fruit or pod of this, esp. when edible.

leguminous / luh-**gyoo**-muh-nuhs / *adj.* of the family of plants that bear their seeds in pods, e.g. peas and beans.

legwork *n.* work which involves a lot of walking, travelling, or physical activity.

lei / lay / *n.* (in Polynesian countries) a garland of flowers worn round the neck.

Leichhardt / **luy**-kaht /, (Friedrich Wilhelm) Ludwig (1813–?48), Australian naturalist and explorer (born in Germany) who disappeared without a trace when attempting to cross the continent of Australia from east to west in 1848. ☐ **Leichhardt pine** a northern Australian coastal tree yielding an edible fruit and a close-grained softwood.

leisure / **lezh**-uh / *n.* free time; the enjoyment of free time. ☐ **at leisure** not occupied; in an unhurried way. **at one's leisure** when one has time.

leisured *adj.* having plenty of leisure.

leisurely / **lezh**-uh-lee / *adj. & adv.* unhurried, relaxed. ☐ **leisureliness** *n.*

leitmotif / **luyt**-moh-teef / *n.* (also **leitmotiv**) a theme associated with a particular person or idea etc. throughout a musical, literary, or cinematic work.

lemming *n.* a small rodent of Arctic regions, one species of which migrates in large numbers and is said to rush into the sea and drown.

lemon *n.* **1** a yellow oval citrus fruit with acidic juice. **2** the tree that bears it. **3** its pale yellow colour. **4** *colloq.* a person or thing regarded as a failure. ☐ **lemon gum** (also **lemon-scented gum**) an Australian tree *Eucalyptus citriodora* with a smooth powdery white bark and strongly lemon-scented leaves. **lemon ironwood** a Qld tree *Backhousia citriodora* having strongly lemon-scented foliage right down to the ground, masses of white flowers, and a hard bark. ☐☐ **lemony** *adj.*

lemonade *n.* a drink made from fresh lemon juice; a synthetic aerated substitute for this.

lemur / **lee**-muh / *n.* a monkey-like animal of Madagascar.

lend *v.* (**lent**, **lending**) **1** give or allow the use of (a thing) temporarily on the understanding that it or its equivalent will be returned. **2** provide (money) temporarily in return for payment of interest. **3** contribute as a temporary help or effect etc. (*lend dignity to the occasion*). ☐ **lend a hand** help. **lend an ear** listen. **lend itself to** be suitable for. ☐☐ **lender** *n.*

length *n.* **1** measurement or extent from end to end. **2** the amount of time occupied by something (*the length of our holiday*). **3** the distance a thing extends, used as a unit of measurement; the length of a horse or boat etc. as a measure of the lead in a race. **4** the degree of thoroughness in an action (*went to great lengths*). **5** a piece of cloth or other material from a larger piece (*a length of wire*). ☐ **at length 1** after a long time. **2** taking a long time. **3** in detail.

lengthen *v.* make or become longer.

lengthways *adv. & adj.* (also **lengthwise**) in the direction of the length of something.

lengthy *adj.* (**lengthier**, **lengthiest**) very long; long and boring. ☐ **lengthily** *adv.* **lengthiness** *n.*

lenient / **lee**-nee-uhnt / *adj.* merciful, not severe (esp. in awarding punishment), mild. ☐ **leniently** *adv.* **lenience** *n.*

Lenin (original name: Vladimir Ilyich Ulyanov) (1870–1924), Russian revolutionary statesman, premier and virtual dictator of the Communist State which he established after the fall of the Tsar.

Leningrad a city of the former USSR on the Gulf of Finland, the Russian capital under the name St Petersburg until 1918, recently renamed St Petersburg.

Lennon, John (1940–80), English singer, guitarist, and songwriter, a member of the Beatles.

lens *n.* (*pl.* **lenses**) **1** a piece of glass or glass-like substance with one or both sides curved, for use in optical instruments. **2** a combination of lenses used in photography etc. **3** the transparent part of the eye, behind the iris.

Lent *n.* a period of fasting and penitence from Ash Wednesday to Holy Saturday (Easter Eve) in commemoration of Christ's fasting in the wilderness. ☐ **Lenten** *adj.*

lent *see* LEND.

lentil *n.* **1** a pea-like plant yielding edible biconvex seeds. **2** these seeds, esp. used as food with the husk removed (see DHAL).

lento *adj.* & *adv.* (in music) slow or slowly.

Leo / lee-oh / *n.* the fifth sign of the zodiac, the Lion.

Leonardo da Vinci / dah **vin**-chee / (1452–1519), Italian painter and designer, whose most famous paintings include the *Last Supper* fresco and the *Mona Lisa*.

leonine / lee-uh-nuyn / *adj.* of or like a lion.

leopard / **lep**-uhd / *n.* a large African and South Asian flesh-eating animal of the cat family (also called a *panther*), having a yellowish coat with dark spots or a black coat.

leopardess *n.* a female leopard.

leotard / **lee**-uh-tahd / *n.* a close-fitting one-piece garment worn by dancers, gymnasts, etc.

leper *n.* **1** a person with leprosy. **2** a person who is shunned; an outcast (*social leper*).

lepidopterous / lep-uh-**dop**-tuh-ruhs / *adj.* of the group of insects that includes moths and butterflies. ☐ **lepidopterist** *n.*

leprechaun / **lep**-ruh-kawn / *n.* (in Irish folklore) a small sprite resembling a little old man.

leprosy *n.* an infectious disease affecting skin and nerves, causing disfigurement and deformities. ☐ **leprous** *adj.*

leptospermum / lep-toh-**sper**-muhm / *n.* = TEA-TREE.

lerp *n. Aust.* **1** a whitish, edible, very sweet, waxy secretion produced by insect larvae (of psyllids) on the leaves of certain eucalypts, esp. mallees. **2** = MANNA (sense 3). (¶ Wemba-wemba)

lesbian *n.* a homosexual woman. • *adj.* of lesbians; of homosexuality in women. ☐ **lesbianism** *n.* (¶ From Lesbos: *see* SAPPHO.)

■ **Usage** See usage note at GAY.

Lesbos / **lez**-bos / the largest of the Greek islands, off the western coast of Turkey.

lese-majesty / leez / *n.* **1** an insult to a sovereign or ruler; treason. **2** *humorous* presumptuous behaviour.

lesion / **lee**-zhuhn / *n.* a physical change in the tissue or functioning of an organ of the body, caused by injury or disease.

Lesotho / luh-**soo**-too / an independent kingdom entirely surrounded by the Republic of South Africa.

less *adj.* **1** not so much, a smaller quantity (*eat less meat*). **2** smaller in amount or degree etc. (*of less importance*). • *adv.* to a smaller extent. • *n.* a smaller amount or quantity etc. (*will not take less*). • *prep.* minus, deducting (*a year less three days; was paid $1,000, less tax*).

■ **Usage** The word *less* is used of things that are measured by amount (e.g. in *eat less butter*; *use less fuel*). Its use of things measured by number is often regarded as incorrect (e.g. in *we need less workers*; correct usage is *fewer workers*).

lessee / le-**see** / *n.* a person who holds a property by lease.

lessen *v.* make or become less.

lesser *adj.* not so great as the other (*the lesser evil*).

lesson *n.* **1** a thing to be learnt by a pupil. **2** an amount of teaching given at one time (*give lessons in French*). **3** an example or experience by which one can learn (*let this be a lesson to you!*). **4** a passage from the Bible read aloud during a church service.

lessor / le-**saw**, **les**-aw / *n.* a person who lets a property on lease.

lest *conj.* **1** in order not to, to avoid the risk that (*lest he forget*). **2** that (*were afraid lest we should be late*).

■ **Usage** *Lest* must be followed by the subjunctive (example 1 above) or by *should* (example 2).

Lesueur's rat-kangaroo *n.* = BOODIE.

let[1] *n.* **1** stoppage (*without let or hindrance*). **2** (in tennis etc.) an obstruction of a ball or player, requiring the ball to be served again.

let[2] *v.* (**let**, **letting**) **1** allow to, not prevent or forbid (*let me see it*). **2** cause to (*let us know what happens*). **3** allow or cause to pass in, out, up, etc. (*let the dog in; let the rope down*). **4** allow the use of (rooms or land) for payment (*house to let*). **5** used as an auxiliary verb in requests or commands (*let's try; let us pray*), assumptions (*let x equal 7*), and challenges (*let him do his worst*). • *n.* the letting of property etc. (*a long let*). ☐ **let alone 1** leave; refrain from interfering with or doing. **2** never mind (*we can't afford one, let alone three; I'm too tired to walk, let alone run*). **let be** leave; refrain from interfering with or doing. **let down 1** let out air from (a balloon or tyre etc.). **2** fail to support or satisfy, disappoint. **3** lengthen (a garment) by adjusting the hem. **let-down** *n.* a disappointment. **let fly** release or emit violently (*let fly a punch; let fly a stream of abuse*). **let oneself go 1** behave freely or spontaneously. **2** neglect one's usual standards of appearance, hygiene, etc. **let off 1** fire (a gun); cause (a bomb) to explode; ignite (a firework). **2** excuse from doing (duties etc.); give little or no punishment to. **let off steam** release one's pent-up energy or feelings. **let on** *colloq.* reveal a secret. **let out 1** release from restraint or obligation. **2** make (a garment) looser by adjusting the seams. **3** let (rooms etc.) to tenants. **let-out** *n.* a way of escaping an obligation. **let slip 1** reveal (a secret) accidentally. **2** miss (an opportunity). **let up** *colloq.* become less intense; relax one's efforts. **let-up** *n.* a reduction in intensity; relaxation of effort.

lethal / lee-thuhl / *adj.* causing or able to cause death. ☐ **lethally** *adv.*

lethargy / leth-uh-jee / *n.* extreme lack of energy or vitality. ☐ **lethargic** / luh-**thah**-jik / *adj.* **lethargically** *adv.*

Lethe / lee-thee / *Gk myth.* a river in Hades; its water when drunk made the souls of the dead forget their life on earth.

let's = let us.

letter *n.* **1** a symbol representing a sound used in speech. **2** a written or printed message, usu. sent by post. • *v.* inscribe letters on; draw or inscribe letters. ☐ **letter bomb** a terrorist explosive device in the form of a postal packet. **letter of credit** a letter from a bank authorising the bearer to draw money from another bank. **letter of the law** the law's exact requirements (as opposed to its spirit or true purpose). **letter stick** = MESSAGE STICK. **letter-winged kite** an Australian bird of prey with an underwing pattern looking like the letter 'W' or 'M'. **man** (or **woman**) **of letters** a scholar or author. **to the letter** paying strict attention to every detail.

letterbox *n.* **1** a receptacle for receiving regular deliveries of mail, esp. at a private residence. **2** a postbox. • *v.* make unsolicited deliveries of advertising material etc. to (letterboxes in a suburb, town, etc.).

lettered *adj.* well-read, well-educated.

letterhead *n.* a printed heading on stationery; stationery with this.

letterpress *n.* **1** the printed words in an illustrated book. **2** printing from raised type.

lettuce *n.* a plant with broad crisp leaves used in salads.

leucocyte / loo-kuh-suyt, lyoo- / *n.* a white blood cell.

leukaemia / loo-kee-mee-uh, lyoo- / *n.* (also **leukemia**) a disease in which the white blood cells multiply uncontrollably.

Leunig / loo-nig /, Michael (1945–), Australian cartoonist.

Levant / luh-vant / *n.* the countries and islands in the eastern part of the Mediterranean Sea. ☐ **Levantine** / luh-**van**-tuyn, lev-uhn-tuyn / *adj.* & *n.*

levee / lev-ee / *n.* an embankment put up to prevent a river flooding, or one built up by the river itself.

level *n.* **1** a horizontal line or plane joining points of equal height. **2** a measured height or value etc., position on a scale (*the level of alcohol in the blood*). **3** relative position in rank or class or authority (*decisions at Cabinet level*). **4** a flat surface, layer, or area. **5** an instrument for testing a horizontal line. • *adj.* **1** horizontal. **2** (of ground) flat, without hills or hollows. **3** on a level with; at the same height, rank, or position on a scale. **4** steady, uniform, (of a voice) not changing in tone. • *v.* (**levelled**, **levelling**) **1** (also foll. by *out*) make or become level, even, or uniform. **2** flatten (an area or its buildings) by demolition; raze. **3** aim (a gun or missile). **4** direct (an accusation or criticism) at a person. ☐ **do one's level best** *colloq.* make all possible efforts. **level crossing** a place where a road and a railway cross each other at the same level. **level-headed** mentally well-balanced, sensible. **level pegging** equal scores or achievements. **level playing field** (esp. in international trade, commerce, etc.) equality of opportunity etc. for all participants, without (esp. government subsidised) advantages for some. **on the level** *colloq.* with no dishonesty or deception.

leveller *n.* **1** something that removes social distinctions (*unemployment is a great leveller*). **2** a person or thing that levels.

lever / lee-vuh / *n.* **1** a bar or other device pivoted on a fulcrum or fixed point in order to lift something or force something open. **2** a projecting handle used to operate machinery etc. • *v.* use a lever; lift or move by means of this.

leverage *n.* **1** the action or power of a lever. **2** power, influence.

leveret / lev-uh-ruht / *n.* a young hare.

leviathan / luh-**vuy**-uh-thuhn / *n.* something of enormous size and power. (¶ Named after a sea monster in the Bible.)

Levis / lee-vuyz / *n.pl. trademark* denim jeans.

levitate *v.* rise or cause to rise and float in the air in defiance of gravity. ☐ **levitation** *n.*

levity / lev-uh-tee / *n.* a humorous attitude, esp. towards matters that should be treated with respect.

levy *v.* (**levied**, **levying**) **1** impose or collect (a payment etc.) by authority or by force. **2** enrol (troops etc.). **3** wage (war). • *n.* **1** levying. **2** the payment etc. levied. **3** (**levies**) troops enrolled.

lewd *adj.* **1** indecent, treating sexual matters in a vulgar way. **2** lascivious. ☐ **lewdly** *adv.* **lewdness** *n.*

Lewis[1], C(live) S(taples) (1898–1963), English literary scholar, whose writings include Christian and moral themes as well as fantasy and science fiction.

Lewis[2], Wally (full name: Walter James Lewis) (1959–), AM, Australian Rugby League footballer, captain of the Australian team 1984–89.

lexical *adj.* **1** of the words of a language. **2** of a lexicon or dictionary.

lexicography / lek-suh-**kog**-ruh-fee / *n.* the process of compiling dictionaries. ◻ **lexicographer** *n.* **lexicographical** *adj.*

lexicology / lek-suh-**kol**-uh-jee / *n.* the study of words and their form, history, and meaning. ◻ **lexicologist** *n.*

lexicon *n.* **1** a dictionary, esp. of certain ancient languages such as Greek and Hebrew. **2** the vocabulary of a person, language, branch of knowledge, etc.

lexis *n.* **1** words, vocabulary. **2** the total stock of words in a language.

ley / lay, lee / *n.* (in full **ley line**) a hypothetical straight line connecting prehistoric sites etc.

LF *abbr.* low frequency.

l.h. *abbr.* left hand.

Lhasa / **lah**-suh / the capital of Tibet.

Li *symbol* lithium.

liability *n.* **1** being liable. **2** a person or thing that is a troublesome responsibility; a handicap. **3** (**liabilities**) debts, obligations.

liable / **luy**-uh-buhl / *adj.* **1** held responsible by law; legally obliged to pay a tax or penalty. **2** (foll. by *to*) exposed or open to (something undesirable) (*she is liable to colds*). **3** (foll. by *for*) answerable. **4** likely (*the cliff is liable to crumble*).

■ **Usage** The use of *liable* in sense 4, though common, is considered incorrect by some people.

liaise / lee-**ayz** / *v.* (often foll. by *with*) act as a link or go-between.

liaison / lee-**ay**-zon / *n.* **1** communication and cooperation (e.g. between units of an organisation). **2** an illicit sexual relationship. **3** the binding or thickening agent of a sauce.

liana / lee-**ah**-nuh / *n.* a thick vine found in tropical forests.

liar *n.* a person who tells lies.

Lib. *abbr.* Liberal.

lib *n. colloq.* (in names of political movements) liberation (*Women's Lib*).

libation / luy-**bay**-shuhn / *n.* (*literary*) **1** a drink poured out in offering to a god. **2** the pouring out of this. **3** *jocular* a celebratory drink.

libel / **luy**-buhl / *n.* **1** a published false statement that damages a person's reputation. **2** the act of publishing it (*was charged with libel*). **3** a statement or anything that brings discredit on a person or thing (*the program is a libel on him*). •*v.* (**libelled**, **libelling**) utter or publish a libel against. ◻ **libellous** *adj.*

liberal *adj.* **1** giving generously. **2** ample, given in large amounts. **3** not strict or literal (*a liberal interpretation of the rules*). **4** (of education) broadening the mind in a general way rather than training it in technical subjects. **5** tolerant, open minded, esp. in religion and politics. **6** (**Liberal**) of the Liberal Party. •*n.* **1** a person who is tolerant or open-minded, esp. in religion and politics. **2** (**Liberal**) a member of the Liberal Party. ◻ **liberalism** *n.*

liberalise *v.* (also **-ize**) make less strict. ◻ **liberalisation** *n.*

Liberal Party a major Australian political party supporting private enterprise (and opposed to socialism) and located to the right of the political spectrum.

liberate *v.* **1** set free. **2** free (a country etc.) from an oppressor or enemy. **3** (often as **liberated** *adj.*) free (a person) from rigid social conventions. **4** *colloq.* steal. ◻ **liberation** *n.* **liberator** *n.*

Liberia / luy-**beer**-ree-uh / a republic on the coast of West Africa. ◻ **Liberian** *adj.* & *n.*

libertarian / lib-uh-**tair**-ree-uhn / *n.* a person who favours absolute liberty of thought and action. ◻ **libertarianism** *n.*

libertine / **lib**-uh-teen, -tuyn / *n.* a person who is not restrained by conventional moral standards, esp. in sexual relations.

liberty *n.* **1** freedom from captivity, slavery, imprisonment, or oppression. **2** the right or power to do as one chooses. **3** a right or privilege granted by authority. **4** the setting aside of convention, improper familiarity. ◻ **at liberty 1** (of a person) not imprisoned, free. **2** allowed (*you are at liberty to leave*). **take liberties 1** behave too familiarly towards a person. **2** (foll. by *with*) treat (facts, rules, etc.) carelessly or superficially (*he is taking liberties with the truth*).

Liberty, Statue of a statue on an island at the entrance to New York harbour, a symbol of welcome to immigrants, representing a draped female figure carrying a book of laws in her left hand and holding aloft a torch in her right.

libidinous / luh-**bid**-uh-nuhs / *adj.* lustful.

libido / luh-**bee**-doh / *n.* (*pl.* **libidos**) emotional energies and urges, esp. those associated with sexual desire. ◻ **libidinal** *adj.*

Libra / **lee**-bruh, **lib**-ruh / *n.* the seventh sign of the zodiac, the Scales. ◻ **Libran** *adj.* & *n.*

librarian *n.* a person in charge of or assisting in a library. ◻ **librarianship** *n.*

library / **luy**-bruh-ree / *n.* **1** a collection of books for reading or borrowing. **2** a room or building where these are kept. **3** a similar collection of records, films, computer programs, etc.

libretto / luh-**bret**-oh / *n.* (*pl.* **librettos** or **libretti**) the words of an opera or other long musical work. ◻ **librettist** *n.*

Libreville / **lee**-bruh-vil / the capital of Gabon.

Libya a republic in North Africa, bordering on the Mediterranean Sea. ◻ **Libyan** *adj.* & *n.*

lice *see* LOUSE.

licence *n.* **1** an official permit to own or do something or to carry on a trade. **2** permission. **3** disregard of rules or customs etc.; lack of due restraint in behaviour. **4** a writer's or artist's exaggeration, or disregard of rules etc., for the sake of effect (*poetic licence*).

license *v.* **1** grant a licence to (*licensed to sell tobacco*). **2** authorise the use of (premises) for a certain purpose.

licensee n. a person who holds a licence, esp. to sell alcoholic drinks.

licentiate / luy-**sen**-shee-uht / n. one who holds a certificate showing that he or she is competent to practise a certain profession (*Licentiate in Dental Surgery*).

licentious / luy-**sen**-shuhs / adj. disregarding the rules of conduct, esp. in sexual matters. □ **licentiousness** n.

lichee alternative spelling of LYCHEE.

lichen / **luy**-kuhn / n. a small slow-growing plant found on rocks, tree trunks, etc., usu. green, grey, or yellow in colour. □ **lichenous** adj.

lich-gate n. (also **lych-gate**) a roofed gateway to a churchyard.

licit / **lis**-uht / adj. formal allowed, not forbidden. □ **licitly** adv.

lick v. **1** pass the tongue over; take up or make clean by doing this. **2** (of waves or flames) move like a tongue; touch lightly. **3** colloq. defeat; thrash. • n. **1** an act of licking with the tongue. **2** a blow with a stick etc. **3** a slight application (of paint etc.). **4** colloq. a fast pace (*we were going at quite a lick*). □ **lick a person's boots** be servile towards him or her. **lick into shape** make presentable or efficient. **lick one's wounds** remain in hiding, recovering after a defeat.

licking n. colloq. **1** a defeat. **2** a thrashing.

licorice alternative spelling of LIQUORICE.

lid n. **1** a hinged or removable cover for a box or pot etc. **2** an eyelid. □ **put the lid on** colloq. **1** form a climax to. **2** put a stop to. □□ **lidded** adj.

lie[1] n. **1** a statement that the speaker knows to be untrue (*tell a lie*). **2** a thing that deceives. • v. (**lied, lying**) **1** tell a lie or lies. **2** be deceptive. □ **give the lie to** show that (something) is untrue. **lie detector** an instrument that can supposedly show whether a person is lying by testing for physical changes caused by tension.

lie[2] v. (**lay, lain, lying**) **1** be in or adopt a horizontal position on a surface; be at rest on something. **2** (of a thing) rest flat on a surface (*snow lay on the ground*). **3** exist, be kept, or remain in a specified state (*machinery lay idle*). **4** be situated (*the mirrnyong lies to the east*). **5** exist or be found (*the remedy lies in education*). • n. the way or position in which something lies. □ **how the land lies** what the situation is. **lie in** colloq. stay in bed late in the morning. **lie-in** such a stay. **lie in state** be displayed in a public place of honour before burial or cremation. **lie low** conceal oneself or one's intentions. **take lying down** accept (an insult etc.) without protest.

■ **Usage** The transitive use of *lie* (meaning *lay*) as in *lie her on the bed* is incorrect in standard English. *See also* the note at LAY[3].

Liechtenstein / **lik**-tuhn-styun / a small independent principality between Austria and Switzerland. □ **Liechtensteiner** n.

lied / leed / n. (pl. **lieder**) a German song, esp. of the Romantic period and usu. for solo voice and piano.

lief / leef / adv. archaic gladly, willingly (*I would as lief stay as go*).

liege / leej / n. hist. (also **liege lord**) one's feudal superior; one's king.

lien / lee-uhn / n. Law the right to hold another person's property until a debt on it (e.g. for repair) is paid.

lieu / lyoo-, loo / n. □ **in lieu** instead, in place (*accepted a cheque in lieu of cash*).

lieutenant / lef-**ten**-uhnt / n. **1** an army officer. **2** / luh-**ten**-uhnt / a naval officer. **3** a deputy, a chief assistant. □ **lieutenancy** n.

life n. (pl. **lives**) **1** the capacity for activity, growth, and change in animals and plants that ends at death. **2** living things (*plant life; is there life on Mars?*). **3** a living form or mode (*portrait is drawn from life*). **4** liveliness, interest (*full of life*). **5** the period for which a person or organism is, has been, or will be alive (*all my life*). **6** this state of existence (*lost their lives*). **7** colloq. a life sentence. **8** a person's or people's activities, fortunes, or manner of existence (*in private life; love life*). **9** the activities and pleasures of the world (*we do see life!*). **10** a biography. **11** a period during which something exists or continues to function (*the battery has a life of two years*). □ **life assurance** = LIFE INSURANCE. **life cycle** the series of changes that characterise the life of an organism or thing. **life insurance** insurance for a sum of money to be paid after a set period or on the death of the insured person if earlier. **life jacket** a jacket of buoyant or inflatable material to keep a person afloat in water. **life sciences** biology and related subjects. **life-support** adj. (of equipment) providing and maintaining suitable conditions for life in unnatural circumstances, e.g. severe illness, space travel, etc. **not on your life** colloq. most certainly not.

lifebelt n. a belt of buoyant or inflatable material to keep a person afloat in water.

lifeblood n. **1** blood, as necessary for staying alive. **2** a vital factor or influence.

lifeboat n. **1** a small boat carried on a ship for use if the ship has to be abandoned at sea. **2** a boat specially constructed for going to the help of people in danger at sea along a coast.

lifebuoy n. a buoyant device to keep a person afloat.

lifeguard n. = LIFESAVER (sense 1).

lifeless adj. **1** without life, dead or never having had life. **2** unconscious. **3** lacking vitality. □ **lifelessly** adv. **lifelessness** n.

lifelike adj. exactly like a real person or thing.

lifeline n. **1** a rope etc. used in rescuing people, e.g. one attached to a lifebelt. **2** a diver's signalling line. **3** a sole means of communication or transport. **4** (**Life Line**) a confidential 24-hour

lifelong *adj.* continued all one's life.

lifer *n. colloq.* a person sentenced to life imprisonment.

lifesaver *n.* **1** (in full **surf lifesaver**) an expert swimmer who supervises surfing beaches etc., esp. to rescue swimmers from drowning. **2** a person or thing that is of great help; a boon.

lifespan *n.* the length of time for which a person or creature lives, or for which a thing exists or is functional.

lifestyle *n.* the way of life of a particular person or group.

lifetime *n.* **1** the duration of a person's life or of a thing's existence. **2** *colloq.* a very long time.

lift *v.* **1** raise to a higher level or position. **2** take up from the ground or from its resting place. **3** dig up (e.g. potatoes etc. at harvest, or plants for storing). **4** *colloq.* steal; copy from another source. **5** (of fog etc.) disperse. **6** remove or abolish (restrictions). • *n.* **1** lifting; being lifted. **2** a free ride in another person's vehicle. **3** an apparatus for transporting people or goods from one floor of a building to another. **4** a ski lift or chair lift. **5** transport (of goods etc.) by air (*an airlift*). **6** the upward pressure that air exerts on an aircraft in flight. **7** a feeling of elation (*the praise gave me a lift*). ☐ **lift-off** the vertical take-off of a rocket or spacecraft.

ligament *n.* a piece of the tough flexible tissue that holds bones together or keeps organs in place in the body.

ligature / lig-uh-chuh / *n.* **1** a thing used in tying, esp. in surgical operations. **2** a tie in music. **3** joined printed letters such as œ. • *v.* tie with a ligature.

light¹ *n.* **1** the energy that stimulates the sense of sight and makes things visible. **2** the presence, amount, or effect of this. **3** a source of light, esp. an electric lamp (*leave the light on*). **4** (often as **lights**) a traffic light. **5** a flame or spark; something used to produce this. **6** the bright parts of a picture etc. **7** mental or spiritual insight. **8** the way something or someone is regarded (*sees the matter in a different light*). **9** a window or opening to admit light. • *adj.* **1** full of light, not in darkness. **2** pale (*light blue*). • *v.* (**lit** *or* **lighted**, **lighting**) **1** set burning; begin to burn. **2** cause to give out light. **3** provide with light; guide with a light. **4** brighten. ☐ **bring** (*or* **come**) **to light** *Aust.* reveal (or be revealed), make (or become) known. **in the light of** taking into account. **light bulb** = LIGHT GLOBE. **light globe** (also **light bulb**) a glass globe containing an inert gas and a metal filament, providing light when an electric current is passed through it. **light meter** an exposure meter. **light pen** a pen-shaped device for drawing on or highlighting parts of a computer screen. **light up 1** put lights on at dusk. **2** make or become bright with light or colour. **3** (of a person's face or eyes) suddenly become animated, shine. **4** begin to smoke a cigarette or pipe. **light year** the distance light travels in one year (about 6 million million miles).

light² *adj.* **1** having little weight, not heavy; easy to lift, carry, or move. **2** of less than average weight, amount, or force (*light rain*). **3** (of work) needing little physical effort. **4** carrying or suitable for carrying small loads (*light aircraft*). **5** (of sleep or a sleeper) easily disturbed. **6** (of food) easy to digest. **7** moving easily and quickly. **8** cheerful, free from worry (*with a light heart*). **9** not profound or serious, intended as entertainment (*light music*). • *adv.* lightly, with little load (*we travel light*). • *v.* (**lit** *or* **lighted**, **lighting**) (foll. by *on* or *upon*) find accidentally (*I lit on this book*). • *n. colloq.* beer of light alcoholic strength. ☐ **light-fingered** apt to steal. **light-footed** nimble. **light-headed** feeling slightly faint, dizzy; delirious. **light-hearted 1** cheerful, without cares. **2** too casual, not treating a thing seriously. **light industry** industry producing small or light articles. **light on** *colloq.* not well supplied with. **make light of** treat as unimportant. ☐☐ **lightish** *adj.* **lightly** *adv.* **lightness** *n.*

lighten¹ *v.* **1** shed light on. **2** make or become brighter. **3** produce lightning.

lighten² *v.* **1** make or become lighter in weight. **2** relieve or be relieved of care or worry. **3** reduce (a penalty).

lighter¹ *n.* a device for lighting cigarettes etc.

lighter² *n.* a flat-bottomed boat used in a harbour for loading and unloading ships and transporting goods.

lighthouse *n.* a tower or other structure containing a beacon light to warn or guide ships.

lighting *n.* equipment for providing light to a room or building or street etc.; the light itself.

lightning *n.* a flash of bright light produced by natural electricity, between clouds or a cloud and the ground. • *adj.* very quick (*with lightning speed*). ☐ **lightning conductor** (also **lightning rod**) a metal rod or wire fixed to an exposed part of a building etc., to divert lightning into the earth. **lightning fence** a wire fence strung from widely spaced posts (and thus quickly erected).

lightweight *n.* **1** a person of less than average weight. **2** a boxing weight (57–60 kg) between welterweight and featherweight. **3** a person of little influence. • *adj.* not having great weight or influence.

ligneous / lig-nee-uhs / *adj.* **1** like wood. **2** (of plants) woody.

lignite / lig-nuyt / *n.* a brown coal of woody texture.

lignotuber *n. Botany* a short thick rounded woody part of a stem usu. found underground and covered with modified buds.

lignum / lig-nuhm / *n.* any of several Australian plants which form tangled impenetrable thickets. ☐ **lignum vitae** / vee-tuy, vuy-tee / a tall rainforest tree of Qld and NSW yielding a durable timber.

like[1] *adj.* **1** having some or all the qualities or appearance etc. of, similar. **2** characteristic of (*it was just like him to do that*). **3** in a suitable state or the right mood for something (*it looks like rain; we felt like a walk*). **4** such as, for example (*in subjects like music*). •*prep.* in the manner of, to the same degree as (*he swims like a fish*). •*conj. colloq.* **1** in the same manner as, to the same degree as (*do it like I do*). **2** as if (*she doesn't act like she belongs here*). •*adv. colloq.* **1** likely (*as like as not they'll refuse*). **2** so to speak (*did a quick getaway, like*). •*n.* one that is like another, a similar thing (*shall not see his like again*). □ **and the like** and similar things. **the likes of** *colloq.* people like (*we don't want the likes of you here*).

like[2] *v.* **1** find pleasant or satisfactory. **2** wish for or be inclined to (*I'd like to think it over*). •*n.pl.* (**likes**) the things one likes or prefers.

likeable *adj.* (also **likable**) pleasant, easy for a person to like.

likelihood *n.* being likely, probability.

likely *adj.* (**likelier**, **likeliest**) **1** such as may reasonably be expected to occur or be true etc. (*he is likely to be late; rain is likely*). **2** seeming to be suitable (*the likeliest place*). **3** showing promise of being successful (*a likely lad*). •*adv.* probably (*is very likely true*). □ **not likely!** *colloq.* certainly not. □□ **likeliness** *n.*

■ **Usage** When used as an adverb, *likely* must be preceded by *more*, *most*, or *very*. Use without the qualifying adverb is standard only in American English, e.g. *They'll likely not come.*

liken *v.* point out the resemblance of (one thing to another) (*he likened the heart to a pump*).

likeness *n.* **1** being like, a resemblance. **2** a copy, portrait, or picture.

likewise *adv.* **1** moreover, also. **2** similarly (*do likewise*).

liking *n.* **1** what one likes, one's taste (*is it to your liking?*). **2** (foll. by *for*) a fondness, a taste (*a liking for it*).

lilac *n.* **1** a shrub with fragrant purplish or white flowers. **2** pale purple. •*adj.* lilac-coloured.

liliaceous / lil-ee-**ay**-shuhs / *adj.* lily-like; of the lily family.

Lilith a female demon of Jewish folklore, who tries to kill newborn children. In the Talmud she is the first wife of Adam, dispossessed by Eve. (¶ Hebrew, = night monster.)

Lillee, Dennis (Keith) (1949–), Australian test cricketer, a fast bowler.

lil-lil *n. Aust.* an Aboriginal weapon used both as a missile and in close combat. (¶ Probably Wembawemba *liawil* (*lia* 'tooth' + *wil* 'having').)

lilliputian / lil-uh-**pyoo**-shuhn / *adj.* very small. •*n.* a very small person or thing. (¶ Named after the inhabitants of Lilliput, a country in Swift's *Gulliver's Travels*, who were only six inches tall.)

lilly-pilly *n.* (also **lilli-pilli**) **1** an Australian rainforest tree having glossy dark green foliage and pink edible fruits; widely cultivated. **2** the fruit of this tree.

lilo / **luy**-loh / *n.* (*pl.* **lilos**) *trademark* a type of inflatable plastic mattress.

Lilongwe / lee-**long**-way / the capital of Malawi.

lilt *n.* a light pleasant rhythm; a song or tune having this.

lilting *adj.* having a light pleasant rhythm.

lily *n.* **1** a plant growing from a bulb, with large white, yellow, orange, or purple flowers. **2** a plant of this family. □ **like a lily on a dustbin** (*or* **garbage bin** etc.) *Aust.* out of place, incongruous. **lily-livered** cowardly. **lily of the valley** a spring flower with small fragrant white bell-shaped flowers. **lily-trotter** = LOTUS BIRD.

Lima / **lee**-muh / the capital of Peru.

lima bean / **lee**-muh, **luy**- / *n.* **1** a tropical American bean plant with large flat white edible seeds. **2** the seed of this plant.

limb *n.* **1** an arm, leg, or wing. **2** a main branch of a tree. **3** an arm of a cross. □ **out on a limb** isolated, stranded.

limber[1] *adj.* flexible, agile. •*v.* make limber. □ **limber up** exercise in preparation for athletic activity.

limber[2] *n.* the detachable front part of a gun carriage. •*v.* attach a limber to.

limbo[1] *n.* (*pl.* **limbos**) **1** (in some Christian theology) the supposed abode of those unbaptised souls not admitted to heaven but not condemned to punishment. **2** an intermediate state or condition (e.g. awaiting a decision), a condition of being neglected or forgotten.

limbo[2] *n.* (*pl.* **limbos**) a West Indian dance in which the dancer bends backwards to pass under a horizontal bar which is progressively lowered.

lime[1] *n.* a white substance (calcium oxide) used in making cement and as a fertiliser. •*v.* treat with lime.

lime[2] *n.* **1** a round green fruit like a lemon but smaller and more acid. **2** (also **lime green**) its colour. □ **lime juicer** *Aust. hist.* = LIMEY (sense 2).

lime[3] *n.* (in full **lime tree**) a tree with smooth heart-shaped leaves and fragrant yellow flowers, a linden.

limelight *n.* (**the limelight**) the glare of publicity. (¶ Named after the brilliant light, obtained by heating lime, formerly used to illuminate the stages of theatres.)

limerick *n.* a type of humorous five-line poem with the rhyme scheme *aabba*. (¶ Named after *Limerick*, a town in Ireland.)

limestone *n.* a kind of rock (mainly calcium carbonate) from which lime is obtained by heating.

limewood *n.* a eucalypt, esp. the *ghost gum*, which has a white bark yielding a chalky powder when touched.

limey *n. colloq.* (*pl.* **limeys**) **1** a British person (originally a sailor) or ship. **2** *Aust.* a British immigrant to Australia, a pom. (¶ Named after *lime juice*, which was formerly issued to British sailors as a drink to prevent scurvy.)

liminal / **lim**-uh-nuhl / *adj.* **1 a** of or relating to a transitional or initial stage. **b** marginal, insignificant. **2** occupying a position on, or on both sides of, a boundary or threshold. ☐ **liminality** *n.* (¶ Latin *limin-*, *limen* 'threshold'.)

limit *n.* **1** the point, line, or level beyond which something does not continue. **2** the greatest amount allowed (*the speed limit*). • *v.* **1** set or act as a limit to. **2** (foll. by *to*) restrict to a specified amount (*I'm limited to two drinks*). ☐ **be the limit** *colloq.* be intolerable.

limitation *n.* **1** limiting; being limited. **2** a limit (of ability etc.) (*knows his limitations*).

limited *adj.* **1** confined within limits. **2** few, scanty. **3** (after the name of a company) limited company. ☐ **limited edition** a production of a limited number of copies. **limited company** (also **limited liability company**) a company whose members are liable for its debts only to a specified extent.

limo / **lim**-oh / *n.* (*pl.* **limos**) *colloq.* a limousine.

limousine / **lim**-uh-zeen, lim-uh-**zeen** / *n.* a large luxurious car.

limp *v.* walk or proceed lamely. • *n.* a limping walk. • *adj.* **1** not stiff or firm or rigid. **2** lacking strength or energy, wilting. ☐ **limply** *adv.* **limpness** *n.*

limpet *n.* a small shellfish that sticks tightly to rocks.

limpid *adj.* (of liquids etc.) clear, transparent. ☐ **limpidity** *n.*

linage / **luy**-nij / *n.* **1** the number of lines in printed or written matter. **2** payment by the line.

linchpin *n.* **1** a pin passed through the end of an axle to keep the wheel in position. **2** a person or thing that is vital to an organisation or plan etc.

Lincoln, Abraham (1809–65), 16th president of the USA 1860–65, noted for his policy of emancipation of slaves.

linctus *n.* a soothing syrupy cough mixture.

Lindbergh / **lind**-berg /, Charles (Augustus) (1902–74), American aviator who made the first solo transatlantic flight (20/21 May 1927).

linden *n.* a lime tree.

Lindsay[1], Joan (1896–1984), Australian artist and writer, best known for her novel *Picnic at Hanging Rock* which was made into a film.

Lindsay[2], Norman (Alfred William) (1879–1969), Australian artist and writer, author of *The Magic Pudding*, a novel for children.

line[1] *n.* **1** a long continuous mark on a surface. **2** a wrinkle, crease, etc. **3** a continuous extent of length without breadth. **4** a contour or outline; a thing's shape. **5** a limit or boundary (*finishing line*). **6** a row of people or things. **7** a row of words on a page. **8** (**lines**) the words of an actor's part. **9** a short letter or note (*drop me a line*). **10** a length of cord, rope, etc., esp. for a specified use (*fishing line*). **11** telephone wire or electrical cable; connection by this (*a bad line*). **12** a single track of a railway, a branch of a railway system (*the Geelong line*). **13** a transport service along a particular route; the name of the company providing this. **14** a connected series of persons following one another in time; a succession (*the line of popes from St. Peter to John Paul II*). **15** an approach or course of action (*along these lines; don't take that line with me!*). **16** a type of activity or business (*what line are you in?*). **17** a type of goods (*a new line of sportswear*). **18** a connected series of military encampments (*enemy lines*). • *v.* **1** mark with lines. **2** arrange in a line (*line them up*). ☐ **come** (*or* **bring**) **into line** conform (or cause to conform). **get a line on** *colloq.* discover information about. **in line** so as to form a straight line. **in line for** likely to get (e.g. promotion). **in line with** in accordance with. **line dancing** group dancing in which the participants, arranged in a line, go through a series of set movements. **line-drawing** a drawing in which an image is created using lines. **line of fire** the path of gunfire, a missile, etc. **line-out** *n.* (in Rugby) parallel lines of opposing forwards formed when the ball is thrown in. **line printer** a machine that prints output from a computer a line at a time. **line-up** *n.* a line of people formed for inspection etc. **on the line** 1 at risk. **2** speaking on the telephone. **out of line** **1** not in line. **2** beyond the accepted bounds of one's position or power.

line[2] *v.* **1** cover the inside surface of (a thing) with a layer of different material. **2** be the lining of. ☐ **line one's pockets** (*or* **purse**) make money, esp. by underhand or dishonest methods.

lineage / **lin**-ee-ij / *n.* ancestry, the line of descendants of an ancestor.

lineal / **lin**-ee-uhl / *adj.* of or in a line, esp. as a descendant. ☐ **lineally** *adv.*

lineaments / **lin**-ee-uh-muhnts / *n.pl.* distinctive features or characteristics, esp. of a face.

linear / **lin**-ee-uh / *adj.* **1** of a line; of length. **2** arranged in a line. ☐ **linearity** *n.*

lineation / lin-ee-**ay**-shuhn / *n.* a division into (or an arrangement in) lines.

linen *n.* **1** cloth made of flax. **2** shirts, sheets, tablecloths, etc. which were formerly made of this.

liner *n.* **1** a large passenger or cargo ship travelling on a regular route. **2** a removable lining (*nappy-liners*).

linesman *n.* **1** an official assisting the referee in certain games, esp. in deciding whether or where a ball crosses a line. **2** (also **lineman**) a person who repairs and maintains telephone or electrical etc. lines. **3** a surf lifesaver whose duty is to handle the line being taken out to a swimmer in difficulties.

ling *n.* (*pl.* the same) a long slender marine food fish of southern Australian waters.

lingam / ling-guhm / n. (also **linga**) an erect phallus as the symbol of the Hindu god Siva (*see also* YONI).

linger v. **1** stay a long time, esp. as if reluctant to leave. **2** dawdle. **3** remain alive although continually growing weaker.

lingerie / lon-*zh*uh-ray / n. women's underwear and nightclothes.

lingo n. (*pl.* **lingos** *or* **lingoes**) *colloq.* **1** a foreign language. **2** the vocabulary of a special subject or group. **3** *Aust.* (in Aboriginal English) an Aboriginal language.

lingua franca / ling-gwuh **frang**-kuh / n. a common language used by people whose native languages are different.

lingual / ling-gwuhl / *adj.* **1** of or formed by the tongue. **2** of speech or languages. ◻ **lingually** *adv.*

linguist / ling-gwuhst / n. a person who is skilled in languages or linguistics.

linguistic / ling-**gwis**-tik / *adj.* of language or linguistics. • n. (**linguistics**) the study of languages and their structure. ◻ **linguistically** *adv.*

liniment / lin-uh-muhnt / n. a liquid etc. for rubbing on the body to relieve muscular pain.

lining n. a layer of material which lines a surface etc.

link n. **1** one ring or loop of a chain. **2** a connecting part. **3** a person who is a connection between others. **4** a cuff link. • v. join; make or be a connection between. ◻ **link up** (usu. foll. by *with*) connect or combine. **link-up** n. an act or result of linking up.

linkage n. linking; a link or system of links.

linkman n. a person providing continuity in a broadcast program or between programs.

links n. (treated as *sing.* or *pl.*) a golf course.

Linnaeus / li-**nee**-uhs /, Carolus (Latinised name of Carl von Linné) (1707–78), Swedish naturalist, who established the system of classifying plants by giving each one a Latin name in two parts (the *genus* or group name, and *species* identifying the individual plant).

linnet / lin-uht / n. a brown-grey European finch.

lino / **luy**-noh / n. linoleum.

linocut n. a design cut in relief on a layer of thick linoleum; a print made from this.

linoleum / li-**noh**-lee-uhm / n. a kind of floor covering made by pressing a thick coating of powdered cork and linseed oil etc. on to a canvas backing.

linotype / **luy**-noh-tuyp / n. *trademark* a machine that produces a line of type as a single strip of metal.

linseed n. the seed of flax. ◻ **linseed oil** oil extracted from linseed and used in paint and varnish.

lint n. **1** a soft absorbent material for dressing wounds, consisting of linen or cotton with a raised nap on one side. **2** fluff.

lintel n. a horizontal piece of timber or stone etc. over a door or other opening.

lion n. **1** a large powerful flesh-eating animal of the cat family; a male lion. **2** (**the Lion**) a sign of the zodiac, Leo. **3** a brave or celebrated person. ◻ **the lion's share** the largest or best part of something. (¶ In the fable the lion demanded most (or, in one version, all) of the prey in return for his help in the kill.)

lioness n. a female lion.

lionise v. (also **-ize**) treat (a person) as a celebrity.

lip n. **1** either of the fleshy edges of the opening of the mouth. **2** *colloq.* impudent talk. **3** the edge of a cup or other hollow container or of an opening. **4** a projecting part of such an edge shaped for pouring. • v. touch with the lips; apply the lips to. ◻ **lip-read** v. understand (speech) from watching the movements of a speaker's lips. **lip-service** service that is proffered but not performed; insincere expressions of support or approval. ◻ ◻ **lipped** *adj.*

lipid n. any of a group of fat-like compounds including fatty acids, oils, waxes, and steroids.

liposuction n. a technique in cosmetic surgery for removing excess fat from under the skin by suction.

lipstick n. a stick of cosmetic for colouring the lips.

liquefy v. (**liquefied**, **liquefying**) make or become liquid. ◻ **liquefaction** n.

liqueur / li-**kyoor** / n. a strong sweet alcoholic spirit with fragrant flavouring.

liquid n. a substance like water or oil that flows freely but is not a gas. • *adj.* **1** in the form of a liquid. **2** having the clearness of water. **3** (of sounds) flowing clearly and pleasantly (*the bellbird's liquid notes*). **4** (of assets) easily converted into cash. ◻ **liquid crystal** a thick liquid with some of the molecular properties of a crystal. **liquid crystal display** a visual display in electronic devices, consisting of a matrix of liquid crystals whose reflective properties change as an electric signal is applied.

liquidate v. **1** pay or settle (a debt). **2** close down (a business) and divide its assets among its creditors. **3** get rid of, esp. by killing. ◻ **liquidator** n.

liquidation n. liquidating, esp. of a firm. ◻ **go into liquidation** (of a business) be closed down and have its assets divided, esp. in bankruptcy.

liquidise v. (also **-ize**) cause to become liquid; crush into a liquid pulp.

liquidiser n. (also **-izer**) a machine for liquidising fruit and vegetables.

liquidity / luh-**kwid**-uh-tee / n. **1** the state of being liquid. **2** the availability of liquid assets.

liquor / lik-uh / n. **1** an alcoholic (esp. distilled) drink. **2 a** juice produced in cooking. **b** a liquid in which food has been boiled.

liquorice / lik-uh-ris, lik-rish / *n*. (also **licorice**) **1** a black substance used in medicine and as a sweet. **2** the plant from whose root it is obtained.

lira / leer-ruh / *n*. (*pl*. **lire**) the unit of money in Italy and Turkey.

Lisbon the capital of Portugal.

lisle / luyl / *n*. a fine smooth cotton thread used esp. for stockings.

lisp *n*. a speech defect in which s is pronounced like th (as in *thin*) and z like th (as in *they*). • *v*. speak or utter with a lisp.

lissom / lis-uhm / *adj*. lithe, agile.

list[1] *n*. **1** a series of names, items, figures, etc. written or printed. **2** (**lists**) the palisades enclosing an area for a tournament; the scene of a contest. • *v*. make a list of; enter (a name etc.) in a list. ▫ **enter the lists** make or accept a challenge, esp. in a controversy. **listed building** a building of architectural or historical importance officially protected from demolition or alteration. **list price** the published or advertised price of goods.

list[2] *v*. (of a ship) lean over to one side. • *n*. a listing position, a tilt.

listen *v*. **1** concentrate in order to hear something or someone. **2** pay attention. **3** (foll. by *to*) respond to a person, request, advice, etc. ▫ **listen in 1** overhear a conversation, esp. by telephone. **2** listen to a radio broadcast. **listen out** (often foll. by *for*) seek to hear by waiting alertly (*listening out for the postie*).

listener *n*. **1** a person who listens. **2** a person listening to a radio broadcast.

Lister, Joseph (1827–1912), English surgeon, inventor of antiseptic techniques in surgery.

listing *n*. a list or catalogue; an item on a list.

listless *adj*. without energy or vitality, showing no enthusiasm. ▫ **listlessly** *adv*. **listlessness** *n*.

Liszt / list /, Franz (Ferenc) (1811–86), Hungarian composer and noted pianist.

lit see LIGHT[1], LIGHT[2].

lit. *abbr*. **1** literal(ly). **2** literary. **3** literature. **4** litre. **5** little.

Li (Tai) Po / lee tuy **poh** / (701–62), a major Chinese poet, whose favourite themes include wine, friendship, and the beauties of nature.

litany *n*. **1** a form of prayer consisting of a series of supplications to God, recited by a priest and with set responses by the congregation. **2** a long monotonous recital (*a litany of complaints*).

litchi alternative spelling of LYCHEE.

lite / luyt / *adj*. applied to low-fat or low-sugar versions of manufactured food or drink products.

literacy / lit-uh-ruh-see / *n*. the ability to read and write.

literal *adj*. **1** taking words in their most basic sense without allowing for figurative or metaphorical use of language. **2** corresponding exactly to a given form of words (*literal translation*). **3** unimaginative, matter of fact. ▫ **literally** *adv*. **literalness** *n*.

literalism *n*. insistence on a literal interpretation; adherence to the letter. ▫ **literalist** *n*. **literalistic** *adj*.

literary / lit-uh-ruh-ree, lit-ruh-ree / *adj*. **1** of or concerned with literature. **2** well informed about literature. **3** (of a word or idiom) used chiefly by writers; formal.

literate / lit-uh-ruht / *adj*. able to read and write. • *n*. a literate person.

literati / lit-uh-**rah**-tee / *n.pl*. learned people.

literature *n*. **1** written works, esp. those novels, poems, plays, etc. valued for their artistic worth. **2** the writings of a country or a period, or on a particular subject (*Australian literature; medieval literature; there is a considerable literature on Australian orchids*). **3** *colloq*. printed pamphlets or leaflets etc. (*some literature about coach tours*).

lithe / luyth / *adj*. flexible, supple.

lithic *adj*. of, like, or made from stone.

lithium / lith-ee-uhm / *n*. a soft silver-white metallic element (symbol Li), the lightest known metal.

litho / **luy**-thoh / *n*. *colloq*. the lithographic process.

lithograph *n*. a picture etc. printed by lithography.

lithography / li-**thog**-ruh-fee / *n*. a process of printing using a smooth surface treated so that ink will adhere only to the design to be printed and not to the rest of the surface. ▫ **lithographic** *adj*.

lithophyte / lith-uh-fuyt / *n*. a plant that grows on stone.

lithosphere / **lith**-uh-sfeer / *n*. **1** the layer including the earth's crust and upper mantle. **2** solid earth.

Lithuania a republic in eastern Europe between Latvia and Poland, formerly a republic of the USSR.

Lithuanian *adj*. of Lithuania or its people or language. • *n*. **1** a person from Lithuania. **2** the language of Lithuania.

litigant / lit-uh-guhnt / *n*. a person who is involved in a lawsuit, one who goes to law.

litigation / lit-uh-**gay**-shuhn / *n*. a lawsuit; the process of going to law.

litigious / luh-**tij**-uhs / *adj*. **1** unreasonably fond of going to law; given to litigation. **2** of lawsuits. **3** giving matter for a lawsuit.

litmus *n*. a blue colouring matter that is turned red by acids and can be restored to blue by alkalis. ▫ **litmus paper** paper stained with this, used to test whether a solution is acid or alkaline. **litmus test** *colloq*. the real or ultimate test.

litotes / luy-**toh**-teez / *n*. an ironic understatement, e.g. *I shan't be sorry* = I shall be glad.

litre / **lee**-tuh / *n*. a metric unit of capacity equal to 1,000 cubic centimetres or 1 cubic decimetre (1.76 pints).

litter *n*. **1** odds and ends of rubbish left lying about. **2** the young animals brought forth at a birth. **3** a means of transport consisting of a couch in a frame carried on the shoulders of bearers. **4** granulated material for use by pets, esp. cats, as an indoor toilet. **5** straw put down as bedding for animals. • *v.* **1** make untidy by scattering odds and ends; scatter as litter. **2** give birth to (a litter of young). **3** provide (a horse etc.) with litter as bedding; spread straw etc. on (a floor).

litterbug *n. colloq.* a person who drops litter, esp. in a public place.

little *adj.* **1** small in size, amount, duration, etc. **2** (**a little**) a small amount of (*add a little salt*). **3** trivial (*argues about every little thing*). **4** only a small amount (*had little sleep*). **5** operating or existing only on a small scale (*little shopkeepers*). **6** smaller than others of its kind (*the little hand of the clock*). **7** young, younger (*a little boy; my little sister*). • *n.* **1** only a small amount (*got little in return*). **2** (**a little**) a definite though small amount, distance, or period of time. • *adv.* **1** only to a small extent (*a little known fact; little more than a rumour*). **2** (**a little**) rather (*I'm a little deaf*). **3** hardly (*little did they know*). ☐ **little lunch** (also **playlunch**) *Aust.* light refreshment eaten during a mid-morning break at school. **the little house** *Aust.* an outdoor toilet.

littley *n.* (also **littlie**) (*pl.* **littlies**) *Aust.* a child.

littoral *adj.* of or on the shore. • *n.* a region lying along the shore.

liturgy / lit-uh-jee / *n.* **1** a fixed form of public worship; a ritual. **2** the Eucharistic office of the Orthodox Church. ☐ **liturgical** / li-**ter**-ji-kuhl / *adj.* **liturgically** *adv.*

live[1] / luyv / *adj.* **1** alive. **2** (of a broadcast) heard or seen while taking place rather than being recorded and edited. **3** (of a recording) made in front of an audience rather than in a studio. **4** of current interest or importance (*a live issue*). **5** (of a match, ammunition, etc.) unused. **6** (of a wire etc.) charged with or carrying electricity. **7** glowing or burning (*live coals*). • *adv.* in the form of a live broadcast (*the show went out live*). ☐ **live wire** a highly energetic person.

live[2] / liv / *v.* **1** have life, be or remain alive. **2** have one's home (*she lives up the road*). **3** feed, subsist (*living on fruit*). **4** depend on for survival (*lives on a pension; lives by his wits*). **5** spend or pass (*live a full life*). **6** express in one's life (*lives his faith*). **7** lead one's life in a specified way (*live quietly*). **8** enjoy life to the full (*you haven't lived*). ☐ **lived-in** *adj.* **1** inhabited; (of a room) used frequently. **2** (of a person's face) worn by weather, worry, etc. **live down** live in such a way that (a past guilt or scandal etc.) becomes forgotten. **live it up** go on a pleasure spree. **live together 1** live in the same house etc. **2** coexist peacefully. **3** (esp. of a couple not married to each other) share a home and have a sexual relationship. **live up to** fulfil (*did not live up to his principles*). **live with 1** live together with. **2** tolerate (*you will have to learn to live with it*).

liveable / liv-uh-buhl / *adj.* (also **livable**) **1** (also **liveable-in**) (of a house etc.) fit to live in. **2** (of one's life) worth living. **3** (also **liveable-with**) (of a person, idea, etc.) easy to live with.

livelihood / luyv-lee-huud / *n.* a means of living; a way in which a person earns a living.

livelong / liv-long / *adj.* for its entire length. ☐ **the livelong day** all day.

lively *adv.* (**livelier, liveliest**) full of life or energy, vigorous and cheerful, full of action. ☐ **look lively** move more quickly or energetically. ☐☐ **liveliness** *n.*

liven / luy-vuhn / *v.* (often foll. by *up*) make or become lively (*liven it up; things livened up*).

liver[1] *n.* **1** a large organ in the abdomen, secreting bile. **2** the liver of certain animals, used as food.

liver[2] *n.* a person who lives in a specified way (*a clean liver*).

liverish *adj.* **1** suffering from a disorder of the liver. **2** irritable, glum.

livery *n.* **1** a distinctive uniform worn by servants etc. **2** a distinctive guise or marking (*birds in their winter livery*). **3** the distinctive colour scheme in which a company's vehicles etc. are painted.

lives see LIFE.

livestock *n.* animals kept for use or profit, e.g. cattle or sheep on a farm.

livid *adj.* **1** of the colour of lead, bluish-grey (*a livid bruise*). **2** *colloq.* furiously angry.

living *adj.* **1** contemporary, now alive. **2** (of a likeness) exact, true to life. **3** (of a language) still in vernacular use. • *n.* **1** being alive. **2** a livelihood. ☐ **living room** a room for general use during the day. **living wage** a wage on which it is possible to live. **living will** a written statement of a person's desire not to be kept alive by artificial means in the event of terminal illness or accident. **within living memory** within the memory of people who are still alive.

Livy (Titus Livius) (59 BC–AD 17), Roman historian, who wrote a history of Rome from its foundation to his own time.

lizard *n.* **1** a reptile with a rough or scaly hide, four legs, and a long tail. **2** *Aust. colloq.* a flathead. ☐ **starve** (or **stiffen**) **the lizards!** *colloq.* an exclamation of surprise or exasperation.

Ljubljana / loo-**blyah**-nuh / the capital of Slovenia.

ll. *abbr.* lines.

'll *abbr.* (usu. after pronouns) shall, will (*I'll; that'll*).

llama / lah-muh / *n.* a South American animal related to the camel, kept as a beast of burden and for its soft woolly hair.

LLB *abbr.* Bachelor of Laws.

LLD *abbr.* Doctor of Laws.

Lloyd Webber, Andrew, Baron Lloyd-Webber of Sydmonton (1948–), English composer, whose works include the musical plays *Evita*, *Cats*, and *The Phantom of the Opera*.

lo *interj. archaic* look. ☐ **lo and behold** *humorous* an expression used to introduce something unexpected or surprising.

load *n.* **1** something carried. **2** the amount carried (*a truckload of bricks*). **3** a commitment or responsibility. **4** (often as **loads**) a lot (*loads of money; what a load of rubbish!*). **5** the amount of power carried by an electric circuit or supplied by a generating station. •*v.* **1** put a load on or aboard (a vehicle etc.); place (a load) aboard a vehicle etc.; (of a vehicle etc.) take a load aboard (*the plane is now loading*); enter a vehicle etc. (*the fans loaded into the coach*). **2** (often foll. by *with*) burden, load heavily. **3** put ammunition into (a firearm). **4** insert (a cassette, film, computer program, etc.) into a device; fill (a tape recorder, camera, computer, etc.). **5** tamper with (dice, a roulette wheel, etc.) by weighting; give bias to. ◻ **get a load of** *colloq.* take notice of.

loaded *adj.* **1** *colloq.* very rich. **2** *colloq.* under the influence of drink or drugs. **3** (of dice, a roulette wheel, etc.) weighted, given bias. **4** (of a question or statement) having some hidden implication.

loader *n.* a gun, machine, truck, etc. loaded in a certain way (*breech-loader; front-loader*).

loading *n.* **1** *Aust.* a payment to employees in addition to the award wage or salary, in acknowledgment of special skills, or as a holiday bonus, etc. **2** esp. *Aust.* the freight carried by a vehicle. **3** an extra charge added to an insurance premium because of poor risk.

loaf[1] *n.* (*pl.* **loaves**) **1** a mass of bread shaped in one piece. **2** minced or chopped meat moulded into an oblong shape. **3** *colloq.* the head (*use your loaf!*). ◻ **loaf sugar** a sugar loaf as a whole or cut into lumps.

loaf[2] *v.* **1** spend time idly; hang about. **2** (foll. by *away*) waste (time etc. idly) (*loafed away the morning*). •*n.* an act or spell of loafing. **2** *colloq.* an undemanding job. ◻ **loafer** *n.*

loam *n.* **1** rich soil containing clay, sand, and decayed vegetable matter. **2** (**loams**) *Aust.* particles of gold found by loaming. •*v.* *Aust.* search for gold by washing loam. ◻ **loamy** *adj.*

loan *n.* **1** something lent, esp. a sum of money. **2** lending, being lent (*books on loan*). •*v.* lend. ◻ **loan shark** *colloq.* a person who lends money at extremely high rates of interest.

loanword *n.* a word adopted, usu. with little modification, from a foreign language (e.g. *morale, naïve*).

loath / lohth / *adj.* (also **loth**) reluctant (*was loath to depart*).

loathe / lohth / *v.* feel great hatred and disgust for.

loathing *n.* hatred, disgust.

loathsome *adj.* arousing loathing, repulsive.

loaves *see* LOAF.

lob *v.* (**lobbed**, **lobbing**) **1** send or strike (a ball) slowly or in a high arc in cricket or tennis etc. **2** (often foll. by *in(to), on to, up,* etc.) *Aust. colloq.* arrive without ceremony; turn up. •*n.* a lobbed ball in tennis etc.; a stroke producing this result.

lobar / **loh**-buh / *adj.* of a lobe, esp. of the lung (*lobar pneumonia*).

lobate / loh-bayt / *adj.* having a lobe or lobes.

lobby[1] *n.* **1** a porch or entrance hall; an anteroom. **2 a** a body of people lobbying an MP etc. or seeking to influence legislation (*the anti-abortion lobby*). **b** an organised rally of lobbying members of the public; the cause supported by such members of the public. •*v.* (**lobbied**, **lobbying**) mount a campaign to influence (an MP or other person).

lobby[2] *n.* (esp. in Qld) a yabby.

lobbyist *n.* a person who lobbies an MP etc., esp. professionally.

lobe *n.* **1** a rounded flattish part or projection (esp. of the brain, liver, and lung). **2** the lower soft part of the ear. ◻ **lobed** *adj.*

lobelia / luh-**bee**-lee-uh / *n.* a garden plant with blue, red, white, or purple flowers.

lobotomised / luh-**bot**-uh-muyzd / *adj.* (also -**ized**) **1** *colloq.* stupefied; stupid. **2** that has undergone lobotomy.

lobotomy / luh-**bot**-uh-mee / *n.* an incision into the frontal lobe of the brain, formerly used in some cases of mental disorder. ◻ **lobotomise** *v.* (also -**ize**).

lobster *n.* **1** *Aust.* = CRAYFISH. **2** a northern Atlantic shellfish with eight legs and two long claws. **3** the flesh of either as food.

local *adj.* **1** belonging to a particular place or neighbourhood (*local history; the local paper*). **2** affecting a particular place, not general (*local disturbances*). •*n.* **1** an inhabitant of a particular place. **2** *colloq.* the local hotel. ◻ **local anaesthetic** one affecting a specific area of the body and not causing unconsciousness. **local area network** (*abbr.* **LAN**) a communication network linking a number of computers in the same locality, typically a building. **local call** a telephone call to a nearby place. **local colour** details characteristic of the scene in which a novel etc. is set, added to make it seem more real. **local government** the system of administration of a city, town, municipality, shire, etc. by the elected representatives of people who live there.

locale / loh-**kahl** / *n.* the scene of an event or occurrence.

localise *v.* (also -**ize**) **1** make local not general, confine within a particular area (*a localised infection*). **2** invest with the characteristics of a particular place.

locality / loh-**kal**-uh-tee / *n.* a thing's position, the site or neighbourhood of something.

locate *v.* **1** discover the place where (a thing) is (*locate the electrical fault*). **2** assign to or establish in a particular location (*the town hall is located in the city centre*).

■ **Usage** In standard English, it is not acceptable to use *locate* to mean merely 'find' as in *I can't locate my keys.*

location *n.* **1** a particular place or position. **2** the act of locating or the process of being located. **3** a

loc. cit. natural (rather than studio-based) setting for a film or broadcast (*filmed entirely on location*).

loc. cit. *abbr.* in the book etc. that has previously been mentioned; in the passage already cited. (¶ Latin *loco citato*.)

loch / lok / *n. Scottish* a lake or narrow inlet of the sea.

loci *see* LOCUS.

lock[1] *n.* **1** a mechanism for fastening shut a door or lid etc., with a bolt that cannot be opened without a key or similar device. **2** a section of a canal or river enclosed by sluice gates, for raising or lowering boats by changing the water level. **3** the turning of a vehicle's front wheels; the maximum extent of this. **4** the interlocking or jamming of parts. **5** a wrestling hold that prevents an opponent's limb from moving. **6** (in full **lock forward**) a player in the second row of a Rugby scrum. **7** a mechanism for exploding the charge in a gun. •*v.* **1** fasten or be able to be fastened with a lock. **2** (often foll. by *up* or *away*) secure in a place fastened by a lock; store away securely or inaccessibly (*his capital is locked up in land*). **3** bring or come into a rigidly fixed position, jam. **4** (foll. by *in*) hold fast (in sleep, a struggle, an embrace, etc.). ☐ **lock on to** (of a missile or guidance system) automatically find and track (a target). **lock out 1** keep out by locking a door. **2** (of an employer) subject (employees) to a LOCKOUT. **lock, stock, and barrel** completely, including everything. **lock-up** *adj.* able to be locked up (*a lock-up garage*). *n.* **1** premises that can be locked up. **2** a room or building where prisoners can be detained temporarily. **3 a** the locking up of premises for the night. **b** the time of doing this. **5** *Aust.* the confinement of journalists etc., previewing confidential government documents, esp. budget papers, before they are made public.

lock[2] *n.* **1** a portion of hair that hangs together. **2** (**locks**) the hair of the head.

locker *n.* a small cupboard or compartment where things can be stowed safely, esp. for an individual's use in a public place.

locket *n.* a small ornamental case holding a portrait or lock of hair etc., worn on a chain round the neck.

Lockett, Tony (full name: Anthony Howard Lockett) (1966–), Australian Rules footballer who in 1999 became the code's highest goal scorer.

lockjaw *n.* a form of tetanus in which the jaws become rigidly closed.

lockout *n.* an employer's exclusion of employees from the workplace until a dispute is ended.

locksmith *n.* a maker and mender of locks.

locomotion *n.* moving, the ability to move from place to place.

locomotive *n.* an engine for drawing a train along rails. •*adj.* of locomotion (*locomotive power*).

locum tenens / loh-kum **tee**-nenz, **ten**-uhnz / *n.* (*pl.* **locum tenentes** / tuh-**nen**-teez /) (also **locum**) a deputy acting for a doctor or clergyman in his or her absence.

locus / **loh**-kuhs, **lok**-uhs / *n.* (*pl.* **loci** / **loh**-suy /) **1** the exact place of something. **2** *Maths* the line or curve etc. formed by all points satisfying certain conditions or by movement of a point or line etc.

locust / **loh**-kuhst / *n.* **1** an African or Asian grasshopper that migrates in swarms and eats all vegetation. **2** a similar destructive Australian grasshopper. **3** *US* & *Aust. colloq.* a cicada.

locution / luh-**kyoo**-shuhn / *n.* **1** a word, phrase, or idiom. **2** a style of speech.

Loddon a river, about 340 km long, in central Vic.

lode *n.* a vein of metal ore.

lodestar *n.* a star used as a guide in navigation, esp. the pole star.

lodestone *n.* **1** a magnetic oxide of iron. **2** a piece of this used as a magnet. **3** a thing that attracts.

lodge *n.* **1** a small makeshift shelter; a hut. **2** a building accommodating skiers etc. during the season (*ski lodge*). **3** (**The Lodge**) *Aust.* the official residence of the prime minister in Canberra. **4** the members or meeting place of a branch of a secret society such as the Freemasons. •*v.* **1** provide with temporary accommodation. **2** live as a lodger. **3** deposit; be or become embedded (*the bullet lodged in his brain*). **4** present formally for attention (*lodged a complaint*).

lodger *n.* a person paying for accommodation in another's house.

lodging *n.* **1** temporary accommodation (*a lodging for the night*). **2** (**lodgings**) a room or rooms (not in a hotel) rented for lodging in.

loess / **loh**-uhs, lers / *n.* a layer of fine-grained fertile soil found esp. in the basins of large rivers.

loft *n.* **1** an attic. **2** a room over a stable. **3** a gallery or upper level in a church or hall (*the organ-loft*). **4** a pigeon house. **5** a backward slope in the face of a golf club. **6** a lofted stroke. •*v.* send (a ball) in a high arc.

lofty *adj.* (**loftier**, **loftiest**) **1** (of things) very tall, towering. **2** (of thoughts or aims etc.) noble. **3** haughty (*a lofty manner*). ☐ **loftily** *adv.* **loftiness** *n.*

log[1] *n.* **1** a length of tree trunk that has fallen or been cut down; a short piece of this cut for firewood. **2** *hist.* a floating device for gauging a ship's speed. **3** a detailed record of a ship's voyage or an aircraft's flight; any similar record. **4** = LOGBOOK. **5** *Aust.* a set of claims for an increase in wages etc., esp. as lodged by a trade union with an industrial tribunal. •*v.* (**logged**, **logging**) **1** enter (facts) in a logbook. **2** achieve (a certain distance, number of hours worked, etc.) as recorded in a logbook (*the pilot had logged 200 hours*). **3** fell trees (in a forest etc.) for timber, woodchips, etc.; fell (an area) for this reason (*logging old-growth* forests). ☐ **log on** *or* **off** (also **log in** *or* **out**) open or close one's online access to a computer system.

log² *n.* a logarithm (*log tables*).

loganberry *n.* a large dark red fruit, hybrid of a blackberry and a raspberry.

logarithm / **log**-uh-ri*th*-uhm / *n.* one of a series of numbers set out in tables which make it possible to work out arithmetic problems by adding and subtracting numbers instead of multiplying and dividing. ☐ **logarithmic** *adj.*

logbook *n.* **1** a book containing a detailed record or log. **2** a record kept by truck drivers etc. of hours driven etc.

logger *n.* a person engaged in the industry of felling forest etc. trees for timber etc.

loggerheads *n.pl.* ☐ **at loggerheads** disagreeing or quarrelling.

loggia / **loh**-jee-uh, **loj**-ee-uh / *n.* an open-sided gallery or arcade.

logging *n.* the work of cutting down forest etc. trees for timber, the woodchip industry, etc.

logic / **loj**-ik / *n.* **1** the science of reasoning. **2** a particular system or method of reasoning. **3** a chain of reasoning regarded as good or bad. **4** the ability to reason correctly. **5** the principles used in designing a computer or any of its units; the circuit(s) involved in this. ☐ **logic bomb** a set of instructions secretly included in a computer program so that if a particular set of conditions ever occurs, the instructions will be put into operation and cause data to be wiped or the system to crash.

logical / **loj**-i-kuhl / *adj.* **1** of or according to logic, correctly reasoned. **2** (of an action etc.) in accordance with what seems reasonable or natural. **3** capable of reasoning correctly. ☐ **logically** *adv.* **logicality** / loj-uh-**kal**-uh-tee / *n.*

logician / luh-**jish**-uhn / *n.* a person who is skilled in logic.

Logie *n. Aust.* any of the statuettes awarded annually since 1958 for excellence in acting etc. in an Australian television production. (¶ John Logie Baird (1888–1946), the inventor of television.)

logistics / luh-**jis**-tiks / *n.pl.* the organisation of a large complex operation, such as a military campaign. ☐ **logistic** *adj.* **logistical** *adj.* **logistically** *adv.*

logjam *n.* **1** a crowded mass of logs in a river. **2** a deadlock. **3** a backlog.

logo / **loh**-goh / *n.* (*pl.* **logos**) a printed symbol used by an organisation as its emblem.

Logos / **log**-os / *n.* (in Christian theology) the Word of God, or second person of the Trinity, incarnate in Jesus Christ according to the fourth Gospel.

logrunner *n.* either of two Australian rainforest birds, esp. the chowchilla.

loin *n.* **1** (**loins**) the side and back of the body between the ribs and the hip bone. **2** a joint of meat that includes the vertebrae of this part.

loincloth *n.* a piece of cloth worn round the body at the hips so as to enclose the genitals, esp. as the only garment.

loiter *v.* linger or stand about idly; proceed slowly with frequent stops. ☐ **loiter with intent** linger in a place in order to commit a crime. ☐☐ **loiterer** *n.*

LOL *abbr.* (esp. in electronic communications) laughing out loud.

loll *v.* **1** stand, sit, or lean back in a lazy or relaxed manner. **2** hang loosely (*a dog with its tongue lolling out*).

lollipop *n.* a large round usu. flat boiled sweet on a small stick. ☐ **lollipop man** *or* **lady** *colloq.* a warden using a circular sign on a pole to stop traffic for schoolchildren to cross the road.

lollop *v.* (**lolloped**, **lolloping**) *colloq.* flop about, move in clumsy bounds.

lolly *n. colloq.* **1** *Aust.* a small shaped piece of confectionery made esp. with sugar; a sweet. **2** *colloq.* the head. **3** *colloq.* money. ☐ **do one's lolly** *colloq.* lose one's temper. **lolly-pink** *n.* & *adj. Aust.* shocking pink. **lolly water** *Aust. colloq.* soft drink.

Lomé / loh-**may** / the capital of Togo.

London the capital of England and of the United Kingdom. ☐ **London fog** *Aust. colloq.* a worker who loafs on the job (i.e. who will not lift).

lone *adj.* **1** solitary, without companions (*a lone horseman*). **2** isolated. **3** single (*a lone parent*). ☐ **play a lone hand** take action without the support of others. **lone wolf** a person who prefers to do this or to be alone.

lonely *adj.* (**lonelier**, **loneliest**) **1** solitary, without companions. **2** sad because one lacks friends or companions. **3** (of places) far from inhabited places, remote, not often frequented (*a lonely road*). ☐ **loneliness** *n.*

loner *n.* one who prefers not to associate with others.

lonesome *adj.* lonely; causing loneliness.

long¹ *adj.* **1** having great length in space or great duration in time. **2** having a certain length or duration (*two metres long; two hours long*). **3** seeming to be longer than it really is (*ten long hours*). **4** lasting, going far into the past or future (*a long friendship*). **5** (foll. by *on*) *colloq.* having plenty of (a quality) (*long on talk, short on ideas*). **6** of elongated shape. **7** (of vowel sounds) having a pronunciation longer than that of a corresponding 'short' vowel (the *a* in *cane* is long, in *can* it is short). **8** (of odds) reflecting a low level of probability. •*adv.* **1** for a long time, by a long time (*long before*). **2** throughout a specified time (*all day long*). •*n.* a long period of time (*it won't take long*). ☐ **as** (*or* **so**) **long as** provided that, on condition that. **in the long run** in the end, over a long period. **long-drawn** (also **long-drawn-out**) prolonged. **long face** a dismal expression. **long in the tooth** *colloq.* old. **long johns** *colloq.* underpants with long legs. **long jump** an athletic competition of jumping as far as possible along the ground in one leap. **long paddock** *Aust.* a public road, the grassy sides of which are used for grazing stock during a drought etc. **long-range** *adj.* **1** having a long range. **2** relating to a period far into the future (*long-range weather forecast*). **long service leave** a period of paid leave granted to an employee who has served a specified period of continuous employment. **long shot** a wild guess or venture; a bet at long odds. **long-sighted 1** able to see clearly only what is at a distance. **2** far-sighted. **long tom 1** a long trough used for washing gold-bearing material in order to separate the gold. **2** any of several Australian sea fish having long needle-like jaws. **long wave** a radio wave of frequency less than 300 kHz. **long-winded** talking or writing at tedious length. □ □ **longish** *adj.*

long² *v.* (often foll. by *for*) feel a longing.

longa / **long**-guh / *prep. Aust.* (in Aboriginal English) belonging to; near; about; with.

longbow *n.* a large bow drawn by hand and shooting a long feathered arrow.

longeron / **lon**-juh-ruhn / *n.* a lengthwise structural part of an aircraft's fuselage.

longevity / lon-**jev**-uh-tee / *n.* long life.

longhand *n.* ordinary writing, contrasted with shorthand, typing, or printing.

longing *n.* an intense persistent wish.

longitude / **long**-guh-tyood / *n.* the distance east or west (measured in degrees) from the meridian of Greenwich.

longitudinal / long-guh-**tyoo**-duh-nuhl / *adj.* **1** of longitude. **2** of or in length, measured lengthwise. □ **longitudinally** *adv.*

longneck *n. Aust. colloq.* a 750 ml bottle of beer (as distinct from a stubby etc.).

longstop *n.* **1** *Cricket* **a** a position directly behind the wicketkeeper. **b** a fielder in this position. **2** a last resort.

longueur / long-**ger** / *n.* **1** a tedious passage in a book etc. **2** a tedious stretch of time. (¶ French, = length.)

longways *adv.* (also **longwise**) lengthways.

loo *n. colloq.* a toilet.

loofah / **loo**-fuh / *n.* the dried pod of a kind of gourd, used as a rough sponge.

look *v.* **1** use one's sight, turn one's eyes in a particular direction (*look at that!*). **2** turn one's eyes on, examine (*looked me up and down; looked him in the eye*). **3** search (*I'll look in the morning; looking for some new shoes*). **4** direct one's attention to examine or investigate (*look at the facts; when one looks deeper*). **5** have a specified appearance (*you look nice; things are looking hopeful*). **6** face (a particular direction) (*the room looked across the lake*). **7** indicate (a specified emotion) in one's face and bearing (*he looks miserable*). • *n.* **1** the act of looking, a gaze or glance. **2** an inspection or search (*have a look at the telly—it's playing up*). **3** (**looks**) the appearance of one's face, esp. when attractive (*good looks; losing his looks*). **4** appearance (*the house had a run-down look*). **5** a style, a fashion (*this year's look; the wet look*). □ **look down on** (or **look down one's nose at**) regard with contempt. **look forward to** be waiting eagerly (or sometimes with anxiety etc.) for an expected thing or event. **look-in** *n.* a chance of participation or success. **look into** investigate. **look on** be a spectator. **look sharp** make haste. **look to 1** consider, be concerned about (*look to the future*). **2** rely on (*we're looking to you for support*). **3** intend (*I'm looking to have it ready for tomorrow*). **look up 1** search for information about (*look up words in a dictionary*). **2** improve in prospects (*things are looking up*). **3** go to visit (*look us up*). **look up to** admire and respect as superior.

lookalike *n.* a person or thing closely resembling another (*a Marilyn Monroe lookalike*).

looker *n. colloq.* an exceptionally attractive person of either sex.

looking glass *n.* a mirror.

lookout *n.* **1** looking out, a watch. **2** one who keeps watch; a place from which watch is kept. **3** *Aust.* an elevated place from which a particular scenic attraction may be viewed. **4** a prospect of luck (*it's a poor lookout for us*). **5** a person's own concern (*that's his lookout*).

loom *n.* an apparatus for weaving cloth. • *v.* **1** come into view dimly but appear close and threatening. **2** (of a future event) seem ominously close.

loon *n.* **1** a diving bird with a loud wild cry. **2** *colloq.* a crazy person.

loony *colloq. n.* a lunatic. • *adj.* crazy. □ **loony bin** a mental home or hospital.

loop *n.* **1** the shape produced by a curve that crosses itself. **2** anything shaped roughly like this. **3** an attachment or fastener shaped like this. **4** a complete circuit for electrical current. **5** a set of computer operations repeated until some specified condition is satisfied. **6** an endless strip of tape or film allowing continuous repetition. **7** a contraceptive coil. **8** a strip of fabric etc. attached to a garment or object so that it can be hung on a peg. • *v.* **1** form into a loop or loops. **2** fasten or join with a loop or loops. **3** enclose in a loop. **4** (also **loop the loop**) (of an aircraft) fly in a vertical loop.

loophole *n.* **1** a way of evading a rule or contract etc., esp. through an omission or inexact wording in its provisions. **2** a narrow vertical slit in the wall of a fort etc.

loose *adj.* **1** detached or detachable from its place, not rigidly fixed (*a loose handle*). **2** freed from bonds or restraint; (of an animal) not tethered or shut in. **3** not fastened, packed, or contained in something (*loose papers*). **4** not organised strictly (*a loose confederation*). **5** slack, relaxed, not tense or tight (*loose skin; loose bowels*). **6** not compact or dense (*a loose weave*). **7** inexact, vague (*a loose translation*). **8** morally lax (*loose living*). • *adv.*

loosen

loosely (*loose-fitting*). • *v.* **1** release. **2** untie or loosen. **3** fire (a missile). ☐ **at a loose end** unoccupied. **loose-leaf** *adj.* (of a notebook etc.) with each leaf separate and removable. **on the loose 1** escaped from captivity. **2** enjoying oneself without restraint. ☐ ☐ **loosely** *adv.* **looseness** *n.*

loosen *v.* make or become loose or looser. ☐ **loosen up 1** relax. **2** limber up.

loot *n.* **1** goods taken from an enemy or by theft. **2** *colloq.* money. • *v.* **1** plunder; take as loot. **2** steal (goods) or rob (premises) left unprotected, esp. after rioting. ☐ **looter** *n.*

lop *v.* (**lopped**, **lopping**) cut away branches or twigs; cut off.

lope *v.* run with a long bounding stride. • *n.* a long bounding stride.

lopsided *adj.* with one side lower, smaller, or heavier than the other.

loquacious / luh-**kway**-shuhs / *adj.* talkative. ☐ **loquacity** / luh-**kwas**-uh-tee / *n.*

loquat / **loh**-kwot / *n.* **1** a tree of the rose family, bearing small yellow egg-shaped fruits. **2** this fruit.

Lorca, Federico García (1898–1936), Spanish poet and playwright.

lord *n.* **1** a master or ruler. **2** *Brit.* a man entitled to the title *Lord*. **3** (**Lord**) God or Christ. • *interj.* (**Lord**) an expression of surprise, dismay, etc. ☐ **lord it over** domineer.

Lord Howe Island an island off the east coast of Australia, 702 km north-east of Sydney. Among the island's fauna is the Lord Howe Island woodhen, one of the world's rarest birds.

lordly *adj.* (**lordlier**, **lordliest**) **1** haughty, imperious. **2** suitable for a lord (*a lordly mansion*).

Lord Mayor the title of the mayor in some large cities.

Lord's a cricket ground in London.

lordship *n.* (foll. by *over*) dominion, rule.

Lord's Prayer the prayer taught by Christ to his disciples, beginning 'Our Father'.

lore *n.* a body of traditions and knowledge on a particular subject or possessed by a particular group (*herbal lore; Aboriginal lore*).

Lorelei / **law**-ruh-luy / a rock or cliff on the Rhine with an unusual echo, in German legend the home of a siren of the same name whose song lured boatmen to destruction.

lorgnette / law-**nyet** / *n.* a pair of spectacles or opera glasses on a long handle.

lorikeet / **lo**-ruh-keet, lo-ruh-**keet** / *n.* any of various small (and usu. mainly green) nectar-feeding parrots of northern and eastern Australia.

lory *n.* (*pl.* **lories**) any of various brightly-coloured parrots occurring in Australasia, the Malay Archipelago, etc.

lose *v.* (**lost**, **losing**) **1** be deprived of or cease to have, esp. through negligence. **2** be deprived of (a person) by death. **3** become unable to find, follow, or understand (*lose one's way*). **4** cease to have, control, or maintain (*lost my balance; lost his temper; we're losing height*). **5** be defeated in a contest, lawsuit, etc. **6** succeed in getting rid of (*lose weight; lost our pursuers*). **7** forfeit (*lost his deposit*). **8** waste time or effort (*lost half an hour in the traffic*). **9** suffer loss, be worse off (*we lost on the deal*). **10** cause (a person) the loss of (*delay lost them the contract*). **11** (of a clock) become slow (*it loses two minutes a day*). ☐ **lose oneself in** become engrossed in. **lose out** *colloq.* be unsuccessful; not get a full chance or advantage. **losing battle** one in which defeat seems certain.

loser *n.* **1** a person or thing that loses, esp. a contest (*he's a bad loser*). **2** *colloq.* a person who regularly fails.

loss *n.* **1** losing; being lost. **2** a person or thing lost. **3** money lost in a business transaction; the excess of outlay over returns. **4** a disadvantage or suffering caused by losing something (*a great loss to me*). ☐ **be at a loss** be puzzled, be unable to know what to do or say.

lost *see* LOSE. • *adj.* **1** strayed or separated from its owner (*a lost dog*). **2** (usu. foll. by *in*) engrossed (*lost in thought*). ☐ **be lost on** be unnoticed or unappreciated by (*subtlety is lost on him*). **be lost without** be extremely dependent on (*I'm lost without my diary*). **get lost!** *colloq.* go away! **lost cause 1** a hopeless effort or undertaking. **2** a person one can no longer help or influence.

Lot (in the Bible) the nephew of Abraham, who was allowed to escape from the destruction of Sodom (Genesis 19). His wife, who disobeyed orders and looked back, was turned into a pillar of salt.

lot *n.* **1** (**a lot** or **lots**) a large number or amount (*a lot of people; lots of gravy*). **2** (**a lot** or **lots**) much (*smiles a lot; lots to do*). **3** (**the lot**) everything (*I'll take the lot*). **4** a group of people or things (*a rowdy lot; that lot's going in the bin*). **5** one of a set of things used in making a chance selection; this method of selection (*was chosen by lot*). **6** a share or responsibility resulting from this. **7** a person's destiny or fortune. **8** a plot of land, or one used for a specified purpose (*parking lot*). **9** an article or group of articles for sale, esp. at an auction. ☐ **a lot** (*or* **a whole lot**) *colloq.* very much (*a whole lot better*). **bad lot** a person of bad character. **draw** (*or* **cast**) **lots** use lots to make a chance selection. **throw in one's lot with** decide to join and share the fortunes of.

loth alternative spelling of LOATH.

Lothario / luh-**thah**-ree-oh, -**thair**-ree-oh / *n.* (*pl.* **Lotharios**) a libertine. (¶ Named after a character in Rowe's play *The Fair Penitent* (1703).)

lotion *n.* a medicinal or cosmetic liquid applied to the skin.

lottery *n.* **1** a system of raising money by selling numbered tickets and giving prizes to the holders of numbers drawn at random. **2** something where the outcome is governed by luck.

lotto *n.* a game resembling bingo but with numbers drawn instead of called.

lotus / loh-tuhs / *n.* (*pl.* **lotuses**) **1** a kind of tropical water lily, esp. as used symbolically in Hinduism and Buddhism. **2** a mythical fruit inducing a state of lazy and luxurious dreaminess. □ **lotus bird** a wading bird of eastern and northern Australia, having long toes which enable it to walk on floating leaves etc. Also called *jacana*, *lily-trotter*. **lotus-eater** a person living a life of lazy enjoyment. **lotus position** a cross-legged position adopted in yoga and for meditating.

loud *adj.* **1** noisy, having a high volume. **2** clamorous, insistent (*loud complaints*). **3** (of behaviour) aggressive; coarse. **4** (of colours etc.) unpleasantly bright, gaudy. •*adv.* loudly. □ **loud hailer** a portable electronic device for amplifying one's voice. □□ **loudly** *adv.* **loudness** *n.*

loudspeaker *n.* an apparatus that converts electrical impulses into sound.

Louis / loo-ee / the name of 18 kings of France, including Louis XIV (reigned 1643–1715), known as the Sun King, whose reign represented the high point of French power in Europe.

lounge *v.* loll, sit or stand about idly. •*n.* **1** (usu. **lounge room**) a sitting room in a private house. **2** a public room (in a hotel) for sitting in. **3** a place in an airport etc. with seats for waiting passengers. □ **lounge suit** a man's ordinary suit for day wear.

lour / lowuh / *v.* (also **lower**) **1** frown or scowl. **2** (of clouds or the sky etc.) look dark and threatening.

Lourdes / loord / a town in SW France where in 1858 a peasant girl, Bernadette Soubirous (later St Bernadette), claimed to have had visions of the Virgin Mary. It is now a major centre of pilgrimage.

louse *n.* **1** (*pl.* **lice**) a small insect that lives as a parasite on animals or plants. **2** (*pl.* **louses**) *colloq.* a contemptible person. •*v.* **1** delouse. **2** *Aust. Mining* pick over (waste material) looking for fragments of the mineral sought. □ **louse up** *colloq.* make a mess of.

lousy / low-zee / *adj.* (**lousier, lousiest**) **1** *colloq.* very bad; disgusting; ill; stingy. **2** *colloq.* well provided; teeming (with) (*he's lousy with money; lousy with tourists*). **3** trifling (*he donated a lousy five dollars*). **4** infested with lice. □ **lousy jack** a mostly grey and very noisy bird which builds its nest of mud and lives in family groups of usu. twelve in wooded parts of eastern Australia. Also called *apostle*.

lout *n.* a rough, crude, or ill-mannered person (usu. a man). □ **loutish** *adj.*

Louvre / loovr / the national museum and art gallery of France, in Paris.

louvre / loo-vuh / *n.* one of a set of overlapping slats arranged to admit air but exclude light or rain.

louvred / loo-vuhd / *adj.* fitted with louvres.

lovable *adj.* (also **loveable**) easy to love.

love *n.* **1** an intense feeling of deep affection or fondness. **2** a great liking (*his love of music*). **3** sexual passion or excitement. **4** sexual relations. **5** a person one loves (*my love; come on, love*). **6** *colloq.* a person one is fond of (*he's a love*). **7** *colloq.* a form of address (*morning, love*). **8** affectionate greetings (*give him my love*). **9** (in certain games) nil, no score (*love thirty*). •*v.* **1** feel a deep affection or fondness for. **2** have a great liking for (*I love Chinese food*). **3** enjoy greatly, find pleasure or satisfaction in, esp. as a habit (*children love dressing up; he loves to find fault*). □ **fall in love** (often foll. by *with*) **1** suddenly and intensely begin to love (a person). **2** begin to live or greatly enjoy (a thing, place etc.). **love affair 1** a romantic or sexual relationship, esp. outside marriage. **2** a feeling of growing fondness and pleasure (*my love affair with Greece*). **love bite** a bruise made by a partner's biting during lovemaking. **love creeper** an Australian twining plant bearing racemes of blue flowers. **love-hate** *adj.* (of a relationship etc.) marked by intense feelings of both love and hate for the same person or thing. **love nest** a secluded, intimate place used by (esp. illicit) lovers. **make love** (often foll. by *to* or *with*) have sexual intercourse (with).

lovebird *n.* **1** *Aust.* a budgerigar. **2** a small African etc. parrot that seems to show great affection for its mate.

loveless *adj.* without love (*a loveless marriage*).

lovelorn *adj.* pining with love; forsaken by one's lover.

lovely *adj.* (**lovelier, loveliest**) **1** beautiful, attractive. **2** *colloq.* delightful (*having a lovely time*). □ **lovely and** *colloq.* delightfully (*lovely and warm*). □□ **loveliness** *n.*

lovemaking *n.* sexual play, esp. sexual intercourse.

lover *n.* **1** someone who is in love with another person. **2** a person with whom another is having sexual relations. **3** (**lovers**) an unmarried couple in love or having sexual relations. **4** one who likes or enjoys something (*lover of music; music lovers*).

lovesick *adj.* languishing because of love.

lovey-dovey *adj. colloq.* fondly affectionate; sentimental.

loving *adj.* feeling or showing love; affectionate. □ **lovingly** *adv.*

low[1] *adj.* **1** not high or tall (*a low wall*). **2** not elevated in position; close to the ground or to sea level (*low hills; low altitude*). **3** below others in importance (*a low priority; lowest of the low*). **4** less than normal (*low prices*). **5** greatly reduced in amount or quantity (*low on fuel*). **6** below the normal level or position (*low neckline*). **7** sad, depressed (*feeling low*). **8** not loud or high-pitched (*a low voice*). **9** unfavourable (*a low opinion*). **10** mean, common (*low cunning*). •*n.* **1** a low level or figure (*share prices reached a new low*). **2** an area of low barometric pressure. •*adv.* **1** in or at or to a low level or position. **2** in or to a low degree. **3** in a low tone; (of sound) at a low pitch. ☐ **low-down** *adj*. mean, dishonourable; *n. colloq*. the true facts, inside information. **low frequency** (in radio) 30 to 300 kilohertz. **low gear** a gear such that the driven end of a transmission revolves more slowly than the driving end. **low-key** *adj*. restrained, not intense or emotional. **low-level** *adj*. **1** (of a computer language) close in form to machine code. **2** close to the ground or to sea level (*low-level airstrike*). **low-pitched** (of a voice or sound) low; (of a roof) having only a slight slope. **low pressure 1** a low degree of activity or exertion. **2** an atmospheric condition with the pressure below average. **low profile** avoidance of attention or publicity. **low-rise** *adj*. (of a building) having few storeys. **low season** the period when a resort etc. has relatively few visitors. **low-tech** *adj*. of or using technology based on the effective use of cheap, simple components and local resources. **low tide** the tide at its lowest level; the time when this occurs. **low water** low tide.

low² *n*. the deep sound made by cattle, a moo. • *v*. make this sound.

lowan / loh-uhn / *n. Aust*. = MALLEE FOWL. (¶ Wemba-wemba)

lowbrow *adj*. not intellectual or cultured. • *n*. a lowbrow person.

Low Church the section of the Anglican Church that attaches little importance to ritual, priestly authority, and the sacraments.

Low Countries the Netherlands, Belgium, and Luxembourg.

lower¹ *adj*. **1** less high in place or position. **2** situated below another part (*lower lip*). **3** situated on less high land to the south (*Lower Egypt*). **4** (of an animal or plant) not highly developed, primitive. • *adv*. in or to a lower position etc. • *v*. **1** let or haul down. **2** make or become lower. ☐ **lower case** (of letters) not capitals. **lower house** (*or* **chamber**) **1** the larger body (in a two-house legislature) directly responsible for law making (as opposed to UPPER HOUSE). **2** = HOUSE OF REPRESENTATIVES. **3** = LEGISLATIVE ASSEMBLY.

lower² alternative spelling of LOUR.

lowest *adj*. least high in position or status. ☐ **lowest common denominator 1** *Maths* the lowest common multiple of the denominators of several fractions. **2** the least attractive or positive features of a group or community. **lowest common multiple** *Maths* the lowest amount that is a multiple of two or more given numbers.

lowland *n*. low-lying land. • *adj*. of or in lowland.

lowlight *n*. a monotonous or dull period; a feature of little prominence (*one of the lowlights of the evening*).

lowly *adj*. (**lowlier**, **lowliest**) of humble rank or condition. ☐ **lowliness** *n*.

lowset / loh-set / *Aust. adj*. (of a house, unit, etc., esp. in northern Australia) built close to the ground or on a concrete slab. • *n*. such a house.

loyal *adj*. true or faithful in one's commitment to one's friends, beliefs, etc. ☐ **loyally** *adv*. **loyalty** *n*.

lozenge *n*. **1** a four-sided diamond-shaped figure. **2** a small tablet or sweet to be dissolved in the mouth.

LP *abbr*. a long-playing record.

LPG *abbr*. liquefied petroleum gas.

L-plate *n*. a sign bearing the letter 'L', fixed to a vehicle that is being driven by a learner.

Lr *symbol* lawrencium.

LSD *n*. a powerful hallucinogenic drug (= lysergic acid diethylamide).

Ltd *abbr*. Limited.

Lu *symbol* lutetium.

Luanda / loo-an-duh / the capital of Angola.

luau / loo-ow / *n*. a Hawaiian party or feast usu. accompanied by some form of entertainment.

lubber *n*. a clumsy fellow, a lout. ☐ **lubberly** *adj*.

lube / loob / *n. US & Aust. colloq*. a grease and oil change for a motor vehicle.

lubra / loo-bruh / *n. Aust. offens*. an Aboriginal woman. (¶ Perhaps from a Tas. Aboriginal language.)

lubricant / loo-bruh-kuhnt / *n*. a substance used to reduce friction.

lubricate / loo-bruh-kayt / *v*. **1** oil or grease (machinery etc.) so that it moves easily. **2** make slippery. ☐ **lubrication** *n*. **lubricator** *n*.

lubricious *adj*. (also **lubricous**) **1** slippery, evasive. **2** lewd. ☐ **lubricity** *n*.

lucerne / loo-sern, loo-suhn / *n*. alfalfa, a clover-like plant used for fodder and, when very young, as a health food.

lucid / loo-suhd / *adj*. **1** clearly expressed, easy to understand. **2** sane. ☐ **lucidly** *adv*. **lucidity** / loo-sid-uh-tee / *n*.

Lucifer / loo-suh-fuh / *n*. **1** Satan, the Devil. **2** the morning star (the planet Venus). **3** (**lucifer**) *archaic* a friction match.

luck *n*. **1** chance thought of as the bringer of good or bad fortune. **2** the events etc. (favourable or unfavourable) that it brings. **3** good fortune (*it will bring you luck*). ☐ **no such luck** *colloq*. unfortunately not.

luckless *adj*. unlucky.

lucky *adj*. (**luckier**, **luckiest**) having or bringing or resulting from good luck. ☐ **luckily** *adv*.

Lucky Country, the (a chiefly ironic) name for Australia as a land of opportunity. (¶ The title of a book by Donald Horne (1964).)

lucrative / loo-kruh-tiv / *adj*. profitable, producing much money. ☐ **lucrativeness** *n*.

lucre / loo-kuh / *n. derog*. money; money-making as a motive for action. ☐ **filthy lucre** *humorous* money.

Luddite / lud-uyt / *n*. **1** *hist*. a member of the bands of English workers (1811–16) who destroyed newly introduced machinery which they thought would cause unemployment. **2** a person who opposes the introduction of new technology (such as computers etc.) or new working methods. (¶ Probably named after Ned Lud, a person who destroyed some machinery c.1779.) ❑ **Luddism** n. **Ludditism** n.

luderick / **loo**-duh-rik / n. a highly valued brown or silvery-green marine and estuarine food fish of eastern Australia. (¶ Ganay)

ludicrous / **loo**-duh-kruhs / adj. absurd, ridiculous, laughable. ❑ **ludicrously** adv.

luff v. steer (a ship) nearer the wind.

Luftwaffe / **luuft**-vah-fuh / n. the German air force before and during the Second World War.

lug v. (**lugged, lugging**) **1** drag or carry with great effort. **2** pull hard. • n. **1** a hard or rough pull. **2** a projection on an object by which it may be carried or fixed in place etc.

luggage n. suitcases and bags etc. containing a traveller's belongings.

lugger n. a small ship with four-cornered sails.

lugubrious / luh-**goo**-bree-uhs / adj. dismal, mournful. ❑ **lugubriously** adv.

Luke, St **1** an evangelist, traditionally the author of the third Gospel and the Acts of the Apostles. **2** the third Gospel.

lukewarm adj. **1** only slightly warm. **2** not enthusiastic (got a lukewarm reception).

lull v. **1** soothe or send to sleep. **2** calm (a person) or allay (suspicion etc.), esp. by deception. **3** (of a storm or noise) lessen, become quiet. • n. a temporary period of quiet or inactivity.

lullaby n. a soothing song sung to send a child to sleep.

lulu / **loo**-loo / n. colloq. a remarkable or excellent person or thing.

lumbago / lum-**bay**-goh / n. rheumatic pain in the muscles of the lower back.

lumbar adj. of or in the lower back. ❑ **lumbar puncture** the extraction of spinal fluid from the lower back for diagnosis, using a hollow needle.

lumber n. **1** disused or inconvenient articles of furniture etc. **2** partly prepared timber. • v. **1** (usu. foll. by with) leave (a person etc.) with something unwanted or unpleasant. **2** fill up (space) inconveniently. **3** move in a heavy clumsy way. **4** cut and prepare forest timber. **5** Aust. colloq. arrest; imprison.

lumberjack n. US & Canada = LOGGER.

luminary / **loo**-muh-nuh-ree / n. **1** a natural light-giving body, esp. the sun or moon. **2** an eminent or influential person.

luminescent / loo-muh-**nes**-uhnt / adj. emitting light without being hot. ❑ **luminescence** n.

luminous / **loo**-muh-nuhs / adj. emitting light, glowing in the dark. ❑ **luminosity** / loo-muh-**nos**-uh-tee / n.

lump n. **1** a hard or compact mass, usu. one without a regular shape. **2** a tumour; a swelling or bruise. **3** a heavy, dull, or clumsy person. • v. put or consider together, treat as alike (lump them all together). ❑ **lump in the throat** a feeling of pressure there caused by emotion. **lump it** colloq. put up with something one dislikes. **lump sum** a single payment covering a number of items, or paid all at once rather than by instalments.

lumpectomy n. surgical removal of a lump of tissue from the breast.

lumpish adj. heavy and clumsy or stupid.

lumpy adj. (**lumpier, lumpiest**) full of lumps; covered in lumps. ❑ **lumpily** adv. **lumpiness** n.

lunacy n. **1** insanity. **2** great folly.

lunar adj. of the moon. ❑ **lunar month 1** the interval between new moons (about 29½ days). **2** four weeks.

lunate / **loo**-nayt / adj. crescent-shaped.

lunatic n. **1** an insane person. **2** one who is extremely foolish or reckless. • adj. insane; extremely foolish or reckless. ❑ **lunatic asylum** archaic a mental home or mental hospital. **lunatic fringe** a few eccentric or fanatical members of a political or other group.

lunation / loo-**nay**-shuhn / n. the interval between new moons, about 29½ days.

lunch n. a meal taken in the middle of the day. • v. **1** eat lunch. **2** entertain to lunch.

luncheon n. formal lunch.

lunette / loo-**net** / n. **1** an arched aperture in a dome to admit light. **2** a crescent-shaped or semicircular space or alcove meant to contain a statue etc. **3** Catholic Church a crescent-shaped holder for the consecrated Host in a monstrance. **4** Aust. a crescent-shaped dune, formed on the lee side of a lake basin in parts of arid Australia.

lung n. either of the two organs used for breathing by humans and most other vertebrates.

lunge n. **1** a sudden forward movement of the body towards something; a thrust. **2** a long rope on which a horse is held by its trainer while it is made to canter in a circle. • v. (**lunged, lunging**) **1** (often foll. by at or out) make a lunge. **2** exercise (a horse) on a lunge.

lungfish n. (in full **Queensland lungfish**) a unique freshwater Australian fish remarkable in that it has both lungs and gills.

lunula / **loo**-nyuh-luh / n. (pl. **lunulae** / -lee /) a crescent-shaped mark, esp. the white area at the base of the fingernail.

lupine / **loo**-puyn / adj. of or like wolves.

lupus / **loo**-puhs / n. a skin disease producing ulcers, esp. tuberculosis of the skin.

lurch n. an unsteady swaying movement to one side. • v. make such a movement, stagger. ❑ **leave in the lurch** abandon (a person etc.) in an awkward situation.

lure / loor, lyoor / n. **1** something that attracts or entices. **2** its power of attracting. **3** a bait or decoy for wild animals. • v. entice, attract (a person) by the promise of pleasure or gain; attract (an animal) with a bait etc.

lurex n. trademark **1** a type of yarn containing glittering metallic threads. **2** fabric made from this.

lurgy / **ler**-gee / n. (pl. **lurgies**) (esp. in the phrase **the dreaded lurgy**) jocular an unspecified illness.

lurid / **loo**-ruhd / adj. **1** in glaring colours or combinations of colour. **2** sensationally and shockingly vivid (*the lurid details*). ☐ **luridly** adv. **luridness** n.

Lurie, Morris (1938–), Australian writer acclaimed esp. for his short stories.

Luritja / luh-**rich**-uh / n. a dialect of the WESTERN DESERT LANGUAGE.

lurk v. **1** hide or wait stealthily; prowl. **2** lie hidden, waiting or as if waiting to attack. **3** be latent or lingering (*a lurking suspicion*). •n. Aust. colloq. **1** a dodge, racket, or scheme. **2** a job.

Lusaka / loo-**sah**-kuh / the capital of Zambia.

luscious / **lush**-uhs / adj. **1** richly sweet in taste or smell. **2** voluptuously attractive. ☐ **lusciously** adv. **lusciousness** n.

lush adj. **1** (of vegetation) growing thickly and strongly. **2** luxurious (*lush furnishings*). **3** colloq. excellent. **4** colloq. good-looking, sexually attractive. ☐ **lushly** adv. **lushness** n.

lust n. **1** intense sexual desire. **2** any intense desire for something (*lust for power*). •v. (usu. foll. by *after* or *for*) feel lust. ☐ **lustful** adj. **lustfully** adv.

lustre / **lus**-tuh / n. **1** the soft brightness of a smooth or shining surface. **2** glory, distinction (*her success adds lustre to our town*). **3** a metallic glaze on pottery and porcelain. ☐ **lustrous** / **lus**-truhs / adj.

lusty adj. (**lustier**, **lustiest**) strong and vigorous, full of vitality. ☐ **lustily** adv. **lustiness** n.

lute / loot, lyoot / n. a guitar-like instrument with a pear-shaped body, popular in the 14th–17th centuries.

lutenist n. a lute player.

lutetium / loo-**tee**-shuhm / n. a metallic element (symbol Lu).

Luther / **loo**-thuh /, Martin (1483–1546), a German Catholic friar who became the founder of the Protestant Reformation in Germany. ☐ **Lutheran** adj. & n. **Lutheranism** n.

luthier / **loo**-tee-uh, **lyoo**- / n. a maker of stringed instruments, esp. those of the violin family.

lux n. the SI unit of illumination.

Luxembourg 1 a grand duchy lying between France and Germany. **2** its capital city. ☐ **Luxembourger** n.

Luxor a city of Egypt, site of the southern complex of monuments of ancient Thebes.

luxuriant / lug-**zhoo**-ree-uhnt / adj. **1** (of plants etc.) growing profusely. **2** exuberant. ☐ **luxuriance** n.

■ **Usage** Do not confuse with *luxurious*.

luxuriate / lug-**zhoo**-ree-ayt / v. feel great enjoyment, enjoy as luxury (*luxuriating in the warm sun*).

luxurious / lug-**zhoo**-ree-uhs / adj. supplied with luxuries, very comfortable. ☐ **luxuriously** adv. **luxuriousness** n.

■ **Usage** Do not confuse with *luxuriant*.

luxury / **luk**-shuh-ree / n. **1** surroundings and food, dress, etc. that are choice and costly. **2** luxuriousness; self-indulgence. **3** something costly that is enjoyable but not essential.

Lw symbol lawrencium.

lycanthrope / luy-kuhn-**throhp** / n. **1** a werewolf. **2** an insane person who believes that he or she is a wolf (or other animal).

lycanthropy / luy-**kan**-thruh-pee / n. **1** the mythical transformation of a person into a wolf at certain periods (see also WEREWOLF). **2** a form of madness involving the delusion of being a wolf.

lych-gate alternative spelling of LICH-GATE.

lychee / **luy**-chee / n. (also **lichee**, **litchi**) **1** a sweet white fleshy fruit with a brown skin. **2** the tree from which this is obtained, originally Chinese.

lycra n. trademark an elastic fabric used esp. for close-fitting clothing.

lye n. **1** water made alkaline with wood ashes. **2** any alkaline solution for washing things.

lying see LIE^1, LIE^2.

lymph / limf / n. **1** a colourless fluid containing white blood cells. **2** this fluid used as a vaccine. ☐ **lymph gland** (or **node**) any of the small glands in the **lymphatic system** (network of vessels carrying lymph) that protect against infection. ☐☐ **lymphatic** adj.

lymphoma / lim-**foh**-muh / n. (pl. **lymphomas** or **lymphomata**) a tumour of the lymph glands.

lynch / linch / v. (of a mob) kill (a suspected wrongdoer) without a legal trial. ☐ **lynch law** the procedure followed when a person is lynched. ☐☐ **lynching** n.

lynx / lingks / n. (pl. **lynx** or **lynxes**) a wild cat with spotted fur, tufted ears, and a short tail.

Lyons, Dame Enid (Muriel) (1897–1981), Australian politician, one of the first two women to be elected to the House of Representatives.

Lyons, Joseph (Aloysius) (1879–1939), Australian politician, Labor premier of Tas., then United Australia Party prime minister 1932–39, husband of Enid Muriel Lyons.

lyre n. an ancient musical instrument with strings fixed in a U-shaped frame.

lyrebird n. either of two species of ground-dwelling bird of forest in south-east mainland Australia, noted for its remarkable power of mimicry, and for the long lyre-shaped tail displayed by the male (*Albert lyrebird*; *superb lyrebird*).

lyric / **li**-rik / adj. **1** (of poetry) expressing the poet's thoughts and feelings, usually briefly and in stanzas; songlike. **2** (of a voice) light in timbre (*lyric tenor*; *lyric soprano*). •n. **1** a lyric poem. **2** (**lyrics**) the words of a song.

lyrical / **li**-ri-kuhl / adj. **1** lyric; using language suitable for lyric poetry. **2** songlike. **3** colloq.

expressing oneself enthusiastically (*waxing lyrical about Australian wildflowers*). ☐ **lyrically** *adv.*

lyricism / li-ruh-siz-uhm / *n.* an artist's expression of emotion in an imaginative and beautiful way; the quality of being lyric.

lyricist *n.* a writer of (esp. popular) lyrics.

lyssavirus / **lis**-uh-vuy-ruhs / *n.* a virus with a number of sub-types, including the classic rabies virus, and a virus discovered in fruit bats in Australia in 1996.

M

M *abbr.* (also **M.**) **1** mega-. **2** (of a film) classified as 'for Mature audiences only', and (on television) not to be broadcast before 8.30 p.m. • *n.* (as a Roman numeral) 1,000.

m *abbr.* (also **m.**) **1** metre(s). **2** mile(s). **3** million(s). **4** minute(s). **5** male; masculine. **6** married. **7** milli-.

'm *abbr. colloq.* am (*I'm sorry*).

MA *abbr.* Master of Arts.

ma'am / mam, mahm / *n.* madam (used in addressing a woman formally).

Mabo[1], Eddie (Koiki) (1939–92), an Australian Mer (Murray) Islander in the Torres Strait, a skilled exponent and teacher of Meriam song and dance, a member of the Aboriginal Arts Board of the Australia Council, known Australia-wide today because in 1982 he began legal proceedings to establish the Mer people's traditional ownership of their land and his name was given to the benchmark judgment of the High Court of Australia in 1992 (*see* MABO[2]).

Mabo[2] / **mah**-boh / *n.* (in full **the Mabo decision**) *Aust.* the High Court judgment of 1992 recognising continuous possession of their lands by the Torres Strait Mer (Murray) Islanders before these lands were annexed by Qld, a judgment which refuted the legal fiction that Australia was TERRA NULLIUS (territory belonging to no-one) when the whites took possession of it and dispossessed the Aborigines. This judgment is of continuing significance. (*See also* NATIVE TITLE.)

mac *n.* (also **mack**) *colloq.* a mackintosh.

macabre / muh-**kah**-buh, -bruh, -**kahbr** / *adj.* gruesome, suggesting death.

macadam / muh-**kad**-uhm / *n.* **1** layers of broken stone used in road making, each layer being rolled hard before the next is put down. **2** = TARMACADAM.

macadamia / ma-kuh-**day**-mee-uh / *n.* an eastern Australian rainforest tree cultivated for its large edible nut; this nut.

macadamise / muh-**kad**-uh-muyz / *v.* (also -**ize**) surface with macadam.

macaque / muh-**kak**, -**kahk** / *n.* a monkey of India and SE Asia, with prominent cheek pouches.

macaroni *n.* **1** short thick tubes of pasta. **2** *Aust.* nonsense, baloney.

macaroon *n.* a small light cake or biscuit made with egg whites, ground almonds, coconut, etc.

Macarthur[1], Elizabeth (?1767–1850), a pioneering Australian pastoralist, instrumental in establishing the fine-wool industry with her Spanish merino breeding program.

Macarthur[2], John (1766–1834), a pioneering Australian pastoralist, husband of Elizabeth Macarthur; he spent forced periods in England as a result of disputes with Governors Hunter and King and because of his role in the rum rebellion.

McAuley, James (Phillip) (1917–76), AM, Australian poet and critic, one of the instigators of the Ern Malley Hoax.

macaw / muh-**kaw** / *n.* a brightly coloured American parrot with a long tail.

Macbeth (*c.*1005–57), King of Scotland 1040–57.

McBride, William (Griffith) (1927–), AO, Australian gynaecologist whose medical research established that the drug thalidomide taken during pregnancy causes birth defects.

McCarthyism *n.* **1** anti-Communist persecution, verging on public hysteria, prevalent in the US in the decade following the Second World War. **2** any similar witch hunt (e.g. for whistle-blowers etc.) in a government or other organisation etc. (¶ Named after the American senator J.R. McCarthy (1909–57).)

Maccabiah Games / mak-uh-**bee**-uh / an Olympic-style sporting competition for Jewish athletes, held every four years in the year following the Olympics.

McCartney, Sir (James) Paul (1942–), English guitarist, singer, and songwriter, a member of the Beatles.

macchiato / mak-ee-**ah**-toh / *n.* a short black coffee with a small amount of milk or cream.

McCoy / muh-**koi** / *n.* ▫ **the real McCoy** *colloq.* the real thing, the genuine article.

McCubbin, Frederick (1855–1917), Australian landscape painter and member of the Heidelberg School.

McCullough / muh-**kul**-uhk /, Colleen (Margaretta) (1937–), Australian writer. Her novels include *The Thorn Birds* (1977).

McDonald, Garry (1948–), Australian television and film actor, esp. noted for his performances in *The Norman Gunston Show* and *Mother and Son*.

MacDonnell Ranges an extensive series of parallel ranges stretching 400 km east-west across the south-central region of the NT, the highest peak being Mount Zeil (1519 m).

mace[1] *n.* **1** a ceremonial staff, esp. that symbolising the Speaker's authority in the House of Representatives. **2** *hist.* a heavy war club with a metal head and spikes.

**mace² ** *n.* a spice made from the dried outer covering of nutmeg.

mace³ *n.* (also **mace gas**) *trademark* a chemical spray designed to be sprayed on a person, crowd, etc., that offers violence: the chemical incapacitates them by causing temporary extreme irritation esp. to the eyes.

macédoine / mas-uh-**dwahn** / *n.* a mixture of chopped fruits or vegetables, often served set in jelly.

Macedon / **mas**-uh-duhn / ancient Macedonia.

Macedonia / mas-uh-**doh**-nee-uh / **1** an ancient country at the NE end of the Greek peninsula. **2** a republic of former Yugoslavia. ☐ **Macedonian** *adj.* & *n.*

macerate / **mas**-uh-rayt / *v.* make or become soft by steeping in a liquid. ☐ **maceration** *n.*

McEwen, Sir John (1900–80), Australian Country Party statesman, caretaker prime minister for three weeks in 1967–68.

mach / mahk / *n.* (in full **mach number**) the ratio of the speed of a body to the speed of sound in the same medium; a body travelling at *mach one* is travelling at the speed of sound, *mach two* is twice this. (¶ Named after the Austrian physicist Ernst Mach (1838–1916).)

machete / muh-**shet**-ee / *n.* a broad heavy knife.

machiavellian / mak-ee-uh-**vel**-ee-uhn / *adj.* elaborately cunning or deceitful. ☐ **machiavellianism** *n.* (¶ Named after Niccolo dei Machiavelli (1469–1527), an Italian statesman who advised the use of any means, however unscrupulous, that would strengthen the State.)

machicolation / muh-chik-uh-**lay**-shuhn / *n.* an opening between the supports of a projecting parapet through which missiles could be hurled down on attackers.

machinate / **mak**-uh-nayt / *v.* scheme cunningly. ☐ **machination** *n.*

machine *n.* **1** an apparatus for applying mechanical power, having several interrelated parts. **2** something operated by such apparatus, e.g. a bicycle or aircraft. **3** a complex controlling system of an organisation (*the party machine*). • *v.* make, produce, or work on (a thing) with a machine; stitch with a sewing machine. ☐ **machine code** (*or* **language**) a computer language to which a particular computer can respond directly without further translation. **machine-gun** *n.* an automatic gun giving rapid continuous fire. *v.* shoot at with a machine-gun. **machine-independent** (of software etc.) capable of use on any computer. **machine-readable** in a form that a computer can respond to. **machine tool** a power-driven machine such as a lathe or a grinding machine used in engineering to shape metals, plastics, etc.

machinery *n.* **1** machines. **2** a mechanism. **3** an organised system for doing something.

machinist *n.* a person who makes or works machinery; one who operates machine tools.

machismo / muh-**chiz**-moh, -**kiz**- / *n.* virility or masculine pride; a show of this.

macho / **mach**-oh / *adj.* aggressively masculine.

macintosh alternative spelling of MACKINTOSH.

McKay¹ Heather (Pamela) (1941–), AO, Australian squash player, the first women's world squash champion. She was undefeated for eighteen years.

McKay² Hugh Victor (1865–1926), Australian inventor who patented the Sunshine Harvester (after which the city of Sunshine in the Melbourne metropolitan area was named).

Mackellar, Dorothea (1885–1968), Australian poet, best known for her poem 'My Country' which contains the line 'I love a sunburnt country'.

mackerel *n.* (*pl.* **mackerel** *or* **mackerels**) **1** a silvery-greenish marine food fish of southern Australian waters. **2** a food fish of the North Atlantic.

McKern, Leo (Reginald) (1920–), AO, Australian stage, television, and film actor, best known for his lead role in the television series *Rumpole of the Bailey*.

Mackerras, Sir (Alan) Charles (1925–), Australian conductor.

McKillop, Blessed Mary Helen (Mother Mary of the Cross) (1842–1909), Australian nun who founded the Sisters of St Joseph of the Sacred Heart and worked all her life for the education of poor children. Beatified in Sydney in 1995 by Pope John Paul II, she is Australia's first Blessed.

mackintosh *n.* (also **macintosh**) **1** a raincoat. **2** waterproof material of rubber and cloth.

Maclean Donald Duart (1913–83), British Foreign Office official and Soviet spy.

McLuhan / muh-**kloo**-uhn /, (Herbert) Marshall (1911–80), Canadian writer, noted for his studies of mass communications.

McMahon, Sir William ('Billy') (1908–88), Australian Liberal statesman, prime minister 1971–72.

Macquarie¹ a river in NSW, flowing from the Great Dividing Range 960 km north-west to join the River Darling. ☐ **Macquarie perch** a freshwater Australian fish highly valued for its fine flesh.

Macquarie² Lachlan (1762–1824), Scottish governor of NSW, 1810–21, his term being noted for extensive building and road making etc., and for a humane treatment of Aborigines and convicts.

Macquarie Island an island in the sub-Antarctic region, 800 nautical miles south-east of Tas., containing a scientific base and a sanctuary for the island's rare flora and fauna, including the endemic royal penguin.

macramé / muh-**krah**-may, -**krah**-mee / *n.* **1** the art of knotting cord to make decorative articles. **2** items made in this way.

macro- *comb. form* **1** large, large scale. **2** long.

macrobiotic / mak-roh-buy-**ot**-ik / *adj.* of or following a dietary system comprising wholefoods grown in close harmony with the patterns of nature.

macrocosm / **mak**-ruh-koz-uhm / *n.* **1** the universe. **2** any great whole.

macroeconomics *n.* the study of the economy as a whole. ◻ **macroeconomic** *adj.*

macromolecule *n.* a molecule containing a very large number of atoms.

macron / **mak**-ron / *n.* a mark placed over a long or stressed vowel (for example, ō).

macropidia / mak-roh-**pid**-ee-uh / *n.* a WA kangaroo paw bearing spikes of green flowers densely covered in jet black hairs. Also called *black kangaroo paw.*

macropod / **mak**-ruh-pod / *n.* any plant-eating marsupial such as the kangaroo and the wallaby.

macroscopic / mak-ruh-**skop**-ik / *adj.* **1** visible to the naked eye. **2** regarded in terms of large units. ◻ **macroscopically** *adv.*

macrozamia / mak-roh-**zay**-mee-uh / *n.* any of several Australian cycads with long dark-green palm-like leaves and pineapple-like cones bearing highly nutritious but toxic seeds, edible only after being treated in a special way (as was traditionally done by the Aborigines). Also called *wild pineapple, burrawang.*

macula *n.* (*pl.* **maculae**) a dark spot on the skin. ◻ **maculation** *n.*

mad *adj.* (**madder, maddest**) **1** having a disordered mind, not sane. **2** (of an animal) rabid. **3** extremely foolish (*a mad scheme*). **4** wildly enthusiastic (*is mad about footy*). **5** *colloq.* very annoyed. **6** frenzied (*a mad scramble*). **7** wildly light-hearted (*had a mad time celebrating*). ◻ **like mad** *colloq.* with great haste, energy, or enthusiasm. **mad cow disease** *see* BSE. ◻◻ **madness** *n.*

Madagascar an island republic off the SE coast of Africa.

madam *n.* **1** a word used in speaking politely to a woman, or prefixed to the name of her office in formal address (*Madam Chair*). **2** *colloq.* a woman in charge of a brothel.

Madame / muh-**dahm** / *n.* (*pl.* **Mesdames** / may-dahm /) the title of a French-speaking woman, = Mrs *or* madam.

madcap *adj.* wildly impulsive. • *n.* a wildly impulsive person.

madden *v.* make mad or angry; irritate.

made *see* MAKE. ◻ **have** (*or* **have got**) **it made** *colloq.* be sure of success. **made to measure** tailor-made; made for a particular person. **made-up 1** wearing make-up. **2** invented, not true. **3** already prepared, ready-made (*made-up salad dressing*).

Madeira the largest of a group of islands (**the Madeiras**) in the Atlantic Ocean off NW Africa which are in Portuguese possession but partly autonomous. • *n.* a fortified white wine produced in Madeira. ◻ **Madeira cake** a rich plain sponge cake.

Mademoiselle / mad-mwuh-**zel** / *n.* (*pl.* **Mesdemoiselles** / mayd-mwuh-**zel** /) the title of a French-speaking girl or unmarried woman, = Miss *or* madam.

madhouse *n. colloq.* **1** *archaic* a mental home or mental hospital. **2** a scene of confused uproar.

madison / **mad**-uh-suhn / *n. Cycling* a long-distance track race for teams of riders. (¶ Named after *Madison* Square Garden, USA, where such races originated.)

madly *adv.* **1** in a mad manner. **2** *colloq.* passionately. **3** *colloq.* extremely.

mado / **may**-doh / *n.* a small sea fish found near wharves and inlets of eastern Australia. (¶ Perhaps from a NSW Aboriginal language.)

Madonna[1] *n.* **1** (**the Madonna**) the Virgin Mary. **2** (**madonna**) a picture or statue of her. ◻ **madonna lily** a tall lily with white flowers.

Madonna[2] (full name: Madonna Louise Veronica Ciccone) (1958–), American singer and film actor.

Madras / muh-**dras**, muh-**drahs** / a seaport on the east coast of India.

Madrid the capital of Spain.

madrigal / **mad**-ri-guhl / *n.* a part-song for voices, usu. without instrumental accompaniment.

maelstrom / **mayl**-struhm / *n.* **1** a great whirlpool. **2** a confused state.

maenad / **mee**-nad / *n.* **1** a bacchante. **2** a frenzied woman.

maestro / **muy**-stroh / *n.* (*pl.* **maestri** *or* **maestros**) **1** a great musical composer, teacher, or conductor. **2** a master of any art.

Mae West *n. colloq.* an inflatable life jacket. (¶ Named after an American film actor (1892–1980) noted for her large bust.)

Mafia / **maf**-ee-uh, **mah**-fee-uh / *n.* **1** (**the Mafia**) an organised group of criminals originating in Sicily, aiming to influence business and politics in Italy and the USA. **2** (**mafia**) a network of people regarded as exerting hidden influence.

Mafioso / maf-ee-**oh**-soh, mah-fee- / *n.* (*pl.* **Mafiosi**) a member of the Mafia.

mag[1] *n. colloq.* a magazine.

mag[2] *Aust. colloq. v.* prattle, talk incessantly. • *n.* gossip or chat.

magazine *n.* **1** a paper-covered illustrated periodical publication containing articles or stories etc. by a number of writers. **2** a store for arms, ammunition, or explosives. **3** a chamber for holding cartridges to be fed into the breech of a gun. **4** a similar device in a camera or slide projector.

mage *n.* **1** (now used primarily in fantasy literature) a wizard. **2** *archaic* a wise and learned person.

Magellan / muh-**jel**-uhn /, Ferdinand (c.1480–1521), Portuguese explorer, who reached South America and rounded the continent through the strait which now bears his name.

magenta / muh-**jen**-tuh / n. & adj. bright purplish red.

maggie Aust. colloq. = MAGPIE (sense 1).

maggot n. a larva, esp. of the blowfly. ◻ **maggoty** adj.

maggotty adj. (also **maggoty**) Aust. colloq. angry; bad-tempered.

Magi / **may**-juy / n.pl. **1** see MAGUS. **2** (in Christian belief) the 'wise men' from the East who brought offerings to the infant Christ at Bethlehem.

magic n. **1** the supposed art of controlling events or effects etc. by supernatural power. **2** witchcraft. **3** conjuring tricks. **4** a mysterious and enchanting quality (*the magic of a spring day*). • adj. of magic; used in producing magic (*magic words*). • v. (**magicked**, **magicking**) **1** change or create by or as if by magic. **2** (foll. by *away*) cause to disappear by or as if by magic. ◻ **magic eye** a photoelectric device that is able to detect movement, used to operate burglar alarms, automatic doors, etc. **magic pudding** Aust. a never-ending or endlessly renewable resource. (¶ From Norman Lindsay's children's story *The Magic Pudding* (1918), in which a pudding instantly renews itself as slices are cut out of it.) ◻◻ **magical** adj. **magically** adv.

magician / muh-**jish**-uhn / n. **1** a person who is skilled in magic. **2** a conjuror.

magisterial / maj-uh-**steer**-ree-uhl / adj. **1** of a magistrate. **2** having or showing authority, imperious. ◻ **magisterially** adv.

magistracy / **maj**-uhs-truh-see / n. **1** the office of magistrate. **2** magistrates collectively.

magistrate n. an official with authority to administer the law, hear and judge minor cases, and hold preliminary hearings. ◻ **magistrates' court** a court where such cases and hearings are held.

magma n. a fluid or semi-fluid material under the earth's crust, from which igneous rock is formed by cooling.

Magna Carta / **kah**-tuh / (also **Magna Charta**) the charter establishing people's rights concerning personal and political liberty, forced from King John by the English in 1215.

magnanimous / mag-**nan**-uh-muhs / adj. noble and generous in one's conduct, not petty. ◻ **magnanimously** adv. **magnanimity** / mag-nuh-**nim**-uh-tee / n.

magnate / **mag**-nayt, -nuht / n. a wealthy and influential person, esp. in business.

magnesia / mag-**nee**-zhuh, -shuh, -zee-uh / n. a white powder that is a compound of magnesium, used as an antacid and mild laxative.

magnesium / mag-**nee**-zee-uhm / n. a chemical element (symbol Mg), a silvery-white metal that burns with an intensely bright flame.

magnet n. **1** a piece of iron or steel etc. that can attract iron and that points north and south when suspended. **2** a person or thing that exerts a powerful attraction.

magnetic adj. **1** having the properties of a magnet. **2** produced or acting by magnetism. **3** having the power to attract people (*a magnetic personality*). ◻ **magnetic anthill** Aust. a wall-like nest constructed by the magnetic termites of Australia, with the long axis of the nest pointing roughly north-south. **magnetic disk** a computer disk. **magnetic field** the area of force around a magnet. **magnetic mine** an underwater mine detonated by the approach of a mass of metal, e.g. a ship. **magnetic needle** a piece of magnetised steel that points north and south, used as an indicator on the dial of a compass. **magnetic north** the direction indicated by a compass needle, at a slight angle to that of true north. **magnetic pole** either of the two points, in the region of the geographical North and South Poles, indicated by the needle of a magnetic compass. **magnetic resonance imaging** a form of medical imaging using the nuclear magnetic resonance of protons in the body. **magnetic storm** disturbance of the earth's magnetic field by charged particles from the sun etc. **magnetic tape** a strip of plastic coated with magnetic particles for recording sound or other signals. **magnetic termite** Aust. a termite of northern Australia which builds a nest like a brick wall (see MAGNETIC ANTHILL). ◻◻ **magnetically** adv.

magnetise v. (also **-ize**) **1** give magnetic properties to. **2** attract as a magnet does. **3** exert attraction on (a person or people). ◻ **magnetisation** n.

magnetism n. **1** the properties and effects of magnetic substances. **2** the scientific study of these. **3** great charm and attraction (*personal magnetism*).

magnetite n. magnetic iron oxide, a valuable source of iron ore.

magneto / mag-**nee**-toh / n. (pl. **magnetos**) a small electric generator using permanent magnets, esp. one used to produce electricity for the spark in the ignition system of an engine.

Magnificat n. a canticle beginning 'My soul doth magnify (i.e. praise) the Lord', the words of the Virgin Mary at the Annunciation, used at vespers.

magnification n. **1** magnifying. **2** the amount by which a lens etc. magnifies things.

magnificent adj. **1** splendid in appearance etc. **2** excellent in quality. ◻ **magnificently** adv. **magnificence** n.

magnify v. (**magnified**, **magnifying**) **1** make (an object) appear larger than it really is, as a lens or microscope does. **2** exaggerate. **3** *archaic* praise (*My soul doth magnify the Lord*). ◻ **magnifying glass** a lens (often mounted in a frame) that magnifies things. ◻◻ **magnifier** n.

magnitude *n.* **1** largeness, size. **2** importance. **3** the degree of brightness of a star. ◻ **of the first magnitude** very important.

magnolia / mag-**noh**-lee-uh / *n.* a tree cultivated for its large wax-like usu. white or pale pink flowers.

magnox *n.* a magnesium-based alloy used to enclose uranium fuel elements in some nuclear reactors.

magnum *n.* a wine bottle twice the normal size.

magnum opus *n.* a great work of art, literature, etc.; an artist's greatest work. (¶ Latin)

magpie *n.* **1** a black and white bird, widespread in Australia, having an extremely melodious carolling call. **2** an unrelated noisy European etc. crow with black and white plumage. **3** a chatterer. **4** a person who collects objects at random. ◻ **magpie lark** a black and white bird, widespread in Australia, which has a loud piping call and which builds a mud nest in a tree.

magsman *n. Aust.* **1** a confidence trickster. **2** a talker; a raconteur.

magus / **may**-guhs / *n.* (*pl.* **magi** / **may**-juy /) **1** a priest of ancient Persia. **2** a sorcerer. **3** *see* MAGI.

mag wheel *n. colloq.* a magnesium alloy wheel for a car.

Magyar / **mag**-yah / *n.* **1** a member of a people originally from western Siberia, now predominant in Hungary. **2** their language, Hungarian. • *adj.* of the Magyars.

Mahabharata / mah-huh-**bah**-ruh-tuh / one of the two great Sanskrit epics of the Hindus (the other is the Ramayana), dating in its present form from *c.*AD 400 and containing almost 100,000 stanzas.

maharaja / mah-huh-**rah**-juh / *n.* (also **maharajah**) the former title of certain Indian princes.

maharani / mah-huh-**rah**-nee / *n.* (also **maharanee**) *hist.* a maharaja's wife or widow.

maharishi / mah-huh-**rish**-ee / *n.* a great Hindu sage or spiritual leader.

Mahathir bin Mohamad (1925–), YAB Dato' Seri, Dr, prime minister of Malaysia from 1981.

mahatma / muh-**haht**-muh / *n.* (in India etc.) a title of respect for a person regarded with reverence.

Mahayana / muh-huh-**yah**-nuh / *n.* (also **Mahayana Buddhism**) one of the two major Buddhist traditions, now practised especially in China, Tibet, Japan, and Korea. See THERAVADA.

Mahdi / **mah**-dee / *n.* **1** the title of a spiritual and temporal leader expected by Muslims. **2** a claimant of this title, esp. a former leader of insurrection in the Sudan. ◻ **Mahdist** *n.*

mah-jong *n.* (also **mah-jongg**) a Chinese game for four people, played with pieces called tiles.

Mahler / **mah**-luh /, Gustav (1860–1911), Austrian composer, conductor, and pianist.

mahogany / muh-**hog**-uh-nee / *n.* **1 a** a reddish-brown wood used for furniture. **b** the colour of this. **c** any of various tropical trees yielding this wood. **2** *Aust.* any eucalypt, esp. jarrah, that produces a similar wood. ◻ **mahogany glider** a rare and endangered mahogany-brown marsupial of coastal woodland in north-east Qld.

mahout / muh-**howt** / *n.* (in India etc.) an elephant driver.

maid *n.* **1** *archaic* a maiden, a girl. **2** a woman servant doing indoor work.

maiden *n. archaic* a girl or young unmarried woman; a virgin. • *adj.* **1** unmarried (*maiden aunt*). **2** (of a horse) not yet having won a prize. **3** first (*a maiden speech; maiden voyage*). ◻ **maiden name** a woman's surname before she marries. **maiden over** an over in cricket in which no runs are scored. ◻◻ **maidenly** *adj.* **maidenhood** *n.*

maidenhair *n.* a fern with fine hairlike stalks and delicate foliage.

maidenhead *n.* **1** virginity. **2** the hymen.

maidservant *n.* a female servant.

mail¹ *n.* **1** letters, parcels, etc. carried by post; the postal service; one complete delivery or collection of mail. **2** messages distributed by a computer system; email. **3** *colloq.* information, a rumour (*the mail is that the government is planning a new tax*). • *v.* send by post or by email. ◻ **mailing list** a list of people to whom advertising matter etc. is to be posted. **mailman** a person who delivers the mail; a postman.

mail² *n.* body-armour made of metal rings or chains.

maim *v.* wound or injure so that some part of the body is useless.

main *adj.* principal, most important; greatest in size or extent. • *n.* **1** the main pipe, channel, or cable in a public system for conveying water, gas, or (usu. **mains**) electricity. **2** *literary* the high seas. ◻ **in the main** for the most part, on the whole.

main clause *Grammar* a clause that can be a complete sentence in its own right.

mainframe *n.* **1** the central processing unit of a large computer. **2** a large computer as distinct from a microcomputer etc.

mainland *n.* **1** any large continuous extent of land, excluding neighbouring islands. **2** the continent of Australia (as opposed to any of the offshore islands and esp. Tas.). • *adj.* of a mainland (*mainland Aussies*).

mainlander *n.* a person who lives on a mainland.

mainline *v. colloq.* take or inject drugs intravenously. ◻ **mainliner** *n.*

mainly *adv.* for the most part, chiefly.

mainmast *n.* the principal mast of a sailing ship.

mainsail *n.* (in a square-rigged ship) the lowest sail on the mainmast; (in a fore-and-aft rigged ship) a sail set on the after part of the mainmast.

mainspring *n.* **1** the principal spring of a watch or clock etc. **2** the chief force motivating the actions of a person or group.

mainstay *n.* **1** the strong cable that secures a mainmast. **2** the chief support (*he is my mainstay in this time of trouble*).

mainstream *n. & adj.* (of) the dominant trend of opinion or style etc.

maintain *v.* **1** cause to continue, keep in existence. **2** keep in repair (*the house is well maintained*). **3** support, provide for, bear the expenses of (*maintains his aged parents*). **4** assert as true.

maintenance *n.* **1** maintaining; being maintained. **2** keeping equipment etc. in repair. **3** provision of the means to support life. **4** financial provision for a spouse after separation or divorce.

maintop *n.* a platform above the head of the lower mainmast.

maiolica / muh-**yol**-uh-kuh / *n.* (also **majolica**) white pottery decorated with metallic colours.

maisonette / may-zuh-**net** / *n.* **1** *Aust.* a semi-detached house. **2** esp. *Brit.* a flat on more than one floor.

maître d'hôtel / may-truh doh-**tel** / *n.* **1** the manager of a hotel. **2** the head waiter.

maize *n.* **1** a tall cereal plant bearing grain on large cobs. **2** its grain.

majestic *adj.* stately and dignified, imposing. □ **majestically** *adv.*

majesty *n.* **1** impressive stateliness. **2** sovereign power. **3** the title used in speaking of or to a king or queen (*His or Her or Your Majesty*).

Major, John (Roy) (1943–), British Conservative statesman, prime minister 1990–97.

major *adj.* **1** greater, very important. **2** (of a surgical operation) serious or life-threatening. **3** (in music) of or based on a scale which has a semitone next above the third and seventh notes and a whole tone elsewhere. **4** of full legal age. • *n.* **1** an army officer below lieutenant colonel and above captain. **2** a person of full legal age. **3** a university student's main subject or course. **4** *Aust. Rules* a goal. • *v.* (foll. by *in*) study or qualify in (a subject) as one's main subject (*majored in English*). □ **major general** an army officer next below lieutenant general.

major-domo / may-juh-**doh**-moh / *n.* (*pl.* **major-domos**) the head steward of a great household.

majority *n.* **1** the greatest part of a group or class. **2** the number by which votes for one party etc. exceed those for the next or for all combined. **3** (in law) full age (*attained his majority*). □ **majority rule** the principle that the largest group, race, etc. should have the most power. **majority verdict** a verdict supported by more than half of a jury but not unanimous.

Major Mitchell cockatoo *n.* a pink and white cockatoo with a scarlet crest and a central yellow band, occurring in arid and semi-arid Australia. Also called *Leadbeater's cockatoo*. (¶ T.L. Mitchell, explorer (1792–1855).)

Majuro / muh-**joo**-roh / the capital of the Marshall Islands.

makarrata / mak-uh-**rah**-tuh / *n.* peace-making; a ceremonial Aboriginal ritual symbolising the restoration of peace after a dispute. (¶ Yolngu)

make *v.* (**made**, **making**) **1** construct, create, or prepare from parts or from other substances. **2** draw up as a legal document or contract (*make a will*). **3** establish (laws, rules, or distinctions). **4** arrange ready for use (*make the beds*). **5** cause to exist, produce (*make difficulties*). **6** result in, amount to (*two and two make four*). **7** cause to be or become (*it made me happy; the pope made him a cardinal*). **8** *Aust.* initiate (an Aboriginal boy) ceremonially into manhood, esp. in the phrase *make a (young) man*. **9** frame in the mind (*made a decision*). **10** succeed in arriving at or achieving a position (*we made Melbourne by midnight*). **11** *colloq.* catch (a train etc.). **12** form, serve for (*this makes pleasant reading; it makes a useful seat*). **13** gain or acquire (*make a profit; make friends*). **14** consider to be (*what do you make the time?*). **15** cause or compel (*he made me do it*). **16** perform (an action etc.) (*make an attempt*). **17** ensure the success of (*wine can make the meal; this made my day*). **18** (foll. by *to* + infinitive) act as if intending to do something (*he made to go*). • *n.* **1** making; the way a thing is made. **2** the origin of manufacture (*our own make of shoes*). □ **be the making of** be the main factor in the success of. **have it made** *colloq.* be sure of success. **make believe** *v.* pretend. **make-believe** *adj.* pretended. *n.* pretence. **make do** manage with something that is not really satisfactory. **make for 1** proceed towards a place or thing, try to reach. **2** tend to bring about (*it makes for domestic harmony*). **3** attack. **make good 1** become successful or prosperous. **2** pay compensation; repair (damage). **3** achieve (a purpose) (*he made good his escape*). **make it** achieve what one wanted, be successful. **make it up** become reconciled after a quarrel. **make it up to** compensate. **make love** *see* LOVE. **make off** go away hastily. **make off with** carry away; steal. **make out 1** write out (a cheque etc.). **2** manage to see or read (*made out a shadowy figure*). **3** understand the nature of (*I can't make him out*). **4** assert, claim, or pretend to be (*made him out to be a fool*). **5** *colloq.* fare (*how did you make out?*). **make over 1** transfer the ownership of. **2** convert for a new purpose. **make up 1** form or constitute; put together, prepare (medicine etc.). **2** invent (a story etc.). **3** compensate (for a loss or mistake). **4** complete (an amount) by supplying what is lacking. **5** apply cosmetics to. **make-up** *n.* **1** cosmetics applied to the skin, esp. of the face. **2** the way something is made up, its composition or constituent parts; a person's character and temperament. **make up one's mind** decide. **make up to** curry favour with. **on the make** *colloq.* intent on gain.

makeover *n.* a complete transformation or remodelling, esp. a person's hairstyle, make-up, or clothes.

maker *n.* **1** a person who makes something. **2** (**Maker**) God. **3** *archaic* a poet.

makeshift *n.* a temporary or improvised substitute. • *adj.* serving as this.

makings *n.* **1** earnings, profit. **2** ingredients. **3** *US & Aust. colloq.* paper and tobacco as materials for rolling a cigarette. ☐ **have the makings of** have the essential qualities for becoming (*he has the makings of a good athlete*).

mal- *comb. form* **1** bad, badly (*malpractice, maltreat*). **2** faulty, faultily (*malfunction*). **3** not (*maladroit*).

Malabo / muh-**lah**-boh / the capital of Equatorial Guinea.

malacca / muh-**lak**-uh / *n.* a brown cane made from the stem of a palm tree.

malachite / **mal**-uh-kuyt / *n.* a green mineral that can be polished.

maladjusted *adj.* (of a person) not well adjusted to his or her own circumstances. ☐ **maladjustment** *n.*

maladminister *v.* manage (business or public affairs) badly or improperly. ☐ **maladministration** *n.*

maladroit / mal-uh-**droit**, **mal**- / *adj.* clumsy, bungling. ☐ **maladroitly** *adv.* **maladroitness** *n.*

malady / **mal**-uh-dee / *n.* an illness, a disease.

Malagasy / mal-uh-**gas**-ee / *adj.* of Madagascar. • *n.* **1** a native or inhabitant of Madagascar. **2** the official language of Madagascar (related to Malay).

malaise / muh-**layz** / *n.* a feeling of illness or mental uneasiness.

malapropism / **mal**-uh-prop-iz-uhm / *n.* a comical confusion of words, e.g. *what are you incinerating?* (for *insinuating*). (¶ Named after Mrs Malaprop in Sheridan's play *The Rivals* (1775), who made mistakes of this kind.)

malaria / muh-**lair**-ree-uh / *n.* a disease causing fever which recurs at intervals, transmitted by mosquitoes. ☐ **malarial** *adj.*

malarkey / muh-**lah**-kee / *n. colloq.* (also **malarky**) humbug, nonsense.

Malawi / muh-**lah**-wee / a republic in south central Africa. ☐ **Malawian** *adj. & n.*

Malay / muh-**lay** / *adj.* of a people living in Malaysia and Indonesia. • *n.* **1** a member of this people. **2** their language.

Malaya a group of States forming part of Malaysia. ☐ **Malayan** *adj. & n.*

Malay Archipelago a large group of islands, including Sumatra, Java, Borneo, the Philippines, and New Guinea, lying SE of Asia and north of Australia.

Malaysia / muh-**lay**-*zh*uh / a federal monarchy in SE Asia. ☐ **Malaysian** *adj. & n.*

Malcolm X (original name: Malcolm Little) (1925–65), American Black civil rights leader who was assassinated.

malcontent / **mal**-kuhn-tent / *n.* a person who is discontented and inclined to rebel.

Maldives / **mawl**-divz / (formerly **Maldive Islands**) a republic consisting of a group of coral islands SW of Sri Lanka. ☐ **Maldive fish** hard dried tuna, used powdered in Sri Lankan etc. cooking. ☐ **Maldivian** / mawl-**div**-ee-uhn / *adj. & n.*

Male / **mah**-lay / the capital of the Maldives.

male *adj.* **1** of the sex that can beget offspring by fertilising egg cells produced by the female. **2** (of plants) having flowers that contain pollen-bearing organs and not seeds. **3** of a man or men (*male voice choir*). **4** (of parts of machinery etc.) designed to enter or fill a corresponding hollow (female) part. • *n.* a male person, animal, or plant. ☐ **male chauvinist** a man who believes that men are superior to women. **male menopause** *colloq.* a crisis of potency, confidence, etc. supposed to afflict some middle-aged men.

malediction / mal-uh-**dik**-shuhn / *n.* a curse.

maledictory / mal-uh-**dik**-tuh-ree / *adj.* expressing a curse.

malefactor / **mal**-uh-fak-tuh / *n.* a criminal, a wrongdoer. ☐ **malefaction** / mal-uh-**fak**-shuhn / *n.*

malevolent / muh-**lev**-uh-luhnt / *adj.* wishing harm to others. ☐ **malevolently** *adv.* **malevolence** *n.*

malfeasance / mal-**fee**-zuhns / *n. formal* improper or unprofessional behaviour.

malformation *n.* faulty formation. ☐ **malformed** *adj.*

malfunction *n.* faulty functioning. • *v.* function faultily.

Mali / **mah**-lee / an inland republic in West Africa. ☐ **Malian** *adj. & n.*

malibu / **mal**-uh-boo / *n.* (also **malibu board**) a lightweight surfboard.

malice *n.* a desire to harm or cause difficulty to others; ill will. ☐ **malice aforethought** *Law* the intention to commit a crime.

malicious / muh-**lish**-uhs / *adj.* feeling, showing, or caused by malice. ☐ **maliciously** *adv.*

malign / muh-**luyn** / *adj.* **1** harmful (*a malign influence*). **2** showing malice. **3** (of a tumour etc.) malignant. • *v.* say unpleasant and untrue things about (*maligning an innocent person*). ☐ **malignity** / muh-**lig**-nuh-tee / *n.*

malignant / muh-**lig**-nuhnt / *adj.* **1** (of a tumour) growing uncontrollably; cancerous. **2** feeling or showing great ill will. ☐ **malignantly** *adv.* **malignancy** *n.*

malinger / muh-**ling**-guh / *v.* pretend to be ill in order to avoid work. ☐ **malingerer** *n.*

mall / mawl, mal / *n.* **1** a sheltered walk or promenade. **2** esp. *US & Aust.* a shopping precinct.

mallard / **mal**-ahd / *n.* (*pl.* **mallard**) a wild duck, the male of which has a glossy green head.

malleable / **mal**-ee-uh-buhl / *adj.* **1** able to be hammered or pressed into shape. **2** easy to influence, adaptable. ◻ **malleably** *adv.* **malleability** *n.*

mallee / **mal**-ee / *n. Aust.* **1** any of many eucalypts, characteristically small and having several trunks or stems arising from a common base. **2** (also **mallee scrub**) a vegetation community characterised by the presence of such trees. **3** (also **mallee country**, **desert**, **district**, **land**) any of the semi-arid areas of Australia (esp. in Vic.) of which the principal natural vegetation is mallee scrub. ◻ **fit** (*or* **strong**) **as a mallee bull** *colloq.* fighting fit (or extremely strong). **mallee fowl** (also **mallee hen**, **lowan**, **gnow**) a mottled grey, brown, and white bird of dry, southern, inland Australia which builds its nest in large mounds. **mallee roller** a heavy roller, usu. a tree trunk, drawn by horses or bullocks and used to crush and flatten mallee scrub. **mallee root** (also **mallee stump**) the large woody rootstock of a mallee eucalypt, highly valued as firewood for the intense heat it gives. (¶ Probably Wemba-wemba.)

mallet[1] *n.* **1** a hammer, usu. of wood. **2** a similarly shaped instrument with a long handle, for striking the ball in croquet or polo.

mallet[2] *n.* any of several WA eucalypts with very hard flexible wood and tannin-rich bark. (¶ Nyungar *malard*.)

malnutrition *n.* weakness resulting from the lack of foods necessary for health.

malodorous / mal-**oh**-duh-ruhs / *adj.* stinking.

Malory / **mal**-uh-ree /, Sir Thomas (d. 1471), English writer, whose major work deals with the legends of King Arthur.

Malouf, David (1934–), AO, Australian novelist and poet. His novel *The Great World* (1990) won the Miles Franklin Award.

malpractice *n.* **1** wrongdoing. **2** improper or negligent professional behaviour, esp. by a doctor.

malt *n.* **1** grain (usu. barley) that has been allowed to sprout and then dried, used for brewing, distilling, or vinegar-making. **2** any liquor made from malt, as beer, malt whisky, etc. • *v.* make or be made into malt. ◻ **malty** *adj.*

Malta an island republic in the Mediterranean Sea.

Maltese *n.* **1** (*pl.* **Maltese**) a person from Malta. **2** the language of Malta. • *adj.* of Malta or its people or language. ◻ **Maltese cross** a cross with four equal arms broadening outwards, often indented at the ends.

Malthusian *adj.* of the doctrine that the population should be restricted to prevent it increasing beyond its ability to feed itself. ◻ **Malthusianism** *n.* (¶ Named after Thomas Malthus (1766–1834), English clergyman who propounded the theory.)

maltose *n.* sugar made from starch by enzymes in malt, saliva, etc.

maltreat *v.* ill-treat. ◻ **maltreatment** *n.*

maluka / muh-**loo**-kuh / *n.* (also **maluga**) *Aust.* a person in charge, a boss. (¶ Djingulu *marluga* 'old man'.)

Malvinas / mal-**vee**-nuhs / (in full **Islas Malvinas**) the Argentinian name for what the British call the Falkland Islands.

Malyangaba / **mah**-lyah-ngah-pu / *n.* an Aboriginal language of a wide area in eastern SA west of Lake Frome and stretching into northern NSW.

mamba *n.* a poisonous black or green South African snake.

mambo *n.* (*pl.* **mambos**) a Latin American dance like the rumba.

Mameluke / **mam**-uh-luuk / *n.* a member of a military group ruling in Egypt 1254–1811.

mammal *n.* a member of the class of animals that suckle their young. ◻ **mammalian** / ma-**may**-lee-uhn / *adj.*

mammary / **mam**-uh-ree / *adj.* of the human female breasts or the milk-secreting organs of other mammals. ◻ **mammary gland** a milk-secreting gland.

mammogram *n.* an image obtained by mammography.

mammography *n.* an X-ray technique for screening the breasts for tumours etc.

Mammon *n.* wealth personified, regarded as a god or evil influence.

mammoth *n.* a large extinct type of elephant with a hairy coat and curved tusks. • *adj.* huge.

man *n.* (*pl.* **men**) **1** an adult human male. **2** a human being. **3** mankind. **4** an individual male person considered as an expert or one's assistant or opponent etc. (*if you want a good teacher, he's your man*). **5** a person of unspecified sex, an individual person (*every man for himself*). **6** a manly person (*is he man enough to do it?*). **7** a husband (*man and wife*). **8** *colloq.* a boyfriend or lover. **9** a male servant, employee, or workman. **10** an ordinary soldier etc., not an officer. **11** a human being of a specified type or historical period (*Peking man; Renaissance man*). **12** each of the set of small objects moved on a board in playing board games such as chess and draughts. • *v.* (**manned**, **manning**) supply with people for service or to operate something (*man the pumps*). ◻ **man Friday** *see* FRIDAY. **man-hour** the amount of work that one person can do in an hour, considered as a unit. **man in the street** the ordinary average person (as distinct from an expert). **man of letters** a scholar or author. **man-of-war** (*pl.* **men-of-war**) a warship. **man on the land** a person who owns or manages a rural property, esp. as representative of those engaged in rural occupations. **man to man** with frankness. **to a man** all without exception.

mana / mah-nuh / n. **1** power; authority; prestige. **2** supernatural or magical power. (¶ Maori)

manacle / man-uh-kuhl / n. each of a pair of fetters for the hands. • v. fetter with manacles.

manage v. **1** have under effective control. **2** be the manager of (a business etc.). **3** operate (a tool or machinery) effectively. **4** succeed in doing or producing something (often with inadequate means); be able to cope (*managed without help*). **5** contrive to persuade (a person) to do what one wants, e.g. by use of tact or flattery. ▫ **manageable** *adj.*

management n. **1** managing; being managed. **2** the process of managing a business; people engaged in this.

manager n. **1** a person who is in charge of the affairs of a business etc. **2** one who deals with the business affairs of a sports team or entertainer etc. **3** one who manages affairs in a certain way (*she is a good manager*). ▫ **managing director** one having executive control or authority. ▫▫ **managerial** / man-uh-jeer-ree-uhl / *adj.*

Managua / muh-**nah**-gwuh / the capital of Nicaragua.

Manama / man-**ah**-muh / the capital of Bahrain.

mañana / man-**yah**-nuh / adv. tomorrow; (indicating procrastination) at some time in the future. (¶ Spanish)

manatee / man-uh-tee / n. a large tropical aquatic mammal that feeds on plants.

manchester n. *Aust.* **1** household linen. **2** the department (of a shop) in which this is sold. (¶ Abbreviation of *Manchester wares*, cotton goods originally manufactured at Manchester in England.)

Manchu / man-**choo** / n. **1** a member of a Tartar people who conquered China and founded the last imperial dynasty (1644–1912). **2** their language, now spoken in part of NE China.

Manchuria / man-**choo**-ree-uh / a region forming the NE portion of China.

mandala / man-duh-luh / n. a circular religious symbol representing the universe.

mandarin / man-duh-ruhn, -rin / n. **1** a high-ranking influential official. **2** (also / man-duh-reen /) a small flattened orange with a loose skin. **3** (**Mandarin**) the language formerly used by officials and educated people in China; any of the varieties of this spoken as a common language in China, esp. the northern variety (the official language of China). ▫ **mandarin collar** a high upright collar not quite meeting in front.

mandate n. **1** authority given to someone to perform a certain task, esp. the authority supposed to be given by electors to a government. **2** an official command or instruction. • v. **1** give a mandate to, delegate authority to (a representative, group, organisation, etc.). **2** command, require by mandate.

mandatory / man-duh-tuh-ree, -tree / *adj.* obligatory, compulsory. ▫ **mandatorily** *adv.*

Mandela / man-**del**-uh /, Nelson (Rolihlahla) (1918–), South African statesman, civil rights leader, leader of the African National Congress. He was president 1994–99. In 1993 he was awarded the Nobel Peace Prize.

mandible / man-duh-buhl / n. **1** a jaw, esp. the lower one. **2** either of the parts of a bird's beak. **3** the corresponding part in insects etc.

mandolin / **man**-duh-lin / n. a musical instrument rather like a small lute, played with a plectrum.

mandrake n. a poisonous narcotic plant with white or purple flowers, large yellow fruit, and a root once thought to resemble the human form and to shriek when uprooted.

mandrel n. **1** (in a lathe) the shaft to which work is fixed while being turned etc. **2** a cylindrical rod round which metal or other material is forged or shaped.

mandrill n. a large baboon of West Africa.

mane n. **1** the long hair on a horse's or lion's neck. **2** *colloq.* a person's long hair.

manège / ma-**nay**zh / n. (also **manege**) **1** a riding school. **2** horsemanship. **3** the movements of a trained horse.

Manet / ma-**nay** /, Édouard (1832–83), French painter.

manful *adj.* brave, resolute. ▫ **manfully** *adv.*

manganese / **mang**-guh-neez / n. a chemical element (symbol Mn), a hard brittle grey metal; its black oxide.

mange / maynj / n. a skin disease affecting hairy animals, caused by a parasite.

manger n. a long open trough or box in a stable etc. for horses or cattle to eat from.

mangle n. a machine for wringing wet clothes etc. • v. **1** press (clothes etc.) in a mangle. **2** damage by cutting or crushing roughly, mutilate.

mango n. (*pl.* **mangoes** *or* **mangos**) a tropical fruit with very sweet yellowish flesh; the tree that bears it.

mangosteen / **mang**-guh-steen / n. a white juicy-pulped fruit with a thick reddish-brown rind.

mangrove n. a tropical or semi-temperate tree or shrub growing in shore mud and swamps, with many tangled roots above ground. ▫ **mangrove crab** the large edible Australian mud crab. **mangrove heron** (also **mangrove bittern**) a predominantly grey or brown bird of esp. mangrove stands in warmer coastal Australia. **mangrove jack** a marine and estuarine food fish usu. found amongst mangrove roots in northern Australia.

mangy / **mayn**-jee / *adj.* (**mangier, mangiest**) **1** having mange. **2** squalid; shabby.

manhandle v. **1** move (a thing) by human effort alone. **2** treat roughly.

Manhattan Project the code name for an American project set up in 1942 to develop an atomic bomb.

manhole *n.* a covered opening through which a person can enter a sewer etc. to inspect or repair it.

manhood *n.* **1** the state of being a man rather than a child or woman. **2** manly qualities, courage. **3** the penis. **4** a man's sexual potency. **5** the men of a country.

manhunt *n.* an organised search for a criminal.

mania / **may**-nee-uh / *n.* **1** a mental illness marked by excitement and violence. **2** extreme enthusiasm for something (*a mania for sport*).

-mania *comb. form* **1** denoting a special type of mental abnormality or obsession (*megalomania*). **2** denoting extreme enthusiasm or admiration (*bibliomania*).

maniac / **may**-nee-ak / *n.* **1** a person behaving wildly; an idiot. **2** an obsessive enthusiast. **3** a person affected with mania (sense 1).

maniacal / muh-**nuy**-uh-kuhl / *adj.* of or like a mania or a maniac. ◻ **maniacally** *adv.*

manic / **man**-ik / *adj.* **1** of or affected with mania. **2** *colloq.* wildly excited; frenzied; excitable. ◻ **manic-depressive** *adj.* of a mental disorder with alternating bouts of excitement and depression. *n.* a person suffering from this disorder. ◻ **manically** *adv.*

manicure *n.* cosmetic care of the hands and fingernails. • *v.* apply such treatment to. ◻ **manicurist** *n.*

manifest *adj.* clear and unmistakable. • *v.* **1** show (a thing) clearly, give signs of (*the crowd manifested its approval by cheering*). **2** *reflexive* (of a thing) reveal itself. **3** (of a ghost) appear. • *n.* a list of cargo or passengers carried by a ship or aircraft etc. ◻ **manifestly** *adv.* **manifestation** *n.*

manifesto *n.* (*pl.* **manifestos**) a public declaration of policy, esp. by a political party.

manifold *adj.* of many kinds, varied. • *n.* a pipe or chamber (in a mechanism) with several openings that connect with other parts.

manikin *n.* (also **mannikin**) **1** a little man; a dwarf. **2** an anatomical model of the human body.

Manila / muh-**nil**-uh / the capital of the Philippines.

manila / muh-**nil**-uh / *n.* strong brown paper used for envelopes, folders, etc.

manioc / **man**-ee-ok / *n.* cassava.

manipulable / muh-**nip**-yuh-luh-buhl / *adj.* able to be manipulated.

manipulate / muh-**nip**-yuh-layt / *v.* **1** handle, manage, or use (a thing) skilfully. **2** arrange or influence cleverly or craftily; alter or adjust (figures, data, etc.) to suit one's purposes. **3** move about (part of a patient's body) to reduce stiffness, pain, etc. ◻ **manipulation** *n.* **manipulator** *n.*

manipulative / muh-**nip**-yuh-luh-tiv / *adj.* tending to exploit a situation, a person, etc., for one's own ends. ◻ **manipulatively** *adv.*

mankind *n.* **1** / man-**kuynd** / human beings in general, the human race. **2** / **man**-kuynd / male people as distinct from female.

manly *adj.* **1** having qualities popularly associated with a man (e.g. strength and courage). **2** suitable for a man. ◻ **manliness** *n.*

Mann, Thomas (1875–1955), German novelist whose works include *Death in Venice* (1912) and *Dr Faustus* (1947).

manna *n.* **1** (in the Bible) a substance miraculously supplied as food to the Israelites in the wilderness after the exodus from Egypt. **2** something unexpected and delightful. **3** a white, sugary, edible substance exuded by many eucalypts. **4** *Aust.* = LERP. ◻ **manna gum** *Aust.* any of several eucalypts yielding manna (sense 3).

manned *see* MAN. • *adj.* (of a spacecraft etc.) containing a human crew (*manned flights*).

mannequin / **man**-uh-kuhn, -kwuhn / *n.* **1** a person who models clothes. **2** a window dummy; a dummy for a person who makes or designs clothes.

manner *n.* **1** the way a thing is done or happens. **2** a person's bearing or way of behaving towards others. **3** kind, sort (*all manner of things*). **4** (**manners**) social behaviour; polite social behaviour (*has no manners*). ◻ **in a manner of speaking** so to speak (used to qualify or weaken what one says).

mannered *adj.* **1** having manners of a certain kind (*well-mannered*). **2** full of mannerisms (*a mannered style*).

mannerism *n.* a distinctive personal habit or way of doing something; excessive use of these in art etc.

mannerly *adj.* well-mannered, polite.

mannish *adj.* **1** (of a woman) masculine in appearance, clothes, or manner. **2** characteristic of or suitable for a man.

Mannix, Daniel (1864–1963), an Australian Catholic prelate (born in Ireland), Archbishop of Melbourne from 1917 until his death, who was outspoken on many political issues.

manoeuvre / muh-**noo**-vuh / *n.* **1** a planned and controlled movement of a vehicle or a body of troops etc. **2** a skilful or crafty proceeding, a trick (*the manoeuvres of politicians to achieve their purposes*). **3** (**manoeuvres**) large-scale exercises of troops or ships (*on manoeuvres*). • *v.* **1** move a thing's position or course etc. carefully (*manoeuvred the car into the garage*). **2** perform manoeuvres. **3** guide skilfully or craftily (*manoeuvred the conversation towards money*). ◻ **manoeuvrable** *adj.* **manoeuvrability** *n.*

manometer / muh-**nom**-uh-tuh / *n.* a pressure gauge for gases and liquids.

manor *n. Brit.* a large country house (also **manor house**) or the landed estate belonging to it. ◻ **manorial** / muh-**naw**-ree-uhl / *adj.*

manpower *n.* **1** power supplied by human physical effort. **2** the number of people working

manqué / mong-kay / *adj.* that might have been but is not what is specified (*a publisher is an author manqué*). (¶ French, = missed.)

manse *n.* a church minister's house.

manservant *n.* (*pl.* **menservants**) a male servant.

Mansfield, Katherine (original name: Kathleen Mansfield Beauchamp) (1888–1923), New Zealand writer of short stories.

mansion / **man**-shuhn / *n.* a large grand house.

manslaughter *n.* the act of killing a person unlawfully but not intentionally, or by negligence.

mantel *n.* a mantelpiece.

mantelpiece *n.* a structure of wood, marble, etc. above and around a fireplace.

mantilla / man-**til**-uh / *n.* a lace veil worn by Spanish women over the hair and shoulders.

mantis *n.* (*pl.* **mantis** or **mantises**) (in full **praying mantis**) an insect resembling a grasshopper, which holds its forelegs like hands folded in prayer.

mantissa *n.* the part of a logarithm after the decimal point.

Mantjiltjara / **mahn**-chil-jah-ru / *n.* a dialect of the WESTERN DESERT LANGUAGE.

mantle *n.* **1** a loose sleeveless cloak. **2** something likened to this, a covering (*a mantle of secrecy*). **3** a fragile gauzy cover fixed round the flame of a gas lamp, producing a strong light when heated. **4** the region between the crust and the core of the earth. • *v.* envelop or cover as if with a mantle (*mist mantled the peak; he was mantled in gloom*).

mantra *n.* **1** a special word or phrase repeated as an aid to concentration in Hindu or Buddhist meditation, yoga, etc. **2** a Vedic hymn.

Manu / **mun**-oo / *Hindu myth.* the first man, survivor of the great flood, and father of the human race.

manual *adj.* **1** of the hands. **2** done or operated by the hand(s), not automatic (*manual labour; manual gear change*). • *n.* **1** a reference book. **2** an organ keyboard that is played with the hands, not with the feet. **3** *colloq.* a vehicle with manual transmission. ▫ **manually** *adv.*

manufacture *v.* **1** make or produce (goods) on a large scale by machinery. **2** invent (*manufactured an excuse*). • *n.* the process of manufacturing. ▫ **manufacturer** *n.*

manure *n.* a fertiliser, esp. dung. • *v.* apply manure to.

manuscript / **man**-yuh-skript / *n.* **1** something written by hand, not typed or printed. **2** an author's work as written or typed, not a printed book.

Manx *adj.* of the Isle of Man. • *n.* **1** the Celtic language of the Manx people. **2** (**the Manx**) Manx people.

many *adj.* (**more**, **most**) great in number, numerous. • *n.* many people or things.

Maoism / **mow**-iz-uhm / *n.* the doctrines of Mao Zedong. ▫ **Maoist** *n.* & *adj.*

Maori / **mow**-ree / *n.* **1** (*pl.* **Maori** or **Maoris**) a member of the indigenous people of New Zealand. **2** their language. **3** (also **Maori wrasse**) *Aust.* a brightly coloured fish of southern Australia, the markings on which are supposed to resemble Maori tattoos. • *adj.* of or concerning the Maori or their language.

Maoriland *n.* esp. *Aust.* New Zealand. ▫ **Maorilander** *n.*

Maoritanga / **mow**-ree-tung-uh / *n.* **1** being Maori. **2** Maori traditions and culture.

Maori Wars the wars fought intermittently in 1845–48 and 1860–72 between Maoris and the colonial government of New Zealand over the enforced sale of Maori lands to Europeans (*see* WAITANGI).

Mao Zedong / mow dzee-**duung** / (also **Mao Tse-tung** / mow tsee-**tuung** /) (1893–1976), Chinese Communist statesman, founder of the People's Republic of China (1949) and its president until 1959; he retained his all-powerful position as chairman of the Communist Party until his death.

map *n.* **1** a representation of the earth's surface or a part of it, or of the sky showing the positions of the stars etc. **2** a diagram of a route etc. • *v.* (**mapped**, **mapping**) **1** make a map of. **2** *Maths* associate each element of (a set) with one element of (another set). ▫ **map out** plan in detail. **off the map** very distant or remote. **put a thing on the map** make it become famous or important. **wipe a thing off the map** obliterate it.

maple *n.* **1** a tree of the Northern hemisphere with broad leaves, grown for ornament or for its wood or sugar. **2** (in full **Queensland maple**) an unrelated Australian tree yielding an attractive, usu. pinkish, cabinet timber; its wood. ▫ **maple leaf** a leaf of Canadian maple, esp. as the emblem of Canada. **maple syrup** a syrup produced from the sap of the sugar maple etc.

Maputo / muh-**poo**-toh / the capital of Mozambique.

maquette / muh-**ket** / *n.* a preliminary sketch or model.

Maquis / mah-**kee** / *n.* (*pl.* **Maquis**) **1** the French resistance movement during the German occupation (1940–45). **2** a member of this.

mar *v.* (**marred**, **marring**) damage, spoil; disfigure.

marabou / **ma**-ruh-boo / *n.* **1** a large African stork. **2** its down used as a trimming.

maracas / muh-**rak**-uhz / *n.pl.* a pair of club-like gourds containing beans, beads, etc., held in the hands and shaken as a musical instrument.

Maradona, Diego (Armando) (1960–), Argentine soccer player.

Maralinga a site, about 850 km north-west of Adelaide at the northern edge of the Nullarbor Plain, used in 1956–57 by the British to explode and test nuclear weapons. The serious effects of

maramie / **ma**-ruh-mee / *n. Aust.* a freshwater crayfish. (¶ Wiradhuri)

marara / muh-**rah**-ruh / *n.* **1** any of three large rainforest trees of Qld and NSW: the rose marara or scrub rosewood; the brush marara or red carabeen; the rose-leaf marara. **2** the close-grained pink wood of these trees. (¶ Perhaps from a Qld Aboriginal language.)

maraschino / ma-ruh-**skee**-noh, -**shee**-noh / *n.* a strong sweet liqueur made from small black Dalmatian cherries. □ **maraschino cherry** a cherry preserved in this.

marathon *n.* **1** a long-distance running race, usu. of 26 miles 385 yards (42.195 km). **2** a long-lasting or difficult test of endurance (*a TV-watching marathon*). • *adj.* of a marathon; of long distance or duration (*the delegates emerged weary after marathon talks*). (¶ Named after Marathon in Greece, where an invading Persian army was defeated in 490 BC; a man who fought at the battle ran to Athens, announced the victory, and died.)

maraud / muh-**rawd** / *v.* make a plundering raid (on); plunder systematically (*the Vikings marauded throughout Europe*). □ **marauder** *n.* **marauding** *adj.*

marble *n.* **1** crystalline limestone that can be polished, used in sculpture and building. **2** a piece of sculpture in marble. **3** a small ball made of glass or clay etc. used in children's games. • *adj.* like marble, hard and smooth and white or mottled. □ **lose one's marbles** *colloq.* lose one's mental faculties, go mad.

marbled *adj.* having a veined or mottled appearance; (of meat) with alternating layers of lean and fat. □ **marbling** *n.*

marcasite / **mah**-kuh-suyt / *n.* crystallised iron pyrites; a piece of this used in jewellery.

March *n.* the third month of the year. □ **March hare** a hare in the breeding season when it leaps about and behaves wildly (*mad as a March hare*).

march *v.* **1** walk in a military manner with regular paces; walk in an organised column. **2** walk purposefully (*marched up to the manager*). **3** cause to march or walk (*he was marched off*). **4** progress steadily (*time marches on*). • *n.* **1** marching; the distance covered by marching troops etc.; a protest or demonstration. **2** progress (*the march of events*). **3** a piece of music suitable for marching to. □ **get one's marching orders** to be told to go; be dismissed. **march past** a ceremonial march past a saluting point. □ □ **marcher** *n.*

marches *n.pl.* border regions.

marchioness / mah-shuh-**nes**, **mah**- / *n.* **1** the wife or widow of a marquess. **2** a woman holding the rank of marquess in her own right.

Marconi / mah-**koh**-nee /, Guglielmo (1874–1937), Italian electrical engineer, a pioneer of radio communication.

Marco Polo (*c.*1254–*c.*1324), Venetian traveller, famous for his account of his travels in China and central Asia.

Mardi Gras / mah-dee-**grah** / *n.* **1** Shrove Tuesday in some Catholic countries; celebrations held on this day. **2** *Aust.* a carnival or fair held at any time of the year.

mardo *n. Aust.* the yellow-footed marsupial mouse. (¶ Nyungar)

mare[1] *n.* the female of a horse or related animal. □ **mare's nest** a discovery that is thought to be important etc. but turns out to be false or worthless.

mare[2] / **mah**-ray / *n.* (*pl.* **maria** / **mah**-ree-uh / *or* **mares**) a large dark flat area on the moon, once thought to be a sea; a similar area on Mars.

margarine / mah-juh-**reen** / *n.* a substance (originally a butter substitute) made by emulsifying vegetable oils or animal fats with milk etc.

margin *n.* **1** an edge or border. **2** a blank space round printed or written matter on a page. **3** an amount over and above the essential minimum (*was defeated by a narrow margin; margin of safety*). **4** (in commerce) the difference between cost price and selling price (*profit margins*). **5** an increment to a basic wage, paid for an employee's particular skill.

marginal *adj.* **1** written in a margin (*marginal notes*). **2** of or at an edge. **3** very slight in amount (*its usefulness is marginal*). **4** (of a parliamentary seat) where an MP has only a small majority. • *n.* a marginal parliamentary electorate. □ **marginal cost** the cost added by making one extra item, copy, etc. □ □ **marginally** *adv.*

marginalia / mah-juh-**nay**-lee-uh / *n.pl.* notes written in a margin.

marginalise *v.* (also **-ize**) **1** treat (a person, a social group, an issue, etc.) as insignificant. **2** push (a person or a social group) from the centre or mainstream towards the periphery of interest, power, society, etc. □ **marginalisation** *n.*

Margu / **mahr**-goo / *n.* an Aboriginal language of Croker Island and the mainland of the extreme north of the NT.

marguerite / mah-guh-**reet** / *n.* any of several flowers of the daisy family.

maria *see* MARE[2].

Marian / **mair**-ree-uhn / *adj.* of or pertaining to the Virgin Mary (*Marian vespers*).

Marie Antoinette / mah-ree ahn-twah-**net** / (1755–93), queen of France (as the wife of Louis XVI), executed during the French Revolution.

marigold *n.* a garden plant with golden or bright yellow flowers.

marijuana / ma-ruh-**wah**-nuh / *n.* (also **marihuana**) the dried leaves, stems, and flowering

marimba / muh-**rim**-buh / n. **1** a xylophone of Africa and Central America. **2** a modern orchestral instrument evolved from this.

marina / muh-**ree**-nuh / n. a harbour for yachts and pleasure boats.

marinade / ma-ruh-**nayd**, -**nahd** / n. a seasoned flavoured liquid in which meat, fish, etc. is soaked before being cooked.

marinara / ma-ruh-**nah**-ruh / adj. designating an Italian sauce made from tomatoes, onions, herbs, etc., usu. combined with seafood.

marinate v. soak (meat, fish, etc.) in a marinade.

marine / muh-**reen** / adj. **1** of or living in the sea (*marine animals*). **2** of shipping, nautical (*marine insurance*). **3** for use at sea. • n. **1** a country's shipping (*the merchant marine*). **2** a member of a body of troops trained to serve on land or sea.

Mariner / **ma**-ruh-nuh / a series of US planetary probes (1962–77), of which 11 and 12 were renamed Voyager 1 and 2.

mariner / **ma**-ruh-nuh / n. a sailor, a seaman.

marionette / ma-ree-uh-**net** / n. a puppet worked by strings.

marital / **ma**-ruh-tuhl / adj. of marriage; of or between husband and wife. ☐ **maritally** adv.

maritime / **ma**-ruh-tuym / adj. **1** living, situated, or found near the sea. **2** of seafaring or shipping (*maritime law*).

marjoram / **mah**-juh-ruhm / n. a herb with fragrant leaves, used in cooking.

Mark, St **1** an evangelist, traditional author of the second Gospel. **2** the second Gospel.

mark[1] n. **1** a line or area that differs in appearance from the rest of a surface, esp. one that spoils it. **2** a distinguishing feature or characteristic. **3** something that indicates the presence of a quality or feeling (*as a mark of respect*). **4** a symbol placed on a thing to indicate its origin, ownership, or quality. **5** a written or printed symbol (*punctuation marks*). **6** a lasting impression (*poverty had left its mark*). **7** a unit awarded for the merit or quality of a piece of work or a performance (*got high marks*). **8** a target, a standard to be aimed at (*not up to the mark*). **9** (usu. **Mark**) (foll. by a number) a particular design or model of a car, aircraft, etc. (*an old Mark 2 Cortina*). **10** a line or object serving to indicate position. **11** *Aust. Rules* the catching before it reaches the ground of a ball kicked at least ten metres. **12** a runner's starting point in a race. • v. **1** make a mark on. **2** distinguish with a mark, characterise. **3** assign marks of merit to. **4** notice, watch carefully (*mark my words!*). **5** keep close to (an opposing player) in football etc. so as to prevent him or her receiving the ball. **6** *Aust. Rules* take the ball in a fair catch. ☐ **make one's mark** make a significant achievement, become famous. **mark down 1** notice and remember the place etc. of. **2** reduce the price of. **mark-down** n. a reduction in price. **mark off** separate by a boundary. **mark out** mark the boundaries of; destine, single out (*marked her out for promotion*). **mark time 1** move the feet rhythmically as if in marching but without advancing. **2** occupy time in routine work without making progress. **mark up 1** increase the price of. **2** mark or correct (text etc.). **mark-up** n. **1** the amount a seller adds to the cost price of an article to determine selling price. **2** the corrections made in marking up text.

mark[2] = DEUTSCHMARK.

marked adj. clearly noticeable (*a marked improvement*). ☐ **a marked man** one who is singled out, e.g. as an object of vengeance. ☐☐ **markedly** adv.

marker n. **1** a person or tool that marks; one who records the score in games etc. **2** a broad felt-tipped pen. **3** something that serves to mark a position.

market n. **1** a gathering for the sale of goods or livestock. **2** a space or building used for this. **3** the conditions or opportunity for buying or selling (*found a ready market*). **4** a place where goods may be sold; a particular class of buyers (*foreign markets; the teenage market*). **5** the trade in a specified commodity (*the wool market*). **6** the stock market. • v. offer for sale; promote the sale of (products) by advertising etc. ☐ **market forces** the influences of business, supply and demand, etc. on prices, wages, jobs, etc. without interference or control from government. **market garden** a farm where vegetables and fruit are grown for market. **market price** the current price; the going rate. **market research** study of consumers' needs and preferences. **market value** the amount for which something can be sold, its current value. **on the market** offered for sale. ☐☐ **marketer** n. **marketing** n.

marketable adj. able or fit to be sold. ☐ **marketability** n.

marketeer n. a marketer (*black marketeer*).

marketplace n. **1** an open space where a market is held in a town. **2** the commercial world.

marking n. **1** a mark or marks. **2** the colouring of an animal's skin, feathers, or fur.

marksman n. (also **markswoman**) a person who is a skilled shot, esp. with a pistol or rifle. ☐ **marksmanship** n.

marl n. a soil consisting of clay and lime, a valuable fertiliser. ☐ **marly** adj.

marlin n. (*pl.* **marlin** or **marlins**) a long-nosed sea fish.

marlinspike n. (also **marlinespike**) a pointed metal tool used to separate strands of rope or wire.

marlock n. any of several small mallee-like eucalypts forming stands. (¶ Probably Nyungar *malag* or *malug*.)

marloo / **mah**-loo / n. (in WA) a red kangaroo. (¶ Western Desert language)

Marlowe / **mah**-loh /, Christopher (1564–93), English dramatist and poet.

marmalade *n.* a jam made from citrus fruit, esp. oranges.

marmoreal / mah-**maw**-ree-uhl / *adj.* of or like marble.

marmoset / **mah**-muh-zet / *n.* a small bushy-tailed monkey of tropical America.

marmot / **mah**-muht / *n.* a small burrowing animal of the squirrel family.

marocain / **ma**-ruh-kayn / *n.* a ribbed crêpe dress fabric.

Maronite / **ma**-ruh-nuyt / *n.* a member of a Christian sect of Syrian origin, living chiefly in Lebanon, and in communion with the Catholic Church.

maroon[1] / muh-**rohn**, -**roon** / *n.* a brownish-red colour. • *adj.* brownish-red.

maroon[2] / muh-**roon** / *v.* abandon or isolate (a person), e.g. on an island or in a deserted place.

marque / mahk / *n.* a make of motor car, as opposed to a specific model.

marquee / mah-**kee** / *n.* a large tent used for a party or an exhibition etc.

marquess / **mah**-kwuhs / *n.* a British nobleman ranking between a duke and an earl.

marquetry / **mah**-kuh-tree / *n.* inlaid work in wood or ivory etc.

marquis / **mah**-kwuhs / *n.* a French nobleman ranking between a duke and a count.

marquise / mah-**keez** / *n.* the wife or widow of a marquis; a woman holding the rank of marquis in her own right.

marram / **ma**-ruhm / *n.* a shore grass that binds sand.

marri *n.* a WA eucalypt with esp. red flowers, often cultivated. (¶ Nyungar)

marriage *n.* **1** the legal union of a man and woman for cohabitation and often procreation. **2** the act or ceremony of being married. **3** a close union; a combination. ☐ **marriage celebrant** a man or woman empowered to perform a marriage, esp. in a non-religious ceremony. **marriage certificate** a certificate confirming that two people are legally married. **marriage guidance** advice given by authorised counsellors about marital problems.

marriageable *adj.* old enough or fit for marriage. ☐ **marriageability** *n.*

married *adj.* **1** united in marriage. **2** of marriage (*married name; married life*). • *n.* (usu. in *plural*) a married person (*young marrieds*).

marron / **ma**-ruhn / (*pl.* **marron** *or* **marrons**) a large freshwater crayfish of WA. (¶ Nyungar)

marrow *n.* **1** the soft fatty substance in the cavities of bones. **2** the large fruit of a plant of the gourd family, used as a vegetable. **3** the essential part. ☐ **to the marrow** right through (*I'm chilled to the marrow*).

marrowbone *n.* a bone containing edible marrow.

marry *v.* (**married**, **marrying**) **1** unite or give or take in marriage. **2** take a husband or wife in marriage (*he never married*). **3** unite, combine. **4** pair (socks etc). ☐ **marry off** find a spouse for. **marry up** link, join.

marrying *adj.* likely or inclined to marry (*he's not the marrying kind*).

Mars 1 *Rom. myth.* the god of war, identified with Ares. **2** one of the planets, with a characteristic red colour.

Marsala / mah-**sah**-luh, muh- / *n.* a dark sweet fortified wine of a kind originally made in Sicily.

Marseillaise / mah-suh-**layz** / *n.* the national anthem of France.

marsh *n.* low-lying watery ground. ☐ **marsh gas** methane. ☐☐ **marshy** *adj.*

marshal *n.* **1** an officer of high or the highest rank (*Field Marshal*). **2** an official with responsibility for arranging certain public events or ceremonies. **3** an official at a race. • *v.* (**marshalled**, **marshalling**) **1** arrange in proper order. **2** cause to assemble. **3** usher (*marshalled him into the governor's office*). ☐ **marshalling yard** a railway yard in which goods trains etc. are assembled for dispatch.

Marshall, Alan (1902–84), AM, Australian writer, best known for his autobiographical novel *I Can Jump Puddles* which has been filmed in Australia and in Europe.

Marshall Islands a country consisting of two chains of islands in the NW Pacific.

marshmallow *n.* a soft sticky sweet made from sugar, egg white, and gelatine.

marsupial / mah-**soo**-pee-uhl / *n.* an animal such as the kangaroo, the female of which gives birth to an undeveloped foetus which is then carried in a pouch until fully developed. • *adj.* of or like a marsupial. ☐ **marsupial lion** a large, extinct, carnivorous Australian marsupial. **marsupial mole** a small, blind, burrowing marsupial of arid Australia. **marsupial mouse** any of many small carnivorous marsupials widespread in Australia (e.g. the DUNNART, the MULGARA) some of which are also known as bush mice and pouched mice. **marsupial rat** a small carnivorous marsupial of arid central Australia.

marsupium / mah-**soo**-pee-uhm / *n.* (*pl.* **marsupia**) **1** the pouch of a marsupial. **2** a pouch for similar use in other animals, e.g. a receptacle for eggs in certain crustaceans.

mart *n.* a market.

marten *n.* a weasel-like carnivore of Canada etc. with thick soft fur.

Martial / **mah**-shuhl / (Latin name: Marcus Valerius Martialis) (AD *c.*40–*c.*104), Roman writer of epigrams.

martial / **mah**-shuhl / *adj.* of war, warlike (*martial music*). ☐ **martial arts** fighting sports such as judo and karate. **martial law** military rule imposed on a country, suspending ordinary law.

Martian / **mah**-shuhn / *adj.* of the planet Mars. • *n.* (in science fiction etc.) an inhabitant of Mars.

martin *n.* **1** a kind of European swallow. **2** *Aust.* any swallow-like migratory bird in Australia.

martinet / mah-tuh-**net** / *n.* a person who demands strict obedience.

martini / mah-**tee**-nee / *n.* a cocktail of gin and vermouth.

Martuthunira / **mahr**-too-too-ni-ru / *n.* an Aboriginal language of a large area of north-west WA.

martyr *n.* **1** a person who undergoes death or great suffering in support of a belief, cause, or principle. **2** a person who makes a show of suffering to get sympathy. **3** (foll. by *to*) a constant sufferer from (an ailment) (*is a martyr to migraine*). • *v.* put to death or torment as a martyr. ☐ **martyrdom** *n.*

marvel *n.* **1** a wonderful thing. **2** (foll. by *of*) a wonderful example of (a quality) (*the house was a marvel of neatness and comfort*). • *v.* (**marvelled, marvelling**) be filled with wonder.

marvellous *adj.* astonishing, excellent. ☐ **marvellously** *adv.*

Marx, Karl (Heinrich) (1818–83), German political philosopher and economist, founder of modern Communism.

Marx Brothers an American family of film comedians, consisting of Chico (1891–1961), and his brothers Harpo (1893–1964), Groucho (1895–1977), and Zeppo (1900–79).

Marxism *n.* the political and economic theory of Karl Marx, predicting the overthrow of capitalism and common ownership of the means of production in a classless society. ☐ **Marxist** *adj.* & *n.*

Mary[1] (in the Bible) **1** the Blessed Virgin Mary, mother of Jesus Christ. **2** St Mary Magdalene (= of Magdala in Galilee), a follower of Christ.

Mary[2] *n.* (*pl.* **Marys**) (also **mary**) *Aust.* (in Aboriginal English) **1** an Aboriginal woman. **2** (also **white Mary**) a white woman.

Mary, Queen of Scots (1542–87), queen of Scotland 1542–67, beheaded after the discovery of a Catholic plot against her cousin, Elizabeth I of England.

marzipan / mah-zuh-pan / *n.* a paste of ground almonds and sugar, made into small cakes or sweets or used to coat large cakes.

Masada / muh-**sah**-duh / a fortress on a steep hill west of the Dead Sea, famous as the Jewish stronghold during the revolt against Roman rule, where in AD 73 the defenders committed mass suicide rather than surrender.

Masai / **mah**-suy, ma-**suy** / *n.* (*pl.* **Masai** or **Masais**) **1** a member of a pastoral people of Kenya and Tanzania. **2** their language.

masala / muh-**sah**-luh / *n.* **1** any of various spice mixtures ground into a paste or powder for use in Indian cookery. **2** a dish flavoured with this.

mascara *n.* a cosmetic for darkening the eyelashes.

mascarpone / mas-kuh-**poh**-nee / *n.* a soft triple-cream Italian cheese used esp. in desserts.

mascot *n.* a person, animal, or thing supposed to bring good luck.

masculine *adj.* **1** of, like, or suitable for men; having the qualities or appearance considered characteristic of a man. **2** having the grammatical form of the male gender (*'hero' is a masculine noun, 'heroine' is the corresponding feminine noun*). • *n.* a masculine word or gender. ☐ **masculinity** *n.*

masculist *n.* a person who upholds the rights of men in the same way as a feminist upholds those of women. • *adj.* upholding men's rights.

maser / **may**-zuh / *n.* a device for amplifying microwaves.

Maseru / muh-**sair**-roo / the capital of Lesotho.

mash *n.* **1** grain or bran etc. cooked in water to form a soft mixture, used as animal food. **2** *colloq.* mashed potatoes. **3** a mixture of malt and hot water used in brewing. • *v.* beat or crush into a soft mixture.

mask *n.* **1** a covering worn over the face (or part of it) as a disguise or for protection. **2** a carved or moulded replica of a face (*death mask*). **3** a respirator worn over the face to filter air for breathing or to supply gas for inhaling. **4** disguise, pretence (*throw off the mask*). **5** a screen used in photography to exclude part of the image. • *v.* **1** cover with a mask. **2** disguise, screen, or conceal. ☐ **masking tape** adhesive tape used when painting to protect areas where paint is not wanted.

masochist / **mas**-uh-kist / *n.* **1** a person who derives sexual excitement and satisfaction from his or her own pain or humiliation. **2** one who enjoys what seems to be painful or tiresome. ☐ **masochism** *n.* **masochistic** *adj.*

mason *n.* **1** a person who works or builds with stone. **2** (**Mason**) a Freemason. ☐ **Masonic** *adj.* (in sense 2).

masonry *n.* stonework; the work of a mason.

masque / mahsk / *n.* a musical drama with mime, esp. in the 16th and 17th centuries.

masquerade / mah-skuh-**rayd**, mas-kuh- / *n.* a false show or pretence. • *v.* pretend to be what one is not (*masqueraded as a policeman*).

mass[1] *n.* **1** a coherent unit of matter with no specific shape. **2** a large quantity or heap, an unbroken extent (*the garden was a mass of flowers*). **3** (in technical usage) the quantity of matter a body contains (called *weight* in non-technical usage). **4** (**the mass**) the majority. **5** (**the masses**) the common people. • *adj.* on a large scale (*mass hysteria*). • *v.* gather or assemble into a mass. ☐ **mass media** = the media; *see* MEDIA (sense 2). **mass meeting** one attended by a large number of people. **mass noun** *Grammar* a noun that is not normally countable and not used with the indefinite article, e.g. *bread*. **mass number** the total number of protons and neutrons in a nucleus. **mass-produce** manufacture in large numbers of identical articles by standardised processes. **mass production** manufacturing in this way.

mass² *n.* (usu. **Mass**) (esp. in the Catholic Church) **1** the central act of worship during which, when the celebrant priest pronounces the words of consecration, bread and the wine are each changed into the substance of the body and the blood of Christ. See TRANSUBSTANTIATION. **2** the liturgy used in this; a musical setting for the words of it.

massacre *n.* slaughter of a large number of people or animals. • *v.* slaughter in large numbers.

massage / mas-ah*zh*, muh-sah*zh*, -sah*j* / *n.* rubbing and kneading the body for pleasure or to lessen pain or stiffness. • *v.* **1** treat in this way. **2** adjust (figures, statistics, etc.) to give an acceptable result. **3** flatter (a person's ego etc.). ☐ **massage parlour 1** an establishment providing massage of various kinds. **2** *euphemistic* a male or female brothel.

masseur / ma-ser / *n.* a man who practises massage professionally.

masseuse / ma-serz / *n.* a woman who practises massage professionally.

massif / mas-eef, ma-seef / *n.* mountain heights forming a compact group.

massive *adj.* **1** large and heavy or solid. **2** unusually large. **3** exceptionally large (*a massive improvement*). ☐ **massively** *adv.* **massiveness** *n.*

mast *n.* **1** a long upright pole that supports a ship's sails. **2** a tall pole from which a flag is flown. **3** a tall steel structure for the aerials of a radio or television transmitter. ☐ **before the mast** serving as an ordinary seaman (quartered in the forecastle). ☐☐ **masted** *adj.*

mastectomy / mas-tek-tuh-mee / *n.* surgical removal of a breast.

master *n.* **1** a person who has control or ownership of people or things. **2** the captain of a merchant ship. **3** a male teacher, a schoolmaster. **4** (**Master**) the holder of a usu. postgraduate university degree as *Master of Arts* etc. **5** a respected teacher. **6** a person with very great skill, a great artist. **7** a chess player of proved ability at international level. **8** a document, film, disk, etc. from which a series of copies is made. **9** (**Master**) a title prefixed to the name of a boy who is not old enough to be called *Mr.* • *v.* **1** overcome, bring under control. **2** acquire knowledge or skill in. ☐ **master class** a class given by a famous musician, artist, etc. **master key** a key that opens a number of locks, each also opened by a separate key. **master stroke** an outstandingly skilful act of policy etc. **master switch** a switch controlling the supply of electricity etc. to an entire system.

masterful *adj.* **1** domineering. **2** (of a person) very skilful. ☐ **masterfully** *adv.*

masterly *adj.* (of an achievement or ability) worthy of a master, very skilful.

mastermind *n.* **1** a person with outstanding mental ability. **2** the person directing an enterprise. • *v.* plan and direct (*masterminded the whole scheme*).

Master of Ceremonies *n.* a person in charge of a social or other occasion, who introduces the events or performers.

masterpiece *n.* **1** an outstanding piece of workmanship. **2** a person's best piece of work.

mastery *n.* **1** complete control, supremacy. **2** thorough knowledge or skill (*his mastery of Arabic*).

masthead *n.* **1** the highest part of a ship's mast. **2** the title details of a newspaper at the head of its front or editorial page.

mastic *n.* **1** a gum or resin exuded from certain trees. **2** a type of cement.

masticate *v.* chew (food). ☐ **mastication** *n.* **masticatory** *adj.*

mastiff *n.* a large strong dog with drooping ears.

mastitis / mas-tuy-tuhs / *n.* inflammation of the breast or udder.

mastodon / mas-tuh-don / *n.* a large extinct animal resembling the elephant.

mastoid *adj.* shaped like a breast. • *n.* **1** = MASTOID PROCESS. **2** (usu. as **mastoids**) inflammation of the mastoid process. ☐ **mastoid process** a cone-shaped bump on the temporal bone behind the ear.

masturbate *v.* excite oneself (or another person) sexually by stimulating the genitals with the hand. ☐ **masturbation** *n.* **masturbator** *n.* **masturbatory** *adj.*

mat¹ *n.* **1** a piece of material used as a floor covering, a doormat. **2** a small pad or piece of material placed under an ornament or vase etc. on or under a hot dish, to protect the surface on which it stands. **3** a thick pad for landing on in gymnastics etc. • *v.* (**matted, matting**) make or become entangled to form a thick mass (*matted hair*). ☐ **on the mat** *colloq.* being reprimanded.

mat² alternative spelling of MATT.

Matabele / mat-uh-bee-lee / *n.* (*pl.* **Matabele**) a member of a Bantu-speaking people of Zimbabwe.

matador / mat-uh-daw / *n.* a performer whose task is to fight and kill the bull in a bull-fight.

Mata Hari / mah-tuh hah-ree / (original name: Margaretha Geertruida Zelle) (1876–1917), Dutch dancer, courtesan, and secret agent, who worked for both the French and the German intelligence services before being executed by the French as a spy.

match¹ *n.* a short piece of wood or pasteboard with a combustible tip.

match² *n.* **1** a contest in a game or sport. **2** a person or animal with abilities equalling those of one met in contest (*meet one's match; you are no match for him*). **3** a person or thing exactly like or corresponding to another. **4** a marriage. **5** a person considered as a partner for marriage. • *v.* **1**

matchbox (foll. by *against* or *with*) place in competition (*the teams were matched against each other*). **2** equal in ability or skill etc. **3** be alike or correspond in colour, quality, quantity, etc. (*his socks don't match*). **4** find something similar to (*I want to match this wool*). **5** put or bring together as corresponding (*matching unemployed workers with vacant posts*). ☐ **match play** Golf scoring by counting the holes won by each side (as opposed to the number of strokes taken). **match point** the stage in a match when one side will win if it gains the next point; this point.

matchbox *n.* a box for holding matches.

matchless *adj.* unequalled.

matchmaker *n.* a person who is fond of scheming to bring about marriages. ☐ **matchmaking** *adj.* & *n.*

matchstick *n.* the stem of a match.

matchwood *n.* **1** wood that splinters easily. **2** wood reduced to splinters.

mate[1] *n.* **1** a very close friend. **2** an acquaintance or fellow worker. **3** a form of address, esp. to another man, implying equality and goodwill. **4** *Aust.* a form of address implying irony or even hostility (*watch it, mate!*). **5** each of a mated pair of birds or animals. **6** *colloq.* a partner in marriage. **7** a fellow member or sharer (*team-mate; room-mate*). **8** an officer on a merchant ship ranking next below the master. **9** a worker's assistant (*plumber's mate*). • *v.* **1** put or come together as a pair or as corresponding. **2** put (two birds or animals) together so that they can breed; come together in order to breed. **3** associate with as a friend.

mate[2] *n.* a situation in chess in which the capture of a king cannot be prevented. • *v.* put into this situation.

material *n.* **1** the substance or things from which something is or can be made or with which something is done (*writing materials; select those regarded as officer material*). **2** cloth, fabric. **3** facts, information, or events etc. to be used in composing something (*gathering material for a book on poverty*). • *adj.* **1** of matter; consisting of matter; of the physical (as opposed to spiritual) world (*material things; had no thought of material gain*). **2** of bodily comfort (*our material well-being*). **3** important, significant, relevant (*at the material time; he is material to our success*).

materialise *v.* (also **-ize**) **1** appear or become visible; arrive (*the boy failed to materialise*). **2** become a fact, happen (*if the threatened strike materialises*). ☐ **materialisation** *n.*

materialism *n.* **1** excessive concern with material possessions rather than spiritual or intellectual values. **2** belief that only the material world exists. ☐ **materialist** *n.* **materialistic** *adj.*

materially *adv.* **1** substantially, considerably. **2** in respect of matter; physically.

matériel / muh-teer-ree-**el** / *n.* **1** materials and equipment needed or used in a business etc. (as opposed to PERSONNEL). **2** materials and equipment in warfare.

maternal / muh-**ter**-nuhl / *adj.* **1** of a mother, of motherhood. **2** motherly. **3** related through one's mother (*maternal uncle*). ☐ **maternally** *adv.*

maternity / muh-**ter**-nuh-tee / *n.* **1** motherhood. **2** of or suitable to or caring for women in pregnancy or childbirth (*maternity dress; maternity ward*).

mateship *n.* *Aust.* **1** the bond between equal partners or close friends. **2** comradeship. **3** comradeship as an ideal.

matey *Aust. colloq. adj.* (**matier**, **matiest**) sociable; familiar, friendly. • *n.* (as a form of address) **1** close comrade, mate. **2** *Aust.* implying irony or even hostility (*just watch it, matey!*). ☐ **mateyness** *n.* **matily** *adv.*

mathematician *n.* a person who is skilled in mathematics.

mathematics *n.* **1** (usu. treated as *sing.*) the science of number, quantity, and space. **2** (treated as *pl.*) the use of mathematics in calculation (*his mathematics are weak*). ☐ **mathematical** *adj.* **mathematically** *adv.*

maths *n. colloq.* mathematics.

matilda / muh-**til**-duh / *n. Aust.* a bushman's bundle; a swag. ☐ **waltz matilda** carry one's swag; travel the road. (*See also* WALTZING MATILDA.)

matinée / **mat**-uh-nay / *n.* (also **matinee**) an afternoon performance at a theatre or cinema. ☐ **matinée coat** (*or* **jacket**) a baby's short coat.

matins *n.* **1** the first of the canonical hours in the Catholic Church; the service for this, said or chanted at midnight or daybreak. **2** (also **mattins**) (treated as *sing.* or *pl.*) morning prayer, esp. in the Anglican Church.

Matisse / ma-**tees** /, Henri (Émile Benoît) (1869–1954), French painter and sculptor.

matriarch / **may**-tree-ahk, **mat**-ree- / *n.* a woman who is head of a family or tribe. ☐ **matriarchal** / may-tree-**ah**-kuhl, mat-ree- / *adj.*

matriarchy / **may**-tree-ah-kee, **mat**-ree- / *n.* **1** a social organisation in which the mother is head of the family and descent is through the female line. **2** a society in which women have most of the authority.

matrices *see* MATRIX.

matricide / **may**-truh-suyd, **mat**-ruh- / *n.* **1** the act of killing one's mother. **2** a person who is guilty of this. ☐ **matricidal** *adj.*

matriculate / muh-**trik**-yuh-layt / *v.* be formally admitted to a university or the like.

matriculation *n.* **1** matriculating. **2** a secondary school examination to qualify for this.

matrilineal / ma-truh-**lin**-ee-uhl / *adj.* of or based on kinship with the mother or the female line of ancestors.

matrimony / **mat**-ruh-muh-nee / n. marriage. ◻ **matrimonial** / mat-ruh-**moh**-nee-uhl / adj. **matrimonially** adv.

matrix / **may**-triks / n. (pl. **matrices** / **may**-truh-seez / or **matrixes**) 1 a mould in which something is cast or shaped. 2 a place in which a thing is developed. 3 rock in which gems, fossils, etc., are embedded. 4 an array of mathematical quantities etc. in rows and columns. 5 (in computers) an interconnected array of circuit elements that resembles a lattice or grid.

matron n. 1 a married woman, esp. one who is staid and middle-aged or elderly. 2 a woman nurse and housekeeper at a school etc. 3 a former term for the woman in charge of nursing in a hospital or other institution. ◻ **matron of honour** a married woman as the chief attendant of the bride at a wedding.

■ Usage In sense 3, *Director of Nursing* is now the official term.

matronly adj. like or suitable for a staid married woman.

matt adj. (also **mat**) (of a colour or surface) having a dull finish, not shiny. • n. (in full **matt paint**) paint giving a dull flat finish.

matter n. 1 that which occupies space in the visible world, as opposed to spirit, mind, or qualities etc. 2 a specified substance (*colouring matter; reading matter*). 3 a discharge from the body; pus. 4 material for thought or expression; the content of a book or speech as distinct from its form (*subject matter*). 5 a situation or business being considered (*it's a serious matter; a matter for complaint*). • v. be of importance (*it doesn't matter*). ◻ **a matter of** approximately; amounting to (*a matter of 40 years*). **a matter of course** an event etc. that follows naturally or is to be expected. **matter-of-fact** adj. strictly factual and not imaginative or emotional; down-to-earth. **for that matter** as far as that is concerned. **no matter 1** (foll. by *when*, *how*, etc.) regardless of. **2** it is of no importance. **the matter** the thing that is amiss, the trouble or difficulty (*what's the matter?*).

Matterhorn a spectacular Alpine peak on the Swiss-Italian border.

Matthew, St 1 an Apostle, to whom the first Gospel is ascribed. 2 the first Gospel.

matting n. mats; material for making these.

mattock n. an agricultural tool like a pickaxe, with an adze and a chisel edge.

mattress n. a stuffed or air-filled or water-filled cushion the size of a bed.

maturate / **mat**-yoo-rayt / v. 1 come or bring to maturation, mature. 2 (of a boil etc.) come to a head.

maturation / mat-yoo-**ray**-shuhn / n. 1 the process of maturing, ripening. 2 the formation of pus.

mature adj. 1 having reached full growth or development. 2 having or showing fully developed mental powers, capable of reasoning and acting sensibly. 3 ripe; seasoned. 4 (of wine) having reached a good stage of development. 5 (of a bill of exchange, life assurance policy, etc.) due for payment. • v. make or become mature. ◻ **maturely** adv. **maturity** n.

matutinal / mat-yoo-**tuy**-nuhl, muh-**tyoo**-tuh-nuhl / adj. *formal* of or occurring in the morning.

matzo n. (pl. **matzos**) a wafer of unleavened bread, traditionally eaten at Passover.

maudlin adj. sentimental in a silly or tearful way, esp. from drunkenness.

maul v. 1 tear the flesh of; claw. 2 treat roughly, injure by rough handling. 3 damage by criticism. • n. 1 (in Rugby) a loose scrum. 2 a brawl. 3 a heavy hammer.

maunder v. talk in a rambling way.

Maundy n. the ceremony in which the pope, bishops, and priests wash and kiss the feet of the poor on Maundy Thursday to commemorate Christ's washing of the Apostles' feet at the Last Supper. ◻ **Maundy Thursday** the Thursday before Easter Sunday.

Mauritania / mo-ruh-**tay**-nee-uh / a republic in north-west Africa. ◻ **Mauritanian** adj. & n.

Mauritius / muh-**rish**-uhs / an independent country consisting of an island in the Indian Ocean. ◻ **Mauritian** adj. & n.

mausoleum / maw-suh-**lee**-uhm / n. a magnificent tomb. (¶ Named after that erected at Halicarnassus in Asia Minor for King Mausolus in the 4th century BC.)

mauve / mohv / adj. & n. pale purple.

maverick / **mav**-uh-rik / n. 1 an unconventional or independent-minded person. 2 an unbranded calf or yearling.

maw n. 1 the stomach of an animal. 2 *colloq*. the stomach of a greedy person. 3 the jaws or throat of a voracious animal.

mawkish adj. sentimental in a sickly way. ◻ **mawkishly** adv. **mawkishness** n.

Mawson[1] an Australian research base in Antarctica, named after Sir Douglas Mawson.

Mawson[2], Sir Douglas (1882–1958), English-born Australian scientist and Antarctic explorer.

max. abbr. maximum. ◻ **to the max** *colloq*. to the utmost; extremely.

maxi n. *colloq*. a full-length skirt, coat, yacht, etc.

maxi- *comb. form* very large or long.

maxilla n. (pl. **maxillae**) 1 a jaw, esp. the upper one. 2 a corresponding part in insects etc. ◻ **maxillary** adj.

maxim n. a general truth or rule of conduct, e.g. 'waste not, want not'.

maxima see MAXIMUM.

maximal adj. greatest possible. ◻ **maximally** adv.

maximise v. (also **-ize**) make as large or as great as possible. ◻ **maximisation** n.

■ Usage *Maximise* should not be used in standard English to mean 'to make as good as possible' or 'to make the most of'.

maximum *n.* (*pl.* **maxima**) the greatest or greatest possible number, amount, or intensity etc. • *adj.* greatest, greatest possible.

May *n.* the fifth month of the year. ☐ **May Day** 1 May, kept as an international holiday in honour of workers.

may *auxiliary v.* (*see also* MIGHT²) expressing possibility (*it may be true*), permission (*you may go*), wish (*may he live to regret it*), uncertainty (*whoever it may be*), or irony (*who are you, may I ask?*).

Maya / mah-yuh / *n.* **1** (*pl.* **Maya** or **Mayas**) a member of an American Indian people living in Mexico until the 15th century. **2** their language. ☐ **Mayan** *adj.* & *n.*

maya / mah-yuh / *n.* **1** (in Hinduism) illusion, magic. **2** (in Hindu and Buddhist philosophy) the power by which the universe becomes manifest; the material world, regarded as illusory.

maybe *adv.* perhaps, possibly.

mayday *n.* an international radio signal of distress. (¶ Representing the pronunciation of French *m'aidez*, = help me.)

Mayflower the ship in which, in 1620, the Pilgrim Fathers sailed from Plymouth to establish the first colony in New England on the coast of North America.

mayhem *n.* destruction; havoc.

Mayi-Kulan / muy-yee-kuu-lahn / *n.* an Aboriginal language of north-west Qld.

Mayi-Kutuna / muy-yee-kuu-too-nu / *n.* an Aboriginal language of north-west Qld to the west of the speakers of Mayi-Kulan.

Mayi-Yapi / muy-yee-yah-pee / *n.* an Aboriginal language of north-west Qld between the speakers of Mayi-Kutuna and Mayi-Kulan.

mayn't = may not.

mayonnaise / may-uh-**nayz** / *n.* **1** a creamy sauce made with egg yolks, oil, and vinegar. **2** a dish with a dressing of this (*egg mayonnaise*).

mayor *n.* the head of the local council of a city or town etc. ☐ **mayoral** / mair-ruhl / *adj.*

mayoralty / mair-ruhl-tee / *n.* the office of mayor; its duration.

mayoress *n.* **1** a mayor's wife, or other lady performing her ceremonial duties. **2** a woman mayor.

maypole *n.* a tall pole, with ribbons attached to its top, around which some people dance on the first day of May (springtime in the Northern hemisphere).

Mazdaism / maz-duh-iz-uhm / *n.* Zoroastrianism, worship of Ahura Mazda.

maze *n.* **1** a complicated network of paths etc. **2** a network of paths and hedges designed as a puzzle in which to try and find one's way. **3** a labyrinth. **4** a state of bewilderment.

mazurka / muh-**zer**-kuh / *n.* a lively Polish dance in triple time; music for this.

MB *abbr.* **1** Bachelor of Medicine. **2** *Computing* (often **Mb**) megabyte.

Mbabane / uhm-bah-**bah**-nee / the capital of Swaziland.

Mbeki / uhm-**bek**-ee /, Thabo (Mvuyelwa) (1942–) South African statesman who became president in 1999.

MC *abbr.* **1** Master of Ceremonies. **2** Military Cross.

MCC *abbr.* Marylebone Cricket Club in London, until 1969 the governing body that made the rules of cricket.

MD *abbr.* Doctor of Medicine. (¶ Latin *Medicinae Doctor*.)

Md *symbol* mendelevium.

ME *abbr.* myalgic encephalomyelitis (*see* CHRONIC FATIGUE SYNDROME).

me¹ *pron.* **1** the objective case of I. **2** *colloq.* = I (*it's me*).

me² *n.* (also **mi**) *Music* the third note of a major scale.

mea culpa / mee-uh kul-puh, may-uh **kuul**-puh / *n.* & *interj.* an acknowledgment of error, guilt, etc. (¶ Latin, = by my fault.)

mead *n.* an alcoholic drink of fermented honey and water.

meadow *n.* (chiefly in Northern hemisphere use) a field of grass, esp. one used for hay.

meagre / **mee**-guh / *adj.* **1** scanty in amount. **2** lean, thin.

meal¹ *n.* **1** an occasion when food is eaten. **2** the food itself. ☐ **make a meal of** make (a task) seem unnecessarily laborious. **meals on wheels** a service that delivers hot meals by car to elderly or disabled people. **meal-ticket** *colloq.* a person or thing that is a source of maintenance or income (*she's his meal-ticket*).

meal² *n.* **1** coarsely-ground grain or pulse. **2** any powdery substance made by grinding (*almond meal*).

Meale, Richard (Graham) (1932–), AM, Australian composer whose works include the opera *Voss*.

mealy *adj.* **1** like or containing meal, dry and powdery. **2** (of a complexion) pale. ☐ **mealy-mouthed** *adj.* afraid to speak plainly.

mean¹ *v.* (**meant**, **meaning**) **1** have as one's purpose or intention. **2** design or destine for a purpose (*it was meant for you; are we meant to go this way?*). **3** intend to convey (a sense) or to indicate or refer to (a thing) (*I mean Richmond in Melbourne*). **4** (of words) have as an equivalent in the same or another language ('*maybe*' *means 'perhaps'; 'nauta' means 'sailor'*). **5** entail, involve (*it means catching the early train*). **6** be likely or certain to result in (*this means war*). **7** be of a specified importance (*the honour means a lot to me*). ☐ **mean business** *colloq.* be ready to take action, not merely talk. **mean well** have good intentions.

mean² *adj.* **1** not generous, miserly. **2** ignoble, small-minded. **3** (of capacity, understanding etc.) inferior, poor. **4** shabby; inadequate (*a mean hovel*). **5** unkind, spiteful (*a mean trick*). **6** vicious or aggressive in behaviour. **7** *colloq.* skilful, formidable (*a mean fighter*). ☐ **no mean** a very good; considerable (*she's no mean runner; requiring no mean effort*). ☐☐ **meanly** *adv.* **meanness** *n.*

mean³ *adj.* (of a point or quantity) equally far from two extremes, average. • *n.* a middle point, condition, or course etc.

meander / mee-**an**-duh / *v.* **1** (of a stream) follow a winding course, flowing slowly and gently. **2** wander in a leisurely way. • *n.* a winding course.

meanie *n.* (also **meany**) *colloq.* a miserly or unkind person.

meaning *n.* what is meant; significance. • *adj.* full of meaning, expressive (*gave him a meaning look*).

meaningful *adj.* full of meaning, significant. ☐ **meaningfully** *adv.*

meaningless *adj.* having no meaning or significance. ☐ **meaninglessly** *adv.*

means *n.pl.* **1** (often treated as *sing.*) that by which a result is brought about (*transported the goods by means of trucks*). **2** resources; money or other wealth considered as a means of supporting oneself (*has private means*). ☐ **by all means** certainly. **by no means** definitely not; not at all (*it is by no means certain*). **means test** an official inquiry into a person's income in order to determine his or her eligibility for a pension or other assistance from public funds etc. **means-test** *v.* subject to or base on a means test.

meant *see* MEAN¹.

meantime *n.* the intervening period (*in the meantime*). • *adv.* meanwhile.

meanwhile *adv.* **1** in the intervening period of time. **2** at the same time, while something else takes place.

measles *n.* an infectious disease producing small red spots on the whole body.

measly *adj. colloq.* meagre, contemptible (*donated a measly two dollars*).

measure *n.* **1** the size or quantity of something, found by measuring. **2** extent, amount (*he is in some measure responsible; had a measure of success*). **3** a unit, standard, or system used in measuring (*the metre is a measure of length*). **4** a device used in measuring, e.g. a container or a marked rod. **5** the rhythm or metre of poetry; the time of a piece of music; a bar of music. **6** suitable action taken for a particular purpose; a law or proposed law (*measures to stop tax evasion*). **7** a layer of rock or mineral. • *v.* **1** find the size, quantity, or extent of something by comparing it with a fixed unit or with an object of known size. **2** be of a certain size (*it measures two metres by four*). **3** mark or deal out a measured quantity (*measured out their rations*). **4** estimate (a quality etc.) by comparing it with some standard. ☐ **beyond measure** very much, very great (*kindness beyond measure*). **for good measure** in addition to what was needed; as a finishing touch. **measure up to** reach the standard required by. ☐☐ **measurable** *adj.*

measured *adj.* **1** rhythmical, regular in movement (*measured tread*). **2** carefully considered (*in measured language*).

measureless *adj.* not measurable, infinite.

measurement *n.* **1** measuring. **2** size etc. found by measuring and expressed in units.

meat *n.* **1** animal flesh as food. **2** informative matter; the chief part (*the meat of the report*). **3** the edible part of fruit, nuts, eggs, shellfish, etc. **4** (in Aboriginal English) a totem; a totemic animal. ☐ **meat in the sandwich** the innocent victim of a conflict or clash of interests who is vulnerable to both sides. ☐☐ **meatless** *adj.*

meat ant *n. Aust.* a mound-building Australian ant, having a red head and purplish body, and capable of inflicting a painful bite. Also called *red ant, red meat ant.* ☐ **game as a meat ant** courageous and tenacious.

meat axe *n.* a butcher's cleaver. ☐ **mad as a meat axe** *Aust.* **1** extremely angry. **2** crazy; eccentric.

meat pie *n.* stewed meat in a square or oval pastry-case. ☐ **as Australian as meat pie** *Aust.* thoroughly Australian.

meatworks *n. Aust.* an abattoir. ☐ **meatworker** *n.*

meaty *adj.* (**meatier**, **meatiest**) **1** like meat. **2** full of meat, fleshy. **3** substantial; full of interest or information; satisfying (*a meaty book; a meaty problem*).

Mecca 1 a city in Saudi Arabia, the birth-place of Mohammed and chief place of Muslim pilgrimage. **2** any place that people with particular interests are eager to visit.

mechanic *n.* a skilled worker who uses or repairs machines or tools.

mechanical *adj.* **1** of machines or mechanisms. **2** worked or produced by machinery. **3** (of a person or action) like a machine, as if acting or done without conscious thought. **4** (of work) needing little or no thought. **5** of or belonging to the science of mechanics. ☐ **mechanical engineer** a person qualified in the design and construction of machines. **mechanical engineering** the work of a mechanical engineer. ☐☐ **mechanically** *adv.*

mechanics *n.* **1** the scientific study of motion and force. **2** the science of machinery. **3** (treated as *pl.*) the processes by which something is done or functions (*the mechanics of local government*).

mechanise / **mek**-uh-nuyz / *v.* (also **-ize**) **1** equip with machines, use machines in or for. **2** give a mechanical character to. ☐ **mechanisation** *n.*

mechanism   **medium**

mechanism *n.* **1** the way a machine works. **2** the structure of parts of a machine. **3** the process by which something is done (*the mechanism of government; no mechanism for complaints*).

medal *n.* a small flat metal disc bearing a design and commemorating an event or given as an award. • *v.* (**medalled, medalling**) **1** decorate or honour with a medal. **2** *colloq.* (in a sporting contest) win a medal.

medallion / muh-**dal**-yuhn / *n.* **1** a large medal. **2** a large circular ornamental design, e.g. on a carpet.

medallist *n.* one who wins a medal as a prize (*gold medallist*).

meddle *v.* **1** interfere in people's affairs. **2** tinker. ☐ **meddler** *n.*

meddlesome *adj.* often meddling.

Medea / muh-**dee**-uh / *Gk myth.* a sorceress, daughter of Aeetes king of Colchis. She helped Jason to obtain the Golden Fleece, and married him, but was deserted in Corinth and avenged herself by killing their two children.

medevac / **med**-ee-vak / *n.* **1** a military helicopter for transporting wounded soldiers etc. to hospital. **2** a helicopter for transporting people to hospital, esp. from remote areas. • *v.* transport (a person) by a medevac.

media / **mee**-dee-uh / *n.pl.* **1** *see* MEDIUM. **2** (**the media**) newspapers and broadcasting, by which information is conveyed to the general public.

■ **Usage** This word is commonly used with a singular verb (e.g. *the media is biased*), but this is not generally accepted as it is the plural of *medium* and should therefore have a plural verb.

mediaeval alternative spelling of MEDIEVAL.

medial / **mee**-dee-uhl / *adj.* situated in the middle, intermediate between two extremes. ☐ **medially** *adv.*

median / **mee**-dee-uhn / *adj.* situated in or passing through the middle. • *n.* **1** a median point or line etc. **2** a medial number or point in a series. ☐ **median strip** a strip of ground, paved or landscaped etc., dividing a street or highway.

mediant / **mee**-dee-uhnt / *n. Music* the third note of a diatonic scale of any key.

mediate / **mee**-dee-ayt / *v.* **1** act as negotiator or peacemaker between the opposing sides in a dispute. **2** bring about (a settlement) in this way. ☐ **mediation** *n.* **mediator** *n.*

medic *n. colloq.* a medical practitioner or student.

medical *adj.* of or involving the science of medicine; of this as distinct from surgery. • *n. colloq.* a medical examination. ☐ **medical certificate** a certificate giving the results of a medical examination, stating whether a person is fit for work etc. **medical examination** examination by a doctor to determine a person's state of health. **medical practitioner** a physician or surgeon. ☐ ☐ **medically** *adv.*

medicament / muh-**dik**-uh-muhnt, **med**-i-kuh-muhnt / *n.* any medicine or ointment etc.

Medicare *n.* the Federal system of basic health care for all Australians, introduced in 1984 by the Labor government and partly financed by a levy on taxable incomes.

medicate *v.* **1** treat medically. **2** impregnate with medicine (*medicated lozenges*).

medication *n.* **1** medicine, drugs, etc. **2** treatment using drugs.

Medici / me-**dee**-chee / the name of an Italian family prominent esp. in Florence and Tuscany in the 15th–17th centuries.

medicinal / muh-**dis**-uh-nuhl / *adj.* of medicine; having healing properties. ☐ **medicinally** *adv.*

medicine / **med**-suhn, **med**-uh-suhn / *n.* **1** the scientific study of the prevention and cure of diseases and disorders of the body. **2** this as distinct from surgery. **3** a substance used to treat a disease etc., esp. one taken by mouth. ☐ **medicine man** a person believed to have powers of healing, esp. among Australian Aborigines. **take one's medicine** submit to something unpleasant.

medico *n.* (*pl.* **medicos**) *colloq.* a medical practitioner or medical student.

medieval / med-ee-**ee**-vuhl / *adj.* (also **mediaeval**) **1** of the Middle Ages. **2** *colloq.* old-fashioned.

medifraud *n. Aust.* **1** the practice (usu. by doctors) of making fraudulent claims against a medical insurance scheme. **2** an instance of this.

Medina / me-**dee**-nuh / a city in Saudi Arabia, the second holiest city of Islam (after Mecca), which contains Mohammed's tomb.

mediocre / mee-dee-**oh**-kuh / *adj.* **1** of medium quality, neither good nor bad. **2** second-rate. ☐ **mediocrity** / mee-dee-**ok**-ruh-tee / *n.*

meditate *v.* **1** think deeply and quietly; engage in religious contemplation. **2** plan in one's mind (*he meditated revenge*). ☐ **meditation** *n.*

meditative / **med**-uh-tuh-tiv, -tay-tiv / *adj.* meditating; accompanied by meditation. ☐ **meditatively** *adv.*

Mediterranean *adj.* of or characteristic of the Mediterranean Sea or the regions bordering on it (*Mediterranean cooking*). • *n.* (in full **Mediterranean Sea**) the sea bordered by southern Europe, SW Asia, and northern Africa.

medium *n.* (*pl.* **media** or **mediums**) **1** a middle quality or degree of intensiveness etc. between extremes. **2** a substance or surroundings in which something exists, moves, or is transmitted (*air is the medium through which sound travels*). **3** an environment. **4** a liquid (e.g. oil or water) in which pigments are mixed for use in painting. **5** an agency or means by which something is done (*the use of television as a medium for advertising*). **6** the material or form used by an artist or composer (*sculpture is his medium*). **7** (*pl.* **mediums**) a person who claims to be able to communicate with the spirits of the dead. • *adj.* intermediate between two extremes or amounts, average, moderate. ☐ **medium wave** a radio wave having a wavelength between 300 kHz and 3 MHz.

■ Usage See the entry for *media*.

medlar *n.* **1** a fruit like a small brown apple that is not edible until it begins to decay. **2** the tree that bears it.

medley *n.* (*pl.* **medleys**) **1** an assortment of things. **2** a collection of tunes or songs played or performed as one piece. **3 a** a swimming race in which each competitor swims set distances in different strokes. **b** (in full **medley relay**) a relay race between swimming teams in which each team member swims a different stroke.

medulla / muh-**dul**-uh / *n.* **1** the marrow within a bone; the substance of the spinal cord. **2** the hindmost section of the brain. **3** the central part of certain organs, e.g. that of the kidney. **4** the soft internal tissue of plants. ☐ **medullary** *adj.*

Medusa / muh-**dyoo**-suh / *Gk myth.* one of the Gorgons, slain by Perseus who cut off her head.

medusa / muh-**dyoo**-suh / *n.* (*pl.* **medusae** or **medusas**) a jellyfish.

meek *adj.* quiet and obedient, making no protest. ☐ **meekly** *adv.* **meekness** *n.*

meerkat *n.* a South African mongoose.

meerschaum / **meer**-shuhm / *n.* a tobacco pipe with a bowl made from a white clay-like substance.

meet[1] *v.* (**met**, **meeting**) **1** come face to face with, come together (e.g. socially or for discussion). **2** come into contact, touch. **3** go to a place to be present at the arrival of (*I will meet your train*). **4** make the acquaintance of, be introduced. **5** come together as opponents in a contest or battle. **6** find oneself faced (with a thing); experience or receive (*met with difficulties; met his death*). **7** deal with (a problem); satisfy (a demand etc.); pay (the cost or what is owing). • *n.* **1** a meeting of athletes etc. for a competition. **2** *colloq.* an assignation, a date, esp. with someone of the opposite sex. ☐ **meet the case** be adequate or satisfactory. **meet the eye** (*or* **ear**) be visible (or audible).

meet[2] *adj. archaic* suitable, proper.

meeting *n.* **1** coming together. **2** an assembly of a society, committee, etc.; the persons assembled (*addressed the meeting*). **3** a race meeting.

meg *n.* one megabyte of computer memory or storage.

mega / **meg**-uh / *colloq. adj.* **1** excellent. **2** enormous. • *adv.* extremely.

mega- *comb. form* **1** large. **2** one million (*megavolts, megawatts*). **3** *colloq.* extremely; very big (*mega-stupid*).

megabucks *n. colloq.* a large amount of money.

megabyte *n. Computing* a measure of how much data a disk or memory can hold, = 1,048,576 (i.e. 2^{20}) bytes.

megacycle *n.* **1** one million cycles as a unit of wave frequency. **2** *colloq.* megahertz.

Megaera / muh-**jeer**-ruh / *Gk myth.* one of the Furies.

megafauna *n.* the large or macroscopic animals or animal life, esp. the large vertebrates, of a given area, habitat, or epoch.

megaflop *n.* **1** *Computing* a processing speed of a million floating-point operations per second. **2** *colloq.* complete failure.

megahertz *n.* a unit of frequency of electromagnetic waves, = one million cycles per second.

megalith / **meg**-uh-lith / *n.* a huge stone used in the building of prehistoric monuments. ☐ **megalithic** / meg-uh-**lith**-ik / *adj.*

megalomania / meg-uh-luh-**may**-nee-uh / *n.* **1** a form of madness in which a person has exaggerated ideas of his or her own importance etc. **2** an obsessive desire to do things on a grand scale. ☐ **megalomaniac** *n.* & *adj.*

megalosaurus *n.* (*pl.* **megalosauruses**) a large flesh-eating dinosaur with stout hind legs and small front limbs.

megaphone *n.* a funnel-shaped device used for amplifying a speaker's voice.

megapode *n.* a bird, native to Australasia, that builds a mound of debris for the incubation of its eggs, e.g. a mallee fowl.

megastar *n. colloq.* an entertainer etc. who has reached the height of fame and fortune, a 'star' greater than a superstar.

megaton / **meg**-uh-tun / *n.* a unit of explosive power equal to that of one million tons of TNT.

megavolt *n.* a unit of electromotive force equal to one million volts.

megawatt *n.* a unit of electrical power equal to one million watts.

megohm *n.* a unit of electrical resistance equal to one million ohms.

Meillon, John (1934–89), Australian stage, television, and film actor.

meiosis / muy-**oh**-suhs / *n.* **1** the process of division of the nuclei of cells in which gametes are formed each containing half the normal number of chromosomes. **2** litotes.

Meir / may-**eer** /, Golda (original name: Goldie Mabovich) (1898–1978), Israeli stateswoman, prime minister 1969–74.

Meistersinger / **muy**-stuh-sing-uh / *n.* a member of one of the guilds of German lyric poets and musicians that flourished in the 14th–17th centuries.

meitnerium / muyt-**neer**-ree-uhm / *n.* a very unstable chemical element (symbol Mt) made by high-energy atomic collisions.

Mekong / mee-**kong** / the major river of SE Asia, flowing from Tibet along the Burma–Laos and Thailand–Laos borders and across Cambodia and Vietnam to the South China Sea.

melaleuca / mel-uh-**loo**-kuh / *n.* any tree or shrub of the large, essentially Australian genus

melancholia

Melaleuca with ball or bottlebrush flowers of white, yellow, purple, or red, many species being cultivated as ornamentals.

melancholia / mel-uhn-**koh**-lee-uh / *n.* mental depression.

melancholy / **mel**-uhn-kol-ee / *n.* **1** mental depression; thoughtful sadness. **2** an atmosphere of gloom. • *adj.* sad, gloomy, depressing. ◻ **melancholic** / mel-uhn-**kol**-ik / *adj.*

Melanesia / mel-uh-**nee**-zhuh / *a* group of islands in the SW Pacific containing the Bismarck Archipelago, the Solomon Islands, Santa Cruz, Vanuatu, New Caledonia, Fiji, and the intervening islands. ◻ **Melanesian** *adj.* & *n.*

melange / may-**lon**zh / *n.* a mixture, a medley.

melanin / **mel**-uh-nuhn / *n.* a dark pigment found in skin and hair.

melanoma / mel-uh-**noh**-muh / *n.* a malignant skin tumour.

Melba, Dame Nellie (original name: Helen Porter Mitchell) (1861–1931), Australian operatic soprano who won worldwide fame. ◻ **do a Melba** *Aust.* **1** return from retirement. **2** make several 'final' farewell appearances. **Melba sauce** a sauce made from puréed raspberries. **Melba toast** very thin crisp toast. **peach Melba** vanilla ice cream and peaches topped with a liqueur or Melba sauce.

Melbourne / **mel**-buhn / the capital of the State of Victoria and second-largest city in Australia (earlier *Bearbrass*, *Bearport*, *Bearheap*, and *Bearbury*, all variations of the Wuywurung name for the area *Berrern* or *Bararing*).

Melbourne Cup a horse race of 3,200 m run on the first Tuesday in November at Flemington racecourse since 1861, one of the world's great handicap races.

Melburnian / mel-**ber**-nee-uhn / *n.* a native of Melbourne. • *adj.* of or relating to Melbourne.

meld *v.* merge, blend.

Meldrum, 'Molly' (full name: Ian Alexander Meldrum) (1946–), AM, Australian commentator on rock music etc., for many years the host of the television program *Countdown*.

mêlée / **mel**-ay, muh-**lay** / *n.* (also **melee**) **1** a confused fight or skirmish. **2** a muddle. **3** *Aust. Rules* an incident (which brings detriment to the game) in which four or more players are involved.

melisma / muh-**liz**-muh / *n.* (*pl.* **melismata** / -muh-tuh / *or* **melismas**) *Mus.* a group of notes sung to one syllable of text.

mellifluous / muh-**lif**-loo-uhs / *adj.* sweet-sounding. ◻ **mellifluously** *adv.* **mellifluousness** *n.*

mellow *adj.* **1** sweet and rich in flavour. **2** (of sound or colour) soft and rich, free from harshness or sharp contrast. **3** made kindly and sympathetic by age or experience. **4** genial, jovial (e.g. through the effects of alcohol). **5** (of wines) well-matured, smooth. • *v.* make or become mellow. ◻ **mellowly** *adv.* **mellowness** *n.*

melodeon / muh-**loh**-dee-uhn / *n.* (also **melodion**) **1** a kind of harmonium. **2** a small accordion in which the notes are produced by pressing buttons.

melodic / muh-**lod**-ik / *adj.* of melody. ◻ **melodically** *adv.*

melodious / muh-**loh**-dee-uhs / *adj.* full of melody. ◻ **melodiously** *adv.*

melodrama / **mel**-uh-drah-muh / *n.* **1** a play full of suspense in a sensational and emotional style. **2** plays of this kind. **3** a situation in real life resembling this. ◻ **melodramatic** / mel-uh-druh-**mat**-ik / *adj.* **melodramatically** *adv.* **melodramatics** *n.pl.*

melody *n.* **1** sweet music, tunefulness. **2** a song or tune (*old Irish melodies*). **3** the main part in a piece of harmonised music.

melon *n.* the large sweet fruit of various gourds. ◻ **melon blindness** *Aust.* an illness of horses characterised by blindness and possibly caused by eating paddymelon. **melon hole** *Aust.* = GILGAI.

melt *v.* **1** make into or become liquid by heat. **2** (of food) be softened or dissolved easily (*it melts in the mouth*). **3** make or become gentler through pity or love. **4** dwindle or fade away; pass slowly into something else (*one shade of colour melted into another*). **5** (often foll. by *away*) (of a person) depart unobtrusively. ◻ **melt down** melt completely; melt (metal articles) in order to use the metal as raw material. **melting point** the temperature at which a solid melts. **melting pot 1** a place where races, theories, etc. are mixed. **2** an imaginary pool where ideas are mixed or reconstructed.

meltdown *n.* **1** the melting of (and consequent damage to) a structure, e.g. the overheated core of a nuclear reactor. **2** a disastrous event, esp. a rapid fall in share prices.

Melville, Herman (1819–91), American novelist and poet, author of *Moby Dick*.

Melville Island an island of 5,800 sq. km off the north coast of Australia, separated from Bathurst Island by Apsley Strait, and from the mainland by Clarence Strait, its Aboriginal name being Yermalner. Together with Bathurst Island it is the homeland of the Tiwi peoples who regained ownership of it in 1978.

member *n.* **1** a person or thing that belongs to a particular group of society. **2** (**Member**) (in full **Member of Parliament**) a person formally elected to take part in the proceedings of a parliament. **3** a part of a complex structure. **4** a part of the body, esp. a limb. **5** the penis. **6** used in the title awarded to a person admitted to (usu. the lowest grade of) certain honours (*Member of the Order of Australia*).

membership *n.* **1** being a member. **2** the total number of members.

membrane / **mem**-brayn / *n.* thin flexible skin-like tissue, esp. that covering or lining organs or other structures in animals and plants. ☐ **membranous** / mem-bruh-nuhs / *adj.*

meme / meem / *n.* an element of a culture or system of behaviour that may be considered to be passed from one individual to another by non-genetic means, esp. imitation. ☐ **memetic** *adj.*

memento / muh-**men**-toh / *n.* (*pl.* **mementoes** *or* **mementos**) a souvenir of a person or event.

memento mori *n.* a warning or reminder of death (e.g. a skull). (¶ Latin, = remember you must die.)

memo / **mem**-oh, **mee**-moh / *n.* (*pl.* **memos**) a memorandum.

memoir / **mem**-wah / *n.* **1** (**memoirs**) a written account of events that one has lived through or of the life or character of a person whom one knew (*write one's memoirs*). **2** an essay on a learned subject.

memorabilia *n.pl.* souvenirs and collectors' items relating to a particular period, event, famous person, etc. (*a sale of Beatles memorabilia*).

memorable / **mem**-uh-ruh-buhl / *adj.* worth remembering; easy to remember. ☐ **memorably** *adv.* **memorability** *n.*

memorandum / mem-uh-**ran**-duhm / *n.* (*pl.* **memorandums** *or* **memoranda**) **1** a note or record of events written as a reminder, for future use. **2** an informal written communication from one person to another in an office or organisation.

memorial *n.* an object, institution, or custom established in memory of an event or person. • *adj.* serving as a memorial.

memorise *v.* (also **-ize**) learn (a thing) so as to know it from memory.

memory *n.* **1** the ability to keep things in one's mind or to recall them at will. **2** remembering; a thing remembered (*memories of childhood*). **3** the length of time over which people's memory extends (*within living memory*). **4** the storage capacity of a computer. ☐ **from memory** remembered without the aid of notes etc. **in memory of** in honour of (a person or thing that is remembered with respect).

men *see* **MAN**. ☐ **men's business** *Aust.* an Aboriginal ritual open only to initiated males. **men's country** (also **men's site**) *Aust.* a site set apart for conducting men's business.

menace *n.* **1** something that seems likely to bring harm or danger; a threatening quality. **2** an annoying or troublesome person or thing. • *v.* threaten with harm or danger. ☐ **menacingly** *adv.*

ménage / may-**nahzh** / *n.* a household.

ménage à trois / ah **trwah** / *n.* (*pl.* **ménages à trois** pronounced the same) an arrangement in which three people live or have a relationship together, typically a married couple and the lover of one of them. (¶ French, = household of three.)

menagerie / muh-**naj**-uh-ree / *n.* a collection of wild animals in captivity, for exhibition.

menarche / **men**-ah-kee / *n.* the onset of first menstruation.

mend *v.* **1** make whole (something that is damaged), repair. **2** make or become better (*mend one's manners*). • *n.* a repaired place. ☐ **on the mend** improving in health or condition.

mendacious / men-**day**-shuhs / *adj.* untruthful, telling lies. ☐ **mendaciously** *adv.* **mendacity** / men-**das**-uh-tee / *n.*

Mendel / **men**-duhl /, Gregor Johan (1822–84), Moravian monk, founder of the science of genetics. ☐ **Mendelian** / men-**dee**-lee-uhn / *adj.*

mendelevium / men-duh-**lee**-vee-uhm / *n.* an artificially produced radioactive metallic element (symbol Md).

Mendelssohn / **men**-duhl-suhn /, (Jakob Ludwig) Felix (1809–47), German composer.

mendicant / **men**-duh-kuhnt / *adj.* begging; depending on alms for a living. • *n.* **1** a beggar. **2** a mendicant friar.

menfolk *n.pl.* men in general; the men of one's family.

menhir / **men**-heer / *n.* a tall upright stone set up in prehistoric times.

menial / **mee**-nee-uhl / *adj.* lowly, degrading (*menial tasks*). • *n.* a domestic servant; a person who does humble tasks. ☐ **menially** *adv.*

Meninga, Mal(colm Norman) (1960–), AO, Australian Rugby League player with the Canberra Raiders who also represented Australia in 41 Tests, 19 as captain.

meninges / muh-**nin**-jeez / *n.pl.* the three membranes that enclose the brain and spinal cord.

meningitis / men-uhn-**juy**-tuhs / *n.* inflammation of the meninges.

meningococcus / muh-nin-joh-**kok**-uhs, -ning-goh- / *n.* (*pl.* **meningococci** / **kok**-suy, **kok**-see /) a bacterium involved in some forms of meningitis. ☐ **meningococcal** *adj.*

meniscus / muh-**nis**-kuhs / *n.* (*pl.* **menisci** / muh-**nis**-uy /) **1** the curved upper surface of liquid in a tube, caused by surface tension. **2** a lens that is convex on one side and concave on the other.

menopause / **men**-uh-pawz / *n.* the time of life during which a woman finally ceases to menstruate (usu. between 45 and 55) (see also MALE MENOPAUSE). ☐ **menopausal** *adj.*

menorah / muh-**naw**-ruh / *n.* a seven-branched Jewish candelabrum.

Mensa an organisation admitting as members people who pass an intelligence test showing that they have a high IQ.

menses / **men**-seez / *n.pl.* **1** the blood etc. discharged in menstruation. **2** the time of menstruation.

menstrual / **men**-stroo-uhl / *adj.* of or in menstruation. ☐ **menstrual cycle** the process of ovulation and menstruation.

menstruate / men-stroo-ayt / v. experience the discharge of blood from the womb that normally occurs in women between puberty and middle age at approximately monthly intervals. □ **menstruation** n.

mensuration / men-shuh-**ray**-shuhn / n. **1** measuring. **2** the mathematical rules for finding lengths, areas, and volumes.

mental adj. **1** of the mind; existing in or performed by the mind (*mental arithmetic*). **2** caring for the mentally ill (*mental hospital*). **3** *colloq.* suffering from a disorder of the mind, mad. □ **mental age** the level of a person's mental development expressed as the age at which this level is reached by an average person. **mental block** an inability to remember something (etc.) due to subconscious factors. **mental deficiency** lack of normal intelligence through imperfect mental development. □□ **mentally** adv.

Mental as Anything Australian pop and rock group formed in 1976.

mentality / men-**tal**-uh-tee / n. a person's mental ability or characteristic attitude of mind.

menthol n. a solid white substance obtained from peppermint oil or made synthetically, used as a flavouring and to relieve pain.

mentholated adj. treated with or containing menthol.

mention v. **1** speak or write about briefly; refer to by name. **2** (usu. as **mention in dispatches**) award a minor military honour to (a person) in war. • n. mentioning, being mentioned; a reference. □ **not to mention** and as another important thing; let alone.

mentor / **men**-taw / n. a trusted adviser.

menu / **men**-yoo / n. **1** a list of dishes to be served or available in a restaurant etc. **2** a list of options, displayed on a screen, from which users select what they require a computer to do.

Menuhin / **men**-yoo-in /, Yehudi, Baron (1916–99), American-born British violinist.

Menzies / **men**-zeez /, Sir Robert (Gordon) (1894–1978), Australian Liberal statesman, prime minister 1939–41 and 1949–66. In his first term he represented the United Australia Party. In 1944 he set in motion procedures which were to lead to the formation of the Liberal Party in the following year. He is Australia's longest-serving prime minister.

meow (also **miaow**) = MEW.

mephistophelean / mef-is-tuh-**fee**-lee-uhn / adj. fiendish. (¶ From MEPHISTOPHELES.)

Mephistopheles / mef-is-**tof**-uh-leez / (in the legend of Faust) the demon to whom Faust sold his soul.

mercantile / **mer**-kuhn-tuyl / adj. trading; of trade or merchants.

Mercator projection / mer-**kay**-tuh / (also **Mercator's projection**) a map of the world projected so that lines of latitude and longitude are straight lines with lines of latitude the same length as the equator. (¶ Named after its inventor G. Mercator (1512–94), Flemish geographer.)

mercenary / **mer**-suh-nuh-ree, -suhn-ree / adj. **1** working merely for money or other reward; grasping. **2** (of professional soldiers) hired to serve a foreign country. • n. a professional soldier serving a foreign country. □ **mercenarily** adv. **mercenariness** n.

mercer n. a dealer in textile fabrics.

mercerised adj. (also **-ized**) (of cotton fabric or thread) treated with caustic alkali to give greater strength and a slight gloss.

merchandise n. goods or commodities bought and sold; goods for sale. • v. **1** buy and sell; trade. **2** advertise or promote (goods, an idea, a person, etc.).

merchant n. **1** a wholesale trader, esp. with foreign countries. **2** a retail trader. **3** *colloq.*, usu. *derog.* a person who is fond of a specified activity etc. or is noted for a particular behaviour (*speed merchants; a panic merchant*). □ **merchant bank** a bank dealing in commercial loans and the financing of businesses. **merchant navy** shipping employed in commerce. **merchant ship** a ship carrying merchandise.

merchantable adj. saleable, marketable.

merchantman n. a merchant ship.

merciful adj. **1** showing mercy. **2** giving relief from pain or suffering (*a merciful death*).

mercifully adv. **1** in a merciful way. **2** fortunately; thank goodness.

merciless adj. showing no mercy. □ **mercilessly** adv.

mercurial / mer-**kyoo**-ree-uhl / adj. **1** of or caused by mercury (*mercurial eczema*). **2** having a lively temperament. **3** liable to sudden changes of mood.

Mercury 1 *Rom. myth.* the messenger of the gods, identified with Hermes. **2** the innermost planet of the solar system.

mercury n. a chemical element (symbol Hg), a heavy silvery normally liquid metal, used in thermometers and barometers etc. □ **mercuric** / mer-**kyoo**-rik / adj. **mercurous** adj.

mercy n. **1** refraining from inflicting punishment or pain on an offender or enemy etc. who is in one's power. **2** a disposition to behave in this way (*a tyrant without mercy*). **3** a merciful act; a thing to be thankful for (*it's a mercy no one was killed*). • interj. an exclamation of surprise or fear (*mercy on us!*). □ **at the mercy of** wholly in the power of; liable to danger or harm from. **mercy killing** euthanasia.

mere[1] adj. nothing more or better than what is specified (*a mere boy; mere words*). □ **merely** adv.

mere[2] n. poetic a lake.

merest adj. very small or insignificant (*the merest trace of colour*).

meretricious / me-ruh-**trish**-uhs / adj. showily attractive but cheap or insincere.

merfolk n. the race of mermaids and mermen.

merge *v.* **1** unite or combine into a whole (*the two companies merged*). **2** pass slowly into something else, blend or become blended.

merger *n.* the combining of two commercial companies etc. into one.

Meriam Mir / me-ree-uhm **meer** / *n.* a language of the eastern Torres Strait Islands of Mer (Murray), Dauar, Darnley, and Stephens.

meridian / muh-**rid**-ee-uhn / *n.* **1** a circle of constant longitude, passing through a given place and the North and South Poles. **2** a corresponding line on a map or globe. **3** the point or period of highest development; one's prime of life. **4** *Acupuncture* any of the pathways in the body along which energy is said to flow. □ **meridional** *adj.*

meringue / muh-**rang** / *n.* **1** a mixture of sugar and beaten egg white, baked crisp. **2** a small cake of this.

merino / muh-**ree**-noh / *n.* (*pl.* **merinos**) **1** (in full **merino sheep**) a breed of sheep with long fine wool. **2** fine soft woollen yarn or fabric. **3** (also **pure merino**) *Aust. hist.* a free settler in Australia (as opposed to a convict: *see* LEGITIMATE *n.*).

merit *n.* **1** the quality of deserving to be praised, excellence. **2** a feature or quality that deserves praise (*judge it on its merits*). **3** intrinsic rights and wrongs (*the merits of a case*). • *v.* (**merited**, **meriting**) deserve.

meritocracy / me-ruh-**tok**-ruh-see / *n.* **1** government or control by people of high ability, selected by some form of competition. **2** these people.

meritorious / me-ruh-**taw**-ree-uhs / *adj.* having merit, deserving praise.

Merlin (also **Myrddin**) (in legends of King Arthur) a wizard who aided King Arthur.

merlin *n.* a small falcon.

mermaid *n.* an imaginary sea creature, a woman with a fish's tail in place of legs.

merman *n.* the male equivalent of a mermaid.

merry *adj.* (**merrier**, **merriest**) **1** cheerful and lively, joyous. **2** *colloq.* slightly drunk. □ **make merry** be festive. **merry-go-round 1** a fairground ride with revolving model horses, cars, etc. **2** a cycle of bustling activity. □ □ **merrily** *adv.* **merriment** *n.*

merrymaking *n.* lively festivities, fun.

mésalliance / may-**zal**-ee-ons / *n.* a marriage with a person of lower social position. (¶ French)

Mesdames *see* MADAME.

Mesdemoiselles *see* MADEMOISELLE.

mesembryanthemum / mez-uhm-bree-**an**-thuh-muhm / *n.* **1** a low-growing South African plant with fleshy leaves and bright daisy-like flowers opening in sunlight. **2** *Aust.* pigface.

mesh *n.* **1** one of the spaces between threads in a net, sieve, etc. **2** network fabric. **3** (**meshes**) a network; a trap or snare. • *v.* **1** (of a toothed wheel etc.) engage with another or others. **2** be harmonious. **3** catch in a net. □ **in mesh** (of the teeth of wheels) engaged.

mesmerise *v.* (also **-ize**) hypnotise; dominate the attention or will of; fascinate, spellbind. □ **mesmerism** *n.* **mesmeric** *adj.*

mesolithic / mes-oh-**lith**-ik / *adj.* of the part of the Stone Age between the palaeolithic and neolithic periods. • *n.* this period.

meson / **mez**-on, **mee**-zon / *n.* an unstable elementary particle intermediate in mass between a proton and an electron.

Mesopotamia / mes-uh-puh-**tay**-mee-uh / a region of SW Asia between the rivers Tigris and Euphrates, now within Iraq.

mesosphere / **mes**-oh-sfeer, **mee**-zoh- / *n.* the region of the earth's atmosphere from the top of the stratosphere to an altitude of about 80 km.

Mesozoic / mes-oh-**zoh**-ik, mee-**zoh**- / *adj.* of the geological era between the Palaeozoic and Cainozoic, lasting from about 248 to 65 million years ago and marked by the development of dinosaurs and the first mammals, birds, and flowering plants. • *n.* this era.

mess *n.* **1** a dirty or untidy condition; an untidy collection of things; something spilt. **2** a difficult or confused situation, trouble. **3** any disagreeable substance or concoction; any domestic animal's excreta. **4** *colloq.* a person who looks untidy, dirty, or slovenly; a person whose life has gone awry. **5** (in the armed forces) a group who take meals together; the place where such meals are eaten. • *v.* **1** (often foll. by *up*) make untidy or dirty. **2** (often foll. by *up*) muddle or bungle (business etc.) (*messed it up*). **3** (foll. by *with*) interfere with. **4** take one's meals with a military or other group (*they mess together*). □ **mess about** (*or* **around**) **1** potter; fiddle; waste time. **2** *colloq.* make things awkward for (a person) by being indecisive, inconsistent, etc. **3** fool around. **4** (foll. by *with*) *colloq.* associate with as mate. **mess kit** a soldier's cooking and eating utensils.

message *n.* **1** a spoken or written communication. **2** the moral of a book etc. (*a film with a message*). **3** (**messages**) *Scottish* & *Aust.* shopping or similar things to be done. □ **message stick** *Aust.* a piece of wood with symbolic patterns which convey a message from one Aboriginal community to another and which may also indicate the bearer's standing or totem.

Messenger, Herbert Henry ('Dally') (1883–1959), Australian Rugby player (Union and League), called 'the Master'.

messenger *n.* the bearer of a message.

Messiaen / **mes**-yan /, Olivier (1908–92), French composer and organist.

Messiah / muh-**suy**-uh / *n.* **1** the expected deliverer and ruler of the Jewish people, whose coming was prophesied in the Old Testament. **2** Christ, regarded by Christians as this.

Messianic / mes-ee-**an**-ik / *adj.* of the Messiah.

Messieurs *see* MONSIEUR.

messmate *n.* **1** *Aust.* a rough-barked eucalypt of south-east Australia. **2** a person with whom one regularly takes meals, esp. in the armed forces.

Messrs / mes-uhz / *abbr.* plural of Mr.

messy *adj.* (**messier, messiest**) **1** untidy or dirty, slovenly. **2** causing a mess (*a messy job*). **3** complicated and difficult to deal with (*a messy situation*). ☐ **messily** *adv.* **messiness** *n.*

met *see* MEET[1].

metabolise / muh-**tab**-uh-luyz / *v.* (also **-ize**) process (food) in metabolism.

metabolism / muh-**tab**-uh-liz-uhm / *n.* the process by which food is built up into living material or used to supply energy in a living organism. ☐ **metabolic** / met-uh-**bol**-ik / *adj.*

metacarpus / met-uh-**kah**-puhs / *n.* (*pl.* **metacarpi**) the part of the hand between the wrist and the fingers; the set of bones in this. ☐ **metacarpal** *adj.*

metafiction *n.* a kind of fiction which self-consciously comments on its own fictional status.

metal *n.* **1** any of a class of mineral substances such as gold, silver, copper, iron, uranium, etc., or an alloy of any of these. **2** the molten material for making glass. **3** blue metal. • *adj.* made of metal. • *v.* (**metalled, metalling**) **1** cover or fit with metal. **2** make or mend (a road) with blue metal. ☐ **metal detector** an electronic device for locating buried metal items.

metalanguage *n.* **1** a form of language used to discuss or describe a language. **2** a system of propositions about propositions.

metallic / muh-**tal**-ik / *adj.* **1** of or like metal. **2** (of sound) like metals struck together, sharp and ringing. **3** shiny (*metallic blue*). ☐ **metallic starling** a bird of Qld rainforests, having glossy black plumage with a metallic green and purple sheen. **metallic sun orchid** an Australian terrestrial orchid having 15 or more large blue-green flowers shot with a metallic iridescence. ☐ **metallically** *adv.*

metalliferous / met-uh-**lif**-uh-ruhs / *adj.* (of rocks etc.) containing metal.

metallography / met-uh-**log**-ruh-fee / *n.* the scientific study of the internal structure of metals.

metalloid *n.* an element that is midway between a metal and a non-metal, e.g. boron, silicon, and germanium.

metallurgy / **met**-uh-ler-jee, muh-**tal**-uh-jee / *n.* **1** the scientific study of the properties of metals and alloys. **2** the art of working metals or of extracting them from their ores. ☐ **metallurgical** / met-uh-**ler**-ji-kuhl / *adj.* **metallurgist** *n.*

metalwork *n.* **1** the art of working in metal. **2** metal objects. ☐ **metalworker** *n.*

metamorphic / met-uh-**maw**-fik / *adj.* **1** (of rock) having had its structure or other properties changed by natural agencies (such as heat and pressure), as in the transformation of limestone into marble. **2** of metamorphosis. ☐ **metamorphism** *n.*

metamorphose / met-uh-**maw**-fohz / *v.* change in form or character.

metamorphosis / met-uh-**maw**-fuh-suhs / *n.* (*pl.* **metamorphoses**) a change of form or character (whether by natural or magical means).

metaphor / **met**-uh-faw / *n.* the application of a word or phrase to something that it does not apply to literally, in order to indicate a comparison with the literal usage (see panel).

metaphorical / met-uh-**fo**-ri-kuhl / *adj.* in a metaphor, not literal. ☐ **metaphorically** *adv.*

metaphysical *adj.* **1** of metaphysics. **2** (of esp. 17th-century English poetry) subtle and complex in imagery.

metaphysics / met-uh-**fiz**-iks / *n.* **1** a branch of philosophy that deals with the nature of existence and of truth and knowledge. **2** the philosophy of mind.

metastasis / me-**tas**-tuh-suhs / *n.* (*pl.* **metastases**) the transfer of disease from one part of the body to another.

metatarsus / met-uh-**tah**-suhs / *n.* (*pl.* **metatarsi**) the part of the foot between the ankle and the toes; the set of bones in this. ☐ **metatarsal** *adj.*

metathesis / muh-**tath**-uh-suhs / *n.* **1** the transposition of sounds or letters in a word (*Old English 'brid' became 'bird' by metathesis*). **2** an instance of this.

mete / meet / *v.* ☐ **mete out** give as what is due (*mete out punishment to wrongdoers*).

meteor / **mee**-tee-uh, **mee**-tee-aw / *n.* a bright moving body seen in the sky, formed by a small mass of matter from outer space that becomes luminous from compression of air as it enters the earth's atmosphere.

meteoric / mee-tee-**o**-rik / *adj.* **1** of meteors. **2** rapid; dazzling (*a meteoric rise to fame*).

meteorite / **mee**-tee-uh-ruyt / *n.* a fallen meteor, a fragment of rock or metal reaching the earth's surface from outer space.

Metaphor

A metaphor is a figure of speech that goes further than a simile, either by saying that something is something else that it could not normally be called, e.g.
   The moon was a ghostly galleon tossed upon cloudy seas.
or by suggesting that something appears, sounds, or behaves like something else, e.g.
   burning ambition   *blindingly obvious*
   the long arm of the law   *a glaring error*
   The government bulldozed the bill through parliament.

meteoroid / mee-tee-uh-roid / n. a body moving through space, of the same nature as those which become visible as meteors when they enter the earth's atmosphere.

meteorology / mee-tee-uh-**rol**-uh-jee / n. the scientific study of atmospheric conditions, esp. in order to forecast weather. ☐ **meteorological** adj. **meteorologist** n.

meter n. a device designed to measure and indicate the quantity of a substance supplied, or the distance travelled and fare payable, or the time that has elapsed, etc. • v. (**metered**, **metering**) measure by meter.

methadone n. a narcotic pain-killing drug, used as a substitute for morphine or heroin.

methanal = FORMALDEHYDE.

methane / mee-thayn, meth-ayn / n. a colourless flammable gas that occurs in coal mines and marshy areas.

methanol n. a colourless flammable liquid hydrocarbon, used as a solvent.

methinks v. archaic I think.

metho n. Aust. colloq. **1** methylated spirits. **2** a person addicted to drinking methylated spirits or who does so out of sheer poverty; a derelict. **3** (Metho) a Methodist.

method n. **1** a procedure or way of doing something. **2** orderliness (he's a man of method). **3** (also **Stanislavski method**) a technique of acting based on the actor's complete emotional identification with the character.

methodical / muh-**thod**-i-kuhl / adj. orderly, systematic. ☐ **methodically** adv.

Methodist n. a member of a Protestant denomination originating in the 18th century Wesleyan evangelical movement. ☐ **Methodism** n.

methodology / meth-uh-**dol**-uh-jee / n. **1** the science of method and procedure. **2** the methods used in a particular activity. ☐ **methodological** adj. **methodologically** adv.

methought v. archaic I thought.

Methuselah / muh-**thoo**-zuh-luh / a Hebrew patriarch, grandfather of Noah, said to have lived for 969 years.

methyl / **meth**-uhl, mee-thuyl / n. a chemical unit present in methane and in many organic compounds. ☐ **methyl alcohol** = METHANOL.

methylated spirit(s) n. alcohol (treated to make it unfit for drinking) used as a solvent and a fuel.

meticulous / muh-**tik**-yuh-luhs / adj. giving or showing great attention to detail, very careful and exact. ☐ **meticulously** adv. **meticulousness** n.

métier / **met**-ee-ay / n. one's trade, profession, or field of activity; what one does best. (¶ French)

metonymy / muh-**ton**-uh-mee / n. using a word denoting an attribute or adjunct of a thing (e.g. *crown* is an adjunct of a *king*) in place of the word for the thing itself; thus *allegiance to the crown* instead of *to the king*; *addicted to the bottle* instead of *to alcohol*.

metre n. **1** a unit of length in the metric system (about 39.4 inches). **2** rhythm in poetry; a particular form of this. **3** the basic rhythm of a piece of music.

metric adj. **1** of or using the metric system. **2** of poetic metre. ☐ **metric system** a decimal system of weights and measures, using the metre, litre, and gram as units. **metric ton** (also **metric tonne**) a tonne (1,000 kilograms, 2,205 lb).

metrical adj. **1** of or composed in rhythmic metre, not prose (*metrical psalms*). **2** of or involving measurement (*metrical geometry*). ☐ **metrically** adv.

metricate v. change or adapt to the metric system of measurement. ☐ **metrication** n.

metro n. (pl. **metros**) colloq. an underground railway, esp. in Paris.

metronome / **met**-ruh-nohm / n. a device that sounds a click repeatedly at a selected interval, used to indicate tempo for a person practising music.

metropolis / muh-**trop**-uh-luhs / n. the chief city of a country or region.

metropolitan / met-ruh-**pol**-uh-tuhn / adj. of a metropolis. • n. **1** a bishop having authority over the bishops of a province. **2** an inhabitant of a metropolis.

mettle n. courage or strength of character. ☐ **on one's mettle** determined to show one's courage or ability.

mettlesome adj. spirited, courageous.

MeV abbr. mega-electronvolt(s).

mew n. the characteristic cry of a cat, gull, etc. • v. make this sound.

mewl v. (also **mule**) **1** whimper. **2** mew like a cat.

mews n. (usu. treated as *sing.*) a group of what were formerly stables in a small square, now converted into houses.

Mexico a federal republic in Central America. ☐ **Mexico City** the capital of Mexico.

Mexican n. **1** a native or national of Mexico; a person of Mexican descent. **2** Aust. colloq. a person from a southern state. • adj. of Mexico or its people. ☐ **Mexican wave** a wave-like movement produced when successive sections of a seated crowd of spectators stand, raise their arms, and sit down again. (¶ First observed at World Cup football matches in Mexico City in 1986.)

mezzanine / **mez**-uh-neen, mez-uh-**neen** / n. an extra storey between ground floor and first floor, often in the form of a wide balcony.

mezzo / **met**-soh / adv. (in music) half; moderately (*mezzo forte*). • n. (in full **mezzo-soprano**) a voice between soprano and contralto; a singer with this voice. ☐ **mezzo forte** adj. & adv. fairly loud(ly). **mezzo piano** adj. & adv. fairly soft(ly).

mezzotint / **met**-soh-tint / n. **1** a method of engraving in which the plate is roughened to give areas of shadow and smoothed to give areas of light. **2** a print produced by this.

mf abbr. (in music) MEZZO FORTE.

Mg *symbol* magnesium.
mg *abbr.* milligram(s).
MHA *abbr. Aust.* Member of the House of Assembly.
MHR *abbr. Aust.* Member of the House of Representatives.
MHz *abbr.* megahertz.
mi alternative spelling of ME^2.
mia-mia / muy-uh-muy-uh, mee-uh-mee-uh / *n. Aust.* **1** = GUNYAH. **2** any temporary shelter erected by a traveller. (¶ From an Aboriginal language, but the precise etymology is uncertain: perhaps from Wathawurung.)
miaow (also **meow**) = MEW.
miasma / mee-**az**-muh, muy- / *n.* (*pl.* **miasmata** or **miasmas**) *archaic* unpleasant or unwholesome air.
mica / muy-kuh / *n.* a mineral substance used as an electrical insulator.
Micawber / muh-**kaw**-buh / *n.* a person who is perpetually hoping that something good will turn up while making no effort. ◻ **Micawberish** *adj.* **Micawberism** *n.* (¶ Name of a character in Dickens's novel *David Copperfield*, for whom the model was Dickens's father.)
mice *see* MOUSE.
Michael, St, one of the archangels. Feast day, 29 September (Michaelmas Day).
Michaelmas / mik-uhl-muhs / *n.* a Christian festival in honour of St Michael (29 September).
Michelangelo / muy-kuhl-**an**-juh-loh / (full name: Michelangelo Buonarroti) (1475–1564), Italian sculptor, painter, architect, and poet, whose most famous works include the decoration of the ceiling of the Sistine chapel in the Vatican.
Michell, Keith (1928–), Australian stage and television actor.
mick *n.* **1** *colloq. offens.* a Catholic. **2** *colloq. offens.* an Irishman. **3** *Aust.* = MICKEY^1. **4** *Aust.* (in two-up) the reverse side of a coin; the tail.
mickery *n.* (also **mickerie**) *Aust.* **1** a natural soak or hollow in (often) sandy soil where water collects, on or below the surface of the ground, often several metres below. **2** an excavated and formed soak, esp. in a dry river bed. (¶ Wangganguru)
mickey^1 *n.* (also **micky**, **mick**) *Aust.* a bull calf, usu. unbranded and frequently wild.
mickey^2 *n.* (also **micky**) *colloq.* ◻ **chuck** (or **throw**) **a mickey** *Aust.* have a tantrum. **take the mickey** (**out of**) tease, mock, ridicule.
mickey^3 (also **micky**) *Aust.* = NOISY MINER.
mickey finn *colloq.* **1** an alcoholic drink secretly laced with a narcotic etc. drug. **2** the drug itself.
mickey mouse *adj. colloq.* **1** of inferior quality; trivial; ridiculous; less than serious (*got a degree doing mickey mouse subjects*). **2** (of music, art, etc.) trite. (¶ Mickey Mouse, a cartoon character created by Walt Disney.)
micro / muy-kroh / *n.* (*pl.* **micros**) *colloq.* a microcomputer; a microprocessor.

micro- / muy-kroh / *comb. form* **1** very small (*microchip*). **2** on a small or local scale (*microeconomics*). **3** one-millionth of a unit (*microgram*).
microbe *n.* a micro-organism, esp. one that causes disease or fermentation. ◻ **microbial** *adj.* **microbic** *adj.*
microbiology *n.* the study of micro-organisms. ◻ **microbiologist** *n.*
microchip *n.* a very small piece of silicon or similar material made so as to work like a complex wired electric circuit.
microcircuit *n.* an integrated circuit or other small electrical circuit.
microclimate *n.* the climatic conditions of a very small area, e.g. inside a glasshouse.
microcomputer *n.* a small computer with a microprocessor as the central processor.
microcosm / muy-kruh-koz-uhm / *n.* a world in miniature; something regarded as resembling something else on a very small scale. ◻ **microcosmic** *adj.*
microdot *n.* a photograph of a document etc. reduced to the size of a dot.
micro-economics *n.* a branch of economics dealing with individual commodities, producers, etc. (as opposed to MACRO-ECONOMICS).
micro-electronics *n.* the design, manufacture, and use of microchips and microcircuits. ◻ **micro-electronic** *adj.*
microfiche / muy-kroh-feesh / *n.* (*pl.* **microfiche** or **microfiches**) a sheet of microfilm in a form suitable for filing like an index card.
microfilm *n.* a length of film on which written or printed material is photographed in greatly reduced size. • *v.* photograph on this.
micromesh *n.* fine-meshed material, esp. nylon.
micrometer / muy-**krom**-uh-tuh / *n.* an instrument for measuring small lengths or angles.
micron / muy-kron / *n.* one-millionth of a metre.
Micronesia / muy-kruh-**nee**-*zh*uh / part of the western Pacific Ocean including the Mariana, Caroline, and Marshall Islands, Nauru, and Kiribati.
micro-organism *n.* an organism that cannot be seen by the naked eye, e.g. bacteria, viruses, and protozoa.
microphone *n.* an instrument for picking up sound waves for recording, amplifying, or broadcasting.
microprocessor *n.* an integrated circuit containing all the functions of a computer's central processing unit.
microscope *n.* an instrument with lenses that magnify objects or details too small to be seen by the naked eye.
microscopic *adj.* **1** of the microscope. **2** too small to be visible without the aid of a microscope. **3** extremely small. ◻ **microscopically** *adv.*
microscopy / muy-**kros**-kuh-pee / *n.* use of microscopes.

microsecond *n.* one-millionth of a second.

microsurgery *n.* intricate surgery using a microscope to see the tissue and instruments involved.

microtone *n. Music* an interval smaller than a semitone.

microwave *n.* **1** an electromagnetic wave of length between about 30 cm and 1 mm. **2** (in full **microwave oven**) an oven using such waves to heat food very quickly. • *v.* cook (food) in a microwave oven. ◻ **microwave proof** (also **microwave safe**) (of dishes etc.) able to be used in a microwave oven.

micturition / mik-chuh-**rish**-uhn / *n.* urination.

mid[1] *adj.* in the middle of, middle (*in mid-air; to mid-August*). ◻ **mid-life** *n.* middle age. **mid-life crisis** a crisis of self-confidence in early middle age. **mid-off** *Cricket* a fielder near the bowler on the off side; this position. **mid-on** *Cricket* a fielder near the bowler on the on side; this position.

mid[2] *prep. poetic* = AMID.

Midas / **muy**-duhs / ◻ **the Midas touch** the ability to make money in all one's activities. (¶ Named after a legendary king in Asia Minor, whose touch turned all things to gold.)

midday *n.* the middle of the day, noon.

midden *n.* **1** a dunghill. **2** a rubbish heap. **3** = MIRRNYONG.

middle *adj.* **1** at an equal distance from extremes or outer limits. **2** occurring halfway between beginning and end. **3** intermediate in rank or quality; moderate in size etc. (*a man of middle height*). • *n.* **1** a middle point, position, time, area, or quality etc. **2** the waist. • *v.* **1** place in the middle of. **2** *Cricket* strike the ball squarely in the middle of the bat. ◻ **middle age** the period between youth and old age, about 45 to 60.

middle-aged *adj.* of middle age. **middle C** the note C that occurs near the middle of the piano keyboard; (in notation) the note between the treble and bass staves. **middle class** the class of society between the upper and working classes, including business and professional people.

middle-class *adj.* of or relating to the middle class. **middle distance 1** (of a landscape) the part between the foreground and the background. **2** (in athletics) a race distance of esp. 400 or 800 metres. **middle ear** the cavity behind the eardrum. **middle name 1** the name between first name and surname. **2** *colloq.* a person's most characteristic quality (*tact is my middle name*).

middle-of-the-road *adj.* **1** favouring a moderate policy, avoiding extremes. **2** of general appeal. **middle-sized** of medium size.

Middle Ages about AD 1000–1453 (the capture of Constantinople by the Turks) or (in a wider sense) 5th c. (the fall of the Roman Empire) to 1453.

Middle Australia the middle class in Australia, esp. as supposed to indicate a social, political, etc. norm.

middlebrow *colloq. adj.* having or appealing to only moderately intellectual (or conventional) tastes. • *n.* a middlebrow person.

Middle East the area covered by countries from Egypt to Iran inclusive.

Middle English the English language as it was from around 1150 to 1500.

middleman *n.* **1** any of the traders handling a commodity between producer and consumer. **2** an intermediary.

middleware *see* -WARE.

middleweight *n.* a boxing weight between light heavyweight and welterweight, in amateur boxing 71–75 kg.

middling *adj.* moderately good. • *adv.* moderately well.

middy *n. Aust.* a medium-sized measure of beer; the glass containing this.

midfield *n.* the part of a football ground away from the goals. ◻ **midfielder** *n.*

midge *n.* a small biting gnatlike insect.

midget *n.* an extremely small person or thing. • *adj.* extremely small.

Midhaga / **mit**-hah-gu / *n.* an Aboriginal language of a vast area of south-west Qld.

MIDI *n.* (also **midi**) an interface allowing electronic musical instruments, synthesisers, and computers to be connected and used together. (¶ Abbreviation of *m*usical *i*nstrument *d*igital *i*nterface.)

midi system *n.* a compact hi-fi system made up of stacking components.

midnight *n.* twelve o'clock at night; the time near this. ◻ **midnight sun** the sun visible at midnight in polar regions during the summer.

Midnight Oil an Australian rock group led by Peter GARRETT.

Midrash *n.* (*pl.* **Midrashim**) an ancient Jewish commentary on part of the Hebrew scriptures.

midriff *n.* the front part of the body just above the waist.

midshipman *n. US & Aust.* the rank of a naval cadet training to be an officer.

midst *n.* the middle. ◻ **in our** (*or* **your** *or* **their**) **midst** among us (or you or them).

midstream *n.* the middle of a stream, river, etc. • *adv.* (also **in midstream**) in the middle of an action etc. (*abandoned the project midstream*).

midway *adv.* halfway between places.

midwicket *n.* a position in cricket on the leg side opposite the middle of the pitch.

midwife *n.* a person trained to assist women in childbirth. ◻ **midwifery** / mid-**wif**-uh-ree / *n.*

mien / meen / *n.* a person's manner or bearing.

miffed *adj. colloq.* offended, put out.

migaloo / **mig**-uh-loo / *n. Aust.* a white person. (¶ Perhaps Mayi-Kutuna.)

might[1] *n.* great strength or power (*with all one's might*). ◻ **with might and main** with all one's power.

might² ** *auxiliary v.* used as the past tense of MAY, esp. expressing: **1 possibility (*it might be true*). **2** permission (*we told him that he might go*). **3** a request (*you might call at the butcher's*). **4** a complaint (*you might have offered*). ☐ **might as well** expressing lukewarm agreement (*might as well give it a go*).

mightn't = might not.

mighty *adj.* (**mightier, mightiest**) **1** having or showing great strength or power. **2** very great in size. • *adv. colloq.* very (*mighty difficult*). ☐ **mightily** *adv.* **mightiness** *n.*

mignonette / min-yuh-**net** / *n.* **1** an annual plant with fragrant greyish-green flowers. **2** a kind of small lettuce.

migraine / **muy**-grayn, **mee**-grayn / *n.* a severe form of recurring headache that usu. affects only one side of the head and is often accompanied by nausea and visual disturbance.

migrant / **muy**-gruhnt / *adj.* migrating. • *n.* **1** a person who leaves his or her own country to take up permanent residence in another. **2** an animal, esp. a bird, that changes its habitation seasonally.

migrate / muy-**grayt** / *v.* **1** leave one place and settle in another. **2** (of animals) go periodically from one place to another, living in each place for part of a year. ☐ **migration** *n.*

migratory / **muy**-gruh-tuh-ree, -tree / *adj.* of or involving migration; migrating.

mihrab / **mee**-rahb / *n.* a niche or slab in a mosque, used to show the direction of Mecca.

mikado / muh-**kah**-doh / *n.* (*pl.* **mikados**) *hist.* an emperor of Japan.

mike *n. colloq.* a microphone.

mil *n.* one-thousandth of an inch.

milch *adj.* giving milk (*a milch cow*).

mild *adj.* **1** moderate in intensity, character, or effect; not severe or harsh or drastic. **2** (of a person) gentle in manner. **3** not strongly flavoured. ☐ **mild steel** steel that is strong and tough and not readily tempered. ☐☐ **mildly** *adv.* **mildness** *n.*

mildew *n.* a destructive minute fungus that forms a white coating on plants and on things exposed to damp. • *v.* taint or be tainted with mildew. ☐ **mildewy** *adj.*

mile *n.* **1** (in the imperial system) a measure of length, 1,760 yards (about 1.609 kilometres). *See also* NAUTICAL MILE. **2** (usu. as **miles**) *colloq.* a great distance or amount (*miles too big*).

mileage *n.* (also **milage**) **1** distance measured in miles. **2** the distance a vehicle travels per unit of fuel. **3** travelling expenses at a fixed rate per mile. **4** *colloq.* benefit (*he gets a lot of mileage out of his family name*).

Miles Franklin Award an annual literary award for a published novel depicting some aspect of Australian life. One of the most prestigious literary awards in Australia, it is given from the estate of Miles Franklin.

milestone *n.* **1** a stone set up beside a road to show the distance in miles to a given point. **2** a significant event or stage in life or history.

milieu / mee-**lyer** / *n.* (*pl.* **milieux** pronounced the same, *or* **milieus**) a person's environment or social surroundings.

militant *adj.* prepared to take aggressive action in support of a cause. • *n.* a militant person. ☐ **militancy** *n.*

militarise *v.* (also **-ize**) **1** make military or warlike. **2** equip with military resources. **3** imbue with militarism. ☐ **militarisation** *n.*

militarism / **mil**-uh-tuh-riz-uhm / *n.* aggressive military policy; strong military spirit. ☐ **militarist** *n.* **militaristic** *adj.*

military *adj.* of soldiers or the army or all armed forces (*military service*). • *n.* (**the military**) (treated as *sing.* or *pl.*) the army.

militate / **mil**-uh-tayt / *v.* (usu. foll. by *against*) serve as a strong influence (*several factors militated against the success of our plan*).

■ **Usage** Do not confuse with *mitigate*.

militia / muh-**lish**-uh / *n.* a military force, esp. one consisting of civilians trained as soldiers and available to supplement the regular army in an emergency. ☐ **militiaman** *n.*

milk *n.* **1** a white fluid secreted by female mammals as food for their young. **2** the milk of cows, goats, or sheep, used as food. **3** a milklike liquid, e.g. that squeezed from the grated flesh of a coconut. • *v.* **1** draw milk from (a cow, goat etc.). **2** extract venom from a snake, spider, etc., or sap from (a tree etc.). **3** exploit or get money undeservedly from. ☐ **milk bar** a local shop selling milk, confectionery, sandwiches, and also, often, basic grocery items etc. (*see also* MIXED BUSINESS). **milk opal** *Aust.* a variety of white or milky blue-white or green-white Australian opal. **milk tooth** any of the first (temporary) teeth in young mammals.

milker *n.* **1** a person who milks an animal; a milking machine. **2** an animal that gives milk.

milkmaids *n.* an Australian plant of the lily family bearing umbels of scented milky flowers.

milkman *n.* a person who delivers milk to customers' houses.

milko *n.* (also **milk-oh**) *colloq.* a milkman.

milkshake *n.* a drink of whisked milk, ice cream, flavouring, etc.

milksop *n.* a weak or timid boy or man.

milky *adj.* (**milkier, milkiest**) **1** of or like milk. **2** made with milk; containing a lot of milk. **3** (of a gem or liquid) cloudy, not clear. ☐ **milky mangrove** a mangrove tree of tropical and sub-tropical Australia having an irritant milky sap. Also called *blind-your-eye*. **milky pine** a tall rainforest tree of north-eastern Qld having a milky sap and soft, whitish wood. ☐☐ **milkiness** *n.*

Milky Way the broad faintly luminous band of stars crossing the sky, the Galaxy.

mill *n.* **1** machinery for grinding cereal grains; a building fitted with this. **2** any machine for grinding or crushing a solid substance into powder or pulp (*coffee mill*). **3** a machine or a building fitted with machinery for processing material of certain kinds (*cotton mill; paper mill; saw mill*). • *v.* **1** grind or crush in a mill. **2** produce in a mill. **3** produce regular markings on the edge of (a coin) (*silver coins with a milled edge*). **4** cut or shape (metal) with a rotating tool. **5** (often foll. by *about* or *around*) (of people or animals) move about in a confused mass. ☐ **go** (*or* **put**) **through the mill** undergo or subject to training, experience, or suffering. **mill-wheel** the wheel that drives a watermill.

millennium / muh-**len**-ee-uhm / *n.* (*pl.* **millenniums** *or* **millennia**) **1** a period of 1,000 years. **2** the thousand-year reign of Christ on earth prophesied in the Bible. **3** a period of great happiness and prosperity for everyone. ☐ **millennium bug** a flaw in computing systems relying on a two-digit indication of a year, where the number 00 (as in 2000) is always interpreted as 1900. ☐ **millennial** *adj.*

millepede alternative spelling of MILLIPEDE.

Miller[1], Arthur (1915–), American playwright, whose works include *Death of a Salesman* and *The Crucible*.

Miller[2], (Alton) Glenn (1904–44), American trombonist, arranger, and band leader.

Miller[3], Harry M(aurice) (1934–), Australian theatrical entrepreneur.

miller *n.* a person who owns or runs a mill, esp. a flour mill.

millet *n.* **1** a cereal plant producing a large crop of small seeds. **2** its seeds, used as food.

milli- *comb. form* **1** thousand. **2** one-thousandth.

milliard *n.* one thousand million.

■ Usage *milliard* is now largely superseded by *billion*.

millibar *n.* one-thousandth of a bar as a unit of pressure in meteorology.

milligram *n.* (also **milligramme**) one-thousandth of a gram.

millilitre *n.* one-thousandth of a litre.

millimetre *n.* one-thousandth of a metre (0.04 inch).

milli milli *n.* (also **milli**) *Aust.* (in Aboriginal English) a written message. (¶ From the English word 'mail'.)

milliner *n.* a person who makes or sells women's hats.

millinery *n.* **1** a milliner's work. **2** women's hats sold in a shop.

million *adj. & n.* **1** one thousand thousand (1,000,000) (*a few million*). **2** a million dollars. **3** (**millions**) *colloq.* an enormous number. ☐ **millionth** *adj. & n.*

millionaire *n.* a person who has over a million dollars, etc.

millipede *n.* (also **millepede**) a small crawling creature like a centipede but with two pairs of legs on each segment of its body.

millisecond *n.* one-thousandth of a second.

millpond *n.* water retained in a dam by a mill to operate a water-wheel. ☐ **like a millpond** (of water) very calm and flat.

millstone *n.* **1** each of a pair of circular stones between which cereal grains are ground. **2** a great burden that impedes progress (*a millstone round one's neck*).

Milne, A(lan) A(lexander) (1882–1956), British writer, author of the *Winnie the Pooh* children's books.

Milne Bay a bay at the eastern tip of mainland New Guinea. It was the site of a decisive battle in 1942, in which Australian troops inflicted the first defeat on the Japanese in the Second World War.

Milosevic / muh-**los**-uh-vich /, Slobodan (1941–), Yugoslavian statesman who became president of Serbia in 1989 and was president of Yugoslavia 1997–2000.

milt *n.* **1** the sperm-filled reproductive gland or the sperm of a male fish. **2** the spleen in mammals.

Milton, John (1608–74), English poet, author of the epics *Paradise Lost* and *Paradise Regained*.

mimbar *n.* a pulpit in a mosque.

mime *n.* **1** acting with gestures and without words; a performance using this. **2** (also **mime artist**) a mime actor. • *v.* act with mime. ☐ **mimer** *n.*

mimesis / muh-**mee**-suhs, muy- / *n.* **1** a close external resemblance of an animal to another that is distasteful or harmful to predators of the first, or of an animal to its immediate surroundings, e.g. a leaf, twig, etc. **2** the representation of the real world in art, poetry, etc.

mimetic / muh-**met**-ik / *adj.* of or using imitation or mimicry.

mimi / **mee**-mee / *n. Aust.* a category of Aboriginal spirit people, executed in red and characterised by their elongated and slender form, depicted in ancient rock and bark paintings of western Arnhem Land. ☐ **Mimi Art** the name for this form of Aboriginal painting.

mimic *v.* (**mimicked**, **mimicking**) **1** copy the appearance or ways of (a person etc.) playfully or for entertainment. **2** pretend to be; (of things) resemble closely. • *n.* a person who is clever at mimicking others. ☐ **mimicry** *n.*

mimosa / muh-**moh**-zuh, -suh / *n.* any of several usu. tropical trees or shrubs, esp. *Mimosa pudica* with clusters of small ball-shaped fragrant flowers and sensitive leaflets which droop when touched.

mina alternative spelling of MYNA.

minaret / min-uh-**ret** / *n.* a tall slender tower on or beside a mosque, with a balcony from which a muezzin calls Muslims to prayer.

minatory / **min**-uh-tuh-ree / *adj.* threatening.

mince v. **1** cut into small pieces in a machine with revolving blades. **2** walk or speak in an affected way, trying to appear refined. • n. minced meat. ❏ **mince pie** a pie containing mincemeat. **not to mince matters** (*or* **one's words**) speak bluntly. ❏❏ **mincer** n.

mincemeat n. a mixture of currants, raisins, sugar, spices, etc., used in pies. ❏ **make mincemeat of** defeat utterly; destroy utterly in argument.

mind n. **1** the ability to be aware of things and to think and reason, originating in the brain. **2** concentration, attention (*keep your mind on the job*). **3** remembrance (*keep it in mind*). **4** opinion (*change one's mind; to my mind he's a genius*). **5** a way of thinking and feeling (*the word 'leg' shocked the Victorian mind*). **6** sanity, normal mental faculties (*in one's right mind; out of one's mind*). • v. **1** take care of, attend to (*minding the baby*). **2** feel annoyance or discomfort at, object to (*she doesn't mind the cold*). **3** bear in mind; give heed to or concern oneself about (*never mind the expense; mind your own business*). **4** remember and take care (*mind you lock the door*). **5** be careful about (*mind the step*). ❏ **blow one's mind** *colloq.* make one utterly enchanted, wild with delight (*this music will really blow your mind*). **have a good** (*or* **half a**) **mind to** feel tempted or inclined to. **in two minds** undecided. **mind-bending** strongly influencing the mind. **mind-blowing** *colloq.* **1** mind-boggling, overwhelming. **2** (of drugs) causing hallucinations. **mind-boggling** unbelievable, amazing. **mind-reader** a thought-reader. **mind's eye** the faculty of imagination. **on one's mind** constantly in one's thoughts, causing worry. **to my mind** in my opinion.

minded adj. **1** having a mind of a certain kind (*independent-minded*). **2** having certain interests (*politically minded*). **3** inclined or disposed to do something (*he could do it if he were so minded*).

minder n. **1** one whose job is to attend to or take care of a person or thing (*child minder*). **2** *colloq.* a bodyguard. **3** *colloq.* a person employed to advise or protect a politician, a famous person, etc. **4** *Aust. Rules* a player whose main task is to keep in check an esp. brilliant opposing player.

mindi / **min**-duy / n. *Aust.* (in Aboriginal mythology) a hairy snake large enough to swallow an emu whole. (¶ Wemba-wemba *mirnday*)

mindic / **min**-dik / adj. *Aust.* (in Aboriginal English) ill, sick. (¶ Nyungar)

mindful adj. taking thought or care of something (*mindful of his public image*). ❏ **mindfully** adv.

mindless adj. **1** lacking intelligence; brutish (*mindless violence*). **2** not requiring thought or skill (*mindless work*). **3** heedless of (advice etc.). ❏ **mindlessly** adv. **mindlessness** n.

mindset n. an attitude or frame of mind.

mine[1] adj. & *possessive pron.* of or belonging to me; the thing(s) belonging to me.

mine[2] n. **1** an excavation in the earth for extracting metal or coal etc. **2** an abundant source of something (*a mine of information*). **3** a receptacle filled with explosive, placed in the ground or in water ready to explode when something strikes it or passes near it. • v. **1** dig for minerals; extract (metal or coal etc.) in this way. **2** lay explosive mines in (an area). **3** search, delve into (books etc.) for information (*mined the resources of the National Library*).

minefield n. **1** an area where explosive mines have been laid. **2** *colloq.* a subject or situation full of difficulties and dangers.

miner[1] n. a person who works in a mine.

miner[2] n. any of several related Australian honey-eaters with yellow bill and legs, esp. the noisy miner and the bell miner (or bellbird).

mineral n. **1** an inorganic substance that occurs naturally in the earth. **2** an ore or other substance obtained by mining. • adj. of or containing minerals. ❏ **mineral water** water that is found naturally, containing dissolved mineral salts or gases; an artificial imitation of this.

mineralogy / min-uh-**ral**-uh-jee / n. the scientific study of minerals. ❏ **mineralogical** adj. **mineralogist** n.

Minerva *Rom. myth.* the goddess of handicrafts, identified with Athene.

minestrone / min-uh-**stroh**-nee / n. a beef etc. soup containing vegetables and pasta.

minesweeper n. a ship for clearing away explosive mines laid in the sea.

Ming n. porcelain belonging to the time of the Ming dynasty in China (1368–1644).

mingle v. **1** mix, blend. **2** go about among people; mix socially (*mingled with the crowd*).

mingy adj. *colloq.* mean, stingy.

mini n. **1** *colloq.* a miniskirt. **2** (**Mini**) *trademark* a make of small car.

mini- *comb. form* miniature, small of its kind (*minibus; mini-budget*).

miniature / **min**-uh-chuh / adj. very small; made or represented on a small scale. • n. **1** a very small and detailed portrait. **2** a small-scale copy or model of something.

miniaturise v. (also **-ize**) make miniature, produce in a very small version. ❏ **miniaturisation** n.

miniaturist n. a person who paints miniatures.

minicomputer n. a computer of medium power, bigger than a microcomputer but not as big as a mainframe.

minim n. **1** a note in music, lasting half as long as a semibreve. **2** one-sixtieth of a fluid drachm, about one drop.

minima see MINIMUM.

minimal adj. very small, the least possible. ❏ **minimally** adv.

minimalism n. the use of simple, basic forms in design, art, etc.; including only the minimum. ❏ **minimalist** adj. & n.

minimise *v.* (also **-ize**) **1** reduce to a minimum. **2** estimate at the smallest possible amount; re-present at less than the true value or importance.

minimum *n.* (*pl.* **minima**) the lowest or the lowest possible number, amount, intensity, etc. • *adj.* that is a minimum. ▫ **minimum wage** the lowest wage permitted by law or agreement.

minion / **min**-yuhn / *n. derog.* a follower or underling of a powerful person, esp. a servile or unimportant one.

miniseries *n.* (*pl.* the same) a short series of television programs on the same theme etc., usu. shown on consecutive days.

miniskirt *n.* a very short skirt.

minister *n.* **1** a person at the head of a government department (*Minister for Defence*). **2** a diplomatic representative usu. ranking below ambassador. **3** a clergyman, esp. in the various Protestant Churches. • *v.* attend to people's needs (*nurses ministered to the wounded*). ▫ **ministerial** / min-uh-**steer**-ree-uhl / *adj.*

ministration *n.* **1** (usu. as **ministrations**) help or service. **2** ministering; supplying of help, justice, etc.

ministry *n.* **1** a government department headed by a minister. **2** a period of government under one prime minister; his or her body of ministers. **3** the profession or functions of a religious minister; his or her period of tenure.

mink *n.* **1** a small stoatlike animal of the weasel family. **2** its fur. **3** a coat made of this.

minke / **ming**-kee / *n.* a small whale with a pointed snout.

min-min *n. Aust.* a will-o'-the-wisp. (¶ Perhaps from an Aboriginal language.)

minnerichi / min-uh-**rich**-ee / *n.* (also **minnaritchi**) the red mulga, a small SA wattle which typically has thin, peeling curls of reddish bark. (¶ Perhaps from a SA Aboriginal language.)

minnow / **min**-oh / *n.* a small European freshwater fish of the carp family.

Minoan / mi-**noh**-uhn / *adj.* of the Bronze Age civilisation of Crete (about 3000–1000 BC). • *n.* a person of this civilisation. (¶ Named after *Minos*, a legendary king of Crete.)

Minogue, Kylie (Ann) (1968–), Australian pop singer and actor.

minor *adj.* **1** lesser, less important (*minor roads; a minor operation*). **2** (in music) of or based on a scale which has a semitone next above the second, fifth, and seventh notes. • *n.* **1** a person under full legal age. **2** *Aust. Rules* a behind. ▫ **minor orders** *see* ORDER. **minor planet** an asteroid. **minor premiers** *Sport* the team at the top of the ladder before the finals begin.

Minorite / **muy**-nuh-ruyt / *n.* a Franciscan friar or Friar Minor.

minority *n.* **1** the smaller part of a group or class. **2** a small group differing from others in race, religion, sexual orientation, etc. **3** the state of having less than half the votes or support (*in the minority*). **4** (in law) the state of being under full age (*during his minority*).

Minotaur / **min**-uh-taw / *Gk myth.* a creature, half man and half bull, kept in the labyrinth in Crete and eventually slain by Theseus.

minster *n.* **1** the church of a monastery. **2** any large or important church.

minstrel *n.* **1** a travelling singer and musician in the Middle Ages. **2** an entertainer with a blacked face singing songs of supposedly African-American origin.

minstrelsy *n.* a medieval minstrel's art or poetry.

mint[1] *n.* **1** a place authorised to make a country's coins. **2** a vast amount (*left him a mint of money*). • *v.* **1** make (coins) by stamping metal. **2** invent or coin (a word etc.). ▫ **in mint condition** fresh and unsoiled as if newly from the mint.

mint[2] *n.* **1** a plant with fragrant leaves that are used for flavouring sauces and drinks etc. **2** peppermint; a sweet flavoured with this. ▫ **mint bush** any shrub of the large Australian genus *Prostanthera*, many of which are cultivated as ornamentals for their strongly minty leaves and profusion of white, blue, or purple flowers. ▫▫ **minty** *adj.*

mintie *n. Aust. trademark* **1** a peppermint-flavoured sweet, having the advertising slogan 'It's moments like these you need Minties'. **2** this slogan used allusively as an emblem of consolation (*there are some crises when even minties won't help*).

minuet / min-yoo-**et** / *n.* a slow stately dance in triple time; music suitable for this.

minus / **muy**-nuhs / *prep.* **1** reduced by the subtraction of (*seven minus three equals four*; 7−3 = 4). **2** *colloq.* without, deprived of (*returned minus his shoes*). • *adj.* less than zero (= negative), less than the amount or number indicated (*a minus quantity*; *temperatures of minus ten degrees*; *alpha minus*). • *n.* **1** = MINUS SIGN. **2** a disadvantage. ▫ **minus sign** a symbol (−), indicating subtraction or a negative value.

minuscule / **min**-uh-skyool / *adj.* extremely small or unimportant.

minute[1] / **min**-uht / *n.* **1** one-sixtieth of an hour. **2** the distance covered in one minute (*ten minutes from the shops*). **3** moment (*expecting her any minute*). **4** (**the minute**) *colloq.* the present time (*not here at the minute*). **5** (**the minute**) as soon as (*see me the minute you get back*). **6** the sixtieth of a degree used in measuring angles. **7** (**minutes**) an official record of the proceedings of an assembly or committee etc. made during a meeting. **8** an official memorandum. • *adj.* taking a very short time (*minute noodles*). • *v.* make a note of; record in the minutes of an assembly's proceedings. ▫ **up to the minute** completely up to date.

minute[2] / muy-**nyoot** / *adj.* **1** extremely small. **2** very detailed and precise (*a minute examination*). ▫ **minutely** *adv.*

minutiae / muy-**nyoo**-shee-ee / n.pl. very small details.

minx n. a cheeky or mischievous girl.

Miocene / **muy**-uh-seen / Geol. adj. of the fourth epoch of the Tertiary period. • n. this epoch.

mips abbr. Computing a million instructions per second.

miracle n. **1** a remarkable and welcome event that seems impossible to explain by the laws of nature and is therefore attributed to a supernatural agency. **2** a remarkable example or specimen (*it's a miracle of ingenuity*). ☐ **miracle play 1** = MYSTERY PLAY. **2** a medieval play dealing with the life of a saint.

miraculous adj. **1** of or like a miracle. **2** supernatural. **3** remarkable, surprising. ☐ **miraculously** adv.

mirage / muh-**rah**zh / n. **1** an optical illusion caused by atmospheric conditions, esp. making sheets of water seem to appear in a desert or on a hot road. **2** any illusory thing.

mire n. **1** swampy ground, bog. **2** mud or sticky dirt. • v. **1** plunge in mire. **2** involve in difficulties. **3** spatter with mire, soil.

mirin / **mi**-ruhn / n. a Japanese rice wine used in cooking.

mirrnyong / **mer**-nyong / n. (also **mirrnyong heap**) a mound of ashes, shells, and other debris, accumulated in a place used by Aborigines for cooking, and often of archaeological significance; a kitchen midden. (¶ Probably from a Vic. Aboriginal language.)

mirr'n-yong alternative spelling of MURNONG.

mirror n. **1** a piece of glass backed with amalgam so that reflections can be seen in it. **2** anything reflecting or illuminating a state of affairs etc. • v. reflect in or as if in a mirror. ☐ **mirror dory** a marine food fish of southern Australia with a brilliantly silvered and mirror-like circular body.

mirror image a reflection or copy in which the right and left sides of the original are reversed.

mirror site Computing a site on a network which stores some or all of the contents from another site.

mirth n. merriment, laughter. ☐ **mirthful** adj. **mirthless** adj.

mis- comb. form badly, wrongly.

misadventure n. **1** a piece of bad luck. **2** Law an accident without crime or negligence (*death by misadventure*).

misalliance n. an unsuitable alliance, esp. a marriage.

misandry / muh-**san**-dree / n. the hatred of men (i.e. the male sex).

misanthrope / **miz**-uhn-throhp / n. (also **misanthropist**) / muh-**zan**-thruh-puhst / a person who hates mankind or avoids people in general. ☐ **misanthropic** adj. **misanthropically** adv. **misanthropy** n.

misapply v. (**misapplied**, **misapplying**) apply wrongly. ☐ **misapplication** n.

misapprehend / mis-ap-ruh-**hend** / v. misunderstand. ☐ **misapprehension** n.

misappropriate / mis-uh-**proh**-pree-ayt / v. take dishonestly, esp. for one's own use. ☐ **misappropriation** n.

misbegotten adj. **1** contemptible, disreputable. **2** illegitimate, bastard.

misbehave v. behave badly. ☐ **misbehaviour** n.

misc. abbr. miscellaneous.

miscalculate v. calculate incorrectly. ☐ **miscalculation** n.

miscarriage / mis-**ka**-rij / n. **1** abortion occurring without being induced. **2** a mistake or failure to achieve the correct result (*a miscarriage of justice*).

miscarry v. (**miscarried**, **miscarrying**) **1** (of a pregnant woman) have a miscarriage. **2** (of a scheme etc.) go wrong, fail.

miscast v. (**miscast**, **miscasting**) cast (an actor) in an unsuitable role.

miscegenation / mi-sej-uh-**nay**-shuhn / n. interbreeding of races, esp. of whites with non-whites.

miscellaneous / mis-uh-**lay**-nee-uhs / adj. **1** of various kinds (*miscellaneous items*). **2** of mixed composition or character (*a miscellaneous collection*).

miscellany / muh-**sel**-uh-nee / n. a collection of various items; a mixture.

mischance n. misfortune.

mischief n. **1** conduct (esp. of children) that is annoying or does slight damage but is not malicious. **2** a tendency to tease or cause annoyance playfully (*full of mischief*). **3** harm or damage (*did a lot of mischief*).

mischievous / **mis**-chuh-vuhs / adj. (of a person) full of mischief; (of an action) brought about by mischief. ☐ **mischievously** adv.

miscible / **mis**-uh-buhl / adj. able to be mixed. ☐ **miscibility** n.

misconceive / mis-kuhn-**seev** / v. **1** misunderstand, interpret incorrectly. **2** (as **misconceived** adj.) badly planned, organised, etc.

misconception / mis-kuhn-**sep**-shuhn / n. a wrong interpretation.

misconduct / mis-**kon**-dukt / n. bad, improper, or unprofessional behaviour.

misconstrue / mis-kuhn-**stroo** / v. misinterpret. ☐ **misconstruction** n.

miscopy v. (**miscopied**, **miscopying**) copy incorrectly.

miscount v. count incorrectly. • n. an incorrect count.

miscreant / **mis**-kree-uhnt / n. a wrongdoer, a villain.

misdeal v. (**misdealt**, **misdealing**) make a mistake in dealing playing cards. • n. an incorrect dealing.

misdeed n. a wrong or improper act, a crime.

misdemeanour / mis-duh-**mee**-nuh / n. (also **misdemeanor**) a misdeed, wrongdoing.

misdiagnose v. diagnose incorrectly. ☐ **misdiagnosis** n.

misdial v. dial (a telephone number etc.) incorrectly.

misdirect v. direct incorrectly. ☐ **misdirection** n.

mise en scène / meez on **sen** / n. **1** the scenery and properties for a play. **2** the surroundings of an event. (¶ French)

miser n. a person who hoards money and spends as little as possible. ☐ **miserly** adj. **miserliness** n.

miserable adj. **1** full of misery, feeling very unhappy or uncomfortable. **2** surly and discontented, disagreeable. **3** unpleasant (*miserable weather*). **4** wretchedly poor in quality or surroundings etc. (*a miserable attempt; miserable slums*). **5** *Scottish & Aust.* stingy, mean (*he refused to donate a cent—could anyone be more miserable?*). ☐ **miserably** adv.

misère / mi-**zair** / n. (in solo whist etc.) a declaration undertaking to win no tricks.

misericord / mi-**ze**-ri-cord / n. **1** a shelving projection on the under side of a hinged seat in a choir stall serving (when the seat is turned up) to help support a person standing. **2** an apartment in a monastery in which some relaxations of discipline are permitted. **3** a dagger for dealing the death stroke.

misery n. **1** a feeling of great unhappiness or discomfort. **2** something causing this. **3** *colloq.* a discontented or disagreeable person.

misfire v. **1** (of a gun) fail to go off correctly. **2** (of an engine etc.) fail to start, fail to function correctly. **3** fail to have the intended effect (*the joke misfired*). • n. a failure of this kind.

misfit n. **1** a garment etc. that does not fit. **2** a person who is not well suited to his or her environment. • v. fit badly (*a misfitting garment; misfitted to his job*).

misfortune n. bad luck; an unfortunate event.

misgive v. (**misgave**, **misgiven**, **misgiving**) fill with misgivings (*his heart misgave him*).

misgiving n. (often as **misgivings**) a feeling of doubt or slight fear or mistrust.

misgovern v. govern badly.

misguided adj. mistaken in one's opinions or actions; ill-judged. ☐ **misguidedly** adv.

mishandle v. deal with (a thing) badly or inefficiently.

mishap / **mis**-hap / n. an unlucky accident.

mishear v. (**misheard**, **mishearing**) hear incorrectly.

mishit v. (**mishit**, **mishitting**) hit (a ball) faultily or badly. • n. a faulty or bad hit.

mishmash n. a confused mixture.

Mishnah n. the collection of decisions on Jewish legal and ritual observance that form the main text of the Talmud.

misinform v. give wrong information to.

misinterpret v. interpret incorrectly. ☐ **misinterpretation** n.

misjudge v. form a wrong opinion of; estimate incorrectly. ☐ **misjudgment** (also **misjudgement**) n.

miskey v. key (data) wrongly.

mislay v. (**mislaid**, **mislaying**) lose temporarily.

mislead v. (**misled**, **misleading**) lead astray; cause (a person) to gain a wrong impression of something. ☐ **misleading** adj.

mismanage v. manage (affairs) badly or wrongly. ☐ **mismanagement** n.

mismatch v. match unsuitably or incorrectly. • n. a bad match.

misnomer / mis-**noh**-muh / n. a name or description that is wrongly applied to something.

miso / **mee**-soh / n. a paste made from fermented soya beans and barley or rice malt, used in Japanese cookery.

misogamy / muh-**sog**-uh-mee / n. a hatred of marriage. ☐ **misogamist** n.

misogynist / muh-**soj**-uh-nuhst / n. a person who hates women. ☐ **misogynistic** adj. **misogyny** n.

misplace v. **1** put (a thing) in the wrong place; lose temporarily. **2** place (one's confidence etc.) unwisely. **3** use (words or action) in an unsuitable situation (*misplaced humour*). ☐ **misplacement** n.

misprint n. an error in printing. • v. print wrongly.

mispronounce v. pronounce incorrectly. ☐ **mispronunciation** n.

misquote v. quote incorrectly. ☐ **misquotation** n.

misread v. (**misread** / mis-**red** /, **misreading**) read or interpret incorrectly.

misremember v. remember imperfectly or incorrectly.

misrepresent v. represent in a false or misleading way. ☐ **misrepresentation** n.

misrule n. bad government. • v. govern badly.

miss[1] v. **1** fail to hit, reach, or catch (an object). **2** fail to see, hear, or understand etc. (*we missed the signpost; I missed that remark*). **3** fail to catch (a train etc.) or keep (an appointment) or meet (a person); fail to seize (an opportunity). **4** hit, lack. **5** notice the absence or loss of (*the child was not missed until the next day*). **6** feel regret at the absence or loss of (*old Smith won't be missed*). **7** avoid (*go this way and you'll miss the traffic*). **8** (of an engine etc.) misfire. • n. failure to hit or attain what is aimed at. ☐ **miss out** omit. **miss out on 1** fail to get or experience (*missed out on a prize*). **2** fail to attend (*missed out on the party*).

miss[2] n. **1** a girl or unmarried woman. **2** (**Miss**) a title used of or to a girl or unmarried woman. **3** a title used to address a female teacher etc.

missal n. *Catholic Church* **1** a book containing the texts for the Mass throughout the year. **2** a book of prayers.

misshapen adj. badly shaped, distorted.

missile *n.* an object or weapon suitable for throwing or firing at a target; a weapon directed by remote control or automatically.

missing *adj.* **1** lost, not in its place (*two pages are missing*). **2** not present (*he's always missing when there's work to be done*). **3** absent from home and with one's whereabouts unknown (*she's listed as a missing person*). **4** (of a soldier etc.) neither present after a battle nor known to have been killed. □ **missing link 1** a thing lacking to complete a series. **2** a type of animal supposed to have existed between the anthropoid apes and the development of man.

mission *n.* **1** a task or goal assigned to a person or a group; a journey undertaken as part of this. **2** a person's vocation. **3** *Aust.* an Aboriginal settlement administered by a religious community; such a settlement administered by a government agency or by Aborigines themselves. **4** a military or scientific expedition. **5** a body of persons sent, esp. to a foreign country, to conduct negotiations or to propagate a religious faith. **6** a missionary post.

missionary *adj.* of or concerned with religious missions. • *n.* a person doing missionary work. □ **missionary position** a position for sexual intercourse with the woman lying on her back and the man lying facing her on top.

missis *n.* (also **missus**) *colloq.* **1** wife (*how's the missis?*). **2** a form of address to a woman, used without her name.

Mississippi the greatest river of North America, flowing south from Minnesota to the Gulf of Mexico.

missive *n.* a written message, a letter.

misspell *v.* (**misspelt** or **misspelled**, **misspelling**) spell incorrectly.

misspend *v.* (**misspent**, **misspending**) spend badly or unwisely (*regrets his misspent youth*).

misstate *v.* state wrongly. □ **misstatement** *n.*

missus *n.* **1** alternative spelling of MISSIS. **2** *Aust.* (in Aboriginal English) the wife of a boss or manager.

mist *n.* **1** water vapour near the ground in drops smaller than raindrops, clouding the atmosphere less thickly than fog does. **2** condensed vapour clouding a window etc. **3** a dimness or blurring of vision caused by tears etc. **4** something resembling mist in its form or effect. • *v.* (usu. foll. by *up* or *over*) cover or become covered with mist or as with mist (*the windscreen misted up*).

mistake *n.* an incorrect idea or opinion; something incorrectly done or thought. • *v.* (**mistook**, **mistaken**, **mistaking**) **1** misunderstand the meaning or intention of. **2** choose or identify wrongly (*mistake one's vocation; she is often mistaken for her sister*).

mistaken *adj.* **1** wrong in one's opinion or judgment. **2** based on or resulting from this (*mistaken loyalty; mistaken identity*). □ **mistakenly** *adv.*

mister *n. colloq.* a form of address to a man, used without his name.

mistime *v.* say or do (a thing) at the wrong time.

mistletoe *n.* **1** a parasitic European plant with white berries. **2** a similar Australian plant, usu. to be seen hanging from the branches of eucalypts. □ **mistletoe bird** a small bird of mainland Australia that has a steel-blue body and a scarlet and white breast and feeds mainly on mistletoe berries.

mistook *see* MISTAKE.

mistral / **mis**-truhl / *n.* a cold north or north-west wind in southern France etc.

mistreat *v.* treat badly. □ **mistreatment** *n.*

mistress *n.* **1** a woman who is in a position of authority or control. **2** the female head of a household. **3** the female owner of a dog or other animal. **4** a female teacher. **5** a man's female lover with whom he has a continuing illicit sexual relationship. **6** *Aust. hist.* a woman to whom a convict is assigned.

mistrial *n.* a trial invalidated by an error in procedure etc.

mistrust *v.* be suspicious of; feel no confidence in. • *n.* suspicion; lack of confidence. □ **mistrustful** *adj.* **mistrustfully** *adv.*

misty *adj.* (**mistier**, **mistiest**) **1** full of mist. **2** indistinct in form or idea etc. □ **mistily** *adj.* **mistiness** *n.*

misunderstand *v.* (**misunderstood**, **misunderstanding**) form an incorrect interpretation or opinion of (a person's words or actions).

misunderstanding *n.* **1** failure to understand correctly. **2** a slight disagreement or quarrel.

misuse *v.* / mis-**yooz** / **1** use wrongly or incorrectly. **2** treat badly. • *n.* / mis-**yoos** / (also **misusage**) wrong or incorrect use.

Mitchell[1], Dame Roma Flinders (1913–2000), AC, Australian jurist and university teacher who in 1965 became the first woman judge in Australia. In 1991 she was appointed governor of SA, the first woman to hold viceregal office in Australia.

Mitchell[2], Sir Thomas Livingstone (1792–1855), Australian surveyor and explorer (born in Scotland) who led four expeditions in eastern Australia in the 1830s. □ **Mitchell grass** (also **Mitchell**) any of the hardy tussock-forming perennial grasses of arid and semi-arid Australia providing valuable fodder.

mite *n.* **1** a very small spider-like animal found on plants, in cheese, etc. **2** a very small contribution (*offered a mite of comfort*). **3** a very small creature; a small child. • *adv.* somewhat (*he's a mite shy*).

Mithras / **mith**-ras / *Persian myth.* the god of light, also worshipped in the ancient Roman world. □ **Mithraic** *adj.* **Mithraism** *n.*

mitigate / **mit**-uh-gayt / *v.* make less intense or serious. □ **mitigating circumstances** facts that partially excuse wrongdoing. □□ **mitigation** *n.*

mitosis

■ **Usage** Do not confuse with *militate*.

mitosis / muh-**toh**-suhs, muy- / *n.* a type of cell division that results in two nuclei each having the same number and kind of chromosomes as the parent nucleus.

mitre / **muy**-tuh / *n.* **1** the tall deeply cleft headdress worn by bishops and abbots, esp. as a symbol of office. **2** a joint or join of two pieces of wood or cloth etc. with their ends evenly tapered so that together they form a right angle. • *v.* (**mitred**, **mitring**) **1** join in this way (*mitred corners*). **2** bestow a mitre on (*a mitred abbot*).

mitt *n.* **1** a mitten. **2** *colloq.* the hand or the fist.

Mitta Mitta a river, about 170 km long, in eastern Vic.

mitten *n.* a glove that has no partition between the fingers; a glove leaving the fingers and thumb-tip exposed.

Mitty, Walter, the hero of a story (by James Thurber) who indulged in extravagant daydreams of his own triumphs.

mix *v.* **1** put different things together so that the substances etc. are no longer distinct. **2** be capable of being blended (*oil will not mix with water*). **3** combine, be able to be combined (*mix business with pleasure; drinking and driving don't mix*). **4** (of a person) be sociable or harmonious (*you must learn to mix*). **5** combine (two or more sound signals) into one. • *n.* **1** a mixture. **2** a mixture prepared commercially from suitable ingredients for making something (*cake mix; concrete mix*). ▫ **be mixed up in** (or **with**) be involved in. **mix it** *colloq.* start fighting. **mix up 1** mix thoroughly. **2** confuse. **mix-up** *n.* a misunderstanding; confusion.

mixed *adj.* **1** composed of various qualities or elements. **2** containing people from various races or social backgrounds. **3** for people of both sexes (*mixed bathing*). ▫ **mixed blessing** a thing that has advantages and also disadvantages. **mixed business** *Aust.* a small shop, often associated with a milk bar, selling groceries and other goods. **mixed doubles** a doubles game in tennis with a man and woman as partners on each side. **mixed economy** an economic system combining private and state enterprise. **mixed farming** with both crops and livestock. **mixed farmer** one who farms in such a way. **mixed marriage** a marriage between people of different race or religion. **mixed metaphor** a combination of metaphors that do not work together; e.g. *this tower of strength will forge ahead*. **mixed-up** *colloq.* mentally or emotionally confused; not well-adjusted socially.

mixer *n.* **1** a device that mixes or blends things (*food mixer*). **2** a person who gets on in a certain way with others (*a good mixer*). **3** a drink to be mixed with another (stronger) drink. **4** a device that receives two or more separate signals from microphones etc. and combines them in a single output.

mixture *n.* **1** mixing; being mixed. **2** something made by mixing, a combination of things, ingredients, or qualities etc. (*cough mixture; he's a mixture of kindness and intolerance*).

mizen *n.* (also **mizzen**) a mizen-sail. ▫ **mizen-mast** the mast that is next aft of the mainmast. **mizen-sail** the lowest sail, set lengthways, on a mizen-mast.

ml *abbr.* millilitre(s).

MLA *abbr.* Member of the Legislative Assembly.

MLC *abbr.* Member of the Legislative Council.

Mlle *abbr.* (*pl.* **Mlles**) Mademoiselle.

mm *abbr.* millimetre(s).

Mme *abbr.* (*pl.* **Mmes**) Madame.

Mn *symbol* manganese.

mnemonic / nuh-**mon**-ik / *adj.* aiding the memory. • *n.* a verse or other aid to help one remember facts. ▫ **mnemonically** *adv.*

Mo *symbol* molybdenum.

mo *n.* (*pl.* **mos**) *colloq.* **1** a moment (*half a mo*). **2** *Aust.* moustache.

moa *n.* an extinct flightless New Zealand bird resembling the ostrich.

moan *n.* **1** a low mournful sound, usu. indicating physical or mental suffering or pleasure. **2** a grumble. • *v.* **1** utter a moan; say with a moan. **2** (of wind etc.) make a sound like a moan. **3** grumble.

moat *n.* a deep wide ditch surrounding a castle, town, etc., usu. filled with water.

mob *n.* **1** a large disorderly crowd of people. **2** the common people, the rabble. **3** *colloq.* a gang. **4** esp. *Aust.* **a** a number (or class) of people showing a specified characteristic, identity, etc. (*it took eleven ships to bring that first mob to Oz*). **b** *colloq.* the friends one usu. associates with. **5** *Aust.* (in Aboriginal English) one's extended family; one's own particular clan or people. **6** a flock or herd. • *adv.* (**mobs**) *Aust. colloq.* much (*it'll be mobs easier*). • *v.* (**mobbed**, **mobbing**) crowd round in great numbers either to attack or to admire. ▫ **mob rule** rule imposed and enforced by the mob. **mobs of** *Aust. colloq.* lots of (*mobs of water on the track; mobs of fish in the creek*).

mobile / **moh**-buyl / *adj.* **1** movable, not fixed; able to move or be moved easily and quickly. **2** (of the features of the face) readily changing expression. **3** (of a library, a business, etc.) accommodated in a vehicle so as to serve various places. **4** (of a person) able to change social status (*a suburb for the upwardly mobile*). • *n.* a decorative structure that may be hung so that its parts move freely. ▫ **mobile phone** a portable cellular telephone for use in a car etc. ▫▫ **mobility** / moh-**bil**-uh-tee / *n.*

mobilise / **moh**-buh-luyz / *v.* (also **-ize**) **1** assemble (troops) for service; prepare for war or other emergency. **2** assemble for a particular

mobster 531 **module**

purpose (*they mobilised support from all parties*). ☐ **mobilisation** *n.*

mobster *n. colloq.* a gangster.

moccasin / **mok**-uh-suhn / *n.* a soft leather shoe, stitched round the vamp.

mocha / **mok**-uh / *n.* a kind of coffee; flavouring made with this.

mock *v.* **1** make fun of by imitating, mimic. **2** scoff or jeer; defy contemptuously. **3** (foll. by *up*) construct (a model etc.). • *adj.* sham, imitation (*a mock battle*). ☐ **mock orange** a shrub with strongly scented white flowers. **mock turtle soup** soup made from calf's head or other meat, to resemble turtle soup. **mock-up** *n.* a model of something, to be used for testing or study. ☐☐ **mockingly** *adv.*

mocker[1] *n.* a person who mocks. ☐ **put the mockers on** *colloq.* bring bad luck to.

mocker[2] *n. Aust. colloq.* clothing (*wear ordinary mocker*). ☐ **mockered up** dressed up (*all mockered up and nowhere to go*).

mockery *n.* **1** ridicule, contempt. **2** a ridiculous or unsatisfactory imitation, a travesty. **3** a ridiculously futile action etc.

mockingbird *n.* a bird that mimics the notes of other birds.

mod *adj. colloq.* modern (esp. in style of dress). ☐ **mod cons** modern conveniences (*a house with all the mod cons*).

modal *adj.* **1** of mode or form, not substance. **2** *Grammar* of the mood of a verb; (of an auxiliary verb, e.g. *would*) used to express the mood of another verb. **3** denoting a style of music using a particular mode. ☐ **modality** / moh-**dal**-uh-tee / *n.*

mode *n.* **1** the way in which a thing is done. **2** the current fashion. **3** (in music) each of a number of traditional scale systems.

model *n.* **1** a three-dimensional reproduction of something, usu. on a smaller scale. **2** a design or style of structure, e.g. of a car (*this year's model*). **3** a garment by a well-known designer; a copy of this. **4** a person or thing regarded as excellent of its kind and worthy of imitation. **5** a person employed to pose for an artist. **6** a person employed to display clothes by wearing them. • *adj.* excellent of its kind, exemplary. • *v.* (**modelled, modelling**) **1** make a model of (a thing) in clay or wax etc.; shape (clay etc.) into a model. **2** design or plan (a thing) in accordance with a model (*the new method is modelled on the old one*). **3** work as an artist's model or as a fashion model; display (clothes) in this way.

modem / **moh**-dem / *n.* a device which enables communication between one computer system and others over a telephone line. (¶ Blend of *mo*dulator + *dem*odulator.)

moderate *adj.* / **mod**-uh-ruht / **1** medium in amount, intensity, or quality etc. **2** keeping or kept within reasonable limits, not extreme or excessive. **3** not holding extremist views. **4** fairly large or good. **5** average, limited (*moderate success*). • *n.* / **mod**-uh-ruht / a person with moderate views in politics etc. • *v.* / **mod**-uh-rayt / **1** make or become moderate or less intense etc. **2** act as moderator of or to. ☐ **moderately** *adv.* **moderateness** *n.*

moderation *n.* moderating; moderateness. ☐ **in moderation** in moderate amounts.

moderato *adj. & adv. Music* at a moderate speed.

moderator *n.* **1** an arbitrator, a mediator; a presiding officer. **2** a Presbyterian or Uniting Church minister presiding over a church court or assembly. **3** a substance used in nuclear reactors to slow down neutrons.

modern *adj.* **1** of the present or recent times (*modern history*). **2** in current fashion, not antiquated. **3** (of artistic or literary forms) new and experimental, not following traditional styles. • *n.* a person of modern times or with modern tastes or style. ☐ **modern dance** an expressive style of dancing distinct from classical ballet. **modern English** the English language from about 1500 onwards. ☐☐ **modernity** / muh-**der**-nuh-tee / *n.*

modernise *v.* (also **-ize**) make modern, adapt to modern ideas or tastes etc. ☐ **modernisation** *n.*

modernism *n.* modern ideas or methods, esp. the rejection of realism and traditionalism in the art and literature of the first half of the 20th century. ☐ **modernist** *n. & adj.*

modest *adj.* **1** not vain, not boasting about one's merits or achievements. **2** rather shy, not putting oneself forward. **3** moderate in size or amount etc.; not showy or splendid in appearance. ☐ **modestly** *adv.* **modesty** *n.*

modicum / **mod**-uh-kuhm / *n.* a small amount.

modification *n.* **1** modifying or being modified. **2** a change made.

modificatory *adj.* modifying.

modifier *n.* **1** a person or thing that modifies. **2** *Grammar* a word (esp. an adjective or a noun used attributively) that qualifies the sense of another word, e.g. the adjective *good* and the noun *family* in *a good family car.*

modify *v.* (**modified, modifying**) **1** make less severe or harsh or violent. **2** make partial changes in (*some clauses in the agreement have been modified*). **3** (in grammar) qualify by describing (*adjectives modify nouns*).

modish / **moh**-dish / *adj.* fashionable. ☐ **modishly** *adv.* **modishness** *n.*

modular *adj.* consisting of independent units.

modulate *v.* **1** adjust or regulate; moderate. **2** vary the tone or pitch of (one's voice). **3** pass from one key to another in music. **4** alter the amplitude, frequency, or phase of (a carrier wave) so as to convey a particular signal. ☐ **modulation** *n.*

module / **mod**-yool / *n.* **1** a unit or standard used in measuring. **2** a standardised part or an independent unit in furniture, buildings, an electronic system, or a spacecraft etc.

modulus / **mod**-yuh-luhs / *n.* (*pl.* **moduli**) a constant factor or ratio.

modus operandi / moh-duhs op-uh-**ran**-duy, -dee / *n.* (*pl.* **modi operandi**) a method of working. (¶ Latin)

modus vivendi / moh-duhs vi-**ven**-duy, -dee / *n.* (*pl.* **modi vivendi**) **1** a way of living or coping. **2** an arrangement that enables parties who are in dispute to carry on instead of having their activities paralysed until the dispute has been settled. (¶ Latin, = way of living.)

Mogadishu / mog-uh-**dish**-oo / the capital of Somalia.

moggie *n.* (also **moggy**, **mog**) *colloq.* a cat.

Mogul / **moh**-guhl / *n.* **1** a member of a Mongolian dynasty in India in the 16th–19th centuries. **2** (**mogul**) *colloq.* an important or influential person. • *adj.* of the Moguls.

moguls *n.pl.* a form of competitive skiing on a ski field with a series of humps over which competitors race against the clock.

mohair *n.* **1** the fine silky hair of the angora goat, or a mixture of it with wool or cotton. **2** yarn or fabric made from this.

Mohammed / muh-**ham**-uhd / (also **Muhammad**) (*c.* 570–632), the founder of the Islamic faith and community.

Mohammedan (also **Muhammadan**) *n.* & *adj.* = MUSLIM.

■ **Usage** The term *Mohammedan* is not used by Muslims, and is often regarded as offensive.

Mohican / moh-**hee**-kuhn / *n.* a member of a warlike tribe of North American Indians. • *adj.* (**mohican**) (of a hairstyle) in which the sides of the head are shaved and the remaining strip of hair is worn stiffly erect and often brightly coloured.

moiety / **moi**-uh-tee / *n. formal* **1** half. **2** each of two parts of something. **3** a form of social organisation in which an Aboriginal people is divided into one of two units, esp. on the basis of lineal descent, each unit being a moiety.

moist *adj.* slightly wet, damp; (of eyes) having a hint of tears.

moisten / **moi**-suhn / *v.* make or become moist.

moisture *n.* water or other liquid diffused through a substance or present in the air as vapour or condensed on a surface.

moisturise *v.* (also -**ize**) make (the skin) less dry by use of certain cosmetics. ☐ **moisturiser** *n.*

moke *n. Aust. colloq.* a horse; sometimes an inferior one.

moksa *n.* (in Hinduism) liberation from the chain of births impelled by the law of karma; the bliss attained by this.

molar / **moh**-luh / *n.* any of the teeth at the back of the jaw that have broad tops and are used for grinding food in chewing. • *adj.* of these teeth.

molasses / muh-**las**-uhz / *n.* uncrystallised syrup drained from raw sugar.

Moldova / mol-**doh**-vuh, **mol**-duh-vuh / (also **Moldavia** / mol-**day**-vee-uh/) **1** a republic of eastern Europe bordering on Romania and Ukraine. **2** a former principality on the Danube. ☐ **Moldovan** *adj.* & *n.*

mole *n.* **1** a small permanent dark spot on the human skin. **2** a small burrowing animal with dark velvety fur and very small eyes. **3** a person working within an organisation who secretly passes confidential information to another organisation or country. **4** a structure built out into the sea as a breakwater or causeway. **5** *Chem.* a unit of amount of a substance equal to the quantity containing as many elementary units as there are atoms in 0.012 kg of carbon-12. **6** *colloq. offens.* a girl or woman.

molecular / muh-**lek**-yuh-luh / *adj.* of, relating to, or consisting of molecules. ☐ **molecular weight** = RELATIVE MOLECULAR MASS.

molecule / **mol**-uh-kyool / *n.* **1** the smallest unit (usu. consisting of a group of atoms) into which a substance can be divided while still retaining the substance's chemical qualities. **2** a small particle.

molehill *n.* a small mound of earth thrown up by a burrowing mole. ☐ **make a mountain out of a molehill** behave as if a small difficulty were a very great one.

moleskin *n.* **1** strong cotton cloth, the surface of which has been shaved before dyeing (with the result that it looks like the skin of a mole). **2** (**moleskins**) trousers made of moleskin, part of the customary dress of Australian stockmen, gold diggers, etc., from the early 19th century onwards.

molest / muh-**lest** / *v.* **1** annoy or pester (a person). **2** attack or interfere with (a person), esp. sexually. ☐ **molestation** *n.* **molester** *n.*

Molière / **mol**-ee-air / (real name: Jean-Baptiste Poquelin) (1622–73), French comic dramatist.

moll *n. colloq.* **1** a prostitute. **2** a gangster's female companion. **3** the girlfriend of a bikie, a surfie, etc.

mollify *v.* (**mollified**, **mollifying**) appease; soothe the anger of. ☐ **mollification** *n.*

mollusc / **mol**-uhsk / *n.* any of a group of animals which have soft bodies and hard shells (e.g. snails, oysters, mussels) or no shell (e.g. slugs, octopuses).

mollycoddle *v.* coddle excessively, pamper. • *n.* a mollycoddled person.

molly-dook *n.* (also **molly-dooker**) *Aust. colloq.* a left-handed person. ☐ **molly-dooked** *adj.*

Moloch / **moh**-lok / *n.* **1 a** a Canaanite idol to whom children were sacrificed. **b** a tyrannical object of sacrifices. **2** (**moloch**) the spiny slow-moving grotesque Australian reptile, *Moloch horridus*. Also called *mountain devil*, *thorny devil*.

Molotov cocktail *n.* an improvised incendiary bomb, usu. a bottle filled with inflammable liquid. (¶ Named after the Russian statesman V.M. Molotov (1890–1986).)

molten / **mohl**-tuhn / *adj.* melted, made liquid by very great heat.

molto *adv. Music* very.

moly *n.* a mythical herb with white flowers and black roots, endowed with powerful magic properties.

molybdenum / muh-**lib**-duh-nuhm / *n.* a metallic element (symbol Mo), used as a strengthening agent in steels and other alloys.

moment *n.* **1** a very brief portion of time. **2** an exact point of time (*at that very moment*). **3** importance (*these are matters of great moment*). ▫ **moment of truth** a time of test or crisis. (¶ From a Spanish phrase referring to the final sword-thrust in a bullfight.)

momentary / **moh**-muhn-tree / *adj.* lasting only a moment. ▫ **momentarily** *adv.*

momentous / muh-**men**-tuhs / *adj.* of great importance. ▫ **momentously** *adv.* **momentousness** *n.*

momentum / muh-**men**-tuhm / *n.* (*pl.* **momenta**) **1** impetus gained by movement (*the sledge gathered momentum as it ran downhill*). **2** strength or continuity derived from an initial effort (*the campaign is gaining momentum*).

Monaco / **mon**-uh-koh / **1** a principality on the French Riviera. **2** its capital city. ▫ **Monegasque** / mon-nay-**gask** / *adj.* & *n.*

monad *n.* **1** the number one; a unit. **2** *Philosophy* the ultimate unit of being (e.g. a soul, an atom, a person, God). ▫ **monadic** *adj.*

Mona Lisa / moh-nuh **lee**-zuh / a painting (now in the Louvre) by Leonardo da Vinci of a woman with an enigmatic smile.

monandry / muh-**nan**-dree / *n.* the custom of having only one husband at a time.

monarch / **mon**-uhk, -ahk / *n.* a ruler with the title of king, queen, emperor, or empress. ▫ **monarchic** / muh-**nah**-kik / *adj.* **monarchical** *adj.*

monarchist / **mon**-uh-kuhst / *n.* a person who favours government by a monarch or a constitutional monarchical system of government. ▫ **monarchism** *n.*

monarchy / **mon**-uh-kee / *n.* **1** a form of government in which a monarch is the supreme ruler. **2** a country with this form of government. ▫ **monarchical** or **monarchial** *adj.*

Monash, Sir John (1865–1931), Australian soldier and engineer who served as commanding officer in Egypt, Gallipoli, and France in the First World War.

monastery / **mon**-uh-stree / *n.* the residence of a religious community, esp. of monks living in seclusion.

monastic / muh-**nas**-tik / *adj.* **1** of or like monasteries. **2** of or like monks or nuns or their way of life; solitary and celibate (*the monastic vows of poverty, chastity, and obedience*). • *n.* a monk or other follower of a monastic rule. ▫ **monastically** *adv.*

monasticism / muh-**nas**-tuh-siz-uhm / *n.* the way of life practised by monks or nuns.

monaych / **mon**-uych / *n. Aust.* (in Aboriginal English) a police officer; the police. (¶ Nyungar *manaj* 'white cockatoo'.)

Moncrieff, Gladys (1892–1976), Australian singer of light opera who gained the affectionate title 'Our Glad'.

Monday *n.* the day of the week following Sunday. • *adv. colloq.* on Monday. **2** (**Mondays**) on Mondays; each Monday.

Mondayitis *n. colloq.* a 'disease', the chief symptom of which is a reluctance to resume work after the weekend break.

Monderup bell *n.* a small WA shrub with reddish flowers and large, spectacular scarlet bracts streaked with white.

Monet / **mon**-ay /, Claude (Oscar) (1840–1926), French painter, one of the founders of Impressionism.

monetarism / **mun**-uh-tuh-riz-uhm / *n.* an economic theory based on the belief that only control of the money supply can successfully lower the rate of inflation or the level of unemployment. ▫ **monetarist** *n.* & *adj.*

monetary / **mun**-uh-tuh-ree, -tree / *adj.* **1** of a country's currency (*our monetary system*). **2** of or involving money (*its monetary value*). ▫ **monetarily** *adv.*

money *n.* **1** coins and banknotes. **2** (**moneys** or **monies**) sums of money. **3** wealth (*there's money in it; he married into money*). ▫ **for my money** in my opinion; for my preference. **money-back** *adj.* (of a guarantee) promising to return a customer's money if he or she is not satisfied. **money-grubber** one who is greedily intent on making money. **money market** trade in short term stocks, loans, etc. **money-spinner** (also **moneymaker**) an idea, thing, business, etc. that produces a lot of money.

moneyed / **mun**-eed / *adj.* wealthy.

moneylender *n.* a person who lends money in return for payment of interest.

mong / mung / *n. colloq.* any dog (not necessarily one of mixed breed). (¶ Abbreviation of *mongrel*.)

monger alternative spelling of MUNGA.

-monger *comb. form* **1** a dealer or trader (*fishmonger; ironmonger*). **2** (usu. *derog.*) a person who promotes, encourages, or spreads something (*warmonger; scaremonger*).

Mongol / **mong**-guhl / *adj.* Mongolian. • *n.* a Mongolian person.

Mongolia / mong-**goh**-lee-uh / a republic north of China, formerly extending to eastern Europe. ▫ **Mongolian** *adj.* & *n.*

mongolism / **mong**-guh-liz-uhm / *n.* Down syndrome.

■ **Usage** The term *Down syndrome* is now preferred.

Mongoloid / **mong**-guh-loid / *adj.* **1** resembling the Mongols in racial characteristics, having yellowish skin, a broad flat face, and straight black hair. **2** (**mongoloid**) (often *offens.*) having the characteristic symptoms of Down syndrome. • *n.* a Mongoloid or mongoloid person.

mongoose / **mong**-goos / *n.* (*pl.* **mongooses**) a stoat-like tropical animal that can attack and kill venomous snakes.

mongrel / **mung**-gruhl / *n.* **1** a dog of no definable type or breed. **2** an animal or plant resulting from crossing different breeds or types. **3** *colloq.* **a** a despicable person. **b** an exasperating or infuriating thing (*can't get this mongrel of a car to start*). • *adj.* **1** of mixed origin, nature, or character. **2** *colloq.* an intensifier expressing abuse (*mongrel idiot lost us the match*).

moniker / **mon**-uh-kuh / *n. colloq.* (also **monicker, monniker**) a person's name or nickname.

monism / **mon**-iz-uhm / *n. Philosophy* **1** a theory denying the duality of matter and mind (Cf. DUALISM sense 2). **2** the doctrine that there is only one supreme being. □ **monist** *n. & adj.*

monitor *n.* **1** a device used for observing or testing the operation of something. **2** a television screen used in a studio to select or verify the picture being broadcast. **3** a visual display unit, a computer screen. **4** a person who listens to and reports on foreign broadcasts etc. **5** a pupil who is given special duties in a school. **6** a detector of radioactive contamination. **7** a large lizard of Australia, Asia, and Africa, supposed to give warning of the approach of crocodiles. • *v.* keep watch over; record or test or control the working of.

monitory *adj. literary* giving a warning. • *n.* (*pl.* **monitories**) a letter of admonition from the pope or a bishop.

monk *n.* a member of a community of men living apart from the world under the rules of a religious order, esp. under the vows of poverty, chastity, and obedience.

monkey *n.* (*pl.* **monkeys**) **1** an animal of a group closely related to man, esp. one of the small long-tailed species. **2** a mischievous person, esp. a child. • *v.* (**monkeyed, monkeying**) **1** (often foll. by *about* or *around*) fool around. **2** (often foll. by *with*) tamper; play mischievous tricks. □ **monkey business** *colloq.* mischief; underhand dealings. **monkey tricks** *colloq.* mischief. **monkey wrench** a wrench with an adjustable jaw.

monkshood *n.* a poisonous plant with blue hood-shaped flowers.

mono *adj.* monophonic. • *n.* (*pl.* **monos**) monophonic sound or recording.

mono- *comb. form* one, alone, single.

monobrow / **mon**-uh-brow / *n. colloq.* **1** two eyebrows which meet to form a continuous line. **2** a person whose behaviour, attitudes, etc., are considered to be neanderthal.

monochromatic / mon-uh-kruh-**mat**-ik / *adj.* **1** (of light or other radiation) containing only one colour or wavelength. **2** (of a picture) monochrome.

monochrome / **mon**-uh-krohm / *adj.* done in only one colour or in black and white.

monocle / **mon**-uh-kuhl / *n.* an eyeglass for one eye only. □ **monocled** *adj.*

monocotyledon / mon-oh-kot-uh-**lee**-duhn / *n.* a flowering plant that has a single cotyledon. □ **monocotyledonous** *adj.*

monoecious / muh-**nee**-shuhs / *adj.* **1** *Botany* with unisexual male and female organs on the same plant. **2** *Zoology* with both male and female organs in the same individual, hermaphrodite.

monogamy / muh-**nog**-uh-mee / *n.* the system of being married to only one person at a time. □ **monogamous** *adj.*

monogram / **mon**-uh-gram / *n.* two or more letters (esp. a person's initials) combined in one design. □ **monogrammed** *adj.*

monograph / **mon**-uh-grahf, -graf / *n.* a scholarly treatise on a single subject.

monogyny / muh-**noj**-uh-nee / *n.* the custom of having only one wife at a time.

monolingual *adj.* speaking or using only one language.

monolith / **mon**-uh-lith / *n.* a large single upright block of stone.

monolithic / mon-uh-**lith**-ik / *adj.* **1** consisting of one or more monoliths. **2** like a monolith in being single and massive (*a monolithic organisation*).

monologue / **mon**-uh-log / *n.* a long speech by one performer in a play or by one person in a group.

monomania / mon-uh-**may**-nee-uh / *n.* an obsession with one idea or interest. □ **monomaniac** *n. & adj.*

monophonic / mon-uh-**fon**-ik / *adj.* (of sound reproduction) using only one transmission channel.

monoplane *n.* an aeroplane with only one set of wings.

monopolise *v.* (also **-ize**) take exclusive control or use of (*monopolise the conversation*). □ **monopolisation** *n.*

monopolist / muh-**nop**-uh-luhst / *n.* one who has or advocates a monopoly. □ **monopolistic** *adj.*

monopoly / muh-**nop**-uh-lee / *n.* **1** exclusive possession or control of the trade in a commodity or service. **2** sole possession or control of anything.

monorail *n.* a railway in which the track consists of a single rail.

monosodium glutamate *n.* a substance added to foods to enhance their flavour.

monosyllable / **mon**-uh-sil-uh-buhl / *n.* a word of one syllable. □ **monosyllabic** / mon-uh-suh-**lab**-ik / *adj.*

monotheism / mon-oh-thee-iz-uhm / *n*. the doctrine that there is only one God. ☐ **monotheist** *n*. **monotheistic** *adj*.

monotone / **mon**-uh-tohn / *n*. a level, unchanging sound or tone of voice.

monotonous / muh-**not**-uh-nuhs / *adj*. lacking in variety or variation; tiring or boring because of this. ☐ **monotonously** *adv*.

monotony / muh-**not**-uh-nee / *n*. a monotonous condition.

monotreme / **mon**-uh-treem / *n*. a mammal (*see* PLATYPUS, ECHIDNA), found only in Australia and New Guinea, which lays large yolky eggs through a common opening for urine, faeces, etc. (¶ From Greek words meaning 'a single hole'.)

monovalent / mon-oh-**vay**-luhnt / *adj*. univalent.

monoxide / muh-**nok**-suyd / *n*. an oxide with one atom of oxygen.

Monroe[1] / muhn-**roh**, **mun**-roh /, James (1758–1831), 5th president of the USA, who formulated the Monroe Doctrine, which opposed interference of European countries in the affairs of the Americas.

Monroe[2] / muhn-**roh**, **mun**-roh /, Marilyn (original name: Norma Jean Mortenson, later Baker) (1926–62), American film actor, promoted as a sex symbol.

Monrovia / mon-**roh**-vee-uh / the capital of Liberia.

Monseigneur / mon-sen-**yer** / *n*. (*pl*. **Messeigneurs** / me-sen-**yer** /) a title of honour given to an eminent Frenchman, esp. a prince, cardinal, archbishop, or bishop.

Monsieur / muh-**syer** / *n*. (*pl*. **Messieurs** / me-**syer** /) the title of a Frenchman, = Mr *or* sir.

Monsignor / mon-**see**-nyuh, mon-sin-**yaw** / *n*. (*pl*. **Monsignori**) a title of honour conferred on some Catholic priests.

monsoon *n*. **1** a seasonal wind blowing in South Asia. **2** the rainy season accompanying the SW monsoon.

mons pubis *n*. the rounded mass of flesh covered with pubic hair just above a man's penis. (¶ Latin, = mountain of the pubes.)

monster *n*. **1** an imaginary creature, usu. large and frightening, made up of incongruous elements. **2** an animal or plant that is very abnormal in form. **3** anything of huge size. **4** an extremely cruel or wicked person. • *adj*. huge. • *v. Aust*. attack (a person, policy, etc.); put pressure on (*the prime minister monstered the opposition's policy document*).

monstrance / mon-struhns / *n*. (in the Catholic Church) a framed open or transparent holder in which the consecrated Host is exposed for veneration.

monstrosity / mon-**stros**-uh-tee / *n*. **1** a huge or outrageous thing. **2** monstrousness. **3** = MONSTER *n*. (sense 2).

monstrous / **mon**-struhs / *adj*. **1** like a monster; abnormally formed. **2** huge. **3** outrageous, very wrong or absurd. **4** atrocious. ☐ **monstrously** *adv*.

mons veneris *n*. the rounded mass of flesh covered with pubic hair just above a woman's vulva. (¶ Latin, = mountain of Venus.)

Montague Island a small island (2.5 km long) off the south coast of NSW, a National Trust Flora and Fauna Reserve. Marine life is strictly protected in its surrounding waters.

montage / mon-**tah**zh / *n*. **1** the process of making a composite picture or piece of music etc. by putting together pieces from other pictures, designs, or compositions. **2** a picture etc. produced in this way. **3** the combination of short disconnected shots in cinematography to compress background information or provide atmosphere etc.

monte / **mon**-tee / *n. Aust. colloq*. a certainty (*he's a monte for the captaincy*).

Monte Carlo one of the three communes of Monaco, famous as a gambling resort and as the terminus of a car rally.

Montenegro / mon-tuh-**nee**-groh / a republic of the former Yugoslavia.

Montessori / mon-tuh-**saw**-ree /, Maria (1870–1952), Italian educationist who devised a system of guided play.

Monteverdi / mon-tuh-**vair**-dee /, Claudio (1567–1643), Italian Renaissance composer of sacred and secular music.

Montevideo / mon-tuh-vuh-**day**-oh / the capital of Uruguay.

Montezuma / mon-tuh-**zyoo**-muh, -**zoo**- / (1466–1520), the last ruler of the Aztec empire in Mexico.

month *n*. **1** (in full **calendar month**) any of the twelve portions into which a year is divided; the period between the same dates in successive months. **2** a period of 28 days or of four weeks. ☐ **a month of Sundays** *colloq*. a very long time.

monthly *adj*. happening, published, payable, etc. once a month. • *adv*. once a month. • *n*. a monthly magazine etc.

monty / **mon**-tee / *n*. ☐ **the full monty** *colloq*. the full amount expected, desired, or possible. (¶ Origin unknown: perhaps from the phrase *the full Montague Burton*, a 'Sunday-best three-piece suit' made by a tailor named Montague Burton; perhaps from the full cooked English breakfast insisted upon by Field Marshall Montgomery ('Monty') (1887–1976) for his troops during the Second World War.)

monument *n*. **1** anything (esp. a structure) designed or serving to celebrate a person, event, etc. **2** a structure that is preserved because of its historical importance.

monumental *adj*. **1** of or serving as a monument. **2** (of a literary work) massive and of permanent importance. **3** extremely great (*a* *monumental blunder*). ☐ **monumental mason** a maker of tombstones etc.

moo *n.* the low deep sound made by a cow. • *v.* make this sound.

mooch *v. colloq.* **1** walk about slowly and aimlessly. **2** cadge; steal.

mood *n.* **1** a temporary state of mind or spirits. **2** the feeling or tone conveyed by a literary or artistic work (*the visual mood of a film*). **3** a fit of bad temper or depression (*he's in one of his moods*). **4** a grammatical form of a verb that shows whether it is a statement (e.g. *he stopped*) or a command (e.g. *stop!*) or a wish etc. (*if I were a rich man*). ☐ **in the mood** in a willing state of mind.

moody *adj.* (**moodier, moodiest**) gloomy, sullen; liable to be like this. ☐ **moodily** *adv.* **moodiness** *n.*

Moog / moog / *n. trademark* (in full **Moog synthesiser**) an electronic instrument with a keyboard, for producing a wide variety of musical sounds.

mook-mook / muuk-muuk / *n.* (in full **mook-mook owl**; also **muk-muk**) an owl, e.g. the barking owl of all except the arid regions of Australia. (¶ Perhaps from a NT Aboriginal language.)

moolah / moo-luh / *n. colloq.* money.

Moomba / moom-buh / *n.* a festival (with a parade, associated sporting and cultural events, etc.) held annually in Melbourne from 1955. (¶ From Wemba-wemba, Wuywurung, etc. *mum* 'anus'; *ba* 'at, in, on'; but popularly understood to mean 'Let's get together and have fun.')

moon *n.* **1** the natural satellite of the earth, made visible by light that it reflects from the sun. **2** this when it is visible (*there's no moon tonight*). **3** a natural satellite of any planet. **4** something desirable but unlikely to be attained (*cry for the moon*; *promised us the moon*). • *v.* move, look, or pass time dreamily or listlessly. ☐ **moon-face** a round face; a person with such. **over the moon** *colloq.* ecstatic, greatly excited or pleased. ☐☐ **moonless** *adj.*

moonbeam *n.* a ray of moonlight.

Moonie *n. colloq. derog.* a member of the Unification Church.

Moonlight (in full **Captain Moonlight**) (original name: Andrew George Scott) (1842–80), Anglican preacher in Australia who became a bushranger and leader of a gang of boys, the youngest being 15. Scott and one of the boys were hanged at Darlinghurst Gaol in January 1880.

moonlight *n.* light from the moon. • *v. colloq.* **1** have two paid jobs, one during the day and the other in the evening. **2** (chiefly as **moonlighting**) *Aust.* muster wild cattle by moonlight.

moonlighter *n.* **1** in the 2 senses of MOONLIGHT *verb*. **2** a marine food fish with a silver head and body with six vertical black bands, occurring near rocky reefs of southern Australia.

moonlit *adj.* lit by the moon.

moonscape *n.* the surface of the moon; a landscape resembling this.

moonshine *n.* **1** foolish ideas. **2** *colloq.* illicitly distilled or smuggled alcoholic liquor.

moonstone *n.* a semi-precious stone, a form of feldspar with a pearly appearance.

moonstruck *adj.* **1** slightly mad. **2** romantically infatuated.

moony *adj.* listless, dreamy.

Moor *n.* a member of a Muslim people of NW Africa. ☐ **Moorish** *adj.*

moor[1] *n. Brit.* a stretch of open uncultivated land with low shrubs (e.g. heather).

moor[2] *v.* secure (a boat or other floating thing) to a fixed object.

Moore, Henry (1898–1986), English sculptor.

moorhen *n.* **1** any of several Australian waterfowl, esp. the Tas. native hen, the black-tailed native hen, and the mallee fowl. **2** a small European waterbird.

Moorhouse, Frank (1938–), AM, Australian writer, a leading exponent of short fiction.

moorings *n.pl.* **1** cables etc. by which something is moored. **2** a place where a boat is moored.

moose *n.* (*pl.* **moose**) a large animal of North America closely related to or the same as the European elk.

moot *adj.* debatable, undecided (*that's a moot point*). • *v.* raise (a question) for discussion. • *n. hist.* an assembly.

mop *n.* **1** a bundle of yarn or soft material fastened at the end of a stick, used for cleaning floors. **2** a small device of similar shape for various purposes (*dish mop*). **3** mopping or being mopped (*give it a mop*). **4** a thick mass of hair. • *v.* (**mopped, mopping**) **1** clean or wipe with a mop etc. **2** wipe (*he mopped his brow*). ☐ **mop up 1** wipe up with a mop etc. **2** finish off a task; clear (an area) of the remnants of enemy troops etc. after a victory.

mope *v.* **1** be in low spirits and listless. **2** wander about listlessly. • *n.* a person who mopes. ☐ **mopy** *adj.*

moped / moh-ped / *n.* a motorised bicycle with an engine capacity below 50 cc.

mopoke / moh-pohk / *n. Aust.* **1** = BOOBOOK. **2** = FROGMOUTH. **3** a tedious or stupid person. • *v.* (of a mopoke) call (*the bird mopoked all night*).

moppet *n. colloq.* (as a term of endearment) a baby or young child.

moquette / moh-**ket**, mo- / *n.* a material with raised loops or cut pile used for carpets and upholstery.

moraine / maw-**rayn** / *n.* a mass of debris carried down and deposited by a glacier.

moral *adj.* **1** of or concerned with the goodness and badness of human character or with the principles of what is right and wrong in conduct (*moral philosophy*). **2** virtuous. **3** capable of understanding and living by the rules of morality. **4** based on people's sense of what is right or just.

not on legal rights and obligations (*we had a moral obligation to help*). **5** psychological, mental, not physical or concrete (*moral courage; moral support*). • *n.* **1** a moral lesson or principle. **2** (**morals**) a person's moral habits, esp. in sexual conduct. **3** a moral certainty (*she's an absolute moral for the post of managing director*). ☐ **moral certainty** esp. *Aust.* a probability so great as to allow no reasonable doubt. **moral philosophy** the branch of philosophy concerned with ethics. **moral victory** a triumph, although nothing concrete is obtained by it. ☐☐ **morally** *adv.*

morale / muh-**rahl** / *n.* the state of a person's or group's spirits and confidence.

moralise *v.* (also **-ize**) talk or write about the principles of right and wrong and conduct etc.; make moral judgments.

moralist *n.* a person who expresses or teaches moral principles. ☐ **moralistic** *adj.*

morality / muh-**ral**-uh-tee / *n.* **1** moral principles or rules. **2** a particular system of morals (*commercial morality*). **3** being moral, conforming to moral principles; goodness or rightness. ☐ **morality play** a drama popular in the 15th and 16th centuries illustrating a moral lesson with characters that represent virtues and vices and usu. dramatising the fall and redemption of a representative Christian.

Morant, Harry Harbord (1865–1902), Australian horseman and soldier (born in England) who published bush ballads in the *Bulletin* under the pseudonym 'The Breaker', and who was executed during the Boer War.

morass / muh-**ras** / *n.* **1** a marsh, a bog. **2** an entanglement, something that confuses or impedes people.

moratorium / mo-ruh-**taw**-ree-uhm / *n.* (*pl.* **moratoriums or moratoria**) **1** legal authorisation to debtors to postpone payment. **2** a temporary ban or suspension on some activity (*a moratorium on logging old growth forests in Australia*). **3** *hist.* the campaign of protest against Australian participation with the US in the Vietnam War.

Morauta / muh-**row**-tuh /, Sir Mekere (1946–), Papua New Guinea statesman. The leader of the People's Democratic Movement, he became prime minister in 1999.

moray / mo-ray, maw- / *n.* **1** a tropical eel of northern Australia valued as a food fish. **2** an eel found in the Mediterranean and valued for food.

morbid *adj.* **1** (of the mind or ideas) unwholesome, preoccupied with gloomy or unpleasant things. **2** caused by or indicating disease, unhealthy (*a morbid growth*). ☐ **morbidly** *adv.* **morbidity** / maw-**bid**-uh-tee / *n.*

morbillivirus / maw-**bil**-uh-vuy-ruhs, -**bil**-ee- / *n.* any of a group of viruses causing diseases such as measles, rinderpest, and canine distemper.

mordant / **maw**-duhnt / *adj.* **1** characterised by a biting sarcasm (*mordant wit*). **2** corrosive. **3** fixing colouring matter. • *n.* a mordant acid or substance.

mordent / **maw**-duhnt / *n. Music* an ornament consisting of one rapid alternation of a written note with the note immediately below it.

More, Sir Thomas (1478–1535), English statesman and Catholic saint, Lord Chancellor of England 1529–32.

more *adj.* greater in quantity or intensity etc. • *n.* a greater quantity or number. • *adv.* **1** in a greater degree. **2** again (*once more*). ☐ **more or less** in a greater or less degree; approximately.

moreish *adj.* (also **morish**) *colloq.* (of food) so tasty that it causes a desire for more.

morel / muh-**rel** / *n.* an edible mushroom with a dark conical cap pitted with irregular holes.

morello / muh-**rel**-oh / *n.* (*pl.* **morellos**) a bitter dark cherry.

moreover *adv.* besides, in addition to what has already been said.

mores / **maw**-rayz / *n.pl.* the customs or conventions of a community.

Moreton Bay the bay on which Brisbane stands. ☐ **Moreton Bay bug** a marine crustacean of northern Australia highly valued for its edible tail flesh. **Moreton Bay fig 1** a tree to 40 m with large buttresses and globular edible fruits, widely planted as an ornamental and shade tree. **2** *colloq.* (also shortened to **Moreton Bay**) an informer to the police. (¶ Rhyming slang on *fizgig* 'an informer'.)

Morgan[1], Daniel ('Mad Dog Morgan') (1830–65), Australian bushranger notorious for his brutality.

Morgan[2], Sally (Jane) (1951–), AM, Australian Aboriginal writer and artist.

morganatic / maw-guh-**nat**-ik / *adj.* (of a marriage) between a man of high rank and a woman of low rank who retains her former status, their children having no claim to the father's possessions or title.

morgue / mawg / *n.* **1** a mortuary. **2** (in a newspaper office) a room containing files of miscellaneous information serving as a reference library.

moribund / **mo**-ruh-bund / *adj.* in a dying state.

morish alternative spelling of MOREISH.

Mormon / **maw**-muhn / *n.* a member of a religious organisation (the Church of Jesus Christ of Latter-Day Saints) founded in the USA in 1830 by Joseph Smith. ☐ **Mormonism** *n.*

morn *n. poetic* morning.

mornay *n.* a cheese-flavoured white sauce.

morning *n.* **1** the early part of the day, ending at noon or at the midday meal. **2** sunrise, dawn (*when morning broke*). **3** (used as *adj.*) taken or occurring in the morning (*morning coffee*). ☐ **morning after** *colloq.* a hangover. **morning glory 1** a twining plant with trumpet-shaped flowers that often close after one morning. Also called *convolvulus*. **2** (also **morning glory cloud**) a huge dark cloud which suddenly covers the sky of a morning in the Qld and NT Gulf Country and just as suddenly disappears. **morning sickness** sickness felt in the morning during the early months of pregnancy. **morning star** a bright star or planet (esp. Venus) seen in the east before sunrise.

Mornington Island a large island in the Gulf of Carpentaria, home to the Lardil and Gayardilt Aboriginal people.

Morocco a kingdom in North Africa. ☐ **Moroccan** *adj.* & *n.*

morocco *n.* a fine flexible leather made (originally in Morocco) from goatskins.

moron / **maw**-ron / *n.* **1** *colloq.* a very stupid person. **2** an adult with intelligence equal to that of an average child of 8–12 years. ☐ **moronic** / muh-**ron**-ik / *adj.*

Moroni / muh-**roh**-nee / the capital of Comoros.

morose / muh-**rohs** / *adj.* sullen, gloomy, and unsociable. ☐ **morosely** *adv.* **moroseness** *n.*

morph / mawf / *n.* a variant form of an animal or plant. (¶ Greek, = form)

morpheme *n.* *Linguistics* a meaningful unit of language that cannot be further divided (e.g. *in*, *come*, *-ing* are morphemes forming *incoming*).

Morpheus / **maw**-fee-uhs / *Rom. myth.* the god of dreams, son of Somnus (god of sleep).

morphia / **maw**-fee-uh / *n.* morphine.

morphine / **maw**-feen / *n.* a drug made from opium, used for relieving pain.

morphing / **maw**-fing / *n.* a technique that changes a film image into a numerical code, enabling it to be manipulated by a computer so that the effect can be created of transforming an image smoothly into a different one.

morphology / maw-**fol**-uh-jee / *n.* the study of the forms of things, esp. of animals and plants and of words and their structure. ☐ **morphological** *adj.*

morrel / **mo**-ruhl, muh-**rel** / *n.* any of several eucalypts of SW Australia which yield a very strong reddish or blackish timber. (¶ Nyungar, probably *murril*)

Morris, William (1834–96), English writer, artist, and designer.

morris dance *n.* a traditional English folk dance, of various forms, usu. performed by people in costume, often with ribbons and bells. (¶ *morys*, variant of MOORISH)

Morrison, James (1962–), AM, Australian jazz musician.

morrison *n.* (also **feather flower**) any shrub of the (Western) Australian genus *Verticordia* with brilliant red, yellow, pink, etc. feathery blooms.

morrow *n.* *poetic* (usu. preceded by *the*) the following day.

Morse, Helen (1946–), Australian film and stage actor.

morse *n.* (in full **Morse code**) a code in which letters of the alphabet are represented by combinations of short and long sounds or flashes of light (dots and dashes). (¶ Devised by S.F.B. Morse (1791–1872), American pioneer of the use of the electric telegraph.)

morsel *n.* a small quantity; a small amount or piece of food.

mortal *adj.* **1** subject to death. **2** causing death, fatal (*a mortal wound*). **3** deadly, lasting until death (*mortal enemies; in mortal combat*). **4** intense (*in mortal fear*). **5** *colloq.* without exception (*sold every mortal thing*). • *n.* a person who is subject to death, a human being. ☐ **mortal sin** (in Catholic teaching) a grave sin that deprives the soul of sanctifying grace and causes a state of spiritual death. ☐☐ **mortally** *adj.*

mortality / maw-**tal**-uh-tee / *n.* **1** being mortal, subject to death. **2** loss of life on a large scale. **3** a number of deaths in a given period. ☐ **mortality rate** the death rate.

mortar *n.* **1** a mixture of lime or cement with sand and water, for joining bricks or stones. **2** a bowl-shaped container in which substances are pounded with a pestle. **3** a short cannon for firing shells at a high angle. • *v.* **1** plaster or join (bricks etc.) with mortar. **2** bombard with mortar shells.

mortarboard *n.* **1** an academic cap with a stiff flat square top. **2** a flat board for holding mortar.

mortgage / **maw**-gij / *v.* give someone a claim on (property) as security for payment of a debt or loan. • *n.* **1** mortgaging. **2** an agreement giving a claim of this kind. **3** the amount of money borrowed or lent against the security of a property in this way. ☐ **have a mortgage on** *colloq.* **1** be certain to win (*he has a mortgage on the marathon*). **2** have an exclusive claim to (*you haven't a mortgage on suffering*). **mortgage belt** *Aust.* a suburb etc. in which most people are in the process of paying off a mortgage on their home, such people being regarded as politically volatile. ☐ **mortgageable** *adj.*

mortgagee / maw-guh-**jee** / *n.* a person or firm (e.g. a building society) to whom property is mortgaged.

mortgager / **maw**-guh-juh / *n.* (also **mortgagor** / maw-guh-**jaw** /) one who mortgages his or her property.

mortice alternative spelling of MORTISE.

mortician / maw-**tish**-uhn / *n.* an undertaker.

mortify *v.* (**mortified**, **mortifying**) **1** cause (a person) to feel greatly shamed, humiliated, or sorry. **2** subdue with discipline or self-denial. **3** (of flesh) become gangrenous. ☐ **mortification** *n.*

mortise / **maw**-tuhs / *n.* (also **mortice**) a hole in one part of a wooden structure into which the end of another part is inserted so that the two are held together. • *v.* cut a mortise in; join with a mortise. ☐ **mortise lock** a lock that is set into (not on) the framework of a door.

mortuary / **maw**-chuh-ree / *n.* a place where dead bodies may be kept temporarily.

morwong / moh-wong, maw-wong / *n.* (frequently abbreviated to **mowie**) *Aust.* **1** a marine food fish of southern Australia and New Zealand which has a distinctive elongated ray of the pectoral fin. **2** a jackass fish. (¶ Possibly from an Aboriginal language.)

Mosaic / moh-**zay**-ik / *adj.* of Moses or his teaching (*Mosaic Law*).

mosaic / moh-**zay**-ik / *n.* **1** a pattern or picture made by placing together small pieces of glass or stone etc. of different colours. **2** a thing consisting of different elements placed together. ▫ **mosaic disease** (also **mosaic**) a virus disease causing leaf-mottling in plants, esp. tobacco, maize, and sugar cane.

Moscow the capital of Russia.

moselle / moh-**zel** / *n.* a light medium-dry white wine from the Moselle valley in Germany; a similar Australian wine.

Moses[1] Hebrew patriarch who led the Jews from bondage in Egypt towards the Promised Land, and gave them the Ten Commandments.

Moses[2], Anna Mary Robertson ('Grandma') (1860–1961), American painter, who began painting at the age of 75.

mosey *v.* (often foll. by *along*) *colloq.* go in a slow, leisurely way.

mosh *colloq. v.* dance to rock music in a violent manner involving colliding with others and headbanging. ▫ **mosh pit** an area where moshing occurs, esp. in front of the stage at a rock concert.

Moslem = MUSLIM.

mosque / mosk / *n.* a Muslim place of worship.

mosquito / muh-**skee**-toh / *n.* (*pl.* **mosquitoes**) a kind of gnat, the female of which bites and sucks blood.

moss *n.* a small flowerless plant that forms a dense growth on moist surfaces or in bogs. ▫ **moss stitch** a pattern formed of alternating plain and purl stitches in knitting.

Mossad / mo-**sad** / *n.* the Israeli secret service. (¶ Hebrew, = institution.)

mossie / **moz**-ee / *n.* (also **mozzie**) *Aust.* a mosquito.

mossy *adj.* (**mossier**, **mossiest**) like moss; covered in moss.

most *adj.* **1** greatest in quantity or intensity etc. **2** the majority of (*most people think so*). • *n.* the greatest quantity or number; the majority. • *adv.* **1** in the greatest degree. **2** very (*a most amusing book*). ▫ **at most** (*or* **at the most**) not more than. **for the most part** in most cases; in most of its extent. **the most** *colloq.* the best of all (*he is the most*).

mostly *adv.* for the most part.

mote *n.* a speck of dust.

motel / moh-**tel** / *n.* a roadside hotel which provides accommodation in self-contained units for motorists.

motet / moh-**tet** / *n.* a short religious choral work.

moth *n.* **1** an insect resembling a butterfly but usu. flying at night. **2** a small similar insect that lays its eggs in cloth or fur fabrics on which its larvae feed. ▫ **moth-eaten** *adj.* **1** damaged by moth larvae. **2** antiquated, decrepit.

mothball *n.* a small ball of naphthalene etc. placed in stored clothes to keep away moths. ▫ **in mothballs** stored out of use for a considerable time.

mother *n.* **1** a female parent. **2** a quality or condition that gives rise to another (*necessity is the mother of invention*). **3** (in full **Mother Superior**) the head of a female religious community. • *v.* look after in a motherly way. ▫ **mother country** a country in relation to its colonies. **mother-in-law** (*pl.* **mothers-in-law**) the mother of one's wife or husband. **mother of** the greatest of its kind (*the mother of all battles*). **mother-of-pearl** a pearly substance lining the shells of oysters and mussels etc. **mother tongue** one's native language.

motherboard *n.* a printed circuit board containing the principal components of a microcomputer or other electronic device, to which other boards may be connected.

motherhood *n.* the state of being a mother. • *adj.* platitudinously endorsing that which everyone accepts as worthy (*the party's election platform consisted mostly of motherhood statements*).

motherland *n.* one's native country.

motherless *adj.* **1** lacking a mother. **2** (in full **motherless broke**) *Aust. colloq.* destitute (*found himself utterly motherless and desperate*). • *adv.* (in full **stone motherless**) *Aust.* completely and utterly (*the horse ran stone motherless last*; *I'm stone motherless broke*).

motherly *adj.* like a mother, showing a mother's kindliness and tenderness. ▫ **motherliness** *n.*

Mother's Day a day in honour of mothers, in Australia the second Sunday in May.

Mother Teresa *see* TERESA, MOTHER.

mothproof *adj.* (of clothes) treated so as to repel moths. • *v.* treat (clothes) in this way.

motif / moh-**teef**, **moh**-tuhf / *n.* **1** a recurring design, feature, or theme in a literary, artistic, or musical work. **2** a decorative design or pattern (*wallpaper with a Chinese motif*).

motile *adj. Biology* capable of moving (*motile spores*). ▫ **motility** *n.*

motion *n.* **1** moving, change of position. **2** a particular manner of moving (*he walked with a jaunty motion*). **3** a gesture (*made a motion of dismissal*). **4** a formal proposal that is to be discussed and voted on at a meeting. **5** emptying of the bowels; faeces. • *v.* make a gesture directing (a person) to do something (*motioned him to sit beside her*). ▫ **go through the motions** do something in a perfunctory or insincere manner.

motionless *adj.* not moving.

motivate *v.* **1** give a motive or incentive to, be the motive of (*she was motivated by kindness*). **2**

stimulate the interest of, inspire. □ **motivation** *n.* **motivator** *n.*

motivated *adj.* having a great deal of incentive.

motive *n.* **1** that which induces a person to act in a certain way. **2** = MOTIF. • *adj.* producing movement or action (*motive power*).

mot juste / moh *zhoost* / *n.* (*pl.* *mots justes* pronounced the same) the most appropriate word or phrase. (¶ French)

motley *adj.* **1** multicoloured. **2** made up of various sorts (*a motley collection*). • *n.* *archaic* a jester's particoloured costume.

motocross *n.* a motorcycle race over rough ground.

motor *n.* **1** a machine that supplies motive power for a vehicle or boat etc. or for another device with moving parts; an internal-combustion engine. **2** a motor car. • *adj.* **1** giving or producing motion. **2** driven by a motor (*motor boat; motor mower*). **3** of or for motor vehicles (*the motor show*). **4** relating to muscular movement or the nerves activating it. • *v.* go or convey in a motor car. □ **motor bike** *colloq.* a motor cycle. **motor car** a short-bodied motor vehicle for a driver and passengers. **motor vehicle** a vehicle with a motor engine, for use on ordinary roads.

motorcade *n.* a procession or parade of motor vehicles.

motorcycle *n.* a two-wheeled motor vehicle without pedal propulsion. □ **motorcyclist** *n.*

motorise *v.* (also **-ize**) **1** equip with a motor or motors. **2** equip (troops) with motor vehicles.

motorist *n.* the driver of a car.

motorway *n.* a road specially constructed and controlled for fast motor traffic.

Motown *n.* popular music with elements of rhythm and blues, associated with Detroit, USA.

motser *n.* (also **motzer**) *Aust. colloq.* **1** a large amount of money (*spent a motser on the wedding*). **2** a certainty (*she's a motser to win the seat*).

motte *n.* a mound forming the site of an ancient castle or camp etc.

mottlecah / **mot**-uhl-kah / *n. Aust.* a small eucalypt with silvery blue leaves, salmon-red new stems, and the largest flowers of any eucalypt, crimson, 8 cm in diameter, followed by large grey gumnuts. (¶ Probably Nhanta.)

mottled *adj.* marked or patterned with irregular patches of colour.

motto *n.* (*pl.* **mottoes**) **1** a short sentence or phrase adopted as a rule of conduct or as expressing the aims and ideals of a family, country, institution, etc. (often accompanying a coat of arms). **2** a sentence inscribed on an object. **3** a maxim, verse, or riddle inside a paper cracker.

mould *n.* **1** a hollow container into which a substance is poured or pressed to harden into a desired shape. **2** a pudding etc. made in a mould. **3** character or type (*in heroic mould*). **4** a fine furry growth of very small fungi, forming on things that lie in moist warm air. **5** soft fine loose earth that is rich in organic matter (*leaf-mould*). • *v.* **1** cause to have a certain shape; produce by shaping. **2** guide or control the development of (*mould his character*).

moulder *v.* decay into dust, rot away.

moulding *n.* a moulded object, esp. an ornamental strip of plaster or wood etc. decorating or outlining something.

mouldy *adj.* (**mouldier, mouldiest**) **1** covered with mould; smelling of mould. **2** stale, out of date (*mouldy jokes*). **3** *colloq.* dull, miserable. □ **mouldiness** *n.*

moult / mohlt / *v.* (of a bird, animal, or insect) shed feathers, hair, or skin etc. before a new growth. • *n.* the process of moulting.

mound *n.* **1** a mass of piled-up earth or stones; a small hill. **2** a heap or pile. **3** a large quantity (*a mound of things to do*). • *v.* heap up in a mound or mounds. □ **mound spring** (also **mud spring**) a natural spring of artesian water, rising out of a mound of mud, in many areas of east-central Australia.

mount *v.* **1** ascend, go upwards; rise to a higher level. **2** get or put on to a horse, bicycle, etc. for riding. **3** increase in amount or intensity (*the death toll mounted; excitement was mounting*). **4** put into place on a support; fix in position for use or display or study (*mounted the statue on the pedestal; mounted the specimen on a slide*). **5** take action to effect (something) (*mount an offensive*). **6** (of a male animal) get on (a female) for copulation. **7** arrange (a play, exhibition, etc.). **8** place on guard (*mount sentries round the palace*). • *n.* **1** a horse for riding. **2** (also **mounting**) something on which a thing is mounted for support or display etc. **3** (*archaic* except before a name) a mountain or hill (*Mount Kosciuszko*).

mountain *n.* **1** a mass of land that rises to a great height. **2** a large heap or pile; a huge quantity (*a mountain of work*). □ **mountain ash** any of several eucalypts, esp. *E. regnans* of Vic. and Tas., favouring cool, moist, mountain gullies. **mountain bike** a sturdy bike with thick tyres and many gears for riding over rough ground. **mountain devil** a small spiny lizard *Moloch horridus* of arid Australia. **mountain range** a continuous line of mountains. **mountain shrimp** a small freshwater crustacean of mountain waters in Tas. which is almost identical with fossil shrimps 200 million years old.

mountaineer *n.* a person who is skilled in mountain climbing. □ **mountaineering** *n.*

mountainous *adj.* **1** full of mountains (*mountainous country*). **2** huge.

mountebank / **mown**-tuh-bangk / *n.* a swindler or charlatan.

mounted *adj.* serving on horseback (*mounted police*).

mounting *n.* = MOUNT *n.* (sense 2).

Mount Isa / **uy**-zuh / a city on the Leichhardt River in north-western Qld, about 1,867 km

mourn v. feel or express sorrow for a person who has died or regret for a thing that is lost or past.

mourner n. a person who mourns, esp. at a funeral.

mournful adj. sorrowful, showing grief. ☐ **mournfully** adv. **mournfulness** n.

mourning n. black or dark clothes worn as a conventional sign of bereavement.

mouse n. (pl. **mice**) **1** a small rodent with a long thin tail. **2** a shy or timid person. **3** (pl. **mouses**) a small hand-held device with one or more buttons for controlling the cursor on a computer screen. • v. (of a cat, owl, etc.) hunt mice. ☐ **mouse spider** any of several very large, black, burrowing spiders widespread in mainland Australia.

mouser n. a cat as a hunter of mice.

mousetrap n. **1** a trap for catching mice. **2** colloq. cheese of poor quality.

moussaka / muu-**sah**-kuh / n. (also **mousaka**) a Greek dish of layers of minced meat, eggplant, etc., usu. topped with cheese sauce.

mousse / moos / n. **1** a dessert of cream or a similar substance flavoured with fruit or chocolate. **2** meat or fish purée mixed with cream etc. and shaped in a mould. **3** a frothy creamy substance, e.g. one used for styling hair. • v. apply mousse to (the hair).

moustache / muh-**stahsh** / n. hair left to grow on a man's upper lip.

mousy adj. **1** quiet and shy or timid. **2** nondescript light brown.

mouth n. / mowth / (pl. **mouths** / mow*th*z /) **1** the opening through which food is taken into an animal's body. **2** colloq. talkativeness; impudence; a loud-mouthed person, or one who puts foot into mouth whenever it is opened. **3** the opening of a bag, cave, cannon, trumpet, etc. **4** the place where a river enters the sea. • v. / mow*th* / **1** form (words) with the lips without speaking them aloud. **2** utter or speak insincerely or without understanding (*mouthing platitudes*). ☐ **mouth off** colloq. **1** speak wildly or thoughtlessly, usu. out of anger or frustration. **2** boast. **3** criticise offensively. **mouth organ** = HARMONICA. **mouth-to-mouth** adj. (of resuscitation) in which a person breathes into a subject's lungs through the mouth.

mouth-watering 1 (of food) looking or smelling delicious, appetising. **2** tempting, alluring.

mouthful n. **1** an amount that fills the mouth. **2** a small quantity of food etc. **3** a lengthy word or phrase; one that is difficult to say. **4** colloq. something important or tactless etc. that is said.

mouthguard n. Sport a guard worn to protect the teeth, gums, etc., worn esp. by boxers and players of contact sports.

mouthpiece n. **1** the part of a musical instrument or telephone that is placed between or near the lips. **2** (often *derog.*) a person who speaks on behalf of another or others. **3** = MOUTHGUARD

movable adj. (also **moveable**) **1** able to be moved. **2** variable in date from year to year (*Easter is a movable feast*). **3** *Law* (of property) of the nature of a chattel, as distinct from land or buildings. • n. an article of furniture that may be removed from a house, as distinct from a fixture.

move v. **1** change or cause to change in position, place, or posture. **2** be or cause to be in motion. **3** change one's place of residence. **4** cause (bowels) to empty. **5** make progress (*the work moves slowly*). **6** (of merchandise) sell; be sold (*these items are not moving well*). **7** make a move in a board game. **8** provoke a reaction or emotion in (*I felt very moved*). **9** (cause to) change one's attitude (*nothing will move me on this issue*). **10** prompt or incline, motivate (*what moved them to invite us?*). **11** put forward formally for discussion and decision at a meeting. **12** make a formal request or application (*moved for an adjournment*). **13** initiate some action (*unless the employers move quickly, there will be a strike*). **14** live or be active in a particular group (*she moves in the best circles*). • n. **1** the act or process of moving. **2** a change of house, premises, etc. **3** the moving of a piece in a board game; a player's turn to do this. **4** a calculated action done to achieve some purpose. ☐ **get a move on** colloq. hurry. **move in** take up residence in a new home. **move over** (or **up**) alter position in order to make room for another.

moveable alternative spelling of MOVABLE.

movement n. **1** moving; being moved. **2** action, activity (*watch every movement*). **3** the moving parts in a mechanism, esp. of a clock or watch. **4** a series of combined actions by a group to achieve some purpose; the group itself (*the Women's Lib movement*). **5** a trend (*the movement towards more casual styles in fashion*). **6** market activity in some commodity (*the movement in stocks and shares*). **7** one of the principal divisions in a long musical work.

mover n. **1** a person, animal, or thing that moves or dances, esp. in a specified way. **2** a person who moves a proposition. **3** (also **prime mover**) an originator.

movie n. a film for viewing in a cinema or on video.

moving adj. affecting the emotions (*a moving story*). ☐ **moving staircase** an escalator.

mow / moh / v. (**mowed**, **mown**, **mowing**) cut (grass or grain etc.) with a scythe or a machine. ☐ **mow down** kill or destroy at random or in great numbers.

mower n. a person or machine that mows.

mowie / **moh**-ee / n. Aust. =MORWONG.

Mozambique / moh-zam-**beek** / a republic in East Africa. ☐ **Mozambican** n.

Mozart / **moht**-saht /, Wolfgang Amadeus (1756–91), Austrian composer.

mozz (also **moz**) *Aust. colloq. n.* a jinx, a malign influence. • *v.* jinx, deter (*tried to mozz him as he was about to take the kick*). ▫ **put the mozz on** jinx, cause bad luck to.

mozzarella / mot-suh-**rel**-uh / *n.* soft Italian curd cheese, used esp. in pizzas etc.

mozzie alternative spelling of MOSSIE.

mozzle *n. Aust. colloq.* luck, fortune (*had rotten mozzle at the races*).

MP *abbr.* Member of Parliament.

■ **Usage** Note the placing or absence of an apostrophe in *MPs* (= Members of Parliament), *an MP's salary, MPs' salaries.*

mp *abbr.* (in music) mezzo piano.

MPEG *n. Computing* an international standard for encoding and compressing video images. (¶ From Motion Pictures Experts Group.)

Mr *n.* (*pl.* **Messrs**) the title prefixed to a man's name or to the name of his office (*Mr Marchesini; Mr Speaker*).

MRI *abbr.* magnetic resonance imaging.

Mrs *n.* (*pl.* **Mrs**) the title prefixed to a married woman's name.

MS *abbr.* **1** (*pl.* **MSS**) manuscript. **2** multiple sclerosis.

Ms / miz, muhz / *n.* the title of a married or unmarried woman, used to avoid indicating marital status (in keeping with MR).

MSc *abbr.* Master of Science.

MS-DOS *abbr. trademark* Microsoft disk operating system.

MSG *abbr.* monosodium glutamate.

Msgr *abbr.* Monsignor.

Mt *abbr.* Mount. • *symbol* meitnerium.

mu / myoo / *n.* **1** the twelfth letter of the Greek alphabet (M, μ). **2** a symbol (μ) = MICRO- (sense 2).

Mubarak / moo-**bah**-rak /, (Muhammad) Hosni (Said) (1928–), Egyptian statesman, president since 1981.

much *adj.* existing in great quantity. • *n.* a great quantity. • *adv.* **1** in a great degree (*much to my surprise*). **2** approximately (*much the same*). **3** for a large part of one's time (*he is not here much*). ▫ **I thought as much** I thought so. **much as** even though, however much (*I can't go, much as I should like to*). **much of a muchness** very alike, very nearly the same.

mucilage / myoo-suh-lij / *n.* **1** a sticky substance secreted by certain plants. **2** an adhesive gum.

muck *n.* **1** farmyard manure. **2** *colloq.* dirt, filth; anything disgusting. **3** *colloq.* untidy things, a mess. **4** *colloq.* rubbish, nonsense. • *v.* (often foll. by *up*) make dirty, mess. ▫ **make a muck of** *colloq.* bungle. **muck about** (*or* **around**) *colloq.* potter or fool about. **muck about** (*or* **around**) **with** *colloq.* fool or interfere with (a person or thing); associate constantly with (a person). **muck in** *colloq.* share tasks or expenses equally. **muck in with** *colloq.* share a bed or living quarters with (*can I muck in with you for tonight?*). **muck out** remove manure from (*mucking out the stables*). **muck up** *colloq.* **1** spoil (*mucked up his chances*). **2** misbehave. **muck-up** a shambles, a fiasco.

muckrake *v.* search out and reveal scandal. ▫ **muckraker** *n.* **muckraking** *n.*

mucky *adj.* (**muckier**, **muckiest**) covered with muck, dirty.

mucous / **myoo**-kuhs / *adj.* of or like mucus; covered with mucus. ▫ **mucous membrane** the moist skin lining the nose, mouth, throat, etc.

mucus / **myoo**-kuhs / *n.* the moist slimy substance produced by a mucous membrane.

MUD *abbr.* multi-user dungeon, a virtual reality tool on the Internet, used esp. for role-playing games.

mud *n.* wet soft earth. ▫ **mud crab** (also **mangrove crab**) an extremely large swimming crab, occurring along muddy shores of estuaries in northern Australia, highly prized as food. **mud-eye** *Aust.* the larva of a dragonfly, used by anglers as bait. **mud map** *Aust.* a diagram or sketch of a route, region, etc., containing only those features essential to its purpose, originally one drawn with a stick in soft earth. **mud pack** a cosmetic paste applied thickly to the skin and removed after a short period of time. **mud-slinger** *colloq.* a person who engages in mud-slinging. **mud-slinging** *colloq.* speaking evil of someone, trying to damage someone's reputation.

mudbrick *n.* a brick made from baked mud. • *adj.* made of mudbricks (*a mudbrick house*).

muddie *n.* (also **muddy**) *Aust. colloq.* a mud crab.

muddle *v.* **1** bring into a state of confusion and disorder. **2** confuse (a person) mentally. **3** confuse or mistake (one thing for another). • *n.* a muddled condition, disorder. ▫ **muddle-headed** liable to muddle things, mentally confused. **muddle on** (*or* **along**) work in a haphazard way. **muddle through** succeed in the end in spite of inefficiency. ▫▫ **muddler** *n.*

muddy *adj.* (**muddier**, **muddiest**) **1** like mud; full of mud. **2** (of colour, liquid, or sound) not clear or pure. **3** (of thoughts) vague, confused. **4** (of the complexion) drab, not clear. • *v.* (**muddied**, **muddying**) make muddy. ▫ **muddiness** *n.*

mudflap *n.* a flap hanging behind the wheel of a vehicle, to catch mud and stones etc. thrown up from the road.

mudflat *n.* a stretch of muddy land uncovered at low tide.

mudguard *n.* a curved cover above the wheel of a cycle etc. to protect the rider from the mud it throws up.

mudlark *n. Aust.* **1** = MAGPIE LARK. **2** a horse that is able to race well on a wet and heavy track.

Mudrooroo (original name: Colin Johnson) (1938–), Australian writer, novelist, and poet who changed his name in 1988 as a bicentennial protest.

mudskipper *n.* (also **mudhopper**) any of several small related fish of tropical northern Australia with modified pectoral and ventral fins which enable it to move about on mudflats.

Mueller / **myoo**-luh /, Baron Sir Ferdinand (Jakob Heinrich) von (1825–96), German botanist and explorer who settled in Australia in 1847. He did important early work on Australian flora. He was one of the founders of Melbourne University.

muesli / **myoo**-zlee / *n.* a breakfast food of mixed crushed cereals, dried fruit, nuts, etc., eaten with milk.

muezzin / moo-**ez**-uhn / *n.* a man who proclaims the hours of prayer for Muslims, usu. from a minaret.

muff *n.* **1** a covering of furry material for keeping the hands or ears warm. **2** *coarse colloq.* the female external genitals. • *v. colloq.* bungle or blunder; miss (a catch, a ball, etc.). ◻ **muff diver** *coarse colloq.* a person who performs cunnilingus.

muffin *n.* **1** a light flat round spongy cake, eaten toasted and buttered. **2** a cup-shaped cake made from dough or batter.

muffle *v.* **1** wrap or cover for warmth or protection. **2** wrap up or pad in order to deaden its sound (*muffle the drums*). **3** deaden, make less loud or less distinct.

muffler *n.* **1** a scarf worn round the neck for warmth. **2** something used to muffle sound in some musical instruments. **3** the silencer of a motor vehicle.

mufti *n.* plain clothes worn by a person who also wears uniform (*in mufti*). ◻ **mufti day** *Aust.* a day on which school students pay (a small sum, usu. towards fund-raising) for the privilege of wearing casual clothes to school instead of the prescribed uniform.

mug *n.* **1** a large drinking-vessel (usu. with a handle) for use without a saucer. **2** its contents. **3** *colloq.* the face or mouth. **4** *colloq.* a person who is easily deceived. • *adj. colloq.* stupid (*mug lair*). • *v.* (**mugged**, **mugging**) **1** attack and rob (a person), esp. in a public place. **2** orig. *Aust. colloq.* (often foll. by *up*) kiss, cuddle. ◻ **a mug's game** *colloq.* an activity that is unlikely to bring profit or reward. **mug lair** see LAIR². **mug shot** *colloq.* a photograph of a face, esp. for police records. ◻◻ **mugger** *n.*

Mugabe / muh-**gah**-bee /, Robert (Gabriel) (1924–), African statesman, first prime minister (1980) of an independent Zimbabwe, president from 1987.

mugga *n.* an eastern Australian eucalypt with black bark (deeply furrowed and red beneath the surface), grey leaves, and pink or red flowers. Also called *red ironbark*. (¶ Wiradhuri)

muggins *n. colloq.* (often used to refer to oneself) a gullible person (*so muggins had to pay as usual*).

muggy *adj.* (**muggier**, **muggiest**) oppressively humid (*a muggy day; muggy weather*). ◻ **mugginess** *n.*

Muhammad alternative spelling of MOHAMMED.

mujahidin / moo-jah-huh-**deen** / *n.pl.* (also **mujahedin**, **mujahedeen**) guerrilla fighters in Islamic countries, esp. Muslim fundamentalists. (¶ Arabic, = one who fights a war.)

mulatto / myoo-**lat**-oh / *n.* (*pl.* **mulattos** or **mulattoes**) a person who has one white and one black parent.

Mulba *n. Aust.* an Aborigine (used in the Pilbara region of WA). (¶ Panyjima)

■ **Usage** *See* KOORI.

mulberry *n.* **1** a purple or white fruit rather like a blackberry. **2** the tree that bears it. **3** dull purplish red.

mulch *n.* a mixture of wet straw, leaves, etc., spread on the ground to protect plants or retain moisture. • *v.* cover with a mulch.

mulct *v.* extract money from (a person) by fines or taxation or by fraudulent means.

mule *n.* **1** an animal that is the offspring of a male donkey and a female horse, or (in general use) of a female donkey and a male horse (cf. HINNY), known for its stubbornness. **2** a stupidly stubborn person.

mules *v.* (frequently as **mulesing**, **mulesed**) *Aust.* cut away the loose folds of skin in the crutch area of a sheep in order to reduce the risk of blowfly strike and maggot infestation. (¶ J.H.W. Mules, Australian sheep farmer (1876–1946) who first began this practice.)

muleteer / myoo-luh-**teer** / *n.* a mule driver.

mulga / **mul**-guh / *n.* (also **mulga bush**, **mulga tree**, **mulga wood**) *Aust.* **1** any of several wattles of dry inland Australia yielding a distinctive brown and yellowish timber; the wood of these trees, much used in the manufacture of Australian souvenirs. **2** (**the mulga**) the outback; remote, sparsely populated country. • *adj.* **1** of the mulga tree. **2** of the mulga. **3** characterised by the presence of mulga (*mulga country; mulga flats; mulga scrub*). **4** rustic, countrified (*mulga lifestyle*). ◻ **mulga ant** an ant of inland Australia which builds a mud nest and then thatches the nest with mulga leaves. **mulga apple** a large edible gall, soft and sweet, produced by the mulga tree. **mulga Bill** a bush simpleton. **mulga madness** odd behaviour supposedly caused by living in the outback. **mulga parrot** (or **parakeet**) a predominantly green parrot of mulga country with brilliant yellow, blue, and red markings. **mulga snake** a large, fierce, and highly venomous snake. **mulga wire 1** = BUSH TELEGRAPH. **2** an Aboriginal smoke signal as a means of long-distance communication; the message so conveyed. (¶ Kamilaroi, Yuwaalaraay, etc.)

mulgara / **mul**-guh-ruh / n. a small carnivorous marsupial which inhabits burrows in sandy regions of drier Australia. (¶ Probably Wangganguru *mardagura*.)

mulish / **myoo**-lish / adj. stubborn. ☐ **mulishly** adv. **mulishness** n.

mull v. heat (wine or beer) with sugar and spices, as a drink. ☐ **mull over** think over, ponder.

mullah / **mul**-uh / n. a Muslim who is learned in Islamic theology and law.

mulla mulla *Aust.* = PUSSY TAIL. (¶ Probably Panyjima.)

mullet / **mul**-uht / n. (*pl.* **mullet**) an edible sea fish. ☐ **like a stunned mullet** *Aust. colloq.* dazed, uncomprehending. **mullet haircut** a type of (usu. male) haircut with the hair short at the top and front and long at the back.

mulligatawny / mul-uh-guh-**taw**-nee / n. a highly seasoned soup flavoured like curry, originally from India.

mullion / **mul**-yuhn / n. an upright bar between the panes of a window.

mullock / **mul**-uhk / *Aust.* n. **1** (also **mullock dump**, **mullock heap**) the refuse left after mining (esp. goldmining). **2** rubbish, nonsense (*made mullock of the opposition*; *spoke a lot of mullock*). • v. *colloq.* perform (a task etc.) in a slovenly way. ☐ **poke mullock at** *colloq.* deride, ridicule. ☐ ☐ **mullocky** adj.

mullocker n. *Aust.* **1** a person who clears away mining refuse. **2** a careless or clumsy person.

mulloway / **mul**-uh-way / n. a very large food fish occurring in marine and estuarine waters of Australia. (¶ Yaralde)

mullygrub n. *Aust.* a witchetty grub.

mullygrubber n. (also **grubber**) *Aust. Cricket* a ball delivered so that it does not bounce after it hits the ground but rolls along instead.

multi- *comb. form* many. ☐ **multi-access** adj. (of a computer) able to serve several terminals at the same time.

multicoloured adj. with many colours.

multicultural adj. of or involving several cultural or ethnic groups within a society (*multicultural Australia*).

multiculturalism n. **1** the existence of many culturally distinct groups within a society. **2** a theory or policy supporting this.

multifarious / mul-tuh-**fair**-ree-uhs / adj. very varied, of many kinds (*his multifarious duties*). ☐ **multifariously** adv.

multigrade adj. (usu. *attrib.*) an engine oil etc. meeting the requirements of several standard grades.

multigrain n. (in full **multigrain bread**) wheat bread containing whole grains of various cereals.

multilateral / mul-tee-**lat**-uh-ruhl / adj. (of an agreement etc.) involving three or more parties. ☐ **multilaterally** adv. **multilateralism** n.

multimedia n. the combined use of text, sound, video, and animation on a compact disc. • adj. (of art, education, etc.) using more than one medium of expression, communication, etc.

multinational adj. (of a business company) operating in several countries. • n. a multinational company.

multiple adj. having several or many parts, elements, or components. • n. a quantity that contains another (a *factor*) a number of times without remainder (*30 is a multiple of 10*). ☐ **multiple-choice** adj. (of an exam question) providing several possible answers from which the correct one must be chosen. **multiple sclerosis** a chronic progressive disease of the nervous system in which patches of tissue in the brain or spinal cord become damaged and harden, causing paralysis, speech difficulties, etc.

multiplex adj. having many parts or forms; consisting of many elements.

multiplicand n. a quantity to be multiplied by another (cf. MULTIPLIER).

multiplication n. multiplying, being multiplied. ☐ **multiplication sign** a sign (×) (as in 2×3) indicating that one quantity is to be multiplied by another. **multiplication tables** a series of lists showing the results when a number is multiplied by each number (esp. 1 to 12) in turn.

multiplicity / mul-tuh-**plis**-uh-tee / n. a great variety.

multiplier n. the number by which a quantity is multiplied (cf. MULTIPLICAND).

multiply v. (**multiplied**, **multiplying**) **1** (in mathematics) take a specified quantity a specified number of times and find the quantity produced (*multiply 6 by 4 and get 24*). **2** make or become many; increase in number by breeding.

multiracial / mul-tee-**ray**-shuhl / adj. composed of people of many races (*a multiracial society*).

multiskilling n. (within an industry etc.) the training of employees to perform tasks requiring a number of skills.

multi-storey adj. (of a building) having several (esp. similarly designed) storeys. • n. *colloq.* a multi-storey car park.

multitasking n. *Computing* the performance of a number of different tasks simultaneously.

multitude n. a great number of things or people.

multitudinous / mul-tuh-**tyoo**-duh-nuhs / adj. very numerous.

mum n. *colloq.* mother. • adj. *colloq.* silent (*keep mum*). ☐ **mum's the word** say nothing about this.

Mumbai / muum-**buy** / the Hindi name (official from 1995) for BOMBAY.

mumble v. speak or utter indistinctly. • n. indistinct speech. ☐ **mumbler** n.

mumbo-jumbo n. **1** meaningless ritual. **2** words or actions that are deliberately obscure in order to mystify or confuse people.

mummer n. a disguised actor in a traditional play or mime.

mummify v. (**mummified**, **mummifying**) preserve (a corpse) by embalming it as in ancient Egypt. □ **mummification** n.

mummy[1] n. colloq. mother.

mummy[2] n. **1** the body of a person or animal embalmed for burial so as to preserve it, esp. in ancient Egypt. **2** a dried-up body preserved from decay by an accident of nature.

mumps n. a virus disease that causes painful swellings in the neck.

munch v. chew steadily and vigorously.

munchies n.pl. colloq. snacks between meals.

mundane / mun-**dayn** / adj. **1** dull, routine. **2** worldly, not spiritual. □ **mundanely** adv. **mundanity** n.

mundarda / mun-**dah**-duh / n. a WA pygmy possum which resembles a minute ball of soft, red-brown hair, generally found in the tops of grass trees. (¶ Nyungar)

Mundey, Jack (full name: John Bernard Mundey) (1932–), AO, Australian trade union leader and environmentalist, noted for his introduction of 'green bans'.

Munduwalawa / muun-doo-wah-lah-wah /, Ginger Riley (1939–), Australian Aboriginal artist of the NT who has exhibited widely in Australia and overseas.

mung n. (in full **mung bean**) a plant, native to India, producing small pea-like beans that can be cooked or sprouted to produce bean sprouts.

munga n. (also **monger**, **munger**) Aust. colloq. food.

mungite / mung-guyt / n. the sweet, nectar-rich flowering spike of a banksia. (¶ Nyungar, probably *manggayit* 'sweet substance').

municipal / myoo-**nis**-uh-puhl / adj. of a municipality or its self-government. □ **municipally** adv.

municipality / myoo-nuh-suh-**pal**-uh-tee / n. a town or district having local self-government; the governing body of this area.

munificent / myoo-**nif**-uh-suhnt / adj. splendidly generous. □ **munificently** adv. **munificence** n.

muniment / myoo-nuh-muhnt / n. (usu. in pl.) **1** a document kept as evidence of rights or privileges etc. **2** an archive.

munitions / myoo-**nish**-uhnz / n.pl. military weapons, ammunition, equipment, etc.

munjon / mun-juhn / n. (also **munjong**) Aust. **1** an Aborigine who has had little contact with white society. **2** an Aborigine brought up in white society and unfamiliar with the traditional way of life. (¶ Yindjibarndi *manyjangu* 'stranger'.)

muntry n. Aust. the edible fruit of a prostrate kunzea; the plant itself. (¶ Yaralde)

munyeroo / mun-yuh-**roo** / n. (also **munyeru**) Aust. either of two succulent plants of the portulaca family, both the seeds and the leaves of which are used as food. (¶ Diyari)

muon / **myoo**-on / n. an unstable elementary particle like an electron, but with a much greater mass.

mural / **myoo**-ruhl / adj. of or on a wall. • n. a wall painting, a fresco.

Murchison a river in WA, rising near Peak Hill and flowing about 640 km south-west to the Indian Ocean.

murder n. **1** the intentional and unlawful killing of one person by another. **2** colloq. something very difficult or unpleasant. • v. **1** kill (a person) unlawfully and intentionally. **2** colloq. ruin by bad performance or pronunciation etc. □ **murder bird** (also **barking owl**) = SCREAMING-WOMAN BIRD. □ □ **murderer** n. **murderess** n.

murderous adj. **1** involving murder; capable of or intent on murder. **2** very angry, suggesting murder (*a murderous look*).

Murdoch, (Keith) Rupert (1931–), AC, Australian-born entrepreneur whose business interests include newspapers, film and television companies, and publishing.

murk n. darkness, poor visibility.

murky adj. (**murkier**, **murkiest**) **1** dark, gloomy. **2** (of liquid) muddy, full of sediment. **3** secretly scandalous (*his murky past*). □ **murkily** adv. **murkiness** n.

murlonga / mer-**long**-guh / n. (also **myrnonga**) Aust. a white man who sexually exploits Aboriginal women. (¶ Possibly from an Aboriginal language.)

murmur n. **1** a low continuous sound. **2** a low abnormal sound made by the heart. **3** softly spoken words. **4** a subdued expression of feeling (*murmurs of discontent*). • v. make a murmur; speak or utter in a low voice.

murnong / **mer**-nong / n. (also **myrrnong**, **mirr'n-yong**) a sweet, milky, edible tuber, tasting like coconut, of a temperate Australian perennial herb: these were a staple food for Aborigines in Vic. (¶ Wathawurung and Wuywurung.)

Murphy, Graeme (Lloyd) (1950–), AM, Australian dancer and choreographer.

Murphy's law a humorous expression of the apparent perverseness of things (roughly, 'anything that can go wrong will go wrong').

murrain / **mu**-rayn / n. an infectious disease of cattle.

Murray[1] the principal river of Australia, flowing from NSW westward to the Southern Ocean in SA. □ **Murray cod** a large, groper-like, greenish food fish of the Murray-Darling river system. **Murray grey** an Australian breed of grey beefcattle. **Murray Valley** n. used atrributively to designate: **1** a severe variety of encephalitis. **2** the mosquito-borne virus that causes it. **Murray whaler** see WHALER (sense 3).

Murray[2], Les(lie Allan) (1938–), AO, Australian poet.

Murray Island an island (also called Mer) in Torres Strait, traditional homeland of the Meriam people. (*See* MABO¹, MABO².)

Murri / **mu**-ree / *n. Aust.* an Aborigine, esp. one from Qld. (¶ Kamilaroi *mari* 'an Aboriginal person'.)

■ Usage *See* KOORI.

Murrumbidgee a river of 2,160 km rising in south-east NSW on the western side of the Snowy Mountains and flowing west to become a tributary of the Murray. □ **Murrumbidgee whaler** *see* WHALER (sense 3).

Mururoa / moo-ruh-**roh**-uh / an atoll in the southern Pacific, site of French testing of nuclear devices from 1966 onwards to increasing protests worldwide.

Muscat / **mus**-kuht / the capital of Oman.

muscat / **mus**-kuht / *n.* **1** a sweet usu. fortified white wine made from musk-flavoured grapes. **2** this grape.

muscatel / mus-kuh-**tel** / *n.* **1** muscat. **2** a raisin from a muscat grape.

muscle *n.* **1** a band or bundle of fibrous tissue able to contract and relax and so produce movement in an animal body. **2** a part of the body made chiefly of such tissue. **3** muscular power. **4** strength (*trade unions with plenty of muscle*). □ **muscle-bound** having well-developed or over-developed muscles. **muscle in** *colloq.* force one's way.

Muscovite / **mus**-kuh-vuyt / *adj.* of Moscow. • *n.* a native or inhabitant of Moscow.

muscular *adj.* **1** of or affecting the muscles. **2** having well-developed muscles. □ **muscular dystrophy** a hereditary condition causing progressive wasting of the muscles. □□ **muscularity** / mus-kyoo-**la**-ruh-tee /.

musculature *n.* the system of muscles of a body or organ.

Muse *n. Gk* & *Rom. myth.* each of the nine sister goddesses presiding over branches of learning and the arts.

muse *v.* ponder; say meditatively.

museum *n.* a building in which objects of historical or scientific interest are stored and exhibited. □ **museum piece 1** a fine specimen suitable for a museum. **2** *derog.* an antiquated person or thing.

mush *n.* **1** soft pulp. **2** feeble sentimentality.

mushie *n. Aust. colloq.* a mushroom.

mushroom *n.* **1** an edible fungus with a stem and domed cap. **2** pale creamy brown. **3** *colloq.* a person who is deliberately kept in the dark, i.e. ignorant of the true facts etc. • *v.* **1** spring up rapidly in large numbers. **2** rise and spread in the shape of a mushroom. **3** gather mushrooms. □ **mushroom cloud** a mushroom-shaped cloud from a nuclear explosion.

mushy *adj.* (**mushier**, **mushiest**) **1** as or like mush; soft. **2** feebly sentimental. □ **mushiness** *n.*

music *n.* **1** the art of arranging the sounds of voices or instruments in a pleasing sequence. **2** the sounds produced; a written or printed score for this. **3** any pleasant series of sounds, e.g. birdsong. □ **music hall** a style of variety entertainment, popular during the late 19th century, including singing, comic turns, dance acts, etc.; a theatre where this took place. **music stick** = CLAP STICK.

musical *adj.* **1** of music (*musical instruments*). **2** fond of, sensitive to, or skilled in music. **3** accompanied by music; set to music. • *n.* a musical film or play. □ **musical box** a box with a mechanical device that produces music by means of a toothed cylinder which strikes a comb-like metal plate. **musical chairs 1** a party game in which the players compete in successive rounds for a decreasing number of chairs. **2** a series of changes or political manoeuvring etc. □□ **musically** *adv.* **musicality** *n.*

musician *n.* a person who plays or composes music; one whose profession is music. □ **musicianship** *n.*

musicology *n.* the study of the history and forms of music. □ **musicologist** *n.*

musk *n.* **1** a substance secreted by the male musk deer or certain other animals, or produced artificially, used as the basis of perfumes. **2** the smell of musk. **3** an Australian shrub of the *Olearia* family having a strong musky aroma. □ **musk deer** a small hornless deer of Central Asia. **musk ox** a shaggy North American ox with curved horns. **musk rose** a rambling rose that has a musky fragrance.

musket *n.* a long-barrelled gun formerly used by infantry.

musketeer *n.* a soldier armed with a musket.

muskrat *n.* a large rat-like water animal of North America, valued for its fur.

muskwood *n.* an eastern Australian rainforest tree, the timber of which has a musk-like scent.

musky *adj.* smelling like musk. □ **muskiness** *n.*

Muslim / **muuz**-luhm / (also **Moslem**) *n.* one who believes in the Islamic faith. • *adj.* of Muslims or their faith.

muslin / **muz**-luhn / *n.* thin cotton cloth.

muso / **myoo**-zoh / *n.* (*pl.* **musos**) *colloq.* a musician, esp. a professional.

muss *v.* (often foll. by *up*) **1** disarrange, dishevel (*she mussed up his hair*). **2** ruin, spoil.

mussel *n.* a bivalve mollusc, the marine variety of which is edible.

Mussolini / muus-uh-**lee**-nee /, Benito (1883–1945), Italian Fascist dictator who took his country into the Second World War on Germany's side.

Mussorgsky / muh-**sawg**-skee /, Modest (Petrovich) (1839–81), Russian composer.

must¹ *auxiliary v.* used to express necessity or obligation (*you must go*), certainty (*night must fall*), or insistence (*I must repeat, all precautions were taken*). • *n. colloq.* a thing that should not be overlooked or missed.

must² *n.* grape juice undergoing fermentation; new wine.

must³ *adj.* (of esp. a male elephant or a camel) in a state of frenzy. • *n.* this state.

mustang / **mus**-tang / *n.* a small wild horse of Mexico and California.

mustard *n.* **1** a plant with yellow flowers and with black or yellowish sharp-tasting seeds in long pods, the former used mainly in Asian cooking. **2** the yellow seeds ground and made into paste as a condiment in western cuisine. **3** a brownish-yellow colour. ◻ **mustard gas** a poison gas that burns the skin, used in chemical weapons.

muster *v.* **1** assemble (troops) for inspection. **2** assemble; gather together. **3** summon (*muster one's strength*). **4** *Aust.* round up (livestock). • *n.* **1** an assembly of troops. **2** *Aust.* a rounding up of livestock. **3** *Aust. colloq.* the number of people attending a meeting. **4** *Aust.* an assembly of people at a country music festival etc.; such an event. ◻ **pass muster** be accepted as adequate. **tarpaulin muster** see TARPAULIN.

musterer *n. Aust.* a person who musters livestock.

mustering *n. Aust.* the action of gathering (frequently widely dispersed) livestock together in one place. ◻ **mustering plant** the working animals, equipment, personnel, etc. that are involved in mustering.

mustn't = must not.

musty *adj.* (**mustier, mustiest**) **1** smelling or tasting mouldy or stale. **2** antiquated. ◻ **mustily** *adv.* **mustiness** *n.*

mutable / **myoo**-tuh-buhl / *adj.* liable to change, fickle. ◻ **mutability** *n.*

mutagen / **myoo**-tuh-juhn / *n.* something causing genetic mutation, e.g. radiation. ◻ **mutagenic** *adj.*

mutant / **myoo**-tuhnt / *n.* a living thing that differs basically from its parents as a result of genetic change. • *adj.* differing in this way.

mutate / myoo-**tayt** / *v.* undergo or cause to undergo mutation.

mutation *n.* **1** a change or alteration in form. **2** a genetic change which, when transmitted to offspring, gives rise to heritable variations. **3** a mutant.

mutatis mutandis / myoo-tah-tis myoo-**tan**-dis / *adv.* when the necessary alteration of details has been made (in comparing things). (¶ Latin)

mute *adj.* **1** silent, refraining from speaking. **2** not having the power of speech, dumb. **3** not expressed in words (*in mute adoration*). **4** (of a letter) not pronounced (*the b in 'debt' is mute*). **5** (of colour) subdued. • *n.* **1** a dumb person. **2** a device fitted to a musical instrument to deaden its sound. • *v.* **1** deaden or muffle the sound of. **2** make less intense. ◻ **mutely** *adv.* **muteness** *n.*

mutilate *v.* **1** deprive (a person or animal) of a limb or organ; destroy the use of (a limb or organ). **2** cut out or damage part of (a book etc.). ◻ **mutilation** *n.* **mutilator** *n.*

mutineer / myoo-tuh-**neer** / *n.* a person who mutinies.

mutinous / **myoo**-tuh-nuhs / *adj.* rebellious, ready to mutiny. ◻ **mutinously** *adv.*

mutiny / **myoo**-tuh-nee / *n.* open rebellion against authority, esp. by members of the armed forces against their officers. • *v.* (**mutinied, mutinying**) engage in mutiny.

mutt *n.* **1** *colloq.* a stupid person. **2** a dog.

mutter *v.* **1** speak or utter in a low unclear tone. **2** utter subdued grumbles. • *n.* muttering; muttered words.

mutton *n.* **1** the flesh of sheep as food, usu. from an animal older than a lamb or hogget (*see also* UNDERGROUND MUTTON). **2** the flesh of a goat as food.

muttonbird *n. Aust.* **1** a brownish-black petrel breeding in south-east Australia, esp. on Bass Strait islands, and once indiscriminately harvested for the fat, feathers, and edible flesh. **2** any of several other birds of similar appearance or usefulness. **3** (also **muttonbird eater**) *colloq.* a Tasmanian. • *v.* catch muttonbirds as food or to prepare their flesh and by-products for the market. ◻ **muttonbird gales 1** seasonal gales coinciding with the annual arrival of flocks of muttonbirds to nest on islands in Bass Strait and on the coast of Tas. **2** the vast flocks of incoming muttonbirds themselves. ◻◻ **muttonbirder** *n.*

muttonhead *n. colloq.* a stupid person.

mutual / **myoo**-choo-uhl / *adj.* **1** (of a feeling or action) felt or done by each towards or to the other (*mutual affection; mutual aid*). **2** having the same specified relationship to each other (*mutual enemies*). **3** *colloq.* common to two or more people (*our mutual friend*). ◻ **mutually** *adv.*

■ **Usage** Some people object to the use in sense 3, although it is often found; the alternative word 'common' could be taken to mean 'ill-bred'.

muu-muu / **moo**-moo / *n.* a woman's loose brightly-coloured dress. (¶ Hawaiian)

muzak / **myoo**-zak / *n. trademark* piped music in public places; recorded light music as a background.

muzzle *n.* **1** the projecting nose and jaws of certain animals (e.g. dogs). **2** the open end of a firearm. **3** a strap or wire etc. put over an animal's head to prevent it from biting or feeding. • *v.* **1** put a muzzle on (an animal). **2** silence, prevent (a person or newspaper etc.) from expressing opinions freely.

muzzlewood *n.* a small eucalypt of south-eastern Australia, the wood of which was used to make muzzles for unweaned calves to prevent them suckling.

MW *abbr.* **1** megawatt(s). **2** medium wave.

my *adj.* **1** of or belonging to me. **2** used in forms of address (*my dear*), or exclamations of surprise etc. (*my God!*).

myalgia / muy-**al**-juh / *n.* pain in the muscles. ☐ **myalgic** *adj.*

myall / **muy**-uhl, -awl / *n. Aust.* **1** (also **warrigal**) an Aborigine living in a traditional manner (esp. as distinct from one accustomed to, or living among, whites). **2** a person placed in an unfamiliar environment (*the pom tourists were complete myalls in the bush—lost themselves within 10 minutes*). **3** any of several wattles with a silvery foliage. • *adj.* **1** (of an Aborigine) living in a traditional manner. **2** (of an animal or plant) wild (*a myall bullock*). (¶ Dharuk *mayal* or *miyal* 'a stranger, an Aborigine from another tribe'.)

Myanmar / mee-an-**mah** / the official name (since 1989) of Burma.

mycelium *n.* (*pl.* **mycelia**) the vegetative part of a fungus consisting of fine threadlike parts.

Mycenaean / muy-suh-**nee**-uhn / *adj.* of the late Bronze Age civilisation in Greece (*c.*1500–1100 BC) depicted in the poems of Homer; remains of this civilisation were found at Mycenae in the Peloponnese and elsewhere. • *n.* a member of this civilisation.

mycology / muy-**kol**-uh-jee / *n.* the study of fungi. ☐ **mycologist** *n.*

myelin *n.* a white substance which forms a protective sheath around certain nerve-fibres.

myeloma *n.* (*pl.* **myelomas** *or* **myelomata**) a malignant tumour of the bone marrow.

Myer family an Australian family important in the retail industry.

myna / **muy**-nuh / *n.* (also **mynah**, **mina**) a talking bird of the starling family, introduced to Australia from Asia and now common.

myopia / muy-**oh**-pee-uh / *n.* short-sightedness.

myopic / muy-**op**-ik / *adj.* short-sighted. ☐ **myopically** *n.*

myoporum / muy-uh-**poh**-ruhm / = BOOBIALLA.

myriad / **mi**-ree-uhd / *literary n.* (often as **myriads**) a vast number. • *adj.* innumerable.

myriapod / **mi**-ree-uh-pod / *n.* a small crawling creature with many legs, such as a centipede or millipede.

myrmidon / **mer**-mid-uhn / *n.* a henchman.

myrrh / mer / *n.* a gum resin used in perfumes, medicine, and incense.

Myrtaceae / mer-**tay**-see-ay / *n.* the myrtle family, a large and varied family of plants including esp. the eucalypts, melaleucas, and leptospermums (tea-trees).

myrtaceous / mer-**tay**-shuhs / *adj.* belonging to the Myrtaceae or myrtle family.

myrtle / **mer**-tuhl / *n.* **1** an evergreen European shrub with dark leaves and scented white flowers. **2** (in full **myrtle beech**; also **Tasmanian myrtle**) a tall tree of Vic. and Tas. (not myrtaceous) with small, shiny, dark green leaves and valuable timber; the wood of this tree. **3** = SWAN RIVER MYRTLE.

myself *pron.* **1** the emphatic and reflexive form of *I* and *me* (*I went myself; I cut myself*). **2** in my normal state (*not myself today*). ☐ **by myself** *see* ONESELF.

mysterious *adj.* **1** full of mystery, puzzling or obscure. **2** (of a person) delighting in mystery. ☐ **mysteriously** *adv.*

mystery *n.* **1** a matter that remains unexplained or secret. **2** the quality of being unexplained or obscure (*its origins are wrapped in mystery*). **3** the practice of making a secret of things. **4** a religious truth that is beyond human powers to understand. **5** a decade of the rosary. **6** a story or play that deals with a puzzling crime. ☐ **mystery play** a medieval play based on biblical events.

mystic / **mis**-tik / *adj.* **1** of hidden or symbolic meaning, esp. in religion (*mystic ceremonies*). **2** inspiring a sense of mystery and awe. • *n.* a person who seeks to obtain union with God by spiritual contemplation and self-surrender.

mystical / **mis**-ti-kuhl / *adj.* **1** of mystics or mysticism. **2** having spiritual meaning, value, or symbolism. ☐ **mystically** *adv.*

mysticism / **mis**-tuh-siz-uhm / *n.* **1** mystical quality. **2** being a mystic.

mystify *v.* (**mystified**, **mystifying**) **1** bewilder, cause (a person) to feel puzzled. **2** wrap in mystery. ☐ **mystification** *n.*

mystique / mis-**teek** / *n.* an aura of mystery or mystical power.

myth / mith / *n.* **1** a traditional story containing ideas or beliefs about ancient times or natural events. **2** such stories collectively (*in myth and legend*). **3** an imaginary person or thing. **4** an idea that forms part of the beliefs of a group but is not founded on fact.

mythical / **mith**-i-kuhl / *adj.* **1** of myths, existing in myths. **2** imaginary, fancied. ☐ **mythically** *adv.*

mythology / mi-**thol**-uh-jee / *n.* **1** a body of myths (*Aboriginal mythology; Greek mythology*). **2** the study of myths. ☐ **mythological** *adj.* **mythologist** *n.*

mythopoeia / mith-oh-**pee**-uh / *n.* the making of myths. ☐ **mythopoeic** *adj.*

myxo *n. Aust.* = MYXOMATOSIS.

myxomatosis / mik-suh-muh-**toh**-suhs / *n.* an infectious and usu. fatal virus disease of rabbits, introduced into Australia to exterminate these introduced creatures who were assuming plague proportions.

N

N *abbr.* (also **N.**) **1** North; Northern. **2** New. **3** newton(s). **4** nuclear. • *symbol* nitrogen.

n *n.* an indefinite number. • *abbr.* (also **n.**) **1** name. **2** neuter. ☐ **to the nth degree** to the utmost.

'n *conj.* (also **'n'**) *colloq.* and.

Na *symbol* sodium.

n/a *abbr.* (also **n.a.**) **1** not applicable. **2** not available.

naan = NAN².

nab *v.* (**nabbed**, **nabbing**) *colloq.* **1** catch (a wrongdoer) in the act, arrest. **2** seize, grab.

nabarlek / **nah**-buh-lek / *n.* a small wallaby of WA and Arnhem Land. (¶ Gunwinygu)

Nabokov / nuh-**boh**-kof, **nab**-uh-kof /, Vladimir Vladimirovich (1899–1977), Russian-born novelist and poet, author of *Lolita*.

nacho *n.* (*pl.* **nachos**) a tortilla chip, usu. topped with melted cheese and chilli etc.

nacre / **nay**-kuh / *n.* mother-of-pearl obtained from shellfish. ☐ **nacreous** / **nay**-kree-uhs / *adj.*

nadir / **nay**-deer / *n.* **1** the point of the celestial sphere directly under the observer (opposite to the zenith). **2** the lowest point; the time of deepest depression.

nads *n.pl. colloq.* the testicles. (¶ Abbreviation of *gonads*.)

naevus / **nee**-vuhs / *n.* (*pl.* **naevi** / **nee**-vuy /) **1** a birthmark consisting of a red patch on the skin. **2** = MOLE (sense 1).

naff *colloq. adj.* tasteless; vulgar; ridiculous. • *v.* (**naff off**) go away, scram.

nag¹ *v.* (**nagged**, **nagging**) **1** make scolding remarks to, find fault continually. **2** (of pain or worry) be felt persistently.

nag² *n. colloq.* a horse, esp. a decrepit one.

naga *n. Aust.* a loin cloth (as worn by Aborigines). (¶ Wuna *naga* 'dress, covering'.)

Nagasaki / nag-uh-**sah**-kee / Japanese city, target of the second atomic bomb attack (9 August 1945); *see also* HIROSHIMA.

naiad / **nuy**-ad / *n.* a water nymph.

nail *n.* **1** the layer of horny substance over the outer tip of a finger or toe. **2** a small metal spike driven in with a hammer to hold things together or as a peg or protection or ornament. • *v.* **1** fasten with a nail or nails. **2** catch or arrest (*the police haven't nailed him yet*). **3** secure or get hold of (a person or thing) (*nailed him to a definite date*). **4** keep (a person, attention, etc.) fixed (*terror nailed him to the spot*). **5** expose or discover (a lie or a liar). ☐ **nail-biter** *colloq.* a highly suspenseful situation (*the match was a real nail-biter*). **nail down 1** bind (a person) to a promise etc. **2** define precisely. **3** fasten (a thing) with nails. **nail-tailed wallaby** *Aust.* any of three species of small wallaby, members of which have a horny nail at the tip of the tail.

Nairobi / nuy-**roh**-bee / the capital of Kenya.

naïve / nuy-**eev** / *adj.* (also **naive**) showing a lack of experience or of informed judgment. ☐ **naïvely** *adv.* **naïvety** *or* **naïveté** / nuy-**ee**-vuh-tee / *n.*

naked *adj.* **1** without clothes on, nude. **2** without the usual coverings, ornamentation, or protection (*a naked sword*). **3** undisguised (*the naked truth*). ☐ **naked eye** the eye unassisted by a telescope or microscope etc. ☐☐ **nakedly** *adv.* **nakedness** *n.*

Namatjira / nam-uht-**jeer**-ruh /, Albert (1902–59), Australian Aboriginal artist, famous for his landscapes of the Australian inland.

namby-pamby *adj.* lacking positive character, feeble; sentimental. • *n.* a person of this kind.

name *n.* **1** a word or words by which a person, animal, place, or thing is known or indicated. **2** a reputation (*it has got a bad name; made a name for himself*). **3** a famous person (*the film has some big names in it*). • *v.* **1** give a name to. **2** state the name(s) of. **3** nominate or appoint to an office etc. **4** mention or specify. ☐ **have to one's name** possess. **in all but name** in effect, although not so called (*she is manager in all but name*). **in name only** not in reality, although so called (*he is manager in name only*). **name-dropping** mention of famous people's names in order to impress others by implying that one is familiar with such people. ☐☐ **nameable** *adj.*

nameless *adj.* **1** having no name or no known name. **2** not mentioned by name, anonymous (*others who shall be nameless*). **3** too bad to be named (*nameless horrors*).

namely *adv.* that is to say, specifically.

namesake *n.* a person or thing with the same name as another.

Namibia / nuh-**mib**-ee-uh / a republic in SW Africa. ☐ **Namibian** *adj.* & *n.*

namma alternative spelling of GNAMMA.

Namoi / **nam**-oi / a river, some 850 km long, in northern NSW.

nan¹ *n.* (also **nana**, **nanna**) *colloq.* grandmother.

nan² / nahn / *n.* (also **naan**) a type of flat leavened Indian bread cooked esp. in a clay oven.

nana / **nah**-nuh / *n. colloq.* an idiot, a fool. ☐ **do one's nana** *Aust.* lose one's temper. **off one's nana** *Aust.* mentally deranged.

Nanak / **nah**-nuhk / (known as Guru Nanak) (1469–1539), Indian religious leader and founder of Sikhism.

Nandi (in Hinduism) the bull of Siva, which is his vehicle and symbolises fertility.

nankeen / nang-**keen** / n. a kind of cotton cloth, originally made in Nanking (Nanjing) in China from naturally yellow cotton. ☐ **nankeen kestrel** a small, mainly Australian, hovering kestrel with a red-brown (supposedly nankeen) back. Also called *sparrowhawk*.

nanna = NAN¹.

nanny n. **1** a child's nurse. **2** *colloq.* grandmother. **3** (in full **nanny goat**) a female goat.

nannygai / **nan**-ee-guy / n. a short-bodied, reddish, sea fish of southern Australia, valued as food. (¶ Probably from a NSW Aboriginal language.)

nano- / **nan**-oh / *comb. form* denoting a factor of 10^{-9} or one thousand millionth (*a nanosecond*).

nanometre n. one thousand-millionth of a metre.

nanosecond n. one thousand-millionth of a second.

nanotechnology n. the branch of technology that deals with dimensions and tolerances of less than 100 nanometres, esp. the manipulation of individual atoms and molecules.

nap¹ n. a short sleep or doze, esp. during the day. • v. (**napped, napping**) sleep lightly or briefly. ☐ **catch a person napping** catch a person off his or her guard. ☐☐ **napper** n.

nap² n. **1** short raised fibres on the surface of cloth (esp. velvet) or leather. **2** a soft downy surface, e.g. on leaves. **3** *Aust.* blankets, bedding; a swag.

napalm / **nay**-pahm / n. a jelly-like petrol substance used in incendiary bombs and flame-throwers. • v. attack with napalm bombs etc. (*napalmed the village*).

nape n. the back of the neck.

naphtha / **naf**-thuh / n. an inflammable oil obtained from coal or petroleum.

naphthalene / **naf**-thuh-leen / n. a strong-smelling white substance obtained from coal tar, used in dyes and as a moth repellent.

napkin n. **1** a square piece of cloth or paper used at meals to protect one's clothes or for wiping one's lips or fingers. **2** a baby's nappy.

Napoleon the name of three rulers of France, including Napoleon I, emperor 1804–15. ☐ **Napoleonic** *adj.*

nappy n. a piece of towelling or other absorbent material wrapped around a baby's bottom to absorb or retain urine and faeces. ☐ **nappy valley** *Aust. colloq.* a suburb (esp. a new one) in which a large number of young families live.

narcissism / **nah**-suh-siz-uhm / n. abnormal self-love or self-admiration. (¶ *See* NARCISSUS.)

narcissist / **nah**-suh-sist / n. a person who is given to narcissism. ☐ **narcissistic** / nah-suh-**sis**-tik / *adj.*

narcissus / nah-**sis**-uhs / n. (pl. **narcissi**) any of a group of flowers including jonquils and daffodils. (¶ *Narcissus*, an extremely beautiful young man in Greek myth who fell in love with his own reflection in a pool and lay there adoring himself until he died: he was then changed into the flower which bears his name.)

narcosis / nah-**koh**-suhs / n. a state of sleep or drowsiness, esp. one produced by drugs.

narcotic / nah-**kot**-ik / *adj.* (of a drug, e.g. morphine) causing sleep or drowsiness. • n. a narcotic drug.

nard n. **1** a plant yielding an aromatic balsam. **2** = SPIKENARD.

nardoo / nah-**doo** / n. *Aust.* a clover-like perennial fern of mainland Australia occurring on or near water, the pea-sized spores of which are ground into flour by Aborigines and used as food. Also called *clover fern*. (¶ Yandruwandha and many other Aboriginal languages.)

nark *colloq.* n. **1** a nagging or whingeing person. **2** *Aust.* an annoying person or thing. **3** a police informer or decoy. • v. **1** annoy by nagging or whingeing. **2** act as a police informer or decoy.

Nar Nar Goon / nah nah **goon** / n. *Aust.* any small, insignificant place. • *adj.* of such a place; insignificant. (¶ The name of a small, remote town in Vic.)

narrate / nuh-**rayt** / v. tell (a story); give an account of; utter or write a narrative. ☐ **narration** n. **narrator** n.

narrative / **na**-ruh-tiv / n. a spoken or written account of something. • *adj.* in the form of narrative.

narrow *adj.* **1** of small width in proportion to length. **2** having or allowing little space (*within narrow bounds*). **3** with little scope or variety, small (*a narrow circle of friends*). **4** with little margin (*a narrow escape; a narrow majority*). **5** searching; precise; exact (*a narrow scrutiny*). **6** narrow-minded. • n. (usu. in *plural*) the narrow part of a strait, river, pass, etc. • v. make or become narrower; contract; lessen. ☐ **narrow-leaved peppermint** *Aust.* a eucalypt with slender foliage having a strong peppermint aroma, this being one of the species used for the commercial distillation of oil (*see* CINEOL). **narrow-leaved red ironbark** *Aust.* a medium-sized eucalypt, the most widespread of the ironbarks, having hard, furrowed bark thickly covered with oozings of red gum, and long, slender leaves. **narrow-minded** rigid in one's views and sympathies, not tolerant. ☐☐☐ **narrowly** *adv.* **narrowness** n.

narthex / **nah**-theks / n. **1** a railed-off antechamber or porch etc. at the western entrance of some early Christian churches, used by catechumens, penitents, etc. **2** a similar antechamber in a modern church.

narwhal / **nah**-wuhl / n. an Arctic animal related to the whale, the male of which has a long tusk with a spiral groove.

nary *adj. colloq.* not a; no (*nary a one*). (¶ *ne'er a*)

NASA / **nas**-uh / *abbr.* (also **Nasa**) National Aeronautics and Space Administration, a body

nasal responsible for organising US research in extraterrestrial space.

nasal / **nay**-zuhl / *adj.* **1** of the nose. **2** (of a voice or speech) sounding as if the breath came out through the nose. ☐ **nasally** *adv.*

nasalise *v.* (also **-ize**) speak nasally; give a nasal sound to. ☐ **nasalisation** *n.*

nascent / **nas**-uhnt, **nay**-suhnt / *adj.* beginning to be or develop (*Australia is considered to be a nascent Republic*). ☐ **nascency** *n.*

nashi *n.* a type of apple-like Japanese pear.

nasho *n. Aust. hist.* **1** compulsory military training introduced in Australia under the National Service Act of 1951. **2** a person who undergoes this.

nasi goreng / nah-see gaw-**reng** / *n.* an Indonesian dish consisting of spiced fried rice containing prawns, slivers of beef, crisp fried onions, and chillies, and garnished with strips of omelette and cucumber.

Nassau / **nas**-aw / the capital of the Bahamas.

nasturtium / nuh-**ster**-shuhm / *n.* a trailing plant with bright orange, yellow, or red flowers and round flat edible leaves.

nasty *adj.* (**nastier**, **nastiest**) **1** highly unpleasant (*nasty weather; a nasty smell*). **2** annoying (*my car has a nasty habit of breaking down*). **3** difficult to negotiate; dangerous (*a nasty hairpin bend; a nasty illness*). **4** unkind, spiteful. **5** violent; offensive (*turns nasty when he's drunk*). **6** disgustingly dirty, filthy; obscene. ☐ **nastily** *adv.* **nastiness** *n.*

Natal / nuh-**tahl** / (also **KwaZulu Natal**) the eastern coastal province of South Africa.

natal / **nay**-tuhl / *adj.* of or from one's birth.

natch *adv. colloq.* naturally.

Nathan, Trent (Hugh Robert) (1940–), AM, Australian fashion designer.

nation *n.* **1** a community of people of mainly common descent and history and speaking the same language or related languages. **2** a community of peoples forming a sovereign State or inhabiting a territory and unified by a national language and government.

national *adj.* of a nation, common to or characteristic of a whole nation. • *n.* **1** a citizen or subject of a particular country (*Australian nationals*). **2** a fellow countryman. ☐ **national anthem** a song of loyalty or patriotism adopted by a nation (in Australia ADVANCE AUSTRALIA FAIR). **national park** an area of natural beauty protected by the Federal or a State government for the use and enjoyment of the public. **national service** a period of compulsory service in a country's armed forces. ☐☐ **nationally** *adv.*

nationalise *v.* (also **-ize**) convert (industries etc.) from private to government ownership. ☐ **nationalisation** *n.*

nationalism *n.* **1** patriotic feeling or principles or efforts. **2** a movement favouring independence for a country that is controlled by or forms part of another. ☐ **nationalist** *n.* **nationalistic** *adj.*

nationality *n.* **1** the condition of belonging to a particular nation. **2** an ethnic group forming a part of one or more political nations.

National Party of Australia a political party formed to represent rural interests.

National Trust an organisation dedicated to the conservation, often by acquisition, of the natural and cultural environment.

nationwide *adj.* extending over the whole of a nation.

native *adj.* **1** belonging to a person or thing by nature; inborn, natural. **2** of one's birth (*one's native land*). **3** (usu. foll. by *to*) belonging to a specified place (*the kangaroo is native to Australia*). **4** of the natives of a place (*the native customs of England*). **5** (of an Australian plant or animal) supposedly resembling one found elsewhere (*native cherry; native bee*). • *n.* **1** a person who was born in a specified place (*a native of Melbourne*). **2** a local inhabitant of a place. **3** *offens.* a member of a non-white native people, e.g. the Aborigines, as regarded by colonial settlers. **4** *hist.* a white person born in Australia (as opposed to e.g. a person living in Australia who was born elsewhere). **5 a** an indigenous animal or plant. **b** an animal or plant peculiar to Australia or to a particular State or region of Australia. ☐ **native bee** any of several small, stingless Australian bees producing honey stored in a comb, often in the hollow of a tree-trunk. **native bread** the large, heavy, tuber-like, underground food-storage body of an Australian fungus, roasted and eaten by Aborigines. **native cat** = QUOLL. **native cherry** a small, cypress-like Australian tree bearing small, sweet, edible fruit. Also called *ballart*, *cherry ballart*. **native companion** *Aust.* a brolga. **native cranberry** any of several Australian plants with edible fruits, esp. the prostrate astroloma bearing a drupe with a sweet pulp. **native frangipani** a small tree of Australian rainforests with fragrant creamy yellow flowers: often grown in gardens. **native title 1** the right of indigenous people to own their traditional land. **2** the right of the Aboriginal and Islander people of Australia to own their traditional land, a right which the High Court of Australia recognised in 1992, thus effectively quashing the colonial fiction of TERRA NULLIUS (*see also* MABO).

Native American *n.* member of a group of indigenous peoples of North and South America and the Caribbean Islands. Also called AMERICAN INDIAN. • *adj.* of or relating to these peoples.

nativity *n.* **1** (esp. as **the Nativity**) Christ's birth; the festival celebrating this (25 December). **2** birth.

NATO / **nay**-toh / *abbr.* (also **Nato**) North Atlantic Treaty Organisation, an association of European and North American States formed in 1949 for the purposes of collective security.

Nats *n.pl. colloq.* **1** the National Party of Australia; its members collectively. **2** (in various sports, esp. motor racing) national championships (*Summer Nats*).

natter *colloq. v.* chat. • *n.* a chat.

natty *adj.* (**nattier, nattiest**) *colloq.* neat and trim, smart, esp. in dress. ☐ **nattily** *adv.*

natural *adj.* **1** of, existing in, or produced by nature (*natural landscape*). **2** in accordance with the course of nature, normal (*a natural death*). **3** (of a person) having certain inborn qualities or abilities (*a natural leader*). **4** not looking artificial; not affected in manner etc. **5** not surprising, to be expected. **6** *Music* (of a note) neither sharp nor flat (*B natural*). • *n.* **1** a person or thing that seems to be naturally suited for something. **2** *Music* a natural note; the sign for this (♮). ☐ **natural gas** gas found in the earth's crust, not manufactured. **natural history** the study of animal and vegetable life. **natural number** a whole number greater than 0. **natural resources** materials or conditions occurring in nature which may be exploited economically. **natural science** any of the sciences which study the natural or physical world. **natural selection** survival of the organisms that are best adapted to their environment while the less well adapted ones die out. ☐☐ **naturally** *adv.* **naturalness** *n.*

naturalise *v.* (also **-ize**) **1** admit (a person of foreign birth) to full citizenship of a country. **2** adopt (a foreign word or custom) into the language or customs of a country. **3** introduce and acclimatise (an animal or plant) into a country or region where it is not native. **4** cause to appear natural, esp. (of a plant) as if growing wild (*daffodil bulbs suitable for naturalising*). ☐ **naturalisation** *n.*

naturalism *n.* **1** realism in art and literature; drawing or representing things as they are in nature. **2** a theory of the world that excludes the supernatural or spiritual; a moral or religious system based on this. ☐ **naturalistic** *adj.*

naturalist *n.* **1** an expert in natural history. **2** a supporter of naturalism.

nature *n.* **1** (often **Nature**) the world with all its features and living things; the physical power that produces these. **2** a kind, sort, or class (*things of this nature; the request was in the nature of a command*). **3** the complex of qualities and characteristics innate in a person or animal (*it's not in her nature to be cruel*). **4** heredity as influencing or determining character (as opposed to NURTURE *n.*, sense 2). **5** a thing's essential qualities, its characteristics (*it is the nature of iron to rust*). ☐ **call of nature** *colloq.* a need to urinate or defecate. **nature reserve** an area of land managed so as to preserve its flora, fauna, physical features, etc. **nature strip** *Aust.* **1** (in some Australian towns) a piece of publicly-owned land (usu. lawn) between the front boundary of a property (and the footpath, if there is one) and the street. **2** a median strip between two lanes of traffic, usu. grassed or planted with shrubs etc. **nature trail** a signposted path through the countryside where interesting natural objects can be seen.

naturist *n.* a nudist. ☐ **naturism** *n.*

naturopathy / nach-uh-**rop**-uh-thee / *n.* the treatment of illness etc. without drugs, usu. involving diet, exercise, massage, etc. ☐ **naturopath** *n.* **naturopathic** *adj.*

naught *n. archaic* nothing, = NOUGHT.

naughty *adj.* (**naughtier, naughtiest**) **1** behaving badly, disobedient. **2** improper; shocking or amusing people by mild indecency. ☐ **naughtily** *adv.* **naughtiness** *n.*

Nauru / nuh-**roo** / an island republic in the SW Pacific. ☐ **Nauruan** *adj.* & *n.*

nausea / **naw**-zee-uh, -see-uh / *n.* **1** an inclination to vomit. **2** disgust.

nauseate / **naw**-zee-ayt, -see-ayt / *v.* affect with nausea.

nauseous / **naw**-zee-uhs, -see-uhs / *adj.* **1** causing or feeling nausea. **2** disgusting.

nautical *adj.* of sailors or seamanship. ☐ **nautical mile** a unit of 1,852 metres (approx. 2,025 yards).

nautilus / **naw**-tuh-luhs / *n.* (*pl.* **nautiluses** *or* **nautili**) a mollusc with a spiral shell divided into compartments.

naval *adj.* of a navy, of ships.

nave *n.* the body of a church apart from the chancel, aisles, and transepts.

navel / **nay**-vuhl / *n.* **1** the small hollow in the centre of the abdomen where the umbilical cord was attached. **2** the central point of something. ☐ **navel orange** a large orange with a navel-like formation at the top.

navigable / **nav**-i-guh-buhl / *adj.* **1** (of rivers or seas) suitable for ships to sail in. **2** (of a ship etc.) able to be steered and sailed. ☐ **navigability** *n.*

navigate *v.* **1** sail in or through (a sea or river etc.). **2 a** direct the course of (a ship, aircraft), using maps and instruments; **b** (in a car etc.) assist the driver by map reading etc. ☐ **navigation** *n.* **navigator** *n.*

navvy *n.* a labourer employed in making roads, railways, canals, etc. where digging is necessary.

navy *n.* **1** (often as **the Navy**) a country's warships and auxiliaries. **2** the officers and personnel of these. **3** (in full **navy blue**) very dark blue like that used in naval uniform.

nawab / nuh-**wahb** / *n.* **1** the title of a distinguished Muslim in Pakistan. **2** *archaic* the title of a governor or nobleman in India.

nay *adv.* **1** *archaic* no. **2** or rather; and even; and more than that (*large, nay, huge*). • *n.* (in parliament etc.) a 'no' vote or voter (*the 'nays' have it*).

Nazarene / naz-uh-**reen**, **naz**- / *n*. **1** (**the Nazarene**) Christ. **2** (esp. in Jewish or Muslim use) a Christian. **3** a native or inhabitant of Nazareth. □ **Nazism** *n*.

Nazareth a town of Galilee in Israel, where Christ spent his youth.

Nazi / **naht**-see / *n*. (*pl*. **Nazis**) **1** a member of the National Socialist party in Germany, brought to power by Hitler. **2** *derog*. a person holding extreme racist or authoritarian views or behaving brutally. **3** a person belonging to any organisation similar to that of the Nazis. • *adj*. of the Nazis. □ **Nazism** *n*.

NB *abbr*. note well. (¶ From the Latin *nota bene*.)

Nb *symbol* niobium.

NCO *abbr*. non-commissioned officer.

Nd *symbol* neodymium.

N'Djamena / uhn-jah-**may**-nah / the capital of Chad.

NE *abbr*. **1** north-east. **2** north-eastern.

Ne *symbol* neon.

Neanderthal / nee-**an**-duh-thahl / *adj*. **1** of the extinct type of human being living in the Old Stone Age in Europe, with a retreating forehead and massive brow ridges. **2** (also **neanderthal**) primitive; archaic; hidebound (*his views are positively neanderthal*). • *n*. (also **neanderthal**) a person whose views are hidebound, fixed on the past (*the neanderthals of the extreme right and left*).

neap *n*. (in full **neap tide**) the tide when there is the least rise and fall of water, halfway between spring tides.

Neapolitan / nee-uh-**pol**-uh-tuhn / *adj*. of Naples. • *n*. a native or inhabitant of Naples.

near *adv*. **1** at, to, or within a short distance or interval. **2** nearly (*as near as I can guess*). • *prep*. near to. • *adj*. **1** with only a short distance or interval between (*in the near future*). **2** closely related, intimate. **3** (of a part of a vehicle, horse, or road) on the left side (*near hind leg*). **4** with little margin (*a near escape*). **5** similar (to) (*this one is nearer the original*). • *v*. draw near. □ **near-sighted** short-sighted. **near thing** something achieved or missed by only a narrow margin; a narrow escape. □□ **nearness** *n*.

nearby *adj*. near in position (*a nearby house*). • *adv*. not far away; close.

nearly *adv*. almost. □ **not nearly** nothing like, far from (*not nearly enough*).

nearside *n*. the side of a vehicle that is normally nearest the kerb, in Australia the left side (cf. OFFSIDE).

neat *adj*. **1** simple and clean and orderly in appearance. **2** done or doing things in a precise and skilful way. **3** undiluted (*neat whisky*). **4** *colloq*. good, pleasing, excellent. □ **neatly** *adv*. **neatness** *n*.

neaten *v*. make or become neat.

Nebuchadnezzar / neb-yoo-kuhd-**nez**-uh / king of Babylon 605–562 BC, who captured and destroyed Jerusalem in 586 BC.

nebula / **neb**-yuh-luh / *n*. (*pl*. **nebulae** / neb-yoo-lee /) a bright or dark patch in the sky caused by a distant galaxy or a cloud of dust or gas. □ **nebular** *adj*.

nebuliser / **neb**-yuh-luy-zuh / *n*. (also **-izer**) a device for producing a fine spray of liquid.

nebulous / **neb**-yuh-luhs / *adj*. indistinct, having no definite form (*nebulous ideas*).

necessarily *adv*. as a necessary result, inevitably.

necessary *adj*. **1** essential in order to achieve something. **2** unavoidable, happening or existing by necessity (*the necessary consequence*). • *n*. **1** (**the necessary**) *colloq*. money or action needed for a purpose. **2** (**necessaries**) things without which life cannot be maintained or is exceedingly harsh.

necessitate / nuh-**ses**-uh-tayt / *v*. make necessary, involve as a condition or result.

necessitous / nuh-**ses**-uh-tuhs / *adj*. needy.

necessity / nuh-**ses**-uh-tee / *n*. 1 the state or fact of being necessary (*the necessity of adequate food*). 2 a necessary thing. 3 the compelling power of circumstances. 4 a state of need or great poverty or hardship.

neck *n*. **1** the narrow part of the body connecting the head to the shoulders. **2** the part of a garment round this. **3** the length of a horse's head and neck as a measure of its lead in a race. **4** the flesh of an animal's neck as food. **5** the narrow part of anything (esp. of a bottle or cavity); a narrow connecting part or channel. • *v*. *colloq*. (of couples) kiss and caress each other lovingly. □ **neck and neck** running level in a race. **neck of the woods** *colloq*. a specified place (*what are you doing in this neck of the woods?*).

neckerchief *n*. a square of cloth worn round the neck.

neckful *n*. *colloq*. more than enough (*I've had a neckful of these whingers*).

necklace *n*. (also **necklet**) an ornament of precious stones, metal, beads, etc. worn round the neck.

neckline *n*. the outline formed by the edge of a garment at or below the neck.

necro- *comb. form* corpse.

necromancy / **nek**-ruh-man-see / *n*. **1** the art of predicting events by allegedly communicating with the dead. **2** magic. □ **necromancer** *n*.

necrophilia *n*. a morbid and esp. sexual attraction to corpses. □ **necrophiliac** *n*.

necrophobia *n*. an intense fear of death or dead bodies.

necropolis / nuh-**krop**-uh-luhs / *n*. a cemetery, esp. an ancient one.

necrosis / nuh-**kroh**-suhs / *n*. the death of tissue caused by disease or injury, esp. as one of the symptoms of gangrene or pulmonary tuberculosis. □ **necrotic** / nuh-**krot**-ik / *adj*.

nectar *n*. **1** a sweet fluid produced by plants and collected by bees for making honey. **2** *Gk myth*. the drink of the gods. **3** pure fruit juice. **4** any delicious drink.

nectarine / **nek**-tuh-ruhn, -**reen** / n. a kind of peach that has a thin skin with no down.

nectary / **nek**-tuh-ree / n. the nectar-secreting part of a plant or flower.

neddy n. colloq. a horse.

ned 'em v. Aust. colloq. (in the game of two-up) throw two heads.

Ned Kelly Aust. n. **1** a person who is unscrupulous in seeking personal gain or who resists authority. **2** rhyming slang the belly. • adj. unscrupulous, esp. in seeking profit etc. (*tycoons with the Ned Kelly syndrome*). • v. **1** bushrange. **2** shoot (a bird etc.) unsportingly (*fearless shooters Ned Kellying ducks while they are resting on the water*). ☐ **game as Ned Kelly** fearless in the face of odds. (¶ *See* KELLY, Ned.)

née / nay / adj. (also **nee**) born (used in giving a married woman's maiden name) (*Mrs Jane Smith, née Jones*).

need n. **1** a circumstance in which a thing or course of action is required (*there is no need to worry*). **2** a situation of great difficulty or misfortune (*a friend in need*). **3** lack of necessaries, poverty. **4** a requirement, a thing necessary for life (*my needs are few*). • v. **1** be in need of, require. **2** be under a necessity or obligation (*need you ask?*). ☐ **if need be** if necessary. **must needs** (or **needs must**) archaic of necessity (*must needs do it*).

needful adj. necessary. ☐ **needfully** adv.

needle n. **1** a small thin piece of polished steel with a point at one end and a hole for thread at the other, used in sewing. **2** a long thin piece of smooth metal or plastic etc. with one or both ends pointed, used in knitting by hand. **3** the pointer of a compass or dial. **4** the sharp hollow end of a hypodermic syringe. **5** a stylus on a record player. **6** an obelisk (*Cleopatra's Needle*). **7** a pointed rock or peak. **8** one of the long thin leaves of pine trees. **9** (**the needle**) colloq. a fit of bad temper or nervousness. • v. colloq. **1** goad (*needled him into taking action*). **2** irritate; make digs at; heckle; harass. ☐ **needle exchange** a program in Australia through which intravenous drug users (who usu. share needles) can exchange their used hypodermic syringes for sterile ones at no charge, a program designed to halt the spread of blood-borne disease.

needless adj. not needed, unnecessary; uncalled for. ☐ **needlessly** adv.

needlepoint n. a kind of fine embroidery on canvas.

needlework n. sewing or embroidery.

needn't = need not.

needy adj. (**needier**, **neediest**) lacking the necessaries of life, extremely poor. ☐ **neediness** n.

neenish tart n. Aust. a small sweet pastry case filled with mock cream, topped with brown and white or pink and white icing.

ne'er adv. poetic never. ☐ **ne'er-do-well** a good-for-nothing person.

nefarious / nuh-**fair**-ree-uhs / adj. wicked. ☐ **nefariously** adv.

negate / nuh-**gayt** / v. nullify, disprove. ☐ **negation** n.

negative adj. **1** expressing or implying denial, refusal, or prohibition (*a negative answer*). **2** (of a person or attitude) not positive, lacking positive qualities or characteristics; pessimistic. **3** marked by the absence of qualities (*a negative reaction; a negative result from the Aids test*). **4** (of a quantity) less than zero, minus. **5** of, containing, or producing the kind of electric charge carried by electrons. • n. **1** a negative statement, reply, or word. **2** a negative quality or quantity. **3** *Photography* a developed film or plate containing an image with black and white reversed, or with colours replaced by complementary ones, from which a positive picture may be obtained. • v. **1** veto. **2** disprove. **3** contradict (a statement). **4** neutralise (an effect). ☐ **negative gearing** a scheme under which the interest payments on the borrowing for an investment exceed the net revenue from that investment, the loss being set against other sources of income to reduce the borrower's tax liability. **negative pole** the south-seeking pole of a magnet. **negative sign** the sign (−). ☐☐ **negatively** adv.

negativism n. a negative attitude; extreme scepticism.

neglect v. **1** pay no attention or not enough attention to. **2** fail to take proper care of. **3** omit to do something, e.g. through carelessness or forgetfulness. • n. neglecting; being neglected. ☐ **neglectful** adj.

negligée / **neg**-luh-zhay / n. (also **negligee**, **négligé**) a woman's light flimsy ornamental dressing gown.

negligence / **neg**-luh-juhns / n. lack of proper care or attention; culpable carelessness. ☐ **negligent** adj. **negligently** adv.

negligible / **neg**-luh-juh-buhl / adj. very small in amount etc. and not worth taking into account. ☐ **negligibly** adv.

negotiable / nuh-**goh**-shuh-buhl / adj. **1** able to be modified after discussion (*the salary is negotiable*). **2** able to be negotiated.

negotiate / nuh-**goh**-shee-ayt / v. **1** try to reach an agreement, compromise, or arrangement by discussion; arrange in this way (*negotiated a treaty*). **2** get over or through (an obstacle or difficulty) successfully. **3** get or give money in exchange for (a cheque or bonds etc.). ☐ **negotiation** n. **negotiator** n.

Negress n. a female Negro.

■ **Usage** Offensive; the term *black* is usu. preferred.

Negro n. (pl. **Negroes**) a member of a black-skinned race that originated in Africa.

Negroid

■ **Usage** Offensive; the term *black* is usu. preferred.

Negroid *adj.* having the physical characteristics that are typical of black people. • *n.* a black person.

Nehru / nay-roo /, Pandit Jawaharlal (1889–1964), Indian statesman, first prime minister of an independent India 1947–64.

neigh / nay / *n.* the long high-pitched cry of a horse. • *v.* make this cry.

neighbour *n.* (also **neighbor**) **1** a person who lives near or next to another. **2** a fellow human being. **3** a person or thing situated near or next to another (*my neighbour at dinner*). • *v.* adjoin, border on.

neighbourhood *n.* (also **neighborhood**) **1** a district. **2** the people living in it. □ **in the neighbourhood of** somewhere near, approximately. **neighbourhood watch** organised local vigilance by householders in order to discourage crime in their neighbourhood.

neighbouring *adj.* (also **neighboring**) living or situated near by.

neighbourly *adj.* (also **neighborly**) like a good neighbour, kind and friendly. □ **neighbourliness** *n.*

Neilson, John Shaw (1872–1942), Australian lyric poet.

neither / nuy-*th*uh, nee-*th*uh / *adj.* & *pron.* not either (*neither of them likes it*). • *adv.* & *conj.* **1** not either (*she neither knew nor cared*). **2** also not (*you don't know and neither do I*). □ **be neither here nor there** be of no importance or relevance.

nelia / nee-lee-uh / *n.* any of several small wattles of inland Australia. (¶ Ngiyambaa)

nelly *n.* □ **nervous Nelly** *Aust.* a timid or cautious person. **not on your nelly** *colloq.* certainly not.

nelson *n.* a hold in wrestling in which the arm is passed under the opponent's arm from behind and the hand applied to the neck (**half nelson**), or both arms and hands are applied (**full nelson**).

nematode / nem-uh-tohd / *n.* a worm with a slender unsegmented cylindrical shape.

nem. con. *adv.* unanimously. (¶ From the Latin *nemine contradicente* = with nobody disagreeing.)

nemesis / nem-uh-suhs / *n.* (*pl.* **nemeses** / -seez /) **1** the infliction of deserved and unavoidable punishment. **2** a person who brings this about (*he was my nemesis*). (¶ Named after Nemesis, goddess of retribution in Greek mythology.)

neo- *comb. form* new, recent, a new form of (*neo-fascism; neo-Nazis*).

neoclassical *adj.* of or in a style of art, literature, or music that is based on or influenced by classical style. □ **neoclassicism** *n.*

neodymium / nee-uh-**dim**-ee-uhm / *n.* a metallic element (symbol Nd), used in certain alloys.

neolithic / nee-uh-**lith**-ik / *adj.* of the later part of the Stone Age.

neologism / nee-**ol**-uh-jiz-uhm / *n.* a newly coined word ('*hairologist*' *for* '*barber*' *is a barbarous neologism*).

neo-mort *n.* a person who is brain-dead but whose other organs (heart, lungs, etc.) are kept artificially functioning.

neon / **nee**-on / *n.* a chemical element (symbol Ne), a kind of gas used in illuminated signs because it glows orange-red when electricity is passed through it.

neonatal *adj.* of or for the newly born.

neophyte / nee-uh-fuyt / *n.* **1** a new convert. **2** (in the Catholic Church) a novice of a religious order. **3** a beginner.

Nepal / nuh-**pawl** / a kingdom north-east of India. □ **Nepalese** / nep-uh-**leez** / *adj.* & *n.* (*pl.* **Nepalese**).

Nepean / nuh-**pee**-uhn / a river, 145 km long, forming part of the Hawkesbury River system, NSW.

nepenthes / nuh-**pen**-theez / *n.* an insectivorous pitcher plant of wet places in northern Qld, having very large pitchers up to 20 cm in length.

nephew / **nev**-yoo, **nef**- / *n.* the son of one's brother or sister or of one's spouse's brother or sister.

nephritic *adj.* **1** of or in the kidneys. **2** of nephritis.

nephritis / nuh-**fruy**-tuhs / *n.* inflammation of the kidneys.

ne plus ultra / nay / *n.* the furthest point attainable; the acme of a thing's perfection (*that ne plus ultra of my childhood—skinny dipping in the sea*). (¶ Latin, = not beyond this point.)

nepotism / **nep**-uh-tiz-uhm / *n.* favouritism shown to relatives in appointing them to jobs.

Neptune 1 *Rom. myth.* the god of water and of the sea, identified with the sea god Poseidon. **2** the third-largest of the planets.

neptunium / nep-**tyoo**-nee-uhm / *n.* a radio-active metallic element (symbol Np).

nerd *n. colloq.* a foolish, feeble, or uninteresting person.

nereid / **neer**-ree-uhd / *n.* (*pl.* **nereides** / nuh-**ree**-uh-deez /) a sea nymph.

Nero (AD 37–68), Roman emperor AD 54–68.

nerve *n.* **1** any of the fibres or bundles of fibres carrying impulses of sensation or of movement between the brain or spinal cord and all parts of the body. **2** courage, coolness in danger (*lose one's nerve*). **3** *colloq.* impudent boldness (*had the nerve to ask for more*). **4** (**nerves**) nervousness; a condition in which a person suffers from mental stress and easily becomes anxious or upset. • *v.* **1** brace (oneself) to face danger etc. (*nerved himself for the ordeal*). **2** give strength, vigour, or courage to. □ **nerve centre** a centre of control from which instructions are sent out. **nerve gas** a poison gas that affects the nervous system. **nerve-racking** inflicting great mental strain.

nerveless *adj.* **1** incapable of effort or movement (*the knife fell from his nerveless fingers*). **2** confident, not nervous (*she seemed quite nerveless as she climbed Mt Arapiles*).

nervous *adj.* **1** of the nerves or nervous system (*a nervous disorder*). **2** excitable, easily agitated; timid. **3** uneasy (*a nervous laugh*). ☐ **nervous breakdown** a period of loss of mental and emotional stability. **nervous system** the system of nerves throughout the body. ☐☐ **nervously** *adv.* **nervousness** *n.*

nervy *adj.* (**nervier**, **nerviest**) nervous, easily agitated, uneasy. ☐ **nerviness** *n.*

NESB *abbr.* non-English-speaking background.

nescient / **nes**-ee-uhnt / *adj. literary* (foll. by *of*) not having knowledge (of a specified thing). ☐ **nescience** *n.*

nest *n.* **1** a structure or place in which a bird lays its eggs and shelters its young. **2** a place where certain creatures (e.g. mice, wasps) live, or produce and keep their young. **3** a snug place. **4** a secluded shelter or retreat. **5** a place fostering something undesirable (*a nest of vice*). **6** a set of similar articles designed to fit inside each other in a series (*a nest of tables*). • *v.* **1** make or have a nest. **2** (of objects) fit together or inside one another. **3** *Computing* make (a set of procedures, commands, etc.) operate within each other in a program. **4** take wild birds' nests or eggs (*arrested while nesting in the bush*). ☐ **nest egg** a sum of money saved for future use.

nestle *v.* **1** curl up or press oneself comfortably into a soft place. **2** press oneself against another in affection. **3** lie half-hidden or sheltered.

nestling *n.* a bird too young to leave the nest.

net¹ *n.* **1** open-work material of thread, cord, wire, etc. woven or joined at intervals. **2** a piece of this used for a particular purpose, e.g. covering or protecting something, catching fish, dividing a tennis court, or surrounding a goal. **3** = NETWORK. **4** (also *adj.*) (of) the Internet. • *v.* (**netted**, **netting**) **1** cover, catch, or confine with or as if with a net. **2** hit (a ball) into the net, esp. of a goal.

net² *adj.* (also **nett**) **1** remaining when nothing more is to be taken away. **2** (of an effect etc.) positive, excluding unimportant effects or those that cancel each other out (*the net result*). • *v.* (**netted**, **netting**) obtain or yield as net profit. ☐ **net profit** profit after tax etc. has been deducted. **net weight** the weight of contents only, excluding wrapping.

netball *n.* a team game in which a ball has to be thrown so that it falls into a net hanging from a ring on a high post.

nether / **neth**-uh / *adj. archaic* lower. ☐ **nether regions** (*or* **world**) hell; the underworld.

Netherlands, the a kingdom (often called Holland) in Europe. ☐ **Netherlander** *n.*

netiquette / **net**-uh-kuht / *n.* the unwritten code governing the customary behaviour of users of the Internet. (¶ Blend of INTERNET + ETIQUETTE.)

netizen *n.* a person who uses the Internet, esp. a habitual or keen one. (¶ Blend of INTERNET + CITIZEN.)

Netscape *n. trademark* a browser used to access and display documents on the World Wide Web.

netsurf *v.* spend time exploring various sites on the Internet.

nett alternative spelling of NET².

netting *n.* fabric of netted thread, cord, wire, etc.

nettle *n.* a common wild plant with hairs on its leaves that sting and redden the skin when they are touched. • *v.* irritate, provoke. ☐ **nettle rash** an eruption on the skin with red patches like those made by nettle stings.

network *n.* **1** an arrangement or pattern with intersecting lines (*a network of railways*). **2** a chain of people connected professionally or socially (*a spy network*). **3** a group of broadcasting stations connected for the simultaneous broadcast of a program. **4** a chain of interconnected computers. **5** a system of connected electrical conductors. • *v.* **1** broadcast on a network. **2** establish contact with other people, groups, etc. (esp. through a computer network) for the interchange of ideas or information or for the pleasure of personal contact.

neume / nyoom / *n.* (also **neum**) *Music* a sign in plainsong indicating a note or group of notes to be sung to a syllable.

neural / **nyoo**-ruhl / *adj.* of nerves.

neuralgia / nyoo-**ral**-juh / *n.* sharp intermittent pain along the course of a nerve, esp. in the head or face. ☐ **neuralgic** *adj.*

neurasthenia / nyoo-ruhs-**thee**-nee-uh / *n.* a general (not medical) term for lasting fatigue, listlessness, emotional disturbance, etc. ☐ **neurasthenic** *adj. & n.*

neuritis / nyoo-**ruy**-tuhs / *n.* inflammation of a nerve or nerves.

neuro- / **nyoo**-roh / *comb. form* a nerve or the nerves.

neurology / nyoo-**rol**-uh-jee / *n.* the scientific study of nerve systems and their diseases. ☐ **neurological** *adj.* **neurologist** *n.*

neuron / **nyoo**-ron / *n.* (also **neurone** / **nyoo**-rohn /) a nerve cell.

neurosis / nyoo-**roh**-suhs / *n.* (*pl.* **neuroses**) a mental disorder producing depression or abnormal behaviour.

neurosurgery *n.* surgery performed on the nervous system. ☐ **neurosurgeon** *n.* **neurosurgical** *adj.*

neurotic / nyoo-**rot**-ik / *adj.* **1** of or caused by a neurosis. **2** *colloq.* (of a person) subject to abnormal anxieties or obsessive behaviour. • *n.* a neurotic person. ☐ **neurotically** *adv.*

neurotransmitter *n.* a chemical substance released from a nerve fibre that effects the transfer of an impulse to another nerve or muscle.

neuter / nyoo-tuh / *adj.* **1** (of a noun) neither masculine nor feminine. **2** (of plants) without male or female parts. **3** (of insects) sexually undeveloped, sterile. • *n.* **1** a neuter word. **2** a neuter plant or insect. **3** a non-fertile or castrated animal. • *v.* castrate.

neutral *adj.* **1** not supporting or assisting either side in a dispute or conflict. **2** belonging to a country or person etc. that is neutral (*neutral ships*). **3** having no positive or distinctive characteristics; not definitely one thing or the other. **4** sexually undeveloped; asexual. **5** (of colours) not strong or positive; grey or beige. **6** (of a gear) in which the engine is disconnected from the moving parts. **7** *Chem.* neither acid nor alkaline. **8** *Electricity* neither positive nor negative. • *n.* **1** a neutral person or country; one who is a subject of a neutral country. **2** grey or beige colour. **3** neutral gear. ☐ **neutrally** *adv.* **neutrality** / nyoo-**tral**-uh-tee / *n.*

neutralise *v.* (also **-ize**) **1** make neutral. **2** make ineffective by means of an opposite force or effect. **3** exempt or exclude (a place) from hostilities. ☐ **neutralisation** *n.*

neutrino / nyoo-**tree**-noh / *n.* (*pl.* **neutrinos**) elementary particle with zero electric charge and probably zero mass.

neutron / **nyoo**-tron / *n.* an elementary particle of about the same mass as a proton but with no electric charge, present in the nuclei of all atoms except those of ordinary hydrogen. ☐ **neutron bomb** a nuclear bomb that kills people by intense radiation but does little damage to buildings etc.

never *adv.* **1** at no time, on no occasion. **2** not at all (*never fear*). **3** *colloq.* surely not (*you never left the key in the lock!*). **4** not (*never a care in the world*). • *interj. colloq.* surely not.

nevermore *adv.* at no future time.

never-never *n.* **1** *Aust.* the far interior of Australia; the remote outback. **2** *colloq.* hire purchase. • *adj. Aust.* of the remote outback of Australia (*never-never country*). ☐ **on the never-never** *colloq.* on the hire purchase system (*bought all their furniture on the never-never*).

nevertheless *adv.* & *conj.* in spite of this.

Nevin, Robyn (Anne) (1942–), AM, Australian stage, film, and television actor.

new *adj.* **1** of recent origin or arrival (*a New Australian*). **2** not existing before; recently made, invented, discovered, or experienced. **3** still in original condition; not worn or used. **4** renewed; reformed; reinvigorated (*a new life; the new order; felt like a new man*). **5** unfamiliar, unaccustomed (*it was new to me; I am new to the job*). **6** recently changed or renewed, different (*the new manager*). **7** (in place names) discovered or founded later than and named after (*New South Wales*). • *adv.* newly, recently, just (*new-laid*). • *n. Aust.* a light beer, made by the bottom fermentation method and so called because it was regarded as a 'new' style when introduced (cf. OLD *n.*). ☐ **new blood** a new member or members admitted to a society, company, etc. **new broom** *see* BROOM. **new chum** *Aust.* **1** *hist.* a convict newly arrived in Australia. **2** *hist.* a newly arrived colonist to Australia (as opposed to an OLD CHUM). **3** (of the present) an immigrant to Australia who has newly arrived. **4** a novice; a person inexperienced in something. **new economy** an economy based primarily on information technology, esp. the Internet. Cf. OLD ECONOMY. **new moon** the moon when it is seen in the evening as a crescent; (on calendars) the precise moment when the moon is in conjunction with the sun and is not visible. **new style** dating reckoned by the Gregorian Calendar. **new year** the first few days of January. ☐ ☐ **newish** *adj.* **newness** *n.*

New Age *n.* a set of beliefs replacing traditional Western culture with alternative approaches to religion, medicine, the environment, etc. • *adj.* (also **new age**) of or pertaining to the New Age. ☐ **New Ageist** *n.* **New Ager** *n.*

New Australian *n.* an immigrant to Australia, esp. one whose first language is not English. • *adj.* of or pertaining to New Australians.

newbie / **nyoo**-bee / *n. colloq.* a person who is new to an occupation, activity, etc., esp. a person new to the Internet or computing.

New Caledonia an island east of Australia in the SW Pacific, in French possession.

Newcombe, John (David) ('Newk') (1944–), AO, Australian tennis player who was Wimbledon champion in 1967, 1970, and 1971. He was non-playing coach of the Australian Davis Cup team 1994–2000.

newcomer *n.* a person who has recently arrived or started an activity.

newel / **nyoo**-uhl / *n.* **1** (also **newel post**) a post that supports the handrail of a stair at the top or bottom of a staircase. **2** the centre pillar of a winding stair.

New England **1** an extensive tableland area (about 27,000 sq. km) of northern NSW averaging about 1,000 metres above sea level. **2** an area on the NE coast of the US.

newfangled *adj. derog.* objectionably new in method or style.

New Guinea an island in the western South Pacific, off the north coast of Australia, the second largest island in the world (following Greenland). It is divided into two parts; the western half comprises part of Irian Jaya, a province of Indonesia, the eastern half forms part of the country of Papua New Guinea.

New Holland *hist.* the name formerly given to the Australian continent (or any part of it), sometimes including Tas. ☐ **New Holland honeyeater** a honeyeater of southern mainland

Australia and Tas., having black and white plumage with bright yellow on the wings and tail.

newie *n. Aust. colloq.* **1** = NEW CHUM (senses 3 & 4). **2** anything new (*sold his car and bought a newie*).

newly *adv.* recently, freshly.

New Right *n.* a loose association of right-wing organisations and individuals advocating extreme free-market policies, reductions in government expenditure on social welfare etc., privatisation of public services, curtailment of trade unionism, etc.

news *n.* **1** information about recent events. **2** a broadcast report of this. **3** newsworthy information (*when a man bites a dog, that's news*). **4** (foll. by *to*) information not previously known (to a person) (*that's news to me*). ❏ **news agency** an organisation that collects and distributes news items.

newsagent *n.* a shopkeeper who sells newspapers. ❏ **newsagency** *n.*

newscast *n.* a broadcast news report. ❏ **newscaster** *n.*

newsflash *n.* a single item of important news, broadcast urgently and often interrupting other programs.

newsgroup *n.* a topic-based group on the Internet to which users subscribe and then receive all mail on the particular topic.

newsletter *n.* an informal printed report giving information that is of interest to members of a club etc.

New South Wales the most populous State in Australia. ❏ **New South Wales Christmas bush** a highly decorative shrub with white flowers, the calyx lobes of which enlarge and turn bright red in summer. **New South Welshman** a native of or resident in the State of New South Wales.

newspaper *n.* **1** a printed publication, usu. issued daily or weekly, containing news reports, advertisements, articles on various subjects, etc. **2** the sheets of paper forming this (*wrapped it in newspaper*).

newspeak / **nyoo**-speek / *n.* ambiguous euphemistic language used esp. in political propaganda. (¶ The name of an artificial official language in George Orwell's *Nineteen Eighty-Four*.)

newsprint *n.* low-quality paper on which newspapers are printed.

newsreader *n.* a person who reads out broadcast news bulletins.

newsreel *n.* a short cinema film of recent events.

newsworthy *adj.* important or interesting enough to be mentioned as news.

newsy *adj. colloq.* full of news.

newt / nyoot / *n.* a small lizard-like creature of Europe that can live in water or on land.

New Testament *n. see* TESTAMENT.

Newton[1], Bert (full name: Albert Watson Newton) (1938–), Australian television compere and entertainer.

Newton[2], Sir Isaac (1642–1727), English mathematician and physicist, the greatest single influence on theoretical physics until Einstein.

newton *n.* a unit of force. (¶ Named after Sir Isaac Newton.)

Newton-John, Olivia (1948–), Australian singer of country and pop. She has also acted in films, notably in *Grease*.

new wave *n.* **1** a new trend etc. which discards established ideas in the arts, fashion, religion, etc. **2** (**New Wave**) a style of rock music which grew out of punk rock and developed a more sophisticated character of its own. • *adj.* **1** of such a new trend (*a new wave marriage ceremony*). **2** belonging to such a style of rock music.

New World *n.* the Americas.

New Year's Day *n.* 1 January.

New Year's Eve *n.* 31 December.

New Zealand a nation in the South Pacific east of Australia, consisting of two major islands and several smaller ones. ❏ **New Zealander** *n.*

next *adj.* **1** lying, living, or being nearest to something. **2** coming nearest in order, time, or sequence; soonest encountered (*ask the next person you meet*). • *adv.* **1** in the nearest place or degree (*place yours next to mine*). **2** on the first or soonest occasion (*when next we meet*). • *n.* the next person or thing. ❏ **next door** in the next house or room. **next-door** *adj.* living or situated next door (*my next-door neighbour*). **next of kin** one's closest relative. **next to** almost (*next to nothing left*).

nexus *n.* (*pl.* **nexus**) **1** a bond, link, or connection. **2** a connected group or series.

Ngaanyatjara / **ngah**-nyah-jah-ru / *n.* a dialect of the WESTERN DESERT LANGUAGE.

Ngamini / **ngah**-min-ee / *n.* an Aboriginal language of the region of Goyder's Lagoon, SA.

Ngarigo / **ngah**-rig-oh / *n.* an Aboriginal language of an area stretching from Canberra through Cooma and the Monaro district, over the Snowy Mountains to Omeo in Vic.

Ngarluma / **ngahr**-loo-mu / *n.* an Aboriginal language of the north-west region of WA.

Ngiyambaa / **ngyem**-pu / *n.* an Aboriginal language of the region around the Bogan, Lachlan, and Darling Rivers of NSW.

Ngunnawal / **nun**-uh-wul / *n.* an Aboriginal language of the ACT and an area of NSW to the north of the ACT.

Nhangka / **nahng**-ku / *n.* an Aboriginal language of southern SA.

Nhanta / **nhahn**-tu / *n.* an Aboriginal language of the Geraldton region of WA.

Ni *symbol* nickel.

niacin = NICOTINIC ACID.

Niagara a river forming the US–Canada border between Lakes Erie and Ontario, famous for its spectacular waterfalls.

Niamey / nyah-**may** / the capital of Niger.

nib *n.* the point of a pen.

nibble *v.* **1** take small quick or gentle bites. **2** eat in small amounts (*don't nibble between meals*). **3** show interest in (an offer etc.) but without being definite. • *n.* **1** a small quick bite. **2** a very small amount of food. **3** (**nibbles**) cautious expressions of interest, esp. in something offered for sale. **4** *Computing* half a byte (four 'bits') of information. ◻ **nibbler** *n.*

nibblies *n.pl. Aust. colloq.* titbits as snacks; munchies.

Nibelungenlied / **nee**-buh-luung-uhn-leet / a 13th-century Germanic poem telling of the life and death of Siegfried, a prince of the Netherlands.

nibs *n.* ◻ **his nibs** *colloq.* a mock title used with reference to an important or self-important person.

nicad / **nuy**-kad / *adj.* nickel and cadmium. • *n.* a nickel and cadmium battery.

Nicaragua / nik-uh-**rah**-gwuh, -**rag**-yoo-uh / a republic in Central America. ◻ **Nicaraguan** *adj. & n.*

nice *adj.* **1** pleasant, satisfactory. **2** (of a person) kind, good-natured. **3** *ironically* difficult, bad (*this is a nice mess*). **4** fine or subtle (*nice distinctions*). **5** fastidious. ◻ **nicely** *adv.* **niceness** *n.*

Nicene Creed / **nuy**-seen / *n.* a formal statement of Christian belief based on that adopted at the Council of Nicaea (AD 325).

nicety / **nuy**-suh-tee / *n.* **1** a subtle distinction or detail. **2** precision. ◻ **to a nicety** exactly.

niche / neesh / *n.* **1** a shallow recess, esp. in a wall. **2** a position in life or employment to which the holder is well suited (*has found his niche*). **3** a position from which an entrepreneur exploits a gap in the market; a profitable corner of the market.

Nicholls, Sir Douglas (Ralph) (1906–88), Australian Aboriginal pastor and spokesman for Aborigines, governor of South Australia 1976–77.

Nicholson, Jack (full name: John Joseph Nicholson) (1937–), American actor. He won best actor Oscars for *One Flew Over the Cuckoo's Nest* (1975) and *As Good As It Gets* (1997).

nick *n.* **1** a small cut or notch. **2** *colloq.* a prison. **3** *colloq.* condition (*it's in good nick*). • *v.* **1** make a nick in. **2** *colloq.* steal. **3** *colloq.* catch or arrest (a criminal). **4** *Aust. colloq.* go (somewhere) on the spur of the moment; slip (away, out, etc.), esp. for a short while (*I'll nick over to the milk bar*). ◻ **get nicked!** *Aust. colloq.* get lost!. **in the nick of time** only just in time. **nick off** *Aust. colloq.* depart.

nick off! *Aust. colloq.* clear out!, scram!

nickel *n.* **1** a chemical element (symbol Ni), a hard silvery-white metal used in alloys. **2** *US* a 5-cent coin. ◻ **nickel silver** an alloy of nickel, zinc, and copper. **nickel steel** a type of stainless steel with chromium and nickel.

nickname *n.* a familiar or humorous name given to a person or thing instead of or as well as the real name. • *v.* give a nickname to.

Nicosia / nik-uh-**see**-uh / the capital of Cyprus.

nicotine / **nik**-uh-teen, -tin / *n.* a poisonous alkaloid found in tobacco. ◻ **nicotinic acid** a vitamin of the B group obtained from nicotine.

nictitate *v.* blink. ◻ **nictitating membrane** a transparent third eyelid in amphibians, birds, and some other animals. ◻ **nictitation** *n.*

niece *n.* the daughter of one's brother or sister or of one's spouse's brother or sister.

Nietzsche / **nee**-chuh /, Friedrich Wilhelm (1844–1900), German philosopher of Polish descent, who divided mankind into a small dominant 'master-class' and a large dominated 'herd'.

nifty *adj. colloq.* **1** smart, stylish. **2** excellent, clever.

Niger 1 / **nuy**-jer / a river of West Africa, flowing into the Gulf of Guinea. **2** / nee-**zhair** / a landlocked republic of West Africa, lying mainly in the Sahara.

Nigeria a federal republic in West Africa. ◻ **Nigerian** *adj. & n.*

niggard *n.* a stingy person. ◻ **niggardly** / nig-uhd-lee / *adj.* **niggardliness** *n.*

nigger *n.* **1** *offens.* a black or dark-skinned person. **2** *Aust.* = LUDERICK.

niggerhead *n. Aust.* **1** a large (frequently blackened and rounded) block of coral deposited on a reef by a storm. **2** a kind of small, tufted grass of mainland Australia, having blackish seed heads.

niggle *v.* **1** fuss over details, find fault in a petty way. **2** nag. • *n.* **1** a trifling complaint or criticism; a worry or an annoyance. **2** a twinge of pain (*a niggle in my tooth*). ◻ **niggling** *adj.* **niggly** *adj.*

nigh / nuy / *adv. & prep. archaic* near.

night *n.* **1** the dark hours between sunset and sunrise. **2** nightfall. **3** darkness of night. **4** a specified or appointed night; an evening on which a performance or other activity occurs (*the first night of the play*). ◻ **night-life** entertainment available in a city at night. **night parrot** a rare, nocturnal, ground-dwelling parrot of arid and semi-arid Australia, having predominantly green, yellow, and black plumage. **night school** classes provided in the evening for people who are at work during the day.

nightcap *n.* **1** *hist.* a soft cap for wearing in bed. **2** an alcoholic or hot drink taken at bedtime.

nightclub *n.* a club that is open at night, providing food, drink, and entertainment.

nightdress *n.* a woman's or child's loose garment for wearing in bed.

nightfall *n.* the coming of darkness at the end of the day.

nightgown *n.* a nightdress or nightshirt.

nightie *n. colloq.* a nightdress.

Nightingale, Florence (1820–1910), British nurse and medical reformer who became famous

nightingale during the Crimean War, where she became known as the 'Lady of the Lamp'.

nightingale *n.* a small reddish-brown European thrush, the male of which sings melodiously, esp. at night.

nightjar *n.* any of various night-flying birds, esp. the spotted nightjar and the owlet nightjar of Australia.

nightly *adj.* **1** happening, done, or existing etc. in the night. **2** happening every night. • *adv.* every night.

nightmare *n.* **1** a bad dream. **2** *colloq.* a terrifying or very unpleasant experience. ❒ **nightmarish** *adj.*

nightshade *n.* any of several wild plants with poisonous berries, esp. 'deadly nightshade' from which the drug atropine is extracted.

nightshirt *n.* a long shirt for wearing in bed by men or boys.

nightspot *n.* a nightclub.

nightwatchman *n.* **1** a person employed to keep watch at night in a building that is closed. **2** *Cricket* an inferior batsman sent in when a wicket falls near the close of a day's play.

nihilism / nuy-uh-liz-uhm / *n.* **1** rejection of all religious and moral principles. **2** the theory that nothing has real existence. ❒ **nihilist** *n.* **nihilistic** *adj.*

Nijinsky / nuh-*zh*in-skee /, Vaslav Fomich (1890–1950), Russian dancer and choreographer.

-nik *suffix* forming nouns denoting a person associated with a specified thing or quality (*beatnik*; *refusenik*).

Nikkei index / **nik**-ay / *n.* an index of shares traded on the Tokyo Stock Exchange.

nil *n.* nothing.

Niland, D' Arcy (Francis) (1917–67), Australian writer and journalist, esp. known for his novel *The Shiralee*.

Nile a river flowing from east central Africa through Egypt to the Mediterranean Sea.

nimble *adj.* **1** able to move quickly, agile. **2** (of the mind or wits) able to think quickly. ❒ **nimbly** *adv.* **nimbleness** *n.*

nimbus *n.* (*pl.* **nimbi** or **nimbuses**) **1** the halo of a saint etc. **2** a rain cloud.

nimby *adj.* selfishly objecting to the siting of unpleasant developments (new prisons, hospitals, airports, etc.) in one's own locality, although happy to have them sited elsewhere. • *n.* a person who objects in this way. (¶ From the initials of *not in my back yard*.)

nincompoop *n.* a foolish person.

nine 1 *adj.* & *n.* one more than eight (9, IX). **2** *n.* (also **niner**) a keg formerly containing nine gallons of beer, now 40.5 litres. ❒ **dressed** (**up**) **to the nines** dressed very elaborately.

ninefold *adj.* & *n.* **1** nine times as much or as many. **2** consisting of nine parts.

ninepins *n.* the game of skittles played with nine objects to be knocked down by rolling a ball.

nineteen *adj.* & *n.* one more than eighteen (19, XIX). ❒ **talk nineteen to the dozen** *see* DOZEN. ❒❒ **nineteenth** *adj.* & *n.*

ninety *adj.* & *n.* **1** nine times ten (90, XC). **2** (**nineties**) the numbers from 90 to 99, esp. the years of a century or of a person's life. ❒ **ninetieth** *adj.* & *n.*

Nineveh / **nin**-uh-vuh / the capital of Assyria from *c.*700 BC to 612 BC.

ningaui / ning-**gow**-ee / *n.* any of three species of very small marsupials of the genus *Ningaui* of dry inland Australia. (¶ Tiwi)

ning-nong *n.* esp. *Aust. colloq.* a fool.

ninja (also **Ninja**) *n.* a Japanese warrior trained in 'ninjutsu', the art of stealth or invisibility which was developed in feudal Japan and later practised more widely as a martial art. • *adj.* of the ninjas or their techniques.

ninny *n.* a foolish person.

ninth *adj.* & *n.* **1** next after eighth. **2** one of nine equal parts of a thing. ❒ **ninthly** *adv.*

niobium / nuy-**oh**-bee-uhm / *n.* a metallic element (symbol Nb) used in alloys.

Nip *n. colloq. offens.* a Japanese person.

nip[1] *v.* (**nipped**, **nipping**) **1** pinch or squeeze sharply; bite quickly with the front teeth. **2** (often foll. by *off*) break off by doing this (*nip off the side-shoots*). **3** pain or harm with biting cold (*a nipping wind*). **4** *colloq.* go quickly (*nip down to the milk bar*). **5** (foll. by *over*) *colloq.* pay a short visit (to) (*nip over for a chat*). **6** *Aust. colloq.* cadge (*nipped him for a loan*) (*see* BITE *n.* & *v.*). • *n.* **1** a sharp pinch, squeeze, or bite. **2** biting coldness (*a nip in the air*). ❒ **nip and tuck 1** neck and neck. **2** (in a game) with one team matching the other's scores throughout. **3** a cosmetic surgical operation. **nip in the bud** destroy at an early stage of development.

nip[2] *n.* a small drink of spirits.

nipper *n.* **1** *colloq.* a young child. **2** *Aust. colloq.* a youth employed to do odd jobs (e.g. tea-making) in a labouring gang. **3** the claw of a crab etc.; any of several small shrimp-like burrowing shellfish used as bait. **4** (**nippers**) pincers or forceps for gripping or cutting things. **5** *Aust.* a junior lifesaver.

nipple *n.* **1** a small projection in the centre of a male or female mammal's breasts, containing (in females) the outlets of the milk-secreting organs. **2** the teat of a feeding bottle. **3** a nipple-like projection.

Nipponese / nip-uh-**neez** / *adj.* & *n.* (*pl.* **Nipponese**) Japanese.

nippy *adj. colloq.* **1** nimble, quick. **2** bitingly cold. ❒ **nippiness** *n.*

nirvana / ner-**vah**-nuh, neer- / *n.* the final goal of Buddhism, a transcendent state in which there is no suffering, no desire, no sense of self (*atman*), with release from the effects of karma.

Nissen hut *n.* a tunnel-shaped hut of corrugated iron with a cement floor.

nit [1] *n.* **1** the egg of a louse or other parasite; the insect laying this. **2** *colloq.* a stupid person. ◻ **nit-picking** fault-finding in a petty way.

nit [2] *interj. Aust. colloq.* used as a warning that someone is approaching. ◻ **keep nit** keep watch; act as guard. ◻◻ **nitkeeper** *n.*

nitrate *n.* / nuy-trayt / **1** a salt or ester of nitric acid. **2** potassium or sodium nitrate used as a fertiliser. • *v.* / nuy-**trayt** / treat, combine, or impregnate with nitric acid. ◻ **nitration** *n.*

nitre / nuy-tuh / *n.* saltpetre.

nitric / **nuy**-trik / *adj.* of or containing nitrogen. ◻ **nitric acid** a colourless caustic highly corrosive acid.

nitride *n.* a binary compound of nitrogen.

nitrify *v.* **1** impregnate with nitrogen. **2** convert into nitrites or nitrates. ◻ **nitrification** *n.*

nitrite *n.* any salt or ester of nitrous acid.

nitrobenzene / nuy-truh-**ben**-zeen / *n.* a poisonous yellow oil used as a solvent and in making certain dyes.

nitrogen / **nuy**-truh-juhn / *n.* a chemical element (symbol N), a colourless odourless gas forming about four-fifths of the atmosphere. ◻ **nitrogenous** / nuy-**troj**-uh-nuhs / *adj.*

nitroglycerine / nuy-troh-**glis**-uh-reen, -ruhn / *n.* a powerful explosive made by adding glycerine to a mixture of nitric and sulphuric acids.

nitrous / **nuy**-truhs / *adj.* of or containing nitrogen. ◻ **nitrous oxide** a colourless gas used as an anaesthetic, laughing-gas.

nitty-gritty *n. colloq.* the basic facts or realities of a matter.

nitwit *n. colloq.* a stupid person.

nix *colloq. n.* **1** nothing. **2** a denial or a refusal. • *v.* cancel; reject (*the board nixed the project*).

Nixon, Richard (Milhous) (1913–94), 37th president of the USA 1969–74, the first president to resign from office (as a result of the Watergate scandal).

No [1] *symbol* nobelium.

No [2] alternative spelling of NOH.

No. *abbr.* (also **no.**) number.

no *adj.* **1** not any (*there is no excuse*). **2** not a, quite other than (*she is no fool*). **3** hardly any (*did it in no time*). • *adv.* **1** used as a denial or refusal of something. **2** not at all (*no better than before*). • *n.* (*pl.* **noes**) **1** a denial or refusal. **2** (**noes**) 'no' voters or votes (*the noes have it*). ◻ **no-ball** *Cricket* an unlawfully delivered ball. **no-claim** (*or* **no-claims**) **bonus** a reduction of an insurance premium after an agreed period without a claim. **no-go area** an area to which entry is forbidden to certain people or groups. **no-hoper** *orig. Aust. colloq.* an incompetent person, a failure. **no man's land** an area not firmly assigned to any one owner; a space between the fronts of two opposing armies in war. **no-name** designating a product not sold under a company's brand name (*a tin of no-name asparagus tips*). **no-no** *n. colloq.* something that is to be avoided at all costs, that is completely 'not on' (*smoking in a restaurant ought to be a no-no*). **no one** no person, nobody. **no way** *colloq.* **1** that is impossible. **2** I will not agree etc. **no-win** *adj.* designating a situation in which success is impossible (cf. WIN-WIN).

Noah 1 a Hebrew patriarch, said to have made the ark which saved his family and specimens of every animal from the flood sent by God to destroy the world. **2** *Aust. colloq.* a shark. (¶ Sense 2 is an abbreviation of *Noah's ark*, rhyming slang.)

nob *colloq. n.* **1** the head. **2** a person of wealth or high social position. **3** a two-headed coin, esp. in the game of two-up.

nobble *v. colloq.* **1** tamper with (a racehorse) to prevent its winning. **2** try to influence (e.g. a jury or judge) by underhand means. **3** steal. **4** seize, catch.

nobbler *n. Aust. colloq.* a measure of spirits or the glass in which this is served.

nobby *n. Aust.* an irregularly shaped opal. • *adj.* (of a beast) lean, and therefore having protuberant bones, joints, etc.

nobelium / noh-**bee**-lee-uhm / *n.* a radioactive metallic element (symbol No).

Nobel prize / noh-**bel** / any of six international prizes awarded annually for outstanding achievements in physics, chemistry, physiology or medicine, literature, economics, and the promotion of peace, from the bequest of Alfred Nobel (1833–96), the Swedish inventor of dynamite.

nobility / noh-**bil**-uh-tee / *n.* **1** nobleness of mind, character, behaviour, etc. **2** (**the nobility**) (in Britain etc.) titled people.

noble *adj.* **1** possessing excellent qualities, esp. character; free from pettiness or meanness. **2** imposing in appearance (*a noble edifice*). **3** belonging to the aristocracy. • *n.* a nobleman or noblewoman. ◻ **noble gas** any of a group of gaseous elements that almost never combine with other elements. ◻◻ **nobleness** *n.* **nobly** *adv.*

nobleman *n.* (*feminine* **noblewoman**) a member of the nobility.

noblesse oblige / noh-bles oh-**bleezh** / privilege entails responsibility. (¶ French.)

nobody *pron.* no person. • *n.* a person of no importance.

nock *n.* a notch on a bow or arrow for the bow-string. • *v.* set an arrow to the bowstring.

nocturn / **nok**-tern / *n. Catholic Church* a part of matins originally said at night.

nocturnal / nok-**ter**-nuhl / *adj.* **1** of or in the night. **2** active in the night (*nocturnal animals*). ◻ **nocturnal emission** an involuntary ejaculation of semen during sleep at night. ◻◻ **nocturnally** *adv.*

nocturne / **nok**-tern / *n.* a short romantic piece of music.

nod *v.* (**nodded**, **nodding**) **1** move the head down and up again quickly as a sign of agreement or casual greeting; indicate (agreement etc.) in this

node 562 **nonconformist**

way. **2** let the head fall forward in drowsiness; be drowsy. **3** (of plumes, flowers, etc.) bend downwards and sway. **4** make a mistake due to a momentary lack of alertness. • *n.* a nodding movement in agreement or greeting. □ **a nodding acquaintance** a slight acquaintance with a person or subject. **get the nod** be chosen or approved. **give the nod to** approve; permit. **land of Nod** sleep. **nodding blue lily** see STYPANDRA. **nodding greenhood** an Australian orchid, commonest of the greenhoods, having large, nodding, translucent, pale green flowers striped a deeper green, with crimson at the tips. **nod off** fall asleep.

node *n.* **1** a knob-like swelling. **2** the point on the stem of a plant where a leaf or bud grows out. **3** either of two points at which a planet's orbit intersects the plane of the ecliptic or the celestial equator. **4** the point of minimum disturbance in a standing wave system. **5** a point at which a curve intersects itself. **6** a component in a computer network. □ **nodal** *adj.*

nodule / **nod**-yool, **noj**-ool / *n.* a small rounded lump, a small node. □ **nodular** *adj.*

Noel / noh-**el** / *n.* (in carols) Christmas.

nog[1] *n.* an egg-flip.

nog[2] *n. Aust. colloq. offens.* an Asian, originally a Vietnamese soldier.

noggin *n.* **1** a small mug. **2** a small measure of alcohol, usu. ¼ pint. **3** *colloq.* the head.

nogging *n.* brickwork in a wooden frame.

Noh / noh / *n.* (also **No**) a form of traditional Japanese drama.

noise *n.* **1** a sound, esp. one that is loud, harsh, or confused or undesired. **2** (in *plural*) conventional remarks; speechlike sounds without actual words (*made sympathetic noises*). • *v.* make public (*noised it abroad*). □ **noiseless** *adj.* **noiselessly** *adv.*

noisette / nwah-**zet** / *n.* a small round piece of meat etc. (¶ French)

noisome / **noi**-suhm / *adj. literary* **1** harmful. **2** evil-smelling; objectionable.

noisy *adj.* (**noisier, noisiest**) making much noise; full of noise (*noisy kids; a noisy street*). □ **noisy friar bird** see LEATHERHEAD. **noisy miner** an eastern Australian honeyeater, a mostly grey and white bird with black face-markings, and given to very noisy calls. **noisy pitta** a rainforest bird of north-east Qld, having a loud, whistling call. Also called *anvil bird*. □ □ **noisily** *adv.* **noisiness** *n.*

Nolan, Sir Sidney (Robert) (1917–92), AC, Australian artist internationally known for his paintings of events from Australian history and of the Australian outback.

nomad / **noh**-mad / *n.* **1** a member of a tribe that roams from place to place seeking pasture for its animals. **2** any wanderer. □ **nomadism** *n.* **nomadic** / nuh-**mad**-ik / *adj.*

nom de plume / nom duh **ploom** / *n.* (*pl.* **noms de plume** pronounced the same) a writer's pseudonym. (¶ French, = pen name.)

nomenclature / nuh-**men**-kluh-chuh, **noh**-muhn-klay-chuh / *n.* a system of names, e.g. those used in a particular science.

nominal / **nom**-uh-nuhl / *adj.* **1** in name only, not real or actual (*nominal ruler of that country*). **2** (of an amount or sum of money) very small but charged or paid as a token that payment is required (*a nominal fee*). **3** of, like, or as a noun. □ **nominal value** the face value of a coin etc. □ □ **nominally** *adv.*

nominalism *n.* the doctrine that universals or general ideas are merely names without any corresponding reality. □ **nominalist** *n.* **nominalistic** *adj.*

nominate / **nom**-uh-nayt / *v.* **1 a** *Aust.* put one's name forward as standing for election. **b** propose (a candidate) for election. **2** appoint as a place or date for a meeting etc. □ **nomination** *n.* **nominator** *n.*

nominative / **nom**-uh-nuh-tiv / *n. Grammar* the form of a noun used when it is the subject of a verb.

nominee / nom-uh-**nee** / *n.* a person who is nominated by another.

non- *comb. form* not.

non-Aboriginal *adj.* not Aboriginal. • *n.* a non-Aboriginal person.

nonagenarian / noh-nuh-juh-**nair**-ree-uhn, non-uh- / *n.* a person who is in his or her nineties.

nonagon *n.* a plane figure with nine sides and angles.

non-aligned / non-uh-**luynd** / *adj.* not in alliance with another (esp. major) power. □ **non-alignment** *n.*

non-Catholic *adj.* not Roman Catholic. • *n.* a non-Catholic person.

nonce *n.* □ **for the nonce** for the time being. **nonce word** a word coined for one occasion only.

nonchalant / **non**-shuh-luhnt / *adj.* not feeling or showing anxiety or excitement, calm and casual. □ **nonchalantly** *adv.* **nonchalance** *n.*

non-combatant / non-**com**-buh-tuhnt / *n.* **1** a member of an army etc. whose duties do not involve fighting, e.g. a doctor or chaplain. **2** a civilian during a war.

non-commissioned *adj.* (of an officer, such as a corporal etc.) not holding a commission.

noncommittal / non-kuh-**mit**-uhl / *adj.* not committing oneself, not showing what one thinks or which side one supports.

non compos *adj.* (in full **non compos mentis**) not in one's right mind. (¶ Latin, = not in control of one's mind.)

non-conductor *n.* a substance that does not conduct heat or electricity.

nonconformist *n.* a person who does not conform to prevailing principles. □ **non-conformity** *n.*

non-contributory *adj.* not involving payment of contributions (*a non-contributory pension scheme*).

nondescript / **non**-duh-skript / *adj.* lacking in distinctive characteristics and therefore not easy to classify. • *n.* a nondescript person or thing.

none[1] / nun / *pron.* **1** not any. **2** no person(s), no one (*none can tell*). • *adv.* by no amount, not at all (*is none the worse for it*). ◻ **none other** no other person. **none the less** *see* NONETHELESS. **none too** not very, not at all (*he's none too pleased*).

■ **Usage** In sense 1, *none* may be followed by either a singular or a plural verb. The singular construction is preferred (*none of the candidates has failed*), but the plural is very common (*none of them are required*).

none[2] / nohn / *n.* (also in *pl.*) **1** the office of the fifth of the canonical hours of prayer, originally said at the ninth hour (3 p.m.). **2** this hour.

nonentity / non-**en**-tuh-tee / *n.* a person or thing of no importance.

nonetheless *adv.* (also **none the less**) nevertheless.

non-event *n.* an event that was expected or intended to be important but proves to be disappointing.

non-existent *adj.* not existing.

non-ferrous *adj.* (of a metal) not iron or steel.

non-fiction *n.* literature other than fiction (e.g. a biography, a historical work, etc.).

non-flammable *adj.* not inflammable, unable to be set on fire.

■ **Usage** *See* the note under INFLAMMABLE.

nong *n.* (also **ning-nong**) *Aust. colloq.* a foolish or stupid person.

non-indigenous *adj.* not native or belonging naturally to (a region, country, etc.).

non-interference = NON-INTERVENTION.

non-intervention *n.* the (esp. political) policy of not becoming involved in others' affairs.

non-nuclear *adj.* **1** not involving nuclei or nuclear energy. **2** (of a nation etc.) not having nuclear weapons.

nonpareil / **non**-puh-rel, non-puh-**rayl** / *adj.* unrivalled, unique. • *n.* an unrivalled person or thing.

non-party *adj.* not belonging to or supported by a political party.

nonplus / non-**plus** / *v.* (**nonplussed**, **nonplussing**) perplex completely. • *n.* a state of complete perplexity (*at a nonplus*).

non-proliferation *n.* limitation of the increase in number esp. of nuclear weapons.

non-resident *adj.* **1** not living on the premises (*a non-resident caretaker*). **2** (of a job) not requiring the holder to live in. • *n.* a person not staying at a hotel etc. (*open to non-residents*).

non-resistance *n.* the policy or practice of not resisting authority.

nonsense *n.* **1** words put together in a way that does not make sense. **2** absurd or foolish talk, ideas, or behaviour. ◻ **nonsensical** / non-**sen**-suh-kuhl / *adj.* **nonsensically** *adv.*

non sequitur / non **sek**-wi-ter / *n.* a conclusion that does not logically follow from the evidence given. (¶ Latin, = it does not follow.)

non-starter *n.* **1** a horse which is entered for a race but does not run in it. **2** *colloq.* a person or scheme that is unlikely to succeed and not worth considering.

non-stick *adj.* coated with a substance that does not allow things to stick to it (*a non-stick frypan*).

non-stop *adj.* **1** (of a train etc.) not stopping at intermediate places. **2** not ceasing (*non-stop chatter*). • *adv.* without stopping or pausing.

non-verbal *adj.* not involving words or speech.

non-violence *n.* the avoidance of violence, esp. as a principle. ◻ **non-violent** *adj.*

non-voting *adj.* (of shares) not entitling the holder to a vote.

noodle[1] *n.* **1** (**noodles**) pasta in narrow strips. **2** a foolish person. **3** *colloq.* the head.

noodle[2] *v. Aust.* search (an opal-mining dump) for opals that may have been unwittingly discarded. ◻ **noodler** *n.*

nook *n.* a secluded place or corner, a recess.

noolbenger / **nool**-beng-guh / *n.* an Australian honey possum which has a long snout and a brush-tipped tongue. (¶ Nyungar)

noon *n.* twelve o'clock in the day, midday.

noonday *n.* midday.

Noongah alternative spelling of NYOONGAH.

Noonuccal, Oodgeroo (1920–93), Australian Aboriginal poet and activist for Aboriginal rights. In the 1980s she discarded her English name (Kath Walker) in favour of her Aboriginal name.

noose *n.* **1** a loop of rope etc. with a knot that tightens when pulled. **2** a snare; a tie or bond. • *v.* catch with a noose; enclose in a noose.

nor *conj.* **1** and not; and not either (*neither one thing nor the other; not a man nor a child was to be seen*). **2** and no more; neither ('*I cannot go.*' — '*Nor can I.*').

nor[1] *adj.* & *adv.* (esp. in compounds) = NORTH; *nor'wester*.

Nordic *adj.* **1** of or relating to a physical type of northern Germanic people who are often tall, blond, and blue-eyed, with a long head. **2** of Scandinavia, Finland, or Iceland. **3** (of skiing) involving cross-country work and jumping. • *n.* a Nordic person.

Norfolk Island / **naw**-fuhk / an Australian territory situated some 1,670 km north-east of Sydney. The island was used as a penal settlement for convicts (1788–1814 and 1825–56). ◻ **Norfolk Island pine** a tall coniferous tree with a symmetrical, conical shape; widely planted elsewhere in Australia.

nori / naw-ree / *n.* an edible seaweed, eaten either fresh or dried in sheets. (¶ Japanese)

nork *n.* (usu. in *pl.*) *Aust. colloq.* a woman's breast.

norm *n.* **1** a standard, pattern, or type considered to be representative of a group. **2** a standard amount of work etc. to be done or produced. **3** customary behaviour.

Norm *n. Aust.* the satirical 'norm' of the Australian male, an overweight and unfit slob who takes no exercise and spends all his leisure hours watching sport on television and drinking beer. (¶ A cartoon character invented for the *Life. Be In It!* campaign on television.)

normal *adj.* **1** conforming to what is standard or usual. **2** free from mental or emotional disorders. **3** (of a line) at right angles, perpendicular. • *n.* **1** the normal value or standard etc. **2** a line at right angles. □ **normal distribution** a function that represents the distribution of many random variables as a symmetrical bell-shaped graph. □□ **normalcy** *n.* **normally** *adv.* **normality** *n.*

normalise *v.* (also **-ize**) make or become normal; cause to conform. □ **normalisation** *n.*

Norman[1] *n.* **1** a native or inhabitant of medieval Normandy. **2** a descendant of the people of mixed Scandinavian and Frankish origin established there in the 10th century. **3** a style of architecture with rounded arches and heavy pillars developed by the Normans. • *adj.* **1** of the Normans. **2** of their style of architecture. □ **Norman Conquest** the conquest of England by the Normans under William the Conqueror in 1066. **Norman French** French as spoken by the Normans or (after 1066) in English lawcourts etc.

Norman[2], Greg(ory John) (the 'Great White Shark') (1955–), AO, Australian golfing champion, now based in the US.

Norman[3], Jessye (1945–), American operatic soprano.

Normandy a region of NW France bordering on the English Channel, home of the Normans.

normative / naw-muh-tiv / *adj.* of or establishing a norm.

Norn *n. Scand. myth.* any of the three virgin goddesses of fate or destiny.

norne *n.* a black, highly venomous Australian tiger snake which feeds largely on frogs and small animals. (¶ Nyungar)

Norse *adj.* of ancient Norway or Scandinavia. • *n.* **1** the Norwegian language. **2** the Scandinavian group of languages.

Norseman *n.* a Viking.

north *n.* **1** the point or direction to the left of a person facing east. **2** the northern part of something. • *adj.* **1** towards or in the north. **2** (of a wind) blowing from the north. • *adv.* towards or in the north. □ **north pole** (of a magnet) the pole that is attracted to the north.

North America the northern half of the American land mass (*see* AMERICA).

northbound *adj.* travelling or leading northwards.

north-east *n.* the point or direction midway between north and east. • *adj.* of, towards, or coming from the north-east. • *adv.* towards, in, or near the north-east. □ **north-easterly** *adj.* & *n.* **north-eastern** *adj.*

northeaster *n.* a north-east wind.

northerly *adj.* **1** in or towards the north. **2** (of a wind) blowing from the north. • *n.* a northerly wind.

northern *adj.* of or in the north. □ **northern lights** the aurora borealis.

northerner *n.* a native or inhabitant of the north.

Northern hemisphere the half of the earth north of the equator.

Northern Ireland a unit of the UK comprising six NE districts (and former counties) of the island Ireland.

northernmost *adj.* furthest north.

Northern Territory a self-governing territory in central north Australia; capital Darwin. □ **Northern Territorian** = TERRITORIAN.

North Pole the northernmost point of the earth.

North Star the pole star.

northward *adj.* & *adv.* (also **northwards**) towards the north.

north-west *n.* the point or direction midway between north and west. • *adj.* of, towards, or coming from the north-west. • *adv.* towards, in, or near the north-west. □ **north-westerly** *adj.* & *adv.* **north-western** *adj.*

northwester *n.* a north-west wind.

North West Shelf an area of continental shelf off the north-west coast of Australia containing a huge natural gas field.

Norway a kingdom in northern Europe.

Norwegian *adj.* of Norway or its people or language. • *n.* **1** a native or inhabitant of Norway. **2** the language of Norway.

nor'wester *n.* **1** = NORTHWESTER. **2** an inhabitant of north-west Australia.

Nos. *abbr.* (also **nos.**) numbers.

nose *n.* **1** the organ at the front of the head in man and animals, containing the nostrils and used for breathing and smelling. **2** a sense of smell. **3** the ability to detect things of a particular kind (*has a nose for scandal*). **4** the odour or perfume of wine etc. **5** the front end or projecting front part of something, e.g. of a car or aircraft. • *v.* **1** (often foll. by *about, around,* etc.) pry, eavesdrop, search, etc. **2** (often foll. by *out*) search by using one's sense of smell; discover (secrets etc.) by prying. **3** smell at; rub with the nose; push the nose against or into. **4** push one's way cautiously ahead (*the car nosed past the obstruction*). □ **by a nose** by a very narrow margin. **get up a person's nose** *colloq.* annoy him or her. **on the nose** *colloq.* **1** having an offensive smell (because rotten) (*the meat's on the nose*). **2** *Aust.* (of a person, behaviour, etc.) distasteful, offensive.

nosebag n. a bag containing fodder, for hanging on a horse's head.

nosedive n. **1** a steep downward plunge by an aircraft. **2** any sudden drop or plunge. • v. make a nosedive.

nosegay n. a small bunch of sweet-scented flowers; a posy.

nosh colloq. n. food, esp. a snack. • v. eat. ☐ **nosh-up** n. colloq. a large meal, a good feed.

noshery n. colloq. a restaurant (or similar place where a meal may be had).

Nossal, Sir Gustav (Joseph Victor) (1931–), AC, Australian medical scientist (born in Austria) specialising in immunology.

nostalgia / nos-**tal**-jee-uh, -juh / n. sentimental memory of or a longing for things of the past. ☐ **nostalgic** / nos-**tal**-jik / adj. **nostalgically** adv.

Nostradamus / nos-truh-**dah**-muhs /, Michel de Notredame (1503–66), Provençal astrologer whose extensive prophecies were widely believed in the mid-16th century at the French court.

nostril n. either of the two openings in the nose through which air is admitted.

nostrum / **nos**-truhm / n. **1** a quack remedy. **2** a pet scheme, esp. for political or social reform.

nosy adj. (**nosier**, **nosiest**) colloq. inquisitive, prying. ☐ **nosy parker** a prying busybody; a stickybeak. ☐☐ **nosily** adv. **nosiness** n.

not adv. expressing a negative, denial, or refusal. ☐ **not at all** a polite reply to thanks. **not on** adj. colloq. not to be tolerated, totally unacceptable (domestic violence is just not on).

notable adj. worthy of notice, remarkable, eminent. • n. an eminent person. ☐ **notability** n. **notably** adv.

notary / **noh**-tuh-ree / n. (in full **notary public**, pl. **notaries public**) a solicitor or other public official who is legally authorised to witness the signing of documents and to perform other formal transactions. ☐ **notarial** adj.

notation n. a system of signs or symbols representing numbers, quantities, musical notes, etc.

notch n. **1** a V-shaped cut or indentation. **2** each of the levels in a graded system (everyone moved up a notch). **3** a nick made on a stick etc. in order to keep count. • v. **1** make a notch or notches in. **2** (usu. foll. by up) record, score (notched up another win).

note n. **1** a brief record of something, written down to aid the memory. **2** a short or informal letter, a memorandum; a formal diplomatic communication. **3** an observation (usu. unwritten) of experiences etc. (let us compare notes). **4** a short comment on or explanation of a word or passage in a book etc. **5** a written or printed promise to pay money; a banknote ($50 notes). **6** a tone of definite pitch made by a voice, instrument, engine, etc. **7** a written sign representing the pitch and duration of a musical sound. **8** any of the keys on a piano etc. **9** a significant sound or indication of feelings etc. (a note of optimism). **10** eminence, distinction (a family of note). **11** notice, attention (take note of what he says). • v. **1** notice, pay attention to. **2** (often foll. by down) write down, record.

notebook n. a small book with blank pages for making notes.

notecase n. a wallet for holding banknotes.

noted adj. famous, well-known.

notelet n. a piece of small folded ornamental notepaper, for informal letters.

notepaper n. paper for writing letters on.

noteworthy adj. worthy of notice, remarkable.

nothing n. **1** no thing, not anything. **2** no amount, nought. **3** non-existence; what does not exist. **4** a person or thing of no importance. • adv. not at all, in no way (it's nothing like as good). ☐ **for nothing 1** without payment, free. **2** without a reward or result. **nothing doing** colloq. a statement of refusal or failure.

nothingness n. **1** non-existence (faded into nothingness). **2** worthlessness, triviality (the nothingness of my life).

notice n. **1** news or information of what has happened or is about to happen. **2** a formal announcement that one is to end an agreement or leave a job at a specified time (gave her a month's notice). **3** written or printed information; instructions displayed publicly. **4** attention, observation (it escaped my notice). **5** an account or review in a newspaper. • v. **1** perceive, become aware of; take notice of. **2** remark upon, speak of. ☐ **at short notice** with little warning. **take notice** show signs of interest; pay attention.

noticeable adj. easily seen or noticed. ☐ **noticeably** adv.

noticeboard n. a board on which notices may be displayed.

notifiable adj. (of a disease etc.) that must be reported to the health authorities.

notify v. (**notified**, **notifying**) **1** inform or give formal notice to (a person). **2** make (a thing) known. ☐ **notification** n.

notion n. **1** an idea or opinion, esp. one that is vague or probably incorrect. **2** an understanding or intention (has no notion of discipline).

notional / **noh**-shuh-nuhl / adj. hypothetical; assumed to be correct or valid for a particular purpose (an estimate based on notional figures). ☐ **notionally** adv.

notorious / noh-**taw**-ree-uhs / adj. well-known, esp. in an unfavourable way. ☐ **notoriously** adv. **notoriety** / noh-tuh-**ruy**-uh-tee / n.

Notre-Dame / not-ruh-**dahm** / the cathedral church of Paris, dedicated to the Virgin Mary.

notwithstanding prep. in spite of. • adv. nevertheless.

Nouakchott / nwak-**shot** / the capital of Mauritania.

nougat / **noo**-gah / n. a chewy sweet made of nuts, sugar or honey, and egg white.

nought / nawt / *n.* **1** the figure 0. **2** *poetic* or *archaic* nothing.

noun *n.* a word (other than a pronoun) or a group of words used to name or identify a person, place, or thing (see panel).

nourish / **nu**-rish / *v.* **1** keep (a person, animal, or plant) alive and well by means of food. **2** foster or cherish (a feeling etc.). ☐ **nourishment** *n.*

nous / nows / *n.* **1** *colloq.* common sense; gumption. **2** *Philosophy* the mind or intellect.

nouveau riche / noo-voh **reesh** / *n.* (*pl.* **nouveaux riches** pronounced the same) a person who has acquired wealth only recently, esp. one who makes a display of it. • *adj.* of, pertaining to, or characteristic of such a person (*houses hideous with nouveau riche vulgarity*). (¶ French, = new rich.)

nouvelle cuisine / noo-vel kwi-**zeen** / *n.* a style of cooking that avoids traditional rich sauces and emphasises fresh ingredients and attractive presentation. (¶ French, = new cookery.)

nova / **noh**-vuh / *n.* (*pl.* **novae** or **novas**) a star that suddenly becomes much brighter for a short time.

novel *n.* a book-length fictional story. • *adj.* of a new kind (*a novel experience*).

novelese / nov-uh-**leez** / *n. derog.* a style of writing like that of inferior novels.

novelette *n.* a short novel, esp. a light romantic one.

novelist *n.* a writer of novels.

novella / nuh-**vel**-uh / *n.* a short novel, longer or more complex than a short story.

novelty *n.* **1** the quality of being new, novel. **2** a new or unusual thing or occurrence. **3** a small toy or trinket.

November *n.* the eleventh month of the year.

novena / noh-**vee**-nuh, nuh- / *n.* (in the Catholic Church) a devotion consisting of special prayers or services on nine successive days.

novice / **nov**-uhs / *n.* **1** a beginner. **2** one who has been accepted into a religious order for a trial period and has not yet taken any vows.

noviciate / nuh-**vish**-ee-uht / *n.* (also **novitiate**) **1** the period of being a novice in a religious order. **2** the novices' quarters in a monastery or convent.

now *adv.* **1** at the time when or of which one is writing or speaking. **2** by this time (*it was now clear that. . .*). **3** immediately (*must go now*). **4** (with no reference to time, giving various tones to a sentence) surely, I wonder, I am telling you, etc. (*now why didn't I think of that?*). • *conj.* as a consequence of the fact, simultaneously with it (*now that you have come, we'll start; I do remember, now you mention it*). • *n.* the present time (*they ought to be here by now*). ☐ **for now** until a later time (*goodbye for now*). **now and again** (or **now and then**) occasionally.

nowadays *adv.* at the present time (contrasted with years ago).

nowhere *adv.* not anywhere. • *pron.* no place. ☐ **in the middle of nowhere** *colloq.* remote from urban life; in the outback. **nowhere near** not nearly.

Nowra, Louis (1950–), Australian playwright.

noxious / **nok**-shuhs / *adj.* unpleasant and harmful.

nozzle *n.* the vent or spout of a hose etc. through which a stream of liquid or air is directed.

Np *symbol* neptunium.

NSW *abbr.* New South Wales.

NT *abbr.* **1** (the) Northern Territory. **2** New Testament.

nth *see* N.

Noun

A noun is the name of a person or thing. There are four kinds:

1 common nouns (the words for articles and classes of creatures), e.g.

shoe	in	*The red shoe was left on the shelf.*
box	in	*The large box stood in the corner.*
plant	in	*The plant grew to two metres.*
horse	in	*A horse galloped by.*

2 proper nouns (the names of people, places, ships, institutions, and animals, which always begin with a capital letter), e.g.

Kylie	HMAS Melbourne	Skippy
Adelaide	Railway Hotel	Australian Institute of Sport

3 abstract nouns (the words for qualities, things we cannot see or touch, and things which have no physical reality), e.g.

truth	absence	love
explanation	warmth	experience

4 collective nouns (the words for groups of things), e.g.

committee	squad	the Cabinet
herd	swarm	the clergy
majority	team	the public

Nouns are said to be used *attributively* (i.e. like an *adjective*) when they precede the word described, although their function is not fully adjectival (e.g. *model* in *a model student*; *the student is very model* is not acceptable usage).

nu *n.* the thirteenth letter of the Greek alphabet (N, v).

nuance / **nyoo**-ons / *n.* a subtle difference in meaning; a subtle shade of meaning, feeling, colour, etc.

nub *n.* **1** (also **nubble**) a small knob or lump. **2** the central point or core of a matter or problem. ☐ **nubbly** *adj.*

Nubia / **nyoo**-bee-uh / a region of southern Egypt and northern Sudan. ☐ **Nubian** *adj. & n.*

nubile / **nyoo**-buyl / *adj.* (of a young woman) marriageable or sexually attractive. ☐ **nubility** / nyoo-**bil**-uh-tee / *n.*

nuclear *adj.* **1** of a nucleus. **2** of or using nuclear energy (*nuclear weapons*). ☐ **nuclear bomb** a bomb using the release of energy by nuclear fission or fusion or both. **nuclear energy** energy that is released or absorbed during reactions taking place in the nuclei of atoms. **nuclear family** a father, mother, and their child or children regarded as a basic social unit. **nuclear fission** the splitting of a heavy nucleus spontaneously or on impact with another particle, with the release of energy. **nuclear-free zone** an area (usu. the territory of a local government council in Australia) designated and signposted as such to declare that it is free of nuclear material and that the passage of nuclear material through that area is prohibited. **nuclear fuel** a source of nuclear energy. **nuclear fusion** the union of atomic nuclei to form a heavier nucleus with the release of energy. **nuclear physics** the branch of physics dealing with atomic nuclei and their reactions. **nuclear power 1** power generated by a nuclear reactor. **2** a country that has nuclear weapons. **nuclear reactor** *see* REACTOR. **nuclear test** the testing of nuclear weapons by nuclear powers, e.g. by Britain in Australia in the 1950s (*see* MARALINGA), or by France in MURUROA, both sites being well away from the home territory of the testers. **nuclear weapon** any weapon using the release of energy by nuclear fission or fusion or both. **nuclear winter** a prolonged period of extreme cold and darkness which, according to some scientists, would be a global consequence of a nuclear war because a thick layer of smoke and dust particles in the atmosphere would shut out the sun's rays.

nucleate / **nyoo**-klee-ayt / *v.* form or form into a nucleus. • *adj.* having a nucleus.

nucleic acid / nyoo-**klee**-ik, **klay**-ik / *n.* a complex organic molecule of either of the two types (DNA and RNA) present in all living cells.

nucleon *n.* a proton or neutron.

nucleonics / nyoo-klee-**on**-iks / *n.* the branch of science and engineering that deals with the practical uses of nuclear energy. ☐ **nucleonic** *adj.*

nucleus / **nyoo**-klee-uhs / *n.* (*pl.* **nuclei** / **nyoo**-klee-uy /) **1** the central part or thing round which others are collected. **2** something established that will receive additions (*this collection of books will form the nucleus of a new library*). **3** the central positively charged portion of an atom. **4** the central part of a seed or of a plant or animal cell.

nuddy *n. colloq.* ☐ **in the nuddy** in the nude, naked.

nude / nyood / *adj.* naked, bare, unclothed. • *n.* **1** a painting, sculpture, etc. of a naked human figure. **2** a naked person. ☐ **in the nude** not clothed, naked. ☐ ☐ **nudity** *n.*

nudge *v.* **1** poke (a person) gently with the elbow to attract attention quietly. **2** push slightly or gradually. • *n.* this movement.

nudist / **nyoo**-duhst, **noo**- / *n.* a person who advocates or practises being naked (esp. in a special private reserve, on a declared 'nude beach', etc.) in the belief that this is beneficial to healthy living. ☐ **nudism** *n.*

nugatory / **nyoo**-guh-tuh-ree, -tree / *adj.* **1** futile, trivial. **2** inoperative, not valid.

nugget / **nug**-uht / *n.* **1** a lump of gold etc. as found in the earth. **2** a lump of anything. **3** something small and valuable (*nuggets of information*). **4** *Aust.* a small, stocky animal or person. **5** *Aust.* an unbranded calf.

nuggetty *adj.* (also **nuggety**) **1** (of gold) occurring as nuggets. **2** rich in nuggets (*discovered a nuggetty gully*). **3** (of a person) compactly built, stocky; tough.

nuisance *n.* **1** a person, thing, or circumstance causing trouble or annoyance. **2** anything harmful or offensive to the community or to a member of it and for which a legal remedy exists. ☐ **nuisance value** the advantage arising from the capacity to harass or frustrate.

nuke *colloq. n.* a nuclear weapon. • *v.* **1** attack with nuclear weapons. **2** defeat, destroy, or get rid of, as if with a nuclear weapon (*nuked the opposition; nuked him from the program*).

Nuku'alofa / noo-koo-uh-**loh**-fuh / the capital of Tonga.

null *adj.* **1** (esp. as **null and void**) having no legal force (*declared the agreement null and void*). **2** non-existent; amounting to nothing. **3** *Computing* **a** empty; having no elements (*null list*). **b** all the elements of which are zeros (*null matrix*). **4** without character or expression. ☐ **nullity** *n.*

nulla (also **nullah**) = NULLA-NULLA.

nulla-nulla *n. Aust.* a hardwood club, used by Aborigines in fighting and hunting. • *v.* strike (a person etc.) with a nulla-nulla. (¶ Dharuk)

Nullarbor Plain an arid limestone plateau, covering about 270,000 sq. km, lying north of the Great Australian Bight. (¶ Latin *nulla arbor* 'not a tree'.)

nullify *v.* (**nullified**, **nullifying**) **1** make (a thing) null. **2** cancel or neutralise the effect of. ☐ **nullification** *n.*

numb *adj.* deprived of the power to feel or move (*numb with cold*). • *v.* make numb. ☐ **numbly** *adv.* **numbness** *n.*

numbat *n.* the banded anteater, a small, termite-eating marsupial, now occurring only in south-west WA and rare, having a long pointed snout and red to grey-brown fur with light stripes across the back and rump: the faunal emblem of WA. (¶ Nyungar)

number *n.* **1** a symbol or word indicating how many, a numeral. **2** a numeral identifying a person or thing (e.g. a telephone or a house in a street) by its position in a series. **3** a single issue of a magazine. **4** a song or piece of music, esp. as an item in a theatrical performance. **5** *colloq.* a person or thing (such as a garment or car) regarded familiarly or affectionately (*an attractive little number*). **6** a group of people (*among our number*). **7** a total of people or things. **8** (**numbers**) very many. **9** the category 'singular' or 'plural' in grammar. • *v.* **1** count, find out how many. **2** amount to. **3** assign a number to (each in a series); distinguish in this way. **4** include or regard as (*I number him among my friends*). ❑ **a number of** several. **number crunching** *colloq.* the process of making complicated calculations, esp. by computer. **without number** innumerable.

numberless *adj.* innumerable.

numberplate *n.* a plate on a motor vehicle bearing its registration number.

numbskull *n.* a stupid person.

numerable *adj.* able to be counted.

numeracy *n.* being numerate, being able to do basic mathematics (cf. LITERACY).

numeral / **nyoo**-muh-ruhl / *n.* a symbol that represents a certain number, a figure.

numerate / **nyoo**-muh-ruht / *adj.* having a good basic knowledge and understanding of mathematics; able to do basic arithmetic etc. (cf. LITERATE).

numeration / nyoo-muh-**ray**-shuhn / *n.* **1** numbering. **2** calculation.

numerator / **nyoo**-muh-ray-tuh / *n.* the number written above the line in a vulgar fraction, showing how many of the parts indicated by the denominator are to be taken (e.g. 2 in ⅔).

numerical / nyoo-**me**-ri-kuhl / *adj.* of a number or series of numbers (*placed in numerical order*). ❑ **numerically** *adv.*

numerology / nyoo-muh-**rol**-uh-jee / *n.* the study of the supposed occult significance of numbers.

numerous / **nyoo**-muh-ruhs / *adj.* **1** many (*received numerous gifts*). **2** consisting of many (*a numerous family*).

numinous / **nyoo**-muh-nuhs / *adj.* **1** indicating the presence of a divinity. **2** spiritual; awe-inspiring.

numismatics / nyoo-muhz-**mat**-iks / *n.* the study of coins and similar objects (e.g. medals). ❑ **numismatic** *adj.* **numismatist** / nyoo-**miz**-muh-tuhst / *n.*

numskull = NUMBSKULL.

nun *n.* a member of a religious community of women living under certain vows, esp. poverty, chastity, and obedience.

nunchaku / nun-**chak**-oo, -**chuk**-uh / *n.* (*pl.* same or **nunchakus**) Japanese martial arts weapon consisting of two hardwood sticks joined together by a chain, rope, or thong. (¶ Japanese)

nunciature / **nun**-see-uh-chuh / *n.* the office or tenure of a nuncio.

nuncio / **nun**-see-oh / *n.* (*pl.* **nuncios**) an ambassador of the pope accredited to a civil government.

Nunga / **nang**-guh / *n.* (also **Nanga**) *Aust.* an Aborigine (the word used by Aborigines in the southern part of SA). (¶ Nhangka)

■ **Usage** *See* KOORI.

nunnery *n.* a religious house of nuns, a convent.

nuptial / **nup**-shuhl / *adj.* of marriage; of a wedding ceremony. • *n.pl.* (**nuptials**) a wedding.

Nureyev / nyoo-**ray**-ef /, Rudolf (1939–93), Russian ballet dancer, who defected to the West in 1961.

nurse *n.* **1** a person trained to care for sick, injured, or infirm people. **2** = NURSEMAID. **3** a sexually imperfect bee, ant, etc., caring for a young brood; a worker. • *v.* **1** work as a nurse; look after in this way. **2** feed or be fed at the breast. **3** hold carefully. **4** give special care or attention to. **5** harbour or foster (a grievance etc.). ❑ **nursing home** a privately run hospital or home for invalids or old people.

nurseling alternative spelling of NURSLING.

nursemaid *n.* a woman employed to take charge of young children.

nursery *n.* **1** a room set apart for young children. **2** a place where young plants are reared for sale. ❑ **nursery rhyme** a simple traditional song or rhyme for children. **nursery slopes** gentle slopes suitable for beginners at a ski resort.

nurseryman *n.* one who owns or works in a plant nursery.

nursling *n.* (also **nurseling**) a baby or young animal that is being suckled.

nurture / **ner**-chuh / *v.* **1** nourish and rear. **2** bring up. • *n.* **1** nurturing; nourishment. **2** sociological factors such as upbringing, education, etc. which influence or determine personality (as opposed to NATURE, sense 4).

nut *n.* **1** a fruit consisting of a hard shell round an edible kernel. **2** this kernel. **3** *colloq.* the head. **4** *colloq.* a crazy or eccentric person. **5** *colloq.* an enthusiast; a fanatic (*he's become a real nut over model planes*). **6** a small piece of metal with a threaded hole through it for screwing on the end of a bolt to secure it. **7** a small lump of a solid substance, e.g. coal or butter. **8** (**nuts**) *coarse colloq.* the testicles. ❑ **do one's nut** *colloq.* be extremely angry. **nuts and bolts** *colloq.* the practical details. **nut out** plan, figure out (*we need to nut out the details*).

nutcase *n. colloq.* a crazy person.

nutcracker *n.* (usu. as **nutcrackers**) a device for cracking nuts.

nutmeg *n.* the hard fragrant seed of a SE Asian tree, ground or grated as spice.

nutrient / **nyoo**-tree-uhnt / *n.* a substance that provides nourishment. • *adj.* nourishing.

nutriment / **nyoo**-truh-muhnt / *n.* nourishing food.

nutrition / nyoo-**trish**-uhn / *n.* **1** providing or receiving nourishing substances. **2** food, nourishment. **3** the study of nutrients and nutrition. □**nutritional** *adj.* **nutritionally** *adv.*

nutritious / nyoo-**trish**-uhs / *adj.* nourishing, efficient as food. □**nutritiousness** *n.*

nutritive / **nyoo**-truh-tiv / *adj.* nourishing, nutritious.

nuts *adj. colloq.* crazy; eccentric. □ **be nuts about** (*or* **on** *or* **over**) *colloq.* be very fond of or enthusiastic about.

nutshell *n.* the hard outer shell of a nut. □ **in a nutshell** expressed in the briefest possible way.

nutter *n. colloq.* = NUT (senses 4 & 5).

nutty *adj.* **1** full of nuts. **2** tasting like nuts. **3** *colloq.* crazy. □**nuttiness** *n.*

nuytsia / **noit**-see-uh / *n.* a parasitic tree with a profuse and spectacular display of brilliant golden flowers in summer. Also called *Western Australian Christmas tree*.

nuzzle *v.* **1** press or rub gently with the nose. **2** nestle; lie snug or cuddle up with a person or thing.

NW *abbr.* **1** north-west. **2** north-western.

Nyangumarda / **nyahng**-oo-mahr-du / *n.* an Aboriginal language of an area north of Port Hedland in WA.

Nyawaygi / **nyah**-wuy-gee / *n.* an Aboriginal language of an area south of Ingham in northern Qld.

nyctalopia / nik-tuh-**loh**-pee-uh / *n.* the inability to see in dim light or at night. Also called *night blindness*.

nylon *n.* **1** a synthetic fibre of great lightness and strength. **2** fabric made from this. **3** (**nylons**) stockings made of nylon.

nymph / nimf / *n.* **1** (in mythology) a semi-divine maiden associated with nature and living in the sea or woods etc. **2** *poetic* a beautiful young woman. **3** a young insect that resembles its parents in form.

nympho / **nim**-foh / *n.* (*pl.* **nymphos**) *colloq.* a nymphomaniac.

nymphomania / nim-fuh-**may**-nee-uh / *n.* excessive and uncontrollable sexual desire in a woman. □**nymphomaniac** *n. & adj.*

Nyoongah / **nyuung**-uh, **nyoong**-uh / *n.* (also **Noongah**) an Aborigine (a word used by Aborigines in the south-west of WA). (¶ Nyungar)

■ **Usage** *See* Koori.

nystagmus / nuhs-**tag**-muhs / *n.* abnormal continual rapid involuntary movement of the eyeballs.

Nyungar / **nyuung**-u / *n.* an Aboriginal language of a large extent of south-west WA, including present-day Perth, Albany, and Esperance.

NZ *abbr.* New Zealand.

O

O *interj.* **1** = OH. **2** prefixed to a name in the vocative (*O God*). •*symbol* oxygen. •*n.* (**0**) nought, zero. •*abbr.* (also **O.**) Old.

o' *prep.* of (*six o'clock; will-o'-the-wisp*).

-o *suffix colloq.* (esp. in Australia) added to: **1** shortened forms, as *garbo* garb(age collector), *journo* journ(alist), *arvo* af(ternoon). **2** one-syllable forms, as *milko* milkman, *smoko* a smoke, *goodo*, *weirdo*. **3** (esp. as a mark of familiarity or affection) personal names, as *Johnno*, *Tommo*.

oaf *n.* (*pl.* **oafs**) an awkward lout; a stupid person. □ **oafish** *adj.*

oak *n.* **1** an acorn-bearing European tree with lobed leaves; its wood. **2** any of many Australian trees thought to resemble the oak (usu. in the appearance of the timber), esp. the casuarina or she-oak; the wood of these trees. □ **oaken** *adj.*

Oakley, Barry (Kingham) (1931–), Australian writer of plays, novels, and short stories.

oakum *n.* loose fibre obtained by picking old rope to pieces.

OAM *abbr.* Medal of the Order of Australia.

oar *n.* **1** a pole with a flat blade at one end, used to row or steer a boat. **2** a rower. □ **put one's oar in** interfere.

oarsman *n.* a male rower.

oarsmanship *n.* skill in rowing.

oarswoman *n.* a female rower.

oasis / oh-**ay**-suhs / *n.* (*pl.* **oases** / oh-**ay**-seez /) **1** a fertile spot in a desert, where water is found. **2** an area or period of calm in the midst of turbulence.

oast *n.* a kiln for drying hops. □ **oast house** a building containing this.

oat *n.* **1** a hardy cereal plant grown for food. **2** (**oats**) its grain. □ **sow one's wild oats** lead a life of excess (esp. by being sexually promiscuous) while young.

oath *n.* **1** a solemn undertaking or declaration, naming God or a revered object as witness. **2** a use of the name of God etc. as a swear word; a curse. □ **on** (*or* **under**) **oath** having made a solemn oath.

oatmeal *n.* **1** meal prepared from oats, used to make porridge etc. **2** a greyish-fawn colour flecked with brown.

OAU *abbr.* Organisation of African Unity.

ob. *abbr.* (before the date of a person's death) he or she died. (¶ Latin *obiit*.)

obbligato / ob-luh-**gah**-toh / *n.* (*pl.* **obbligatos**) an important accompanying part in a musical composition.

obdurate / **ob**-dyoo-ruht / *adj.* stubborn and unyielding. □ **obduracy** *n.*

obedient *adj.* doing what one is told to do, willing to obey. □ **obediently** *adv.* **obedience** *n.*

obeisance / oh-**bay**-suhns / *n.* **1** a deep bow or curtsy. **2** homage, deference. □ **obeisant** *adj.*

obelisk / **ob**-uh-lisk / *n.* **1** a tall pillar, usu. with four sides and a tapering top, set up as a monument or landmark. **2** = OBELUS.

obelus / **ob**-uh-luhs / *n.* (*pl.* **obeli** / **ob**-uh-luy /) a dagger-shaped reference mark (†).

Oberammergau / oh-buh-**ram**-uh-gow / a village in the Bavarian Alps of south-west Germany. It is the site of the most famous of the few surviving passion plays, which has been performed every tenth year (with few exceptions) from 1634.

obese / oh-**bees** / *adj.* very fat. □ **obesity** *n.*

obey *v.* (**obeyed**, **obeying**) do what is commanded by (a person, law, instinct, etc.); be obedient.

obfuscate / **ob**-fuhs-kayt / *v.* **1** make (a subject) obscure. **2** bewilder. □ **obfuscation** *n.*

obituary / uh-**bich**-uh-ree / *n.* a notice of a person's death, esp. in a newspaper, often with a short account of his or her life and achievements.

object *n.* / **ob**-jekt / **1** something solid that can be seen or touched. **2** a person or thing to which some action or feeling is directed (*an object of pity*). **3** a purpose, an intention (*the object of our mission*). **4** (in grammar) a noun or its equivalent acted upon by a transitive verb or by a preposition (see panel on next page). •*v.* / uhb-**jekt** / say that one is not in favour of something, protest. □ **no object** not acting as a restriction or limitation (*expense is no object*). **object lesson** a striking practical illustration of some principle. □□ **objector** *n.*

objectify *v.* present as an object; express in concrete form.

objection *n.* **1** a feeling of disapproval or opposition; a statement of this. **2** a reason for objecting; a drawback in a plan etc.

objectionable *adj.* **1** unpleasant, offensive. **2** open to objection. □ **objectionably** *adv.*

objective / uhb-**jek**-tiv / *adj.* **1** having real existence outside the mind, not subjective. **2** not influenced by personal feelings or opinions (*an objective account of the problem*). **3** (in grammar) (of a case or word) expressed as the object of a verb or preposition; *see* OBJECT (sense 4). •*n.* something one is trying to achieve, reach, or capture. □ **objectively** *adv.* **objectivity** *n.*

objet d'art / ob-*zhay* **dah** / *n.* (*pl.* **objets d'art** pronounced the same) a small decorative object. (¶ French, = object of art.)

oblate / **ob**-layt / *adj.* (of a spheroid) flattened at the poles.

oblation / oh-**blay**-shuhn / *n.* an offering to a divine being.

obligate / **ob**-luh-gayt / *v.* oblige (a person) legally or morally to do a specified thing.

obligation *n.* **1** being obliged to do something. **2** what one must do in order to comply with an agreement or law etc., one's duty. □ **day of obligation** *Catholic Church* a day on which attendance at Mass is compulsory under the Commandments of the Church.

obligatory / uh-**blig**-uh-tuh-ree, -tree / *adj.* required by law, rule, or custom; compulsory not optional.

oblige *v.* **1** compel by law, agreement, custom, or necessity. **2** help or gratify by performing a small service (*oblige me with a loan*). □ **be obliged to a person** be indebted to him or her for some service. **much obliged** thank you.

obliging *adj.* courteous and helpful. □ **obligingly** *adv.*

oblique / uh-**bleek** / *adj.* **1** slanting. **2** expressed indirectly, not going straight to the point (*an oblique reply*). □ **oblique angle** an acute or obtuse angle. □□ **obliquely** *adv.* **obliqueness** *n.*

obliterate / uh-**blit**-uh-rayt / *v.* blot out, destroy leaving no trace. □ **obliteration** *n.*

oblivion / uh-**bliv**-ee-uhn / *n.* **1** the state of being forgotten. **2** the state of being oblivious.

oblivious / uh-**bliv**-ee-uhs / *adj.* (often foll. by *of* or *to*) forgetful, unaware, or unconscious of something (*oblivious of her surroundings*).

oblong *n.* a rectangular shape with one pair of sides longer than the other. • *adj.* having this shape.

obloquy / **ob**-luh-kwee / *n.* **1** abuse intended to damage a person's reputation. **2** shame, etc. caused by this abuse.

obnoxious / uhb-**nok**-shuhs, ob- / *adj.* offensive, objectionable. □ **obnoxiously** *adv.*

oboe / **oh**-boh / *n.* a woodwind instrument of treble pitch. □ **oboist** *n.*

obscene / uhb-**seen** / *adj.* **1** offensive or indecent, esp. sexually (*an obscene film*). **2** offensive or repugnant, esp. morally (*an obscene amount of money*). □ **obscenely** *adv.*

obscenity / uhb-**sen**-uh-tee / *n.* **1** being obscene. **2** an obscene action or word etc.

obscurantism / ob-skyuh-**ran**-tiz-uhm / *n.* opposition to knowledge and enlightenment. □ **obscurantist** *n.* & *adj.*

obscure *adj.* **1** dark, indistinct. **2** remote from people's observation. **3** not famous (*an obscure poet*). **4** not easily understood, not clearly expressed. • *v.* make obscure, conceal from view. □ **obscurely** *adv.* **obscurity** *n.* **obscuration** *n.*

obsequies / **ob**-suh-kweez / *n.pl.* funeral rites.

obsequious / uhb-**see**-kwee-uhs / *adj.* servile, sickeningly respectful. □ **obsequiously** *adv.* **obsequiousness** *n.*

observance *n.* **1** the keeping of a law, rule, or custom etc. **2** the keeping or celebrating of a religious rite or festival or of a holiday.

observant *adj.* quick at noticing things. □ **observantly** *adv.*

observation *n.* **1** observing; being observed. **2** a comment or remark. □ **observational** *adj.*

observatory / uhb-**zer**-vuh-tuh-ree, -tree / *n.* a building designed and equipped for scientific observation of the stars or weather.

observe *v.* **1** see and notice; watch carefully. **2** follow or keep (rules etc.). **3** keep or celebrate (*not all countries observe New Year's Day*). **4** make a remark (*observed that grammar was going to the dogs*).

observer *n.* **1** a person who observes. **2** an interested spectator. **3** a person attending a conference, meeting, etc. in order to note what happens rather than to participate.

obsess / uhb-**ses**, ob- / *v.* occupy the thoughts of (a person) continually; totally preoccupy (*obsessed by fears of death*).

obsession / uhb-**sesh**-uhn, ob- / *n.* **1** obsessing; being obsessed. **2** a persistent idea that dominates

---

Object
There are two types of object:
1. A direct object is the person or thing directly affected by the verb and can usually be found by asking the question 'whom or what?' after the verb, e.g.
    The electors chose Mr Smith.
    Charles wrote a letter.
2. An indirect object is usually a person or thing receiving something from the subject of the verb, e.g.
    He gave me *the pen.*
    (*me* is the indirect object, and *the pen* is the direct object.)
    I sent my bank *a letter.*
    (*my bank* is the indirect object, and *a letter* is the direct object.)
    Note that the indirect object can usually be rewritten with the preposition *to*: *he gave the pen to me*; *I sent a letter to my bank*.
Sentences containing an indirect object usually contain a direct object as well, but it is not always expressed, e.g.
    Pay me.
'Object' on its own usually means a direct object.

a person's thoughts and affects his or her behaviour. ☐ **obsessional** *adj.*

obsessive *adj.* of, causing, or showing obsession. ☐ **obsessively** *adv.* **obsessiveness** *n.*

obsidian *n.* a dark glassy rock formed from lava.

obsolescent / ob-suh-**les**-uhnt / *adj.* **1** (of a word) going out of use. **2** (of equipment etc.) becoming out of date. ☐ **obsolescence** *n.*

obsolete / **ob**-suh-leet / *adj.* **1** (of a word) no longer in use. **2** (of equipment etc.) discarded; antiquated.

obstacle *n.* a person or thing that obstructs progress.

obstetrician / ob-stuh-**trish**-uhn / *n.* a specialist in obstetrics.

obstetrics / uhb-**stet**-riks, ob- / *n.* the branch of medicine and surgery that deals with childbirth. ☐ **obstetric** *adj.*

obstinate *adj.* **1** keeping firmly or stubbornly to an opinion or course of action against advice. **2** persistent, not yielding to treatment (*an obstinate cough*). ☐ **obstinately** *adv.* **obstinacy** *n.*

obstreperous / uhb-**strep**-uh-ruhs, ob- / *adj.* noisy, unruly. ☐ **obstreperously** *adv.*

obstruct *v.* **1** block; make movement along or through (a place) difficult or impossible (*obstructing the road*). **2** prevent or hinder the movement or progress of (*obstructing the police*).

obstruction *n.* **1** obstructing; being obstructed. **2** a thing that obstructs. **3** (in sport) the act of unlawfully obstructing another player. **4** (in medicine) a blockage in a bodily passage, esp. in an intestine.

obstructionist *n.* a person who seeks to obstruct proceedings, legislation, etc.

obstructive *adj.* causing or intended to cause obstruction.

obtain *v.* **1** get, come into possession of (a thing) by effort or as a gift. **2** be established or in use as a rule or custom (*this custom still obtains in some districts*). ☐ **obtainable** *adj.*

obtrude / uhb-**trood**, ob- / *v.* **1** force (oneself or one's ideas) on others. **2** be or become obtrusive. ☐ **obtrusion** *n.*

obtrusive / uhb-**troo**-siv, ob- / *adj.* obtruding oneself; unpleasantly noticeable. ☐ **obtrusively** *adv.*

obtuse / uhb-**tyoos**, ob- / *adj.* **1** of blunt shape, not sharp or pointed. **2** stupid, slow at understanding. ☐ **obtuse angle** an angle of more than 90° but less than 180°. ☐ **obtusely** *adv.* **obtuseness** *n.*

obverse / **ob**-vers / *n.* **1** the side of a coin or medal etc. that bears the head or the principal design. **2** the counterpart or opposite of something. **3** the front or top side of a thing.

obviate / **ob**-vee-ayt / *v.* get round or do away with (an inconvenience or need).

obvious *adj.* easy to see, recognise, or understand. ☐ **obviously** *adv.* **obviousness** *n.*

OC *abbr.* Officer Commanding.

ocarina / ok-uh-**ree**-nuh / *n.* a small egg-shaped musical wind instrument with a mouthpiece and holes for the fingers.

occasion *n.* **1** the time at which a particular event takes place. **2** a special event (*this is quite an occasion*). **3** a suitable time for doing something, an opportunity. **4** a need, reason, or cause (*had no occasion to be alarmed*). • *v.* cause (*his remarks occasioned some surprise*). ☐ **on occasion** when the need arises, occasionally.

occasional *adj.* **1** happening from time to time but not regular or frequent (*occasional showers*). **2** used or meant for a special event (*occasional verses*). ☐ **occasional table** a small table for use as required. ☐ ☐ **occasionally** *adv.*

Occident / **ok**-suh-duhnt / *n.* (**the Occident**) the West as opposed to the Orient.

occidental / ok-suh-**den**-tuhl / *adj.* western. • *n.* a native of the West.

occiput / **ok**-si-put / *n.* the back of the head. ☐ **occipital** / ok-**sip**-uh-tuhl / *adj.*

occlude *v.* **1** stop up, obstruct (pores, a passage, etc.). **2** *Chem.* absorb and retain (gases). ☐ **occluded front** a front formed when a cold front overtakes a warm front, driving warm air upwards and producing a long period of steady rain. ☐ ☐ **occlusion** *n.*

occult / **ok**-ult, uh-**kult** / *adj.* **1** involving the supernatural; mystical; magical (*occult powers*). **2** secret, esoteric (*occult rituals*). • *n.* (**the occult**) the knowledge and study of supernatural phenomena.

occupant *n.* a person occupying a place, dwelling, or position. ☐ **occupancy** *n.*

occupation *n.* **1** occupying; being occupied. **2** taking or holding possession by force, esp. of a defeated country or district. **3** an activity that keeps a person busy; one's employment.

occupational *adj.* of or caused by one's occupation (*an occupational hazard*). ☐ **occupational health** (also **occupational health and safety**) programs designed to maintain and improve the health and safety of workers in their place of work. **occupational therapy** a program of mental or physical activity designed to assist recovery from illness or injury.

occupier *n.* a person living in a house as its owner or tenant.

occupy *v.* (**occupied**, **occupying**) **1** dwell in, inhabit. **2** take military possession of (a country or strategic position etc.). **3** place oneself in (a building etc.) forcibly or without authority as a protest. **4** take up or fill (space or a position). **5** hold as one's official position (*he occupies the post of manager*). **6** keep (a person or his or her time) busy.

occur *v.* (**occurred**, **occurring**) **1** come into being as an event or process. **2** be found to exist in some place or conditions (*kangaroo paws occur naturally only in Western Australia*). ☐ **occur to** come into the mind of.

occurrence / uh-**ku**-ruhns / *n.* **1** occurring. **2** an incident or event.

ocean *n.* **1** the seas surrounding the continents of the earth, esp. one of the very large named areas of this (*the Atlantic, Pacific, Indian, Arctic, and Antarctic Oceans*). **2** (often in *pl.*) *colloq.* a very large expanse or amount (*we have oceans of time*).

Oceania / oh-shee-**ah**-nee-uh, oh-see- / *the* islands of the Pacific Ocean and adjacent seas. ☐ **Oceanian** *adj.* & *n.*

oceanic / oh-shee-**an**-ik, oh-see- / *adj.* of the ocean. • *n.* (**Oceanic**) a branch of the language that includes Melanesian and Polynesian.

oceanography / oh-shuh-**nog**-ruh-fee / *n.* the scientific study of the ocean. ☐ **oceanographer** *n.*

Oceanus / oh-**see**-uh-nuhs, oh-see-**ay**-, oh-see-**ah**- / *Gk myth.* the son of Uranus (Heaven) and Gaia (Earth), and father of the ocean nymphs (Oceanids) and river gods. He is the personification of the great river encircling the whole world.

ocelot / **os**-uh-lot / *n.* a leopard-like cat of Central and South America.

ochre / **oh**-kuh / *n.* **1** a yellow, red, or brownish mineral consisting of clay and iron oxide, used as a pigment. **2** pale brownish-yellow. ☐ **ochreous** *adj.* **ochrous** *adj.*

ock *n. Aust.* = OCKER *n.*

ocker *Aust. n.* a rough, boorish, aggressively Australian male. • *adj.* characterised by brash vulgarity, boorishness, crassness, etc. (*the ocker attitude to women*). • *v.* behave as an ocker. ☐ **ockerisation** *n.* **ockerised** *adj.*

ockerdom *n. Aust.* ockers collectively; their social impact.

ockerism *n. Aust.* behaviour characteristic of an ocker.

ocky / **ok**-ee / *n. Aust. colloq.* an octopus. ☐ **ocky** (*or* **ockie**) **strap** = OCTOPUS STRAP.

o'clock *adv.* of the clock (used in specifying the hour) (*six o'clock*).

octagon / **ok**-tuh-guhn / *n.* a geometric figure with eight sides. ☐ **octagonal** / ok-**tag**-uh-nuhl / *adj.*

octahedron / ok-tuh-**hee**-druhn, -**hed**-ruhn / *n.* a solid geometric shape with eight faces.

octane / **ok**-tayn / *n.* a hydrocarbon compound occurring in petrol. ☐ **high-octane** *adj.* (of fuel) having a high octane number and therefore good antiknock properties. **octane number** (*or* **rating**) a measure of the antiknock properties of a petrol.

octave / **ok**-tuhv / *n.* **1** a series of eight consecutive notes on a scale, between and including the upper and lower note. **2** the interval between the upper and lower note. **3** each of these two notes. **4** these two notes played together. **5** a verse of eight lines.

octavo / ok-**tay**-voh / *n.* (*pl.* **octavos**) **1** the size of a book or page given by folding a sheet of standard size three times to form eight leaves. **2** a book or page of this size.

octet / ok-**tet** / *n.* **1** a musical composition for eight performers; these performers. **2** a group of eight. **3** the first eight lines of a sonnet.

octo- *comb. form* eight.

October *n.* the tenth month of the year.

octogenarian / ok-toh-juh-**nair**-ree-uhn / *n.* a person who is in his or her eighties. • *adj.* of this age.

octopus *n.* (*pl.* **octopuses**) a sea animal with a soft saclike body, eight long tentacles with suckers, and strong beaklike jaws. ☐ **octopus strap** *Aust.* a rubber strap with metal hooks at each end, used to secure luggage, surfboards, etc. to a roof rack or trailer.

ocular / **ok**-yuh-luh / *adj.* of, for, or by the eyes; visual. • *n.* the eyepiece of an optical instrument.

oculist / **ok**-yuh-luhst / *n.* a specialist in the treatment of diseases and defects of the eyes.

OD *colloq. n.* a drug overdose. • *v.* (**OD'd**, **OD'ing**) take a drug overdose.

odalisque / **oh**-duh-lisk / *n. archaic* a female slave in a harem.

odd *adj.* **1** unusual, strange, eccentric (*a very odd idea*). **2** casual, occasional (*odd jobs; at odd moments; earned the odd dollar*). **3** unexpected, unconnected (*picks up odd bargains*). **4** additional to a round number stated (*won fifty-odd dollars*). **5** (of a number) not even, not divisible by two. **6** bearing such a number (*no parking on odd dates*). **7** remaining from a pair or set (*an odd sock*). **8** (of a pair) mismatched (*wearing odd socks*). **9** detached from a set or series (*a few odd volumes*). **10** (following a number) somewhat more than (*forty-odd people*). ☐ **oddly** *adv.* **oddness** *n.*

oddball *n.* (also **oddbod**) *colloq.* an eccentric person.

oddity *n.* **1** strangeness. **2** an unusual person, thing, or event.

oddment *n.* **1** something left over, an isolated article. **2** (**oddments**) miscellaneous articles.

odds *n.pl.* **1** the probability that a certain thing will happen; this expressed as a ratio (*the odds are that it will rain; the odds are 5 to 1 against throwing a six*). **2** the ratio between amounts staked by parties to a bet (*gave odds of 3 to 1*). **3** an equalising allowance given to a weaker competitor. ☐ **at odds with** in disagreement or conflict with. **odds-on** with success more likely than failure; with betting odds in favour of its success (*the odds-on favourite*). **over the odds** above the normal price etc.

ode *n.* a poem expressing noble feelings, often addressed to a person or celebrating an event.

Odin / **oh**-din / *Scand. myth.* the supreme god and creator.

odious / **oh**-dee-uhs / *adj.* hateful, detestable. ☐ **odiously** *adv.* **odiousness** *n.*

odium / **oh**-dee-uhm / *n.* widespread hatred or disgust incurred by a person or associated with an

odometer action (*the resumption of nuclear testing earned worldwide odium*).

odometer / oh-**dom**-uh-tuh / *n.* an instrument for measuring the distance travelled by a wheeled vehicle.

O'Donoghue, Lowitja (also Lois) (1932–), AM, Australian Aboriginal leader, chair of ATSIC 1990–99.

odoriferous / oh-duh-**rif**-uh-ruhs / *adj.* bearing an odour (usu. an agreeable one).

odour / **oh**-duh / *n.* (also **odor**) a smell. □ **in good** (*or* **bad**) **odour** in good (or bad) repute or favour. □□ **odorous** *adj.* **odourless** *adj.*

Odysseus / uh-**dee**-see-uhs / *Gk myth.* king of Ithaca (called Ulysses by the Romans) whose ten-year journey home after the Trojan Wars is the subject of the *Odyssey*.

odyssey / **od**-uh-see / *n.* (*pl.* **odysseys**) **1** a long adventurous journey. **2** (***Odyssey***) a Greek epic poem telling of the wanderings of Odysseus.

OECD *abbr.* Organisation for Economic Cooperation and Development.

OED *abbr.* Oxford English Dictionary.

oedema / uh-**dee**-muh / *n.* (also **edema**) an accumulation of excess fluid in body tissues, causing swelling.

Oedipus complex / **ee**-duh-puhs / *n.* a child's, esp. a boy's, subconscious sexual desire for the parent of the opposite sex and the wish to exclude the parent of the same sex. □ **Oedipal** *adj.* (¶ Named after Oedipus in Greek legend, who, unaware of his own identity, unknowingly killed his father and married his mother.)

o'er *prep.* & *adv. poetic* over.

oesophagus / uh-**sof**-uh-guhs / *n.* (also **esophagus**) (*pl.* **oesophagi** *or* **oesophaguses**) the canal from the mouth to the stomach; the gullet.

oestrogen / **ee**-struh-juhn, **es**-truh- / *n.* (also **estrogen**) a sex hormone responsible for developing and maintaining female bodily characteristics.

oestrus / **ee**-struhs / *n.* (also **estrus, oestrum**) the recurring period of sexual receptivity in many female mammals. □ **oestrous** *adj.*

œuvre / **er**-vruh / *n.* the total works of a writer, musician, artist, etc.

of *prep.* used to indicate relationships: **1** originating from or caused by (*the works of Shakespeare; died of starvation*). **2** containing or made from (*built of bricks*). **3** belonging to or connected with (*the car of the future; items of clothing; chief of police*). **4** identified or specified as (*the city of Adelaide; a pint of milk; a giant of a man*). **5** removed or separated from (*north of the border; got rid of them; robbed her of $100*). **6** referring to (*beware of the dog; accused of murder; short of money*). **7** specifying an object (*a love of music; in search of happiness*). **8** dividing, classifying, or including (*part of the story; this sort of thing*). **9** representing a quality or condition (*a woman of good taste; a boy of sixteen; on the point of leaving*).

■ **Usage** *Of* should not be used instead of *have* in constructions such as *You should have asked*; *He couldn't have known*, although in rapid speech they sound the same.

off *adv.* **1** away, at or to a distance (*drove off; 3 kilometres off*). **2** out of position, not touching or attached, separate (*take the lid off*). **3** disconnected, not functioning, no longer obtainable, cancelled (*turn the gas off; the wedding is off; take the day off*). **4** to the end, completely, so as to be clear (*finish off; sell them off*). **5** situated as regards money or supplies (*well off*). **6** (in a theatre) behind or at the side(s) of the stage (*noises off*). **7** (of food) beginning to decay. • *prep.* **1** from, away from, not on (*fell off a ladder*). **2** not attracted to or involved with for the time being (*off his food; off duty*). **3** leading from, not far from (*in a street off Bennelong Avenue*). **4** deducted from (*$5 off the price*). **5** at sea a short distance from (*sank off Cape York Peninsula*). • *adj.* **1** (of a part of a vehicle, horse, or road) on the right-hand side (*the off front wheel*). **2** of the side of a cricket field to the right-hand side of the wicketkeeper, opposite the leg side. **3** *colloq.* annoying; unfair; in bad taste (*that's really off*). **4** *colloq.* somewhat unwell (*feeling a bit off*). **5** (of the period) not spent at work (*his off day; off hours*). **6** worse than usual; bad (*it's been an off year for the tourist industry*). • *n.* **1** the off side in cricket. **2** the start of a race etc. (*ready for the off*). □ **off and on** now and then. **off chance** a slight possibility. **off colour 1** unwell. **2** indelicate or indecent. **off-key 1** out of tune. **2** not quite appropriate. **off-line** *Computing adj.* not online; *adv.* with a delay between the production of data and its processing; not under direct computer control. **off-peak** in or used outside times when demand is greatest (*off-peak electricity*). **off-putting** repellent, disconcerting. **off season** the time when business etc. is slack. **off-stage** *adj.* & *adv.* not on the stage; not visible to the audience. **off white** white with a grey or yellowish tinge.

■ **Usage** Avoid the use of *off of* for the preposition *off* (e.g. *picked it up off of the floor*).

offal *n.* **1** the less valuable edible parts of an animal, esp. the entrails and internal organs. **2** rubbish, scraps.

offbeat *adj.* unusual, unconventional. • *n. Music* an unaccented beat in a bar.

offcourse / **of**-kaws / *adj. Aust.* (of betting etc.) taking place away from a racecourse (opp. ONCOURSE).

offcut *n.* a remnant of timber, paper, etc.

Offenbach / **of**-uhn-bahk /, Jacques (1819–80), German composer, resident in France from 1833.

offence *n.* **1** breaking of the law, an illegal act. **2** a feeling of annoyance or resentment (*take offence*).

offend *v.* **1** cause offence or displeasure to. **2** do wrong (*offend against the law*). □ **offender** *n.*

offensive *adj.* **1** causing offence, insulting (*offensive remarks*). **2** disgusting, repulsive (*an offensive smell*). **3** used in attacking, aggressive (*offensive weapons*). • *n.* an aggressive action or campaign (*go on the offensive; the UN offensive against Iraq; a big peace offensive*). □ **offensively** *adv.* **offensiveness** *n.*

offer *v.* (**offered**, **offering**) **1** present (a thing) so that it may be accepted, rejected, or considered. **2** state what one is willing to do, pay, or give. **3** show for sale. **4** provide, give opportunity (*the job offers prospects of promotion*). **5** show an intention (*the dog didn't offer to bark*). • *n.* **1** an expression of willingness to give, do, or pay something. **2** an amount offered (*offers above $500*).

offering *n.* a gift or contribution etc. that is offered.

offertory *n.* **1** (in the Mass etc.) the offering of the bread and wine to God by the priest before the consecration. **2** money collected in a religious service.

offhand *adj.* (of behaviour etc.) casual or curt. • *adv.* without previous thought or preparation (*I couldn't say offhand*). □ **offhanded** *adj.* **offhandedly** *adv.* **offhandedness** *n.*

office *n.* **1** a room or building used as a place of business, esp. for clerical and administrative work. **2** the staff working there. **3** a particular room or area of a business (*post office; our Hobart office*). **4** (**Office**) the premises, staff, or authority of certain government departments (*the Taxation Office*). **5** a position of authority or trust, the holding of an official position (*hold office*). **6** an authorised form of Christian worship (*the Office for the Dead*). **7** (in full **divine office**) the daily recital by all in major orders of the prayers, psalms, readings from Scripture, etc. in the breviary. **8** (usu. as **offices**) a piece of kindness or a service (*through the good offices of his friends*).

officer *n.* **1** a person holding a position of authority or trust, an official (*customs officers*). **2** a person who holds authority in the army, navy, air force, etc., or on a passenger ship. **3** a policeman or policewoman. **4** (**Officer**) a member of the grade below Companion in the Order of Australia.

official *adj.* **1** of an office or position of authority (*in his official capacity*). **2** suitable for or characteristic of officials and bureaucracy (*official red tape*). **3** properly authorised (*the news is official*). • *n.* a person holding office. □ **officially** *adv.*

officialdom *n.* officials collectively.

officialese *n. derog.* the formal long-winded language used in official documents.

officiate / uh-**fish**-ee-ayt / *v.* act in an official capacity, be in charge.

officious / uh-**fish**-uhs / *adj.* **1** exerting authority aggressively; bossy. **2** intrusive in correcting, offering help, etc. □ **officiously** *adv.*

offing *n.* □ **in the offing** not far away in distance or future time.

offload *v.* get rid of (something unwelcome or unpleasant) by passing responsibility to someone else.

offprint *n.* a printed copy of an article etc. originally forming part of a larger publication.

offset *v.* (**offset**, **offsetting**) counter balance or compensate for (*this win offsets all my losses*). • *n.* **1** an offshoot. **2** a method of printing in which the ink is transferred to a rubber surface and from this to paper (*offset lithography*).

offshoot *n.* **1** a side shoot. **2** a subsidiary product, organisation, etc.

offshore *adj.* & *adv.* **1** at sea some distance from the shore. **2** (of wind) blowing from the land towards the sea.

offside *adj.* & *adv.* **1** (of a player in soccer etc.) in a position (usu. ahead of the ball) that is not allowed if it affects play. **2** (of a bullock team) of or pertaining to the right-hand side. **3** (foll. by *with*) incurring hostility or opposition from (*found himself offside with most of the staff*). **4** opposed; hostile (*don't get her offside—we need her support*). • *n.* the side of a vehicle that is normally furthest from the kerb. • *v. Aust.* act as an offsider.

offsider *n. Aust.* **1** a partner; an assistant (originally a bullock driver's assistant). **2** a friend, a mate.

offspring *n.* (*pl.* **offspring**) **1** the child or children of a person. **2** the young of an animal. **3** a result or outcome.

oft *adv. archaic* often.

often *adv.* **1** frequently, many times, at short intervals. **2** in many instances.

ogee / **oh**-jee / *n.* **1** the line of a double continuous curve, as in S. **2** a moulding with such a section.

ogham / **og**-uhm / *n.* (also **ogam**) **1** an ancient British and Irish alphabet of twenty characters formed by parallel strokes on either side of or across a continuous line. **2** an inscription in this alphabet. **3** each of its characters.

ogive / **oh**-juyv / *n.* **1** a diagonal groin or rib of a vault. **2** a pointed arch.

ogle / **oh**-guhl / *v.* look flirtatiously or lustfully (at). • *n.* such a look.

O'Grady, John Patrick (1907–81), Australian humorous writer, whose novel *They're a Weird Mob*, written under the pseudonym 'Nino Culotta', was an instant success.

ogre *n.* **1** a cruel or man-eating giant in fairy tales and legends. **2** a terrifying person. □ **ogreish** / **oh**-guh-rish / *or* **ogrish** *adj.*

ogress *n.* a female ogre.

oh *interj.* **1** an exclamation of surprise, pain, entreaty, etc.

ohm *n.* a unit of electrical resistance. (¶ Named after the German physicist G.S. Ohm (1789–1854).)

oil *n.* **1** a thick slippery liquid that will not dissolve in water and is often inflammable. **2** petroleum; a form of this used as fuel (*oil heater*). **3** (also **oils**) oil paint. **4** an oil painting. **5** (**the oil**) *Aust.* information, news (*what's the oil on...?*). • *v.* apply oil to, lubricate or treat with oil. ☐ **oil paint** paint made by mixing powdered pigment in oil. **oil painting 1** the practice or technique of using oil paint. **2** a picture painted using oil paints. **oil rig** a structure equipped for drilling oil wells and extracting oil. **oil slick** a patch of oil, esp. on the sea. **oil tanker** a ship for transporting fuel oil in bulk. **oil up** *Aust. colloq.* **1** give information or news to (*oiled him up on the latest developments*). **2** flatter. **oil well** a well yielding mineral oil. **the dinkum** (*or* **good** *or* **straight**) **oil** *Aust.* reliable information.

oilcloth *n.* strong fabric treated with oil to make it waterproof.

oiled *adj. colloq.* drunk.

oilfield *n.* an area where oil is found in the ground or beneath the sea.

oilskin *n.* **1** cloth waterproofed by treatment with oil. **2** (**oilskins**) waterproof clothing made of this.

oily *adj.* (**oilier**, **oiliest**) **1** of or like oil; covered in oil; containing much oil. **2** unpleasantly smooth in manner; trying to win favour by flattery. ☐ **oiliness** *n.*

ointment *n.* a smooth greasy paste rubbed on the skin as a medicine or cosmetic.

OK[1] (also **okay**) *colloq. adj.* all right, satisfactory. • *adv.* well, satisfactorily. • *n.* (*pl.* **OKs**) approval, agreement to a plan etc. • *v.* (**OK'd**, **OK'ing**) give one's approval or agreement to. (¶ Originally US: probably abbreviation of *orl* (or *oll*) *korrect*, jocular form of 'all correct')

okapi / oh-**kah**-pee / *n.* (*pl.* **okapis**) an animal of Central Africa, like a giraffe but with a shorter neck and a striped body.

okay alternative spelling of OK.

O'Keefe, Johnny (full name: John Michael O'Keefe) (1935–78), Australian rock'n'roll singer.

okra / **ok**-ruh / *n.* a tropical plant with long ridged seed pods that are used as a vegetable and to thicken soups and stews. Also called *gumbo*, *ladies' fingers*.

old *adj.* **1** having lived or existed for a long time. **2** made long ago; used, established, or known for a long time. **3** shabby from age or wear. **4** of a specified age (*ten years old; a ten-year-old*). **5** belonging to the past; not recent or modern (*in the old days*). **6** former, original (*in its old place*). **7** skilled through long experience (*an old campaigner*). **8** *colloq.* used for emphasis in friendly or casual mention (*good old Charlie*). • *n.* (**the olds**) (esp. in teenage use) *colloq.* one's parents. ☐ **of old** of, in, or from former times (*we know him of old*). **old age** the period of a person's life from about 65 or 70 onwards. **old-age pension** a means-tested pension paid by the government to people above a certain age. **old-age pensioner** a person receiving this. **old boy** a former male pupil of a school. **old chum** *Aust. hist.* an immigrant with experience of life in Australia, esp. in the outback (as opposed to a NEW CHUM, sense 2). **old economy** an economy based primarily on industry, manufacturing, etc. Cf. NEW ECONOMY. **old-fashioned 1** in a fashion that is no longer in style. **2** having the ways or tastes of former times. **old girl** a former female pupil of a school. **old gold** dull gold colour. **old guard** the original or most conservative members of a group. **old-growth forest** a forest still in its original condition (as opposed to one that has been logged and replanted). **old hand 1** a person who has had long experience of an activity, occupation, or place. **2** *Aust. hist.* a convict with long experience of life in an Australian penal colony; an ex-convict. **3** *Aust. hist.* an immigrant with some experience of life in Australia. **old hat** *colloq.* tediously familiar or outdated. **old maid 1** *offens.* an elderly unmarried woman. **2** *derog.* a prim and fussy person of either sex. **old-maidish** fussy and prim. **old man** *see* separate entry. **old master 1** a great painter of former times (esp. the 13th–17th centuries in Europe). **2** a painting by such a painter. **old people** *Aust.* **1** Aborigines who live in the traditional manner. **2** elderly Aborigines regarded by their descendants as repositories of traditional knowledge. **old school** traditional attitudes or those people having them. **old stager** an experienced person, an old hand. **old-time** *adj.* belonging to former times. **old-timer** a person with long experience or standing. **old wife** an edible Australian fish, silvery with black stripes and supposedly venomous dorsal fins, which grunts like an old wife when caught (or so the story goes). **old wives' tale** an old and superstitious or foolish belief. ☐☐ **oldish** *adj.* **oldness** *n.*

Old Dart *n. Aust.* Britain, esp. England. (¶ British dialect pronunciation of *dirt*.)

olden *adj. archaic* old; of old.

Old English *n.* = ANGLO-SAXON (sense 2).

oldie *n. colloq.* **1** an old person or thing. **2** a thing that is old or familiar esp. an old song, tune, or film. **3** (**oldies**) (esp. in teenage use) one's parents.

old man *colloq. n.* **1** one's employer, husband, or father. **2** (in full **old man kangaroo**) a fully grown male kangaroo. • *adj.* of exceptional size or duration or intensity etc. (*old man crocodile; old man drought*). ☐ **old man saltbush** either of two shrubs of arid Australia, having grey-green foliage, used as fodder. **old man's beard** an Australian clematis, a vigorous climber with silvery young foliage, perfumed starry white flowers, and silvery beard-like hairs around the fruits.

Old Testament *see* TESTAMENT.

Old World Europe, Asia, and Africa, as distinct from the Americas.

oleaginous / oh-lee-**aj**-uh-nuhs / *adj.* **1** like oil; producing oil. **2** oily in texture. **3** obsequious, ingratiating.

oleander / oh-lee-**an**-duh, ol-ee- / *n.* a poisonous evergreen shrub originally of Mediterranean regions, with red, white, or pink flowers.

olearia / oh-lee-**air**-ree-uh, ol-ee- / *n.* any of a large genus of shrubs (about 80 of the 100 or so species of which are endemic to Australia), having daisy flowers in white, blue, pink, or mauve. Also called *daisy bush*.

olfactory / ol-**fak**-tuh-ree / *adj.* concerned with smelling (*olfactory organs*).

Olga, **Mount** (also called **the Olgas**) = KATA TJUTA.

oligarch / **ol**-uh-gahk / *n.* a member of an oligarchy.

oligarchy / **ol**-uh-gah-kee / *n.* **1** a form of government in which power is in the hands of a few people. **2** these people. **3** a country governed in this way. ◻ **oligarchic** *adj.* **oligarchical** *adj.*

Oligocene / **ol**-uh-guh-seen / *adj.* of the third geological epoch of the Tertiary period. •*n.* this period.

oligopoly / ol-uh-**gop**-uh-lee / *n.* a state of limited competition between a small number of producers or sellers. ◻ **oligopolist** *n.* **oligopolistic** / ol-uh-gop-uh-**lis**-tik / *adj.*

Oliphant, Sir Mark (full name: Marcus Laurence Elwin Oliphant) (1901–2000), AC, Australian nuclear physicist, governor of South Australia 1971–76.

olive *n.* **1** a small oval fruit with a hard stone and bitter pulp from which an oil (*olive oil*) is obtained. **2** the evergreen tree that bears it. **3** = OLIVE GREEN. •*adj.* **1** = OLIVE GREEN. **2** (of the complexion) yellowish-brown. ◻ **olive branch** something done or offered to show one's desire to make peace. **olive green** dull yellowish green. **olive oil** an oil extracted from olives used esp. in cookery.

Olivier / uh-**liv**-ee-ay /, Laurence (Kerr), Baron Olivier of Brighton (1907–89), English stage and film actor and director.

olivine / **ol**-uh-veen / *n.* a mineral that is usu. olive green in colour.

Olsen, John (1928–), AO, Australian artist, well known for his mural in the Sydney Opera House.

Olympia / uh-**lim**-pee-uh / a plain in Greece, in the western Peloponnese. In ancient Greece it was the site of the chief sanctuary of the god Zeus, the place where the original Olympic Games were held, after which the site is named.

Olympiad / uh-**lim**-pee-ad / *n.* **1** a period of four years between Olympic Games, used by the ancient Greeks in dating events. **2** a staging of the modern Olympic Games. **3** a regular international contest in chess etc.

Olympian / uh-**lim**-pee-uhn / *adj.* **1** of Olympus; celestial. **2** (of manners etc.) majestic and imposing. **3** Olympic. •*n.* **1** any of the Greek gods dwelling on Olympus. **2** a person of superhuman attainments or great calm.

Olympic / uh-**lim**-pik / *adj.* of the Olympic Games. •*n.pl.* (**the Olympics**) the Olympic Games.

Olympic Games an ancient Greek sporting and cultural festival held at Olympia every four years and revived since 1896 as a four-yearly international athletic and sports meeting.

Olympus / uh-**lim**-puhs / a mountain in NE Greece, the home of the gods in Greek mythology.

om *n.* (in Buddhism and Hinduism etc.) a mystic syllable considered the most sacred mantra.

O'Malley, King (?1858–1953), Australian Labor politician (believed to have been born in Canada), elected to the first Commonwealth parliament after Federation, responsible for the founding of the Commonwealth and Reserve banks and for founding Canberra.

Oman / oh-**mahn** / a sultanate in Arabia. ◻ **Omani** / oh-**mah**-nee / *adj.* & *n.* (*pl.* **Omanis**).

Omar Khayyám / oh-mah kuy-**ahm** / (d. 1123), Persian poet, mathematician, and astronomer. He is remembered for his *rubáiyát* (quatrains), translated and adapted by Edward Fitzgerald in *The Rubáiyát of Omar Khayyám* (1859).

omasum / oh-**may**-suhm / *n.* (*pl.* **omasa**) the third stomach of a ruminant.

ombudsman / om-**buhdz**-muhn / *n.* an official appointed by a government to investigate complaints by individuals against public authorities.

omega / **oh**-muh-guh, oh-**mee**-guh / *n.* **1** the last (24th) letter of the Greek alphabet (Ω, ω). **2** the last of a series; the final development.

omelette / **om**-luht / *n.* a dish of beaten eggs cooked in a frying pan and served plain or with a savoury or sweet filling.

omen / **oh**-muhn / *n.* an event regarded as a prophetic sign of good or evil.

omicron / oh-**muy**-kruhn, **om**-ee-kron / *n.* the fifteenth letter of the Greek alphabet (Ο, ο).

ominous / **om**-uh-nuhs / *adj.* **1** looking or seeming as if trouble is at hand (*an ominous silence*). **2** giving or being an omen, predictive. ◻ **ominously** *adv.*

omission *n.* **1** omitting; being omitted. **2** something that has been omitted or not done.

omit *v.* (**omitted**, **omitting**) **1** leave out, not insert or include. **2** leave undone, neglect or fail to do.

omni- *comb. form* **1** all; of all things. **2** in all ways or places.

omnibus *n.* **1** *formal* a bus. **2** a volume containing a number of books or stories previously published separately. •*adj.* comprising several items (*omnibus edition*).

omnipotent / om-**nip**-uh-tuhnt / *adj.* having unlimited or very great power. ☐ **omnipotence** *n.*

omnipresent *adj.* present everywhere. ☐ **omnipresence** *n.*

omniscient / om-**nis**-ee-uhnt / *adj.* knowing everything, having very extensive knowledge. ☐ **omniscience** *n.*

omnivorous / om-**niv**-uh-ruhs / *adj.* **1** feeding on both plants and animal flesh. **2** reading, observing, etc. everything that comes one's way.

on *prep.* **1** supported by, attached to, covering, or around (*sat on a chair; a fly on the wall; rings on her fingers*). **2** about one's person (*have you got a pen on you?*). **3** at or during a specified time or event (*on 11 March; on my birthday*). **4** immediately after or before (*I was met on my arrival*). **5** as a result of (*on further investigation*). **6** in a specified group or location (*on the committee; on the Continent*). **7** living or operating by means of (*living on a grant; lives on chips; runs on diesel*). **8** close to or alongside (*a house on the sea; lives on the main road*). **9** against (*marched on Rome; pulled a gun on me*). **10** with a specified basis or reason (*on good authority; arrested on suspicion of murder*). **11** concerning or about (*a book on computers*). **12** involved in a specified process (*on holiday; on strike*). **13** using (a drug) (*on antibiotics; on heroin*). **14** played or broadcast by means of (*a tune on the piano; a program on television*). **15** so as to affect (a person, group, etc.) (*walked out on her; burst in on them*). **16** paid for by (*this round is on me*). **17** added to (*disaster on disaster; ten cents on every glass of beer*). • *adv.* **1** (so as to be) covering or in contact (*put your boots on*). **2** in the appropriate direction; towards something (*looked on from the balcony; come on in*). **3** forward (*head on; side on*). **4** further forward or advanced (*time is getting on; later on*). **5** continuing in an activity (*the band played on; keeps on complaining*). **6** operating or active (*leave the light on; the search is on*). **7** due to take place as planned (*is the party still on?*). **8** (of a person making an offer or challenge) accepted (*you're on!*). **9** (of an idea or suggestion) unacceptable or impracticable (*it's just not on*). **10** being broadcast or performed (*a good film on tonight*). **11** (of an actor) on stage; (of an employee) on duty. • *adj.* of the part of a cricket field to the striker's side and in front of the wicket. • *n. Cricket* the on side. ☐ **be on to** realise the significance of (a thing) or the intentions of (a person). **on for young and old** *Aust.* (of an argument, fight, party, etc.) lacking restraint, with everyone drawn in, participating. **on to** to a position on (*see* ONTO). **on with** *Aust.* having a (esp. sexual) relationship with.

onager / **on**-uh-juh / *n.* a wild ass.

onanism / **oh**-nuh-niz-uhm / *n. literary* **1** masturbation. **2** coitus interruptus.

onball *adj. Aust. Rules* (of a player) following the ball rather than playing in a set position. ☐ **onballer** *n.*

once *adv.* **1** on one occasion only (*only read it once*). **2** at some time in the past (*I once had a car*). **3** ever or at all (*once a thief, always a thief*). **4** multiplied by one. • *conj.* as soon as (*once he had gone she cheered up*). • *n.* one time or occasion (*just this once*). ☐ **all at once 1** suddenly. **2** all together. **at once 1** immediately. **2** simultaneously. **for once** on one particular occasion, even if at no other time. **once and for all** finally, esp. after hesitation. **once-over** *n. colloq.* a quick inspection. **once upon a time** at some unspecified time in the past.

oncer *n. colloq.* **1** a thing that occurs only once. **2** *Aust.* a person elected as a member of parliament (esp. in a marginal seat), who is considered unlikely to hold the seat for more than one term.

oncogene / **ong**-kuh-jeen / *n.* a gene which can transform a cell into a cancer cell.

oncology / ong-**kol**-uh-jee / *n.* the scientific study of tumours. ☐ **oncologist** *n.*

oncoming *adj.* approaching.

oncost / **on**-kost / *n.* an overhead expense, esp. a cost of employing labour additional to the salary payable (e.g. insurance, superannuation, payroll tax, etc.).

oncourse *adj. Aust.* (of betting etc.) taking place at a racecourse (opp. OFFCOURSE).

one *adj.* **1** single in number. **2** a particular person or thing of the kind described (*that's a nasty one*). **3** particular but undefined (*one thing led to another; one day*). **4** only (*the one thing I can't stand*). **5** forming a unity. **6** identical, the same (*of one mind*). **7** *Aust.* (in Aboriginal English) a, an. • *n.* **1** the smallest whole number. **2** a single thing or person (*the red shirt and the green one*). **3** a joke or story (*the one about the parson and the cocky*). **4** *colloq.* a drink (*have one on me*). **5** (**ones**) *Aust.* a call in two-up indicating that the coins have fallen unmatched. • *pron.* **1** a person of a specified kind (*loved ones*). **2** any person; the speaker or writer as representing people in general (*one doesn't want to seem mean*). ☐ **at one** in agreement. **for one** being one, even if the only one (*I for one don't believe it*). **one-armed bandit** a poker machine. **one-dayer** a one-day cricket match. **one-eyed** strongly biased towards (a thing or a person) (*she's a one-eyed supporter of Labor*). **one-horse** *adj. colloq.* small or insignificant (*a one-horse town*). **one-horse race** a contest in which one competitor is far superior to all the others. **one-liner** a joke or witty remark consisting of a single short sentence. **one-night stand 1** a single performance in a place by actors, musicians, etc. **2** a sexual liaison which lasts only the one occasion; the person with whom one has this liaison. **one-off** *adj.* made or done as the only one, not reproduced or repeated; *n.* a one-off event, object, achievement, etc. **one-pub** *adj. Aust.* (of a town etc.) small, uninteresting, one-horse. **one-upmanship** the practice or skill of maintaining a psychological advantage over others. **one-way** *adj.* allowing movement or travel in one direction only (*one-way street; one-way ticket*).

O'Neill, Susan ('Susie') (1973–), OAM, Australian swimmer. She won the 200 metres butterfly at the 1996 Olympic Games and the 200 metres freestyle at the 2000 Olympic Games. She also won ten gold medals in three Commonwealth Games.

oneness *n.* **1** singleness. **2** uniqueness. **3** agreement. **4** sameness.

onerous / **oh**-nuh-ruhs / *adj.* burdensome.

oneself *pron.* the emphatic and reflexive form of *one* (*do it oneself; ask oneself*). ☐ **be oneself** act in one's normal manner. **by oneself** alone; unaided.

ongoing *adj.* continuing to exist or progress.

onion *n.* a vegetable with an edible rounded bulb that has a strong smell and strong flavour. ☐ **oniony** *adj.*

onka *n.* (in full **onkaparinga**) *Aust. rhyming slang* a finger.

Onkaparinga / ong-kuh-puh-**ring**-guh / *n.* **1** a river in SA, part of Adelaide's water supply. **2** (**onkaparinga**) *trademark* a type of blanket. (¶ Gaurna).

onkus *adj. Aust. colloq.* **1** disagreeable; distasteful. **2** not functioning properly; out of order.

online *adj.* & *adv. Computing* directly controlled by or connected to a central processor allowing information to be sent, received, or processed immediately.

onlooker *n.* a spectator. ☐ **onlooking** *adj.*

only *adj.* **1** existing alone, with no others of its or their kind (*the only coat I've got; an only child*). **2** the best, with no others worth considering (*it's the only place to eat*). • *adv.* **1** solely, merely, with nothing or no one else (*I'm only looking; it's only me*). **2** no longer ago than (*saw him only yesterday*). **3** not until (*arrives only on Monday*). **4** with no better result than (*hurried home only to find her gone*). • *conj.* but, except that (*I would go, only I'm too tired*). ☐ **only too** extremely (*we'll be only too pleased*).

o.n.o. *abbr.* or nearest offer.

onomatopoeia / on-uh-mat-uh-**pee**-uh / *n.* the formation of words that imitate or suggest the sounds that they stand for, e.g. *cuckoo*, *plop*, *sizzle*. ☐ **onomatopoeic** *adj.*

onrush *n.* an onward rush.

onscreen *adj.* & *adv.* **1** appearing on a cinema, television, or computer screen. **2** within the range of a film camera; being filmed.

onset *n.* **1** a beginning (*the onset of winter*). **2** an attack or assault.

onshore *adj.* **1** (of wind) blowing from the sea towards the land. **2** on land.

onside *adj.* & *adv.* **1** (of a player in a field game) not offside. **2** cooperative, agreeing (*we need him to be onside with us on this*).

onslaught / **on**-slawt / *n.* a fierce attack.

onto *prep.* to a position on.

■ **Usage** Many people prefer not to use *onto*, and write *on to* in all cases. Note that *onto* cannot be used where *on* is an adverb, e.g. *we walked on to the river* (= continued walking until we reached it).

ontology / on-**tol**-uh-jee / *n.* a branch of philosophy dealing with the nature of being. ☐ **ontological** *adj.*

onus / **oh**-nuhs / *n.* (*pl.* **onuses**) the duty or responsibility of doing something.

onward *adj.* & *adv.* (also **onwards**) with an advancing motion; further on.

onya *interj. Aust. colloq.* = good on you! (*see* GOOD) (*onya, Bill!—that was beaut*).

onyx / **on**-iks / *n.* a stone like marble with different colours in layers.

Oodgeroo Noonuccal *see* NOONUCCAL.

oodles *n. colloq.* a great quantity.

Oodnagalahbi / ood-nuh-guh-**lah**-bee / *n. Aust.* an imaginary place or town in Australia, utterly remote and backward (*see also* BULLAMAKANKA, WOOP WOOP).

oolite / **oh**-uh-luyt / *n.* a granular form of limestone. ☐ **oolitic** *adj.*

oomph *n. colloq.* **1** energy, enthusiasm. **2** sex appeal.

oont / uunt / *n. esp. Aust.* a camel.

oops *interj.* an exclamation on falling or making an obvious mistake etc.

ooroo = HOOROO.

ooze *v.* **1** (of liquid) trickle or flow out slowly. **2** (of a substance or wound etc.) exude a liquid; allow to trickle out slowly. **3** show (a feeling) freely (*ooze confidence*). • *n.* wet mud or slime; a bog or a marsh.

op *n. colloq.* an operation.

op. *abbr.* opus.

opacity / oh-**pas**-uh-tee / *n.* being opaque.

opal *n.* a semiprecious stone usu. of a milky or bluish colour with iridescent reflections. ☐ **opal dirt** *Aust.* the type of earth in which opal occurs.

opalescent / oh-puh-**les**-uhnt / *adj.* iridescent like an opal. ☐ **opalescence** *n.*

opaline / **oh**-puh-luyn / *adj.* opal-like, opalescent.

opaque / oh-**payk** / *adj.* **1** not transparent, not allowing light to pass through. **2** (of a statement etc.) not clear.

op art *n.* art in a style using geometric patterns and optical effects to give an illusion of movement. (¶ The word *op* is short for *optical*.)

op. cit. *abbr.* in the work already quoted. (¶ Latin *opere citato*.)

OPEC / **oh**-pek / *abbr.* Organisation of Petroleum Exporting Countries.

open *adj.* **1** not closed or blocked up; not sealed or locked. **2** not enclosed or confined (*the open road*). **3** uncovered or unprotected (*open drain;*

open goal). **4** undisguised, public (*open hostility*). **5** spread out, unfolded. **6** with wide spaces between solid parts (*open texture*). **7** honest, direct, open-minded. **8** (of a government) conducted in an informative manner receptive to enquiry, criticism, etc. from the public. **9** admitting visitors or customers, ready for business. **10** not restricted to particular categories of people, or to members (*open scholarship; open meeting*). **11** (foll. by *to*) available (*three options are open to us; I'm open to offers*). **12** vulnerable (*open to abuse*). **13** (of a return ticket) not restricted in the date of travel. •*n.* an open championship or competition. •*v.* **1** make or become open or more open. **2** (of a door, room etc.) give access as specified (*opened on to a patio*). **3** begin or establish, make a start (*open a business; opened fire*). **4** ceremonially declare (a building etc.) to be open to the public. ☐ **in the open air** not inside a house or building. **open-air** taking place in the open air. **open-and-shut** perfectly straightforward. **open book 1** a person whose motives, feelings, etc. are transparent, easily read. **2** anything that is easily understood. **open-cut** *adj.* (of a mine or mining) with removal of the surface layers and working from above, not from shafts. **open day 1** a day when the public may visit a place that is not normally open to them. **2** a day when a university etc. puts itself, its courses, etc., on display for prospective students. **open-door** *adj.* open, accessible to all (*open-door management*). **open-ended** with no fixed limit (*an open-ended discussion*). **open go** Aust. = OPEN SLATHER. **open-heart surgery** surgery with the heart exposed and with blood circulating temporarily through a bypass. **open house** hospitality to all comers. **open letter** a letter of comment or protest addressed to a person by name but printed in a newspaper. **open mind** a mind that is unprejudiced or undecided. **open-minded** accessible to new ideas, unprejudiced. **open-plan** *adj.* (of a house, office, etc.) having large undivided rooms. **open prison** a prison with few physical restraints on the prisoners. **open question** a matter on which no final verdict has yet been made or on which none is possible. **open secret** a supposed secret which is known to many. **open slather** *Aust. colloq.* **1** freedom to operate without impediment, a free rein. **2** a free-for-all. **open verdict** a verdict that does not specify whether a crime is involved in the case of a person's death. **the open 1** open space; open country; open air. **2** public notice; general attention (*bring the matter out into the open*). ☐☐ **openness** *n.*

opener *n.* **1** a device for opening tins, bottles, etc. **2** *colloq.* the first item on a program etc. **3** *Cricket* an opening batsman.

opening *n.* **1** a space or gap; a place where something opens. **2** the beginning of something. **3** an opportunity; a vacancy (for a job). •*adj.* initial, first (*opening remarks*).

openly *adv.* without concealment, publicly, frankly.

opera *n.* **1** a play in which the words are sung to a musical accompaniment. **2** dramatic works of this kind. **3** an opera house. •*n.pl. see* OPUS. ☐ **opera glasses** small binoculars for use at the opera or theatre. **opera house 1** a theatre for operas. **2** (**the Opera House**) the Sydney Opera House.

operable *adj.* **1** able to be operated. **2** able to be treated by a surgical operation.

operate *v.* **1** be in action; produce an effect (*the new tax operates to our advantage*). **2** control the functioning of (*he operates the lift*). **3** perform a surgical operation. **4** conduct a military or similar operation. ☐ **operating system** the basic software that enables a computer program to be run. **operating theatre** a room for surgical operations.

operatic *adj.* **1** of or like an opera or an opera singer. **2** in opera (*an operatic soprano.*)

operation *n.* **1** operating; being operated. **2** the way a thing works. **3** a piece of work, something to be done. **4** strategic military activities in war or during manoeuvres. **5** an act of surgery performed on a patient.

operational *adj.* **1** of, engaged in, or used in operations. **2** able to function (*is the system operational yet?*).

operative *adj.* **1** having an effect, working or functioning. **2** having the main relevance ('*may*' *is the operative word*). **3** of surgical operations. •*n.* a worker, esp. a skilled one.

operator *n.* **1** a person who operates a machine; one who engages in business or runs a business etc. **2** one who makes connections of lines at a telephone exchange. **3** *colloq.* a person acting in a specified way (*a smooth operator*). **4** a symbol or function denoting an operation in maths, computing, etc.

operculum / oh-**per**-kyuh-luhm, uh- / *n.* (*pl.* **opercula**) a flap covering the gills of a fish; any other flap-like cover on a plant or animal.

operetta *n.* a short or light opera.

ophidian / oh-**fid**-ee-uhn / *n.* a member of a suborder of reptiles including snakes. •*adj.* **1** of this order. **2** snakelike.

ophthalmia / of-**thal**-mee-uh / *n.* inflammation of the eye, conjunctivitis.

ophthalmic / of-**thal**-mik / *adj.* of or for the eyes and its diseases.

ophthalmology / of-thal-**mol**-uh-jee / *n.* the study of the eye and its diseases. ☐ **ophthalmologist** *n.*

ophthalmoscope / of-**thal**-muh-skohp / *n.* an instrument for examining the retina and other parts of the eye.

opiate / oh-pee-uht / *n.* **1** a sedative drug containing opium. **2** a thing that soothes the feelings or dulls activity.

opine / oh-**puyn** / *v. literary* express or hold as one's opinion.

opinion *n.* **1** an unproven belief or judgment; a view held as probable. **2** what one thinks on a particular point (*your opinion on capital punishment*). **3** a judgment or observation given by an expert. **4** an estimation (*have a low opinion of him*). ☐ **opinion poll** an assessment of public opinion made by questioning a representative sample of people.

opinionated *adj.* having strong opinions and holding them obstinately.

opium *n.* an addictive drug made from the juice of certain poppies and used in medicine as a sedative and painkiller.

opossum / uh-**pos**-uhm / *n.* **1** a tree-living American marsupial. **2** = POSSUM.

■ **Usage** In Australia and New Zealand, *opossum* has now been replaced by *possum*.

opp. *abbr.* opposite.

Oppenheimer / **op**-uhn-huy-muh /, Julius Robert (1904–67), American theoretical physicist who led the team which designed and built the first atomic bomb during the Second World War.

opponent *n.* a person or group opposing another.

opportune / **op**-uh-tyoon / *adj.* **1** (of time) suitable or favourable for a purpose. **2** (of an action or event) well-timed. ☐ **opportunely** *adv.*

opportunist / op-uh-**tyoo**-nuhst / *n.* one who grasps opportunities, often in an unprincipled way. ☐ **opportunism** *n.*

opportunistic / op-uh-tyoo-**nis**-tik / *adj.* **1** exploiting chances offered by immediate circumstances without reference to a general plan or moral principle. **2** (of a plant or animal) able to spread quickly into a previously unexploited habitat. **3** (of a micro-organism or an infection caused by it) rarely affecting patients, except in unusual circumstances, typically when the immune system is depressed.

opportunity *n.* a time or set of circumstances that are suitable for a particular purpose. ☐ **opportunity shop** a shop (run by a charitable organisation) in which donated second-hand goods, esp. clothes, are sold.

opposable *adj.* **1** (of the thumb in primates) facing and able to touch the fingers of the same hand and so grip objects. **2** able to be opposed.

oppose *v.* **1** show resistance to, argue or fight against. **2** place opposite; place be in opposition to. **3** represent (things) as contrasting. ☐ **as opposed to** in contrast with.

opposite *adj.* **1** having a position on the other or further side, facing. **2** of a contrary kind, as different as possible from (*opposite opinion; opposite directions*). • *n.* an opposite thing, person, or term. • *adv.* facing, on the other side (*lives opposite*). • *prep.* **1** facing (*sat opposite me*). **2** in a complementary role to (another actor etc.) (*she played opposite Laurence Olivier*). ☐ **opposite number** a person holding a similar position to oneself in another group or organisation. **the opposite sex** either sex in relation to the other.

opposition *n.* **1** resistance, being hostile or in conflict or disagreement. **2** the people who oppose a proposal etc.; one's competitors or rivals. **3** placing or being placed opposite; contrast. **4** (**the Opposition**) the chief parliamentary party opposed to the one that is in office.

oppress *v.* **1** govern harshly, treat with continual cruelty or injustice. **2** weigh down with cares or unhappiness. ☐ **oppression** *n.* **oppressor** *n.*

oppressive *adj.* **1** oppressing. **2** difficult to endure. **3** (of weather) sultry and tiring. ☐ **oppressively** *adv.* **oppressiveness** *n.*

opprobrious / uh-**proh**-bree-uhs / *adj.* (of language) showing scorn or reproach, abusive.

opprobrium / uh-**proh**-bree-uhm / *n.* great disgrace brought by shameful conduct.

oppugn / uh-**pyoon** / *v.* dispute the truth or validity of.

op shop *n.* (also **opp shop**) *Aust.* = OPPORTUNITY SHOP.

opt *v.* (often foll. by *for*) make a choice. ☐ **opt out** choose not to participate.

optic *adj.* of the eye or the sense of sight. • *n.* (**optics**) the scientific study of light and vision.

optical *adj.* **1** of the sense of sight. **2** aiding sight. **3** relating to optics. ☐ **optical character reader** a computer device enabling written and printed material to be scanned optically and then stored. **optical character recognition** a process by which written and printed material is scanned electronically and letters and numbers are recognised by a computer. **optical fibre** thin glass fibre used in fibre optics to transmit signals. **optical illusion 1** an image which deceives the eye. **2** the mental misinterpretation that this causes. ☐☐ **optically** *adv.*

optician / op-**tish**-uhn / *n.* **1** a maker or seller of spectacles and other optical equipment. **2** a person trained in the detection and correction of poor eyesight.

optimal *adj.* best or most favourable (*achieved the optimal result*).

optimise *v.* (also **-ize**) make the best or most effective use of. ☐ **optimisation** *n.*

optimism *n.* a tendency to take a hopeful view of things, or to expect that results will be good. ☐ **optimist** *n.*

optimistic *adj.* showing optimism, hopeful. ☐ **optimistically** *adv.*

optimum *adj.* best, most favourable. • *n.* (*pl.* **optima**) the best or most favourable conditions or amount etc.

option *n.* **1** freedom to choose (*had no option but to go*). **2** a thing that is or may be chosen (*none of*

optional | 582 | **order**

the options is satisfactory). **3** the right to buy or sell something at a certain price within a limited time. ☐ **keep** (*or* **leave**) **one's options open** avoid committing oneself so that one still has a choice.

optional *adj.* not compulsory. ☐ **optionally** *adv.*

optometrist / op-**tom**-uh-truhst / *n.* a person who tests eyes for defects of vision and provides the required corrective lenses. ☐ **optometry** *n.*

opulent / **op**-yuh-luhnt / *adj.* **1** wealthy, rich. **2** abundant, luxuriant. ☐ **opulently** *adv.* **opulence** *n.*

opus / oh-puhs, op-uhs / *n.* (*pl.* **opera** / **op**-uh-ruh /) a musical composition numbered as one of a composer's works (usu. in order of publication) (*Beethoven opus 15*).

or *conj.* **1** as an alternative (*are you coming or not?*). **2** also known as (*hydrophobia or rabies*). ☐ **or else 1** otherwise (*run or else you'll be late*). **2** *colloq.* expressing a warning or threat (*do what you're told or else*).

oracle *n.* **1** one of the places where the ancient Greeks consulted their gods for advice or prophecy. **2** the usu. ambiguous reply given. **3** a person or thing regarded as a source of wisdom or knowledge. ☐ **oracular** / uh-**rak**-yuh-luh / *adj.*

oracy / **o**-ruh-see, **aw**- / *n.* the ability to express oneself fluently in speech.

oral / **o**-ruhl, **aw**- / *adj.* **1** spoken not written (*oral evidence*). **2** of the mouth; done or taken by mouth (*oral sex; oral contraceptives*). • *n. colloq.* a spoken (not written) examination. ☐ **orally** *adv.*

orange *n.* **1** a round juicy citrus fruit with reddish-yellow peel. **2** reddish yellow. • *adj.* orange-coloured. ☐ **orange-bellied parrot** a rare, chiefly coastal parrot of south-eastern Australia, having grass-green plumage above and a brilliant orange undersurface. **orange blossom** flowers of the orange tree, traditionally worn by brides. **orange horseshoe bat** a tropical northern Australian bat with bright orange fur.

orang-utan / uh-rang-uh-**tan**, uh-**rang**-uh-tan / *n.* (also **orang-outang**) a large reddish-haired long-armed anthropoid ape of Borneo and Sumatra.

oration / o-**ray**-shuhn, uh- / *n.* a long speech, esp. of a ceremonial kind.

orator / **o**-ruh-tuh / *n.* a person who makes public speeches; one who is good at public speaking.

oratorio / o-ruh-**taw**-ree-oh / *n.* (*pl.* **oratorios**) a musical composition for solo voices, chorus, and orchestra, usu. with a biblical theme and performed without costume, scenery, or action.

oratory / **o**-ruh-tuh-ree, -tree / *n.* **1** the art or skill of public speaking. **2** a small chapel or place for private worship. ☐ **oratorical** *adj.*

orb *n.* **1** a sphere or globe. **2** an ornamental globe surmounted by a cross, forming part of coronation regalia. **3** *poetic* the eye.

orbicular / aw-**bik**-yuh-luh / *adj. formal* spherical, circular.

orbit *n.* **1** the curved path of a planet, satellite, or spacecraft etc. round another body. **2** a person's range of action, sphere of influence. • *v.* move in an orbit; travel in an orbit round (a body). ☐ **orbiter** *n.*

orbital / **aw**-buh-tuhl / *adj.* **1** (of a road) passing round the outside of a city. **2** of an orbit (*orbital velocity*). ☐ **orbitally** *adv.*

orc *n.* a fierce goblin; a monster; an ogre.

orca *n.* **1** a killer whale. **2** a large sea animal or sea monster.

orchard / **aw**-chuhd / *n.* a piece of land planted with fruit trees.

orchardist *n.* a commercial fruit grower.

orchestra *n.* **1** a large body of people playing various musical instruments, including stringed and wind instruments and percussion. **2** (in full **orchestra pit**) the part of a theatre where they sit, in front of the stalls and lower than the stage. ☐ **orchestral** / aw-**kes**-truhl / *adj.*

orchestrate / **aw**-kuh-strayt / *v.* **1** compose or arrange (music) for performance by an orchestra. **2** coordinate (things) deliberately (*an orchestrated series of protests*). ☐ **orchestration** *n.*

orchid / **aw**-kuhd / *n.* any of various plants which (usually) bear flowers in fantastic shapes and brilliant colours.

orchitis / aw-**kuy**-tuhs / *n.* inflammation of the testicles.

ordain *v.* **1** confer the sacrament of holy orders on; appoint to the priesthood or the ministry. **2** (of God or fate) destine (*has ordained us to die*). **3** appoint or decree authoritatively (*ordained that he should resign*).

ordeal / aw-**deel** / *n.* **1** a difficult experience that tests a person's character or power of endurance. **2** *hist.* the testing of an accused person by subjecting him or her to severe pain, with survival taken as divine proof of innocence.

order *n.* **1** the way in which things are placed in relation to one another; tidiness. **2** a proper or customary sequence (*alphabetical order*). **3** a condition in which every part or unit is in its right place or in a normal or efficient state (*in good working order; out of order*). **4** the condition brought about by good and firm government and obedience to the laws (*law and order*). **5** a system of rules or procedure. **6** a command, an instruction given with authority. **7** a request to supply goods; the goods themselves. **8** a written direction (esp. to a bank or post office) to pay money, or giving authority to do something (*a postal order; an estate agent's order to view property*). **9** a rank or class in society (*the lower orders*). **10** a kind, sort, or quality (*showed courage of the highest order*). **11** (**Order**) a community of monks, friars, priests, or nuns, bound by a common rule of life (*the Franciscan Order*). **12** any of the grades of the Christian ministry. **13** (**orders**) the status of a member of the clergy (*women are now being admitted to Anglican* *orders*). **14** a company of people distinguished by a particular honour (*the Order of Australia*). **15** a style of ancient Greek or Roman architecture distinguished by the type of column used. **16** a scientifically classified group of plants or animals. • *v.* **1** put in order, arrange methodically. **2** issue a command to, command that (something shall be done). **3** give an order for (goods etc.); direct a waiter to serve (certain food). □ **in order to** (*or* **that**) with the intention that, with the purpose of. **major orders** (in the Christian ministry) the higher grades of ordination: bishop, priest, deacon, subdeacon. **minor orders** (in the Christian ministry) grades of ordination below subdeacon. **of** (*or* **in**) **the order of** approximately. **on order** (of goods) ordered but not yet received. **to order** according to the buyer's instructions.

orderly *adj.* **1** well arranged, in good order, tidy. **2** methodical (*an orderly mind*). **3** obedient, well-behaved (*an orderly crowd*). • *n.* **1** a soldier who carries orders or does errands for a senior officer. **2** a male attendant in a hospital. □ **orderliness** *n.*

Order of Australia *n.* an order of merit established in 1975 to reward achievement and merit to Australia and humanity at large. It has civil and military divisions, consisting of companions (AC), officers (AO), members (AM), and medallists (OAM). Awards are made by the governor-general on the recommendations of the Council of the Order from nominations which may be submitted by any person or organisation in Australia. The awards AK (Knight of the Order of Australia) and AD (Dame of the Order of Australia) are no longer made.

ordinal *n.* (in full **ordinal number**) a number defining a thing's position in a series (e.g. *first*, *fifth*, *twentieth*).

ordinance *n.* a rule made by authority, a decree.

ordinand / aw-duh-nuhnd / *n.* a candidate for ordination, esp. to the priesthood.

ordinary *adj.* usual, customary, not exceptional. • *n.* *Catholic Church* parts of the Mass that do not vary from day to day (as opposed to the PROPER). □ **in the ordinary way** if the circumstances were not exceptional. □ □ **ordinarily** *adv.* **ordinariness** *n.*

ordinate / aw-duh-nuht / *n.* (in mathematics) a coordinate measured usu. vertically.

ordination *n.* the act of conferring holy orders on an ordinand.

ordnance *n.* military supplies and materials; the government service dealing with these.

Ordovician / aw-doh-**vish**-ee-uhn / *Geol. adj.* of the second period of the Palaeozoic era. • *n.* this period.

Ord River a river in the far north of WA. □ **Ord River Irrigation Scheme** a scheme for providing irrigation by damming the Ord (completed 1972). The Ord Dam is the largest artificial lake in Australia, covering an area of 740 sq. km.

ordure / aw-dyoor / *n. literary* dung.

ore *n.* solid rock or mineral, found in the earth's crust, from which metal or other useful or valuable substances can be extracted (*iron ore*).

oread / aw-ree-ad / *n.* (in Greek and Roman mythology) a mountain nymph.

oregano / o-ruh-**gah**-noh / *n.* dried wild marjoram used as a seasoning.

organ *n.* **1** a musical instrument consisting of pipes that sound notes when air is forced through them, operated by keyboards and pedals. **2** a distinct part of an animal or plant body, adapted for a particular function (*digestive organs*). **3** (esp. *jocular*) the penis. **4** a medium of communication (e.g. a newspaper) giving the views of a particular group. □ **organ bird** either of two Australian birds having an extremely melodious song: the pied butcherbird and the magpie. **organ-grinder 1** a person who plays a barrel organ. **2** (in full **organ-grinder lizard**) any of many Australian lizards having a characteristic waving movement of a forelimb as if turning the handle of a barrel organ.

organdie / aw-guhn-dee / *n.* a kind of fine translucent usu. stiffened muslin.

organic / aw-**gan**-ik / *adj.* **1** of or affecting an organ or organs of the body (*organic diseases*). **2** of or formed from living things (*organic matter*). **3** produced without the use of artificial fertilisers or pesticides (*organic vegetables; organic gardening*). **4** organised or arranged as a system of related parts (*the business forms an organic whole*). □ **organic chemistry** chemistry of carbon compounds, present in all living matter.

organisation *n.* (also **-ization**) **1** organising; being organised. **2** an organised body of people; an organised system. □ **organisational** *adj.*

Organisation for Economic Cooperation and Development an organisation formed in 1961 (replacing the Organisation for European Economic Cooperation) to assist the economy of its member nations and to promote world trade. Its members include the industrialised countries of western Europe together with Australia, Japan, New Zealand, and the US.

Organisation of the Petroleum Exporting Countries an association of the thirteen major oil-producing countries, founded in 1960 to coordinate policies.

organise *v.* (also **-ize**) **1** arrange in an orderly or systematic way. **2** make arrangements for (*organise a picnic*). **3** provide; take responsibility for (*who will organise the sandwiches?*). **4** enlist (a person or group) in a trade union, political party, etc.; form (a trade union etc.) (*organised the workers*). **5** make organic, make into living tissue. □ **organiser** *n.*

organism / aw-guh-niz-uhm / *n.* a living being, an individual animal or plant.

organist *n.* one who plays the organ.

organochlorine *n.* any of a large group of pesticides and other synthetic organic compounds with chlorinated aromatic molecules.

organophosphorous *adj.* denoting synthetic organic compounds containing phosphorus, esp. pesticides and nerve gases of this kind.

organza / aw-**gan**-zuh / *n.* thin stiff transparent dress fabric of silk or synthetic fibre.

orgasm / **aw**-gaz-uhm / *n.* **a** sexual climax characterised by feelings of pleasure centred in the genitals and (in men) experienced as an accompaniment to ejaculation. **b** an instance of this. •*v.* experience a sexual orgasm. ◻ **orgasmic** / aw-**gaz**-mik / *adj.*

orgy / **aw**-jee / *n.* **1** a wild party, esp. one involving excessive drinking and indiscriminate sexual activity. **2** excessive indulgence in an activity (*an orgy of destruction*). ◻ **orgiastic** *adj.*

oriel window / **aw**-ree-uhl, o- / a projecting window in an upper storey.

orient / **aw**-ree-uhnt, o- / *n.* (**the Orient**) the East; countries east of the Mediterranean, esp. East Asia. •*v.* **1** place or determine the position of (a thing) with regard to the points of the compass. **2** face or direct (towards a certain direction). ◻ **orient oneself** get one's bearings; become accustomed to a new situation.

oriental / aw-ree-**en**-tuhl, o- / (often **Oriental**) *adj.* of the Orient, of the eastern or Asian world or its civilisation. •*n.* a native of the Orient.

orientate / o-ree-en-tayt, **aw**- / *v.* orient.

■ **Usage** Many people object to *orientate* as an unnecessary duplication of *orient*, but the variant form has been in existence since the mid 19th c.

orientation / o-ree-en-**tay**-shuhn / *n.* **1** orienting; being oriented. **2** position relative to surroundings. **3** an introduction to a subject or situation; a briefing or short course.

orienteering / aw-ree-en-**teer**-ring, o- / *n.* the competitive sport of finding one's way on foot across rough country by map and compass.

orifice / **o**-ruh-fuhs / *n.* an opening, esp. the mouth of a cavity, a bodily aperture, etc.

origami / o-ruh-**gah**-mee / *n.* the Japanese art of folding paper into decorative shapes.

origin *n.* **1** the point, source, or cause from which a thing begins its existence ('*kangaroo' is a word of Aboriginal origin*). **2** (often as **origins**) a person's ancestry or parentage (*a man of humble origins*).

original *adj.* **1** existing from the beginning, earliest. **2** inventive, creative; new in character or design (*an original idea*). **3** not a copy or a translation; by the artist rather than being a reproduction (*the original Greek text; an original Rembrandt*). •*n.* **1** the first form of something, the thing from which another is copied. **2** an eccentric or unusual person. ◻ **original Australian** an Aboriginal person. **original sin** the condition of innate wickedness thought to be common to all humanity because of the sin of Adam and Eve. ◻◻ **originally** *adv.* **originality** *n.*

originate *v.* **1** give origin to, cause to begin. **2** have origin, begin (*from what country did the custom originate?*). ◻ **origination** *n.* **originator** *n.*

oriole / **aw**-ree-ohl / *n.* any bird of the genus *Oriolus*, many of which have striking plumage, esp. the yellow oriole of Australia.

Orion / uh-**ruy**-uhn / **1** Gk myth. a giant and hunter, said to have been turned into a constellation on his death. **2** a constellation containing many bright stars including **Orion's belt**, three stars in a short line.

orison / **o**-ruh-zuhn / *n.* (usu. in *pl.*) archaic a prayer.

ormolu / **aw**-muh-loo / *n.* **1** gilded bronze or a gold-coloured alloy of copper, used in decorating furniture. **2** articles made of or decorated with this.

ornament *n.* **1** a decorative object or detail. **2** decoration, adornment (*rich in ornament*). **3** a person or thing that adds distinction (*she's an ornament to the legal profession*). •*v.* decorate, be an ornament to. ◻ **ornamentation** *n.* **ornamental** *adj.*

ornate / aw-**nayt** / *adj.* elaborately ornamented.

ornithology / aw-nuh-**thol**-uh-jee / *n.* the scientific study of birds. ◻ **ornithologist** *n.* **ornithological** *adj.*

ornithorhynchus / aw-nuh-thuh-**ring**-kuhs / *Aust.* = PLATYPUS.

orotund / **o**-ruh-tund / *adj.* **1** (of the voice) full, round, imposing. **2** (of writing, style, etc.) pompous; pretentious.

orphan *n.* a child whose parents are dead. •*v.* make (a child) an orphan (*children orphaned by war*).

orphanage *n.* an institution where orphans are housed and cared for.

Orpheus Gk myth. a poet, singer and lyre player so skilled that he could charm wild beasts. He went to the underworld after the death of his wife Eurydice and, singing, secured her release from the dead, but he subsequently lost her because he failed to obey the condition that he must not look back at her until they had reached the world of the living.

orrery / **o**-ruh-ree / *n.* a clockwork model of the solar system.

orris / **o**-ruhs / *n.* a kind of iris that has a fragrant root which is dried for use in perfumery and medicine.

Orstralia / aw-**stray**-lee-uh / *n.* (also **Orstralier**) a representation for satiric effect of an exaggerated, esp. British, pronunciation of 'Australia' (*the Queen of Australia calls it 'Orstralia'*).

orthodontics / aw-thuh-**don**-tiks / *n.* (also **orthodontia**) correction of irregularities in the teeth and jaws. ◻ **orthodontist** *n.* **orthodontic** *adj.*

orthodox *adj.* **1** of or holding conventional or widely accepted beliefs, esp. in religion or morals. **2** (also **Orthodox**) (of Judaism) strictly traditional. **3** generally approved, conventional (*orthodox medicine*). ◻ **orthodoxy** *n.*

Orthodox Church the Eastern or Greek Church (recognising the Patriarch of Constantinople as its head), and the national Churches of Russia, Romania, etc., in communion with it.

orthography / aw-**thog**-ruh-fee / *n.* spelling, esp. with reference to its correctness. ◻ **orthographic** *adj.* **orthographical** *adj.*

orthopaedics / aw-thuh-**pee**-diks / *n.* (also **orthopedics**) the branch of surgery dealing with the correction of deformities in bones or muscles. ◻ **orthopaedic** *adj.* **orthopaedist** *n.*

Orwell, George (real name: Eric Arthur Blair) (1903–50), English novelist and essayist, whose novels include *Animal Farm* and *Nineteen Eighty-Four*.

oryx / **o**-riks / *n.* a large African antelope with straight horns.

OS *abbr.* **1** outsize. **2** *Computing* operating system.

Os *symbol* osmium.

Oscar *n.* any of the statuettes awarded by the US Academy of Motion Picture Arts and Sciences for excellence in film acting, directing, etc.

oscillate / **os**-uh-layt / *v.* **1** move to and fro like a pendulum. **2** vary between extremes of opinion or condition etc. **3** (of an electric current) undergo high-frequency alternations. ◻ **oscillation** *n.* **oscillator** *n.*

oscilloscope / o-**sil**-uh-skohp / *n.* a device for showing oscillations as a display on the screen of a cathode-ray tube.

O'Shane, Pat(ricia June) (1941–), AM, Australian Aboriginal barrister (the first such), head of the NSW Department of Aboriginal Affairs 1981–86 (the first woman and the first Aborigine to head a government department in Australia), appointed Magistrate in 1986 (the first Aborigine to be so appointed).

osier / **oh**-zee-uh / *n.* **1** a kind of willow with flexible twigs used in basketwork. **2** a twig from this.

Osiris / uh-**suy**-ruhs / *Egyptian myth.* • a god connected with fertility. He is known chiefly through the story of his death at the hands of his brother Seth and his subsequent resurrection.

Oslo / **oz**-loh / the capital of Norway.

osmium / **oz**-mee-uhm / *n.* a hard metallic element (symbol Os) used chiefly in alloys with platinum etc.

osmosis / oz-**moh**-suhs / *n.* the passage of fluid through a porous partition into a more concentrated solution. ◻ **osmotic** / oz-**mot**-ik / *adj.*

osprey / **os**-pray, -pree / *n.* (*pl.* **ospreys**) a large bird preying on fish in inland waters.

osseous / **os**-ee-uhs / *adj.* **1** of bone. **2** having bones, bony.

ossify *v.* (**ossified**, **ossifying**) **1** change into bone; make or become hard like bone. **2** make or become rigid and unprogressive (*their ideas had ossified*). ◻ **ossification** *n.*

ostensible / os-**ten**-suh-buhl / *adj.* pretended, put forward as a reason etc. to conceal the real one (*their ostensible motive was humanitarian*). ◻ **ostensibly** *adv.*

ostensive / os-**ten**-siv / *adj.* showing something directly.

ostentation *n.* a pretentious display of wealth etc. intended to impress people. ◻ **ostentatious** / os-ten-**tay**-shuhs / *adj.* **ostentatiously** *adv.*

osteoarthritis *n.* a form of arthritis in which the joints degenerate.

osteopathy / os-tee-**op**-uh-thee / *n.* the treatment of disease or illness by manipulation of the bones and muscles. ◻ **osteopath** *n.* **osteopathic** *adj.*

osteoporosis / os-tee-oh-puh-**roh**-suhs / *n.* a painful condition in which the bones become brittle, often caused by hormonal changes or calcium deficiency.

ostler / **os**-luh / *n. hist.* a person in charge of stabling horses at an inn.

ostracise / **os**-truh-suyz / *v.* (also **-ize**) refuse to associate with, exclude from a group or from society. ◻ **ostracism** *n.*

ostrich *n.* **1** a swift-running flightless African bird, said to bury its head in the sand when pursued, in the belief that it then cannot be seen. **2** a person who refuses to face an awkward truth.

other *adj.* **1** alternative, additional, being the remaining one or set of two or more (*has no other income; try the other shoe; my other friends*). **2** further, additional (*some other examples*). **3** not the same (*my reasons are quite other*). •*n.* & *pron.* the other person or thing (*where are the others?*). • *adv.* otherwise (*cannot react other than angrily*). ◻ **other than 1** apart from; except (*has no friends other than me*). **2** different from (*wouldn't want her to be other than she is*). **the other day** etc., a few days etc. ago. **other-worldly 1** of another world. **2** dreamy, remote, impractical.

othersider = TOTHERSIDER.

otherwise *adv.* **1** in a different way (*could not have done otherwise*). **2** in other respects (*is otherwise correct*). **3** if circumstances were different; or else (*write it down, otherwise you'll forget*). **4** as an alternative (*otherwise known as Jacko*). •*adj.* in a different state, not as supposed (*the truth is quite otherwise*).

otiose / **oh**-tee-ohs, -ohz / *adj.* serving no practical purpose; not required.

otitis / oh-**tuy**-tuhs / *n.* inflammation of the ear.

Ottawa the capital of Canada.

otter *n.* a fish-eating water animal with webbed feet, a flat tail, and thick brown fur.

Ottoman *adj.* of the Turkish dynasty founded by Osman or Othman (1259–1326), his branch of the Turks, or the empire ruled by his descendants (late 13th–early 20th century). • *n.* **1** a Turk of the Ottoman period. **2** (**ottoman**) a long cushioned seat without back or arms, sometimes a storage box with a padded top.

Ouagadougou / wah-guh-**doo**-goo / the capital of Burkina Faso.

oubliette / oo-blee-**et** / *n.* a secret dungeon with a trapdoor entrance.

ouch *interj.* an exclamation of sudden pain.

ought *auxiliary v.* expressing duty, rightness, advisability, or strong probability.

oughtn't = ought not.

ouija / **wee**-juh, -jee / *n.* trademark (in full **ouija board**) a board marked with the alphabet and other signs, used with a movable pointer to indicate messages from the spirits in seances.

ounce *n.* **1** a unit of weight equal to one-sixteenth of a pound (about 28 grams). **2** a very small amount (*hasn't an ounce of common sense*).

our *adj.* of or belonging to us.

Our Father the Lord's Prayer.

Our Lady the Virgin Mary.

Our Lord Christ.

ours *possessive pron.* belonging to us; the thing(s) belonging to us.

ourselves *pron.* **1** the emphatic and reflexive form of *we* and *us* (*we did it ourselves; hurt ourselves*). **2** in our normal state (*not ourselves today*). ☐ **be ourselves** *see* ONESELF. **by ourselves** *see* ONESELF.

oust / owst / *v.* drive out, eject from office or a position or employment etc.

out[1] *adv.* **1** away from or not in a place (*keep out; the tide is out*). **2** dispersed (*share it out; spread out*). **3** indicating a need for alertness (*look out*). **4** not in one's home, place of work, etc. **5** to or at an end; completely (*write it out; die out; tired out*). **6** (of a fire etc.) no longer burning. **7** in error (*3% out*). **8** *colloq.* unconscious, asleep. **9** (of a jury) deciding on a verdict. **10** (of workers) on strike. **11** (of a secret) revealed. **12** (of a flower) open. **13** (of a book, record, etc.) just published or on sale. **14** (of a star) visible after dark. **15** no longer in fashion. **16** (in a game or sport) dismissed, at the end of one's turn. **17** not worth considering (*that idea is definitely out*). **18** (of a stain etc.) removed (*it won't wash out*). • *prep. colloq.* out of (*looked out the window*). • *n.* a means of escape; an excuse (*he has an out for every contingency*). • *v.* **1** come or go out (*the truth will out*). **2** suspend from a team (*he was outed for two matches*). **3** publicly reveal (a well-known person) to be homosexual (*he was outed by some sections of the gay press*). ☐ **out and away** by far (*he is out and away the best Australian bat*). **out-and-out** thorough, complete (*an out-and-out bigot*). **out bush** *Aust.* into or in an area of back country or outback country. **out of 1** from within. **2** not within (*I was never out of Oodnadatta*). **3** from among (*nine people out of ten*). **4** beyond the range of (*out of reach*). **5** so as to be without; lacking (*was swindled out of his money; out of sugar*). **6** from (*get money out of him*). **7** because of (*asked out of curiosity*). **8** by the use of (material) (*what did you make it out of?*). **9** at a specified distance from (*a kilometre out of Kalgoorlie*). **out of date** no longer fashionable, current, or valid (*this passport is out of date*). **out-take** a film or tape sequence rejected in editing. **out to** acting with the intention of (*out to cause trouble*). **out to it** *colloq.* **1** asleep. **2** unconscious. **3** utterly exhausted. **out with it** say what you are thinking.

out[2] *colloq.* a particle (used to form compound verbs and compound adjectives) indicating the utmost degree of a specified behaviour, emotion, etc., e.g. 'veg out' (intensified form of the verb to VEG); 'stressed out' (intensified form of *stressed*) (*see also* -OUT).

out- *comb. form* **1** out of, away from, outward (*outcast*). **2** external, separate (*outhouse*). **3** more than, so as to exceed (*outbid, outgrow, out-talk*).

-out *comb. form colloq.* used in compound nouns which are formed from compound verbs ending in 'out' (*see* OUT[2]) to indicate the utmost degree of a specified behaviour, emotion, etc. (*a wipe-out; a wimp-out*).

outback *Aust. n.* (also **Outback**) (preceded by *the*) remote and uninhabited or sparsely inhabited inland areas of Australia. • *adv.* out, in, or to areas remote from a major centre of population (*they live outback*). • *adj.* of or relating to remote parts of Australia. ☐ **the Great** (**Australian**) **Outback** the outback, esp. as romanticised in some Australian literature.

outbacker *n. Aust.* a person living in the outback.

outbackery *n. Aust.* the cultivation of attitudes and values supposedly characteristic of those who live in the outback.

outbalance *v.* outweigh.

outbid *v.* (**outbid**, **outbidding**) bid higher than (another person).

outboard *adj. & adv.* on or towards the outside of a ship, aircraft, or vehicle. ☐ **outboard motor** a portable motor attached to the rear of a boat.

outbreak *n.* a sudden breaking out of anger, war, disease, etc.

outbuilding *n.* a shed, barn, etc. detached from a main building.

outburst *n.* a bursting out, esp. of strong or violent emotion.

outcast *n.* a person who has been driven out of a group or rejected by society. • *adj.* rejected; homeless.

outclass *v.* surpass greatly.

outcome *n.* the result or effect of an event etc.

outcrop *n.* **1** part of an underlying layer of rock that projects on the surface of the ground. **2** a noticeable manifestation of something (*a sudden outcrop of strikes*).

outcry *n.* a strong public protest.

outdated *adj.* out of date; obsolete.

outdistance *v.* get far ahead of (a person) in a race etc.

outdo *v.* (**outdid, outdone, outdoing**) do better than (another person etc.); surpass.

outdoor *adj.* **1** of or for use in the open air. **2** enjoying open-air activities (*she's not an outdoor type*).

outdoors *adv.* in or to the open air. • *n.* the open air. ▫ **the great outdoors** nature, esp. as in the bush.

outer *adj.* further from the centre or from the inside; exterior, external. • *n.* **1** an external or further out thing or part. **2** *Aust.* **a** an uncovered area for non-members at a racecourse or sports ground. **b** (in two-up) the periphery of the ring. ▫ **on the outer** excluded from the group; rejected. **outer space** the universe beyond the earth's atmosphere.

outermost *adj.* furthest outward, most remote.

outface *v.* disconcert (a person) by one's confident manner or by staring.

outfall *n.* an outlet where water falls or flows out.

outfield *n.* the outer part of a cricket or baseball field.

outfit *n.* **1** a set of equipment. **2** a set of clothes to be worn together. **3** *colloq.* an organisation, a group of people regarded as a unit. • *v.* provide with an outfit, esp. of clothes.

outflank *v.* **1** get round the flank of (an enemy). **2** outmanoeuvre, outwit.

outflow *n.* an outward flow; the amount that flows out.

outfox *v.* outwit.

outgoing *adj.* **1** sociable, friendly. **2** retiring from office (*the outgoing president*). **3** going out. • *n.pl.* (**outgoings**) expenditure.

outgrow *v.* (**outgrew, outgrown, outgrowing**) **1** grow too big for (clothes etc.). **2** grow out of (childish behaviour etc.). **3** grow faster or taller than.

outgrowth *n.* **1** something that grows out of another thing. **2** a natural development, an effect.

outhouse *n.* **1** a building (e.g. a shed or barn) belonging to but separate from a house. **2** an outdoor toilet.

outing *n.* **1** a pleasure trip, an excursion. **2** the act of publicising the fact that a well-known person is gay.

outlandish *adj.* looking or sounding strange or foreign. ▫ **outlandishly** *adv.* **outlandishness** *n.*

outlast *v.* last longer than.

outlaw *n.* **1** a fugitive from the law. **2** *hist.* a person formally deprived of the protection of the law. **3** *Aust.* an intractable horse. • *v.* **1** make illegal; proscribe. **2** declare (a person) an outlaw.

outlay *n.* what is spent on something. • *v.* spend.

outlet *n.* **1** a way out for water or steam etc. **2** a means or occasion for giving vent to one's feelings or energies. **3** a market for goods; a shop (*a retail outlet*).

outline *n.* **1** a line or lines showing the shape or boundary of something. **2** a statement or summary of the chief facts about something. • *v.* draw or describe in outline; mark the outline of. ▫ **in outline** giving only an outline.

outlive *v.* live longer than.

outlook *n.* **1** a view on which one looks out (*a pleasant outlook over the lake*). **2** a person's mental attitude or way of looking at something. **3** future prospects.

outlying *adj.* situated far from a centre, remote.

outmanoeuvre *v.* outdo in manoeuvring.

outmatch *v.* be more than a match for.

outmoded / owt-**moh**-duhd / *adj.* no longer fashionable or acceptable.

outnumber *v.* exceed in number.

outpace *v.* go faster than.

outpatient *n.* a person who visits a hospital for treatment but does not remain resident there.

outpost *n.* **1** a detachment of troops stationed at a distance from the main army. **2** any distant branch or settlement.

outpouring *n.* an intense expressing of one's emotions.

output *n.* **1** the amount produced (by a machine, worker etc.). **2** the electrical power etc. delivered by a machine or apparatus. **3** the printout or results from a computer. • *v.* (**output** or **outputted, outputting**) (of a computer) supply (results).

outrage *n.* **1** an act that shocks public opinion. **2** great anger. **3** violation of rights (*safe from outrage*). • *v.* commit an outrage against; shock and anger greatly.

outrageous *adj.* greatly exceeding what is moderate or reasonable, shocking. ▫ **outrageously** *adv.*

outrank *v.* be of higher rank than.

outré / **oo**-tray / *adj.* eccentric; unseemly. (¶ French)

outrider *n.* a mounted guard or motorcyclist riding ahead of or beside a car, a procession, etc.

outrigger *n.* **1** a spar or framework projecting from the side of a ship or canoe to give stability. **2** a boat fitted with this.

outright *adv.* **1** completely, entirely, not gradually (*bought the house outright*). **2** openly, frankly (*told him outright*). • *adj.* **1** thorough, complete (*an outright fraud*). **2** undisputed (*the outright winner*).

outrun *v.* (**outran, outrun, outrunning**) **1** run faster or further than. **2** go beyond (a specified point or limit).

outsell *v.* (**outsold, outselling**) sell or be sold in greater quantities than.

outset *n.* ▫ **at** (*or* **from**) **the outset** from the beginning.

outshine *v.* (**outshone, outshining**) surpass in splendour or excellence.

outside *n.* the outer side, surface, or part. • *adj.* **1** of or coming from the outside. **2** not in the main building (*an outside toilet*). **3** (of a player in football etc.) positioned nearest to the edge of the field (*outside left*). **4** (of a chance etc.) remote, very unlikely. **5** (of an estimate etc.) greatest possible (*the outside price*). •*adv.* on or at or to the outside. •*prep.* on the outer side of; at or to the outside of; other than (*has no interests outside his work*). ☐ **at the outside** (of amounts) at most. **outside broadcast** one that is not made from a studio. **outside chance** a remote possibility. **outside interest** a hobby etc. not connected with one's work.

outsider *n.* **1** a non-member of a certain group or profession. **2** a competitor thought to have little chance.

outsize *adj.* much larger than average. •*n.* an unusually large person or thing, esp. a garment.

outskirts *n.pl.* the outer districts or outlying parts, esp. of a town.

outsmart *v. colloq.* outwit.

outsource / **owt**-saws / *v.* **1** obtain (goods etc.) by contract from an outside source. **2** contract (work) out. ☐ **outsourcing** *n.*

outspoken *adj.* speaking or spoken without reserve, very frank. ☐ **outspokenly** *adv.* **outspokenness** *n.*

outspread *adj.* spread out.

outstanding *adj.* **1** conspicuous. **2** exceptionally good. **3** (of a debt) not yet paid or settled. **4** still to be dealt with (*outstanding correspondence*). ☐ **outstandingly** *adv.*

outstation *n. Aust.* **1** (on a grazing property) a subordinate station at some distance from the main establishment. **2** an autonomous Aboriginal community at some distance from the centre on which it depends for services and supplies. ☐ **outstation movement** the campaign among Aboriginal people to move out of mission stations, government reserves, towns, etc. and establish autonomous communities in remote areas, esp. on traditional tribal lands.

outstay *v.* stay longer than (*outstayed his welcome*).

outstretched *adj.* stretched out.

outstrip *v.* (**outstripped**, **outstripping**) **1** outrun. **2** surpass.

outvote *v.* defeat by a majority of votes.

outward *adj.* **1** situated on the outside. **2** going towards the outside. **3** in one's expression or actions etc. as distinct from one's mind or spirit. •*adv.* (also **outwards**) towards the outside. ☐ **outward bound** travelling away from home.

outwardly *adv.* on the outside.

outweigh *v.* be greater in weight, value, importance, or significance than.

outwit *v.* (**outwitted**, **outwitting**) get the better of (a person) by one's cleverness or craftiness.

outworn *adj.* worn out, obsolete (*outworn beliefs*).

ouzo / **oo**-zoh / *n.* a Greek drink of aniseed-flavoured spirits.

ova *see* OVUM.

oval *n.* **1** a rounded symmetrical shape longer than it is broad. **2** a sports ground (not necessarily of this shape). •*adj.* having this shape.

ovary / **oh**-vuh-ree / *n.* **1** either of the two organs in which egg cells are produced in female animals. **2** part of the pistil in a plant, from which fruit is formed. ☐ **ovarian** / oh-**vair**-ree-uhn / *adj.*

ovate / **oh**-vayt / *adj.* egg-shaped, oval.

ovation / oh-**vay**-shuhn / *n.* enthusiastic applause.

oven *n.* an enclosed chamber in which things are cooked or heated.

ovenproof *adj.* suitable for use in an oven; heat-resistant.

Ovens a river in north-eastern Vic., rising near Mt Hotham and flowing some 200 km north-west to join the Murray River near Corowa.

ovenware *n.* dishes for cooking food in the oven.

over *adv.* **1** with movement outwards and downwards from the brink or from an upright position (*knocked me over*). **2** with movement from one side to the other or so that a different side is showing (*turn it over*). **3** across a street or other space or distance (*she is over here from New Zealand*). **4** passing above or across something (*climb over; fly over*). **5** so as to cover or touch a whole surface (*the lake froze over; paint it over*). **6** changing or transferring from one hand, side, etc. to another (*went over to the enemy; hand it over*). **7** (in radio conversation) it is your turn to speak. **8** besides, in addition or excess (*left over*). **9** with repetition (*ten times over*). **10** thoroughly, with detailed consideration (*think it over*). **11** at an end, finished (*the crisis is over; it is over between us*). •*n.* a series of 6 balls bowled in cricket. •*prep.* **1** in or to a position higher than. **2** out and downwards from (*fell over the cliff*). **3** so as to cover (*hat over his eyes*). **4** above and across, so as to clear (*the bridge over the Murrumbidgee*). **5** throughout the length or extent of, during (*over the years; stayed over the weekend*). **6** so as to visit or examine all parts (*saw over the house; went over the plan again*). **7** transmitted by (*heard it over the radio*). **8** while engaged with (*we can talk over dinner*). **9** concerning (*quarrelling over money*). **10** more than (*it's over a mile away; is he over 18?*). **11** in superiority or preference to (*the Socceroos' victory over England*). **12** recovered from (*I'm over it now*). •*adj.* **1** upper, outer. **2** superior. **3** extra. ☐ **over and above** besides.

over- *comb. form* **1** above (*overlay*). **2** too much, excessively (*over-anxious*).

overact *v.* act one's part in an exaggerated manner.

overall *n.* **1** a garment worn to protect other clothing, which it covers. **2** (**overalls**) a one-piece garment covering body and legs, worn as protective clothing. •*adj.* **1** including everything, total. **2** taking all aspects into account. •*adv.* in all parts, taken as a whole.

overarm *adj.* & *adv.* with the hand raised above the shoulder.

overawe *v.* overcome with awe.

overbalance *v.* lose balance and fall.

overbear *v.* (**overbore**, **overborne**, **overbearing**) **1** bear down by weight or force or emotion. **2** repress by power or authority.

overbearing *adj.* domineering; overpowering.

overblown *adj.* **1** pretentious or inflated (*an overblown style of writing*). **2** (of a flower etc.) past its prime.

overboard *adv.* from a ship into the water. ❑ **go overboard** *colloq.* **1** be very enthusiastic. **2** behave immoderately.

overburden *v.* burden excessively.

overcast *adj.* (of the sky) covered with cloud. •*v.* (**overcast**, **overcasting**) stitch over (an edge) to prevent it from fraying.

overcharge *v.* **1** charge too high a price. **2** fill too full.

overcoat *n.* a warm outdoor coat.

overcome *v.* (**overcame**, **overcome**, **overcoming**) **1** win a victory over, succeed in subduing. **2** be victorious. **3** make helpless or weak (*overcome by gas fumes; overcome by grief*). **4** find a way of dealing with (a problem etc.).

overcompensate *v.* **1** (usu. foll. by *for*) compensate excessively for. **2** try excessively hard to make amends.

overdo *v.* (**overdid**, **overdone**, **overdoing**) **1** do (a thing) excessively. **2** cook (food) too long. ❑ **overdo it** (*or* **things**) work too hard, exhaust oneself; exaggerate.

overdose *n.* too large a dose of a drug etc. •*v.* give or take an overdose.

overdraft *n.* **1** overdrawing of a bank account. **2** the amount by which an account is overdrawn.

overdraw *v.* (**overdrew**, **overdrawn**, **overdrawing**) **1** draw more from (a bank account) than the amount credited. **2** (as **overdrawn** *adj.*) having drawn more money than is in one's account.

overdress *v.* dress too formally.

overdrive *n.* **1** a mechanism providing an extra gear above the normal top gear in a vehicle. **2** a state of great activity (*now that it's election time, the politicians are going into overdrive*). •*v.* **1** overwork or drive to exhaustion. **2** drive (cattle) too hard.

overdue *adj.* past the expected time for payment, arrival, return, etc.

overestimate *v.* form too high an estimate of. •*n.* too high an estimate. ❑ **overestimation** *n.*

overexpose *v.* **1** expose to the public for too long. **2** expose (film) for too long. ❑ **overexposure** *n.*

overfish *v.* catch so many fish from (a certain area) that next season's supply is reduced.

overflow *v.* / oh-vuh-**floh** / **1** flow over (the edge, limits, or banks etc.). **2** (of a crowd) spread beyond the limits of (a room etc.). •*n.* / **oh**-vuh-floh / **1** what overflows. **2** an outlet for excess liquid.

overfly *v.* (**overflew**, **overflown**, **overflying**) fly over or beyond (a place or territory).

overfond *adj.* having too great a fondness (*an overfond parent*).

overgraze *v.* allow stock to graze land so extensively that it is seriously damaged, with consequent erosion etc.

overgrown *adj.* **1** having grown too large. **2** covered with weeds etc. ❑ **overgrowth** *n.*

overhang *v.* (**overhung**, **overhanging**) jut out over. •*n.* an overhanging part.

overhaul *v.* **1** examine and make any necessary repairs or changes. **2** overtake. •*n.* an examination and repair etc.

overhead *adv.* & *adj.* above the level of one's head; in the sky. •*n.pl.* (**overheads**) the expenses involved in running a business.

overhear *v.* (**overheard**, **overhearing**) hear accidentally or without the speaker's knowledge or intention.

overheat *v.* **1** make or become too hot or too intensive. **2** cause inflation (in) by placing excessive pressure on resources at a time of expanding demand. **3** (as **overheated** *adj.*) excessively excited (*an overheated discussion*).

overjoyed *adj.* filled with very great joy.

overkill *n.* **1** a surplus of capacity for destruction above what is needed to defeat or destroy an enemy. **2** more energy, resources, etc. used than is required to achieve an aim. **3** excess.

overland *adv.* & *adj.* by land, not by sea. •*v. Aust.* drive (large mobs of stock) overland, esp. for a very great distance. ❑ **overland fish** (*or* **trout**) *Aust.* a lizard or snake, esp. when used for human consumption.

overlander *n. Aust.* a drover who drives large mobs of stock over a very great distance.

overlanding *n. Aust.* the driving of stock over very large distances.

overlap *v.* (**overlapped**, **overlapping**) **1** extend beyond the edge of (a thing) and partly cover it (*overlapping tiles*). **2** coincide partially (*our holidays overlap*). •*n.* overlapping; an overlapping part or amount.

overlay *v.* / oh-vuh-**lay** / *v.* (**overlaid**, **overlaying**) **1** cover with a surface layer. **2** lay one thing over another. •*n.* / **oh**-vuh-lay / a thing laid over another.

overleaf *adv.* on the other side of a leaf (page) of a book etc. (*see overleaf for the diagram*).

overlie *v.* (**overlay**, **overlain**, **overlying**) lie on top of; smother by doing this.

overload *v.* / oh-vuh-**lohd** / **1** load excessively (with baggage, work, etc.). **2** put too great a demand on (an electrical circuit etc.) •*n.* / **oh**-vuh-lohd / an excessive quantity or demand.

overlook *v.* **1** have a view of or over (a place) from above. **2** oversee. **3** fail to observe or consider. **4** take no notice of, allow (an offence) to go unpunished.

overlord *n.* a supreme lord.

overly *adv.* excessively; too.

overman *v.* (**overmanned, overmanning**) provide with too many people as workers or crew etc.

over-much *adv.* too much.

overnight *adv.* **1** for a night (*stayed overnight*). **2** during the night. **3** instantly (*won't happen overnight*). • *adj.* **1** done or used overnight (*overnight bag*). **2** instant (*an overnight success*).

overpass *n.* a road that crosses another by means of a bridge.

overplay *v.* give too much importance to. ☐ **overplay one's hand** take unjustified risks by overestimating one's strength.

overpower *v.* overcome by greater strength or numbers.

overpowering *adj.* (of heat or feelings) extremely intense.

overprint *v.* / oh-vuh-**print** / **1** print (a photograph) darker than was intended. **2** print further matter on (an already printed surface, e.g. a postage stamp); print (further matter) thus. • *n.* / **oh**-vuh-print / material that is overprinted.

overqualified *adj.* too highly qualified for a particular job or type of work.

overrate *v.* **1** have too high an opinion of. **2** assess the rates of (a place) too highly.

overrated *adj.* not as good as it is generally believed to be.

overreach *v.* outwit. ☐ **overreach oneself** fail through being too ambitious.

overreact *v.* respond more strongly than is justified. ☐ **overreaction** *n.*

override *v.* (**overrode, overridden, overriding**) **1** set aside (an order) by having, or behaving as if one had, superior authority. **2** prevail over (*considerations of safety override all others*). **3** intervene and cancel the operation of (an automatic mechanism), esp. to take manual control.

overrule *v.* **1** set aside (a decision etc.) by using one's authority. **2** reject a proposal of (a person) in this way.

overrun *v.* (**overran, overrun, overrunning**) **1** spread over and occupy or injure (*the place is overrun with mice*). **2** exceed (a limit or time allowed) (*the broadcast overran its allotted time*).

overseas *adv.* & *adj.* across or beyond the sea, abroad.

oversee *v.* (**oversaw, overseen, overseeing**) officially supervise; superintend.

overseer *n.* **1** a person who supervises others, esp. workers. **2** *Aust. hist.* a convict who supervises the work of a party of convicts. **3** *Aust.* a person who manages a rural property.

over-sensitive *adj.* excessively sensitive; too easily hurt or quick to react.

overservicing *n.* the practice by some doctors of providing more medical services than their patients require in order that greater claims may be made by these doctors on the government medical fund. ☐ **overservice** *v.*

oversexed *adj.* having unusually strong sexual desires.

overshadow *v.* **1** cast a shadow over. **2** make (a person or thing) seem unimportant in comparison (*men's sports always overshadow women's in the Australian media*).

overshoot *v.* (**overshot, overshooting**) pass beyond (a target or limit) (*the plane overshot the runway*). ☐ **overshoot the mark** go beyond what is intended or proper.

oversight *n.* **1** supervision. **2** an unintentional omission or mistake.

oversimplify *v.* (**oversimplified, oversimplifying**) misrepresent (a problem etc.) by stating it in terms that are too simple. ☐ **oversimplification** *n.*

oversize *adj.* (also **oversized**) of greater than the usual size.

overspill *n.* **1** what spills over or overflows. **2** the surplus population of a town etc., who seek accommodation in other districts.

overstate *v.* state too strongly; exaggerate. ☐ **overstatement** *n.*

overstay *v.* stay longer than (*overstay one's welcome*).

oversteer *v.* (of a car etc.) have a tendency to turn more sharply than was intended. • *n.* this tendency.

overstep *v.* (**overstepped, overstepping**) go beyond (a permitted or acceptable limit). ☐ **overstep the mark** violate conventional behaviour etc.

overstock *v.* **1** provide more cattle or sheep than one's land can feed. **2** stock with too many items.

overstretch *v.* **1** stretch too much or too far. **2** make excessive demands on (a person, resources, etc.).

overstrung *adj.* **1** (of a piano) with strings in sets crossing each other obliquely. **2** (of a person, nerves, etc.) too highly strung; tense.

oversubscribed *adj.* with applications for (an issue of shares etc.) in excess of the number offered.

overt / oh-**vert** / *adj.* done or shown openly (*overt hostility*). ☐ **overtly** *adv.*

overtake *v.* (**overtook, overtaken, overtaking**) **1** catch up with and pass (a person or vehicle). **2** (of misfortune etc.) come suddenly upon.

overtax *v.* **1** levy excessive taxes on. **2** put too heavy a burden or strain on (*don't overtax your strength*).

overthrow *v.* / oh-vuh-**throh** / (**overthrew, overthrown, overthrowing**) cause the downfall of (*overthrew the government*). • *n.* / **oh**-vuh-throh / **1** downfall, defeat. **2** a fielder's throwing of a ball beyond an intended point.

overtime *adv.* in addition to regular working hours. •*n.* **1** time worked in this way. **2** payment for this.

overtone *n.* **1** an additional quality or implication (*overtones of malice in his comments*). **2** (in music) any of the tones above the lowest in a harmonic series.

overture *n.* **1** an orchestral composition forming a prelude to an opera or ballet etc. **2** a composition resembling this. **3** (**overtures**) a friendly approach showing willingness to begin negotiations; a formal proposal or offer.

overturn *v.* **1** turn over; cause to turn over. **2** reverse or overthrow.

overview *n.* a general survey.

overweening *adj.* arrogant, presumptuous, conceited.

overweight *adj.* weighing more than is normal, required, or permissible.

overwhelm *v.* **1** make helpless with emotion. **2** overcome completely, esp. by force of numbers. **3** bury or drown beneath a huge mass.

overwhelming *adj.* **1** too great to resist (*an overwhelming desire to laugh*). **2** by a great number (*an overwhelming majority*).

overwork *v.* **1** work or cause to work so hard that one becomes exhausted. **2** make excessive use of (*an overworked phrase*). •*n.* excessive work causing exhaustion.

overwrought / oh-vuh-**rawt** / *adj.* in a state of nervous agitation.

Ovid / **ov**-uhd / (Latin name: Publius Ovidus Naso) (43 BC–AD 17), Roman poet in the age of Augustus.

oviduct / **oh**-vee-dukt / *n.* a canal through which ova pass from the ovary.

oviform *adj.* egg-shaped.

ovine / **oh**-vuyn / *adj.* of or like sheep. ◻ **ovine Johne's disease** the form of Johne's disease affecting sheep.

oviparous / oh-**vip**-uh-ruhs / *adj.* producing young from eggs that are expelled from the body and then hatched (cf. VIVIPAROUS).

ovoid / **oh**-void / *adj.* egg-shaped.

ovulate / **ov**-yuh-layt / *v.* produce or discharge an ovum or ova from an ovary. ◻ **ovulation** *n.*

ovule / **ov**-yool / *n.* a small part in a plant's ovary that develops into a seed when fertilised.

ovum / **oh**-vuhm / *n.* (*pl.* **ova**) a female egg-cell capable of developing into a new individual when fertilised.

ow *interj.* an exclamation of sudden pain.

owe *v.* **1** be under an obligation to pay or repay (money, gratitude, etc.), be in debt (*I owe you $50; I still owe for my car*). **2** have a duty to render (*owe allegiance to Australia*). **3** (usu. foll. by *to*) have (a thing) as a result of the work or action of another person or cause (*we owe this discovery to Newton; he owes his success to luck*).

owing *adj.* owed and not yet paid. ◻ **owing to 1** caused by (*the cancellation was owing to ill health*). **2** because of (*couldn't come owing to the bushfires*).

owl *n.* a bird of prey with a large head, large eyes, and a hooked beak, usu. flying at night. ◻ **owlish** *adj.*

owlet *n.* a small or young owl. ◻ **owlet nightjar** a small nocturnal bird with grey or brown plumage and barred wing and tail feathers, widespread in Australia.

own *adj.* belonging to oneself or itself; not another's. •*v.* **1** have as one's property, possess. **2** *Aust.* (in Aboriginal English) have a spiritual responsibility (for a place). **3** acknowledge that one is the author, possessor, father, etc. of (*I own him as my son*). **4** *archaic* confess (*he owns he did not know; he owned to a prejudice against Asians*). ◻ **come into one's own** receive one's due; achieve recognition. **own goal 1** *Soccer* a goal scored by mistake against the scorer's own side. **2** an act etc. that has the unintended effect of harming one's own interests. **own up** confess, admit that one is guilty.

owner *n.* **1** a person who owns something. **2** = TRADITIONAL OWNER. ◻ **ownership** *n.*

ox *n.* (*pl.* **oxen**) **1** a large usu. horned ruminant used for draught, milk, and meat. **2** a castrated male of a domesticated species of cattle.

■ **Usage** The term *ox* is little used in Australia, *bullock* being preferred.

oxalic acid *n.* a very poisonous acid found in sorrel and rhubarb leaves.

oxalis *n.* any of several clover-like exotic plants introduced to Australia, one species of which has been declared a noxious weed in SA, Tas., and Vic.

Oxford English Dictionary the largest dictionary of the English language, prepared in Oxford and originally issued in instalments between 1884 and 1928 under the title *A New English Dictionary on Historical Principles* (NED).

oxhide *n.* **1** the hide of an ox. **2** leather made from this.

oxidant *n.* an oxidising agent.

oxidation *n.* the process of combining or causing to combine with oxygen.

oxide *n.* a compound of oxygen and one other element.

oxidise *v.* (also **-ize**) **1** combine or cause to combine with oxygen. **2** coat with an oxide. **3** make or become rusty. ◻ **oxidation** *n.*

Oxley, John (Joseph William Molesworth) (?1785–1828), Australian explorer (born in England), surveyor, and pioneer settler in the Bowral area.

oxtail *n.* the tail of an ox, used to make soup or stew.

oxyacetylene / ok-see-uh-**set**-uh-leen / *adj.* using a mixture of oxygen and acetylene, esp. in the cutting and welding of metals.

oxygen *n.* a chemical element (symbol O), a colourless odourless tasteless gas essential to plant and animal life, existing in air and combining with hydrogen to form water. ☐ **oxygen tent** a tentlike cover over a patient's bed supplying air rich in oxygen.

oxygenate *v.* supply, treat, or mix with oxygen. ☐ **oxygenation** *n.*

oxymoron / ok-see-**maw**-ron / *n.* putting together words which seem to contradict one another, e.g. *bitter-sweet*.

oxytocin / ok-see-**toh**-suhn / *n.* a hormone controlling contractions of the womb, used in synthetic form to induce labour in childbirth.

oyster *n.* **1** a kind of shellfish used as food, some types of which produce pearls inside their shells. **2** *colloq.* an uncommunicative or secretive person. • *adj.* **1** *colloq.* (abbreviation of *oyster-like*) unforthcoming; secretive (*he was questioned closely, but remained oyster*). **2** oyster white. ☐ **oyster blenny** a small marine fish of eastern Australia which usu. shelters in empty oyster-shells. **oyster white** greyish white.

oystercatcher *n.* a wading sea bird which feeds on shellfish.

Oz *colloq. n.* **1** Australia. **2** an Australian. • *adj.* (also **oz**) Australian.

oz. *abbr.* ounce(s).

ozone / **oh**-zohn / *n.* **1** a form of oxygen with a sharp smell, formed by an electrical discharge in the atmosphere. **2** *colloq.* **a** invigorating air at the seaside; **b** an exhilarating influence. ☐ **ozone depletion** a reduction of ozone concentration in the ozone layer caused by atmospheric pollution and the build-up in the atmosphere of ozone-depleting chemicals such as CFCs. **ozone-friendly** (of a product etc.) not containing chemicals destructive to the ozone layer. **ozone hole** an area of the ozone layer in which serious ozone depletion has occurred through atmospheric pollution. **ozone layer** a layer of ozone in the earth's upper atmosphere that absorbs most of the sun's harmful ultraviolet radiation. **ozone-unfriendly** (of a product etc.) containing chemicals destructive to the ozone layer.

Ozzie alternative spelling of Aussie.

P

P *abbr.* (on road signs) parking. •*symbol* phosphorus.

p *abbr.* (also **p.**) **1** page. **2** *Music* piano (softly). **3** *Brit.* penny, pence.

PA *abbr.* public address system.

Pa *symbol* protactinium.

pa *n. colloq.* father.

p.a. *abbr.* per annum, yearly.

pabulum / **pab**-yuh-luhm / *n.* food, esp. for the mind.

pace *n.* **1** a single step made in walking or running. **2** the distance passed in this. **3** a style of walking or running. **4** speed in walking or running. **5** the rate of progress in some activity. •*v.* **1** walk with a slow or regular pace. **2** walk to and fro across (a room etc.). **3** (foll. by *out*) measure by pacing. **4** set the pace for (a runner etc.). □ **keep pace (with)** advance at an equal rate (to). **pace bowler** *Cricket* a fast bowler. **put a person through his (or her) paces** test his (or her) ability.

pace / **pah**-chay, **pay**-see / *prep.* although (a named person) may not agree; with due respect to. (¶ Latin)

pacemaker *n.* **1** a runner who sets the pace in a race. **2** a device which supplies electrical signals to the heart in order to stimulate contractions.

pacesetter *n.* a leader (in a race, in business, etc.), one who sets the pace others are forced to follow.

pachyderm / **pak**-ee-derm / *n.* a thick-skinned mammal, esp. an elephant or rhinoceros.

Pacific *n.* (in full **Pacific Ocean**) the world's largest ocean, separating North and South America from Asia and Australia. •*adj.* **1** of the Pacific Ocean. **2** (**pacific**) peaceful; making or loving peace.

Pacific Rim (usu. prec. by *the*) the countries and regions bordering the Pacific Ocean, esp. the small nations of eastern Asia.

pacifist / **pas**-uh-fist / *n.* a person who totally opposes war, believing that disputes should be settled by peaceful means. □ **pacifism** *n.*

pacify / **pas**-uh-fuy / *v.* (**pacified**, **pacifying**) **1** calm and quieten. **2** establish peace in. □ **pacification** *n.* **pacificatory** *adj.* **pacifier** *n.*

pack¹ *n.* **1** a collection of things wrapped or tied together for carrying. **2** a BACKPACK. **3** a complete set of playing cards (usu. 52). **4** a group of hounds, wild animals, etc. **5** a gang of people; an organised group of Cub Scouts or Brownies. **6 a** *Aust. Rules* a group of players contesting the ball. **b** *Rugby* a team's forwards. **c** *Sport* the main body of competitors following the leader or leaders esp. in a race. **7** a large amount or collection (*a pack of lies*). **8** a face pack. **9** pack ice. •*v.* **1** put (things) into a container for transport or storing; fill with things in this way. **2** be able to be packed (*this dress packs easily*). **3** cram, press, or crowd together into; fill (a space) in this way (*the hall was packed out; fans packed the stadium; packed a lot into a few hours; a booklet packed with information*). **4** cover or protect (a thing) with something pressed tightly on, in, or round it. **5** *colloq.* carry (a gun etc.); be capable of delivering (a forceful punch). **6** (of animals or Rugby forwards) form a pack. □ **packed lunch** a lunch of sandwiches etc. prepared and packed to be eaten at school, at work, etc. **pack ice** crowded pieces of floating ice in the sea. **pack in** *colloq.* stop doing, give up (*packed in his job*). **pack it** *colloq.* lose one's nerve, be terrified (*was packing it at the thought of speaking in public*). **pack it in** *colloq.* **1** end or stop it. **2** break down, cease functioning (*the car's packed it in*). **pack off** send (a person) away. **pack rape** the rape of one person by a pack of men. **pack up 1** put one's things together in readiness for departing or stopping work. **2** *Aust. colloq.* (of machinery etc.) break down. **3** *Aust.* retire from an activity, a contest, etc. **send packing** dismiss abruptly. □□ **packer** *n.*

pack² *v.* select (a jury or committee) fraudulently so that their decisions will be in one's favour.

package *n.* **1** a parcel; a box in which things are packed. **2** (in full **package deal**) a set of items or proposals considered as a whole. **3** *Computing* a piece of software designed for a wide range of users. •*v.* put together in a package. □ **package holiday** (or **tour**) one offering travel, hotels, etc. at an inclusive price. □□ **packager** *n.*

packaging *n.* wrapping or containers for goods.

Packer, Kerry (Francis Bullmore) (1937–), AC, Australian multi-media magnate.

packer *n.* a person or thing that packs, esp. a dealer who prepares and packs food.

packet *n.* **1** a small package. **2** *colloq.* a considerable sum of money. **3** a mailboat.

packhorse *n.* a horse for carrying loads.

packing *n.* material used as padding to pack esp. fragile articles.

pact *n.* an agreement, a treaty.

pad¹ *n.* **1** a thick piece of soft material used to protect, add bulk, absorb fluid, etc. **2** a set of sheets of blank paper fastened together at one edge. **3** the fleshy underpart of an animal's foot or at the end of a finger. **4** a flat surface for helicopter take-off or rocket launching. **5** a guard for the leg and ankle in sports. **6** *colloq.* a person's home; a flat or bedsitter. **7** the floating leaf of a water lily. • *v.* (**padded, padding**) **1** provide with a pad or padding; stuff. **2** lengthen (a piece of writing or speech) by adding unnecessary material. □ **padded cell** a room with padded walls in a mental hospital. **pad down** *colloq.* sleep; spend a night or nights (*can I pad down with you tonight?*).

pad[2] *v.* (**padded, padding**) **1** walk with soft steady steps. **2** travel or tramp along (a road etc.) on foot. • *n.* **1** the sound of soft footfalls. **2** *Aust.* a track or trail made by animals (*followed the kangaroo pads*).

padding *n.* **1** soft material used to pad things. **2** unnecessary material used to lengthen or fill out (a book etc.).

paddle[1] *n.* **1** a short oar with a broad blade, used without a rowlock. **2** an instrument shaped like this. **3** a fin or a flipper. **4** one of the boards on a paddle wheel or mill wheel. • *v.* **1** propel by using a paddle or paddles. **2** row gently. □ **paddle boat** (*or* **steamer**) a boat propelled by a paddle wheel. **paddle wheel** a wheel, with boards round its rim, attached to the side of a boat as a means of propulsion.

paddle[2] *v.* **1** walk with bare feet in shallow water. **2** dabble (the feet or hands) in shallow water. • *n.* a spell of paddling.

paddock *n.* **1 a** *Aust.* a piece of land (usu. of considerable size) fenced, defined by natural boundaries, or otherwise considered distinct, as a section of a rural property. **b** *Brit.* a small field. **2** = SADDLING PADDOCK (*see* SADDLE). **3** a turf enclosure (for spectators at a racecourse) adjacent to the saddling paddock. **4** a playing field. • *v.* **1** confine (livestock) in a paddock. **2** *Aust.* fence or enclose an area to turn it into a paddock.

Paddy *n.* (*pl.* **Paddies**) *colloq. often offens.* an Irishman. □ **Paddy's market** *Aust.* any of various markets where cheap or second-hand goods are sold; a FLEA MARKET.

paddy[1] *n. colloq.* a rage, a temper.

paddy[2] *n.* **1** (in full **paddy field**) a field where rice is grown. **2** rice that is still growing or in the husk.

paddymelon[1] / **pad**-ee-mel-uhn / *n.* (also **pademelon**) **1** any of several small wallabies inhabiting dense vegetation in moist forests of eastern Australia. **2** (occasionally) any of several other, usu. small, macropods. (¶ Dharuk *badimaliyan*, altered by folk etymology to *paddymelon*.)

paddymelon[2] *n.* (also **pademelon**) any of several cucurbits, esp. the trailing or climbing annual African plant naturalised in inland Australia, bearing a bristly, melon-like fruit, and widely regarded as a weed. (¶ Probably from an erroneous association with PADDYMELON[1].)

paddy wagon *n.* *US & Aust.* a secure van used by police for transporting prisoners.

padlock *n.* a detachable lock with a U-shaped bar that fastens through the loop of a staple or ring. • *v.* fasten with a padlock.

padre / **pah**-dray / *n. colloq.* a minister or priest; a chaplain in the armed forces.

paean / **pee**-uhn / *n.* a song of praise or triumph.

paederast alternative spelling of PEDERAST.

paediatrician / pee-dee-uh-**trish**-uhn / *n.* (also **pediatrician**) a specialist in paediatrics.

paediatrics / pee-dee-**at**-riks / *n.* (also **pediatrics**) the branch of medicine dealing with children and their diseases. □ **paediatric** *adj.*

paedophile / **pee**-duh-fuyl, **ped**-uh-fuyl / *n.* (also **pedophile**) an adult who displays paedophilia.

paedophilia / pee-duh-**fil**-ee-uh, ped-uh- / *n.* (also **pedophilia**) sexual attraction felt by an adult towards a child.

paella / puy-**el**-uh / *n.* a Spanish dish of rice, saffron, chicken, seafood, etc. cooked and served in a large shallow pan.

paeony alternative spelling of PEONY.

pagan / **pay**-guhn / *adj.* **1** heathen. **2** holding the belief that deity exists in natural forces; nature-worshipping, esp. in contrast to believing in Christianity, Judaism, etc. • *n.* a pagan person. □ **paganism** *n.*

Paganini / pag-uh-**nee**-nee /, Niccolò (1782–1840), Italian violinist and composer.

page[1] *n.* **1** a leaf in a book, newspaper, etc. **2** one side of this.

page[2] *n.* **1** a uniformed boy or man employed to go on errands, act as door attendant, etc. **2** a boy as a personal attendant of a bride etc. • *v.* summon (a person) by making an announcement or using a pager. □ **page-boy 1** a page. **2** a woman's hairstyle with the hair reaching to the shoulder and rolled under at the ends.

pageant / **paj**-uhnt / *n.* an elaborate procession, play, or tableau, esp. on a historical theme. □ **pageantry** *n.*

pager *n.* a radio device with a beeper, used to contact the wearer.

paginate *v.* number the pages of (a book etc.). □ **pagination** *n.*

pagoda / puh-**goh**-duh / *n.* a Hindu or Buddhist temple, esp. a pyramid-shaped tower with many tiers.

paid see PAY. • *adj.* receiving money in exchange for goods or services (*a paid assistant; paid holidays*). □ **paid-up** having paid one's subscription to a trade union, a club, etc; or having done what is required to be recognised as a full member of a particular group (*a paid-up feminist*). **put paid to** *colloq.* destroy the hopes, chances, or activities of.

pail *n.* a bucket.

pain *n.* **1** an unpleasant feeling caused by injury or disease of the body. **2** mental suffering. **3** (**pains**) careful effort, trouble taken (*got nothing for my pains*). **4** a pain in the neck. • *v.* cause pain to. □ a

pain in the neck *colloq.* an annoying or tiresome person or thing.

pained *adj.* distressed and annoyed (*a pained look*).

painful *adj.* **1** causing pain. **2** (of a part of the body) suffering pain. **3** causing trouble or difficulty; laborious (*a painful climb*). □ **painfully** *adv.*

painkiller *n.* a drug for lessening pain.

painless *adj.* not causing pain. □ **painlessly** *adv.*

painstaking *adj.* careful, thorough.

paint *n.* colouring matter for applying in liquid form to a surface. •*v.* **1** cover or decorate with paint. **2** make a picture or portray using paint(s). **3** describe vividly (*he's not as black as he is painted*). □ **painted burrowing frog** a frog of south-east Australia, grey or green with dark brown to olive patches. **paint the town red** *colloq.* go out and enjoy oneself flamboyantly. **paint up** *Aust.* (in Aboriginal English) *n.* the decoration of the body for ceremonial purposes. *v.* decorate the body with a paint up.

paintball *n.* a game in which participants simulate military combat using airguns to shoot capsules of paint at each other.

painter *n.* **1** a person who paints; an artist or decorator. **2** a rope attached to the bow of a boat for tying it up.

paintwork *n.* a painted surface.

pair *n.* **1** a set of two things or people, a couple. **2** something consisting of two joined corresponding parts (*a pair of scissors*). **3** the other member of a pair (*can't find a pair to this sock*). **4** either or both of two MPs of opposite parties who agree not to vote on certain occasions. •*v.* **1** (often foll. by *off*) arrange or be arranged in couples. **2** (of animals) mate. **3** partner (a person) with a member of the opposite sex. **4** *Parliament* form a pair.

paisley *adj.* having a pattern of curved feather-shaped figures with much detail.

Pajamal / **buy**-chah-mahl / *n.* an Aboriginal language of the regions west of Darwin.

pakapoo / pak-uh-**poo** / *n. Aust.* a Chinese gambling game played with slips of paper marked with columns of Chinese characters. □ **like** (etc.) **a pakapoo ticket** difficult to decipher or make sense of.

pakeha / pah-kuh-hah, -kee-hah / *n. NZ* a white person (as opposed to a Maori).

Pakistan / pak-uh-**stahn**, pah-kuh- / *n.* a republic in southern Asia. □ **Pakistani** *adj. & n.* (*pl.* **Pakistanis**).

pakora / puh-**kaw**-ruh / *n.* a piece of cauliflower, carrot, or other vegetable, coated in seasoned batter and deep-fried. (¶ Hindustani)

pal *n. colloq.* a friend. □ **pal up** (**palled**, **palling**) become friends.

palace *n.* **1** the official residence of a sovereign, president, archbishop, or bishop. **2** a splendid building. □ **palace revolution** (*or* **coup**) the (usu. non-violent) overthrow of a sovereign, government, etc. by a bureaucracy.

Palaeocene / **pal**-ee-uh-seen, **pay**-lee-uh- / *adj. Geol.* of the first epoch of the Tertiary period. •*n.* this epoch.

palaeography / pal-ee-**og**-ruh-fee, pay-lee- / *n.* the study of ancient writing and documents. □ **palaeographer** *n.* **palaeographic** *adj.*

palaeolithic / pal-ee-oh-**lith**-ik, pay-lee-oh- / *adj.* of the early part of the Stone Age. •*n.* this period.

palaeontology / pal-ee-on-**tol**-uh-jee, pay-lee- / *n.* the study of life in the geological past. □ **palaeontologist** *n.*

Palaeozoic / pal-ee-oh-**zoh**-ik, pay-lee-oh- / *adj.* of the geological era between the Precambrian and Mesozoic, marked by the appearance of plants and animals. •*n.* this era.

palais / **pal**-ay / *n.* a public dance hall.

palanquin / pal-uhn-**keen** / *n.* (also **palankeen**) a covered litter for one passenger, used in India etc.

palatable / **pal**-uh-tuh-buhl / *adj.* **1** pleasant to the taste. **2** (of an idea) acceptable.

palate / **pal**-uht / *n.* **1** the roof of the mouth. **2** the sense of taste. **3** a mental taste or inclination; a liking.

palatial / puh-**lay**-shuhl / *adj.* like a palace; spacious and splendid. □ **palatially** *adv.*

palaver / puh-**lah**-vuh / *n. colloq.* **1** tedious fuss and bother. **2** profuse or idle talk. **3** cajolery. **4** an affair or business. •*v.* **1** talk lengthily, esp. to little purpose. **2** flatter; wheedle.

Palawa / **pal**-uh-wah / *n.* a Tasmanian Aborigine. (¶ The name of a Tasmanian Aboriginal people.)

pale[1] *adj.* **1** (of a person's face) having little colour, lighter than normal. **2** (of colour or light) faint, not bright or vivid. •*v.* **1** grow or make pale. **2** (often foll. by *before*, *beside*) seem feeble in comparison (with) (*her beauty paled beside that of her sister*). □ **palely** *adv.* **paleness** *n.*

pale[2] *n.* **1** a stake forming part of a fence. **2** a boundary. □ **beyond the pale** outside the bounds of acceptable behaviour.

Palestine a territory in the Middle East on the eastern coast of the Mediterranean sea. □ **Palestine Liberation Organisation** *see* PLO. □ □ **Palestinian** *adj. & n.*

palette / **pal**-uht / *n.* **1** a thin board on which an artist mixes colours when painting. **2** the range of colours used by an artist. □ **palette knife 1** an artist's knife for mixing or spreading paint. **2** a kitchen knife with a flexible blade for spreading or smoothing soft substances.

Pali / **pah**-lee / *n.* a language, closely related to Sanskrit, in which many sacred Buddhist texts are written.

palimony *n. colloq.* an allowance paid by one partner of a separated unmarried couple to the other. *See* ALIMONY.

palimpsest / **pal**-uhmp-sest / *n.* **1** writing material or a manuscript on which the original writing has been removed to make room for other writing. **2** a monumental brass turned and re-engraved on the reverse side.

palindrome / **pal**-uhn-drohm / *n.* a word or phrase that reads the same backwards as forwards, e.g. *rotator, nurses run*.

paling *n.* **1** fencing made of wooden posts or railings. **2** one of its uprights.

palisade / pal-uh-**sayd** / *n.* a fence of pointed stakes.

pall / pawl / *n.* **1** a cloth spread over a coffin. **2** = PALLIUM. **3** something forming a dark heavy covering (*a pall of smoke*). • *v.* become uninteresting or boring.

palladium / puh-**lay**-dee-uhm / *n.* a rare white metallic element (symbol Pd), used as a catalyst and in jewellery.

pallbearer *n.* a person helping to carry the coffin or walking beside it at a funeral.

pallet *n.* **1** a mattress stuffed with straw. **2** a hard narrow bed; a makeshift bed. **3** a portable platform for carrying or storing goods.

palliasse / **pal**-ee-as / *n.* a straw mattress.

palliate / **pal**-ee-ayt / *v.* **1** make less intense or severe. **2** excuse (an offence etc.).

palliative / **pal**-ee-uh-tiv / *adj.* reducing the bad effects of something. • *n.* something that does this. ☐ **palliative care** care of the terminally ill and their families, usu. by a hospice etc.

pallid / **pal**-uhd / *adj.* pale, esp. from illness. ☐ **pallid cuckoo** an Australian cuckoo with a melodious five-note call.

pallium / **pal**-ee-uhm / *n.* a shoulder band of white lambswool with a hanging band front and back, decorated with black crosses, worn by the pope as a symbol of authority and given by him as an honour to some archbishops.

pallor / **pal**-uh / *n.* paleness.

pally *adj. colloq.* friendly.

palm *n.* **1** the inner surface of the hand between the wrist and the fingers; this part of a glove. **2** a palm tree. • *v.* **1** conceal in one's hand. **2** *Aust. Rules* (in a ball up or throw-in) direct (the ball) to a team mate with the open palm (*the ruckman palmed the ball to his rover*). ☐ **palm cockatoo** a large, slaty-black cockatoo of Cape York Peninsula. **palm off 1** get (a thing) accepted fraudulently (*palmed it off on them*). **2** cause (a person) to accept unwillingly or unknowingly (*palmed him off with my old car*). **palm tree** a tree growing in warm climates, with no branches and a mass of pointed or fan-shaped leaves at the top. ☐☐ **palmar** *adj.* (in sense 1 of noun).

palmate / **pal**-mayt, -muht / *adj.* shaped like a hand with the fingers spread out.

Palmer[1] a river rising in north Qld and flowing through the hinterland of Cooktown. It was the location of the richest alluvial goldfield in Qld in the late 19th c.

Palmer[2], (Edward) Vance (1885–1959), Australian writer (esp. of novels), editor, and critic, husband of Nettie Palmer.

Palmer[3], Nettie (Janet Gertrude) (1885–1964), Australian poet and critic, wife of Vance Palmer.

palmetto / pal-**met**-oh / *n.* (*pl.* **palmettos**) any of various small palm trees with fan-shaped leaves.

palmistry / **pah**-muh-stree / *n.* telling a person's future or character by examining the lines in the palm of his or her hand. ☐ **palmist** *n.*

Palm Sunday the Sunday before Easter, on which Jesus' entry into Jerusalem is celebrated by processions in which branches of palms are carried.

palmy / **pah**-mee / *adj.* (**palmier**, **palmiest**) **1** full of palms. **2** flourishing (*in their former palmy days*).

palmyra / pal-**muy**-ruh / *n.* an Asian palm yielding a sap which is boiled down to make one of the most valued kinds of jaggery.

palomino / pal-uh-**mee**-noh / *n.* (*pl.* **palominos**) a golden or cream-coloured horse with a light-coloured mane and tail.

palpable / **pal**-puh-buhl / *adj.* **1** able to be touched or felt (*a palpable lump in her breast*). **2** easily perceived, obvious (*a palpable lie*). ☐ **palpably** *adv.*

palpate / pal-**payt** / *v.* examine by feeling with the hands, esp. as part of a medical examination. ☐ **palpation** *n.*

palpitate / **pal**-puh-tayt / *v.* **1** pulsate, throb rapidly. **2** (of a person) quiver with fear or excitement.

palpitation *n.* **1** throbbing, quivering. **2** (often as **palpitations**) increased heartbeat due to agitation or disease.

palsied / **pawl**-zeed / *adj.* affected with palsy.

palsy / **pawl**-zee / *n.* paralysis, esp. with involuntary tremors.

paltry / **pawl**-tree / *adj.* (**paltrier**, **paltriest**) worthless, trivial, contemptible (*donated a paltry 50 cents*).

pampas / **pam**-puhs / *n.* (treated as *sing.* or *pl.*) vast grassy plains in South America. ☐ **pampas grass** a tall ornamental grass with feathery plumes.

pamper *v.* overindulge (a person, a taste, etc.); spoil (a person) with luxury.

pamphlet / **pam**-fluht / *n.* a leaflet or booklet containing information. • *v.* (**pamphleted**, **pamphleting**) distribute pamphlets to (*pamphleted the area for Labor*).

Pan *Gk myth.* the horned and goat-legged god of flocks and herds.

pan[1] *n.* **1** a metal or earthenware vessel with a handle, used for cooking. **2** any similar shallow container, e.g. the bowl of a pair of scales. **3** a depression in the ground (*a salt pan*). • *v.* (**panned, panning**) **1** wash (gravel) in a pan in search of gold. **2** *colloq.* criticise severely. ☐ **pan-fry** fry in a pan in shallow fat. **pan out 1** (of gravel) yield gold. **2** (of circumstances or events) work out well or in a specified way.

pan² *n.* **1** a leaf of the betel. **2** this enclosing lime and areca-nut parings, chewed in India, Sri Lanka, etc.

pan³ *v.* (**panned, panning**) **1** swing (a camera) horizontally to give a panoramic effect or follow a moving object. **2** (of a camera) swing in this way.

pan- *comb. form* all-, of the whole of a continent, racial group etc. (*pan-African; pan-American*).

panacea / pan-uh-**see**-uh / *n.* a remedy for all kinds of diseases or troubles.

panache / puh-**nash** / *n.* a confident stylish manner.

Panama / pan-uh-**mah** / a republic in Central America. ☐ **Panama Canal** a canal across the isthmus of Panama, connecting the Atlantic and Pacific Oceans. **Panama City** the capital of Panama. ☐☐ **Panamanian** / pan-uh-**may**-nee-uhn / *adj.* & *n.*

panama / pan-uh-**mah** / *n.* a straw hat with a brim and indented crown.

panatella / pan-uh-**tel**-uh / *n.* a long thin cigar.

pancake *n.* **1** a thin round cake of batter fried on both sides, sometimes rolled up with filling. **2** make-up in the form of a flat cake. • *v.* (of an aircraft) make a pancake landing. ☐ **pancake landing** an emergency landing in which an aircraft lands horizontally with the undercarriage still retracted.

pancetta / pan-**chet**-uh / *n.* an Italian bacon in tissue-thin slices, often spicy hot.

Panchen Lama / **pun**-chuhn lah-muh / a Tibetan lama ranking next after the Dalai Lama.

panchromatic / pan-kroh-**mat**-ik / *adj.* sensitive to all colours of the visible spectrum (*panchromatic film*).

pancreas / **pang**-kree-uhs / *n.* a gland near the stomach discharging a digestive secretion into the duodenum and insulin into the blood. ☐ **pancreatic** / pang-kree-**at**-ik / *adj.*

panda *n.* **1** (also **giant panda**) a large rare bearlike black and white animal living in the mountains of SW China. **2** (also **red panda**) a reddish-brown racoon-like animal of India.

pandanny / pan-**dan**-ee / *n.* a palm-like shrub or tree of the heath family, endemic to Tas., having pink or white flowers in sprays.

pandanus / pan-**dan**-uhs / *n.* **1** a screw pine of Qld and NSW, having spined leaves and large fruits resembling a pineapple. **2** a screw pine of esp. Malaysia.

pandemic / pan-**dem**-ik / *adj.* (of a disease) occurring over a whole country or the whole world; widespread.

pandemonium / pan-duh-**moh**-nee-uhm / *n.* uproar; confusion and chaos.

pander *v.* (foll. by *to*) gratify (weakness or a person's wishes) (*pandering to the public interest in scandal*). • *n.* a pimp.

pandit = PUNDIT (sense 1).

Pandora *Gk myth.* the first woman, who opened a store-jar which let loose all the evils which have since beset the human race. ☐ **Pandora's box** something that once begun will generate many unmanageable problems.

pandorea / pan-duh-**ree**-uh / *n.* either of two climbers: **1** from Qld and NSW, having large trumpet-flowers, rosy pink with a maroon centre. **2** = WONGA-WONGA VINE.

pane *n.* a single sheet of glass in a window or door.

panegyric / pan-uh-**ji**-rik / *n.* a speech or piece of writing praising a person or thing.

panel *n.* **1** a strip of board or other material forming a separate section of a wall, door, or cabinet; a section of the metal bodywork of a vehicle; a distinct section of a surface. **2** a strip of material set lengthwise in a garment. **3** a group of people assembled to discuss or decide something. **4** a list of jurors; a jury. • *v.* (**panelled, panelling**) cover or decorate with panels. ☐ **panel beater** a person who beats out the metal panels of vehicles.

panel van *Aust.* a motor vehicle similar in size and shape to a station wagon, having two doors, a single row of seats in front, a flat tray in the rear, and usu. with closed sides.

panelling *n.* **1** a series of panels in a wall. **2** wood used for making panels.

panellist *n.* a member of a panel (esp. in broadcasting).

pang *n.* a sudden sharp feeling of pain or painful emotion (*pangs of jealousy*).

pangolin / pang-**goh**-luhn / *n.* a scaly anteater.

panic *n.* sudden uncontrollable terror, infectious fear. • *v.* (**panicked, panicking**) affect or be affected with panic. • *adj.* characterised or caused by panic (*panic buying*). ☐ **panic merchant** *colloq.* a person prone to panic for the slightest of reasons or for no reason at all. **panic stations** *colloq.* a state of emergency. **panic-stricken, panic-struck** affected with panic. ☐☐ **panicky** *adj.* (¶ From the Greek god Pan.)

panic button *n. colloq.* an imaginary button needing to be pressed in a situation which gives rise to panic. ☐ **hit the panic button** it's time to react or panic because this is an emergency.

panicle *n.* a loose branching cluster of stalked flowers with the youngest flowers at the top.

pani puri / pah-nee **poo**-ree / *n.* (in Indian cookery) a puff-pastry ball filled with spiced mashed potato and tamarind juice and fried.

pannier *n.* a large basket, bag, or box, esp. one of a pair carried on either side of a pack animal, bicycle, or motor cycle.

pannikin *n.* a small metal drinking vessel. ☐ **pannikin boss** *Aust.* a person who has only a small degree of authority but who acts as if he or she had complete power.

panoply / **pan**-uh-plee / *n.* a splendid array.

panorama *n.* **1** a view of a wide area; a picture or photograph of this. **2** a view of a constantly changing scene or series of events. ☐ **panoramic** / pan-uh-**ram**-ik / *adj.*

pan pipes *n.pl.* a musical instrument made of a series of pipes of graduated lengths fixed together. (¶ Named after the Greek god Pan.)

pansy *n.* **1** a garden plant of the violet family, with large richly-coloured petals. **2** *colloq. offens.* **a** an effeminate man. **b** a male homosexual.

pant *v.* **1** breathe with short quick breaths. **2** utter breathlessly. **3** (usu. foll. by *for*) be extremely eager. •*n.* a panting breath.

pantaloons *n.pl.* baggy trousers gathered at the ankles.

pantheism / **pan**-thee-iz-uhm / *n.* **1** the belief that God is in everything. **2** worship that accepts all gods. ☐ **pantheist** *n.* **pantheistic** *adj.*

pantheon / **pan**-thee-uhn / *n.* **1** a temple dedicated to all the gods. **2** the gods of a people collectively. **3** a building in which illustrious dead are buried or have memorials.

panther *n.* **1** a leopard, esp. a black one. **2** *US* a puma.

panties *n.pl. colloq.* underpants for women and girls.

pantihose *n.* (also **pantyhose**) (usu. treated as *pl.*) women's tights.

pantograph *n.* **1** an instrument with jointed rods for copying drawings on a different scale. **2** a jointed framework conveying a current to an electric vehicle from overhead wires.

pantomime *n.* **1** a Christmas theatre show based on a fairy tale. **2** expressive movements of the face and body used to convey a story or meaning. **3** *colloq.* a ridiculous situation.

pantry *n.* **1** a room in which crockery, cutlery, table linen, etc. are kept. **2** a larder.

pants *n.pl.* **1** underpants or knickers. **2** trousers or slacks. ☐ **caught with one's pants down** caught in an embarrassing situation.

Panyjima / **pun**-juh-muh / *n.* an Aboriginal language of a large area of the north-west of WA.

pap *n.* **1** soft or semi-liquid food for infants or invalids. **2** light or trivial reading matter. **3** *archaic* a nipple.

papa *n. archaic* father.

papacy / **pay**-puh-see / *n.* the position or authority of the pope; the system of Church government by popes.

papal / **pay**-puhl / *adj.* of the pope or the papacy. ☐ **papal infallibility** (in the Catholic Church) the doctrine that in specified circumstances the pope is incapable of error when pronouncing on matters of faith and morals.

paparazzo / pap-uh-**raht**-soh / *n.* (*pl.* **paparazzi**) a freelance photographer who intrusively pursues celebrities to photograph them.

papaw / **pa**-paw / = PAWPAW.

papaya = PAWPAW.

paper *n.* **1** a substance manufactured in thin sheets from wood fibre etc., used for writing or printing on or for wrapping things. **2** a newspaper. **3** wallpaper. **4** a set of examination questions (*the biology paper*). **5** (**papers**) official documents, identification, etc. (*a ship's papers*). **6** an essay or dissertation, esp. one read to a learned society. •*adj.* **1** made of paper. **2** only theoretical; not actual (*paper profits*). •*v.* **1** cover (walls etc.) with wallpaper. **2** (foll. by *over*) try to hide (faults etc.). ☐ **on paper** in writing; in theory, when judged from written or printed evidence (*the scheme looks good on paper*). **paper clip** a piece of bent wire for holding sheets of paper together. **paper daisy** any of several Australian plants bearing a daisy flower head with stiff, papery, petal-like bracts (*see* HELICHRYSUM, HELIPTERUM). **paper money** banknotes as distinct from coins. **paper talk** *Aust.* (in Aboriginal English) a written message; a letter. **paper tiger** a person or thing that seems threatening but can do no harm. **paper yabber** *Aust.* = PAPER TALK.

paperback *n.* a book bound in a flexible paper binding, not in a stiff cover.

paperbark *n.* **1** any of several Australian trees of the genus *Melaleuca* having a papery, often peeling bark. **2** the bark of these trees.

paperweight *n.* a small heavy object placed on top of loose papers to keep them in place.

paperwork *n.* routine clerical or administrative work.

papery *adj.* like paper in texture; thin and flimsy.

papier mâché / pay-puh **mash**-ay / *n.* paper pulp used for making boxes and ornaments. (¶ French, = chewed paper.)

papilla *n.* (*pl.* **papillae**) a small protuberance at the base of a hair, feather, or tooth. ☐ **papillary** *adj.*

papist / **pay**-puhst / *n. offens.* a Catholic.

papoose / puh-**poos** / *n.* a North American Indian baby.

pappadam / **pup**-uh-dum / *n.* (also **poppadam**) a thin, crisp, fried lentil wafer eaten with rice and curry.

paprika / puh-**pree**-kuh / *n.* a red pepper; a ground condiment made from this (*sweet paprika; hot paprika*).

pap smear *n.* (also **cervical smear**) a smear taken from the cervix or vagina and used in the pap test. ☐ **pap test** a cervical smear test to detect cancer in an early stage. (¶ G.N. *Papanicolaou* (1883–1962), the scientist who invented this procedure.)

Papua New Guinea / **pah**-poo-uh / an independent country in the Pacific off the NE coast of Australia.

papyrus / puh-**puy**-ruhs / n. (pl. **papyri**) **1** a reed-like water plant with thick fibrous stems. **2** a type of paper made from this plant by the ancient Egyptians. **3** a manuscript written on this.

par n. **1** an average or normal amount, degree, condition, etc. (*feeling below par*). **2** (in golf) the number of strokes that a first-class player should normally require for a hole or course. **3** the face value of stocks and shares. **4** (in full **par of exchange**) the recognised value of one country's currency in terms of another's. □ **on a par with** on an equal footing with; similar to. **par for the course** *colloq*. what is normal or expected in any given circumstances.

para n. *colloq*. a paragraph.

parable n. a story told to illustrate a moral lesson; an allegory.

parabola / puh-**rab**-uh-luh / n. a curve like the path of an object that is thrown into the air and falls back to earth; an open plane curve formed by the intersection of a cone with a plane parallel to its side. □ **parabolic** / pa-ruh-**bol**-ik / adj.

paracetamol / pa-ruh-**see**-tuh-mol / n. a drug used to relieve pain and reduce fever.

parachute n. a rectangular or umbrella-shaped device that allows a person to jump from an aircraft and descend safely; a similar device used as a brake. • v. descend or drop (supplies) by parachute. □ **parachutist** n.

parade n. **1** a public procession or display. **2** a ceremonial assembly of troops for inspection, roll-call, etc. **3** a boastful display (*makes a parade of his virtues*). **4** a public square, promenade; sometimes used in the name of a street. • v. **1** march ceremonially; walk in procession through (streets etc.). **2** (of troops) assemble for parade. **3** display boastfully. □ **on parade** taking part in a parade.

paradigm / **pa**-ruh-duym / n. an example, pattern, or model that serves as an explanation. □ **paradigmatic** / pa-ruh-dig-**mat**-ik / adj.

paradise n. **1** heaven. **2** the garden of Eden. **3** a place or state of complete happiness. □ **paradise parrot** a predominantly brown, red, and turquoise parrot of central eastern Australia, now possibly extinct. **paradise rifle bird** a rainforest bird of eastern Australia, having velvety black plumage with iridescent blue-green markings. □□ **paradisaical** / pa-ruh-duh-**say**-uh-kuhl / adj. **paradisal** / **pa**-ruh-duy-suhl / adj. **paradisiacal** / par-ruh-duh-**suy**-uh-kuhl / adj. **paradisical** / pa-ruh-**dis**-i-kuhl / adj.

paradox / **pa**-ruh-doks / n. **1** a statement which seems contradictory or absurd, but which expresses a truth. **2** a person or thing having contradictory qualities. □ **paradoxical** / pa-ruh-**doks**-i-kuhl / adj. **paradoxically** adv.

paraffin n. an oil obtained from petroleum or shale, used as a fuel. □ **liquid paraffin** a tasteless form of this used as a mild laxative. **paraffin wax** paraffin in solid form.

paragliding n. a sport resembling hang-gliding, using a wide parachute-like canopy attached to the body by a harness, allowing a person to glide after jumping from or being hauled to a height. □ **paraglide** v. **paraglider** n.

paragon / **pa**-ruh-guhn / n. a model of excellence; an apparently perfect person or thing.

paragraph n. one or more sentences forming a distinct section of a piece of writing and beginning on a new (often indented) line. • v. arrange in paragraphs.

Paraguay / **pa**-ruh-gwuy / an inland republic in South America. □ **Paraguayan** / pa-ruh-**gwuy**-uhn / adj. & n.

parakeeliya / pa-ruh-**keel**-yuh / n. (also **parakeelya**, **junga**) any of several purple-flowered herbs of arid inland Australia, having thick, succulent, edible leaves, and seeds which may be ground into a paste and eaten (*see also* MUNYEROO). (¶ Guyani)

parakeet / **pa**-ruh-keet / n. a small parrot, usu. with a long tail.

paralanguage elements or factors in communication that are ancillary to language proper, e.g. intonation and gesture.

parallax / **pa**-ruh-laks / n. an apparent difference in the position or direction of an object when it is viewed from different points. □ **parallactic** / pa-ruh-**lak**-tik / adj.

parallel adj. **1** (of lines or planes) continually at the same distance from each other or from another line or plane (*parallel lines; the road runs parallel to the railway*). **2** (of circumstances) similar; having features that correspond. **3** (of processes) occurring or performed simultaneously. • n. **1** a person or situation that is comparable or similar to another. **2** a comparison (*drew a parallel between the two situations*). **3** (in full **parallel of latitude**) an imaginary line on the earth's surface, or a corresponding line on a map, parallel to the equator. • v. (**paralleled**, **paralleling**) **1** be parallel to. **2** mention something parallel or corresponding; compare. □ **in parallel** (of electronic circuits) arranged so as to join at common points at each end. **parallel bars** a pair of parallel rails on posts for gymnastics. □□ **parallelism** n.

parallelepiped / pa-ruh-lel-uh-**puy**-ped, pa-ruh-luh-**lep**-uh-ped / n. a solid body of which each face is a parallelogram.

parallelogram / pa-ruh-**lel**-uh-gram / n. a plane four-sided figure with its opposite sides parallel to each other.

Paralympics n.pl. an international athletic competition, modelled on the Olympic Games, for paraplegics and other disabled athletes.

paralyse v. **1** affect with paralysis; make unable to move or act normally. **2** bring to a standstill.

paralysis n. **1** inability to move normally, esp. when caused by disease or injury to nerves. **2** powerlessness; inability to function normally.

paralytic / pa-ruh-**lit**-ik / *adj.* **1** affected with paralysis. **2** *colloq.* very drunk.

Paramaribo / pa-ruh-**ma**-ree-boh / the capital of Suriname.

paramedic *n.* a paramedical worker, esp. a member of an ambulance crew with advanced medical training.

paramedical *adj.* supplementing and supporting medical work.

parameter / puh-**ram**-uh-tuh / *n.* **1** *Maths* a quantity that is constant in the case considered but varies in different cases. **2** a variable quantity or quality that restricts or gives a particular form to the thing it characterises. **3** a specification that is used in a computer program or routine and that can be given a different value whenever this is repeated. **4** a limit or boundary, esp. of a subject of discussion.

paramilitary *adj.* organised like a military force but not part of the official armed services. • *n.* a member of a paramilitary organisation.

paramount *adj.* chief in importance; supreme.

paramour / pa-ruh-**maw** / *n.* a married person's secret or illicit lover.

paranoia / pa-ruh-**noi**-uh / *n.* **1** *Psychol.* a mental disorder in which a person has delusions, e.g. of grandeur or persecution. **2** an abnormal tendency to suspect and mistrust others.

paranoiac = PARANOID.

paranoid / **pa**-ruh-noid / *adj.* of, like, or suffering from paranoia. • *n.* a person suffering from paranoia.

paranormal *adj.* (of occurrences or powers) operating according to laws and influences that cannot be explained scientifically; supernatural.

parapente / **pa**-ruh-pont / *n.* **1** the activity of gliding by means of an aerofoil parachute launched from high ground. **2** the parachute used in this activity. • *v.* glide using an aerofoil parachute.

parapet / **pa**-ruh-puht / *n.* a low protective wall along the edge of a balcony, roof, or bridge.

paraphernalia / pa-ruh-fuh-**nay**-lee-uh / *n.* (treated as *pl.* or *sing.*) miscellaneous articles or pieces of equipment.

paraphrase / **pa**-ruh-frayz / *v.* express the meaning of (a passage) in other words. • *n.* rewording in this way; a reworded passage.

paraplegia / pa-ruh-**plee**-juh / *n.* paralysis of the legs and part of the trunk.

paraplegic / pa-ruh-**plee**-jik / *adj.* of or suffering from paraplegia. • *n.* a person suffering from paraplegia.

parapsychology / pa-ruh-suy-**kol**-uh-jee / *n.* the study of mental phenomena that seem to be beyond normal mental abilities (e.g. clairvoyance and telepathy).

parasailing *n.* the sport of gliding through the air attached to an open parachute and towed by a speedboat.

parascending *n.* a sport in which the participant is attached to a parachute and towed through the air behind a speedboat or vehicle until he or she gains sufficient height to parachute down.

parasite *n.* **1** an animal or plant that lives on or in another and feeds on it. **2** a person who lives off another and gives nothing in return. ☐ **parasitic** / pa-ruh-**sit**-ik / *adj.*

parasol *n.* a light umbrella giving shade from the sun.

paratha / puh-**rah**-thuh / *n.* (in esp. Indian cookery) a piece of flat unleavened bread fried on a griddle.

paratrooper *n.* a member of the paratroops.

paratroops *n.pl.* parachute troops.

parboil *v.* boil (food) until it is partly cooked.

Parcae / **pah**-kee, **pah**-see / *Rom. myth.* the Roman name for the Fates.

parcel *n.* **1** something wrapped up in a package for posting or carrying. **2** a quantity of something considered as a distinct unit; a piece of land. • *v.* (**parcelled**, **parcelling**) **1** (foll. by *up*) wrap up as a parcel. **2** (foll. by *out*) divide into portions (*parcelled it out*).

parch *v.* make hot and dry or thirsty.

parchment *n.* **1** a heavy paper-like material made from animal skins. **2** a manuscript written on this. **3** high-grade paper resembling parchment.

pardalote / **pah**-duh-loht / *n.* any of several small, colourful, spotted, finch-like birds of all Australian States, esp. the diamond bird.

pardon *n.* **1** forgiveness for an offence, discourtesy, or error (*I beg your pardon*). **2** cancellation of the punishment incurred through a crime or conviction (*a free pardon*). • *v.* (**pardoned**, **pardoning**) **1** forgive; overlook (a slight discourtesy, error, etc.) kindly. **2** release from the legal consequences of an offence etc. ☐ **pardonable** *adj.*

pare / pair / *v.* **1** trim by cutting away the edges. **2** (often foll. by *down* or *away*) reduce little by little (*pared down their expenses*).

parent *n.* **1** a person who has or adopts a child; a father or mother. **2** an animal or plant from which others are derived. **3** the source or origin of something. • *v.* be a parent (of). ☐ **parent company** a company of which others are subsidiaries. ☐☐ **parenthood** *n.*

parentage / **pair**-ruhn-tij / *n.* ancestry, lineage; descent from parents.

parental / puh-**ren**-tuhl / *adj.* of parents (*parental guidance*).

parenthesis / puh-**ren**-thuh-suhs / *n.* (*pl.* **parentheses**) **1** an additional word, phrase, or sentence inserted into a sentence or paragraph and marked off by brackets, dashes, or commas. **2** either of a pair of round brackets (like these) used for this. ☐ **in parenthesis** between brackets as a parenthesis; as an aside or digression in a speech.

parenthetic / pa-ruhn-**thet**-ik / *adj.* **1** of or as a parenthesis. **2** inserted as an aside or digression. ☐ **parenthetical** *adj.* **parenthetically** *adv.*

parenting *n.* bringing up children.

Parer / **pair**-ruh /, Damien (1912–44), Australian photographer renowned for his films of troops in action in the Second World War, esp. *Jungle Warfare on the Kokoda Front* which won an Oscar. He was killed while filming the American invasion of Pelelieu.

par excellence / par **ek**-suh-luhns / *adv.* being a supreme example of its kind (*the short story par excellence*). (¶ French)

parfait / **pah**-fay / *n.* **1** a rich iced pudding of whipped cream, eggs, etc. **2** layers of ice cream, meringue, etc., served in a tall glass. (¶ French)

pariah / puh-**ruy**-uh / *n.* a social outcast.

parietal / puh-**ruy**-uh-tuhl / *n.* either of the **parietal bones**, those forming part of the sides and top of the skull.

parings / **pair**-ringz / *n.pl.* strips that have been cut off.

Paris[1] the capital of France. ☐ **Parisian** / puh-**riz**-ee-uhn / *adj.* & *n.*

Paris[2] *Gk myth.* a young Trojan prince whose abduction of Helen (the wife of the king of Sparta) provoked the Trojan War.

parish *n.* **1** an area within a diocese, having its own church and priest or minister. **2** the people of a parish. ☐ **parish priest** a Catholic priest in charge of a parish.

parishioner / puh-**rish**-uh-nuh / *n.* an inhabitant of a parish.

parity / **pa**-ruh-tee / *n.* **1** equality; equal status or pay. **2** equivalence of one currency with another; being valued at par.

Park, (Rosina) Ruth (Lucia) (1923–), AM, New Zealand-born Australian writer.

park *n.* **1** a public garden or recreation ground in a city or town. **2** a similar area set aside for various sports. **3** a large area of land kept in its natural state for the public benefit (*a national park*). **4** a large protected area where wild animals are kept in captivity (*a wildlife park*). **5** a parking area for vehicles (*a car park*). • *v.* **1** position and leave (a vehicle) temporarily. **2** *colloq.* deposit temporarily (*just park it on the table*). ☐ **parking meter** a coin-operated meter allocating a length of time for which a vehicle may be parked beside it. **parking ticket** a notice of a fine for parking illegally.

parka *n.* **1** a long canvas jacket with fur round the hood. **2** a hooded skin jacket worn by Eskimos.

parkers *n.pl. Aust. colloq.* the parking lights on a motor vehicle.

Parkes, Sir Henry (1815–96), Australian politician (born in England) who pressed strongly for federation in Australia and was known as 'The Father of Federation'.

Parkinson's disease *n.* a disease of the nervous system causing trembling and weakness of the muscles. (¶ Named after the surgeon J. Parkinson, who described it in 1817.)

Parkinson's law *n.* the humorous notion that work expands to fill the time available for its completion. (¶ Formulated by the writer C.N. Parkinson (1909–93).)

parkland *n.* open grassland with groups of trees.

parlance / **pah**-luhns / *n.* the vocabulary or expressions of a particular subject or group (*medical parlance*).

parley *n.* (*pl.* **parleys**) a discussion to settle a dispute. • *v.* (**parleyed**, **parleying**) hold a parley.

parliament / **pah**-luh-muhnt / *n.* **1** an assembly that makes the laws of a country. **2** (**Parliament**) **a** the national legislature of Australia, consisting of the House of Representatives and the Senate. **b** the legislature of an Australian State.

parliamentarian / pah-luh-muhn-**tair**-ree-uhn / *n.* a member of a parliament, esp. an expert in its procedures.

parliamentary / pah-luh-**men**-tuh-ree, -tree / *adj.* **1** of parliament; enacted by parliament. **2** (of language, behaviour) polite; acceptable according to the rules of a parliament. ☐ **parliamentary privilege** freedom of speech granted to MPs during a meeting of parliament with consequent immunity from prosecution in a civil case as a result of what is said in parliament.

parlour *n.* (also **parlor**) **1** *archaic* a sitting room in a private house. **2** a room in a hotel, convent, etc., in which residents may relax, receive guests, etc. **3** a shop providing specific items (*beauty parlour; ice cream parlour*).

parlourmaid *n.* a maid who waits on a household at meals.

parlous / **pah**-luhs / *adj. formal* (of a state of affairs) difficult or dangerous.

parma wallaby *n.* a greyish-brown wallaby of NSW, having a white throat and white cheek stripe. (¶ Dharawal)

parmesan / **pah**-muh-zuhn / *n.* a hard dry cheese made originally at Parma in Italy, usu. grated.

Parnassus a mountain of central Greece, in antiquity sacred to the Muses. ☐ **Parnassian** *adj.*

parochial / puh-**roh**-kee-uhl / *adj.* **1** of a church parish. **2** showing interest only in local affairs; limited, narrow. ☐ **parochially** *adv.* **parochialism** *n.*

parody / **pa**-ruh-dee / *n.* **1** a comic imitation of a well-known person, literary work, style of writing, etc. **2** a feeble imitation, a travesty. • *v.* (**parodied**, **parodying**) write a parody of; mimic humorously. ☐ **parodist** *n.*

parole / puh-**rohl** / *n.* **1** temporary or permanent release of a prisoner before his or her sentence has expired, on the promise of good behaviour. **2** such a promise. • *v.* release (a prisoner) on parole.

parotid / puh-**rot**-uhd / *adj.* situated near the ear. • *n.* (in full **parotid gland**) the salivary gland in front of the ear.

paroxysm / **pa**-ruhk-siz-uhm / n. a spasm; a sudden attack or outburst of pain, rage, laughter, etc. ◻ **paroxysmal** / pa-rok-**siz**-muhl / adj.

parquet / **pah**-kay, -kee / n. flooring of wooden blocks arranged in a pattern.

parquetry / **pah**-kuh-tree / n. the use of wooden blocks to make floors or to inlay furniture.

parricide / **pa**-ruh-suyd / n. **1** the act of killing one's own parent or other near relative. **2** a person who is guilty of this.

parrot n. **1** any of various birds (e.g. the Australian cockatoo) with a short hooked bill, often brightly coloured plumage, and the ability to mimic the human voice. **2** a person who mechanically repeats another's words or actions. • v. (**parroted**, **parroting**) repeat mechanically. ◻ **parrot-fashion** adv. (learning or repeating) mechanically, by rote.

parrotfish n. any (usu. brightly coloured) fish of Australian coastal waters having fused teeth resembling a parrot's beak.

parry v. (**parried**, **parrying**) **1** ward off (a blow) using a weapon, one's arm, etc. to block the thrust. **2** deal skilfully with (an awkward question). • n. an act of parrying.

parse / pahz / v. identify the grammatical form and function of (the words in a sentence).

parsec / **pah**-sek / n. a unit of distance used in astronomy; about 3.25 light years.

Parsee / pah-**see** / n. a descendant of the Persians who fled to India from Muslim persecution in the 7th–8th century; a Zoroastrian.

parsimonious / pah-suh-**moh**-nee-uhs / adj. stingy; too careful with money. ◻ **parsimoniously** adv. **parsimony** / **pah**-suh-muh-nee / n.

parsley n. a herb with crinkly aromatic leaves used for flavouring and garnishing food.

parsnip n. a plant with a large yellowish tapering root used as a vegetable.

parson n. any (esp. Protestant) clergyman. ◻ **parson's nose** the rump of a cooked fowl.

parsonage n. the house of a parson.

Parsons, Geoffrey (Penwill) (1930–95), AO, Australian pianist and renowned accompanist.

part n. **1** some but not all of something. **2** a section or portion (*a story broadcast in three parts; this part of the country; parts of the body*). **3** (**parts**) the genitals. **4** (**parts**) abilities (*a man of many parts*). **5** a component of a machine or structure. **6** each of several equal portions of a whole (*three parts sugar to two parts butter*). **7** one's share or duty (*I've done my part; I want no part in it*). **8** an integral element (*feel part of the family*). **9** the role of a character in a play. **10** the tune or line of music assigned to a particular voice or instrument. • v. **1** separate or divide into parts (*the crowd parted to let me through*). **2** cause to separate (*they were fighting so fiercely I couldn't part them*). **3** leave one another's company. **4** separate (the hair on one's head) to make a parting. • adv. **1** in part; partly (*part iron and part wood*). **2** partly descended from another race. ◻ **part of speech** one of the grammatical classes into which words are divided (in English, noun, adjective, pronoun, verb, etc.). **part-song** a song with three or more voice parts. **part-time** adj. & adv. for only part of the working week. **part-timer** one employed in part-time work.

partake v. (**partook**, **partaken**, **partaking**) **1** (foll. by *of* or *in*) participate; take a share or part. **2** (foll. by *of*) eat or drink (something).

parterre / pah-**tair** / n. **1** a level space in a formal garden, occupied by flower beds. **2** the pit of a theatre.

parthenogenesis / pah-thuh-noh-**jen**-uh-suhs / n. reproduction without fertilisation, esp. in invertebrates and lower plants.

Parthenon / **pah**-thuh-non / the temple of Athene Parthenos built on the Acropolis at Athens in 447–432 BC.

Parthian / **pah**-thee-uhn / adj. of the ancient kingdom of Parthia, SE of the Caspian Sea, or its people. • n. a native of Parthia. ◻ **Parthian shot** a sharp remark made by a person as he or she departs. (¶ The horsemen of Parthia were renowned for firing arrows at the enemy while retreating.)

partial / **pah**-shuhl / adj. **1** in part but not complete or total (*a partial eclipse*). **2** biased, unfair. ◻ **be partial to** have a strong liking for. ◻◻ **partially** adv.

partiality / pah-shee-**al**-uh-tee / n. **1** bias, favouritism. **2** a strong liking.

participant / pah-**tis**-uh-puhnt / n. one who participates.

participate / pah-**tis**-uh-payt / v. take part or share in something. ◻ **participation** n. **participator** n.

participle / **pah**-tuh-suh-puhl / n. a word formed from a verb (e.g. *going, gone; burning, burnt*) and used in compound verb forms (*she is going* or *has gone*) or as an adjective (*a going concern*). ◻ **past participle**, e.g. *burnt, frightened, wasted*. **present participle**, e.g. *burning, frightening, wasting*. ◻◻ **participial** / pah-tuh-**sip**-ee-uhl / adj.

particle n. **1** a very small portion of matter. **2** the smallest possible amount (*he hasn't a particle of sense*). **3** a minor part of speech or a common prefix or suffix, e.g. *non-, un-, -ness*.

particoloured adj. (also **particolored**) of more than one colour; variegated; multicoloured.

particular adj. **1** relating to one person or thing as distinct from others, individual (*this particular case*). **2** special, exceptional (*took particular trouble*). **3** insisting on high standards; fussy (*is very particular about what he eats*). • n. a detail; a piece of information (*gave particulars of the stolen property*). ◻ **in particular 1** particularly (*we liked this one in particular*). **2** specifically (*did nothing in particular*). ◻◻ **particularity** / puh-tik-yuh-**la**-ruh-tee / n.

particularise v. (also **-ize**) specify, name specially or one by one. □□ **particularisation** n.

particularly adv. **1** especially, very. **2** specifically (*particularly asked for vegetarian food*).

parting n. **1** leave-taking. **2** a line where hair is combed away in different directions. □ **parting shot** = PARTHIAN SHOT.

partisan / pah-tuh-**zan**, **pah**-tuh-zuhn / n. **1** a strong and often uncritical supporter of a person, cause, etc. **2** a guerrilla. •*adj.* **1** of partisans. **2** biased. □ **partisanship** n.

partition / pah-**tish**-uhn / n. **1** division into parts, esp. (*Politics*) of a country. **2** a structure that divides a room or space; a thin wall. •*v.* **1** divide into parts; share out in this way. **2** divide (a room) with a partition.

partitive adj. *Grammar* (of a word or form) denoting part of a group or quantity. •*n.* a partitive word or form, e.g. *some*, *any*.

partly adv. to some extent but not completely or wholly.

partner n. **1** one who shares with another or others in some activity, esp. in a business where he or she shares risks and profits. **2** either of two people dancing together or playing on the same side in a game. **3** either member of a married or unmarried couple. •*v.* be the partner of. □ **partnership** n.

partook *see* PARTAKE.

partridge n. a game bird (of Europe or Asia) with brown feathers and a plump body.

parturition / pah-chuh-**rish**-uhn, -tyoo- / n. *formal* giving birth to young, childbirth.

party n. **1** a social gathering, usu. of invited guests. **2** a number of people travelling or working together as a unit (*a search party*). **3** a political group organised on a national basis to put forward its policies and candidates for office. **4** the person(s) forming one side in an agreement or dispute. **5** a person who participates in, knows of, or supports an action or plan etc. (*refused to be a party to the conspiracy*). **6** *humorous* a person. •*adj.* **1** of a political party (*party politics*). **2** of or for a celebration etc. (*party pies; party clothes*). •*v.* (**parties**, **partied**) enjoy oneself at a party or other lively gathering, typically with drinking and music. □ **party hack** a person who has dutifully served a political party for a long time, esp. as a dogsbody, a drudge. **party line 1** a shared telephone line. **2** the set policy of a political party.

Parvati / **pah**-vuh-tee / (in Hinduism) a benevolent goddess, wife of Siva.

parvenu / **pah**-vuh-noo, -nyoo / n. an upstart.

parvenue n. a female upstart.

pas / pah / n. (*pl.* same) a step in dancing, esp. in classical ballet. □ **pas de deux** a dance for two in ballet.

Pascal / pas-**kahl** / n. *Computing* a programming language, used esp. in education. (¶ Named after Blaise Pascal (1623–62), French mathematician, scientist, and religious philosopher, because he built a calculating machine.)

pascal / **pas**-kuhl / n. a unit of pressure. (¶ Named after Blaise Pascal (1623–62).)

paschal / **pas**-kuhl / adj. **1** of the Jewish Passover. **2** of Easter.

pash *colloq.* n. **1** an infatuation (*has a pash on the boy next door*). **2** *Aust.* a kiss and cuddle. •*v. Aust.* to kiss and cuddle.

paspalum / pas-**pay**-luhm / n. a robust pasture grass native to southern America, now naturalised and widespread in non-arid regions of Australia.

pass v. (**passed**, **passing**) **1** go, proceed, or move onward or past something. **2** cause to move across, over, or past. **3** be transferred from one person to another (*his property passed to his eldest son*). **4** hand or transfer; (in football etc.) send the ball to another player. **5** discharge (esp. faeces or urine) from the body. **6** change from one state into another. **7** come to an end. **8** happen, be done or said (*we heard what passed between them*). **9** occupy (time). **10** circulate, be accepted or currently known in a certain way. **11** be tolerated or allowed. **12** examine and declare satisfactory; approve (a law etc.), esp. by vote. **13** achieve the required standard in performing (a test). **14** go beyond. **15** utter; pronounce as a decision (*passed some remarks; pass judgment*). **16** (in cards) refuse one's turn (e.g. in bidding). •*n.* **1** passing, esp. of an examination or at cards; a university degree without honours. **2** a movement made with the hand(s) or something held. **3** a permit to go into or out of a place or to be absent from one's quarters. **4** transference of the ball to another player in football etc. **5** a critical state of affairs (*things have come to a pretty pass*). **6** a narrow road or path over a mountain range. □ **make a pass at** *colloq.* make sexual advances to. **pass off** (foll. by *as*) offer or dispose of (a thing) under false pretences (*passed it off as his own*). **2** evade or dismiss (an awkward remark etc.) lightly. **pass over** disregard; ignore the claims of (a person) to promotion etc. **pass water** urinate.

passable adj. **1** able to be passed. **2** fairly good but not outstanding. □ **passably** adv.

passage n. **1** the process of passing. **2** the right to pass through. **3** a journey by sea or air. **4** a way through, a passageway. **5** a tube-like structure through which air or secretions pass in the body. **6** a particular section of a literary or musical work.

passageway n. a narrow path, alley, or corridor.

passbook n. a book recording deposits and withdrawals from a bank or building society account.

passé / pah-**say** / adj. old-fashioned; past its prime. (¶ French)

passenger n. **1** a person (other than the driver, pilot, or crew) travelling in a vehicle, ship, or aircraft. **2** a member of a team etc. who does no work.

passer-by *n.* (*pl.* **passers-by**) a person who happens to be going past.

passerine / **pas**-uh-reen / *adj.* of perching birds, whose feet are adapted for gripping. • *n.* a bird of this kind.

passim / **pas**-uhm / *adv.* throughout or at many points in a book, article, etc. (¶ Latin, = everywhere.)

passing *adj.* **1** not lasting long (*a passing interest*). **2** casual, incidental (*a passing reference*). • *n.* the end of something; a death.

passion *n.* **1** strong emotion, esp. anger or intense sexual love. **2** great enthusiasm for something (*he has a passion for knitting*); the object arousing this (*playing footy is her passion*). **3** (**the Passion**) **a** the suffering of Christ during his last days. **b** a narrative of this from the Gospels. **c** a musical setting of any of these narratives. □ **passion flower** a climbing plant with flowers thought to resemble the crown of thorns and symbolise the Passion of Christ.

passionate *adj.* **1** full of passion, showing or moved by strong emotion. **2** (of emotion) intense. □ **passionately** *adv.*

passionfruit *n.* the edible fruit of some kinds of passion flower.

passive *adj.* **1** acted upon and not active. **2** not resisting, submissive. **3** lacking initiative or forceful qualities. **4** (of substances) inert, not active. • *n.* the form of a verb used when the subject of the sentence receives the action, e.g. *was seen* in *he was seen there*. □ **passive resistance** non-violent resistance by refusal to cooperate. **passive smoking** breathing in smoke from other people's cigarettes etc., identified as a health risk. **passive smoker** a non-smoker whose health is put at risk by involuntarily inhaling the exhaled tobacco smoke of smokers in the vicinity. □□ **passively** *adv.* **passiveness** *n.* **passivity** / pas-**siv**-uh-tee / *n.*

Passover *n.* a Jewish festival commemorating the Exodus of the Israelites from slavery in Egypt and their entry into the Promised Land.

passport *n.* **1** an official document identifying the holder as a citizen of a particular country and entitling him or her to travel abroad under its protection. **2** (foll. by *to*) a thing that enables one to obtain something (*such ability is a passport to success*).

password *n.* a secret prearranged word, phrase, or string of characters used as a code to gain admission, as proof of identity, etc.

past *adj.* **1** belonging or referring to the time before the present; (of time) gone by. **2** *Grammar* (of a tense or form) expressing a past action or state. • *n.* **1** time that is gone by; past events. **2** a person's past life, esp. if discreditable (*a man with a past*). **3** *Grammar* the past tense. • *prep.* **1** beyond in time or place (*it's past 2 a.m.; lives just past the pub*). **2** beyond the limits, power, range, or stage of (*past belief; she's past caring what happens*). • *adv.* beyond in time or place; up to and further (*drove past*). □ **past master** an expert.

pasta / **pas**-tuh, **pah**-stuh / *n.* dried flour paste used in various shapes in cooking (e.g. lasagne, spaghetti).

paste *n.* **1** a moist fairly stiff mixture, esp. of a powder and a liquid. **2** an adhesive. **3** food rendered to a smooth, moist mixture for use as a spread or in cooking (*anchovy paste; tomato paste*). **4** a hard glasslike substance used in making imitation gems. • *v.* **1** fasten or coat with paste. **2** *colloq.* beat or thrash.

pasteboard *n.* thin board made of layers of paper or wood fibres pasted together.

pastel / **pas**-tuhl / *n.* **1** a chalk-like crayon. **2** a drawing made with this. **3** a light delicate shade of colour.

pastern / **pas**-tuhn / *n.* the part of a horse's foot between fetlock and hoof.

Pasternak / **pas**-ter-nak /, Boris Leonidovich (1890–1960), Russian poet and novelist, author of *Doctor Zhivago*.

Pasteur / pas-**ter** /, Louis (1822–95), French chemist and bacteriologist, whose work led to the process now known as pasteurisation.

pasteurise / **pahs**-chuh-ruyz / *v.* (also **-ize**) sterilise (milk etc.) partially by heating and then chilling it. □ **pasteurisation** *n.* (¶ Named after Louis Pasteur.)

pasticceria / pas-tuh-**chair**-ree-uh / *n.* an Italian cake and pastry shop.

pastiche / pas-**teesh** / *n.* **1** a musical or other composition made up of selections from various sources. **2** a work composed in the style of a well-known author, composer, etc.

pastie alternative spelling of PASTY[1].

pastille / pas-**teel** / *n.* a small flavoured sweet for sucking; a lozenge.

pastime *n.* something done to pass time pleasantly; a recreation, a hobby.

pasting *n.* a beating or a thrashing.

pastor / **pahs**-tuh / *n.* **1** a minister, esp. of a Protestant church. **2** a person exercising spiritual guidance.

pastoral / **pahs**-tuh-ruhl / *adj.* **1** of shepherds, flocks, or herds. **2** of, pertaining to, or engaged in stock-raising as distinct from crop-raising; (of land) used for or suitable for stock-raising. **3** (of a poem, picture, etc.) portraying (esp. romanticised) country life. **4** of a pastor; concerned with spiritual guidance. • *n.* **1** a pastoral poem, picture, etc. **2** a letter from a bishop to the clergy or people of his diocese. □ **pastoral company** *Aust.* a commercial enterprise engaged in large-scale stock-raising. **pastoral district** *Aust.* an area in which the principal industry is stock-raising. **pastoral lease** *Aust.* an agreement under which an area of land is held on condition that it is used for stock-raising; the land so held. **pastoral property** (also **pastoral run**) *Aust.* a stock-raising establishment.

pastoralist / pahs-tuh-ruhl-uhst / n. Aust. the owner of a substantial stock-raising establishment or of a number of such establishments (see also GRAZIER).

pastrami / pas-**trah**-mee / n. seasoned smoked beef.

pastry n. **1** dough made of flour, fat, and water, used for making pies etc. **2** a cake etc. made of sweetened or filled pastry. ☐ **pastry cook** a cook who specialises in pastry.

pasturage / pahs-chuh-rij / n. **1** pasture-land. **2** the pasturing of cattle or sheep.

pasture n. **1** grassland suitable for grazing. **2** grass on such land. • v. put (animals) to graze in a pasture; (of animals) graze.

pasty[1] / pahs-tee, pas-tee / n. (also **pastie**) an individual portion of pastry wrapped around a filling of meat and vegetables.

pasty[2] / **pays**-tee / adj. **1** of or like paste. **2** unhealthily pale (pasty-faced). ☐ **pastiness** n.

Pat. abbr. Patent.

pat[1] v. (**patted**, **patting**) **1** tap gently with a flat palm, esp. in affection, sympathy, etc.; strike gently with the hand or a flat surface. **2** flatten or shape by doing this. • n. **1** a patting movement. **2** the sound of this. **3** a small mass (of butter or other soft substance) formed by patting. • adv. & adj. known and ready for any occasion (had his answer pat). ☐ **have off pat** know or have memorised perfectly.

pat[2] n. orig. Aust. rhyming slang ☐ **on one's pat** on one's own (short for PAT MALONE).

patch n. **1** a piece of material or metal etc. put over a hole to mend it. **2** a piece of plaster or a pad placed over a wound etc. to protect it. **3** a piece of material impregnated with a drug (e.g. nicotine) and stuck on a part of the body for absorption through the skin. **4** an area on a surface, differing in colour or texture from the rest. **5** a small area of anything (patches of fog). **6** a short period (went through a bad patch last summer). **7** a stretch of land, road, etc. **8** a number of plants growing in one place (the cabbage patch). **9** a scrap, a remnant. • v. **1** put a patch or patches on. **2** (of material) serve as a patch for. **3** piece (things) together. ☐ **patch test** a test for allergy by applying patches of different allergenic substances to the skin.

patchouli / puh-**choo**-lee / n. a fragrant plant of India etc., the leaves of which yield an essential oil; the powerful perfume made from this.

patchwork n. (often used as adj.) **1** needlework in which assorted small pieces of cloth are joined, often in a pattern (a patchwork quilt). **2** anything made of assorted pieces.

patchy adj. (**patchier**, **patchiest**) **1** having patches, existing in patches (patchy fog). **2** uneven in quality. ☐ **patchily** adv.

pate / payt / n. humorous or archaic the head.

pâté / **pat**-ay, **pah**-tay / n. paste of mashed and spiced liver, meat, etc. ☐ **pâté de foie gras** / duh fwah **grah** / pâté made from the liver of a force-fed and fatted goose.

patella / puh-**tel**-uh / n. (pl. **patellae**) the kneecap.

paten / **pat**-uhn / n. a metal plate on which the consecrated Host or bread is placed during the Mass etc.

patent / **pay**-tuhnt / n. **1** an official document conferring a right or title, esp. the sole right to make, use, or sell an invention. **2** an invention or process protected in this way. • adj. **1** obvious, plain, unconcealed (her patent dislike of him). **2** protected by patent. • v. obtain a patent for (an invention). ☐ **patent leather** leather with a glossy varnished surface. **patent medicine** a medicine made under a patent and available without a prescription.

patentee / pay-tuhn-**tee** / n. a person who takes out or holds a patent.

patently adv. clearly, obviously (he was patently jealous).

paternal / puh-**ter**-nuhl / adj. **1** of a father; of fatherhood. **2** fatherly. **3** related through one's father (paternal grandmother). ☐ **paternally** adv.

paternalism / puh-**ter**-nuh-liz-uhm / n. the policy of governing in a paternal way, providing for people's needs but giving them no responsibility. ☐ **paternalistic** adj.

paternity / puh-**ter**-nuh-tee / n. **1** fatherhood, being a father. **2** descent from a father. ☐ **paternity test** a test to determine from blood samples whether a man may be the father of a particular child.

paternoster / pah-tuh-**nos**-tuh / n. **1** the Lord's Prayer, esp. in Latin. **2** a rosary bead which indicates that this prayer be said.

Paterson, Banjo (full name: Andrew Barton Paterson) (1864–1941), Australian poet who portrayed an optimistic and idealised bush Australia, author of 'The Man from Snowy River', 'Clancy of the Overflow', and 'Waltzing Matilda'.

Paterson's curse n. a European herb with bluish-purple flowers naturalised in Australia and growing rampantly; variously regarded as a noxious weed, useful drought fodder, or a valuable source of honey. Paterson's curse is known as Salvation Jane in SA, and Lady Campbell weed in WA. In NSW it is sometimes facetiously referred to as the Riverina bluebell. (¶ Probably R.E. Paterson, Australian grazier (d.1918).)

path n. **1** a track by which people pass on foot. **2** a line along which a person or thing moves (flight path). **3** a course of action.

Pathan / puh-**tahn** / n. a member of a people living in parts of Afghanistan and Pakistan.

pathetic / puh-**thet**-ik / adj. **1** arousing pity, sadness, or contempt. **2** miserably inadequate. ☐ **pathetic fallacy** crediting non-human things with human emotions and responses. ☐☐ **pathetically** adv.

pathfinder *n.* an explorer, a pioneer.

pathogen *n.* something causing disease. ☐ **pathogenic** *adj.*

pathological / path-uh-**loj**-i-kuhl / *adj.* **1** of pathology. **2** of or caused by a physical or mental disorder (*a pathological fear of spiders*). ☐ **pathologically** *adv.*

pathology / puh-**thol**-uh-jee / *n.* **1** the study of diseases of the body. **2** abnormal changes in body tissue, caused by disease. ☐ **pathologist** *n.*

pathos / **pay**-thos / *n.* a quality that arouses pity or sadness.

pathway *n.* a path or its course.

patience *n.* **1** calm endurance of hardship, inconvenience, delay, etc. **2** perseverance. **3** a card game for one player.

patient *adj.* having or showing patience. • *n.* a person receiving or seeking medical or surgical treatment. ☐ **patiently** *adv.*

patina / **pat**-uh-nuh, puh-**tee**-nuh / *n.* **1** a green incrustation on the surface of old bronze. **2** a gloss on the surface of esp. woodwork, produced by age.

patio / **pat**-ee-oh / *n.* (*pl.* **patios**) a paved, usu. roofless area adjoining a house and used for outdoor living, entertainment, etc.

patisserie / puh-**tis**-uh-ree / *n.* **1** fancy pastries. **2** a shop selling these.

Pat Malone ☐ **on one's Pat Malone** orig. *Aust. rhyming slang* on one's own; alone.

Patna the capital of Bihar. ☐ **Patna rice** rice with long firm grains.

patois / **pat**-wah / *n.* (*pl.* **patois** / **pat**-wahz /) a regional dialect, differing from the literary language.

patriarch / **pay**-tree-ahk, **pat**-ree- / *n.* **1** the male head of a family or tribe. **2** (**the Patriarchs**) men named in the Bible as the ancestors of mankind or of the tribes of Israel. **3** a chief bishop in an Orthodox Church (*the Patriarch of Antioch; the Ecumenical Patriarch*). **4 a** the pope (*Patriarch of Rome*). **b** any bishop ranking immediately below the pope (*the Patriarch of Venice*). **5** the head of a Uniate Church. **6** a venerable old man. ☐ **patriarchal** / pay-tree-**ah**-kuhl, pat-ree- / *adj.*

patriarchy *n.* a male-dominated social system with descent through the male line.

patrician / puh-**trish**-uhn / *n. hist.* a member of the nobility in ancient Rome. • *adj.* aristocratic; of the ancient Roman nobility.

patricide / **pat**-ruh-suyd / *n.* **1** the crime of killing one's father. **2** a person who is guilty of this. ☐ **patricidal** *adj.*

Patrick, St (5th century), the patron saint of Ireland. Feast day, 17 March.

patrimony / **pat**-ruh-muh-nee / *n.* property inherited from one's father or ancestors; a heritage.

patriot / **pay**-tree-uht, **pat**-ree- / *n.* a patriotic person.

patriotic / pay-tree-**ot**-ik, pat-ree- / *adj.* loyally supporting one's country. ☐ **patriotically** *adv.*

patriotism / **pay**-tree-uh-tiz-uhm, **pat**-ree- / *n.*

patrol *v.* (**patrolled**, **patrolling**) walk or travel around (an area or building) to see that all is secure and orderly. • *n.* **1** patrolling (*on patrol*). **2** the guards or police, ship(s), or aircraft whose job is to patrol an area.

patron / **pay**-truhn / *n.* **1** a person who gives encouragement or financial support to an activity or cause. **2** a regular customer of a shop, restaurant, etc. ☐ **patron saint** a saint regarded as giving special protection to a person, place, or activity.

patronage / **pat**-ruh-nij / *n.* **1** support given by a patron. **2** the control of appointments to office, privileges, etc. **3** patronising behaviour.

patronise / **pat**-ruh-nuyz / *v.* (also **-ize**) **1** act as a patron towards, support or encourage. **2** be a regular customer at (a shop etc.). **3** treat in a condescending way.

patronising *adj.* (also **-zing**) condescending. ☐ **patronisingly** *adv.*

patronymic / pat-ruh-**nim**-ik / *n.* a person's name taken from the name of the father or a male ancestor (e.g. *Johnson, O'Brien, Ivanovich*).

patter[1] *v.* **1** make a series of light quick taps. **2** run with short quick steps. • *n.* a series of light quick tapping sounds.

patter[2] *n.* rapid and often glib or deceptive speech, e.g. that used by a conjuror or salesman. • *v.* talk or repeat glibly.

pattern *n.* **1** an arrangement of lines, shapes, or colours; a decorative design. **2** a model, design, or instructions for making something (*a knitting pattern*). **3** an excellent example, a model (*he's a pattern of elegance*). **4** the regular form or order in which a series of actions or qualities occur (*behaviour patterns*). • *v.* **1** model according to a pattern. **2** decorate with a pattern.

patty *n.* a small pie or pasty.

paucity / **paw**-suh-tee / *n.* smallness of supply or quantity.

Paul, St (original name: Saul) (1st century AD), the first Christian missionary, whose journeys are described in the Acts of the Apostles.

paunch *n.* a large stomach or belly. ☐ **paunchy** *adj.*

pauper *n.* a very poor person.

pause *n.* **1** a temporary stop or silence. **2** *Music* a mark (⌒) over a note or rest that is to be lengthened. • *v.* make a pause. ☐ **give pause to** cause (a person) to hesitate.

pav *n. Aust. colloq.* = PAVLOVA.

pavane / puh-**vahn**, -**van** / *n.* a stately dance; the music for this.

Pavarotti, Luciano (1935–), Italian operatic tenor.

pave *v.* cover (a road or path etc.) with a hard surface. ☐ **pave the way** prepare the way (for changes etc.).

pavement *n.* a paved path for pedestrians beside a road.

paver *n.* **1** a person who paves a road etc. **2** a paving stone, a paving tile.

pavilion *n.* **1** a decorative shelter in a park etc. **2** a large tent at a show, a fair, etc. **3** a building on a sports ground for use by players and spectators.

Pavlov / **pav**-lov /, Ivan Petrovich (1849–1936), Russian physiologist, noted for his study of conditioned reflexes in dogs.

Pavlova / pav-**loh**-vuh /, Anna (1881–1931), Russian ballerina.

pavlova / pav-**loh**-vuh / *n.* an Australian dessert: a large, soft-centred meringue cake topped with cream and fruit, traditionally passionfruit. (¶ Named after Anna Pavlova.)

Pavlovian / pav-**loh**-vee-uhn / *adj.* **1** reacting predictably to a stimulus. **2** of such a stimulus or response.

paw *n.* **1** the foot of an animal that has claws. **2** *colloq.* a person's hand. • *v.* **1** strike with a paw. **2** scrape (the ground) with a hoof. **3** *colloq.* fondle (a person) awkwardly or indecently.

pawl *n.* a lever with a catch that engages with the notches of a ratchet.

pawn[1] *n.* **1** a chess piece of the smallest size and value. **2** a person whose actions are controlled by others.

pawn[2] *v.* **1** deposit (a thing) with a pawnbroker as security for money borrowed. **2** pledge or wager (one's life, honour, etc.). • *n.* something deposited as a pledge.

pawnbroker *n.* a person licensed to lend money on the security of personal property deposited. ☐ **pawnbroking** *n.*

pawnshop *n.* a pawnbroker's place of business.

pawpaw *n.* (also **papaw, papaya**) a tropical fruit like a long melon with orange flesh.

pax / paks / *n.* **1** the kiss of peace, esp. at Mass. **2** (as *interj.*) *colloq.* a call for a truce (used esp. by schoolchildren). (¶ Latin, = peace)

pay *v.* (**paid, paying**) **1** give (money) in return for goods or services. **2** give what is owed as wages, a debt, ransom, etc.; undergo (a penalty). **3** bear the cost of something. **4** be profitable or worthwhile (*it would pay you to get a computer*). **5** bestow, render, or express (*pay attention; paid a call on his uncle; paid them a compliment*). **6** acknowledge the validity of a remark, repartee, etc.; acknowledge that one has been outwitted (*I'll pay that*). • *n.* **1** payment. **2** wages. ☐ **pay-as-you-earn** (also **PAYE**) *n.* a method of collecting income tax by deducting it at source from wages, interest, etc. **pay-back 1** *Aust.* (in Aboriginal English) an act of revenge, as sanctioned by traditional Aboriginal practice; the code governing this. **2** any act of revenge. **pay claim** a demand for an increase of wages. **pay off 1** pay in full and be free from (a debt) or discharge (an employee). **2** yield good results (*the risk paid off*). **pay-off** *colloq.* **1** payment. **2** reward or retribution. **3** a climax, esp. of a joke or story. **pay out 1** punish or be revenged on (a person). **2** let out (a rope) by slackening it. **pay television** (also **cable television**) a television channel or service to which viewers pay a monthly fee in order to receive its programs (as opposed to free-to-air television). ☐ ☐ **payer** *n.*

payable *adj.* which must or may be paid.

PAYE *abbr.* = PAY-AS-YOU-EARN.

payee / pay-**ee** / *n.* a person to whom money is paid or is to be paid.

payload *n.* **1** the part of an aircraft's load from which revenue is derived (e.g. passengers or cargo). **2** the total weight of bombs carried by an aircraft or rocket; the explosive warhead carried by a rocket etc.

paymaster *n.* an official who pays troops, workers, etc.

payment *n.* **1** paying. **2** money paid. **3** reward, compensation.

payola / pay-**oh**-luh / *n.* (esp. *US*) *colloq.* a bribe offered to one who promotes a commercial product by dishonestly making use of his or her position or influence.

payroll *n.* a list of a firm's employees receiving regular pay.

payslip *n.* a note given to an employee when paid detailing the amount of pay, and of tax etc. deducted.

PB *abbr.* = PERSONAL BEST.

Pb *symbol* lead.

PC *abbr.* (also **pc**) personal computer.

p.c. *abbr.* **1** per cent. **2** postcard.

PCB *abbr.* **1** polychlorinated biphenyl; a toxic compound formed as a waste product of industrial processes. **2** *Computing* printed circuit board.

Pd *symbol* palladium.

pd. *abbr.* paid.

PE *abbr.* physical education.

pea *n.* **1** a climbing plant bearing seeds in pods; its seed used as a vegetable. **2** a similar plant (*sweet pea; chickpea*). **3** (in full **Darling pea**) a perennial of SA, NSW, and Qld bearing profuse pea-flowers and causing poisoning when eaten by stock. **4** *Aust. colloq.* **a** (in horse racing) a favourite. **b** a person favoured to win a job etc. over other applicants (*she's the pea for the post of managing director*). ☐ **pea-eater 1** an animal poisoned by eating Darling pea. **2** *colloq.* an idiot, a brainless person (as brainless as an animal which eats Darling pea). **pea-struck** *Aust.* (of an animal) poisoned by eating Darling pea. **pea green** bright green. **pea-souper** *colloq.* a thick yellowish fog.

peabrain *n. colloq.* a stupid person. ☐ **pea-brained** *adj.*

peace *n.* **1** a state of freedom from war; ending of war. **2** a state of harmony between people; freedom from civil disorder (*a breach of the peace*). **3** quiet, calm. ☐ **peace offering** something offered to show that one is willing to make peace.

peaceable *adj.* **1** not quarrelsome, desiring to be at peace with others. **2** peaceful, without strife (*a peaceable settlement*). ☐ **peaceably** *adv.*

peaceful *adj.* **1** characterised by peace; tranquil. **2** not infringing peace (*peaceful coexistence*). ☐ **peacefully** *adv.* **peacefulness** *n.*

peacemaker *n.* a person who brings about peace.

peacenik *n.* a committed pacifist, esp. one who joins demonstrations etc.

peach[1] *n.* **1** a round juicy fruit with downy yellowish-pink skin and a rough stone. **2** the tree that bears this. **3** *colloq.* a person or thing that is greatly admired (*he's a peach*). **4** yellowish-pink colour. •*adj.* yellowish-pink. ☐ **peach Melba** *see* MELBA. ☐☐ **peachy** *adj.*

peach[2] *v. colloq.* turn informer; inform (on or against a person).

peacock *n.* **1** a large male bird, native to India, with greenish-blue plumage and long tail-feathers that can be spread upright like a fan. **2** a vain or ostentatious person. •*v.* (of a person) strut like a peacock, displaying oneself. ☐ **peacock blue** *n. & adj.* (as *adj.* usu. with hyphen) shiny greenish blue.

peafowl *n.* (*pl.* the same) peacock, peahen.

peahen *n.* the drab female of a peacock.

peak *n.* **1** a pointed top, esp. of a mountain. **2** the mountain itself. **3** a projecting part of the edge of a cap. **4** the point of highest value, achievement, intensity, etc. (*at the peak of his career; peak hours; peak viewing on TV*). •*v.* reach its peak in value or intensity etc. ☐ **peak body** (*or* **council**) an organisation setting policy for, coordinating the activities of, or representing the interests of, a number of other organisations with similar interests. **peak hour** the time of the most intense traffic etc. **peak load** the maximum of electric power demand.

peaked *adj.* (of features) thin, drawn, pinched.

peal *n.* **1** the loud ringing of bells. **2** a set of bells with different notes. **3** a loud burst of thunder or laughter. •*v.* sound or cause to sound in a peal.

peanut *n.* **1** a plant bearing pods that ripen underground, containing seeds used for food and oil. **2** this seed. **3** (**peanuts**) *colloq.* a trivial or contemptibly small amount, esp. of money. **4** *colloq.* **a** an insignificant, worthless person. **b** a short person. ☐ **peanut butter** a paste of ground roasted peanuts.

pear *n.* **1** a rounded fleshy fruit that tapers towards the stalk. **2** the tree that bears this.

pearl *n.* **1** a round lustrous white solid formed inside the shells of certain oysters, valued as a gem. **2** something resembling this. **3** something valued because of its excellence or beauty. •*v.* fish for pearls. •*adj.* (of an electric light bulb) made of opaque glass. ☐ **pearl barley** barley grains ground small. **pearl perch** a greenish to silvery-grey marine food fish of reefs off the Qld coast.

pearled *adj.* formed into or covered with pearl-like drops.

pearler[1] *n.* **1** a person who dives or fishes for pearls. **2** a boat used in pearl fishing.

pearler[2] alternative spelling of PURLER.

Pearl Harbor a harbour on the island of Oahu, Hawaii, site of an American naval base attacked by the Japanese on 7 December 1941, an event which brought America into the Second World War.

pearly *adj.* like pearls, adorned with pearls; lustrous. ☐ **pearly nautilus** = NAUTILUS.

Pearson, Noel (1965–), Australian Aboriginal lawyer and Aboriginal rights activist.

peasant / **pez**-uhnt / *n.* **1** (in some countries) a farm labourer or small farmer. **2** *derog.* a lout, a boor.

peasantry *n.* peasants.

pease *n.pl. archaic* peas.

peat *n.* vegetable matter decomposed by the action of water in bogs etc. and partly carbonised, used in horticulture. ☐ **peaty** *adj.*

peatmoss *n.* any of various mosses, of the genus *Sphagnum*, which form peat as they decay: much used in horticulture for potting mixes etc.

pebble *n.* a small stone worn smooth esp. by the action of water. ☐ **pebbly** *adj.*

pec *n.* (usu. in *pl.*) *colloq.* a pectoral muscle.

pecan / pee-kuhn, pee-**kan** / *n.* the smooth pinkish-brown nut of a kind of hickory.

peccadillo / pek-uh-**dil**-oh / *n.* (*pl.* **peccadilloes** *or* **peccadillos**) a trivial offence; a venial sin.

peccary / **pek**-uh-ree / *n.* a wild pig of tropical America.

peck[1] *v.* **1** strike or nip or pick up with the beak. **2** kiss lightly and hastily. **3** *colloq.* eat listlessly; nibble at (food) without much interest. •*n.* **1** a stroke or nip made with the beak. **2** a light hasty kiss. ☐ **pecking order** a system of rank or status in which people dominate those below themselves and are dominated by those above (as observed among domestic fowls).

peck[2] *n.* (in the imperial system) a measure of capacity for dry goods, = 2 gallons or 8 quarts.

pecked *adj. Aust.* (of ancient Aboriginal rock engravings) characterised by many pecked strokes or marks.

pecker[1] *n.* **1** that which pecks; a beak. **2** *colloq.* courage; spirit. ☐ **keep your pecker up** *colloq.* keep up your spirits; be cheerful.

pecker[2] *n. coarse colloq.* the penis.

peckish *adj. colloq.* hungry.

pectin *n.* a gelatinous substance found in ripe fruits etc., causing jams to set.

pectoral / **pek**-tuh-ruhl / *adj.* **1** of, in, or on the chest or breast (*pectoral muscles*). **2** worn on the breast (*a bishop's pectoral cross*). •*n.* a pectoral muscle or fin.

peculate / **pek**-yuh-layt / *v.* embezzle (money). ☐ **peculation** *n.* **peculator** *n.*

peculiar *adj.* **1** strange, eccentric. **2** belonging exclusively to a particular person, place, or thing

(*clothing peculiar to the early 19th century*). **3** particular, special (*a point of peculiar interest*).
peculiarity *n.* **1** being peculiar. **2** a characteristic (*meanness is his peculiarity*). **3** something unusual, an eccentricity.
peculiarly *adv.* **1** in a peculiar way. **2** especially (*peculiarly annoying*).
pecuniary / puh-**kyoo**-nyuh-ree / *adj.* of or in money (*pecuniary aid*).
pedagogue / **ped**-uh-gog / *n. derog.* or *archaic* a teacher. ☐ **pedagogic** *adj.*
pedal *n.* a lever operated by the foot. • *v.* (**pedalled**, **pedalling**) **1** work the pedal(s) of. **2** move or operate by means of pedals; ride a bicycle.
pedant / **ped**-uhnt / *n. derog.* a person who insists unimaginatively on strict observance of formal rules and details, or who is obsessed by theory to the exclusion of practical application. ☐ **pedantry** / **ped**-uhn-tree / *n.* **pedantic** / puh-**dan**-tik / *adj.* **pedantically** *adv.*
Pedder, Lake a former lake in south-west Tas., now drowned and serving as a water storage for the Gordon River hydroelectric power scheme.
peddle *v.* **1** sell (goods) as a pedlar. **2** advocate or promote (ideas etc.). **3** sell (drugs) illegally.
peddler *n.* a person who sells drugs illegally.
pederast / **ped**-uh-rast / *n.* (also **paederast**) an adult male who has anal intercourse with an under-age male. ☐ **pederasty** *n.*
pedestal *n.* a base supporting a column, statue, etc. ☐ **put a person on a pedestal** admire or respect him or her greatly.
pedestrian *n.* a person who is walking, esp. in a street. • *adj.* **1** of walking; of or for pedestrians. **2** unimaginative, dull. ☐ **pedestrian crossing** a street crossing where pedestrians have priority over traffic.
pedestrianise *v.* (also -**ize**) convert (a street or area) for the use of pedestrians only.
pediatrician, pediatrics alternative spelling of PAEDIATRICIAN, PAEDIATRICS.
pedicure / **ped**-uh-kyoor / *n.* care or treatment of the feet and toenails.
pedigree *n.* a line of ancestors, esp. a distinguished one. • *adj.* (of animals) having a recorded line of descent that shows pure breeding (*pedigree dogs*). ☐ **pedigreed** *adj.*
pediment / **ped**-uh-muhnt / *n.* a triangular part crowning the front of a building, esp. over a portico.
pedlar *n.* **1** a person who goes from house to house selling small articles. **2** (usu. foll. by *of*) a spreader (of gossip etc.).
pedometer / puh-**dom**-uh-tuh / *n.* a device that calculates the distance a person walks by counting the number of steps taken.
pedophile alternative spelling of PAEDOPHILE.
pedophilia alternative spelling of PAEDOPHILIA.
peduncle / puh-**dung**-kuhl / *n.* the stalk of a flower, fruit, or cluster. ☐ **peduncular** *adj.*

pee *colloq. v.* (**pees**, **peed**) urinate. • *n.* **1** urination. **2** urine.
peek *v.* peep slyly, glance. • *n.* a quick or sly look.
peel *n.* the skin of certain fruits and vegetables. • *v.* **1** remove the peel of. **2** strip away, pull off (a skin or covering). **3** come off in strips or layers; lose skin or bark etc. in this way. ☐ **peel off 1** veer away from a formation. **2** strip off one's clothes. ☐ ☐ **peeler** *n.*
peeler *n.* (also **potato peeler**) a small instrument with double, swivelling blades, used in the kitchen for peeling vegetables etc.
peelings *n.pl.* strips of skin peeled from potatoes etc.
peen *n.* the wedge-shaped or curved end of a hammer head, opposite the striking face.
peep[1] *v.* **1** look through a narrow opening; look quickly or surreptitiously. **2** come briefly or partially into view, show slightly. • *n.* a brief or surreptitious look.
peep[2] *n.* a high chirping sound like that made by young birds. • *v.* make this sound.
peephole *n.* a small hole to look through.
peeping Tom *n.* a man who furtively watches someone undressing or engaging in sexual activities. (¶ From the name of the tailor said to have peeped at Lady Godiva when she rode naked through Coventry.)
peer[1] *v.* look searchingly or with difficulty.
peer[2] *n.* **1** one who is the equal of another in rank, quality, ability, etc.; a contemporary. **2** *Brit.* (feminine **peeress**) a member of the nobility. ☐ **peer group** a group of people of the same age, status, social background, etc.
peerage *n. Brit.* **1** the nobility. **2** the rank of peer or peeress.
peerless *adj.* without equal; superb.
peeve *colloq. v.* annoy. • *n.* a cause of annoyance; a feeling of irritation. ☐ **peeved** *adj.*
peevish *adj.* irritable. ☐ **peevishly** *adv.*
peewee *n.* (also **peewit**) *Aust.* = MAGPIE LARK.
peg *n.* **1** a wooden or metal pin or bolt for fixing, hanging, or marking things. **2** a clothes peg. **3** a wooden screw for tightening or loosening the strings of a violin etc. **4** a drink or measure of spirits. • *v.* (**pegged**, **pegging**) **1** fix or mark by means of a peg or pegs. **2** keep (wages or prices) at a fixed amount. ☐ **off the peg** (of clothes) ready-made. **peg it** (*or* **a thing specified**) **on a person** hang the blame (or a thing specified) on a person (*tried to peg it on me; pegged the theft on the boy next door*). **peg leg** *n. colloq.* **1** an artificial leg; a person with this. **2** *Aust.* a disease of cattle attributed to phosphorus deficiency.
Pegasus / **peg**-uh-suhs / **1** *Gk myth.* an immortal winged horse. **2** a northern constellation.
peggy *n. Aust. colloq.* an unskilled worker responsible for tea-making etc.
pejorative / puh-**jo**-ruh-tiv / *adj.* expressing disapproval; disparaging, derogatory. • *n.* a derogatory word. ☐ **pejoratively** *adv.*

Peking / pee-**king** / variant of BEIJING.

Pekingese *n.* (*pl.* **Pekingese**) a dog with short legs, flat face, and long silky hair.

pekoe / **pee**-koh / *n.* a superior grade of black tea.

pelagic / puh-**laj**-ik / *adj.* **1** of or performed on the open sea (*pelagic whaling*). **2** (of marine life) belonging to the upper layers of the open sea.

pelargonium / pel-uh-**goh**-nee-uhm / *n.* a plant with showy flowers and often fragrant leaves (often erroneously called 'geranium').

pelf *n. humorous* or *derog.* money, wealth.

pelican *n.* a large waterbird with a pouch in its long bill for storing fish.

pellagra / puh-**lag**-ruh, **lay**-gruh / *n.* a deficiency disease causing cracking of the skin, often ending in insanity.

pellet *n.* **1** a small compressed ball of paper, bread, etc. **2** a piece of small shot. **3** a pill.

pellicle *n.* a thin skin or membrane, a thin layer.

pell-mell *adv.* & *adj.* in a hurried disorderly manner; headlong.

pellucid / puh-**loo**-sid / *adj.* very clear.

pelmet / **pel**-muht / *n.* a valance or ornamental strip above a window to conceal a curtain rail.

peloton / **pel**-uh-ton / *n.* the main field or group of cyclists in a race. (¶ French, = small ball.)

pelt *n.* an animal skin, esp. with the fur or hair still on it. • *v.* **1** throw missiles at. **2** (of rain etc.) come down fast. **3** run fast. □ **at full pelt** as fast as possible.

pelvic *adj.* of the pelvis. □ **pelvic inflammatory disease** (also **PID**) an inflammation of the female genital tract, esp. the fallopian tubes.

pelvis *n.* the basin-shaped cavity at the lower end of the body formed by the right and left hip bones etc. and including the genital region. □ **pelvic** *adj.*

Pemulwuy (?–1802), an Aborigine who from 1790 to 1802 led his people in resistance to the British invaders in what is now the area of Sydney, including attacks on British settlements at Toongabbie and Parramatta. He was ambushed in 1802, after which his head was cut off and sent to England in a cask of spirits. He is regarded by many as a patriot, the first inhabitant of this country to give his life resisting a foreign invader.

pen[1] *n.* **1** a small fenced enclosure, esp. for cattle, sheep, poultry, etc. **2** *Aust.* a division in a shearing shed; a job as a shearer. **3** any place of confinement; a prison. • *v.* (**penned, penning**) shut in or as if in a pen.

pen[2] *n.* a device with a metal point for writing with ink. • *v.* (**penned, penning**) write (a letter etc.). □ **pen-name** *n.* an author's pseudonym. **pen-pushing** *colloq.* clerical work.

pen[3] *n.* a female swan.

penal / **pee**-nuhl / *adj.* **1** of or involving punishment, esp. according to law. **2** (of an offence) punishable by law. **3** extremely severe, punishing (*penal taxation*). □ **penal colony** (also **convict colony**) *Aust. hist.* an Australian Colony regarded primarily as a place of penal servitude for convicts from Britain. **penal settlement** (also **penal station, convict settlement**) *Aust. hist.* any of several places in Australia where convicts from Britain were confined. □□ **penally** *adv.*

penalise *v.* (also **-ize**) **1** subject (a person) to a penalty or disadvantage. **2** make or declare (an action) penal. □ **penalisation** *n.*

penalty *n.* **1** a punishment for breaking a law, rule, or contract. **2** a disadvantage, loss, etc., esp. as a result of one's own actions (*paid the penalty for his carelessness*). **3** a disadvantage to which a sports player or team must submit for breaking a rule. □ **penalty rate** *Aust.* an increased rate of pay for overtime or in recognition of abnormal conditions.

penance / **pen**-uhns / *n.* **1** an act performed as an expression of penitence. **2** (in the Catholic and Orthodox Church) a sacrament including confession, absolution, and an act of penitence. □ **do penance** perform a penance.

pence *see* PENNY.

penchant / **pen**-shuhnt / *n.* a liking or inclination (*he has a penchant for sword-and-sorcery films*). (¶ French)

pencil *n.* **1** an instrument for drawing or writing, usu. a thin stick of graphite enclosed in a cylinder of wood. **2** something used or shaped like this. • *v.* (**pencilled, pencilling**) write or draw or mark with a pencil. □ **pencil in** enter (a suggested date, estimate, etc.) provisionally. **pencil pine** any of various conifers which grow tall, thin, and pencil-shaped.

penda *n.* any of several related trees of south-eastern Qld valued for their very hard wood; the wood of these trees. (¶ Probably from Gabi-gabi.)

pendant *n.* **1** a hanging ornament, esp. one attached to a necklace or bracelet. **2** a light-fitting or ornament hanging from a ceiling.

pendent *adj.* hanging. □ **pendency** *n.*

pending *adj.* **1** waiting to be decided or settled. **2** about to come into existence (*patent pending*). • *prep.* **1** during (*pending these negotiations*). **2** until (*pending his return*).

pendulous / **pen**-dyoo-luhs / *adj.* hanging downwards; hanging so as to swing freely.

pendulum / **pen**-dyoo-luhm / *n.* a weight hung so that it can swing freely, esp. a rod with a weighted end that regulates the movement of a clock.

Penelope / puh-**nel**-uh-pee / *Gk myth.* the wife of Odysseus, who remained faithful to him during his long years of absence.

penetrable / **pen**-uh-truh-buhl / *adj.* able to be penetrated. □ **penetrability** *n.*

penetrate *v.* **1** make a way into or through, pierce. **2** enter and permeate. **3** see into or through (*our eyes could not penetrate the darkness*). **4** discover or understand (*penetrated their secrets*). **5** be absorbed by the mind (*my hint didn't penetrate*). □ **penetration** *n.*

penetrating *adj.* **1** having or showing great insight. **2** (of a voice or sound) loud and carrying; piercing.

penetrative / pen-uh-truh-tiv / *adj.* able to penetrate; penetrating.

penetrometer / pen-uh-**trom**-uh-tuh / *n.* an instrument for determining the consistency or hardness of a substance by measuring the depth or rate of penetration of a rod or needle driven into it by a known force.

penfriend *n.* (also **penpal**) a friend with whom a person corresponds, usu. without meeting.

penguin *n.* a flightless black and white sea bird of the Southern hemisphere, with wings developed into flippers for swimming underwater.

Penguin Award any of the annual awards for excellence made by the Television Society of Australia.

penicillin / pen-uh-**sil**-uhn / *n.* an antibiotic of the kind obtained from mould fungi.

penile / **pee**-nuyl / *adj.* of or concerning the penis.

peninsula / puh-**nin**-syoo-luh, -shuh-luh / *n.* a piece of land that is almost surrounded by water or projecting far into the sea. ☐ **peninsular** *adj.*

penis / **pee**-nuhs / *n.* the male organ of copulation and (in mammals) urination.

penitent *adj.* feeling regret that one has done wrong. •*n.* **1** a penitent person. **2** a person doing penance under the direction of a confessor. ☐ **penitently** *adv.* **penitence** *n.*

penitential / pen-uh-**ten**-shuhl / *adj.* of penitence or penance.

penitentiary / pen-uh-**ten**-shuh-ree / *n.* US a federal or State prison. •*adj.* **1** of penance. **2** of reformatory treatment.

penknife *n.* (*pl.* **penknives**) a small folding knife (orig. for sharpening quills into pens).

pennant / **pen**-uhnt / *n.* **1** a long tapering flag, esp. one flown on a ship. **2** = PENNON. **3** a flag as a symbol of success in sports, the flag of a championship etc.

penne / **pe**-nay / *n.* pasta in the form of short wide tubes. (¶ *Italian*)

penniless *adj.* having no money; destitute.

pennon *n.* **1** a long narrow triangular or swallow-tailed flag. **2** a long pointed streamer on a ship.

penny *n.* (*pl.* **pennies** for separate coins, **pence** for a sum of money) **1** a British coin and monetary unit equal to one-hundredth of a pound. **2** *hist.* a bronze coin equal to one-two-hundred-and-fortieth of a pound. **2** a very small sum of money (*it won't cost you a penny*). ☐ **penny farthing** an old type of bicycle with a very large front wheel and a small rear one.

pennyroyal *n.* a creeping mint cultivated for its supposed medicinal properties.

pennyworth *n.* a very small amount (orig. the amount a penny would have bought).

penology / pee-**nol**-uh-jee / *n.* the scientific study of crime, its punishment, and prison management. ☐ **penological** *adj.*

pension / **pen**-shuhn / *n.* a periodic payment made by a government to people who are above a certain age, to widows, or to the disabled. •*v.* pay a pension to. ☐ **pension off 1** dismiss or allow to retire with a pension. **2** cease to employ or use.

pensionable *adj.* **1** entitled to receive a pension. **2** (of a job) entitling a person to receive a pension.

pensioner *n.* a person who receives a retirement or other pension.

pensive *adj.* deep in thought. ☐ **pensively** *adv.* **pensiveness** *n.*

pent *adj.* (often foll. by *in* or *up*) shut in a confined space; shut in (*pent-up anger*).

penta- *comb. form* five.

pentacle / **pen**-tuh-kuhl / *n.* a figure used as a symbol, esp. in magic, e.g. a pentagram.

pentagon / **pen**-tuh-guhn, -gon / *n.* **1** a geometric figure with five sides. **2** (**the Pentagon**) a five-sided building near Washington, headquarters of the US Department of Defense.

pentagonal / pen-**tag**-uh-nuhl / *adj.* five-sided.

pentagram / **pen**-tuh-gram / *n.* a five-pointed star, used as a mystic symbol.

pentameter / pen-**tam**-uh-tuh / *n.* a line of verse with five metrical feet.

pentangle / **pen**-tang-guhl / *n.* = PENTAGRAM.

Pentateuch / **pen**-tuh-tyook / *n.* the first five books of the Old Testament.

pentathlon / pen-**tath**-luhn / *n.* an athletic contest in which each competitor takes part in the five events it includes.

Pentecost / **pen**-tuh-kost / *n.* **1** the Jewish harvest festival, fifty days after the second day of the Passover. **2** Whit Sunday.

pentecostal / pen-tuh-**kos**-tuhl / *adj.* of or designating Christian sects which emphasise divine gifts such as miraculous healing of the sick, are usu. fundamentalist in outlook, and the members of which express religious fervour by clapping, shouting, dancing, glossolalia, etc.

penthouse *n.* a flat (esp. a luxurious one) on the roof or top floor of a tall building.

penultimate / puh-**nul**-tuh-muht / *adj. & n.* last but one.

penumbra / puh-**num**-bruh / *n.* (*pl.* **penumbras** or **penumbrae**) a partly shaded region around the complete shadow of an opaque body, esp. that around the shadow of the earth or moon in an eclipse; a partial shadow. ☐ **penumbral** *adj.*

penurious / puh-**nyoo**-ree-uhs / *adj.* **1** poverty-stricken. **2** stingy, mean.

penury / **pen**-yuh-ree / *n.* **1** extreme poverty. **2** dearth, scarcity.

peony / **pee**-uh-nee / *n.* (also **paeony**) a garden plant with large round red, pink, or white flowers.

people *n.pl.* **1** human beings in general. **2** the persons belonging to a place or forming a group or social class; the subjects or citizens of a State. **3**

People's Republic of China / **perennial**

(**the people**) ordinary persons, those not having special rank or position; these as an electorate (*the people will reject it*). **4** a person's parents or other relatives (*my people disapprove*). **5** (treated as *sing.*) the persons composing a community, tribe, race, or nation (*the English-speaking peoples; a warlike people*). • *v.* fill (a place) with people, populate.

People's Republic of China the official name (since 1949) of CHINA.

pep *n. colloq.* vigour, energy, spirit. □ **pep pill** a pill containing a stimulant drug. **pep talk** a talk urging the hearer(s) to great effort or courage. **pep up** (**pepped**, **pepping**) *colloq.* fill with vigour, enliven.

pepino / puh-**pee**-noh / *n.* a spiny plant grown for its elongated fruit tasting of melon.

pepper *n.* **1** a hot-tasting powder made from the dried berries of certain plants, used to season food. **2** a capsicum grown as a vegetable. • *v.* **1** sprinkle with pepper. **2** pelt with small missiles. **3** sprinkle here and there (*a speech peppered with jokes*). □ **pepper mill** a mill for grinding peppercorns by hand. **pepper tree** (also **peppercorn, peppercorn tree, pepperina**) the introduced South American tree *Schinus molle*, bearing small, red, aromatic fruit, and widely planted as a shade tree, esp. near homesteads in inland Australia.

peppercorn *n.* **1** the dried berry from which pepper is made. **2** = PEPPER TREE. □ **peppercorn rent** a very low rent, virtually nothing.

pepperina (also **pepperina tree**) = PEPPER TREE.

peppermint *n.* **1** a mint grown for its strong fragrant oil, used in medicine, sweets, etc. **2** a sweet flavoured with this. **3** any of many small to large eucalypts of south-eastern Australia, the leaves of which yield aromatic, peppermint-like essential oils; any of several other Australian plants, esp. the tree or shrub *Agonis* of WA, having peppermint-scented foliage.

pepperoni *n.* an Italian beef and pork sausage seasoned with pepper.

peppery *adj.* **1** like pepper, containing much pepper. **2** hot-tempered.

pepsin *n.* an enzyme contained in gastric juice, helping to digest food.

peptic *adj.* of digestion. □ **peptic ulcer** an ulcer in the stomach or duodenum.

peptide *n.* a compound consisting of a chain of amino acids, chemically linked.

per *prep.* **1** for each (*70 cents per litre*). **2** (in full **as per**) in accordance with (*as per instructions; as per usual*). **3** by means of (*per post*). □ **per annum** for each year. **per capita** for each person. **per cent** in or for every hundred (*three per cent*).

perambulate / puh-**ram**-byuh-layt / *v.* **1** walk through, over, or round (an area), travel through and inspect. **2** walk about. □ **perambulation** *n.*

perambulator *n. archaic* a pram.

perceive *v.* become aware of, see or notice.

percentage / puh-**sen**-tij / *n.* **1** the rate or proportion per hundred. **2** a proportion or part. **3** *colloq.* personal benefit or advantage (*there's no percentage in pursuing the matter*). • *adj.* (in tennis, football, etc.) pertaining to a style of play which avoids risk-taking and concentrates on achieving a higher percentage of orthodox strokes etc. than the opposing player or team.

percentile *n.* each of 99 points at which a range of data is divided to make 100 groups of equal size.

perceptible *adj.* able to be perceived. □ **perceptibly** *adv.* **perceptibility** *n.*

perception *n.* perceiving; ability to perceive.

perceptive *adj.* having or showing insight and sensitive understanding. □ **perceptively** *adv.* **perceptiveness** *n.*

perceptual *adj.* of or involving perception.

Perceval / **per**-suh-vuhl / a legendary figure associated with the story of the Holy Grail.

perch[1] *n.* **1** a bird's resting place, e.g. a branch or rod. **2** a high place or narrow ledge used as a resting place, viewing point, etc. **3** a measure of length equal to 5½ yards. • *v.* rest or place on or as if on a perch.

perch[2] *n.* (*pl.* **perch** or **perches**) **1** an edible European freshwater fish with spiny fins. **2** any of many similar freshwater or marine food fish found in Australia.

perchance *adv. archaic* perhaps.

percipient / puh-**sip**-ee-uhnt / *adj.* perceiving; perceptive. □ **percipience** *n.*

percolate / **per**-kuh-layt / *v.* **1** filter or cause to filter, esp. through small holes. **2** prepare (coffee) in a percolator. **3** (of news, ideas, etc.) spread gradually. □ **percolation** *n.*

percolator *n.* a coffee-making pot, in which boiling water circulates repeatedly up a central tube and downwards through ground coffee held in a perforated drum.

percussion / per-**kush**-uhn / *n.* **1** the striking of one object against another. **2** percussion instruments in an orchestra. □ **percussion cap** a small metal or paper device containing explosive powder that explodes when it is struck, used as a detonator or in a toy pistol. **percussion instrument** a musical instrument (e.g. drum, cymbals) played by striking. □□ **percussionist** *n.* **percussive** *adj.*

perdition / puh-**dish**-uhn / *n.* eternal damnation.

peregrination / pe-ruh-gruh-**nay**-shuhn / *n. archaic* travelling; a journey.

peregrine / **pe**-ruh-gruhn / *n.* (in full **peregrine falcon**) a falcon that can be trained to hunt and catch small animals and birds.

peremptory / puh-**remp**-tuh-ree / *adj.* imperious; insisting on obedience. □ **peremptorily** *adv.* **peremptoriness** *n.*

perennial / puh-**ren**-ee-uhl / *adj.* **1** lasting a long time or for ever; constantly recurring (*a perennial* *problem*). **2** (of a plant) living for several years. • *n.* a perennial plant. ☐ **perennially** *adv.*

perentie / puh-**ren**-tee / *n.* a giant monitor lizard, the largest of the Australian lizards (often 2 m long), of rocky country in arid central and western Australia. (¶ Diyari)

Peres, Shimon (1923–), prime minister of Israel 1984–86, 1995–96. He shared the 1994 Nobel Peace Prize with Yitzhak Rabin and Yasser Arafat.

perestroika / pe-ruh-**stroi**-kuh / *n.* (in the former USSR) the restructuring of the Russian economic and political system under Gorbachev. (¶ Russian, = restructuring.)

perfect *adj.* / **per**-fekt / **1** complete, having all its essential qualities. **2** faultless; excellent. **3** exact, precise (*a perfect circle*). **4** entire, total (*a perfect stranger*). **5** *Grammar* of a tense of a verb used to denote an action or event that is completed, e.g. *he has gone.* • *v.* / puh-**fekt** / **1** make perfect; improve. **2** carry through; complete. ☐ **perfect pitch** the ability to recognise or sing any given note.

perfection *n.* **1** making or being perfect. **2** a person or thing considered perfect.

perfectionist *n.* a person who is satisfied with nothing less than what he or she thinks is perfect. ☐ **perfectionism** *n.*

perfectly *adv.* **1** in a perfect way. **2** completely, quite (*perfectly satisfied*).

perfidious / per-**fid**-ee-uhs / *adj.* treacherous, disloyal. ☐ **perfidiously** *adv.* **perfidy** / **per**-fuh-dee / *n.*

perforate *v.* **1** make a hole or holes through, esp. a row of tiny holes so that part(s) can be torn off easily. **2** penetrate. ☐ **perforation** *n.*

perforce *adv. archaic* by force of circumstances; necessarily.

perform *v.* **1** carry into effect, accomplish, do; go through (a particular proceeding). **2** function (*the car performed well when tested*). **3** act in a play etc.; play an instrument, sing, do tricks, etc. before an audience. **4** *Aust. colloq.* display anger or bad temper. ☐ **performer** *n.*

performance *n.* **1** the act, process, or manner of performing. **2** the performing of a play or other entertainment. **3** *colloq.* a fuss; an emotional scene. ☐ **performance art** a form of visual art combining static elements with dramatic performance. **performance artist** a person presenting performance art. **performing arts** drama, music, dance, etc.

perfume *n.* **1** a sweet smell. **2** a fragrant liquid for giving a pleasant smell, esp. to the body. • *v.* give a sweet smell to; apply perfume to.

perfumery / puh-**fyoo**-muh-ree / *n.* perfumes; the preparation of these.

perfunctory / puh-**fungk**-tuh-ree / *adj.* done as a duty or routine but without much care or interest. ☐ **perfunctorily** *adv.* **perfunctoriness** *n.*

pergola / per-**goh**-luh, **per**-guh-luh / *n.* **1** *Aust.* a horizontal wooden framework with vertical supports and a decking floor, attached to a house and usu. with climbing plants trained over it, used for recreation. **2** an arbour or covered walk formed of climbing plants trained over trelliswork.

perhaps *adv.* it may be; possibly.

perianth / **pe**-ree-anth / *n.* the outer part of a flower.

pericardium *n.* (*pl.* **pericardia**) the membranous sac enclosing the heart.

pericarp / **pe**-ree-kahp / *n.* a seed-vessel such as a pea pod.

perigee / **pe**-ruh-jee / *n.* the point in the orbit of the moon or any planet when it is nearest to earth (as opposed to APOGEE).

perihelion / pe-ree-**hee**-lee-uhn / *n.* (*pl.* **perihelia**) the point in a planet's or comet's orbit when it is closest to the sun.

peril *n.* serious danger.

perilous *adj.* full of risk, dangerous. ☐ **perilously** *adv.*

perimeter / puh-**rim**-uh-tuh / *n.* **1** the outer edge or boundary of a closed geometric figure or of an area. **2** the length of this.

perinatal *adj.* relating to the time immediately before and after birth.

perineum / pe-ruh-**nee**-uhm / *n.* the region of the body between the anus and the scrotum or vulva. ☐ **perineal** *adj.*

period *n.* **1** a length or portion of time. **2** a time with particular characteristics (*the colonial period*). **3** the time allocated for a lesson in school. **4** an occurrence of menstruation. **5** a complete sentence. **6** a full stop in punctuation. **7** *colloq.* used at the end of a statement to indicate finality (*I'm not going, period!*). • *adj.* (of furniture, dress, or architecture) belonging to a past age.

periodic *adj.* occurring or appearing at intervals. ☐ **periodic table** a table of the elements in order of their atomic numbers, in which chemically related elements tend to appear in the same column or row.

periodical *adj.* periodic. • *n.* a magazine etc. published at regular intervals. ☐ **periodically** *adv.*

periodicity / peer-ree-uh-**dis**-uh-tee / *n.* being periodic, the tendency to recur at intervals.

periodontics *n.* the branch of dentistry concerned with the gums and structures surrounding the teeth. ☐ **periodontal** *adj.*

periodontitis / pe-ree-oh-don-**tuy**-tuhs / *n.* inflammation of the tissue around the teeth, often causing shrinkage of the gums and loosening of the teeth.

peripatetic / pe-ree-puh-**tet**-ik / *adj.* going from place to place; itinerant. • *n.* a peripatetic person.

peripheral / puh-**rif**-uh-ruhl / *adj.* **1** of or on the periphery. **2** of minor but not central importance to something. • *n.* any input, output, or storage device that can be controlled by the central processing unit of a computer (e.g. a magnetic tape, floppy disk, line printer).

periphery / puh-**rif**-uh-ree / n. **1** the boundary of a surface or area; the region immediately inside or beyond this. **2** the fringes of a subject.

periphrasis / puh-**rif**-ruh-suhs / n. (pl. **periphrases**) a roundabout way of speaking, a circumlocution; a roundabout phrase. ☐ **periphrastic** / pe-ruh-**fras**-tik / adj.

periscope n. an apparatus with a tube and mirror(s) by which a person in a trench, a submerged submarine, or at the back of a crowd etc., can see things that are otherwise out of sight. ☐ **periscopic** adj.

perish v. **1** suffer destruction; become extinct; die a violent or untimely death. **2** suffer from cold, hunger, thirst, heat, etc. **3** rot, lose or cause (rubber or other fabric) to lose its normal qualities. • n. Aust. a period of extreme privation, esp. as caused by lack of water (suffered badly during the perish). ☐ **do a perish** Aust. **1** suffer a period of extreme privation; be without sustenance (esp. water). **2** die (of thirst). **3** suffer hardship or privation of any kind, not always of an extreme nature (doing a perish for a tinny).

perishable adj. liable to decay or go bad in a short time. • n.pl. (**perishables**) perishable foods.

perisher n. colloq. **1** a freezing cold day. **2** an annoying child.

Peris-Kneebone, Nova (1971–), OAM, Australian athlete. She won a gold medal as a member of the hockey team at the 1996 Olympics, and a gold medal in the 200 metres at the 1998 Commonwealth Games.

peristalsis / pe-ruh-**stal**-suhs / n. the involuntary muscular wavelike movement by which the contents of the digestive tract are propelled along it. ☐ **peristaltic** adj.

peritoneum / pe-ruh-tuh-**nee**-uhm / n. (pl. **peritoneums** or **peritonea**) the membrane lining the inside of the abdominal cavity. ☐ **peritoneal** adj.

peritonitis / pe-ruh-tuh-**nuy**-tuhs / n. inflammation of the peritoneum.

perjure / **per**-juh / v. ☐ **perjure oneself** give false evidence while on oath. ☐☐ **perjurer** n.

perjured adj. **1** involving perjury (perjured evidence). **2** guilty of perjury.

perjury / **per**-juh-ree / n. the deliberate giving of false evidence while on oath.

perk n. colloq. a perquisite. ☐ **perk up 1** regain or cause to regain courage, confidence, or vitality. **2** smarten up. **3** raise (the head etc.) briskly or jauntily.

Perkins[1], Charles (Nelson) (1936–2000), AO, Australian Aboriginal activist. In 1984 he became secretary of the Department of Aboriginal Affairs, the first Aborigine to head a Commonwealth department.

Perkins[2], Kieren (John) (1973–), OAM, Australian swimmer. He won gold medals in the 1500 metres freestyle at the 1992 and 1996 Olympics, and a silver medal in the same event at the 2000 Olympics.

perky adj. (**perkier**, **perkiest**) lively and cheerful. ☐ **perkily** adv. **perkiness** n.

perm n. a permanent wave. • v. give a perm to.

permaculture / **per**-muh-kul-chuh / n. the development of agricultural ecosystems intended to be complete and self-sustaining.

permafrost n. the permanently frozen subsoil in polar regions.

permanent adj. lasting or meant to last indefinitely. ☐ **permanent head** the senior executive officer of a public service department; the secretary of such a department. **permanent wave** a long-lasting artificial wave in the hair. ☐☐ **permanently** adv. **permanence** n. **permanency** n.

permanganate / per-**mang**-guh-nayt / n. a salt of an acid containing manganese.

permeable / **per**-mee-uh-buhl / adj. able to be permeated by fluids etc. ☐ **permeability** n.

permeate / **per**-mee-ayt / v. pass, flow, or spread into every part of. ☐ **permeation** n.

Permian / **per**-mee-uhn / adj. Geol. of the final period of the Palaeozoic era. • n. this period.

permissible adj. such as may be permitted; allowable. ☐ **permissibly** adv. **permissibility** n.

permission n. consent or authorisation to do something.

permissive adj. **1** giving permission. **2** tolerant, allowing much freedom in social conduct and sexual matters (the permissive society). ☐ **permissiveness** n.

permit v. / puh-**mit** / (**permitted**, **permitting**) **1** give permission or consent to; authorise. **2** give opportunity, make possible (weather permitting). • n. / **per**-muht / a written order giving permission, esp. for entry.

permutation / per-myuh-**tay**-shuhn / n. **1** variation of the order of a set of things. **2** any one of these arrangements. **3** a selection of specified items from a larger group, to be arranged in a number of combinations.

pernicious / puh-**nish**-uhs / adj. very harmful or destructive. ☐ **pernicious anaemia** defective formation of red blood cells through lack of vitamin B.

pernickety adj. colloq. fastidious, scrupulous; too fussy.

peroration / pe-ruh-**ray**-shuhn / n. **1** the rhetorical ending of a speech. **2** a lengthy speech.

peroxide n. a compound containing the maximum proportion of oxygen, esp. hydrogen peroxide which is used as an antiseptic or to bleach hair. • v. bleach (the hair) with hydrogen peroxide.

perpendicular adj. **1** at a right angle (90°) to another line or surface. **2** upright, at right angles to the horizontal. **3** (of a cliff etc.) having a vertical face. **4** (**Perpendicular**) of the style of English Gothic architecture in the 14th–15th centuries,

perpetrate with vertical tracery in large windows. • *n.* a perpendicular line or direction. ◻ **perpendicularly** *adv.* **perpendicularity** *n.*

perpetrate / per-puh-trayt / *v.* commit (a crime or error); be guilty of (a blunder etc.). ◻ **perpetration** *n.* **perpetrator** *n.*

perpetual *adj.* **1** lasting for a long time, not ceasing. **2** *colloq.* frequent, often repeated (*this perpetual quarrelling*). ◻ **perpetual motion** the motion of a hypothetical machine which would continue for ever unless subject to an external force or to wear. ◻◻ **perpetually** *adv.*

perpetuate *v.* preserve from being forgotten or from going out of use (*his invention will perpetuate his memory*). ◻ **perpetuation** *n.*

perpetuity / per-puh-**choo**-uh-tee, -**tyoo**- / *n.* the state or quality of being perpetual. ◻ **in perpetuity** for ever.

perplex *v.* **1** bewilder, puzzle. **2** make more complicated.

perplexedly / puh-**pleks**-uhd-lee / *adv.* in a perplexed way.

perplexity *n.* bewilderment; a thing that perplexes.

perquisite / per-kwuh-zuht / *n.* a profit, allowance, or privilege given in addition to wages or salary.

■ **Usage** *Perquisite* is sometimes confused with *prerequisite*, which means 'a thing required as a precondition'.

Perry, Joseph Henry (1862–1943), Australian pioneer film-maker whose film *Soldiers of the Cross* (1900) is claimed to be the first full-length film in the world.

perry *n.* an alcoholic drink made from the fermented juice of pears.

per se *adv.* by or in itself; intrinsically. (¶ Latin)

persecute *v.* **1** subject to constant hostility or cruel treatment, esp. because of religious or political beliefs. **2** harass. ◻ **persecution** *n.* **persecutor** *n.*

Persephone / per-**sef**-uh-nee / *Gk myth.* the daughter of the cereal-goddess Demeter, carried off by Pluto and made queen of the Underworld, but allowed to return to earth for part of each year.

Perseus / **per**-see-uhs / *Gk myth.* the son of Zeus and Danae, who cut off the head of Medusa and rescued Andromeda.

persevere *v.* continue steadfastly, esp. in something that is difficult or tedious. ◻ **perseverance** *n.*

Persia the ancient and now the alternative name of Iran.

Persian *adj.* of Persia or its people or language. • *n.* **1** a native or inhabitant of Persia. **2** the language of Persia (preferred terms for the language are *Iranian* and *Farsi*). **3** (in full **Persian cat**) a cat of a breed that has long silky fur.

Persian Gulf an arm of the Arabian Sea, between the Arabian peninsula and mainland Asia.

persiflage / per-suh-flah*zh* / *n.* banter.

persimmon / per-**sim**-uhn / *n.* **1** the edible sweet tomato-like fruit of an American or East Asian tree. **2** this tree.

persist *v.* **1** (often foll. by *in*) continue firmly or obstinately. **2** continue to exist (*the custom persists in some areas*). ◻ **persistent** *adj.* **persistently** *adv.* **persistence** *n.*

person *n.* **1** an individual human being. **2** the living body of a human being (*offences against the person*). **3** (in Christianity) God as the Father (*First Person*), the Son (*Second Person*), or the Holy Spirit (*Third Person*). **4** *Grammar* any of the three classes of personal pronouns and verb forms, referring to the person speaking (*first person*, = I, me, we, us), or spoken to (*second person*, = thou, thee, you), or spoken of (*third person*, = he, him, she, her, it, they, them). **5** (in *combinations*) used to replace *-man* or *-woman* in occupations etc. open to either sex (*salesperson*). ◻ **in person** physically present. **person with Aids** *see* PWA.

persona / per-**soh**-nuh / *n.* (*pl.* **personae**) **1** the personality that a person presents to other people. **2** an author's assumed character in his or her writing.

personable / **per**-suh-nuh-buhl / *adj.* attractive in appearance and personality.

personage / **per**-suhn-ij / *n.* a person, esp. one of importance or distinction.

persona grata / per-soh-nuh **grah**-tuh / *n.* (*pl.* **personae gratae**) a person who is acceptable, esp. a diplomat acceptable to a foreign government. ◻ **persona non grata** one who is not acceptable. (¶ Latin)

personal *adj.* **1** one's own (*will give it my personal attention*). **2** designed for use by one person only (*a personal stereo*). **3** of one's private life (*a personal matter*). **4** making critical remarks about a person's appearance or private affairs (*let's not become personal*). **5** done or made etc. in person (*several personal appearances*). **6** of the body and clothing (*personal hygiene*). **7** existing as a person (*a personal God*). ◻ **personal best** esp. *Sport* one's best performance, esp. one's fastest time over a measured distance. **personal computer** a computer designed for use by a single individual (*abbr.* **PC**). **personal identification number** *see* PIN. **personal pronoun** *see* PRONOUN.

personalise *v.* (also **-ize**) **1** make personal, esp. by marking as one's own property. **2** personify.

personality *n.* **1** a person's own distinctive character. **2** a person with distinctive qualities, esp. pleasing ones. **3** a celebrity. **4** (**personalities**) personal remarks of a critical or hostile kind.

personally *adv.* **1** in person, not through an agent (*showed us round personally*). **2** as a person, in a personal capacity (*we don't know him personally*). **3** in a personal manner (*don't take it personally*). **4** as regards oneself (*personally, I like it*).

personate *v.* impersonate. ☐ **personation** *n.*

personify / per-**son**-uh-fuy / *v.* (**personified**, **personifying**) **1** represent (an idea) in human form or (a thing) as having human characteristics (*Justice is personified as a blindfolded woman holding a pair of scales*). **2** embody in one's life or behaviour (*he was meanness personified*). ☐ **personification** *n.*

personnel / per-suh-**nel** / *n.* **1** the body of people employed in any work; staff. **2** the department (in a business firm etc.) dealing with employees and their problems and welfare.

Persoonia / puh-**soh**-nee-uh / *n.* a genus of plants (related to banksias) endemic to Australia (*see* GEEBUNG).

perspective *n.* **1** the art of drawing solid objects on a flat surface so as to give the impression of depth, solidity, etc. **2** the apparent relationship between visible objects as to position, distance, etc. **3** a view of a visible scene or of facts and events. **4** a mental picture of the relative importance of things (*you need to have the right perspective*). ☐ **in** (*or* **out of**) **perspective 1** drawn or viewed according to (or not according to) the rules of perspective. **2** with its relative importance understood (or not understood) (*keep things in perspective*).

perspex *n. trademark* a tough transparent plastic material.

perspicacious / per-spuh-**kay**-shuhs / *adj.* showing great insight. ☐ **perspicaciously** *adv.* **perspicacity** / per-spuh-**kas**-uh-tee / *n.*

■ **Usage** *Perspicacious* is sometimes confused with *perspicuous*.

perspicuous / puh-**spik**-yoo-uhs / *adj.* expressed or expressing things clearly. ☐ **perspicuity** / per-spuh-**kyoo**-uh-tee / *n.*

■ **Usage** *Perspicuous* is sometimes confused with *perspicacious*.

perspiration *n.* **1** sweat. **2** sweating.

perspire *v.* sweat.

persuade *v.* cause (a person) to believe or do something by reasoning; convince or induce. ☐ **persuadable** *adj.* **persuasible** *adj.*

persuader *n.* **1** a person who persuades. **2** *Aust. jocular* a bullock driver's or jockey's whip.

persuasion *n.* **1** persuading, being persuaded. **2** persuasiveness. **3** religious belief, or the group or sect holding it (*people of the same persuasion*). **4** *colloq. jocular* any group or party (*the male persuasion*).

persuasive *adj.* good at persuading people. ☐ **persuasively** *adv.* **persuasiveness** *n.*

pert *adj.* **1** cheeky, saucy. **2** lively, jaunty. ☐ **pertly** *adv.* **pertness** *n.*

pertain / puh-**tayn** / *v.* (usu. foll. by *to*) **1** be relevant (*evidence pertaining to the case*). **2** belong as part (*the house and lands pertaining to it*).

Perth the capital city of the State of Western Australia. (¶ Named in honour of George Murray, Britain's secretary of state for war and the colonies, who was born in *Perthshire*, Scotland.)

pertinacious / per-tuh-**nay**-shuhs / *adj.* holding firmly to an opinion or course of action, persistent and determined. ☐ **pertinaciously** *adv.* **pertinacity** / per-tuh-**nas**-uh-tee / *n.*

pertinent *adj.* pertaining, relevant. ☐ **pertinently** *adv.* **pertinence** *n.* **pertinency** *n.*

perturb *v.* **1** disturb greatly, make anxious or uneasy. **2** throw into confusion. ☐ **perturbation** *n.*

Peru a republic in South America on the Pacific coast. ☐ **Peruvian** / puh-**roo**-vee-uhn / *adj.* & *n.*

peruse / puh-**rooz** / *v.* **1** read or study carefully. **2** browse, read casually. ☐ **perusal** / puh-**roo**-zuhl / *n.*

perv (also **perve**) *colloq. n.* **1** a sexual pervert. **2** *Aust.* **a** a person who watches or observes another (or others) with erotic or sexual interest. **b** the act of so watching or observing. •*v. Aust.* (frequently with *on*) **1** observe (an other or others) with erotic or sexual interest. **2** observe anything with interest, fascination, etc. (*tourists perving on our fairy penguins*).

pervade *v.* spread or be present throughout, permeate (*a pervading atmosphere of optimism*). ☐ **pervasion** *n.*

pervasive / puh-**vay**-siv / *adj.* pervading; able to pervade. ☐ **pervasiveness** *n.*

perve alternative spelling of PERV.

perverse / puh-**vers** / *adj.* **1** obstinately doing something different from what is reasonable or required; intractable. **2** indicating or characterised by a tendency of this kind (*a perverse satisfaction*). **3** perverted; wicked. ☐ **perversely** *adv.* **perverseness** *n.* **perversity** *n.*

perversion *n.* **1** perverting; being perverted. **2** a perverted form of something. **3 a** a preference for a form of sexual activity that is not the norm. **b** such an activity.

pervert *v.* / puh-**vert** / **1** turn (a thing) from its proper course or use (*pervert the course of justice*). **2** lead astray (a person, a person's mind, etc.) from what is deemed to be right opinion or conduct or (esp. religious) beliefs; corrupt. **3** misapply or misconstrue (words etc.). **4** (as **perverted** *adj.*) showing perversion. •*n.* / **per**-vert / a perverted person; one showing what is deemed to be a perversion of sexual instincts.

pervious / **per**-vee-uhs / *adj.* **1** permeable, allowing something to pass through. **2** accessible, receptive (*pervious to new ideas*).

peseta / puh-**say**-tuh / *n.* the unit of money in Spain.

pesky / pes-kee / adj. (**peskier, peskiest**) colloq. troublesome, annoying.

peso / pay-soh / n. (pl. **pesos**) the unit of money in several Latin-American countries, and in the Philippines.

pessary / pes-uh-ree / n. 1 a device placed in the vagina to prevent displacement of the womb or as a contraceptive. 2 a vaginal suppository.

pessimism n. 1 a tendency to take a gloomy view of things or to expect the worst. 2 Philosophy the belief that this world is as bad as it could be or that all things tend to evil (as opposed to OPTIMISM). ☐ **pessimist** n.

pessimistic adj. showing pessimism. ☐ **pessimistically** adv.

pest n. 1 a troublesome or annoying person or thing. 2 an insect or animal that is destructive to plants, stored food, etc.

pester v. make persistent requests; annoy with frequent requests or questions.

pesticide n. a substance for destroying harmful insects.

pestiferous / pes-**tif**-uh-ruhs / adj. 1 noxious; pestilent. 2 harmful; pernicious; bearing moral contagion.

pestilence n. archaic a deadly epidemic disease, esp. bubonic plague.

pestilent adj. 1 deadly. 2 harmful or morally destructive. 3 annoying, troublesome. ☐ **pestilential** / pes-tuh-**len**-shuhl / adj.

pestle n. a club-shaped instrument for pounding substances in a mortar.

pesto / pes-toh / n. an Italian sauce of crushed basil leaves, pine nuts, garlic, parmesan cheese, and olive oil, usu. served with pasta.

pet[1] n. 1 a tame animal kept for companionship or amusement. 2 a darling or favourite. •adj. 1 kept or treated as a pet (pet lamb). 2 of or for pet animals (pet food). 3 (often jocular) favourite (that's my pet hate). 4 expressing fondness or familiarity (a pet name). •v. (**petted, petting**) 1 treat with affection, stroke, pat. 2 fondle erotically.

pet[2] n. a fit of ill temper (he's in a pet).

petal n. any of the coloured outer parts of a flower head. ☐ **petalled** adj. **petal-like** adj.

petard / puh-**tahd** / n. archaic a small bombshell. ☐ **hoist with one's own petard** injured by one's own schemes against others.

Peter, St (d. c.AD 67), prominent among the Apostles of Christ, founder and first bishop of the Church in Rome where he was martyred and where his tomb is reputed to be (in St Peter's basilica); in Catholic belief he was the first of the popes. ☐ **Peter's pence 1** hist. an annual tax of one penny, formerly paid to the Papal See. **2** (since 1860) an annual voluntary contribution by Catholics all over the world to the pope.

peter[1] v. ☐ **peter out** (originally of a vein of ore etc.) diminish gradually and cease to exist.

peter[2] n. colloq. a prison cell; a prison.

peter[3] n. colloq. a cash register; a till. ☐ **tickle the peter** Aust. steal, embezzle (esp. by ringing up false amounts).

Peter Pan 1 the hero of J.M. Barrie's play of the same name (1904), a boy who never grew up. **2** a man who retains boyish features or who behaves boyishly or is immature.

pethidine / peth-uh-deen / n. a soluble synthetic drug, chemically similar to morphine, used for relieving pain.

petiole / pet-ee-ohl / n. a slender stalk joining a leaf to a stem.

petis n. = TRASI. (¶ Indonesian)

petit / pet-ee / adj. ☐ **petit bourgeois** / boor-zhwah, boo- / a member of the lower middle classes. **petit mal** a mild form of epilepsy with only momentary loss of consciousness (cf. GRAND MAL). **petit point** / pet-ee point / embroidery on canvas using small stitches. (¶ French, = small.)

petite / puh-**teet** / adj. (of a woman) of small dainty build.

petition n. 1 an earnest request. 2 a formal document appealing to an authority for a right or benefit etc., esp. one signed by a large number of people. 3 a formal application made to a court of law for a writ, order, etc. •v. make or address a petition to. ☐ **petitioner** n.

Petrarch / pet-rahk / (Italian name: Francesco Petrarca) (1304–74), Italian lyric poet and scholar.

petrel n. a seabird that flies far from land.

Petri dish / pee-tree / n. a shallow covered dish used in laboratories for growing bacteria.

petrify v. (**petrified, petrifying**) 1 change or cause to change into a stony mass. 2 paralyse or stun with astonishment, fear, etc. ☐ **petrification** n. **petrifaction** n.

petrochemical n. a chemical substance obtained from petroleum or natural gas.

petrodollar n. a notional unit of currency earned by a country that exports petroleum.

petrol n. an inflammable liquid made from petroleum, used as fuel in internal-combustion engines. •adj. concerned with the supply of petrol (petrol pump).

petroleum / puh-**troh**-lee-uhm / n. a mineral oil found underground, refined for use as fuel (e.g. petrol, paraffin) or for use in dry-cleaning etc. ☐ **petroleum jelly** a greasy translucent substance obtained from petroleum, used as a lubricant.

petrolhead n. Aust. colloq. a person who is a motor car (or motor car racing) fanatic.

Petrophile / puh-**trof**-uh-lee / n. a genus of plants endemic to WA (see CONESTICKS).

Petrov Affair a case concerning Vladimir and Evdokia Petrov, husband and wife, who confessed to spying for the USSR while employed at the USSR embassy in Canberra and were granted political asylum in 1954. The event led to a lengthy royal commission into Communist Party activity in Australia, and contributed to the split in the Australian Labor Party in 1955.

petticoat *n.* a woman's or girl's dress-length undergarment hanging from the shoulders or waist. • *adj.* (often *derog.*) feminine; associated with women.

pettifog *v.* (**pettifogged**, **pettifogging**) **1** practise legal trickery. **2** quibble or wrangle about trivial points. □ **pettifogger** *n.* **pettifoggery** *n.*

pettifogging *adj.* trivial, paying too much attention to unimportant details.

pettish *adj.* peevish, irritably impatient. □ **pettishness** *n.*

Petty, Bruce (Leslie) (1929–), AM, Australian cartoonist and film director.

petty *adj.* (**pettier**, **pettiest**) **1** unimportant, trivial (*petty details*). **2** minor, on a small scale. **3** small-minded (*petty spite*). □ **petty cash** a small amount of money kept by an office etc. for minor payments. **petty officer** an NCO in the navy. □□ **pettily** *adv.* **pettiness** *n.*

petulant / **petch**-uh-luhnt, **pet**-yoo- / *adj.* peevish. □ **petulantly** *adv.* **petulance** *n.*

petunia *n.* a garden plant (native to tropical America) with large funnel-shaped flowers in many colours.

pew *n.* **1** a long bench-like seat with a back and sides, usu. in a church. **2** *colloq.* a seat (*take a pew*).

pewter *n.* **1** a grey alloy of tin with lead or other metal, used for making mugs and dishes etc. **2** articles made of this.

peyote / pay-**oh**-tee / *n.* **1** a Mexican cactus. **2** a hallucinogenic drug made from this.

pfennig *n.* a German coin worth one hundredth of a mark.

PGR *abbr.* parental guidance recommended; a film classification indicating that parents should decide whether the film is suitable for their children.

pH / pee-**aych** / *n.* a measure of the acidity or alkalinity of a solution.

■ **Usage** An alkaline solution or soil has a pH of greater than 7, while an acid solution has a pH of less than 7. Most plants prefer a soil close to neutral, pH 7, while Australian natives generally prefer a pH of 5.5 to 7.

phaeton / **fay**-tuhn / *n.* an old type of open horse-drawn carriage with four wheels.

phagocyte / **fag**-uh-suyt / *n.* a leucocyte or other cell that can absorb foreign matter (e.g. bacteria) in the body.

phaius / **fuy**-uhs / *n.* any of three Australian orchids, esp. *Phaius tancarvilliae*, having the largest flowers of any Australian orchid in brown, white, and purple.

phalanger / fuh-**lan**-juh / *n.* any of various Australian tree-dwelling marsupials, including cuscuses and possums, having thick woolly fur, webbed hind feet, and, frequently, prehensile tails.

phalanx *n.* (*pl.* **phalanxes** *or* **phalanges**) **1** a number of people forming a compact mass or banded together for a common purpose. **2** an ancient Greek line of battle with infantry in close ranks.

phalaris / fuh-**lah**-ruhs / *n.* fodder of the grass genus *Phalaris*.

phallic / **fal**-ik / *adj.* **1** of, relating to, or resembling a phallus. **2** denoting the stage of male sexual development characterised by pre-occupation with the penis.

phallocentric / fal-oh-**sen**-trik / *adj.* centred on the phallus, esp. as a symbol of male superiority or dominance.

phallocrat / **fal**-oh-krat / *n.* a person who advocates, or assumes the existence of, a male-dominated society; a man who argues that because he is male he is superior to women. □ **phallocracy** *n.*

phallus / **fal**-uhs / *n.* (*pl.* **phalluses** *or* **phalli**) **1** a penis, esp. when erect. **2** an image of an erect penis as a symbol of natural generative power. □ **phallicism** *n.*

phantasm / **fan**-taz-uhm / *n.* a phantom, an illusion. □ **phantasmal** *adj.*

phantasmagoria / fan-taz-muh-**gaw**-ree-uh / *n.* a shifting scene of real or imagined figures. □ **phantasmagoric** *adj.*

phantom *n.* **1** a ghost, an apparition. **2** something without reality, as seen in a dream or vision. □ **phantom limb** the continuing sensation of the presence of a limb which has been amputated. **phantom pregnancy** symptoms of pregnancy in a person not actually pregnant.

Pharaoh / **fair**-roh / *n.* the title of a king of ancient Egypt.

Pharisee *n.* **1** a member of an ancient Jewish sect, distinguished by strict observance of the traditional and written law. **2** (**pharisee**) a self-righteous person; a hypocrite. □ **pharisaic** / fa-ruh-**say**-ik / *adj.* **pharisaical** *adj.* **pharisaism** / **fa**-ruh-say-iz-uhm / *n.*

Phar Lap an Australian racehorse (foaled in New Zealand) which won the 1930 Melbourne Cup.

pharmaceutical / fah-muh-**syoo**-ti-kuhl / *adj.* **1** of or engaged in pharmacy. **2** of the use or sale of medicinal drugs.

pharmaceutics / fah-muh-**syoo**-tiks / = PHARMACY (sense 1).

pharmacist / **fah**-muh-suhst / *n.* a person qualified to prepare and dispense medicinal drugs, a chemist.

pharmacology / fah-muh-**kol**-uh-jee / *n.* the study of medicinal drugs and their effects on the body. □ **pharmacological** *adj.* **pharmacologist** *n.*

pharmacopoeia / fah-muh-kuh-**pee**-uh / *n.* **1** a book containing a list of medicinal drugs with directions for their use. **2** a stock of medicinal drugs.

pharmacy / **fah**-muh-see / *n.* **1** the preparation and dispensing of medicinal drugs. **2** a chemist's shop.

Pharos / fair-ros / a large lighthouse, one of the Seven Wonders of the World, erected *c.*280 BC on the island of Pharos off the coast of Egypt and destroyed in 1375.

pharyngitis / fa-ruhn-**juy**-tuhs / *n.* inflammation of the pharynx.

pharynx / **fa**-ringks / *n.* the cavity at the back of the nose and throat. ❑ **pharyngeal** / fa-rin-**jee**-uhl / *adj.*

phascogale / **fas**-kuh-gayl, fas-kuh-**gah**-lee / *n.* either of two species of largely tree-dwelling Australian carnivorous marsupials: the tuan or the wambenger.

phase *n.* **1** a stage in a process of change or development. **2** any of the forms in which the moon or a planet appears, as part or all of its disc is seen illuminated (new moon, first quarter, full moon, last quarter). **3** *Physics* a stage in a recurring sequence, esp. the wave form of alternating electric currents or light. **4** a difficult or unhappy period, esp. in adolescence. •*v.* carry out (a program etc.) in stages. ❑ **in phase** having the same phase at the same time; happening together. **out of phase** not in phase. **phase in** (*or* **out**) bring gradually into (or out of) use.

phatic *adj.* (of speech, an utterance, etc.) used to convey general sociability rather than to communicate a specific meaning, e.g. 'lovely day!', 'how are you?'.

PhD *abbr.* Doctor of Philosophy; a higher degree awarded for a piece of original research usu. taking three or more years to complete.

pheasant / **fez**-uhnt / *n.* **1** a long-tailed game bird, originally from Asia. **2** its flesh as food. ❑ **pheasant coucal** / **koo**-kuhl / (also **coucal**, **swamp pheasant**) a very large, long-tailed, nest-building cuckoo of northern and eastern Australia.

phenobarbitone / fee-noh-**bah**-buh-tohn / *n.* a narcotic and sedative barbiturate drug used esp. to treat epilepsy.

phenol / **fee**-nol / *n.* a hydroxyl derivative of benzene, used as an antiseptic and disinfectant.

phenomenal / fuh-**nom**-uh-nuhl / *adj.* **1** extraordinary, remarkable. **2** of the nature of a phenomenon. ❑ **phenomenally** *adv.*

phenomenalism *n. Philosophy* **1** the doctrine that human knowledge is confined to the appearances presented to the senses. **2** the doctrine that appearances are the foundation of all knowledge.

phenomenon / fuh-**nom**-uh-nuhn / *n.* (*pl.* **phenomena**) **1** a fact, occurrence, or change perceived by any of the senses or by the mind (*snow is a common phenomenon in winter*). **2** a remarkable person or thing, a wonder.

■ **Usage** Note that *phenomena* is a plural but is often used mistakenly for the singular. This should be avoided.

pheromone / **fe**-ruh-mohn / *n.* a substance, secreted by an animal, that is detected by others of the same species and produces a (sexual etc.) response in them.

phew / fyoo / *interj.* an exclamation of relief, surprise, discomfort, etc.

phi / fuy / *n.* the twenty-first letter of the Greek alphabet (Φ, φ).

phial / **fuy**-uhl / *n.* a small glass bottle, esp. for perfume or liquid medicine.

philadelphus *n.* any highly-scented deciduous flowering shrub of the genus *Philadelphus*, esp. the mock orange.

philander / fuh-**lan**-duh / *v.* (of a man) flirt or have casual love affairs. ❑ **philanderer** *n.*

philanthropic / fil-uhn-**throp**-ik / *adj.* **1** benevolent. **2** concerned with human welfare and the reduction of suffering. ❑ **philanthropically** *adv.*

philanthropist / fuh-**lan**-thruh-puhst / *n.* a philanthropic person.

philanthropy / fuh-**lan**-thruh-pee / *n.* love of mankind, benevolence; philanthropic acts and principles.

philately / fuh-**lat**-uh-lee / *n.* stamp-collecting. ❑ **philatelist** *n.*

-phile / fuyl / *comb. form* forming nouns and adjectives denoting fondness for what is specified (*bibliophile*; *Francophile*).

philharmonic / fil-ah-**mon**-ik / *adj.* (in names of symphony orchestras and music societies) devoted to music.

Philip[1], Prince, Duke of Edinburgh (1921–), husband of Elizabeth II of England.

Philip[2], St, an apostle.

Philip II (?382–336 BC), King of Macedonia, father of Alexander the Great.

philippic / fuh-**lip**-ik / *n.* a bitter verbal attack. (¶ Originally applied to the speeches made by the Greek orator Demosthenes attacking Philip II of Macedonia.)

Philippine *adj.* of or relating to the Philippine Islands or their people; Filipino.

Philippines, the a republic in SE Asia consisting of a chain of islands, the chief of which are Luzon and Mindanao.

philistine / **fil**-uh-stuyn / *n.* **1** (**Philistine**) a member of a people in ancient Palestine who were enemies of the Israelites. **2** an uncultured person, one whose interests are material and commonplace and ocker. •*adj.* hostile or indifferent to culture, ocker. ❑ **philistinism** *n.*

Phillip, Arthur (1738–1814), commander of the First Fleet and first Governor of NSW.

Phillip Island an island of some 100 sq. km, lying across the entrance to Westernport, Vic., and developed primarily as a tourist resort.

Phillips screw *n. trademark* a screw with a cross-shaped slot in the head, turned with a Phillips screwdriver. ❑ **Phillips screwdriver** a screwdriver with a cross-shaped point.

philo- *comb. form* (also **phil-** before a vowel or *h*) denoting a liking for what is specified (*philosophy*). (¶ Greek *philos* 'loving, fond of'.)

philodendron / fil-uh-**den**-druhn / *n.* (*pl.* **philodendrons** *or* **philodendra**) a tropical evergreen climber cultivated as a house plant.

philology / fuh-**lol**-uh-jee / *n.* the study of languages and their development. ☐ **philological** *adj.* **philologist** *n.*

philosopher *n.* **1** an expert in philosophy. **2** one who expounds a particular philosophical system. **3** one who speaks or behaves philosophically. ☐ **philosophers' stone** (also **philosopher's stone**) the supreme object of alchemy, a substance able to change other metals into gold or silver.

philosophical *adj.* (also **philosophic**) **1** of philosophy. **2** calmly reasonable, bearing unavoidable misfortune unemotionally. ☐ **philosophically** *adv.*

philosophise *v.* (also **-ize**) reason like a philosopher; moralise.

philosophy *n.* **1** the search, by logical reasoning, for understanding of the basic truths and principles of the universe, life, and morals, and of human perception and behaviour and an understanding of these. **2** a particular system or set of beliefs reached by such a search; a system of principles for the conduct of life. **3** advanced learning in general (*a Doctor of Philosophy*). **4** calm endurance of misfortune.

philtre / **fil**-tuh / *n.* a magic potion; a love potion supposed to excite sexual love in the drinker.

phimosis / fuy-**moh**-suhs / *n.* constriction of the foreskin of the penis, making it difficult to draw back.

phlebitis / fluh-**buy**-tuhs / *n.* inflammation of the walls of a vein.

phlegm / flem / *n.* **1** thick mucus in the throat and bronchial passages, ejected by coughing. **2** *archaic* one of the four bodily humours.

phlegmatic / fleg-**mat**-ik / *adj.* **1** not easily excited or agitated. **2** sluggish, apathetic. ☐ **phlegmatically** *adv.*

phloem / **floh**-em / *n.* tissue conducting sap in plants.

phlox / floks / *n.* (*pl.* **phlox** *or* **phloxes**) a plant with reddish, purple, or white flowers.

Phnom Penh / nom **pen** / the capital of Cambodia.

-phobe *comb. form* forming nouns denoting a person with a specified abnormal or morbid fear or hatred (*xenophobe; homophobe*).

phobia / **foh**-bee-uh / *n.* a lasting abnormal or morbid fear or hatred of something. ☐ **phobic** *adj.* & *n.*

-phobia *comb. form* forming nouns denoting a specified abnormal or morbid fear or hatred (*agoraphobia; homophobia*).

-phobic *comb. form* forming adjectives indicating a specified phobia (*homophobic*).

Phoenician / fuh-**nee**-shuhn / *n.* a member of an ancient Semitic people of the eastern Mediterranean. • *adj.* of the Phoenicians.

phoenix / **fee**-niks / *n.* a mythical bird of the Arabian desert, said to live for hundreds of years and then burn itself on a funeral pyre, rising from its ashes to live for another cycle.

phone *colloq. n.* a telephone. • *v.* telephone. ☐ **phone-in** a broadcast program during which the listeners or viewers telephone the studio etc. and participate. **phone sex** a commercial sexual service, via a telephone, whereby a caller listens to or participates in talk of an explicitly sexual nature, for the purpose of sexual arousal.

phonecard *n.* a card containing prepaid units for use in a card phone.

phoneme / **foh**-neem / *n.* a unit of significant sound in a language (e.g. the sound of *c* in *cat*, which differs from the *b* in *bat* and distinguishes the two words). ☐ **phonemic** / foh-**nee**-mik / *adj.*

phonetic / fuh-**net**-ik / *adj.* **1** representing each speech sound by a particular symbol which is always used for that sound (*the phonetic alphabet*). **2** (of spelling) corresponding to pronunciation. **3** of phonetics. • *n.* (**phonetics**) (usu. treated as *sing.*) speech sounds; the study of these. ☐ **phonetically** *adv.*

phonetician / foh-nuh-**tish**-uhn / *n.* an expert in phonetics.

phoney *adj.* (also **phony**) (**phonier, phoniest**) *colloq.* sham, not genuine; insincere. • *n. colloq.* a phoney person or thing. ☐ **phoniness** *n.*

phonic / **fo**-nik, **foh**- / *adj.* of sound; of vocal sounds. • *n.* (**phonics**) a method of teaching reading based on sounds.

phonology / fuh-**nol**-uh-jee / *n.* the study of the sounds in a language. ☐ **phonological** *adj.*

phony alternative spelling of PHONEY.

phosphate / **fos**-fayt / *n.* a salt or ester of phosphoric acid; an artificial fertiliser composed of or containing this.

phosphor / **fos**-fuh / *n.* a synthetic fluorescent or phosphorescent substance.

phosphoresce / fos-fuh-**res** / *v.* be phosphorescent.

phosphorescent / fos-fuh-**res**-uhnt / *adj.* luminous, glowing with a faint light without burning or perceptible heat. ☐ **phosphorescence** *n.*

phosphoric / fos-**fo**-rik / *adj.* of or containing phosphorus.

phosphorus / **fos**-fuh-ruhs / *n.* a chemical element (symbol P) existing in several forms, esp. as a poisonous whitish waxy substance burning slowly at ordinary temperatures and hence luminous in the dark, and a reddish form used in matches, fertilisers, etc. ☐ **phosphorous** *adj.*

photo *n.* (*pl.* **photos**) a photograph. ☐ **photo finish** a very close finish of a race, photographed to decide the winner.

photochemistry *n.* the study of the chemical effects of light.

photocopier *n.* a machine for photocopying documents etc.

photocopy *n.* a copy (of a document etc.) made by photographing the original. •*v.* (**photocopied**, **photocopying**) make a photocopy of.

photoelectric *adj.* of or using the electrical effects of light. ◻ **photoelectric cell** an electronic device which emits an electric current when light falls on it, used e.g. to measure light for photography or to cause a door to open when someone approaches it. ◻ **photoelectricity** *n.*

photofit = IDENTIKIT.

photogenic / foh-toh-**jen**-ik, -**jee**-nik / *adj.* **1** looking attractive in photographs. **2** *Biology* producing or emitting light.

photograph / **foh**-tuh-grahf, -graf / *n.* a picture formed by the chemical action of light or other radiation on a sensitive surface. •*v.* **1** take a photograph of. **2** come out in a certain way when photographed (*it photographs badly*).

photographer / fuh-**tog**-ruh-fuh / *n.* a person who takes photographs.

photographic / foh-tuh-**graf**-ik / *adj.* **1** of or used in or produced by photography. **2** (of the memory) recalling accurately what was seen. ◻ **photographically** *adv.*

photography / fuh-**tog**-ruh-fee / *n.* the taking and processing of photographs.

photogravure / foh-toh-gruh-**vyoor** / *n.* a picture produced from a photographic negative transferred to a metal plate and etched in.

photojournalism *n.* the relating of news by photographs, esp. in magazines.

photolithography / foh-toh-li-**thog**-ruh-fee / *n.* lithography with plates made photographically.

photometer / foh-**tom**-uh-tuh / *n.* an instrument for measuring light. ◻ **photometric** *adj.* **photometry** *n.*

photon / **foh**-ton / *n.* an indivisible unit of electromagnetic radiation.

photosensitive *adj.* reacting to light.

photostat *n. trademark* **1** a photocopier. **2** a photocopy. •*v.* (**photostat**) (**photostatted**, **photostatting**) make a photostat of.

photosynthesis / foh-toh-**sin**-thuh-suhs / *n.* the process by which green plants use sunlight to convert carbon dioxide (taken from the air) and water into complex substances. ◻ **photosynthesise** *v.* **photosynthetic** *adj.*

phototropic / foh-toh-**trop**-ik / *adj.* (of the movement or growth of a plant) responding to the direction from which light falls on it. ◻ **phototropism** *n.*

phrase *n.* **1** a group of words forming a unit, esp. as an idiom or a clever way of saying something. **2** a group of words (usu. without a finite verb) forming a unit within a sentence or clause (see panel). **3** the way something is worded (*we didn't like his choice of phrase*). **4** *Music* a short distinct passage forming a unit in a melody. •*v.* **1** express in words. **2** divide (music) into phrases, esp. in performance. ◻ **phrasal** *adj.*

phraseology / fray-zee-**ol**-uh-jee / *n.* wording, the way something is worded.

phreak / freek / *v.* **1** use an electronic device to obtain (a telephone call) without payment. **2** *Computing* illegally access (communication networks) to obtain free services etc. (¶ Alteration of FREAK, after *phone*.)

phrenetic alternative spelling of FRENETIC.

phrenology / fruh-**nol**-uh-jee / *n.* study of the external shape of a person's skull as a supposed indication of character and abilities. ◻ **phrenological** *adj.*

phut *n.* a sound like air escaping in a short burst. ◻ **go phut** *colloq.* come to nothing, break down.

phwoah / fwaw / *exclam. colloq.* expressing desire or attraction, esp. of a sexual nature.

phylactery / fuh-**lak**-tuh-ree / *n.* a small leather box containing Hebrew texts, worn by Jews at weekday morning prayer.

phyllo alternative spelling of FILO.

phyllode / **fil**-ohd / *n.* a flattened leaf-stalk that resembles (and functions as) a true leaf, as in many Australian wattles.

phylum / **fuy**-luhm / *n.* (*pl.* **phyla**) any of the larger groups into which plants and animals are divided, containing species with the same general form.

physic / **fiz**-ik / *n. archaic* medicine.

Phrase

A phrase is a group of words that has meaning but does not have both a subject and a predicate (unlike a clause or sentence). It can be:

1 a noun phrase, functioning as a noun, e.g.
   'my friend Tom' in *I went to see my friend Tom.*
   'The only ones they have' in *The only ones they have are too small.*
2 an adjective phrase, functioning as an adjective, e.g.
   'very pleased indeed' in *I was very pleased indeed.*
   'better than mine' in *This one is better than mine.*
3 an adverb phrase, functioning as an adverb, e.g.
   'in their car' in *They drove off in their car.*
   'ten days ago' in *I was there ten days ago.*

physical *adj.* **1** of the body (*physical fitness; a physical examination*). **2** of matter or the laws of nature (as opposed to moral, spiritual, or imaginary things) (*the physical world*). **3** of physics. •*n.* (in full **physical examination**) a medical examination. □ **physical chemistry** a branch of chemistry in which physics is used to study substances and their reactions. **physical geography** a branch of geography dealing with the natural features of the earth's surface (e.g. mountains, lakes, rivers). **physical science** science concerned with inanimate natural objects. □□ **physically** *adv.*

physician / fuh-**zish**-uhn / *n.* a doctor, esp. one who practises medicine (as distinct from surgery) or is a specialist in this (as distinct from a general practitioner).

physicist / **fiz**-uh-sist / *n.* an expert in physics.

physics / **fiz**-iks / *n.* **1** the scientific study of the properties and interactions of matter and energy. **2** these properties etc.

physio *n. colloq.* **1** physiotherapy. **2** physiotherapist.

physiognomy / fiz-ee-**on**-uh-mee / *n.* **1** the form of a person's face, body, expression, etc. **2** the external features of a landscape etc.

physiology / fiz-ee-**ol**-uh-jee / *n.* **1** the study of the bodily functions of living organisms and their parts. **2** these functions. □ **physiological** / fiz-ee-uh-**loj**-i-kuhl / *adj.* **physiologist** *n.*

physiotherapy / fiz-ee-oh-**the**-ruh-pee / *n.* treatment of a disease, injury, deformity, or weakness by massaging, exercises, heat, etc. □ **physiotherapist** *n.*

physique / fuh-**zeek** / *n.* a person's physical build and muscular development.

pi / puy / *n.* the sixteenth letter of the Greek alphabet (Π, π), used as a symbol for the ratio of the circumference of a circle to its diameter (approximately 3.14159).

Piaf / pee-**ahf** / , Edith (original name: Edith Giovanna Gassion) (1915–63), French singer and songwriter.

pia mater / puy-uh **may**-tuh, pee-uh **mah**-tuh / *n.* a delicate membrane surrounding the brain and spinal cord.

pianissimo *adv.* (in music) very softly.

pianist *n.* a person who plays the piano.

piano[1] / pee-**an**-oh / *n.* (*pl.* **pianos**) a musical instrument in which metal strings are struck by hammers operated by pressing the keys of a keyboard. □ **piano accordion** an accordion in which the melody is played on a small piano-like keyboard.

piano[2] / **pyah**-noh / *adv.* (in music) softly.

pianoforte / pee-an-oh-**faw**-tay / *n. formal* a piano.

pianola / pee-uh-**noh**-luh / *n. trademark* an automatic piano operated by a perforated paper roll.

piazza / pee-**at**-suh, -**aht**-suh / *n.* a public square in a town. (¶ Italian)

pica / **puy**-kuh / *n.* **1** a size of letters in typewriting (10 per inch). **2** a unit of length for measuring printing-type, about 4.2 mm.

picador / **pik**-uh-daw / *n.* a mounted man with a lance in bullfighting.

picaresque / pik-uh-**resk** / *adj.* (of a style of fiction) dealing with the episodic adventures of a rogue etc. who is the hero.

■ **Usage** *Picaresque* is sometimes used to mean 'transitory' or 'roaming', but this is considered incorrect in standard English.

Picasso, Pablo (1881–1973), Spanish painter, living in France, highly inventive and a founder of cubism.

picayune / pik-uh-**yoon** / *colloq. n.* an insignificant person or thing. •*adj.* mean; petty, contemptible.

piccabeen / **pik**-uh-been / *n.* a tall palm of Qld and NSW with long pinnate leaves, lilac flowers, and red fruits: the green heart of the palm was eaten by Aborigines and the expanded leaf-base used as a water carrier. Also called *bangalow*. (¶ Yagara *bigi* for the palm and the water carrier; the *-been* may have been added from English.)

piccaninny *n.* (often *offens.*) **1** *Aust.* an Aboriginal child. **2** a black child. □ **piccaninny dawn** (also **piccaninny daylight**) *Aust.* the approach of dawn, infant dawn. **piccaninny twilight** *Aust.* the last glow of the setting sun.

piccolo *n.* (*pl.* **piccolos**) a small flute sounding an octave higher than the ordinary one.

pick[1] *v.* **1** use a pointed instrument, the fingers, beak, etc. to make a hole in or remove bits from (a thing). **2** detach (a flower or fruit) from the plant bearing it. **3** select carefully; choose (*pick a winner*). **4** eat (food) in small bites, nibble without appetite. **5** *colloq.* victimise, harass (*three drunken louts picked me outside the pub*). •*n.* **1** the act or an instance of picking. **2** selection (*have first pick*). **3** (usu. foll. by *of*) the best part (*the pick of the bunch*). **4** = GREEN PICK (see GREEN). **5** = PICKING. □ **pick a person's pocket** steal its contents while he or she is wearing the garment. **pick on** single out, esp. as a target for nagging or harassment. **pick up 1** lift or take up. **2** call for and take with one, take aboard (passengers or freight etc.). **3** (of police etc.) catch, find and take into custody. **4** get or acquire by chance or casually. **5** meet casually and become acquainted with, esp. for sexual purposes. **6** detect by scrutiny, or with a telescope, radio, etc. (*picked up most of the mistakes; picked up a distress signal*). **7** (of one's health, the weather, share prices, etc.) recover, improve, etc. **8** accept the responsibility of paying (a bill etc.) (*I'll pick up the tab*). **9** resume, take up anew (*picked up where we left off*).

pick-up *n.* **1** picking up. **2** a person one gets casually acquainted with, esp. for sexual purposes.

pick   623   **piece**

3 (also **pick-up truck**) a small open motor truck. **4** the part carrying the stylus in a record player. ☐☐ **pickable** *adj.*

pick[2] *n.* **1** a pickaxe. **2** a plectrum.

pickaxe *n.* a tool consisting of a curved iron bar with sharpened ends mounted at right angles to its handle, used for breaking hard ground, stones, etc. • *v.* break (the ground etc.) with a pickaxe; work with a pickaxe.

picker *n.* **1** a person or thing that picks (*pickers wanted in the orchard*). **2** = PICKER-UP. ☐ **picker-up** *Aust. Shearing* a shed hand who gathers up the shorn fleeces and places them on a table for skirting, classing, etc.

picket *n.* **1** one or more persons stationed by strikers outside their place of work to dissuade others from entering. **2** (also **picquet, piquet**) an out post of troops; a party of sentries. **3** a pointed stake set into the ground, e.g. as part of a fence. • *v.* (**picketed, picketing**) **1** station or act as a picket during a strike; place guard on (a factory etc.) in this way. **2** post as a military picket. **3** secure or enclose with a stake or stakes. ☐ **picket line** a line of workers on strike at their workplace, which line others are asked not to go past.

picking *n.* (also **pick**) *Aust.* sparse pasture.

pickings *n.pl.* **1** scraps of good food etc. remaining. **2** odd gains or perquisites; profits from pilfering.

pickle *n.* **1** food (esp. a vegetable) preserved in vinegar or brine. **2** vinegar or brine used for this. **3** *colloq.* a plight; a mess. • *v.* preserve in pickle.

pickled *adj. colloq.* drunk.

pickpocket *n.* a thief who picks people's pockets.

picky *adj. colloq.* extremely fastidious.

picnic *n.* **1** an informal meal taken in the open air for pleasure; an excursion for this. **2** *colloq.* something very agreeable or easily done (*the exam was a picnic; it was no picnic organising the meeting*). **3** *Aust. colloq.* an awkward, disorganised, frightening, etc. occasion or experience (*it was some picnic in the trenches; I'm in for a picnic if I get home late*). • *v.* (**picnicked, picnicking**) take part in a picnic. ☐ **picnic races** (also **picnic race meeting**) *Aust.* a day of horse racing, usu. in a rural district, the primary purpose of which is to be an informal social get-together. ☐☐ **picnicker** *n.*

pico- *comb. form* denoting a factor of 10^{-12} (*picometre*).

Pict *n.* a member of an ancient people of northern Britain. ☐ **Pictish** *adj.*

pictograph *n.* (also **pictogram**) **1** a pictorial symbol used as a form of writing. **2** a chart using pictures to represent statistical information. ☐ **pictographic** *adj.*

pictorial *adj.* **1** of or expressed in a picture or pictures. **2** illustrated by pictures. • *n.* a newspaper or magazine in which pictures are the main feature. ☐ **pictorially** *adv.*

picture *n.* **1** a representation of a person or people or object(s) etc. made by painting, drawing, or photography. **2** a portrait. **3** something that looks beautiful (*the garden is a picture*). **4** a scene; the total impression produced on one's sight or mind (*the picture looks bleak*). **5** a written or spoken description (*his novel draws a vivid picture of moral decay*). **6** (esp. *ironical*) a perfect example (*he was the picture of innocence*). **7** a person or thing resembling another closely (*he's the picture of his mother*). **8** (**the pictures**) cinema; a cinema film. **9** the image on a television screen. • *v.* **1** represent in a picture. **2** describe vividly. **3** form a mental picture of (*picture yourself on a deserted beach*). ☐ **in the picture** *colloq.* fully informed. **picture window** a large window of one pane of glass, usu. facing an attractive view.

picturesque / pik-chuh-**resk** / *adj.* **1** forming a striking and pleasant scene (*a picturesque valley*). **2** (of words or a description) very expressive, vivid.

PID *see* PELVIC INFLAMMATORY DISEASE.

piddle *colloq. v.* **1** urinate. **2** (foll. by *about, around*) work or act in a trifling way (*stop piddling around and get the job done*). • *n.* **1** urination. **2** urine.

piddling *adj. colloq.* trivial, trifling.

piddly *adj. colloq.* trivial, trifling.

pidgin / **pij**-uhn / *n.* a simplified language containing vocabulary from two or more languages, used between people not having a common language. ☐ **Australian pidgin** a pidgin used in colonial Australia, in which English was combined with one or more Aboriginal languages. **pidgin English** a pidgin in which the chief language is English, used orig. between Chinese and Europeans. (¶ A Chinese pronunciation of the word *business*.)

pie *n.* a baked dish of meat, fruit, etc. enclosed in or covered with pastry or other crust. ☐ **pie chart** a diagram representing quantities as sectors of a circle. **pie-eater** *Aust. colloq.* **1** a person of little account. **2** an Australian. (¶ From the ubiquitous Australian meat pie.) **pie in the sky** a prospect (considered unrealistic) of future happiness. **pie night** (in full **beer and pie night**) *Aust.* a social occasion in many sports clubs etc.

piebald *adj.* (of a horse etc.) with irregular patches of white and black or other dark colour. • *n.* a piebald animal.

piece *n.* **1** one of the distinct portions of which a thing is composed or into which it is divided or broken. **2** one of a set of things (*a three-piece suite*). **3** something regarded as a unit (*a fine piece of work*). **4** a musical, literary, or artistic composition. **5** a coin (*a ten-cent piece*). **6** one of the set of objects used to make moves in board games; a chessman other than a pawn. **7** an item or instance (*a piece of news; a piece of impudence*). **8** *colloq. offens.* a woman. • *v.* (usu. foll. by *together*) form into a whole; put together; join.

☐ **go to pieces** lose one's strength or ability; collapse emotionally. **of a piece** of the same kind, consistent.

pièce de résistance / pyes duh ray-**zis**-tons / *n.* (*pl.* **pièces de résistance** pronounced the same) **1** the principal dish at a meal. **2** the most important or remarkable item. (¶ French)

piecemeal *adj.* & *adv.* done piece by piece; gradually; unsystematically.

piecework *n.* work paid according to the quantity done, not by the time spent on it.

pied / puyd / *adj.* **1** particoloured. **2** (as applied to birds) black and white. ☐ **pied butcherbird** a black and white bird of mainland Australia with an extremely beautiful song. Also called *organ bird*. **pied currawong** one of the three species of currawong, a black and white bird of eastern Australia with a ringing, bell-like call. Also called *crow-shrike, bell magpie*.

Pied Piper (in German legend) a piper who rid the town of Hamelin of its rats by luring them away with his music and, when refused the promised fee, lured away all the children.

pier / peer / *n.* **1** a structure built out into the sea, a lake, etc., to serve as a breakwater, landing stage, or promenade. **2** each of the pillars supporting an arch or bridge. **3** solid masonry between windows etc.

pierce *v.* **1** go into or through like a sharp-pointed instrument; make a hole in (a thing) in this way (*had his ear pierced*). **2** (of cold, grief, etc.) affect keenly or sharply (*grief pierced his heart*). **3** force one's way into or through (*pierced their way through the jungle*).

piercing *adj.* **1** (of a glance, intuition, light, pain, cold, etc.) penetrating sharply. **2** (of a voice or sound) shrilly audible.

Pierrot / **peer**-roh / a male character from French pantomime with a whitened face and loose white clown's costume.

pietà / pee-uh-**tah**, pee-**ay**-tah / *n.* a representation of the Virgin Mary holding the dead body of Christ on her lap.

pietism / **puy**-uh-tiz-uhm / *n.* pious sentiment; exaggerated or affected piety.

piety / **puy**-uh-tee / *n.* the quality of being pious; a pious act.

piffle *colloq. n.* nonsense, worthless talk. • *v.* talk or act feebly; trifle.

piffling *adj. colloq.* trivial, worthless.

pig *n.* **1** a domestic or wild animal with short legs, cloven hooves, and a broad blunt snout. **2** *colloq.* a greedy, dirty, or unpleasant person; a difficult or unpleasant thing. **3** *colloq. offens.* a police officer. **4** *colloq.* a Rugby Union forward. **5** an oblong mass of metal from a smelting-furnace; pig-iron. **6** (**pigs**) *colloq.* (an abbreviation of *pig's bum, pig's eye*, etc.) a derisive retort (*pigs!; pigs to you, mate!*). ☐ **buy a pig in a poke** buy a thing without seeing it or knowing whether it will be satisfactory. **home on the pig's back** *Aust. colloq.* assured of success. **make a pig of oneself** overeat. **pig dog** *Aust.* a dog bred to hunt the feral pig. **pig fish** any of several marine fish of northern and eastern Australia having an elongated 'snout'. **pig-footed bandicoot** a bandicoot (probably now extinct) of drier southern and central Australia having only two well-developed toes on the fore foot. **pig iron** crude iron from a smelting furnace. **pig out** (**on**) *colloq.* eat gluttonously. **pig-root** *Aust.* (of a horse or other animal) kick upwards with the hind legs while the forelegs are firmly planted and the head is held down. **pig-rooter** *Aust.* an animal that pig-roots. **pig's arse** (or **bum** or **eye**, etc.) *colloq.* a derisive retort; frequently as a strong negative; also an expression of sympathy etc. ('*My house caught fire.*' —'*Pig's arse, mate!*'). **pig's ear** *colloq.* beer. (¶ Rhyming slang.) **ride** (or **fly**) **on the pig's back** *colloq.* be extremely successful or fortunate.

pigeon *n.* **1** a bird of the dove family. **2** any of various Australian birds including bronzewings (flock bronzewing, crested pigeon, etc.) and fruit pigeons (purple-crowned pigeon, wompoo pigeon), with many of the smaller species being called 'doves' (peaceful dove, bar-shouldered dove). **3** a person who is easily duped or swindled. **4** *colloq.* a person's business or responsibility (*that's your pigeon*). (¶ From a Chinese pronunciation of the word *business*.) ☐ **pigeon-hole** *n.* one of a set of small compartments in a desk or on a wall, used for holding papers, letters, etc. *v.* **1** put away for future consideration or indefinitely. **2** classify mentally as belonging to a particular group or kind. **pigeon-toed** *adj.* having the toes turned inwards.

pigface *n. Aust.* any of several succulent, prostrate, perennial plants of coastal and dry inland Australia, having showy daisy-like flowers in various colours; so called because the ripe fruit bears resemblance to a pig's head.

piggery *n.* **1** a pig-breeding establishment. **2** a pigsty.

piggish *adj.* like a pig; dirty or greedy.

piggy *adj.* like a pig; (of features etc.) like those of a pig (*piggy eyes*).

piggyback *n.* a ride on a person's shoulders and back. • *adv.* carried in this way. • *adj.* (of an article etc.) attached to another article. • *v.* attach an article to another (*it's unsafe to piggyback plugs*).

pigheaded *adj.* stubborn, obstinate.

Pig Island *Aust. colloq. n.* (also **Pig Islands**) New Zealand. • *adj.* (**Pig-Island**) of or pertaining to New Zealand. ☐ **Pig Islander** *n.* (¶ Allusion to the wild pigs introduced by Captain James Cook.)

piglet *n.* a young pig.

pigment *n.* colouring matter. • *v.* colour (skin or other tissue) with natural pigment.

pigmentation *n.* **1** the natural colouring of plants, animals, etc. **2** the excessive colouring of tissue by the deposition of pigment.

pigmy alternative spelling of PYGMY.

pigskin *n.* leather made from the skin of a pig.

pigsty n. **1** a partly-covered pen for pigs. **2** a very dirty or untidy place.

pigswill n. kitchen refuse fed to pigs.

pigtail n. long hair worn hanging in a plait at the back of the head.

pigweed n. Aust. = MUNYEROO.

pike[1] n. **1** hist. a weapon with a pointed metal head on a long wooden shaft. **2** (pl. **pike**) a large voracious freshwater fish of the Northern hemisphere with a long narrow snout; any of several voracious Australian sea fish with elongated head and sharp teeth.

pike[2] v. Aust. colloq. **1** (foll. by on) let a person down (piked on me after all his promises). **2** (foll. by out) go back on (one's word, a deal, etc.) (he piked out on our bargain).

pike[3] n. a jackknife position in diving or gymnastics, with the legs straight and forming an angle with the body at the hips. ☐ **with pike** colloq. with greater difficulty involving added skill, toil, etc. ('Did you get your degree?' — 'Yes, mate, with pike!').

pikelet n. Aust. a small, thickish pancake eaten buttered. Also called *drop scone*.

piker n. Aust. **1** a cautious, timid, or mean and miserly person. **2** colloq. a person who lets others down or who welshes on an agreement, promise, etc. **3** a person who does not pull his or her weight; a shirker. **4** a bullock living in the wild.

pikestaff n. the wooden shaft of a pike. ☐ **plain as a pikestaff** quite plain or obvious.

pilaff, pilaf = PILAU.

pilaster / puh-**las**-tuh / n. a rectangular column, esp. an ornamental one that projects from a wall into which it is set.

Pilate, Pontius (1st century AD), the Roman governor of Judaea who presided at the trial of Jesus Christ.

pilau / puh-**low** / n. (also **pilaff, pilaf**) a Middle Eastern or Indian dish of rice boiled with meat, vegetables, spices, etc.

Pilbara / **pil**-buh-ruh / a vast region in northwest WA some 1,200 km north-east of Perth, renowned for its high temperatures and low rainfall, mineral mining, salt production, and Aboriginal art; the rocks which form the Pilbara are some of the most ancient in Australia.

pilchard n. **1** a small sea fish of the herring family found in the Atlantic and the Mediterranean. **2** a related sea fish of southern Australian waters.

pile[1] n. a heavy beam of metal, concrete, or timber driven vertically into the ground as a foundation or support for a building or bridge.

pile[2] n. **1** a number of things lying one upon another. **2** a funeral pyre. **3** colloq. a large quantity (a pile of work). **4** colloq. a large quantity of money (made a pile). **5** a large imposing building. **6** Physics a nuclear reactor. • v. **1** heap, stack, or load. **2** crowd (they all piled into one car). ☐ **pile it on** colloq. exaggerate. **pile up 1** accumulate. **2** cause (a vehicle) to crash. **pile-up** a collision of several motor vehicles.

pile[3] n. the projecting surface on velvet, carpets, etc.

piledriver n. a machine for driving piles into the ground.

piles n.pl. haemorrhoids.

pilfer v. steal small items or in small quantities.

Pilger, John (1939–), Australian journalist, internationally known for his documentary films on human rights abuses.

pilgrim n. a person who travels to a sacred place as an act of religious devotion.

pilgrimage n. a pilgrim's journey; a journey made to a place as a mark of respect (e.g. to a person's birthplace).

Pilipino / pil-uh-**pee**-noh / n. the national language of the Philippines, based on Tagalog.

pill n. **1** a small solid medicinal substance for swallowing whole. **2** (**the pill**) colloq. a contraceptive pill. **3** an unpleasant or painful necessity (a bitter pill). **4** colloq. an obnoxious or painfully boring person.

pillage v. plunder. • n. plunder. ☐ **pillager** n.

pillar n. **1** a vertical structure used as a support or ornament. **2** something resembling this in shape (a pillar of rock). **3** a person regarded as one of the chief supporters of something (a pillar of the community). ☐ **from pillar to post** from one place or situation to another.

pillbox n. **1** a small round box for holding pills. **2** a hat shaped like this. **3** a small concrete shelter for a gun emplacement.

pillion n. a saddle for a passenger behind the driver of a motor cycle. ☐ **ride pillion** ride on this as a passenger.

pillory n. a wooden framework with holes for the head and hands, into which offenders were formerly locked for exposure to public ridicule. • v. (**pilloried, pillorying**) **1** hold up to public ridicule or scorn. **2** put into the pillory as a punishment.

pillow n. a cushion used (esp. in bed) for supporting the head. • v. rest or prop up on or as if on a pillow.

pilot n. **1** a person who operates the controls of an aircraft. **2** a person qualified to take charge of ships entering or leaving a harbour or travelling through certain waters. **3** a guide. • v. (**piloted, piloting**) **1** act as pilot of. **2** conduct as a test or pilot project. • adj. experimental; testing (on a small scale) how a scheme etc. will work (a pilot project). ☐ **pilot bird** a reddish-brown, chiefly terrestrial bird of SE mainland Australia, having a penetrating whistle: once thought to pilot its frequent companion, the lyrebird. **pilot light 1** a small jet of gas kept alight to light a larger burner when this is turned on. **2** an electric indicator light.

pimelea / puh-**mee**-lyuh, puy- / n. any shrub of the mainly Australian genus *Pimelea*, the ones usu. cultivated having terminal heads of flowers surrounded by prominent bracts, their colours ranging from white to deep pink (*see also* QUALUP BELL). Also called *rice flower*.

pimento / puh-**men**-toh / *n.* (*pl.* **pimentos**) **1** allspice; the West Indian tree yielding this. **2** = PIMIENTO.

pi meson = PION.

pimiento *n.* (*pl.* **pimientos**) a sweet red capsicum.

pimp *n.* **1** a man who lives off the earnings of a prostitute or brothel. **2** *Aust.* an informer, a telltale, a sneak. • *v.* be a pimp.

pimple *n.* a small hard inflamed spot on the skin.

pimply *adj.* covered with pimples, esp. on the face.

PIN *abbr.* personal identification number; a number allocated by a bank etc. to a customer, e.g. for use with a card for obtaining cash from a machine.

■ **Usage** The variant *PIN number* is common, even though the element *number* is redundant. The reason is probably that it is more readily understood than *PIN* in examples such as *He'd forgotten his PIN.*

pin *n.* **1** a short thin stiff piece of metal with a sharp point and a round head, used for fastening fabrics or papers together or (with an ornamental head) as a decoration. **2** a peg of wood or metal used for various purposes. **3** a stick with a flag on it, placed in a hole on a golf course to mark its position. **4** a drawing pin, hairpin, ninepin, or safety pin. **5** (**pins**) *colloq.* legs (*quick on his pins*). • *v.* (**pinned**, **pinning**) **1** fasten with a pin or pins. **2** transfix with a weapon or arrow etc. and hold fast; restrict and make unable to move (*he was pinned under the wreckage*). **3** (foll. by *on*) put (blame, responsibility, hopes, etc.) on (a person) (*pinned the blame on her*). ☐ **pin down 1** establish clearly. **2** make (a person) agree to keep to a promise or arrangement, or declare his or her intentions definitely. **3** restrict the actions of (an enemy etc.). **pins and needles** a tingling sensation. **pin-tuck** a very narrow ornamental tuck. **pin-up** *colloq.* a picture of a sexually attractive or famous person, for pinning on a wall; the subject of this.

pinafore *n.* **1** an apron. **2** (in full **pinafore dress**) a dress without collar or sleeves, worn over a blouse or jumper.

pinball *n.* a game in which balls are shot across a sloping board to strike pins or targets.

pinboard *n.* a board made from cork on which notices etc. are pinned for display.

pince-nez / **pans**-nay / *n.* (*pl.* **pince-nez**) a pair of glasses with a spring that clips on the nose and no side-pieces. (¶ French, = pinch-nose.)

pincers *n.pl.* **1** a tool for gripping and pulling things, consisting of a pair of pivoted jaws with handles that are pressed together to close them. **2** the front claw-like parts of lobsters etc. ☐ **pincer movement** an attack in which forces converge from each side on an enemy position.

pinch *v.* **1** squeeze tightly or painfully between two surfaces, esp. between finger and thumb. **2** (usu. as **pinched** *adj.*) having a drawn appearance from feeling unpleasantly cold or hungry. **3** stint, be niggardly (*pinching and scraping*). **4** *colloq.* steal. **5** *colloq.* arrest. • *n.* **1** pinching, squeezing. **2** stress or pressure of circumstances (*began to feel the pinch*). **3** as much as can be held between the tips of the thumb and forefinger. ☐ **at a pinch** in an emergency.

pinchbeck *n.* an alloy of copper and zinc used as imitation gold in cheap jewellery. • *adj.* sham.

pincushion *n.* **1** a small pad into which pins are stuck to keep them ready for use. **2** (in full **blue pincushion** or **Austral pincushion**) a small Australian shrub producing many heads of cornflower-blue flowers. **3** (in full **pincushion hakea**) a shrub or small tree of WA producing abundant pincushion-like red flower heads with protruding white styles resembling pins stuck in.

pindan *n.* **1** (also **pindan country**) arid, sandy country characteristic of stretches of northern WA. **2** (also **pindan scrub**) the low, scrubby vegetation occurring in such country. **3** any of several plants typifying such vegetation, esp. a small wattle. (¶ Bardi *bindan* 'the bush'.)

pine¹ *n.* **1** an evergreen coniferous tree with needle-shaped leaves growing in clusters. **2** any of several such trees native to Australia, e.g. the Huon pine. **3** its wood. **4** = CYPRESS PINE. **5** = PINEAPPLE. ☐ **pine cone** the fruit of the pine. **pine nut** the edible seed of various pine trees.

pine² *v.* **1** waste away through grief or yearning. **2** feel an intense longing.

pineapple *n.* **1** a large juicy tropical fruit with yellow flesh and a tough prickly segmented skin. **2** the plant that bears it. ☐ **get the rough** (or **wrong**) **end of the pineapple** *colloq.* get the worse of a deal, bargain, etc.; receive rough or hostile treatment.

Pine Gap a classified joint defence space research facility (near Alice Springs) of the Australian and US governments, run by the US Central Intelligence Agency.

ping *n.* **1** a single short high ringing sound. **2** *Aust.* a high-pitched explosive sound in the engine of a motor vehicle, caused by faulty combustion. • *v.* **1** make or cause to make this sound. **2** *Sport* penalise (a player).

ping pong *n.* table tennis.

pinhead *n.* **1** a very small thing or spot. **2** *colloq.* a stupid person. **3** the head of a pin.

pinion¹ / **pin**-yuhn / *n.* a bird's wing, esp. the outer segment. • *v.* **1** clip the wings of (a bird) to prevent it from flying. **2** restrain (a person) by holding or binding his or her arms or legs.

pinion² / **pin**-yuhn / *n.* a small cog wheel that engages with a larger one or with a rack.

pink[1] *n.* **1** a pale red colour. **2** a garden plant with fragrant white or pink flowers. **3** the best or most perfect condition (*the pink of perfection*). **4** a person with mildly socialist tendencies (*the closet pinks in the Liberal Party*). • *adj.* **1** of pale red colour. **2** *colloq.* mildly left-wing. ☐ **in the pink** *colloq.* in very good health. ☐☐ **pinkish** *adj.* **pinkness** *n.*

pink[2] *v.* **1** pierce slightly (with a sword etc.). **2** cut a zigzag edge on. **3** ornament (leather etc.) with perforations. **4** *Aust.* shear a sheep so closely that the skin shows. ☐ **pinking shears** dressmaker's scissors with serrated blades for cutting a zigzag edge.

pink-eye[1] *n.* **1** a contagious fever in horses. **2** a contagious ophthalmia in humans and some livestock.

pink-eye[2] *n.* (also **pink bells**) *Aust.* = TETRATHECA.

pink-eye[3] *n.* (also **pink-hi**) **1** = WALKABOUT. **2** (in extended use) a holiday; a festivity. (¶ Yindjibarndi, possibly *binggayi* 'holiday' or *binigayi* 'go'.)

pink-eye[4] *n. Aust. colloq.* **1** = PINKY (sense 2). **2** a drinking bout.

pinko *adj. colloq.* drunk.

pinky *n.* (also **pinkie**) *Aust.* **1** = BILBY. **2** *colloq.* a cheap or home-made (fortified) wine. (¶ Sense 1 from Gaurna *binggu*; sense 2: origin unknown.)

pinnace / **pin**-uhs / *n.* a ship's small boat.

pinnacle *n.* **1** a pointed ornament on a roof. **2** a peak. **3** the highest point (*the pinnacle of his fame*).

pinnate *adj.* (of a compound leaf) having leaflets on either side of the leaf-stalk.

pinot / **pee**-noh / *n.* a variety of grape used in winemaking.

pinpoint *n.* **1** the point of a pin. **2** something very small or sharp. • *adj.* precise, accurate (*with pinpoint accuracy*). • *v.* locate or identify precisely.

pinprick *n.* a small annoyance.

pinstripe *n.* **1** (often *attrib.*) a very narrow stripe in (esp. worsted or serge) cloth (*pinstripe suit*). **2** (in *sing* or *pl.*) a pinstripe suit (*came wearing his pinstripes*).

pint *n.* a measure of capacity for liquids etc., ⅛ of a gallon (0.568 litre). ☐ **pint-sized** *adj. colloq.* very small.

pintle / **pin**-tuhl / *n.* a pin or bolt, esp. one on which another part turns.

Pintupi / **pin**-tuh-pee / *n.* a dialect of the Aboriginal language called the Western Desert language, spoken over about one and a quarter million square kilometres of arid country, mostly in WA.

Pinyin / pin-**yin** / *n.* a system of romanised spelling for transliterating Chinese.

pion *n.* (also **pi meson**) a sub-atomic particle with a mass many times greater than that of an electron.

pioneer / puy-uh-**neer** / *n.* a person who is one of the first to enter or settle in a new region or to investigate a new subject or method. • *v.* be a pioneer; take part in (a course of action etc.) that leads the way for others to follow.

piosphere / **puy**-uh-sfeer / *n. Aust.* an ecological system defined as the area around a watering point, in an arid zone, in which the grazing animals interact (*the piosphere effect*).

pious *adj.* **1** devout in religion. **2** too virtuous, sanctimonious. ☐ **piously** *adv.* **piousness** *n.*

pip *n.* **1** one of the small seeds of an apple, pear, orange, etc. **2** a spot on a domino, dice, or playing card. **3** a star (indicating rank) on the shoulder of an army officer's uniform. **4** a diamond-shaped segment on the surface of a pineapple. **5** a short high-pitched sound, usu. one produced mechanically (*the six pips of the time signal*). **6** a disease of poultry and other birds. **7** (**the pip**) *colloq.* a feeling of disgust, depression, or bad temper (*he gives me the pip*). • *v.* (**pipped**, **pipping**) *colloq.* **1** hit with a shot. **2** defeat. ☐ **pip at the post** defeat at the last moment.

pipe *n.* **1** a tube through which something can flow. **2** a wind instrument consisting of a single tube. **3** each of the tubes by which sound is produced in an organ. **4** (**the pipes**) bagpipes. **5** a boatswain's whistle; its sounding. **6** a narrow tube with a bowl at one end in which tobacco burns for smoking. • *v.* **1** convey (water etc.) through pipes. **2** transmit (music or a broadcast program etc.) by wire or cable. **3** play (music) on a pipe. **4** lead, bring, or summon by sounding a pipe. **5** utter in a shrill voice. **6** decorate (a dress etc.) with piping. **7** force (icing, cream, etc.) through an aperture to make ornamental shapes. ☐ **pipe down** *colloq.* become less noisy or less insistent. **pipe up** begin to play, sing, or speak.

pipeclay *n. Aust.* a fine white clay which forms a paste when mixed with water and is used as ritual body paint by Aborigines.

pipedream *n.* an impractical hope or scheme. (¶ Originally as experienced when smoking an opium pipe.)

pipeline *n.* **1** a pipe for conveying oil etc. over a distance. **2** a channel of supply or information. ☐ **in the pipeline** on the way; in the process of being prepared.

piper *n.* a person who plays a pipe or bagpipes.

pipette / pi-**pet** / *n.* a slender tube, usu. filled by suction, used in a laboratory for transferring or measuring small quantities of liquids.

pipi *n.* an edible marine bivalve of southern Australian coasts, often used as bait. Also called *ugari*.

piping *n.* **1** pipes; a length of pipe. **2** a pipelike fold (often enclosing a cord) decorating edges or seams of clothing or upholstery. **3** a decorative line of icing etc. piped on food. ☐ **piping hot** (of water or food) very hot. **piping shrike** *Aust.* a magpie, the faunal emblem of SA.

pipit *n.* a small bird resembling a lark, found Australia-wide.

pippin *n.* a variety of apple.

pipsqueak *n. colloq.* a small, unimportant, or contemptible person or thing.

piquant / **pee**-kuhnt / *adj.* **1** pleasantly sharp in taste or smell. **2** pleasantly stimulating or exciting to the mind. □ **piquancy** *n.*

pique / peek / *v.* (**piqued**, **piquing**) **1** hurt the pride or self-respect of. **2** stimulate (*their curiosity was piqued*). •*n.* a feeling of hurt pride.

piracy / **puy**-ruh-see / *n.* **1** robbery of ships at sea. **2** hijacking. **3** infringement of copyright; use of material without authorisation.

Pirandello / pi-ruhn-**del**-oh /, Luigi (1867–1936), Italian dramatist and novelist.

piranha / puh-**rah**-nuh / *n.* a fierce tropical South American freshwater fish, with sharp teeth.

pirate *n.* **1** a person on a ship who unlawfully attacks and robs another ship at sea. **2** a ship used by pirates. **3** (often used as *adj.*) infringing another's copyright or business rights, or broadcasting without authorisation (*a pirate radio station*). •*v.* reproduce (a book, video, or computer software) or trade (goods) without due authorisation. □ **piratical** *adj.*

pirouette / pi-roo-**et** / *n.* a dancer's spinning movement while balanced on tiptoe. •*v.* perform a pirouette.

pirri *n.* (also **pirrie**) *Aust.* an Aboriginal leaf-shaped engraving tool made of stone or quartz. (¶ Arabana *birri* 'fingernail', extended to anything pointed.)

Pisa / **pee**-zuh / a city in northern Italy, noted for its 'Leaning Tower', the campanile of its cathedral (12th century).

piscatorial / pis-kuh-**taw**-ree-uhl / *adj.* of fishing or fishermen.

Pisces / **puy**-seez / *n.* the twelfth sign of the zodiac, the Fishes. □ **Piscean** *adj.* & *n.*

piscina / puh-**see**-nuh, -**suy**-nuh / *n.* (*pl.* **piscinae** or **piscinas**) **1** a stone basin near the altar in a church, used for rinsing the chalice etc. used in the Mass. **2** a fish pond.

piscine / **pis**-een / *adj.* of or concerning fish.

piss *colloq. v.* **1** urinate. **2** wet by urinating (*pissed the bed*). •*n.* **1** the act of urinating. **2** urine. **3** *Aust.* alcoholic drink, esp. beer. •*adv.* (as an intensifier) extremely (*piss-awful; piss-weak*). □ **piss about** (*or* **around**) mess about, fool around. **piss in a person's pocket** ingratiate oneself with, crawl to him or her. **piss oneself 1** receive a sudden severe fright (*pissed himself when the car skidded*). **2** laugh extravagantly (*pissed himself*). **piss-up** *n.* a beer-drinking spree. **piss-weak 1** highly unsatisfactory or disappointing. **2** despicable; underhand (*that was a piss-weak thing you did*). **3** gutless, cowardly. **take the piss out of a person 1** ridicule. **2** humble, puncture the pretensions of.

pissant / **pis**-ant / *n. colloq.* □ **game as a pissant** *Aust.* brave; foolhardy. **pissant around** *Aust.* mess around; waste time doing nothing useful.

pissed *adj. colloq.* drunk.

pisser *n. colloq.* **1** a person who pisses. **2** a men's urinal or toilet. **3** *Aust.* a hotel (*down at the pisser with his mates*). **4 a** an extraordinary person or thing. **b** an annoying or disappointing thing.

pisspot *n. Aust.* a heavy drinker; an alcoholic.

pistachio / puhs-**tah**-shee-oh / *n.* (*pl.* **pistachios**) a nut with an edible green kernel.

piste / peest / *n.* a ski run of compacted snow.

pistil *n.* the female organs of a flower, comprising ovary, style, and stigma. □ **pistillate** *adj.*

pistol *n.* a small handgun.

piston *n.* **1** a sliding disc or cylinder fitting closely inside a tube in which it moves up and down as part of an engine or pump. **2** the sliding valve in a trumpet or other brass wind instrument.

pit[1] *n.* **1** a hole in the ground, esp. one from which material is dug out (*gravel pit*). **2** a coalmine. **3** a depression in the skin or in any surface. **4** orchestra pit. **5** a sunken area in a workshop floor, giving access to the underside of motor vehicles. **6** an area at the side of a racetrack where cars are serviced and refuelled during a race. •*v.* (**pitted**, **pitting**) **1** make pits or depressions in, become marked with hollows (*pitted with craters; a face pitted by acne*). **2** (usu. foll. by **against**) set (one's wits, strength, etc.) in competition (*pitted her strength against mine*). **3** (usu. as **pitted** *adj.*) remove stones from (olives, cherries, etc.). □ **the pits** *colloq.* the worst or most despicable person, place, situation, or thing. **pit of the stomach** the depression between the ribs below the breastbone.

pit[2] *n.* the stone of a fruit. •*v.* (**pitted**, **pitting**) remove pits from (fruit).

pita alternative spelling of PITTA[2].

pit-a-pat *n.* (also **pitter-patter**) a quick tapping sound. •*adv.* with this sound.

Pitcairn Islands a British dependency comprising a group of islands in the South Pacific, north-east of New Zealand, settled in 1790 by mutineers from HMS *Bounty*.

pitch[1] *n.* a dark resinous tarry substance that sets hard, used for caulking seams of ships etc. •*v.* coat with pitch. □ **pitch-black** (also **pitch-dark**) *adj.* completely black, with no light at all.

pitch[2] *v.* **1** throw or fling. **2** erect and fix (a tent or camp). **3** set at a particular degree, slope, or level (*pitched their hopes high*). **4** fall heavily. **5** (in cricket) cause the ball to strike the ground near the wicket in bowling; (of a bowled ball) strike the ground. **6** (in baseball) throw (the ball) to the batter. **7** (of a ship or vehicle) plunge forward and backward alternately. •*n.* **1** the act or process of pitching. **2** the steepness of a slope. **3** the intensity of a quality etc. **4** the degree of highness or lowness of a musical note or a voice. **5** a place at which a street performer or hawker etc. is stationed. **6** a playing field for football, hockey, etc.; the area between and near the wickets in cricket. **7** a

pitchblende

salesman's persuasive talk; spiel. ☐ **pitched battle** a battle fought by troops in prepared positions, not a skirmish. **pitched roof** a sloping roof. **pitch in** *colloq.* **1** set to (eat, work, etc.) vigorously. **2** contribute (money etc.) for a cause. **3** join in, participate. **pitch into** *colloq.* attack or reprimand vigorously.

pitchblende *n.* a mineral ore (uranium oxide) that yields radium.

pitcher *n.* **1** the baseball player who delivers the ball to the batter. **2** a large jug. ☐ **pitcher plant 1** any of several usu. insect-eating plants having leaves in the form of pitchers in which to trap insects. **2** (also **Albany pitcher plant**) a Western Australian insect-eating plant with large pitchers, now on the endangered species list.

pitchfork *n.* a long-handled fork with two prongs, used for pitching hay. • *v.* **1** lift or move (a thing) with a pitchfork. **2** thrust (a person) forcibly into a position or office.

pitchi *n. Aust.* = COOLAMON. (¶ Western Desert language (and neighbouring languages).)

piteous *adj.* deserving or arousing pity. ☐ **piteously** *adv.*

pitfall *n.* an unsuspected danger or difficulty.

pith *n.* **1** the spongy tissue in the stems of certain plants or lining the rind of oranges etc. **2** the essential part (*the pith of the argument*).

pithead / **pit**-hed / *n.* the top of a mine shaft; the area surrounding that.

pithy *adj.* (**pithier**, **pithiest**) **1** like pith; containing much pith. **2** brief and full of meaning (*pithy comments*).

pitiable *adj.* deserving or arousing pity or contempt. ☐ **pitiably** *adv.*

pitiful *adj.* pitiable. ☐ **pitifully** *adv.*

pitiless *adj.* showing no pity. ☐ **pitilessly** *adv.*

Pitjantjatjara / **pich**-uhn-ja-ru, **pich**-uhn-ju-ja-ru / *n.* a dialect of the Western Desert language.

piton / **pee**-ton / *n.* a peg with a hole through which a rope can be passed, driven into rock as a support in rock-climbing.

pitta[1] *n.* any of various passerine birds of Australia, India, etc., often with vivid colouring.

pitta[2] *n.* (also **pita**) a flat hollow unleavened bread which can be split and filled with salad etc., originally from Greece and the Middle East.

pittance *n.* a very small allowance or wage.

Pitta-pitta / **pit**-u-pit-u / *n.* an Aboriginal language of the Boulia district of central Qld.

pitter-patter = PIT-A-PAT.

pittosporum / puh-**tos**-puh-ruhm / *n.* a large genus of trees and shrubs, nine or so species of which are native to Australia, having usu. cream to yellow fragrant flowers and orange fruit.

Pitt Street farmer *n.* (also **Collins Street farmer**) *Aust. derog.* a person whose interests are in the city but who buys rural property, farms, etc., usu. as a tax write-off. (¶ *Pitt Street, Collins Street*, the principal business streets in Sydney and Melbourne respectively.)

place

pituitary / puh-**tyoo**-uh-tuh-ree, -tree / *n.* (also **pituitary gland**) a small ductless gland at the base of the brain, with important influence on growth and bodily functions.

pituri / **pich**-uh-ree / *n.* a shrub widespread in arid, sandy, central Australia, the leaves being traditionally chewed by Aborigines for their powerful narcotic effect, as well as being crushed and placed in waterholes to stun food animals, esp. emus. (¶ Yandruwandha)

piturine *n.* an alkaloid extracted from pituri.

pity *n.* **1** a feeling of sorrow for another person's suffering. **2** a cause for regret (*what a pity*). • *v.* (**pitied**, **pitying**) feel (sometimes contemptuous) pity for (*pitied them deeply; I pity you if you think that*).

pivot *n.* **1** a central point or shaft etc. on which something turns or swings. **2** a pivoting movement. **3** a crucial person, point, etc. • *v.* (**pivoted**, **pivoting**) turn or place to turn on a pivot.

pivotal *adj.* **1** of a pivot. **2** vitally important.

pixel *n.* any of the minute illuminated areas which make up an image displayed on a screen.

pixie *n.* (also **pixy**) a small supernatural being in fairy tales.

pizza / **peet**-suh / *n.* an Italian dish of a layer of dough baked with a savoury topping.

pizzazz / puh-**zaz** / *n.* (also **pizazz**) *colloq.* **1** zest, liveliness. **2** showiness.

pizzeria / peet-suh-**ree**-uh / *n.* a pizza restaurant.

pizzicato / pit-see-**kah**-toh / *adv.* plucking the strings of a musical instrument (instead of using the bow).

pizzle / **piz**-uhl / *n. esp. Aust.* the penis of an animal, esp. a bull, formerly used as a whip.

pl. *abbr.* **1** plural. **2** (usu. **Pl.**) place.

placable / **plak**-uh-buhl / *adj.* able to be placated, forgiving. ☐ **placability** *n.*

placard *n.* a poster or other notice for displaying. • *v.* post up placards on (a wall etc.).

placate / pluh-**kayt** / *v.* pacify, conciliate. ☐ **placatory** *adj.*

place *n.* **1** a particular part of space or of an area. **2** a particular town, district, building, etc. (*one of the places we visited*). **3** (in names) a short street; a square or the buildings round it. **4** one's home or dwelling (*come over to my place*). **5** the part one has reached in a book etc. (*lose one's place*). **6** a proper position for a thing; a position in a series; one's rank or position in a community; a duty appropriate to this. **7** a position of employment. **8** a space or seat or accommodation for a person (*keep me a place on the train*). **9** (in racing) a position among placed competitors, esp. second or third. **10** the position of a figure after a decimal point etc. (*correct to 3 decimal places*). • *v.* **1** put into a particular place, rank, position, or order; find a place for. **2** locate, identify in relation to circumstances etc. (*I know his face but can't place him*). **3** put or give (*placed an order with the firm*). ☐ **be placed** (in a race) be among the first three.

placebo / pluh-**see**-boh / n. (pl. **placebos**) a harmless substance given as if it were medicine, to humour a patient or as a dummy pill etc. in a controlled experiment.

placement n. placing; a position.

placenta / pluh-**sen**-tuh / n. an organ that develops in the womb during pregnancy and supplies the developing foetus with nourishment. □ **placental** adj.

placid adj. calm and peaceful, not easily made anxious or upset. □ **placidly** adv. **placidity** / pluh-**sid**-uh-tee / n.

placket n. an opening or slit in a garment for fastenings or access to a pocket.

plage / plahzh / n. **1** *Astronomy* an unusually bright region on the sun. **2** a sea beach, esp. at a fashionable resort.

plagiarise / **play**-juh-ruyz / v. (also **-ize**) take and use (another person's ideas, writings, or inventions) as one's own. □ **plagiarism** n. **plagiarist** n.

plague / playg / n. **1** a deadly contagious disease. **2** an infestation of a pest (*a plague of caterpillars*). **3** *colloq.* a nuisance. •v. (**plagued**, **plaguing**) annoy, pester.

plaice n. (pl. **plaice**) a European flatfish used as food.

plaid / plad / n. tartan cloth.

plain adj. **1** unmistakable, easy to see or hear or understand. **2** not elaborate or intricate, not luxurious, without flavouring etc. (*plain cooking; plain water*). **3** straightforward, candid (*some plain speaking*). **4** ordinary; homely in manner, without affectation. **5** lacking beauty. •adv. plainly, simply (*it's plain stupid*). •n. **1** a large area of level country. **2** the basic stitch in knitting, made by pushing the point of the working needle away from the knitter. □ **plain clothes** civilian clothes as distinct from uniform or official dress. **plain turkey** (also **plains turkey**) *Aust.* **1** a large, nomadic, often solitary game bird of mainland Australia. **2** (the nickname for) a SWAGGIE. **plain wanderer** (also **plains wanderer**) a terrestrial bird of south-east mainland Australia. □□ **plainly** adv. **plainness** n.

plainchant n. (also **Gregorian chant**) unaccompanied liturgical music (for High Mass etc.) chanted in unison in medieval modes and in free rhythm corresponding to the accentuation of the Latin words (esp. in monasteries etc.).

plainsong = PLAINCHANT.

plaint n. **1** *Law* a charge, an accusation. **2** *archaic* a complaint or lamentation.

plaintiff n. the party that brings an action in a court of law (opposed to the DEFENDANT).

plaintive adj. sounding sad. □ **plaintively** adv.

plait / plat / v. weave or twist (three or more strands) into one rope-like length. •n. something plaited.

plan n. **1** a drawing showing the relative position and size of parts of a building etc. **2** a map of a town or district. **3** a drawing or diagram showing a structure or object as viewed from above (cf. ELEVATION). **4** a method or course of action thought out in advance (*it all went according to plan*). •v. (**planned**, **planning**) **1** make a plan or design of. **2** arrange a method etc. for, make plans.

planchette / plahn-**shet**, plan- / n. a small board on castors with a vertical pencil, said to write messages from spirits on paper when people place their fingers on the board.

plane[1] n. a tall spreading tree with broad leaves.

plane[2] n. **1** a flat or level surface. **2** an imaginary surface of this kind. **3** a level of thought, existence, or development (*on the same plane as a savage*). **4** an aeroplane. •adj. lying in a plane, level (*a plane figure; a plane surface*).

plane[3] n. **1** a tool with a blade projecting from the base, used for smoothing the surface of wood by paring shavings from it. **2** a similar tool for smoothing metal. •v. smooth or pare with a plane.

planet n. a celestial body orbiting round a star; the earth. □ **planetary** adj.

planetarium / plan-uh-**tair**-ree-uhm / n. (pl. **planetariums** or **planetaria**) a room with a domed ceiling on which lights are projected to show the appearance of the stars and planets.

plangent / **plan**-juhnt / adj. *literary* (of sounds) **1** resonant, reverberating. **2** loud and mournful.

plank n. **1** a long flat piece of timber. **2** one of the policies in a political program. •v. **1** provide, cover, or floor with planks. **2** *colloq.* (usu. foll. by *down*) **a** put down or deposit (a thing or person) roughly or violently; **b** pay (money) on the spot (*planked down $5*).

planking n. a structure or floor of planks.

plankton n. the forms of organic life (chiefly microscopic) that float in the sea or fresh water.

planner n. **1** a person who plans new towns etc. **2** a person who makes plans. **3** a list, table, etc. with information helpful in planning.

planning n. making plans, esp. with reference to the controlled design of buildings and development of land. □ **planning permission** formal approval for the construction or alteration of a building or structure, esp. as granted by a local council.

plant n. **1** a living organism that makes its own food from inorganic substances and has neither the power of movement nor special organs of sensation and digestion. **2** a small plant (distinguished from a tree or shrub). **3** a factory or its machinery and equipment. **4** *Aust.* the working animals, equipment, vehicles, personnel, employed by a drover, stockman, etc., on the move. **5** *colloq.* someone or something deliberately placed so as to incriminate a person. •v. **1** put (plants or seeds) into ground or soil for growing. **2** set or place firmly in position (*planted his foot on the ladder*). **3** station (a person) as a spy. **4** take up a position (*planted myself by the*

Plantagenet

entrance). **5** cause (an idea etc.) to be established (*planted a doubt in his mind*). **6** deliver (a blow, a kiss, etc.) with deliberate aim. **7** *Aust.* hide (articles, cattle, etc.) after stealing. **8** *colloq.* place (something incriminating) in a place where it will be discovered. ◻ **plant out** transfer (a plant) from a pot or frame to open ground; set out (seedlings) at intervals.

Plantagenet / plan-**taj**-uh-nuht / *n.* any of the kings of England from Henry II to Richard III (1154–1485).

plantain / **plahn**-tuhn, **plan**- / *n.* **1** a variety of banana plant. **2** the starchy fruit of this containing less sugar than the dessert varieties and chiefly used in cooking.

plantation *n.* **1** an area planted with trees etc. **2** an estate on which cotton, tobacco, tea, etc. is cultivated.

planter *n.* **1** a person who owns or manages a plantation. **2** a decorative container for plants.

plaque / plahk, plak / *n.* **1** a flat plate fixed on a wall as an ornament or memorial. **2** a substance that forms on teeth, encouraging the growth of harmful bacteria.

plash *n.* **1** a splash; a plunge. **2** a puddle. •*v.* **1** splash. **2** strike the surface of (water).

plasma / **plaz**-muh / *n.* (also **plasm**) **1** the colourless fluid part of blood, lymph, or milk, in which corpuscles or globules of fat are suspended; this taken from blood for transfusions. **2** = PROTOPLASM. **3** a kind of gas containing positively and negatively charged particles in approximately equal numbers. ◻ **plasmatic** *adj.* **plasmic** *adj.*

plaster *n.* **1** a soft mixture of lime, sand, and water, etc. applied to walls and ceilings to dry as a smooth hard surface. **2** plaster of Paris; a cast made of this fitted round a broken limb etc. **3** sticking plaster; a piece of this. •*v.* **1** cover (a wall etc.) with plaster or a similar substance. **2** coat or daub; cover thickly. **3** make smooth with a fixative etc. (*his hair was plastered down*). **4** *colloq.* hit repeatedly, thrash; bomb or shell heavily. ◻ **plaster cast 1** a cast of a statue etc. made in plaster. **2** plaster moulded round a broken limb etc. to keep it rigid. **plaster of Paris** white paste made from gypsum, used for making moulds or casts. ◻◻ **plasterer** *n.*

plasterboard *n.* board with a core of plaster, used for making partitions etc.

plastered *adj. colloq.* drunk.

plastic / **plas**-tik / *n.* **1** a synthetic resinous substance that can be given any permanent shape, e.g. by moulding it under pressure while heated. **2** = PLASTIC MONEY. •*adj.* **1** made of plastic (*plastic bag*). **2** able to be shaped or moulded (*clay is a plastic substance*). **3** giving form to clay or wax etc. **4** (of people) artificial in manner, false, etc. (*the socialite set, full of plastic people*). ◻ **plastic arts** arts involving modelling, e.g. sculpture or ceramics. **plastic bullet** a solid plastic cylinder fired as a riot-control device rather than to kill.

plastic explosive a soft putty-like explosive. **plastic money** *colloq.* credit cards as opposed to cash or cheques. **plastic surgeon** a specialist in **plastic surgery**, the repairing or replacing of damaged or unsightly skin, muscle, etc. ◻◻ **plasticity** / plas-**tis**-uh-tee / *n.*

plasticine *n. trademark* a soft plastic material used, esp. by children, for modelling.

plasticise / **plas**-tuh-suyz / *v.* (also **-ize**) make or become plastic. ◻ **plasticiser** *n.*

plat du jour / plah doo **zhoor** / *n.* a dish specially featured on a day's menu. (¶ French, = dish of the day)

plate *n.* **1** an almost flat usu. circular utensil from which food is eaten or served; its contents. **2** a similar shallow vessel for the collection of money in church etc. **3** *Aust.* a contribution of cakes, sandwiches, etc., brought by each invitee to a party, social gathering, etc. **4** dishes and other domestic utensils made of gold, silver, or other metal. **5** plated metal; objects made of this. **6** a silver or gold cup as a prize for a horse race etc.; the race itself. **7** a flat thin sheet of metal, glass, or other rigid material. **8** this coated with material sensitive to light or other radiation, for use in photography etc. **9** a flat piece of metal on which something is engraved or bearing a name, registration number, etc. **10** an illustration on special paper in a book. **11** a thin flat structure or formation in a plant or animal body. **12** a piece of plastic material moulded to the shape of the gums or roof of the mouth for holding artificial teeth; *colloq.* a denture. **13** each of several rigid layers of rock thought to form the earth's crust. •*v.* **1** cover with plates of metal. **2** coat (metal) with a thin layer of silver, gold, or tin. ◻ **plate glass** thick glass of fine quality for shop windows etc. **plate tectonics** the study of the earth's surface based on the concept of moving plates forming its structure. ◻◻ **plateful** *n.*

plateau / **plat**-oh / *n.* (*pl.* **plateaux** or **plateaus**) **1** an area of fairly level high ground. **2** a state in which there is little variation following an increase (*the firm's export trade reached a plateau*).

platelet *n.* a small colourless disc found in the blood and involved in clotting.

platen / **plat**-uhn / *n.* **1** a plate in a printing press which presses the paper against the type. **2** the roller of a typewriter, against which the paper is held.

platform *n.* **1** a level surface raised above the surrounding ground or floor, esp. one from which a speaker addresses an audience. **2** a raised area along the side of the line at a railway station, where passengers get on and off trains. **3** a floor area at the entrance to a bus or tram. **4** the declared policy or program of a political party.

platinum *n.* a chemical element (symbol Pt), a silver-white metal that does not tarnish. ◻ **platinum blonde** (also **platinum blond**) a woman (or man) with silvery-blond(e) hair.

platitude / **plat**-uh-tyood / *n*. a commonplace remark, esp. one uttered solemnly as if it were new. ☐ **platitudinous** / plat-uh-**tyood**-uh-nuhs / *adj*.

Plato / **play**-toh / (*c*.429–*c*.347 BC), Greek philosopher, a disciple of Socrates.

Platonic / pluh-**ton**-ik / *adj*. **1** of Plato or his doctrines. **2** (**platonic**) (of love or friendship) not sexual.

platoon *n*. a subdivision of a military company.

platter *n*. a large flat dish or plate.

platypus / **plat**-uh-puus / *n*. (also **duck-billed platypus**) (*pl*. **platypuses**) an amphibious, burrowing, egg-laying mammal of freshwater lakes and watercourses of eastern Australia, having thick brown fur, a ducklike bill with leathery skin, webbed feet, and a broad, flat tail: in summer the male carries venom in a hollow spur on each hind leg. ☐ **platypus frog** = GASTRIC BROODING FROG.

■ **Usage** The plural of *platypus* is *platypuses* and not *platypi*. The *-pus* element is from Greek *pous* 'foot', the plural of which is *podes* (cf. ANTIPODES). In scientific and conservationist contexts the word sometimes appears with zero inflection in the plural: *there are six platypus in this section of the river*.

platypussary / plat-uh-**puus**-uh-ree / *n*. (*pl*. **platypussaries**) *Aust*. an enclosure or building in which platypuses are kept.

plaudit / **plaw**-duht / *n*. (usu. as **plaudits**) a round of applause; an emphatic expression of approval.

plausible / **plaw**-zuh-buhl / *adj*. **1** (of a statement etc.) reasonable or probable but not proved. **2** (of a person) persuasive but deceptive. ☐ **plausibly** *adv*. **plausibility** *n*.

Plautus / **plaw**-tus /, Titus Maccius (*c*.250–184 BC), Roman comic dramatist.

play *v*. **1** occupy oneself in a game or other recreational activity. **2** take part in (a game); compete against (a player or team); occupy (a specified position) in a game; assign (a player) to a particular position. **3** move (a piece), put (a card) on the table, or strike (a ball etc.) in a game. **4** act in a drama etc.; act in real life the part of (*play the politician; play the fool*). **5** perform (a part in a process). **6** perform on (a musical instrument); perform (a piece of music). **7** cause (a tape, CD, etc.) to produce sound. **8** move lightly or irregularly; emit light, water, etc. (*fountains gently playing*). **9** allow (a hooked fish) to exhaust itself by pulling against the line. **10** (foll. by *on*) perform (a trick or joke etc.) on (a person). **11** gamble, gamble on. ● *n*. **1** playing. **2** activity, operation (*other influences came into play*). **3** a literary work written for performance on the stage, television, or radio. **4** free movement (*bolts should have 1 cm of play*). **5** gambling. ☐ **play along** pretend to cooperate. **play back** play (what has recently been recorded) on a tape recorder etc. **play ball** *colloq*. cooperate. **play by ear 1** perform (music) without having seen a written score. **2** (also **play it by ear**) proceed step by step, going by one's instinct or by results. **play it cool** *colloq*. be relaxed; pretend to be indifferent. **play lunch** (also **little lunch**) *Aust*. a snack taken by children to school to eat during the pre-lunch mid-morning break; the break itself. **play off 1** play an extra match to decide a drawn position. **2** oppose (one person against another) in order to serve one's own interests. **play-off** *n*. a match played to decide a draw or tie. **play the market** speculate in stocks etc. **play up 1** be mischievous and unruly, annoy by doing this. **2** cause trouble, go wrong (*my leg's playing up*). **play up to** try to win the favour of (a person) by flattery etc. **play with fire** take foolish risks.

playback *n*. playing back sound; a device for doing this.

playboy *n*. a rich pleasure-seeking man.

player *n*. **1** a person who takes part in a game. **2** a performer on a musical instrument. **3** an actor. **4** a record player.

playful *adj*. **1** full of fun. **2** in a mood for play, not serious. ☐ **playfully** *adv*. **playfulness** *n*.

playing card *n*. each of a pack or set of 52 oblong cards used to play a variety of games, marked on one side to show one of 13 ranks in one of 4 suits.

plaything *n*. **1** a toy. **2** a person used merely as an object of amusement or pleasure.

playing field *n*. a field used for outdoor team games. ☐ **level playing field** a supposedly efficient free trade environment where no participant receives a subsidy or other unfair market advantage.

playwright *n*. a person who writes plays, a dramatist.

plaza / **plah**-zuh / *n*. an open square in a city or town.

plea *n*. **1** a formal statement (esp. of 'guilty' or 'not guilty') made by or on behalf of a person charged in a lawcourt. **2** an appeal or entreaty (*a plea for mercy*). **3** an excuse (*on the plea of ill health*).

plead *v*. (**pleaded**, **pleading**) **1** put forward as a plea in a lawcourt. **2** address a lawcourt as an advocate; put forward (a case) in court. **3** make an appeal or entreaty. **4** put forward as an excuse (*pleaded a previous engagement*). ☐ **plead with** entreat.

pleasant *adj*. **1** pleasing, giving pleasure to the mind or feelings or senses. **2** having an agreeable manner. ☐ **pleasantly** *adv*. **pleasantness** *n*.

pleasantry *n*. **1** an inconsequential remark made as part of a polite conversation. **2** a mild joke.

please *v*. **1** give pleasure to, make (a person etc.) feel satisfied or glad. **2** think fit; have the desire (*take as many as you please*). **3** (short for *may it*

pleased

please you) used in polite requests (*come in, please*). □ **if you please 1** *formal* please. **2** an ironical phrase, pointing out unreasonableness (*and so, if you please, we're to get nothing!*). **please oneself** do as one chooses.

pleased *adj.* feeling or showing pleasure or satisfaction.

pleasurable *adj.* causing pleasure. □ **pleasurably** *adv.*

pleasure *n.* **1** a feeling of satisfaction or joy, enjoyment. **2** a source of pleasure (*it's a pleasure to talk to him*). **3** choice, desire (*at your pleasure*). **4** sensual gratification (*a life of pleasure*). • *v.* give (esp. sexual) pleasure to. • *adj.* done or used for pleasure (*a pleasure trip*). □ **with pleasure** willingly, gladly.

pleat *n.* a flat fold made by doubling cloth on itself. • *v.* make a pleat or pleats in.

pleb *n. colloq.* often *derog.* a coarse uncultured person.

plebeian / pluh-**bee**-uhn / *adj.* **1** of the lower social classes. **2** uncultured, vulgar (*plebeian tastes*). • *n.* **1** a member of the lower classes, esp. in ancient Rome. **2** a coarse uncultured person.

plebiscite / **pleb**-uh-suht, -suyt / *n.* a vote by all the people of a country etc. on an important public matter.

plectrum *n.* (*pl.* **plectrums** or **plectra**) a small piece of plastic etc. for plucking the strings of a musical instrument; a corresponding mechanical part of a harpsichord etc.

pledge *n.* **1** a thing deposited as security for payment of a debt or fulfilment of a contract etc., and liable to be forfeited in case of failure. **2** a token of something (*as a pledge of his devotion*). **3** a toast drunk to someone's health. **4** a solemn promise (*under pledge of secrecy*). • *v.* **1** deposit (an article) as a pledge. **2** promise solemnly. **3** drink to the health of.

Pleiades / **pluy**-uh-deez / *n.pl.* the 'Seven Sisters', a group of seven stars in the constellation Taurus.

Pleistocene / **play**-stuh-seen / *adj. Geol.* of the first of the two epochs forming the Quaternary period. • *n.* this epoch: during the late Pleistocene Australia's giant marsupials were still alive but became extinct shortly after.

plenary / **plee**-nuh-ree / *adj.* **1** attended by all members (*a plenary session of the assembly*). **2** entire, unqualified (*a plenary indulgence*).

plenipotentiary / plen-uh-puh-**ten**-shuh-ree / *n.* an envoy with full powers to take action on behalf of the government he or she represents. • *adj.* having these powers.

plenitude / **plen**-uh-tyood / *n. literary* **1** fullness, completeness. **2** abundance.

plenteous / **plen**-tee-uhs / *adj. literary* plentiful.

plentiful *adj.* in large quantities or numbers, abundant. □ **plentifully** *adv.*

plenty *n.* quite enough, as much as one could need or desire. • *adv. colloq.* quite, fully (*it's plenty big enough*).

plough

plenum / **plee**-nuhm / *n.* a full or complete assembly.

pleonasm / **plee**-uh-naz-uhm / *n.* the use of more words than are needed to give the sense (e.g. *see with one's eyes*). □ **pleonastic** *adj.*

plethora / **pleth**-uh-ruh / *n.* an over-abundance; a glut.

pleura / **ploo**-ruh / *n.* (*pl.* **pleurae**) the membrane surrounding the lungs.

pleurisy / **ploo**-ruh-see / *n.* inflammation of the pleura, causing painful breathing. □ **pleuritic** *adj.*

plexus *n.* (*pl.* **plexus** or **plexuses**) a network of nerves or vessels.

pliable *adj.* **1** bending easily, flexible. **2** easily influenced. □ **pliability** *n.*

pliant / **pluy**-uhnt / *adj.* pliable. □ **pliancy** *n.*

pliers *n.pl.* pincers having jaws with flat surfaces that can be brought together for gripping small objects, bending wire, etc.

plight *n.* a serious and difficult situation. • *v. archaic* pledge. □ **plight one's troth** *archaic* promise to marry.

Plimsoll line / **plim**-suhl / *n.* (also **Plimsoll mark**) marking on a ship's side showing the limit of legal submersion under various conditions.

plinth *n.* a block or slab forming the base of a column; the base supporting a vase, statue, etc.

Pliny 'the Elder' (Gaius Plinius Secundus) (23–79), Roman statesman, author of the encyclopedic *Natural History*.

Pliocene / **pluy**-uh-seen / *adj. Geol.* of the final epoch of the Tertiary period. • *n.* this epoch.

PLO *abbr.* Palestine Liberation Organisation, a political and military organisation campaigning for the rights of Palestinian Arabs in the Middle East.

plod *v.* (**plodded**, **plodding**) **1** walk doggedly or laboriously, trudge. **2** work at a slow but steady rate. • *n.* plodding. □ **plodder** *n.*

plonk[1] *v.* place or drop down heavily. • *adv. colloq.* exactly (*hit him plonk on the nose*). • *n.* a heavy thud.

plonk[2] *n. Aust. colloq.* cheap or inferior wine.

plonko *n. Aust. colloq.* an addict of cheap or inferior wine.

plop *n.* a sound like that of something dropping into water without a splash.

plot *n.* **1** a small measured piece of land. **2** the story in a play, novel, or film. **3** a conspiracy, a secret plan. • *v.* (**plotted**, **plotting**) **1** make a plan or map of. **2** mark on a chart or diagram. **3** plan secretly, contrive a secret plan. □ **plotter** *n.*

plough / plow / *n.* **1** an implement for cutting furrows and turning the soil. **2** an implement resembling a plough (*snow plough*). **3** (**the Plough**) a constellation also called the Great Bear. • *v.* **1** turn (earth) or cut (a furrow) with a plough. **2** progress laboriously (*ploughed through the snow; ploughing through the book*). **3** advance violently; get into or consume with vigour (*the*

ploughman

truck ploughed into the barrier; he's ploughing into the pâté. □ **plough back 1** turn (growing grass etc.) into the soil to enrich it. **2** reinvest (profits) in the business that produced them.

ploughman *n.* a person who guides a plough.

ploughshare *n.* the cutting blade of a plough.

plover / **pluv**-uh / *n.* a wading bird: those with facial wattles are called lapwings, and smaller forms are called dotterels.

ploy *n.* a cunning manoeuvre to gain an advantage.

pluck *v.* **1** pick (a flower or fruit); pull out (a hair or feather etc.). **2** strip (a bird) of its feathers. **3** pull at or twitch. **4** sound (the string of a musical instrument) by pulling and then releasing it with the finger(s) or a plectrum. **5** plunder, rob, swindle. •*n.* **1** plucking, a pull. **2** courage, spirit. **3** an animal's heart, liver, and lungs as food.

plucky *adj.* (**pluckier, pluckiest**) showing pluck, brave. □ **pluckily** *adv.*

plug *n.* **1** something fitting into and stopping or filling a hole or cavity. **2** a device with metal pins that fit into a socket to make an electrical connection. **3** *colloq.* a spark plug. **4** *colloq.* a piece of free publicity for an idea, product, etc. **5** a cake of compressed tobacco. •*v.* (**plugged, plugging**) **1** put a plug into, stop with a plug. **2** *colloq.* shoot or hit (a person etc.). **3** *colloq.* advertise (a song, product, policy, etc.) by constant commendation. □ **plug away** (**at**) work steadily (at). **plug in** connect electrically by inserting a plug into a socket. **pull the plug on** (a person, a scheme, etc.) *colloq.* ruin; make ineffective.

plughole *n.* **1** a hole, esp. in a sink or bath, which can be closed by a plug. **2** an electric socket. □ **gone down the plughole** = GONE DOWN THE GURGLER (*see* GURGLER).

plum *n.* **1** a fleshy fruit with sweet pulp and a flattish pointed stone. **2** the tree that bears it. **3** any of several Australian trees or shrubs bearing edible plum-like fruit (e.g. *black plum, Burdekin plum, Davidson plum*). **4** *archaic* a dried grape or raisin used in cooking (*plum pudding*). **5** reddish-purple colour. **6** (usu. used as *adj.*) very good; highly desirable (*a plum job*). □ **have a plum in one's mouth** have an affected (esp. 'pommy') pronunciation. **plum pine** (also **she pine**) an Australian rainforest climber having a small seed at the head of an edible egg-shaped receptacle that looks like a bluish-black plum. **plum sauce** a sweet tangy Chinese sauce made from plums, chillies, vinegar, spices, etc.

plumage / **ploo**-mij / *n.* a bird's feathers.

plumb / plum / *n.* a piece of lead tied to the end of a cord, used for finding the depth of water or testing whether a wall etc. is vertical. •*adv.* **1** exactly (*plumb in the middle*). **2** *colloq.* completely (*plumb stupid*). **3** vertically. •*adj.* vertical. •*v.* **1** measure the depth of (water) with a plumb; determine depth. **2** test (an upright surface) to determine the vertical. **3** reach; experience (an intense feeling) (*plumb the depths of misery*). **4** get to the bottom of (a matter). □ **out of plumb** not vertical. **plumb line** a cord with a plumb attached.

plumber / **plum**-uh / *n.* a person whose job is to fit and repair plumbing.

plumbing / **plum**-ing / *n.* **1** a system of water pipes, cisterns, and drainage pipes in a building. **2** the work of a plumber.

plume / ploom / *n.* **1** a feather, esp. a large one used for ornament. **2** an ornament of feathers or similar material. **3** something resembling this (*a plume of smoke*). •*v.* (of a bird) preen (itself or its feathers). □ **plume oneself** pride oneself, esp. on something trivial.

plumed *adj.* used as a distinguishing epithet in the names of birds (*plumed egret*).

plummet *n.* **1** a plumb or plumb line. **2** a weight attached to a fishing line to keep a float upright.
•*v.* (**plummeted, plummeting**) fall or plunge steeply.

plummy *adj.* **1** full of or like plums. **2** (of the voice) sounding affectedly rich in tone or English ('pommy') in pronunciation.

plump[1] *adj.* having a full rounded shape. •*v.* (often foll. by *up* or *out*) make or become plump (*plumped up the cushion*). □ **plumpness** *n.*

plump[2] *v.* drop or plunge abruptly (*plumped down*). •*adv.* with a sudden or heavy fall. □ **plump for** choose, decide on.

plumy *adj.* **1** plumelike, feathery. **2** adorned with plumes.

plunder *v.* rob (a place or person) forcibly or systematically, steal or embezzle. •*n.* **1** the taking of goods or money in this way. **2** the goods etc. acquired. □ **plunderer** *n.*

plunge *v.* **1** thrust or go forcefully into something. **2** descend suddenly. **3** jump or dive into water. **4** change the circumstances of (a person) suddenly; embark impetuously on a new course (*plunged the world into war*). **5** immerse completely. **6** diminish rapidly (*prices have plunged*). **7** (of a ship) thrust its bows down into the water; pitch. •*n.* **1** a plunging movement; a dive. **2** (also **betting plunge**) a sudden and coordinated series of bets placed on a horse etc. □ **take the plunge** take a bold decisive step.

plunger *n.* **1** the part of a mechanism that works with a plunging or thrusting movement. **2** a rubber cup on a handle for removing blockages by alternate thrusting and suction. **3** a jug for making coffee by separating the grounds from the liquid with a plunging action.

pluperfect / ploo-**per**-fekt / *adj. Grammar* of the tense of a verb used to denote an action completed before some past point of time, e.g. *we had arrived.*

plural / **ploo**-ruhl / *n.* the form of a noun or verb used with reference to more than one person or thing (*the plural of 'child' is 'children'*). •*adj.* **1** of this form. **2** of more than one. □ **plurality** *n.*

pluralise *v.* (also **-ize**) make or become plural.
pluralism *n.* **1** a form of society with many minority groups and cultures; multiculturalism. **2** the holding of more than one office at a time. ◻ **pluralist** *n.* **pluralistic** *adj.*
plurality *n.* **1** the state of being plural. **2** a large number, the greater number, a majority.
plus *prep.* **1** with the addition of (*two plus four equals six*; 2 + 4 = 6). **2** (of temperature) above zero (*plus 2°*). **3** *colloq.* with, having gained, possessing (*arrived plus dog*). • *adj.* **1** (after a number) at least; more than the amount indicated (*we're expecting thirty plus*). **2** (after a grade etc.) slightly better than (*B plus*). **3** above zero, positive. • *n.* **1** = PLUS SIGN. **2** an advantage (*experience will be a plus*). • *conj.* also, furthermore (*they arrived late, plus they wanted a meal*). ◻ **plus fours** knickerbockers worn esp. by golfers. (¶ So named because the length is increased by 4 inches to produce the overhang.) **plus sign** the symbol (+), indicating addition or a positive value.

■ **Usage** The use of *plus* as a conjunction, as in *They arrived late, plus they wanted a meal*, is considered incorrect by some people.

plush *n.* a kind of cloth with long soft nap, used in furnishings. • *adj.* **1** made of plush. **2** plushy.
plushy *adj. colloq.* luxurious. ◻ **plushiness** *n.*
Plutarch / **ploo**-tahk / (Lucius Mestrius Plutarchus) (*c.*46–*c.*120), Greek Platonist philosopher and biographer.
Pluto / **ploo**-toh / **1** *Gk myth.* a title of Hades, lord of the Underworld. **2** the ninth planet of the solar system.
plutocracy / ploo-**tok**-ruh-see / *n.* **1** government by the wealthy. **2** a wealthy élite.
plutocrat / **ploo**-tuh-krat / *n.* a person who is powerful because of his or her wealth. ◻ **plutocratic** *adj.*
plutonic *adj. Geol.* formed as igneous rock by solidification below the earth's surface.
plutonium / ploo-**toh**-nee-uhm / *n.* a chemical element (symbol Pu), a radioactive substance used in nuclear weapons and reactors.
pluvial / **ploo**-vee-uhl / *adj.* of or caused by rain, rainy.
ply[1] *n.* **1** a thickness or layer of wood or cloth etc. **2** a strand in yarn (*3-ply wool*). **3** plywood.
ply[2] *v.* (**plied**, **plying**) **1** use or wield (a tool or weapon). **2** work steadily at (*ply one's trade*). **3** keep offering or supplying (*plied her with questions*). **4** go to and fro regularly (*the boat plies between the two harbours*). **5** (of a taxi driver etc.) look for custom (*ply for hire*).
plywood *n.* strong thin board made by gluing layers with the grain crosswise.
PM *abbr.* **1** prime minister. **2** postmortem.
Pm *symbol* promethium.
p.m. *abbr.* after noon. (¶ From the Latin *post meridiem*.)
PMS *abbr.* premenstrual syndrome.

PMT *abbr.* premenstrual tension.
pneumatic / nyoo-**mat**-ik / *adj.* filled with or operated by compressed air (*pneumatic drills*). ◻ **pneumatically** *adv.*
pneumonia / nyoo-**moh**-nyuh / *n.* inflammation of one or both lungs. ◻ **pneumocystis carinii pneumonia** (**PCP**) a fatal form of pneumonia which esp. affects the immunocompromised (such as people with Aids).
PNG *abbr.* Papua New Guinea.
PO *abbr.* post office.
Po *symbol* polonium.
po *n.* (*pl.* **pos**) *colloq.* a chamber pot.
poach[1] *v.* **1** cook (an egg removed from its shell) in boiling water. **2** cook (fish, fruit, etc.) by simmering in a small amount of liquid.
poach[2] *v.* **1** catch (game or fish) illegally. **2** trespass or encroach on something that belongs to another person; take (another's ideas, staff, etc.). ◻ **poacher** *n.*
pobblebonk *n.* either of two Australian frogs having a loud, single-note call.
pock *n.* (also **pock-mark**) **1** one of the small pus-filled spots that erupt on the skin in chickenpox or smallpox. **2** a scar left by this. ◻ **pock-marked** marked by scars or pits.
pocket *n.* **1** a small baglike part sewn into a garment for holding money or small articles. **2** one's financial resources; what one can afford (*beyond my pocket*). **3** a pouchlike compartment in a suitcase, on a car door, etc. **4** any of the pouches at the edges of a billiard or snooker table, into which balls are driven. **5** an isolated group or area (*small pockets of resistance*). **6** a cavity in the earth containing ore, esp. gold. **7** *Aust. Rules* a side position, as back pocket, forward pocket. • *adj.* **1** of a size or shape suitable for carrying in a pocket (*pocket calculators*). **2** smaller than the usual size (*a pocket dictionary*). • *v.* **1** put into one's pocket. **2** take for oneself (esp. dishonestly). **3** (in billiards and snooker) drive (a ball) into a pocket. **4** submit to (an injury or affront) (*pocketed the insults*). **5** suppress or hide (one's feelings) (*pocketing his pride*). ◻ **in a person's pocket** intimate with him or her; completely under his or her control. **pocket bread** = PITTA[2]. **pocket knife** a penknife. **pocket money** money for small expenses; money allowed regularly to children.
pocketbook *n.* **1** a notebook. **2** a small folding case for money or papers carried in a pocket.
pocketful *n.* (*pl.* **pocketfuls**) the amount that a pocket will hold.
poco *adv. Music* a little; rather (*poco adagio*). (¶ Italian)
pod[1] *n.* a long seed vessel like that of a pea or bean. • *v.* (**podded**, **podding**) **1** bear or form pods. **2** remove (peas etc.) from their pods.
pod[2] *n.* a small herd of whales, seals, etc.
poddy *n. Aust.* **1** a calf old enough to wean and fatten; an unbranded calf. **2** a calf (less frequently a lamb or a foal) which is being handfed. • *adj.*

hand-fed. • *v.* feed (a young animal) by hand. ☐ **poddy-dodge** steal unbranded cattle. **poddy-dodger** a thief of unbranded cattle. **poddy-rear** = PODDY *v.*

poddy mullet *n.* Aust. any of several food fish, esp. the young of the sea mullet. (¶ Probably an alteration of Yagara *budinba* or *bunba*.)

Podgorica / pod-**gaw**-rit-suh / the capital of Montenegro.

podgy *adj.* (**podgier**, **podgiest**) short and fat; chubby.

podiatry / puh-**duy**-uh-tree / *n.* the treatment of the feet and their ailments. ☐ **podiatrist** *n.*

podium / **poh**-dee-uhm / *n.* (*pl.* **podiums** or **podia**) a pedestal or platform.

Poe, Edgar Allan (1809–49), American short-story writer, poet, and critic, famous for his macabre tales.

poem *n.* a literary composition in verse, esp. one expressing deep feeling in an imaginative way.

poesy / **poh**-uh-zee / *n. archaic* poetry.

poet *n.* a writer of poems.

poetaster / poh-uh-**tas**-tuh / *n.* a trivial or inferior poet.

poetic *adj.* of or like poetry; of poets. ☐ **poetic justice** suitable and well-deserved punishment or reward.

poetical *adj.* poetic, written in verse (*poetical works*). ☐ **poetically** *adv.*

Poet Laureate *n.* (in the UK) a poet officially appointed to write poems for State occasions.

poetry *n.* **1** poems; a poet's art or work. **2** a quality that pleases the mind as poetry does (*the poetry of motion*).

po-faced *adj.* solemn-faced; not showing amusement.

pogo *n.* (also **pogo stick**) a stiltlike toy with a spring, used for jumping about on.

pogrom / **pog**-ruhm, -rom / *n.* an organised massacre (orig. of Jews in Russia 1905–06).

pohutukawa / poh-hoo-tuh-**kah**-wuh / *n.* an evergreen tree from New Zealand with brilliant crimson flowers, often cultivated in Australia. Also called *New Zealand Christmas tree*.

poignant / **poi**-nyuhnt / *adj.* **1** arousing sympathy; deeply moving to the feelings; keenly felt (*poignant grief*). **2** sharp or pungent in taste or smell. **3** pleasantly piquant. ☐ **poignantly** *adv.* **poignancy** *n.*

poinsettia / poin-**set**-ee-uh / *n.* a plant with large usu. scarlet petal-like bracts.

point *n.* **1** the tapered or sharp end of something, the tip. **2** a projection, a promontory of land. **3** (in geometry) that which has position but not magnitude, e.g. the intersection of two lines. **4** a dot used as a punctuation mark; a decimal point. **5** a particular place, position, stage, or moment. **6** each of the directions marked on a compass. **7 a** a unit of measurement, value, or scoring; **b** Aust. Rules a behind. **8** a detail; an item being discussed (*we differ on several points*). **9** a distinctive feature (*it has its good points*). **10** the essential thing; the main issue; the important feature of a story or remark (*come to the point*). **11** effectiveness, purpose, value (*there's no point in wasting time*). **12** a fielder in cricket near the batsman on the off side; this position. **13** an electrical socket (*power points*). **14** (**points**) electrical contacts in the distributor of a vehicle. **15** (**points**) the tapering movable rails by which a train is directed from one line to another. **16** the tip of the toes in ballet. • *v.* **1** (usu. foll. by *to* or *at*) direct or aim (a finger, weapon, etc.) (*pointed a gun at her*). **2** (foll. by *at* or *towards*) be directed or aimed to (*a telescope pointed at the stars*). **3** (foll. by *to*) direct attention to; indicate; be evidence of (*it all points to a conspiracy*). ☐ **a case in point** one that is relevant to what has just been said. **point-blank** *adj.* **1** (of a shot) aimed or fired at very close range. **2** (of a remark) direct, straightforward (*a point-blank refusal*). *adv.* directly; bluntly (*refused point-blank*). **point duty** traffic control by a police officer at a road junction. **point of order** a query in a debate as to whether correct procedure is being followed. **point of view** a way of looking at an issue. **point out** indicate; draw attention to. **point the bone** Aust. **1** (in Aboriginal ritual practice) point a bone at a person whose death is willed. **2** (in extended use) jinx (*someone must have pointed the bone at me—I didn't get the job*). **to the point** relevant; relevantly.

pointed *adj.* **1** tapering or sharpened to a point. **2** (of a remark or manner) direct; cutting. ☐ **pointedly** *adv.*

pointer *n.* **1** a thing that points or is used to point to something; an indicator on a dial or scale. **2** *colloq.* a hint or indication.

pointillism / **pwan**-tuh-liz-uhm, **poin**- / *n.* a technique of impressionist painting using tiny dots of pure colour which become blended in the viewer's eye. ☐ **pointillist** *n.* & *adj.*

pointing *n.* **1** Aust. (in Aboriginal ritual practice) the ceremony of pointing the bone at a person whose death is willed. **2** the cement filling the joints of brickwork.

pointless *adj.* having no purpose, point, or meaning. ☐ **pointlessly** *adv.*

poise *v.* **1** balance or be balanced. **2** hold suspended or supported. • *n.* **1** balance, the way something is poised. **2** a dignified and self-assured manner.

poised *adj.* **1** (of a person) having poise; dignified and self-assured. **2** ready for action (*poised to strike*).

poison *n.* **1** a substance that can cause death or injury when absorbed by a living thing. **2** a harmful influence (*the poison of racial prejudice*). **3** (also **poison plant**) Aust. any of several plants poisonous to stock, esp. the *poison pea*. • *v.* **1** give poison to; kill with poison. **2** treat (a weapon) with poison. **3** infect (air, water, etc.) with poison (*rivers poisoned by factory effluents*). **4** corrupt or pervert (*poisoned their minds*). **5** spoil or destroy (a person's pleasure etc.). • *adj. Aust.* (in Aboriginal English) characterising a party in an avoidance relationship (*poison uncle*). ☐ **poison pea** any of several (mainly WA) plants having striking pea-flowers: considered a menace in the wild because their foliage is poisonous to stock. **poison-pen letter** a malicious or libellous anonymous letter. ☐☐ **poisoner** *n.*

poisonous *adj.* **1** containing or having the effect of poison. **2** likely to corrupt people (*a poisonous influence*).

poke[1] *v.* **1** push, prod, or lever with the end of a finger, stick, etc. **2** (usu. foll. by *out* or *up*) thrust or be thrust forward; protrude (*the bone was poking out of his flesh*). **3** produce by poking (*poked a hole in it*). **4** thrust forward, esp. obtrusively (*poked his way into the crowd*). **5** (often foll. by *about* or *around*) potter. **6** (foll. by *into*) pry (*stop poking into my affairs*). **7** *coarse colloq.* have sexual intercourse with. **8** (foll. by *up*) confine in a poky place (*I'm poked up in this tiny flat*). • *n.* **1** a poking movement, a thrust or nudge. **2** *coarse colloq.* an act of sexual intercourse.

poke[2] *n. Brit. dialect* a bag or sack. ☐ **buy a pig in a poke** see PIG.

poker *n.* **1** a metal rod for poking a fire. **2** a card game in which bluff is used as players bet on whose hand of cards has the highest value. ☐ **poker-face** an expression that does not reveal thoughts or feelings. **poker machine** *Aust.* a coin-operated gaming machine which pays according to the combination of symbols appearing on the edges of the wheels spun by the operation of a lever or by pressing a button.

pokie *n.* (also **pokey**) (usu. as **the pokies**) *Aust. colloq.* POKER MACHINE (*I'm off to play the pokies*).

poky *adj.* (**pokier**, **pokiest**) small and cramped (*poky little rooms*). ☐ **pokiness** *n.*

Poland a republic in eastern Europe.

polar *adj.* **1** of or near the North Pole or South Pole. **2** of one of the poles of a magnet. **3** directly opposite in character or tendency. ☐ **polar bear** a white bear living in the Arctic regions. **polar circle** each of the circles parallel to the equator at 23° 27′ from either pole; the Arctic or Antarctic circle.

Polaris *n.* **1** the North Star or pole star. **2** an intermediate-range nuclear missile, fired from a submarine.

polarise *v.* (also **-ize**) **1** confine similar vibrations (of light waves etc.) to a single direction or plane. **2** give polarity to. **3** set or become set at opposite extremes of opinion (*public opinion had polarised*). ☐ **polarisation** *n.*

polarity / poh-**la**-ruh-tee / *n.* **1** the possessing of negative and positive poles. **2** the electrical condition of a body (positive or negative). **3** the state of having two opposite opinions, tendencies, etc.

polaroid *n. trademark* **1** a material that polarises the light passing through it, used in sunglasses to protect the eyes from glare. **2** a camera that prints a photograph as soon as it has been taken. **3** (**polaroids**) sunglasses with polaroid lenses.

Pole *n.* a Polish person.

pole[1] *n.* **1** a long slender rounded piece of wood or metal, esp. one used as a support. **2** = PERCH[1] (sense 3). **3** a wooden shaft fitted to the front of a vehicle and attached to the yokes or collars of draught animals. • *v.* **1** push off or propel (a punt, boat, etc.) with a pole. **2** = POLE-FISH. ☐ **pole-fish** *v.* (also **pole**) fish (esp. for tuna), using a pole, a short line, and a barbless lure. **pole-fishing** *n.* this activity. **pole position 1** the most favourable position on the starting-grid in a motor race. **2** any favourable starting position (*she has the pole position in the race for promotion*). **pole vault** *n.* a vault, or the sport of vaulting, over a high crossbar with the help of a pole held in the hands. **pole-vault** *v.* perform this vault.

pole[2] *n.* **1** (in full **north pole**, **south pole**) either extremity of the earth's or other body's axis; either of two points in the sky about which the stars appear to rotate. **2** each of the two points of a magnet which attract or repel magnetic bodies. **3** the positive or negative terminal of an electric cell or battery. **4** each of two opposed principles. ☐ **be poles apart** differ greatly. **pole star 1** a star in the Little Bear, near the North Pole in the sky. **2** a thing serving as a guide.

■ **Usage** The spelling is *North Pole* and *South Pole* when used as geographical designations.

poleaxe *n.* **1** a battleaxe with a long handle. **2** a butcher's implement for slaughtering cattle. • *v.* **1** strike down with or as if with a poleaxe. **2** (esp. as **poleaxed** *adj.*) *colloq.* dumbfound, overwhelm.

polecat *n.* a small European brownish-black fetid mammal of the weasel family.

polemic / puh-**lem**-ik / *n.* **1** a forceful oral or written controversy or argument; an attack on some belief, opinion, etc. **2** (**polemics**) the art or practice of aggressive disputation. • *adj.* (also **polemical**) involving controversial dispute. ☐ **polemically** *adv.*

polenta / puh-**len**-tuh / *n.* **1** maize flour as used in Italian cookery; cornmeal. **2** a paste or dough made from this flour, which is boiled and then fried or baked. (¶ Italian)

poler *n.* **1** each of the pair of bullocks attached to the pole of a vehicle (and leaving most of the pulling to the others in front). **2** a shirker, a sponger, a person who does not pull his or her weight. **3** a person who hoists tuna fish on board with a pole.

poley *Aust. adj.* hornless; dehorned. • *n.* **1** a dehorned or hornless bullock or cow. **2** a type of saddle which does not have knee-pads.

police *n.* **1** a civil force responsible for the keeping of public order; its members. **2** a force with similar functions (*military police*). • *v.* **1** keep order by means of police; provide with police. **2** keep in order, administer, control (*the problem of policing the new law*). ☐ **police officer** a policeman or policewoman. **police State** a country (usu. a totalitarian State) controlled by political police. **police station** the office of a local police force.

policeman *n.* (*feminine* **policewoman**) a member of a police force. ☐ **policeman bird** *Aust.* = JABIRU. **policeman fly** *Aust.* any of many small wasps which swoop down on flies and capture them as food for the wasp larvae.

policy[1] *n.* **1** the plan of action adopted by a person or organisation. **2** wisdom, prudence.

■ Usage Do not confuse with *polity*.

policy[2] *n.* a contract of insurance; the document containing this.

policyholder *n.* a person or body holding an insurance policy.

polio / **poh**-lee-oh / *n.* poliomyelitis.

poliomyelitis / poh-lee-oh-muy-uh-**luy**-tuhs / *n.* an infectious disease caused by a virus, producing temporary or permanent paralysis.

Polish / **poh**-lish / *adj.* of Poland or its people or language. • *n.* the language of Poland.

polish / **pol**-ish / *v.* **1** make or become smooth and glossy by rubbing. **2** refine or improve by correcting or putting finishing touches. • *n.* **1** a substance used for polishing. **2** smoothness and glossiness. **3** elegance and refinement. ☐ **polish off** finish off. **polish up** (often foll. by *on*) revise or improve (a skill etc.) (*need to polish up on my Japanese*).

polished *adj.* elegant, refined, perfected (*polished manners; a polished performance*).

Politburo / **pol**-it-byoo-roh / *n.* the principal policy-making committee of a Communist Party, esp. in the former USSR.

polite *adj.* **1** having good manners, socially correct. **2** refined (*polite society*). ☐ **politely** *adv.* **politeness** *n.*

politic / **pol**-uh-tik / *adj.* showing good judgment, prudent. • *v.* (**politicked**, **politicking**) engage in politics. ☐ **the body politic** the State or similar organised system.

political *adj.* **1** of or engaged in politics. **2** of the way a country is governed (*its political system*). **3** concerned with power, policy, status, etc. rather than with principle (*a political decision*). ☐ **political asylum** refuge in foreign territory for people fleeing from political persecution. **political correctness** avoidance of expressions or actions that may be considered discriminatory or pejorative to any minority or disadvantaged group. **politically correct** exhibiting political correctness (*is it politically correct to talk of God the 'Father'?*). **political prisoner** a person imprisoned for a political offence. ☐☐ **politically** *adv.*

politician *n.* an MP or other political representative.

politicise *v.* (also **-ize**) **1** engage in or talk politics. **2** give a political character to. ☐ **politicisation** *n.*

politics *n.* (treated as *sing.* or *pl.*) **1** the science and art of governing a country. **2** political affairs or life. **3** manoeuvring for power etc. within a group (*office politics*). **4** (usu. treated as *pl.*) political principles or affairs or tactics.

polity / **pol**-uh-tee / *n.* **1** the form or process of civil government. **2** an organised society, a State.

■ Usage Do not confuse with *policy*.

polka *n.* a lively dance for couples, of Bohemian origin; the music for this. ☐ **polka dots** round dots evenly spaced to form a pattern on fabric.

poll / pohl / *n.* **1** voting at an election; the counting of votes; the number of votes recorded (*a heavy poll*). **2** the place where voting is held. **3** (in full (**public**) **opinion poll**) an estimate of public opinion made by questioning a representative sample of people. **4** *archaic* the head. • *v.* **1** vote at an election. **2** (of a candidate) receive as votes. **3** cut off the top of (a tree), esp. make a pollard of. **4** (esp. as **polled** *adj.*) cut the horns off (cattle). ☐ **polling booth** a compartment in which a voter stands to mark the ballot-paper. **polling station** a building, often a school, used for voting at an election. **poll tax** a tax on each (or on each adult) person.

pollard / **pol**-uhd / *n.* **1** a tree that is polled so as to produce a close head of young branches. **2** an animal that has cast or lost its horns; an ox or sheep or goat of a hornless breed. • *v.* make (a tree) into a pollard.

pollen *n.* a fine dustlike grains discharged from the male part (anther) of a flower, containing the fertilising element.

pollie alternative spelling of POLLY.

pollinate *v.* shed pollen on; fertilise (a stigma) with pollen. ☐ **pollination** *n.* **pollinator** *n.*

Pollock, Jackson (1912–56), American abstract expressionist painter.

pollster *n.* a person conducting a public opinion poll.

pollutant *n.* a substance causing pollution.

pollute *v.* **1** contaminate (the environment), esp. by adding harmful or offensive substances. **2** corrupt (*polluting the mind*). ☐ **polluter** *n.* **pollution** *n.*

Pollux **1** *Gk myth.* the immortal twin brother of Castor (who was mortal), sons of Zeus and Leda. **2** a bright star in the constellation Gemini.

polly *n.* (also **pollie**) *Aust. colloq.* a politician.

polo *n.* a game like hockey, played by teams on horseback with long-handled mallets. ☐ **poloneck** a high turned-over collar on a jumper.

polocrosse / **poh**-loh-kros / *n.* a game played on horseback between two teams of six, in which players pass and catch a ball using netted sticks.

polonaise / pol-uh-**nayz** / *n.* a stately dance of Polish origin; music for this or in this style.
polonium / puh-**loh**-nee-uhm / *n.* a radioactive metallic element (symbol Po).
polony / puh-**loh**-nee / *n.* a sausage of partly cooked pork etc.
Pol Pot (1925–98), Cambodian Communist leader, prime minister 1976–79, leader of the Khmer Rouge guerrilla forces.
poltergeist / **pol**-tuh-guyst / *n.* a ghost or spirit that throws things about noisily.
poltroon / pol-**troon** / *n. archaic* a coward.
Polwarth / **pol**-wuhth / *n.* a breed of Australian sheep; an animal of this breed.
poly- *comb. form* **1** many (as in *polyhedron*). **2** (in names of plastics) polymerised.
polyandry / **pol**-ee-an-dree / *n.* polygamy in which a woman has more than one husband at a time. ◻ **polyandrous** *adj.*
polyanthus *n.* (*pl.* **polyanthuses**) a flowering plant cultivated from hybridised primulas.
polychromatic / pol-ee-kroh-**mat**-ik / *adj.* **1** many-coloured. **2** (of radiation) consisting of more than one wavelength.
polychrome / **pol**-ee-krohm / *adj.* painted, printed, or decorated in many colours.
polyester *n.* a polymerised substance, esp. as a synthetic resin or fibre.
polygamy / puh-**lig**-uh-mee / *n.* the system of having more than one wife or (less usu.) husband at a time. ◻ **polygamous** *adj.* **polygamist** *n.*
polyglot / **pol**-ee-glot / *adj.* knowing, using, or written in several languages. • *n.* a person who knows several languages.
polygon / **pol**-ee-gon / *n.* a geometric figure with many (usu. five or more) sides. ◻ **polygonal** / puh-**lig**-uh-nuhl / *adj.*
polygraph / **pol**-ee-grahf, -graf / *n.* a machine for reading the pulse rate and other variable physical features, used as a lie detector.
polygyny / puh-**lij**-uh-nee / *n.* polygamy in which a man has more than one wife at a time.
polyhedron / pol-ee-**hee**-druhn / *n.* (*pl.* **polyhedra**) a solid figure with many (usu. seven or more) faces. ◻ **polyhedral** *adj.*
polymath / **pol**-ee-math / *n.* a person with deep knowledge of many subjects.
polymer / **pol**-uh-muh / *n.* a compound of one or more large molecules formed from repeated units of smaller molecules.
polymerise / **pol**-uh-muh-ruyz / *v.* (also **-ize**) combine or become combined into a polymer. ◻ **polymerisation** *n.*
polymorphous *adj.* (also **polymorphic**) passing through various forms in successive stages of development.
Polynesia / pol-uh-**nee**-zhuh / the islands of the central and western Pacific Ocean, including New Zealand, Hawaii, and Samoa. ◻ **Polynesian** *adj.* & *n.*

polynomial / pol-uh-**noh**-mee-uhl / *adj.* (of an algebraic expression) consisting of three or more terms. • *n.* a polynomial expression.
polyp / **pol**-uhp / *n.* **1** a simple organism with a tube-shaped body, e.g. one of the organisms of which coral is composed. **2** a small growth on a mucous membrane, e.g. in the nose.
polyphony / puh-**lif**-uh-nee / *n.* contrapuntal music. ◻ **polyphonic** / pol-uh-**fon**-ik / *adj.*
polypropylene *n.* (also **polypropene**) any polymer of propylene, including thermoplastic materials used for films, fibres, or moulding materials.
polystyrene / pol-ee-**stuy**-reen / *n.* a plastic, a polymer of styrene, used for packaging and insulating.
polysyllabic / pol-ee-suh-**lab**-ik / *adj.* having many syllables (*polysyllabic words*).
polytechnic *n.* an institution of higher education offering courses in many (esp. vocational) subjects at degree level or below.
polytheism / **pol**-ee-thee-iz-uhm / *n.* belief in or worship of more than one god. ◻ **polytheist** *n.* **polytheistic** *adj.*
polythene *n.* a tough light plastic.
polyunsaturated *adj.* (of a fat or oil) having a chemical structure capable of further reaction and (unlike animal and dairy fats) not thought to contribute to the formation of cholesterol in the blood.
polyurethane / pol-ee-**yoo**-ruh-thayn / *n.* a synthetic resin or plastic used esp. in paints or foam.
polyvinyl / pol-ee-**vuy**-nuhl / *adj.* made from polymerised vinyl. ◻ **polyvinyl chloride** a plastic used for electrical insulation and as fabric (*abbr.* **PVC**).
pom *n. Aust.* = POMMY. ◻ **the poms** the British, esp. the English.
pomade / puh-**mahd**, -**mayd** / *n.* a scented dressing for the hair and the skin of the head.
pomander / puh-**man**-duh / *n.* a ball of sweet-smelling substances or a round container for this.
pome *n.* a firm-fleshed fruit in which the carpels from the central core enclose the seeds, e.g. the apple, pear, and quince.
pomegranate / **pom**-uh-gran-uht, **pom**-ee- / *n.* **1** a tropical fruit with tough rind, reddish pulp, and many seeds. **2** the tree that produces it. **3** (also **pommygranate**, **pommygrant**) *Aust. hist.* Australian term for a British immigrant to Australia (now replaced by POM and POMMY).
pomelo / **pom**-uh-loh / *n.* a citrus fruit resembling a grapefruit.
pommel / **pum**-uhl, **pom**- / *n.* **1** a knob on the handle of a sword. **2** an upward projection at the front of a saddle. • *v.* (**pommelled**, **pommelling**) = PUMMEL.
pommified *adj. Aust. derog.* **1** (of an Australian) affecting an English manner, esp. in speech. **2**

pommy characterised or influenced by an English model (*pommified behaviour*).

pommy (also **pommie**) *Aust. colloq. n.* **1** a British (esp. English) person, esp. a recent immigrant to Australia. **2** an inhabitant of the British Isles (esp. of England). • *adj.* of or pertaining to a pommy; British; English. (¶ Probably an abbreviation of POMEGRANATE rhyming slang for *immigrant*.)

Pommyland *n. Aust. colloq.* Britain, esp. England.

pomp *n.* **1** stately and splendid display. **2** specious glory, vainglory.

Pompeii / pom-**pay**-ee / an ancient town SE of Naples, buried in volcanic ash from the eruption of Vesuvius in AD 69.

pompom *n.* (also **pompon**) **1** a decorative tuft or ball. **2** a form of flower with small tightly-clustered petals.

pompous *adj.* **1** full of ostentatious dignity and self-importance. **2** (of language) pretentious, pommified. ☐ **pompously** *adv.* **pomposity** / pom-**pos**-uh-tee / *n.*

ponce *n.* **1** a man who lives off a prostitute's earnings, a pimp. **2** *offens.* a homosexual or effeminate man. •*v.* act as a ponce. ☐ **poncy** *adj.*

poncho *n.* (*pl.* **ponchos**) a blanket-like piece of cloth with a slit in the centre for the head, worn as a cloak.

pond *n.* a small area of still water formed naturally or artificially.

ponder *v.* **1** be deep in thought. **2** think something over thoroughly.

ponderable *adj.* having an appreciable weight or significance.

ponderous *adj.* **1** heavy, unwieldy. **2** laborious in style. ☐ **ponderously** *adv.*

pong *colloq. n.* a stink. •*v.* stink. ☐ **pongy** *adj.*

poniard / **pon**-yuhd, -yahd / *n. archaic* a dagger.

pontiff *n.* (in full **supreme** or **sovereign pontiff**) the pope.

pontifical / pon-**tif**-uh-kuhl / *adj.* papal. ☐ **pontifically** *adv.*

Pontifical Mass high Mass celebrated by a bishop or one higher in rank.

pontificate *v.* / pon-**tif**-uh-kayt / **1 a** play the pontiff; pretend to be infallible. **b** be pompously dogmatic. **2** officiate as bishop, esp. at mass. •*n.* / pon-**tif**-uh-kuht / the office of pope or bishop; the period of this. ☐ **pontificator** *n.*

pontoon *n.* **1** a flat-bottomed boat. **2** each of a number of floats used to support a temporary bridge. **3** a card game in which players try to acquire cards with face value totalling 21.

pony *n.* **1** a horse of any small breed. **2** a small glass for beer; the beer in this. ☐ **pony-tail** hair drawn back and tied at the back of the head so that it hangs down.

poo *colloq. n.* faeces. •*v.* (**pooed**, **pooing**) **1** defecate. **2** soil with faeces (*the baby has pooed its nappy*).

pooch *n. colloq.* a dog.

poodle *n.* a dog with a curly coat often clipped in a pattern.

poof / puuf / *n., adj., & v.* = POOFTER.

poofter / **puuf**-tuh / *colloq. offens. n.* **1** a male homosexual. **2** a man whose manner or behaviour does not conform with that conventionally regarded as masculine; anyone not an OCKER. **3** a general term of abuse for any man. • *adj.* pertaining to a poofter (however defined). • *v.* behave in a poofter manner (however defined). ☐ **poofter basher** *Aust.* a male who victimises homosexuals, usu. operating as one of a gang, and usu. inflicting physical violence on the victims. **poofter bashing** *Aust.* such activity.

poofy / **puuf**-ee / *adj. colloq.* unmanly; not macho; arty.

pooh *interj.* an exclamation of impatience, contempt, or disgust at a bad smell. •*n.* = POO. ☐ **pooh-pooh** *v.* dismiss (a suggestion) scornfully; ridicule.

pool[1] *n.* **1** a small area of still water. **2** a shallow patch of liquid; a puddle. **3** a swimming pool. **4** a deep place in a river.

pool[2] *n.* **1** a common fund, e.g. that containing the total stakes in a gambling venture. **2** a common supply of vehicles, commodities, or services for sharing among a number of people (*a typing pool*). **3** an arrangement between competing parties to fix prices and share business. **4** a game resembling snooker. •*v.* **1** put into a common fund (*pooled their resources*). **2** share in common. **3** *Aust. colloq.* involve (a person) in a scheme etc. often by deception; implicate (a person); inform on (a person). ☐ **the pools** football pools.

poon[1] *v.* (foll. by *up*) *Aust.* dress to impress, usu. with sexual success in view. ☐ **pooned up** *adj.*

poon[2] *n. Aust. colloq.* a simpleton, a fool.

poonce / puuns / *Aust. colloq. offens. n.* **1** a man who is not, or is thought not to be, macho or aggressively masculine (*in some circles, if you're not an ocker, you must be a poonce*). **2** a homosexual male. **3** a general term of abuse for any man. •*v.* (**pooncing**, **poonced**) (often foll. by *around*) act or behave like a poonce. ☐ **pooncy** *adj.*

poop[1] / poop / *n.* **1** the stern of a ship. **2** a raised deck at the stern.

poop[2] / poop / *colloq. n.* **1** faeces. **2** an act of defecation or breaking wind. •*v.* **1** defecate; break wind. **2** (esp. as **pooped** *adj.*) exhaust; tire out.

poor *adj.* **1** having little money or means. **2** deficient in something (*poor in minerals; poor in judgment*). **3** scanty, inadequate, less good than is expected (*a poor crop; he is a poor driver*). **4** deserving pity or sympathy, unfortunate (*you poor thing!*). ☐ **poorness** *n.*

Poor Clare *n.* a member of an order of Franciscan nuns founded by St Clare of Assisi c.1212.

poorly *adv.* in a poor way, badly. •*adj.* unwell (*feeling poorly*).

POP *abbr. Computing* **1** point of presence, denoting equipment that acts as access to the Internet. **2** a post office protocol, denoting the way email software obtains mail from a mail server.

pop *n.* **1** a small sharp explosive sound. **2** *colloq.* an individual item (*bought these ducks at a dollar a pop*). **3** a fizzy non-alcoholic drink. • *v.* (**popped, popping**) **1** make or cause to make a pop. **2** put, come, or go quickly or suddenly (*pop it in the oven; popped out to the shop; pop over for a quick visit*). **3** *colloq.* swallow or inject as a drug. **4** *colloq.* pawn. ❑ **pop-eyed** with bulging eyes; wide-eyed (with surprise etc.). **pop-up 1** involving parts that come upwards automatically (*pop-up toaster*). **2** *Computing* (of a menu) able to be superimposed on the screen being worked on and suppressed (or called up) rapidly.

pop² *adj.* in a popular modern style. • *n.* pop music. ❑ **pop art** art that uses themes drawn from popular culture. **pop culture** commercial culture based on popular taste. **pop music** highly successful commercial music (e.g. rock music) appealing particularly to younger people.

popcorn *n.* kernels of maize heated so that they burst to form fluffy balls.

pope *n.* (as title **Pope**) the bishop of Rome, head of the Catholic Church (*the pope; Pope John XXIII; we have a new pope*).

popinjay *n.* a fop; a conceited person.

popish *adj. offens.* of Catholicism or the papal system.

poplar *n.* a tall slender tree, often with leaves that quiver easily. ❑ **poplar gum** a partly deciduous eucalypt of northern Australia.

poplin *n.* a plain woven fabric usu. of cotton.

poppadam alternative spelling of PAPPADAM.

poppet *n. colloq.* a term of endearment for a small child.

popping crease *n.* a line marking the limit of the batsman's position in cricket.

poppy *n.* a plant with large esp. scarlet flowers on tall stems.

poppycock *n. colloq.* nonsense.

Poppy Day *n.* Remembrance Day, on which artificial poppies are worn.

populace / **pop**-yuh-luhs / *n.* the general public.

popular *adj.* **1** liked or enjoyed by many people. **2** of or for the general public. **3** (of a belief etc.) held by many people (*popular superstitions*). **4** adapted to the understanding, taste, etc. of the general public (*popular science; the popular press*). ❑ **popular front** a political party or coalition combining left-wing or progressive groups. ❑ **popularly** *adv.* **popularity** *n.*

popularise *v.* (also **-ize**) **1** make generally liked. **2** present (a subject) so that it can be understood by ordinary people. ❑ **popularisation** *n.*

populate *v.* supply with inhabitants (e.g. people, plants, animals); form the population of.

population *n.* **1** the inhabitants of a place, country, etc.; any specified group within this (*the Greek population of Melbourne*). **2** the total number of these or of any group of living things (*a population of 2 million; the total penguin population*). **3** the act or process of supplying with inhabitants (*pressing ahead with the re-population of forest areas*). ❑ **population explosion** a sudden large increase of population.

populist *n.* a person who claims to support the interests of ordinary people.

populous *adj.* thickly populated.

porcelain / **paw**-suh-luhn / *n.* **1** a hard fine translucent ceramic. **2** objects made of this.

porch *n.* a covered entrance to a building.

porcine / **paw**-suyn / *adj.* of or like a pig.

porcupine *n.* **1** a rodent (of Europe etc.) with a body and tail covered with erectile spines. **2** *Aust.* = ECHIDNA. **3** *Aust.* = PORCUPINE GRASS. **4** (as *adj.*) denoting any of various animals or other organisms with spines. ❑ **porcupine grass** (also **porcupine**) *Aust.* = SPINIFEX.

pore *n.* one of the tiny openings on an animal's skin or on a leaf, through which moisture may pass (e.g. as sweat). ❑ **pore over** study (a thing) with close attention; think intently about (a problem etc.).

pork *n.* unsalted pig flesh as food. ❑ **pork barrel** *n.* government funds allocated so as to derive political benefit, esp. at election time. *v.* (**pork barrelled, pork barrelling**) (of a government) allocate funds to (a particular region, electorate, etc.) in the hope of obtaining votes.

porky *adj.* **1** *colloq.* fat. **2** of or like pork.

porn *n. colloq.* pornographic books, videos, etc.; pornography.

porno *colloq. n.* **1** pornography. **2** a person who enjoys pornography. • *adj.* pornographic.

pornographer / paw-**nog**-ruh-fuh / *n.* a person who writes pornographic literature, makes pornographic videos etc., or sells pornography.

pornography / paw-**nog**-ruh-fee / *n.* the portrayal of explicit sexual activity in literature, films, etc., intended to stimulate erotic feelings; the books, magazines, videos, etc. containing this. ❑ **pornographic** *adj.*

porous / **paw**-ruhs / *adj.* **1** containing pores. **2** letting through fluid or air. ❑ **porosity** / paw-**ros**-uh-tee / *n.*

porphyry / **paw**-fuh-ree / *n.* a rock containing crystals of minerals. ❑ **porphyritic** *adj.*

porpoise / **paw**-puhs / *n.* a sea mammal resembling a dolphin, with a blunt rounded snout. • *v.* move through the water like a porpoise, alternately rising above it and submerging.

porridge *n.* a food made by boiling oatmeal or other cereal to a thick paste in water or milk.

port¹ *n.* **1** a harbour. **2** a town with a harbour, esp. one where goods are imported or exported.

port² *n.* **1** an opening in a ship's side for entrance, loading, etc. **2** a porthole. **3** a socket or aperture in an electronic circuit, esp. in a computer network, where connections can be made with peripheral equipment.

port³ *n.* the left-hand side (when facing forward) of a ship or aircraft. •*v.* turn (the helm) to port.

port⁴ *n.* a sweet, usu. dark red, fortified wine.

port⁵ *n. colloq.* (esp. in Qld) **1** a suitcase, travelling bag, or school satchel. **2** (**ports**) baggage. **3** a shopping bag, sugar bag, etc.

portable *adj.* **1** able to be carried or shifted (*a portable computer*). **2** (of rights, benefits, etc.) able to be transferred or adapted (esp. with a change in job etc.) (*portable superannuation*). **3** = MACHINE-INDEPENDENT (*see* MACHINE). •*n.* a portable building, typewriter, television set, etc. ◻ **portability** *n.*

portage *n.* the carrying of a boat, goods, etc. overland between two navigable waters.

portal *n.* an imposing doorway or gateway.

Port Arthur an inlet in south-eastern Tas. and the site of a notoriously cruel penal settlement for male convicts from 1830 to 1877, now part of the National Estate. In 1996 a lone gunman killed 37 people here.

Port-au-Prince / pawt-oh-**prins**, -**prans** / the capital of Haiti.

portcullis *n.* a strong heavy vertical grating that can be lowered to block the gateway to a fortress.

portend / paw-**tend** / *v.* foreshadow; be an omen of.

portent / **paw**-tent / *n.* an omen, a significant sign of something to come.

portentous / paw-**ten**-tuhs / *adj.* ominous, being a sign of some extraordinary (usu. terrible) event.

Porter¹, Cole (1891–1964), American composer and songwriter.

Porter², Hal (1911–84), AM, Australian writer, best known for his autobiographical *The Watcher on the Cast-Iron Balcony*.

Porter³, Peter (Neville Frederick) (1929–), AM, Australian poet, now living in England.

porter *n.* **1** a gatekeeper or doorman of a large building. **2** a person employed to carry luggage or other goods. **3** a dark brown bitter beer brewed from charred or browned malt (apparently originally made esp. for porters).

porterage *n.* the services of a porter; the charge for this.

portfolio *n.* (*pl.* **portfolios**) **1 a** a case for holding loose sheets of paper or drawings; **b** samples of an artist's work. **2** a set of investments held by one investor. **3** the position of a minister of state or member of a cabinet.

porthole *n.* a window-like structure in the side of a ship or aircraft.

portico / **paw**-tuh-koh / *n.* (*pl.* **porticoes** or **porticos**) a structure consisting of a roof supported on columns, usu. forming a porch to a building.

portion *n.* **1** a part or share of something. **2** the amount of food allotted to one person. **3** one's destiny or lot. •*v.* divide up and distribute in portions (*portion it out*).

Port Jackson the port of Sydney including Sydney Harbour, Middle Harbour, and North Harbour. ◻ **Port Jackson fig** a shrub to large tree having shiny leaves rusty on the underside and small fruits; often cultivated as an indoor plant. **Port Jackson pine** a tall, attractive, cypress pine tree of southern Australia, growing in a slender column and having an extremely formal appearance. **Port Jackson shark** a small, harmless, primitive shark of southern Australia which feeds on shellfish.

Portland cement cement made from chalk and clay.

Port Lincoln a city in SA and the principal port of the Eyre Peninsula. ◻ **Port Lincoln parrot** = TWENTY EIGHT.

Port Louis / **loo**-uhs, **loo**-ee / the capital of Mauritius.

portly *adj.* (**portlier**, **portliest**) stout and dignified. ◻ **portliness** *n.*

portmanteau / pawt-**man**-toh / *n.* (*pl.* **portmanteaux** or **portmanteaus**) a trunk for clothes that opens into two equal parts. ◻ **portmanteau word** a word combining the sounds and meanings of two others, e.g. *motel* (motor + hotel), *brunch* (breakfast + lunch).

Port Moresby the capital of Papua New Guinea.

Port of Spain the capital of Trinidad and Tobago.

Porto Novo / **noh**-voh / the capital of Benin.

Port Phillip *hist.* the name given to that part of the Colony of New South Wales which in 1851 became the Colony of Victoria. ◻ **Port Phillip Bay** the large inlet on the south coast of Vic., near which the city of Melbourne now stands.

portrait *n.* **1** a picture of a person or animal. **2** a description in words. ◻ **portraitist** *n.*

portraiture *n.* **1** making portraits. **2** a portrait.

portray / paw-**tray** / *v.* **1** make a picture of. **2** describe in words or represent in a play etc. (*she is portrayed as a pathetic character*). ◻ **portrayal** *n.*

Portugal a republic in SW Europe.

Portuguese *adj.* of Portugal or its people or language. •*n.* **1** (*pl.* **Portuguese**) a native of Portugal. **2** the language of Portugal. ◻ **Portuguese man-of-war** a dangerous jellyfish with a large crest and tentacles that have a poisonous sting. Also called *bluebottle*.

portulaca / paw-chuh-**lak**-uh / *n.* any of several plants of the genus of the same name, having thick, succulent leaves and brightly coloured flowers (*see* MUNYEROO).

pose *v.* **1** take up a position for a portrait or photograph etc. **2** take a particular attitude for effect. **3** (foll. by *as*) pretend to be (*posed as an* *expert*). **4** put forward; present (*pose a question*). • *n.* **1** an attitude in which a person is posed. **2** an affectation, a pretence.

Poseidon / puh-**suy**-duhn / *Gk myth.* the god of earthquakes and the sea.

poser *n.* **1** = POSEUR. **2** a puzzling question or problem.

poseur / poh-**zer** / *n.* a person who behaves affectedly.

posh *colloq. adj.* **1** smart, stylish; luxurious and expensive. **2** superior, supposedly upper-class. • *adv.* in a supposedly upper-class way (*talk posh*). ☐ **poshly** *adv.* **poshness** *n.*

posit / **poz**-uht / *v.* assume as a fact, postulate.

position *n.* **1** the place occupied by a person or thing. **2** the proper place for something (*in or out of position*). **3** an advantageous location (*manoeuvring for position*). **4** the way in which a thing or its parts are placed or arranged. **5** a situation in relation to others (*this puts me in a difficult position*). **6** a point of view (*what is their position on French nuclear testing?*). **7** rank or status; social standing. **8** paid employment, a job. • *v.* place in a certain position.

positive *adj.* **1** explicit; definite, with no doubt (*we have positive proof*). **2** holding an opinion confidently. **3** *colloq.* clear, out-and-out (*it's a positive miracle*). **4** constructive and helpful (*some positive suggestions*). **5** indicating the presence of qualities or features tested for (*the result of the test for Aids was positive*). **6** (of a number) greater than zero. **7** containing or producing the kind of electrical charge produced by rubbing glass with silk; lacking electrons. **8** (of a photograph) having the lights and shades or colours as in the actual scene photographed, not as in a negative. **9** *Grammar* (of an adjective or adverb) in the primary form (e.g. *big*) as distinct from the comparative (*bigger*) or superlative (*biggest*). • *n.* a positive quality, quantity, photograph, etc. ☐ **positive discrimination** the policy of deliberately favouring members of an under-privileged or disadvantaged group. **positive pole** the north-seeking pole of a magnet. **positive sign** the sign (+). ☐☐ **positively** *adv.* **positiveness** *n.*

positivism *n.* a philosophical system recognising only facts and observable phenomena. ☐ **positivist** *n.* & *adj.*

positron / **poz**-uh-tron / *n. Physics* an elementary particle with the mass of an electron and a charge the same as an electron's but positive.

posse / **pos**-ee / *n.* **1** a group of law enforcers; a strong force or company. **2** *colloq.* a gang of youths.

possess *v.* **1** have or own. **2** occupy or dominate the mind of (*he's possessed by a devil*). ☐ **be possessed of** own, have. ☐☐ **possessor** *n.*

possession *n.* **1** possessing; being possessed. **2** a thing possessed. ☐ **take possession of** become the owner of; take.

possessive *adj.* **1** wanting to retain what one possesses; reluctant to share. **2** of or indicating possession (*the possessive form of a word*), e.g. *John's*, *the baker's*. • *n.* (in full **possessive case**) a grammatical case of nouns and pronouns expressing possession. ☐ **possessive pronoun** see PRONOUN. ☐☐ **possessively** *adv.* **possessiveness** *n.*

possibility *n.* **1** the fact or condition of being possible. **2** something that may exist or happen (*thunder is a possibility today*). **3** the capability of being used or of producing good results (*the plan has distinct possibilities*).

possible *adj.* capable of existing, happening, or of being done or used. • *n.* a candidate etc. who may be successful (*he's a possible for the team*).

possibly *adv.* **1** in accordance with possibility (*can't possibly do it*). **2** perhaps.

possie / **poz**-ee / *n.* (also **possy**) *Aust. colloq.* a position of supposed advantage to the occupant (*secured a good possie along the route of the procession; has a possy in the bank with little work and decent pay*).

possum *n.* **1** any of many chiefly herbivorous, long-tailed, tree-dwelling, mainly Australian marsupials, some of which are gliding animals (e.g. *brush-tailed possum, flying possum*). **2** *Aust.* a mildly scornful term for a person. **3** *Aust.* an affectionate mode of address. ☐ **play possum** pretend to be asleep or unconscious when threatened etc.; feign ignorance. **possum banksia** a small WA banksia with very large, woolly, browny-grey flowers which remain woolly even after they die and resemble possums on the bush. **stir the possum** *Aust.* excite interest or controversy; liven things up.

post[1] *n.* **1** a piece of timber or metal set upright and used as a support or marker. **2** the starting post or winning post in a race. • *v.* **1** put up (a notice). **2** announce by means of a notice (*the ship was posted as missing*). ☐ **post and rail fence** esp. *Aust.* a wooden fence consisting of two or more horizontal rails morticed into upright posts.

post[2] *n.* **1** the place where a soldier is on duty (*the sentries are at their posts*). **2** a place occupied by soldiers; the soldiers occupying this. **3** a position of paid employment (*got a post with a textile firm*). • *v.* **1** place or station (*we posted sentries*). **2** appoint to a post or command.

post[3] *n.* **1** the official conveyance of letters and parcels (*sent by post*). **2** the letters etc. conveyed; a single collection or delivery of these. **3** the place where letters etc. are collected, dealt with: a postbox, a post office. • *v.* **1** put (a letter etc.) in the post. **2** enter in an official ledger. ☐ **keep a person posted** keep him or her informed. **post office 1** a building where postal business is carried on. **2** the organisation responsible for postal services. **post office box** a numbered place in a post office where letters are kept until called for.

post[4] *n.* (in some Australian universities) a supplementary examination, chiefly for candidates who missed the first through illness.

post- *comb. form* after in time or order.

postage *n.* the charge for sending something by post. □ **postage stamp** a small adhesive stamp for sticking on things to be posted, showing the amount paid.

postal *adj.* **1** of the post. **2** by post (*a postal vote*). □ **postal order** a money order issued by the Post Office. **postal vote** *Aust.* a vote cast in an election before polling day and sent to the returning officer by post within a specified period.

postbox *n.* a public box where letters are posted.

postcard *n.* a card for sending by post without an envelope.

postcode *n.* a group of figures included in a postal address to assist sorting.

post-coital *adj.* occurring after sexual intercourse. □ **post-coital triste** a feeling of let-down etc. that can occur after sexual intercourse.

post-colonial *adj.* occurring or existing after the end of colonial rule.

postdate *v.* **1** put a date on (a document or cheque) that is later than the actual one. **2** occur later than.

poster *n.* **1** a large sheet of paper announcing or advertising something, for display in a public place. **2** *Aust. Rules* a kick for goal which hits one of the goal posts and hence scores only a point.

poste restante / pohst res-**tahnt** / *n.* a department in a post office where letters are kept until called for. (¶ French, = letters remaining.)

posterior *adj.* **1** later; coming after in series, order, or time. **2** situated behind or at the back. • *n.* the buttocks.

posterity / pos-**te**-ruh-tee / *n.* **1** future generations. **2** a person's descendants.

postern / **pos**-tuhn, **poh**-stuhn / *n.* a back or side entrance.

postgraduate *adj.* (of studies) carried on after taking a first degree. • *n.* a student engaged on such studies.

post-haste *adv.* with great speed or haste.

posthumous / **pos**-chuh-muhs, -tyoo- / *adj.* **1** happening or awarded after a person's death. **2** published after the author's death (*a posthumous novel*). **3** (of a child) born after its father's death. □ **posthumously** *adv.*

postie *n. colloq.* a postman or postwoman.

postilion / pos-**til**-yuhn / *n.* (also **postillion**) a rider on a near-side horse drawing a coach when there is no coach-driver.

post-Impressionism *n.* a movement in French painting in the late 19th century seeking to express the individual artist's conception of the objects represented. □ **post-Impressionist** *n.* & *adj.*

posting *n.* **1 a** an appointment to a job, esp. one abroad or in the armed services. **b** the location of such an appointment. **2** *Computing* a message entered into a network communications system.

postman *n.* (*feminine* **postwoman**) a person employed to deliver and collect letters and parcels.

postmark *n.* an official mark on mail giving the place and date of posting. • *v.* mark with a postmark.

postmaster *n.* (*feminine* **postmistress**) an official in charge of a post office.

post-modern *adj.* (in the arts etc.) of the movement reacting against modernism, esp. by drawing attention to former conventions. □ **post-modernism** *n.* **post-modernist** *n.* & *adj.*

post-mortem *adv.* & *adj.* after death. • *n.* **1** an examination made after death to determine its cause. **2** *colloq.* a detailed discussion of something that is over (as a game, an election, etc.).

postnatal *adj.* existing or occurring after birth or childbirth.

postpone *v.* rearrange (an event) so that it takes place at a later time (*postpone the meeting*). □ **postponement** *n.*

postprandial *adj. formal* or *humorous* taking place after lunch or after dinner.

postscript *n.* **1** a note added at the end of a letter, after the signature, and introduced by 'PS'. **2** an afterthought, a sequel. **3** (**Postscript**) *trademark* a programming language used esp. in word processing and desktop publishing to control page layout.

post-structuralism *n.* a movement in literature, psychology, linguistics, etc., modifying the principles of structuralism and questioning the concepts of form and representation.

post-traumatic stress disorder *n.* a nervous disorder occurring after an event that has caused severe emotional and/or physical stress and producing such symptoms as depression, withdrawal, and the tendency to relive the event which caused the initial stress: associated e.g. with survivors of a massacre in a shopping mall, etc., and esp. with many Vietnam veterans.

postulant / **pos**-chuh-luhnt, **pos**-tyoo- / *n.* a candidate for admission to a religious order.

postulate *v.* / **pos**-chuh-layt, -tyoo- / **1** assume (a thing) to be true, esp. as a basis for reasoning. **2** claim. • *n.* / **pos**-chuh-luht, -tyoo- / something postulated. □ **postulation** *n.*

postulator *n. Catholic Church* a person who presents and argues the case for a dead person's canonisation or beatification (as opposed to the DEVIL'S ADVOCATE).

posture / **pos**-chuh / *n.* **1** the way a person stands, sits, or walks. **2** a condition or state (of affairs etc.) (*a more diplomatic posture*). • *v.* assume a mental or physical attitude, esp. for effect. □ **postural** *adj.* **posturer** *n.*

posy *n.* a small bunch of flowers.

pot[1] *n.* **1** a rounded vessel for holding liquids or solids, or for cooking in; a teapot, flowerpot, etc. **2** the contents of a pot (*there's no jam – he ate the whole pot*). **3** the total amount bet in a game etc. **4** *colloq.* a large amount (*pots of money*). **5** =

POTSHOT. **6** = POT BELLY. **7** = CHAMBER POT. **8** *Aust.* a medium-to-large glass for beer; the beer it contains. •*v.* (**potted**, **potting**) **1** plant in a pot. **2** pocket (a ball) in billiards etc. **3** abridge (*a potted edition*). **4** shoot; kill with a pot shot. **5** seize or secure (*potted the trophy*). **6** make pots (as a potter). ☐ **go to pot** *colloq.* deteriorate, become ruined. **pot belly** a belly that bulges out. **pot-bound** (of a plant) with roots filling a flower-pot tightly and lacking room to spread. **pot luck** whatever is available (e.g. food) (*take pot luck with us*). **pot plant** a plant grown in a flowerpot; a house plant. **pot roast** a piece of meat cooked slowly in a covered dish.

pot² *n. colloq.* marijuana.

potable / poh-tuh-buhl / *adj.* drinkable.

potage / po-**tah***zh* / *n.* thick soup. (¶ French)

potash *n.* any of various salts of potassium, esp. potassium carbonate.

potassium / puh-**tas**-ee-uhm / *n.* a soft silvery-white metallic element (symbol K).

potation / poh-**tay**-shuhn / *n.* drinking; a drink.

potato *n.* (*pl.* **potatoes**) **1** a plant with starchy edible tubers. **2** one of these tubers used as a vegetable. ☐ **potato cake** = POTATO SCALLOP. **potato chip** = CHIP *n.* (sense 3). **potato crisp** = CRISP *n.* **potato peeler** = PEELER. **potato scallop** a slice of potato (or flattened pounded potato) battered and fried.

potboiler *n.* a piece of art, writing, etc. done merely to make money.

potch *n. Aust.* **1** an opal that has little or no play of colour and is of no value. **2** the opal-bearing material that is found in association with precious opal.

potent / poh-tuhnt / *adj.* **1** powerful, strong (*potent drugs; a potent argument*). **2** (of a male) capable of having an erection of the penis and of ejaculating viable sperm. ☐ **potency** *n.*

potentate / **poh**-tuhn-tayt / *n.* a monarch or ruler.

potential / puh-**ten**-shuhl / *adj.* capable of coming into being or of being developed or used (*a potential source of energy*). •*n.* **1** an ability or capacity for development or use. **2** *Physics* the quantity determining the energy of mass in a gravitational field or of charge in an electric field. ☐ **potential difference** the difference of electric potential between two points, measured in volts. ☐ **potentially** *adv.* **potentiality** *n.*

pother *n. literary* a commotion.

pothole *n.* **1** a deep cylindrical hole formed in rock (e.g. in limestone) by the action of water; an underground cave. **2** a hole in the surface of a road.

potion / **poh**-shuhn / *n.* a liquid medicine, poison, or drug.

potoroo / po-tuh-**roo** / *n.* a small, long-nosed, nocturnal macropod inhabiting areas of dense ground vegetation of south-eastern (and formerly south-western) Australia. Also called *rat-kangaroo*. (¶ Probably from Dharuk *badaru*.)

pot-pourri / poh-**poor**-ree, poh-puh-**ree** / *n.* **1** a scented mixture of dried petals and spices. **2** a literary or musical medley.

potsherd / **pot**-sherd / *n.* a broken piece of earthenware, esp. in archaeology.

potshot *n.* **1** a random shot from a gun. **2** a gibe (esp. oral). **3** an attempt.

pottage *n. archaic* a soup; a stew.

potter¹ *n.* a person who makes ceramic pots, vases, etc. ☐ **potter's wheel** a horizontal revolving disc to carry clay for shaping.

potter² *v.* **1** (often foll. by *about* or *around*) work on trivial tasks in a leisurely and enjoyable way (*I like pottering around in my garden*). **2** go slowly, dawdle.

pottery *n.* **1** vessels and other objects made of fired clay. **2** a potter's work or workshop.

potting mix *n.* a specially formulated mixture of materials in which to grow pot plants.

potty *adj.* (**pottier**, **pottiest**) *colloq.* crazy. •*n. colloq.* a chamber pot for a child.

pouch *n.* **1** a small bag or detachable outside pocket. **2** a baggy area of skin under the eyes. **3** a pocket-like receptacle in which marsupials carry their young; a similar structure in various animals, e.g. in the cheeks of rodents. ☐ **pouched mouse** any of several small, carnivorous, Australian marsupials, esp. the dunnart and the phascogale.

pouffe / poof / *n.* a large firm cushion used as a low seat or footstool.

poulterer *n.* a dealer in poultry and game.

poultice / **pohl**-tuhs / *n.* a soft heated mass applied to an inflamed area of skin.

poultry / **pohl**-tree / *n.* domestic fowls (ducks, geese, turkeys, chickens, etc.), esp. as a source of food.

pounce *v.* **1** spring or swoop down on and grasp; attack suddenly. **2** seize eagerly on a mistake, remark, etc. •*n.* a pouncing movement.

Pound, Ezra (Weston Loomis) (1885–1972), American poet and critic.

pound¹ *n.* **1** a measure of weight in the imperial system, 16 oz avoirdupois (0.4536 kg) or 12 oz troy (0.3732 kg). **2** the unit of money of the UK and certain other countries.

pound² *n.* **1** a place where stray animals, or motor vehicles left in unauthorised places, are taken and kept until claimed. **2** *Aust.* a natural basin surrounded by high rocky terrain (*Wilpena pound*). •*v.* enclose (cattle etc.) in a pound.

pound³ *v.* **1** crush or beat with repeated blows. **2** make one's way heavily (*pounding along*). **3** (of the heart) beat quickly and heavily. ☐ **pound out** produce with or as with heavy blows (*pounding out 'Waltzing Matilda' on the piano*).

pounder *n.* (usu. in combinations) **1** a thing or person weighing a specified number of pounds (*a five-pounder*). **2** a gun firing a shell of a specified number of pounds.

pour v. **1** flow or cause to flow in a stream or shower. **2** pour tea etc. into cups. **3** rain heavily. **4** come or go in large numbers (*refugees poured out of the country; letters poured in*). **5** (foll. by *out*) say or write rapidly (*he poured out his story*).

poussin / **poo**-san / n. a young chicken bred for eating.

pout v. push out one's lips; (of lips) be pushed out, esp. as a sign of annoyance or sulking. • n. a pouting expression.

pouter n. a kind of pigeon that can inflate its crop greatly.

poverty n. **1** being poor; want of the necessities of life. **2** scarcity, lack (*poverty of invention in his novel*). **3** inferiority, poorness (*the poverty of sandy soils*). □ **poverty line** the minimum income needed for the necessities of life. **poverty-stricken** extremely poor. **poverty trap** a situation in which an increase of income incurs a loss of government benefits, making real improvement impossible.

POW abbr. prisoner of war.

powder n. **1** a mass of fine dry particles. **2** a medicine or cosmetic in this form. **3** gunpowder. • v. apply powder to. □ **powder one's nose** *euphemistic* (of a female) go to the toilet. **powder room** a women's toilet in a public building.

powdered adj. made into powder.

powdery adj. like powder.

power n. **1** the ability to do something. **2** vigour, energy, strength. **3** a property, quality, or function (*great heating power*). **4** control, influence (*the party in power*). **5** what one has authority to do (*their powers are defined by law*). **6** an influential person, country, or organisation. **7** *colloq.* a large amount (*did me a power of good*). **8** (in mathematics) the product of a number multiplied by itself a given number of times (*2 to the power of 3 = 8*). **9** mechanical or electrical energy as opposed to manual labour (*power tools*). **10** the electricity supply (*a power failure*). **11** the magnifying capacity of a lens. • v. **1** equip with mechanical or electrical power. **2** *colloq.* travel with great speed or strength. □ **power dressing** wearing clothes calculated to proclaim one's position of power, esp. in contexts in which one's power would not otherwise be given due weight. **power of attorney** authority to act for another person in legal and financial matters. **power point** a socket on a wall where electrical appliances can be connected to the mains. **power station** a building where electrical power is generated. **power steering** hydraulic etc. mechanism for aiding steering in a motor vehicle.

powerful adj. having great power, strength, or influence. □ **powerful owl** a large owl of eastern Australia, having a deep, resonant, two-note hoot. □□ **powerfully** adj.

powerhouse n. **1** a power station. **2** a person or thing of great energy.

powerless adj. without power to take action; wholly unable.

powwow n. a meeting for discussion. • v. hold a powwow.

pox n. **1** a virus disease leaving pock-marks. **2** *colloq.* syphilis or any other venereal disease.

pp abbr. *Music* pianissimo.

pp. abbr. pages.

p.p. abbr. (also **pp**) by proxy, through an agent (Latin *per procurationem*); used in signatures.

■ **Usage** The correct sequence is A p.p. B, where B is signing on behalf of A.

P-plate n. *Aust.* a sign bearing the letter P (for 'provisional') which by law must be attached to the front and rear of a motor vehicle to indicate that the driver has only a provisional licence.

PPP abbr. *Computing* point to point protocol, a protocol that allows a computer to use a telephone line and a modem.

PPS abbr. post-postscript, = an additional postscript.

PR abbr. **1** public relations. **2** proportional representation.

Pr *symbol* praseodymium.

pr. abbr. pair.

practicable adj. able to be done. □ **practicability** n.

practical adj. **1** involving activity as distinct from study or theory (*has had practical experience*). **2** suitable for use (*an ingenious but not very practical invention*). **3** (of people) clever at doing and making things (*a practical handyman*). **4** virtual (*he has practical control of the firm*). • n. a practical examination; practical study. □ **practical joke** a humorous trick played on a person. □□ **practicality** / prak-ti-**kal**-uh-tee / n.

practically adv. **1** in a practical way. **2** virtually, almost.

practice n. **1** action as opposed to theory (*it works well in practice*). **2** a habitual action, custom (*it is our practice to supply good material*). **3** repeated exercise to improve one's skill. **4** the professional work, business, or place of business of a doctor, lawyer, etc.

practician n. a person who works at a profession etc., a practitioner.

practise v. **1** do something repeatedly to improve one's skill. **2** do something actively (*a practising Catholic; practise what you preach*).

practised adj. experienced, expert.

practitioner / prak-**tish**-uh-nuh / n. a professional or practical worker, esp. in medicine.

prad n. *Aust. colloq.* a horse.

Praed, Rosa (Caroline) (1851–1935), Australian novelist (writing as 'Mrs Campbell Praed') whose upbringing on family pastoral stations in Qld is reflected in her fiction.

pragmatic / prag-**mat**-ik / *adj.* treating things from a practical point of view (*a pragmatic approach to the problem*). ❑ **pragmatically** *adv.*

pragmatism / **prag**-muh-tiz-uhm / *n.* **1** treating things in a pragmatic way. **2** philosophy that evaluates assertions solely by their practical consequences. ❑ **pragmatist** *n.*

Prague / prahg / the capital of the Czech Republic (formerly of Czechoslovakia).

Praia the capital of Cape Verde Islands.

prairie *n.* a large treeless tract of grassland. ❑ **prairie oyster** a raw egg seasoned and swallowed whole.

praise *v.* **1** express approval or admiration of. **2** honour (God) in words. • *n.* praising, approval.

praiseworthy *adj.* deserving praise.

praline / **prah**-leen, **pray**- / *n.* a sweet made by browning nuts in boiling sugar.

pralltriller / **prahl**-tril-uh / *n.* a musical ornament consisting of one rapid alternation of the written note with the note immediately above it.

pram *n.* a four-wheeled conveyance for a baby, pushed by a person walking.

prance *v.* **1** (of horses) raise the forelegs and spring from the hind legs. **2** walk or behave in an elated or arrogant manner.

prandial / **pran**-dee-uhl / *adj. formal* or *jocular* of dinner or lunch.

prang *colloq. v.* crash (esp. a car); damage (a car etc.) by impact; have a crash. • *n.* a crash.

prank *n.* a practical joke, a piece of mischief.

prankster *n.* a person who plays pranks.

praseodymium / pray-zee-uh-**dim**-ee-uhm / *n.* a metallic element (symbol Pr).

prat *n. colloq.* **1** a silly or foolish person. **2** the bum, the buttocks.

prate *v.* **1** chatter, talk too much; talk foolishly. **2** tell or say in a prating manner.

pratincole / **prat**-ing-kohl, **pray**-ting- / *n.* a small, long-legged, browny-red bird of open plains in northern and central Australia etc. which runs with great speed along the ground and has a swallow-like flight.

prattle *v.* chatter in a childish way. • *n.* childish chatter.

prawn *n.* **1** any of several, often large, marine crustaceans, several species of which are highly prized as food. **2** *Aust. colloq.* a fool. • *v.* fish for prawns. ❑ **come the raw prawn** (often foll. by *with*) *Aust. colloq.* attempt to deceive (a person); misrepresent a situation (*don't come the raw prawn with me, mate!*).

prawnie *n. Aust. colloq.* a prawn fisherman.

praxis *n.* **1** accepted practice or custom. **2** the practising of an art or skill.

pray *v.* **1** say prayers. **2** entreat. **3** *archaic* please (*pray be seated*). ❑ **praying mantis** *see* MANTIS.

prayer *n.* **1** a solemn request or thanksgiving to God or to an object of worship. **2** a set form of words used in this (*the Lord's Prayer*). **3** a religious service (*morning prayer*). **4** the act of praying. **5** entreaty to a person. ❑ **prayer mat** a small carpet on which Muslims kneel to pray. **prayer shawl** = TALLITH. **prayer wheel** a revolving cylindrical box inscribed with or containing prayers, used esp. by Tibetan Buddhists.

pre- *comb. form* before, beforehand.

preach *v.* **1** deliver (a sermon or religious address). **2** advocate or encourage (a practice, quality, etc.) (*they preached economy*). **3** give moral advice in an obtrusive way. ❑ **preacher** *n.*

preachify *v. colloq.* preach or moralise tediously.

preachy *adj. derog.* inclined to preach or moralise.

preamble / pree-**am**-buhl / *n.* an introductory or preliminary statement.

preamp = PREAMPLIFIER.

preamplifier *n.* an electronic device that amplifies a weak signal and transmits it to the main amplifier.

prearrange *v.* arrange beforehand. ❑ **prearrangement** *n.*

Precambrian / pree-**kam**-bree-uhn / *adj.* of the earliest geological era, preceding the Cambrian period and Palaeozoic era. • *n.* this era.

precarious / pruh-**kair**-ree-uhs / *adj.* unsafe, not secure. ❑ **precariously** *adv.* **precariousness** *n.*

precast *adj.* (of concrete) cast in its final shape before use.

precaution *n.* something done in advance to avoid a risk (*take precautions*). ❑ **precautionary** *adj.*

precede / pree-**seed** / *v.* come, go, or place before in time or order.

precedence / **pres**-uh-duhns, pree-**see**- / *n.* priority in time or order. ❑ **take precedence** have priority.

precedent / **pree**-suh-duhnt, **pres**-uh- / *n.* a previous case that is taken as an example to be followed.

precentor / pruh-**sen**-tuh / *n.* a person who leads the singing or (in a synagogue) the prayers of a congregation.

precept / **pree**-sept / *n.* a command; a rule of conduct.

preceptor / pruh-**sep**-tuh / *n.* a teacher, an instructor. ❑ **preceptorial** / pree-sep-**taw**-ree-uhl / *adj.*

precession / pree-**sesh**-uhn / *n.* the slow movement of the axis of a spinning body round another axis. ❑ **precession of the equinoxes** the apparent slow backward movement of the equinoctial points along the ecliptic; the resulting earlier occurrences of the equinoxes in each successive year.

precinct / **pree**-singkt / *n.* **1** an enclosed or specially defined area around a place or building etc. **2** an area where traffic is prohibited in a town (*a pedestrian precinct*). **3** *US* an administrative subdivision of a county, city, or ward. **4** (**precincts**) the area surrounding a place.

preciosity / pres-ee-**os**-uh-tee / n. affected refinement, esp. in choice of words.

precious adj. **1** of great value or worth. **2** affectedly refined. **3** colloq. ironic considerable (did him a precious lot of good). **4** expressing irritation or scorn (you can keep your precious flowers!). • adv. colloq. very (there's precious little money left). ☐ **precious metals** gold, silver, and platinum. **precious stone** a valuable mineral used in jewellery, e.g. a diamond or ruby. ☐☐ **preciously** adv. **preciousness** n.

precipice / **pres**-uh-puhs / n. a very steep or vertical cliff or rock-face.

precipitant adj. = PRECIPITATE adj. • n. Chem. a substance that causes another substance to precipitate. ☐ **precipitance** n. **precipitancy** n.

precipitate v. / pruh-**sip**-uh-tayt / **1** cause to happen suddenly or prematurely (this action precipitated a crisis). **2** send rapidly into a certain state or condition (precipitated the country into war). **3** throw down headlong. **4** Chem. cause (a substance) to be deposited in solid form from a solution. **5** condense (vapour) into drops which fall as rain, dew, etc. • n. / pruh-**sip**-uh-tuht / a substance precipitated from a solution; moisture condensed from vapour (e.g. rain, dew). • adj. / pruh-**sip**-uh-tuht / headlong, hasty; rash (a precipitate departure). ☐ **precipitately** adv.

precipitation n. **1** rain or snow; the amount of this. **2** precipitating or being precipitated.

precipitous / pruh-**sip**-uh-tuhs / adj. **1** like a precipice, steep. **2** hasty, precipitate.

précis / **pray**-see / n. (pl. **précis** / **pray**-seez /) a summary. • v. (**précises** / **pray**-seez /, **précised** / **pray**-seed /, **précising** / **pray**-see-ing /) make a précis of.

precise adj. **1** exact; correctly and clearly stated. **2** taking care to be exact (she is very precise).

precisely adv. **1** in a precise manner, exactly. **2** (as a reply) I agree entirely.

precision / pruh-**sizh**-uhn / n. **1** great accuracy. **2** (used as adj.) adapted for precision (precision tools).

preclude / pree-**klood** / v. **1** exclude; prevent (precluded from taking part). **2** make impossible; remove (I say this so as to preclude all doubt).

precocious / pruh-**koh**-shuhs / adj. **1** (of a child) having developed certain abilities earlier than is usual. **2** (of abilities or knowledge) showing such development. **3** (of a plant) flowering or fruiting earlier than usual. ☐ **precociously** adv. **precociousness** n. **precocity** / pruh-**kos**-uh-tee / n.

precognition / pree-kog-**nish**-uhn / n. (supposed) foreknowledge, esp. of a supernatural kind.

pre-coital adj. preceding sexual intercourse. ☐ **pre-coitally** adv.

preconceived adj. (of an idea or opinion) formed before full knowledge or evidence is available.

preconception n. **1** a preconceived idea. **2** a prejudice.

precondition n. a condition that must be fulfilled before something else can happen.

precursor / pree-**ker**-suh / n. **1** a person or thing that precedes another, a forerunner. **2** a thing that precedes a later and more developed form (rocket bombs were the precursors of space probes).

pre-date v. exist or occur at an earlier time than.

predator / **pred**-uh-tuh / n. a predatory animal.

predatory / **pred**-uh-tuh-ree, -tree / adj. **1** (of animals) preying upon others. **2** (of a person or nation etc.) plundering or exploiting others.

predecease / pree-duh-**sees** / v. die earlier than (another person).

predecessor / **pree**-duh-ses-uh / n. **1** the former holder of a position. **2** an ancestor. **3** a thing to which another has succeeded (the new plan will share the fate of its predecessor).

predestination n. the doctrine that God has determined in advance all that happens, including who is to be saved and who damned.

predestine v. destine beforehand, appoint as if by fate.

predetermine v. determine in advance, predestine. ☐ **predetermination** n.

predeterminer n. a word or phrase that occurs before a determiner, generally quantifying the noun group, e.g. both, all, a lot of.

predicament / pruh-**dik**-uh-muhnt / n. a difficult or unpleasant situation.

predicate n. / **pred**-uh-kuht / Grammar the part of a sentence that says something about the subject, e.g. 'is short' in life is short. • v. / **pred**-i-kayt / assert that (a thing) belongs as a quality or property (we cannot predicate honesty of his motives).

predicative / pruh-**dik**-uh-tiv / adj. Grammar (of an adjective or noun) forming or contained in the predicate, e.g. 'old' in the dog is old, but not 'old' in the old dog died ('old' is ATTRIBUTIVE here).

predict v. forecast, prophesy. ☐ **prediction** n. **predictor** n.

predictable adj. able to be predicted; expected. ☐ **predictably** adv. **predictability** n.

predilection / pree-duh-**lek**-shuhn / n. a special liking, a preference.

predispose v. **1** influence in advance (circumstances predispose us to be lenient). **2** make susceptible or liable, e.g. to a disease.

predisposition n. a state of mind or body that makes a person liable to act or behave in a certain way, or to be subject to certain diseases (a predisposition to bronchitis).

predominant adj. predominating. ☐ **predominantly** adv. **predominance** n.

predominate v. **1** be greater than others in number or intensity etc., be the main element. **2** (foll. by over) have or exert control.

pre-eminent adj. excelling others, outstanding. ☐ **pre-eminently** adv. **pre-eminence** n.

pre-empt *v.* obtain (a thing) before anyone else can do so; forestall.

■ **Usage** *Pre-empt* is sometimes used to mean *prevent*, but this is considered incorrect by many people.

pre-emption *n.* purchase of property etc. by one person before the opportunity is offered to others.
pre-emptive *adj.* **1** pre-empting. **2** (of military action) intended to prevent attack by disabling the enemy first (*a pre-emptive strike*).
preen *v.* (of a bird) smooth (its feathers) with its beak. □ **preen oneself 1** groom or admire oneself. **2** congratulate or pride oneself.
prefab *n. colloq.* a prefabricated building.
prefabricate *v.* **1** manufacture (a building) in sections that are ready for assembly on a site. **2** produce in a mechanical way (*she prefabricated romantic novelettes by the dozen*). **3** concoct beforehand (*prefabricated his excuse*). □ **prefabrication** *n.*
preface / **pref**-uhs / *n.* **1** an introductory statement at the beginning of a book or speech. **2** the introduction to the central part of the Mass etc. • *v.* **1** provide or introduce with a preface. **2** lead up to (an event) (*the music that prefaced the ceremony*).
prefatory / **pref**-uh-tuh-ree, -tree / *adj.* serving as a preface; preliminary (*prefatory remarks*).
prefect *n.* **1** a senior pupil in a school, authorised to maintain discipline. **2** the chief administrative official of a district in France, Japan, and other countries.
prefecture / **pree**-fek-chuh / *n.* the office or district of authority of a prefect.
prefer *v.* (**preferred**, **preferring**) **1** choose as more desirable; like better. **2** put forward (an accusation etc.) for consideration by an authority (*they preferred charges of forgery against him*). **3** promote (a person).
preferable / **pref**-uh-ruh-buhl / *adj.* more desirable. □ **preferably** *adv.*
preference / **pref**-uh-ruhns / *n.* **1** preferring; being preferred. **2** a thing preferred. **3** a prior right, esp. to the payment of debts. **4** the favouring of one person or country etc. rather than another. **5** *Aust.* (in a system of preferential voting) the numerical ranking given by a voter to a candidate on a ballot paper. • *v. Aust.* direct preferences to (a candidate or party). □ **first preference** the first choice, as expressed by a voter on a ballot paper. **preference against** *Aust.* direct preferences against (a candidate or party). **preference shares** (*or* **stock**) those on which dividend is paid before profits are distributed to holders of ordinary shares.
preferential / pref-uh-**ren**-shuhl / *adj.* giving or receiving preference (*preferential treatment*). □ **preferential voting** a system of voting in which the voter marks the candidates in order of preference. □□ **preferentially** *adv.*
preferment *n. formal* promotion.
prefigure *v.* **1** represent beforehand by a figure or type (*Abel prefigured Christ*). **2** imagine beforehand. □ **prefiguration** *n.* **prefigurative** *adj.*
prefix *n.* (*pl.* **prefixes**) **1** a word or syllable (e.g. *co-, ex-, non-, out-, pre-*) placed in front of a word to change its meaning. **2** a title (e.g. *Mr*) before a name. • *v.* **1** put as a prefix. **2** add as an introduction.
pregnant *adj.* **1** having a child or young developing in the womb. **2** full of meaning, significant (*a pregnant pause*). □ **pregnant with** full of (*a situation pregnant with danger*). □□ **pregnancy** *n.*
prehensile / pree-**hen**-suyl / *adj.* (of an animal's foot, tail, etc.) able to grasp things.
prehistoric *adj.* **1** of the ancient period before written records of events were made. **2** *colloq.* completely out of date. □ **prehistorically** *adv.*

■ **Usage** The prehistoric era is divided into a Stone Age, Bronze Age, and Iron Age.

prehistory *n.* prehistoric events or times.
prejudge *v.* form a judgment before full information is available.
prejudice *n.* **1** an unreasoning opinion or like or dislike of something (*racial prejudice*). **2** harm to someone's rights. • *v.* **1** cause (a person) to have a prejudice. **2** cause harm to (*it may prejudice our rights*). □ **without prejudice** *Law* without detriment (to an existing right or claim). □□ **prejudiced** *adj.*
prejudicial / prej-uh-**dish**-uhl / *adj.* harmful to someone's rights or claims.
prelacy / **prel**-uh-see / *n.* **1** church government by prelates. **2** prelates collectively; the rank of prelate.
prelate / **prel**-uht / *n.* a high ranking member of the clergy, e.g. a cardinal, an archbishop, etc.
prelim *n. colloq.* any event which precedes a main one (e.g. an examination, a sports match, etc.).
preliminary *adj.* coming before a main action or event and preparing for it (*some preliminary negotiations*). • *n.* a preliminary action, event, or examination.
preliterate *adj.* of or relating to a society or culture that has not yet developed the use of writing.
preloved *adj. colloq.* second-hand, pre-owned.
prelude / **prel**-yood / *n.* **1** an action or event that precedes another and leads up to it. **2** an introductory section of a poem or piece of music; a short piece, esp. for the piano.
premarital / pree-**ma**-ruh-tuhl / *adj.* existing or (esp. of sexual relations) occurring before marriage (*premarital sex*).
premature / prem-uh-chuh, -**choor** / *adj.* **1** happening before the proper time; too early. **2** (of a baby) born three or more weeks before the expected time. □ **prematurely** *adv.*

pre-med *n. colloq.* premedication.

premedication *n.* medication to prepare (a patient) for a surgical operation.

premeditated / pree-**med**-uh-tay-tuhd / *adj.* planned beforehand (*a premeditated crime*). ☐ **premeditation** *n.*

premenstrual / pree-**men**-stroo-uhl / *adj.* of the time immediately before each menstruation (*premenstrual tension*). ☐ **premenstrual syndrome** (also **PMS**) a syndrome experienced by some women prior to menstruation and characterised by any of several symptoms such as tension, headaches, irritability, etc.

premier / **prem**-ee-uh, **prem**-yuh / *adj.* **1** first in importance, order, or time. **2** of earliest creation (*New South Wales is the premier State*). •*n.* **1** (also **Premier**) **a** the chief minister of a State government in Australia. **b** (in some countries) prime minister. **2** (**premiers**) *Aust.* the sporting team which wins a premiership. ☐ **minor premiers** the team leading the points table before the finals series begins. ☐☐ **premiership** *n.*

première / **prem**-ee-air / *n.* the first public performance of a play or film. •*v.* give a première of.

premiership *n.* **1** the office or tenure of a premier. **2** an organised competition among sporting clubs; the winning of this.

premise *n.* (also **premiss**) *Logic* a statement on which reasoning is based.

premises / **prem**-uh-suhz / *n.pl.* a house or other building with its grounds and outbuildings etc. (*not allowed on the premises*).

premiss alternative spelling of PREMISE.

premium / **pree**-mee-uhm / *n.* **1** an amount or instalment to be paid for an insurance policy. **2** a sum added to interest, wages, price, etc.; a bonus. **3** a sum added to ordinary charges. **4** a reward or prize. •*adj.* of the best quality and therefore more expensive (*premium mince*). ☐ **at a premium 1** above the nominal or usual price; highly valued or esteemed. **2** scarce and in demand.

premolar / pree-**moh**-luh / *n.* a tooth between the canines and the molars.

premonition / prem-uh-**nish**-uhn, pree-muh- / *n.* a feeling that something (bad) is going to happen. ☐ **premonitory** / pree-**mon**-uh-tuh-ree, -tree / *adj.*

prenatal *adj.* of the period before childbirth.

prenuptial *adj.* existing or occurring before marriage. ☐ **prenuptial contract** *Law* a contract between two persons intending to marry each other, setting out the terms and conditions of their marriage, esp. as to property and financial matters.

preoccupation *n.* **1** the state of being preoccupied. **2** a thing that fills one's thoughts.

preoccupied *adj.* deep in thought; inattentive because of this.

preoccupy *v.* (of a thought etc.) dominate the mind of (a person) to the exclusion of all else.

preordain *v.* ordain or determine beforehand.

prep *n. colloq.* **1** preparation. **2** homework. ☐ **prep school** a preparatory school.

preparation *n.* **1** preparing; being prepared. **2** a thing done to make ready for something. **3** a substance or mixture prepared for use, e.g. as medicine.

preparatory / pruh-**pa**-ruh-tuh-ree, -tree / *adj.* **1** preparing for something (*preparatory training*). **2** introductory. •*adv.* in a preparatory way. ☐ **preparatory school** a private primary school.

prepare *v.* make or get ready. ☐ **be prepared to** be ready and willing to (do something).

preparedness / pruh-**pair**-ruhd-nuhs / *n.* readiness.

preponderant / pruh-**pon**-duh-ruhnt / *adj.* greater in number, importance, or power; predominant. ☐ **preponderantly** *adv.* **preponderance** *n.*

preponderate / pruh-**pon**-duh-rayt / *v.* (often foll. by *over*) be greater than others in number or intensity etc.

preposition *n. Grammar* a word used with a noun or pronoun to show place, position, time, or means (see panel). ☐ **prepositional** *adj.*

prepossessing *adj.* attractive; making a good impression.

Preposition

A preposition is used in front of a noun or pronoun to form a phrase. It often describes the position of something, e.g. *under the chair*, or the time at which something happens, e.g. *in the evening*, or the means by which something happens, e.g. *by train*.

Prepositions in common use are:

about	*behind*	*into*	*through*
above	*beside*	*like*	*till*
across	*between*	*near*	*to*
after	*by*	*of*	*towards*
against	*down*	*off*	*under*
along	*during*	*on*	*underneath*
among	*except*	*outside*	*until*
around	*for*	*over*	*up*
as	*from*	*past*	*upon*
at	*in*	*round*	*with*
before	*inside*	*since*	*without*

preposterous / pruh-**pos**-tuh-ruhs / *adj.* utterly absurd, outrageous. ☐ **preposterously** *adv.*

prepuce / **pree**-pyoos / *n.* **1** the FORESKIN. **2** a similar fold of skin at the tip of the clitoris.

prequel / **pree**-kwuhl / *n.* a story, film, etc., whose events or concerns precede those of an existing work.

Pre-Raphaelite / pree-**raf**-uh-luyt / *n.* a member of a group of 19th-century artists who produced work in the style of Italian artists of before the time of Raphael. • *adj.* of the Pre-Raphaelites.

prerequisite / pree-**rek**-wuh-zuht / *adj.* required as a condition or in preparation for something else. • *n.* a prerequisite thing.

prerogative / pruh-**rog**-uh-tiv / *n.* a right or privilege.

Pres. *abbr.* president.

presage *n.* / **pres**-ij / **1** an omen. **2** a presentiment. • *v.* / pruh-**sayj** / **1** foreshadow, be an advance sign of. **2** predict.

Presbo / **prez**-boh / *Aust. colloq. n.* a Presbyterian. • *adj.* Presbyterian.

presbyopia / prez-bee-**oh**-pee-uh / *n.* the condition of being long-sighted, caused by loss of elasticity in the lens of the eye. ☐ **presbyopic** *adj.*

presbyter / **prez**-buh-tuh / *n.* (in some Churches) an elder.

Presbyterian / prez-buh-**teer**-ree-uhn / *adj.* (of a Protestant church) governed by elders who are all of equal rank. • *n.* a member of the Presbyterian Church. ☐ **Presbyterianism** *n.*

presbytery / **prez**-buh-tuh-ree, -tree, **pres**-puh- / *n.* **1** the eastern part of a chancel; the sanctuary. **2** a body of presbyters. **3** the house of a Catholic priest.

preschool *adj.* of the time before a child is old enough to go to school. • *n.* kindergarten.

prescient / **pres**-ee-uhnt / *adj.* having foreknowledge or foresight. ☐ **prescience** *n.*

prescribe *v.* **1** advise the use of (a medicine etc.), esp. by an authorised prescription. **2** lay down as a course or rule to be followed.

■ **Usage** Do not confuse with *proscribe*.

prescript / **pree**-skript / *n.* a law or command.

prescription *n.* **1** a doctor's written instruction for the supply of a medicine; the medicine itself. **2** prescribing.

prescriptive *adj.* **1** laying down rules. **2** prescribed by custom.

preselection *n.* esp. *Aust.* the choice of a candidate for a forthcoming election by (local) members of a political party.

presence *n.* **1** being present in a place (*your presence is required*). **2** a person's bearing, impressiveness of bearing (*has a fine presence*). **3** a person or thing that is or seems to be present in a place (*felt a presence in the room*). ☐ **presence of mind** ability to act quickly and sensibly in an emergency. **Real Presence** (in Catholic & Orthodox belief) the actual presence of Christ's body and blood in the consecrated bread and wine.

present[1] / **prez**-uhnt / *adj.* **1** being in the place in question (*no one else was present*). **2** being dealt with or discussed (*in the present case*). **3** existing or occurring now (*the present prime minister*). **4** *Grammar* expressing an action etc. now going on or habitually performed (*the present tense*). • *n.* present time, the time now passing.

present[2] / **prez**-uhnt / *n.* a gift.

present[3] / pruh-**zent** / *v.* **1** give as a gift or award. **2** introduce (a person) to another or others. **3** bring (a play, new product, etc.) to the public. **4** (of a compère, broadcaster, etc.) introduce (a show). **5** show, reveal (*presented a brave front to the world*). **6** send (a cheque) to the bank or (a bill) to a customer for payment. ☐ **present arms** hold a rifle etc. vertically in front of the body as a salute. **present oneself** appear or attend, e.g. for an examination. ☐ ☐ **presenter** *n.*

presentable *adj.* fit to be presented to someone; neat and tidy.

presentation *n.* **1** presenting; being presented. **2** something that is presented. **3** the way in which something is presented. **4** a demonstration or display; a lecture; an exhibition or theatrical performance.

presentiment / pruh-**zen**-tuh-muhnt, -**sen**- / *n.* a feeling of something that is about to happen, a foreboding.

presently *adv.* **1** soon, after a short time. **2** now.

preservation *n.* preserving; being preserved.

preservative *adj.* preserving things. • *n.* a substance that preserves perishable foods, wood, etc.

preserve *v.* **1** keep safe; keep in an unchanged condition. **2** keep from decay; treat (food) so that it can be kept for future use. **3** prepare (fruit) by boiling it with sugar, for long-term storage. • *n.* **1** (also **preserves**) preserved fruit; jam. **2** a thing, a place, etc. that is preserved. **3** activities or interests regarded as belonging to a particular person. ☐ **preserver** *n.*

pre-set *v.* (**pre-set**, **pre-setting**) set (a device etc.) beforehand; settle or decide beforehand.

preside *v.* be president or chairman; be in authority or control.

president *n.* **1** the head of a club, society, or council. **2** the head of a republic. ☐ **presidency** *n.* **presidential** / prez-uh-**den**-shuhl / *adj.*

Presley / **prez**-lee /, Elvis (Aaron) (1935–77), American rock and roll singer.

press[1] *v.* **1** apply weight or force steadily to (a thing). **2** squeeze juice from. **3** make by pressing. **4** flatten or smooth; iron (clothes etc.). **5** exert pressure on (an enemy etc.); urge, entreat, or demand (*press for a 35-hour week*). **6** offer insistently (*they pressed sweets upon us*). **7** insist upon (*don't press that point*). **8** throng closely. **9** embrace or caress by squeezing. • *n.* **1** pressing (*give it a press*). **2** a throng of people. **3** hurry, pressure of affairs (*the press of modern life*). **4** an instrument or machinery for compressing, flattening, or shaping something. **5** a printing press; a printing or publishing firm. **6** newspapers and periodicals, the people involved in writing or producing these (*a press photographer; read it in the press*). **7** publicity in newspapers etc (*got a good press*). **8** (**Press**) a printing or publishing company (*Oxford University Press Australia*). **9** a large cupboard with shelves for linen etc. ☐ **be pressed for** have barely enough of (*we are pressed for time*). **press conference** an interview given to journalists by a person who wishes to publicise something. **press gallery** a gallery for reporters, esp. in a legislative assembly; the reporters authorised to attend such a gallery. **press release** a statement issued to newspapers. **press stud** a small fastener for clothes etc., with two parts that are pressed together. **press-up** an exercise in which a person lies face downwards and presses down on the hands to lift the shoulders and trunk.

press² *v. archaic* force to serve in the army or navy. ☐ **press gang** a group which coerces people into doing something. **press-gang** force into doing something. **press into service** bring into use as a makeshift.

pressie / **prez**-ee / *n.* = PREZZIE.

pressing *adj.* **1** urgent (*a pressing need*). **2** urging something strongly (*a pressing invitation*). • *n.* a thing made by pressing; a record, CD, or series of these made at one time.

pressure *n.* **1** the exertion of continuous force upon something. **2** the force exerted; that of the atmosphere (*pressure is high in eastern areas*). **3** a compelling or oppressive influence (*is under pressure to resign; the pressures of business life*). • *v.* pressurise (a person etc.). ☐ **pressure cooker** a vessel designed for cooking things quickly under high pressure. **pressure group** a group (representing an industry etc.) applying esp. political pressure to serve its own interests by trying to influence public policy making (*a pressure group of the logging industry*). **pressure point** a point where an artery can be pressed against a bone to inhibit bleeding. **pressure suit** an inflatable suit which maintains body pressure and supplies air, worn by those flying in high altitudes or in outer space.

pressurise *v.* (also -**ize**) **1** try to compel (a person) into some action. **2** keep (a closed compartment, e.g. an aircraft cabin) at a constant atmospheric pressure. ☐ **pressurised water reactor** a nuclear reactor in which the coolant is water at high pressure. ☐☐ **pressurisation** *n.*

prestidigitator / pres-tuh-**dij**-uh-tay-tuh / *n. formal* a conjuror. ☐ **prestidigitation** *n.*

prestige / pres-**teezh** / *n.* **1** respect or good reputation gained from success, power, etc. **2** (as *adj.*) having or conferring prestige (*a prestige job*).

prestigious / pres-**tij**-uhs / *adj.* having or bringing prestige.

presto *adv.* (esp. in music) very quickly. ☐ **hey presto!** a conjuror's words used at a moment of sudden change.

Preston, Margaret (Rose) (1875–1963), Australian artist, known for her still-life pictures of Australian native flowers; one of the first artists to recognise and be influenced by the decorative beauty of Aboriginal bark paintings.

prestressed *adj.* (of concrete) strengthened by stretched wires within it.

presumably *adv.* as may reasonably be presumed; I presume.

presume *v.* **1** take for granted; suppose to be true. **2** take the liberty of doing something, venture (*may we presume to advise you?*). **3** (foll. by *on*) make unscrupulous use of, take unwarranted liberties because of (*they are presuming on her good nature*).

presumption *n.* **1** supposing a thing to be true; something presumed. **2** presumptuous behaviour.

presumptive *adj.* giving grounds for presumption (*presumptive evidence*).

presumptuous / pruh-**zump**-choo-uhs / *adj.* behaving with impudent boldness; acting without authority. ☐ **presumptuously** *adv.* **presumptuousness** *n.*

presuppose *v.* **1** take for granted. **2** require as a prior condition (*effects presuppose causes*). ☐ **presupposition** *n.*

pre-tax *adj.* before tax has been deducted (*pre-tax profits*).

pretence *n.* **1** pretending, make-believe. **2** a claim, e.g. to merit or knowledge. **3** pretentiousness.

pretend *v.* **1** create a false appearance or impression, either playfully or deceitfully. **2** (foll. by *to*) lay claim to (*he pretended to the title*). **3** imagine to oneself in play (*pretended it was night*). • *adj. colloq.* in pretence (*pretend money*).

pretender *n.* **1** a person who pretends. **2** a person who claims a throne, title, etc.

pretension *n.* **1** (often foll. by *to*) **a** an assertion of a claim. **b** a justifiable claim (*has some pretensions to be included*). **2** pretentiousness.

pretentious / pruh-**ten**-shuhs / *adj.* making an excessive claim to great merit or importance; too showy; pompous. ☐ **pretentiously** *adv.* **pretentiousness** *n.*

preterite / **pret**-uh-ruht / *adj. Grammar* expressing a past action or state. • *n.* a preterite tense or form.

preternatural / pree-tuh-**nach**-uh-ruhl / *adj.* extraordinary, unusual; supernatural.

pretext / **pree**-tekst / *n.* a reason put forward to conceal one's true reason.

Pretoria / pruh-**taw**-ree-uh / the capital of Transvaal and administrative capital of South Africa.

prettify v. (**prettified**, **prettifying**) make (a thing) look superficially attractive.

pretty adj. (**prettier**, **prettiest**) **1** attractive in a delicate way without being truly beautiful. **2** considerable (*cost me a pretty penny*). •adv. fairly, moderately (*pretty good*). ▫ **pretty face** = WHIPTAIL WALLABY. **pretty much** (or **nearly** or **well**) almost. **pretty-pretty** adj. too pretty or dainty. ▫▫ **prettily** adv. **prettiness** n.

pretzel / pret-suhl / n. a crisp stick- or knot-shaped biscuit flavoured with salt.

prevail v. **1** be victorious, gain the mastery. **2** be more usual or frequent than others; occur generally (*the prevailing wind*). **3** (foll. by *on* or *upon*) persuade.

prevalent / prev-uh-luhnt / adj. occurring generally; widespread. ▫ **prevalently** adv. **prevalence** n.

prevaricate / pruh-**va**-ruh-kayt / v. speak evasively or misleadingly. ▫ **prevarication** n. **prevaricator** n.

■ Usage *Prevaricate* is often confused with *procrastinate* which means 'to defer or put off action'.

prevent v. (often foll. by *from*) stop from happening or doing something; hinder; make impossible (*the weather prevented me from going*). ▫ **prevention** n. **preventable** (also **preventible**) adj.

■ Usage The use of *prevent* without 'from' as in *prevented me going* is informal. An acceptable alternative is *prevented my going*.

preventative adj. & n. = PREVENTIVE.

preventive (also **preventative**) adj. preventing something, esp. disease (*preventive medicine; took preventive action*). •n. a preventive agent, measure, drug, etc. ▫ **preventive medicine** the branch of medicine concerned with the prevention of disease.

preview n. an advance showing of a film, play, etc. before it is shown to the general public.

previous adj. **1** coming before in time or order. **2** *colloq.* done or acting prematurely; hasty (*you have been a little too previous*). ▫ **previously** adv.

prey / pray / n. **1** an animal that is hunted by another for food. **2** a person or thing that falls victim to an enemy, fear, disease, etc. •v. (**preyed**, **preying**) (foll. by *on* or *upon*) **1** seek or take as prey. **2** have a harmful influence on (*the problem preyed on his mind*). ▫ **bird** (or **beast**) **of prey** one that kills and eats other birds or animals.

prezzie (also **pressie**) n. *colloq.* a gift (*Chrissie prezzies*).

Priam / pruy-am / Gk myth. the king of Troy at the time of the Trojan War.

Priapus / pruy-uh-puus / the Greek and Roman god of fertility (represented as having a huge erect penis) and later the guardian god of gardens as well.

priapic / pruy-**ap**-ik / adj. phallic; characterised by a big penis. ▫ **priapism** *Med.* a persistent erection of the penis. (¶ From PRIAPUS.)

price n. **1** the amount of money for which a thing is bought or sold. **2** the odds in betting. **3** what must be given or done in order to achieve something (*peace at any price*). •v. fix or estimate the price of. ▫ **at a price** at a high cost. **price control** the establishment by a government of a maximum price for specified goods and services. **price-cutting** the lowering of prices, usu. in a price war. **price fixing** the maintaining of prices at a certain level by collusion between competing sellers. **price tag 1** a label on an item showing its price. **2** the cost of an undertaking.

priceless adj. **1** invaluable; beyond price. **2** *colloq.* very amusing or absurd.

pricey adj. (**pricier**, **priciest**) *colloq.* expensive.

Prichard, Katharine Susannah (1883–1969), Australian novelist, poet, and playwright, a founding member of the Communist Party of Australia.

prick v. **1** pierce slightly, make a tiny hole in. **2** worry; make one feel guilty (*my conscience is pricking me*). **3** feel a tingling sensation. •n. **1** pricking; a mark or puncture made by this. **2** pain caused as by pricking. **3** mental pain (*pricks of remorse*). **4** *colloq.* the penis. **5** *derog.* a contemptible man. ▫ **prick out** plant out (seedlings) in small holes pricked in soil. ▫▫ **pricker** n.

prickle n. **1** a small thorn. **2** one of the hard pointed spines on an echidna etc. **3** a tingling sensation. •v. feel or cause a sensation of tingling.

prickly adj. (**pricklier**, **prickliest**) **1** having prickles. **2** (of a person) irritable, touchy. **3** tingling. ▫ **prickly heat** an itchy inflammation of the skin causing a tingling sensation, common in hot countries. **prickly moses** any of several Australian wattles with prickles. **prickly pear** a cactus native to arid America (but widespread as a pest in Australia) with barbed bristles and large pear-shaped edible fruit. ▫▫ **prickliness** n.

pride n. **1** pleasure or satisfaction at one's actions, qualities, possessions, etc. **2** a person or thing that is a source of pride. **3** a proper sense of what is fitting for one's position or character; self-respect. **4** an unduly high opinion of one's own worth. **5** the best condition, the prime (*in the pride of young manhood*). **6** a group (of lions). ▫ **pride oneself on** be proud of (*prided himself on his skill at embroidery*). **pride of place** the most prominent position.

prie-dieu / pree-**dyer** / n. (*pl.* **prie-dieux** pronounced the same) a desk at which one kneels to pray.

priest n. **1 a** an ordained minister of the Catholic and Orthodox Churches empowered to offer sacrifice, administer the sacraments, etc. (ranking

priestess 654 **princess**

above a deacon and below a bishop); **b** an ordained minister in some Protestant Churches (esp. the High section of the Anglican Church). **2** a person appointed to perform religious rites in a non-Christian religion.

priestess *n.* a female priest of a non-Christian religion.

priesthood *n.* (**the priesthood**) the office or position of priest; priests in general.

priestly *adj.* of, like, or suitable for a priest.

prig *n.* a self-righteous person. ☐ **priggish** *adj.* **priggishness** *n.*

prim *adj.* (**primmer, primmest**) stiffly formal and precise; disliking what is rough or improper. ☐ **primly** *adv.* **primness** *n.*

prima ballerina / **pree**-muh / *n.* the chief female dancer in a ballet or ballet company.

primacy / **pruy**-muh-see / *n.* **1** pre-eminence. **2** the office of a primate of the Church.

prima donna *n.* (*pl.* **prima donnas**) **1** the chief female singer in an opera or opera company. **2** a temperamental and self-important person of either sex.

prima facie / pruy-muh **fay**-see / *adj.* & *adv.* at first sight, based on a first impression (*made out a prima facie case against him*). (¶ Latin)

primal / **pruy**-muhl / *adj.* **1** primitive, primeval. **2** chief, fundamental.

primary *adj.* **1** earliest in time or order; first in a series (*the primary meaning of a word*). **2** most important; chief. ☐ **primary colours** those colours from which all others can be made by mixing, (of paint) red, yellow, and blue, (of light) red, green, and blue. **primary education** (or **school**) education (or school) for children from the age of approximately 5 to 11. **primary feather** a large flight feather of a bird's wing. **primary industry** agriculture, sheep and cattle raising, fishing, forestry, etc., as distinct from manufacturing industry. **primary producer** a person who is engaged in primary industry. **primary source** a literary text, historical document, etc., on which a thesis, essay, etc. is based (as opposed to a SECONDARY SOURCE) (*Shakespeare's 'Macbeth' is the primary source in this thesis and the secondary sources include E.F.C. Ludowyk's 'Understanding Shakespeare'*). ☐☐ **primarily** / **pruy**-muh-ruh-lee, pruy-**mair**- / *adv.*

primate / **pruy**-mayt / *n.* **1** a member of the highly developed order of animals that includes apes, monkeys, and man. **2** / **pruy**-muht / the chief bishop of a country; an archbishop.

prime[1] *adj.* **1** chief, most important (*the prime cause*). **2** first-rate, excellent (*prime beef*). **3** basic, fundamental. • *n.* **1** the state of greatest perfection, the best part (*in the prime of life*). **2** *Eccl.* **a** the second canonical hour of prayer, appointed for the first hour of the day (i.e. 6 a.m.). **b** the office of this. **c** *archaic* this time. ☐ **prime minister** the head of a parliamentary government. **prime mover 1** the initial natural or mechanical source of motive power. **2** the author of a fruitful idea. **3** a person who is the main organiser of, or motive force behind, a project etc. **4** the powerful motor of a semitrailer. **prime number** a number (e.g. 2, 3, 5, 7, 11) that can be divided exactly only by itself and 1. **prime time** the time at which a TV or radio audience is at its largest.

prime[2] *v.* **1** prepare (a thing) for use or action (*prime a gun for firing*). **2** prepare (a surface) for painting by coating it with a substance that prevents the first coat of paint from being absorbed. **3** equip (a person) with information. **4** ply (a person) with food or drink in preparation for something.

primed *adj. colloq.* drunk.

primer / **pruy**-muh / *n.* **1** a substance used to prime a surface for painting. **2** an elementary textbook.

primeval / pruy-**mee**-vuhl / *adj.* of the earliest times of the world; ancient. ☐ **primevally** *adv.*

■ **Usage** The spelling *primaeval* is still occasionally encountered: *primeval* is preferred.

primitive *adj.* **1** of or at an early stage of civilisation (*primitive man*). **2** simple or crude, using unsophisticated techniques (*primitive tools*). ☐ **primitively** *adv.*

primogeniture / pruy-moh-**jen**-uh-chuh / *n.* **1** the fact of being a first-born child. **2** the system by which the eldest child (esp. the eldest son) inherits all his parents' property.

primordial / pruy-**maw**-dee-uhl / *adj.* existing at or from the beginning, primeval.

primp *v.* make (the hair etc.) tidy; smarten (oneself).

primrose *n.* **1** a European wild plant bearing pale yellow flowers in spring. **2** pale yellow. ☐ **primrose path** a life of ease and pleasure (with supposed disastrous consequences in the next life).

primula / **prim**-yuh-luh / *n.* a perennial plant of the family which includes the primrose and polyanthus.

primus / **pruy**-muhs / *n. trademark* a portable cooking stove burning vaporised oil.

prince *n.* **1** a male member of a royal family other than the reigning king. **2** a ruler, esp. of a small nation. **3** a nobleman of various countries.

princeling *n.* a young or petty prince.

princely *adj.* **1** of or worthy of a prince; (of a nation) ruled by a prince. **2** splendid, generous.

Prince of Wales a title usu. conferred on the heir apparent to the British throne.

princess *n.* **1** the wife of a prince. **2** a female member of a royal family other than a queen. ☐ **princess parrot** a delicately pastel-coloured parrot of arid inland central and western Australia.

principal *adj.* first in rank or importance, chief. • *n.* **1** the person with highest authority in an organisation; the head of certain schools or colleges. **2** a person who takes a leading part in an activity, play, etc. **3** the leading player in each section of an orchestra. **4** a person for whom another acts as agent (*I must consult my principal*). **5** a capital sum as distinguished from the interest or income on it. □ **principal boy** the leading male part in a pantomime, traditionally played by a woman.

■ Usage Do not confuse with *principle*.

principality / prin-suh-**pal**-uh-tee / *n.* a nation ruled by a prince.

principally *adv.* for the most part; chiefly.

principle *n.* **1** a basic truth or a general rule used as a basis of reasoning or a guide to behaviour. **2** a personal code of right conduct (*a man of principle; has no principles*). **3** a general or scientific law shown in the way something works. □ **in principle** in theory; as regards the main elements but not necessarily the details. **on principle** because of the principles of conduct one accepts (*we refused on principle*).

■ Usage Do not confuse with *principal*.

principled *adj.* based on or having (esp. praiseworthy) principles of behaviour.

prink *v.* **1** smarten (oneself) up, dress oneself up. **2** (of a bird) preen.

print *v.* **1** press (a mark or design etc.) on a surface. **2** produce (a book, newspaper, etc.) by applying inked type to paper. **3** express or publish in print. **4** write (letters) without joining them up. **5** produce a positive picture from (a photographic negative or transparency) by transmission of light. **6** (often foll. by *out*) produce a printed copy of (a document stored on computer). • *n.* **1** a mark or indentation left where something has pressed on a surface (*footprint; fingerprints*). **2** printed lettering or writing; words in printed form. **3** a printed picture or design. **4** printed cotton fabric. □ **in print 1** in printed form. **2** available from a publisher. **out of print** no longer available from the publisher. **printed circuit** an electric circuit with thin strips of conducting material on a flat insulating sheet. **printing press** a machine for printing. **print journalism** journalism intended for the print media rather than for television or radio. **print journalist** one who works for the print media. **print media** newspapers, journals, magazines (as opposed to electronic media).

printer *n.* **1** a person whose job or business is the printing of books, newspapers, etc. **2** a machine that prints, esp. one linked to a computer.

printout *n.* material produced in printed form from a computer or teleprinter.

prion / **pruy**-on / *n.* any of several bluey-grey and white migratory seabirds with a serrated bill that feed on plankton while skimming the surface of southern seas.

prior[1] *adj.* earlier, coming before another or others in time, order, or importance. • *adv.* **prior to** before (*prior to that date*).

prior[2] *n.* **1** the superior of certain monasteries of friars (e.g. the Dominicans). **2** (in an abbey) the deputy of an abbot.

prioress *n.* a nun holding an office equivalent to that of a prior.

prioritise *v.* (also **-ize**) give priority to. □ **prioritisation** *n.*

priority *n.* **1** being earlier or more important; precedence in rank etc., the right to be first. **2** something that is (or that a person considers to be) more important than other things (*he has got his priorities wrong*).

priory *n.* a monastery governed by a prior or a prioress.

prise *v.* (also **prize**) force out or open by leverage.

prism *n.* **1** a solid geometric shape with ends that are similar, equal, and parallel. **2** a transparent body of this form, usu. triangular and made of glass, that breaks up light into the colours of the rainbow.

prismatic / priz-**mat**-ik / *adj.* **1** of or like a prism. **2** (of colours) formed or distributed as if by a prism, rainbow-like.

prison *n.* **1** a building used to confine people who are convicted or awaiting trial. **2** imprisonment as a punishment. **3** any place in which a person feels imprisoned or confined (*home's a prison to many women*).

prisoner *n.* **1** a person kept in prison. **2** a person who is in custody and on trial for a criminal offence (*prisoner at the bar*). **3** a captive. □ **prisoner of conscience** *see* CONSCIENCE. **prisoner of war** an enemy captured in a war.

prissy *adj.* prim, prudish. □ **prissily** *adv.* **prissiness** *n.*

pristine / **pris**-teen / *adj.* **1** in its original condition; unspoilt. **2** spotless; fresh and clean as if new (*a pristine layer of snow*). **3** ancient, primitive.

■ Usage Some people consider the use in sense 2 incorrect.

privacy / **pruy**-vuh-see, **priv**-uh- / *n.* being private, seclusion.

private *adj.* **1** of or belonging to a particular person; personal (*private property*). **2** not holding public office (*speaking as a private citizen*). **3** not to be made known publicly, confidential. **4** (of a place) secluded. **5** not open to the public (*a private road*). **6** (of education or medical treatment) conducted outside the publicly funded system, at the individual's expense (*a private school; private patient*). • *n.* **1** a soldier of the lowest rank. **2** (**privates**) *colloq.* one's genitals. □ **in private** in the presence only of the person(s) directly concerned, not in public. **private bill** a parliamentary bill based on a petition from, and affecting, an individual or corporation only. **private company** a company with restricted membership and no public share issue. **private enterprise** businesses not under government control. **private eye** *colloq.* a private investigator. **private hotel** a (unlicensed) hotel that is not obliged to accept all comers. **private investigator** a detective engaged privately, outside an official police force. **private means** an income from investments etc., not as an earned salary. **private member** an MP not holding a government appointment. **private member's bill** a bill introduced by a private member, not part of government legislation. **private parts** the genitals. **private practice** a medical practice that is not part of the public health service. **private practitioner** a doctor who is in private practice. **private school** (also **independent school**) a fee-charging school not supported mainly by government funding (cf. PUBLIC SCHOOL sense 1). **private sector** the part of a country's economy that is free of direct government control. **private soldier** an ordinary soldier, other than officers. □□ **privately** *adv.*

privateer / pruy-vuh-**teer** / *n.* **1 a** an armed vessel owned and commanded by private persons commissioned by a government to act against a hostile nation. **b** its commander. **2** *Motor Racing* a competitor who races as a private individual rather than as a member of a team.

privation / pruy-**vay**-shuhn / *n.* loss or lack of the comforts or necessities of life.

privatise / **pruy**-vuh-tuyz / *v.* (also **-ize**) transfer (a business) from government to private ownership. □ **privatisation** *n.*

privet / **priv**-uht / *n.* a bushy evergreen European shrub used for hedges and now a serious pest in the Australian bush.

privilege *n.* **1** a special right, advantage, or immunity granted to one person or group. **2** (in full **parliamentary privilege**) *see* PARLIAMENTARY. **3** *Law* the right of a lawyer, priest, doctor, etc. to refuse to disclose communications made by a client, penitent, patient etc. in the course of a professional relationship. **4** a special benefit or honour (*it's a privilege to meet you*). •*v.* grant a privilege to, give priority to; exempt (a person from a liability etc.).

privileged *adj.* having a privilege or privileges.

privy *adj. archaic* hidden, secret. •*n.* a toilet, esp. an outside one. □ **be privy to** share in the secret of (a person's plans etc.).

prize¹ *n.* **1** something that can be won in a competition; an award given as a symbol of victory or superiority. **2** something striven for or worth striving for. **3** a ship or property captured at sea during a war. •*adj.* **1** to which a prize is awarded (*prize poem*). **2** excellent of its kind (*prize cattle*). **3** outstanding (*a prize idiot*). •*v.* value highly.

prize² alternative spelling of PRISE.

prizefight *n.* a boxing match fought for a prize of money. □ **prizefighter** *n.*

pro¹ *n.* (*pl.* **pros**) *colloq.* **1** a professional. **2** a prostitute.

pro² *adj.* & *prep.* (of an argument or reason) for, in favour (of). •*n.* (*pl.* **pros**) a reason for or in favour; a person who votes etc. in favour of something. □ **pros and cons** reasons for and against something.

pro- *prefix* **1** favouring or supporting (the opposite of ANTI-). **2** acting as a substitute or deputy for (*pro-vice-chancellor*). □ **pro-choice** *adj.* in favour of a woman's right to choose whether or not to have an abortion. **pro-choicer** *n.* a person who is pro-choice. **pro-life** *adj.* opposed to legal abortion. **pro-lifer** *n.* a member or supporter of the pro-life movement (*see also* RIGHT-TO-LIFER). **pro-life movement** a movement which, on moral grounds, seeks the banning of legal abortions whatever the circumstances, or in most circumstances (*see also* RIGHT-TO-LIFE).

proactive *adj.* (of a person, policy, etc.) taking the initiative.

prob *n. colloq.* a problem.

probability *n.* **1** being probable. **2** something that is probable. **3** a ratio expressing the chances that a certain event will occur. □ **in all probability** most probably.

probable *adj.* likely to happen or be true. •*n.* a probable candidate, member of a team, etc. □ **probably** *adv.*

probate / **proh**-bayt / *n.* **1** the official process of proving that a will is valid. **2** a copy of a will with a certificate that it is valid, handed to executors.

probation *n.* **1** the testing of a person's behaviour or abilities, esp. those of a new employee. **2** the supervision of (esp. young) offenders by an official (**probation officer**) as an alternative to imprisonment. □ **on probation** undergoing probation. □□ **probationary** *adj.*

probationary licence *n.* **1** a restricted licence to drive issued to a driver after a court-imposed period of disqualification. **2** = PROVISIONAL LICENCE.

probationer *n.* a person who is undergoing a probationary period of testing.

probative / **proh**-buh-tiv / *adj. formal* providing proof.

probe *n.* **1** a device for exploring an otherwise inaccessible place or object; a blunt-ended surgical instrument for exploring a wound. **2** (in full **space probe**) an unmanned exploratory spacecraft transmitting information about its environment. **3** a penetrating investigation. •*v.* **1** explore with a probe. **2** make a penetrating investigation of.

probity / **proh**-buh-tee / *n.* honesty, integrity.

problem *n.* **1** a difficult situation that needs to be resolved. **2** something that is hard to understand or accomplish or deal with. **3** a puzzle or question for solution; an exercise. **4** (as *adj.*) causing problems (*a problem child*).

problematic *adj.* (also **problematical**) difficult to deal with or understand. ☐ **problematically** *adv.*

proboscis / pruh-**bos**-kuhs, -**boh**-suhs / *n.* (*pl.* **probosces**) **1** a long flexible snout, e.g. an elephant's trunk. **2** an elongated mouth-part in certain insects, used for sucking things.

procedure *n.* a series of actions done or appointed to be done in order to accomplish something. ☐ **procedural** *adj.*

proceed / pruh-**seed** / *v.* **1** go forward or onward, make one's way. **2** continue, carry on an activity (*please proceed with your work*). **3** (foll. by *against*) start a lawsuit. **4** come forth, originate (*the evils that proceed from war*).

proceedings *n.pl.* **1** a lawsuit (*start proceedings for divorce*). **2** what takes place at a formal meeting. **3** a published report of discussions (*proceedings of the conference of Australian linguists*).

proceeds / **proh**-seedz / *n.pl.* the amount of money produced by a sale or performance.

process[1] / **proh**-ses / *n.* **1** a series of actions or operations used in making or achieving something. **2** a series of changes, a natural function (*the digestive process*). **3** a course of events or time (*the process of growing old*). **4** a lawsuit; a summons or writ. **5** a natural projection on the body or a plant. • *v.* **1** put through a manufacturing or other process. **2** (usu. as **processed** *adj.*) treat (food, esp. to prevent decay) (*processed cheese*). **3** *Computing* perform operations on (data) by means of a program.

process[2] / pruh-**ses** / *v.* go in procession.

procession *n.* a number of people, vehicles, etc. going along in an orderly line, esp. in the course of a religious ceremony. ☐ **procession caterpillar** an Australian caterpillar with slender hairs that can cause severe skin irritation: so called because they appear in large numbers, moving in a long single file.

processional *adj.* **1** of processions. **2** used, carried, or sung in processions. • *n.* a processional hymn; a book containing processional hymns.

processor *n.* a machine that processes things, esp.: **1** a central processor. **2** a food processor.

proclaim *v.* **1** announce officially, declare publicly. **2** make known unmistakably as being (*your accent proclaims you a New Zealander*). ☐ **proclamation** *n.*

proclivity / pruh-**kliv**-uh-tee / *n.* a tendency, an inclination.

procrastinate / proh-**kras**-tuh-nayt / *v.* postpone action. ☐ **procrastination** *n.* **procrastinator** *n.*

■ *Usage Procrastinate* is often confused with *prevaricate* which means 'to be evasive, quibble'.

procreate / **proh**-kree-ayt / *v.* produce (offspring) by the natural process of sexual intercourse. ☐ **procreation** *n.* **procreative** *adj.* **procreator** *n.*

procrustean / proh-**krus**-tee-uhn / *adj.* seeking to enforce conformity by ruthless or violent methods. (¶ Named after Procrustes, a robber in Greek legend, who made his victims fit a standard-sized bed by stretching them (if they were too short) or cutting bits off their legs (if they were too tall).)

proctor *n.* either of two disciplinary officials at certain universities. ☐ **proctorial** *adj.*

procumbent *adj.* lying on the face; prostrate.

procure *v.* **1** obtain by care or effort; acquire. **2** bring about (*procured their dismissal*). **3** obtain (a female or male) for sexual use. ☐ **procurement** *n.*

procurer *n.* one who procures something, esp. one who obtains women or men for a client's sexual pleasure or who obtains clients for a female or male prostitute; a pimp.

procuress / pruh-**kyoo**-res / *n.* a female procurer.

prod[1] *v.* (**prodded**, **prodding**) **1** poke. **2** urge or stimulate into action. • *n.* **1** a poke or a thrust. **2** a stimulus to action. **3** any pointed instrument, e.g. a goad.

prod[2] *colloq.* (also **proddie**, **proddy**) *n.* a Protestant. • *adj.* Protestant.

prodigal *adj.* **1** recklessly wasteful or extravagant. **2** (foll. by *of*) lavish with (*he is prodigal of good advice*). • *n.* **1** a recklessly extravagant person. **2** (in full **prodigal son**) a wanderer who has returned home. ☐ **prodigality** / prod-ee-**gal**-uh-tee / *n.*

prodigious / pruh-**dij**-uhs / *adj.* **1** marvellous, amazing (*a prodigious achievement*). **2** enormous (*spent a prodigious amount*). ☐ **prodigiously** *adv.*

prodigy / **prod**-uh-jee / *n.* **1** a person with exceptional qualities or abilities; a child with abilities very much beyond his or her age. **2** a marvellous thing, a wonderful example of something.

produce *v.* / pruh-**dyoos** / **1** bring forward for inspection, consideration, or use (*will produce evidence*). **2** bring (a play or performance etc.) before the public. **3** bear, yield, or bring into existence (offspring, fruit, a harvest, etc.). **4** cause or bring about (a reaction, a sensation, etc.) (*produced some surprise when he played the violin with his feet*). **5** manufacture. **6** (in geometry) extend (a line). • *n.* / **prod**-yoos / **1** an amount or thing produced. **2** agricultural and natural products (*dairy produce*). ☐ **producible** *adj.*

producer *n.* **1** a person producing articles, agricultural products, etc. (contrasted with a CONSUMER). **2** one who directs the acting of a play. **3** one who is responsible for control of expenditure, schedule, and quality in the production of a film or a broadcast program.

product *n.* **1** something produced, esp. by a natural process or by agriculture or manufacture. **2** *Maths* the result obtained by multiplying two quantities together.

production *n.* **1** producing; being produced. **2** a thing produced, esp. a play or film. **3** the amount produced. □ **production line** a sequence of machines and workers through which things pass during manufacture.

productive *adj.* able to produce things, esp. in large quantities. □ **productively** *adv.* **productiveness** *n.*

productivity *n.* productiveness; efficiency in industrial production. □ **productivity bargaining** *Aust.* the process of negotiating a deal between unions and employers whereby wage increases are granted in exchange for work practices which result in increased productivity.

proem / **proh**-em / *n.* a preface etc. to a book or speech; a beginning or prelude.

Prof. *abbr.* Professor.

profane / pruh-**fayn** / *adj.* **1** not concerned with religion; not sacred. **2** irreverent, blasphemous; (of language) vulgar, coarse; shocking in the circumstances. • *v.* treat (esp. a sacred thing) with irreverence or lack of due respect; violate or debase (such a thing) (*many developers profane Aboriginal sacred sites in pursuit of a fast buck*). □ **profanely** *adv.*

profanity *n.* **1** profane act or language; blasphemy. **2** a swear word.

profess *v.* **1** state that one has (a quality or feeling etc.); pretend (*she professed ignorance of this law*). **2** affirm one's faith in or allegiance to. **3** take the vows of a religious order at the end of the novitiate.

professed *adj.* **1** avowed, openly acknowledged by oneself (*a professed Buddhist; a professed homosexual*). **2** falsely claiming to be something (*a professed friend*). **3** (of a monk, friar, nun, etc.) having taken the vows of a religious order. □ **professedly** *adv.*

profession *n.* **1** an occupation, esp. one that involves knowledge and training in a branch of advanced learning (*the dental profession*). **2** the people engaged in an occupation of this kind. **3** a declaration or avowal (*made professions of undying love*). **4** a declaration of belief in a religion (*made profession of Hinduism*). **5** the taking of vows in a religious order; the ceremony at which this is done. □ **the oldest profession** *jocular* prostitution.

professional *adj.* **1** of or belonging to a profession or its members. **2** having or showing the skill of a professional; worthy of a professional (*professional conduct*). **3** doing a certain kind of work to make a living (as opposed to AMATEUR) (*a professional boxer*). **4** *derog.* engaged in a specified activity, esp. fanatically (*a professional agitator*). • *n.* **1** a person working or performing for payment. **2** someone highly skilled, esp. in some branch of advanced learning. □ **professionally** *adv.*

professionalism *n.* the qualities or skills of a profession or professionals.

professor *n.* (often as a title) **1** a university teacher of the highest rank; the holder of a university chair. **2** (in the US) any lecturer at a university. □ **professorship** *n.* **professorial** / prof-uh-**saw**-ree-uhl / *adj.*

proffer / **prof**-uh / *v.* offer (a gift, services, etc.). • *n. literary* an offer.

proficient / pruh-**fish**-uhnt / *adj.* doing something correctly and competently; skilled. □ **proficiently** *adv.* **proficiency** *n.*

profile / **proh**-fuyl / *n.* **1** a side view, esp. of the human face; a drawing or other representation of this. **2** a short account of a person's character or career. • *v.* represent in profile; give a profile of. □ **keep a low profile** avoid being noticed; avoid attention.

profit *n.* **1** an advantage or benefit obtained from doing something. **2** money gained in a business transaction, the excess of returns over outlay. • *v.* (**profited**, **profiting**) **1** bring advantage to. **2** obtain an advantage or benefit. □ **profit margin** profit after the deduction of costs. **profit-sharing** allowing a company's employees to share directly in its profits.

profitable *adj.* bringing profit or benefits. □ **profitably** *adv.* **profitability** *n.*

profiteer *n.* a person who makes excessive profits, esp. by taking advantage of times of difficulty or scarcity; or one who does so illegally or on the black market. • *v.* make excessive profits.

profiterole / pruh-**fit**-uh-rohl / *n.* a small hollow cake of choux pastry, usu. filled with cream and covered with chocolate.

profligate / **prof**-luh-guht / *adj.* **1** recklessly wasteful or extravagant. **2** licentious, dissolute. • *n.* a profligate person. □ **profligacy** *n.*

pro forma *adv.* & *adj.* as a matter of form. • *n.* a standard form or other document. (¶ Latin)

profound *adj.* **1** deep, intense (*takes a profound interest in it*). **2** having or showing great knowledge of or insight into a subject. **3** requiring much study or thought. □ **profoundly** *adv.* **profundity** *n.*

profuse / pruh-**fyoos** / *adj.* **1** lavish, extravagant (*profuse gratitude*). **2** plentiful, copious (*a profuse variety; profuse bleeding*). □ **profusely** *adv.* **profuseness** *n.*

profusion / pruh-**fyoo**-zhuhn / *n.* abundance, a plentiful supply (*a profusion of roses*).

progenitor / pruh-**jen**-uh-tuh / *n.* an ancestor.

progeny / **proj**-uh-nee / *n.* **1** offspring, descendants. **2** an outcome.

progesterone / pruh-**jes**-tuh-rohn / *n.* a hormone that prevents ovulation and prepares the uterus for pregnancy.

progestogen *n.* any of a group of hormones (including progesterone) that maintain pregnancy.

prognosis / prog-**noh**-suhs / *n.* (*pl.* **prognoses**) a forecast or advance indication, esp. of the course of a disease.

prognostic / prog-**nos**-tik / *n.* **1** a prediction. **2** an advance indication. •*adj.* making or giving this.

prognosticate / prog-**nos**-tuh-kayt / *v.* **1** predict. **2** be an advance indication of. ◻ **prognostication** *n.* **prognosticator** *n.*

program / **proh**-gram / (also **programme**, except in computing contexts) *n.* **1** a list of events, performers, etc., at a public function, concert, etc. **2** a radio or television broadcast. **3** a plan of events (*program is dinner and an early night*). **4** a course or series of studies, lectures, etc. **5** (always **program**) a series of coded instructions which controls the operation of a computer etc. •*v.* (**programmed**, **programming**) **1** make a program or definite plan of. **2** (always **program**) express (a problem) or instruct (a computer) by means of a program. ◻ **programmable** *adj.* **programmatic** / -gruh-**mat**-ik / *adj.* **programmer** *n.* (in sense 5 of *n.*).

■ **Usage** While either spelling of this word is acceptable in non-computing contexts, the spelling *program* should be used in senses to do with computing.

progress *n.* / **proh**-gres / **1** forward or onward movement. **2** an advance or development; an improvement. •*v.* / pruh-**gres** / **1** move forward or onward. **2** advance, develop, or improve. ◻ **in progress** taking place, in the course of occurring. ◻◻ **progression** *n.*

progressive *adj.* **1** making continuous forward movement. **2** proceeding steadily or in regular degrees (*a progressive improvement*). **3** (of a card game, dance, etc.) with a periodic change of partners. **4** (of a disease) gradually increasing in its effect. **5** advancing in social conditions or efficiency (*a progressive company*). **6** favouring rapid progress or reform (*a progressive policy*). •*n.* (also **Progressive**) one who favours a progressive political policy. ◻ **progressively** *adv.* **progressiveness** *n.*

prohibit *v.* (**prohibited**, **prohibiting**) formally forbid; prevent. ◻ **prohibitor** *n.*

prohibition *n.* **1** forbidding or being forbidden. **2** (usu. **Prohibition**) a ban on the manufacture and sale of alcohol, esp. in the USA 1920–33.

prohibitive *adj.* preventing or intended to prevent the use, abuse, or purchase of something (*prohibitive prices*). ◻ **prohibitively** *adv.*

project *v.* / pruh-**jekt** / **1** extend outward from a surface (*a projecting balcony*). **2** cast or throw outward. **3** cause (a picture or shadow) to fall on a surface. **4** imagine (a thing or oneself) in another situation or having another person's feelings. **5** plan (a scheme or course of action). **6** represent (a solid thing) on a plane surface, as maps of the earth are made. •*n.* / **proj**-ekt / **1** a plan or scheme. **2** a detailed study, piece of research, etc. by a student.

projectile / pruh-**jek**-tuyl / *n.* a missile (e.g. a bullet, arrow, or rocket) that can be projected forcefully.

projection *n.* **1** projecting; being projected. **2** something that projects from a surface. **3** a thing that is projected. **4** a representation of the surface of the earth on a plane surface. **5** an estimate of future situations or trends based on a study of present ones.

projectionist *n.* a person who operates a projector.

projector *n.* an apparatus for projecting photographs or film on to a screen.

Prokofiev / pruh-**kof**-ee-ef /, Sergei Sergeevich (1891–1953), Russian composer.

prolactin *n.* a hormone that stimulates milk production after childbirth.

prolapse / **proh**-laps / *v.* (of an organ of the body) slip forward or down out of its place. •*n.* (also **prolapsus**) the prolapsing of an organ of the body.

prolegomenon / pro-luh-**gom**-uh-nuhn / *n.* (*pl.* **prolegomena**) the preface to a book etc., esp. when critical or discursive.

proletarian / proh-luh-**tair**-ree-uhn / *adj.* of the proletariat. •*n.* a member of the proletariat.

proletariat / proh-luh-**tair**-ree-uht / *n.* the working class, esp. those without capital and dependent on selling their labour (contrasted with the BOURGEOISIE).

proliferate / pruh-**lif**-uh-rayt / *v.* produce new growth or offspring rapidly, multiply. ◻ **proliferation** *n.*

proliferous / pruh-**lif**-uh-ruhs / *adj.* **1** (of a plant) producing many leaf or flower buds; growing luxuriantly. **2** spreading by proliferation.

prolific / pruh-**lif**-ik / *adj.* producing many offspring or much output (*a prolific writer*). ◻ **prolifically** *adv.*

prolix / **proh**-liks / *adj.* lengthy, tediously wordy. ◻ **prolixity** / proh-**lik**-suh-tee / *n.*

prologue / **proh**-log / *n.* **1** an introduction to a poem or play. **2** an act or event serving as an introduction.

prolong / pruh-**long** / *v.* lengthen (a thing) in extent or duration. ◻ **prolongation** / proh-long-**gay**-shuhn / *n.*

prolonged *adj.* continuing for a long time; tedious.

prom *n. colloq.* a prom concert. ◻ **prom concert** (in full **promenade concert**) a concert at which the audience, or part of it, can stand, sit on the floor, or move about.

promenade / prom-uh-**nahd**, -**nayd** / *n.* **1** (also **esplanade**) a paved public walk (esp. along a sea front). **2** a walk, ride, or drive, taken esp. for display or pleasure. •*v.* go or take for a promenade.

Promethean *adj.* daring or inventive. (¶ From PROMETHEUS.)

Prometheus / pruh-**mee**-thee-uhs / *Gk myth.* a Titan who, because he stole fire from the gods to give it to a fire-less human race, was punished by being chained to a rock where an eagle fed on his ever regrowing liver.

promethium / pruh-**mee**-thee-uhm / *n.* a radioactive metallic element (symbol Pm).

prominent *adj.* **1** jutting out, projecting. **2** conspicuous. **3** important, well-known (*prominent citizens*). ☐ **prominently** *adv.* **prominence** *n.*

promiscuous / pruh-**mis**-kyoo-uhs / *adj.* **1** having frequent, esp. casual, sexual relations with many people. **2** mixed and indiscriminate; without order (*a promiscuous jumble of books for sale*). ☐ **promiscuously** *adv.* **promiscuity** / prom-uhs-**kyoo**-uh-tee / *n.*

promise *n.* **1** a declaration that one will give or do a certain thing. **2** a sign of future success or good results (*his work shows promise*). •*v.* **1** make a promise. **2** make (a thing) seem likely (*it promises to be a good investment*). **3** *colloq.* assure (*I promise you, it won't be easy*). **4** (*archaic* except in Aboriginal traditional society) betroth (*she is promised to another*).

Promised Land 1 Canaan, the land promised by God to Abraham and his descendants. **2** any place of expected happiness.

promising *adj.* likely to turn out well. ☐ **promisingly** *adv.*

promissory / **prom**-uh-suh-ree / *adj.* conveying a promise. ☐ **promissory note** a signed promise to pay a sum of money.

promo / **proh**-moh / *n.* (*pl.* **promos**) *colloq.* a film or other thing used to promote a product, advertise a program, etc.

promontory / **prom**-uhn-tuh-ree, -tree / *n.* high land jutting out into the sea; a headland.

promote *v.* **1** raise (a person) to a higher rank or office. **2** encourage the progress of (*promote friendship between nations*). **3** publicise (a product) in order to sell it. **4** finance or organise (*promoted the new show*).

promoter *n.* a person who promotes, esp. a sporting event, a theatrical production, etc.

promotion *n.* **1** promoting; being promoted. **2** an advertising campaign; a special offer. ☐ **promotional** *adj.*

prompt *adj.* **1** made, done, or doing something without delay. **2** punctual. •*adv.* punctually. •*v.* **1** stimulate (a person) to action. **2** cause (a feeling, thought, or action). **3** assist by supplying forgotten words to (an actor or speaker). •*n.* **1** an act of prompting; something said to prompt an actor or speaker. **2** a prompter. **3** a sign on a computer screen showing that the system is ready for input. ☐ **prompt side** the side of the stage where the prompter sits, usu. to the actor's right as he or she faces the audience. ☐☐ **promptitude** *n.* **promptly** *adv.* **promptness** *n.*

prompter *n.* (also **prompt**) a person (out of sight of the audience) who prompts actors on the stage.

promulgate / **prom**-uhl-gayt / *v.* make widely known; promote. ☐ **promulgation** *n.* **promulgator** *n.*

prone *adj.* **1** lying face downwards (cf. SUPINE). **2** likely to do or suffer something (*prone to feelings of jealousy; strike-prone industries*). ☐ **proneness** *n.*

prong *n.* each of the projecting pointed parts at the end of a fork, antler, etc.; a tine. •*v.* pierce or stab with a fork; turn up (soil) with a fork.

pronoun / **proh**-nown / *n.* a word used as a substitute for a noun (see panel).

pronounce *v.* **1** utter (a speech sound) correctly or in a certain way (*Australians pronounce English quite differently from other speakers of the language*). **2** declare formally (*I now pronounce you man and wife; the wine was pronounced excellent*).

pronounced *adj.* **1** definite, noticeable (*he walks with a pronounced limp*). **2** forthright, decided (*he has pronounced views on Aboriginal land rights*).

pronouncement *n.* a declaration.

pronto *adv. colloq.* immediately, quickly.

Pronoun

A pronoun is used as a substitute for a noun or a noun phrase, e.g.
   He *was upstairs.*   Did you see *that?*
   Anything *can happen now.*   It's *lovely weather.*
Using a pronoun often avoids repetition, e.g.
   I found Jim—he *was outside.*
   (instead of *I found Jim—Jim was outside.*)
   Where are your keys?—I've got them.
   (instead of *Where are your keys?—I've got my keys.*)
Types of pronoun:
1. demonstrative pronouns: *this, that, these, those.*
2. interrogative pronouns: *who? what? which?* etc.
3. personal pronouns: *I, me, we, us, thou, thee, you, ye, he, him, she, her, it, they, them.*
4. possessive pronouns: *my, your,* etc.
5. reflexive pronouns: *myself, oneself,* etc.
6. relative pronouns: *who, whom, whose, what, which, that.*

pronunciation *n.* **1** the way a word is pronounced. **2** the way a person pronounces words.

proof *n.* **1** a fact or thing that shows or helps to show that something is true or exists. **2** a demonstration of the truth of something (*in proof of my statement*). **3** a standard of strength for distilled alcohol (*80% proof*). **4** a trial impression of printed matter, produced so that corrections can be made. • *adj.* able to resist or withstand penetration or damage (*bullet-proof; proof against the severest weather*). • *v.* **1** make a proof of (printed matter etc.). **2** make (a fabric) proof against water or bullets.

proofreader *n.* a person employed to read and correct proofs. □ **proofreading** *n.*

prop[1] *n.* **1** a rigid support. **2** a person or thing providing support or help. **3** *Aust.* a horse's action of propping. **4** *Rugby* a forward at either end of the front row of a scrum. • *v.* (**propped, propping**) **1** support with or as if with a prop (*prop it up*). **2** esp. *Aust.* (of a horse) come to a dead stop, with the forelegs rigid, when moving at speed. **3** *Aust.* (of a person) stay, stop, remain (*I'll prop here for a bit*).

prop[2] *n. colloq.* **1** a stage property. **2** (**props**) a person in charge of theatrical properties.

prop[3] *n. colloq.* an aircraft propeller.

prop[4] *abbr.* proprietor.

propaganda *n.* **1** organised propagation of a doctrine, religion, cause, etc., by use of publicity, selected information, etc. **2** (usu. *derog.*) the ideas etc. so propagated (*neo-Nazi propaganda; vicious anti-Semitic propaganda*). □ **propagandise** *v.* **propagandist** *n.* & *adj.*

propagate *v.* **1** breed or reproduce (a plant, animal, etc.) from parent stock (*propagating plants from cuttings*). **2** spread (news or ideas). **3** transmit (*the vibrations are propagated through the rock*). □ **propagation** *n.*

propagator *n.* **1** a person or thing that propagates. **2** a small box that can be heated, used for germinating seeds or raising seedlings.

propane (or **proh**-payn) *n.* a hydrocarbon found in petroleum and used as a fuel.

propel *v.* (**propelled, propelling**) drive or push forward; urge on.

propellant *n.* **1** a thing that propels. **2** an explosive that fires bullets etc. from a firearm. **3** a substance used as a reagent in a rocket engine etc. to provide thrust. **4** compressed gas in an aerosol can used to thrust the contents out in the form of a spray.

propeller *n.* a revolving device with blades for propelling a ship or aircraft.

propensity / pruh-**pen**-suh-tee / *n.* a tendency or inclination (*a propensity to laziness*).

proper *adj.* **1** suitable, appropriate; correct; according to rules (*the proper way to hold the bat*). **2** strictly so called (*we drove from the suburbs to the city proper*). **3** *colloq.* thorough, complete (*a proper fool you made me look*). • *n.* that part of the Mass etc. which varies from day to day (as distinct from the ORDINARY *n.*). □ **proper fraction** one that is less than unity, with the numerator less than the denominator, e.g. ¾. **proper noun** the capitalised name for an individual person, place, country, etc., e.g. *Kylie, Kosciuszko*.

properly *adv.* **1** fittingly, suitably. **2** accurately, correctly. **3** rightly (*he very properly refused her*). **4** with decency; respectably (*behave properly*). **5** *colloq.* thoroughly (*properly ashamed of himself*).

property *n.* **1** a thing or things owned. **2** real estate, someone's land (*their property borders on ours*). **3** a movable object (other than furniture or scenery) used on stage. **4** a quality or characteristic (*it has the property of dissolving grease*). □ **common property** a thing known by most people (*the secret affairs of the royals have now become common property*).

prophecy / **prof**-uh-see / *n.* **1** the power of prophesying (*the gift of prophecy*). **2** a statement that tells what will happen.

prophesy / **prof**-uh-suy / *v.* (**prophesied, prophesying**) declare beforehand (what will happen) as if by divine inspiration.

prophet *n.* **1** a person who foretells the future. **2** a teacher or interpreter of the supposed will of God. □ **the Prophet** Mohammed.

prophetess *n.* a female prophet.

prophetic *adj.* **1** prophesying the future. **2** of a prophet or prophets. □ **prophetically** *adv.*

prophylactic / prof-uh-**lak**-tik / *adj.* tending to prevent a disease or misfortune. • *n.* **1** a preventive medicine or action. **2** a condom.

prophylaxis / prof-uh-**lak**-suhs / *n.* preventive treatment against a disease.

propinquity / pruh-**ping**-kwuh-tee / *n.* **1** nearness in position. **2** close kinship. **3** similarity.

propitiate / pruh-**pish**-ee-ayt / *v.* win the favour or forgiveness of; placate. □ **propitiation** *n.* **propitiator** *n.* **propitiatory** / pruh-**pish**-ee-uh-tuh-ree / *adj.*

propitious / pruh-**pish**-uhs / *adj.* favourable, giving a good omen or a suitable opportunity. □ **propitiously** *adv.*

proponent / pruh-**poh**-nuhnt / *n.* a person who puts forward a theory or proposal.

proportion *n.* **1** a fraction or share of a whole. **2** a ratio (*the proportion of skilled workers to unskilled*). **3** the correct relation in size, amount, or degree between one thing and another or between parts of a thing. **4** (**proportions**) size, dimensions (*a termites' nest of huge proportions*). • *v.* give correct proportions to; make (one thing) proportionate to another.

proportional *adj.* in correct proportion, corresponding in size or amount or degree. □ **proportional representation** an electoral system in which each party has a number of seats in proportion to the number of votes for its candidates. □□ **proportionally** *adv.*

proportionate *adj.* in proportion, corresponding (*the cost is proportionate to the quality*). □ **proportionately** *adv.*

proposal *n.* **1** the proposing of something. **2** the thing proposed. **3** an offer of marriage.

propose *v.* **1** put forward for consideration. **2** have and declare as one's intention (*we propose to wait*). **3** nominate as a candidate. **4** make a proposal of marriage. □ **propose a toast** ask people formally to drink a toast. □□ **proposer** *n.*

proposition *n.* **1** a statement, an assertion. **2** a proposal; a scheme proposed. **3** *colloq.* an undertaking; something to be dealt with (*not an attractive proposition*). **4** a proposal or request for sexual intercourse. • *v. colloq.* put a proposal to (a person); suggest sexual intercourse to (*he propositioned her*).

propound *v.* put forward for consideration.

proppy *adj. Aust.* (of a horse) disposed to be restive when ridden; inclined to prop.

proprietary / pruh-**pruy**-uh-tuh-ree, -tree / *adj.* **1** manufactured and sold by one particular firm, usu. under a patent (*proprietary medicines*). **2** of an owner or ownership. □ **proprietary company** *Aust.* a private company. **proprietary name** (also **proprietary term**) the name of a product etc. registered by its owner as a trademark and not usable by another without permission.

proprietor / pruh-**pruy**-uh-tuh / *n.* a holder of property; the owner of a business.

proprietorial / pruh-pruy-uh-**taw**-ree-uhl / *adj.* of or indicating ownership.

proprietress *n.* a female proprietor.

propriety / pruh-**pruy**-uh-tee / *n.* **1** being proper or suitable. **2** correctness of behaviour or morals. **3** (**proprieties**) the details or rules of correct conduct.

propulsion *n.* the process of propelling or being propelled.

propylene *n.* a gaseous hydrocarbon used in the manufacture of chemicals.

pro rata / proh **rah**-tuh / *adj.* proportional (*if costs increase, there will be a pro rata increase in prices*). • *adv.* proportionally (*prices will increase pro rata*). (¶ Latin = according to the rate.)

prorogue / pruh-**rohg** / *v.* (**prorogued**, **proroguing**) **1** discontinue the meetings of (a parliament etc.) without dissolving it. **2** (of a parliament etc.) have its meetings discontinued in this way. □ **prorogation** / proh-ruh-**gay**-shuhn / *n.*

prosaic / proh-**zay**-ik, pruh- / *adj.* **1** like prose, lacking poetic beauty. **2** unimaginative, plain, and ordinary. □ **prosaically** *adv.*

proscenium / pruh-**see**-nee-uhm / *n.* (*pl.* **prosceniums** or **proscenia**) the part of a theatre stage in front of the curtain, with its enclosing arch.

prosciutto / pruh-**shoo**-toh / *n.* Italian cured ham, usu. served raw and very thinly sliced as an hors d'oeuvre.

proscribe *v.* **1** forbid by law. **2** reject or denounce as dangerous etc. **3** outlaw (a person); banish, exile (*he was proscribed from the club*). □ **proscription** *n.* **proscriptive** *adj.*

■ **Usage** Do not confuse with *prescribe*.

prose *n.* **1** written or spoken language not in verse form. **2** a passage of prose for translation into another language. **3** dull or matter-of-fact quality (*the prose of daily life*). • *v.* talk tediously (*prosing on about his private life*).

prosecute *v.* **1** take legal proceedings against (a person) for a crime. **2** carry on or conduct (*prosecuting their trade*). □ **prosecutor** *n.*

prosecution *n.* **1** prosecuting; being prosecuted. **2** the party prosecuting another for a crime.

proselyte / **pros**-uh-luyt / *n.* a person converted, esp. recently, from one opinion, religion, party, etc. to another.

proselytise / **pros**-uh-luh-tuyz / *v.* (also **-ize**) try to convert people to one's beliefs or opinions.

proselytism / **pros**-uh-luh-tiz-uhm / *n.* **1** being a proselyte. **2** proselytising.

Proserpine / pruh-**ser**-puh-nee / *Rom. myth.* the Roman name for Persephone.

prosody / **pros**-uh-dee, **proz**- / *n.* the study of verse forms and poetic metres. □ **prosodic** *adj.* **prosodist** *n.*

prospect *n.* / **pros**-pekt / **1** an extensive view of a landscape etc.; a mental view of matters. **2** something one is expecting (*I don't relish the prospect of telling him*). **3** (usu. as **prospects**) a chance of success or advancement (*a job with no prospects*). **4** a possible customer or client; a person likely to be successful. • *v.* / pruh-**spekt** / explore in search of something (*prospecting for gold*). □ **prospector** *n.*

prospective / pruh-**spek**-tiv / *adj.* expected to be or to occur; future, possible (*prospective customers*).

prospectus / pruh-**spek**-tuhs / *n.* (*pl.* **prospectuses**) a printed document describing and advertising the chief features of a school, a business, a forthcoming book, etc.

prosper *v.* be successful, thrive.

prosperous *adj.* financially successful. □ **prosperously** *adv.* **prosperity** *n.*

prostanthera / pros-**tan**-thuh-ruh / *n.* an Australian mint bush (*see* MINT²).

prostate / **pros**-tayt / *n.* (in full **prostate gland**) a large gland round the urethra at the base of the bladder in males, releasing a fluid forming part of the semen. □ **prostatic** / pros-**tat**-ik / *adj.*

■ **Usage** Do not confuse with *prostrate*.

prosthesis / pros-**thee**-suhs / *n.* (*pl.* **prostheses**) **1** an artificial part supplied to remedy a deficiency, e.g. a false breast, leg, tooth, etc. **2** the branch of surgery dealing with prostheses. □ **prosthetic** *adj.*

prosthetics / pros-**thet**-iks / n. = PROSTHESIS 2.

prostitute n. **1** a woman or girl who engages in sexual activity for payment. **2** (usu. **male prostitute**) a man or boy who engages in sexual activity, esp. with homosexual men, for payment. • v. **1** make a prostitute of (*prostitute oneself*). **2** put to an unworthy use, esp. for money (*prostituting their artistic abilities*). ☐ **prostitution** n.

prostrate adj. / **pros**-trayt / **1** lying face downwards, esp. in submission. **2** lying horizontally. **3** overcome, exhausted (*prostrate with grief*). **4** (of a plant) growing (usu. flat) along the ground. • v. / pros-**trayt** / **1** throw (esp. a person) flat on the ground. **2** throw (oneself) down in submission etc. **3** overcome; make physically weak (*prostrated by the heat*). ☐ **prostration** n.

prosy / **proh**-zee / adj. tedious, prosaic, dull. ☐ **prosily** adv. **prosiness** n.

protactinium / proh-tak-**tin**-ee-uhm / n. a radioactive metallic element (symbol Pa).

protagonist / proh-**tag**-uh-nuhst / n. **1** the chief person in a drama. **2** one of the chief contenders in a contest. **3** an advocate or champion of a cause etc. (*a protagonist of women's rights*).

■ **Usage** The use of *protagonist* in sense 3 to mean 'an advocate or champion of a cause etc.' is considered incorrect in standard English. The word contains the Greek prefix *proto-* meaning 'first', not the prefix *pro-* meaning 'in favour of'.

protea / **proh**-tee-uh / n. a South African shrub with many species, having spectacular flowerheads.

protean / **proh**-tee-uhn, -**tee**-uhn / adj. variable, versatile; taking many forms. (¶ PROTEUS.)

protect v. **1** keep from harm or injury; defend, guard. **2** shield (home industry) from competition by imposing import duties on foreign goods.

protection n. **1** protecting or being protected. **2** a thing, person, or animal that protects (*bought a dog as protection*). **3** = PROTECTIONISM. **4** colloq. protection from violence etc. obtained by payment to gangsters or terrorists. ☐ **protection money** money paid for protection from violence.

protectionism n. the economic theory or practice of protecting home industries by imposing import duties on foreign goods. ☐ **protectionist** n. & adj.

protective adj. protecting, giving protection. ☐ **protective custody** the detention of a person for his or her own protection. ☐☐ **protectively** adv.

protector n. **1** a person or thing that protects something. **2** (**Protector**) *Aust. hist.* an official responsible for the Aboriginal population of a particular district. ☐ **protectorship** n.

protectorate n. **1** a nation that is under the official protection and partial control of a stronger one; this relation. **2** (**Protectorate**) *Aust. hist.* the office or district of a Protector of Aborigines.

protégé / **prot**-uh-zhay, **proh**-tuh- / n. a person who is helped and protected by another.

protégée n. a female protégé.

protein / **proh**-teen / n. an organic compound containing nitrogen, occurring in plant and animal tissue and forming an essential part of the food of animals.

pro tem adv. & adj. colloq. for the time being, temporarily. (¶ From the Latin *pro tempore*.)

Proterozoic adj. *Geol.* of the later part of the Precambrian era.

protest n. / **proh**-test / a statement or action showing one's disapproval. • adj. (usu. publicly) demonstrating objection to something (*thousands joined the protest march against nuclear testing*). • v. / pruh-**test** / **1** express one's strong disapproval (*protesting against nuclear testing*). **2** declare firmly or solemnly (*protested their innocence*). ☐ **under protest** unwillingly. ☐☐ **protester** n.

Protestant / **prot**-uhs-tuhnt / n. a member of any of the Christian groups that separated from the Catholic Church at the Reformation, or any group subsequently splitting from or descending from these. • adj. of the Protestants or their forms of religion etc. ☐ **Protestantism** n.

protestation / prot-uh-**stay**-shuhn / n. **1** a firm declaration (*protestations of loyalty*). **2** a protest.

Proteus / **proh**-tee-uhs / *Gk myth.* a minor sea god who had the power of prophecy but who would assume different shapes to avoid answering questions.

protium n. the most common isotope of hydrogen.

protocol / **proh**-tuh-kol / n. **1** official, esp. diplomatic, formality and etiquette, esp. as observed on State occasions etc. **2** the first or original draft of an agreement (esp. between States) in preparation for a treaty. **3** the formal statement of a transaction. **4** *Computing* a set of rules governing the exchange or transmission of data electronically between devices.

protomartyr n. the first martyr in any cause (*Pemulwuy is probably the Aborigines' protomartyr*).

proton / **proh**-ton / n. an elementary particle with a positive electric charge equal to that of an electron.

protoplasm / **proh**-tuh-plaz-uhm / n. the living part of a cell, consisting of a nucleus enclosed in cytoplasm. ☐ **protoplasmic** adj.

prototype / **proh**-tuh-tuyp / n. a first or original example of something from which others are developed; a trial model (e.g. of an aircraft). ☐ **prototypic** / pro-tuh-**tip**-ik / adj. **prototypical** adj.

protozoan / proh-tuh-**zoh**-uhn / n. (also **protozoon**) (pl. **protozoa** or **protozoans**) a minute usu. microscopic animal, such as the amoeba.

protract / pruh-**trakt** / v. prolong in duration (*protracted talks*). ☐ **protraction** n.

protractor n. an instrument for measuring angles, usu. a semicircle marked off in degrees.

protrude v. project from a surface; stick out. ☐ **protrusion** n. **protrusive** adj.

protuberance n. a protuberant part.

protuberant / pruh-**tyoo**-buh-ruhnt / adj. bulging outwards from a surface.

proud adj. **1** feeling or showing justifiable pride. **2** marked by such feeling (*a proud day for us*). **3** full of self-respect and independence (*too proud to ask for help*). **4** having an unduly high opinion of one's own qualities or merits. ☐ **do proud** treat with lavish generosity or honour (*they did us proud*). ☐☐ **proudly** adv.

prove v. (**proved** or **proven**, **proving**) **1** give or be proof of. **2** establish the validity of (a will). **3** be found to be (*it proved to be a good thing*). **4** (of dough) rise because of the action of yeast, before being baked. ☐ **prove oneself** show that one has the required character or abilities. ☐☐ **provable** adj.

■ Usage In Australian English it is not standard to use *proven* as the past participle (e.g. *his worth has been proven*). It is, however, common in certain expressions, such as *of proven ability*.

provedore / **prov**-uh-daw / n. (also **providore**, **provedor**) a supplier of provisions to a ship, a canteen, etc.

provenance / **prov**-uh-nuhns / n. **1** the place of origin or history, esp. of a work of art. **2** the origin (*do you know the provenance of the word 'kangaroo'?*).

provender / **prov**-uhn-duh / n. **1** fodder. **2** *jocular* food.

proverb n. a short well-known saying stating a general truth, e.g. *many hands make light work*.

proverbial / pruh-**ver**-bee-uhl / adj. **1** of or like a proverb; mentioned in a proverb (*the proverbial ill wind*). **2** well-known, notorious (*his meanness is proverbial*). ☐ **proverbially** adv.

provide v. **1** give or supply (*they will provide office space; provided me with an opportunity*). **2** (usu. foll. by *for*) take care of (a person) by supplying money, food, etc. (*has to provide for his family*). **3** make suitable preparation for something (*try to provide against emergencies*). ☐ **provider** n.

provided conj. (often foll. by *that*) on the condition or understanding (that) (*I shall come provided (that) the rest of your family agree*).

providence n. **1** timely preparation; forethought; thrift. **2** God's or nature's care and protection. **3** (**Providence**) God in this aspect.

provident adj. showing wise forethought for future needs or events; thrifty.

providential / prov-uh-**den**-shuhl / adj. fortunate, lucky; by divine intervention. ☐ **providentially** adv.

providing conj. = PROVIDED.

province n. **1** one of the principal administrative divisions in certain countries. **2** a sphere of action; business (*estimates of expenditure are the treasurer's province*). **3** a branch of learning etc. (*in the province of aesthetics*). ☐ **the provinces** the areas of a country outside its capital city, often regarded as uncultured or unsophisticated.

provincial / pruh-**vin**-shuhl / adj. **1** of a province or provinces (*provincial government*). **2** having only limited interests and narrow-minded views (*provincial attitudes*). • n. **1** a native or inhabitant of a province or of the provinces. **2** an unsophisticated or uncultured person. ☐ **provincialism** n.

provision n. **1** providing; preparation of resources etc. for future need (*made provision for their old age*). **2** (**provisions**) food and drink. **3** a statement or clause in a treaty or contract stipulating something (*under the provisions of his will*). • v. supply with provisions of food etc.

provisional adj. arranged or agreed upon temporarily but possibly to be altered later. ☐ **provisional licence** *Aust.* an initial licence to drive a motor vehicle, requiring (for a specified period, e.g. 3 years) the display of P-plates on any vehicle driven, and imposing certain restrictions (e.g. in Vic. the driver must be alcohol-free whenever driving). **provisional tax** an advance payment anticipating tax on income not taxed at source. ☐☐ **provisionally** adv.

proviso / pruh-**vuy**-zoh / n. (pl. **provisos**) something insisted upon as a condition of an agreement.

provisory / pruh-**vuy**-zuh-ree / adj. **1** conditional. **2** making provision for something.

provocation n. **1** provoking; being provoked. **2** a cause of annoyance.

provocative / pruh-**vok**-uh-tiv / adj. **1** arousing or likely to arouse anger, interest, or sexual desire. **2** deliberately annoying or controversial. ☐ **provocatively** adv.

provoke v. **1** make angry. **2** rouse or incite (a person) to action. **3** produce as a reaction or effect (*the joke provoked laughter*). **4** tempt; allure. ☐ **provoking** adj.

provost / **prov**-uhst / n. **1** the head of certain schools, colleges, etc. **2** the head of a chapter etc. of certain religious foundations.

prow n. the projecting front part of a ship or boat.

prowess / **prow**-es, prow-**es** / n. great ability or daring.

prowl v. roam (a place) esp. stealthily or restlessly or in search of prey, plunder, etc. • n. prowling. ☐ **prowler** n.

prox. abbr. proximo.

proximate / **prok**-suh-muht / adj. **1** nearest, next before or after. **2** approximate.

proximity / prok-**sim**-uh-tee / *n*. **1** nearness in space or time. **2** neighbourhood (*in the proximity of the station*).

proximo *adj*. (in commerce) of the next month (*the 3rd proximo*). (¶ Latin, = in the next.)

proxy *n*. a person authorised to represent or act for another; the use of such a person (*voted by proxy*).

prude / prood / *n*. a person of extreme or exaggerated propriety; one who is easily shocked by sexual matters. ☐ **prudery** *n*.

prudent *adj*. wise and cautious. ☐ **prudently** *adv*. **prudence** *n*.

prudential / proo-**den**-shuhl / *adj*. showing or involving prudence. ☐ **prudentially** *adv*.

prudish / **proo**-dish / *adj*. like a prude, showing prudery. ☐ **prudishness** *n*.

prune[1] *n*. a dried plum.

prune[2] *v*. **1** trim and shape by cutting away branches or shoots. **2** shorten or reduce and improve (a speech, book, etc.) by removing unnecessary parts. **3** reduce (costs etc.).

prunus *n*. a shrub or tree of the plum family, esp. purple-leaved varieties grown as garden ornamentals.

prurient / **proo**-ree-uhnt / *adj*. having or exciting sexual or lustful thoughts or curiosity. ☐ **prurience** *n*.

Prussian *adj*. of Prussia, a former country of north Europe. • *n*. a native of Prussia. ☐ **Prussian blue** a deep blue.

prussic acid *n*. a highly poisonous acid, hydrocyanic acid.

pry *v*. (**pried**, **prying**) inquire or investigate or peer impertinently and often furtively (into a person's private affairs etc.), snoop.

PS *abbr*. postscript.

psalm / sahm / *n*. a sacred song, esp. one of those in the Book of Psalms in the Old Testament.

psalmist / **sah**-muhst / *n*. a writer of psalms.

psalmody / **sahm**-uh-dee, **sal**-muh- / *n*. the practice or art of singing psalms, hymns, etc., esp. in public worship.

psalter / **sawl**-tuh, **sol**- / *n*. a copy of the Book of Psalms.

psaltery *n*. an early instrument like a dulcimer but played by plucking the strings.

psephology / se-**fol**-uh-jee / *n*. the study of trends in elections and voting. ☐ **psephologist** *n*.

pseudo / **syoo**-doh / *colloq. adj*. pretentious (esp. intellectually); false, insincere. • *n*. such a person; a poseur.

pseudo- *comb. form* false.

pseudonym / **syoo**-duh-nim / *n*. a fictitious name used by an author.

pseudonymous / syoo-**don**-uh-muhs / *adj*. writing or written under a false name. ☐ **pseudonymity** / syoo-duh-**nim**-uh-tee / *n*. **pseudonymously** *adv*.

psi / psuy / *n*. the twenty-third letter of the Greek alphabet (Ψ, ψ).

psittacosis *n*. an infectious viral disease, esp. of parrots, also affecting humans.

psoriasis / suh-**ruy**-uh-suhs / *n*. a skin disease causing red scaly patches.

psst *interj*. (also **pst**) a whispered exclamation to attract someone's attention.

psych / suyk / *v. colloq*. **1** (often foll. by *out*) intimidate or frighten (a person), esp. for one's own advantage. **2** (usu. foll. by *out*) analyse (a person's motivation etc.) for one's own advantage (*can't psych him out*). **3** (foll. by *out*) go under the influence of some drug, esp. marijuana. ☐ **psych up** make (oneself or another person) ready psychologically for a game, an ordeal, etc.

psyche / **suy**-kee / *n*. the human soul, spirit, or mind.

psychedelic / suy-kuh-**del**-ik / *adj*. **1** (of a drug) producing hallucinations. **2** vivid, colourful, and bold; involving abstract patterns.

psychiatry / suy-**kuy**-uh-tree, suh- / *n*. the study and treatment of mental disease. ☐ **psychiatric** / suy-kee-**at**-rik / *adj*. **psychiatrist** *n*.

psychic / **suy**-kik / *adj*. **1** of the soul or mind. **2** (of a person) considered to have occult powers such as telepathy, clairvoyance, etc. **3** (of a faculty, phenomenon, etc.) inexplicable by natural laws. • *n*. a person considered to have psychic powers; a medium. ☐ **psychically** *adv*.

psychical / **suy**-kik-uhl / *adj*. **1** concerning psychic phenomena or faculties (*psychical research*). **2** of the soul or mind. ☐ **psychically** *adv*.

psycho / **suy**-koh / *colloq. n*. (*pl*. **psychos**) a psychopath; an insane or eccentric person; a weirdo. • *adj*. psychopathic; highly eccentric.

psychoanalyse *v*. treat (a person) by psychoanalysis.

psychoanalysis *n*. a method of examining or treating mental conditions that involves bringing to light certain things in a person's unconscious mind that may be influencing behaviour and mental state. ☐ **psychoanalytic** *adj*. **psychoanalytical** *adj*.

psychoanalyst *n*. a specialist in psychoanalysis.

psychodrama *n*. **1** a form of psychotherapy in which patients act out events from their past. **2** a play or film etc. in which psychological elements are the main interest.

psychokinesis / suy-koh-kuh-**nee**-suhs / *n*. the movement of objects supposedly by telepathy or mental effort alone.

psychological *adj*. **1** of or affecting the mind and its workings. **2** of psychology. **3** *colloq*. (of an ailment etc.) existing only in the mind, imaginary (*his backache is purely psychological*). ☐ **psychological block** mental inability or inhibition caused by emotional factors. **psychological moment** the best time for achieving a particular effect or purpose. **psychological warfare** actions or propaganda designed to weaken an enemy's morale. ☐☐ **psychologically** *adv*.

psychology *n.* **1** the study of the mind (as deduced from behaviour) and how it works. **2** mental characteristics etc. of a person or group. **3** mental aspects of an activity, situation, etc. (*the psychology of crime*). ☐ **psychologist** *n.*

psychopath / **suy**-kuh-path / *n.* **1** a person suffering from a severe mental disorder, esp. with aggressive antisocial behaviour. **2** *colloq.* a mentally or emotionally unstable person. ☐ **psychopathic** / suy-kuh-**path**-ik / *adj.*

psychopathology / suy-koh-puh-**thol**-uh-jee / *n.* the scientific study of mental disorders.

psychopathy / suy-**kop**-uh-thee / *n.* psychopathic or psychologically abnormal behaviour.

psychosexual *adj.* of or involving the psychological aspects of the sexual impulse.

psychosis / suy-**koh**-suhs / *n.* (*pl.* **psychoses**) a severe mental disorder affecting the whole personality, esp. when resulting in delusions and loss of contact with external reality.

psychosomatic / suy-koh-suh-**mat**-ik / *adj.* **1** of or involving both the mind and the body. **2** (of an illness) caused or aggravated by mental stress. ☐ **psychosomatically** *adv.*

psychotherapy / suy-koh-**the**-ruh-pee / *n.* treatment of mental disorders by the use of psychological methods. ☐ **psychotherapeutic** *adj.* **psychotherapist** *n.*

psychotic / suy-**kot**-ik / *adj.* of or suffering from a psychosis. • *n.* a person suffering from a psychosis.

PT *abbr.* physical training.

Pt *symbol* platinum.

pt *abbr.* **1** pint. **2** part. **3** point.

Pte *abbr.* Private (in the army).

pteridophyte / **te**-ruh-duh-fuyt / *n.* a flowerless plant, e.g. ferns, clubmosses, etc.

pterodactyl / te-ruh-**dak**-tuhl / *n.* a large extinct birdlike reptile with wings.

pterostylis / te-roh-**stuy**-luhs / *n.* any of several Australian terrestrial orchids bearing deeply hooded flowers and often forming colonies (*see* GREENHOOD).

ptilotus / tuh-**loh**-tuhs / *see* PUSSY TAIL.

PTO *abbr.* please turn over.

Ptolemaic / tol-uh-**may**-ik / *adj.* of Ptolemy or his theories (*see* PTOLEMY).

Ptolemy / **tol**-uh-mee / (2nd century), Greek astronomer and geographer, who conceived a theory that the earth was the stationary centre of the universe.

ptomaine / tuh-**mayn**, toh- / *n.* any of various substances (some of which are poisonous) that occur in rotting animal and vegetable matter.

PTSD *abbr.* post-traumatic stress disorder.

Pty *abbr.* proprietary.

Pu *symbol* plutonium.

pub *n. colloq.* a hotel. ☐ **pub crawl** a drinking tour of several hotels in the one outing.

puberty / **pyoo**-buh-tee / *n.* the stage at which a person's reproductive organs mature and he or she becomes capable of producing offspring. ☐ **pubertal** *adj.*

pubes[1] / **pyoo**-beez / *n.* (*pl.* **pubes**) **1** the lower part of the abdomen at the front of the pelvis, covered with hair at puberty. **2** the hair, scanty at first, which appears in this region at puberty. **3** / pyoobz / *colloq.* pubic hair.

pubes[2] the plural of PUBIS.

pubescence *n.* **1** the beginning of puberty. **2** a soft down on plants, insects, etc. ☐ **pubescent** *adj.*

pubic / **pyoo**-bik / *adj.* of the pubes or pubis (*pubic hair*).

pubis / **pyoo**-buhs / *n.* (*pl.* **pubes** / **pyoo**-beez /) either of the pair of bones forming the sides of the pelvis.

public *adj.* **1** of or concerning the people as a whole (*public holiday*). **2** open to or shared by all (*public library*). **3** done or existing openly (*public apology*). **4** (of a service, funds, etc.) provided by or concerning the government (*public transport; public expenditure*). **5** of or involved in the affairs, esp. the government or the entertainment, of the community (*a distinguished public career; public figures*). • *n.* **1** members of the community in general or a particular section of this (*the Australian public; the reading public; my public*). **2** *Aust. colloq.* a pupil of a public school (*the majority of Aussie students are publics*). ☐ **go public 1** become a public company. **2** reveal one's plans etc. **public address system** a system of loudspeakers to make something audible over a wide area. **public company** a company that sells shares on the open market. **public convenience** a public toilet. **public enemy** a notorious wanted criminal. **public figure** a famous person. **public health** the provision by government of adequate sanitation, drainage, hygienic living conditions and environment etc. to protect the public from disease. **public housing** government-owned housing made available, usu. at a low rent, to those on a low income. **public lending right** the right of authors to payment when their books are lent by public libraries. **public opinion** the views generally prevalent among the general public. **public ownership** ownership by the nation, a State, etc., of the means of production, distribution, or exchange. **public prosecutor** a law officer conducting prosecutions on behalf of the government or in the public interest. **public relations** the promotion of a favourable public image, esp. by a company, political party, etc. **public school 1** a school established and maintained at public expense as part of a system of public (and usu. free) education (as opposed to PRIVATE SCHOOL). **2** (occasionally, imitating the Brit. system) a private school. **public sector** the part of a country's economy that is owned and controlled by the government. **public servant** *Aust.* **1** *hist.* a convict assigned to public labour. **2** a member of the public service. **public service**

Aust. the permanent professional branches of (State or Commonwealth) administration, excluding military and judicial branches and elected politicians. **public utility** an organisation supplying water, gas, electricity, transport, etc. to the community. **public works** building operations etc. done by or for a government on behalf of the community.

publican *n.* the keeper of a hotel.

publication *n.* **1** publishing; being published. **2** something published, e.g. a book or newspaper.

publicise *v.* (also **-ize**) bring to the attention of the public; advertise.

publicist / pub-luh-suhst / *n.* **1** a writer on or an expert in current public affairs. **2** a publicity agent or public relations officer.

publicity *n.* **1** public attention directed upon a person or thing. **2** the process of drawing public attention to a person or thing; the material used for this.

publicly *adv.* in public, openly.

publish *v.* **1** prepare and issue copies of (a book etc.) to the public. **2** make generally known. **3** announce formally.

publisher *n.* a person or firm that publishes books, newspapers, etc.

Puccini / puu-**chee**-nee /, Giacomo (1858–1924), Italian operatic composer.

puce / pyoos / *adj.* & *n.* dark red or purple-brown.

puck[1] *n.* a mischievous or evil sprite. ❑ **puckish** *adj.* **puckishness** *n.*

puck[2] *n.* a hard rubber disc used in ice hockey.

pucker *v.* (often foll. by *up*) gather or cause to gather into wrinkles, folds, or bulges (*puckered her eyebrows*). • *n.* a wrinkle or bulge made in this way.

pudding *n.* **1** a sweet cooked dish. **2** the sweet course of a meal; dessert. **3** a savoury dish (*steak and kidney pudding*). **4** any of various sausages stuffed with oatmeal, blood, etc. (*black pudding*). **5** *colloq.* a fat, stupid, or lazy person. ❑ **puddingy** *adj.*

puddle *n.* **1** a small pool of rainwater or other liquid on a surface. **2** wet clay and sand used as a watertight covering for embankments etc. • *v.* **1** stir (molten iron) to expel carbon and produce wrought iron. **2** work (clay and sand) into a wet mixture. **3** work (clayey gold-bearing or opal-bearing material) with water in a tub so as to separate out (the gold or opal). ❑ **puddler** *n.* **puddling** *n.* **puddly** *adj.*

pudendum / pyoo-**den**-duhm / *n.* (*pl.* **pudenda**) (usu. in *pl.*) the genitals, esp. of a woman. ❑ **pudendal** *adj.* (¶ Latin = that of which one should be ashamed.)

pudgy *adj.* (**pudgier**, **pudgiest**) podgy, plump.

puerile / pyoor-ruyl / *adj.* childish, immature (*asking puerile questions*). ❑ **puerility** / pyoo-**ril**-uh-tee / *n.*

puerperal / pyoo-**er**-puh-ruhl / *adj.* of or caused by childbirth. ❑ **puerperal fever** fever following childbirth, caused by infection of the lining of the uterus or vagina.

Puerto Rico / pwer-tuh **ree**-koh / an island in the West Indies. ❑ **Puerto Rican** *adj.* & *n.*

puff *n.* **1** a short light breath or wind; smoke or vapour sent out by this. **2** a powder puff. **3** a cake of puff pastry or choux pastry filled with cream etc. (*cream puffs*). **4** an over-enthusiastic review or advertisement. • *v.* **1** send out a puff or puffs; blow (smoke etc.) in puffs; smoke (a pipe etc.) in puffs. **2** breathe hard, pant. **3** (usu. in passive; often foll. by *out*) exhaust (*I'm completely puffed; I'm puffed out*). **4** make or become inflated, swell. **5** (usu. as **puffed up** *adj.*) make proud or boastful (*puffed up with conceit*). **6** advertise with extravagant praise. ❑ **puff pastry** light flaky pastry. **puff sleeve** (or **puffed sleeve**) a sleeve that is very full at the shoulder.

puffball *n.* a fungus with a ball-shaped spore-case that bursts open when ripe.

puffin *n.* a black and white seabird of the N. Atlantic and N. Pacific with a large brightly coloured bill.

puffy *adj.* (**puffier**, **puffiest**) puffed out, swollen. ❑ **puffiness** *n.*

puftaloon / puf-tuh-**loon** / *n. Aust.* a small fried cake, usu. spread with jam, sugar, or honey.

pug *n.* a dog of a dwarf breed with a broad flat nose and wrinkled face. ❑ **pug-nosed** (of a person) having a short flattish nose.

Pugh, Clifton (Ernest) (1924–90), AO, Australian artist, known esp. for his paintings inspired by the bush and for his portraits.

pugilist / **pyoo**-juh-luhst / *n.* a professional boxer. ❑ **pugilism** *n.* **pugilistic** *adj.*

pugnacious / pug-**nay**-shuhs / *adj.* eager to fight; aggressive. ❑ **pugnaciously** *adv.* **pugnacity** / pug-**nas**-uh-tee / *n.*

puissance *n.* **1** / pwee-suhns / *literary* or *archaic* power; might. **2** / pwee-**sawns** / (in show-jumping) a test of a horse's ability to jump high obstacles. ❑ **puissant** *adj.*

pukamani pole / **poo**-kuh-mah-nee / *n. Aust.* a carved and painted mortuary pole up to 4 metres in height, many of which surround the graves of the Tiwi people of Bathurst and Melville Islands.

puke *v. colloq.* vomit.

pukka / **puk**-uh / *adj. colloq.* real, genuine.

pulchritude / **pul**-kruh-tyood, **puul**- / *n. literary* beauty. ❑ **pulchritudinous** *adj.*

pull *v.* **1** exert force upon (a thing) so as to move it towards oneself or towards the source of the force. **2** remove by pulling (*pull the cork*). **3** propel (a boat) by pulling on its oars. **4** (in cricket) strike the ball to the leg side; (in golf) hit the ball widely to the left. **5** exert a pulling or driving force (*the engine is pulling well*). **6** attract (*attractions that pull the crowds*). **7** damage (a muscle) by straining or twisting it awkwardly. **8** draw (beer, liquor) from a barrel. **9** check the speed of (a horse), esp. to lose a race; (of a horse) strain against the bit. **10** *colloq.* achieve or accomplish (esp. something shady or illicit) (*what are you trying to pull?*). • *n.* **1** the act of pulling; the force exerted by this. **2** a means of exerting influence (*he has a lot of pull with the politicians*). **3** an attraction or attention-getter (*the Australian Ballet was a big pull overseas*). **4** a deep draught of a drink; a draw at a pipe etc. **5** a prolonged effort in walking etc. (*the long pull up the hill*). ▫ **pull a fast one** *see* FAST¹. **pull a person's leg** tease him or her. **pull back** retreat or withdraw; cause to do this. **pull-back** a withdrawal (of troops etc.). **pull-down 1** that may be, or is designed to be, pulled down. **2** *Computing* (of a menu) appearing below a menu title when selected. **pull in 1** (of a train) enter and stop at a station. **2** (of a vehicle) move into a slower lane; move to the side of the road and stop. **3** *colloq.* take into custody. **4** obtain as wages or profit. **5** draw crowds (*the new show is really pulling them in*). **pull off** succeed in achieving (something). **pull (oneself or someone) off** *coarse colloq.* masturbate (oneself or another). **pull oneself together** regain one's self-control. **pull one's punches** avoid using one's full force. **pull one's weight** do one's fair share. **pull out 1** withdraw or cause to withdraw. **2** (of a train) move out of a station. **3** (of a vehicle) move away from the side of a road, or from behind another vehicle to overtake it. **pull-out** a middle section of a magazine etc., detachable by pulling. **pull over** (of a vehicle) pull in. **pull rank** make unfair use of one's senior rank in demanding obedience or a privilege. **pull round** recover or cause to recover from illness. **pull strings** use one's influence, often secretly. **pull through** come or bring successfully through an illness or difficulty. **pull together** cooperate. **pull up 1** stop or cause (a person, vehicle, etc.) to stop. **2** reprimand.

pullet *n.* a young domestic hen less than one year old.

pulley *n.* (*pl.* **pulleys**) a wheel over which a rope or belt passes, used in lifting things or to drive a circular belt.

pullover *n.* a knitted garment (with no fastenings) for the upper part of the body, put on over the head.

pullulate / **pul**-yuh-layt / *v.* **1** (of a seed, shoot, etc.) sprout, bud. **2** swarm, teem; breed prolifically. **3** develop; spring up. **4** (foll. by *with*) abound.

pulmonary / **pul**-muh-nuh-ree, puul- / *adj.* of or affecting the lungs.

pulp *n.* **1** the soft moist part of fruit. **2** the soft tissue inside a tooth. **3** any soft moist mass of material, esp. of wood-fibre, rags, etc. as used for making paper. • *v.* reduce to pulp; become pulpy. ▫ **pulp magazines** (also **pulp fiction**) cheap popular magazines or books (originally printed on rough paper). ▫▫ **pulpy** *adj.*

pulpit / **puul**-pit / *n.* a raised enclosed platform in a church, used by a preacher.

pulpwood *n.* timber suitable for making paper pulp.

pulsar *n.* a source (in space) of radio signals that pulsate in a rapid regular rhythm.

pulsate / pul-**sayt** / *v.* expand and contract rhythmically; vibrate; quiver. ▫ **pulsation** *n.* **pulsator** *n.*

pulse¹ *n.* **1** the rhythmical throbbing of the arteries as blood is propelled along them; this as felt in the wrists, temples, etc. **2** any steady throb. **3** a single beat or throb. **4** a general feeling or opinion. • *v.* pulsate.

pulse² *n.* the edible seed of peas, beans, lentils, etc.

pulverise *v.* (also **-ize**) **1** crush or crumble into powder. **2** defeat thoroughly. ▫ **pulverisation** *n.*

puma / **pyoo**-muh / *n.* a large greyish brown American animal of the cat family.

pumice / **pum**-uhs / *n.* (in full **pumice stone**) a light porous kind of lava used for removing hard skin or as powder for polishing.

pummel *v.* (**pummelled**, **pummelling**) strike repeatedly, esp. with the fists.

pump¹ *n.* a machine or device for forcing liquid, air, or gas into or out of something. • *v.* **1** raise, move, or inflate by means of a pump. **2** use a pump. **3** empty by using a pump (*pump the ship dry*). **4** move vigorously up and down; shake (a person's hand) vigorously. **5** pour or cause to pour forth as if by pumping. **6** question (a person) persistently to obtain information. ▫ **pump iron** *colloq.* exercise with weights. **the sets are pumping** *Surfing* the waves are very good.

pump² *n.* a light shoe for dancing etc.

pumpernickel *n.* German wholemeal rye bread.

pumpkin *n.* a large round orange-coloured fruit used as a vegetable or made into a pie (*see* GRAMMA). ▫ **pumpkin beetle** an Australian insect that is a serious pest on pumpkins and similar plants.

pun *n.* a humorous use of a word to suggest another that sounds the same, e.g. 'the sole has no feet and therefore no sole, poor soul'. • *v.* (**punned**, **punning**) make a pun or puns.

Punch a character in the puppet show **Punch and Judy**, a bullying puppet with a humped back and hooked nose. ▫ **as pleased as Punch** extremely pleased.

punch¹ *v.* strike, esp. with a closed fist. • *n.* **1** a blow with the fist. **2** *colloq.* vigour, effective force; fizz, potency (*a speech with plenty of punch in it; the lemonade has lost its punch*). ▫ **pack a punch 1** (of a person) have the ability to deliver a telling blow with the fist. **2** (of an alcoholic drink) be very potent. **3** have great force or impact, esp. adversarial (*the editorial against nuclear testing packed quite a punch*). **punch-drunk** stupefied

punch from or as if from being punched. **punch-up** *colloq.* a fight with fists, a brawl.

punch[2] *n.* a device for making holes in metal, leather, or paper, or for stamping a design on material. •*v.* perforate with a punch; make (a hole etc.) with a punch.

punch[3] *n.* a drink made of wine or spirits mixed with fruit juices, spices, etc., and served chilled or hot.

punchline *n.* words that give the point of a joke or story.

Punch-McGregor, Angela (1953–), Australian actor of stage, television, and film.

punchy *adj.* **1** punch-drunk. **2** having vigour, forceful.

punctilio / pungk-**til**-ee-oh / *n.* (*pl.* **punctilios**) **1** a delicate point of ceremony or honour. **2** the etiquette of such points. **3** petty formality.

punctilious / pungk-**til**-ee-uhs / *adj.* very careful to carry out duties correctly; conscientious. □ **punctiliously** *adv.* **punctiliousness** *n.*

punctual *adj.* arriving or doing things at the appointed time, neither early nor late. □ **punctually** *adv.* **punctuality** *n.*

punctuate *v.* **1** insert punctuation marks in. **2** interrupt at intervals (*his speech was punctuated with cheers*).

punctuation *n.* punctuating; the marks used for this. □ **punctuation mark** any of the marks (e.g. full stop, comma, question mark) used in written or printed material.

puncture *n.* a small hole made by something sharp, esp. one made accidentally in a tyre. •*v.* **1** make a puncture in; suffer a puncture. **2** reduce the pride or confidence of (*punctured his conceit*). **3** *Aust.* exhaust, tire out.

pundit *n.* **1** (also **pandit**) a Hindu learned in Sanskrit, and in the philosophy, theology, etc. of India. **2** (often *ironical*) an expert.

pungent / **pun**-juhnt / *adj.* **1** having a strong sharp taste or smell. **2** (of remarks) penetrating, biting. **3** mentally stimulating. □ **pungently** *adv.* **pungency** *n.*

punish *v.* **1** cause (an offender) to suffer for his or her offence. **2** inflict a punishment for (*vandalism should be severely punished*). **3** treat roughly, test severely (*the race was run at a punishing pace*).

punishable *adj.* liable to be punished, esp. by law (*punishable offences*).

punishment *n.* **1** punishing; being punished. **2** a penalty for an offence. **3** *colloq.* severe treatment.

punitive / **pyoo**-nuh-tiv / *adj.* **1** inflicting or intended to inflict punishment. **2** (of taxation etc.) extremely severe. **3** *Law* (of damages etc.) vindictive.

punk *n.* **1** (in full **punk rock**) an anti-establishment and deliberately outrageous style of rock music, popular in the late 1970s. **2** (in full **punk rocker**) a follower of this. **3** a young hooligan or petty criminal, a lout. **4** *colloq.* a worthless person or thing. •*adj. colloq.* worthless; rotten; of very poor quality.

punkari / **pung**-kuh-ree / *n.* a white-eyed duck of all Australian States. (¶ Yaralde)

punnet / **pun**-uht / *n.* a small container for small fruit such as strawberries or for seedlings.

punster *n.* a person who makes puns, esp. habitually.

punt[1] *v.* **1** bet on a horse etc. **2** speculate in shares etc. □ **take** (*or* **have**) **a punt** *Aust.* **1** wager, place a bet. **2** try, have a go at (something).

punt[2] *v.* **1** *Aust. Rules* kick the ball, after it has dropped from the hands and before it reaches the ground. **2** make a similar kick in soccer, Rugby, etc. •*n.* (in full **punt kick**) a kick of this kind.

punt[3] *n.* a flat-bottomed boat propelled by pushing a pole on the river-bottom. •*v.* **1** propel (a punt) with a pole in this way. **2** carry or travel in a punt. □ **punter** *n.*

punter *n.* a person who gambles or lays a bet.

punty *n.* (also **punty bush**) any Australian shrub of the genus *Cassia*, having delicate pinnate leaves and showy yellow flowers. (¶ Western Desert language)

puny / **pyoo**-nee / *adj.* (**punier**, **puniest**) **1** undersized. **2** weak, feeble; petty (*a puny attempt at humour*).

pup *n.* **1** a young animal, esp. a dog or seal. **2** an unpleasant or arrogant young man or boy. •*v.* (**pupped**, **pupping**) give birth to pups. □ **be sold a pup** be cheated.

pupa / **pyoo**-puh / *n.* (*pl.* **pupae** / **pyoo**-pee /) a chrysalis. □ **pupal** *adj.*

pupate / pyoo-**payt** / *v.* become a pupa. □ **pupation** *n.*

pupil *n.* **1** a person taught by another. **2** an opening in the centre of the iris of the eye, through which light passes to the retina.

puppet *n.* **1** a kind of doll that can be made to move by various means as an entertainment. **2** a person who is entirely controlled by another. •*adj.* controlled or manipulated by external agencies (*a puppet government*). □ **puppet State** a country that is nominally independent but actually under the control of another.

puppeteer *n.* a person who works puppets.

puppetry *n.* manipulation of puppets.

puppy *n.* **1** a young dog. **2** a conceited or arrogant young man. □ **puppy fat** temporary fatness of a child or adolescent. **puppy love** romantic adolescent love.

purblind / **per**-bluynd / *adj.* **1** partially blind, dim-sighted. **2** stupid, dim-witted.

Purcell / per-**sel**, **per**-suhl /, Henry (1659–95), English composer. He composed the first English opera, *Dido and Aeneas* (1689).

purchase *v.* buy. •*n.* **1** buying. **2** something bought. **3** a firm hold to pull or raise something or prevent it from slipping; leverage. □ **purchaser** *n.*

purdah / **per**-duh / n. **1** the system in some Muslim or Hindu communities of keeping women from the sight of men or strangers by means of a veil or curtain. **2** a curtain in a house, used for this purpose.

pure adj. **1** not mixed with any other substance; free from impurities. **2** mere, nothing but (*pure nonsense*). **3** free from evil or sin. **4** chaste. **5** dealing with theory only, not with practical applications (*pure mathematics*). ☐ **pure merino** see MERINO (sense 3). ☐☐ **pureness** n.

purée / **pyoo**-ray, **pyoor**- / n. pulped fruit, vegetables, etc. •v. make into purée.

purely adv. **1** in a pure way. **2** entirely; only (*came purely out of interest*).

purgation / per-**gay**-shuhn / n. **1** purification. **2** purging of the bowels. **3** spiritual cleansing, esp. of a soul in purgatory.

purgative / **per**-guh-tiv / adj. **1** purifying. **2** strongly laxative. •n. a purgative thing; a strong laxative.

purgatory / **per**-guh-tuh-ree, -tree / n. **1** (in Catholic and Orthodox belief) a place or condition in which souls undergo purification by temporary punishment. **2** a place or condition of suffering. ☐ **purgatorial** / per-guh-**taw**-ree-uhl / adj.

purge / perj / v. **1** empty the bowels of (a person) by means of a purgative. **2** rid (an organisation) of undesirable members. **3** atone for (an offence, esp. contempt of court). •n. **1** purging. **2** a purgative.

purify v. (**purified**, **purifying**) make pure, cleanse from impurities. ☐ **purifier** n. **purification** n. **purificatory** adj.

Purim / **puu**-rim, poo-**reem** / n. a Jewish festival commemorating the defeat of Haman's plot to massacre the Jews.

purist n. a stickler for correctness, esp. in language. ☐ **purism** n.

puritan n. **1** (**Puritan**) a member of the party of English Protestants in the 16th and 17th centuries who regarded the Reformation of the English Church under Elizabeth I as incomplete and sought to simplify and regulate forms of worship. **2** a strict person who regards many forms of pleasure as sinful. •adj. **1** (**Puritan**) of the Puritans. **2** characteristic of a puritan.

puritanical / pyoo-ruh-**tan**-i-kuhl / adj. (usu. scornful) excessively religious or moral in behaviour. ☐ **puritanically** adv.

purity n. pureness.

purl[1] n. a knitting stitch formed by inserting the needle with its point towards the knitter. •v. make this stitch.

purl[2] v. (of a brook) flow with a swirling motion and babbling sound.

purler n. (also **pearler**) colloq. **1** a headlong fall. **2** Aust. something surpassing good or otherwise remarkable (of its kind) (*played a pearler of an innings; the PM's speech was a purler*).

purlieu / **per**-lyoo / n. **1** one's bounds, limits, or usual haunts. **2** (**purlieus**) outskirts, an outlying region.

purloin / per-**loin** / v. formal or humorous steal.

purple n. **1** a colour obtained by mixing red and blue. **2** the office or rank of a cardinal or bishop, with reference to the scarlet or purple official dress. •adj. of this colour. •v. become purple. ☐ **purple coral pea** Aust. = HARDENBERGIA. **purple passage** a very ornate passage in a literary work. **purple patch 1** Aust. a run of luck or success. **2** = PURPLE PASSAGE. ☐☐ **purplish** adj.

purport n. / **per**-pawt / the meaning or intention of something said or written. •v. / per-**pawt** / pretend, be intended to seem (*this purports to be Gough Whitlam's autograph*). ☐ **purportedly** adv.

purpose n. **1** an intended result (*this will serve our purpose*). **2** intention to act, determination. •v. intend (*this is what he purposes*). ☐ **on purpose** by intention, not by chance. **to no purpose** with no result.

purposeful adj. having or showing a particular purpose; with determination. ☐ **purposefully** adv. **purposefulness** n.

purposeless adj. having no aim or plan.

purposely adv. on purpose.

purposive / **per**-puh-siv / adj. having or done with a purpose; purposeful; resolute.

purr v. **1** (of a cat) make a low vibrant sound expressing contentment. **2** (of machinery etc.) run smoothly and quietly. **3** (of a person) express pleasure; utter purringly. •n. a purring sound.

purse n. **1** a small pouch for carrying money. **2** money, funds; a sum of money as a prize. •v. pucker or contract (*pursed his lips primly*).

purser n. a ship's officer in charge of accounts, esp. on a passenger ship.

pursuance n. performance or carrying out of something (*in pursuance of my duties*).

pursuant adv. (foll. by *to*) in accordance with.

pursue v. (**pursued**, **pursuing**) **1** follow or chase. **2** afflict continually (*was pursued by misfortunes*). **3** continue, proceed along (*we pursued our course*). **4** engage in (*pursuing her hobby*). ☐ **pursuer** n.

pursuit n. **1** pursuing (*in pursuit of the dingo*). **2** an activity or occupation pursued (*the pursuit of pleasure; her pursuit is dentistry*).

purulent / **pyoo**-ruh-luhnt / adj. of, containing, or discharging pus. ☐ **purulence** n.

purvey / per-**vay** / v. (**purveyed**, **purveying**) supply (food etc.) as a trader. ☐ **purveyor** n.

purview / **per**-vyoo / n. **1** the scope or range of a document, scheme, occupation, etc. **2** the range of physical or mental vision.

pus n. thick yellowish matter produced from infected tissue.

push v. **1** exert force upon (a thing) so as to move it away from oneself or from the source of the force. **2** thrust or cause to thrust outwards.

extend by effort (*the frontier was pushed further north*). **4** move forward or make (one's way) by pushing. **5** make a vigorous effort in order to succeed or to surpass others. **6** press (a person) to do something; harass (*pushing me to join their crazy church*). **7** urge the use or adoption of (goods or ideas etc.), e.g. by advertisement. **8** *colloq.* sell (illegal drugs). • *n.* **1** the act of pushing; the force exerted by this. **2** a vigorous effort; a military attack made in order to advance. **3** enterprise, self-assertion, determination to get on (*I admire her push*). **4** the use of influence to advance a person. **5** *Aust.* a group of people having a common interest or background (*the old-boy network or private school push*). ☐ **at a push** *colloq.* just about; if a big effort were made. **be pushed for** *colloq.* have barely enough of (*I'm pushed for time*). **give** (or **get**) **the push** *colloq.* dismiss or be dismissed (from one's job etc.); reject or be rejected (*got the push from his girlfriend*). **push around** treat contemptuously and unfairly; bully. **push-button** *adj.* operated by pressing a button. **push off** *colloq.* go away. **push polling** a political election campaign tactic in which damaging allegations are made about a candidate (usu. by telephone) in the guise of market research etc. **push-start** *v.* start (a motor vehicle) by pushing it along to turn the engine. *n.* a start made in this way. **push the envelope** see ENVELOPE. **push through** get (a proposal) accepted quickly. **push-up** a press-up. ☐☐ **pusher** *n.*

pushbike *n.* a bicycle worked by pedalling.
pusher *n.* **1** a person who sells illegal drugs. **2** *Aust.* a collapsible pram on wheels for very small children. Also called *stroller*.
pushing *adj.* (of a person) **1** pushy. **2** *colloq.* having nearly reached (a specified age) (*pushing forty*).
pushover *n. colloq.* **1** something that is easily done. **2** a person who is easily convinced.
pushy *adj.* too assertive and determined; not patient or considerate.
pusillanimous / pyoo-suh-**lan**-uh-muhs / *adj.* timid, cowardly. ☐ **pusillanimity** / pyoo-suh-luh-**nim**-uh-tee / *n.*
puss *n. colloq.* a cat.
pussy *n.* **1** (also **pussy-cat**) *colloq.* a cat. **2** *coarse colloq.* **a** a woman's genitals. **b** *offens.* women in general, considered sexually. ☐ **pussy tail** *Aust.* any of many Australian shrubs of the genus *Ptilotus* having soft, fluffy flower heads. Also called *ptilotus*, *mulla mulla*.
pussyfoot *v. colloq.* **1** move stealthily. **2** act too cautiously; avoid committing oneself.
pustule / **pus**-tyool / *n.* a pimple or blister containing pus. ☐ **pustular** *adj.*
put *v.* (**put**, **putting**) **1** move (a thing) to a specified place; cause to occupy a certain place or position; send. **2** cause to be in a certain state or relationship (*put the machine out of action; put her at her ease*). **3** subject (*put it to the test*). **4** estimate (*I put the cost at $400*). **5** express or state (*put it tactfully*). **6** impose as a tax etc. **7** place as an investment or bet (*put his money into land*). **8** lay (blame) on. **9** (of ships) proceed (*put to sea*). • *n.* a throw of the shot. ☐ **put about 1** spread (information, a rumour, etc.). **2** *Nautical* turn round; put (a ship) on the opposite tack. **put across** communicate (an idea etc.). **put away** *colloq.* **1** put into prison or a mental home. **2** consume as food or drink. **put back 1** return to its former place. **2** change to a later time. **put by** save for future use. **put down 1** suppress by force or authority. **2** snub. **3** have (an animal) destroyed. **4** enter (a person's name) on a list. **5** reckon or consider (*put him down as a fool*). **6** attribute (*put it down to nervousness*). **put-down** *n.* a snub. **put forward 1** suggest, propose. **2** change to an earlier time. **put in 1** make (an appearance). **2** enter (a claim). **3** spend (time) working. **put in for** apply for. **put it on** *colloq.* pretend an emotion. **put off 1** postpone; postpone an engagement with (a person). **2** make excuses and try to avoid. **3** dissuade, repel (*the smell puts me off*). **put on 1** stage (a play etc.). **2** increase (*putting on weight*). **3** cause to operate (*put the radio on*). **put-on** *n.* a deception or hoax. **put out 1** disconcert, annoy, or inconvenience (a person). **2** extinguish (a light or fire). **3** dislocate (a joint). **put over** = PUT ACROSS. **put the hard word on** (a person) *colloq.* **1** pressure (him or her) for sex. **2** pressure (him or her) for a loan. **put through 1** complete (a business transaction) successfully. **2** connect by telephone. **3** cause to undergo (*put it through severe tests*). **put up 1** construct or build. **2** raise the price of. **3** provide or contribute (*the firm will put up the money*). **4** offer for sale. **5** display (a notice). **6** present as an idea or proposal. **7** give or receive accommodation (*they put up no resistance*). **put-up** *adj.* concocted fraudulently (*a put-up job*). **put up to** encourage (a person) to do something wrong (*who put him up to it?*). **put up with** endure, tolerate.
putative / **pyoo**-tuh-tiv / *adj.* reputed, supposed (*his putative father*).
Putin / **poo**-tin /, Vladimir (1952–), Russian statesman. He became president of Russia in 2000.
putrefy / **pyoo**-truh-fuy / *v.* (**putrefied**, **putrefying**) rot, decay or cause to decay. ☐ **putrefaction** / pyoo-truh-**fak**-shuhn / *n.*
putrescent / pyoo-**tres**-uhnt / *adj.* decaying, rotting. ☐ **putrescence** *n.*
putrid / **pyoo**-truhd / *adj.* **1** decomposed, rotting. **2** foul-smelling. **3** corrupt. ☐ **putridity** *n.*
putsch / puuch / *n.* an attempt at political revolution; a violent uprising.
putt / put / *v.* strike (a golf ball) lightly to make it roll along the ground. • *n.* a stroke of this kind. ☐ **putting green** (in golf) a smooth area of grass round a hole.

putter *n.* a golf club used in putting.

putto / **puut**-oh / *n.* (*pl.* **putti**) the representation of a naked boy (esp. as a cherub or a cupid) in (esp. Renaissance) art.

putty *n.* a soft paste that sets hard, used for fixing glass in window frames, filling holes, etc. • *v.* cover, fix, join, or fill with putty. ☐ **putty in someone's hands** (of a person) easily influenced or manipulated. **up to putty** *Aust. colloq.* worthless (*these cheap secateurs are up to putty*).

puzzle *n.* **1** a question that is difficult to answer; a problem. **2** a problem or toy designed to test one's knowledge, ingenuity, or patience. **3** a person or situation that is difficult to work out, confusing. • *v.* confuse (a person); cause doubt and uncertainty to. ☐ **puzzle over** be uncertain and think hard about. **puzzle out** solve or understand by patient thought or ingenuity. ☐☐ **puzzlement** *n.*

puzzler *n.* a puzzling problem.

PVC *abbr.* polyvinyl chloride.

PWA *abbr.* person with Aids.

■ **Usage** PWA is the official designation and should be used instead of *Aids patient, Aids sufferer, or Aids victim.*

pyaemia / puy-**ee**-mee-uh / *n.* (also **pyemia**) blood poisoning with formation of abscesses in the internal organs of the body.

pycnantha / pik-**nan**-thuh / = GOLDEN WATTLE.

Pygmalion / pig-**may**-lee-uhn / *Gk myth.* a king of Cyprus who made an ivory statue of a beautiful woman and loved it so deeply that at his request Aphrodite gave it life.

pygmy / **pig**-mee / *n.* (also **pigmy**) **1** a person or thing of unusually small size. **2** a member of a dwarf Black people of equatorial Africa. • *adj.* very small. ☐ **pygmy possum** *Aust.* any of several small (mouse-sized) mainly nocturnal marsupials of northern, eastern, and southern Australia.

pyjamas *n.pl.* a loose-fitting jacket and trousers for sleeping in. ☐ **pyjama cricket** *Aust.* one-day cricket (from the coloured uniforms worn by the players).

pylon *n.* a tall metal structure for carrying overhead electricity cables.

Pyongyang the capital of North Korea.

pyorrhoea / puy-uh-**ree**-uh / *n.* (also **pyorrhea**) a disease of the tooth-sockets causing discharge of pus and loosening of the teeth.

pyramid *n.* a structure with a flat (usu. square) base and sloping sides that meet at the top, esp. one built by the ancient Egyptians as a tomb or by the Aztecs and Mayas as a platform for a temple. ☐ **pyramid selling** a system of selling goods in which agency rights are sold to an increasing number of distributors at successively lower levels, with only those at the very bottom of the pyramid actually selling any goods. ☐☐ **pyramidal** / pi-**ram**-i-duhl / *adj.*

pyre / puyuh / *n.* a pile of wood etc. for burning a corpse at a funeral.

Pyrenees *n.pl.* a range of mountains between France and Spain. ☐ **Pyrenean** / pi-ruh-**nee**-uhn / *adj.*

pyrethrum / puy-**ree**-thruhm / *n.* **1** a chrysanthemum with finely divided leaves. **2** an insecticide made from its dried flowers.

pyretic / puy-**ret**-ik / *adj.* of or producing fever.

pyrex *n. trademark* a hard heat-resistant glass.

pyrexia / puy-**rek**-see-uh / *n. Med.* fever.

pyrites / puy-**ruy**-teez / *n.* a mineral that is a sulphide of iron (*iron pyrites*) or copper and iron (*copper pyrites*).

pyromania / puy-roh-**may**-nee-uh / *n.* an uncontrollable impulse to set things on fire. ☐ **pyromaniac** *n. & adj.*

pyrotechnic / puy-roh-**tek**-nik / *adj.* of or like fireworks. • *n.pl.* (**pyrotechnics**) **1** the art of making fireworks. **2** a firework display. **3** any loud or brilliant display.

Pyrrhic victory / **pi**-rik / *n.* a victory gained at too great a cost, like that of Pyrrhus (king of Epirus) over the Romans in 279 BC.

Pythagoras / puy-**thag**-uh-ruhs / (late 6th century BC), Greek philosopher and mathematician. ☐ **Pythagoras' theorem** the mathematical theorem that the square on the hypotenuse of a right-angled triangle is equal to the sum of the squares on the other two sides. ☐☐ **Pythagorean** *adj. & n.*

Pythia / **pith**-ee-uh / *n.* the priestess of Apollo at Delphi in ancient Greece, who delivered the oracles.

python / **puy**-thuhn / *n.* a large tropical snake that squeezes its prey so as to suffocate it.

pyx / piks / *n.* **1** a vessel in which the consecrated Host is kept within the tabernacle. **2** a small, flat, circular box in which the Host is carried to a sick person for communion.

Q

Q *abbr.* (also **Q.**) question.

Qantas / **kwon**-tuhs / an Australian international airline. (¶ Abbreviation of Queensland and Northern Territory Aerial Services.)

Qatar / ka-**tah** / a monarchy (sheikdom) on the west coast of the Persian Gulf. ☐ **Qatari** *adj.* & *n.* (*pl.* **Qataris**).

QC *abbr.* = QUEEN'S COUNSEL.

QED *abbr.* quod erat demonstrandum. (¶ Latin, = which was the thing that had to be proved.)

Q fever *n.* an often acute febrile disease, first identified and described in Australia, caused by a parasitic micro-organism of the type that causes typhus etc. (¶ Q = query: many wrongly believe that Q = Queensland.)

Qld *abbr.* Queensland.

qr. *abbr.* quarter(s).

q. t. *n.* ☐ **on the q. t.** *colloq.* on the quiet, secretly.

qua / kwah, kway / *conj.* in the capacity or character of (*put his duty qua citizen above other loyalties*). (¶ Latin)

quack[1] *n.* the harsh cry of a duck. •*v.* utter this sound.

quack[2] *n.* **1** a person who falsely claims to have medical skill or to have remedies which will cure disease etc. **2** *colloq.* a doctor. ☐ **quackery** *n.*

quad / kwod / *n. colloq.* **1** a quadrangle. **2** a quadruplet. **3** quadraphonics. •*adj.* quadraphonic.

Quadragesima / kwod-ruh-**jes**-uh-muh / *n.* the first Sunday in Lent.

quadrangle / **kwod**-rang-guhl / *n.* **1** a four-sided plane figure, esp. a square or a rectangle. **2** a four-sided court, orig. in colleges. ☐ **quadrangular** *adj.*

quadrant / **kwod**-ruhnt / *n.* **1** a quarter of a circle or of its circumference. **2** an instrument with an arc of 90° marked off in degrees, for measuring angles.

quadraphonic / kwod-ruh-**fon**-ik / *adj.* (also **quadrophonic**) (of sound reproduction) using four transmission channels. •*n. pl.* (**quadraphonics**) quadraphonic transmission. ☐ **quadraphonically** *adv.*

quadrate *n.* a rectangular object. •*v.* make square.

quadratic / kwod-**rat**-ik / *n.* (also **quadratic equation**) an equation involving the square (and no higher power) of one or more of the unknown quantities or variables.

quadrella / kwod-**rel**-uh / *n. Aust.* a form of betting on horse races etc. in which the better must select the winners of four specified races.

quadrennial / kwod-**ren**-ee-uhl / *adj.* **1** lasting for four years. **2** happening every fourth year.

quadri- *comb. form* four.

quadriceps / **kwod**-ruh-seps / *n.* the four-headed muscle at the front of the thigh.

quadrilateral / kwod-ruh-**lat**-uh-ruhl / *n.* a geometric figure with four sides. •*adj.* having four sides.

quadrille / kwuh-**dril** / *n.* a square dance for four couples; the music for this.

quadriplegia / kwod-ruh-**plee**-juh / *n.* paralysis of both arms and both legs. ☐ **quadriplegic** *adj.* & *n.*

quadroon *n.* a person of one quarter black blood.

quadruped / **kwod**-ruh-ped / *n.* a four-footed animal, esp. a mammal.

quadruple *adj.* **1** consisting of four parts; involving four people or groups (*a quadruple alliance*). **2** four times as much as (*we shall need quadruple that number of lights*). **3** (of time in music) having four beats in a bar. •*v.* multiply or become multiplied by four (*costs had quadrupled*).

quadruplet / kwo-**droo**-pluht / *n.* each of four children born at one birth.

quadruplicate *adj.* / kwo-**droo**-pluh-kuht / fourfold; of which four copies are made. •*v.* / kwo-**droo**-pluh-kayt / multiply by four.

quaff / kwof / *v.* drink (a thing) in long draughts.

quagmire / **kwog**-muy-uh, **kwag**- / *n.* **1** a bog or marsh. **2** a complex or dangerous situation.

quail *n.* (*pl.* **quail** or **quails**) a small European game bird related to the partridge (and now farmed in Australia). •*v.* flinch, show fear.

quaint *adj.* attractive through being unusual or old-fashioned. ☐ **quaintly** *adv.* **quaintness** *n.*

quake *v.* shake or tremble from unsteadiness; shake with fear. •*n.* **1** a quaking movement. **2** an earthquake.

Quaker *n.* a member of the Society of Friends (*see* SOCIETY). ☐ **Quakerism** *n.*

Quaky Isles *n. pl. Aust. colloq.* New Zealand.

qualification *n.* **1** qualifying; being qualified. **2** a thing that qualifies a person to do something. **3** something that restricts a meaning (*this statement needs certain qualifications*).

qualificatory *adj.* of, giving, or involving qualifications.

qualify *v.* (**qualified**, **qualifying**) **1** make or become competent, eligible, or legally entitled to do something. **2** make (a statement etc.) less general or extreme; limit its meaning (*'in all cases' needs to be qualified as 'in all known cases'; we gave it only qualified approval*). **3** describe, attribute

qualitative / kwol-uh-tuh-tiv / *adj.* of or concerned with quality rather than quantity.

some quality to (*adjectives qualify nouns*). ☐ **qualifier** *n.*

quality *n.* **1** a degree or level of excellence (*goods of high quality*). **2** general excellence. **3** a characteristic, something that is special in a person or thing (*she has the quality of inspiring confidence*). ☐ **quality control** maintenance of standards in products or services by testing samples.

qualm / kwahm / *n.* **1** a misgiving; a pang of conscience. **2** a sudden feeling of sickness or faintness.

Qualup bell / kway-luhp / *n.* a WA pimelea, a small shrub bearing bracts streaked with crimson or purple.

quamby / kwom-bee / *n. Aust.* a camp; a temporary shelter. • *v. hist.* lie down (esp. for the night etc.); stop; die. (¶ Probably Wuywurung *guwambi* 'a sleeping place'.)

quandary / kwon-duh-ree, -dree / *n.* a state of perplexity; a difficult situation.

quandong / kwon-dong / *n. Aust.* **1** a shrub or small tree of dry country in southern Australia bearing a bright red edible fruit with a wrinkled stone that contains an edible kernel. **2** a large rainforest tree of eastern Qld and eastern NSW bearing a globular blue edible fruit. **3** *colloq.* **a** a person who exploits or imposes on another. **b** a country bumpkin. (¶ Wiradhuri *guwandhaang*.)

quango *n.* (*pl.* **quangos**) an administrative body with financial support from and senior appointments made by the government but not controlled by it. (¶ From *quasi-autonomous non-governmental organisation*.)

quanta *see* QUANTUM.

quantify / kwon-tuh-fuy / *v.* (**quantified**, **quantifying**) determine the quantity of; express as a quantity. ☐ **quantification** *n.* **quantifiable** *adj.*

quantitative / kwon-tuh-tuh-tiv / *adj.* of or concerned with quantity (*quantitative analysis*).

quantity *n.* **1** an amount or number of things; a specified or considerable amount or number. **2** ability to be measured through having size, weight, amount, or number. **3** a thing that has this ability; a figure or symbol representing it. ☐ **quantity surveyor** a person who measures and prices building work.

quantum / kwon-tuhm / *n.* (*pl.* **quanta**) **1** *Physics* a minimum amount of a physical quantity (such as energy) which can exist in a given situation. **2** the amount required, desired, or allowed. ☐ **quantum leap** (*or* **jump**) a sudden great advance. **quantum mechanics** (also **quantum theory**) a theory of physics based on the assumption that energy exists in indivisible units.

quarantine / kwo-ruhn-teen / *n.* **1** isolation imposed on persons, animals, or plants to prevent infection or contagion and the introduction to a country of plant diseases or pests. **2** the period of this isolation. • *v.* put into quarantine.

quark *n. Physics* any of a group of hypothetical components of elementary particles.

quarrel *n.* **1** a violent disagreement; breaking of friendly relations. **2** a cause for complaint against a person (*we have no quarrel with him*). • *v.* (**quarrelled**, **quarrelling**) **1** engage in a quarrel. **2** disagree or complain (*we are not quarrelling with this decision*).

quarrelsome *adj.* liable to quarrel with people.

quarrion / kwo-ree-uhn / *n.* (also **quarrian**, **quarry hen**) a name for the cockatiel, the crested, predominantly grey parrot widespread in mainland Australia. (¶ Wiradhuri *guwarraying*.)

quarry *n.* **1** an intended prey or victim being hunted. **2** something that is sought or pursued. **3** an open excavation from which stone or slate etc. is obtained. • *v.* (**quarried**, **quarrying**) **1** obtain (stone etc.) from a quarry. **2** search laboriously in order to extract information. ☐ **quarry hen** = QUARRION. **quarry tile** an unglazed floor tile.

quart *n.* a measure of capacity for liquids in the imperial system, 2 pints or a quarter of a gallon (0.946 litre). ☐ **quart pot** (also **quart**) *Aust.* a tin vessel (orig. of a quart capacity) used for boiling water etc., esp. out bush.

quarter *n.* **1** each of the four equal parts into which a thing is divided. **2** a quarter of a US or Canadian dollar, 25 cents. **3** a fourth part of a year. **4** a fourth part of a lunar month. **5** a point of time 15 minutes before or after every hour. **6** a direction or point of the compass. **7** a district or division of a town (*the residential quarter*). **8** a person or group regarded as a possible source of help or information (*got no sympathy from that quarter*). **9** mercy towards an enemy or opponent (*gave no quarter*). **10** (**quarters**) lodgings, accommodation. **11** each of the four parts into which a carcass is divided; (in *pl.*) hindquarters. **12** (in Australian Rules, netball, etc.) each of the four equal periods into which a match is divided. • *v.* **1** divide into quarters; *hist.* divide (the body of an executed person) in this way. **2** put (soldiers etc.) into lodgings. **3** (in heraldry) place (a symbol) in one of the divisions of a shield or coat of arms. ☐ **quarter acre block** *Aust.* **1** a standard suburban building block, formerly approximately a quarter of an acre in size. **2** this as an emblem of material security. **quarter-final** a match or round preceding a semifinal. **quarter horse** a small stocky horse noted for agility and speed over short distances (originally usu. a quarter of a mile). **quarter-tone** *Music* half a semitone.

quarterback *n.* a player in American football who directs attacking play.

quarterdeck *n.* the part of the upper deck of a ship nearest the stern, usu. reserved for the ship's officers.

quarterly *adj.* & *adv.* produced or occurring once in every quarter of a year. • *n.* a quarterly periodical.

quartermaster *n.* **1** (in the army) a regimental officer in charge of stores and assigning quarters etc. **2** a naval petty officer in charge of steering and signals.

quarterstaff *n.* a stout pole 2 to 2.5 metres long formerly used as a weapon.

quartet *n.* **1** a group of four instruments or voices; a musical composition for these. **2** a set of four.

quarto *n.* (*pl.* **quartos**) the size of a book or sheet of paper given by folding a sheet of standard size twice to form four leaves.

quartz / kwawtz / *n.* a hard mineral occurring in various forms. ☐ **quartz clock** (*or* **watch**) one operated by electric vibrations of a quartz crystal.

quasar / **kway**-zah / *n.* a starlike object that is the source of intense electromagnetic radiation.

quash *v.* **1** annul; reject (by legal authority) as not valid (*quashed the conviction*). **2** suppress or crush (a rebellion etc.).

quasi- / **kway**-zuy, **kwah**-zee / *comb. form* seeming to be something but not really so (*a quasi-scientific explanation*).

quassia / **kwosh**-uh / *n.* a South American tree with bitter bark, wood, and root, used to make a medicinal tonic and insecticide.

quaternary / kwuh-**ter**-nuh-ree / *adj.* **1** having four parts. **2** (**Quaternary**) *Geol.* of the second period of the Cainozoic era. • *n.* (**Quaternary**) this period.

quatrain / **kwot**-rayn / *n.* a stanza or poem of four lines.

quatrefoil / **kat**-ruh-foil / *n.* **1** a leaf or flower with four lobes. **2** (in architecture) an ornament resembling this.

quattrocento / kwat-roh-**chen**-toh, kwot-roh- / *n.* Italian art of the 15th century.

quaver *v.* **1** tremble, vibrate. **2** speak in a trembling voice. • *n.* **1** a quavering sound. **2** a note in music, lasting half as long as a crotchet.

quay / kee / *n.* an artificial landing place alongside which ships can be tied up for loading and unloading.

queasy *adj.* (**queasier**, **queasiest**) **1** feeling slightly sick. **2** having a digestion that is easily upset. **3** (of the conscience etc.) uneasy; squeamish. ☐ **queasiness** *n.*

queen *n.* **1** (as a title, usu. **Queen**) a woman who is a sovereign. **2** a king's wife. **3** a woman, place, or thing regarded as supreme (*Venice, the queen of the Adriatic*). **4** a playing card bearing a picture of a queen. **5** *colloq. offens.* a male homosexual. **6** a piece in chess. **7** a fertile female of a bee or ant etc. • *v.* convert (a pawn in chess) to a queen when it reaches the opponent's end of the board. ☐ **queen bee 1** a fertile female bee. **2** a woman who behaves as if she is the most important person in a group. **queen-size** *adj.* extra large, but smaller than king-size. ☐☐ **queenly** *adj.*

Queen-Anne *adj.* in the style of furniture and architecture popular in the early 18th century, characterised by careful proportions, lack of ornament, and the curved cabriole leg.

Queensberry Rules the standard rules of boxing.

Queen's Counsel *n.* an appointment bestowed on a barrister by an attorney-general in recognition of excellence as an advocate etc.

Queensland a State comprising the NE part of Australia. ☐ **Queensland blue** a variety of pumpkin having a deep blue-grey skin. **Queensland bottle tree** *see* BOTTLE. **Queensland cane toad** *see* CANE. **Queensland groper** = GROPER[1]. **Queensland heeler** a blue heeler (*see* BLUE). **Queensland maple** a rainforest tree of north-eastern Qld yielding a valuable timber much used in furniture making; its wood. Also called *silkwood*. **Queensland nut** = MACADAMIA. **Queensland trumpeter** the javelin fish (*see* JAVELIN). **Queensland walnut** a tall rainforest tree of north-eastern Qld yielding a valuable timber much used in furniture making; its wood.

Queenslander *n.* **1** a native or resident of Queensland. **2** a highset weatherboard house, of a style built in Queensland from the 1870s onwards.

queer *adj.* **1** strange, odd, eccentric. **2** causing one to feel suspicious; of questionable character. **3** slightly ill or faint (*felt queer*). **4** *colloq. offens.* homosexual. • *n. colloq. offens.* a homosexual. • *v.* spoil. ☐ **in Queer Street** *colloq.* in difficulties, in debt or trouble. **queer a person's pitch** *colloq.* spoil his or her chances. ☐☐ **queerly** *adv.* **queerness** *n.*

quell *v.* suppress, reduce to submission (*quelled the rebellion*).

quench *v.* **1** extinguish (a fire or flame). **2** satisfy (one's thirst) by drinking. **3** cool (a heated thing) by water. **4** stifle or suppress (desire, lust, etc.).

quenda / **kwen**-duh / *n.* the small marsupial *Isoodon obesulus* of southern Australia. Also called *southern brown bandicoot*. (¶ Nyungar)

quern *n.* a hand mill for grinding corn.

querulous / **kwe**-ruh-luhs / *adj.* complaining peevishly. ☐ **querulously** *adv.*

query *n.* **1** a question. **2** a question mark. • *v.* (**queried**, **querying**) ask a question or express doubt about.

quest *n.* **1** a search. **2** the thing being sought, esp. by a medieval knight and in modern fantasy literature. • *v.* (often foll. by *for*) (esp. in modern fantasy literature) go about or travel in search of something. ☐ **quester** *n.* (also **questor**).

question *n.* **1** a sentence requesting information or an answer. **2** something being discussed or for discussion; a problem requiring solution. **3** the raising of doubt (*whether we shall win is open to question*). • *v.* **1** ask questions of (a person). **2** express doubt about. ☐ **in question** being

questionable referred to or discussed; being disputed (*his honesty is not in question*). **no question of** no possibility of. **out of the question** completely impracticable. **question mark 1** a punctuation mark (?) placed after a question (see panel). **2** a doubt as to validity etc. (*there's a question mark about the whole project*). **question time** a period in Parliament when MPs may question ministers. □ □ **questioner** *n.* **questioning** *adj.* & *n.*

questionable *adj.* open to doubt or suspicion. □ **questionably** *adv.*

questionnaire / kwes-chuh-**nair**, kes- / *n.* a list of questions seeking information about people's opinions or customs etc.

queue *n.* a line or series of people, computer programs, vehicles, etc. awaiting their turn to be attended to or to proceed. • *v.* (**queued**, **queuing** or **queueing**) wait in a queue (*queuing up*). □ **queue-jump** push forward out of turn in a queue.

quibble *n.* a petty objection. • *v.* make petty objections. □ **quibbler** *n.*

quiche / keesh / *n.* an open tart, usu. with a savoury egg filling.

quick *adj.* **1** taking only a short time. **2** able to notice, learn, or think quickly. **3** (of temper) easily roused. **4** *archaic* alive (*the quick and the dead*). • *n.* **1** the sensitive flesh below the nails. **2** *Cricket* a fast bowler. • *adv.* quickly (*quick-drying*). □ **be cut to the quick** have one's feelings deeply hurt. **quick-fire** rapid, in quick succession. **quick fix** a rapid (esp. inadequate) solution to a problem. **quick smart** *Aust.* very quickly. **quick-witted** quick at understanding a situation or making jokes. □ □ **quickly** *adv.*

quicken *v.* **1** make or become quicker. **2** stimulate, make or become livelier (*our interest quickened*). **3** reach a stage in pregnancy when the foetus makes movements that can be felt by the mother.

quickie *n. colloq.* **1** something done or made quickly or hastily. **2 a** a hasty drink. **b** a hasty act of sex. **3** *Cricket* a fast bowler.

quicklime = LIME[1].

quicksand *n.* **1** an area of loose wet deep sand into which heavy objects will sink. **2** a treacherous situation etc.

quicksilver *n.* mercury.

quickstep *n.* a ballroom dance with quick steps; music for this.

quid *n.* (*pl.* **quid**) *colloq.* (in Britain and formerly in Australia) one pound, £1. □ **make a quick quid** *Aust.* make money, often by dubious means. **make a quid** *Aust.* earn money. **not for quids** under no circumstances. (**not**) **the full quid** *Aust.* (not) in possession of one's mental faculties. **quids in** in a position of profit.

quiddity *n.* **1** the essence of a thing. **2** a quibble.

quid pro quo *n.* (*pl.* **quid pro quos**) a thing given or done in return for something else. (¶ Latin, = something for something.)

quiescent / kwee-**es**-uhnt / *adj.* inactive, quiet. □ **quiescence** *n.*

quiet *adj.* **1** with little or no sound, not loud or noisy. **2** with little or no movement. **3** free from disturbance or vigorous activity, peaceful. **4** silent (*be quiet!*). **5** unobtrusive, done in a restrained manner (*had a quiet laugh about it*). **6** (of colours or dress etc.) subdued, not showy. • *n.* quietness. • *v.* make or become quiet, calm. □ **just quietly** *Aust.* confidentially; just between you and me. **on the quiet** unobtrusively; secretly. □ □ **quietly** *adv.* **quietness** *n.*

quieten *v.* make or become quiet.

quietism / **kwuy**-uh-tiz-uhm / *n.* a passive contemplative attitude to life, as a form of religious mysticism. □ **quietist** *n.* & *adj.*

quietude / **kwuy**-uh-tyood / *n.* quietness.

quietus / kwuy-**ee**-tuhs / *n.* release from life; final riddance, death.

quiff *n.* a curl of hair on the forehead; a tuft of hair brushed upward above the forehead.

quill *n.* **1** one of the large feathers on a bird's wing or tail. **2** (in full **quill pen**) an old type of pen made from this. **3** each of an echidna's or porcupine's spines. **4** the hollow stem of a feather.

quilt[1] *n.* a padded bed covering. • *v.* line with padding and fix with patterns of stitching. □ **quilter** *n.*

quilt[2] *v. Aust. colloq.* thrash; clout.

quin *n. colloq.* a quintuplet.

quince *n.* **1** a hard yellowish pear-shaped fruit used for making jam. **2** the tree bearing it. □ **get on a person's quince** *Aust. colloq.* irritate or exasperate him or her beyond measure.

quincentenary / kwin-sen-**tee**-nuh-ree / *n.* a 500th anniversary.

quincunx *n.* five objects (esp. trees) in the shape of a square or rectangle with one in each corner and one in the middle.

quinella *n.* a form of betting in horse racing etc. in which the gambler must select the first two place-getters in a race, not necessarily in the correct order.

quinine / **kwin**-een, kwuh-**neen** / *n.* a bitter-tasting drug obtained from cinchona bark, used to treat malaria and in tonics.

Question mark ?

A question mark is used instead of a full stop at the end of a sentence to show that it is a question, e.g.
  Have you seen the film yet?
  You didn't lose my purse, did you?
It is not used at the end of a reported question, e.g.
  I asked you whether you'd seen the film yet.

Quinkan / kwing-kuhn / *n.* **1** a category of spirit people depicted in rock paintings of northern Qld. **2** the galleries in the Quinkan reserve (100 km west of Cooktown) which contain these figures as well as paintings of birds, animals, fish, etc., an important Aboriginal art site. (¶ Kuku-Yalanji *guwin-gan* 'ghost, spirit'.)

quinquennial / kwin-**kwen**-ee-uhl / *adj.* **1** lasting for five years. **2** happening every fifth year. ☐ **quinquennially** *adv.*

quinquereme / **kwing**-kwuh-reem / *n.* an ancient Roman galley with five rows of oarsmen on each side.

quinsy / **kwin**-zee / *n.* a severe inflammation of the throat, often with an abscess on one of the tonsils.

quintessence / kwin-**tes**-uhns / *n.* **1** an essence of a substance. **2** the essence or essential part of a theory, speech, condition, etc. **3** a perfect example of a quality. ☐ **quintessential** / kwin-tuh-**sen**-shuhl / *adj.* **quintessentially** *adv.*

quintet *n.* **1** a group of five instruments or voices; a musical composition for these. **2** a set of five.

quintuple / **kwin**-tyoo-puhl / *adj.* **1** consisting of five parts; involving five people. **2** five times as much. • *v.* multiply by five.

quintuplet / kwin-**tup**-luht / *n.* each of five children born at one birth.

quip *n.* a witty or sarcastic remark. • *v.* (**quipped**, **quipping**) utter as a quip.

quire *n.* a set of 25 (formerly 24) sheets of paper.

quirk *n.* **1** a peculiarity of a person's behaviour. **2** a trick of fate. ☐ **quirky** *adj.*

quisling / **kwiz**-ling / *n.* a traitor, esp. one who collaborates with an enemy occupying his or her country. (¶ Named after V. Quisling (1887–1945), a pro-Nazi Norwegian leader in the Second World War.)

quit *v.* (**quitted** or **quit**, **quitting**) **1** go away from, leave (*gave him notice to quit*). **2** give up or abandon (a task etc.). **3** cease (*quit grumbling*). • *adj.* (foll. by *of*) rid (*glad to be quit of the trouble*).

quitch *n.* (in full **quitch grass**) couch grass.

quite *adv.* **1** completely, entirely (*quite finished*). **2** to some extent, somewhat (*quite a long time*). **3** really, actually (*it's quite a change*). **4** (as an answer) I agree (*quite so*). ☐ **quite a few** a considerable number. **quite something** a remarkable thing or person.

Quito / **kee**-toh / the capital of Ecuador.

quits *adj.* even with; on even terms as a result of retaliation or repayment. ☐ **call it quits** *colloq.* **1** acknowledge that things are now even; agree to cease quarrelling. **2** cease work for a time.

quitter *n. colloq.* a person who gives up too easily; a shirker.

quiver[1] *n.* a case for holding arrows.

quiver[2] *v.* shake or vibrate with a slight rapid motion. • *n.* a quivering movement or sound.

quixotic / kwik-**sot**-ik / *adj.* chivalrous and unselfish to an extravagant or impractical extent. ☐ **quixotically** *adv.* (¶ Named after Don *Quixote*, hero of a Spanish story (1605–15) by CERVANTES.)

quiz *n.* (pl. **quizzes**) **1** a series of questions testing people's knowledge, as a form of entertainment. **2** an interrogation or examination. • *v.* (**quizzed**, **quizzing**) examine by questioning.

quizzical / **kwiz**-i-kuhl / *adj.* **1** done in a questioning way. **2** gently amused. ☐ **quizzically** *adv.*

quoin / koin / *n.* **1** an external angle of a building. **2** a cornerstone.

Quotation marks ' ' " "

Also called inverted commas, quotation marks are used:
1 around a direct quotation (there is legitimate variety of opinion whether the quotation marks come before or after other punctuation marks), e.g.
   He said, 'That is nonsense'.
   He said, 'That is nonsense.'
   'That', he said, 'is nonsense'.
   'That,' he said, 'is nonsense.'
2 around a quoted word or phrase, e.g.
   What does 'integrated circuit' mean?
3 around a word or phrase to which the writer wishes to draw attention, e.g.
   Joan Sutherland was known as 'La Stupenda'.
   He said he had enough 'bread' to buy a car.
4 around the title of a book chapter, song, poem, magazine article, television program, etc. (but not a book of the Bible), e.g.
   'Waltzing Matilda' by Banjo Paterson.
   In printing, word processing, etc., it is more usual to use italics for titles of books, novels, plays, long poems, etc., although these would appear in quotation marks if hand-written.
5 as double quotation marks around a quotation within a quotation, e.g.
   He asked, 'Do you know what "integrated circuit" means?'
There is legitimate variety of opinion as to how quotation marks should be used. For example, some people prefer the use of double quotation marks (in which case, at point 5, the quotation within a quotation would be in single quotation marks: "Do you know what 'integrated circuit' means?").

quoit / koit / *n.* a ring of metal, rubber, or rope thrown to encircle a peg in the game of **quoits**.

quokka / **kwok**-uh / *n.* a small short-tailed wallaby of SW WA, including Rottnest and Bald Islands, having long, greyish-brown fur. (¶ Nyungar)

quoll / kwol / *n.* an Australian native cat, a carnivorous, long-tailed spotted marsupial. (¶ Guugu Yimidhirr *dhigul*.)

quondam *adj.* that once was; former (*his quondam friend*).

quorate / **kwaw**-ruht, -rayt / *adj.* having or constituting a quorum.

quorum / **kwaw**-ruhm / *n.* the minimum number of people that must be present at a meeting before its proceedings are valid.

quota *n.* **1** a fixed share that must be done, contributed, or received. **2** the maximum number or amount of people or things that may be admitted e.g. to a country or institution or allowed as exports.

quotable *adj.* worth quoting.

quotation *n.* **1** quoting; being quoted. **2** a passage quoted. **3** an amount stated as the current price of stocks or commodities. **4** a contractor's statement of the sum for which he or she is willing to do a job. ☐ **quotation marks** punctuation marks (either single '' or double " ") enclosing words quoted or put round a slang or similar word (see panel on previous page).

quote *v.* **1** repeat or write out words from a book or speech (*quote from the Bible; quoting Shakespeare*). **2** mention in support of a statement (*can you quote a recent example?*). **3** state the price of (goods or services); give a quotation or estimate. **4** (in dictation etc.) begin the quotation, open the inverted commas (cf. UNQUOTE).
• *n. colloq.* **1** a passage quoted. **2** a price quoted. **3** (**quotes**) quotation marks.

quoth / kwohth / *v. archaic* (only used in 1st and 3rd person singular and always placed before the subject) said (*quoth I; quoth the dragon*).

quotidian / kwo-**tid**-ee-uhn / *adj.* **1** daily; (of a fever) recurring every day. **2** everyday, commonplace.

quotient / **kwoh**-shuhnt / *n.* the result obtained when one amount is divided by another (e.g. 3 in '$12 \div 4 = 3$').

q.v. *abbr.* which see (used as an indication that the reader should look at the reference given). (¶ From the Latin *quod vide*.)

qwerty *adj.* denoting the standard layout of English-language keyboards, with these letters as the first keys on the top row of letters.

R

R *abbr.* (also **R.**) **1** (in names) River. **2** (of a film) not suitable for persons under 18.

r. *abbr.* **1** right. **2** radius.

Ra[1] / rah / *Egyptian myth.* the sun god, the supreme Egyptian deity, the creator of all life.

Ra[2] *symbol* radium.

RAAF *abbr.* Royal Australian Air Force.

Rabat the capital of Morocco.

rabbi / rab-uy / *n.* (*pl.* **rabbis**) **1** the religious leader of a Jewish congregation. **2** a Jewish scholar or teacher, esp. of the law.

rabbinical / ruh-**bin**-i-kuhl / *adj.* of rabbis or Jewish doctrines or law.

rabbit *n.* **1** a burrowing animal with long ears and a short fluffy tail. **2** *colloq.* a person who is a poor performer at a game, esp. a poor batsman. •*v.* (**rabbited**, **rabbiting**) **1** hunt rabbits. **2** (often foll. by *on*) *colloq.* talk pointlessly; chatter at length. **3** *Aust. Rules* duck down in the path of an opposing player, so causing him to trip or fall. ▫ **rabbit-eared bandicoot** *Aust.* = BILBY. **rabbit-oh** *Aust.* a person who sells rabbits as food; a rabbiter. **rabbit punch** a short chop with the edge of the hand on the back of a person's neck. **rabbit-rat** *Aust.* **1** either of two rodents of northern Australia, having long ears and a long, brushy tail. **2** = BILBY. **3** = STICK-NEST RAT.

rabble *n.* **1** a disorderly crowd; a mob. **2** a contemptible or inferior set of people. **3** (**the rabble**) *offens.* the lowest stratum of society (as viewed from higher up the social scale). ▫ **rabble-rouser** a person who stirs up the rabble or a crowd, esp. to agitate for social change.

Rabelais / rab-uh-lay /, François (*c.* 1494–1553), French satirist.

Rabelaisian / rub-uh-**lay**-zee-uhn / *adj.* **1** of or like Rabelais or his writings. **2** marked by exuberant imagination and coarse humour.

rabid / **rab**-uhd / *adj.* **1** furious; fanatical (*rabid hate; a rabid feminist*). **2** affected with rabies. ▫ **rabidly** *adv.* **rabidity** / ruh-**bid**-uh-tee / *n.*

rabies / **ray**-beez / *n.* a contagious fatal virus disease affecting dogs and similar animals, transmitted to humans by the bite of an infected animal and causing madness; hydrophobia.

Rabin / ruh-**been** /, Yitzhak (1922–95), Israeli statesman, prime minister from 1992 until his assassination in 1995. In 1994 he was awarded the Nobel Peace Prize, together with Yasser Arafat and Shimon Peres.

raccoon alternative spelling of RACOON.

race[1] *n.* **1** a contest of speed in reaching a certain point or in doing or achieving something. **2** (**the races**) a series of races for horses or dogs at fixed times on a regular course. **3** a strong fast current of water. **4** a channel of a stream etc. **5** *Aust.* a narrow, fenced passageway through which stock pass, singly, for branding, dipping, etc. **6** a passageway along which football players etc. run to enter the field. •*v.* **1** compete in a race; have a race with. **2** move or cause to move or operate at full speed. ▫ **race off a person** *colloq.* have sex with him or her. ▫ **racer** *n.*

race[2] *n.* **1** any of the great divisions of humankind with certain inherited physical characteristics in common; a number of people related by common descent. **2** a genus, species, breed, or variety of animals or plants. ▫ **race riot** an outbreak of violence due to antagonism between different races in the same country. **race relations** relations between members of different races in the same country. **the human race** human beings collectively.

racecaller *n. Aust.* a person who broadcasts a description of a horse race in progress.

racecourse *n.* a ground where horse races are run.

racegoer *n.* a person who frequents horse races.

racehorse *n.* a horse bred or kept for racing. ▫ **racehorse goanna** any of several extremely swift-moving goannas of central and northern Australia.

raceme / ruh-**seem** / *n.* flowers evenly spaced along a central stem, with the ones at the base opening first.

racetrack *n.* **1** = RACECOURSE. **2** a motor-racing circuit.

raceway *n.* **1** a track or channel along which something runs. **2 a** a track for trotting, pacing, or harness racing. **b** a racecourse. **c** a track for motor racing.

Rachmaninov / rak-**man**-uh-nof /, Sergei (Vasilevich) (1873–1943), Russian composer and pianist, resident in the US from 1917.

racial / **ray**-shuhl / *adj.* of or based on race. ▫ **racially** *adv.*

racism / **ray**-siz-uhm / *n.* **1** belief in the superiority of a particular race; prejudice based on this. **2** antagonism towards people of other races. ▫ **racist** *n.* & *adj.*

rack *n.* **1** a framework with bars or pegs for holding things or for hanging things on. **2** a bar or rail with teeth or cogs into which those of a wheel or gear etc. fit. **3** an instrument of torture on which people were tied and stretched. **3** a joint of lamb etc. including the front ribs. •*v.* **1** inflict great torment on (*was racked with pain*). **2** draw off (wine or beer) from the lees. ☐ **rack off** *colloq.* leave, go. **rack off!** *Aust. colloq.* get lost! **rack railway** a mountain railway having a cogged rail with which a cogged wheel on the train engages.

racket[1] alternative spelling of RACQUET.

racket[2] *n.* **1** a din, a noisy fuss. **2** a business or other activity in which dishonest methods are used. **3** *colloq.* a dodge; a sly game. **4** *colloq.* a legitimate activity, a line of business (*what's your racket?*). • *v.* move about noisily; engage in wild social activities (*racketing about*).

racketeer *n.* a person who runs a dishonest business. ☐ **racketeering** *n.*

raconteur / rak-on-**ter** / *n.* a person who is good at telling entertaining stories.

racoon *n.* (also **raccoon**) (*pl.* **racoon** or **racoons**) a North American animal with a bushy tail, sharp snout, and greyish-brown fur.

racquet / **rak**-uht / *n.* (also **racket**) **1** a stringed bat used in tennis and similar games. **2** (**racquets**) a game like squash for 2 or 4 people, played in a court of four plain walls. ☐ **racquet abuse** (of a tennis player) throwing the racquet about in anger or frustration, an act which can be penalised.

racy *adj.* (**racier**, **raciest**) **1** spirited and vigorous in style (*a racy description of his adventures*). **2** risqué. **3** of distinctive quality (*a racy wine*). ☐ **racily** *adv.* **raciness** *n.*

rad[1] *n.* a unit of absorbed dose of ionising radiation.

rad[2] *adj. colloq.* really good or exciting, cool, awesome.

radar *n.* **1** a system for detecting the presence, position, or movement of objects by sending out short radio waves which they reflect. **2** apparatus used for this. ☐ **radar detector** a device (now usu. illegal) in a motor vehicle for detecting a radar trap ahead. **radar trap** a device using radar to detect vehicles travelling faster than the speed limit.

raddle *n.* red ochre. • *v.* **1** colour with raddle or too much rouge. **2** *Aust.* mark (an imperfectly shorn sheep) with a red dye.

raddled *adj.* worn out.

radial / **ray**-dee-uhl / *adj.* of rays or radii; having spokes or lines etc. that radiate from a central point. • *n.* a radial-ply tyre. ☐ **radial-ply** *adj.* (of a tyre) having fabric layers with cords lying radial to the hub of the wheel (cf. CROSS-PLY). ☐ ☐ **radially** *adv.*

radian / **ray**-dee-uhn / *n.* an SI unit of plane angle; the angle at the centre of a circle formed by the radii of an arc equal in length to the radius.

radiant *adj.* **1** giving out rays of light. **2** looking very bright and happy; (of beauty) dazzling. **3** transmitting heat by radiation; (of heat) transmitted in this way. ☐ **radiantly** *adv.* **radiance** *n.*

radiata pine *n.* a Californian conifer cultivated in plantations in Australia for its softwood timber.

radiate *v.* **1** spread outwards (esp. in lines or rays) from a central point. **2** send out (light or heat etc.) in rays; be sent out as radiation. **3** give out a feeling of (*she radiated confidence*).

radiation *n.* **1** radiating; being radiated. **2** the sending out of the rays and atomic particles characteristic of radioactive substances; these rays and particles. ☐ **radiation sickness** sickness caused by exposure to radiation, such as gamma rays. **radiation therapy** the treatment of cancer etc. using radiation, e.g. X-rays or ultraviolet light.

radiator *n.* **1** a usu. portable electrical appliance for warming a room by radiating heat from red-hot bars. **2** a device for heating a room etc., consisting of a metal case through which hot water or steam circulates. **3** an engine-cooling device in a motor vehicle or aircraft.

radical *adj.* **1** going to the root or foundation of something, fundamental. **2** drastic, thorough (*radical changes*). **3** desiring radical reforms; holding extreme political views; revolutionary. **4** *colloq.* excellent, outstanding, cool. • *n.* **1** a person desiring radical reforms or holding extremist views. **2** a group of atoms forming part of a compound and remaining unaltered during the compound's ordinary chemical changes. **3** = FREE RADICAL (see FREE). **4** the root of a word. **5** a mathematical quantity forming or expressed as the root of another. ☐ **radically** *adv.* **radicalism** *n.*

radicchio / ruh-**dee**-kee-oh / *n.* (*pl.* **radicchios**) a variety of chicory with reddish-purple leaves.

radicle *n.* an embryo root (e.g. of a pea or bean).

radii see RADIUS.

radio *n.* (*pl.* **radios**) **1** the process of sending and receiving messages etc. by invisible electromagnetic radiation. **2** an apparatus for sending or receiving messages in this way; a transmitter or receiver. **3** sound broadcasting; a sound-broadcasting station (*Radio Australia*). • *adj.* **1** of or using radio. **2** of or involving stars etc. from which radio waves are received or reflected (*radio astronomy*). • *v.* (**radioed**, **radioing**) send, signal, or communicate with by radio. ☐ **radio-controlled** controlled from a distance by radio signals. **radio frequency** the frequency band of telecommunication, ranging from 10^4 to 10^{11} or 10^{12} Hz. **radio-telephone** a telephone operating by radio signals rather than electronic signals sent along cables. **radio telescope** an instrument used to detect radio emissions from the sky, whether from natural celestial objects or from artificial satellites.

radioactive *adj.* of or showing radioactivity.

radioactivity *n.* the property of having atoms that break up spontaneously and send out radiation capable of penetrating opaque bodies and producing electrical and chemical effects.

radiocarbon *n.* a radioactive form of carbon that is present in organic materials and is used in carbon dating (*see* CARBON).

radiogram *n.* **1** an old-fashioned piece of furniture incorporating a radio and a record player. **2** a picture obtained by X-rays etc. **3** a telegram sent by radio.

radiograph *n.* **1** an instrument recording the intensity of radiation. **2** = RADIOGRAM (sense 2).

radiography / ray-dee-**og**-ruh-fee / *n.* the production of X-ray photographs. □ **radiographer** *n.*

radioisotope *n.* a radioactive isotope that decays spontaneously.

radiology / ray-dee-**ol**-uh-jee / *n.* the scientific study of X-rays and other high-energy radiation, esp. as used in medicine. □ **radiologist** *n.*

radiophonic *adj.* relating to electronically produced sound, music, etc.

radioscopy *n.* examination by X-rays of opaque objects.

radiotherapy *n.* treatment of disease etc. by X-rays or similar forms of radiation.

radish *n.* **1** a plant with a crisp root that is eaten raw. **2** its root.

radium *n.* a radioactive metallic element (symbol Ra), obtained from pitchblende etc., used esp. in radiotherapy.

radius *n.* (*pl.* **radii** / **ray**-dee-uy / *or* **radiuses**) **1** a straight line extending from the centre of a circle or sphere to its circumference. **2** the length of this line; the distance from a centre (*within a radius of 20 kilometres*). **3** the thicker of the two long bones in the forearm; the corresponding bone in animals.

radix / **ray**-diks / *n.* (*pl.* **radices**) a number or symbol used as the basis of a numeration scale (e.g. ten in the decimal system).

radon / **ray**-don / *n.* a chemical element, a radioactive gas (symbol Rn).

Rafferty, Chips (original name: John William Pilbeam Goffage) (1909–71), Australian film actor and producer, esp. known for films in which he typified the Australian bushman.

Rafferty's rules *n. pl. Aust.* no rules at all (i.e. anything goes).

raffia *n.* soft fibre from the leaves of a palm tree, used for tying plants, making mats, etc.

raffish *adj.* vulgarly flashy, disreputable, or rakish. □ **raffishness** *n.*

raffle *n.* a lottery with an object as the prize, esp. as a method of raising money for a charity. • *v.* offer (a thing) as the prize in a raffle.

raft *n.* **1** a flat floating structure used esp. as a substitute for a boat. **2** a large collection (*presented a raft of proposals to the board*).

rafter *n.* each of the sloping beams forming the framework of a roof.

rag[1] *n.* **1** a torn or worn piece of fabric. **2** (**rags**) old torn clothes. **3** rags used as material for stuffing things, making paper etc. **4** *colloq. derog.* a newspaper. □ **rag-and-bone man** an itinerant dealer in old clothes, furniture, etc. **rag-bag 1** a bag for scraps of fabric etc. **2** a miscellaneous collection. **rag trade** *colloq.* the clothing business.

rag[2] *v.* (**ragged**, **ragging**) **1** tease, play rough jokes on (a person). **2** engage in rough play; be noisy and riotous. • *n.* **1** a prank, esp. one performed by students. **2** a rowdy celebration; a noisy disorderly scene.

rag[3] *n.* a piece of ragtime music.

raga / **rah**-guh / *n.* (in Indian music) **1** any of various patterns of notes used as a basis for melodies and improvisations. **2** a piece of music using a particular raga.

ragamuffin *n.* **1** a child in ragged dirty clothes. **2** = RAGGA.

rage *n.* **1** violent anger; a fit of this. **2** the violent action of a natural force (*felt the full rage of the cyclone*). **3** esp. *Aust. colloq.* a lively, usu. frenetic social occasion (*the party was a rage*). • *v.* **1** be full of anger. **2** (often foll. by *at, against*) speak furiously or madly. **3** (of a storm or battle etc.) be violent; continue furiously. **4** esp. *Aust. colloq.* enjoy oneself with no holds barred; party on with total abandon (*we raged till dawn*). □ **all the rage** very popular or fashionable.

rager *n.* esp. *Aust. colloq.* a person who enjoys himself or herself at a party etc. with total abandon.

ragga *n.* (also **ragamuffin**) a style of pop music derived from reggae but with faster more electronic elements; a follower of this style.

ragged / **rag**-uhd / *adj.* **1** torn, frayed. **2** wearing torn clothes. **3** jagged. **4** faulty, lacking finish, smoothness, or uniformity (*a ragged performance*). □ **raggedly** *adv.* **raggedness** *n.*

raging *n. colloq.* enjoying oneself with total abandon at a party etc. • *adj.* extreme; very painful (*raging thirst; a raging headache*).

raglan *n.* a sleeve that continues to the neck and is joined to the body of the garment by sloping seams.

Ragnarök / **rahg**-nuh-rok / *n. Scand. myth.* the great battle between the gods and the powers of evil at the end of the world when the gods and all humans will be destroyed.

ragout / ra-**goo** / *n.* meat stewed with vegetables and highly seasoned.

ragtag and bobtail *n.* riff-raff, common people.

ragtime *n.* a form of jazz music with much syncopation.

raid *n.* **1** a rapid surprise attack, esp. **a** in warfare. **b** in order to commit a crime, steal, or do harm. **2** a surprise visit by police etc. to arrest suspected people or seize illicit goods. • *v.* **1** make a raid on. **2** make a foray for food etc. (*raided the fridge*). □ **raider** *n.*

rail[1] *n.* **1** a horizontal or sloping bar forming part of a fence or barrier or for hanging things on. **2** one of the metal lines on which trains or trams run. **3** railways as a means of transport (*travel by*

rail *rail*). • *v.* fit or enclose with a rail (*rail it off*). ☐ **go off the rails** *colloq.* become disorganised, out of control or crazy.

rail² *n.* a small wading bird, including the Australian *buff-banded rail* etc.

rail³ *v.* (often foll. by *at* or *against*) complain or protest strongly; rant (*railing at him*).

railing *n.* a fence of rails supported on upright metal bars.

raillery *n.* good-humoured joking or teasing.

railroad *n.* esp. *US* a railway. • *v.* rush or force into hasty action (*railroaded him into accepting*).

railway *n.* **1** a set of rails on which trains run. **2** a system of transport using these; the organisation required for its working.

raiment *n. archaic* clothing.

rain *n.* **1** condensed moisture of the atmosphere falling in drops. **2** a fall of this. **3** (**the rains**) the rainy season. **4** a shower of things (*a rain of petals from the trees above*). **5** a large or overwhelming quantity (*a rain of bullets*). • *v.* send down rain; fall as or like rain. ☐ **rain bird** a bird whose call is said to foretell rain, as the Australian channel-billed cuckoo and the grey currawong. **rain check 1** esp. *US* a ticket for an outdoor event allowing a refund or readmission should the event be interrupted by rain. **2** a voucher (issued to a shopper) promising that an article advertised in a sale, but which is temporarily out of stock, will be made available later at the sale price. **take a rain check** *colloq.* defer one's acceptance of an offer until convenient.

rainbow *n.* an arch of colours formed in rain or spray by the sun's rays. • *adj.* many-coloured. ☐ **rainbow bird** (also **rainbow bee-eater**) a migratory bee-eater of mainland Australia and islands to the north, having blue, green, and orange plumage. **rainbow lorikeet** an Australian bird with blue head, green wings, and orange or red breast. **rainbow trout** a large trout, originally from North America, introduced into rivers in Australia.

Rainbow Serpent (also **Rainbow Snake**, **Rainbow Spirit**) a widely venerated Spirit of Aboriginal sacred lore, esp. associated with the fashioning of the earth in the Dreamtime.

raincoat *n.* a water-resistant coat.

raindrop *n.* a single drop of rain.

rainfall *n.* the total amount of rain falling within a given area in a given time.

rainforest *n.* thick forest in tropical areas where there is heavy rainfall.

rainmaker *n. Aust.* a highly esteemed Aborigine (usu. a man) who is skilled in performing the ceremonies to bring down rain.

rainmaking *n. Aust.* the rituals and ceremonies, usu. elaborate, often long-lasting, and varying from place to place, which often invoke the Rainbow Spirit, and are used by Aboriginal rainmakers to bring down rain when needed.

rainwater *n.* water collected from fallen rain, not obtained from wells etc.

rainy *adj.* (**rainier, rainiest**) in or on which much rain falls. ☐ **save for a rainy day** save (money etc.) for a time when one may need it.

raise *v.* **1** bring to or towards a higher or upright position. **2** increase the amount or level of (*raise prices*). **3** cause, rouse, or produce (*raise doubts; raise a laugh; raise a loan*). **4** breed, rear, or grow (*raise sheep; raise a family*). **5** put forward (*raise objections*). • *n.* an increase in wages or salary.

raisin *n.* a dried grape.

raison d'être / ray-zon **det**-ruh / *n.* (*pl. raisons d'être* pronounced the same) the reason for or purpose of a thing's existence. (¶ French)

raj / rahj / *n.* the period of British rule in India.

rajah / **rah**-juh / *n.* (also **raja**) *hist.* an Indian king or prince.

raja yoga / **rah**-juh / *n.* a form of yoga intended to achieve control over the mind and emotions.

rake¹ *n.* **1** a long-handled tool with prongs used for drawing together hay, fallen leaves, etc. or for smoothing loose soil. **2** an implement resembling this, used e.g. by a croupier at a gaming table. • *v.* **1** gather or smooth with a rake. **2** search (*have been raking through old records*). **3** direct gunfire along (a line) from end to end; direct one's eyes or a camera in this way. ☐ **rake-off** *n. colloq.* a commission or share of (esp. illicit) profits. **rake up 1** revive the memory of (an unpleasant incident). **2** *colloq.* find, collect (*can you rake up enough money for the trip?*). **3** reveal, expose (*the press raking up all these scandals about the British royals*).

rake² *n.* a slope (e.g. of a ship's mast or funnel, or of a driver's seat). • *v.* set at a sloping angle.

rake³ *n. archaic* a man of fashion who lives an irresponsible and immoral life.

rakish *adj.* dashing, jaunty, and perhaps immoral. ☐ **rakishly** *adv.* **rakishness** *n.*

rallentando *adv.* & *adj. Music* with a gradual decrease in speed.

rally¹ *v.* (**rallied, rallying**) **1** bring or come together for a united effort. **2** rouse or revive; recover one's strength after illness. **3** (of share prices etc.) increase after falling. • *n.* **1** an act of rallying; a recovery of energy or spirits. **2** (in tennis etc.) a lengthy series of strokes before a point is scored. **3** a mass meeting of people with a common interest. **4** a driving competition for cars or motorcycles over public roads. ☐ **rally-cross** *Motor Racing* motor racing over roads and cross-country.

rally² *v.* (**rallied, rallying**) tease, ridicule in a good-humoured way.

ralph *colloq. v.* vomit. • *n.* an act of vomiting.

RAM *abbr. Computing* random-access memory; a temporary working memory that can be read from and written to. Data in RAM is held only while electrical power remains available to it.

ram *n.* **1** an uncastrated male sheep. **2** (**the Ram**) a sign of the zodiac, Aries. **3** a battering ram. **4** a striking or plunging device in various machines. • *v.* (**rammed**, **ramming**) **1** force or drive into place by pressure. **2** crash against. ◻ **ram raid** a robbery in which a shop window is rammed with a vehicle and looted. **ram-raid** carry out a ram raid.

Rama the Hindu model of the ideal man, the seventh incarnation of the God Vishnu.

Ramadan / **ram**-uh-dan, **rum**-uh-dahn / *n.* the ninth month of the Muslim year, when Muslims fast between sunrise and sunset.

Ramayana / rah-**mah**-yuh-nuh / *n.* a Sanskrit epic poem composed *c.* 300 BC which tells how Rama rescued his wife Sita from Ravana, the ten-headed demon king of Sri Lanka.

ramble *v.* **1** walk for pleasure. **2** talk or write disconnectedly; wander from the subject. • *n.* a walk taken for pleasure.

rambler *n.* **1** a person who rambles; one who goes for a ramble. **2** a climbing rose.

rambling *adj.* **1** wandering. **2** speaking, spoken, or written disconnectedly, wandering from one subject to another. **3** (of a plant) straggling, climbing. **4** (of a house, street, village, etc.) extending in various directions irregularly.

Rambo 1 the violent hero of David Morrell's novel *First Blood* (popularised in film). **2** any macho male type who advocates or carries out violence and aggression. ◻ **Ramboesque** *adj.* **Rambo-like** *adj.* **Ramboism** *n.*

rambutan / **rum**-boo-tahn / *n.* a Malaysian tree bearing bright red roundish edible fruit covered with soft spines and having very sweet flesh.

Rameau, Jean-Philippe (1683–1764), French composer.

ramekin / **ram**-uh-kuhn / *n.* a small mould for baking and serving an individual portion of food.

Rameses see RAMSES.

ramification *n.* (usu. as **ramifications**) **1** an arrangement of branching parts; a part of a complex structure. **2** a consequence; an indirect result.

ramify *v.* (**ramified**, **ramifying**) form or cause to form into branching parts.

Ramos Horta / rah-mos **haw**-tuh /, José (1949–), East Timorese activist who, with Bishop Carlos Belo, won the 1996 Nobel Peace Prize.

ramp *n.* **1** a slope joining two levels. **2** a movable set of stairs put beside an aircraft. **3** a ridge across a road which causes vehicles to slow down; a speed hump. **4** *Aust.* a cattle grid. **5** *colloq.* a swindle, esp. one involving exorbitant prices. **6** *colloq.* a search made of a prisoner or of his cell. • *v.* **1** furnish or build with a ramp. **2** storm, rage, rush about wildly. **3** *colloq.* search (a prisoner or his cell).

rampage *v.* / ram-**payj** / rush about wildly or destructively. • *n.* / **ram**-payj / violent behaviour. ◻ **on the rampage** rampaging.

rampant *adj.* **1** unrestrained, flourishing excessively (*disease was rampant in the poorer districts*). **2** (in heraldry) (of an animal) standing on one hind leg with the opposite foreleg raised (*a lion rampant*). **3** violent (*rampant wild boars*). **4** fanatical (*rampant racists*). ◻ **rampancy** *n.*

rampart *n.* a broad bank of earth built as a fortification, usu. topped with a parapet.

rampe / **rum**-pay / *n.* the leaves of a pandanus tree used as a flavouring in curries etc. (¶ Sinhalese)

ramrod *n.* an iron rod formerly used for ramming a charge into muzzle-loading guns. ◻ **like a ramrod** (of a person) excessively rigid, formal, or unbending.

Ramses / **ram**-seez / (also **Rameses**) the name of 11 Egyptian pharaohs, of whom the most famous are **Ramses II** 'the Great' (d. *c.* 1225 BC) and **Ramses III** (d. *c.* 1167 BC).

ramshackle *adj.* tumbledown, rickety.

RAN *abbr.* Royal Australian Navy.

ran *see* RUN.

ranch *n.* a cattle-breeding establishment, esp. in the US and Canada. ◻ **rancher** *n.*

rancid / **ran**-suhd / *adj.* smelling or tasting rank and unpleasant like stale fat. ◻ **rancidity** / ran-**sid**-uh-tee / *n.*

rancour / **rang**-kuh / *n.* (also **rancor**) bitter feeling or ill will. ◻ **rancorous** *adj.*

rand *n.* the unit of money in South Africa.

R & D *abbr.* research and development.

random *adj.* done, made, or taken etc. at random (*a random choice*). ◻ **at random** without a particular aim, purpose, or principle. **random-access** *Computing* (of a memory or file) having all parts directly accessible, so that it need not be read sequentially; *see also* RAM. **random breath-test** measurement of the amount of alcohol in the breath of a motorist chosen randomly from a line of traffic. ◻◻ **randomly** *adv.*

randy *adj.* (**randier**, **randiest**) lustful, sexually aroused. ◻ **randiness** *n.*

ranee alternative spelling of RANI.

rang *see* RING[2].

range *n.* **1** a line or tier or series of things, esp. mountains (*the Great Dividing Range*). **2** an extent, the limits between which something operates or varies (*a voice of astonishing range; the whole range of politics*). **3** the distance over which one can see or hear, or to which a sound, signal, or missile can travel; the distance that a ship or aircraft etc. can travel without refuelling. **4** the distance to a thing being aimed at or looked at (*at close range*). **5** (esp. *US*) a large open stretch of grazing ground. **6** a place with targets for shooting practice. **7** an electric or gas stove. • *v.* **1** arrange in a row or ranks or in a specified way (*they were ranged in ascending order of height*). **2** extend, reach (*her knowledge ranged from astrology to zoology*). **3** vary between limits (*their ages ranged from ten to twenty*). **4** rove, wander;

rangefinder — **rarefied**

traverse in all directions (*the searchers ranged the forest*). **5** (esp. of a bird or animal) be found over a specified district (*the noisy friar bird ranges from South Australia to Queensland*).

rangefinder *n.* a device for calculating the distance of an object to be shot at or photographed.

rangehood *n.* a canopy or hood above a stove or cooktop, fitted with a fan to extract smells, smoke, etc.

rangeland *n.* **1** *US* an extensive area of open country used for grazing livestock. **2** *Aust.* a large area of usu. arid or semi-arid land which is unsuitable for intensive agricultural use because of unreliable rainfall, poor soils, etc., often grazed by domestic or feral stock.

ranger *n.* **1** a keeper of a national park etc. **2** *Aust. hist.* a bushranger. **3** (**Ranger**) a senior Guide.

Rangoon / rang-**goon** / (from 1989 officially called **Yangon**) the capital of Burma (from 1989 officially called Myanmar).

rangy / **rayn**-jee / *adj.* tall and thin.

rani / **rah**-nee / *n.* (also **ranee**) *hist.* a rajah's wife or widow.

rank[1] *n.* **1** a line of people or things. **2** a place where taxis stand to await hire. **3** a place in a scale of quality or value etc.; a position or grade (*ministers of Cabinet rank*). **4** high social position (*people of rank*). **5** (**the ranks**) ordinary soldiers, not officers. •*v.* **1** arrange in a rank. **2** assign a rank to. **3** have a certain rank or place (*he ranks among the great statesmen*). ☐ **close ranks** maintain solidarity. **the rank and file** the ordinary people of an organisation.

rank[2] *adj.* **1** growing too thickly and coarsely. **2** (of land) full of weeds. **3** foul-smelling. **4** unmistakably bad; out-and-out (*rank injustice*).

rankle *v.* cause lasting and bitter annoyance or resentment.

ransack *v.* **1** search thoroughly or roughly. **2** rob or pillage (a place).

ransom *n.* the release of a captive in return for payment demanded by the captors; the payment itself. •*v.* **1** obtain the release of (a captive) in return for payment. **2** hold (a captive) to ransom. ☐ **hold to ransom** hold (a captive) and demand ransom for his or her release; demand concessions from (a person etc.) by threatening some damaging action.

rant *v.* preach or make a speech etc. loudly and theatrically. •*n.* a piece of ranting. ☐ **rant and rave** express anger noisily and violently.

rap[1] *n.* **1** a quick sharp blow or knock. **2** *colloq.* blame, punishment; a criminal charge. **3** *colloq.* a chat. •*v.* (**rapped**, **rapping**) **1** strike quickly and sharply. **2** reprimand. **3** *colloq.* (also **rap on**) chat. ☐ **not care** (or **give**) **a rap** not care at all. **take the rap** *colloq.* suffer the consequences.

rap[2] *n.* **1** a rhythmic monologue, often in rhyming sentences, recited to rap music. **2** (in full **rap music**) a style of popular music which accompanies the rapper. **3** (in full **rap dancing**) energetic dancing associated with rap music. •*v.* perform rap music; talk, sing, or dance in the style of rap. ☐ **rapper** a person who raps.

rap[3] *Aust. colloq. n.* praise, commendation (*the coach gave him a rap after his good game*). •*v.* to praise.

rapacious / ruh-**pay**-shuhs / *adj.* greedy and grasping; plundering and robbing others. ☐ **rapaciously** *adv.* **rapacity** / ruh-**pas**-uh-tee / *n.*

rape[1] *n.* **1** the crime of forcing a person to have sexual intercourse against his or her will. **2** violent assault or plunder, forcible interference. **3** destruction, destructive exploitation (*the rape of Australian rainforests*). •*v.* commit rape on (in all senses of the noun).

rape[2] *n.* a plant grown as fodder and for its seed from which oil is obtained.

Raphael, (Italian name: Raffaello Sanzio) (1483–1520), Italian Renaissance painter and architect.

rapid *adj.* **1** quick, swift. **2** acting or completed in a short time. **3** (of a slope) descending steeply. •*n.* (**rapids**) a swift current in a river, caused by a steep downward slope in the river bed. ☐ **rapid eye movement** *see* REM. ☐☐ **rapidly** *adv.* **rapidity** / ruh-**pid**-uh-tee / *n.*

rapier / **ray**-pee-uh / *n.* a thin light double-edged sword used for thrusting.

rapine / **ra**-peen, -puyn / *n.* plundering.

rapist / **ray**-puhst / *n.* a person who commits rape.

rapport / ra-**paw** / *n.* a harmonious and understanding relationship between people; a feeling of being in harmony (with something) (*established a rapport with his neighbours; Aborigines have a strong rapport with the land*).

rapprochement / ruh-**prosh**-mon, -muhnt / *n.* a resumption of friendly relations, esp. between countries. (¶ French)

rapscallion *n.* a rascal.

rapt *adj.* **1** very intent and absorbed, enraptured. **2** *Aust. colloq.* overjoyed, delighted. ☐ **raptly** *adv.*

raptor *n.* a bird of prey.

raptorial / rap-**taw**-ree-uhl / *adj.* (of an animal, esp. a bird) predatory.

rapture *n.* intense delight. ☐ **rapturous** *adj.* **rapturously** *adv.*

rare[1] *adj.* **1** seldom found; very uncommon. **2** *colloq.* exceptionally good (*had a rare time*). **3** of low density; thin (*the rare atmosphere in the Himalayas*). ☐ **rare earth** a lanthanide element, any of a group of metallic elements with similar chemical properties. ☐☐ **rarely** *adv.* **rareness** *n.*

rare[2] *adj.* (of meat) cooked very lightly so that the inside is still red.

rarebit = WELSH RAREBIT.

rarefied / **rair**-ruh-fuyd / *adj.* **1** (of air etc.) less dense than is normal; thin, like that on high mountains. **2** very subtle; highly intellectual; select.

raring / **rair**-ring / *adj. colloq.* enthusiastic (*raring to go*).

rarity / **rair**-ruh-tee / *n*. **1** rareness. **2** something uncommon; a thing valued because it is rare.

Ras al Khaimah / ras al **kuy**-muh / an emirate belonging to the federation of United Arab Emirates.

rascal *n*. **1** a dishonest person. **2** a mischievous person. ◻ **rascally** *adj*.

rase alternative spelling of RAZE.

rash *n*. **1** an eruption of spots or patches on the skin. **2** a sudden widespread phenomenon (*a rash of strikes*). ● *adj.* acting or done without due consideration of the possible consequences or risks. ◻ **rashly** *adv.* **rashness** *n*.

rasher *n*. a slice of bacon or ham.

rasp *n*. **1** a coarse file with raised sharp points on its surface. **2** a rough grating sound. **3** *Aust.* an Aboriginal musical instrument consisting of e.g. a woomera with numerous notches, this being played like a violin with a special kind of stick. ● *v.* **1** scrape with a rasp. **2** make a rough grating sound (*a rasping voice; he rasped out orders*).

raspberry *n*. **1** an edible sweet red conical berry. **2** the bush that bears it. **3** *colloq.* a vulgar sound or expression of disapproval or rejection. ◻ **raspberry jam** a WA wattle yielding a durable timber having a fragrance of raspberry jam.

Rasputin / ras-**pyoo**-tin /, Grigori Efimovich (1871–1916), Russian religious fanatic, who exerted great influence over the Tsar and his family during the First World War.

Rastafarian / ras-tuh-**fair**-ree-uhn / *n*. (also **Rasta**) a member of a Jamaican sect regarding Emperor Haile Selassie (1892–1975) of Ethiopia as God and their true homeland as Africa. ● *adj.* of Rastafarians.

rat *n*. **1** a rodent resembling a mouse but larger. **2** an unpleasant or treacherous person. **3** a turncoat, a deserter. **4** (**rats!**) an exclamation of annoyance etc. ● *v.* (**ratted, ratting**) **1** hunt or kill rats. **2** *colloq.* withdraw treacherously from an undertaking; break a promise (*he ratted on us*). **3** *colloq.* inform (on); desert, betray; be a scab (sense 2). **4** *Aust. colloq.* rob (a person); steal (money etc.). ◻ **rat-kangaroo** *see* KANGAROO. **rat race** a fiercely competitive struggle to maintain one's position in work or life.

ratable alternative spelling of RATEABLE.

ratatouille / ra-tuh-**too**-ee / *n*. a Provençal dish of stewed vegetables (chiefly eggplants, tomatoes, zucchinis, onions, and peppers). (¶ French)

ratbag *n. Aust. colloq.* **1** an obnoxious person. **2** a troublemaker. **3** an eccentric or unconventional person. **4** (also *as adj.*) a person who is rigid or extreme in (esp. left-wing) political views etc. (*lunatic-left ratbag; ratbag fringe of the Labor Party*).

ratchet / **rach**-uht / *n*. **1** a series of notches on a bar or wheel in which a catch engages to prevent backward movement. **2** the bar or wheel bearing these.

rate *n.* **1** a standard of reckoning, obtained by expressing the quantity or amount of one thing with respect to another (*moving at a rate of 100 kilometres per hour*). **2** a measure of value or charge or cost (*postal rates*). **3** pace of working, change, etc. (*worked at a steady rate; prices are increasing at a great rate*). **4** (**rates**) a tax on land and buildings levied by local governments, the money gained being used for local services. ● *v.* **1** estimate the worth or value of. **2** assign a value to. **3** rank or be regarded in a certain way (*that rates as his worst performance*). **4** consider, regard as (*I rate him among my mates*). **5** deserve (*that joke didn't rate a laugh*). **6** levy rates on (property); value (property) for the purpose of assessing rates. **7** scold angrily. **8** place (a film etc.) in a category relative to its suitability for viewing. ◻ **at any rate** in any possible case, no matter what happens; at least. **at this** (*or* **that**) **rate** if this is true or a typical specimen.

rateable *adj.* (also **ratable**) liable to rates (*see* RATE *n.* sense 4). ◻ **rateable value** the value at which a business etc. is assessed for rates.

ratepayer *n*. a person liable to pay rates.

rather *adv.* **1** slightly; more so than not (*rather dark*). **2** more precisely; as a better alternative; as opposed to (*he is lazy rather than incompetent*). **3** more willingly, by preference (*would rather not go*). ◻ **had rather** would rather.

ratify *v.* (**ratified, ratifying**) confirm or accept (an agreement, treaty, etc.), esp. by signing it. ◻ **ratification** *n*.

rating *n*. **1** the classification assigned to a person or thing in respect of quality, popularity, etc. **2** the estimated standing of a person as regards credit etc. **3** the relative popularity of a broadcast program as determined by the estimated size of the audience. **4** (**ratings**) (*as adj.*) pertaining to the calculation of the rating of broadcast programs (*we should see some good programs now—it's ratings week*). **5** a non-commissioned sailor. **6** an angry reprimand.

ratio / **ray**-shee-oh / *n.* (*pl.* **ratios**) the relationship between two amounts reckoned as the number of times one contains the other.

ratiocinate / rat-ee-**oh**-suh-nayt, rash-ee- / *v. literary* reason, esp. in a formal way. ◻ **ratiocination** *n*.

ration *n*. a fixed quantity (esp. of food) allowed to one person. ● *v.* **1** limit (food etc.) to a fixed ration; allow (a person) only a certain amount.

rational *adj.* **1** able to reason. **2** sane. **3** based on reasoning, using reason or logic and rejecting explanations that involve the supernatural etc. ◻ **rationally** *adv.* **rationality** / rash-uh-**nal**-uh-tee / *n*.

rationale / rash-uh-**nahl** / n. the logical basis of something; the fundamental reason for it.

rationalise v. (also **-ize**) **1** make logical and consistent (*tried to rationalise English spelling*). **2** put forward a rational explanation of (*tried to rationalise their fears*). **3** make (a process or an industry) more efficient by reorganising so as to eliminate waste of labour, time, or materials. □ **rationalisation** n.

rationalism n. using rational explanations as the basis of belief and knowledge; a belief in reason rather than religion as a guiding principle in life. □ **rationalist** n. & adj. **rationalistic** adj.

ratshit adj. esp. Aust. colloq. **1** useless; of no worth or value. **2** ill, unwell (*feeling ratshit*). **3** abominable, awful (*that film was ratshit*).

rattan / ruh-**tan** / n. **1** a climbing palm with long thin jointed pliable stems, used for furniture-making. **2** a piece of this stem used as a walking stick etc.

rattle v. **1** make or cause to make a rapid series of short sharp hard sounds esp. by shaking. **2** move with a rattling noise. **3** (often foll. by *along*) move or travel briskly. **4** (usu. foll. by *off*) utter rapidly (*rattled off the prayer*). **5** (usu. foll. by *on*) chatter idly. **6** colloq. alarm, agitate, or fluster (*the question rattled him*). • n. **1** a rattling sound. **2** a device or toy for making a rattling sound.

rattlesnake n. a poisonous American snake with a rattling structure of horny rings on its tail.

rattling adj. **1** that rattles. **2** vigorous, brisk (*a rattling pace*). • adv. colloq. very (*a rattling good story*).

ratty adj. (**rattier**, **rattiest**) **1** infested with rats. **2** colloq. irritable, bad-tempered. **3** Aust. colloq. mad; eccentric.

raucous / **raw**-kuhs / adj. loud and harsh-sounding. □ **raucously** adv. **raucousness** n.

raunchy adj. (**raunchier**, **raunchiest**) colloq. coarse, earthy; sexually boisterous; randy. □ **raunchily** adv. **raunchiness** n.

ravage v. do great damage to; devastate. • n. pl. (**ravages**) damage, devastation.

rave v. **1** talk wildly or furiously; talk nonsensically in delirium. **2** (foll. by *about*, *over*) talk with great enthusiasm, go into raptures. • n. **1** an act or instance of raving. **2** colloq. a very enthusiastic review of a book or play etc. **3** colloq. a craze. **4** a long, lively conversation. **5** (also **rave party**) an all-night party with loud rock music attended by large numbers of young people (*see also* WAREHOUSE PARTY). □ **rave it up** colloq. enjoy oneself freely. **rave on** colloq. talk tediously and at length (*what's he, raving on about?*).

ravel v. (**ravelled**, **ravelling**) **1** tangle; become tangled. **2** fray out. **3** (usu. foll. by *out*) disentangle, unravel.

raven n. **1** a large bird with glossy black feathers and a hoarse cry, found in many parts of the world. **2** any of three Australian birds of the crow family: the Australian raven, the forest raven, the little raven. • adj. (esp. of hair) glossy black.

ravening / **rav**-uh-ning / adj. hungrily seeking prey.

ravenous / **rav**-uh-nuhs / adj. **1** very hungry. **2** voracious. **3** rapacious. □ **ravenously** adv.

raver n. **1** colloq. an uninhibited pleasure-loving person. **2** a person attending a rave-party.

ravine / ruh-**veen** / n. a deep narrow gorge or cleft between mountains.

raving n. (usu. as **ravings**) wild or delirious talk. • adj. & adv. as an intensifier (*raving mad; a raving beauty*).

ravioli / rav-ee-**oh**-lee / n. small square pasta cases containing meat or other savoury fillings.

ravish v. **1** rape. **2** fill with delight, enrapture. □ **ravishment** n.

ravishing adj. very beautiful. □ **ravishingly** adv.

raw adj. **1** not cooked. **2** in its natural state, not yet or not fully processed or manufactured (*raw hides*). **3** crude in artistic quality, lacking finish. **4** inexperienced, untrained (*raw recruits*). **5 a** stripped of skin; with the flesh exposed, unhealed. **b** sensitive to the touch from being so exposed. **c** abnormally sensitive (*touched a raw nerve*). **6** (of an edge of cloth) not a selvage and not hemmed. **7** (of weather) damp and chilly. □ **come the raw prawn** *see* PRAWN. **in the raw 1** naked. **2** in a raw state; crude, without a softening or refining influence (*life in the raw*). **touch on the raw** upset (a person) by raising a sensitive issue. **raw deal** unfair treatment. **raw material** any material from which something is made. □□ **rawness** n.

rawhide n. **1** untanned leather. **2** a rope or whip of this.

Ray / ruy /, Satyajit (1921–92), Indian film director.

ray n. **1** a single line or narrow beam of light or other radiation. **2** a trace of something good (*a ray of hope*). **3** one of a set of radiating lines, parts, or things. **4** the marginal floret of a composite flower, e.g. a daisy. **5** a large edible marine fish with a flat body and a long slender tail. **6** (also **re**) (in music) the second note of a major scale.

rayon n. a synthetic fibre or fabric made from cellulose.

raze v. (also **rase**) destroy completely, tear down to the ground.

razoo / rah-**zoo** / n. (also **brass razoo**) Aust. a non-existent coin of trivial value (the word being used in negative contexts only). □ **not have a brass razoo** colloq. have no money at all. **not worth a brass razoo** colloq. worth nothing.

razor n. an instrument with a sharp blade used for shaving. □ **razor gang** a parliamentary committee established to examine ways of reducing government expenditure.

razorback n. a narrow, steep-sided ridge of land.

razzamatazz n. (also **razzmatazz**) colloq. showy publicity or display.

razzle-dazzle n. (also **razzle**) colloq. **1** excitement, bustle. **2** a spree. **3** extravagant publicity.
Rb symbol rubidium.
RC abbr. Roman Catholic.
Rd abbr. Road.
RDA abbr. recommended daily allowance (of vitamins, minerals, etc.).
Re symbol rhenium.
re[1] / ree / prep. in the matter of; about, concerning (in business correspondence).
re[2] alternative spelling of RAY (sense 6).
re- comb. form **1** again (as in redecorate, revisit). **2** back again, with return to a previous state (as in re-enter, reopen).

■ **Usage** A hyphen is normally used when the word begins with *e* (*re-enact*), or to distinguish the compound from a more familiar one-word form (*re-cover* = cover again).

reach v. **1** stretch out or extend. **2** go as far as, arrive at. **3** stretch out one's hand in order to touch or take something (*reached for his gun*). **4** establish communication with (*you can reach me by phone*). **5** achieve (*reached a speed of 100 km/h; reached a conclusion*). **6** sail with the wind blowing at right angles to the ship's course. •n. **1** an act of reaching. **2** the distance over which a person or thing can reach; the extent covered by one's mental abilities. **3** a continuous extent of a river between two bends or of a canal between two locks. □ **reachable** adj.
react v. respond to a stimulus; cause or undergo a reaction.
reaction n. **1** a response to a stimulus or act or situation etc. **2** a chemical change produced by two or more substances acting upon each other. **3** the occurrence of one condition after a period of the opposite (*the permissiveness of the 1960s was a reaction to decades of conservatism*). **4** a tendency to oppose change or reform, esp. in politics. **5** a bad physical response to a drug.
reactionary adj. opposed to (esp. political) change or reform; conservative. •n. a person who favours reactionary policies.
reactivate v. restore to a state of activity. □ **reactivation** n.
reactive adj. **1** showing reaction. **2** reacting rather than taking the initiative. **3** susceptible to chemical reaction.
reactor n. (also **nuclear reactor**) an apparatus for the controlled production of nuclear energy.
read / reed / v. (**read** / red /, **reading**) **1** be able to understand the meaning of (written or printed words or symbols) (*I'm reading Shakespeare; can't read music*). **2** speak (written words etc.) aloud (*read to the children*). **3** carry out a course of study (*she's reading Philosophy at Melbourne University*). **4** interpret mentally, find implications (*don't read too much into it*). **5** have a certain wording (*the sign reads 'Keep Left'*). **6** (of a computer) copy, extract, or transfer (data). **7** (of a measuring instrument) indicate or register (*the thermometer reads 30°*). •n. colloq. **1** a session of reading (*had a nice quiet read*). **2** a book etc. in regard to its readability (*an interesting read*). □ **read between the lines** discover a hidden or implicit meaning. **read-only memory** Computing a memory read at high speed but not capable of being changed by program instructions. **read up** study (a subject) by reading. **read-write** Computing capable of reading existing data and allowing alterations or further input (cf. *read-only memory*). **take as read** treat (a thing) as if it has been agreed. **well read** adj. (of a person) having knowledge of a subject, esp. literature, through reading. **you wouldn't read about it** Aust. exclamation expressing incredulity.
readable adj. **1** pleasant and interesting to read. **2** legible. □ **readability** n.
reader n. **1** a person who reads. **2** (also **Reader**) a university lecturer of the highest grade below professor. **3** a book containing passages for practice in reading. **4** a device for producing an image that can be read from microfilm etc. **5** a publisher's employee who reports on submitted manuscripts.
readership n. **1** the readers of a newspaper etc.; the number of these. **2** (also **Readership**) the position of Reader at a university.
readily adv. **1** without reluctance, willingly. **2** without difficulty.
readiness n. being ready.
reading n. **1** the act of one who reads. **2** books etc. intended to be read. **3** (comb. form) used for reading (*reading lamp; reading room*). **4** literary knowledge (*a person of wide reading*). **5** an entertainment at which a play, poems, etc. are read. **6** the amount that is indicated or registered by a measuring instrument. **7** an interpretation or view taken (*what is your reading of the facts?*). **8** each of the successive occasions on which a bill must be presented to a legislature for acceptance.
readjust v. **1** adjust (a thing) again. **2** adapt oneself again. □ **readjustment** n.
ready adj. (**readier, readiest**) **1** in a fit state for immediate action or use. **2** willing (*always ready to help a friend*). **3** about or inclined to do something (*looked ready to collapse*). **4** quick (*a ready wit*). **5** easily available (*found a ready market*). •adv. beforehand (*ready-mixed concrete*). •v. make ready, prepare. □ **ready-made** adj. (of clothes) made in standard shapes and sizes, not to individual customers' orders; (of opinions or excuses etc.) not original. **ready reckoner** a collection of answers to calculations commonly needed in business etc.
reafforest = REFOREST. □ **reafforestation** n.
Reagan / **ray**-guhn /, Ronald (Wilson) (1911–), American statesman, 40th president of the USA 1981–89. He was a film actor before entering politics.

reagent / ree-**ay**-juhnt / *n.* a substance used to produce a chemical reaction.

real *adj.* **1** existing as a thing or occurring as a fact, not imaginary. **2** genuine, not imitation (*real pearls*). **3** true, complete (*there's no real cure*). **4** (of income or value etc.) with regard to its purchasing power. **5** consisting of immovable property such as land or houses (*real estate*). •*adv. colloq.* really, very (*it's real hard*). ▫ **for real** *colloq.* definite; genuine (*are you for real?*); seriously, in earnest (*this time he's playing for real*). **get real** *colloq.* wake up (to oneself, to facts, etc.). **real estate** immovable property such as land and houses. **real tennis** the original form of tennis played on an indoor court. **real-time** *adj.* (of a computer system) able to respond immediately to input data, as in an air-traffic-control system. **real wage** (usu. in *pl.*) income reckoned by purchasing power rather than monetary or nominal value.

realign *v.* **1** align again. **2** regroup in politics etc. ▫ **realignment** *n.*

realise *v.* (also **-ize**) **1** be fully aware of, accept as a fact (*realised his mistake*). **2** convert (a hope or plan) into a fact (*our hopes were realised*). **3** present as real (*the story was powerfully realised on stage*). **4** convert (securities or property) into money by selling. **5** obtain or bring in as profit; (of goods) fetch as a price. ▫ **realisation** *n.*

realism *n.* **1** (in art and literature) representing things as they are in reality. **2** the attitude of a realist.

realist *n.* a person whose ideas and practices are based on facts not on ideals or illusions.

realistic *adj.* **1** true to nature, closely resembling what is imitated or portrayed. **2** facing facts, based on facts not on ideals or illusions. **3** (of wages, or prices) high enough to pay the worker or seller adequately. ▫ **realistically** *adv.*

reality *n.* **1** the quality of being real; resemblance to an original. **2** all that is real, the real world as distinct from imagination or fantasy (*lost his grip on reality*). **3** something that exists or that is real (*the realities of the situation*).

really *adv.* **1** in fact. **2** truly; very (*a really nice girl*). **3** an expression of mild protest, interest, or surprise.

realm / relm / *n.* **1** a kingdom. **2** a field of activity or interest (*the realm of myth*).

realty / ree-uhl-tee / *n.* real estate.

ream *n.* **1** a quantity of paper (about 500 sheets) of the same size. **2** (**reams**) a great quantity of writing (*wrote reams for the assignment*).

reap *v.* **1** cut (grain or a similar crop) as a harvest. **2** receive as the consequence of actions (*reaped great benefit from their training*).

reaper *n.* **1** a person who reaps. **2** a reaping machine. **3** (**the Reaper** *or* **the Grim Reaper**) death personified.

reappraisal / ree-uh-**pray**-zuhl / *n.* a new appraisal.

rear¹ *n.* **1** the back part of something. **2** *colloq.* the buttocks. •*adj.* situated at or in the rear. ▫ **bring up the rear** come last.

rear² *v.* **1** bring up (children); breed and look after (animals); cultivate (crops). **2** build or set up (a monument etc.). **3** (of a horse etc.) raise itself on its hind legs. **4** (of a building, a mountain, etc.) extend to a great height.

rearguard *n.* a body of troops whose job is to protect the rear of the main force. ▫ **rearguard action** a defensive stand or struggle, esp. when losing.

rearm *v.* arm again, esp. with improved weapons. ▫ **rearmament** *n.*

rearmost *adj.* furthest back.

rearrange *v.* arrange in a different way or order. ▫ **rearrangement** *n.*

rearward *adj.* to the rear. •*adv.* (also **rearwards**) towards the rear.

reason *n.* **1** a motive, cause, or justification. **2** the ability to think, understand, and draw conclusions. **3** sanity (*lost his reason*). **4** good sense or judgment; what is right, practical, or possible (*will do anything within reason*). •*v.* **1** use one's ability to think and draw conclusions (*reasoned that the burglar was familiar with the house*). **2** try to persuade someone (*reasoned with the rebels; reasoned him out of his fears*).

■ **Usage** The phrase *the reason is …* should not be followed by *because* (which means the same thing). Correct usage is *We are unable to come; the reason is that we both have flu* (not *the reason is because we have flu*).

reasonable *adj.* **1** ready to use or listen to reason; sensible (*a reasonable person*). **2** in accordance with reason, not absurd, logical. **3** moderate, not expensive or extortionate (*reasonable prices*). ▫ **reasonably** *adv.* **reasonableness** *n.*

reassure / ree-uh-**shaw** / *v.* restore confidence to; remove the fears or doubts of. ▫ **reassurance** *n.* **reassuring** *adj.*

rebate¹ / **ree**-bayt / *n.* a reduction in the amount to be paid, a partial refund. •*v.* pay back as a rebate.

rebate² *n.* a step-shaped channel cut along the edge of a piece of wood etc. to receive another piece or the glass of a window etc. •*v.* **1** join or fix with a rebate. **2** make a rebate in.

rebel *v.* / ruh-**bel** / (**rebelled**, **rebelling**) **1** refuse to continue allegiance to an established government; take up arms against it. **2** resist authority or control; refuse to obey. **3** feel or display repugnance (*my stomach rebelled at the thought of eating a live witchetty grub*). •*n.* / **reb**-uhl / a person or thing that rebels.

rebellion *n.* open resistance to authority, esp. organised armed resistance to an established government.

rebellious *adj.* **1** rebelling, insubordinate. **2** (of a thing) unmanageable (*couldn't do a thing with his hair, it was so rebellious*). ▫ **rebelliously** *adv.* **rebelliousness** *n.*

rebirth *n.* a return to life or activity, a revival.

reboot *v.* start up (a computer) again; switch it off and on again.

rebound *v.* / ruh-**bownd** / **1** spring back after an impact. **2** have an adverse effect upon the originator. •*n.* / **ree**-bownd / an act or instance of rebounding. ▫ **on the rebound 1** (of a hit or catch) made to a ball that is rebounding. **2** while still recovering from an emotional shock, esp. rejection by a lover.

rebuff *n.* an unkind or contemptuous refusal, a snub. •*v.* give a rebuff to.

rebuild *v.* (**rebuilt**, **rebuilding**) build again after destruction or demolition.

rebuke *v.* reprove sharply or severely. •*n.* a sharp or severe reproof.

rebus / **ree**-buhs / *n.* (*pl.* **rebuses**) a representation of a name or word by means of pictures etc. suggesting its parts (*a picture of a man with his chains falling off while he stands next to a cloak may well be a rebus for 'Fremantle'; the letters IOU are a rebus for 'I owe you'*).

rebut / ruh-**but** / *v.* (**rebutted**, **rebutting**) refute or disprove (evidence or an accusation). ▫ **rebuttal** *n.*

rec *n.* recreation. ▫ **rec leave** *Aust. colloq.* a period of leave from work for recreational purposes.

recalcitrant / ruh-**kal**-suh-truhnt / *adj.* disobedient; resisting authority or discipline. ▫ **recalcitrance** *n.*

recall *v.* **1** summon (a person) to return from a place. **2** bring back into the mind, remember or cause to remember. **3** (of a manufacturer) withdraw from sale or take back an article etc. found to be faulty. •*n.* recalling, being recalled.

recant / ruh-**kant** / *v.* formally withdraw one's former statement or belief, rejecting it as wrong or heretical. ▫ **recantation** *n.*

recap[1] / **ree**-kap / *colloq. v.* (**recapped**, **recapping**) recapitulate. •*n.* a recapitulation.

recap[2] *v.* / ree-**kap** / partially replace the worn tread of (a tyre). •*n.* / **ree**-kap / such a tyre.

recapitulate / ree-kuh-**pich**-uh-layt / *v.* state again the main points of what has been said. ▫ **recapitulation** *n.*

recapture *v.* **1** capture (a person or thing that has escaped or been lost to an enemy). **2** succeed in experiencing (a former state or emotion) again. • *n.* recapturing.

recast *v.* (**recast**, **recasting**) **1** cast again (a play, a net, votes, etc.). **2** put into a different form (*recast the question in different words*). •*n.* **1** an act or instance of recasting. **2** the new form etc. of a thing after recasting.

recede *v.* **1** go or shrink back from a certain point; seem to go away from the observer (*the floods receded; the shore receded as we sailed away*). **2** slope backwards (*a receding chin*). **3** decline in force or value. **4** (of a man's hair) cease to grow at the front, sides, etc.

receipt / ruh-**seet** / *n.* **1** receiving; being received (*on receipt of your letter*). **2** a written acknowledgment that something has been received or that money has been paid. **3** (**receipts**) an amount (of money) or quantity received (*the receipts from the concert were good*). •*v.* mark (a bill) as having been paid.

receive *v.* **1** acquire, accept, or take in (something offered, sent, or given). **2** experience; be treated with (*it received close attention*). **3** have conferred or inflicted on one (*received a doctorate; received a kick in the groin*). **4** take the force, weight, or impact of. **5** serve as a receptacle for (*the room receives little light*). **6** consent to hear (a confession etc.) or consider (a petition). **7** accept (stolen goods knowingly). **8** greet or welcome, esp. in a specified manner (*received them with chilly courtesy*). **9** admit to membership (*were received into the Catholic Church*). **10** convert (broadcast signals) into sound or pictures. ▫ **be on the receiving end** be the one who has to submit to something unpleasant.

receiver *n.* **1** a person or thing that receives something. **2** one who accepts stolen goods while knowing them to be stolen. **3** a person appointed usu. by a court to administer the property of a bankrupt person or company, or property subject to litigation. **4** a radio or television apparatus that receives broadcast signals and converts them into sound or a picture. **5** the part of a telephone that is held to the ear.

receivership *n.* the office of receiver; the state of being dealt with by a receiver (*in receivership*).

receiving *n.* the crime of accepting stolen goods while knowing them to be stolen.

recent *adj.* not long past, happening or begun in a time shortly before the present. ▫ **recently** *adv.*

receptacle *n.* something for holding or containing what is put into it.

reception *n.* **1** receiving; being received. **2** the way something is received (*the speech got a cool reception*). **3** an assembly held to receive guests (*wedding reception*). **4** a place where hotel guests or a firm's clients are received on arrival. **5** the receiving of broadcast signals, the efficiency of this (*reception was poor*). ▫ **reception room** a room where visitors are received.

receptionist *n.* a person employed to receive and direct callers or clients.

receptive *adj.* able or quick or willing to receive knowledge, ideas, or suggestions etc. ▫ **receptiveness** *n.* **receptivity** *n.*

receptor *n.* an organ of the body that is able to respond to a stimulus (such as light or pressure) and transmit a signal through a sensory nerve.

recess / ruh-**ses**, **ree**-ses / *n.* **1** a part or space set back from the line of a wall etc.; a small hollow

recession | 690 | **reconciliation**

place inside something. **2** temporary cessation from business, a time of this (*while parliament is in recess*). **3** the midmorning or midafternoon break between school classes. •*v.* make a recess in or of (a wall etc.); set back.

recession *n.* **1** receding from a point or level. **2** a temporary decline in economic activity or prosperity.

recessional *n.* a hymn sung while clergy and choir withdraw after a church service.

recessive *adj.* **1** tending to recede. **2** (of an inherited characteristic) appearing in an offspring only when not masked by a dominant characteristic inherited from one parent.

recharge *v.* charge (a battery or gun etc.) again. □ **rechargeable** *adj.*

recherché / ruh-**shair**-shay / *adj.* **1** devised or selected with care. **2** rare or exotic. **3** far-fetched. (¶ French)

rechristen *v.* christen again; give a new name to.

recidivist / ruh-**sid**-uh-vist / *n.* a person who constantly commits crimes and seems unable to be cured; a persistent offender. □ **recidivism** *n.*

recipe *n.* **1** directions for preparing a dish in cookery. **2** a way of achieving something (*a recipe for disaster*).

recipient / ruh-**sip**-ee-uhnt / *n.* a person who receives something.

reciprocal / ruh-**sip**-ruh-kuhl / *adj.* **1** given or received in return (*reciprocal help*). **2** given or felt by each towards the other, mutual (*reciprocal desire*). **3** corresponding but the other way round (*I thought he was a waiter, while he made the reciprocal mistake and thought that I was*). •*n.* Maths an expression or function so related to another that their product is unity (*½ is the reciprocal of 2*). □ **reciprocally** *adv.*

reciprocate / ruh-**sip**-ruh-kayt / *v.* **1** give and receive; make a return for something done, given, or felt. **2** (of a machine part) move backward and forward alternately. □ **reciprocation** *n.*

reciprocity / res-uh-**pros**-uh-tee / *n.* a reciprocal condition or action; the giving of privileges in return for similar privileges.

recital *n.* **1** reciting. **2** a long account of a series of events. **3** a musical entertainment given by one performer or group.

recitation *n.* **1** reciting. **2** a thing recited.

recitative / res-uh-tuh-**teev** / *n.* a narrative or conversational part of an opera or oratorio, sung in a rhythm imitating that of ordinary speech.

recite *v.* **1** repeat (a passage) aloud from memory, esp. before an audience. **2** state (facts) in order.

reckless *adj.* wildly impulsive, rash. □ **recklessly** *adv.* **recklessness** *n.*

reckon *v.* **1** count up. **2** include in a total or as a member of a particular class. **3** have as one's opinion, feel confident (*I reckon we'll win*). **4** (foll. by *on*) rely or base one's plans on (*we reckoned on your support*). □ **day of reckoning** the time when one must atone for one's actions or be punished.

reckon with (*or* **without**) take (or fail to take) into account.

reclaim *v.* **1** take action so as to recover possession of. **2** make (flooded or waste land) usable, e.g. by draining or irrigating it. □ **reclamation** / rek-luh-**may**-shuhn / *n.*

recline *v.* have or put one's body in a horizontal or relaxed leaning position.

recluse / ruh-**kloos** / *n.* a person who lives alone and avoids mixing with people.

recognisance / ruh-**kog**-nuh-zuhns / *n.* a pledge made to a lawcourt or magistrate that a person will observe some condition (e.g. keep the peace) or appear when summoned; a sum of money pledged as surety for this.

recognise *v.* (also -**ize**) **1** know again, identify from one's previous knowledge or experience. **2** realise or admit the nature of (*recognised the hopelessness of the situation*). **3** acknowledge or accept formally as genuine or valid (*many objected to the fact that Australia recognised Indonesia's annexation of East Timor*). **4** show appreciation of (ability or service etc.) by giving an honour or reward. **5** (of a chairman in a formal debate) allow (a particular person) the right to speak next. □ **recognisable** *adj.* **recognisably** *adv.*

recognition *n.* recognising; being recognised (*a presentation in recognition of his services*).

recoil *v.* **1** move or spring back suddenly; rebound after an impact. **2** (of a gun) be driven backwards by its discharge. **3** draw oneself back in fear or disgust. **4** have an adverse effect on the originator. •*n.* the act or sensation of recoiling.

recollect *v.* remember. □ **recollection** *n.*

recombinant / ree-**kom**-buh-nuhnt / *adj.* (of a gene etc.) formed by recombination. •*n.* a recombinant organism or cell. □ **recombinant DNA** DNA that has been recombined using constituents from different sources.

recommence / ree-kuh-**mens** / *v.* begin again. □ **recommencement** *n.*

recommend *v.* **1** advise (a course of action or a treatment etc.). **2** praise as worthy of employment, favour, or trial etc. **3** (of qualities or conduct) make acceptable or desirable (*this plan has much to recommend it*). □ **recommendation** *n.*

recompense / **rek**-uhm-pens / *v.* repay or reward, compensate. •*n.* payment or reward etc. in return for something.

reconcile / **rek**-uhn-suyl / *v.* **1** restore friendship between (people) after an estrangement or quarrel. **2** induce (a person or oneself) to accept an unwelcome fact or situation (*this reconciled him to living far from home*). **3** bring (facts or statements etc.) into harmony or compatibility when they appear to conflict. □ **reconcilable** *adj.*

reconciliation / re-kuhn-sil-ee-**ay**-shuhn / *n.* **1** the action or an act of reconciling. **2** the action or an act of reconciling a person to oneself or another, or estranged parties to one another. **3** the

recondite / rek-uhn-duyt, ruh-kon- / *adj.* (of a subject) obscure; (of an author) writing about an obscure subject.

recondition / ree-kuhn-**dish**-uhn / *v.* overhaul, replace any worn parts, and make any necessary repairs to.

reconnaissance / ruh-**kon**-uh-suhns / *n.* an exploration or examination of an area to obtain information about it (esp. for military purposes).

reconnoitre / rek-uh-**noi**-tuh / *v.* make a reconnaissance of (an area); make a preliminary survey.

reconsider *v.* consider again, esp. with the possibility of changing one's former decision. □ **reconsideration** *n.*

reconstitute *v.* **1** reconstruct; reorganise. **2** add water to (dried food) to restore it to its previous condition. □ **reconstitution** *n.*

reconstruct *v.* **1** construct or build again. **2** create or enact (past events) again, e.g. in investigating the circumstances of a crime. □ **reconstruction** *n.*

record *n.* / **rek**-awd / **1** information preserved in a permanent form, esp. in writing. **2** a document etc. bearing this. **3** a disc bearing recorded sound. **4** facts known about a person's past (*has a good record of service*). **5** (in full **police record**) a list of a person's previous criminal convictions. **6** the best performance (esp. in sport) or the most remarkable event etc. of its kind that is known (*he holds the high jump record*). •*adj.* / **rek**-awd / best, highest, or most extreme hitherto recorded (*a record crop*). •*v.* / ruh-**kawd** / **1** set down in writing or other permanent form. **2** preserve (sound or visual scenes, esp. television pictures) on disc or tape etc. for later reproduction. **3** register (a vote, a protest, etc.). **4** (of a measuring-instrument) register. □ **for the record** so that facts may be recorded. **off the record** stated unofficially or not for publication. **on record** preserved in written records. **record-breaking** surpassing all previous records. **recorded delivery** a postal delivery in which a receipt is obtained from the recipient as proof of delivery. **record player** an apparatus for reproducing sound from discs on which it is recorded.

recorder *n.* **1** a person who records something; an apparatus for recording, esp. a video or tape recorder. **2** a wooden or plastic wind instrument with holes covered by the fingers, held downwards from the mouth as it is played.

recording *n.* **1** a process by which audio or video signals are recorded for later reproduction. **2** the disc or tape etc. produced. **3** the recorded material.

recordist *n.* a person who records sound.

recount / ruh-**kownt** / *v.* narrate; tell in detail (*recounted his adventures*).

re-count *v.* / ree-**kownt** / count again. •*n.* / ree-kownt / a second counting, esp. of election votes to check the totals.

recoup / ruh-**koop** / *v.* **1** recover what one has lost or its equivalent (*recoup one's losses*). **2** reimburse or compensate (*recoup him for his losses*). □ **recoupment** *n.*

recourse / ruh-**kaws** / *n.* a source of help. □ **have recourse to** turn to (a person or thing) for help.

recover *v.* **1** regain possession, use, or control of. **2** obtain as compensation (*sought to recover damages from the company*). **3** return to a normal condition after illness or unconsciousness. □ **recover oneself** regain consciousness or calmness, or one's balance. □□ **recoverable** *adj.* **recovery** *n.*

recreant / **rek**-ree-uhnt / *literary adj.* **1** craven, cowardly. **2** treacherous, false. •*n.* **1** a coward. **2** a traitor.

recreate / ree-kree-**ayt** / *v.* create again, reproduce.

recreation / rek-ree-**ay**-shuhn / *n.* **1** the process or means of entertaining oneself or relaxing. **2** a pleasurable activity. □ **recreational** *adj.*

recriminate *v.* make recriminations.

recrimination *n.* an angry retort or accusation made in retaliation.

recriminatory *adj.* making recriminations.

recrudesce / ree-kroo-**des** / *v. formal* (of a disease or sore or discontent) break out again, esp. after a dormant period. □ **recrudescent** *adj.* **recrudescence** *n.*

recruit / ruh-**kroot** / *n.* **1** a person who has just joined the armed forces and is not yet trained. **2** a new member of a group. •*v.* **1** form (an army or other group) by enlisting recruits. **2** enlist (a person) as a recruit. **3** refresh (*recruit one's strength*). □ **recruitment** *n.*

rectal *adj.* of or by means of the rectum.

rectangle *n.* a four-sided geometric figure with four right angles, esp. one with adjacent sides unequal in length.

rectangular *adj.* shaped like a rectangle.

rectifier *n.* a device that converts alternating current to direct current.

rectify *v.* (**rectified**, **rectifying**) **1** put right, correct (*rectify the error*). **2** purify or refine, esp. by distillation. **3** convert (alternating current) to direct current. □ **rectifiable** *adj.* **rectification** *n.*

rectilinear / rek-tuh-**lin**-ee-uh / *adj.* **1** bounded by straight lines (*a rectilinear figure*). **2** in or forming a straight line.

rectitude *n.* moral goodness; correctness of behaviour or procedure.

recto *n.* (*pl.* **rectos**) **1** the right-hand page of an open book. **2** the front of a leaf of a manuscript etc. (cf. VERSO).

rector *n.* **1** (in the Anglican Church) a clergyman in charge of a parish. **2** (in the Catholic Church) the priest in charge of a church or religious institution. **3** the head of some universities, schools, and colleges. ☐ **rectorship** *n.*

rectory *n.* the house of a rector.

rectum *n.* the final section of the large intestine, terminating at the anus.

recumbent *adj.* lying down, reclining.

recuperate / ree-**koo**-puh-rayt, ruh- / *v.* **1** recover, regain (one's health or strength) after illness or exhaustion. **2** recover (losses). ☐ **recuperation** *n.* **recuperative** *adj.*

recur *v.* (**recurred, recurring**) happen again, keep occurring. ☐ **recurring decimal** a decimal fraction in which the same figures are repeated indefinitely, e.g. 3.999… or 4.014014…

recurrent / ree-**ku**-ruhnt, ruh- / *adj.* recurring (*a recurrent problem*). ☐ **recurrence** *n.*

recusant / **rek**-yuh-zuhnt / *n.* a person who refuses to submit to authority or to comply with a regulation. • *adj.* of or being a recusant. ☐ **recusancy** *n.*

recycle *v.* convert (waste material) into a form in which it can be reused. ☐ **recyclable** *adj.*

red *adj.* (**redder, reddest**) **1** of the colour of blood. **2** (of the face) flushed with anger or shame; (of the eyes) bloodshot or reddened with weeping. **3** (of the hair) reddish-brown, ginger. **4** *colloq.* communist or socialist. • *n.* **1** red colour. **2** red clothes or material. **3** red wine. **4** *colloq.* a communist or socialist. ☐ **in the red** having a debit balance, in debt. **red ant** = MEAT ANT. **red-bellied black snake** a highly venomous and dangerous eastern Australian snake, having a red belly, black scales, and a tendency to rear and puff up its neck in the manner of its relative the cobra. **red-blooded** virile, full of vigour. **red box** *Aust.* any of several eucalypts yielding a red timber. **red bream** a young snapper. **red card** such a card shown by a football referee to a player who is being sent off the field. **red carpet** privileged treatment given to an important visitor. **red cedar** *Aust.* a large, deciduous rainforest tree, highly valued for its deep red timber, and now rare because of extensive logging. **red cell** (also **red corpuscle**) an erythrocyte, a blood cell which contains haemoglobin and carries oxygen and carbon dioxide to and from the tissues. **red emperor** a red and white marine fish of northern Australia. **red flag 1** a flag used as a warning of danger. **2** the symbol of socialist revolution. **red gum** *Aust.* any of many Australian eucalypts yielding a ruby-red timber, esp. the widespread river red gum. **red hand** *Aust.* the impression of a human hand made with red ochre on rock, a frequent motif in ancient Aboriginal painting. **red-handed** in the act of crime (*caught red-handed*). **red hat 1** a cardinal's hat. **2** the symbol of a cardinal's office (*was elevated to the red hat*). **red herring** a misleading clue; something that draws attention away from the matter under consideration. **red-hot** *adj.* **1** so hot that it glows red. **2** *colloq.* highly exciting. **3** (of news) fresh, completely new. **4** intensely excited. **5** (of prices) extremely low (*red-hot specials*). **6** (of anger) violent, quick to flare up. **7** *colloq.* (of a person) performing at the peak of ability. **red-hot favourite** (of a horse, athlete, team, etc.) highly favoured to win (a race etc.). **red ironbark** *Aust.* any of several Australian ironbarks having bark which is red under the surface and yielding a durable red timber, esp. the mugga. **red kangaroo** a very large kangaroo widely distributed in drier inland Australia, having red to blue-grey fur above and white below. Also called *marloo* in WA. **red lead** red oxide of lead, used as a pigment. **red-letter day** a day that is memorable because of a success, happy event, etc. **red-light district** a district containing many brothels. **red mallee** any of several eucalypts of drier southern Australia having red branchlets or other parts. **red meat** meat that is red when raw (e.g. beef, kangaroo, lamb). **red mulga** *Aust.* = MINNERICHI. **red-necked wallaby** a wallaby of eastern Australia with a reddish patch at the back of the neck. Also called *Bennett's wallaby* in Tas. **red oak** a Qld rainforest tree (of the same family as banksias, grevilleas, etc.) having dark green leaves and spikes of white flowers. **red pepper 1** the ripe red fruit of the capsicum plant. **2** cayenne pepper. **red shift** displacement of the spectrum to longer wavelengths in the light coming from receding galaxies. **red steer** *Aust.* a destructive fire, esp. a bushfire. **red tape** excessive bureaucracy or formalities in official transactions. ☐ ☐ **reddish** *adj.* **redness** *n.*

redback *n.* (in full **redbacked spider**) a small, common, black, Australian spider, the female having a pea-sized body with a red abdominal band and a highly toxic bite.

redbreast *n.* a robin.

Red Centre, the (also **the Red Heart**) central Australia (so called because of the reddish colour of iron oxide in the soil and rocks).

Red Crescent the equivalent of the Red Cross in Muslim countries.

Red Cross an international organisation for the treatment of the sick and wounded in war and for helping those affected by large-scale natural disasters.

redcurrant *n.* a small round edible berry; the bush bearing it.

redden *v.* **1** make or become red. **2** blush.

redecorate *v.* decorate (a room etc.) again or differently. ☐ **redecoration** *n.*

redeem *v.* **1** buy back, recover (a thing) by payment or by doing something. **2** clear (a debt etc.) by paying it off (*redeem the mortgage*). **3** convert (tokens etc.) into goods or cash. **4** obtain the freedom of (a person) by payment. **5** save from damnation or from the consequences of sin. **6** make up for faults or deficiencies (*it has one redeeming feature*). ☐ **redeem oneself** make up for one's former fault. ☐ ☐ **redeemable** *adj.*

redeemer n. **1** one who redeems something. **2** (**the Redeemer**) Christ.
redemption n. redeeming; being redeemed.
redeploy v. send (troops or workers etc.) to a new place or task. □ **redeployment** n.
redevelop v. (**redeveloped**, **redeveloping**) replan or rebuild (an urban area). □ **redevelopment** n.
redfin n. a European freshwater food fish, naturalised in streams etc. of southern Australia.
redfish n. any of several Australian fish, esp. the nannygai.
redhead n. a person with reddish hair.
rediffusion n. relaying of broadcast programs, esp. by cable from a central receiver.
Red Indian n. offens. a Native American, a North American Indian. □ **Red Indian fish** a scarlet Australian marine fish with a dorsal fin said to resemble the feathers of a Native American's headdress.
redirect v. direct or send to another place; readdress (a letter etc.). □ **redirection** n.
rediscover / ree-duh-**skuv**-uh / v. discover again. □ **rediscovery** n. (pl. **rediscoveries**).
redistribute / ree-duh-**strib**-yoot / v. **1** distribute again or differently. **2** change electoral boundaries in order to even out the number of voters in all the electorates. □ **redistribution** n.
redneck n. derog. **1** an ultra right-wing working-class white person in the southern USA. **2** a similar ultra-conservative person elsewhere.
redo / ree-**doo** / v. (**redid**, **redone**, **redoing**) **1** do again. **2** redecorate.
redolent / **red**-uh-luhnt / adj. (foll. by of) **1** smelling strongly (a massage oil redolent of wattle and boronia). **2** suggestive of, full of memories of (an Australian homestead redolent of the past). □ **redolence** n.
redouble v. **1** double again. **2** make or become more intense (redoubled their efforts).
redoubt / ruh-**dowt** / n. a temporary or outer fortification with no defences flanking it.
redoubtable adj. formidable, esp. as an opponent.
redound v. come back as an advantage or disadvantage; accrue (this will redound to our credit).
redress / ruh-**dres** / v. set right, rectify (redress the balance). • n. reparation, amends for a wrong done (has no chance of redress for this damage).
redskin n. offens. a Native American, an American Indian.
reduce v. **1** make or become less. **2** make lower in rank or status. **3** slim. **4** subdue; bring by force or necessity into a specified state or condition (was reduced to despair; reduced to begging). **5** convert into a simpler or more general form (reduce the fraction to its lowest terms; the problem may be reduced to two main elements). **6** restore (a fractured or dislocated bone) to its proper position. **7** Chem. combine or cause to combine with hydrogen; undergo or cause to undergo addition of electrons; convert (oxide) into metal. **8** (in cookery) boil off excess liquid from (a sauce) to thicken it. □ **reduced circumstances** poverty after a period of prosperity. □□ **reducible** adj.
reductio ad absurdum n. proof that a premise is false by showing that its logical consequence is absurd. (¶ Latin)
reduction n. **1** reducing; being reduced. **2** the amount by which something is reduced, esp. in price.
reductive adj. causing reduction.
redundant adj. **1** superfluous. **2** (of workers) no longer needed and therefore unemployed. **3** (of apparatus etc.) being a duplicate in case of failure of the corresponding part or unit. □ **redundancy** n.
reduplicate v. double (a letter or syllable or word) exactly or with a slight change, e.g. *bye-bye, goody-goody, super-duper*. □ **reduplication** n.
redwood n. **1** a very tall evergreen coniferous tree of California. **2** its reddish wood.
re-echo v. (**re-echoed**, **re-echoing**) echo; echo repeatedly, resound.
reed n. **1** a water or marsh plant with tall straight hollow stems. **2** its stem. **3** a vibrating part (often a strip of cane) that produces the sound in certain wind instruments. □ **reed warbler** a widespread, predominantly brown Australian bird of reedy wetlands, having a highly melodious voice.
re-educate v. educate again, esp. to change a person's views.
reedy adj. (**reedier**, **reediest**) **1** full of reeds. **2** like a reed in slenderness or (of grass) thickness. **3** (of the voice) having the thin high tone of a reed instrument. □ **reediness** n.
reef[1] n. **1** a ridge of rock or coral etc. at or near the surface of the sea. **2** a lode of ore; the bedrock surrounding this.
reef[2] n. each of several strips at the top or bottom of a sail that can be drawn in to reduce the area of sail exposed to the wind. • v. shorten (a sail) by drawing in a reef or reefs. □ **reef-knot** a symmetrical double knot that is very secure.
reefer n. colloq. a marijuana cigarette.
reefer jacket n. **1** a thick double-breasted jacket. **2** a sportscoat usu. with gold or silver buttons.
reek n. a foul or stale smell. • v. (often foll. by of) **1** smell strongly and unpleasantly. **2** have unpleasant or suspicious associations (this reeks of bribery).
reel n. **1** a cylinder or similar device on which something is wound; the amount (of thread etc.) held by a reel. **2** a device for winding and unwinding a line as required, esp. in fishing and surf lifesaving. **3** a lively folk-dance, esp. of Scottish or Irish origin. • v. **1** wind on or off a reel. **2** pull (a thing) in using a reel. **3** stand, walk, or run unsteadily. **4** be shaken mentally or physically. **5** rock from side to side, or swing violently. □ **reel**

off say, recite, or write very rapidly and without apparent effort.

reelman n. Aust. the member of a surf lifesaving team who controls the reel.

re-emphasise v. (also **-ize**) place renewed emphasis on.

re-enact v. act out (a past event). ☐ **re-enactment** n.

re-entry n. the act of entering again, esp. of a spacecraft returning into the earth's atmosphere.

Rees, Lloyd (Frederic) (1895–1988), AC, Australian landscape artist.

reeve n. Brit. hist. **1** the chief magistrate of a town or district. **2** an official supervising a landowner's estate. •v. (**rove** or **reeved, reeving**) (in nautical use) **1** thread (a rope or rod etc.) through a ring or other opening. **2** fasten (a rope or block etc.) in this way.

ref n. **1** colloq. a referee in sports. **2** (in commerce) reference, reference number.

reface v. put a new facing on (a building).

refectory / ruh-**fek**-tuh-ree / n. the dining room of a monastery, college, etc.

refer v. (**referred, referring**) (usu. foll. by *to*) **1** make an allusion, direct people's attention by words (*I wasn't referring to you*). **2** send on or direct (a person) to some authority, specialist, or source of information. **3** turn to (a thing) for information (*we referred to the list of rules*). **4** (of a statement etc.) be relevant; relate (*these figures refer to last year*). **5** return (a document) to its sender. ☐ **referred pain** one felt in a part of the body other than its true source. ☐ **referable** adj.

referee n. **1** an umpire, esp. in soccer and boxing. **2** a person to whom disputes are referred for decision, an arbitrator. **3** a person willing to testify to the character or ability of someone applying for a job. •v. (**refereed, refereeing**) act as referee (for).

reference n. **1** the act of referring. **2** something that can be referred to as an authority or standard. **3** a statement referring to or mentioning something (*made no reference to recent events*). **4** a direction to a book or page or file etc. where information can be found; the book or passage etc. cited in this way. **5** a testimonial. **6** a person willing to testify to someone's character, ability, or financial circumstances. ☐ **in** (or **with**) **reference to** in connection with, about. **reference book** a book providing information for reference but not designed to be read straight through. **terms of reference** the points referred to an individual or to a body of persons for decision or report; the scope of an inquiry etc.

referendum n. (pl. **referendums** or **referenda**) the referring of a question to the people of a country etc. for direct decision by a general vote; a vote taken in this way.

referent n. the idea or thing that a word etc. symbolises.

referral / ruh-**fer**-ruhl / n. referring; being referred.

reffo n. Aust. hist. a refugee to Australia from Europe; any migrant to Australia other than from Britain.

refill v. / ree-**fil** / fill again. •n. / **ree**-fil / **1** a second or later filling. **2** the material used for this; a thing that replaces something used up. ☐ **refillable** adj.

refinance v. **1** finance again; provide with further capital. **2** renegotiate the terms of (a debt) esp. to obtain better terms, more capital, etc.

refine v. **1** remove impurities or defects from. **2** make elegant or cultured.

refinement n. **1** refining; being refined. **2** elegance of behaviour or manners etc. **3** an added improvement or development (*the oven has automatic cleaning and other refinements*). **4** a piece of subtle reasoning, a fine distinction.

refiner n. one whose business is to refine crude oil, metal, sugar, etc.

refinery n. a factory where crude substances are refined.

refit v. / ree-**fit** / (**refitted, refitting**) renew or repair the fittings of. •n. / **ree**-fit / a refitting.

reflate v. cause reflation of (a financial system).

reflation n. the process of restoring a financial system to its previous condition when deflation has been carried out too fast or too far. ☐ **reflationary** adj.

reflect v. **1** throw back (light, heat, or sound). **2** be thrown back in this way. **3** (of a mirror etc.) show an image of. **4** correspond to (a thing) because of its influence (*improved methods of agriculture were soon reflected in larger crops*). **5** bring (credit or discredit). **6** (usu. foll. by *on, upon*) bring discredit on (*this failure reflects upon the whole industry*). **7** think deeply, consider; remind oneself of past events.

reflection n. (also **reflexion**) **1** reflecting; being reflected. **2** reflected light or heat etc.; a reflected image. **3** discredit; a thing that brings this. **4** deep thought; an idea or statement produced by this.

reflective adj. **1** reflecting. **2** thoughtful (*in a reflective mood*). ☐ **reflectively** adv.

reflector n. **1** a thing that reflects light or heat or images. **2** a red fitment on the back of a vehicle that reflects the lights of vehicles behind it.

reflex / **ree**-fleks / n. **1** a reflex action. **2** a reflected light or image. ☐ **reflex action** an involuntary or automatic movement in response to a stimulus. **reflex angle** an angle of more than 180°.

reflexion alternative spelling of REFLECTION.

reflexive adj. (of a word or form) referring back to the subject of the verb, in which the action of the verb is performed on its subject, e.g. *he washed himself*. •n. a reflexive word or form. ☐ **reflexive pronoun** any of the pronouns *myself, himself, itself, themselves*, etc.

reflexology *n.* the practice of massaging points on the feet, hands, and head to relieve tension and treat illness. ☐ **reflexologist** *n.*

refloat *v.* set (a stranded ship) afloat again.

reflux / ree-**fluks** / *n.* a backward flow.

reforest *v.* replant (former forest land) with trees. ☐ **reforestation** *n.*

reform *v.* make or become better by removal or abandonment of imperfections or faults. • *n.* **1** the removal of faults or abuses, esp. moral, political, or social. **2** a change to improve something. ☐ **reform school** an institution for the reform of young offenders. ☐☐ **reformative** *adj.*

re-form *v.* form again.

reformation / ref-uh-**may**-shuhn / *n.* **1** reforming; being reformed; a great change for the better in public affairs. **2** (**the Reformation**) *hist.* the 16th-century movement for reform of certain doctrines and practices of the Catholic Church, resulting in the establishment of Protestant Churches.

reformatory / ruh-**faw**-muh-tuh-ree, -tree / *adj.* reformative. • *n.* **1** *hist.* an institution where young offenders are sent to be reformed. **2** = REFORM SCHOOL.

reformer *n.* a person who advocates or brings about (esp. political or social) reform.

reformism *n.* the policy of reform rather than abolition or revolution. ☐ **reformist** *n.* & *adj.*

refract / ree-**frakt** / *v.* bend (a ray of light) at the point where it enters water or glass etc. obliquely. ☐ **refraction** *n.* **refractive** *adj.*

refractor *n.* a refracting medium or lens. **2** a telescope using a lens to produce an image.

refractory *adj.* **1** resisting control or discipline, stubborn (*a refractory child*). **2** (of a disease etc.) not yielding to treatment. **3** (of a substance) resistant to heat; hard to fuse or work.

refrain *n.* **1** the lines of a song that are repeated at the end of each verse. **2** the main part of a song, after the verse. • *v.* (foll. by *from*) keep oneself from doing something (*please refrain from smoking*).

refrangible / ree-**fran**-juh-buhl, ruh- / *adj.* able to be refracted.

refresh *v.* **1** restore the strength and vigour of (a person etc.) by food, drink, or rest. **2** stimulate (the memory) by reminding.

refresher *n.* **1** an extra fee paid to counsel while a case is proceeding in a lawsuit. **2** a drink. ☐ **refresher course** a course of instruction enabling a qualified person to keep abreast of recent developments in the subject.

refreshing *adj.* **1** restoring strength and vigour. **2** welcome and interesting because of its novelty.

refreshment *n.* **1** refreshing; being refreshed. **2** (usu. in *pl.*) food and drink when not regarded as constituting a meal.

refrigerant *n.* a substance used for cooling things in refrigeration. • *adj.* refrigerating.

refrigerate *v.* make extremely cold, esp. in order to preserve and store food. ☐ **refrigeration** *n.*

refrigerator *n.* a cabinet or room in which food is stored at a very low temperature.

refuel *v.* (**refuelled**, **refuelling**) replenish the fuel supply of (esp. a ship or aircraft).

refuge *n.* shelter from pursuit, danger, or trouble; a person or place giving this.

refugee *n.* a person who has left home and seeks refuge elsewhere e.g. from war, persecution, or some natural disaster.

refulgent / ruh-**ful**-juhnt / *adj. literary* shining; gloriously bright. ☐ **refulgence** *n.*

refund *v.* / ruh-**fund** / pay back (money received, or expenses that a person has incurred). • *n.* / **ree**-fund / money refunded, repayment.

refurbish *v.* make clean or bright again; restore and redecorate. ☐ **refurbishment** *n.*

refusal *n.* refusing; being refused. ☐ **first refusal** the right to accept or refuse something before the choice is offered to others.

refuse[1] / ruh-**fyooz** / *v.* **1** indicate that one is unwilling to accept, give, or do something (*I refused to go; she refused my request; the car refused to start*). **2** (of a horse) be unwilling to jump (a fence).

refuse[2] / **ref**-yoos / *n.* what is rejected as worthless, waste material.

refusenik *n.* **1** *archaic* a Soviet Jew who had been refused permission to emigrate to Israel. **2** any person who has been refused official permission to do something. **3** a person who refuses to follow instructions, esp. as a form of protest.

refutable / ruh-**fyoot**-uh-buhl / *adj.* able to be refuted.

refute *v.* **1** prove that (a statement or opinion or person) is wrong. **2** deny; contradict (without argument) (*I absolutely refute your accusation*). ☐ **refutation** / ref-yoo-**tay**-shuhn / *n.*

■ **Usage** The use of *refute* in sense 2 is generally considered incorrect. It is often confused in this sense with *repudiate*.

regain *v.* **1** obtain possession, use, or control of (a thing) again after losing it. **2** reach again (*regained the shore*).

regal / **ree**-guhl / *adj.* like or fit for a monarch. ☐ **regally** *adv.* **regality** / ruh-**gal**-uh-tee / *n.*

regale / ruh-**gayl** / *v.* feed or entertain well (*regaled them with stories of the campaign*).

regalia / ruh-**gay**-lyuh / *n. pl.* **1** the emblems of royalty used at coronations. **2** the emblems of an order (e.g. the Order of Australia) or of a certain rank or office.

regard *v.* **1** look steadily at. **2** consider to be (*we regard the matter as serious*). **3** concern or have a connection with (*he is innocent as regards the first charge*). • *n.* **1** a steady gaze. **2** heed, consideration (*acted without regard to the safety of others*). **3** respect (*we have a great regard for him as our chairman*). **4** a point or reference (*in this regard*).

regardful

5 (**regards**) kindly greetings conveyed in a message (*give him my regards*). ☐ **as regards** about, concerning; in respect of. **in** (*or* **with**) **regard to** regarding, in respect of.

regardful *adj.* (usu. foll. by *of*) mindful of.

regarding *prep.* concerning, with reference to (*laws regarding picketing*).

regardless *adj.* paying no attention to something (*regardless of expense*). • *adv.* nonetheless (*there were hazards, but they carried on regardless*).

regatta *n.* a number of boat or yacht races organised as a sporting event.

regency *n.* **1** being a regent; a regent's period of office. **2** a group of people acting as regent. **3** (**Regency**) the period 1811–20 in England, when George (later George IV) acted as regent; the style of furniture etc. of this period.

regenerate *v.* / ree-**jen**-uh-rayt, ruh- / **1** give new life or vigour to. **2** reform spiritually or morally. **3** *Biology* regrow or cause (new tissue) to regrow. • *adj.* / ree-**jen**-uh-ruht / spiritually born again, reformed. ☐ **regeneration** *n.* **regenerative** *adj.*

regent *n.* a person appointed to administer a country while the monarch is too young or is absent or incapacitated. • *adj.* **1** acting as regent (*Prince Regent*). **2** used in the names of some Australian birds, e.g. *regent honeyeater, regent parrot*. ☐ **regent bird** (*or* **bowerbird**) a bowerbird of dense rainforests in near-coastal Qld and NSW, the male having brilliant golden and black plumage.

reggae / **reg**-ay / *n.* a West Indian style of music with a strongly accented subsidiary beat.

reggo / **rej**-oh / *n.* alternative spelling of REGO.

regicide / **rej**-uh-suyd / *n.* **1** the killing of a king. **2** a person guilty of or involved in this.

regime / ray-**zheem** / *n.* **1** a method or system of government. **2** (usu. *derog.*) a particular government. **3** a regimen.

regimen / **rej**-uh-muhn / *n.* a prescribed course of exercise, way of life, and esp. diet.

regiment *n.* **1** a permanent unit of an army, usu. divided into companies, troops, or battalions. **2** an operational unit of artillery, tanks, armoured cars, etc. **3** a large array or number of things. • *v.* organise (people, work, data, etc.) rigidly into groups or into a pattern. ☐ **regimentation** *n.*

regimental *adj.* of an army regiment. • *n. pl.* (**regimentals**) the uniform of an army regiment.

Regina / ruh-**juy**-nuh / *n.* (after the name) a reigning queen (*Elizabeth Regina*). (¶ Latin, = queen.)

region *n.* **1** a geographical area or division, having definable boundaries or characteristics. **2** an administrative division of a country. **3** a part of the body (*genital region*). ☐ **in the region of** approximately. ☐☐ **regional** *adj.* **regionally** *adv.*

regionalism *n.* **1** the theory or practice of regional rather than central systems of admin-

696

regretful

istration or economic, cultural, or political affiliation. **2** a linguistic feature peculiar to a particular region and not part of the standard language of a country.

register *n.* **1** an official list of names, items, etc. **2** the book or other document(s) in which this is kept. **3** a mechanical device for indicating or recording speed, force, numbers, etc. automatically. **4** a cash register. **5** an adjustable plate for widening or narrowing an opening, e.g. for regulating the draught in a fire grate. **6** exact correspondence of position (*out of register*). **7** the range of a human voice or of a musical instrument. **8** a set of organ pipes; a sliding device controlling this. **9** a particular style of language (e.g. informal, literary) used in appropriate circumstances. **10** *Computing* a memory location having specific properties and quick access time. • *v.* **1** enter or cause to be entered in a particular register. **2** set down (a name, fact, complaint, etc.) formally in writing; present for consideration. **3** pay an annual fee on a motor vehicle. **4** commit (a letter etc.) to registered post. **5** notice and remember. **6** (of an instrument) indicate or record something automatically. **7** make an impression on a person's mind (*his name did not register with me*). **8** express (an emotion) on one's face or by gesture. ☐ **registered post** a postal service with special precautions for safety and compensation in case of loss.

registrar / **rej**-uhs-trah / *n.* **1** an official with responsibility for keeping written records or registers. **2** a chief administrator in a university or college. **3** a doctor undergoing hospital training to be a specialist.

registration *n.* **1** registering; being registered. **2** the annual fee payable by the owner of a motor vehicle. ☐ **registration number** a combination of letters and numbers identifying a motor vehicle. **registration plate** a vehicle number plate.

registry *n.* a place where written records or registers are kept. ☐ **registry office** an office where civil marriages are conducted and births, marriages, and deaths are recorded.

rego / **rej**-oh / *n.* & *adj.* (also **reggo** pronounced the same) *Aust. colloq.* **1** motor vehicle registration. **2** an instance of registering (*footy rego day*).

regress *v.* / ruh-**gres** / go back to an earlier or worse or more primitive form or state. • *n.* / **ree**-gres / regressing. ☐ **regression** *n.* **regressive** *adj.*

regret *n.* a feeling of sorrow for the loss of a person or thing, or of disappointment or repentance. • *v.* (**regretted, regretting**) feel regret about.

regretful *adj.* feeling regret. ☐ **regretfully** *adv.*

■ **Usage** *Regretfully* should be used only when 'in a regretful manner' is meant, e.g. *She shook her head regretfully*, and not where *regrettably* is meant, e.g. *Regrettably, he cannot be here tonight*.

regrettable *adj.* (of events or conduct) undesirable, unwelcome; deserving censure. ☐ **regrettably** *adv.*

■ **Usage** See Usage Note at REGRETFUL.

regroup *v.* **1** form into new groups; arrange again differently. **2** reorganise (people, troops etc.) after a setback etc.; prepare for a fresh start or attack.

regular *adj.* **1** acting, recurring, or done in a uniform manner, or constantly at a fixed time or interval (*his pulse is regular*). **2** conforming to a principle or to a standard of procedure. **3** even, symmetrical (*a regular pentagon*). **4** usual, normal, habitual (*has no regular occupation*). **5** belonging to the permanent armed forces of a country (*regular soldiers*). **6** (used before or after the noun) bound by religious rule; belonging to a religious or monastic order. **7** (of a verb or noun etc.) having inflections that are of a normal type. **8** *colloq.* complete, out-and-out (*it's a regular mess*). **9** (of a person) defecating or menstruating at predictable times. • *n.* **1** a member of the permanent armed forces of a country. **2** *colloq.* a regular customer or client etc. (*most pubs have their regulars*). ☐ **regularly** *adv.* **regularity** *n.*

regularise *v.* (also **-ize**) **1** make regular. **2** make lawful or correct (*the company wishes to regularise the situation*). ☐ **regularisation** *n.*

regulate *v.* **1** control or direct by means of rules and restrictions. **2** adjust or control (a thing) so that it works correctly or according to one's requirements. ☐ **regulator** *n.*

regulation *n.* **1** regulating; being regulated. **2** a rule or restriction. • *adj.* **1** in accordance with regulations; of the correct type etc. (*students must wear the regulation uniform*). **2** *colloq.* usual (*downed his regulation tinnie before tea*).

regurgitate / ree-**ger**-juh-tayt, ruh- / *v.* **1** bring (swallowed food) up again to the mouth. **2** reproduce, rehash (information etc.). ☐ **regurgitation** *n.*

rehabilitate *v.* **1** restore (a person) to a normal life by training, after a period of illness or imprisonment. **2** restore to former privileges or reputation or a proper condition. ☐ **rehabilitation** *n.*

rehash *v.* / ree-**hash** / put (old material) into a new form with no great change or improvement. • *n.* / **ree**-hash / **1** rehashing. **2** something made of rehashed material (*the program was a rehash of old newsreels*).

rehearsal *n.* **1** rehearsing. **2** a practice or trial performance.

rehearse *v.* **1** practise before performing in public. **2** train (a person) by doing this. **3** say over, give an account of (*rehearsing his grievances*).

rehouse / ree-**howz** / *v.* provide with accommodation elsewhere.

Reich / ruyk / *n.* the former German State. ☐ **Third Reich** Germany under the Nazi regime (1933–45).

Reid, Sir George Houston (1845–1918), Australian statesman, prime minister 1904–05.

reign / rayn / *n.* **1** a sovereign's rule; the period of this. **2** the controlling or dominating effect of a person or thing (*a reign of terror*). • *v.* **1** be a king or queen. **2** be supreme, dominate; prevail (*silence reigned*). **3** (as **reigning** *adj.*) (of a champion) currently holding the title.

reiki / **ray**-kee / *n.* a healing technique based on the principle that the therapist can channel energy into the patient by means of touch. (¶ Japanese, = universal life energy.)

reimburse *v.* repay, refund. ☐ **reimbursement** *n.*

rein *n.* (also **reins**) **1** a long narrow strap fastened to the bit of a bridle and used to control a horse. **2** a means of control (*he has no rein on his lust*). • *v.* **1** (often foll. by *in*) check or control with (or as with) reins. **2** govern, restrain, control. ☐ **give free rein to** allow freedom to (*give one's imagination free rein*).

reincarnate *v.* / ree-in-**kah**-nayt / bring back (a soul after death) into another body. • *adj.* / ree-in-**kah**-nat / reincarnated. ☐ **reincarnation** *n.*

reindeer *n.* (*pl.* **reindeer** or **reindeers**) a deer with large antlers, living in Arctic regions.

reinforce *v.* strengthen or support by additional persons or material or an added quantity. ☐ **reinforced concrete** concrete with metal bars or wire embedded in it to increase its strength.

reinforcement *n.* **1** reinforcing; being reinforced. **2** a thing that reinforces. **3** (**reinforcements**) additional personnel, equipment, etc.

reinstate *v.* replace in a former position; restore (a person etc.) to former privileges. ☐ **reinstatement** *n.*

reissue *v.* issue (a thing) again. • *n.* something reissued, e.g. a new issue of a book.

reiterate / ree-**it**-uh-rayt / *v.* say or do again or repeatedly. ☐ **reiteration** *n.*

reject *v.* / ruh-**jekt** / **1** refuse to accept; put aside or send back as not to be chosen, used, or done etc. **2** react against (*the body may reject the transplanted tissue*). **3** fail to give due affection to (*the child was rejected by both his parents*). • *n.* / **ree**-jekt / a person or thing that is rejected, esp. as being below standard. ☐ **rejection** *n.*

rejig *v.* (**rejigged**, **rejigging**) **1** re-equip (a factory etc.) for a new type of work. **2** *colloq.* rearrange.

rejoice *v.* feel or show great joy.

rejoin[1] / ree-**join** / *v.* join again; reunite; join (a companion etc.) again.

rejoin[2] / ruh-**join** / *v.* say in answer; retort.

rejoinder *n.* something said in answer or retort.

rejuvenate / ree-**joo**-vuh-nayt, ruh- / *v.* restore youthful appearance or vigour to. ☐ **rejuvenation** *n.*

relapse / ruh-**laps** / v. fall back into a previous condition, or into a worse state after improvement. • n. (also / **ree**-laps /) relapsing, esp. after partial recovery from illness.

relate v. **1** narrate; tell in detail. **2** (often foll. by *to*) connect (two things) in thought or meaning. **3** (foll. by *to*) have reference to; be concerned with. **4** (foll. by *to*) establish a sympathetic or successful relationship with (a person or thing) (*learning to relate to children*).

related *adj.* having a common descent or origin.

relation *n.* **1** the way in which one thing is related to another; a similarity, correspondence, or contrast between people, things, or events. **2** being related. **3** a person who is a relative. **4** narrating, being narrated. **5** (**relations**) dealings with others (*the country's foreign relations*). **6** (**relations**) sexual intercourse (*I've had relations with him*).

relationship *n.* **1** the state of being related; a connection or association. **2** an emotional (esp. sexual) association between two people.

relative *adj.* **1** considered in relation or proportion to something else (*the relative merits of the two plans; lived in relative comfort*). **2** having a connection with (*facts relative to the matter in hand*). **3** *Grammar* (esp. of a pronoun) referring or attached to an earlier noun, clause, or sentence (*'who' in 'the man who came to dinner' is a relative pronoun*). • n. **1** a person who is related to another by parentage, descent, or marriage. **2** *Grammar* a relative pronoun or adverb. ☐ **relative atomic mass** the ratio of the average mass of one atom of an element to one twelfth of the mass of an atom of carbon-12. **relative density** the ratio between the mass of a substance and that of the same volume of a substance used as a standard (usu. water or air). **relative molecular mass** the ratio of the average mass of one molecule of an element or compound to one twelfth of the mass of an atom of carbon-12. ☐☐ **relatively** *adv.*

relativity *n.* **1** relativeness. **2** one of two theories developed by Einstein: (**special theory of relativity**) based on the principle that all motion is relative and that light has a constant speed; (**general theory of relativity**) a theory extending this to gravitation and accelerated motion. **3** the relative differences in wages between occupational groups (*the union movement is concerned to maintain relativities*).

relax v. **1** become or cause to become less tight or tense. **2** make or become less strict (*relax the rules*). **3** make or become less anxious or formal; cease work or effort and indulge in recreation. ☐ **relaxation** *n.*

relay *n.* / **ree**-lay / **1** a fresh set of people or animals taking the place of others who have completed a spell of work (*operating in relays*). **2** a fresh supply of material to be used or worked on. **3** a relay race. **4** a relayed message or transmission. **5** an electronic device that receives and passes on a signal, often strengthening it. • v. / ree-**lay** / (**relayed**, **relaying**) receive and pass on or retransmit (a message, broadcast, etc.). ☐ **relay race** a race between teams in which each person in turn covers a part of the total distance.

re-lay v. (**re-laid**, **re-laying**) lay again.

release v. **1** set free. **2** remove from a fixed position; allow to fall, fly, etc. (*released an arrow*). **3** issue (a film) for general exhibition; make (information or a recording etc.) available to the public. • n. **1** releasing; being released. **2** a handle or catch that unfastens a device or machine part. **3** a news item released to the public (*a press release*). **4** a new film, recording, etc. issued for sale or public showing.

relegate / **rel**-uh-gayt / v. **1** send or consign to a less important place or condition. **2** transfer (a sports team) to a lower division of a league etc. ☐ **relegation** *n.*

relent v. abandon one's harsh intentions and be more lenient.

relentless *adj.* **1** not relenting. **2** unceasing in its severity (*the relentless pressure of business life*). ☐ **relentlessly** *adv.* **relentlessness** *n.*

relevant / **rel**-uh-vuhnt / *adj.* related to the matter in hand. ☐ **relevance** *n.*

reliable *adj.* **1** able to be relied on. **2** consistently good in quality or performance. ☐ **reliably** *adv.* **reliability** *n.*

reliance *n.* **1** relying. **2** trust or confidence. ☐ **reliant** *adj.*

relic / **rel**-ik / *n.* **1** something that survives from an earlier age. **2** a surviving trace of a custom or practice. **3** part of a saint's body or belongings kept after his or her death as an object of reverence. **4** (**relics**) remnants, residue.

relict / **rel**-ikt / *n.* **1** *archaic* a person's widow. **2** a geological or other object surviving in a primitive form.

relief *n.* **1** ease given by reduction or removal of pain, anxiety, or a burden. **2** something that relaxes tension or breaks up monotony (*a humorous scene serving as comic relief*). **3** assistance given to people in special need (*drought relief*). **4** a person taking over another's turn of duty. **5** the raising of the siege of a besieged town. **6** a method of carving or moulding in which the design projects from the surface. **7** a piece of carving etc. done in this way. **8** a similar effect achieved by the use of colour or shading. ☐ **relief map** a map showing hills and valleys either by shading or by their being moulded in relief.

relieve v. **1** give relief to; bring or be a relief to. **2** introduce variation into, make less monotonous. **3** (foll. by *of*) take a thing from (a person) (*the thief had relieved him of his watch*). **4** raise the siege of (a town). **5** (foll. by *of*) release (a person) from a duty or task by taking his or her place or providing a substitute. ☐ **relieve oneself** urinate or defecate.

religion *n.* **1** belief in and worship of a superhuman controlling power, esp. a god or gods. **2** a particular system of faith and worship (*the Zoroastrian religion*). **3** a controlling influence on a person's life (*footie is her religion*). **4** life under monastic vows.

religiosity *n.* (usu. *derog.*) the state of being obtrusively religious or too religious.

religious *adj.* **1** of religion (*a religious service*). **2** believing firmly in a religion and paying great attention to its practices. **3** of or belonging to a monastic order. **4** very conscientious (*with religious attention to detail*). •*n.* (*pl.* **religious**) a person bound by monastic vows. ▫ **religiously** *adv.*

relinquish *v.* **1** give up or cease from (a plan, habit, or belief etc.). **2** surrender possession of. **3** relax one's hold of; let go (*relinquished the reins*). ▫ **relinquishment** *n.*

reliquary / **rel**-i-kwuh-ree / *n.* a receptacle for a relic or relics of a saint.

relish *n.* **1** great enjoyment of food or other things. **2** an appetising flavour. **3** an attractive quality (*gardening loses its relish in winter*). **4** a strong-tasting substance or food eaten with plainer food to add flavour. •*v.* enjoy greatly.

relive *v.* live (an experience etc.) over again, esp. in the imagination.

rellie *n.* (also **relo**) *Aust. colloq.* (usu. in *pl.*) a relative (*all the rellies will be here for Christmas*).

relocate / ree-loh-**kayt** / *v.* **1** move (a person or thing) to a new place. **2** move to a new place (esp. to live or work). ▫ **relocation** *n.*

reluctant *adj.* unwilling, grudging one's consent. ▫ **reluctantly** *adv.* **reluctance** *n.*

rely *v.* (**relied**, **relying**) (foll. by *on*) trust confidently, depend on for help etc.

REM *abbr.* rapid eye movement; movement of the eyeballs during sleep, indicating a period of dreaming.

remain *v.* **1** be there after other parts have been removed or used or dealt with. **2** be in the same place or condition during further time, continue to be (*remained at home*; *remained faithful*).

remainder *n.* **1** the remaining people, things, or part. **2** the quantity left after subtraction or division. **3** (usu. in *pl.*) copies of a book left unsold when demand has almost ceased. •*v.* dispose of unsold copies of (a book) at a reduced price (*his novel has been remaindered*).

remains *n. pl.* **1** what remains after other parts or things have been removed or used. **2** ancient buildings or objects that have survived when others are destroyed; relics (*ancient Roman remains in Italy*). **3** a dead body (*his mortal remains*).

remake *v.* / ree-**mayk** / (**remade**, **remaking**) make again. •*n.* / **ree**-mayk / something remade, esp. a new version of an old film.

remand *v.* return (a prisoner) to custody while further evidence is sought. •*n.* remanding, being remanded. ▫ **on remand** held in custody pending trial. **remand centre** a place where accused people are sent to await trial.

remark *n.* **1** a written or spoken comment. **2** noticing (*worthy of remark*). **3** commenting (*let it pass without remark*). •*v.* **1** make a remark, say. **2** notice.

remarkable *adj.* worth noticing, exceptional, unusual. ▫ **remarkably** *adv.*

remarry *v.* (**remarried**, **remarrying**) marry again. ▫ **remarriage** *n.*

Rembrandt / **rem**-brant / (full name: Rembrandt Harmensz van Rijn) (1606–69), Dutch painter.

remediable / ruh-**mee**-dee-uh-buhl / *adj.* able to be remedied.

remedial / ruh-**mee**-dee-uhl / *adj.* **1** providing a remedy for a disease or deficiency (*remedial exercises*). **2** (of teaching) for slow or disadvantaged pupils. ▫ **remedially** *adv.*

remedy *n.* something that cures or relieves a disease or that puts a matter right. •*v.* (**remedied**, **remedying**) be a remedy for, put right.

remember *v.* **1** keep in one's mind. **2** recall knowledge or experience to one's mind; be able to do this. **3** think of (a person), esp. in making a gift (*remembered me in his will*). **4** mention as sending greetings (*remember me to your mother*).

remembrance *n.* **1** remembering; being remembered; memory. **2** something that reminds people, a memento or memorial.

Remembrance Day 11 November, when those killed in the two World Wars and in later conflicts are commemorated.

remind *v.* cause to remember or think of something.

reminder *n.* a thing that reminds someone; a note written to remind someone.

reminisce / rem-uh-**nis** / *v.* think or talk about past events and experiences.

reminiscence / rem-uh-**nis**-uhns / *n.* **1** thinking or talking about past events. **2** an account of what one remembers (*wrote his reminiscences*). **3** a thing that is reminiscent of something else.

reminiscent / rem-uh-**nis**-uhnt / *adj.* **1** inclined to reminisce (*she was in a reminiscent mood*). **2** (foll. by *of*) having characteristics that recall something to one's mind (*his style is reminiscent of Picasso's*). ▫ **reminiscently** *adv.*

remiss / ruh-**mis** / *adj.* negligent (*you have been remiss in your duties*).

remission *n.* **1** forgiveness (of sins etc.). **2** the remitting of a debt or penalty; the shortening of a convict's prison sentence for good behaviour. **3** reduction of the force or intensity of something (*slight remission of the pain*).

remit *v.* (**remitted**, **remitting**) **1** cancel (a debt); refrain from inflicting (a punishment). **2** make or become less intense (*nothing will remit his rage*; *your pain will remit in time*). **3** send (money, a document, etc.) to a person or place (*please remit the interest to my home address*). **4** postpone. **5** forgive (sins).

remittance *n.* **1** the sending of money to a person. **2** the money sent. ☐ **remittance man** *Aust. hist.* a British immigrant to Australia financially supported by his family overseas (usu. with the implication that the family was prepared to pay to keep him away from Britain).

remittent *adj.* (of a fever or disease) abating at intervals.

remix *v.* / ree-**miks** / **1** mix again. **2** (of a recording) alter the relative sound levels of the various performers etc. •*n.* / **ree**-miks / a remixed recording.

remnant *n.* **1** a small remaining quantity or trace of something. **2** a small piece of cloth left when the rest of the roll has been used or sold.

remodel *v.* (**remodelled**, **remodelling**) model again or differently; reconstruct or reorganise.

remonstrance / ruh-**mon**-struhns / *n.* remonstrating, a protest.

remonstrate / **rem**-uhn-strayt / *v.* make a protest (*remonstrated with him about his behaviour*).

remontant / ruh-**mon**-tuhnt / *adj.* (esp. of a rose) blooming more than once a year. •*n.* a remontant rose.

remorse *n.* **1** deep regret for one's wrong-doing. **2** compassion, pity. ☐ **remorseful** *adj.* **remorsefully** *adv.*

remorseless *adv.* relentless; without compassion. ☐ **remorselessly** *adv.*

remote *adj.* **1** far away in place or time (*the remote past*). **2** far from civilisation (*a remote country town*). **3** not close in relationship or connection (*a remote ancestor; remote causes*). **4** slight (*I haven't the remotest idea*). **5** aloof; not friendly. ☐ **remote control** control of an apparatus from a distance, usu. by means of signals transmitted from a radio or electronic device; such a device. ☐ ☐ **remotely** *adv.* **remoteness** *n.*

removal *n.* **1** removing; being removed. **2** the transfer of furniture etc. to a different house.

removalist *n.* (often in *pl.*) *Aust.* a person or a firm whose work is the transferring of furniture etc. for those moving house.

remove *v.* **1** take off or away from the place occupied (*remove the lid carefully; remove your clothes*). **2** convey to another place; change the situation of. **3** dismiss from office. **4** get rid of (*this removes the last of my doubts*). •*n.* **1** a stage or degree; a degree of difference (*this is several removes from the truth*). ☐ **removable** *adj.* **remover** *n.*

removed *adj.* **1** distant, remote (*an Aboriginal dialect not far removed from Pitjantjatjara*). **2** *Aust.* (of Aboriginal children) forcibly taken from their parents and put into a mission or other institution (*saying sorry to removed children for years of pain is not enough*). ☐ **cousin once removed** a cousin's child or parent. **cousin twice removed** a cousin's grandchild or grandparent.

remunerate / ruh-**myoo**-nuh-rayt / *v.* pay (a person) for services rendered. ☐ **remuneration** *n.* **remunerative** *adj.*

Remus / **ree**-muhs / *Rom. myth.* the twin brother of ROMULUS.

Renaissance / ruh-**nay**-suhns, -sons / *n.* **1** the revival of art and literature in Europe (influenced by classical forms) in the 14th–16th centuries; the period of this. **2** (**renaissance**) any similar revival.

renal / **ree**-nuhl / *adj.* of the kidneys.

rename *v.* give a fresh name to.

renascent / ruh-**nas**-uhnt / *adj.* springing up anew; being reborn. ☐ **renascence** *n.*

rend *v.* (**rent**, **rending**) tear, wrench.

render *v.* **1** give, esp. in return or exchange or as something due (*a reward for services rendered*). **2** present or send in (*account rendered*). **3** cause to become (*rendered him helpless*). **4** give a performance of (a play or character or piece of music); represent, portray (*rendered his likeness faithfully*). **5** translate (*rendered into English*). **6** melt down (fat). **7** cover (stone or brick) with a coat of plaster.

rendezvous / **ron**-day-voo / *n.* (*pl.* **rendezvous** / **ron**-day-vooz /) **1** a prearranged meeting. **2** a prearranged or regular meeting place. •*v.* (**rendezvouses** / ron-day-**vooz** /, **rendezvoused** / ron-day-**vood** /, **rendezvousing** / ron-day-**voo**-ing /) meet at a rendezvous.

rendition / ren-**dish**-uhn / *n.* **1** a performance of a dramatic role or musical piece etc. **2** a translation.

Rene, Roy (original name: Henry Van der Sluys) (1892–1954), Australian comedian, creator of the clown-character 'Mo'.

renegade / **ren**-uh-gayd / *n.* someone who deserts from a group, cause, or faith.

renege / ree-**neg**, ruh- / *v.* **1** (often foll. by *on*) go back on (one's word etc.), fail to keep (a promise etc.). **2** (in card games) fail to follow suit when able to do so.

renew *v.* **1** restore to its original state. **2** replace with a fresh supply (*the tyres need renewing*). **3** get or make or give again (*renewed their acquaintance*). **4** arrange for a continuation or continued validity of (*renew one's subscription*). ☐ **renewal** *n.*

renewable *adj.* **1** able to be renewed. **2** (of a fuel or source of energy) not depleted by utilisation.

rennet / **ren**-uht / *n.* **1** curdled milk found in the stomach of an unweaned calf. **2** a substance made from the stomach membrane of a calf or from certain fungi, used to curdle milk in making cheese or junket.

Renoir / ruh-**nwah**, ren-wah /, Pierre Auguste (1841–1919), French Impressionist painter.

renounce v. **1** give up (a claim or right etc.) formally (*renounced his title*). **2** reject; refuse to abide by (an agreement etc.).

renovate / **ren**-uh-vayt / v. repair; renew. ▫ **renovation** n. **renovator** n.

renown / ruh-**nown** / n. fame.

renowned adj. famous, celebrated.

rent[1] *see* RENT. • n. a tear in a garment etc.

rent[2] n. payment made periodically for the use of land or accommodation or for equipment such as a telephone. • v. **1** pay rent for temporary use of. **2** allow to be used in return for payment of rent. ▫ **rent boy** *colloq.* a young male prostitute.

rental n. **1** the amount paid or received as rent. **2** renting.

renumber v. change the numbering of.

renunciation / ruh-nun-see-**ay**-shuhn / n. renouncing; giving something up.

reorder v. **1** order again; order further supplies of. **2** put into a different sequence. • n. a renewed or repeated order for goods.

reorganise v. (also **-ize**) organise in a new way. ▫ **reorganisation** n.

reorient v. **1** change or adjust (a person's ideas or outlook). **2** help (a person) find his or her bearings again.

reorientate = REORIENT. ▫ **reorientation** n.

rep n. *colloq.* **1** a business firm's travelling representative. **2** the elected representative of a group of employees (*union rep; shearers' rep*). **3** repertory; a repertory theatre or company.

repackage v. **1** package again or differently. **2** present in a new form (*he needs to be repackaged if he's ever to be elected*).

repaint v. paint again or differently; restore the paint or colouring of. • n. **1** repainting. **2** a repainted thing.

repair v. **1** restore to good condition after damage or the effects of wear and tear. **2** put right, make amends for. **3** go (*he repaired to a monastery*). • n. **1** the act or process of repairing something. **2** condition as regards being repaired (*keep it in good repair*). ▫ **repairable** adj. **repairer** n.

reparable / **rep**-uh-ruh-buhl / adj. (of a loss etc.) able to be made good.

reparation / rep-uh-**ray**-shuhn / n. **1** making amends. **2** (**reparations**) compensation for war damage, demanded by the victor from a defeated enemy.

repartee / rep-ah-**tee** / n. a witty reply; the ability to make witty replies.

repast / ruh-**pahst** / n. *formal* a meal.

repatriate / ree-**pat**-ree-ayt / v. return (a person) to his or her own country. • n. / ree-**pat**-ree-uht / a repatriated person.

repatriation n. **1** repatriating. **2** *Aust.* the rehabilitation of former service personnel, including the provision of pensions, loans, medical care, etc.

repay v. (**repaid**, **repaying**) **1** pay back (money). **2** do, make, or give in return (*repaid kindness with kindness; the book repays close study*). ▫ **repayment** n.

repayable adj. able or needing to be repaid.

repeal v. withdraw (a law) officially. • n. the repealing of a law.

repeat v. **1** say, do, or occur again. **2** say aloud (something heard or learnt) (*repeat the oath after me*). **3** (of food) produce a taste in one's mouth after being eaten due to belching. **4** supply a further consignment of (*we cannot repeat this article*). • n. **1** repeating. **2** (often as *adj.*) something that is repeated (*this prescription has two repeats; a repeat broadcast; tonight's film on telly is a repeat*). **3** *Music* a passage intended to be repeated; the mark indicating this. ▫ **repeat oneself** say or do the same thing again.

repeatable adj. able to be repeated; suitable for being repeated.

repeatedly adv. again and again.

repeater n. **1** a person or thing that repeats. **2** a firearm which fires several shots without reloading. **3** a watch or clock which repeats its last strike when required. **4** a device for the retransmission of an electrical message.

repechage / **rep**-uh-chahj / n. (in rowing etc.) an extra contest in which the runners-up in the elimination heats compete for a place in the final.

repel v. (**repelled**, **repelling**) **1** drive away; ward off (*repelled the attackers; this spray repels insects*). **2** refuse to accept (*repelled all offers of help*). **3** be impossible for (a substance) to penetrate (*the surface repels moisture*). **4** push away from itself by an unseen force (*one north magnetic pole repels another*). **5** be repulsive or distasteful to (*racist remarks repel me*).

repellent adj. **1** repelling, arousing distaste. **2** not penetrable by a specified substance (*the fabric is water-repellent*). • n. a substance that repels something (*insect repellent*).

repent v. feel regret about (what one has done or failed to do). ▫ **repentance** n. **repentant** adj.

repercussion / ree-puh-**kush**-uhn / n. **1** the recoil of something after impact. **2** an echo. **3** an indirect effect or reaction following an event or act (*consider the repercussions of this move*).

repertoire / **rep**-uh-twah / n. **1** a stock of songs, plays, acts, etc. that a person or company knows and is prepared to perform. **2** a stock of techniques etc. (*his familiar repertoire of excuses*).

repertory / **rep**-uh-tuh-ree, -tree / n. **1** a repertoire. **2** performance of various plays for short periods by one company. **3** repertory theatres collectively. **4** a store or collection, e.g. of jokes, information, instances, etc. ▫ **repertory company** (*or* **theatre**) a theatrical company that performs plays from a repertoire.

répétiteur / re-pet-uh-**ter** / n. **1** a tutor or coach of musicians, esp. opera singers. **2** a person who supervises ballet rehearsals etc.

repetition *n.* repeating, being repeated; an instance of this. ☐ **repetition strain injury** = REPETITIVE STRAIN INJURY.

repetitious / rep-uh-**tish**-uhs / *adj.* characterised by (esp. tedious or unnecessary) repetition.

repetitive / ruh-**pet**-uh-tiv / *adj.* repetitious. ☐ **repetitive strain injury** (also **repetition strain injury**; *abbr.* **RSI**) painful damage to tendons etc. caused by work which involves repetitive muscular movements over long periods of time. ☐☐ **repetitively** *adv.*

rephrase *v.* express using different words.

repine / ruh-**puyn** / *v.* fret, be discontented.

replace *v.* **1** put back in place. **2** take the place of (*personal computers have largely replaced typewriters; replaced him as leader*). **3** find or provide a substitute for. ☐ **replaceable** *adj.*

replacement *n.* **1** replacing or being replaced. **2** a person or thing that replaces another.

replant *v.* transfer (a plant etc.); plant (ground) again.

replay *v.* / ree-**play** / play (a match or recording etc.) again. • *n.* / **ree**-play / the replaying of a match, a recorded incident in a game, etc.

replenish *v.* **1** fill (a thing) again (*replenish your glasses*). **2** renew (a supply etc.). ☐ **replenishment** *n.*

replete / ruh-**pleet** / *adj.* **1** well stocked or supplied. **2** well-fed, gorged. ☐ **repletion** *n.*

replica / **rep**-li-kuh / *n.* **1** an exact copy, esp. a duplicate of a work, made by the original artist. **2** a copy or model, esp. on a smaller scale.

replicate / **rep**-luh-kayt / *v.* make a replica of; reproduce; repeat. ☐ **replication** *n.*

reply *v.* (**replied**, **replying**) answer; say in answer. • *n.* **1** replying. **2** what is replied, an answer.

report *v.* **1** give an account of (something seen, done, or studied); tell as news. **2** make a formal accusation about (an offence or offender). **3** make an official or formal statement about (*the committee reported its findings*). **4** present oneself to a person when one arrives or returns. **5** be responsible to a certain person as one's superior or supervisor. **6** act as a reporter. • *n.* **1** a spoken or written account of something seen, done, or studied. **2** a description for publication or broadcasting. **3** a periodical statement about a pupil's or employee's work and conduct. **4** rumour, a piece of gossip (*report has it that…*). **5** an explosive sound like that made by a gun. ☐ **reported speech** a speaker's words as reported by another person (e.g. Tom said, 'I will go' becomes in reported speech Tom said that he would go).

reportage / re-paw-**tah**zh, ruh-**paw**-tij / *n.* the reporting of news for the press etc.; a particular style of doing this.

reportedly *adv.* according to reports.

reporter *n.* a person employed to report news etc. for publication or broadcasting.

repose / ruh-**pohz** / *n.* **1** rest, sleep. **2** a peaceful state or effect, tranquillity. • *v.* **1** rest, lie. **2** place (trust etc.) (*he reposes all his trust in her*).

reposeful *adj.* inducing or showing repose. ☐ **reposefully** *adv.*

repository *n.* **1** a place where things are stored or may be found (e.g. a warehouse, a museum). **2** a receptacle. **3** (often foll. by *of*) a book, a person, etc. regarded as a store of information etc. **4** a recipient of secrets etc.

repossess *v.* regain possession of (goods on which credit payments have not been kept up). ☐ **repossession** *n.*

repot / ree-**pot** / *v.* move (a potted plant) to another, esp. larger, pot.

reprehend / rep-ruh-**hend** / *v.* rebuke.

reprehensible / rep-ruh-**hen**-suh-buhl / *adj.* deserving rebuke. ☐ **reprehensibly** *adv.*

represent / rep-ruh-**zent** / *v.* **1** show (a person, thing, or scene) in a picture or play etc. **2** describe or declare to be (*representing himself as an expert*). **3** state in polite protest or remonstrance (*we must represent to them the risks involved*). **4** symbolise (*in Roman numerals C represents 100*). **5** be an example or embodiment of (*the election results represent the views of the electorate*). **6** act as a deputy, agent, or spokesman for (*she is representing the prime minister*). **7** / ree-pruh-**zent** / present or submit (a cheque) again for payment.

representation *n.* **1** representing or being represented. **2** something that represents another, e.g. a picture or diagram. **3** (**representations**) statements made in the form of an appeal, protest, or allegation (*the welfare lobby made representations to the government*).

representational *adj.* (in art) portraying a subject as it appears to the eye.

representative *adj.* **1** typical of a group or class (*he's truly representative of the Australian ocker*). **2** containing examples of a number of types (*a representative selection*). **3** consisting of elected representatives; based on representation by these (*representative government*). • *n.* **1** a sample or specimen or typical embodiment of something. **2** a person's or firm's agent. **3** a person chosen to represent another or others, or to take part in a legislative assembly on their behalf. **4** the elected agent of a trade union.

repress *v.* **1** check; restrain; keep under; suppress; quell (*he can't repress his anger; repressed the rebellion*). **2** *Psychol.* actively (but unknowingly) exclude from the conscious mind or suppress into the unconscious (an unacceptable memory, impulse, or desire). **3** (usu. as **repressed** *adj.*) subject (a person) to the suppression of his or her thoughts or impulses (*many gays feel repressed*). ☐ **repression** *n.*

repressive *adj.* serving or intended to repress a person or thing. ☐ **repressively** *adv.*

reprieve / ruh-**preev** / *n.* **1** postponement or cancellation of a punishment, esp. of the death sentence. **2** temporary relief from danger; postponement of trouble. • *v.* give a reprieve to.

reprimand / **rep**-ruh-mahnd, -mand / *n.* a rebuke, esp. a formal or official one. • *v.* give a reprimand to.

reprint *v.* / ree-**print** / print again in the same or a new form. • *n.* / **ree**-print / the reprinting of a book; a book reprinted; the quantity reprinted.

reprisal / ruh-**pruy**-zuhl / *n.* an act of retaliation.

reprise / ruh-**preez** / *n.* **1** a repeated passage in music. **2** a repeated song etc. in a musical performance.

reproach *v.* express disapproval to (a person) for a fault or offence. • *n.* **1** reproaching; an instance of this. **2** a thing that brings disgrace or discredit. ▫ **above** (*or* **beyond**) **reproach** deserving no blame; perfect.

reproachful *adj.* full of or expressing reproach. ▫ **reproachfully** *adv.*

reprobate / **rep**-ruh-bayt / *n.* an immoral or unprincipled person. • *adj.* immoral; bad. • *v.* express or feel disapproval of; censure.

reprobation / rep-ruh-**bay**-shuhn / *n.* strong condemnation.

reproduce *v.* **1** produce a copy of (a picture etc.). **2** cause to be seen or heard again or to occur again. **3** have a specified quality when reproduced (*some colours don't reproduce well*). **4** produce (offspring). ▫ **reproducible** *adj.*

reproduction *n.* **1** reproducing; being reproduced. **2** a copy of a painting etc. ▫ **reproduction furniture** furniture made in imitation of an earlier style.

reproductive *adj.* of or belonging to reproduction (*the reproductive system*).

reproof *n.* an expression of condemnation for a fault or offence.

reprove *v.* rebuke, reprimand, tell off.

Reps, the *Aust. colloq.* = HOUSE OF REPRESENTATIVES.

reptile *n.* a member of the class of cold-blooded animals with a backbone and relatively short legs or no legs at all, e.g. snakes, lizards, crocodiles, tortoises. ▫ **reptilian** / rep-**til**-ee-uhn / *adj.* & *n.*

republic *n.* a nation in which the supreme power is held by the people or their elected representatives, or by an elected or nominated president, not by a king or queen.

republican *adj.* of, like, or advocating a republic (*the growing republican movement in Australia*). • *n.* a person advocating or supporting republican government. ▫ **republicanism** *n.*

repudiate / ruh-**pyoo**-dee-ayt / *v.* **1** reject or disown utterly (*repudiated by his family; repudiated his religion*). **2** deny (*repudiated the accusation*). ▫ **repudiation** *n.* **repudiator** *n.*

■ Usage *See* note at *refute*.

repugnant / ruh-**pug**-nuhnt / *adj.* **1** extremely distasteful, disgusting (*racism is utterly repugnant*). **2** contradictory (*a vacuum is repugnant to nature*). ▫ **repugnance** *n.*

repulse *v.* **1** drive back (an attacking force). **2** rebuff (friendly advances or their maker). **3** reject (an offer or help etc.) firmly. • *n.* repulsing or being repulsed; a rebuff.

repulsion *n.* **1** repelling; being repelled. **2** a feeling of strong distaste, revulsion.

repulsive *adj.* **1** causing aversion or loathing; disgusting. **2** repelling things (*a repulsive force*). ▫ **repulsively** *adv.* **repulsiveness** *n.*

reputable / **rep**-yuh-tuh-buhl / *adj.* having a good reputation, respected. ▫ **reputably** *adv.*

reputation *n.* **1** what is generally said or believed about a person or thing (*she has a reputation for honesty*). **2** public recognition for one's abilities or achievements (*built up a reputation*).

repute / ruh-**pyoot** / *n.* reputation (*I know him by repute*).

reputed / ruh-**pyoo**-tuhd / *adj.* said or thought to be (*his reputed father*). ▫ **reputedly** *adv.*

request *n.* **1** the act of asking for something (*at my request*). **2** a thing asked for. • *v.* make a request for. ▫ **by** *or* **on request** in response to a request.

requiem / **rek**-wee-uhm / *n.* **1** (**Requiem**) *Catholic Church* a special Mass for the repose of the souls of the dead. **2** a musical setting for this (*Mozart's Requiem*). (¶ From the Introit which begins this Mass *Requiem aeternam dona eis, Domine* 'Give them eternal rest, O Lord'.)

requiescat / rek-wee-**es**-kat / *n.* (in full **requiescat in pace** / **pah**-chay /) a wish or prayer, esp. in obituaries, on tombstones, etc., that a dead person's soul may rest in peace. (¶ Latin (from the Requiem Mass) = 'may he (or she) rest in peace'.)

require *v.* **1** need, depend on for success or fulfilment etc. (*cars require regular servicing*). **2** order, insist on (an action or measure). **3** wish to have (*will you require dinner?*).

requirement *n.* a thing required; a need.

requisite / **rek**-wuh-zuht / *adj.* required by circumstances, necessary to success (*she has all the requisite skills for the job*). • *n.* a thing needed for some purpose (*he has none of the requisites for the job*).

requisition *n.* an official order laying claim to the use of property or materials; a formal written demand for something that is needed. • *v.* (esp. of the military or a public authority) demand the use or supply of, esp. by a requisition order.

requite / ruh-**kwuyt** / *v.* **1** make a return for (a service) or to (a person). **2** avenge (a wrong or injury etc.). ▫ **requital** *n.*

reredos / **reer**-dos / *n.* an ornamental screen covering the wall above the back of an altar.

re-route / ree-**root** / *v.* (**re-routed, re-routeing**) send or carry by a different route.

rerun *v.* / ree-**run** / (**reran, rerunning**) run (a race, film, computer program, etc.) again. • *n.*

/ **ree**-run / **1** an act of rerunning. **2** a repeat of a film etc. **3** a repetition (of events) (*this match is nothing but a rerun of last week's*).

resale *n.* sale to another person of something one has bought. • *adj.* pertaining to the sale of something previously bought (*resale value; resale prospects*).

rescind / ruh-**sind** / *v.* repeal or cancel (a law or rule etc.). □ **rescission** / ruh-si*zh*-uhn / *n.*

rescript / **ree**-skript / *n.* **1** a pope's written reply to an appeal for a decision. **2** any papal decision. **3** an official edict or announcement.

rescue *v.* save from attack, capture, danger, etc. • *n.* rescuing, being rescued. □ **rescuer** *n.*

research / ruh-**serch**, **ree**-serch / *n.* careful study and investigation, esp. in order to discover new facts or information. • *v.* do research into (*the subject has been fully researched*). □ **research and development** (*abbr.* **R & D**) work directed towards the innovation, introduction, and improvement of products and processes. □ **researcher** *n.*

■ **Usage** The second pronunciation given, with the stress on the first syllable (originally US), is becoming more common in Australian English, and while some regard it as incorrect, it is now generally accepted as a variant in Australian English.

reseat / **ree**-seet / *v.* **1** (also *refl.*) seat (oneself, a person, etc.) again. **2** provide with a fresh seat or seats. **3** realign or repair in order to fit (a tap, nail, etc.) into its former correct position.

resemble *v.* be like (another person or thing). □ **resemblance** *n.*

resent / ruh-**zent** / *v.* feel displeased and indignant about; feel insulted by (something said or done). □ **resentment** *n.*

resentful *adj.* feeling resentment. □ **resentfully** *adv.*

reservation *n.* **1** reserving; being reserved. **2** a reserved seat or accommodation etc.; a record of this (*our hotel reservations*). **3** a limitation on one's agreement or acceptance of an idea (*we accept the plan in principle but have certain reservations; without reservation*). **4** an area of land set apart by a government for some special purpose or for the exclusive use of certain people, e.g. American or Canadian Indians.

reserve *v.* **1** put aside or order for a later occasion or for special use. **2** retain (*the company reserves the right to offer a substitute*). **3** postpone (*reserve judgment*). • *n.* **1** something reserved for future use; an extra amount or stock kept available for use when needed. **2** (also **reserves**) forces outside the regular armed services and liable to be called out in an emergency. **3** an extra player chosen in case a substitute should be needed in a team. **4** (**reserves**) *Aust.* a sporting club's second-grade team. **5** land set aside for recreational use, as a public park, etc. **6** *Aust.* land set aside for the exclusive use of Aborigines (*Arnhem Land Reserve*). **7** land set aside for the protection of fauna and flora (*wildlife reserve; nature reserve*). **8** a limitation on one's agreement or acceptance of an idea etc. (*I accept her without reserve*). **9** a reserve price. **10** a tendency to avoid showing one's feelings; lack of friendliness. □ **in reserve** in a state of being unused but available. **reserve bank** a country's central bank, responsible for the administration of the monetary policy of that country (*the Reserve Bank of Australia*). **reserve price** the lowest price that will be accepted for something sold at an auction or exhibition.

reserved *adj.* **1** (of a person) reticent; slow to reveal emotion or opinions; uncommunicative. **2** set apart, destined for a particular use.

reservist *n.* a member of a country's reserve forces.

reservoir / **rez**-uh-vwah / *n.* **1** a natural or artificial lake that is a source of water. **2** a container for a supply of fuel or other liquid. **3** a supply or collection of information etc.

reset *v.* set (a bone, gems, a clock, etc.) again or differently.

resettle *v.* **1** settle again (*let the dust resettle*). **2** move or be moved elsewhere to live. □ **re-settlement** *n.*

reshuffle *v.* **1** shuffle (cards) again. **2** change the posts or responsibilities of (a group of people, e.g. government ministers). • *n.* reshuffling (*a Cabinet reshuffle*).

reside *v.* **1** have one's home (in a certain place). **2** be present or vested in a person (*supreme authority resides in the military in that country; the potential for good resides in all human beings*).

residence *n.* **1** a place where one lives. **2** a house (*desirable residence for sale*). **3** residing (*take up residence*). □ **in residence** living or working at a specified place, esp. for the performance of specialist duties, and usu. for a specified time (*writer in residence at the Australian National University*). □ **residency** *n.*

resident *adj.* **1** residing, in residence. **2** having quarters at one's workplace etc. (*resident caretaker*). **3** located in; inherent (*powers of feeling are resident in the nerves*). **4** (of birds etc.) non-migratory. • *n.* **1** a permanent inhabitant of a place, not a visitor. **2** (at a hotel) a person staying overnight.

residential / rez-uh-**den**-shuhl / *adj.* **1** containing or suitable for private houses (*a residential area*). **2** connected with or based on residence (*residential qualifications for voters*).

residual / ruh-**zid**-yoo-uhl / *adj.* left over as a residue. □ **residually** *adv.*

residuary / ruh-**zid**-yoo-uh-ree / *adj.* **1** residual. **2** of the residue of an estate.

residue / **rez**-uh-dyoo / *n.* the remainder, what is left over.

residuum / ruh-**zid**-yoo-uhm / *n.* (*pl.* **residua**) a residue, esp. after combustion or evaporation.

resign *v.* give up or surrender (one's job, property, claim, etc.). ☐ **resign oneself to** be ready to accept and endure, accept as inevitable.

resignation *n.* **1** resigning. **2** a statement conveying that one wishes to resign. **3** a resigned attitude or expression.

resigned *adj.* showing patient acceptance of an unwelcome task or situation. ☐ **be resigned to** resign oneself to. ☐ ☐ **resignedly** / ruh-**zuy**-nuhd-lee / *adv.*

resile / ruh-**zuyl** / *v.* **1** show resilience. **2** (usu. foll. by *from*) withdraw from a course of action etc.

resilient / ruh-**zil**-ee-uhnt / *adj.* **1** springing back to its original form after being bent or stretched; springy. **2** (of a person) readily recovering from shock or depression etc. ☐ **resiliently** *adv.* **resilience** *n.*

resin / **rez**-uhn / *n.* **1** a sticky substance that oozes from pine trees and many other plants, used in making varnish etc. **2** a similar substance made synthetically, used in making plastics. ☐ **resinous** *adj.*

resist *v.* **1** oppose; use force to prevent something from happening or being successful. **2** regard (a plan or idea) unfavourably. **3** be undamaged or unaffected by; prevent from penetrating (*pans that resist heat*). **4** refrain from accepting or yielding to (*I managed to resist his advances*). ☐ **resistible** *adj.*

resistance *n.* **1** resisting; the power to resist something. **2** an influence that hinders or stops something. **3** the property of not conducting heat or electricity; the measure of this. **4** (also **Resistance**) a secret organisation resisting the authorities, esp. in an enemy-occupied country. ☐ **the line of least resistance** the easiest method or course.

resistant *adj.* offering resistance, capable of resisting (*heat-resistant plastics*).

resistivity / re-zis-**tiv**-uh-tee / *n.* the power of a specified material to resist the passage of electric current.

resistor *n.* a device having resistance to the passage of electric current.

resit / ree-**sit** / *v.* (**resat**, **resitting**) sit (an examination) again after a failure.

reskill / ree-**skil** / *v.* teach, or equip with, new skills.

resolute / **rez**-uh-loot / *adj.* showing great determination. ☐ **resolutely** *adv.* **resoluteness** *n.*

resolution *n.* **1** the quality of being resolute, great determination. **2** a mental pledge, something one intends to do (*New Year resolutions*). **3** a formal statement agreed on by a legislative body or public meeting. **4** the solving of a problem. **5** the process of separating something or being separated into constituent parts. **6** *Music* the process of causing discord to pass into concord. **7** the degree of detail visible in a photographic or television image.

resolve *v.* **1** decide firmly. **2** (foll. by *that*) (of an assembly or meeting) pass a resolution by vote. **3** solve or settle (a problem or doubts etc.). **4** separate into constituent parts. •*n.* **1** something one has decided to do, a resolution (*and she kept her resolve*). **2** great determination.

resolved *adj.* (of a person) resolute.

resonant / **rez**-uh-nuhnt / *adj.* **1** resounding, echoing. **2** tending to emphasise or prolong sound, esp. by vibration. ☐ **resonance** *n.*

resonate / **rez**-uh-nayt / *v.* produce or show resonance; resound. ☐ **resonator** *n.*

resort / ruh-**zawt** / *v.* **1** turn for help; adopt as an expedient (*resorted to violence*). **2** go often or as a customary practice or in large numbers to (*many resort to the beaches in summer*). •*n.* **1** an expedient or measure; resorting to this (*compulsion is our only resort; without resort to violence*). **2** a place frequented esp. for holidays or for a specified purpose or quality (*seaside resort; health resort*).

resound / ruh-**zownd** / *v.* **1** (of a voice or sound etc.) fill a place with sound; produce echoes. **2** (of a place) be filled with sound; echo. **3** (of a reputation etc.) be much talked of (*even Woop Woop resounded with his praise*). **4** (foll. by *through*) produce a sensation (*the scandal resounded through New South Wales*).

resounding *adj.* (of an event etc.) notable (*a resounding victory*). ☐ **resoundingly** *adv.*

resource *n.* **1** something to which one can turn for help or support or to achieve one's purpose. **2** a means of relaxation or amusement. **3** ingenuity, quick wit. **4** (**resources**) available assets (*we pooled our resources*). **5** (**resources**) a source of wealth to a country (*natural resources such as minerals*).

resourceful *adj.* clever at finding ways of doing things. ☐ **resourcefully** *adv.* **resourcefulness** *n.*

respect *n.* **1** admiration felt towards a person or thing that has good qualities or achievements; politeness arising from this. **2** attention, consideration (*showing respect for people's feelings*). **3** relation, reference (*this is true with respect to English but not to French*). **4** a particular detail or aspect (*in this one respect*). **5** (**respects**) polite greetings (*pay one's respects*). •*v.* feel or show respect for. ☐ **respecter** *n.*

respectable *adj.* **1** of good social standing; honest and decent; proper in appearance or behaviour. **2** of a moderately good standard or size etc., not bringing disgrace or embarrassment (*a respectable score*). ☐ **respectably** *adv.* **respectability** *n.*

respectful *adj.* showing respect. ☐ **respectfully** *adv.* **respectfulness** *n.*

respecting *prep.* concerning, with respect to.

respective *adj.* of or relating to each as an individual (*go to your respective seats*).

respectively *adv.* for each separately in the order mentioned (*she and I gave $20 and $10 respectively*).

respiration *n.* **1** breathing. **2** (in living organisms) the absorption of oxygen and release of energy and carbon dioxide.

respirator *n.* **1** a device worn over the nose and mouth to filter or purify the air. **2** an apparatus for giving artificial respiration.

respiratory / res-**pi**-ruh-tree, **res**-pruh-tree / *adj.* of or involving respiration.

respire *v.* breathe; (of plants) perform the process of respiration.

respite / **res**-puht, **res**-puyt / *n.* **1** an interval of rest or relief. **2** delay permitted before an obligation must be fulfilled or a penalty suffered.

resplendent *adj.* brilliant with colour or decorations. ☐ **resplendently** *adv.*

respond *v.* **1** answer. **2** (foll. by *to*) act or behave in answer to or because of (*the horse responds to the bridle; the disease did not respond to treatment*).

respondent *n.* the defendant in a lawsuit, esp. in an appeal case or divorce case.

response *n.* **1** an answer. **2** any part of the liturgy said or sung in answer to the priest. **3** an act, feeling, or movement produced by a stimulus or by another's action. ☐ **response time** the time between the performance of an action by a user and a response from a computer etc.

responsibility *n.* **1** being responsible. **2** authority; managerial freedom (*a job with more responsibility*). **3** a person or thing for which one is responsible; duty, commitment (*the food is my responsibility*). **4** the capacity for rational conduct (*diminished responsibility*).

responsible *adj.* **1** legally or morally obliged to take care of something or to carry out a duty; liable to be blamed for loss or failure. **2** having to account for one's actions (*you will be responsible to the prime minister himself*). **3** capable of rational conduct; trustworthy (*a responsible person*). **4** involving important duties (*a responsible position*). **5** being the cause of something (*the plague was responsible for many deaths*). ☐ **responsibly** *adv.*

responsive *adj.* **1** responding warmly and favourably to an influence; sympathetic. **2** answering (*the responsive calls of the two magpies*). ☐ **responsiveness** *n.*

respray *v.* spray again (esp. a vehicle with paint). • *n.* the act or process of respraying.

rest[1] *v.* **1** be still; stop moving or working, esp. to regain one's vigour. **2** cause or allow to do this (*sit down and rest your feet*). **3** (of a problem or subject) be left without further investigation or discussion (*let the matter rest*). **4** place or be placed for support (*his head resting on my lap; the roof rests on four arches*). **5** (foll. by *on*) rely on, be based on (*the case rests on evidence of identification*). **6** repose in or justly be ascribed to (a person) (*the responsibility rests entirely in you; the blame rests with the builder*). **7** (of a look) alight, be directed (*his gaze rested on his son*). • *n.* **1** inactivity or sleep as a way of regaining one's vigour; a period of this. **2** a prop or support for an object. **3** an interval of silence between notes in music; a sign indicating this. ☐ **be resting** (of an actor) be out of work. **rest area** an area off a highway where a motorist can stop for a time, these areas being sometimes provided with tables, toilet facilities, gas barbecues, etc. **rest home** a place where old or convalescent people are cared for. **rest room** a toilet in a public building.

rest[2] *v.* **1** remain in a specified state (*rest assured, it will be a success*). • *n.* (**the rest**) the remaining part; the others. ☐ **rest with** be left in the hands or charge of (*it rests with you to suggest terms*).

restaurant / **res**-tuh-ront / *n.* a place where meals can be bought and eaten.

restaurateur / res-tuh-ruh-**ter** / *n.* a restaurant keeper.

■ **Usage** The word *restaurateur* is frequently (wrongly) spelt *restauranteur* under the influence of the word *restaurant*.

rested *adj.* refreshed by resting.

restful *adj.* giving rest or a feeling of rest; quiet and relaxing. ☐ **restfully** *adv.* **restfulness** *n.*

restitution *n.* **1** restoration of a thing to its proper owner or its original state. **2** reparation for injury or damage.

restive *adj.* fidgety, restless; resisting control. ☐ **restively** *adv.* **restiveness** *n.*

restless *adj.* **1** unable to rest or to be still. **2** without rest or sleep (*a restless night*). ☐ **restless flycatcher** a black and white busy bird of mainland Australia, having harsh notes which sound like the grinding of a razor or scissors. Also called *razor grinder, scissors grinder*. ☐ **restlessly** *adv.* **restlessness** *n.*

restoration *n.* **1** restoring; being restored. **2** the act or process of bringing something back to its original condition. **3** a model, drawing, or reconstruction of an extinct animal, ruined building, etc. ☐ **the Restoration** the re-establishment of the monarchy in Britain in 1660; the literary period following this (*Restoration comedy*).

restorative / ruh-**sto**-ruh-tiv / *adj.* tending to restore health or strength. • *n.* a restorative food or medicine or treatment.

restore *v.* **1** bring back to its original state, e.g. by repairing or rebuilding. **2** bring back to good health or vigour. **3** give back to the original owner etc.; put back in its former position, reinstate. ☐ **restorer** *n.*

restrain *v.* hold back from movement or action; keep under control; confine, imprison. ☐ **restraining order** a court order placing certain restrictions on a person (e.g. that a husband must

restrained *adj.* showing restraint.

restraint *n.* **1** restraining; being restrained. **2** something that restrains, a limiting influence. **3** avoidance of exaggeration; moderation; self-control; reserve of manner. **4** confinement; a state of limited freedom.

restrict *v.* put a limit on; subject to limitations. □ **restriction** *n.*

restricted *adj.* withheld from general circulation or disclosure; limited, out of bounds to certain people (*a restricted publication; restricted films may not be viewed by persons under 18; a restricted area*).

restrictive *adj.* restricting. □ **restrictive practice** an industrial agreement that limits competition or output.

restructure *v.* give a new structure to; rebuild; rearrange.

restump / ree-**stump** / *v. Aust.* replace the supporting stumps of (a house, building, etc.)

result *n.* **1** that which is produced by an activity or operation, an effect. **2** a statement of the score or the name of the winner etc. in a sporting event, examination, competition, etc. **3** an answer or formula obtained by calculation. • *v.* **1** (often foll. by *from*) occur as a result (*the troubles that resulted from the merger*). **2** (often foll. by *in*) have a specified result (*the match resulted in a draw*).

resultant *adj.* occurring as a result (*the resultant profit*).

resume *v.* **1** get, take, or occupy again (*resume one's seat*). **2** begin to speak or work or use again. □ **resumption** *n.*

resumé / **rez**-yuh-may / *n.* (also **résumé**, **resume**) **1** a summary. **2** = CURRICULUM VITAE.

resumptive *adj.* resuming.

resurface *v.* **1** lay a new surface on (a road etc.). **2** return to the surface. **3** turn up again.

resurgence / ri-**ser**-juhns / *n.* a rise or revival after defeat, destruction, or disappearance etc. □ **resurgent** *adj.*

resurrect *v.* bring back into use (*resurrect an old custom*).

resurrection *n.* **1** rising from the dead. **2** (**the Resurrection**) **a** that of Christ; **b** the rising of the dead at the Last Judgment. **3** revival after disuse.

resuscitate / ruh-**sus**-uh-tayt / *v.* **1** bring back from unconsciousness. **2** revive (a custom, institution, etc.). □ **resuscitation** *n.*

retail *n.* the selling of goods to the general public. • *adj.* & *adv.* in the retail trade. • *v.* **1** sell or be sold in the retail trade. **2** recount, relate details of (*retailed all the latest gossip*). □ **retail price index** an index of the variation in prices of retail goods. □ □ **retailer** *n.*

retain *v.* **1** keep in one's possession or use. **2** continue to have; not lose (*the fire had retained its heat*). **3** keep in one's memory (*she retained a clear impression of the building*). **4** keep in place; hold fixed (*a retaining wall*). **5** book the services of (a barrister). □ **retaining wall** a wall supporting and confining a mass of earth or water.

retainer *n.* **1** a fee paid to secure a person's services. **2** a faithful servant (*old retainer*). **3** a person or thing that retains.

retake *v.* / ree-**tayk** / (**retook, retaken, retaking**) **1** take (an exam, photograph, etc.) again. **2** recapture. • *n.* / **ree**-tayk / **1** an act of filming a scene or recording music etc. again; the film or recording obtained in this way. **2** an act of taking an exam etc. again.

retaliate / ruh-**tal**-ee-ayt / *v.* repay an injury, attack, insult, etc. with a similar one. □ **retaliation** *n.* **retaliatory** / ruh-**tal**-yuh-tree / *adj.*

retard / ruh-**tard** / *v.* delay, slow the progress of. □ **retardant** *n.* **retardation** *n.*

retarded *adj.* backward in mental or physical development.

retch *v.* strain one's throat as if vomiting. • *n.* such a motion or the sound of it.

retell *v.* (**retold, retelling**) tell (a story etc.) again.

retention *n.* **1** retaining or being retained. **2** the ability to retain (in the mind) things experienced or learned; memory. **3** the condition of retaining urine or other body fluid that would normally be expelled.

retentive *adj.* able to retain things (*a retentive memory*). □ **retentiveness** *n.*

rethink / ree-**thingk** / *v.* (**rethought, rethinking**) think about again; plan again and differently. • *n.* / **ree**-thingk / reassessment; rethinking.

reticent / **ret**-uh-suhnt / *adj.* not revealing one's thoughts and feelings readily. □ **reticently** *adv.* **reticence** *n.*

reticulate / ruh-**tik**-yuh-layt / *v.* (**reticulating**) **1** divide or be divided in fact or appearance into a network. **2** supply (esp. water for the purpose of irrigation) through a network of pipes. • *adj.* / ruh-**tik**-yuh-luht / reticulated. □ **reticulation** / -**lay**-shuhn / *n.*

retina / **ret**-uh-nuh / *n.* (*pl.* **retinas** or **retinae**) a layer of membrane at the back of the eyeball, sensitive to light.

retinol / **ret**-uh-nol / *n.* a vitamin found in green and yellow vegetables, egg yolk, and fish-liver oil, essential for growth and for vision in dim light. Also called *vitamin A*.

retinue / **ret**-uh-nyoo / *n.* a number of attendants accompanying an important person.

retire *v.* **1** give up one's regular work because of advancing age; cause (an employee) to do this. **2** withdraw, retreat. **3** go to bed or to one's private room. □ **retire into oneself** become uncommunicative or unsociable. □ □ **retiree** *n.*

retired *adj.* **1** having retired from work. **2** withdrawn from society or from observation, secluded.

retirement *n.* **1** the act or an instance of retiring; the period of one's life as a retired person. **2**

seclusion. ☐ **retirement pension** = OLD-AGE PENSION (*see* OLD). **retirement village** a complex of usu. self-contained and separate dwellings in which retired people live.

retiring *adj.* shy, avoiding company.

retort¹ *v.* **1** make a quick or witty or angry reply. **2** repay (an attack or an insult) in kind. • *n.* retorting; a reply of this kind.

retort² *n.* **1** a vessel (usu. of glass) with a long downward-bent neck, used in distilling liquids. **2** a receptacle used in making gas or steel.

retouch *v.* improve (a picture or photograph) by making minor alterations.

retrace *v.* **1** go back over (one's steps etc.). **2** trace back to a source or a beginning. **3** recall the course of (a thing) in one's memory. ☐ **retraceable** *adj.*

retract *v.* **1** pull (a thing) back or in (*the snail retracts its horns*). **2** withdraw (a statement or promise). ☐ **retractable** *adj.* **retraction** *n.* **retractor** *n.*

retractile / ruh-**trak**-tuyl / *adj.* (of a part of the body) retractable.

retrain *v.* train again or for something different, esp. for new work.

retread *v.* / ree-**tred** / **1** (**retrod, retrodden**) tread (a path etc.) again. **2** (**retreaded**) put a fresh tread on (a tyre) by moulding rubber to a used foundation. • *n.* / **ree**-tred / **1** a retreaded tyre. **2** *Aust. colloq.* **a** a retired person who is re-engaged in the workforce. **b** a person (esp. a politician) who regains office, position, etc. after a forced absence.

retreat *v.* withdraw when faced with defeat, danger, or difficulty; go away to a place of shelter. • *n.* **1** retreating; the military signal for this. **2** a military bugle call at sunset. **3** a place of shelter or seclusion. **4** a short period of seclusion (in a monastery etc.) for prayer and meditation.

retrench *v.* **1** *Aust.* sack an employee (or employees) in order to reduce costs, because of a downturn in profits etc. **2** cut down expenses; introduce economies. **3** reduce the amount of (costs). ☐ **retrenchment** *n.*

retrial *n.* the trying of a lawsuit again.

retribution / ret-ruh-**byoo**-shuhn / *n.* a deserved punishment.

retributive / ruh-**trib**-yuh-tiv / *adj.* happening or inflicted as retribution.

retrieve *v.* **1** regain possession of. **2** extract (information stored in a computer etc.). **3** recover by investigation or effort of memory. **4** (of a dog) find and bring back (killed game, a thrown stick, etc.). **5** rescue (esp. from a bad state); restore to a flourishing state (*retrieve one's fortunes*). **6** set right (a loss or error or a bad situation). • *n.* possibility of recovery (*beyond retrieve*). ☐ **retrievable** *adj.* **retrieval** *n.*

retriever *n.* a dog of a breed traditionally used to retrieve game.

retro / **ret**-roh / *adj. colloq.* imitative of a style or fashion from the recent past.

retroactive *adj.* (esp. of new laws) effective as from a past date. ☐ **retroactively** *adv.*

retrograde *adj.* **1** going backwards (*retrograde motion*). **2** reverting to a less good condition (*it would be a retrograde step to bring back capital punishment*). • *v.* **1** move backwards, recede. **2** revert, esp. to a less good condition.

retrogress / ret-truh-**gres** / *v.* move backwards; deteriorate. ☐ **retrogression** *n.* **retrogressive** *adj.*

retrorocket *n.* an auxiliary rocket discharging its exhaust in the opposite direction to the main rockets, used for slowing a spacecraft.

retrospect *n.* a survey of a past time or events. ☐ **in retrospect** when one looks back on a past event or situation.

retrospection *n.* looking back, esp. on the past.

retrospective *adj.* **1** looking back on the past. **2** applying to the past as well as the future (*the law could not be made retrospective*). • *n.* an exhibition, recital, etc. showing an artist's development over his or her lifetime. ☐ **retrospectively** *adj.*

retroussé / ruh-**troo**-say / *adj.* (of the nose) turned up at the tip. (¶ French, = tucked up.)

retroverted / ret-**roh**-ver-tuhd / *adj.* (esp. of the womb) turned backwards. ☐ **retroversion** *n.*

retrovirus / **ret**-roh-vuy-ruhs / *n.* any of a group of RNA viruses (including the Aids viruses or HIV) which form DNA during the replication of their RNA, and so transfer genetic material into the DNA of host cells.

retry *v.* (**retried, retrying**) try (a lawsuit or a defendant) again.

retsina / ret-**see**-nuh / *n.* Greek white wine flavoured with resin.

retune *v.* **1** tune (a musical instrument) again or differently. **2** tune (a radio etc.) to a different frequency. **3** tune (an engine) again to make it run more efficiently.

return *v.* **1** come or go back. **2** bring, put, or send back. **3** pay back or reciprocate (*return good for evil*). **4** say in reply, retort (*to the charge that he was a fool, he wittily returned, 'I am not!'*). **5** yield (a profit). **6** (of an electorate) elect as an MP, government, etc. • *n.* **1** coming or going back. **2** bringing, giving, putting, or sending back. **3** the proceeds or profits of a transaction (*brings a good return on one's investment*). **4** a return ticket. **5** a return match or game. **6** a formal report, e.g. of a set of transactions (*income-tax return*). ☐ **returning officer** the official conducting an election in a constituency and announcing the result. **return match** (*or* **game**) a second match or game between the same opponents. **return ticket** a ticket for a journey to a place and back to one's starting point. ☐☐ **returnable** *adj.*

Returned and Services League of Australia *see* RSL.

reunify *v.* restore (esp. separated territories) to a political unity. ☐ **reunification** *n.*

reunion *n.* **1** reuniting; being reunited. **2** a social gathering of people who were formerly associated.

reunite *v.* unite again after separation.

reusable *adj.* able to be reused.

reuse *v.* / ree-**yooz** / use again. • *n.* / ree-**yoos** / using or being used again.

rev *n.* a revolution of an engine. • *v.* (**revved, revving**) **1** (of an engine) revolve. **2** (often foll. by *up*) **a** cause (an engine) to run quickly, esp. when starting **b** inject life, vim, vigour, etc. (into a person, a flagging party, etc.).

Rev. *abbr.* Reverend.

revalue *v.* **1** reassess the value of. **2** give a new (higher) value to (a currency). □ **revaluation** *n.*

revamp *v.* / ree-**vamp** / renovate, improve; give a new appearance to. • *n.* / ree-vamp / an act or instance of revamping.

Revd *abbr.* Reverend.

reveal *v.* make known; uncover and allow to be seen.

reveille / ruh-**val**-ee / *n.* a military waking signal sounded on a bugle or drums.

revel *v.* (**revelled, revelling**) **1** (foll. by *in*) take great delight (*some people revel in gossip*). **2** have a good time; be festive. • *n.* (in *sing.* or *pl.*) lively festivities or merrymaking. □ **reveller** *n.*

revelation *n.* **1** revealing, making known something that was secret or hidden. **2** something revealed, esp. something surprising.

revelry *n.* revelling; revels.

revenge *n.* **1** punishment or injury inflicted in return for what one has suffered. **2** a desire to inflict this. • *v.* avenge. □ **be revenged** (*or* **revenge oneself**) get satisfaction by inflicting vengeance. □ **revengeful** *adj.* **revengefully** *adj.*

revenue / **rev**-uh-nyoo / *n.* **1** income, esp. of a large amount, from any source. **2** a country's annual income from taxes, duties, etc.

reverberate / ruh-**ver**-buh-rayt / *v.* **1** echo, resound. **2** (of an event etc.) produce a continuing effect, shock, etc. (*news of the disaster reverberated through Australia*). □ **reverberant** *adj.* **reverberation** *n.* **reverberative** *adj.*

revere / ruh-**veer** / *v.* feel deep respect or religious veneration for.

reverence *n.* **1** a feeling of awe and respect or veneration (*hold in reverence; feel reverence for*). **2** the capacity for revering (*lacks reverence*). • *v.* feel or show reverence towards.

reverend *adj.* (esp. as the title of a clergyman) deserving reverence.

Reverend Mother the Mother Superior of a convent.

reverent *adj.* feeling or showing reverence. □ **reverently** *adj.*

reverential *adj.* full of respect, awe, and admiration. □ **reverentially** *adv.*

reverie / **rev**-uh-ree / *n.* a daydream; daydreaming.

revers / ruh-**veer** / *n.* (*pl.* **revers** / ruh-**veerz** /) a turned-back front edge of the neck of a jacket or bodice.

reversal *n.* reversing; being reversed.

reverse *adj.* facing or moving in the opposite direction; opposite in character or order; upside down. • *v.* **1** turn the other way round or up, or inside out. **2** convert to the opposite kind or effect (*reversed the tendency*). **3** annul (a decree or decision etc.). **4** move in the opposite direction; travel backwards; make (something) move or work backwards. • *n.* **1** the reverse side or effect. **2** the opposite of the usual manner (*the name was printed in reverse*). **3** a piece of misfortune; a setback or defeat. **4** reverse gear. □ **reverse gear** a gear used to make a vehicle travel backwards. **reverse the charges** make the recipient (not the caller) pay for a telephone call.

reversible *adj.* able to be reversed; (of a garment) able to be worn with either side turned outwards.

reversion *n.* **1 a** a return to a previous state, habit, etc. **b** *Biology* a return to an ancestral type. **2** the legal right to possess something when its present holder relinquishes it; the returning of a right or property in this way. □ **reversionary** *adj.*

■ **Usage** Note that *reversion* does not mean *reversal*.

revert *v.* **1** return to a former condition, habit or type. **2** return to a subject in talk or thought. **3** (of property etc.) return or pass to another owner by reversion.

revhead *n.* *Aust. colloq.* a person with a passionate interest in cars.

review *n.* **1** a general survey of past events or of a subject. **2** a re-examination or reconsideration (*the salary scale is under review*). **3** a ceremonial inspection of troops or a fleet etc. **4** a published report assessing the merits of a book, play, etc. • *v.* **1** survey. **2** re-examine or reconsider. **3** inspect (troops or a fleet etc.) ceremonially. **4** write a review of (a book, play, etc.). □ **reviewer** *n.*

■ **Usage** Do not confuse with *revue*.

revile *v.* criticise angrily in abusive language.

revise *v.* **1** re-examine and alter or correct (esp. written or printed matter). **2** go over (work already studied) in preparation for an examination.

revision *n.* **1** revising; being revised. **2** a revised edition or form.

revisionist / ruh-**vizh**-uh-nuhst / *n.* a person who insists on modifying theories or practices that are considered authoritative. □ **revisionism** *n.*

revisory *adj.* revising; of revision.

revitalise *v.* (also -**ize**) give new life and vitality to.

revival *n.* **1** reviving; being revived. **2** a new production of an old play etc. **3** something brought back into use or fashion (*revival of paganism; Gothic revival*). **4** a reawakening of religious fervour; a special effort with meetings etc. to promote this.

revivalist *n.* a person who organises or conducts meetings to promote religious fervour. ☐ **revivalism** *n.*

revive *v.* **1** come or bring back to life, consciousness, or strength (*this music revives old memories; the doctor managed to revive him*). **2** come or bring back into use, activity, or fashion etc. (*some ultra right-wing elements want to revive the 'White Australia' policy*).

revivify *v.* restore the vigour of; bring back to life. ☐ **revivification** *n.*

revocable / **rev**-uh-kuh-buhl / *adj.* able to be revoked.

revoke / ree-**vohk** / *v.* **1** withdraw or cancel (a decree or licence etc.). **2** fail to follow suit in a card game when able to do so. • *n.* revoking in a card game. ☐ **revocation** *n.*

revolt *v.* **1** take part in a rebellion. **2** be in a mood of protest or defiance. **3** feel strong disgust (*revolted against giving his children the strap*). **4** cause a feeling of strong disgust in (a person) (*the decision to resume nuclear testing revolted most Australians*). • *n.* **1** an act or state of rebelling; a state of insurrection. **2** a sense of disgust. **3** a mood of protest or defiance (*there was revolt in the air at the student meeting*).

revolting *adj.* disgusting, horrible. ☐ **revoltingly** *adv.*

revolution *n.* **1** the overthrow of a government or social order, esp. by force. **2** any complete change of method, conditions, etc. (*a revolution in the treatment of burns*). **3** revolving, rotation; a single complete orbit or movement of this kind.

revolutionary *adj.* **1** of political revolution. **2** involving a great change (*Darwin's revolutionary theory of evolution*). • *n.* a person who begins or supports a political revolution.

revolutionise *v.* (also **-ize**) alter (a thing) completely (*the discovery will revolutionise our lives*).

revolve *v.* **1** turn or cause to turn round, rotate. **2** move in a circular orbit. **3** turn over (a problem etc.) in one's mind. **4** (foll. by *around*) have as its chief concern, be centred upon (*our lives revolve around the baby*).

revolver *n.* a pistol with a revolving mechanism that makes it possible to fire it a number of times without reloading.

revue *n.* an entertainment consisting of a series of items such as sketches and songs.

■ **Usage** Do not confuse with *review*.

revulsion *n.* **1** a feeling of strong disgust. **2** a sudden violent change of feeling (*a revulsion of public feeling in favour of the accused woman*).

reward *n.* **1** something given or received in return for what is done or for a service or merit. **2** a sum of money offered for the detection of a criminal or return of lost property etc. • *v.* give a reward to.

rewarding *adj.* (of an occupation, activity, etc.) well worth doing; satisfying.

rewind *v.* (**rewound, rewinding**) wind (a film or tape etc.) back to the beginning. • *n.* rewinding.

rewire *v.* renew the electrical wiring of.

reword *v.* change the wording of.

rework *v.* revise; remake.

rewrite *v.* (**rewrote, rewritten, rewriting**) write (a thing) again in a different form or style. • *n.* **1** rewriting (*this essay needs a rewrite*). **2** a thing rewritten.

Rex *n.* (after the name) reigning king (*George Rex*). (¶ Latin)

Reykjavik / **ray**-kyuh-vik / the capital of Iceland.

rezone / ree-**zohn** / *v.* alter the planning restrictions of (a property, neighbourhood, piece of land, etc.)

Rf *symbol* rutherfordium.

Rh *abbr.* Rhesus. • *symbol* rhodium.

r.h. *abbr.* right hand.

rhapsodise *v.* (also **-ize**) talk or write about something in an ecstatic way.

rhapsody *n.* **1** an ecstatic written or spoken statement. **2** a romantic musical composition in an irregular form.

rhea *n.* a South American flightless ostrich-like bird.

rhenium / **ree**-nee-uhm / *n.* a rare metallic element occurring naturally in molybdenum ores (symbol Re).

rheostat / **ree**-uh-stat / *n.* an instrument used to control the current in an electrical circuit by varying the amount of resistance in it.

rhesus / **ree**-suhs / *n.* (in full **rhesus monkey**) a small monkey common in northern India. ☐ **rhesus factor** (also **Rh factor**) a substance present in the blood of most people and some animals, causing a blood disorder in a newborn baby whose blood is **rhesus positive** (= containing this substance) while its mother's blood is **rhesus negative** (= not containing it).

rhetoric / **ret**-uh-rik / *n.* **1** the art of using words impressively, esp. in public speaking. **2** language used for its impressive sound; affected or exaggerated expressions.

rhetorical / ruh-**to**-ri-kuhl / *adj.* expressed in a way that is designed to be impressive. ☐ **rhetorical question** something phrased as a question only for dramatic effect and not to seek an answer, e.g. *who cares?* (= nobody cares). ☐ ☐ **rhetorically** *adv.*

rheumatic / roo-**mat**-ik / *adj.* of or affected with rheumatism. • *n.* **1** a person suffering from rheumatism. **2** (**rheumatics**) *colloq.* rheumatic pains. ☐ **rheumatic fever** a serious form of rheumatism with fever, chiefly in children. ☐ ☐ **rheumaticky** *adj. colloq.* **rheumatically** *adv.*

rheumatism / roo-muh-tiz-uhm / *n.* a disease causing pain in the joints, muscles, or fibrous tissue, esp. rheumatoid arthritis.

rheumatoid / roo-muh-toid / *adj.* having the character of rheumatism. ☐ **rheumatoid arthritis** a disease causing inflammation and stiffening of the joints.

rhinestone *n.* an imitation diamond.

rhino *n.* (*pl.* **rhino** *or* **rhinos**) *colloq.* a rhinoceros.

rhinoceros *n.* (*pl.* **rhinoceros** *or* **rhinoceroses**) a large thick-skinned animal of Africa and south Asia, with a horn or two horns on its nose. ☐ **rhinoceros beetle** a black Australian scarab beetle having a horned head resembling that of a rhinoceros.

rhizome / ruy-zohm / *n.* a rootlike stem growing along or under the ground and sending out both roots and shoots.

rho *n.* the seventeenth letter of the Greek alphabet (P, ρ).

Rhodes Scholar *n.* the holder of any of a number of **Rhodes Scholarships** tenable at Oxford University by students from certain overseas countries: some 500 Australians have been Rhodes Scholars to date. (¶ Cecil John Rhodes (1853–1902), South African millionaire and imperialist.)

rhodium / roh-dee-uhm / *n.* a metallic element (symbol Rh), used in alloys to increase hardness.

rhododendron / roh-duh-**den**-druhn / *n.* an evergreen shrub with large clusters of trumpet-shaped flowers, native to S. Asia, but widely cultivated elsewhere (cf. AZALEA).

rhomboid / rom-boid / *adj.* (also **rhomboidal**) like a rhombus. • *n.* a quadrilateral of which only the opposite sides and angles are equal.

rhombus / rom-buhs / *n.* a geometric figure shaped like the diamond on playing cards.

rhotic / roh-tik / *adj.* of or relating to a dialect or variety of English (e.g. in Scotland and Canada) in which r is pronounced before a consonant (as in *hard*) and at the ends of words (as in *far*).

rhubarb *n.* **1** a garden plant with fleshy reddish leaf-stalks cooked as a dessert. **2** *colloq.* nonsense (*gave us a heap of rhubarb about why he was late*). **3** *colloq.* indistinct conversation or hubbub (from the stage convention of repeatedly using the word 'rhubarb' by actors playing a crowd). **4** *colloq.* a heated dispute.

rhyme *n.* **1** the similarity of sound between words or syllables or the endings of lines of verse (e.g. *line/mine/pine*; *visit/is it*). **2** a poem with rhymes. **3** a word providing a rhyme to another. • *v.* form a rhyme; have rhymes. ☐ **rhyming slang** slang in which words are replaced by words that rhyme with them, e.g. *Noah's Ark* = 'shark', often with the rhyming word omitted (as in SEPTIC[2], sense 2). **without rhyme or reason** with no sensible or logical reason.

rhymester / ruym-stuh / *n.* a writer of (esp. simple) rhymes.

rhythm / rith-uhm / *n.* **1** the pattern produced by emphasis and length of notes in music or by long and short or stressed syllables in words. **2** a movement with a regular succession of strong and weak elements (*the rhythm of the heart beating*). **3** a constantly recurring sequence of events. ☐ **rhythm and blues** popular music with a blues theme and a strong rhythm. **rhythm method** contraception by avoiding sexual intercourse near the time of ovulation (which recurs regularly). **rhythm section** piano (or guitar etc.), bass, and drums in a dance or jazz band. ☐☐ **rhythmic** *adj.* **rhythmical** *adj.* **rhythmically** *adv.*

rib *n.* **1** each of the curved bones round the chest. **2** a cut of meat from this part of an animal. **3** a curved structural part resembling a rib. **4** each of the hinged rods forming the framework of an umbrella. **5** a knitting stitch of alternating plain and purl stitches producing a raised pattern of vertical lines. • *v.* (**ribbed, ribbing**) **1** support (a structure) with ribs. **2** knit in rib. **3** *colloq.* tease. ☐ **rib-tickler** something amusing; a joke.

ribald / rib-uhld / *adj.* humorous in a vulgar or disrespectful way; somewhat obscene.

ribaldry / rib-uhl-dree / *n.* ribald talk or behaviour.

riband / rib-uhnd / *n.* a ribbon.

ribbed *adj.* **1** with raised ridges. **2** knitted in rib.

ribbing *n.* **1** ribs or a riblike structure. **2** *colloq.* the act or an instance of teasing.

ribbon *n.* **1** a narrow band of ornamental material used for decoration or for tying something. **2** a ribbon of special colour or pattern worn to indicate the award of a medal or order etc. **3** a long narrow strip of anything (*typewriter ribbon*). **4** (**ribbons**) ragged strips. ☐ **ribbon development** the building of houses along a main road, extending outwards from a town. **ribbon fern** an epiphytic rainforest fern of Qld and NSW, having extremely long, hanging, glossy, ribbon-like fronds. **ribbon gum** any of several Australian eucalypts having bark which tends to hang from the trunk in ribbons as it is shed.

ribcage *n.* the framework of ribs round the chest.

riboflavin *n.* (also **riboflavine**) a vitamin of the B complex found in liver, milk, and eggs.

ribonucleic acid *n.* a nucleic acid in living cells, involved in protein synthesis.

rice *n.* **1** a kind of grass *Oryza sativa* (in numerous varieties) grown in marshes esp. in Asia, producing starchy seeds that are used as food. **2** these seeds. ☐ **glutinous rice** a variety of true rice which is sticky when cooked and is essential to some Asian cuisines. **rice flower** *Aust.* = PIMELEA. **rice paper** edible paper made from the pith of an oriental tree, used for painting and in cookery. **rice wine** a wine made from fermented rice. **wild rice** the slender, black-husked, edible grain of a North American grass growing in water; unrelated to true rice.

rich *adj.* **1** having much wealth. **2** having a large supply of something (*the country is rich in natural resources*). **3** splendid, made of costly materials, elaborate (*rich furniture*). **4** producing or produced abundantly (*rich soil; a rich harvest*). **5** (of food) containing a large proportion of fat, butter, eggs, etc. **6** (of a mixture in an internal-combustion engine) containing more than the normal proportion of fuel. **7** (of colour, sound, or smell) pleasantly deep or strong (*a rich voice; a rich aroma*). **8** highly amusing or outrageous; (of humour) earthy; indecent. ☐ **richness** *n.*

Richard *n.* (also **richard**) ☐ **have had the Richard** *Aust. colloq.* be finished; be irreparably damaged (*he's had the Richard—she's left him for good; I think the car's had the richard*). (¶ Probably a variant of *have had the dick.*)

Richards, Mark (1957–), OAM, Australian surfer, world champion 1979–82.

Richardson[1], Henry Handel (pseudonym of Ethel Florence Lindesay Robertson, née Richardson) (1870–1946), Australian novelist, author of *The Getting of Wisdom* and *The Fortunes of Richard Mahony*.

Richardson[2], Marilyn (Ann) (1936–), Australian operatic soprano.

richea / **rich**-ee-uh / *n.* a shrub or tree, chiefly of Tas. (esp. PANDANNY), with pink or white flowers and with highly ornamental palm-like foliage.

riches *n. pl.* a great quantity of money, property, or valuable possessions.

richly *adj.* **1** in a rich way. **2** thoroughly (*the book richly deserves its success*).

Richter scale / **rik**-tuh / a scale of 0 to 10 for measuring the strength of earthquakes. (¶ Named after the American seismologist C.F. Richter (1900–85).)

rick[1] *n.* a stack of hay etc.

rick[2] *n.* a slight sprain or strain (of the neck, back, etc.). • *v.* sprain or strain slightly.

rickets *n.* a children's disease caused by deficiency of vitamin D, resulting in softening and deformity of the bones.

rickety *adj.* **1** insecure or shaky in construction (*rickety stairs*). **2** feeble (*feeling a bit rickety after my operation*). **3** suffering from rickets. ☐ **ricketiness** *n.*

rickshaw *n.* a light two-wheeled hooded vehicle used in some Asian countries, pulled along by one or more people.

ricochet / **rik**-uh-shay / *v.* (**ricocheted** / **rik**-uh-shayd /, **ricocheting** / **rik**-uh-shay-ing /) rebound from a surface as a missile does when it strikes with a glancing blow. • *n.* a rebound of this kind; a hit made by it.

ricotta / ruh-**kot**-uh / *n.* a soft Italian cheese.

rid *v.* (**rid, ridding**) free (a person or place) from something unpleasant or unwanted (*rid the house of mice; was glad to be rid of him*). ☐ **be** (or **get**) **rid of** cause to go away; *colloq.* succeed in selling.

riddance *n.* getting rid of something. ☐ **good riddance** an expression of relief at getting rid of something.

ridden *see* RIDE. • *adj.* full of or dominated by (*rat-ridden cellars; guilt-ridden*).

riddle[1] *n.* **1** a question or statement designed to test ingenuity or give amusement in finding its answer or meaning. **2** something puzzling or mysterious. • *v.* speak in riddles.

riddle[2] *n.* a coarse sieve for gravel or cinders etc. • *v.* **1** pass (gravel etc.) through a riddle (*riddle the ashes*). **2** pierce with many holes (*riddled the car with bullets*). **3** permeate thoroughly (*be riddled with disease*).

ride *v.* (**rode, ridden, riding**) **1** travel in or be carried on a bicycle, vehicle, horse, etc. **2 a** sit on and manage a horse. **b** *Aust.* traverse (a station boundary) in order to inspect or maintain. **3** be supported on, float or seem to float (*the ship rode at anchor; the moon was riding high*). **4** yield to (a blow) so as to reduce its impact (*he rode the punch*). **5** give a ride to (*he rode me home*). **6** torment; harass (*they ride him out of spite*). **7** domineer; impose (authority, rules, restrictions, etc.) on (*you are riding the boy too hard*). • *n.* **1** a spell of riding; a journey in a vehicle (*only a short ride into town*). **2** the feel of a ride (*the car gives a smooth ride*). **3** a piece of equipment on which people ride at a fairground etc. ☐ **for the ride** for fun; as an observer only (*I'm in it only for the ride*). **let it ride** take no further action. **ride high** be elated or successful. **ride on** depend on (*everything rides on whether she will agree to the deal*). **ride up** (of a garment) work upwards when worn. **take for a ride** *colloq.* deceive or swindle.

rider *n.* **1** a person who rides a horse or bicycle etc. **2** an additional clause supplementing a statement etc.; an expression of opinion added to a verdict.

ridge[1] *n.* **1** a narrow raised strip; a line where two upward-sloping surfaces meet. **2** a long narrow hilltop, mountain range, or watershed. **3** the top part or crest of anything, esp. when long and narrow (*ridge of the spine; riding the ridge of the wave*). **4** an elongated region of high barometric pressure. ☐ **ridge pole** a horizontal pole supporting the top of a tent.

ridge[2] *adj.* (also **ridgy-didge**) *Aust. colloq.* all right, genuine, dinkum.

ridgecapping / **rij**-kap-ing / *n.* **1** a line of angled tiles etc. covering the ridge of a roof. **2** the process of installing or repairing these tiles etc.

ridged *adj.* formed into ridges.

ridicule *n.* the process of making a person or thing appear ridiculous. • *v.* subject to ridicule; make fun of.

ridiculous *adj.* **1** deserving to be laughed at, esp. in a scornful way. **2** not worth serious consideration, preposterous. ☐ **ridiculously** *adv.*

riding[1] *n.* the sport or pastime of riding horses.

riding[2] *n.* an electoral division of a shire.

Ridley, John (1806–87), Australian inventor (born in England) of the first workable combined harvester and stripper.

riesling / **rees**-ling, **reez**- / n. a kind of grape; a medium-dry white wine made from this.

rife adj. **1** occurring frequently, widespread (*crime was rife in the city*). **2** (foll. by *with*) abounding in, full of (*the country was rife with rumours of war*).

riff n. a short repeated phrase in jazz etc.

riffle v. **1** turn (pages) in quick succession, leaf through quickly. **2** shuffle (playing cards) rapidly by flexing and combining two halves of the pack.

riff-raff n. the rabble; disreputable people.

rifle n. a gun, usu. fired from the shoulder, with a long barrel cut with spiral grooves to make the bullet spin and so travel more accurately. •v. **1** search and rob (*rifled the safe*). **2** search messily for something mislaid etc. (*rifled through all the cupboards*). ▫ **rifle bird** any of three Australian birds of paradise, the male having velvety black plumage with metallic patches. (¶ Possibly from colour resemblance to the uniform of the Rifle Brigade, or from its call sounding like a rifle shot.)

rifle fish a northern Australian fish, so called because it ejects a stream of water from its mouth to shoot down flying insects etc.

rift n. **1** a cleft in earth or rock. **2** a crack or split; a break in cloud. **3** a disagreement; a breach in friendly relations. ▫ **rift valley** a steep-sided valley formed by subsidence of the earth's crust.

rig[1] v. (**rigged**, **rigging**) **1** provide with clothes or equipment (*rigged them out*). **2** fit (a ship) with spars, ropes, sails, etc. **3** set up (a structure) quickly or with makeshift materials. •n. **1** the way a ship's masts and sails etc. are arranged. **2** equipment for a special purpose, e.g. for drilling an oil well (*a test rig; an oil rig*). **3** *US & Aust.* a large truck; a semitrailer. **4** *colloq.* style of dress; uniform (*in full rig*). ▫ **rig-out** n. *colloq.* an outfit of clothes.

rig[2] v. (**rigged**, **rigging**) manage or control fraudulently (*the election was rigged*).

Riga / **ree**-guh / the capital of Latvia.

rigatoni / rig-uh-**toh**-nee / n. **1** pasta made in short hollow fluted tubes. **2** an Italian dish consisting largely of this and usu. a sauce.

rigger n. **1 a** a person who rigs or who arranges rigging. **b** a person who erects and maintains scaffolding etc. **2** a worker on an oil rig.

rigging n. the ropes etc. used to support masts and control the sails on a ship.

right adj. **1** (of conduct or actions etc.) morally or socially correct, in accordance with justice (*do the right thing*). **2** proper, correct, true (*the right answer*). **3** suitable; preferable (*the right person for the job*). **4** healthy or normal (*the engine doesn't sound right*). **5** *colloq.* real; complete (*made a right old mess of it*). **6** of the right-hand side. **7** esp. *Aust. colloq.* **a** in good shape; all right ('*Want another chop?*' —'*No, I'm right thanks, mate*'). **b** (as **are you right?** *or* **you right?**) (in shopping) are you being served?; may I help you? •n. **1** that which is correct or just; fair treatment (often in *pl.*) (*the rights and wrongs of the issue*). **2** justification or fair claim (*has no right to speak*). **3** legal or moral entitlement (*Aboriginal land rights*). **4** the right-hand part or region. **5** *Boxing* the right hand; a blow with this. **6** (often **Right**) a conservative political group or section (originally the more conservative section of a European legislature, seated on the president's right); conservatives collectively. •v. **1** restore to a proper or correct or upright position (*managed to right the boat*). **2** set right, make amends or take vengeance for (*the fault will right itself; right a wrong*). •adv. **1** on or towards the right-hand side (*turn right*). **2** straight (*go right on*). **3** *colloq.* immediately (*I'll be right back*). **4** all the way (*sank right to the bottom*). **5** exactly (*right in the middle*). **6** completely (*am right out of vegemite*). **7** rightly (*you did right to come*). **8** all right; that is correct; I agree. ▫ **by right** (*or* **rights**) if right were done. **on the right side** of in the favour of or liked by (a person). **right angle** an angle of 90°. **at right angles** placed at or turning through a right angle. **right-angled** having a right angle. **right arm** one's most reliable helper. **right away** immediately. **right hand** the hand that in most people is used more than the left, on the east side of the body when facing north. **right-hand** adj. of or towards this side of a person or the corresponding side of a thing. **right-hand man** a person's indispensable or chief assistant. **right-handed 1** naturally using the right hand for writing etc. **2** (of a blow or tool) made with or operated by the right hand. **3** (of a screw) be tightened by turning towards the right. **right-hander** a right-handed person or blow. **right of way** the right to pass over another's land, a path that is subject to such a right; the right to proceed, while another vehicle must wait. **right on!** *colloq.* an expression of strong approval or encouragement. **right-to-life** adj. of or pertaining to a movement opposing legal abortion. **right-to-lifer** a person who opposes abortion absolutely or would allow it only in the most extreme circumstances. **right wing** the more conservative or reactionary section of a political party or system. **right-winger** a member of the right wing. **she'll be right** *Aust. colloq.* don't worry, all will be well. **she's right** *Aust. colloq.* all is under control ('*Do you need a hand?*' —'*No, she's right, mate, thanks!*'). **too right** *colloq.* an expression of agreement.

righten v. make right or correct.

righteous adj. **1** doing what is morally right; making a show of this. **2** morally justifiable (*full of righteous indignation*). ▫ **righteously** adv. **righteousness** n.

rightful adj. in accordance with what is just or proper or legal. ▫ **rightfully** adv.

rightist *n.* a member of the right wing of a political party. •*adj.* of the right wing in politics etc. ☐ **rightism** *n.*

rightly *adv.* justly, correctly, properly, justifiably.

rightness *n.* being just, correct, proper, or justifiable.

righto *interj.* (also **rightio**, **righty-o**) *colloq.* an expression of agreement.

rightward *adv.* & *adj.* towards or facing the right. ☐ **rightwards** *adv.*

rigid *adj.* **1** stiff, not bending or yielding. **2** strict, inflexible (*rigid rules*). ☐ **rigidly** *adv.* **rigidity** / ruh-**jid**-uh-tee / *n.*

rigmarole / **rig**-muh-rohl / *n.* **1** a long rambling statement. **2** a complicated formal procedure.

rigor mortis *n.* stiffening of the body after death. (¶ Latin)

rigorous / **rig**-uh-ruhs / *adj.* **1** strict, severe (*rigorous discipline*). **2** thorough, detailed (*a rigorous search*). **3** harsh, unpleasant (*a rigorous climate*). ☐ **rigorously** *adv.*

rigour / **rig**-uh / *n.* (also **rigor**) **1** severity, strictness. **2** harshness of weather or conditions (*the rigours of famine*).

Rig-veda / rig-**vay**-duh / *Hinduism* a sacred text containing a collection of hymns in early Sanskrit. It was composed in the 2nd millennium BC, and is the oldest and most important of the four Vedas.

rile / ruyl / *v. colloq.* annoy, irritate.

rill *n.* a small stream.

rim *n.* **1** the edge or border of something more or less circular. **2** the outer edge of a wheel, on which a tyre is fitted. •*v. coarse colloq.* perform anilingus (on).

rime *n.* frost.

rimless *adj.* (of spectacles) made without frames.

rimmed *adj.* edged, bordered (*red-rimmed eyes*).

Rimsky-Korsakov, Nikolai Andreievich (1844–1908), Russian composer.

rind / ruynd / *n.* a tough outer layer or skin on fruit, cheese, bacon, etc.

ring¹ *n.* **1** the outline of a circle. **2** something shaped like this, a circular band, esp. as worn on the finger. **3** an enclosure for a circus, sports event, betting at races, two-up game, cattle-show etc. **4** (**the ring**) bookmakers collectively. **5** traders, spies, politicians, etc., combined illicitly for profit etc. (*a drug ring*). •*v.* **1** enclose with a ring, encircle. **2** *Aust.* beat (one's fellow-shearers) by shearing the most sheep in a given period (*ring the shed*). **3** put a ring on (a bird etc.) to identify it. ☐ **ring binder** a loose-leaf binder with ring-shaped clasps. **ring finger** the third finger, esp. of the left hand, on which a wedding ring is worn. **ring-pull** *adj.* (of a can) having a seal that can be broken by pulling the attached ring. **ring road** a bypass encircling a town.

ring² *v.* (**rang**, **rung**, **ringing**) **1** give out a loud clear resonant sound, esp. like that of a bell when struck (*a shot rang out; ringing laughter; the telephone rang*). **2** cause (a bell) to do this; signal by ringing (*bells rang out the old year*). **3** be filled with sound (*the stadium rang with cheers*). **4** telephone (a person). **5** convey a specified impression (*his words rang true*). •*n.* **1** the act of ringing a bell. **2** a ringing sound or tone. **3** a tone or feeling of a particular kind (*it has the ring of truth*). **4** *colloq.* a telephone call. ☐ **ring a bell** *colloq.* arouse a vague memory, sound faintly familiar. **ring the changes** vary things. **ring up 1** telephone (a person). **2** record (an amount) on a cash register.

ringbark *v.* **1** kill (a tree) by cutting a ring of bark from around the trunk. **2** (esp. as **ringbarked** *adj.*) *colloq.* circumcise a male person.

ringer¹ *n.* a person who rings bells. ☐ **be a ringer** (*or* **dead ringer**) **for** look exactly like (a person).

ringer² *n. Aust.* **1** a shearer with the highest tally of sheep shorn in a given period. **2** a person who excels (at any activity etc.). **3** a stockman, esp. as employed in droving.

ringie / **ring**-ee / *n. Aust. colloq.* = RINGKEEPER.

ring in *Aust. v.* **1** substitute (a horse) fraudulently for another in a race. **2** (in two-up) substitute (a double-headed or double-tailed coin) for a genuine coin. •*n.* **1** a fraudulent substitution, esp. of one horse for another in a race; a horse etc. so substituted. **2** a person or thing that is not of a kind with others in a group or set.

ringkeeper *n.* (also **ringie**) *Aust.* the person in charge of a two-up game.

ringleader *n.* a person who leads others in wrongdoing or in opposition to authority.

ringlet *n.* a long tubular curl of hair.

ringmaster *n.* the person in charge of a circus performance.

ringneck *n.* any of several predominantly green Australian parrots having a narrow yellow collar on the plumage of the neck.

ringside *n.* the area immediately beside a boxing or circus ring etc. ☐ **ringside seat** a position from which one has a clear view of the scene of action.

ringtail *n.* (in full **ringtail possum** *or* **ringtailed possum**) any of several Australian possums with a long prehensile tail which curls into a ring at the end.

ringworm *n.* a skin disease producing round scaly patches on the skin, caused by a fungus.

rink *n.* **1** an area of ice for skating or curling etc. **2** an enclosed area for roller skating. **3** a building containing either of these. **4** a strip of bowling green. **5** a team in bowls or curling.

rinse *v.* **1** wash lightly with water. **2** wash out soap or impurities from. •*n.* **1** rinsing. **2** a solution washed through hair to tint it.

riot *n.* **1** a violent disturbance by a crowd of people. **2** loud uncontrolled revelry. **3** a profuse display of something (*a riot of colour*). **4** *colloq.* a very amusing thing or person. •*v.* take part in a riot or in disorderly revelry. ☐ **read the Riot Act** caution or reprimand sternly. **run riot 1** throw off

riotous *adj.* **1** disorderly, unruly. **2** boisterous, unrestrained (*riotous laughter*). ☐ **riotously** *adv.*

RIP *abbr.* may he (*or* she *or* they) rest in peace. (¶ From the Latin, *requiescat* (or *requiescant*) *in pace* in a Requiem Mass.)

rip[1] *v.* (**ripped**, **ripping**) **1** tear apart, remove by pulling roughly. **2** become torn. **3** rush along. •*n.* ripping; a torn place. ☐ **let rip** *colloq.* **1** express emotion (esp. anger) without restraint. **2** speak violently or obscenely. **rip into** esp. *Aust. colloq.* **1** criticise or scold severely. **2** engage in (a task, activity, etc.) with energy and speed (*ripped into the housework; ripped into the chocolates*). **rip off** *colloq.* defraud; steal. **rip-off** *n. colloq.* **1** a swindle or fraud. **2** financial exploitation; an exorbitant charge or price. *adj.* financially exploitative; swindling, cheating (*a rip-off merchant*). **rip-roaring** *adj.* **1** wildly noisy or boisterous (*got a rip-roaring welcome*). **2** excellent, first-rate (*a rip-roaring performance*). ☐ **ripper** *n.*

rip[2] *n.* a stretch of rough water caused by meeting currents.

riparian / ruy-**pair**-ree-uhn / *adj.* of or on a river bank.

ripcord *n.* a cord for pulling to release a parachute from its pack.

ripe *adj.* **1** (of grain, fruit, cheese, etc.) matured and ready to be gathered, used, eaten or drunk. **2** mature, fully developed (*ripe in judgment*). **3** (of a person's age) advanced (*lived to a ripe old age*). **4** ready; prepared or able to undergo something (*the time is ripe for revolution; the land is ripe for development*). ☐ **ripely** *adv.* **ripeness** *n.*

ripen *v.* make or become ripe.

riposte / ruh-**post** / *n.* **1** a quick retort. **2** a quick return thrust in fencing. •*v.* deliver a riposte.

ripped / ript / *adj.* **1** torn. **2** *colloq.* intoxicated by a drug. **3** *colloq.* having the muscles showing prominently.

ripper esp. *Aust. colloq. n.* something (or someone) exciting admiration, enthusiasm, etc. (*the party was a ripper; had a ripper of a day; he's a real ripper*). •*adj.* excellent, admirable, great (*a ripper day for the beach; a ripper bloke*). ☐ **you little ripper!** an exclamation of enthusiastic admiration for a person or thing.

ripple *n.* **1** a small wave or series of waves. **2** something resembling this in appearance or movement. **3** a gentle sound that rises and falls (*a ripple of laughter; a ripple of applause*). •*v.* form or cause ripples; show or sound like ripples. ☐ **ripply** *adj.*

ripsaw *n.* a coarse saw for sawing wood along the grain.

Rip van Winkle a character in a story (by Washington Irving) who slept for 20 years and awoke to find the world completely changed.

rise *v.* (**rose**, **risen**, **rising**) **1** come or go upwards; grow or extend upwards. **2** get up from lying, sitting, or kneeling; get out of bed. **3** (of a meeting, Parliament, etc.) come to the end of a session; adjourn. **4** become upright or erect. **5** come to life again after death (*Christ is risen*). **6** rebel (*rise in revolt*). **7** (of the wind) begin to blow more strongly. **8** (of the sun etc.) become visible above the horizon. **9** increase in amount, number, or intensity (*prices are rising; her spirits rose*). **10** achieve a higher position or status (*rose to the rank of colonel*). **11** (of bread or cake etc.) swell by the action of yeast or other raising agent. **12** have its origin, begin or begin to flow (*the river rises in the mountains*). •*n.* **1** rising, an upward movement. **2** an upward slope; a small hill. **3** an increase in amount, number, or intensity; an increase in wages. **4** an upward movement in rank or status. ☐ **get** (*or* **take**) **a rise out of** *colloq.* draw (a person) into a display of annoyance or into making a retort. **give rise to** cause. **rising damp** moisture absorbed upwards from the ground into a wall.

riser *n.* **1** a person or thing that rises (*an early riser*). **2** a vertical piece between treads of a staircase.

risible *adj.* laughable; ludicrous.

rising *n.* a revolt.

risk *n.* **1** the possibility of meeting danger or suffering harm or loss; exposure to this. **2** a person or thing causing a risk or regarded (e.g. by an insurance company) in relation to risk (*not a good risk*). •*v.* expose to the chance of injury or loss; accept the risk of.

risky *adj.* (**riskier**, **riskiest**) full of risk. ☐ **riskily** *adv.* **riskiness** *n.*

risotto / ruh-**zot**-oh / *n.* (*pl.* **risottos**) an Italian dish of rice cooked in stock with chopped meat or cheese and vegetables.

risqué / **ris**-kay / *adj.* (of a story etc.) slightly indecent. (¶ French)

rissole *n.* a compressed mixture of minced meat and spices, mixed with or coated in breadcrumbs and fried.

rit. *abbr.* (in music) ritardando.

ritardando = RALLENTANDO.

rite *n.* **1** a religious or other solemn ritual (*burial rites; rites of human sacrifice*). **2** a body of customary observances characteristic of a Church (*the Roman rite*). ☐ **rite of passage** an event marking a significant change or stage in life, e.g. puberty, marriage.

ritual *n.* **1** the series of actions used in a religious or other ceremony. **2** a procedure regularly followed (*feeding the magpies was one of his daily rituals*). •*adj.* of or done as a ritual or rite (*ritual murder*). ☐ **ritually** *adv.* **ritualistic** *adj.*

ritzy *adj.* (**ritzier**, **ritziest**) *colloq.* high-class, luxurious, ostentatiously smart. (¶ From *Ritz*, the name of luxurious hotels, named after C. Ritz (1850–1918), Swiss hotel owner.)

rival *n.* **1** a person or thing competing with another (*beat all his rivals*). **2** a person or thing that can equal another in quality (*he has no rival*). • *adj.* being a rival or rivals. • *v.* (**rivalled, rivalling**) be comparable to, seem or be as good as. ☐ **rivalry** *n.*

riven / **riv**-uhn / *adj.* split; torn violently.

river *n.* **1** a large natural stream of water flowing in a channel. **2** a great flow (*rivers of blood*). ☐ **river oak** *Aust.* any of several casuarinas which grow near watercourses, esp. the large *Casuarina cunninghamiana*. **river red gum** *Aust.* any of several eucalypts which grow near watercourses. **river rose** = DOG ROSE (*see* DOG).

riverfront *n.* an area of ground alongside a river.

Riverina a rural district of south-west NSW bounded on the north and south by the Lachlan and Murray rivers respectively, with the Murrumbidgee river flowing through the central part.

rivet / **riv**-uht / *n.* a nail or bolt for holding two pieces of metal together, its headless end being beaten or pressed down to form a head when it is in place. • *v.* (**riveted, riveting**) **1** fasten with a rivet. **2** flatten (the end of a bolt) when it is in place. **3** fix, make immovable (*she stood riveted to the spot*). **4** (esp. as **riveting** *adj.*) fascinate; hold one's attention (*a riveting performance*). ☐ **riveter** *n.*

Riviera / riv-ee-**air**-ruh / the region along the Mediterranean coast, of SE France, Monaco, and NW Italy. • *n.* (**riviera**) a region thought to resemble this.

rivulet / **riv**-yuh-luht / *n.* a small stream.

Riyadh / ree-**ahd** / the capital of Saudi Arabia.

Rn *symbol* radon.

RNA *abbr.* ribonucleic acid.

Roach, Archie (full name: Archibald William Roach) (1955–), Aboriginal Australian award-winning singer and songwriter.

roach[1] *n.* (*pl.* **roach** or **roaches**) a small European freshwater fish related to the carp, introduced into Australian rivers.

roach[2] *n.* a cockroach.

road *n.* **1** a way with a prepared surface by which people, animals, or vehicles may pass between places. **2** one's way or route (*our road takes us via Wantabadgery*). **3** a way of reaching or achieving something (*the road to success*). ☐ **on the road** travelling, esp. as a firm's representative, drover, itinerant performer, or swagman. **road gang** *Aust. hist.* a detachment of convicts detailed to work at road construction. **road hog** *colloq.* a reckless or inconsiderate driver. **road-holding** *n.* the stability of a moving vehicle; its ability to travel round bends at speed. **road plant** *Aust.* equipment etc. for road repairs. **road rage** hostility, physical violence, etc., directed at the driver of a motor vehicle by another driver etc. **road test** a test of a vehicle by using it on a road. **road-test** *v.* test in this way. **road toll** the number of people killed in motor vehicle accidents. **road train** *Aust.* a group of several long trailers (usu. carrying cattle) pulled along the road by a prime mover.

roadblock *n.* a barrier set up to stop and examine traffic.

roadhouse *n.* a petrol station-cum-restaurant on a major road.

roadie *n. colloq.* a person who helps members of a touring band with their equipment.

roadshow *n.* **1** performances given by a touring company, esp. a group of pop musicians. **2** the company giving such performances from town to town. **3** a television or radio series broadcasting each program from a different venue.

roadside *n.* the border of a road.

roadster *n.* an open car without rear seats.

roadway *n.* a road; the part of this intended for vehicles.

roadworks *n. pl.* the construction or repair of roads.

roadworthy *adj.* (of a vehicle) fit to be used on a road. • *n.* **1** (in full **roadworthy certificate**) an official certificate indicating that a motor vehicle has passed a roadworthiness test (*my car has got its roadworthy*). **2** (in full **roadworthy test**) an official test of a motor vehicle's roadworthiness. ☐ **roadworthiness** *n.*

roam *v.* ramble, wander; travel unsystematically about. • *n.* a wander.

roan *adj.* (of an animal) having a coat thickly sprinkled with white or grey hairs. • *n.* a roan horse or other animal.

roar *n.* **1** a long deep loud sound, like that made by a lion; a similar sound as made by a person in pain or rage or excitement. **2** the loud sound made by thunder, an engine, a bushfire, waves, etc. **3** loud laughter. • *v.* **1** give a roar. **2** express in this way (*the crowd roared its approval; roared with laughter*). **3** drive a vehicle at high speed, esp. with the engine roaring. ☐ **roaring forties** stormy ocean tracts between latitudes 40° and 50° S. **roaring success** a great success. **roaring trade** very brisk trade. ☐ **roarer** *n.*

roast *v.* **1** cook (meat etc.) in an oven or by exposure to heat. **2** expose to great heat. **3** criticise severely, denounce. • *adj.* roasted (*roast beef*). • *n.* **1** roast meat; a joint of meat for roasting. **2** the process of roasting (in all senses).

roasting *adj.* very hot. • *n.* severe criticism.

rob *v.* (**robbed, robbing**) **1** steal from; commit robbery. **2** deprive of what is due or normal (*robbing us of our sleep*). ☐ **robber** *n.*

robbery *n.* **1** the act of robbing. **2** *colloq.* an excessive charge or cost. ☐ **robbery under arms** *Aust. hist.* the committing of armed robbery by one who has escaped into, or lives in, the bush; bushranging.

robe *n.* **1** a long loose garment, esp. a ceremonial one. **2** a dressing gown. **3** a wardrobe. • *v.* dress in a robe.

Roberts[1], Julia (full name: Julie Fiona Roberts) (1967–), American actor. Her films include *Pretty Woman* (1990) and *Erin Brockovich* (2000).

Roberts[2], Tom (1856–1931), Australian artist (born in England), one of the founders of the Heidelberg school.

Robeson / rohb-suhn /, Paul (Bustill) (1898–1976), African-American bass singer, actor, and political activist.

robin *n*. **1** = ROBIN REDBREAST (senses 1 & 2). **2** any of many small, active, Australian etc. birds, some having a brightly coloured breast, e.g. *pink-breasted robin, yellow robin*. ☐ **robin redbreast 1** a small European bird with a red breast. **2** any of various red-breasted Australian robins, esp. the scarlet robin. **3** an Australian shrub (*Melaleuca lateritia*) having bright orange-red bottlebrush flowers.

Robin Hood a semi-legendary English medieval outlaw, said to have robbed the rich and helped the poor.

robot / roh-bot / *n*. **1** a machine resembling or functioning like a human. **2** a machine automatically completing a mechanical process. **3** a person who seems to act like a machine.

robotic / roh-**bot**-ik / *adj*. of or using robots. •*n*. (**robotics**) the study and development of robots; the use of robots in industry.

robust / roh-**bust**, **roh**- / *adj*. strong, vigorous. ☐ **robustly** *adv*. **robustness** *n*.

roc *n*. a gigantic bird of Arabian legend.

rock[1] *n*. **1** the hard part of the earth's crust, underlying the soil. **2** a mass of this forming a hill etc.; a large stone or boulder. **3** a hard sweet made in cylindrical sticks. **4** used as a distinguishing epithet in the names of Australian fauna and flora (e.g. *rock flathead, rock ringtail, rock fern*). ☐ **get one's rocks off 1** *coarse colloq*. **a** masturbate. **b** have sexual intercourse. **2** *colloq*. obtain thrills etc. (*gets his rocks off by abseiling down rocks*). **on the rocks** *colloq*. **1** short of money. **2** (of a marriage, business, etc.) in difficulties, about to collapse. **3** (of a drink) served neat with ice cubes. **rock art** *Aust*. Aboriginal rock painting. **rock-bottom** *adj*. (of prices etc.) the very lowest. *n*. the very lowest level. **rock chopper** *Aust. colloq. offens.* a Catholic. (¶ From *rock chopper* 'a navvy'; influenced by the initials R.C. for 'Roman Catholic'.) **rock crystal** transparent colourless quartz. **rock-garden** = ROCKERY. **rock hole** = GNAMMA. **rock painting** *Aust.* any of very many traditional Aboriginal paintings on the walls of caves, rock shelters, etc., some of them estimated to be at least 3,000 years old. **rock plant** a plant growing on or among rocks (or, in the garden, planted in a rockery). **rock python** any of several Australian constricting snakes, including Australia's largest python, the Amethystine. **rock salt** common salt as a solid mineral. **rock shelter** *Aust.* an Aboriginal cave dwelling. **rock spider** *Aust. colloq*. a child molester. **rock wallaby** any of several small wallabies with long bushy tails, inhabiting rocky ranges and rock-strewn outcrops of mainland Australia. **the Rocks** a rocky area of Sydney, west of Sydney Cove, famed for its historic buildings and historical associations.

rock[2] *v*. **1** move or be moved gently to and fro; sway or shake. **2** disturb greatly by shock (*the scandal rocked the country*). •*n*. **1** a rocking movement. **2** modern music with a heavy beat popular with young people, performed by bands or solo singers. ☐ **rock and roll** (also **rock 'n' roll**) a style of popular dance music originating in the 1950s with a strong beat and elements of blues.

Rockefeller / rok-uh-fel-uh /, John Davison (1839–1937), American industrialist and philanthropist.

rocker *n*. **1** a thing that rocks something or is rocked. **2** each of the curved bars on which a rocking chair etc. is mounted. **3** a rocking chair. **4** a devotee of rock music. ☐ **off one's rocker** *colloq*. crazy.

rockery *n*. a construction of stones with soil between them for growing rock plants on.

rocket *n*. **1** a firework or signalling device that rises into the air when ignited and then explodes. **2** a structure that flies by expelling gases that are the products of combustion, used to propel a warhead or spacecraft; a missile, spacecraft, etc. propelled by this. **3** *colloq*. a severe reprimand. •*v*. (**rocketed, rocketing**) **1** move rapidly upwards or away. **2** increase rapidly (*prices have rocketed*).

rocketry *n*. the science or practice of using rockets for propelling missiles or spacecraft.

rockhopper *n*. *Aust.* a person who fishes from coastal rocks. ☐ **rockhop** *v*.

rocking chair *n*. a chair mounted on rockers or with springs so that it can be rocked by the sitter.

rocking horse *n*. a toy horse mounted on rockers or springs. ☐ **as rare as rocking-horse manure** extremely rare.

rockmelon *n*. a melon with fragrant orange flesh; a cantaloupe.

rocky *adj*. (**rockier, rockiest**) **1** of or like rock. **2** full of rocks. **3** unsteady, unstable (*a rocky relationship*). ☐ **rockily** *adv*. **rockiness** *n*.

rococo / ruh-**koh**-koh / *adj*. **1** of an ornate style of decoration common in Europe in the 18th century. **2** (of literature, music, architecture, etc.) highly ornate. •*n*. this style.

rod *n*. **1** a slender straight round stick or metal bar. **2** a cane for flogging people; the use of this. **3** a fishing rod. **4** a former measure of length equal to 5½ yards.

rode *see* RIDE.

rodent *n*. an animal (e.g. rat, mouse, squirrel) with strong front teeth used for gnawing.

rodeo / **roh**-dee-oh, roh-**day**-oh / *n*. (pl. **rodeos**) an exhibition of cowboy-like skills in handling animals.

rodomontade / rod-uh-mon-**tayd** / *n.* boastful talk or behaviour.

roe[1] *n.* **1** (also **hard roe**) a mass of eggs in a female fish's ovary. **2** (also **soft roe**) a male fish's milt.

roe[2] *n.* (*pl.* **roe** *or* **roes**) (also **roe deer**) a kind of small deer.

roentgen / **ront**-yuhn / *n.* (also **röntgen**) a unit of ionising radiation. (¶ Named after RÖNTGEN.)

rogaine / **roh**-gayn / *n. Aust.* a rogaining event.

rogaining *n. Aust.* a sport similar to orienteering, held over a greater time and distance. □ **rogainer** *n.*

rogan josh / roh-guhn **johsh** / *n.* (also **roghan josh**) a dish of curried meat (usu. lamb) cooked in a rich sauce.

roger / **roj**-uh / *interj.* **1** your message has been received and understood (used in radio communication etc.). **2** *colloq.* I agree.

rogue *n.* **1** a dishonest or unprincipled person. **2** a mischievous person. **3** a wild animal driven away from the herd or living apart from it (*a rogue elephant*). **4** an inferior or defective specimen among many acceptable ones. □ **roguery** *n.*

roguish *adj.* mischievous, affectedly playful. □ **roguishly** *adv.* **roguishness** *n.*

role *n.* **1** an actor's part. **2** a person's or thing's function. □ **role model** a person regarded by others as an ideal to be copied. **role playing** (also **role play**) an exercise in which participants act the part of another character; this as an aid in teaching, psychotherapy, etc. **role-playing game** a game in which players take on the roles of imaginary characters who take part in adventures in a (usu. fantasy) setting.

roll *v.* **1** move or cause to move along in contact with a surface, either on wheels or by turning over and over. **2** turn on an axis or over and over; revolve. **3** form into a cylindrical or spherical shape. **4** flatten by means of a roller (*roll out the pastry*). **5** walk unsteadily (*he rolled out of the pub*). **6** move or pass steadily (*the years rolled on*). **7** undulate (*rolling hills*). **8** make a long continuous vibrating sound (*the thunder rolled; rolls his rs*). **9** start functioning or moving (*the cameras rolled*). **10** throw dice. **11** *colloq.* **a** overturn (a car etc.) while in motion; **b** (of a car etc. in motion) overturn. **12** *colloq.* **a** soundly defeat (*Cabinet rolled his proposal*); **b** rob (esp. a helpless victim) (*got rolled in the park at night*). • *n.* **1** a cylinder formed by turning flexible material over and over upon itself without creasing it. **2** something having this shape, an undulation (*rolls of fat*). **3** a small individual portion of bread baked in a rounded shape. **4** an official list or register. **5** a rolling movement. **6** (esp. as **a roll in the hay**) *colloq.* sexual intercourse etc. **7** a long steady vibrating sound. □ **be on a roll** *colloq.* experience a bout of success or progress. **roll-call** the calling of a list of names, to check that all are present. **rolled gold** a thin coating of gold applied to a base metal by rolling. **rolled oats** husked and crushed oats. **rolling mill** a machine or factory for rolling metal into various shapes. **rolling pin** a cylinder used to flatten pastry or dough. **rolling-stock** railway engines, carriages, and wagons. **rolling strike** industrial action (against an employer or within an industry) that takes place in different places in succession or is engaged in by consecutive groups, each for a limited period. **roll-neck** *adj.* (of a sweater) having a high turned-over neck. **roll of honour** a list of people whose achievements are honoured, esp. the dead in war. **roll-on** *adj.* (of deodorant etc.) applied by means of a ball that rotates in the neck of a container. **roll one's swag** (*or* **bluey**) *Aust.* pack (one's belongings, swag, etc.) preparatory to departure. **roll over 1** invest a lump-sum superannuation payout in a government-approved investment fund, thus deferring the payment of lump-sum tax. **2** (of a witness in a corruption investigation) admit one's guilt and provide evidence of corruption. **roll up** *v.* **1** *Aust. colloq.* arrive casually; appear on the scene. **2** wind or make into a roll. *n. Aust.* the number of persons attending a meeting etc. **strike off the rolls** debar (esp. a solicitor) from practising his or her profession.

roller *n.* **1** a cylinder used for flattening or spreading things, or on which something is wound. **2** a long swelling wave. □ **roller coaster** a big dipper at an amusement park etc. **roller skate** *n.* a metal frame with four small wheels on two tracks, fitted to shoes for gliding on a hard surface. *v.* move on roller skates. **roller skater** a person who roller skates.

rollerblade *n. trademark* a roller skate with the four wheels on one track. Also called *in-line skate*. • *v.* skate using a pair of these. □ **rollerblader** *n.*

rollicking *adj.* full of boisterous high spirits.

Rolling Stones a British rock group formed in 1962, with Mick Jagger (1943–) as the lead vocalist.

rollmop *n.* a rolled uncooked pickled herring fillet.

rollover *n.* **1** *Econ.* the extension or transfer of a debt or other financial relationship. **2** *Aust.* an investment in a rollover fund. **3** *colloq.* the overturning of a vehicle etc. □ **rollover fund** *Aust.* an investment fund which can accept eligible termination payments and is approved for concessional tax treatment.

roly-poly *n.* **1** a pudding consisting of suet pastry spread with jam, rolled up, and boiled or baked. **2** any of several plants, usu. of arid and semi-arid Australia, which break off at ground level and roll along in the wind. • *adj.* plump, podgy.

ROM *abbr. Computing* read-only memory (*see* READ).

rom. *abbr.* roman (type).

romaji / **roh**-muh-jee / *n.* a system of romanised spelling used to transliterate Japanese.

Roman *adj.* **1** of ancient or modern Rome. **2** of the ancient Roman republic or empire. **3** of the largest section of the Christian Church which has its chief See in Rome and acknowledges the pope as its head. • *n.* **1** a member of the ancient Roman republic or empire. **2** a native or inhabitant of Rome. **3** (**Romans**) (in full the **Epistle to the Romans**) an epistle of St Paul to the Church at Rome. **4** (**roman**) plain upright type (not italic), like that used for the definitions in this dictionary. □ **Roman Catholic** *see* CATHOLIC. **Roman Empire** a powerful empire established by Augustus in 27 BC, eventually extending into western and southern Europe, northern Africa, and SW Asia. It was divided by Theodosius in AD 395. **Roman nose** a nose with a high bridge. **Roman numerals** letters representing numbers (I = 1, V = 5, X = 10, L = 50, C = 100, D = 500, M = 1,000).

romance / roh-**mans**, ruh- / *n.* **1** a type of literature concerning romantic love, stirring action, etc.; a work of this kind. **2** a romantic situation, event, or atmosphere. **3** a love affair; mutual attraction in this; sentimental or idealised love. **4** a medieval, esp. verse, tale of chivalry, common in the Romance languages. **5** a picturesque exaggeration or falsehood. • *v.* **1** exaggerate or distort the truth in an imaginative way. **2** court, woo. □ **Romance languages** the group of European languages descended from Latin (French, Italian, Spanish, etc.).

Romanesque / roh-muh-**nesk** / *n.* a style of art and architecture in Europe in about 900–1200, with massive vaulting and round arches. • *adj.* of this style.

Romania (also **Rumania**) a republic in eastern Europe.

Romanian (also **Rumanian**) *n.* **1** a person from Romania. **2** the language of Romania. • *adj.* of Romania or its people or language.

Roman Rite *n.* **1** (also **Latin Rite**) the tradition of sacrament and canon law in the Roman Catholic Church. **2** the most usual form of the Roman Catholic Mass.

romantic *adj.* **1** of, characterised by, or suggestive of an idealised, sentimental, or fantastic view of reality; remote from experience (*a romantic picture; a romantic setting*). **2** inclined towards or suggestive of romance in love. **3** (of a person) imaginative, visionary, idealistic. **4** (of style in art, music, etc.) concerned more with feeling and emotion than with form and aesthetic qualities. **5** (also **Romantic**) of the 18th–19th century romantic movement or style in the European arts. **6** (of a project etc.) unpractical, fantastic. • *n.* a person who enjoys romantic situations etc. □ **romantically** *adv.*

romanticise *v.* (also -**ize**) **1** make romantic; exaggerate (*a highly romanticised account*). **2** indulge in romantic thoughts or actions.

romanticism *n.* (also **Romanticism**) the romantic style in art, music, etc. □ **romanticist** *n.*

Romany / **rom**-uh-nee, **roh**-muh- / *n.* **1** a gypsy. **2** the language of the gypsies. • *adj.* of gypsies or the Romany language.

Rome 1 the capital of Italy. **2** the ancient Roman republic or empire. **3** Catholicism (*our vicar has gone over to Rome*).

Romeo *n.* (*pl.* **Romeos**) a romantic or passionate male lover or seducer. (¶ Named after the hero of Shakespeare's romantic tragedy *Romeo and Juliet*.)

romp *v.* **1** play about in a lively way, as children do. **2** *colloq.* get along easily. • *n.* a spell of romping. □ **romp in** (or **romp home**) *colloq.* win easily.

rompers *n. pl.* (also **romper suit**) a child's one-piece garment covering the legs and trunk.

Romulus *Rom. myth.* the founder of Rome, exposed at birth with his twin brother Remus and found and suckled by a she-wolf.

rondeau / **ron**-doh / *n.* (*pl.* **rondeaux** pronounced the same or / **ron**-dohz /) a short poem with only two rhymes throughout and the opening words used twice as a refrain.

rondel *n.* a rondeau.

rondo *n.* (*pl.* **rondos**) a piece of music with a theme that recurs several times.

Röntgen / **ront**-yuhn /, Wilhelm Conrad von (1845–1923), German physicist, the discoverer of X-rays.

röntgen alternative spelling of ROENTGEN.

roo *Aust. n.* (also **'roo**) a kangaroo. • *adj.* pertaining to a kangaroo (*roo dog; roo shooter*). □ **roo bar** a kangaroo bar (*see* KANGAROO).

rood *n.* **1** a crucifix, esp. one raised on the middle of a rood-screen. **2** a quarter of an acre. □ **Holy Rood** *archaic* the Cross of Christ. **rood-screen** a carved wooden or stone screen separating the nave from the chancel in a church.

roof *n.* **1** a structure covering the top of a building. **2** the top of a car, tent, cave, etc. • *v.* cover with or as with a roof; be the roof of. □ **roof of the mouth** the palate. **roof rack** a framework for carrying luggage etc. on the roof of a vehicle.

roofing *n.* material used for a roof.

rooftop *n.* the outer surface of a roof. □ **shout it from the rooftops** make a thing embarrassingly public.

rook *n.* **1** a European black crow that nests in colonies. **2** a chess piece with a top shaped like battlements. • *v.* swindle, charge (a person) an extortionate price.

rookery *n.* **1** a colony of rooks; a place where these nest. **2** a colony or breeding place of penguins or seals.

rookie *n. colloq.* a new recruit.

room *n.* **1** space that is or could be occupied by something. **2** a part of a building enclosed by walls or partitions; the people present in this (*the room fell silent*). **3** opportunity or scope or ability to allow something (*there is room for improvement*). □ **room mate** a person sharing a

roomy *adj.* (**roomier**, **roomiest**) having plenty of room, spacious. ☐ **roominess** *n.*

Roosevelt / **roh**-zuh-velt /, Franklin D(elano) (1882–1945), 32nd president of the USA 1932–1945, whose 'New Deal' lifted America out of the 1930s depression.

roost *n.* a place where birds perch or where they settle for sleep. • *v.* (of birds) perch; settle for sleep. ☐ **come home to roost** (of an action) react unfavourably on the doer.

rooster *n.* a male domestic fowl.

root[1] *n.* **1** the part of a plant that supports it in the earth and absorbs water and nourishment from the soil. **2** (**roots**) a person's emotional attachment to a place in which the person or his or her family has lived for a long time. **3** an edible root, a plant with this (e.g. carrot, turnip). **4** the part of a bodily organ or structure that is embedded in tissue (*the root of a tooth*). **5** a source or basis (*the root of all evil; get to the root of the matter*). **6** a number in relation to a given number which it produces when multiplied by itself once (= SQUARE ROOT) or a specified number of times (*2 is the cube root of 8*, i.e. $2 \times 2 \times 2 = 8$). **7** *Aust. coarse colloq.* **a** an act of sexual intercourse. **b** a sexual partner. • *v.* **1** take root; cause to do this. **2** cause to stand fixed and unmoving (*was rooted to the spot by fear*). **3** establish deeply and firmly (*the feeling is deeply rooted*). **4** (esp. as **rooted** *adj.*) *colloq.* ruin; exhaust; frustrate (*the telly's rooted; I'm rooted after all that digging*). **5** *Aust. coarse colloq.* have sexual intercourse (with). ☐ **root canal 1** the pulp-filled cavity in the root of a tooth. **2** (in full **root canal therapy**) a procedure to replace infected pulp with an inert material. **root out** (*or* **up**) **1** drag or dig up by the roots. **2** eradicate; get rid of (*root out the troublemakers; root out heresy*). **strike** (*or* **take**) **root 1** begin to grow and take nourishment from the soil. **2** (of an idea etc.) become established. ☐ ☐ **rooter** *n.* **rootless** *adj.*

root[2] *v.* **1** (of an animal) turn up ground with its snout or beak in search of food. **2** rummage; find or extract by doing this (*root out some facts and figures*). ☐ **root for** *colloq.* support actively by applause etc., barrack for (*rooting for their team*).

rootstock *n.* **1** a rhizome. **2** a plant into which a graft is inserted.

rope *n.* **1** strong thick cord; a length of this. **2** a quantity of similar things strung together (*a rope of pearls*). **3** execution by hanging. • *v.* **1** fasten, secure, or catch with rope. **2** fence off with rope. ☐ **rope in** (*or* **into**) persuade to take part in an activity. **rope ladder** a ladder made of two ropes connected by crosspieces. **the ropes** the procedure for doing something (*know the ropes*).

ropeable *adj. Aust.* requiring to be restrained; furious; bad-tempered.

ropy *adj.* (also **ropey**) (**ropier**, **ropiest**) *colloq.* poor in quality. ☐ **ropiness** *n.*

rorqual / **raw**-kwuhl / *n.* a whale with a dorsal fin.

Rorschach test / **raw**-shahk / *n.* a personality test based on a person's interpretation of a standard set of ink blots.

rort *Aust. n.* **1** an act of fraud or sharp practice (*knows all the tax rorts*). **2** *colloq.* a wild party; an escapade. • *v.* **1** engage in sharp practice (*he's expert at rorting the system*). **2** manipulate (a ballot, records, etc.) fraudulently; rig (*a splinter group tried to rort the union election*). ☐ **rorter** *n.*

rosaceous / roh-**zay**-shuhs / *adj.* of the large family of plants including the rose.

rosary *n.* **1** *Catholic Church* a repeated sequence of prayers, to be said while meditating on the birth, death, resurrection, etc. of Christ. **2** a string of beads for keeping count of these prayers as they are recited.

Rose, Lionel (Edmund) (1948–), Aboriginal Australian boxer who won the world bantamweight title in 1968.

rose[1] *n.* **1** a bush or shrub bearing ornamental usu. fragrant flowers. **2** its flower. **3** any Australian flowering plant resembling this (*desert rose*). **4** deep pink colour. **5** the perforated sprinkling nozzle of a watering can etc. • *adj.* deep pink. ☐ **rose-breasted cockatoo** *Aust.* = GALAH. **rose hip** the fruit of a rose. **rose of the west** a small eucalypt of WA with silvery blue rounded leaves and extremely large cardinal-red flowers powdered with bright gold. **rose water** a fragrant liquid perfumed with roses. **rose window** a circular patterned window in a church.

rose[2] *see* RISE.

rosé / roh-**zay** / *n.* a light pink wine. (¶ French, = pink.)

roseate / **roh**-zee-uht / *adj.* deep pink, rosy.

Roseau / roh-**zoh** / the capital of Dominica.

rosebowl *n.* a bowl for cut roses, esp. as a prize in a competition.

rosella[1] / roh-**zel**-uh / *n. Aust.* **1** any of several brightly coloured parrots, with white, yellow, or red cheek-patches. **2** a sheep which is losing its wool (and said to resemble a rosella parrot which has lost some of its feathers) and is therefore easy to shear.

rosella[2] *n. Aust.* **1** a tall shrub or small tree of NSW, Qld, and the NT, having large pinky red (sometimes yellow) flowers and edible young growth and buds, used as a food plant and as an ornamental. Also called *native hibiscus*. **2** the fruit of this, often used for jam.

rosemary / **rohz**-muh-ree / *n.* an evergreen shrub with fragrant leaves used for flavouring food.

Rosetta stone a basalt stone found in Egypt in 1799, dating from *c.*200 BC, with parallel inscriptions in hieroglyphs, demotic Egyptian, and Greek, providing the key to the decipherment of ancient Egyptian texts.

rosette *n.* **1** a rose-shaped ornament of ribbon etc., esp. as a supporter's badge or as a prize in a competition. **2** a rose-shaped carving.

rosewood *n.* any of several Australian trees having a fragrant (often reddish) timber used for making furniture.

Rosh Hashana *n.* the Jewish New Year.

rosin / roz-uhn / *n.* a kind of resin. •*v.* (**rosined, rosining**) rub (esp. a violin bow etc.) with rosin.

Ross, Sir James Clark (1800–62), English polar explorer, after whom the Ross Sea, Ross Barrier, and Ross Island in the Antarctic are named.

Rossini / ruh-**see**-nee /, Gioacchino Antonio (1792–1868), Italian composer of operas.

Ross River virus *n.* **1** a mosquito-borne virus causing a non-fatal disease characterised by a rash, and joint and muscle pain. **2** (also **Ross River fever**) this disease. (¶ Ross River, near Townsville.)

roster / **ros**-tuh / *n.* a list showing people's turns of duty etc. •*v.* place on a roster.

rostrum / **ros**-truhm / *n.* (*pl.* **rostra** or **rostrums**) a platform for public speaking or for an orchestral conductor.

rosy *adj.* (**rosier, rosiest**) **1** rose-coloured, deep pink. **2** promising, hopeful (*a rosy future*). ▫ **rosily** *adv.* **rosiness** *n.*

rot *v.* (**rotted, rotting**) **1** (of animal or vegetable matter) lose its original form by chemical action caused by bacteria or fungi etc.; decay. **2** perish or become weak through lack of use or activity. •*n.* **1** rotting; rottenness. **2** *colloq.* nonsense. **3** a series of failures (*the rot set in*).

Rotarian / roh-**tair**-ree-uhn / *n.* a member of a Rotary Club.

rotary *adj.* rotating; acting by rotating (*a rotary drill*). •*n.* a rotating machine. ▫ **rotary hoe** a machine with many rotating spikes for breaking up soil prior to planting a lawn etc.; *v.* break up the ground with a rotary hoe. **rotary hoist** = CLOTHES HOIST.

Rotary Club a local branch of an international association (**Rotary International**) formed by businesspeople for the purpose of rendering service to the community.

rotate *v.* **1** turn round an axis or central point; revolve. **2** arrange or deal with in a recurrent series. **3** take turns; be used in turn (*the crews rotate every three weeks*). ▫ **rotatable** *adj.* **rotator** *n.*

rotation *n.* **1** an act or instance of rotating or being rotated. **2** regular succession (*each member will act as chair by rotation*). **3** the growing of different crops in regular order to avoid exhausting the soil. ▫ **rotational** *adj.*

rotatory / **roh**-tuh-tuh-ree, ruh-**tay**-tuh-ree / *adj.* rotating.

rote *n.* ▫ **by rote** by memory without thought of the meaning. **rote learning** mechanical or habitual repetition (in order to memorise).

ROTFL *abbr.* (esp. in electronic communications) rolling on the floor laughing. (¶ Acronym)

Rothschild the name of a family of European Jewish bankers, who first established a banking-house in Frankfurt at the end of the 18th century.

roti / **roh**-tee / *n.* a round flat unleavened bread of India and Sri Lanka, often with grated coconut in it.

rotisserie / roh-**tis**-uh-ree / *n.* **1** a restaurant etc. where meat is roasted or barbecued. **2** a revolving spit for roasting or barbecuing meat.

rotor *n.* **1** a rotating part of a machine. **2** a horizontally-rotating vane of a helicopter.

rotten *adj.* **1** rotting; rotted; breaking easily or falling to pieces from age or use. **2** morally or politically corrupt. **3** *colloq.* **a** ill-advised, worthless (*a rotten idea*). **b** unpleasant (*rotten weather*). **c** ill (*feeling rotten*). **d** very drunk. ▫ **rottenly** *adv.* **rottenness** *n.*

rotter *n. colloq.* a nasty or contemptible person.

Rottnest Island a small island north-west of Fremantle, WA. It was named Rottenest (i.e. 'rat nest') because the small wallabies or quokkas on the island were mistaken for rats.

Rottweiler / **rot**-wuy-luh / *n.* a dog of a tall black-and-tan breed, used as a guard dog.

rotund / roh-**tund** / *adj.* **1** rounded, plump, podgy. **2** (of voice, literary style, etc.) sonorous, grandiloquent. ▫ **rotundity** *n.*

rotunda / ruh-**tun**-duh / *n.* a circular domed building or hall.

rouble / **roo**-buhl / *n.* (also **ruble**) the unit of money in Russia.

roué / **roo**-ay / *n.* a debauchee, esp. an elderly one; a rake. (¶ French)

rouge / roozh / *n.* a reddish cosmetic for colouring the cheeks. •*v.* colour with rouge.

rough *adj.* **1** having an uneven or irregular surface, coarse in texture, not level or smooth. **2** not gentle or restrained or careful; violent (*rough weather*). **3** lacking finish or delicacy; not perfected or detailed. •*adv.* roughly; in rough conditions. •*n.* **1** something rough; rough ground. **2** hardship (*take the rough with the smooth*). **3** an unfinished state. **4** a rough drawing or design etc. **5** a ruffian or hooligan. •*v.* **1** make rough. **2** shape or plan or sketch roughly (*roughed out a scheme*). ▫ **a bit rough** *colloq.* **1** unfair, unreasonable (*that decision by the umpire was a bit rough*). **2** lacking taste; unseemly (*that joke was a bit rough in the circumstances*). **rough diamond 1** a diamond not yet cut. **2** a person of good nature but lacking polished manners. **rough it** do without ordinary comforts. **rough justice** treatment that is only approximately fair or not fair at all. **rough spin** *Aust.* a rough trot. **rough trot** *Aust.* a period of difficulty or misfortune (*she's had a rough trot recently*). ▫▫ **roughish** *adj.* **roughness** *n.*

roughage *n.* indigestible material in plants used as food (e.g. bran, green vegetables, and certain fruits) that stimulates the action of the intestines.

roughcast *n.* plaster of lime and gravel, used for covering the outsides of buildings. • *adj.* (of a plan etc.) roughly formed, preliminary. • *v.* (**roughcast**, **roughcasting**) **1** coat with roughcast. **2** prepare in outline.

roughen *v.* make or become rough.

roughie / **ruf**-ee / *n. Aust. colloq.* **1** (in horse racing etc.) **a** a rank outsider. **b** an outsider with some chance of winning (*my roughie for the Melbourne Cup is 'Darling Drin'*). **2** an unfair or unreasonable act; a 'swiftie'.

roughly *adv.* **1** in a rough manner. **2** approximately (*roughly 200 people*). ☐ **roughly speaking** in an approximate sense (*it is, roughly speaking, a square*).

Roughsey, Dick (Goobalathaldin) (1920–85), Aboriginal Australian artist and writer, noted for his award-winning children's books, esp. *Giant Devil Dingo*, *The Rainbow Serpent*, and *The Quinkins*.

roughshod *adj.* (of a horse) having shoes with the nail heads left projecting to prevent slipping. ☐ **ride roughshod over** treat inconsiderately or arrogantly.

roughy / **ruf**-ee / *n. Aust.* **1** = TOMMY ROUGH. **2** a small, reef-dwelling, Australian food fish.

roulade / roo-**lahd** / *n.* **1** a rolled piece of meat, sponge, etc. with a filling. **2** a quick succession of notes, usu. sung to one syllable.

roulette / roo-**let** / *n.* a gambling game in which a small ball falls at random into one of the compartments on a revolving disc.

round *adj.* **1** having a curved shape or outline; shaped like a circle, sphere, or cylinder. **2** full, complete (*a round dozen*). **3 a** candid, outspoken (*a round assertion of her independence*); **b** harsh; unstinting (*received nothing but round abuse for her pains*). • *n.* **1** a round object. **2** a circular or recurring course or series (*the daily round; a round of talks*). **3** a route on which things are to be inspected or delivered (*a doctor's rounds; milk round*). **4** a musical composition for two or more voices in which each sings the same melody but starts at a different time. **5** a single shot or volley of shots from one or more firearms; ammunition for this. **6** one stage in a competition or struggle; one section of a boxing match; one circuit of a golf course playing all the holes once. **7** a drink for each person in a group. **8** a sandwich made of two slices of bread. **9** a separate or distinct outburst (of applause, jeering, etc.). • *prep.* **1** so as to circle or enclose. **2** at points on or near the circumference of (*sat round the table*). **3** having as its axis or central point (*the earth moves round the sun*). **4** visiting in a series or all over, to all points of interest in (*went round the cafés; were shown round the museum*). **5** on or to the further side of (*the shop round the corner*). • *adv.* **1** in a circle or curve; by a circuitous route. **2** so as to face in a different direction. **3** round a place or group; in every direction. **4** to a person's house etc. (*I'll be round in an hour*). • *v.* **1** make or become round. **2** make into a round figure or number (*round it up to 100*). **3** travel round (*the car rounded the corner*). ☐ **in the round** (of sculpture) with all sides shown, not attached to a background; (of a theatre) with seats on all sides of the stage. **round about 1** near by. **2** approximately. **round brackets** brackets of the form ( ). **round figure** (or **number**) one without odd units. **round off** bring (a thing) into a complete state; finish off. **round on** make an attack or retort in retaliation, esp. unexpectedly. **round robin 1** a statement signed by a number of people (often with signatures in a circle to conceal who signed first). **2** a tournament in which each competitor plays every other. **round the clock** continuously throughout day and night. **round trip** a trip to one or more places and back again. **round up** gather (animals, people, or things) into one place. **round-up** *n.* **1** a systematic rounding up. **2** a summary (of news etc.). ☐☐ **roundish** *adj.* **roundness** *n.*

roundabout *n.* **1** a merry-go-round at a fairground. **2** a road junction with a circular structure round which traffic has to pass in the same direction. • *adj.* indirect, not using the shortest or most direct route or phrasing etc. (*heard the news in a roundabout way*).

rounder *n.* the unit of scoring in rounders.

rounders *n.* a team game played with bat and ball, in which players have to run round a circuit.

Roundhead *n. Brit. hist.* a supporter of the Parliament party in the English Civil War. (¶ So called because they wore their hair cut short at a time when long hair was in fashion for men.)

roundly *adv.* **1** thoroughly, severely (*was roundly scolded*). **2** in a rounded shape.

roundsman *n. Aust.* a journalist covering a specific subject (*the paper's political roundsman*).

Round Table *n.* **1** the round table at which King Arthur and his knights sat so that none might have precedence. **2** (**round table**) an assembly for discussion, esp. at a conference or in a situation where those who are not normally equals meet as equals (often as *adj.*: *round-table talks*).

roundworm *n.* a worm with a rounded body, esp. as found in the human intestine.

rouse[1] / rowz / *v.* **1** cause (a person) to wake; wake up. **2** cause to become active or excited. **3** anger (*he's terrible when roused*).

rouse[2] / rows / *v. Aust.* **1** scold (*Mum really rouses when I come home late*). **2** (foll. by *at* or *on*) berate, tongue-lash.

rouseabout / row-suh-bowt / *Aust. n.* **1** an unskilled labourer or odd jobber on a farm, in a shearing shed, etc. **2** any unskilled worker or odd jobber. • *v.* work as a rouseabout.

rousie / **row**-see / *n. colloq.* a rouseabout.

rousing *adj.* vigorous, stirring.
Rousseau¹ / roo-**soh** /, Henri Julien (1844–1910), French painter noted for his bold naïve style.
Rousseau² / roo-**soh** /, Jean-Jacques (1712–78), Swiss-born French philosopher.
roust / rowst / *v.* **1** (usu. foll. by *on* or *at*) *Aust.* scold, 'go crook at'. **2** (often foll. by *up*, *out*) **a** rouse, stir up. **b** root out. ◻ **roust around** rummage.
roustabout *n.* a rouseabout.
rout¹ *n.* utter defeat; a disorderly retreat of defeated troops. • *v.* defeat completely; put to flight.
rout² *v.* **1** fetch or force out (*routed him out of bed*). **2** rummage.
route / root / *n.* the course or way taken to get to a place. • *v.* (**routed**, **routeing**) send by a certain route.
routine / roo-**teen** / *n.* **1** a standard course of procedure; a series of acts performed regularly in the same way. **2** a set sequence of movements in a dance or other performance. **3** a sequence of instructions to a computer. • *adj.* in accordance with routine. ◻ **routinely** *adv.*
roux / roo / *n.* a mixture of heated fat (esp. butter) and flour used as a basis for a sauce.
rove¹ *v.* **1** wander without settling; roam, ramble. **2** (of eyes) look about. **3** act as a rover (sense 2).
rove² see REEVE.
rover *n.* **1** a wanderer. **2** *Aust. Rules* one of three players making up the ruck, usu. small, fast, and adept at securing possession of the ball.
row¹ / roh / *n.* **1** a number of people or things in a line. **2** a line of seats across a theatre etc.
row² / roh / *v.* **1** propel (a boat) using oars. **2** carry in a boat that one rows. • *n.* a spell of rowing; an excursion in a rowing boat. ◻ **rower** *n.*
row³ / row / *colloq. n.* **1** a loud noise. **2** a quarrel, a heated argument. **3** a severe reprimand. • *v.* quarrel or argue heatedly.
rowdy / row-dee / *adj.* (**rowdier**, **rowdiest**) noisy and disorderly. • *n.* a rowdy person. ◻ **rowdily** *adv.* **rowdiness** *n.* **rowdyism** *n.*
Rowe, Normie (full name: Norman John Rowe) (1947–), AM, Australian pop singer.
rowel / row-uhl / *n.* a spiked revolving disc at the end of a spur.
rowlock / rol-uhk, rul- / *n.* a device on the side of a boat for holding an oar in place.
royal *adj.* **1** of, suitable for, or worthy of a king or queen. **2** belonging to the family of a king or queen; in the service or under the patronage of royalty. **3** splendid, first-rate; of exceptional size etc. • *n. colloq.* a member of a (esp. Brit.) royal family (*the antics of the younger royals*). ◻ **royal blue** deep vivid blue. **royal bluebell** a small perennial herb *Wahlenbergia gloriosa* of higher altitudes in SE mainland Australia, having large royal blue flowers held erect: the floral emblem of the ACT. Also called *Austral bluebell*, *wahlenbergia*. **royal flush** see FLUSH. **royal hakea** an erect WA hakea having round, stiff, spiky leaves brilliantly variegated with red, green, and cream. **royal icing** hard icing for cakes, made with icing sugar and egg white. **royal jelly** a substance secreted by worker bees and fed to future queen bees; believed by some people to be beneficial to health. **royal 'we'** the use of 'we' instead of 'I' by a single person (as by a sovereign). ◻ ◻ **royally** *adv.*
royal commission *n.* a commission of inquiry appointed by the representative of the Crown at the request of the government; the committee so appointed.
royalist *n.* **1** a person who favours monarchy. **2** (**Royalist**) a supporter of the monarchy in the English Civil War.
royalty *n.* **1** being royal. **2** a royal person; royal people. **3** payment to an author etc. for each copy of the book sold or for each public performance of his or her work; payment to a patentee for the use of the patent. **4** payment by a mining or oil company to the owner of the land used.
RPI *abbr.* = RETAIL PRICE INDEX.
rpm. *abbr.* revolutions per minute.
RSI *abbr.* = REPETITIVE STRAIN INJURY.
RSL *abbr.* Returned and Services League of Australia, an organisation providing assistance to returned Australian servicemen and servicewomen and their families.
RSPCA *abbr.* Royal Society for the Prevention of Cruelty to Animals.
RSVP *abbr.* (in an invitation) please reply. (¶ From the French, *répondez s'il vous plaît*.)
Ru *symbol* ruthenium.
rub *v.* (**rubbed**, **rubbing**) **1** press something against (a surface) and slide it to and fro; apply in this way. **2** polish or clean by rubbing; make or become dry, smooth, or sore etc. in this way. • *n.* **1** the act or process of rubbing. **2** a difficulty or impediment (*there's the rub*). ◻ **rub down 1** dry, smooth, or reduce the level of (a thing) by rubbing. **2** massage (an athlete etc.), esp. after strenuous exercise. **rub-down** *n.* an instance of rubbing down; a massage. **rub off** (usu. foll. by *on*) be removed or transferred by or as if by rubbing (*his attitudes have rubbed off on me*). **rub out 1** remove (marks etc.) by using a rubber. **2** *Aust. colloq.* (of a sportsperson) suspend (*he was rubbed out for 3 weeks for kicking in danger*).
rubato *n.* (*pl.* **rubatos** or **rubati**) (in music) a temporary disregarding of strict tempo.
rubber¹ *n.* **1** a tough elastic substance made from the latex of certain plants or synthetically. **2** a piece of this or other substance for rubbing out pencil or ink marks. **3** *colloq.* a condom. ◻ **rubber band** a loop of thin rubber for holding papers etc. together. **rubber duckie** *colloq.* an inflated rubber boat with motor, used in surf rescue work etc. **rubber plant** a tropical plant with large leathery leaves, often grown as a house plant. **rubber**

stamp 1 a device for imprinting a mark on to a surface. **2** a person who mechanically gives approval to the actions of another person or group. **rubber-stamp** v. approve automatically without due consideration. □□ **rubberiness** n.

rubber² n. a match of three or five successive games between the same sides or persons at whist, bridge, cricket, tennis, etc.

rubberise v. (also **-ize**) treat or coat with rubber.

rubbery adj. **1** like rubber. **2** (of figures, financial statements, etc.) unreliable; to be regarded with some suspicion.

rubbing n. a reproduction made of a memorial brass or other relief design by placing paper over it and rubbing with pigment.

rubbish n. **1** waste or worthless material. **2** nonsense. • v. criticise severely, disparage. • adj. Aust. (in Aboriginal English) inferior, worthless (*rubbish language*). □ **rubbishy** adj.

rubbity n. (in full **rubbity-dub**) Aust. rhyming slang a pub.

rubble n. waste or rough fragments of stone or brick etc.

rubella n. German measles.

Rubens / roo-buhnz /, Sir Peter Paul (1577–1640), Flemish painter.

Rubicon / roo-buh-kon / □ **cross the Rubicon** take a decisive step that commits one to an enterprise. (¶ The river Rubicon, in NE Italy, was the ancient boundary between Gaul and Italy; by crossing it into Italy Julius Caesar committed himself to war against the Senate and Pompey.)

rubicund / roo-buh-kund / adj. (of the complexion) red, ruddy.

rubidium / roo-**bid**-ee-uhm / n. a soft silvery metallic element (symbol Rb).

Rubik's cube n. a cube-shaped puzzle formed of coloured sections which are rotated until each face is a single colour.

ruble alternative spelling of ROUBLE.

rubric / roo-brik / n. **1** a heading or passage in red or in special lettering. **2** explanatory words. **3** an established custom or rule. **4** directions for the conduct of divine service in a liturgical book. **5** (often **rubrics**) instructions to candidates on an examination paper.

ruby n. **1** a red precious stone. **2** deep red colour. • adj. deep red. □ **ruby wedding** the 40th anniversary of a wedding.

ruche / roosh / n. a gathered trimming. • v. gather (fabric) ornamentally.

ruck n. **1** (**the ruck**) the main body of competitors (in a race) not likely to overtake the leaders. **2** a crowd or mass of undistinguished people or things. **3** Aust. Rules **a** a group of three players (two followers and a rover) who do not have fixed positions but follow the play; **b** = RUCKMAN. **4** Rugby a loose scrum. **5** a crease or wrinkle. • v. **1** Aust. Rules (of the two followers) play as one of the ruck. **2** crease or wrinkle. □ **ruck rover** Aust. Rules a tall and agile player chosen for his ability to combine the roles of ruckman and rover.

ruckman n. Aust. = FOLLOWER (sense 3).

rucksack n. a bag worn slung by straps from both shoulders and resting on the back, used esp. by walkers and climbers.

ruckus n. colloq. a row, a commotion.

ruction n. pl. colloq. **1** a disturbance or tumult. **2** (**ructions**) heated arguments or protests.

Rudd, Steele (1868–1935), pseudonym of Arthur Hoey Davis, Australian writer who created the characters of Dad and Dave.

rudder n. a vertical piece of metal or wood hinged to the stern of a boat or rear of an aeroplane and used for steering.

ruddy adj. (**ruddier**, **ruddiest**) **1** reddish; (of a person's face) having a fresh healthy reddish colour. **2** colloq. bloody, damned, wretched. □ **ruddily** adv. **ruddiness** n.

rude adj. **1** impolite, showing no respect or consideration. **2** primitive, roughly made (*rude stone implements*). **3** vigorous, hearty (*rude health*). **4** violent, startling (*a rude awakening*). **5** colloq. indecent, lewd (*rude jokes*). □ **rudely** adv. **rudeness** n.

rudiment / roo-duh-muhnt / n. **1** a part or organ that is incompletely developed. **2** (**rudiments**) basic or elementary principles (*learning the rudiments of chemistry*). □ **rudimentary** / roo-duh-**men**-tuh-ree, -tree / adj.

rue n. an evergreen European shrub with bitter leaves formerly used in medicine. • v. (**rued**, **ruing**) repent or regret (*he'll live to rue the day*).

rueful adj. showing good-humoured regret. □ **ruefully** adv. **ruefulness** n.

ruff¹ n. **1** a deep starched pleated frill worn around the neck in the 16th century. **2** a projecting or coloured ring of feathers or fur round the neck of a bird or animal. **3** (*feminine* = **reeve**) a wading bird, the male having a very large ruff during the mating season.

ruff² v. trump in a card game. • n. trumping.

ruffian n. a violent lawless person.

ruffle v. **1** disturb the smoothness or evenness of. **2** upset the calmness or even temper of (a person); become ruffled. **3** gather (lace etc.) into a ruffle. **4** (often foll. by *up*) (of a bird) erect (its feathers) in anger, display, etc. • n. a gathered ornamental frill, esp. round the wrist or neck.

rufous / roo-fuhs / adj. (esp. of birds and animals) reddish-brown (*rufous owl; rufous rat-kangaroo*).

rug n. **1** a thick floor-mat. **2** a thick warm blanket or coverlet. □ **pull the rug from under** remove the support of (a theory etc.); weaken. **rug rat** colloq. a small child. **rug up** wear extra clothes as protection against the cold.

Rugby n. (in full **Rugby football**) a kind of football played with an oval ball which may be kicked or carried. □ **Rugby League** a professional form of the game with teams of 13.

Rugby Union an originally amateur form with teams of 15. (¶ Named after *Rugby* School in England, where it was first played.)

rugged *adj.* **1** having an uneven surface or an irregular outline, craggy. **2** rough but kindly and honest (*a rugged individualist*). ☐ **ruggedly** *adv.* **ruggedness** *n.*

rugger *n. colloq.* Rugby football. ☐ **ruggerbugger** *colloq. derog.* a player or supporter of Rugby football, esp. an aggressive one.

ruin *n.* **1** severe damage or destruction. **2** complete loss of one's fortune, resources, or prospects. **3** the remains of something decayed or destroyed (*the house was a ruin; the ruins of Pompeii*). **4** a cause of ruin. •*v.* **1** damage (a thing) so severely that it is useless; bring into a ruined condition. **2** spoil, damage (*rain ruined the barbecue*). ☐ **ruination** *n.*

ruinous *adj.* **1** bringing or likely to bring ruin (*ruinous expense*). **2** in ruins, ruined (*the house is in a ruinous condition*). ☐ **ruinously** *adv.*

rule *n.* **1** a statement of what can, must, or should be done. **2** the general custom or normal state of things (*seaside holidays became the rule*). **3** exercise of authority, control, governing (*countries that were under French rule*). **4** a straight often jointed measuring device used by carpenters etc. **5** (**Rule**) the code of discipline of a religious order (*the Dominican Rule*). **6** (**Rules**) *colloq.* = AUSTRALIAN RULES. **7** (usu. **Rules** or **Old Rule**) *Aust.* (in Aboriginal English) the body of Aboriginal religious belief and social custom. •*v.* **1** have authoritative control over people or a country; govern. **2** keep (a person or feeling etc.) under control, dominate. **3** be the prevailing custom or usual condition (*cheerful chaos rules in our house*). **4** hold sway (*footy rules in the Australian sporting scene*). **5** give a decision as judge or other authority (*the chairman ruled that the question was out of order*). **6** draw (a line) using a ruler or other straight edge; mark parallel lines on (paper etc.). ☐ **as a rule** usually. **go through the rules** *Aust.* (in Aboriginal English) (of a boy) be initiated. **rule of thumb** a rough practical method. **rule out** exclude as irrelevant or ineligible.

ruler *n.* **1** a person who rules by authority. **2** a straight strip of wood, plastic, etc. used for measuring or drawing straight lines.

ruling *n.* an authoritative decision.

rum *n.* alcoholic spirit distilled from sugar cane or molasses. •*adj. colloq.* strange, odd.

Rumania, Rumanian alternative spelling of ROMANIA, ROMANIAN.

rumba *n.* a ballroom dance of Cuban origin; music for this.

rumble *v.* **1** make a deep heavy continuous sound, like thunder. **2** utter in a deep voice. •*n.* **1** a rumbling sound. **2** *colloq.* a fight; an argument.

rumblings *n. pl.* early indications of some state of things or incipient change (*rumblings of discontent*).

rumbustious *adj. colloq.* boisterous, noisy, uproarious.

ruminant / **roo**-muh-nuhnt / *n.* an animal that chews the cud. •*adj.* **1** ruminating. **2** meditative.

ruminate / **roo**-muh-nayt / *v.* **1** chew the cud. **2** meditate, ponder. ☐ **rumination** *n.*

ruminative / **roo**-muh-nuh-tiv / *adj.* meditative, pondering.

rummage *v.* search by turning things over or disarranging them. •*n.* a search of this kind.

rummy *n.* a card game in which players try to form sets and sequences of cards.

rumour (also **rumor**) *n.* information spread by word of mouth but not certainly true. ☐ **be rumoured** be spread as a rumour.

rump *n.* **1** the buttocks; the corresponding part of a bird. **2** a cut of meat from an animal's hindquarters.

rumple *v.* make or become crumpled; make (something smooth) untidy.

rumpus *n. colloq.* an uproar; an angry dispute or brawl; a disturbance. ☐ **rumpus room** a room which does not have to be kept tidy or quiet, set aside for recreation in a house; esp. a children's playroom.

Rum Rebellion a rebellion by officers of the NSW Corps against Governor Bligh's attempts to curb their monopolistic trading activities (esp. in liquor): on 26 January 1808 the officers arrested Bligh and deposed him as Governor.

run *v.* (**ran**, **run**, **running**) **1** move with quick steps, never having both or all feet on the ground at once. **2** go or travel smoothly or swiftly; (of fish) appear in large numbers; go up river from the sea. **3** compete in a race, contest, or election (*ran for president*). **4** spread rapidly or beyond the intended limit (*the dye has run*). **5** flow or cause to flow, exude liquid (*the water runs into the barrel; run a bath for me; smoke makes my eyes run*). **6** function, be in action (*left the engine running*). **7** travel or convey from point to point (*the bus runs every hour; we'll run you home*). **8** extend (*a fence runs round the property*). **9** be current, operative, or valid (*the lease runs for 20 years*). **10** pass or cause to pass (into a specified condition) (*supplies are running low; run a temperature*). **11** cause to run, go, extend, or function. **12** manage, organise (*who runs the country?*). **13** own and use (a vehicle etc.). **14** (of a newspaper) print as an item. **15** *Aust.* provide pasture (for sheep, cattle, etc.); raise (livestock) (*runs a few thousand sheep on her property*). **16** *Aust.* round up (wild cattle, horses, etc.) (*spent a few weeks running brumbies*). **17** *Aust.* (in Aboriginal English) live, usu. in the bush, in the traditional way (*he was running in the bush*). **18** *Aust.* (in Aboriginal English) (of an idea, belief, ceremony, etc.) prevail (*the law runs right down to the Alice*). •*n.* **1** an act or spell or course of running. **2** a point scored in cricket or baseball. **3** a ladder in a stocking or knitted fabric. **4** a continuous stretch, sequence, or spell (*a run of* *bad luck*). **5** a general demand for goods etc. (*there has been a run on king prawns; a run on the dollar*). **6** a large number of fish, esp. going up river from the sea. **7** an average type or class of things (*the general run of customers*). **8** an enclosure where domestic animals can range. **9** *Aust.* **a** a tract (usu. extensive) of land used as pasture. **b** an extensive tract of land used for the raising of stock and containing the requisite improvements such as dwellings, yards, etc. **10** a bird's or other animal's regular track (*lyrebird's run*). **11** a track for some purpose (*a ski run*). **12** *Aust.* (in Aboriginal English) the traditional territory of an Aboriginal people. **13** *Aust.* **a** *Shearing* an uninterrupted period worked during a day; the period of employment as a shearer. **b** the period of any employment (*brickies wanted—long run*). **14** (foll. by *of*) permission to make unrestricted use of something (*he has the run of the house*). **15** (**the runs**) *colloq.* diarrhoea. ❑ **on the run 1** fleeing from pursuit. **2** hurrying about from place to place. **run across 1** happen to meet or find. **2** (foll. by *to*) make a brief journey or a flying visit (to a place). **run after 1** pursue at a run. **2** pursue, esp. sexually. **run away** leave quickly or secretly. **run away with 1** elope with (a person). **2** win a prize etc.) easily. **3** accept (an idea) too hastily. **run down 1** stop because not rewound. **2** reduce the numbers of. **3** knock down with a moving vehicle or ship. **4** discover after searching (*ran him down at last in Woolloomooloo*). **5** speak of in a slighting way. **run-down** *adj.* weak or exhausted; *n.* a detailed analysis. **run in** *colloq.* **1** arrest and take into custody. **2** run (a new engine) carefully into good working order. **3** *Aust.* pursue and confine (cattle or sheep). **run-in** *n. colloq.* a quarrel. **run into** collide with; happen to meet. **run off 1** flee. **2** produce (copies etc.) on a machine. **3** decide (a race etc.) after heats or a tie. **4** (cause to) flow away. **5** write or recite fluently. **run-of-the-mill** *adj.* ordinary, not special. **run out 1** (of time or a stock of something) become used up, (of a person) have used up one's stock. **2** put down the wicket of (a running batsman). **run over 1** knock down or crush with a vehicle. **2** study or repeat quickly. **run through** study or repeat quickly. **run to 1** have the money, resources, or ability for. **2** (of a person) have a tendency to (*runs to fat*). **run up 1** raise (a flag) on a mast. **2** allow (a bill) to mount. **3** make quickly by sewing (*ran up some curtains*). **run-up** *n.* the period leading to an event.

runabout *n.* a small car, boat, or aircraft.

run-around *n. colloq.* deceit or evasion. ❑ **give a person the run-around** put off or lead astray (a person) with evasions or deceits.

runaway *n.* **1** a fugitive. **2** a bolting animal; a vehicle out of control. • *adj.* **1** having run away or become out of control. **2** won easily (*a runaway victory*).

rune / roon / *n.* **1** any of the letters in an alphabet used by early Germanic peoples. **2** a similar mark used as a mystical or magical symbol. ❑ **runic** *adj.*

rung[1] *n.* one of the crosspieces of a ladder etc.
rung[2] *see* RING[2].

runnel *n.* **1** a brook. **2** a gutter.

runner *n.* **1** a person or animal that runs; one taking part in a race. **2 a** a messenger. **b** *Sport* a messenger who conveys the coach's instructions to players on the field. **3** a creeping stem that grows from the main stem and takes root. **4** a groove, rod, or roller for a thing to move on; each of the long strips on which a sledge etc. slides. **5** a long narrow strip of carpet, or of ornamental cloth for a table etc. **6** (in *pl.*) *Aust.* running shoes, sneakers. ❑ **runner bean** a climbing bean.

runner-up (*pl.* **runners-up**) a person or team finishing second in a competition.

running *see* RUN. • *adj.* **1** performed while running (*a running jump*). **2** following each other without interval (*for four days running*). **3** continuous (*a running battle; running commentary*). ❑ **in** (or **out of**) **the running** with a good chance (or with no) chance of winning. **make the running** set the pace. **running postman** a prostrate Australian plant with trifoliate leaves and vivid scarlet and gold pea-flowers.

runny *adj.* **1** semi-liquid. **2** tending to flow or to exude fluid.

runt *n.* an undersized person or animal (*the runt of the litter*).

runway *n.* a prepared surface on an airfield, on which aircraft take off and land.

rupee / roo-**pee** / *n.* the unit of money in India, Pakistan, Sri Lanka, and certain other countries.

rupiah / roo-**pee**-uh / *n.* the unit of money in Indonesia.

rupture *n.* **1** breaking; a breach; disagreement followed by parting in a relationship. **2** an abdominal hernia. • *v.* **1** burst or break (tissue etc.); become burst or broken. **2** affect with a hernia.

rural *adj.* in, of, or suggesting the country; pastoral or agricultural (as distinct from URBAN) (*rural seclusion; rural electorate; rural property; rural school*).

rusa / **roo**-suh / *n.* (in full **rusa deer**) a large deer of the Indonesian archipelago, introduced to Australia in the latter half of the 19th c. and now common in limited locations. Also called *Timor deer* and *Javan rusa*.

ruse / rooz / *n.* a deception or trick.

Rush, Geoffrey (1947–), Australian actor who won an Oscar for his performance in *Shine* (1996).

rush[1] *n.* a marsh plant with a slender pithy stem used for making mats, chair seats, baskets, etc.

rush[2] *v.* **1** go, come, or convey with great speed. **2** act hastily; force into hasty action. **3** attack with a sudden assault. **4** *Aust. hist.* occupy (a place) by a rush of goldminers. •*n.* **1** rushing; an instance of this. **2** a period of great activity. **3** a sudden great demand for goods etc. **4** a sudden migration of large numbers (esp. to a newly-discovered goldfield). **5** (**rushes**) *colloq.* the first prints of a cinema film before it is cut and edited. •*adj.* done with haste or with minimum delay (*a rush job*). ▫ **rush hour** the time(s) each day when traffic is busiest.

Rushdie, (Ahmed) Salman (1947–), Indian-born British novelist.

rusk *n.* a biscuit, esp. one for babies.

russet *adj.* soft reddish-brown. •*n.* russet colour.

Russia (official name **Russian Federation**) a country in northern Asia and eastern Europe.

Russian *adj.* of Russia (or more widely the former USSR) or its people or language. •*n.* **1** a native or inhabitant of Russia or the former USSR. **2** the language of Russia, the official language of the former USSR. ▫ **Russian roulette 1** an act of bravado in which a person holds to his or her head a revolver of which one (unknown) chamber contains a bullet, and pulls the trigger. **2** any potentially dangerous enterprise.

Russo- *comb. form* Russian; Russian and (*Russo-Japanese*).

rust *n.* **1** a reddish-brown or yellowish-brown coating formed on iron or other metal by the effect of moisture, and gradually corroding it. **2** reddish-brown. **3** a plant disease with rust-coloured spots; the fungus causing this. **4** an impaired state brought about by disuse (*his skills have gone to rust*). •*v.* **1** affect or be affected with rust. **2** lose quality or efficiency by lack of use. ▫ **rust belt** a declining industrial area.

rustbucket *n. colloq.* a motor vehicle greatly affected by rust or otherwise dilapidated.

rustic *adj.* **1** having the qualities ascribed to country people or country life, simple and unsophisticated. **2** made of rough timber or untrimmed branches (*a rustic seat*). **3** of rude or rough workmanship. •*n.* a country person, esp. a simple or unsophisticated one. ▫ **rusticity** / rus-tis-uh-tee / *n.*

rusticate *v.* **1** settle in the country and live a rural life. **2** make or become rustic. ▫ **rustication** *n.*

rustle *v.* **1** make a sound like that of paper being crumpled; cause to do this. **2** steal (horses or cattle). •*n.* a rustling sound. ▫ **rustle up** *colloq.* prepare or produce quickly (*rustle up a meal*). ▫ ▫ **rustler** *n.*

rustproof *adj.* not susceptible to corrosion by rust. •*v.* make rustproof.

rusty *adj.* (**rustier**, **rustiest**) **1** affected with rust. **2** rust-coloured. **3** stiff with age or disuse. **4** (of knowledge etc.) having lost quality or efficiency by lack of use (*my Latin is rusty*). ▫ **rustiness** *n.*

rut[1] *n.* **1** a deep track made by wheels in soft ground. **2** a dull tedious routine or way of life (*getting into a rut*).

rut[2] *n.* the periodic sexual excitement of a male deer, goat, etc. •*v.* (**rutted**, **rutting**) be affected with this.

ruthenium / roo-**thee**-nee-uhm / *n.* a metallic element (symbol Ru), used in certain alloys to increase hardness.

Rutherford, Sir Ernest, 1st Baron (1871–1937), British physicist, born in New Zealand, widely regarded as the founder of nuclear physics.

rutherfordium / ru-*th*uh-**faw**-dee-uhm / *n.* a very unstable chemical element made by high-energy atomic collisions (symbol Rf).

ruthless *adj.* having no pity or compassion. ▫ **ruthlessly** *adv.* **ruthlessness** *n.*

rutile / **roo**-tuyl / *n.* a mineral form of titanium dioxide.

rutted *adj.* marked with ruts.

rutty *adj.* full of ruts.

Rwanda / roo-**an**-duh, ruh-**wan**-duh / a republic in East Africa. ▫ **Rwandan** *adj.* & *n.*

rye *n.* **1** a cereal used for making flour or as food for cattle. **2** (in full **rye whisky**) a whisky made from rye.

ryebuck / **ruy**-buk / *adj.* chiefly *Aust. colloq.* good, excellent.

ryegrass *n.* forage grass or coarse lawn grass.

S

S[1] *abbr.* siemens. • *symbol* sulphur.

S[2] *abbr.* (also **S.**) **1** Saint. **2** South, Southern.

s. *abbr.* **1** second(s). **2** *hist.* shilling(s). (¶ Sense 2 originally short for the Latin *solidus*.)

-s' *comb. form* denoting the possessive case of plural nouns and sometimes of singular nouns ending in *s* (*the boys' shoes; Charles' book*).

's *abbr.* **1** is; has (*he's coming; she's got it*). **2** us (*let's go*).

-'s *comb. form* denoting the possessive case of singular nouns and of plural nouns not ending in *s* (*Tom's book; the book's cover; children's shoes*).

SA *abbr.* **1** South Australia. **2** South Australian.

Sabah / **sah**-bah / a State of Malaysia, comprising North Borneo and some offshore islands.

sabbath *n.* **1** a religious day of rest kept by Christians on Sunday, Jews on Saturday, and Muslims on Friday. **2** (in full **witches' sabbath**) a supposed general midnight meeting of witches with the Devil.

sabbatical / suh-**bat**-i-kuhl / *adj.* (of leave) granted at intervals to a university teacher for study or travel, usu. every seventh year. • *n.* a period of sabbatical leave.

Sabin / **say**-buhn /, Albert Bruce (1906–93), Russian-born American biologist who developed an oral vaccine against poliomyelitis.

sable *n.* a small weasel-like animal of Arctic and adjacent regions, valued for its dark brown fur. • *adj.* black; gloomy.

sabot / **sab**-oh / *n.* a shoe hollowed out from one piece of wood, or with a wooden sole.

sabotage / **sab**-uh-tah*zh* / *n.* deliberate damage to machinery, materials, etc. in order to prevent work or plans going ahead. • *v.* commit sabotage on; destroy or spoil (*sabotaged my plans*).

saboteur / sab-uh-**ter** / *n.* a person who commits sabotage.

sabre / **say**-buh / *n.* **1** a cavalry sword with a curved blade. **2** a light fencing sword with a tapering blade. ☐ **sabre-rattling** a display or threat of force. **sabre-toothed** designating any of various extinct mammals having long, sabre-shaped upper canine teeth.

sac *n.* a bag-like part in an animal or plant.

saccharin / **sak**-uh-ruhn / *n.* a very sweet substance used as a substitute for sugar.

saccharine / **sak**-uh-reen / *adj.* intensely and unpleasantly sweet or sentimental (*a novel of saccharine romance*).

sacerdotal / sak-uh-**doh**-tuhl, sas- / *adj.* of priests or priestly office.

sachet / **sash**-ay / *n.* **1** a small bag filled with a sweet-smelling substance for laying among clothes etc. **2** a sealed plastic or paper pack containing a single portion of a substance (e.g. shampoo).

sack[1] *n.* **1** a large bag of strong coarse fabric; this with its contents. **2** (**the sack**) *colloq.* dismissal from one's employment or position (*got the sack*). **3** (**the sack**) *colloq.* bed. • *v.* **1** put into a sack or sacks. **2** *colloq.* dismiss from a job. ☐ **hit the sack** go to bed. ☐☐ **sackful** *n.* (*pl.* **sackfuls**).

sack[2] *v.* plunder (a captured town etc.) in a violent destructive way. • *n.* the act or process of sacking a place.

sackbut *n.* an early form of trombone.

sackcloth *n.* **1** coarse fabric for making sacks. **2** clothing for penance or mourning (*sackcloth and ashes*). (¶ From the ancient custom of wearing sackcloth and sprinkling ashes on one's head in penitence or mourning.)

sacking *n.* material for making sacks; sackcloth.

sacral / **say**-kruhl / *adj.* **1** of the sacrum. **2** of or for sacred rites.

sacrament *n.* **1** a Christian ceremony which is an outward and visible sign of God's gift of an inward and spiritual grace, namely the seven rites of baptism, confirmation, the Eucharist, penance (confession and absolution), extreme unction, ordination (to the priesthood), and matrimony, as practised by the Catholic and Orthodox Churches, but restricted by most Protestants to baptism and the Eucharist. **2** (also **the Blessed Sacrament**) the Eucharist; the consecrated Host. ☐ **sacramental** *adj.*

sacramental *n.* an observance analogous to but not reckoned among the sacraments, e.g. the use of holy water or the sign of the cross.

sacred *adj.* **1** associated with or dedicated to a god; regarded with reverence because of this. **2** dedicated to some person or purpose (*sacred to the memory of those who fell in battle*). **3** connected with religion, not secular (*sacred music*). **4** sacrosanct. ☐ **sacred cow** an idea or institution which its supporters will not allow to be criticised. (¶ The phrase refers to Hindu respect for the cow as a sacred animal.) **sacred site** *Aust.* a place venerated by Aborigines because of its spiritual significance to them.

Sacred College the cardinals of the Catholic Church.

Sacred Heart *n. Catholic Church* **1** the heart of Christ as an object of devotion. **2** an image representing this.

sacrifice *n.* **1** the slaughter of a person or an animal or the presenting of a gift to win the favour of a god. **2 a** Christ's offering of himself in the Crucifixion for the redemption of the human species. **b** the Mass as a re-presentation of Christ's sacrifice on the Cross. **3** the giving up of a valued thing for the sake of another that is more worthy. **4** the thing offered or given up. •*v.* **1** offer or give up as a sacrifice. **2** give up (a thing) in order to achieve something else. □ **sacrificial** / sak-ruh-**fish**-uhl / *adj.*

sacrilege / **sak**-ruh-lij / *n.* disrespect or damage to something regarded as sacred. □ **sacrilegious** / sak-ruh-**lij**-uhs / *adj.*

sacristan / **sak**-ruh-stuhn / *n.* the person in charge of the contents of a church, esp. the sacred vessels etc.

sacristy / **sak**-ruh-stee / *n.* the place in a church where the vestments, sacred vessels, etc., are kept and the celebrant can prepare for a service.

sacrosanct / **sak**-roh-sangkt / *adj.* sacred or respected and therefore secure from violation or damage.

sacrum / **say**-kruhm / *n.* (*pl.* **sacra** or **sacrums**) the triangular bone that forms the back of the pelvis.

sad *adj.* (**sadder**, **saddest**) **1** showing or causing sorrow; unhappy. **2** regrettable (*a sad miscalculation*). **3** shameful, deplorable (*is in a sad state*). □ **sadly** *adv.* **sadness** *n.*

sadden *v.* make sad.

saddle *n.* **1** a seat for a rider on a horse, bicycle, etc. **2** a saddle-shaped thing; a ridge of high land between two peaks. **3** a joint of meat consisting of the two loins. •*v.* **1** put a saddle on (an animal). **2** burden (a person) with a task. □ **saddling paddock** (or **enclosure**) *Aust.* an enclosure in which horses are saddled before a race.

saddleback *n.* **1** the roof of a tower with two opposite gables. **2** a hill with a concave upper outline.

saddlebag *n.* **1** each of a pair of bags laid across the back of a horse etc. **2** a bag attached to a bicycle saddle etc.

saddler *n.* one who makes or sells saddles and harnesses.

saddlery *n.* a saddler's goods or business.

Sade / sahd /, Donatien Alphonse François, Comte de (known as the Marquis de Sade) (1740–1814), French writer. The word *sadism* owes its origin to his name, referring to the cruel sexual practices which he described in his writings.

sadhu / **sah**-doo / *n.* (in India) a holy man, sage, or ascetic.

sadism / **say**-diz-uhm, **sad**-iz- / *n.* **1** the condition or state of deriving (esp. sexual) pleasure from inflicting pain, suffering, humiliation, etc. **2** *colloq.* enjoyment of cruelty to others. □ **sadist** *n.* **sadistic** / suh-**dis**-tik / *adj.* **sadistically** *adv.*

sadomasochism *n.* sadism and masochism in one person. □ **sadomasochist** *n.* **sadomasochistic** *adj.*

s.a.e. *abbr.* stamped (self-)addressed envelope.

safari / suh-**fah**-ree / *n.* (*pl.* **safaris**) an expedition, esp. in Africa, to observe or hunt wild animals (*go on safari*). □ **safari jacket** a belted jacket in linen or similar fabric.

safe *adj.* **1** free from risk or danger, not dangerous. **2** providing security or protection. **3** reliable, certain (*missed a safe catch*). **4** cautious, unenterprising (*a safe performance of the piano concerto*). •*adv.* safely (*play safe*). •*n.* a strong lockable cabinet etc. for valuables. □ **on the safe side** allowing a margin of security against risks. **safe conduct** the right to pass through a district without risk of arrest or harm (e.g. in time of war); a document guaranteeing this. **safe period** (in birth control) the time in a woman's menstrual cycle when sexual intercourse is least likely to result in conception. **safe sex** sexual activity in which precautions (esp. the use of a condom) are taken against sexually transmitted diseases, esp. Aids (cf. UNSAFE SEX). □□ **safely** *adv.* **safeness** *n.*

safeguard *n.* a means of protection. •*v.* protect.

safety *n.* being safe, freedom from risk or danger. □ **safety belt** a seat belt; a belt or strap worn to prevent injury. **safety catch** a device that prevents a mechanism from being operated accidentally or dangerously; a locking device on a gun trigger. **safety curtain** a fireproof curtain that can be lowered to cut off a theatre stage from the auditorium. **safety fuse 1** a protective fuse (*see* FUSE[1]). **2** a fuse containing a slow-burning composition for firing detonators from a distance. **safety match** a match that will light only on a special surface. **safety net 1** a net placed to catch an acrobat etc. in case of a fall. **2 a** a safeguard against possible hardship or adversity. **b** *Aust.* welfare measures etc. which protect the disadvantaged. **safety pin** a brooch-like pin with a guard covering the point. **safety ramp** a road for a vehicle to turn into if unable to negotiate a bend, a descent, etc. **safety razor** a razor with a guard to prevent the blade from cutting the skin. **safety valve 1** a valve that opens automatically to relieve excessive pressure in a steam boiler. **2** a means of releasing anger, excitement, etc. harmlessly.

Safety House *adj.* of or pertaining to a scheme which provides that certain houses occupied by adults can be entered by children who are being sexually or otherwise harassed in the street (*this is a Safety House zone*). •*n.* a house so designated.

safflower *n.* a thistle-like European plant yielding a red dye and an oil.

saffron *n.* **1** the orange-coloured stigmas of a kind of crocus, used for colouring and flavouring food. **2** the colour of these. □ **saffron thistle** an introduced Mediterranean annual, now naturalised, and proclaimed a noxious weed, in all Australian States.

sag v. (**sagged**, **sagging**) **1** sink or curve down in the middle under weight or pressure. **2** (of a garment) hang loosely and unevenly; (of a part of the body) droop. **3** fall in price. • n. sagging.

saga / **sah**-guh / n. **1** a long heroic story, esp. medieval Icelandic or Norwegian. **2** a series of connected novels concerning a family's history etc. **3** a long involved story.

sagacious / suh-**gay**-shuhs / adj. showing insight or wisdom. ☐ **sagaciously** adv. **sagacity** / suh-**gas**-uh-tee / n.

sage[1] n. a herb with fragrant greyish-green leaves used to flavour food.

sage[2] adj. profoundly wise; having wisdom gained from experience. • n. (often *ironic*) a profoundly wise man. ☐ **sagely** adv.

Sagittarius / saj-uh-**tair**-ree-uhs / n. the ninth sign of the zodiac, the Archer. ☐ **Sagittarian** adj. & n.

sago n. a starchy food in the form of hard white grains, used in puddings, obtained from the pith of a palm tree (the **sago palm**).

Sahara a great desert of North Africa extending from the Atlantic to the Red Sea.

sahib / **sah**-ib, sahb / n. a former title of address to European men in India.

said *see* SAY.

sail n. **1** a piece of fabric spread on rigging to catch the wind and drive a ship or boat along. **2** a journey by ship or boat (*Haifa is three days' sail from Naples*). **3** something resembling a sail in function (*the sails of a windmill*). • v. **1** travel on water by use of sails or engine power. **2** start on a voyage (*we sail next week*). **3** travel on or over (water) in a ship or boat (*sailed the seas*). **4** control the navigation of (a ship); set (a toy boat) afloat. **5** move swiftly and smoothly; walk in a stately manner. **6** (usu. foll. by *through*) progress or succeed easily (*sailed through the exams*). ☐ **sail close to the wind 1** sail as nearly against the wind as possible. **2** come close to indecency or dishonesty. **sail into** *colloq.* attack physically or verbally.

sailboard n. a board with a mast and sail, used in windsurfing. ☐ **sailboarder** n. **sailboarding** n.

sailcloth n. **1** canvas for sails. **2** a strong canvas-like dress material.

sailor n. **1** a person who works as a member of a ship's crew; a member of a country's navy, esp. one below the rank of officer. **2** a traveller considered as liable or not liable to seasickness (*I'm not a good sailor*).

sailplane n. a glider designed for soaring.

saint n. **1** a canonised person, i.e. one officially declared (in the Catholic and Orthodox Churches) to be in heaven and to be worthy of veneration. **2** (**Saint** or **St**, *pl.* **Saints**, **Sts** or **SS**) the title(s) of such a person or persons. **3** a very good, patient, or unselfish person. ☐ **sainthood** n. **saintlike** adj.

St Andrew's Cross spider n. an Australian spider (the female having an abdomen banded in gold and red) which aligns its legs in pairs along the St Andrew's cross-shaped (×) centrepiece of its web.

St Bernard (in full **St Bernard dog**) n. a very large dog of a breed originally kept by monks in the Alps to rescue travellers.

St John Ambulance an organisation providing first aid, nursing, ambulance, and welfare services.

St Kitts and Nevis / **nee**-vis / a State consisting of two adjoining islands in the West Indies.

St Lucia / **loo**-shuh / an island State of the West Indies.

saintly adj. (**saintlier**, **saintliest**) like a saint, very virtuous. ☐ **saintliness** n.

St Peter's Basilica the great metropolitan church of the See of Rome in the Vatican City, the largest church in Christendom, with a dome designed by Michelangelo, and containing the tomb of the Apostle St Peter.

St Petersburg (formerly **Leningrad**) a major city and port in Russia.

Saint-Saëns / san-**sons** /, (Charles) Camille (1835–1921), French composer.

St Vincent an island State in the West Indies.

St Vincent de Paul Society an international Catholic lay charitable organisation for helping the poor and needy, named after the Saint (1581–1660) and established in Australia in 1854.

St Vitus's dance n. a disease causing the limbs to twitch uncontrollably.

sake[1] n. ☐ **for Christ's** (or **God's** or **goodness'** or **Heaven's** or **Pete's** etc.) **sake** an expression of impatience, entreaty, anger, etc. **for the sake of** (or **for one's sake**) out of consideration for; in the interest of; because of; in order to please, honour, get, or keep (*for my own sake as well as yours; for the sake of uniformity*).

sake[2] / **sah**-kee, -kay / n. a Japanese alcoholic drink made from rice.

Sakti / **shuk**-tee / n. (also **sakti**, **Shakti**) *Hinduism* **1** the female principle, esp. when personified as the wife of a god. **2** the goddess as supreme deity (Devi).

salaam / suh-**lahm** / n. **1** an Oriental salutation meaning 'Peace'. **2** a Muslim greeting consisting of a low bow with the right palm on the forehead. **3** (**salaams**) respectful compliments. • v. make a salaam to.

salacious / suh-**lay**-shuhs / adj. (of writings, pictures, talk, etc.) tending to cause sexual desire; indecently erotic. ☐ **salaciously** adv. **salaciousness** n. **salacity** / suh-**las**-uh-tee / n.

salad n. a cold dish consisting of one or more vegetables (usu. raw), often with a dressing. ☐ **salad days** a period of youth and inexperience. **salad dressing** a mixture of oil and vinegar or lemon juice with flavourings, poured over salads.

salamander / **sal**-uh-man-duh / n. **1** a lizard-like animal related to the newt. **2** (in mythology) a lizard-like animal living in fire.

salami / suh-**lah**-mee / n. a strongly flavoured Italian sausage.

sal ammoniac n. ammonium chloride, a white crystalline salt.

salaried adj. receiving a salary.

salary n. a fixed payment made by an employer at regular intervals to a person doing other than manual or mechanical work. ☐ **salary cap** Football the maximum amount that the administration of some football codes allows a club to spend on recruiting players and paying their salaries.

sale n. **1** selling; being sold. **2** an instance of this; the amount sold (*made a sale; our sales were enormous*). **3** an event at which goods are sold. **4** disposal of a shop's stock at reduced prices. ☐ **sales talk** (*or* **pitch**) persuasive talk designed to make people buy goods or accept an idea. **sales tax** a tax levied on the retail price of goods.

saleable adj. fit for sale; likely to find a purchaser. ☐ **saleability** n.

Salesian / suh-**lee**-zhuhn / n. a member of a Catholic religious order engaged in teaching, named after St Francis de Sales (1567–1622), French bishop of Geneva. • adj. of this order.

salesman n. a man employed to sell goods.

salesmanship n. skill in selling.

salesperson n. a salesman or saleswoman.

saleswoman n. a woman employed to sell goods.

saleyard n. Aust. **1** an enclosure in which livestock is sold. **2** (also **saleyards**) a set of such enclosures.

salicylic acid / sal-uh-**sil**-ik / n. a chemical used as a fungicide and in aspirin and dyes.

salient / **say**-lee-uhnt / adj. prominent; most noticeable (*the salient features of the plan*). • n. a projecting part, esp. of a battle-line.

salination / sal-uh-**nay**-shuhn / n. (also **salinisation**) an increase in the salt content of soil (caused by bad land management, poor irrigation methods, etc.) resulting in progressive infertility (*see* SCALDED EARTH).

saline / **say**-luyn / adj. **1** containing salt or salts. **2** tasting of salt. **3** of chemical salts. **4** of the nature of a salt. • n. a saline solution, esp. a medicine. ☐ **salinity** / suh-**lin**-uh-tee / n.

saliva / suh-**luy**-vuh / n. the colourless liquid discharged into the mouth by various glands, assisting in chewing and digestion.

salivary / suh-**luy**-vuh-ree / adj. of or producing saliva (*salivary glands*).

salivate / **sal**-uh-vayt / v. produce saliva, esp. in excess or in greedy anticipation. ☐ **salivation** n.

Salk, Jonas Edward (1914–95), American microbiologist, who developed the first effective vaccine against poliomyelitis.

sallee alternative spelling of SALLY[2].

sallow[1] adj. (of a person's skin or complexion) yellowish. ☐ **sallowness** n.

sallow[2] n. a willow tree, esp. of a low-growing or shrubby kind.

sally[1] n. **1** a sudden rush forward in attack; a sortie. **2** an excursion. **3** a lively or witty remark. • v. (**sallied**, **sallying**) (usu. foll. by *out* or *forth*) set out on a walk, journey etc.; make a military sally.

sally[2] n. (also **sallee**) any of several eucalypts and wattles resembling the willow.

salmagundi / sal-muh-**gun**-dee / n. (*pl.* **salmagundis**) **1** a dish of chopped meat, anchovies, eggs, onions, etc., and seasoning. **2** a general mixture; a miscellaneous collection of articles, subjects, qualities, etc.

salmon n. **1** (*pl.* **salmon** *or* **salmons**) a large fish of the Northern hemisphere with pinkish flesh, valued for food and sport and now introduced into Australia. **2** any of several marine and freshwater food fish abundant in southern Australian waters. **3** salmon-pink colour. ☐ **salmon gum** a WA eucalypt having a silky-smooth, salmon-pink trunk. **salmon-pink** orange-pink in colour like the flesh of salmon. **salmon trout 1** a large silver-coloured trout resembling a salmon. **2** the young of some Australian salmon, having brown trout-like markings on the upper surface.

salmonella n. (*pl.* **salmonellae**) food poisoning caused by bacteria; the bacterium itself.

Salome / suh-**loh**-mee / the daughter of Herod Antipas (son of Herod the Great) and Herodias, who asked for John the Baptist to be beheaded.

salon / **sal**-on / n. **1** a room or establishment where a hairdresser, beautician, etc. works. **2** *hist*. an assembly of eminent people in the home of a lady of fashion.

Salonica / suh-**lon**-i-kuh / *see* THESSALONIKI.

saloon n. **1** a public room for a specified purpose (*billiard saloon*). **2** a public room on a ship. **3** a saloon car. ☐ **saloon bar** a more comfortable bar in a hotel. **saloon car** a car with a closed body and no partition behind the driver.

salsa n. **1** dance music of Cuban origin with jazz and rock elements. **2** (esp. in Latin American cookery) a spicy sauce served with meat or as a dip.

salsify / **sal**-suh-fuy / n. a plant with a long fleshy root cooked as a vegetable and thought to taste of oyster.

SALT *abbr.* Strategic Arms Limitations Talks (*or* Treaty), aimed at the reduction of nuclear armaments.

salt / sawlt, solt / n. **1** sodium chloride obtained from mines or by evaporation of sea water, used to flavour and preserve food. **2** a chemical compound of a metal and an acid. **3** (**salts**) a substance resembling salt in form, esp. a laxative. **4** piquancy, wit. • adj. tasting of salt; impregnated with or preserved in salt. • v. **1** season with salt. **2**

preserve in salt. **3** put aside for the future (*salt it away*). ❑ **salt lick** a place where animals go to lick rock or earth impregnated with salt. **salt pan 1** a dried-up salt lake. **2** a vessel or hollow by the sea where salt is obtained from sea water by evaporation. **take with a grain** (*or* **pinch**) **of salt** not believe wholly. **worth one's salt** competent; deserving one's position.

saltbush *n.* any of various shrubs or herbs typically dominating tracts of saline and alkaline land in drier Australia, e.g. *berry saltbush, bladder saltbush, old man saltbush*.

saltie *n. Aust. colloq.* a saltwater crocodile.

saltimbocca / sal-**tuhm**-**bok**-uh / *n.* a traditional Italian dish consisting of rolled pieces of veal and ham cooked with sage and other herbs and wine.

saltire / **sal**-tuyuh / *n.* an X-shaped cross dividing a shield into four compartments.

saltpetre / solt-**pee**-tuh / *n.* a salty white powder (potassium nitrate) used in gunpowder, medicines, and preserving meat.

saltwater *adj.* of or living in the sea. ❑ **saltwater crocodile** a large crocodile of coastal and near-coastal north and north-eastern Australia, inhabiting estuarine, sea, and fresh water. **saltwater people** an Aboriginal people who live by the sea (opp. FRESHWATER PEOPLE).

salty *adj.* (**saltier, saltiest**) **1** containing or tasting of salt. **2** (of wit etc.) piquant. ❑ **saltiness** *n.*

salubrious / suh-**loo**-bree-uhs / *adj.* health-giving, healthy. ❑ **salubrity** *n.*

salutary / **sal**-yoo-tuh-ree, -tree / *adj.* producing a beneficial effect (*learned a salutary lesson from that experience*).

salutation / sal-yoo-**tay**-shuhn / *n.* a word or gesture of greeting; an expression of respect.

salute *n.* **1** a formal military movement of the body, or a signal by guns or flags, as a sign of respect. **2** a gesture of respect, greeting, or polite recognition. **3** = GREAT AUSTRALIAN SALUTE. • *v.* **1** perform a salute; greet with this. **2** express respect or admiration for.

Salvador *see* EL SALVADOR. ❑ **Salvadorean** / sal-vuh-**daw**-ree-uhn / *adj. & n.*

salvage *n.* **1** rescue of a wrecked or damaged ship or its cargo; rescue of property from fire or other disaster. **2** the goods or property saved. **3** the saving and use of waste paper, scrap metal, etc. **4** the items saved. • *v.* **1** save from a wreck etc. **2** retrieve or preserve (something favourable) in adverse circumstances (*she salvaged her pride*). ❑ **salvageable** *adj.*

salvation *n.* **1** saving of the soul from sin; the state of being saved. **2** preservation from loss or calamity; a person or thing that preserves from these (*the loan was our salvation*). ❑ **salvation Jane** (chiefly in SA) = PATERSON'S CURSE.

Salvation Army a worldwide Christian organisation founded on military lines to do charitable work and spread its form of Christianity.

salve[1] *n.* **1** a soothing ointment. **2** something that soothes an uneasy conscience or wounded feelings. • *v.* soothe (conscience etc.).

salve[2] *v.* save from a wreck or fire. ❑ **salvable** *adj.*

salver *n.* a tray (usu. of metal) on which letters, cards, or refreshments are placed.

Salve Regina / sal-vay ruh-**jee**-nuh / *n.* a hymn said or sung after compline and after the Divine Office from Trinity Sunday to Advent, the opening words meaning 'hail (holy) queen'.

Salvo *n.* (*pl.* **Salvoes** *or* **Salvos**) *Aust.* **1** a member of the Salvation Army. **2** (in *pl.*) the Salvation Army.

salvo[1] *n.* (*pl.* **salvoes** *or* **salvos**) **1** the firing of a number of guns simultaneously, esp. as a salute. **2** a round of applause.

salvo[2] *n.* (*pl.* **salvos**) a saving clause; a quibble or reservation (*she gave her consent, with the salvo that…*).

sal volatile / sal vuh-**lat**-uh-lee / *n.* a strong-smelling solution of ammonium carbonate used as a remedy for faintness. (¶ Latin)

Salyut / **sal**-yuut / any of a series of manned space stations launched by the former USSR.

Samaritan *n.* (in full **good Samaritan**) someone who readily gives help to a person in distress. (¶ Named after the parable of the Good Samaritan in the Bible.)

samarium / suh-**mair**-ree-uhm / *n.* a metallic element of the lanthanide series (symbol Sm).

samba *n.* a ballroom dance of Brazilian origin; music for this.

sambal / **sam**-bahl / *n.* in Malaysian and Indonesian cuisines, a condiment used as an accompaniment to rice and curry etc. and in cooking. ❑ **sambal bajak** a paste made from chillies and various spices. **sambal rujak** a paste made from chillies, tamarind, shrimp paste, etc. **sambal ulek** (also **sambal oelek**) a paste made from chillies and salt etc.

sambo *n. Aust. colloq.* a sandwich.

sambol / **sam**-bawl / *n.* (in Sri Lankan, South Indian, etc. cuisines) any of a variety of relishes eaten with rice and curry, e.g. grated coconut mixed with chilli powder, ground Maldive fish, chopped onion, lime juice, and salt.

same *adj.* **1** being of one kind, not changed or changing or different. **2** previously mentioned. **3** (**the same**) the same person or thing (*would do the same again*). **4** (**the same**) in the same manner (*we still feel the same about it*). • *pron. & adj. colloq.* = THE SAME (senses 3 and 4 above) (*same for me, please*). ❑ **all the same** immaterial; of no consequence (*it's all the same to me*). **all** (*or* **just**) **the same** nevertheless.

sameness *n.* being the same; lack of variety.

Samoa / suh-**moh**-uh / 1 a group of islands in Polynesia, divided between American Samoa and the state of Samoa. 2 a country consisting of the western islands of Samoa. ☐ **Samoan** adj. & n.

samosa / suh-**moh**-suh / n. a fried triangular pastry containing spiced vegetables or meat.

samovar / **sam**-uh-vah / n. a metal urn with an interior heating-tube to keep water at boiling point for making tea. (¶ Russian)

samoyed / **sam**-oid / n. a dog of a white Arctic breed.

sampan n. a small flat-bottomed boat used in China etc.

samphire / **sam**-fuyuh / n. a plant with fragrant fleshy edible leaves, growing on cliffs.

sample n. a small separated part showing the quality of the whole; a specimen. • v. test by taking a sample or getting an experience of. ☐ **sample bag** = SHOW BAG (see SHOW).

sampler n. a thing that takes samples. 2 a piece of embroidery worked in various stitches to display skill in needlework. 3 a compact disc providing samples of the output of an orchestra, a group, a recording company, etc.

sampling n. 1 the taking of a sample or samples. 2 in electronic music, the technique or process of taking a piece of digitally encoded sound and re-using it, often in a modified form, as part of a composition or recording.

samsara / sam-**sah**-ruh / n. *Hinduism* the endless cycle of death and rebirth to which life in the material world is bound.

Samson (probably 11th century BC) an Israelite leader famous for his strength, betrayed by Delilah to the Philistines. • n. a person of great strength. ☐ **Samson fish** any of several Australian marine fish noted for their strength, esp. in game-fishing contexts.

samurai / **sam**-uh-ruy / n. (pl. **samurai**) 1 a Japanese army officer. 2 a member of the former military caste in Japan.

Sana'a / sah-**nah** / the capital of the Yemen Arab Republic.

sanatorium n. (pl. **sanatoriums** or **sanatoria**) an establishment for treating chronic diseases (e.g. tuberculosis) or convalescents.

sanctify v. (**sanctified**, **sanctifying**) 1 consecrate; treat as holy. 2 free (a person) from sin. 3 justify; sanction (*a custom sanctified by tradition*). ☐ **sanctification** n.

sanctimonious / sangk-tuh-**moh**-nee-uhs / adj. too righteous or pious (*a sanctimonious hypocrite*). ☐ **sanctimoniously** adv. **sanctimoniousness** n. **sanctimony** n.

sanction n. 1 permission or approval. 2 (esp. in pl.) action taken by a country to penalise and coerce a country or organisation that has violated a law or code of practice or basic human rights. • v. 1 give sanction or approval to; authorise. 2 attach a penalty or reward to (a law).

sanctity n. sacredness, holiness.

sanctuary n. 1 a sacred place. 2 the holiest part of a temple; the part of a chancel containing the altar. 3 an area where birds or wild animals are protected. 4 refuge; a place of refuge (*seek sanctuary*).

sanctum n. 1 a holy place. 2 a person's private room.

Sanctus n. the hymn beginning 'Sanctus, sanctus, sanctus' ('Holy, holy, holy') which concludes the Preface of the Mass; the music for this.

Sand, George (pseudonym of Amandine-Aurore Lucille Dupin, Baronne Dudevant) (1804–76), French novelist, advocate of women's rights.

sand n. 1 very fine loose fragments resulting from the wearing down of rock, found in deserts, seashores, river beds, etc. 2 (**sands**) grains of sand; an expanse of sand; a sandbank. 3 light brown colour like that of sand. • v. 1 smooth or polish with sand or sandpaper. 2 sprinkle or cover with sand. ☐ **sand crab** (also **blue swimmer**, **sandie**) an edible blue crab widely distributed in sheltered estuaries and inlets of Australia. **sand dune** (*or* **hill**) loose sand formed into a mound by wind. **sand goanna** Aust. = BUNGARRA. **sand mullet** Aust. = TALLEGALANE. **sand whiting** a marine fish frequenting estuary sand flats etc. of eastern Australia, highly prized as a food fish.

sandal n. a light shoe with straps over the foot.

sandalled adj. wearing sandals.

sandal tree n. any of several trees yielding sandalwood.

sandalwood n. the scented wood of a sandal tree; a perfume made from this.

sandbag n. a bag filled with sand, used to protect a wall or building (e.g. in war, or as a defence against rising flood-water). • v. (**sandbagged**, **sandbagging**) 1 protect with sandbags. 2 hit as if with a sandbag.

sandbank n. (also **sandbar**) a deposit of sand forming a shallow area in the sea or a river.

sandblast v. roughen, clean, or treat with a jet of sand driven by compressed air or steam. • n. this jet. ☐ **sandblaster** n.

sander n. a power tool for sanding things.

sanderling n. a small migrant sandpiper (from Siberia) of Australian sandy coastal regions.

sandfly n. any of various small blood-sucking flies found among and near sand, and often transmitting diseases to humans.

Sandgroper n. Aust. colloq. a Western Australian.

sandie n. Aust. colloq. = SAND CRAB (see SAND).

Sandinista / san-duh-**nees**-tuh / n. a member of a revolutionary guerrilla organisation in Nicaragua, in power 1979–90. (¶ Named after A.C. Sandino (1893–1934), Nicaraguan nationalist leader.)

sandman n. the personification of tiredness causing children's eyes to smart towards bedtime.

sandpaper n. paper with a coating of sand or other abrasive substance, used for smoothing or

sandpiper

polishing surfaces. •*v.* smooth or polish with sandpaper. ☐ **sandpaper fig** any of several Australian fig trees with extremely harsh, rough-textured leaves.

sandpiper *n.* any of many wading birds, generally migrants from the Northern hemisphere, frequenting wet sandy areas in Australia.

sandpit *n.* a shallow pit containing sand for children to play in.

sandshoe *n.* a light canvas shoe with a rubber sole used primarily for sport (formerly for wearing on the sand).

sandstone *n.* rock formed of compressed sand.

sandstorm *n.* a storm with clouds of sand raised by the wind.

sandwich *n.* two or more slices of bread with a filling between. •*v.* insert (a thing) between two others. ☐ **be the meat in the sandwich** be the innocent victim in the middle of a conflict between two opposing parties, neither of whom the victim wishes to side with or against.

sandy *adj.* (**sandier**, **sandiest**) **1** like sand; covered with sand. **2** (of hair) reddish-yellow. ☐ **sandy blight** (also **sand blight**) *Aust.* acute conjunctivitis, usu. contagious, characterised by granular follicles on the inner surface of the eyelids, and common in arid Australia (*see* TRACHOMA). ☐☐ **sandiness** *n.*

sane *adj.* **1** having a sound mind; not mad. **2** showing good judgment; sensible and practical. ☐ **sanely** *adv.* **saneness** *n.*

sang *see* SING.

sanger / **sang**-uh / *n.* (also **sango**) *Aust. colloq.* a sandwich.

sangfroid / sahng-**frwah** / *n.* calmness in danger or difficulty. (¶ French, = cold blood.)

sangha / **sung**-guh / *n.* the Buddhist monastic order, including monks, nuns, and novices.

sanguinary / **sang**-gwuh-nuh-ree / *adj.* **1** full of bloodshed. **2** bloodthirsty.

sanguine / **sang**-gwuhn / *adj.* **1** hopeful, optimistic (*they are not very sanguine about their chances of winning*). **2** (of the complexion) ruddy.

sanitary / **san**-uh-tuh-ree, -tree / *adj.* **1** of hygiene; hygienic. **2** of sanitation. ☐ **sanitary pad** (*or* **napkin**) an absorbent pad worn during menstruation.

sanitation *n.* arrangements to protect public health, esp. by drainage and the efficient disposal of sewage.

sanitise *v.* (also **-ize**) **1** make hygienic. **2** *colloq.* censor (information) to make it more acceptable. ☐ **sanitisation** *n.*

sanity *n.* the state or condition of being sane.

San José / hoh-**zay** / the capital of Costa Rica.

San Juan / wahn / the capital of Puerto Rico.

sank *see* SINK.

San Marino / muh-**ree**-noh / a small independent republic in NE Italy.

San Salvador the capital of El Salvador.

sanserif / san-**se**-rif / *n.* (also **sans-serif**) a form of typeface without serifs.

Sanskrit *n.* the ancient language of the Hindus in India, one of the oldest known Indo-European languages.

Santa Claus a person said to bring children presents on Christmas Eve. (¶ From the Dutch name *Sante Klaas* = St Nicholas.)

Santiago / san-tee-**ah**-goh / the capital of Chile.

Santo Domingo / duh-**ming**-goh / the capital of the Dominican Republic.

São Tomé / sow to-**may** / the capital of **São Tomé and Principe** / **prin**-chi-pay /, a republic consisting of two islands off the west coast of Africa.

sap *n.* **1** the liquid that circulates in plants, carrying food to all parts. **2** vigour, vitality. **3** *colloq.* a weak or foolish person. **4** a trench or tunnel made to get closer to an enemy. •*v.* (**sapped**, **sapping**) **1** exhaust (strength) gradually. **2** drain of sap. **3** dig saps; undermine.

sapient / **say**-pee-uhnt / *adj. literary* wise; pretending to be wise. ☐ **sapience** *n.*

sapling *n.* a young tree.

sapper *n.* **1** a soldier (esp. a private) of the Royal Australian Engineers. **2** a person who digs saps.

Sapphic / **saf**-ik / *adj.* **1** of Sappho or her poetry. **2** lesbian.

sapphire *n.* **1** a transparent blue precious stone. **2** its colour. •*adj.* bright blue.

Sappho / **saf**-oh / (early 7th century BC) Greek lyric poet from the island of Lesbos. Many of her poems express her love for young girls in her circle, and have given rise to her association with female homosexuality, from which the words *lesbian* and *Sapphic* derive.

sappy *adj.* **1** full of sap. **2** young and vigorous. **3** *colloq.* silly (*sappy sort of thing to do*).

saprophyte / **sap**-ruh-fuyt / *n.* a fungus or similar plant living on dead or decayed organic matter. ☐ **saprophytic** / sap-ruh-**fit**-ik / *adj.*

saraband / **sa**-ruh-band / *n.* a slow Spanish dance; the music for this.

Saracen / **sa**-ruh-suhn / *n.* an Arab or Muslim of the time of the Crusades.

Sarajevo / sa-ruh-**yay**-voh / a city in former Yugoslavia, capital of Bosnia-Herzegovina.

saratoga / sa-ruh-**toh**-guh / *n. Aust.* a large-scaled freshwater fish.

sarcasm / **sah**-kaz-uhm / *n.* ironically scornful language.

sarcastic / sah-**kas**-tik / *adj.* using or showing sarcasm. ☐ **sarcastically** *adv.*

sarcoma / sah-**koh**-muh / *n.* (*pl.* **sarcomas** *or* **sarcomata**) a malignant tumour of connective tissue.

sarcophagus / sah-**kof**-uh-guhs / *n.* (*pl.* **sarcophagi**) a stone coffin, often decorated with carvings.

sardine *n.* a young pilchard or similar small fish, often tinned as food tightly packed in oil.

sardonic / sah-**don**-ik / *adj.* humorous in a grim or sarcastic way. ☐ **sardonically** *adv.*

sardonyx / sah-duh-niks / *n.* onyx with alternate layers of white and yellow or orange.

sargasso / sah-**gas**-oh / *n.* (*pl.* **sargassos** *or* **sargassoes**) (also **sargassum**, *pl.* **sargassa**) a seaweed with berry-like air vessels, found floating in masses.

sarge *n. colloq.* sergeant.

sari / sah-ree / *n.* (*pl.* **saris**) a length of cloth draped round the body, traditionally worn by women of the Indian subcontinent.

Sarich engine *n. trademark* an orbital engine, named after its Australian inventor Ralph Sarich (1938–).

sarky *adj. colloq.* sarcastic.

sarong / suh-**rong** / *n.* **1** an ankle-length tube of cloth worn tucked around the waist by men in Sri Lanka and other Asian countries. **2** a Malay and Javanese skirt-like garment worn by both sexes, consisting of a strip of cloth worn tucked round the waist or under the armpits.

sarsaparilla / sah-suh-puh-**ril**-uh, sahs-puh- / *n.* **1** a preparation of the dried roots of various plants, esp. smilax, used to flavour drinks and medicines; formerly used as a tonic. **2** (also **false sarsaparilla**) *Aust.* = HARDENBERGIA. **3** (also **native sarsaparilla**) a climber of Qld and NSW, having strongly flavoured leaves formerly used in the bush etc. as a substitute for tea.

sarsen / **sah**-suhn / *n.* a sandstone boulder carried by ice during a glacial period.

sarsenet / **sahs**-nuht / *n.* a soft silk fabric used mainly for linings.

sartorial / sah-**taw**-ree-uhl / *adj.* of tailoring; of men's clothing (*sartorial elegance*).

Sartre / sahtr /, Jean-Paul (1905–80), French existentialist philosopher, novelist, and dramatist.

sarvo *adv. Aust. colloq.* this afternoon.

sash[1] *n.* a long strip of cloth worn round the waist or over one shoulder and across the body.

sash[2] *n.* either of the frames holding the glass in a sash window. ☐ **sash cord** strong cord used for attaching a weight to each end of a sash so that it can be balanced at any height. **sash window** a window sliding up and down in grooves.

sashimi / sa-**shee**-mee / *n.* a Japanese dish of slices of raw fish served with grated horseradish and soy sauce.

sassafras / **sas**-uh-fras / *n.* **1** a small N. American tree with aromatic bark. **2** a medicinal preparation from its leaves or bark. **3** any of several Australian trees having pungently aromatic bark and spicily fragrant leaves.

sassy *adj.* (**sassier**, **sassiest**) esp. *US colloq.* impudent, cheeky.

sat *see* SIT.

Satan the Devil; Lucifer.

satanic / suh-**tan**-ik / *adj.* of Satan; devilish, hellish. ☐ **satanically** *adv.*

Satanism *n.* worship of Satan, using distorted forms of Christian worship. ☐ **Satanist** *n.* & *adj.*

satay / **sat**-ay, **sah**-tay / *n.* an Indonesian and Malaysian dish consisting of small pieces of meat grilled on a skewer and usu. served with a satay sauce. •*adj.* cooked and served in this way (*chicken satay; satay lamb*). ☐ **satay sauce** a spicy sauce containing peanuts, chilli, etc.

satchel *n.* a small shoulder bag for carrying light articles (esp. schoolbooks).

sate / sayt / *v.* (**sating**) **1** gratify (desire or a desirous person) to the full. **2** cloy, surfeit, weary with overabundance, satiate (*sated with sexual pleasure*).

satellite *n.* **1** a heavenly body revolving round a planet; an artificial body placed in orbit to revolve similarly. **2** (in full **satellite State**) a country that is subservient to another and follows its lead. •*adj.* transmitted by satellite (*satellite television*). ☐ **satellite dish** a dish-shaped aerial for receiving satellite television. **satellite town** a smaller town dependent on a larger one near it.

Sati / **sut**-ee / (in Hinduism) the wife of Siva, reborn as Parvati.

satiable / say-shuh-buhl / *adj.* able to be satiated.

satiate / **say**-shee-ayt / *v.* satisfy fully; glut or cloy with an excess of something. ☐ **satiation** *n.*

satiety / suh-**tuy**-uh-tee / *n. formal* the condition or feeling of being sated.

satin *n.* a silky material woven in such a way that it is glossy on one side only. •*adj.* smooth as satin. ☐ **satin bowerbird** a bowerbird of eastern Australia, the mature male having glossy black plumage shot through with a rich blue satiny sheen. ☐☐ **satiny** *adj.*

satinwood *n.* **1** (in full **Ceylon satinwood**) a tree native to Sri Lanka (Ceylon) yielding a golden satiny timber with a beautiful grain. **2** any of several eastern Australian trees (unrelated to *Ceylon satinwood*) yielding a glossy, usu. yellowish timber.

satire *n.* **1** ridicule, irony, or sarcasm in speech or writing. **2** a novel, play, etc. that ridicules people's hypocrisy or foolishness in this way.

satirical / suh-**ti**-ri-kuhl / *adj.* using satire, criticising in a humorous or sarcastic way. ☐ **satirically** *adv.*

satirise / **sat**-uh-ruyz / *v.* (also -**ize**) attack with satire; describe satirically.

satirist / **sat**-uh-ruhst / *n.* a person who writes satires or uses satire.

satisfaction *n.* **1** satisfying; being satisfied. **2** something that satisfies a desire or gratifies a feeling. **3** compensation for injury or loss (*demand satisfaction*).

satisfactory *adj.* satisfying expectations or needs; adequate. ☐ **satisfactorily** *adv.*

satisfy *v.* (**satisfied, satisfying**) **1** give (a person) what he or she wants or needs; make pleased or contented. **2** put an end to (a demand or craving) by giving what is required (*satisfy*

satsuma

one's hunger). **3** adequately fulfil or comply with conditions etc.) (*satisfied all the legal requirements*). **4** provide with sufficient proof, convince (*the police are satisfied that his death was accidental*).

satsuma / sat-**soo**-muh / *n.* a small variety of orange similar to a mandarin.

saturate *v.* **1** make thoroughly wet, soak. **2** cause to absorb or accept as much as possible (*the market for used cars is saturated*). **3** cause (a substance) to combine with or absorb the greatest possible amount of another substance. **4** (as **saturated** *adj.*) (of molecules of fat) containing the greatest number of hydrogen atoms. **5** overwhelm (enemy defences etc.) by concentrated bombing. ☐ **saturation** *n.*

saturation point *n.* the stage beyond which no more can be absorbed or accepted.

Saturday *n.* the day of the week following Friday. • *adv. colloq.* **1** on Saturday. **2** (**Saturdays**) on Saturdays; each Saturday.

Saturn 1 *Rom. myth.* a god of agriculture. **2** a large planet of the solar system, with 'rings' composed of small icy particles.

saturnalia / sat-uh-**nay**-lee-uh / *n.* (*pl.* **saturnalia** *or* **saturnalias**) **1** wild revelry; an orgy. **2** (usu. **Saturnalia**) an ancient Roman festival of Saturn in December, the predecessor of Christmas. ☐ **saturnalian** *adj.*

saturnine / **sat**-uh-nuyn / *adj.* (of a person or looks) having a gloomy forbidding appearance.

satyr / **sat**-uh / *n.* **1** *Gk & Rom. myth.* a woodland god in human form but having a goat's ears, tail, and legs. **2** a grossly lustful man.

sauce *n.* **1** a liquid or semi-liquid preparation served with food to add flavour or richness (*mint sauce; tomato sauce*). **2** something adding piquancy, excitement. **3** *colloq.* impudence, cheek. • *v.* (**saucing**) **1** give piquancy or excitement to. **2** *colloq.* be impudent to; cheek. ☐ **sauce boat** a shallow jug for serving sauces, gravy, etc.

saucepan *n.* a metal cooking pan with a long handle, used over heat.

saucer *n.* **1 a** a small shallow curved dish on which a cup stands. **b** a similar dish on which to stand a plant pot etc. **2** something shaped like this (*a flying saucer*). ☐ **saucerful** *n.* (*pl.* **saucerfuls**).

saucy *adj.* (**saucier**, **sauciest**) **1** impudent, cheeky. **2** smart-looking, jaunty (*a saucy hat*). ☐ **saucily** *adv.* **sauciness** *n.*

Saudi / **sow**-dee / *n.* (*pl.* **Saudis**) a native or inhabitant of Saudi Arabia.

Saudi Arabia a kingdom in SW Asia, occupying most of the Arabian peninsula. ☐ **Saudi Arabian** *adj. & n.*

sauerkraut / **sowuh**-krowt / *n.* a German dish of chopped pickled cabbage.

Saul (11th century BC) the first king of Israel.

sauna / **saw**-nuh / *n.* a Finnish-style steam bath; a building or room with this.

saving

saunter *v.* walk in a leisurely way, stroll. • *n.* a leisurely walk or walking-pace.

saurian / **saw**-ree-uhn / *adj.* of or like a lizard. • *n.* a lizard.

sausage *n.* **1** minced seasoned meat enclosed in a cylindrical edible skin. **2 a** a sausage-shaped object. **b** *Aust. colloq.* the penis. ☐ **sausage meat** meat prepared for this or as a stuffing etc. **sausage roll** sausage meat enclosed in a cylindrical roll of pastry. **sausage sizzle** *Aust.* a fund-raising or social event for clubs, groups of employees, etc., at which barbecued sausages etc. are sold or provided.

sauté / **soh**-tay / *adj.* fried quickly in a small amount of fat (*sauté potatoes*). • *v.* (**sautéd** *or* **sautéed**, **sautéing**) cook in this way.

sauterne / soh-**tern** / *n.* (also **sauternes** pronounced the same) a sweet white (originally French) wine.

Sauvage / suh-**vahzh** /, Louise (1973–), OAM, Australian athlete who represented Australia in wheelchair events at the 1992, 1996 and 2000 Paralympic Games, winning nine gold medals.

sav *n. Aust. colloq.* a saveloy.

savage *adj.* **1** in a primitive or wild state (*savage tribes; savage terrain; savage animals*). **2** fierce; cruel (*a savage attack; savage criticism*). **3** *colloq.* very angry (*in a savage mood*). • *n.* **1 a** *offens.* a member of a primitive tribe. **b** *Aust. hist.* (in 19th century white use) an Australian Aborigine. **2** a cruel or barbarous person. • *v.* **1** attack savagely, maul (*the dog savaged the cat*). **2** attack verbally (*the prime minister savaged the opposition*). ☐ **savagely** *adv.* **savagery** *n.*

Savage Garden Australian pop duo consisting of Darren Hayes (1972–) and Daniel Jones (1973–).

savannah / suh-**van**-uh / *n.* (also **savanna**) a grassy plain in hot regions, with few or no trees.

savant / **sav**-uhnt / *n.* a learned person.

save[1] *v.* **1** rescue; keep from danger, harm, or capture. **2** free from the power of sin. **3** avoid wasting (*save fuel*). **4** keep for future use or enjoyment; put aside (money) for future use. **5** make unnecessary; relieve (a person) from (trouble, expense, etc.) (*did it to save you a journey*). **6** (in sports) prevent an opponent from scoring. • *n.* the act of saving in soccer etc. • *prep.* except (*in all cases save one*). ☐ **savable** *or* **saveable** *adj.*

save[2] (*archaic* or *poetic*) *prep.* except; but. • *conj.* (often foll. by *for*) except; but.

saveloy / **sav**-uh-loi / *n.* a seasoned red pork sausage, dried and smoked, and sold ready to eat.

saver *n.* **1** a person who saves (money). **2** (often as *comb. form*) something that saves (*a real timesaver*). **3** *Racing* a hedging bet; a bet laid to insure against loss on another (more risky) bet.

saving *adj.* **1** that delivers, rescues, or preserves from peril etc. **2** (often in *comb.*) making economical use of (*labour-saving*). • *n.* **1** anything that is saved. **2** an economy (*a saving in expenses*). **3** (**savings**) money put aside for future use. • *prep.* except (*I'll have all saving the red one*). ☐ **saving grace** a good quality that redeems a person or thing whose other qualities are not good. **savings bank** a bank paying interest on deposits from individual members of the public, dealing in housing loans, etc. (cf. TRADING BANK).

saviour *n.* **1** a person who rescues or delivers people from harm or danger. **2** (**the** or **our Saviour**) Christ.

savoir-faire / sav-wahr-**fair** / *n.* knowledge of how to behave in any situation that may arise; social tact. (¶ French, = knowing how to do.)

savory / **say**-vuh-ree / *n.* a herb used in cooking.

savour *n.* **1** the taste or smell of something. **2** the power to arouse enjoyment (*felt that life had lost its savour*). • *v.* **1** have a certain taste or smell. **2** taste or smell (a thing) with enjoyment. **3** (foll. by *of*) give a certain impression (*the reply savours of impertinence*).

savoury *adj.* **1** having an appetising taste or smell. **2** having a salt or piquant and not sweet flavour. • *n.* **1** a bite-sized salty or spicy snack; a canapé. **2** a savoury dish served as an appetiser or at the end of a dinner. ☐ **savouriness** *n.*

savoy *n.* a cabbage with wrinkled leaves.

savvy *colloq. n.* common sense, understanding. • *v.* understand.

saw[1] *n.* **1** a hand tool with a toothed blade used to cut esp. wood with a to-and-fro movement. **2** a power tool with a toothed rotating disk or moving band, for cutting. • *v.* (**sawed**, **sawn** or **sawed**, **sawing**) **1** cut with a saw. **2** make a to-and-fro movement like that of sawing.

saw[2] *n.* an old saying, a maxim.

saw[3] *see* SEE[1].

sawdust *n.* powdery fragments of wood produced when timber is sawn.

sawfish *n.* a large tropical sea fish having a bladelike snout with jagged edges.

sawfly *n.* an insect whose larvae are injurious to plants.

sawmill *n.* a factory with power-operated saws where timber is cut into planks.

sawn *see* SAW[1]. ☐ **sawn-off** *adj.* (of a gun) with part of the barrel removed by sawing.

sawyer *n.* a person who saws timber.

sax *n. colloq.* a saxophone.

Saxon *n.* **1** a member of a Germanic people who conquered parts of England in the 5th–6th centuries. **2** (usu. **Old Saxon**) their language. • *adj.* of the Saxons or their language.

saxophone *n.* a brass wind instrument with a reed in the mouthpiece, and with keys operated by the player's fingers.

saxophonist / sak-**sof**-uh-nuhst / *n.* a person who plays the saxophone.

say *v.* (**said**, **saying**) **1** utter or recite in a speaking voice. **2** state, express in words; have a specified wording (*the notice says 'keep out'*). **3** give as an argument or excuse (*there's much to be said on both sides*). **4** give as one's opinion or decision (*I say we should accept*). **5** suppose as a possibility; take (a specified amount) as being near enough (*let's allow, say, an hour for the meeting*). **6** convey artistically (inner meaning etc.) (*what is the poem saying?*). • *n.* the power to decide (*has no say in the matter*). ☐ **go without saying** be too obvious to need mention. **say so 1** the power to decide something; a command. **2** a mere assertion without proof.

saying *n.* a well-known phrase or proverb.

Sb *symbol* antimony.

SBS *abbr.* **1** *Aust.* Special Broadcasting Service. **2** sick building syndrome.

Sc *symbol* scandium.

sc. *abbr.* **1** scilicet. **2** scene (*Act V, sc. 2*).

s.c. *abbr.* small capitals: LIKE THIS.

scab *n.* **1** a crust forming over a wound or sore as it heals. **2** *derog.* (often also as *adj.*) a person who refuses to join a strike, who tries to break a strike by working, or who refuses to join a union. **3** a skin disease or plant disease that causes scab-like roughness. **4** *colloq.* a dislikeable or contemptible person. • *v.* (**scabbed**, **scabbing**) **1** form a scab; heal by doing this. **2** *derog.* act as a scab (sense 2). **3** *Aust. colloq.* cadge, borrow.

scabbard *n.* the sheath of a sword or dagger.

scabby *adj.* **1** having scabs (on the skin). **2** non-union. **3** *colloq.* despicable, contemptible.

scabies / **skay**-beez / *n.* a contagious skin disease causing itching.

scabrous / **skay**-bruhs / *adj.* **1** (of the surface of a plant or animal) rough, scaly. **2** indecent, salacious (*scabrous gossip*).

scad *n.* a fish of tropical and subtropical seas.

scads *n.pl. colloq.* a large amount; lots (*she paid scads for it; scads of places we can go to for a holiday*).

scaffold *n.* **1** a wooden platform for the execution of criminals. **2** scaffolding. • *v.* fit scaffolding to (a building).

scaffolding *n.* **1** a temporary structure of poles and planks providing workers with platforms to stand on while building or repairing a house etc. **2** the poles etc. from which this is made.

scalar / **skay**-luh / *adj.* (in mathematics) having magnitude but not direction. • *n.* a scalar quantity.

scald / skawld / *v.* **1** injure with hot liquid or steam. **2** heat (milk) to near boiling point. **3** clean (pans etc.) with boiling water. • *n.* an injury to the skin by scalding.

scalded earth *n.* (also **scalded land**, **country**, etc.) *Aust.* land that is now bare of vegetation because of soil erosion or salination, esp. because of bad farming practices, indiscriminate clearing, etc.

scale[1] *n.* **1** each of the thin overlapping plates of horny membrane or hard substance that protect the skin of many fish and reptiles. **2** something

scale resembling this (e.g. on a plant); a flake of skin. **3** a white deposit formed inside a boiler or kettle etc. in which hard water is regularly used. **4** tartar formed on teeth. **5** = SCALE INSECT. • *v.* **1** remove scales or scale from. **2** form or come off in scales or flakes. ☐ **scale insect** any of various sap-sucking insect pests which cling to plants and secrete a shield-like scale as a covering.

scale[2] *n.* **1** (**scales**) an instrument for weighing things. **2** (also **scale-pan**) each of the dishes on a simple balance. **3** (**the Scales**) a sign of the zodiac, Libra. ☐ **tip** (*or* **turn**) **the scales** be the decisive factor in a situation.

scale[3] *n.* **1** an ordered series of units, degrees, qualities, etc. for measurement or classification. **2** an arrangement of notes in music, ascending or descending by fixed intervals. **3** the ratio of the actual measurements of something to those of a drawing, map, or model of it; a line with marks showing this (*the scale is 1 centimetre to the kilometre; a scale model*). **4** the relative size or extent of something (*entertainment on a grand scale*). • *v.* **1** climb (*scaled the cliff*). **2** represent in measurements or extent in proportion to the size of the original. ☐ **to scale** in exact proportion throughout. **scale up** (*or* **down**) make larger (or smaller) in proportion.

scale[4] *v. Aust. colloq.* **1** avoid paying what is due, esp. a fare. **2** defraud, cheat. ☐ **scaler** *n.*

scalene / skay-leen / *adj.* (esp. of a triangle) having unequal sides.

scallion / skal-yuhn / *n.* a shallot or spring onion.

scallop / skol-uhp / *n.* **1** an edible mollusc with two hinged fan-shaped shells. **2** either shell of this, often used for cooking and serving food. **3** each of a series of semicircular curves used as an ornamental edging. **4** a potato scallop (*see* POTATO). • *v.* (**scalloped, scalloping**) **1** cook in a scallop shell. **2** ornament with scallops. ☐ **scalloping** *n.* (in sense 3 of noun).

scallywag *n.* (used esp. of a child) a scamp, a rascal.

scaloppine / skal-uh-**pee**-nee / *n.* an Italian dish consisting of escalopes of meat (esp. veal) sautéed or fried.

scalp *n.* **1** the skin of the head excluding the face. **2** this with the hair, formerly cut as a trophy from an enemy's head by American Indians. **3** this cut from a noxious animal in order to obtain a bounty. • *v.* **1** take the scalp of. **2** resell (shares etc.) at a high or quick profit. **3** buy tickets for a pop concert, sporting event, etc., in order to sell them later at a highly inflated price. ☐ **scalper** *n.*

scalpel / skal-puhl / *n.* a surgeon's small sharp knife.

scaly *adj.* (**scalier, scaliest**) covered in scales or scale (*see* SCALE[1]). ☐ **scaly-breasted lorikeet** an eastern Australian lorikeet having green plumage, yellow breast feathers scalloped with green so that they look like scales, and bright orange-red underwings.

scam *n. colloq.* **1** a fraudulent trick; a swindle. **2** an illegal business racket.

scamp *n.* a rascal. • *v.* do (work, a job, etc.) carelessly, hurriedly, or inadequately.

scamper *v.* **1** run hastily; run and skip playfully. **2** (usu. foll. by *through*) perform (a task etc.) in a hurried and skimpy manner (*scampered through her homework; do it thoroughly—don't scamper*). • *n.* a scampering run.

scampi / **skam**-pee / (treated as *pl.* or *sing.*) large European prawns.

scan *v.* (**scanned, scanning**) **1** look at all parts of (a thing) intently. **2** glance at quickly and not thoroughly. **3** sweep a radar or electronic beam over (an area) in search of something. **4** resolve (a picture) into elements of light and shade for television transmission. **5** obtain an image of (part of the body) using a scanner. **6** read a barcode on packaging etc. **7** (of a document scanner) read a document or picture in order to reproduce it in computer-readable form etc. **8** analyse the rhythm of (a line of verse). **9** (of verse) be correct in rhythm. • *n.* **1** scanning. **2** an image obtained by scanning.

scandal *n.* **1** something shameful or disgraceful. **2** gossip about other people's faults and wrongdoing.

scandalise *v.* (also **-ize**) shock by something shameful or disgraceful.

scandalmonger *n.* a person who invents or spreads scandal.

scandalous *adj.* shameful, disgraceful; containing scandal (*scandalous reports*). ☐ **scandalously** *adv.*

Scandinavia Norway, Sweden, and Denmark (sometimes also Finland, Iceland, and the Faeroe Islands) considered as a unit. ☐ **Scandinavian** *adj.* & *n.*

scandium *n.* a metallic element (symbol Sc).

scanner *n.* **1** a device for scanning or systematically examining all parts of something. **2** (in medicine) a machine using X-ray, ultrasound, etc. to examine internal areas of the body. **3** (in full **document scanner** *or* **optical scanner**) a machine for reproducing a document etc. in computer-readable form etc.

scansion / **skan**-shuhn / *n.* the scanning of lines of verse; the way verse scans.

scant *adj.* scanty, insufficient (*was treated with scant courtesy*).

scanty *adj.* (**scantier, scantiest**) **1** of small amount or extent (*scanty vegetation*). **2** barely enough. ☐ **scantily** *adv.* **scantiness** *n.*

scapegoat *n.* a person who is made to bear blame or punishment that should rightly fall on others. (¶ Named after the goat which, in ancient Jewish religious custom, was allowed to escape into the wilderness after the high priest had symbolically laid the sins of the people upon it.)

scapula / **skap**-yuh-luh / *n.* (*pl.* **scapulae** / **skap**-yuh-lee / *or* **scapulas**) the shoulder blade.

scapular / **skap**-yuh-luh / *adj.* of the scapula. • *n.* **1** a monastic outer garment consisting of two long strips of cloth hanging down the breast and back and joined across the shoulders. **2** a miniature version of this worn under their clothing by lay persons affiliated to a monastic order.

scar[1] *n.* **1** a mark left where a wound or sore has healed, or on a plant from which a leaf has fallen. **2** a mark left by damage. **3** a lasting effect produced by grief etc. • *v.* (**scarred**, **scarring**) mark with a scar; form a scar or scars.

scar[2] *n.* a steep craggy part of a mountainside or cliff.

scarab / **ska**-ruhb / *n.* **1** a kind of beetle. **2** the sacred dung beetle of ancient Egypt. **3** a gem carved as a beetle, used in ancient Egypt as a charm.

scarce *adj.* not enough to supply a demand or need; rare. • *adv. archaic or literary* scarcely. ☐ **make oneself scarce** *colloq.* go away; keep out of the way.

scarcely *adv.* **1** only just, almost not (*she is scarcely 17 years old; I scarcely know him*). **2** not, surely not (*you can scarcely expect me to believe that*).

scarcity *n.* being scarce; a shortage.

scare *v.* frighten or become frightened suddenly. • *n.* a sudden fright; alarm caused by a rumour (*a bomb scare*).

scarecrow *n.* **1** a human figure dressed in old clothes, set up to scare birds away from crops. **2** *colloq.* a badly-dressed, grotesque-looking, or very thin person.

scaremonger *n.* a person who spreads alarming rumours. ☐ **scaremongering** *n.*

scarf[1] *n.* (*pl.* **scarves** *or* **scarfs**) **1** a long strip of material worn for warmth or ornament round the neck. **2** a square of material worn round the neck or over the head.

scarf[2] *n.* (*pl.* **scarfs**) a joint made by thinning the ends of two pieces of timber etc., so that they overlap without an increase of thickness, and fastening them with bolts etc. • *v.* join in this way.

scarifier *n.* esp. *Aust.* a machine with prongs for loosening soil without turning it, and for removing thatch etc. from a lawn.

scarify / **ska**-ruh-fuy, **skair**- / *v.* (**scarified**, **scarifying**) **1** esp. *Aust.* loosen the surface of (soil etc.). **2** make slight cuts in (skin or tissue) surgically. **3** hurt by severe criticism. **4** *colloq.* scare.

Scarlatti / skah-**lat**-ee /, Alessandro (1660–1725) and his son Domenico (1685–1757), Italian composers.

scarlet *adj.* **1** of brilliant red tinged with orange. **2** used as a distinguishing epithet in the names of fauna and flora (e.g. *scarlet honeyeater*, *scarlet running postman*). • *n.* **1** scarlet colour. **2** a scarlet substance or material; scarlet clothes. ☐ **scarlet fever** an infectious fever caused by bacteria, producing a scarlet rash. **scarlet hat** a cardinal's tasselled hat as a symbol of rank. **scarlet running postman** *Aust.* = RUNNING POSTMAN (*see* RUNNING).

scarp *n.* a steep slope on a hillside.

scarper *v. colloq.* run away. ☐ **do a scarper** make a quick getaway.

scarves *see* SCARF[1].

scary *adj.* (**scarier**, **scariest**) frightening.

scat[1] *v.* (esp. as *interj.*) *colloq.* go away quickly.

scat[2] *n.* wordless jazz singing using the voice as an instrument. • *v.* (**scatted**, **scatting**) sing in this way.

scat[3] *n.* excrement.

scathing / **skay**-*th*ing / *adj.* witheringly scornful. ☐ **scathingly** *adv.*

scatology *n.* an excessive interest in faeces or obscene things. ☐ **scatological** *adj.*

scatter *v.* **1** throw or put here and there; cover in this way. **2** go or send in different directions. **3** (as **scattered** *adj.*) wide apart or sporadic (*scattered settlements*). • *n.* scattering; the extent over which something is scattered.

scatterbrain *n.* a person who is unable to concentrate or do things systematically. ☐ **scatterbrained** *adj.*

scatty *adj.* (**scattier**, **scattiest**) *colloq.* scatterbrained; crazy. ☐ **scattily** *adv.* **scattiness** *n.*

scavenge *v.* **1** (of an animal) search for decaying flesh etc. as food. **2** search for usable objects or material among rubbish or discarded things. ☐ **scavenger** *n.*

scenario / suh-**nah**-ree-oh, -**nair**- / *n.* (*pl.* **scenarios**) **1** the outline of a film, play, etc. **2** a possible sequence of events suggested for consideration.

■ **Usage** *Scenario* should not be used to mean 'situation', as in *it was an unpleasant scenario*.

scene *n.* **1** the place of an actual or fictional event (*the scene of the crime*). **2** a piece of continuous action in a play or film; a subdivision of an act. **3** an incident thought of as resembling this. **4** a dramatic outburst of temper or emotion; a stormy argument (*made a scene*). **5** stage scenery. **6** a landscape or view as seen by a spectator (*the rural scene before us*). **7** *colloq.* an area of action, a way of life (*the drug scene; not my scene*). ☐ **behind the scenes 1** backstage. **2** in secret.

scenery *n.* **1** the general appearance of a landscape. **2** picturesque features of a landscape. **3** structures used on a theatre stage to represent features in the scene of the action.

scenic / **see**-nik / *adj.* **1** having picturesque scenery (*the scenic road to Lorne*). **2** of natural scenery (*flatness is the main scenic feature*). **3** of or on a theatre stage. ☐ **scenically** *adv.*

scent *n.* **1** the characteristic pleasant smell of something. **2** a sweet-smelling liquid made from essence of flowers or aromatic chemicals; perfume. **3** a perceptible smell left by an animal, by which it can be traced. **4** clues leading to a discovery. • *v.* **1** discover by sense of smell (*the dog scented a rat*). **2** begin to suspect the presence or existence of (*she scented danger*). **3** put scent on (a thing); make fragrant. ☐ **scented** *adj.*

sceptic / **skep**-tik / *n.* **1** a sceptical person; one who doubts the truth of religions or religious doctrines. **2** a philosopher who questions the possibility of knowledge. ☐ **scepticism** / **skep**-tuh-siz-uhm / *n.*

sceptical / **skep**-ti-kuhl / *adj.* inclined to disbelieve things; doubting or questioning the truth of claims or statements etc. ☐ **sceptically** *adv.*

sceptre / **sep**-tuh / *n.* a staff carried by a king or queen as a symbol of sovereignty.

schadenfreude / **shah**-duhn-froi-duh / *n.* the malicious enjoyment of another's misfortunes. (¶ German)

schedule / **shed**-yool, **she**-jool, **sked**-yool / *n.* **1** a program or timetable of planned events or of work. **2** a list of rates or prices. • *v.* include in a schedule, appoint for a certain time (*the train is scheduled to stop at Werribee*). ☐ **on schedule** punctual according to the timetable. **schedule fee** (also **scheduled fee**) *Aust.* a government approved fee for a medical service (esp. with regard to the payment of medical benefits) (*most doctors charge above the scheduled fee*).

schema *n.* (*pl.* **schemata** *or* **schemas**) a summary, outline, or diagram.

schematic / skee-**mat**-ik / *adj.* in the form of a diagram or chart. • *n.* a diagram, esp. of an electronic circuit. ☐ **schematically** *adv.*

schematise / **skee**-muh-tuyz / *v.* (also **-ize**) put into schematic form; formulate in regular order. ☐ **schematisation** *n.*

scheme / skeem / *n.* **1** a plan of work or action. **2** a secret or underhand plan. **3** an orderly planned arrangement (*a colour scheme*). • *v.* make plans; plan in a secret or underhand way. ☐ **schemer** *n.* **scheming** *adj.*

Schepisi, Fred(erick Alan) (1939–), Australian film director who has made films in Australia, Britain, and the United States.

scherzo / skairt-soh / *n.* (*pl.* **scherzos**) a lively vigorous musical composition or independent section of a longer work.

schism / siz-uhm, shiz-, skiz- / *n.* division into opposing groups because of a difference in belief or opinion, esp. in a religious body. ☐ **schismatic** *adj.* & *n.*

schist / shist / *n.* a crystalline rock formed in layers.

schizo / skit-soh / *adj.* & *n.* (*pl.* **schizos**) *colloq.* = SCHIZOPHRENIC.

schizoid / skit-soid / *adj.* resembling or suffering from schizophrenia. • *n.* a schizoid person.

schizophrenia / skit-suh-**free**-nee-uh / *n.* a mental disorder in which a person becomes unable to act or think in a rational way, often with delusions and withdrawal from social relationships.

schizophrenic / skit-suh-**fren**-ik / *adj.* of or suffering from schizophrenia. • *n.* a schizophrenic person.

schlock / shlok / *n. colloq.* inferior goods; trash.

schlong / shlong / *n. colloq.* a penis. (¶ Yiddish, = snake.)

schmaltz / shmawlts, shmalts / *n. colloq.* sugary sentimentality, esp. in music or literature.

schmuck *n. colloq.* a foolish or contemptible person. (¶ Yiddish, = penis.)

schnapper / **snap**-uh / alternative spelling of SNAPPER.

schnapps / shnaps / *n.* any of various strong spirits drunk in northern Europe.

schnitzel / shnit-suhl / *n.* an escalope of veal.

schnook *n. colloq.* a foolish or contemptible person.

Schoenberg / **shern**-berg /, Arnold (1874–1951), Austrian composer, living in the USA from 1933, who invented serial composition and developed atonality and the twelve-tone technique.

scholar *n.* **1** a person with great learning in a particular subject. **2** a person who is skilled in academic work. **3** a person who holds a scholarship. ☐ **scholarly** *adj.*

scholarship *n.* **1** a financial award for a student etc., given for scholarly achievement and to enable him or her to continue study. **2** great learning in a particular subject. **3** the methods and achievements characteristic of scholars and academic work.

scholastic / skuh-**las**-tik / *adj.* of schools or education; academic. ☐ **scholastically** *adv.*

scholasticism *n. hist.* medieval western church philosophy, based on the Church Fathers and Aristotle.

school[1] *n.* **1** an institution for educating or giving instruction, esp. for children. **2** its buildings; its pupils. **3** the time during which teaching is done there (*school ends at 3.30 p.m.*). **4** the department of one branch of study in a university (*the history school*). **5** experience that gives discipline or instruction (*learned his tactics in the school of hard knocks*). **6** a group or succession of philosophers, artists, etc. following the same teachings or principles (*the Heidelberg school of artists in Australia*). **7** a group of drinkers, gamblers, etc. (*a two-up school*). • *adj.* of or for use in an educational school (*school uniform; school books*). • *v.* send to school; educate; train or accustom; discipline. ☐ **school leaver** a person finishing secondary school (esp. considered as joining the job market). **school sores** *Aust.* = IMPETIGO.

school / 741 / **scope**

school[2] *n.* a shoal, e.g. of fish or whales. ◻ **school prawn** an Australian prawn occurring in large shoals and commercially fished. **school shark** a medium-sized shark of southern and eastern Australian waters occurring in schools and commercially fished, its flesh being sold as flake etc.

schoolboy *n.* a boy at school. ◻ **schoolboy humour** (esp. as applied to an adult) puerile humour.

schoolgirl *n.* a girl at school.

schoolhouse *n.* a school building, esp. in a rural or outback region of Australia.

schoolie *n. Aust. colloq.* **1** a schoolteacher. **2** a secondary school student, esp. one who has just completed year 12. **3** a school prawn. **4** a school shark. ◻ **schoolies' week** (esp. in Qld) a period of post-exam celebrations for year 12 students.

schooling *n.* education, training.

School of the Air *Aust.* a government educational program using a two-way radio system to enable children in the Australian outback to participate in a 'classroom' learning situation with a teacher or teachers.

schooner / skoo-nuh / *n.* **1** a sailing ship with two or more masts. **2** *US & Aust.* a large beer glass; the beer contained in it.

Schroeder / **shrer**-duh /, Gerhardt (1944–), German statesman who became chancellor in 1999.

Schubert / **shoo**-bert /, Franz (1797–1828), Austrian composer.

Schumann / **shoo**-mahn /, Robert Alexander (1810–56), German composer.

schwa / shwah / *n.* **1** an indistinct unstressed vowel sound as in the word 'another'. **2** the symbol ə / / (or in this dictionary / uh /) representing this.

sciatic / suy-**at**-ik / *adj.* **1** of the hip or the sciatic nerve. **2** suffering from or liable to sciatica. ◻ **sciatic nerve** the largest nerve in the human body, running from pelvis to thigh.

sciatica / suy-**at**-i-kuh / *n.* neuralgia of the hip and thigh, pain in the sciatic nerve.

science *n.* **1** a branch of knowledge requiring systematic study and method, esp. one of those dealing with substances, animal and vegetable life, and natural laws. **2** an expert's skilful technique (*with skill and science*). ◻ **science fiction** stories based on imaginary future scientific discoveries, changes of the environment, or space travel and life on other planets (cf. FANTASY, sense 4).

scientific *adj.* **1** of or used in a science (*scientific apparatus*). **2** of scientists. **3** using careful and systematic study, observations, and tests of conclusions etc. ◻ **scientifically** *adv.*

scientism *n. derog.* **1** an excessive belief in, or application of, scientific method. **2** an uncritical belief in science as an absolute authority or as a panacea for all human ills.

scientist *n.* an expert in or student of a science.

Scientology *n. trademark* a religious system founded in 1951 by the American science fiction novelist L. Ron Hubbard (1911–86). ◻ **Scientologist** *n.*

sci-fi / **suy**-fuy / *n. & adj. colloq.* science fiction.

scilicet / **suy**-luh-set, **sil**-uh- / *adv.* that is to say (used esp. in explaining an ambiguity). (¶ Latin)

scimitar / **sim**-uh-tuh / *n.* a short curved oriental sword.

scintilla / sin-**til**-uh / *n.* a trace (*not a scintilla of evidence*).

scintillate / **sin**-tuh-layt / *v.* **1** sparkle, give off sparks. **2** be brilliant (*a scintillating discussion*). ◻ **scintillation** *n.*

sciolism / **suy**-uh-liz-uhm / *n.* superficial knowledge; a display of this. ◻ **sciolist** *n.* **sciolistic** *adj.*

scion / **suy**-uhn / *n.* **1** a shoot of a plant cut for grafting or planting. **2** a descendant; a younger member of a family.

scissors *n.pl.* a cutting instrument made of two blades with handles for the thumb and fingers.

sclerosis / skluh-**roh**-suhs / *n.* a diseased condition in which soft tissue (e.g. of arteries) hardens; *see also* MULTIPLE SCLEROSIS. ◻ **sclerotic** / skluh-**rot**-ik / *adj.*

scoff[1] *v.* jeer, speak contemptuously. •*n.* a taunt; mocking words.

scoff[2] *colloq. v.* eat (food) greedily. ◻ **scoff-out** *n.* a lavish or appetising meal.

scold *v.* rebuke; tell off harshly. ◻ **scolding** *n.*

sconce *n.* **1** an ornamental wall bracket for holding a candle or electric light. **2** *colloq.* the head.

scone / skon / *n.* **1** a small soft cake of flour, fat, and milk, baked quickly and eaten buttered. **2** *Aust. colloq.* the head. ◻ **do one's scone** *Aust. colloq.* become angry. **off one's scone** *Aust. colloq.* crazy; insane.

scoop *n.* **1** a deep shovel-like tool for taking up and moving grain, sugar, etc. **2** a ladle. **3** a device with a small round bowl and a handle used for serving ice cream etc. **4** the excavating part of a digging machine etc. **5** a scooping movement. **6** the quantity taken up by a scoop. **7** a piece of news discovered and published by one newspaper in advance of its rivals. **8** a large profit made quickly. •*v.* **1** lift or hollow with or as if with a scoop. **2** forestall (a rival newspaper) with a news scoop. **3** secure (a large profit etc.), esp. suddenly.

scoot *v. colloq.* go away hastily.

scooter *n.* **1** a child's toy vehicle with a footboard on wheels and a long steering handle. **2** (in full **motor scooter**) a lightweight motorcycle with a protective shield at the front.

scope *n.* **1** the range of something (*the subject is outside the scope of this inquiry*). **2** opportunity, outlet (*a kind of work that gives scope for her abilities*). •*v.* **1** look at carefully. **2** weigh up. ◻ **scoping study** a preliminary study for a project that identifies issues and alternatives, makes comparisons with similar projects, etc.

scorbutic / skaw-**byoo**-tik / *adj.* of, like, or affected with scurvy.

scorch *v.* **1** burn or become burnt on the surface; make or become discoloured in this way. **2** *colloq.* (of a motorist) travel at an excessive speed. • *n.* **1** a mark made by scorching. **2** *colloq.* a spell of fast driving (*went for a scorch and got nabbed by the cops*). ☐ **scorched earth policy** the policy of burning crops etc., and removing and destroying anything that might be of use to an invading enemy.

scorcher *n. colloq.* a very hot day.

scorching *adj. colloq.* **1** (of the weather) very hot. **2** (of criticism etc.) harsh, severe.

score *n.* **1** the number of points made by each player or side in a game or competition. **2** a record of this, a reckoning. **3** a reason or motive (*rejected on that score*). **4** a set of twenty. **5** (**scores**) a great many (*scores of things*). **6** a line or mark cut into something. **7** a copy of a musical composition showing the notes on sets of staves. **8** the music for a film, musical, etc. **9** a record of money owing. **10** the state of affairs; the present situation (*asked him what the score was*). • *v.* **1** gain (a point or points) in a game etc.; make a score. **2** keep a record of the score. **3** be worth as points in a game (*a goal scores 6 points*). **4** achieve (*scored a great success*). **5** have an advantage (*he scores by knowing the language well*). **6** make a clever retort that puts an opponent at a disadvantage. **7** cut a line or mark(s) into (a thing). **8** write out as a musical score; arrange (a piece of music) for instruments. **9** *colloq.* obtain drugs illegally. **10** *colloq.* make a sexual conquest. ☐ **know the score** *colloq.* be aware of the essential facts. **score out** (*or* **through**) cancel by drawing a line through (words etc.). ☐☐ **scorer** *n.*

scoreboard *n.* a large board for displaying the score in a game.

scoria / **skaw**-ree-uh / *n.* (*pl.* **scoriae**) **1** cellular lava or fragments of it. **2** the slag or dross of metals. ☐ **scoriaceous** / skaw-ree-**ay**-shuhs / *adj.*

scorn *n.* strong contempt. • *v.* **1** feel or show strong contempt for. **2** reject or refuse scornfully (*would scorn to ask for favours*).

scornful *adj.* (often foll. by *of*) feeling or showing scorn. ☐ **scornfully** *adv.*

Scorpio *n.* the eighth sign of the zodiac, the Scorpion. ☐ **Scorpian** *adj.* & *n.*

scorpion *n.* **1** a small animal of the spider group with pincers and a jointed stinging tail. **2** (**the Scorpion**) a sign of the zodiac, Scorpio.

Scot *n.* a native of Scotland; a person of Scottish descent.

Scotch (also **Scottish** *or* **Scots**) *adj.* of Scotland or Scottish people or their form of English. • *n.* **1** (preceded by *the*) the people of Scotland. **2** the Scottish dialect. **3** (**Scotch**) Scotch whisky, the kind distilled in Scotland esp. from malted barley.

■ **Usage** Modern Scots prefer to use the words *Scots* and *Scottish*, not *Scotch*, except in a few compound nouns, e.g. *Scotch whisky*.

scotch *v.* put an end to (*scotched the rumour*).

scot-free *adj.* & *adv.* unharmed; not punished.

Scotland the country forming the northern part of Great Britain.

Scots *adj.* Scottish. • *n.* the Scottish dialect.

Scott[1], Andrew George. See MOONLIGHT, Captain.

Scott[2], Robert Falcon (1868–1912), English explorer of the Antarctic, who died on the return journey from the South Pole.

Scott[3], Rose (1847–1925), Australian feminist, social reformer, and writer.

Scott[4], Sir Walter (1771–1832), Scottish novelist and poet.

Scottish *adj.* of Scotland or its people or their form of the English language.

scotty *adj. colloq.* irritable, bad-tempered.

scoundrel *n.* a dishonest or unprincipled person; a rogue.

scour *v.* **1** clean by rubbing with something abrasive. **2** clear out (a channel or pipe etc.) by the force of water flowing through it. **3** remove grease, dirt, etc. from (wool etc.) by washing. **4** travel over (an area) in search of something; search thoroughly. • *n.* scouring; the action of water on a channel etc. ☐ **scourer** *n.*

scoured *n.* scoured wool.

scourge / skerj / *n.* **1** a whip for flogging. **2** a person or thing regarded as a cause of suffering, esp. on a large scale. • *v.* **1** flog with a whip. **2** afflict greatly; punish.

scout[1] *n.* **1** a person sent out to gather information, e.g. about an enemy's movements or strength. **2** a search for information etc. **3** = TALENT SCOUT (*see* TALENT). **4** (also **Scout**) a member of the Scout Association, an (originally boys') organisation intended to develop character by outdoor activities. **5** a fellow, a person (*she's a good scout*). • *v.* **1** (often foll. by *for*) go about searching for information etc. **2** (foll. by *around*) make a search (*scouted around to see if he could find any tracks*). **3** (often foll. by *out*) explore (territory etc.) (*I'll scout out the lie of the land*). ☐ **scouting** *n.*

scout[2] *v.* reject (an idea etc.) with scorn.

scowl *n.* a sullen or angry frown. • *v.* make a scowl.

Scrabble *n. trademark* a game played on a board in which words are built up from letters printed on small square counters.

scrabble *v.* (often foll. by *about*, *at*) **1** make a scratching movement or sound with the hands or feet. **2** grope busily or struggle to find or obtain something. • *n.* an act of scrabbling.

scrag *n.* **1** the bony part of an animal's carcass as food; neck of mutton or the less meaty end (**scrag-end**) of this. **2** a skinny person or animal.

scraggy

- *v.* (**scragged**, **scragging**) *colloq.* **1** seize roughly by the neck; handle roughly or beat up. **2** strangle, hang.

scraggy *adj.* (**scraggier**, **scraggiest**) lean and bony. ☐ **scragginess** *n.*

scram *v.* (**scrammed**, **scramming**) *colloq.* go away.

scramble *v.* **1** clamber, crawl, climb, etc., esp. hurriedly and awkwardly. **2** struggle eagerly to do or obtain something. **3** (of aircraft or their crew) take off quickly in an emergency or to attack an invading enemy. **4** mix together indiscriminately. **5** cook (egg) by stirring and heating it in a pan until it thickens. **6** make (a radio broadcast, telephone conversation, etc.) unintelligible except to a person with a special receiver, by altering the frequencies on which it is transmitted. **7** (as **scrambled**) *colloq.* roundly defeat (*the poms were well and truly scrambled by the Aussies in pyjama cricket*). • *n.* **1** a climb or walk over rough ground. **2** an eager struggle to do or obtain something. **3** a motorcycle race over rough ground. **4** an emergency take-off by aircraft.

scrambler *n.* an electronic device for scrambling telephone conversations.

scrap[1] *n.* **1** a small detached piece of something, a fragment; a remnant. **2** rubbish, waste material; discarded metal suitable for being reprocessed. • *v.* (**scrapped**, **scrapping**) discard as useless. ☐ **scrap heap 1** a heap of waste material. **2** the state of being discarded as useless.

scrap[2] *colloq. n.* a fight or rough quarrel. • *v.* (**scrapped**, **scrapping**) fight; quarrel.

scrapbook *n.* a blank book for sticking cuttings, drawings, etc. in.

scrape *v.* **1** make (a thing) clean, smooth, or level by passing the hard edge of something across it. **2** pass (an edge) across in this way. **3** remove by doing this (*scrape mud off shoes*). **4** excavate by scraping (*scrape a hole*). **5** damage by scraping. **6** make the sound of scraping. **7** pass along or through something with difficulty, with or without touching it. **8** obtain or amass with difficulty or by careful saving (*scraped a pass in the exam; scrape a living*). **9** be very economical. • *n.* **1** a scraping movement or sound. **2** a scraped mark or injury. **3** *colloq.* an awkward situation resulting from rashness. **4** *colloq.* a fight. ☐ **scrape through** get through a testing situation with great difficulty.

scraper *n.* a device used for scraping.

scrapings *n.pl.* fragments produced by scraping.

scrappy *adj.* (**scrappier**, **scrappiest**) **1** made up of scraps or odds and ends or disconnected elements. **2** incomplete; carelessly arranged or put together. **3** *colloq.* aggressive; quarrelsome. ☐ **scrappily** *adv.* **scrappiness** *n.*

scrapyard *n.* a place where metal scrap, old vehicles, etc. are collected for recycling.

scratch *v.* **1** make a shallow mark or wound on (a surface) with something sharp. **2** form by scratching (*scratched a hole in the ground*). **3** scrape with the fingernails to relieve itching. **4** make a thin scraping sound. **5** obtain with difficulty (*scratch a living; scratched up a meal*). **6** cancel by drawing a line through (*scratch it out*). **7** withdraw from a race or competition (*was obliged to scratch; scratched his horse*). • *n.* **1** a mark or wound made by scratching. **2** a spell of scratching (*had a good scratch*). **3** a line from which competitors start in a race when they receive no handicap. • *adj.* **1** collected from whatever is available (*a scratch team*). **2** with no handicap given (*a scratch race*). ☐ **from scratch 1** from the very beginning. **2** with no advantage or preparation. **scratch along** *colloq.* make a living with difficulty. **scratch ticket** = SCRATCHIE (sense 1). **up to scratch** up to the required standard.

scratchie *n.* esp. *Aust. colloq.* **1** an instant lottery ticket requiring the surface to be scratched off to reveal symbols etc. which indicate if a prize has been won. **2** a safety match.

scratchy *adj.* (**scratchier**, **scratchiest**) **1** tending to make scratches or a scratching sound. **2** (of a drawing etc.) untidy, careless. **3** tending to cause itching. **4** *colloq.* ill-tempered; peevish. **5** *colloq.* out of practice (*my piano playing is a bit scratchy, but I'll try*). • *n.* esp. *Aust. colloq.* = SCRATCHIE (senses 1 & 2). ☐ **scratchily** *adv.* **scratchiness** *n.*

scrawl *n.* bad handwriting; something written in this. • *v.* write in a scrawl. ☐ **scrawly** *adj.*

scrawny *adj.* (**scrawnier**, **scrawniest**) scraggy and thin.

scream *v.* **1** make a long piercing cry of pain, terror, annoyance, or excitement. **2** utter in a screaming tone. **3** (of the wind or a machine etc.) make a loud piercing sound. **4** be blatantly obvious, esp. of colours. • *n.* **1** a screaming cry or sound. **2** *colloq.* an extremely amusing person or thing.

screamer *n.* **1** a person or thing that screams. **2** (in full **two-pot screamer**) *Aust. colloq.* a person who has a very low tolerance of alcohol. **3** *colloq.* a person or thing that is spectacularly funny. **4** *colloq.* an outstanding specimen of anything (*hit a screamer to the boundary; the party was a screamer*). **5** *Aust. Rules* a spectacular overhead mark.

screamingly *adv.* so as to cause screams of laughter (*screamingly funny*).

screaming-woman bird *n.* (also **murder bird**) the Australian barking owl, a bird (of all except the arid parts of Australia) having a call like a woman's scream or sometimes like a hoarse bark.

scree *n.* a mass of loose stones on a mountainside.

screech *n.* a harsh high-pitched scream or sound. • *v.* make a screech. ☐ **screech owl** an owl that makes a screeching cry (not a hoot), esp. a barn owl.

screed *n.* **1** a tiresomely long list, letter, or other document. **2** a strip of plaster, wood, etc. fixed to a wall or floor as a guide to the correct thickness of a coat of plaster or concrete to be laid. **3** a finishing layer of mortar, cement, etc. • *v.* level by means of a screed; apply (material) as a screed.

screen *n.* **1** an upright structure used to conceal, protect, or divide something. **2** anything serving a similar purpose (*under the screen of night*). **3** a windscreen. **4** = **FLY SCREEN**. **5** a blank surface on which pictures, cinema films, or television transmissions etc. are projected. **6** a large sieve or riddle, esp. one used for sorting grain or coal etc. into sizes. • *v.* **1** shelter, conceal, or protect. **2** protect (a person) from discovery or deserved blame by diverting suspicion from him or her. **3** show (images or a cinema film etc.) on a screen. **4** pass (grain or coal etc.) through a screen. **5** examine systematically in order to discover something, e.g. a person's suitability for a post, or the presence or absence of a substance or disease. □ **screen door** a door fitted with a fly screen. **screen printing** a process like stencilling, with ink or dye forced through a prepared sheet of fine fabric. **screen saver** *Computing* a program which, after a set time, replaces an unchanging screen display with a moving image to prevent damage to the screen. **screen test** a test of a person's suitability for taking part in a film.

screenplay *n.* the script of a film.

screenwriter *n.* a person who writes for the cinema.

screw *n.* **1** a metal pin with a spiral ridge or thread round its length, used for holding things together by being twisted in under pressure, or secured by a nut. **2** a thing turned like a screw and used for tightening something or exerting pressure. **3** (in full **screw propeller**) a propeller, esp. of a ship or motor boat. **4** the act of screwing. **5** *colloq.* a prison warder. **6** *coarse colloq.* an act of sexual intercourse; one's partner in this. **7** *colloq.* wages, a living (*earning a good screw*). **8** *colloq.* a miser. • *v.* **1** fasten or tighten with a screw or screws; fasten by twisting like a screw. **2** turn (a screw); twist or become twisted. **3** oppress; extort (*screwed a promise out of her*). **4** *colloq.* extort money from (*how much did they screw you for?*). **5** *coarse colloq.* have sexual intercourse (with). **6** swindle. □ **put the screws on** *colloq.* put pressure on, intimidate. **screw cap** (*or* **top**) a cap that screws on to the opening of a container. **screw up 1** contract (one's eyes); twist (one's face) out of the natural expression, e.g. in disgust. **2** summon up (one's courage). **3** *colloq.* bungle, mismanage; spoil (an event, opportunity, etc.). **4** *colloq.* upset, disturb mentally. **screw-up** *colloq.* a bungle, a mess.

screwball *n. colloq.* a crazy person.

screwdriver *n.* **1** a tool with a tip that fits into the head of a screw to turn it. **2** a cocktail of vodka and orange juice.

screwed *adj.* **1** twisted. **2** *colloq.* drunk.

screwy *adj.* (**screwier**, **screwiest**) *colloq.* crazy, eccentric; ridiculous, absurd.

scribble *v.* **1** write hurriedly or carelessly. **2** make meaningless marks. • *n.* something scribbled; hurried or careless writing; scribbled meaningless marks.

scribbly gum *n. Aust.* any of several smooth-barked eucalypts having characteristic scribbles on the bark formed by the burrowing larvae of the scribbly gum moth.

scribe *n.* **1** an ancient or medieval copyist of manuscripts. **2** an ancient Jewish record keeper or professional theologian and jurist. **3** a pointed instrument for making marks on wood, metal, etc. **4** *colloq.* a writer, esp. a journalist. □ **scribal** *adj.*

scrim *n.* a loosely-woven cotton fabric.

scrimmage *n.* a confused struggle; a skirmish. • *v.* engage in this.

scrimp *v.* use sparingly, skimp.

scrip *n.* **1** a provisional certificate of money subscribed, entitling the holder to dividends; such certificates collectively. **2** an extra share or shares (in a business company) issued instead of a dividend (*a scrip issue*). **3** a doctor's prescription.

script *n.* **1** handwriting. **2** a style of printed or typewritten characters resembling this. **3** the text of a play, film, or broadcast talk. **4** a candidate's written answer-paper in an examination. **5** a doctor's prescription. • *v.* write a script for (a film etc.).

scripture *n.* **1** any sacred writings. **2** (**Scripture** *or* **the Scriptures**) the sacred writings of the Christians (the Old and New Testaments) or the Jews (the Old Testament). □ **scriptural** *adj.*

scriptwriter *n.* a person who writes scripts for films, TV, etc. □ **scriptwriting** *n.*

scrofula / skrof-yuh-luh / *n.* a disease causing glandular swellings. □ **scrofulous** *adj.*

scroll *n.* **1** a roll of paper or parchment, esp. written on. **2** a book in ancient roll form. **3** an ornamental design resembling a scroll or in spiral form. • *v.* (often foll. by *down* or *up*) move gradually upwards or downwards through the text of a computer document, viewing successive sections on the screen. □ **scroll bar** a long thin section at the edge of a computer display by which material can be scrolled using a mouse.

scrooge *n.* a miser. (¶ Named after a character in Dickens's novel *A Christmas Carol.*)

scrotum / skroh-tuhm / *n.* (*pl.* **scrota** *or* **scrotums**) the pouch of skin that encloses the testicles in most male mammals, behind the penis. □ **scrotal** *adj.*

scrounge *v. colloq.* cadge; borrow; get without paying. □ **scrounge around** (*or* **about**) **for** hunt or rummage for (something). □□ **scrounger** *n.*

scrub / **sculpture**

scrub[1] *n.* **1** generally low and apparently stunted forms of vegetation, often thick, and frequently growing in poor soil; areas of land in Australia covered with this. **2** (**the scrub**) *Aust.* country areas in general (as opposed to *the city*). •*adj.* **1** of a small or dwarf variety (*scrub pine*). **2** *US* & *Aust.* (of livestock) of inferior breed or physique (*scrub horses*). **3** *Aust.* as a distinguishing epithet in the names of flora and fauna (e.g. *scrub bloodwood*; *scrub wattle*; *scrub robin*; *scrub wallaby*). □ **scrub-bash** *Aust.* **1** = SCRUB-DASH. **2** make a track through the scrub; travel cross-country. **scrub-dash** *Aust.* ride at speed through thick scrub, esp. in pursuit of wild or straying cattle. **scrub fire** *Aust.* a bushfire which burns mainly scrub and undergrowth. **scrub fowl** (also **scrub hen**, **jungle fowl**) a grey-brown bird of northern coastal Australia which nests in a huge mound (up to 12 metres across and up to 5 metres high) which it builds from soil and leaves. **scrub itch** a skin irritation caused by the parasitic larvae of mites, affecting humans in northern tropical Australia. **scrub plain** an expanse of relatively flat country covered in scrub vegetation and small mallees. **scrub running** the rounding up of wild livestock. **scrub tick** any of several burrowing ticks that attack humans and animals and can cause paralysis and death in dogs etc.

scrub[2] *v.* (**scrubbed**, **scrubbing**) **1** rub hard with something coarse or bristly; clean in this way with a wet brush. **2** *colloq.* cancel, scrap (*we'll have to scrub our plans*). •*n.* scrubbing, being scrubbed (*give it a scrub*). □ **scrub up** (of a surgeon etc.) clean the hands and arms by scrubbing, before an operation.

scrubber *n.* **1** *colloq. offens.* a promiscuous woman. **2** *Aust.* (of cattle) a beast which has been bred in, or has strayed and established itself in, the scrub. **3** *colloq.* a person of rough or unkempt appearance. **4** an apparatus for purifying gases.

scrubby *adj.* (**scrubbier**, **scrubbiest**) **1** covered with scrub; consisting of or in the form of scrub. **2** small, undersized. **3** mean or shabby.

scruff[1] *n.* the back of the neck as used to grasp, lift, or drag a person or animal. •*v. Aust.* seize and hold (a calf) for branding, castrating, etc., without the use of a rope.

scruff[2] *n. colloq.* a scruffy person.

scruffy *adj.* (**scruffier**, **scruffiest**) shabby, slovenly, untidy. □ **scruffily** *adv.* **scruffiness** *n.*

scrum *n.* a scrummage. □ **scrum-half** a half-back who puts the ball into the scrum.

scrummage *n.* (in Rugby football) the grouping of the forwards of each side to push against each other and seek possession of the ball thrown on the ground between them.

scrumptious *adj. colloq.* delicious; delightful.

scrumpy *n. colloq.* rough cider.

scrunch *v.* crunch or crumple. •*n.* a crunching sound.

scrunchy *n.* (also **scrunchie**) (*pl.* **scrunchies**) a circular band of fabric-covered elastic used for fastening the hair.

scruple *n.* a feeling of doubt or hesitation produced by one's conscience or principles. •*v.* hesitate because of scruples (*did not scruple to steal from the till*).

scrupulous / skroo-pyuh-luhs / *adj.* **1** very conscientious; painstakingly careful and thorough. **2** strictly honest or honourable. □ **scrupulously** *adv.*

scrutineer *n.* an electoral official or representative of a political party who scrutinises ballot papers as they are counted.

scrutinise *v.* (also **-ize**) look at or examine carefully.

scrutiny *n.* a careful look or examination of something.

SCSI / skuz-ee / *n. Computing* a standard way of connecting peripheral devices. [Acronym from *s*mall *c*omputer *s*ystems *i*nterface.]

scuba *n.* an aqualung. (¶ Acronym from *s*elf-*c*ontained *u*nderwater *b*reathing *a*pparatus.)

scuba-diving *n.* swimming underwater using a scuba. □ **scuba-dive** *v.* **scuba-diver** *n.*

scud *v.* (**scudded**, **scudding**) move along straight, fast, and smoothly (*clouds were scudding across the sky*). •*n.* **1** clouds or spray driven by the wind; a short shower of driving rain. **2** (usu. **Scud**) a type of long-range surface-to-surface guided missile originally developed in the former USSR.

scuff *v.* **1** scrape or drag (one's feet) in walking. **2** mark or wear away by doing this. **3** scrape (a thing) with one's foot or feet. •*n.* a mark made by scuffing.

scuffle *n.* a confused struggle or fight at close quarters. •*v.* take part in a scuffle.

scull *n.* **1** each of a pair of small oars used by a single rower. **2** an oar that rests on the stern of a boat, worked with a twisting movement. **3** a small boat propelled with a scull or a pair of sculls. **4** (**sculls**) a sculling race. •*v.* **1** propel (a boat) with sculls. **2** (also **skol**) *colloq.* drink (a glass etc. of alcoholic liquor) in a single draught; finish one's drink quickly (*scull your drink and let's go*).

sculler *n.* **1** one who uses a scull or sculls. **2** a boat for sculling.

scullery *n.* (chiefly *Brit.*) a back kitchen; a room where dishes etc. are washed up.

Scullin, James Henry (1876–1953), Australian Labor statesman, prime minister 1929–32.

scullion *n. archaic* a cook's boy assistant; one who washes dishes.

sculpt *v.* (also **sculp**) sculpture.

sculptor *n.* a person who makes sculptures.

sculpture *n.* **1** the art of carving in wood or stone or producing shapes in cast metal. **2** a work made in this way. •*v.* represent in sculpture; decorate with sculptures. □ **sculptural** *adj.*

Sculthorpe, Peter (Joshua) (1929–), AO, Australian composer.

scum *n.* **1** impurities that rise to the surface of a liquid; a film of material floating on the surface of water. **2** a worthless part; worthless person or persons (*scum of the earth*). • *v.* (**scummed, scumming**) **1** remove the scum from. **2** form a scum. □ **scummy** *adj.*

scumbag *n.* coarse *colloq.* a contemptible person.

scuncheon *n.* the inside face of a door-jamb or window frame.

scunge / skunj / *n. Aust. colloq.* **1** dirt; scum; mess. **2** a dirty or disagreeable person. **3** a person who is tight with money or who habitually cadges. □ **scungy** *adj.*

scungies / **skun**-jeez / *n.pl. Aust. colloq.* stretch sports briefs worn under boardshorts, netball skirt, etc.

scupper *n.* an opening in a ship's side to carry off water from the deck. • *v.* **1** sink (a ship) deliberately. **2** *colloq.* wreck (plans etc.).

scurf *n.* **1** flakes of dry skin, esp. from the scalp; dandruff. **2** any dry scaly matter on a surface. □ **scurfy** *adj.*

scurrilous / sku-ruh-luhs / *adj.* **1** grossly or indecently abusive. **2** coarsely humorous. □ **scurrilously** *adv.* **scurrility** / sku-**ril**-uh-tee / *n.*

scurry *v.* (**scurried, scurrying**) move hurriedly with quick short steps; scamper. • *n.* **1** scurrying, a rush. **2** a flurry of rain or snow.

scurvy *n.* a disease caused by lack of vitamin C in the diet. • *adj.* paltry; dishonourable, contemptible.

scut *n.* a short tail, esp. that of a hare, rabbit, or deer.

scutter *colloq. v.* scurry. • *n.* a scurrying movement or sound.

scuttle[1] *n.* **1** = COAL SCUTTLE. **2** a small opening with a lid, on a ship's deck or side or in a roof or wall. • *v.* let water into (a ship) to sink it.

scuttle[2] *v.* scurry; hurry away. • *n.* a scuttling run; a hasty departure.

scuttlebutt *n.* **1** a water butt on the deck of a ship, for drinking from. **2** *colloq.* rumour, gossip.

scuzzy *adj. colloq.* disgusting, abhorrent.

Scylla / sil-uh / *Gk myth.* a female sea monster who devoured men from ships when they tried to navigate the narrow channel between her cave and the whirlpool Charybdis.

scythe / suyth / *n.* an implement with a curved blade and a long handle, used for cutting long grass or grain. • *v.* cut with a scythe.

SE *abbr.* **1** south-east. **2** south-eastern.

Se *symbol* selenium.

sea *n.* **1** the expanse of salt water that covers most of the earth's surface. **2** any part of this as opposed to dry land or fresh water; a named section of it partly enclosed by land (*the Tasman Sea*). **3** a large inland lake of either salt or fresh water (*the Sea of Galilee*). **4** the waves of the sea; the movement or state of these (*a heavy sea*). **5** a vast expanse of something (*a sea of faces*). **6** used attributively in the names of fish (e.g. *sea garfish*; *sea mullet*). □ **at sea 1** in a ship on the sea. **2** (also **all at sea**) perplexed, confused. **sea anemone** a tube-shaped sea animal with petal-like tentacles round its mouth. **sea change** a significant or unexpected transformation. **sea cow 1** a herbivorous mammal which lives in the sea, e.g. the dugong. **2** a walrus. **sea dog** an old sailor. **sea green** *adj.* & *n.* bluish-green. **sea horse 1** a small upright fish with a horse-like head. **2** a mythical creature with a horse's head and a fish's tail. **sea legs** ability to walk steadily and avoid seasickness at sea. **sea level** the level corresponding to that of the surface of the sea halfway between high and low water. **sea lion 1** any of several large, eared seals of the Pacific region. **2** a large, eared seal of coastal areas and esp. islands from WA to SA, the male having a white mane of hair on its nape. **sea mile** a unit varying between 1,842 metres and 1,861 metres. **sea urchin** a sea animal with a round spiny shell.

seaboard *n.* **1** seashore or coastline. **2** coastal region.

seaborgium / see-**baw**-gee-uhm / *n.* an unstable chemical element (symbol Sg) made by high-energy atomic collisions. (¶ Named after G. Seaborg (1912–99), American nuclear chemist.)

seafarer *n.* **1** a sailor. **2** a traveller by sea.

seafaring *adj.* & *n.* working or travelling on the sea, esp. as one's regular occupation.

seafood *n.* (often used also as *adj.*) fish or shellfish from the sea eaten as food (*a seafood restaurant*).

seagoing *adj.* (of ships) fit for crossing the sea.

seagull *n.* a gull.

seal[1] *n.* an amphibious fish-eating sea mammal with flippers. • *v.* hunt for seals. □ **seal leopard** (also **leopard seal**) a large seal of Antarctic regions, having spotted fur and feeding on penguins.

seal[2] *n.* **1** a gem or piece of metal etc. with an engraved design that is pressed on wax or other soft material to leave an impression. **2** this impression or a piece of wax bearing it, attached to a document as a guarantee of authenticity, or to an envelope, box, etc. to show that (while the seal is unbroken) the contents have not been tampered with. **3** a mark, event, action, etc. serving to confirm or guarantee something (*gave it their seal of approval*). **4** a small decorative paper sticker resembling a postage stamp. **5** a substance or fitting used to close an opening and prevent air or liquid from passing through it. • *v.* **1** affix a seal to. **2** stamp or certify as authentic in this way. **3** close securely so as to prevent penetration; coat or surface with a protective substance or sealant; stick down (an envelope etc.). **4** surface (a road) with tar, bitumen, etc. **5** settle or decide (*his fate was sealed*).

sealant *n.* a substance used for coating a surface to make it watertight or airtight.

sealing *n.* hunting seals.

sealing wax *n.* a substance that is soft when heated but hardens when cooled, used for sealing letters or for impressing with a raised design.

seam *n.* **1** the line or groove where two edges of cloth, wood, etc. join. **2** a surface line such as a wrinkle or scar. **3** a layer of coal etc. in the ground. • *v.* **1** join by means of a seam. **2** mark with a wrinkle or scar etc. ☐ **seam bowler** a bowler in cricket who makes the ball bounce off its seam.

seaman *n.* **1** a sailor, esp. one below the rank of officer. **2** a person who is skilled in seafaring.

seamanship *n.* skill in seafaring.

seamer *n.* a seam bowler.

seamstress / sem-struhs, seem- / *n.* (also **sempstress**) a woman who sews, esp. for a living.

seamy *adj.* (**seamier**, **seamiest**) **1** sordid, disreputable. **2** showing seams.

seance / say-ons / *n.* a meeting at which a spiritualist attempts to make contact with spirits of the dead.

seaplane *n.* an aeroplane designed to alight on and take off from water.

seaport *n.* a town with a harbour.

sear *v.* **1** scorch esp. with a hot iron; cauterise. **2** (as **searing** *adj.*) burning; severe and sharp (*a searing pain*). **3** brown (meat) quickly at a high temperature to retain its juices in cooking.

search *v.* **1** look through or go over (a place, a person, etc.) in order to find something. **2** examine thoroughly (*search your conscience*). • *n.* the act or process of searching. ☐ **search me!** *colloq.* I do not know. **search party** a group of people conducting an organised search. **search warrant** a warrant allowing officials to enter a building and search it. ☐☐ **searcher** *n.*

searching *adj.* (of a scrutiny or examination) thorough.

searchlight *n.* an outdoor electric lamp with a powerful beam that can be turned in any direction.

seascape *n.* a picture or view of the sea.

Sea Scout *n.* a member of the maritime branch of the Scout Association.

seashell *n.* the shell of a mollusc living in salt water.

seashore *n.* the land next to the sea.

seasick *adj.* made sick or queasy by the motion of a ship. ☐ **seasickness** *n.*

season *n.* **1** each of the climatic divisions of the year (spring, summer, autumn, winter). **2** a section of the year with distinct characteristics of temperature and rainfall (*the wet season*). **3** the time of year when something is common or plentiful, or when an activity takes place (*the footy season*). • *v.* **1** give extra flavour to (food) by adding salt, pepper, spices, etc. **2** bring (wood etc.) into a fit condition for use by drying, treating, or allowing to mature; become seasoned in this way. **3** make (people) competent by training and experience (*a seasoned campaigner*). ☐ **in season 1** (of food) available as a freshly-gathered crop at the normal time of year. **2** (of an animal) on heat. **out of season** (of food) not in season. **season ticket** a ticket that allows a person to travel between certain destinations, or to attend performances etc., for a specified period.

seasonable *adj.* **1** suitable for the season (*seasonable weather*). **2** timely, opportune. ☐ **seasonably** *adv.*

■ **Usage** Do not confuse with *seasonal*.

seasonal *adj.* of a season or seasons, varying according to these (*accommodation charges are seasonal; fruit picking is seasonal work*).

■ **Usage** Do not confuse with *seasonable*.

seasoning *n.* salt, pepper, herbs, spices, etc. added to food.

seat *n.* **1** a thing made or used for sitting on. **2** a place where one sits. **3** the right to occupy a seat, esp. as an elected member of parliament; such a member's electorate (*the seat of Wills*). **4** the horizontal part of a chair etc. on which a sitter's buttocks rest. **5** the part supporting another part in a machine. **6** the buttocks; the part of a skirt or trousers covering these. **7** the place where something is based or located (*the university is a seat of learning*). **8** the manner in which a person sits on a horse etc. • *v.* **1** cause to sit (*seat them in the front row*). **2** provide sitting accommodation for (*the hall seats 500*). **3** put (machinery) on its support. ☐ **seated** *adj.*

seatbelt *n.* a strap securing a person to a seat in a vehicle or aircraft, for safety.

-seater *comb. form* having a specified number of seats.

seating *n.* **1** seats collectively. **2** sitting accommodation.

seaward *adv.* (also **seawards**) towards the sea. • *adj.* going or facing towards the sea.

seaweed *n.* a plant that grows in the sea or on rocks on a shore.

seaworthy *adj.* (of a ship) in a fit state for a sea voyage. ☐ **seaworthiness** *n.*

sebaceous / suh-**bay**-shuhs / *adj.* secreting an oily or greasy substance (*sebaceous glands*).

sebum / **see**-buhm / *n.* the oily substance secreted by sebaceous glands.

sec *n. colloq.* a short time (*wait a sec*). • *abbr.* secant.

sec. *abbr.* second(s).

secant / **see**-kuhnt / *n. Maths* **1** the ratio of the hypotenuse to the shorter side adjacent to an acute angle (in a right-angled triangle). **2** a line cutting a curve at one or more points.

secateurs / sek-uh-**terz**, sek-uh-**tuhz** / *n.pl.* clippers used with one hand for pruning plants.

secede / suh-**seed** / v. withdraw formally from a political federation or religious body.

secession / suh-**sesh**-uhn / n. seceding. ☐ **secessionist** n. & adj.

seclude v. keep (a person) apart from others.

secluded adj. (of a place) screened or sheltered from view.

seclusion / suh-**kloo**-zhuhn / n. secluding; being secluded, privacy.

second[1] / **sek**-uhnd / adj. **1** next after first. **2** another after the first (*a second chance*). **3** of a secondary kind, subordinate, inferior (*second quality; the second eleven*). **4** such as to be comparable to (*a second Gough Whitlam*). **5** alternate (*every second week*). • n. **1** something that is second; the second day of a month. **2** second-class honours in a university degree. **3** second gear. **4** an attendant of a person taking part in a duel or boxing match. **5** a sixtieth part of a minute of time or angular measurement. **6** *colloq.* a short time (*wait a second*). **7** (**seconds**) goods rated second-class in quality, having some flaws. **8** (**seconds**) *colloq.* a second helping of food; a second course at a meal. • adv. **1** in second place, rank, or position. **2** second class (*travelling second*). • v. **1** assist. **2** state formally that one supports a motion that has been put forward by another person as a means of bringing it to be voted on. ☐ **second childhood** childishness caused by mental weakness in old age. **second class** a group of persons or things, or a standard of accommodation etc., less good than first class (but better than third); (used adverbially) in or by second-class accommodation etc. (*we travelled second class*). **second-class** adj. of second or inferior quality; of or using less good accommodation etc. than first-class. **second cousin** *see* COUSIN. **second-degree burn** a burn causing blistering but not scars. **second fiddle** a subsidiary or secondary role (*had to play second fiddle to his brother*). **second-generation** adj. denoting the offspring of a first generation, esp. of immigrants to Australia, but also of machines etc. (*a second-generation computer*). **second-guess** v. *colloq.* **1** anticipate by guesswork. **2** criticise with hindsight. (**at**) **second hand** obtained indirectly, not from the original source. **second-hand** (also **secondhand**) adj. & adv. **1** bought after use by a previous owner. **2** dealing in used goods (*a second-hand shop*). **3** at second hand, obtained or experienced in this way. **second lieutenant** an army officer immediately below lieutenant. **second name** a surname. **second nature** a habit or characteristic that has become automatic (*secrecy is second nature to him*). **second person** *see* PERSON. **second-rate** adj. not of the best quality, mediocre; rated second-class. **second sight** the supposed power to foresee future events. **second string** an alternative course of action or means of livelihood etc., invoked if the main one is unsuccessful. **second thoughts** a change of mind after reconsideration. **second wind** recovery of one's ease of breathing after having become out of breath; renewed energy. ☐☐ **seconder** n.

second[2] / suh-**kond** / v. transfer (a person) temporarily to another post or department. ☐ **secondment** n.

secondary adj. **1** coming after what is primary (*the secondary stress in the word 'segregate' falls on the syllable '-gate'*). **2** of lesser importance or rank etc. than the first. **3** derived from what is primary or original (*secondary sources*). **4** (of education or school) following primary. ☐ **secondary boycott** *Aust.* an attempt to influence the outcome of an industrial dispute through action against an employer not directly involved in the dispute. **secondary colours** colours obtained by mixing two primary colours. **secondary industry** an industry which produces manufactured goods (as opposed to PRIMARY INDUSTRY). **secondary school** a school providing education after primary school and before university etc. **secondary source** a critical book, journal, article, etc., used as supporting evidence in the discussion of a PRIMARY SOURCE (*Shakespeare's 'Macbeth' is the primary source in this thesis, and the secondary sources include E.F.C. Ludowyk's 'Understanding Shakespeare'*). ☐ **secondarily** adv.

Second Fleet n. *hist.* a fleet of convict-carrying ships from Britain reaching Sydney in June 1790 (*see* FIRST FLEET). ☐ **Second Fleeter** a British convict arriving in Sydney on the Second Fleet.

secondly adv. furthermore; as a second consideration.

secrecy n. **1** being kept secret. **2** keeping things secret (*was pledged to secrecy*).

secret adj. **1** kept or intended to be kept from the knowledge or view of others, to be known only by specified people. **2** working or operating secretly. • n. **1** something kept or intended to be kept secret. **2** a mystery, a thing no one properly understands (*the secrets of nature*). **3** a method for attaining something (*the secret of good health*). ☐ **secret agent** a spy acting for a country. **secret ballot** one in which individual voters' choices are not made public. **secret men's business** *Aust.* **1** (in Aboriginal culture) ceremony and ritual open only to men. **2** typically male activities, talk, interests, etc. **secret police** a police force operating in secret for political purposes. **secret sacred** *Aust.* (in Aboriginal culture) of or pertaining to rites, songs, objects, etc., the knowledge of which is limited to particular persons or groups. **secret service** a government department responsible for conducting espionage. **secret society** a society whose members are sworn to secrecy about it. **secret women's business** *Aust.* **1** (in Aboriginal culture) ceremony and ritual open only to women. **2** typically female activities, talk, interests, etc. ❑ ❑ **secretly** *adv.*

secretaire / sek-ruh-**tair** / *n.* an escritoire.

secretarial / sek-ruh-**tair**-ree-uhl / *adj.* of or involving the work of a secretary.

secretariat / sek-ruh-**tair**-ree-uht / *n.* **1** an administrative office or department, esp. a government one. **2** its members or premises.

secretary / **sek**-ruh-tuh-ree, -tree / *n.* **1** a person employed to help deal with correspondence, typing, filing, making appointments, etc. **2** an official in charge of the correspondence and records of an organisation. **3** the head of a public service department. ❑ **secretary-general** the principal administrator of a large organisation.

secrete / suh-**kreet** / *v.* **1** hide or conceal (an object) (*secreted the roll of film in his underpants*). **2** form and send out (a substance) into the body, either for excretion or for use within the body (*the liver secretes bile*). ❑ **secretor** *n.*

secretion / suh-**kree**-shuhn / *n.* **1** secreting; being secreted. **2** a substance secreted by an organ or cell of the body.

secretive / **see**-kruh-tiv / *adj.* inclined to make or keep secrets; uncommunicative. ❑ **secretive envelope** an envelope through which one cannot see the contents. ❑ ❑ **secretively** *adv.* **secretiveness** *n.*

secretory / suh-**kree**-tuh-ree / *adj.* of bodily secretion.

sect *n.* **1** a group sharing (usu. unorthodox) religious, political, or philosophical doctrines. **2** a religious denomination, esp. an exclusive one.

sectarian / sek-**tair**-ree-uhn / *adj.* **1** of or belonging to a sect or sects. **2** narrow-mindedly putting the beliefs or interests of one's sect before more general interests. • *n.* a member of a sect. ❑ **sectarianism** *n.*

section *n.* **1** a distinct part or portion of something. **2** a distinct group or subdivision of a larger body of people (*the poorer section of the community; the wind section of an orchestra*). **3** a subdivision of a book, document, statute, etc. **4** the process of cutting or separating something surgically (*caesarian section*). **5** a plane surface formed by cutting a solid. **6** the representation of the internal structure of something as if cut across along a vertical or horizontal plane. **7** a fare stage on a bus or tram. • *v.* arrange in or divide into sections.

sectional *adj.* **1** of a social group (*sectional interests*). **2** partisan (*the Aussie team can rely on sectional support whenever it plays in Australia*). **3** made in sections. **4** local rather than general.

sector *n.* **1** any of the parts into which a battle area is divided for the purpose of controlling operations. **2** a similar division of an activity (*the private sector of industry*). **3** a section of a circular area between two lines drawn from its centre to its circumference. **4** *Computing* a subdivision of a track on a magnetic disk. ❑ **sectoral** *adj.*

secular / **sek**-yuh-luh / *adj.* **1** concerned with worldly affairs rather than spiritual ones; not involving religion (*secular State; secular music*). **2** (of education) not concerned with religion or religious belief; excluding religious instruction. **3** (of priests) not members of a monastic community. • *n.* a priest who does not belong to a monastic or other religious Order. ❑ **secularise** (also -**ize**) *v.* **secularity** / sek-yuh-**la**-ruh-tee / *n.*

secularism / **sek**-yuh-luh-riz-uhm / *n.* **1** the attitude or belief that religions or religious doctrines should have no place or say in the conduct of a public education system and in the civil affairs and policies of a nation. **2** *Philosophy* the doctrine that religion, religious dogmas, etc., have no place in the formulation of a system of ethics.

secure *adj.* safe (esp. against attack); certain not to slip or fail, reliable. • *v.* **1** make secure. **2** fasten securely. **3** obtain (*secured good seats for the rock concert*). **4** guarantee by pledging something as security (*the loan is secured on landed property*). ❑ **securely** *adv.*

security *n.* **1** a state or feeling of being secure; something that gives this. **2** the safety of a country or organisation against espionage, theft, or other danger. **3** a thing that serves as a guarantee or pledge (*offered the deeds of his house as security for the loan*). **4** a certificate showing ownership of financial stocks, bonds, or shares. ❑ **security blanket 1** an official sanction on information in the interest of security. **2** a blanket or other familiar object given as a comfort to a child.

Security Council a permanent body of the UN established to maintain world peace, consisting of five permanent members (China, France, UK, USA, Russia) and ten members elected for two-year terms.

sedan / suh-**dan** / *n.* **1** an enclosed car with four or more seats. **2** (in full **sedan chair**) an enclosed chair for one person (used in the 17th–18th centuries), mounted on two poles and carried by two bearers.

sedate / suh-**dayt** / *adj.* calm and dignified, not lively. • *v.* put (a person) under sedation. ❑ **sedately** *adv.* **sedateness** *n.*

sedation *n.* the act of calming, esp. by giving sedatives.

sedative / **sed**-uh-tiv / *adj.* having a calming or soothing effect. • *n.* a sedative drug or influence.

sedentary / **sed**-uhn-tuh-ree, -tree / *adj.* **1** spending much time seated (*sedentary workers*). **2** requiring much sitting (*sedentary work*). **3** (of a person) disinclined to exercise.

sedge *n.* a grass-like plant growing in marshes or near water.

sediment *n.* **1** fine particles of solid matter suspended in a liquid or settling to the bottom of it. **2** solid matter (e.g. sand, gravel) that is carried by water or wind and settles on land.

sedimentary / sed-uh-**men**-tuh-ree, -tree / *adj.* **1** of or like sediment. **2** (of rock) formed from layers of sediment carried by water or wind.

sedition / suh-**dish**-uhn / *n.* words or actions that make people rebel against authority. ☐ **seditious** / suh-**dish**-uhs / *adj.*

seduce / suh-**dyoos** / *v.* **1** persuade (esp. into wrongdoing) by offering temptations (*was seduced into betraying his country*). **2** entice (a person) into sexual intercourse. **3** tempt (*seduced by the aroma of freshly ground coffee*). ☐ **seducer** *n.*

seduction *n.* **1** seducing; being seduced. **2** a tempting and attractive feature (*the seductions of rural life*).

seductive *adj.* tending to seduce, alluring. ☐ **seductively** *adj.* **seductiveness** *n.*

sedulous / **sej**-yuh-luhs / *adj.* **1** diligent and persevering. **2** (of an action etc.) deliberately and consciously continued; painstaking (*a sedulous attempt to seduce him*). ☐ **sedulously** *adv.* **sedulity** *n.*

see[1] *v.* (**saw**, **seen**, **seeing**) **1** perceive with the eyes; have or use the power of doing this. **2** perceive with the mind, understand (*I see what you mean*). **3** have a certain opinion about (*as I see it*). **4** consider; take time to do this (*must see what can be done; let me see, how can we fix it?*). **5** watch; be a spectator of (*went to see a film*). **6** look at for information (*see page 310*). **7** meet; be near and recognise (*I saw your mother in town*). **8** discover (*see who is at the door*). **9** experience, undergo (*saw service during the war*). **10** grant or obtain an interview with, consult (*I must see the doctor about my wrist*). **11** escort, conduct (*see her to the door*). **12** make sure (*see that this letter goes today*). ☐ **see through 1** understand the true nature of, not be deceived by. **2** finish (a project) completely. **see-through** *adj.* transparent.

see[2] *n.* the position or district of a bishop or archbishop.

seed *n.* (*pl.* **seeds** or **seed**) **1** a fertilised ovule of a plant, capable of developing into a plant like its parent. **2** seeds as collected for sowing (*to be kept for seed*). **3** semen; milt. **4** something from which a tendency or feeling etc. can develop (*sowing the seeds of doubt in their minds*). **5** a seeded player. • *v.* **1** plant seeds in; sprinkle with seeds. **2** place particles in (a cloud) to cause condensation and produce rain. **3** remove seeds from (fruit). **4** so position (a strong competitor in a knockout competition) that he or she will not meet other strong competitors in early rounds. ☐ **go** (or **run**) **to seed 1** cease flowering as seed develops. **2** deteriorate in appearance or efficiency. **seed pearl** a very small pearl. **seed potato** a potato kept for seed. ☐☐ **seedless** *adj.*

seedbed *n.* **1** a bed of fine soil in which seeds are sown. **2** a place of development (*a seedbed of rebellion*).

seedling *n.* a very young plant growing from a seed rather than from a cutting etc.

seedy *adj.* (**seedier**, **seediest**) **1** full of seeds. **2** looking shabby and disreputable. **3** *colloq.* feeling slightly ill. ☐ **seedily** *adv.* **seediness** *n.*

seeing *see* SEE[1]. ☐ **seeing that** in view of the fact that, because.

seek *v.* (**sought**, **seeking**) make a search or inquiry for; try to find, obtain, or do. ☐ **seek out** seek specially, make a special effort to meet and address (a person).

Seekers, the an Australian folk and pop group, formed in 1962, with Judith Durham (1943–) as lead singer.

seem *v.* appear to be or to exist or to be true.

seeming *adj.* having an appearance of being something but not necessarily being this in fact. ☐ **seemingly** *adv.*

seemly *adj.* proper, suitable, in accordance with accepted standards of good taste. ☐ **seemliness** *n.*

seen *see* SEE[1].

See of Rome the papacy, the Holy See.

seep *v.* ooze slowly out or through.

seepage / **see**-pij / *n.* seeping; the amount that seeps out.

seer *n.* **1** a prophet, a person who sees visions. **2** one who sees.

seersucker *n.* fabric woven with a puckered surface.

see-saw *n.* **1** a long board balanced on a central support so that when a child sits on each end the two can go up and down alternately. **2** an up-and-down change that is constantly repeated. **3** a close contest with alternating advantage. • *v.* **1** play on a see-saw; make this movement. **2** vacillate in policy, emotion, etc.

seethe *v.* **1** bubble or surge as in boiling. **2** be very angry or resentful.

segment *n.* / **seg**-muhnt / a part cut off or marked off as separable from the other parts of a thing. • *v.* / seg-**ment** / divide into segments. ☐ **segmental** / seg-**men**-tuhl / *adj.*

segmented / seg-**men**-tuhd / *adj.* divided into segments. ☐ **segmentation** *n.*

Segovia / se-**goh**-vee-uh /, Andrés (1893–1987), Spanish guitarist and composer.

segregate / **seg**-ruh-gayt / *v.* **1** put apart from the rest, isolate. **2** separate (people) according to their race. ☐ **segregation** *n.* **segregationist** *n.* & *adj.*

segue / **seg**-way / esp. *Music v.* (**segues**, **segued**, **seguing**) (usu. foll. by *into*) go on without a pause. • *n.* an uninterrupted transition from one song or melody to another.

Seidler, Harry (1923–), AC, Australian architect (born in Austria).

seigneur / say-**nyer** / *n.* a feudal lord. ☐ **seigneurial** *adj.*

seine / sayn / *n.* a large fishing net that hangs vertically with floats at the top and weights at the bottom, the ends being drawn together to enclose fish as it is hauled ashore. •*v.* fish or catch with a seine.

seismic / **suyz**-mik / *adj.* **1** of an earthquake or earthquakes. **2** of or using vibrations produced artificially by explosions, e.g. to explore the structure of underground rock formations (*seismic survey*). □ **seismically** *adv.*

seismogram / **suyz**-muh-gram / *n.* the record given by a seismograph.

seismograph / **suyz**-muh-grahf, -graf / *n.* an instrument for detecting, recording, and measuring earthquakes.

seismography / suyz-**mog**-ruh-fee / *n.* the study or recording of seismic effects. □ **seismographer** *n.* **seismographic** *adj.*

seismology / suyz-**mol**-uh-jee / *n.* the study of earthquakes. □ **seismological** *adj.* **seismologist** *n.*

seize *v.* **1** take hold of (a thing) forcibly, suddenly, or eagerly. **2** take possession of (a thing) forcibly or by legal right (*police seized the bags of marijuana*). **3** have a sudden overwhelming effect on (*panic seized us*). **4** seize up. **5** (often foll. by *on*, *upon*) take advantage of (an opportunity etc.); comprehend quickly or clearly. □ **seize up 1** (of a moving part or the machine containing it) become stuck or jammed. **2** (of part of the body) become stiff.

seizure / **see**-zhuh / *n.* **1** seizing; being seized. **2** a sudden attack of epilepsy or apoplexy etc., a stroke.

seldom *adv.* rarely, not often.

select *v.* **1** pick out as best or most suitable. **2** *Aust.* = FREE-SELECT (*see* FREE). •*adj.* **1** chosen for excellence. **2** (of a society) exclusive, admitting only certain people as members. □ **select committee** a small parliamentary committee appointed to make a special investigation.

selection *n.* **1** selecting, being selected. **2** the people or things selected. **3** a collection of things from which a choice can be made (*they stock a large selection of goods*). **4** *Biology* the process in which environmental and genetic influences determine which types of organism thrive better than others, regarded as a factor in evolution. **5** *Aust.* = FREE-SELECTION (*see* FREE). **6** a small or medium-sized rural property.

selective *adj.* **1** choosing; involving choice. **2** chosen or choosing carefully. **3** able to select. **4** (of memory etc.) selecting what is convenient. □ **selectively** *adv.* **selectivity** *n.*

selector *n.* **1** a person who selects; a member of a committee selecting a sports team. **2** a device that selects the appropriate gear or circuit etc. in machinery. **3** *Aust.* = FREE-SELECTOR (*see* FREE). **4** a farmer who owns a small to medium-sized property.

selenium / suh-**lee**-nee-uhm / *n.* a chemical element (symbol Se) that is a semiconductor and has various applications in electronics.

self *n.* (*pl.* **selves**) **1** a person as an individual. **2** a person's special nature (*she is her old self again*). **3** one's own interests, advantage, or pleasure (*always puts self first*). **4** (*humorous* or in commerce) myself, herself, itself, etc. (*the cheque is payable to self*).

self- *comb. form* of, to, or done by oneself or itself.

self-abuse *n. archaic* masturbation.

self-addressed *adj.* (of an envelope for containing a reply) addressed to oneself.

self-adhesive = SELF-STICKING.

self-aggrandisement *n.* the process of enriching oneself or making oneself powerful.

self-appointed *adj.* designated or described as such by oneself, not by others.

self-assembly *adj.* (of furniture etc.) to be made by the buyer from a kit.

self-assertive *adj.* confident or aggressive in promoting oneself, one's rights, etc. □ **self-assertion** *n.*

self-assured *adj.* self-confident. □ **self-assurance** *n.*

self-aware *adj.* conscious of one's feelings, motives, etc. □ **self-awareness** *n.*

self-catering *adj.* (of holiday accommodation etc.) with cooking facilities provided, but no food.

self-centred *adj.* thinking chiefly of oneself or one's own affairs, selfish.

self-confessed *adj.* openly admitting (or inadvertently revealing) oneself to be (*a self-confessed liar*).

self-confident *adj.* having confidence in one's own abilities. □ **self-confidence** *n.*

self-conscious *adj.* embarrassed or unnatural in manner from knowing that one is being observed by others. □ **self-consciously** *adv.* **self-consciousness** *n.*

self-contained *adj.* **1** complete in itself; (of accommodation) having all the necessary facilities and not sharing these. **2** (of a person) able to do without the company of others.

self-control *n.* ability to control one's behaviour and not act emotionally. □ **self-controlled** *adj.*

self-deception *n.* the deceiving of oneself, esp. about one's motives or feelings. □ **self-deceit** *n.*

self-defeating *adj.* (of a course of action etc.) achieving the opposite of what was intended; doomed to failure because of internal inconsistencies.

self-defence *n.* defence of oneself, or of one's rights or good reputation etc., against attack.

self-denial *n.* deliberately going without the things one would like to have, esp. so as to discipline oneself or do penance; asceticism.

self-deprecation *n.* the act of disparaging or belittling oneself. □ **self-deprecating** *adj.*

self-destruct *v.* (of a spacecraft, bomb, etc.) destroy itself automatically, esp. when pre-set to do so.

self-destruction *n.* **1** the process or an act of destroying itself or oneself or one's chances, happiness, etc. **2** an act of self-destructing. □ **self-destructive** *adj.*

self-determination *n.* **1 a** a nation's right to determine its own allegiance, government, etc. **b** a people's right to determine its future development, cultural priorities, etc. **2** the ability to act with free will, as opposed to fatalism etc.

self-discipline *n.* the ability to control one's feelings, apply oneself to a task, etc.

self-discovery *n.* the process of acquiring insight into oneself, one's character, desires, etc.

self-doubt *n.* a lack of confidence in oneself.

self-educated *adj.* educated by one's own reading etc., without formal instruction.

self-effacing *adj.* modest, retiring, timid. □ **self-effacement** *n.*

self-employed *adj.* working as a freelance or for one's own business etc. and not for an employer. □ **self-employment** *n.*

self-esteem *n.* one's good opinion of oneself; contentment with oneself, one's personality, etc. (*he suffers from low self-esteem*).

self-evident *adj.* obvious; clear without proof or explanation or further evidence.

self-examination *n.* **1** the study of one's own conduct, motives, etc. **2** the examining of one's body for signs of illness.

self-explanatory *adj.* so easy to understand that it needs no further explanation.

self-expression *n.* the expression of one's feelings, thoughts, etc., esp. in writing, painting, music, dancing, etc.

self-fertilisation *n.* the fertilisation of plants by their own pollen, not from others (as opposed to CROSS-FERTILISATION). □ **self-fertile** *adj.* **self-fertilise** *v.*

self-flattery *n.* a high, esp. exaggerated, opinion of oneself; conceit. □ **self-flattering** *adj.*

self-fulfilling *adj.* (of a prophecy, forecast, etc.) bound to come true as a result of actions brought about by the prophecy etc. having been made.

self-fulfilment *n.* the fulfilment of one's hopes, ambitions, etc.

self-governing *adj.* (of a country) governing itself. □ **self-government** *n.*

self-hatred *n.* (also **self-hate**) a very low opinion or hatred of oneself, esp. of one's actual self when contrasted with one's imagined or idealised self.

self-help *n.* (often also as *adj.*) the use of one's own abilities, resources, etc. to solve one's problems etc. (*they formed a self-help group*).

self-image *n.* one's conception of oneself, esp. in relation to others.

self-important *adj.* having a high opinion of one's own importance, pompous. □ **self-importance** *n.*

self-imposed *adj.* (of a task etc.) imposed on and by oneself, not externally (*self-imposed exile*).

self-improvement *n.* improvement of oneself or one's life etc. by one's own efforts.

self-induced *adj.* induced by oneself or itself (*his vomiting was self-induced*).

self-indulgent *adj.* **1** greatly indulging one's own desires for comfort and pleasure. **2** (of a work of art etc.) lacking economy and control. □ **self-indulgence** *n.*

self-inflicted *adj.* administered to oneself.

self-interest *n.* one's own personal advantage (esp. when associated with disregard for others). □ **self-interested** *adj.*

selfish *adj.* acting or done according to one's own interests and needs without regard for others; keeping things for oneself and not sharing. □ **selfishly** *adv.* **selfishness** *n.*

self-justification *n.* the justifying or excusing of oneself, one's actions, etc.

self-knowledge *n.* understanding of oneself, one's motives, etc.

selfless *adj.* disregarding oneself or one's own interests; unselfish. □ **selflessly** *adv.* **selflessness** *n.*

self-love *n.* **1** selfishness; self-indulgence. **2** *Philosophy* regard for one's own well-being and happiness.

self-made *adj.* having risen from poverty or obscurity and achieved success by one's own efforts (*a self-made man*).

self-opinionated *adj.* stubbornly sticking to one's opinions.

self-perpetuating *adj.* reproducing itself or continuing without help or intervention.

self-pity *n.* pity for oneself, feeling extremely sorry for oneself.

self-pollination *n.* the pollination of a flower by pollen from the same plant (as opposed to CROSS-POLLINATION). □ **self-pollinate** *v.* **self-pollinating** *adj.*

self-portrait *n.* a portrait of himself or herself by an artist; an account of himself or herself by a writer.

self-possessed *adj.* calm and dignified. □ **self-possession** *n.*

self-preservation *n.* protection of oneself from harm or injury; the instinct to ensure one's own survival.

self-proclaimed *adj.* proclaimed by oneself or itself to be such (*a self-proclaimed messiah*).

self-publishing *n.* publishing one's own work at one's own expense (without the aid of a commercial publisher) (cf. VANITY PUBLISHING).

self-raising *adj.* (of flour) containing a raising agent and for use without additional baking powder.

self-realisation *n.* **1** development of one's abilities etc. **2** this as an ethical principle.

self-regard *n.* **1** proper regard for oneself. **2** selfishness; conceit.

self-reliant *adj.* independent, relying on one's own abilities and resources. □ **self-reliance** *n.*

self-respect *n.* proper regard for oneself and one's own dignity and principles etc. ☐ **self-respecting** *adj.*

self-restraint *n.* self-control.

self-righteous *adj.* smugly sure of one's own righteousness, virtue, etc. (*self-righteous moralisers; a self-righteous little wowser*). ☐ **self-righteously** *adv.* **self-righteousness** *n.*

self-sacrifice *n.* sacrifice of one's own interests and desires so that others may benefit. ☐ **self-sacrificing** *adj.*

selfsame *adj.* the very same (*died in the selfsame house where he was born*).

self-satisfied *adj.* excessively and unjustifiably complacent about oneself; conceited. ☐ **self-satisfaction** *n.*

self-sealing *adj.* **1** (of a tyre) automatically able to seal small punctures. **2** (of an envelope) = SELF-STICKING.

self-seed *v.* (of a plant) propagate itself by sowing its own seed. ☐ **self-seeder** *n.*

self-seeking *adj.* & *n.* seeking to promote one's own interests rather than those of others.

self-service (also **self-serve**) *adj.* (of a garage, shop, restaurant, etc.) with customers serving themselves and paying at a checkout etc. • *n.* a self-service garage, shop, restaurant, etc.

self-serving *adj.* pandering to one's own interests (*a self-serving politician*).

self-starter *n.* **1** an electric device for starting an internal-combustion engine. **2** an ambitious person who can act on his or her own initiative.

self-sticking *adj.* (also **self-stick**) (of an envelope, label, postage stamp, etc.) adhesive without having to be moistened.

self-styled *adj.* using a name or description one has adopted without right (*one of these self-styled fast safe drivers*).

self-sufficient *adj.* **1** needing nothing; independent. **2** (of a person, nation etc.) able to supply one's needs for a commodity, esp. food, from one's own resources. **3** content with one's own opinion; arrogant. ☐ **self-sufficiency** *n.*

self-supporting *adj.* **1** financially self-sufficient. **2** staying up or standing without external aid.

self-taught *adj.* having taught oneself without formal teaching.

self-willed *adj.* obstinately doing what one wishes, stubborn.

self-worth = SELF-ESTEEM.

sell *v.* (**sold**, **selling**) **1** transfer the ownership of (goods etc.) in exchange for money. **2** keep a stock of (goods) for sale, be a dealer in. **3** promote sales of (*the author's name alone will sell many copies*). **4** (of goods) find buyers (*the book is selling well*). **5** be on sale at a certain price (*it sells for $21.50*). **6** persuade a person into accepting (a thing) (*tried to sell him the idea*). **7** betray or prostitute for money etc. (*sell one's country; sell one's honour*). • *n.* **1** the manner of selling something (*the soft sell*). **2** *colloq.* a deception, a disappointment (*what a sell!*). ☐ **sell-by date** the date by which something should be sold, after which it may no longer be fresh or safe. **selling point** an advantageous feature. **sell out 1** dispose of (all one's stock etc.) by selling. **2** betray. **sell-out 1** the selling of all tickets for a show etc.; a great commercial success. **2** a betrayal. **sell short** underestimate the value or worth of; make (a person or thing) seem insignificant. **sold on** enthusiastic about (*he's sold on the idea of Australia becoming a Republic*).

seller *n.* **1** a person who sells something. **2** a thing that sells well or badly (*that face cream made of processed dingo dung was a brilliant seller*). ☐ **seller's market** a state of affairs when goods are scarce and prices are high.

sellotape *n. trademark* an adhesive usu. transparent tape. • *v.* fix or seal with this.

selvage *n.* (also **selvedge**) **1** an edge of cloth so woven that it does not unravel. **2** a tape-like border along the edge of cloth, intended to be removed or hidden.

selves *see* SELF.

semantic / suh-**man**-tik / *adj.* of meaning and connotations in language; of semantics. • *n.* (**semantics**) the branch of linguistics concerned with meanings. ☐ **semantically** *adv.*

semaphore / **sem**-uh-faw / *n.* **1** a system of signalling by holding the arms in certain positions to indicate letters of the alphabet. **2** a device with mechanically moved arms, used for signalling on railways. • *v.* signal by semaphore. ☐ **semaphore crab** a burrowing crab of eastern Australia which moves its claws in the manner of semaphoring.

semblance / **sem**-bluhns / *n.* **1** an outward appearance (either real or pretended); a show (*spoke with a semblance of friendship*). **2** a resemblance or likeness to something.

semen / **see**-muhn / *n.* the whitish reproductive fluid of males, containing spermatozoa in suspension, and ejaculated by the penis; sperm. (¶ Latin, = seed.)

semester / suh-**mes**-tuh / *n.* a half-year course or term in universities, schools, etc.

semi *n.* (*pl.* **semis**) *colloq.* **1** a semi-detached house. **2** *Aust.* a semitrailer. **3** a semifinal.

semi- *comb. form* **1** half (*semicircle*). **2** partly; in some degree or particular (*semi-official; semi-detached*).

semibreve / **sem**-ee-breev / *n.* the longest note in common use in music, equal to two minims in length.

semicircle *n.* half of a circle; something arranged in this shape. ☐ **semicircular** *adj.*

semicolon / sem-ee-**koh**-luhn / *n.* the punctuation mark (;) used to separate parts of a sentence where there is a more distinct break than that represented by a comma (see panel on next page).

semiconductor *n.* a substance that (in certain conditions) conducts electricity but not as well as most metals do. ☐ **semiconductor memory** (also **solid-state memory**) a memory device used in digital equipment, esp. computers.

semi-conscious *adj.* partly or imperfectly conscious.

semi-detached *adj.* (of a house) being one of a pair of houses that have one wall in common but are detached from other houses. • *n.* such a house.

semifinal *n.* the match or round between any two of the last four competitors or teams in a competition. ☐ **semifinalist** *n.*

semillon / sem-ee-yon / *n.* **1** a variety of white grape. **2** a white table wine made from this.

seminal / sem-uh-nuhl / *adj.* **1** of seed or semen. **2** giving rise to new developments (*seminal ideas*). **3** (of books etc.) highly original and influential. ☐ **seminal fluid** semen. (¶ Latin, related to SEMEN.)

seminar / sem-uh-nah / *n.* **1** a small discussion class at a university etc. **2** a short intensive course of study. **3** a small conference of specialists.

seminary / sem-uh-nuh-ree / *n.* a training college for Catholic priests, rabbis, etc. ☐ **seminarist** *n.*

semiotics / sem-ee-o-tiks / *n.* the branch of linguistics concerned with signs and symbols. ☐ **semiotic** *adj.*

semi-permeable *adj.* (of a membrane) allowing small molecules to pass through.

semi-precious *adj.* (of a gemstone) less valuable than those called precious.

semi-professional *adj.* **1** (of a footballer, musician, etc.) paid for an activity but not relying on it for a living. **2** involving semi-professionals. • *n.* a semi-professional person.

semiquaver *n.* a note in music equal to half a quaver.

semi-skilled *adj.* having or requiring some training but less than that needed for skilled work.

Semite / see-muyt, sem-uyt / *n.* a member of the group of races that includes the Jews and Arabs and formerly the Phoenicians and Assyrians.

Semitic / suh-mit-ik / *adj.* **1** of the Semites, esp. the Jews. **2** of languages of the family including Hebrew and Arabic.

semitone *n.* the smallest interval used in classical European music, half of a tone.

semitrailer *n.* an articulated vehicle consisting of a prime mover and a long trailer, the trailer having wheels at the back but supported at the front by the towing vehicle.

semi-tropical *adj.* subtropical.

semivowel *n.* **1** a sound that is intermediate between a vowel and a consonant (e.g. that of *w* or *y*). **2** a letter representing this.

semolina *n.* hard round grains left when wheat has been ground and sifted, used to make puddings and pasta.

sempstress = SEAMSTRESS.

Semtex *n. trademark* a soft plastic explosive.

Sen. *abbr.* **1** senior. **2** senator.

senate / sen-uht / *n.* **1** (**Senate**) the upper house of the Australian Federal Parliament. **2** a legislative body, esp. the upper and smaller assembly in some countries. **3** the governing body of certain universities. **4** the governing council in ancient Rome.

senator / sen-uh-tuh / *n.* a member of a senate. ☐ **senatorial** / sen-uh-taw-ree-uhl / *adj.*

send *v.* (**sent**, **sending**) **1** order, cause, or enable to go to a certain destination; have (a thing) conveyed. **2** send a message or letter (*she sent to say she was coming*). **3** cause to move, go, or become (*sent his temperature up; the sermon sent us to sleep*). **4** *colloq.* put into ecstasy, excite (*her trumpet playing really sends me*). ☐ **send down 1** expel from a university. **2** send to prison. **send her down, Hughie** *see* HUGHIE. **send-off** *n.* a demonstration of goodwill etc. at a person's departure. **send up** *colloq.* make fun of (a thing) by imitating it. **send-up** *n. colloq.* a humorous imitation. ☐☐ **sender** *n.*

Senegal / sen-uh-gahl / a republic in West Africa. ☐ **Senegalese** / sen-uh-guh-leez / *adj.* & *n.* (*pl.* **Senegalese**).

senescent / suh-nes-uhnt / *adj.* growing old. ☐ **senesce** *v.* **senescence** *n.*

seneschal / sen-uh-shuhl / *n.* the steward of a medieval great house.

senhor / sen-yaw / *n.* a title used of or to a Portuguese-speaking man.

senhora / sen-yaw-ruh / *n.* a title used of or to a Portuguese-speaking woman, esp. a married woman.

senhorita / sen-yuh-ree-tuh / *n.* a title used of or to a Portuguese-speaking (esp. unmarried) woman.

senile / see-nuyl, sen-uyl / *adj.* suffering from bodily or mental weakness because of old age; (of

---

Semicolon ;

A semicolon is used:
1 between clauses that are too short or too closely related to be made into separate sentences; such clauses are not usually connected by a conjunction, e.g.
   To err is human; to forgive, divine.
   In the area north of the city there is a large industrial area with little private housing; further east is the university.
2 between items in a list which themselves contain commas, if it is necessary to avoid confusion, e.g.
   Dining room, 1 table, 6 chairs; kitchen, 1 table, 2 cupboards; bedroom, 1 bed, 1 wardrobe, 2 chairs.

illness etc.) characteristic of elderly people. ❑ **senile dementia** an illness of older people with loss of memory and lack of control over bodily functions. ❑❑ **senility** / suh-**nil**-uh-tee / n.

senior adj. **1** older in age. **2** added to a father's name to distinguish him from a son with the same name (Tom Brown senior). **3** higher in rank or authority. **4** for older children, esp. over the age of 11 (senior school). • n. **1** a senior person; a member of a senior school. **2** a person older than oneself (he is three years my senior). ❑ **senior citizen** an elderly person, one who has retired. **senior cits** colloq. n.pl. elderly people collectively. adj. (also **senior cit**) pertaining to elderly people (senior cit outing). ❑❑ **seniority** n.

senna n. the dried pods or leaves of a tropical tree, used as a laxative (see CASSIA).

señor / sen-**yaw** / n. (pl. **señores**) the title used of or to a Spanish-speaking man.

señora / sen-**yaw**-ruh / n. the title used of or to a Spanish-speaking woman, esp. one who is married.

señorita / sen-yuh-**ree**-tuh / n. the title used of or to a young (esp. unmarried) Spanish-speaking woman.

sensation n. **1** an awareness or feeling produced by stimulation of a sense organ or of the mind. **2** ability to feel such stimulation (loss of sensation in the fingers). **3** a condition of eager interest, excitement, or admiration aroused in a number of people; a person or thing arousing this.

sensational adj. **1** producing or intended to produce eager interest, excitement, or admiration in many people. **2** colloq. wonderful. ❑ **sensationally** adv.

sensationalise v. (also **-ize**) portray events etc. (esp. in media reporting) as being more lurid, salacious, etc. than they really are.

sensationalism n. **1** the use of or interest in the sensational. **2** the process of sensationalising. ❑ **sensationalist** n. & adj.

sense n. **1** any of the special powers by which a living thing becomes aware of things; the faculties of sight, hearing, smell, taste, and touch, by which the external world is perceived. **2** ability to perceive or feel or be conscious of a thing; awareness or recognition of something (has no sense of shame). **3** the power of making a good judgment; practical wisdom (had the sense to get out of the way). **4** the way in which a word or phrase or passage etc. is to be understood; its meaning. **5** possession of a meaning or of reasonableness. **6** (**senses**) sanity, ability to think (bring him to his senses, if you can). • v. **1** perceive by one of the senses. **2** become aware of (a thing) by getting a mental impression (sensed that he was unwelcome). **3** realise (you must travel for days before you can really sense the vast emptiness of the Australian outback). **4** (of a machine) detect. ❑ **in a sense** (or **in one sense**) if the statement is understood in a particular way (what you say is true in a sense). **sense organ** any of the organs (e.g. the eye or ear) by which the body becomes aware of stimuli from the external world.

senseless adj. **1** not showing good sense, pointless, foolish. **2** unconscious. ❑ **senselessness** n.

sensibility n. **1** the capacity to feel (lost all sensibility in his toes). **2** the ability to feel things mentally, sensitiveness; delicacy of feeling; an exceptional degree of this. **3** (**sensibilities**) a tendency to feel offended etc. (ruffled his sensibilities).

■ **Usage** This word does not mean 'possession of good sense'.

sensible adj. **1** having or showing good sense. **2** perceptible by the senses (sensible phenomena). **3** great enough to be perceived (a sensible difference). **4** (foll. by of) aware (was sensible of his peril). **5** (of clothing) practical rather than fashionable (sensible shoes). ❑ **sensibleness** n. **sensibly** adv.

sensitise v. (also **-ize**) make sensitive or abnormally sensitive. ❑ **sensitisation** n.

sensitive adj. **1** acutely susceptible to external stimuli or mental impressions; having sensibility (plants are sensitive to light; a highly sensitive part of the body; the sight of starving African children shocked his sensitive nature). **2** alert and considerate about other people's feelings. **3** easily hurt or offended. **4** (of an instrument etc.) readily responding to or recording slight changes of condition. **5** (of a subject) requiring tactful treatment. ❑ **sensitive plant** a plant whose leaves curve downwards and leaflets fold together when touched, esp. Neptunia gracilis of mainland Australia, and the naturalised Mimosa pudica. ❑❑ **sensitively** adv. **sensitivity** n.

sensor n. a device (e.g. a photoelectric cell) that reacts to a certain stimulus.

sensory / **sen**-suh-ree / adj. of the senses, receiving or transmitting sensations (sensory nerves).

sensual / **sen**-shoo-uhl / adj. **1** of physical, esp. sexual, pleasure. **2** enjoying this or giving this, voluptuous. **3** showing sensuality (sensual lips). ❑ **sensually** adv. **sensualism** n.

■ **Usage** See the note under sensuous.

sensuality / sen-shoo-**al**-uh-tee / n. (esp. sexual) gratification of the senses.

sensuous / **sen**-shoo-uhs / adj. affecting or appealing to the senses, esp. by beauty or delicacy rather than sensually (the sensuous colours of this painting; the sensuous quality of Keats's poetry). ❑ **sensuously** adv.

■ **Usage** This word does not have the sexual overtones that sensual can have.

sent see SEND.

sentence n. **1** a set of words containing a verb, which is complete in itself and conveys a statement, question, exclamation, or command (see panel). **2** the punishment awarded by a lawcourt to a person convicted in a criminal trial; declaration of this. • v. pass sentence on (a person); condemn (to punishment).

sententious /sen-**ten**-shuhs/ adj. putting on an air of wisdom; pompously moralising. ☐ **sententiously** adv. **sententiousness** n.

sentient /**sen**-shuhnt, **sen**-tee-uhnt/ adj. capable of perceiving and feeling things (*sentient beings*). ☐ **sentience** n.

sentiment /**sen**-tuh-muhnt/ n. **1** a mental attitude produced by one's feeling about something; an opinion (*the sentiment of pity; public sentiment is divided on this issue*). **2** emotion as opposed to reason (*bought it out of sentiment*). **3** mawkish tenderness; a display of this.

sentimental /sen-tuh-**men**-tuhl/ adj. **1** showing or influenced by romantic or nostalgic feeling. **2** characterised by emotions as opposed to reason. ☐ **sentimentalise** (also -**ize**) v. **sentimentally** adv. **sentimentalist** n. **sentimentality** /sen-tuh-men-**tal**-uh-tee/ n.

sentinel n. a sentry or lookout.

sentry n. a soldier posted to keep watch and guard something.

Seoul /sohl/ the capital of South Korea.

sepal /**see**-puhl, **sep**-uhl/ n. one of the leaf-like parts forming the calyx of a flower.

separable /**sep**-uh-ruh-buhl/ adj. able to be separated. ☐ **separably** adv. **separability** n.

separate adj. /**sep**-uh-ruht, **sep**-ruht/ forming a unit by itself, not joined or united with others. • n.pl. (**separates**) /**sep**-uh-ruhts/ individual items of outer clothing for wearing together in various combinations. • v. /**sep**-uh-rayt/ **1** divide, make separate; keep apart. **2** be between (*Bass Strait separates Tasmania from mainland Australia*). **3** become separate; go different ways; withdraw oneself from a union; cease to live together as a married or de facto couple. ☐ **separately** adv. **separateness** n.

separation n. **1** separating; being separated. **2** a legal arrangement by which a couple remain married but live apart. ☐ **separation of powers** *Politics* the vesting of the legislative, executive, and judiciary powers of government in separate bodies, thus ensuring their independence.

separatist /**sep**-uh-ruh-tuhst/ n. a person who favours separation from a larger unit, e.g. so as to achieve political independence. ☐ **separatism** n.

separator n. a machine that separates things (e.g. cream from milk).

Sephardi /suh-**fah**-dee/ n. (pl. **Sephardim**) a Jew of Spanish or Portuguese descent, as distinct from an Ashkenazi. ☐ **Sephardic** adj.

sepia /**see**-pee-uh/ n. **1** brown colouring matter originally made from the black fluid of the cuttlefish, used in inks and paints. **2** rich reddish-brown colour. • adj. of sepia colour.

seppo /**sep**-oh/ Aust. colloq. n. an American. • adj. American (*seppo surfboards*).

sepsis n. a septic condition.

September n. the ninth month of the year.

septet n. a group of seven instruments or voices; a musical composition for these.

septic[1] adj. infected with harmful micro-organisms that cause pus to form.

septic[2] n. **1** = SEPTIC TANK. **2** (also **seppo**) Aust. colloq. an American (see SEPTIC TANK, sense 2).

septicaemia /sep-tuh-**see**-mee-uh/ n. (also **septicemia**) blood poisoning. ☐ **septicaemic** adj.

septic tank n. **1** a tank in which sewage is disintegrated through bacterial activity. **2** Aust. rhyming slang 'Yank', an American.

septuagenarian /sep-choo-uh-juh-**nair**-ree-uhn/ n. a person in his or her seventies.

septum n. (pl. **septa**) a partition between two cavities, e.g. that in the nose between the nostrils.

septuple /**sep**-tyoo-puhl/ adj. sevenfold. • n. a sevenfold quantity.

sepulchral /suh-**pul**-kruhl/ adj. **1** of a tomb (*sepulchral monument*). **2** looking or sounding dismal, funereal (*a sepulchral voice*).

sepulchre /**sep**-uhl-kuh/ n. a tomb, esp. one cut in rock or built of stone or brick. • v. **1** place in a sepulchre. **2** serve as a sepulchre for.

sepulture /**sep**-uhl-chuh/ n. burying, placing in a grave.

sequel n. **1** what follows or arises out of an earlier event. **2** a novel or film etc. that continues the story of an earlier one.

Sentence

A sentence is the basic unit of language in use and expresses a complete thought. There are three types of sentence, each starting with a capital letter, and each normally ending with a full stop, a question mark, or an exclamation mark:

Statement:	*You're happy.*
Question:	*Is it raining?*
Exclamation:	*I wouldn't have believed it!*

A sentence, especially a statement, often has no punctuation at the end in a public notice, a newspaper headline, or a legal document, e.g.

Government cuts public spending

A sentence normally contains a subject and a verb, but may not, e.g.

What a mess!   *Where?*   *In the sink.*

sequence

sequence *n.* **1** the following of one thing after another in an orderly or continuous way. **2** a series without gaps, a set of things that belong next to each other in a particular order. **3** a section dealing with one scene or topic in a film. **4** (**Sequence**) a hymn said or sung after the Gradual or Alleluia that precedes the Gospel (*that great Sequence from the Mass for the Dead, the 'Dies Irae'*). ▫ **sequent** *adj.*

sequencer *n.* a programmable electronic device for storing sequences of musical notes and transmitting them to an electronic musical instrument. ▫ **sequencing** *n.*

sequential / suh-**kwen**-shuhl / *adj.* **1** forming a sequence, following in succession. **2** occurring as a result. ▫ **sequential file** *Computing* a set of data which must be read in the same order as it is written. ▫▫ **sequentially** *adv.*

sequester / suh-**kwes**-tuh, see- / *v.* **1** (esp. as **sequestered** *adj.*) seclude, isolate. **2** confiscate.

sequestrate / suh-**kwes**-trayt, see- / *v.* **1** confiscate. **2** take temporary possession of (a debtor's estate etc.). ▫ **sequestration** *n.* **sequestrator** *n.*

sequin / **see**-kwuhn / *n.* a circular spangle ornamenting clothing or other material. ▫ **sequinned** or **sequined** *adj.*

sequoia / suh-**kwoi**-uh / *n.* a coniferous tree of California, growing to a great height.

seraglio / suh-**rah**-lee-oh / *n.* (*pl.* **seraglios**) **1** a harem. **2** *hist.* a Turkish palace.

serang / suh-**rang** / *n. Aust.* a person in authority. (¶ Hindi)

seraph *n.* (*pl.* **seraphim** *or* **seraphs**) a member of the highest order of angels in Christian belief. ▫ **seraphic** *adj.*

Serb *n.* a native or inhabitant of Serbia. • *adj.* Serbian.

Serbia a republic in SE Europe, formerly part of Yugoslavia.

Serbian *n.* **1** a Serb. **2** the dialect of the Serbs. • *adj.* of Serbia or its people or language.

Serbo-Croat / ser-boh-**kroh**-at / *n.* (also **Serbo-Croatian**) the Slavic language of the Serbs and Croats (written in the Cyrillic alphabet by the Serbs who generally belong to the Orthodox Church, and in the Roman alphabet by the mainly Catholic Croats).

sere[1] *n.* a sequence of animal or plant communities in an ecological system.

sere[2] *adj.* (also **sear**) *literary* (esp. of a plant etc.) withered, dried up.

serenade *n.* **1** a song or tune performed at night, esp. beneath a lover's window. **2** an orchestral suite for a small ensemble. • *v.* sing or play a serenade to. ▫ **serenader** *n.*

serendipity / se-ruhn-**dip**-uh-tee / *n.* the making of pleasant discoveries by accident; the knack of doing this. ▫ **serendipitous** *adj.* (¶ Coined by Horace Walpole (1754) from *Serendip*, the former name of Sri Lanka (Ceylon).)

sermonise

serene *adj.* **1** (of the weather, sky, sea, etc.) clear and calm. **2** (of a person, a mood, etc.) tranquil, unperturbed. ▫ **serenely** *adv.* **serenity** / suh-**ren**-uh-tee / *n.*

serf *n.* a farm labourer who was forced to work for his landowner in the Middle Ages and was not allowed to leave the land on which he worked. **2** an oppressed person, a drudge. ▫ **serfdom** *n.*

serge *n.* a strong twilled worsted fabric used for making clothes.

sergeant *n.* / **sah**-juhnt / **1** a non-commissioned army officer ranking above corporal. **2** a police officer ranking just below inspector. ▫ **sergeant baker** a crimson, purple, and white marine food-fish of all Australian States. **sergeant major** (in full **regimental sergeant major**) a warrant officer assisting the adjutant of a regiment or battalion.

serial *n.* a story presented in a series of instalments. • *adj.* of or forming a series. ▫ **serial composition** serialism. **serial killer** a person who commits a sequence of murders with no apparent motive. **serial number** a number that identifies one item in a series of things. ▫▫ **serially** *adv.*

serialise *v.* (also *-ize*) produce as a serial. ▫ **serialisation** *n.*

serialism *n.* a technique of musical composition using the twelve notes of the chromatic scale arranged in a fixed order.

seriatim / seer-ree-**ay**-tim, se-ree- / *adv.* point by point; taking one subject etc. after another in regular order.

series *n.* (*pl.* **series**) **1** a number of similar things occurring or arranged in order. **2** a set of stamps or coins etc. issued at one time or in one reign.

serif / **se**-ruhf / *n.* a slight projection finishing off the stroke of a printed letter (as in T, contrasted with sanserif T).

serio-comic *adj.* partly serious and partly comic.

serious *adj.* **1** solemn and thoughtful, not smiling. **2** sincere, in earnest; not casual or light-hearted (*made a serious attempt*). **3** important (*this is a serious decision*). **4** causing great concern, not slight (*serious illness*). **5** (of music, literature, etc.) intellectual in content or appeal; not popular. ▫ **seriousness** *n.*

seriously *adv.* **1** in a serious manner (esp. introducing a sentence, implying that irony etc. is now to cease). **2** to a serious extent. **3** *colloq.* very, really (*seriously rich*).

serjeant-at-arms *n.* an official of an Australian parliament with ceremonial duties.

sermon *n.* **1** a talk on a religious or moral subject, esp. one delivered during a religious service. **2** a long moralising talk.

sermonise *v.* (also *-ize*) give a long moralising talk.

serotonin / se-ruh-**toh**-nuhn / n. Biology a compound present in blood platelets and serum, which constricts the blood vessels and acts as a neurotransmitter.

serous / seer-ruhs / adj. of, like, or producing serum.

serpent n. 1 a snake, esp. a large one. 2 a sly or treacherous person.

serpentine adj. 1 of or like a serpent. 2 twisting and curving (*a serpentine road*). 3 cunning, treacherous.

serrated / suh-**ray**-tuhd / adj. having a series of small projections like the teeth of a saw. □ **serration** n.

serried / se-reed / adj. (of ranks of soldiers, rows of trees, etc.) pressed together; without gaps; close.

serum / seer-ruhm / n. (pl. **sera** or **serums**) 1 the thin yellowish fluid that remains from blood when the rest has clotted. 2 this taken from an immunised animal and used for inoculations. 3 any watery fluid from animal tissue (e.g. in a blister).

servant n. 1 a person employed to do domestic work in a household or as a personal attendant. 2 a devoted follower or employee (*a faithful servant of the company*). 3 (in full **assigned servant**) *Aust. hist.* a convict assigned to be the servant of a private person in Australia.

serve v. 1 perform services for (a person or community etc.), work for (*served his country*). 2 be employed or performing a spell of duty (*served in the Navy*). 3 be suitable for, do what is required (*it will serve our purpose; it will serve*). 4 provide a facility for (*the area is served by a number of buses*). 5 spend time in; undergo (*served his apprenticeship; served a prison sentence*). 6 (of a male animal) copulate with. 7 set out (food etc.) for others to consume; attend to (customers in a shop). 8 (of a quantity of food) be enough for (*this recipe serves six people*). 9 set the ball in play at tennis etc. 10 assist the priest officiating in a religious service. 11 deliver (a legal writ etc.) to the person named (*served him with the writ; served the writ on him*). 12 treat in a certain way (*she was most unjustly served*). • n. 1 a service in tennis etc.; a person's turn for this; the ball served. 2 *Aust. colloq.* a severe reprimand (*got a serve from his wife for not doing the dishes*). 3 chiefly *Aust. colloq.* a serving or helping of food. □ **serve a person right** be his or her deserved punishment.

server n. 1 a person who serves. 2 a utensil for serving food. 3 (in full **altar server**) the celebrant's assistant at Mass etc. 4 *Computing* **a** a program which manages shared access to a centralised resource or service in a network. **b** a device on which such a program is run.

servery n. a room or counter from which meals are served.

service n. 1 employment as a servant. 2 the occupation or process of working for an employer or of assisting others. 3 a department of people employed by the government or by a public organisation (*public service*). 4 a system or arrangement that performs work for customers or supplies public needs (*laundry services are available; the bus service*). 5 a branch of the armed forces (*the services*). 6 use, assistance; a helpful or beneficial act (*did me a service; be of service*). 7 a religious ceremony. 8 the serving of a legal writ. 9 the serving of food or goods; provision of help for customers or clients (*quick service*). 10 a service charge. 11 a set of dishes, plates, etc. for serving a meal (*a dinner service*). 12 the act or manner or turn of serving in tennis etc.; the game in which one serves (*lost his service*). 13 maintenance and repair of a car or of machinery or appliances at intervals. 14 the serving of a mare etc. by a male animal. • v. 1 maintain or repair (a piece of machinery etc.). 2 supply with service(s). 3 pay the interest on (*the amount needed to service this loan*). □ **service industry** an industry providing services (e.g. tourism) not goods. **service road** a road giving access to houses etc. but not intended for through traffic. **service station** an establishment selling petrol etc. and/or repairing motor vehicles.

serviceable adj. 1 usable. 2 suitable for ordinary use or wear; hard-wearing. □ **serviceably** adv. **serviceability** n.

serviceman n. 1 a man in the armed services. 2 a man providing service or maintenance.

servicewoman n. a woman in the armed services.

serviette n. a table-napkin.

servile / ser-vuyl / adj. 1 suitable for a servant; menial (*servile tasks*). 2 excessively submissive; lacking independence (*servile flattery*). □ **servility** / ser-**vil**-uh-tee / n.

serving n. a helping of food for one person.

servitude n. 1 the condition of being forced to work for others and having no freedom. 2 (also **penal servitude**) *Aust. hist.* compulsory labour to which a convict (later, a prisoner) in Australia was sentenced.

servo n. (pl. **servos**) 1 (in full **servo-mechanism**) a powered mechanism producing motion at a higher level of energy than the input level. 2 (in *comb.*) involving this (*servo-assisted*). 3 *Aust. colloq.* = SERVICE STATION.

servo- *comb. form* power-assisted.

sesame / ses-uh-mee / n. 1 a plant of tropical Asia with seeds that are used as food or as a source of oil. 2 its seeds. □ **open sesame** a magic phrase for obtaining access to something that is usu. inaccessible. (¶ These words were used, in one of the Arabian Nights stories, to cause a hidden door to open.)

sesqui- / ses-kwee / *comb. form* denoting 1½ (*sesquicentennial*). (¶ Latin)

sessile / ses-uyl / adj. 1 (of a flower, leaf, eye, etc.) attached directly at the base without a stalk. 2 fixed in one position; immobile.

session *n.* **1** a period devoted to an activity (*recording session*). **2** *colloq.* a period spent drinking. **3** the assembly of a parliament, court, etc.; a single meeting for this; the period during which these are regularly held. **4** the division (usu. into two) of the academic year. ☐ **in session** assembled for business. ☐☐ **sessional** *adj.*

sestet /ses-tet/ *n.* **1** the last six lines of a sonnet. **2** a sextet.

set *v.* (**set, setting**) **1** put or place; cause to stand in position. **2** put in contact with (*set pen to paper*). **3** fix in position; adjust the hands of (a clock) or the mechanism of (a mousetrap etc.). **4** represent as happening in a certain place, or at a certain time (*the story is set in Egypt in 2000 BC*). **5** provide a tune for (*set it to music*). **6** make or become hard, firm, or established. **7** fix, decide, or appoint (*set a date for the wedding*). **8** arrange (a broken bone) so that it will heal. **9** fix (hair) while it is damp so that it will dry in the desired style. **10** place (a jewel) in a surrounding framework (*the bracelet is set with emeralds*). **11** (of blossom) form into fruit; (of fruit) develop from blossom. **12** establish (*set a new record for the high jump*). **13** offer or assign as something to be done (*set them a task*). **14** prescribe (a book etc.) for study; formulate (an examination paper). **15** put into a specified state (*set them free; set it swinging*). **16** have a certain movement (*the current sets strongly eastwards*). **17** be brought towards or below the horizon by the earth's movement (*the sun sets*). • *n.* **1** a number of people or things regarded as a group or unit (*the jet set; a teaset*). **2** a group of games forming part of a match in tennis etc. **3** *Surfing* a series of waves followed by a lull. **4** (in mathematics) a collection of things having a common property. **5** a radio or television receiver. **6** the way something is set or arranged (*the set of his shoulders*). **7** the process or style of setting hair. **8** the scenery in use for a play or film. **9** *Aust. colloq.* a grudge. **10** a slip or shoot for planting (*onion sets*). • *adj.* **1** prescribed or determined in advance (*a set menu*). **2** fixed, unchanging (*set in his ways*). **3** (of a phrase or speech etc.) having invariable wording; not extempore. **4** prepared for action. **5** (of a book etc.) prescribed for a course, an examination, etc. ☐ **be set on** be determined about. **have** (or **take**) **a set on** (or **against**) **a person** *Aust. colloq.* have a grudge against him or her. **set about** begin (a task); attack with blows or words. **set back 1** halt or slow the progress of. **2** *colloq.* cost (*it set me back $50*). **set-back** *n.* something that sets back progress. **set forth 1** begin a journey. **2** expound. **set in** become established (*depression had set in*). **set off 1** begin a journey; start (*set off a chain reaction*). **2** ignite or cause to explode. **3** improve the appearance of (a thing) by providing a contrast. **set out 1** declare or make known (*set out the terms of the agreement*). **2** begin a journey. **3** make a start with the intention of doing something. **set piece 1** a formal or elaborate arrangement, esp. in art or literature. **2** a pre-arranged movement in a team game at a free-kick, scrum, etc. **set sail** hoist sail(s); begin a voyage. **set square** a draughtsman's right-angled triangular plate for drawing lines in a certain relation to each other. **set theory** the study of sets in mathematics, without regard to the nature of their individual constituents. **set to** begin doing something vigorously, esp. fighting, arguing, or eating. **set-to** *n.* a fight; an argument. **set up 1** place in view. **2** arrange; begin or create a business etc.); establish in some capacity; begin making (a loud sound). **3** supply (*set yourself up with a computer*). **4** *colloq.* lead on in order to fool, cheat, or incriminate (a person). **set-up** *n.* **1** the structure of an organisation. **2** an instance of setting a person up (*see* SET UP, sense 4).

settee *n.* a long upholstered seat with a back, for two or more people.

setter *n.* **1** a person or thing that sets something. **2** a dog of a long-haired breed that is trained to stand rigid when it scents game.

setting *n.* **1** the way or place in which something is set. **2** music for the words of a song etc. **3** the period, place, etc., of a story, drama, etc. **4** a set of cutlery or crockery for one person.

settle[1] *v.* **1** place (a thing) so that it stays in position. **2** establish or become established more or less permanently; make one's home. **3** sink or come to rest (*dust settled on the shelves; let the earth settle after digging*). **4** resolve (*settled the dispute*). **5** make or become calm or orderly. **6** pay (a debt, bill, claim, etc.). **7** bestow legally (*settled all his property on his wife*). **8 a** colonise. **b** establish colonists in. **c** *Aust. hist.* establish oneself, esp. as a farmer, on land not previously occupied by non-Aboriginal inhabitants. ☐ **settle down** become settled after wandering, movement, disturbance, etc. **settle up** pay what is owing.

settle[2] *n.* a wooden seat for two or more people, with a high back and arms.

settlement *n.* **1** settling; being settled. **2** a business or financial arrangement. **3** an amount or property settled legally on a person. **4 a** a place occupied by settlers. **b** a small community, esp. in outback areas etc. **c** *Aust.* an Aboriginal community. **d** *Aust. hist.* the British community established in Australia in 1788 and as subsequently enlarged; the Aboriginal lands so occupied by them. **e** *Aust. hist.* the act by the British of settling in Australia and dispossessing the Aborigines of their traditional lands.

settler *n.* **1** a person who goes to live permanently in a previously unoccupied land. **2 a** *hist.* a British person who settled in Australia on land belonging to and occupied by Aborigines; a (small) farmer. **b** (as **old settler**) one of the earliest British colonists in Australia or in a particular district (of Australia).

seven *adj.* & *n.* one more than six (7, VII). ☐ **chuck** (*or* **throw**) **a seven** *Aust. colloq.* **1** faint; die. **2** lose one's temper. **3** vomit. **seven deadly sins** *see* DEADLY. **seven seas** all the oceans of the world: the Arctic, Antarctic, North and South Atlantic, North and South Pacific, and Indian Oceans.

sevenfold *adj.* & *adv.* **1** seven times as much or as many. **2** consisting of seven parts.

seventeen *adj.* & *n.* one more than sixteen (17, XVII). ☐ **seventeenth** *adj.* & *n.*

seventh *adj.* & *n.* **1** next after sixth. **2** each of seven equal parts of a thing. ☐ **seventh heaven** a state of intense delight. ☐☐ **seventhly** *adv.*

Seventh-day Adventist a member of a sect of Protestants who observe the sabbath on Saturday; they originally expected the second coming of Christ in 1844 and still preach that his return is imminent.

seventy *adj.* & *n.* **1** seven times ten (70, LXX). **2** (**seventies**) the numbers from 70 to 79, esp. the years of a century or of a person's life. ☐ **seventieth** *adj.*

Seven Wonders of the World the seven most spectacular man-made structures of the ancient world, traditionally the pyramids of Egypt, the Hanging Gardens of Babylon, the Mausoleum of Halicarnassus, the temple of Diana at Ephesus, the Colossus of Rhodes, the statue of Zeus at Olympia in Greece, and the Pharos of Alexandria.

sever / sev-uh / *v.* (**severed**, **severing**) **1** divide, break, or make separate, esp. by cutting (*severed an artery*). **2** break off or away; separate (*severed our friendship*). **3** end the employment contract (of a person).

several *adj.* **1** a few, more than two but not many. **2** separate, individual (*we all went our several ways*). • *pron.* several people or things.

severally *adv.* separately.

severance / sev-uh-ruhns / *n.* severing; being severed. ☐ **severance pay** an amount of money paid to an employee on termination of his or her contract.

severe / suh-**veer** / *adj.* **1** strict, without sympathy, imposing harsh rules on others. **2** intense, forceful (*severe gales*). **3** making great demands on endurance or energy or ability etc. (*the pace was severe*). **4** plain and without decoration (*a severe style of dress*). ☐ **severely** *adv.* **severity** / suh-**ve**-ruh-tee / *n.*

Seville orange / sev-il, suh-**vil** / *n.* a bitter orange used for making marmalade. (¶ Named after *Seville* in Spain.)

sew / soh / *v.* (**sewed**, **sewn** *or* **sewed**, **sewing**) fasten, join, make, etc. by passing thread through material, using a needle or a sewing machine. ☐ **sew up 1** join or enclose by sewing. **2** (esp. as **sewn up**) *colloq.* satisfactorily arrange or finish; gain control of; be more than likely to win (*the plans are sewn up; Geelong has sewn up the game with that goal*).

sewage *n.* waste matter from houses, factories, etc. ☐ **sewage farm**, **sewage works** a place where sewage is purified.

sewer / soo-uh / *n.* a pipe for carrying away sewage.

sewerage *n.* a system of sewers; drainage by this.

sewing *n.* material or work to be sewn. ☐ **sewing machine** a machine for sewing or stitching things.

sewn *see* SEW.

sex *n.* **1** either of the two main groups (male and female) into which living things are placed according to their reproductive functions; the fact of belonging to one of these. **2** sexual feelings or impulses or their manifestation. **3** sexual intercourse (*had sex with the guy next door*). **4** (as *adj.*) of or relating to sex or sexual differences (*sex education; sex antagonism; the sex urge*). • *v.* judge the sex of (*to sex chickens*). ☐ **safe sex** *see* SAFE. **sex act** = SEXUAL INTERCOURSE. **sex appeal** sexual attractiveness. **sex change** an apparent change of sex by hormone treatment and surgery. **sex drive** the urge to seek satisfaction of one's sexual needs. **sex education** education about sex, esp. with regard to safe sex practices and contraception. **sex life** a person's sexual activities. **sex maniac** *colloq.* a person obsessed with sex or enjoying having lots of sexual activity. **sex object** a person regarded not as a person but solely as an object of sexual gratification. **sex offender** a person who commits a sexual crime. **sex symbol** a person who is for many people an epitome of sexual attraction. **sex therapist** a professional practitioner of sex therapy. **sex therapy** therapy dealing with a person's psychological etc. problems in sexual relationships or in having sexual intercourse. **sex worker** a person who offers himself or herself for sexual activity on payment; a prostitute. **unsafe sex** *see* UNSAFE.

sexagenarian / sek-suh-juh-**nair**-ree-uhn / *n.* a person in his or her sixties.

sexational *adj.* (also **sexsational**) *colloq.* sexually sensational.

sexcapade *n. colloq.* a sexual escapade.

sexed *adj.* having specified sexual characteristics or impulses (*highly sexed*).

sexism *n.* **1** prejudice or discrimination, esp. against women, on the grounds of sex. **2** the institutionalisation and dissemination of sexist attitudes.

sexist *adj.* **1** (of a mindset) based on a stereotypical view of people according to their gender or sexual preference. **2** (of behaviour, language, etc.) discriminatory or exploitative on the basis of gender. • *n.* a person who holds such views or exhibits such behaviour.

sexless *adj.* **1** neither male nor female. **2** lacking sexual desire or attractiveness.

sexology *n.* study of human sexual relationships. ☐ **sexological** *adj.* **sexologist** *n.*

sexpert *n. colloq.* a sexologist or sex therapist.

sexploitation *n.* the exploitation of sex for commercial reasons, esp. in films.

sextant *n.* an instrument used in navigating and surveying, for finding one's position by measuring the altitude of the sun etc.

sextet *n.* a group of six instruments or voices; a musical composition for these.

sexton *n.* a person who takes care of a church and churchyard.

sextuple / **seks**-tyoo-puhl / *adj.* sixfold. • *n.* a sixfold quantity.

sextuplet / seks-**tup**-luht, seks-**tyoo**-pluht / *n.* each of six children born at one birth.

sexual *adj.* **1** of sex or the sexes or the relationship or feelings etc. between them. **2** (of reproduction) occurring by fusion of male and female cells. ☐ **sexual harassment** the subjection of a person to unwelcome sexual advances, actions, words, etc., esp. in the workplace. **sexual intercourse** physical contact between individuals involving sexual stimulation, esp. the insertion of a male's erect penis into a female's vagina, followed by rhythmic movement and usu. ejaculation of semen; copulation. **sexual orientation** or **sexual preference**) one's basic sexual drive, i.e. whether towards the opposite sex or to one's own sex or to both sexes. **sexually transmitted disease** (*abbr.* **STD**) any disease which can be transmitted by sexual contact, e.g. Aids, syphilis, gonorrhoea, etc. ☐☐ **sexually** *adv.*

sexuality / sek-shoo-**al**-uh-tee, seks-yoo- / *n.* **1** the fact of belonging to one of the sexes; one's sexual orientation or preference. **2** possession of sexual powers, capacity for sexual feelings; sexual feelings, desires, etc. collectively; the expression of these.

sexy *adj.* (**sexier**, **sexiest**) **1** sexually attractive, sexually stimulating, or sexually aroused. **2** *colloq.* (of a project etc.) exciting, trendy. ☐ **sexily** *adv.* **sexiness** *n.*

Seychelles / say-**shelz** / a republic consisting of a group of islands in the Indian Ocean. ☐ **Seychellois** / say-**shel**-wah / *adj.* & *n.*

Seymour, Alan (1927–), Australian writer, best known for his play *The One Day of the Year.*

SF *abbr.* science fiction.

sf *abbr.* sforzando.

sforzando *adj.* & *adv. Music* with sudden emphasis.

Sg *symbol* seaborgium.

SGML *abbr. Computing* standard generalised markup language, a form of generic coding used for producing printed material in electronic form.

Sgt *abbr.* sergeant.

sh *interj.* hush.

shabby *adj.* (**shabbier**, **shabbiest**) **1** worn and threadbare, not kept in good condition; (of a person) poorly dressed. **2** unfair, dishonourable (*a shabby trick*). ☐ **shabbily** *adv.* **shabbiness** *n.*

shack *n.* a roughly-built hut or cabin; a small holiday house. ☐ **shack up with** *colloq.* live with (a person) as a lover.

shackle *n.* **1** one of a pair of iron rings joined by a chain, for fastening a prisoner's wrists or ankles. **2** (**shackles**) restraints, impediments (*grumbled about the shackles of marriage*). • *v.* **1** put shackles on. **2** impede or restrict (*shackled by tradition*).

Shackleton, Sir Ernest Henry (1874–1922), Irish-born explorer of the Antarctic.

shade *n.* **1** comparative darkness or coolness where something blocks rays of light. **2** the darker part of a picture. **3** a colour; a degree or depth of colour (*in shades of blue*). **4** a different variety (*all shades of opinion*). **5** a small amount (*she's a shade better today*). **6** *literary* a ghost. **7** a screen used to block light or heat; a cover for a lamp. **8** (**shades**) sunglasses. • *v.* **1** block the rays of. **2** give shade to; make dark. **3** pass gradually into another colour or variety (*the blue here shades into green; where socialism shaded into communism*). **4** darken, esp. with parallel lines to show shadow etc. in a drawing etc. ☐ **put in the shade** cause to appear inferior by contrast; outshine. **shades of** a reminder of (esp. something unpleasant) (*shades of Hitler!*).

shadecloth *n.* a network fabric, usu. made of plastic, used in shadehouses etc., esp. to provide tender plants with (differing degrees of) protection from the summer sun.

shadehouse *n.* a structure, usu. roofed and sided with shadecloth, in which sensitive plants may be shaded from the summer sun.

shading *n.* light and shade shown on a map or drawing by parallel lines etc.

shadow *n.* **1** shade. **2** a patch of this with the shape of the body that is blocking the rays. **3** a person's inseparable attendant or companion; bosom friend, constant mate. **4** a person secretly following another to spy etc. **5** a slight trace (*shadow of doubt*). **6** gloom; an ongoing threat (*the news cast a shadow over the proceedings; living under the shadow of war*). **7** a weak or insubstantial remnant (*a shadow of his former self*). **8** (used as *adj.*) denoting members of the opposition party holding posts parallel to those of the government (*the shadow cabinet; the shadow Treasurer*). • *v.* **1** cast shadow over. **2** follow and watch secretly. ☐ **shadow-boxing** boxing against an imaginary opponent as a form of training.

shadowy *adj.* **1** full of shadows. **2** like a shadow; vague and indistinct.

shady *adj.* (**shadier**, **shadiest**) **1** giving shade; situated in the shade. **2** disreputable; not completely honest (*shady dealings*). ☐ **shadily** *adv.* **shadiness** *n.*

shaft *n.* **1** a spear or arrow; its long slender stem. **2** a remark aimed or striking like an arrow (*shafts of wit*). **3** a ray (of light); a bolt (of lightning). **4**

any long narrow straight part of something, e.g. of a supporting column or a golf club. **5** a large axle. **6** each of a pair of long bars between which a horse is harnessed to draw a vehicle. **7** a vertical or sloping passage or opening giving access to a mine or providing an outlet for air, smoke, etc. **8** *colloq.* harsh or unfair treatment (*gave him the shaft*). •*v. colloq.* treat harshly or unfairly (*he was shafted by his best friend*).

shag[1] *n.* **1** a rough mass of hair or fibre. **2** a strong coarse tobacco. **3** a cormorant. •*adj.* (of a carpet) having a long rough pile. ☐ **shag on a rock** *Aust. colloq.* emblem of isolation, deprivation, etc. (*living all alone like a shag on a rock*).

shag[2] *v. coarse colloq.* **1** have sexual intercourse with. **2** masturbate oneself or another. **3** (as **shagged** *adj.*) (often foll. by *out*) exhausted, tired out. ☐ **shag wagon** (also **shaggin' wagon**) *Aust.* a panel van fitted out for sleeping in, as a convenient place in which to engage in sexual intercourse etc.

shagger *n. Aust. coarse colloq.* (often *derog.*) a sexually promiscuous male. ☐ **shagger's back** a pain in the back, jocularly attributed to injury during sexual intercourse.

shaggy *adj.* (**shaggier, shaggiest**) **1** having long rough hair or fibre. **2** rough, thick, and untidy; unkempt (*shaggy hair*). ☐ **shaggy-dog story** a long rambling joke, amusing only by its pointlessness. ☐☐ **shagginess** *n.*

shagreen / shuh-**green** / *n.* **1** untanned leather with a granulated surface. **2** sharkskin used for rasping and polishing things.

shah *n.* the title of the former monarch of Iran.

shake *v.* (**shook, shaken, shaking**) **1** move quickly and jerkily up and down or to and fro. **2** dislodge by doing this (*the dog shook himself and we were drenched*). **3** shock or disturb; upset the calmness of (*we were shaken by the news*). **4** weaken or impair (*shook his faith in God*). **5** (of a voice) tremble or falter. **6** shake hands (*let's shake on it*). **7** *Aust. colloq.* steal (something); rob (a person). •*n.* **1** shaking; being shaken. **2** a jolt or shock. **3** (**the shakes**) *colloq.* a fit of trembling. **4** a milk shake. **5** a moment (*shall be there in two shakes*). ☐ **shake-a-leg** *Aust.* a style of traditional Aboriginal dancing. **shake down 1** become adjusted to new conditions. **2** sleep in an improvised bed. **3** extort money from. **shake up 1** mix by shaking. **2** restore to shape by shaking. **3** rouse from sluggishness or a set habit. **shake-up** *n.* an upheaval; a drastic reorganisation.

shakedown *n.* **1** a makeshift bed. esp. made up on the floor. **2** an act of extortion. ☐ **shakedown merchant** a confidence man (*see* CONFIDENCE).

shaker *n.* **1** a person or thing that shakes something. **2** a container in which cocktails are mixed by being shaken. **3** *Aust.* a machine in which gold-bearing gravel, sand, etc. is agitated to separate out alluvial gold without the need of water.

Shakespeare, William (1564–1616), English playwright and poet, born at Stratford-upon-Avon in Warwickshire. ☐ **Shakespearian** or **Shakespearean** *adj.*

shaky *adj.* (**shakier, shakiest**) **1** shaking, unsteady, trembling. **2** unreliable, wavering. ☐ **shakily** *adv.* **shakiness** *n.*

Shaky Isles *Aust. colloq.* New Zealand (from the frequency there of earthquakes).

shale *n.* stone that splits easily into fine pieces. ☐ **shaly** *adj.*

shall *auxiliary v.* (*past* **should**) (*archaic* **shalt**, used with *thou*) **1** (in the 1st person singular, *I*, and the 1st person plural, *we*) expressing the simple future tense (*I shall return soon; we shall see the moon any moment now*). **2** (in the 2nd person singular, *thou*, 2nd person plural, *we*, 3rd person singular, *he*, *she*, or *it*, and 3rd person plural *they*) expressing a strong assertion, command, or obligation, rather than the simple future (cf. WILL[1]) (*thou shalt not steal; you shall obey; she shall marry the man I choose for her; they shall go to church whether they want to or not*). **3** (in 2nd-person questions) expressing an enquiry, esp. to avoid the form of a request (cf. WILL[1]) (*shall you go to Oodnadatta?*). ☐ **shall I?** (*or* **shall we?**) do you want me (*or* us) to? (*shall I go?; shall we dance?*).

■ **Usage** The distinction between the use of *shall* in the 1st person (expressing the simple future) and *shall* in the 2nd and 3rd persons (expressing determination etc.) remains valid, but in common (esp. *colloquial*) usage *shall* is used to express determination etc. in all persons, and *will* is used in all persons to express the simple future, with an increasing tendency for the emphatic use of *will* to replace *shall*.

shallot / shuh-**lot** / *n.* a plant of the onion family that forms a cluster of small bulbs each slightly bigger than a large clove of garlic.

■ **Usage** In Australia the term *shallot* is sometimes applied to a *spring onion*.

shallow *adj.* **1** not deep. **2** not thinking or thought out deeply; not capable of deep feelings. •*n.* (often in *pl.*) a shallow place. •*v.* make or become shallow. ☐ **shallowly** *adv.* **shallowness** *n.*

shalom / shuh-**lom** / *n.* & *interj.* a Jewish expression of greeting or leave-taking.

shalt *see* SHALL.

sham *n.* a pretence; a thing, feeling, or person that is not genuine. •*adj.* pretended, not genuine. •*v.* (**shammed, shamming**) pretend; pretend to be, simulate (*he's always shamming; she's shamming sleep*).

shaman / **shah**-muhn, **shay**- / *n.* a person regarded as having direct access to the spirit world, which is usually contacted during a trance. ☐ **shamanism** *n.*

shamble v. walk or run in an awkward or lazy way. • n. **1** a shambling movement. **2** (**shambles**) (treated as *sing.*) a mess, a muddle; a butcher's slaughterhouse; a scene of chaos or carnage.

shambolic / sham-**bol**-ik / adj. *colloq.* chaotic, very disorganised.

shame n. **1** a painful mental feeling aroused by a sense of having done something wrong or ridiculous. **2** ability to feel this (*he has no shame*). **3** something regrettable, a pity (*it's a shame you can't come*). • v. bring shame on, make ashamed; compel by arousing feelings of shame (*they were shamed into contributing more*). • adj. *Aust.* (in Aboriginal English) self-conscious; embarrassed. ▫ **shame job** *Aust.* (in Aboriginal English) an act occasioning embarrassment.

shamefaced adj. looking ashamed.

shameful adj. causing shame, disgraceful. ▫ **shamefully** adv.

shameless adj. having or showing no feeling of shame; impudent. ▫ **shamelessly** adv.

shammy n. a chamois leather.

shampoo n. **1** a liquid used to wash hair. **2** a liquid or chemical for cleaning carpets or upholstery, or for washing a car. **3** shampooing (*a shampoo and set*). • v. wash or clean with a shampoo.

shamrock n. a clover-like plant with three leaves on each stem, the national emblem of Ireland.

shandy n. a mixed drink of lemonade or ginger beer.

shanghai / **shang**-huy / v. (**shanghaied**, **shanghaiing**) **1** *hist.* abduct (a male) using force, fraud, or drugs and make him serve as a sailor on an undermanned ship. **2** trick or force (a person) into doing something against his or her will. **3** *Aust.* shoot with a catapult. **4** *colloq.* steal. • n. *Aust.* a (child's) catapult. (¶ Named after *Shanghai*, a seaport in China.)

shank n. **1** the leg. **2** the leg from knee to ankle; the corresponding part of an animal's leg (esp. as a cut of meat). **3** a long narrow part of something; a shaft. ▫ **shanks's mare** (or **pony**) one's own legs as a means of transport.

Shankar, Ravi (1920–), Indian sitar player and composer.

shan't = shall not.

shantung n. a soft untreated Chinese silk.

shanty[1] n. **1** a hut or cabin. **2** a crudely built shack. **3** (in full **grog shanty**) *Aust. hist.* a roughly constructed unlicensed public house, esp. on an Australian goldfield. **4** a small tavern, usu. in a rural area. ▫ **shanty town** an area with makeshift housing of rough shacks.

shanty[2] n. (in full **sea shanty**) a sailors' traditional work song.

shape n. **1** an area or form with a definite outline. **2** the form or condition in which something appears (*a monster in human shape*). **3** the proper form or condition of something (*get it into shape*). **4** a pattern or mould. • v. **1** give a certain shape to. **2** develop into a certain shape or condition (*the plans are shaping up well*). **3** adapt or modify (one's plans or ideas etc.). ▫ **shape up** show promise; make good progress; perform better (*shape up or get out*). **take shape** take on a definite form.

shapeless adj. **1** having no definite shape. **2** not shapely. ▫ **shapelessly** adv.

shapely adj. (**shapelier**, **shapeliest**) having a pleasing shape; well proportioned. ▫ **shapeliness** n.

shard n. a broken piece of pottery or glass.

share n. **1** a part given to an individual out of a larger amount which is being divided; the part one is entitled to have or do. **2** any of the equal parts forming a business company's capital and entitling the holder to a proportion of the profits. • v. **1** give portions of (a thing) to two or more people (*share it out*). **2** give away part of (*would share his last crust*). **3** have a share of; use, possess, endure, or benefit from (a thing) jointly with others (*share a bed; we share the credit*). ▫ **go shares** share things equally.

share farmer n. one of two or more people contributing part of the resources required to produce a crop etc., and receiving a proportional share of the profits. ▫ **share farm** v. **share farming** n.

shareholder n. a person who owns a share or shares in a business company.

shareware n. computer programs available on trial to any user free of charge (but if used regularly a fee should be paid to the author).

shariah / shuh-**ree**-uh / n. the sacred law of Islam, prescribing religious and other duties.

Sharjah an emirate, a member state of the United Arab Emirates.

shark n. **1** a large voracious sea fish with a triangular fin on its back, some kinds of which attack swimmers. **2** a person who ruthlessly extorts money from others, a swindler or profiteer. • v. **1** *colloq.* obtain by swindling; steal. **2** *Aust. Rules* interrupt (steal) a ball being passed between two of one's opponents. ▫ **shark patrol** *Aust.* the patrol of surfing beaches by boat or aircraft to warn swimmers of the presence of sharks.

sharkskin n. **1** the skin of a shark. **2** wool, silk, or rayon fabric with a smooth slightly shiny finish.

sharp adj. **1** having a fine edge or point that is capable of cutting or piercing. **2** narrowing to a point or edge (*a sharp ridge*). **3** steep, angular, not gradual (*a sharp slope; a sharp turn*). **4** well-defined, distinct (*in sharp focus*). **5** severe or intense (*a sharp pain*). **6** (of weather etc.) cuttingly cold (*a sharp wind*). **7** (of tastes and smells) producing a smarting sensation. **8** (of a voice or sound) shrill and piercing. **9** (of words or temper etc.) harsh (*a sharp tongue*). **10** quick to see or hear or notice things; intelligent. **11** unscrupulous (*sharp practices*). **12** (in music)

sharpen

above the correct pitch; a semitone higher than the specified pitch (*C sharp; F sharp*). •*adv.* **1** punctually (*at six o'clock sharp*). **2** suddenly (*pulled up sharp*). **3** at a sharp angle (*turn sharp right at the junction*). **4** above the correct pitch in music (*was singing sharp*). •*n.* **1** (in music) a note that is a semitone higher than the corresponding one of natural pitch; a sign (♯) indicating this. **2** *colloq.* a swindler. ☐ **sharp practice** business dealings that are dishonest or dubious. ☐☐ **sharpish** *adj.* **sharply** *adv.* **sharpness** *n.*

sharpen *v.* make or become sharp. ☐ **sharpener** *n.*

sharper *n.* a swindler, esp. at cards.

sharpshooter *n.* a skilled marksman.

shashlik / **shash**-lik / *n.* an eastern European and Asian kebab of mutton and garnishings, usu. served on a skewer.

Shastra / **shahs**-truh / *n.* any of the sacred writings of the Hindus.

shastri / **shahs**-tree / *n.* a scholar or teacher of the Shastras.

shat *see* SHIT.

shatter *v.* **1** break violently into small pieces. **2** destroy utterly (*shattered our hopes*). **3** disturb or upset the calmness of (*we were shattered by the news*).

shave *v.* **1** scrape (growing hair) off the skin with a razor. **2** cut thin slices from the surface of (wood etc.). **3** graze gently in passing. **4** reduce or remove (*shave ten per cent off our estimates*). •*n.* the shaving of hair from the face. ☐ **close shave** *colloq.* a narrow escape.

shaven *adj.* shaved.

shaver *n.* **1** a person or thing that shaves. **2** an electric razor. **3** *colloq.* a young lad.

Shavian / **shay**-vee-uhn / *adj.* of G.B. Shaw. •*n.* an admirer of Shaw.

shavings *n.pl.* thin strips of wood etc. shaved off the surface of a piece.

Shaw, George Bernard (1856–1950), Irish playwright and critic.

shawl *n.* a large piece of fabric worn round the shoulders or head, or wrapped round a baby.

shawm / shawm / *n.* a medieval double-reed wind instrument with a sharp penetrating tone.

she *pron.* **1** the female person or animal mentioned; a thing (e.g. a vehicle, ship, or aircraft) personified as female. **2** (in Australia) applied to things to which the female sex is not conventionally attributed, = it; the state of affairs; etc. ('*Bet you five to one.*' —'*She's on!*'; *she's starting to get a bit chilly; she's a beaut ditch—best I ever dug*) (cf. RIGHT; SWEET). **3** (as *adj.*) *Aust.* used in the names of some trees, apparently indicative of the perceived inferiority of the timber (*she-oak; she pine*). •*n.* **1** a female; a woman. **2** a female animal (*she-goat*).

s/he *pron.* a written representation of 'he or she', used to indicate either sex.

sheep

sheaf *n.* (*pl.* **sheaves**) **1** a bundle of stalks of wheat etc. tied together after reaping. **2** a bundle of arrows, papers, or other things laid lengthwise together.

shear *v.* (*past* **sheared** *or* (*Aust.* esp. in shearers' use) **shore**; *past participle* **shorn** *or* **sheared**; **shearing**) **1** clip the wool off (a sheep etc.). **2** remove or take off by cutting. **3** cut with scissors or shears etc. **4** *Aust.* be employed as a shearer (*he shore from one end of Australia to the other*). **5** strip bare, deprive (*shorn of his glory*). **6** break or distort, or become broken or distorted. •*n.* **1** (**shears**) a large scissor-shaped instrument for cutting or clipping. **2** a type of fracture or distortion produced by pressure, in which each successive layer (e.g. of a mass of rock) slides over the next.

shearer *n. Aust.* an itinerant worker hired seasonally to shear sheep.

Shearers' Strike industrial action by shearers in 1891 and 1894 against the pastoralists' attempts to employ non-union labour at cheaper rates, significant in the history of unionism in Australia.

shearing *n.* the act or the season of shearing sheep. ☐ **shearing board** *see* BOARD (*n.* sense 6.).

shearing shed *Aust.* a large building in which sheep are shorn and the fleeces are processed and packed.

shearwater *n.* any of various long-winged seabirds, usu. flying near to the surface of the water, many of which migrate to Australian waters, often breeding on coastal islands.

sheath *n.* (*pl.* **sheaths** / sheeths, shee*thz* /) **1** a close-fitting covering; a cover for a blade or tool. **2** a covering for wearing on the penis during sexual intercourse as a contraceptive; a condom. **3** a close-fitting dress. ☐ **sheath knife** a dagger-like knife carried in a sheath.

sheathe / shee*th* / *v.* **1** put into a sheath. **2** encase in a covering.

sheaves *see* SHEAF.

shebang / shuh-**bang** / *n. colloq.* matter or affair (*I'm fed up with the whole shebang*).

shed[1] *n.* **1** a one-storeyed building for storing things, sheltering livestock, for use as a workshop, etc. **2** *Aust.* = SHEARING SHED. **3** (also as *adj.*) *Aust.* the gang of shearers working in a particular shed (*the shed went on strike; he topped the shed tally and was declared the ringer*). ☐ **shed hand** *Aust.* an unskilled worker in a shearing shed.

shed[2] *v.* (**shed**, **shedding**) **1** lose (a thing) by a natural falling off (*trees shed their leaves*). **2** take off (*shed one's clothes*). **3** allow to pour forth (*shed tears*). **4** get rid of (*the company is shedding 200 jobs; shed your inhibitions*). ☐ **shed light on** help to explain.

she'd = **1** she had. **2** she would.

sheen *n.* gloss, lustre.

sheep *n.* (*pl.* **sheep**) a grass-eating animal with a thick fleecy coat, kept for its fleece and meat. ☐ **like sheep** (of people) easily led or influenced.

sheepdog

on (*or* **off**) **the sheep's back** *Aust.* used in allusion to wool as the source of Australia's prosperity (*politicians often claimed that Australia lives off the sheep's back*). **separate the sheep from the goats** divide into superior and inferior groups. **sheep bush** *Aust.* = WILGA. **sheep cocky** *Aust.* a sheep farmer on a small scale. **sheep dip** a preparation or a place for cleansing sheep of vermin by dipping. **sheep run** *Aust.* a tract of land (usu. extensive) used for grazing sheep. **sheep-sick** *adj. Aust.* (of land) degraded as a result of over-grazing sheep. **sheep station** *Aust.* an extensive establishment for the raising of sheep.

sheepdog *n.* a dog of a breed often trained to guard and herd sheep.

sheepish *adj.* bashful, embarrassed; ashamed. □ **sheepishly** *adv.* **sheepishness** *n.*

sheepskin *n.* **1** a coat or rug made of sheep's skin with the wool on. **2** leather made from sheep's skin used in bookbinding etc.

sheer[1] *adj.* **1** pure, absolute (*sheer luck*). **2** (of a rock etc.) having a vertical or almost vertical surface. **3** (of fabric) very thin, transparent. • *adv.* directly, straight up or down (*the cliff rises sheer from the sea*).

sheer[2] *v.* **1** swerve from a course. **2** (foll. by *off* or *away*) turn away, esp. from a person or topic that one dislikes or wishes to avoid.

sheet[1] *n.* **1** a large rectangular piece of fabric, used as part of bedclothes. **2** a large thin piece of any material (e.g. glass, metal). **3** a piece of paper. **4** a wide expanse of water, snow, flame, etc. • *v.* **1** provide or cover with sheets. **2** form into sheets. **3** (of rain etc.) fall in sheets. □ **sheet lightning** a lightning flash with its brightness diffused by reflection. **sheet music** music published on loose sheets of paper and not bound into a book.

sheet[2] *n.* a rope or chain attached to the lower corner of a sail, to secure or adjust it. □ **sheet anchor 1** an emergency reserve anchor. **2** a person or thing on which one depends for security or stability.

sheikh / sheek, shayk / *n.* (also **sheik**) **1** the leader of an Arab family, tribe, or village. **2** a Muslim leader. □ **sheikhdom** *n.*

sheila *n. Aust. colloq.* a girl, a young woman; a girlfriend.

shekel / **shek**-uhl / *n.* **1** *hist.* a silver coin and unit of weight in ancient Israel etc. **2** the unit of money in modern Israel. **3** (**shekels**) *colloq.* money, riches.

sheldrake *n.* (*pl.* **sheldrake** *or* **sheldrakes**) a male shelduck.

shelduck *n.* (*pl.* **shelduck** *or* **shelducks**) a wild duck with bright plumage, including the Australian shelduck.

shelf *n.* (*pl.* **shelves**) **1** a flat rectangular piece of wood, glass, etc. fastened horizontally for things to be placed on. **2 a** something resembling this, a ledge or step-like projection in a cliff-face etc. **b** a reef or sandbank. □ **on the shelf 1** (of an unmarried woman) *offens.* past the age when she is regarded as likely to be sought in marriage. **2** (esp. of a retired person) put aside as if no longer useful or wanted. **shelf life** the time for which a stored item remains usable. **shelf mark** a number marked on a book to show its place in a library.

shell *n.* **1** the hard outer covering of eggs, nut-kernels, and of animals such as snails, crabs, and tortoises. **2** the walls of an unfinished or burnt-out building or ship. **3** any structure that forms a firm framework or covering. **4** a light rowing boat for racing. **5** a metal case filled with explosive, to be fired from a large gun. **6** a group of electrons in an atom, with almost equal energy. **7** a mere semblance or outer form without substance (*he's just a shell of his former self*). • *v.* **1** remove the shell of (*shell peas*). **2** fire explosive shells at. □ **shell out** *colloq.* pay out (money). **shell shock** a nervous breakdown resulting from exposure to battle conditions.

she'll = she will; she shall. □ **she'll be right** *Aust. colloq.* everything will be fine.

shellac / shuh-**lak** / *n.* thin flakes of a resinous substance used in making varnish. • *v.* (**shellacked**, **shellacking**) varnish with shellac.

Shelley[1], Mary (Wollstonecraft) (1797–1851), English novelist, author of *Frankenstein*.

Shelley[2], Percy Bysshe (1792–1822), English Romantic poet who eloped with and later married Mary Wollstonecraft Shelley.

shellfish *n.* a water animal that has a shell, esp. one of edible kinds such as oysters, crabs, and prawns.

Shelta *n.* an ancient secret language used by Irish Gypsies, tinkers, etc.

shelter *n.* **1** something that serves as a shield or barrier against attack, danger, heat, wind, etc. **2** a structure built to keep rain etc. off people (*a bus shelter*). **3** refuge; a shielded condition (*seek shelter from the rain*). • *v.* **1** provide with shelter. **2** protect from blame, trouble, or competition. **3** find or take shelter. □ **sheltered workshop** a building etc. designed to provide work for people with disabilities. **shelter shed** *Aust.* a roofed structure, usu. partly enclosed, affording protection (in school playgrounds etc.) from inclement weather, and providing a place for eating lunch etc.

shelve *v.* **1** arrange on a shelf or shelves. **2** fit (a wall or cupboard etc.) with shelves. **3** put aside for later consideration. **4** slope (*the river bottom shelves here*).

shelves *see* SHELF.

shelving *n.* shelves; material for making these.

shemozzle *n. colloq.* **1** a rumpus; a brawl. **2** a muddle.

shenanigans / shuh-**nan**-uh-guhnz / *n.pl. colloq.* **1** high-spirited behaviour. **2** trickery; carryings-on.

she-oak *n.* **1** any of various Australian trees or shrubs of the casuarina family. **2** the wood of these trees, the grain of which resembles that of English oak, although the wood itself is considered inferior (*see* SHE, sense 3).

shepherd *n.* **1** a person who looks after sheep. **2** *Aust. hist.* a miner who holds a claim (on a goldfield) but does not work it, waiting instead to see if neighbouring claims yield gold. • *v.* **1** tend (sheep etc.). **2** guide (followers etc.). **3** marshal or drive (a crowd etc.) like sheep. **4** *Aust. hist.* effect token occupation (by, e.g., digging small pits) of a goldmining claim in order to comply with the regulations governing possession, but put off hard work on it until neighbouring claims prove to be rich. **5** guard or keep under close surveillance. **6** *Aust. Rules* guard a team-mate in possession of the ball by blocking opponents. □ **shepherd's pie** a dish of minced meat topped with mashed potato.

shepherdess *n.* a woman who looks after sheep.

Sheraton / she-ruh-tuhn / *n.* a late 18th-century style of English furniture, named after its designer Thomas Sheraton (1751–1806).

sherbet *n.* **1** (esp. in Arab countries) a cooling drink of weak sweet fruit juice. **2** a fizzy sweet drink or the powder from which this is made. **3** *Aust. colloq.* beer.

sheriff *n.* **1** *Brit.* the chief executive officer of the Crown in a county, administering justice etc. **2** *Aust.* an officer of the Supreme Court of Australia who enforces judgments and the execution of writs, and attends to other administrative matters. **3** *US* the chief law-enforcing officer of a county.

Sherpa *n.* a member of a Himalayan people living on the borders of Nepal and Tibet.

sherry *n.* a fortified wine, originally from southern Spain.

she's = **1** she is. **2** she has.

Shetland *adj.* of a group of about 100 Scottish islands NE of the Orkneys. □ **Shetland pony** a pony of a very small rough-coated breed.

shew *v. archaic* = SHOW.

Shi'a / sheer / (also **Shia**) *n.* **1** smaller of the two main branches of Islam (the other being Sunni), found esp. in Iran. **2** a Shi'ite. • *adj.* of or relating to Shi'a. (¶ Arabic, = a party (of Ali, Muhammad's cousin and son-in-law).)

shiatsu / shee-**at**-soo / *n.* Japanese therapy in which pressure is applied with the hands to specific points on the body.

shibboleth / **shib**-uh-leth / *n.* an old slogan, doctrine, or principle that is still considered essential by a party or sect etc. (¶ From a story in the Bible, in which 'shibboleth' was a kind of password.)

shicer / **shuy**-suh / *n. Aust.* **1** an unproductive claim, mine, or goldfield. **2** *colloq.* a cheat, a swindler.

shickered / shik-uhd / *adj.* (also **shicker**) *Aust. colloq.* drunk. □ **on the shicker** drunk.

shield *n.* **1** a piece of armour carried on the arm to protect the body. **2** a person or thing giving protection. **3** a shield-shaped trophy. **4** a protective plate or screen in machinery etc. **5** a large rigid area of the earth's crust, usu. of Precambrian rock, unaffected by later displacements of the crust. • *v.* protect or screen; protect from discovery. □ **shield fern** (also **mother shield fern**) a common Australian fern, having large dark green fronds, and producing small new fern plants at the extremities of mature fronds.

shift *v.* **1** (cause to) change or move from one position to another. **2** change form or character. **3** transfer (blame or responsibility etc.). **4** *colloq.* move quickly. **5** remove (*can't shift this stain*). • *n.* **1** a change of place, form, character, etc. **2** a set of workers who start work as another set finishes; the time for which they work (*the night shift*). **3** a piece of evasion. **4** a scheme for achieving something. **5** an unwaisted dress or petticoat. **6** a key on a keyboard used to switch between lower and upper case etc. **7** a gear lever in a vehicle; the mechanism for this. □ **shifting spanner** (also **shifter**) an adjustable spanner.

shiftless *adj.* lazy; lacking resourcefulness. □ **shiftlessness** *n.*

shifty *adj.* (**shiftier**, **shiftiest**) evasive, not straightforward in manner or character; untrustworthy. □ **shiftily** *adv.* **shiftiness** *n.*

shiitake / shuh-**tah**-kay / *n.* (in full **shiitake mushroom**) an edible mushroom cultivated in Japan and China on oak logs etc.

Shi'ite / **shee**-uyt / *n.* a member of the Shi'a sect, one of the two major sects in Islam, centred chiefly in Iran (the other being the Sunni sect in most other Muslim countries).

shilling *n. hist.* a former coin of Australia, Britain, etc., worth one twentieth of a pound.

shilly-shally *v.* (**shilly-shallied**, **shilly-shallying**) be unable to make up one's mind.

shimmer *v.* shine with a soft light that appears to quiver. • *n.* a shimmering effect.

shin *n.* **1** the front of the leg below the knee. **2** the lower part of the foreleg in cattle, esp. as a cut of beef. • *v.* (**shinned**, **shinning**) climb using arms and legs.

shindig *n. colloq.* **1** a lively noisy party. **2** a shindy.

shindy *n. colloq.* a din; a brawl.

shine *v.* (**shone** (in sense 5 **shined**), **shining**) **1** give out or reflect light, be bright, glow. **2** (of the sun etc.) be visible and not obscured by clouds. **3** excel in some way (*does not shine in maths; a shining example*). **4** direct the light of (*shine the torch on it*). **5** *colloq.* polish. • *n.* **1** brightness. **2** a high polish. □ **take a shine to** *colloq.* take a liking to.

shiner *n. colloq.* a black eye.

shingle *n.* **1** a rectangular slip of wood used as a roof tile. **2** small round pebbles, esp. on the seashore. • *v.* roof with shingles. □ **a shingle**

short *Aust. colloq.* mentally deficient; stupid, dull. (¶ From sense 1 of the noun.)

shingleback *Aust.* = BOBTAIL (sense 2).

shingles *n.* a painful disease caused by a virus, with a rash often encircling the body.

Shinto *n.* (also **Shintoism**) a Japanese religion revering ancestors and nature spirits.

shiny *adj.* (**shinier**, **shiniest**) shining, rubbed until glossy. • *n.* = SHINY BUM. □ **shiny bum** (also **shiny arse**) *Aust. colloq.* an office worker, administrator, or public servant. □ □ **shininess** *n.*

ship *n.* a large seagoing vessel. • *v.* (**shipped**, **shipping**) **1** put, take, or send on a ship. **2** transport.

shipboard *adj.* used or occurring on board a ship.

shipmate *n.* a sailor working on the same ship as another.

shipment *n.* **1** the putting of goods on a ship. **2** the amount shipped; a consignment.

shipping *n.* **1** ships. **2** transporting goods by ship or by other means; the cost of this.

shipshape *adv.* & *adj.* in good order, tidy.

shipwreck *n.* **1** the destruction of a ship by storm or striking a rock etc.; a ship so destroyed. **2** the ruin of hopes, dreams, etc. • *v.* inflict shipwreck on (a ship, a person's hopes, etc.); suffer shipwreck. □ **shipwrecked** *adj.*

shipwright *n.* **1** a shipbuilder. **2** a ship's carpenter.

shipyard *n.* a shipbuilding establishment.

shiralee / **shi**-ruh-lee / *n. Aust. colloq.* a swag.

shiraz / shuh-**raz**, -**rahz** / *n.* (also **Shiraz**) **1** a black grape variety used in winemaking. **2** the red wine made from such grapes. (¶ *Shiraz*, a city in Iran.)

shire *n.* **1** *Aust.* a rural administrative district, with its own local council, in some Australian States. **2** *Brit.* a county.

shirk *v.* avoid (a duty or work etc.) selfishly or unfairly. □ **shirker** *n.*

shirr *v.* gather (cloth) with parallel elastic threads run through it. □ **shirring** *n.*

shirt *n.* a garment of cotton or silk etc. for the upper part of the body. □ **keep one's shirt on** *colloq.* keep one's temper. **shirt tail** the curved part of a shirt below the waist.

shirtfront *Aust. Rules n.* a fierce tackle usu. delivered by the shoulder to the chest of an opponent. • *v.* (also **shirt-front**) deliver such a tackle.

shirtsleeve *n.* the sleeve of a shirt. □ **in one's shirtsleeves** without one's jacket on.

shirty *adj.* (**shirtier**, **shirtiest**) *colloq.* annoyed, angry. □ **shirtily** *adv.* **shirtiness** *n.*

shish kebab / **shish** kuh-**bab** / *n.* a dish consisting of pieces of marinated meat (usu. lamb) and vegetables grilled and served on skewers.

shit *coarse colloq. n.* **1** faeces. **2** an act of defecating. **3** a contemptible person or thing. **4** nonsense; lies. **5** (**the shits**) **a** diarrhoea. **b** a state of extreme anger or annoyance. **6** marijuana. • *interj.* an exclamation of anger, frustration, etc. • *v.* (**shitted** *or* **shat** *or* **shit**, **shitting**) empty the bowels, defecate. □ **get one's shit together** organise oneself; manage one's affairs. **in the shit** in trouble; in a difficult situation. **not give a shit** not care at all. **shit-hot** excellent. **shit-kicker 1** an unskilled worker; a performer of menial tasks. **2** a person of little consequence. **shit stirrer** a person who enjoys causing trouble or discord. **up shit creek** in a predicament. **when the shit hits the fan** when the disastrous consequences of something become public.

shithouse *coarse colloq. n.* a toilet. • *adj.* bad; awful.

shitless *predic.adj. coarse colloq.* □ **be scared shitless** be extremely frightened.

shitty *Aust. coarse colloq. adj.* **1** bad-tempered, angry. **2** disgusting, contemptible. **3** bad, awful. • *n.* a fit of bad temper.

Shiva / **shee**-vuh / = SIVA.

shiver[1] *v.* tremble slightly, esp. with cold or fear. • *n.* **1** a momentary shivering movement. **2** (**the shivers**) an attack of shivering. □ **shivery** *adj.*

shiver[2] *v.* shatter. • *n.pl.* (**shivers**) shattered fragments.

shivoo / shuh-**voo** / *n. Aust. colloq.* a party or celebration; a revel. (¶ A corruption of French *chez vous* = at your place.)

shoal[1] *n.* a great number, esp. of fish swimming together. • *v.* form shoals.

shoal[2] *n.* **1** a shallow place; an underwater sandbank. **2** (**shoals**) hidden dangers or difficulties. • *v.* (of water) become shallower.

shock[1] *n.* **1** the effect of a violent impact or shake. **2** a violent shake of the earth's crust in an earthquake. **3** a sudden violent effect upon a person's mind or emotions (e.g. by news of a disaster). **4** an acute state of weakness caused by physical injury or pain or by mental shock. **5** an electric shock (*see* ELECTRIC). • *v.* **1** affect with great indignation, horror, or disgust. **2** give an electric shock to. **3** cause an acute state of weakness in (a person or animal). □ **shock absorber** a device for absorbing vibration in a vehicle. **shock tactics** sudden violent action taken to achieve one's purpose. **shock therapy** (*or* **treatment**) treatment of psychiatric patients by means of an electric shock or a drug causing a similar effect. **shock troops** troops specially trained for violent assaults. **shock wave** a sharp wave of increased atmospheric pressure, caused by an explosion or by a body moving faster than sound.

shock[2] *n.* a bushy untidy mass of hair.

shocker *n. colloq.* **1** a shocking person or thing. **2** a very bad specimen (*his performance was a shocker; had a shocker of a day*).

shocking *adj.* **1** causing great shock, indignation, or disgust; scandalous. **2** *colloq.* very bad (*shocking weather*). ☐ **shocking pink** very bright pink. ☐☐ **shockingly** *adv.*

shod *see* SHOE. • *adj.* having shoes of a specified kind (*sensibly shod*).

shoddy *adj.* (**shoddier, shoddiest**) **1** of poor quality or workmanship. **2** base, mean (*got shoddy treatment from the authorities*). ☐ **shoddily** *adv.* **shoddiness** *n.*

shoe *n.* **1** an outer covering for a person's foot, with a fairly stiff sole. **2** a horseshoe. **3** an object like a shoe in appearance or use. **4** the part of a brake that presses against the wheel or its drum in a vehicle. • *v.* (**shod, shoeing**) fit with a shoe or shoes. ☐ **be in a person's shoes** be in his or her situation or difficulty.

shoehorn *n.* a curved implement for easing one's heel into the back of a shoe.

shoelace *n.* a cord for fastening shoes.

shoemaker *n.* a person whose trade is making or mending boots and shoes.

shoestring *n.* a shoelace. ☐ **on a shoestring** with only a small amount of money.

shogun / **shoh**-guhn / *n. hist.* the hereditary commander of the army in feudal Japan.

shone *see* SHINE.

shonky (also **shonkie**) *Aust. colloq. adj.* (**shonkier, shonkiest**) **1** unreliable; unsound; dishonest (*the budget figures are shonky; a shonky used-car salesman*). **2** out of sorts; unwell (*feeling a bit shonky today*). • *n.* a person who engages in sharp practice.

shoo *interj.* an exclamation used to frighten birds, animals, etc. away. • *v.* (**shooed, shooing**) utter the word 'shoo!'; drive away by this.

shook *see* SHAKE. • *adj. colloq.* **1** (**shook up**) emotionally or physically disturbed; greatly upset (*am all shook up*). **2** (**shook on**) *Aust.* keen on; enthusiastic about (*Aussies are not too shook on the pommy climate*).

shoot *v.* (**shot, shooting**) **1** fire (a gun, missile, etc.). **2** kill or wound with a bullet, arrow, etc. **3** hunt with a gun for sport. **4** move or send out swiftly or violently (*the car shot past*). **5** (of a plant) put forth buds or shoots. **6** slide (the bolt of a door) into or out of its fastening. **7** take a shot at goal. **8** photograph or film. **9** *Surfing* ride (a wave). **10** (of a boat) pass swiftly through (rapids etc.). • *interj.* say what you have to say. • *n.* **1** a young branch or new growth of a plant. **2** an expedition for shooting game. **3** *Surfing* **a** a breaking wave which carries a surfer towards the beach. **b** the act of riding such a wave. **4** = CHUTE (senses 1 & 2). ☐ **shoot one's bolt** *colloq.* **1** do all that is in one's power and have nothing left. **2** (of a man) ejaculate (semen), esp. prematurely.

shooting gallery 1 a place used for shooting at targets with rifles etc. **2** *colloq.* **a** a place where addictive drugs may be illicitly obtained and injected. **b** *Aust.* an establishment providing a safe environment for the injection of illicit drugs.

shooting star a small meteor appearing like a star, moving rapidly, and then disappearing.

shoot-out *colloq.* **1** a decisive gun battle. **2** (in full **penalty shoot-out**) *Soccer* a tie-breaker decided by each side taking a specified number of penalty shots. **shoot up 1** rise suddenly; (of a person) grow rapidly. **2** *colloq.* inject oneself with a drug. ☐☐ **shooter** *n.*

shop *n.* **1** a place where goods or services are on sale. **2** an act of going shopping (*went for a shop in the city*). **3** a place for manufacture or repair. **4** one's own work or profession as a subject of conversation (*she is always talking shop*). • *v.* (**shopped, shopping**) **1** go to shops to buy things. **2** *colloq.* inform against (a person), esp. to the police. ☐ **shop around** look for the best bargain. **shop floor 1** the production area in a factory. **2** workers as distinct from management. **shop-soiled** soiled or faded from being on display in a shop. **shop steward** a trade-union official elected by fellow workers as their representative. **shop talk** talk about one's occupation or business. ☐☐ **shopper** *n.*

shopaholic *n. colloq.* a compulsive shopper.

shopkeeper *n.* a person who owns or manages a shop.

shoplifter *n.* a person who steals goods on display in a shop. ☐ **shoplifting** *n.*

shopping *n.* **1** buying goods in shops. **2** the goods bought. ☐ **shopping centre** an area where shops are concentrated. **shopping jeep** a shopping bag set on a wheeled frame.

shore[1] *n.* the land along the edge of the sea or a lake.

shore[2] *v.* prop or support with a length of timber set at a slant. • *n.* a support of this kind.

shore[3] *v. archaic* (or esp. in sheep-shearing contexts *Aust.*) = the *past tense* of SHEAR.

shoreline *n.* the line of a shore.

shorn *see* SHEAR.

shornie *n. Aust.* a newly-shorn sheep.

short *adj.* **1** measuring little from end to end in space or time. **2** seeming to be shorter than it really is (*for one short hour*). **3** not lasting; not going far into the past or future (*a short memory*). **4** insufficient, having an insufficient supply (*water is short; we are short of water*). **5** *colloq.* having little of a certain quality (*he's short on tact*). **6** concise, brief (*the Shorter Oxford Dictionary*). **7** curt, uncivil (*was short with him*). **8** (of vowel sounds) relatively brief or light (*see* LONG[1], sense 7). **9** (of an alcoholic drink) small and concentrated, made with spirits. **10** (of temper) easily lost. **11** (of pastry) rich and crumbly. • *adv.* suddenly, abruptly (*stopped short*). • *n.* **1** a short film. **2** a short circuit. • *v.* = SHORT-CIRCUIT (sense 1). ☐ **for short** as an abbreviation (*Frederick is called Freddie for short*). **get** (or **have**) **by the short hairs** (or **by the short and curlies**) *colloq.* have (a person) at one's mercy or at a complete

shortage   769   **shovel**

disadvantage. **short and curlies** (usu. male) pubic hair. **short-change** v. give insufficient change; cheat (a person). **short circuit** a connection (usu. a fault) in an electrical circuit in which current flows by a shorter route than the normal one. **short-circuit** v. **1** cause a short circuit in. **2** bypass. **short cut** a route or method that is quicker than the usual one. **short for** an abbreviation of (*'Fred' is short for 'Frederick'*). **short-handed** having an insufficient number of workers or helpers. **short leg** *Cricket* **1** a fielding position near the batsman on the leg side. **2** a fielder in this position. **short list** a list of selected candidates from whom the final choice will be made. **short-list** v. put on a short list. **short odds** nearly even odds in betting. **short of 1** without going so far as (*will do anything for her short of having her to stay*). **2** distant from; having failed to reach (*two miles short of home*). (*See also* sense 4 of *adj.*) **short of a sheet of bark** *Aust. colloq.* mentally deficient; stupid. **short shrift** curt treatment. **short-sighted 1** able to see clearly only what is close. **2** lacking foresight. **short soup** a Chinese soup made from chicken stock and wontons. **short-staffed** with insufficient staff. **short story** a story with a full developed theme but much shorter than a novel. **short-tempered** easily becoming angry. **short-term** *adj.* of or for a short period. **short wave** a radio wave of frequency greater than 3 MHz. ☐☐**shortish** *adj.* **shortness** *n.*

shortage *n.* a lack of something that is needed.

shortbread *n.* a rich sweet biscuit.

shortcake *n.* shortbread.

shortcoming *n.* failure to reach a required standard; a fault.

shortcrust pastry *n.* crumbly pastry with an even texture.

shorten *v.* make or become shorter.

shortening *n.* fat used to make pastry etc.

shortfall *n.* a deficit.

shorthand *n.* a system of rapid writing using special symbols.

shorthorn *n.* one of a breed of cattle with short horns.

shortly *adv.* **1** in a short time, not long, soon (*coming shortly; shortly afterwards*). **2** in a few words. **3** curtly.

shorts *n.pl.* trousers reaching to the knees or higher up the thigh.

shorty *n.* (also **shortie**) (*pl.* **shorties**) *colloq.* **1** a person shorter than average. **2** a short garment, esp. a nightdress etc. (*shorty pyjamas*).

Shostakovich / shos-tuh-**koh**-vich /, Dmitri (1906–75), Russian composer.

shot *see* SHOOT. • *adj.* (of fabric) woven or dyed so that different colours show at different angles. • *n.* **1** the firing of a gun etc.; the sound of this. **2** a person with regard to skill in shooting (*he's a good shot*). **3** (*pl.* **shot**) a single missile for a cannon or gun, a non-explosive projectile. **4** lead pellets for firing from small guns. **5** a heavy metal ball thrown as a sport. **6** the launching of a rocket or spacecraft (*moonshot*). **7** a stroke in tennis, cricket, billiards, etc. **8** an attempt to hit something or reach a target. **9** an attempt to do something (*have a shot at this crossword*). **10** an injection. **11** *colloq.* a measure of spirits. **12** a photograph; the scene photographed; a single continuous photographed scene in a cinema film. ☐ **like a shot** without hesitation; willingly. **shot in the arm** a stimulus, an encouragement. **shot in the dark** a mere guess. **shot-put** an athletic contest in which a shot is thrown.

shotgun *n.* a gun for firing small shot at close range. ☐ **shotgun wedding** a wedding that has been enforced, esp. because the bride is pregnant.

should *auxiliary v.*, used to express **1** duty or obligation (*you should have told me*). **2** an expected future event (*they should be here by ten*). **3** a possible event (*if you should happen to see him*). **4** with *I* and *we* to form a polite statement or a conditional clause (*I should like to come; I should say it's about right*).

shoulder *n.* **1** the part of the body at which an arm, foreleg, or wing is attached; the part of the human body between this and the neck. **2** the part of a garment covering a shoulder. **3** a strip of land bordering a road. **4** part of anything resembling a shoulder in form or function (*the shoulder of a mountain*). • *v.* **1** push with one's shoulder; make one's way thus. **2** put or carry on one's shoulders. **3** take (blame or responsibility) upon oneself. ☐ **shoulder arms** hold a rifle with the barrel against one's shoulder. **shoulder blade** either of the two large flat bones at the top of the back.

shouldn't = should not.

shouse *n. Aust. colloq.* a toilet. (¶ Abbreviated form of *shithouse.*)

shout *n.* **1** a loud cry calling attention or expressing joy, excitement, or disapproval. **2** *Aust.* **a** the purchase of a round of drinks (or for a person). **b** the round of drinks itself. **c** one's turn to buy a round of drinks etc. (*your shout, I think*). • *v.* **1** utter a shout; say or express loudly. **2** *Aust.* **a** buy a round of drinks for an assembled company (*shouted them a beer; I'm shouting*). **b** buy a drink for a person (*I'll shout you a beer*). **c** buy or give as a treat etc. (*shouted all the kids an ice cream*).

shove / shuv / *n.* a rough push. • *v.* **1** push roughly. **2** *colloq.* put (*shove it in the drawer*). ☐ **shove off 1** push a boat so that it moves from the shore. **2** *colloq.* go away.

shovel *n.* **1** a tool for scooping up earth etc., shaped like a spade with the edges turned up. **2** (part of) a machine with a similar form or function. • *v.* (**shovelled, shovelling**) **1** shift or clear with or as if with a shovel. **2** scoop or thrust roughly (*shovelling food into his mouth*). ☐ **shovel-nosed lobster** any of several Australian marine crustaceans, valued as food, having a flattened appearance and shovel-shaped ends of the main feelers, including the Moreton Bay bug and the Balmain bug. **shovel-spear** an Aboriginal weapon with a killing head made of salvaged iron etc. (or, previous to the arrival of whites, of razor-sharp stone). □□ **shovelful** *n.*

shoveller *n.* (also **shoveler**) a duck of southwestern and eastern Australia with a broad shovel-like beak.

show *v.* (**showed**, **shown**, **showing**) **1** allow or cause to be seen; offer for inspection or viewing. **2** demonstrate; point out; prove; cause (a person) to understand (*show us how it works*). **3** conduct (*show them in*). **4** present an image of (*this picture shows the hotel*). **5** treat in a certain way (*showed us much kindness*). **6** be able to be seen (*the lining is showing*). **7** *colloq.* appear, come when expected (*he failed to show*). • *n.* **1** showing; being shown. **2** a display (*a spectacular show of wattle blossom this year*). **3** a collection of things shown for public entertainment or a competition (*a flower show*). **4** an annual exhibition of livestock, produce, etc., with entertainments, etc., in a city or town (*the Melbourne Show*). **5** *colloq.* any business or undertaking (*he runs the whole show*). **6** an outward appearance, an insincere display (*under a show of friendship*). **7** *colloq.* an opportunity; a chance (*he hasn't a show of winning*). **8** a discharge of blood from the vagina at the start of childbirth. □ **show-and-tell** a method used in teaching young children, by which they are encouraged to bring objects to school and describe them to their classmates. **show bag** (also **sample bag**) a bag of goods, esp. trade or company samples, available at annual shows etc. **show business** the entertainment or theatrical profession. **show off** display well, proudly, or ostentatiously; try to impress people. **show-off** *n.* a person who tries to impress others. **show pony** *Aust. colloq.* a person who gives more attention to appearances than to performance (*he's the show pony of the political arena*). **show-stopper** a spectacular act in a show receiving prolonged applause. **show trial** a judicial trial designed to frighten or impress the public. **show up 1** make or be clearly visible. **2** expose or humiliate. **3** *colloq.* appear, come when expected.

showbiz *colloq.* = SHOW BUSINESS.

showcase *n.* **1** a glass case for exhibiting items. **2** an event designed to show someone or something to advantage. • *v.* display in or as if in a showcase.

showdown *n.* a final test or confrontation.

shower *n.* **1** a brief fall of rain or snow etc. **2** a brisk flurry of arrows, bullets, etc. **3** a dust storm (*Darling shower*; *Wimmera shower*). **4** a sudden influx of letters or gifts etc. **5** a device set over a bath or in a cabinet in the bathroom (a shower recess) from which water is sprayed so as to wash a person's body; a wash under this. **6** (in full **shower party** or **shower tea**) a party for giving (a 'shower' of) presents to a prospective bride. • *v.* **1** pour down or come in a shower. **2** send or give (many letters or gifts etc.) to. **3** take a shower (in a shower recess etc.). □ **I** (**he**, **they**, etc.) **didn't come down in the last shower** *Aust. colloq.* an indication that one is not without experience, that one is not a fool.

showery *adj.* (of weather) with many showers.

showing *n.* the evidence or quality that a person shows (*on today's showing, he will fail*).

showground *n.* a venue providing facilities for equestrian events, rodeos, agricultural shows, etc.

showjumping *n.* the sport of riding and jumping horses around a course of fences. □ **showjumper** *n.*

showman *n.* **1** an organiser of circuses or similar entertainments. **2** a skilled performer. **3** a person skilled in publicity, esp. self-advertisement. □ **showmanship** *n.*

shown *see* SHOW.

showpiece *n.* **1** an item of work presented for exhibition or display. **2** an outstanding example or specimen.

showroom *n.* a room in which goods are displayed for inspection.

showy *adj.* (**showier**, **showiest**) **1** making a good display. **2** brilliant, gaudy. □ **showily** *adv.* **showiness** *n.*

shrank *see* SHRINK.

shrapnel *n.* **1 a** an artillery shell containing bullets or pieces of metal which it scatters as it explodes. **b** the pieces it scatters. **2** *Aust. colloq.* small change.

shred *n.* **1** a small piece torn or cut from something. **2** a small amount (*not a shred of evidence*). • *v.* (**shredded**, **shredding**) tear or cut into shreds.

shredder *n.* a machine (esp. in an office) designed to reduce (esp. confidential) documents to unreadable shreds.

shrew *n.* **1** a small mouselike animal of Europe etc. **2** a sharp-tempered scolding woman. □ **shrewish** *adj.* (in sense 2).

shrewd *adj.* having sound judgment and common sense; clever. □ **shrewdly** *adv.* **shrewdness** *n.*

shrewdie *n.* (also **shrewdy**) esp. *Aust. colloq.* a shrewd or cunning person.

shriek *n.* a shrill cry or scream. • *v.* make a shriek; utter with a shriek.

shrift *n.* *archaic* confession and absolution. □ **short shrift** *see* SHORT.

shrike *n.* **1** a bird (of Africa, Europe, etc.) with a strong hooked beak that impales its prey on thorns. **2** any of three Australian birds: *shrike thrush* (with an extremely melodious song), *shrike tit*, *cuckoo-shrike*.

shrill *adj.* piercing and high-pitched in sound. • *v.* sound or utter in a shrill way. □ **shrilly** *adv.* **shrillness** *n.*

shrimp *n.* **1** a small edible shellfish, pink when boiled; a prawn. **2** *colloq.* a very small person. •*v.* try to catch shrimps. ☐ **shrimp paste** = TRASI.

shrine *n.* **1** esp. *Catholic Church* **a** a chapel, church, altar, etc., sacred to a saint, holy person, relic, etc. **b** the tomb of a saint etc. **2** a place associated with or containing memorabilia of a particular person, event, etc. **3** a Shinto place of worship.

shrink *v.* (**shrank**, **shrunk** *or* (esp. as *adj.*) **shrunken**, **shrinking**) **1** make or become smaller, esp. by the action of moisture, heat, or cold (*it shrank in the wash*). **2** draw back so as to avoid something; be unwilling to do something (e.g. because of shame or dislike). •*n. colloq.* (in full **headshrinker**) a psychiatrist. ☐ **shrink fit** an extremely tight fit formed by shrinking one metal part round another.

shrinkage *n.* **1** the process of shrinking; the amount by which something shrinks. **2** (in commerce) loss by theft, wastage, etc.

shrink-wrap *v.* package (an article) by enclosing it in clinging transparent plastic film. • *n.* the plastic film used for this purpose.

shrive *v.* (**shrove**, **shriven**) *archaic* hear the confession of and give absolution to (a penitent).

shrivel *v.* (**shrivelled**, **shrivelling**) shrink and wrinkle from great heat or cold or lack of moisture.

shroud *n.* **1** a sheet or garment in which a dead body is wrapped for burial. **2** something that conceals (*wrapped in a shroud of secrecy*). **3** one of a set of ropes supporting the mast of a ship. •*v.* **1** wrap in a shroud; conceal in wrappings. **2** hide; cover; obscure (*his past life is shrouded in mystery*).

Shroud of Turin (also **Holy Shroud of Turin**) the winding sheet in which the dead body of Christ was supposedly wrapped and which shows the image of a bearded and bleeding man, preserved in Turin Cathedral, Italy: this has been the subject of much controversy.

shrove *see* SHRIVE.

shrovetide *n.* Shrove Tuesday and the two days preceding it when it was formerly customary to be shriven.

Shrove Tuesday the day before Ash Wednesday. Also called *Pancake Day.*

shrub *n.* a woody plant smaller than a tree, usu. with several main stems. ☐ **shrubby** *adj.*

shrubbery *n.* an area planted with shrubs.

shrug *v.* (**shrugged**, **shrugging**) raise (the shoulders) as a gesture of indifference, doubt, or helplessness. •*n.* this movement. ☐ **shrug off** dismiss (a thing) as unimportant.

shrunk *see* SHRINK.

shrunken *adj.* having shrunk.

shudder *v.* **1** shiver violently with horror, fear, or cold. **2** make a strong shaking movement. •*n.* a shuddering movement. ☐ **the shudders** *colloq.* a state of shuddering.

shuffle *v.* **1** walk without lifting the feet clear of the ground. **2** rearrange; change the order of (cards, papers, etc.). **3** keep shifting one's position. **4** get rid of (a burden etc.) shiftily (*shuffled off the responsibility on to others; shuffled out of it*). •*n.* **1** a shuffling movement, walk, or dance. **2** shuffling of cards etc. **3** a rearrangement (*the latest Cabinet shuffle*).

shun *v.* (**shunned**, **shunning**) avoid, keep away from.

shunt *v.* **1** move (a train) on to a side track. **2** divert onto an alternative course. •*n.* **1** shunting; being shunted. **2** *colloq.* a collision of vehicles, esp. one behind another (*a rear-end shunt*). **3** *Electricity* a conductor joining two points of a circuit, through which current may be diverted. **4** (in surgery) an alternative path for the circulation of the blood. ☐ **shunter** *n.*

shush / shuush / *interj.* & *v. colloq.* hush.

shut *v.* (**shut**, **shutting**) **1** move or be moved into a closed position; seal. **2** (of a shop, office, etc.) close for business. **3** bring or fold the parts of (a thing) together (*shut the book*). **4** keep in or out by shutting a door etc. (*shut out the noise*). **5** trap a finger or dress etc. by shutting something on it. ☐ **shut down** cease working or business, either for the day or permanently; cause to do this. **shut-down** *n.* this process. **shut-eye** *n. colloq.* sleep. **shut off** stop the flow of (water or gas etc.). **shut up 1** shut securely; shut all the doors and windows of (a house). **2** put away in a box etc. **3** *colloq.* stop talking or making a noise; cause to do this, silence. **shut up shop** close a business or shop.

Shute, Nevil (original name: Nevil Shute Norway) (1899–1960), Australian novelist (born in England), best known for *A Town Like Alice* and *On the Beach.*

shutter *n.* **1** a panel or screen that can be closed over a window. **2** a device that opens and closes the aperture of a camera lens to allow light to fall on the film.

shuttered *adj.* **1** fitted with shutters. **2** with the shutters closed.

shuttle *n.* **1** a holder carrying the weft-thread to and fro across the loom in weaving. **2** a holder carrying the lower thread in a sewing machine. **3** a bus, aircraft, etc. used in a shuttle service. **4** = SPACE SHUTTLE. •*v.* move, travel, or send to and fro. ☐ **shuttle diplomacy** diplomacy that involves travelling between countries involved in a dispute. **shuttle service** a transport service operating to and fro over a relatively short distance.

shuttlecock *n.* a cork with a ring of feathers, or a similar plastic device, struck to and fro in badminton.

shy[1] *adj.* (**shyer**, **shyest**) **1** (of a person) timid and lacking self-confidence in the presence of others. **2** (of behaviour) showing shyness (*a shy smile*). **3** (of an animal) timid and avoiding observation. **4** disliking or fearing (*work-shy*). **5** (often foll. by *of*, *on*) *colloq*. having lost; short of (*shy of three dollars*). • *v.* (**shied**, **shying**) jump or move suddenly in alarm. ☐ **shyly** *adv.* **shyness** *n.*

shy[2] *v.* (**shied**, **shying**) fling or throw (a stone etc.). • *n.* a throw.

shylock *n.* a hard-hearted money lender. (¶ Name of a character in Shakespeare's *Merchant of Venice*.)

shyster / **shuy**-stuh / *n. colloq.* a person who acts unscrupulously or unprofessionally.

SI *abbr.* Système International d'Unités; the international system of units of measurement. (¶ French)

Si *symbol* silicon.

Siamese *adj.* of Siam (now called Thailand) or its people or language. • *n.* (*pl.* **Siamese**) **1** a native of Siam. **2** the language of Siam. **3** (in full **Siamese cat**) a cat of a breed that has short cream-coloured fur with darker face, ears, tail, and feet. ☐ **Siamese twins** identical twins whose bodies are joined in some way at birth.

sib *n.* **1** a brother or sister (cf. SIBLING). **2** a blood relative.

Siberia a region of eastern Russia, noted for its harsh winters. ☐ **Siberian** *adj.*

sibilant *adj.* having a hissing sound. • *n.* one of the speech sounds that sound like hissing, e.g. *s*, *sh*. ☐ **sibilance** *n.*

sibling *n.* a child in relation to another or others of the same parent; a brother or sister.

sibyl / **sib**-uhl / *n.* (in ancient times) a woman acting as the reputed mouthpiece of a god, uttering prophecies and oracles.

sibylline / **sib**-uh-luyn / *adj.* issuing from a sibyl; oracular, mysteriously prophetic.

sic[1] / sik / *adv.* used or spelt in that way. (¶ Latin, = thus.)

■ **Usage** This word is placed in brackets after a word that seems odd or is wrongly spelt, to show that one is quoting it exactly as it was given.

sic[2] alternative spelling of SICK[2].

Sicily a large island in the Mediterranean Sea, off the 'toe' of Italy. ☐ **Sicilian** *adj.* & *n.*

sick[1] *adj.* **1** physically or mentally unwell. **2** likely to vomit (*feel sick*). **3** distressed; disgusted (*their attitude makes me sick*). **4** bored with something through having already had too much of it (*I'm sick of cricket*). **5** finding amusement in misfortune or in morbid subjects (*sick jokes*). • *v. colloq.* vomit (*sicked it up*). • *n. colloq.* vomit. ☐ **sick building** a large building whose infrastructure (e.g. air-conditioning system) has deteriorated to such an extent that it causes illness in those who work or live there. **sick building syndrome** (*abbr.* **SBS**) **1** the set of adverse environmental conditions found in a sick building. **2** the set of symptoms (headaches, dizziness, etc.) experienced by those who live or work there.

sick leave leave of absence because of illness.
sick pay pay given to an employee who is absent through illness. **sick up** vomit.

sick[2] *v.* (also **sic**) **1** (of a dog) set upon, attack (a person etc.). **2** (usu. in *imperative*) incite a dog to attack (a person etc.) (*sick him, Rover!*).

sickbay *n.* a room, cabin, etc. for people who are ill at school, on board ship, etc.

sickbed *n.* the bed of a sick person.

sicken *v.* **1** begin to be ill (*be sickening for a disease*). **2** make or become distressed or disgusted.

sickening *adj.* annoying; disgusting.

sickie *n. Aust. colloq.* a day's sick leave, esp. as taken without sufficient medical reason (*think I'll take a sickie today*).

sickle *n.* a tool with a curved blade and a short handle, used for reaping etc. **2** something shaped like this, e.g. the crescent moon. ☐ **sickle cell** a sickle-shaped blood cell, esp. as found in a type of severe hereditary anaemia.

sickly *adj.* (**sicklier**, **sickliest**) **1** often ill (*a sickly child*). **2** unhealthy-looking. **3** causing ill health (*a sickly climate*). **4** causing sickness or distaste (*a sickly smell*; *sickly sentimentality*).

sickness *n.* **1** illness. **2** a disease. **3** vomiting or a tendency to vomit. ☐ **sickness country** (*or* **site**) *Aust.* (in Aboriginal belief) an area of spiritual significance where spirit-beings may cause illness, esp. to those disturbing or profaning the area.

side *n.* **1** any of the more or less flat inner or outer surfaces of an object, esp. as distinct from the top and bottom, front and back, or ends. **2** any of the bounding lines of a plane figure such as a triangle or square. **3** either of the two halves into which an object can be divided by a line down its centre. **4** the part near the edge and away from the centre of something. **5** a slope of a hill or ridge. **6** the region next to a person or thing (*he stood at my side*). **7** one aspect or view of something (*study all sides of the problem*). **8** one of two opposing groups, teams, etc. **9** the line of descent through father or mother (*his mother's side of the family*). **10** *Aust.* (in two-up) the body of players as distinct from the spinner and the ringkeeper. • *adj.* at or on the side (*side door*). • *v.* take the side of a person in a dispute (*he sided with his son*). ☐ **on the side** as a sideline; as a surreptitious or illicit activity. **on the ... side** rather, somewhat (*prices are on the high side*). **side effect** a secondary (usu. undesirable) effect. **side issue** an issue that is not the main one. **side road** a road leading off a main road; a minor road. **side-saddle** *n.* a saddle for a woman rider to sit on with both legs on the same side of the horse, not astride. *adv.* sitting in this way. **side-whiskers** whiskers on the cheeks.

sideboard *n.* **1** a flat-topped piece of dining-room furniture with drawers and cupboards for china etc. **2** (**sideboards**) *colloq.* hair grown by a man down the sides of his face.

sideburns *n.pl.* sideboards.

sidecar *n.* a passenger compartment attached to the side of a motorcycle.

sidekick *n. colloq.* a close friend or associate; a subordinate member of a pair or group.

sidelight *n.* **1** light from one side (not front or back). **2** each of a pair of small lights at the front of a vehicle. **3** a light at either side of a moving ship. **4** incidental information.

sideline *n.* **1** something done in addition to one's main work or activity. **2** (**sidelines**) the lines bounding a football pitch etc. at its sides; the space just outside these; a place for spectators. ▢ **on the sidelines** not directly concerned.

sidelong *adv.* & *adj.* to one side, sideways (*a sidelong glance*).

sidereal / suy-**deer**-ree-uhl / *adj.* of or measured by the stars.

sideshow *n.* **1** a small show or stall forming part of a fair, exhibition, etc. **2** a minor incident or issue.

sidestep *n.* a step to the side. •*v.* (**sidestepped, sidestepping**) **1** avoid by stepping sideways. **2** evade (a question, responsibility, etc.).

sidestroke *n.* a swimming stroke in which the swimmer lies sideways, paddles with the arms, and makes a scissors-like kick with the legs.

sideswipe *n.* **1** a glancing blow on or from the side. **2** incidental criticism. •*v.* hit (as if) with a sideswipe.

sidetrack *v.* divert from the main course or issue.

sideways *adv.* & *adj.* **1** to or from one side. **2** with one side facing forward (*sat sideways*).

Sidhe / shee / *n.pl. Irish myth.* **1** the gods of ancient Ireland, the faerie. **2** (*sing.*) a mound or hill inside which the Sidhe dwell; fairyland; faerie.

siding *n.* **1** a short track by the side of a railway, used for shunting. **2** *Aust.* a slope or declivity.

sidle / **suy**-duhl / *v.* move in a timid, furtive, or cringing manner; edge.

SIDS *abbr.* sudden infant death syndrome; cot death.

siege *n.* the surrounding and blockading of a town or fortified place, to capture it or the people inside. ▢ **lay siege to** begin besieging.

Siegfried / **seeg**-freed / the hero of the first part of the *Nibelungenlied*, who forged the sword *Nothung*, killed the dragon Fafner, and won the Valkyrie Brunhild as his wife.

siemens / **see**-muhnz / *n.* the SI unit of electrical conductance, the reciprocal of the ohm. (¶ Named after E.W. von Siemens (1816–92).)

sienna / see-**en**-uh / *n.* a kind of earth used as colouring matter. ▢ **burnt sienna** reddish-brown. **raw sienna** yellowish-brown.

sierra / see-**air**-ruh / *n.* a long jagged mountain-chain, esp. in Spain or Spanish America.

Sierra Leone / see-air-ruh lee-**ohn** / a republic in West Africa. ▢ **Sierra Leonean** *adj.* & *n.*

siesta / see-**es**-tuh / *n.* an afternoon nap or rest, esp. in hot countries.

sieve / siv / *n.* a utensil consisting of a frame with mesh, used for straining, sifting, or pulping food or other material. •*v.* put through a sieve.

sift *v.* **1** sieve. **2** sprinkle lightly from a perforated container. **3** examine carefully and select or analyse. **4** (of snow or light) fall as if from a sieve.

sig *n. Computing* a short personalised message at the end of an email message.

sigh *n.* a long audible breath expressing sadness, tiredness, relief, etc. •*v.* **1** give a sigh; express with a sigh. **2** (of wind etc.) make a similar sound.

sight *n.* **1** the faculty of seeing; ability to see. **2** seeing, being seen (*lost sight of it*). **3** the range over which a person can see or an object can be seen (*within sight of the Harbour Bridge*). **4** a thing seen or visible or worth seeing, a display (*the tulips at Canberra's annual Floriade are always a wonderful sight*). **5** something regarded as unsightly or looking ridiculous (*he looks a sight in those clothes*). **6** *colloq.* a great quantity (*a darned sight better*). **7** a device looked through to help aim or observe with a gun or telescope etc.; aim or observation using this. •*v.* **1** get a sight of (*we sighted land*). **2** aim or observe by using the sight in a gun, telescope, etc. ▢ **lower** (or **raise**) **one's sights** become less (or more) ambitious. **play music at sight** play without preliminary practice or study of the score. **sight-read** *v.* play or sing music at sight. **sight screen** a large movable usu. white structure placed to help the batsman see the ball in cricket. **sight unseen** without previous inspection.

sighted *adj.* having sight, not blind.

sightless *adj.* blind.

sightseeing *n.* visiting places of interest in a place. ▢ **sightseer** *n.*

sigma *n.* the eighteenth letter of the Greek alphabet (Σ, σ, or, when final, ς).

sign *n.* **1** something perceived that suggests the existence of a fact or quality or condition (*it shows signs of being a success*). **2** a mark with a special meaning, a symbol. **3** a signboard or other visual object used similarly; a notice. **4** an action or gesture conveying information or a command etc. **5** any of the twelve divisions of the zodiac; a symbol representing one of these. •*v.* **1** make a sign (*signed to me to come*). **2** write (one's name) on a document etc. to guarantee that it has one's authority or consent (*signed the letter; sign here*). **3** convey by signing a document (*signed away her right to the house*). **4** engage or be engaged as an employee by signing a contract of employment. **5** use sign language. ▢ **sign language 1** a series of gestures used by deaf or dumb people for communication. **2** any of several elaborate gesture systems used by Australian Aborigines when speech has to be avoided for ritual reasons.

sign off (in broadcasting) announce the end of one's program or transmission. **sign of the cross** a Christian sign made in blessing or prayer, by tracing a cross from the forehead to the chest and to each shoulder, or in the air. **sign on 1** sign a contract (of employment etc.). **2** register as a player for a sports team. **sign up 1** engage (a person). **2** enrol. **3** enlist in the armed forces.

signage / **suy**-nij / *n*. signs collectively, esp. commercial or public display signs.

signal *n*. **1** a sign, object, or gesture giving information or a command; a message made up of such signs. **2** an act or event that immediately produces a general reaction (*his arrival was the signal for an outburst of cheering*). **3** a sequence of electrical impulses or radio waves transmitted or received. **4** a device on a railway giving instructions or warnings to train drivers etc. •*v*. (**signalled, signalling**) make a signal or signals; direct, communicate with, or announce in this way. •*adj*. remarkably good or bad (*a signal success*). ❑ **signal box** a small railway building with signalling apparatus. ❑ ❑ **signaller** *n*. **signally** *adv*.

signalise *v*. (also **-ize**) make noteworthy.

signatory / **sig**-nuh-tuh-ree, -tree / *n*. any of the parties signing a treaty or other agreement.

signature *n*. **1** a person's name or initials written by himself or herself in signing something. **2** a key signature or time signature in music. **3** a section of a book made from one sheet folded and cut, often marked with a letter or figure as a guide to the binder. ❑ **signature tune** a tune used to announce a particular program or performer.

signet / **sig**-nuht / *n*. a person's seal used with or instead of a signature. ❑ **signet ring** a finger-ring with an engraved design, formerly used as a seal.

significance *n*. **1** what is meant by something (*what is the significance of this symbol?*). **2** being significant, importance (*the event is of no significance*).

significant *adj*. **1** having a meaning. **2** full of meaning (*a significant glance*). **3** important, noteworthy (*significant developments*). ❑ **to three**, **four**, etc. **significant figures** (of a number) expressed to the specified degree of accuracy, with the final figure rounded up or down, ignoring zeros at the beginning; e.g. 7.63186 to four significant figures is 7.632. ❑ ❑ **significantly** *adv*.

signification *n*. **1** the act of signifying. **2** the exact meaning or sense, esp. of a word or phrase.

signify *v*. (**signified, signifying**) **1** be a sign or symbol of. **2** have as a meaning. **3** make known (*signified her approval*). **4** be of importance, matter (*it doesn't signify*).

signor / **see**-nyaw / *n*. the title used of or to an Italian-speaking man.

signora / see-**nyaw**-ruh / *n*. the title used of or to an Italian-speaking woman.

signorina / see-nyaw-**ree**-nuh / *n*. the title used of or to an Italian-speaking young woman (esp. one who is unmarried).

signpost *n*. a post at a road junction etc. showing the names of places along each of the roads. •*v*. provide with a post or posts of this kind.

signwriter *n*. a person who paints signboards etc.

Sihanouk / **see**-uh-nuuk /, Norodom (1922–), Cambodian king 1941–55 and since 1993, prime minister 1955–60, and head of state 1960–70 and 1975–76.

Sikh / seek / *n*. a member of an Indian religious sect, combining elements of Hinduism and Islam. ❑ **Sikhism** *n*.

silage / **suy**-lij / *n*. green fodder stored and fermented in a silo; storage in a silo.

silence *n*. **1** absence of sound. **2** avoidance or absence of speaking or of making a sound. **3** avoidance of mentioning something, refusal to betray a secret. •*v*. make silent, esp. by force or superior argument.

silencer *n*. a device for reducing the sound made by a gun or a vehicle's exhaust etc.

silent *adj*. **1** not speaking, not making or accompanied by a sound. **2** (of a letter) written but not pronounced, e.g. *b* in *doubt*. **3** saying or recording nothing on some subject (*the records are silent on the incident*). ❑ **silent cop** *Aust. colloq*. a small raised dome marking the centre of a traffic intersection etc. **silent majority** people of moderate opinions who rarely make themselves heard. **silent partner** a partner not sharing in the actual work of a firm. ❑ ❑ **silently** *adv*.

silhouette / sil-oo-**et** / *n*. **1** a dark shadow or outline seen against a light background. **2** a profile portrait in solid black. •*v*. show as a silhouette (*she was silhouetted against the screen*).

silica / **sil**-i-kuh / *n*. a compound of silicon occurring as quartz or flint and in sandstone and other rocks. ❑ **silica gel** hydrated silica in the form of granules, used as a drying agent. ❑ ❑ **siliceous** / suh-**lee**-shuhs / *adj*.

silicate / **sil**-uh-kayt / *n*. any of the insoluble compounds of silica.

silicon / **sil**-uh-kuhn / *n*. a chemical element (symbol Si), found widely in the earth's crust in its compound forms. ❑ **silicon chip** a microchip made of silicon.

silicone / **sil**-uh-kohn / *n*. any of the organic compounds of silicon, widely used in paints, varnish, and lubricants.

Silicon Valley an area with a high concentration of electronics industries, esp. the Santa Clara valley south-east of San Francisco.

silicosis / sil-uh-**koh**-suhs / *n*. an abnormal condition of the lungs caused by inhaling dust that contains silica.

silk *n*. **1** the fine strong soft fibre produced by a silkworm in making its cocoon, or by certain other insects or spiders. **2** thread or cloth made from it; fabric resembling this. **3** (**silks**) clothing made from silk. **4** *colloq*. a Queen's Counsel, entitled to wear a silk gown. **5** fine soft strands like threads of silk. ❑ **silk-screen printing** = SCREEN PRINTING.

silken *adj*. made of or like silk.

Silk Road a trade route from China through Central Asia to Europe, used in ancient times by traders in silk (now a tourist route by rail).

silkworm *n.* a caterpillar which feeds on mulberry leaves and spins its cocoon of silk.

silky *adj.* (**silkier**, **silkiest**) as soft, fine, or smooth as silk. ☐ **silky oak** any of various usu. rainforest trees of northern and eastern Australia yielding an oak-like timber of silky texture, esp. the tall, commonly cultivated *Grevillea robusta* which has masses of golden-orange flowers; the wood of these trees. ☐ ☐ **silkily** *adv.* **silkiness** *n.*

sill *n.* a strip of stone, wood, or metal at the base of a window or door.

sillabub alternative spelling of SYLLABUB.

silly *adj.* (**sillier**, **silliest**) **1** lacking good sense, foolish, unwise. **2** feeble-minded. **3** (in Aboriginal English) (esp. of a drunken person) mad, crazy. **4** (of a fieldsman's position in cricket) close to the batsman (*silly mid-on*). • *n. colloq.* a foolish person. ☐ **silliness** *n.*

silo / **suy**-loh / *n.* (*pl.* **silos**) **1** a pit or tower for storing grain, cement, etc. **2** a pit or airtight barn etc. in which green crops are kept for fodder. **3** an underground place where a missile is kept ready for firing.

silt *n.* sediment deposited by water in a channel or harbour etc. • *v.* (often foll. by *up*) block or become blocked with silt (*the harbour is silted up*).

Silurian / suy-**lyoo**-ree-uhn / *adj. Geol.* of the third period of the Palaeozoic era. • *n.* this period.

silvan alternative spelling of SYLVAN.

silver *n.* **1** a chemical element (symbol Ag), a shiny white precious metal. **2** coins made of this or of an alloy resembling it. **3** silver dishes or ornaments; household cutlery of any metal. **4** a silver medal (awarded as second prize). **5** the colour of silver. • *adj.* **1** made of silver; coloured like silver. **2** used as a distinguishing epithet in the names of: fish (*silver dory* etc.), birds (*silvereye* etc.), and flora, indicating wood colour (*silver ash* etc.) or foliage colour (*silver wattle* etc.). • *v.* **1** coat or plate with silver. **2** give a silvery appearance to; become silvery; (of hair) turn grey or white. ☐ **silver birch** a birch tree with silver-coloured bark. **silver jubilee** a 25th anniversary. **silver perch** an Australian freshwater food and game fish that makes a grunting noise when caught. Also called *grunter*. **silver-plated** coated with silver. **the silver screen** cinema films; the film industry. **silver wattle** *Aust.* any of several wattles having a silvery foliage. **silver wedding** the 25th anniversary of a wedding.

silverbeet *n.* esp. *Aust.* a kind of beet with edible broad white leaf-stalks and green blades.

silverchair Australian rock group, formed in 1992, comprising Daniel Johns (1979–), Ben Gillies (1979–), and Chris Joannou (1979–).

silvereye *n.* a small Australian bird having yellowy-green plumage and a conspicuous white eye ring.

silverfish *n.* a small silvery wingless insect, thoroughly destructive of books, paper, etc.

silverside *n.* a joint of beef cut from the haunch, below topside.

silversmith *n.* a person whose trade is making articles in silver.

silvertail *Aust. adj.* socially prominent; having social aspirations; privileged. • *n.* a person who is socially prominent or who displays social aspirations; a privileged person. ☐ **silvertailed** *adj.*

silverware *n.* articles made of silver.

silvery *adj.* **1** like silver in colour or appearance. **2** having a clear gentle ringing sound.

silviculture *n.* (also **sylviculture**) the cultivation of forest trees.

simian / **sim**-ee-uhn / *adj.* like an ape or monkey. • *n.* an ape or monkey.

similar *adj.* (often foll. by *to*) **1** like, alike, resembling something but not the same. **2** of the same kind, nature, or amount. ☐ **similarly** *adv.* **similarity** / sim-uh-**la**-ruh-tee / *n.*

simile / **sim**-uh-lee / *n.* a figure of speech in which one thing is compared to another (see panel).

similitude / suh-**mil**-uh-tyood / *n.* similarity.

simmer *v.* **1** keep (a pan or its contents) almost at boiling point; be kept like this; boil very gently. **2** be in a state of excitement or anger which is only just kept under control. ☐ **simmer down** become less excited or agitated.

Simon, St (1st century AD), one of the twelve Apostles.

simony / **suy**-muh-nee, **sim**-uh- / *n.* the buying or selling of ecclesiastical privileges.

simoom / suh-**moom** / *n.* a hot dry dust-laden desert wind.

Simile

A simile is a figure of speech involving the comparison of one thing with another of a different kind, using *as* or *like*, e.g.
   The water was as clear as glass.
   Cherry blossom lay like driven snow upon the lawn.
Everyday language is rich in similes:
   with *as*:   *as mad as a cut snake*   *as Australian as meat pie*
                as poor as a church mouse   *as fit as a mallee bull*
   with *like*:   *spread like wildfire*   *go down like a lead balloon*
                drink like a fish   *like a bull in a china shop*

simper *v.* smile in a silly or affected way. • *n.* an affected smile.

simple *adj.* **1** understood or done easily; not difficult. **2** of one element or kind, not compound. **3** not elaborate, showy or luxurious; plain. **4** foolish; inexperienced. **5** feeble-minded. **6** of humble rank (*simple ordinary people*). ☐ **simple fracture** a fracture of a bone without a wound on the skin. **simple interest** interest paid only on the original capital, not on the interest added to it. Cf. COMPOUND INTEREST.

simpleton *n.* a foolish or easily-deceived person; a halfwit.

simplicity *n.* being simple.

simplify *v.* (**simplified**, **simplifying**) make simple, make easy to do or understand. ☐ **simplification** *n.*

simplistic *adj.* excessively or affectedly simple; too simple for accuracy etc. ☐ **simplistically** *adv.*

simply *adv.* **1** in a simple manner. **2** absolutely, without doubt. **3** merely.

Simpson[1], John (full name: John Simpson Kirkpatrick) (1892–1915), Australian soldier (born in England) who enlisted in the Australian Imperial Force and was landed at Gallipoli on 25 April 1915. There, using a stray donkey, he transported the wounded to the aid stations under heavy fire until he himself was killed. He has become part of the Anzac legend as 'The Man with the Donkey'.

Simpson[2], Bob (full name: Robert Baddeley Simpson) (1936–), AM, Australian cricketer. A batsman and leg-spin bowler, he played in 62 tests. He was coach of the Australian team 1986–96.

Simpson[3], Wallis (Warfield) (1896–1986), a twice-divorced American woman who married the Duke of Windsor, formerly King Edward VIII.

Simpson Desert a vast arid area in the southeast of the NT and extending into parts of Qld to the east and SA to the south. Spinifex, cane grass, mulga, and coolibahs are characteristic of the region.

simulate *v.* **1** reproduce the conditions of (a situation), for study, testing, training etc.; produce a computer model (of a process). **2** pretend to have or feel. **3** imitate the form or condition of. ☐ **simulation** *n.* **simulator** *n.*

simulated *adj.* (of furs, pearls, etc.) manufactured to look like natural products.

simulcast / **sim**-uhl-kahst / *v.* broadcast (a program) simultaneously on radio and television or on two or more channels. • *n.* a program broadcast in this way.

simultaneous / sim-uhl-**tay**-nee-uhs / *adj.* occurring or operating at the same time. ☐ **simultaneously** *adv.* **simultaneity** / sim-uhl-tuh-**nay**-uh-tee / *n.*

sin[1] *n.* **1** the breaking of a religious or moral law; an act which does this. **2** an offence against good taste or propriety etc. **3** something contrary to common sense (*it's a sin to stay indoors on this fine day*). • *v.* (**sinned**, **sinning**) commit a sin. ☐ **live in sin** *archaic* cohabit without marrying.

sin[2] *abbr.* sine.

Sinatra / suh-**nah**-truh /, Frank (full name: Francis Albert Sinatra) (1915–98), American singer and film actor.

sin bin *colloq. n.* **1** (in ice hockey, rugby league, etc.) a penalty box, i.e. a place where a player sent off the field for an infringement of the rules spends a specified period of time. **2** *Aust.* = SHAGWAGON. • *v.* (**sin-bin**) **1** penalise (a player) by sending to the sin bin. **2** remove from office etc. pending an inquiry etc. (*the shadow minister was sin-binned and had to sit on the back bench*).

since *adv., prep.,* & *conj.* **1** after (a certain event or past time), between then and now. **2** ago, before now (*it happened long since*). **3** for the reason that; because (*since we have no money, we can't buy it*).

sincere *adj.* free from pretence or deceit; genuine, honest. ☐ **sincerely** *adv.* **sincerity** / sin-**se**-ruh-tee / *n.*

sine / suyn / *n.* (in a right-angled triangle) the ratio of the length of a side opposite one of the acute angles to the length of the hypotenuse.

sinecure / **suy**-nuh-kyoor / *n.* an official position that gives the holder profit or honour with no work attached.

sine die / suy-nee **duy**-ee, see-nay **dee**-ay / *adv.* indefinitely, with no appointed date (*the business was adjourned sine die*). (¶ Latin, = without a day.)

sine qua non / see-nay kwah **nohn** / *n.* an indispensable condition or qualification. • *adj.* indispensable, absolutely essential. (¶ Latin, = without which not.)

sinew / **sin**-yoo / *n.* **1** tough fibrous tissue uniting muscle to bone. **2** a tendon. **3** (**sinews**) muscles; strength. ☐ **sinewy** *adj.*

sinful *adj.* full of sin, wicked. ☐ **sinfully** *adv.* **sinfulness** *n.*

sing *v.* (**sang**, **sung**, **singing**) **1** make musical sounds with the voice, esp. in a set tune. **2** perform (a song). **3** make a humming, buzzing, or whistling sound (*the kettle sings*). **4** *colloq.* turn informer. **5** *Aust.* (of an Aborigine) **a** impart supernatural powers to (an object) by incantation (*sang the spear; singing the sea cow*). **b** bring a (frequently malign) supernatural influence to bear on (a person or thing) by incantation (*sang the white man*). ☐ **sing out** *colloq.* say, call out (*sing out if you want any more*). **sing the cattle** (of stockmen) soothe cattle by 'singing'.

Singapore a republic in SE Asia consisting of the island of Singapore (and about 54 smaller islands) lying just off the southern tip of the Malay Peninsula to which it is linked by a causeway carrying a road and a railway. ☐ **Singaporean** *adj.* & *n.*

singe / sinj / *v.* (**singed**, **singeing**) burn slightly; burn the ends or edges of. • *n.* a slight burn.

singer *n.* a person who sings, esp. as a professional.

single

single *adj.* **1** one only, not double or multiple. **2** designed for one person or thing (*a single bed*). **3** taken separately (*every single thing*). **4** unmarried. **5** (of a ticket) valid for a one-way journey only, not to return. **6** (of a flower) having only one circle of petals. •*n.* **1** one person or thing, a single one. **2** a room etc. for one person. **3** a single ticket. **4** a pop record with one piece of music on each side. **5** a hit for one run in cricket. **6** (**singles**) a game with one player on each side. **7** (**singles**) unmarried men and women, esp. those looking for a partner (*a club for singles*). •*v.* (foll. by *out*) choose or distinguish from others (*singled him out*). ☐ **single-breasted** *adj.* (of a coat) fastening but not overlapping widely across the breast. **single combat** a duel. **single figures** any number from 1 to 9 inclusive. **single file** a line of people one behind the other. **single-handed** without help from others. **single-minded** with one's mind set on a single purpose. **single parent** a person bringing up a child or children alone. ☐☐ **singly** *adv.*

singlet *n.* a sleeveless vest.

singleton / sing-guhl-tuhn / *n.* one card only of a suit in a player's hand; a single person or thing.

singsong *adj.* with a rise and fall of the voice in speaking. •*n.* an informal singing of well-known songs by a group of people.

singular *n.* the form of a noun or verb used with reference to one person or thing (*the singular is 'man', the plural is 'men'*). •*adj.* **1** of this form. **2** uncommon; extraordinary (*spoke with singular shrewdness*). ☐ **singularly** *adv.* **singularity** / sing-gyuh-**la**-ruh-tee / *n.*

Sinhalese / sing-huh-leez / *n.* (also **Sinhala** / sing-huh-luh /) (*pl.* same) **1** a member of an Indo-Aryan people now forming the majority of the population of Sri Lanka. **2** the Indo-European language of this people. •*adj.* of this people or their language.

sinister *adj.* **1** suggestive of evil. **2** involving wickedness, criminal (*sinister motives*). **3** ominous (*a sinister sound*).

sink *v.* (**sank**, **sunk** *or* (as *adj.*) **sunken**, **sinking**) **1** fall slowly downwards, come gradually to a lower level or pitch. **2** become wholly or partly submerged in water etc.; (of a ship) go to the bottom of the sea. **3** pass into a less active condition (*she sank into sleep*). **4** lose value or strength etc. gradually; (of a sick person) approach death. **5** cause (a plan, a person, etc.) to fail. **6** cause or allow to sink (*the dog sank its teeth into my thigh*). **7** dig (a well) or bore (a shaft). **8** *colloq.* consume (an alcoholic drink) (*sank a few tinnies*). **9** send (a ball) into a pocket or hole in billiards, golf, etc. **10** invest (money). **11** overlook or forget (*they decided to sink their differences*). •*n.* **1** a fixed basin with a drainage pipe and water supply, in a kitchen etc. **2** a cesspool. **3** a place of vice. ☐ **sink in** penetrate; become understood. **sinking fund** a fund set aside for the purpose of wiping out a country's or business company's debt gradually.

sinker *n.* a weight used to sink a fishing line or a line used in taking soundings.

sinner *n.* a person who sins.

Sinn Fein / shin **fayn** / *n.* a nationalist political party in Ireland, linked to the Irish Republican Army. (¶ Irish, = we ourselves.)

Sino- / suy-noh- / *comb. form* Chinese and (*Sino-Japanese; Sino-Tibetan*).

sinology / suy-**nol**-uh-jee / *n.* the study of the Chinese language, literature, history, etc. ☐ **sinologist** *n.*

sinuous / **sin**-yoo-uhs / *adj.* with many curves, undulating. ☐ **sinuously** *adv.* **sinuosity** *n.*

sinus / **suy**-nuhs / *n.* (*pl.* **sinuses**) a cavity in bone or tissue, esp. that in the skull connecting with the nostrils.

sinusitis / suy-nuh-**suy**-tuhs / *n.* inflammation of a sinus.

sip *v.* (**sipped**, **sipping**) take a sip; drink in small mouthfuls. •*n.* **1** the act of sipping. **2** a small mouthful of liquid.

siphon / **suy**-fuhn / *n.* **1** a pipe or tube in the form of an upside-down U, used for forcing liquid to flow from one container to another by utilising atmospheric pressure. **2** a bottle from which aerated water is forced out through a tube by pressure of gas. •*v.* (often foll. by *off*) **1** flow or draw out through a siphon. **2** divert, take, or set aside (funds, resources, etc.).

sir *n.* **1** a polite form of address to a man. **2** (**Sir**) a title prefixed to the name of a knight or baronet (*Sir John Moore; Sir J. Moore; Sir John*). •*v.* address as sir (*don't sir me*).

sire *n.* **1** the male parent of an animal, esp. a stallion. **2** *archaic* a father or male ancestor. •*v.* (of an animal) be the sire of, beget.

siren *n.* **1** a device that makes a loud prolonged sound as a signal. **2** a dangerously fascinating woman. (¶ Named after the Sirens in Greek legend, women who lived on an island and by their singing lured seafarers to destruction on the rocks.)

sirenian / suy-**ree**-nee-uhn / *n.* a member of a group of large plant-eating animals that live in water, e.g. the dugong and the manatee. •*adj.* of this group.

Sirius / si-ree-uhs / *n.* the Dog Star, the brightest of the fixed stars, apparently following on the heels of the hunter Orion.

sirloin *n.* the upper (best) part of loin of beef.

sirocco / suh-**rok**-oh / *n.* (also **scirocco**) (*pl.* **siroccos**) a hot wind that reaches Italy from Africa.

sis *n. colloq.* **1** sister. **2** sissy.

sisal / **suy**-suhl / *n.* **1** rope fibre made from the leaves of a tropical plant. **2** the plant itself.

sissy *n.* (also **cissy**) *colloq.* an effeminate boy; a cowardly person. •*adj.* effeminate; cowardly.

sister *n.* **1** a daughter of the same parents as another person. **2** *Aust.* (in Aboriginal English) a female relative of the same generation as the speaker; (loosely) a female Aborigine. **3** a fellow woman; one who is a fellow member of a trade union, feminist group, profession, etc. **4** a nun; (**Sister**) the title of a nun. **5** a female hospital nurse in authority over others. ☐ **sister city** either of a pair of cities in different countries which have established close cultural etc. links. **sister-in-law** (*pl.* **sisters-in-law**) the sister of one's husband or wife; the wife of one's brother. ☐☐ **sisterly** *adj.*

sisterhood *n.* **1** the relationship of sisters. **2** an order of nuns; a society of women doing religious or charitable work. **3** the community of feeling between women.

Sisters of St Joseph of the Sacred Heart an Australian teaching order of nuns founded by Mother Mary MACKILLOP in 1866.

Sistine / **sis**-teen / *adj.* of any of the popes called Sixtus, esp. Sixtus IV. ☐ **Sistine Chapel** a chapel in the Vatican, built by Sixtus IV (pope 1471–84), containing Michelangelo's painted ceiling and his fresco of the Last Judgment.

Sisyphean / sis-uh-**fee**-uhn / *adj.* (of toil) endless and fruitless. (¶ From SISYPHUS.)

Sisyphus / **sis**-uh-fuhs / *Gk myth.* a king of Corinth whose punishment in Hades for his misdeeds was to roll a large stone up a hill from which it continually rolled back before the summit was reached.

sit *v.* (**sat**, **sitting**) **1** take or be in a position in which the body rests more or less upright on the buttocks (*we were sitting gossiping*). **2** cause to sit, place in a sitting position (*sat him down*). **3** pose for a portrait. **4** (of birds) perch. **5** (of birds) remain on the nest to hatch eggs. **6** be situated, lie. **7** be a candidate for (*sit an examination*). **8** occupy a seat as a member of a committee etc. **9** (of Parliament or a lawcourt or committee) be in session. **10** (of clothes) fit in a certain way (*the coat sits badly on the shoulders*). **11** babysit. ☐ **sit back** relax one's efforts. **sit down 1** take a seat after standing; cause to sit. **2** *Aust.* (in Aboriginal English) be (in a place); settle (somewhere) permanently. **sit-down** *adj.* **1** (of a meal) eaten sitting at a table. **2** (of a protest etc.) with demonstrators occupying their workplace or sitting down on the ground in a public place. **sit-down** *n.* **1** a spell of sitting. **2** a sit-down protest etc. **3** *Aust.* (in Aboriginal English) a rest; a stay. **sit-in** *n.* occupation of a building etc. as a form of protest. **sit in on** be present as an observer at (a meeting etc.). **sit on** *colloq.* **1** delay action concerning (*the Government has been sitting on the report*). **2** *colloq.* repress or snub (*he wants sitting on*). **sit on the fence** avoid taking sides in a dispute. **sit out 1** take no part in (a dance etc.). **2** stay till the end of (esp. an ordeal) (*had to sit the concert out*). **sit tight** *colloq.* remain firmly where one is; take no action and not yield.

Sita / **see**-tah / (in the Ramayana) the wife of Rama. She is the Hindu model of an ideal woman.

sitar / si-**tah** / *n.* an Indian musical instrument resembling a long-necked lute.

sitcom *n. colloq.* a situation comedy.

site *n.* **1** the ground on which a town or building stood, stands, or is to stand. **2** the place where some activity or event takes place or took place (*an Aboriginal sacred site; the site of the battle*). • *v.* locate, provide with a site.

Sitsky, Larry (1934–), AM, Australian pianist and composer.

sittella / suh-**tel**-uh / *n.* (also **sitella**) a small tree-living bird of mainland Australia, usu. grey or brown and white-streaked.

sitter *n.* **1** a person who is seated. **2** one who is sitting for a portrait. **3** a babysitter. **4** *colloq.* an easy catch or shot; something easy to do.

sitting see SIT. • *adj.* **1** (of an animal) not running; (of a game bird) not flying (*shot a sitting pheasant*). **2** (of a member of parliament etc.) current. • *n.* **1** a continuous period spent on one activity (*finished the book in one sitting*). **2** the time during which an assembly is engaged in business. **3** a session during which a meal is served.

situate *v.* place or put in a certain position.

situation *n.* **1** a place (with its surroundings) that is occupied by something. **2** a set of circumstances. **3** a position of employment. ☐ **situation comedy** a broadcast comedy in which humour derives from characters' misunderstandings and embarrassments in everyday situations.

Siva / **see**-vuh, **shee**-vuh / (also **Shiva**) one of the gods of the Hindu Trinity, usu. depicted with a third eye in the middle of his forehead, wearing a crescent moon and a necklace of skulls.

six *adj.* & *n.* one more than five (6, VI). ☐ **six-pack 1** a pack of six cans, stubbies, etc., esp. of beer. **2** *colloq.* a set of well-developed abdominal muscles. **3** *Volleyball* a blow delivered to the face of an opponent by a spiked ball.

sixfold *adj.* & *adv.* **1** six times as much or as many. **2** consisting of six parts.

sixpence *n. hist.* the sum of six pennies; a coin worth this.

sixteen *adj.* & *n.* one more than fifteen (16, XVI). ☐ **sixteenth** *adj.* & *n.*

sixth *adj.* & *n.* **1** next after fifth. **2** one of six equal parts of a thing. ☐ **sixth sense** a supposed extra power of perception other than the five physical ones; intuition. ☐☐ **sixthly** *adv.*

sixty *adj.* & *n.* six times ten (60, LX). • *n.pl.* (**sixties**) the numbers from 60 to 69, esp. the years of a century or of a person's life. ☐ **sixtieth** *adj.* & *n.*

sizable alternative spelling of SIZEABLE.

size[1] *n.* **1** the measurements or extent of something. **2** any of the standard measurements

size in which things are made and sold. •*v.* group or sort according to size. ▫ **size up** estimate the size of; *colloq.* form a judgment of (a person or situation etc.).

size[2] *n.* a gluey solution used to glaze paper, stiffen textiles, etc. •*v.* treat with size.

sizeable *adj.* (also **sizable**) large or fairly large.

sizzle *v.* **1** make a hissing sound like that of frying. **2** *colloq.* be very hot; be angry or resentful. •*n.* **1** a sizzling sound. **2** *Aust.* = SAUSAGE SIZZLE (*see* SAUSAGE).

SJ *abbr.* Society of Jesus.

ska *n.* a type of fast pop music, originally from Jamaica.

skate[1] *n.* (*pl.* **skate** *or* **skates**) a large flat sea fish used as food.

skate[2] *n.* **1** an ice skate. **2** a roller skate. **3** = SKATEBOARD. •*v.* glide over ice or a hard surface wearing skates; perform (a specified figure) in this way. ▫ **skater** *n.*

skateboard *n.* a short narrow board on two pairs of trucks, for riding on while standing. ▫ **skateboarding** *n.* **skateboarder** *n.*

skating rink *n.* **1** a stretch of artificial ice used for skating. **2** a smooth floor used for roller skating.

sked *colloq. n.* a schedule. •*v.* (**skedded**, **skedding**) to schedule.

skedaddle *v. colloq.* go away quickly.

skeet *n.* a shooting sport in which a clay target is thrown from a trap to simulate the flight of a bird.

skeeter *n. colloq.* a mosquito.

skeg *n.* **1** the fin underneath the rear of a surfboard. **2** *Aust. colloq.* a surfie; a person who surfs frequently.

skeghead *Aust.* = SKEG (sense 2).

skein / skayn / *n.* **1** a loosely-coiled bundle of yarn or thread. **2** a number of wild geese etc. in flight.

skeletal / **skel**-uh-tuhl / *adj.* of or like a skeleton.

skeleton *n.* **1** the framework of bones supporting an animal body. **2** the shell or other hard structure covering or supporting an invertebrate animal. **3** a very lean person or animal. **4** any supporting structure or framework, e.g. of a building. **5** an outline of a literary work etc. •*adj.* reduced to a minimum (*a skeleton crew; a skeleton staff*). ▫ **skeleton in the cupboard** a discreditable secret. **skeleton key** a key made so as to fit many locks.

skerrick *n.* (usu. with *negative*) esp. *Aust. colloq.* the smallest bit (*not a skerrick left*).

sketch *n.* **1** a rough or unfinished drawing or painting. **2** a brief account of something. **3** a short usu. comic play. •*v.* make a sketch or sketches; make a sketch of; outline briefly. ▫ **sketch map** a roughly-drawn map.

sketchbook *n.* a pad of drawing paper for sketching on.

sketchy *adj.* (**sketchier**, **sketchiest**) rough and not detailed or careful. ▫ **sketchily** *adv.* **sketchiness** *n.*

skew *adj.* slanting, askew. •*n.* a slant. •*v.* **1** make skew, turn or twist round. **2** distort (*his account is somewhat skewed*). ▫ **on the skew** askew.

skewbald *adj.* (of an animal) with irregular patches of white and another colour (strictly, not including black; cf. PIEBALD).

skewer *n.* a pin thrust through meat to hold it together while it is cooked. •*v.* pierce or hold in place with a skewer or other pointed object.

skew-whiff *adj. & adv. colloq.* askew.

ski / skee / *n.* (*pl.* **skis**) one of a pair of long narrow strips of wood etc. fixed under the feet for travelling over snow. •*v.* (**ski'd** *or* **skied**, **skiing**) travel on skis. ▫ **ski-jump** a steep snow-covered slope levelling off before a sharp drop to allow skiers to leap through the air. **ski lift** a device for carrying skiers up a slope, usu. on seats slung from an overhead cable. **ski run** a slope suitable for skiing down as a sport. ▫ ▫ **skier** *n.*

skid *v.* (**skidded**, **skidding**) (of a vehicle or its wheels) slide on slippery ground; cause (a vehicle) to do this. •*n.* **1** a skidding movement. **2** a log or plank etc. used to make a track over which heavy objects may be dragged or rolled. **3** a runner on a helicopter, for use when landing. **4** a wedge or a wooden or metal shoe that acts as a braking device on the wheel of a cart. ▫ **on the skids** *colloq.* about to be discarded or defeated. **skid row** a slum area where vagrants live.

skidlid *n. colloq.* a crash helmet worn by motorcyclists etc.

skiff *n.* a small light boat for rowing or sculling.

skilful *adj.* having or showing great skill. ▫ **skilfully** *adv.*

skill *n.* ability to do something well; technique, expertise.

skilled *adj.* **1** skilful. **2** (of work) needing great skill; (of a worker) highly trained or experienced in such work.

skillet *n.* a frying pan.

skillion / skil-yuhn / *n.* (also **skilling**) *Aust.* a lean-to attached to a dwelling and providing additional accommodation (esp. as a kitchen). ▫ **skillion roof** a sloping roof characteristic of a lean-to building.

skim *v.* (**skimmed**, **skimming**) **1** take (floating matter) from the surface of a liquid; clear (a liquid) in this way. **2** move or throw lightly and quickly over a surface; glide through air. **3** (often foll. by *over*) deal with or treat (a matter) superficially. **4** read quickly, noting only the chief points (*skim through a newspaper*). •*n.* skimming. ▫ **skim milk** (also **skimmed milk**) milk from which the cream has been removed.

skimp *v.* supply, use, or do less than is needed.

skimpy *adj.* (**skimpier**, **skimpiest**) **1** scanty, meagre, insufficient. **2** greatly concerned to

skin economise; stingy. •*n. colloq.* (in WA) a scantily clad barmaid. ◻ **skimpily** *adv.* **skimpiness** *n.*

skin *n.* **1** the flexible covering of the body. **2** an animal's skin removed from its body, with or without the hair still attached. **3** a vessel for water or wine, made from an animal's whole skin. **4** a person's complexion. **5** an outer layer or covering, esp. of a fruit, a sausage, etc. **6** the film that forms on the surface of certain liquids. **7** *Aust.* one of two units into which an Aboriginal people is divided, usu. on the basis of lineal descent, each skin being associated with a totemic bird, animal, or insect; a moiety. **8** a prize in a sporting competition. •*v.* (**skinned**, **skinning**) **1** remove the skin from. **2** graze (part of the body). **3** *colloq.* swindle. ◻ **by the skin of one's teeth** only just, barely. **skin cancer** a cancer occurring on the skin, caused by overexposure of unprotected skin to sunlight, the deadliest form of such cancers being melanoma. **skin-deep** superficial. **skin diver** one who engages in skin diving. **skin diving** the sport of swimming deep under water with flippers and breathing apparatus. **skin graft** the surgical transplanting of skin; the skin transferred in this way. **skin-tight** (of a garment) very close-fitting.

skinflint *n.* a miserly person.

skinful *n. colloq.* enough alcohol to make a person very drunk. ◻ **have had a skinful 1** be drunk. **2** be weary of; be fed up with (*I've had a skinful of those kids today*).

skinhead *n.* a youth with a shaven head, esp. one of an aggressive gang.

skink *n.* any small lizard of the family Scincidae, including numerous Australian species usu. ranging in size from about 30 to 70 mm, but including the large land mullet and the blue-tongue (about 300 mm).

skinny *adj.* (**skinnier**, **skinniest**) (of a person or animal) very thin. •*n.* (also **skinnyfish**) any of several food fish of northern Australia and elsewhere, having a notably compressed body. ◻ **skinny-dip** *colloq. v.* swim in the nude. *n.* an act or instance of skinny-dipping. **skinny-dipper** a person who skinny-dips. ◻◻ **skinniness** *n.*

skins golf *n.* a form of golf in which prize money is awarded to the winner of each hole: if a hole is not won outright, the prize money jackpots to the next hole, and so on.

skint *adj. colloq.* having no money left.

skip[1] *v.* (**skipped**, **skipping**) **1** move along lightly, esp. by taking two steps with each foot in turn. **2** jump with a skipping rope. **3** pass quickly from one subject or point to another. **4** omit in reading or dealing with a thing. **5** *colloq.* go away hastily or secretly. •*n.* a skipping movement. ◻ **skipping rope** (also **skip rope**) a length of rope, turned over the head and under the feet as a person jumps.

skip[2] *n.* **1** a cage or bucket in which people or materials are raised and lowered in mines and quarries. **2** a large metal container for holding and carrying away builders' rubbish etc.

skip[3] *n. Aust. derog.* an Australian of British descent. (¶ From *Skippy*, the name of a kangaroo in an Australian TV series for children.)

skipper *n.* the captain of a ship, aircraft, or sports team. •*v.* be captain of.

skippy *n.* (in WA and Tas.) a silvery marine food fish of southern Australia.

skirl *n.* the shrill sound characteristic of bagpipes. •*v.* make this sound.

skirmish *n.* a minor fight or conflict. •*v.* take part in a skirmish.

skirt *n.* **1** a woman's garment hanging from the waist; this part of a garment. **2** the flap of a saddle. **3** the hanging part round the base of a hovercraft. **4** a cut of beef from the lower flank. **5** (also **bit of skirt**) *colloq. offens.* a woman regarded as an object of sexual desire. •*v.* (often foll. by *around*) **1** go or be situated along the edge of. **2** avoid dealing directly with (an issue etc.). **3** *Aust.* trim the skirtings from (a fleece).

skirting *n.* (also **skirting board**) a narrow board round the wall of a room, close to the floor.

skirtings *n.pl. Aust.* the trimmings or inferior parts of a fleece.

skit *n.* a short play or piece of writing that is a humorous imitation of a serious one; a piece of humorous mimicry.

skitch *v. Aust. colloq.* = SOOL.

skite *Aust. colloq. v.* boast, brag. •*n.* **1** a braggart, a boaster. **2** boasting. ◻ **skiter** *n.*

skittish *adj.* frisky. ◻ **skittishly** *adv.* **skittishness** *n.*

skittle *n.* **1** (**skittles**) a game of trying to knock down a group of wooden pins by rolling a ball at them. **2** a pin used in this game. •*v.* knock over in the manner of skittles; defeat (*he skittled the Opposition in debate*).

skivvy *n. US & Aust.* a thin, high-necked, long-sleeved garment.

skol / skol, skohl / *n.* used as a toast in drinking. •*v.* (also **scull**) *colloq.* **1** drink (a glass etc. of alcoholic liquor) in a single draught. **2** finish one's drink quickly (*skol your beer and let's go*).

skua / skyoo-uh / *n.* a predatory seabird like a large gull which pursues other birds and forces them to disgorge the fish they have caught.

skulduggery *n.* trickery; unscrupulous behaviour.

skulk *v.* loiter or move stealthily; lurk, hide (out of cowardice or to shirk duty).

skull *n.* the bony framework of the head; the part of this protecting the brain. ◻ **skull and crossbones** a picture of a skull with two thigh bones crossed below it as an emblem of death or piracy.

skullcap *n.* a small, round, close-fitting cap with no peak, covering the crown of the head only, and worn by popes, bishops, etc.

skunk *n.* **1** a black bushy-tailed American animal about the size of a cat, able to spray a foul-smelling liquid from its anal glands. **2** *colloq.* a contemptible person.

sky *n.* the region of the clouds or upper air. • *v.* (**skied**, **skying**) hit (a ball) to a great height. ☐ **sky blue** *adj.* & *n.* bright clear blue. **sky-high** *adj.* & *adv.* very high.

skydiving *n.* the sport of performing acrobatic movements in the sky under free fall before opening a parachute. ☐ **skydiver** *n.*

skyjack *v. colloq.* hijack (an aircraft).

skylark *n.* a lark of Eurasia and N. Africa that sings while soaring. • *v.* play about light-heartedly.

skylight *n.* a window in a roof or ceiling.

skyline *n.* the outline of hills, buildings, etc. seen against the sky.

skyrocket *n.* a rocket that rises high into the air before exploding. • *v.* (esp. of prices) rise sharply.

skyscraper *n.* a very tall building.

skysurfing *n.* the sport of jumping from an aircraft and surfing through the air on a board before landing by parachute.

skyward *adv.* (also **skywards**) towards the sky. • *adj.* moving skyward.

slab *n.* **1** a flat broad fairly thick piece of something solid, esp. stone. **2** (also as *adj.*) *Aust.* a thick, rough-hewn plank of wood used for building purposes, esp. in the bush (*a slab hut; a slab fence*). **3** a large flat piece of chocolate, bread, etc. **4** *Aust. colloq.* a carton of 24 cans of beer. **5** a mortuary table.

slack *adj.* **1** loose, not tight or tense. **2** slow, sluggish; negligent. **3** (of trade or business) with little happening; not busy. • *n.* the slack part of a rope etc. (*haul in the slack*). • *v.* **1** slacken. **2** be idle or lazy about work. ☐ **slack off 1** loosen. **2** reduce one's level of activity; reduce speed. ☐☐ **slackly** *adv.* **slackness** *n.*

slacken *v.* make or become slack. ☐ **slacken off** = SLACK OFF.

slacker *n.* a lazy person; a shirker.

slacks *n.pl.* informal trousers.

slag *n.* **1** solid non-metallic waste matter left when metal has been separated from ore by smelting. **2** volcanic scoria. • *v.* **1** form slag. **2** (often fol. by *off*) *colloq.* criticise, insult, slander. **3** *Aust. colloq.* spit. ☐ **slag heap** a mound of waste matter from a mine etc. ☐☐ **slaggy** *adj.*

slain *see* SLAY.

slake *v.* **1** satisfy or make less strong (*slake one's thirst*). **2** combine (lime) chemically with water.

slalom / **slay**-luhm, **slah**- / *n.* **1** a ski race down a zigzag course. **2** an obstacle race in canoes.

slam *v.* (**slammed**, **slamming**) **1** shut forcefully with a loud noise; put down loudly. **2** put or do suddenly (*slammed the brakes on*). **3** *colloq.* criticise severely. **4** *colloq.* hit. • *n.* **1** a slamming noise. **2** the winning of 12 or 13 tricks in the game of bridge. ☐ **grand slam** the winning of all 13 tricks in the game of bridge; the winning of all of a group of championships in tennis or golf etc.

slam dunk *Basketball* a play in which a player jumps and thrusts the ball forcefully down into the basket. **slam-dunk** perform a slam dunk.

slander *n.* **1** a false statement uttered maliciously that damages a person's reputation. **2** the crime of uttering this. • *v.* utter a slander about. ☐ **slanderous** *adj.* **slanderously** *adv.*

slang *n.* words, phrases, or particular meanings of these, that are used very informally, often by a specific group or profession, and are not regarded as standard. • *v.* use abusive language to. ☐ **slanging match** a prolonged exchange of insults. ☐☐ **slangy** *adj.*

slanguage / **slang**-gwij / *n.* (also **slangwidge** or **Australian slanguage**) a distinctively Australian expression, esp. of the more colourful variety; Australian colloquial speech.

slant *v.* **1** slope. **2** (often as **slanted** *adj.*) present (news etc.) in a biased way or from a particular point of view. • *n.* a slope. **2** the way something is presented, an attitude or bias.

slanter (also **slinter**) *Aust. colloq. n.* a trick; a fraudulent stratagem. • *adj.* crooked, dishonest.

slantwise *adv.* in a slanting position.

slap *v.* (**slapped**, **slapping**) **1** strike with the open hand or with something flat. **2** lay forcefully (*slapped the money on the counter*). **3** place hastily or carelessly (*slapped paint on the walls*). • *n.* a blow with the open hand or with something flat. • *adv.* with a slap; directly (*ran slap into him*). ☐ **slap bang** *adv. colloq.* **1** violently, headlong. **2** precisely, exactly (*landed slap bang in the middle*). **slap-up** *adj. colloq.* first-class, lavish (*a slap-up meal*).

slapdash *adj.* hasty and careless. • *adv.* in a slapdash way.

slapstick *n.* boisterous comedy based on actions rather than words.

slash *v.* **1** make a sweeping stroke with a sword, knife, etc.; cut or gash in this way. **2** reduce (prices etc.) drastically. **3** criticise vigorously. • *n.* **1** a slashing cut; a wound made by this. **2** *Printing* an oblique stroke; a solidus.

slat *n.* one of the thin narrow strips of wood, metal, or plastic overlapping to form a screen, e.g. in a Venetian blind.

slate *n.* **1** a kind of rock that is easily split into flat smooth plates. **2** a piece of this used as roofing material or (formerly) for writing on. **3** the bluish-grey colour of slate. **4** a list of nominees for office etc. • *v.* **1** cover or roof with slates. **2** *colloq.* criticise severely; scold (*her book was slated by the media*). ☐ **a clean slate** a record of good conduct with nothing discreditable. **on the slate** *colloq.* recorded as a debt; on credit. ☐☐ **slaty** *adj.*

slater *n.* a woodlouse or similar crustacean, usu. grey or brown and oval-shaped.

slather / **sla**-*th*uh / *v.* spread thickly (*slathered his toast with peanut butter*). ☐ **open slather** *Aust.* **1** unrestricted scope for action (*gave him open*

slattern *n.* a slovenly woman. ☐ **slatternly** *adj.*

slaughter *n.* **1** the killing of animals for food. **2** the ruthless killing of a great number of people or animals; a massacre. • *v.* **1** kill (animals) for food. **2** kill ruthlessly or in great numbers. **3** *colloq.* defeat utterly. ☐ **slaughterer** *n.*

slaughterhouse *n.* = ABATTOIR.

Slav *n.* a member of any of the peoples of East and Central Europe who speak a Slavonic language.

slave *n.* **1** a person who is the property of another and obliged to work for him or her. **2** one who is dominated by another person or by an influence (*a slave to duty*). **3** a mechanism directly controlled by another mechanism. • *v.* work very hard. ☐ **slave labour** forced labour. **slave trade** the procuring, transporting, and selling of slaves, esp. (formerly) African blacks.

slaver / slav-uh / *v.* **1** have saliva flowing from the mouth. **2** (foll. by *over*) drool over. • *n.* **1** dribbling saliva. **2** fulsome flattery; drivel, nonsense.

slavery / slay-vuh-ree / *n.* **1** the condition of a slave. **2** the practice of having slaves (*to abolish slavery*). **3** very hard work, drudgery.

Slavic / slah-vik, slav-ik / *adj.* & *n.* = SLAVONIC.

slavish / slay-vish / *adj.* **1** like a slave, excessively submissive. **2** showing no independence or originality (*a slavish imitator of the style of Patrick White*). ☐ **slavishly** *adv.* **slavishness** *n.*

Slavonic / sluh-**von**-ik / *adj.* **1** of the group of languages including Russian and Polish. **2** of the Slavs. ■ *n.* this group of languages.

slay *v.* (**slew**, **slain**, **slaying**) *literary* kill.

sleaze *colloq. n.* **1** sleaziness. **2** a person of low moral standards. **3** (*attrib.*) characterised by sleaziness (*the annual sleaze ball*). • *v.* live, behave, etc., in a sleazy fashion.

sleazy *adj.* (**sleazier**, **sleaziest**) *colloq.* dirty and slovenly; squalid, slummy. ☐ **sleazily** *adv.* **sleaziness** *n.*

sled *n.* = SLEDGE¹. • *v.* (**sledded**) ride on a sled. ☐ **sledding** *n.*

sledge¹ *n.* a narrow cart with runners, used for travelling on snow. • *v.* (**sledged**) travel or convey by sledge. ☐ **sledging** *n.*

sledge² *v.* orig. *Aust.* **1** *Cricket* (of a fielder) attempt to break the concentration of (a batsman) by abusive language, needling, etc. **2** act in this way in other contexts. ☐ **sledging** *n.*

sledgehammer *n.* a large heavy hammer used with both hands.

sleek *adj.* **1** smooth and glossy (*sleek hair*). **2** looking well-fed and thriving. **3** ingratiating, slick, in speech, behaviour, etc. • *v.* make sleek by smoothing. ☐ **sleekly** *adv.* **sleekness** *n.* **sleeky** *adj.*

sleep *n.* **1** the natural recurring condition of rest in animals, with the eyes closed and muscles relaxed. **2** a spell of this (*a long sleep*). **3** the inert condition of hibernating animals. • *v.* (**slept**, **sleeping**) **1** be in a state of sleep. **2** stay somewhere for a night's sleep. **3** provide with sleeping accommodation (*the cottage sleeps four*). ☐ **sleep around** *colloq.* be sexually promiscuous. **sleep in** sleep late. **sleeping bag** a padded bag for sleeping in, esp. while camping. **sleeping car** or **sleeping carriage** a railway coach fitted with berths or beds. **sleeping partner** a partner in a business firm who does not take part in its actual work. **sleeping pill** a pill to help a person to sleep. **sleeping sickness** a disease transmitted by the bite of the tsetse fly and characterised by changes in the central nervous system leading to apathy, coma, and death. **sleep off** remedy by sleeping (*slept off his hangover*). **sleep on it** delay deciding about something until the next day. **sleep-out** *n.* a verandah or porch (often glassed in or partitioned off) or an outbuilding, providing sleeping accommodation. **sleep through** fail to be woken by (*slept through the earthquake*). **sleep with** have sexual intercourse with.

sleeper *n.* **1** one who sleeps. **2** each of the beams on which the rails of a railway etc. rest. **3** a sleeping car; a berth in this. **4** a ring worn in a pierced ear to keep the hole from closing. **5** a thing (or person) that is suddenly successful after being undistinguished. **6** an issue etc. which is not currently of concern but which has the potential to achieve prominence at any time.

sleepless *adj.* **1** unable to sleep; without sleep. **2** continually active; tireless (*sleepless pursuit of the facts*). ☐ **sleeplessly** *adv.* **sleeplessness** *n.*

sleepout *n.* *Aust.* a verandah or porch (often glassed in or partitioned off) or an outbuilding, providing sleeping accommodation.

sleepwalk *v.* walk about while asleep. ☐ **sleepwalker** *n.*

sleepy *adj.* (**sleepier**, **sleepiest**) **1** feeling or showing a desire to sleep. **2** inactive, without stir or bustle (*a sleepy little town*). ☐ **sleepy lizard** any of several Australian lizards noted for their sluggish habits, including the bobtail and the blue-tongue. Also called *boggi.* ☐ ☐ **sleepily** *adv.* **sleepiness** *n.*

sleepyhead *n.* a sleepy person.

sleet *n.* snow and rain falling at the same time; hail or snow that melts while falling. • *v.* send down sleet (*it is sleeting*). ☐ **sleety** *adj.*

sleeve *n.* **1** the part of a garment covering the arm. **2** a tube enclosing a rod or another tube. **3** the cover of a gramophone record. ☐ **up one's sleeve** concealed but available for use; in reserve. ☐ ☐ **sleeved** *adj.* **sleeveless** *adj.*

sleigh / slay / *n.* a sledge, esp. a passenger vehicle drawn by horses.

sleight of hand / slyut / *n.* great skill in using the hands to perform conjuring tricks etc.

slender *adj.* **1** slim and graceful. **2** small in amount, scanty (*slender means*).

slept *see* SLEEP.

Slessor, Kenneth (Adolf) (1901–71), Australian poet. His poems include 'Five Bells' (1939).

sleuth / slooth / n. a detective. • v. **1** investigate crime etc. **2** poke and pry (*sleuthing into my private life*).

slew[1] v. (also **slue**) turn or swing round.

slew[2] see SLAY.

slewed adj. colloq. drunk.

slice n. **1** a piece cut from something. **2** a portion or share (*slice of the profits*). **3** a long-handled kitchen utensil with a broad flat perforated blade. **4** a slicing stroke in golf, tennis, etc. • v. **1** cut into slices. **2** (foll. by *off*) cut off. **3** cut cleanly or easily. **4** strike (a ball) so that it spins away or travels at an angle. ☐ **slicer** n.

slick adj. **1** skilful or efficient (*a slick performance*). **2** superficially or pretentiously smooth and dextrous; glib (*a slick salesman*). **3** sleek, smooth (*a slick appearance; slick hair*). **4** slippery. • n. **1** a large patch of oil etc., esp. on the sea. **2** *Motor Racing* a smooth tyre. • v. **1** (usu. foll. by *back*, *down*) flatten (one's hair etc.) **2** (usu. foll. by *up*) make sleek or smart.

slide v. (**slid**, **sliding**) **1** move or cause to move along a smooth surface with the same area in continuous contact with this. **2** move or cause to move quietly or unobtrusively (*slid his hand into mine*). **3** pass gradually into a condition or habit. **4** (foll. by *over*) barely touch upon (a delicate subject etc.) (*I shall slide over your, shall we say, sleeping around*). • n. **1** the act of sliding. **2** a rapid decline. **3** a smooth surface for sliding on. **4** a chute for goods etc. or for children to play on. **5** a sliding part of a machine or instrument. **6** a small glass plate on which things are placed for examination under a microscope. **7** a mounted picture or transparency for showing on a blank surface by means of a projector. ☐ **slide rule** a ruler with a sliding central strip, marked with logarithmic scales and used for making calculations. **sliding scale** a scale of fees, taxes, wages, etc. that varies in accordance with the variation of some standard.

slight adj. **1** not much, not great; not thorough. **2** (**the slightest**) any whatever (*if there were the slightest chance*). **3** slender, not heavily built. • v. treat or speak of (a person etc.) as not worth one's attention; insult by lack of respect or courtesy. • n. an insult given in this way. ☐ **slightly** adv. **slightness** n.

slim adj. (**slimmer**, **slimmest**) **1** of small girth or thickness, not heavily built. **2** small, insufficient (*only a slim chance of success*). • v. (**slimmed**, **slimming**) **1** make oneself slimmer by dieting, exercise, etc. **2** reduce in numbers or scale (*slim down the workforce*). ☐ **slimly** adv. **slimness** n. **slimmer** n.

slime n. a slippery thick mud or liquid substance.

slimy adj. (**slimier**, **slimiest**) **1** like slime; covered or smeared with slime. **2** disgustingly dishonest, meek, or flattering. ☐ **slimily** adv. **sliminess** n.

sling[1] n. **1** a belt, strap, etc. looped round an object to support or lift it. **2** a bandage looped round the neck to form a support for an injured arm. **3** a looped strap used to throw a stone or other missile. **4** *Aust. colloq.* a tip or a bribe. • v. (**slung**, **slinging**) **1** suspend or lift with a sling. **2** hurl (a stone) with a sling. **3** *colloq.* throw. **4** *Aust. colloq.* pay a tip or a bribe (*sling him $50 and she'll be apples*). ☐ **sling off at** *Aust.* ridicule; disparage; mock; be scathingly critical of (*I wasn't slinging off at your religion, even though it's utterly stupid*). **sling** (*or* **swing**) **the billy** *Aust.* prepare to make tea, esp. as an act of hospitality to visitors (*see* BILLY).

sling[2] n. a sweetened drink of gin (or other spirits) and water.

slink v. (**slunk**, **slinking**) move in a stealthy, guilty, or shamefaced way.

slinky adj. **1** moving in a slinking way. **2** smooth and sinuous. **3** (of clothes) close-fitting.

slinter alternative spelling of SLANTER.

slip[1] v. (**slipped**, **slipping**) **1** slide accidentally; lose one's balance in this way. **2** go, put, or be put with a smooth movement, esp. without being observed. **3** detach or release. **4** escape; become detached from (*the ship slipped her moorings; it slipped my memory*). **5** place or slide stealthily or casually (*slipped him a coin*). **6** (foll. by *on*, *off*) pull (a garment) easily or hastily on or off. **7** (foll. by *into*) wear (*think I'll slip into something more comfortable*). • n. **1** the act of slipping. **2** a careless or slight error. **3** a loose covering or garment; a petticoat; a pillowcase. **4** a slipway. **5** a fieldsman in cricket stationed on the off side just behind the wicket; this position; (**the slips**) this part of the field. ☐ **slip-knot** a knot that can slide easily or be undone by pulling. **slip of the pen** (*or* **tongue**) a small mistake in what is written (or said). **slipped disc** a displaced disc between vertebrae, causing back pain. **slip up** *colloq.* make a mistake. **slip-up** n. *colloq.* a mistake. ☐☐ **slippage** n.

slip[2] n. **1** a small piece of paper. **2** a cutting taken from a plant for grafting or planting. ☐ **a slip of a** small and slim (*a slip of a girl*).

slipper n. a light loose comfortable shoe for indoor wear.

slippery adj. **1** smooth and difficult to hold; causing slipping by its wetness or smoothness. **2** (of a person) not to be trusted (*a slippery customer*). ☐ **slippery dip** *Aust.* a slide in a children's playground. ☐☐ **slipperiness** n.

sliprail n. *Aust.* a fence rail, forming one of a set which can be slipped out so as to leave an opening.

slipshod adj. careless; badly done or arranged.

slipstream n. a current of air driven backward by a vehicle moving forward.

slipway n. a sloping structure used as a landing stage or on which ships are built or repaired.

slit n. a narrow straight cut or opening. • v. (**slit**, **slitting**) **1** cut a slit in. **2** cut into strips.

slither v. **1** slide unsteadily (as on an icy surface). **2** move with a sinuous motion (*the snake slithered across the floor*). ◻ **slithery** adj.

sliver / **sliv**-uh / n. a thin strip cut or split from wood or glass etc.

Sloane Ranger n. (also **Sloane**) a fashionable upper-class conventional young person. (¶ Named after *Sloane* Square in London and the Lone *Ranger*, hero of Western stories and films.)

slob n. colloq. derog. a lazy, untidy person.

slobber v. **1** slaver or dribble. **2** (foll. by *over*) behave with repulsively excessive affection. • n. slaver.

slog v. (**slogged**, **slogging**) **1** hit hard and usu. wildly. **2** work or walk hard and steadily. • n. **1** a hard random hit. **2** a spell of hard steady work or walking.

slogan n. a word or phrase adopted as a motto; a short catchy phrase used in advertising.

sloop n. a sailing ship with one mast.

slop v. (**slopped**, **slopping**) **1** spill over or cause to spill; splash liquid on. **2** plod clumsily, esp. through mud or puddles etc. • n. **1** (also **slops**) weak unappetising drink or liquid food. **2** a quantity of slopped liquid. **3** (**slops**) household liquid refuse; dregs from tea cups. **4** (**slops**) US & Aust. colloq. beer; alcoholic liquor generally.

slope v. lie, turn, or place at an angle from the horizontal or vertical. • n. **1** a sloping surface or direction; a stretch of rising or falling ground. **2** the amount by which something slopes. ◻ **slope off** colloq. go away, esp. to evade work etc.

sloppy adj. (**sloppier**, **sloppiest**) **1** (of the ground) wet with rain, full of puddles. **2** (of food etc.) watery and disagreeable. **3** careless, untidy (*sloppy work practices*). **4** foolishly sentimental, maudlin. **5** (of a garment) ill-fitting or untidy; badly made. ◻ **sloppy joe** a loose, (deliberately) overlarge jumper. ◻◻ **sloppily** adv. **sloppiness** n.

slosh v. **1** colloq. hit (*sloshed him one*). **2** pour (liquid) clumsily. **3** splash; move with a splashing sound. • n. **1** colloq. a blow. **2** a splashing sound. **3** slush.

sloshed adj. colloq. drunk.

slot n. **1** a narrow opening through which something is to be put. **2** a groove, channel, or slit into which something fits. **3** a position in a series or scheme (*the program has its regular slot*). • v. (**slotted**, **slotting**) **1** make a slot or slots in. **2** put into a slot. ◻ **slot machine** a machine operated by a coin put in a slot.

sloth / slohth / n. **1** laziness. **2** a slow-moving animal of tropical America that hangs upside down in trees.

slothful adj. lazy. ◻ **slothfully** adv.

slouch v. stand, sit, or move in a lazy awkward way, not with an upright posture. • n. **1** a slouching movement or posture. **2** colloq. an incompetent or slovenly worker etc. ◻ **slouch hat 1** Aust. a hat with a wide flexible brim. **2** a hat with the left brim turned up, worn by an Australian soldier; this as an emblem of patriotism, courage, etc.

slough[1] / slow / n. a swamp or marshy place.

slough[2] / sluf / v. shed (*a snake sloughs its skin periodically*). • n. a snake's cast skin; dead tissue that drops away.

Slough of Despond a state of hopeless depression. (¶ From John Bunyan's *Pilgrim's Progress* (1678–84).)

Slovak / **sloh**-vak / n. a native or the language of the Slovak Republic. • adj. of the Slovaks or their language. ◻ **Slovak Republic** the eastern of the two republics into which the former Czechoslovakia is divided.

sloven / **sluv**-uhn / n. a slovenly person.

Slovenia / sluh-**vee**-nee-uh / a republic of former Yugoslavia. ◻ **Slovenian** adj. & n.

slovenly / **sluv**-uhn-lee / adj. careless and untidy; not methodical. • adv. in a slovenly manner. ◻ **slovenliness** n.

slow adj. **1** not quick or fast. **2** (of a clock) showing a time earlier than the correct one. **3** (of a person) not able to understand or learn easily. **4** lacking liveliness, sluggish (*business is slow today*). **5** tending to cause slowness (*a slow racetrack*). • adv. slowly (*go slow*). • v. reduce one's speed or the speed of (a vehicle etc.); reduce one's pace of life (*slow down; slow up*). ◻ **slow motion** (of a film) making movements appear to be performed much more slowly than in real life. **slow-worm 1** a small European legless lizard. **2** any of the small, wormlike, burrowing snakes of mainland Australia. **3** any of many legless lizards of mainland Australia. ◻◻ **slowish** adj. **slowly** adv. **slowness** n.

slowcoach n. a person who is slow in actions or work.

sludge n. **1** thick greasy mud; something resembling this. **2** sewage. ◻ **sludgy** adj.

slue alternative spelling of SLEW[1].

slug[1] n. **1** a small slimy animal like a snail without a shell. **2** a roundish lump of metal; a bullet of irregular shape; a pellet for firing from an airgun. **3** a mouthful of drink (esp. spirits). **4** a roundish lump of metal, esp. a nugget of gold, found on or just below the surface.

slug[2] v. (**slugged**, **slugging**) **1** strike with a hard heavy blow. **2** Aust. charge an exorbitant price; impose an exorbitant tax. • n. **1** a hard blow. **2** Aust. an exorbitant price or tax. ◻ **slug it out** fight it out.

sluggard n. a slow or lazy person.

sluggish adj. slow-moving; not alert or lively. ◻ **sluggishly** adv. **sluggishness** n.

sluggoes / **slug**-ohz / n.pl. (also **sluggos**) Aust. colloq. a man's brief swimming costume.

sluice / sloos / n. **1** (also **sluice gate**, **sluice valve**) a sliding gate or other contrivance for controlling the volume or flow of water in a stream etc. **2** the water controlled by this. **3**

slum (**sluice way**) an artificial water channel, esp. for washing ore. **4** a place where objects are rinsed. **5** the act of rinsing. •v. **1** provide or wash with a sluice or sluices. **2** flood, scour, or rinse with a flow of water. **3** (of water) rush out (as if) from a sluice.

slum n. **1** an overcrowded, run-down district with buildings of poor quality. **2** a house unfit for human habitation. ◻ **slum it** colloq. put up with uncomfortable conditions for a short period. ◻◻ **slummy** adj.

slumber n. sleep, esp. of a specified kind (a fitful slumber). •v. **1** sleep, esp. in a specified manner (slumbering peacefully). **2** be idle or inactive (as if in a slumber). **3** be quiet and peaceful (a slumbering outback township).

slump n. a sudden great fall in prices or in the demand for goods etc. •v. **1** undergo a slump. **2** sit or flop down heavily and slackly.

slung see SLING[1].

slunk see SLINK.

slur v. (**slurred**, **slurring**) **1** write or pronounce indistinctly with each letter or sound running into the next. **2** mark (notes) with a slur in music; perform in the way indicated by this. **3** pass lightly over (a fact etc.). **4** speak ill of. •n. **1** a slurred letter or sound. **2** a curved line placed over notes in music to show that they are to be sung to one syllable or played smoothly without a break. **3** discredit (a slur on his reputation).

slurp colloq. v. make a noisy sucking sound in eating or drinking. •n. this sound.

slurry / slu-ree / n. thin mud; thin liquid cement; liquid manure.

slush n. **1** partly melted snow on the ground. **2** silly sentimental talk or writing. •v. squelch, splash; make a squelching or splashing sound. ◻ **slush fund** a fund of money for corrupt purposes such as bribing officials.

slushy adj. (**slushier**, **slushiest**) **1** like slush. **2** mawkishly sentimental. •n. (also **slusher**) Aust. an assistant to a cook, esp. in a shearing gang.

slut n. offens. a slovenly or promiscuous woman. ◻ **sluttish** adj.

sly adj. (**slyer**, **slyest**) **1** done or doing things in an unpleasant cunning and secret way. **2** mischieving and knowing (with a sly smile). **3** Aust. illicit, illegal (esp. of the retailing of alcoholic liquor—see SLY GROGGER). ◻ **on the sly** secretly. ◻◻ **slyly** adv. **slyness** n.

sly grog n. Aust. colloq. alcoholic liquor sold by an unlicensed vendor. ◻ **sly grogger** a person who sells alcoholic liquor without a licence. **sly grogging** this practice. **sly grog shop 1** a place where sly grog is sold. **2** (also **sly grog shanty**, **sly grog tent**) hist. a venue for the sale of sly grog, esp. on the Australian goldfields.

Sm symbol samarium.

smack[1] n. **1** a slap. **2** a hard hit. **3** a loud kiss. •v. slap, hit hard. •adv. colloq. **1** with a smack. **2** suddenly; directly; violently (went smack through the window). **3** exactly (smack in the centre).

smack[2] n. a slight flavour or trace of something (add a smack of chilli; he has just a smack of snobbishness in his character). •v. have a flavour or suggestion of something (his manner smacks of conceit; this ice cream smacks too much of garlic).

smack[3] n. a boat with a single mast used for coasting or fishing.

smack[4] n. colloq. a hard drug, esp. heroin.

smacker n. colloq. **1** a loud kiss. **2** a dollar (can you hit me with ten smackers?).

small adj. **1** not large or big. **2** not great in size, importance, number, etc. **3** of the smaller kind (the small intestine). **4** doing things on a small scale (a small farmer). **5** petty. •n. the most slender part of something (the small of the back). •adv. in a small size or way; into small pieces (chop it small). ◻ **look** (or **feel**) **small** be humiliated. **small beer** something trivial. **small change** coins as opposed to notes. **small fry** unimportant people; children. **small hours** the hours soon after midnight. **small-minded** narrow or selfish in outlook. **small of the back** the part at the back of the waist. **small print** matter printed in small type; limitations (in a contract etc.) stated inconspicuously in this way. **small screen** television (as opposed to the cinema). **small talk** social conversation on unimportant subjects. **small-time** unimportant, minor (small-time crooks). **small-town** adj. relating to or characteristic of a small town; unsophisticated; provincial. ◻◻ **smallness** n.

smallgoods n.pl. Aust. cooked meats and meat products of the sort sold in a delicatessen.

smallpox n. an acute contagious disease (now eliminated) caused by a virus, with pustules that often left disfiguring scars.

small-scaled snake n. an extremely venomous large snake of eastern central Australia, having the most potent snake venom in the world. Also called fierce snake and inland taipan.

smarmy adj. colloq. trying to win favour by flattery or excessive politeness. ◻◻ **smarmily** adv. **smarminess** n.

smart adj. **1** well-groomed, neat. **2** brightly coloured, newly painted, etc. **3** stylish, fashionable (in all the smart restaurants). **4** (of a device) capable of some independent and seemingly intelligent action (e.g. through having a built-in microprocessor) (a smart card). **5** clever, ingenious, quickwitted. **6** quick, brisk (set a smart pace). **7** painfully severe; sharp; vigorous. •v. feel a stinging pain (bodily or mental). •n. a stinging pain. ◻ **smart alec** (also **smart aleck**) colloq. a conceited know-all. **smart arse** = SMART ALEC. **smart bomb** (or **missile** or **weapon** etc.) a bomb (or other weapon) which is able to track and 'lock on to' its target; a laser-guided weapon. **smart card** a plastic bankcard with an embedded microprocessor, used in conjunction with an electronic card reader to provide such services as the automatic transfer of funds between bank accounts, etc. **smart money** money invested by people with expert knowledge. **smart quotes** *Computing* quotation marks which are automatically interpreted as opening or closing marks (i.e. as inverted or raised commas). □□ **smartly** *adv.* **smartness** *n.*

smarten *v.* (usu. foll. by *up*) make or become smarter.

smash *v.* **1** break or become broken suddenly and noisily into pieces. **2** strike or move with great force; crash. **3** strike (a ball) forcefully downwards in tennis etc. **4** overthrow or destroy (*police smashed the drug ring*). • *n.* **1** the act or sound of smashing. **2** a collision. □ **smash hit** *colloq.* an extremely successful play, song, etc. **smash-up** *n.* a violent collision.

smashed *adj. colloq.* affected by alcohol or other drugs.

smasher *n. colloq.* a beautiful or pleasing person or thing.

smashing *adj. colloq.* excellent.

smattering *n.* a slight superficial knowledge of a language or subject.

smear *v.* **1** spread with a greasy, sticky, or dirty substance. **2** try to damage the reputation of. • *n.* **1** something smeared on a surface; a mark made by this. **2** a specimen of material smeared on a microscope slide for examination. **3** an attempt to damage a reputation (*a smear campaign*). □ **smear test** = CERVICAL SMEAR. □□ **smeary** *adj.*

smegma *adj.* a sebaceous secretion which collects esp. under the foreskin of the penis.

smell *n.* **1** the faculty of perceiving things by the sense organs of the nose. **2** the quality that is perceived in this way. **3** an unpleasant quality of this kind. **4** an act of smelling something. • *v.* (**smelt** *or* **smelled**, **smelling**) **1** perceive the smell of; detect or test by one's sense of smell. **2** give off a smell. **3** give off an unpleasant smell. □ **smelling salts** a strong-smelling substance sniffed to relieve faintness.

smelly *adj.* (**smellier**, **smelliest**) having a strong or unpleasant smell.

smelt[1] *see* SMELL.

smelt[2] *v.* heat and melt (ore) so as to obtain the metal it contains; obtain (metal) in this way. □ **smelter** *n.*

smelt[3] *n.* (*pl.* **smelt** *or* **smelts**) **1** any of several small marine and freshwater food fish of south-eastern Australia. **2** a small silvery European fish related to salmon.

smidgen *n.* (also **smidgin**) *colloq.* a very small amount.

smile *n.* a facial expression indicating pleasure or amusement with the corners of the mouth turned up. • *v.* **1** give a smile; express by smiling. **2** look bright or favourable (*fortune smiled on us*).

smiley / **smuy**-lee / *adj.* smiling, cheerful. • *n.* (*pl.* **smileys** *or* **smilies**) *colloq.* a symbol which, when viewed sideways, represents a smiling face, formed by the characters :-) and used in electronic communications to indicate that the writer is pleased or joking.

smirch *v.* **1** smear or soil. **2** bring discredit upon (a reputation). • *n.* a smear; a blot (on one's character etc.).

smirk *n.* a self-satisfied smile. • *v.* give a smirk.

smite *v.* (**smote**, **smitten**, **smiting**) **1** hit hard. **2** have a sudden effect on (*his conscience smote him*).

Smith, Dick (full name: Richard Harold Smith) (1944–), AO, Australian businessman, adventurer, aviator, and publisher.

Smith Brothers, Sir Keith (1890–1955) and Sir Ross (1892–1922), Australian pioneer aviators who in 1919 flew together from England to Australia in 27 days and 20 hours to win the £10,000 prize offered by the Australian government.

Smith Family a voluntary Australian welfare organisation established in Sydney in 1922, the largest of its kind in Australia. Operating in NSW, Vic., and the ACT, it provides material and financial help to the needy.

smith *n.* **1** a blacksmith. **2** a worker in a specified metal (*a goldsmith*). **3** a craftsman (*a wordsmith*).

smithereens *n.pl.* small fragments.

smithy *n.* a blacksmith's workshop, a forge.

smitten *see* SMITE. □ **smitten with** (*or* **by**) affected by (a disease, desire, fascination, etc.) (*smitten with cholera; smitten with regret; smitten by her beauty*).

smock *n.* **1** a loose shirtlike garment, often decorated with smocking and embroidery. **2** a loose overall. • *v.* ornament with smocking.

smocking *n.* a decoration of close gathers stitched into a square or criss-cross pattern.

smog *n.* fog polluted by smoke.

smoke *n.* **1** the visible vapour given off by a burning substance. **2** the act of smoking tobacco. **3** *colloq.* a cigarette or cigar. **4** (**the Smoke** *or* **the Big Smoke**) *Aust. colloq.* a large city, e.g. Sydney. • *v.* **1** give out smoke or steam or other visible vapour. **2** (of a fireplace) send smoke into a room instead of up the chimney. **3** darken with smoke (*smoked glass*). **4** preserve by treating with smoke (*smoked salmon*). **5** draw into the mouth the smoke from a cigarette, cigar, or tobacco pipe; do this as a habit (*we don't smoke*). □ **smoke-free 1** free from smoke. **2** where smoking tobacco is not permitted. **smoke out 1** drive out by means of smoke. **2** drive out of hiding etc. **3** *Aust.* (in Aboriginal English) ritually cleanse (a person or place) of unwelcome spirits, esp. after death, by the use of smoke. **smoking ceremony** *Aust.* (in Aboriginal culture) a ceremony in which smoke is used for ritual purposes, esp. after a death.

smokeless *adj.* **1** free from smoke. **2** producing little or no smoke (*smokeless fuel*).

smoker *n.* **1** a person who smokes tobacco as a habit. **2** an Australian parrot with smoky yellow plumage and a long dark tail.

smokescreen *n.* **1** a mass of smoke used to conceal the movement of troops. **2** something intended to conceal or disguise one's activities.

smokestack *n.* a tall chimney; the funnel of a locomotive or steamer.

smoko *n.* (also **smoke-o**, **smoke-oh**) *Aust. colloq.* **1** a teabreak; a brief rest from work (orig. time to have a cigarette etc.). **2** the food eaten at such a break.

smoky *adj.* (**smokier**, **smokiest**) **1** emitting, filled with, or obscured by smoke. **2** stained with or coloured like smoke. **3** having the flavour of smoked food. **4** greyish (*smoky blue*).

smooch *colloq. v.* **1** kiss and caress. • *n.* a spell of smooching.

smoodge / smooj / (also **smooge**) *Aust. colloq. v.* **1** behave amorously by kissing, fondling, etc. **2** behave in a fawning or ingratiating manner. • *n.* **1** a session of smoodging. **2** an act or instance of ingratiation.

smoodger *n. Aust. colloq.* a flatterer, a sycophant.

smooth *adj.* **1** having an even surface with no projections, free from roughness. **2** not hairy (*he has a smooth body*). **3** not wrinkled (*a smooth complexion*). **4** (of liquids) of even consistency; without lumps. **5** not harsh in sound or taste. **6** moving evenly without jolts or bumping (*a smooth ride*). **7** pleasantly polite but perhaps insincere. • *adv.* smoothly (*the course of true love never did run smooth*). • *v.* **1** make or become smooth. **2** remove problems or dangers from (*smooth a person's path*). • *n.* **1** a smoothing touch or stroke (*gave his hair a smooth*). **2** the easy part of life (*take the rough with the smooth*). ☐ **smooth-tongued** pleasantly polite or convincing but insincere. ☐☐ **smoothly** *adv.* **smoothness** *n.*

smoothie *n.* **1** a charming but perhaps insincere person. **2** *esp. US & Aust.* a smooth thick drink consisting of fresh fruit (esp. banana), puréed with milk, yoghurt, soymilk, or ice cream.

smorgasbord / smaw-guhs-bawd / *n.* **1** Swedish hors d'oeuvres; a buffet meal with a variety of dishes to choose from. **2** a wide variety or choice in general (*given this smorgasbord of options being put to them, the public is bound to be confused*).

smote *see* SMITE.

smother *v.* **1** suffocate or stifle. **2** die of suffocation. **3** have difficulty breathing. **4** put out (a fire) by covering it. **5** cover densely or thickly (*the flowerbed is smothered in weeds*). **6** (foll. by *in*, *with*) overwhelm or cover with (kisses, gifts, kindness, etc.). **7** (often foll. by *up*) restrain or suppress (*she smothered her anger*; *smothered up his feelings*).

smoulder *v.* **1** burn slowly with smoke but no flame. **2** burn inwardly with concealed anger or jealousy etc. **3** (of feelings) exist in a suppressed state. • *n.* a smouldering.

smudge *n.* a dirty or blurred mark. • *v.* **1** make a smudge on or with. **2** become smudged or blurred. ☐ **smudgy** *adj.*

smug *adj.* (**smugger**, **smuggest**) self-satisfied. ☐ **smugly** *adv.* **smugness** *n.*

smuggle *v.* **1** convey secretly. **2** bring (goods) into or out of a country illegally, esp. without paying customs duties. ☐ **smuggler** *n.* **smuggling** *n.*

smut *n.* **1** a small flake of soot; a small black mark made by this. **2** indecent talk, pictures, or stories. **3** a disease of cereal plants in which parts of the plant turn to black powder. • *v.* (**smutted**, **smutting**) mark with smuts.

smutty *adj.* (**smuttier**, **smuttiest**) **1** marked with smuts. **2** (of talk, pictures, or stories) indecent.

Sn *symbol* tin.

snack *n.* **1** a small, casual, or hurried meal. **2** a small amount of food eaten between meals. **3** *Aust. colloq.* something which is easy to accomplish, a pushover. ☐ **snack bar** a place where snacks are sold.

snaffle *n.* a horse's bit without a curb. • *v.* **1** put a snaffle on. **2** *colloq.* take for oneself; steal. **3** (often foll. by *up*) acquire quickly (*the early customers snaffled up the best bargains*).

snag[1] *n.* **1** a jagged projection. **2** a tear in fabric that has caught on a snag. **3** an unexpected difficulty (*negotiations have hit a snag*). • *v.* (**snagged**, **snagging**) catch, tear, or be caught on a snag.

snag[2] *n. Aust. colloq.* a sausage.

snag[3] *n. colloq.* a sensitive new-age guy. (¶ Acronym)

snagger *n. Aust. colloq.* a slow, inexperienced, or inept shearer.

snail *n.* a soft-bodied animal with a spiral shell. ☐ **snail mail** airmail or surface mail (as distinct from EMAIL). **snail's pace** a very slow pace.

snake *n.* **1** a reptile with a long narrow body and no legs. **2** (also **snake in the grass**) a treacherous person. • *v.* move or twist like a snake (*a road snaking through the hills*). ☐ **snake charmer** an entertainer who seems to make snakes move to music. **snake flower** a traditional term for any deep purple or blackish purple Australian flower. **snake lizard** any of various small Australian lizards and skinks having reduced or absent limbs and so often mistaken for snakes.

Snake Gully *Aust.* an imaginary place, perceived as remote and backward.

snakewood *n.* a traditional term for any Australian tree having twisted branches, as the wattle *Acacia grasbyi* of WA.

snaky *adj.* **1** of or like a snake. **2** winding, sinuous. **3** cunning, treacherous. **4** *Aust. colloq.*

angry; irritable (*he became very snaky when I asked him where he had been*).

snap *v.* (**snapped, snapping**) **1** make or cause to make a sharp cracking sound. **2** break suddenly or with a cracking sound. **3** bite or try to bite with a snatching movement. **4** take or accept eagerly (*snapping up bargains*). **5** speak with sudden irritation. **6** move smartly (*snapped to attention*). **7** take a snapshot of. •*n.* **1** the act or sound of snapping. **2** a small crisp brittle biscuit (*brandy snaps*). **3** (in full **cold snap**) a sudden brief spell of cold weather. **4** a snapshot. **5** a card game in which players call 'snap' when two similar cards are exposed. **6** vigour, liveliness (*has plenty of snap in him*). **7** *colloq.* an easy task (*the exam was a snap*). **8** *Aust. Rules* a quickly taken kick at goal. •*adv.* with a snapping sound. •*adj.* sudden; done or arranged at short notice (*a snap election*). □ **snap out of it** *colloq.* make oneself recover quickly from a bad mood.

snapper *n.* (also **schnapper**) any of several usu. pinkish-coloured marine fish valued as food.

snappish *adj.* bad-tempered and inclined to snap at people. □ **snappishly** *adv.*

snappy *adj.* (**snappier, snappiest**) *colloq.* **1** brisk, vigorous. **2** neat and elegant (*a snappy dresser*). □ **make it snappy** *colloq.* be quick. □□ **snappily** *adv.*

snapshot *n.* a photograph taken informally or casually.

snare *n.* **1** a trap for catching birds or animals, usu. with a noose. **2** something liable to entangle a person or expose him or her to danger or failure. **3** each of the strings of gut or hide stretched across a side drum to produce a rattling effect. **4** (in full **snare drum**) a drum with snares. •*v.* trap in a snare.

snarl[1] *v.* **1** growl angrily with the teeth bared. **2** speak in a bad-tempered way. •*n.* the act or sound of snarling.

snarl[2] *v.* tangle; become entangled. •*n.* a tangle. □ **snarl up** make or become jammed or tangled (*traffic was snarled up*). **snarl-up** *n. colloq.* a traffic jam; a muddle.

snatch *v.* **1** seize quickly or eagerly. **2** take quickly or when a chance occurs (*snatched a few hours' sleep*). •*n.* **1** the act of snatching. **2** a fragment of a song, or talk, etc. (*caught snatches of their conversation*). **3** (in weightlifting) the rapid raising of a weight from the floor to above the head. **4** *coarse colloq.* a woman's genitals. □ **in** (or **by**) **snatches** in fits and starts.

snazzy *adj. colloq.* smart, stylish. □ **snazzily** *adv.* **snazziness** *n.*

sneak *v.* **1** go or convey furtively. **2** *colloq.* steal furtively. **3** *colloq.* tell tales; turn informer. •*n.* **1** a mean-spirited underhand person. **2** *colloq.* a tell-tale; an informer. •*adj.* acting or done without warning (*a sneak attack*). □ **sneaky** *adj.*

■ **Usage** The form *snuck* for the past or past participle should not be used in formal contexts. It arose in American English in the 19th century and remains non-standard in Australian and British English.

sneakers *n.pl.* soft-soled canvas shoes.

sneaking *adj.* persistent but not openly acknowledged (*a sneaking feeling; a sneaking affection*).

sneer *n.* a scornful expression or remark. •*v.* show contempt by a sneer; say with a sneer.

sneeze *n.* a sudden audible involuntary expulsion of air through the nose and mouth. •*v.* give a sneeze. □ **not to be sneezed at** *colloq.* not to be despised; worth having.

sneezeweed *n. Aust.* any of several aromatic herbs which cause sneezing, esp. when the leaves are crushed.

snib *v.* (**snibbed, snibbing**) bolt, fasten, or lock (a door etc.). •*n.* a lock, catch, or fastening, for a door or window.

snick *n.* **1** a small cut or notch. **2** a batsman's light glancing stroke. •*v.* **1** cut a snick in. **2** hit with a light glancing stroke.

snicker *v.* snigger. •*n.* a snigger.

snide *adj.* sneering in a sly way (*made a snide remark about her boyfriend's sexual orientation*).

sniff *v.* **1** draw up air audibly through the nose. **a** draw (a scent, drug, liquid, or air) in through the nose. **b** try the smell of by sniffing. **3** show disdain etc. by sniffing. •*n.* the act or sound of sniffing. □ **sniff at** show contempt for (*sniffed at the offer*).

sniffer *n.* a person who sniffs, esp. a drug etc. (often in *comb.*: *a glue sniffer*). □ **sniffer dog** a dog trained to sniff out drugs or explosives.

sniffle *v.* sniff slightly or repeatedly. •*n.* **1** the act or sound of sniffling. **2** (also **the sniffles**) a cold in the head.

snifter *n. colloq.* a small drink of alcohol.

snig *v.* (**snigged, snigging**) *Aust.* haul (a log) with ropes or chains. □ **snig track** (also **snigging track**) a track along which timber is snigged.

snigger *n.* a sly or suppressed giggle. •*v.* give a snigger.

snip *v.* (**snipped, snipping**) cut with scissors or shears in small quick strokes. •*n.* **1** the act or sound of snipping. **2** a piece snipped off. **3** *colloq.* a bargain; a certainty; something very easy to do.

snipe *n.* (*pl.* **snipe** or **snipes**) a wading bird with a long straight bill, frequenting marshes, some species migrating from Asia and Russia to northern and eastern Australia in spring. •*v.* **1** fire shots from a hiding place. **2** (often foll. by *at*) make sly critical remarks attacking a person or thing. □ **snipe shooting** *Aust. hist.* (in white usage, a euphemistic description of) the practice of killing Aborigines. Also called *dispersing the natives.* □□ **sniper** *n.*

snippet *n.* **1** a small piece cut off. **2** a fragment of information or news; a brief extract.

snitch *colloq. v.* **1** steal. **2** (often foll. by *on*) inform on a person. •*n.* an informer.

snitchy *adj. Aust. colloq.* angry; bad-tempered.

snivel *v.* (**snivelled**, **snivelling**) **1** cry or complain in a miserable whining way. **2** run at the nose. •*n.* **1** an act of snivelling. **2** running mucus. ❏ **sniveller** *n.*

snob *n.* **1** a person who has an exaggerated respect for social position, wealth, etc., and who despises people whom he or she considers inferior. **2** a person who despises those supposedly inferior in intellect, taste, etc. (*he's an intellectual snob*). **3** *Aust.* = COBBLER (sense 4). ❏ **snobbery** *n.* **snobby** *adj.*

snobbish *adj.* of or like a snob. ❏ **snobbishly** *adv.* **snobbishness** *n.*

snog *colloq. v.* (**snogged**, **snogging**) kiss and caress. •*n.* a kissing session.

snood *n.* a loose bag-like ornamental net in which the hair is held at the back.

snook *n.* **1** *colloq.* a contemptuous gesture with thumb to nose and fingers spread out. **2** = BARRACUDA. ❏ **cock a snook** make this gesture; show cheeky contempt.

snooker *n.* **1** a game played on a billiard table with 15 red and 6 other coloured balls. **2** a position in snooker where a direct shot would lose points. •*v.* **1** subject to a snooker. **2** *colloq.* thwart, defeat.

snoop *colloq. v.* pry inquisitively. •*n.* the act of snooping. ❏ **snooper** *n.* **snoopy** *adj.*

snooty *adj.* (**snootier**, **snootiest**) *colloq.* haughty and snobbish. ❏ **snootily** *adv.*

snooze *n.* a nap. •*v.* take a snooze.

snore *n.* a snorting or grunting sound made during sleep. •*v.* make such sounds. ❏ **snorer** *n.*

snorkel *n.* **1** a breathing tube to enable a person to swim under water. **2** a device by which a submerged submarine can take in and expel air.

snorkelling *n.* swimming with the aid of a snorkel.

snort *n.* **1** a rough sound made by forcing breath suddenly through the nose, usu. expressing annoyance or disgust. **2** *colloq.* **a** a small alcoholic drink. **b** an inhaled dose of a (usu. illegal) powdered drug. •*v.* **1** make a snort; express or say with a snort. **2** *colloq.* inhale (cocaine etc.).

snorter *n. colloq.* **1** something very impressive or difficult. **2** something vigorous or violent (*a real snorter of a gale*).

snot *n. colloq.* mucous discharge from the nose.

snotty *adj. colloq.* **1** running or covered with nasal mucus. **2** snobbish. **3** mean, nasty.

snottygobble *n.* any of several (chiefly WA) trees or shrubs yielding an edible fruit.

snout *n.* **1** an animal's long projecting nose or nose and jaws. **2** the projecting front part of something. **3** *colloq.* an informer. ❏ **have a snout on** (*or* **against**) *Aust. colloq.* be ill-disposed towards; have an aversion to.

snow *n.* **1** crystals of ice that form from atmospheric vapour and fall to earth in light white flakes. **2** a fall or layer of snow. **3** something resembling snow. **4** flickering white spots on a television screen caused by interference or a weak signal. **5** *colloq.* cocaine. •*v.* **1** send down snow (*it is snowing*). **2** scatter or fall like snow. ❏ **snow chains** chains placed around the driving wheels of a motor vehicle when it has to negotiate an icy road or climb so that the wheels may have extra traction. **snowed under 1** covered with snow. **2** overwhelmed with a mass of work. **snowed up** snow-bound; blocked with snow. **snow gum** *n.* of several eucalypts of SE Australia occurring both above and below the snowline, and having a smooth, usu. whitish trunk. **snow-in-summer** *Aust.* any of several trees and shrubs with such abundant masses of white flowers that the tree seems covered with snow, esp. *Melaleuca linariifolia*. **snow job** *colloq.* an attempt to cover up, or distract (a person's attention from), the truth or unwelcome facts etc. **snow pea** (also **sugar pea**, **sugar pod**) a variety of pea, used esp. in Asian cooking, eaten whole including the pod. **snow-white** pure white.

snowball *n.* snow pressed into a small compact mass for throwing in play. •*v.* grow quickly in size or intensity, as a snowball does when rolled in more snow (*opposition to nuclear testing snowballed rapidly*).

snowboard *n.* a wide ski resembling a large skateboard without wheels, used for sliding downhill on snow. •*v.* ride a snowboard down a slope. ❏ **snowboarder** *n.* **snowboarding** *n.*

snowdrop *n.* a small flower growing from a bulb, with hanging white flowers blooming in early spring.

snowfall *n.* a fall of snow; the amount that falls.

snowflake *n.* a flake of snow.

snowline *n.* the level above which snow never melts entirely.

snowman *n.* a figure made in snow in the shape of a human.

snowshoe *n.* a racquet-shaped device attached to each shoe to prevent a person from sinking into deep snow.

snowstorm *n.* a storm in which snow falls.

snowy *adj.* (**snowier**, **snowiest**) **1** with snow falling (*snowy weather*). **2** covered with snow. **3** as white as snow.

Snowy Mountains a series of mostly granite mountains in south-eastern NSW, part of the Australian Alps, which includes Australia's highest mountain, Mt Kosciuszko (2,228 m).

Snowy River a river, some 435 km in length, which rises on the north-eastern slopes of Mt Kosciuszko in NSW and enters the sea at Marlo near Orbost in Vic.

Snr *abbr.* Senior.

snub v. (**snubbed, snubbing**) reject or humiliate (a person) by speaking sharply or behaving coldly. • n. treatment of this kind. □ **snub nose** a short turned-up nose.

snuff[1] n. powdered tobacco for sniffing up the nostrils.

snuff[2] n. the charred part of a candle wick. • v. **1** put out (a candle) by covering or pinching the flame. **2** (foll. by *out*) put an end to (hopes etc.). □ **snuff it** *colloq.* die.

snuffle v. sniff in a noisy way; breathe noisily through a partly blocked nose. • n. a snuffling sound.

snug adj. (**snugger, snuggest**) **1** cosy. **2** (of a garment) close-fitting. **3** (of an income etc.) allowing comfortable living. □ **snugly** adv.

snuggery n. a snug place, a cosy room or den.

snuggle v. nestle, cuddle.

so[1] adv. & conj. **1** to the extent or in the manner or with the result indicated (*it was so dark that we could not see*). **2** very (*we are so pleased*). **3** for that reason (*and so they ran away*). **4** also (*if you go, so shall I*). • pron. that; the same thing (*do you think so?; and so say all of us*). □ **and so on** and others of the same kind. **or so** or about that number or amount (*two hundred or so*). **so-and-so** n. (pl. **so-and-so's**) **1** a person or thing that need not be named. **2** *colloq.* (to avoid using a vulgar word) an unpleasant or objectionable person. **so-called** adj. called by that name or description but perhaps not correctly. **so-so** adj. & adv. *colloq.* only moderately good or well. **so that** in order that; with the result that. **so to speak** an expression of reserve or apology for an exaggeration etc.; in a manner of speaking. **so what?** that fact has no importance.

so[2] alternative spelling of SOH.

soak v. **1** place or lie in a liquid so as to become thoroughly wet. **2** (of liquid) penetrate gradually; (of rain etc.) drench. **3** absorb (*soak it up with a sponge; soak up knowledge*). **4** *colloq.* extract a lot of money from (a person). • n. **1** the act or process of soaking; a prolonged spell in a bath. **2** *colloq.* a heavy drinker. **3** *Aust.* a hollow in (often sandy) soil where water collects, on or below the surface of the ground; a waterhole.

soaking adj. (in full **soaking wet**) wet through (*I'm soaking*).

soap n. **1** a substance used for washing and cleaning things, made of fat or oil combined with an alkali. **2** *colloq.* a soap opera. • v. apply soap to. □ **soap opera** a sentimental broadcast serial with a domestic setting. (¶ A type of broadcast originally sponsored by soap manufacturers in the USA.) **soap tree** a rainforest tree of Qld and NSW having edible red fleshy fruit and leaves which can be used as a substitute for soap.

soapbox n. a makeshift stand for a speaker in the street.

soapie n. **1** a young fish, esp. a jewfish. **2** *colloq.* a soap opera.

soapstone n. steatite.

soapy adj. **1** like soap. **2** covered or impregnated with soap. **3** *colloq.* trying to win favour by flattery or excessive politeness. □ **soapiness** n.

soar v. **1** rise high in flight. **2** rise very high (*prices soared*).

sob n. an uneven drawing of breath in weeping. • v. (**sobbed, sobbing**) weep or utter with sobs. □ **sob story** *colloq.* a story or explanation meant to arouse sympathy.

sober adj. **1** not drunk; not given to drink. **2** serious and self-controlled; not frivolous. **3** (of colour) not bright or conspicuous. • v. (often foll. by *down, up*) make or become sober. □ **soberly** adv.

Sobers, Gary (full name: Sir Garfield St Aubrun Sobers) (1936–), West Indian cricketer, captain of the test team 1965–72.

sobriety / suh-**bruy**-uh-tee / n. being sober.

sobriquet / **soh**-bruh-kay / n. (also **soubriquet**) a nickname.

soccer n. a form of football played by sides of 11 in which players (except the goalkeepers) must not touch the ball with their hands or arms (except at throw-ins). • v. esp. *Aust. Rules* kick (a ball) so that it travels along the ground. (¶ Alteration of *Association Football*.)

Socceroos / sok-uh-**rooz** / n.pl. **1** the Australian international soccer team. **2** (**Socceroo**) a member of this team.

sociable / **soh**-shuh-buhl / adj. fond of company; characterised by friendly companionship. □ **sociably** adv. **sociability** n.

social adj. **1** living in an organised community, not solitary. **2** of society or its organisation; of the relationships of people living in an organised community (*social problems*). **3** of or designed for companionship and sociability (*a social club*). **4** sociable. • n. a social gathering, esp. of a school, a club, etc. □ **social climber** a person seeking to gain a higher rank in society. **social democracy** a political system favouring a mixed economy and democratic social change. **social science** the study of human society and social relationships. **social security** government financial assistance for those who are unemployed, ill, disabled, etc. **social welfare** services provided by the government for disadvantaged groups, esp. education, health, and housing. **social worker** a person trained to help people with social problems. □□ **socially** adv.

socialise v. (also **-ize**) **1** mix socially; behave sociably. **2** organise on socialistic principles. □ **socialisation** n.

socialism n. a political and economic theory advocating that the community as a whole should own and control the means of production, transport, property, etc.; a social system based on this. □ **socialist** n. & adj. **socialistic** adj.

socialite / **soh**-shuh-luyt / n. a person who is prominent in fashionable society.

society *n.* **1** an organised community; the system of living in this. **2** the socially advantaged members of a community (*one needs to be wealthy to be in society*). **3** company, companionship (*always enjoy his society*). **4** a group of people organised for some common purpose (*music society; building society*).

Society Islands a group of islands in French Polynesia, including Tahiti, named by Captain Cook in honour of the Royal Society.

Society of Friends a Christian sect (also called **Quakers**) with no written creed or ordained ministers, whose members believe in the 'Inner Light' or Christ's direct working in the soul and have a strong commitment to pacifism.

Society of Jesus see JESUIT.

socio- *comb. form* of society or sociology and (*socio-economic; socio-political*).

sociology / soh-see-**ol**-uh-jee / *n.* the scientific study of human society or of social problems. □ **sociological** *adj.* **sociologist** / soh-see-**ol**-uh-juhst / *n.*

sock[1] *n.* a short stocking not reaching the knee. □ **pull one's socks up** *colloq.* make an effort to do better.

sock[2] *colloq. v.* hit hard. • *n.* a hard blow. □ **sock it to** *colloq.* attack or address (a person or people) forcefully.

socket *n.* **1** a hollow into which something fits. **2** a device into which an electric plug, bulb, etc. is inserted to make a connection.

Socratic *adj.* of Socrates or his philosophy. □ **Socratic irony** a pose of ignorance assumed in order to entice others into making statements that can then be challenged. **Socratic method** the investigation of truth by discussion or question and answer.

Socrates / **sok**-ruh-teez / (469–399 BC), Athenian moral philosopher.

sod[1] *n.* **1** turf; a piece of turf. **2** the surface of the ground. **3** *Aust.* a damper, esp. one that has not risen.

sod[2] *colloq. n.* **1** an unpleasant or awkward person or thing. **2** a person (*you lucky sod!*). □ **sod off** go away. (¶ An abbreviation of SODOMITE.)

soda *n.* **1** a compound of sodium in common use, esp. sodium carbonate (*washing soda*), bicarbonate (*baking soda*), or hydroxide (*caustic soda*). **2** soda water. **3** a sweet effervescent drink. **4** *Aust. colloq.* **a** an easy victim. **b** a simple task; a pushover. □ **soda water** water made fizzy by being charged with carbon dioxide under pressure.

sodden *adj.* **1** saturated; soaked through. **2** (of bread etc.) heavy and moist. **3** stupid or dull etc. with drunkenness.

sodium / **soh**-dee-uhm / *n.* a chemical element (symbol Na), a soft silver-white metal. □ **sodium bicarbonate** a white crystalline compound used in baking powder etc. **sodium chloride** common salt. **sodium hydroxide** a strongly alkaline compound used in soap; caustic soda.

Sodom a town of ancient Palestine, said to have been destroyed (along with Gomorrah) by fire from heaven for the wickedness of its inhabitants.

sodomise / sod-uh-muyz / *v.* (also **-ize**) practise or commit sodomy on or with (a person).

sodomite *n.* a person who practises sodomy.

sodomy / **sod**-uh-mee / *n.* **1** anal intercourse with a male or female. **2** = BESTIALITY (sense 2).

sofa *n.* a long upholstered seat with a back and arms. □ **sofa bed** a sofa that can be converted into a bed.

Sofia / **soh**-fee-uh / the capital of Bulgaria.

soft *adj.* **1** not hard or firm. **2** not rough or stiff. **3** not loud. **4** gentle, soothing. **5** not physically robust; feeble. **6** easily influenced, tender-hearted. **7** *colloq.* easy, comfortable (*a soft job; soft living*). **8** (of currency) likely to drop suddenly in value. **9** (of water) free from mineral salts that prevent soap from lathering. **10** (of colour or light) not bright or dazzling; (of an outline) not sharp. **11** (of consonants) not hard (*see* HARD, sense 11). **12** *Politics* moderate (*Labor's soft Left*). • *adv.* softly. □ **soft-boiled** (of eggs) boiled but without allowing the yolk to set. **soft-core** *adj.* (of pornography) not highly obscene. **soft drink** a non-alcoholic drink. **soft drug** a drug that is not likely to cause addiction (*marijuana is said to be a soft drug*). **soft fruit** small stoneless fruits such as strawberries and currants. **soft furnishings** curtains, cushions, rugs, etc. **soft-hearted** compassionate. **soft option** the easier alternative. **soft on 1** lenient towards. **2** romantically attracted to. **soft palate** the rear of the roof of the mouth. **soft pedal** *n.* a piano pedal that softens the tone. **soft-pedal** *v. colloq.* refrain from emphasising; be restrained. **soft roe** *see* ROE[1]. **soft sell** restrained sales talk. **soft soap** *n. colloq.* persuasive talk; flattery. **soft-soap** *v. colloq.* persuade with flattery. **soft spot** a feeling of affection towards a person or thing. **soft touch** *colloq.* a person who is easy to persuade or from whom it is easy to obtain money. □ □ **softly** *adv.* **softness** *n.*

softball *n.* a form of baseball using a large soft ball.

soften *v.* make or become soft or softer. □ **soften up** make weaker by attacking repeatedly; make less able to resist (salesmanship etc.) by making preliminary approaches. □ □ **softener** *n.*

softie *n.* (also **softy**) *colloq.* a person who is physically weak or not hardy, or who is soft-hearted.

softly-softly *adj.* (also **softly, softly**) (of strategy) cautious and cunning.

software *n.* computer programs (as distinct from *hardware*).

softwood *n.* wood from coniferous trees, which is easily sawn.

softy alternative spelling of SOFTIE.

soggy *adj.* **1** sodden. **2** moist and heavy in texture. ☐ **soggily** *adv.* **sogginess** *n.*

soh *n.* (also **so, sol**) *Music* the fifth note of a major scale.

soil *n.* **1** the loose upper layer of earth in which plants grow. **2** ground as territory (*on Australian soil*). •*v.* **1** make or become dirty. **2** defile; discredit. •*n.* **1** a dirty mark. **2** filth; refuse; sewage.

soirée / swah-ray / *n.* a social gathering in the evening, e.g. for music.

soixante-neuf / swah-zon **nerf** / *n. coarse colloq.* mutual oral stimulation of the genitals. (¶ French, = sixty-nine.)

sojourn / **soh**-jern, so-jern / *n.* a temporary stay. •*v.* stay at a place temporarily.

Sol *n. Rom. myth.* the sun, esp. as a personification.

solace / **sol**-uhs / *n.* comfort in distress; something that gives this. •*v.* give solace to.

solar / **soh**-luh / *adj.* **1** of or derived from the sun (*solar energy*). **2** reckoned by the sun (*solar time*). ☐ **solar battery** (or **cell**) a device converting solar radiation into electricity. **solar day** the interval between meridian transits of the sun. **solar heating** heating derived from solar energy. **solar panel** a panel that absorbs the sun's rays to power a heating system etc. **solar plexus** the network of nerves at the pit of the stomach; this area. **solar system** the sun with the heavenly bodies that revolve round it. **solar year** the time taken for the earth to travel once round the sun.

solarium / suh-**lair**-ree-uhm / *n.* (*pl.* **solaria**) a room with sunlamps or enclosed with glass so that people can benefit from exposure to sunlight.

sold *see* SELL. ☐ **sold on** *colloq.* enthusiastic about.

solder / **sohl**-duh / *n.* a soft alloy used to cement metal parts together. •*v.* join with solder. ☐ **soldering iron** a tool used hot for applying solder.

soldier *n.* a member of an army, esp. a private or NCO. •*v.* serve as a soldier. ☐ **soldier ant** a wingless ant or termite with a large head and jaws for fighting in defence of its colony, esp. the **bulldog ant** (or **bull ant**) a large Australian ant capable of inflicting a painful sting. **soldier crab** a small Australian crab occurring in large numbers on sandy tidal flats, so called because of the way they move across the sand in large groups resembling formations of troops. **soldier of fortune** a person ready to serve any country or person for money. **soldier settlement** *Aust.* a scheme by which Australian ex-service personnel were given land grants, usu. of previously uncultivated land; this land.

soldierly *adj.* like a soldier.

soldiery *n.* soldiers collectively or as a class.

sole[1] *n.* **1** the undersurface of a foot. **2** the part of a shoe or stocking that covers this (often excluding the heel). **3** the lower surface of an object. •*v.* put a sole on (a shoe).

sole[2] *n.* (*pl.* **sole** *or* **soles**) any of various flatfish (including those occurring in Australian waters) used as food.

sole[3] *adj.* **1** one and only (*our sole objection is this*). **2** belonging exclusively to one person or group (*we have the sole right to sell these cars*). ☐ **sole parent** = SINGLE PARENT (*see* SINGLE). ☐☐ **solely** *adv.*

solecism / **sol**-uh-siz-uhm / *n.* **1** a mistake in grammar or idiom, e.g. *they done their homework; its a hot day; for sale: fresh ladies finger's.* **2** an offence against good manners or etiquette. ☐ **solecistic** / sol-uh-**sis**-tik / *adj.*

solemn *adj.* **1** not smiling or cheerful. **2** dignified and impressive (*a solemn occasion*). **3** formal; accompanied by a religious or other ceremony. ☐ **solemnly** *adv.* **solemnity** / suh-**lem**-nuh-tee / *n.*

solemnise / **sol**-uhm-nuyz / *v.* (also **-ize**) **1** celebrate (a festival etc.). **2** perform (a marriage ceremony) with formal rites. ☐ **solemnisation** *n.*

solenoid / **sol**-uh-noid / *n.* a coil of wire that becomes magnetic when an electric current is passed through it.

sol-fa / **sol**-fah / *n.* a system of syllables representing musical notes.

solicit / suh-**lis**-uht / *v.* **1** seek to obtain, ask earnestly (*solicit votes*). **2** (of a prostitute) offer sexual services; look for business, esp. in a public place. ☐ **solicitation** *n.*

solicitor *n.* a lawyer qualified to advise clients, represent them in the lower courts, and instruct barristers. ☐ **solicitor-general** (*pl.* **solicitors-general**) **1** (in Australia) the principal legal adviser and counsel to the Australian government. **2** (in some other countries) a law officer below an attorney-general.

solicitous / suh-**lis**-uh-tuhs / *adj.* anxious and concerned about a person's welfare or comfort. ☐ **solicitously** *adv.*

solicitude / suh-**lis**-uh-tyood / *n.* solicitous concern.

solid *adj.* **1** keeping its shape, firm; not liquid or gas. **2** not hollow. **3** of the same substance throughout (*solid silver*). **4** continuous, without a break (*for two solid hours*). **5** strongly constructed, not flimsy. **6 a** having three dimensions. **b** concerned with solids (*solid geometry*). **7** sound and reliable (*there are solid arguments against it*). **8** unanimous; undivided; determined (*the miners are solid on this issue*). **9** *Aust. colloq.* severe; unreasonable (*they'll be solid on him for that mistake; got detention for a week—a bit solid, I reckon*). •*n.* **1** a solid substance or body or food. **2** a body or shape with three dimensions. •*adv.* solidly (*jammed solid*). ☐ **solid state** a state of matter in which the constituent atoms or molecules occupy fixed positions with respect to each other and cannot move freely (other states are the liquid, gas, and plasma states). **solid-state** *adj.* using transistors (which make use of the electronic properties of solids) instead of valves. □□ **solidly** *adv.* **solidity** / suh-**lid**-uh -tee / *n.* **solidness** *n.*

Solidarity an organisation which began as an independent trade-union movement in Poland and became involved in government following political reform and elections.

solidarity *n.* unity resulting from common interests, feelings, or sympathies.

solidify / suh-**lid**-uh-fuy / *v.* (**solidified**, **solidifying**) make or become solid.

solidus *n.* (*pl.* **solidi**) an oblique stroke (/).

soliloquise / suh-**lil**-uh-kwuyz / *v.* (also -**ize**) utter a soliloquy.

soliloquy / suh-**lil**-uh-kwee / *n.* a speech in which a person expresses his or her thoughts aloud without addressing anyone.

solipsism / **sol**-ip-siz-uhm / *n.* the theory that the self is all that exists or can be known. □ **solipsist** *n.*

solitaire / sol-uh-tair / *n.* **1** a diamond or other gem set by itself. **2** a game for one person, in which marbles or pegs are removed from their places on a special board after jumping others over them. **3** a card game for one person.

solitary *adj.* **1** alone, without companions. **2** single (*a solitary example*). **3** not frequented, lonely (*a solitary valley*). •*n.* **1** a recluse. **2** *colloq.* solitary confinement. □ **solitary confinement** isolation in a separate prison cell as a punishment. □□ **solitarily** *adv.*

solitude *n.* being solitary.

solo *n.* (*pl.* **solos**) **1** (*pl.* **solos** or **soli**) a musical composition or passage or a dance, performed by one person. **2** a pilot's flight in an aircraft without an instructor or companion. **3** (in full **solo whist**) a type of whist in which one person may oppose the others. •*adj.* & *adv.* unaccompanied, alone (*for solo flute; flying solo*). •*v.* (**soloes**, **soloed**) perform a solo.

soloist *n.* a person who performs a solo.

Solomon king of Israel *c.*970–930 BC, son of David, famous for his wisdom and magnificence. □ **Song of Solomon** (also called the **Song of Songs** or **Canticles**) a book of the Old Testament, an anthology of love poems ascribed to Solomon but dating from a much later period.

Solomon Islands a nation consisting of a group of islands in the South Pacific.

solstice / **sol**-stuhs / *n.* either of the times in the year when the sun is furthest from the equator; the point reached by the sun at these times (**summer solstice** about 22 December; **winter solstice** about 21 June, in the Southern hemisphere).

soluble / **sol**-yuh-buhl / *adj.* **1** able to be dissolved in liquid. **2** (of a problem) able to be solved. □ **solubly** *adv.* **solubility** / sol-yuh-**bil**-uh-tee / *n.*

solute *n.* a dissolved substance.

solution *n.* **1** a liquid in which something is dissolved. **2** dissolving or being dissolved into liquid form. **3** the process of solving a problem etc.; the answer found.

solve *v.* find the answer to (a problem or puzzle) or the way out of (a difficulty). □ **solvable** *adj.* **solver** *n.*

solvent *adj.* **1** having enough money to pay one's debts. **2** able to dissolve another substance. •*n.* a liquid used for dissolving something. □ **solvency** *n.*

Solzhenitsyn / sol-*zh*uh-**nit**-sin /, Alexander (1918–), Russian novelist, imprisoned and later deported to the West (1974) for his criticisms of the former Soviet regime, awarded the Nobel Prize for literature in 1970.

Somalia / suh-**mah**-lee-uh / a republic in East Africa. □ **Somali** *adj.* & *n.* (*pl.* **Somalis**).

somatic / soh-**mat**-ik / *adj.* of the body; physical as distinct from mental or spiritual. □ **somatically** *adv.*

sombre / **som**-buh / *adj.* dark, gloomy, dismal. □ **sombrely** *adv.* **sombreness** *n.*

sombrero / som-**brair**-roh / *n.* (*pl.* **sombreros**) a felt or straw hat with a very wide brim, worn esp. in Latin America.

some *adj.* & *pron.* **1** an unspecified quantity (*buy some apples*). **2** an amount that is less than the whole (*some of them were late*). **3** an unspecified person or thing (*some fool locked the door; come round some time*). **4** a considerable quantity (*that was some years ago*). **5** approximately (*waited some 20 minutes*). **6** *colloq.* remarkable (*that was some party!*). •*adv. colloq.* to some extent (*do it some more*).

somebody *n.* & *pron.* **1** an unspecified person. **2** a person of importance.

someday *adv.* at some time in the future.

somehow *adv.* **1** in some unspecified or unexplained manner (*I never liked him, somehow*). **2** by one means or another (*must get it finished somehow*).

someone *n.* & *pron.* somebody.

somersault / **sum**-uh-sawlt, -solt / *n.* **1** an acrobatic movement in which a person rolls head over heels on the ground or in the air. **2** a complete about-turn (*the government has done a somersault on immigration policy*). •*v.* turn a somersault.

something *n.* & *pron.* **1** an unspecified thing (*passed by a tiny town called Worra- something; something must have happened*). **2** a notable person or thing (*he's really something; the party was quite something*). □ **something else** *colloq.* an excellent or remarkable person or thing. **something like** approximately (*it cost something like $10*). **something of** to some extent (*something of an expert*).

-something *comb. form* an indeterminate age between twenty and thirty, thirty and forty, etc; a person of this age (*this sort of music appeals mostly* to lively twenty-somethings). •adj. of or belonging to such a person or the group as a whole (*a thirty-something businesswoman*).

sometime *adj.* former (*her sometime friend*). •*adv.* **1** at some time. **2** formerly.

sometimes *adv.* at some times, occasionally.

somewhat *adv.* to some extent (*it is somewhat difficult*).

somewhere *adv.* at, in, or to an unspecified place or position (*must have dropped it somewhere; she must be somewhere around 30*). •*pron.* some unspecified place. ☐ **get somewhere** *colloq.* achieve some success.

Somme a river of north-eastern France, flowing into the English Channel, the scene of a First World War battle (1916) in which more than a million soldiers were killed.

somnambulist / som-**nam**-byoo-luhst / *n.* a sleepwalker. ☐ **somnambulism** *n.* **somnambulant** *adj.*

somnolent / **som**-nuh-luhnt / *adj.* **1** sleepy, drowsy. **2** inducing drowsiness (*a most somnolent sermon*). ☐ **somnolence** *n.*

son *n.* **1** a boy or man in relation to his parents. **2** a male descendant. **3** a form of address to a boy or young man. ☐ **son-in-law** (*pl.* **sons-in-law**) a daughter's husband.

sonar / **soh**-nuh / *n.* a device for detecting objects under water by reflection of sound waves.

sonata / suh-**nah**-tuh / *n.* a musical composition for one instrument or two, usu. with three or four movements.

sonatina / son-uh-**tee**-nuh / *n.* a simple or short sonata.

son et lumière / son ay loo-mee-**air** / *n.* an entertainment given at night, a dramatic account of the history of a building or place, with lighting effects and recorded sound. (¶ French, = sound and light.)

song *n.* **1** singing. **2** a musical composition for singing. **3** the cry of some birds. ☐ **going for a song** being sold very cheaply. **on song** *colloq.* in good form; performing well. **song cycle 1** a set of musically linked songs on a romantic theme. **2** *Aust.* (in Aboriginal culture) a series of linked songs, usu. dealing with the journeyings of an ancestral being or beings. **song line** *Aust.* (in Aboriginal culture) the 'map' drawn by the journeyings of an ancestral being or beings; a dreaming track.

songman *n.* (*feminine* **songwoman**) *Aust.* an Aborigine who memorises and performs the sacred and other traditional songs of a community.

songster *n.* **1** a singer. **2** a bird with a melodious voice, such as the brown songlark and the rufous songlark, both widespread throughout Australia.

sonic *adj.* of or involving sound waves. ☐ **sonic barrier** = SOUND BARRIER. **sonic boom** (*or* **bang**) a loud noise heard when the shock wave caused by an aircraft travelling at supersonic speed reaches the hearer.

sonky *adj. Aust. colloq.* foolish; gawky.

sonnet *n.* a poem of 14 lines with lengths and rhymes in accordance with any of several patterns.

sonny *n. colloq.* a form of address to a boy or young man.

sonorous / **son**-uh-ruhs / *adj.* **1** resonant, giving a deep powerful sound. **2** (of language, style, etc.) imposing, grand.

sook / suuk / *n. Aust. colloq.* **1** a timid, bashful person; a crybaby. **2** a timid racehorse. **3** a hand-reared calf. ☐ **sooky** *adj.*

sool / sool / *v. esp. Aust. colloq.* **1** (of a dog) attack or worry (an animal). **2** (often as a command) incite or goad a dog to attack. **3** (often foll. by *on*) urge, excite to go after (*sooled his dog on the feral pig; who sooled the priest on me?*).

soon *adv.* **1** in a short time, not long after the present or a specified time. **2** early, quickly (*spoke too soon*). **3** readily or willingly (*I would sooner go; I would as soon stay*). ☐ **as soon as** at the moment that, as early as; as readily or willingly as.

soot / suut / *n.* the black powdery substance that rises in the smoke of coal or wood etc. •*v.* cover with soot.

sooth *n. archaic* truth.

soothe *v.* calm (a person, feelings, etc.); ease (pain etc.). ☐ **soothing** *adj.*

soothsayer *n.* a person who foretells the future.

sooty / **suut**-ee / *adj.* (**sootier**, **sootiest**) **1** full of soot; covered with soot. **2** like soot, black. **3** used as a distinguishing epithet in the names of some birds (*sooty owl; sooty oystercatcher*).

sop *n.* **1** a piece of bread dipped in liquid before being eaten or cooked. **2** a concession made to pacify or bribe a troublesome person. **3** *colloq.* a coward; a weak or stupid person. •*v.* (**sopped**, **sopping**) **1** dip (a thing) in liquid. **2** soak up (liquid) with something absorbent.

sophism / **sof**-iz-uhm / *n.* a clever but false or misleading argument.

sophist / **sof**-uhst / *n.* a person who uses sophistry. (¶ Named after the Sophists, Greek philosophers of the 5th century BC, who taught rhetoric and skilled reasoning.)

sophisticate *v.* / suh-**fis**-tuh-kayt / make sophisticated. •*n.* / suh-**fis**-tuh-kuht / a sophisticated person.

sophisticated / suh-**fis**-tuh-kay-tuhd / *adj.* **1** characteristic of fashionable life and its ways; experienced in this and lacking natural simplicity. **2** complicated, elaborate (*sophisticated electronic devices*). ☐ **sophistication** *n.*

sophistry / **sof**-uhs-tree / *n.* clever and subtle but misleading reasoning.

Sophocles / **sof**-uh-kleez / (*c.*496–406 BC), Greek tragic playwright.

soporific / sop-uh-**rif**-ik / *adj.* tending to cause sleep. •*n.* a soporific drug or influence. ☐ **soporifically** *adv.*

sopping *adj.* very wet, drenched.

soppy *adj.* (**soppier**, **soppiest**) *colloq.* sentimental in a sickly way; silly; infatuated (*a soppy romantic novel; is soppy about him*). □ **soppily** *adv.* **soppiness** *n.*

soprano / suh-**prah**-noh / *n.* (*pl.* **sopranos**) **1** the highest female or boy's singing voice. **2** a singer with such a voice; a part written for it.

sorbet / **saw**-bay / *n.* **1** an iced dessert made with fruit, liqueurs, etc. **2** a frozen dessert made with fruit juice, egg whites, etc.

sorcerer *n.* **1** a male magician, a wizard. **2** *Aust.* = KORADJI.

sorceress *n.* a female magician, a witch.

sorcery *n.* a sorcerer's art or practices.

sordid *adj.* **1** dirty, squalid. **2** (of motives or actions) not honourable; mercenary. □ **sordidly** *adv.* **sordidness** *n.*

sore *adj.* **1** causing or suffering pain. **2** causing mental pain or annoyance (*a sore subject*). **3** *archaic* dire, serious (*in sore need*). **4** distressed, vexed. • *n.* **1** a sore place, esp. where the skin is raw. **2** a source of distress or annoyance. • *adv. archaic* grievously, severely (*was sore distressed*). □ **sore loser** a bad loser, one who is unsporting in defeat. □ □ **soreness** *n.*

sorely *adv.* seriously, very (*I was sorely tempted*).

sorghum / **saw**-guhm / *n.* a tropical cereal grass.

sorority / suh-**ro**-ruh-tee, -**raw**-ruh-tee / *n.* (*pl.* **sororities**) *US* a female students' society in a university or college. (¶ Latin *soror* 'sister'.)

sorrel / **so**-ruhl / *n.* **1** a herb with sharp-tasting leaves used in salads. **2** light reddish-brown; a horse of this colour.

sorrow *n.* **1** mental suffering caused by loss or disappointment. **2** something that causes this. • *v.* feel sorrow; grieve.

sorrowful *adj.* **1** feeling or showing sorrow. **2** distressing, lamentable. □ **sorrowfully** *adv.*

sorry *adj.* (**sorrier**, **sorriest**) **1** pained, regretful, penitent. **2** feeling pity or sympathy for. **3** wretched (*in a sorry plight*). **4** *Aust.* (in Aboriginal English) of or relating to mourning (*a sorry camp*). • *interj.* an expression of apology. □ **sorry business** *Aust.* (in Aboriginal English) mortuary rites. **sorry camp** *Aust.* (in Aboriginal English) a mourning camp. **sorry cut** *Aust.* (in Aboriginal English) an incision signifying ritual mourning.

sort *n.* **1** a particular kind or variety (*this sort of person; these sorts of events; arrange them by sorts*). **2** (foll. by *of*) roughly of the kind specified (*she is some sort of doctor*). **3** *colloq.* **a** a person of a specified kind (*he's a decent sort*). **b** a sexually attractive person. • *v.* arrange according to sort, size, destination, etc. □ **good sort** *colloq.* **1** an attractive person of either sex. **2** a friendly, reliable person of either sex. **of a sort** (*or* **of sorts**) not fully deserving the name given (*a holiday of sorts*). **out of sorts** slightly unwell; in a bad mood. **sort of** *colloq.* somewhat, rather. **sort out 1** disentangle; select from others. **2** *colloq.* deal with or punish.

sortie / **saw**-tee / *n.* **1** an attack by troops, esp. from a besieged place. **2** a flight of an aircraft on a military operation. • *v.* (**sortied**, **sortieing**) make a sortie.

SOS *n.* **1** the international code-signal of extreme distress. **2** (*pl.* **SOSs**) an urgent appeal for help or response.

sostenuto *adv.* & *adj. Music* in a sustained or prolonged way. (¶ Italian)

sot *n.* a drunkard. □ **sottish** *adj.*

sotto voce / sot-oh **voh**-chee, -chay / *adv.* in an undertone (*she cursed me sotto voce*). • *adj.* spoken in an undertone. (¶ Italian)

sou / soo / *n.* **1** a former French coin of low value. **2** *colloq.* a very small amount of money (*haven't a sou*).

soubrette / soo-**bret** / *n.* a pert maidservant or similar character in comedy.

soubriquet / **soo**-bruh-kay / = SOBRIQUET.

soufflé / **soo**-flay / *n.* a light spongy sweet or savoury dish made with beaten egg white.

sough / sow / *v.* make a moaning or whispering sound as the wind does in trees. • *n.* this sound.

sought *see* SEEK. □ **sought-after** *adj.* much sought for purchase or use etc.

soul *n.* **1** the spiritual or immaterial part of a person, often regarded as immortal. **2** a person's mental, moral, or emotional nature (*his whole soul revolted from it*). **3** a personification or pattern (*she is the soul of discretion*). **4** a person (*there's not a soul in sight*). **5** a person regarded with familiarity, pity, etc. (*poor soul*). **6** a person regarded as an animating or essential part (*he was the life and soul of the party*). **7** soul music. □ **soul-destroying** deadeningly monotonous or depressing. **soul music** African-American music with rhythm and blues, gospel, and rock influences.

soulful *adj.* **1** having or showing deep feeling. **2** emotional. □ **soulfully** *adv.*

soulless *adj.* **1** lacking sensitivity or noble qualities. **2** dull, uninteresting.

sound[1] *n.* **1** vibrations that travel through the air and are detectable (at certain frequencies) by the ear. **2** the sensation produced by these vibrations; a particular kind of it. **3** the mental impression produced by a statement or description etc. (*we don't like the sound of the new scheme*). • *v.* **1** produce or cause to produce sound (*sound the trumpet*). **2** utter, pronounce (*the 'h' in 'hour' is not sounded*). **3** give an impression when heard (*it sounds like a screaming-woman bird; the news sounds good*). **4** test by noting the sound produced (*the doctor sounds a patient's lungs with a stethoscope*). □ **sound barrier** the high resistance of air to objects moving at speeds near that of sound. **sound bite** a very short, snappy extract from an interview, speech, etc., used e.g. as part of a news broadcast to convey a forceful message.

sound centre a set of equipment comprising radio, compact disc player, video, etc. **sound effects** sounds (other than speech or music) made artificially for use in a play or film etc. **sound mixer 1** a person who combines sounds from various sources (for a film, radio broadcast, etc.). **2** equipment for mixing sound. **sound off 1** express one's opinions loudly and freely. **2** exaggerate, boast (*sounding off about his new car*). **sound out** question cautiously. **sound system** a hi-fi, PA system, or other equipment for sound reproduction. **sound wave** a wave by which sound is transmitted through the air etc.

sound[2] *adj.* **1** healthy, not diseased or damaged. **2** (of an opinion, policy, etc.) correct, logical, well-founded (*sound reasoning*). **3** financially secure (*a sound investment*). **4** thorough (*a sound thrashing; sound sleep*). •*adv.* soundly (*is sound asleep*). ☐ **soundly** *adv.* **soundness** *n.*

sound[3] *v.* **1** test or measure the depth or quality of the bottom of (the sea or a river etc.). **2** (often foll. by *out*) inquire (esp. discreetly) into the opinions or feelings of (a person). **3** examine with a probe. **4** (of a whale or fish) dive to the bottom. •*n.* a surgeon's probe. ☐ **sounder** *n.*

sound[4] *n.* a narrow passage (of water) connecting two seas, a sea and a lake, or the mainland and an island.

soundbox *n.* the hollow body of a stringed musical instrument, providing resonance.

sounding *n.* **1** measurement of the depth of water (*see* SOUND[3]). **2** (**soundings**) discreet enquiries. ☐ **sounding balloon** a balloon used to obtain information about the upper atmosphere. **sounding board 1** a person or group used as a trial audience to test opinion. **2** a means of causing opinions etc. to be more widely known (*used his students as a sounding board*). **3** a canopy directing sound towards an audience.

soundproof *adj.* not able to be penetrated by sound. •*v.* make soundproof.

soundtrack *n.* **1** a strip on cinema film or recording tape for recording sound. **2** the sound itself.

soup *n.* liquid food made by boiling meat, vegetables, etc. •*v.* (usu. foll. by *up*) *colloq.* **1** increase the power of (an engine). **2** enliven (*a souped-up version of his original song; this party needs souping up*). ☐ **in the soup** *colloq.* in difficulties. **soup kitchen** a place where soup and other food is supplied free to the needy.

soupçon / **soop**-son / *n.* a very small quantity; a trace (*add a soupçon of chilli*). (¶ French)

soupy *adj.* (**soupier**, **soupiest**) **1** like soup. **2** soppily sentimental.

sour *adj.* **1** tasting sharp like vinegar. **2** not fresh; tasting or smelling sharp or unpleasant from fermentation or staleness. **3** (of soil) excessively acid, deficient in lime. **4** bad-tempered, disagreeable (*gave me a sour look*). •*v.* make or become sour (*was soured by misfortune*). ☐ **go** (or **turn**) **sour 1** turn out badly (*the job turned sour on him*). **2** lose one's keenness (*went sour on the idea*). **sour cream** cream deliberately fermented by adding bacteria. **sour grapes** resentful disparagement of something one cannot personally acquire. (¶ From the fable of the fox who wanted some grapes but found that they were out of reach and so pretended that they were sour and undesirable anyway.) ☐☐ **sourly** *adv.* **sourness** *n.*

source *n.* **1** the place from which something comes or is obtained. **2** the starting point of a river.

sourpuss *n. colloq.* a sour-tempered person.

soursob *n.* (also **soursobs**, **soursops**) any of several perennial herbs of the genus *Oxalis*, esp. the S. African species *Oxalis pes-caprae* which is naturalised in all Australian States and declared a noxious weed in some.

soursop *n.* **1** a small tropical tree *Annona muricata* now cultivated in Qld. **2** the large edible heart-shaped fruit of this tree, having soft spines on its skin.

souse / sows / *v.* **1** steep in pickle (*soused herrings*). **2** plunge or soak in liquid; drench, throw (liquid) over a thing. •*n.* **1** a pickle made with salt. **2** a plunge or a drench in liquid. **3** *colloq.* a drunkard.

soused *adj. colloq.* drunk.

soutane / soo-**tahn**, -**tan** / *n.* the cassock worn by a Catholic priest.

south *n.* **1** the point or direction opposite north. **2** the southern part of something. •*adj.* **1** towards or in the south. **2** (of a wind) blowing from the south. •*adv.* towards or in the south. ☐ **South Pole** the southernmost point of the earth. **south pole** (of a magnet) the pole that is attracted to the south. **South Sea** (also **South Seas**) the southern Pacific Ocean.

South Africa a republic occupying the southernmost part of the continent of Africa. ☐ **South African** *adj.* & *n.*

South America the southern half of the American land mass (*see* AMERICA).

South Australia a State comprising the central southern part of Australia. ☐ **South Australian** *adj.* & *n.*

southbound *adj.* travelling or leading southwards.

south-east *n.* the point or direction midway between south and east. •*adj.* of, towards, or coming from the south-east. •*adv.* towards, in, or near the south-east. ☐ **south-easterly** *adj.* & *n.* **south-eastern** *adj.*

southeaster *n.* a south-east wind.

southerly / **suth**-uh-lee / *adj.* **1** in or towards the south. **2** (of a wind) blowing from the south. •*n.* a southerly wind. ☐ **southerly buster** *Aust.* a sudden strong cool wind from the south, affecting the south-eastern coast of Australia; a cool change.

southern *adj.* of or in the south. ☐ **southern lights** *Aust.* the aurora australis.

Southern Cross *n.* **1** a southern constellation in the shape of a cross, and represented on the flags of Australia and New Zealand. **2** *Aust.* = EUREKA FLAG (see EUREKA). **3** a WA perennial with attractive flowers which, with their bracts, form a perfect white cross. ☐ **land of the Southern Cross** Australia.

southerner *n.* **1** a native or inhabitant of the south. **2** the often derisive epithet used by Queenslanders and Northern Territorians to designate a person normally resident in a southern State.

Southern hemisphere *n.* the half of the earth south of the equator.

southernmost *adj.* furthest south.

Southern Ocean the body of water surrounding the continent of Antarctica.

South Korea a republic in Asia, occupying the southern part of the peninsula of Korea.

southpaw *n. colloq.* a left-handed person, esp. in boxing. ●*adj.* left-handed.

southward *adj.* & *adv.* (also **southwards**) towards the south.

south-west *n.* the point or direction midway between south and west. ●*adj.* of, towards, or coming from the south-west. ●*adv.* towards, in, or near the south-west. ☐ **south-westerly** *adj.* & *n.* **south-western** *adj.*

southwester *n.* a south-west wind.

souvenir / soo-vuh-**neer** / *n.* something bought or kept as a reminder of an incident or a place visited. ●*v. colloq.* steal (esp. a small item) to use as a souvenir (*souvenired an ashtray from the motel*).

souvlaki / soov-**lah**-kee / *n.* a Greek dish of pieces of meat (esp. lamb) grilled on a skewer.

sou'wester *n.* **1** a waterproof hat with a broad flap at the back. **2** a south-west wind.

sovereign / **sov**-ruhn / *n.* **1** a king or queen who is the supreme ruler of a country. **2** *hist.* a British gold coin, nominally worth £1. ●*adj.* **1** supreme (*sovereign power*). **2** possessing sovereign power, independent (*sovereign States*). **3** very effective (*a sovereign remedy*). ☐ **sovereignty** *n.*

soviet / **soh**-vee-uht, **sov**-ee-uht / *n.* **1** a citizen of the former USSR. **2** (**Soviet**) an elected council in the former USSR. ●*adj.* of the former Soviet Union.

Soviet Union *hist.* the Union of Soviet Socialist Republics.

sow[1] / soh / *v.* (**sowed**, **sown** *or* **sowed**, **sowing**) **1** plant or scatter (seed) for growth; plant seed in (a field etc.). **2** implant or spread (feelings or ideas). ☐ **sow one's wild oats** (of a young person) behave wildly or promiscuously.

sow[2] / sow / *n.* a fully-grown female pig.

Soweto / suh-**wet**-oh, -**way**-toh / a group of townships near Johannesburg in South Africa.

soy *n.* **1** (in full **soy bean**) the soya bean. **2** (in full **soy sauce**) a sauce made by fermenting soya beans in brine.

soya *n.* **1** (in full **soybean** *or* **soya bean**) a bean (originally from SE Asia) from which an edible oil and flour are obtained, often used to replace animal protein. **2** (in full **soya sauce**) = SOY (sense 2).

Soyuz / soi-**yuuz** / *n.* any of a series of manned spacecraft launched by the former USSR.

sozzled *adj. colloq.* very drunk.

SP *abbr. Aust. Racing* starting price; the final odds of a horse or greyhound at the start of a race.

spa / spah / *n.* **1** a curative mineral spring; a resort with such a spring. **2** (also **spa bath**) = JACUZZI. **3** (also **spa pool**) a usu. outdoor pool, usu. attached to a swimming pool, with massaging underwater jets of water.

space *n.* **1** the boundless expanse in which all objects exist and move. **2** a portion of this, an area or volume for a particular purpose (*the box takes too much space; parking spaces*). **3** an interval between points or objects, an empty area (*separated by a space of 3 metres; there's a space for your signature*). **4** the area of paper used in writing or printing something (*would take too much space to explain in detail*). **5** an outdoor urban recreation area (*open space*). **6** a large unoccupied region (*the wide open spaces*). **7** outer space (*see* OUTER). **8** an interval of time (*within the space of an hour*). **9** freedom to think, be oneself, etc. (*I need my own space*). **10** *Music* each of the blanks between the lines of a staff. ●*v.* **1** set or arrange at intervals. **2** put spaces between. **3** (as **spaced** *adj.*) (often foll. by *out*) *colloq.* **a** euphoric, esp. from taking drugs. **b** acting strangely, as if from taking drugs. ☐ **space age** the era of space travel. **space-age** *adj.* very modern (*space-age technology*). **space out** spread out (more) widely. **space probe** an unmanned rocket with instruments to detect conditions in outer space. **space shuttle** a spacecraft for repeated use e.g. between earth and a space station. **space station** an artificial satellite used as a base for operations in space. **space-time** (**continuum**) fusion of the concepts of space and time, with time as a fourth dimension.

spacecraft *n.* (*pl.* **spacecraft**) a vehicle for travelling in outer space.

spaceman *n.* a person who travels in outer space; an astronaut.

spaceship *n.* a spacecraft.

spacesuit *n.* a sealed pressurised suit allowing the wearer to leave a spacecraft and move about in outer space.

spacewoman *n.* a female astronaut.

spacious / **spay**-shuhs / *adj.* providing much space, roomy. ☐ **spaciousness** *n.*

spade *n.* **1** a tool for digging ground, with a broad metal blade and a wooden handle. **2** a playing card of the suit (**spades**) marked with

spadework

black figures shaped like an inverted heart with a short stem. • *v.* dig over (ground) with a spade. □□ **spadeful** *n.* (*pl.* **spadefuls**).

spadework *n.* hard work done in preparation for something.

spaghetti / spuh-**get**-ee / *n.* pasta made in solid strands, between macaroni and vermicelli in thickness. □ **spaghetti Bolognese** / bol-uh-**nayz** / spaghetti with a meat and tomato sauce. **spaghetti western** a cowboy film made cheaply in Italy.

Spain a kingdom in SW Europe.

spam¹ *n. trademark* a tinned meat product made mainly from ham. (¶ Blend of *spiced* + *ham*)

spam² *n.* junk electronic mail, esp. mass mailings to news groups. • *v.* send electronic junk mail to.

span¹ *n.* **1** the extent from end to end or across. **2** the distance (reckoned as 23 cm or 9 inches) between the tips of a person's thumb and little finger when these are stretched apart. **3** the distance or part between the uprights supporting an arch or bridge. **4** the distance between the tips of the wings of an aeroplane or the outspread wings of a bird. • *v.* (**spanned, spanning**) extend across, bridge.

span² *see* SPICK AND SPAN.

spanakopita / span-uh-kuh-**pit**-uh / *n.* (in Greek cookery) a double crust pie of filo pastry filled with spinach and feta cheese. (¶ Modern Greek, = spinach pie.)

spandrel *n.* the space between the curve of an arch and the surrounding rectangular moulding or framework, or between the curves of adjoining arches and the moulding above.

spangle *n.* one of many thin pieces of glittering material ornamenting a dress etc. • *v.* cover with spangles or sparkling objects. □ **spangled drongo** a bird of northern and eastern Australia, having glossy black plumage with iridescent blue-green spangles or spots. **spangled grunter** a food fish widespread in Australian waters, having a spangled skin (*see* GRUNTER, sense 3).

Spaniard *n.* a native of Spain.

spaniel *n.* a dog with long drooping ears and a silky coat.

Spanish *adj.* of Spain or its people or language. • *n.* **1** the language of Spain and Spanish America. **2** (**the Spanish**) (as *pl.*) Spanish people.

Spanish Main *hist.* the NE coast of South America and adjoining parts of the Caribbean Sea.

spank *v.* slap on the buttocks with the open hand, a slipper, etc., as punishment. • *n.* such a slap.

spanking *adj.* **1** brisk, lively (*a spanking pace*). **2** *colloq.* striking; excellent. • *adv. colloq.* very (*spanking new*). • *n.* a slapping on the buttocks.

spanner *n.* a tool for gripping and turning the nut on a bolt etc. □ **throw a spanner in the works** sabotage a scheme.

spar¹ *n.* **1** a strong pole used for a ship's mast, boom, etc. **2** the main lengthwise beam of an aeroplane wing.

spar² *n.* any of several kinds of non-metallic mineral that split easily.

spar³ *v.* (**sparred, sparring**) **1** box, esp. for practice. **2** quarrel or argue. □ **sparring partner 1** a boxer employed to give another boxer practice. **2** a person with whom one enjoys frequent arguments.

spare *v.* **1** be merciful towards, refrain from hurting or harming. **2** use with great restraint. **3** part with; afford to give (*we can't spare him until next week; can you spare me a moment?*). • *adj.* **1** additional to what is usu. needed or used; in reserve for use when needed (*a spare wheel; spare time*). **2** thin; lean. **3** small in quantity. • *n.* = SPARE PART. □ **spare part** a duplicate part, esp. as a replacement. **spare ribs** closely-trimmed ribs of pork (or beef) with little flesh on them. **spare tyre 1** an extra tyre carried for emergencies. **2** *colloq.* a roll of fat round the waist. □□ **sparely** *adv.* **spareness** *n.*

sparing / **spair**-ring / *adj.* economical, not generous or wasteful. □ **sparingly** *adv.*

spark *n.* **1** a fiery particle thrown off by a burning substance or caused by friction. **2** a flash of light produced by an electrical discharge. **3** a short burst or flash of genius, wit, generosity, energy, etc. **4** a small amount (*showed a spark of interest; not a spark of life*). **5** (also **bright spark**) a lively young person. • *v.* **1** give off a spark or sparks. **2** (often foll. by *off*) stir up, trigger off (*sparked off a heated debate*). □ **spark plug** a device producing an electrical spark to fire the mixture in an internal-combustion engine.

sparkle *v.* **1** shine brightly with (or as if with) tiny flashes of light (*his eyes sparkled*). **2** show brilliant wit or liveliness. **3** (of wine etc.) effervesce. • *n.* a sparkling light; brightness; liveliness.

sparkler *n.* a hand-held sparkling firework.

sparrow *n.* (also **house sparrow**) a small brownish-grey bird, introduced into eastern Australia.

sparrowhawk *n.* **1** (in full **collared sparrowhawk**) a predominantly brown bird of prey having a rufous mark around the neck, widespread in Australia. **2** *Aust.* = NANKEEN KESTREL.

sparse *adj.* thinly scattered, not dense. □ **sparsely** *adv.* **sparsity** *n.* **sparseness** *n.*

Sparta a city in the southern Peloponnese in Greece, whose citizens in ancient times were renowned for hardiness. □ **Spartan** *adj.* & *n.*

spartan *adj.* (of conditions) simple and sometimes harsh, without comfort or luxuries. (¶ *See* SPARTA.)

spasm *n.* **1** a strong involuntary contraction of a muscle. **2** a convulsive movement or emotion etc. (*a spasm of coughing; a spasm of grief*). **3** a brief spell of an activity (*does his gardening in spasms*).

spasmodic — special

spasmodic / spaz-**mod**-ik / *adj.* **1** occurring at irregular intervals. **2** of or like a spasm; characterised by spasms. ☐ **spasmodically** *adv.*

spastic *adj.* **1** physically disabled because of a condition (esp. cerebral palsy) in which there are faulty links between the brain and the motor nerves, causing jerky or involuntary movements. **2** *Aust. colloq. offens.* drunk. • *n.* **1** a person who is spastic (sense 1). **2** *colloq. offens.* **a** a stupid or incompetent person. **b** *Aust.* a drunk.

■ **Usage** The use of the word *spastic* in the medical sense may be considered offensive as a result of its use as an offensive slang term. To avoid offence, the term *cerebral palsy* should be used, e.g. *She suffers from cerebral palsy* rather than *She is a spastic.*

spat[1] *see* SPIT[1].

spat[2] *n.* **1** a short gaiter covering the instep and ankle, formerly worn by men. **2** *colloq.* a petty quarrel. • *v.* (**spatted**, **spatting**) quarrel pettily.

spat[3] *n.* the spawn of shellfish, esp. the oyster. • *v.* (of an oyster etc.) spawn; shed (spawn).

spatchcock *n.* an extremely small chicken (or very small game bird) split open and grilled.

spate / spayt / *n.* a sudden flood or rush (*a spate of orders*). ☐ **in spate** (of a river) flowing strongly at an abnormally high level.

spathe / spay*th* / *n.* a large petal-like part of a flower, surrounding a central spike.

spatial / **spay**-shuhl / *adj.* of or relating to space; existing in space. ☐ **spatially** *adv.*

spätlese / shpet-**lay**-zuh, **spat**-layz / *n.* a white wine made from grapes picked later than the general harvest and therefore very sweet.

spatter *v.* scatter or fall in small bits or drops; splash. • *n.* a splash or splashes; the sound of spattering.

spatula / **spa**-chuh-luh / *n.* a tool with a broad blunt flexible blade for spreading, mixing, etc. **2** a strip of stiff material used by a doctor for pressing the tongue down or to one side.

spawn *n.* **1** the eggs of fish or frogs or shellfish. **2** *derog.* human offspring. **3** the thread-like matter from which fungi grow (*mushroom spawn*). • *v.* **1** deposit spawn; produce from spawn. **2** generate, esp. in large numbers (*the reports spawned by that committee*). **3** *derog.* (of people) produce offspring (esp. in large numbers). ☐ **spawner** *n.*

spay *v.* sterilise (a female animal) by removing the ovaries.

speak *v.* (**spoke**, **spoken**, **speaking**) **1** utter words in an ordinary voice (not singing); hold a conversation; make a speech; express in words. **2** use or be able to use (a specified language) in speaking (*he can speak Dyirbal well enough to be understood*). **3** make a polite or friendly remark (*she always speaks when we meet*). **4** be evidence of something (*it speaks volumes for his patience; the facts speak for themselves*). ☐ **so to speak** if I may express it this way. **speak up** speak more loudly; speak out. **speak with** (*or* **in**) **tongues** *see* GLOSSOLALIA.

-speak *comb. form* jargon (*computerspeak; marketing-speak; teenspeak*).

speaker *n.* **1** a person who speaks; one who makes a speech. **2** a person who speaks a specified language (*a Japanese speaker*). **3** a loudspeaker. **4** (**the Speaker**) the person presiding over a legislative assembly, as the House of Representatives.

speaking *n.* **1** an act or instance of uttering words etc. • *adj.* **1** (of a portrait) lifelike; true to its subject (*a speaking likeness*). **2** speaking or capable of speaking a specified foreign language (*French-speaking*). **3** with a reference, or from a point of view, specified (*roughly speaking; professionally speaking*).

spear *n.* **1** a weapon for hurling, with a long shaft and a pointed tip. **2** *Aust.* a lance-like Aboriginal weapon, made of wood and usu. headed with razor-sharp shaped quartz etc., often impelled by means of a woomera. **3** a pointed stem, e.g. of asparagus. • *v.* **1** pierce with or as if with a spear (*speared an olive*). **2** *Aust.* dismiss from employment; fire. ☐ **spear grass** any of many Australian grasses bearing a seed with a spear-like husk, capable of working its way into the soil, clothing, flesh, etc., and often injurious to stock. **spear-thrower** = WOOMERA.

speargun *n.* a gun used to propel a spear in underwater fishing.

spearhead *n.* the foremost part of an attacking or advancing force. • *v.* be the spearhead of.

spearmint *n.* a common garden mint used in cookery and to flavour chewing gum etc.

spearwood *n.* any of several Australian plants furnishing a hard wood traditionally used by Aborigines for making spears, esp. YARRAN.

spec *colloq. n.* **1** speculation. **2** a detailed description of a design, materials used, etc.; a specification. • *adj.* speculative; without a firm order or contract (*a spec-builder; a spec-house*). ☐ **on spec** as a speculation or gamble; on the off chance.

special *adj.* **1** of a particular kind; for a particular purpose, not general (*a special key; special training*). **2** exceptional in amount, quality, or intensity (*take special care of it*). **3** in which a person specialises (*Statistics is her special field*). • *n.* **1** a special person or thing, e.g. a special train, edition of a newspaper, dish on a menu, etc. **2** an item bought at a reduced price. ☐ **on special** (of goods etc.) available at a reduced price. **special correspondent** a journalist reporting on a specific subject. **special effects** (in TV, film, etc.) illusions created by props, camerawork, etc. **special pleading** (in Law) pleading with particular reference to the circumstances of a case, as opposed to general pleading; (in popular use) persuasive but unfair reasoning. **special school** a school for children with learning

specialise 800 **speech**

difficulties or for children who are exceptionally gifted. □ □ **specially** *adv.* **specialness** *n.*

specialise *v.* (also **-ize**) **1** (often foll. by *in*) study a subject etc. with special intensity; become a specialist. **2** devote oneself to an interest, skill, etc. (*he specialises in insulting people*). **3** (often foll. by *in*) have a product etc. to which one devotes special attention (*the shop specialises in sports goods*). **4** adapt for a particular purpose (*specialised organs such as the ear*). □ **specialisation** *n.*

specialist *n.* an expert in a special branch of a subject, esp. of medicine.

speciality / spesh-ee-**al**-uh-tee / *n.* a special quality, characteristic, or product; an activity in which a person specialises.

specialty / **spesh**-uhl-tee / = SPECIALITY.

specie / **spee**-shee / *n.* coin as opposed to paper money.

species / **spee**-sheez, -seez / *n.* (*pl.* **species**) **1** a group of animals or plants within a genus, differing only in minor details from the others. **2** a kind or sort. **3** (in the Mass etc.) the visible form of the consecrated bread and wine, the substance of either being the body and blood of Christ.

speciesism *n.* the assumption of human superiority over other creatures, leading to the exploitation of animals.

specific / spuh-**sif**-ik / *adj.* **1** particular, clearly distinguished from others (*the money was given for a specific purpose*). **2** expressing oneself in exact terms, not vague (*please be specific about your requirements*). **3** of or concerning a species (*the specific name for a plant*). • *n.* a specific aspect or influence; a remedy for a specific disease or condition. □ **specific gravity** = RELATIVE DENSITY. □ □ **specifically** *adv.*

specification *n.* **1** specifying; being specified. **2** the details describing something to be done or made.

specify *v.* (**specified**, **specifying**) mention (details, ingredients, etc.) clearly and definitely; include in a list of specifications.

specimen *n.* **1** a part or individual taken as an example of a whole or of a class, esp. for experiments. **2** a quantity of a person's urine etc. taken for testing. **3** *colloq.* usu. *derog.* a person of a specified sort.

specious / **spee**-shuhs / *adj.* seeming good or sound at first sight but lacking real merit (*specious reasoning*). □ **speciously** *adv.*

speck[1] *n.* **1** a small spot or stain. **2** a particle (*a speck of dirt*). **3** *Aust.* a particle of gold. **4** anything very small (by comparison, through the effect of distance, etc.). **5** *Aust. derog.* Tasmania. • *v.* (esp. as **specked** *adj.*) *Aust.* **1 a** marked with specks. **b** (of gold etc.) found on the surface. **2 a** search for surface gold, opal, etc. (*specking in Coober Pedy*). **b** search (the ground) for gold or opal (*specked the entire Steiglitz area*). **c** discover (particles of gold etc.) (*specked some small nuggets*).

speck[2] *n.* bacon or pork fat for larding meat etc.

specker *n. Aust.* a person who searches for surface deposits of gold, opal, etc.

speckle *n.* a small spot, a speck, esp. as a natural marking on the skin, on a bird's egg, etc.

speckled *adj.* marked with speckles.

specs *n.pl. colloq.* spectacles.

spectacle *n.* **1** a striking or impressive sight (*a magnificent spectacle*). **2** a ridiculous sight (*made a spectacle of himself*). **3** (**spectacles**) a pair of lenses set in a frame, worn in front of the eyes.

spectacled *adj.* **1** wearing spectacles. **2** (of an animal) having facial markings resembling spectacles (*spectacled flycatcher; spectacled hare wallaby*).

spectacular *adj.* striking, impressive, amazing. • *n.* an event intended to be spectacular, esp. a film or play. □ **spectacularly** *adv.*

spectator *n.* a person who watches a show, game, incident, etc.

spectra *see* SPECTRUM.

spectral *adj.* **1** of or like a spectre. **2** of the spectrum. □ **spectrally** *adv.*

spectre / **spek**-tuh / *n.* **1** a ghost. **2** a haunting fear of future trouble (*the spectre of defeat*).

spectrometer / spek-**trom**-uh-tuh / *n.* a spectroscope that can be used for measuring spectra.

spectroscope / **spek**-truh-skohp / *n.* an instrument for producing and examining spectra. □ **spectroscopic** *adj.*

spectroscopy / spek-**tros**-kuh-pee / *n.* the examination and investigation of spectra.

spectrum *n.* (*pl.* **spectra**) **1** the bands of colour as seen in a rainbow, forming a series according to their wavelengths. **2** a similar series of bands of sound. **3** an entire range of related qualities, ideas, etc. (*their views reflected the wide range of the Australian political spectrum*).

specula *see* SPECULUM.

speculate *v.* **1** form opinions without definite knowledge or evidence. **2** buy or sell goods or stocks and shares etc. in the hope of making a profit but with risk of loss. □ **speculation** *n.* **speculator** *n.*

speculative / **spek**-yuh-luh-tiv / *adj.* **1** of or based on speculation (*speculative reasoning*). **2** involving financial speculation and risk of loss. □ **speculatively** *adv.*

speculum / **spek**-yuh-luhm / *n.* (*pl.* **specula**) **1** a medical instrument for looking inside cavities of the body. **2** a mirror of polished metal in a telescope.

sped *see* SPEED.

speech *n.* **1** the act, power, or manner of speaking. **2** words spoken; a spoken communication to an audience. **3** the language of a nation, group, etc. (*varieties of Australian speech*). □ **speech recognition** *Computing* the interpretation by a computer of spoken material.

speechify

speech therapy treatment to improve speech defects.

speechify *v. colloq.* make a long or boring speech.

speechless *adj.* silent; unable to speak because of great emotion. ◻ **speechlessly** *adv.*

speed *n.* **1** the rate at which something moves or operates. **2** rapidity of movement. **3** the sensitivity of photographic film to light; the power of a lens to admit light. **4** *colloq.* an amphetamine drug. •*v.* (**sped** (in senses 3 and 4 **speeded**), **speeding**) **1** move or pass quickly. **2** send quickly (*speed you on your way*). **3** travel at an illegal or dangerous speed. **4** (foll. by *up*) move or work at greater speed. ◻ **speed limit** the maximum permitted speed on a road etc. ◻◻ **speeder** *n.*

speedo *n.* (*pl.* **speedos**) *colloq.* a speedometer.

speedometer / spee-**dom**-uh-tuh / *n.* a device in a motor vehicle, showing its speed.

speedos *n.pl. trademark* a brief (orig. nylon) man's or woman's swimming costume.

speedway *n.* **1** an arena for motorcycle racing. **2** a road or track reserved for fast traffic.

speedy *adj.* (**speedier**, **speediest**) **1** moving quickly. **2** done without delay. ◻ **speedily** *adv.*

Speewah / spee-wah / *n.* (also **Speewa**) *Aust. colloq.* **1** an imaginary station or place used as a setting for tall stories of the outback. **2** such a story.

speleology / spee-lee-**ol**-uh-jee / *n.* the exploration and scientific study of caves. ◻ **speleological** *adj.* **speleologist** *n.*

spell[1] *n.* **1** words supposed to have magic power; their magical effect. **2** fascination, attraction (*the spell of eastern countries*).

spell[2] *v.* (**spelt** *or* **spelled**, **spelling**) **1** put in their correct sequence the letters that form (a word). **2** (of letters) form as a word (*c a t spells 'cat'*). **3** result in (*these changes spell ruin*). ◻ **spell out 1** spell aloud. **2** state explicitly; explain in detail. ◻◻ **speller** *n.*

spell[3] *n.* **1** a short period of time (*sit down for a spell*). **2** a period of a certain type of weather (*a cold spell*). **3** a period of a certain activity (*took a spell at digging*). **4** *Aust.* a period of rest from work etc.; a holiday. •*v.* **1** rest. **2** relieve or take the place of (a person) in work etc. so that he or she may have a break. **3** cause (an animal etc.) to rest; allow (land) to lie fallow.

spellbound *adj.* with the attention held as if by a spell; entranced, fascinated.

spellchecker *n.* (also **spelling checker**) *Computing* a facility for checking the spelling of any word or all of the words of a computer document against a specified dictionary or dictionaries. ◻ **spellcheck** *n. & v.*

spelling *n.* **1** the way a word is spelt. **2** the ability to spell (*his spelling is atrocious*).

spelt *see* SPELL[2].

spencer *n.* a woman's (usu. woollen) sleeved singlet worn for extra warmth.

801

sphinx

Spencer Gulf an inlet on the coast of SA, separating the Eyre and Yorke Peninsulas. It is about 320 km long and 85 km wide at its entrance.

spend *v.* (**spent**, **spending**) **1** pay out (money) in buying something. **2** use up (*don't spend too much time on it*). **3** pass (*spend a holiday in Greece*). ◻ **spend a penny** *colloq.* urinate or defecate. ◻◻ **spender** *n.*

spendthrift *n.* a person who spends extravagantly and wastefully. •*adj.* extravagant.

Spenser, Edmund (*c.*1552–99), English poet, author of *The Faerie Queene*.

spent *see* SPEND. •*adj.* used up, having lost its force or strength (*the storm is spent*).

sperm *n.* **1** (*pl.* **sperms** *or* **sperm**) a sperm-atozoon. **2** semen. ◻ **sperm bank** a store of semen for artificial insemination. **sperm count** the number of spermatozoa in one ejaculation or in a measured amount of semen. **sperm whale** a large whale yielding spermaceti.

spermaceti / sper-muh-**set**-ee / *n.* a white waxy substance from a sperm whale, used in ointments, soap, etc.

spermatozoon / sper-muh-tuh-**zoh**-uhn / *n.* (*pl.* **spermatozoa**) a mature actively motile reproductive cell in semen, capable of fertilising an ovum.

spermicide / **sper**-muh-suyd / *n.* a substance able to kill spermatozoa. ◻ **spermicidal** *adj.*

spew *v.* (also **spue**) **1** vomit. **2** (often foll. by *out*) (cause to) gush out. **3** *colloq.* become extremely angry; be upset (*he's spewing because he can't go on the trip*).

sphagnum / **sfag**-nuhm / *n.* (in full **sphagnum moss**) any of various mosses of the genus *Sphagnum* growing in bogs and peat, widely used in horticulture (*see* PEATMOSS).

■ **Usage** The pronunciation / **spag**-nuhm / is sometimes heard but is considered incorrect by many people.

sphere / sfeer / *n.* **1** a perfectly round solid geometric figure. **2** something shaped like this. **3** a field of action or influence or existence; a person's place in society (*it took him out of his sphere*).

spherical / **sfe**-ruh-kuhl / *adj.* shaped like a sphere. ◻ **spherically** *adv.*

spheroid / **sfeer**-royd / *n.* a sphere-like but not perfectly spherical solid. ◻ **spheroidal** *adj.*

sphincter / **sfingk**-tuh / *n.* a ring of muscle surrounding an opening in the body and able to close it by contracting, esp. in the anus (*anal sphincter*).

sphinx *n.* **1** (**the Sphinx**) *Gk myth.* a winged monster at Thebes that killed all who could not answer a riddle. **2** any of the ancient stone statues in Egypt with a recumbent lion's body and a human or animal's head, esp. the one at Giza. **3**

spic alternative spelling of SPICK.

spice *n.* **1** a plant substance, esp. ground seeds or roots, with a strong taste or smell, used for flavouring food, e.g. cinnamon, cloves, pepper, etc. **2** a thing that adds zest or excitement (*variety is the spice of life*). • *v.* **1** flavour with spice. **2** (foll. by *with*) enhance (*a book spiced with malice*).

spick *n.* (also **spic**, **spik**) *Aust. colloq. offens.* a person of European, esp. Latin, descent.

spick and span *adj.* neat and clean; new-looking.

spicy *adj.* (**spicier**, **spiciest**) **1 a** like spice; flavoured with spice. **b** hot to the taste. **2** (of stories) slightly scandalous or improper. □ **spiciness** *n.*

spider *n.* **1** an animal (not an insect) with a segmented body and eight jointed legs, spinning webs to trap insects. **2** *Aust.* a soft drink to which ice cream has been added. • *v.* **1** move in a scuttling manner suggestive of a spider. **2** (as **spidering** *adj.*) spiderlike in form, manner, or movement (*streets spidering in all directions*). □ **spider flower** *Aust.* any of several species of grevillea having spidery flowers, esp. the grey spider flower, having woolly grey 'spiders', the pink spider flower, and the red spider flower.

spider orchid 1 any of several terrestrial Australian orchids of the genus *Caladenia*, having long, narrowed sepals and petals. **2** (in full **tree spider orchid**) an Australian dendrobium, having many racemes of spidery yellow-green flowers bordered in red.

spidery *adj.* having long thin angular lines like a spider's legs (*spidery handwriting*).

spiel / speel, shpeel / *colloq. n.* a glib or lengthy speech, usu. intended to persuade; a sales pitch. • *v.* **1** speak glibly; hold forth. **2** reel off (a sales pitch etc.).

Spielberg, Steven (1947–), American film director.

spieler *n. colloq.* **1** a person who spiels. **2** *Aust.* a person who engages in sharp practice; a swindler.

spigot / **spig**-uht / *n.* a peg or plug used to stop the vent-hole of a cask or a device to control the flow of a tap.

spik alternative spelling of SPICK.

spike *n.* **1** a sharp projecting point; a pointed piece of metal. **2 a** any of several metal points in the sole of a running shoe to prevent slipping. **b** (**spikes**) spiked running shoes. **3** a pointed metal rod standing on a base and used for filing rejected news items, bills, etc. **4** a long cluster of flowers on a central stem (*my cymbidiums are in spike*). **5** *Volleyball* a forceful attacking hit over the net. • *v.* **1** put spikes on or into. **2** fix (bills etc.) on a spike. **3** *colloq.* **a** lace (a drink) with alcohol etc. **b** contaminate with something added. **4** *colloq.* reject (a newspaper story). **5** scotch (a rumour etc.). **6** *Volleyball* hit the ball forcefully over the net with an overarm action.

spikenard / **spuyk**-nahd / *n.* **1** a tall sweet-smelling Indian plant. **2** a fragrant ointment formerly made from this.

spikey *n. Aust. colloq.* the long-spined flathead, a marine food fish of south-eastern and western Australia, having a long sharp spine on each side of the head.

spiky *adj.* (**spikier**, **spikiest**) **1** like a spike; having or sticking up in spikes. **2** *colloq.* touchy, irritable. □ **spikily** *adv.* **spikiness** *n.*

spill[1] *n.* a thin strip of wood or of twisted paper used for lighting a fire etc.

spill[2] *v.* (**spilt** *or* **spilled**, **spilling**) **1** cause or allow (a liquid, a powder, etc.) to run over the edge of its container, esp. accidentally. **2** (of liquid etc.) become spilt. **3** *colloq.* make known (*spilt the news*). **4** throw (a person etc.) from a vehicle, saddle, etc. **5** (foll. by *into*, *out* etc.) (esp. of a crowd) tumble out quickly from a place etc. (*the fans spilled into the street*). • *n.* **1** spilling; being spilt. **2** a tumble, esp. from a horse, a bicycle, etc. **3** *Aust.* the vacating of all or several posts of a parliamentary party, esp. after one important change of office. □ **spill over** overflow. □□ **spiller** *n.*

spillage *n.* **1** spilling. **2** the amount spilt.

spin *v.* (**spun**, **spinning**) **1** turn or cause to turn rapidly on its axis. **2** draw out and twist (raw cotton or wool etc.) into threads. **3** (of a spider or silkworm) make from a fine threadlike material emitted from the body (*spinning its web*). **4** (esp. of the head) be dizzy or in a whirl. **5** impart spin to (a ball). **6 a** toss (a coin). **b** *Aust.* toss (the coins) in a game of two-up. • *n.* **1** a spinning movement. **2** a rotating dive of an aircraft. **3** a secondary twisting motion, e.g. of a ball in flight. **4** *colloq.* a short (often fast) drive in a vehicle. **5** *Aust.* (in two-up) the act of tossing the coins. **6** *Aust. colloq.* (with a qualifying word) a (good, bad, fair, rough, etc.) run of luck (*she's had a rough spin*). **7** favourable bias or slant to a news story. □ **spin a yarn** tell a story; fabricate a story, explanation, excuse, etc. **spin bowler** *Cricket* a bowler who spins the ball. **spin doctor** a person employed to promote a favourable impression of political events to the media. **spin-drier** (also **spin-dryer**) a machine with a rapidly rotating drum in which moisture is removed from washed articles. **spin-dry** *v.* dry in a spin-drier. **spin-off** *n.* a benefit or product produced incidentally from a larger process. **spin out 1** cause to last a long time; prolong (*we need to spin out our resources; spinning out the agony*). **2** (of a vehicle) skid out of control. **3** *colloq.* freak out; cause (a person) to freak out. **spin out at** *colloq.* abuse or attack (a person) orally.

spina bifida / spuy-nuh **bif**-uh-duh / *n.* an abnormal congenital condition in which certain bones of the spine are not properly developed and the spinal cord protrudes.

spinach / **spin**-ich, -ij / *n.* a vegetable with dark green leaves.

spinal *adj.* of the spine. ☐ **spinal column** the spine. **spinal cord** the rope-like mass of nerve fibres enclosed within the spinal column.

spindle *n.* **1** a slender rod on which thread is wound in spinning. **2** a pin or axis that revolves or on which something revolves.

spindly *adj.* long or tall and thin.

spindrift *n.* spray blown along the surface of the sea.

spine *n.* **1** the backbone. **2** any of the sharp needle-like projections on certain plants (e.g. cacti) and animals (e.g. echidnas). **3** the part of a book where the pages are hinged. **4** a sharp ridge or projection, esp. of a mountain range. ☐ **spine-bash** *v.* & *n. Aust. colloq.* rest; sleep; loaf. **spine-basher** *Aust. colloq.* a person who spine-bashes. **spine-chiller** a spine-chilling book, film, etc. **spine-chilling** causing a thrill of terror.

spinebill *n.* either of two small Australian honeyeaters having a long, spine-like bill.

spineless *adj.* **1** having no backbone. **2** lacking determination or strength of character. ☐ **spinelessness** *n.*

spinet / spuh-**net**, spin-uht / *n.* a small harpsichord with oblique strings.

spinifex / **spin**-uh-feks / *n. Aust.* any of many tussocky, often spiny, perennial grasses, in Australia growing in arid and semi-arid areas, or on coastal sand dunes. Also called *porcupine*, *porcupine grass*. ☐ **spinifex country** (also **spinifex plain**) vast areas associated with spinifex. **spinifex parrot 1** = NIGHT PARROT. **2** = PRINCESS PARROT (*see* PRINCESS). **spinifex people** Aboriginal people of parts of central Australia. **spinifex pigeon** a reddish-brown pigeon of central and northern Australia, having a distinctive upright crest. **spinifex rat** a hare-wallaby of arid and semi-arid Australia. **spinifex snake 1** an extremely venomous green snake of spinifex country. **2** a harmless legless lizard occurring in spinifex country.

spinnaker / **spin**-uh-kuh / *n.* a large triangular extra sail on a racing yacht.

spinner *n.* **1** a person or thing that spins. **2** a spin bowler; a spun ball. **3** (in fishing) a revolving bait or lure. **4** *Aust.* the player who tosses the coins in two-up. **5** = SPINNERET. ☐ **come in spinner** *Aust.* (in two-up) the call which signals to the spinner that all bets have been placed and that it is time to toss the coins.

spinneret *n.* the spinning organ in a spider, silk-worm, etc.

spinney / **spin**-ee / *n.* (*pl.* **spinneys**) a small wood; a thicket.

spinning *n.* the act of spinning yarn. ☐ **spinning gum** (also **spinning-wheel gum**) a small eucalypt of NSW, Vic., and Tas., having silvery circular juvenile leaves which completely surround the stem, and which, when dead, spin around the stem in the slightest breeze. **spinning wheel** a household device for spinning fibre into yarn, with a spindle driven by a wheel.

spinster *n.* an unmarried woman.

spiny *adj.* **1** full of spines, prickly. **2** used as a distinguishing epithet in the names of fauna and flora, e.g. *spiny-cheeked honeyeater*; *spiny emex*. **3** perplexing, thorny (*a spiny problem*). ☐ **spiny anteater** *Aust.* = ECHIDNA.

spiracle / **spuy**-ruh-kuhl / *n.* **1** any of the openings through which an insect breathes. **2** the blowhole of a whale etc.

spiral *adj.* advancing or ascending in a continuous curve that winds round a central point or axis. • *n.* **1** a spiral line; a thing of spiral form. **2** a continuous increase or decrease in two or more quantities alternately because of their dependence on each other (*the wage-price spiral*). • *v.* (**spiralled**, **spiralling**) **1** move in a spiral course. **2** (of prices, wages, etc.) rise or fall continuously. ☐ **spirally** *adv.*

spire *n.* a pointed structure in the form of a tall cone or pyramid, esp. on a church.

spirit *n.* **1** a person's mind, feelings, or soul as distinct from the body. **2** a ghost. **3** a person's nature. **4** a person with specified mental or moral qualities (*a few brave spirits went swimming*). **5** the characteristic quality or mood of something (*the spirit of the times*). **6** the real purpose (of a law) as distinct from a strict interpretation of its words. **7** liveliness, readiness to assert oneself (*answered with spirit*). **8** (**spirits**) a person's feeling of cheerfulness or depression. **9** a strong distilled alcoholic drink, e.g. whisky or gin. • *v.* carry off swiftly and secretly (*spirited him away*). ☐ **spirit gum** quick-drying gum for attaching false hair. **spirit level** a glass tube nearly filled with liquid and containing an air bubble, used to test whether something is level.

spirited *adj.* **1** full of spirit, lively; ready to assert oneself. **2** having spirits of a specified kind; in a specified mood (*high-spirited*). ☐ **spiritedly** *adv.*

spiritless *adj.* lacking vigour or energy.

spiritual *adj.* **1** of or concerning the spirit as opposed to matter (*a spiritual relationship*). **2** religious, divine, inspired (*the spiritual life*). **3** refined, sensitive. • *n.* (also **Negro spiritual**) a religious folk song of American blacks. ☐ **spiritually** *adv.* **spirituality** *n.*

spiritualism *n.* **1** belief in (and the supposed practice of) communication with the dead, esp. through mediums. **2** the belief that the spirit exists as distinct from matter, or that spirit is the only reality (cf. MATERIALISM). ☐ **spiritualist** *n.* **spiritualistic** *adj.*

spirituous *adj.* (of alcoholic drink) **1** very alcoholic. **2** distilled as well as fermented.

spit[1] *v.* (**spat** or **spit**, **spitting**) **1** eject from the mouth; eject saliva. **2** (of a cat) make a noise like spitting when angry or hostile; (of a person) show anger (*spitting with fury*). **3** (of a fire etc.) throw out sparks etc. explosively. **4** fall lightly (*it's spitting with rain*). •*n*. **1** spittle. **2** the act of spitting. ☐ **spit and polish** cleaning and polishing of equipment etc., esp. by soldiers. **spit the dummy** *Aust. colloq.* **1** be very angry. **2** give up (contesting, participating, etc.) prematurely. **spitting distance** *colloq.* a very short distance. **spitting image** the exact likeness or double of another person or thing. **the spit** (*or* **the dead spit** *or* **the very spit**) = SPITTING IMAGE.

spit[2] *n.* **1** a long thin metal spike thrust through meat to hold it while it is roasting over a fire etc. **2** a long narrow strip of land projecting into the sea. •*v.* (**spitted, spitting**) pierce with or as if with a spit. ☐ **spit roast** *n.* **1** meat roasted on a spit. **2** an occasion when spit-roasting occurs (*invited to a spit roast*). **spit-roast** *v.* cook (a piece of meat) on a spit.

spite *n.* a malicious desire to hurt, annoy, or humiliate another person. •*v.* hurt or annoy etc. from spite. ☐ **in spite of** not being prevented by (*we enjoyed ourselves in spite of the weather*).

spiteful *adj.* full of spite; showing or caused by spite. ☐ **spitefully** *adv.* **spitefulness** *n.*

spitfire *n.* **1** a fiery-tempered person. **2** the large dark green larva of a sawfly, often as one of a huge cluster esp. on eucalypts, and prone to spit forth a sticky greenish fluid when disturbed.

spittle *n.* saliva, esp. that ejected from the mouth.

spittoon *n.* a vessel for spitting into.

spiv *n. Aust. colloq.* a man, esp. a flashily-dressed one, living from illicit or unscrupulous dealings.

splash *v.* **1** cause (liquid) to fly about in drops; wet with such drops. **2** (of liquid) be splashed. **3** move or fall with splashing (*we splashed through the puddles*). **4** decorate with irregular patches of colour etc. **5** display prominently (*the news was splashed across the Sunday papers*). **6** (often foll. by *out*) spend (money) freely; be extravagant. •*n.* **1** splashing; a sound or mark made by this. **2** a quantity of liquid splashed. **3** a prominent news feature, sensation, etc. **4** a patch of colour or light. **5** a striking or ostentatious display or effect.

splashdown *n.* the landing of a spacecraft on the sea.

splat *colloq. n.* a sharp sound of something squashy hitting a hard surface (*his brains hit the wall with a splat*). •*adv.* with a splat. •*v.* (**splatted, splatting**) fall or hit with a splat.

splatter *v.* splash noisily. •*n.* a noisy splashing sound.

splay *v.* spread apart; bend outwards; slant (the sides of an opening).

splayd *n. Aust. trademark* a fork with a spoon-shaped bowl and the cutting edge of a knife, a three-in-one table utensil.

spleen *n.* **1** an organ of the body situated at the left of the stomach and involved in maintaining the proper condition of the blood. **2** bad temper, peevishness (*vented their spleen; a fit of spleen*).

splendid *adj.* **1** magnificent, displaying splendour. **2** excellent (*a splendid achievement*). ☐ **splendidly** *adv.*

splendiferous *adj. colloq.* splendid.

splendour *n.* (also **splendor**) brilliance; magnificent display or appearance, grandeur.

splenetic / spluh-**net**-ik / *adj.* bad-tempered, peevish. ☐ **splenetically** *adv.*

splenic / **splen**-ik, **splee**-nik / *adj.* of or in the spleen.

splice *v.* **1** join (two ends of rope) by untwisting and interweaving the strands of each. **2** join (pieces of film or timber etc.) by overlapping the ends. •*n.* a join made by splicing.

splint *n.* a strip of rigid material bound to an injured part of the body to prevent movement, e.g. while a broken bone heals. •*v.* secure with a splint.

splinter *n.* a thin sharp piece of wood or stone etc. broken off from a larger piece. •*v.* break or become broken into splinters. ☐ **splinter group** a small group that has broken away from a larger one, e.g. in a political party. ☐☐ **splintery** *adj.*

split *v.* (**split, splitting**) **1** break or become broken into parts, esp. lengthwise or along the grain of wood etc. **2** divide into parts; divide and share. **3** come apart, tear (*this coat has split at the seams*). **4** divide or become divided into hostile groups. **5** *colloq.* leave, esp. suddenly (*I've got to split*). **6** (usu. foll. by *on*) *colloq.* betray, inform (*split on his mates*). •*n.* **1** splitting; being split. **2** the place where something has split or torn. **3** a disagreement; a schism. **4** *colloq.* a share (*here's your split of our winnings*). **5** a dish of split fruit with cream or ice cream etc. (*banana split*). **6** (**splits**) an acrobatic position in which the legs are stretched in opposite directions and at right angles to the trunk. ☐ **split hairs** make trivial distinctions; quibble. **split-level** *adj.* (of a building) having adjoining rooms at a level midway between successive storeys in other parts. **split pea** a dried pea split in half. **split personality 1** an alteration or dissociation of personality occurring in some mental illnesses, e.g. a person seeming to have two or more alternating personalities. **2** *colloq.* schizophrenia. **split screen** a screen, usu. associated with a computer, on which two or more separate images are displayed simultaneously. **split second** a very brief moment. **split-second** *adj.* extremely rapid; accurate to a very small fraction of time (*split-second timing*). **split stuff** *Aust.* timber sawn into lengths and then split. **split the difference** decide on an amount halfway between two proposed amounts. **split up** split, separate; (of a couple) cease to live together.

split infinitive *n.* an infinitive (e.g. *to like*) with a word or words placed between *to* and the verb, e.g. *he seems to really like it*.

splitting

■ **Usage** Some people oppose the use of the split infinitive under any circumstances, while others approve of it in cases where it avoids stylistic awkwardness. Occasionally a split infinitive neatly avoids ambiguity, e.g. the difference in meaning between *he failed to entirely understand the issue* and **1** *he entirely failed to understand the issue* and **2** *he failed to understand the issue entirely*.

splitting *adj.* (of a headache) severe, feeling as if it will split one's head.

splodge *colloq. n.* a daub, blot, or smear. • *v.* make a splodge on. ☐ **splodgy** *adj.*

splosh *colloq. v.* splash. • *n.* **1** a splashing sound. **2** a splash of water etc. **3** money.

splotch = SPLODGE.

splurge *n.* **1** a sudden extravagance; a spending spree. **2** an ostentatious display. • *v.* make a splurge, spend money freely.

splutter *v.* **1** speak, say, or express in a hurried, vehement, or choking manner. **2** speak or utter (words, threats, etc.) rapidly or incoherently. **3** emit sparks, hot oil, etc., with spitting sounds. • *n.* a spluttering speech or sound.

spoil *v.* (**spoilt** or **spoiled**, **spoiling**) **1** damage; make or become useless or unsatisfactory. **2** (of food) go bad. **3** harm the character of (a person) by lack of discipline, excessive generosity, or pampering. **4** render (a ballot paper) invalid by improper marking. **5 a** prevent or obstruct the success of (a person, undertaking, etc.) in sport etc. (often as **spoiling tactics**). **b** *Aust. Rules* punch the ball away from a player attempting to take a mark. • *n.* (usu. as **spoils**) **1** plunder; benefits gained by a victor. **2** profitable advantages of an official position. ☐ **be spoiling for** desire eagerly (*he is spoiling for a fight*).

spoilage *n.* **1** paper spoilt in printing. **2** the spoiling of food etc. by decay.

spoilsport *n.* a person who spoils others' enjoyment.

spoke[1] *n.* each of the rods that connect the centre of a wheel to its rim. ☐ **put a spoke in a person's wheel** thwart his or her intentions.

spoke[2], **spoken** see SPEAK.

spokesman *n.* (*feminine* **spokeswoman**) a person who speaks on behalf of a group.

spokesperson *n.* (*pl.* **spokespersons** or **spokespeople**) a spokesman or spokeswoman.

spoliation / spoh-lee-**ay**-shuhn / *n.* pillaging.

spondee *n. Poetry* a metrical foot with two long or stressed syllables.

sponge / spunj / *n.* **1** a sea animal with a porous structure. **2** the skeleton of this, or a substance of similar texture, used for washing, cleaning, or padding. **3** a sponge cake. **4** sponging; a wash with a sponge. **5** a person who sponges on others; an act of such sponging. **6** *colloq.* a heavy drinker. • *v.* **1** wipe or wash with a sponge. **2** (often foll. by *out*, *away*, etc.) wipe off or efface (as) with a sponge. **3 a** (often foll. by *on* or *off*) live as a parasite, be meanly dependent upon (a person or persons) (*sponges shamelessly on his relatives*). **b** obtain (a drink, a cigarette, etc.) by cadging. ☐ **sponge bag** a waterproof bag for toilet articles. **sponge cake** a cake with a light, open texture.

sponger *n.* a parasitic person.

spongiform *adj.* of or like a sponge, esp. the sea animal.

spongy *adj.* (**spongier**, **spongiest**) like a sponge in texture, soft and springy. ☐ **sponginess** *n.*

sponsor *n.* **1** a person who makes himself or herself responsible for another who is undergoing training etc. **2** a godparent at baptism or (esp. in the Catholic Church) a person who presents a candidate for confirmation. **3** a person who puts forward a proposal, e.g. for a new law. **4 a** a person or firm that provides funds for a musical, artistic, or sporting event. **b** a business organisation that promotes a broadcast program in return for advertising time. **5** a person who subscribes to charity in return for a specified activity by another person. • *v.* act as sponsor for. ☐ **sponsorship** *n.*

spontaneous / spon-**tay**-nee-uhs / *adj.* resulting from natural impulse; not caused or sug-gested from outside; not forced. ☐ **spontaneous combustion** the bursting into flame of a substance because of heat produced by its own rapid oxidation and not by flame etc. from an external source. **spontaneous generation** the supposed production of living from non-living matter. ☐ ☐ **spontaneously** *adv.* **spontaneity** / spon-tuh-**nee**-uh-tee, spon-tuh-**nay**- / *n.*

spoof[1] / spoof / *n. colloq.* a hoax; a humorous imitation or parody. ☐ **spoofer** *n.*

spoof[2] / spuuf / *n. Aust. coarse colloq.* semen. • *v.* ejaculate semen.

spoofy / **spuuf**-ee / *adj. Aust. coarse colloq.* **1** of or like semen. **2** covered with semen; stained with semen.

spook / spook / *colloq. n.* **1** a ghost. **2** a spy, esp. in the secret service. • *v.* **1** frighten, unnerve. **2** take fright; become alarmed. ☐ **spooked** *adj.*

spooky *adj. colloq.* ghostly, eerie. ☐ **spookily** *adv.* **spookiness** *n.*

spool *n.* a reel on which something is wound, e.g. yarn or photographic film. • *v.* wind or become wound on a spool.

spoon *n.* **1** a utensil consisting of a rounded bowl and a handle, used for eating, stirring, or measuring things. **2** the amount it contains. • *v.* **1** take or lift with a spoon. **2** hit (a ball) feebly upwards. **3** *colloq.* kiss and cuddle.

spoonbill *n.* a wading bird with a very broad flat tip to its bill.

spoonerism *n.* an interchange of the initial sounds of two words, usu. as a slip of the tongue, e.g. *he's a boiled sprat* (= spoiled brat); *you have hissed my mystery lectures*. (¶ Named after the Rev. W.A. Spooner (1844–1930), said to have made such errors in speaking (e.g. 'our queer old Dean' when he was referring to Queen Victoria).)

spoonfeed v. (**spoonfed**, **spoonfeeding**) **1** feed with liquid food from a spoon. **2** give excessive help to (a person etc.) so that the recipient does not need to make any effort.

spoonful n. (pl. **spoonfuls**) as much as a spoon will hold.

spoor n. the track or scent left by an animal.

sporadic / spuh-**rad**-ik / adj. occurring here and there or occasionally; scattered. ☐ **sporadically** adv.

spore n. one of the tiny reproductive cells of plants such as fungi and ferns.

sport n. **1** a competitive activity; a game or pastime involving physical exertion; these collectively. **2** (**sports**) athletic activities; a meeting for competition in these (*the school sports*). **3** amusement, fun (*we said it in sport*). **4** *colloq.* **a** a fair or generous person (*she's a real sport*). **b** a person with a specified attitude to games, rules, etc. (*a bad sport at tennis*). **c** *US & Aust.* a familiar form of address, esp. between males (*what's yours, sport?*). **5** an animal or plant that is strikingly different from its parent(s). • v. **1** play, amuse oneself. **2** wear or display (*he sported a gold tie pin*). ☐ **be a sport 1** abide by the rules, play fair. **2** be generous in agreeing to a request or plea (*come on, be a sport and give me a hand*). **make sport of** ridicule. **sports car** an open low-built fast car. **sports coat** (or **jacket**) a man's jacket for informal wear (not part of a suit).

sporting adj. **1** interested in sport; concerned with sport (*a sporting type; the sporting news*). **2** generous, fair (*a sporting offer*). ☐ **a sporting chance** a reasonable chance of success.

sportive adj. playful. ☐ **sportively** adv.

sportscast n. a sporting broadcast or telecast.

sportsground n. an area reserved for organised sport, usu. with accommodation for spectators and facilities for players.

sportsman n. **1** a man who takes part in sports, esp. professionally. **2** a fair and generous person.

sportsmanlike adj. behaving fairly and generously.

sportsperson n. (pl. **sportspersons** or **sportspeople**) a sportsman or sportswoman.

sportswear n. clothes for sports or informal wear.

sportswoman n. a woman who takes part in sports, esp. professionally.

sporty adj. *colloq.* **1 a** fond of sport. **b** (esp. of clothes) suitable for wearing for sport or for casual outdoor use. **2** loud and vulgar, rakish, showy. ☐ **sportily** adv. **sportiness** n.

spot n. **1** a roundish area different in colour from the rest of the surface; a roundish mark. **2** a pimple. **3** a moral blemish or stain. **4** a particular place (*this is the spot where hundreds of Aborigines were massacred by whites*). **5** a particular part of one's body or aspect of one's character (*yes, that's the spot to rub; has a blind spot about racism*). **6** one's esp. regular position in an organisation, program, etc. (*has a regular spot in ABC TV's 'Gardening Australia'*). **7** a slot for advertising on radio or television. **8** *colloq.* a small amount of something (*a spot of leave*). **9** a drop (*a few spots of rain*). **10** *colloq.* a drink of alcoholic liquor (not necessarily small). **11** a spotlight. **12** (usu. as *adj.*) money paid or goods delivered immediately after a sale (*paid spot cash*). **13** *Aust. colloq.* $100. • v. (**spotted**, **spotting**) **1** *colloq.* pick out; catch sight of; recognise (*spotted the winner in every race; spotted her in the crowd*). **2** watch for and take note of (talent etc.). **3** mark or become marked with spots. **4** rain slightly (*it's spotting*). **5** stain or blemish (*one's or a person's reputation etc.*). **6** (of a bushfire) break out in patches ahead of the main fire (*tried to prevent the bushfire from spotting*). ☐ **in a spot** *colloq.* in difficulties. **on the spot 1** at the scene of an event. **2** *colloq.* in a position demanding response or action (*the questions put him on the spot*). **3** without delay or change of place, then and there (*on the spot fine*). **4** without moving forwards or backwards (*jogging on the spot*). **5** (of a person) wide awake, equal to the situation, in good form at a game etc. **spot check** a check made suddenly on something chosen at random. **spot on** *colloq.* adj. **1** precise; on target. **2** excellent (being just what was wanted). adv. precisely; exactly. interj. **3** that is exactly right! **4** that is just what was required!; excellent! ☐☐ **spotter** n.

spotless adj. free from stain or blemish, perfectly clean. ☐ **spotlessly** adv.

spotlight n. **1** a beam of light directed on a small area; a lamp giving this. **2** full publicity or attention. • v. (**spotlighted**, **spotlighting**) **1** direct a spotlight on. **2** draw attention to, make conspicuous.

spotted adj. **1** marked or decorated with spots. **2** used as a distinguishing epithet in the names of fauna and flora, e.g. *spotted harrier, spotted emu bush*.

spotter n. **1** (often in *combinations*) a person who spots people or things (*talent spotter*). **2** (in full **spotter plane**) a light aircraft used to locate bushfires, sharks, etc.

spotty adj. (**spottier**, **spottiest**) **1** marked with spots. **2** patchy, irregular. ☐ **spottiness** n.

spouse n. a person's husband or wife.

spout n. **1** a projecting tube or lip used for pouring from a teapot, kettle, jug, etc., or on a fountain, roof gutter, etc. **2** = SPOUTING (sense 1). **3** a jet of liquid. • v. **1** come or send out forcefully as a jet of liquid. **2** (often foll. by *off*) utter or speak lengthily, boastfully, or angrily. ☐ **up the spout** *colloq.* **1** useless, ruined, broken down. **2** pregnant.

spouting n. **1** (also **spout**) a downpipe for carrying rainwater from a roof. **2** such pipes collectively.

sprain v. injure (a joint or its muscles or ligaments) by wrenching it violently. • n. an injury caused in this way.

sprang see SPRING.

sprat n. a small edible marine fish (often dried and used in Asian cooking).

sprawl v. **1** sit, lie, or fall with the arms and legs spread out loosely. **2** (of handwriting, a plant, a town, etc.) spread out in an irregular or straggling way. • n. **1** a sprawling attitude, movement, or arrangement. **2** straggling urban expansion (*urban sprawl*).

spray[1] n. **1** a single shoot or branch with its leaves, twigs, and flowers. **2** a bunch of cut flowers etc. arranged decoratively. **3** an ornament in similar form.

spray[2] n. **1** water or other liquid dispersed in very small drops. **2** a liquid preparation for spraying with an aerosol etc. **3** a device for spraying liquid. **4** a quantity of small particles, e.g. bullets, flying through the air. • v. **1** send out (liquid) or be sent out in very small drops; wet with liquid in this way. **2** direct a spray of bullets at. ☐ **spray gun** a device for spraying paint or other liquid. ☐☐ **sprayer** n.

spread v. (**spread**, **spreading**) **1** open out, unroll or unfold. **2** become longer or wider (*the stain began to spread*). **3** cover the surface of, apply as a layer (*spread the bread with jam*). **4** be able to be spread (*it spreads like butter*). **5** make or become more widely distributed, known, felt, or suffered (*spread the news; panic spread*). **6** distribute over a period (*spread the payments over 12 months*). • n. **1** spreading; being spread. **2** the extent, expanse, or breadth of something. **3** expansion. **4** a bedspread. **5** *colloq.* a lavish meal. **6** the range of something. **7** a sweet or savoury paste for spreading on bread. ☐ **spread eagle** the figure of an eagle with legs and wings extended, as an emblem. **spread-eagle** v. **1** spread out (a person's body) in this way. **2** defeat utterly.

spreadsheet n. a computer program that manipulates figures in tabulated form; used in financial planning and accounting.

spree n. **1** a lively extravagant outing (*a shopping spree*). **2** a bout of fun or drinking etc.

sprig n. **1** a small branch, a shoot. **2** an ornament or decoration in this form. **3** (usu. *scornful*) a youth or young man (*a sprig of the British nobility playing at being a jackeroo*).

sprightly adj. (**sprightlier**, **sprightliest**) lively, full of energy. ☐ **sprightliness** n.

spring v. (**sprang**, **sprung**, **springing**) **1** jump; move rapidly or suddenly in a single movement. **2** move rapidly by or as by the action of a coiled spring (*the branch sprang back*). **3** grow or issue; arise; come into being (*weeds sprang up; their discontent springs from distrust of their leaders; new houses springing up; nothing springs to mind*). **4** (usu. foll. by *from*) originate (from ancestors) (*he springs from a convict on the Second Fleet*). **5** a become warped or split. **b** split or crack (wood or a wooden implement). **6** *colloq.* arrange the escape of (a prisoner). **7** cause to operate suddenly (*sprang the trap*). **8** produce or develop suddenly or unexpectedly (*sprang a surprise on us*). **9** *Aust. colloq.* discover or come upon (something or someone, usu. a concealed object or someone engaged in an illicit activity) (*police sprang a marijuana plantation in the forest; they got sprung snogging behind the shelter shed*). • n. **1** the act of springing, a jump. **2** a recoil. **3** an elastic device (usu. of bent or coiled metal) that reverts to its original position after being compressed or stretched. **4** elasticity (*a mattress with plenty of spring*). **5** a place where water or oil comes up naturally from the ground; the flow of this. **6** the season in which new vegetation begins to appear, from September to November in Australia. ☐ **spring balance** a device that measures weight by the tension of a spring. **spring chicken 1** a young fowl for eating. **2** a youthful person (*he's no spring chicken*). **spring-clean** v. clean one's home thoroughly. **spring equinox** the equinox about 22 September in the southern hemisphere. Also called *vernal equinox*. **spring onion** a form of onion with a very small bulb, often eaten raw. **spring roll** a Chinese pancake filled with vegetables (and sometimes meat) and fried. **spring tide** the tide when there is the largest rise and fall of water, occurring shortly after the new and full moon.

springboard n. **1** a flexible board for giving impetus to a person who jumps on it, used in gymnastics and in diving. **2** a source of impetus or help in an activity.

springbok n. (*pl.* **springbok** or **springboks**) a South African gazelle that can spring high into the air. **2** (**Springboks**) a South African national sporting (esp. Rugby) team or touring party.

springer n. **1** the part of an arch where the curve begins; the lowest stone of this. **2** a cow or heifer near to calving.

springtime n. the season of spring.

springy adj. (**springier**, **springiest**) able to spring back easily after being squeezed or stretched. ☐ **springiness** n.

sprinkle v. scatter or fall in small drops or particles; scatter small drops etc. on (a surface). • n. **1** the action or an act of sprinkling. **2** (foll. by *of*) a quantity sprinkled, a sprinkling (*add a sprinkle of chilli powder*). **3** a light shower of rain.

sprinkler n. a device for sprinkling a lawn or extinguishing fires.

sprinkling n. **1** something sprinkled. **2** a few here and there (*only a sprinkling of people at the show*).

sprint v. run at full speed, esp. over a short distance. • n. a run of this kind; a similar spell of maximum effort in swimming, cycling, etc. ☐ **sprinter** n.

sprit n. a small spar reaching diagonally from a mast to the upper outer corner of a sail.

sprite *n.* an elf, fairy, or goblin.

sprocket *n.* each of a series of teeth on a wheel, engaging with links on a chain.

sprout *v.* **1** begin to grow or appear; put forth shoots. **2** cause to spring up as a growth (*has sprouted horns*). •*n.* **1** the shoot of a plant. **2** a Brussels sprout (*see* BRUSSELS). **3** a beansprout.

spruce¹ *adj.* neat and trim in appearance, smart. •*v.* smarten (*spruce oneself up*). ☐ **sprucely** *adv.* **spruceness** *n.*

spruce² *n.* a fir with dense foliage; its wood.

spruik / sprook / *v. Aust.* hold forth in public; deliver a harangue, esp. to advertise a show etc. ☐ **spruiker** *n.* **spruiking** *n.*

sprung *see* SPRING. •*adj.* fitted with springs (*a sprung mattress*).

spry *adj.* (**spryer**, **spryest**) active, nimble, lively. ☐ **spryly** *adv.* **spryness** *n.*

spud *n.* **1** *colloq.* a potato. **2** a small narrow spade for digging up weeds or cutting their roots. •*v.* (**spudded**, **spudding**) dig with a spud. ☐ **spud cocky** a potato farmer.

spumante / spyoo-**man**-tee / *n.* Italian sparkling white wine.

spume *n.* froth, foam. •*v.* foam. ☐ **spumy** *adj.*

spun *see* SPIN.

spunk *n. colloq.* **1** courage, mettle, spirit. **2** *coarse colloq.* semen. **3** *Aust.* a sexually attractive person. ☐ **spunk rat** *Aust. colloq.* an attractive and sexually promiscuous young male.

spunky *colloq. adj.* **1** brave, spirited. **2** *Aust.* highly attractive sexually. •*n. Aust.* = SPUNK (sense 3).

spur *n.* **1** a pricking device with a projecting point or toothed wheel, worn on a horse-rider's heel. **2** a stimulus or incentive. **3** something shaped like a spur; a hard projection on a cock's leg; a slender hollow projection on a flower. **4** a ridge projecting from a mountain. **5** a branch road or railway. •*v.* (**spurred**, **spurring**) **1** urge on (one's horse) by pricking it with spurs. **2** urge on, incite, stimulate (*he spurred the men to greater effort*). ☐ **on the spur of the moment** on an impulse. **spur-winged plover** a wading bird of eastern and southern Australia, having a yellow claw-like projection on the shoulder of each wing, and a loud call said to be like a dingo's howl. Also called *masked lapwing*.

spurious / **spyoor**-ree-uhs / *adj.* not genuine or authentic.

spurn *v.* reject scornfully.

spurt *v.* **1** gush, send out (a liquid) suddenly. **2** increase one's speed suddenly. •*n.* **1** a sudden gush. **2** a short burst of activity; a sudden increase in speed.

sputnik / **spuut**-nik / *n.* a Russian artificial satellite orbiting the earth.

sputter *v.* **1** make a series of quick explosive sounds, esp. when being heated. **2** speak or utter (words, threats, etc.) rapidly or incoherently. •*n.* a sputtering sound.

sputum / **spyoo**-tuhm / *n.* spittle; matter that is spat out.

spy *n.* (*pl.* **spies**) a person who secretly collects and reports information, esp. for a government or organisation. •*v.* (**spied**, **spying**) **1** see, catch sight of. **2** be a spy, keep watch secretly. **3** pry.

sq. *abbr.* square.

squab / skwob / *n.* a young (esp. unfledged) pigeon or other bird, esp. as food.

squabble *v.* quarrel in a petty or noisy way. •*n.* a quarrel of this kind.

squad *n.* a small group sharing a task etc., esp. of soldiers or police (*drug squad*).

squadron *n.* **1** a basic tactical and administrative unit of an air force. **2** a detachment of warships employed on a particular duty. **3** an organised group etc., esp. a cavalry division of two companies. ☐ **squadron leader** a commander of a RAAF squadron, next below wing commander.

squalid *adj.* **1** dirty and unpleasant, esp. because of neglect or poverty. **2** morally degrading. ☐ **squalidly** *adv.*

squall / skwawl / *n.* **1** a harsh cry or scream, esp. of a baby. **2** a sudden storm of wind, esp. with rain, snow, or sleet. •*v.* utter a squall. ☐ **squally** *adj.*

squalor *n.* a filthy or squalid state.

squander *v.* spend (money, time, etc.) wastefully.

square *n.* **1** a geometric figure with four equal sides and four right angles. **2** an area or object shaped like this. **3** a four-sided area surrounded by buildings. **4** an area within a military barracks etc. for drill. **5** an L-shaped or T-shaped instrument for obtaining or testing right angles. **6** the product obtained when a number is multiplied by itself (*9 is the square of 3*). **7** *colloq.* a person considered old-fashioned or conventional. •*adj.* **1** of square shape. **2** right-angled (*the desk has square corners*). **3** of or using units that express the measure of an area (e.g. *one square metre* is an area equal to that of a square with sides one metre long). **4** of comparatively broad sturdy shape (*a man of square frame*). **5** properly arranged; tidy (*get things square*). **6** (also **all square**) equal, with no balance of advantage or debt etc. on either side. **7** straightforward, uncompromising (*a square refusal*). **8** fair, honest (*a square deal*). **9** *colloq.* old-fashioned, conventional. •*adv.* squarely, directly (*hit him square on the jaw*). •*v.* **1** make right-angled (*square the corners*). **2** mark with squares (*squared paper*). **3** place evenly or squarely (*he squared his shoulders*). **4** multiply (a number) by itself (*3 squared is 9*). **5** settle or pay (*that squares the account*). **6** *colloq.* secure the cooperation of (a person) by payment or bribery (*try and square the umpire*). **7** be or make consistent (*his story doesn't square with yours*). ☐ **square brackets** brackets of the form [ ]. **square dance** a dance in which four couples face inwards from four sides. **square-eyed** *colloq.* affected by, or given to, excessive viewing of

squash

television. **square leg** a fielder in cricket on the batsman's leg side and nearly in line with the wicket; this position. **square meal** a large satisfying meal. **square-rigged** with the principal sails at right angles to the length of the ship. **square root** a number of which the given number is the square (*see* noun, sense 6) (*3 is the square root of 9*). **square the circle 1** construct a square equal in area to a given circle. **2** do what is impossible. **square up to** assume a boxer's fighting attitude; face and tackle (a difficulty) resolutely. □□ **squarely** *adv*. **squareness** *n*.

squash[1] *v*. **1** crush; squeeze or become squeezed flat or into pulp. **2** pack tightly; squeeze into a small space. **3** suppress (*squashed the rebellion*). **4** silence with a crushing reply. •*n*. **1** a crowd of people squashed together. **2** the sound of something being squashed. **3** a drink made of crushed fruit. **5** (in full **squash racquets**) a game played with racquets and a small ball in a closed court. □ **squashy** *adj*.

squash[2] *n*. a gourd used as a vegetable; the plant that bears it.

squat *v*. (**squatted**, **squatting**) **1** sit on one's heels or crouch with knees drawn up closely. **2** (of an animal) crouch close to the ground. **3** *colloq*. sit. **4** *Aust. hist.* occupy a tract of Crown land in order to graze cattle or sheep. **5** be a squatter; occupy as a squatter. •*n*. **1** a squatting posture. **2** occupying a place as a squatter; the place itself. •*adj*. short and thick, dumpy.

squatter *n*. **1** one who sits in a squatting posture. **2** *Aust. hist.* a person who occupies a tract of Crown land in order to graze livestock, having title by licence or lease. **3** *Aust. hist.* a person, esp. an ex-convict, who occupies Crown land without legal title. **4** *Aust.* a sheep farmer, esp. on a large scale; such a person as being of an elevated socio-economic status. **5** a person who takes temporary possession of an unoccupied building for living in, without authority. □ **squatter's chair** (also **squatter's delight**) *Aust.* an outdoor reclining chair consisting of a light wooden frame from which a length of canvas is suspended and having a leg rest.

squattocracy / skwo-**tok**-ruh-see / *n*. *Aust*. wealthy farmers as an interest group or as a socio-economic group.

squaw *n*. *offens*. a North American Indian woman or wife.

■ **Usage** Until relatively recently, the word *squaw* was used neutrally with the above meaning. With changes in the social climate of the second half of the 20th century, however, the derogatory attitudes of the past towards American Indian women have meant that the word cannot be used without being offensive.

squawk *n*. **1** a loud harsh cry, esp. of a bird. **2** *colloq*. a complaint. •*v*. **1** utter a squawk. **2** *colloq*. complain.

809

squiffy

squeak *n*. a short high-pitched cry or sound. •*v*. **1** utter or make a squeak. **2** *colloq*. become an informer. □ **a narrow squeak** *colloq*. a narrow escape.

squeaker *n*. *Aust*. a name applied to the bettong, to various birds with a squeaky call (esp. the grey currawong), and to various cicadas.

squeaky *adj*. (**squeakier**, **squeakiest**) making a squeaking sound. □ **squeaky clean** *colloq*. **1** completely clean. **2** above criticism; beyond reproach. □□ **squeakily** *adv*. **squeakiness** *n*.

squeal *n*. a long shrill sound, esp. a cry of a child or a pig. •*v*. **1** make this cry or sound. **2** *colloq*. protest sharply. **3** *colloq*. become an informer.

squeamish *adj*. **1** easily nauseated; slightly sick. **2** easily shocked; prudish. **3** excessively scrupulous about principles. □ **squeamishly** *adv*. **squeamishness** *n*.

squeegee / skwee-jee / *n*. a tool with a rubber blade, used for sweeping or squeezing away water or moisture from windows etc.

squeeze *v*. **1** exert pressure on, esp. to extract moisture or juice; extract (moisture etc.) by squeezing. **2** force into or through (*we squeezed six people into the car; she squeezed through the gap*). **3** produce or obtain by pressure or compulsion (*squeeze a promise from them*). **4** extort money etc. from; harass in this way (*heavy taxation is squeezing small firms*). •*n*. **1** squeezing; being squeezed. **2** an affectionate clasp or hug. **3** a small amount of liquid produced by squeezing (*a squeeze of lemon juice*). **4** a crowd or crush (*we all got in, but it was a tight squeeze*). **5** hardship or difficulty caused by shortage of money or time etc. **6** restrictions on borrowing etc. during a financial crisis.

squeezer *n*. a device for squeezing juice from fruit.

squelch *v*. **1** make a sucking sound as of someone treading in thick mud; move with a squelching sound. **2** disconcert, silence (*she squelched him with a look*). **3** stamp on; crush flat; put an end to (*squelched a snail underfoot; squelched her hopes*). •*n*. an act of squelching; the sound of squelching.

squib *n*. **1** a small hissing firework that finally explodes. **2** *Aust*. a racehorse lacking stamina. **3** a spineless person, a coward. •*v*. *Aust*. **1** (often with *it* as object) evade (a difficulty or responsibility); shirk through fear or cowardice (*he squibbed the challenge; he should have taken tough action but he squibbed it*). **2** fail to act; back down; give in (*when the going got tough, he squibbed*). **3** (foll. by *on*) betray or let down (*he squibbed on his mates*). □ **damp squib** *see* DAMP.

squid *n*. (*pl*. **squid** or **squids**) a sea creature related to the cuttlefish, with ten arms round the mouth; used as food.

squidgy *adj*. *colloq*. squashy, soggy.

squiffy *adj*. *colloq*. slightly drunk.

squiggle *n.* a short curly line, esp. in handwriting. ☐ **squiggly** *adv.*

squillion *n. colloq.* **1** a large number of millions. **2** (**squillions**) a large amount of money.

squint *v.* **1** have an eye that is turned abnormally from the line of gaze of the other; be cross-eyed. **2** look at a thing with the eyes turned sideways or half shut, or through a narrow opening. •*n.* **1** a squinting position of the eyeballs. **2** a stealthy or sideways glance. **3** *colloq.* a look (*take a squint at this*). •*adj. colloq.* askew.

squire *n.* **1** *Brit.* a country gentleman, esp. the chief landowner in a district. **2** *hist.* a youth who, in training for knighthood, acts as an attendant to a knight. **5** *Aust.* a young snapper. •*v.* (of a man) escort or accompany (a woman).

squirm *v.* **1** wriggle or writhe. **2** feel embarrassment or uneasiness. •*n.* a squirming movement.

squirrel *n.* **1** a small, bushy-tailed, usu. tree-living animal of Europe, Asia, etc. **2** a person who hoards small objects. •*v.* (**squirrelled**, **squirrelling**) **1** (often foll. by *away*) put away in a hoard. **2** (often foll. by *around*) bustle about busily. ☐ **squirrel glider** a gliding possum of eastern mainland Australia. **squirrel grip** esp. *Aust. colloq.* the gripping and squeezing of another person's testicles (so called because a squirrel gathers 'nuts').

squirt *v.* **1** eject (liquid etc.) in a jet. **2** be ejected in this way. **3** splash with a squirted substance. •*n.* **1** a syringe. **2** a jet of liquid etc.; a small quantity squirted. **3** *colloq.* an unimportant but self-assertive person; a short person.

squish *n.* a slight squelching sound. •*v.* move with a squish. ☐ **squishy** *adj.*

squizz *Aust. colloq. n.* a look; an inspection (*take a squizz at this!; he's gone to have a squizz at the workmen*). •*v.* look (at); inspect.

Sr *symbol* strontium.

Sri Lanka a republic consisting of a large island (formerly called Ceylon) south of India. ☐ **Sri Lankan** *adj. & n.*

SS *abbr.* **1** Saints. **2** steamship. **3** *hist.* the Nazi special police force. (¶ German *Schutz-Staffel.*)

St *abbr.* **1** Saint. **2** Street.

stab *v.* (**stabbed**, **stabbing**) **1** pierce or wound with a pointed tool or weapon. **2** aim a blow with or as if with a pointed weapon. **3** cause a sensation of being stabbed (*a stabbing pain*). •*n.* **1** the act of stabbing; a blow, thrust, or wound made by stabbing. **2** a sensation of being stabbed (*she felt a stab of fear*). **3** *colloq.* an attempt (*go on—have a stab at it!*). ☐ **a stab in the dark** a guess; a gamble. **stab in the back** *n.* a treacherous or slanderous attack; *v.* betray. **stab kick** (also **stab pass**) *Aust. Rules* a fast, low kick to a team-mate.

stabilise / **stay**-buh-luyz / *v.* (also **-ize**) make or become stable. ☐ **stabilisation** *n.*

stabiliser *n.* (also **-izer**) **1** a device to prevent a ship from rolling or to aid in keeping a child's bicycle upright. **2** an arrangement for stabilising an amount, effect, etc. **3** a food additive for preserving texture.

stability / stuh-**bil**-uh-tee / *n.* being stable.

stable[1] *adj.* **1** firmly fixed or established; not readily changing or fluctuating; not easily destroyed or decomposed. **2** (of a person) not easily upset or disturbed. ☐ **stably** *adv.*

stable[2] *n.* **1** a building in which horses are kept. **2** an establishment for training racehorses; the horses from a particular establishment. **3** racing cars, products, or people originating from or working for the same establishment (*all these magazines come from the same stable*). •*v.* put or keep in a stable.

stabling *n.* accommodation for horses.

staccato / stuh-**kah**-toh / *adj. & adv.* (esp. in music) with each sound or note sharply detached or separated from the others; not running on smoothly.

stack *n.* **1** an orderly pile or heap. **2** a haystack. **3** *colloq.* a large quantity (*have stacks of work to do*). **4** a number of aircraft in a queue for landing. **5** a tall factory chimney; a chimney or funnel on a steamer etc. **6** the part of a library where books are compactly stored, esp. one to which the public does not have direct access. •*v.* **1** pile in a stack or stacks. **2** arrange (cards) secretly for cheating. **3** manipulate (circumstances etc.) to suit one; manipulate the proceedings of a meeting by ensuring the attendance of many of one's supporters. **4** instruct (aircraft) to fly round the same point at different altitudes while waiting to land. **5** *colloq.* crash (a motor vehicle). ☐ **stack it on** *colloq.* exaggerate (one's feelings etc.). **stack on** *colloq.* turn on; produce (*stacked on a bonzer party for her 21st*). **stacks on the mill** *colloq.* a situation (in Australian Rules, Rugby, children's games, etc.) where several players are piled up chaotically one on top of the other (with the ball at the very bottom of the pile).

stackhat *n. trademark* a safety helmet used by skateboarders, cyclists, etc.

stadium *n.* (*pl.* **stadiums** or **stadia**) a sports ground surrounded by tiers of seats for spectators.

staff *n.* **1** a stick or pole used as a weapon, support, symbol of authority, etc. **2** a body of officers assisting a commanding officer and concerned with an army, regiment, or fleet etc. as a whole. **3** the people employed in a particular business or organisation; those in authority in a school. **4** a stave in music. •*v.* provide (an institution etc.) with staff.

staffer *n.* a member of a staff, esp. of a newspaper.

staffroom *n.* a room for staff, esp. in a school.

stag *n.* **1** a fully-grown male deer. **2** *Aust.* a beast castrated after maturity when the sexual organs have fully grown; an inferior bullock. •*adj.* of or for males only (*stag party; stag turn*). ☐ **go stag** (of a man) attend a mixed party etc. unaccompanied by a woman. **stag party** (also **stag night**) a party for men only, held for a man who is

stage

about to marry. **stag turn** a stag party or other all-male event.

stage *n.* **1** a platform on which plays etc. are performed before an audience. **2** the theatrical profession. **3** a raised floor or platform, e.g. on scaffolding. **4** a point or period in the course or development of something (*the talks have reached a critical stage*). **5** a section of a space rocket with a separate engine, jettisoned when its fuel is exhausted. • *v.* **1** present (a play etc.) on the stage. **2** arrange and carry out (*decided to stage a sit-in*). ☐ **stage fright** nervousness on facing an audience. **stage-manage** *v.* organise things as or like a stage manager. **stage manager** the person responsible for the scenery and other practical arrangements in the production of a play. **stage whisper** a whisper that is meant to be overheard.

stagecoach *n. hist.* a large closed horse-drawn coach running on a regular route by stages.

stagey alternative spelling of STAGY.

stagflation *n.* a state of inflation without a corresponding increase in demand and employment.

stagger *v.* **1** move or go unsteadily, as if about to fall. **2** shock deeply; amaze (*we were staggered by the news*). **3** arrange (events, hours of work, etc.) so that they do not coincide. **4** place or organise in a zigzag or alternating arrangement. • *n.* **1** an unsteady tottering movement. **2** (**staggers**) **a** a disease, esp. of horses and cattle, causing staggering. **b** (usu. **the staggers**) giddiness. ☐ **stagger weed** *Aust.* a European annual herb, naturalised in temperate Australia, and noxious to stock.

staggering *adj.* bewildering, astonishing (*the total cost is staggering*). ☐ **staggering bob** *Aust. colloq.* **1** a newly-born calf. **2** veal.

staghorn *n.* an extremely large epiphytic fern of NSW, Qld, and elsewhere, having long, pendulous, much-divided leaves resembling the horns of a stag.

staging *n.* **1** the presentation of a play etc. **2** scaffolding; a temporary platform or support.

stagnant *adj.* **1** (of water) not flowing, still and stale. **2** showing no activity (*business was stagnant*). ☐ **stagnancy** *n.*

stagnate / stag-**nayt**, **stag**-nayt / *v.* **1** be stagnant. **2** (of a person) become dull through inactivity. ☐ **stagnation** *n.*

stagy **stay**-jee / *adj.* (also **stagey**) theatrical and exaggerated in style or manner.

staid / stayd / *adj.* steady and serious in manner, tastes, etc.; sedate.

stain *v.* **1** discolour or become discoloured by a substance. **2** spoil, damage (*it stained his good reputation*). **3** colour with a pigment that penetrates. • *n.* **1** a mark caused by staining. **2** a blemish (*without a stain on his character*). **3** a liquid used for staining things. ☐ **stained glass** pieces of glass, either dyed or superficially coloured, set in a framework (usually of lead) to form decorative or pictorial designs.

stainless *adj.* free from stains or blemishes. ☐ **stainless steel** steel containing chromium making it resistant to rust and tarnishing.

stair *n.* **1** each of a flight of fixed indoor steps. **2** (**stairs**) a set of these.

staircase *n.* a flight of stairs (often with banisters) and its supporting structure.

stairway *n.* a staircase.

stairwell *n.* a shaft or space for a staircase.

stake *n.* **1** a stick or post sharpened at one end for driving into the ground. **2** the post to which a person was bound for execution by being burnt alive. **3** money etc. wagered on the result of a race or other event. **4** something invested in an enterprise and giving a share or interest in it. **5** (**stakes**) (in horse races) money offered as a prize; the race itself. **6** (**stakes**) (with defining word) a particular business or way of life in which success is attained through competition (*beauty stakes; fashion stakes*). • *v.* **1** fasten, support, or mark with stakes. **2** wager or risk (money etc.) on an event. **3** *colloq.* give financial or other support to. ☐ **at stake** being risked, depending on the outcome of an event. **pull** (**up**) **stakes** depart; go to live elsewhere. **stake a claim** claim or obtain a right to something. **stake out** *colloq.* place under surveillance.

stakeholder *n.* **1** an independent party with whom each of those who make a wager deposits the money etc. wagered. **2** a person with an interest or concern in something, esp. a business.

stalactite / **stal**-uhk-tuyt / *n.* a deposit of calcium carbonate hanging like an icicle from the roof of a cave etc.

Stalag / **stal**-ag / *n. hist.* a German prison camp, esp. for non-commissioned officers and privates.

stalagmite / **stal**-uhg-muyt / *n.* a deposit like a stalactite but standing like a pillar on the floor of a cave etc.

stale *adj.* **1** lacking freshness; dry, musty. **2** uninteresting because not new (*stale jokes*). **3** having one's ability to perform spoilt by too much practice. • *v.* make or become stale. ☐ **stalely** *adv.* **staleness** *n.*

stalemate *n.* **1** a drawn position in chess, in which a player can make no move without putting the king in check. **2** a deadlock, a drawn contest. • *v.* bring to a position of stalemate or deadlock.

Stalin / **stah**-lin / , Joseph (original name: Joseph Dzhugashvili) (1879–1953), Russian dictator. (¶ His adopted name means 'man of steel'.)

Stalinism *n.* a rigid centralised authoritarian form of socialism associated with Stalin. ☐ **Stalinist** *n.* & *adj.*

stalk[1] / stawk / *n.* **1** the main stem of a plant. **2** a stem attaching a leaf, flower, or fruit to another stem. **3** a similar support of a part or organ in animals or of a device.

stalk² / stawk / v. **1** track or pursue (game or an enemy) stealthily. **2** stride or walk in a haughty manner. **3** move silently or threateningly through (a place) (*fear stalked the land*). **4** harass or persecute (a person) with unwanted and obsessive attention. ☐ **stalking horse 1** a horse used to conceal a hunter. **2** a person or thing used to conceal one's real intentions or actions. ☐☐ **stalker** n.

stall¹ n. **1** a booth or table in a market etc. displaying goods for sale. **2** a stable or shed; a compartment for one animal in this. **3** (**stalls**) the seats in a theatre nearest to the stage. **4** a compartment for one horse at the start of a race. **5** stalling of an engine or aircraft. •v. **1** (of an engine) stop suddenly because of an overload or insufficient fuel. **2** (of an aircraft) begin to drop because the speed is too low for the plane to respond to its controls. **3** cause (an engine or aircraft) to stall.

stall² v. use delaying tactics in order to gain time; stave off (a person or request) in this way.

stallion / stal-yuhn / n. an uncastrated male horse, esp. one kept for breeding.

stalwart / stawl-wuht / adj. **1** sturdy. **2** courageous, resolute, reliable (*stalwart supporters of the Geelong footy team*). •n. a stalwart person, esp. a loyal comrade.

stamen / stay-muhn / n. the male fertilising organ of flowering plants, bearing pollen.

stamina / stam-uh-nuh / n. staying power, ability to withstand prolonged physical or mental strain.

stammer v. **1** speak haltingly, esp. with involuntary pauses or rapid repetitions of the same syllable, often because of a speech impairment. **2** (often foll. by *out*) utter (words) in this way through fear etc. (*stammered out his excuse to the headmaster*). •n. stammering speech; a tendency to stammer. ☐ **stammerer** n.

stamp v. **1** bring one's foot down heavily on the ground. **2** walk with loud heavy steps. **3** strike or press with a device that leaves a mark or pattern etc.; cut or shape in this way. **4** fix a postage or other stamp to. **5** give a certain character to (*this achievement stamps him as a genius*). •n. **1** the act or sound of stamping. **2** an instrument for stamping a pattern or mark; the mark itself. **3** a piece of paper for affixing to an envelope or document to indicate that postage or duty has been paid. **4** a distinguishing mark, a clear indication (*the story bears the stamp of truth*). ☐ **stamp duty** a duty imposed on certain legal documents. **stamping ground** *colloq.* a person's or animal's usual haunt. **stamp on** crush by stamping; quell. **stamp out** extinguish by stamping; suppress (a rebellion etc.) by force.

stampede n. **1** a sudden rush of a herd of frightened animals. **2** a rush of people under a sudden common impulse. •v. take part or cause to take part in a stampede; cause to act hurriedly.

stance n. **1** the position in which a person or animal stands; a player's attitude for making a stroke. **2** a standpoint; an attitude of mind (*has taken a hostile stance towards the proposal*).

stanch v. (also **staunch**) restrain the flow of (blood etc.) or the flow from (a wound).

stanchion / stahn-shuhn, stan-chuhn / n. an upright bar or post forming a support.

stand v. (**stood, standing**) **1** have, take, or keep an upright position, esp. on the feet or on a base. **2** be of a specified height (*stands 175 cm tall*). **3** be situated (*a village once stood here*). **4** place; set upright (*stand it against the wall*). **5** remain firm or valid or in a specified condition (*the offer still stands; the thermometer stood at 36°*). **6** take a specified attitude (*he stood aloof*). **7** act in a specified capacity (*stood proxy*). **8** remain stationary or unused. **9** offer oneself for election (*she stood for parliament*). **10** undergo (*he stood trial for murder*). **11** steer a specified course in sailing. **12** put up with, endure (*I can't stand that noise*). **13** provide at one's own expense (*stood him a drink*). •n. **1** a stationary condition. **2** a position taken up (*took his stand near the door; his stand on the monarchy is ultra-conservative*). **3** resistance to attack, the period of this (*made a stand*). **4** a halt to give a performance (*the band did a one-night stand*). **5** a rack or pedestal etc. on which something may be placed. **6** a raised structure with seats at a sports ground etc. **7** a table, booth, or other (often temporary) structure where things are exhibited or sold. **8** a standing place for vehicles (*taxi stand*). **9** a witness box. **10** a group of growing plants (*a stand of trees*). ☐ **stand by 1** look on without interfering. **2** support or side with (a person) in a difficulty or dispute. **3** stand ready for action. **4** keep to (a promise or agreement). **stand down 1** withdraw from a position or candidacy. **2** terminate (a person's employment), esp. as a result of the effects of a strike. **stand for 1** represent (*'ALP' stands for 'Australian Labor Party'*). **2** *colloq.* tolerate. **stand in** deputise. **stand-in** n. a person who takes the place of another; a substitute or deputy. **stand off 1** remain at a distance. **2** lay off (employees) temporarily. **stand-off** adj. (of a missile) launched by an aircraft but having a long range and its own guidance system. n. a deadlock or stalemate in negotiations etc. **stand-off half** *Rugby* a player who forms a link between the scrum-half and the three-quarters. **stand on** insist on formal observance of (*stand on ceremony*). **stand out 1** be prominent or outstanding. **2** (foll. by *for*) persist in opposition or in one's demands (*they stood out for a ten per cent rise*). **3** (foll. by any of various similes) be conspicuous (*it stands out like a sore thumb*). **stand over 1** stand close to (a person) to watch, control, intimidate, etc. **2** *Aust.* intimidate or threaten; extort money (from someone). **stand to 1** stand ready for action. **2** abide by. **3** be likely

standard | **starfish**

or certain to. **stand up 1** be valid (*that argument won't stand up*). **2** *colloq.* fail to keep an appointment with (*he stood me up*). **stand-up** *adj.* (of a collar) not turned down; (of a fight) vigorous, actual; (of a meal) eaten while standing; (of a comedian) telling jokes to an audience. **stand up to** resist courageously; remain durable in (hard use or wear).

standard *n.* **1** a thing, quality, or specification by which something may be tested or measured. **2** the required level of quality (*rejected as being below standard*). **3** the average quality (*the standard of her work is high*). **4** a distinctive flag. **5** an upright support or pipe. **6** a shrub that has been grafted on a tall upright stem (*a standard rose*). **7** a tune or song of established popularity. • *adj.* **1** serving as or conforming to a standard (*standard measures of length*). **2** of average or usual quality, not of special design etc. (*the standard model of this car*). **3** of recognised merit or authority (*the standard book on spiders*). **4** (of language) of the type used by educated speakers; regarded as correct. ☐ **standard bearer 1** a soldier who carries a standard. **2** a prominent leader in a cause. **standard deviation** *Statistics* a quantity calculated to indicate the extent of deviation for a group as a whole. **standard lamp** a household lamp set on a tall pillar on a base. **standard of living** the level of material comfort enjoyed by a person or group. **standard time** uniform time for places in approximately the same longitude, established in a country or region by law or custom.

standardise *v.* (also **-ize**) cause to conform to a standard. ☐ **standardisation** *n.*

standby *n.* (*pl.* **standbys**) **1** (often *attrib.*) a person or thing ready if needed in an emergency etc. **2** readiness for duty (*on standby*). **3** the state of waiting to secure an unreserved place for a journey or performance, allocated on the basis of earliest availability.

standing *adj.* **1** upright. **2** (of a jump) performed without a run. **3** permanent, remaining effective or valid (*a standing invitation*). **4** (of water) stagnant. • *n.* **1** status (*people of high standing*). **2** past duration (*a friendship of long standing*). ☐ **standing committee** a committee (of a parliament, a university, etc.) which is appointed to deal with a particular issue or area of responsibility, and which is permanent for the duration of the appointing body. **standing joke** an object of permanent ridicule. **standing order** an instruction to a banker to make regular payments, or to a newsagent etc. for a regular supply of a periodical etc. **standing orders** rules governing the procedures of a committee, parliament, etc. **standing ovation** a rousing ovation conferred by an audience risen from their seats.

standoffish *adj.* cold, aloof, distant in manner.

standover *n.* (also **standover merchant**) *Aust.* a person who engages in intimidatory tactics.

standpoint *n.* a point of view.

standstill *n.* a stoppage, inability to proceed.

Stanislavsky, Konstantin (1863–1938), Russian director, actor, and teacher of acting. ☐ **Stanislavski method** *see* METHOD.

stank *see* STINK.

stannary *n.* a tin-mine.

stanza *n.* a verse of poetry.

staphylococcus / staf-uh-luh-**kok**-uhs / *n.* (*pl.* **staphylococci** / -**kok**-uy /) a bacterium occurring in grape-like clusters, and sometimes causing pus formation usu. in the skin and mucous membranes. ☐ **staphylococcal** *adj.*

staple[1] *n.* **1** a U-shaped piece of metal or wire for holding something in place. **2** a piece of wire driven into papers to fasten them. • *v.* secure with a staple or staples. ☐ **stapler** *n.*

staple[2] *adj.* principal, standard (*rice is their staple food*). • *n.* **1** a principal or important article of commerce (*the staples of Australian industry*). **2** the chief element or main component (e.g. of a diet). **3** the fibre of cotton or wool etc. with regard to its quality (*cotton of fine staple*).

star *n.* **1** a celestial body appearing as a point of light in the night sky. **2** (in astronomy) any large light-emitting gaseous ball, such as the sun. **3** a celestial body regarded as influencing a person's fortunes (*thank your lucky stars*). **4** a figure, object, or ornament with rays or radiating points; an asterisk; a star-shaped mark indicating a category of excellence (*a five-star motel*). **5** a brilliant person; a famous or principal performer. • *adj.* outstanding (*he's my star pupil*). • *v.* (**starred**, **starring**) **1** put an asterisk or star symbol beside (a name or item). **2** present or perform as a star actor. ☐ **star anise** a star-shaped seed pod with an aniseed flavour, used in Asian cooking. **star-studded** featuring many famous performers. **star turn** the principal item in an entertainment.

starboard / **stah**-buhd / *n.* the right-hand side (when facing forward) of a ship or aircraft. • *v.* turn this way.

starch *n.* **1** a white carbohydrate that is an important element in human food. **2** a preparation for stiffening fabrics. **3** stiffness of manner. • *v.* stiffen with starch.

starchy *adj.* (**starchier**, **starchiest**) **1** of or like starch. **2** containing much starch. **3** stiff and formal in manner. ☐ **starchiness** *n.*

stardom *n.* being a star actor or performer.

stare *v.* **1** gaze fixedly with the eyes wide open. **2** (of the eyes) be wide open with a fixed gaze. **3** reduce (a person) to a specified condition by staring (*stared me into silence*). • *n.* a staring gaze. ☐ **stare a person in the face** be glaringly obvious or clearly imminent (*ruin stared him in the face*).

starfish *n.* a star-shaped sea creature.

stark *adj.* **1** desolate; bare; cheerless (*stark prison conditions*). **2** sharply evident (*in stark contrast*). **3** absolute (*stark lunacy*). • *adv.* completely, wholly (*stark naked*). ☐ **starkly** *adv.* **starkness** *n.*

starkers *adj. colloq.* **1** stark naked. **2** mad, insane.

starlet *n.* a promising young performer, esp. a woman.

starlight *n.* light from the stars.

starling *n.* **1** a gregarious bird with blackish speckled lustrous plumage, introduced into, and now common in, eastern Australia. **2** = METALLIC STARLING (*see* METALLIC).

starlit *adj.* lit by starlight.

Star of David the six-pointed star used as a Jewish and Israeli symbol.

starry *adj.* (**starrier, starriest**) **1** set with stars. **2** shining like stars. ☐ **starry-eyed** romantically enthusiastic; enthusiastic but impractical; euphoric.

Stars and Stripes the national flag of the USA.

start *v.* **1** begin or cause to begin; (of an engine) begin running. **2** set in motion or action (*he started a bushfire*). **3** cause or enable (a person) to make a beginning (*started me in business*). **4** (foll. by *present participle*) provoke (a person) into (*he started me crying*). **5** begin a journey. **6** make a sudden movement from pain, surprise etc. **7** spring suddenly (*started from his seat*). **8** (of timber) spring from its proper position. • *n.* **1** the beginning of a journey, activity, or race; the place where a race starts. **2** an opportunity for or assistance in starting; an advantage gained or allowed in starting; the amount of this (*I'll give you a 10-second start*). **3** a sudden movement of surprise or pain etc. ☐ **starting block** a shaped block for a runner's feet at the start of a race. **starting price** the final odds on a horse etc. at the start of a race. **start out** begin, begin a journey; intend when starting (*started out to write a short story but turned it into a novel instead*).

starter *n.* **1** a person or thing that starts something. **2** a horse or competitor at the start of a race (*list of probable starters*). **3** the first course of a meal. ☐ **for starters** *colloq.* to start with.

startle *v.* surprise or alarm.

startling *adj.* **1** surprising. **2** alarming (*startling news*).

starve *v.* **1** die or suffer acutely from lack of food; cause to do this. **2** suffer or cause to suffer for lack of something (*was starved of affection*). **3** *colloq.* feel very hungry. ☐ **starve the bardies!** (*or* **crows!** *or* **lizards!** *or* **roan bullock!** etc.) *Aust. colloq.* an exclamation of exasperation, astonishment, etc. (more often to be met with now in caricatures of Australian speech than in Australian speech itself). ☐ **starvation** *n.*

starveling / **stahv**-ling / *n.* a starving or ill-fed person or animal.

Star Wars *colloq.* the US Strategic Defense Initiative (*see* STRATEGIC).

stash *colloq. v.* (often foll. by *away*) hide away; hoard. • *n.* a hiding place; a hidden store of things.

stasis / **stay**-suhs / *n.* (*pl.* **stases** / **stay**-seez /) **1** inactivity, stagnation. **2** a state of equilibrium. **3** stoppage of circulation.

state *n.* **1** the existing condition or position of a person or thing (*his health is in a precarious state*; *in a bad state of repair*). **2** an excited or agitated condition of mind (*he got into a state*). **3** an untidy condition (*what a state this room is in!*). **4** a grand imposing style (*arrived in state*). **5** (often **State**) a political community under one government (*the State of Israel*) or forming part of a federal republic (*States of the USA*) or forming part of a federal union (*the States of the Commonwealth of Australia*). **6** civil government (*matters of state*). • *adj.* **1** of, for, or run by the State. **2** involving ceremony, used or done on ceremonial occasions (*a State banquet*). • *v.* **1** express in spoken or written words. **2** fix or specify (*must be inspected at stated intervals*). ☐ **lie in state** *see* LIE². **State aid** *Aust.* financial assistance from the government of an Australian State, esp. as given to private schools. **state of emergency** a national situation of danger or disaster, with normal constitutional procedures suspended. **state of play** (*or* **affairs** *or* **things**) present circumstances; the current situation. **state of the art** the current stage of esp. technological development. **state-of-the-art** *adj.* absolutely up-to-date (*state-of-the-art weaponry*). **State rights** administrative and legislative responsibilities reserved to an Australian State. **state school** *Aust.* a school largely managed and funded by the public authorities. **the States** the USA.

stateless *adj.* (of a person) not a citizen or subject of any country.

stately *adj.* (**statelier, stateliest**) dignified, imposing, grand. ☐ **stateliness** *n.*

statement *n.* **1** stating. **2** something stated. **3** a formal account of facts; a written report of a financial account.

State of Origin a term applied to annual interstate Rugby League and Australian Rules football games where the members of each team have been born in the State they represent. State of Origin matches developed in both codes in the 1980s.

stateroom *n.* **1** a state apartment. **2** a passenger's private compartment on a ship.

statesperson *n.* a statesman or a stateswoman.

statesman *n.* (feminine **stateswoman**) a distinguished and extremely capable politician or diplomat. ☐ **statesmanlike** *adj.* **statesmanship** *n.*

static *adj.* **1** (of force) acting by weight without motion (as opposed to *dynamic*). **2** not moving, stationary. **3** not changing. • *n.* **1** atmospherics. **2** (in full **static electricity**) electricity present in a body and not flowing as current. **3** (**statics**) (usu.

treated as *sing.*) a branch of physics that deals with bodies at rest or forces in equilibrium.

station *n.* **1** a place where a person or thing stands or is stationed. **2** an establishment or building where a public service is based or which is equipped for certain activities (*the fire station; an agricultural research station*). **3** a military or naval base; its inhabitants. **4** a broadcasting establishment with its own frequency. **5** a stopping place on a railway with buildings. **6** position in life, status (*she had ideas above her station*). **7** *Aust.* **a** an extensive sheep or cattle raising establishment. **b** a large tract of grazing land. **c** = HOME STATION (*see* HOME). **8** *Aust. hist.* **a** an outpost of colonial government, esp. as established for the employment of convict labour on public works (*convict station*; *penal station*). **b** a reserve for Aborigines, esp. as established by a religious mission or a government agency. •*adj.* of or pertaining to a sheep or cattle station (*station boss; station hand*). •*v.* put at or in a certain place for a purpose (*the regiment was stationed in Darwin*). ☐ **station wagon** *US* & *Aust.* a car with passenger area extended, with space for luggage behind the back seat (which can be lowered to make extra luggage space), and with a rear door.

stationary *adj.* **1** not moving; not movable. **2** not changing in condition or quantity etc.

■ **Usage** Do not confuse with *stationery*.

stationer *n.* one who sells writing materials (paper, pens, ink, etc.).

stationery *n.* writing paper, envelopes, and other articles sold by a stationer.

■ **Usage** Do not confuse with *stationary*.

stationmaster *n.* an official in charge of a railway station.

Stations of the Cross a series of locations on Christ's traditional route in Jerusalem from Pilate's house to Calvary, followed by pilgrims; a series of 14 paintings or sculptures, distributed round the interior of a Catholic church and representing events in Christ's Passion, before each of which prayers are said, esp. in Lent.

statistic / stuh-**tis**-tik / *n.* **1** an item of information expressed in numbers. **2** (**statistics**) the science of collecting, classifying, and interpreting information based on the numbers of things. ☐ **statistical** *adj.* **statistically** *adv.*

statistician / stat-uhs-**tish**-uhn / *n.* an expert in statistics.

statuary / **sta**-choor-ree / *n.* statues collectively.

statue *n.* a sculptured, cast, or moulded figure of a person or animal.

statuesque / sta-choo-**esk** / *adj.* like a statue in size or dignity or stillness.

stature / **sta**-chuh / *n.* **1** the natural height of the body. **2** greatness gained by ability or achievement.

status / **stay**-tuhs / *n.* (*pl.* **statuses**) **1** a person's position or rank in relation to others; a person's or thing's legal position. **2** high rank or prestige. ☐ **status symbol** a possession or activity etc. regarded as evidence of a person's high status.

status quo / stay-tuhs **kwoh** / *n.* the existing state of affairs (*maintain the status quo*). (¶ Latin, = the state in which.)

statute / **sta**-choot, **stat**-yoot / *n.* **1** a law passed by Parliament or a similar body. **2** one of the rules of an institution (*the University Statutes*).

statutory *adj.* fixed, done, or required by statute. ☐ **statutory authority** *Aust.* an organisation established by parliament, having specially defined powers, considerable independence, and direct responsibility to parliament. **statutory declaration** a written and signed declaration witnessed by a justice of the peace etc., stating e.g. that an item has been lost or damaged, a document has been read, etc. ☐ ☐ **statutorily** *adv.*

staunch[1] *adj.* firm in attitude, opinion, or loyalty. ☐ **staunchly** *adv.*

staunch[2] alternative spelling of STANCH.

stave *n.* **1** one of the curved strips of wood forming the side of a cask or tub. **2** (also **staff**) a set of five parallel horizontal lines on which music is written. •*v.* (**stove** *or* **staved, staving**) dent or break a hole in (*stove it in*). ☐ **stave off** ward off permanently or temporarily (*we staved off disaster*).

Stawell Gift / stawl / a professional handicap footrace run over 120 metres and held annually in the town of Stawell, Vic. It began in 1878 and is claimed to be the oldest event of its kind in the world.

stay[1] *n.* **1** a rope or wire supporting or bracing a mast, spar, pole, etc. **2** any prop or support.

stay[2] *v.* **1** continue to be in the same place or state (*stay here; stay awake; stay away*). **2** remain or dwell temporarily, esp. as a guest or visitor. **3** satisfy temporarily (*we stayed our hunger with a sandwich*). **4** postpone (*stay judgment*). **5** pause in movement, action, or speech. **6** show endurance, e.g. in a race or task (*stay the course*). •*n.* **1** a period of temporary dwelling or visiting (*made a short stay in Athens*). **2** a postponement, e.g. of carrying out a judgment (*was granted a stay of execution*). ☐ **staying power** endurance. **stay put** *colloq.* remain where it is placed; remain where one is.

stayer *n.* a person or animal with great staying power.

stays *n.pl. archaic* a corset.

STD *abbr.* **1** subscriber trunk dialling. **2** sexually transmitted disease.

Stead, Christina (Ellen) (1902–83), Australian novelist, best known for *The Man Who Loved Children* (1940).

stead / sted / *n.* ☐ **in a person's** (*or* **thing's**) **stead** instead of this person or thing. **stand a**

person in good stead be of great advantage or service to him or her.

steadfast / **sted**-fahst / *adj.* firm and not changing or yielding (*a steadfast refusal*). □ **steadfastly** *adv.* **steadfastness** *n.*

steady *adj.* (**steadier, steadiest**) **1** firmly supported or balanced. **2** uniform and regular (*a steady pace*). **3** behaving in a serious and dependable manner, not frivolous or excitable. • *n. colloq.* a regular boyfriend or girlfriend. • *adv.* steadily. • *v.* (**steadied, steadying**) make or become steady. □ **go steady** *colloq.* go out with a person as a regular boyfriend or girlfriend. **steady on!** slow!; stop! □□ **steadily** *adv.* **steadiness** *n.*

steak *n.* **1** a thick slice of meat or fish, cut for grilling or frying etc. **2** beef from the front of an animal, cut for stewing or braising. □ **steak tartare** a dish consisting of raw minced beefsteak mixed with raw egg, onion, and seasonings and shaped into small cakes or patties.

steal *v.* (**stole, stolen, stealing**) **1** take another person's property without right or permission (*stole my car; stole my ideas*). **2** obtain by surprise or a trick or surreptitiously (*stole a kiss; stole a look at her*). **3** move secretly or without being noticed (*stole out of the room*). **4** gain insidiously or artfully (*stole the lead from their business rivals by using slick advertising*). • *n. colloq.* an easy task or a good bargain. □ **steal a march on** gain an advantage over (a person). **steal the show** outshine other performers.

stealth / stelth / *n.* secrecy; a secret procedure. □ **Stealth bomber** a US airplane which because of its shape and angles is difficult to be detected by enemy radar or other sensing devices.

stealthy / **stel**-thee / *adj.* (**stealthier, stealthiest**) acting or done in a quiet, secret, or furtive way. □ **stealthily** *adv.* **stealthiness** *n.*

steam *n.* **1** invisible gas into which water is changed by boiling, used as motive power. **2** the mist that forms when steam condenses in the air. **3** energy or power (*run out of steam*). • *v.* **1** give out steam or vapour. **2** cook or treat by steam. **3** move by the power of steam (*the ship steamed down the river*). **4** (foll. by *ahead, away,* etc.) *colloq.* travel fast or with vigour, outdistance. **5** (usu. foll. by *up*) cover or be covered with condensed steam (*the windows are all steamed up*). • *adj.* **1** powered by steam (*steam engine; steam hammer*). **2** emitting steam (*steam iron*). □ **steamed up** *colloq.* excited or angry.

steamboat *n.* a steam-driven boat, esp. a paddle-wheel craft.

steamer *n.* **1** a steamboat. **2** a container in which things are cooked or treated by steam.

steamroller *n.* **1** a heavy slow-moving engine with a large roller, used in road-making. **2** a crushing power or force. • *v.* (also **steamroll**) **1** crush or break down (opposition etc.) as with a steamroller; ride roughshod over; overwhelm. **2** (foll. by *through*) force (a measure etc.) through a legislature etc. by forcibly overriding all opposition. **3** (foll. by *into*) force (a person) into a course of action, a situation, etc.

steamship *n.* a steam-driven ship.

steamy *adj.* (**steamier, steamiest**) **1** like steam; full of steam. **2** *colloq.* erotic; sexually explicit. □ **steaminess** *n.*

steatite / **stee**-uh-tuyt / *n.* a greyish talc that feels smooth and soapy.

steed *n. poetic* a horse.

steel *n.* **1** a very strong alloy of iron and carbon. **2** a tapered steel rod for sharpening knives. • *v.* make hard or resolute (*steel oneself; steel one's heart*). □ **steel wool** a mass of fine steel shavings used as an abrasive.

steelworks *n.pl.* (usu. treated as sing.) a factory producing steel. □ **steelworker** *n.*

steely *adj.* (**steelier, steeliest**) like steel in colour or hardness; severe, determined; cold, ruthless. □ **steeliness** *n.*

steelyard *n.* a weighing apparatus with a graduated arm along which a weight slides.

steep[1] *v.* **1** soak or be soaked in liquid. **2** permeate thoroughly (*the story is steeped in mystery*). **3** make deeply acquainted with (a subject etc.) (*she is steeped in Australian literature*).

steep[2] *adj.* **1** sloping sharply. **2** (of a rise or fall) rapid (*a steep drop in prices*). **3** *colloq.* **a** (of a price, demand, etc.) exorbitant, unreasonable (*that's a bit steep!*). **b** (of a story etc.) exaggerated; incredible. • *n.* a steep slope or precipice. □ **steeply** *adv.* **steepness** *n.*

steepen *v.* make or become steeper.

steeple *n.* a tall tower with a spire on top, rising above the roof of a church.

steeplechase *n.* **1** a horse race across country or on a course with hedges and ditches to jump. **2** a footrace with similar obstacles, either cross-country or on an athletics track. • *v.* take part in a steeplechase. □ **steeplechaser** *n.* **steeplechasing** *n.*

steeplejack *n.* a person who climbs tall chimneys, steeples, etc. to do repairs etc.

steer[1] *v.* **1** direct or guide (one's course, other people, a conversation, etc.) in a specified direction. **2** guide (a vehicle or boat etc.) with its wheel, rudder, etc. □ **steer clear of** take care to avoid.

steer[2] *n.* a bullock.

steerage *n.* **1** steering. **2** *archaic* the cheapest passenger accommodation in a ship, situated below decks.

steering *n.* the mechanism by which a vehicle or boat etc. is steered. □ **steering committee** a committee deciding the order of business, the general course of operations, etc.

stegosaurus / steg-uh-**saw**-ruhs / *n.* (*pl.* **stegosauruses**) a plant-eating dinosaur with a double row of pointed bony plates along its back.

stein / stuyn / *n.* a large earthenware mug, esp. for beer. (¶ German)

stela / stee-luh / n. (pl. **stelae**) (also **stele** / steelee or steel /) Archaeol. an upright slab or pillar, usu. shaped and inscribed, as a gravestone or memorial.

stellar adj. of a star or stars.

stem n. **1** the main central part (usu. above the ground) of a tree, shrub, or plant. **2** a slender part supporting a fruit, flower, or leaf. **3** any slender upright part, e.g. that of a wineglass between bowl and foot. **4** the main part of a noun or verb, from which other parts or words are made e.g. by altering the endings. **5** the curved piece at the fore end of a ship; a ship's bows. • v. (**stemmed**, **stemming**) stop the flow of; check. ☐ **stem from** arise from, have as its source.

stench n. a foul smell.

stencil n. **1** a sheet of metal or card etc. with a design cut out, which can be painted or inked over to produce a design on the surface below. **2** a waxed sheet from which a stencil is made by a typewriter. **3** the decoration or lettering etc. produced by a stencil. • v. (**stencilled**, **stencilling**) produce or ornament by means of a stencil. ☐ **stencil art** Aust. a form of ancient Aboriginal art on rock, depicting patterns of hands, human figures, animals, etc., and created by holding the object to be depicted against a rock surface and spraying mouthfuls of liquid pigment around the object, so creating a negative image.

stenographer / stuh-**nog**-ruh-fuh / n. a person who can write shorthand.

stenography / stuh-**nog**-ruh-fee / n. shorthand.

stentorian / sten-**taw**-ree-uhn / adj. (of a voice) extremely loud. (¶ Stentor, the name of a herald in Homer's Iliad.)

step v. (**stepped**, **stepping**) **1** lift and set down the foot as in walking. **2** move a short distance in this way. **3** (often foll. by into) achieve something easily (step into the job). • n. **1** a complete movement of one foot in stepping. **2** the distance covered by this. **3** a short distance. **4** a series of steps forming a pattern in dancing. **5** the sound of a step (I recognised your step). **6** each of a series of things done in some process. **7** a level surface for placing the foot on in climbing up or down. **8** (**steps**) a stepladder. ☐ **in step 1** stepping in time with other people in marching or dancing. **2** conforming to what others are doing. **out of step** not in step. **step in** intervene. **step on it** colloq. hurry. **step out** walk briskly, stride. **step up** increase. **watch your step** be careful.

step- comb. form related by remarriage of one parent. ☐ **stepchild**, **stepdaughter**, **stepson** the child of one's wife or husband, by an earlier marriage. **stepbrother**, **stepsister** the child of one's stepfather or stepmother. **stepfather**, **stepmother**, **step-parent** the husband or wife of one's parent, by a later marriage.

Stephen, St (d. c.AD 35), the first Christian martyr.

stepladder n. a short folding ladder with flat steps.

steppe / step / n. a huge grassy plain with few trees, in Russia and elsewhere.

stepping stone n. **1** a raised stone providing a place to step on in crossing a stream etc. **2** a means or stage of progress towards achieving something.

stereo / **ste**-ree-oh, **steer**-ree-oh / n. (pl. **stereos**) **1** stereophonic sound or recording. **2** a stereophonic hi-fi system. **3** a stereoscope. • adj. **1** = STEREOPHONIC. **2** = STEREOSCOPIC.

stereophonic / ste-ree-uh-**fon**-ik, steer- / adj. (of sound reproduction) using two transmission channels to give the effect of naturally-distributed sound. ☐ **stereophonically** adv. **stereophony** / -**of**-uh-nee / n.

stereoscope / **ste**-ree-uh-skohp, **steer**- / n. a device for giving a stereoscopic effect.

stereoscopic / ste-ree-uh-**skop**-ik, steer- / adj. giving a three-dimensional effect, e.g. in photographs. ☐ **stereoscopically** adv.

stereotype / **ste**-ree-uh-tuyp, **steer**- / n. **1** a person or thing regarded as a conventional type rather than an individual; a preconceived and over-simplified idea of the characteristics which typify a person, situation, etc. (the common stereotype of the young Australian male as a bronzed, well-muscled surfie). **2** a printing plate cast from a mould. • v. standardise as a stereotype.

sterile / **ste**-ruyl / adj. **1** unable to produce fruit or young; barren. **2** free from living microorganisms; absolutely clean (a sterile needle). **3** unproductive (a sterile discussion). ☐ **sterility** / stuh-**ril**-uh-tee / n.

sterilise / **ste**-ruh-luyz / v. (also -**ize**) **1** make sterile or free from micro-organisms. **2** make unable to produce offspring, esp. by removal or obstruction of reproductive organs. ☐ **sterilisation** n.

sterling n. **1** British money. **2** Aust. hist. a non-convict, British-born resident of Australia (as opposed to CURRENCY). • adj. **1** (of precious metal) genuine, of standard purity. **2** excellent, of solid worth (her sterling qualities). **3** Aust. hist. of or pertaining to non-convict, British-born residents of Australia (as distinct from CURRENCY) (the currency lads despised the new-chum sterling class). ☐ **sterling silver** silver of 92.25% purity.

stern[1] adj. strict and severe, not lenient or cheerful or kindly. ☐ **sternly** adv. **sternness** n.

stern[2] n. the rear end of a boat or ship.

sternum n. (pl. **sterna** or **sternums**) the breastbone.

steroid / **ste**-roid, **steer**- / n. **1** any of a group of organic compounds that includes certain hormones and other bodily secretions. **2** this used (often illegally) as a performance-enhancing drug by athletes etc.

sterol / **ste**-rol / n. a naturally occurring steroid alcohol.

stertorous / **ster**-tuh-ruhs / *adj.* making a snoring or rasping sound.

stet *v.* (placed beside a word that has been crossed out or altered by mistake) ignore the alteration. (¶ Latin, = let it stand.)

stethoscope / **steth**-uh-skohp / *n.* an instrument for listening to sounds within the body, e.g. breathing and heartbeats.

stetson *n.* an American cowboy hat with a very wide brim and a high crown.

stevedore / **stee**-vuh-daw / *n.* a person employed in loading and unloading ships.

Stevenson, Robert Louis (1850–94), Scottish-born writer, whose novels include *Treasure Island* and *Kidnapped*.

stew *v.* **1** cook by simmering for a long time in a closed vessel. **2** fret; be anxious. **3** *colloq.* swelter. **4** (as **stewed** *adj.*) *colloq.* drunk. • *n.* a dish (esp. of meat) made by stewing. ☐ **in a stew** *colloq.* in a state of great agitation.

steward *n.* **1** one whose job is to arrange for the supply of food to a club etc. **2** a passengers' attendant and waiter on a ship, aircraft, or train. **3** any of the officials managing a race meeting or show etc.

stewardess *n.* a woman attendant and waitress on a ship or aircraft.

stick[1] *n.* **1** a short relatively slender piece of wood. **2** a walking stick. **3** the implement used to hit the ball in hockey, polo, etc. **4** a gear lever. **5** punishment by caning or beating. **6** a slender more or less cylindrical piece of a substance, e.g. sealing wax, rhubarb, dynamite. **7** *colloq.* adverse criticism (*can't take a bit of stick*). **8** *colloq.* a person (*he's not a bad old stick*). ☐ **cop some stick** *colloq.* receive much adverse criticism. **stick insect** an insect with a twiglike body. **stick-nest rat** an Australian rodent (esp. on Franklin Island, SA) which builds a dwelling of sticks containing a soft nest or burrow. **the sticks** *Aust.* **1** remote rural areas; the Australian outback. **2** *Aust. Rules* the goalposts.

stick[2] *v.* (**stuck, sticking**) **1** thrust (a thing or its point) into something; stab (*stuck a finger in my eye; stuck him with a stiletto*). **2** thrust, put forward, protrude (the head, hand, etc.) in, into, over, out, etc. (*his foot was stuck in the hole; stuck her head out of the window and yelled*). **3** fix or be fixed by means of a pointed object (or as if by such) (*stick the skewer through the cubes of meat; we're stuck on the horns of a dilemma*). **4** *colloq.* put (*stick the parcel on the table*). **5** fix or be fixed by glue or suction etc. or as if by these (*stick a label on it; the scene stuck in my memory for weeks*). **6** fix or be fixed in one place and unable to move (*the car is stuck in the mud; the words stuck in her throat; the drawer is stuck*). **7** *colloq.* remain in the same place (*they stuck indoors all day*). **8** *colloq.* (of an accusation) be established as valid (*we couldn't make the charges stick*). **9** *colloq.* endure, tolerate (*couldn't stick his whingeing any longer*). **10** *colloq.* impose a difficult or unpleasant task upon (*we were stuck with the job of clearing up*). ☐ **be stuck for** be at a loss for or in need of. **be stuck on** *colloq.* be infatuated with. **be stuck with** *colloq.* be unable to get rid of. **get stuck into** *colloq.* **1** lay into; make a physical assault on (a person). **2** make a verbal assault on (a person); vehemently scold or criticise. **3** attack (a task, a meal, etc.) with gusto. **stick at nothing** be absolutely ruthless. **sticking plaster** a strip of adhesive material for covering small wounds. **stick-in-the-mud** an old-fashioned or unadventurous person. **stick it!** *coarse colloq.* an expression of contemptuous rejection. **stick it out** endure in spite of difficulty or unpleasantness. **stick one's neck out** be rashly bold. **stick out 1** (cause to) protrude. **2** (foll. by any of various similes etc.) be conspicuous (*sticks out like udders on a bull*). **stick out for** persist in one's demands (*stick out for a pay rise*). **stick to** remain faithful to (a friend or promise etc.); abide by and not alter (*he stuck to his story*). **stick to one's guns** *see* GUN. **stick up** *v. Aust. hist.* (of an armed Australian bushranger) stop by force and rob (a person or persons) on the road; rob (a building, coach, etc.) under threat of violence (*see also* BAIL[2]) (*a bushranger stuck up the gold escort*). **stick-up** *n. colloq.* a robbery using a gun. **stick up for** defend, stand up for. **stick up to** be assertive in the face of; offer resistance to.

sticker *n.* **1** an adhesive label or sign. **2** a person who persists in his or her efforts.

stickler *n.* a person who insists on something (*a stickler for punctuality*).

sticky *adj.* (**stickier, stickiest**) **1** sticking or tending to stick to what is touched. **2** (of weather) hot and humid. **3** *colloq.* difficult, awkward (*a sticky situation*). **4** *colloq.* very unpleasant (*he'll come to a sticky end*). • *n.* = STICKYBEAK. ☐ **sticky tape** adhesive tape. **sticky wicket** *colloq.* difficult circumstances. ☐☐ **stickily** *adv.* **stickiness** *n.*

stickybeak *Aust. colloq. n.* (also **sticky**) **1** an inquisitive or prying person; a person who sticks his or her nose (beak) into others' affairs. **2** an inquisitive (esp. surreptitious) look (*having a stickybeak at what the neighbours are up to*). • *v.* pry, snoop (*stickybeaks all the time*).

stiff *adj.* **1** not bending, moving, or changing shape easily. **2** (of a muscle, limb, or person) aching owing to exertion, injury, etc. **3** not fluid; thick and hard to stir (*a stiff dough*). **4** difficult (*a stiff examination*). **5** formal in manner, not sociable or friendly. **6** (of a price or penalty) high, severe. **7** (of a breeze) blowing briskly. **8** (of a drink or dose) strong. **9** *Aust. colloq.* **a** bad, hard (*stiff luck*). **b** unlucky (*a bit stiff, us getting wiped out by the Windies!*). • *adv. colloq.* to an extreme degree (*bored stiff*). • *n. colloq.* **1** a corpse. **2** an erection of the penis. ☐ **stiff with** *colloq.* full of; packed with (*the place was stiff with cops*). ☐☐ **stiffly** *adv.* **stiffness** *n.*

stiffen *v.* make or become stiff. ☐ **stiffener** *n.*

stiffie *n.* (also **stiffy**) *colloq.* an erection of the penis; an erect penis.

stifle *v.* **1** suffocate; feel unable to breathe for lack of air. **2** restrain or suppress (*stifled a yawn*). ❑ **stifling** *adj.*

stigma *n.* **1** a mark of shame, a stain on a person's good reputation. **2** the part of a pistil that receives the pollen in pollination.

stigmata / stig-**muh**-tuh, stig-**mah**-tuh / *n.pl.* marks corresponding to those left on Christ's body by the nails and spear at his Crucifixion, supernaturally imposed on the bodies of some saintly persons (*the stigmata of Father Pio*).

stigmatic / stig-**mat**-ik / *n.* a person bearing stigmata.

stigmatise / **stig**-muh-tuyz / *v.* (also **-ize**) brand as something disgraceful.

stile *n.* an arrangement of steps allowing people but not animals to climb over a fence or wall.

stiletto *n.* (*pl.* **stilettos**) **1** (in full **stiletto heel**) a high pointed heel on a shoe; a shoe with such a heel. **2** a dagger with a narrow blade. **3** a pointed device for making eyelet-holes etc.

still *adj.* **1** without moving, without or almost without motion or sound. **2** (of drinks) not sparkling or fizzy. • *n.* **1** silence and calm (*in the still of the night*). **2** an apparatus for distilling spirits. **3** a photograph as distinct from a motion picture, esp. a single shot from a cinema film. • *v.* make or become still (*to still the waves*). • *adv.* **1** without or almost without moving. **2** then or now or for the future as before (*the Pyramids are still standing*). **3** nevertheless. **4** in a greater amount or degree (*that would be still better; better still*). ❑ **still life** a painting of lifeless things such as cut flowers or fruit. ❑❑ **stillness** *n.*

stillbirth *n.* the birth of a dead child.

stillborn *adj.* **1** born dead. **2** (of an idea or plan) abortive; not able to succeed.

stilt *n.* **1** either of a pair of poles with a rest for the foot, enabling the user to walk above the ground. **2** each of a set of piles or posts supporting a building etc. **3** any of several long-legged Australian wading birds with a very thin bill.

stilted *adj.* stiffly or artificially formal (*written in stilted language*).

stilton *n.* *trademark* a cheese, often strong-tasting, with blue veins.

stimulant *adj.* stimulating. • *n.* a stimulant drug or drink; a stimulating event etc.

stimulate *v.* **1** make more vigorous or active. **2** apply a stimulus to. ❑ **stimulation** *n.* **stimulator** *n.*

stimulative / **stim**-yuh-luh-tiv / *adj.* stimulating.

stimulus *n.* (*pl.* **stimuli**) something that rouses a person or thing to activity or that produces a reaction in the body.

sting *n.* **1** a sharp-pointed part or organ of an insect etc., used for wounding and often injecting poison; a similar sharp-pointed hair on certain plants. **2** infliction of a wound by a sting; the wound itself. **3** any sharp bodily or mental pain (*the sting of remorse*). **4** *colloq.* **a** a swindle. **b** a police undercover operation. • *v.* (**stung**, **stinging**) **1** wound or affect with a sting; be able to do this. **2** feel sharp pain; stimulate sharply as if by a sting (*I was stung into answering rudely*). **3** *colloq.* cheat (a person) by over-charging; extort money from. **4** *colloq.* cadge from (a person) (*stung me for $20*). ❑ **stinging nettle** a nettle that stings. **stinging tree** *Aust.* = GYMPIE.

stingaree / **sting**-uh-ree / *Aust.* = STINGRAY.

stinger *n.* **1** a stinging animal or thing. **2** = STING *n.* (sense 1). **3** *Aust.* = STINGING TREE (*see* STING). **4** *Aust.* = BOX JELLYFISH (*see* BOX[1]). **5** a sharp, stinging blow.

stingray *n.* a broad flatfish with a poisonous spine at the base of its tail.

stingy / **stin**-jee / *adj.* (**stingier**, **stingiest**) grudging, mean. ❑ **stingily** *adv.* **stinginess** *n.*

stink *n.* **1** an offensive smell. **2** *colloq.* a row or fuss (*kicked up a stink about it*). • *v.* (**stank** or **stunk**, **stunk**, **stinking**) **1** give off an offensive smell. **2** (often foll. by *out*) fill (a place) with a stink (*his socks stank out the entire house*). **3** (foll. by *out* etc.) drive (a person) out etc. by a stink (*his socks stank me out of his bedroom*). **4** seem very unpleasant or unsavoury or dishonest (*the whole business stinks*).

stinkbird *n.* either of two Australian songbirds which have a strong scent-trail: the striated field-wren and the rufous fieldwren.

stinker *n.* *colloq.* **1** an objectionable person or thing. **2** a difficult task. **3** an unpleasantly hot day.

stinkfish *n.* any of several Australia sea fish having a disagreeable odour and taste, some of which are poisonous.

stinking *adj.* **1** that stinks. **2** *colloq.* very objectionable. • *adv.* *colloq.* extremely and usu. objectionably (*stinking rich*).

stinkwood *n.* any of several trees or shrubs esp. of south-eastern Australia, the leaves of which smell unpleasant when crushed, and the wood of which emits a highly offensive stink when burned.

stint *v.* restrict to a small allowance, be niggardly (*don't stint on food*). • *n.* **1** a limitation of supply or effort (*gave help without stint*). **2** a fixed or allotted amount of work (*did her stint*). **3** any of various small sandpipers which migrate to Australia from the Northern hemisphere during spring to early summer.

stipend / **stuy**-pend / *n.* a fixed regular allowance or salary.

stipendiary / stuy-**pen**-dyuh-ree / *adj.* receiving a stipend. ❑ **stipendiary magistrate** a paid professional magistrate. **stipendiary steward** *Aust.* a paid official who controls the running of horseraces etc., esp. the enforcement of rules.

stipple *v.* **1** paint, draw, or engrave in small dots (not in lines or strokes). **2** roughen the surface of (cement etc.). • *n.* stippling; this effect.

stipulate *v.* demand or insist on as part of an agreement. ◻ **stipulation** *n.*

stir *v.* (**stirred, stirring**) **1** move or cause to move (*not a leaf stirred*). **2** mix or move (a substance) by moving a spoon etc. round and round in it. **3 a** rouse (oneself), esp. from a lethargic state. **b** rise from sleep (*is he stirring yet?*). **c** (foll. by *out of* or *from*) leave (*hasn't stirred out of his room all day*). **4** arouse, excite, or stimulate (*the story stirred their interest; was stirred to anger*). **5** *Aust. colloq.* **a** cause trouble for its own sake. **b** provoke (a person) into exhibiting exasperation etc. (*he's only stirring you, silly*). ● *n.* **1** the act or process of stirring (*give the soup a stir*). **2** a commotion or excitement (*the news caused a stir*). **3** *colloq.* prison. ◻ **stir-fry** *v.* fry rapidly while stirring. *n.* a stir-fried dish. **stir the possum** *see* POSSUM. **stir up** stimulate; cause; rouse (*stir up trouble*).

Stirling, Sir James (1791–1865), Scottish naval officer and lieutenant-governor of the first settlement in WA, at the Swan River, 1829–39.

Stirling Range a range of peaks in south-western WA. The highest peak is Bluff Knoll (1,073 metres).

stirrer *n.* **1** a thing or person that stirs. **2** *Aust. colloq.* a person who provokes (another) to exasperation; a troublemaker; an agitator.

stirring *adj.* exciting, stimulating.

stirrup *n.* a support for a rider's foot, hanging from the saddle.

stirry *adj.* (of a bullock etc.) bad-tempered; restive.

stitch *n.* **1** (in sewing, knitting, etc.) a single complete movement of a needle or hook. **2** the loop of thread made in this way; each of the loops of material used in sewing up a wound. **3 a** particular method of arranging the thread (*cross stitch; purl stitch*). **4** the least bit of clothing (*without a stitch on*). **5** a sudden sharp pain in the muscles at the side of the body, often caused by running. ● *v.* sew, join, or close with stitches. ◻ **in stitches** *colloq.* laughing uncontrollably.

stoat *n.* the ermine of Europe etc., esp. when its fur is brown.

stobie pole *n.* (in SA) a pole of steel and concrete carrying electricity lines. (¶ J.C. Stobie, Australian engineer (1895–1953).)

stock *n.* **1** an amount of something available for use. **2** the total of goods kept by a trader. **3** farm animals or equipment. **4** a line of ancestry (*comes of convict stock*). **5** the capital of a business company; a portion of this held by an investor (differing from *shares* in that it is not issued in fixed amounts). **6** a person's standing in the opinion of others (*his stock is high*). **7** liquid made by stewing bones, meat, fish, or vegetables, used as a basis for making soup, sauce, etc. **8** a garden plant with fragrant flowers. **9** the lower and thicker part of a tree trunk. **10** a growing plant into which a graft is inserted. **11** a plant from which cuttings are taken. **12** a part serving as the base, holder, or handle for the working parts of an implement or machine (*the stock of a rifle*). ● *adj.* **1** kept in stock and regularly available. **2** hackneyed, conventional (*a stock argument*). ● *v.* **1** keep (goods) in stock. **2** provide with goods, livestock, or a supply of something (*a well-stocked library*). ◻ **in stock** available in a shop etc. without needing to be obtained specially. **out of stock** sold out. **stock agent** *Aust.* a person who deals in the buying and selling of livestock. **stock and station** *adj. Aust.* relating to firms or their employees dealing in farm land, products, and supplies (*a stock and station agent*). **stock car** an ordinary car strengthened for use in racing where deliberate collisions are allowed. **stock exchange** a place where stocks and shares are publicly bought and sold; an association of dealers conducting such business according to fixed rules. **stock horse** *Aust.* a horse trained to work with cattle etc. **stock-in-trade** *n.* **1** all the stock and other requisites for carrying on a trade or business. **2** a person's characteristic behaviour or qualities. **stock market** the stock exchange; transactions there. **stock route** *Aust.* a strip of Crown land reserved as a right of way for travelling stock. **stock saddle** *Aust.* a heavy saddle made for a stock horse. **stock-still** motionless. **stock up** assemble a stock of goods etc. **take stock** review a situation etc.

stockade *n.* **1** a protective fence of upright stakes. **2** *Aust. hist.* a structure in which convict gangs, working in outlying districts, were accommodated. ● *v.* fortify with a stockade.

stockbreeder *n.* a farmer who breeds livestock. ◻ **stockbreeding** *n.*

stockbroker = BROKER (sense 2). ◻ **stockbroking** *n.*

stockholder *n.* **1** an owner of stocks or shares. **2** *Aust.* a sheep or cattle farmer.

Stockholm the capital of Sweden.

stocking *n.* a close-fitting covering for the foot and part or all of the leg. ◻ **stocking stitch** alternate rows of plain and purl in knitting, giving a plain smooth surface on one side.

stockman *n. Aust.* a person employed to tend livestock, esp. cattle. ◻ **stockman-cut** *n.* a narrow-legged style of trousers. **stockman's hat** a broad-brimmed felt hat.

stockpile *n.* an accumulated stock of goods or materials etc. kept in reserve. ● *v.* accumulate a stockpile of.

stockpot *n.* a pot for cooking stock for soup etc.

stocks *n.pl.* **1** *hist.* a wooden framework with holes for the legs of a seated person, used like the pillory. **2** a framework on which a ship rests during construction.

stocktaking *n.* **1** making an inventory of stock in a shop. **2** reviewing of one's position and resources.

stockwhip *n.* a long whip used in the handling of cattle.

stocky *adj.* (**stockier**, **stockiest**) short and solidly built. ▢ **stockily** *adv.* **stockiness** *n.*

stockyard *n.* an enclosure with pens etc. for the sorting or temporary keeping of cattle.

stodge *n. colloq.* heavy fattening food.

stodgy *adj.* (**stodgier**, **stodgiest**) **1** (of food) heavy and filling; indigestible. **2** dull, uninteresting; heavy-going. ▢ **stodgily** *adv.* **stodginess** *n.*

stoic / **stoh**-ik / *n.* a stoical person. (¶ Named after the Stoics, Greek and Roman philosophers of the 3rd century BC onwards, who taught that goodness is based on knowledge and that the truly wise man is indifferent to changes of fortune.

stoical / **stoh**-i-kuhl / *adj.* calm and not excitable; bearing difficulties or discomfort without complaining. ▢ **stoically** *adv.*

stoicism / **stoh**-uh-siz-uhm / *n.* being stoical.

stoke *v.* (often foll. by *up*) **1** put fuel on (a furnace or fire etc.). **2** *colloq.* eat large quantities of food.

stoked *adj. colloq.* **1** affected by alcohol or drugs. **2** (often foll. by *on*) thrilled, excited, elated (*he's really stoked on surfing*).

stokehold *n.* a compartment in which a steamship's fires are tended.

Stoker, Bram (full name: Abraham Stoker) (1847–1912), Irish novelist, author of *Dracula*.

stoker *n.* **1** a person who stokes a furnace etc. **2** mechanical device for doing this.

stole[1] *n.* **1** a clerical vestment consisting of a long strip of material worn round the neck with the ends hanging down in front. **2** a woman's wide scarf-like garment worn round the shoulders.

stole[2] *see* STEAL.

stolen *see* STEAL. ▢ **stolen generation** (also **stolen generations**) *Aust.* the Aboriginal people who were removed from their families as children and placed in institutions or fostered by white families.

stolid *adj.* not feeling or showing emotion; not excitable. ▢ **stolidly** *adv.* **stolidity** / stuh-**lid**-uh-tee / *n.*

stoma *n.* (*pl.* **stomas** or **stomata**) **1** a minute pore in the epidermis of a leaf. **2** a small mouthlike opening in some lower animals. **3** *Surgery* a small mouthlike artificial opening made in a person's stomach.

stomach *n.* **1** the internal organ in which the first part of digestion occurs. **2** the lower front of the body. **3** appetite for food. **4** appetite or spirit for danger or an undertaking etc. (*had no stomach for the fight*). • *v.* endure or tolerate (*can't stomach all that violence*). ▢ **stomach pump** a syringe for emptying the stomach or forcing liquid into it.

stomp *v.* tread heavily. • *n.* a lively jazz dance with heavy stomping.

Stone, Emma Constance (1856–1902), Australian physician, the first woman to be registered as a medical practitioner in Australia.

stone *n.* **1** a small piece of rock. **2** stones or rock as a substance or material, e.g. for building. **3** a piece of stone shaped for a particular purpose, e.g. a tombstone or millstone. **4** a precious stone (*see* PRECIOUS). **5** a small piece of hard substance formed in the bladder, kidney, or gall bladder. **6** the hard case round the kernel of certain fruits. **7** (*pl.* **stone**) a unit of weight in the imperial system, = 14lb (or approx. 6.35 kg). • *adj.* made of stone. • *v.* **1** pelt with stones. **2** remove the stones from (fruit). ▢ **stone country** *Aust.* = GIBBER PLAIN (*see* GIBBER[2]). **stone fruit** a fruit (e.g. plum, peach, cherry) containing a single stone. **stone's throw** a short distance. **stone the crows!** *Aust.* an exclamation of surprise, disgust, etc. (more often to be met with now in caricatures of Australian speech than in Australian speech itself).

stone- *comb. form* completely (*stone-cold, stone-dead, stone-deaf*).

Stone Age the very early period of civilisation when weapons and tools were made of stone not metal.

stoned *adj. colloq.* **1** drunk. **2** under the influence of drugs.

stonefish *n.* any of several highly venomous fish of northern Australia and elsewhere in the tropics, having dorsal fins capable of inflicting a painful and potentially fatal sting, and resembling a large lump of weathered rock.

Stonehenge a megalithic monument in southern England, dating from the Bronze Age.

stonemason *n.* a person who cuts and dresses stone or builds in stone.

stonewall *v.* obstruct (a discussion or investigation) with evasive answers etc. ▢ **stonewalling** *n.*

stoneware *n.* items of pottery made from a mixture of clay and stone that will withstand heat.

stonewashed *adj.* (esp. of denim) washed with abrasives to give a worn, faded look.

stonework *n.* stone(s) forming a building or other structure.

stonkered *adj. Aust. colloq.* **1** utterly exhausted. **2** utterly confounded or defeated. **3** very drunk.

stony *adj.* (**stonier**, **stoniest**) **1** full of stones. **2** hard as stone, unfeeling; not responsive (*a stony gaze*). ▢ **stonily** *adv.*

stood *see* STAND.

stooge *colloq. n.* **1** a comedian's assistant, used as a target for jokes. **2** a subordinate who does routine or unpleasant work. **3** an unquestioningly loyal or obsequious subordinate, a lackey. **4** a person whose actions are entirely controlled by another. • *v.* act as a stooge.

stook / stook, stuuk / *n.* a group of sheaves of grain stood on end in a field. • *v.* arrange in stooks.

stool *n.* **1** a movable seat without arms or a back. **2** a footstool. **3** (**stools**) faeces. ▢ **stool pigeon** a person acting as a decoy, esp. to trap a criminal. **2** a police informer.

stoop v. **1** bend forwards and down. **2** condescend; lower oneself morally (*he would never stoop to speak to those he considered his inferiors; he wouldn't stoop to cheating*). •n. a posture of the body with shoulders bent forwards (*he walks with a stoop*).

stop v. (**stopped**, **stopping**) **1** put an end to (movement, progress, operation, etc.). **2** cease motion or working. **3** *colloq.* stay (*will you stop for tea?*). **4** keep back, refuse to give or allow (*the cost will be stopped out of your wages*). **5** (in full **stop payment of** *or* **on**) order the bank not to honour (a cheque) when it is presented for payment. **6** close by plugging or obstructing (*stop the holes; stop them up*). **7** fill a cavity in (a tooth). **8** press down a string or block a hole in a musical instrument to obtain the desired pitch. •n. **1** stopping; being stopped, a pause or check (*ran without a stop; put a stop to it*). **2** a place where a train or bus etc. stops regularly. **3** a punctuation mark, esp. a full stop. **4** an obstruction or device that stops or regulates movement or operation. **5** a row of organ pipes providing tones of one quality; the knob or lever controlling these. **6** a key or lever regulating pitch in a wind instrument. **7** any of the standard sizes of aperture in an adjustable lens. ▫ **pull out all the stops** make all possible efforts. **stop-go** alternate stopping and progressing, esp. of the economy. **stop off** (*or* **over**) break one's journey. **stop press** late news inserted in a newspaper after printing has begun.

stopcock n. a valve in a pipe to regulate the flow of liquid or gas.

stopgap n. a temporary substitute.

stopoff n. a stopover.

stopover n. a break in one's journey, esp. for one or more nights.

stoppage n. **1** stopping; being stopped. **2** an obstruction.

stopper n. a plug for closing a bottle etc. •v. close with a stopper.

stopwatch n. a watch that can be stopped and started, used to time races etc.

stopwork meeting n. *Aust.* a meeting (to consider working conditions, possible strike action, etc.) that employees must stop working to attend.

storage n. **1 a** the storing of goods etc. **b** the method of or space for storing. **c** the cost of storing. **2** the storing of data in a computer etc.

store n. **1** a stock or supply of something available for use. **2** a large shop; a general store. **3** a warehouse where things are stored. **4** a device in a computer or calculator for storing and retrieving information. •v. **1** collect and keep for future use. **2** put into a store. **3** put (furniture etc.) into a warehouse for temporary keeping. **4** stock with something useful. **5** enter or retain (data) for retrieval. ▫ **in store 1** being stored; kept available for use. **2** destined to happen, imminent (*there's a surprise in store for you*). **set store by** value greatly.

storehouse n. a place where things are stored.

storekeeper n. **1** a person in charge of a store or stores. **2** a shopkeeper.

storeman n. a person responsible for stored goods.

storey n. (pl. **storeys**) one horizontal level of a building that contains more than one such level (*a house of three storeys*). ▫ **storeyed** adj.

stork n. **1** a large long-legged European wading bird with a long straight bill, humorously pretended to be the bringer of babies. **2** = JABIRU.

storm n. **1** a violent disturbance of the atmosphere with strong winds and usu. thunder, rain, or dust, etc. **2** a violent shower of missiles or blows. **3** a great outbreak of applause, anger, criticism etc. **4** a violent military attack. •v. **1** (of wind or rain) rage, be violent. **2** behave very angrily; rage (*stormed out of the room; stormed at us for being late*). **3** attack or capture by storm (*they stormed the citadel*). ▫ **storm bird** any of several Australian birds, the movements or cries of which are supposed to presage a storm, esp. the channel-billed cuckoo. **storm in a teacup** great agitation over a trivial matter. **storm petrel** (also **stormy petrel**) **1** a small black and white N. Atlantic petrel. **2** any of various small migratory seabirds, often seen in Australian waters, brownish-grey with some white on their underparts. **take by storm** capture by a violent attack; captivate rapidly.

stormwater n. surface water in abnormal quantity resulting from heavy falls of rain.

stormy adj. (**stormier**, **stormiest**) **1** affected by storms (*a stormy night; stormy coasts*). **2** (of wind etc.) violent as in a storm. **3** full of violent anger or outbursts (*a stormy interview*). ▫ **stormily** adv. **storminess** n.

story n. **1** an account of an incident either true or invented. **2** *Aust.* (in Aboriginal English) an account of the sacred events associated with a dreaming site. **3** (in full **storyline**) the plot of a novel or play etc. **4** a report of an item of news; material for this. **5** *colloq.* a lie. **6** explanation (*so what's your story this time?*).

storyteller n. **1** a person who tells stories. **2** *colloq.* a liar. ▫ **storytelling** n. & adj.

Stott Despoja / stot **des**-poi-yuh /, Natasha (Jessica) (1969–), Australian politician. In 2000 she became leader of the Australian Democrats.

stoup / stoop / n. a stone basin for holy water, esp. in the wall of a church.

stoush / stowsh / *Aust. colloq.* n. a brawl, a fight. •v. hit; fight with.

stout adj. **1** of considerable thickness or strength (*a stout stick*). **2** (of a person) solidly built and rather fat. **3** brave and resolute (*a stout heart*). •n. a strong dark beer brewed with roasted malt or barley. ▫ **stoutly** adv. **stoutness** n.

stove[1] *n.* a closed apparatus burning fuel or using electricity for heating or cooking.
stove[2] *see* STAVE.
Stow, (Julian) Randolph (1935–), Australian novelist and poet. His novel *To the Islands* (1958) won the Miles Franklin Award.
stow *v.* place in a receptacle for storage. ◻ **stow away 1** put away in storage or in reserve. **2** conceal oneself as a stowaway.
stowage *n.* **1** stowing; being stowed. **2** space available for this. **3** the charge for it.
stowaway *n.* a person who hides on a ship or aircraft etc. so as to travel free.
Stowe, Harriet Beecher (1811–96), American novelist, author of *Uncle Tom's Cabin*.
strabismus / struh-**biz**-muhs / *n. Med.* a squint.
Stradbroke Island either of two islands located east of Brisbane in Moreton Bay.
straddle *v.* **1** sit or stand across (a person or thing) with the legs or supports wide apart. **2** stand with the legs wide apart. **3** be situated on both sides of (*the town straddles the border*). • *n.* an act or instance of straddling.
Stradivarius / strad-uh-**vair**-ree-uhs / *n.* a violin or other stringed instrument made by Antonio Stradivari (*c.*1644–1737), Italian violin maker, or his followers.
strafe / strahf, strayf / *v.* bombard, attack with gunfire.
straggle *v.* **1** grow or spread in an irregular or untidy manner. **2** go or wander separately; drop behind others. • *n.* a body or group of straggling or scattered persons or things. ◻ **straggler** *n.*
straggly *adj.* straggling.
straight *adj.* **1** extending or moving continuously in one direction, not curved or bent. **2** correctly arranged; tidy. **3** in unbroken succession (*ten straight wins*). **4** candid, not evasive; honest. **5** *colloq.* (of a person) **a** conventional. **b** heterosexual, not gay. **6** not modified or elaborate; without additions; (of alcoholic drinks) not diluted. • *adv.* **1** in a straight line. **2** direct, without delay (*went straight home*). **3** straightforwardly (*told him straight*). • *n.* **1** the straight part of something, e.g. the last section of a racecourse. **2** *colloq.* **a** a conventional person. **b** a heterosexual person. **3** a sequence of five cards in poker. ◻ **go straight** live an honest life after being a criminal. **straight away** without delay. **straight face** one without a smile even though amused. **straight man** a comedian's stooge. **straight off** *colloq.* without hesitation or deliberation etc. ◻◻ **straightness** *n.*
straightaway = STRAIGHT AWAY (*see* STRAIGHT).
straighten *v.* make or become straight.

■ **Usage** Do not confuse *straightened* with *straitened*.

straightforward *adj.* **1** honest, frank. **2** (of a task etc.) without complications. ◻ **straightforwardly** *adv.* **straightforwardness** *n.*

strain[1] *v.* **1** stretch tightly; make taut. **2** injure by overuse or excessive demands (*strained a muscle; strained their loyalty*). **3** make an intense effort. **4** apply (a meaning or rule etc.) beyond its true application. **5** pass through a sieve or similar device to separate solids from a liquid; (of liquid) filter. • *n.* **1** straining; being strained; the force exerted. **2** an injury caused by straining a muscle etc. **3** a severe demand on one's mental or physical strength or on one's resources; exhaustion caused by this. **4** a stretch of fencing wire between two strainers. **5** a passage from a tune. **6** the tone or style of something written or spoken (*continued in a more cheerful strain*).
strain[2] *n.* **1** a line of descent of animals, plants, or micro-organisms; a variety or breed of these (*a new strain of flu virus*). **2** a slight or inherited tendency in character (*there's a strain of insanity in the family*).
strained *adj.* **1** (of behaviour or manner) constrained, artificial. **2** (of a relationship) characterised by distrust or unpleasant tension.
strainer *n.* **1** a utensil for straining liquids. **2** *Aust.* **a** a device for keeping wire etc. taut. **b** (also **strainer post**) a strong post against which the wires of a fence are tightened.
strait *n.* **1** (also **straits**) a narrow stretch of water connecting two seas. **2** (**straits**) a difficult state of affairs (*in dire straits*).
straitened *adj.* poverty-stricken (*in straitened circumstances*).

■ **Usage** Do not confuse with *straightened*.

straitjacket *n.* **1** a strong jacket-like garment with long sleeves for restraining a violent prisoner or mental patient. **2** a situation or measure that severely restricts one's actions. • *v.* **1** restrain by a straitjacket. **2** restrict severely.
strait-laced *adj.* very prim, puritanical.
strand *n.* **1** one of the threads or wires etc. twisted together to form a rope, yarn, or cable. **2** a single thread or strip of fibre. **3** a lock of hair. **4** a string (of pearls etc.). **5** an element, a component (*when I consider the next strand in his argument...*). **6** a foreshore; a beach. • *v.* run or cause to run aground.
stranded *adj.* left in difficulties, e.g. without funds or means of transport.
strange *adj.* **1** not familiar or well known; not one's own, alien (*in a strange land*). **2** unusual, surprising (*it's strange that you haven't heard*). **3** (foll. by *to*) unaccustomed (*she is strange to the work*). ◻ **strangely** *adv.* **strangeness** *n.*
stranger *n.* **1** a person in a place or company etc. to which he or she does not belong; a person one does not know. **2** one who is unaccustomed to a certain experience or task (*a stranger to poverty*).
strangle *v.* **1** kill or be killed by squeezing the throat. **2** restrict or prevent the proper growth, operation, or utterance of. ◻ **strangler** *n.*

stranglehold *n.* **1** a throttling hold in wrestling. **2** a deadly grip. **3** complete and exclusive control.

strangulate *v.* compress (a vein or intestine etc.) so that nothing can pass through it.

strangulation *n.* **1** strangling; being strangled. **2** strangulating; being strangulated.

strap *n.* **1** a strip of leather, fabric, etc., often with a buckle, for holding things in place. **2** a shoulder strap. **3** a loop for grasping to steady oneself in a moving vehicle. **4** (**the strap**) punishment by beating with a leather strap. • *v.* (**strapped**, **strapping**) **1** secure with a strap or straps. **2** bind (an injury) (*strap it up*). **3** beat with a strap.

straphanger *n. colloq.* a standing passenger in a bus, train, etc.

strapless *adj.* without shoulder straps.

strapped *adj. colloq.* short of something (*strapped for cash*).

strapper *n. esp. Aust.* a person who grooms racehorses.

strapping *adj.* tall, sturdy, and healthy-looking.

strasbourg / **straz**-berg / *n.* (also **stras** / straz /) a spiced sausage.

strata *pl.* of STRATUM. ▫ **strata title** *Aust.* the registered ownership of a certain amount of space (rather than ground area) in a multi-storey building, a complex of home units, etc.

■ **Usage** See STRATUM.

stratagem / **strat**-uh-juhm / *n.* a cunning plan or scheme; a piece of trickery.

strategic / struh-**tee**-jik / *adj.* **1** of strategy. **2** giving an advantage (*a strategic position*). **3** (of materials) essential in war. ▫ **strategic weapons** missiles etc. that can reach an enemy's home territory (as distinct from *tactical weapons* which are for use in a battle or at close quarters). ▫▫ **strategically** *adv.*

Strategic Defense Initiative a former US defence proposal (popularly known as 'Star Wars') in which enemy weapons would be destroyed in space by lasers, missiles, etc. directed from satellites.

strategist / **strat**-uh-juhst / *n.* an expert in strategy.

strategy / **strat**-uh-jee / *n.* **1** the planning and directing of a campaign or war. **2** a plan or policy to achieve something (*our economic strategy*).

stratified *adj.* arranged in strata, grades, layers, etc. ▫ **stratification** *n.*

stratigraphy / struh-**tig**-ruh-fee / *n.* Geol. & Archaeol. **1** the order and relative proportions of strata. **2** the scientific study of these. ▫ **stratigraphic** *adj.* (also **stratigraphical**).

stratosphere / **strat**-uh-sfeer / *n.* a layer of the earth's atmosphere between about 10 and 60 km above the earth's surface.

stratum / **strah**-tuhm, **stray**- / *n.* (*pl.* **strata**) **1** one of a series of layers, esp. of rock in the earth's crust. **2** a social level or class (*the various strata of society*).

■ **Usage** The word *strata* is a plural; it is incorrect to speak of *a strata* or *this strata*, or of *stratas*.

Strauss[1] / strows /, Johann (II) (1825–99), Austrian composer, famous for his waltzes (son of Johann I (1804–49), composer of dance music).

Strauss[2] / strows /, Richard (1864–1949), German composer.

Stravinsky / struh-**vin**-skee /, Igor (1882–1971), Russian-born composer.

straw *n.* **1** dry cut stalks of grain used as material for bedding, packing, fodder, etc. **2** a single stalk or piece of this. **3** a narrow tube of paper or plastic for sucking up liquid in drinking. **4** a pale yellow colour. ▫ **clutch at straws** try any remedy in desperation. **straw poll** (or **vote**) an unofficial poll as a test of general feeling.

strawberry *n.* a soft juicy edible red fruit with seeds on the surface; the plant that bears it. ▫ **strawberry mark** a reddish birthmark.

strawflower *Aust.* = HELICHRYSUM.

stray *v.* **1** leave one's group or proper place with no settled destination or purpose; roam. **2** go aside from a direct course; depart from a subject. • *adj.* **1** having strayed. **2** isolated, occurring here and there not as one of a group (*hit by a stray bullet*). • *n.* a person or domestic animal that has strayed; a stray thing.

streak *n.* **1** a thin line or band of a different colour or substance from its surroundings. **2** an element in a person's character (*has a jealous streak*). **3** a spell or series (*had a long winning streak*). **4** *colloq.* a tall, thin person. • *v.* **1** mark with streaks. **2** move very rapidly. **3** run stark naked in public (e.g. onto the field during a cricket match) as a humorous or defiant act or for a bet.

streaker *n.* a person (usu. male and young and sometimes intoxicated) who streaks (*v.* sense 3).

streaky *adj.* full of streaks; (of bacon etc.) with alternate layers or streaks of fat and lean. ▫ **streakily** *adv.* **streakiness** *n.*

stream *n.* **1** a flowing body of water, esp. a small river. **2** a flow of any liquid or of a mass of things or people (*a stream of complaints; a stream of visitors*). **3** (in certain schools) a section into which children with the same level of ability are placed. **4** the current or direction of something moving (*against the stream*). • *v.* **1** flow or move as a stream. **2** emit a stream of; run with liquid (*the wound streamed blood; with streaming eyes*). **3** (of hair, ribbons, etc.) be blown at full length in the wind. **4** arrange (schoolchildren) in streams. ▫ **on stream** in operation or production. **stream of consciousness** **1** *Psychology* a person's thoughts and conscious reactions to events, perceived as a continuous flow. **2** a literary style depicting events as such a flow in the mind of a character.

streamer *n.* **1** a long narrow flag. **2** a long narrow ribbon or strip of paper.

streamline *v.* **1** give a streamlined form to. **2** make more efficient by simplifying, removing superfluities, etc.

streamlined *adj.* having a smooth even shape that offers the least resistance to movement through air or water.

Streep, Meryl (original name: Mary Louise Streep) (1949–), American film actor.

street *n.* a public road in a city or town with buildings along one or both sides. •*v. colloq.* outdistance (other competitors). ▫ **on the streets 1** living by prostitution. **2** homeless. **street credibility** (also **street cred**) a personal image of being fashionable, confident, and successful in modern city life. **street kid** a homeless young person in an urban area. **up** (or **right up**) **one's street** *colloq.* within one's field of knowledge or interests.

Streeton, Sir Arthur (Ernest) (1867–1943), Australian painter, a member of the Heidelberg School.

streetwalker *n.* a prostitute who stands in or walks along a street waiting for a customer.

streetwise *adj.* (of street kids etc.) knowing how to survive in modern urban life; knowing how to survive on the streets.

Streisand, Barbra (Joan) (1942–), American singer and film actor.

strength *n.* **1** the quality of being strong (physically, mentally, morally, etc.); the intensity of this. **2** a source of strength; the particular respect in which a person or thing is strong. **3** the number of people present or available; the full complement (*the department is below strength*). ▫ **in strength** in large numbers (*supporters were present in strength*). **on the strength of** on the basis of, using (a fact etc.) as one's support. **that's about the strength of it** that's what it amounts to.

strengthen *v.* make or become stronger.

strenuous *adj.* **1** energetic, making great efforts. **2** requiring great effort (*a strenuous task*). ▫ **strenuously** *adv.* **strenuousness** *n.*

streptococcus *n.* (*pl.* **streptococci**) any of a group of bacteria that cause serious infections. ▫ **streptococcal** *adj.*

streptomycin / strep-tuh-**muy**-sin / *n.* an antibiotic drug.

stress *n.* **1** a force acting on or within a thing and tending to distort it, e.g. by pressing, pulling, or twisting. **2** mental or physical distress caused by difficult circumstances. **3** = EMPHASIS (senses 1 and 3). •*v.* **1** lay emphasis on. **2** cause mechanical or physical or mental stress. ▫ **stressed out** *colloq.* suffering greatly from stress, anxiety, etc.

stressful *adj.* causing stress. ▫ **stressfully** *adv.*

stretch *v.* **1** pull out tightly or into a greater length or size. **2** be able to be stretched without breaking; tend to become stretched (*knitted fabrics stretch*). **3** be continuous from a point or between points (*the wall stretches right round the prime minister's Lodge*). **4** thrust out one's limbs and tighten the muscles. **5** make great demands on the abilities of (a person). **6** strain to the utmost or beyond a reasonable limit (*stretch the truth; you are stretching our friendship*). •*n.* **1** stretching; being stretched. **2** a continuous expanse or tract; a continuous period of time. **3** *colloq.* a period of service or imprisonment. **4** the straight side of a racetrack, esp. leading to the winning post. •*adj.* able to be stretched (*stretch fabrics*). ▫ **at a stretch** without interruption. **at full stretch** (or **fully stretched**) working to the utmost of one's powers. **stretch a point** agree to something beyond the limit of what is normally allowed. **stretch one's legs** go for a walk.

stretcher *n.* **1** a framework of poles, canvas, etc. for carrying a sick or injured person in a lying position. **2** *Aust.* a collapsible bed usu. made of canvas etc. on a frame. **3** any of various devices for stretching things or holding things taut. **4** a board against which a rower braces his or her feet. **5** a brick in a wall laid horizontally with its long side showing. •*v.* remove (a person, esp. an injured player from the field) on a stretcher (*stretchered him off the ground*).

stretto / **stret**-oh / *adv. Music* in quicker time. (¶ Italian)

strew *v.* (**strewed**, **strewn** or **strewed**, **strewing**) scatter over a surface; cover with scattered things.

'strewth alternative spelling of 'STRUTH.

stria / **struy**-uh / *n.* (*pl.* **striae** / **struy**-ee /) *Geol.* a slight ridge or furrow.

striate / **struy**-ayt / *v.* mark with slight ridges, furrow (*the wind has striated the dunes*). ▫ **striation** *n.*

striated / struy-**ay**-tuhd / *adj.* **1** (also **striate** / **struy**-uht /) marked with striae. **2** (as a distinguishing epithet in the names of birds etc.) marked with ridges, stripes, etc., streaked. ▫ **striated pardalote** a small bird of all Australian States, having a black crown sometimes striated with white.

stricken *adj.* affected or overcome by an illness, shock, or grief.

Strickland, Shirley (Barbara) (married name: Shirley Barbara de la Hunty) (1925–), AO, Australian athlete who won gold medals in the 80 metres hurdles at the 1952 and 1956 Olympic Games.

strict *adj.* **1** precisely limited or defined, without exception or deviation (*a strict interpretation of the law*). **2** requiring complete obedience or exact performance; not lenient or indulgent (*a strict teacher*). **3** complete, total (*I mention this in strictest confidence*). ▫ **strictly speaking** if one uses words in their exact sense. ▫▫ **strictly** *adv.* **strictness** *n.*

stricture n. **1** severe criticism or condemnation. **2** abnormal constriction of a tube-like part of the body.

stride v. (**strode, stridden, striding**) **1** walk with long steps. **2** stand astride. • n. **1** a single long step, the length of this. **2** a person's manner of striding. **3** progress (*has made great strides towards independence*). **4 strides** colloq. trousers. ☐ **get into one's stride** settle into a fast and steady pace of work. **take in one's stride** do without needing a special effort.

strident / **struy**-duhnt / adj. loud and harsh. ☐ **stridently** adv. **stridency** n.

strife n. **1** a conflict, a struggle or clash (*the terrible strife in Bosnia*). **2** Aust. colloq. trouble of any kind; difficulty.

strike v. (**struck, striking**) **1** bring or come into sudden hard contact with; knock with a blow or stroke. **2** attack suddenly; (of a disease) afflict. **3** (of lightning) descend upon and blast. **4** produce (sparks or a sound etc.) by striking something; produce (a musical note) by pressing a key; make (a coin or medal) by stamping metal etc.; ignite (a match) by friction. **5** bring into a specified state by or as if by striking (*he was struck blind*). **6** indicate (the hour) or be indicated by a sound (*the clock struck two*). **7** reach (gold or mineral oil etc.) by digging or drilling. **8** occur to the mind of; produce a mental impression on (*an idea struck me; she strikes me as being efficient*). **9** lower or take down (a flag or tent etc.). **10** stop work in protest about a grievance. **11** penetrate or cause to penetrate; fill with sudden fear etc. **12** proceed in a certain direction (*strike north-west through the forest*). **13** reach or achieve (*strike a balance; strike a bargain*). **14** assume (an attitude) suddenly and dramatically. **15 a** insert (the cutting of a plant) in soil etc. to take root. **b** (of a plant or cutting etc.) put forth (roots). • n. **1** an act or instance of striking. **2** an attack, esp. from the air. **3** a workers' refusal to work, in protest about a grievance. **4** a sudden discovery of gold or oil etc. ☐ **on strike** (of workers) striking. **strike bowler** Cricket a frontline bowler used for comparatively short spells to an attacking field, esp. with the new ball. **strike me lucky** (or **blue** or **dead** or **fat** or **pink** or **roan** etc.) Aust. colloq. a mild oath. **strike off** cross off; remove (a person) from a professional register because of misconduct. **strike out** (or **through**) cross out. **strike up 1** begin playing or singing. **2** start (a friendship etc.). **struck on** colloq. infatuated with; sexually aroused by.

strikebreaker n. a person who works while fellow employees are on strike or who is employed in place of strikers.

striker n. **1** a person or thing that strikes. **2** a worker who is on strike. **3** a soccer player whose main function is to score goals.

striking adj. sure to be noticed, attractive and impressive. ☐ **strikingly** adv.

Strine n. a comic transliteration of Australian pronunciation characterised by excessive elision etc., e.g. *Emma Chisit* = 'How much is it?', *Gloria Some* = 'glorious home'. • adj. Australian (*the Strine language*). (¶ The alleged pronunciation of the word 'Australian' in Strine.)

string n. **1** narrow cord. **2** a length of this used to fasten or lace something, or interwoven in a frame to form the head of a racquet. **3** a piece of catgut, wire, etc. stretched on a musical instrument, producing a note by vibration. **4** a strip of tough fibre on a bean pod etc. **5** a set of objects strung together or of people or events coming after one another; a series or line. **6** Computing a one dimensional array of characters. **7** a condition that is insisted upon (*the offer has no strings attached*). **8** (**strings**) stringed instruments; their players. • v. (**strung, stringing**) **1** fit or fasten with string(s). **2** thread (beads etc.) on a string. **3** furnish or adorn with something suspended (*a hall strung with streamers*). **4** trim the tough fibre from (beans). ☐ **highly-strung** see HIGHLY. **pull strings** see PULL. **string along with** colloq. keep company with. **string course** a projecting horizontal line of bricks etc. round a building. **string out** spread out in a line; cause to last a long time. **string up** kill by hanging.

stringed adj. (of musical instruments) having strings.

stringent / **strin**-juhnt / adj. (of a rule) strict, precise. ☐ **stringently** adv. **stringency** n.

stringer n. **1** a lengthwise structural part in a framework, esp. in a ship or aircraft; one of the side pieces of a staircase. **2** a newspaper correspondent who is not on the regular staff.

stringy adj. **1** like string. **2** (of beans etc.) having a strip of tough fibre.

stringybark n. Aust. **1** any of many eucalypts chiefly of south-eastern mainland Australia, having thick, rough, long-fibred bark. **2** the bark or wood of these trees. • adj. of or pertaining to stringybarks (*stringybark forest; stringybark cockatoo*). ☐ **stringybark cockatoo** a farmer of small means.

strip v. (**stripped, stripping**) **1** remove the clothes or covering from (a person or thing) (*they grabbed him and stripped him; stripped the orange of its peel*). **2** (often foll. by *off*) undress oneself (*he stripped naked and jumped into bed; let's strip off and have a skinny-dip*). **3** deprive (a person), e.g. of property or titles. **4 a** leave bare of accessories or fittings (*stripped the room of all its contents*). **b** deprive (a plant etc.) of its foliage or fruit (*the storm stripped the trees*). **5** remove (paint) or remove paint from (a surface) with solvent etc. **6** damage the thread of (a screw) or the teeth of (a gear wheel). **7** (often foll. by *down*) take apart (a machine, engine, etc.) in order to overhaul it. **8** sell off (the assets of a company) for profit. • n. **1** an act of stripping naked, esp. in striptease. **2** a long narrow piece or area (*use a strip of cloth; a*

stripe / *strip of land*). **3** the identifying outfit worn by the members of a sports team while playing. ☐ **strip cartoon** = COMIC STRIP. **strip light** a long tubular fluorescent light. **strip search** *n.* a search involving the removal of all a person's clothes. **strip-search** *v.* conduct such a search.

stripe *n.* **1** a long narrow band on a surface, differing in colour or texture from its surroundings. **2** a chevron on a sleeve, indicating the wearer's military rank.

striped *adj.* marked with stripes.

stripling *n.* a youth who has not yet fully emerged into manhood.

stripper *n.* **1** a person or thing that strips something. **2** a device or solvent for removing paint etc. **3** *Aust.* a machine used to harvest grain. **4** a striptease performer.

striptease *n.* entertainment in which the performer undresses slowly and erotically.

stripy *adj.* striped.

strive *v.* (**strove**, **striven**, **striving**) **1** make great efforts. **2** carry on a conflict.

strobe *n. colloq.* a stroboscope. ☐ **strobe lighting** an electric light that flashes on and off rapidly and automatically, used at discos, pop concerts, etc.

stroboscope / stroh-buh-skohp / *n.* **1** *Physics* an instrument for determining speeds of rotation etc. by shining a bright light at intervals so that a rotating object appears stationary. **2** a lamp made to flash intermittently, esp. for this purpose. ☐ **stroboscopic** / -skop-ik / *adj.*

strode *see* STRIDE.

stroganoff / strog-uh-nof / *n.* a dish of strips of beef cooked in a sauce containing sour cream.

stroke *n.* **1** the act or process of striking something. **2** a single movement or action or effort, a successful or skilful effort (*he hasn't done a stroke of work; a stroke of genius; a stroke of luck*). **3** each of a series of repeated movements; a particular sequence of these (e.g. in swimming). **4** one hit at the ball in various games; (in golf) this used as a unit of scoring. **5** (in full **stroke oar**) the oarsman nearest the stern of a racing boat, setting the time of the stroke. **6** a mark made by a movement of a pen or paintbrush etc. **7** the sound made by a clock striking (*on the stroke of ten*). **8** an attack of apoplexy or paralysis. **9** an act or spell of stroking. • *v.* **1** pass one's hand gently along the surface of (hair, fur, a person's body, etc.). **2** act as stroke to (a boat or crew).

stroll *v.* walk in a leisurely way. • *n.* a leisurely walk.

stroller *n.* **1** a person who strolls. **2** a folding chair on wheels, in which a child can be pushed along.

strong *adj.* **1** having power of resistance to being broken, damaged, captured etc. **2** capable of exerting great power, physically powerful; powerful through numbers, resources, or quality. **3** concentrated, having a large proportion of flavouring or colouring; (of a drink) containing much alcohol. **4** having a considerable effect on one of the senses or the emotions (*a strong smell; strong acting by John Gielgud*). **5** having a specified number of members (*an army 5000 strong*). **6** (of language) **a** indicating anger or excited feeling. **b** vulgar; coarse. **7** *Grammar* (of verbs) changing the vowel in the past tense (as *ring/rang, strike/struck*), not adding a suffix (as *float/floated*). • *adv.* strongly, vigorously (*going strong*). ☐ **come on strong** behave aggressively. **the strong of** *Aust. colloq.* the point or meaning of; the truth of (*we'll never get the strong of why they split*). ☐ ☐ **strongly** *adv.*

strongbox *n.* a small strongly made chest for valuables.

strongfish *Aust.* = TILLYWURTI.

stronghold *n.* **1** a fortified place; a secure refuge. **2** a centre of support for a cause etc.

strongroom *n.* a room, esp. in a bank, for keeping valuables safe from fire and theft.

strontium / stron-tee-uhm / *n.* a chemical element (symbol Sr), a soft silver-white metal. ☐ **strontium-90** a radioactive isotope of strontium that is found in nuclear fallout and concentrates in bones and teeth when taken into the body.

strop *n.* a strip of leather on which a razor is sharpened. • *v.* (**stropped**, **stropping**) sharpen on or with a strop.

strophe / stroh-fee / *n.* **1** the first section of an ancient Greek choral ode or of one division of it. **2** a group of lines forming a section of a lyric poem.

stroppy *adj. colloq.* bad-tempered, awkward to deal with.

strove *see* STRIVE.

struck *see* STRIKE.

structural *adj.* of a structure or framework. ☐ **structurally** *adv.*

structuralism *n.* the theory that societies, languages, works of literature, etc. can be understood only by analysis of their structure (rather than their function). ☐ **structuralist** *n.* & *adj.*

structure *n.* **1** the way in which something is constructed or organised. **2** a supporting framework or the essential parts of a thing. **3** a constructed thing; a complex whole; a building. • *v.* construct; organise. ☐ **structured programming** *Computing* the method of dividing a computer program into small, separately testable, units.

strudel / stroo-duhl / *n.* a thin pastry in leaves, rolled round a sweet filling (esp. apple) and baked.

struggle *v.* **1** move one's limbs or body in a vigorous effort to get free. **2** make a vigorous effort under difficulties. **3** try to overcome an opponent or problem etc. **4** (esp. as **struggling** *adj.*) have difficulty in gaining recognition or a living (*a struggling artist*). • *n.* a spell of struggling;

strum 828 **stuffy**

a determined effort under difficulties; a hard contest.

strum v. (**strummed**, **strumming**) play (chords) on (a guitar, piano, etc.), esp. casually or unskilfully or as a very basic accompaniment; play (a tune etc.) in this way. • n. the sound made by strumming.

strumpet n. archaic a prostitute.

strung see STRING.

strut n. **1** a bar of wood or metal inserted into a framework to strengthen and brace it. **2** a strutting walk. • v. (**strutted**, **strutting**) walk in a pompous self-satisfied way.

'struth interj. (also **'strewth**) colloq. an exclamation of surprise. (¶ Abbreviation of 'God's truth'.)

strychnine / **strik**-neen / n. a bitter highly poisonous substance, used in very small doses as a stimulant.

stub n. **1** the remnant of a pencil, cigarette, etc. **2** the counterfoil of a cheque, receipt, etc. **3** the stump (of a tree, tooth, etc.). • v. (**stubbed**, **stubbing**) **1** strike against a hard object (stub one's toe). **2** (foll. by out) extinguish (a cigarette) by pressing the end against something hard.

stubble n. **1** the lower ends of the stalks of cereal plants left in the ground after the harvest. **2** short stiff hair or bristles, as on the face of a man who has not recently shaved. ☐ **stubble quail** a bird of chiefly southern mainland Australia, usu. found in stubble etc., and much sought after as a game bird. ☐☐ **stubbly** adj.

stubborn adj. obstinate, not easy to control or deal with. ☐ **stubbornly** adv. **stubbornness** n.

stubby adj. (**stubbier**, **stubbiest**) short and thick. • n. Aust. **1** (also **stubbie**) a small (375 ml) squat bottle of beer. **2** (**stubbies**) trademark a pair of short shorts for men's casual wear. ☐ **stubby cooler** (also **stubby holder**) Aust. a casing made of insulating material in which a stubby is held while the contents are being drunk.

stucco n. plaster or cement used for coating walls or moulding to form architectural decorations. ☐ **stuccoed** adj.

stuck see STICK. • adj. **1** unable to move or make progress. **2** (of an animal) that has been stabbed or had its throat cut. ☐ **stuck-up** colloq. conceited; snobbish.

stud[1] n. **1** a short large-headed nail; a rivet; a small knob projecting from a surface. **2** a small piece of jewellery for wearing in pierced ears or nostrils. **3** a device like a button on a shank, used e.g. to fasten a detachable shirt collar or double buttonholes in a shirt front. **4** a post (in the frame of a building) to which laths are nailed. • v. (**studded**, **studding**) decorate with studs or precious stones set into a surface; strengthen with studs.

stud[2] n. **1** a number of horses, cattle, etc., kept for breeding. **2** (in full **stud farm**) a place where horses, cattle, etc. are bred. **3** (in full **stud horse**) a stallion. **4** a good-looking young man, esp. one noted for sexual prowess. ☐ **at stud** (of a male horse) available for breeding on payment of a fee.

student n. a person engaged in studying something, a pupil at a university, college, etc. • adj. studying in order to become (a student nurse).

studied adj. carefully and intentionally contrived (she answered with studied indifference).

studio n. (pl. **studios**) **1** the workroom of a painter, sculptor, photographer, etc. **2** a place where cinema films are made. **3** a room from which radio or television programs are regularly broadcast or in which recordings are made.

studious adj. **1** involving study; habitually spending much time in studying. **2** deliberate, painstaking (studious politeness). ☐ **studiously** adv. **studiousness** n.

study n. **1** the process of studying. **2** its subject; a thing that is investigated. **3** a musical composition designed to develop a player's skill. **4** a preliminary drawing (charcoal study of a male torso). **5** a room in a house used for work that involves writing, reading, etc. • v. (**studied**, **studying**) **1** give one's attention to acquiring knowledge of (a subject). **2** look at carefully (we studied the map). **3** give care and consideration to. ☐ **in a brown study** in a reverie; absorbed in one's thoughts.

stuff n. **1** material; fabric. **2** unnamed things, belongings, subject-matter, activities, etc. (leave your stuff in the hall; westerns are kids' stuff). **3** particular knowledge or activity (he knows his stuff). **4** what a person is made of: capabilities or inward character (he hasn't the right stuff in him to control 200 men). **5** colloq. valueless matter, trash (stuff and nonsense!). • v. **1** pack (a receptacle) tightly (stuff a cushion with feathers; his head is stuffed with obnoxious racist notions). **2** (foll. by in, into) force or cram (a thing) (stuffed his underwear into the pocket of the holdall). **3** fill the empty parts etc. of (a bird or animal) with material to restore its original shape, e.g. for exhibition in a museum. **4** fill with savoury stuffing. **5** fill (a person or oneself) with food; eat greedily. **6** colloq. dispose of as unwanted (you can stuff the job). ☐ **get stuffed!** coarse colloq. an exclamation of dismissal, contempt, etc. **not give a stuff** colloq. not care at all. **stuffed shirt** colloq. a pompous person. **stuff it** colloq. a coarse expression of contempt, rejection, defiance, etc. **stuff up** v. colloq. ruin, bungle. **stuff-up** n. colloq. a bungled action; a ruined event etc.; a mess.

stuffed adj. **1** colloq. ruined; exhausted (I'm stuffed). **2** (often foll. by up) blocked, congested (my nose is all stuffed up).

stuffing n. **1** padding used to stuff cushions etc. **2** a savoury mixture put as a filling into poultry, vegetables, etc. before cooking.

stuffy adj. (**stuffier**, **stuffiest**) **1** lacking fresh air or sufficient ventilation. **2** (of the nose) blocked so

stultify that breathing is difficult. **3** prim, straitlaced; formal, pompous; boring, conventional. ☐ **stuffily** *adv.* **stuffiness** *n.*

stultify *v.* (**stultified**, **stultifying**) impair or make ineffective, esp. through routine (*a boring job that stultifies the brain*). ☐ **stultification** *n.*

stum *n.* unfermented grape juice, must.

stumble *v.* **1** strike one's foot on something and lose one's balance. **2** walk with frequent stumbles. **3** make a blunder or frequent blunders in speaking or playing music etc. • *n.* an act of stumbling. ☐ **stumble across** or **on** discover accidentally. **stumbling block** an obstacle; a difficulty.

stumer / **styoo**-muh, **stoo**- / *colloq. n.* a worthless cheque. ☐ **come a stumer** *Aust.* lose one's money.

stumered / **styoo**-muhd, **stoo**- / *adj. Aust. colloq.* without any money.

stump *n.* **1** the base of a tree remaining in the ground when the rest has been cut down. **2** a corresponding remnant e.g. of a broken tooth or an amputated limb. **3 a** one of the three uprights of a wicket in cricket. **b** (**stumps**) the end of the day's play. **4** (esp. in Qld) one of the piles supporting a dwelling. • *v.* **1** walk stiffly or noisily. **2** (of a wicket-keeper) put out (a batsman) by dislodging the bails while he is out of the crease. **3** be too difficult for, baffle (*the question stumped him*). ☐ **beyond the black stump** *see* BLACK STUMP. **stump-grub** *v. Aust.* remove the stumps of felled trees (from a paddock etc.) by manual or mechanical means. **stump-jump plough** *Aust.* a plough specially designed for use on land which has not been stump-grubbed. **stump up** *colloq.* pay or produce (the money required).

stumpy *adj.* (**stumpier**, **stumpiest**) short and thick. ☐ **stumpy tail** (also **stump-tailed lizard**, **stumpy-tailed skink**, **stumpy** etc.) *Aust.* = BOBTAIL (sense 2). ☐☐ **stumpiness** *n.*

stun *v.* (**stunned**, **stunning**) **1** knock senseless. **2** daze or shock.

stung *see* STING.

stunk *see* STUNK.

stunner *n. colloq.* a highly attractive and sexually desirable male or female; a thing of outstanding excellence.

stunning *adj. colloq.* extremely attractive or impressive. ☐ **stunningly** *adv.*

stunt[1] *v.* hinder the growth or development of.

stunt[2] *n. colloq.* something unusual or difficult done as a performance or to attract attention.

stuntman *n.* a person employed to take an actor's place in performing esp. dangerous stunts.

stupa / **stoo**-puh / *n.* a round usu. domed Buddhist monument, usu. containing a sacred relic.

stupefy *v.* (**stupefied**, **stupefying**) **1** dull the wits or senses of. **2** stun with astonishment. ☐ **stupefaction** *n.*

stupendous / styoo-**pen**-duhs / *adj.* amazing, exceedingly great. ☐ **stupendously** *adv.*

stupid / **styoo**-puhd / *adj.* **1** not intelligent or clever, slow at learning or understanding. **2** in a state of stupor (*he was knocked stupid*). **3** uninteresting, boring (*this is a stupid film*). ☐ **stupidly** *adv.* **stupidity** *n.*

stupor / **styoo**-puh / *n.* a dazed or almost unconscious condition brought on by shock, drugs, drink, etc.

sturdy *adj.* (**sturdier**, **sturdiest**) **1** robust; strongly built. **2** vigorous (*sturdy resistance*). ☐ **sturdily** *adv.* **sturdiness** *n.*

sturgeon *n.* (*pl.* **sturgeon** or **sturgeons**) a large shark-like fish (of the Northern hemisphere) with flesh that is valued as food and roe that is made into caviare.

Sturt, Charles (1795–1869), Australian explorer (born in India) who led several expeditions into the interior of Australia. ☐ **Sturt's desert pea** a trailing plant of sandy soils in arid parts of all States except Vic. and Tas., bearing masses of extremely large brilliant red pea-flowers with a shiny black boss: the floral emblem of South Australia. Also called *clianthus*. **Sturt's desert rose** a shrub of arid central Australia bearing large, bluish-mauve hibiscus-like flowers with a dark red basal splotch: the floral emblem of the Northern Territory.

stutter *v.* stammer, esp. by repeating the first consonants of words. • *n.* stuttering speech; a tendency to stutter.

sty[1] *n.* (*pl.* **sties**) a pigsty.

sty[2] *n.* (also **stye**) (*pl.* **sties** or **styes**) an inflamed swelling on the edge of the eyelid.

Stygian / **stij**-ee-uhn / *adj. literary* of or like the Styx or Hades; gloomy, murky.

style *n.* **1** the manner of writing, speaking, or doing something (contrasted with the subject-matter or the thing done). **2** shape or design (*a new style of coat*). **3** elegance, distinction. **4** a narrow extension of the ovary in a plant, supporting the stigma. • *v.* design, shape, or arrange, esp. in a fashionable style. ☐ **in style** elegantly; luxuriously.

stylidium / stuy-**lid**-ee-uhm / = TRIGGER PLANT.

stylised *adj.* (also **-ized**) made to conform to a conventional, non-realistic style.

stylish *adj.* in fashionable style, elegant. ☐ **stylishly** *adv.* **stylishness** *n.*

stylist *n.* **1** a person who achieves or aims at a good style in what he or she does. **2** a hairdresser or designer.

stylistic *adj.* of literary or artistic style. ☐ **stylistically** *adv.*

stylus *n.* (*pl.* **styluses**) **1** a needle-like device following a groove in a gramophone record to reproduce the sound. **2** a pointed writing tool.

stymie / **stuy**-mee / *n.* **1** the situation in golf where an opponent's ball is between a player's ball and the hole. **2** something that blocks or thwarts one's activities. • *v.* (**stymied, stymieing**) **1** subject to a stymie in golf. **2** block or thwart the activities of.

stypandra / stuy-**pan**-druh / *n.* a tufted perennial plant of southern and eastern Australia, having starry, bright blue flowers with golden anthers borne on slender, nodding stalks. Also called *nodding blue lily*.

styptic / **stip**-tik / *adj.* checking the flow of blood by causing blood vessels to contract. • *n.* a styptic substance.

styrene *n.* a liquid hydrocarbon used in plastics.

Styx / stiks / *Gk myth.* one of the rivers of the Underworld, over which Charon ferried the souls of the dead.

suasion / **sway**-zhuhn / *n. formal* persuasion (*moral suasion*).

suave / swahv / *adj.* smooth-mannered; sophisticated. ☐ **suavely** *adv.* **suavity** *n.*

sub *n. colloq.* **1** a submarine. **2** a subscription. **3** a substitute. **4** a sub-editor. • *v.* **1** (usu. foll. by *for*) act as a substitute (*I'm subbing for the boss*). **2** sub-edit.

sub- *comb. form* **1** under (as in *substructure*). **2** subordinate, secondary (as in *subsection*).

subaltern / **sub**-uhl-tuhn / *n.* a second lieutenant.

subantarctic *adj.* of regions immediately north of the Antarctic Circle.

sub-aqua *adj.* (of sport etc.) taking place under water.

subaquatic *adj.* underwater.

subarctic *adj.* of regions bordering on the Arctic Circle.

sub-artesian *adj.* (of bore water) rising but not to the surface.

subatomic *adj.* (of a particle of matter) occurring in an atom; smaller than an atom.

subbie *n.* (also **subby**) *Aust. colloq.* a subcontractor.

subcommittee *n.* a committee formed for a special purpose from some members of the main committee.

subconscious *adj.* of the part of the mind that influences our attitudes, behaviour, etc. without us being aware of it. • *n.* this part of the mind. ☐ **subconsciously** *adv.*

subcontinent *n.* **1** a large land mass, smaller than a continent. **2** a large geographically or politically independent part of a continent.

subcontract / **sub**-**kuhn**-**trakt** / *v.* give or accept a contract to carry out all or part of another contract. • *n.* / sub-**kon**-trakt / a secondary contract, esp. to supply materials. ☐ **subcontractor** *n.* / sub-kuhn-**trak**-tuh /

subculture *n.* a distinct cultural group within a larger culture, often having beliefs or interests at variance with those of the larger culture.

subcutaneous / sub-kyoo-**tay**-nee-uhs / *adj.* under the skin.

subdivide *v.* divide into smaller parts after a first division. ☐ **subdivision** *n.*

subdominant *n. Music* the fourth note of the diatonic scale of any key.

subdue *v.* **1** overcome, bring under control. **2** make quieter or less intense (*subdued lighting*).

sub-edit *v.* (**sub-edited, sub-editing**) prepare (material) as a sub-editor.

sub-editor *n.* **1** an assistant editor. **2** a person who prepares material for printing in a book or newspaper etc.

subgroup *n.* a subset of a group; a group within a larger group.

subheading *n.* a subordinate heading.

subhuman *adj.* less than human; not fully human.

subincise / sub-in-**suyz** / *v. Aust.* (in Aboriginal initiation ritual) slit the underside of the penis to make a permanent opening into the urethra (*see also* WHISTLECOCK). ☐ **subincision** *n.*

subject *adj.* / **sub**-jekt / **1** not politically independent (*subject peoples*). **2** owing obedience to, under the authority of (*we are all subject to the laws of the land*). • *n.* / **sub**-jekt / **1** a person owing allegiance to and under the protection of a national government; a member of a specified nation (*Australian subjects*). **2** the person or thing that is being discussed, described, represented, etc. **3** a field of study (*his subject is Australian Literature*). **4** *Grammar* the word or words in a sentence that name who or what does the action or undergoes what is stated by the verb. **5** *Music* a theme; a leading phrase or motif. • *v.* / suhb-**jekt** / **1** bring (a country) under one's control. **2** cause to undergo or experience (*subjecting the metal to severe tests*). ☐ **subject matter** the matter treated in a book or speech etc. **subject to 1** liable to (*trains are subject to delay during fog*). **2** depending upon as a condition (*subject to your approval; subject to contract*). ☐ **subjection** *n.*

subjective / suhb-**jek**-tiv / *adj.* **1** existing in a person's mind and not produced by things outside it, not objective. **2** depending on personal taste or views etc. **3** *Grammar* of the subject. ☐ **subjectively** *adv.* **subjectivity** *n.*

subjoin *v.* add at the end.

sub judice / sub **joo**-duh-see / *adv.* under judicial consideration, not yet decided (and, for this reason, not to be commented upon). (¶ Latin, = under a judge.)

subjugate / **sub**-juh-gayt / *v.* subdue or bring (a country etc.) into subjection. ☐ **subjugation** *n.* **subjugator** *n.*

subjunctive *adj. Grammar* of the form of a verb used in expressing what is imagined or wished or possible, e.g. '*were*' in *if I were you*. • *n.* a subjunctive form.

sublease *n.* a lease granted by a tenant to a subtenant. • *v.* lease by a sublease.

sublet *v.* (**sublet, subletting**) let (accommodation etc. that one holds by lease) to a subtenant.

sublimate / **sub**-luh-mayt / v. **1** divert the energy of (an emotion or impulse arising from a primitive instinct, esp. sexual) into a culturally higher activity. **2** *Chem.* sublime (a substance); purify. □ **sublimation** n.

sublime adj. **1** of the most exalted, noble, or impressive kind. **2** extreme, lofty, like that of a person who does not fear the consequences (*with sublime indifference*). •v. **1** *Chem.* convert (a solid substance) into a vapour by heat (and usu. allow it to solidify again). **2** undergo this process. **3** purify; make sublime. □ **sublimely** adv. **sublimity** / suh-**blim**-uh-tee / n.

subliminal / suh-**blim**-uh-nuhl / adj. below the threshold of consciousness; (of advertising, messages, etc.) containing a hidden picture, message, etc. that influences people without them being consciously aware of it. □ **subliminally** adv.

sub-machine gun n. a hand-held lightweight machine gun.

submarine adj. under the surface of the sea (*submarine cables*). •n. a ship that can operate under water. □ **submariner** / sub-**ma**-ruh-nuh / n.

submediant n. *Music* the sixth note of the diatonic scale of any key.

submerge v. **1** place below water or other liquid; flood. **2** inundate with work, problems, etc. **3** (of a submarine) dive, go below the surface. □ **submergence** n. **submersion** n.

submersible adj. able to be submerged. •n. a ship or other craft that can operate under water.

submicroscopic adj. too small to be seen by an ordinary microscope.

submission n. **1** submitting; being submitted. **2** something submitted; a theory etc. submitted by counsel to a judge or jury. **3** being submissive, obedience.

submissive adj. submitting to power or authority, willing to obey. □ **submissively** adv. **submissiveness** n.

submit v. (**submitted**, **submitting**) **1** yield (oneself) to the authority or control of another, surrender. **2** subject (a person or thing) to a process. **3** present for consideration or decision (*submitted her thesis*).

subnormal adj. **1** less than normal. **2** below the normal standard of intelligence.

subordinate adj. / suh-**baw**-duh-nuht / **1** of lesser importance or rank. **2** working under the control or authority of another person. •n. / suh-**baw**-duh-nuht / a person in a subordinate position. •v. / suh-**baw**-duh-nayt / make subordinate, treat as of lesser importance than something else. □ **subordinate clause** a clause acting as an adjective, adverb, or noun in a main sentence. □□ **subordination** n.

suborn / suh-**bawn** / v. induce (a person) by bribery or other means to commit perjury or some other unlawful act.

sub-plot n. a secondary plot in a play.

subpoena / suh-**pee**-nuh / n. a writ commanding a person to appear in a lawcourt. •v. (**subpoenaed** or **subpoena'd**, **subpoenaing**) summon with a subpoena.

sub rosa adv. & adj. in confidence, in secrecy. (¶ Latin, = under the rose, which was an emblem of secrecy.)

subroutine n. a self-contained section of a computer program, for performing a specific task but not itself a complete program.

subscribe v. (usu. foll. by *to*) **1** pay (a sum of money) esp. regularly for membership of an organisation, receipt of a magazine, etc.; arrange to receive a magazine etc. regularly. **2** express one's agreement (*we cannot subscribe to such a racist view*).

subscriber n. **1** a person who subscribes. **2** one who rents a telephone. □ **subscriber trunk dialling** a system of dialling numbers for trunk calls instead of asking an operator to obtain these.

subscript adj. written below the line. •n. a subscript number or character (e.g. 2 as in H_2O).

subscription n. **1** subscribing. **2** money subscribed. **3** a fee for membership of a society etc.

subsection n. a division of a section.

subsequent adj. following in time or succession; coming after. □ **subsequently** adv.

subserve / suhb-**serv** / v. serve as a means in furthering (a purpose, action, etc.).

subservient adj. **1** subordinate. **2** servile, obsequious. □ **subserviently** adv. **subservience** n.

subset n. *Maths* a set of which all the elements are contained in another set.

subshrub n. a low growing or small shrub.

subside v. **1** sink to a lower or to the normal level. **2** (of land) sink, e.g. because of mining operations underneath. **3** become less active or intense (*the excitement subsided*). □ **subsidence** / suhb-**suy**-duhns / n.

subsidiary adj. **1** of secondary importance. **2** (of a business company) controlled by another. •n. a subsidiary thing.

subsidise v. (also **-ize**) pay a subsidy to or for; support by subsidies.

subsidy n. a grant paid to an industry or cause needing help, or to keep down the price at which commodities are sold.

subsist v. exist or continue to exist; keep oneself alive (*they managed to subsist on a diet of nuts and berries*).

subsistence n. subsisting; a means of doing this. □ **subsistence farming** farming in which almost all the crops etc. are consumed by the farmer's household with no surplus for sale.

subsistence level merely enough to supply the bare necessities of life.

subsoil n. soil lying immediately beneath the surface layer.

subsonic *adj.* (of speed) less than the speed of sound; (of aircraft) flying at subsonic speeds, not supersonic. ☐ **subsonically** *adv.*

substance *n.* **1** matter with more or less uniform properties; the material of which something consists. **2** the essence of something spoken or written (*we agree with the substance of this argument*). **3** reality, solidity (*a ghost has no substance*). **4** *archaic* wealth and possessions (*a woman of substance*). **5** the essential nature of a thing, that which makes it what it is (as opposed to its *accidents* such as colour, shape, external appearances, etc.). **6** an intoxicating or narcotic chemical or drug, esp. an illegal one (*substance abuse*).

substandard *adj.* below the usual or required standard.

substantial *adj.* **1** of solid material or structure. **2** of considerable amount, intensity, or validity (*a substantial fee; substantial reasons*). **3** possessing much property or wealth (*substantial farmers*). **4** in essentials, virtual (*we are in substantial agreement*). ☐ **substantially** *adv.*

substantiate / suhb-**stan**-shee-ayt / *v.* support (a statement or claim etc.) with evidence; prove. ☐ **substantiation** *n.*

substantive *adj.* / **sub**-stuhn-tiv, sub-**stan**-tiv / **1** genuine, actual, real. **2** not slight; substantial. • *n.* / **sub**-stuhn-tiv / *Grammar* a noun.

substation *n.* a subordinate station, e.g. for the distribution of electric current.

substitute *n.* a person or thing that acts or serves in place of another. • *v.* (often foll. by *for*) **1** put or use as a substitute. **2** *colloq.* serve as a substitute. • *adj.* acting as a substitute. ☐ **substitution** *n.*

substratum / sub-**strah**-tuhm, -**stray**- / *n.* (*pl.* **substrata**) an underlying layer or substance.

subsume *v.* (usu. foll. by *under*) include (an instance, idea, category, etc.) in a particular rule or classification etc. (*many differing Aboriginal dialects are subsumed under the one name 'The Western Desert language'*). ☐ **subsumable** *adj.* **subsumption** *n.*

subtenant *n.* a person who rents accommodation etc. from its tenant. ☐ **subtenancy** *n.*

subterfuge / **sub**-tuh-fyooj / *n.* a trick or excuse used to avoid blame or defeat; trickery.

subterranean / sub-tuh-**ray**-nee-uhn / *adj.* underground.

subtext *n.* an underlying theme.

subtitle *n.* **1** a subordinate title. **2** a caption on a cinema film, television program, etc. giving a translation of foreign dialogue or a summary of speech for people with hearing difficulties. • *v.* provide with a subtitle.

subtle / **sut**-uhl / *adj.* **1** slight and difficult to detect or analyse. **2** (of colour, scent, etc.) faint, delicate. **3** making or able to make fine distinctions, having acute perception (*a subtle mind*). **4** ingenious, crafty. ☐ **subtly** *adv.* **subtlety** *n.*

subtonic *n. Music* the note below the tonic, the seventh note of the diatonic scale of any key.

subtotal *n.* the total of part of a group of figures.

subtract *v.* deduct, remove (a part, quantity, or number) from a greater one. ☐ **subtraction** *n.*

subtropical *adj.* of regions bordering on the tropics. ☐ **subtropics** *n.pl.*

suburb *n.* a residential district lying outside the central part of a city.

suburban *adj.* **1** of a suburb or suburbs. **2** having only limited interests and narrow-minded views.

suburbanite *n.* a person who lives in a suburb.

suburbia *n.* (often *derog.*) suburbs, their inhabitants, and their way of life.

subvention / suhb-**ven**-shuhn / *n.* a subsidy; a grant of money from a government etc.

subversion *n.* the action or practice of subverting (esp. a government); an instance or result of this.

subversive *adj.* tending to subvert (esp. a government). • *n.* a subversive person. ☐ **subversively** *adv.* **subversiveness** *n.*

subvert / suhb-**vert** / *v.* overthrow the authority of (a religion or government etc.) by weakening people's trust or belief.

subway *n.* **1** an underground passage, e.g. for pedestrians to cross below a road. **2** *esp. US* an underground railway.

subzero *adj.* (of temperatures) below zero.

succeed *v.* **1** be successful. **2** come next to in time or order; follow; take the place previously filled by (*Pope John XXIII succeeded Pope Pius XII; he succeeded to the throne*).

success *n.* **1** a favourable outcome; doing what was desired or attempted; the attainment of wealth, fame, or position. **2** a person or thing that is successful.

successful *adj.* having success. ☐ **successfully** *adv.*

succession *n.* **1** following in order; a series of people or things following each other. **2** succeeding to the throne or office or to an inheritance or position; the right of doing this; the sequence of people with this right. ☐ **in succession** one after another.

successive *adj.* following one after another, in an unbroken series. ☐ **successively** *adv.*

successor *n.* a person or thing that succeeds another.

succinct / suhk-**singkt** / *adj.* concise; expressed briefly and clearly. ☐ **succinctly** *adv.* **succinctness** *n.*

succour / **suk**-uh / *n.* (also **succor**) help given in time of need. • *v.* give such help.

succubus / **suk**-yuh-buhs / *n.* (*pl.* **succubi** / -buy /) a female demon believed to have sexual intercourse with sleeping men.

succulent / **suk**-yuh-luhnt / *adj.* **1** juicy; palatable. **2** (of plants) having thick fleshy leaves or stems. • *n.* a succulent plant. ☐ **succulence** *n.*

succumb / suh-**kum** / v. **1** (often foll. by *to*) give way to something overpowering (*he succumbed to the temptation*). **2** die (from) (*he succumbed to his injuries*).

such adj. **1** of the same kind or degree (*people such as these*). **2** of the kind or degree described (*there's no such person*). **3** so great or intense (*it gave her such a fright*). •*pron.* that, the action or thing referred to (*such being the case, we can do nothing*). ❑ **and such** and things or people of that kind (*bought sandwiches and such; there were priests and such all over the place*). **as such** as what has been specified; in itself (*interested in getting a good photograph, not in the castle as such*). **such-and-such** adj. particular but not now specified (*says he will arrive at such-and-such a time but is always late*). **such as** for example.

suchlike adj. colloq. of the same kind. ❑ **and suchlike** and things or people of that kind.

suck v. **1** draw (liquid or air etc.) into the mouth; draw liquid etc. from (a thing) in this way. **2** squeeze in the mouth using the tongue. **3** draw in (*plants suck moisture from the soil; the canoe was sucked into the whirlpool; was sucked into the fray*). **4** (also **sux**) colloq. be contemptible or disgusting etc. (*homework sucks; sucking sux*). **5** = SUCK UP (sense 1) (*sucking the boss for all he's worth*). •*n.* an act or period of sucking. **2** (**sucks**) (esp. as *interj.*) colloq. **a** an expression of disappointment. **b** an expression of derision or amusement at another's discomfiture (*sucks to you!*). **3** = SOAK n. (sense 3). ❑ **suck in 1** absorb. **2** colloq. involve (a person) esp. against his or her will (*sucked him in to keep guard while they robbed the house*). **3** colloq. deceive (*don't be sucked in by his padre-like manner*). **suck up 1** (often foll. by *to*) Aust. colloq. behave in a flattering, servile way towards (a person) to gain advantage. **2** absorb.

sucker n. **1** a person or thing that sucks. **2** an organ of certain animals, or a device of rubber etc., that can adhere to a surface by suction. **3 a** a shoot coming up from the roots or underground stem of a tree or shrub. **b** an adventitious growth (esp. of eucalypts) from a branch or trunk that has been severed or bruised. **4** colloq. a person who is easily deceived, a dupe. ❑ **be a sucker for** colloq. be always unable to resist the attractions of.

sucker-bash Aust. colloq. v. cut down suckers or new growth on newly-cleared land. •*n.* an act or instance of sucker-bashing. ❑ **sucker-basher** n.

suckhole colloq. n. a sycophant, a crawler. •*v.* toady, crawl to.

suckle v. **1** feed (young) at the breast or udder. **2** (of young) take milk in this way.

suckling n. a child or animal that is not yet weaned.

sucky adj. colloq. fawning, toadying, given to sucking up to (bosses etc.).

Sucre / **soo**-kray / the legal capital and seat of the judiciary of Bolivia.

sucrose / **soo**-krohz / n. sugar obtained from plants such as sugar cane or sugar beet.

suction n. **1** sucking. **2** production of a partial or complete vacuum so that external atmospheric pressure forces fluid or other substance into the vacant space or causes adhesion of surfaces (*vacuum cleaners work by suction*).

Sudan / soo-**dahn**, -**dan** / a republic in north-east Africa. ❑ **Sudanese** / soo-duh-**neez** / adj. & n. (pl. **Sudanese**).

sudden adj. happening or done quickly, unexpectedly, or without warning. ❑ **sudden death** colloq. decision of a drawn or tied contest by the result of the next game or point. **sudden infant death syndrome** (also **SIDS**) = COT DEATH. ❑❑ **suddenly** adv. **suddenness** n.

sudorific / soo-duh-**rif**-ik / adj. causing sweating. •*n.* a sudorific drug.

Sudra / **soo**-druh / n. a member of the lowest of the four great Hindu classes or varnas, the labourer class, with the traditional function of serving the other three varnas.

suds n.pl. a froth of soap and water. ❑ **sudsy** adj.

sue v. (**sued**, **suing**) **1** begin legal proceedings against. **2** make an entreaty (*sue for peace*).

suede / swayd / n. leather with the flesh side rubbed so that it has a velvety nap.

suet n. hard fat from round the kidneys of cattle and sheep, used in cooking. ❑ **suety** adj.

Suez an isthmus connecting Egypt to the Sinai peninsula, site of the **Suez Canal**, a canal connecting the Mediterranean with the Red Sea.

suffer v. **1** undergo or be subjected to (pain, grief, damage, etc.). **2** feel pain or grief; be subjected to damage or a disadvantage. **3** permit. **4** tolerate (*she does not suffer fools gladly*). ❑ **sufferer** n. **suffering** n.

sufferance n. ❑ **on sufferance** tolerated but only grudgingly or because there is no positive objection.

suffice / suh-**fuys** / v. be enough; meet the needs of.

sufficient adj. enough. ❑ **sufficiently** adv. **sufficiency** n.

suffix n. (pl. **suffixes**) a letter or combination of letters added at the end of a word to make another word (e.g. *y* added to *rust* to make *rusty*) or as an inflection (e.g. *ing* added to *suck* to make *sucking*).

suffocate v. **1** kill by stopping the breathing. **2** cause discomfort to (a person) by making breathing difficult. **3** be suffocated. ❑ **suffocation** n.

suffrage / **suf**-rij / n. the right to vote in political elections.

suffragette / suf-ruh-**jet** / n. a woman who, in the early 20th century, campaigned for women to have the right to vote in political elections.

suffuse / suh-**fyooz** / v. (of colour or moisture) spread throughout or over (*a blush suffused his cheeks*). ❑ **suffusion** n.

Sufi / **soo**-fee / n. a Muslim ascetic mystic. ❑ **Sufic** adj. **Sufism** n.

sugar *n.* **1** a sweet crystalline substance obtained from the juices of various plants, esp. from sugar cane and sugar beet. **2** *Chem.* a soluble crystalline carbohydrate, e.g. glucose. •*v.* sweeten or coat with sugar. □ **sugar ant** any of several related stingless Australian ants, esp. one with an orange thorax and legs and a black head. **sugar bag** *Aust.* **1** (in Aboriginal English) **a** the honey of the wild Australian stingless bee; its honeycomb or hive. **b** a bee of any kind; the honey from such a bee. **c** = HONEY ANT (*see* HONEY). **2** a bag of fine sacking, orig. made for containing sugar, and used subsequently for a variety of purposes (e.g. as a shopping bag, a small swag, etc.). **sugar beet** beet from which sugar is extracted. **sugar cane** a tropical grass with tall jointed stems from which sugar is obtained. **sugar cocky** (also **cane cocky**) *Aust.* the proprietor of a sugar cane farm. **sugar daddy** *colloq.* a rich older man who lavishes gifts on, or maintains, a young woman or a young man in return for sexual favours. **sugar glider** a gliding possum of northern and eastern Australia including Tas., feeding on nectar, insects, etc. **sugar gum** *Aust.* any of several eucalypts, esp. *E. cladocalyx* of southern SA, widely planted as a windbreak. **sugar pea** = SNOW PEA (*see* SNOW). **sugar soap** an abrasive compound for cleaning or removing paint.

sugarwood *n.* a myoporum of eastern Australia, having a rough bark which often exudes a sugary substance, and providing an extremely sweet-smelling, sandalwood-like timber; the wood of this tree.

sugary *adj.* **1** containing or resembling sugar. **2** sweet; excessively sweet or sentimental in style or manner. □ **sugariness** *n.*

suggest *v.* **1** cause (an idea or possibility) to be present in the mind. **2** propose (a plan or theory).

suggestible *adj.* **1** easily influenced by people's suggestions. **2** that may be suggested. □ **suggestibility** *n.*

suggestion *n.* **1** suggesting; being suggested. **2** something suggested. **3** a slight trace (*he speaks with a suggestion of a French accent*).

suggestive *adj.* **1** conveying a suggestion. **2** tending to convey an indecent or improper meaning. □ **suggestively** *adv.* **suggestiveness** *n.*

Suharto (1921–), General, president of Indonesia 1968–98.

suicidal *adj.* **1** of suicide. **2** (of a person) liable to commit suicide. **3** destructive to one's own interests. □ **suicidally** *adv.*

suicide *n.* **1** the intentional killing of oneself; an instance of this. **2** a person who commits suicide. **3** an act that is destructive to one's own interests (*political suicide*). •*v.* commit suicide. □ **commit suicide** kill oneself intentionally. **suicide pact** an agreement between people to commit suicide together.

sui generis / soo-uy **jen**-uh-ris, soo-ee, syoo-uy / *adj.* (the only one) of its own kind; unique. (¶ Latin)

suit *n.* **1** a set of clothing to be worn together, esp. a jacket and trousers or skirt. **2** clothing for use in a particular activity (*a diving suit*). **3** any of the four sets (spades, hearts, diamonds, clubs) into which a pack of cards is divided. **4** a lawsuit. **5** a petition, esp. to a person in authority. **6** *archaic* the seeking of a woman's hand in marriage. •*v.* **1** satisfy, meet the requirements of. **2** be convenient or right for. **3** give a pleasing appearance or effect upon (*red doesn't suit her*). **4** adapt, make suitable (*suit your style to your audience*). □ **suit oneself** do as one pleases.

suitable *adj.* right for the purpose or occasion. □ **suitably** *adv.* **suitability** *n.*

suitcase *n.* a rectangular case for carrying clothes, usu. with a hinged lid and a handle.

suite *n.* **1** a set of things belonging together, esp.: **a** a set of rooms in a hotel etc. **b** a sofa and armchairs etc. of the same design. **2** a set of attendants, a retinue. **3** a set of musical pieces or extracts.

suitor *n.* **1** a man who is courting a woman. **2** a person bringing a lawsuit.

sukiyaki / suu-kee-**yah**-kee / *n.* a Japanese dish of sliced meat simmered with vegetables and sauce.

sulfa, sulfate, sulfur, etc. alternative spelling of SULPHA, SULPHATE, SULPHUR, etc.

sulk *v.* be sulky. •*n.* **1** (also **the sulks**) a fit of sulkiness. **2** a person who sulks. □ **sulker** *n.*

sulky *adj.* (**sulkier, sulkiest**) **1** sullen or silent because of resentment or bad temper. **2** *Aust.* (in Aboriginal English) angry, threatening. •*n.* a light two-wheeled horse-drawn vehicle for one, esp. used in trotting races. □ **sulkily** *adv.* **sulkiness** *n.*

sullen *adj.* **1** gloomy and unresponsive from resentment or bad temper. **2** dark and dismal (*sullen skies*). □ **sullenly** *adv.* **sullenness** *n.*

Sullivan, Sir Arthur (1842–1900), English composer, noted for the comic operas produced with librettist W.S. Gilbert.

sully *v.* (**sullied, sullying**) stain or blemish; spoil (*sullied his reputation*).

sulpha *adj.* sulphonamide (*sulpha drugs*).

sulphate *n.* a salt of sulphuric acid.

sulphide *n.* a binary compound of sulphur.

sulphite *n.* a salt or ester of sulphurous acid.

sulphonamide / sul-**fon**-uh-muyd / *n.* any of a class of antibiotic drugs containing sulphur.

sulphur *n.* **1** a chemical element (symbol S), a pale yellow substance that burns with a blue flame and a stifling smell, used in industry and medicine. **2** yellow with a slight greenish tinge. □ **sulphur-crested cockatoo** *Aust.* = WHITE COCKATOO.

■ **Usage** In general use the standard Australian spelling is *sulphur* and the standard US spelling is *sulfur*. In chemistry, however, the *sulfur* spelling is now the standard form in all related words in the field in Australian and US contexts.

sulphureous / sul-**fyoo**-ree-uhs / *adj.* of or like sulphur.

sulphuric / sul-**fyoo**-rik / *adj.* containing a proportion of sulphur. ❑ **sulphuric acid** a strong oily highly corrosive acid.

sulphurous / sul-fuh-ruhs / *adj.* **1** of or like sulphur. **2** containing a proportion of sulphur. ❑ **sulphurous acid** a weak acid used as a reducing and bleaching acid.

sultan *n.* the ruler of certain Muslim countries.

sultana *n.* **1** a seedless raisin; a small pale yellow grape producing this. **2** the wife, mother, sister, or daughter of a sultan.

sultanate *n.* the territory of a sultan.

sultry *adj.* (**sultrier**, **sultriest**) **1** hot and humid. **2** (of a person) passionate and sensual. ❑ **sultriness** *n.*

sum *n.* **1** a total. **2** an amount of money. **3** a problem in arithmetic. • *v.* (**summed**, **summing**) find the sum of. ❑ **in sum** briefly, in summary. **sum total** a total. **sum up 1** give the total of. **2** summarise. **3** (of a judge) summarise the evidence or argument. **4** form an opinion of (*sum a person up*). **summing-up 1** a judge's review to a jury of the evidence presented. **2** a recapitulation of the main points of an argument etc.

summarise *v.* (also **-ize**) make or be a summary of.

summary *n.* a statement giving the main points of something briefly. • *adj.* **1** brief, giving the main points only (*a summary account*). **2** done or given without delay or attention to detail or formal (legal etc.) procedure (*summary justice*). ❑ **summary offence** a minor offence that can be tried in a magistrate's court without a jury. ❑ ❑ **summarily** *adv.*

summation / suh-**may**-shuhn / *n.* finding of a total or sum; summing up.

summer *n.* the warmest season of the year. ❑ **summer pudding** a pudding of fresh berry-fruit pressed in a bread case. **summer school** a course of summer lectures etc. held esp. at a university. **summer solstice** the solstice occurring about 22 December.

summertime *n.* the season of summer.

summery *adj.* like summer; suitable for summer.

summit *n.* **1** the highest point of something; the top of a mountain. **2** (in full **summit meeting**, **talks**, etc.) **a** a meeting between heads of governments. **b** a conference of national leaders, organisations, etc., called upon to discuss and make recommendations about issues of national importance (*tax summit; youth unemployment summit*).

summon *v.* **1** send for (a person); order to appear in a lawcourt. **2** call together; order to assemble (*summon a meeting*). **3** gather together (one's strength or courage). **4** call upon (a person etc.) to do something (*summoned her to assist*).

summons *n.* (*pl.* **summonses**) a command to do something or appear somewhere; an order to appear in a lawcourt. • *v.* serve with a summons.

■ **Usage** It is equally correct to use *summon* as a verb with this meaning.

sumo / **soo**-moh / *n.* Japanese wrestling in which a person is considered defeated if he touches the ground except with his feet or fails to keep within a marked area.

sump *n.* **1** an inner casing holding lubricating-oil in a petrol engine. **2** a hole or low area into which waste liquid drains.

sumptuous *adj.* splendid and costly-looking. ❑ **sumptuously** *adv.* **sumptuousness** *n.*

sun *n.* **1** the star round which the earth travels and from which it receives light and warmth. **2** this light or warmth (*let the sun in*). **3** any fixed star with or without planets. • *v.* (**sunned**, **sunning**) bask in the sun; expose to the sun. ❑ **sunless** *adj.*

sunbake *v. Aust.* sunbathe. • *n.* (a period of) basking in the sun.

sunbathe *v.* expose one's body to the sun, esp. to tan the body. ❑ **sunbather** *n.*

sunbeam *n.* **1** a ray of sunlight. **2** an item of cutlery or crockery laid on the table but not used, and so not needing to be washed.

sunbird *n.* any of various small birds with brilliant and variegated plumage found in tropical and sub-tropical regions of Australia etc. (*yellow-bellied sunbird*).

sunblock *n.* a cream that protects the skin from the sun's harmful ultraviolet rays.

sunburn *n.* inflammation of the skin caused by exposure to sun. ❑ **sunburnt** *adj.* (also **sunburned**).

suncream = SUNBLOCK.

sundae / **sun**-day / *n.* a dish of ice cream and crushed fruit, nuts, syrup, etc.

Sunday *n.* the first day of the week, a Christian holiday and day of worship (*see also* BIG SUNDAY under BIG). • *adv. colloq.* **1** on Sunday. **2** (**Sundays**) *colloq.* on Sunday; each Sunday (*Sundays he works on the house he is building*). ❑ **Sunday business** *Aust.* (in Aboriginal English) religious matters—*see also* BUSINESS (sense 6), BUSINESS GROUND.

sunder *v.* break or tear apart, sever.

sundew *n.* a genus (about 70 species in Australia) of small, insect-consuming plants having extremely sticky hairs on the leaves, each hair tipped with a globule of nectar which gleams jewel-like in the sun and attracts insects.

sundial *n.* a device that shows the time by the shadow of a pointer on a dial.

sundown *n.* sunset. ❑ **sundown way** *Aust.* (in Aboriginal English) the west.

sundowner *n. Aust.* an itinerant, ostensibly seeking work, who times his arrival (at a station etc.) to coincide with the end of the day's work and the provision of food and bed; a loafer, a sponger.

sundry *adj.* various, several. • *n.* **1** (**sundries**) various small items not named individually. **2** *Cricket esp. Aust.* an extra; a run scored otherwise than off the bat. □ **all and sundry** everyone.

sunfish *n.* any of various almost spherical fish of Australian waters and elsewhere.

sunflower *n.* a tall plant bearing very large flowers with golden petals round a dark centre, producing seeds that yield an edible oil.

sung *see* SING.

sunglasses *n.pl.* glasses with tinted lenses to protect the eyes from sunlight or glare.

sunk *see* SINK.

sunken *adj.* **1** lying below the level of the surrounding area. **2** (of cheeks etc.) hollow.

sunlamp *n.* a lamp producing ultraviolet rays for therapy, to tan the skin, etc.

sunlight *n.* light from the sun.

sunlit *adj.* lit by sunlight.

Sunna / **suun**-uh, **sun**- / *n.* the traditional portion of Islamic law, based on Mohammed's words or acts but not written by him.

Sunni / **sun**-ee / *n.* **1** one of the two major groups in Islam (the other is Shi'a), comprising the main community in most Muslim countries other than Iran. **2** (also **Sunnite**) a member of this group.

sunnies *n.pl. Aust. colloq.* sunglasses.

sunny *adj.* (**sunnier**, **sunniest**) **1** bright with sunlight, full of sunshine. **2** (of a person or mood) cheerful. □ **sunnily** *adv.*

sunrise *n.* the rising of the sun; the time of this. □ **sunrise industry** any newly established industry, esp. in electronics, telecommunications, etc., regarded as signalling prosperity. **sunrise way** *Aust.* (in Aboriginal English) the east.

sunscreen *n.* = SUNBLOCK.

sunset *n.* **1** the setting of the sun; the time of this. **2** the western sky full of colour at sunset. □ **sunset clause** (or **provision**) a provision for an agency or program to be disbanded or terminated at the end of a fixed period unless formally reviewed.

sunshade *n.* **1** a parasol. **2** an awning.

sunshine *n.* **1 a** direct sunlight uninterrupted by cloud. **b** an area lit by the sun. **2** cheerfulness. □ **sunshine wattle** a dense wattle of NSW, Vic., and Tas., having deep yellow flowers which 'light up' the gloom of winter.

Sunshine coast the name given to a section of the coast of Qld extending from Caloundra to Noosa Heads which has become popular with holidaymakers and retirees.

Sunshine State Queensland.

sunspot *n.* **1** one of the dark patches sometimes observed on the sun's surface. **2** *Aust.* a horny growth on the skin, caused by excessive exposure to sunlight; keratosis.

sunstroke *n.* illness caused by too much exposure to sun.

suntan *n.* a brownish skin colour caused by exposure to the sun. □ **suntanned** *adj.*

sup *v.* (**supped**, **supping**) **1** take (liquid) by sips or spoonfuls. **2** eat supper. • *n.* a mouthful of liquid.

super *n. colloq.* **1** a superintendent. **2** a supernumerary. **3** *Aust.* superphosphate. **4** *Aust.* superannuation. **5 a** petrol of a high-octane grade. **b** leaded petrol (as opposed to *unleaded petrol*). • *adj. colloq.* excellent, superb.

super- *comb. form* **1** over, beyond (as in *superstructure, superhuman*). **2** extremely (as in *superabundant*). **3** extra good or large of its kind (as in *supertanker*).

superabundant *adj.* very abundant, more than enough. □ **superabundance** *n.*

superannuant *n. Aust.* a recipient of a superannuation pension.

superannuate *v.* **1** discharge (an employee) into retirement with a pension. **2** discard as too old for use.

superannuation *n.* **1** superannuating. **2** a pension paid on retirement to a worker who has contributed to a superannuation scheme; payment(s) contributed towards this during employment.

superb *adj.* of the most impressive or splendid kind, excellent. □ **superb blue wren** (also **superb fairy wren**) a small bird of south-eastern Australia, the breeding male having brilliant light-and-dark-blue plumage. **superb lyrebird** a greyish-brown lyrebird of south-eastern Australia, the male having a magnificent lyre-shaped tail display, dark on the outside and silvery on the inside, and a superb song, including uncanny mimicry of forest sounds and the songs and calls of other birds. □□ **superbly** *adv.*

supercharge *v.* **1** charge (the atmosphere etc.) with energy, emotion, etc. **2** use a supercharger on.

supercharger *n.* a device supplying air or fuel to an internal-combustion engine at above atmospheric pressure to increase the power of the engine.

supercilious / soo-puh-**sil**-ee-uhs / *adj.* with an air of superiority, haughty and scornful. □ **superciliously** *adv.* **superciliousness** *n.*

supercomputer *n.* a powerful computer capable of dealing with complex mathematical problems.

superconductivity *n.* the property of certain metals, at temperatures near absolute zero, of having no electrical resistance, so that once a current is started it flows without a voltage to keep it going. □ **superconductive** *adj.* **superconductor** *n.*

superego / soo-puhr-**ee**-goh / *n. Psychol.* the part of a person's mind that acts like a conscience in directing his or her behaviour.

supererogation / soo-puhr-e-roh-**gay**-shuhn / n. the doing of more than is required by duty (*works of supererogation*).

superficial *adj.* **1** of or on the surface, not deep or penetrating (*a superficial wound; superficial knowledge*). **2** (of a person) having no depth of character or feeling. ▫ **superficially** *adv.* **superficiality** / soo-puh-fish-ee-**al**-uh-tee / *n.*

superfine *adj.* of extra-high quality (*superfine wool*).

superfluity / soo-puh-**floo**-uh-tee / *n.* a superfluous amount.

superfluous / soo-**per**-floo-uhs / *adj.* more than is required. ▫ **superfluously** *adv.*

superhuman *adj.* beyond ordinary human capacity or power.

superimpose *v.* lay or place (a thing) on top of something else. ▫ **superimposition** *n.*

superintend *v.* supervise, direct. ▫ **superintendence** *n.*

superintendent *n.* **1** a person who superintends. **2** a police officer next above the rank of chief inspector.

superior *adj.* **1** higher in position or rank. **2** better or greater in some way; of higher quality. **3** showing that one feels oneself to be better or wiser etc. than others; conceited, supercilious. •*n.* **1** a person or thing of higher rank, ability, or quality. **2** the head of a monastery or other religious community (*Mother Superior*). ▫ **superiority** *n.*

superlative / soo-**per**-luh-tiv / *adj.* **1** of the highest degree or quality (*a man of superlative wisdom*). **2** of a grammatical form that expresses the highest or a very high degree of quality, e.g. *dearest*, *shyest*, *best*. •*n.* a superlative form of a word. ▫ **superlatively** *adv.*

superman *n.* a man of exceptional strength or ability.

supermarket *n.* a large self-service shop selling groceries and household goods.

supernatural *adj.* of or caused by power above the forces of nature; magical; mystical. ▫ **supernaturally** *adv.*

supernova *n.* (*pl.* **supernovae** or **supernovas**) a star that suddenly increases greatly in brightness because of an explosion disrupting its structure.

supernumerary / soo-puh-**nyoo**-muh-ruh-ree / *adj.* **1** in excess of the normal number, extra. **2** engaged for extra work. **3** (of an actor) appearing on stage but not speaking. •*n.* a supernumerary person or thing.

superphosphate *n.* a fertiliser containing soluble phosphates.

superpower *n.* one of the most powerful nations of the world.

superscript *adj.* written or printed just above and to the right of a word, figure, or symbol (e.g. 2 in *snuff*[2]). •*n.* a superscript number or symbol.

supersede / soo-puh-**seed** / *v.* **1** take the place of (*cars have superseded horse-drawn carriages*). **2** put or use in place of (another person or thing). ▫ **supersession** *n.*

supersonic *adj.* of or having a speed greater than that of sound. ▫ **supersonically** *adv.*

superstar *n.* a great star in entertainment etc.

superstition *n.* **1** belief that events can be influenced by supernatural forces; a practice, belief, or religion based on this. **2** a belief that is held by a number of people but without foundation (*the superstition that an umbrella should not be opened inside a house*).

superstitious *adj.* based on or influenced by superstition. ▫ **superstitiously** *adv.* **superstitiousness** *n.*

superstructure *n.* a structure that rests on top of something else; a building as distinct from its foundations.

supertonic *n. Music* the note above the tonic, the second note of the diatonic scale of any key.

supervene / soo-puh-**veen** / *v.* occur as an interruption or a change from some condition or process. ▫ **supervention** / soo-puh-**ven**-shuhn / *n.*

supervise *v.* direct and inspect (work or workers or the operation of an organisation). ▫ **supervision** *n.* **supervisor** *n.*

supervisory / soo-puh-**vuy**-zuh-ree / *adj.* supervising (*supervisory duties*).

superwoman *n.* a woman of exceptional strength or ability.

supine / **soo**-puyn / *adj.* **1** lying face upwards. **2** not inclined to take action, indolent. ▫ **supinely** *adv.*

supper *n.* **1** a late evening snack. **2** a light evening meal taken as part of or following a social event.

supplant *v.* oust and take the place of.

supple *adj.* bending easily, flexible, not stiff. ▫ **supplely** *adv.* **suppleness** *n.*

supplejack *n.* any of several Australian plants having tough, flexible stems, esp. the rainforest tree *Flagellaria indica*, a tree which, unable to support itself, grows along the ground until it encounters a 'host', whereupon it grows upwards with very great vigour.

supplement *n.* / **sup**-luh-muhnt / **1** a thing added as an extra or to make up for a deficiency. **2** a part added to a book etc. to give further information or to treat a particular subject; a set of special pages (esp. a colour magazine) issued with a newspaper. •*v.* / **sup**-luh-ment / provide or be a supplement to. ▫ **supplemental** *adj.* **supplementation** *n.*

supplementary *adj.* serving as a supplement.

suppliant / **sup**-lee-uhnt / *n.* a person asking humbly for something. •*adj.* supplicating.

supplicate *v.* ask humbly for, beseech. ▫ **supplicant** *adj.* & *n.* **supplication** *n.* **supplicatory** *adj.*

supplier *n.* one who supplies something.

supply *v.* (**supplied**, **supplying**) **1** give or provide with (something needed or useful); make available for use. **2** make up for, satisfy (*supply a need*). • *n.* **1** provision of what is needed. **2** a stock or store; an amount of something provided or available (*the water supply; an inexhaustible supply of fish*). **3** a grant of money by parliament for the costs of government (*the Opposition threatened to block supply in the Senate*). **4** (**supplies**) provisions and equipment for an army, an expedition, etc. □ **supply bill** a parliamentary bill which seeks money for general government expenditure until the passing of the appropriation bills. **supply-side** *adj. Economics* describing a policy of low taxation etc. to encourage production and investment.

support *v.* **1** keep from falling or sinking, hold in position, bear the weight of. **2** give strength to, enable to last or continue (*too little food to support life*). **3** supply with necessaries (*he has a family to support*). **4** assist by one's approval or presence or by subscription to funds; be a fan of (a particular sports team). **5** speak in favour of (a resolution etc.). **6** take a secondary part (*the play has a strong supporting cast*). **7** corroborate, bring facts to confirm (a statement etc.). **8** endure or tolerate (*we cannot support such insolence*). • *n.* **1** supporting, being supported (*we need your support*). **2** a person or thing that supports. **3** a secondary act at a pop concert etc. □ **supporter** *n.*

supportive *adj.* providing support and encouragement.

suppose *v.* **1** be inclined to think, accept as true or probable (*I don't suppose they will come*). **2** assume as true for the purpose of argument (*suppose the world were flat*). **3** consider as a proposal (*suppose we try another*). **4** require as a condition, presuppose (*that supposes a mechanism without flaws*). □ **be supposed to** be expected or intended to; have as a duty.

supposed *adj.* believed to exist or to have a certain character or identity (*his supposed brother*).

supposedly / suh-**poh**-zuhd-lee / *adv.* according to supposition; as is generally believed.

supposition *n.* supposing, what is supposed (*the article is based on supposition not on fact*).

suppositious / sup-uh-**zish**-uhs / *adj.* hypothetical, based on supposition.

supposititious / suh-poz-uh-**tish**-uhs / *adj.* substituted for the real person or thing; spurious; hypothetical.

suppository / suh-**poz**-uh-tuh-ree, -tree / *n.* a solid piece of medicinal substance placed in the rectum or vagina and left to melt.

suppress *v.* **1** put an end to the activity or existence of (*suppress the rebellion*). **2** keep (information, feelings, a reaction, etc.) from being known or seen (*suppress the truth; tried to suppress the report; suppressed a yawn*). **3** *Psychol.* keep out of one's consciousness. □ **suppression** *n.* **suppressible** *adj.*

suppressor *n.* a person or thing that suppresses; a device to suppress electrical interference.

suppurate / **sup**-yuh-rayt / *v.* form pus; fester. □ **suppuration** *n.*

supra / **soo**-pruh / *adv.* above or further back in the book etc. (¶ Latin, = above.)

supra- *comb. form* above, over.

supranational *adj.* transcending national limits.

supremacy / soo-**prem**-uh-see / *n.* being supreme; the position of supreme authority or power.

supreme *adj.* **1** highest in authority or rank (*the supreme commander*). **2** highest in importance, intensity, or quality (*supreme courage*). **3** (of a penalty, sacrifice, etc.) involving death. **4** (of food) served in a rich cream sauce (*chicken supreme*). □ **supremely** *adv.*

Supreme Court the highest judicial court in an Australian State.

Supreme Pontiff *see* PONTIFF.

supremo *n.* (*pl.* **supremos**) a person in overall charge.

surcharge *n.* **1** payment demanded in addition to the usual charge. **2** an additional or excessive load. **3** a mark printed over a postage stamp, changing its value. • *v.* **1** make a surcharge on; charge extra. **2** overload. **3** print a surcharge on (a stamp).

surd *n.* a mathematical quantity (esp. a root) that cannot be expressed in finite terms of whole numbers or quantities; an irrational number.

sure *adj.* **1** having sufficient reason for one's beliefs; free from doubts. **2** certain to do something or to happen (*the book is sure to be a success*). **3** undoubtedly true (*one thing is sure*). **4** reliable, secure, unfailing (*there's only one sure way*). • *adv. colloq.* certainly. □ **sureness** *n.*

surely *adv.* **1** in a sure manner, without doubt; securely. **2** used for emphasis (*surely you won't desert us?*). **3** (as an answer) certainly.

surety / **shoor**-ruh-tee / *n.* **1** a guarantee. **2** (esp. in **stand surety for**) a person who makes himself or herself responsible for another person's debts, promises, etc.

surf *n.* **1 a** a swell of the sea breaking on the shore or reefs. **b** the foam caused by this. **2** the surf as a place of recreation. **3** a swim in the surf, esp. with the intention of riding waves; the riding of a wave. • *v.* **1** swim in the surf. **2 a** ride waves on a board. **b** = BODYSURF. **3** surf at (a specified place) (*have you surfed North Narrabeen yet?*). **4** (also **channel surf**) flip rapidly between esp. television channels using a remote control. **5** explore the Internet or other network of electronic data, esp. by moving from site to site in search of information. □ **surf beach** *Aust.* a beach from which people surf. **surf carnival** *Aust.* a competitive display of the skills of a surf lifesaver. **surf club** a surf lifesaving club. **surf lifesaver** *Aust.* a member of a surf lifesaving club. **surf lifesaving club** *Aust.* **1** a voluntary organisation formed to safeguard lives in the surf.

surface 2 the premises of such an organisation. **surf ski** a long narrow board propelled with a paddle by the rider.

surface *n.* 1 the outside of an object. 2 any of the sides of an object. 3 the uppermost area, the top of a table or desk etc. 4 the top of a body of water. 5 the outward appearance of something; the qualities etc. perceived by casual observation (as distinct from deeper or hidden ones) (*all is quiet on the surface, but...*). •*adj.* 1 of or on the surface only; of the surface of the earth or sea (as distinct from in the air or underground, or under water). 2 superficial (*surface politeness*). •*v.* 1 put a particular surface on (*surface a road*). 2 come or bring to the surface. 3 become visible or known. 4 *colloq.* **a** wake after sleep or unconsciousness. **b** arrive (at a place); finally appear. ☐ **surface mail** mail carried by land or sea not by air. **surface tension** the tension of the surface film of a liquid.

surfboard *n.* a long narrow board used in surfing. ☐ **surfboarding** *n.*

surfboat *n.* an oared boat designed for rescue work etc. in the surf.

surfeit / **ser**-fuht / *n.* too much of something (esp. food and drink); a feeling of discomfort arising from this. •*v.* 1 overfeed. 2 cause to take too much of something, satiate, cloy.

surfer *n.* a person who goes surfing.

Surfers Paradise a tourist resort on the Gold Coast, Qld, 75 km south of Brisbane.

surfie (also **surfy**) *n.* esp. *Aust. colloq.* 1 a surfer, esp. a dedicated surfer. 2 *derog.* a person (usu. with bleached hair etc.) who frequents surf beaches, esp. in a gang, and does little or no actual surfing. •*adj.* of or pertaining to a surfie (*surfie chicks*).

surfing *n.* the sport of riding the surf on a board or as a bodysurfer.

surge *n.* 1 a sudden rush. 2 a heavy forward or upward motion. 3 a sudden increase in price, activity, etc. 4 a sudden increase in voltage of an electric current. 5 a swell of the sea. •*v.* 1 move suddenly and powerfully forwards. 2 (of an electric current etc.) increase suddenly. 3 (of the sea etc.) swell.

surgeon *n.* a medical practitioner who performs surgical operations.

surgery *n.* 1 **a** the treatment of injuries and disorders and disease by cutting or manipulation of the affected parts. **b** the branch of medicine concerned with this. **c** an operation performed by a surgeon. 2 the place where or time when a doctor or dentist etc. treats patients.

surgical *adj.* 1 of surgery or surgeons; used in surgery. 2 worn to correct an injury, deformity, etc. ☐ **surgically** *adv.*

Suriname / soo-ruh-**nam** / (also **Surinam**) a republic on the north coast of South America. ☐ **Surinamer** *n.* **Surinamese** *adj.* & *n.* (*pl.* **Surinamese**).

surly *adj.* (**surlier**, **surliest**) bad-tempered and unfriendly. ☐ **surliness** *n.*

surmise / suh-**muyz** / *n.* a guess; a supposition. •*v.* guess; suppose; infer.

surmount *v.* overcome (a difficulty); get over (an obstacle). ☐ **be surmounted by** have on or over the top (*the spire is surmounted by a weather vane*). ☐☐ **surmountable** *adj.*

surname *n.* the name held by all members of a family, as distinct from a first (or personal) name. •*v.* give as a surname.

surpass *v.* do or be better than; excel.

surpassing *adj.* greatly excelling or exceeding others. ☐ **surpassingly** *adv.*

surplice / **ser**-pluhs / *n.* a loose white vestment with full sleeves, worn over the cassock by clergy and choir at a religious service.

surplus / **ser**-pluhs / *n.* an amount left over after what is required has been used, esp. an excess of revenue over expenditure. •*adj.* extra; additional; spare.

surprise *n.* 1 the emotion aroused by something sudden or unexpected. 2 an event or thing that arouses this emotion. 3 the process of catching a person etc. unprepared. 4 (usu. used as *adj.*) unexpected (*a surprise party*). •*v.* 1 cause to feel surprise. 2 capture or attack suddenly and without warning. 3 come upon (a person) unawares (*surprised him in the act*). 4 (foll. by *into*) startle (a person) into action by catching him or her unprepared (*surprised him into consenting*).

surprised *adj.* experiencing surprise. ☐ **be surprised at** be shocked or scandalised by (*we are surprised at your behaviour*).

surprising *adj.* causing surprise. ☐ **surprisingly** *adv.*

surreal *adj.* unreal; dreamlike; bizarre.

surrealism / suh-**ree**-uh-liz-uhm / *n.* a 20th-century movement in art and literature attempting to express what is in the unconscious mind by depicting dreamlike images and unusual combinations of things. ☐ **surrealist** *n.* & *adj.* **surrealistic** *adj.*

surrender *v.* 1 hand over, give into another person's power or control, esp. on demand or under compulsion. 2 give oneself up, accept an enemy's demand for submission. 3 yield to a habit, emotion (*surrendered herself to grief*). 4 give up one's rights under (an insurance policy) in return for a smaller sum payable immediately. •*n.* surrendering; being surrendered.

surreptitious / su-ruhp-**tish**-uhs / *adj.* acting or done stealthily. ☐ **surreptitiously** *adv.*

surrogate / **su**-ruh-guht / *n.* a deputy; a substitute. ☐ **surrogate mother** a woman who bears a child on behalf of another woman, either from her own egg fertilised by the other woman's partner, or from the implantation in her womb of a fertilised egg from the other woman. ☐☐ **surrogacy** *n.*

surround v. **1** come or lie or be all round. **2** place all round; encircle with enemy forces. • n. a border or edging.

surroundings n.pl. the things or conditions around and liable to affect a person or place.

surtitle n. a caption above the stage during an opera, providing a translation of the words being sung.

surveillance / ser-**vay**-luhns / n. supervision or close observation, esp. of a suspected person.

survey v. / ser-**vay** / **1** look at and take a general view of. **2** make a survey of (*the report surveys progress made in the past year*). **3** examine the condition of (a building etc.). **4** measure and map out the size, shape, elevation, etc. of (an area of land). • n. / **ser**-vay / **1** a general look at something. **2** a general examination of a situation or subject; an account of this. **3** the surveying of land etc.; a map or plan.

surveyor n. a person whose job is to survey land or buildings.

survival n. **1** surviving. **2** a person, thing, or practice that has survived from an earlier time.

survive v. **1** continue to live or exist. **2** live or exist longer than; remain alive or in existence after (*she survived her husband by a year; few flowers survived the frost*).

survivor n. one who survives; one who survives another.

sus alternative spelling of SUSS.

susceptibility n. **1** being susceptible. **2** (**susceptibilities**) a person's feelings that may be hurt or offended.

susceptible / suh-**sep**-tuh-buhl / adj. **1** liable to be affected by something (*susceptible to colds*). **2** impressionable, falling in love easily. **3** (foll. by *of*) allowing; admitting of (*a theory not susceptible of proof*). ☐ **susceptibly** adv.

sushi / **soo**-shee, **suu**-shee / n. a Japanese dish of balls of cold rice topped with raw fish etc.

suspect v. / suh-**spekt** / **1** have an impression of the existence or presence of (*we suspected a trap*). **2** have suspicions or doubts about; mistrust (*we suspect their motives*). **3** feel that (a person) is guilty but have little or no proof. **4** imagine or fancy something about (a person or thing) with slight or no proof (*I suspect him of being gay—it's just a feeling I have*). **5** imagine or fancy (something) to be possible or likely (*I suspect the world is going to end next week*). • n. / **sus**-pekt / a person who is suspected of a crime etc. • adj. / **sus**-pekt / suspected, open to suspicion.

suspend v. **1** hang up. **2** keep from falling or sinking in air or liquid etc. (*particles are suspended in the fluid*). **3** postpone (*suspend judgment*). **4** put a temporary stop to. **5** deprive temporarily of a position or a right (*suspended him for three weeks for kicking in danger*). ☐ **suspended animation** a temporary deathlike condition: (*some yogis can put themselves into a state of suspended animation, don't ask me how—my brain's in suspended animation*). **suspended sentence** a sentence of imprisonment that is not enforced subject to good behaviour.

suspender n. an attachment to hold up a sock or stocking by its top. ☐ **suspender belt** a woman's undergarment with suspenders for holding up stockings.

suspense n. a state of anxious uncertainty while awaiting news or an event etc. • adj. inducing suspense (*a suspense novel*).

suspension n. **1** suspending; being suspended. **2** the means by which a vehicle is supported on its axles. **3** a substance consisting of particles suspended in a medium. ☐ **suspension bridge** a bridge suspended from cables that pass over supports at each end.

suspicion n. **1** suspecting; being suspected. **2** a partial or unconfirmed belief. **3** a slight trace (*there's a suspicion of asafoetida in this curry gravy*).

suspicious adj. feeling or causing suspicion. ☐ **suspiciously** adv.

suss (also **sus**) *colloq.* adj. **1** suspicious (*a bit suss the way he always hangs around with you*). **2** suspect (*I think the milk's a bit sus, way past its use-by date*). • v. (**sussed**, **sussing**) **1** suspect of crime (*sussed him of the thefts*). **2** (usu. foll. by *out*) investigate, inspect (*need to suss out the local restaurants*). **3** work out; realise (*sussed that I am gay*). • n. **1** a suspect. **2** suspicion; suspicious behaviour. ☐ **on suss** on suspicion (of having committed a crime) (*stopped and questioned us on suss*).

sustain v. **1** support, bear the weight of, esp. for a long period. **2** keep alive, nourish. **3** keep (a sound, effort, etc.) going continuously. **4** undergo; suffer (*sustained a defeat*). **5** endure without giving way (*this wattle can sustain long periods of dryness*). **6** confirm or uphold the validity of (*the objection was sustained*). **7** substantiate or corroborate (a statement or charge).

sustainable adj. **1** able to be sustained or upheld. **2** (of economic development or the utilisation of natural resources) able to be maintained at a particular level without causing damage to the environment or depletion of the resource. ☐ **sustainably** adv. **sustainability** n.

sustenance / **sus**-tuh-nuhns / n. **1** the process of sustaining life by food. **2** food, nourishment. **3** means of support; livelihood.

Sutherland[1], Dame Joan (1926–), AC, Australian operatic soprano known worldwide as 'La Stupenda'.

Sutherland[2], Margaret (Ada) (1897–1984), AO, Australian composer and musician.

suttee / su-**tee**, **sut**-ee / n. **1** the act or custom (now illegal) of a Hindu widow sacrificing herself on her husband's funeral pyre. **2** a Hindu widow who did this.

suture / soo-chuh / *n*. surgical stitching of a wound; a stitch or thread etc. used in this. •*v*. stitch (a wound).

Suva / soo-vuh / the capital of Fiji.

sux alternative spelling of SUCK *v*. (sense 4) (*I saw 'SEX SUX' written on a wall*).

suzerain / soo-zuh-rayn / *n*. **1** a country or ruler that has some authority over another country which is self-governing in its internal affairs. **2** an overlord in feudal times. □ **suzerainty** *n*.

Suzuki / suh-**zoo**-kee / *adj*. designating, pertaining to, or using a method of teaching the violin (esp. to young children) developed by Shin'ichi Suzuki, Japanese educationalist and violin teacher, and characterised by exercises involving large groups and parental participation.

svelte / svelt / *adj*. (of a person) slender, lissom, graceful.

SW *abbr*. **1** south-west. **2** south-western.

swab / swob / *n*. **1** a mop or absorbent pad for cleansing, drying, or absorbing things. **2** a specimen of a secretion taken with this. •*v*. (**swabbed**, **swabbing**) **1** clean with a swab. **2** take a specimen of saliva etc. from a racehorse etc. to test for the presence of illegal substances. □ **swab up** absorb (moisture) with a swab.

swaddle *v*. swathe (esp. a baby) in wraps or warm garments. □ **swaddling clothes** strips of cloth formerly wrapped round a newborn baby to restrain its movements.

swag *n*. **1** *Aust*. a collection of possessions and daily necessaries carried by a person travelling, usu. on foot, in the bush; esp. the blanket-wrapped roll carried, usu. on the back or across the shoulders, by an itinerant worker; a MATILDA; a BLUEY. **2** *Aust*. a bed roll. **3** *colloq*. the booty of burglars etc. **4** esp. *Aust. colloq*. a large number (*the Australian swimmers came home with a swag of gold medals*). •*v*. (also **swag it**) *Aust*. carry one's swag; travel as a swagman. □ **swagged** *adj*.

swage *n*. **1** a die or stamp for shaping wrought iron. **2** a tool for bending metal etc. •*v*. shape with a swage.

swagger *v*. walk or behave in a self-important manner; strut. •*n*. **1** a swaggering gait or manner. **2** (esp. New Zealand) a swagman. □ **swagger stick** a short cane carried by a military officer.

swaggie *n*. *Aust*. a swagman.

swagman *n*. *Aust*. **1** a person who carries a swag, esp. an itinerant. **2** a tramp.

swain *n*. **1** *archaic* a country youth. **2** *poetic* a young lover or suitor.

swainsona / swayn-**soh**-nuh / *n*. (also **swainsonia**) any plant of a group of herbaceous perennials or annuals, chiefly of drier Australia, having very colourful pea-flowers in a variety of colours (one species, the Darling pea, being very poisonous to stock).

swallow[1] *v*. **1** cause or allow (food etc.) to go down one's throat; work the muscles of the throat as when doing this. **2** take in so as to engulf or absorb (*she was swallowed up in the crowd*). **3** accept meekly; believe readily (*he swallowed the story*). **4** repress (a sound or emotion etc.) (*swallow one's pride*). •*n*. the act of swallowing; the amount swallowed in one movement.

swallow[2] *n*. a small migratory insect-eating bird with a forked tail. □ **swallow dive** *n*. a dive with arms outspread at the start. **swallow-dive** *v*. perform a swallow dive. **swallow-tail 1** a deeply forked tail. **2** a butterfly with such a tail.

swam *see* SWIM.

swami / swah-mee / *n*. (*pl*. **swamis**) a Hindu religious teacher.

swamp *n*. **1** (an area of) waterlogged ground. **2** used in the names of Australian fauna and flora having a swampy or periodically flooded habitat, e.g. *swamp pheasant*, *swamp stringybark*. •*v*. **1** flood; drench or submerge in water. **2** overwhelm with a great mass or number of things (*swamped with paperwork*). □ **swamp lily** a large Australian plant of the lily family with long leaves and very fragrant white flowers, occurring in swampy land. □□ **swampy** *adj*.

swamphen *n*. (also **purple swamphen**) a bird with bright blue (or purple) and black plumage and a red bill, inhabiting wetlands in south-western and eastern Australia.

swan *n*. **1** a large white water bird, proverbial in Europe for its whiteness, with a long slender neck. **2** the black swan, Australia's only representative of this group of birds, a jet-black bird with a red bill, the faunal emblem of Western Australia. •*v*. (**swanned**, **swanning**) *colloq*. move in a leisurely or majestic way or with a superior air (*swanning around*).

swank *colloq*. *n*. boastful behaviour; ostentation. •*v*. show off.

swanky *adj*. *colloq*. marked by swank; ostentatiously smart or showy; stylish, posh (*went to a swanky restaurant*). □ **swankily** *adv*.

Swan River the lower course of the river in WA on which Perth and Fremantle are situated (the upper course of the river being called the *Avon*). □ **Swan River Colony** the infant colony of WA, established on the northern banks of the Swan River in 1829, with Captain James Stirling as its Governor. **Swan River daisy** *see* BRACHYCOME. **Swan River myrtle** a WA shrub of the myrtle family bearing masses of deep rose-red flowers.

swansong *n*. a person's last work or act before death or retirement.

swap (also **swop**) *v*. (**swapping**, **swapped**) exchange or barter. •*n*. **1** an act of swapping. **2** a thing for swapping or a thing swapped.

sward *n*. *literary* an expanse of short grass; turf.

swarm *n*. **1** a large number of insects, birds, small animals, or people moving about in a cluster. **2** a cluster of bees leaving the hive with a queen bee to establish a new home. •*v*. **1** move in a swarm, come together in large numbers. **2** (of bees) cluster in a swarm. **3** (of a place) be crowded or

swarthy / swaw-*thee* / *adj.* (**swarthier, swarthiest**) having a dark complexion.

swashbuckling *adj.* swaggering aggressively. □ **swashbuckler** *n.*

swastika / swos-tik-uh / *n.* **1** an ancient symbol formed by an equal-armed cross with each arm continued at a right angle. **2** this with clockwise continuations adopted by Nazi Germany as its symbol. (¶ Sanskrit)

swat *v.* (**swatted, swatting**) hit hard with something flat; crush (a fly etc.) in this way. •*n.* a swatting blow. □ **swatter** *n.*

swatch / swoch / *n.* **1** a sample, esp. of cloth. **2** a collection of such samples.

swath / swawth / *n.* (also **swathe** / swayth /) **1** the space that a scythe or mowing machine cuts in one sweep or passage. **2** a line of grass or wheat etc. lying after being cut. **3** a broad strip.

swathe / swayth / *v.* wrap in layers of bandage or wrappings or warm garments. •*n.* **1** a bandage or wrapping. **2** *see* SWATH.

sway *v.* **1** (cause to) swing or lean from side to side. **2** influence the opinions or actions of (*his speech swayed many voters*). **3** waver in one's opinion or attitude. •*n.* **1** a swaying movement. **2** influence, power (*hold sway*).

Swaziland / swah-zee-land / a kingdom in SE Africa. □ **Swazi** *adj.* & *n.* (*pl.* **Swazis**).

swear *v.* (**swore, sworn, swearing**) **1** state or promise on oath. **2** *colloq.* state emphatically (*swore he hadn't touched it*). **3** cause to take an oath (*swore him to secrecy*). **4** use obscene or blasphemous language. □ **swear by** *colloq.* have great confidence in. **swear in** admit (a person) to office by making him or her take an oath. **swear word** a profane or indecent word used in anger etc. □□ **swearer** *n.*

sweat *n.* **1** moisture that is given off by the body through the pores of the skin. **2** a state of sweating. **3** *colloq.* a state of great anxiety (*in a sweat*). **4** *colloq.* a laborious task. **5** moisture forming in drops on a surface, e.g. by condensation. •*v.* **1** give out sweat; cause to do this. **2** be in a state of great anxiety. **3** (cause to) work long and hard. □ **no sweat** *colloq.* no problem. **sweated labour** labour of workers enduring long hours, low wages, and poor conditions. **sweat it out** *colloq.* endure it to the end. **sweat on** esp. *Aust. colloq.* anxiously await (an event or person) (*sweating on his arrival*).

sweatband *n.* a band of absorbent material for absorbing sweat.

sweater *n.* a jumper or pullover.

sweatshirt *n.* a long-sleeved cotton sweater with a fleecy lining.

sweatshop *n.* a factory where sweated labour is used.

sweaty *adj.* damp with sweat.

Swede *n.* a native of Sweden.

swede *n.* a large yellow variety of turnip.

Sweden a kingdom in northern Europe.

Swedish *adj.* of Sweden or its people or language. •*n.* the language of Sweden.

sweep[1] *v.* (**swept, sweeping**) **1** clear or clean (a room, an area, etc.) with a broom or as if with a broom (*swept the table clean of crumbs with his hand*). **2** clean a room etc. in this way. **3** (foll. by *aside, away*, etc.) **a** push with or as with a broom (*swept away the broken glass; swept him aside*). **b** dismiss abruptly (*their objections were swept aside*). **4** (foll. by *along, down*, etc.) carry or drive along with force (*I was swept along by the panicked crowd*). **5** move swiftly or majestically (*she swept out of the room*). **6** extend in a continuous line or slope (*the mountains sweep down to the sea*). **7** pass quickly over or along (*winds sweep the hillside; a new fashion is sweeping Australia*). **8** win government by an overwhelming margin (*the Liberals swept into office*). **9** touch with a sweeping motion (*swept the lock of hair off his forehead*). •*n.* **1** the act or movement of sweeping. **2** a sweeping line or slope. **3** a chimney sweep. **4** a sweepstake. □ **make a clean sweep 1** get rid of everything and make a new start. **2** win all the prizes. **sweep all before one** be very successful.

sweep[2] *n.* (*pl.* **sweep** *or* **sweeps**) any of several marine food fish of south-eastern Australia.

sweeper *n.* **1** a person who sweeps a place. **2** a thing that sweeps; a carpet sweeper. **3** *Aust.* a person employed to sweep up wool in a shearing shed. **4** the steerer of a surfboat. **5 a** *Soccer* & *Aust. Rules* a defensive player usu. playing behind the other defenders across the width of the field. **b** *Cricket* a fielder who patrols a wide area of the boundary, usu. square on the off side or leg side.

sweeping *adj.* **1** wide-ranging, comprehensive (*sweeping changes*). **2** (of a statement) generalised; taking no account of individual cases. •*n.pl.* (**sweepings**) dust or scraps collected by sweeping.

sweepstake *n.* **1** a form of gambling on horse races etc. in which the money staked is divided among those who have drawn numbered tickets for the winners. **2** (usu. as **sweep**) *Aust.* a version of this (esp. in association with the Melbourne Cup) in which the participants are allotted horses by chance. **3** a race etc. with betting of this kind.

sweet *adj.* **1** tasting as if containing sugar, not bitter. **2** fragrant. **3** melodious. **4** fresh, (of food) not stale, (of water) not salt. **5** pleasant, gratifying; pretty or charming. **6** having a pleasant nature, lovable. **7** (foll. by *on*) *colloq.* fond of; in love with. **8** *Aust. colloq.* good; all right; advantageously situated. •*n.* **1** a small shaped piece of sweet substance, usu. made with sugar or chocolate. **2** a sweet dish forming one course of a meal. □ **she's sweet** *Aust. colloq.* all is well. **sweet-and-sour** *adj.* cooked in sauce containing sugar and either vinegar or lemon. **sweet pea** a climbing garden plant with fragrant flowers. **sweet potato** a tropical climbing plant with sweet tuberous roots used for food. **sweet-talk** *v. colloq.* persuade by flattery. **sweet tooth** a liking for sweet things. **sweet william** 1 a cultivated dianthus with clusters of vivid fragrant flowers. 2 *Aust.* = GUMMY *n.* (sense 1), so called because of its smell; its flesh used as food. □□ **sweetish** *adj.* **sweetly** *adv.* **sweetness** *n.*

sweetbread *n.* an animal's thymus gland or pancreas used as food.

sweetcorn *n.* maize with sweet-flavoured yellow kernels.

sweeten *v.* make or become sweet or sweeter.

sweetener *n.* 1 a substance used to sweeten food or drink. 2 *colloq.* a bribe.

sweetheart *n.* 1 a lover, boyfriend, girlfriend, etc. 2 a term of affection. □ **sweetheart deal** an agreement arranged privately between trade unions and employers, giving workers benefits etc. beyond what is set down in an industrial award.

sweetie *n. colloq.* 1 a sweet. 2 a sweetheart (esp. as a form of address).

sweetlip *n.* (also **sweetlips**) any of many thick-lipped food fish mainly of Australian tropical waters. □ **sweetlip emperor** a fish of Qld coral reefs.

sweetmeal *n.* sweetened wholemeal.

sweetmeat *n.* 1 a sweet. 2 a very small fancy cake.

swell *v.* (**swelled**, **swollen** *or* **swelled**, **swelling**) 1 make or become larger in size, amount, volume, numbers, or intensity. 2 feel full of joy, pride, etc. (*his heart swelled with pride*). • *n.* 1 the act or state of swelling. 2 the heaving of the sea with waves that do not break. 3 a gradual increase of loudness in music; a mechanism in an organ for obtaining this. 4 *colloq.* a person of social distinction or of a dashing or fashionable appearance. 5 a protuberance. • *adj. colloq.* 1 fine, excellent. 2 smart, fashionable. □ **have a swelled** (*or* **swollen**) **head** *colloq.* be conceited.

swelling *n.* an abnormally swollen place on the body.

swelter *v.* be uncomfortably hot. • *n.* a sweltering condition.

swept *see* SWEEP.

swerve *v.* (cause to) change direction, esp. abruptly. • *n.* a swerving movement or direction.

Swift, Jonathan (1667–1745), Anglo-Irish poet and satirist, author of *Gulliver's Travels*.

swift *adj.* 1 quick, rapid. 2 prompt (*a swift response; was swift to act*). • *n.* a swift-flying insect-eating bird with long narrow wings, migrant to Australia from spring to early autumn. □ **swiftly** *adv.* **swiftness** *n.*

swiftie *n. Aust. colloq.* a piece of sharp practice; an act of deception; a trick. □ **pull a swiftie** perform a piece of sharp practice etc.

swig *colloq. v.* (**swigged**, **swigging**) drink in large draughts; drink copiously or greedily (*swigging beer*). • *n.* a drink or a large swallow.

swill *v.* 1 pour water over or through, wash or rinse. 2 drink in large quantities. • *n.* 1 a rinse (*give it a swill*). 2 a sloppy mixture of waste food fed to pigs.

swim *v.* (**swam**, **swum**, **swimming**) 1 propel the body through water by movements of the limbs, fins, tail, etc. 2 cross (a stretch of water or a distance) by swimming. 3 perform (a particular stroke) by swimming. 4 float on a liquid (*bubbles swimming on the surface*). 5 (foll. by *in*, *with*) be covered or flooded with liquid (*eyes swimming in tears; ate a floater swimming in gravy*). 6 seem to be whirling or waving; have a dizzy sensation (*everything swam before her eyes; my head is swimming*). • *n.* a period or act of swimming. □ **in the swim** *colloq.* active in or knowing what is going on. **swimming costume** a garment worn for swimming. **swimming pool** an artificial pool for swimming in. **swimming togs** see TOG. □□ **swimmer** *n.*

swimmers *n.pl. Aust.* a swimming costume.

swimmingly *adv.* with easy unobstructed progress.

swimsuit *n.* a one-piece swimming costume for women and girls.

swindle *v.* cheat (a person); obtain by fraud. • *n.* a piece of swindling; a fraudulent person or thing. □ **swindler** *n.*

swine 1 (*pl.* **swine**) a pig. 2 (*pl.* **swine** *or* **swines**) *colloq.* **a** a hated person. **b** a difficult or unpleasant thing. □ **swinish** *adj.*

swineherd *n. archaic* a person taking care of pigs.

swing *v.* (**swung**, **swinging**) 1 move to and fro while hanging or supported; cause to do this. 2 hang by its ends. 3 move smoothly; turn to one side or in a curve (*the car swung into the drive*). 4 lift with a swinging movement. 5 revolve (*swung the bullroarer round and round above his head*). 6 change from one opinion or mood etc. to another. 7 influence (voting etc.) decisively. 8 *colloq.* succeed in arranging (something); achieve. 9 *colloq.* **a** (of a person, a party, etc.) be lively etc. **b** (of a person) be up to date, with it. **c** (of a person) be sexually promiscuous. 10 *colloq.* be executed by hanging. • *n.* 1 a swinging movement, action, or rhythm. 2 a seat slung by ropes or chains for swinging in; a spell of swinging in this. 3 the extent to which a thing swings; the amount by which votes, opinions, or points scored etc. change from one side to the other. 4 a kind of jazz with the time of the melody varied while the accompaniment is in strict time. □ **in full swing** with activity at its greatest. **swing both ways** enjoy both homosexual and heterosexual sexual relations. **swinging vote** the collective votes of swinging voters which can have a decisive effect at an election. **swinging voter** a voter who is not committed to a particular political party but swings from party to party at different elections. **swing (or sling) the billy** prepare to make tea, esp. as an act of hospitality for visitors etc. **swing-wing** an aircraft wing that can be moved to slant backwards.

swingeing / **swin**-jing / *adj.* **1** (of a blow) forcible. **2** huge in amount, number, or scope (*a swingeing increase in taxation*).

swinger *n.* **1** a person who swings. **2** *colloq.* a person who is sexually promiscuous.

swipe *v. colloq.* **1** hit with a swinging blow. **2** steal, esp. by snatching. **3** pass (a swipe card) over the electronic device that reads it. •*n.* **1** *colloq.* a swinging blow. **2** an electronic device for reading information from a card (e.g. a credit card) when the card is passed through a slot. ☐ **swipe card** a card which can be used in a swipe.

swirl *v.* move or carry along with a whirling movement. •*n.* a swirling movement.

swish *v.* **1** swing (a scythe, stick, etc.) audibly through the air, grass, etc. **2** move with or make a swishing sound. **3** (foll. by *off*) cut (the tops of plants etc.) in this way (*swished off the dandelion flowers with his switch*). •*n.* a hissing sound. •*adj. colloq.* smart, fashionable.

Swiss *adj.* of Switzerland or its people. •*n.* (*pl.* **Swiss**) a native of Switzerland. ☐ **Swiss Guards** a body of guards at the Vatican, the members of which can be recruited only from Switzerland, and who wear colourful uniforms designed by Michelangelo.

switch *n.* **1** a device for completing and breaking an electric circuit. **2** an exchange, a swap. **3** a flexible shoot cut from a tree; a tapering rod or whip. **4** a tress of real or false hair tied at one end. **5** a shift or change in opinion, methods, policy etc. •*v.* **1** turn (an electrical or other appliance) on or off by means of a switch. **2** exchange (*let's switch chairs*). **3** divert (thoughts or talk) to another subject. **4** change or shift (positions, methods, or policy etc.). **5** whip with a switch. ☐ **switched-on** *adj. colloq.* **1** alert to what is going on, up to date. **2** excited; under the influence of drugs. **switch off** *colloq.* cease to pay attention.

switchback *n.* **1** a railway ride at a funfair with a series of steep descents and ascents. **2** a road or railway with alternate ascents and descents.

switchboard *n.* a panel with a set of switches for making telephone connections or operating electric circuits.

Switzerland a federal republic in central Europe.

swivel *n.* a link or pivot between two parts enabling one of them to revolve without turning the other. •*v.* (**swivelled, swivelling**) turn on or as if on a swivel. ☐ **swivel chair** a chair with a seat that can turn horizontally on a pivot.

swizz *n.* (also **swiz**) *colloq.* **1** something unfair or disappointing. **2** a swindle.

swizzle *n.* **1** *colloq.* a frothy mixed alcoholic drink. **2** *colloq.* = SWIZZ. ☐ **swizzle stick** a stick used for stirring a drink to make it frothy or flat.

swollen *see* SWELL.

swoon *v.* **1** lose consciousness; faint. **2** be so enraptured that one is close to fainting (*swooning over the latest pop star*). •*n.* a faint.

swoop *v.* come down with a rushing movement like a bird upon its prey; make a sudden attack. •*n.* a swooping movement or attack.

swoosh *n.* the noise of a sudden rush of air, liquid, etc. •*v.* move with this noise.

swop alternative spelling of SWAP.

sword / sawd / *n.* a weapon with a long blade and a hilt. ☐ **sword grass** any of several Australian plants having long serrated or sharp-edged leaves capable of inflicting lacerations. **sword of Damocles** *see* DAMOCLES.

swordfish *n.* a large sea fish with a long swordlike upper jaw.

swordsman *n.* a person of skill with a sword. ☐ **swordsmanship** *n.*

swore, sworn *see* SWEAR.

sworn *adj.* open and determined in devotion or enmity (*sworn friends; sworn foes*).

swot *colloq. v.* (**swotted, swotting**) study hard or hurriedly. •*n.* (usu. *derog.*) a person who studies hard.

swum *see* SWIM.

swung *see* SWING.

swy *n. Aust.* **1** *hist.* an Australian two-shilling coin. **2** two-up.

sybarite / **sib**-uh-ruyt / *n.* a person who is excessively fond of comfort and luxury. ☐ **sybaritic** / sib-uh-**rit**-ik / *adj.*

sycamore / **sik**-uh-maw / *n.* **1** (in Europe) a large tree of the maple family. **2** (in US) a plane tree. **3** (in Egypt etc.) a kind of fig tree.

sycophant / **sik**-uh-fant / *n.* a person who tries to win favour by flattering people; a toady, a crawler. ☐ **sycophancy** *n.* **sycophantic** / sik-uh-**fan**-tik / *adj.* **sycophantically** *adv.*

Sydney the name of the capital city of the State of New South Wales (the Aboriginal name for the area being *Warrane*). ☐ **Sydney or the bush 1** all or nothing. **2** used allusively with reference to the extremes of urban and rural life.

Sydney Harbour Bridge a bridge (affectionately known as the Coathanger) which spans Sydney Harbour and is one of Australia's most famous landmarks. It was opened in 1932.

Sydney–Hobart Yacht Race an annual yacht race from Sydney to Hobart, beginning on Boxing Day, in which yachts compete for line and handicap honours. It was first held in 1945.

Sydney Opera House a spectacular building on Sydney Harbour resembling a series of scallop shells, completed in 1973, one of Australia's most famous landmarks.

Sydneysider a person native to or resident in the city of Sydney.

syllabary / sil-uh-buh-ree / *n.* a list of characters representing syllables and serving the purpose, in some languages or stages of writing, of an alphabet.

syllabic / suh-**lab**-ik / *adj.* of or in syllables. ☐ **syllabically** *adv.*

syllabify *v.* divide into syllables. ☐ **syllabification** *n.*

syllable / **sil**-uh-buhl / *n.* one of the units of sound into which a word can be divided (see panel). ☐ **in words of one syllable** expressed very plainly or bluntly.

syllabus / **sil**-uh-buhs / *n.* (*pl.* **syllabuses** or **syllabi**) an outline of the subjects that are included in a course of study.

syllepsis / suh-**lep**-suhs / *n.* a figure of speech in which a word is applied to two others in different senses (e.g. *he took the oath and his seat*) or to two others of which it grammatically suits only one (e.g. *neither you nor he knows*).

syllogism / **sil**-uh-jiz-uhm / *n.* a form of reasoning consisting of two propositions (premises) from which a conclusion may be validly or invalidly drawn: e.g. *All Aussies are human beings* (major premise); *John is an Aussie* (minor premise); *therefore John is a human being* (valid conclusion); *All Aussies are human beings*; *John is a human being; therefore John is an Aussie* (invalid conclusion); *All Aussies are ockers*; *Johnno's an Aussie; therefore Johnno's an ocker* (valid in *form* if the major premise were true). ☐ **syllogistic** / sil-uh-**jis**-tik / *adj.*

sylph / silf / *n.* **1** an elemental spirit of the air. **2** a slender, graceful woman or girl.

sylvan *adj.* (also **silvan**) **1** of the woods. **2** having woods; rural.

sylviculture alternative spelling of SILVICULTURE.

symbiosis / sim-bee-**oh**-suhs, sim-buy- / *n.* **1** an association of two different organisms living attached to each other or one within the other, usu. to the advantage of both. **2** a similar relationship between people or groups. ☐ **symbiotic** / sim-bee-**ot**-ik, sim-buy- / *adj.*

symbol *n.* **1** a thing regarded as suggesting something or embodying certain characteristics (*white is a symbol of purity*). **2** a mark or sign with a special meaning, for example a mathematical sign, a punctuation mark, or a printed note in music.

symbolic *adj.* of, using, or used as a symbol. ☐ **symbolically** *adv.*

symbolise *v.* (also **-ize**) **1** be a symbol of. **2** represent by means of a symbol. ☐ **symbolisation** *n.*

symbolism *n.* **1** use of symbols to express things. **2** an artistic movement using symbols to express ideas. ☐ **symbolist** *n.*

symmetrical / suh-**met**-ri-kuhl / *adj.* able to be divided into parts that are the same in size and shape and similar in position on either side of a dividing line or round a centre. ☐ **symmetrically** *adv.*

symmetry / **sim**-uh-tree / *n.* **1** being symmetrical. **2** pleasing proportion between parts of a whole.

sympathetic *adj.* **1** feeling, expressing, or resulting from sympathy. **2** likeable (*he's not a sympathetic character*). **3** (often foll. by *to*) showing approval or support (*he is sympathetic to our plan*). **4** (of a pain etc.) caused by a pain or injury to someone else or in another part of the body (*he began to feel sympathetic labour pains when his wife went into labour*). ☐ **sympathetic magic** a type of magic that seeks to achieve its effect by performing an associated action or using an associated thing. ☐☐ **sympathetically** *adv.*

sympathise *v.* (also **-ize**) **1** feel or express sympathy. **2** agree with a sentiment or opinion. ☐ **sympathiser** *n.*

sympathy *n.* **1** sharing another person's emotions or sensations. **2** a feeling of pity or tenderness towards one suffering pain, grief, or trouble. **3** liking for each other produced in people who have similar opinions or tastes. ☐ **be in sympathy with** feel approval of (an opinion or desire).

symph *n. colloq.* a symphony orchestra (*the Sydney symph*).

symphonic / sim-**fon**-ik / *adj.* of or like a symphony. ☐ **symphonic poem** an orchestral piece, usu. descriptive or rhapsodic. ☐ **symphonically** *adv.*

symphony / **sim**-fuh-nee / *n.* a long musical composition (usu. in several movements) for a full orchestra. ☐ **symphony orchestra** a large orchestra playing symphonies etc.

symposium / sim-**poh**-zee-uhm / *n.* (*pl.* **symposia**) a meeting for discussion of a particular subject; a conference.

symptom *n.* **1** a physical or mental sign of disease or injury. **2** a sign of the existence of something (*crime is often a symptom of social inequality*).

Syllable

A syllable is the smallest unit of speech that can normally occur alone, such as *a*, *at*, *ta*, or *tat*. A word can be made up of one or more syllables.

   cat, *fought*, and *twinge* each have one syllable;
   rating, *deny*, and *collapse* each have two syllables;
   excitement, *superman*, and *telephoned* each have three syllables;
   Victorian and *complicated* each have four syllables;
   examination and *uncontrollable* each have five syllables.

symptomatic / simp-tuh-**mat**-ik / *adj.* serving as a symptom.

synaesthesia / sin-uhs-**thee**-zee-uh / *n.* (also **synesthesia**) **1** *Psychol.* the production of a mental sense-impression relating to one sense by the stimulation of another sense. **2** a sensation produced in a part of the body by stimulation of another part. ☐ **synaesthetic** *adj.*

synagogue / **sin**-uh-gog / *n.* **1** a building for Jewish worship and instruction. **2** a Jewish congregation.

synapse *n.* a junction of two nerve cells in the body.

sync / sink / (also **synch**) *colloq. n.* synchronisation. •*v.* synchronise. ☐ **in** (or **out of**) **sync** (often foll. by *with*) according or agreeing well (or badly) (with).

synchromesh / **sing**-kroh-mesh / *n.* a device that makes parts of a gear revolve at the same speed while they are being brought into contact.

synchronic / sing-**kron**-ik / *adj.* concerned with a subject as it exists at a particular time, not with its historical antecedents (as opposed to DIACHRONIC). ☐ **synchronically** *adv.*

synchronise / **sing**-kruh-nuyz / *v.* (also -**ize**) **1** occur or exist at the same time. **2** operate at the same rate and simultaneously. **3** cause to occur or operate at the same time; cause (clocks etc.) to show the same time. ☐ **synchronised swimming** a form of swimming in which participants make ballet-like co-ordinated leg and arm movements in time to music. ☐☐ **synchronisation** *n.* **synchroniser** *n.*

synchronism / **sing**-kruh-niz-uhm / *n.* **1** being or treated as synchronous or synchronic. **2** synchronising.

synchronous / **sing**-kruh-nuhs / *adj.* **1** existing or occurring at the same time. **2** operating at the same rate and simultaneously.

syncopate / **sing**-kuh-payt / *v.* **1** change the beats or accents in (a passage of music) so that strong beats become weak (and vice versa). **2** *Grammar* shorten (a word) by dropping interior sounds or letters, as *pacifist* for 'pacificist', *idolatry* for 'idolatory', etc. ☐ **syncopation** *n.*

syncope / **sing**-kuh-pee / *n.* **1** a faint; fainting. **2** *Grammar* syncopation.

syncretic / sing-**kret**-ik / *adj.* combining different beliefs or principles.

syncretise / **sing**-kruh-tuyz / *v.* (also -**ize**) combine (different beliefs or principles).

syndic / **sin**-dik / *n.* **1** a government official in various countries. **2** a business agent of certain universities and corporations.

syndicate *n.* / **sin**-duh-kuht / **1** an association of people or firms combining to carry out a business or commercial undertaking. **2** an agency supplying material simultaneously to a number of different newspapers etc. **3** a group of people who combine to gamble, organise crime, etc. •*v.* / sin-duh-kayt / **1** combine into a syndicate. **2** publish through an association that acquires stories, articles, cartoons, etc. for simultaneous publication in numerous newspapers and periodicals. ☐ **syndication** *n.*

syndrome / **sin**-drohm / *n.* **1** a set of symptoms that together indicate the presence of a disease or abnormal condition. **2** a combination of opinions, emotions, behaviour, etc. that are characteristic of a particular condition.

synecdoche / si-**nek**-duh-kee / *n.* a figure of speech in which a part is made to represent the whole or vice versa (e.g. *new faces at the club; Australia beat England by six wickets*).

synergy / **sin**-uh-jee / *n.* interaction or cooperation of two or more organisations, substances, or other agents to produce a combined effect greater than the sum of their separate effects. (¶ Greek, = working together.)

synod / **sin**-uhd / *n.* a council attended by clergy, church officials, and sometimes lay people to discuss questions of policy, teaching, etc.

synonym / **sin**-uh-nim / *n.* a word or phrase with a meaning similar to that of another in the same language (see panel).

synonymous / suh-**non**-uh-muhs / *adj.* (often foll. by *with*) **1** equivalent in meaning. **2** associated with, suggestive of (*his name was synonymous with terror*).

synopsis / suh-**nop**-suhs / *n.* (*pl.* **synopses**) a summary; a brief general survey.

synoptic / suh-**nop**-tik / *adj.* of or forming a synopsis.

Synoptic Gospels the gospels of Matthew, Mark, and Luke, describing events from a similar point of view.

synovia / suy-**noh**-vee-uh / *n.* a thick sticky fluid lubricating joints etc. in the body. ☐ **synovial** *adj.*

Synonym

A synonym is a word that has the same meaning as, or a similar meaning to, another word:
cheerful, happy, merry, and *jolly*
are synonyms that are quite close to each other in meaning, as are
lazy, indolent, and *slothful*
In contrast, the following words all mean 'a person who works with another', but their meanings vary considerably:

colleague	*conspirator*
collaborator	*accomplice*
ally	*partner*

syntax / **sin**-taks / *n.* the way in which words are arranged to form phrases and sentences; the rules governing this. ❑ **syntactic** / sin-**tak**-tik / *adj.* **syntactically** *adv.*

synthesis / **sin**-thuh-suhs / *n.* (*pl.* **syntheses**) **1** the combining of separate parts or elements to form a complex whole. **2** the combining of substances to form a compound. **3** artificial production of a substance that occurs naturally in plants or animals.

synthesise / **sin**-thuh-suyz / *v.* (also **-ize**) make by synthesis.

synthesiser *n.* an electronic (usu. keyboard) instrument that can produce a variety of sounds imitating musical instruments, speech, etc.

synthetic *adj.* **1** made by synthesis; manufactured as opposed to produced naturally (*synthetic rubber*). **2** (of emotions etc.) affected, insincere; artificial (*decorated in synthetic Federation style*). • *n.* a synthetic substance or fabric (e.g. nylon). ❑ **synthetically** *adv.*

syphilis / **sif**-uh-luhs / *n.* a contagious venereal disease progressing from infection of the genitals via the skin and mucous membrane to the bones, muscles, and brain. ❑ **syphilitic** *adj.*

Syria a republic in the Middle East. ❑ **Syrian** *adj.* & *n.*

Syriac / **si**-ree-ak / *n.* an ancient language based on a form of Aramaic and still used as the liturgical language of certain Eastern Churches.

syringe / suh-**rinj** / *n.* a device for drawing in liquid and forcing it out again in a fine stream. • *v.* wash out or spray with a syringe.

syrinx / **si**-ringks / *n.* the part of a bird's throat where its song is produced.

syrup *n.* **1** a thick sweet liquid; water in which sugar is dissolved. **2** excessive sentimentality. ❑ **syrupy** *adj.*

system *n.* **1** a set of connected things or parts that form a whole or work together (*a railway system; the nervous system; the solar system*). **2** an animal body as a whole (*too much alcohol poisons the system*). **3** a set of rules, principles, or practices forming a particular philosophy or form of government etc. **4** a method of classification, notation, or measurement (*the metric system*). **5** a method of choosing one's procedure in gambling etc. **6** *Computing* a group of related hardware units or programs or both, esp. when dedicated to a single application. **7** orderliness, being systematic. ❑ **systems analysis** analysis of a complex process etc. in order to decide how a computer may be used to increase efficiency etc. **systems analyst** an expert in systems analysis. **systems operator** *Computing* a person who controls or monitors the operation of complex esp. electronic systems. **systems programmer** a person who specialises in low-level computer software and machine-support tasks.

systematic *adj.* **1** methodical, according to a plan and not casually or at random. **2** regular, deliberate (*a systematic liar*). ❑ **systematically** *adv.*

systematise / **sis**-tuh-muh-tuyz / *v.* (also **-ize**) arrange according to a system. ❑ **systematisation** *n.*

systemic / sis-**tem**-ik / *adj.* **1** of or affecting the body as a whole. **2** (of an insecticide etc.) entering a plant via the roots or shoots and passing into the tissues. ❑ **systemically** *adv.*

systemise (also **-ize**) = SYSTEMATISE. ❑ **systemisation** *n.*

systole / **sis**-tuh-lee / *n.* the rhythmical contraction of chambers of the heart, alternating with diastole to form the pulse. ❑ **systolic** / sis-**tol**-ik / *adj.*

Szechuan (also **Szechwan**) a province of west central China (now called **Sichuan**) noted for its distinctive cuisine characterised by being spicily hot to the taste through the use of Szechuan pepper and chilli.

T

T *symbol* tritium. ☐ **to a T** exactly; perfectly; in every respect.

t. *abbr.* (also **t**) **1** ton(s). **2** tonne(s).

Ta *symbol* tantalum.

ta *interj. colloq.* thank you.

TAB / tab, tee-ay-bee / *n. Aust.* **1** acronym of *Totalisator Agency Board*, the government agency which controls off-course betting. **2** a branch of this body (*the local TAB*). • *adj.* of or related to TAB betting (*TAB dividend*).

tab[1] *n.* **1** a small projecting flap or strip by which something can be grasped, hung, fastened, or identified. **2** *colloq.* a bill at a restaurant etc. • *v.* (**tabbed**, **tabbing**) provide with tabs. ☐ **keep a tab** (or **tabs on**) *colloq.* keep account of; keep under observation. **pick up the tab** *colloq.* pay the bill.

tab[2] = TABULATOR (sense 2).

tabard / **tab**-uhd / *n.* **1** a short tunic open at the sides, worn by a herald, emblazoned with royal arms. **2** *hist.* a knight's short emblazoned garment worn over armour.

tabasco *n.* **1** a hot-tasting pepper. **2** (**Tabasco**) *trademark* a sauce made from this.

tabby *n.* a cat with grey or brownish fur and dark stripes.

tabernacle *n.* **1** *hist.* a tent used as a sanctuary for the Ark of the Covenant by the Israelites during the Exodus. **2** (in the Catholic Church) a niche or receptacle over the main altar, having a lockable door concealed by a veil, used for reserving the consecrated Host(s). **3** a meeting place for worship used by nonconformist sects.

tabla *n.* a pair of small Indian drums played with the hands.

table *n.* **1** a piece of furniture consisting of a flat top supported on one or more legs. **2 a** food provided in a household (*she keeps a good table*); **b** a group seated for dinner etc. **3** a list of facts or figures arranged in columns. **4** a multiplication table. • *v.* submit (a motion or report in Parliament etc.) for discussion. ☐ **on the table** offered for consideration or discussion. **table tennis** a game played with bats and a light hollow ball on a table with a net across it. **turn the tables** *see* TURN. **under the table 1** *colloq.* very drunk. **2** = UNDER THE COUNTER (*see* COUNTER).

tableau / **tab**-loh / *n.* (*pl.* **tableaux** / **tab**-lohz /) **1** a silent motionless group of people etc. arranged to represent a scene. **2** a dramatic or picturesque scene.

tablecloth *n.* a cloth spread over a table, esp. for meals.

table d'hôte / **tah**-buhl doht / *n.* a meal consisting of a set menu at a fixed price, esp. in a hotel (cf. À LA CARTE). (¶ French, = host's table.)

tableland *n.* a plateau of land.

tablespoon *n.* **1** a large spoon esp. for serving food and as a measurement in cooking. **2** the amount (4 teaspoons or 20 ml) held by this. ☐ **tablespoonful** *n.* (*pl.* **tablespoonfuls**).

tablet *n.* **1** a panel bearing an inscription, esp. one fixed to a wall as a memorial. **2** a small flattish piece of a solid substance (e.g. soap). **3** a small amount of medicine in solid form; a pill.

tableware *n.* dishes, plates, etc., for meals.

tabloid *n.* a newspaper (usu. popular or sensational in style) with pages that are half the size of those of larger newspapers.

taboo *n.* (also **tabu**) a ban or prohibition on something that is regarded by religion or custom as not to be done, touched, or used. • *adj.* prohibited by a taboo (*taboo words*). • *v.* place under a taboo.

tabor / **tay**-buh / *n.* a small drum formerly used to accompany a pipe.

tabouli / tuh-**boo**-lee / *n.* (also **tabbouleh**) a Syrian and Lebanese salad made with bulgur, parsley, onion, mint, lemon juice, oil, and spices.

tabu alternative spelling of TABOO.

tabular / **tab**-yuh-luh / *adj.* arranged or displayed in a table or list.

tabula rasa / tab-yuh-luh **rah**-zuh / *n.* **1** an erased tablet. **2** an absence of preconceived ideas or predetermined goals. (¶ Latin, = scraped tablet.)

tabulate / **tab**-yuh-layt / *v.* arrange (facts or figures) in a table or list. ☐ **tabulation** *n.*

tabulator *n.* **1** a person or thing that tabulates facts or figures. **2** (also **tab**) a device on a typewriter or computer keyboard for advancing to a series of set positions in tabular work.

tachograph / **tak**-uh-grahf, -graf / *n.* a device that automatically records the speed and travel time of a motor vehicle in which it is fitted.

tachometer / ta-**kom**-uh-tuh / *n.* an instrument for measuring the speed of a vehicle etc. or of the rotation of its engine.

tacit / **tas**-uht / *adj.* implied or understood without being put into words (*he gave tacit consent*). ☐ **tacitly** *adv.*

taciturn / **tas**-uh-tern / *adj.* habitually saying very little, uncommunicative. ☐ **taciturnity** / tas-uh-**ter**-nuh-tee / *n.*

Tacitus / tas-uh-tuhs / (full name Publius (or Gaius) Cornelius Tacitus) (AD c.56–c.120), Roman historian.

tack n. **1** a small nail with a broad head. **2** a long stitch used to hold fabric in position temporarily. **3** a rope for securing the corner of some sails; the corner to which this is fastened. **4** the direction of a ship's course as determined by the position of its sails; a temporary oblique course to take advantage of a wind. **5** a course of action or policy (*changed tack*). **6** riding saddles, bridles, etc. • v. **1** nail with a tack or tacks. **2** stitch with tacks. **3** (foll. by *on*) add as an extra thing (*a service charge was tacked on to the bill*). **4** sail a zigzag course to take advantage of a wind; make a tack or tacks.

tacker n. Aust. a small boy.

tackle n. **1** a set of ropes and pulleys for lifting weights or working a ship's sails. **2** equipment for a task or sport (*fishing tackle*). **3** the act of tackling in football. • v. **1** try to deal with (a problem or difficulty). **2** grapple with (an opponent). **3** confront (a person) in discussion or argument (*tackled him about his behaviour*). **4** intercept (an opponent running with the ball). ☐ **tackler** n.

tacky adj. (**tackier**, **tackiest**) **1** (of paint or varnish etc.) slightly sticky, not quite dry. **2** colloq. in poor taste, cheap; tatty, shabby. ☐ **tackiness** n.

taco / **tah**-ko, **tak**-oh / n. (pl. **tacos**) a Mexican dish of a folded or rolled tortilla with a savoury filling of meat etc.

tact n. **1** skill in dealing with others, esp. in delicate situations. **2** intuitive perception of the right thing to do or say.

tactful adj. having or showing tact. ☐ **tactfully** adv.

tactic n. **1** a piece of tactics. **2** (**tactics**) (treated as *sing.* or *pl.*) the art of placing or manoeuvring forces skilfully in a battle. **3** (**tactics**) manoeuvring; the procedure(s) adopted in order to achieve something.

tactical adj. **1** of tactics (*a tactical retreat*). **2** (of bombing etc.) done in immediate support of armed forces (cf. STRATEGIC). **3** planning or planned skilfully. ☐ **tactical weapons** see STRATEGIC WEAPONS. ☐☐ **tactically** adv.

tactician / tak-**tish**-uhn / n. an expert in tactics.

tactile / **tak**-tuyl / adj. **1** of or using the sense of touch (*tactile organs*). **2** perceived by touch; tangible. ☐ **tactility** n.

tactless adj. lacking in tact. ☐ **tactlessly** adv. **tactlessness** n.

tad colloq. n. a small amount. ☐ **a tad** a little; slightly (*feeling a tad off-colour*).

taddie n. colloq. a tadpole.

Tadjikistan / tah-jee-ki-**stahn** / a mountainous republic in central Asia (formerly part of the USSR).

tadpole n. the larva of a frog or toad etc. at the stage when it lives in water and has gills and a tail.

tae kwon do / tuy kwon **doh** / n. a modern Korean martial art similar to karate. (¶ Korean, = art of hand and foot fighting.)

TAFE / tayf / n. Aust. **1** a system of tertiary education offering courses mainly in technical and vocational subjects. **2** an institution offering such courses. (¶ Acronym of *Technical and Further Education*.)

taffeta n. a shiny silklike fabric.

taffrail / **taf**-rayl / n. a rail round the stern of a ship.

tag¹ n. **1** a metal or plastic point at the end of a shoelace etc. **2** a label tied to something to show its price etc. **3** a loop or flap for handling or hanging a thing; a loose or ragged end. **4** a stock phrase or much-used quotation (*the tag 'feminist' is often loosely applied*). **5** the personal signature (a nickname etc.) of a graffiti artist. **6** *Computing* a character or set of characters appended to an item of data in order to identify it. • v. (**tagged**, **tagging**) **1** label with a tag. **2** (often foll. by *on*) attach, add as an extra thing (*a postscript was tagged on to her letter*). **3 a** colloq. follow closely. **b** *Aust. Rules* follow (one's opponent) closely. **4** *Computing* label (an item of data) for later retrieval etc. ☐ **tag along** colloq. go along with another or others, accompany passively. **tag end** the last remaining bit; the last part.

tag² n. a children's chasing game. • v. touch (someone) in a game of tag.

Tagalog n. **1** a member of the principal people of the Philippines. **2** their language.

tagliatelle / tal-yuh-**tel**-ee / n. pasta in narrow ribbon-shaped strips.

tahina / tah-**hee**-nuh / n. (also **tahini**) a Middle Eastern paste or sauce made from sesame seeds.

Tahiti / tah-**hee**-tee / one of the Society Islands in the South Pacific, administered by France. ☐ **Tahitian** / tah-**hee**-shuhn / adj. & n.

t'ai chi / tuy **chee** / n. (in full **t'ai chi ch'uan**) a Chinese martial art and system of exercises with slow controlled movements.

tail¹ n. **1 a** the hindmost part of an animal, esp. when extending beyond the rest of the body; an oxtail as food. **b** a person's buttocks. **2** something resembling this in its shape or position; the rear part of anything, e.g. of a procession. **3** a luminous trail following a comet. **4 a** the inferior, weaker, or last part of anything, esp. in a sequence. **b** *Cricket* the end of the batting order, with the weakest batsmen. **5** the part of a shirt or coat below the waist at the back. **6** colloq. a person following or shadowing another. **7** (**tails**) a tailcoat; evening dress with this. **8** (**tails**) the reverse of a coin as a choice when tossing; the side that does not bear the head. **9** *coarse colloq*. **a** the female genitals. **b** sexual intercourse. • v. **1** remove the stalks of (fruit). **2** colloq. follow closely, shadow. **3** dock the tail (of a lamb etc.) **4** *Aust.* follow, herd, and tend (livestock). ☐ **on a person's tail** following closely. **tail away** = TAIL

OFF. **tail end** the hindmost or very last part. **tail light** a light at the back of a vehicle, train, or bicycle. **tail off** become fewer, smaller, or slighter; (of remarks etc.) end inconclusively. **tail them** *Aust.* (in two-up) toss the coins so that they fall tails uppermost. **tail wind** a following wind.

tail² *n.* limitation of ownership, esp. of an estate limited to a person and his or her heirs. ☐ **in tail** under such a limitation.

tailcoat *n.* a man's coat with a long divided flap at the back, worn as part of formal dress.

tailgate *n.* **1** a hinged or removable flap at the rear of a truck etc. **2** the rear door of a station wagon or hatchback. • *v.* drive dangerously close to the vehicle in front.

tailless *adj.* having no tail.

tailor *n.* **1** a maker of clothes, esp. men's outer garments to measure. **2** (also **taylor**) a marine food fish of Australian waters. • *v.* **1** make (clothes) as a tailor; make in a simple smoothly-fitting design. **2** make or adapt for a special purpose (*the new factory is tailored to our needs*). ☐ **tailor made 1** made by a tailor. **2** perfectly suited for the purpose.

tailorbird *n. Aust.* the golden-headed warbler, a bird which stitches leaves etc. together with spiderwebs to form its nest.

tailplane *n.* the horizontal surface of the tail of an aeroplane.

tailspin *n.* **1** an aircraft's spiral dive with the tail making wider circles than the front. **2** a state of chaos or panic.

taint *n.* a trace of some bad quality, decay, or infection. • *v.* **1** affect with a taint; become tainted. **2** (foll. by *with*) affect slightly (*tainted with remorse*).

taipan / **tuy**-pan / *n.* a long-fanged brownish snake of northern Australia (and New Guinea), the longest (2–4 metres) and perhaps deadliest of Australian venomous snakes. (¶ Wik-Mungkan)

Taipei / tuy-**pay** / *the capital of Taiwan.*

Taiwan / tuy-**wahn** / an island republic off the SE coast of China, regarded by China as one of its provinces. ☐ **Taiwanese** *adj.* & *n.*

Taj Mahal / tahj muh-**hahl** / a mausoleum at Agra in northern India, completed *c.*1648 by the Mogul emperor Shah Jahan in memory of his favourite wife.

take *v.* (**took, taken, taking**) **1** lay hold of, get into one's hands. **2** get possession of, capture, win (*took many prisoners; took first prize*). **3 a** be successful or effective (*the brain transplant did not take*). **b** (of a plant, seed, cutting, etc.) begin to grow. **4** remove from its place (*someone has taken my bicycle*). **5** subtract. **6** make use of, indulge in (*take this opportunity; take a holiday; take the train*). **7** occupy (a position), esp. as one's right. **8** obtain after fulfilling necessary conditions (*take a degree; take lodgings*). **9** require (*it takes a strong man to lift that; these things take time*). **10** cause to come or go with one; carry or remove (*take the letters to the post*). **11** be affected by; catch (*the sticks took fire*). **12** experience or exert (a feeling or effort) (*took pity on him; take care*). **13** find out and record (*take his name*). **14** interpret in a certain way; understand; accept (*we take it that you are satisfied; I take your point*). **15** perform, deal with (*take a decision; take an examination*). **16** photograph (a person or thing). • *n.* **1** an amount of game or fish etc. caught. **2** a scene or film sequence photographed continuously at one time. **3** *colloq.* a swindle. ☐ **be taken with** find attractive (*is very much taken with him*). **on the take** *colloq.* taking bribes; receiving money etc. by illicit means. **take after** resemble (a parent etc.). **take-all** a disease of wheat and other cereals caused by a fungus producing rootrot. **take-home pay** the amount remaining after tax etc. has been deducted from wages. **take in 1** accept into one's house etc. **2** include. **3** make (a garment etc.) smaller. **4** understand. **5** deceive or cheat (a person). **6** *colloq.* visit (a place) en route. **take it out on** work off one's frustration by attacking or maltreating (a person etc.). **take off** *v.* **1 a** remove (clothing) from the body. **b** remove or lead away. **c** withdraw (transport, a show, etc.). **2** deduct (part of an amount). **3** depart, esp. hastily. **4** mimic humorously. **5** begin a jump. **6** leave the ground and become airborne. **7** (of a scheme, enterprise, etc.) become successful. **8** have (a period) away from work. **9** (of prices etc.) rise steeply or suddenly. **take-off** *n.* **1** a piece of humorous mimicry. **2** the process of taking off in flying. **take on 1** acquire; undertake (work or responsibility); engage (an employee). **2** agree to play against (a person in a game). **3** *colloq.* show great emotion, make a fuss. **take out 1** escort on an outing. **2** be emotionally involved with (*is he taking anyone out at the moment?*). **3** obtain or get (an insurance policy, licence, summons, etc.) issued. **take over** take control of (a business etc.). **take to 1** adopt as a habit or course. **2** have recourse to. **3** adapt oneself to. **4** develop a liking for. **5** *colloq.* attack. **take up 1** start doing as a hobby or business. **2** occupy (time or space). **3** resume at the point where something was left; investigate (a matter) further. **4** shorten (a garment). **5** accept (an offer etc.). **6** *Aust. hist.* acquire (land) from the Crown as owner or as tenant (*took up a selection*). **take up with** begin to associate with.

takeaway *adj.* (of food) bought at a restaurant for eating elsewhere. • *n.* **1** this food. **2** a restaurant selling this.

takeover *n.* assumption of control (esp. of a business).

taker *n.* **1** a person who takes a bet, accepts an offer, etc. **2** a potential buyer (*I think we have a taker for the house*).

taking *adj.* attractive, captivating. • *n.pl.* (**takings**) the amount of money taken in a shop, at a show, etc.

talc *n.* **1** talcum powder. **2** a form of magnesium silicate used as a lubricator.

talcum *n.* **1** = TALC (sense 2). **2** (in full **talcum powder**) talc powdered and usu. perfumed, applied to the skin to make it feel smooth and dry.

tale *n.* **1** a narrative or story. **2** a report spread by gossip.

talent *n.* **1** special or very great ability; people who have this. **2** a unit of money used in certain ancient countries. **3** *colloq.* attractive members of the opposite sex (*eyeing up the local talent*). ❏ **talent scout** (*or* **spotter**) a person whose job is to find talented people, esp. in sport or entertainment.

talented *adj.* having talent.

talisman / **tal**-uhz-muhn / *n.* (*pl.* **talismans**) an object supposed to bring good luck. ❏ **talismanic** *adj.*

talk *v.* **1** convey or exchange ideas by spoken words. **2** have the power of speech. **3** influence by talking (*talked him into going to Spain*). **4** give away information (*we have ways of making you talk*). **5** gossip (*people will talk*). **6** have influence (*money talks*). • *n.* **1** talking, conversation, discussion. **2** an informal lecture. **3** rumour, gossip; its theme (*there is talk of a general election*). **4** talking or promises etc. without action or results. ❏ **talk down 1** silence (a person) by talking loudly or persistently. **2** bring (a pilot or aircraft) to a landing by radio instructions from the ground. **3** depress the economy generally, the value of (a currency), or the price of (a commodity) by making tactical public statements (*he was accused of talking down the Australian dollar*) (cf. TALK UP). **talk down to** speak to in condescendingly simple language. **talk over** discuss at length. **talk over a person's head** use language, knowledge, etc. which the addressee cannot understand. **talk shop** *v.* talk about one's occupation. **talk show** an interview program on radio or television. **talk up 1** discuss favourably; praise or advocate. **2** raise the economy generally, the value of (a currency), or the price of (a commodity) by making tactical public statements (cf. TALK DOWN).

talkative *adj.* talking very much.

talkback *n.* (often used as *adj.*) *Aust.* **1** a system of two-way communication by loudspeaker. **2** a broadcast program in which the listeners telephone the presenter and participate (*talkback radio*).

talkfest *n.* a lengthy discussion, conference, etc., at which much is said but little is achieved (cf. GABFEST).

talkie *n. colloq.* an early film with a soundtrack.

talking *adj.* **1** that talks, or is able to talk (*a talking parrot*). **2** expressive (*he has such talking eyes*). • *n.* in the senses of TALK *v.* ❏ **talking book** a recorded reading of a book, esp. for the blind. **talking point** a topic for discussion. **talking-to** *colloq.* a reproof, a reprimand.

tall *adj.* **1** of more than average height. **2** having a certain height (*about 175 cm tall*). ❏ **tall order** *colloq.* a difficult task. **tall story** *colloq.* one that is difficult to believe (and probably untrue). ❏❏ **tallish** *adj.* **tallness** *n.*

tallboy *n.* a tall chest of drawers.

tallegalane / tuh-**leg**-uh-layn / *n.* a small marine and estuarine food fish of southern Australia, excluding Tas. Also called *sand mullet*. (¶ Possibly from an Aboriginal language.)

Tallinn the capital of Estonia.

tallith / **tal**-it / *n.* a scarf worn by Jews esp. at prayer.

tallow *n.* animal fat used to make candles, soap, lubricants, etc. ❏ **tallow wood** a tall eucalypt of Qld and NSW; the greasy, extremely durable wood of this tree.

tall poppy *n. Aust.* a person who is conspicuously successful and whose distinction frequently attracts envious notice or hostility. ❏ **tall-poppy syndrome** the Australian habit of denigrating or 'cutting down' those who are successful or who are high achievers etc.

tally *n.* **1** the reckoning of a debt or score; the total score or amount. **2** *Aust.* the number of sheep shorn by an individual shearer in a specified period. • *v.* (**tallied**, **tallying**) correspond (*see that the goods tally with what we ordered; the two witnesses' stories tallied*). ❏ **tally room** *Aust.* a centre at which votes are counted or posted in an election.

tally-walka / **tal**-ee-**waw**-kuh / *n.* (also **tally-walker**) *Aust.* a branch of a river which separates from and then rejoins the main river further on; an anabranch. (¶ Baagandji)

Talmud / **tal**-muud / *n.* a collection of ancient writings on Jewish civil and ceremonial law and tradition. ❏ **Talmudic** / tal-**muud**-ik / *adj.*

talon / **tal**-uhn / *n.* a claw, esp. of a bird of prey.

talus / **tay**-luhs / *n.* (*pl.* **tali**) the ankle bone supporting the tibia (the shin bone).

tamar alternative spelling of TAMMAR.

tamarillo / tam-uh-**ril**-oh / *n.* esp. *Aust.* the egg-shaped acidic red fruit of a South American shrub, used stewed as a dessert, etc. Also called *tree tomato*.

tamarind / **tam**-uh-rind / *n.* **1** a tropical tree bearing fruit with acid pulp. **2** its pulp, used esp. in Asian curries and to make a refreshing cordial.

tambour / **tam**-boor, -baw / *n.* **1** a drum. **2** a circular frame for holding fabric taut while it is being embroidered.

tambourine / tam-buh-**reen** / *n.* a percussion instrument consisting of a small hoop fitted with jingling metal discs and often a drum-like skin.

tame *adj.* **1** (of animals) domesticated; not wild or shy. **2** docile. **3** insipid; dull (*tame entertainment*). • *v.* **1** make tame; domesticate. **2** subdue, curb; humble; break the spirit of. ❏ **tamely** *adv.* **tameness** *n.* **tameable** *adj.*

tamer *n.* a person who tames and trains wild animals (*lion-tamer*).

Tamil / tam-uhl / *n.* **1** a member of a Dravidian people indigenous to south India and Sri Lanka. **2** their language. • *adj.* of this people or their language.

Tamil Tiger *n.* (also **Tiger**) a member of the Liberation Tigers for Tamil Eelam, a Sri Lankan guerrilla organisation founded in 1972 that seeks the establishment of an independent state (Eelam) in the north-east of the country for the Tamil community.

tammar / tam-uh / *n.* (also **tamar** or **tammar wallaby**) a greyish-brown wallaby of southern Australia. (¶ Nyungar)

Tammuz / ta-muuz / *n.* a Babylonian or Syrian deity, the lover of Astarte, corresponding to the Greek Adonis. He became the personification of the seasonal decay and revival of crops.

tam-o'-shanter *n.* a beret with a soft full top.

tamp *v.* pack or ram down tightly.

tamper *v.* (foll. by *with*) **1** meddle or interfere with, alter without authority. **2** influence illegally, bribe (*tamper with a jury*).

tampon *n.* a plug of absorbent material inserted into the body, esp. used by women to absorb menstrual blood.

tan *v.* (**tanned**, **tanning**) **1** convert (animal hide) into leather by treating it with tannic acid or mineral salts etc. **2** make or become brown by exposure to sun. **3** *colloq.* thrash. • *n.* **1** = SUNTAN. **2** yellowish brown. **3** the bark (of wattle trees etc.) bruised and used to tan hides. • *adj.* yellowish-brown. • *abbr. Maths* tangent.

Tanami Desert / tan-uh-muy / a large desert (3,750,000 ha) in the central west of the NT.

tanbark *n.* bark (which had been used in the tanning process) broken up into chips and used as a mulch in gardens etc.

tandava / tahn-duh-vuh / *n.* a vigorous and masculine style of Indian dancing, associated with Siva.

tandem *n.* **1** a bicycle with seats and pedals for two or more people one behind another. **2** an arrangement of people or things one behind another. • *adv.* one behind another. ☐ **in tandem 1** arranged in this way. **2** together; alongside each other (*the issues have to be dealt with in tandem*).

tandoor / tan-door / *n.* a clay oven used in some Indian cooking.

tandoori / tan-**door**-ree / *n.* food spiced and cooked over charcoal in a tandoor; (often as *adj.*) (*tandoori chicken*).

tang *n.* **1** a strong flavour or smell. **2** a characteristic quality (*the unmistakable tang of gum logs burning*). **3** a slight hint or trace of some quality (*after decades in Australia his speech still has a pommy tang*). **4** a projection on the blade of a knife or chisel etc. by which it is held firm in its handle.

T'ang the name of a dynasty which ruled in China from 618 to *c.*906.

tangelo / tan-juh-loh / *n.* a hybrid citrus fruit, a cross between a tangerine and a grapefruit or a pomelo; the tree bearing this fruit.

tangent / tan-juhnt / *n.* **1** a straight line that touches the outside of a curve but does not intersect it. **2** the ratio of the two sides (other than the hypotenuse) opposite and adjacent to an acute angle in a right-angled triangle. ☐ **go off at a tangent** diverge suddenly from a line of thought etc. or from the matter in hand.

tangential / tan-**jen**-shuhl / *adj.* **1** of or along a tangent. **2** divergent. **3** peripheral (*the issue you raise is quite tangential to the purpose of this meeting*). ☐ **tangentially** *adv.*

tangerine / tan-juh-**reen** / *n.* **1** a small orange similar to a mandarin. **2** a deep orange-yellow colour.

tangible / **tan**-juh-buhl / *adj.* **1** able to be perceived by touch. **2** clear and definite, real (*tangible advantages*). • *n.* (usu. in *pl.*) a tangible thing, esp. an asset. ☐ **tangibly** *adv.* **tangibility** *n.*

tangle *v.* **1** twist or become twisted into a confused mass. **2** entangle. **3** (foll. by *with*) become involved in conflict with (*don't you tangle with me*). • *n.* a tangled mass or condition. ☐ **tangly** *adj.*

tanglefoot *n.* **1** a deciduous shrub or small tree having wiry, tangled branches, and occurring in the mountains of Tas. **2** any of several other Australian plants of similar habit.

Tangney, Dame Dorothy (Margaret) (1911–85), Australian Labor member of parliament, the first woman to be elected to the Senate (1943).

tango *n.* (*pl.* **tangos**) a slow South American ballroom dance with gliding steps; music for this. • *v.* dance the tango.

tangy / **tang**-ee / *adj.* (**tangier**, **tangiest**) having a strong sharp flavour or smell.

tank *n.* **1** a large container for liquid or gas. **2** a reservoir; a dam. **3** a heavily armoured tracked vehicle carrying guns. • *v.* (usu. foll. by *up*) fill the petrol tank of a vehicle. ☐ **tanked** (also **tanked up**) *colloq.* drunk.

tankard *n.* a large one-handled drinking vessel, usu. of silver or pewter and often with a lid.

tanker *n.* a ship, aircraft, or road vehicle for carrying oil or other liquid in bulk.

tanner *n.* a person who tans animal hides.

tannery *n.* a place where hides are tanned.

tannic *adj.* of tannin. ☐ **tannic acid** tannin.

tannin *n.* **1** any of various organic compounds found in wattle-tree barks etc., used in leather production. **2** a compound, deriving from grape skins, seeds, stalks, and from oak barrels, which gives certain red wines a desirable astringency. **3** a compound in the leaves which gives (esp. strong or overbrewed) tea an astringent quality.

tansy / **tan**-zee / *n.* (*pl.* **tansies**) a plant with aromatic leaves, formerly used in medicine.

tantalise v. (also **-ize**) **1** tease or torment by the sight of something that is desired but kept out of reach or withheld. **2** raise and then dash the hopes of. (¶ From Tantalus.)

tantalum / **tan**-tuh-luhm / n. a hard white metallic element (symbol Ta). □ **tantalic** adj.

Tantalus / **tan**-tuh-luhs / Gk myth. a king condemned to stand in Hades surrounded by water and fruit that receded when he tried to reach them.

tantamount / **tan**-tuh-mownt / adj. (foll. by to) equivalent (*what you say is tantamount to blackmail*).

Tantanoola tiger / **tan**-tuh-noo-luh / n. Aust. a fabulous tiger-like animal, first reported at Tantanoola, SA, in 1889, and (allegedly) sighted thereafter in Vic. as well.

tantra n. each of a class of Hindu, Buddhist, or Jain sacred texts that deal with mystical and devotional practices. □ **tantric** adj. **tantrism** n.

tantrum n. an outburst of bad temper, esp. in a child.

Tanzania / tan-zuh-**nee**-uh / a republic in E. Africa (formerly called Tanganyika). □ **Tanzanian** adj. & n.

Taoism / **tow**-iz-uhm, **tah**-oh-iz-uhm / n. a Chinese religious and philosophical system whose central concept and goal is the Tao, the code of behaviour in harmony with the natural order. □ **Taoist** n.

tap[1] n. **1** a device for drawing liquid or gas from a cask or pipe in a controllable flow. **2** a device for cutting a screw-thread inside a cavity. **3** a connection for tapping a telephone. • v. (**tapped**, **tapping**) **1** fit a tap into (a cask) to draw out its contents. **2** draw off (liquid) by means of a tap. **3** draw sap from (a tree) by cutting into it. **4** obtain supplies or information from. **5** cut a screw-thread inside (a cavity). **6** discover and exploit (*we need to tap the skills of young Australians*). **7** make a connection in (a circuit etc.) so as to divert electricity or fit a listening device for overhearing telephone calls. □ **on tap** (of liquid or gas) ready to be drawn off by a tap; *colloq.* freely available. **tap root** the chief root of a plant, growing straight downwards.

tap[2] v. (**tapped**, **tapping**) **1** strike with a quick light blow; knock gently on (a door etc.). **2** strike (an object) lightly against something (*tapped me on the shoulder*). **3** (often foll. by *out*) make by a tap or taps (*tapped out the rhythm*). • n. **1** a quick light blow or tap; the sound of this. **2** *colloq.* (in a negative context) the slightest amount (*hasn't done a tap of work*). **3** a metal attachment on a tap-dancer's shoe. **5** (in full **tap kick**) *Rugby* a light kick of the ball to restart play and retain possession. □ **tap dance** n. a dance in which an elaborate rhythm is tapped with the feet wearing shoes with metal taps. **tap-dance** v. perform a tap dance.

tapas n.pl. small savoury (esp. Spanish) snacks.

tape n. **1** a narrow strip of woven cotton etc. used for tying, fastening, or labelling things; a piece of this stretched across a racetrack at the finishing line. **2** a narrow continuous strip of paper or other flexible material; adhesive tape; insulating tape; magnetic tape. **3** a tape measure. **4** a tape recording. • v. **1** tie or fasten with tape. **2** record on magnetic tape. □ **have a person** or **thing taped** *colloq.* understand fully; have an effective method of dealing with it. **tape deck** a machine for playing and recording audiotapes. **tape measure** a strip of tape or flexible metal marked in centimetres or inches etc. for measuring length. **tape recorder** an apparatus for recording sounds or computer data on magnetic tape and playing back the recording or reproducing the data. **tape-record** v. record on a tape recorder. **tape recording** a recording made on magnetic tape.

tapenade / **tap**-uh-nahd / n. a Provençal savoury paste or dip, made from black olives, capers, and anchovies.

taper n. a slender candle, burnt to give a light or to light other candles etc. • v. make or become gradually narrower. □ **taper off** make or become gradually less (*interest in the monarchy has tapered off*).

tapestry / **tap**-uhs-tree / n. a piece of strong material with a picture or design woven into it or embroidered on it, used for hanging on walls or as an upholstery fabric.

tapeworm n. a flat worm with a segmented body that can live as a parasite in the intestines of humans and other animals.

tapioca / tap-ee-**oh**-kuh / n. a starchy substance in hard white grains obtained from cassava and used for making puddings.

tapir / **tay**-puh / n. a pig-like animal of Central and South America and Malaysia with a flexible snout.

tappet n. a projection in a piece of machinery that causes a certain movement by tapping against something, used e.g. to open and close a valve.

tar n. **1** a thick dark flammable liquid obtained by distilling wood, coal, or peat etc. **2** a similar substance formed by burning tobacco. **3** *colloq.* a sailor. • v. (**tarred**, **tarring**) coat with tar. □ **tar tree** a tree of northern Australia which exudes a tar-like sap.

taramasalata / ta-ruh-ma-suh-**lah**-tuh / n. (also **taramosalata**) a pinkish pâté made from the roe of mullet or smoked cod, with olive oil, seasoning, etc.

tarantella / ta-ruhn-**tel**-uh / n. a rapid whirling South Italian dance. (¶ Italian: the dance was once thought to be a cure for a tarantula bite.)

tarantula / tuh-**ran**-chuh-luh / n. **1** Aust. = HUNTSMAN (sense 2). **2** a large hairy tropical spider. **3** a large black spider of southern Europe.

tarboy n. Aust. a shearers' worker employed chiefly to apply a disinfectant (originally tar) to a wound accidentally inflicted on a sheep.

tardy *adj.* (**tardier, tardiest**) **1** slow to act or move or happen. **2** behind time. ☐ **tardily** *adv.* **tardiness** *n.*

tare[1] / tair / *n.* a vetch, esp. as an injurious weed in grain fields.

tare[2] / tair / *n.* **1** an allowance made to the purchaser for the weight of the container in which goods are packed. **2** the weight of a vehicle without fuel or load.

target *n.* **1** the object or mark that a person tries to hit in shooting etc.; a disc painted with concentric circles for this purpose. **2** a person or thing against which criticism or scorn etc. is directed. **3** persons or a social group aimed at by advertisers for marketing etc. **4** an objective, a minimum result aimed at (*export targets*). •*v.* (**targeted, targeting**) **1** aim (a weapon etc.) at a target. **2** plan or schedule (a thing) so as to attain an objective.

tariff *n.* **1** a list of fixed charges, esp. for rooms and meals etc. at a hotel. **2** duty to be paid on imports or exports.

tarmac *n. trademark* **1** tarmacadam. **2** an airport runway etc. surfaced with tarmacadam. •*v.* (**tarmacked, tarmacking**) surface with tarmacadam.

tarmacadam *n.* stone, gravel, etc., bound with bitumen, used in surfacing roads etc.

tarn *n.* a small mountain lake.

tarnish *v.* **1** lose or cause (metal) to lose its lustre by exposure to air or damp. **2** stain or blemish (a reputation etc.). •*n.* loss of lustre; a stain or blemish.

taro / ta-roh, tah- / *n.* (*pl.* **taros**) a tropical plant with edible tuberous roots.

tarot / ta-roh / *n.* a game played with a pack of 78 cards which are also used for fortune-telling.

tarpaulin / tah-**paw**-luhn / *n.* **1** canvas made waterproof, esp. by being tarred. **2** a sheet of this used as a covering. ☐ **tarpaulin muster** *Aust.* the collecting of a pool of money, to be used either to buy drinks etc. for the contributors or to provide assistance to some other person or cause (*the workers held a tarpaulin muster for the bushfire victims*).

tarragon / ta-ruh-guhn / *n.* a bushy herb with narrow fragrant leaves used in salads, stuffings, vinegar, etc.

tarry[1] / **tah**-ree / *adj.* of, like, or smeared with tar.

tarry[2] / ta-ree / *v.* (**tarried, tarrying**) *archaic* delay in coming or going.

tarsal *adj.* of the tarsus. •*n.* one of the tarsal bones.

tarsus *n.* (*pl.* **tarsi**) the group of bones that make up the ankle and upper foot.

tart[1] *adj.* **1** sharp-tasting, acid. **2** sharp in manner, biting (*a tart reply*). ☐ **tartly** *adv.* **tartness** *n.*

tart[2] *n.* **1** a pie containing fruit or sweet filling. **2** an open pastry case containing jam etc. **3** *colloq.* a prostitute; a promiscuous woman. **4** *colloq. offens.* any girl or woman. ☐ **tart up** *colloq.* dress or decorate gaudily or with cheap smartness; smarten up (*tarting himself up for the social; tarted up his car with purple paint and silver cushions*).

tartan *n.* **1** the distinctive pattern of a Scottish Highland clan, with coloured stripes crossing at right angles. **2** fabric woven in such a pattern.

Tartar *n.* **1** a member of a group of Asiatic peoples of Siberia and eastern Europe. **2** the Turkic language of these peoples. **3** (**tartar**) a person who is violent-tempered or difficult to deal with.

tartar *n.* **1** a hard chalky deposit that forms on the teeth. **2** a reddish deposit that forms on the side of a cask in which wine is fermented. ☐ **cream of tartar** *see* CREAM. **tartar sauce** (also **sauce tartare, tartare sauce**) a cold sauce of mayonnaise, chopped gherkins, capers, etc.

tartaric / tah-**ta**-rik / *adj.* of or derived from tartar. ☐ **tartaric acid** a natural acid found esp. in unripe grapes, used in baking powders etc.

tartlet *n.* a small pastry tart.

Tartarus / **tah**-tuh-ruhs / *Gk myth.* the part of the underworld where the wicked suffer punishment.

tartrazine / **tah**-truh-zeen / *n.* a bright yellow dye from tartaric acid, used as a food colouring.

tarwhine / **tah**-wuyn / *n.* a marine food fish of Qld, NSW, and WA, silvery-grey with gold flecks along its body. (¶ Probably Dharuk *darrawayin*.)

Tarzan the hero of novels by the American author Edgar Rice Burroughs (1875–1950) and subsequent films. He is a man of powerful physique reared by apes in the jungle.

Tas. / taz / *abbr.* **1** Tasmania. **2** Tasmanian.

task *n.* a piece of work to be done. •*v.* make great demands on (a person's powers etc.). ☐ **take to task** rebuke. **task force** a group and resources specially organised for a particular task.

taskmaster *n.* a person who makes others work hard.

Tasman, Abel Janszoon (1603–59), Dutch explorer, after whom Tasmania (which he named Van Diemen's Land) is named.

Tasmania / taz-**may**-nee-uh / an island State of the Commonwealth of Australia off the south-eastern coast of Australia.

Tasmanian *adj.* of or pertaining to the island or State of Tasmania. •*n.* **1** a person native to or resident in Tasmania. **2 a** a member of an Aboriginal people of Tasmania, dispossessed of their land by the whites and systematically massacred or forcibly evicted to small islands in Bass Strait (*see* William LANNEY, TRUGANINI). **b** a descendant of these first Tasmanians. ☐ **Tasmanian blue gum** a medium-sized eucalypt (*E. globulus*) of southern Vic. and Tas., having grey-blue juvenile foliage and dark green adult foliage: the floral emblem of Tas. **Tasmanian devil** a carnivorous marsupial, coloured black with white markings, mainly carrion-eating and of fierce appearance, and occurring only in Tas. **Tasmanian tiger** a carnivorous marsupial having sandy brown fur with dark brown stripes across the back and rump: now probably extinct. Also called *marsupial wolf* and *thylacine*. **Tasmanian trumpeter** a fish of primarily Tas. waters, highly valued as a food fish (*see* TRUMPETER). **Tasmanian waratah** a telopea endemic to Tas. bearing bright red flower heads.

Tasmanoid *adj.* of, allied to, or resembling the ethnological type of the Aborigines of Tas. (cf. AUSTRALOID).

Tasman Sea the sea (part of the South Pacific) between Australia and New Zealand.

Tass the official news agency of the former Soviet Union.

tassel *n.* **1** a bunch of threads tied at one end and hanging loosely, used as an ornament. **2** the tassel-like head of certain plants (e.g. maize). □ **tassel fern** an epiphytic plant of Qld (a survival from the Carboniferous period), having long bright green tassels on the ends of hanging stems.

tasselled *adj.* ornamented with a tassel or tassels.

Tassie / taz-ee / *n. Aust. colloq.* **1** Tasmania. **2** a Tasmanian. •*adj.* Tasmanian.

taste *n.* **1** the sensation caused in the mouth by things placed in it. **2** the faculty of perceiving this. **3** a small quantity of food or drink taken as a sample; a slight experience of something (*a taste of fame*). **4** a liking (*she has always had a taste for foreign travel; add sugar to taste*). **5** the ability to perceive and enjoy what is beautiful or harmonious or to know what is fitting for an occasion etc.; a choice made according to this (*the remark was in bad taste*). •*v.* **1** discover or test the flavour of (a thing) by taking it into the mouth. **2** be able to perceive flavours (*I cannot taste with a cold*). **3** have a certain flavour (*it tastes sour*). **4** experience (*taste the joys of freedom*). □ **taste bud** one of the small projections on the tongue by which flavours are perceived.

tasteful *adj.* showing good taste. □ **tastefully** *adv.* **tastefulness** *n.*

tasteless *adj.* **1** having no flavour. **2** showing bad taste (*tasteless decorations*). □ **tastelessly** *adv.* **tastelessness** *n.*

taster *n.* **1** a person employed to judge teas or wines etc. by tasting them. **2** a small sample.

tasting *n.* a gathering at which food or drink (esp. wine) is tasted and evaluated.

tasty *adj.* (**tastier**, **tastiest**) having a strong pleasant flavour; appetising. □ **tastily** *adv.* **tastiness** *n.*

Taswegian / taz-**wee**-juhn / *jocular* or *derog. n.* a person native to or resident in Tasmania. •*adj.* Tasmanian. (¶ *Tas*(manian), *-wegian* as in *Norwegian*, etc., pointing to the supposed 'foreignness' of Tasmanians.)

tattered *adj.* ragged, torn into tatters.

tatters *n.pl.* rags; irregularly torn pieces. □ **in tatters 1** torn in many places. **2** (of a negotiation, plan, argument, etc.) destroyed, ruined.

tatting *n.* **1** a kind of lace made by hand with a small shuttle. **2** the process of making this.

tattle *v.* chatter or gossip idly; reveal information in this way. •*n.* idle chatter or gossip.

tattler *n.* any of various sandpipers with a vociferous cry, some of which migrate to Australia from the Northern hemisphere in spring to autumn.

tattoo^1 *n.* **1** an evening drum or bugle signal calling soldiers back to their quarters. **2** an elaboration of this with music and marching, as an entertainment. **3** a drumming or tapping sound.

tattoo^2 *v.* mark (skin) with indelible patterns by puncturing it and inserting a dye; make (a pattern) in this way. •*n.* a tattooed pattern. □ **tattooer** *n.* **tattooist** *n.*

Tatts *n. Aust.* **1** a large-scale lottery. **2** = TATTSLOTTO. (¶ Abbreviation of *Tattersall's Sweep*, the name of a lottery established in 1881 by George Adams, licensee of Tattersall's Hotel, Sydney; the lottery was later based in Melbourne.)

Tattslotto *n. trademark Aust.* a large-scale lottery in which the main prizewinner must select the 6 drawn numbers (out of a total of 45 numbers).

tatty *adj.* (**tattier**, **tattiest**) *colloq.* **1** shabby and untidy. **2** tawdry, cheap. **3** (of a place, building, etc.) badly cared for, dirty, run down (*a tatty restaurant*). □ **tattily** *adv.* **tattiness** *n.*

tau / tow, taw / *n.* the nineteenth letter of the Greek alphabet (T, τ).

taught *see* TEACH.

taunt *v.* jeer at, try to provoke with scornful remarks or criticism. •*n.* a taunting remark.

taupe / tawp, tohp / *n.* grey with a tinge of another colour, usu. brown.

Taurus / **taw**-ruhs / *n.* the second sign of the zodiac, the Bull. □ **Taurean** *adj.* & *n.*

taut *adv.* **1** (of a rope etc.) stretched firmly, not slack. **2** (of nerves etc.) tense. □ **tautly** *adv.* **tautness** *n.*

tauten *v.* make or become taut.

tautology / taw-**tol**-uh-jee / *n.* **1** saying of the same thing again in different words, esp. as a fault of style, as in 'free, gratis, and for nothing'. **2** a statement which is so obviously true that it does not need stating (*they are either coming or they aren't*). □ **tautological** / taw-tuh-**loj**-i-kuhl / *adj.* **tautologous** / taw-**tol**-uh-guhs / *adj.*

tavern *n.* a place where alcoholic liquor is sold to be drunk on the premises and which does not provide accommodation.

taverna *n.* a Greek restaurant.

taw *n.* **1** a large marble. **2** (usu. **taws**) a game of marbles. **3** the line from which the players throw their marbles. □ **back to taws** *Aust. colloq.* back to the beginning.

tawdry / **taw**-dree / *adj.* (**tawdrier**, **tawdriest**) showy or gaudy but without real value. ☐ **tawdrily** *adv.* **tawdriness** *n.*

tawny *adj.* brownish-yellow or brownish-orange. ☐ **tawny frogmouth** a mottled grey to brown nocturnal Australian bird having a low, soft call often mistaken for that of the mopoke.

tax *n.* **1** a sum of money to be paid by people or businesses to a government, used for public purposes. **2** something that makes a heavy demand (*a tax on one's strength*). • *v.* **1** impose a tax on; deduct tax from (income etc.). **2** make heavy demands on (*taxes my patience*). **3** accuse in a challenging or reproving way (*taxed him with having left the door unlocked*). ☐ **tax avoidance** reducing the amount of tax payable by financial manoeuvring. **tax-deductible** (of expenses) legally deductible from income before tax assessment. **tax evasion** illegal non-payment or underpayment of tax. **tax file number** *Aust.* a unique identifying number assigned by tax authorities to each taxpayer. **tax haven** a country where income tax etc. is low. **tax return** a form to complete giving a declaration of income and expenditure for a particular year so that tax can be assessed.

taxa *pl.* of TAXON.

taxable *adj.* able or liable to be taxed.

taxation *n.* the imposition or payment of tax.

taxi *n.* (*pl.* **taxis**) (in full **taxi-cab**) a car that plies for hire, usu. with a meter to record the fare payable. • *v.* (**taxied, taxiing**) **1** go or convey in a taxi. **2** (of aircraft) move along ground or water under its own power, esp. before or after flying. ☐ **taxi rank** a place where taxis wait to be hired.

taxidermy / **tak**-suh-der-mee / *n.* the art of preparing, stuffing, and mounting the skins of animals in lifelike form. ☐ **taxidermist** *n.*

taximeter / **tak**-see-mee-tuh / *n.* an automatic device indicating the fare payable, fitted to a taxi.

taxman *n.* an inspector or collector of taxes.

taxon *n.* (*pl.* **taxa**) any taxonomic group.

taxonomy / taks-**on**-uh-mee / *n.* the scientific process of classifying living things. ☐ **taxonomic** *adj.* **taxonomically** *adv.* **taxonomist** *n.*

taxpayer *n.* a person who pays tax (esp. income tax).

Taylor[1], Mark (Anthony) (1964–), Australian cricketer. A batsman, he was captain of the test team 1994–99.

Taylor[2], Squizzy (original name: Leslie Taylor) (1888–1927), a crime 'boss' of the underworld in Melbourne in the 1920s.

TB *abbr.* tuberculosis.

Tb *symbol* terbium.

T-bone *n.* a T-shaped bone, esp. in a steak from the thin end of the loin.

tbsp. *abbr.* tablespoonful.

Tc *symbol* technetium.

T-cell *n.* = T-LYMPHOCYTE.

Tchaikovsky / chuy-**kof**-skee /, Pyotr Ilyich (1840–93), Russian composer.

tchuringa alternative spelling of CHURINGA.

Te *symbol* tellurium.

te *n.* (also **ti**) the seventh note of a major scale in music.

tea *n.* **1** (in full **tea plant**) an evergreen shrub of the camellia family. **2** its dried leaves. **3** the hot drink that is made by infusing these in boiling water. **4** an infusion of other leaves etc. (*camomile tea; beef tea*). **5 a** morning tea. **b** afternoon tea. **6** the main meal of the day eaten in the evening. ☐ **tea bag** a small porous bag of tea for infusion in a pot or cup. **tea break** an interruption of work allowed for drinking tea etc. **tea chest** a light cubical chest lined with thin sheets of lead or tin, in which tea is exported. **tea leaves** leaves of tea, esp. after infusion. **tea towel** a towel for drying washed dishes. **tea-tree** any of about 40 species (as well as numerous cultivars) of the genus *Leptospermum* widespread throughout Australia, having white, pink, or red flowers and highly aromatic foliage; the common name derives from the fact that early settlers used the leaves of some species as a tea-substitute. **tea-tree fence** *Aust.* a fence made from tea-tree stakes. **tea-tree stake** *Aust.* a thin branch of a tea-tree, used for fencing.

teach *v.* (**taught, teaching**) **1** impart information or skill to (a person) or about (a subject etc.). **2** do this for a living. **3** put forward as a fact or principle (*taught forgiveness*). **4** communicate, instruct in (*suffering taught me patience*). **5** cause to adopt (a practice etc.) by example or experience; *colloq.* deter by punishment etc. (*that will teach you not to meddle*).

teachable *adj.* **1** able to learn by being taught. **2** (of a subject) able to be taught.

teacher *n.* a person who teaches others, esp. in a school.

teaching *n.* what is taught; a doctrine (*the teachings of the Buddha*).

teacup *n.* a cup from which tea or other hot liquids are drunk.

teak *n.* **1** the strong heavy wood of a tall evergreen tree of Sri Lanka, India, etc., used for making furniture and in shipbuilding. **2** any of several Australian trees yielding a durable timber resembling teak, esp. *crow's ash.*

teal *n.* (*pl.* **teal**) a small freshwater duck, e.g. *Australian grey teal; chestnut teal.*

Teale, Leonard (George) (1922–94), AO, Australian actor in television and film.

team *n.* **1** a set of players forming one side in certain games and sports. **2** a set of people working together. **3** a set of draught animals. • *v.* **1** (usu. foll. by *up*) join in a team or in common action (*teamed up with them*). **2** (foll. by *with*) match or coordinate (clothes). ☐ **team spirit** willingness to act for the good of one's group rather than oneself.

teamster *n.* a driver of a team of animals.
teamwork *n.* organised cooperation.
teapot *n.* a pot with a handle, lid, and spout, in which tea is made and from which it is poured.
tear[1] / tair / *v.* (**tore, torn, tearing**) **1** pull forcibly apart or away or to pieces. **2** make (a hole or a split) in this way. **3** become torn, be able to be torn (*paper tears easily*). **4** subject (a person etc.) to conflicting desires or demands (*torn between love and duty*). **5** *colloq.* go or leave hurriedly (*tore across the road; I've got to tear*). • *n.* a hole or split caused by tearing. ☐ **tear apart 1** search (a place) exhaustively. **2** criticise forcefully. **3** destroy; divide utterly; distress greatly. **tear into** *colloq.* **1** severely reprimand. **2** start (an activity) vigorously.

tear[2] / teer / *n.* a drop of the salty water that appears in or flows from the eye as the result of grief or irritation by fumes etc. ☐ **tear duct** a drain for carrying tears to the eye or from the eye to the nose. **tear gas** a gas that causes severe irritation of the eyes. **tear jerker** *colloq.* a sentimental story etc. calculated to make people cry.

tearaway *n.* an impetuous or unruly young person.
teardrop *n.* a single tear.
tearful *adj.* crying or about to cry; sad. ☐ **tearfully** *adv.*
tearing / tair-ring / *adj.* extreme, violent; overwhelming (*in a tearing hurry*).
tearoom *n.* **1** a small restaurant, café, etc. where tea is served. **2** a room, esp. in an office, with facilities for staff to make tea and coffee, eat lunch, etc. **3** *US colloq.* a public toilet used as a meeting place by homosexuals.
tease *v.* **1** try to provoke in a playful or unkind way by jokes or questions or petty annoyances. **2** allure, esp. sexually, while withholding satisfaction. **3** pick (wool etc.) into separate strands. **4** brush or comb (one's hair) towards the scalp to impart fullness. • *n.* **1** a person who is fond of teasing others. **2** an act of teasing.
teaser *n. colloq.* a problem that is difficult to solve.
teaspoon *n.* **1** a small spoon for stirring tea. **2** the amount held by this as a measure in cooking (5 ml). ☐ **teaspoonful** *n.* (*pl.* **teaspoonfuls**).
teat *n.* **1** a nipple on an animal's milk-secreting organ. **2** a device of rubber etc. on a feeding-bottle, through which the contents are sucked.
tech *n.* (also **tec**) *colloq.* **1** a technical college or school. **2** (esp. in the phrase **high-tech**) technology.
technetium / tek-**nee**-shuhm / *n.* an artificially produced radioactive element (symbol Tc).
technical *adj.* **1** of the mechanical arts and applied sciences (*a technical education; technical college*). **2** of a particular subject or craft etc. or its techniques (*the technical terms of chemistry; technical skill*). **3** (of a book etc.) requiring specialised knowledge, using technical terms. **4** due to a mechanical failure (*a technical hitch*). **5** in a strict legal sense (*technical assault*). ☐ **technical foul** a deliberate foul to prevent a certain score by the opposition. **technical knockout** a ruling by a referee that a boxer is unfit to continue and has lost the fight. ☐ ☐ **technically** *adv.*

technicality / tek-nuh-**kal**-uh-tee / *n.* **1** being technical. **2** a technical word, phrase, or point (*he was acquitted on a technicality*).
technician / tek-**nish**-uhn / *n.* an expert in the techniques of a particular subject or craft.
Technicolor *n.* **1** *trademark* a process of producing cinema films in colour. **2** (**technicolour** *or* **technicolor**) vivid or artificial brilliant colour. ☐ **technicolour yawn** *Aust. colloq.* an act or instance of vomiting.
technique / tek-**neek** / *n.* the method of doing or performing something (esp. in an art or science); skill in this.
techno / **tek**-noh / *n.* a style of popular music making extensive use of electronic instruments and synthesised sound (also in *comb.*: *techno-funk; techno-rock*).
technocracy / tek-**nok**-ruh-see / *n.* the rule or control of society or industry by an elite of technical experts.
technocrat / **tek**-nuh-krat / *n.* **1** an exponent or advocate of technocracy. **2** a member of a technically skilled elite. ☐ **technocratic** *adj.*
technology *n.* **1** the scientific study of mechanical arts and applied sciences (e.g. engineering). **2** these subjects, their practical application in industry etc. ☐ **technological** *adj.* **technologically** *adv.* **technologist** *n.*
technophile *n.* a person who is enthusiastic about new technology.
technophobe *n.* a person who fears, dislikes, or avoids new technology.
tectonics / tek-**ton**-iks / *n.* the scientific study of the earth's structural features.
teddy *n.* (in full **teddy bear**) a soft toy bear.
Te Deum / tay **day**-uhm / *n.* an ancient Latin hymn of praise beginning 'Te Deum laudamus' (= we praise thee O God), regularly chanted at matins as well as on special occasions of thanksgiving or celebration.
tedious / **tee**-dee-uhs / *adj.* tiresome because of its length or slowness or dullness; boring. ☐ **tediously** *adv.* **tediousness** *n.*
tedium / **tee**-dee-uhm / *n.* tediousness.
tee *n.* **1** the cleared space from which a player strikes the ball in golf at the beginning of play for each hole. **2** a small pile of sand or piece of wood etc. on which the ball is placed for being struck. **3** the mark aimed at in quoits, bowls, and curling. • *v.* (**teed, teeing**) place (a ball) on a tee in golf. ☐ **tee off 1** play the ball from the tee. **2** *colloq.* start, begin. **tee up** *colloq.* make ready; arrange (*have you teed up the barbie yet?*).

teem *v.* **1** (foll. by *with*) be full of (*the river was teeming with fish*). **2** be present in large numbers (*yabbies teem in this dam*). **3** (of water or rain etc.) flow in large quantities, pour.

teen = TEENAGE.

teenage *adj.* of or characteristic of teenagers.

teenaged *adj.* in one's teens.

teenager *n.* a person in his or her teens.

teens *n.pl.* the period when one is between 13 and 19 years old.

teensy *adj.* (**teensier**, **teensiest**) *colloq.* = TEENY.

teeny *adj.* (**teenier**, **teeniest**) *colloq.* tiny. □ **teeny-bopper** a young teenager following the latest fashions in clothes, music, etc. **teeny-weeny** (also **teensy-weensy**) very tiny.

teepee alternative spelling of TEPEE.

tee shirt alternative spelling of T-SHIRT.

teeter *v.* totter; stand or move unsteadily.

teeth see TOOTH.

teethe *v.* (of a baby) have its first teeth beginning to grow through the gums. □ **teething troubles** problems arising in the early stages of an enterprise.

teetotal *adj.* abstaining completely from alcoholic drinks. □ **teetotaller** *n.*

Teflon *n. trademark* a non-stick coating for pots and pans used in cooking.

Tegucigalpa / tay-goo-thee-**gahl**-pah / the capital of Honduras.

Tehran / tay-**rahn** / the capital of Iran.

Teilhard de Chardin / tay-yah duh shah-**dan** /, Pierre (1881–1955), French Jesuit philosopher and palaeontologist, best known for his evolutionary theory, blending science and theology, that man is evolving mentally and socially towards a perfect spiritual state.

Te Kanawa / te **kah**-nuh-wuh /, Dame Kiri (1944–), AC, New Zealand operatic soprano.

tektite *n.* a small roundish glassy object occurring in various parts of the earth, believed to have been formed as molten debris in meteorite impacts (in Australia called an AUSTRALITE).

telco / **tel**-koh / *n.* (*pl.* **telcos**) a telecommunications company.

tele- *comb. form* **1** at or to a distance (*telescope*). **2** television (*telecast*). **3** by telephone (*telesales*).

telecast *n.* a television broadcast. • *v.* transmit by television. □ **telecaster** *n.*

telecommunications *n.pl.* the means of communication over long distances, as by cable, telegraph, telephone, radio, or television.

teleconference *n.* a conference with participants in different locations linked by telecommunication devices. □ **teleconferencing** *n.*

teledex / **tel**-uh-deks / *n. Aust.* a mechanically-opened index for recording esp. frequently-called telephone numbers.

telegenic / tel-uh-**jen**-ik / *adj.* having an appearance or manner that looks pleasing on television.

telegram *n.* a message sent by telegraph.

telegraph *n.* a system or apparatus for sending messages to a distance, esp. by transmission of electrical impulses along wires. • *v.* **1** send (a message) or communicate with (a person) by telegraph. **2** give advance indication of (*he telegraphed his punch so I was able to avoid it*).

telegraphic *adj.* **1** of or by telegraphs or telegrams. **2** using few words; concise. □ **telegraphically** *adv.*

telegraphist / tuh-**leg**-ruh-fuhst / *n.* a person whose job is to send and receive messages by telegraph.

telegraphy / tuh-**leg**-ruh-fee / *n.* communication by telegraph.

telekinesis / tel-ee-kuy-**nee**-suhs, -kuh-**nee**- / *n.* the supposed paranormal force by which a person can move things without touching them and without using ordinary physical means.

Telemann / **tel**-uh-mahn /, Georg Philipp (1681–1767), German composer.

telemarketing *n.* attempting to sell goods or services by unsolicited telephone calls.

telemetry / tuh-**lem**-uh-tree / *n.* the process of recording the readings of an instrument at a distance, usu. by means of radio.

telemovie *n.* a movie made esp. for television.

teleology / tee-lee-**ol**-uh-jee, tel-ee- / *n.* **1** *Philosophy* the explanation of phenomena by the purpose they serve rather than by postulated causes. **2** *Theology* the doctrine that there is evidence of design and purpose in nature. □ **teleological** / tee-lee-uh-**loj**-i-kuhl / *adj.*

telepath / **tel**-uh-path / *n.* a telepathic person.

telepathic / tel-uh-**path**-ik / *adj.* of or using telepathy; able to communicate by telepathy. □ **telepathically** *adv.*

telepathy / tuh-**lep**-uh-thee / *n.* the supposed communication from one mind to another without the use of speech, writing, or gestures etc.

telephone *n.* **1** a system of transmitting sound (esp. speech) to a distance, esp. by using optical or electrical signals. **2** an instrument used in this, with a receiver and mouthpiece. **3** a system of communication using a network of telephones. • *v.* send (a message) or speak to (a person) by telephone. □ **telephonic** / tel-uh-**fon**-ik / *adj.* **telephonically** *adv.*

telephonist / tuh-**lef**-uh-nuhst / *n.* an operator in a telephone exchange or at a switchboard.

telephony / tuh-**lef**-uh-nee / *n.* the process of transmitting sound by telephone.

telephotography *n.* photographing distant objects using a telephoto lens.

telephoto lens *n.* a lens producing a large image of a distant object that is photographed.

teleprinter *n.* a device for transmitting, receiving, and printing telegraph messages.

teleprompter *n.* a device beside a television or cinema camera that slowly unrolls a speaker's script out of sight of the audience (cf. AUTOCUE).

telescope *n.* an optical instrument using lenses or mirrors or both to make distant objects appear larger when viewed through it. • *v.* **1** make or become shorter by sliding overlapping sections one inside another. **2** compress or become compressed forcibly. **3** condense so as to occupy less space or time.

telescopic *adj.* **1** of a telescope; magnifying like a telescope. **2** visible only through a telescope (*telescopic stars*). **3** capable of being telescoped (*telescopic umbrella*). ☐ **telescopic sight** a telescope fitted to a rifle for magnifying the image of the target. ☐☐ **telescopically** *adv.*

teleshopping *n.* the ordering of goods by customers using a telephone or direct computer link.

teletext *n.* a system in which news and information can be selected and produced on a television screen.

telethon *n.* a very long television program broadcast to raise money for charity.

televangelist / tel-ee-**van**-juh-luhst / *n.* a Protestant evangelical preacher who buys television time to promote his or her doctrines and to solicit funds from viewers.

televise *v.* transmit by or broadcast on television.

television *n.* **1** a system for reproducing on a screen visual images transmitted with sound by radio signals or cable. **2** (in full **television set**) an apparatus with a screen for receiving these signals. **3** televised programs; television as a medium of communication. ☐ **televisual** *adj.*

telex *n.* **1** an international system of telegraphy in which printed messages are transmitted and received by teleprinters using public transmission lines. **2** a message sent or received by telex. • *v.* send (a message) or communicate with (a person) by telex.

Tell, William, a legendary hero (traditionally placed in the 14th century) of the liberation of Switzerland, who was required to hit with an arrow an apple placed on the head of his son.

tell *v.* (**told**, **telling**) **1** make known, esp. in spoken or written words. **2** give information to. **3** utter (*tell the truth*). **4** reveal a secret (*promise you won't tell*). **5** (foll. by *on*) *colloq.* inform against (*he went and told on me, the sneak!*). **6** direct or order (*tell them to wait*). **7** decide or determine (*how do you tell which button to press?*). **8** distinguish (*I can't tell him from his brother*). **9** produce a noticeable effect (*the strain began to tell on him*). ☐ **tell off** *colloq.* scold. **tell-tale** *n.* a person who reveals secrets to another. *adj.* revealing or indicating something (*a tell-tale blush*).

teller *n.* **1** a person who tells or gives an account of something. **2** a person appointed to count votes. **3** a bank cashier.

telling *adj.* having a noticeable effect, striking (*a telling argument*).

tellurium / te-**lyoor**-ree-uhm / *n.* an element (symbol Te) chemically related to sulphur and selenium, used in semiconductors.

telly *n. colloq.* television; a television set.

Telnet *n. trademark Computing* a program which allows a user to access another computer system.

telopea / tuh-**loh**-pee-uh / *n.* a shrub or tree of the Australian genus of the same name, confined to NSW, Vic., and Tas. (*see* WARATAH).

Telstra the Australian Government's telecommunications company.

temerity / tuh-**me**-ruh-tee / *n.* audacity, rashness.

temp *colloq. n.* a temporary employee. • *v.* work as a temp.

tempeh / **tem**-pay / *n.* an Indonesian dish made by deep-frying fermented soy beans.

temper *n.* **1** the state of the mind as regards calmness or anger (*in a good temper*). **2** a fit of anger (*in a temper*). **3** calmness under provocation (*keep one's temper*). **4** a tendency to have fits of anger (*have a temper*). **5** the condition of a tempered metal as regards hardness and elasticity. • *v.* **1** bring (metal) to the required degree of hardness and elasticity by heating and then cooling. **2** bring (clay etc.) to the required consistency by moistening and mixing. **3** moderate or soften the effects of (*temper justice with mercy*). **4** tune or modulate (a piano, harpsichord, etc.) so as to distance intervals correctly. **5** (in Asian cooking) season (cooked rice etc.) with fried onions and spices etc.

tempera *n.* a method of painting with powdered colours mixed with egg yolk or size, used in Europe chiefly in the 12th–15th centuries.

temperament *n.* **1** a person's or animal's nature and character (*a nervous temperament; an artistic temperament*). **2** the adjustment of intervals in tuning a piano etc. so as to fit the scale for use in all keys.

temperamental *adj.* **1** of temperament. **2** not having a calm temperament, having fits of excitable or moody behaviour. **3** *colloq.* (of esp. a machine) unreliable, unpredictable. ☐ **temperamentally** *adv.*

temperance *n.* **1** self-restraint in one's behaviour or in eating and drinking. **2** total abstinence from alcoholic drinks.

temperate *adj.* **1** self-restrained in one's behaviour, moderate. **2** (of climate) having a mild temperature without extremes of heat and cold. ☐ **temperate zone** the regions of the earth lying south of the Arctic Circle to the tropic of Cancer and north of the Antarctic Circle to the tropic of Capricorn. ☐☐ **temperately** *adv.*

temperature *n.* **1** the intensity of heat or cold in a body or room or country etc. **2** a measure of this shown by a thermometer. **3** an abnormally high temperature of the body (*have a temperature*).

tempest *n.* a violent storm.

tempestuous / tem-**pes**-choo-uhs / *adj.* stormy, full of commotion. ☐ **tempestuously** *adv.*

tempi *see* TEMPO.

template *n.* a piece of thin board or metal used as a pattern or guide in cutting, drilling, or shaping.

temple[1] *n.* a building dedicated to the presence or service of a god or gods.

temple[2] *n.* the flat part at each side of the head between forehead and ear.

tempo *n.* (*pl.* **tempos** *or* **tempi**) **1** the speed or rhythm of a piece of music (*in waltz tempo*). **2** the pace of any movement or activity (*the tempo of the war is quickening*).

temporal / **tem**-puh-ruhl / *adj.* **1** secular, of worldly affairs as opposed to spiritual. **2** of or denoting time. **3** of the temples of the head (*the temporal artery*). ☐ **temporal power** the power of an ecclesiastic, esp. the pope, in temporal matters.

temporary *adj.* lasting or meant to last for a limited time only, not permanent. •*n.* a person employed temporarily. ☐ **temporarily** *adv.*

temporise *v.* (also -**ize**) compromise temporarily, or avoid giving a definite answer or decision, in order to gain time.

tempt *v.* **1** persuade or try to persuade (esp. into doing something wrong or unwise) by the prospect of pleasure or advantage. **2** arouse a desire in, attract. **3** risk provoking (fate or Providence) by deliberate rashness. ☐ **tempter** *n.* **temptress** *n.*

temptation *n.* **1** tempting; being tempted. **2** something that tempts or attracts.

tempting *adj.* attractive, inviting (*a tempting offer*). ☐ **temptingly** *adv.*

tempura / tem-**poo**-ruh / *n.* a Japanese dish of seafood or vegetables fried in batter.

ten *adj.* & *n.* **1** one more than nine (10, X). **2** *colloq.* a thing or person of the best quality, attractiveness, etc. (on a scale of 1 to 10) (*he's a ten in my book, a spunk*).

tenable / **ten**-uh-buhl / *adj.* **1** able to be defended against attack or objection (*a tenable position*). **2** (of an office) able to be held for a certain time or by a certain class of person etc. ☐ **tenability** *n.*

tenacious / tuh-**nay**-shuhs / *adj.* **1** holding or clinging firmly to something (e.g. rights, principles, life, etc.); not easily relinquishing. **2** (of memory) retentive. **3** sticking firmly together or to an object or surface. ☐ **tenaciously** *adv.* **tenacity** / tuh-**nas**-uh-tee / *n.*

tenancy *n.* **1** the use of land or buildings as a tenant. **2** the period of this.

tenant *n.* **1** a person who rents land or buildings from a landlord. **2** (in law) an occupant or owner of land or a building. •*v.* occupy as a tenant (*my garden is tenanted by magpies and skinks*). ☐ **tenant in common** a person who owns property in common with another or others, each of whom has a distinct, separately transferable interest.

tenantry *n.* the tenants of land or buildings on one estate.

Ten Commandments, the (in the Bible) the ten rules of correct behaviour given by God to Moses.

tend *v.* **1** take care of or look after (a person or thing). **2** be likely to behave in a certain way or to have a certain characteristic. **3** have a certain influence (*recent laws tend to increase customers' rights*). **4** take a certain direction (*the track tends upwards*).

tendency *n.* **1** the way a person or thing tends to be or behave (*a tendency towards fatness; homicidal tendencies*). **2** the direction in which something moves or changes; a trend (*an upward tendency*).

tendentious / ten-**den**-shuhs / *adj.* (of a speech or piece of writing etc.) aimed at helping a cause, not impartial. ☐ **tendentiously** *adv.*

tender[1] *adj.* **1** not tough or hard; easy to chew (*tender meat*). **2** easily damaged, delicate (*tender plants; of tender age*). **3** sensitive, painful when touched. **4** easily moved to pity or sympathy (*a tender heart*). **5** loving, gentle. ☐ **tender mercies** *ironic* bad treatment. ☐ ☐ **tenderly** *adv.* **tenderness** *n.*

tender[2] *v.* **1** offer formally (*tender one's resignation*). **2** make a tender (for goods or work). •*n.* a formal offer to supply goods or carry out work at a stated price. ☐ **legal tender** currency that must, by law, be accepted in payment. **put out to tender** ask for competitive tenders for (work).

tender[3] *n.* **1** a person who tends or looks after something. **2** a vessel or vehicle travelling to and from a larger one to convey stores or passengers etc. **3** a truck attached to a steam locomotive, carrying fuel and water etc.

tenderfoot *n.* (*pl.* **tenderfoots** *or* **tenderfeet**) a newcomer; an inexperienced person.

tenderise *v.* (also -**ize**) make more tender (esp. meat by beating, marinating, etc.). ☐ **tenderiser** *n.*

tendinitis / ten-duh-**nuy**-tuhs / *n.* (also **tendonitis**) the inflammation of a tendon.

tendon *n.* a strong band or cord of tissue connecting a muscle to some other part.

tendril *n.* **1** a thread-like part by which a climbing plant clings to a support. **2** a slender curl of hair etc.

Tendulkar / ten-**duul**-kuh /, Sachin (Ramesh) (1973–), Indian cricketer. He is the leading run scorer in one-day internationals.

tenebrous *adj. literary* dark, gloomy.

tenement / **ten**-uh-muhnt / *n.* **1** (in law) land or other permanent property held by a tenant (*lands and tenements*). **2** a flat or room rented for living in. **3** a large block of flats.

tenet / ten-uht / n. a firm belief, principle, or doctrine.

tenfold adj. & adv. ten times as much or as many.

Tennant, Kylie (1912–88), AO, Australian novelist and playwright.

tennis n. either of two ball games for 2 or 4 players, played with racquets over a net with a soft ball on an open court (**lawn tennis**) or with a hard ball in a walled court (**real tennis**). □ **tennis elbow** a sprain caused by overuse of the forearm muscles.

Tennyson, Alfred, 1st Baron (1809–92), English poet.

teno n. Aust. colloq. = TENOSYNOVITIS.

tenon / ten-uhn / n. a projection shaped to fit into a mortise.

tenor / ten-uh / n. **1** the general routine or course of something (*disrupting the even tenor of his life*). **2** the general meaning or drift (*the tenor of his lecture*). **3** the highest ordinary adult male singing-voice, between baritone and countertenor or alto; a singer with this voice. **4** a musical instrument with approximately the range of a tenor voice (*tenor recorder*). □ **tenor clef** the clef which places middle C on the second highest line of the staff.

tenosynovitis / ten-oh-suy-nuh-**vuy**-tuhs / n. (also **repetitive strain injury**, **RSI**) an injury esp. of a wrist tendon resulting from repetitive strain.

tenpin bowling n. a game in which ten pins or skittles are bowled at in a special alley.

tense[1] n. any of the forms of a verb that indicate the time of action etc. as past, present, or future (*'came' is the past tense of 'come'*).

tense[2] adj. **1** stretched tightly, strained (*is the wire tense enough?*). **2** with muscles tight in attentiveness for what may happen. **3** unable to relax, edgy. **4** causing tenseness (*a tense moment*). • v. make or become tense. □ **tensely** adv. **tenseness** n.

tensile / ten-suyl / adj. **1** of or relating to tension. **2** capable of being stretched. □ **tensile strength** resistance to breaking under tension. □ □ **tensility** / ten-**sil**-uh-tee / n.

tension n. **1** stretching; being stretched. **2** tenseness, the condition when feelings are tense. **3** the effect produced by forces pulling against each other. **4** electromotive force, voltage (*high-tension cables*). **5** (in knitting etc.) the number of stitches and rows to a unit of measurement (e.g. 10 cm); the tightness of the stitches.

tent n. **1** a portable shelter or dwelling made of canvas etc. **2** a tentlike enclosure, e.g. supplying oxygen to a patient. • v. (also **tent up**) form a shape suggesting a tent. □ **tent embassy** Aust. any of several embassies set up by Aborigines, esp. outside Parliament House in Canberra, to draw attention to the denial of rights to Aboriginal people, the last being set up in 1992; called 'embassy' as a reflection of the feeling by many Aborigines that they are foreigners in their own country as long as land rights etc. are denied them.

tentacle n. a slender flexible part extending from the body of certain animals (e.g. snails, octopuses), used for feeling, grasping, or moving. □ **tentacled** adj.

tentative / ten-tuh-tiv / adj. hesitant, not definite, done as a trial (*a tentative suggestion*). □ **tentatively** adv.

tenter n. a machine for stretching cloth to dry in shape during manufacture.

tenterhook n. each of the hooks that hold cloth stretched for drying on a tenter during its manufacture. □ **on tenterhooks** in a state of suspense or strain because of uncertainty.

tenth adj. & n. **1** next after ninth. **2** one of ten equal parts of a thing. □ **tenthly** adv.

tenuous / ten-yoo-uhs / adj. **1** very thin in form or consistency (*watched the spider weave its tenuous threads*). **2** having little substance or validity, very slight (*tenuous distinctions; a tenuous claim to fame*). □ **tenuously** adv. **tenuity** / tuh-**nyoo**-uh-tee / n.

tenure / ten-yuh / n. **1** the holding of office or of land, property, or accommodation; the period or manner of this (*freehold tenure; during his tenure of office*). **2** guaranteed permanent employment, esp. as a teacher, lecturer, or public servant. □ **tenured** adj.

tenuto / tuh-**nyoo**-toh / Music adv. & adj. (of a note etc.) sustained, given its full time value (cf. LEGATO, STACCATO). • n. (pl. **tenutos**) a note or chord played tenuto. (¶ Italian, = held.)

Tenzing Norgay (1914–86), Sherpa mountaineer who, with Sir Edmund Hillary, was the first to reach the summit of Mount Everest (1953).

tepee / **tee**-pee / n. (also **teepee**) a N. American Indian's conical tent.

tepid adj. **1** slightly warm, lukewarm. **2** unenthusiastic (*received some tepid applause*). □ **tepidly** adv. **tepidity** / tuh-**pid**-uh-tee / n.

teppan-yaki / tep-uhn-**yah**-kee / n. a Japanese dish of meat or fish fried with vegetables on a hot steel plate forming the centre of the dining table.

tequila / tuh-**kee**-luh / n. a Mexican liquor made from agave.

TER abbr. Aust. tertiary entrance rank.

teraglin / tuh-**rag**-luhn / n. (also **trag**) a marine fish of eastern Australia, valued as a food fish. (¶ Possibly from an Aboriginal language.)

terbium n. a metallic element (symbol Tb).

tercentenary / ter-sen-**tee**-nuh-ree / n. a 300th anniversary.

teredo / tuh-**ree**-doh / n. (pl. **teredos**) a mollusc that bores into submerged timber.

Teresa / tuh-**ree**-zuh /, Mother (1910–97), Catholic nun, born of Albanian parents in the former Yugoslavia, who founded the Missionaries of Charity, an order noted for its work among the poor and the dying in Calcutta, India, and throughout the world, including Australia; awarded the Nobel Peace Prize in 1979.

tergiversate / ter-juh-ver-sayt, ter-**jiv**-uh-sayt / *v.* **1** change one's party or principles. **2** make conflicting or evasive statements. ☐ **tergiversation** *n.* **tergiversator** *n.*

teriyaki *n.* a Japanese dish of marinated and grilled meat or fish.

term *n.* **1** the time for which something lasts; a fixed or limited time (*during his term of office; a term of imprisonment*). **2** completion of this (*a pregnancy approaching term*). **3** one of the periods during which instruction is given in a school, college, or university or in which a lawcourt holds sessions, alternating with holidays or vacations. **4** *Aust. Rules* etc.) = QUARTER (sense 12). **5** each of the quantities or expressions in a mathematical series or ratio etc. **6** a word or phrase considered as the name or symbol of something (*'the nick' is a slang term for 'prison'*). **7** (**terms**) language or the manner of its use (*we protested in strong terms*). **8** (**terms**) stipulations made, conditions offered or accepted (*peace terms*). **9** (**terms**) payment offered or asked (*hire purchase on easy terms*). **10** (**terms**) a relation between people (*on friendly terms*). • *v.* call by a certain term or expression (*this music is termed Gregorian chant*). ☐ **come to terms** reconcile oneself to a difficulty etc. (*came to terms with his handicap*). **in terms of** referring to, regarding. **terms of reference** *see* REFERENCE.

termagant / **ter**-muh-guhnt / *n.* a shrewish bullying woman.

terminable *adj.* able to be terminated.

terminal *adj.* **1** of, forming, or situated at the end or boundary of something. **2** forming or undergoing the last stage of a fatal disease (*terminal cancer*). **3** of or done each term (*terminal examinations*). • *n.* **1** a terminating point or part. **2** a terminus for railway trains or long-distance buses; a building (at an airport or in a town) where air passengers arrive and depart. **3** a point of connection in an electric circuit or device. **4** an apparatus with a VDU and keyboard for transmitting messages to and from a computer or communications system etc. ☐ **terminal velocity** a velocity of a falling body such that the resistance of the air etc. prevents any further increase of speed under gravity. ☐☐ **terminally** *adv.*

terminate *v.* **1** bring or come to an end. **2** end (a pregnancy) before term by artificial means. ☐ **terminator** *n.*

termination *n.* **1** terminating or being terminated. **2** an induced abortion. **3** an ending or result.

terminology *n.* **1** the technical terms of a particular subject. **2** the proper use of words as names or symbols. ☐ **terminological** *adj.* **terminologist** *n.*

terminus *n.* (*pl.* **termini** *or* **terminuses**) the end of something; the last station or stop at the end of a railway or bus route.

termite *n.* a small antlike social insect that is very destructive to timber.

tern *n.* a seabird with long pointed wings and a forked tail.

ternary *adj.* composed of three parts.

Terpsichore / terp-**sik**-uh-ree / *Gk* & *Rom. myth.* the Muse of lyric poetry and dance.

Terra Australis Incognita / te-ruh os-trah-luhs in-kog-**nee**-tuh / *n.* the name for a landmass south of Africa, India, and Asia which Classical writers and early cartographers hypothesised had to be there, as a result of which Australia later came to be called sometimes 'Terra Australis' or 'The (Great) Southland'. (¶Latin, = unknown southern land.)

terrace *n.* **1** a raised level place; one of a series of these into which a hillside is shaped for cultivation. **2** a flight of wide shallow steps, e.g. for spectators at a sports ground. **3** a paved area beside a house. **4** a row of houses joined to each other by party walls. • *v.* form into a terrace or terraces. ☐ **terrace house** a house forming one of a terrace.

terracotta *n.* **1** brownish-red unglazed pottery. **2** its colour.

terra firma *n.* dry land; the ground. (¶ Latin)

terrain / tuh-**rayn** / *n.* a stretch of land with regard to its natural features.

terra incognita / in-kog-**nee**-tuh / *n.* an unexplored region. (¶Latin, = unknown land.)

terra nullius / te-ruh **nul**-ee-uhs / *n.* **1** 'land belonging to no-one', hence, in international law, land which could be occupied for the first time by another country and so brought under that country's ownership. **2** the fiction that, prior to white settlement, Australia belonged to no-one (in spite of more than 40,000 years of Aboriginal occupation) and hence could be legally taken over by the British, a fiction effectively quashed by the Mabo decision of the High Court of Australia in 1992 (*see* MABO[1], MABO[2], and NATIVE TITLE).

terrapin / **te**-ruh-puhn / *n.* an edible North American freshwater tortoise.

terrarium / tuh-**rair**-ree-uhm / *n.* (*pl.* **terrariums** *or* **terraria**) **1** a place for keeping small land animals such as lizards, snakes, etc. **2** a sealed transparent globe etc. containing growing plants.

terrazzo / tuh-**rat**-soh, -**raht**-soh / *n.* (*pl.* **terrazzos**) a flooring material of stone chips set in concrete and given a smooth surface.

terrene / tuh-**reen** / *adj.* of the earth, earthly; terrestrial.

terrestrial / tuh-**res**-tree-uhl / *adj.* **1** of the earth. **2 a** of or on dry land. **b** *Zoology* living on or in the ground (as opposed to AQUATIC, ARBOREAL, AERIAL). **c** *Botany* growing in the soil (as opposed to epiphytic etc.: *see* EPIPHYTE).

terrible *adj.* **1** appalling, distressing. **2** extreme, hard to bear (*the heat was terrible*). **3** *colloq.* very bad (*I'm terrible at tennis*). ◻ **terribly** *adv.*

terrier *n.* a small hardy active dog.

terrific *adj. colloq.* **1** of great size or intensity (*a terrific storm*). **2** excellent (*you did a terrific job*). ◻ **terrifically** *adj.*

terrified *adj.* feeling terror.

terrify *v.* (**terrified**, **terrifying**) fill with terror. ◻ **terrifying** *adj.* **terrifyingly** *adv.*

terrine / tuh-**reen** / *n.* **1** pâté or a similar food. **2** an earthenware dish holding this.

territorial *adj.* **1** of territory or a district (*territorial rights*). **2** tending to defend one's territory (*the Australian magpie is a very territorial bird*). ◻ **territorial waters** the sea within a certain distance of a country's coast and subject to its control. ◻◻ **territorially** *adv.*

Territorian *n.* a person native to or resident in the NT.

territory *n.* **1** land under the control of a country, State, city, etc. **2** (**Territory**) an organised division of a country, esp. one not yet admitted to the full rights of a State (*the Australian Capital Territory; the Northern Territory*). **3** an area for which a person has responsibility. **4** a sphere of action or thought, a province (*sorry I can't help you—defence matters aren't in my territory*). **5** an area claimed or dominated by one person, group, or animal and defended against others. ◻ **Territory rig** *Aust.* = DARWIN RIG (*see* DARWIN[1]). **the Territory** *Aust.* the Northern Territory.

terror *n.* **1** extreme fear. **2** a terrifying person or thing. **3** *colloq.* a formidable person; a troublesome person or thing, esp. a child.

terrorise *v.* (also **-ize**) fill with terror; coerce by terrorism. ◻ **terrorisation** *n.*

terrorism *n.* the use of violence and terror to coerce a government or community to grant specific political demands. ◻ **terrorist** *n.*

terry *n.* a cotton fabric used for towels and nappies, with raised loops left uncut.

terse *adj.* concise; curt. ◻ **tersely** *adv.* **terseness** *n.*

tertiary / **ter**-shuh-ree / *adj.* **1** coming after secondary, of the third rank or stage etc. **2** (of education) above secondary level. **3** (**Tertiary**) *Geol.* of the first period of the Cenozoic era with evidence of the development of mammals and flowering plants. • *n.* (**Tertiary**) **1** the Tertiary period. **2** a member of the third order of a monastic body. ◻ **tertiary entrance rank** *Aust.* a score out of 100 assigned to a matriculating student by education authorities which determines eligibility for tertiary courses.

terylene *n. trademark* a synthetic textile fibre.

TESL *abbr.* teaching of English as a second language.

tesla / **tes**-luh / *n.* the SI unit of magnetic induction. (¶ Named after the American scientist N. Tesla (1856–1943).)

tessellated / **tes**-uh-lay-tuhd / *adj.* (of a pavement) made from small flat pieces of stone in various colours arranged in a pattern, resembling a mosaic.

tessellation *n.* an arrangement of shapes fitting together, esp. in a repeated pattern.

tessera *n.* (*pl.* **tesserae**) a small square block used in mosaics.

tessitura / tes-uh-**tyoor**-ruh / *n.* the range of a singing voice or vocal part.

test *n.* **1** an examination or evaluation of the qualities or abilities of a person or thing. **2** a means or procedure for making this. **3** a minor examination (esp. in a school). **4** a test match. **5** the shell of some invertebrates. • *v.* subject to a test. ◻ **test case** a lawsuit providing a decision which is taken as applying to similar cases in the future. **test drive** a drive taken in order to judge the performance of a car. **test-drive** *v.* take a test drive in (a car). **test match** a cricket or Rugby match between teams of certain countries, usu. one of a series in a tour. **test tube** a tube of thin glass with one end closed, used in laboratories. **test-tube baby** *colloq.* one conceived by in vitro fertilisation.

testa *n.* (*pl.* **testae**) the (usu. hard) protective outer covering of a seed.

testaceous *adj.* having a hard continuous shell.

testacy / **tes**-tuh-see / *n.* the state of being testate.

testament *n.* **1** (usu. in **last will and testament**) a will. **2** *colloq.* a written statement of one's beliefs. **3** (usu. foll. by *to*) evidence, proof (*his action is a testament to his loyalty*). **4** a covenant. ◻ **New Testament** the books of the Bible telling of the life and teaching of Christ and his earliest followers. **Old Testament** the books of the Bible telling of the history of the Jews and their beliefs.

testamentary *adj.* of or given in a person's will.

testate / **tes**-tayt / *adj.* having left a valid will at death.

testator / tes-**tay**-tuh / *n.* a person who has made a will.

testatrix *n.* a woman who has made a will.

testes *see* TESTIS.

testicle *n.* a male reproductive organ in which sperm-bearing fluid is produced; (in man) each of the two enclosed in the scrotum.

testify *v.* (**testified**, **testifying**) **1** bear witness to (a fact etc.); give evidence. **2** be evidence of.

testimonial *n.* **1** a formal statement testifying to a person's character, abilities, or qualifications. **2** something given to a person to show appreciation of his or her services or achievements.

testimony *n.* **1** a declaration or statement (esp. one made under oath). **2** evidence in support of something.

testis *n.* (*pl.* **testes** / **tes**-teez /) a testicle.

testosterone / tes-**tos**-tuh-rohn / *n.* a male sex hormone formed in the testicles.

testy *adj.* easily annoyed, irritable. ◻ **testily** *adv.* **testiness** *n.*

tetanus / tet-uh-nuhs / *n.* a disease in which the muscles contract and stiffen (as in lockjaw), caused by bacteria that enter the body.

tetchy *adj.* peevish, irritable. ◻ **tetchily** *adv.* **tetchiness** *n.*

tete-a-tete / tayt-ah-**tayt** / *n.* (also **tête-à-tête**) a private conversation between two people. •*adv.* & *adj.* (of two people) together in private. (¶ French, = head to head.)

tether *n.* a rope or chain by which an animal is fastened. •*v.* fasten (an animal) with a tether. ◻ **at the end of one's tether** having reached the limit of one's endurance.

tetrad *n.* a group of four.

tetragon *n.* a plane figure with four angles and sides.

tetrahedron / tet-ruh-**hee**-druhn / *n.* (*pl.* **tetrahedra** *or* **tetrahedrons**) a solid with four faces; a pyramid with three triangular faces and a triangular base.

tetralogy *n.* a group of four related novels, plays, etc.

tetratheca / tet-ruh-**thee**-kuh / *n.* any of several small Australian heath-like shrubs having nodding, bell-like, pink, mauve, or purple flowers with a black spot or eye in the centre of the bell. Also called *black-eyed Susan.*

Teutonic / tyoo-**ton**-ik / *adj.* **1** of the Germanic peoples (Teutons) or their languages. **2** German.

text *n.* **1** the wording of something written or printed. **2** the main body of a book or page etc. as distinct from illustrations or notes. **3** a sentence from Scripture used as the subject of a sermon. **4** a book or play etc. prescribed for study. **5** data in textual form, esp. as stored, processed, or displayed in a word processor etc. ◻ **text editor** *Computing* a system or program allowing the user to enter and edit text. **text processing** *Computing* the manipulation of text, esp. converting it from one format into another.

texta / **tek**-stuh / *n.* (in full **textacolour**) *Aust. trademark* a pen with a writing point made of felt or fibre.

textbook *n.* a book of information for use in studying, esp. a standard account of a subject. • *adj.* **1** exemplary, accurate. **2** instructively typical (*the batsman made a textbook stroke for four*).

textile *n.* a woven or machine-knitted fabric. • *adj.* of weaving or cloth.

textual *adj.* of, in, or concerning a text (*textual errors; textual commentary*). ◻ **textually** *adv.*

texture *n.* the way a fabric or other substance feels to the touch; its thickness, firmness, or solidity. ◻ **textural** *adj.* **texturally** *adv.*

textured *adj.* **1** having a certain texture (*coarse-textured*). **2** (of a vegetable protein) provided with a texture resembling meat. **3** (of yarn or fabric) crimped, curled, or looped.

Th *symbol* thorium.

Thai / tuy / *adj.* of Thailand or its people or language. •*n.* **1** (*pl.* **Thai** *or* **Thais**) a native or inhabitant of Thailand. **2** the language of Thailand.

Thailand / **tuy**-land / a kingdom in SE Asia (formerly known as Siam).

thalidomide / thuh-**lid**-uh-muyd / *n.* a sedative drug found (in 1961) to have caused malformation of the limbs of babies whose mothers took it during pregnancy.

thallium / **thal**-ee-uhm / *n.* a chemical element (symbol Tl), a soft white poisonous metallic substance.

than *conj.* used to introduce the second element in a comparison (*his brother is taller than he is; I am taller than him*).

■ **Usage** With reference to the last example, it is also legitimate to say *I am taller than he,* but this is much more formal.

thanatology / than-uh-**tol**-uh-jee / *n.* the study of death and dying and their associated phenomena and practices.

thank *v.* **1** express gratitude to. **2** hold (a person) responsible (*he has only himself to thank*). •*n.pl.* (**thanks**) expressions of gratitude; *colloq.* thank you. ◻ **thanks to** on account of, as the (good or bad) result of (*thanks to my foresight; thanks to your pig-headedness*). **thank you** a polite expression of thanks.

thankful *adj.* feeling or expressing gratitude.

thankfully *adv.* **1** in a thankful way. **2** we are thankful (*thankfully it has stopped raining*).

■ **Usage** The use of *thankfully* in sense 2 is extremely common, but it is still considered incorrect by some people. The main reason is that other such adverbs, e.g. *regrettably, fortunately,* etc., can be converted to the form *it is regrettable, it is fortunate,* etc., but *thankfully* converts to *one is thankful (that).* Like *hopefully, thankfully* first became popular in America in the 1960s, and its use is also best restricted to informal contexts.

thankless *adj.* **1** not likely to win thanks; unappreciated (*a thankless task*). **2** ungrateful. ◻ **thanklessly** *adv.* **thanklessness** *n.*

thanksgiving *n.* an expression of gratitude, esp. to God.

Than Shwe / than **shwee** / (1933–), Burmese statesman who became prime minister in 1992.

that *adj.* & *pron.* (*pl.* **those**) the person or thing referred to or pointed to or understood; the further or less obvious one of two. •*adv.* so, to such an extent (*I'll go that far*). •*relative pron.* used to introduce a clause that is essential in order to define or identify something (*the book that I sent you; the man that she married*). •*conj.* introducing a dependent clause (*we hope that all will go well*). ◻ **that's that** that is settled or finished.

■ **Usage** As a relative pronoun *that* usu. specifies or identifies something referred to, whereas *who* or *which* need not: compare *the book that you sent me is lost* with *the book, which you sent me, is lost*.

thatch *n.* **1** a roof or roof covering made of straw, reeds, etc. **2** a matted layer of plant debris etc. on a lawn. **3** *colloq.* a thick growth of hair on the head. • *v.* roof or cover with thatch; make (a roof) of thatch. □ **thatcher** *n.*

Thatcher, Margaret (Hilda), Baroness (1925–), British Conservative politician, first woman prime minister of the UK 1979–90.

thaw *v.* **1** pass into a liquid or unfrozen state after being frozen. **2** become warm enough to melt ice etc. or to lose numbness. **3** become less cool or less formal in manner. **4** cause to thaw. • *n.* **1** thawing; weather that thaws ice etc. **2** *Politics* a lessening of hostility, tension etc. (between nations etc.).

Thawa / **tah**-wu / *n.* an Aboriginal language of south-eastern NSW.

the *adj.* (called the *definite article*) **1** applied to a noun standing for a specific person or a thing (*the prime minister; the man in grey*), or representative of all of a kind (*diseases of the eye; the rich*), or an occupation or pursuit etc. (*too fond of the bottle*). **2** used to emphasise excellence or importance (with *the* stressed) (*do you mean the Whitlam?*). **3** *colloq.* my, our, your, etc. (*the wife*). **4** (of prices) per (*oysters at $5 the dozen*). **5** *Aust.* used with the names of some towns (esp. in northern Australia), often with omission of a secondary element of the name, as *the Alice, the Isa, the Tennant* (for Alice Springs, Mount Isa, Tennant Creek). **6** (foll. by a defining adjective) which is, who are, etc. (*Pope John the Twenty-third*). • *adv.* in that degree, by that amount (*all the better; the more the merrier*).

theatre *n.* **1** a building or outdoor structure for the performance of plays and similar entertainments. **2** a room or hall for lectures etc. with seats in tiers. **3** an operating theatre. **4** a scene of important events (*Belgium was the theatre of war*). **5** the writing, acting, and producing of plays.

theatrical *adj.* **1** of or for the theatre. **2** (of behaviour) exaggerated and designed to make a showy effect. • *n.pl.* (**theatricals**) theatrical performances (*amateur theatricals*). □ **theatrically** *adv.* **theatricality** *n.*

Thebes / theebz / **1** an ancient city of Upper Egypt that was the capital *c.*1550–1290 BC. **2** a city of Greece, NW of Athens, leader of the whole of Greece for a short period in the 4th century BC. □ **Theban** *adj.* & *n.*

thee *pron.* the objective case of **thou**.

theft *n.* stealing.

their *adj.* of or belonging to them.

theirs *possessive pron.* **1** of or belonging to them, the thing(s) belonging to them. **2** as a third person singular indefinite, meaning 'his or her' (*has any person here lost their keys?*).

■ **Usage** It is incorrect to write *their's* (*see* the note under ITS).

theism / **thee**-iz-uhm / *n.* belief in the existence of gods or a god, esp. a god supernaturally revealed to man (as opposed to ATHEISM). □ **theist** *n.* **theistic** *adj.*

Thelymitra / thel-ee-**mit**-ruh / *n.* a genus of (mainly Australian) terrestrial orchids with large, highly colourful flowers (often blue, a colour rare among orchids) in a terminal raceme, most species being known as 'sun orchids' because the flowers open only in the sun.

them *pron.* **1** the objective case of *they* (*we saw them*). **2** *colloq.* = they (*it's them all right*). • *demonstrative adj. colloq.* = those (*them next-door moggies are after them maggies again*).

■ **Usage** The use of *them* as a demonstrative adjective is not acceptable in standard English.

thematic / thee-**mat**-ik / *adj.* of or according to a theme or themes. □ **thematically** *adv.*

theme / theem / *n.* **1** the subject about which a person speaks, writes, or thinks. **2** a melody which is repeated or on which variations are constructed. □ **theme park** an amusement park in which all the activities etc. are related to a particular subject.

themselves *pron.* **1** the emphatic form of *they* and *them*, used in the same ways as *himself* and *herself*. **2** the reflexive form of *them*. □ **be themselves** act in their normal, unconstrained manner (*they are quite themselves again*).

then *adv.* **1** at that time (*was then too busy; the then existing laws*). **2 a** next; after that (*then she told me to come in*). **b** and also (*then, there are the children to consider*). **c** after all (*it is a problem, but then that is what we are here for*). **3 a** in that case, therefore (*if that's yours, then this must be mine*). **b** if what you say is true (*but then why did you take it?*). **c** (implying grudging or impatient concession) if you must have it so (*all right then, have it your own way*). • *adj.* of that time (*the then Premier*). • *n.* that time (*from then on*).

thence *adv.* **1** from that place (*we're cycling to Geelong, and thence to Ballarat*). **2** from that time, thenceforth (*became a monk and thence was lost to the world*). **3** for that reason (*thence it would follow that …*).

■ **Usage** The formulation *from thence*, as in *travelled to Rome and from thence to Venice*, is considered incorrect by some people as the sense 'from' is already present in 'thence'.

thenceforth, thenceforward *adv. colloq.* from then on.

theocracy / thee-**ok**-ruh-see / *n.* **1** government by God or a god directly or through priests. **2** a country governed in this way.

theodolite / thee-**od**-uh-luyt / n. a surveying instrument with a rotating telescope used for measuring horizontal and vertical angles.

theologian / thee-uh-**loh**-juhn / n. an expert in theology.

theology / thee-**ol**-uh-jee / n. the study of religion; a system of religion. ☐ **theological** adj. **theologically** adv.

theorem n. **1** a mathematical statement to be proved by a chain of reasoning. **2** a rule in algebra etc., esp. one expressed as a formula.

theoretical adj. based on theory not on practice or experience. ☐ **theoretically** adv.

theoretician / theer-uh-**tish**-uhn / n. a person who deals with the theoretical (not practical) parts of a subject.

theorise v. (also **-ize**) form a theory or theories.

theorist n. a person who theorises.

theory n. **1** a set of ideas formulated (by reasoning from known facts) to explain something (*Darwin's theory of evolution*). **2** an opinion or supposition. **3** ideas or suppositions in general (contrasted with *practice*). **4** a statement of the principles on which a subject is based (*theory of music*).

theosophy / thee-**os**-uh-fee / n. any of several systems of philosophy that aim at a direct knowledge of God by means of spiritual ecstasy and contemplation, esp. a modern movement following Hindu and Buddhist teachings and seeking universal brotherhood, founded in 1875 in New York by the Russian adventuress H.P. Blavatsky. ☐ **theosophical** adj. **theosophist** n.

therapeutic / the-ruh-**pyoo**-tik / adj. **1** of the relief or healing of disease etc., curative. **2** soothing, conducive to well-being (*finds singing in the shower therapeutic*). • n. (**therapeutics**) (usu. treated as *sing.*) medical treatment of disease. ☐ **therapeutically** adv.

therapist n. a specialist in a certain kind of therapy.

therapy n. **1** the treatment of physical or mental disorders, other than by surgery. **2** physiotherapy; psychotherapy.

Theravada / the-ruh-**vah**-duh / n. the most ancient form of Buddhism, practised in Sri Lanka and parts of SE Asia.

there adv. **1** in, at, or to that place. **2** at that point in a process or series of events. **3** in that matter (*I can't agree with you there*). **4** used for emphasis in calling attention (*hey, you there!*). **5** used to introduce a sentence where the verb comes before its subject (*there was plenty to eat*). • n. that place (*we live near there*). • interj. an exclamation of satisfaction or dismay (*there! what did I tell you!*) or used to soothe a child etc. (*there, there!*).

thereabouts adv. (also **thereabout**) **1** somewhere near there. **2** somewhere near that number or quantity or time etc.

thereafter adv. after that.

thereby adv. by that means.

therefore adv. for that reason.

therein adv. formal in that place; in that respect.

thereof adv. formal of that, of it.

thereto adv. formal to that, to it.

thereupon adv. in consequence of that; immediately after that.

therm n. a unit of heat in the imperial system, used esp. in measuring a gas supply (= 100,000 British thermal units, 1.055×10^8 joules).

thermal adj. **1** of heat; using or operated by heat. **2** warm or hot (*thermal springs*). **3** promoting the retention of heat (*thermal underwear*). • n. a rising current of hot air (used by birds, gliders, etc. to gain height). ☐ **thermal unit** a unit for measuring heat.

thermionic valve / ther-mee-**on**-ik / n. a vacuum tube in which a flow of electrons is emitted by heated electrodes, used in radio etc.

thermo- *comb. form* denoting heat.

thermocouple n. a device for measuring temperatures by means of the thermoelectric voltage developing between two pieces of wire of different metals joined to each other at each end.

thermodynamics n. a branch of physics dealing with the relation between heat and other forms of energy. ☐ **thermodynamic** adj. **thermodynamically** adv.

thermoelectric adj. producing electricity by difference of temperature.

thermometer n. an instrument for measuring temperature, esp. a graduated glass tube containing mercury or alcohol which expands when heated.

thermonuclear adj. **1** of nuclear reactions that occur only at very high temperatures. **2** (of weapons) using such reactions.

thermoplastic adj. becoming soft and plastic when heated and hardening when cooled. • n. a thermoplastic substance.

thermos n. (in full **thermos flask**) *trademark* a vacuum flask.

thermosetting adj. (of plastics) setting permanently when heated.

thermosphere n. the region of the atmosphere beyond the mesosphere.

thermostat n. a device that automatically regulates temperature by cutting off and restoring the supply of heat to a piece of equipment or a room etc. ☐ **thermostatic** adj. **thermostatically** adv.

thesaurus / thuh-**saw**-ruhs / n. (*pl.* **thesauri** / thuh-**saw**-ruy / or **thesauruses**) **1** a book that lists words in groups of synonyms and related concepts. **2** *Computing* a list of similes, definitions, etc., used with a word processing system.

these *see* THIS.

Theseus / **thee**-see-uhs / *Gk myth.* the national hero of Athens, whose exploits include the slaying of the Minotaur in Crete.

thesis / **thee**-suhs / *n.* (*pl.* **theses** / -seez /) **1** a statement or theory put forward and supported by arguments. **2** a lengthy written essay submitted by a candidate for a university degree.

thespian / **thes**-pee-uhn / *adj.* of drama or the theatre. •*n.* an actor or actress. (¶ Named after Thespis, Greek tragic dramatist of the 6th century BC.)

Thessalonian / thes-uh-**loh**-nee-uhn / *adj.* of ancient Thessalonia (modern Salonica), a city in NE Greece.

Thessaloniki / thes-uh-luh-**nee**-kee / (also **Salonica**) a major port in NE Greece and the second largest city in Greece, the capital of the present-day Greek region of Macedonia.

theta / **thee**-tuh / *n.* the eighth letter of the Greek alphabet (Θ, θ).

they *pron.* **1** the people or things mentioned. **2** people in general (*they say the play is a success*). **3** those in authority (*they are increasing income tax*). **4** used informally instead of 'he or she' (*anyone can come if they want to*).

■ **Usage** The use of *they* instead of 'he or she' (see sense 4 above) is common in spoken English and increasingly so in written English, although still deplored by some people. It is particularly useful when the sex of the person is unspecified or unknown and the writer wishes to avoid the accusation of sexism that can arise from the use of *he*. Similarly, *their* can replace 'his' or 'his or her' and *themselves* 'himself' or 'himself or herself', e.g. *Everyone must provide their own lunch*; *Did anyone hurt themselves in the accident?*

they'd = they had; they would.
they'll = they will.
they're = they are.
they've = they have.

thiamine / **thuy**-uh-meen / *n.* (also **thiamin**) vitamin B₁, important in energy production and for healthy muscles and nerves, found in unrefined cereals, yeast extract, liver, and beans.

thick *adj.* **1** of great or specified distance between opposite surfaces. **2** (of a line etc.) broad not fine. **3** made of thick material (*a thick coat*). **4** crowded or numerous; dense (*a thick forest; thick fog*). **5** densely covered or filled (*her roses were thick with aphids*). **6** (of a liquid or paste) relatively stiff in consistency, not flowing easily. **7** (of the voice) not sounding clear. **8** (of an accent) very noticeable. **9** *colloq.* stupid. **10** *colloq.* on terms of close association or friendliness (*her parents are very thick with mine*). •*adv.* thickly (*blows came thick and fast*). •*n.* the busiest part of a crowd, fight, or activity (*in the thick of it*). ☐ **thick as a brick** (*or* **as a log of wood** *or* **as two short planks**) *colloq.* extremely dim-witted, stupid. **thick ear** *colloq.* an ear that is swollen as the result of a blow. **thick head** a feeling of muzziness, esp. from a hangover. **thick-skinned** not sensitive to criticism or snubs. ☐☐ **thickish** *adj.* **thickly** *adv.*

thicken *v.* **1** make or become thicker or of a stiffer consistency. **2** become more complicated (*the plot thickens*). ☐ **thickener** *n.*

thicket *n.* a number of shrubs and small trees etc. growing close together.

thickhead *n.* **1** *colloq.* a stupid person. **2** *Aust.* = WHISTLER. ☐ **thickheaded** *adj.*

thickness *n.* **1** the quality of being thick; the extent to which something is thick. **2** a layer (*use three thicknesses of cardboard*). **3** the part between opposite surfaces (*steps cut in the thickness of the wall*).

thickset *adj.* **1** with parts set or growing close together (*a thickset hedge*). **2** having a stocky or burly body.

thief *n.* (*pl.* **thieves**) one who steals, esp. secretly. ☐ **thievish** *adj.* **thievery** *n.*

thieve *v.* be a thief; steal (a thing).

thigh *n.* the part of the human leg between hip and knee; the corresponding part in other animals. ☐ **thigh bone** = FEMUR.

thimble *n.* a small metal or plastic cap worn on the end of the finger to protect it and push the needle in sewing.

thimbleful *n.* (*pl.* **thimblefuls**) a very small quantity of liquid to drink.

Thimphu / **tim**-poo / the capital of Bhutan.

thin *adj.* (**thinner**, **thinnest**) **1** of small thickness or diameter. **2** (of a line etc.) narrow, not broad. **3** made of thin material (*a thin dress*). **4** lean, not plump. **5** not dense; not plentiful (*thin hair*). **6** having units that are not crowded or numerous. **7** (of a liquid or paste) flowing easily, not thick. **8** lacking strength or substance or an important ingredient, feeble (*a thin voice*). **9** (of an excuse etc.) flimsy or transparent. •*adv.* thinly (*cut the bread thin*). •*v.* (**thinned**, **thinning**) **1** (often foll. by *down*) make or become thinner. **2** (often foll. by *out*) make or become less dense or crowded or numerous (*thin out the seedlings*). ☐ **thin end of the wedge** a thing of little importance in itself, but likely to lead to more serious developments. ☐☐ **thinly** *adv.* **thinness** *n.*

thine *possessive pron. archaic* of or belonging to thee; the thing(s) belonging to thee. •*adj.* (before a vowel) = THY; *thine eyes*.

thing *n.* **1** whatever is or may be an object of perception or knowledge or thought. **2** an unnamed object or item (*there are only a few things on my list*). **3** an inanimate object as distinct from a living creature. **4** (in pity or contempt) a creature (*poor thing!*). **5** an act, fact, idea, or task etc. (*a difficult thing to do*). **6** (**the thing**) what is conventionally proper or is fashionable; what is important or suitable (*the latest thing in computers; just the thing*). **7** (**things**) personal belongings, clothing (*pack your things*). **8** (**things**) implements or utensils (*my painting things*). **9** (**things**) circumstances or conditions (*things began to improve*). **10** *colloq.* one's special interest or concern (*that's just not my thing*).

thingummyjig *n.* (also **thingumabob, thingummybob**) *colloq.* a person or thing whose name one has forgotten or does not know.

thingy (also **thingo**) *colloq.* = THINGUMMYJIG.

think *v.* (**thought, thinking**) **1** exercise the mind in an active way, form connected ideas. **2** have as an idea or opinion (*we think we shall win*). **3** form as an intention or plan (*can't think what to do next; I'm thinking of becoming a monk because I like the costume*). **4** take into consideration (*think how nice it would be*). **5** call to mind, remember (*can't think where I put it; I think of him constantly*). **6** be of the opinion, judge (*it is thought to be a fake*). • *n. colloq.* an act of thinking (*must have a think about that*).

thinker *n.* a person who thinks deeply or in a specified way (*an original thinker*).

thinking *adj.* using thought or rational judgment about things (*all thinking people*).

thinktank *n. colloq.* a group of experts providing advice and ideas, esp. on national and commercial problems.

thinner *n.* a substance for thinning paint.

thinnish *adj.* rather thin.

third *adj.* next after second. • *n.* **1** something that is third. **2** third-class honours in a university degree. **3** third gear. **4** one of three equal parts of a thing. □ **third age** the period in life of active retirement; old age. **third degree** long and severe questioning, esp. by police to get information or a confession. **third-degree burn** a burn of the most severe kind, affecting lower layers of tissue. **third man** *Cricket* a fielder positioned near the boundary behind the slips. **third party** another person etc. besides the two principal ones involved. **third-party insurance** that in which the insurer gives protection to the insured against liability for damage or injury to any other person. **third person** *see* PERSON. **third-rate** *adj.* very inferior in quality. □□ **thirdly** *adv.*

Third Reich the Nazi regime in Germany, 1933–45.

Third World the developing countries of Asia, Africa, and Latin America.

thirst *n.* **1** the feeling caused by a desire or need to drink. **2** a strong desire (*a thirst for adventure*). • *v.* feel a thirst.

thirsty *adj.* (**thirstier, thirstiest**) **1** feeling thirst. **2** (of land, a season, etc.) dry or parched. **3** (often foll. by *for* or *after*) eager. **4** *colloq.* causing thirst (*thirsty work*). □ **thirstily** *adv.*

thirteen *adj.* & *n.* one more than twelve (13, XIII). □ **thirteenth** *adj.* & *n.*

thirty *adj.* & *n.* **1** three times ten (30, XXX). **2** (**thirties**) the numbers from 30 to 39, esp. the years of a century or of a person's life. □ **thirtieth** *adj.* & *n.*

this *adj.* & *pron.* (*pl.* **these**) the person or thing close at hand or touched, or just mentioned or about to be mentioned; the nearer or more obvious one of two. • *adv.* to such an extent (*we're surprised he got this far*). □ **this and that** various things.

thistle *n.* a prickly plant usu. with globular heads of purple flowers.

thistledown *n.* the very light fluff on thistle seeds by which they are carried by the wind.

thither *adv. archaic* to or towards that place.

thole *n.* (in full **thole-pin**) a peg set in the gunwale of a boat to serve as a rowlock.

-thon *see* -ATHON.

Thomas[1], Dylan (Marlais) (1914–53), Welsh poet who wrote in English.

Thomas[2], St (1st century AD), an Apostle, who refused to believe that Christ had risen from the dead unless he could see and touch his wounds. □ **doubting Thomas** a sceptical person.

Thomas Aquinas *see* AQUINAS.

Thomism / **toh**-miz-uhm / *n.* the doctrine of Thomas Aquinas or of his followers. □ **Thomist** *n.*

Thompson, Jack (full name: John Payne Thompson) (1940–), AM, Australian television and film actor.

thong *n.* **1** a narrow strip of hide or leather used as a fastening or lash etc. **2** *US* & *Aust.* a flat-soled sandal held on the foot by a bifurcated thong passing between the first and second toes.

Thor *Scand. myth.* the god of thunder and the weather. Thursday is named after him.

thorax / **thaw**-raks / *n.* (*pl.* **thoraces** / **thaw**-ruh-seez / *or* **thoraxes**) the part of the body between the head or neck and the abdomen. □ **thoracic** / thaw-**ras**-ik / *adj.*

thorium / **thaw**-ree-uhm / *n.* a radioactive metallic element (symbol Th), with a variety of industrial uses and important also as a nuclear fuel.

thorn *n.* **1** a sharp pointed projection on a plant. **2** a thorny tree or shrub. □ **thornless** *adj.*

thornbill *n.* any of various small, plump, Australian birds, often with a freckled forehead, e.g. *yellow thornbill, chestnut-rumped thornbill*.

Thornton, Sigrid (1959–), Australian television and film actor.

thorny *adj.* (**thornier, thorniest**) **1** having many thorns. **2** like a thorn. **3** troublesome, difficult (*a thorny problem*). □ **thorny devil** *Aust.* = MOUNTAIN DEVIL (*see* MOUNTAIN). (¶ From the thorn-like spines with which it is covered.)

thorough *adj.* **1** complete in every way; doing things or done with great attention to detail. **2** absolute (*a thorough nuisance*). □ **thoroughly** *adv.* **thoroughness** *n.*

thoroughbred *adj.* (esp. of a horse) bred of pure or pedigree stock. • *n.* a thoroughbred animal.

thoroughfare *n.* a public way open at both ends. □ **no thoroughfare** (as a notice) this road is private or is obstructed.

thoroughgoing *adj.* thorough.

Thorpe, Ian (James) (1982–), OAM, Australian swimmer. At the 2000 Olympics he won gold medals in the 400 metres freestyle, the 4×100 metres freestyle relay, and the 4×200 metres freestyle relay.

those see THAT.

Thoth / thohth, toht / *Egyptian myth.* a moon god, the god of wisdom, justice, and writing, and patron of the sciences.

thou[1] / thow / *pron. archaic* (in speaking to one person) you.

thou[2] / thow / *n.* (*pl.* **thou** or **thous**) *colloq.* **1** thousand. **2** one thousandth.

though *conj.* in spite of the fact that, even supposing (*it's true, though hard to believe*). • *adv. colloq.* however (*she's right, though*).

thought see THINK. • *n.* **1** the process or power of thinking. **2** a way of thinking that is characteristic of a particular class, nation, or period (*in modern thought*). **3** meditation; consideration (*deep in thought*). **4** an idea or chain of reasoning produced by thinking. **5** an intention (*we had no thought of giving offence*).

thoughtful *adj.* **1** thinking deeply; often absorbed in thought. **2** (of a book, writer, or remark etc.) showing signs of careful thought. **3** showing thought for the needs of others, considerate. ☐ **thoughtfully** *adv.* **thoughtfulness** *n.*

thoughtless *adj.* **1** not alert to possible effects or consequences. **2** inconsiderate. ☐ **thoughtlessly** *adv.* **thoughtlessness** *n.*

thousand *adj.* & *n.* ten hundred (1000, M). ☐ **thousandth** *adj.* & *n.*

thousandfold *adj.* & *adv.* one thousand times as much or as many.

thrall / thrawl / *n.* **1** a slave (of a person, a power, an influence, etc.). **2** slavery. ☐ **in thrall** in bondage; enslaved.

thrash *v.* **1** beat severely with a stick or whip. **2** defeat thoroughly in a contest. **3** thresh. **4** (foll. by *about* or *around*) make violent movements. • *n.* (in full **thrash metal**) a style of rock music which includes elements of heavy metal combined with punk rock. ☐ **thrash out** discuss thoroughly.

thread *n.* **1** a thin length of any substance, esp. a length of spun cotton or wool etc. **2** a continuous link or aspect of a thing (*lose the thread of an argument; pick up the threads of one's life*). **3** the spiral ridge of a screw. • *v.* **1** pass a thread through the eye of (a needle). **2** pass (a strip of film etc.) through or round something into the proper position for use. **3** put (beads) on a thread. **4** cut a thread on (a screw). ☐ **thread one's way** make one's way through a crowd or streets etc.

threadbare *adj.* **1** (of cloth) with the nap worn off and threads visible. **2** (of a person) wearing threadbare or shabby clothes. **3** poor, meagre (*a threadbare existence*). **4** hackneyed, stale, feeble or insubstantial (*a threadbare justification for logging old-growth forests; a threadbare excuse*).

threadworm *n.* a small threadlike worm, esp. one sometimes found in the rectum of children.

threat *n.* **1** an expression of one's intention to punish or harm a person or thing. **2** an indication of something undesirable (*there's a threat of rain*). **3** a person or thing regarded as liable to bring danger or catastrophe (*machinery was seen as a threat to people's jobs*).

threaten *v.* **1** make a threat or threats against (a person etc.); try to influence by threats. **2** be a warning of (*the clouds threatened rain*). **3** (foll. by *to*) seem likely to be or do something undesirable (*the scheme threatens to be expensive*). **4** be a threat to (*the dangers that threaten us*).

threatened *adj.* (of a species etc.) likely to become extinct.

three *adj.* & *n.* one more than two (3, III). ☐ **three-cornered** triangular; (of a contest) between three parties. **three-cornered jack** *Aust.* = DOUBLEGEE. **three-D** (also **3-D**) *adj.* three-dimensional; a three-dimensional realisation or state (*saw the film in 3-D*). **three-dimensional** *adj.* having or appearing to have three dimensions (length, breadth, depth). **three-quarter** *adj.* consisting of three-quarters of a whole. *n. Rugby* a player with a position just behind the half-backs. **three-quarters** three parts out of four. **three-ring circus 1** a circus with three rings for simultaneous performances. **2** an extravagant display. **3** a chaotic mess. **the three Rs** reading, writing, and arithmetic, as the basis of elementary education.

threefold *adj.* & *adv.* **1** three times as much or as many. **2** consisting of three parts.

threepence / **thruup**-uhns / *n. hist.* the sum of three pence. ☐ **threepenny** *adj.*

threescore *n. archaic* sixty.

threesome *n.* **1** three people together, a trio. **2** an activity (e.g. sex) in which three persons take part. **3** a game etc. for three, esp. in golf.

three-way *adj.* involving three directions or participants.

threnody / **thren**-uh-dee / *n.* a song of lamentation, esp. on a person's death.

thresh *v.* **1** beat out or separate (grain) from husks of corn. **2** make violent movements (*threshing about*). ☐ **thresher shark** a shark of Australian waters having a very strong upper lobe to its tail which it uses to lash fish into groups for ease in feeding. ☐☐ **thresher** *n.*

threshold *n.* **1** a piece of wood or stone forming the bottom of a doorway. **2** the entrance of a house etc. **3** the point of entry or beginning of something (*on the threshold of discovering a cure for Aids*). **4** the lowest limit at which a stimulus becomes perceptible. **5** the highest limit at which pain etc. is bearable.

threw see THROW.

thrice *adv. archaic* three times.

thrift *n.* **1** economical management of money or resources. **2** the sea pink.

thriftless *adj.* not thrifty, wasteful.

thrifty *adj.* (**thriftier, thriftiest**) practising thrift, economical. ☐ **thriftily** *adv.*

thrill *n.* **1** a wave or nervous tremor of emotion or sensation (*a thrill of joy*). **2** a thrilling experience (*abseiling is a thrill*). • *adj.* (of a crime) committed solely for the thrill of carrying it out (*a wave of thrill killings in America*). • *v.* **1** feel or cause to feel a thrill (*I thrilled to his touch; a voice that thrilled millions*). **2** (as **thrilled**) *colloq.* extremely pleased or delighted (*thrilled to bits to see him again*).

thriller *n.* an exciting story, play, or film, esp. one involving crime.

thrips *n.* (*pl.* **thrips**) a very small sap-sucking insect that is harmful to plants.

thrive *v.* (**throve** *or* **thrived**, **thrived** *or* **thriven**, **thriving**) **1** grow or develop well and vigorously. **2** prosper, be successful (*a thriving industry*).

throat *n.* **1** the front of the neck. **2** the passage in the neck through which food passes to the oesophagus and air passes to the lungs. **3** a narrow passage or funnel.

throaty *adj.* **1** uttered deep in the throat. **2** hoarse. ☐ **throatily** *adv.* **throatiness** *n.*

throb *v.* (**throbbed, throbbing**) **1** (of the heart or pulse etc.) beat with more than usual force or rapidity. **2** vibrate or sound with a persistent rhythm; hurt in this way (*a throbbing wound*). • *n.* throbbing.

throes *n.pl.* severe pangs of pain. ☐ **in the throes of** struggling with the task of (*in the throes of spring-cleaning*).

thrombosis / throm-**boh**-suhs / *n.* (*pl.* **thromboses**) formation of a clot of blood in a blood vessel or organ of the body.

throne *n.* **1** the special ceremonial chair or seat used by a monarch or bishop etc. **2** sovereign power (*came to the throne*). • *v.* enthrone.

throng *n.* a crowded mass of people. • *v.* **1** come or go or press in a throng. **2** fill (a place) with a throng.

throttle *n.* a valve controlling the flow of fuel or steam etc. to an engine; the lever or pedal operating this. • *v.* **1** choke or strangle. **2** control (an engine or steam etc.) with a throttle.

through *prep.* **1** from end to end or side to side of; entering at one side and coming out at the other. **2** between or among (*scuffling through fallen leaves*). **3** from beginning to end of; so as to have finished or completed (*read through the letter; went through some hard times*). **4** past (traffic lights) (*went through the red light*). **5** throughout (*toured through Australia; the disease spread through his body*). **6** by reason of; by the means or fault of (*lost it through carelessness*). • *adv.* **1** through something (*go through to the lounge; they would not let us through*). **2** throughout, thoroughly (*wet through*). **3** with a connection made to a desired telephone etc. (*you're through*). **4** finished (*wait till I'm through with these papers*). **5** having no further dealings (*I'm through with him forever*). • *adj.* going through something; (of traffic) passing through a place without stopping; (of travel or passengers etc.) going to the end of a journey without a change of line or vehicle etc.; (of a road) open at both ends. ☐ **through and through** through again and again; thoroughly, completely.

throughout *prep.* & *adv.* right through, from beginning to end of (a place, course, or period).

throughput *n.* the amount of material processed, esp. in manufacturing or computing.

throve *see* THRIVE.

throw *v.* (**threw, thrown, throwing**) **1** send with some force through the air or in a certain direction. **2** hurl to the ground (*the horse threw its rider*). **3** *colloq.* disconcert (*the question threw me*). **4** put (clothes etc.) on or off hastily or casually. **5** cause (dice) to fall to the table; obtain (a number) by this. **6** shape (rounded pottery) on a potter's wheel. **7** turn, direct, or move (a part of the body) quickly (*threw his head back*). **8** cause to be in a certain state (*they were thrown out of work; thrown into confusion*). **9** move (a switch or lever) so as to operate it. **10** have (a fit or tantrum). **11** give (a party). **12** lose (a contest, race, etc.) intentionally, esp. for a bribe. **13** *Cricket* bowl (a ball) with an illegitimate sudden straightening of the arm. • *n.* **1** the act of throwing. **2** the distance something is or may be thrown. ☐ **throw a wobbly** (*or* **wobbler**) *colloq.* have a fit of annoyance, temper, or panic. **throw in** **1** include (a thing) without additional charge. **2** put in (a remark) casually or as an addition. **throw-in** *n.* the throwing in of a ball at Rugby etc. after it has gone out of play over the touch line. **throw in the towel** (*or* **sponge**) admit defeat or failure; give up hope. (¶ From the practice of admitting defeat in a boxing match by throwing into the air the sponge used between rounds.) **throw it in** *colloq.* **1** give up, accept defeat (*this job's the pits—think I'll throw it in*). **2** cease working, call a halt (*I'm throwing it in for a while*). **throw off** **1** manage to get rid of or become free from (*throw off a cold*). **2** write or utter in an offhand manner. **3** confuse, disconcert (*don't be thrown off by his comments*). **throw off at** *Aust. colloq.* ridicule or criticise. **throw oneself at** seek blatantly as a sexual partner. **throw oneself into** engage vigorously in. **throw out** **1** throw away. **2** put out suddenly or forcibly; expel (a troublemaker etc.). **3** reject (a proposed plan etc.). **throw over** desert or abandon. **throw the book at** *colloq.* make all possible charges against (a person). **throw up** **1** bring to notice (*his researches threw up some interesting facts*). **2** give up (*throw up one's job*). **3** vomit. **4** erect hastily.

throwaway *adj.* **1** meant to be thrown away after one use. **2** spoken in a deliberately casual way (*a throwaway remark*). **3** disposed to throwing things away (*we live in a throwaway society*).

throwback *n.* an animal etc. showing characteristics of an ancestor that is earlier than its parents.

throwing *n.* the action of THROW *v.* ☐ **throwing club** *Aust.* an Aboriginal weapon meant for hurling, with a clublike, sometimes barbed, head opposite the handle. **throwing stick** *Aust.* **1** an Aboriginal weapon made from a thin, peeled branch of wood. **2** = WOOMERA. **3** = BOOMERANG.

thrum[1] *v.* (**thrummed, thrumming**) **1** play (a stringed instrument) monotonously or unskilfully. **2** (often foll. by *on*) drum idly. •*n.* a thrumming sound.

thrum[2] *n.* the uneven end of a warp-thread left when the finished web is cut away.

thrush[1] *n.* **1** any of various songbirds, esp. the song thrush (introduced into Australia from Europe). **2** any of several Australian birds having a melodious song, including the *shrike thrush* and the *ground thrush*.

thrush[2] *n.* **1** an infection in which a minute fungus produces white patches in the mouth and throat, esp. in children. **2** a similar disease of the vagina.

thrust *v.* (**thrust, thrusting**) **1** push forcibly; make (one's way) forcibly. **2** make a forward stroke with a sword etc. **3** put forcibly into a position or condition, force the acceptance of (*some have greatness thrust upon them*). **4** (as **thrusting** *adj.*) aggressive, ambitious. •*n.* **1** a sudden or forcible push or lunge. **2** the propulsive force produced by a jet or rocket engine. **3** a strong attempt to penetrate an enemy's line or territory. **4** a hostile remark aimed at a person. **5** an attack with the point of a weapon. **6** (often foll. by *of*) the chief theme or gist of remarks etc.

thud *n.* a low dull sound like that of a blow or something that does not resound. •*v.* (**thudded, thudding**) make a thud; fall with a thud.

thug *n.* a vicious or brutal ruffian. ☐ **thuggery** *n.* **thuggish** *adj.*

thulium / **thyoo**-lee-uhm / *n.* a metallic element (symbol Tm).

thumb *n.* **1** the short thick finger set apart from the other four. **2** the part of a glove covering this. •*v.* wear or soil, or turn pages etc., with the thumbs (*a well-thumbed book*). ☐ **be all thumbs** be very clumsy at handling things. **thumb a lift** obtain a lift by signalling with one's thumb, hitchhike. **thumb index** a set of notches on the edges of a book's leaves, marked with letters etc. to enable the user to open the book directly at a particular section. **thumb one's nose** cock a snook (*see* SNOOK). **thumbs down** an indication of rejection. **thumbs up** an indication of satisfaction or approval. **under a person's thumb** completely under his or her influence.

thumbnail *n.* **1** the nail of the thumb. **2** (used as *adj.*) concise, brief (*a thumbnail sketch*). **3** *Computing* a miniature picture to be clicked on if the full-sized picture is required.

thumbscrew *n.* a former instrument of torture for crushing the thumb.

thump *v.* **1** beat, strike, or knock heavily (esp. with the fist). **2** throb strongly (*my heart was thumping*). **3** tread heavily. **4** pound (the keys of a piano) heavily, unmusically, or (as a child would) meaninglessly. •*n.* a heavy blow; a dull sound made by this.

thumping *adj. colloq.* very big (*a thumping lie; a thumping majority*).

thunder *n.* **1** the loud noise accompanying lightning. **2** any similar noise (*thunders of applause*). •*v.* **1** sound with thunder (*it thundered*). **2** make a noise like thunder, sound loudly (*the train thundered past*). **3** utter loudly; make a forceful attack in words (*thundered against immorality from the pulpit*). ☐ **steal a person's thunder** use his or her ideas or words etc. before he or she is able to do so. (¶ From the remark of a dramatist (*c.*1710) when the stage thunder intended for his play was taken and used for another.) ☐☐ **thundery** *adj.*

thunderbird *n.* either of two Australian birds, the golden whistler or the rufous whistler, whose call is popularly regarded as presaging a thunderstorm.

thunderbolt *n.* **1** a flash of lightning accompanying thunder. **2** an imaginary destructive missile thought of as sent to earth with a lightning flash by a god. **3** a very startling event or statement.

thunderclap *n.* a clap of thunder.

thundercloud *n.* a cloud charged with electricity and producing thunder and lightning.

thundering *adj. colloq.* very big (*a thundering nuisance*).

thunderous *adj.* like thunder.

thunderstorm *n.* a storm accompanied by thunder.

thunderstruck *adj.* amazed.

thurible / **thyoo**-ruh-buhl / *n.* a censer.

thurifer / **thyoo**-ruh-fuh / *n.* the acolyte who carries the thurible at Mass etc.

Thursday *n.* the day of the week following Wednesday. •*adv. colloq.* **1** on Thursday. **2** (**Thursdays**) on Thursdays; each Thursday.

Thursday Island an island in Torres Strait (called Waiben by the Muralag Aborigines), the administrative and commercial centre of the Torres Strait Islands.

thus *adv. formal* **1** in this way, like this (*hold the wheel thus*). **2** as a result of this (*he was the eldest son and thus heir to the title*). **3** to this extent (*thus far*).

thwack *v.* strike with a heavy blow. •*n.* a heavy blow; the sound of this.

thwart *v.* prevent (a person) from doing what he or she intends; prevent (a plan etc.) from being accomplished. •*n.* a rower's bench across a boat.

thy *adj. archaic* of or belonging to thee.

thylacine / **thuy**-luh-seen / *n.* = TASMANIAN TIGER (*see* TASMANIAN).

thyme / tuym / *n.* any of several herbs with fragrant leaves.

thymol *n.* a substance obtained from oil of thyme, used as an antiseptic.

thymus *n.* (*pl.* **thymi**) a gland near the base of the neck.

thyroid *n.* (in full **thyroid gland**) a large ductless gland at the front of the neck, secreting a hormone which regulates the body's growth and development. ◻ **thyroid cartilage** the large cartilage of the larynx forming the Adam's apple.

thyself *pron.* corresponding to *thee* and *thou*, used in the same ways as *himself* and *herself*.

Ti *symbol* titanium.

ti alternative spelling of TE.

Tiananmen Square / **tyen**-uhn-muhn / a square in the centre of Beijing, the largest public open space in the world. It attracted worldwide attention in spring 1989 when it was occupied by hundreds of thousands of student-led protesters of the emerging pro-democracy movement. The demonstration ended when government troops and tanks opened fire on the unarmed protesters, killing over 2,000. (¶ The name means 'The Square of Heavenly Peace'.)

tiara / tee-**ah**-ruh / *n.* **1** a woman's jewelled ornamental crescent-shaped headdress. **2** (in full **papal tiara**) the pope's diadem, pointed at the top and surrounded by three crowns.

Tibet / tuh-**bet** / a former country north of India; a self-governing region of China since 1965.

Tibetan *n.* **1** a native of Tibet. **2** the language of Tibet. •*adj.* of Tibet or its people or language.

tibia *n.* (*pl.* **tibiae**) the inner of the two bones extending from the knee to the ankle; the shin bone. ◻ **tibial** *adj.*

tic *n.* an involuntary spasmodic twitching of the muscles, esp. of the face.

tich = TITCHY.

tick[1] *n.* **1** a regularly repeated clicking sound, esp. that of a watch or clock. **2** *colloq.* a moment. **3** a mark (often ✓) placed against an item in a list etc. to show that it has been checked or is correct. •*v.* **1** (of a clock etc.) make a series of ticks. **2** put a tick beside (an item). **3** (of a mechanism etc.) work, function (*take it apart to see how it ticks*). ◻ **tick off** *colloq.* reprimand. **tick over 1** (of an engine) idle. **2** (of activities) continue in a routine way.

tick[2] *n.* any of several blood-sucking mites or parasitic insects.

tick[3] *n.* the case of a mattress or pillow, holding the filling.

tick[4] *n. colloq.* credit (*buying on tick*).

ticker *n. colloq.* **1** a watch. **2** a teleprinter. **3** the heart; courage. ◻ **ticker tape** paper tape from a teleprinter etc.; this or similar material thrown in long strips from windows to greet a celebrity.

ticket *n.* **1** a written or printed piece of card or paper that entitles the holder to a certain right (e.g. to travel by train or bus etc. or to a seat in a cinema etc.). **2** *Aust.* a document certifying that the bearer is a member of a trade union (*no ticket, no start*). **3** *Aust. hist.* = TICKET-OF-LEAVE. **4** a label attached to a thing and giving its price or other particulars. **5** an official notification of a traffic offence (*parking ticket*). **6** a list of the candidates put forward by one party in an election. **7** (**the ticket**) *colloq.* the correct or desirable thing (*that's the ticket!*). •*v.* (**ticketed**, **ticketing**) put a ticket on (an article for sale etc.). ◻ **have tickets on oneself** *Aust. colloq.* be conceited.

ticket-of-leave *n. Aust. hist.* a permit entitling a convict in Australia to live and work as a private individual within a stipulated area until the expiration or remission of his or her sentence. ◻ **ticket-of-leaver** a convict who has been granted a ticket-of-leave.

ticking *n.* strong fabric (often striped) used for covering mattresses, pillows, etc.

tickle *v.* **1** touch or stroke (a person) lightly in some very sensitive spot so as to excite the nerves, titillate, and, usu., produce laughter and involuntary movements. **2** feel this sensation (*my nose is tickling*). **3** amuse, please (a person's vanity or sense of humour etc.) (*tickled by his antics*). •*n.* an act of tickling; a tickling sensation. ◻ **tickled pink** *or* **to death** *colloq.* extremely amused or pleased. **tickle the peter** *see* PETER[3]. ◻◻ **tickly** *adj.*

ticklish *adj.* **1** sensitive to tickling. **2** (of a problem or person) requiring careful handling. ◻ **ticklishness** *n.*

tidal *adj.* of or affected by a tide or tides. ◻ **tidal wave 1** a great ocean wave, e.g. one caused by an underwater earthquake. **2** a great wave of enthusiasm or indignation etc. ◻◻ **tidally** *adv.*

Tidbinbilla / tid-bin-**bil**-uh / a deep space tracking station located near Canberra in the ACT.

tidbit variant of TITBIT.

tiddler *n. colloq.* **1** a small fish. **2** an unusually small thing, esp. a child.

tiddly *adj. colloq.* **1** very small. **2** slightly drunk.

tide *n.* **1** the regular rise and fall in the level of the sea, caused by the attraction of the moon and the sun. **2** water as moved by this. **3** a trend of opinion, fortune, or events (*the rising tide of discontent*). **4** a time or season (*Eastertide*). •*v.* float with the tide. ◻ **tide over** help (a person) through a difficult period by providing what is needed.

tidings *n.pl. literary* news.

tidy *adj.* (**tidier**, **tidiest**) **1** neat and orderly in arrangement or in one's ways. **2** *colloq.* fairly large, considerable (*left a tidy fortune when he died*). •*n.* a receptacle for holding small objects, waste scraps of food, etc. (*a kitchen tidy*). •*v.* (**tidied**, **tidying**) (often foll. by *up*) make tidy. ◻ **tidily** *adv.* **tidiness** *n.*

tie *v.* (**tied**, **tying**) **1** attach, fasten, or bind with a cord or something similar. **2** arrange (a string, ribbon, shoelace, necktie, etc.) to form a knot or bow; form (a knot or bow) in this way. **3** unite (notes in music) with a tie. **4** achieve the same score as another competitor (*they tied for second place*). **5** restrict or limit to certain conditions or to an occupation or place etc. (*is tied to his job; is tied to the house*). •*n*. **1** a cord etc. used for fastening or by which something is tied. **2** a strip of material worn round the neck, passing under the collar and knotted at the front with the ends hanging down. **3** something that unites things or people, a bond (*family ties*). **4** something that restricts a person's freedom of action (*children are a real tie*). **5** a curved line (in a musical score) over two notes of the same pitch, indicating that the second is not sounded separately. **6** equality of score between two or more competitors. **7** a sports match between any pair from a group of competing players or teams in an elimination competition. ▫ **fit to be tied** *colloq.* very angry, ropeable. **tie break** (also **tie breaker**) a means of deciding the winner when competitors have tied. **tie-dyeing** a method of producing dyed patterns by tying parts of a fabric so that they are protected from the dye. **tie in** *v.* bring into or have a close association or agreement. **tie-in** *n.* a connection or association. **tie pin** an ornamental pin for holding a tie in place. **tie up 1** fasten with a cord etc. **2** invest or reserve (capital etc.) so that it is not readily available for use; make restrictive conditions about (a bequest etc.). **3** occupy (a person) so that he or she has no time for other things (*I'm tied up all this week*). **4** bring to a satisfactory conclusion. **tie-up** *n.* a connection, a link.

tier / teer / *n.* **1** any of a series of rows, ranks, or units of a structure placed one above the other. **2** (often as **tiers**) (in Tas. and SA) a forested mountain range, esp. one of a series.

tiered *adj.* / teerd / arranged in tiers.

tiff *n.* a petty quarrel.

tiffin *n.* (in India, Sri Lanka, etc.) a light meal at midday or in the afternoon.

tiger *n.* **1** a large Asian animal of the cat family, with yellowish and black stripes. **2** *Aust.* = TASMANIAN TIGER (*see* TASMANIAN). **3** a fierce, energetic, or formidable person. **4** (**Tigers**, in full **the Tamil Tigers**) *see* TAMIL TIGER. ▫ **tiger cat** *n.* any of several animals resembling the tiger (e.g. the ocelot). **2** *Aust.* a large, carnivorous marsupial of eastern Australia, having brown fur with white spots on the body and tail, the largest of the marsupial cats. **tiger country** *Aust.* the remote and inaccessible parts of Australia. **tiger flathead** *Aust.* a marine food fish, predominantly brown with darker bands or blotches, an important commercial species. **tiger prawn** *Aust.* a very large prawn of esp. northern Australia, having dark vertical stripes, valued as food. **tiger snake** *Aust.* either of two highly venomous snakes, usu. with distinctive bands of lighter and darker colouring.

tight *adj.* **1** fixed or fastened or drawn together firmly and hard to move or undo. **2** fitting closely; made so that a specified thing cannot penetrate (*a tight joint; water tight*). **3** too closely fitting (*these shoes are a bit tight*). **4** with things or people arranged closely together (*a tight little group*). **5** tense, stretched so as to leave no slack. **6** *colloq.* drunk. **7** with no time, resources, etc. to spare (*a tight schedule*). **8** (of money or materials) not easily obtainable; (of the money market) in which money and credit are severely restricted; (of a program, regulation, etc.) strictly enforced, stringent. **9** stingy (*tight with his money*). •*adv.* tightly (*hold tight*). ▫ **tight-fisted** stingy. **tight-lipped** keeping the lips compressed firmly together to restrain one's emotion or comments; grim-looking. ▫▫ **tightly** *adv.* **tightness** *n.*

tighten *v.* make or become tighter. ▫ **tighten one's belt** live more frugally.

tightrope *n.* a rope stretched tightly high above the ground, on which acrobats perform.

tights *n.pl.* a thin close-fitting garment covering the feet, legs, and lower part of the body, worn by women and also by male and female ballet dancers, acrobats, etc.

tigress *n.* a female tiger.

tike alternative spelling of TYKE.

tiki / tee-kee / *n.* a large wooden or small ornamental greenstone image representing a human figure. (¶ Maori)

tikka / tik-uh, tee-kuh / *n.* an Indian dish of kebabs marinated in a spice mixture.

tilde / til-duh / *n.* a mark (˜) put over a letter, e.g. over a Spanish *n* when pronounced *ny* as in *señor*.

tile *n.* **1** a thin slab of baked clay or other material used in rows for covering roofs, walls, or floors. **2** any of the small flat pieces used in mah-jong. •*v.* cover with tiles. ▫ **on the tiles** *colloq.* out having a good time, esp. drinking a lot.

tiler *n.* a person who makes or lays tiles.

tiling *n.* a surface made of tiles.

till^1 *v.* prepare and use (land) for growing crops.

till^2 *prep.* **1** up to or as late as (*wait till six o'clock*). **2** up to the time of (*faithful till death*). •*conj.* **1** up to the time when (*wait till I return*). **2** so long that (*I laughed till I cried*).

■ Usage In all senses, *till* can be replaced by *until*. However, see the note at UNTIL.

till^3 *n.* a drawer for holding money in a shop, bank, etc., usu. with a device for recording transactions.

tillage *n.* **1** the tilling of land. **2** tilled land.

tiller *n.* a horizontal bar by which the rudder of a small boat is turned in steering.

tilly *n. Aust. colloq.* = UTE.

tillywurti / til-ee-**wer**-tee / *n.* (also **tilliwurty**) a greyish marine food fish of southern Australia. Also called *butterfish, dusky morwong, strongfish*. (¶ Probably from a SA Aboriginal language.)

tilt *v.* **1** move or cause to move into a sloping position. **2** (foll. by *at*) **a** run or thrust with a lance in jousting; **b** attack with argument or satire. **3** (foll. by *with*) engage in a contest. • *n.* **1** an act or instance of tilting. **2** a sloping position. **3** an attack, esp. with argument or satire (*he's having a tilt at religion again*). ☐ **full tilt** (*or* **at full tilt**) at full speed; with full force. **tilt at windmills** battle with enemies who are only imaginary. (¶ From the story of Don Quixote who attacked some windmills, thinking they were giants.)

tilth *n.* **1** tillage, cultivation. **2** the condition of tilled soil.

timber *n.* **1** wood prepared for use in building or carpentry. **2** trees suitable for this. **3** a piece of wood or a wooden beam used in constructing a house or ship.

timbered *adj.* **1** (of a building) constructed of timber or with a timber framework. **2** (of land) wooded.

timberline *n.* the level of land above which no trees grow.

timbre / **tam**-buh / *n.* the distinctive character of the sound produced by a particular voice or instrument, apart from its pitch and volume.

timbrel *n.* a tambourine.

Timbuktu **1** a town of Mali in Africa. **2** any distant or very remote place.

time *n.* **1** all the years of the past, present, and future. **2** the passing of these taken as a whole (*time will show who is right*). **3** a portion of time associated with certain events, conditions, or experiences (*about the time the Second Fleet arrived; in times of hardship; have a good time*). **4** a portion of time between two points; the point or period allotted, available, or suitable for something (*the time it takes to do this; now is the time to buy; lunch time*). **5** the point of time when something must occur or end. **6** an occasion or instance (*the first time we saw him; I told you three times*). **7** a point of time stated in hours and minutes of the day (*the time is exactly two o'clock*). **8** any of the standard systems by which time is reckoned (*Greenwich Mean Time*). **9** measured time spent in work etc.; the rate paid for this period (*put them on part time; paid time and a half*). **10** tempo in music, rhythm depending on the number and accentuation of beats in a bar. **11** (**times**) expressing multiplication (*five times six is thirty; three times as old*). **12** (in *combinations* with various senses of the noun): *time-basis, time bomb, time-honoured, time-waster,* etc. • *v.* **1** choose the time or moment for, arrange the time of (*timed his entrance perfectly; the concert is timed to start at six*). **2** measure the time taken by (a race or runner or a process etc.). ☐ **at times** sometimes. **do time** *colloq.* serve a prison sentence. **for the time being** until some other arrangement is made. **in time 1** not late. **2** eventually, sooner or later. **on time** punctually. **time-and-motion** *adj.* concerned with measuring the efficiency of industrial or other operations. **time bomb** a bomb that can be set to explode after a certain interval. **time capsule** a container holding objects typical of the present time, buried for future discovery. **time exposure** a photographic exposure in which the shutter is left open for more than a second or two and not operated at an automatically-controlled speed. **time lag** an interval of time between two connected events. **time limit** a limit of time within which something must be done. **time on** *Aust. Rules* time added to the normal playing time of each quarter to compensate for interruptions to play. **time payment** hire purchase. **time-server** *derog.* a person who changes his or her opinion to suit the current fashion, circumstances, etc. **time-sharing** *n.* **1** operation of a computer system by two or more users so that each user appears to have exclusive use at the same time. **2** (also **time-share**) the joint ownership and right to use a holiday home for a limited time each year. **time sheet** a record of hours worked. **time signal** an audible indication of the exact time of day. **time signature** an indication of the speed and rhythm of a piece of music following the clef. **time switch** a switch that can be set to act automatically at a certain time. **time warp** **1** (in science fiction) an imaginary distortion of space in relation to time, whereby persons or objects of one age can be moved to another. **2** a state in which the styles, attitudes, etc. of a past period are retained (*caught in a 1950s time warp*). **time zone** a region (between two lines of longitude) where a common standard time is used.

timekeeper *n.* **1** a person who records time, esp. in a game. **2** a watch or clock in respect of its accuracy of operation (*a good timekeeper*).

timeless *adj.* **1** not to be thought of as having duration. **2** not affected by the passage of time.

timely *adj.* occurring at just the right time (*a timely warning*). ☐ **timeliness** *n.*

timepiece *n.* a clock or watch.

timer *n.* a person who times something; a timing device.

timetable *n.* a list showing the time at which certain events are scheduled to take place, esp. the arrival and departure of transport or a sequence of lessons. • *v.* include in or arrange to a timetable; schedule.

timid *adj.* easily alarmed, not bold, shy. ☐ **timidly** *adv.* **timidity** / tuh-**mid**-uh-tee / *n.*

timing *n.* **1** the way an action or process is timed or regulated, esp. in relation to others (*an actor with a superb sense of timing; the batsman has lost his timing*). **2** the control of the opening and closing of valves in an internal-combustion engine.

Timor / **tee**-maw / the largest of the Lesser Sunda Islands, in the southern Malay Archipelago. The island was formerly divided into Dutch West Timor and Portuguese East Timor. In 1950 West

Timor was absorbed into the newly formed Republic of Indonesia. In 1975 East Timor (chief town, Dili) declared itself independent but was invaded and occupied by Indonesia in 1976. *See* EAST TIMOR and DILI MASSACRE. ❑ **Timor pony** a small stocky Australian horse of a breed produced from Timor. **Timor Sea** the part of the Indian Ocean between Timor and north-western Australia. ❑❑ **Timorese** *adj.* & *n.*

timorous / **tim**-uh-ruhs / *adj.* timid. ❑ **timorously** *adv.* **timorousness** *n.*

timothy *n. Aust. colloq.* a brothel.

timpani / **tim**-puh-nee / *n.pl.* (also **tympani**) kettledrums. ❑ **timpanist** *n.*

tin *n.* **1** a chemical element (symbol Sn), a silvery-white metal. **2** iron or steel sheets coated with tin. **3** a container made of tin plate; one in which food is sealed for preservation. •*v.* (**tinned**, **tinning**) **1** coat with tin. **2** seal in a tin for preservation. ❑ **tin arse** *Aust. colloq.* an exceptionally lucky person. **tin-arsed** *Aust. colloq.* extremely lucky. **tin can** a tin for preserving food, esp. an empty one. **tin foil** a thin sheet of tin, aluminium, or tin alloy, used for wrapping food. **tin god** a person who is unjustifiably given great veneration; a self-important person. **tin lid** *Aust. colloq.* a kid, a child. (¶ Rhyming slang.) **tin-pan alley** the world of composers and publishers of popular music. (¶ Originally the name given to a district in New York where many songwriters and music publishers were based.) **tin plate** sheet iron or steel coated thinly with tin.

tincture *n.* **1** a solution consisting of a medicinal substance dissolved in alcohol (*tincture of quinine*). **2** a slight tinge or trace of some element or quality. •*v.* tinge.

tinder *n.* any dry substance that catches fire easily. ❑ **tinder box** a metal box formerly used in kindling a fire, containing dry material that caught fire from a spark produced by flint and steel.

tine *n.* any of the points or prongs of a fork, antler, or comb.

tinea / **tin**-ee-uh / *n.* any of several fungal diseases of the skin, e.g. *athlete's foot*.

ting *n.* a sharp ringing sound. •*v.* make a ting.

tinge / tinj / *v.* (**tinged**, **tingeing**) **1** colour slightly (*tinged with pink*). **2** give a slight trace of some element or quality to (*their admiration was tinged with envy*). •*n.* a slight colouring or trace.

tingle *v.* have a slight pricking or stinging sensation. •*n.* this sensation. ❑ **tingly** *adj.*

tinker *n.* a travelling mender of pots and pans. •*v.* work at something in an amateurish or desultory way, trying to repair or improve it (*stop tinkering with the clock*).

tinkle *n.* **1** a series of short light ringing sounds. **2** *colloq.* a telephone call. •*v.* make or cause to make a tinkle.

tinnie *Aust. colloq.* alternative spelling of TINNY *n.*

tinnitus / tuh-**nuy**-tuhs / *n.* a condition causing repeated ringing or other sounds in the ears.

tinny *adj.* **1** of or like tin; (of metal objects) not looking strong or solid. **2** having a metallic taste or a thin metallic sound. **3** *Aust. colloq.* lucky (*how tinny can you get?*). •*n.* (also **tinnie**) *Aust. colloq.* **1 a** a can of beer. **b** the contents of such a can (*drank two tinnies*). **2** a small boat with an aluminium hull.

tinpot *adj. derog.* worthless, inferior.

tinsel *n.* a glittering metallic substance used in strips or threads to give an inexpensive sparkling effect. ❑ **tinsel lily** (also **blue tinsel lily**) a shrub of WA, western Vic., and eastern SA, having needle-like leaves and numerous vivid blue to blue-purple star flowers having a highly metallic gloss. ❑❑ **tinselled** *adj.* **tinselly** *adj.*

tinsnips *n.pl.* clippers for cutting sheet metal.

tint *n.* **1** a variety of a particular colour. **2** a slight trace of a different colour (*red with a bluish tint*). **3** a kind of hair dye; the application of this (*having a tint*). •*v.* **1** apply or give a tint to, colour slightly. **2** apply a polyester film to glass etc. (in order to screen out glare etc.). **3** colour (in order to shade light etc.) (*tinted spectacles*).

tintack *n.* (also **tin-tack**) an iron tack. ❑ **get down to tintacks** deal with the central issues, get down to the core (of a matter).

T-intersection *n.* (also **T-junction**) a junction where one road or pipe etc. meets another but does not cross it, forming the shape of a T.

tintinnabulation *n.* a ringing or tinkling of bells.

tiny *adj.* (**tinier**, **tiniest**) very small. ❑ **tinily** *adv.* **tininess** *n.*

tip[1] *n.* **1** the very end of a thing, esp. of something small or tapering. **2** the summit or apex of a thing (*the tip of the iceberg*). **3** a small part or piece fitted to the end of something (*a walking stick with a rubber tip*). •*v.* (**tipped**, **tipping**) provide with a tip. ❑ **tip of the iceberg** the small evident part of something much larger.

tip[2] *v.* (**tipped**, **tipping**) **1** tilt or topple; cause to do this. **2** discharge (the contents of a truck or jug etc.) by doing this. **3** strike or touch lightly. **4** name as a likely winner of a contest etc. **5** make a small present of money to (a person), esp. in acknowledgment of his or her services. **6** *colloq.* guess (*the kids haven't yet tipped that it's me in the Santa suit*). •*n.* **1** a small present of money. **2** private or special information (e.g. about horse races or the stock market) likely to profit the receiver. **3** a small but useful piece of advice. **4** a slight tilt or push. **5** a place where rubbish etc. is tipped. ❑ **tip off** give an advance warning or hint or inside information to (a person). **tip-off** *n.* advance or inside information etc. **tip a person the wink** give him or her a private signal or piece of information. **tip the balance** (*or* **scales**) *see* SCALE[2]. **tip truck** a road haulage vehicle that tips at the back to discharge its load.

tipper *n.* **1** a person who gives a tip. **2** a tip truck.

tippet *n.* a small cape or collar of fur etc. with ends hanging down in front.

tipple *v.* drink (wine or spirits etc.); be in the habit of drinking. • *n. colloq.* alcoholic drink.

tipster *n.* a person who gives tips about horse races etc.

tipsy *adj.* slightly drunk. ☐ **tipsily** *adv.* **tipsiness** *n.*

tiptoe *v.* (**tiptoed**, **tiptoeing**) walk very quietly with heels not touching the ground. ☐ **on tiptoe** **1** on the tips of one's toes. **2** eagerly expectant, anxious (*am on tiptoe for the results*). **3** stealthy, furtive.

tiptop *adj. colloq.* excellent, very best (*tiptop quality*).

tirade / tuy-**rayd** / *n.* a long angry or violent piece of criticism or denunciation.

Tiranë / tee-**rah**-nuh / the capital of Albania.

tire *v.* **1** make or become tired. **2** (foll. by *of*) become bored with; lose interest in (*he soon tired of looking after his pets*).

tired *adj.* **1** feeling that one would like to sleep or rest. **2** (of a joke, idea, etc.) used or suggested so often that it has become dull and uninteresting. ☐ **tired of** having had enough of (a thing or activity) and feeling impatient or bored. ☐ ☐ **tiredly** *adv.* **tiredness** *n.*

tireless *adj.* not tiring easily, having inexhaustible energy. ☐ **tirelessly** *adv.*

tiresome *adj.* **1** wearisome, tedious. **2** annoying (*don't be tiresome*).

tiro / **tuy**-roh / *n.* (*pl.* **tiros**) (also **tyro**) a beginner, a novice.

'tis *archaic* = it is.

tissue / **tish**-oo, **tis**-yoo / *n.* **1** the substance forming an animal or plant body; a particular kind of this (*muscular tissue*). **2** tissue paper. **3** a disposable piece of soft absorbent paper used as a handkerchief etc. **4** fine gauzy fabric. **5** something thought of as an interwoven series (*a tissue of lies*). **6** (also **tisher**) *colloq.* (chiefly in Tas.) a cigarette paper. ☐ **tissue paper** *n.* very thin soft paper used for wrapping and packing things.

tit *n.* **1** any of several small birds. **2** *colloq.* a nipple or teat. **3** *coarse colloq.* a woman's breast. ☐ **tit for tat** blow for blow; retaliation.

Titan / **tuy**-tuhn / *n.* **1** *Gk myth.* any of the older gods who preceded the Olympians, a race of giants who were the offspring of Heaven and Earth. **2** (often **titan**) a person of great size, strength, or importance.

Titanic / tuy-**tan**-ik / a British passenger liner, believed to be unsinkable, that struck an iceberg in the Atlantic on its maiden voyage in 1912 and sank with the loss of 1,490 lives.

titanic / tuy-**tan**-ik / *adj.* gigantic, immense.

titanium / tuy-**tay**-nee-um / *n.* a grey metallic element (symbol Ti), used in alloys for parts of aircraft, space vehicles, etc.

titbit *n.* (also **tidbit**) a choice bit of something, e.g. of food or of gossip or information.

titch *n. colloq.* **1** a small person. **2** a small amount.

tithe / tuy*th* / *n.* **1** one tenth of the annual produce of agriculture etc., formerly taken as a tax by the church. **2** a tenth part. • *v.* (**tithed**, **tithing**) **1** subject to tithes. **2** pay tithes.

Titian / **tish**-uhn / (Italian name: Tiziano Vecellio) (*c.*1488–1576), Italian painter. • *adj.* & *n.* (**titian**) bright golden auburn (as a colour of hair, favoured by Titian in his paintings).

titillate / **tit**-uh-layt / *v.* **1** excite or stimulate, esp. sexually. **2** tickle. ☐ **titillation** *n.*

titivate / **tit**-uh-vayt / *v. colloq.* smarten up; put the finishing touches to. ☐ **titivation** *n.*

title *n.* **1** the name of a book, poem, or picture etc. **2** a word used to show a person's rank or office (e.g. *professor, cardinal, captain*) or used in speaking of or to a person (e.g. *Your Eminence, Mrs, Doctor*). **3** the legal right to ownership of property; a document conferring this. **4** a championship in sport (*the world heavyweight title*). • *v.* give a title to (a book etc.). ☐ **title deed** a legal document proving a person's title to a property. **title page** a page at the beginning of a book giving the title, author's name, and other particulars. **title role** the part in a play etc. from which the title is taken, e.g. the part of Hamlet in the play of that name.

Tito / **tee**-toh / (original name: Josip Broz) (1892–1980), statesman of the former Yugoslavia, leader of the Communist resistance movement during the Second World War, afterwards head of the new government and president from 1953.

titrate / tuy-**trayt** / *v.* calculate the amount of a constituent in (a substance) by using a standard reagent. ☐ **titration** *n.*

ti-tree erroneous alternative spelling of TEA-TREE (see TEA).

titter *v.* laugh in a furtive or restrained way; giggle • *n.* a furtive or restrained laugh; a giggle.

tittle-tattle = TATTLE.

titular / **tich**-uh-luh, **tit**-yuh-luh / *adj.* **1** of or belonging to a title (*the book's titular hero*). **2** existing, or being, in name or title only, but without real authority (*the titular head of the State*).

Tiwi / **tee**-wee / *n.* **1** an Aboriginal language spoken on Melville and Bathurst Islands. **2** an Aboriginal inhabitant of these islands.

tizz *n.* (also **tizzy**) *colloq.* a state of nervous agitation or confusion (*in a tizz*).

tizzy *adj. Aust.* gaudy, showy, in bad taste. • *v.* (usu. foll. by *up*; often as **tizzied up** *adj.*) (try to) improve the appearance of, esp. in a gaudy or showy manner (*all tizzied up for the party; he's tizzying up his car*).

tjukurpa / **tyoo**-koor-pu / *n. Aust.* = DREAMING.

T-junction = T-INTERSECTION.

tjuringa alternative spelling of CHURINGA.

Tl *symbol* thallium.

TLC *abbr. colloq.* tender loving care.

T-lymphocyte *n.* a lymphocyte of a type produced or processed by the thymus gland and active in the immune system, esp. the cell-mediated immune response. Also called *T-cell*. (¶ *T* for *thymus*.)

Tm *symbol* thulium.

tmesis / **tmee**-suhs / *n.* (*pl.* **tmeses**) *Grammar* the separation of parts of a compound word by an intervening word or words (esp. in Australian colloquial speech with 'bloody' as the intervener) (*kanga-bloody-roos at the billa-bloody-bong*).

TNT *abbr.* trinitrotoluene, a powerful explosive.

to *prep.* **1** in the direction of; so as to approach or reach (a place, position, or state etc.) (*walked to the station; rose to power; was sent to prison; back to back*). **2** as far as; not falling short of (*patriotic to the core; from noon to 2 o'clock; goods to the value of $10; cooked to perfection*). **3** as compared with; in respect of (*won by 3 goals to 2; made to measure; his remarks were not to the point*). **4** for (a person or thing) to hold, possess, or be affected etc. by (*give it to me; spoke to her; kind to animals; accustomed to it*). **5** (with a verb) forming an infinitive, or expressing purpose or consequence etc. (*he wants to go; does it to annoy; I meant to call but forgot to*). • *adv.* **1** to or in the normal or required position; to a closed or almost closed position (*push the door to*). **2** into a state of consciousness (*when she came to*). **3** into a state of activity (*set to*). ◻ **to and fro** backwards and forwards. **to-die-for** *adj. colloq.* gorgeous, wonderful (*a to-die-for babe*). **toing and froing** going to and fro; repeatedly changing one's mind, decision, etc., vacillating.

toa / toh-uh / *n. Aust.* an Aboriginal direction marker made of gypsum, wood, and feathers, and used to indicate precisely where a departing group had gone to. (¶ Diyari)

toad *n.* **1** a froglike animal, an amphibian living chiefly on land. **2** a repulsive person.

toadfish *n. Aust.* any of many self-inflating, usu. poisonous and spiny, marine and estuarine fish.

toado *Aust. colloq.* = TOADFISH.

toadstool *n.* a fungus (esp. a poisonous one) with a round top and a slender stalk.

toady *n.* **1** a person who flatters and behaves obsequiously to another in the hope of gain or advantage. **2** *Aust.* = TOADFISH. • *v.* (**toadied**, **toadying**) behave servilely to, fawn upon. ◻ **toadyism** *n.*

to and from *n.* (*pl.* **to and froms**) *Aust. colloq.* a pom. (¶ Rhyming slang.)

toast *n.* **1** sliced bread browned on both sides by radiant heat. **2** the person or thing in whose honour a company is requested to drink; an instance of drinking in this way. **3** a celebrated person of the moment (*she's the toast of the town*). • *v.* **1** brown the surface of (bread etc.) by placing it close to radiant heat. **2** warm (one's feet, oneself, etc.) at a fire etc. **3** honour or pledge good wishes to (a person or thing) by drinking.

toaster *n.* an electrical device for toasting bread.

toastmaster *n.* (*feminine* **toastmistress**) a person responsible for announcing toasts at a reception, ceremonial dinner, etc.

tobacco *n.* **1** a plant of the genus *Nicotiana* with narcotic leaves used esp. for smoking; its leaves after being prepared for smoking etc. **2** (also **native tobacco**) any of several Australian plants of the genus *Nicotiana*, the leaves of which were traditionally dried and chewed by Aborigines and were also highly valued as items of trade.

tobacconist *n.* a dealer in tobacco products.

Tobago / tuh-**bay**-goh / an island in the West Indies (*see* TRINIDAD). ◻ **Tobagan** *adj.* & *n.*

Tobagonian / toh-buh-**goh**-nee-uhn / *adj.* & *n.*

-to-be *adj.* soon to become (*the bride-to-be*).

toboggan / tuh-**bog**-uhn / *n.* a long light narrow sledge curved upwards at the front, used for sliding downhill. • *v.* ride on a toboggan. ◻ **tobogganer** *n.* **tobogganing** *n.*

toccata / tuh-**kah**-tuh / *n.* a musical composition for a keyboard instrument, designed to exhibit the performer's touch and technique.

tocsin *n.* an alarm bell or signal.

today *n.* this present day or age. • *adv.* **1** on this present day. **2** at the present time.

toddle *v.* **1** (of a young child) walk with short unsteady steps. **2** *colloq.* walk, stroll. **3** *colloq.* (usu. foll. by *off* or *along*) depart.

toddler *n.* a child who is just learning to walk.

toddy *n.* **1** a sweetened drink of spirits and hot water. **2** the sap from the flowers of some kinds of palm (palmyra, coconut, etc.) drunk fresh (**sweet toddy**) or fermented, or distilled to make arrack.

to-do *n.* a fuss or commotion.

toe *n.* **1** one of the divisions (five in humans) of the front part of the foot. **2** the part of a shoe or stocking that covers the toes. **3** the lower end or tip of a tool etc. **4** *Aust. colloq.* strength, speed (*Aussie fast bowlers have lots of toe*). • *v.* (**toed**, **toeing**) touch or reach with the toes. ◻ **on one's toes** alert. **toe-hold 1** a slight foothold. **2** a small beginning or advantage. **toe the line** conform (esp. under compulsion).

toenail *n.* the nail on each toe.

toe-rag *n.* (also **toe-ragger**) *colloq.* a term of contempt for a person. (¶ Formerly = a tramp or vagrant, from the rag wrapped around the foot in place of a sock.)

toey *adj. Aust. colloq.* **1** restless, eager to go. **2** touchy, bad-tempered.

toff *n. colloq. derog.* a person of wealth and social prestige. ◻ **toffy** *adj.*

toffee *n.* a sweet made with heated butter and sugar etc. ◻ **toffee apple** a toffee-coated apple on a stick. **toffee-nosed** *colloq. derog.* snobbish, pretentious.

tofu / **toh**-foo / *n.* a soft white curd made from soya bean milk, used in cooking.

tog *colloq. v.* (**togged**, **togging**) (foll. by *up* or *out*) dress. • *n.* (**togs**) **1** *Aust.* (when unqualified) a swimming costume. **2** (when qualified) clothes as

toga /**toh**-guh/ n. a loose flowing outer garment worn by citizens in ancient Rome.

together adv. **1** in or into company or conjunction; towards each other; so as to unite (*were at school together; let's bring them together; tied them together; put two and two together*). **2** one with another (*talking together*). **3** simultaneously (*both shouted together*). **4** in an unbroken succession (*he is away for weeks together*). • adj. colloq. well-organised; self-assured; emotionally stable (*he's really together since he stopped drinking*). ☐ **together with** as well as, and also.

specified (*footy togs; shearing togs; he's just hired his wedding togs*).

togetherness n. being together; feeling of belonging together.

toggle n. **1** a fastening device consisting of a short piece of wood or metal etc. secured by its centre and passed through a loop or hole. **2** *Computing* a switch action that is operated the same way but has the opposite effect on successive occasions.

Togo /**toh**-goh/ a republic in West Africa. ☐ **Togolese** adj. & n. (pl. **Togolese**).

togs see TOG.

toil v. **1** work long hours or laboriously. **2** move laboriously (*we toiled up the hill*). • n. hard or laborious work.

toiler n. a hard worker; a battler.

toilet n. **1** a large receptacle for urine and faeces, usu. with running water and a flush mechanism as a means of disposal; the room or compartment containing one or more of these. **2** the process of dressing and grooming oneself.

toiletries n.pl. articles or preparations used in washing and grooming.

toilette /twah-**let**/ = TOILET (sense 2).

toils n.pl. a snare or net; power that acts as does a snare or net (*I'm caught in his toils*).

toilsome adj. involving toil, laborious.

tokay /toh-**kay**/ n. a sweet Hungarian wine; a similar wine from elsewhere.

token n. **1** a sign, symbol, or evidence of something (*a token of our esteem*). **2** a keepsake or memorial of friendship etc. **3** a voucher or coupon that can be exchanged for goods (*book token*). **4** a device like a coin bought for use in coin-operated machines etc. • adj. **1** perfunctory (*a token effort*). **2** conducted briefly to demonstrate strength of feeling (*a token strike*). **3** serving to acknowledge a principle only (*a token payment*). **4** chosen by tokenism to represent a group (*the token woman on the committee*). ☐ **by the same token** similarly; moreover.

tokenism n. making only a token effort or granting only small concessions, esp. to minority or suppressed groups.

Tok Pisin /tok **pis**-uhn, **piz**-uhn/ n. a variety of pidgin spoken in Papua New Guinea. (¶ Tok Pisin, = pidgin talk.)

Tokyo /**toh**-kee-oh/ the capital of Japan.

told see TELL¹. ☐ **all told** counting everything or everyone (*we were 16 all told*).

tolerable adj. **1** able to be tolerated, endurable. **2** fairly good, passable. ☐ **tolerably** adv. **tolerableness** n.

tolerance n. **1** a willingness or ability to tolerate a person or thing; a disposition to be patient with or indulgent to the opinions or practices of others; freedom from bigotry in judging the conduct of others; forbearance. **2** the permitted variation in the measurement or weight etc. of an object. **3** the ability to tolerate the effects of a drug etc. after use or continued use.

tolerant adj. having or showing tolerance. ☐ **tolerantly** adv.

tolerate v. **1** show tolerance; permit without protest or interference. **2** bear (pain etc.); be able to take (a medicine) or undergo (radiation etc.) without harm.

toleration n. the process or practice of tolerating or being tolerated, esp. the allowing of religious differences without discrimination.

Tolkien /**tol**-keen/, J(ohn) R(onald) R(euel) (1892–1973), British philologist, Professor of English at Oxford, and author of *The Hobbit* and the seminal fantasy trilogy *The Lord of the Rings*.

toll¹ /tohl/ n. **1** a tax or duty paid for the use of a public road or bridge etc. **2** the loss or damage caused by a disaster or incurred in achieving something (*the death toll in the earthquake*). ☐ **take its toll** be accompanied by loss or injury etc. **toll bridge** a bridge at which a toll is charged. **toll-free** adj. & adv. (esp. of a telephone call) without charge (*a toll-free number; call toll-free*). **toll gate** a gate across a road to prevent anyone passing until the toll has been paid.

toll² /tohl/ v. **1** ring (a bell) with slow strokes, esp. for a death or funeral. **2** (of a bell) sound in this way; indicate by tolling. • n. the stroke of a tolling bell.

tollway n. (also **tollroad**) a road maintained by the tolls collected on it.

Tolstoy, Count Leo Nikolaevich (1828–1910), Russian writer, author of *War and Peace* and *Anna Karenina*.

toluene /**tol**-yoo-een/ n. a liquid hydrocarbon derivative of benzene, used in explosives etc.

tom n. (in full **tomcat**) a male cat.

tomahawk n. **1** a North American Indian war axe. **2** *Aust.* a hatchet. • v. **1** strike, cut, or kill with a tomahawk. **2** *Aust.* shear (a sheep) roughly.

tomato /tuh-**mah**-toh / n. (pl. **tomatoes**) **1** a glossy red or yellow fruit eaten as a vegetable. **2** the plant bearing this.

tomb /toom/ n. **1** a grave or other place of burial. **2** a vault or stone monument in which one or more people are buried.

tomboy n. a girl who enjoys activities traditionally or stereotypically associated with boys. ☐ **tomboyish** adj.

tombstone n. a memorial stone over a grave.

Tom Collins *n. Aust.* a gossip; a rumour-monger. (¶ A mythical 19th-century Australian character: see FURPHY, Joseph.)

Tom, Dick, and Harry *n.* ordinary people, people taken at random.

tome / tohm / *n.* a book or volume, esp. a large heavy one.

tomfoolery *n.* foolish behaviour.

tommy gun *n.* a sub-machine gun.

tommyrot *n. colloq.* nonsense, rubbish.

tommy rough *n.* (also **tommy ruff**) a marine fish of Australian waters, highly valued as food. Also called *herring*.

tomogram / **tom**-uh-gram / *n.* a record obtained by tomography.

tomography / tuh-**mog**-ruh-fee / *n.* a method of radiography displaying details in a selected plane within the body or other object. ☐ **tomographic** *adj.*

tomorrow *n.* **1** the day after today. **2** the near future. •*adv.* on the day after today; at some future date.

tomtit *n.* any of several small Australian birds, esp. a thornbill.

tom-tom *n.* **1** an African or Asian drum beaten with the hands. **2** a deep-toned drum used in jazz bands.

ton / tun / *n.* **1** (in full **long ton**) a unit of weight in the imperial system equal to 2,240 lb. (1,016.05 kg). **2** (in full **short ton**) a unit of weight, esp. in the US, equal to 2,000 lb. (907.19 kg). **3** (in full **metric ton**) = TONNE. **4** (in full **displacement ton**) a unit of measurement in the imperial system of a ship's weight or volume. **5** (usu. as **tons**) *colloq.* a large number or amount (*tons of money*). **6** *colloq.* **a** a speed of 100 km/h in a motor vehicle or on a motorcycle. **b** $100. **c** a score of 100. ☐ **hit the ton** *colloq.* **1** score 100 runs in cricket. **2** reach a speed of 100 km/h in a motor vehicle or on a motorcycle.

tonal / **toh**-nuhl / *adj.* **1** of a tone or tones. **2** of tonality. ☐ **tonally** *adv.*

tonality / toh-**nal**-uh-tee / *n.* **1** the character of a melody, depending on the scale or key in which it is composed. **2** the colour scheme of a picture.

tone *n.* **1** a musical or vocal sound, esp. with reference to its pitch, quality, and strength. **2** a modulation of the voice expressing a particular feeling or mood (*a cheerful tone; an aggressive tone*). **3 a** the manner of expression in writing or speaking. **b** (in literary criticism) the author's attitude to his or her subject matter or audience; the distinctive mood created by this. **4** any one of the five intervals between one note and the next which, together with two semitones, make up an octave. **5** proper firmness of the organs and tissues of the body (*muscle tone*). **6** a tint or shade of a colour; the general effect of colour or of light and shade in a picture. **7** the general spirit or character prevailing (*set the tone with a dignified speech; the tone of the gathering was somewhat raunchy*). •*v.* **1** give a particular tone of sound or colour to. **2** (often foll. by *with, in with*) harmonise in colour (*the curtains tone in with the wallpaper*). **3** give proper firmness to (muscles, organs, or skin etc.). ☐ **tone-deaf** unable to perceive accurately differences of musical pitch. **tone down** make or become softer in tone of sound or colour; make (a statement) less strong or harsh. **tone up** make or become stronger in tone (*exercise tones up the body*).

toneless *adj.* without positive tone, not expressive. ☐ **tonelessly** *adv.*

toner *n.* a substance similar to ink used in a photocopier, laser printer, etc.

Tonga / **tong**-uh, -guh / a kingdom consisting of a group of islands in the Pacific, also called the Friendly Islands. ☐ **Tongan** *adj.* & *n.*

tongs *n.pl.* an instrument with two arms joined at one end, used for grasping and holding things.

tongue *n.* **1** the fleshy muscular organ in the mouth, used in tasting, licking, swallowing, and (in man) speaking. **2** the tongue of an ox etc. as food. **3** the ability to speak or a manner of speaking (*have lost one's tongue; a persuasive tongue*). **4** a language (*his native tongue is German*). **5** a thing like a tongue in shape or position, esp.: **a** a long low promontory. **b** a strip of leather etc. under the laces in a shoe. **c** the clapper of a bell. **d** the pin of a buckle. **e** a projecting strip on a board etc. fitting into the groove of another. **f** a tapering jet of flame. •*v.* **1** produce staccato or other effects in a wind instrument by use of the tongue. **2** touch, lick, etc. with the tongue. ☐ **speak with tongues** see GLOSSOLALIA. **tongue-and-groove** planking or boarding with a projecting strip down one side and a groove down the other, allowing pieces to be fitted together. **tongue-in-cheek** *adj.* ironic. *adv.* insincerely or ironically. **tongue-tied 1** silent because of shyness or embarrassment. **2** unable to speak normally because the ligament connecting the tongue to the base of the mouth is abnormally short. **tongue-twister** a sequence of words that is difficult to pronounce quickly and correctly, e.g. *she'll chew, chew, chew, till her jaws drop off.*

tonic *n.* **1** a medicine with an invigorating effect, taken after illness or weakness. **2** anything that restores people's energy or good spirits. **3** a keynote in music. **4** tonic water. •*adj.* having the effect of a tonic, toning up the muscles etc. ☐ **tonic sol-fa** the system of syllables *doh, ray, me, fah, soh, la, te* used (esp. in teaching singing) to represent the notes of the musical scale, with *doh* always denoting the tonic or keynote. **tonic water** carbonated water flavoured with quinine.

tonight *n.* **1** the present evening or night. **2** the evening or night of today. •*adv.* on the present evening or night or that of today.

tonk *n. Aust. colloq.* **1** a male who in speech or manner appears to set himself up above his fellows. **2** a fool.

tonnage / **tun**-ij / *n.* **1** the carrying capacity of a ship, expressed in tons. **2** the charge per ton for carrying cargo or freight.

tonne / ton, tun / *n.* (also **metric ton** *or* **metric tonne**) 1,000 kilograms.

■ **Usage** When the metric system was introduced into Australia, the preferred pronunciation for *tonne* was the first given above (to distinguish it from the imperial *ton*). Both pronunciations, however, are now common.

tonsil *n.* either of two small organs at the sides of the throat near the root of the tongue. □ **tonsillar** *adj.*

tonsillectomy *n.* surgical removal of tonsils.

tonsillitis *n.* inflammation of the tonsils.

tonsure / **ton**-shuh / *n.* **1** a shaving of the crown or all of the head of a person entering certain priesthoods or monastic orders. **2** the part of the head shaven in this way. • *v.* give a tonsure to.

too *adv.* **1** to a greater extent than is desirable, permissible, or possible for a specified or understood purpose (*too large to fit; too hard*). **2** *colloq.* very (*he's not too well today*). **3** also (*I'm coming too*). **4** moreover (*the food was bad, and expensive too*). □ **none too** rather less than (*feeling none too good*).

too-hard basket *n.* an imaginary basket into which one 'puts' matters, problems, etc., which are too difficult to deal with at the moment.

took *see* TAKE.

tool *n.* **1** a thing (usu. something held in the hand) for working on something. **2** a simple machine, e.g. a lathe. **3** anything used in an occupation or pursuit (*a dictionary is a useful tool*). **4** a person used as a mere instrument by another. **5** *coarse colloq.* a penis. • *v.* **1** dress (stone) with a chisel. **2** cut a design on (leather). **3** (foll. by *up*) provide oneself or equip (a factory etc.) with necessary tools. **4** *colloq.* (foll. by *along, around*, etc.) drive or ride in a casual or leisurely way (*tooling along*).

toolache / too-**lay**-chee / *n.* a large wallaby, formerly of south-eastern SA and adjacent Vic., much exploited for its attractive fur and now probably extinct. (¶ Yaralde)

toolmaker *n.* a person who makes precision tools. □ **toolmaking** *n.*

toopong alternative spelling of TUPONG.

toot[1] / toot / *n.* a short sound as made by the horn of a car, a trumpet, etc. • *v.* **1** sound (a car horn, a trumpet, etc.) with a short sharp sound. **2** give out such a sound (*stop tooting, I'm coming*).

toot[2] / tuut / *n. Aust. colloq.* = TOILET (sense 1).

tooth *n.* (*pl.* **teeth**) **1** each of the hard white bony structures rooted in the gums, used for biting and chewing things. **2** a similar structure in the mouth or alimentary canal of certain invertebrate animals. **3** a toothlike part or projection, e.g. on a gear, saw, comb, or rake. **4** (often foll. by *for*) a liking for a particular type of food. **5** (**teeth**) force, effectiveness (*stronger penalties will give the anti-racism laws teeth*). □ **in the teeth of** in spite of; in opposition to; directly against (the wind).

tooth-billed catbird a bowerbird of rainforest in north-eastern Qld, having a double notch at the tip of its bill, used for collecting leaves for the bower, and a wailing cat-like call.

toothache *n.* an ache in a tooth or teeth.

toothbrush *n.* a brush for cleaning the teeth.

toothed *adj.* **1** having teeth. **2** having teeth of a certain kind (*sharp-toothed*).

toothless *adj.* **1** lacking teeth. **2** lacking the means of compulsion or enforcement; ineffectual (*a toothless law*).

toothpaste *n.* paste for cleaning the teeth.

toothpick *n.* a small pointed piece of wood etc. for removing food from between the teeth.

toothy *adj.* having or showing many or large teeth (*a toothy smile*).

tootle *v.* **1** toot gently or repeatedly. **2** *colloq.* (usu. foll. by *along, around*, etc.) go in a casual or leisurely way (*tootling along*).

top[1] *n.* **1** the highest point or part of something; the upper surface. **2** the highest rank, degree, or position (*he is at the top of his profession*). **3** the utmost degree of intensity (*shouted at the top of his voice*). **4** a thing forming the upper part of something, e.g. the creamy part of milk; a garment covering the upper part of the body. **5** the covering or stopper of a bottle or tube. **6** top gear. **7** (**tops**) *colloq.* a person or thing of the best quality (*she's tops at cricket; he's the tops*). • *adj.* **1 a** highest in position (*top shelf*). **b** highest in degree (*at top speed*). **c** highest in importance (*he's got the top job*). **d** greatest in amount (*paid top prices; top dollar*). **2** *colloq.* excellent, first-rate (*he's a top bloke*). • *v.* (**topped, topping**) **1** provide with a top, a cap, a covering, etc. (*a cake topped with icing*). **2** reach the top of (a hill etc.). **3** be higher than, surpass; be at the top of (*she topped the honours list*). **4** add as a final thing or finishing touch. **5** remove the top of (a plant or fruit). **6** (in golf) strike (the ball) above its centre. □ **over the top 1** over the parapet of a trench (and into battle). **2** beyond what is normally acceptable (*that joke was over the top*). **the top** northern Australia. **top brass** *colloq.* the highest-ranking officials. **top dog** *colloq.* the master or victor. **top dollar** *colloq.* the highest price (*paid top dollar for the horse*). **top drawer** the highest social position (*out of the top drawer*). **top dress** *v.* apply fertiliser on the top of soil without ploughing it in. **top dressing** this process; the substance used. **top-flight** *adj.* of the highest rank; most successful. **top gear** the highest gear, allowing parts to revolve fast. **top hat** a man's tall stiff black or grey hat worn with formal dress. **top-heavy** overweighted at the top and therefore in danger of falling over. **top-level** *adj.* of the highest level of importance etc. (*a top-level meeting of Pacific nations*). **top-notch** *adj. colloq.* first-rate. **top up 1** fill up (a

top partly full container). **2** top up something for (a person) (*may I top you up with sherry?*). **top-up** *n.* an addition; something that serves to top up. **up top** (also **Up Top**) *Aust.* **1** northern Australia. **2** in northern Australia.

top² *n.* a toy that spins on its point when set in motion by hand or by a string or spring etc.

topaz / toh-paz / *n.* a semiprecious stone of various colours, esp. yellow.

topcoat *n.* **1** an overcoat. **2** an outer coat of paint etc.

Top End *n.* (also **top end**) the northern part of the Northern Territory.

Top Ender *n.* (also **top ender**) a person native to or resident in the northern part of the Northern Territory.

toper / toh-puh / *n.* a habitual drunkard. ▫ **tope** *v.*

topiary / toh-pee-uh-ree / *n.* the art of clipping shrubs etc. into ornamental shapes.

topic *n.* the subject of a discussion or written work.

topical *adj.* **1** having reference to current events. **2** (of an ailment, medicine, etc.) affecting or applied externally to a part of the body. ▫ **topically** *adv.* **topicality** / top-i-**kal**-uh-tee / *n.*

topknot *n.* a tuft, crest, or knot of ribbon etc. on top of the head.

topless *adj.* **1** (of a woman's garment) leaving the breasts bare. **2** (of a woman) wearing such a garment. **3** (of a place) employing bare-breasted women (*a topless bar*).

topmost *adj.* highest.

topography / tuh-**pog**-ruh-fee / *n.* the features of a place or district, the position of its rivers, mountains, roads, buildings, etc. ▫ **topographical** / top-uh-**graf**-i-kuhl / *adj.*

topology *n.* the study of geometrical properties unaffected by changes of shape or size. ▫ **topological** *adj.*

topping *n.* a thing that tops another thing, esp. sauce on ice-cream or on a dessert etc.

topple *v.* **1** fall headlong or as if top-heavy, totter and fall. **2** cause to do this. **3** overthrow, cause to fall from authority (*the crisis toppled the government*).

topside *n.* a joint of beef cut from the upper part of the haunch.

topsoil *n.* the top layer of soil as distinct from the subsoil.

topspin *n.* a spinning motion given to a ball in cricket, tennis etc.

topspinner *n. Cricket* **1** a ball delivered with a forward and upward spin so that it does not break much after it bounces but accelerates upwards and takes the batsman by surprise. **2** a bowler who bowls topspinners.

topsy-turvy *adv.* & *adj.* **1** in or into a state of great disorder. **2** upside down.

toque / tohk / *n.* a chef's hat.

tor *n.* a hill or rocky peak.

Torah *n.* the will of God as revealed in Mosaic law; the Pentateuch; a scroll containing this.

torc *n.* (also **torque**) *hist.* a necklace of twisted metal not completely joined into a circle, esp. of the ancient Gauls and Britons.

torch *n.* **1** a small hand-held electric lamp powered by a battery or electric power cell, contained in a case. **2** a burning stick of resinous wood, or of combustible material fixed on a stick and ignited, used as a light. **3** a blowlamp. •*v.* purposely set fire to (*torched the house*). ▫ **carry a torch for** be filled with unreturned love for (a person). **torch song** a popular song of unrequited love.

tore see TEAR¹.

toreador / **to**-ree-uh-daw / *n.* a Spanish bull-fighter.

torment *n.* / **taw**-ment / **1** severe physical or mental suffering. **2** something causing this. •*v.* / taw-**ment** / **1** subject to torment. **2** tease or try to provoke by annoyances etc. (*enjoyed tormenting the teacher*). ▫ **tormentor** *n.*

torn see TEAR¹.

tornado / taw-**nay**-doh / *n.* (*pl.* **tornadoes**) **1** a violent and destructive whirlwind advancing in a narrow path. **2** a whirlwind of cheers, hisses, missiles, etc.

torpedo *n.* (*pl.* **torpedoes**) a cigar-shaped explosive underwater missile, launched against a ship from a submarine or surface ship or from an aircraft. •*v.* **1** destroy or attack with a torpedo. **2** ruin or wreck (a policy or conference etc.) suddenly (*torpedoed the project with just a few words*).

torpid *adj.* sluggish, inactive, apathetic; numb; (of a hibernating animal) dormant. ▫ **torpidly** *adv.* **torpidity** / taw-**pid**-uh-tee / *n.*

torpor / **taw**-puh / *n.* a torpid condition.

torque / tawk / *n.* **1** a force causing rotation of a mechanism. **2** = TORC.

torr *n.* (*pl.* **torr**) a unit of pressure. (¶ Named after Evangelista Torricelli (1608–47), Italian scientist.)

Torrens system / **to**-ruhnz / (also **Torrens title**) a system of land ownership in which title to land derives from the registration of documents by a public official. (¶ R. Torrens (1814–84), premier of South Australia for one month in 1857.)

torrent *n.* **1** a rushing stream of water or lava. **2** a downpour of rain. **3** a violent flow (*a torrent of abuse*).

torrential / tuh-**ren**-shuhl / *adj.* like a torrent.

Torres Strait / **to**-ruhz / a stretch of water between Cape York Peninsula, Qld, and the southern coast of Papua New Guinea. ▫ **Torres Strait Islander** an inhabitant of any of the Torres Strait Islands. **Torres Strait Islands** a group of more than 70 islands in the Torres Strait, in Australian possession, inhabited by people Melanesian in origin. Islander interest in secession from Australia, to gain political independence and re-establish traditional culture, has been growing since the 1980s. **Torres Strait Creole** (also **Torres Strait Broken**) a language with its own distinctive grammar and syntax that developed from the pidgin English of the SW Pacific and spread among the Torres Strait Islands in the early 20th century.

torrid / **to**-rid / *adj.* **1** (of the weather) very hot and dry; (of land etc.) parched by such weather. **2** intense, passionate (*torrid love scenes*). ☐ **torrid zone** the part of the earth between the tropics of Cancer and Capricorn.

torsion / taw-shuhn / *n.* **1** twisting, esp. of one end of a thing while the other is held fixed. **2** the state of being spirally twisted.

torso / taw-soh / *n.* (*pl.* **torsos**) **1** the trunk of the human body. **2** a statue lacking head and limbs.

tort *n. Law* any private or civil wrong (other than breach of contract) for which the wronged person may claim damages.

tortelli / taw-**tel**-ee / *n.* an Italian dish of small pasta parcels stuffed with a cheese or vegetable mixture etc.

tortellini / taw-tuh-**lee**-nee / *n.pl.* small squares of pasta stuffed with meat, cheese, etc. (tortelli), rolled and shaped into rings; an Italian dish of these and a sauce.

tortilla / taw-**tee**-yuh / *n.* a thin flat orig. Mexican maize cake eaten hot with or without a filling.

tortoise / **taw**-tuhs / *n.* a slow-moving four-footed reptile with its body enclosed in a hard shell, living on land or in fresh water.

tortoiseshell / **taw**-tuhs-shel / *n.* the semi-transparent mottled yellowish-brown shell of certain turtles, used for making combs etc. •*adj.* having such colouring.

tortuous / taw-choo-uhs / *adj.* **1** full of twists and turns (*followed a tortuous route*). **2** devious, not straightforward (*a tortuous mind; a tortuous argument*). ☐ **tortuously** *adv.* **tortuosity** / taw-choo-**os**-uh-tee / *n.*

■ Usage *Tortuous* should not be confused with *torturous* which means 'involving torture, excruciating'.

torture / **taw**-chuh / *n.* **1** the infliction of severe pain as a punishment or means of coercion. **2** a method of torturing. **3** severe physical or mental pain. •*v.* **1** inflict torture upon; subject to great pain or anxiety. **2** force out of its natural position or shape (*tea-trees tortured by storms to shapes like serpents interlaced*). **3** twist, deform, pervert (words, language, meaning, etc.) (*some sects torture Scripture to make it support their doctrines*). ☐ **torturer** *n.* **torturous** *adj.*

Tory *n.* **1** a member of the Conservative Party in Britain. **2** *derog.* a member or supporter of the political right; an extreme conservative. •*adj.* Conservative or conservative.

tosh *n. colloq.* nonsense.

toss *v.* **1** throw up (a ball etc.), esp. with the hand. **2** throw lightly, carelessly (*tossed her letter away*). **3** send (a coin) spinning in the air to decide something according to the way it lands. **4** throw or roll about from side to side restlessly or with an uneven motion (*was tossing and turning all night*). **5** coat (food) by gently shaking it in dressing etc. •*n.* **1** a tossing action or movement. **2** the result obtained by tossing a coin. **3** a fall (from a bicycle, a horse, etc.). ☐ **toss off 1** drink off at a draught. **2** finish or compose rapidly or without much thought or effort (*tossed off three symphonies and a five-act opera in one afternoon*). **3** *coarse colloq.* masturbate (oneself or another male). **toss up** toss a coin to decide a choice etc. **toss-up** *n.* **1** the tossing of a coin. **2** an even chance (*it's a toss-up as to which party will win the next election*).

tot[1] *n.* **1** a small child. **2** *colloq.* a small quantity of alcoholic drink, esp. spirits.

tot[2] *v.* (**totted**, **totting**) (foll. by *up*) *colloq.* add up (*tot this up; it tots up to $20*).

total *adj.* **1** including everything or everyone, comprising the whole (*the total number of votes*). **2** utter, complete (*in total darkness*). •*n.* the total number or amount, a count of all the items. •*v.* (**totalled**, **totalling**) **1** reckon the total of. **2** amount to.

totalisator *n.* (also **-izator**) a device automatically registering the number and amount of bets staked on a race, with a view to dividing the total amount among those backing the winner; a system of betting based on this.

totalise *v.* (also **-ize**) find the total of.

totalitarian / toh-tal-uh-**tair**-ree-uhn / *adj.* of a dictatorial one-party government in which no rival parties or loyalties are permitted. •*n.* a person who favours this or a similar system. ☐ **totalitarianism** *n.*

totality / toh-**tal**-uh-tee / *n.* **1** the quality of being total. **2** a total number or amount.

totally *adv.* completely; absolutely.

tote[1] *n.* esp. *Aust. colloq.* a totalisator.

tote[2] *v. colloq.* carry, convey (*toting a gun; toting his friend from place to place*).

totem / **toh**-tuhm / *n.* **1** a natural object, esp. an animal, adopted among N. American Indians as the emblem of a clan or family. **2** an image of this. **3** *Aust.* (in Aboriginal culture) a natural object similarly adopted. ☐ **totem pole** a pole on which totems of N. American Indians are carved or hung.

tother *adj.* & *pron.* (also **t'other**) *colloq.* the other.

tothersider / tuth-uh-**suy**-duh / *n. Aust.* a person from the other side: (in WA) a person from an eastern State; (in Tas.) a person from mainland Australia.

totter *v.* **1** walk unsteadily. **2** (of a building etc.) shake as if about to collapse. **3** (of a system of government etc.) be about to fall. •*n.* an unsteady or shaky walk or movement. ☐ **tottery** *adj.*

toucan / too-kan / n. a tropical American fruit-eating bird with an immense beak.

touch v. **1** be or come together so that there is no space between; meet (another object) in this way. **2** put one's hand etc. on (a thing) lightly. **3** press or strike lightly. **4** draw or paint with light strokes (*touch the details in*). **5** move or meddle with; harm (*leave your things here, no one will touch them*). **6** have to do with in the slightest degree, attempt (*the firm doesn't touch business of that kind*). **7** eat or drink even a little of (*she hasn't touched her breakfast*). **8** reach (*the speedometer touched 120*). **9** equal in excellence (*no other cloth can touch it for quality*). **10** affect slightly. **11** rouse sympathy or other emotion in. **12** *colloq.* persuade to give money as a loan or gift (*touched him for $20*). • n. **1** the act or fact of touching. **2** the faculty of perceiving things or their qualities through touching them. **3** small things done in producing a piece of work (*put the finishing touches*). **4** a manner or style of workmanship; a person's special skill (*he hasn't lost his touch*). **5** a musician's manner of playing keys or strings (*he has a sensitive touch*). **6** a relationship of communication or knowledge (*we've lost touch with her*). **7** a slight trace (*there's a touch of frost in the air; a touch of flu*). **8** the part of a Rugby etc. field outside the touchlines. **9** *colloq.* the act of obtaining money from a person. ☐ **touch down** (of an aircraft) land. **touch football** a game based on rugby, played with an oval ball by teams of seven, with touching instead of tackling. **touch screen** a computer display which can detect pressure from a finger etc. **touch-typing** typing without looking at the keys. **touch wood** touch something made of wood in superstitious or humorous hope that this will avert bad luck.

touchable *adj.* able to be touched.

touchdown n. **1** the act of touching down by an aircraft. **2** *Rugby* the act or an instance of touching the ground with the ball behind the opponent's goal in order to score a try.

touché / too-**shay** / *interj.* an acknowledgment that one's opponent has made a hit in fencing or a valid accusation or criticism in a discussion. (¶ French, = touched.)

touched *adj.* **1** caused to feel warm sympathy or gratitude. **2** slightly mad.

touching *adj.* rousing kindly feelings or sympathy or pity. • *prep.* concerning (*touching your request …*). ☐ **touchingly** *adv.*

touchline n. (in various sports) either of the lines marking the side boundaries of the pitch.

touchstone n. a standard or criterion by which something is judged. (¶ Alloys of gold and silver were formerly tested by being rubbed against a fine-grained stone such as black jasper.)

touchy *adj.* (**touchier**, **touchiest**) **1** apt to take offence; over-sensitive. **2** apt to cause offence (*this is a touchy issue*). ☐ **touchily** *adv.* **touchiness** n.

tough *adj.* **1** difficult to break or cut or to chew. **2** able to endure hardship, not easily hurt, damaged, or injured. **3** unyielding, stubborn, resolute. **4** difficult (*a tough job*). **5** *colloq.* (of luck etc.) hard, unpleasant. **6** vicious, rough and violent. • n. a rough and violent person (*young toughs*). • *adv. colloq.* in an uncompromising, aggressive, or unyielding manner (*play it tough, you guys*). ☐ **tough it** (*or* **tough it out**) *colloq.* endure or withstand difficult circumstances. ☐ ☐ **toughly** *adv.* **toughness** n.

toughie n. *colloq.* a tough person or problem.

toughen v. make or become tough.

toupee / **too**-pay / n. an artificial patch of hair worn to cover a bald spot.

tour n. **1** a journey from place to place as a holiday; a sightseeing excursion. **2** a walk round; an inspection (*made a tour of the garden*). **3** a spell of duty on military or diplomatic service. **4** a series of performances, matches, etc., at different places. • v. make a tour of.

tour de force / toor duh **faws** / n. (*pl.* **tours de force** pronounced the same) an outstandingly skilful performance or achievement. (¶ French)

tourism n. **1** visiting places as a tourist. **2** the business of providing accommodation and services etc. for tourists.

tourist n. a person who is travelling or visiting a place for recreation. ☐ **tourist class** the lowest class of passenger accommodation in a ship or aircraft etc.

touristy *adj.* (usu. *derog.*) designed to attract tourists; visited by many tourists.

tourmaline / **toor**-muh-leen / n. a mineral of various colours, possessing unusual electric properties and used as a gem.

tournament / **taw**-nuh-muhnt / n. **1** a contest of skill between a number of competitors, involving a series of matches. **2** *hist.* a pageant in which jousting between knights (with blunted weapons etc.) took place.

tournedos / **toor**-nuh-doh / n. (*pl.* **tournedos** / -dohz /) a small round thick cut from a fillet of beef.

tourney n. a tournament. • v. (**tourneys**, **tourneyed**) take part in a tournament.

tourniquet / **taw**-nuh-kay / n. a device or a strip of material drawn tightly round a limb to stop the flow of blood from an artery by compressing it.

tousle / **tow**-zuhl / v. make (hair etc.) untidy by ruffling it (*she tousled his hair lovingly*).

tout / towt / v. **1** try busily to obtain orders for one's goods or services (*touting for custom*). **2** pester people to buy. **3 a** (foll. by *for*) US & Aust. solicit for (support, votes, etc.). **b** try to sell (*touting vacuum cleaners door-to-door; is busy touting his mate as next captain*). **4** spy out the movements and condition of racehorses in training. **5** (as **touted** *adj.*) vaunted, extolled (*the much touted free heroin trial for addicts*). • n. a person who touts things.

tout de suite / too duh **sweet** / *adv.* immediately; at once. (¶ French)

tow[1] / toh / *n.* short coarse fibres of flax or hemp, used for making yarn etc. ☐ **tow-headed** *adj.* having very light-coloured hair.

tow[2] / toh / *v.* pull (a boat, vehicle, etc.) along behind one. • *n.* towing, being towed. ☐ **tow bar** a bar fitted to a car for towing a caravan etc. **tow truck** a truck specially designed to tow broken-down or accident-damaged motor vehicles.

toward / tuh-**wawd** / *prep.* = TOWARDS. • *adj.* / **toh**-uhd / *archaic* about to take place; in process (*I've come to see what is toward*).

towards *prep.* **1** in the direction of (*walked towards the sea*). **2** in relation to, regarding (*the way he behaved towards his children*). **3** for the purpose of achieving or promoting (*efforts towards peace*). **4** as a contribution to (*put the money towards a new bicycle*). **5** near, approaching (*towards the end of our journey*).

towel *n.* a piece of absorbent cloth or paper for drying oneself or wiping things dry. • *v.* (**towelled, towelling**) **1** wipe or dry with a towel (*towelled himself and the kids*). **2** (also foll. by *up*) *colloq.* thrash or beat (a person) (*I towelled him up in 3 sets*).

towelling *n.* fabric for making towels.

tower *n.* **1** a tall usu. square or circular structure, either standing alone (e.g. as a fort) or forming part of a church or castle or other large building. **2** a tall structure housing machinery etc. (*cooling tower; control tower*). • *v.* be of great height; be taller or more eminent than others (*he towered above everyone*).

towering *adj.* **1** very tall, lofty. **2** (of rage etc.) extreme, intense.

Tower of Babel *see* BABEL.

town *n.* **1 a** a densely populated built-up defined area, larger than a township (esp. one that has not been created a city), and having local government; its inhabitants. **b** any densely populated area, esp. as opposed to the country. **c** *Aust.* any small cluster of dwellings and other buildings recognised as a distinct place, even if remote and rural. **2** the central business and shopping area serving, and contrasted with, the surrounding suburbs. ☐ **town camp** *Aust.* an Aboriginal camp within or near a town. **town clerk** an official responsible for the administration of a local government area. **town hall** a building containing local government offices and usu. a hall for public events. **town house 1** (esp. *Brit.*) the town residence esp. of a person with a house in the country. **2** a terrace house or a house in a planned group in a town, usu. of a stylish modern type, and usu. with strata title. **town planning** preparation of plans for the regulated growth and improvement of towns.

townie *n.* (also **towny**) *derog.* a town dweller as distinct from a country dweller.

Townsend, Mt a peak in south-eastern NSW near Mt Kosciuszko, at 2,209 metres the second highest mountain in Australia.

township *n.* a small town or village.

towpath / **toh**-pahth / *n.* a path beside a river or canal used for towing a boat by horse.

towri / **tow**-ree / *n.* *Aust.* = COUNTRY (sense 6). (¶ Kamilaroi)

toxaemia / tok-**see**-mee-uh / *n.* (also **toxemia**) **1** blood poisoning. **2** a condition in pregnancy in which blood pressure is abnormally high.

toxic *adj.* **1** of or related to poison (*toxic symptoms*). **2** poisonous (*toxic gas*). **3** caused by poison (*toxic anaemia*). ☐ **toxic shock syndrome** a potentially fatal blood poisoning disease caused by bacteria in the vagina, and often associated with the use of tampons. ☐☐ **toxicity** / tok-**sis**-uh-tee / *n.*

toxicology *n.* the study of poisons. ☐ **toxicological** *adj.* **toxicologist** *n.*

toxin *n.* a poisonous substance of animal or vegetable origin, esp. one formed in the body by micro-organisms.

toxophily / tok-**sof**-uh-lee / *n.* archery.

toy *n.* **1** a thing to play with, esp. for a child. **2** (often as *adj.*) a model or miniature replica of a thing, esp. as a plaything (*toy guns should be banned*). **3** a thing regarded as providing amusement, esp. for an adult (*my husband's driving the family crazy with his latest toy, a camcorder*). • *adj.* **1** (of a dog) of a very small breed. • *v.* (foll. by *with*) **1 a** handle or finger idly (*toyed with his earring*). **b** nibble at food etc. unenthusiastically (*toyed with his fricassee of tiger snake*). **2** consider as a vague possibility; trifle, amuse oneself, flirt (*toyed with the idea of a trip to Antarctica; he toyed quite callously with her emotions*).

toyboy *n.* *colloq.* an attractive young man who is kept or used as a sexual plaything or partner by an older woman or man.

trac *n.* *Aust. colloq.* a refractory prisoner.

trace[1] *n.* **1** a track or mark left behind. **2** a visible or other sign of what has existed or happened (*hardly a trace remains of the Aboriginal languages of Tasmania*). **3** a very small quantity (*found a trace of blood in his urine*). **4** a track or footprint (*dingo traces everywhere*). **5** the track recorded by a self-recording instrument etc. • *v.* **1** follow or discover by observing marks, tracks, pieces of evidence, etc. **2** mark out, sketch the outline of, form (letters etc.) laboriously. **3** copy (a map or drawing etc.) on translucent paper placed over it or by using carbon paper below. ☐ **trace element** a chemical element required only in minute amounts by living organisms for normal growth. ☐☐ **traceable** *adj.*

trace[2] *n.* each of the two side straps, chains, or ropes by which a horse draws a vehicle. ☐ **kick over the traces** (of a person) become insubordinate or reckless.

tracer *n.* **1** a person or thing that traces. **2** a bullet that leaves a trail of smoke etc. by which its course can be observed. **3** a radioactive substance that can be traced in its course through the human body by the radiation it produces.

tracery *n.* **1** an openwork pattern in stone (e.g. in a church window). **2** a decorative pattern of lines resembling this.

trachea / truh-**kee**-uh / *n.* (*pl.* **tracheae**) the windpipe.

tracheotomy / trak-ee-**ot**-uh-mee / *n.* an opening made surgically into the trachea to relieve an obstruction.

trachoma / truh-**koh**-muh / *n.* a contagious disease of the eye causing grainy inflammation of the inner surface of the eyelids and leading eventually to blindness.

tracing *n.* a copy of a map or drawing etc. made by tracing it. ☐ **tracing paper** *n.* translucent paper for making tracings.

track[1] *n.* **1** a mark or series of marks left by a moving person, animal, or thing. **2** a course taken. **3** a course of action or procedure (*you're on the right track; an effective vaccine for Aids is a long way down the track*). **4 a** a rough path, esp. one beaten by use. **b** *Aust.* the route followed by a drover. **c** *Aust.* the Sturt Highway between Darwin and Alice Springs. **5** a racecourse; a prepared course for runners etc. **6** a section of a CD, record, or tape containing one song, section of music, etc. **7** (in a computer etc.) the path followed by a head over the surface of a magnetic or optical recording medium. **8** a continuous line of railway. **9** a continuous band round the wheels of a tank or tractor etc. **10** a metal or plastic strip designed to carry the sliding fittings from which a curtain is hung. • *v.* **1** follow the track of (an animal, person, spacecraft, etc.); (foll. by *down*) find by doing this. **2** (of wheels) run so that the back wheel is exactly in the front wheel's track. **3** (of electric current) leak excessively between insulated points, e.g. in damp conditions. **4** (of a film camera) follow (a moving object) while filming. **5** deposit (dirt etc.) with one's feet (*you're tracking mud all over my new carpet*). ☐ **make tracks** *colloq.* leave, depart. **track events** running events as distinct from field events. **track mate** a male travelling companion. **track pants** loose pull-on trousers worn while exercising or to keep warm before and after athletics etc. events. **track record** a person's past performance. **track shoe** a runner's spiked shoe. **track with** *Aust. colloq.* **1** keep company with (a member of the opposite sex). **2** (of males) associate with, be mates with (*see also* TRACK MATE). ☐☐ **tracker** *n.*

track[2] *v.* **1** tow (a boat) by rope etc. from a bank. **2** drag after oneself by means of a string etc. (*a small boy tracking a wheeled toy along the footpath*).

tracker dog *n.* a police dog tracking by scent.

trackie daks *pl.* (also **trackies**) *Aust.* = TRACK PANTS.

tracksuit *n.* a warm loose-fitting suit worn for exercising etc.

tract *n.* **1** a large stretch of land. **2** a system of connected parts in an animal body along which something passes (*the digestive tract*). **3** a short treatise, esp. in pamphlet form; a pamphlet, esp. propagandist, on a religious subject etc.

tractable *adj.* **1** (of a person) easy to manage or deal with, docile. **2** (of material etc.) pliant, malleable. ☐ **tractability** *n.*

traction *n.* **1** pulling or drawing a load along a surface. **2** a continuous pull on a limb etc. in medical treatment. **3** the grip of a tyre on a road, a wheel on a rail, etc.

tractor *n.* **1** a powerful motor vehicle for pulling farm machinery or other heavy equipment. **2** a device supplying traction.

trad *colloq. adj.* traditional. • *n.* traditional jazz.

trade *n.* **1** exchange of goods for money or other goods. **2** business of a particular kind (*the tourist trade*). **3** a skilled craft practised to earn a living (*he's a butcher by trade; learn a trade*). **4** the people engaged in a particular trade (*we sell cars to the trade, not to private buyers*). **5** a swap. • *v.* **1** engage in trade, buy and sell. **2** exchange (goods etc.) in trading; swap. **3** exchange insults, blows, etc. ☐ **trade in** give (a used article) as partial payment for another article. **trade-in** *n.* an article given in this way. **trademark 1** a manufacturer's or trader's registered emblem or name etc. used to identify goods. **2** a distinctive characteristic etc. (*bluntness is his trademark*). **trade name** a name given by a manufacturer to a proprietary article or material; the name by which a thing is known in the trade; the name under which a person or firm trades. **trade-off** *n.* a balancing factor; an exchange as a compromise. **trade on** make great use of for one's own advantage (*trading on his brother's reputation*). **trade secret 1** a technique used in the trade but kept from being generally known. **2** *jocular* any secret. **trade union** an organised association of workers in a trade, profession, etc., formed to protect and further their rights and interests. **trade unionist** an active member of a trade union. **trade wind** one of the winds blowing continually towards the equator over most of the tropics, from the NE in the Northern hemisphere and from the SE in the Southern hemisphere. ☐☐ **trader** *n.*

tradesman, tradeswoman *n.* = TRADES-PERSON.

tradesperson *n.* a person engaged in trade, a shopkeeper or supplier.

trading *n.* buying and selling. ☐ **trading bank** a bank that handles a range of business transactions, issues cheques in its own name, etc. (cf. SAVINGS BANK). **trading post** a store in a remote or sparsely populated region.

tradition *n.* **1** the handing down of beliefs or customs from one generation to another, esp. without writing. **2** a belief or custom handed down in this way; a long-established custom or method of procedure.

traditional *adj.* **1** of or based on tradition. **2** (of jazz) in the style of the early 20th century. **3** *Aust.* (of Aboriginal society, now chiefly that of central and northern Australia) characterised by social practices and religious beliefs that prevailed before European settlement. □ **traditional owner** *Aust.* an Aborigine who is a member of a local descent group having certain rights in a tract of land. □□ **traditionally** *adv.*

traditionalist *n.* a person who follows or upholds traditional beliefs etc. □ **traditionalism** *n.* **traditionalist** *adj.*

traduce / truh-**dyoos** / *v.* misrepresent in an unfavourable way. □ **traducement** *n.*

traffic *n.* **1** vehicles, ships, or aircraft moving along a route. **2** trading, esp. when illegal or morally wrong (*drug traffic*). **3** dealings between people etc. (*had no traffic with them*). **4** messages etc. transmitted through a communications system; the volume of this. • *v.* (**trafficked, trafficking**) **1** (usu. foll. by *in*) deal in something, esp. illegally. **2** deal in; barter. □ **traffic jam** traffic banked up and at a standstill because of an accident etc. **traffic lights** an automatic signal of coloured lights controlling traffic at junctions etc. □□ **trafficker** *n.*

trag *n.* (*pl.* **trag** or **trags**) *Aust.* = TERAGLIN.

tragedian / truh-**jee**-dee-uhn / *n.* **1** a writer of tragedies. **2** (*feminine* **tragedienne**) an actor in tragedy.

tragedy *n.* **1** a serious play with unhappy events or a sad ending, esp. with the downfall of the protagonist. **2** the branch of drama that consists of such plays. **3** an event that causes great sadness, a calamity.

tragic *adj.* **1** of or in the style of tragedy (*he was a great tragic actor*). **2** sorrowful. **3** causing great sadness, calamitous. □ **tragic irony** a device, originally in Greek tragedy, by which words carry a tragic, esp. prophetic, meaning to the audience, unknown to the character speaking. □□ **tragically** *adv.*

tragicomedy / traj-ee-**kom**-uh-dee / *n.* a play (or a situation) with both tragic and comic elements. □ **tragicomic** *adj.*

trail *v.* **1** drag or be dragged along behind. **2** hang or float loosely; (of a plant) grow lengthily downwards or along the ground. **3** move wearily; lag or straggle. **4** be losing in a game or other contest. **5** diminish, become fainter (*her voice trailed away*). **6** follow the trail of, track. • *n.* **1** something that trails or hangs trailing. **2** a line of people or things following behind something. **3** a mark left where something has passed (*a snail's slimy trail*). **4** a track or scent followed in hunting. **5** a beaten path, esp. through a wild region. □ **trail bike** a light motorcycle designed to be used in rough terrain. **trailing edge** the rear edge of a moving body.

trailblazer *n.* **1** a person who makes a new track through wild country. **2** a person who pioneers a new idea, project, system, etc.

trailer *n.* **1** a vehicle designed to be towed by another, esp. the large rear section of a semitrailer, or a small open cart attached to a car. **2** a short extract from a film, radio program, etc. used to advertise it. **3** a person or thing that trails.

train *n.* **1** a railway engine with a series of linked carriages or trucks. **2** a number of people or animals moving in a line (*a camel train*). **3** a body of followers, a retinue (*a train of admirers*). **4** a series or sequence of things (*a train of events; a train of thought*). **5** part of a long dress or robe that trails on the ground behind the wearer. • *v.* **1** bring to a desired standard of efficiency or behaviour etc. by instruction and practice. **2** undergo such a process (*she trained as a secretary*). **3** make or become physically fit for a sport by exercise and diet. **4** aim (a gun or camera etc.) (*trained his gun on the doorway*). **5** cause (a plant) to grow in the required direction. □ **in train** in preparation (*put matters in train for the election*).

trainee *n.* a person being trained.

trainer *n.* **1** a person who trains; one who trains racehorses or athletes etc. **2** an aircraft, or a device simulating one, used to train pilots. **3** a soft running shoe.

traipse *v. colloq.* trudge, tramp wearily. • *n.* a tedious journey on foot.

trait / tray, trayt / *n.* a distinguishing feature or characteristic.

traitor *n.* a person who behaves disloyally; one who betrays his or her country. □ **traitorous** / **tray**-tuh-ruhs / *adj.*

trajectory / truh-**jek**-tuh-ree / *n.* the path of a bullet or rocket etc. or of a body moving under certain forces.

tram *n.* a public passenger vehicle running on rails laid in the road.

tramlines *n.pl.* rails for a tram.

trammel *n.* **1** a triple dragnet for catching fish. **2** (**trammels**) things that hamper one's activities. • *v.* (**trammelled, trammelling**) hamper.

trammie *n. Aust. colloq.* the driver or conductor of a tram.

tramp *v.* **1** walk with heavy steps. **2** travel on foot across (an area) (*tramping the hills*). **3** trample (*tramp it down*). **4** *Aust. colloq.* dismiss (a person) from employment. • *n.* **1** the sound of heavy footsteps. **2** a long walk. **3** a person who goes from place to place as a vagrant. **4** *colloq. derog.* a promiscuous person (used esp. of a woman).

trample *v.* tread repeatedly with heavy or crushing steps; crush or harm in this way.

trampoline / **tram**-puh-leen / *n.* a sheet of strong canvas attached by springs to a horizontal frame, used for gymnastic jumping. □ **trampolining** *n.*

trance *n.* **1** a sleeplike state, e.g. that induced by hypnosis. **2** such a state as supposedly entered into by a medium. **3** rapture, ecstasy.

trannie *n.* (also **tranny**) *colloq.* **1** a transistor radio. **2** a transvestite. **3** a transsexual.

tranquil *adj.* calm and undisturbed, not agitated. □ **tranquilly** *adv.* **tranquillity** *n.*

tranquillise *v.* (also **-ize**) make tranquil, calm.

tranquilliser *n.* (also **-izer**) a drug used to relieve anxiety and make a person feel calm.

transact *v.* perform or carry out (business). □ **transactor** *n.*

transaction *n.* **1** transacting. **2** business transacted. **3** (**transactions**) published reports of discussions, papers read, etc. at meetings of a learned society.

transceiver / tran-**see**-vuh / *n.* a combined radio transmitter and receiver.

transcend / tran-**send** / *v.* **1** go or be beyond the range of (human experience, belief, or powers of description etc.). **2** surpass.

transcendent / tran-**sen**-duhnt / *adj.* **1** going beyond the limits of ordinary experience, surpassing. **2** (of God) existing apart from the material universe. □ **transcendence** *n.* **transcendency** *n.*

transcendental / tran-sen-**den**-tuhl / *adj.* **1** *Philosophy* not based on experience; intuitive, innate in the mind. **2** abstract; obscure; visionary. □ **transcendentally** *adv.*

transcendentalism *n.* transcendental philosophy. □ **transcendentalist** *n.*

Transcendental Meditation *n.* a method of detaching oneself from problems, anxiety, etc., by silent meditation and repetition of a mantra.

transcontinental *adj.* extending or travelling across a continent.

transcribe *v.* **1** copy in writing; write out (shorthand etc.) in ordinary characters. **2** record (sound) for later reproduction or broadcasting. **3** arrange (music) for a different instrument etc. □ **transcriber** *n.* **transcription** *n.*

transcript *n.* a written or recorded copy.

transducer *n.* a device that converts waves etc. from one system and conveys related waves to another (e.g. a radio receiver, which receives electromagnetic waves and sends out sound waves).

transept *n.* the part that is at right angles to the nave in a cross-shaped church; either arm of this (*the north and south transepts*).

transexual alternative spelling of TRANSSEXUAL.

transfer *v.* / trans-**fer** / (**transferred**, **transferring**) **1** convey, move, or hand over (a thing) from one place or person etc. to another. **2** convey (a drawing or pattern etc.) from one surface to another. **3** change from one station, route, or form of transport to another during a journey. **4** change to another group or occupation etc. (*she has transferred to the sales department*). **5** change (meaning) by extension or metaphor. • *n.* / trans-fer / **1** transferring, being transferred. **2** a document that transfers property or a right from one person to another. **3** a design that is or can be transferred from one surface to another; paper bearing such a design. □ **transfer fee** a fee paid for transfer, esp. of a professional footballer to another club.

transference / **trans**-fer-ruhns / *n.* transferring; being transferred.

transferral / trans-**fer**-ruhl / *n.* transferring; being transferred.

transfiguration *n.* **1** change of form or appearance. **2** (**the Transfiguration**) the Christian festival (6 August) commemorating Christ's appearance in radiant glory to three of his disciples.

transfigure *v.* make a great change in the appearance of, esp. to something nobler or more beautiful (*her face was transfigured by happiness*).

transfix *v.* **1** pierce with or impale on something sharp-pointed. **2** make (a person) motionless with horror or astonishment.

transform *v.* **1** make a great change in the appearance or character of (*the caterpillar is transformed into a butterfly*). **2** change the voltage of (electric current). **3** become transformed. □ **transformation** *n.*

transformer *n.* an apparatus for reducing or increasing the voltage of alternating current.

transfuse *v.* **1** give a transfusion of (a fluid) to a person or animal. **2** permeate (*purple dye transfused the water; was transfused with gratitude*).

transfusion *n.* an injection of blood or other fluid into a blood vessel to replace lost fluid.

transgenic / tranz-**jen**-ik / *adj.* (of an animal or plant) having genetic material artificially introduced from another species.

transgress *v.* **1** break (a rule or law etc.); go beyond (a limitation). **2** *archaic* sin. □ **transgression** *n.* **transgressor** *n.*

transient / **tran**-zee-uhnt / *adj.* passing quickly, not lasting or permanent. • *n.* a temporary visitor or worker etc. □ **transience** *n.*

transistor *n.* **1** a semiconductor device with three electrodes, performing the same functions as a thermionic valve but smaller and using less power. **2** (in full **transistor radio**) a portable radio set equipped with transistors.

transistorise *v.* (also **-ize**) equip with transistors rather than valves.

transit *n.* **1** the process of going, conveying, or being conveyed (*the goods were delayed in transit*). **2** a passage or route (*the overland transit*). **3** the apparent passage of a heavenly body across the disc of the sun or a planet or across the meridian of a place (*to observe the transit of Venus*). • *v.* (**transited**, **transiting**) make a transit across. □ **transit camp** a camp for temporary accommodation of soldiers or refugees etc. **transit lounge** a lounge at an airport for (usu. international) passengers waiting between flights. **transit visa** a visa allowing the holder to pass through a country but not to stay there.

transition / tran-**zish**-uhn / *n.* the process of changing from one state or style etc. to another (*the transition from childhood to adult life*). □ **transitional** *adj.* **transitionally** *adv.*

transitive *adj.* (of a verb) used with a direct object, e.g. *ride* in *ride a bike*. □ **transitively** *adv.*

transitory *adj.* existing only for a short time, not lasting. □ **transitorily** *adv.* **transitoriness** *n.*

translate *v.* **1** express in another language or in simpler words, or in code for use in a computer. **2** be able to be translated (*the poems don't translate well*). **3** interpret (*we translated his silence as disapproval*). **4** move or change, esp. from one person, place, or condition to another (*was translated body and soul into heaven*). □ **translatable** *adj.* **translation** *n.* **translator** *n.*

transliterate *v.* represent (letters or words) in the closest corresponding letters of a different alphabet. □ **transliteration** *n.*

translucent / tranz-**loo**-suhnt / *adj.* allowing light to pass through but not transparent. □ **translucence** *n.* **translucency** *n.*

transmigration *n.* migration. □ **transmigration of the soul** the supposed passing of a person's soul into another body after death. □ □ **transmigrate** *v.*

transmissible *adj.* able to be transmitted.

transmission *n.* **1** transmitting; being transmitted. **2** the broadcasting of a radio or television program. **3** the gear by which power is transmitted from engine to axle in a motor vehicle.

transmit *v.* (**transmitted, transmitting**) **1** send or pass on from one person, place, or thing to another (*transmit the message; the disease is transmitted by mosquitoes*). **2** allow to pass through or along, be a medium for (*iron transmits heat*). **3** send out (a signal or program etc.) by telegraph wire or radio waves.

transmittable *adj.* able to be transmitted.

transmitter *n.* a person or thing that transmits; a device or equipment for transmitting electric or radio signals.

transmogrify *v.* (**transmogrified, transmogrifying**) *humorous* transform, esp. in a magical or surprising way (*the Prince, to his great annoyance, was transmogrified into an ordinary human being*). □ **transmogrification** *n.*

transmute *v.* **1** *hist.* change (a base metal like lead) into gold by alchemy. **2** cause (a thing) to change in form, nature, or substance. □ **transmutation** *n.*

transnational *adj.* extending beyond national boundaries. • *n.* a transnational company.

transoceanic *adj.* **1** on or from the other side of the ocean. **2** crossing the ocean.

transom *n.* **1** a horizontal bar of wood or stone across the top of a door or window. **2** (in full **transom window**) a window above the transom of a door or larger window; a fanlight.

transparency / trans-**pair**-ruhn-see / *n.* **1** being transparent. **2** a photographic slide.

transparent / trans-**pair**-ruhnt / *adj.* **1** allowing light to pass through so that objects behind can be seen clearly. **2** easily understood; (of an excuse or motive etc.) of such a kind that the truth behind it is easily perceived. **3** clear and unmistakable (*a man of transparent honesty*). □ **transparently** *adv.*

transpire *v.* **1** (of information etc.) leak out, become known (*no details of the contract were allowed to transpire*). **2** *colloq.* happen (*these events transpired a hundred years ago*). **3** (of plants) give off watery vapour from the surface of leaves etc. □ **transpiration** *n.*

■ **Usage** The use in sense 2 is considered incorrect by some people.

transplant *v.* / trans-**plahnt**, -**plant** / **1** remove and replant or establish elsewhere. **2** transfer (living tissue or an organ) from one part of the body or one person or animal to another. **3** be able to be transplanted. • *n.* / **trans**-plahnt, -plant / **1** transplanting of tissue or an organ. **2** something transplanted. □ **transplantation** *n.*

transponder *n.* a device for receiving a radio signal and automatically transmitting a different signal.

transport *v.* / trans-**pawt** / **1** convey (a person, goods, etc.) from one place to another. **2** *Aust. hist.* deport (a person sentenced in the British Isles) to a penal colony in Australia. **3** carry away by strong emotion (*she was transported with joy*). • *n.* / **trans**-pawt / **1** the act or process of conveying people, goods, etc., from place to place. **2** means of conveyance (*have you got transport?*). **3** the condition of being carried away by strong emotion (*in transports of rage*). **4** *Aust. hist.* a person sentenced in the British Isles to a term of servitude in a penal colony in Australia. □ **transportation** *n.*

transportable *adj.* able to be transported.

transporter *n.* a vehicle used to transport other vehicles, heavy machinery, etc. □ **transporter bridge** a bridge carrying vehicles on a suspended moving platform.

transpose *v.* **1** cause (two or more things) to change places; change the position of (a thing) in a series. **2** put (a piece of music) into a different key. □ **transposition** *n.*

transputer *n.* a microprocessor with integral memory designed for parallel processing. (¶ A blend of TRANSISTOR + COMPUTER.)

transsexual *adj.* (also **transexual**) having the physical characteristics (genitals etc.) of one sex and an overwhelming psychological identification

transubstantiation with the other sex. •*n.* **1** a transsexual person. **2** a person whose sex has been changed by surgery.

transubstantiation *n.* the Catholic doctrine that the *substance* of the Eucharistic elements (bread and wine) is converted by consecration wholly into the *substance* of the body and blood of Christ, only the appearance and taste (the *accidents*) of bread and wine still remaining.

transuranic / tranz-yoo-**ran**-ik / *adj.* belonging to a group of radioactive elements whose atoms are heavier than those of uranium.

transverse *adj.* lying or acting in a crosswise direction. □ **transversely** *adv.*

transvestite *n.* a person, esp. a male, who wears the clothes of the opposite sex, esp. as a sexual stimulus. □ **transvestism** *n.*

Transylvania / tran-sil-**vay**-nee-uh / a large tableland region in Romania, associated with the legend of Dracula.

trap[1] *n.* **1 a** an enclosure or device, often baited, for catching animals, usu. by affording a way in but not a way out. **b** a device with bait for killing vermin, esp. a mousetrap. **2** a trick betraying a person into speech or an act (*is this question a trap?*). **3** an arrangement to catch an unsuspecting person, esp. a speeding motorist. **4** a golf bunker. **5** a device for hurling an object (e.g. a clay pigeon) into the air to be shot at. **6** a device for preventing the passage of water or steam or silt etc.; a U-shaped or S-shaped section of a pipe that holds liquid and so prevents foul gases from coming up from a drain. **7** a two-wheeled carriage drawn by a horse. **8** a trapdoor. **9** *colloq.* the mouth (*shut your trap*). **10** (**traps**) percussion instruments, esp. in a jazz band. **11** (usu. in *pl.*) *Aust. colloq.* a police officer. •*v.* (**trapped**, **trapping**) **1** catch (an animal) in a trap. **2** catch or catch out (a person) by means of a trick etc. **3** stop or retain in or as in a trap. **4** provide (a place) with traps. □ **go round the traps 1** inspect a series of traps (on a farm etc.) to see what has been caught. **2** *Aust. colloq.* make a tour of inspection in general; visit one's regular haunts, esp. to elicit information. **3** *colloq.* (**been round the traps**) possessed of the necessary information; experienced in the ways of the world.

trap[2] *n.* (in full **trap-rock**) dark volcanic rock.

trapdoor *n.* a door in a floor, ceiling, or roof. □ **trapdoor spider** any of many large burrowing spiders which dig a nest in the shape of a tube, concealing the entrance at the top with a hinged flap which opens and shuts as does a trapdoor.

trapeze *n.* a horizontal bar hung by ropes as a swing for acrobatics; a similar device which enables a person to lean safely out of a small sailing boat.

trapezium / truh-**pee**-zee-uhm / *n.* (*pl.* **trapeziums** or **trapezia**) a quadrilateral in which two opposite sides are parallel and the other two are not.

trapezoid / **trap**-ee-zoid / *n.* a quadrilateral in which no sides are parallel.

trapper *n.* a person who traps animals, esp. for furs.

trappings *n.pl.* **1** ornamental accessories, symbols of status, etc. (*he had all the trappings of high office but very little power*). **2** the harness of a horse, esp. when ornamental.

Trappist *n.* a monk of a branch of the Cistercian Order founded at La Trappe in France, noted for the extreme austerity of its rule which includes the vow of perpetual silence. •*adj.* of this Order.

trash *n.* **1** worthless or waste stuff, rubbish. **2** a worthless person or persons. □ **trash and treasure** *Aust.* **1** cheap or second-hand goods, esp. as sold at a fête or informal market. **2** such a market selling these goods. □□ **trashy** *adj.*

trasi / **trah**-see / *n.* a hard dark pungent paste made from dried prawns and available in slabs, an essential ingredient in many SE Asian recipes. Also called *blachan*.

trattoria / trat-uh-**ree**-uh / *n.* an Italian restaurant.

trauma / **traw**-muh / *n.* **1** a wound or injury. **2** emotional shock producing a lasting effect upon a person.

traumatic / traw-**mat**-ik / *adj.* **1** of or causing trauma. **2** *colloq.* (of an experience) very unpleasant. □ **traumatically** *adv.*

traumatise *v.* (also **-ize**) cause (a person) to suffer trauma or distress.

travail / **trav**-ayl / *n.* **1** *literary* painful or laborious effort. **2** *archaic* the pains of childbirth. •*v.* **1** *literary* make a painful or laborious effort. **2** *archaic* undergo the pains of childbirth.

travel *v.* (**travelled**, **travelling**) **1** go from one place or point to another, make a journey. **2** journey along or through; cover (a distance) in travelling. **3** go from place to place as a salesperson. **4** *colloq.* withstand a long journey (*some wines travel badly*). **5** *colloq.* move at high speed (*the car was certainly travelling*). •*n.* **1** travelling, esp. in foreign countries. **2** the range, rate, or method of movement of a machine part. □ **travel agency** an agency making arrangements for travellers. **travel agent** a person or firm acting as a travel agency. **travel sickness** a feeling of nausea caused by motion when travelling.

travelled *adj.* experienced in travelling.

traveller *n.* **1** a person who travels or is travelling. **2** a travelling salesperson. □ **traveller's cheque** a cheque for a fixed amount, sold by a bank etc. and usu. able to be cashed in various countries.

traveller's joy *Aust.* = OLD MAN'S BEARD (*see* OLD).

travelling salesperson = COMMERCIAL TRAVELLER.

travelogue / **trav**-uh-log / *n.* a film or illustrated lecture about travel.

Travers, P(amela) L(yndon) (1906–96), Australian-born writer, esp. of books for children, best known for the six fantasy novels in her *Mary Poppins* series (1934–88).

traverse / truh-**vers**, **trav**-uhs / *n*. **1** a thing (esp. part of a structure) that lies across another. **2** a zigzag course or road; each leg of this. **3** a lateral movement across something. •*v*. **1** travel or lie across (*traversed the country; a pit traversed by a beam*). **2** ☐ **traversal** *n*.

travesty / **trav**-uhs-tee / *n*. a grotesque misrepresentation or imitation (*his trial was a travesty of justice*). •*v*. (**travestied, travestying**) make or be a travesty of.

trawl *n*. a large wide-mouthed fishing net dragged along the bottom of the sea etc. by a boat. •*v*. **1** fish with a trawl. **2** catch by trawling.

trawler *n*. a boat used in trawling; a person who trawls.

tray *n*. **1** a flat utensil, usu. with a raised edge, on which articles are carried. **2** a shallow lidless box for papers or small articles, sometimes as a drawer in a cabinet etc. **3** *Aust*. the flat open part of a truck on which goods are carried.

treacherous *adj*. **1** behaving with or showing treachery. **2** not to be relied on, not giving a firm support (*the roads were icy and treacherous*). ☐ **treacherously** *adv*. **treacherousness** *n*.

treachery *n*. betrayal of a person or cause; an act of disloyalty.

treacle *n*. **1** a syrup produced when sugar is refined. **2 a** molasses. **b** golden syrup. **3** cloying sentimentality or flattery (*I can't take your treacle any more*).

treacly *adj*. **1** like treacle. **2** excessively sweet or sentimental.

tread *v*. (**trod, trodden, treading**) **1** set one's foot down; walk or step. **2** press or crush with the feet; make (a path or trail or mark etc.) by walking. **3** press down into the ground with the feet (*trod dirt into the carpet*). •*n*. **1** the manner or sound of walking (*a heavy tread*). **2** the top surface of a step or stair. **3** the part of a wheel or tyre etc. that touches the ground. ☐ **tread the boards** be an actor. **tread water** keep oneself upright in water by making treading movements with the legs.

treadle / **tred**-uhl / *n*. a lever worked by the foot to drive a wheel, e.g. in a lathe or sewing machine.

treadmill *n*. **1** a wide mill-wheel turned by the weight of people (or animals) treading on steps fixed round its edge, formerly worked by prisoners as a punishment. **2** a device worked by treading an endless belt, used for testing reactions to exertion. **3** monotonous routine work.

treason *n*. violation by a subject of allegiance to his or her country, e.g. by giving military information to the enemy at a time of war.

■ **Usage** The term *high treason*, originally distinguished from *petty treason*, now means the same as *treason*.

treasonable *adj*. involving or guilty of treason.

treasure *n*. **1** precious metals or gems; a hoard of these (*buried treasure*). **2** a highly valued object (*art treasures*). **3** a beloved or highly valued person. •*v*. value highly, keep or store as precious (*a treasured possession*). ☐ **treasure trove 1** treasure found hidden and of unknown ownership. **2** any collection or source of valuable things etc. (*the old Aborigine was a treasure trove of information about his near-extinct language*).

treasurer *n*. **1** a person in charge of the funds of an institution or club etc. **2** (also **Treasurer**) the cabinet minister responsible for the Treasury.

treasury *n*. a place where treasure is stored; something regarded as containing things of great value or interest (*the book is a treasury of useful information*). ☐ **the Treasury** the department managing the public revenue of a nation; the offices and officers of this.

treat *v*. **1** act or behave towards (a person or thing) in a certain way (*treated him roughly; treat it as a joke*). **2** present or deal with (a subject) (*recent events are treated in detail*). **3** give medical or surgical treatment to (*treated him for sunstroke*). **4** subject (a substance or thing) to a chemical or other process. **5** entertain (a person) at one's own expense; buy, give, or allow to have as a treat (*treated myself to a taxi*). **6** (foll. by *with*) negotiate terms (*treating with their enemies to secure a ceasefire*). •*n*. **1** something that gives great pleasure, esp. something special or unexpected. **2** a meal, entertainment, etc., designed to do this. **3** the treating of others to something at one's own expense (*it's my treat*). ☐ **a treat** extremely good or well (*he looks a treat; the project has come on a treat*).

treatise / **tree**-tuhs / *n*. a written work dealing formally and systematically with one subject.

treatment *n*. **1** the process or manner of dealing with a person or thing (*his treatment of me was atrocious*). **2** something done in order to relieve or cure an illness or abnormality etc. ☐ **the treatment** *colloq*. the customary way of dealing with a person, a situation, etc. (*got the full treatment*).

treaty *n*. **1** a formal agreement between two nations, concerning cessation of hostilities, trade, human rights, etc. **2** a formal agreement between people, esp. for the purchase of property.

treble *adj*. **1** three times as much or as many. **2** (of a boy's voice before puberty, a musical instrument, etc.) high-pitched, soprano. •*n*. **1** a treble quantity or thing. **2** a hit in the narrow ring between the two middle circles of a dartboard, scoring treble. **3** a bet where winnings and stakes from a race are restaked on a second and then a third race. **4** a high-pitched or soprano voice (esp.

that of a boy before puberty), or of an instrument, etc. **5** the high-frequency output of a radio, record player, etc. • *v.* make or become three times as much or as many (*costs had trebled*). ☐ **treble clef** *Music* a clef placing the G above middle C on the second lowest line of the stave. ☐ ☐ **trebly** *adv.*

Treblinka / tre-**bling**-kuh / a Nazi concentration camp in Poland in the Second World War, where a great many of the Jews of the Warsaw ghetto were murdered.

tree *n.* **1** a perennial plant with a woody, self-supporting main stem or trunk without branches for some distance above the ground. **2** a shrub having a tree-like shape or form (*tree dahlia; tree tomato*). **3** a framework of wood for various purposes (*shoe-tree*). **4** = FAMILY TREE. • *v.* (**trees, treed**) **1** force to take refuge in a tree (*I was treed by a dog for three hours*). **2** establish with trees (*a thickly treed block*). ☐ **tree duck** *see* WHISTLING DUCK. **tree fern** any of many Australian ferns which are tree-like, having a tall woody trunk and a canopy of arching green fronds often several metres in length. **tree kangaroo** (also **tree-climbing kangaroo**) any of various wallaby-like macropods inhabiting jungle areas of north-eastern Qld and New Guinea, and adapted to living and foraging in trees. **tree line** = TIMBERLINE. **tree rat** a tree-dwelling rodent of northern Australia. **tree ring** a ring, in the cross section of a tree, from one year's growth. **tree surgeon** a person who prunes trees, treats damaged trees to preserve them, etc. **tree tomato** = TAMARILLO. ☐ ☐ **treeless** *adj.* **treey** *adj.*

treecreeper *n.* any of many small birds of Australia (and elsewhere), creeping up tree trunks and feeding on insects in tree bark.

trefoil / **tref**-oil / *n.* **1** a plant with three leaflets, e.g. clover. **2** an ornament or design shaped like this, esp. in tracery windows.

trek *n.* a long arduous journey or walk (*it's quite a trek to the supermarket*). • *v.* (**trekked, trekking**) **1** travel or make one's way arduously. **2** make a long journey by foot. ☐ **trekker** *n.*

trellis *n.* (in full **trelliswork**) a light framework of bars, used to support climbing plants.

trematode / **trem**-uh-tohd / *n.* a parasitic flatworm.

tremble *v.* shake involuntarily from fear or cold etc.; quiver. • *n.* a trembling or quivering movement, a tremor.

trembly *adj. colloq.* inclined to tremble; agitated.

tremendous *adj.* **1** immense. **2** *colloq.* excellent (*gave a tremendous performance*). ☐ **tremendously** *adv.* **tremendousness** *n.*

tremolo / **trem**-uh-loh / *n.* (*pl.* **tremolos**) **1** a tremulous effect in playing stringed and keyboard instruments or singing, esp. by the rapid reiteration of a note. **2** a device in an organ etc. producing a tremulous effect.

tremor / **trem**-uh / *n.* **1** a slight shaking or trembling movement, a vibration. **2** (in full **earth tremor**) a slight earthquake. **3** a thrill of fear or other emotion.

tremulous / **trem**-yuh-luhs / *adj.* **1** trembling from nervousness or weakness (*spoke in a tremulous voice*). **2** quivering or vibrating. ☐ **tremulously** *adv.*

trench *n.* a long narrow hole cut in the ground, e.g. for drainage or to give troops shelter from enemy fire. • *v.* dig trenches in (ground). ☐ **trench coat** a belted coat or raincoat with pockets and flaps like those of a military uniform coat.

trenchant / **tren**-chuhnt / *adj.* (of comments or policies etc.) penetrating, strong and effective (*made some trenchant criticisms*). ☐ **trenchantly** *adv.* **trenchancy** *n.*

trencher *n.* **1** *hist.* a wooden platter for serving food. **2** a stiff square academic cap; a mortarboard.

trend *n.* the general direction and tendency (esp. of events, fashion, or opinion). • *v.* **1** bend or turn away in a specified direction. **2** have a general tendency.

trendoid / **tren**-doid / (*colloq. derog.*) *n.* a person who is ultra-trendy in dress, lifestyle, etc. • *adj.* ultra-trendy.

trendsetter *n.* a person who leads the way in fashion etc.

trendy (*colloq.* often *derog.*) *adj.* (**trendier, trendiest**) fashionable, 'with it'. • *n.* a trendy person. ☐ **trendily** *adv.* **trendiness** *n.*

trepan / truh-**pan** / *n.* a cylindrical saw formerly used by surgeons for removing part of the skull.

trepidation / trep-uh-**day**-shuhn / *n.* a state of fear and anxiety, nervous agitation.

trespass *v.* **1** enter a person's land or property unlawfully. **2** intrude or make use of unreasonably (*I don't want to trespass on your time*). **3** *archaic* sin or do wrong (*as we forgive them that trespass against us*). • *n.* **1** the act of trespassing. **2** *archaic* sin, wrongdoing. ☐ **trespasser** *n.*

tress *n.* **1** a long lock of hair. **2** (**tresses**) the hair of the head, esp. of a woman or girl.

trestle *n.* **1** each of a pair or set of supports on which a board is rested to form a table; (in full **trestle table**) the table itself. **2** (in full **trestlework**) an open braced framework for supporting a bridge.

trevally / truh-**val**-ee / *n.* (*pl.* **trevally** or **trevallies**) *Aust.* any of several marine fish, many of which are fished commercially.

trey *n.* (in full **trey-bit**) *hist.* an Australian threepenny coin.

tri- *comb. form* three, three times, triple.

triad / **truy**-ad / *n.* **1** a group of three connected persons or things (esp. notes in a chord). **2** (also **Triad**) a Chinese secret society, usu. criminal. ☐ **triadic** / truy-**ad**-ik / *adj.*

triage / **tree**-ahj / *n.* **1** the act of sorting according to quality. **2** the assignment of degrees of urgency

trial to decide the order of treatment of wounds, illnesses, etc.

trial *n.* **1** an examination in a lawcourt by a judge to decide on the guilt or innocence of an accused person. **2** the process of testing qualities or performance by use and experience. **3** a sports match etc. to test the ability of players who may be selected for a team. **4** a test of individual ability on a motor cycle over rough ground or on a road. **5** a person or thing that tries one's patience or endurance; a hardship (*he's such a trial; the trials of old age*). • *v.* (**trialled**, **trialling**) **1** subject to or undergo a test to assess performance. **2** *Aust.* perform in a specified manner in a test. ☐ **on trial 1** being tried in a court of law. **2** being tested; to be chosen or retained only if suitable. **trial and error** the process of trying repeatedly and learning from one's failures. **trial run** a preliminary operational test.

triangle *n.* **1** a geometric figure with three sides and three angles. **2** something shaped like this; a percussion instrument consisting of a steel rod bent into this shape and struck with another steel rod. **3** *Aust. hist.* a tripod to which a convict (later any prisoner) was tied before being flogged. **4** a relationship of three people, esp. one involving sexual rivalry.

triangular *adj.* **1** shaped like a triangle. **2** involving three people (*a triangular contest*).

triangulate *v.* **1** divide into triangles. **2** measure or map out (an area) in surveying by means of calculations based on a network of triangles. ☐ **triangulation** *n.*

triantelope / truy-**an**-tuh-lohp / *n. Aust.* = HUNTSMAN (sense 2). (¶ A corruption of TARANTULA.)

Triassic / truy-**as**-ik / *Geol. adj.* of the earliest period of the Mesozoic era. • *n.* this period.

triathlon / truy-**ath**-lon / *n.* an athletic contest in which competitors take part in three events (swimming, cycling, and running).

tribal *adj.* of a tribe or tribes.

tribalism *n.* tribal organisation.

tribe *n.* **1 a** a group of families or communities, linked by social, religious, or blood ties, and usu. having a common culture and dialect and a recognised leader. **b** the name applied, originally by colonists in Australia (and often misleadingly), to a traditional Aboriginal community. **2** (usu. *derog.* or *jocular*) a set or class of people, esp. of one profession etc. or family (*he despises the whole tribe of politicians; the whole tribe is gathering at our place for Christmas*).

tribesman *n.* (*feminine* **tribeswoman**) a member of a tribe.

tribology / truy-**bol**-uh-jee / *n.* the study of friction, wear, lubrication, and the design of bearings.

tribulation / trib-yuh-**lay**-shuhn / *n.* great affliction; a cause of this.

tribunal / truy-**byoo**-nuhl / *n.* **1** a board of officials appointed by a government to make a judgment or act as arbitrators on a particular problem. **2** a court of justice.

tribune[1] / **trib**-yoon / *n.* **1** (in ancient Rome) an official chosen by the people to protect their liberties; an officer in periodic command of a legion. **2** a leader of the people.

tribune[2] *n.* **1** a bishop's throne in a basilica. **2** the apse containing this. **3** a dais, a rostrum.

tributary *n.* a river or stream that flows into a larger river or into a lake. • *adj.* flowing in this way.

tribute *n.* **1** something said, done, or given as a mark of respect or admiration. **2** (foll. by *to*) an indication of the effectiveness of (*his recovery is a tribute to the doctor's skill*). **3** payment that one country or ruler was formerly obliged to pay to a more powerful one.

trice *n.* ☐ **in a trice** in an instant.

triceps / **truy**-seps / *n.* the large muscle at the back of the upper arm, which straightens the elbow.

triceratops *n.* / truy-**se**-ruh-tops / a dinosaur with three horns on the forehead and a wavy-edged collar round the neck.

trichinosis / trik-uh-**noh**-suhs / *n.* a disease caused by hairlike worms usu. ingested in meat.

trichology / tri-**kol**-uh-jee / *n.* the study of hair and its diseases. ☐ **trichologist** *n.*

trick *n.* **1** something done in order to deceive or outwit someone. **2** a deception or illusion (*a trick of the light*). **3** a particular technique, knack; the exact or best way of doing something (*he has the trick of making perfect soufflés; the trick is in frying the rice in ghee before boiling it*). **4** a feat of skill done for entertainment (*conjuring tricks*). **5** a mannerism (*he has a trick of repeating himself*). **6** a mischievous, foolish, or discreditable act; a practical joke. **7** the cards played in one round of a card game; the round itself; a point gained as a result of this. **8** *colloq.* a male or female prostitute's client; a casual sexual partner. • *v.* **1** deceive or persuade by a trick, mislead. **2** (often foll. by *out of*) swindle (*tricked out of his savings*). **3** (foll. by *into*) cause to do something by using trickery (*he was tricked into marriage; tricked me into agreeing*). **4** foil, baffle; take by surprise. **5** (foll. by *out* or *up*) deck or decorate. ☐ **trick or treat** a phrase said by children who call at houses at Hallowe'en asking to be given sweets etc. and threatening to do mischief if these are not provided.

trickery *n.* the use of tricks; deception.

trickle *v.* **1** flow or cause to flow in a thin stream. **2** come or go slowly or gradually (*people trickled into the hall*). • *n.* a small amount coming or going slowly (*a trickle of information*).

trickster *n.* a person who tricks or cheats people.

tricksy *adj.* full of tricks, playful.

tricky adj. (**trickier**, **trickiest**) **1** crafty, deceitful. **2** requiring skilful handling (*a tricky task*). □ **trickily** adv. **trickiness** n.

tricolour / trik-uh-luh, truy-ku-luh / n. (also **tricolor**) a flag with three colours in stripes, esp. those of France and Ireland.

tricycle n. a three-wheeled pedal-driven vehicle.

trident / **truy**-duhnt / n. **1** a three-pronged spear. **2** (**Trident**) a submarine-launched ballistic missile.

Tridentine / truy-**den**-tuyn / adj. of the Council of Trent, held at Trento in Italy 1545–63, esp. as the basis of Catholic doctrine and orthodoxy.

tried see TRY.

triennial / truy-**en**-ee-uhl / adj. **1** lasting for three years. **2** happening every third year. □ **triennially** adv.

trier n. **1** a person who tries hard, one who always does his or her best. **2** a tester.

trifecta / truy-**fek**-tuh / n. US & Aust. a form of betting in which the first three places in a race must be predicted in the correct order.

trifle n. **1** something of only slight value or importance. **2** a very small amount, esp. of money (*it cost a mere trifle*). **3** (**a trifle**) somewhat, rather (*he seems a trifle angry*). **4** a dish made of sponge cake soaked in wine or jelly etc. and topped with custard and cream. • v. **1** talk or act frivolously. **2** (foll. by *with*) treat or deal with frivolously; flirt heartlessly with. **3** (foll. by *away*) waste (time, energies, money, etc.) frivolously.

trifling adj. **1** unimportant, petty. **2** frivolous.

triforium / truy-**faw**-ree-uhm / n. (pl. **triforia**) an arcade or gallery above the arches of the nave, choir, and transepts in a church.

trig n. *colloq.* trigonometry. □ **trig point** a reference point on high ground, used in triangulation.

trigger n. **1** a lever or catch for releasing a spring, esp. so as to fire a gun. **2** an event, occurrence, etc. that sets off a chain reaction. • v. (often foll. by *off*) start; set (an action or process) in motion (*the announcement triggered off riots*). □ **trigger plant** (or **flower**) any of numerous Australian plants in the genus *Stylidium*, the flowers (white to deep rose-red) having a unique device for pollination: an insect alighting on a flower triggers a hammer which springs down and hits the insect on the back, dusting it with pollen, the hammer automatically resetting itself after a while.

trigonometry / trig-uh-**nom**-uh-tree / n. the branch of mathematics dealing with the relationship of sides and angles of triangles etc. □ **trigonometric** adj. **trigonometrical** adj.

trike n. *colloq.* a tricycle.

trilateral / truy-**lat**-uh-ruhl / adj. having three sides or three participants.

trilby n. a man's soft felt hat with a lengthwise dent in the crown and a narrow brim.

trilingual / truy-**ling**-gwuhl / adj. speaking or using three languages.

trill n. **1** a vibrating sound made by the voice (pronouncing *r* with the tongue vibrating) or in birdsong. **2** quick alternation of two notes in music that are a tone or semitone apart. • v. sound or sing with a trill.

triller n. either of two Australian birds with a distinctive trilling call (*varied triller; white-winged triller*).

trillion n. **1** a million million (10^{12}). **2** (now less often) a million million million (10^{18}). □ **trillionth** adj. & n.

trilobite / **truy**-luh-buyt / n. a marine creature of Palaeozoic times, an invertebrate with a segmented body and jointed limbs, now only found as a fossil.

trilogy / **tril**-uh-jee / n. a group of three related literary or operatic works.

trim adj. (**trimmer**, **trimmest**) neat and orderly; having a smooth outline or compact structure. • v. (**trimmed**, **trimming**) **1** make neat or of the required size or form, esp. by cutting away irregular or unwanted parts (*trim the joint of fat; will you trim my hair?*). **2** remove or reduce by cutting (*the hedge needs trimming*). **3** reduce the size, amount, or number of; eliminate (*wasteful expenditure etc.*) (*we need to trim the budget*). **4** ornament (*help me trim the Christmas tree*). **5** make (a boat or aircraft) evenly balanced by arranging the position of its cargo or passengers etc. **6** arrange (sails) to suit the wind. **7** associate oneself with currently prevailing views, esp. to advance oneself (*he trims to every popular notion*). **8** hold a middle course in politics or opinion. • n. **1** condition as regards readiness or fitness (*in perfect trim*). **2** the trimming on a dress or furniture etc.; the colour or type of upholstery and other fittings in a car. **3** the trimming of hair etc. **4** the balance or the even horizontal position of a boat in the water or an aircraft in the air. □ **trimly** adv. **trimness** n. **trimmer** n.

trimaran / **truy**-muh-ran / n. a vessel like a catamaran, with three hulls side by side.

trimmer n. Aust. *colloq.* a striking or outstanding person or thing.

trimming n. **1** something added as an ornament or decoration on a dress or furniture etc. **2** (**trimmings**) the usual accompaniments of something, esp. of the main course of a meal (*rice and curry and all the trimmings*).

Trinidad an island in the West Indies, forming part of the republic of **Trinidad and Tobago**. □ **Trinidadian** / trin-uh-**day**-dee-uhn / adj. & n.

trinitrotoluene (also **trinitrotoluol**) = TNT.

trinity n. **1** being three. **2** a group of three. **3** (**the Trinity**) the three persons of the Christian Godhead (Father, Son, Holy Spirit), each being God, although there is only one God not three.

trinket n. a small fancy article or piece of jewellery.

trinomial / truy-**noh**-mee-uhl / *adj.* consisting of three terms. • *n.* a scientific name or an algebraic expression consisting of three terms.

trio / **tree**-oh / *n.* (*pl.* **trios**) **1** a group or set of three. **2** a group of three singers or players; a musical composition for these.

trip *v.* (**tripped**, **tripping**) **1** walk, run, or dance with quick light steps; (of rhythm) run lightly. **2** *colloq.* have a long visionary experience caused by a drug. **3** (often foll. by *up*) stumble, catch one's foot on something and fall; cause to do this. **4** (often foll. by *up*) make a slip or blunder; cause to do this. **5** release (a switch or catch) so as to operate a mechanism. • *n.* **1** a journey or excursion, esp. for pleasure. **2** a stumble or blunder. **3** a device for tripping a mechanism. **4** *colloq.* a drug-induced hallucinatory experience.

tripartite / truy-**pah**-tuyt / *adj.* **1** consisting of three parts. **2** shared by or involving three parties.

tripe *n.* **1** the first or second stomach of a ruminant (esp. a bullock) as food. **2** *colloq.* nonsense; something worthless.

Tripitaka / trip-ee-**tah**-kuh / *n.* the sacred canon of Theravada Buddhism, written in the Pali language.

triple *adj.* **1** consisting of three parts; involving three people or groups. **2** three times as much or as many. • *v.* make or become three times as much or as many. • *n.* a threefold number or amount; a set of three. ❑ **triple antigen** *Aust.* a vaccine administered, usu. in infancy, as protection against diphtheria, whooping cough, and tetanus. **triple crown** the official tiara of the pope. **triple jump** an athletic contest comprising a hop, a step, and a long jump. **triple time** (in music) rhythm with three beats to the bar. ❑ ❑ **triply** *adv.*

triplet *n.* **1** one of three children or animals born at one birth. **2** a set of three things, esp. three equal musical notes played in the time of two.

triplex *adj.* triple, threefold.

triplicate *adj.* / **trip**-luh-kuht / existing in three parts, copies, or examples; tripled. • *n.* / **trip**-luh-kuht / each of a set of three copies or corresponding parts. • *v.* / **trip**-luh-kayt / **1** make in three copies. **2** multiply by three; triple. ❑ **in triplicate** in three copies.

tripod / **truy**-pod / *n.* a three-legged stand for a camera or surveying instrument etc.; a stool, table, or utensil resting on three feet or legs.

Tripoli the capital of Libya.

triptych / **trip**-tik / *n.* a picture or carving on three panels fixed or hinged side by side, esp. as an altarpiece.

tripwire *n.* a wire stretched close to the ground, actuating a trap or warning device etc. when disturbed.

trireme / **truy**-reem / *n.* an ancient Greek warship with three banks of oarsmen on each side.

trisect / truy-**sekt** / *v.* divide into three equal parts. ❑ **trisection** *n.*

trite / truyt / *adj.* (of a phrase or opinion) commonplace, hackneyed. ❑ **tritely** *adv.* **triteness** *n.*

tritium *n.* a radioactive isotope of hydrogen (symbol T).

Triton / **truy**-tuhn / *Gk myth.* **1** the son of Poseidon. **2** a minor sea god, usu. represented as a man with a fish's tail carrying a trident and a shell-trumpet.

triumph *n.* **1** the fact of being successful or victorious; joy at this. **2** a great success or achievement. **3** a supreme example (*a triumph of engineering*). • *v.* be successful or victorious; rejoice at one's success etc.

triumphal / truy-**um**-fuhl / *adj.* of or celebrating a triumph (*a triumphal arch*).

■ **Usage** Do not confuse *triumphal* with *triumphant.*

triumphalism *n.* excessive exultation over the victories of one's own party, country, etc. ❑ **triumphalist** *adj. & n.*

triumphant / truy-**um**-fuhnt / *adj.* **1** victorious, successful. **2** rejoicing at success etc. ❑ **triumphantly** *adv.*

■ **Usage** Do not confuse *triumphant* with *triumphal.*

triumvirate / truy-**um**-vuh-ruht / *n.* a ruling group of three persons, esp. in ancient Rome.

triune / **truy**-yoon / *adj.* three in one, esp. with reference to the Trinity.

trivalent / truy-**vay**-luhnt / *adj. Chem.* having a valence of three.

trivet / **triv**-uht / *n.* an iron stand, esp. a tripod, for a kettle or pot etc.

trivia *n.pl.* trivial things.

trivial *adj.* **1** of only small value or importance; trifling. **2** (of a person etc.) concerned only with trivial things. ❑ **trivially** *adv.* **triviality** / triv-ee-**al**-uh-tee / *n.*

trivialise *v.* (also **-ize**) treat (something) as being trivial; demean. ❑ **trivialisation** *n.*

trochee / **troh**-kee / *n.* a metrical foot consisting of one long or stressed syllable followed by one short or unstressed syllable. ❑ **trochaic** / truh-**kay**-ik / *adj.*

trochus / **troh**-kuhs / *n.* (in full **trochus shell**) a mollusc with a conical shell.

trod, trodden *see* TREAD.

troglodyte / **trog**-luh-duyt / *n.* **1** a cave dweller in ancient times. **2** *colloq. derog.* **a** a wilfully obscurantist or old-fashioned person. **b** a boorish or obnoxious person.

troika / **troi**-kuh / *n.* **1** a Russian vehicle with a team of three horses abreast. **2** this team. **3** a group of three people, esp. as an administrative council.

Troilus (in medieval legend) the forsaken lover of Cressida.

Trojan *adj.* of Troy or its people. •*n.* **1** a native or inhabitant of Troy. **2** (**trojan**) a person who works, fights, endures, etc., courageously. ☐ **Trojan Horse 1** *Gk myth.* the hollow wooden horse used by the Greeks (who concealed warriors inside it) to enter Troy. **2** a person or device planted to bring about an enemy's downfall. **3** a computer program designed to sabotage a computer system: it appears to be part of a legitimate program, but once it has been carried successfully into the system, it breaks the system's security and begins to erase data or to retrieve confidential data for access by unauthorised persons. **Trojan War** *Gk myth.* the ten-year siege of Troy by the Greeks, ending in its capture after the trick of the wooden horse. **work like a Trojan** work with great energy and endurance.

troll / trohl / *v.* fish by drawing bait along in the water. •*n. Scand. myth.* a member of a race of supernatural beings formerly thought of as giants but now as grotesque dwarfs dwelling in caves.

trolley *n.* (*pl.* **trolleys**) **1** a table, stand, or basket on wheels or castors for serving food, transporting luggage etc., gathering purchases in a supermarket etc. **2** a low truck running on rails.

trollop *n.* a disreputable woman; a prostitute.

trombone *n.* a large brass wind instrument with a sliding tube. ☐ **trombonist** *n.*

trompe l'oeil / tromp **ler**-ee / *n.* a painting on a wall etc. designed to give an illusion of reality. (¶ French, = deceives the eye.)

troop *n.* **1** a company of people or animals, esp. when moving. **2** a cavalry unit commanded by a captain; a unit of artillery. **3** a unit of three or more Scout patrols. **4** (**troops**) soldiers, armed forces. •*v.* **1** assemble or go as a troop or in great numbers. **2** carry or parade (a colour or flag) in a ceremonial manner before assembled troops (*trooping the colour*).

trooper *n.* **1** a private in a cavalry or armoured unit. **2** *hist.* a mounted police officer in Australia, esp. on the goldfields. **3** = TROUPER.

trophy *n.* **1** something taken in war or hunting etc. as a souvenir of success. **2** a cup etc. awarded as a prize or token of victory.

tropic *n.* **1** a line of latitude 23°27′ north of the equator (**tropic of Cancer**) or the same latitude south of it (**tropic of Capricorn**). **2** (**the tropics** or **the Tropics**) the region between these, with a hot climate. •*adj.* = TROPICAL.

tropical *adj.* of, found in, or like the tropics; very hot; luxuriant.

troposphere / **trop**-uh-sfeer / *n.* the layer of atmospheric air extending about 6–10 km upwards from the earth's surface.

troppo *adj. Aust. colloq.* mentally disturbed, allegedly as a result of spending too much time in the tropics; mad, crazy. ☐ **go troppo** become disturbed in this way.

trot *n.* **1** the running action of a horse etc. with legs moving as in a walk. **2** (of a person) a slowish run. **3** (**trots**) a race meeting at which the program consists of trotting and pacing races (*see* TROTTING). **4** (**the trots**) *colloq.* diarrhoea. **5** *Aust.* an uninterrupted sequence, esp. in a game of chance; a run of good or bad luck. •*v.* (**trotted**, **trotting**) **1** (of a horse) proceed at a steady pace, faster than a walk, lifting each diagonal pair of legs alternately. **2** (of a person) run at a moderate pace, esp. with short strides. **3** *colloq.* walk or go (*trot round to the milk bar*). **4** cause (a horse or person) to trot. **5** traverse (a distance) at a trot. ☐ **on the trot** *colloq.* **1** continually busy (*kept him on the trot*). **2** in succession (*for five weeks on the trot*). **trot out** *colloq.* produce, bring out for inspection or approval etc. (*trotted out the same old excuse*).

troth *see* PLIGHT.

Trotsky, Leon (original name: Lev Davidovich Bronstein) (1879–1940), Russian leader and revolutionary urging worldwide socialist revolution.

Trotskyist *n.* a supporter of Trotsky; a radical left-wing Communist. ☐ **Trotskyism** *n.* **Trotskyite** *n.*

trotter *n.* **1** a horse of a special breed trained for trotting. **2** an animal's foot as food (*pigs' trotters*).

trotting *n.* a form of horse racing in which a horse pulls a two-wheeled vehicle (a sulky) and its driver and is obliged to trot: *see* TROT *v.* (sense 1). Also called *harness racing.*

troubadour / **troo**-buh-daw / *n.* a lyric poet in southern France etc. in the 11th–13th centuries, singing mainly of chivalry and courtly love.

trouble *n.* **1** difficulty, inconvenience; distress, vexation; misfortune. **2** a cause of any of these. **3** conflict, public unrest; (**the Troubles**) rebellions and unrest in Ireland in 1919–23 and in Northern Ireland from 1968. **4** unpleasantness involving punishment or rebuke. **5** faulty functioning of a mechanism or of the body or mind (*engine trouble; kidney trouble*). •*v.* **1** cause trouble, distress, pain, or inconvenience to. **2** be disturbed or worried, be subjected to inconvenience or unpleasant exertion (*don't trouble about it*). ☐ **trouble spot** a place where trouble frequently occurs.

troublemaker *n.* a person who habitually stirs up trouble. ☐ **troublemaking** *n.*

troubleshooter *n.* **1** a person who acts as a mediator in disputes. **2** a person who traces and corrects faults in machinery or in an organisation. ☐ **troubleshooting** *n.*

troublesome *adj.* giving trouble; causing annoyance.

trough / trof / *n.* **1** a long narrow open receptacle, esp. for holding water or food for animals. **2** a channel for conveying liquid. **3** a depression between two waves or ridges. **4** an elongated region of low atmospheric pressure.

trounce *v.* **1** thrash; punish severely. **2** defeat heavily.

troupe / troop / *n.* a company of actors or acrobats etc.

trouper / **troo**-puh / *n.* **1** a member of a theatrical troupe. **2** a loyal and supportive friend, helper, etc. (*a good trouper*).

trousers *n.pl.* a two-legged outer garment reaching from the waist usu. to the ankles. ☐ **trouser suit** a woman's suit of jacket and trousers.

trousseau / **troo**-soh / *n.* (*pl.* **trousseaus** or **trousseaux** / **troo**-sohz /) a bride's collection of clothing etc. to begin married life.

trout *n.* (*pl.* **trout** or **trouts**) **1** any of several mainly Northern hemisphere freshwater fish, famed as food, some of which have been introduced into Australian waters. **2** any of several Australian food fish unrelated to the Northern hemisphere trout (e.g. the *salmon trout*).

trove *n.* = TREASURE TROVE.

trowel *n.* **1** a small tool with a flat blade for spreading mortar etc. **2** a small garden tool with a curved blade for lifting plants or scooping things. • *v.* (**trowelled, trowelling**) apply or spread (mortar etc.) with a trowel.

Troy a city in Asia Minor, (also called **Ilium**) besieged for ten years by Greek forces in their attempt to recover Helen, wife of Menelaus, who had been abducted by the Trojan prince Paris. The city was believed to have been a figment of Greek legend until its site was discovered in the 1870s.

troy *n.* (in full **troy weight**) an imperial system of weights used for precious metals and gems, in which 1 pound = 12 ounces or 5,760 grains.

truant *n.* **1** a child who stays away from school without leave. **2** a person who avoids work etc. • *adj.* (of a person, conduct, thoughts, etc.) shirking, idle, wandering. • *v.* play truant. ☐ **play truant** stay away as a truant. ☐☐ **truancy** *n.*

truce *n.* a temporary agreement to stop fighting or arguing.

truck *n.* **1** a large powerful motor vehicle for transporting goods etc. **2** an open railway wagon for freight. ☐ **fall off the back of a truck** *see* FALL. **have no truck with** have no dealings with.

truckie *n. Aust. colloq.* a long-distance truck driver.

trucking *n.* the act or the business of driving a truck.

truckle *v.* submit obsequiously (*refusing to truckle to bullies*). ☐ **truckle bed** a low bed on wheels so that it can be pushed under another.

truculent / **truk**-yuh-luhnt / *adj.* defiant and aggressive. ☐☐ **truculently** *adv.* **truculence** *n.*

trudge *v.* walk laboriously; traverse (a distance) in this way. • *n.* a trudging walk.

true *adj.* **1** in accordance with fact. **2** in accordance with correct principles or an accepted standard; genuine and not false (*he was the true heir*). **3** exact, accurate; (of the voice etc.) in good tune. **4** accurately placed, balanced, or shaped. **5** loyal, faithful. • *adv.* truly, accurately. ☐ **true blue** *adj.* **1** extremely loyal. **2** extremely orthodox or conservative. **3** *Aust.* genuine (*a true-blue Aussie*). *n. Aust.* an Australian. **true north** north according to the earth's axis, not magnetic north.

truffle *n.* **1** a rich-flavoured edible fungus that grows underground. **2** a soft sweet made of a chocolate mixture.

Truganini / truug-uh-**nee**-nee / (nicknamed **Lalla(h) Rooke** by whites) (1803–1876), a Tasmanian Aborigine, daughter of Mangana, chief of the Bruny Island people, popularly regarded by non-Aborigines as 'the last of the Tasmanian Aborigines'. After her death in Hobart, her corpse was exhumed and given to the Royal Society of Tas. in 1878. It was exhibited at the Melbourne Exhibition in 1888. It remained on public exhibition in Tas. until 1947. After protests from the Aboriginal community, the Tas. Government finally allowed her skeleton to be cremated in 1976, the centenary of her death.

trugo / **troo**-goh / *n.* a game in which a disc is struck towards a goal with a mallet.

truism / **troo**-iz-uhm / *n.* a statement that is obviously true, esp. one that is so hackneyed that it is not worth making, e.g. *nothing lasts for ever*.

truly *adv.* **1** truthfully. **2** sincerely, genuinely (*we are truly grateful*). **3** faithfully, loyally.

trump *n.* **1** a playing card of a suit temporarily ranking above others; (**trumps**) this suit (*hearts are trumps*). **2** *colloq.* a very helpful or loyal person. **3** *Aust. colloq.* a person in authority. **4** *archaic* a trumpet blast. • *v.* **1** take (a card or trick) with a trump; play a trump. **2** *colloq.* outdo. ☐ **trump card 1** a card of the trump suit. **2** a valuable resource, esp. kept in reserve; a means of getting what one wants. **trump up** invent (an excuse or accusation etc.).

trumpery *adj.* showy but worthless; trashy. • *n.* worthless finery; worthless things; rubbish.

trumpet *n.* **1** a brass wind instrument with a bright penetrating tone, consisting of a narrow straight or curved tube flared at the end. **2** something shaped like this. • *v.* (**trumpeted, trumpeting**) **1** blow a trumpet. **2** (of an enraged elephant) make a loud resounding sound with its trunk. **3** proclaim loudly.

trumpeter *n.* **1** a person who plays or sounds a trumpet. **2** any of several food fish of south-eastern Australian waters, reputed to make a trumpeting sound when taken out of the water. ☐ **trumpeter whiting** any of several food fish of the whiting family, inhabiting the northern, eastern, and western waters of Australia.

truncate / trung-**kayt** / *v.* cut the top or the end from; shorten. ☐ **truncation** *n.*

truncheon / **trun**-chuhn / *n.* a short thick stick carried as a weapon by police.

trundle *v.* roll or move along, esp. heavily or noisily, esp. on, or as on, wheels (*trundling a wheelbarrow; a bus trundled up*).

trunk *n.* **1** the main stem of a tree. **2** the body apart from head and limbs. **3** a large box with a hinged lid for transporting or storing clothes etc. **4** the long flexible nose of an elephant. **5** (**trunks**) close-fitting shorts worn by men or boys for swimming, boxing, etc. □ **trunk line** a main line or route of a railway, telephone system, etc.

truss *n.* **1** a bundle of hay or straw. **2** a compact terminal cluster of flowers or fruit. **3** a framework of beams or bars supporting a roof or bridge etc. **4** a padded belt or other device worn to support a hernia. • *v.* **1** tie or bind securely (*truss him up; truss a chicken*). **2** support (a roof or bridge etc.) with trusses.

trust *n.* **1** firm belief in the reliability, truth, or strength etc. of a person or thing. **2** confident expectation. **3** responsibility arising from trust placed in the person given authority (*a position of trust*). **4** property legally entrusted to a person with instructions to use it for another's benefit or for a specified purpose. **5** an organisation founded to promote or preserve something (*the National Trust of Australia*). **6** an association of business firms, formed to reduce or defeat competition (*anti-trust legislation*). • *v.* **1** have or place trust in, treat as reliable. **2** entrust. **3** hope earnestly (*I trust he is not hurt*). □ **in trust** held as a trust (*see* sense 4). **take on trust** accept without investigation (*don't take the statement on trust*). **trust area** *Aust.* land which is owned or administered by an Aboriginal land trust.

trustee *n.* **1** a person who holds and administers property in trust for another. **2** a member of a group of people managing the business affairs of an institution.

trustful *adj.* full of trust or confidence. □ **trustfully** *adv.*

trusting *adj.* having trust, trustful. □ **trustingly** *adv.*

trustworthy *adj.* worthy of trust, reliable. □ **trustworthiness** *n.*

trusty *adj. archaic* trustworthy (*his trusty sword*).

truth / trooth / *n.* (*pl.* **truths** / troo*th*z, trooths /) **1** the quality of being true. **2** something that is true.

truthful *adj.* **1** habitually telling the truth. **2** true (*a truthful account of what happened*). □ **truthfully** *adv.* **truthfulness** *n.*

try *v.* (**tried, trying**) **1** attempt, make an effort to do something. **2** use, do, or test the possibilities of something to discover whether it is satisfactory or useful (*try your strength; try soap and water; try giving it a kick*). **3** try to open (a door or window) to discover whether it is locked. **4** be a strain on (*you are trying my patience*). **5** examine and decide (a case or issue) in a lawcourt; hold a trial of (a person) (*he was tried for murder*). • *n.* **1** an attempt. **2** *Rugby* a touchdown, scoring points and entitling the scoring side to a kick at goal. □ **try it on** *colloq.* do something to discover whether it will be tolerated. **try-on** *colloq.* an experimental action of this kind; an attempt to deceive. **try on** put (a garment) on to see whether it fits and looks good.

■ **Usage** The use of *try* and foll. by a verb (e.g. *try and be early; don't try and get the better of me*) is common in colloquial speech, but is considered incorrect by some people, and should be avoided in formal writing: say instead, *try to be early*, etc.

trying *adj.* putting a strain on one's temper or patience; annoying.

tryst / trist / *n. archaic* a meeting, esp. of lovers in secret.

tsar / zah / *n.* (also **czar**) the title of the former emperors of Russia.

tsetse fly / tset-see, tet- / *n.* a tropical African fly that feeds on blood and transmits disease (esp. sleeping sickness) by its bite.

T-shirt *n.* (also **tee shirt**) a casual short-sleeved cotton top with no collar, having the form of a T when spread out.

tsk-tsk! (an alveolar click formed by suction; also *jocular* **tisk-tisk!**) (also **tsk!**) *interj.* a sound expressing commiseration; an exclamation of disapproval or irritation ('*I'm henpecked.*' —'*Tsk-tsk!*' *said his mate sympathetically;* '*Tisk-tisk!*' *he said,* '*you shouldn't be doing that, you naughty boy!*'). • *v.* make this sound or utter this exclamation; say disapprovingly (*he tsk-ed his displeasure; don't you tsk-tsk at me in that tone of voice!*).

tsp *abbr.* (*pl.* **tsps**) teaspoonful.

T-square *n.* a T-shaped instrument for measuring or obtaining right angles.

tsunami / tsoo-**nah**-mee / *n.* **1** a series of long high sea waves caused by earth-movement. **2** an exceptionally large tidal wave. (¶ Japanese)

tuan / **tyoo**-uhn / *n. Aust.* **1** = PHASCOGALE. **2** = FLYING POSSUM (*see* FLYING). (¶ Wathawarung *duwan* 'small gliding possum'.)

tuart / **tyoo**-aht / *n.* **1** a medium to large eucalypt of coastal SW WA, the flowers of which, rich in nectar, produce a much-valued honey. **2** the strong, hard, yellowish wood of this tree. (¶ Nyungar)

tub *n.* **1** an open flat-bottomed usu. round container used for washing, planting, etc. **2** a tub-shaped (usu. plastic) carton. **3** *colloq.* a bath. **4** *colloq.* a clumsy, slow boat. • *v.* (**tubbed, tubbing**) plant, bathe, or wash in a tub.

tuba / **tyoo**-buh / *n.* a large low-pitched brass wind instrument.

tubby *adj.* (**tubbier, tubbiest**) short and fat. □ **tubbiness** *n.*

tube *n.* **1** a long hollow cylinder. **2** anything shaped like this. **3** a cylinder of flexible material usu. with a screw cap, holding a semi-liquid substance (*a tube of toothpaste*). **4** a hollow cylindrical organ in the body (*Fallopian tubes*). **5** (**the tube**) *Brit. colloq.* the underground railway system in London. **6** (**the tube**) *colloq.* television. **7** a cathode ray tube in a television set. **8** a thermionic valve. **9** *Aust. colloq.* a can of beer. **10** *Surfing* the hollow curve of a breaking wave. **11** the inflatable part of a pneumatic tyre. □ **have one's tubes tied** (of a woman) be made sterile by having the fallopian tubes surgically blocked.

tuber *n.* a short thick rounded root (e.g. of a dahlia) or underground stem (e.g. of a potato), producing buds from which new plants will grow.

tubercle / **tyoo**-buh-kuhl / *n.* a small rounded projection or swelling, esp. as characteristic of tuberculosis.

tubercular / tuh-**ber**-kyuh-luh / *adj.* of or affected with tuberculosis.

tuberculosis / tuh-ber-kyuh-**loh**-suhs / *n.* an infectious wasting disease in which tubercles appear on body tissue, esp. in the lungs.

tuberose / **tyoo**-buh-rohz / *n.* a tropical plant with fragrant white funnel-shaped flowers.

tuberous *adj.* of or like a tuber; bearing tubers.

tubestock *n. Aust.* cultivated, esp. native, plant seedlings in tubes.

tubing *n.* tubes; a length of tube.

tubular *adj.* tube-shaped; (of furniture) made of tube-shaped pieces. □ **tubular bells** an orchestral instrument of hanging brass tubes struck with a hammer.

tubule / **tyoo**-byool / *n.* a small tube in a plant or animal body.

tuck *n.* a flat fold stitched in a garment etc. to make it smaller or as an ornament. • *v.* **1** put a tuck or tucks in (a garment etc.). **2** turn (ends or edges etc.) or fold (a part) in, into, or under something so as to be concealed or held in place (*tucked his shirt into his trousers*). **3** cover snugly and compactly (*tucked him up in bed*). **4** stow (a thing) away in a specified place or in a specified way (*tucked it in a drawer; tucked it out of sight*). **5** draw together into a small space (*tucked its head under its wing*). □ **tuck in** *colloq.* eat heartily. **tuck-in** *n. colloq.* a large meal. **tuck into** (or **tuck it away**) *colloq.* eat (food) heartily. **tuck shop** a canteen, esp. in a school, selling snacks, lunches, drinks, etc.

Tucker[1], Albert (1914–99), AO, Australian painter, pioneer of expressionist and surrealist painting in Australia.

Tucker[2], James (*c.*1808–88), Australian convict and writer (born in England): he is credited with having written three plays and the important early convict novel *Ralph Rashleigh*.

tucker[1] *n. Aust.* **1** food. **2** the means of subsistence. • *v.* **1** eat, take a meal. **2** supply (a person) with food (*he tuckered us for the trip*). □ **make tucker** earn just enough for the bare means of subsistence (*with the few opals I find I just make tucker*). **tucker bag** a bag for provisions, esp. as carried by a swagman etc. (*what's that jolly jumbuck you've got in your tucker bag?*). **tucker box** a box for the storing or conveyance of provisions, esp. as used by a swagman etc. (*the dog shat in the tucker box five miles from Gundagai*).

tucker[2] *v.* (esp. in *passive*; often foll. by *out*) *colloq.* tire, exhaust (*I'm tuckered after all that hard yakka*).

tuckeroo / tuk-uh-**roo** / *n.* a small to medium tree of northern and eastern Australia, cultivated as an ornamental. (¶ Probably Yagara.)

Tuckwell, Barry (Emmanuel) (1931–), AC, Australian virtuoso French horn player and conductor, the leading exponent of the instrument in the world.

Tudawali, Robert (1930–67), Australian Aboriginal film and television actor, famous for his lead role in *Jedda*.

Tudor *adj.* of the royal family of England 1485–1603 or this period; of the architectural style of this period.

Tuesday the day of the week following Monday. • *adv. colloq.* **1** on Tuesday. **2** (**Tuesdays**) on Tuesdays; each Tuesday.

tufa / **tyoo**-fuh / *n.* **1** porous limestone rock formed round springs of mineral water. **2** = TUFF.

tuff *n.* rock formed from volcanic ashes.

tuffet *n.* a clump of grass; a small mound.

tuft *n.* a bunch of threads, grass, feathers, hair, etc. held or growing together at the base. □ **tufty** *adj.*

tufted *adj.* having a tuft or tufts; (of a bird) having a tuft of projecting feathers on its head.

Tu Fu / too **foo** / (712–70), a major (according to some, the greatest) Chinese poet, noted for his bitter satiric poems attacking social injustice and corruption.

tug *v.* (**tugged, tugging**) **1** pull vigorously or with great effort. **2** tow by means of a tugboat. • *n.* **1** a vigorous pull. **2** a sudden strong emotion (*felt a tug as I watched him go*). **3** a small powerful boat for towing others. □ **tug of war 1** a contest in which two teams hold a rope at opposite ends and pull until one hauls the other over a central point. **2** a decisive or severe contest or struggle.

tugboat *n.* a tug (= TUG *n.* sense 3).

tuition / tyoo-**ish**-uhn / *n.* teaching, esp. if paid for; the fee for this.

tula *n.* (also **tuhla, tula adze**) *Aust.* an Aboriginal tool, having a curved wooden handle and a sharp stone chisel-edge, used for woodworking. (¶ Arabana)

tulip *n.* **1** a garden plant growing from a bulb, with a large cup-shaped flower on a tall stem. **2** *Aust.* = TULIPWOOD. □ **tulip oak** *Aust.* = BOOYONG.

tulipwood *n.* (also **tulip**) **1** a medium rainforest tree of NSW and Qld, having perfumed flowers and red and yellow fruit; often cultivated as an ornamental. **2** the beautifully figured wood of this tree, highly prized for cabinetmaking etc.

tulle / tyool / *n.* a fine silky net used for veils and dresses.

tumble *v.* **1** fall (or cause to fall) suddenly or headlong. **2** fall in value or amount. **3** roll over and over in a disorderly way. **4** move or rush in a hasty careless way (*tumbled into bed*). **5** throw or push carelessly in a confused mass. **6** rumple or disarrange. **7** (often foll. by *to*) *colloq.* realise or grasp the meaning of something (*I eventually tumbled to their plan*). **8** perform acrobatic feats, esp. somersaults. • *n.* **1** a tumbling fall. **2** an untidy state. **3** a somersault or other acrobatic feat. ☐ **tumble-drier** (also **tumble-dryer**) a machine for drying washing in a heated drum that rotates; **tumble-dry** *v.*

tumbledown *adj.* falling or fallen into ruin, dilapidated.

tumbler *n.* **1** a drinking glass with no handle or foot. **2** an acrobat.

tumbleweed *n. US & Aust.* a plant that forms a globular bush which breaks off in late summer and is tumbled about by the wind.

tumbrel *n.* (also **tumbril**) *archaic* an open cart, esp. used to carry condemned people to the guillotine during the French Revolution.

tumescent / tyoo-**mes**-uhnt / *adj.* **1** becoming tumid; swelling. **2** beginning to swell and harden as a response to sexual stimulation (*his nipples were tumescent; a tumescent penis*). ☐ **tumescence** *n.*

tumid / **tyoo**-muhd / *adj.* **1** (of parts of the body) **a** swollen, inflated. **b** enlarged, rigid, as a response to sexual stimulation (*tumid nipples; a tumid penis*). **2** (of style) pompous. ☐ **tumidity** *n.*

tummy *n. colloq.* the stomach.

tumour / **tyoo**-muh / *n.* (also **tumor**) an abnormal mass of new tissue growing on or in the body.

tumult / **tyoo**-mult / *n.* **1** an uproar. **2** a state of confusion and agitation (*her mind was in a tumult*).

tumultuous / tyoo-**mul**-choo-uhs / *adj.* noisy; crowded, confused, and disorderly. ☐ **tumultuously** *adv.*

tumulus / **tyoo**-myuh-luhs / *n.* (*pl.* **tumuli**) an ancient burial mound.

tun *n.* a large cask for wine or beer etc.

tuna / **tyoo**-nuh / *n.* (*pl.* **tuna** or **tunas**) **1** any of various large edible sea fish of tropical and warm waters (including a number of Australian varieties). **2** its flesh as food.

tundra *n.* the vast level treeless Arctic regions where the subsoil is frozen.

tune *n.* a melody. • *v.* **1** put (a musical instrument) in tune. **2** tune in (a radio receiver etc.). **3** adjust (an engine) to run smoothly. ☐ **in tune 1** playing or singing at the correct musical pitch. **2** (usu. foll. by *with*) harmonising or in sympathy with one's company, surroundings, etc. **out of tune** not in tune. **to the tune of** *colloq.* to the considerable sum of (*received compensation to the tune of $5000*). **tune in** set a radio receiver to the right wavelength. **tune up 1** (of an orchestra) bring instruments to the correct pitch. **2** bring to the most efficient condition.

tuneful *adj.* melodious, having a pleasing tune. ☐ **tunefully** *adv.*

tuneless *adj.* not melodious, without a tune. ☐ **tunelessly** *adv.*

tuner *n.* **1** a person who tunes pianos etc. **2** a radio receiver, esp. as part of a hi-fi system.

tungoo / **tung**-goo, **tung**, also **tungo** / *n.* (also **tungo**) central Australian name for the BOODIE. (¶ Western Desert language)

tungsten / **tung**-stuhn / *n.* a chemical element (symbol W), a heavy grey metallic substance used for the filaments of electric lamps and in making steel.

tunic *n.* **1** a close-fitting jacket worn as part of a uniform. **2** a woman's light hip-length garment. **3** a loose garment reaching to the hips or knees.

tuning fork *n.* a steel device like a two-pronged fork, which produces a note of fixed pitch when struck.

Tunis / **tyoo**-nuhs / the capital of Tunisia.

Tunisia / tyoo-**niz**-ee-uh / a republic in North Africa. ☐ **Tunisian** *adj.* & *n.*

tunnel *n.* an underground passage dug by an animal; a passage for a road or railway through a hill or under a river etc. • *v.* (**tunnelled**, **tunnelling**) dig a tunnel; make a tunnel through. ☐ **tunnel vision 1** vision which is poor outside the centre of the normal field of vision. **2** *colloq.* an inability to grasp the wider implications of a situation.

tup *n.* a male sheep, a ram. • *v.* (of a ram) copulate with (a ewe) (*an old black ram is tupping your white ewe*).

tupong / **too**-pong / *n.* (also **toopong**) a small, chiefly marine food fish of south-eastern Australia. Also called *congolli*. (¶ Kuurn Kopan Noot)

tuppence = TWOPENCE.

turban *n.* **1** a man's headdress of a scarf wound round a cap, worn esp. by Muslims and Sikhs. **2** a woman's hat resembling this.

turbid *adj.* **1** (of liquids) muddy, not clear. **2** confused, disordered (*a turbid imagination*). ☐ **turbidity** / ter-**bid**-uh-tee / *n.*

■ **Usage** *Turbid* is sometimes confused with *turgid* which means 'swollen, inflated; pompous'.

turbine / **ter**-buyn / *n.* a machine or motor driven by a wheel that is turned by a flow of water or gas (*gas turbines*).

turbocharger *n.* a supercharger driven by a turbine powered by the engine's exhaust gases.

turbojet *n.* **1** a turbine engine that delivers its power in the form of a jet of hot gases. **2** an aircraft driven by this instead of by propellers.

turboprop *n.* **1** a jet engine in which a turbine is used as a turbojet and also to drive a propeller. **2** an aircraft driven by this.

turbulent / **ter**-byuh-luhnt / *adj.* **1** in a state of commotion or unrest; (of air or water) moving violently and unevenly. **2** unruly, riotous. ☐ **turbulently** *adv.* **turbulence** *n.*

turd *n. coarse colloq.* **1** a ball or lump of excrement (*dog turds*). **2** a contemptible person.

tureen / tyoo-**reen** / *n.* a deep covered dish from which soup is served.

turf *n.* (*pl.* **turfs** *or* **turves**) **1** short grass and the surface layer of earth bound together by its roots. **2** a piece of this cut from the ground. **3** a slab of peat for fuel. **4** (**the turf**) horse racing; a racecourse. • *v.* lay (ground) with turf. ☐ **turf out** *colloq.* throw out.

turgid / **ter**-juhd / *adj.* **1** swollen or distended and not flexible (*his belly is quite turgid*). **2** (of language or style) pompous, not flowing easily. ☐ **turgidly** *adv.* **turgidity** / ter-**jid**-uh-tee / *n.*

■ **Usage** *Turgid* is sometimes confused with *turbid* which means 'muddy, not clear; confused'.

Turk *n.* **1** a native or inhabitant of Turkey. **2** a member of a Central Asian people from whom the Ottomans derived, speaking a Turkic language (*see* TURKI). **3** *offens.* a ferocious or wild person.

Turkey a republic in western Asia.

turkey *n.* (*pl.* **turkeys**) **1** a large bird reared for its flesh. **2** its flesh as food. **3** *Aust.* = BRUSH TURKEY (*see* BRUSH²). **4** *Aust.* = PLAIN TURKEY (sense 1)—*see* PLAIN. **5** *colloq.* a stupid or inept person. ☐ **head over turkey** head over heels. **talk turkey** *colloq.* talk frankly; get down to business. **turkey bush 1** a tea-tree of Cape York, Qld, having gnarled and twisted limbs, smooth purple bark, and white flowers. **2** (also **Ellangowan poison bush, emu bush**) any of many shrubs of the mainland Australian genus *Eremophila*, the leaves of some species being poisonous to stock and the berries of others being relished by emus. (¶ *Turkey bush* a common Australian name for any low, branching bush or tree on which brush turkeys may roost.) **turkey-bush scrub** a name applied to vast areas of Cape York Peninsula covered by turkey bushes. **turkey lolly** sugar syrup spun into threadlike brittle strands (often mistakenly called *fairy floss*): a confection originating in India. **turkey nest** (in full **turkey nest dam** *or* **turkey nest tank**) *Aust.* a reservoir built in flat country where there is no natural run-off, having high earthen walls and so resembling the mound of the brush turkey.

Turki / **ter**-kee / *adj.* of a group of languages and peoples including Turkish. • *n.* this group. ☐ **Turkic** *adj.*

Turkish *adj.* of Turkey or its people or language. • *n.* the language of Turkey. ☐ **Turkish bath** a hot-air or steam bath followed by washing or massage; a building for this. **Turkish delight** a sweet consisting of lumps of flavoured gelatine coated in powdered sugar.

Turkistan (also **Turkestan**) a vast region of central Asia east of the Caspian Sea, inhabited mainly by Turkic peoples.

Turkmenistan a republic of western central Asia, lying between the Caspian Sea and Afghanistan.

turmeric / **ter**-muh-rik / *n.* **1** a tropical Asian plant of the ginger family. **2** its aromatic powdered rhizome used as a spice in Sri Lankan and Indian curries, rice dishes, etc., or for yellow dye.

turmoil / **ter**-moil / *n.* a state of great disturbance or confusion.

turn *v.* **1** move or cause to move round a point or axis. **2** change or cause to change in position so that a different side becomes uppermost or outermost. **3** give a new direction to, take a new direction (*the river turns north at this point; turn the hose on them; our thoughts turned to Christmas*). **4** go or move or travel round, go to the other side of (*turn the corner*). **5** pass (a certain hour or age) (*it's turned midnight; I have no desire to turn 40*). **6** cause to go, send or put (*turn the horse into the field*). **7** change or become changed in nature, form, or appearance etc. (*the prince turned into a frog, a change very much for the better; turned the book into a play*). **8** make or become sour (*the milk has turned*). **9** make or become nauseated (*it turns my stomach*). **10** shape in a lathe. **11** give an elegant form to (*he knows how to turn a compliment*). **12** translate (*turn it into French*). **13** *colloq.* change one's religion (esp. of an Anglican becoming a Catholic) (*some Anglican priests are thinking of turning*). • *n.* **1** turning; being turned; a turning movement. **2** a change of direction or condition etc.; the point at which this occurs. **3** an angle; a bend or corner in a road. **4** character or tendency (*he's of a mechanical turn of mind*). **5** service of a specified kind (*did me a good turn*). **6** an opportunity or obligation etc. that comes to each of a number of people or things in succession (*wait your turn*). **7** a short performance in an entertainment. **8** *colloq.* an attack of illness; a momentary nervous shock. **9** *colloq.* a display of anger, peevishness, etc.; a fuss etc. **10** *Aust. colloq.* a party. ☐ **to a turn** so as to be cooked perfectly. **turn-about** an abrupt change of policy etc. **turn it up!** *colloq.* fair go!; you must be joking! **turn off 1** enter a side road. **2** stop the flow or operation of by turning a tap or switch. **3** *colloq.* cause to lose interest. **turn-off** *n.* **1** a turning off a road. **2** *colloq.* something that causes disgust or loss of interest. **turn of speed** ability to go fast. **turn on 1** start the flow or operation of by turning a tap or switch. **2** *colloq.* excite (a person) sexually or with drugs etc. (*he really turns me on*). **3** (of events etc.) depend on. **turn-on** *n. colloq.* a person or thing that causes sexual excitement. **turn out 1** expel. **2** turn off (an electric light etc.). **3** equip or dress (*well turned out*). **4** produce by work. **5** empty and search or clean (*turn out the attic*). **6** prove to be, be eventually (*we'll see how things turn out*). **turn over 1** hand over; transfer. **2** consider carefully (*turn it over in your mind*). **turn round** unload and reload (a ship, aircraft, etc.) so that it is ready to leave again. **turn the corner** pass a critical point safely, e.g. in an illness. **turn the tables** reverse a situation and put oneself in a superior position. **turn turtle** capsize. **turn up 1** discover or reveal; be found; make one's appearance; happen or present itself. **2** increase the volume or flow of (sound, gas, or heat etc.) by turning a knob or tap. **turn-up** *n.* **1** a turned-up part, esp. at the lower end of trouser legs. **2** *colloq.* an unexpected event. **a turn-up for the books** *colloq.* an unexpected turn of fortune; a surprise.

turnaround *n.* **1 a** unloading and reloading between trips. **b** receiving, processing, and sending out again; progress through a system. **2** the reversal of an opinion or tendency.

turncoat *n.* a person who changes his or her principles or allegiances etc.

Turner, Ethel (Sibyl) (1872–1958), Australian writer (born in England), noted esp. for her novel *Seven Little Australians*.

turner *n.* a person who works with a lathe.

turning point *n.* a point at which a decisive change takes place.

turnip *n.* **1** a plant with a round white root. **2** its root as a vegetable.

turnkey *n. archaic* a jailer.

turnout *n.* **1** the number of people attending a meeting, voting at an election, etc. **2** a set or display of equipment, clothes, etc.

turnover *n.* **1** turning over. **2** a small pie of pastry folded over a filling. **3** the amount of money turned over in a business. **4** the rate at which goods are sold. **5** the rate at which workers leave and are replaced (*a rapid turnover of staff*).

turnpike *n. hist.* a toll gate.

turnstile *n.* a device for admitting people to a building etc. one at a time, with barriers that revolve as each person passes through.

turntable *n.* **1** a circular revolving plate on which records are played. **2** a circular revolving platform for turning a railway locomotive.

Turon / **tyoo**-ron / a river in NSW, a tributary of the Macquarie. The valley of the Turon was a major goldfield in the 1850s and 1860s.

turpentine / **ter**-puhn-tuyn / *n.* **1** an oil distilled from the resin of certain trees, used for thinning paint and as a solvent. **2** a tall tree of NSW and Qld having a resin in its timber which acts as a preservative; the reddish timber of this tree, valued for its durability even in sea water. **3** a turpentine bush. ☐ **turpentine bush** any of several very resinous or aromatic Australian shrubs.

turpitude / **ter**-puh-tyood / *n.* depravity, wickedness.

turps *n. colloq.* **1** oil of turpentine. **2** *Aust.* any alcoholic liquor. ☐ **on the turps** *Aust.* drinking alcoholic liquor to excess.

turquoise / **ter**-kwoiz / *n.* **1** a greenish-blue semiprecious stone. **2** a greenish-blue colour. • *adj.* of this colour.

turret *n.* **1** a small tower-like projection on a building or defensive wall. **2** a low revolving structure protecting a gun and gunners in a ship, aircraft, fort, or tank. **3** a rotating holder for various dies and cutting tools in a lathe or drill etc. ☐ **turreted** *adj.*

turrum / **tu**-ruhm / *n.* any of several large marine fish of northern Australia valued as game fish. (¶ Possibly from an Aboriginal language.)

turtle *n.* a sea-creature resembling a tortoise, with flippers used in swimming; its flesh used for soup. ☐ **turn turtle** *see* TURN. **turtle dove** a wild dove of Europe, Asia, etc. (two species of which, the *spotted turtle dove* and the *laughing turtle dove*, have been introduced into Australia), noted for its soft cooing and for its affection towards its mate and young. **turtle-neck** a high round close-fitting neck on a knitted garment.

Tuscan *n.* **1** an inhabitant of Tuscany. **2** the form of Italian spoken in Tuscany; standard Italian. • *adj.* of Tuscany or the Tuscans.

Tuscany a region of west central Italy; capital Firenze (Florence).

tush *n.* **1** a long pointed tooth, esp. a canine tooth of a horse. **2** an elephant's short tusk.

tusk *n.* one of the pair of long pointed teeth that project outside the mouth in the elephant, walrus, etc.

tusker *n.* an animal, esp. an elephant, with well-developed tusks.

tussle *n.* a struggle, a conflict. • *v.* take part in a tussle.

tussock *n.* a tuft or clump of grass. ☐ **tussocky** *adj.*

tut = TUT-TUT.

Tutankhamen / too-tuhn-**kah**-muhn / (also **Tutankhamun**) (*c.*1370–1352 BC), an Egyptian pharaoh who came to the throne while still a boy, whose tomb and its rich contents were found virtually intact in 1922.

tute *n. colloq.* a tutorial.

tutelage / **tyoo**-tuh-lij / *n.* **1** guardianship. **2** the state or duration of being under this. **3** tuition.

tutelary / **tyoo**-tuh-luh-ree / *adj.* **1 a** serving as a guardian. **b** of a guardian (*tutelary authority*). **2** giving protection to a place, a person etc. (*tutelary saint*).

tutor *n.* **1** a private teacher. **2** a university teacher directing the studies of assigned undergraduates, usu. in small groups. • *v.* act as tutor to, teach.

tutorial / tyoo-**taw**-ree-uhl / *adj.* of or as a tutor. • *n.* a period of tuition given by a college or university tutor.

Tutsi / **tuut**-see / *n.* (*pl.* **Tutsi** *or* **Tutsis**) a member of a Bantu-speaking people who form a minority

tutti of the population of Rwanda and Burundi but who formerly dominated the Hutu majority.

tutti *adv.* & *adj. Music* with all voices or instruments together.

tut-tut *interj.* (also **tut**) an exclamation of impatience, annoyance, or rebuke. • *v.* express disapproval with this exclamation.

Tutu, Desmond (Mpilo) (1931–), South African Anglican archbishop and anti-apartheid activist, winner of the Nobel Peace Prize in 1984.

tutu / **too**-too / *n.* a ballet dancer's short skirt made of layers of stiffened projecting frills.

Tuvalu / too-**vah**-loo / an independent country of the Commonwealth consisting of a group of nine islands in the western Pacific. ☐ **Tuvaluan** *adj.* & *n.*

tuxedo / tuk-**see**-doh / *n.* (*pl.* **tuxedos** or **tuxedoes**) a dinner jacket; evening dress including this.

TV *abbr.* **1** television. **2** transvestite.

twaddle *n.* silly writing or talk; nonsense. • *v.* indulge in this.

Twain, Mark (pseudonym of Samuel Langhorne Clemens) (1835–1910), American writer, author of *The Adventures of Tom Sawyer* and *The Adventures of Huckleberry Finn.*

twain *adj.* & *n. archaic* two.

twang *n.* **1** a sharp ringing sound like that made by a tense wire when plucked. **2** a nasal intonation in speech. • *v.* make or cause to make a twang.

'twas *archaic* = it was.

twat / twot / *n. coarse colloq.* **1** a contemptible person; an idiot (*silly twat!*). **2** the female genitals.

tweak *v.* **1** pinch and twist sharply; pull with a sharp jerk. **2** make fine adjustments to (a mechanism). **3** *Cricket* (esp. of a left-arm leg-spinner) impart spin (to the ball). • *n.* a sharp pinch, twist, or pull.

twee *adj.* (**tweer** / **twee**-uh /, **tweest** / **twee**-uhst /) affectedly dainty or quaint. ☐ **tweely** *adv.* **tweeness** *n.* (¶ A childish pronunciation of SWEET.)

tweed *n.* **1** a twilled usu. woollen material, often woven of mixed colours. **2** (**tweeds**) **a** clothes made of tweed. **b** *colloq.* trousers.

'tween *archaic* = BETWEEN.

tweet *n.* the chirp of a small bird. • *v.* make a tweet.

tweeter *n.* a small loudspeaker for accurately reproducing high-frequency signals.

tweezers *n.pl.* small pincers for picking up small objects, plucking out individual hairs, etc.

twelfth *adj.* & *n.* **1** next after eleventh. **2** any of twelve equal parts of a thing. ☐ **twelfth man** a reserve member of a cricket team. ☐☐ **twelfthly** *adv.*

Twelfth Day 6 January, the twelfth day after Christmas, the festival of the Epiphany.

Twelfth Night 5 January, the Eve of Epiphany, formerly the last day of Christmas festivities.

twelve *adj.* & *n.* **1** one more than eleven (12, XII). **2** twelve o'clock. ☐ **twelve apostles** lousy jacks (*see* LOUSY). **twelve-note** *adj.* (also **twelve-tone**) (of music) using the twelve chromatic notes of the octave arranged in a chosen order without a conventional key.

twelvefold *adj.* & *adv.* **1** twelve times as much or as many. **2** consisting of twelve parts.

twenty *adj.* & *n.* **1** twice ten (20, XX). **2** (**twenties**) the numbers from twenty to twenty-nine, esp. the years of a century or of a person's life, or degrees of temperature. ☐ **twenty-eight** a parrot of south-western WA with predominantly green plumage, black head, red bar on forehead, and yellow collar: its call resembles the word 'twenty-eight' in sound. Also called *Port Lincoln parrot.* **twenty-twenty vision 1** normal good vision. **2** *colloq.* clear perception, understanding, or hindsight. **twenty-two** a line across the ground 22 metres from either goal in hockey and Rugby football; the space enclosed by this. ☐☐ **twentieth** *adj.* & *n.*

'twere *archaic* = it were.

twerp *n.* (also **twirp**) *colloq.* a stupid or objectionable person.

twice *adv.* **1** two times, on two occasions. **2** in a double amount or degree (*twice as strong*).

twiddle *v.* twirl or handle aimlessly; twist (a thing) quickly to and fro. • *n.* **1** a slight twirl. **2** a twirled mark or sign. ☐ **twiddly** *adj.*

twig *n.* a very small thin branch of a tree or shrub. • *v.* (**twigged, twigging**) *colloq.* realise or grasp (the meaning of something) (*he hasn't yet twigged what is going on*). ☐ **twiggy** *adj.*

twilight *n.* **1** light from the sky when the sun is below the horizon (esp. after sunset); the period of this. **2** a faint light. **3** a period of decline or destruction. • *adj.* of or relating to or resembling twilight (*twilight hour; his twilight years*). ☐ **twilight of the gods** *Scand. myth.* the destruction of the gods and of the world in conflict with the powers of evil. **twilight zone** an area or concept which is undefined or halfway between two other areas or concepts.

twilit *adj.* dimly lit by twilight.

twill *n.* a textile fabric woven so that parallel diagonal lines are produced.

'twill *archaic* = it will.

twin *n.* **1** either of two children or animals born at one birth. **2** either of two people or things that are exactly alike. **3** (**the Twins**) a sign of the zodiac, Gemini. • *adj.* being a twin or twins (*twin brothers*). • *v.* (**twinned, twinning**) **1 a** join intimately together. **b** (foll. by *with*) combine as a pair. **2** give birth to twins. ☐ **twin beds** a pair of single beds.

twine *n.* strong thread or string made of strands of fibre twisted together. • *v.* **1** form (a string etc.) by twisting strands; weave (a garland etc.). **2** (often foll. by *with*) garland (a brow etc.). **3** (often

twinge foll. by *round* or *about*) coil or wind. **4** (of a plant) grow round and support etc.

twinge / twinj / *n*. a sharp brief local pain or a pang.

twink *n. colloq.* (in the male gay community) a slim, attractive male in his late teens or early twenties.

twinkle *v.* **1** shine with a light that flickers rapidly, sparkle. **2** (of the eyes) be bright or sparkling with amusement. **3** (of the feet in dancing etc.) move with short rapid movements. •*n.* a twinkling light, look, or movement. ☐ **in a twinkle** (*or* **in the twinkling of an eye**) in an instant.

twinset *n.* a woman's matching jumper and cardigan. ☐ **twinset and pearls** *colloq.* (of a woman) conservative in dress and attitudes.

twirl *v.* twist lightly or rapidly. •*n.* **1** a twirling movement. **2** a twirled mark or sign; a flourish made with a pen.

twirp alternative spelling of TWERP.

twist *v.* **1** wind (strands etc.) round each other so as to form a single cord; interweave. **2** make by doing this. **3** pass or coil round something. **4** give a spiral form to, e.g. by turning the ends in opposite directions. **5** take a spiral or winding form or course; turn or bend round (*the road twisted and turned; he twisted round in his seat*). **6** rotate or revolve; cause to do this. **7** wrench out of its normal shape (*I twisted my ankle*). **8** distort the meaning of (*tried to twist his words into an admission of guilt*). **9** (as **twisted** *adj.*) (of a person's mind) emotionally unbalanced; perverted. **10** dance the twist. •*n.* **1** twisting; being twisted. **2** something formed by twisting; a turn in a twisting course. **3** (**the twist**) a popular 1960s dance with vigorous twisting of the body and hips. **4** a peculiar tendency of mind or character. **5** an unexpected development of events, esp. in a story etc. (*a surprising twist at the end*). ☐ **round the twist** *colloq.* crazy. ☐☐ **twisty** *adj.*

twister *n. colloq.* **1** an untrustworthy person, a swindler. **2** a tornado.

twit *v.* (**twitted**, **twitting**) reproach or taunt, usu. good-humouredly. •*n. colloq.* a foolish person.

twitch *v.* **1** pull with a light jerk (*twitched aside the curtain*). **2** (of features, muscles, etc.) quiver or contract spasmodically. •*n.* **1** a sudden involuntary contraction or movement. **2** a sudden pull or jerk. **3** *colloq.* a state of nervousness.

twitcher *n. colloq.* a birdwatcher who tries to see as many species as possible.

twitchy *adj. colloq.* nervous. ☐ **twitchiness** *n.*

twitter *v.* **1** (esp. of a bird) make a series of light chirping sounds. **2** talk rapidly in an anxious or nervous way. •*n.* **1** an act of twittering. **2** *colloq.* a tremulously excited state. ☐ **twittery** *adj.*

'twixt *archaic* = BETWIXT.

two *adj.* **1** one more than one (2, II). **2** (in Aboriginal English) both. •*n.* **1** one more than one (2, II). **2** two o'clock. ☐ **put two and two together** infer from known facts. **two-dimensional 1** having or appearing to have length and breadth but no depth. **2** lacking substance; superficial. **two-edged 1** having two cutting edges. **2** cutting both ways, having two interpretations. **two-faced** insincere, deceitful. **two-handed 1** having, using, or requiring the use of two hands. **2** (of a card game) for two players. **two-piece** a suit of clothes or a swimsuit consisting of two separate parts. **two-ply** *adj.* made of two strands or layers. **two-pot screamer** *Aust. colloq.* a person who is easily or quickly affected by alcoholic liquor. **two-step** a dance in march or polka time. **two-stroke** *adj.* (of an engine) having its power cycle completed in one up-and-down movement of the piston. **two-time** *v. colloq.* be unfaithful to (a lover); double-cross. **two-timer** *n.* a person who two-times. **two-tooth** *Aust.* (meat from) a sheep from one to two years old, having two full-grown permanent teeth. **two-way** *adj.* **1** involving two directions or two participants. **2** *Aust.* (in Aboriginal English) involving both Aboriginal and European culture (*two-way medicine; a two-way school*). **3** (of a radio) capable of transmitting and receiving signals.

two-bob esp. *Aust. colloq. n.* (formerly) a sum of two shillings. •*adj.* cheap; of little consequence. ☐ **have two-bob each way** arrange one's affairs so that one cannot lose; hedge one's bets. **mad as a two-bob watch** completely crazy; idiotic.

twofold *adj. & adv.* **1** twice as much or as many. **2** consisting of two parts.

twopence / *tup*-uhns / *n.* (also **tuppence**) **1** *hist.* the sum of two pence. **2** (esp. with *negative*) a thing of little value; a small amount (*I wouldn't give tuppence for his chances*).

twosome *n.* two people together, a couple or pair.

'twould *archaic* = it would.

two-up *n.* *Aust.* a gambling game, institutionalised in Australia, in which two coins are tossed in the air after bets have been placed on a showing of two heads or two tails. •*adj.* of or pertaining to this game. ☐ **two-up ring** the site of a two-up game. **two-up school 1** a group of people who have assembled to play two-up. **2** a place where such an assemblage is regularly held.

tycoon *n.* a wealthy and influential businessman or industrialist, a magnate. (¶ Japanese, = great lord.)

tying *see* TIE.

tyke *n.* (also **tike**) **1** a dog. **2** a small child. **3** *Aust. colloq.* a Catholic. (¶ Sense 3 is probably an alteration of *Teague*, a nickname for an Irishman.)

Tyler, Wat (d. 1381), the leader of the Peasants' Revolt in England.

tympani alternative spelling of TIMPANI.

tympanum / **tim**-puh-nuhm / *n.* (*pl.* **tympanums** *or* **tympana**) **1** the middle ear. **2** the eardrum. **3** *Archit.* a recessed triangular area, esp. over a doorway.

type *n.* **1** a class of people or things that have characteristics in common, a kind. **2** a typical example or instance. **3** a person, thing, or event exemplifying a class or group (*he's the perfect type of the Australian ocker; he's not the marrying type*). **4** *colloq.* a person of specified character (*a quiet type; he's not my type*). **5** *Theology* a foreshadowing in the Old Testament of a thing, person, or event in the New Testament (*Jonah in the whale's belly is a type of Christ in the tomb*). **6** (in *combinations*) made of, resembling, or functioning as (*a ceramic-type material; a cheddar-type cheese*). **7** a letter or figure etc. used in printing; a set, supply, kind, or size of these (*printed in large type*). •*v.* **1** classify according to type. **2** write using a typewriter or keyboard. **3** typecast.

typecast *v.* (**typecast**, **typecasting**) cast (an actor) repeatedly in the kind of part which he or she has the reputation of playing or which seems to fit his or her personality.

typeface *n.* a set of printing types in one design.

typescript *n.* a typewritten document.

typesetter *n.* **1** a person who sets type for printing. **2** a machine for doing this. ☐ **typeset** *v.* **typesetting** *n.*

typewriter *n.* a machine for producing characters similar to those of print by pressing keys which cause raised metal letters etc. to strike the paper, usu. through an inked ribbon.

typewritten *adj.* written with a typewriter.

typhoid *n.* (in full **typhoid fever**) a serious infectious feverish disease that attacks the intestines, caused by bacteria taken into the body in food or drink.

typhoon / tuy-**foon** / *n.* a violent hurricane in the western Pacific or East Asian seas.

typhus *n.* an infectious disease with fever, a purple rash, headaches, and usu. delirium.

typical *adj.* **1** having the distinctive qualities of a particular type of person or thing, serving as a representative specimen (*a typical outback pub; a typical Kiwi*). **2** characteristic (*he answered with typical curtness; typical of him to refuse*). ☐ **typically** *adv.*

typify / **tip**-uh-fuy / *v.* (**typified**, **typifying**) be a representative specimen of.

typist *n.* a person who types, esp. one employed to do so.

typo *n.* (*pl.* **typos**) *colloq.* a printing error.

typography / tuy-**pog**-ruh-fee / *n.* **1** the art or practice of printing. **2** the style or appearance of printed matter. ☐ **typographical** / tuy-puh-**graf**-i-kuhl / *adj.*

tyrannical / tuh-**ran**-i-kuhl / *adj.* as or like a tyrant, obtaining obedience by force or threats. ☐ **tyrannically** *adv.*

tyrannise / **ti**-ruh-nuyz / *v.* (also **-ize**) rule as or like a tyrant.

tyrannosaurus / tuh-ran-uh-**saw**-ruhs / *n.* (*pl.* **tyrannosauruses**) (also **tyrannosaur**) a very large dinosaur that walked on its hind legs.

tyrannous / **ti**-ruh-nuhs / *adj.* tyrannical.

tyranny / **ti**-ruh-nee / *n.* **1** government by a tyrannical ruler. **2** oppressive or tyrannical use of power.

tyrant / **tuy**-ruhnt / *n.* a ruler or other person who uses power in a harsh or oppressive way, insisting on absolute obedience.

tyre *n.* a rubber covering fitted round the rim of a wheel to absorb shocks, usu. filled with air.

tyro alternative spelling of TIRO.

tzatziki / tsat-**see**-kee / *n.* a Greek side dish of yoghurt with cucumber, garlic, and often mint.

U

U *symbol* uranium. • *adj.* / yoo / *colloq.* upper-class, supposedly characteristic of upper-class speech or behaviour. • *n.* / oo / in Burma (Myanmar) a title of respect before a man's proper name.

UAE *abbr.* United Arab Emirates.

UAI *abbr. Aust.* Universities Admission Index.

ubiquitous / yoo-**bik**-wuh-tuhs / *adj.* being everywhere; widespread. ▫ **ubiquity** *n.*

U-boat *n.* a German submarine, esp. in the Second World War.

u.c. *abbr.* upper case.

udder *n.* a baglike milk-secreting organ of a cow, ewe, or female goat, with two or more teats.

uey / **yoo**-ee / *n.* (also **U-ie, uy, youee**) *Aust. colloq.* a U-turn (*did an illegal uey and was nabbed*).

ufella / **yoo**-fel-uh / *pron.* (*pl.* **ufellas**) *Aust.* (in Aboriginal English) = YOU.

UFO (also **ufo**) *abbr.* & *n.* (*pl.* **ufos**) unidentified flying object, a term often applied to supposed vehicles ('flying saucers') piloted by beings from outer space.

Uganda / yoo-**gan**-duh / a republic in East Africa. ▫ **Ugandan** *adj.* & *n.*

ugari / yoo-guh-ree / *n.* (also **yugari**) Qld name for the PIPI. (¶ Yagara)

ugh / uh, ug / *interj.* **1** an exclamation of disgust or horror (*she punctuated my story with expressive ughs*). **2** the sound of a cough or grunt.

ugh boot *n.* (also **ug boot**) *Aust.* trademark a boot made of sheepskin with the wool on the inside.

ugli *n.* (*pl.* **uglis** or **uglies**) trademark a citrus fruit that is a hybrid of grapefruit and tangerine.

uglify *v.* make ugly.

ugly *adj.* (**uglier, ugliest**) **1** unpleasant to the eye, ear, or mind, etc. (*an ugly scar; an ugly sneer*). **2** unpleasantly suggestive; discreditable (*ugly rumours*). **3** hostile and threatening (*the crowd was in an ugly mood*). **4** morally repulsive (*an ugly vice*). ▫ **ugly customer** an unpleasantly formidable person. **ugly duckling** a person who at first seems unpromising but later becomes much admired or very able. (¶ Like the cygnet in the brood of ducks in Hans Andersen's story.) ▫▫ **uglily** *adv.* **ugliness** *n.*

UHF *abbr.* ultrahigh frequency.

U-ie alternative spelling of UEY.

UK *abbr.* United Kingdom.

Ukraine / yoo-**krayn** / a republic in eastern Europe to the north of the Black Sea, formerly a republic of the USSR. ▫ **Ukrainian** *adj.* & *n.*

ukulele / yoo-kuh-**lay**-lee / *n.* a small four-stringed Hawaiian guitar.

Ulan Bator / oo-lahn **bah**-taw / the capital of Mongolia.

ulcer *n.* **1** an open sore on the surface of the body or one of its organs. **2** a corrupting influence etc ▫ **ulcerous** *adj.*

ulcerate *v.* cause an ulcer in or on; become affected with an ulcer. ▫ **ulceration** *n.*

Ulm, Charles Thomas Philippe (1898–1934) Australian pioneer airman who broke several records as co-pilot with Charles KINGSFORD SMITH.

ulna / **ul**-nuh / *n.* the thinner and longer of the two long bones in the forearm; the corresponding bone in an animal's foreleg or a bird's wing. ▫ **ulnar** *adj.*

Ulster 1 a former province of Ireland comprising the present Northern Ireland and the counties of Cavan, Donegal, and Monaghan (which are now in the Republic of Ireland). **2** (used loosely) = NORTHERN IRELAND.

ult. *abbr.* ultimo.

ulterior *adj.* **1** not obvious or admitted; hidden, secret (*ulterior motives*). **2** situated beyond.

ultimate *adj.* **1** last or last possible, final (*the ultimate deterrent*). **2** basic, fundamental (*the ultimate cause*). **3** difficult to better; being the 'last word' in its class (*the 'Oxford English Dictionary' is the ultimate dictionary*). • *n.* **1** (**the ultimate**) the best (*the ultimate in dictionaries*). **2** a final or basic fact or principle. ▫ **ultimately** *adv.*

ultimatum / ul-tuh-**may**-tuhm / *n.* (*pl.* **ultimatums** or **ultimata**) a final demand or statement of terms, rejection of which may lead to hostility or conflict.

ultimo *adj.* (in commerce) of last month (*the 3rd ultimo*). (¶ Latin, = in the last (*mense* month).)

ultra *adj.* extreme, esp. in religion or politics. • *n.* a person who is such.

ultra- *comb. form* **1** extremely, excessively (*ultra-conservative; ultra-modern*). **2** beyond; on the other side of (*ultrasonic*).

ultra-high *adj.* (of frequency) in the range of 300 to 3000 MHz.

ultralight *n.* a small lightweight usu. one-seater aircraft whose fuselage is in an open framework without an enclosed cockpit.

ultramarine / ul-truh-muh-**reen** / *adj.* & *n.* bright deep blue.

ultramicroscope *n.* a kind of optical microscope used to detect particles smaller than a wavelength of light.

ultramicroscopic *adj.* **1** too small to be seen with an ordinary microscope. **2** of or involving the use of the ultramicroscope.

ultramontane *adj.* **1** situated beyond the Alps. **2** supporting the supreme authority of the pope. • *n.* **1** a person from the other side of the Alps. **2** a supporter of the supreme authority of the pope.

ultrasonic / ul-truh-**son**-ik / *adj.* (of sound waves) with a pitch above the upper limit of normal human hearing. • *n.* (**ultrasonics**) the science and application of ultrasonic waves. ☐ **ultrasonically** *adv.*

ultrasound *n.* **1** ultrasonic waves. **2** (also as *adj.*) the use of such waves as a diagnostic medical procedure.

ultraviolet *adj.* **1** (of radiation) having a wavelength that is slightly shorter than that of visible light rays at the violet end of the spectrum. **2** of or using this radiation (*an ultraviolet lamp*). ☐ **ultraviolet protection factor** (of sunscreen, clothing, etc.) the degree of protection against the harmful ultraviolet rays of the sun.

ultra vires / ul-truh **vuy**-reez, uul-trah **veer**-rayz / *adv. & adj.* beyond one's legal power or authority. (¶ Latin)

ululate / **yoo**-luh-layt / *v.* howl, wail. ☐ **ululation** *n.*

Uluru / oo-luh-**roo** / a vast red sandstone rock mass (formerly called 'Ayers Rock') in the south-west of the NT. It is an Aboriginal sacred site, the Pitjantjatjara people believing that ten different sacred beings created the rock's topography. In 1985 inalienable freehold title to the rock and Uluru National Park surrounding it was handed over to the traditional Aboriginal owners, since when the park has been administered by a special board which supervises the increasing volume of tourism while protecting Aboriginal sacred sites and safeguarding the rights of the owners.

Uluru-Kata Tjuta National Park / kah-tuh **joo**-tuh / a World Heritage listed park occupying 132,566 ha on the edge of the Gibson and Great Victoria deserts, 463 km south-west of Alice Springs.

Ulysses / yoo-**lis**-eez / the Roman name for Odysseus. ☐ **Ulysses butterfly** a large swallowtail butterfly of northern Qld and elsewhere, having brilliant blue, black-bordered wings.

um *interj.* expressing hesitation or a pause in speech.

umbel / **um**-buhl / *n.* a flower cluster with stalks springing from a common centre to form a flat or curved surface. ☐ **umbellate** *adj.*

umbelliferous / um-buh-**lif**-uh-ruhs / *adj.* bearing umbels.

umber *n.* a natural colouring matter like ochre but darker and browner. ☐ **burnt umber** reddish-brown.

umbilical / um-**bil**-uh-kuhl, um-buh-**luy**-kuhl / *adj.* of the navel. ☐ **umbilical cord 1** the long cordlike structure connecting the placenta to the navel of a foetus. **2** an essential connecting line or cable.

umbilicus / um-**bil**-uh-kuhs, um-buh-**luy**-kuhs / *n.* (*pl.* **umbilici** / -suy / or **umbilicuses**) the navel.

umbra *n.* (*pl.* **umbrae** / **um**-bree / *or* **umbras**) the dark central part of the shadow cast by the earth or the moon in an eclipse, or of a sunspot.

umbrage / **um**-brij / *n.* a feeling of being offended. ☐ **take umbrage** take offence.

umbrella *n.* **1** a collapsible ribbed canopy mounted on a central pole or stick, used as protection against rain, strong sun, etc. **2** protection, patronage. **3** (usu. used as *adj.*) coordinating or supervising (*an umbrella organisation*). ☐ **umbrella fern** any of several ferns of eastern Australia and elsewhere, the fronds of which produce an umbrella-like appearance. **umbrella tree** a tree of Qld and the NT, having jade-green leaflets radiating umbrella-like from a single point, red leaf stalks, and scarlet flowers. Also called *schefflera*.

umlaut / **uum**-lowt / *n.* **1** a mark (¨) used over a vowel, esp. in German, to indicate a change in its pronunciation. **2** such a vowel change, e.g. German *Mann*, *Männer*, English *man*, *men*.

Umm al Qaiwain / kuy-**wayn** / an emirate belonging to the federation of United Arab Emirates.

umpire *n.* **1** a person enforcing rules and settling disputes in various sports. **2** a person chosen to arbitrate between disputants, or to see fair play. • *v.* act as umpire in (a game or dispute etc.).

umpteen *adj. colloq.* very many. ☐ **umpteenth** *adj.*

umpy *n.* (also **umpie**, **ump**) *colloq.* an umpire.

UN *abbr.* United Nations.

un- *comb. form* **1** not (as in *uncertain*, *uncertainty*). **2** reversing the action indicated by the simple verb (as in *unlock* = release from being locked).

■ **Usage** The number of words with this prefix is almost unlimited, and many of those whose meaning is obvious are not listed below.

'un / uhn / *pron. colloq.* one (*that's a good'un*).

unabashed *adj.* not abashed, brazen. ☐ **unabashedly** *adv.*

unabated *adj.* not abated; undiminished.

unable *adj.* not able; lacking ability.

unabridged *adj.* complete; not abridged.

unaccompanied *adj.* **1** not accompanied. **2** without musical accompaniment.

unaccomplished *adj.* **1** not accomplished; uncompleted (*all these unaccomplished tasks*). **2** lacking accomplishment, skill, expertise (*some quite unaccomplished singing*).

unaccountable *adj.* **1** unable to be explained or accounted for. **2** unpredictable or strange in behaviour. **3** not accountable for one's actions etc. ☐ **unaccountably** *adv.*

unaccounted *adj.* (often foll. by *for*) unexplained; not included in an account.

unaccustomed *adj.* **1** (usu. foll. by *to*) not accustomed. **2** unusual (*an unaccustomed silence*).

unadorned *adj.* plain.

unadulterated *adj.* **1** pure. **2** complete, utter (*unadulterated nonsense*).

unadvised *adj.* **1** indiscreet; rash. **2** without advice. ☐ **unadvisedly** *adv.*

unaffected *adj.* **1** not affected (*he was completely unaffected by the hullabaloo*). **2** free from affectation. ☐ **unaffectedly** *adv.*

Unaipon, David (1873–1967), Australian Aboriginal writer and inventor. He worked on many inventions and patented a modified handpiece for shearing. He was the first Aborigine to have a book published in Australia, his chief work being *Native Legends* (1929). ☐ **David Unaipon Award** an award for Aboriginal and Torres Strait Islander writers, instituted in 1988.

unalienated *adj.* (of land) not transferred in respect of ownership.

unaligned *adj.* **1** = NON-ALIGNED. **2** not physically aligned.

unalike *adj.* not alike; different (*they are not unalike in their attitude to racism*).

unalloyed / un-uh-**loid**, un-**al**-oid / *adj.* not alloyed; pure (*unalloyed joy*).

unambiguous *adj.* not ambiguous; forthright, clear, or definite in meaning (*his opposition to racism is quite unambiguous*). ☐ **unambiguously** *adv.*

unanimous / yoo-**nan**-uh-muhs / *adj.* all agreeing in an opinion or decision; (of an opinion or decision etc.) held or given by everyone. ☐ **unanimously** *adv.* **unanimity** / yoo-nuh-**nim**-uh-tee / *n.*

unannounced *adj.* not announced; without warning (of arrival etc.).

unanswerable *adj.* **1** unable to be disputed or disproved (*an unanswerable case*). **2** unable to be answered (*unanswerable questions*). ☐ **unanswerably** *adv.*

unappealing *adj.* unattractive.

unapproachable *adj.* **1** not approachable; remote, inaccessible. **2** (of a person) unfriendly.

unarmed *adj.* not armed, without weapons.

unashamed *adj.* **1** feeling no guilt. **2** bold, blatant. ☐ **unashamedly** *adv.*

unasked *adj.* & *adv.* not asked; without being requested.

unassailable *adj.* unable to be attacked or challenged; impregnable. ☐ **unassailably** *adv.*

unassuming *adj.* modest, unpretentious.

unattached *adj.* **1** not attached to another thing, person, or organisation. **2** not engaged, married, or involved in a relationship.

unattended *adj.* **1** (of a child, a vehicle, etc.) having no person in charge of it. **2** (foll. by *to*) not being attended to or dealt with.

unattributable *adj.* (esp. of published information) that cannot be or is not allowed to be attributed to a source etc.

un-Australian *adj.* not in accordance with characteristics, attitudes, etc. said to be typical of the Australian community.

unavailing *adj.* achieving nothing; ineffectual. ☐ **unavailingly** *adv.*

unavoidable *adj.* inevitable. ☐ **unavoidably** *adv.*

unaware *adj.* **1** (usu. foll. by *of* or *that*) not aware (*unaware of his presence*). **2** insensitive; unperceptive. • *adv.* = UNAWARES. ☐ **unawareness** *n.*

unawares *adv.* **1** unexpectedly (*met them unawares*). **2** inadvertently (*dropped it unawares*).

unbacked *adj.* **1** having no back or no backing. **2** (in betting) having no backers.

unbalanced *adj.* **1** (of wheels, a mechanism, etc.) not in proper balance. **2** emotionally or mentally unstable. **3** biased (*an unbalanced report*).

unbar *v.* (**unbarred**, **unbarring**) **1** unlock, open. **2** remove a bar from (a gate etc.).

unbearable *adj.* not bearable, unable to be endured. ☐ **unbearably** *adv.*

unbeatable *adj.* impossible to defeat or surpass.

unbeaten *adj.* not defeated; (of a record etc.) not surpassed.

unbecoming *adj.* **1** not suited to the wearer (*an unbecoming hat*). **2** not fitting; indecorous (*it's quite unbecoming for you to visit him so often*).

unbeknown *adj.* (also **unbeknownst**) (foll. by *to*) without the knowledge of (*they did it unbeknown to us*).

unbelief *n.* lack of belief, esp. religious belief. ☐ **unbeliever** *n.* **unbelieving** *adj.*

unbelievable *adj.* not believable, incredible. ☐ **unbelievably** *adv.*

unbend *v.* (**unbent**, **unbending**) **1** change or become changed from a bent position. **2** become relaxed or affable.

unbending *adj.* **1** inflexible. **2** firm, austere; refusing to alter one's demands. **3** relaxing from strain, activity, or formality.

unbiased *adj.* (also **unbiassed**) not biased, impartial.

unbidden *adj.* not commanded or invited (*arrived unbidden*).

unblinking *adj.* **1** not blinking. **2** steadfast; not hesitating (*an unblinking determination*). **3** stolid; cool, unemotional (*an unblinking response to the charges*). ☐ **unblinkingly** *adv.*

unblushing *adj.* **1** shameless. **2** frank.

unbolt *v.* release (a door etc.) by drawing back the bolt.

unborn *adj.* not yet, or never to be, born (*his unborn child; unborn hopes*).

unbosom *v.* ☐ **unbosom oneself** reveal one's thoughts or feelings; unburden oneself.

unbounded *adj.* boundless, without limits (*unbounded optimism*).

unbridle *v.* **1** remove a bridle from (a horse). **2** remove constraints from (one's tongue, a person, etc.).

unbridled *adj.* unrestrained (*unbridled insolence*).

unbroken *adj.* **1** not broken. **2** untamed (*an unbroken horse*). **3** uninterrupted (*unbroken sleep; unbroken sunshine*). **4** not beaten (*an unbroken record*).

unbuckle *v.* release the buckle of (a strap, shoe, etc.).

unburden *v.* remove a burden from. ☐ **unburden oneself** relieve oneself or one's conscience, esp. by confessing or disclosing something (*he unburdened himself to her*).

unbutton *v.* **1** unfasten (a shirt etc.) by taking the buttons out of the buttonholes. **2** unbutton the clothes of (a person). **3** *colloq.* relax from tension or formality; become communicative (*he had a drink and began to unbutton*).

uncalled-for *adj.* (of a remark, action, etc.) rude, unnecessary.

uncanny *adj.* **1** seemingly supernatural; strange or frightening. **2** extraordinary, beyond what is normal (*they predicted the results with uncanny accuracy*). ☐ **uncannily** *adv.* **uncanniness** *n.*

unceasing *adj.* not ceasing; continuous. ☐ **unceasingly** *adv.*

unceremonious *adj.* **1** abrupt; discourteous (*an unceremonious dismissal*). **2** lacking ceremony or formality; informal (*he gave his workers a warm and unceremonious welcome to his house*). ☐ **unceremoniously** *adv.*

uncertain *adj.* **1** not known or knowing certainly (*uncertain what it means; the result is uncertain*). **2** not to be depended on (*his aim is uncertain*). **3** changeable, erratic (*an uncertain temper*). **4** not fully confident or assured, tentative (*his approach was uncertain*). ☐ **in no uncertain terms** clearly and forcefully. ☐ ☐ **uncertainly** *adv.* **uncertainty** *n.*

unchallengeable *adj.* not challengeable; unassailable.

uncharitable *adj.* **1** making severe or unsympathetic judgments about people or acts. **2** not generous.

uncharted *adj.* not mapped or surveyed.

unchecked *adj.* **1** not checked. **2** unrestrained (*unchecked violence*).

uncial / **un**-see-uhl / *adj.* of or written in a script with rounded unjoined letters resembling modern capitals, found in manuscripts of the 4th–8th centuries. • *n.* an uncial letter, style, or manuscript.

uncircumcised *adj.* not circumcised.

uncivil *adj.* ill-mannered, impolite. ☐ **uncivilly** *adv.*

uncivilised *adj.* (also **-ized**) **1** not civilised. **2** rough, uncultured.

unclad *adj.* not clad; naked.

unclasp *v.* **1** loosen the clasp(s) of. **2** release the grip of (a hand etc.).

unclassified *adj.* **1** not classified. **2** (of government information) not secret.

uncle *n.* **1** a brother or brother-in-law of one's father or mother. **2** *Aust.* (in Aboriginal English) a male of one's parents' generation; a community elder.

unclean *adj.* **1** not clean. **2** unchaste. **3** religiously impure; forbidden.

unclear *adj.* **1** (of a liquid) not clear. **2** not easy to understand. **3** (of a person) uncertain (*I'm unclear as to what you mean*).

unclench *v.* **1** release (clenched hands etc.). **2** (of hands etc.) become relaxed or open.

Uncle Sam *colloq.* a personification of the federal government or citizens of the US.

unclothe *v.* **1** remove the clothes from. **2** expose; reveal. ☐ **unclothed** *adj.*

unclouded *adj.* **1** clear, bright. **2** untroubled (*unclouded serenity*).

uncluttered *adj.* not cluttered; austere, simple.

uncoloured *adj.* **1** having no colour. **2** not influenced; impartial. **3** not exaggerated.

uncomfortable *adj.* **1** not comfortable. **2** uneasy, disquieting (*an uncomfortable silence*).

uncommitted *adj.* **1** not committed. **2** not attached to any specific political cause or group.

uncommon *adj.* **1** not common, unusual. **2** remarkably great etc. (*has an uncommon fear of spiders*).

uncommunicative *adj.* not inclined to give information or an opinion etc., silent.

uncomplaining *adj.* not complaining; resigned. ☐ **uncomplainingly** *adv.*

uncomplimentary *adj.* insulting.

uncompromising / un-**kom**-pruh-muy-zing / *adj.* not allowing or seeking compromise, inflexible. ☐ **uncompromisingly** *adv.*

unconcern *n.* lack of concern; indifference; apathy. ☐ **unconcerned** *adj.* **unconcernedly** *adv.*

unconditional *adj.* not subject to conditions or limitations; complete (*unconditional surrender*). ☐ **unconditionally** *adv.*

unconditioned reflex *n.* an instinctive response to a stimulus.

unconfined *adj.* not confined; boundless.

unconnected *adj.* **1** not physically joined. **2** not connected or associated. **3** (of speech etc.) disconnected; not joined in order or sequence (*unconnected ideas*). **4** not related by family ties.

unconscionable / un-**kon**-shuh-nuh-buhl / *adj.* **1** having no conscience. **2** against one's conscience. **3** unreasonably excessive (*an unconscionable length of time*). ☐ **unconscionably** *adv.*

unconscious *adj.* **1** not conscious, not aware (*fell unconscious; unconscious of any change*). **2** done or spoken etc. without conscious intention (*unconscious prejudice*). • *n.* the unconscious mind, that part of the mind whose content is not normally accessible to the conscious mind but which is found to affect behaviour, emotions, etc. ☐ **unconsciously** *adv.* **unconsciousness** *n.*

unconsidered *adj.* **1** not considered; disregarded. **2** (of a response etc.) immediate; not premeditated.

unconstitutional *adj.* in breach of a political constitution or procedural rules. ☐ **unconstitutionally** *adv.*

uncontrolled *adj.* not controlled; unrestrained; unchecked.

unconventional *adj.* not bound by convention or custom; unusual; unorthodox. ☐ **unconventionality** *n.*

unconvincing *adj.* not convincing, unable to convince; (of an excuse, attempt, etc.) feeble, unimpressive.

uncool *adj. colloq.* not stylish or fashionable.

uncoordinated *adj.* **1** not coordinated. **2** (of a person's movements etc.) clumsy.

uncountable *adj.* **1** inestimable, immense (*uncountable wealth*). **2** (of a noun) not used in the plural or with the indefinite article (e.g. *milk*).

uncounted *adj.* **1** not counted. **2** very many; innumerable.

uncouth / un-**kooth** / *adj.* awkward or clumsy in manner; boorish; uncultured; rough. ☐ **uncouthly** *adv.* **uncouthness** *n.*

uncover *v.* **1** remove the covering from. **2** reveal or expose (*their deceit was uncovered*).

uncritical *adj.* **1** not critical; complacently accepting. **2** not in accordance with the principles of criticism.

unction / ungk-shuhn / *n.* **1 a** anointing with oil etc., esp. as a religious rite (*extreme unction*). **b** the oil etc. so used. **2** soothing words or thought. **3** excessive or insincere flattery. **4** emotional fervency; the pretence of this.

unctuous / ungk-choo-uhs / *adj.* having an oily manner, smugly earnest or virtuous; unpleasantly flattering. ☐ **unctuously** *adv.* **unctuousness** *n.*

uncured *adj.* **1** not cured (*he prayed for a miracle but he's still uncured*). **2** (of ham etc.) not salted or smoked.

uncut *adj.* **1** not cut. **2** (of a book) with the pages sealed or untrimmed; (of a book, film, etc.) complete, uncensored; (of a gem) not shaped by cutting; (of fabric) with the loops of the pile not cut. **3** *colloq.* (of the penis, or of a male) uncircumcised. **4** *colloq.* (of drugs, esp. heroin) undiluted, unadulterated.

undead *adj.* (esp. of a vampire etc. in fiction) technically dead but still animate. • *n.* (prec. by *the*; treated as *pl.*) those who are undead.

undeceive *v.* free (a person) from a mistaken belief, deception, or error.

undecided *adj.* **1** not yet settled or certain (*the point is still undecided*). **2** not yet having made up one's mind.

undeclared *adj.* **1** not publicly announced or acknowledged (*an undeclared war*). **2** (esp. of taxable income or dutiable goods) not declared.

undefined *adj.* **1** not defined. **2** not clearly marked; vague, indefinite.

undemanding *adj.* not demanding; easily done or satisfied (*this book makes undemanding reading*).

undemonstrative *adj.* not emotionally expressive; reserved.

undeniable *adj.* impossible to deny, undoubtedly true. ☐ **undeniably** *adv.*

under *prep.* **1** in or to a position lower than; below; beneath (*under the table*). **2** less than (*it's under a kilometre from here*). **3** inferior to, of lower rank than (*no one under a bishop*). **4** governed or controlled by (*the firm prospered under him; under oath*). **5** undergoing (*the road is under repair*). **6** in accordance with (*it is permissible under our agreement*). **7** designated or indicated by (*writes under an assumed name*). **8** in the category of (*file it under 'Estimates'*). **9** (of land) planted with (*50 hectares under wheat*). **10** powered by (sail, steam, etc.). • *adv.* **1** in or to a lower position or subordinate condition (*kept him under*). **2** in or into a state of unconsciousness (*they will put you under before they operate*). **3** below a certain quantity, rank, or age etc. (*children of five and under*). • *adj.* lower, situated underneath (*the under layers*). ☐ **under age** (also **under-age**) *adj.* carried on by a person not old enough, esp. for some legal right (*under-age drinking*). **under way** in motion; in progress.

under- *comb. form* **1** below, beneath (*underseal*). **2** lower, subordinate (*under-manager*). **3** insufficient, incompletely (*undercooked*).

underachieve *v.* do less well than was expected, esp. academically. ☐ **underachiever** *n.*

underarm *adj.* & *adv.* **1** in the armpit. **2** (in cricket etc.) bowling or bowled with the hand brought forward and upwards and not raised above shoulder level. **3** (in tennis) with the racquet moved similarly.

underbelly *n.* the undersurface of an animal, vehicle, etc., esp. as being vulnerable to attack.

underbid *v.* (**underbid**, **underbidding**) **1** make a lower bid than (another person). **2** bid less than is justified in the game of bridge.

undercarriage *n.* an aircraft's landing wheels and their supports; the supporting frame of a vehicle.

undercharge *v.* **1** charge too low a price. **2** give too little charge to (an electric battery, a gun, etc.).

underclass *n.* the lowest social group in a community, consisting of its least privileged members (e.g. the poor and the unemployed).

underclothes *n.pl.* underwear.

underclothing *n.* underclothes collectively.

undercoat *n.* **1** a layer of paint under a finishing coat; the paint used for this. **2** (in animals) a coat of hair under another. •*v.* apply an undercoat of paint.

undercook *v.* cook insufficiently.

undercover *adj.* **1** doing things secretly, done secretly. **2** engaged in spying by working among those to be spied on (*undercover agents*).

undercurrent *n.* **1** a current that is below a surface or below another current. **2** an underlying feeling, influence, or trend (*an undercurrent of hostility in the crowd*).

undercut *v.* (**undercut, undercutting**) **1** cut away the part below. **2** sell or work for a lower price than (another person). **3** render unstable or less firm; undermine. •*n.* **1** the underside of sirloin. **2** a hairstyle in which the hair is cut very short from the nape of the neck upwards to a certain extent at the back and sides and the rest is left long; not tapered.

underdaks *n.pl. Aust. colloq.* underpants, briefs.

underdeveloped *adj.* **1** not fully developed; immature. **2** (of a country) not having reached its full economic potential. ▫ **underdevelopment** *n.*

underdog *n.* **1** an oppressed person. **2** the loser or the expected loser in a fight, sporting competition, etc.

underdone *adj.* **1** undercooked. **2** (of a sportsperson etc.) not at the peak of fitness or preparedness.

underemployed *adj.* not fully employed.

underestimate *v.* / un-duhr-**es**-tuh-mayt / make too low an estimate of. •*n.* / un-duhr-**es**-tuh-muht / an estimate that is too low. ▫ **underestimation** *n.*

underexpose *v.* expose (film etc.) for too short a time or with insufficient light. ▫ **underexposure** *n.*

underfed *adj.* not sufficiently fed.

underfelt *n.* felt for laying under a carpet.

underfoot *adv.* **1** on the ground, under one's feet. **2** so as to obstruct or inconvenience.

undergarment *n.* a piece of underwear.

undergo *v.* (**underwent, undergone, undergoing**) experience, endure, be subjected to (*the new aircraft underwent intensive trials*).

undergraduate *n.* a university student studying for a first degree.

underground *adv.* / un-duh-**grownd** / **1** under the ground. **2** in secret; into secrecy or hiding. •*adj.* / **un**-duh-grownd / **1** under the surface of the ground. **2** secret, subversive. **3** artistically or morally unconventional or experimental (*underground literature*). •*n.* / **un**-duh-grownd / **1** an underground railway. **2** a secret subversive group or activity. ▫ **underground mutton** *Aust. jocular* rabbit as food. **underground orchid** either of two completely subterranean orchids (the only such in the world), having dark-coloured flowers and living on decayed vegetable matter, one endemic in south-western WA, the other in eastern Australia.

undergrowth *n.* dense shrubs etc., esp. in a forest.

underhand *adj.* / **un**-duh-hand / **1** done or doing things in a sly or secret way. **2** (in cricket etc.) underarm. •*adv.* / un-duh-**hand** / in an underhand manner. ▫ **underhanded** *adj.*

underlay[1] *v.* (**un-duh-lay** / (**underlaid, underlaying**) lay something under (a thing) as a support or in order to raise it. •*n.* / **un**-duh-lay / a thing so laid (esp. felt, rubber, etc., under a carpet).

underlay[2] / un-duh-**lay** / *see* UNDERLIE.

underlie *v.* (**underlay, underlain, underlying**) **1** lie or exist beneath. **2** be the basis of (a theory etc.), be the facts that account for (*the underlying reasons for her behaviour*).

underline *v.* **1** draw a line under (a word etc.) to give emphasis, to indicate that italic type should be used, etc. **2** emphasise, stress.

underling *n.* a subordinate.

undermentioned *adj.* mentioned at a later place in a book etc.

undermine *v.* **1** injure (a person, reputation, health, etc.) secretly or insidiously. **2** weaken, injure, or wear out (health, confidence, etc.) imperceptibly or insidiously. **3** wear away the base of (*the banks were undermined*). **4** make an excavation under.

undermost *adj.* & *adv.* furthest underneath.

underneath *prep.* beneath, below; on the inside of (a thing). •*adv.* at, in, or to a position underneath something. •*n.* a lower surface or part. •*adj.* lower.

underpants *n.pl.* a man's undergarment covering the genitals and buttocks.

underpart *n.* a lower or subordinate part.

underpass *n.* a road etc. that passes under another; a subway.

underpay *v.* (**underpaid, underpaying**) pay too little to (a person) or in discharge of (a debt).

underpin *v.* (**underpinned, underpinning**) **1** support (a building) from beneath, with masonry etc. **2** support or strengthen (a theory, relationship, etc.).

underplant *v.* (usu. foll. by *with*) plant or cultivate the ground about (a tall plant) with smaller ones.

underplay *v.* **1** make little of. **2** (of an actor) perform with deliberate restraint.

underprivileged *adj.* less privileged than others, not enjoying the normal standard of living or rights in a community.

underproof *adj.* containing less alcohol than proof spirit does.

underrate *v.* have too low an opinion of. ▫ **underrated** *adj.*

underscore *v.* underline; emphasise.

undersell *v.* (**undersold, underselling**) **1** sell at a lower price than (another seller). **2** fail to communicate forcefully enough the virtues of (a thing or person, esp. oneself through a lack of confidence in oneself).

undersexed *adj.* having less than the normal degree of sexual desires.

undershoot *v.* (**undershot**, **undershooting**) (of an aircraft) land short of (*the plane undershot the runway*).

undershot *adj.* (of a lower jaw) projecting beyond the upper jaw.

underside *adj.* the side or surface underneath.

undersigned *adj.* who has or have signed at the bottom of this document (*we, the undersigned*).

undersized *adj.* of less than the usual size.

underslung *adj.* **1** supported from above. **2** (of a vehicle chassis) hanging lower than the axles.

underspend *v.* (**underspent**, **underspending**) spend too little.

understaffed *adj.* having less than the necessary number of staff.

understand *v.* (**understood**, **understanding**) **1** perceive the meaning of (words, a person, a language, a subject, etc.) (*I understand you better than you think; I can't understand trigonometry*). **2** know the significance or cause of (*don't understand why he came*). **3** sympathise with, know how to deal with (*I quite understand your difficulty; ask her, she understands*). **4** become aware from information received, draw as a conclusion (*I understand she is in Paris; am I to understand that you refuse?*). **5** supply (a missing word or words) mentally (*before 'ready?' the words 'are you' are understood*).

understandable *adj.* able to be understood. ❑ **understandably** *adv.*

understanding *n.* **1** the ability to understand or think; intelligence. **2** an individual's perception of a situation etc. **3** tolerance or sympathy. **4** harmony in opinion or feeling (*I think I've disturbed the good understanding between them*). **5** an informal or preliminary agreement (*reached an understanding*). • *adj.* having or showing insight, good judgment, or sympathy. ❑ **understandingly** *adv.*

understate *v.* **1** express (an idea) in very restrained terms. **2** represent (an amount) as being less than it really is. ❑ **understated** *adj.* **understatement** *n.*

understeer *v.* (of a car etc.) have a tendency to turn less sharply than was intended. • *n.* this tendency.

understorey *n.* (*pl.* **understoreys**) **1** a layer of vegetation beneath the main canopy of a forest. **2** the plants forming this.

understudy *n.* a person who studies the part in a play or the duties etc. of another in order to be able to take his or her place at short notice. • *v.* (**understudied**, **understudying**) act as understudy to; learn (a part etc.) as understudy.

undersubscribed *adj.* without sufficient subscribers, participants, etc.

undertake *v.* (**undertook**, **undertaken**, **undertaking**) **1** agree or promise to do something, make oneself responsible for (*undertook the cooking*). **2** guarantee (*we cannot undertake that you will make a profit*).

undertaker *n.* one whose business is to prepare the dead for burial or cremation and make arrangements for funerals.

undertaking *n.* **1** work etc. undertaken, an enterprise. **2** a promise or guarantee.

undertone *n.* **1** a low or subdued tone (*they spoke in undertones*). **2** a colour that modifies another (*pink with mauve undertones*). **3** an underlying quality or feeling (*a threatening undertone*).

undertow / **un**-duh-toh / *n.* a current below the surface of the sea, moving in an opposite direction to the surface current.

undervalue *v.* put too low a value on; underestimate.

underwater *adj.* situated, used, or done beneath the surface of water. • *adv.* beneath the surface of water.

underwear *n.* clothes worn under others, esp. next to the skin; underclothes.

underweight *adj.* weighing less than is normal, required, or permissible.

underwent *see* UNDERGO.

underwhelm *v. jocular* fail to impress. (¶ Alteration of OVERWHELM.)

underworld *n.* **1** professional criminals and their associates. **2** (in mythology) the abode of the dead under the earth.

underwrite *v.* (**underwrote**, **underwritten**, **underwriting**) **1** sign and accept liability under (an insurance policy, esp. for ships), guaranteeing payment in the event of loss or damage. **2** undertake to finance (an enterprise). **3** undertake to buy all the unsold stock in (a company etc.). ❑ **underwriter** *n.*

undescended *adj.* (of a testicle) remaining in the abdomen instead of descending normally into the scrotum.

undeserved *adj.* not deserved as reward or punishment. ❑ **undeservedly** / un-duh-**zer**-vuhd-lee / *adv.*

undesirable *adj.* not desirable, objectionable. • *n.* a person who is undesirable to a community. ❑ **undesirably** *adv.* **undesirability** *n.*

undetermined *adj.* **1** not yet decided. **2** undiscovered.

undies *n.pl. colloq.* underwear; underpants.

undigested *adj.* **1** not digested. **2** (of information, facts, etc.) not properly arranged or considered.

undine / **un**-deen / *n.* a female water spirit.

undiplomatic *adj.* tactless.

undivided *adj.* not divided or shared; whole, entire (*I had his undivided attention*).

undo *v.* (**undid**, **undone**, **undoing**) **1** unfasten (a coat, button, parcel, etc.); unfasten the clothing of

undoing

(a person). **2** annul, cancel the effect of (*cannot undo the past*). **3** ruin the prospects, reputation, or morals of.

undoing *n.* bringing or being brought to ruin; a cause of this (*drink was his undoing*).

undone *adj.* **1** not fastened (*your fly is undone*). **2** not done (*left the work undone*). **3** *archaic* brought to ruin or destruction (*I am undone, alas!*).

undoubted *adj.* certain, beyond doubt or dispute. □ **undoubtedly** *adv.*

undreamed *adj.* (also **undreamt**) (often foll. by *of*) not imagined, not thought to be possible (*an undreamed of coincidence*).

undress *v.* **1** take off one's clothes; take the clothes off (another person). **2** *Aust. jocular* shear (a sheep). •*n.* **1** being naked or scantily clad. **2** ordinary or casual dress, esp. as opposed to full dress or uniform.

undressed *adj.* **1** not, or no longer, dressed. **2** (of food) without a dressing. **3** (of leather etc.) not treated.

undue *adj.* **1** excessive, disproportionate (*undue severity*). **2** not suitable or proper (*undue influence on an impressionable mind*). □ **unduly** *adv.*

undulate / **un**-dyoo-layt / *v.* have or cause to have a wavy movement or appearance. □ **undulation** *n.*

undying *adj.* never-ending; lifelong (*undying love*).

unearned *adj.* not earned. □ **unearned income** income from interest on investments or rent from property rather than from working.

unearth *v.* **1** uncover or obtain from the ground by digging. **2** bring to light, find by searching.

unearthly *adj.* **1** not earthly. **2** supernatural, mysterious and frightening. **3** *colloq.* absurdly early or inconvenient (*getting up at this unearthly hour*). □ **unearthliness** *n.*

uneasy *adj.* **1** not comfortable (*passed an uneasy night*). **2** not confident, worried. **3** worrying (*an uneasy suspicion that all was not well*). □ **uneasily** *adv.* **unease** *n.* **uneasiness** *n.*

uneconomic *adj.* not profitable.

uneconomical *adj.* not economical; wasteful.

unedifying *adj.* distasteful, degrading.

unemployable *adj.* unfit for paid employment, e.g. because of lack of abilities or qualifications. □ **unemployability** *n.*

unemployed *adj.* **1** having no employment, temporarily without a paid job. **2** not in use. □ **the unemployed** *n.* (treated as *pl.*) those who are without a paid job.

unemployment *n.* **1** the condition of being unemployed. **2** the lack of employment in a country, region, etc. □ **unemployment benefit** a regular government payment made to an unemployed person.

unencumbered *adj.* **1** not encumbered with a burden etc. **2** (of an estate) having no liabilities (e.g. a mortgage). **3** (of a motor vehicle) not subject to financial obligation.

unendurable *adj.* too bad to be borne.

unequal *adj.* **1** not equal. **2** (of work or achievements etc.) not of the same quality throughout. **3** not with equal advantage to both sides, not well matched (*an unequal contest*). **4** (foll. by *to*) unable to deal with the demands of a particular job or task. □ **unequally** *adv.*

unequalled *adj.* superior to all others.

unequivocal / un-ee-**kwiv**-uh-kuhl, un-uh- / *adj.* clear and unmistakable, not ambiguous. □ **unequivocally** *adv.*

unerring *adj.* making no mistake (*with unerring accuracy*). □ **unerringly** *adv.*

UNESCO / yoo-**nes**-koh / *abbr.* (also **Unesco**) United Nations Educational, Scientific & Cultural Organisation. (¶Acronym)

unethical *adj.* not ethical, unscrupulous in business or professional conduct. □ **unethically** *adv.*

uneven *adj.* **1** not level or smooth. **2** varying, not uniform. **3** unequal (*an uneven contest*). □ **unevenly** *adv.* **unevenness** *n.*

unexampled *adj.* having no precedent (*an unexampled opportunity*).

unexceptionable *adj.* with which no fault can be found; entirely satisfactory (*unexceptionable behaviour*). □ **unexceptionably** *adv.*

■ **Usage** Do not confuse with *unexceptional*.

unexceptional *adj.* not exceptional, quite ordinary.

■ **Usage** Do not confuse with *unexceptionable*.

unexpected *adj.* not expected, surprising. □ **unexpectedly** *adv.*

unexpressed *adj.* not spoken about or made known (*unexpressed fears*).

unexpurgated *adj.* (esp. of a text etc.) not expurgated; complete.

unfailing *adj.* not failing or dwindling; constant, reliable (*unfailing resources; his unfailing good humour*).

unfair *adj.* **1** not equitable or honest (*obtained by unfair means; unfair business practices*). **2** not impartial or according to the rules (*an unfair decision; unfair play*). □ **unfairly** *adv.* **unfairness** *n.*

unfaithful *adj.* **1** not loyal; not keeping to one's promise. **2** having committed adultery. □ **unfaithfully** *adv.* **unfaithfulness** *n.*

unfamiliar *adj.* **1** strange, unknown (*unfamiliar territory*). **2** (foll. by *with*) not used to or acquainted with (*being a pom, I'm unfamiliar with many Australian words and expressions*). □ **unfamiliarity** *n.*

unfasten *v.* **1** make or become loose. **2** open the fastening(s) of (*unfasten your seat belts*). **3** detach (*unfasten the lifeboats*).

unfathomable *adj.* incapable of being fathomed or fully understood (*the Trinity is an unfathomable mystery to me*).

unfazed *adj. colloq.* untroubled; not disconcerted.

unfeeling *adj.* **1** lacking the power of sensation or sensitivity. **2** unsympathetic, not caring about others' feelings. ◻ **unfeelingly** *adv.* **unfeelingness** *n.*

unfettered *adj.* **1** released from fetters. **2** not subject to the usual controls or limitations (*unfettered corporate greed*).

unfinancial *adj.* **1** insolvent. **2** not having paid a subscription (*some members are unfinancial*).

unfit *adj.* **1** unsuitable (*he's unfit for the job*). **2** not in perfect health or physical condition. •*v.* (often foll. by *for*) make unsuitable (*his known belief that women must be subservient to their husbands unfits him to try this case of rape in marriage*).

unfitting *adj.* not suitable, unbecoming.

unflagging *adj.* tireless, persistent.

unflappable *adj. colloq.* remaining calm in a crisis, not getting into a flap. ◻ **unflappability** *n.*

unfledged *adj.* **1** (of a person) inexperienced. **2** (of a young bird) not yet fledged.

unfold *v.* **1** open the fold or folds of, spread (a thing) or become spread out. **2** reveal (thoughts etc.) (*unfolded his desire for me*). **3** become opened out (*watched the bud unfold in slow motion*). **4** develop (*as the story unfolded*).

unforced *adj.* **1** easy, natural. **2** not compelled or constrained.

unforeseen *adj.* not foreseen; unexpected.

unforgettable *adj.* not able to be forgotten; memorable, wonderful.

unfortunate *adj.* **1** having bad luck. **2** unsuitable, regrettable (*a most unfortunate choice of words*). **3** miserable, unhappy. •*n.* an unfortunate person. ◻ **unfortunately** *adv.*

unfounded *adj.* (of beliefs, fears, etc.) without good reasons or evidence (*unfounded fears; an unfounded rumour*).

unfreeze *v.* (**unfroze**, **unfrozen**, **unfreezing**) **1** thaw, cause to thaw. **2** remove restrictions on (financial assets etc.).

unfriendly *adj.* **1** not friendly. **2** unhelpful or harmful (used esp. as a *comb. form* in compound adjectives, in which the preceding noun names the person or thing hindered or harmed, e.g. *environment-unfriendly*). ◻ **environment unfriendly** (of a person, organisation, product, etc.) harmful to the environment, not ecologically sound. **ozone-unfriendly** see OZONE. **user-unfriendly** see USER.

unfrock *v.* dismiss (a priest) from office.

unfurl *v.* unroll, spread out (a sail, an umbrella, etc.); become unrolled.

unfurnished *adj.* **1** (usu. foll. by *with*) not supplied. **2** without furniture (*an unfurnished flat*).

ungainly *adj.* awkward-looking, clumsy, ungraceful. ◻ **ungainliness** *n.*

Ungarinyin / **uung**-ah-rin-yin / *n.* an Aboriginal language of the Ngarinyin people in the north Kimberley region of WA.

unget-at-able *adj. colloq.* difficult or impossible to reach, inaccessible.

ungodly *adj.* **1** impious, wicked. **2** *colloq.* outrageous, very inconvenient (*phoning at this ungodly hour*). ◻ **ungodliness** *n.*

ungovernable *adj.* uncontrollable, violent (*an ungovernable temper*).

ungracious *adj.* not courteous; grudging (*an ungracious apology*). ◻ **ungraciously** *adv.*

ungrammatical *adj.* contrary to the rules of grammar.

ungreen *adj.* not concerned with the protection of the environment; harmful to the environment (*the ungreen attitudes of some loggers; the ungreen practices of some industries*).

unguarded *adj.* **1** not guarded. **2** thoughtless, incautious (*in an unguarded moment*).

unguent / **ung**-gwuhnt / *n.* an ointment or lubricant.

ungulate / **ung**-gyuh-luht, -layt / *adj.* having hooves. •*n.* a mammal that has hooves.

unhallowed *adj.* **1** not consecrated. **2** unholy, wicked.

unhand *v. literary* or *jocular* take one's hands off (a person), let go of (*unhand me, villain!—I'm a good girl, I am*).

unhappy *adj.* (**unhappier**, **unhappiest**) **1** not happy, sad. **2** unfortunate (*the decision to merge proved to be an unhappy one*). **3** unsuitable. ◻ **unhappily** *adv.* **unhappiness** *n.*

UNHCR *abbr.* United Nations High Commission for Refugees, an agency of the United Nations set up in 1951 to aid, protect, and monitor refugees.

unhealthy *adj.* (**unhealthier**, **unhealthiest**) **1** not having good health. **2** harmful to health (*smoking is utterly unhealthy*). **3** unwholesome (*unhealthy fumes from the factory*). **4** morally dangerous (*he has an unhealthy influence over them*). **5** psychologically unwholesome (*he has an unhealthy interest in instruments of torture*). **6** *colloq.* physically dangerous (*this place is going to be unhealthy for you, mate, if you're still here in five minutes!*). •*v.* ◻ **unhealthily** *adv.* **unhealthiness** *n.*

unheard *adj.* not heard. ◻ **unheard-of** *adj.* not previously known of or done.

unhinge *v.* cause to become mentally unbalanced (*the shock unhinged his mind*).

unholy *adj.* (**unholier**, **unholiest**) **1** wicked, irreverent. **2** *colloq.* very great, outrageous (*making an unholy row*). **3** unnatural (*an unholy alliance*). ◻ **unholiness** *n.*

unhoped-for *adj.* not hoped for or expected.

unhorse *v.* throw or drag (a rider) from a horse.

uni / **yoo**-nee / *n.* orig. *Aust. colloq.* university. •*adj.* pertaining to a university (*uni courses*).

Uniat / yoo-nee-at, -uht / *adj.* (also **Uniate**) of the Churches in eastern Europe, North Africa, and SW Asia that acknowledge the pope's supremacy but retain their own liturgy etc. • *n.* a member of such a Church.

unicameral / yoo-nee-**kam**-uh-ruhl / *adj.* having only one legislative chamber.

UNICEF / **yoo**-nuh-sef / *abbr.* United Nations Children's (originally International Children's Emergency) Fund, established to help governments to meet the long-term needs of the welfare of mothers and children.

unicellular / yoo-nee-**sel**-yuh-luh / *adj.* (of an organism) consisting of one cell.

unicorn *n.* a mythical animal resembling a white horse with a single long straight (and usu. spiralled) horn projecting from its forehead.

unicycle *n.* a single-wheeled cycle, used esp. by acrobats. ◻ **unicyclist** *n.*

unification *n.* unifying; being unified.

Unification Church a religious sect founded in Korea by Sun Myung Moon whose members are sometimes known as Moonies. Moon claims Messianic status, believing that he was chosen by God to save humankind from Satanism and regarding Communists as Satan's representatives.

uniform *n.* distinctive clothing intended to identify the wearer as a member of the armed forces, the police, a particular school, etc. • *adj.* **1** always the same, not varying (*planks of uniform thickness*). **2** conforming to the same standard, rules, etc. ◻ **uniform resource locator** an address on the World Wide Web, e.g. *http://www.anu.edu.au/ANDC*. ◻ **uniformly** *adv.* **uniformity** / yoo-nuh-**faw**-muh-tee / *n.*

uniformed *adj.* wearing a uniform.

unify *v.* (**unified**, **unifying**) form into a single unit, unite.

unilateral / yoo-nee-**lat**-uh-ruhl / *adj.* one-sided, done by or affecting one person or group or country etc. and not another. ◻ **unilaterally** *adv.* **unilateralism** *n.*

unimaginable *adj.* impossible to imagine.

unimaginative *adj.* lacking imagination; stolid, dull. ◻ **unimaginatively** *adv.*

unimpeachable *adj.* completely trustworthy, not open to doubt or question (*unimpeachable honesty*). ◻ **unimpeachably** *adv.*

unimproved *adj.* **1** not made better. **2** (of land) not used for agriculture or building; not developed. ◻ **unimproved capital value** (of land) the value placed on a residential block etc., excluding any improvements, buildings, etc., usu. for the purpose of assessing rates.

uninformed *adj.* **1** ignorant. **2** not informed or instructed.

uninhabitable *adj.* not suitable for habitation.

uninhabited *adj.* not inhabited.

uninhibited *adj.* not inhibited, having no inhibitions; extroverted.

uninspired *adj.* not inspired; commonplace, not outstanding. ◻ **uninspiring** *adj.*

unintelligible *adj.* not intelligible, impossible to understand. ◻ **unintelligibly** *adv.*

uninterested *adj.* not interested; showing or feeling no concern (cf. DISINTERESTED).

uninviting *adj.* unattractive, repellent.

union *n.* **1** uniting; being united. **2** a whole formed by uniting parts; an association formed by the uniting of people or groups. **3** a trade union. **4** marriage. **5** concord, agreement (*their minds were in perfect union*). **6** (**Union**) a university social club. **7** Rugby Union. **8** *Maths* the totality of the members of two or more sets. ◻ **union bashing** *colloq.* a media or government campaign against trade unions.

unionise *v.* (also **-ize**) organise into or cause to join a trade union. ◻ **unionisation** *n.*

unionist *n.* a member of a trade union; a supporter of trade unions. ◻ **unionism** *n.*

Union Jack *n.* **1** the national ensign of the United Kingdom. **2** = DOUBLE DRUMMER (see DOUBLE).

Union of Soviet Socialist Republics the full name of the former Soviet Union.

unique / yoo-**neek** / *adj.* **1** being the only one of its kind (*this vase is unique*). **2** unusual, remarkable (*a unique opportunity; this makes it even more unique*). ◻ **uniquely** *adv.*

■ **Usage** In sense 1, *unique* cannot be qualified by adverbs such as *absolutely*, *most*, *quite*, etc. Many people regard the use in sense 2 as illogical and incorrect.

unisex / **yoo**-nee-seks / *adj.* **1** (of clothing, hairstyles, etc.) designed for people of both sexes. **2** catering to both sexes (*unisex hair salon; unisex toilet*).

unison *n.* ◻ **in unison 1** (of musical instruments or voices) sounding or singing together at the same pitch or at pitches differing by one or more octaves. **2** in agreement or concord (*acted in unison*).

unit *n.* **1** an individual thing, person, or group regarded as single and complete, or as the smallest part of a complex whole (*the family as the unit of society*). **2** a quantity chosen as a standard in terms of which other quantities may be expressed, or for which a stated charge is made. **3 a** a measure of educational attainment credited to a student for successfully completing one section of an academic course (*he has six units towards the degree*). **b** such a section of an academic course (*enrolled in three units this year*). **4** a part or group with a specified function within a complex machine or organisation. **5** a piece of furniture, esp. one designed to be fitted with others like it. **6** *US & Aust.* = HOME UNIT. ◻ **unit cost** the cost of producing one item. **unit price** the price charged for each unit of goods supplied. **unit trust** a company investing contributions from many people in various securities and paying them all a dividend in proportion to their holdings.

Unitarian / yoo-nuh-**tair**-ree-uhn / *n.* a member of a Christian sect maintaining that God is one person, not a Trinity. ❑ **Unitarianism** *n.*

unitary *adj.* **1** of a unit or units. **2** marked by unity or uniformity.

unite *v.* **1** join together, make or become one. **2** agree or combine or cooperate (*they all united in condemning the nuclear tests*).

United Arab Emirates a State formed from sheikhdoms lying along the Persian Gulf.

United Kingdom Great Britain and Northern Ireland.

United Nations an organisation of about 150 countries set up in 1945 to promote international peace, security, and cooperation.

United States (of America) a country (occupying most of the southern half of North America and including also Alaska and Hawaii) consisting of 50 States and the Federal District of Columbia.

Uniting Church *n.* (also **Uniting Church in Australia**) an Australian Church, formed in 1977 from the Methodist Church of Australasia, part of the Presbyterian Church of Australia, and part of the Congregational Union of Australia.

unity *n.* **1** the state of being one or a unit. **2** a thing forming a complex whole. **3** the number one in mathematics. **4** harmony, agreement in feelings, ideas, or aims etc. (*dwell together in unity*). ❑ **unity ticket** *Aust.* (in a trade-union election) an alliance of candidates, of differing political or ideological persuasion, united for electoral advantage.

univalent / yoo-nee-**vay**-luhnt / *adj.* having a valency of one.

univalve / **yoo**-nee-valv / *n.* a shellfish with a shell consisting of only one part (valve).

universal *adj.* of, for, or done by all persons or things in the world or in the class concerned; applicable to all cases (*the feeling was universal; met with universal approval*). • *n.* **1** a term, characteristic, or concept of general application. **2** a universal joint. ❑ **universal joint** (*or* **coupling**) a joint that connects two shafts in such a way that they can be at any angle to each other. **universal suffrage** the right of voting in a political election extending to all adults. **universal time** that used for astronomical reckoning at all places. ❑❑ **universally** *adv.* **universality** *n.*

universe *n.* **1** all existing things, including the earth and its creatures and all the heavenly bodies; the cosmos. **2** all human beings.

university *n.* an educational institution of advanced learning and research which awards degrees; the members of this.

UNIX *n. trademark Computing* an operating system developed in the early 1970s with the aim of improving communication between different brands of computers.

unkempt *adj.* untidy, dishevelled.

unkind *adj.* not kind; harsh, cruel. ❑ **unkindly** *adv.* **unkindness** *n.*

unknown *adj.* not known, not identified. • *n.* an unknown person, thing, or quantity. ❑ **unknown to** without the knowledge of. **unknown quantity** a mysterious or unfamiliar person or thing.

Unknown Soldier an unidentified soldier ceremonially buried to symbolise all of a nation's armed forces killed in war.

unladen *adj.* not laden. ❑ **unladen weight** the weight of a vehicle etc. when not loaded with goods.

unleaded *adj.* (of petrol) containing no added lead compounds.

unlearn *v.* discard and forget (habits, knowledge, false information, etc.) deliberately.

unleash *v.* **1** set free from a leash or restraint. **2** set (a thing) free so that it can attack or pursue something.

unleavened / un-**lev**-uhnd / *adj.* not leavened; (of bread) made without yeast or other raising agent.

unless *conj.* if not, except when (*we shall not move unless we are obliged to*).

unlettered *adj.* illiterate; not well educated.

unlicensed *adj.* not licensed, esp. to sell alcohol or drive a motor vehicle.

unlike *adj.* **1** not like, different. **2** not characteristic of (*such behaviour is quite unlike him*). • *prep.* differently from (*behaves quite unlike anyone else*).

unlikely *adj.* **1** not likely to happen or be true (*an unlikely tale*). **2** not likely to be successful (*the most unlikely candidate*).

unlimited *adj.* not limited; very great in number or quantity.

unlined *adj.* **1** without a lining. **2** (of paper etc.) not marked with lines. **3** (of a face etc.) without wrinkles.

unlisted *adj.* not included in a list; not in a published list of telephone numbers; (of a company) not listed on a stock exchange.

unload *v.* **1** remove (a load) from (a vehicle etc.); remove cargo. **2** remove the ammunition from (a gun etc.). **3** dispose of stocks, shares, etc., by selling off. **4** *colloq.* **a** give vent to feelings etc.; unburden oneself (*unloaded his grief; unloaded his problems on me*). **b** divulge information etc. (*threatened to unload it all on the police*). **c** get rid of a thing that is unwanted or an embarrassment, esp. by sale (*unloaded the stolen towels on a clergyman's wife at a dollar a pop*). **d** get rid of an unwanted person, esp. by dumping him or her on someone else (*tried to unload some of his visiting relatives on me*).

unlock *v.* **1** release the lock of (a door etc.); release or disclose by unlocking. **2** release thoughts, feelings, etc. from (one's mind etc).

unlooked-for *adj.* unexpected.

unloose *v.* (also **unloosen**) set loose; set free.

unlucky *adj.* not lucky, wretched, having or bringing bad luck. ☐ **unluckily** *adv.*

unmade *adj.* **1** (of a bed) not yet arranged ready for use. **2** not yet made; uncreated. ☐ **unmade road** *Aust.* a vehicular way which has not been sealed with bitumen etc.

unman *v.* (**unmanned**, **unmanning**) **1** deprive of the supposedly manly qualities (e.g. self-control, courage). **2** make effeminate.

unmanned *adj.* **1** (esp. of a spacecraft etc.) operated without a crew. **2** without staff or personnel, empty (*left the office unmanned*).

unmarked *adj.* **1** not marked; with no mark of identification (*an unmarked police car*). **2** not noticed.

unmask *v.* **1** remove the mask from; remove one's mask. **2** expose the true character of.

unmentionable *adj.* so bad, embarrassing, or shocking that it may not be spoken of. • *n.* (**unmentionables**) *jocular* undergarments.

unmet *adj.* (of a demand, goal, etc.) not achieved or fulfilled.

unmistakable *adj.* clear and obvious, not able to be mistaken for another. ☐ **unmistakably** *adv.*

unmitigated / un-**mit**-in-gay-tuhd / *adj.* not modified, absolute (*an unmitigated success*).

unmoral *adj.* not concerned with morality (cf. IMMORAL).

unmoved *adj.* not moved; not changed in one's purpose; not affected by emotion.

unmusical *adj.* **1** not pleasing to the ear. **2** unskilled in or indifferent to music.

unna *contraction Aust.* (in Aboriginal English) isn't it?

unnatural *adj.* **1** not natural or normal. **2** lacking natural feelings of affection. **3** artificial. **4** affected. ☐ **unnaturally** *adv.*

unnecessary *adj.* **1** not necessary. **2** more than is necessary (*with unnecessary care*). ☐ **unnecessarily** *adv.*

unnerve *v.* cause to lose courage or determination.

unnumbered *adj.* **1** not marked with a number. **2** not counted. **3** countless.

unobtrusive / un-uhb-**troo**-siv / *adj.* not obtrusive, not making oneself or itself noticed. ☐ **unobtrusively** *adv.*

unofficial *adj.* not officially authorised or confirmed. ☐ **unofficially** *adv.*

unorganised *adj.* (also -**ized**) **1** not organised; not formed into an orderly and regulated whole. **2** (of workers) not members of, or organised into, a trade union.

unpalatable *adj.* **1** not pleasant to the taste. **2** (of an idea, suggestion, etc.) disagreeable, distasteful.

unparalleled *adj.* not equalled; supreme (*unparalleled enthusiasm*).

unparliamentary *adj.* contrary to parliamentary custom. ☐ **unparliamentary language** oaths, insults, abuse, etc.

unperson *n.* a person whose name or existence is ignored or denied, esp. by a government.

unpick *v.* undo the stitching of.

unplaced *adj.* not placed as one of the first three in a race etc.

unplayable *adj.* (of a ball in games) too fast etc. to be returned; that cannot be played.

unpleasant *adj.* not pleasant, disagreeable. ☐ **unpleasantly** *adv.* **unpleasantness** *n.*

unplug *v.* (**unplugged**, **unplugging**) **1** disconnect (an electrical device) by removing its plug from the socket. **2** unstop.

unplugged / un-**plugd** / *adj. colloq.* (of a band, performance, etc.) without full amplification etc.

unplumbed *adj.* **1** not plumbed. **2** not fully investigated or understood.

unpolished *adj.* **1** not made smooth or bright by polishing; rough. **2** without refinement; crude.

unpopular *adj.* not popular, not liked or enjoyed by people in general. ☐ **unpopularly** *adv.* **unpopularity** *n.*

unpractical *adj.* **1** not practical. **2** (of a person) without practical skill.

unpractised *adj.* **1** not experienced or skilled. **2** not put into practice.

unprecedented / un-**pres**-uh-den-tuhd, -**pree**-suh- / *adj.* for which there is no precedent; unparalleled.

unprepossessing / un-pree-puh-**zes**-ing / *adj.* unattractive, not making a good impression.

unpretentious / un-pruh-**ten**-shuhs / *adj.* not pretentious; simple, modest, unassuming.

unprincipled *adj.* without good moral principles, unscrupulous.

unprintable *adj.* too offensive or indecent to be printed.

unprofessional *adj.* **1** contrary to professional standards of behaviour. **2** unskilled, amateurish. **3** not belonging to a profession. ☐ **unprofessionally** *adv.*

unpromising *adj.* not likely to turn out well.

unprompted *adj.* not prompted, spontaneous.

unprotected / un-pruh-**tek**-tuhd / *adj.* **1** not protected. **2** (of sexual intercourse) performed without a condom.

unputdownable *adj. colloq.* (of a book) gripping, compulsively readable.

unqualified *adj.* **1** (of a person) not legally or officially qualified to do something (*an unqualified medical practitioner*). **2** not restricted or modified (*gave it our unqualified approval*). **3** not competent (*I'm unqualified to say*).

unquestionable *adj.* not questionable, too clear to be doubted. ☐ **unquestionably** *adv.*

unquestioned *adv.* not disputed or doubted.

unquestioning *adj.* **1** asking no questions. **2** (of obedience etc.) absolute.

unquote *v.* (in dictation etc.) end the quotation, close the inverted commas (cf. QUOTE sense 4) (*Churchill said (quote) 'We shall never surrender' (unquote)*).

unravel v. (**unravelled, unravelling**) **1** disentangle. **2** undo (knitted fabrics). **3** probe and solve (a mystery etc.). **4** become unravelled.

unread / un-**red** / adj. **1** (of a book etc.) not read. **2** (of a person) not well-read.

unreadable adj. **1** too bad, dull, or difficult to read. **2** illegible. **3** not able to be interpreted (*an unreadable expression on his face*).

unreal adj. **1** not real, existing in the imagination only. **2** US & Aust. colloq. **a** incredibly good. **b** incredibly bad. □ **unreality** / un-ree-**al**-uh-tee / n.

unreason n. lack of reasonable thought or action.

unreasonable adj. **1** not reasonable in one's attitude etc. **2** excessive, going beyond the limits of what is reasonable or just. □ **unreasonably** adv.

unrecognised adj. (also **-ized**) **1** not recognised. **2** not given sufficient acknowledgment.

unregenerate / un-ruh-**jen**-uh-ruht / adj. obstinately wrong or bad.

unrelated adj. **1** not connected by blood (*he and I are quite unrelated*). **2** not standing in relationship or connection (*these three murders are quite unrelated*).

unrelenting adj. **1** not relenting or yielding. **2** unmerciful. **3** not abating or relaxing (*unrelenting pursuit of the fugitives*).

unrelieved adj. **1** lacking the relief given by contrast or variation; monotonously uniform (*unrelieved gloom; a plain black dress unrelieved by any touches of colour*). **2** not aided or assisted.

unremitting / un-ruh-**mit**-ing / adj. not relaxing or ceasing, persistent.

unrepeatable adj. **1** that cannot be done or offered etc. again (*unrepeatable bargains*). **2** too obscene to be said again.

unrequited / un-ruh-**kwuy**-tuhd / adj. (of love) not returned or rewarded.

unreserved adj. **1** not reserved (*unreserved seats*). **2** without reservation or restriction, complete (*he has my unreserved support*). □ **unreservedly** / un-ruh-**zer**-vuhd-lee / adv.

unresolved adj. **1** uncertain how to act, irresolute, undecided. **2** (of questions etc.) undetermined, undecided, unsolved.

unrest n. disturbance or dissatisfaction (*industrial unrest*).

unrighteous adj. not righteous; unjust, wicked.

unrivalled / un-**ruy**-vuhld / adj. having no equal, incomparable.

unroll v. open or become opened after being rolled.

unruffled adj. **1** (of a person) not agitated or disturbed; calm. **2** not physically ruffled or choppy (*the sea was as calm and unruffled as a pond*).

unruly / un-**roo**-lee / adj. not easy to control or discipline, disorderly. □ **unruliness** n.

unsaddle v. **1** remove the saddle from (a horse). **2** unseat (a rider).

unsafe adj. **1** not safe. **2** not to be trusted to; unreliable. **3** Law (of a verdict, conviction, etc.) likely to constitute a miscarriage of justice. □ **unsafe sex** n. sexual intercourse etc. entered into without proper precaution (esp. the use of a condom) against contracting Aids and other sexually transmitted diseases (cf. SAFE SEX). (**unsafe-sex**) (of or pertaining to unsafe sex (*too many, especially the young, still use unsafe-sex practices*). □ **unsafely** adv. **unsafeness** n.

unsaid / un-**sed** / see UNSAY. •adj. not spoken or expressed (*many things were left unsaid*).

unsatisfactory adj. not satisfactory; poor, unacceptable.

unsaturated adj. Chem. (of a fat or oil) capable of further reaction by combining with hydrogen.

unsavoury adj. **1** disagreeable to the taste, smell, or feelings; disgusting. **2** disagreeable, unpleasant (*an unsavoury character lurking by those trees*). **3** morally offensive (*an unsavoury reputation*).

unsay v. (**unsaid, unsaying**) take back or retract (*what's said can't be unsaid*).

unscathed / un-**skayth**d / adj. without suffering any injury.

unschooled adj. **1** uneducated, untaught. **2** untrained, undisciplined. **3** not made artificial by education or training: natural, spontaneous.

unscientific adj. not in accordance with scientific principles or methods. □ **unscientifically** adv.

unscramble v. **1** sort out from a disordered or confused state. **2** make (a scrambled transmission) intelligible.

unscreened adj. **1** not passed through a screen or sieve. **2** not checked, esp. for security or medical problems. **3** not having a screen. **4** (of a film etc.) not yet shown on a screen.

unscrew v. loosen (a screw or nut etc.) by turning it; unfasten by turning or removing screws, or by twisting.

unscrupulous / un-**skroo**-pyuh-luhs / adj. without moral scruples, unprincipled. □ **unscrupulously** adv. **unscrupulousness** n.

unseasonable adj. **1** not appropriate to the time or occasion. **2** untimely, inopportune. □ **unseasonably** adv.

unseasonal adj. not typical of or appropriate to the time or season (*unseasonal weather*).

unseasoned adj. **1** not flavoured with salt, herbs, etc. **2** (esp. of timber) not matured.

unseat v. **1** dislodge (a rider) from horseback or from a bicycle etc. **2** remove from a parliamentary seat (*was unseated at the last election*).

unseeded adj. (of a tennis player etc.) not seeded.

unseeing adj. **1** unobservant. **2** blind.

unseemly adj. not seemly, improper; indecent. □ **unseemliness** n.

unseen *adj.* **1** not seen; invisible. **2** (of translation or a piece of music) done or performed without previous preparation, esp. at an examination. •*n.* an unseen translation.

unselfish *adj.* not selfish, considering the needs of others before one's own; sharing. ☐ **unselfishly** *adv.* **unselfishness** *n.*

unsettle *v.* **1** make uneasy; disturb the calm or stability of. **2** derange (*the shock unsettled his mind*).

unsettled *adj.* **1** not peaceful or orderly; disturbed; restless (*dangerous and unsettled times*). **2** (of weather etc.) changeable, variable. **3** still in a state of flux, not yet come to rest (*the dust was still unsettled, eddying about in thick swirls*). **4** open to change or further discussion; not determined or decided (*a few unsettled matters remain on the agenda*). **5** (of a bill etc.) unpaid. **6** not settled or stable in character (*had an unsettled childhood because of constant shifts of school*). **7** unbalanced, mentally disturbed. **8** unpopulated or sparsely populated by settlers.

unshakeable *adj.* not able to be shaken, firm, unwavering.

unsheathe *v.* remove (a knife etc.) from a sheath.

unshod *adj.* not wearing or equipped with shoes.

unshrinking *adj.* not flinching or hesitating; fearless.

unsighted *adj.* **1** not sighted or seen. **2** prevented from seeing, esp. by an obstruction.

unsightly *adj.* not pleasant to look at, ugly (*unsightly sores all over his hands*). ☐ **unsightliness** *n.*

unskilled *adj.* **1** not needing special skill or training (*unskilled work does not pay good wages*). **2** lacking special skill or training (*it is difficult for unskilled young people to get a job*).

unsociable *adj.* not sociable, disliking company. ☐ **unsociably** *adv.*

unsocial *adj.* **1** not suitable for society. **2** outside the normal working day (*unsocial hours*). **3** not conforming to standard social practices; antisocial. ☐ **unsocially** *adv.*

unsolicited / un-suh-**lis**-uh-tuhd / *adj.* not asked for; given or done voluntarily (*as publishers we receive hundreds of unsolicited manuscripts*).

unsophisticated *adj.* not sophisticated; simple and natural or naïve.

unsought *adj.* **1** not searched out or sought for. **2** unasked; without being requested.

unsound *adj.* **1 a** not physically healthy; diseased; weak. **b** not mentally healthy; not sane. **2** (of fruit, timber, goods, etc.) not in sound or good condition; rotten. **3** lacking in firmness or solidity (*the foundations of this building are unsound*). **4** not soundly based on reason; ill-founded (*your conclusion is unsound*). **5** of doubtful financial viability (*an unsound business*). **6** (of sleep) broken or disturbed. ☐ **of unsound mind** insane.

unsparing / un-**spair**-ring / *adj.* **1** giving freely and lavishly (*unsparing in one's efforts*). **2** merciless (*unsparing in his revenge*).

unspeakable *adj.* **1** unable to be described in words (*unspeakable terror*). **2** indescribably bad or objectionable (*he whispered something unspeakable in my ear*).

unsporting *adj.* not fair or generous.

unstable *adj.* **1** not stable, tending to change suddenly. **2** mentally or emotionally unbalanced. ☐ **unstably** *adv.*

unsteady *adj.* not steady; unstable. ☐ **unsteadily** *adv.* **unsteadiness** *n.*

unstick *v.* (**unstuck, unsticking**) separate (a thing stuck to another). ☐ **come unstuck** *colloq.* come to grief, fail.

unstinting *adj.* given freely and lavishly.

unstressed *adj.* **1** (of a syllable) not pronounced with a stress. **2** not subjected to stress.

unstring *v.* (**unstrung**) **1** remove or relax the string(s) of (a bow, a harp, etc.). **2** remove (beads etc.) from a string. **3** (esp. as **unstrung** *adj.*) unnerve.

unstructured *adj.* without a formal structure; informal.

unstuck *see* UNSTICK.

unstudied *adj.* natural in manner, not affected (*with unstudied elegance*).

unsubstantial *adj.* not substantial, flimsy; having little or no factual basis.

unsuccessful *adj.* not successful. ☐ **unsuccessfully** *adv.*

unsuited *adj.* **1** not fit (for a purpose) (*he is unsuited for the job*). **2** not adapted (to a specified thing) (*he said that his hands were unsuited to such rough work*).

unsung *adj.* not acknowledged or honoured (*unsung heroes*).

unsure *adj.* **1** not sure. **2** unsafe; liable to yield or give way (*the ground is unsure; unsure foundations*). **3** dependent on chance or accident; uncertain, precarious (*all I am sure of is that life is unsure*). **4** lacking in confidence, uncertain, subject to doubt (*feeling quite unsure of himself*). **5** unreliable; untested (*an unsure scheme for beating the odds in gambling*).

unswerving *adj.* **1** steady, constant (*unswerving loyalty*). **2** not turning aside.

unsworn *adj.* **1** (of a person) not subjected to or bound by an oath or affirmation. **2** not confirmed by an oath or affirmation (*an unsworn statement by the accused*).

untangle *v.* free from a tangle, disentangle (*untangle the string; I'll leave you to untangle this mess*).

untapped *adj.* not tapped, not yet made use of (*the country's untapped resources*).

untaught *adj.* **1** not instructed by teaching. **2** not acquired by teaching.

untenable / un-**ten**-uh-buhl / *adj.* (of a theory or position) not tenable; not able to be held,

unthinkable *adj.* unimaginable, inconceivable; too unlikely or undesirable to be considered.

unthinking *adj.* thoughtless, done or said etc. without consideration. ☐ **unthinkingly** *adv.*

untidy *adj.* (**untidier**, **untidiest**) not neat or orderly. ☐ **untidily** *adv.* **untidiness** *n.*

untie *v.* (**untied**, **untying**) **1** undo (a knot, a package, etc.). **2** release from bonds or attachment.

until *prep.* & *conj.* up to (a specified time or event) (*until last year we had never been overseas; he resided there until his decease*).

■ **Usage** Used in preference to *till* when it stands first or in formal contexts.

untimely *adj.* **1** happening at an unsuitable time. **2** (of death) premature. ☐ **untimeliness** *n.*

unto *prep. archaic* to.

untold *adj.* **1** not told. **2** not counted; too much or too many to be counted (*untold misery*).

untouchable *adj.* not able to be touched, not allowed to be touched. • *n.* a member of the lowest Hindu group (non-caste) in India, held to defile members of a higher caste on contact.

■ **Usage** Use of the term, and the social restrictions which accompany it, were declared illegal in India in 1949 and in Pakistan in 1953.

untouched *adj.* **1** not touched. **2** not affected physically; not harmed, modified, used, or tasted. **3** not affected by emotion. **4** not discussed.

untoward / un-tuh-**wawd** / *adj.* **1** inconvenient, awkward (*if nothing untoward happens*). **2** at variance with good conduct or propriety; unseemly (*untoward behaviour*). **3** difficult to control, manage, etc. (*untoward material to work with*).

untrammelled *adj.* not hampered.

untried *adj.* **1** not yet tried or tested. **2** inexperienced.

untrue *adj.* **1** not true, contrary to facts. **2** not faithful or loyal (*untrue to his wife and to his principles*). **3** deviating from an accepted standard (*your aim's untrue; your scales are untrue*).

untruth *n.* **1** an untrue statement, a lie. **2** lack of truth. ☐ **untruthful** *adj.* **untruthfully** *adv.*

unused *adj.* **1** / un-**yoozd** / **a** not in use. **b** never having been used. **2** / un-**yoost** / (foll. by *to*) not accustomed (*unused as I am to public speaking …*).

unusual *adj.* **1** not usual. **2** exceptional, remarkable. ☐ **unusually** *adv.*

unutterable *adj.* too great or too intense to be expressed in words; beyond description (*unutterable joy; an unutterable idiot*). ☐ **unutterably** *adv.*

unvarnished *adj.* **1** not varnished. **2** (of a statement or a person) plain and straightforward (*the unvarnished truth; an unvarnished liar*).

unveil *v.* **1** remove a veil from; remove one's veil. **2** remove concealing drapery from, as part of a ceremony (*unveiled the portrait*). **3** disclose, make publicly known.

unversed *adj.* (usu. foll. by *in*) not experienced or skilled (*I'm quite unversed in these matters— you'll have to show me what to do*).

unvoiced *adj.* **1** not spoken. **2** (of a consonant) not voiced (e.g. t, p, k).

unwaged *adj.* unemployed; not receiving a wage (*are we supposed to do unwaged work?*). • *n.* (**the unwaged**) the unemployed (*the waged have no idea what we the unwaged go through day after day*).

unwarrantable *adj.* indefensible; unjustifiable.

unwarranted *adj.* unauthorised; unjustified.

unwary / un-**wair**-ree / *adj.* not cautious; not aware of possible danger etc. ☐ **unwarily** *adv.* **unwariness** *n.*

unwearying *adj.* **1** persistent. **2** not causing or producing weariness.

unwelcome *adj.* not welcome or acceptable; unpleasing.

unwell *adj.* not in good health.

unwholesome *adj.* **1** harmful to health or to moral well-being. **2** unhealthy, insalubrious. **3** unhealthy-looking. ☐ **unwholesomeness** *n.*

unwieldy / un-**weel**-dee / *adj.* awkward to move or control because of its size, shape, or weight. ☐ **unwieldiness** *n.*

unwilling *adj.* not willing, reluctant, hesitating to do something. ☐ **unwillingly** *adv.* **unwillingness** *n.*

unwind *v.* (**unwound**, **unwinding**) **1** draw out or become drawn out after having been wound. **2** relax after a period of work or tension.

unwitting *adj.* **1** not knowing, ignorant, unaware (*an unwitting offender*). **2** unintentional. ☐ **unwittingly** *adv.*

unwonted / un-**wohn**-tuhd / *adj.* not customary or usual (*spoke with unwonted rudeness*). ☐ **unwontedly** *adv.*

unworldly *adj.* **1** spiritually-minded, not materialistic. **2** unsophisticated, naïve. ☐ **unworldliness** *n.*

unworthy *adj.* **1** not worthy, lacking worth or excellence. **2** not deserving (*he is unworthy of this honour*). **3** unsuitable to the character of a person or thing (*such conduct is unworthy of a future king*). **4** (of words, actions, etc.) hurtful or injurious to reputation; unseemly; offensive (*an unworthy suggestion*). ☐ **unworthily** *adv.* **unworthiness** *n.*

unwritten *adj.* **1** not written. **2** (of a law etc.) based on custom or judicial decision, not on statute.

unyielding *adj.* **1** firm in texture, not yielding. **2** firm in resisting persuasion, threats, etc.

unzip v. (**unzipped**, **unzipping**) **1** open or become opened by the undoing of a zip. **2** *Computing* decompress (a file) that has previously been compressed.

up *adv.* **1** at, in, or towards a higher place or position (*jumped up in the air*). **2** to or in a place regarded as higher, e.g. the north or a capital city (*up in Queensland; went up to Sydney; up the country*). **3** to or in an erect or required position or condition (*stand up; wound up the watch*). **4** in a stronger or leading position (*they are two goals up; I am $10 up on the transaction*). **5** *colloq.* ahead etc. as indicated (*went up front*). **6** higher in price or value (*our costs are up; shares are up*). **7** completely (*burn up; eat up*). **8** more loudly or clearly (*speak up*). **9** so as to be inflated (*pump up the tyres*). **10** to the place or time in question or where the speaker etc. is (*went straight up to the door; I've been fine up till now; a child came up to me*). **11** out of bed, having risen (*are you up yet?; the sun is up*). **12** in or into a condition of activity, efficiency, or progress (*getting up steam; stirred up trouble; house is up for sale*). **13** (of a computer) running and available for use. **14** apart, into pieces (*tore it up*). **15** into a compact state, securely (*pack it up; tie it up*). **16** *colloq.* (of the penis) to a state of erection (*he can't get it up any longer*). **17** finished (*your time is up*). **18** happening (esp. of something unusual or undesirable) (*something is up*). **19** (usu. foll. by *before*) appearing for trial etc. (*up before the magistrate; up for drink driving*). • *prep.* **1** upwards along, through, or into; from bottom to top of (*went halfway up the hill; flames roaring up the chimney; climbed up the ladder*). **2** along (*went up the road*). **3** at a higher part of (*fix it further up the wall*). **4** towards the source of (a river). • *adj.* **1** directed upwards (*an up stroke*). **2** of travel towards a particular place (*pressed the 'up' button in the lift*). • *n.* a spell of good fortune (*I'm on an up at the moment; he has his ups and downs*). • *v.* (**upped**, **upping**) *colloq.* **1** begin to do something suddenly or unexpectedly (*he upped and went*). **2** increase (*they promptly upped the price*). □ **be up oneself** *colloq.* have an inflated opinion of oneself. **up against 1** close to. **2** in or into contact with. **3** *colloq.* confronted with (a problem, challenge, etc.). **up-and-coming** *adj. colloq.* promising; progressing. **up for 1** available for; standing for (office etc.) (*up for sale; up for election*). **2** under consideration for (*up for a medal*). **3** *colloq.* liable to pay. **up-market** *adj.* & *adv.* of or directed at the upper end of the market; classy and pricey. **up to 1** until (*busy up to 7 o'clock*). **2** below or equal to (*I can take up to four passengers*). **3** occupied with, doing (*what is he up to?*). **4** required as a duty or obligation from (*it's up to us to help her*). **5** capable of (*I don't feel up to a long walk*). **up to date** *adj.* (**up-to-date** when placed before the noun) **1** in current fashion. **2** in accordance with what is now known or required (*bring the files up to date; up-to-date equipment*). **up yours!** *coarse colloq.* an expression of contemptuous rejection.

Upanishad / oo-**pah**-nee-shahd / *n.* each of a series of Hindu sacred treatises based on the Vedas, written in Sanskrit *c.*800–200 BC. The Upanishads mark the transition from ritual sacrifice to a mystical concern with the nature of reality.

upbeat *n.* an unaccented beat in music. • *adj. colloq.* cheerful, encouraging.

upbraid *v.* chide, reproach.

upbringing *n.* a person's rearing and education during childhood.

upcoming *adj.* forthcoming; about to happen.

up-country *n.* country which is inland and away from a major centre of population. • *adj.* situated in, belonging or related to, such country (*jackerooing on an up-country station*). • *adv.* in or to such country.

update *v.* / up-**dayt** / bring up to date. • *n.* / **up**-dayt / updating; updated information.

upend *v.* set or rise up on end; overturn.

UPF *abbr.* ultraviolet protection factor.

Upfield, Arthur William (1892–1964), Australian writer (born in England) of more than 30 detective novels, most of which are set in the outback and feature the part-Aboriginal detective Napoleon Bonaparte ('Bony').

upfront *colloq. adv.* (usu. **up front**) **1** at the front; in front. **2** (of payments) in advance. • *adj.* **1** honest, frank, direct. **2** (of payments) made in advance.

upgrade / up-**grayd** / *v.* **1** raise to a higher grade or rank. **2** improve (equipment etc.). • *n.* / **up**-grayd / **1** an act or instance of upgrading. **2** an upgraded piece of equipment etc.

upheaval *n.* a violent change or disturbance.

uphill *adv.* in an upward direction; further up a slope. • *adj.* **1** going or sloping upwards. **2** arduous, difficult (*an uphill task; an uphill battle to win the election*).

uphold *v.* (**upheld**, **upholding**) **1** support, keep from falling. **2** support a decision, statement, or belief.

upholster *v.* put a fabric covering, padding, springs, etc. on (furniture). □ **upholsterer** *n.*

upholstery *n.* **1** the work of upholstering furniture. **2** the material used for this.

upkeep *n.* **1** keeping something in good condition and repair. **2** the cost of this.

upland *n.* higher or inland parts of a country. • *adj.* of uplands.

uplift *v.* / up-**lift** / **1** raise. **2** elevate emotionally or morally. • *n.* / **up**-lift / **1** being raised. **2** a mentally or morally elevating influence.

upmost = UPPERMOST.

upon *prep.* on (*Christmas is almost upon us*).

upper *adj.* **1** higher in place or position (*the upper atmosphere; upper lip*). **2** ranking above others (*the upper class*). • *n.* **1** the part of a boot or shoe

uppercut

above the sole. **2** *colloq.* an amphetamine or other stimulant. □ **the upper hand** mastery, dominance (*gained the upper hand*). **upper case** capital letters.

uppercut *n.* a blow in boxing, delivered upwards with the arm bent.

Upper House one of the houses of a legislature consisting of two houses, usu. the smaller and less representative, e.g. the Senate in the Federal parliament of Australia.

uppermost *adj.* (also **upmost**) highest in place or rank; predominant. • *adv.* on or to the top or most prominent position.

uppity *adj. colloq.* presumptuous, arrogant.

upright *adj.* **1** in a vertical position. **2** (of a piano) with the strings mounted vertically. **3** strictly honest or honourable. • *n.* **1** a post or rod placed upright, esp. as a support. **2** (**the uprights**) *Aust. Rules* the goalposts. **3** an upright piano. □ **uprightness** *n.*

uprising *n.* a rebellion or revolt.

uproar *n.* a violent outburst of noise and excitement or anger.

uproarious *adj.* very noisy; provoking loud laughter. □ **uproariously** *adv.*

uproot *v.* **1** pull out of the ground together with its roots. **2** force (a person) to leave a native or established place. **3** remove or destroy completely.

uprush *n.* an upward rush (*an uprush of blood to the head*).

upset *v.* / up-**set** / (**upset**, **upsetting**) **1** overturn; become overturned. **2** disrupt (*this will upset their plans*). **3** distress mentally or emotionally. **4** make physically ill (*it has upset my stomach*). • *n.* / **up**-set / **1** an emotional or physical disturbance (*a stomach upset*). **2** a surprising result (in a game etc.).

upshot *n.* an outcome.

upside down *adv.* & *adj.* **1** with the upper part underneath instead of on top. **2** in or into total disorder.

upsilon / uup-suh-lon / *n.* the twentieth letter of the Greek alphabet (Υ, υ).

upsize / **up**-suyz / *v.* esp. *Computing* move (applications, databases, etc.) from a smaller system to a larger one.

upstage *adj.* & *adv.* nearer the back of a theatre stage. • *v.* **1** move upstage to make (another actor) face away from the audience. **2** divert attention from (a person) to onself; outshine.

upstairs *adv.* / up-**stairz** / to or on an upper floor. • *n.* / **up**-stairz / an upper floor. • *adj.* / **up**-stairz / (also **upstair**) situated upstairs.

upstanding *adj.* **1** standing up. **2** strong and healthy. **3** law-abiding, honest.

upstart *n.* a person who has risen suddenly to a high position, esp. one who behaves arrogantly. • *adj.* **1** that is an upstart (*an upstart crow beautified with our feathers*). **2** of or characteristic of an upstart.

urethra

upstream *adj.* & *adv.* in the direction from which a stream flows, against the current.

upsurge *n.* an upward surge, a rise (esp. in feelings etc.).

upswing *n.* an upward movement or trend.

upsy-daisy *interj.* (also **ups-a-daisy**) an expression of encouragement to a child who is being lifted or has fallen.

uptake *n.* ability to understand what is meant (*quick on the uptake; slow on the uptake*).

uptight *adj. colloq.* **1** nervously tense. **2** annoyed.

uptime *n.* time during which a computer system etc. is in operation.

upturn *n.* / **up**-tern / an upward trend in business or fortune etc., an improvement. • *v.* / up-**tern** / turn upwards; turn upside down.

upward *adj.* moving, leading, or pointing towards what is higher or more important or earlier. • *adv.* (also **upwards**) towards what is higher etc. □ **upwards of** more than (*upwards of forty turned up*).

upwardly *adv.* in an upward direction. □ **upwardly mobile** *adj.* able to or aspiring to advance socially or professionally; *n.* a person or people in this position.

upwind *adj.* & *adv.* in the direction from which the wind is blowing.

Ural Mountains / **yoor**-ruhl / (also **Urals**) a mountain range in the former USSR forming a natural boundary between Europe and Asia.

uranium / yoo-**ray**-nee-uhm / *n.* a chemical element (symbol U), a heavy grey metal used as a source of nuclear energy.

Uranus / yoo-**ray**-nuhs / **1** *Gk myth.* the most ancient of the gods, ruler of the universe, overthrown and castrated by his son Cronus. **2** one of the major planets.

urban *adj.* of or situated in a city or town. □ **urban myth** a widely disseminated apocryphal story about modern urban life, often with elements of black comedy.

urbane / er-**bayn** / *adj.* elegant, sophisticated. □ **urbanity** / er-**ban**-uh-tee / *n.*

urbanise *v.* (also **-ize**) change (a place) into a townlike area, remove the rural quality of (a district). □ **urbanisation** *n.*

urchin *n.* **1** a mischievous child, esp. one who is young and (seemingly) not looked after or cared for (*street urchins*). **2** a sea urchin.

Urdu / **er**-doo / *n.* a language related to Hindi but with many Persian words, one of the official languages of Pakistan.

urea / yoo-**ree**-uh, **yoo**-ree-uh / *n.* a soluble colourless compound contained esp. in urine.

ureter / yoo-**ree**-tuh / *n.* either of the two ducts by which urine passes from the kidneys to the bladder.

urethra / yoo-**ree**-thruh / *n.* the duct conveying urine, leading from the bladder to the extremity of the penis (in males) or to the vulva (in females).

urge *v.* **1** drive onward, encourage to proceed (*urging them on; urged the horses into a gallop*). **2** try hard or persistently to persuade (*urged him to accept the job*). **3** (often foll. by *on*) recommend strongly (*urged on them the importance of keeping to the schedule*). **4** adduce forcefully as a reason or justification (*urged the seriousness of the problem*). • *n.* a feeling or desire that urges a person to do something.

urgent *adj.* **1** needing immediate attention, action, or decision. **2** showing that something is urgent (*spoke in an urgent whisper*). ☐ **urgently** *adv.* **urgency** *n.*

urger *n.* **1** a person who urges. **2** *Aust. colloq.* a person who gives (unsolicited) tips at a race meeting (for a consideration); a tout. **3** *Aust. colloq.* a person who takes advantage of others; a petty racketeer.

uric / **yoo**-rik / *adj.* of urine. ☐ **uric acid** a crystalline acid present in urine.

urinal / **yoo**-ruh-nuhl, yoo-**ruy**- / *n.* **1** a sanitary fitting, usu. against a wall, for men to urinate into. **2** a place or receptacle for urination.

urinary / **yoo**-ruh-nuh-ree / *adj.* of urine or its excretion (*urinary organs*).

urinate / **yoo**-ruh-nayt / *v.* discharge urine from the body. ☐ **urination** *n.*

urine / **yoo**-ruhn, -ruyn / *n.* waste fluid secreted by the kidneys, stored in the bladder, and discharged through the urethra.

URL *abbr.* = UNIFORM RESOURCE LOCATOR.

urn *n.* **1** a vase, usu. with a stem and base, esp. one used for holding the ashes of a cremated person. **2** a large metal container with a tap, in which tea or coffee is made or from which it is served.

urogenital / yoo-roh-**jen**-uh-tuhl / *adj.* of the urinary and reproductive systems.

urology / yoo-**rol**-uh-jee / *n.* the branch of medicine that deals with the kidneys and the urinary system. ☐ **urologist** *n.*

Ursa Major the constellation known as the Great Bear or the Plough.

Ursa Minor the constellation known as the Little Bear, containing the pole star.

ursine / **er**-suyn / *adj.* of or like a bear.

Ursuline *n.* a nun of the Order founded by St Angela Merici (1470–1540) for nursing the sick and educating girls, the oldest teaching Order of women in the Catholic Church. • *adj.* of or relating to this Order.

urticaria / er-tuh-**kair**-ree-uh / *n.* nettle rash.

Uruguay / **yoo**-ruh-gwuy / a republic in South America, south of Brazil. ☐ **Uruguayan** *adj.* & *n.*

US *abbr.* United States (of America).

us *pron.* **1** the objective case of *we.* **2** *colloq.* = we (*it's us*). **3** *colloq.* me (*give us a kiss*). ☐ **us mob** *pron. Aust.* (in Aboriginal English) us; we (*that's us mob on the screen now; us mob are not really happy*).

USA *abbr.* United States of America.

usable *adj.* able to be used; fit for use.

usage / **yoo**-sij / *n.* **1** the manner of using or treating something (*it was damaged by rough usage*). **2** a habitual or customary practice, esp. in the way words are used (*modern English usage*).

use *v.* / yooz / **1** cause to act or serve for a purpose; bring into service; avail oneself of (*I rarely use the car; use your discretion*). **2** consume (*my car uses too much oil*). **3** treat in a specified way, behave towards (*they used her shamefully*). **4** exploit for one's own ends (*they are just using you*). • *n.* / yoos / **1** using; being used; application to a purpose (*put it to good use; it's in daily use; worn with use*). **2** the right or power of using something (*lost the use of his legs*). **3** benefit, advantage (*be of use; it's no use talking to him*). **4** custom or usage (*established by long use*). ☐ **use-by date** a date marked on a food package or other perishable goods (usu. preceded by the words 'use by') to show the latest time by which the contents should be used to avoid risk of deterioration.

used[1] / yoozd / *adj.* (of clothes or vehicles) second-hand.

used[2] / yoost / *v.* was or were accustomed to in the past (*I used to smoke; it used not to rain so often*). • *adj.* having become familiar with (a thing) by practice or habit (*he is used to getting up at dawn*).

useful *adj.* **1** able to produce good results, able to be used for some practical purpose. **2** *colloq.* good or skilful (*a useful footballer*). ☐ **usefully** *adv.* **usefulness** *n.*

useless *adj.* **1** serving no useful purpose. **2** *colloq.* extremely poor or bad (*useless at football*). ☐ **uselessly** *adv.* **uselessness** *n.*

user *n.* **1** a person who uses a thing. **2** a person who takes illegal drugs (cf. PUSHER). ☐ **user-friendly** (of a computer etc.) easy for the user to operate; designed with the needs of the non-technical user in mind. **user-unfriendly** (also **user-hostile**) (of a computer etc.) too difficult or complicated for the ordinary non-technical user, not user-friendly.

usher *n.* **1** a person who shows people to their seats in a cinema, church, etc. **2** an officer walking before a person of rank (e.g., in the Senate of the Parliament of Australia, *the Usher of the Black Rod*). **3** an official acting as doorkeeper in a lawcourt. • *v.* **1** lead in or out; escort as an usher. **2** (usu. foll. by *in*) announce, herald, or show in.

usherette *n.* a woman who ushers people to their seats in a cinema or theatre.

USSR *abbr.* Union of Soviet Socialist Republics.

Ustinov / **yoo**-stuh-nof /, Sir Peter (Alexander) (1921–), British stage and film actor, director, and playwright.

usual *adj.* **1** such as happens or is done or used in most instances; customary, habitual. **2** (preceded by *the*, *my*, etc.) *colloq.* a person's usual drink etc. ☐ **as usual** as happens normally. ☐☐ **usually** *adv.*

usurer / **yoo**-zhuh-ruh / *n.* a person who lends money at excessively high interest.

usurp / yoo-**zerp** / *v.* take (power or a position or right) wrongfully. ☐ **usurpation** *n.* **usurper** *n.*

usury / yoo-*zh*uh-ree / *n.* **1** the lending of money at excessively high interest. **2** an excessively high rate of interest. ☐ **usurious** / yoo-*zhoor*-ree-uhs / *adj.*

ute / yoot / *n. Aust. colloq.* = UTILITY (sense 4).

utensil / yoo-**ten**-suhl / *n.* an instrument or container, esp. for kitchen use.

uterine / **yoo**-tuh-ruyn / *adj.* of the uterus.

uterus / **yoo**-tuh-ruhs / *n.* (*pl.* **uteri** /-ruy/) the womb.

Uther Pendragon / **oo**-thuh, **yoo**- / (in Arthurian legend) king of the Britons and father of Arthur.

utilise *v.* (also **-ize**) use, find a use for. ☐ **utilisation** *n.*

utilitarian / yoo-til-uh-**tair**-ree-uhn / *adj.* **1** designed to be useful rather than decorative or luxurious, severely practical. **2** of utilitarianism. • *n.* an advocate of utilitarianism.

utilitarianism *n.* **1** the doctrine that actions are right if they benefit or are useful to most people. **2** the doctrine that the greatest happiness of the greatest number should be the guiding principle of conduct.

utility *n.* **1** usefulness. **2** a useful thing. **3** (in full **public utility**) a company supplying water, gas, or electricity etc. to the community. **4** (in full **utility truck**) a small truck, having a cabin and a tray in the rear used for carrying light loads. **5** (in full **utility player**) (esp. *Aust. Rules*) a player who is able to perform well in a number of positions. • *adj.* basic and standardised (*utility furniture*).

utmost *adj.* furthest, greatest, extreme (*with the utmost care*). • *n.* the furthest point or degree etc. ☐ **do one's utmost** do all that one possibly can.

Utopia / yoo-**toh**-pee-uh / *n.* an imaginary place or state of things where everything is perfect. ☐ **Utopian** *adj.* (also **utopian**). (¶ The title of a book by Saint Sir Thomas More (1516), meaning 'Nowhere'.)

utter[1] *adj.* complete, absolute (*utter bliss*). ☐ **utterly** *adv.*

utter[2] *v.* **1** make (a sound or words) with the mouth or voice; express (*uttered a sigh*). **2** *Law* put (forged money etc.) into circulation.

utterance *n.* **1** the act or power of uttering. **2** something spoken.

uttermost *adj.* & *n.* = UTMOST.

U-turn *n.* **1** the driving of a vehicle in a U-shaped course so as to proceed in an opposite direction. **2** an abrupt reversal of policy.

Utzon, Joern (1918–), AC, Danish architect of the Sydney Opera House.

UV *abbr.* ultraviolet.

uvula / **yoo**-vyuh-luh / *n.* (*pl.* **uvulae**) the small fleshy projection hanging from the back of the roof of the mouth above the throat. ☐ **uvular** *adj.*

uxorious / uk-**saw**-ree-uhs / *adj.* obsessively fond of one's wife.

uy alternative spelling of UEY.

Uzbek / **uuz**-bek / *n.* **1** a native of Uzbekistan. **2** the language of Uzbekistan.

Uzbekistan / uuz-bek-uh-**stahn** / an independent republic (formerly a republic of the USSR) lying south and SE of the Aral Sea.

V

V *n.* (as a Roman numeral) 5. •*abbr.* volt(s). •*symbol* vanadium.

v. *abbr.* **1** verb. **2** verse. **3** versus. **4** very. **5** (as an instruction in a reference to a passage in a book etc.) see, consult. (¶ Sense 5 = Latin *vide*.)

vac *colloq. n.* **1** a vacation. **2** *Aust.* a vacuum cleaner. •*v.* (**vacced**, **vaccing**) *Aust.* use a vacuum cleaner on (*I've just vacced the carpets*).

vacancy *n.* **1** the condition of being vacant; empty space. **2** an unoccupied position of employment (*we have a vacancy for a typist*). **3** unoccupied accommodation (*this motel has no vacancies*). **4** emptiness of mind; idleness, listlessness.

vacant *adj.* **1** empty, not filled or occupied (*a vacant seat; applied for a vacant post*). **2** showing no sign of thought or intelligence, having a blank expression. □ **vacant possession** (of a house etc.) the state of being empty of occupants and available for the purchaser to occupy immediately. □□ **vacantly** *adv.*

vacate / vuh-**kayt** / *v.* cease to occupy (a place or position).

vacation / vuh-**kay**-shuhn / *n.* **1** any of the intervals between terms in universities and lawcourts. **2** a holiday. **3** vacating (*immediate vacation of the house is essential*). •*v.* spend a holiday (*he's vacationing at Surfers Paradise*).

vaccinate / **vak**-suh-nayt / *v.* inoculate with a vaccine to immunise against a disease. □ **vaccination** *n.*

vaccine / **vak**-seen / *n.* **1** a preparation injected or administered orally to give immunity against an infection. **2** a program which protects a computer system against being attacked by malicious software such as a VIRUS or WORM.

vacillate / **vas**-uh-layt / *v.* **1** waver, keep changing one's mind. **2** swing or sway unsteadily. □ **vacillation** *n.* **vacillator** *n.*

vacuole / **vak**-yoo-ohl / *n.* a tiny space in an organ or cell containing air, fluid, etc.

vacuity / vuh-**kyoo**-uh-tee / *n.* **1** emptiness. **2** vacuousness.

vacuous / **vak**-yoo-uhs / *adj.* **1** expressionless (*a vacuous stare*). **2** showing absence of thought or intelligence, inane. □ **vacuously** *adv.* **vacuousness** *n.*

vacuum *n.* (*pl.* **vacuums** *or*, in science, **vacua**) **1** space completely empty of matter; space in a container from which the air has been pumped out. **2** absence of the normal or previous contents, activities, etc. (*the end of the footy season creates a vast vacuum for many Aussies*). **3** *colloq.* a vacuum cleaner. •*v. colloq.* clean with a vacuum cleaner. □ **vacuum cleaner** an electrical appliance that takes up dust, dirt, etc. by suction. **vacuum flask** a flask with a double wall that encloses a vacuum, used for keeping liquids hot or cold. **vacuum-packed** sealed in a pack from which most of the air has been removed. **vacuum tube** a sealed tube with an almost perfect vacuum, allowing free passage of electric current.

vade mecum / vah-day **may**-kuhm / *n.* a handbook or other small useful work of reference carried constantly for use. (¶ Latin, = go with me.)

Vaduz / fah-**duuts** / the capital of Liechtenstein.

vag[1] / vag / *US* & *Aust. colloq. n.* **1** a vagrant. **2** vagrancy. •*v.* (**vagged**, **vagging**) arrest for vagrancy. □ **on** (or **under**) **the vag** *Aust.* on a charge of vagrancy.

vag[2] / vaj / *n. coarse colloq.* the vagina.

vagabond *n.* a wanderer, a vagrant, esp. an idle or dishonest one. •*adj.* **1** having no fixed habitation; wandering. **2** *colloq.* shiftless, idle, good-for-nothing (*your vagabond mates have cleaned out the fridge*).

vagary / **vay**-guh-ree / *n.* a capricious act or idea; a fluctuation (*vagaries of fashion*).

vagina / vuh-**juy**-nuh / *n.* the passage leading from the vulva to the womb in women and female animals. □ **vaginal** *adj.*

vagina dentata / den-**tah**-tuh / *n.* the motif of a vagina with teeth, occurring in folklore and fantasy and said to symbolise male fears of the dangers of sexual intercourse. (¶ Latin, = having teeth.)

vagrant / **vay**-gruhnt / *n.* a person without a settled home or regular work. •*adj.* wandering, roving. □ **vagrancy** *n.*

vague *adj.* **1** not clearly expressed, perceived, or identified. **2** not expressing one's thoughts clearly or precisely. □ **vaguely** *adv.* **vagueness** *n.*

vain *adj.* **1** conceited, esp. about one's looks, abilities, etc. **2** having no value or significance (*vain triumphs*). **3** useless, futile (*in the vain hope of persuading him*). □ **in vain** with no result, uselessly (*we tried, but in vain*). **take God's name in vain** use it irreverently. □□ **vainly** *adv.*

vainglory *n.* extreme vanity; boastfulness. □ **vainglorious** *adj.*

Vaisya / **vuys**-yuh / *n.* a member of the third of the four great Hindu classes (the farmer or merchant class).

Vajpayee / **vahj**-puy-ee /, Atal Bahari (1924–), Indian statesman. He was prime minister in 1996 (for 16 days) and from 1998.

valance / *val*-uhns / *n.* (also **valence**) a short curtain round the base or canopy of a bed, above a window, or under a shelf.

vale *n.* (*archaic* except in place names) a valley.

valediction / val-uh-**dik**-shuhn / *n.* saying farewell; the words used in this.

valedictory / val-uh-**dik**-tuh-ree / *adj.* saying farewell (*a valedictory speech*).

valence / **vay**-luhns / *n.* **1** = VALENCY. **2** alternative spelling of VALANCE.

valencia / vuh-**len**-see-uh / *n.* a variety of orange, widely grown in southern Australia for its sweet juice.

valency / **vay**-luhn-see / *n.* the capacity of an atom to combine with others, measured by the number of hydrogen atoms it can displace or combine with.

Valentine, St, an early Italian saint (a Roman priest, martyred *c.*269), regarded as the patron of lovers. Feast day, 14 February.

valentine *n.* **1** a lover chosen on St Valentine's day (14 February). **2** a card sent on this day (often anonymously) to one's valentine.

valet / **val**-ay, **val**-uht / *n.* a man's personal attendant who takes care of clothes etc. • *v.* (**valeted**, **valeting**) **1** act as valet to. **2** clean or clean out (a car). ▫**valet parking** parking (of one's car) by an attendant as a service provided at an airport, hotel, etc.

valetudinarian / val-uh-tyoo-duh-**nair**-ree-uhn / *n.* a person of poor health or who pays excessive attention to preserving health. • *adj.* of or being a valetudinarian. ▫**valetudinarianism** *n.*

Valhalla / val-**hal**-uh / *Scand. myth.* the hall in which the souls of slain heroes feasted with Odin.

valiant *adj.* brave, courageous. ▫**valiantly** *adv.*

valid / **val**-uhd / *adj.* **1** having legal force, legally acceptable or usable (*a valid passport*). **2** not having reached its expiry date. **3** (of reasoning etc.) sound and to the point, logical. ▫**validly** *adv.* **validity** / vuh-**lid**-uh-tee / *n.*

validate / **val**-uh-dayt / *v.* make valid, confirm. ▫**validation** *n.*

valise / vuh-**leez**, -**lees** / *n.* a small suitcase.

valium *n. trademark* the drug diazepam used as a tranquilliser and relaxant.

Valkyrie / **val**-kuh-ree / *n. Scand. myth.* any of Odin's twelve handmaidens who hovered over battlefields and carried chosen slain warriors to Valhalla.

Valletta / vuh-**let**-tuh / the capital of Malta.

valley *n.* (*pl.* **valleys**) **1** a long low area between hills. **2** a region drained by a river (*the Nile valley*).

valour / **val**-uh / *n.* (also **valor**) bravery, esp. in fighting. ▫**valorous** *adj.*

valuable *adj.* of great value or price or worth. • *n.pl.* (**valuables**) valuable things, esp. small personal possessions. ▫**valuably** *adv.*

valuation *n.* estimation of a thing's value (esp. by a professional valuer) or of a person's merit; the worth so estimated.

value *n.* **1** the amount of money or other commodity or service etc. considered to be equivalent to something else or for which a thing can be exchanged. **2** desirability, usefulness, importance (*he learnt the value of regular exercise*). **3** the ability of a thing to serve a purpose or cause an effect (*the food value of milk; news value*). **4** the amount or quantity denoted by a figure etc.; the duration of a musical sound indicated by a note; the relative importance of each playing card etc. in a game. **5** (in full **value for money**) a good bargain. **6** (**values**) standards or principles considered valuable or important in life (*moral values*). • *v.* **1** estimate the value of, esp. professionally. **2** consider to be of great worth or importance (*I value your advice*). ▫**value-added 1** (of goods etc.) having enhancements etc. added to a basic line, esp. to increase profit margins. **2** (of a company) offering specialised or extended services in a commercial area. **value judgment** a subjective estimate of worth etc.

valueless *adj.* having no value.

valuer *n.* a person who estimates values professionally. ▫**valuer general** a State official who assesses properties for rating purposes etc.

valve *n.* **1** a device for controlling the flow of gas or liquid through a pipe. **2** a structure in the heart or in a blood vessel allowing blood to flow in one direction only. **3** a device for varying the length of the tube in a brass wind instrument. **4** each piece of the shell of molluscs such as oysters. **5** a thermionic valve.

valvular / **val**-vyuh-luh / *adj.* of the valves of the heart or blood vessels.

vamoose *v. colloq.* go away hurriedly.

vamp[1] *n.* the upper front part of a boot or shoe. • *v.* **1** (foll. by *up*) make from odds and ends (*we'll vamp something up*). **2** improvise a musical accompaniment to a song or dance.

vamp[2] *colloq. n.* a seductive woman who uses her sexual attraction to exploit men, an unscrupulous flirt. • *v.* exploit or flirt with (a man) unscrupulously.

vampire *n.* **1** a ghost or reanimated body supposed to leave a grave at night and suck the blood of living people. **2** a person who preys ruthlessly on others. ▫**vampire bat** a tropical bat that bites or is said to bite animals and suck their blood.

van *n.* **1** a small covered vehicle for transporting goods etc. **2** a railway carriage for luggage or goods, or for the use of the guard. **3** the vanguard, the forefront.

vanadium / vuh-**nay**-dee-uhm / *n.* a hard grey metallic element (symbol V) used in certain steels.

Van Allen belt each of two regions of intense radiation partly surrounding the earth at heights of several thousand kilometres. (¶ Named after the American physicist J. Van Allen (1914–) who discovered them.)

vancomycin / vang-koh-**muy**-suhn / *n.* a bacterial antibiotic used against resistant strains of streptococcus and staphylococcus.

vandal *n.* a person who wilfully or maliciously damages property or natural features. ☐ **vandalism** *n.* (¶ Named after the *Vandals*, a Germanic people who ravaged Gaul, Spain, North Africa, and Rome in the 4th–5th centuries, destroying many books and works of art.)

vandalise *v.* (also **-ize**) damage (property etc.) as a vandal.

Vandemonia / van-duh-**moh**-nee-uh / *n. Aust. hist.* Tasmania, esp. as a penal colony. (¶ From *Van Diemen's Land*, the former name of Tasmania.)

Vandemonian / van-duh-**moh**-nee-uhn / *Aust. hist. n.* **1** a person native to or resident in Tasmania. **2** a convict who has served a sentence in Tasmania. • *adj.* **1** of, belonging to, or inhabiting Tasmania. **2** of or pertaining to Tasmania as a penal colony.

Van Diemen's Land / van **dee**-muhnz / *n. hist.* the name given to Tasmania by its discoverer, Abel Tasman, in 1642. (¶ Anthony Van Diemen (1593–1645), governor of the Dutch East Indies.)

vane *n.* **1** a weathervane. **2** the blade of a propeller, sail of a windmill, or similar device acting on or moved by wind or water.

Van Gogh / gof, goh /, Vincent (Willem) (1853–90), Dutch post-Impressionist painter, who used colours for their expressive or symbolic values and vigorous swirling brushstrokes.

vanguard *n.* **1** the foremost part of an advancing army or fleet. **2** the leaders of a movement or fashion etc.

vanilla *n.* **1** a flavouring obtained from the pods of a tropical climbing orchid, or made synthetically. **2** this orchid. ☐ **vanilla lily** a small Australian plant of the lily family bearing umbels of purple flowers strongly scented of vanilla.

vanish *v.* disappear completely; cease to exist. ☐ **vanishing point 1** the point at which receding parallel lines viewed in perspective appear to meet. **2** the state of complete disappearance of something (*some Australian fauna and flora are at vanishing point because of clearance of their habitats*).

vanity *n.* **1** conceit, esp. about one's appearance. **2** a thing about which a person is very vain (*his muscles are his abiding vanity and obsession*). **3** futility, worthlessness, something vain (*the vanity of human achievement*). ☐ **vanity bag** (*or* **case**) a small bag or case used by a woman for carrying cosmetics etc. **vanity publishing** getting one's own work published by paying a commercial publisher for the production costs etc. (cf. SELF-PUBLISHING). **vanity unit** a washbasin set into a flat top with cupboards beneath.

vanquish *v.* conquer; overcome.

vantage *n.* (in tennis) an advantage. ☐ **vantage point** a place from which one has a good view of something.

Vanuatu / van-oo-**ah**-too / a republic consisting of a group of islands in the SW Pacific. ☐ **Ni-Vanuatu** an inhabitant of Vanuatu. ☐☐ **Vanuatuan** (*or* **Ni-Vanuatu**) *n.* & *adj.*

vapid / **vap**-uhd / *adj.* insipid, uninteresting. ☐ **vapidity** / vuh-**pid**-uh-tee / *n.*

vaporise *v.* (also **-ize**) change into vapour. ☐ **vaporisation** *n.* **vaporiser** *n.*

vapour *n.* (also **vapor**) **1** moisture or other substance diffused or suspended in air, e.g. mist. **2** the air-like substance into which certain liquid or solid substances can be converted by heating (*see* GAS). **3** a medicinal inhalant. ☐ **vapour trail** a trail of condensed water from an aircraft etc. ☐☐ **vaporous** *adj.* **vapoury** *adj.*

vapourware *see* -WARE.

variable *adj.* varying, changeable; (of a star) periodically varying in brightness. • *n.* something that varies or can vary, a variable quantity. ☐ **variably** *adv.* **variability** *n.*

variance *n.* ☐ **at variance** disagreeing, conflicting; (of people) in a state of discord.

variant *adj.* differing from something or from a standard (*'gipsy' is a variant spelling of 'gypsy'*). • *n.* a variant form or spelling etc.

variation *n.* **1** varying; the extent to which something varies. **2** a variant. **3** a repetition of a melody in a different (usu. more elaborate) form.

varicoloured / vair-ree-kul-uhd / *adj.* (also **varicolored**) **1** variegated in colour. **2** of various or different colours.

varicose / **va**-ruh-kohs / *adj.* (of a vein) permanently swollen or enlarged. ☐ **varicosity** / va-ruh-**kos**-uh-tee / *n.*

varied *see* VARY. • *adj.* of different sorts, full of variety.

variegated / **vair**-ree-uh-gay-tuhd / *adj.* **1** marked with irregular patches of different colours. **2** having leaves of two or more colours. ☐ **variegation** *n.*

varietal / vuh-**ruy**-uh-tuhl / *adj.* **1** esp. *Botany* & *Zoology* of, forming, or designating a variety. **2** (of wine) made from a single designated variety of grape.

variety *n.* **1** the quality of not being the same or of not being the same at all times. **2** a quantity or range of different things (*for a variety of reasons*). **3** a class of things that differ from others in the same general group; a member of such a class (*several varieties of wallaby*). **4** *Biology* a subdivision of a species. **5** entertainment consisting of a series of short performances of different kinds (e.g. singing, dancing, acrobatics).

various *adj.* **1** of several kinds, unlike one another (*from various backgrounds*). **2** more than one, several, individual and separate (*we met various people*). ☐ **variously** *adv.*

■ **Usage** *Various* (unlike *several*) cannot be used with *of*, as (wrongly) in *various of the guests arrived late.*

varlet *n. archaic* **1** a menial servant. **2** a rascal.

varna *n.* any of the four great Hindu classes (Brahman, Kshatriya, Vaisya, Sudra).

varnish *n.* **1** a liquid that dries to form a hard shiny transparent coating, used on wood or metal etc. **2** nail varnish. **3** a deceptive outward appearance or show. •*v.* **1** coat with varnish. **2** give a deceptively attractive appearance to; gloss over (a fact).

Varuna / **vu**-ruu-nuh / (in Hinduism) the ancient ruler of the universe, later the god of the waters.

vary *v.* (**varied**, **varying**) **1** make or become different (*you can vary the pressure; his temper varies from day to day*). **2** be different or of different kinds (*opinions vary on this point*).

vas / vas / *n.* (*pl.* **vasa** / **vay**-suh /) *Anatomy* a vessel or duct. ☐ **vas deferens** / vas **def**-uh-renz / (*pl.* **vasa deferentia**) each of the ducts through which semen passes from the testicle to the urethra and then out through the penis.

Vasco da Gama *see* GAMA.

vascular / **vas**-kyuh-luh / *adj.* consisting of vessels or ducts for conveying blood or sap within an organism (*vascular system*).

vas deferens *see* VAS.

vase / vahz / *n.* an open usu. tall vessel of glass, pottery, etc. used for holding cut flowers or as an ornament.

vasectomy / vuh-**sek**-tuh-mee / *n.* the surgical removal of part of each VAS DEFERENS, esp. as a method of birth control.

vaseline / **vas**-uh-leen, -**leen** / *n. trademark* petroleum jelly used as an ointment or lubricant.

vassal *n.* **1** *hist.* a feudal tenant of land. **2** (often *derog.* or *jocular*) a humble subordinate. ☐ **vassalage** *n.*

vast *adj.* immense, huge (*a vast expanse of water; it makes a vast difference*). ☐ **vastly** *adv.* **vastness** *n.*

vat *n.* a tank, esp. for holding liquids in brewing, distilling, food manufacture, dyeing, and tanning.

Vatican *n.* **1** the pope's official residence in the Vatican City, Rome, including a great library, archives, and a museum of art. **2** the papal government or papal authority (*the Vatican has decreed that …*). ☐ **Vatican City** a sovereign, independent State in Rome, including the Vatican and St Peter's Basilica. **Vatican Council** either of two ecumenical councils of the Catholic Church attended by all the Catholic and Uniat bishops in the world, the first in 1869–70 and the second in 1962–65.

vaudeville / **vaw**-duh-vil, **vawd**-vil / *n.* **1** a variety entertainment. **2** a light stage play with interspersed songs. ☐ **vaudevillian** / vaw-duh-**vil**-yuhn / *adj.* & *n.*

vault *n.* **1** an arched roof. **2** a vault-like covering (*the vault of heaven*). **3** an underground chamber: **a** used as a place of storage (*a bank vault*). **b** used as a burial chamber beneath a church or in a cemetery. **4** = VAULTING HORSE. **5** an act of vaulting. •*v.* **1** jump or leap, esp. using the hands or with the help of a pole (*vaulted over the gate*). **2** make in the form of a vault; provide with a vault or vaults. ☐ **vaulter** *n.*

vaulting *n.* arched work in a roof or ceiling. ☐ **vaulting horse** a padded structure for vaulting over in a gymnasium.

vaunt *v.* boast; boast of, extol boastfully. •*n.* a boast.

Vaux, James Hardy (1782–?), English petty criminal and writer, transported to Australia three times, who included a valuable dictionary of slang (*Vocabulary of the Flash Language*) in his *Memoirs* (1819).

VC *abbr.* **1** Victoria Cross. **2** vice-chancellor.

VCR *abbr.* video cassette recorder.

VD *abbr.* venereal disease.

VDU *abbr.* visual display unit.

've *colloq.* (esp. after pronouns) = have (*they've finished*).

veal *n.* calf's flesh as food.

vealer *n.* esp. *Aust.* a calf aged less than a year that has been fattened for slaughter.

vector *n.* **1** (in mathematics) a quantity that has both magnitude and direction (e.g. velocity, = speed in a given direction). **2** the carrier of a disease or infection.

Veda / **vay**-duh, **vee**- / *n.* (also **Vedas**) the most ancient and sacred literature of the Hindus.

Vedic / **vay**-dik, **vee**-dik / *adj.* of the Vedas. •*n.* the language of the Vedas, an old form of Sanskrit.

veer *v.* **1** change direction; (of wind) change gradually in a clockwise direction. **2** change in course or opinion etc. •*n.* a change of direction.

veg / vej / *colloq. n.* vegetable(s). •*v.* (also **veg out**) relax; do nothing (*veging out in front of the telly*).

vegan / **vee**-guhn / *n.* a person who does not eat or use animal products. •*adj.* using or containing no animal products.

vegemite / **vej**-uh-muyt / *n. Aust. trademark* **1** a concentrated yeast extract used as a spread. **2** *colloq.* an Australian child (*happy little vegemites*).

vegetable *n.* **1** a plant of which some part is used (raw or cooked) as food, esp. as an accompaniment to meat. **2** a person leading a dull monotonous life. **3** *colloq. offens.* a person who is without mental faculties because of brain damage. •*adj.* **1** of, from, or relating to plant life (*the vegetable kingdom*). **2** of or relating to vegetables as food (*a vegetable curry*). **3** dull, monotonous (*a vegetable existence*).

vegetal / **vej**-uh-tuhl / *adj.* of or like plants.

vegetarian *n.* a person who eats no meat. •*adj.* excluding animal food, esp. meat (*a vegetarian diet*). ☐ **vegetarianism** *n.*

vegetate / **vej**-uh-tayt / *v.* **1** live an uneventful or monotonous life. **2** grow as plants do.

vegetation *n.* **1** plants collectively; plant life. **2** vegetating.

vegetative / **vej**-uh-tuh-tiv / *adj.* **1** concerned with growth and development as distinct from sexual reproduction. **2** of vegetation. **3** *Med.* alive but without apparent brain activity or responsiveness.

vegie *n.* (usu. **vegies** *pl.*) *colloq.* a vegetable.

vehement / **vee**-uh-muhnt / *adj.* showing strong feeling, intense (*a vehement denial*). ▫ **vehemently** *adv.* **vehemence** *n.*

vehicle / **veer**-kuhl, **vee**-i-kuhl / *n.* **1** a conveyance for transporting passengers or goods on land or in space. **2** a means by which something is expressed or displayed (*art can be a vehicle for propaganda; the play was an excellent vehicle for this actor's talents*).

vehicular / vuh-**hik**-yuh-luh / *adj.* of vehicles (*vehicular access*).

veil *n.* **1** a piece of fine net or other fabric worn as part of a headdress or to protect or conceal the face. **2** a piece of linen etc. as part of a nun's headdress, resting on the head and shoulders. **3** a thing that hides or disguises (*met with a veil of silence*). **4** a curtain, esp. that separating the sanctuary in a Jewish temple or that screening the door of the tabernacle on the altar of e.g. a Catholic church. •*v.* **1** cover with a veil. **2** partly conceal (*a veiled threat*). ▫ **draw a veil over** avoid discussing or calling attention to. **take the veil** become a nun.

vein *n.* **1** any of the tubes carrying blood from all parts of the body to the heart. **2** any of the threadlike structures forming the framework of a leaf or of an insect's wing. **3** a narrow strip or streak of a different colour, e.g. in wood, marble, cheese, etc. **4** a long continuous or branching deposit of mineral or ore, esp. in a fissure. **5** a mood or manner (*she spoke in a humorous vein*). ▫ **veined** *adj.*

Velázquez / ve-**las**-kwuhth /, Diego Rodriguez de Silva y (1599–1660), Spanish painter.

Velcro *n.* (also **velcro**) *trademark* a fastener consisting of two strips of fabric which cling when pressed together.

veld / velt / *n.* (also **veldt**) open grassland in South Africa.

vellum *n.* **1** a fine parchment, orig. calfskin; a manuscript on this. **2** smooth writing paper.

velocity *n.* speed, esp. in a given direction.

velodrome / **vel**-uh-drohm / *n.* a place or building with a track for cycle racing.

velour / vuh-**loor** / *n.* (also **velours** pronounced the same) a plushlike fabric.

velvet *n.* **1** a woven fabric (esp. of silk or cotton) with thick short pile on one side. **2** a furry skin covering a growing antler. •*adj.* of, like, or as soft as velvet. ▫ **on velvet** in an advantageous or prosperous position. **velvet glove** outward gentleness of treatment, esp. cloaking firmness. ▫▫ **velvety** *adj.*

velveteen *n.* cotton velvet.

Ven. *abbr.* Venerable (*see* VENERABLE, sense 2).

venal / **vee**-nuhl / *adj.* **1** corrupt; able to be bribed. **2** (of conduct) influenced by bribery. ▫ **venally** *adv.* **venality** / vee-**nal**-uh-tee / *n.*

■ **Usage** Do not confuse with *venial*.

vend *v.* sell or offer (small wares) for sale. ▫ **vending machine** a slot machine where small articles can be obtained. ▫▫ **vendible** *adj.*

vendetta / ven-**det**-uh / *n.* **1** a blood feud. **2** a prolonged bitter quarrel.

vendor *n. Law* a person who sells something, esp. property.

veneer *n.* **1** a thin layer of fine wood covering the surface of a cheaper wood in furniture etc. **2** a superficial show of some good quality (*a veneer of politeness*). •*v.* cover with a veneer.

venerable / **ven**-uh-ruh-buhl / *adj.* **1** worthy of deep respect because of age or associations etc. (*a venerable old man; these venerable ruins*). **2** (**Venerable**) **a** the title of a deceased person proclaimed by the pope as having attained a certain degree of sanctity: the first stage in a process which may lead to beatification or eventual canonisation (*the Venerable Bede*). **b** the title of a high-ranking Buddhist monk or an archdeacon in the Anglican Church. ▫ **venerably** *adv.* **venerability** *n.*

venerate *v.* regard with deep respect. ▫ **veneration** *n.* **venerator** *n.*

venereal / vuh-**neer**-ree-uhl / *adj.* **1** of or relating to sexual desire or sexual intercourse. **2** of or relating to venereal disease. ▫ **venereal disease** (*abbr.* **VD**) any disease contracted chiefly by sexual intercourse with a person already infected. ▫▫ **venereally** *adv.*

Venetian / vuh-**nee**-shuhn / *adj.* of Venice. •*n.* a native, citizen or dialect of Venice. ▫ **venetian blind** a window blind consisting of horizontal slats that can be adjusted to let in or exclude light.

Venezuela / ven-uh-**zway**-luh / a republic on the north coast of South America. ▫ **Venezuelan** *adj.* & *n.*

vengeance *n.* retaliation for hurt or harm done to oneself or to a person etc. whom one supports. ▫ **with a vengeance** to a high or excessive degree (*that is punctuality with a vengeance*).

vengeful *adj.* seeking vengeance. ▫ **vengefully** *adv.* **vengefulness** *n.*

venial / **vee**-nee-uhl / *adj.* (of a sin or fault) pardonable; not serious. ▫ **venial sin** *Theology* a sin not grave enough to bring about a state of spiritual death (as opposed to *mortal sin—see* MORTAL). ▫▫ **venially** *adv.* **veniality** *n.*

■ **Usage** Do not confuse with *venal*.

Venice a city of NE Italy built on numerous islands on a lagoon of the Adriatic Sea.

venison / **ven**-uh-suhn, -zuhn / n. a deer's flesh as food.

Venn diagram n. a diagram using overlapping and intersecting circles etc. to show the relationships between mathematical sets. (¶ Named after J. Venn (1834–1923), British logician.)

venom / **ven**-uhm / n. **1** poisonous fluid secreted by certain snakes, spiders, etc. and injected into a victim by a bite or sting. **2** strong bitter feeling or language; hatred. ☐ **venomous** / **ven**-uh-muhs / adj. **venomously** adv.

venous / **vee**-nuhs / adj. **1** of veins. **2** contained in veins (venous blood). **3** full of veins.

vent n. **1** an opening allowing air, gas, or liquid to pass out of or into a confined space (a smoke vent). **2** a slit in a garment (esp. a coat or jacket) at the bottom of a back or side seam. **3** the anus, esp. of a lower animal. •v. **1** make a vent in. **2** give vent to (vented his anger on the boy). ☐ **give vent to** give an outlet to (feelings etc.), express freely (gave vent to his anger).

ventilate v. **1** cause air to enter or circulate freely in (a room etc.). **2** express (an opinion etc.) publicly so that others may consider and discuss it. **3** Med. admit or force air into (the lungs); oxygenate the blood. ☐ **ventilation** n.

ventilator n. **1** a device for ventilating a room etc. **2** Med. = RESPIRATOR (sense 2).

ventral adj. of or on the abdomen (this fish has a ventral fin). ☐ **ventrally** adv.

ventricle / **ven**-tri-kuhl / n. a cavity or chamber in an organ of the body, esp. one of the two in the heart that pump blood into the arteries by contracting. ☐ **ventricular** adj.

ventriloquist / ven-**tril**-uh-kwist / n. an entertainer who produces voice sounds without moving the lips so that they seem to come from another source, e.g. a dummy. ☐ **ventriloquism** n. **ventriloquise** v. (also -**ize**). **ventriloquy** n.

venture n. **1** the undertaking of a risk; a risky undertaking. **2** a commercial speculation. •v. **1** dare; not be afraid (he ventured to stop them). **2** dare to go, do, or utter (did not venture forth; ventured an opinion). **3 a** expose to risk; stake (a bet etc.) (ventured all he had on one last fling). **b** take risks (nothing ventured, nothing gained). **4** (foll. by on, upon) dare to engage in etc. (ventured on a solo exploration of central Australia).

venturesome adj. ready to take risks, daring.

venue / **ven**-yoo / n. an appointed place of meeting; a place fixed for a sports match, concert, etc.

Venus 1 Rom. myth. the goddess of love, identified with Aphrodite. **2** one of the planets, also known as the morning and evening star. ☐ **Venus flytrap** a flesh-consuming plant with hinged leaves that spring shut on insects.

veracious / vuh-**ray**-shuhs / adj. **1** truthful by nature. **2** (of a statement etc.) true. ☐ **veracity** / vuh-**ras**-uh-tee / n.

verandah n. (also **veranda**) **1** an open-sided roofed structure along one or more sides of a house or commercial building, the main purpose of which is the provision of shelter. **2** Aust. such a structure that is enclosed or partially enclosed and used for relaxation or as additional living space.

verb n. a word indicating action, occurrence, or being (see panel on next page).

verbal adj. **1** of or in words (verbal accuracy). **2** spoken, not written (a verbal statement). **3** of, deriving from, or in the nature of a verb (a verbal noun). •n. colloq. a verbal statement made to the police. •v. (**verballed, verballing**) colloq. (of police) attribute a damaging statement to (a suspect) (he swore that the police had verballed him and that he had never admitted to the crime). ☐ **verbal noun** a noun derived from a verb (e.g. smoking in smoking is dangerous to health). ☐ ☐ **verbally** adv.

verbalise v. (also -**ize**) put into words. ☐ **verbalisation** n.

verbatim / ver-**bay**-tuhm / adv. & adj. in exactly the same words, word for word (copied it verbatim).

verbiage / **ver**-bee-ij / n. an excessive number of words or unnecessarily difficult words used to express an idea.

verbose / ver-**bohs** / adj. using more words than are needed. ☐ **verbosity** / ver-**bos**-uh-tee / n.

verdant adj. (of grass or fields) green, lush. ☐ **verdancy** n.

Verdi / **vair**-dee /, Giuseppe (1813–1901), Italian composer, whose most famous operas include Rigoletto, La Traviata, and Aida.

verdict n. **1** the decision reached by a jury. **2** a decision or opinion given after examining, testing, or experiencing something.

verdigris / **ver**-duh-gree, -grees / n. green rust on copper or brass.

verdure n. green vegetation; its greenness.

verge n. **1** an edge or border. **2** the brink (on the verge of tears; on the verge of ruin). **3** the grass edging of a road etc. •v. **1** (foll. by on) border on, approach closely (verging on the ridiculous). **2** incline downwards or in a specified direction.

verger / **ver**-juh / n. **1** a caretaker and attendant in a church. **2** an official who carries the staff etc. in front of a bishop or other dignitary.

verify v. (**verified, verifying**) **1** check the truth or correctness of (please verify these figures). **2** (of an event etc.) bear out (a prediction or promise). ☐ **verifiable** adj. **verification** n. **verifier** n.

verily adv. archaic in truth.

verisimilitude / ve-ree-suh-**mil**-uh-tyood / n. an appearance of being true or real.

verismo / vuh-**riz**-moh / n. (esp. of opera) realism.

veritable *adj.* real, rightly named (*a veritable feast*). □ **veritably** *adv.*

verity *n.* **1** a fundamental truth. **2** *archaic* the truth of something.

verjuice / **ver**-joos / *n.* an acid liquor obtained from crab apples, sour grapes, etc., used in cooking and formerly in medicine.

vermicelli / ver-muh-**chel**-ee, -**sel**-ee / *n.* pasta made in long slender threads.

vermicide *n.* a substance that kills worms.

vermiculite / ver-**mik**-yuh-luyt / *n.* a hydrous silicate mineral used esp. as a moisture-holding medium in potting mixes etc. to promote plant growth.

vermiform / **ver**-muh-fawm / *adj.* worm-like in shape. □ **vermiform appendix** a small blind tube extending from the caecum in humans and some other mammals.

vermifuge / **ver**-muh-fyooj / *n.* a drug that expels intestinal worms.

vermilion *n.* **1** bright red pigment. **2** cinnabar. • *adj.* bright red.

vermin *n.* (usu. treated as *pl.*) **1** animals harmful to crops, native wildlife, etc., e.g. species introduced to Australia such as rabbits and foxes; disease-carrying species such as rats. **2** parasitic worms or insects, e.g. hookworm, lice, ticks, fleas. **3** people who are unpleasant or harmful to society. □ **verminous** *adj.*

vermouth / **ver**-muhth, ver-**mooth** / *n.* a wine flavoured with aromatic herbs.

vernacular / ver-**nak**-yuh-luh / *n.* **1** the language or dialect of a particular country (*the Mass is now said or sung in the vernacular all over the world, no longer in Latin*). **2** the language of a particular class or group (*shearers' vernacular; in ultra-feminist vernacular, would a manhole mutate into a personhole?*). **3** everyday, colloquial speech. • *adj.* (of language) native; not foreign or formal.

vernal *adj.* of or occurring in spring. □ **vernally** *adv.*

Verne / vern /, Jules (1828–1905), French writer of science fiction.

vernier / **ver**-nee-uh / *n.* a small movable graduated scale for indicating fractions of the main scale on a measuring device.

Veronica, St, a woman of Jerusalem said to have offered her headcloth to Christ on the way to his Crucifixion to wipe blood and sweat from his face. The cloth is said to have retained the image of his features.

verruca / vuh-**roo**-kuh / *n.* (*pl.* **verrucas** or **verrucae** / vuh-**roo**-see /) a wart or wart-like swelling, esp. on the foot.

Versailles / vair-**suy** / a town south-west of Paris, noted for its royal palace built in the 17th century by Louis XIII and XIV.

versatile / **ver**-suh-tuyl / *adj.* **1** adapting easily to different subjects or occupations; skilled in many

---

Verb

A verb says what a person or thing does, and can describe:
  an action, e.g. *run, hit*
  an event, e.g. *rain, happen*
  a state, e.g. *be, have, seem, appear*
  a change, e.g. *become, grow*

Verbs occur in different forms, usually in one or other of their tenses. The most common tenses are:
  the simple present tense: *The boy walks down the road.*
  the continuous present tense: *The boy is walking down the road.*
  the simple past tense: *The boy walked down the road.*
  the continuous past tense: *The boy was walking down the road.*
  the perfect tense: *The boy has walked down the road.*
  the past perfect tense: *The boy had walked down the road.*
  the future tense: *The boy will walk down the road.*
  the future perfect tense: *The boy will have walked down the road.*

Each of these forms is a finite verb, which means that it is in a particular tense and that it changes according to the number and person of the subject, as in
  I am   *you walk*
  we are   *he walks*

An infinitive is the form of a verb that usually appears with 'to', e.g.
  to wander, to look, to sleep

The designation 'absolute' refers to those uses of transitive verbs (i.e. verbs which take an object) in which the object is implied but not stated, e.g.
  smoking kills;
  let me explain.

The designation 'reflexive' refers to a verb which has a reflexive pronoun as its object, e.g.
  she acquitted herself well.

The designation 'passive' refers to the passive voice. Verbs can be in the active voice or the passive voice. 'Voice' shows the relation of the subject to the action. In *He killed the cat* the verb is in the active voice because the subject ('He') is the doer of the action of the verb. In *The cat was killed by him* the verb is in the passive voice because the subject ('The cat') is the recipient of the action of the verb.

verse *n.* **1** poetry. **2** a poem. **3** a group of lines forming a unit in a poem or song. **4** each of the short numbered divisions of a chapter of the Bible.

versed *adj.* ☐ **versed in** experienced or skilled in; having a knowledge of (*he's well versed in Pitjantjatjara*).

versicle / ver-suh-kuhl / *n.* each of the short sentences in a liturgy, said or sung by the priest and alternating with the 'responses' of the congregation.

versify *v.* (**versified, versifying**) express in verse; write verse. ☐ **versification** *n.*

version *n.* **1** a particular person's account of a matter. **2** a particular edition or translation of a book etc. (*the Douay Version of the Bible*). **3** a special or variant form of a thing (*the de luxe version of this car*).

vers libre / vair **leebr, lee**-bruh / *n.* verse with no regular metrical pattern. (¶ French, = free verse.)

verso *n.* (*pl.* **versos**) **1** the left-hand page of an open book. **2** the back of a leaf of a manuscript etc. (cf. RECTO).

versus *prep.* against (esp. in sport and law) (*the Geelong Cats versus the Sydney Swans; the case of Verdi versus Green*).

vertebra / **ver**-tuh-bruh / *n.* (*pl.* **vertebrae** / **ver**-tuh-bree /) any of the individual bones or segments that form the backbone. ☐ **vertebral** *adj.*

vertebrate / **ver**-tuh-bruht, -brayt / *adj.* (of an animal) having a backbone or spinal column. • *n.* such an animal.

vertex *n.* (*pl.* **vertexes** or **vertices** / **ver**-tuh-seez /) the highest point of a hill or structure; the apex of a cone or triangle.

vertical *adj.* **1** perpendicular to the horizontal; moving or placed in this way; upright. **2** in the direction from top to bottom of a picture etc. • *n.* a vertical line, part, or position. ☐ **vertical blind** a window blind of adjustable vertical strips of fabric. ☐ ☐ **vertically** *adv.*

verticordia / ver-tuh-**kaw**-dee-uh / *n.* a genus of highly ornamental plants, containing about 50 species mostly confined to south-western WA, with profuse feathery flowers in brilliant hues. Also called *feather flowers*.

vertiginous / ver-**tij**-uh-nuhs / *adj.* of or causing vertigo.

vertigo / **ver**-tuh-goh / *n.* a sensation of dizziness, esp. caused by heights.

verve / verv / *n.* enthusiasm, liveliness, vigour.

very *adv.* **1** in a high degree, extremely (*very good*). **2** in the fullest sense (*drink it to the very last drop*). **3** exactly (*sat in the very same seat*). • *adj.* **1** itself or herself etc. and no other, actual, truly such (*it's the very thing we need!*). **2** extreme, utter (*at the very end*). ☐ **very high frequency** (in radio) 30–300 megahertz. **very well** an expression of consent.

vesicle / **ves**-i-kuhl / *n.* **1** *Anatomy* & *Zoology* small fluid-filled bladder, sac, etc. **2** an air-filled bubble in some water plants, e.g seaweed. **3** a small cavity in volcanic rock produced by gas bubbles. **4** *Med.* a blister.

vespers *n.pl.* **1** *Catholic Church* **a** the sixth of the seven canonical hours of the breviary. **b** the service for this, said or chanted in the evening. **2** (in the Anglican Church etc.) evensong.

vessel *n.* **1** a hollow structure designed to travel on water and carry people or goods, a ship or boat. **2** a hollow receptacle, esp. for liquid. **3** a tube-like structure in the body of an animal or plant, conveying or holding blood or other fluid.

vest *n.* **1** a waistcoat. **2** (chiefly *Brit.*) a knitted or woven undergarment covering the trunk of the body (cf. SINGLET). • *v.* **1** confer as a firm or legal right (*the power of making laws is vested in Parliament; Parliament is vested with this power*). **2** clothe (oneself), esp. in vestments (*the priest is vesting for Mass*). ☐ **vested interest 1** personal interest in something, usu. with an expectation of gain. **2** *Law* an interest in land or money recognised as belonging to a person.

Vesta *Rom. myth.* the goddess of the hearth and household.

vestal *adj.* **1** chaste, pure. **2** of or relating to the goddess Vesta. ☐ **vestal virgin** (in ancient Rome) a virgin consecrated to Vesta and vowed to chastity.

vestibule / **ves**-tuh-byool / *n.* an entrance hall or lobby of a building.

vestige *n.* **1** a trace, a small remaining bit of what once existed (*not a vestige of the abbey remains*). **2** a very small amount (*not a vestige of truth in it*). **3** a functionless part or organ of a plant or animal that was well developed in ancestors. ☐ **vestigial** / ves-**tij**-uhl / *adj.*

vestment *n.* **1** any of various ceremonial ecclesiastical garments, esp. a chasuble as worn by a priest at Mass. **2** an official or state robe as worn by a lay person.

vestry *n.* = SACRISTY.

Vesuvius / vuh-**soo**-vee-uhs / an active volcano near Naples in Italy.

vet *n.* **1** a veterinary surgeon. **2** a veteran. • *v.* (**vetted, vetting**) examine carefully and critically for faults or errors etc.

vetch *n.* a plant of the pea family, used as fodder for cattle.

veteran *n.* **1** (often used as *adj.*) a person with long experience (in the armed forces or other group) (*a war veteran; a veteran actor*). **2** an ex-serviceman or servicewoman. ☐ **veteran car** a car made before 1916, or (strictly) before 1905.

veterinarian / vet-uh-ruh-**nair**-ree-uhn / *n.* a veterinary surgeon.

veterinary / **vet**-ruhn-ree, **vet**-uh-ruhn-uh-ree / *adj.* of or for the treatment of diseases and injuries of farm and domestic animals. ☐ **veterinary**

surgeon a person who is qualified in such treatment.

veto / **vee**-toh / *n.* (*pl.* **vetoes**) **1** an authoritative rejection or prohibition of something that is proposed. **2** the right to make such a rejection or prohibition unilaterally. • *v.* (**vetoed**, **vetoing**) reject or prohibit authoritatively.

vex *v.* annoy, irritate, cause worry to (a person). □ **vexed question** a problem that is difficult and much discussed.

vexation *n.* **1** vexing; being vexed, a state of irritation or worry. **2** something that causes this.

vexatious / vek-**say**-shuhs / *adj.* **1** causing vexation, annoying. **2** *Law* (of litigation) lacking sufficient grounds and seeking only to annoy the defendant.

VFT *abbr.* very fast train.

VHF *abbr.* very high frequency.

VHS *abbr. trademark* Video Home System, a format for recording and playing video tape.

via / **vuy**-uh / *prep.* by way of, through (*from Canberra to Adelaide via Melbourne; send it via your son*).

viable / **vuy**-uh-buhl / *adj.* **1** feasible, esp. economically; able to exist successfully (*a viable plan; is the newly-created State viable?*). **2** (of a plant, animal, etc.) capable of surviving in a particular climate etc. **3** (esp. of a foetus) sufficiently developed to be able to survive independently. □ **viably** *adv.* **viability** *n.*

viaduct / **vuy**-uh-dukt / *n.* a long bridge-like structure (usu. with a series of arches) for carrying a road or railway over a valley or dip in the ground.

viagra / vuy-**ag**-ruh / *n. trademark* a drug which increases a man's ability to maintain an erection during sexual stimulation.

vial / vuyuhl, **vuy**-uhl / *n.* a small bottle, esp. for liquid medicine.

viands / **vuy**-uhndz, **vee**-uhndz / *n.pl. formal* articles of food.

viaticum / vuy-**at**-i-kuhm / *n.* (*pl.* **viatica**) (esp. in the Catholic Church) the Eucharist as given to a dying person. (¶ Latin, = food for the road or journey.)

vibes / vuybz / *n.pl. colloq.* **1** mental or emotional vibrations; a feeling or atmosphere communicated (*this place has bad vibes*). **2** = VIBRAPHONE.

vibrant / **vuy**-bruhnt / *adj.* vibrating; resonant; lively; (of colours) bright.

vibraphone / **vuy**-bruh-fohn / *n.* a percussion instrument like a xylophone but with electronic resonators underneath the bars, giving a vibrating effect.

vibrate *v.* **1** move rapidly and continuously to and fro. **2** resonate; sound with a rapid slight variation of pitch. **3** (foll. by *with*) quiver, thrill (*his whole body was vibrating with passion*).

vibration *n.* **1** a vibrating movement, sensation, or sound. **2** (**vibrations**) a mental, esp. occult, influence. **3** the atmosphere or feeling in a place, regarded as communicable to people present in it (*'This room is haunted: can't you feel the sinister vibrations?'*).

vibrato / vuh-**brah**-toh / *n.* a vibrating effect in music, with rapid slight variation of pitch.

vibrator / vuy-**bray**-tuh / *n.* a device that vibrates or causes vibration, esp. an instrument for massage or sexual stimulation. □ **vibratory** / **vuy**-bruh-tuh-ree, vuy-**bray**- / *adj.*

viburnum / vuy-**ber**-nuhm, vuh- / *n.* a kind of shrub, usu. with white flowers.

Vic. *abbr.* **1** (the State of) Victoria. **2** Victorian.

vicar *n.* **1** (in the Anglican Church) a clergyman in charge of a parish. **2** (in the Catholic Church) a representative or deputy of a bishop or of the pope.

vicarage *n.* the house of a vicar (sense 1).

vicarious / vuh-**kair**-ree-uhs, vuy- / *adj.* **1** (of feelings or emotions) experienced indirectly, through other people (*received vicarious pleasure as he listened to his friend's account of what he'd done*). **2** acting or done for another (*vicarious suffering*). □ **vicariously** *adv.*

Vicar of Christ the pope as Christ's representative on earth.

vice[1] *n.* **1 a** grossly immoral conduct, great wickedness. **b** a particular form of this, esp. involving child prostitution, drug trafficking, etc. **2** a harmful habit (*smoking isn't one of my vices*). **3** a weakness, an indulgence (*good brandy is my one vice*). □ **vice ring** a group of criminals organising prostitution etc. **vice squad** a police department concerned with prostitution, drugs, gambling etc.

vice[2] *n.* an instrument with two jaws that grip a thing securely so as to leave the hands free for working on it, used esp. in carpentry and metalworking.

vice[3] / **vuy**-see / *prep.* in place of (*Ms Smith has been appointed as chief accountant vice Mr Brown, who has retired*). (¶ Latin, = by change.)

vice- *comb. form* **1** acting as substitute or deputy for (*vice-president*). **2** next in rank to (*vice admiral*).

vice-chancellor *n.* a deputy chancellor; the chief executive officer of a university.

vice-president *n.* an official ranking below and deputising for a president.

viceregal / vuys-**ree**-guhl / *adj.* **1** of a viceroy. **2** *Aust.* of or relating to the governor-general or a State governor.

viceroy *n.* a person governing a colony or province etc. as the sovereign's representative.

vice versa / vuy-see **ver**-suh, vuys / *adv.* the other way round (*we gossip about them and vice versa*). (¶ Latin, = the position being reversed.)

vichyssoise / vish-ee-**swahz** / *n.* a creamy soup of leeks and potatoes, often served chilled.

vicinity / vuh-**sin**-uh-tee / *n.* the surrounding district (*there is no good school in the vicinity*). □ **in the vicinity** (often foll. by *of*) near (to).

vicious / vish-uhs / *adj.* **1** acting or done with evil intentions, brutal, strongly spiteful. **2** (of animals) savage and dangerous, bad-tempered. **3** severe (*a vicious wind*). ◻ **vicious circle** a state of affairs in which a cause produces an effect which itself produces or intensifies the original cause. ◻◻ **viciously** *adv.* **viciousness** *n.*

vicissitude / vuh-**sis**-uh-tyood, vuy- / *n.* a change of circumstances affecting one's life.

Victa *n. Aust.* a two-stroke petrol rotary lawn-mower developed by Mervyn Victor Richardson (1894–1972) in the early 1950s. He called it the Victa, after his middle name.

victim *n.* **1** a person who is injured or killed by another or as the result of an occurrence (*victims of the earthquake*). **2** a prey or dupe (*fell victim to his charm*). **3** a living creature killed and offered as a religious sacrifice.

victimise *v.* (also **-ize**) make a victim of; single out (a person) to suffer ill-treatment or discrimination. ◻ **victimisation** *n.*

victimless crime *n.* activity which has been declared criminal because it is considered by legislators to be offensive to the moral standards of a community, even though there is no victim of that activity, e.g. homosexual activity between consenting adults in private.

victor *n.* the winner in a battle or contest.

Victoria[1] a State of south-eastern Australia, capital Melbourne.

Victoria[2], **Lake** (also **Victoria Nyanza**) the largest lake in Africa, in Uganda, Tanzania, and Kenya.

Victoria Cross / vik-**taw**-ree-uh / *n.* a decoration awarded to members of the Commonwealth armed services for a conspicuous act of bravery, instituted by Queen Victoria in 1856. In 1991 the imperial award was replaced by the Victoria Cross for Australia. (¶ Queen Victoria (1819–1901).)

Victorian *adj.* **1** of or relating to the State of Victoria or its inhabitants. **2 a** belonging to or characteristic of the reign of the British Queen Victoria (1837–1901). **b** narrow-minded and wowserish, prudish, rigidly moral. • *n.* **1** a native or resident of the State of Victoria. **2** a person, esp. a writer, of the time of Queen Victoria.

Victoriana / vik-taw-ree-**ah**-nuh / *n.pl.* articles, esp. collectors' items, of the Victorian period.

victorious *adj.* having gained the victory; triumphant.

victory *n.* success in a battle, contest, or game etc. achieved by gaining mastery over one's opponent or achieving the highest score.

victualler / **vit**-luh / *n.* a person who supplies victuals. ◻ **licensed victualler** a publican etc. licensed to sell alcohol.

victuals / **vit**-uhlz / *n.pl.* food, provisions. • *v.* (**victualled**, **victualling**) **1** supply with victuals. **2** obtain stores.

vicuña / vuh-**kyoo**-nuh, -**koo**-nyuh / *n.* **1** a South American animal related to the llama, with fine silky wool. **2** cloth made from its wool; an imitation of this.

vid *n. colloq.* a video recording, esp. of a film.

vide / **vee**-day, **vuy**-dee / *v. imperative* see, consult (a passage in a book etc.). (¶ Latin.)

videlicet / vee-**del**-uh-set / = VIZ.

video / **vid**-ee-oh / *adj.* **1** of the recording (or reproduction) of moving pictures on magnetic tape. **2** of the broadcasting of television pictures. • *n.* **1** such a recording or broadcasting. **2** a video recorder. **3** (also **vid**) a film on videotape. • *v.* (**videos**, **videoed**) record on videotape (*videoed the wedding*). ◻ **video cassette** a cassette of videotape. **video clip** a short film usu. of a pop star or group performing a song. **video game** a game in which points of light are moved on a television screen by means of an electronic control. **video nasty** *colloq.* a video film depicting scenes of explicit and gratuitous violence, cruelty, etc. **video recorder** (also **video cassette recorder**) a device for recording a television program etc. on magnetic tape for playing back later.

videoconference *n.* the use of television sets linked by telephone lines etc. to enable a group of people to communicate with each other in sound and vision. ◻ **videoconferencing** *n.*

videodisc *n.* a metal-coated disc on which visual material is recorded for reproduction on a television screen.

videotape *n.* magnetic tape for recording television pictures and sound. • *v.* record on this. ◻ **videotape recorder** = VIDEO RECORDER (see VIDEO).

videotext *n.* (also **videotex**) a system that links a television receiver etc. to an electronic news and information service.

vie *v.* (**vied**, **vying**) carry on a rivalry, compete (*vying with each other*).

Vienna the capital of Austria. ◻ **Viennese** *adj.* & *n.* (*pl.* **Viennese**).

Vientiane / vyen-tee-**ahn** / the capital of Laos.

Vietcong / vyet-**kong** / *n.* (*pl.* **Vietcong**) a member of the Communist guerrilla forces in South Vietnam 1954–75, which, with the support of North Vietnamese forces, fought the South Vietnamese government forces and their American and Australian etc. allies and won.

Vietnam a republic in SE Asia with a coastline on the South China Sea. ◻ **Vietnam War** a war between the South Vietnamese Government, aided by the USA (and supported by Australia etc.) and the Communist insurgents (the Vietcong) supported by North Vietnam (1959–75).

Vietnamese *n.* **1** (*pl.* **Vietnamese**) a person from Vietnam. **2** the language of Vietnam. • *adj.* of Vietnam or its people or language.

view *n.* **1** what can be seen from a specified point, fine natural scenery (*the view from the summit*). **2** range of vision (*the ship sailed into view*). **3** visual inspection of something (*we had a private view of the exhibition before it was opened*). **4** a mental survey of a subject etc. **5** a mental attitude, an opinion (*they have strong views about tax reform*). • *v.* **1** survey with the eyes or mind (*different ways of viewing the subject*). **2** inspect; look over (a house etc.) with the idea of buying it. **3** watch television etc. **4** regard or consider (*we view the matter seriously*). ☐ **in view of** having regard to, considering (*in view of the excellence of the work, we do not grudge the cost*). **on view** displayed for inspection. **with a view to** with the hope or intention of.

viewer *n.* **1** a person who views something, esp. television. **2** a device used in inspecting photographic slides etc.

viewfinder *n.* a device on a camera by which the user can see the area that will be photographed through the lens.

viewpoint *n.* a point of view, a standpoint.

vigil / vij-uhl / *n.* **1** staying awake to keep watch at a sick bed etc. or to pray; a period of this (*keep vigil; a long vigil*). **2** the eve of a religious festival. **3** a stationary, peaceful demonstration in support of a particular cause, usu. without speeches.

vigilant / vij-uh-luhnt / *adj.* watchful, on the lookout for possible danger etc. ☐ **vigilantly** *adv.* **vigilance** *n.*

vigilante / vij-uh-**lan**-tee / *n.* a member of a self-appointed group of people who, without legal authority, try to maintain law and order in a community, punish those who commit crimes, etc.

vigneron / vee-nyuh-ron, vin-yuh-ron / *n.* a grower of vines for wine.

vignette / vee-**nyet** / *n.* **1 a** a short description or character sketch. **b** a short evocative episode in a play, film, etc. **2** a photograph or portrait with the edges of the background gradually shaded off. • *v.* shade off in the style of a vignette.

vigoro / **vig**-uh-roh / *n. Aust.* a team game combining elements of baseball and cricket.

vigorous *adj.* full of vigour. ☐ **vigorously** *adv.* **vigorousness** *n.*

vigour *n.* (also **vigor**) **1** active physical or mental strength, energy; flourishing physical condition. **2** forcefulness of language or composition etc.

vihara / vuh-**hah**-ruh / *n.* a Buddhist temple or monastery. (¶ Sanskrit)

Viking / **vuy**-king / *n.* a Scandinavian raider and pirate of the 8th–11th centuries.

Vila / **vee**-luh / the capital of Vanuatu.

vile *adj.* **1** extremely disgusting (*a vile smell*). **2** depraved (*performed some vile acts*). **3** *colloq.* bad (*this vile weather*). ☐ **vilely** *adv.* **vileness** *n.*

vilify / **vil**-uh-fuy / *v.* (**vilified**, **vilifying**) say evil things about. ☐ **vilification** *n.*

villa *n.* **1** (in ancient Rome etc.) a large country house with an estate. **2** (esp. in Mediterranean countries) a country house; a mansion. **3** (in full **villa unit**) = HOME UNIT (*see* HOME).

village *n.* **1** a small country settlement. **2** *Aust.* a shopping centre in a suburb (*Corio village*). ☐ **villager** *n.*

villain / **vil**-uhn / *n.* **1** a person who is guilty or capable of great wickedness; a wrongdoer, a criminal. **2** a character in a story or play whose evil actions or motives are important in the plot. **3** *colloq.* a rascal. ☐ **villainy** *n.* **villainous** / **vil**-uh-nuhs / *adj.*

-ville *comb. form colloq.* forming the names of fictitious places with reference to a particular quality etc. (*dragsville; squaresville*).

villein / **vil**-uhn / *n. hist.* a feudal tenant entirely subject to a lord or attached to a manor. ☐ **villeinage** *n.*

Vilnius the capital of Lithuania.

vim *n. colloq.* vigour, energy.

vina / **vee**-nuh / *n.* an Indian musical instrument with four strings and a half-gourd at each end.

vinaigrette / vin-uh-**gret** / *n.* **1** salad dressing made of oil, wine, vinegar, and seasoning. **2** a small ornamental bottle for holding smelling salts.

Vincent de Paul, St (*c.*1580–1660), a French priest who devoted his life to work among the poor, the sick, and the oppressed, and inspired similar devotion in others. He founded two religious orders to carry on his work, one of secular priests and the other of nuns. (*See also* SAINT VINCENT DE PAUL SOCIETY.)

vindaloo / vin-duh-**loo** / *n.* (also used as *adj.*) a highly spiced hot Indian curry made with meat, fish, or poultry (originating in the Portuguese cuisine of Goa in India) (*chicken vindaloo; a vindaloo curry*).

vindicate / **vin**-duh-kayt / *v.* **1** clear of blame or suspicion. **2** establish the existence, merits, or justice of (something disputed etc.). **3** justify by evidence or argument. ☐ **vindication** *n.* **vindicator** *n.*

vindictive / vin-**dik**-tiv / *adj.* **1** having or showing a desire for revenge. **2** spiteful (*a vindictive remark*). ☐ **vindictively** *adv.* **vindictiveness** *n.*

vine *n.* **1** a climbing or trailing woody-stemmed plant whose fruit is the grape. **2** a slender climbing or trailing stem. ☐ **vine scrub** seasonally dry tropical or sub-tropical rainforest in Australia.

vinegar *n.* a sour liquid made from wine, cider, malt, etc. by fermentation, used in flavouring food and for pickling (*see also* BALSAMIC VINEGAR). ☐ **vinegarish** *adj.* **vinegary** *adj.*

vineyard / **vin**-yahd, -yuhd / *n.* a plantation of vines producing grapes for winemaking.

vino / **vee**-noh / *n. colloq.* wine, esp. of an inferior kind.

vinous / **vuy**-nuhs / *adj.* **1** of, like, or due to wine. **2** addicted to wine.

vintage / **vin**-tij / *n.* **1** the gathering of grapes for winemaking; the season of this. **2** wine made from a particular season's grapes; the date of this as an indication of the wine's quality. **3** the date or period when something was produced or existed (*searched the op shops for clothes of the 60s vintage*). • *adj.* of high or peak quality, esp. from a past period or characteristic of the best period of a person's work (*a CD of vintage Joan Sutherland*). ☐ **vintage car** a car made between 1917 and 1930.

vintner / **vint**-nuh / *n.* a wine merchant.

vinyl / **vuy**-nuhl / *n.* a kind of plastic, esp. polyvinyl chloride.

viol / **vuy**-ohl / *n.* a medieval stringed musical instrument of various sizes, similar to a violin but held vertically.

viola[1] / vee-**oh**-luh / *n.* **1** a stringed musical instrument slightly larger than a violin and of lower pitch. **2** a viola player in an orchestra (*spoke to the violas about their playing*). ☐ **viola da gamba** a large viol, corresponding to the modern cello, held between the player's knees.

viola[2] / **vuyuh**-luh, vuy-**oh**-luh / *n.* a plant of the genus to which pansies and violets belong, esp. a hybrid cultivated variety.

violable *adj.* able to be violated.

violate *v.* **1** break or act contrary to (an oath or treaty etc.). **2** treat (a sacred place) with irreverence or disrespect. **3** disturb (a person's privacy). **4** assault sexually; rape. ☐ **violation** *n.* **violator** *n.*

violence *n.* being violent; violent acts or conduct etc. ☐ **do violence to** act contrary to, be a breach of.

violent *adj.* **1** involving great force, strength, or intensity. **2** involving the unlawful use of force (*violent crime*). **3** (of death) caused by physical violence, not natural. ☐ **violently** *adv.*

violet *n.* **1** a small garden plant, usu. with purple sweet-scented flowers. **2** the colour at the opposite end of the spectrum from red; bluish purple. • *adj.* bluish-purple.

violin *n.* **1** a musical instrument with four strings of treble pitch, played with a bow. **2** a violin player in an orchestra (*spoke to the violins about their playing*). ☐ **violinist** *n.*

violist *n.* **1** / **vuy**-uh-luhst / a person who plays the viol. **2** / vee-**oh**-luhst / a person who plays the viola.

violoncello / vuy-uh-luhn-**chel**-oh / *n.* (*pl.* **violoncellos**) a cello.

VIP *abbr.* very important person.

viper *n.* **1** a small poisonous snake. **2** a malicious or treacherous person.

virago / vuh-**rah**-goh / *n.* (*pl.* **viragos**) a fierce or abusive woman.

viral / **vuy**-ruhl / *adj.* of or caused by a virus.

Virgil / **ver**-jil / (Publius Vergilius Maro) (70–19 BC), Roman poet, whose most famous work was the *Aeneid*.

virgin *n.* **1** a male or female who has never had sexual intercourse. **2** (**the Virgin**) the Virgin Mary, mother of Christ. **3** (**the Virgin**) a sign of the zodiac, Virgo. • *adj.* **1** virginal. **2** spotless, undefiled (*virgin snow*). **3** untouched, in its original state, not yet used (*virgin soil; virgin wool; virgin bush*). **4** (of olive oil etc.) obtained from the first pressing of olives etc. ☐ **virgin birth** (in Christian teaching) the doctrine that Christ had no human father but was conceived by the Virgin Mary by the power of the Holy Spirit.

■ **Usage** Do not confuse this doctrine with that of the IMMACULATE CONCEPTION.

virginal *adj.* **1** of, being, or suitable for a virgin. **2** (also **virginals** *or* **pair of virginals**) a keyboard instrument of the 16th–17th centuries, the earliest form of harpsichord.

virginity *n.* the state of being a virgin.

Virgo / **ver**-goh / the sixth sign of the zodiac, the Virgin. ☐ **Virgoan** *adj.* & *n.*

virile / **vi**-ruyl / *adj.* **1** (of a man) vigorous or strong. **2** marked by strength, force, energy, etc. (*virile poetry*). **3** (of a man) sexually potent. **4** of a man as distinct from a woman or child. ☐ **virility** / vuh-**ril**-uh-tee / *n.*

virology / vuy-**rol**-uh-jee / *n.* the study of viruses. ☐ **virological** *adj.* **virologist** *n.*

virtual *adj.* **1** being so in effect though not in name or according to strict definition (*he is the virtual head of the firm; gave what was a virtual promise*). **2** *Computing* not physically existing as such but made by software to appear to do so (*virtual RAM*). ☐ **virtual memory** *Computing* a memory in which required data is automatically transferred from a secondary data store so that it appears to be in the main memory. **virtual reality 1** image or environment (generated by computer software) with which a user can interact realistically using a helmet with a screen inside, gloves fitted with sensors, etc. **2** the world of IRC, interactive role-playing, etc., as generated by the Internet.

virtually *adv.* in effect, nearly, almost.

virtue *n.* **1** moral excellence, goodness; a particular form of this (*patience is a virtue*). **2** chastity, esp. of a woman. **3** a good quality, an advantage (*the seat has the virtue of being adjustable*). ☐ **by** (*or* **in**) **virtue of** by reason of, because of (*he is entitled to a pension by virtue of his long service*).

virtuoso / ver-choo-**oh**-soh, -zoh / *n.* (*pl.* **virtuosos** *or* **virtuosi**) (also used as *adj.*) a person who excels in the technique of doing something, esp. singing or playing music (*he's a virtuoso on the organ; a virtuoso performance*). ☐ **virtuosity** / ver-choo-**os**-uh-tee / *n.*

virtuous *adj.* having or showing moral virtue. ☐ **virtuously** *adv.* **virtuousness** *n.*

virulent / **vi**-ruh-luhnt / *adj.* **1** (of poison or disease) extremely strong or violent. **2** strongly

virus 936 **vitalise**

and bitterly hostile (*virulent abuse*). ☐ **virulence** *n.*

virus / **vuy**-ruhs / *n.* (*pl.* **viruses**) **1** a very simple microscopic organism (smaller than bacteria) multiplying in living cells and capable of causing disease. **2** such a disease. **3** a computer program or section of programming code which is designed to sabotage a computer system by causing itself to be copied into other parts of the system, often destroying data in the process.

visa / **vee**-zuh / *n.* an official stamp or mark put on a passport by officials of a foreign country to show that the holder may enter their country.

visage / **viz**-ij / *n. literary* a person's face.

vis-à-vis / vee-zah-**vee** / (also **vis-a-vis**) *prep.* **1** in a position facing; opposite to. **2** in relation to (*vis-a-vis the proposed extension* ...). •*adv.* facing one another; opposite. •*n.* a person occupying a corresponding position in another group etc. (*he's my vis-a-vis in the Indonesian Embassy*).

viscera / **vis**-uh-ruh / *n.pl.* the internal organs of the body, esp. the intestines.

visceral / **vis**-uh-ruhl / *adj.* **1** of the viscera. **2** of feelings rather than reason.

viscid / **vis**-uhd / *adj.* (of liquid) thick and gluey.

viscose / **vis**-kohz, -kohs / *n.* **1** cellulose in a viscous state, used in the manufacture of rayon etc. **2** fabric made of this.

viscount / **vuy**-kownt / *n.* a nobleman ranking between earl or count and baron. ☐ **viscountcy** *n.*

viscountess / **vuy**-kown-tes / *n.* **1** a viscount's wife or widow. **2** a woman holding the rank of viscount.

viscous / **vis**-kuhs / *adj.* thick and gluey, not pouring easily. ☐ **viscosity** / vis-**kos**-uh-tee / *n.*

Vishnu / **vish**-noo / one of the major gods of Hinduism, the supreme being, the Preserver in the Hindu trinity comprising Vishnu, Brahma, and Siva.

visibility *n.* **1** being visible. **2** the range or possibility of vision as determined by conditions of light and atmosphere (*visibility was down to 50 metres*).

visible *adj.* **1** able to be seen by the eye. **2** able to be perceived or ascertained; apparent; open (*has no visible means of support; spoke with visible impatience*). ☐ **visibly** *adv.*

Visigoth *n.* a member of the western branch of the Goths, who invaded the Roman Empire in the 3rd–5th centuries.

vision *n.* **1** the faculty of seeing, sight. **2** a thing or person seen in a dream or trance. **3** a supernatural or prophetic apparition (*vision of the Virgin Mary at Fatima*). **4** a thing or idea perceived vividly in the imagination (*the romantic visions of youth*). **5** imaginative insight into a subject or problem etc. (*his work shows vision and flair*). **6** statesmanlike foresight; imaginative planning for the future (*a political party devoid of vision*). **7** a person or sight of unusual beauty. **8** a television or cinema picture, esp. of a specified quality (*poor vision*).

visionary *adj.* **1** given to seeing visions. **2** existing only in the imagination, fanciful, not practical (*wildly visionary schemes*). **3** having vision or foresight (*a visionary plan for urban restructuring*). **4** not real, imagined (*these threats to Australia are merely visionary*). •*n.* **1** a person who sees visions. **2** a person with visionary ideas.

visit *v.* **1** go or come to see (a person or place etc.), socially, on business, or for some other purpose. **2** stay temporarily with (a person) or at (a place). **3** (of a disease, calamity, etc.) attack (*visited by floods and then by cholera*). **4** (in the Bible) inflict punishment for (*why should the sins of the fathers be visited on the children?*). •*n.* **1 a** an act of visiting. **b** a temporary stay. **2** (foll. by *to*) an occasion of going to a doctor etc. **3** a formal or official call. ☐ **visiting medical officer** *Aust.* a specialist in one of the branches of medicine who is contracted to provide services to a public hospital.

visitant *n.* **1** a visitor, esp. a supernatural one; a ghost. **2** a migratory bird that is staying temporarily in an area.

visitation *n.* **1** an official visit, esp. of inspection. **2** trouble or disaster looked upon as punishment from God. **3** (**the Visitation**) a Christian festival on 2 July, commemorating the visit of the Virgin Mary to her kinswoman Elizabeth.

visitor *n.* **1** one who visits a person or place. **2** a migratory bird that lives in an area temporarily or at a certain season.

visor / **vuy**-zuh / *n.* (also **vizor**) **1** the movable front part of a helmet, covering the face. **2** a shield for the eyes, esp. one at the top of a vehicle windscreen.

vista *n.* **1** a view, esp. one seen through a long narrow opening such as an avenue of trees. **2** a mental view of an extensive period or series of remembered or anticipated events (*opened up new vistas to his ambition*).

visual *adj.* of or used in seeing; received through sight. •*n.* (usu. **visuals** *pl.*) a visual image or display; a picture. ☐ **visual aid** a film, picture, model, etc., as an aid to teaching. **visual display unit** (*or* **terminal**) *Computing* a device resembling a television screen on which data can be displayed. ☐☐ **visually** *adv.*

visualise *v.* (also **-ize**) form a mental picture of. ☐ **visualisation** *n.*

vital *adj.* **1** connected with life, essential to life (*vital functions*). **2** essential to the existence, success, or operation of something; extremely important. **3** full of life or activity (*she's a very vital sort of person*). **4** fatal to life or success etc. (*a vital error*). •*n.pl.* (**vitals**) the vital parts of the body (e.g. heart, lungs, brain). ☐ **vitally** *adv.*

vitalise *v.* (also **-ize**) put life or vitality into. ☐ **vitalisation** *n.*

vitality / vuy-**tal**-uh-tee / n. **1** liveliness, vigour, persistent energy. **2** the ability to survive or endure.

vitamin / **vuy**-tuh-min, **vit**-uh- / n. any of a number of organic substances present in many foods and essential to the nutrition of man and other animals (*vitamin A, B, C,* etc.).

vitaminise v. (also -**ize**) add vitamins to (a food, face cream, etc.).

vitiate / **vish**-ee-ayt / v. **1** make imperfect, spoil. **2** weaken the force of, make ineffective (*this admission vitiates your claim*). ▫ **vitiation** n.

viticulture / **vit**-ee-kul-chuh / n. the process of growing grapes.

vitreous / **vit**-ree-uhs / adj. having a glasslike texture or finish (*vitreous enamel*). ▫ **vitreous humour** the clear fluid in the eye between the lens and the retina.

vitrify / **vit**-ruh-fuy / v. (**vitrified, vitrifying**) change into glass or a glasslike substance, esp. by heat. ▫ **vitrifaction** n. **vitrification** n.

vitriol / **vit**-ree-ol / n. **1** sulphuric acid or one of its salts. **2** savagely hostile comments or criticism.

vitriolic / vit-ree-**ol**-ik / adj. (of speech or criticism) caustic, hostile.

vituperate / vuh-**tyoo**-puh-rayt, vuy- / v. use abusive language. ▫ **vituperation** n. **vituperative** adj.

Vitus / **vuy**-tuhs /, St (c.300), a martyr of the persecution in the reign of Diocletian, invoked against epilepsy, chorea (= St Vitus's dance), and rabies.

viva[1] / **vuy**-vuh / colloq. n. a viva voce examination. •v. (**vivaed, vivaing**) examine in a viva.

viva[2] / **vee**-vuh / interj. long live (a person or thing).

vivace / vuh-**vah**-chay / adv. *Music* in a lively manner.

vivacious / vuh-**vay**-shuhs / adj. lively, high-spirited. ▫ **vivaciously** adv. **vivacity** / vuh-**vas**-uh-tee / n.

Vivaldi / vi-**val**-dee /, Antonio (1678–1741), Italian composer and violinist, whose best-known work is *The Four Seasons*.

vivarium / vuh-**vair**-ree-uhm, vuy- / n. (pl. **vivaria** or **vivariums**) a place prepared for keeping animals in conditions as similar as possible to their natural environment, for purposes of study etc.

viva voce / vuy-vuh **voh**-chee / adj. (of an examination in universities) oral. •adv. orally. •n. an oral examination. •v. (**viva-voce**) (**vivavoceed, viva-voceing**) examine orally.

vivid adj. **1** (of light or colour) bright and strong, intense. **2** producing strong and clear mental pictures (*a vivid description*). **3** (of the imagination) creating ideas etc. in an active and lively way. ▫ **vividly** adv. **vividness** n.

viviparous / vuh-**vip**-uh-ruhs / adj. producing young in a developed state from the mother's body, not hatching by means of an egg (cf. OVIPAROUS).

vivisect v. perform vivisection on.

vivisection n. dissection or other painful treatment of living animals for purposes of scientific research, testing the effects of new cosmetics, etc. ▫ **vivisectional** adj. **vivisectionist** n. & adj. **vivisector** n.

vixen n. **1** a female fox. **2** a spiteful woman.

viz. adv. namely (*the case is made in three sizes, viz. large, medium, and small*).

■ **Usage** In reading aloud, the word 'namely' is usu. spoken where 'viz.' (short for Latin *videlicet*) is written.

vizor alternative spelling of VISOR.

VMO abbr. Aust. = VISITING MEDICAL OFFICER.

V-neck n. a V-shaped neckline on a pullover etc.

vocab / **voh**-cab / n. colloq. vocabulary.

vocabulary n. **1** the words used by a particular language. **2** the words used by a particular book, branch of science, author, etc. (*scientific vocabulary; Shakespeare's vocabulary*). **3** a list of these, in alphabetical order with definitions or translations. **4** an individual's stock of words (*he has a highly limited vocabulary*).

vocal / **voh**-kuhl / adj. **1** of, for, or uttered by the voice. **2** expressing one's feelings freely in speech (*he was very vocal about his rights*). •n. **1** (**vocal** or **vocals**) (esp. in pop, rock, etc.) the sung part of a musical composition. **2** (**vocals**) (esp. in pop, rock, etc.) the words of such a sung part. ▫ **vocal cords** the voice-producing part of the larynx. ▫▫ **vocally** adv.

vocalese / voh-kuh-**leez** / n. **1** a style of singing in which the singers put meaningless syllables to what was previously an instrumental piece, imitating the instruments (*they performed a vocalese of Bach's 'Brandenberg Concerto'*). **2** = SCAT[2].

vocalic / voh-**kal**-ik / adj. of or consisting of a vowel or vowels.

vocalise v. / **voh**-kuh-luyz / (also -**ize**) **1** utter; express (*vocalised his indignation*). **2** sing with several notes to one vowel. •n. / voh-kuh-**leez** / a singing exercise using individual syllables or vowel sounds; a vocal passage consisting of a melody without words.

vocalist / **voh**-kuh-luhst / n. a singer, esp. in a pop group.

vocation / voh-**kay**-shuhn / n. **1** a strong feeling of suitability for a particular career. **2** this regarded as a divine call to work in the Church. **3** a person's trade or profession. ▫ **vocational** adj.

vocative n. the grammatical case of a noun etc. used in addressing a person or thing. •adj. of or in this case.

vociferate / vuh-**sif**-uh-rayt / v. say loudly or noisily, shout. ▫ **vociferation** n.

vociferous / vuh-**sif**-uh-ruhs / *adj.* making a great outcry, expressing one's views forcibly and insistently. ☐ **vociferously** *adv.* **vociferousness** *n.*

vodka *n.* alcoholic spirit distilled chiefly from rye, esp. in Russia.

vogue *n.* **1** current fashion (*large hats are the vogue*). **2** popular favour or acceptance (*his novels had a great vogue ten years ago*). ☐ **in vogue** in fashion.

voice *n.* **1** sounds formed in the larynx and uttered by the mouth, esp. human utterance in speaking, singing, etc. **2** ability to produce such sounds (*she has a cold and has lost her voice*). **3** expression of one's opinion etc. in spoken or written words; the opinion itself; the right to express opinion (*gave voice to his indignation; I have no voice in the matter*). **4** *Grammar* any of the sets of forms of a verb that show whether it is active or passive. • *v.* **1** put into words, express (*she voiced her opinion*). **2** (usu. as **voiced** *adj.*) utter with resonance of the vocal cords, not only with the breath (e.g. *b, d*). ☐ **voice box** the larynx.

voice-over *n.* narration (e.g. in a film) by a voice not accompanied by a picture of the speaker. *v.* provide (a television program etc.) with a commentary spoken by an unseen narrator (usu. someone whose voice is well known). **with one voice** unanimously.

voiceless *adj.* **1** dumb, speechless. **2** uttered without vibration of the vocal cords (e.g. *f, p*).

void *adj.* **1** empty, vacant (*the void deeps of space; the position has been void since the sacking of the last incumbent*). **2** not legally valid. • *n.* empty space, emptiness. • *v.* **1** make legally void (*the contract was voided by his death*). **2** excrete (urine or faeces). ☐ **void of** lacking; free from (a bad quality or a good) (*a style void of affectation; he is void of pity*).

voila / vwu-**lah** / *exclam.* there it is; there you are. (¶ French)

voile / voil / *n.* a very fine semi-transparent fabric.

volatile / **vol**-uh-tuyl / *adj.* **1** (of a liquid) evaporating rapidly. **2** (of a person) lively, changing quickly or easily from one mood or interest to another. **3** (of trading conditions) unstable. **4** (of a political situation etc.) liable to erupt into violence. ☐ **volatility** / vol-uh-**til**-uh-tee / *n.*

volatilise / vuh-**lat**-uh-luyz / *v.* (also **-ize**) turn or become turned into vapour. ☐ **volatilisation** *n.*

vol-au-vent / **vol**-oh-von / *n.* a small circular puff pastry case with a savoury filling. (¶ French, = flight in the wind.)

volcanic *adj.* of, like, or from a volcano. ☐ **volcanically** *adv.*

volcano *n.* (*pl.* **volcanoes**) a mountain or hill with openings through which lava, gases, etc. from below the earth's crust are or have been expelled.

volcanology / vol-kuh-**nol**-uh-jee / *n.* (also **vulcanology**) the study of volcanoes. ☐ **volcanological** / -nuh-**loj**-i-kuhl / *adj.* **volcanologist** *n.*

vole *n.* a small plant-eating rodent.

Volga the longest river in Europe, flowing from north-western Russia to the Caspian Sea.

volition / vuh-**lish**-uhn / *n.* use of one's own will in choosing or making a decision (*she did it of her own volition*). ☐ **volitional** *adj.*

volley *n.* (*pl.* **volleys**) **1** simultaneous discharge of a number of missiles; the missiles themselves. **2** a number of questions or curses etc. directed in quick succession at someone. **3** return of the ball in tennis etc. before it touches the ground. • *v.* **1** discharge or fly in a volley. **2** return (a ball) by a volley.

volleyball *n.* a game for two teams of six players who volley a large ball by hand over a high net.

volt *n.* a unit of electromotive force; force sufficient to carry one ampere of current against one ohm resistance. (¶ Named after the Italian physicist Count Alessandro Volta (1745–1824).)

voltage / **vohl**-tij / *n.* electromotive force expressed in volts.

Voltaire / vol-**tair** / (pseudonym of François-Marie Arouet) (1694–1778), French writer of plays, poetry, and histories, an outspoken critic of the civil and ecclesiastical establishments.

voltameter *n.* an instrument for measuring an electric charge.

volte-face / volt-**fahs** / *n.* a complete change of one's attitude towards something.

voltmeter *n.* an instrument measuring electric potential in volts.

voluble / **vol**-yuh-buhl / *adj.* talking very much; speaking or spoken with great fluency. ☐ **volubly** *adv.* **volubility** / vol-yuh-**bil**-uh-tee / *n.*

volume *n.* **1** a book, esp. one of a set. **2** the amount of space (often expressed in cubic units) that a three-dimensional thing occupies or contains. **3** the size or amount of something, a quantity (*the great volume of water pouring over the weir; the volume of business has increased*). **4** the strength or power of sound, loudness (*turn down the volume!*). ☐ **speak volumes** be highly significant (*a look that speaks volumes*).

volumetric / vol-yuh-**met**-rik / *adj.* of or using measurement by volume (*volumetric analysis*). ☐ **volumetrically** *adv.*

voluminous / vuh-**loo**-muh-nuhs / *adj.* **1** (of drapery etc.) large and full (*voluminous skirts*). **2** (of writings) great in quantity; (of a writer) producing many works.

voluntary *adj.* **1** acting, done, or given etc. of one's own free will and not under compulsion. **2** working or done without payment (*voluntary work*). **3** (of an organisation) maintained by voluntary contributions or voluntary workers. **4** (of bodily movements) controlled by the will. • *n.* an organ solo played before, during, or after a church service. ☐ **voluntarily** *adv.* **voluntariness** *n.*

volunteer *n.* **1** a person who offers to do something. **2** a person who enrols for military or other service voluntarily, not as a conscript. • *v.* undertake or offer voluntarily, be a volunteer.

volunteerism *n.* the use or involvement of volunteer labour, esp. in community services.

voluptuary / vuh-**lup**-choo-uh-ree, -tyoo- / *n.* a person who indulges in luxury and sensual pleasure.

voluptuous / vuh-**lup**-choo-uhs, -tyoo- / *adj.* **1** of, tending to, occupied with, or derived from, sensuous or sensual or sexual pleasure (*a voluptuous feast; voluptuous satin sheets; a long, voluptuous embrace*). **2** (of a woman) having a full and attractive figure. ☐ **voluptuously** *adv.* **voluptuousness** *n.*

volute / vuh-**lyoot** / *n.* **1** a spiral stonework scroll as an ornament of esp. Ionic capitals. **2** a twist or turn of a spiral shell. ☐ **voluted** *adj.* **volution** *n.*

vomit *v.* (**vomited, vomiting**) **1** eject (matter) from the stomach through the mouth; be sick. **2** (of a volcano, chimney, etc.) eject violently, belch forth. • *n.* matter vomited from the stomach.

von Mueller, Baron Sir Ferdinand (Jakob Heinrich) (1825–96), Australian botanist and explorer in Australia (born in Germany) who did much scientific research into Australian flora (esp. eucalypts and acacias), designed and was director of the Melbourne Botanic Gardens, and was one of the founders of Melbourne University.

voodoo *n.* a form of religion based on belief in witchcraft and magical rites, as practised esp. in the West Indies. • *v.* (**voodoos, voodooed**) affect by voodoo; bewitch. ☐ **voodooism** *n.* **voodooist** *n.*

voracious / vuh-**ray**-shuhs / *adj.* **1** greedy in eating, very eager (*a voracious reader*). ☐ **voraciously** *adv.* **voracity** / vuh-**ras**-uh-tee / *n.*

vortex *n.* (*pl.* **vortexes** *or* **vortices** / **vaw**-tuh-seez /) **1** a whirling mass of water or air, a whirlpool or whirlwind. **2** a thing viewed as swallowing things which approach it (*the vortex of society*). ☐ **vortical** *adj.*

vorticist / **vaw**-tuh-suhst / *n.* a futurist painter, writer, etc., of a school based on the so-called 'vortices' of modern civilisation. ☐ **vorticism** *n.*

votary / **voh**-tuh-ree / *n.* (*feminine* **votaress**) (usu. foll. by *of*) **1** a person dedicated to the service of God or a god or a cult. **2** a devoted follower of a person, system, occupation, etc.

vote *n.* **1** a formal expression of one's opinion or choice on a matter under discussion, e.g. by ballot or show of hands, or in an election. **2** the total number of votes given by or for a certain group (*that policy will lose us the Labor vote*). **3** (**the vote**) the right to vote, esp. in a parliamentary election. **4** a ticket etc. used for recording a vote. • *v.* **1** express an opinion or choice by a vote. **2** decide by a majority of votes. **3** declare by general consent (*the meal was voted excellent*). **4** suggest, urge (*I vote that we call it a day and go home*). ☐ **voter** *n.*

votive / **voh**-tiv / *adj.* given in fulfilment of a vow (*votive offerings at the shrine*). ☐ **votive Mass** *Catholic Church* a Mass celebrated for a special purpose or occasion.

vouch *v.* (foll. by *for*) guarantee the certainty, accuracy, reliability, etc. of (*I will vouch for his honesty*).

voucher *n.* **1** a document (issued in token of payment made or promised) that can be exchanged for certain goods or services. **2** a receipt.

vouchsafe *v.* give or grant, often in a gracious or condescending manner (*they did not vouchsafe a reply*).

vow *n.* **1** a solemn promise, esp. in the form of an oath to God, a saint, etc. **2** (**vows**) the solemn promises to God by which a monk, nun, or priest, is bound to poverty, chastity, and obedience. **3** a promise of fidelity (*marriage vows*). • *v.* promise or declare solemnly (*they vowed vengeance against their oppressor*).

vowel *n.* **1** a speech sound made without audible stopping of the breath (as opposed to a CONSONANT). **2** a letter or letters representing such a sound, as *a*, *e*, *i*, *o*, *u*, *ee*, etc.

vox populi / voks **pop**-yoo-lee, -luy / *n.* public opinion, popular belief. (¶ Latin, = voice of the people.)

voyage *n.* a journey by water or in space, esp. a long one. • *v.* make a voyage. ☐ **voyager** *n.*

Voyager 1 (in full **HMAS** *Voyager*) either of two Australian navy destroyers, one sunk during the Second World War, the other sunk in collision with HMAS *Melbourne* in 1964. **2** each of two US space probes launched in 1977 to Jupiter, Saturn, Uranus, and Neptune.

voyeur / vwah-**yer**, voi-**er** / *n.* **1** a person who obtains sexual gratification from looking at the sexual actions or organs of others. **2** a spectator, esp. in secret. ☐ **voyeurism** *n.* **voyeuristic** *adj.*

vs *abbr.* versus.

V-sign *n.* **1** a sign of the letter V made with the first two fingers pointing up and the back of the hand facing outwards, as a gesture of abuse. **2** a similar sign made with the palm of the hand facing outwards, as a symbol of victory.

VTR *abbr.* videotape recorder.

Vulcan *Rom. myth.* the god of fire and metal-working, identified with Hephaestus.

vulcanise *v.* (also **-ize**) treat (rubber or similar material) with sulphur at a high temperature in order to increase its elasticity and strength. ☐ **vulcanisation** *n.*

vulcanite *n.* hard black vulcanised rubber.

vulcanology *n.* variant spelling of VOLCANOLOGY.

vulgar *adj.* **1** lacking in refinement or good taste. **2** coarse, indecent. **3** commonly used and incorrect (but not coarse) (*vulgar superstitions*). ❑ **the vulgar tongue** the national or vernacular language. **vulgar fraction** a fraction represented by numbers above and below a line (e.g. ⅔, ⅝), not decimally. ❑ **vulgarly** *adv.*

vulgarian / vul-**gair**-ree-uhn / *n.* a vulgar person, esp. a rich one.

vulgarise *v.* (also **-ize**) **1** cause (a person or manners etc.) to become vulgar. **2** reduce to the level of being usual or ordinary, spoil by making ordinary or too well known. ❑ **vulgarisation** *n.*

vulgarism *n.* **1** a word or expression in coarse or uneducated use (*'he is learning her to drive'* is a *vulgarism for 'he is teaching her'*). **2** a coarse action or habit.

vulgarity *n.* the quality of being vulgar; a vulgar act or expression.

Vulgate / **vul**-gayt, -guht / *n.* the Latin version of the Bible prepared mainly by St. Jerome in the 4th century, the Old Testament being translated directly from the Hebrew; the official Catholic Latin text of this as revised in 1592.

vulnerable / **vul**-nuh-ruh-buhl / *adj.* **1** able to be hurt or wounded. **2** unprotected, exposed to danger, temptation, criticism, etc. ❑ **vulnerably** *adv.* **vulnerability** *n.*

vulpine / **vul**-puyn / *adj.* **1** of or like a fox. **2** crafty, cunning.

vulture *n.* **1** a large bird of prey that lives on the flesh of dead animals. **2** a greedy person seeking to profit from the misfortunes of others.

vulva *n.* the external parts of the female genital organs, esp. the two pairs of labia and the cleft between these.

vv. *abbr.* **1** verses. **2** volumes.

vying *see* VIE.

W

W *abbr.* (also **W.**) **1** watt(s). **2** West; Western. • *symbol* tungsten.

w. *abbr.* **1** wicket(s). **2** wide(s). **3** with.

WA *abbr.* **1** Western Australia. **2** Western Australian; West Australian.

waatgin alternative spelling of WATJIN.

WACA / wak-uh / **1** *abbr.* Western Australian Cricket Association. **2** *n.* the cricket ground of this Association in Perth (*played at the WACA*).

wacker alternative spelling of WHACKER.

wacko *colloq. adj.* crazy; weird. •*n.* (*pl.* **wackos** or **wackoes**) a weird or crazy person.

wacky *adj.* (**wackier**, **wackiest**) *colloq.* crazy, weird. ◻ **wackiness** *n.*

wad / wod / *n.* **1** a lump or bundle of soft material used to keep things apart or in place, stop up a hole, etc. **2** a bundle of documents or banknotes. **3** (**wad** *or* **wads**) a large quantity (esp. of money). •*v.* (**wadded**, **wadding**) line, stuff, or protect with wadding.

wadding *n.* soft fibrous material used for padding, packing, or lining things.

waddle *v.* walk with short steps and a swaying movement (e.g. like a duck or goose). •*n.* a waddling walk.

waddy[1] / wod-ee / (also **waddie**) *n.* (*pl.* **waddies**) *Aust.* **1** an Aboriginal war club made of wood. **2** a club, cudgel, stick, etc. used as a weapon by a person other than an Aborigine. •*v.* strike, beat, or kill (an animal or person) with a waddy; bludgeon (*surrounded the beast and waddied it to death*). ◻ **waddy tree** = WADDYWOOD (sense 1). (¶ Dharuk *wadi* 'tree, stick, club'.)

waddy[2] *n. Aust.* an Aboriginal male. (¶ Western Desert language *wadi* 'an initiated man'.)

waddywood / wod-ee-wuud / *n.* **1** (also **waddy tree**) any of several Australian trees yielding a hard wood used by Aborigines for making waddies, esp. the rare wattle *Acacia peuce* of south-western Qld and the NT. **2** = WHALEBONE TREE. (¶ Probably Midhaga.)

wade *v.* **1** walk through water, mud, etc., esp. with difficulty. **2** (foll. by *through*) progress slowly and with difficulty (*waded through the book; wading through the chores*). ◻ **wade in** *colloq.* intervene; make a vigorous attack. **wade into** *colloq.* attack (a person or task) vigorously.

wader *n.* **1** a long-legged waterbird that wades in shallow water. **2** (**waders**) high waterproof boots worn in fishing etc.

wadgula / wah-dyoo-lah / *n. Aust.* (in Aboriginal English) a white person. (¶ Alteration of *white fellow*.)

wafer *n.* **1** a thin light biscuit. **2** a thin disc of unleavened bread used in the Eucharist, a host. ◻ **wafer-thin** *adj.* very thin.

waffle[1] / wof-uhl / *colloq. n.* vague wordy talk or writing; nonsense. •*v.* talk or write waffle. ◻ **waffler** *n.* **waffly** *adj.*

waffle[2] / wof-uhl / *n.* a small cake made of batter and eaten hot. ◻ **waffle-iron** a utensil with two hinged metal plates used for cooking waffles.

waft / woft / *v.* carry or travel lightly and easily through the air or over water. •*n.* (usu. foll. by *of*) a whiff or smell.

wag[1] *v.* (**wagged**, **wagging**) **1** shake or move briskly to and fro. **2** *Aust.* play truant, be absent from (work etc.) without leave. •*n.* a single wagging movement. ◻ **tongues wag** there is talk.

wag[2] *n.* a person who is fond of making jokes or playing tricks.

Waga-waga / wah-gu-wah-gu / *n.* an Aboriginal language of south-eastern Qld in a vast area roughly bounded by Toowoomba, Biloela, and Condamine.

wage[1] *v.* engage in (*wage war*).

wage[2] *n.* **1** (also **wages**) regular payment to an employee, esp. a manual worker (cf. SALARY). **2** (also **wages**, sometimes treated as *sing.*) requital (*the wages of sin is death*). ◻ **wage earner** a person who works for wages. **wage indexation** the adjustment of wages in relation to movements in the consumer price index.

waged *adj.* receiving a wage; in regular paid employment. •*n.* (**the waged**) the employed.

wager / way-juh / *n.* a bet. •*v.* bet.

wagga / wog-uh / *n. Aust.* (in full **wagga blanket**) an improvised covering, usu. of lengths of sacking etc. sewn together, often padded with whatever scraps of cloth etc. come to hand. (¶ Abbreviation of *Wagga Wagga*, a town in NSW.)

waggish *adj.* of or like a wag; said or done in a joking way. ◻ **waggishly** *adv.* **waggishness** *n.*

waggle *v.* wag. •*n.* a wagging movement. ◻ **waggly** *adj.*

Wagner / vahg-nuh /, (Wilhelm) Richard (1813–83), German composer of operas and music dramas, often based on Germanic myths and legends.

Wagnerian / vahg-neer-ree-uhn / *adj.* of or characteristic of the works of Wagner, esp. with regard to their large dramatic scale.

wagon *n.* (also **waggon**) **1** a four-wheeled vehicle for heavy loads. **2** an open railway truck, e.g. for coal. **3** *colloq.* a station wagon. ◻ **on the**

wagon (*or* **water wagon**) *colloq.* abstaining from alcohol.

wagoner *n.* (also **waggoner**) the driver of a wagon.

wagtail *n.* any of several small birds with a long tail that moves up and down constantly when the bird is standing.

wagyl / **wog**-uhl / *n. Aust.* **1** (in Aboriginal lore) the creator of waterways in Australia; the rainbow serpent. **2** a carpet snake. (¶ Nyungar)

wahlenbergia / wah-luhn-**ber**-jee-uh / *n.* (also **bluebell, royal bluebell**) any of several Australian herbs of the genus of the same name, esp.: **1** *W. gloriosa* (also the **Austral bluebell**) bearing large, dark blue flowers, the floral emblem of the ACT. **2** *W. stricta*, bearing light blue flowers which often carpet large areas of the landscape in blue.

waif *n.* a homeless and helpless person; an unowned or abandoned child.

wail *v.* **1** utter a long sad cry; lament or complain persistently. **2** (of wind etc.) make a sound like a person wailing. • *n.* a wailing cry, sound, or utterance.

wain *n. archaic* a farm wagon.

wainwright *n.* a person who builds and repairs wagons.

wainscot *n.* wooden panelling on the lower part of the wall of a room.

wainscoting *n.* wainscot; material for this.

waist *n.* **1** the part of the human body below the ribs and above the hips. **2** the part of a garment covering this. **3** a narrow part in the middle of a long object.

waistcoat *n.* a close-fitting waist-length sleeveless collarless garment, worn usu. over a shirt and under a jacket.

waisted *adj.* **1** having a waist; narrowed in the middle. **2** having a waist of a specified kind (*thick-waisted*).

waistline *n.* the circumference of the body at the waist.

wait *v.* **1** postpone an action or departure for a specified time or until some expected event occurs (*we waited until evening*). **2** defer (a meal etc.) until a person's arrival (*we waited dinner for them*). **3** be postponed (*this question will have to wait until our next meeting*). **4** wait on people at a meal. • *n.* an act or period of waiting (*we had a long wait for the train*). ◻ **wait on** hand food and drink to (a person) at a meal; fetch and carry for (a person). **wait on!** *Aust.* & *Scottish colloq.* be patient!, wait!, hang on! **wait up** (often foll. by *for*) not go to bed until a person arrives or an event happens.

Waitangi / wuy-**tang**-ee / a treaty signed in 1840 at the settlement of Waitangi in New Zealand, which formed the basis of British annexation of New Zealand. The Maori chiefs of the North Island accepted British sovereignty in exchange for protection, and direct purchase of land from the Maoris was forbidden. Subsequent contraventions of the treaty by the British, esp. their encroachment on lands set aside for the Maoris, led eventually to the MAORI WARS and the final destruction of Maori independence.

wait-a-while *n.* any of several Australian plants which may impede passage with their barbed leaves or prickles, esp. the LAWYER PALM.

waiter *n.* (*feminine* **waitress**; also **waitperson**) a person who serves at table in a hotel or restaurant.

waive *v.* refrain from using or insisting on (one's right, claim, or privilege etc.); forgo or dispense with (*he waived his right to be paid compensation*).

waiver *n.* the waiving of a legal right; a document recording this.

wake[1] *v.* (**woke** *or* **waked**, **woken** *or* **waked**, **waking**) **1** = WAKE UP. **2** disturb with noise; cause to re-echo; evoke. • *n.* a watch kept beside a corpse before burial; lamentations (and sometimes merrymaking) in connection with this. ◻ **wake up 1** cease to sleep; arouse (a person) from sleep. **wake up to** realise (*he woke up to the fact that she meant it*).

wake[2] *n.* **1** the track left on water's surface by a ship etc. **2** air currents left behind an aircraft etc. moving through air. ◻ **in the wake of** behind; following after.

wakeboarding *n.* the sport of riding on a board resembling a surfboard and performing acrobatic manoeuvres while being towed behind a motor boat. ◻ **wakeboarder** *n.*

wakeful *adj.* **1** (of a person) unable to sleep. **2** (of a night etc.) with little sleep. **3** vigilant.

waken *v.* make or become awake.

waking *adj.* being awake (*in his waking hours*).

wale *n.* **1** = WEAL (sense 1). **2** a ridge on corduroy etc. **3** a broad thick timber along a ship's side.

waler *n.* **1** a horse bred in NSW and imported into India. **2** a light, Australian-bred horse.

Wales the country in the west of Great Britain.

Walesa / vuh-**wen**-suh /, Lech (1943–), Polish trade unionist, leader of Solidarity, president 1990–95. He won the 1983 Nobel Peace Prize.

walk *v.* **1** progress by lifting and setting down each foot in turn, never having both or all feet off the ground at once. **2** travel or go on foot; take exercise in this way. **3** go over on foot (*walked the streets*). **4** cause to walk with one; accompany in walking. **5** ride or lead (a horse or dog etc.) at a walking pace. • *n.* **1** a journey on foot, esp. for pleasure or exercise (*went for a walk*). **2** a distance which can be walked in a (usu. specified) time (*ten minutes' walk from here*). **3** the manner or style of walking; a walking pace. **4** a place for walking; a route followed in walking. ◻ **walk-in** *adj.* (of a storage area) large enough to walk into (*a walk-in cupboard*). **walking frame** a metal frame used as a support by people who have difficulty walking. **walking stick** a stick used for support when

walkabout 943 **walnut**

walking. **walking-stick palm** a small palm of south-eastern Qld and north-eastern NSW, having a slender trunk with a knob on the end (used frequently as a walking stick). **walk matilda** = WALTZ MATILDA (see MATILDA). **walk of life** social rank; profession or occupation. **walk-on** *n.* (in full **walk-on part**) a non-speaking role in a play or film; a player of this. **walk out** leave suddenly and angrily; go on strike suddenly. **walk-out** *n.* a sudden angry departure, esp. as a protest or strike. **walk out on** desert, abandon.

walkabout *n.* **1** *Aust. hist.* a person who travels on foot; a swagman. **2** *Aust.* a journey on foot as undertaken by an Aborigine in order to live in the traditional manner (esp. one undertaken as a temporary withdrawal from white society in order to re-establish contact with spiritual resources). **3** an informal stroll among a crowd by a visiting dignitary. □ **go walkabout** *Aust.* **1** (of an Aborigine) take a walkabout (in sense 2). **2** wander around casually. **3** lose concentration etc. (*he went walkabout halfway through the second set and lost it*). **4** *colloq.* (of an article) be lost (probably because of theft) (*my wallet's gone walkabout*).

walkathon *n.* an organised fund-raising walk.

Walker, Kath *see* NOONUCCAL, Oodgeroo.

walker *n.* **1** a person who walks. **2** a framework in which a baby can walk unaided. **3** = WALKING FRAME (*see* WALK).

walkie-talkie *n.* a small portable radio transmitter and receiver.

Walkman *n.* (*pl.* **Walkmans**) *trademark* a personal stereo.

walkover *n.* an easy victory.

walkway *n.* a passage for walking along (esp. one connecting different sections of a building).

wall *n.* **1** a continuous upright structure forming one of the sides of a building or room, or serving to enclose, protect, or divide an area. **2** something thought of as resembling this in form or function; the outermost part of a hollow structure; tissue surrounding an organ of the body etc. • *v.* **1** surround or enclose with a wall (*a walled garden*). **2** (often foll. by *up*) block (a space) by building a wall. □ **drive** *or* **send up the wall** *colloq.* make crazy or furious. **go to the wall** suffer defeat, failure, or ruin (*the weakest goes to the wall*). **up against the wall** in dire difficulty, with no resources or avenues of escape left. **wall bars** a set of parallel bars on the wall of a gymnasium. **wall-eye** an eye with a streaked or opaque white iris. **2** an eye squinting outwards. **wall-to-wall** *adj.* **1** (of a carpet) fitted to cover the whole room. **2** *colloq. derog.* found everywhere, ever-present (*wall-to-wall pop music*).

wallaby / wol-uh-bee / *n.* **1** any of various marsupials of Australia and New Guinea similar to but smaller than a kangaroo (often with a descriptive epithet): *nail-tailed wallaby*; *parma wallaby*; *rock wallaby* etc. **2** *Aust.* an itinerant rural worker; a swagman. **3** (**the Wallabies**) *Aust.* the Australian international Rugby Union team; (**Wallaby**) a member of this team. □ **on the wallaby** *Aust. see* WALLABY TRACK. **wallaby grass** any of many perennial Australian grasses valued as winter fodder. **wallaby rat** (in Tas.) the long-nosed potoroo. (¶ Dharuk)

wallaby track *n.* *Aust.* the route followed by a person who journeys through the country in search of seasonal work. □ **on the wallaby track** (*or* **on the wallaby**) **1** vagrant; unemployed. **2** on the move, not settling down in one place.

Wallace, Alfred Russel (1823–1913), British naturalist, who independently formulated a theory of the origin of species that was identical with that of Darwin. □ **Wallace's line** an imaginary line, proposed by Wallace, marking the boundary between countries with Australasian fauna and those with Asian fauna.

wallaroo / wol-uh-**roo** / *n.* (also **euro**, **hill kangaroo**, **rock kangaroo**) any of several large, stocky kangaroos of rocky or hilly country, esp. the dark, shaggy-haired kangaroo of NSW and southern Qld. (¶ Dharuk *walaru*.)

wallet *n.* a small flat folding case for banknotes or small documents etc.

wallflower *n.* **1** a wild or garden plant of Europe with fragrant flowers, often found clinging to walls etc. **2** *colloq.* a neglected or socially awkward person, esp. a person sitting out at a dance for lack of partners.

wallop *colloq. v.* (**walloped**, **walloping**) **1** thrash, hit hard. **2** defeat convincingly. • *n.* a heavy blow.

walloper *n. colloq.* **1** a person or thing that wallops. **2** *Aust.* a police officer.

walloping *colloq. adj.* **1** big, thumping (*a walloping lie*). **2** severe (*came down with a walloping cold*). • *n.* a thrashing; a decisive defeat.

wallow *v.* **1** roll about in water or mud etc. **2** (usu. foll. by *in*) indulge in unrestrained pleasure, misery, etc. (*wallowing in luxury*). • *n.* **1** the act of wallowing. **2** a place used by buffalo etc. for wallowing.

wallpaper *n.* paper for pasting on the interior walls of rooms. • *v.* decorate with wallpaper.

Wall Street a street in New York City, in or near which the chief American financial institutions are concentrated; the American money market.

wallum / wol-uhm / *n. Aust.* **1** a small, gnarled banksia of south-eastern Qld and eastern NSW. **2** (also **wallum country**) a sandy coastal heathland in which this plant is the predominant species. **b** any area of coastal lowland. (¶ Gabi-gabi)

wally / wol-ee / *n. colloq.* a foolish or inept person.

wally grout *n. Aust. colloq.* a shout, a turn to buy a round of drinks. (¶ Rhyming slang, from Wally Grout (1927–68), Australian test wicketkeeper.)

Walmatjari / wahl-mah-jah-ree / *n.* an Aboriginal language of north-central WA.

walnut *n.* **1** a nut containing an edible kernel with a wrinkled surface. **2** the Northern hemi-

walrus *n.* (*pl.* **walrus** *or* **walruses**) a large amphibious animal of Arctic regions, related to the seal and sea lion and having a pair of long tusks.

Walsh, Adela (Constantia Mary) (1885–1961), Australian (born in England) suffragist, feminist, and leader of the women's anti-war and anti-conscription movement. She openly promoted Japan as a trading partner for Australia and was interned when Japan entered the Second World War in 1942.

waltz *n.* **1** a ballroom dance for couples, with a flowing melody in triple time. **2** music for this. • *v.* **1** dance a waltz. **2** *colloq.* move in a casual, confident manner (*came waltzing in; waltzed him off to Paris*).

'Waltzing Matilda' a song with words by A.B. ('Banjo') Paterson sung to an old Scottish tune he heard in Qld. First sung in public in Winton (Qld) in 1895, it has become the unofficial national song of Australia. (*See* MATILDA.)

wambenger / wom-ben-juh / *n. Aust.* = PHASCOGALE. (¶ Possibly from Nyungar *wambanang*.)

wan / won / *adj.* (**wanner, wannest**) pale; looking exhausted or unhappy. □ **wanly** *adv.* **wanness** *n.*

WAN / wan / *abbr. Computing* wide area network.

wand *n.* **1** a slender rod for carrying in the hand, esp. one associated with the working of magic. **2** a staff as a symbol of office.

wander *v.* **1** go from place to place without a settled route, destination, or purpose. **2** (of a road or river) wind, meander. **3** leave the right path or direction; stray from one's group or from a place. **4** digress from a subject; be inattentive or speak disconnectedly through illness or weakness. • *n.* an act of wandering. □ **wanderer** *n.*

Wandering Jew a legendary person who, because he mocked Christ at the crucifixion, was condemned to wander the world until Christ's second coming.

wanderlust *n.* eagerness for travelling or wandering; restlessness.

wanderoo / won-duh-**roo** / *n.* the hanuman monkey or langur of Sri Lanka.

Wandjina / **won**-jee-nu / *n.* (also **Wondjina**) an Aboriginal ancestral spirit of fertility and rain, found in rock paintings of the Kimberley ranges in WA. (¶ Ungarinyin *wanjina* (of uncertain meaning).)

wandoo / won-**doo** / *n.* **1** the gum *Eucalyptus wandoo* of SW WA, having a smooth mottled white trunk. **2** the very hard, strong, durable wood of this tree. (¶ Nyungar)

wane *v.* **1** (of the moon) show a gradually decreasing area of brightness after being full. **2** decrease in vigour, strength, or importance (*his influence was waning*). • *n.* **1** the process of waning. **2** a defect in a plank etc. when the corners are not square. □ **on the wane** waning.

Wangganguru / wung-gu-**ngoo**-roo / *n.* an Aboriginal language of a vast area of northern SA and extending into the NT.

Wangka-Yutjuru / **wahng**-ku-yuu-chuu-roo / *n.* an Aboriginal language of western Qld.

wangle *colloq. v.* obtain or arrange by using trickery, improper influence, persuasion, etc. • *n.* an act of wangling.

wank *colloq. n.* **1** (usu. applied to a male) a person who deludes himself as to his importance etc.; a fool. **2** a pastime or hobby on which a person is besotted (*hang-gliding is her wank*). **3** rubbish, nonsense (*I've heard the rumour—it's an utter wank*). **4** self-indulgent posturing (*what a wank his farewell speech turned out to be!*). **5** *coarse colloq.* an act or instance of masturbating. • *v. coarse colloq.* masturbate oneself or another. □ **wank** (**oneself** etc.) **1** delude (oneself etc.) as to (one's) importance etc. **2** (usu. foll. by *off*) *coarse colloq.* masturbate (oneself or another).

wanker *n. colloq.* **1** (usu. applied to a male) a person who deludes himself, thinks highly of himself, and shows it in his behaviour; a contemptible or ineffectual person. **2** a person who masturbates.

wanna / **won**-uh / *n.* (also **wonna**) *Aust.* an implement used by Aboriginal women for digging etc. (¶ Nyungar)

wannabe / **won**-uh-bee / *colloq. n.* **1** an avid fan or follower (of a pop star etc.) who models his or her personal appearance, dress, etc. on this hero-worshipped person (*there are Madonna wannabes everywhere*). **2** anyone who wants to be someone else. • *adj.* aspiring, would-be; like a wannabe (*the wannabe prime minister*). (¶ A respelling of *want to be*.)

want *v.* **1** desire, wish for possession of; need or desire (a person). **2** require or need (*your hair wants cutting; you want to be more careful*). **3** lack, have an insufficient supply of. **4** be without the necessities of life (*waste not, want not; want for nothing*). **5** be without or fall short of (*the drawer wants a handle*). **6** (foll. by *in* or *out*) *colloq.* desire to be in or out etc. (*he wants in on the deal; he wanted out of the contract*). • *n.* **1** a desire for something, a requirement (*a man of few wants*). **2** lack or need of something, deficiency (*the plants died from want of water*). **3** lack of the necessities of life (*living in great want*).

wanted *adj.* (of a suspected criminal) being sought by the police.

wanting *adj.* lacking; deficient; not equal to requirements.

wanton / **won**-tuhn / *adj.* **1** licentious; sexually promiscuous. **2** capricious; arbitrary (*wanton destruction*). **3** luxuriant; unrestrained (*wanton profusion*). • *n.* a licentious person. □ **wantonly** *adv.* **wantonness** *n.*

war *n.* **1** armed conflict between countries, ethnic groups, etc. **2** open hostility between people. **3** a strong effort to combat crime, disease, poverty, etc. • *v.* (**warred, warring**) **1** make war. **2** (as **warring** *adj.*) **a** rival; fighting (*warring factions in the Labor Party*). **b** conflicting (*warring principles*). ☐ **war crime** a crime violating the international laws of war. **war cry** a word or cry shouted in attacking or in rallying one's side; the slogan of a political or other party. **war dance** a ceremonial dance performed before battle or after a victory. **war game** a game in which models representing troops etc. are moved about on maps; a training exercise in which sets of armed forces participate in mock opposition to each other. **war memorial** a memorial erected to those who died in a war. **war of nerves** an effort to wear down one's opponent by gradually destroying morale.

warabi / wo-ruh-bee / *n. Aust.* the smallest rock wallaby, restricted to rugged, inhospitable parts of the Kimberley region, WA. (¶ Wunambal)

waratah / wo-ruh-tah / *n.* **1** any of four species of the Australian genus *Telopea*, all highly ornamental shrubs with very large usu. red flowers (*Gippsland waratah; Tasmanian waratah*). **2** (also **New South Wales waratah**) a tall shrub, *Telopea speciosissima*, bearing huge (15 cm in diameter) crimson flowerheads surrounded by large red bracts: this flower is the floral emblem of NSW. (¶ Dharuk)

Waray / wah-ruy / *n.* an Aboriginal language of the northern region of the NT.

warb / wawb / *n.* (also **waub**) *Aust. colloq.* an idle, unkempt, or disreputable person.

warble *v.* sing, esp. with a gentle trilling note as certain birds do. • *n.* a warbling sound.

warbler *n.* a bird that warbles; any of many small Australian birds usu. having a very melodic call (*brown warbler, reed warbler*, etc.).

warby *adj. Aust. colloq.* shabby; decrepit. (¶ From WARB.)

Ward, Frederick ('Captain Thunderbolt') (1835–70), Australian bushranger who began his career as a teenager and who had a reputation for chivalry, never injuring or killing his victims. He was shot dead by troopers in May 1870. Ballads, plays, and novels have been written about him and he has been the subject of two films.

ward *n.* **1** a room with beds for patients in a hospital. **2** an administrative division of a constituency, usu. electing a councillor or councillors etc. **3** a person, esp. a child, under the care of a guardian or (**ward of court**) the protection of a lawcourt. **4** each of the notches and projections in a key (or the corresponding parts in a lock). ☐ **ward off** keep at a distance (a person or thing that threatens danger), fend off.

warden *n.* **1** an official with supervisory duties. **2** the president or governor of a college, school, hospital, youth hostel, etc.

warder *n.* an official in charge of prisoners in a prison.

wardrobe *n.* **1** a large cupboard for storing clothes. **2** a person's stock of clothes. **3** the costume department or the costumes of a theatre, film company, etc.

wardroom *n.* the mess-room for commissioned officers in a warship.

wardship *n.* the state of being a ward; a guardian's care.

ware *n.* **1** manufactured goods (esp. pottery) of the kind specified (*delftware*). **2** (**wares**) articles offered for sale (*traders displayed their wares*).

-ware *comb. form Computing* part of the word *software* in words whose first element describes the software under discussion. ☐ **courseware** software specifically designed for educational use. **fontware** typesetting software or software designed to enable the use of unusual fonts and alphabets. **freeware** software distributed free to users, without support from its developer. **groupware** a related set of software. **middleware** programs which function between an operating system and applications software. **vapourware** software that as yet only exists in the plans of its developers. *See also* SHAREWARE.

warehou / wu-ruh-**hoo** / *n.* a fish of Australian and New Zealand waters.

warehouse *n.* a building for storing goods. • *v.* store temporarily in a repository. ☐ **warehouse party** a large, illicitly organised party for teenagers (usu. held in a warehouse or some other spacious building). Also called a *rave party*.

warfare *n.* making war, fighting; a particular form of this (*guerrilla warfare*).

warfarin / **waw**-fuh-rin / *n.* a water-soluble anticoagulant used in the treatment of stroke victims etc. and also as a rat poison.

warhead *n.* the explosive head of a missile, torpedo, or similar weapon.

Warhol / **waw**-hohl /, Andy (original name: Andrew Warhola) (1930–87), American painter, graphic artist, and film-maker, prominent in the New York pop art of the 1960s.

warlike *adj.* **1** hostile, aggressive (*a warlike people*). **2** of or for war (*warlike preparations*).

warlock *n.* a wizard or sorcerer.

warlord *n.* a regional military ruler with his own army.

Warlpiri / **wahl**-bree / *n.* an Aboriginal language of the central regions of the NT.

warm *adj.* **1** moderately hot, not cold or cool. **2** (of clothes etc.) keeping the body warm. **3** enthusiastic, hearty (*a warm supporter; the speaker got a warm reception*). **4** kindly and affectionate (*she has a warm heart*). **5** animated; heated (*the dispute grew warm*). **6** (of colours) suggesting warmth, containing reddish shades. **7** (in children's games etc.) near the object sought, on the verge of guessing. • *n.* an act of warming, the state of being warmed (*had a nice warm by the* *fire*). • *v.* make or become warm or warmer. ☐ **warm-blooded 1** having blood that remains warm (ranging from 36° to 42°C) permanently. **2** ardent; passionate. **warm down** recover from strenuous physical exercise by doing gentler exercise. **warm front** an advancing mass of warm air. **warm to** become cordial or well-disposed to (a person); become more animated about (a task). **warm up 1** make or become warm; reheat (food etc.). **2** prepare for athletic exercise by practice beforehand. **3** make or become more lively. **4** put (an audience) into a receptive mood before a performance. **warm-up** *n.* a period of preparatory exercise. ☐☐ **warmish** *adj.* **warmly** *adv.* **warmness** *n.*

warmonger / **waw**-mung-guh / *n.* a person who seeks to bring about war. ☐ **warmongering** *n.* & *adj.*

warmth *n.* warmness; the state of being warm.

warn *v.* **1** inform (a person) about a danger or about something that must be reckoned with; advise about action in such circumstances (*we warned them to take waterproof clothing*). **2** give a person cautionary notice regarding conduct etc. (*I shall not warn you again*). ☐ **warn off** tell (a person) to keep away (from).

Warne, Shane (1969–), Australian cricketer. A leg-spin bowler, in 2000 he broke Dennis Lillee's record for an Australian bowler of 355 test wickets.

warning *n.* something that serves to warn. • *adj.* serving as or relating to warning (*a warning frown; warning bell*).

warp / wawp / *v.* **1** cause (timber etc.) to become bent by uneven shrinkage or expansion; become bent in this way. **2** make or become perverted, bitter, or strange (*a mind warped by malice; a warped sense of humour*). • *n.* **1** a warped state, esp. of timber. **2** perversion, bitterness, etc., of the mind. **3** threads stretched lengthwise in a loom, to be crossed by the weft.

warpath *n.* ☐ **on the warpath** *colloq.* angry or hostile about something.

warrant / **wo**-ruhnt / *n.* **1** written authorisation to do something (*the police have a warrant for his arrest*). **2** a justifying reason for an action, belief, or feeling (*I've some warrant for my fear of spiders; you've no warrant for thinking that he's gay*). **3** a written authorisation, money voucher, etc. **4** a certificate of service rank held by a warrant officer. • *v.* **1** serve as a warrant for, justify (*nothing can warrant such rudeness*). **2** prove or guarantee; assure (*he'll be back, I'll warrant you*). ☐ **warrant officer** a member of the armed services ranking between commissioned officers and NCOs.

warranty / **wo**-ruhn-tee / *n.* **1** a guarantee, esp. one given to the buyer of an article. **2** authority or justification for doing something.

warren *n.* **1** a network of rabbit burrows. **2** a building or district with many narrow winding passages.

Warrgamay / **wahr**-gu-muy / *n.* an Aboriginal language of a wide region of north-eastern Qld south of Cairns.

warrigal / **wo**-ruh-guhl / *n. Aust.* **1** = DINGO. **2** = MYALL *n.* (sense 1). **3** (in full **warrigal cabbage**) a plant occurring in Australia and New Zealand, having fleshy leaves used as a vegetable. **4** a wild or untamed horse. • *adj.* wild; untamed. (¶ Dharuk *warrigal* 'wild dingo'.)

warring see WAR *v.*

warrior *n.* **1** a person who is experienced in battle. **2** a fighting man, esp. of primitive peoples.

Warsaw the capital of Poland. ☐ **Warsaw Pact** a treaty of mutual defence and military aid signed at Warsaw in 1955 by the Communist countries of Europe under Russian leadership.

warship *n.* a ship for use in war.

wart *n.* **1** a small hard roundish abnormal growth on the skin, caused by a virus. **2** a similar growth on a plant. ☐ **warts and all** without concealment of blemishes, defects, or unattractive features. ☐☐ **warty** *adj.*

warthog *n.* an African wild pig with two large tusks and wart-like growths on its face.

Warumungu / **wah**-roo-muung-oo / *n.* an Aboriginal language of the central region of the NT.

Warungu / **wah**-roong-oo / *n.* an Aboriginal language of north-eastern Qld.

wary / **wair**-ree / *adj.* (**warier, wariest**) cautious, in the habit of looking out for possible danger or difficulty. ☐☐ **warily** *adv.* **wariness** *n.*

was see BE.

wasabi / wuh-**sah**-bee / *n.* a plant whose thick green root is used in Japanese cookery.

wash *v.* **1** cleanse with water or other liquid. **2** wash oneself; wash clothes etc. **3** be washable; (of fabric or dye) bear washing without damage (*this garment washes well*). **4** flow past or against, go splashing or flowing (*the sea washes the base of the cliffs; waves washed over the deck*). **5** (of moving liquid) carry in a specified direction (*a wave washed him overboard*). **6** sift (ore) by the action of water. **7** coat with a wash of paint or wall colouring etc. **8** (of reasoning etc.) be valid (*that argument won't wash*). • *n.* **1** washing, being washed (*give it a good wash*). **2** the process of laundering. **3** a quantity of clothes etc. that are being washed or to be washed or have just been washed. **4** disturbed water or air behind a moving ship or aircraft etc. **5** liquid to spread over a surface to cleanse, heal, or colour. **6** a lotion or cosmetic (*a mouthwash*). **7** a thin coating of colour painted over a surface. **8** soil swept off by water; alluvium. **9** a sandbank exposed only at low tide. ☐ **come out in the wash** be revealed and resolved or eliminated in the course of time. **washed out** faded by washing; faded-looking; pale, exhausted. **washed up** *colloq.* defeated, having failed. **wash out 1** clean the inside of by washing. **2** cause (an event) to be cancelled

washable *adj.* able to be washed without suffering damage.

washaway *n. esp. Aust.* **1** a removal of earth or of a portion of a road or railway line by flood. **2** the hole or gap or channel caused by this.

washbasin *n.* a basin (usu. fixed to a wall) for washing one's hands and face in.

washboard *n.* **1 a** (formerly) a ribbed board for scrubbing clothes on when washing. **b** this used as a percussion instrument. **2** (in full **washboard stomach**) a stomach with well-defined abdominal muscles.

washer *n.* **1** a person or machine that washes. **2** *Aust.* = FACECLOTH. **3** a ring of rubber or metal etc. placed between two surfaces (e.g. under a nut) to give tightness or prevent leakage.

washing *n.* clothes etc. that are being washed or to be washed or have just been washed. ◻ **washing machine** a machine for washing clothes. **washing soda** sodium carbonate, used (dissolved in water) for washing and cleaning things. **washing-up** the process of washing dishes etc. after use; the dishes etc. for washing.

Washington[1] **1** a State in the NW of the USA, bordering on the Pacific. **2** the administrative capital of the USA, covering the same area as the District of Columbia.

Washington[2], George (1732–99), American military commander and statesman, 1st president of the USA 1789–96.

washup *n.* the end or outcome of a process (*you'll find, in the washup, that my predictions were correct*).

wasn't = was not.

WASP *n.* (also **Wasp**) *derog.* a middle-class white Protestant (*the WASPs believe that they have a God-given right to dominate*). • *adj.* of or pertaining to WASPs. (¶ Acronym from *White Anglo-Saxon Protestant.*)

wasp *n.* a stinging insect with a black and yellow striped body.

waspish *adj.* making sharp or irritable comments. ◻ **waspishness** *n.*

wassail / **wos**-ayl, **wos**-uhl / *archaic n.* making merry (esp. at Christmas) with much drinking. • *v.* (**wassailed, wassailing**) make merry in this way.

wast *archaic* the past tense of *be*, used with *thou*.

wastage *n.* **1** loss by waste. **2** (also **natural wastage**) loss of employees through retirement or resignation, not through declaring them redundant.

waste *v.* **1** use extravagantly or needlessly or without an adequate result (*he is wasted as a teacher*). **2** fail to use (an opportunity). **3** make or become gradually weaker (*wasting away for lack of food; a wasting disease*). **4 a** ravage, devastate (*cities wasted by repeated bombing*). **b** *colloq.* kill, murder (a person). **c** kill ruthlessly in war (*wasted entire villages including women and children*). • *adj.* **1** left over or thrown away because not wanted (*waste products*). **2** not inhabited or cultivated; desolate (*waste ground*). • *n.* **1** an act of wasting or using something ineffectively (*a waste of time*). **2** waste material or food; useless by-products. **3** a waste region; a WASTELAND.

wasted *adj. esp. US & Aust. colloq.* intoxicated (from alcoholic drink or drugs).

wasteful *adj.* using more than is needed, showing waste. ◻ **wastefully** *adv.* **wastefulness** *n.*

wasteland *n.* **1** an expanse of barren or useless land. **2** a place or time considered spiritually or intellectually barren.

waster / **way**-stuh / *n.* **1** a wasteful person. **2** *colloq.* a wastrel.

wastrel / **way**-struhl / *n.* a good-for-nothing person.

watch *v.* **1** look at, keep under observation. **2** be on the alert, take heed (*watch for an opportunity*). **3** be careful about (*have to watch my weight*). **4** (often foll. by *over*) safeguard, exercise protective care. • *n.* **1** the act of watching, esp. to see that all is well; constant observation or attention (*keep watch*). **2** a small portable device indicating the time. **3** a period (usu. 4 hours) for which a division of a ship's company remains on duty; a turn of duty; the part (usu. half) of a ship's company on duty during a watch. ◻ **watch-house** a building, now usu. attached to a police station, in which suspected lawbreakers are held under temporary arrest. **watching brief** the brief of a barrister who is present during a lawsuit to advise a client who is not directly concerned in it.

watch it! *colloq.* **1** be careful! **2** an exclamation of hostile warning, = 'Stop (doing that), or I'll deal with you!' ◻ ◻ **watcher** *n.*

watchdog *n.* **1** a guard dog. **2** a person or organisation acting as a guardian of people's rights, monitoring people's behaviour, morals, etc.

watchful *adj.* watching or observing closely. ◻ **watchfully** *adv.* **watchfulness** *n.*

watchman *n.* a person employed to look after a building etc. at night.

watchword *n.* a word or phrase summarising a guiding principle (*the watchword is vigilance*).

water *n.* **1** a colourless odourless tasteless liquid that is a compound of oxygen and hydrogen. **2** a liquid consisting chiefly of this and found in seas and rivers etc., in rain, and in secretions of organisms, e.g. tears, urine (*pass water*). **3** an expanse of water such as a sea, river, lake, etc.; (**waters**) part of a sea or river (*the southern Australian waters*). **4** (**the waters**) mineral water at a spa etc. **5** a watery infusion or other preparation (*lavender water; soda water*). **6** the level of the tide (*at high water*). **7** the transparency and lustre of a gem (*a diamond of the first water*). **8** (as *adj.*) **a** found in or near water (esp. in the names of Australian fauna and flora): *water goanna; water gum.* **b** of, for, or worked by water (*water trough; water meter; water wheel*). **c** involving, using, or yielding water (*water polo; water vine*). **9** amniotic fluid, released during labour. •*v.* **1** sprinkle with water. **2** supply (plants) with water; give drinking water to (an animal). **3** (of an animal) go to a pool etc. to drink (*emus and kangaroos water at this billabong*). **4** dilute with water. **5** (of a river etc.) supply (a place) with water (*regions watered by the Murrumbidgee*). **6** (of a ship etc.) take in a supply of water. **7** secrete tears or saliva (*make one's mouth water*). ☐ **water buffalo** the common domestic buffalo of India, introduced to Australia and now naturalised in the NT. **water burner** (*or* **scorcher**) *Aust. colloq.* a highly inferior cook. **water cannon** a device for shooting a powerful jet of water to disperse a crowd etc. **Water-carrier** (also **Water-bearer**) a sign of the zodiac, Aquarius. **water chestnut** the corm from a sedge, used in Chinese cookery. **water closet** a toilet that is flushed by water; the room containing this. **water diviner** a person who searches for underground water by holding a rod supposed to dip when over the right spot. **water down** dilute; make less forceful or horrifying. **water dragon** *Aust.* a large green or brown black-barred lizard with a spiny crest on head and back, occurring in or near water in eastern mainland Australia. **water hammer** a knocking noise in a water pipe when a tap is turned off. **water-holding frog** any of several burrowing frogs of drier inland Australia having the ability, when pools etc. begin to dry up, to take in water until its body swells greatly, and also to store water in its burrow. **watering hole 1** a waterhole from which animals drink. **2** *colloq.* a hotel or bar, esp. one frequented by a regular group. **water joey** *Aust.* a person who is employed to carry water and to supply the needs of a group, esp. in the bush etc. **water level 1** the surface of water in a reservoir etc.; the height of this. **2** = WATER TABLE. **water lily** a plant that grows in water, with broad floating leaves and showy flowers. **water main** a main pipe in a water supply system. **water mallee** *Aust.* any of several mallee eucalypts the roots of which when cut yield a considerable quantity of drinkable water. **water polo** a game played by two teams each with seven swimmers, with a ball like a football. **water power** power obtained from flowing or falling water, used to drive machinery or generate electric current. **water rat** (also **beaver rat**) a large aquatic rodent, widespread near water in Australia, having dense soft fur and webbed hind feet. **water-ski** either of a pair of skis on which a person stands for water-skiing. **water-skiing** the sport of skimming over the surface of water, holding a tow line from a motor boat. **water table** the level below which the ground is saturated with water. **water tower** a tower that holds a water-tank at a height to secure pressure for distributing water. **water wings** = FLOATIES.

waterbed *n.* a mattress filled with water and held in a supporting frame.

watercolour *n.* artists' paint in which the pigment is diluted with water (not oil); a picture painted with paints of this kind.

watercolourist *n.* a painter who uses water-colours.

watercourse *n.* a stream, brook, or artificial waterway; the bed of this.

watercress *n.* a cress that grows in streams or ponds, with sharp-tasting leaves, used in salads.

watered *adj.* (of fabric, esp. silk) having an irregular wavy marking.

waterfall *n.* a stream that falls from a height.

waterfowl *n.pl.* birds frequenting water, esp. swimming birds.

waterfront *n.* the part of a town that borders on a river, lake, or sea.

Watergate a political scandal deriving from an incident during the US election campaign of 1972, when the Republican Party supporting President Nixon attempted to bug the offices of the Democratic Party at the Watergate building in Washington, DC. The attempted cover-up and subsequent inquiry forced Nixon's resignation.

waterhole *n.* **1** a shallow dip in the ground where water collects; a pond or pool which may be very large. **2** a cavity in the bed of a water-course, esp. one which retains water when the main stream dries up. **3** a watering hole (*see* WATER).

waterline *n.* the line along which the surface of water touches a ship's side (marked on a ship for use in loading).

waterlogged *adj.* saturated or filled with water.

Waterloo a village in Belgium where in 1815 Napoleon's army was defeated by the British and Prussians. ☐ **meet one's Waterloo** lose a decisive contest.

watermark *n.* **1** a mark showing how high a river or tide rises or how low it falls. **2** a manufacturer's design in some paper, visible when the paper is held against light.

watermelon *n.* a large dark-green melon with red pulp and watery juice.

waterproof *adj.* unable to be penetrated by water. •*n.* a waterproof coat or cape. •*v.* make waterproof.

watershed *n.* **1** a line of high land where streams on one side flow into one river or sea and streams on the other side flow into another. **2** a turning point in the course of events.

waterside *n.* the edge of a river, lake, or sea. ☐ **waterside worker** *Aust.* a person employed to load and unload a ship's cargo; a wharf labourer.

watersider *n. Aust.* a waterside worker.

waterspout *n.* a funnel-shaped column of water between sea and cloud, formed when a whirlwind draws up a whirling mass of water.

watertight *adj.* **1** made or fastened so that water cannot get in or out. **2** (of an excuse or alibi) impossible to set aside or disprove; (of an agreement) leaving no possibility of escape from its provisions.

waterway *n.* **1** a route for travel by water; a canal. **2** a navigable channel.

waterwheel *n.* a wheel turned by a flow of water, used to work machinery.

waterworks *n.* **1** an establishment with pumping machinery etc. for supplying water to a district. **2** *colloq.* crying; tears. **3** *colloq.* the urinary system in the body.

watery *adj.* **1** of or like water. **2** made weak or thin by too much water. **3** full of water or moisture (*watery eyes*). **4** (of colours) pale.

Wathawurung / wut-u-wu-rung / *n.* an Aboriginal language of the west side of Port Phillip Bay, including the present city of Geelong and the town of Bacchus Marsh and extending inland probably as far as the city of Ballarat.

Watjari / **wuch**-u-ree / *n.* an Aboriginal language of west-central WA.

watjin / **wahd**-jin / *n.* (also **waatgin**, **wijen**, **wodgin**) *Aust.* (in Aboriginal English) a white woman. (¶ Alteration of *white gin*: see GIN[3].)

Watson, (John) Chris(tian) (1867–1941), Chilean-born Australian statesman, prime minister 1904. He was Australia's first Labor prime minister.

Watt / wot /, James (1736–1819), Scottish engineer, who greatly improved the steam engine.

watt / wot / *n.* a unit of electric power. ▫ **watt-hour** the energy used when one watt is applied for one hour. (¶ Named after James WATT.)

wattage / **wot**-ij / *n.* an amount of electric power, expressed in watts.

wattle[1] / **wot**-uhl / *n.* **1** any plant of the largest Australian plant genus *Acacia* (of which there are in Australia nearly 800 described species), having long pliant branches used by early settlers for building wattle-and-daub huts: wattles vary in size from prostrate plants to trees over 30 m tall, have foliage consisting either of true leaves or of phyllodes (or both), and bear densely profuse often perfumed ball- or rod-flowers in colours ranging from cream through yellow to deepest gold. One species, *A. pycnantha*, the Australian golden wattle, is the floral emblem of Australia. **2** interlaced rods and split rods and twigs used as material for making fences, walls, etc. • *v.* make (a fence, hut, etc.) of wattle; enclose or fill up with wattles. ▫ **wattle and daub** a network of rods and twigs plastered with clay or mud as a building material. **wattle goat-moth** an Australian moth, the female having a wingspan of about 18 cm and a body the size of a mouse, which lays its eggs on wattles, the larvae being among the insects which are known as witchetty grubs.

wattle[2] / **wot**-uhl / *n.* a red fleshy fold of skin hanging from the head or throat of certain birds, e.g. the turkey.

wattlebird *n.* any of several large Australian honeyeaters with loud harsh calls and sometimes conspicuous facial wattles (*brush wattlebird; red wattlebird; yellow wattlebird*).

Wattle Day *Aust.* an annual celebration of the blossoming of the wattle.

Waugh, Steve (full name: Stephen Rodger Waugh) (1965–), Australian cricketer. A batsman, he became captain of the test team in 1999.

waul (also **wawl**) *v.* give a loud plaintive cry like a cat or a new-born infant. • *n.* such a cry.

wave *n.* **1** a ridge of water between two depressions; a long body of water curling into an arch and breaking on the seashore. **2** something compared to this, e.g. a body of persons in one of successive advancing groups (*wave after wave of attackers*); a temporary increase of an influence or condition (*a wave of anger*); a spell of hot or cold weather (*a heat wave*). **3** a wave-like curve or arrangement of curves, e.g. in a line or in hair. **4** a gesture of waving the hand etc. **5** the wave-like motion by which heat, light, sound, or electricity etc. is spread or carried; a single curve in the course of this, plotted in (a graph) against time. • *v.* **1** move loosely to and fro or up and down, as of a flag, tree, tall grass, etc., in the wind. **2** move (one's hand or something held) to and fro as a signal or greeting. **3** signal or express in this way (*waved him away; waved goodbye*). **4** give a wavy course or appearance to (hair etc.). **5** be wavy. ▫ **make waves** be a disturbing influence. **wave aside** dismiss (an objection etc.) as unimportant. **wave down** signal (a vehicle or its driver) to stop, by waving one's hand.

■ **Usage** Do not confuse with *waive*.

waveband *n.* a range of wavelengths between certain limits.

waveform *n. Physics* a curve showing the shape of a wave at a given time.

wavelength *n.* **1** the distance between successive crests of a wave. **2** the distance between corresponding points in a sound wave or an electromagnetic wave. **3** *colloq.* a particular mode or range of thought (*we don't seem to be on the same wavelength*).

wavelet *n.* a small wave in water (e.g. on a lake).

waver *v.* **1** be or become unsteady; begin to give way (*his courage wavered*). **2** (of light) flicker. **3** show hesitation or uncertainty (*he wavered between faith and agonising doubt*). ▫ **waverer** *n.*

■ **Usage** Do not confuse with *waiver*.

wavy *adj.* (**wavier**, **waviest**) full of waves or wave-like curves. ▫ **waviness** *n.*

wax[1] *n.* **1** beeswax; this used for candles etc. **2** any of various soft sticky substances that melt easily

wax¹ (e.g. obtained from petroleum), used for various purposes such as making candles or polishes. **3** a yellow wax-like substance secreted in the ears. **4** = WAX PLANT. •*v.* **1** coat, polish, or treat with wax. **2** remove unwanted hair from (the legs etc.) using wax; depilate. □ **wax plant 1** a genus of twelve small to medium-sized shrubs endemic to WA, having showy, often highly waxy, white, pink, rose, or purple flowers, esp. the Geraldton wax and the Esperance wax. **2** (occasionally) = HOYA. □□ **waxy** *adj.* **waxiness** *n.*

wax² *v.* **1** (of the moon) show a bright area that is becoming gradually larger until it becomes full. **2** increase in vigour, strength, or importance (*kingdoms waxed and waned*). **3** become (*wax lyrical*).

wax³ *Aust. colloq. v.* share (a football, cricket ball, etc.); go partner with (a person in a game, sport, etc.). •*n.* (as *pl.*) shares. □ **go wax with** (also **go whacks with**) share or go partner with (a person).

waxen *adj.* **1** made of wax. **2** like wax in its paleness or smoothness.

waxhead *n. colloq.* a surfer.

waxwork *n.* an object modelled in wax, esp. a lifelike model of a person.

way *n.* **1** a line of communication between places, e.g. a path or road. **2** the best route, the route taken or intended (*asked the way to Queanbeyan*). **3** a method or style, a person's chosen or desired course of action (*do it my way*). **4** travelling distance (*it's a long way to Bullamakanka, it's a long way to go*). **5** the amount of difference between two states or conditions (*his work is a long way from being perfect*). **6** space free of obstacles so that people can pass (*make way*). **7** the route over which a person or thing is moving or would naturally move (*don't get in the way of the trucks*). **8** a specified direction (*which way is she looking?*). **9** a manner (*she spoke in a kindly way*). **10** a habitual manner or course of action or events (*you'll soon get into our ways*). **11** a talent or skill (*she has a way with flowers*). **12** an advance in some direction, progress (*we made our way to the front*). **13** a respect, a particular aspect of something (*it's a good plan in some ways*). **14** a condition or state (*things are in a bad way*). •*adv. colloq.* far (*the shot was way off the target*). □ **by the way** incidentally. **by way of 1** by means of (*got to where he is by way of bribery and corruption*). **2** as a form of (*did it by way of apology*). **3** passing through, via (*went to Ballarat by way of Geelong*). **give way 1 a** make concessions (*gave way on all the lesser issues*). **b** yield; fail to resist. **2** (often foll. by *to*) concede precedence (to) (*gave way to the car on his right*). **3** (of a structure etc.) be dislodged or broken under a load; collapse (*the scaffolding gave way under their weight*). **4** (foll. by *to*) be superseded by (*this outmoded method must give way to the new*). **5** (foll. by *to*) be overcome by (*he gave way at last to his grief*). **no way** *colloq.* under no circumstances (*no way will I let you use the car*). **out of the way 1** no longer an obstacle or hindrance. **2** disposed of; settled. **3** unusual. **4** (of a place) remote. **way back** *colloq.* a long way back; long ago. **way-out** *adj. colloq.* **1** unusual; eccentric. **2** progressive; avant-garde (*can't stand this way-out art*). **ways and means** methods of achieving something; (in Parliament) a means of providing money.

wayback *Aust. n.* **1** the Australian outback. **2** a person inhabiting or coming from the outback (*gave a lift to a dinkum wayback*). •*adj.* of or pertaining to the outback (*a wealthy wayback grazier*). •*adv.* far away in the outback; in or from a remote area of Australia.

waybill *n.* a list of passengers or goods on a vehicle.

wayfarer *n.* a traveller, esp. on foot. □ **wayfaring** *n.* & *adj.*

waylay *v.* (**waylaid**, **waylaying**) lie in wait for, esp. so as to talk to or rob.

Way of the Cross 1 a devotional religious exercise conducted progressively at each *Station of the Cross* (*see* STATION). **2** the fourteen Stations of the Cross.

wayside *n.* the side of a road or path; land bordering this.

wayward *adj.* **1** childishly self-willed, not obedient or easily controlled. **2** capricious (*a wayward whim*). **3** unaccountable or freakish (*a wayward wind*). □ **waywardness** *n.*

Wb *abbr.* weber(s).

WC *abbr.* (also **wc**) – WATER CLOSET.

we *pron.* **1** used by a person referring to himself or herself and another or others, or speaking on behalf of a nation, group, or organisation. **2** used instead of 'I' by a royal person in formal speech etc. and by the writer of an editorial article in a newspaper etc. **3** (used humorously or condescendingly) you (*and how are we today?*).

weak *adj.* **1** lacking strength, power, or numbers; easily broken, bent, or defeated. **2** lacking vigour, not acting strongly. **3** not convincing or forceful (*the evidence is weak*). **4** dilute, having little of a substance in proportion to the amount of water (*weak tea*). **5** *Grammar* (of verbs) forming the past tense etc. by adding a suffix (as *walk/walked, waste/wasted*), not by changing the vowel (as *ring/rang*).

weaken *v.* make or become weaker.

weakling *n.* a feeble person or animal.

weakly *adv.* in a weak manner. •*adj.* sickly, not robust.

weakness *n.* **1** the state of being weak. **2** a weak point; a defect or fault. **3** inability to resist something, a particular fondness (*she has a weakness for coffee creams*).

weal *n.* **1** a ridge raised on the flesh by a stroke of a rod or whip. **2** *literary* welfare, prosperity (*for the public weal*).

wealth *n.* **1** riches; possession of these. **2** a great quantity (*a book with a wealth of illustrations*).

wealthy *adj.* (**wealthier**, **wealthiest**) having wealth, rich. ◻ **wealthiness** *n.*

wean *v.* **1** accustom (a baby or other young mammal) to take food other than (esp. its mother's) milk. **2** cause (a person) to give up a habit or interest etc. gradually.

weaner *n.* an animal, usu. a lamb or calf, weaned during the current year.

weapon *n.* **1** a thing used as a means of inflicting bodily harm, e.g. a gun, a guided missile, a stick, etc. **2** a means of getting the better of someone in a conflict (*his tears were a devastating weapon*). ◻ **weaponed** *adj.*

weaponry *n.* weapons collectively.

wear *v.* (**wore**, **worn**, **wearing**) **1** have on the body, e.g. as clothing, ornaments, or make-up (*he's wearing shorts; he wears an earring*). **2** have (a certain look) on one's face (*wearing a frown*). **3** *colloq.* accept or tolerate (*the boss won't wear that excuse*). **4** injure the surface of or become injured by rubbing, stress, or use; make (a hole etc.) in this way. **5** (foll. by *down*) exhaust or overcome by persistence (*wore down the opposition*). **6** (often foll. by *out*) exhaust; tire or be tired (*the children have worn me out; I'm utterly worn*). **7** endure continued use (*this fabric wears well*). **8** (of time) pass gradually (*the night wore on*). •*n.* **1** wearing or being worn as clothing (*choose cotton for summer wear*). **2** clothing (*menswear is on the ground floor*). **3** (also **wear and tear**) damage resulting from ordinary use. **4** capacity to endure being used (*there's a lot of wear left in that coat*). ◻ **wear off 1** remove or be removed by wear. **2** become gradually less intense. **wear out** use or be used until no longer usable. ◻ ◻ **wearer** *n.*

wearisome *adj.* tedious; tiring by monotony or length.

weary *adj.* (**wearier**, **weariest**) **1** very tired, esp. from exertion or endurance. **2** (foll. by *of*) tired of something (*weary of war*). **3** tiring; tedious. •*v.* (**wearied**, **wearying**) make or become weary. ◻ **wearily** *adv.* **weariness** *n.*

weasel *n.* a small fierce animal of Europe etc. with a slender body and reddish-brown fur, living on small animals, birds' eggs, etc. ◻ **weasel out** (often foll. by *on*, *of*) default on an obligation, commitment, etc. (*he weaselled out; he weaselled out on her; he weaselled out of his promise*). **weasel word** (usu. in *pl.*) a word that is intentionally ambiguous or misleading.

weather *n.* the condition of the atmosphere with reference to the presence or absence of sunshine, rain, wind, etc. •*adj.* windward (*on the weather side*). •*v.* **1** dry or season by exposure to the action of the weather. **2** become dried, discoloured, worn, etc. in this way. **3** sail to windward of (*the ship weathered the Cape*). **4** come safely through; survive (*the ship weathered the storm; trying to weather the trauma of divorce*). ◻ **keep a weather eye open** be watchful. **under the weather** feeling unwell or depressed. **weather-beaten** affected or worn by exposure to weather. **weather vane** a weathercock.

weatherboard *n.* **1** (also **weatherboarding**) a series of horizontal boards with each overlapping the one below, fixed to the outside wall of buildings. **2** *Aust.* a weatherboarded building, usu. a dwelling. •*adj.* (also **weatherboarded**) (of a building) having weatherboards. •*v.* clad (external walls) with weatherboards.

weathercock *n.* **1** a revolving pointer, often in the shape of a rooster, turning easily in the wind to show from which direction the wind is blowing. **2** an inconstant person.

weatherman *n.* a meteorologist, esp. one who broadcasts a weather forecast.

weatherproof *adj.* unable to be penetrated by rain or wind.

weathershield *n.* a moulded plastic etc. shield over the window esp. on the driver's side of a vehicle, to provide protection against rain, wind, etc.

weave[1] *v.* (**wove**, **woven**, **weaving**) **1** make (fabric etc.) by passing crosswise threads or strips under and over lengthwise ones. **2** form (thread etc.) into fabric in this way. **3** put together into a connected whole; compose (a story etc.) in this way (*wove the incidents into his novel; wove an intricate plot*). •*n.* a style or pattern of weaving (*a loose weave*). ◻ **weaver** *n.*

weave[2] *v.* (**weaved**, **weaving**) move from side to side in an intricate course (*weaving in and out of the traffic*).

Weaver, Jacki (1947–), Australian film, stage, and television actor.

web *n.* **1** the network of fine strands made by a spider etc. **2 a** a network (*a web of deceit*). **b** = WORLD WIDE WEB. **3** skin filling the spaces between the toes of birds such as ducks and animals such as frogs. **4** woven fabric; an amount woven in one piece. ◻ **web-footed** having the toes joined by webs. **web page** (also **webpage**) a document connected to the World Wide Web and viewable by anyone with an Internet connection and browser. **web site** (also **website**) a location connected to the Internet that maintains one or more pages on the World Wide Web. ◻ ◻ **webbed** *adj.*

Webb, Karrie (Ann) (1974–), Australian golfer who has won many international titles.

webbing *n.* strong bands of woven fabric used in upholstery, belts, etc.

webcam *n.* a video camera whose output can be transmitted over an electronic network, esp. the Internet.

webcast *n.* a live video broadcast of an event transmitted over the Internet. *v.* broadcast in this way. ◻ **webcasting** *n.*

weber / vay-buh / *n. Physics* the SI unit of magnetic flux. (¶ Named after the German physicist W.E. Weber (1804–91).)

webmaster *n.* a person who administers a site on the World Wide Web.

wed *v.* (**wedded**, **wedding**) **1** marry. **2** unite (*if we can wed efficiency to economy*). ☐ **wedded to** devoted to and unable to abandon (an occupation or opinion etc.).

we'd = **1** we had. **2** we should. **3** we would.

wedding *n.* a marriage ceremony and festivities. ☐ **wedding breakfast** a meal between a wedding and the departure for the honeymoon.

wedge *n.* **1** a piece of wood or metal etc. thick at one end and tapered to a thin edge at the other, thrust between things to force them apart or prevent free movement etc. **2** a wedge-shaped thing (*a wedge of cake*). **3** anything causing division, separation, etc. (of persons) (*the issue of ordaining women drove a wedge into the faithful*). • *v.* **1** force apart or fix firmly by using a wedge. **2** thrust or pack tightly between other things or people or in a limited space; be immovable because of this. ☐ **thin end of the wedge** *see* THIN. **wedge-tailed eagle** a large eagle, widespread in Australia, having dark brown plumage and a wedge-shaped tail.

wedgebill *n.* either of two conspicuously crested brown and grey songbirds of drier eastern Australia (*chirruping wedgebill*) and drier western Australia (*chiming wedgebill*).

wedgie *n. colloq.* **1** *Aust.* = WEDGE-TAILED EAGLE (*see* WEDGE). **2** a prank in which a person's trousers etc. are pulled up between the buttocks.

wedlock *n.* the married state.

Wednesday *n.* the day of the week following Tuesday. • *adv. colloq.* **1** on Wednesday. **2** (**Wednesdays**) on Wednesdays; each Wednesday.

wee¹ *adj.* little, tiny (*it's a wee bit too long*).

wee² *colloq.* = WEE-WEE.

weebill *n.* an olive-brown to yellowish bird widespread in mainland Australia, Australia's smallest bird.

weed *n.* **1** a wild (or any) plant growing where it is not wanted. **2** (**the weed**) *colloq.* marijuana; tobacco. **3** a thin weak-looking person or horse. • *v.* remove weeds from; uproot weeds. ☐ **weed out** remove (things, persons, weeds, etc.) as inferior, undesirable, or unwanted (*weed out your unwanted books; weed out all but the fittest from the squad*).

weedy *adj.* **1** full of weeds. **2** thin and weak-looking.

wee juggler *n. Aust.* = MAJOR MITCHELL COCKATOO. (¶ Wiradhuri *wijagala*.)

week *n.* **1** a period of seven successive days, esp. one reckoned from midnight at the end of Saturday. **2** the six days other than Sunday; the five days other than Saturday and Sunday (*never go there during the week*). **3** the period for which one regularly works during a week (*a 40-hour week*). **4** (preceded by a specified day) a week after (that day) (*Tuesday week; tomorrow week*). **5** (**weeks**) a long time (*did it weeks ago*).

weekday *n.* a day other than Saturday or Sunday.

weekend *n.* Sunday and all or part of Saturday (or occasionally slightly longer, esp. as a time for a holiday or visit). • *v.* spend a weekend (*we weekended at Hall's Gap*).

weekender *n. Aust.* a house used only for holidaying in or at weekends.

weekly *adj.* happening, published, or payable etc. once a week. • *adv.* once a week. • *n.* a weekly newspaper or magazine.

weelo / wee-loh / *n.* either of two ground-nesting birds formerly widespread in Australia but no longer found in closely settled areas. Also called *curlew, stone curlew, stone plover.* (¶ Nhanta)

weeny *adj. colloq.* tiny.

weep *v.* (**wept**, **weeping**) **1** cry, shed tears. **2** bewail, lament over (*wept for his lost innocence*). **3** shed or ooze moisture in drops (*if you prune the vine now, it will weep badly; a weeping sore*). • *n.* a spell of weeping.

weepie *n. colloq.* a sentimental or emotional play, film, etc.

weeping *adj.* (of a tree) having drooping branches (*weeping gum; weeping myall*).

weepy *adj. colloq.* inclined to weep, tearful.

weero / wee-roh / *n. Aust.* = COCKATIEL. (¶ Yindjibarndi)

weet-weet *n. Aust.* an Aboriginal throwing weapon and toy, consisting of a flexible handle with a wooden or bone knob at the end. (¶ Wuywurung *wij-wij*)

weevil *n.* a destructive beetle feeding esp. on grain.

wee-wee (also **wee**) *colloq.* (esp. in use by or to small children) *v.* urinate. • *n.* urine; an act of urinating. ☐ **do wees** (or **wee-wees**) urinate.

weft *n.* crosswise threads woven under and over the warp to make fabric.

weigh *v.* **1** measure the weight of. **2** have a certain weight. **3** consider the relative importance or value of (*weigh the pros and cons*). **4** have importance or influence (*this evidence weighed with the jury*). **5** be burdensome (*the responsibility weighed heavily upon him*). ☐ **weigh anchor** raise the anchor and start a voyage. **weigh down 1** bring or keep down by its weight. **2** depress or make troubled (*weighed down with cares*). **weigh in 1** (of a boxer before a contest or a jockey after a race) be weighed. **2** (often foll. by *with*) bring one's influence etc. to bear, make a strong contribution to (a discussion etc.) (*she weighed in to stop the squabble before they came to blows; he weighed in with a handy 172 runs*). **weigh-in** *n.* the official weighing of a boxer before a fight. **weigh into** *colloq.* attack (physically or verbally). **weigh one's words** select carefully those words that convey exactly what one means. **weigh up** *colloq.* assess, form an estimate of.

weighbridge *n.* a weighing machine with a plate set in a road etc. onto which vehicles can be driven to be weighed.

weight *n.* **1** an object's mass numerically expressed according to a recognised scale of units. **2** the property of heaviness. **3** a unit or system of units by which weight is measured (*tables of weights and measures; troy weight*). **4** a piece of metal of known weight used with scales for weighing things. **5** a heavy object, esp. one used to bring or keep something down (*the clock is worked by weights*). **6** a load to be supported (*the pillars carry a great weight*). **7** a heavy burden of responsibility or worry. **8** importance, influence, a convincing effect (*the weight of the evidence is against you*). •*v.* **1** attach a weight to; hold down with a weight or weights. **2** burden with a load. **3** bias or arrange the balance of (*the test was weighted in favour of candidates with scientific knowledge*). ☐ **pull one's weight** do one's fair share (of work etc.). **weight-for-age** (of a horse race) in which competitors carry handicap weights according to their age and gender. **weight training** physical training using weights.

weighting *n.* extra pay or allowances given in special cases, e.g. to allow for the higher cost of living in a capital city.

weightless *adj.* having no weight, or with no weight relative to its surroundings; of objects in a spacecraft, apparently unaffected by gravity. ☐ **weightlessness** *n.*

weightlifting *n.* the sport of lifting heavy weights. ☐ **weightlifter** *n.*

weighty *adj.* (**weightier, weightiest**) **1** having great weight, heavy. **2** burdensome. **3** showing or deserving earnest thought. **4** important, influential. ☐ **weightily** *adv.* **weightiness** *n.*

Weir, Peter (Lindsay) (1944–), AM, Australian film director. His films include *Picnic at Hanging Rock, Gallipoli, The Year of Living Dangerously,* and *Dead Poets Society.*

weir /weer/ *n.* a small dam built across a river or canal so that water flows over it, serving to regulate the flow or to raise the level of water upstream.

weird *adj.* **1** uncanny, supernatural. **2** *colloq.* strange, utterly peculiar (*a weird hairdo*). **3** (in fantasy literature) connected with fate or with the powers of magic. ☐ **weirdly** *adv.* **weirdness** *n.*

weirdo *n.* (*pl.* **weirdos**) *colloq.* an odd or eccentric person.

welch alternative spelling of WELSH *v.*

welcome *adj.* **1** received with pleasure (*a welcome guest; welcome news*). **2** ungrudgingly permitted (*anyone is welcome to try it*). •*interj.* a greeting expressing pleasure at a person's coming. •*v.* **1** greet with pleasure or ceremony. **2** be glad to receive (*we welcome this opportunity*). •*n.* a greeting or reception, esp. a glad and kindly one. ☐ **welcomer** *n.*

weld *v.* **1** unite or fuse (pieces of metal or plastic) by hammering or pressure, usu. after softening by heat. **2** make by welding. **3** unite (members of a group etc.) into a whole. •*n.* a joint made by welding. ☐ **welder** *n.*

welfare *n.* **1** well-being; health and prosperity (of a person or community etc.). **2** financial support given by the government to those in need. ☐ **welfare state** a system whereby the nation undertakes to protect the health and well-being of its citizens, esp. those in financial or social need, by means of grants, pensions, etc. **2** a country practising this system. **welfare work** organised efforts to secure the welfare of the poor, the disabled, etc. in the community.

welkin *n.* *poetic* the sky.

well[1] *n.* **1** a shaft dug in the ground to obtain water or oil etc. from below the earth's surface. **2** a spring serving as a source of water. **3** an enclosed space resembling the shaft of a well; a deep enclosed space containing a staircase or lift in a building. **4** (foll. by *of*) a source, esp. a plentiful one (*she's a well of information*). •*v.* (usu. foll. by *up*) rise or spring (*tears welled up in his eyes; his eyes welled with tears*).

well[2] *adv.* (**better, best**) **1** in a good or suitable way, satisfactorily, rightly. **2** thoroughly, carefully (*polish it well*). **3** by a considerable margin (*she is well over forty*). **4** favourably, kindly (*they think well of him*). **5** with good reason, easily, probably (*you may well ask; it may well be our last chance*). **6** profitably (*did well for themselves*). • *adj.* **1** in good health. **2** in a satisfactory state or position (*all's well*). •*interj.* expressing surprise, resignation, etc., or used to introduce a remark when one is hesitating. ☐ **as well** (*or* **as well as**) see AS. **let** (*or* **leave**) **well alone** leave things as they are and not meddle unnecessarily. **well-adjusted 1** mentally and emotionally stable. **2** in a good state of adjustment. **well-advised** prudent (*you'd be well-advised to wait*). **well-appointed** (of a home, motel, etc.) having all the necessary equipment, furnishings, comforts, etc. **well-balanced 1** sane, sensible. **2** equally matched. **well-being** good health, happiness, and prosperity. **well-bred** showing good breeding, well-mannered; (of a horse etc.) of good breed or stock. **well-built** of good construction; (of a person) big, strong, and well-proportioned. **well-connected** associated with influential relatives or persons in positions of power etc. **well-disposed** having kindly or favourable feelings (towards a person or plan etc.). **well-endowed 1** well provided with talent etc. **2** = WELL-HUNG. **well-founded** (of suspicions etc.) based on good evidence. **well-grounded 1** = WELL-FOUNDED. **2** having a good training in or knowledge of the groundwork of a subject. **well-heeled** *colloq.* wealthy. **well-hung** *colloq.* (of a male) having a large penis. **well-meaning** (also **well-meant**) acting or done with good intentions but not having a good effect. **well off** in a satisfactory or good situation; fairly rich. **well-preserved** (of an elderly person) showing little sign of age, looking much younger than his or her years. **well-read** knowledgable through much reading; learned in a subject. **well-rounded** (of a person) having or showing a fully developed personality, ability, etc. **well-spoken** speaking in a polite and correct way. **well-to-do** fairly rich. **well-worn** much worn by use; (of a phrase) overused, hackneyed.

we'll = we shall; we will.

well- (in *combinations*) = WELL² *adv.*

■ Usage A hyphen is normally used in combinations of *well-* when used attributively, but not when used predicatively (e.g. a *well-known person* but *he is well known*).

Weller, Archie (1957–), Australian Aboriginal writer, from whose works two films have been made, *Blackfellas* and *Saturday Night, Saturday Morning*.

wellies *n.pl. colloq.* wellingtons.

Wellington the capital of New Zealand, situated at the south end of the North Island.

wellington *n.* (in full **wellington boot**) a boot of rubber or similar waterproof material, usu. reaching almost to the knee.

wellnigh *adv.* almost (*it's wellnigh impossible*).

Wells, H(erbert) G(eorge) (1866–1946), English novelist, an early writer of science fiction.

Welsh *adj.* of Wales or its people or language. • *n.* **1** the Welsh language. **2** (**the Welsh**) Welsh people. □ **Welsh rabbit** (*or* **rarebit**) melted or toasted cheese on toast. (¶ *Welsh rabbit* is the original name for this dish. The humorous use of *rabbit* was misunderstood and the word was altered to *rarebit* in an attempt to make it sound more understandable, but there is no independent evidence for the word *rarebit*.) □ **Welshman** *n.* **Welshwoman** *n.*

welsh *v.* (also **welch**) **1** (of a bookmaker at a race course) swindle by decamping without paying out winnings. **2** avoid paying one's just debts, break an agreement (*they welshed on us*). **3** inform on, tell tales on; betray (a mate etc.) (*he welshed on his best friend to the cops*). □ **welsher** *n.*

welt *n.* **1** a strip of leather etc. sewn round the edge of the upper of a boot or shoe for attaching it to the sole. **2** a ribbed or strengthened border of a knitted garment, e.g. at the waist. **3** a weal, the mark of a heavy blow. • *v.* raise weals on; thrash.

welter¹ *v.* **1** (of a ship etc.) be tossed to and fro on the waves. **2** (foll. by *in*) wallow, lie soaked in blood etc. • *n.* **1** a state of turmoil. **2** a disorderly mixture (*a welter of inconsistencies in the report*).

welter² *n.* **1** a heavy rider or boxer. **2** a horse race in which the minimum weight for riders is higher than usual.

welterweight *n.* a boxing weight between lightweight and middleweight, in the amateur boxing scale 63.5–67 kg; a boxer of this weight.

Wemba-wemba / **wem**-bu-wem-bu / *n.* a generic term (though a dialect in itself) for the dialects of an Aboriginal language spoken by peoples in Western Vic. and an adjoining portion of NSW: from Bendigo and Ballarat in the east to the SA border in the west, from Balranald and Mildura in the north to Hamilton and Chatsworth in the south.

wen *n.* a benign tumour on the skin esp. of the scalp.

wench *n. archaic* or *jocular* a girl or young woman.

wend *v.* □ **wend one's way** go.

went *see* GO¹.

Wentworth¹, D'Arcy (*c.*1762–1827), Irish medical practitioner who was tried four times in England for highway robbery but always acquitted. He sailed to Sydney as assistant surgeon on the Second Fleet, was surgeon of convicts on Norfolk Island, and later was principal surgeon in Sydney. He was appointed magistrate and superintendent of police and became a foundation director of the Bank of NSW. By the time he died he had accumulated large landholdings.

Wentworth², William Charles (1790–1872), Australian lawyer and statesman, explorer (with Blaxland and Lawson), founder of the University of Sydney, and ardent advocate of self-government for the colony of NSW. He was the son of D'Arcy Wentworth and the convict Catherine Crowley.

wept *see* WEEP.

were *see* BE.

we're = we are.

weren't = were not.

werewolf / **weer**-wuulf, **wair**- / *n.* (*pl.* **werewolves**) (also **werwolf** / **wer**-wuulf /) (in myths and in fantasy literature) a person who at times turns into a wolf.

wert *archaic* the past subjunctive of *be*, used with *thou*.

Wesley, John (1703–91), an Anglican priest who founded Methodism and broke away from the Church of England. His brother Charles (1707–88) was also a member of the movement and the composer of many well-known hymns. □ **Wesleyan** *adj.* & *n.*

West, Morris (Langlo) (1916–99), AO, Australian novelist whose works include *The Devil's Advocate* and *The Shoes of the Fisherman*.

west *n.* **1** the point of the horizon where the sun sets, opposite east; the direction in which this lies. **2** the western part of something. **3** (**the West**) Europe in contrast to Oriental countries; the States of western Europe and N. America. • *adj.* **1** towards or in the west. **2** (of a wind) blowing from the west. • *adv.* **1** towards or in the west. □ **go west** *colloq.* be destroyed, lost, or killed.

West Bank the area on the west side of the River Jordan occupied by Israel in 1967.

westbound adj. travelling or leading westwards.

westering adj. (of the sun, etc.) moving towards the west.

westerly adj. **1** in or towards the west. **2** (of a wind) blowing from the west. • n. a westerly wind.

western adj. **1** of or in the west. **2** used as a distinguishing epithet in the names of esp. Australian fauna (*western black cockatoo, western brown snake, western whipbird*, etc.). • n. a film or story dealing with life in western North America during the wars with the American Indians, or with cowboys etc. ❑ **western bristlebird** a rare, ground-dwelling, brownish bird of south-western WA. **western grey** (in full **western grey kangaroo**) a kangaroo of SW and central southern Australia (distinguished as a species from the eastern grey in 1966). **Western hemisphere** the half of the earth containing the Americas.

Western Australia the largest State in Australia comprising the western part of the continent, capital Perth. ❑ **Western Australian Christmas tree** see NUYTSIA. ❑ **Western** (*or* **West**) **Australian** n. & adj.

Western Church n. the major part of Christendom continuing to derive its authority, doctrine, and ritual from the popes in Rome (cf. EASTERN CHURCH).

Western Desert language n. the name for a single Aboriginal language (with many dialects) spoken over about one and a quarter million square kilometres of central and western Australia (about one sixth of the total area of Australia) including large areas of WA, SA, and the NT.

westerner n. a native or inhabitant of the west.

westernise v. (also **-ize**) make (a person or country) more like the West in ideas and institutions etc. ❑ **westernisation** n.

westernmost adj. furthest west.

Western Samoa see SAMOA.

Western Standard Time an Australian time zone lying on the 120th meridian and covering all of Western Australia.

westie *Aust. colloq. derog.* n. **1** a resident of the western suburbs of Sydney or Melbourne. **2** a person who is regarded as uncultured, lacking style, etc. • adj. of, pertaining to, or belonging to a westie.

West Indies a chain of islands in the Atlantic Ocean off Central America, enclosing the Caribbean Sea. ❑ **West Indian** adj. & n.

Westminster Abbey a church in London, originally the abbey church of a Benedictine monastery.

West Papua see IRIAN JAYA.

Westralia n. *colloq.* Western Australia.

Westralian *colloq.* adj. of or pertaining to Western Australia. • n. a person native to or resident in Western Australia.

westringia / wes-**trin**-jee-uh / n. any of over 20 shrubs of the genus of the same name, endemic to temperate Australia, and having white, blue, or bluey-mauve flowers and whorled leaves, one species being called 'coastal rosemary'.

westward adj. & adv. (also **westwards**) in or towards the west.

wet adj. (**wetter, wettest**) **1** soaked, covered, or moistened with water or other liquid. **2** rainy (*wet weather*). **3** (of paint or ink etc.) recently applied and not yet dry. **4** *colloq.* (of a person) feeble, inept; lacking spunk or zest. **5** of or being a political 'wet'. • v. (**wetted, wetting**) **1** make wet. **2 a** urinate in or on (*he wet the bed*). **b** (*reflexive*) urinate involuntarily (*he's wet himself*). • n. **1** moisture, liquid that wets something. **2 a** rainy weather. **b** (**the wet**) *Aust.* = the WET SEASON. **3** *colloq.* a feeble or inept person; a person lacking spunk etc. **4** *colloq.* a conservative politician with a progressive attitude towards social issues etc. (as opposed to a 'dry' —see DRY n. (sense 2). ❑ **wet behind the ears** immature, inexperienced. **wet blanket** *colloq.* a gloomy person who prevents others from enjoying themselves. **wet dream** an erotic dream in which semen is ejaculated involuntarily. **wet nurse** n. a woman employed to suckle another's child. **wet-nurse** v. **1** act as wet nurse to. **2** look after or coddle as if helpless. **wet season** a period of substantial rainfall, a rainy season, esp. in central and northern Australia (as opposed to the DRY SEASON – see DRY). **wet weekend** *colloq.* a thing regarded as the epitome of boredom, misery, gloom, or which seems never-ending. ❑ ❑ **wetly** adv. **wetness** n.

wether n. a castrated ram.

wetlands n.pl. swamps and marshes.

wetsuit n. a rubber garment worn by divers, windsurfers, etc. to keep warm.

wetting agent n. a substance that helps water etc. to penetrate (soils etc.) or adhere to (leaves etc.).

we've = we have.

whack *colloq.* n. **1** a heavy resounding blow. **2** a share (*he's come for his whack*). • v. **1** strike or beat forcefully with a sharp blow. **2** put (*whack a few more steaks on the barbie; whack your things down over there*). **3** (as **whacked** adj.) **a** tired out. **b** drunk. ❑ **have a whack at** attempt, have a go at. **whack in** insert. **whack off** masturbate (oneself or another).

whacker n. (also **wacker**) *colloq.* a generalised term of abuse; a fool.

whacking *colloq.* adj. very large. • adv. very (*a whacking great semi*).

whacko *colloq. interj.* (also **whacko the diddle oh**) an exclamation of delight or enjoyment. • adj. (also **whacko-the-chook** or **-the diddle-oh** or **-the-goose**) absolutely splendid (*had a whacko-the-chook time at Surfers'*).

whale[1] n. (pl. **whales** or **whale**) **1** a very large sea mammal with a horizontal tail and a blowhole on

whale the top of the head for breathing. **2** *Aust.* = MURRAY COD (*see* MURRAY). •*v.* **1** hunt wales. **2** *Aust.* travel the course of a river as a swagman. ❐ **a whale of a** *colloq.* an exceedingly good (*had a whale of a time*).

whale² *colloq. v.* beat, thrash. ❐ **whale into 1** attack (physically or verbally). **2** begin (working, doing, eating, etc.) energetically.

whalebird = PRION.

whalebone *n.* a horny springy substance from the upper jaw of some kinds of whale, formerly used as a stiffening material in garments etc. ❐ **whalebone tree** a medium-sized tree of rainforests in eastern NSW and eastern Qld, having very springy whalebone-like branches and yielding a hard yellowish timber used by Aborigines for making waddies (*see* WADDY¹) and later by whites for making tool handles etc. Also called *waddywood*.

whaler *n.* **1** a person or ship engaged in hunting whales. **2** any of several sharks of Australian waters (probably so called because they were seen near whales), esp. the large bronze whaler (*blue whaler*; *bronze whaler*; *Swan River whaler*). **3** a swagman whose route follows the course of a river which provides food in the form of whales (*see* WHALE¹ *n.*, sense 2) (*Darling whaler; Murray whaler; Murrumbidgee whaler*).

whaling *n.* hunting whales.

wham *colloq. interj.* expressing forcible impact. •*n.* a forceful hit, stroke, etc. (*give it a wham*). •*v.* (often foll. by *into*) hit with forcible impact (*my car whammed into the tree*).

whammy *n. colloq.* an evil or unlucky influence; a stroke of extreme misfortune (*the crash was a real whammy to them both*).

wharf / wawf / *n.* (*pl.* **wharves** or **wharfs**) a landing-stage where ships may be moored to load and unload. •*v.* **1** moor (a ship) at a wharf. **2** store (goods) on a wharf.

wharfage / **waw**-fij / *n.* accommodation at a wharf; the charge for this.

wharfie *n. Aust. colloq.* waterside worker; wharf labourer.

what *adj.* **1** asking for a statement of amount, number, or kind (*what books have you read?*). **2** *colloq.* which (*what book have you chosen?*). **3** how great or strange or remarkable (*what a fool you are!*). **4** the or any that (*I'll give you what help I can*). •*pron.* **1** what thing or things (*what did you say?; this is what I mean*). **2** a request for something to be repeated because one has not heard or understood. •*adv.* to what extent or degree (*what does it matter?*). •*interj.* an exclamation of surprise. ❐ **give a person what for** *colloq.* punish or scold him or her. **what have you** *colloq.* other similar things (*get all the magazines, papers, and what have you, into this crate*). **what is more** as an additional point, moreover. **what's what** *colloq.* what things are useful or important etc. (*she knows what's what*). **what with** on account of (various causes) (*what with overwork and undernourishment, he fell ill*).

whatever *adj.* **1** of any kind or number (*take whatever books you need*). **2** of any kind at all (*there is no doubt whatever*). •*pron.* anything or everything that; no matter what (*do whatever you like; keep calm, whatever happens*). ❐ **or whatever** or anything similar.

whatnot *n.* **1** *colloq.* something trivial or indefinite. **2** suchlike things (*bought a pav, some lamingtons, and whatnot*). **3** a stand with shelves for small objects.

whatsoever = WHATEVER.

wheat *n.* **1** grain from which flour is made. **2** the plant that produces this. ❐ **wheat cocky** *Aust.* a wheat farmer. **wheat germ** the embryo of the wheat grain, extracted as a source of vitamins.

wheaten *adj.* made from wheat.

wheatmeal *n.* wholemeal flour made from wheat.

wheedle *v.* coax; persuade or obtain by coaxing.

wheel *n.* **1** a disc or circular frame arranged to revolve on a shaft that passes through its centre. **2** something resembling this. **3** a machine etc. of which a wheel is an essential part. **4** motion like that of a wheel or of a line of persons that pivots on one end. **5** (**wheels**) *colloq.* a car. •*v.* **1** push or pull (a bicycle or cart etc. with wheels) along. **2** turn or cause to turn like a wheel; change direction and face another way (*he wheeled round in astonishment*). **3** move in circles or curves. ❐ **at the wheel 1** driving a vehicle or directing a ship's course. **2** in control of affairs (*in this firm she's at the wheel*). **wheel and deal** engage in political or commercial scheming. **wheel clamp** *see* CLAMP *n.* (sense 2). **wheels within wheels** secret or indirect motives and influences interacting with one another.

wheelbarrow *n.* an open container for moving small loads, with a wheel beneath one end and two handles and legs at the other.

wheelbase *n.* the distance between the front and rear axles of a vehicle.

wheelchair *n.* a chair on wheels, for use by a person who cannot walk.

-wheeler *comb. form* a vehicle with a specified number of wheels (*a three-wheeler*).

wheeler-dealer *n.* a scheming person who negotiates political or commercial deals.

wheelhouse *n.* a steersman's shelter.

wheelie *n. colloq.* **1** the stunt of riding a bicycle or motor cycle for a short distance with the front wheel off the ground. **2 a** the stunt of violently accelerating a car so as to cause the drive wheels to spin. **b** such spinning caused by accelerating sharply round a corner etc. ❐ **wheelie bin** a very large bin on wheels for household garbage; a similar bin for recyclable materials. Also called *big bin*.

wheelwright *n.* a maker or repairer of wooden wheels.

wheeze v. breathe with an audible hoarse whistling sound in the chest. •n. **1** the sound of wheezing. **2** colloq. a clever scheme or plan. ☐ **wheezy** adj. **wheeziness** n.

whelk n. any of several sea snails with a spiral shell, esp. one used as food.

whelp n. **1** a young dog, a pup. **2** an ill-mannered child or youth. •v. give birth to (puppies).

when adv. **1** at what time?; on what occasion?; how soon?; how long ago? **2** at which time (*there are times when joking is out of place*). •conj. **1** at the time that, on the occasion that; whenever; as soon as (*come when you like; when I was your age*). **2** although; considering that, since (*why risk it when you know it's dangerous?*). **3** after which; and then; but just then (*I was nearly asleep when the bell rang*). •pron. what time?; which time (*till when can you stay?; since when it has improved*). •n. time, occasion, date (*I'll leave you to fix the where and when*).

whence adv. & conj. formal or archaic from where, from what place or source; from which (*whence did they come?*).

■ **Usage** In questions, *whence* is now replaced by *where … from*. The phrase *from whence* (*the place from whence they came*) is found frequently in translations of the Bible and occurs also in Shakespeare and Dickens, but strictly the word *from* is unnecessary and should be omitted.

whenever conj. & adv. **1** at whatever time; on whatever occasion (*do it whenever you like*). **2** every time that (*whenever he opens his mouth he puts his foot in it*).

whensoever conj. & adv. formal whenever.

where adv. & conj. **1** at or in or to what or which place, position, or circumstances (*where are you going?; go where you like*). **2** in what respect; from what place, source, or origin (*where does it concern us?; where did you hear such nonsense?*). **3** in or at or to the place in which (*leave it where it is*). **4** and there (*we reached Pimbaacla, where the car broke down*). •pron. what place (*where does it fit?*). •n. a place, the scene of something (*see* WHEN n.).

whereabouts adv. in or near what place (*whereabouts are they?*). •n. (treated as *sing.* or *pl.*) a person's or thing's approximate location (*his whereabouts are uncertain*).

whereas conj. **1** (esp. in legal preambles) since it is the fact that. **2** but in contrast (*the Coalition did well, whereas Labor suffered heavy losses*).

whereby adv. by what or which means.

wherefore adv. archaic for what reason?; for this reason. •n. see WHY.

wherein adv. in what; in which.

whereof adv. & conj. of what or which.

wheresoever adv. & conj. formal wherever.

whereupon conj. immediately after which.

wherever adv. in or to whatever place. •conj. in every place that. ☐ **or wherever** colloq. or in any similar place (*it's in the top drawer—or wherever*).

wherewithal n. colloq. the things (esp. money) needed for a purpose.

wherry n. (*pl.* **wherries**) **1** a light rowing boat usu. for carrying passengers. **2** a large light barge.

whet v. (**whetted**, **whetting**) **1** sharpen (a tool) by grinding. **2** stimulate (*whet one's appetite*).

whether conj. introducing an alternative possibility (*we don't know whether she will come or not*).

whetstone n. a shaped stone used for sharpening tools.

whew interj. an exclamation of astonishment, dismay, or relief.

whey / way / n. the watery liquid left when milk forms curds, e.g. in cheese-making.

which adj. & pron. **1** what particular one or ones of a set of things or people (*which Bob do you mean?*). **2** and that (*we invited him to come, which he did very willingly*). •relative pron. the thing or animal referred to (*the house, which is large, is left to his son*).

■ **Usage** As a relative pronoun *which* is used esp. of an incidental description rather than one which defines or identifies something; *see* note at THAT.

whichever adj. & pron. any which; that or those which (*take whichever book you fancy; take whichever you like*).

whicker v. (of a horse) give a soft breathy whinny. •n. **1** such a whinny. **2** a similar human sound (*he gave a little whicker of laughter*).

whiff n. **1** a puff or breath of air, smoke, etc. **2** a slight smell (*caught a whiff of something rotting*). **3** a trace of scandal etc.

whiffle v. (of the wind) blow lightly; shift about (*wind whiffling through the gum trees*).

whiffy adj. (**whiffier**, **whiffiest**) colloq. having a stink (*your socks are whiffier than mine*).

Whig n. Brit. hist. a member of the British reforming and constitutional party succeeded in the 19th c. by the Liberal Party.

while n. a period of time, the time spent in doing something (*a long while ago; we've waited all this while*). •conj. **1** during the time that, as long as (*make hay while the sun shines*). **2** although (*while I admit that he is sincere, I think he is mistaken*). **3** on the other hand (*she is dark, while her sister is fair*). •v. (foll. by *away*) pass (time) in a leisurely or interesting manner. ☐ **between whiles** in the intervals.

whilst adv. & conj. while.

whim n. a sudden fancy or impulse.

whimbrel / **wim**-bruhl / n. a small curlew of Australian coastal waters.

whimp alternative spelling of WIMP.

whimper v. whine softly, make feeble frightened or complaining sounds. •n. a whimpering sound.

whimsical / **wim**-zi-kuhl / adj. **1** impulsive and playful. **2** fanciful, quaint. ☐ **whimsically** adv. **whimsicality** / wim-zi-**kal**-uh-tee / n.

whimsy *n.* **1** a whim; a capricious notion or fancy. **2** capricious or quaint humour.

whine *v.* **1** make a long high complaining wail like that of a dog. **2** make a long high shrill sound resembling this. **3** complain in a petty or feeble way; utter complainingly. • *n.* a whining cry or sound or complaint. ☐ **whiner** *n.* **whiny** *adj.*

whinge *colloq. v.* (**whinged**, **whingeing** or **whinging**) whine, grumble persistently. • *n.* a whining complaint; an act or instance of whingeing (*having a whinge*). ☐ **whingeing pom** (also **whingeing pommy**) *colloq. derog.* a person from Britain (esp. England), esp. a migrant to Australia, who continually complains about life in Australia (*see* POM).

whinny *n.* a gentle or joyful neigh. • *v.* (**whinnied**, **whinnying**) utter a whinny.

whip *n.* **1** a cord fastened to a handle, used for urging animals on or for punishment. **2** an official of a political party in parliament with authority to maintain discipline among members of the party, esp. ensuring attendance and voting in debates. **3** the action of beating cream, eggs, etc. into a froth. • *v.* (**whipped**, **whipping**) **1** strike or urge on with a whip. **2** beat (cream or eggs etc.) into a froth. **3** move or take suddenly (*whipped behind the door; whipped out a knife*). **4** (foll. by *off*) *colloq.* steal. **5** *colloq.* defeat soundly. **6** sew (an edge) with overcast stitches; bind (the end of a rope etc.) with a spiral of cord. ☐ **fair crack of the whip** (also **fair suck of the sauce bottle**) *Aust. n.* an equitable opportunity; a reasonable chance. *interj.* give someone a chance! **whip on** urge into action. **whip-round** *n. colloq.* an informal collection of money from a group of people. **whip snake** any of several slender whip-like snakes of mainland Australia, esp. the widespread venomous *yellow-faced whip snake*. **whip up 1** incite, stir up (*whip up support for the republican cause*). **2** make quickly (*whipped up a dress for the party*).

whipbird *n.* **1** (in full **eastern whipbird**) the predominantly olive-green bird of eastern mainland Australia, uttering a cry like the crack of a stockwhip. Also called *stockwhip bird* and, formerly, *coachman* or *coachwhip*. **2** (in full **western whipbird**) predominantly olive-green bird of coastal heaths and mallee scrubs in parts of southern Australia, lacking the startling whip-crack call of the eastern species.

whipcord *n.* **1** cord made of tightly twisted strands, used e.g. for whiplashes. **2** twilled fabric with prominent ridges.

whiplash *n.* **1** the flexible end of a whip. **2** a blow with a whip. **3** whiplash injury. ☐ **whiplash injury** injury to the neck caused by a sudden jerk of the head (e.g. when travelling in a vehicle that collides with something and stops suddenly).

whippersnapper *n.* **1** a small child. **2** an insignificant person who behaves in a presumptuous way.

whipper snipper *n.* a hand-held machine with a revolving trimming line, used for cutting grass etc. in a domestic garden.

whippet *n.* a small cross-bred dog resembling a greyhound, used for racing.

whipping *n.* a beating or flogging, usu. with a whip. ☐ **whipping boy** a person who is blamed regularly for someone else's mistakes, a scapegoat. (¶ Formerly a lower-class boy educated with a young prince and whipped for the prince's mistakes and wrongdoings.) **whipping side** the last side (of the sheep) to be shorn.

whippoorwill *n.* the American nightjar.

whippy *n.* **1** *Aust.* the base in a game of hide-and-seek. **2** *Aust.* a place in which money is kept, a hiding place for cash. • *adj.* **1** flexible, springy. **2** *colloq.* fleet, speedy.

whipstick *n. Aust.* **1** a form of growth (usu. of mallee eucalypts) characterised by a number of slim, even stems; a tree of this habit. **2** an area of vegetation dominated by such trees (*surveying wildlife out in the whipstick*). **3** (in full **whipstick mallee**, **whipstick scrub**) an area dominated by whipsticks.

whipstock *n.* the handle of a whip.

whiptail wallaby *n.* a light to brownish-grey wallaby of eastern Qld and eastern NSW, having a long, slender, dark-tipped tail.

whirl *v.* **1** swing or spin round and round; cause to have this motion. **2** send or travel swiftly in a curved course. **3** convey or go rapidly (*the car whirled them away*). **4 a** (of the brain, senses, etc.) seem to spin round (*my head's whirling*). **b** (of thoughts etc.) be confused; follow each other in bewildering succession (*dozens of excuses whirled in his mind*). • *n.* **1** a whirling movement. **2** a confused state (*her thoughts were in a whirl*). **3** a bustling activity (*the social whirl*). **4** *colloq.* a try (*give it a whirl*).

whirligig *n.* **1** a spinning or whirling toy. **2** a revolving motion. **3** anything regarded as hectic or constantly changing (*the whirligig of time*).

whirlpool *n.* a current of water whirling in a circle, drawing objects towards its centre.

whirlwind *n.* **1** a mass of air whirling rapidly about a central point. **2** a confused, hectic process (*a whirlwind of activity*). **3** (used as *adj.*) very rapid (*a whirlwind courtship*).

whirly *n.* (also **whirly-whirly**) *Aust.* = WILLY WILLY.

whirr *v.* make a continuous buzzing or vibrating sound like that of a wheel etc. turning rapidly. • *n.* this sound.

whisk *v.* **1** move with a quick light sweeping movement. **2** convey or go rapidly (*he whisked me off to Canberra*). **3** brush or sweep lightly from a surface (*whisk away the crumbs*). **4** wave or lightly brandish (*whisking flies away from his face in the great Australian salute*). **5** take suddenly (*whisked the plate away*). **6** beat (eggs etc.) into a froth. • *n.* **1** a whisking movement. **2** an instrument for beating eggs etc. **3** a bunch of strips of straw etc. tied to a handle, used for flicking flies or dust away.

whisker *n.* **1** each of the long hair-like bristles growing near the mouth of a cat and certain other animals. **2** (**whiskers**) hair growing on a man's face, esp. on the cheek. **3** *colloq.* a very small distance (*within a whisker of it; won by a whisker*). ▫ **have whiskers on it** (of news, a subject, etc.) be no longer novel or fresh. ▫▫ **whiskered** *adj.* **whiskery** *adj.*

whisky *n.* (*Irish* **whiskey**) spirit distilled from malted grain (esp. barley or rye). ▫ **whisky drinker** *colloq.* = CHERRY NOSE (*see* CHERRY). (¶ An abbreviation of *usquebaugh* from Gaelic, = water of life).

whisper *v.* **1** speak or utter softly, using the breath but not the vocal cords. **2** converse privately or secretly; plot or spread (a tale) as a rumour in this way. **3** (of leaves or fabrics etc.) rustle. • *n.* **1** a whispering sound or remark; whispering speech (*spoke in a whisper*). **2** a rumour. ▫ **whisperer** *n.* **whispering** *adj.* & *n.*

whist *n.* a card game usu. for two pairs of players. ▫ **whist drive** a series of games of whist in which a number of people take part.

whistle *n.* **1** a shrill sound made by forcing breath through narrowed lips. **2** a similar sound made by a bird, the wind, a missile, etc. **3** an instrument that produces a shrill sound when air or steam is forced through it. **4** *colloq.* the penis. • *v.* **1** emit a whistle. **2 a** give a signal or express surprise or derision by whistling. **b** (often foll. by *up*) summon or give a signal to (a dog etc.) by whistling. **c** (foll. by *up*) summon by, or as if by, whistling (*I'll whistle up some help*). **3** produce (a tune) by whistling. **4** (foll. by *for*) vainly seek or desire (*she drove off telling him he could whistle for his money*). ▫ **as clean** (or **clear** or **dry**) **as a whistle** very clean (or clear or dry). **blow the whistle on** reveal and so bring to an end (an underhand deal, unacceptable practice, etc.); inform on. **whistle in the dark** pretend to be unafraid. **whistle in** (or **against**) **the wind** make a futile protest. **whistle-stop 1** a small unimportant town on a railway. **2** a brief stop (during a tour made by a politician etc.) e.g. for electioneering. ▫▫ **whistler** *n.*

whistleblower *n.* a person who exposes or brings to public attention an irregularity or a crime, esp. from within an organisation.

whistlecock *Aust. n.* **1** subincision, the slitting of the underside of the penis in order to make a permanent opening into the urethra. **2** an Aboriginal male on whom this procedure has been performed. • *v.* perform this procedure (*they whistlecocked him*).

whistler *n.* **1** any of many small insect-eating Australian birds, typically having a rich whistled song (e.g. the *golden whistler*, the *rufous whistler*). **2** *Aust.* a whistling duck.

whistling *n.* the action or an instance of WHISTLE *v.* • *adj.* that whistles. ▫ **whistling dick** (esp. in Tas.) = GREY THRUSH (*see* GREY). **whistling duck 1 a** a perching duck of northern and eastern Australia having a loud whistling call. **b** a closely related duck of northern and eastern Australia and elsewhere in the Indo-Pacific region. **2** a nomadic whistling duck of various parts of Australia, having a pink patch behind the eye, white underparts with brown bars, and a shovel-shaped bill. **whistling eagle** (also **whistling kite**) a dark and light brown bird of prey of Australia and elsewhere, having a loud whistling call. **whistling tree-frog** either of two frogs of south-eastern mainland Australia having loud, melodious, whistle-like calls.

Whit *adj.* of Whitsuntide or Whit Sunday. • *n.* Whitsuntide.

whit *n.* the least possible amount (*not a whit better*).

White, Patrick (Victor Martindale) (1912–90), Australian novelist and playwright, considered by many to be Australia's greatest novelist. White was the first Australian writer to be awarded a Nobel Prize (1973), and used its prize money to establish the Patrick White Award. His novels include *The Aunt's Story*, *The Tree of Man*, *Voss*, *Riders in the Chariot*, and *The Eye of the Storm*. His plays include *The Ham Funeral* and *The Season at Sarsaparilla*.

white *adj.* **1** of the very lightest colour, like milk or snow. **2** (also **White**) of the human group with light-coloured skin. **3** pale in the face from illness or fear etc. **4** (of hair) having lost its colour, esp. in old age. **5** (of coffee or tea) with milk or cream. **6** used as a distinguishing epithet in the names of Australian fauna, esp. birds (*white-backed magpie, white-breasted robin*, etc.). **7** used as a distinguishing epithet in the names of Australian flora to indicate the colour of bark, wood, flowers, etc. (*white apple, white gum, white waratah*, etc.). **8** (of wine) made with white grapes or dark grapes with the skins removed. • *n.* **1** white colour. **2** a white substance or material; (**whites**) white garments worn in cricket, tennis, etc. **3** (also **White**) a white person. **4** the white part of something (e.g. of the eyeball, round the iris). **5** the transparent substance round the yolk of an egg, turning white when cooked. **6** the white pieces in chess etc.; the player using these. ▫ **white cedar** a tree of Qld and NSW, deciduous, having highly scented lilac flowers and oval fruits favoured by parrots; the attractively figured wood of this tree. Also called *melia*. **white cell** (or **corpuscle**) a leucocyte, a white blood cell. **white cockatoo** (also **sulphur-crested cockatoo**) a very large, predominantly white Australian cockatoo with a curling yellow crest and an extremely raucous call. **white-collar worker** an office worker; one who is not engaged in manual labour. **white death** = WHITE POINTER. **white**

dwarf a small very dense star. **white elephant** a useless possession. **white-eye** = SILVEREYE. **white feather** a symbol of cowardice. **white flag** a symbol of surrender. **white gold** gold mixed with platinum to give a silver-coloured alloy. **white heat 1** the temperature at which heated metal looks white. **2** a state of intense passion or activity (*worked at white heat*). **white-hot** at white heat, hotter than red-hot. **white leghorn 1** a breed of hardy, egg-laying, domestic fowl. **2** *Aust. colloq.* a female player of lawn bowls (who wears a mandatory white uniform). **white lie** a harmless lie (e.g. one told for the sake of politeness). **white magic** magic used for beneficial purposes. **white meat** poultry, veal, rabbit, and pork. **white noise** noise containing many frequencies with equal intensities; a harsh hissing sound. **white pepper** pepper made by grinding a ripe or husked berry. **white pointer** (also **great white shark**, **white death**) *Aust.* a large aggressive shark of warm seas, with a brownish or grey back, white underparts, and large triangular teeth. **white spirit** light petroleum used as a solvent. **white tie** a man's white bow tie worn with full evening dress. **white water** a shallow or foamy stretch of water; rapids. **white wine** golden or pale yellow wine. □□ **whiteness** *n.* **whitish** *adj.*

white ant *n.* **1** a termite. **2** *esp. Aust. colloq.* a saboteur; a person who undermines (a political party, a policy, etc.). •*v.* (**white-ant**) *esp. Aust.* **1** (of termites) destroy (a wooden structure). **2** undermine or sabotage (an enterprise, an organisation, etc.). □ **white-anter** *n.* **white-anting** *n.*

White Australia *n. hist.* Australia as a society into which the immigration of non-whites is restricted. □ **White Australia Policy** *hist.* the policy of restricting immigration into Australia to white persons only. The policy continued until 1958, when entry permits, based chiefly on economic criteria, came into use.

whitebait *n.* (*pl.* **whitebait**) (usu. in *pl.*) any of several fish caught small and eaten whole.

whiteboard *n.* a kind of 'blackboard' made of white plastic, and written on with a felt pen rather than with chalk.

whiteface *n.* any of three small brownish birds of drier southern and central mainland Australia.

white fellow (in Aboriginal English) *n.* (also **white fella**, **white feller**) a non-Aboriginal inhabitant of Australia. •*adj.* (**whitefellow**, **white-fella**, **white-feller**) non-Aboriginal; alien (to the Aborigines) (*whitefellow names like 'Ayers Rock' for Uluru*).

White Friar a Carmelite (so called from his white cloak).

whitegoods *n.pl.* large domestic electrical appliances such as fridges.

whitehead *n. colloq.* a white or white-topped pustule on the skin.

White House the official residence of the US president in Washington, DC; by extension, the president or presidency of the US.

Whiteley, Brett (1939–92), AO, Australian painter, winner of the Archibald Prize, whose works are exhibited in Australia and internationally.

White Monk a monk of the Cistercian Order (so called from the colour of his habit).

whiten *v.* make or become white or whiter. □ **whitener** *n.*

White Paper *n.* a report issued by the government to give information on a subject.

whitewash *n.* **1** a liquid containing quicklime or powdered chalk used for painting walls, ceilings, etc. **2** a means of glossing over mistakes or faults. **3** a sporting match in which an opponent does not score. •*v.* **1** paint with whitewash. **2** clear the reputation of (a person etc.) by glossing over mistakes or faults. **3** defeat (an opponent) without allowing any opposing score.

whitewood *n.* any of many Australian trees yielding a very pale wood.

whither *archaic adv.* to what place (*whither away, lad?*). •*conj.* to the or any place which (*go whither you will*).

whiting *n.* **1** (*pl.* **whiting**) any of several silvery marine fish of Australian waters valued as food, esp. the spotted whiting. **2** a small, unrelated European food-fish with white flesh. **3** ground chalk used in white-washing, plate-cleaning, etc.

Whitlam, (Edward) Gough (1916–), AC, Australian Labor statesman, prime minister 1972–75. While in office he ended compulsory military service in Australia, relaxed the laws for Asian and African immigrants, abolished tertiary education fees, introduced welfare payments to single parents and the homeless, abolished the death penalty, commissioned studies on Aboriginal Land Rights, and introduced other innovative reforms. When, in 1975, the opposition blocked finance bills in the Senate, he refused to call an election and was dismissed by the Governor-General Sir John Kerr under controversial circumstances.

whitlow / **wit**-loh / *n.* a small abscess under or near a fingernail or toenail.

Whitman, Walt (1819–92), American poet whose poetry celebrates democracy, sexuality (homosexuality), the self, and the liberated spirit in union with nature: best known for *Leaves of Grass*.

Whitsun *n.* = WHITSUNTIDE. •*adj.* = WHIT.

Whit Sunday *n.* the seventh Sunday after Easter, commemorating the descent of the Holy Ghost upon the Apostles at Pentecost.

Whitsuntide *n.* the weekend or week including Whit Sunday.

whittle *v.* **1** trim or shape (wood) by cutting thin slices from the surface. **2** (foll. by *down* or *away*) reduce by repeatedly removing various amounts (*our few remaining old growth forests are being whittled away; whittled down the cost*).

whiz (also **whizz**) *v.* (**whizzed**, **whizzing**) **1** make a sound like that of something moving at great speed through air. **2** move very quickly. •*n.* **1** a whizzing sound. **2** (also **wiz**) *colloq.* a person who is remarkable or highly skilled in some respect (*she's a wiz at chess*). ◻ **whiz-bang** (also **whizz-bang**) *adj. colloq.* excellent; spectacular.

whiz kid *n. colloq.* an exceptionally brilliant or successful young person.

WHO *abbr.* World Health Organisation.

who *pron.* **1** what or which person or persons? (*who called?; you know who it was; whom do you wish to see?*). **2** the particular person or persons (*this is the man who wanted to see you*).

whoa *interj.* a command to a horse etc. to stop or stand still.

who'd = **1** who had. **2** who would.

whodunit *n.* (also **whodunnit**) *colloq.* a detective story, play, or film. (¶ Humorous representation of the (incorrect) sentence 'who done it?')

whoever *pron.* any or every person who, no matter who.

whole *adj.* **1** with no part removed or left out (*told them the whole story*). **2** not injured or broken (*there's not a plate left whole*). •*n.* **1** the full or complete amount, all the parts or members (*the whole of Ororoo knows it*). **2** a complete system made up of parts (*the universe is a whole and the earth is part of this*). ◻ **a whole lot** *colloq.* a great amount. **on the whole** considering everything; in respect of the whole though some details form exceptions. **whole number** a number consisting of one or more units with no fractions.

wholefood *n.* food which has not been unnecessarily processed or refined.

wholegrain *adj.* containing or consisting of whole grains (*wholegrain bread*).

wholehearted *adj.* with all possible effort or sincerity; total. ◻ **wholeheartedly** *adv.*

wholemeal *adj.* meal or flour with none of the bran or germ removed.

wholesale *n.* the selling of goods in large quantities to be retailed by others. •*adj.* & *adv.* **1** by wholesale; at a wholesale price. **2** on a large scale (*wholesale destruction*). •*v.* sell in the wholesale trade. ◻ **wholesaler** *n.*

wholesome *adj.* good for physical or mental health or moral condition; showing a healthy condition. ◻ **wholesomeness** *n.*

wholism alternative spelling of HOLISM.

who'll = who will.

wholly *adv.* entirely, with nothing excepted or removed (*he's wholly responsible*).

whom *pron.* the objective case of WHO (*the man whom I saw*).

■ **Usage** *who* is commonly used instead of *whom* in colloquial contexts.

whomever *pron.* the objective case of WHOEVER.

whomsoever *pron.* the objective case of WHOSOEVER.

whoop / hoop, woop / *v.* utter a loud cry of excitement. •*n.* **1** this cry. **2** a long rasping indrawn breath as in whooping cough. ◻ **whoop it up** *colloq.* **1** engage in noisy revelry. **2** make a stir.

whoopee / wuup-**ee** / *interj.* an exclamation of exuberant joy. ◻ **make whoopee** *colloq.* **1** have fun; live it up. **2** make love.

whooping cough / **hoo**-ping / *n.* an infectious disease esp. of children, with a series of short violent coughs followed by a whoop.

whoops / wuups / *interj. colloq.* an exclamation of surprise or apology, esp. on losing balance or making an obvious mistake.

whoosh / wuush / *v.* move or cause to move with a rushing sound (*the skier whooshed past me*). •*n.* a sudden movement accompanied by a rushing sound.

whop *v.* (**whopped**, **whopping**) *colloq.* thrash; defeat decisively.

whopper *n. colloq.* **1** something very large. **2** a big lie.

whopping *adj. colloq.* very large or remarkable (*a whopping great lie*).

whore / haw / *n.* **1** a professional prostitute. **2** *derog.* a promiscuous woman. •*v.* **1** (of a man) resort to a professional prostitute for sex. **2** (usu. foll. by *around*) (of a man or woman) be sexually promiscuous; act in a whorish manner.

whorehouse *n.* a brothel.

whorish *adj.* of or like a whore. ◻ **whorishly** *adv.* **whorishness** *n.*

whorl / werl / *n.* **1** a coiled form; one turn of a spiral. **2** a complete circle formed by ridges in a fingerprint. **3** a ring of leaves or petals round a stem or central point. ◻ **whorled** *adj.*

who's = **1** who is. **2** who has.

■ **Usage** Do not confuse with *whose*.

whose *pron.* & *adj.* of whom, of which (*the people whose house we admired; the house whose owner takes pride in it; whose book is this?*).

■ **Usage** Do not confuse with *who's*.

whosoever = WHOEVER.

why *adv.* **1** for what reason or purpose? **2** on account of which (*the reasons why it happened are not clear*). •*interj.* an exclamation of surprised discovery or recognition (*why, it's you!*). •*n.* reason or explanation (*I need to know the why of it*). ◻ **whys and wherefores** reasons.

Wicca / **wik**-uh / *n.* the religious cult of modern witchcraft. ◻ **Wiccan** *adj.* & *n.*

wick *n.* **1** a length of thread in the centre of a candle, oil-lamp, etc., by which the flame is kept supplied with fuel. **2** *colloq.* the penis. ◻ **get on a person's wick** *colloq.* annoy or irritate a person.

wicked *adj.* **1** morally bad, offending against what is right. **2** spiteful; intending or intended to give pain (*a wicked lie*). **3** *colloq.* very bad or formidable, severe (*wicked weather; a wicked cough*). **4** mischievous (*a wicked grin*). **5** *colloq.* (esp. among young people) excellent. □ **wickedly** *adv.* **wickedness** *n.*

wicker *n.* thin canes or osiers woven together as material for making furniture or baskets etc.

wickerwork *n.* **1** wicker. **2** things made of wicker.

wicket *n.* **1** a wicket door or wicket gate. **2** a set of three stumps and two bails used in cricket, defended by the batsman. **3** the part of a cricket ground between or near the wickets. **4** an instance of a batsman being got out (*the bowler has taken four wickets*). □ **on a good** (or **sticky**) **wicket** *colloq.* in a favourable (or unfavourable) position. **wicket door** (or **gate**) a small door or gate usu. beside or within a larger one for use when this is not open.

wicketkeeper *n.* a fielder in cricket stationed close behind the batsman's wicket.

widdershins *adv.* (also **withershins**) in a direction contrary to the apparent course of the sun (considered unlucky); anticlockwise.

wide *adj.* **1** measuring much from side to side, not narrow (*a wide river*). **2** in width (*one metre wide*). **3** extending far, having great range (*a wide knowledge of art*). **4** open to the full extent (*staring with wide eyes*). **5** at a considerable distance from the point or mark aimed at (*his guess was wide of the mark*). •*adv.* **1** widely. **2** to the full extent (*wide awake*). **3** far from the target etc. (*I'm shooting wide*). •*n.* (in full **wide ball**) a bowled ball in cricket that passes the wicket beyond the batsman's reach and counts one point to the batsman's team. □ **give a wide berth to** *see* BERTH. **wide-angle** *adj.* (of a lens) able to include a wider field of vision than a standard lens does. **wide area network** (also **WAN**) *Computing* a communication network over a broad geographic region and possibly including some local area networks. **wide awake** completely awake; *colloq.* wary, knowing. **wide comb** *see* COMB. **wide-eyed** *adj.* surprised; innocent or naive. **wide open** (of a person or place) exposed or vulnerable (to attack etc.); (of a contest) with no contestant who can be predicted as a certain winner. **wide worker** *Aust.* a sheep dog that controls the movement of sheep while remaining at some distance from them. □□ **wideness** *n* **widish** *adj.*

widely *adv.* **1** to a wide extent; far apart. **2** extensively (*widely read; widely distributed*). **3** by many people (*it is widely thought that* …). **4** considerably; to a large degree (*holds a widely different view*).

widen *v.* make or become wider.

widespread *adj.* found or distributed over a wide area.

widgeon / **wij**-uhn / *n.* (also **wigeon**) any of several wild Australian ducks, esp. the pink-eared duck (*see* WHISTLING).

widow *n.* **1** a woman whose husband has died. **2** a woman whose husband is often away on a specified activity (*she's a golf widow*). •*v.* make into a widow or a widower (*the fighting in Bosnia has widowed thousands*). □ **widow's peak** a V-shaped growth of hair towards the centre of the forehead. □□ **widowhood** *n.*

widowed *adj.* bereft by death of a wife or husband.

widower *n.* a man whose wife has died.

width *n.* **1** wideness. **2** distance or measurement from side to side. **3** a piece of material of full width as woven (*use two widths to make this curtain*).

widthwise *adv.* (also **widthways**) in the direction of the width of something.

wield / weeld / *v.* **1** hold and use (a weapon or tool etc.) with the hands. **2** command or exert (power or authority etc.). □ **wielder** *n.*

wieldy *adj.* (**wieldier**, **wieldiest**) easily wielded, controlled, or handled.

Wiener schnitzel / vee-nuh **shnit**-suhl / *n.* a veal cutlet covered in breadcrumbs, fried, and garnished.

wife *n.* (*pl.* **wives**) **1** a married woman in relation to her husband. **2** *archaic* a woman (*the Wife of Bath*). **3** (in *combinations*) a woman engaged in a specified activity (*housewife; midwife*). □ **wifely** *adj.*

wig *n.* **1** a covering made of real or artificial hair, worn on the head (esp. to conceal baldness, or as part of the costume of a judge or a barrister). **2** the wool which grows above and around the eyes of a sheep. •*v.* **1** provide with a wig. **2** *Aust.* clip the wool from around the eyes of (a sheep). □ **wig tree fern** a tree fern (a cyathea) of the far north of Qld, having curious, curly, wig-like growths at the base of each frond.

wigeon alternative spelling of WIDGEON.

wiggle *v.* move or cause to move repeatedly from side to side, wriggle (*the doctor said, 'See if you can wiggle your toes'*). •*n.* a wiggling movement; a kink in a line etc. □ **wiggly** *adj.*

wight *n. archaic* a person.

wigwam / **wig**-wawm, -wom / *n.* a hut or tent made by fastening skins or mats over a framework of poles, as formerly used by American Indians. □ **a wigwam for a goose's bridle** *Aust.* used as a snubbing reply to an unwanted question. (¶ Originally a *whim-wham* (= a trifling ornament) *for a goose's bridle*, altered by folk etymology.)

wijen alternative spelling of WATJIN.

Wik *n.* an Aboriginal people of the central-eastern area of the Gulf of Carpentaria. □ **the Wik decision** the judgment handed down in 1996 by the High Court of Australia that native title can co-exist with pastoral leases. **Wik-Mungkan** the

Aboriginal language spoken by one of the Wik peoples.

wilco *interj.* = 'will comply', used in signalling etc. to indicate that directions received will be carried out.

wild *adj.* **1** living or growing in its original natural state, not domesticated or tame or cultivated. **2** (in *combinations*) designating Australian flora which, the early settlers felt, resembled European plants, or which acted as substitutes for them (*wild ginger; wild grape; wild hop; wild lemon; wild nutmeg; wild parsnip; wild violet;* etc.). **3** not civilised, barbarous. **4** unrestrained, disorderly, uncontrolled (*wild youth; wild hair*). **5** tempestuous, violent (*a wild and stormy night; wild fighting in the streets*). **6** intensely eager, frantic (*wild excitement; wild delight*). **7** (foll. by *about*) *colloq.* passionately in love with, enthusiastically devoted to (*wild about the boy; he's wild about speleology and snakes*). **8** *colloq.* utterly exciting (*the party was really wild*). **9** *colloq.* furious (*he makes me wild*). **10** extremely foolish or unreasonable (*these wild ideas*). **11** random (*a wild guess*). • *adv.* in a wild manner (*shooting wild*). ◻ **run wild** grow or behave without being checked or restrained. **the wilds** districts far from civilisation. **wild card 1** a card having any value chosen by the player holding it. **2** *Computing* a character that will match any character or combination of characters. **3** a person or thing that can be used in several different ways; a person whose behaviour cannot be predicted. **wild cauliflower** a WA verticordia, having creamy flowers (said to resemble the florets of a cauliflower) completely covering the shrub in spring. **wild colonial boy** *Aust.* **1** a bushranger. **2** a larrikin. **wild-goose chase** a useless search, a hopeless quest. **wild horse 1** = BRUMBY. **2** (**wild horses**) *colloq.* even the most powerful influence etc. (*wild horses wouldn't drag the secret from me*). **wild pineapple** see MACROZAMIA. **wild rice** see RICE. **wild turkey** = PLAIN TURKEY (see PLAIN). ◻◻ **wildly** *adv.* **wildness** *n.*

wildcat *adj.* **1** reckless or impracticable, esp. in business and finance (*wildcat schemes*). **2** (of strikes) sudden and unofficial. • *n.* **1 a** *Aust.* = NATIVE CAT (see NATIVE). **b** the European or American wild cat. **2** a hot-tempered or violent person. **3** an exploratory oil well.

Wilde, Oscar (Fingal O'Flahertie Wills) (1854–1900), Irish dramatist, novelist, poet, and brilliant wit. His relationship with Lord Alfred Douglas resulted in his imprisonment for homosexual offences (1895–97); he died bankrupt and in exile in Paris. Among his best known works are plays such as *The Importance of Being Earnest*, and the novel *The Picture of Dorian Gray*.

wildebeest /ˈwil-duh-beest, vil-/ *n.* (*pl.* **wildebeest** *or* **wildebeests**) a gnu.

wilderness *n.* **1** an uncultivated and still wild region of forest, scrub, bush, desert, etc., a WILDERNESS AREA. **2** a part of a garden left with an uncultivated appearance. **3** (foll. by *of*) a confused assemblage of things. ◻ **in the** (**political**) **wilderness** out of office; out of a former position of political influence and power. **wilderness area** a tract of land that is largely undisturbed by humans and where indigenous plants and animals flourish in their natural environment.

wildfire *n. hist.* a combustible liquid used in war. ◻ **spread like wildfire** (of rumours etc.) spread very fast.

wildflower *n.* **1** the flower of an indigenous plant growing in e.g. a wilderness area (*Western Australian wildflowers; wildflowers of the Little Desert in Victoria*). **2** some of these plants as introduced into garden etc. cultivation (*a bed of Australian wildflowers putting pansies and petunias to shame*).

wildfowl *n.* birds that are hunted as game (e.g. wild ducks).

wildlife *n.* wild animals collectively, esp. as inhabiting a wilderness area.

Wild West the western States of the USA during the period when they were lawless frontier districts.

wile *n.* (usu. in *pl.*) a piece of trickery intended to deceive or attract someone. • *v.* (foll. by *away, into,* etc.) lure, entice (*wiled him into some dubious practices*).

wilful *adj.* **1** done with deliberate intention and not as an accident (*wilful murder*). **2** self-willed, obstinate (*a wilful child*). ◻ **wilfully** *adv.* **wilfulness** *n.*

wilga /ˈwil-guh/ *n.* a small drought-resistant tree of inland Australia, having a spreading crown and pendulous foliage (a favourite fodder for sheep), and bearing creamy flowers. Also called *sheep bush*. (¶ Wiradhuri)

Wilga Mia a red ochre quarry in central Australia which has been mined by Aborigines for several thousands of years. The ochre is the blood of a Dreaming kangaroo which was slain at this site.

wilgie /ˈwil-gee/ *n. Aust.* red ochre used by Aborigines to paint the body on ceremonial occasions. (¶ Nyungar)

Wilkes Land a region of Antarctica with a coast on the Indian Ocean. It is claimed by Australia.

will[1] *auxiliary v.* (**wilt** is used with *thou*) **1** (strictly only in the 2nd and 3rd persons: see SHALL) expressing the future tense in statements, commands, or questions (*they will regret this; you will leave at once!; will you go to the party?*). **2** (in the 1st person) expressing the speaker's determination or intention (*I will do it, whatever you may say*). **3** expressing desire, consent, or inclination (*will you have a drink?; come when you will; the door will not open*). **4** expressing a request as a question (*will you please open the window?*). **5** be able to (*the jar will hold a kilo*). **6** have a habit or tendency to (*accidents will happen*). **7** expressing probability or expectation (*that will be my boyfriend at the door*). ☐ **will do** *colloq.* expressing willingness to carry out a request.

will[2] *n.* **1** the mental faculty by which a person decides on and controls his or her own actions or those of others. **2** will power (*he overcame his shyness by sheer force of will*). **3** determination (*they set to work with a will*). **4** a strong desire or intention (*the will to live*). **5** a person's attitude in wishing good or bad to others (*with the best will in the world*). **6** written directions made by a person for the disposal of his or her property after death. • *v.* **1** exercise one's will-power; influence or compel by doing this (*tried to will his hand to stop shaking; willed her to win*). **2** intend unconditionally (*God has willed it*). **3** bequeath by a will (*she willed her money to a hospital*). ☐ **at will** as or whenever or wherever one pleases (*he comes and goes at will*). **will power** control exercised by one's will, esp. over one's own actions and impulses.

Williams[1], Fred(erick Ronald) (1927–82), Australian painter and etcher.

Williams[2], Harold (1893–1976), Australian operatic baritone.

Williams[3], John (Christopher) (1941–), AO, Australian classical guitarist.

Williams[4], Tennessee (original name: Thomas Lanier Williams) (1911–83), American playwright.

Williamson[1], David (Keith) (1942–), AO, Australian playwright; among his works are *The Removalists*, *Don's Party*, and *The Club*.

Williamson[2], J(ames) C(assius) (1845–1913), Australian theatrical entrepreneur and actor (born in the US), founder of J.C. Williamson Theatres Ltd.

Williamson[3], John (Robert) (1945–), AO, Australian country and folk songwriter and singer.

Williamson[4], Malcolm (Benjamin Graham Christopher) (1931–), AO, Australian composer and organist resident in England, appointed Master of the Queen's Musick in 1975.

willie *n.* (also **willy**) *colloq.* the penis.

willies *n.pl. colloq.* nervous discomfort (*gives me the willies*).

willie wagtail alternative spelling of WILLY WAGTAIL.

willing *adj.* **1** doing readily what is required, having no objection. **2** given or performed willingly (*we received willing help*). ☐ **willingly** *adv.* **willingness** *n.*

will-o'-the-wisp *n.* **1** a phosphorescent light sometimes seen on marshy ground. **2** an elusive person. **3** a hope or aim that lures a person on but can never be fulfilled. (¶ Originally *Will with the wisp*, a *wisp* being a handful of (lighted) hay.)

willow *n.* **1** a tree or shrub with very flexible branches yielding osiers as well as timber for cricket bats etc. **2** any of several Australian trees resembling the willow, including some species of wattle. **3** a cricket bat. ☐ **willow myrtle** a small Australian tree *Agonis flexuosa* (*see* PEPPERMINT, sense 3). **willow-pattern** a conventional Chinese design including a willow tree and a river, done in blue on a white background, esp. on china. **willow wattle** any of several Australian wattles having pendulous foliage and occurring along watercourses, esp. COOBA.

willowy *adj.* **1** (esp. of a person) lithe and slender (*a willowy lad*). **2** having or bordered by willow trees. **3** bendable, pliable.

Wills, William John (1834–61), *see* BURKE, Robert O'Hara.

willy 1 = WILLY WILLY. **2** alternative spelling of WILLIE.

willy-nilly *adv.* whether one desires it or not (*you will do it willy-nilly*). • *adj.* existing or occurring willy-nilly.

willy wagtail *n.* (also **willie wagtail**) a black and white bird, a fantail, widespread in Australia.

willy willy *n.* (also **willy**) *Aust.* a whirlwind or dust storm. (¶ Either from Yindjibarndi *wili-wili* or from Wemba-wemba *wilang-wilang*.)

wilt[1] *see* WILL[1].

wilt[2] *v.* **1** (of plants or flowers) lose freshness and droop. **2** (of a person or a person's spirits, confidence etc.) lose energy, flag, tire, droop (*I'm wilting in this heat; his resolution wilted in the face of all the opposition*). **3** cause to wilt (*this heatwave is wilting all my plants*). • *n.* a plant disease that causes wilting.

wiltja / **wil**-chuh / *n. Aust.* an Aboriginal shelter. (¶ Western Desert language *wilja* 'shelter', 'shade', or 'shadow'.)

wily / **wuy**-lee / *adj.* (**wilier**, **wiliest**) full of wiles; crafty, cunning. ☐ **wiliness** *n.*

Wimbledon a suburb of London containing the headquarters of the All England Lawn Tennis and Croquet Club, and scene of an annual lawn tennis tournament.

wimp[1] *colloq. n.* a feeble or ineffective person. ☐ **wimp out** fail to carry out (an undertaking etc.) through weakness of will, lack of nerve, etc. **wimp-out** *n.* an instance of such a failure. ☐☐ **wimpish** *adj.* **wimpy** *adj.*

wimp[2] *n. Computing* a user-friendly computer system having windows, a mouse, pull-down menus, etc. (¶ Abbreviation of *w*indows, *i*cons, *m*ouse, *p*ull-down menus.)

wimple *n.* a medieval headdress of linen or silk folded round the head and neck, covering all but the front of the face, and worn by some nuns.

win *v.* (**won**, **winning**) **1** be victorious in (a battle, game, race, etc.). **2** obtain or achieve as the result of a battle or contest or bet etc. **3** obtain as a result of effort or perseverance (*he won their confidence*). **4** (foll. by *through*, *free*, etc.) make one's way, or become, as a result of successful effort (*we won free of all the red tape at last*). **5** reach by effort (*the exhausted swimmer won the shore at last*). • *n.* victory in a game or contest. ☐ **win over**

wince persuade, gain the support of. **win through** (*or* **out**) overcome obstacles.

wince *v.* make a slight involuntary movement from pain, distress, embarrassment, etc. • *n.* a wincing movement.

winch *n.* a machine for hoisting or pulling things by means of a cable which winds round a revolving drum or wheel. • *v.* hoist or pull with a winch.

wind[1] *n.* **1** a moving current of air, esp. occurring naturally in the atmosphere. **2** a smell carried by the wind (*the deer we were stalking had got our wind*). **3** gas forming in the stomach or intestines and causing discomfort. **4** breath as needed in exertion, speech, or playing a musical instrument. **5** the wind instruments of an orchestra. **6** empty or boastful talk. • *v.* **1** detect by the presence of a smell (*the wallabies have winded us*). **2** cause to be out of breath (*we were quite winded by the climb*). **3** make (a baby) bring up wind after feeding. **4** renew the wind of by rest (*let's stop and wind the horses*). **5** / wuynd / (*past* & *past participle* **winded** *or* **wound** / wownd /) *poetic* sound (a bugle etc.) by blowing. □ **close to** (*or* **near**) **the wind** verging on indecency or dishonesty. **get** (*or* **have**) **the wind up** *colloq.* feel frightened. **get wind of** hear a hint or rumour of. **in the wind** happening or about to happen. **put the wind up** *colloq.* alarm or frighten. **take the wind out of a person's sails** take away his or her advantage suddenly; frustrate him or her by anticipating arguments etc. **wind cone** = WINDSOCK. **wind instrument** a musical instrument in which sound is produced by a current of air, esp. by the player's breath (e.g. a clarinet or flute). **wind tunnel** a tunnel-like device in which an airstream can be produced to move past models of aircraft etc. for studying the effects of wind. □ **windless** *adj.*

wind[2] / wuynd / *v.* (**wound** / wownd /, **winding**) **1** go or cause to go in a curving, spiral, or twisting course (*the road winds through the hills*). **2** twist or wrap closely round and round upon itself so as to form a ball. **3** wrap, encircle (*wound a bandage round his finger*). **4** haul, hoist, or move by turning a handle or windlass etc. (*wind the car window down*). **5** wind up (a clock etc.). • *n.* **1** a bend or turn in a course. **2** a single turn in winding a clock or string etc. □ **wind down 1** lower by winding. **2** (of a mechanism) unwind. **3** draw gradually to a close (*the party is beginning to wind down*). **4** (of a person) relax. **wind-down** *n. colloq.* a gradual lessening of excitement or intensity. **winding sheet** a sheet in which a corpse is wrapped for burial. **wind up 1** coil the whole of (a length of string etc.). **2** set or keep (a clock etc.) going by tightening its spring. **3** *colloq.* **a** increase the intensity of (feelings etc.), excite (*wound myself up to fever pitch*). **b** provoke or tease (a person). **4** bring or come to an end (*wound up his speech*). **5** settle and finally close the business and financial transactions of (a company going into liquidation). **6** *colloq.* arrive finally; end in a specified state or circumstance (*wound up at Wolloomooloo; he'll wind up in gaol; he wound up owing us $300*). **wind-up** *n.* a conclusion; a finish. *adj.* (of a mechanism) operated by being wound up.

windbag *n. colloq.* a person who talks a lot but says little of any value.

windbreak *n.* a screen or row of trees etc. shielding something from the full force of the wind.

windburn *n.* inflammation of the skin caused by exposure to the wind.

windcheater *n.* a casual wind-resistant jacket.

winder / **wuyn**-duh / *n.* a winding key or mechanism, esp. of a clock, watch, or wind-up toy.

windfall *n.* **1** an apple or pear etc. blown off a tree by the wind. **2** a piece of unexpected good fortune, esp. a sum of money acquired.

Windhoek / **vint**-huuk / *n.* the capital of Namibia.

Windies / **win**-deez / *n.pl.* **1** (nickname for) the West Indies cricket team. **2** (**Windie**) (*singular*) a member of this team.

windjammer *n.* a merchant sailing ship.

windlass / **wind**-luhs / *n.* a device for pulling or hoisting things by means of a rope or chain that winds round an axle. • *v.* hoist or haul with a windlass.

windmill *n.* a mill worked by the action of wind on projecting parts (sails) that radiate from a central shaft. □ **tilt at windmills** *see* TILT.

window *n.* **1** an opening in the wall of a building or in a car etc., usu. of glass in a frame. **2** this glass (*broke the window*). **3** a space for the display of goods behind the window of a shop etc. **4** an aperture in a wall etc. through which customers are served in a bank, ticket-office, etc. **5** an opportunity to learn by observation. **6** *Computing* a rectangular area on a computer screen, usu. with graphics capability, that allows the user to view and control a number of different tasks. **7** an interval during which the positions of planets etc. allow a specified journey by a spacecraft. □ **window dressing** the displaying of goods attractively in a shop window; the adroit presentation of facts etc. so as to create a deceptively favourable impression. **window seat** a seat fixed under a recessed window; a seat next to a window in a train, plane, etc. **window-shopping** looking at goods displayed in shop windows etc. without necessarily intending to buy. **window sill** a sill below a window.

windowpane *n.* a pane of glass in a window.

windpipe *n.* the principal passage by which air reaches the lungs, leading from the throat to the bronchial tubes.

windscreen *n.* the glass in the window at the front of a motor vehicle.

windsock *n.* a tube-shaped piece of canvas open at both ends, flown at an airfield to show the direction of the wind.

Windsor the new name assumed by members of the British royal house in 1917 during the First World War, since they feared that their previous German name (Saxe-Coburg-Gotha) would arouse anti-German feeling in the British people. ☐ **Duke of Windsor** the title conferred on Edward VIII on his abdication in 1936—an event precipitated by his decision to marry a divorced American commoner, Mrs Wallis Simpson.

windsurfing *n.* the sport of surfing on a board to which a sail is fixed. ☐ **windsurf** *v.* **windsurfer** *n.*

windswept *adj.* exposed to or swept back by the wind.

windward *adj.* & *adv.* situated in the direction from which the wind blows. • *n.* the windward side or region. ☐ **get to windward of 1** place oneself there to avoid the smell of. **2** gain an advantage over.

Windward Islands a group of islands in the eastern Caribbean Sea, including Dominica, Martinique, St Lucia, and Barbados.

windy[1] / **win**-dee / *adj.* (**windier, windiest**) **1** with much wind (*a windy night*). **2** exposed to high winds. **3** generating or characterised by flatulence. **4** wordy, full of useless talk. **5** *colloq.* nervous, frightened. ☐ **windily** *adv.* **windiness** *n.*

windy[2] / **wuyn**-dee / *adj.* that winds, winding (*a narrow windy path*).

wine *n.* **1** fermented grape juice as an alcoholic drink. **2** a fermented drink made from other fruits or plants as specified (*ginger wine; elderberry wine*). **3** dark purplish red. • *v.* drink wine; entertain with wine (*they wined and dined us*). ☐ **wine bar** a bar or small restaurant where wine is the main drink available. **wine cask** *Aust.* a plastic or foil-lined container filled with wine, enclosed within a cardboard box, and having a spigot so that wine not drawn off remains under a vacuum. **wine cellar** a cellar for storing wine; the contents of this. **wine vinegar** vinegar made from wine (red or white as specified) as distinct from malt etc.

wineglass *n.* a glass for wine, usu. with a stem and foot.

winepress *n.* a press in which grapes are squeezed in making wine.

wing *n.* **1** each of a pair of projecting parts by which a bird, bat, or insect etc. is able to fly. **2** a corresponding part in a non-flying bird or insect. **3** each of the parts projecting from the sides of an aircraft. **4** a projecting part extending from one end of a building (*lived in the north wing*). **5** *Aust.* a fence, usu. one of a pair, built out from a stockyard and serving to guide stock towards its entrance. **6 a** the flank of a battle array. **b** *Aust.* the flank of a travelling mob of sheep, cattle, etc. **7** either of the players (*left wing, right wing*) in football or hockey etc. whose place is at the extreme end of the forward line (or, in Australian Rules, on either side of the centre position); the side part of the playing area in these games. **8** an air-force unit of several squadrons. **9** a polarised section of a political party in terms of its views (*right wing; left wing; centre-left wing*) etc. **10** (**wings**) the sides of a theatre stage out of sight of the audience (*waiting in the wings*). **11** (**wings**) a pilot's badge in the RAAF etc. • *v.* **1** fly; travel (*a bird winging its way home; winging my way back to Oz*). **2** enable to fly; send in flight (*fear winged my feet; winged an arrow towards them*). **3** wound slightly in the wing or arm. ☐ **on the wing** flying. **take wing** fly away. **under one's wing** under one's protection. **wing case** the horny cover of an insect's wing. **wing commander** an officer of the RAAF, next below group captain. **wing nut** a nut with projections so that it can be turned by thumb and finger. ☐ ☐ **wingless** *adj.*

winged *adj.* having wings.

winger *n.* **1** a wing player in football etc. **2** (in *combinations*) a member of a specified political wing (*left-winger*).

wingspan *n.* (also **wingspread**) the measurement across wings from one tip to the other.

wink *v.* **1** close and open one eye deliberately, esp. as a private signal to someone. **2** (of a light or star etc.) twinkle; (of an indicator) flash on and off. • *n.* **1** an act of winking. **2** a brief period of sleep (*didn't sleep a wink*). ☐ **wink at** pretend not to notice something that should be stopped or condemned.

winkle *n.* an edible sea snail. • *v.* (foll. by *out*) extract, prise out (*winkled the secret out of him*).

winner *n.* **1** a person who wins. **2** something successful (*her latest novel is a winner*).

winning *see* WIN. • *adj.* charming, persuasive (*a winning smile; winning ways*). • *n.pl.* (**winnings**) money won in betting or at cards etc. ☐ **winning post** a post marking the end of a race.

winnow *v.* **1** expose (grain) to a current of air so that the loose dry outer part is blown away; separate (chaff) in this way. **2** sift or separate from worthless or inferior elements (*winnow out the truth from the falsehoods*).

wino / **wuy**-noh / *n.* (*pl.* **winos**) *colloq.* an alcoholic.

winsome *adj.* having an engagingly attractive appearance or manner. ☐ **winsomely** *adv.*

winter *n.* **1** the coldest season of the year, in Australia June, July, August. **2** a bleak or lifeless period (*nuclear winter*). **3** *poetic* a year (esp. of a person's age) (*a man of fifty winters*). • *adj.* characteristic of or fit for winter (*winter winds; winter wear*). • *v.* spend the winter (*we Canberrans like to winter in places like Darwin*). ☐ **winter solstice** the solstice occurring about 21 June.

wintertime *n.* the season of winter.

Winton, Tim(othy John) (1960–), Australian novelist and short story writer. His novel *Cloudstreet* (1991) won the Miles Franklin Award.

wintry *adj.* **1** of or like winter, cold (*wintry weather*). **2** (of a smile etc.) chilly, lacking warmth or vivacity. □ **wintriness** *n.*

win-win *adj.* of or designating a situation in which both sides in a dispute or negotiated settlement etc. (esp. industrial) can be seen as gaining and neither side as being defeated (as opposed to NO-WIN—*see* NO).

winy *adj.* like wine (*a winy taste*).

wipe *v.* **1** clean or dry the surface of by rubbing something over it. **2** remove by wiping (*wipe your tears away*). **3** spread (a substance) thinly over a surface. **4** erase or eliminate completely (*the village was wiped off the map*). **5** erase a magnetic medium (of data); erase data (from such a medium) (*wiped the tape; wiped the recording from the video*). **6** *Aust. colloq.* reject or dismiss (a person or idea) (*my girlfriend wiped me; you can wipe that plan, it's stupid*). • *n.* **1** the act of wiping (*give this plate a wipe*). **2** a piece of specially treated material for wiping (*antiseptic wipes*). □ **wipe the floor with** *colloq.* inflict a humiliating defeat on. **wipe off** cancel or annul (a debt etc.). **wipe out** cancel; destroy completely (*the whole army was wiped out; I've wiped it out of my mind*).

wipe-out *n.* **1** *Surfing* a fall from a surfboard. **2 a** an instance of destruction etc. **b** failure; defeat. **3** the obliteration of one radio signal by another.

wiper *n.* (in full **windscreen wiper**) a rubber strip moving to and fro across a windscreen to remove rain etc.

Wiradhuri / wuh-**raj**-uh-ree / *n.* an Aboriginal language of a vast area from southern NSW to northern Vic.

wire *n.* **1** a strand or slender flexible rod of metal. **2** a barrier or framework etc. made from this. **3** a piece of wire used to carry electric current. **4** *colloq.* a telegram. • *v.* **1** provide, fasten, or strengthen with wire. **2** install wiring in (a house). **3** *colloq.* telegraph. □ **down to the wire** all the way (to the finishing line). **get one's wires crossed** become confused and misunderstood. **the straight wire** *Aust. colloq.* the complete truth. **wire door** *Aust.* = SCREEN DOOR (*see* SCREEN). **wire grass** any of many perennial Australian grasses having a tufted or tussocky habit and stiff, wiry stems. **wire netting** a netting of meshed wire. **wire tapping** the tapping of telephone lines to eavesdrop.

wireless *n.* **1** radio, radio communications. **2** a radio receiver or transmitter.

■ **Usage** Now old-fashioned, especially with reference to broadcasting, and superseded by *radio*.

wirilda / wuh-**ril**-duh / *n.* (in full **wirilda wattle**) a shrub or small tree of southern Australia, having long, narrow, grey-green phyllodes and creamy yellow ball-flowers, often cultivated as an ornamental. (¶ Yaralde)

wiring *n.* a system of wires for conducting electricity in a building or vehicle.

wirra[1] / **wi**-ruh / *n. Aust.* a small cup-like digging scoop of the Aborigines, traditionally made of hardwood. (¶ Western Desert language)

wirra[2] / **wi**-ruh / *n.* a tall, willow-like wattle occurring near watercourses in drier Australia and bearing gold ball-flowers in winter and spring. Also called *cooba, willow wattle*. (¶ Diyari)

wirrah / **wi**-ruh / *n.* either of two marine fish of rocky reefs of SE and SW Australia, often also called 'boot' in reference to its tough and tasteless flesh. (¶ Possibly from an Aboriginal language.)

wirrang / **wi**-rang / *n. Aust.* = ROCK WALLABY (*see* ROCK[1]). (¶ Wiradhuri)

wiry *adj.* (**wirier, wiriest**) **1** like wire. **2** (of a person) lean but strong. □ **wiriness** *n.*

wisdom *n.* **1** being wise, soundness of judgment. **2** prudence; commonsense. **3** wise sayings etc. regarded collectively. □ **wisdom tooth** the hindmost molar tooth on each side of the upper and lower jaws, usu. cut (if at all) after the age of 20.

wise[1] *adj.* **1** having or showing soundness of judgment. **2** prudent, sensible. **3** having knowledge (esp. as specified) (*wise in linguistics*); often in *combinations*: (*streetwise; worldly-wise*). **4** *colloq.* aware, informed (*I'm wise to what is going on*). □ **wise man** a wizard; one of the Magi. **wise up** *colloq.* become aware; learn (about); inform. □□ **wisely** *adv.*

wise[2] *n. archaic* way, manner (*in no wise*).

-wise *comb. form* **1** indicating direction or manner (*clockwise; lengthwise*). **2** with respect to (*businesswise*).

■ **Usage** Fanciful or phrase-based combinations, such as *youth unemployment-wise* (= as regards youth unemployment) should be restricted to informal contexts.

wiseacre / **wuyz**-ay-kuh / *n.* a person who pretends to have great wisdom, a know-all.

wisecrack *colloq. n.* a witty or clever remark. • *v.* make a wisecrack.

wish *n.* **1** a desire, request, or aspiration; an expression of this. **2** a thing desired (*got my wish*). • *v.* **1** have or express as a wish. **2** formulate a wish (*wish when you see a shooting star*). **3** want or demand, usu. so as to bring about what is wanted (*I wish to go now; I wish you to do it; I wish it done at once*). **4** hope or express hope about another person's welfare (*wish me luck; wish him 'good day'*). **5** *colloq.* foist (*the dog was wished on us while its owners were on holiday*). □ **wish for** desire to have; express a wish that one may have (a thing).

wish-fulfilment a tendency for subconscious desires to be satisfied in fantasy.

wishbone *n.* a forked bone between the neck and breast of a bird (pulled by two people, the one who gets the longer part having the supposed right to magic fulfilment of any wish).

wishful *adj.* desiring. ◻ **wishful thinking** a belief that is founded on what one wishes to be true rather than on fact.

wishy-washy *adj.* weak or feeble in colour, character, etc.; (of soup, tea, etc.) weak, watery.

wisp *n.* **1** a small separate bunch or bundle of something (*wisps of hair*). **2** a small streak of smoke or cloud etc. **3** a small thin person. ◻ **wispy** *adj.*

wisteria / wis-**teer**-ree-uh / *n.* (also **wistaria** / wis-**tair**-ree-uh /) a climbing plant with hanging clusters of blue, purple, or white flowers.

wistful *adj.* full of sad or vague longing. ◻ **wistfully** *adv.* **wistfulness** *n.*

wit *n.* **1** the ability to combine words or ideas etc. ingeniously so as to produce clever humour. **2** a witty person. **3** intelligence, quick understanding (*hadn't the wit to see what was needed; use your wits*). ◻ **at one's wits' end** at the end of one's mental resources, not knowing what to do. **have** (*or* **keep**) **one's wits about one** be or remain mentally alert. **to wit** that is to say, namely.

witch *n.* **1** a sorceress, a woman supposed to have dealings with the devil or evil spirits in practising witchcraft. **2** an old hag. **3** a bewitching woman. • *v. archaic* bewitch. ◻ **the witching hour** midnight. **witch doctor** a tribal magician, credited with powers of healing, divination, and protection against the magic of others. **witch hazel** (also **wych hazel**) an astringent lotion obtained from the bark of an American shrub; the shrub itself. **witch-hunt 1** *hist.* the search for and persecution (usu. by burning alive) of supposed witches. **2** a search to find and destroy or persecute people suspected of holding unorthodox or unpopular views (e.g. the witch-hunts against supposed Communists in America in the 1950s).

witchcraft *n.* **1** the practice of magic. **2** bewitching charm.

witchery = WITCHCRAFT.

witchetty / **wich**-uh-tee / *n.* (in full **witchetty grub**) a large (up to 12 cm in length and 2 cm thick), edible, wood-eating larva or pupa of any of several Australian moths and beetles, an important food (raw or roasted) for many Aboriginal peoples since it is rich in iron and fat. Also called *margoo*. (*See also* BARDI). ◻ **witchetty-bush** any of several wattles of drier Australia, esp. *Acacia kempeana*, so named because witchetty grubs are commonly to be found in abundance in its trunk and branches and at its roots. (¶ Probably Adnyamathanha *wityu* 'a hooked stick used to extract such grubs from holes etc. in wood' + *varti* 'a grub or insect'.)

with *prep.* **1** in the company of, among. **2** having, characterised by (*a man with a sinister expression*). **3** using as an instrument or means (*hit it with a hammer*). **4** on the side of, of the same opinion as (*we're all with you on this matter*). **5** in the care or charge of (*leave a message with the receptionist*). **6** in the employment etc. of (*he is with BHP*). **7** at the same time as, in the same way or direction or degree as (*rise with the sun; swimming with the tide*). **8** because of (*shaking with laughter*). **9** feeling or showing (*heard it with calmness*). **10** under the conditions of (*sleeps with the window open*). **11** by addition or possession of (*fill it with water; laden with baggage*). **12** in regard to, towards (*lost my temper with him*). **13** in opposition to (*he argued with me*). **14** in spite of (*with all his roughness, he's very good-natured*). **15** so as to be separated from (*we parted with our luggage reluctantly*). ◻ **get with it** *colloq.* **1** become realistic, aware; awake to (oneself, a situation, etc.). **2** become up to date. **3** cope, concentrate. **I'm not with you** *colloq.* I cannot follow your meaning. **with it** *colloq.* **1** fashionable, trendy. **2 a** expert, well-informed (*she's very with it on car engines*). **b** alert, intelligent, dynamic (*Bill's a live wire—really with it*).

withdraw *v.* (**withdrew, withdrawn, withdrawing**) **1** take back or away (*withdrew troops from the frontier; withdrew my hand*). **2** remove (money deposited) from a bank etc. **3** cancel (a promise or statement etc.). **4** go away from company or from a place (*withdrew to his bedroom*).

withdrawal *n.* **1** withdrawing. **2** the process of ceasing to take drugs to which one is addicted, often with unpleasant reactions (*withdrawal symptoms*). **3** = COITUS INTERRUPTUS (*see* COITUS).

withdrawn *adj.* (of a person) abnormally shy and unsociable; mentally detached.

withe / with, wi*th*, wuy*th* / *n.* (also **withy**) (*pl.* **withes** *or* **withies**) a tough flexible shoot, esp. of willow, used for basketry, binding, etc.

wither *v.* **1** make or become shrivelled; lose or cause to lose freshness and vitality. **2** subdue or overwhelm by scorn (*withered him with a glance*). ◻ **witheringly** *adv.*

withers / **with**-uhz / *n.pl.* the ridge between a horse's shoulder blades.

withershins = WIDDERSHINS.

withhold *v.* (**withheld, withholding**) **1** refuse to give, grant, or allow (*withhold permission*). **2** hold back, restrain (*we could not withhold our laughter*).

within *prep.* **1** inside, enclosed by. **2** not beyond the limit or scope of (*success was within our grasp; he acted within his rights*). **3** not transgressing or exceeding (*within the law; within the speed limit*). **4** in a time no longer than (*we shall finish within an hour*). **5** not further off than (*within 3 kilometres; not within cooee*). • *adv.* inside (*seen from within*).

without *prep.* **1** not having or feeling or showing; free from (*without food; they are without fear*). **2** in the absence of (*cannot live without him; no smoke without fire*). **3** with no action of (*we can't leave without thanking them*). **4** *archaic* outside

withstand *v.* (**withstood**, **withstanding**) endure successfully, resist.

withy / with-ee / = WITHE.

witless *adj.* foolish, unintelligent.

witness *n.* **1** a person who sees or hears something (*there were no witnesses to their quarrel*). **2** a person who gives evidence in a lawcourt. **3** a person who is present at an event in order to testify to the fact that it took place; one who confirms that a signature is genuine by adding his or her own signature. **4** something that serves as evidence (*his tattered clothes were a witness to his poverty*). • *v.* **1** be a witness at or of; sign (a document) as a witness. **2** be the scene or setting of (*this stretch of scrub has witnessed the massacre of Aborigines by whites*). ☐ **witness box** an enclosure from which witnesses give evidence in a lawcourt.

witticism / wit-uh-siz-uhm / *n.* a witty remark.

wittingly *adv.* knowing what one does; intentionally.

witty *adj.* (**wittier**, **wittiest**) full of wit. ☐ **wittily** *adv.* **wittiness** *n.*

wives see WIFE.

wizard *n.* **1** a male skilled in the use of magic powers. **2** a person with amazing abilities (*a financial wizard*). • *adj. colloq.* wonderful, excellent. ☐ **wizardly** *adj.* **wizardry** *n.*

wizened / wiz-uhnd / *adj.* full of wrinkles, shrivelled with age (*a wizened face*).

WO *abbr.* warrant officer.

woad *n.* **1** a blue dye formerly obtained from a plant of the mustard family. **2** this plant.

wobbegong *n. Aust.* = CARPET SHARK (*see* CARPET). (¶ Perhaps from a NSW Aboriginal language.)

wobble *v.* **1 a** sway or vibrate unsteadily from side to side. **b** cause to do this (*stop wobbling the table—I'm trying to write*). **2** quiver (*his huge belly wobbled as he laughed*). **3** stand or go unsteadily; stagger. **4** waver, vacillate; act inconsistently. **5** (of the voice or a sound) quaver, pulsate (*the boy's voice wobbled between gruff and falsetto*). • *n.* **1** a wobbling movement, a quiver. **2** (**wobbles**) *Aust.* an affliction, esp. of cattle, brought about by eating the leaves of certain Australian plants (esp. macrozamia) and characterised by irreversible loss of coordination of the hind limbs.

wobbleboard *n.* a piece of fibreboard, used as a musical instrument, which, when held in both hands and wobbled, produces a low, rhythmic, booming sound.

wobbly *adj.* wobbling, unsteady. ☐ **throw a wobbly** *see* THROW.

wodgil / woj-uhl / *n.* (in full **wodgil scrub**) *Aust.* a vegetation community of tall, shrubby growth dominated by wattles. (¶ Probably from a WA Aboriginal language.)

wodgin alternative spelling of WATJIN.

woe *n.* **1** affliction, bitter grief. **2** (**woes**) calamities. **3** (**woes**) *jocular* problems (*went on and on about his woes at work*). ☐ **woe betide** an expression of warning (*woe betide you if you get it wrong*).

woebegone / woh-buh-gon / *adj.* looking unhappy.

woeful *adj.* **1** full of woe, sad. **2** deplorable (*woeful ignorance*). ☐ **woefully** *adv.*

wog[1] *n. colloq. offens.* a foreigner or migrant, esp. a southern European one.

wog[2] *n. Aust. colloq.* **1 a** an illness or infection, usu. minor (e.g. a cold, an upset stomach). **b** the germ etc. causing this (*I think I've caught a wog*). **2** the name applied to various predatory or disagreeable insects and grubs.

woggle *n.* a leather etc. ring through which the ends of a boy scout's neckerchief are passed at the neck.

wogoit / wog-oit / *n.* the ring-tailed rock possum of northern Australia. (¶ Waray)

wok *n.* a large bowl-shaped frying pan, used esp. in Chinese cookery.

woke, woken *see* WAKE[1].

wolf *n.* (*pl.* **wolves**) **1** a fierce wild animal of Europe, North America, and Asia, of the dog family, feeding on the flesh of other animals and often hunting in packs. **2** a greedy or grasping person. **3** *colloq.* a man who seduces women. • *v.* (often foll. by *down*) eat (food) quickly and greedily. ☐ **cry wolf** raise repeated false alarms (like the shepherd-boy in the fable, so that eventually a genuine alarm is ignored). **wolf in sheep's clothing** a person who appears friendly but is really an enemy. **wolf whistle** a whistle (sliding rapidly up and down the scale) made to a sexually attractive person. ☐☐ **wolfish** *adj.*

wolfram / wuul-fruhm / *n.* tungsten (ore).

wollamai / wol-uh-muy / *n. Aust.* = SNAPPER. (¶ Dharuk)

wollemi pine / wol-uh-muy / *n. Aust.* an ancient conifer, formerly known only from fossils, discovered growing in the Wollemi National Park, NSW, in 1994.

wolverine / wuul-vuh-reen / *n.* a N. American animal, the largest of the weasel family.

wolves *see* WOLF.

woman *n.* (*pl.* **women**) **1** an adult female person. **2** the female sex (*how does woman differ from man?*). **3** *colloq.* a wife or girlfriend. **4** feminine characteristics (*every man needs to bring out the woman in him*). • *adj.* female (*a woman doctor; women friends*). ☐ **women's business** *1 colloq.* the intimate details of women's lives, such as bodily functions, reproductive health, etc., that they may prefer to discuss with other women rather than with men. **2** Australian Aboriginal rituals and cultural knowledge open only to women. **women's camp** (also **women's country**) *Aust.* (in Aboriginal English) a place open only to women. **women's liberation** (also

women's lib) a movement urging the liberation of women from domestic duties and from a subordinate role in society and business, as well as from a subservient status in relation to men. **women's libber** *colloq.* a supporter of women's liberation. **women's refuge** a usu. temporary accommodation for women in danger as a result of domestic violence inflicted on or threatened to them. **women's studies a** academic studies concerning women, their role in society, etc. **b** traditional studies such as history, literature, etc., dealt with from a feminist perspective.

womanhood *n.* **1** female maturity. **2** womanly instinct. **3** womankind.

womanise *v.* (also **-ize**) chase after women; philander. □ **womaniser** *n.*

womanish *adj.* **1** *derog.* effeminate, unmanly. **2** suitable for women but not for men.

womankind *n.* (also **womenkind**) women in general.

womanly *adj.* having or showing qualities that are characteristic of a woman. □ **womanliness** *n.*

womb / woom / *n.* the hollow organ (in woman and other female mammals) in which a child or the young may develop before birth; the uterus.

wombat *n. Aust.* **1** any of several thickset, burrowing, plant-eating marsupials of southern and eastern Australia, the commonest and most widespread of which is the *hairy-nosed wombat.* **2** *colloq.* a slow or stupid person. □ **wombat berry** an Australian climber of the lily family having tubers favoured by wombats, and globular orange berries; often cultivated as an ornamental. **wombat crossing** *Aust.* a pedestrian crossing with a raised speed hump. (¶ Dharuk)

women *see* WOMAN. (*See also* WOMYN.)

womenfolk *n.* women in general; the women of one's family.

womenkind = WOMANKIND.

Women's Electoral Lobby an Australia-wide feminist political lobby which is not aligned to any political party.

womma[1] / **wom**-uh / = HONEY ANT (*see* HONEY). (¶ Yankunytjatjara *wama* 'any sweet substance or delicacy'.)

womma[2] / **wom**-uh / *n.* (also **woma**) *Aust.* a python of arid Australia. (¶ Diyari)

wompoo pigeon / **wom**-poo / *n.* a large green fruit pigeon with purple breast, yellow belly, and grey head, inhabiting near-coastal rainforest in north-eastern Australia. (¶ Imitative of its far-reaching booming call; perhaps a borrowing from an Aboriginal language.)

womyn / **wim**-uhn / *n.pl.* (also **wimmin**) **1** (in writing by or about feminists) women. **2** (**womyn**) (*sing.*) a woman. (¶ A respelling of *women* which is expressly intended to remove from it the 'word' *men.* The use of *womyn* in the singular is rare.)

won *see* WIN.

wonder *n.* **1** a feeling of surprise mingled with admiration, curiosity, or bewilderment. **2** something that arouses this; a remarkable thing. •*adj.* having marvellous or amazing properties etc. (*a wonder drug; a wonder woman*). •*v.* **1** feel wonder or surprise (*I wonder that he wasn't killed*). **2** feel curiosity about; try to form an opinion or decision about (*we're still wondering what to do next*).

wonderful *adj.* marvellous, surprisingly fine or excellent. □ **wonderfully** *adv.*

wonderland *n.* **1** a land or place full of wonderful things. **2** fairyland.

wonderment *n.* a feeling of wonder, surprise.

wondrous *adj. poetic* wonderful. □ **wondrously** *adv.*

wonga[1] / **wong**-guh / *n. Aust.* = CUMBUNGI. (¶ Wemba-wemba)

wonga[2] / **wong**-guh / *n. Aust.* = CORROBOREE. (¶ Pajamal)

wonga bluey *n.* **1** a type of blue woollen cloth used for the clothes of farmers, bushmen, etc. **2** an item of clothing made from this. (¶ *Wonga,* the Vic. town in which this cloth is made.)

wongai / **wong**-guy / *n.* a seashore tree occurring in Cape York Peninsula and on the islands of north-eastern Australia, bearing bright red, sticky, edible fruits. (¶ Kala Lagaw Ya)

wonga-wonga / **wong**-guh-wong-guh / *n.* (also **wonga pigeon, wonga-wonga pigeon**) a large, ground-feeding grey and white pigeon of eastern mainland Australia. (¶ Probably Dharuk.)

wonga-wonga vine *n.* a vigorous twining climber *Pandorea pandorana* of eastern Australia, having glossy leaves and numerous clusters of showy creamy tubular flowers spotted with red, purple, or orange; often cultivated as an ornamental. Also called *pandorea.* (¶ Possibly associated with *wonga-wonga* the pigeon.)

Wongi / **wong**-guy / *n. Aust.* an Aborigine. (¶ Western Desert language)

■ **Usage** *See* KOORI.

wongi / **wong**-gee / *n. Aust.* a conversation; a chat (*invited me over for a wongi*). •*v.* talk; tell (*we wongied till late at night*). (¶ *Wangga* ('speak, talk, language') is common to most WA Aboriginal languages.)

wonguim / **wong**-gwuhm / *n. Aust.* a boomerang which can be made to return to its thrower. (¶ Wathawurung and Wuywurung.)

wonk *n. colloq. derog.* **1** a white person. **2 a** a man deemed to be not macho. **b** *offens.* a gay male.

wonky *adj. colloq.* **1** unwell. **2** crooked, askew. **3** loose, unsteady (*the ladder's a bit wonky, but*). **4** broken, not working; unreliable.

wonna / **won**-nuh / *n. Aust.* an Aboriginal implement used for digging, esp. by women. (¶ Nyungar)

wont / wohnt / *adj. archaic* accustomed (*he was wont to go to bed early*). • *n.* a habit or custom (*he went to bed early, as was his wont*).
won't = will not.
wonted *adj.* habitual, usual.
wonton / won-**ton** / *n.* (in Chinese cookery) a small round dumpling or roll with a savoury filling, usu. eaten boiled in soup.
woo *v.* (**wooed**, **wooing**) **1** *archaic* court (a woman). **2** try to achieve or obtain (*woo success*). **3** seek the favour of; try to coax or persuade (*wooing the voters*).
wood *n.* **1** the tough fibrous substance of a tree and its branches, enclosed by the bark. **2** this cut for use as timber or fuel etc. **3** (also **woods**) (mainly *Brit.* & *US*) trees growing fairly densely over an area of ground. **4** a wooden cask for wine etc. (*matured in wood*). **5** a golf club with a wooden head. □ **can't see the wood for the trees** cannot get a clear view of the whole because of too many details. **have the wood on** (**a person**) *Aust. colloq.* have an advantage over (a person). **out of the wood** (*or* **woods**) clear of danger or difficulty. **take to the woods** *Aust. hist.* become a bushranger. **wood duck 1** (also **maned duck**, **maned goose**) a mainly grey perching duck, having a brown, prominently maned head and a somewhat goose-like stance, occurring in lightly-treed country near water in Australia. **2** *Aust. colloq.* a customer who is easily duped (e.g. by a salesman). **wood pulp** wood fibre prepared for paper-making.

■ **Usage** In Australia *wood* or *woods* (sense 3) has been superseded by BUSH or FOREST.

wood-and-water joey *n. Aust.* **1** an unskilled labourer who performs the menial tasks of an establishment; a general rouseabout. **2** a servile employee.
woodblock *n.* a block from which woodcuts are made.
woodchip *n.* **1** (**woodchips**) fragments of wood. **2** (as *adj.*) of or pertaining to the production or deployment of woodchips (*the woodchip industry*). • *v.* reduce felled trees to woodchips for use in paper-making etc. (*old-growth Australian forests being felled and woodchipped to feed foreign demand*).
woodchop *n.* a woodchopping contest.
woodcraft *n.* **1** *US* & *Aust.* bushmanship. **2** skill in woodwork.
woodcut *n.* **1** an engraving made on wood. **2** a print made from this, esp. as an illustration in a book.
wooded *adj.* covered with growing trees.
wooden *adj.* **1** made of wood. **2** stiff and unnatural in manner, showing no expression or animation. • *v.* strike, knock down (*she woodened him with her handbag*). □ **wooden pear** = WOODY PEAR. **wooden spoon** an imaginary prize for a person or team that comes last in a sporting competition etc., a booby prize. **wooden spooner(s)** a person or team 'awarded' a wooden spoon. □ □ **woodenly** *adv.*
woodheap *n.* (also **woodpile**) a pile or stack of wood, esp. firewood.
woodland *n.* **1** wooded country, woods. **2** *Aust.* forest, usu. dominated by eucalypts, without a dense canopy.
woodpecker *n.* **1** a bird that clings to tree trunks and taps them with its beak to find insects. **2** either of two Australian birds (unrelated to the woodpecker, there being no true woodpeckers in Australia): **a** = TREECREEPER. **b** = SITELLA.
woodpile *n.* = WOODHEAP.
woodser *n. Aust.* = JIMMY WOODSER.
woodshed *n.* a shed where wood for fuel is stored.
woodswallow *n.* any of several predominantly grey insect-eating birds of Australia, having bluish bills tipped in black.
Woodward, Roger (Robert) (1942–), AC, Australian pianist internationally acclaimed for his performances of Beethoven, Chopin, and modern composers, co-founder of the Sydney International Piano Competition.
woodwind *n.* **1** any of the wind instruments of an orchestra that are (or were originally) made of wood, e.g. clarinet, oboe. **2** these collectively.
woodwork *n.* **1** the art or practice of making things from wood. **2** things made from wood, esp. the wooden fittings of a house.
woodworm *n.* the larva of a beetle that bores into wooden furniture and fittings.
woody *adj.* **1** like wood, consisting of wood (*the woody parts of a plant*). **2** (of a region) wooded. □ **woody pear** (also **wooden pear**) any of four tall Australian shrubs (or small trees) related to the waratah, having showy sprays of creamy white flowers followed by large, pear-like, woody fruits. □ □ **woodiness** *n.*
woof[1] *n.* the gruff bark of a dog. • *v.* bark gruffly.
woof[2] = WEFT.
woofer / **wuuf**-uh / *n.* a loudspeaker for reproducing low-frequency signals.
wool *n.* **1** the fine soft hair that forms the fleece of sheep and goats etc. **2** yarn or fabric made from this. **3** a wool-like substance (*steel wool*). □ **pull the wool over someone's eyes** deceive him or her. **wool cheque** *Aust.* the amount received from the sale of a season's wool. **wool classer** *Aust.* a person who grades fleeces according to quality. **wool clip** *Aust.* the annual wool production of a sheep farmer or of a district etc. **wool-gathering** being in a dreamy or absent-minded state. **wool grower** a sheep farmer. **wool press** *Aust.* a hydraulic press which compresses wool into a bale. **wool presser** *Aust.* a person who operates a wool press. **wool scour** *Aust.* a large shed where wool is washed.
Woolf, (Adeline) Virginia (1882–1941), English novelist.

woollen *adj.* made of wool. • *n.pl.* (**woollens**) knitted woollen garments.

woolly *adj.* (**woollier, woolliest**) **1** covered with wool or wool-like hair. **2** like wool; woollen (*woolly clouds; a woolly cardigan*). **3** (of a sound) indistinct. **4** not thinking clearly, not clearly expressed or thought out. • *n. colloq.* **1** a knitted woollen garment, esp. a pullover. **2** *Aust.* a sheep. **3** *Aust.* a sheep farmer. ☐ **woolly bush** *Aust.* any of several plants related to the banksias, having silky hairs on the leaves. **woolly butt** *Aust.* any of several eucalypts having a thick fibrous bark on all (or esp. the lower part) of the trunk. ☐☐ **woolliness** *n.*

woolshed *n. Aust.* a shearing shed.

woolstore *n.* a warehouse in which wool is stored.

Woolworth, Frank Winfield (1852–1919), American businessman who opened a chain of shops in the USA (and later in other countries), selling low-priced goods.

Woomera a town in central SA, housing the personnel involved with a vast military testing ground used in the 1950s for nuclear tests by the British; since 1969 it has housed the personnel of the joint Australian United States Space Communications Station. (¶ Named after the WOOMERA.)

woomera / **wuu**-muh-ruh / *n. Aust.* an Aboriginal implement used for propelling a spear more forcibly; a spear-thrower, throwing stick. (¶ Dharuk)

woop woop / **wuup**-wuup / *n. Aust.* **1** a jocular name for any remote outback region of Australia. **2** (**Woop Woop**) an imaginary remote town in Australia, the epitome of remoteness (*see also* BULLAMAKANKA, OODNAGALAHBI). (¶ A jocular imitation of reduplication in Aboriginal languages to indicate intensity or plurality.)

woozy *adj. colloq.* **1** dizzy or unsteady. **2** slightly drunk. ☐ **wooziness** *n.*

wop *n. colloq. offens.* a person from southern Europe, esp. an Italian. • *adj.* of or pertaining to these peoples.

word *n.* **1** a sound or sounds expressing a meaning and forming one of the basic elements of speech. **2** this represented by letters or symbols. **3** something said, a remark or statement (*may I have a word with you?*). **4** a message, information (*we sent word of our safe arrival*). **5** a promise or assurance (*take my word for it*). **6** a command or spoken signal (*don't fire till I give you the word*). **7** (**words**) the text of a song or an actor's part. **8** a rumour (*the word is that he's about to quit*). **9** the basic unit of the expression of data in a computer. • *v.* phrase, select words to express (*word it tactfully*). ☐ **word blindness** = DYSLEXIA. **word for word** in exactly the same or corresponding words (*translate it word for word*). **word-perfect** having memorised every word perfectly. **word processing** the use of a word processor to produce text. **word processor** a computer program designed for producing and altering text and documents; a computer and printer designed specifically for this purpose. **word up** *v. colloq.* inform (*he worded me up about the situation at home*).

wording *n.* the way something is worded.

wordless *adj.* without words, not expressed in words (*wordless sympathy*).

wordplay *n.* witty use of words, esp. punning.

Wordsworth, William (1770–1850), English poet.

wordy *adj.* using too many words. ☐ **wordily** *adv.* **wordiness** *n.*

wore *see* WEAR.

work *n.* **1** physical or mental activity, esp. as contrasted with play or recreation. **2** something to be undertaken; the materials for this. **3** a thing done or produced by work; the result of action. **4** a piece of literary or musical composition (*one of Mozart's later works*). **5** what a person does to earn a living; employment. **6** doings or experiences of a certain kind (*nice work!*). **7** ornamentation of a specified kind; articles having this; things or parts made of certain materials or with certain tools (*fine filigree work*). **8** (**works**) (treated as *sing.* or *pl.*) a factory. **9** (**works**) the working parts of a machine, clock, etc. **10** (**works**) building operations, road repairs, etc. • *v.* **1** perform work, be engaged in bodily or mental activity. **2** make efforts (*work for peace*). **3** be employed, have a job (*she works in a bank*). **4** operate, do this effectively (*it works by electricity; a tin-opener that really works; that method won't work*). **5** operate (a thing) so as to obtain material or benefit from it (*the mine is still being worked*). **6** purchase with one's labour (*work one's passage*). **7** cause to work or function (*he works his staff very hard; can you work the lift?*). **8** bring about, accomplish (*work miracles*). **9** shape, knead, or hammer etc. into a desired form or consistency (*work the mixture into a paste*). **10** do or make by needlework or fretwork etc. (*work your initials on it*). **11** excite progressively (*worked them into a frenzy*). **12** make (a way); pass or cause to pass slowly or by effort (*the grub works its way into timber; work the stick into the hole*). **13** become through repeated stress or pressure (*the screw had worked loose*). **14** be in motion (*his face worked violently*). **15** ferment (*the yeast began to work*). ☐ **the works** *colloq.* **1** everything. **2** complete or drastic treatment (*gave him the works*). **work back** *Aust.* work overtime. **work experience** temporary experience of employment offered to young people. **work in** find a place for, insert. **work off** get rid of by work or activity. **work on** use one's influence on (a person). **work out 1** find or solve by calculation; be calculated (*it works out at $5 each*). **2** plan the details etc. of (*work out a plan*). **3** have a specified result (*it worked out very well*). **4** engage in physical exercise or training. **work over**

workable

1 examine thoroughly. **2** treat with violence. **work-shy** disinclined to work. **work to rule** follow the rules of one's occupation with excessive strictness in order to cause delay, as a form of industrial protest. **work up 1** bring gradually to a more developed state. **2** (foll. by *to*) advance gradually to a climax etc. (*the skirmish worked up to a violent battle*). **3** elaborate or excite by degrees (*worked up a ravenous appetite*). **4** mingle (ingredients). **5** learn (a subject) by study (*worked up my Bahasa Indonesia*).

workable *adj.* that can be worked, will work, or is worth working (*a workable quarry; a workable scheme*).

workaday *adj.* **1** ordinary, everyday, practical. **2** dull, unimaginative, commonplace; pedestrian.

workaholic *n. colloq.* a person who is addicted to working. (¶ *See* -HOLIC.)

workbench *n.* a bench for woodwork, metalwork, etc.

worker *n.* **1** a person who works; one who works hard or in a specified way (*a slow worker*). **2** a neuter or undeveloped female bee or ant etc. that does the work of the hive or colony but cannot reproduce. **3** a member of the working class. **4** *Aust.* a draught bullock; a draught horse. □ **workers' compensation** *US* & *Aust.* **1** legislation that provides for the compensation of an employee injured in the course of employment. **2** payment to workers made under this legislation.

workforce *n.* the total number of workers employed or available.

workhorse *n.* a hard and willing worker.

working *adj.* **1 a** engaged in work (*a working mother; a working man*). **b** while so engaged (*all his working life; during working hours*). **2** functioning or able to function (*a working model*). • *n.* **1** the activity of work. **2** the act or manner of functioning of a thing (*its working is erratic*). **3** a mine or quarry etc.; a part of this in which work is or has been carried on (*disused mine-workings*). **4** (usu. **workings**) machinery, mechanism. □ **working bee** *Aust.* a gathering of volunteers to perform a (communal) task. **working capital** capital used in the carrying on of business, not invested in its buildings and equipment etc. **working class** the class of people who are employed for wages, esp. in manual or industrial work. **working-class** *adj.* of the working class. **working day** a day on which work is regularly done; the portion of the day spent in working. **working hypothesis** a hypothesis used as a basis for action. **working knowledge** knowledge adequate for dealing with something. **working order** a condition in which a machine etc. works satisfactorily. **working party** a group of people appointed to investigate and report or advise on something.

workload *n.* the amount of work to be done.

workman *n.* **1** a man employed to do manual labour. **2** a person who works in a certain way (*a conscientious workman*).

workmanlike *adj.* characteristic of a good workman, practical.

workmanship *n.* a person's skill in working; the quality of this as seen in something produced.

workmate *n.* a person working with another.

workout *n.* a session of physical exercise.

workplace *n.* a place at which a person works; an office, factory, etc. □ **workplace agreement** *Aust.* an agreement between employers and employees on wages, conditions, etc. (cf. ENTERPRISE BARGAINING).

worksheet *n.* **1** a paper on which work done is recorded. **2** a paper listing questions or activities etc. for students to work through.

workshop *n.* **1** a room or building in which manual work or manufacture is carried on. **2** a place or meeting for concerted discussion or activity (*a dance workshop*). • *v.* put to test or trial in a practical way in a non-public context (esp. of a hitherto unperformed play etc.) (*I learned a lot from seeing parts of my play workshopped by actors*).

workstation *n.* **1** a computer terminal and keyboard; a desk or table with this. **2** the location of an individual worker or stage in manufacturing etc.

world *n.* **1** the universe, all that exists. **2** the earth with all its countries and peoples. **3** a heavenly body like it. **4** a section of the earth (*the western world*). **5** a time, state, or scene of human existence. **6** the people or things belonging to a certain class or sphere of activity (*the sporting world; the insect world; the world of fantasy*). **7** everything, all people (*felt that the world was against him*). **8** material things and occupations (contrasted with spiritual) (*renounced the world and became a nun*). **9** a very great amount (*it will do him a world of good*). • *adj.* affecting many nations, of all nations (*world politics; world champion*). □ **for all the world** (foll. by *like* or *as if*) precisely (*looked for all the world as if they were real*). **man** (*or* **woman**) **of the world** a person who is experienced in the ways of human society. **out of this world** *colloq.* extremely good etc. (*the food was out of this world*). **world-class** of a quality or standard fit to be regarded as high throughout the world. **world music** rock music incorporating elements of traditional music, esp. from the developing world. **world war** a war involving many important nations; **First World War** that of 1914–18; **Second World War** that of 1939–45. **world-weary** bored with human affairs; **world-weariness** *n.*

World Bank the popular name of the International Bank for Reconstruction and Development, set up by the UN to promote the economic development of member countries.

World Cup 1 any of various international sports competitions or the trophies awarded for these. **2** an international competition in soccer, held every fourth year between teams who are winners from regional competitions.

World Health Organisation a UN agency whose aim is the attainment by all peoples of the world of the highest possible level of health.

World Heritage list a list kept by UNESCO of World Heritage Sites. ☐ **World Heritage listing** the process by which sites are nominated by countries to the World Heritage Convention which decides whether or not to declare them World Heritage Sites. **World Heritage Site** a natural or man-made site, area, or structure, recognised as being of outstanding international importance and therefore deserving special conservation and protection.

World Intellectual Property Organisation an organisation, established in 1967 and an agency of the United Nations from 1974, for cooperation between governments in matters concerning patents, trademarks, copyright, etc., and the transfer of technology between countries.

worldly *adj.* **1** of or belonging to life on earth, not spiritual. **2** devoted to the pursuit of pleasure or material gains or advantages. ☐ **worldly goods** property. **worldly wisdom** wisdom and shrewdness in dealing with worldly affairs. **worldly-wise** prudent or shrewd. ☐☐ **worldliness** *n.*

worldwide *adj.* occurring or known in all parts of the world. •*adv.* throughout the world.

World Wide Fund for Nature (*abbr.* **WWF**) an international organisation established (as the World Wildlife Fund) in 1961 to raise funds for projects including the conservation of endangered species or of valuable habitats.

World Wide Web a visually-based system for accessing information (text, graphics, sound, and video) by means of the Internet, which consists of a large number of documents tagged with cross-referencing links by which the user can move between sources.

worm[1] *n.* **1** any of several types of animal with a soft rounded or flattened body and no backbone or limbs. **2** the worm-like larva of certain insects, esp. those that damage fruit or wood. **3** (**worms**) intestinal or other internal parasites. **4** a maggot supposed to eat dead bodies in the grave. **5** an insignificant or contemptible person. **6** the spiral part of a screw. •*v.* **1** move with a twisting movement like a worm; make one's way by wriggling or with slow or patient progress. **2** obtain by crafty persistence (*wormed the secret out of him*). **3** rid (a dog etc.) of parasitic worms. ☐ **worm cast** *n.* a tubular pile of earth sent up by an earthworm on to the surface of the ground. **worm oneself into** insinuate oneself into (*wormed himself into her trust and affections*). **worm's-eye view** humorous a view as seen from below or from a humble position.

worm[2] *n.* a computer program which (like a VIRUS) is designed to sabotage a computer or network of computers and can replicate itself without first being incorporated into another program (cf. Trojan Horse—*see* TROJAN).

worm[3] (also **WORM**) *n. Computing* a class of storage device in which data, once written, cannot be erased or overwritten. (¶ Acronym from *write once read many times*.)

wormeaten *adj.* **1** full of worm-holes; decayed. **2** old and dilapidated.

wormwood *n.* **1** a woody plant with a bitter aromatic taste, used in vermouth and absinthe. **2** bitter mortification; a source of this.

wormy *adj.* full of worms; wormeaten. ☐ **worminess** *n.*

worn *see* WEAR. •*adj.* **1** damaged by use or wear. **2** looking tired and exhausted. **3** (in full **well-worn**) (of a joke etc.) stale; often heard.

worried *adj.* feeling or showing worry.

worrisome *adj.* causing worry.

worry *v.* (**worried**, **worrying**) **1** harass, importune; be a trouble or anxiety to. **2** give way to anxiety; fret. **3** (often foll. by *at*) seize with the teeth and shake or pull about (*a dog worrying at an old rag; a dog worrying sheep*). •*n.* **1** a state of worrying, mental uneasiness. **2** something that causes this. ☐ **not to worry** *colloq.* there is no need to worry. **no worries** (*or* **nurries**) *colloq.* no bother, no trouble; fine; okay (*Can I borrow your car, mate?—No worries*). **worry beads** a string of beads for fiddling with to occupy or calm oneself. **worry for** *Aust.* (in Aboriginal English) be concerned about or preoccupied with (*he worries for his country*). **worry out** obtain (a solution to a problem etc.) by persistent effort. ☐ **worrier** *n.*

worse *adj.* & *adv.* **1** more bad, more badly; more evil or ill. **2** less good, in or into less good health or condition or circumstances. •*n.* something worse (*there's worse to come*). ☐ **none the worse** (often foll. by *for*) not adversely affected (by). **the worse for wear 1** damaged by use; injured or exhausted. **2** *colloq.* drunk. **worse luck!** such is my bad fortune. **worse off** in a worse (esp. financial) position.

worsen *v.* make or become worse.

worship *n.* **1** reverence and respect paid to a god. **2** acts or ceremonies displaying this. **3** adoration of or devotion to a person or thing. •*v.* (**worshipped**, **worshipping**) **1** honour as a deity, pay worship to. **2** take part in an act of worship. **3** idolise, treat with adoration. ☐ **Your** (*or* **His** *or* **Her**) **Worship** a title of respect used to or of a mayor or certain magistrates. ☐☐ **worshipper** *n.*

worst *adj.* & *adv.* most bad, most badly; most evil or ill, least good. •*n.* the worst part, feature, state, event, etc. (*we are prepared for the worst*). •*v.* get the better of, defeat or outdo (*worsted him thrice running*).

worsted / wuus-tuhd / n. fine smooth yarn spun from long strands of wool; fabric made from this.

wort / wert / n. **1** (*archaic* except in names of plants) a plant, a herb (*liverwort*). **2** an infusion of malt before it is fermented into beer.

worth adj. **1** having a specified value (*a book worth $100*). **2** giving or likely to give a satisfactory or rewarding return for, deserving (*the book is worth reading*). **3** possessing as wealth, having property to the value of (*he was worth a million dollars when he died*). • n. **1** value, merit, usefulness (*people of great worth to the community*). **2** the amount of something that a specified sum will buy (*give me ten dollars' worth of petrol*). ☐ **worth while** (also **worth one's while**) worth the time or effort needed (*the scheme isn't worth while; a worthwhile scheme*).

■ Usage *Worth while* is often written as *worthwhile*, and always when preceding the noun that it qualifies.

worthless adj. having no value or usefulness. ☐ **worthlessness** n.

worthwhile adj. worth the time or effort needed (*a worthwhile undertaking*).

■ Usage *See* the note at WORTH.

worthy adj. (**worthier, worthiest**) **1** having great merit; deserving respect or support (*a worthy cause; the cause is worthy of support*). **2** entitled to (esp. condescending) recognition (*a worthy old couple*). **3** (foll. by *of*) **a** deserving (*worthy of mention*). **b** suitable to the dignity etc. of (*words worthy of the occasion*). • n. a worthy person; a person of some distinction. ☐ **worthily** adv. **worthiness** n.

-worthy comb. form forming adjectives meaning: **1** deserving of (*noteworthy*). **2** suitable or fit for (*newsworthy; roadworthy*).

Wotan / vo-tahn / another name for ODIN.

would auxiliary v. used **1** in senses corresponding to WILL[1] in the past tense (*we said we would do it*), conditional statements (*you could do it if you would only try*), questions (*would they like it?*), and polite requests (*would you come in please?*). **2** expressing something to be expected (*that's just what he would do!*) or something that happens from time to time (*occasionally the machine would go wrong*). **3** expressing probability (*she would be about 60 when she died*). ☐ **would-be** adj. desiring or pretending to be (*a would-be humorist*).

■ Usage With the verbs *like, prefer, be glad*, etc., 'I would' and 'we would' are often used informally, but 'I should' and 'we should' are required in formal written English: (*I should like to add that ...; I should prefer not to discuss the matter; we should be glad of some assistance*).

wouldn't colloq. = would not. ☐ **wouldn't it!** Aust. expressing dismay, exasperation, or disgust (*'My Tatts ticket blew out of the train window and it had the winning numbers. Wouldn't it!'— 'Wouldn't it!'*).

wound[1] / woond / n. **1** an injury done to living tissue by a cut, stab, blow, or tear. **2** an injury to a person's reputation or feelings etc. • v. inflict a wound on.

wound[2] / wownd / *see* WIND[2]. ☐ **wound-up** adj. excited; tense; angry.

wove, woven *see* WEAVE[1].

wow[1] interj. an exclamation of astonishment or admiration. • n. colloq. a sensational success. • v. colloq. impress or excite greatly.

wow[2] n. a slow fluctuation of pitch in sound reproduction, perceptible in long notes.

wowse / wowz / v. (esp. as **wowsing**) Aust. preach at or moralise in an annoying holier-than-thou way; behave puritanically (*he wowses at anyone who doesn't spend his life in church*).

wowser / wow-zuh / n. Aust. **1** a puritanical fanatic; a person who tries to inflict his or her rigid or narrow morality on others or would have it inflicted on all society; a kill-joy. **2** a teetotaller. • v. preach at or moralise in an annoying holier-than-thou manner; behave puritanically. • adj. of or pertaining to a wowser; publicly censorious of others and the pleasures they seek (*the wowser mentality*). ☐ **wowserish** adj. **wowserly** adv.

WP abbr. word processor or word processing.

w.p.m. abbr. words per minute.

wrack n. **1** seaweed thrown up on the shore or growing there. **2** destruction; ruin. **3** a wreck or wreckage.

wraith / rayth / n. a ghost; a spectral apparition of a living person supposed to be a sign that he or she will die soon.

wrangle v. have a noisy angry argument or quarrel. • n. an argument or quarrel of this kind.

wrap v. (**wrapped, wrapping**) **1** enclose in soft or flexible material used as a covering. **2** arrange (a flexible covering or a garment etc.) round a person or thing (*wrap a scarf round your neck*). **3** (foll. by *round*) *Computing* (of a line of text) continue on the next visible line when the edge of the screen is reached; (of a block of text) flow round a diagram, picture, etc. inserted in a document. • n. a shawl, scarf, cloak, etc. ☐ **take the wraps off** disclose. **under wraps** in concealment or secrecy. **wrapped up in 1** with one's attention deeply occupied by (*she is completely wrapped up in her children*). **2** deeply involved in (*the country's prosperity is wrapped up in its wool trade*). **wrap up 1** enclose in wrappings; put on warm clothing. **2** colloq. finish off (a matter) (*that about wraps it up for the day; wrapped up the deal in under an hour*).

wraparound n. *Computing* a facility by which a linear sequence of memory locations or screen positions is treated as a continuous circular series.

wrapped *adj.* (also **rapt**) entranced; overjoyed. ☐ **wrapped in** infatuated by (*they are all wrapped in him*).

wrapper *n.* **1** a cover of paper etc. wrapped round something. **2** a loose dressing gown.

wrapping *n.* material used to wrap something.

wrasse / ras / *n.* any of various brightly-coloured sea fish with thick lips and strong teeth, some being good food fish (as the species found on the Great Barrier Reef).

wrath / roth / *n.* extreme anger, indignation.

wrathful *adj.*, full of anger or indignation. ☐ **wrathfully** *adv.*

wreak / reek / *v.* inflict, cause (*wreak vengeance on a person; fog wreaked havoc with the train schedules*).

wreath / reeth / *n.* (*pl.* **wreaths** / reethz /) **1** flowers or leaves etc. fastened into a ring and used as a decoration or placed on a grave etc. as a mark of respect. **2** a curving line of mist or smoke.

wreathe / reeth / *v.* **1** encircle or cover with or as if with a wreath. **2** wind (*the snake wreathed itself round the branch*). **3** move in a curving line (*smoke wreathed upwards*). **4** form (flowers etc.) into a wreath; make a garland.

wreck *n.* **1** the disabling or destruction of something, esp. of a ship by storms or accidental damage. **2** a ship that has suffered a wreck. **3** the remains of a greatly damaged building, vehicle, etc. **4** a person whose physical or mental health has been damaged or destroyed (*a nervous wreck*). **5** a wretched remnant (*tried to survive on the wreck of his fortune*). **6** ruin (*the wreck of all his hopes*). • *v.* **1** seriously damage (a vehicle etc.). **2** ruin (hopes, a life, etc.). **3 a** cause the wreck of (a ship). **b** suffer a shipwreck (*they were wrecked on the Australian shore*).

wreckage *n.* **1** the remains of something wrecked. **2** wrecking.

wrecked *adj.* **1** involved in a shipwreck (*wrecked sailors*). **2** *colloq.* exhausted or ill, esp. after eating, drinking, or merrymaking to excess.

wrecker *n.* **1** a person or thing that wrecks or destroys. **2** a person employed in the demolition or breaking up of damaged vehicles. **3** a firm etc., the business of which is the demolition of houses, buildings. **4** (**wreckers**) a business which sells products from demolished buildings, damaged vehicles, etc. (*you can get some good stuff cheap at the wreckers*).

wren *n.* **1** a small brown European songbird with a short erect tail. **2** (also **fairy wren**) any of many small, ground-frequenting, insectivorous Australian birds, unrelated to the European wren, the males having brightly coloured (esp. blue) plumage (*splendid wren*) and sometimes chestnut shoulder patches (*variegated wren*).

wrench *v.* **1** twist or pull violently round or sideways. **2** twist (the ankle etc.). **3** (often foll. by *off*, *away*, etc.) pull off with a wrench. **4** distort (facts etc.) to suit a theory etc. (*wrenched the evidence to suit his argument*). • *n.* **1** a violent twist or twisting pull. **2** pain caused by parting (*leaving home was a great wrench*). **3** an adjustable tool like a spanner for gripping and turning nuts etc.

wrest / rest / *v.* **1** wrench away (*wrested the pistol from him; wrested the presidency from the incumbent*). **2** obtain by effort or with difficulty (*wrested a confession from him; wrested a meagre living from almost barren soil*).

wrestle *v.* **1** fight (esp. as a sport) by grappling with a person and trying to throw him or her to the ground. **2** fight with (a person) in this way (*police wrestled him to the ground*). **3** (foll. by *with* or *against*) struggle to deal with or overcome (*wrestled with the problem; wrestling against poverty*). • *n.* **1** a wrestling match. **2** a hard struggle. ☐ **wrestler** *n.*

wretch *n.* **1** a very unfortunate or miserable person. **2** a despicable person. **3** (in playful use) a rascal.

wretched / rech-uhd / *adj.* **1** miserable, unhappy. **2** of poor quality, unsatisfactory. **3** causing discomfort or nuisance; displeasing (*this wretched car won't start*). ☐ **wretchedly** *adv.* **wretchedness** *n.*

wrick alternative spelling of RICK[2].

wriggle *v.* **1** (of a worm etc.) twist or turn its body with short writhing movements. **2** (of a person or animal) make similar motions. **3** (foll. by *along*, *through*, etc.) move or go in this way (*wriggled through the gap*). • *n.* a wriggling movement. ☐ **get a wriggle on** *Aust. colloq.* hurry up (*get a wriggle on, mate, we're way behind*). **wriggle out of** avoid (a task etc.) on some pretext; escape from (a difficulty) cunningly. ☐☐ **wriggly** *adj.*

wriggler *n. Aust.* **1** the larva of a mosquito. **2** a worm or snake.

Wright[1], Judith (Arundell) (1915–2000), Australian poet whose chief volumes of poetry include *The Moving Image* (1946), *Woman to Man* (1949), and *Five Senses* (1963). She was also an active conservationist and supporter of Aboriginal land rights.

Wright[2], Orville (1871–1948) and Wilbur (1867–1912), American brothers, pioneers of powered aeroplane flight.

Wrightson, Patricia (1921–), Australian writer, author of many fantasy novels for children in which Aboriginal themes and lore are deftly realised.

wring *v.* (**wrung**, **wringing**) **1** twist and squeeze to remove liquid. **2** remove (liquid) in this way. **3** squeeze with emotion (*wrung his hand*). **4** squeeze and twist forcibly in order to break (*wring the bird's neck*). **5** extract or obtain with effort or difficulty (*wrung a promise from him*). • *n.* a wringing movement, a squeeze or twist. ☐ **wringing wet** so wet that water can be wrung out; extremely wet.

wringer *n.* a device with a pair of rollers for wringing water out of washed clothes etc.

wrinkle *n.* a small crease; a small furrow or ridge in the skin (esp. the kind produced by age). •*v.* make wrinkles in; form wrinkles. ▫ **wrinkly** *adj.*

wrinklie *n.* (also **wrinkly**) *colloq. offens.* an old or middle-aged person.

wrist *n.* **1** the joint connecting hand and forearm. **2** the part of a garment covering this. ▫ **wrist-watch** a watch worn on a strap or band etc. round the wrist.

wristlet *n.* **1** a band or ring worn on the wrist to strengthen, guard, or adorn it. **2** (in full **wristlet watch**) a wrist-watch.

writ[1] / rit / *n.* **1** a formal written command issued by a lawcourt or ruling authority directing a person to act or abstain from acting in some way. **2** a document ordering the election of a member or members of Parliament. **3** *archaic* written matter (*Holy Writ*).

writ[2] *adj. archaic* written. ▫ **writ large** in an emphasised form, clearly recognisable.

write *v.* (**wrote**, **written**, **writing**) **1** make letters or other symbols on a surface, esp. with a pen or pencil on paper. **2** form (letters or words or a message etc.) in this way. **3** compose in written form for publication, be an author (*write music; he's writing a fantasy trilogy*). **4** (foll. by *into*, *out of*) include or exclude (a character or episode) in a story by changing the text (*wrote the nun out of the plot*). **5** (foll. by *to*) write and send a letter (*write to me often*). **6** *colloq.* write to (*I will write you soon*). **7** indicate clearly (*guilt was written all over her face*). **8** enter (data) in or on any computer storage device or medium; transfer from one storage device or medium to another; output. ▫ **write down 1** record in writing. **2** write as if for those considered inferior (*the best writers for teenagers never write down to their readers*). **write off 1** cancel the record of (a bad debt etc.); acknowledge the loss of (an asset). **2** completely destroy (a vehicle etc.). **3** dismiss as insignificant. **write-off** *n.* **1** something written off as lost; a vehicle too badly damaged to be worth repairing. **2** something or someone dismissed as worthless or ineffectual; a failure. **write once read many times** *see* WORM[3]. **write up 1** write an account of; write entries in (a diary etc.). **2** praise in writing.

write-up *n.* a published account of something; a review.

writer *n.* **1** a person who writes or has written something; one who writes in a specified way. **2** a person who writes books etc., an author. ▫ **writer's cramp** cramp in the muscles of the hand.

writhe / ruy*th* / *v.* **1** twist one's body about, as in pain. **2** suffer because of great shame or embarrassment (*writhing under the insult*).

writing *n.* **1** written words etc. (*couldn't decipher the writing on the old tombstone*). **2** handwriting. **3** literary work, a piece of this (*in the writings of Banjo Paterson*). ▫ **the writing on the wall** an event signifying that something is doomed (¶ after the Biblical story of the writing that appeared on the wall of Belshazzar's palace, foretelling his doom).

written *see* WRITE.

wrong *adj.* **1** (of conduct or actions) contrary to justice or to what is right. **2** incorrect, not true. **3** not what is required or suitable (*backed the wrong horse*). **4** (in Aboriginal English) not according to law, esp. marriage laws (*he is wrong for her; wrong marriages*). **5** not in a normal condition, not functioning normally (*there's something wrong with the gearbox*). •*adv.* in a wrong manner or direction, mistakenly (*you guessed wrong*). •*n.* **1** what is morally wrong; a wrong action. **2** injustice, an unjust action or treatment (*they did us a great wrong*). •*v.* **1** do wrong to, treat unjustly (*a wronged wife*). **2** attribute bad motives to (a person) mistakenly. ▫ (**get**) **the wrong end of the pineapple** *see* PINEAPPLE. **on the wrong side of 1** in disfavour with or not liked by (a person). **2** over (a certain age) (*on the wrong side of forty*). **wrong-foot** *v.* catch (a person) off balance or unprepared. **wrong-headed** perverse and obstinate. ▫▫ **wrongly** *adv.* **wrongness** *n.*

wrongdoer *n.* a person who acts illegally or immorally. ▫ **wrongdoing** *n.*

wrongful *adj.* contrary to what is fair, just, or legal (*wrongful arrest*). ▫ **wrongfully** *adv.*

wrong 'un / **rong** uhn / *n. colloq.* **1** a person of bad character. **2** *Cricket* = GOOGLY.

wrote *see* WRITE.

wroth / rohth, roth / *adj. literary* angry.

wrought / rawt / *archaic* = worked. •*adj.* (of metals) beaten out or shaped by hammering. ▫ **wrought iron** iron made by forging or rolling, not cast.

wrung *see* WRING.

wry / ruy / *adj.* (**wryer**, **wryest**) **1** twisted or bent out of shape. **2** twisted into an expression of disgust or disappointment or mockery (*a wry face*). **3** (of humour) dry and mocking. ▫ **wryly** *adv.* **wryness** *n.*

wt *abbr.* weight.

WTO *abbr.* World Trade Organisation, the successor to GATT.

Wuna / **wuur**-nu / *n.* an Aboriginal language of the NT east of Darwin.

Wunambal / **wuu**-nahm-bahl / *n.* an Aboriginal language of the far north of WA.

wurley / **wer**-lee / *n. Aust.* **1** = GUNYAH. **2** any temporary shelter. (¶ Gaurna)

wurrung / **wu**-rung / *n. Aust.* a nail-tailed wallaby having a crescent-shaped white marking on the shoulder: now presumed extinct. Also called *crescent nail-tailed wallaby*. (¶ Probably Nyungar *warang*.)

wurst / werst, verst / *n.* German or Austrian sausage.

wuss / wuus / *n. colloq.* an inept, feeble, or cowardly person; an unmacho male; a wimp. ☐ **wussy** *adj.*

Wuywurung / **wuy**-wu-rung / *n.* an Aboriginal language of the region now occupied by Melbourne and up to as far north as Seymour, and to the north of Westernport, and from the Goulburn River across to Bendigo.

www *abbr.* = WORLD WIDE WEB.

wych hazel alternative spelling of WITCH HAZEL.

WYSIWYG / **wiz**-ee-wig / *n.* (also **wysiwyg**) *Computing* a computer system which displays text and graphics onscreen exactly as they will appear in a printout. • *adj.* denoting such an onscreen display. (¶ Acronym of *what you see is what you get.*)

wyvern / **wuy**-vuhn / *n.* a winged two-legged dragon with a barbed tail.

X

X *n.* (also **x**) (*pl.* **Xs** or **X's**) **1** (as a Roman numeral) ten. **2** (usu. **x**) *Algebra* the first unknown quantity. **3** an unknown or unspecified number or person etc. **4** a cross-shaped symbol used: **a** to mark a position on a chart, diagram, etc. **b** to indicate that an answer etc. is wrong. **c** to mark one's vote in an election. **d** to symbolise a kiss. **e** as a signature by a person who cannot write. ☐ **X-chromosome** a sex chromosome, of which female cells have twice as many as male cells. **X-rated** (of a videotape or film) classified as non-violent erotica for viewing by persons over 18 years of age only.

xanthic / **zan**-thik / *adj.* (usu. in *Botany*) yellowish.

Xanthippe / zan-**thip**-ee / *n.* a shrewish or illtempered woman. (¶ The name of the wife of Socrates.)

xanthophyll / **zan**-thuh-fil, -thoh-fil / *n.* any of various oxygen-containing carotenoids associated with chlorophyll, some of which cause the yellow colour of leaves in autumn.

xanthorrhoea / zan-thuh-**ree**-uh / *n.* any of 17 species of the Australian genus of the same name, varying in form from herb-like plants to small trees of all States, the most typical being *Xanthorrhoea australis*, having a tall trunk surmounted by a crown of grass-like leaves from which arises a flowering spike 4 to 5 metres tall. Also called *blackboy, grass tree, yacca.*

Xavier / **zay**-vyuh / , St Francis (1506–52), a Spanish missionary, one of the original seven Jesuits with St Ignatius Loyola. He set out on a remarkable series of missionary journeys: to India, Malacca, the Moluccas, Sri Lanka, and Japan. He died, exhausted, on his way to China, having made more than 700,000 converts.

Xe *symbol* xenon.

xenon / **zen**-on, **zee**-non / *n.* a chemical element (symbol Xe), a colourless odourless gas.

xenophobe / **zen**-uh-fohb / *n.* a person afflicted with xenophobia.

xenophobia / zen-uh-**foh**-bee-uh / *n.* hatred or fear of foreigners. ☐ **xenophobic** *adj.*

xerography / zeer-**rog**-ruh-fee / *n.* a dry copying process in which powder adheres to areas remaining electrically charged after exposure of the surface to light from the image of the document to be copied. ☐ **xerograph** *n.* **xerographic** *adj.*

Xerox / **zeer**-roks, **ze**- / *n. trade mark* **1** a xerographic process for producing photocopies. **2** a photocopy made in this way. • *v.* (**xerox**) photocopy by a process of this kind.

xi / suy, gzuy / *n.* the fourteenth letter of the Greek alphabet (Ξ, ξ).

Xmas *n. colloq.* = CHRISTMAS. (¶ The *X* represents the Greek letter chi (= ch), the first letter of *Christos* (the Greek word for *Christ*).)

XML *abbr.* extensible markup language. It is a subset of SGML, designed for use on the World Wide Web, and compatible with SGML and HTML.

X-ray *n.* a photograph or examination made by means of a kind of electromagnetic radiation (**X-rays**) that can penetrate solids and make it possible to see into or through them. • *v.* photograph, examine, or treat by this radiation. ☐ **X-ray painting** *Aust.* a style of traditional Aboriginal art native to Arnhem Land which shows complex human and animal figures with their internal organs (spinal column, bones, heart, lungs, etc.) depicted as well as the external form, this being a convention to indicate that a living being is more than mere outer appearance.

xylem / **zuy**-luhm / *n.* the woody tissue of a plant (cf. PHLOEM).

xylograph / **zuy**-luh-grahf, -graf / *n.* a woodcut or a wood engraving (esp. an early one). ☐ **xylography** *n.*

xylophone / **zuy**-luh-fohn / *n.* a musical instrument consisting of flat wooden bars, graduated in length, which produce different notes when struck with small hammers. ☐ **xylophonist** *n.*

Y

Y *n.* (usu. **y**) *Algebra* the second unknown quantity. • *symbol* yttrium. ☐ **Y-chromosome** a sex chromosome occurring only in males. **Y-fronts** *n.pl. trademark* men's or boys' briefs with a Y-shaped seam of overlapping folds at the front, enabling the penis to be taken out for urination.

-y (also **-ey**, **-ie**) *suffix* **1** forming diminutive nouns, pet names, etc. (*granny; Freddie; nightie*). **2** widespread in Australia as a mark of familiarity, added to: **a** usu. monosyllabic forms (*bluey; chalkie; littley; tinny*); etc. **b** the shortened forms of words or collocations (*Aussie; blowey; ocky; tilly*; etc.).

yabber *colloq. n.* (also **yabber-yabber**) *Aust.* talk, conversation; discussion; language (*had a good yabber with the blokes*). • *v.* talk, converse (*those Brits hadn't a clue when we yabbered in Strine*). ☐ **yabbering** *n.* (¶ Probably from an Aboriginal language.)

yabber stick *n. Aust.* = MESSAGE STICK (*see* MESSAGE).

yabby *n.* (also **yabbie**) *Aust.* any of several freshwater crayfish, valued as food. • *v.* fish for yabbies (*we yabbied in the dam*). ☐ **yabbying** *n.* (¶ Wemba-wemba).

yacca / **yak**-uh / *n.* (also **yacka**) *Aust.* = BLACKBOY, GRASS TREE, XANTHORRHOEA. ☐ **yacca gum** the resin exuded by this tree. (¶ Gaurna.)

yacht / yot / *n.* **1** a light sailing vessel for racing. **2** a larger power-driven vessel for cruising. • *v.* race or cruise in a yacht. ☐ **yachtsman** *n.* (*feminine* **yachtswoman**).

yachtie / **yot**-ee / *n. colloq.* a yachting enthusiast.

yack alternative spelling of YAK[2].

yacka alternative spelling of YACCA, YAKKA[1].

yackai / **yak**-uy / *n. Aust.* a call used by an Aborigine (and also later by whites) to command attention (cf. COOEE) or to express emotion such as pain or surprise. • *v.* (**yackais, yackaied, yackaing**) utter such a call. (¶ Wiradhuri)

yacker alternative spelling of YAKKA, YAKKER.

Yadhaykenu / **yah**-*thuy*-kay-noo / *n.* an Aboriginal language of the north of Cape York Peninsula, Qld.

yaffler *n.* (in Tas.) *colloq.* a garrulous person.

Yagan (?–1833), Aboriginal leader and hero of the resistance by his people to white invasion of their homeland in the first years of white settlement on the Swan and Canning Rivers, WA. Yagan was eventually shot, whereupon his head was cut off, smoke-cured for some months, and then sent to England. It was recovered from a mass grave in Liverpool in 1998 and returned to WA for a tribal burial.

Yagara / **yah**-gu-ru / *n.* an Aboriginal language of the Brisbane region of Qld and covering a vast surrounding area.

yahoo[1] / **yah**-hoo / *n. Aust.* **1** the name given by Aborigines to: **a** an evil spirit. **b** a monster in the form of a huge, hairy man. **2** a bird of northern and eastern Australia (the *grey-crowned babbler*) having a loud call sounding like 'ya-hoo'. (¶ Probably from a NSW Aboriginal language.)

yahoo[2] / yah-**hoo** / *n.* a bestial person; a rough, coarse hooligan. • *v.* (**yahooed, yahooing**) behave roughly or like a yahoo. (¶ The name of a race of hairy, man-like brutes in Swift's *Gulliver's Travels.*)

Yahweh / **yah**-way / (also **Yahveh**) the Hebrew name of God in the Old Testament. (¶ Hebrew *YHVH* with added vowels: the word is often mistakenly written out as JEHOVAH.)

yak[1] *n.* a long-haired humped ox of central Asia.

yak[2] *colloq. derog.* (also **yakker, yakkety-yak, yackety-yack**) *n.* trivial or unduly persistent conversation. • *v.* (**yakked, yakkered, yackety-yacked** etc.) engage in this (*yakking to the neighbours; yakkety-yakking all afternoon*). ☐ **yak-yak-yak!** a derisive exclamation intended to indicate that ongoing conversation etc. is trivial or long-winded.

yakka[1] / **yak**-uh / *n.* (also **yacka, yacker, yakker**) *Aust. colloq.* work, toil. ☐ **hard yakka** strenuous labour. (¶ Yagara)

yakka[2] alternative spelling of YACCA.

yakka[3] / **yuk**-uh / *n.* (also **yakkha, yaksha**) *Indian & Sri Lankan etc. myth.* **1** a devil or demon. **2** any of a class of demi-gods or nature spirits, often serving as tutelary guardians, esp. one ministering to Kubera, the Hindu god of wealth.

yakka[4] / **yak**-uh / *n. Aust.* a yellowtail scad, often used as live bait.

yakker *n. colloq.* **1** *derog.* = YAK[2]. **2** *Aust.* = YAKKA[1].

Yale lock *n. trademark* a type of lock with a revolving barrel, used for doors etc.

yam *n.* **1** the edible starchy tuber of a tropical climbing plant; the plant itself. **2** any of several Australian plants (e.g. MURNONG) having an edible tuberous root which formed ☐ a staple food for Aborigines; the plant itself. ☐ **yam daisy** a small plant of temperate Australia with slender leaves and bright yellow daisy-flowers, the tuberous rootstock of which was valued by Aborigines as food. **yam stick** (also **digging**

stick) *Aust.* an Aboriginal tool made from a rod of wood pointed at each end and used (esp. by women and children) to excavate yams etc.

Yama / yam-uh / *Hindu myth.* the first man to die, who became the guardian, judge, and ruler of the dead.

Yammagi / ya-muh-jee / *n. Aust.* an Aborigine. (¶ Watjari *yamaji* 'a person, a man'.)

■ **Usage** *See* KOORI.

yammer *colloq. n.* **1** a lament, a wail, a whinge. **2** voluble talk. •*n.* utter a yammer; talk volubly.

Yamoussoukro / ya-moo-**sook**-roh / the capital of the Ivory Coast.

Yandruwandha / yahn-droo-wahnd-hu / *n.* an Aboriginal language of a vast area of north-eastern SA and south-western Qld.

yandy (also **yandi**, **yandie**) *n. Aust.* (also **yandy dish**) a shallow (wooden) winnowing dish used to separate edible seeds from refuse, or particles of mineral from alluvial material. •*v.* winnow (*he showed us all the alluvial gold he had yandied*). (¶ Yindjibarndi and neighbouring languages *yandi* 'a winnowing dish'.)

yang *n.* (in Chinese philosophy) the active male principle of the universe (complemented by YIN).

Yangon / yang-**gon** / *see* RANGOON.

Yank *n. colloq.* (often *derog.*) an American.

yank *colloq. v.* pull with a sudden sharp tug. •*n.* a sudden sharp tug.

Yankee *n.* **1** = YANK. **2** *US* an inhabitant of the northern States of the USA. ☐ **Yankee Doodle** a national song of the USA, originally used by British troops in the War of American Independence to deride the colonial revolutionaries.

Yankunytjatjara / yahn-kuun-ju-jah-ru / *n.* a dialect of the WESTERN DESERT LANGUAGE.

Yaoundé / ya-**uun**-day / the capital of Cameroon.

yap *n.* a shrill bark. •*v.* (**yapped**, **yapping**) **1** bark shrilly or fussily. **2** *colloq.* talk noisily, foolishly, or complainingly. ☐ **yappy** *adj.* (in sense 1 of verb).

yapunyah / yuh-**pun**-yuh / *n.* (also **napunyah**) either of two species of eucalypt occurring along watercourses in Qld, NSW, and the NT. (¶ Gunya)

Yaralde / **yu**-ruhl-dee / *n.* a single Aboriginal language with dialectal variants spoken over a vast area of south-eastern SA.

yard[1] *n.* **1** a measure of length in the imperial system, = 3 feet or 0.9144 metre. **2** a long pole-like piece of wood stretched horizontally or crosswise from a mast to support a sail.

yard[2] *n.* **1** *US & Aust.* the garden of a house (*playing cricket in the back yard*). **2** an enclosure in which sheep, cattle, etc. are confined for a particular purpose. **3** an enclosed area in which business or work is carried out (*a timber yard; a shipyard*).

yardarm *n.* either end of a yard supporting a sail.

yarding *n. Aust.* **1** the confining of animals in an enclosure. **2** the animals so confined (*a yarding of 1,000 cattle*).

yardstick *n.* a standard of comparison.

yarmulke / **yah**-muul-kuh / *n.* (also **yarmulka**) a skullcap worn by Jewish men.

yarn *n.* **1** any spun thread, esp. for knitting or weaving. **2** a *colloq.* a chat; a talk. **b** a long or rambling story, a traveller's tale or anecdote, esp. one that is exaggerated or invented. •*v.* **1** *colloq.* talk, have a chat. **2** tell yarns or tall tales.

Yarra a river rising east of Melbourne, near Mount Baw Baw, fed by many tributaries from the Great Dividing Range, and flowing west, north, and west, to run through Melbourne to Port Phillip Bay. (¶ The name means 'running water' in many Aboriginal languages.)

yarra / **ya**-ruh / *adj. Aust. colloq.* insane; stupid (*the racket they were making nearly drove me yarra*). (¶ From the name of a psychiatric hospital at Yarra Bend, Vic. (cf. *round the bend* at BEND[1]).)

Yarralumla the official residence in Canberra of the Governor-General of Australia.

yarraman / **ya**-ruh-muhn / *n. Aust.* a horse. (¶ The word is probably from an Aboriginal language, although its exact meaning in that language is unknown: the word was taken into the early pidgin used by white settlers and Aborigines to communicate with each other; each believed that *yarraman* was the word for 'horse' in the other's language.)

yarran / **ya**-ruhn / *n.* **1** a small to medium wattle of inland eastern Australia, having a rough bark, smooth foliage, and an unpleasant odour. **2** the dark brown, durable wood of this tree, used by Aborigines for weapons including boomerangs. (¶ Kamilaroi)

yashmak *n.* a veil concealing the face except for the eyes, worn in public by Muslim women in certain countries.

yate *n.* **1** any of several eucalypts of southern WA yielding a remarkably hard, strong timber. **2** the wood of these trees. (¶ Perhaps from a WA Aboriginal language.)

yaw *v.* (of a ship or aircraft etc.) fail to hold a straight course, turn from side to side. •*n.* a yawing movement or course.

yawl *n.* **1** a sailing boat with two masts. **2** a fishing boat.

yawn *v.* **1** open the mouth wide and draw in breath (often involuntarily), as when sleepy or bored. **2** have a wide opening, form a chasm. •*n.* **1** the act of yawning. **2** *colloq.* something boring (*playing kanga cricket with the kids is a real yawn*).

Yawor / **yah**-wuur / *n.* an Aboriginal language of the north of WA.

yaws *n.* a contagious tropical skin disease causing raspberry-like swellings.

Yb *symbol* ytterbium.

ye[1] *pron. archaic* you (more than one person).

ye[2] *adj. pseudo-archaic* the (*ye olde tea shoppe*). (¶ From the obsolete *y*-shaped letter for *th*.)

yea / yay / *adv. & n. archaic* yes.

yeah / yair / *adv. colloq.* yes.

year *n.* **1** the time taken by the earth to make one complete orbit of the sun, about 365¼ days. **2** (also **calendar year**) the period from 1 January to 31 December inclusive. **3** any period of twelve consecutive months. **4** (**years**) age, time of life (*he looks younger than his years*). **5** *colloq.* a very long time (*it took us years to get served*). **6 a** an academic level or grade (*doing 4th year medicine; she's in year 11 at high school*). **b** a group of students entering college etc. in the same academic year (*she was in my year at Uni*).

yearling / **yeer**-ling / *n.* an animal between 1 and 2 years old.

yearly *adj.* happening, published, or payable etc. once a year; annual. • *adv.* annually.

yearn *v.* be filled with great longing. ☐ **yearning** *n.*

yeast *n.* a fungus that produces alcohol and carbon dioxide while it is developing, used to cause fermentation in making beer and wines and as a raising agent in baking.

yeasty *adj.* **1** of, like, or tasting of yeast; frothy like yeast when it is developing. **2** in a ferment. ☐ **yeastiness** *n.*

Yeats / yayts /, W(illiam) B(utler) (1865–1939), Irish poet and dramatist.

yelka *n.* (also **yulka**) any of several Australian sedges yielding a small edible tuber; the tuber itself. (¶ Aranda)

yell *n.* a loud sharp cry of fright, anger, pain, encouragement, delight, etc.; a shout. • *v.* cry out, shout.

yellow *adj.* **1** of the colour of buttercups and ripe lemons. **2** used as a distinguishing epithet in the names of fauna and flora (e.g. *yellow robin, yellow-faced rock wallaby, yellow-eye mullet, yellow bloodwood*). **3** *colloq.* cowardly. • *n.* **1** yellow colour. **2** a yellow substance or material, yellow clothes. • *v.* make or become yellow. ☐ **yellowbelly** *colloq.* a coward. **yellow box** a medium to tall eucalypt of Qld, NSW, the ACT, and Vic., having an often twisted trunk with yellow tints beneath the bark, and profuse nectar-rich flowers highly valued by apiarists. **yellow fever** a tropical disease with fever and jaundice. **yellow flag** a flag displayed by a ship in quarantine. **yellow gum** any of several eucalypts of SE mainland Australia, having a very smooth, mottled, yellowish trunk. **yellow jacket** (also **yellow jack**) any of several eucalypts of Qld and WA having a yellowish bark. **yellow monday** (*or* **munday** *or* **mundy**) a cicada of south-eastern Australia when yellow (*see* GREENGROCER). **yellow oriole** *see* ORIOLE. **yellow spot** the point of acutest vision in the retina. **yellow streak** *colloq.* cowardice. **yellow stringybark** any of several very rough-barked eucalypts of eastern Vic. and south-eastern NSW, having a yellow timber. **yellow walnut** a tall rainforest tree of north-eastern Qld, having fleshy fruit and yielding a yellow wood with darker streaks. **yellow-wood** any of several large Australian rainforest trees, esp. of the genus *Flindersia*, yielding a golden timber. ☐☐ **yellowish** *adj.* **yellowness** *n.* **yellowy** *adj.*

yellowbelly *n.* a large freshwater food fish with yellowish underparts, native to south-eastern Australia and probably introduced into WA and the NT. Also called *callop, golden perch.*

yellowtail *n.* any of several southern Australian marine food fish having a yellow caudal fin, esp. the jack mackerel and the kingfish.

yelp *n.* a sharp shrill cry of, or as of, a dog in pain or excitement. • *v.* utter a yelp.

Yeltsin, Boris (Nikolayevich) (1931–), Russian statesman, president of Russia 1991–99.

Yemen / **yem**-uhn / a republic in the south and SW of the Arabian peninsula. (North Yemen and South Yemen united in 1990.) ☐ **Yemeni** / yem-uh-nee / *adj. & n.*

Yemmerrawanyea, Kebbarah (*c.*1776–94), a young Aborigine from Port Jackson in NSW who was taken to England by Governor Arthur Phillip (together with another Aborigine BENNELONG) in the hope that he would learn civilised ways and return to 'civilise' his people. England's climate killed him and he was buried in the churchyard at Eltham, Kent. Since 1988 Aborigines have been trying to bring his remains back to Australia for interment, but they have been opposed by the Eltham Society.

yen[1] *n.* (*pl.* **yen**) the unit of money in Japan.

yen[2] *n.* a longing, a yearning. • *v.* (**yenned**, **yenning**) feel a yen.

yeo / yoh / *n.* (also **yoe**) *Aust.* a ewe (*he curses the old snagger with the bare-bellied yeo*).

yeoman / **yoh**-muhn / *n.* (*pl.* **yeomen**) *Brit. hist.* a man who owns and farms a small estate. ☐ **yeoman service** efficient or useful help in need. ☐☐ **yeomanly** *adj.*

Yeoman of the Guard *n.* = BEEFEATER.

Yerevan / yi-ri-**van** / the capital of Armenia.

yes *adv.* **1** it is so, the statement is correct. **2** what you request or command will be done. **3** (as a question) what do you want? **4** (in answer to a summons etc.) I am here. • *n.* the word or answer 'yes'; a 'yes' vote. ☐ **yes-man** a person who always agrees with a superior in a weak or sycophantic way.

yesterday *n.* **1** the day before today. **2** the recent past. • *adv.* on the day before today; in the recent past.

yesteryear *n. literary* last year; the recent past.

yet *adv.* **1** up to this or that time and continuing; still (*there's life in the old dog yet*). **2** by this or that time; so far (*it hasn't happened yet*). **3** besides, in addition (*heard it yet again*). **4** before the matter is done with; eventually (*I'll be even with you yet*). **5** even (*she became yet more excited*). **6** nevertheless (*strange yet true*). • *conj.* nevertheless, but in spite of that (*he worked hard, yet he failed*).

yeti / **yet**-ee / *n.* (*pl.* **yetis**) = ABOMINABLE SNOWMAN (*see* ABOMINABLE).

Yevtushenko / yef-tuh-**sheng**-koh /, Yevgeni (Aleksandrovich) (1933–), Russian poet.

yew *n.* **1** an evergreen tree with narrow dark green leaves and red berries. **2** its springy wood, used formerly as the material for archers' bows.

Yggdrasil / **ig**-druh-sil / *Scand. myth.* an ash tree whose roots and branches connect earth, heaven, and hell.

Yiddish *n.* a language used by Jews of central and eastern Europe, based on a German dialect and with words from Hebrew and various modern languages. • *adj.* of or relating to this language.

Yidiny / **yi**-di-nee / *n.* an Aboriginal language of the Cairns region of northern Qld.

yield *v.* **1** give or return as fruit, gain, or result (*the land yields good crops; the investment yields 15%*). **2** surrender, do what is requested or ordered (*the town yielded; he yielded to persuasion*). **3** be inferior or confess inferiority (*I yield to none in appreciation of his merits*). **4** (of traffic) allow other traffic to have right of way. **5** be able to be forced out of the natural or usual shape, e.g. under pressure. • *n.* the amount yielded or produced; the quantity obtained.

yielding *adj.* **1** compliant, submissive. **2** (of a substance) soft and pliable, able to bend, not stiff or rigid.

yike *n. Aust. colloq.* **1** a quarrel; a fight. **2** a complaint; a gripe (*his constant yike is that no one takes him seriously*).

yin *n.* (in Chinese philosophy) the passive female principle of the universe (complemented by YANG).

Yindjibarndi / yin-jee-**bun**-dee / *n.* an Aboriginal language of the Lower Hamersley Range and the Fortescue River region of WA.

Yingkarta / **ying**-gah-du / *n.* an Aboriginal language of western WA.

Yirawala (*c.*1894–1976), Australian Aboriginal artist, a leading exponent of bark painting.

Yirrkala / **yeer**-kul-uh / *n.* an Aboriginal settlement on Gove Peninsula, NT, since 1976 run by the Yirrkala Town Council composed of representatives from the various clans. Yirrkala has received world-wide recognition as a centre for fine bark paintings and wood carvings.

Yitha-yitha / **yith**-u-yith-u / *n.* an Aboriginal language of south-western NSW and north-western Vic.

YMCA *abbr.* Young Men's Christian Association.

yob *n. colloq.* a lout, a hooligan. ❏ **yobbish** *adj.* (¶ Back slang for BOY.)

yobbo *n.* (*pl.* **yobbos**) *colloq.* = YOB.

yodel / **yoh**-duhl / *v.* (**yodelled, yodelling**) **1** sing so that the voice alternates continually between falsetto and its normal pitch, in the manner of Swiss mountain dwellers. **2** *Aust. colloq.* vomit. • *n.* **1** a yodelling cry. **2** *Aust. colloq.* an act or instance of vomiting. ❏ **yodeller** *n.*

yoe / yoh / alternative spelling of YEO.

yoga / **yoh**-guh / *n.* **1** a Hindu system of meditation and self-control designed to produce mystical experience and spiritual insight. **2** a system of physical exercises and breathing control used in yoga. ❏ **yogic** *adj.*

yoghurt / **yoh**-guht, **yog**-uht / *n.* (also **yogurt**) a food prepared from milk that has been thickened by the action of certain bacteria.

yogi / **yoh**-gee / *n.* a master of yoga; a devotee of yoga.

yohi / **yoh**-wuy / *adv.* (also **youi, youai**) *Aust.* (in Aboriginal English) an affirmative reply, 'yes'. (¶ Yagara)

yoke *n.* **1** a wooden crosspiece fastened over the necks of two bullocks etc. pulling a wagon or plough etc. **2** (*pl.* **yoke** or **yokes**) a pair (of bullocks etc.). **3** a piece of timber shaped to fit a person's shoulders to hold a pail or other load slung from each end. **4** a part of a garment fitting round the shoulders or hips and from which the rest hangs. **5** oppression, burdensome restraint (*throw off the yoke of servitude*). **6** a bond of union, esp. of marriage (*the yoke of wedlock is no joke*). • *v.* **1** harness by means of a yoke (*yoke bullocks to the plough*). **2** couple or unite (a pair) (*yoked to an unwilling partner*). **3** link (one thing) to (another) (*I am yoked to my desk*). **4** match or work together.

yokel / **yoh**-kuhl / *n.* a simple country person, a country bumpkin.

yolk / yohk / *n.* the round yellow internal part of an egg.

Yolngu[1] / **yol**-noo / *n.* (also **Yolnu**) an Aborigine. (¶ Yolngu language *yuulngu*.)

■ **Usage** *See* KOORI.

Yolngu[2] / **yol**-ngoo / *n.* an Aboriginal language of the north-eastern sections of Arnhem Land in the NT.

Yom Kippur / yom ki-**poor** / *n.* the most solemn religious fast day of the Jewish year, the Day of Atonement.

yon *adj.* & *adv. literary* yonder.

yonder *adv.* over there. • *adj.* situated or able to be seen over there.

yoni / **yoh**-nee / *n.* a symbol of the external female genitals venerated by Hindus etc. (*see also* LINGAM).

yonks *n.pl.* (also **yonkers**) *colloq.* a long time, ages (*yonks ago; I haven't seen him in yonkers*).

yonnie *n. Aust. colloq.* a small stone, esp. one used as a missile.

yook / yuuk / *n. Aust.* a native yam. Also called *native potato, wild potato.* (¶ Nyungar)

yore *n.* ❏ **of yore** formerly; of long ago.

yorga / **yaw**-guh / *n. Aust.* a woman, esp. an Aboriginal woman. (¶ Nyungar)

york *v. Cricket* bowl (a batsman) out with a yorker.

yorker *n.* a ball bowled in cricket so that it pitches immediately under the bat.

Yorta Yorta *n.* an Aboriginal people of northern Vic. and southern NSW.

Yothu Yindi an Australian rock band founded by Mandawuy YUNUPINGU in 1986. The band combines contemporary western rock with traditional Aboriginal songs, music, and instruments.

you *pron.* **1** the person(s) addressed. **2** one; anyone; everyone (*you can never tell*). **3** (of a thing) suitable to or characteristic of the person being addressed (*that hat just isn't you; racial intolerance is you to a T!*). ☐ **you-know-what** (*or* **-who**) something (or someone) unspecified but understood (*don't let the kids find out what happened to you-know-who's you-know-what!*).

youai alternative spelling of YOHI.

you'd = **1** you had. **2** you would.

youee alternative spelling of UEY.

youi alternative spelling of YOHI.

you'll = you will; you shall.

Young, Simone (1961–), Australian conductor. She was appointed musical director of Opera Australia from 2001.

young *adj.* **1** having lived or existed for only a short time; not the eldest. **2** not far advanced in time (*the night is young*). **3** youthful, having little experience. **4** *Aust.* (in Aboriginal English) newly initiated. **5** of or characteristic of youth (*young love*). **6** representing youth (*Young Farmers*). **7** distinguishing a son from his father (*young George*). **8** as a familiar or condescending form of address (*listen, young lady*). • *n.* **1** the offspring of animals, before or soon after birth. **2** young people (*the young aren't interested in politics*). ☐ **young blood** comparatively young people with new ideas etc. (*what this firm needs is some young blood*). **young turk** a young person eager for radical change to the established order.

youngie / **yung**-ee / *n. Aust. colloq.* a young person (as opposed to OLDIE).

youngish *adj.* fairly young.

youngling *n.* a young person or animal. • *adj.* youthful.

youngster *n.* a young person, a child.

your *adj.* **1** of or belonging to you. **2** *colloq.* (often *derog.*) much talked of, well known (*none so fallible as your self-styled expert*).

you're = you are.

yours *possessive pron.* **1** belonging to you; the thing(s) belonging to you. **2** used in phrases for ending letters: **Yours** (*or* **Yours ever**) used casually to friends; **Yours faithfully** used for ending business or formal letters beginning 'Dear Sir' or 'Dear Madam'; **Yours sincerely** used in letters to acquaintances and to friends (other than close friends), and often also in business letters addressing a person by name (e.g. beginning 'Dear Mr Brown'), where it is now more frequently used than *Yours truly*; **Yours truly** *a* used to slight acquaintances and in business letters (less formal than *Yours faithfully* but more formal than *Yours sincerely*). **b** *colloq.* = me (*the awkward jobs are always left for yours truly*).

■ **Usage** It is incorrect to write *your's* (*see* the note under *its*).

yourself *pron.* (*pl.* **yourselves**) **1** corresponding to *you*, used in the same ways as HIMSELF, HERSELF, etc. **2** in your normal state of body or mind (*you're quite yourself again*). ☐ **be yourself** *see* ONESELF.

youse / yooz / *pron. colloq.* (used when addressing more than one person) you (*pl.*) (*we were told not to have anything to do with youse; are youse guys coming or not?*).

■ **Usage** This pronoun is often heard in colloquial speech, but its use is regarded as unacceptable in standard speech and it should not be used in formal writing.

youth *n.* (*pl.* **youths** / yoo*th*z /) **1** being young. **2** the period between childhood and maturity; the vigour or lack of experience etc. characteristic of this. **3** a young man (*a youth of 16*). **4** young people collectively (*the youth of the country*). ☐ **youth hostel** any of a chain of cheap lodgings for (esp. young) holidaymakers, esp. walkers and cyclists. **youth hosteller** a person who uses youth hostels. **youth hostelling** staying in youth hostels.

youthful *adj.* **1** young; looking or seeming young. **2** characteristic of young people (*youthful impatience*). ☐ **youthfully** *adv.* **youthfulness** *n.*

you've = you have.

yowie[1] / **yoh**-ee / *n. Aust.* a ewe.

yowie[2] / **yow**-ee / *n. Aust.* an ape-like or humanoid monster supposed to inhabit parts of eastern Australia. (¶ Yuwaalaraay *yuwi* 'a dream spirit'.)

yowl *n.* a loud wailing cry, a howl. • *v.* utter a yowl.

yo-yo *n.* (*pl.* **yo-yos**) **1** a toy consisting of two circular parts with a deep grove between, which can be made to rise and fall on a string. **2** a thing that repeatedly falls and rises. **3** *colloq.* an idiot, a fool. • *v.* (**yo-yoes**, **yo-yoed**, **yo-yoing**) **1** play with a yo-yo. **2** move up and down; fluctuate (*the dollar's yo-yoing badly*).

yr *abbr.* **1** year(s). **2** younger. **3** your.

yrs *abbr.* **1** years. **2** yours.

ytterbium / i-**ter**-bee-uhm / *n.* a metallic element (symbol Yb).

yttrium / **it**-ree-uhm / *n.* a metallic element (symbol Y), compounds of which are used to make red phosphors for colour-television tubes.

Y2K *abbr.* **1** year two thousand. **2** = MILLENNIUM BUG.

yu *n.* an Aboriginal shelter, esp. from the wind. (¶ Western Desert language *yuu* 'a windbreak'.)

yuan / yoo-**ahn** / *n.* (*pl.* **yuan**) the chief unit of money in China.

yuck *interj.* (also **yuk**) *colloq.* an expression of strong dislike, disgust, etc.

yucky *adj.* (also **yukky**) *colloq.* **1** messy, disgusting. **2** sickly, sentimental.

yugari alternative spelling of UGARI.

Yugoslavia / yoo-guh-**slah**-vee-uh / a country in south-eastern central Europe. ☐ **Yugoslav** / yoo-guh-slahv / **Yugoslavian** *adj.* & *n.*

Yuin / **yoo**-uhn / *n.* an Aborigine. (¶ Dharawal and Dhurga *yuwiny.*)

■ Usage *See* KOORI.

yuk, yukky alternative spellings of YUCK, YUCKY.

yule / yool / *n.* (in full **yuletide**) *archaic* the Christmas festival.

yulka alternative spelling of YELKA.

yumcha / yum-**chah** / *n.* a Chinese meal in which diners select from a wide range of dishes served from a trolley.

Yunupingu[1], Galarrwuy (1948–), AM, Australian Aboriginal land rights activist.

Yunupingu[2], Mandawuy (1956–), Australian Aboriginal singer and songwriter. He is the founder of the rock band YOTHU YINDI.

yuppie *n.* (also **yuppy**) *colloq.* (often *derog.*) a young, ambitious, upwardly mobile, professional person working in a city. • *adj.* characteristic of a yuppie or yuppies. ☐ **yuppie flu** = CHRONIC FATIGUE SYNDROME. (¶ From *y*oung *u*rban *p*rofessional.)

Yura / **yoo**-ruh / *n.* an Aborigine; Aboriginal people, esp. of SA. (¶ Adnyamathanha)

■ Usage *See* KOORI.

yurt / yert / *n.* **1** a circular tent of felt, skins, etc., on a collapsible framework, used by nomads in Mongolia and Siberia. **2** a semi-subterranean hut, usu. of timber covered with earth or turf.

Yuwaalaraay / yoo-**wah**-luh-ruy / *n.* an Aboriginal language of northern NSW (between Walgett and Lightning Ridge).

Yuwaaliyaay / yoo-**wah**-luh-yuy / *n.* an Aboriginal language of northern NSW (between Lightning Ridge and Mungindi).

YWCA *abbr.* Young Women's Christian Association.

Z

z *n. Algebra* the third unknown quantity.

zabaglione / zah-buh-**lyoh**-nay / *n.* an Italian dessert of whipped and heated egg yolks, sugar, and (esp. Marsala) wine.

zac *n.* (also **zack**) *Aust. colloq.* **1** *hist.* the Australian sixpenny coin. **2** a five-cent coin. **3** a trifling sum of money (*I won't contribute another zac until I know where my money is going*). **4** a prison term of six months or six years.

Zagreb / **zah**-greb / the capital of Croatia.

Zaire / zuy-**eer** / **1** a major river (also called the Congo) in central Africa, flowing into the Atlantic Ocean. **2** the former name (1971–97) of the Democratic Republic of Congo. □ **Zairean** *adj.* & *n.*

Zambia a landlocked republic in central Africa. □ **Zambian** *adj.* & *n.*

zambuk / **zam**-buk / *n.* (also **zambuck**) *Aust.* a member of the St John Ambulance Brigade, esp. one in attendance at a sporting fixture. (¶ *Zambuk* the proprietary name of an antiseptic ointment.)

zamia / **zay**-mee-uh / (in full **zamia palm**) = MACROZAMIA.

zany *adj.* (**zanier**, **zaniest**) crazily funny. • *n.* a fool, an idiot; a jester.

Zanzibar an island off the coast of East Africa, united with Tanganyika to form the republic of Tanzania.

zap *v.* (**zapped**, **zapping**) *colloq.* **1** hit; attack; knock out, kill (*zapped the enemy; zapped the blowie*). **2** 'destroy' a television commercial by using the remote control device as a gun to kill the sound or (while watching a videotaped film etc.) to fast-forward the tape. **3** move quickly (*I'll zap over to the milk bar and get some*). **4** exhaust (*all this digging has zapped me*). **5** (foll. by *up*) **a** enliven (*this party needs to be zapped up*); **b** make quickly, whip up (*I'll zap up some more sangers in a jiff*). • *interj.* expressing the sound or impact of a bullet, a ray gun, etc., or any sudden event. • *n.* liveliness, energy (*he's lost his zap*).

zapped *adj. colloq.* exhausted.

zapper *n.* the remote control device which operates a VCR etc.

zappy *adj. colloq.* lively; striking and forceful.

Zarathustra / za-ruh-**thuus**-truh / the Old Persian name for Zoroaster.

Zarathustrian alternative spelling of ZOROASTRIAN.

zarzuela / thah-**thway**-luh / *n.* a Spanish dish of various kinds of seafood cooked in a rich sauce.

zeal / zeel / *n.* enthusiasm; hearty and persistent effort.

zealot / **zel**-uht / *n.* an extreme partisan, a fanatic. □ **zealotry** *n.*

zealous / **zel**-uhs / *adj.* full of zeal. □ **zealously** *adv.*

zebra / **zeb**-ruh, **zee**-bruh / *n.* (*pl.* **zebra** or **zebras**) an African animal of the horse family with a body covered by black and white stripes. □ **zebra crossing** a striped street-crossing where pedestrians have precedence. **zebra duck** (also **pink-eared duck**) an Australian duck with zebra-like markings (*see* WIDGEON). **zebra finch** a small bird widespread in much of mainland Australia, having black and white tail-bars.

zebu / **zee**-boo / *n.* (*pl.* **zebu** or **zebus**) a humped ox found in India, East Asia, and Africa, used in Australia for cross-breeding.

zed *n.* **1** the letter Z. **2** *colloq.* a nap, a sleep (*go away!—I'm having a zed*). • *v. colloq.* take a nap, sleep (*he's been zedding all arvo*). □ **push up zeds** *colloq.* sleep, nap.

Zeitgeist / **tsuyt**-guyst / *n.* the spirit of the times. (¶ German)

Zen *n.* a form of Buddhism emphasising the value of meditation and intuition.

Zend *n.* an interpretation of the Avesta, each Zend being part of the **Zend-Avesta**, Zoroastrian scriptures consisting of Avesta (= text) and Zend (= commentary).

zenith / **zen**-uhth / *n.* **1** the part of the sky that is directly above an observer (as opposed to NADIR). **2** the highest point (*his power was at its zenith*).

zephyr / **zef**-uh / *n. literary* a soft gentle wind.

Zeppelin, Ferdinand, Count von (1838–1917), German airship pioneer, whose airships (known as Zeppelins) were used during the First World War.

zero *n.* (*pl.* **zeros**) **1** nought, the figure 0. **2** nothing, nil. **3** the point on the scale of a thermometer etc. from which a positive or negative quantity is reckoned. **4** *colloq.* a nonentity; a dull or boring person. • *adj.* no, not any (*zero growth*). • *v.* (**zeroed**, **zeroing**) adjust (an instrument etc.) to zero. □ **zero hour** the hour at which something (esp. a military operation) is timed to begin; a crucial moment. **zero in on** focus one's aim on; go purposefully towards. **zero option** a disarmament proposal for the total removal of certain types of weapons. **zero-rated** (of goods or services) on which no GST is charged.

zest *n.* **1** keen enjoyment or interest. **2** a pleasantly stimulating quality (*the risk added zest to the adventure*). **3** the coloured part of the peel of an orange or lemon, used as flavouring. ☐ **zestful** *adj.* **zestfully** *adv.* **zesty** *adj.*

zeta / **zee**-tuh / *n.* the sixth letter of the Greek alphabet (Z, ζ).

zeugma / **zyoog**-muh / *n.* a figure of speech using a verb or adjective with two nouns where it is appropriate to only one of these, e.g. *with weeping eyes and hearts* (where what is meant is something like *with weeping eyes and grieving hearts*).

Zeus / zyoos / *Gk myth.* the supreme god, identified with Jupiter.

Zhou Enlai / joh en-**luy** / (formerly **Chou Enlai**) (1898–1976), Chinese Communist statesman, prime minister of China 1949–76.

zidovudine / zuy-doh-**vyoo**-deen / = AZT.

ziggurat / **zig**-uh-rat / *n.* a pyramid-shaped tower in ancient Mesopotamia surmounted by a temple, built in tiers which become smaller in size towards the summit.

zigzag *n.* a line or course that turns right and left alternately at sharp angles. • *adj.* & *adv.* forming or in a zigzag. • *v.* (**zigzagged, zigzagging**) move in a zigzag course. ☐ **to zig when one should have zagged** do the wrong thing; move in the wrong direction; make a mess of things; etc.

zigzag wattle a large wattle of arid Qld, having lance-like leaves, cream flowers, and branches which zigzag from leaf-node to leaf-node.

zilch *n. colloq.* nothing.

zillion *n. colloq.* an indefinite large number.

Zimbabwe / zim-**bahb**-wee / a republic in SE Africa. ☐ **Zimbabwean** *adj.* & *n.*

zinc *n.* a white metallic element (symbol Zn), used in alloys and to coat iron and steel as a protection against corrosion.

zine / zeen / *n.* (also **'zine**) magazine, esp. a fanzine one published on the Internet.

zing *colloq. n.* vigour, energy. • *v.* move swiftly or with a shrill sound (*mozzies zinging past my ears*).

zinnia *n.* a garden plant with showy flowers.

Zion / **zuy**-uhn / *n.* (also **Sion**) **1** ancient Jerusalem; its holy hill. **2** the Jewish people or religion. **3** the Christian Church. **4** the kingdom of heaven.

Zionism / **zuy**-uh-niz-uhm / *n.* a movement founded in 1897 that has sought and achieved the founding of a Jewish homeland in Palestine. ☐ **Zionist** *n.* & *adj.*

zip *n.* **1** a short sharp sound like that of a bullet going through the air. **2** energy, vigour, liveliness. **3** a zip fastener. • *v.* (**zipped, zipping**) **1** open or close with a zip fastener. **2** move with a zip or at high speed. **3** *Computing* compress (a file) so that it takes up less space in storage. ☐ **zip fastener** a fastening device consisting of two flexible strips of material with projections that interlock when brought together by a sliding tab.

zipper *n.* a zip fastener.

zippy *adj.* (**zippier, zippiest**) *colloq.* lively, speedy.

zircon / **zer**-kuhn, -kon / *n.* a bluish-white gem cut from a translucent mineral.

zirconium / zer-**koh**-nee-uhm / *n.* a grey metallic element (symbol Zr), with a variety of uses in industry.

zit *n. colloq.* a pimple.

zither / **zith**-uh / *n.* a musical instrument with many strings stretched over a shallow boxlike body, played by plucking with the fingers of both hands.

zloty / **zlot**-ee / *n.* (*pl.* **zloty** or **zlotys**) the unit of money in Poland.

Zn *symbol* zinc.

zodiac / **zoh**-dee-ak / *n.* (in astrology) **1** a band of the sky containing the paths of the sun, moon, and principal planets, divided into twelve equal parts (called **signs of the zodiac**) each named from a constellation that was formerly situated in it. **2** a diagram of these signs. ☐ **zodiacal** / zuh-**duy**-uh-kuhl, zoh- / *adj.*

Zola / **zoh**-luh /, Émile (1840–1902), French novelist, the leading exponent of naturalism.

zombie *n.* **1** *colloq.* a person who acts mechanically or lifelessly. **2** a corpse said to have been revived by witchcraft.

zone *n.* **1** an area that has particular characteristics or a particular purpose or use; a defined region or area (*danger zone; erogenous zones in the body; a smoke-free zone*). **2** (in full **time zone**) a range of longitudes where a common standard time is used. **3** any of five divisions of the earth bounded by circles parallel to the equator (*see* FRIGID ZONES, TEMPERATE ZONE, TORRID ZONE). • *v.* **1** divide into zones. **2** arrange or distribute by zones; assign to a particular area. ☐ **zonal** *adj.* **zoning** *n.*

zonked *adj. colloq.* exhausted; intoxicated.

zoo / zoo / *v.* a zoological garden.

zoological / zoh-uh-**loj**-i-kuhl, zoo- / *adj.* of zoology. ☐ **zoological garden** (*or* **gardens**) a public garden or park with a collection of animals for exhibition, conservation, and study.

■ **Usage** *See* note at *zoology*.

zoology / zoh-**ol**-uh-jee, zoo- / *n.* the scientific study of animals. ☐ **zoologist** *n.*

■ **Usage** The second pronunciation given for *zoological* and *zoology* (and *zoologist*), with the first syllable pronounced as in *zoo*, although extremely common, is considered incorrect by some people.

zoom *v.* **1** move quickly, esp. with a buzzing sound. **2** rise quickly (*prices had zoomed*). **3** (often foll. by *in* or *in on*) (in photography) alter the size of the image by means of a zoom lens. ☐ **zoom lens** a camera lens that can be adjusted from a long shot to a close-up (and vice versa), giving an effect of going steadily closer to (or further from) the subject.

zoomorphic / zoh-uh-**maw**-fik / *adj.* **1** dealing with, or represented in, animal forms. **2** having gods of animal form. ◻ **zoomorphism** *n.*

zoophyte / **zoh**-uh-fuyt / *n.* a plantlike animal, esp. a coral, sea anemone, or sponge.

Zoroaster / zo-roh-**as**-tuh / the Greek name for the Persian prophet Zarathustra (6th century BC or earlier), founder of Zoroastrianism.

Zoroastrian / zo-roh-**as**-tree-uhn / *n.* a person who believes in **Zoroastrianism**, the ancient Persian religion taught by Zoroaster (or Zarathustra) and his followers, based on the conflict between a spirit of light and good and one of darkness and evil. •*adj.* of Zoroaster or Zoroastrianism.

zot *v. colloq.* **1** kill, swat (*zotted the blowie with my newspaper*). **2** (foll. by *off*) leave or go quickly.

Zr *symbol* zirconium.

zucchetto / tsuu-**ket**-oh, zuu- / *n.* an ecclesiastical skullcap, black for a priest, purple for a bishop, red for a cardinal, white for a pope.

zucchini / zuh-**kee**-nee / *n.* (*pl.* **zucchini** or **zucchinis**) *US* & *Aust.* a small, usu. green variety of vegetable marrow; a courgette.

Zulu *n.* (*pl.* **Zulus**) **1** a member of a Bantu people of South Africa. **2** their language. •*adj.* of this people or language.

zygomaturus / zuy-goh-muh-**tyoo**-ruhs / *n.* a large extinct Australian marsupial of the genus of the same name.

zygote / **zuy**-goht, **zig**-oht / *n.* a cell formed by the union of two gametes.

zymotic / zuy-**mot**-ik / *adj.* of fermentation.

zzz / zuhz / *colloq. n.* a sleep. •*v.* (foll. by *out*) sleep. (¶ From the convention used in comics etc. in which a sleeping person is shown as having a stream of zeds issuing from the mouth.)

Appendix 1 Countries of the world

(Countries are given for linguistic information on the names in use. Some regions and dependent territories are included.)

country	person (name in general use)	related adjective (in general use)
Afghanistan	Afghan	Afghan
Albania	Albanian	Albanian
Algeria	Algerian	Algerian
America *see* United States of America		
Andorra	Andorran	Andorran
Angola	Angolan	Angolan
Anguilla	Anguillan	Anguillan *or* Anguilla
Antigua and Barbuda	Antiguan *or* Barbudan	Antiguan *or* Barbudan, *or* Antigate and Barbuda
Argentina	Argentinian	Argentine *or* Argentinian
Armenia	Armenian	Armenian
Australia	Australian	Australian
Austria	Austrian	Austrian
Azerbaijan	Azerbaijani	Azerbaijani
Bahamas	Bahamian	Bahamian
Bahrain	Bahraini	Bahraini *or* Bahrain
Bangladesh	Bangladeshi	Bangladeshi
Barbados	Barbadian	Barbadian
Belarus (*formerly* Belorussia)	Belorussian *or* Belarussian	Belorussian *or* Belarussian
Belgium	Belgian	Belgian
Belize	Belizean	Belizean
Benin	Beninese	Beninese
Bermuda (*dependent territory*)	Bermudan	Burmudan
Bhutan	Bhutanese	Bhutanese
Bolivia	Bolivian	Bolivian
Bosnia-Herzegovina	Bosnian *or* Herzegovinian	Bosnian *or* Bosnian and Herzegovinian
Botswana	Motswana, *pl.* Batswana	Motswana, *pl.* Batswana
Brazil	Brazilian	Brazilian
Britain *see* Great Britain		
Brunei	Bruneian	Bruneian *or* Brunei
Bulgaria	Bulgarian	Bulgarian
Burkina (*official name* Burkina Faso)	Burkinese	Burkinese

country	person (name in general use)	related adjective (in general use)
Burma *see* Myanmar	Burmese	Burmese
Burundi	Burundian	Burundi
Cambodia (*formerly* Kampuchea)	Cambodian	Cambodian
Cameroon	Cameroonian	Cameroonian
Canada	Canadian	Canadian
Cape Verde Islands	Cape Verdean	Cape Verdean
Cayman Islands (*dependent territory*)	Cayman Islander *or* Caymanian	Cayman Islands
Central African Republic	Central African	Central African Republic
Chad	Chadian	Chadian
Chile	Chilean	Chilean
China	Chinese	Chinese
Colombia	Colombian	Colombian
Comoros	Comoran	Comoran
Congo	Congolese	Congolese
Costa Rica	Costa Rican	Costa Rican
Croatia	Croat *or* Croatian	Croatian
Cuba	Cuban	Cuban
Cyprus	Cypriot	Cypriot *or* Cyprus
Czech Republic	Czech	Czech
Denmark	Dane	Danish
Djibouti	Djiboutian	Djiboutian
Dominica	Dominican	Dominican
Dominican Republic	Dominican	Dominican
East Timor	East Timorese	East Timorese
Ecuador	Ecuadorean	Ecuadorean
Egypt	Egyptian	Egyptian
El Salvador	Salvadorean	Salvadorean
England	Englishman/ Englishwoman	English
Equatorial Guinea	Equatorial Guinean	Equatorial Guinean
Eritrea	Eritrean	Eritrean
Estonia	Estonian	Estonian
Ethiopia	Ethiopian	Ethiopian
Falkland Islands (*dependent territory*)	Falkland Islander	Falkland Islands
Fiji	Fijian	Fijian *or* Fiji
Finland	Finn	Finnish
France	Frenchman/ Frenchwoman	French

country	person (name in general use)	related adjective (in general use)
Gabon	Gabonese	Gabonese
Gambia	Gambian	Gambian
Georgia	Georgian	Georgian
Germany	German	German
Ghana	Ghanaian	Ghanaian *or* Ghana
Gibraltar (*dependent territory*)	Gibraltarian	Gibraltarian *or* Gibraltar
Great Britain	Briton	British
Greece	Greek	Greek
Grenada	Grenadian	Grenadian
Guatemala	Guatemalan	Guatemalan
Guinea	Guinean	Guinean
Guinea-Bissau	Guinean	Guinean
Guyana	Guyanese	Guyanese
Haiti	Haitian	Haitian
Holland *see* Netherlands		
Honduras	Honduran	Honduran
Hong Kong (*special administrative region of China*)	inhabitant of Hong Kong	Hong Kong
Hungary	Hungarian	Hungarian
Iceland	Icelander	Icelandic
India	Indian	Indian
Indonesia	Indonesian	Indonesian
Iran	Iranian	Iranian
Iraq	Iraqi	Iraqi *or* Iraq
Ireland, Republic of	Irishman/Irishwoman	Irish
Israel	Israeli	Israeli *or* Israel
Italy	Italian	Italian
Ivory Coast	Ivorian	Ivorian
Jamaica	Jamaican	Jamaican
Japan	Japanese	Japanese
Jordan	Jordanian	Jordanian
Kampuchea *see* Cambodia		
Kazakhstan	Kazakh	Kazakh
Kenya	Kenyan	Kenyan
Kiribati	I-Kiribati	I-Kiribati
Korea, North	North Korean	North Korean
Korea, South	South Korean	South Korean
Kuwait	Kuwaiti	Kuwaiti *or* Kuwait
Kyrgyzstan	Kyrgyz	Kyrgyz
Laos	Laotian	Laotian

country	person (name in general use)	related adjective (in general use)
Latvia	Latvian	Latvian
Lebanon	Lebanese	Lebanese
Lesotho	Mosotho, *pl.* Basotho	Basotho
Liberia	Liberian	Liberian
Libya	Libyan	Libyan
Liechtenstein	Liechtensteiner	Liechtenstein
Lithuania	Lithuanian	Lithuanian
Luxembourg	Luxembourger	Luxembourg
Macedonia	Macedonian	Macedonian
Madagascar	Madagascan	Malagasy *or* Madagascan
Malawi	Malawian	Malawian
Malaysia	Malaysian	Malaysian
Maldives	Maldivian	Maldivian
Mali	Malian	Malian
Malta	Maltese	Maltese
Marshall Islands	Marshall Islander	Marshallese
Mauritania	Mauritanian	Mauritanian
Mauritius	Mauritian	Mauritian
Mexico	Mexican	Mexican
Micronesia	Micronesian	Micronesian
Moldova	Moldovan	Moldovan
Monaco	Monegasque	Monegasque
Mongolia	Mongolian	Mongolian
Montenegro	Montenegrin	Montenegrin
Montserrat (*dependent territory*)	Montserratian	Monserrat
Morocco	Moroccan	Moroccan
Mozambique	Mozambican	Mozambican *or* Mozambique
Myanmar (*formerly* Burma)	citizen of Myanmar	Myanmar
Namibia	Namibian	Namibian
Nauru	Nauruan	Nauruan
Nepal	Nepalese	Nepalese
Netherlands	Dutchman/ Dutchwoman *or* Netherlander	Dutch *or* Netherlands
New Zealand	New Zealander	New Zealand
Nicaragua	Nicaraguan	Nicaraguan
Niger	Nigerien	Nigerien
Nigeria	Nigerian	Nigerian

country	person (name in general use)	related adjective (in general use)
Northern Ireland	Northern Irish *or* Ulsterman/Ulsterwoman	Northern Irish *or* Northern Ireland *or* Ulster
Norway	Norwegian	Norwegian
Oman	Omani	Omani *or* Oman
Pakistan	Pakistani	Pakistani
Panama	Panamanian	Panamanian
Papua New Guinea	Papua New Guinean	Papua New Guinean
Paraguay	Paraguayan	Paraguayan
Peru	Peruvian	Peruvian
Philippines	Filipino *or* Filipina	Philippine *or* Filipino
Pitcairn Islands (*dependent territory*)	Pitcairn Islander	Pitcairn
Poland	Pole	Polish
Portugal	Portuguese	Portuguese
Puerto Rico	Puerto Rican	Puerto Rican
Qatar	Qatari	Qatari *or* Qatar
Romania	Romanian	Romanian
Russia	Russian	Russian
Rwanda	Rwandan	Rwandan
St Helena (*dependent territory*)	St Helenian	St Helenian *or* St Helena
St Kitts and Nevis	citizen of St Kitts and Nevis	Kittitian *or* Nevisian *or* St Kitts and Nevis
St Lucia	St Lucian	St Lucian *or* St Lucia
St Vincent	Vincentian	Vincentian *or* St Vincent
Samoa	Samoan	Samoan
San Marino	Sammarinese	Sammarinese
São Tomé and Principe	São Toméan	São Toméan
Saudi Arabia	Saudi Arabian *or* Saudi	Saudi Arabian *or* Saudi
Scotland	Scot	Scottish *or* Scots *or* Scotch
Senegal	Senegalese	Senegalese
Serbia	Serb *or* Serbian	Serb *or* Serbian
Seychelles	Seychellois	Seychelles *or* Seychellois
Sierra Leone	Sierra Leonean	Sierra Leonean *or* Sierra Leone
Singapore	Singaporean	Singaporean
Slovak Republic	Slovak	Slovak
Slovenia	Slovene *or* Slovenian	Slovenian
Solomon Islands	Solomon Islander	Solomon Islander
Somalia	Somali	Somali
South Africa	South African	South African
Spain	Spaniard	Spanish
Sri Lanka	Sri Lankan	Sri Lankan

Countries of the World

country	person (name in general use)	related adjective (in general use)
Sudan	Sudanese	Sudanese
Suriname	Surinamer	Surinamese
Swaziland	Swazi	Swazi
Sweden	Swede	Swedish
Switzerland	Swiss	Swiss
Syria	Syrian	Syrian
Taiwan	Taiwanese	Taiwanese
Tajikistan	Tajik	Tajik
Tanzania	Tanzanian	Tanzanian
Thailand	Thai	Thai
Togo	Togolese	Togolese
Tonga	Tongan	Tongan
Trinidad and Tobago	Trinidadian or Tobagan or Tobagonian	Trinidadian or Tobagan or Tobagonian
Tunisia	Tunisian	Tunisian
Turkey	Turk	Turkish
Turkmenistan	Turkmen	Turkmen
Tuvalu	Tuvaluan	Tuvaluan
Uganda	Ugandan	Ugandan
Ukraine	Ukrainian	Ukrainian
United Arab Emirates	Emirian	Emirian
United Kingdom *see also* Great Britain	Briton	British
United States of America	United States citizen *or* American	United States *or* American
Uruguay	Uruguayan	Uruguayan
Uzbekistan	Uzbek	Uzbek
Vanuatu	Vanuatuan *or* Ni-Vanuatu	Vanuatuan *or* Ni-Vanuatu
Vatican City	Vatican citizen	Vatican
Venezuela	Venezuelan	Venezuelan
Vietnam	Vietnamese	Vietnamese
Virgin Islands	Virgin Islander	Virgin Islands
Wales	Welshman/Welshwoman	Welsh
Yemen	Yemeni	Yemeni
Yugoslavia	Yugoslav	Yugoslav
Zambia	Zambian	Zambian
Zimbabwe	Zimbabwean	Zimbabwean *or* Zimbabwe

Appendix 2 Prime Ministers of Australia

Edmund Barton	1901–1903
Alfred Deakin	1903–1904
John C. Watson	1904
George Houston Reid	1904–1905
Alfred Deakin	1905–1908
Andrew Fisher	1908–1909
Alfred Deakin	1909–1910
Andrew Fisher	1910–1913
Joseph Cook	1913–1914
Andrew Fisher	1914–1915
William M. Hughes	1915–1923
Stanley M. Bruce	1923–1929
James H. Scullin	1929–1932
Joseph A. Lyons	1932–1939
Earle C. G. Page	1939
Robert Gordon Menzies	1939–1941
Arthur William Fadden	1941
John Curtin	1941–1945
Francis M. Forde	1945
Joseph Benedict Chifley	1945–1949
Robert Gordon Menzies	1949–1966
Harold Edward Holt	1966–1967
John McEwen	1967–1968
John Grey Gorton	1968–1971
William McMahon	1971–1972
Gough Whitlam	1972–1975
Malcolm Fraser	1975–1983
Robert J. L. Hawke	1983–1991
Paul Keating	1991–1996
John Howard	1996–